THE NORTON HISTORY OF
MODERN EUROPE

The Norton History of Modern Europe

FELIX GILBERT, *General Editor*
Institute for Advanced Study

EUGENE F. RICE, JR.
Columbia University

RICHARD S. DUNN
University of Pennsylvania

LEONARD KRIEGER
Columbia University

CHARLES BREUNIG
Lawrence University

NORMAN RICH
Brown University

W · W · NORTON & COMPANY · INC · NEW YORK

SBN 393 09938 5

Library of Congress Catalog Card No. 72–95530

Cartography by Harold K. Faye

PRINTED IN THE UNITED STATES OF AMERICA

1 2 3 4 5 6 7 8 9 0

Contents

94883

Part VI The End of the European Era, 1890 to the Present

Illustrations

Maps and Charts

Foreword

There is wisdom in the words of a great scholar who, when asked how he became interested in history, replied that he wanted to know "how much man could stand." Consideration of the past will always arouse a personal and emotional response; learning about the manner in which men behave in triumph or in defeat will always touch our emotions.

But such questions and responses do not constitute history as a field of knowledge that provides insights which no other study can grant. Whatever aspect of the past, whatever events or developments a historian studies, his concern is with the historical process as a whole; he places a particular problem in the broader context of which it is part.

In their considerations of the crucial features of the historical process historians have been inclined to stress continuity; the past has been studied for clues about the direction and forms of the historical process in the future. Of course, historians are not prophets. Yet, for centuries people were sure that they had some feeling for the shape of things to come—that the progress from the past showed them the path they were to follow. But to those living in the twentieth century the darkness which conceals the future appears impenetrable. Where are fixed points? The same person who, as a youth, read Jules Verne's story about travel to the moon as a delightful fantasia less real than Homer's epic about the siege of Troy can see, in his old age, men taking steps on the moon. What can be taken for granted when people now circle the globe in scarcely more time than it took to travel from London to Constantinople fifty years ago?

The changes that have taken place in the past few decades have been so revolutionary and rapid that we are most impressed by our distance and remoteness from the past than by the links which connect us with it. Stress on continuity as the most important feature of the historical process no longer has much appeal. Such emphasis seems to seek an escape from the present because, in minimizing the changes from the past, the historian refuses to acknowledge reality. Certainly, continuities between past and present do exist. But if the study of the past is to remain a vital part of man's quest for knowledge, history must be able to answer questions other than those which previous generations asked.

History is concerned with change. It is a quest for the causes of change. Not always have historians considered change to have resulted from or been influenced by the thought and action of man. For Thucydides the political society in which men lived was an organism; changes in this body were symptoms of health or weakness. Christians who wrote histories in late antiquity and in the Middle Ages believed that God directed the events of this world; God was the cause of every change that took place. The interest in man's role in effecting change has developed only in recent centuries; it has given the search for the causes of change a particular form: To what extent is man able to control events?

The problem of the nature and extent of man's capacity for control has many aspects. First of all, it raises the question of man's rule over other men. Since the beginning of the sixteenth century, when Machiavelli asked how power might be acquired, preserved, or lost, the study of history has revealed the complexity of this question, which embraces a variety of possibilities reaching from the application of physical force to the bonds created by common beliefs and common intellectual values. The age of religious wars will always remain significant and instructive in revealing the difficulties in drawing a clear boundary line between political power and intellectual freedom.

The question of control comprises also that of man's mastery over his surroundings; basically, this is the story of scientific discoveries and technological inventions. But scientific progress has been dependent on man's view of himself, on the notions which he has of his position in the universe, and of his potentialities. The formation and acceptance of intellectual and cultural values must be viewed as a determining and limiting condition of man's attitude in any field of human activity. The disequilibrium and unrest which develop when a widening of the geographical horizon or a transformation of the external conditions of life clashes with the accepted image of the world-order is a consequence of this bond between man's empirical and ideal world. The sixteenth century, the age of discoveries and of the Reformation, testifies to this quite as much as our own twentieth century.

Certainly, in our time the problem has become more complex. Inability to handle new issues in the framework of traditionally established institutions, and the breakdown of authority because of unwillingness to look for new answers is now compounded by increasing possibilities for molding opinion, and by a technology which has gained an impetus of its own, so that its devices often are not used by men for clearly described aims but determine the channels into which human activities flow.

Nevertheless, we face old issues in a new form. Thus, when we look now into the past we are more interested in clarifying where we stand by confronting the present with the past than in discovering continuities. Such a shift in concern with the past has influenced the work of the historian in many ways. Although historians have always made comparisons between events and institutions belonging to various periods or different countries, only in recent years have the possibilities of comparative history been systematically explored. Analysis of the similarities between absolutism and totalitarianism, for instance, has sharpened our understanding of the character of both systems. There are other phenomena which have recently emerged as focal points of interest. Close study of the manner in which decisions have been made appears more instructive than the narration of factual events and the establishment of causal connections among them. The nature and the effectiveness of a decision depend on the institutional framework in which it is made, on the completeness or faultiness of the information on which it is based, and on the experiences and influences which have formed the minds of those who make the decision. There is now a new concern with, and a new comprehension of, the interplay of institutional, intellectual, and psychological factors. If such an analysis has been intensified and refined, historians have also gained more knowledge about those factors which are beyond their control. Computers and other technical devices broaden the possibilities of statistical and quantitative analysis and increase their exactitude, enable historians to place events and decisions against the background of demographic developments, economic growth or decline, or changes in social structure. Although the aspects of the past which the historian finds instructive might not be identical with those which historians of former times scrutinized, his task remains the same: to discover where we are and what we can do.

These observations may serve as a justification for the manner in which the following treatment of modern history has been conceived. This work adopts the traditional view that the modern world begins with the Renaissance and Reformation. It is frequently said that the modern world —our own world—was born in the French Revolution. Yet, considering the revolutionary changes which have taken place in our own time, we can no longer be sure of the permanency of the political ideas and of the social forces which emerged in the period of the French Revolution and dominated the following century. It is certain, however, that the more basic problem of the scope of human control over change arose with the decline of belief in a divinely ordered world and with the formation of a secularized world outlook two centuries earlier. There is validity, therefore, in the traditional notion that the Renaissance and Reformation represent a crucial break in the history of the Western world.

The periods into which European developments since the sixteenth century conveniently fall are treated by different authors. Such a procedure is justified because our attention is focused on the varied forms of social organization and development rather than on the links which lead from one to the other. It is important, therefore, to have each period stand out as a unit and to stress those aspects which the various phenomena in a period have in common. Intellectual, political, social, and cultural developments are presented not as streams running parallel to each other but in their interdependence. Because differences in relationships among these developments are integral elements of the particular character of each period, the various authors themselves had to decide on the emphasis they wanted to give to each of these fields of human endeavor within the periods they are treating; the nearer we come to the present, political and social events predominate. This seems to correspond to the structure of our time.

The history of Europe from the sixteenth century to the present have been frequently described; this story cannot claim to be novel. It is dependent on the work which previous historians have done and tries to incorporate the most recent results of research. There is questionable truth to the statement that each generation must write history anew. For while our knowledge of the facts of history steadily increases and widens, the facts themselves do not change. Generations of historians have gathered the material on which future historians can confidently build. What change in the course of time are the questions historians ask, and this new presentation of an old story will fulfill its purpose if it raises—and perhaps answers—some of the questions which are appropriate and urgent to ask in the twentieth century.

Felix Gilbert

Part I

THE FOUNDATIONS OF
EARLY MODERN EUROPE,
1460-1559

Introduction

THE CENTURY OF European history between 1460 and 1559 was a period of rapid, comprehensive change. Like all periods of transition from one firmly contoured civilization to another, its most obvious characteristic is an intricate counterpoint of tradition and innovation, catastrophe and promise. This is why historians of the fifteenth and sixteenth centuries, like historians of the transitional centuries between antiquity and the Middle Ages, have always faced particularly difficult choices of perspective and emphasis. Some historians of fifteenth - and sixteenth-century manners, belief, and institutions have told their story in metaphors of spring and awakening. Others have lingered on the evidence of stagnation, traditionalism, and decay. Their imagery is autumnal. This sort of apparently contradictory appreciation reflects the period's bewildering, and fascinating, mixture of new and old.

Was the shift from old to new a shift from medieval to modern? The answer is yes, though with qualifications. The first concerns the temptation to reduce the medieval to a sociological "type," to find a quintessential medieval science, art, philosophy, religion or system of government and then measure change and innovation by variations from this standard. Such a procedure is not wholly misguided. The selection and ordering of material always stylizes the past to some extent. Otherwise, its history would be unintelligible. At the same time, the comparison of innovation with tradition must remain alert to the diversity of medieval life. For example, it is a common, and sometimes desirable, kind of historical shorthand to use St. Thomas Aquinas' solution of a particular problem to represent the opinion of all medieval philosophers and theologians. To the extent that all or most medieval thinkers shared important assumptions, the views of St. Thomas are typical, and yet Thomism was only one of several thirteenth-century philosophical tendencies. Equally representative contemporaries rejected many Thomist doctrines, and his influence in the fourteenth and fifteenth centuries was largely confined to his own Dominican order; the Church has recognized him as a normative theologian only in modern times. It is also

3

well to remember that claims for innovation in one period often rest on ignorance of the period that preceded it.

The idea of the modern conceals an even greater diversity and ambiguity. Clarity here is important because so many nineteenth- and early twentieth-century scholars saw in the fifteenth and sixteenth centuries—especially in the civilizations of Renaissance Italy and Reformation Germany—the prototypes of modern European civilization. By modern they meant their own day. To later twentieth-century historians, however—self-consciously aware that they are living in another period of transition that is moving even more rapidly than the age of the Renaissance and Reformation—the innovations of Erasmus or Luther, of Henry VIII or Jakob Fugger, of Raphael or Michelangelo look less like the beginnings of the modern world than strands in a fabric of custom and tradition which contemporary innovators have been tearing up for three quarters of a century. Many of the modernisms of the Renaissance and Reformation have become as old-fashioned as medieval Latin or Gothic architecture were in sixteenth-century Rome. It is no longer plausible, therefore, to argue that the Renaissance and Reformation are the beginning of the modern world, if by modern we mean contemporary, or give the word the connotation it has, for instance, in the phrase "modern art," an art, like so much else in twentieth-century culture, based on assumptions and aspirations different from and hostile to those of the Renaissance.

Between modern and fifteenth- and sixteenth-century Europe lie, in any case, the industrial and French revolutions, the development of nationalism, and a profound secularization of culture. Renaissance and Reformation Europe was a pre-industrial, "underdeveloped" society, much closer in its economic life, technology, demographic patterns, communications, and class structure to imperial Rome than to contemporary western Europe or America. Everywhere political and military loyalty was dynastic rather than national. Political ties were overwhelmingly personal and familial, and every man took religion seriously. The age was one of astonishing religious creativity, pullulating with saints, mystics, reformers, and original theologians. Among the laity the temperature of piety was high—for the safety of religious minorities, dangerously high.

In a word, the shift from old to new in the fifteenth and first half of the sixteenth centuries (it had begun earlier in the fourteenth) was not a shift from medieval to modern, but from medieval to *early* modern. Renaissance and Reformation men built the foundations of a new Europe, but one that modern historians now call traditional Europe—Europe before the French and industrial revolutions. It still remains for students of the period to detect the crucial continuities—and discontinuities—in a gradual shift from one mode of perception and of production to another.

CHAPTER 1

Science, Technology, and Discovery

THE DATE 1492 is familiar, and so is 1498, the year Vasco da Gama reached the Malabar Coast of India by sea. Around these dates cluster others hardly less familiar and equally important. During the half century before 1500, Europeans read the first books printed in the West. Firearms created a new kind of warfare between 1450 and 1525. In 1500 Copernicus lectured on mathematics in Rome, and soon after, he began to teach that the earth rotates on its axis and at the same time revolves in orbit around the central sun. Each of these innovations, discoveries, and rediscoveries influenced profoundly the future course of European and world history. Together they transformed Europe's relation to non-European civilizations and to its own past. Until the sixteenth century, Europe was the technical and cultural pupil of Greco-Roman antiquity and of the civilizations of the Near and Far East. The voyages of Columbus and Vasco da Gama coincided with the beginning of the end of that dependence. Europe acquired and exercised, along with political and economic predominance, technical and scientific leadership. Before 1500, Europe imported ideas and techniques; after 1500, Europeans were cultural creditors.

THE INVENTION OF PRINTING

Printing with movable metal type was perfected in Mainz about 1450. Three names recur in the sources, those of Johann Gutenberg (*c.* 1395–1468), Johann Fust (*c.* 1400–1465), and Peter Schöffer (*c.* 1425–1502), Fust's son-in-law. These sources are scanty, often unclear, and sometimes of doubtful authenticity. So it is impossible to determine accurately the contribution of a particular individual to the development of typography and its commercial exploitation. Our relative ignorance about the origins of printing does have advantages, however. It discourages the misguided effort to attribute complex technological innovation to a single man, and forces us to realize that an invention is in any case not the creation of an individual, as is a poem or a painting, but a social

5

product. Like the development of the steam engine or the telegraph, the "invention" of a mechanical process for duplicating texts was multiple and cumulative. It was successfully completed by Mainz printers in the 1450's, but it had important earlier beginnings.

Two Chinese inventions, block printing and paper, are linked with the beginnings of typographic printing in western Europe. Xylography, or block printing, originated in China in the early eighth century. The printer drew in reverse on a block of wood the text or the picture he wished to reproduce, carved the wood so that the graphic pattern stood out in relief, inked the block, and transferred the design to paper. The process is simple in conception; difficult, time-consuming, and wasteful in execution; and ill adapted to the alphabetic writing of the West. Its transmission to the West—probably during the century from 1250 to 1350, when European contact with China was unusually close—had little direct importance for

The Papermaker. *Woodcut by Jost Amman from Hans Sachs' description of the arts, crafts and trades, published in 1568.*

the development of typography. Its indirect importance, on the other hand, was great. It probably suggested the next crucial step: cutting up an old block into its constituent letters and then rearranging these letters to spell out a new text. It certainly diffused the idea of printing and of the printed book, while the lively commercial success starting in the late fourteenth century of printed playing cards (another Chinese invention), religious prints, and crude block books emphasized the magnitude of the market and the potential profit to be got from it.

Paper was indispensable, but for economic rather than technical reasons. Manuscript books were usually copied on parchment (made from split sheepskin) or on vellum (calfskin), and these materials were used also by typographic printers when the aim was magnificence rather than utility. But since a single large book like the Bible required as many as 170 calf skins or 300 sheep skins, the absence of paper soon would have nullified the promise of mechanical duplication: the cheap, rapid production of books in large numbers. Paper manufacture was introduced in Spain during the twelfth century by the Arabs, who had themselves received the technique from China. It spread slowly during the next two centuries to much of Europe: Italy (*c.* 1270), France (*c.* 1340), Germany (*c.* 1390), and Switzerland (1411). In Europe the chief raw material was old rags. Papermakers shredded the rags in a stamping mill driven by waterpower, mixed the macerated flax and hemp fibers with water, and dipped their mold, a large flat wire sieve with a wooden frame, into the liquid pulp. When the pulp was evenly distributed over the wire mesh and the water had run out through the holes, they put the sheets on alternate layers of felt, squeezed them in a press, and then dried and sized them. Hans Sachs (1494–1576), the cobbler-poet and hero of Wagner's *Meistersinger von Nürnberg*, described the process in a poem which accompanies the earliest picture of papermaking:

> I am using old rags in my mill,
> Where flowing water turns the wheel
> That tears the rags and shreds them up.
> Then I soak the pulp in water tub,
> Mold the sheets, on a felt them lay,
> And squeeze them in my press all day.
> I hang them up to let them dry,
> Snow-white and glossy, a treat for every eye.

By the time of Gutenberg's youth, paper was plentiful and sold for approximately one sixth the price of parchment.

Western typography drew upon European methods also, and these were of more immediate technical relevance. Printing, as it was practiced in Mainz by Gutenberg, Fust, and Schöffer, required a suitable ink, a press for transferring the ink to paper, and metal type. To adhere to metal smoothly and evenly, ink must have an oil base. By the early fifteenth century, Flemish artists had begun to paint in oils; a suitable printer's ink, consisting of a pigment (lampblack or powdered charcoal) ground in a linseed-oil varnish, was simply an adaptation of oil paint. The immediate ancestor of the wooden press was also at hand: the press used in paper mills for squeezing water from the damp sheets, a device easily adaptable to printing. Most crucial was the invention of type—the mirror image of each of the letters of the alphabet made in metal by precision casting from matrices. The skills which contributed to the development of typecasting were understandably those connected with the more delicate forms of metallurgy: those of the metal engraver and the designer of coins and medals, of the goldsmith adept at casting small objects, of craftsmen who made punches for stamping letters on bells, pewter vessels, and bookbindings. We must imagine that in many places in Europe during the first half of the fifteenth century ingenious artisans experimented with type, inks, and presses; that many parallel efforts were made to replace the scribe by a mechanical device; that the actual invention of printing—the dramatic fusion (so easy for us to imagine in retrospect, so immensely difficult before it was accomplished) of familiar techniques into a new and workable process—also occurred independently in several places; that, finally, this new process was perfected and first organized as an industry by Gutenberg, Fust, and Schöffer.

What is certain is that the oldest surviving books printed with movable metal type were issued in Mainz. The best among them astonish still by their technical perfection, further evidence that the Mainz printing firms had inherited considerable expertise from earlier experiment and discovery. The great Latin Bible popularly associated with Gutenberg and more cautiously named the forty-two-line Bible by bibliographers (to distinguish it from another early Mainz Bible, printed with thirty-six lines to the pages) was finished in 1455. The craftsmanship of its type and the art of its typesetting and printing are impeccable. Clearly, the Mainz printers had established the technology of printing on firm foundations; and indeed for over three hundred years Gutenberg's successors cut punches, fitted matrices, cast type, composed, and printed substantially as he had done. Nor were later printers to surpass the founders aesthetically. On August 14, 1457, Fust and Schöffer issued the *Psalms*. The volume was printed on vellum. The type, printed in red and black, is noble and fits handsomely on the page. Each psalm, as the printers boasted in a note at the end, is "adorned with the beauty of large initial letters"; the lacy design of these letters, ornamented with flowers and small animals and printed in red and blue, is masterly. Fust and Schöffer's *Psalms* is the oldest signed and dated book printed in Europe that has survived. In its sober magnificence it is also one of the most beautiful.

A page from Fust and Schöffer's Psalms. *The initial "B" begins the second Psalm*: Beatus vir qui non abiit in consilio impiorum: Blessed is the man that walketh not in the counsel of the ungodly.

These first printed books have a further, and curious, characteristic: their pages so closely resemble those of manuscript books as to be virtually indistinguishable to the unpracticed eye. Clearly the printers' technical, aesthetic, and commercial aim was to reproduce exactly the handwritten manuscript. And they did not do so merely through inertia or in order to give their customers a familiar product; the practice suggests rather that the earliest printers had no conception of the unique potentialities of their invention, that they considered printing only a new and particular kind of writing ("the art of writing artificially without reed or pen," as Schöffer put it), and that they thought that what they had to sell consisted simply of less expensive manuscripts in greater numbers. Their difficulty in freeing themselves from traditional conceptions is explained by the fact that although typography was the greatest invention of the Renaissance, its earliest development was shaped almost exclusively by clerical tastes and needs. Its geographical origins were far from Italy, the literary and artistic center of European culture in the fifteenth century. Printing first became a significant business enterprise in a provincial ecclesiastical capital with a population of about three thousand and meager intellectual distinction. Monasteries and cathedral chapters contracted for the Latin Bibles, missals, psalters, and antiphonaries which were the printers' more important productions. The ecclesiastical authorities dominated job printing; for example, a common order was for indulgence forms. The cheaper books, to judge from the earliest publishers' list (that of Peter Schöffer), reflected traditional tastes; biblical digests, works by St. Thomas Aquinas, saints' lives, brief guides to living well and dying well, and for secular diversion, romances of chivalry predominated.

Yet even in Mainz, what was to be the key factor in the astonishingly rapid spread of printing between 1460 and 1500 was clearly evident: the unsatisfied demand for books among the merchants, substantial artisans, lawyers, government officials, doctors, and teachers who lived and worked in towns. The European peasantry was largely illiterate and would remain so for centuries. The needs of the clergy and of those adaptable nobles who were beginning to recognize the importance of a literary education for careers of service to their prince and country had been reasonably well met in the past by workshops where sometimes scores of copyists multiplied books by hand. Indeed, printed books met with a lively resistance for several decades, especially in Italy, from wealthy and cultivated collectors. But among what we must call, loosely but inevitably, the middle classes of the towns, among men who needed to read, write, and calculate in order to manage their businesses and conduct civic affairs, who were being educated in increasing numbers in town and guild schools, and who in the fifteenth century were swelling the arts faculties of the universities, there was a large and ready market for printed books. Underlying the expansion of printing was that expansion of urban population and secular literacy which had begun in the high Middle Ages. As townsmen grew in number, education, wealth, power, and self-consciousness, their intellectual and cultural needs increased. With the unremitting enthusiasm of the bourgeoisie for edification and self-improvement, they eagerly bought entertaining and useful books of all sorts: religious and secular, in Latin and in the vernacular, grammars, dictionaries, and encyclopedias, elementary texts in mathematics, astrology, medicine, and law, local and universal histories, manuals of popular devotion, and Latin classics of proven appeal—Virgil's *Aeneid*, Cicero's *De officiis*, Terence, Pliny, and Seneca. Their demands released the inherent dynamism of typography. The result was a steadily expanding stream of books. Printing spread from Mainz to Strasbourg (1458), Cologne (1465), Augsburg (1468), Nuremberg (1470), Leipzig (1481), and Vienna (1482). German printers, or their pupils, introduced the "divine" art to Italy in 1467, Switzerland and Bohemia in 1468, France and the

THE SPREAD OF PRINTING
THROUGH RENAISSANCE EUROPE

△ Printing centers and dates of first
occurrence of printing

Printers shown thus: CAXTON

NORWAY

Stockholm,
1483

SWEDEN

BALTIC SEA

SCOTLAND

Edinburgh,
1507

DENMARK

Copenhagen, 1490

Odense, 1482

IRELAND

Dublin,
1551

NORTH SEA

POLAND

Elbe R.

Oder R.

ENGLAND

CAXTON

London,
c. 1492

NETHERLANDS

Utrecht, 1470

Leipzig, 1481

GERMANY

Westminster,
1476

English Channel

BELGIUM

Brussels,
1475

Cologne, 1465

Mainz, 1450

BOHEMIA

Pilsen, 1468

ATLANTIC

FUST
SCHÖFFER
GUTENBERG

Nuremberg,
1470

Vienna, 1482

OCEAN

Seine R.

Paris,
1470

Strasbourg,
1458

Rhine R.

Augsburg,
1468

Danube R.

AUSTRIA

Loire R.

Basel,
1468

SWITZ.

HUNGARY

FRANCE

Lyons, 1473

Rhone R.

Milan,
1471

Venice,
1469

Po R.

ADRIATIC

ITALY

Florence,
1482

SEA

CORSICA

Rome
1467

PORTUGAL

SPAIN

Tagus R.

Valencia,
1474

SARDINIA

Naples,
1471

Lisbon,
1489

BALEARIC
ISLANDS

Seville
1478

MEDITERRANEAN

SEA

SICILY

0   500 miles

Netherlands in 1470, Spain, England, Hungary, and Poland between 1474 and 1476, Denmark and Sweden in 1482–1483. By 1500 the presses had issued about six million books in approximately forty thousand editions, more books, probably, than had been produced in western Europe since the fall of Rome.

So vast an increase in the quantity of books inevitably had important cultural consequences. Most striking, perhaps, in the years before the Reformation was the influence of printing on scholarship. Manuscripts, totally dependent on the skill, learning, and care of the scribe, had always been inaccurate and unreliable. Furthermore, this inaccuracy and unreliability was becoming increasingly great as successive generations of scribes copied the errors of their predecessors and added their own. The fundamental contribution of printing to learning was that it halted this progressive corruption and made possible the long and continuing effort to restore the great texts of the past to something approaching their original integrity. Printing gave scholars all over Europe identical texts to work on. Referring precisely to a particular word in a particular line on a particular page, a scholar in Basel could propose an emendation which could be rapidly checked by his colleagues in Rome or Florence. Or another scholar might discover, in a monastic library in Paris, a manuscript whose text would be judged, by increasingly precise and objective criteria, better than any known before. From such corrections and discoveries a critical edition would emerge, to be superseded by another and yet another until something approaching a standard text had been achieved, usually only in the nineteenth or even the twentieth century. The past is sometimes a burden. That we know it as well as we do—and so much of it—we owe to printing.

The way printing made textual criticism a cumulative science is only a specific case of a more general phenomenon. Printing turned intellectual work as a whole into a cooperative instead of a solitary human activity. As the steam-powered machines of the industrial Revolution would multiply the productivity of human physical labor, so printing enlarged the amount of intellectual effort applied to individual problems. In no field were the effects of this novel concentration of brainpower more noticeable than in the natural sciences. Copernicus, for example, had adopted the heliocentric hypothesis early in the sixteenth century, but he did not publish it until 1543. Between 1500 and 1543 he worked on this major scientific problem in intellectual isolation. After 1543 Copernicus' printed book gradually drew a few of the best minds in Europe into a cooperative, controversial study of the problem, and a solution was found much more rapidly than it would have been otherwise. Scientific research—and all scholarship—became, through this new tool of the intellect, a public dialogue, a published exchange of novel results controlled by cooperative critical examination and the repetition of experiments. In this context the invention of printing can be compared only with the invention of writing, on the one hand, and of the computer, on the other.

Printing not only made scholarship fuller and more accurate; it also made it less difficult to acquire. Because of the greater standardization of print, learning to read was easier. Now individuals could afford to own books, where before they had normally been owned almost exclusively by institutions—monasteries, cathedral chapters, and colleges. Medieval students had had to compile their own dictionaries and reference books, and much of their time in the lecture room was spent writing out texts dictated by the teacher. To lecture had been to read a book aloud so the student could take it down; now the student could read the text at home. To learn had been to memorize; printing freed the memory. There was less need to keep a fact in the mind if it could more easily be found on the shelf. In 1580, well over a century after the invention of typography, the French essayist Michel de Montaigne (1533–1592) eloquently restated a principal theme of Renaissance educational theory when he defined the end of education not as a large amount of factual knowledge, but as a trained intelligence, sound judgment, and cultivated taste. For Montaigne the walking encyclopedia was a pedant; but he could legitimately brand him pedant only because printed reference books now served the traditional function of the human memory.

Equally striking, particularly after 1500, was the way printing accelerated the diffusion of images and ideas. The visual arts reached a new and wider public. Engravings, the normal means of reproducing works of art before the invention of photography, carried iconographic and decorative motifs from one region to another, from one artist to another; just as the influence of a man of letters like Erasmus of Rotterdam rapidly touched every intellectual circle in Europe through the printed word, so engravings of works by Michelangelo, for example, made the arrangement and postures of the nudes on the ceiling of the Sistine Chapel the common property of his most distant contemporaries. But it was the spread of Lutheranism that first made frighteningly and triumphantly clear the revolutionary significance of printing for the communication of ideas. The Reformation spread with the same astonishing rapidity as printing itself; it could not have done so without it. Indeed, the role of printing in the early sixteenth century already suggests its double role in the future: through its promise of enlightenment and popular education, potentially revolutionary and hostile to the *status quo*; but when controlled by the state, the most effective agent of manipulation until the invention of radio and television.

This is why the systematic censorship of books, little practiced in the Middle Ages, appeared very soon after the invention of printing, and spread with it. By making reading more democratic, printing spawned the modern censor. Both secular and ecclesiastical authorities censored books, for the prohibition and burning of books were designed to maintain political as well as religious orthodoxy. Alexander VI, pope between 1492 and 1503, clearly expressed the attitude of the Church in a bull of 1501. "The art of printing," he said, "is very useful insofar as it furthers the circulation of useful and tested books; but it can be very harmful if it is permitted to widen the influence of pernicious works. It will therefore be necessary to maintain full control over the printers so that they may be prevented from bringing into print writings which are antagonistic to the Catholic faith or which are likely to cause trouble to believers." Such attitudes became concrete in the lists of prohibited books issued to combat the spread of Lutheranism, lists which culminated in the Roman Index of Prohibited Books (1559). Henry VIII of England ordered the publication of such a catalogue in 1526. Other early indexes were prepared by the universities of Paris and Louvain. The Protestant churches protected the minds of the faithful as zealously as Catholic bishops, while secular princes generally considered religious commitments different from their own not only heretical, but treasonable as well. By 1560 censorship of books in all its forms was universal in western Europe. The struggle between author, printer, and publisher, on the one hand, and ecclesiastical and governmental censors, on the other, had become one aspect of the battle for intellectual liberty and freedom of conscience in an age of fundamental ideological conflict.

THE NEW WARFARE

In no period before our own has the technology of violence been more fertile than in the century between 1450 and 1550. During these years the use of gunpowder to propel missiles transformed the art of war. The new warfare, in turn, shaped the pattern of European political and social change as profoundly as printing altered the conditions of its intellectual life.

Gunpowder became known in the West about the middle of the thirteenth century. The Franciscan scientist Roger Bacon (c. 1214– c. 1292) mentioned it as something already widely known. This is his description of a firecracker:

There is a child's toy of sound and fire made in various parts of the world with powder of saltpetre, sulphur and charcoal of hazelwood. This powder is enclosed in an instrument of parchment the size of a finger, and this can make such a noise that it seriously distresses the ears of men, especially if one is taken unawares, and the terrible flash is also very alarming; if an instrument of large size were used, no one could stand the terror of the noise and flash. If the instrument were made of solid material, the violence of the explosion would be much greater.[1]

[1]Quoted by J. R. Partington, *A History of Greek Fire and Gunpowder* (Cambridge, Eng., 1960), p. 78.

Bacon clearly knew real gunpowder—its composition of suitable proportions of saltpeter, charcoal, and sulfur and its explosive combustion in a proper container. He did not invent it. Gunpowder was invented in China, probably as early as the eleventh century, and like paper and block printing was probably transmitted to Europeans by the Arabs.

The technological discovery, however, which turned gunpowder from a toy into a weapon and transformed warfare and society was that of its use as a propellant. This discovery was made early in the fourteenth century, independently in Europe and China. The first mention of a gun in Europe occurs in a Florentine document of 1326, which names two officers to make iron shot and metal cannon for the defense of castles and villages belonging to the republic. The first representation of a gun—a crude "firepot" designed to propel an arrow—is in an English manuscript dated the same year. By the end of the fourteenth century, firearms were being manufactured all over Europe, ranging from twenty-four-pound guns throwing lead bullets and thirty-four-pound guns throwing arrows to guns weighing over a ton and requiring more than a month to make. By the middle of the fifteenth century, artillery had proved of decisive effect against feudal stone castles and the traditional curtain walls of towns. At the siege of Constantinople by the Ottoman Turks in 1453, Sultan Mahomet II (ruled 1451–1481), who had German and Hungarian cannon founders in his service, was able to deploy against the astonished Byzantines fourteen batteries, each of several great bombards, plus fifty-six smaller cannon of various types. Most spectacular of all were two enormous guns which fired stone balls nearly three feet in diameter and weighing over eight hundred pounds. The guns required seventy oxen each and more than a thousand men to move them from Adrianople, where they were cast, to the Bosporus. The bombardment began early in April. By May 28, seven weeks later (the great cannon took two hours to load and could fire only a few times a day), serious breaches had been made in the most formidable defensive walls in Europe. On May 29 the city was carried by storm. In the meantime, in France, the revolutionary effectiveness of artillery in siege warfare became equally apparent during the final phase of the Hundred Years' War, the French reconquest of Normandy from the English. In the twelfth century, French kings had spent months, sometimes years, trying to pry a recalcitrant vassal out of a stone castle. In 1449–1450 Charles VII conducted sixty successful siege operations in a year and four days. The royal siege train became so respected that many fortified places surrendered the moment the big guns were placed in battery. The complete mastery of efficient cannon over the old fortifications was established.

For over a century and a half after these first decisive successes, artillery remained primarily a siege weapon. One major pitched battle—Marignano in 1515—was indeed largely won by artillery fire; more commonly, however, the limited mobility and the lack of accuracy and firepower of Renaissance cannon restricted their role in the field to mutual bombardment before the real battle was engaged. Battles were transformed not by cannon, but by the emergence of infantry as the "substance and sinew" of armies (the phrase is Machiavelli's) and by the gradual equipment of foot soldiers with portable firearms.

The decisive arm in a medieval army had been the cavalry; a medieval battle was a clash of mounted and armored nobles. By 1530, cavalry formed only one eleventh of the French army and one twelfth of the Spanish (some military theorists argued even more radically that the proportions of foot to horse should be twenty to one); and battles had become clashes of plebeian infantry armed with pikes and arquebuses, with heavy cavalry playing only a subordinate role. Early steps toward this new way of fighting had been taken during the fourteenth and fifteenth centuries by the English and the Swiss. The English contributed the longbow. At the Battle of Crécy in 1346, for the first time in over a thousand years, the sky over a battlefield was thick with missiles; for the first time, unassisted infantry won a major victory over enemies who relied on their superiority in cavalry. The achievement of the Swiss was to develop infantry tactics which permitted masses of unmounted troops to maneuver in the open field, defend themselves against cavalry charges, and engage in shock offensive action themselves. It was their practice to form compact squares of as many as six thousand men, trained to move swiftly and precisely without breaking their formation. Their principal weapon was the pike, a shaft of wood about ten feet long with a sharp iron head. In defensive action, the men stood still. The outer four ranks would cross the heads of their protruding pikes and present to charging cavalry a bristling wall. Horsemen who penetrated the phalanx were jabbed with halberds or twisted from their horses and finished off with swords by men of the inner ranks. By such means, men described with aristocratic disdain by a Milanese ambassador as "rude peasants who feed on cheese and curds" routed the chivalrous knights of the Burgundian dukes (at Morat in 1476) as efficiently as English yokels armed with longbows had defeated the mounted mobility of France at Crécy. Even more important was the fact that Swiss pikemen, unlike English archers or Italian crossbowmen, who were incapable of offensive action, could also attack, becoming charging squares of almost irresistible momentum. In the Middle Ages only cavalry had been able to charge; the Swiss pike phalanx made it possible for infantry to come out into the open and charge as well.

The reinforcement of pikemen with large numbers of foot soldiers carrying firearms was the last and decisive step by which the infantryman succeeded to the position formerly held by the mailed knight. Inefficient handguns (miniature cannon strapped to pike handles) were in use by the beginning of the fifteenth century; but only toward the end of the century did a true infantry firearm, the arquebus, become common, and only in 1521 did the Spaniards introduce the improved arquebus that came to be called the musket. It consisted of an iron barrel sunk in a wooden butt, was about six feet long, weighed fifteen pounds, and fired lead bullets to an effective range of about two hundred yards. After 1500, an ever-increasing number of troops were equipped with arquebuses and muskets. The arquebus supplemented rather than displaced the pike. Pikemen, to be sure, were extremely vulnerable to arquebus and musket fire. On the other hand, the arquebusier was helpless against cavalry once he had fired the single shot he normally had time to get off before the horsemen reached him. He needed the pike to protect him against cavalry, as the pike needed the musket to clear a path for his advance.

The tactics suggested by the mutual dependence of pike and musket were worked out between 1520 and 1525 by the father of modern infantry, the Spanish general Fernando de Avalos, marquis of Pescara (1489–1525), and scored their most dramatic early success at the Battle of Pavia (1525). On this occasion a French army commanded by the king, Francis I (ruled 1515–1547), met a Spanish Imperialist army in a contest for the mastery of northern Italy. The Imperialists had about seventeen

The Capture of Francis I at the Battle of Pavia, February 24, 1525.

thousand infantry and less than a thousand heavy cavalry. The French forces, especially the cavalry, were more numerous. The battle was a disaster for the French cavalry, a triumph for the Spanish musketeers. The slaughter among the French nobility caused by the steady shooting and maneuvering of Pescara's musketeers was fearful. Francis himself was captured. The French are said to have lost eight thousand men; the Imperialists reported their losses at seven hundred. On that day the superiority of the arquebusier to the mailed knight was proved as decisively as three quarters of a century earlier the vulnerability of medieval fortifications to cannon had been proved by the fall of Constantinople.

Between 1450 and 1525, then, a new era in warfare began, the age of gunpowder, or more precisely, the age of missiles (cannonballs and bullets) propelled by gunpowder. The rapid development and spread of these novel methods of destruction were made possible by an exactly contemporary increase in European metal production. Artillery consumed and wasted enormous amounts of metal. In the 1530's a large cannon required three to four tons of bronze. Although gun carriages were made of wood, they were armored with bands of iron and carried heavy iron bolts, chains and hooks. Together, a gun and its carriage weighed over two tons. By the end of the fifteenth century, iron had replaced stone for cannonballs. The barrels of arquebuses and muskets were made of iron. Moreover, the familiar metal weapons and defenses of the past—swords, lances, daggers, arrows, and above all, plate armor for both men and horses—continued in use. Armor, which had been getting heavier since the middle of the fourteenth century, was an effective defensive reply to the arrows of the English longbowmen. But the elaborate, often very beautiful, metal plates which encased the body of the rider and partially shielded his horse were ultimately useless as a defense against the bullet. The first age of gunpowder was also the last, and most extravagant, age of armor.

A supply of metal adequate to meet these accelerating military needs became available in the years after 1460, when a series of technological innovations combined to increase very substantially the output of Europe's mines. More efficient machines to drain mines, and blast furnaces fanned by water-driven bellows (furnaces which for the first time could refine ore into an iron pure enough to be cast as skillfully as bronze), contributed to a fivefold increase of iron production between 1460 and 1530. New techniques for removing silver from the argentiferous copper ores that abounded in central Europe increased the supply of copper even more rapidly, a fact of particular importance because copper was the essential element in cannon manufacture until cast iron came into use in the late sixteenth century. Just as the spread of typography depended on an adequate supply of paper, so the spread of firearms required an adequate supply of copper and iron.

But although the availability of sufficient metal accelerated the extensive adoption of the new weapons, it hardly explains it. We tend, of course, to assume that the inherent purpose of gunpowder is the destruction of human life. Yet it is by no means self-evident that gunpowder should of necessity be employed primarily for war. It was used for firecrackers and for peaceful economic purposes like blasting in mines before it was used to propel bullets. In China, where gunpowder had been known long before it reached Europe, its military uses were not developed to the extent they were in the West. This difference suggests the existence in Renaissance Europe of a very powerful pressure to exploit the new invention for military purposes. This pressure, becoming acute about 1450, came from the larger territorial princes and derived its force from a fundamental political reality of the age: the consolidation in Europe of what would remain the dominant political form of the modern world, the sovereign territorial state. The new weapons and the new warfare benefitted the ruler seeking to organize a large territory. They armored his aggressions at home and abroad. Gunpowder technology became normal in the West because it royalized warfare and helped the prince to establish a monopoly on the use of organized force within his territory.

If in one perspective the effect of firearms was to royalize warfare, in another perspective the effect was to proletarianize it. Contemporaries seem to have been more struck by the second than by the first. "Would to God," wrote a French noble taken prisoner at Pavia, "that this unhappy weapon [the arquebus] had never been invented. I myself would not bear the scars it caused me and which still cripple me today. Nor would so many brave and valiant men have died by the hands of cowards and shirkers who would not dare to look in the face the men they bring down from a distance with their wretched bullets." Gentlemen with pretensions to chivalry were disturbed not so much by the fact that fighting with missiles propelled by gunpowder was making war bloodier than it had ever been before, as by the fact that firearms enabled a base-born man to strike down at a distance the bravest knight. The poet Lodovico Ariosto (1473–1533), who sang of "ladies, knights, arms and loves" at the court of the duke of Este in Ferrara, lamented the evil, devilish invention of the gun: "O wretched and foul invention, how did you ever find place in a human heart? Through you the soldier's glory is destroyed, through you the business of arms is without honor, through you valor and courage are brought low, for often the bad man seems better than the good; through you valor no more, daring no more can come to a test in the field."[2] Here is the reverse of royal profit, the nostalgia for a past when only aristocrats had really fought, and did so—at least in theory—according to a code of honor. Now foot soldiers with pikes and arquebuses fought more decisively, if not better; and they attempted to win not by valorous clash of arms

[2]*Orlando Furioso*, XI, 26, trans. by Allan Gilbert (New York, 1954), Vol. I, p. 156 .

or acts of individual courage, but by disciplined industry and cunning, by ruse, surprise attack, and fraud. "Although in all other affairs it is hateful to use fraud, in the operations of war it is praiseworthy and glorious," wrote Niccolò Machiavelli (1469–1527).[3] In war the amorality of the state supplanted the personal honor of the knight. Gunpowder hastened the decay of chivalry. Its end is symbolized by the death in 1524 of Pierre Terrail, Seigneur de Bayard, *chevalier sans peur and sans reproche*, the last great representative of Christian knighthood. It was his amiable practice to execute on the spot every arquebusier he captured; he was killed by a bullet.

By royalizing warfare, on the one hand, and by proletarianizing it, on the other, the gun helped to tip the balance of power within each European state away from the nobility and in favor of the crown. The process was gradual and complex, and its rate varied in the different parts of Europe. But the long-range effect was everywhere the same: gunpowder technology curbed, and finally extinguished, the freedom of landed magnates to exercise significant independent, organized military and political power. In earlier centuries private armies had been commonplace and private war endemic. In an age when no weapon but starvation or treachery could reliably prevail against a well-placed stone castle, and when the only effective warriors were armored horsemen, the feudal nobles had monopolized the military profession. The new weapons weakened this military basis of independent aristocratic power. Warfare in the age of gunpowder demanded a siege train of hundreds of cannon and thousands of well-equipped and well-trained infantrymen. Both defensive and offensive operations became enormously expensive, technically and financially beyond the means of any private individual—beyond the means, indeed, of all except the rulers of important states. To be sure, noble magnates still went to war. Their numbers, training, and bellicosity remained the most reliable measure of a country's military competence. In some cases with reluctance, in others with cynicism, most commonly with prudent foresight, they adapted themselves successfully to technological change and continued to lead Europe's armies in the sixteenth century as they had in the past. What they could rarely do was to own or control directly an artillery train, or with their own resources, organize, pay, and field effective contingents of foot. This progressive loss of their former direct and independent control over men and arms—a loss qualified by their kings' continued dependence on their military talents, traditions, skill, and experience—was to influence profoundly the relation of magnates to rulers, and more generally, the development of the early modern state.

Gradually the increasing use of firearms modified even men's moral responses to war. A handful of sixteenth-century intellectuals were pacifists

[3]*Discourses*, III, xl.

Mars and Venus. *Painting by Veronese. The goddess of love and concord subdues the god of war and discord. Their coupling produced a daughter, Harmony.* Metropolitan Museum, New York.

and condemned the brutish immorality of all war. A few Christians opposed war on religious grounds, notably the Anabaptists, who quaintly believed that the commandment "Thou shalt not kill" was meant to be observed literally. Everyone agreed that soldiers were detestable. "The whole science of warfare," wrote a Florentine theologian, "has been turned into brigandage, and there is no faith or piety in the men who pursue martial service. They are full of treachery, theft, sacrilege, perjury, blasphemy, cruelty toward even innocent prisoners, drunkenness, gambling, and sodomy."[4] But most men of substance, as they have in every age, defended "just" wars, that is, wars necessary for the preservation of peace, the repelling of aggressive foes, and the prevention of acts of injustice. Commonly, too, war was glorified, for man was thought to possess a balanced capacity for both action and thought, arms and letters. The ideal man developed both. Venus and Mars were a favorite subject of Renaissance painting, their conjunction suggesting the necessary, indeed

[4]St. Antoninus of Florence, *Summa sacrae theologiae.* Quoted by Edward Surtz, *The Praise of Wisdom. A Commentary on the Religious and Moral Problems of St. Thomas More's Utopia* (Chicago, 1957), p. 271.

desirable coexistence of tenderness and violence. War was regarded as the most fitting subject of epic, pageant, romance, and history. War even had an ethical relevance, since it encouraged noble virtues like courage, fortitude, and loyalty. But as the horror of firearms spread, men began to picture war in a more fearful image. In art they revived the Roman war goddess Bellona, associated her with gunpowder, provided her with an arsenal of cannon, muskets, mines, and grenades, and lamented her ruinous brutality. The slow transformation of sensibility by a military technology that erases the poetry of war had begun.

THE ORIGINS OF MODERN SCIENCE

The sensibilities and values of western men were to be even more profoundly molded by the method and pursuit of science.

Only modern western civilization has produced a fully developed science. The breakthrough to such a science, so different and so much more successful than the sciences of the ancient Greeks, the medieval Arabs, the Indians, and the Chinese, occurred between the publication of Copernicus' *On the Revolutions of the Celestial Spheres* in 1543 and the appearance of Newton's *Principia* in 1687. We call it the scientific revolution. This fundamental intellectual mutation, rapid and dauntingly complex, rested, of course, on earlier work. Specifically, it was the fruit of a novel and sophisticated methodology created in the late Middle Ages and in the Renaissance. The new method combined three procedures, one logical, one experimental, and one mathematical. Each of these procedures had been the intellectual tool in a distinct social or scholarly milieu. Their separate histories in the fourteenth and fifteenth centuries form the prehistory of the scientific revolution. Their gradual combination in the early sixteenth century into a fruitful method of discovery laid the foundation for the unparalleled enlargement of man's understanding and mastery of nature achieved by the generations of Galileo and Newton, and is the most important contribution of the Renaissance to the development of modern science.

The logical component of modern scientific method was given its initial form by fourteenth-century scholastics, teachers of logic and philosophy in the arts faculties of the universities of Paris and Oxford, and perfected in the Renaissance by teachers of philosophy and medicine at the universities of Bologna and Padua. They named it the method of resolution and composition. "Resolution" was an inductive movement from observed effects to their cause, a demonstration *a posteriori*. "Composition" was a deductive movement from cause to effect, an *a priori* explanation.

Jacopo Zabarella (1533–1589), the greatest sixteenth-century logician, admirably defined the purpose of this procedure: to lead us in "syllogistic form from known principles by a necessary movement to the knowledge of an unknown conclusion."[5] For example, an investigator observes the phenomenon of shadows. From his empirical observations he constructs a hypothesis to account for them. This is the *a posteriori*, inductive movement from effects to a tentative statement of their cause. But this is only half his task. He must now prove his generalization by checking it against the observed phenomena, more precisely by deducing effects which must follow if the generalization is true and by testing these effects empirically. This is composition, the *a priori* deductive movement from cause to effect. The demonstration took the form of an Aristotelian syllogism reshaped for purposes of scientific investigation. An eclipse of the moon is a striking shadow effect. Describe it as the major term of a syllogism: "The moon in eclipse has an opaque body interposed between it and its source of light." The generalization or cause, previously induced from this and other observations of shadows, follows as the middle term: Whatever has an opaque body interposed between it and its source of light loses its light." Therefore—the syllogism's conclusion—the moon loses its light *because* an opaque body has interrupted its source. The middle term is thus shown to be the cause of the major term in a tight, logical structure of hypothesis and observation.

The method of resolution and composition produced some remarkable results. Fourteenth-century French and English scholastics defined uniform speed. They discovered a form of the theorem describing uniform acceleration: "a moving body uniformly acquiring or losing that increment [of velocity] will traverse in some given time a magnitude completely equal to that which it would traverse if it were moving continuously through the same time with the mean degree [of velocity]."[6] They probed weak points in Aristotle's theory of motion. Aristotle had believed that rest was natural and motion a disturbance of nature. In order for a thing to move, something else must push or pull it. This is mistaken common sense. The difficulty is to explain projectile motion. Why does a rock continue to fly through the air after it has left the thrower's hand? Aristotle had unconvincingly supposed that the rock was moved along by air pushed apart by its progress and forcefully reuniting behind it. The scholastics revived a superior hypothesis, first suggested by a sixth-century Byzantine critic of Aristotle's mechanics, and explained the continuance of projectile motion by a force they called *impetus*, an intrinsic qualitative power infused into the projectile by the projector. Most scholars thought that this force was gradually dissipated like heat, but one or two argued that it was destroyed only by resistance of the medium or by the object's

[5]*In Libros Aristotelis Physicorum commentarii.* Quoted by Neal W. Gilbert, *Renaissance Concepts of Method* (New York, 1960), p. 168.

[6]Marshall Clagett, *The Science of Mechanics in the Middle Ages* (Madison, Wis., 1959), p. 284.

weight, an intimation of the modern definitions of momentum and inertia.

For a century and a half, scholastic physics got no further. One reason for this arrested development was the limited knowledge of mathematics during this period. The late medieval scholastics were far below the highest level of Greek competence in mathematics, and they tended to deny that the abstractions of geometry had any significant link with physical reality; for, they said, there are no observable circles or triangles in nature. Moreover, their method was too exclusively logical. They were reluctant, in practice, to subject their theories to the test of experiment. They considered a hypothesis established if they had logically refuted any argument brought against it. At the same time, many of their more attractive hypotheses were advanced simply to show that a non-Aristotelian explanation was, in fact, logically possible, while they themselves, with an exaggerated respect for authority, continued to believe that Aristotle's explanation was the true one. They were disputatious, and too often preferred the sophistical victory of debate to the empirical search for truth. They calculated, but saw little need to measure.

The habits of experiment and measurement evolved in a social and intellectual milieu wholly different from that of university and clerical scholarship: the studios of Italian artist-engineers of the fifteenth and sixteenth centuries. These men were laymen and superior craftsmen, mechanics who had begun as apprentices educated in a master's workshop. Their thinking was quantitative and causal. Their observation was trained to precision by painting and carving. In order to reproduce nature more accurately they studied birds, flowers, and foliage; learned the optical laws of perspective; used the scalpel and recorded their dissections in brilliant anatomical drawings. In the course of analyzing the proportions of antique ruins and planning their own buildings, measurement became for them a conscious professional discipline. Besides being artists in the limited sense, they were mechanical, military, and hydraulic engineers. They designed cannon, laid out canals and elaborate fountains, built machines for princely theatricals. They made clocks, lutes, and maps, nautical and astronomical instruments. They experimented constantly. They were the real pioneers of empirical research, and their rules of thumb constituted the modest beginnings of the physical laws of modern science.

The greatest of the Italian artist-engineers was Leonardo da Vinci (1452–1519). We know a great deal about him because an impressive collection of his manuscript notes has survived. The notebooks give us a close view of his experimental method and expose both the virtues and the limitations of his scientific work. They record hundreds of experiments. They prove eloquently that for Leonardo experimentalism was a habit, even a philosophy of knowledge. "Wisdom," he wrote, "is the daughter of experiment." "Experience is never at fault." And again: "I

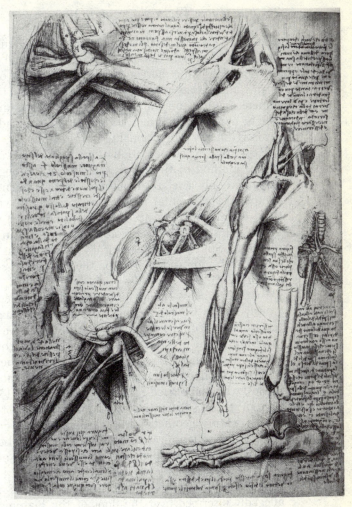

Anatomical Studies (The Shoulder). *Drawing by Leonardo da Vinci. Leonardo dissected more than thirty corpses in his exploration of the human body. Windsor Castle, Royal Library.*

know well that because I have not had a literary education there are some who will think in their arrogance that they are entitled to set me down as uncultured—the fools. . . . They do not see that my knowledge is gained rather from experience than from the words of others: from experience, which has been the master of all those who have written well." The notebooks show him testing his theories by making small scale models and seeing if they work. He knew that experiments must be repeated. His techniques and apparatus were ingenious. But he was a naive empiricist. The scholastics had too much theory; he had too little. And he knew no more mathematics than they. He mentions Archimedes, but he knew him more as a magnificent legend than as a fruitful influence in his work. He was very successful in areas where careful observation and experimental pertinacity are more important than theoretical sophistication—in anat-

omy, for example, or in finding quantitative rules connecting two varia-
bles, one of which can be altered at will and the other observed with
convenience. Thus he conducted experiments on the strength of loaded
beams and struts, placing weights of different sizes on beams of varying
dimensions and on different sites on the beams and observing at what
weight breakage occurred. Ultimately he concluded that the strength of a
beam is directly proportional to its breadth.

Repetitive experimentation alone, however, was not enough, just as the
logical method of the scholastics was not enough. Leonardo's discoveries
explained only a relatively narrow range of phenomena. To organize more
complex experimental results and produce a viable scientific method a
third component was needed: an acquaintance with mathematics, and a
more sophisticated conception of its function in understanding the physical world. Superior mathematical knowledge was the indirect contribution
of a third professional group, the humanist scholars of the sixteenth
century.

By 1500, many Italian humanists knew Greek, and they were prodi-
giously active in discovering, editing, translating, and publishing Greek
texts hitherto unknown in the Latin West. An important phase of this
reappropriation of Greek antiquity was the recovery and renewed understanding of major Greek scientific and mathematical works, those of
Pappus, Apollonius, Diophantus, Hero, and above all, those of Archimedes, which appeared in Latin translation in 1543. Allied to the exploration of these substantive works, knowledge of which transformed sixteenth-century geometry and algebra, was a growing emphasis on the
cultural and scientific importance of mathematics. Humanist educational
practice stressed mathematics at the expense of logic. The professional
teaching of mathematics spread in universities, and there was hardly a
Renaissance writer who did not remind his readers of the sentence
allegedly inscribed over the door of the Platonic Academy: "Let no one
unskilled in geometry enter here." Most important, perhaps, a higher level
of mathematical knowledge and sophistication—encouraged by a widespread enthusiasm for Platonism—began to convince scientists that nature
itself was mathematical in structure, that the circles and triangles of
geometry could, in fact, make intelligible the apparent confusion of
sensible experience.

Why this insistence on the mathematical intelligibility of nature was to
be so important is suggested by Galileo's paradoxical praise of Copernicus
and his supporters for being "able to make reason so conquer sense that,
in defiance of the latter, the former became the mistress of their belief."[7]
Galileo did not mean that the evidence of experience was unimportant.

[7]*Dialogue Concerning the Two Chief World Systems—Ptolemaic and Copernican,*
trans. by Stillman Drake (Berkeley, Calif., 1953), p. 328.

He was suggesting that common sense is deceptive and that the under-brush of empirical fact could better be cleared away by mathematical abstraction than by simple inductions from experience. Almost all science before the sixteenth century had been dominated by naive and direct generalization from sense experience. The result was common-sense expla-nations and empirical rules rather than scientific laws. What was needed in order to formulate scientific laws was the development of a radical habit of abstraction, the will to penetrate the confusing diversity of the visible world and to express its observed regularities in mathematical formulas. This demanded imaginative bravura—the power, for example, to visualize bodies falling in a vacuum or moving in the pure reaches of Archimedean space. It required ruthless simplification and concentration on formulating hypothetical abstractions which could be tested quantita-tively. It meant studying phenomena in their simplest quantitative rela-tions with other phenomena, as mathematical entities rather than as sensible bodies with the inevitable peculiarities and irregularities of nature. It meant a geometrizing of experience. The sixteenth-century recovery of Greek mathematics made this way of thinking possible.

Before 1500 the three components of modern scientific method—the logical, the experimental, and the mathematical—developed in isolation, for the aims, sympathies, intellectual interests, and social positions of the professional groups with which they were connected were too diverse to permit fruitful communication among them. After 1500, the gaps between these groups narrowed rapidly. A successful eclecticism was made possible by interlocking developments of great complexity. One factor, clearly, was printing. The diffusion and wider availability of learned, technical, and mathematical books encouraged the flow of ideas among different professional groups. The cultural ideals of humanism influenced all edu-cated men. Fashion, if nothing else, forcefully imposed newly translated texts on their attention, while an increasing number of scholars learned Greek and began to study Greek science in its original sources. Artist-engi-neers won a higher social position than they had enjoyed before. Their artistic and technological achievements aroused the interests of both liter-ary men and scholastic philosophers and diminished the traditional con-tempt of the academically learned for manual and mechanical operations. Scholars with university training began to write in Latin about gunnery, navigation, and mining. The great mathematician Niccolò Tartaglia (*c.* 1500–1557), for example, devoted much time and energy to problems of ballistics. The physician Georg Bauer (1490–1555), or Agricola, as in humanist fashion he preferred to call himself, was an excellent Latinist, a correspondent of Erasmus and the author both of a book on fossils (*De natura fossilium*, 1546) and of the most important sixteenth-century treatise on mining and metallurgy, the *De re metallica*, published posthu-mously in 1556. Superior craftsmen acquired academic learning. Thus

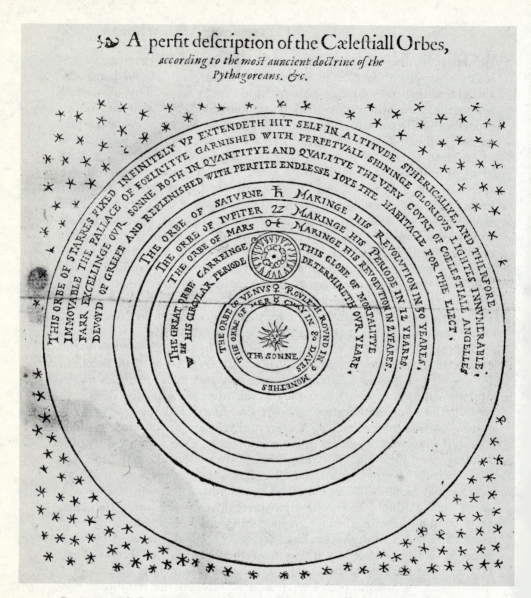

A perfit description of the Cælestiall Orbes,
according to the most auncient doctrine of the Pythagoreans. &c.

THIS ORBE OF STARRES FIXED INFINITELY VP EXTENDETH HIT SELF IN ALTITVDE SPHERICALLYE. AND THERFORE IMMOVABLE THE PALLACE OF FOELICITYE GARNISHED WITH PERPETVALL SHININGE GLORIOVS LIGHTES INNVMERABLE. FARR EXCELLINGE OVR SONNE BOTH IN QVANTITYE AND QVALITYE THE VERY COVRT OF CŒLESTIALL ANGELLES. DEVOYD OF GREEFE AND REPLENISHED WITH PERFITE ENDLESSE IOYE THE HABITACLE FOR THE ELECT.

THE ORBE OF SATVRNE ♄ MARINGE HIS REVOLVTION IN 30 YEARES.

THE ORBE OF IVPITER ♃ MAKINGE HIS REVOLVTION IN 12 YEARES.

THE ORBE OF MARS ♂ MARINGE HIS REVOLVTION IN 2 YEARES.

THE GREAT ORBE CARREINGE ♁ THIS GLOBE OF MORTALITYE WTH HIS CIRCVLAR PERIODE DETERMINETH OVR YEARE.

THE ORBE ☿ VENVS ♀ ROVLETH ROVND IN 9 MONETHES

THE ORBE OF ☿ MER ☿ CVRY IN 8o DAYES

THE SONNE

Copernicus' heliocentric hypothesis. *A sixteenth-century English adaptation of a diagram from the 1543 edition of the* Revolutions of the Celestial Spheres. *Within the sphere of the fixed stars, the orbs of Saturn, Jupiter, Mars, Earth, Venus, and Mercury revolve in circles around the central sun.*

Leonardo learned Latin in middle age and came into direct contact with humanism and traditional university scholarship. From this fusion of professional habits and procedures emerged a new sort of natural philosopher, the *filosofo geometra*, as he was called in Italy, a scientist who combined in his research the syllogistic procedure of the scholastics, the experimental habit of the artist-engineers, and the mathematical knowledge made available by scholars trained in Greek. Nicolaus Copernicus (1473–1543) is a striking early example of this new type. He studied the scholastic Aristotelian tradition at its greatest centers, Padua and Bologna. He learned Greek, and came to believe profoundly in the possibility and importance of discovering simple geometric regularities in nature. And he absorbed the causal thinking and manual dexterity of the artists and engineers; there is some reason to believe, for example, that he painted a self-portrait, and reliable evidence indicates that he built many of his own astronomical instruments.

The same process of decompartmentalization produced a new scientific method. The vulgar empiricist became aware that he could give his multitude of observations theoretical structure by applying to his data the scholastic's method of resolution and composition. The scholastic logician was stimulated to measure and experiment. The mathematician learned to bend his abstract imagination to the demands of the scientific syllogism and the controlled experiment. The result was a powerful intellectual tool, a methodology whose core was the traditional scientific syllogism, but whose middle term now took the form of a mathematical formula, while the consequences deduced from this mathematical hypothesis were rigorously tested by further observation and experiment. With this tool the scientific revolution was made.

Yet even in the middle of the sixteenth century an acute observer could not have predicted revolution. The first major document of the new science, Copernicus' *On the Revolutions of the Celestial Spheres*, appeared in 1543. Those who accepted his views before 1560 can, literally, be counted on the fingers of one hand. Opponents too were few, but they were, like Luther, vigorous: "The fool wants to overturn the whole science of astronomy." The typical attitude was indifference. Yet with the single-minded impetuosity of genius, Copernicus had reconstructed the heavens. Embedded in his largely traditional structure were the novel assertion that the earth rotated annually around the sun and a detailed demonstration that the mathematical consequences of the earth's motion fitted existing knowledge of the heavens. In 1560 most men still pictured the universe as Dante had: closed, tidy, man-measured and man-centered. But with Copernicus' assertion of the earth's status as a planet, the first great step had already been taken toward the Newtonian World Machine.

PORTUGUESE VOYAGES OF EXPLORATION

"The owl of Minerva," said Hegel, "flies only as dusk is falling"; he meant that only toward the end of a historical process can we grasp its full significance. Until very recently the economy and civilization of

Europe dominated the world. The passing of that domination in our own day makes us understand all the more clearly the significance of the Portuguese voyages of exploration. They marked the beginning of European expansion over the world: the political colonization of vast areas, the economic penetration which transformed the earth into Europe's economic hinterland, the Christian imperialism which was only a part of a vast effort to impose European cultural patterns on the whole globe. They began the European age of world history.

At the same time, it should not surprise us that many sixteenth-century Europeans were no more impressed by the importance of the discoveries than they were by the truth of the heliocentric hypothesis. So intelligent a man as Erasmus hardly mentioned them. Luther saw them only as providential channels for the dissemination of the Gospel. Far more books were published about the Turks than about India or China. A French description of the world written in the second half of the sixteenth century does not mention America. As ignorant of their future as we are of ours, the contemporaries of the explorers assessed their discoveries far more narrowly than we do. They measured them in terms of their own immediate personal interest and ambition. Or they judged them by the provincial standards of a closed society intolerant of the foreign values of non-European cultures. In both cases they were blinkered by their particular position in time, at the beginning rather than at the end of an era.

They were all the less likely to magnify the results of expansion because the initial impulse to exploration and discovery was itself narrow and concrete. It is misleading to suppose that important historical events must necessarily have equally important causes. The discoveries are a case in point. They began the extension of European influence throughout the world. But their original motive was more prosaic—a desire, colored by crusading emotion and justified by missionary zeal, to find gold in Africa.

The Portuguese descent of the African coast, which began in 1415 with the capture of Ceuta, was at once an episode in the long struggle of Christianity and Islam and an attempt to reach the sources of an ancient and well-known trade in gold. The capture of Ceuta, a Moslem city at the northern tip of Morocco, was a traditional crusading enterprise; and even after Prince Henry the Navigator (1394–1460), a younger son of King John I of Portugal, had come to see it as the first step in a coherent program of African expansion, hostility to Islam remained a powerful motive behind Portuguese exploration. One of Henry's initial aims, for example, was to measure Mohammedan power in Africa. Another was to contact directly the mysterious Prester John, a Christian ruler of vast and opulent domains whom Europeans had come to identify with the negus, the emperor of Ethiopia, and to draw him into a Christian alliance against the infidel. Later the Portuguese hoped to find Christians in India, the

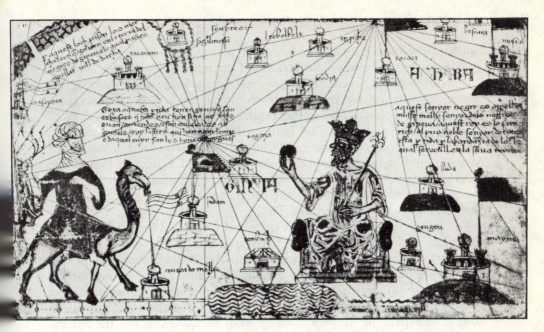

Mansa Musa, King of Guinea. *Detail of the Catalan Atlas, a map drawn on the island of Majorca in 1375. Bibliothèque Nationale, Paris.*

descendants of those traditionally said to have been converted by the apostle Thomas; while for the more numerous Indians who were not Christians their hope was speedy conversion.

But the hopeful blossoms of conversion were nourished by roots of commerce, and the first commercial lure was gold. In 1375 a Spanish Jew had drawn a map of Africa that was to become famous. At the center of the Sahara the map showed the figure of a Negro monarch with a scepter in one hand and a nugget of gold in the other. The legend read: "This Negro lord is called Musa Mali, lord of the Negroes of Guinea. So abundant is the gold which is found in his country that he is the richest and most noble king in all the land." The cartographer's information was perfectly correct as far as it went. Mansa Musa, to give the king his real name, is known from other sources. He made a pilgrimage to Mecca in 1321 and on the way dazzled the Egyptians in Cairo with a prodigal display of wealth. His kingdom was only one of several organized states in the great bend of the Niger River whose wealth and power were based on profits from the gold trade. This trade was a very ancient one, and from at least the tenth century powdered gold had flowed into the Mediterranean world from the West African Sudan (most notably from the region bounded on the north by the Senegal River, on the west by the Falémé, and on the east by the Niger) and from the territories of the Ashanti north of the Gold Coast. The primitive natives of these regions got the gold from river gravels. They traded it to more sophisticated Moslem Negroes for salt, the one absolutely indispensable product they lacked. These, in turn, carried it inland to the great markets on the southern fringe of the Sahara: Niani, the capital of Mansa Musa's kingdom of Mali; the independent city of Jenné, an important center of trade and culture farther up the Niger; and the prosperous commercial centers of Walata and Timbuktu. Here the merchants of the south met their white coreligionists from the north and east, and the gold began the long journey by camel caravan across the Sahara to the Mediterranean ports of the Maghrib—Algiers, Bône, and Tunis.

For centuries merchants from Venice and Genoa, Marseilles and Barcelona, had traded on the Barbary Coast and bought the goods so laboriously transported across the desert from the distant countries of the Negroes, the area already known as Guinea. Prince Henry's fundamental objective—and it was one requiring great imagination in conception, and courage, skill, and tenacity in execution—was to tap the gold trade at its source, to bypass the Moslem middlemen of the Maghrib and the Sahara, to win control of a trade hitherto in infidel, and often hostile, hands. He was all the more anxious to do this because in Portugal, as in all Europe, the precious metals, and especially gold, were notably scarce in the fifteenth century. A monopoly of one of Europe's principal sources of gold would bring with it power and profit. The voyages sponsored by Prince Henry were not, therefore, leaps into a dark unknown. To be sure, they demanded skill in navigation and cartography and innovations in shipbuilding and naval gunnery. And they necessarily involved exploration and an expansion of knowledge. But they rested on earlier knowledge of Africa gathered by an international group of scholars and seamen—Christians, Jews, and Moslems in Henry's service—and their aim was precise: to seek out the gold of the Guinea Negroes.

Prince Henry's will and imagination directed the first stage of the Portuguese advance. Almost every year, voyages were made down the African coast. By 1460, the year of Henry's death, Portuguese sailors had arrived off Guinea. Between 1460 and 1480 they explored the territory and began its commercial exploitation. King John II (ruled 1481–1495), an enthusiastic expansionist, assumed the title of lord of Guinea. Contact was made with the rulers of West Africa. Forts and trading stations were established. By the end of the century the Portuguese had drawn into their hands a very large proportion of the trade once monopolized by African Moslems. Gold now went to Europe by sea, directly to Lisbon and Antwerp, rather than over the old caravan routes to Algiers and Tunis and ultimately to Genoa and Venice. The result in the sixteenth century was severe economic depression for the cities of the Maghrib and a brilliant prosperity for Portugal. Already by the end of the 1440's Portugal commanded enough gold to issue its first national gold coin, the *crusado*. By 1502, an ordinary shipment of gold weighed two thousand ounces and normally twelve or fifteen ships arrived every year, each bringing a similar quantity. But gold was not all. In the 1470's the Portuguese colonized the island of São Tomé off the Cameroons, planted sugarcane, worked the estates with Negro slaves, and shipped sugar to Europe. In return for cheap, loud-colored fabrics, rings, bracelets, and copper dishes, they acquired ivory, ebony, and melegueta pepper (cruder than eastern pepper, but cheaper). Far more lucrative even than their trade in these tropical products was their commerce in slaves. During the second half of the fifteenth century over a thousand slaves a year reached Lisbon from Africa. The slave trade would continue for centuries, remaining profitable long after the gold and silver of Mexico and Peru had reduced the West African supply to insignificance. Until 1530, gold was more important than slaves; after 1530, slaves were more important than gold, and the Guinea coast became significant chiefly as a source of African forced labor for the colonists of the New World.

At what precise moment the Portuguese raised their sights from the gold and slaves of Guinea to the spices of India is unknown. It is probable that by the last decade of his life Prince Henry imagined reaching India by sea. It is certain that by 1480, when the exploitation of the Guinea coast had become continuous and efficient, the principal objective of Portuguese ambition had shifted to the East. New and rapid progress down the African coast was made in the 1480's, reaching its climax in 1487 when Bartholomeu Dias (*c.* 1450–1500) voyaged around the Cape, named "Good Hope, for the promise it gave of finding India, so desired and for so many years sought after." Fulfillment of this promise was delayed for ten more years. Then in 1497 the king of Portugal "dispatched four vessels to make discoveries and go in search of spices."[8] On May 20, 1498, Vasco da Gama (*c.* 1469–1524) anchored off the Malabar Coast.

The twentieth-century American, taking for granted refrigeration, ease and rapidity of transport, and the resulting extraordinary variety of diet, may find perplexing his ancestors' lust for spices. We must remember some of the foods Europeans lacked. They had no rice, no corn, no potatoes; little cheese or butter; fresh fruits and green vegetables only in season, and few of these in the larger cities; almost no sugar. Fresh meat was relatively plentiful at the moment of massive slaughter in the autumn. At other times of the year meat was salted and more than a little high; and since its source was excess work animals, it was hardly of prime quality. The ordinary diet was based on bread and gruel, enlivened by pickled cabbage, turnips, peas, lentils, and onions. The entire art of

---

[8]Álvaro Vehlo, "A Journal of the First Voyage of Vasco da Gama in 1497–9," in *Portuguese Voyages*, ed. by C. D. Ley (London and New York, 1947), p. 3.

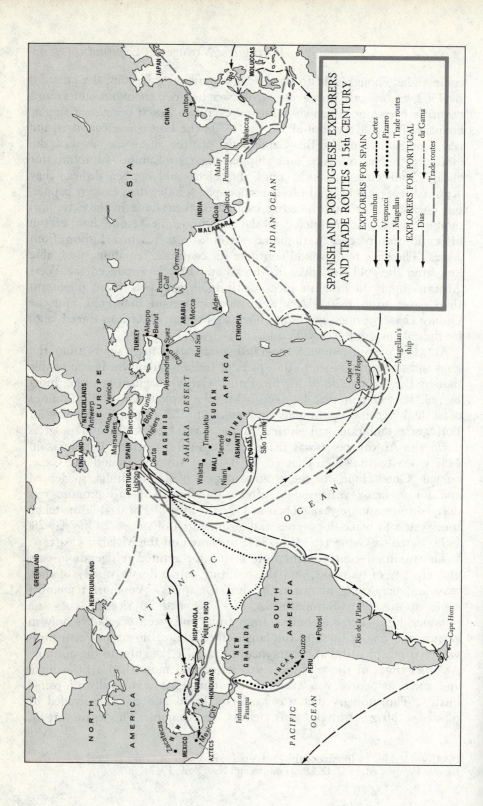

SPANISH AND PORTUGUESE EXPLORERS
AND TRADE ROUTES · 15th CENTURY

EXPLORERS FOR SPAIN

Columbus
Cortez
Vespucci
Pizarro
Magellan
Trade routes

EXPLORERS FOR PORTUGAL

da Gama
Dias
Trade routes

cookery lay in the sauce, and the piquancy of the sauce lay in its spices. Men wanted spices because they teased the palate, disguised the disagreeable or dull, gave variety to the menu. They wanted them for medicines and drugs, for perfumes and for use in religious ceremonies. The result was a most powerful demand for camphor, cinnamon, nutmeg, ginger, mace, cardamon, and above all, for pepper and cloves—all products of Asia and excessively rare in Europe.

When da Gama arrived in Calicut the trade in spices between Europe and the Far East was ancient and well organized. At Malacca, on the western coast of the Malay peninsula, junks from Canton and spice craft from the East Indies met the ships of the Moslem merchants who controlled the trade of the Indian Ocean. The spices were then shipped to the second great area of redistribution and transshipment, the Malabar Coast, especially the city of Calicut. From there the spices took either of two ancient routes to the Mediterranean: to Ormuz, at the entrance to the Persian Gulf, through the gulf, up the Euphrates River to Aleppo and Beirut; or to Aden, through the Red Sea, and then overland to Suez and Alexandria. At Alexandria and Beirut the precious cargoes for the first time passed into the hands of Christian merchants, mostly Venetian, for at the end of the fifteenth century Venice still successfully enforced the monopoly of the Mediterranean spice trade she had imposed during the Middle Ages. Along this vastly extended line of traffic the trade enriched all who touched it, and from the Moslem merchants of the Indian Ocean to the sultans of Egypt and Turkey and the Venetian traders, all had a vested interest in maintaining the old routes.

The arrival of the Portuguese in the Indian Ocean threatened them all; and it became the task of the Portuguese to repeat on a vastly greater scale the strategy they had employed in cornering Sudanese gold—to wrest commercial control of the eastern seas from the Moslems, destroy the Moslem monopoly, divert the traffic in spices from the routes leading to Venice by way of Ormuz, Aden, Beirut, and Alexandria, and instead ship the cargo around the Cape of Good Hope directly to Lisbon. In 1509 they annihilated a large fleet assembled by the Mameluke sultan of Egypt with the connivance of the Venetians. Under the leadership of Affonso de Albuquerque, governor of the Portuguese in India, (1509–1515), they destroyed Calicut, captured Ormuz, and conquered Goa and made it the trading center of the Malabar Coast. Malacca, a commercial nerve center, fell in 1511. These victories of the first twenty years of the sixteenth century laid the foundation of the Portuguese empire in the Indian Ocean and made possible the magnificent flow of spices to Lisbon, and from Lisbon to Antwerp, which began between 1501 and 1504. By 1520 the bridgeheads of European imperialism were firmly planted in the East.

The Portuguese rapidly captured an important share of the European market. In 1515 even Venetians were forced to buy pepper in Lisbon. The opening of a direct sea route to the Indies did not, however, put an immediate end to the Mediterranean spice trade. The flow of spices along the old routes continued. The Portuguese broke the Moslem monopoly of the Indian Ocean, but they never succeeded in establishing a monopoly of their own. Specifically, they failed to capture Aden. It fell in 1538, not to the Portuguese, but to the Turks. The Red Sea became a Turkish lake. In 1560 the amount of pepper and other spices that reached Alexandria and the Mediterranean was still as great as the amount that reached Lisbon. The ultimate triumph of the oceanic route was inevitable; and da Gama's voyage initiated the shift of Europe's center of gravity from the Mediterranean to the Atlantic, from Italy to the Netherlands, England, and France. But the triumph was long delayed. Economic preponderance did not shift decisively to the north until the seventeenth century.

THE NEW WORLD

In 1492, shortly before the Portuguese, having thrust south and east, entered the Indian Ocean, the Spaniards were sailing westward across the Atlantic. The motives of the two were identical: to acquire wealth and save souls. "We came here," said one of Cortes' foot soldiers, "to serve God and the king, and also to get rich."[9] Christopher Columbus (1451–1506), like Henry the Navigator, was touched by the fact that "many people believing in idolatries were lost by receiving doctrine of perdition."[10] He left Spain prepared to smite the heathen, and he did, in fact, convert them in droves to the true and European faith. He also wanted to get rich. His first voyage was a race to India by a mariner convinced that he could reach it more easily and rapidly by crossing the Atlantic than by sailing around Africa. The result was very different from his expectations. The Portuguese had looked first for gold in Guinea, and their search had insensibly led them to the sources of the spice trade. The Spanish looked first for an alternative and better route to the spices, pearls, and treasures of the Indies. They discovered instead a new world, but they found there gold and silver in hitherto unimagined quantities. Consequently, while the Portuguese empire in the East took the form of a loose string of forts and trading stations around the periphery of the Indian Ocean, the Spanish empire in the New World became a vast and settled mining community. Begun in rivalry, the two empires were soon linked by the fact that bullion from America was increasingly used to pay for the spices of the East. The commercial exploitation of Asia was made possible by the discovery of precious minerals in the West.

[9]Quoted by Lewis Hanke, *Bartolomé de las Casas* (The Hague, 1951), p. 9.
[10]*The Journal of Christopher Columbus*, ed. by C. R. Markham (*Works Issued by the Hakluyt Society*, Vol. LXXXVI, London, 1893), p. 16.

After Columbus' first voyage, the exploration and conquest of the New World proceeded with absolutely extraordinary rapidity. As long as he lived, Columbus himself believed that he had reached the Far East. His tenacity of illusion was not shared by many; and as his companions and successors came to realize that what they had come upon was not a goal, but an obstacle, they began a frantic search for a passage to India across or around it. This was the first motive for penetration of the Americas, the spur which led Amerigo Vespucci (1451–1512) to explore the Río de la Plata and Ferdinand Magellan (*c.* 1480–1521) between 1519 and 1521 to discover the southern strait and head westward across a Pacific Ocean which, with mistaken optimism, he thought was an arm of the Indian Ocean and an easy path to the Moluccas, themselves mistakenly believed to lie temptingly close to the Spanish settlements on the Isthmus of Panama. However, by the time Magellan's voyage had made clear the vastness of the Pacific and the hopeless impracticality of tapping the spices of the Moluccas from the West, gold had been discovered in the Caribbean islands and on the mainland. Henceforth, the lust for gold became the prime motive for exploration and colonization in Spanish America.

The geography and chronology of conquest and settlement were dictated by the location of gold and silver deposits and by the availability of Indian labor to work them. Mining was the first economic activity of the Spaniards in the New World; and the necessities of the mine would shape every detail of the political, economic, and social life of Spanish America throughout the colonial period. Gold was found first on the island of Hispaniola, Columbus' main discovery on his first voyage, then in Cuba and Puerto Rico. The central mountain core of these islands was honeycombed with gold-bearing quartz veins. Extraction was simple; gold was dredged from shallow surface diggings, or more often, worked from the sand and gravel of streams. But because a single person had to wash so long to get so little, only the presence of large numbers of docile Indians who could be forced to mine as virtual slaves made placer mining economically viable. When Columbus landed, over a million Indians lived in Hispaniola. By 1510 smallpox epidemics, famine, and the ruthless exploitation inseparable from placer mining had reduced the Indian population by about 90 per cent, to a hundred thousand. Deprived of Indian labor by the catastrophic decline of the native population, a minority of settlers remained on the islands and turned to cattle raising and agriculture, growing sugarcane with Negro slave labor imported from Africa. The surplus majority crossed over to the mainland, to Mexico and then to Peru, in the hope of finding more gold and the Indians to mine it.

The conquests of the Aztec and Inca empires are the epics of the Spanish appropriation of the New World. In 1519, a quarter of a century after Columbus' landfall, drawn by rumors of a wealthy empire on the

The Cerro Rico of Potosí. Unknown artist, about 1584. On the nearer flank of the mountain, llamas loaded with silver ore. In the foreground, reduction of ore by the mercury-amalgamation process. Hispanic Society of America, New York.

mainland, Hernando Cortes (1485–1547) left Cuba for Mexico. By 1532, Spaniards controlled the entire area of high Indian culture in central Mexico, and named it New Spain. A year later, in 1533, a second private freebooting expedition, led by Francisco Pizarro (*c.* 1470–1541) and recruited, promoted, and financed in Panama much as wildcat mining schemes are organized today, occupied Cuzco, the capital of the Inca Empire. Within fifteen years the two great kingdoms of the New World had fallen to a handful of utterly brave and utterly ruthless adventurers. The rewards were great. Spaniards now controlled the most populous areas of the continent, with twenty to twenty-five million inhabitants, ninety per cent of the population of pre-Columbian Central and South America. Cortes amassed an enormous booty of gold and silver ornaments from the Aztec lands; Pizarro seized the hoard of the Incas. But what made the *conquista* supremely important for early modern Europe was the accidental fact that several of the richest silver deposits in the world were within the newly conquered territories of New Spain and the viceroyalty of Peru:

at Zacatecas and Guanajuato, north of Mexico City, discovered between 1543 and 1548, and at Cerro Rico, the fabulous sugarloaf mountain of silver at Potosí, in the Bolivian highlands, discovered in 1545.

With the exploitation of these Mexican and Peruvian silver deposits placer mining gave way to the more elaborate and technically demanding vein mining as the fundamental economic activity of the New World, and silver replaced gold as the principal export of Spanish America to Europe. In the sixteenth century Potosí was the most important mining town in the world. It lay in the shadow of the celebrated Cerro Rico at an altitude of almost three miles above sea level. No temperature above 59 degrees Fahrenheit has ever been recorded there. At the time of the first census, a quarter of a century after the discovery of the lode, Potosí had a population of 120,000, larger than that of any city in Spain, approaching that of Paris and London, the greatest cities in Europe. The city had eighty churches, crawled with gamblers and prostitutes, and its inhabitants produced, in an uproarious atmosphere of violence, exploitation, and conspiracy, astronomical quantities of silver. Potosí and Zacatecas rapidly became the nerve centers of a colonial economy based on silver. The location of silver deposits determined the centers of population, while the nonmining population worked to house, feed, and equip the miners and scoured the country for the forced Indian labor which did the actual digging; in this economic pattern the development of agriculture, stock farming, manufacturing and trade became functions of mining. The colonists, to be sure, sent hides, copper, tobacco, sugar, and indigo to Europe too. But in amount and value, silver and gold far outweighed all other exports. The New World specialized in mining and exported bullion in exchange for manufactured goods. From the European point of view, treasure so far outweighed all other colonial products that the very fleets which sailed between Spain and the Indies were spoken of as the "fleets going to the Indies to bring back the gold and silver of His Majesty and private individuals."

However rich, the Mexican and Peruvian mines would not have made such a great impact on European civilization if they had not been imaginatively worked. Technological innovation was as crucial for silver production in the Renaissance as it was for the production of firearms and books. The best knowledge of mining and metallurgy in sixteenth-century Europe was German, summed up in the most comprehensive metallurgical textbook of the period, Agricola's *De re metallica*, a work much read in the New World. By the mid 1530's scores of Germans were active in American mines; and it was they who introduced into Mexico in 1555–1556 the mercury-amalgamation process, the decisive event in the history of American mining. In this process the ore, finely crushed in a water-powered stamp mill (also introduced by German miners), was mixed with water, mercury, salt, and impure copper sulphate in a spacious

Sixteenth-century mining. *Woodcut from Agricola's* De re metallica, *published in 1556. Shaft (A, D), tunnel (E), mouth of tunnel (F), and drift, a dark tunnel without a mouth open to daylight (B, C). The larger capital investments required by technological innovation imposed an increasingly capitalistic organization on the mining industry in the sixteenth century.*

rock-floored patio, then heaped into piles and allowed to stand until the silver ion chemically separated out of its compounds was amalgamated with the mercury. The amalgam was then washed, pressed into bars, and heated in a furnace, where the mercury volatilized, leaving bars of silver. Apparently this technique of reducing silver ores had been developed by miners in the territories of Venice late in the fifteenth century, but it was not used on a large scale before its introduction into America. There it proved valuable because it greatly increased the yield of silver ores and permitted the profitable exploitation of ores of a much lower grade than was possible with traditional methods. During the fifteen years after the new process reached Potosí in 1571, production quadrupled. Corresponding increases in production occurred at Zacatecas and Guanajuato.

During the sixteenth century, then, a flood of bullion poured into Europe. In the beginning, between 1503 and 1535, shipments were mostly of gold—from Hispaniola, Cuba, Puerto Rico, and Central America—obtained from placer mines or by collecting the golden objects worked and accumulated over the centuries by the pre-Columbian civilizations. After 1535, most bullion came from Mexico and Peru. Silver predominated to an ever greater extent, until by 1570 only 3 per cent of the treasure arriving in Seville was gold. In amount and value, the bullion Europe received increased throughout the century, forming a graphed curve which ascended slowly until 1535, climbed more sharply between 1536 and 1580 with the spoliation of the Incas, the discovery of Zacatecas and Potosí, and the introduction of the amalgamation process, and after 1580 rose precipitously to its peak in the 1590's. By the 1540's, about 1.5 million ounces of silver a year were pouring into Europe; in the 1590's, over 10 million. These figures take on more concrete historical meaning when we compare them with those of the contemporary European output. Most of Europe's silver was mined in Saxony, Bohemia, the Tyrol, and Hungary. Like iron and copper production, silver production there rose rapidly after 1460, to a peak of some 3 million ounces a year in the decade between 1525 and 1535. Before 1540, therefore, Europe produced about twice as much silver as Spanish America. But while the production of American silver was climbing vertiginously during the second half of the century, European production was declining with hardly less impressive rapidity. By the end of the century vastly more silver circulated in Europe than ever before, but it came from Mexico and Peru rather than from central Europe.

The most important sixteenth-century effect of the discoveries was the impact of the massive importation of American gold and silver on European prices. The increasing quantities of bullion in circulation reinforced inflationary pressures caused by a rising population and rapidly pushed up prices. The great price increase began early in the century. By 1560, Spanish prices had doubled. Elsewhere, inflation was more gradual, and its consequences were not felt acutely until the later sixteenth and early seventeenth centuries. But even in the earlier part of the century it hastened profound shifts in the distribution of wealth and economic power. Its role was the more revolutionary because its beginning coincided with a general, rapid expansion of the European economy between 1460 and 1560. In its early stages, the price revolution both stimulated commercial and industrial development and aggravated the social tensions inseparable from the emergence of capitalist modes of production in industry and agriculture. In this perspective, expansion abroad was itself a prolongation of expansion at home, while aggressive thrusts beyond the traditional boundaries of Christendom sharpened patterns of change inherent in the domestic development of the European economy.

CHAPTER 2

The Economic Expansion of Europe

OVER TWO CENTURIES of medieval economic expansion had ended by the beginning of the fourteenth century. The years between 1310 and the 1340's were a period of scarcity and often of famine. The Black Death—which reached Constantinople and the eastern Mediterranean littoral in 1347; Italy, Spain, and France in 1348; Switzerland, Austria, Germany, and Low Countries, and England in 1349; and Scandinavia and Poland in 1350—transformed this subsistence crisis into demographic catastrophe. Fragmentary evidence makes any estimates of the losses impressionistic. The most reliable suggest a reduction of from 12 to 60 per cent in the population, depending on the region, with a global loss for the period between 1348 and 1377 of about 40 per cent. Until far into the fifteenth century, population stagnated at a level well below that of 1347. In response to the fall in population, both prices and the volume of commerce and of industrial and agricultural production also declined or remained stationary. The long depression ended between 1460 and 1500. During the lifetimes of Luther, Copernicus, and Michelangelo, Europeans enjoyed a remarkable prosperity, a resurgence of industrial, commercial, financial, and demographic growth.

A CENTURY OF PROSPERITY

In the first half of the sixteenth century, population growth was large, generalized, and rapid. In most parts of Europe, population continued to increase, probably less rapidly and less uniformly in the second half of the century, until about 1620. The populations of Sicily and the kingdom of Naples doubled. Rome housed 50,000 people in 1526, 100,000 at the end of the century. In villages in the agricultural region south of Paris, the number of inhabitants doubled, tripled, even quadrupled between the end of the fifteenth century and the middle of the sixteenth. Changes in the rural population of the county of Hainaut, one of the seventeen provinces of the Netherlands, show a similar pattern. From 1365 to about 1470, the

42

population declined. Between 1470 and 1540–1541 it swung sharply upward. Antwerp expanded from 20,000 about 1440, to 50,000 about 1500, to 100,000 about 1560. Calculations of the total population of the Empire are wildly approximate, but studies of particular areas confirm a strong upward trend. Similar evidence of demographic vitality, though with important regional variations, can be found in Spain, Portugal, and Switzerland; elsewhere in the Netherlands and France; and in Scandinavia, Poland, and Russia.

A buoyant expansion of industrial production paralleled this growth in population. The quantities of iron, copper, and silver extracted from Europe's mines quadrupled. Very probably the output of the metallurgical industries expanded as rapidly as mining itself. Wholly new enterprises contributed to industrial prosperity. The production of printed books, for example, already so remarkable before 1500, soared in the sixteenth century, and its progress stimulated older industries like papermaking and the manufacture of spectacles. An increasing urban population encouraged building. Much of Rome as we know it today, to take a single instance, was built in the sixteenth century: fifty-four churches, including St. Peter's, sixty palaces, many villas outside the city, hundreds of buildings to house ordinary citizens, and scores of hotels for pilgrims. Thirty new streets were laid out; most of the old streets were paved; almost a hundred miles of ancient aqueducts were rebuilt to bring in drinking water.

The pattern of growth in textile manufacture, Europe's greatest industry ever since the thirteenth century, was more complex. The preeminence of Italy in the manufacture of woolens faded. Florence, which had produced about 100,000 bolts of cloth a year in the late fourteenth century, produced only 30,000 in 1500; but the decline in woolens was probably more than offset, in value if not in volume, by increases in silk production. The old woolen industry of the Netherlands, centered at Ypres, Ghent, and Bruges, was also in decline; but again the progress of a new industry, the manufacture of lighter, cheaper woolen fabrics, made up for the losses in the old. In the meantime, England, which in the Middle Ages had exported raw wool rather than cloth, superseded Italy and the Netherlands to become Europe's chief producer of heavy woolens of the best quality. In 1503–1509 England exported an average of 81,835 bolts of cloth a year and only 5,000 sacks of wool. By 1540–1548 her average yearly exports totaled 122,254 bolts.

These are only examples. They could be multiplied. Everywhere the evidence is the same; industry was booming, and depending on the commodity, production rose from two to five times what it had been before.

The increases in population and production, and the opening of new trade routes, made it profitable for European merchants to exchange a larger volume of goods over greater distances than they had in earlier

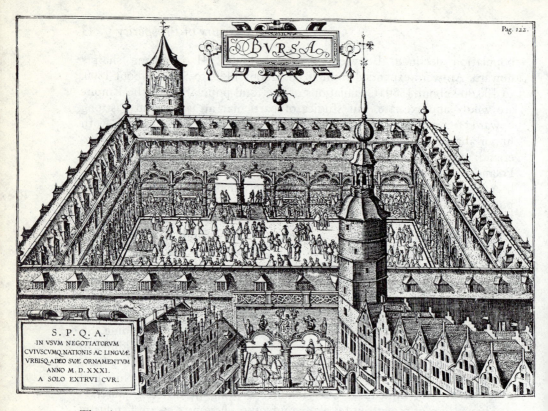

S. P. Q. A.
IN VSVM NEGOTIATORVM
CVIVSCVMQ.NATIONIS AC LINGVÆ
VRBISQ.ADEO SVÆ ORNAMENTVM
ANNO M.D.XXXI.
A SOLO EXTRVI CVR.

The Antwerp Bourse. Engraving from Ludovico Guicciardini's description of the Low Countries, published in 1565. The inscription reads: Erected in 1531 by the senate and people of Antwerp for the use of the merchants of every nation and language and to enhance the beauty of their city.

centuries. Portuguese merchants pushed east from Malacca to the centers of clove and nutmeg cultivation in the Moluccas, and then north to China and Japan. In the West, Seville was becoming the capital of an emerging Atlantic economy. European trade became literally worldwide in 1565 when Spanish galleons began regularly to link Manila and Mexican port of Acapulco. Chinese junks visited Manila every year and traded spices, silks, and procelains for Mexican silver, a traffic reproducing in miniature the exchange forming the basis of intercontinental commerce in the sixteenth century: American silver for eastern spices.

But the romance of intercontinental trade should not obscure the fundamental and more important exchanges of food, raw materials, and manufactured goods among the different regions of Europe itself. England exported its woolens to northern Europe, not to the East. Indians did not drink Portuguese wine; Englishmen did. Spanish wool went to the Netherlands and Italy; Hungarian copper to Germany and France. The market for Venetian goblets and mirrors, Ferrarese ceramics, Flemish tapestries,

Neapolitan silks, the products of the metallurgical industries of Nuremburg and Milan, was overwhelmingly European. And the heaviest volume of trade—economically and in tonnage far more weighty than the domestic trade in luxuries or any extra-European trade—involved the prosaic exchange, by way of Antwerp, Europe's commercial nerve center in the first half of the sixteenth century, of the cereals and forest products of the Baltic for the salt, wine, fish, vegetable oils, fruits, and dyestuffs of France and Spain and of southern and Mediterranean Europe in general. Commercial expansion abroad rested on the vigorous multiplication of commercial exchanges at home.

Bankers too enlarged their field of operations. In the Middle Ages banking had been almost exclusively an Italian monopoly. During the several decades before and after 1500, Frenchmen, Englishmen, and Germans joined Italians in consolidating the position of exchange banking in the economies of France and England, while financiers of many nationalities established banking houses in areas that had had few or none before—in Portugal, in Castile, and above all, in Germany. The organized money market widened, and in most of the great commercial centers, merchant-bankers built exchanges, often called bourses (after the Place de la Bourse in Bruges, a square much older than the banking institution to which it gave its name, and itself named for a Bruges family called, providentially, *de la Bourse, i.e.* "Purse"), where they bought and sold bills of exchange and speculated on currency rates. In 1531 the new Antwerp bourse was opened "to the merchants of every nation and language." The proud inhabitants boasted of its size and beauty and of the thousand merchants who crowded its daily sessions, so colorful in dress and so various in tongue that the bourse seemed a miniature world, a microcosm, bringing together everything to be found in the large one, the macrocosm.

In 1460 the most impressive business organization in Europe was the Medici Bank of Florence. By 1545, the Fugger Company of Augsburg was the largest firm. The Medici Bank (the firm was called a *banco*, but its activities were commercial and industrial as well as financial) had eight branch offices, the Fuggers, twenty-five. The Medici owned three modest textile firms. The Fuggers owned silver mines in the Tyrol and gold mines in Silesia, mined mercury in Spain, and controlled the larger part of copper production in Hungary. The Medici Bank got into financial difficulties—one among several more important reasons for its decline—when its agent at Bruges made a risky loan to the duke of Burgundy. At the time of the imperial election of 1519, Jakob Fugger loaned Charles, the Habsburg candidate, the colossal sum of 543,000 florins with which to bribe the electors, and he got it back with interest. Finally, the capital of the Medici Bank in 1451 was 90,000 florins; that of the Fuggers in 1547 was over ten times as great. The larger scale of economic activity in the sixteenth century is clear.

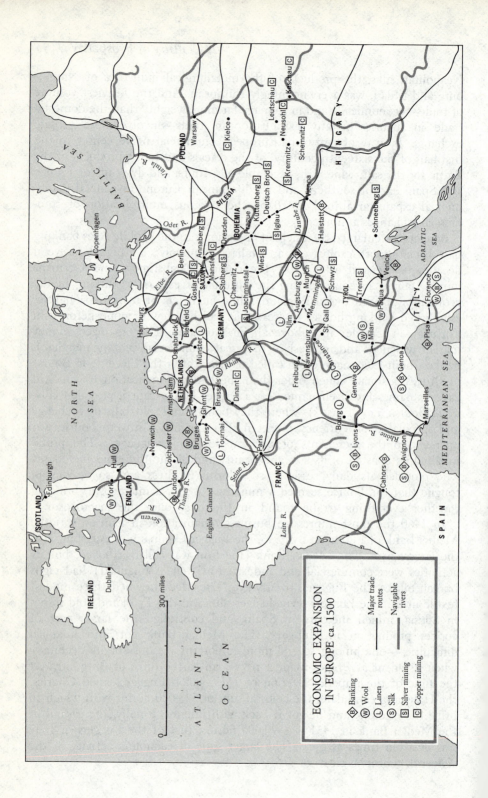

ECONOMIC EXPANSION
IN EUROPE ca. 1500

- Ⓑ Banking
- Ⓦ Wool
- Ⓛ Linen
- Ⓢ Silk
- Ⓢ Silver mining
- Ⓒ Copper mining

—— Major trade routes
—— Navigable rivers

300 miles

THE MERCHANT

The key figure in the expanding economy of Europe between 1460 and 1560 was the merchant. He belonged to an exclusive business elite. The merchant aristocracy of Venice numbered about 1,500 out of a total population of 100,000. In Florence in the same period very probably no more than 2 per cent of the inhabitants were engaged in international trade and banking or held positions of capitalist command in industry. The proportion was not larger elsewhere. In Lyons and Augsburg, Genoa and Seville, London and Antwerp, as in Florence and Venice, most men were shopkeepers, artisans, or wage workers. The merchant's dynamism, economic power, and influence, however, were out of all proportion to his numbers.

Furthermore, the diverse enterprises of the merchant illustrate many characteristics of the economic life of the age. In the high Middle Ages the merchant was usually an itinerant trader who moved his goods in person along the trade routes of the continent. By the early years of the sixteenth century he had been, by and large, a sedentary businessman for many generations. Under improved conditions of transportation, with the greater security for goods and persons enforced by the larger states, with cities like Bruges replacing fairs as centers of international exchange, with the beginning of marine insurance and reasonably rational and enforced codes of commercial law, the merchant became a man in an office. Here a mounting pile of ledgers, with their neat rows of assets and liabilities (recorded in Arabic rather than Roman numerals), informed him at a glance of the conditions of his affairs. From the office he conducted a continuous correspondence with his fellow merchants and with subordinates abroad (his factors), who kept him informed about the state of the market and about the many and varied circumstances, often political or military, affecting the supply and prices of the commodities and currencies he dealt in. Through the factors, who functioned as commission agents, he bought and sold. (Sales were not concluded, as they are today, on the basis of samples. Goods themselves had to be forwarded on speculation to the distant agent for sale, if possible, to local retailers—a system, clearly, that demanded of the merchant the nicest combination of flair and calculation.) He borrowed money and transferred it from place to place by a sophisticated system of bills of exchange. His firm was usually a family partnership, but he often pooled his capital with that of affluent associates for particular ventures: to handle large purchases or loans, to spread the risk in a difficult enterprise, to hire ships and ensure their armed protection. The sixteenth-century merchant was the resident motor of a complex economic machine.

A further characteristic of the early modern merchant, as of his medieval predecessor, was the extreme diversity of his enterprises. For although enough risk had been eliminated from international trade to enable the merchant to stay at home, conditions remained extremely hazardous by modern standards. The merchant therefore sought safety by putting his money into a large variety of separate ventures. Like all merchants until well into the eighteenth century, Renaissance traders dealt in as many commodities as possible, in many different parts of the world, investing only a fraction of their capital in each. Antonio, in Shakespeare's *Merchant of Venice*, expressed a common prudence:

> Believe me, no: I thank my fortune for it,
> My ventures are not in one bottom trusted,
> Nor to one place; nor is my whole estate
> Upon the fortune of this present year:
> Therefore my merchandise makes me not sad.

Even as large a firm as the Medici refused to specialize and dealt in commodities as various as raw wool, woolen cloth, silks, alum, dyestuffs, spices, olive oil, citrus fruits, raw cotton, gold thread, and much else besides.

But in diversifying his business the typical merchant went far beyond simply trading in numerous commodities. The very concept of "merchant" was very different in the sixteenth century from what it is today. We tend to separate industrial, commercial, and financial enterprises and to understand by "merchant" solely a man engaged in trade, commonly retail trade. Few Renaissance merchants engaged in retail trade; that was left to shopkeepers. A merchant occasionally restricted himself to buying and selling on the international market, but such specialization was rare. More often he was also a money changer, and sometimes he was an international banker; he was involved in the economics and problems of transportation; he was an insurance broker; he was an industrialist, large or small; he invested in both urban and rural real estate. In its medieval and early modern usage the word "merchant" implied all of these activities, singly or in combination. The Medici, for example, were merchants. In addition to their purely commercial business they conducted all manner of banking operations, manufactured woolen cloth and silk, and for a time managed the papal alum mines at Tolfa. The Fuggers too were merchants, and the range of their business is even more instructive.

The first Fugger came from the country to Augsburg, a free imperial city of southern Germany, in 1367. He was a weaver, but he traded too, and when he died, he left his heirs a modest inheritance. They continued in trade, dealing almost exclusively, like most Augsburg merchants, in the spices, silks, and woolens of the Venetian trade. But the family fortune

Jakob Fugger. *Drawing by Hans Holbein the Elder. Kupferstichkabinett, Staatliche Museen Preussischer Kulturbesitz, Berlin.*

was really made by the business genius of Jakob Fugger, who became a merchant in 1478 at the age of nineteen and died in 1525, the richest merchant-banker in Europe. He soon turned from the solid Venetian trade to the risky but more profitable fields of international finance, royal moneylending, and mining. Through his loans to Emperor Maximilian I and his grandson Charles V, he became the leading silver and copper merchant in Europe. Among the original Habsburg lands was the Tyrol—as we have seen, since the middle of the fifteenth century one of the principal regions on the continent producing silver, iron, and copper. The Habsburg ruler had important regalian rights in all the mineral wealth of his possessions. All silver mined in the Tyrol, for example, was taxed. The price of a mark of silver (280 grams) was fixed at eight florins. The producers deposited their silver with an officer of the crown and received five florins per mark; the ruler's profit was three florins. As security for his loans to Maximilian, Jakob Fugger got an option on virtually the entire silver production of the Tyrol. He paid the producers, collected and pocketed the tax to the amount of the principal of the loan and the interest on it, and distributed the silver, at a further profit, on the international market.

But the great enterprise of Fugger's life was Hungarian copper. Here, in the rich mining region centered at Neusohl, on the southern slopes of the Carpathians in what is now Slovakia, Jakob and his successors were not only traders but industrial capitalists as well. The firm owned mines and built copper foundries, forges, and refineries. By controlling both Tyrolese and Hungarian production, Fugger cornered a major portion of Europe's copper supply. But this was not all. The Fuggers were papal bankers for much of Germany, Scandinavia, Poland, and Hungary. They managed the sale of the indulgence that was to provoke the anger of Martin Luther. They amassed extensive landed property. In return for further loans, Charles V turned over to them the revenues of the three orders of Spanish chivalry—income derived from enterprises which included mercury mines at Almaden and the wheat and wool of the orders' vast *latifundia*, or landed estates. Their profits on these varied activities had averaged over 50 per cent in each year between 1511 and 1527. To be sure, only the largest companies could imitate the bravura of the Fuggers. But even modest merchants, as a matter of principle and universal practice, responded with unspecialized interest to any chance for profit, whether it happened to be commercial, financial, or industrial.

THE DEVELOPMENT OF INDUSTRIAL CAPITALISM

In his manufacturing undertakings the merchant was becoming an industrial capitalist.

Definitions of capitalism are legion. Most of them are correct; very few are useful. It is correct, for example, to say that capitalism is an economic system which uses capital. It is also correct to define the goal of the system as profit. But since every economic system in every period of history and in every part of the world has involved the use of capital and the pursuit of profits, these definitions are not useful analytical tools. Nor is it particularly useful to call a society capitalistic because some of its members trade or engage in banking operations. Commerce, too, is as old as written records and so is lending and borrowing money, with or without interest. None of these definitions allows us to distinguish among the different forms European economic organization has taken in various historical periods or to distinguish the peculiarities of European economic arrangements from those of non-European cultures. Indeed, they discourage differentiation, periodization, and analysis.

A more fruitful approach is to narrow the meaning of "capitalism," to associate it primarily with industrial production, to understand it as a mode of industrial production—a particular way of producing goods—and to define it by contrasting it with the craft mode of production.

Craft production has dominated every human society except that of the modern West. A typical craftsman is the shoemaker. He buys his own raw material. He makes shoes in his own shop with his own tools. He himself sells the product of his labor to the consumer. He is economically independent and holds each thread of his enterprise in his own hands. The capitalist mode of production splits the single class of artisans into two distinct social groups: entrepreneurs, or capitalists, on the one hand, and wage workers on the other. The capitalist owns and controls the capital invested in the business. He owns the raw material, and owns and markets the final product. He owns the means of production—the plant and the tools. With the help of managers he supervises all stages of production. The worker is economically dependent; he owns only his labor, which he sells to the capitalist in exchange for wages. Capitalism is the form of industrial organization in which this split between the owners of capital and the owners of labor dominates the productive process.

The direction of industrial change between 1460 and 1560 was from the craft mode of production to the capitalist mode of production. But in 1500 capitalist production, at least in its pure form, was still extremely rare. Perhaps the organization of capital and labor closest to it was the Venetian Arsenal. The Arsenal built, repaired, and equipped the warships of the Venetian navy. In 1540 it covered sixty acres of land and water, employed well over a thousand workers, and represented, for the time, an enormous investment. It was probably the largest industrial establishment in Europe before 1560. The ship carpenters and caulkers, the sailmakers, pulleymakers, and ironsmiths employed by the Arsenal worked by the piece or by the day under the supervision of foremen. All the employees were wage workers, and the distinction between master craftsmen and apprentices was hardly more than one of wages. The employer owned the capital invested in the enterprise and controlled the whole process of production. The employer, however, was the Venetian state, not a private capitalist. The government fixed wages and hours. Workers considered the obligation to work in the Arsenal a burden to be avoided if possible, and labor had to be conscripted as for a modern army. It is characteristic of the early modern period that until far into the seventeenth century the best examples of large-scale industrial organization were state-owned factories producing war materiel, enterprises rather closer to the military state factories of the later Roman Empire than to the automobile plants of today. This situation suggests that only governments had the capital necessary to finance the largest undertakings and the coercive power necessary to recruit and control the great number of workers they required. In large-scale industry, state capitalism preceded private capitalism, just as national regulation of industry preceded *laissez-faire*.

The Venetian Arsenal represents one extreme among the various forms of industrial organization in existence during the Renaissance. An independent craftsman, perhaps a shoemaker working in a small cathedral town in the north of France, represents the other. Although craft production in its pure form was less common in 1500 than it had been, say, in the thirteenth century, it remained a very widespread, possibly the most widespread, European industrial type. Tailors, glovemakers, and hatters, like shoemakers, were in most places independent artisans. So were cutlers and coopers, bakers and woodcarvers. They produced for a local market and rarely had more than one or two assistants. Usually they belonged to craft guilds, which set standards of quality, supervised the training of apprentices, and limited competition. Their horizon was limited to the town they lived and worked in. The unit of production was the patriarchal family. Their mentality was that of the shop, the guildhall, and the parish church—traditional, conformist, and petty. Their pride was their independence. They were men of modest property who did not sell their labor to others.

Between the military state factory and the independent artisan stretched a wide variety of industrial types. Three of these intermediate types are of special interest. Two of them had already become important during the later Middle Ages and remained common in the sixteenth century: first, the small industrial enterprise owned by an independent craftsman who, through the gradual freezing of the vertical mobility of the medieval craft guild, had himself become a small-scale industrial capitalist; and second, the larger industrial enterprise, generally for the production of textiles, organized according to the putting-out system and controlled by a merchant who had reduced the master craftsmen in his employ to varying degrees of economic dependence. Both types were located within the walls of towns and were subject to municipal regulation. Both combined elements of craft production and of capitalist production, but craft elements predominated. The particular contribution of the sixteenth century to the development of industrial capitalism was a third transitional combination of craft and capitalist production: a rural putting-out system located outside the walls of towns, beyond the reach of municipal control and regulation. In this type of production, capitalist elements predominated.

In the high Middle Ages the craft guild had been a flexible institution. The master craftsmen who were its members trained apprentices in their domestic workshops. They also employed journeymen, young men who were trained artisans but were not yet ready to set up shop for themselves. The passage from apprenticeship to mastership was regulated but smooth. The average apprentice could look forward to becoming a journeyman and then an independent master craftsman. But increasingly, after 1300, the masters thwarted this expectation. In various ways, especially in crafts where equipment was expensive, they tended to make themselves a hereditary group. In many trades the sons of masters were given special privileges. Guilds raised their standards for the masterwork that every journeyman had to finish as a demonstration of his skill in order to qualify as a master; its production became more and more complicated, time-consuming, and costly. Very high fees were set for those who wanted to become masters. As the mastership became hereditary, so did the condition of the journeyman. A growing number of trained artisans could no longer look forward to becoming masters. Journeymen were being transformed from potentially independent craftsmen into the paid workers of masters who had themselves become small-scale industrial capitalists.

The result was a pronounced class tension in many cities in the first half of the sixteenth century. As the old patriarchal relationship between master and journeyman dissolved, journeymen resisted the exploitation inseparable from their new position in the productive process. They fought for higher wages, better food, shorter hours, and holidays. They went out on strike. In Germany they organized *Brüderschaften* ("brotherhoods"), rudimentary labor unions, and kept in contact with unions of the same trade in other localities. About 1500, when the journeyman tinsmiths in Nuremberg found that the masters of the guild had reduced their wages, they struck and left the city, and through the influence of their union no one was allowed to take their places. In 1503 the journeyman tailors struck in Wesel, on the Rhine, demanding higher wages and better diet and maintaining that "those who work the most should get the most." The masters, on their side, organized against the workers. When the journeyman tailors struck in Mainz, they were fired, and in 1505 the master tailors of Mainz called a meeting of the master tailors of twenty-one Rhineland cities to consider the interest of their trade and the best means of treating with the workmen. They agreed that they would not employ a journeyman who had struck against another master, that a master should not be obliged to give his journeyman more than one helping of meat in the evening, that wine must never be expected in the evening, and at other times must never consist of more than "a small half jug," terms which remind us that the relations between employer and employees in these small businesses were closer to those between a Victorian housewife and her maids than to the struggle between capital and labor in modern industry. Yet there is evidence of really bitter antagonism too. In Lyons and Paris strikes by printing workers occasionally erupted in open violence. The masters won (they always did in this period); and the royal edict issued at Villers-Cotterêts in 1539, forbade "all craftsmen to form brotherhoods or unions, large or small, for any purpose whatever." Royal and municipal authorities considered strikes and unions seditious and regularly suppressed them.

The second form of industrial organization common in the late Middle Ages and combining elements of both craft and capitalist production was the urban putting-out system; it, too, retained much of its former vigor in the early modern period. Textile enterprises producing for the export market, especially numerous in Flanders and in northern and central Italy, normally used this system. Since clothmaking probably employed half as many people as all other industries combined, its predominant form of

FILATOIO DA AQVA. .I.

A water-powered throwing mill. *Engraving from a volume by Vittorio Zonca published in 1607. The machine was introduced in the thirteenth century and was used throughout the Renaissance to twist filaments of raw silk into long threads that were strong enough to weave. Master throwers owned the machine, employed eight or nine journeymen, and worked for the silk merchant on a piece basis.*

organization is of special importance. The Italian silk industry is a clear illustration of the type.

Silk manufacture had been introduced into Europe by the Arabs as early as the tenth century. Until the middle of the fourteenth century, by far the most important European center of silk production was the Tuscan city of Lucca. In the later fourteenth century the industry began to spread all over Italy, so that by 1450 Florence, Milan, Venice, Bologna, Genoa, and Naples were all major centers of silk production. Between 1450 and 1550 the industry's geographical spread continued, over the Alps to Germany and to France and Spain.

In spite of competition from abroad, Italy remained supreme in the manufacture of silk of the first quality. Italians manufactured sheer veils, heavy patterned silks, and brocade velvets with pile of two or three heights, sometimes in one color with delicate traceries, sometimes in three, four, or five colors, and shot with gold and silver thread. The designs of these fabrics make a lively story of cultural interpenetration. They range from Arabic and Byzantine motifs to lotus plants, clouds, and rays of light adapted from Chinese silks, from feudal castles and hunting scenes in the early period to the classical garlands, vine leaves, and grotesques of the sixteenth century. The invariable effect was one of richness, color, and magnificence. This suggests the first important fact about the industry. It was a luxury industry, producing fabrics, wall hangings, banners, and altar cloths for the rich. And it was an export industry, with a clientele in all parts of Europe.

Similarly, its raw materials could not be got locally. In the thirteenth century most of the raw silk used in Lucca was imported from the region of the Caspian Sea; some came from even farther—from Persia and Turkestan. Starting in the fifteenth century, raw silk was produced in western Europe, some in Spain, but most in Italy itself. So rapid was the spread of silkworm cultivation in Sicily and Calabria, Tuscany, Lombardy, and Savoy that by 1550 Italy was self-sufficient in raw silk. But even in the sixteenth century the local manufacturer of Naples or Bologna had to import his raw materials from a certain distance. Moreover, raw silk and the other materials used in the industry—gold and silver thread, good dyes, and alum, the fixative that made the colors permanent—were expensive and required a considerable capital outlay.

The facts that silks were sold on the international market and that the raw materials needed in their manufacture were expensive and not easily obtainable locally opened the industry to control by merchant bankers. The typical Italian silk firm was a family partnership. The head of the firm was a merchant. He and his partners supplied the capital, bought raw silk from merchants who had imported it from the Levant or from another part of Italy and sold the final product through his agents in London, Paris, Augsburg, or Antwerp. This commercial activity determined his relation to the artisans who actually made the cloth. The dyers, for example, worked in small shops and used fairly expensive vats owned by themselves, and they had their own guild. To this extent they remained independent masters. On the other hand, they did not own the silk they dyed, and they performed only a single task in a complex industrial process over which they had no control. The independence of the weavers, who also had their own guild, was similarly limited. Weaving the complex patterns of a luxury silk required great skill and experience and complicated machines—drawlooms—which were expensive to buy and maintain. The weaver's skill and his ownership of his loom solidified his bargaining position. Yet like the dyer he was not an independent craftsman in the full sense, for he did not own the silk thread with which he worked, or sell the fabrics he wove. Both were dependent on the merchant capitalist, who provided and owned the raw material, marketed the final product, and in a loose way supervised the whole process of production. Master craftsmen were becoming pieceworkers. Merchants were becoming industrial capitalists.

Between 1460 and 1560 the dependence of artisan on capitalist in the textile industries increased, and a new type of industrial organization emerged that was to be typical of the early modern period—the *rural* putting-out system. The entrepreneur tightened his hold on the process of production by moving his operations from the city to the countryside. All over Europe a quite new kind of industrial center grew up, unwalled, straggling haphazardly over the countryside from a central marketplace. Enterprising capitalists in the southern Netherlands met the competition of English cloth by importing Spanish wool (by 1536 over thirty thousand bales a year arrived in Antwerp from Spain); making cheaper, lighter fabrics, serges, and worsteds; and locating the new industry in agricultural areas around Ypres and Armentières. Petty towns in Tuscany challenged the old monopoly of Florence, and rural industry spread through the villages of Lombardy and the Venetian mainland. Rouen merchants deserted the city in order to hire cheaply the spare time of peasants and shepherds and their wives and children. The same thing happened in the Netherlands, Germany, and England.

In England the principal cloth-producing regions were Yorkshire, East Anglia, the Cotswolds, and the area along the Avon. The manufacturer of woolen cloth was called a clothier. He was an economic individualist of a novel type. In the rural village where he had his headquarters he was free of municipal taxes and the burdens of public office, unhampered by the old guild and municipal regulations which formerly limited the number of employees he could hire and minutely regulated the quality of his materials and the nature of his manufacturing methods. Here he could hire or contract with whom he pleased, offer whatever wages or piece rates would secure him workers, order their work in any way he liked. He determined the quality, quantity, and price of what he produced in response to the varying demands of the international market. He was free to experiment with machines (such as the gig mill, which mechanized part of the finishing process) in order to reduce labor costs and increase production. The organization of his enterprise marked the beginning of a new stage in the development of capitalist industry.

Basically, the industrial organization of the English sixteenth-century clothier remained the putting-out system, but the system was profoundly modified by its rural location. His new freedom of enterprise and of risk allowed the clothier to extend still further his ownership of the means of production and to group workers in "manufactories," where he could combine under one roof several stages of production that had been kept apart in the past. Thus the large clothier commonly owned a dyehouse where wage workers dyed the wool under his close supervision. He owned a fulling mill, and workshops for stretching and pressing the cloth.

Spinning and weaving were more often put out to large numbers of rural craftsmen working in their own homes. Spinning was very widely distributed over the countryside and was done mostly by women, on a part-time basis. The relation of clothier to spinner was what it had been in the past: the women worked in their own homes and with their own tools on a piece basis for an entrepreneur who owned the raw wool and the finished yarn. On the other hand, important changes were taking place in the relation of clothier to weaver. Often the rural craftsmen could not afford the capital outlay for a loom, and it became common practice for the clothier to own looms and rent them to the weavers. Sometimes the clothier owned a string of houses along a village street and rented these to the weavers as well, obtaining the further advantage of being able to supervise their work more closely. Less often, clothiers concentrated the weaving under a single roof, against the strenuous opposition of the weavers, who were rightly afraid of losing entirely their already limited independence. Some "factories" of this kind employed several hundred workers. Wage work, clearly, was becoming much more common than it had been in the old textile towns, and the separation of capital and labor was becoming more marked. The urban putting-out system was still closer to craft production than to capitalist production; but in the rural putting-out system of the sixteenth century, the capitalist mode of production predominated.

Yet equally characteristic of the age is the still bewildering variety of the ways in which men produced the articles they needed. The complex shift from craft to capitalist production stretched from the twelfth century to the Industrial Revolution and beyond. The rate of change varied enormously from industry to industry, from region to region, and from period to period. In the sixteenth century, as in any other, there existed a spectrum of industrial types, each one, whether traditional or novel, uniquely important to the men whose working lives were organized by it. The expansive years between 1460 and 1560 are particularly important because the balance of tradition and innovation shifted gradually but decisively. A halfway mark in the long transition from craft to capitalist production was reached and passed. Independent craftsmen remained common. Firms were still small; very few employed more than a dozen men. Most men worked at home with their own tools. An artisanal spirit pervaded industry and gave its products the varied individuality of the skillfully handmade. But by 1560 the cleavage between capital and labor, which is—like scientific method and an art based on perspective—a unique peculiarity of western civilization, was firmly and widely established in many parts of industrial Europe.

Rising prices widened the cleavage. Wages lagged behind prices. By 1560, real wages in Spain, France, England, and Germany had fallen from 20 per cent to 50 per cent below their average levels between 1450 and

1500. For wage workers the price rise meant economic regression and a serious fall in living standards. For manufacturers, however, higher prices meant larger profits, and the price revolution was a profit inflation from which they emerged with a larger share of the community's wealth than ever before.

USURY, MORALITY, AND SOCIAL CLIMBING

Grown rich in commerce, banking, and industry, the sixteenth-century merchant-capitalist was a man of individuality and ambitious resource. His life was motivated by a rational search for profit. He operated, however, in a society whose ideals were overwhelmingly religious and aristocratic. He could justify his way of life only in opposition to a traditional clerical distrust and a traditional aristocratic disdain. Any elite develops values that reflect its mode of life and legitimize its interests and ambitions. A gradual secularization of the economic ethic of the churches and the creation of a bourgeois morality performed this value-making function for the merchant class. The process began in Italy about 1400, the work of liberal scholastic theologians and civic humanists; it was continued in northern Europe by bourgeois publicists, Calvinist divines, and the Jesuit order.

Medieval theologians had commonly respected poverty, emphasized the "glittering wretchedness" of wealth, and distrusted merchants. St. Thomas Aquinas (*c.* 1225–1274) expressed perfectly the prejudices of peasants, artisans, and aristocrats when he wrote, "Properly speaking, commerce is the exchange of money for goods with a view to gain. . . . It is justly condemned, for it encourages the passion for money [*cupiditas lucri*], which is without limit and almost infinite. Therefore commerce, considered in itself, has something shameful about it."[1] On this conviction, and on the further assumption that business behavior should obey the same Christian rules as private morality, clerical theorists had built a comprehensive economic ethic. Its most striking prohibition was that of usury, which was defined as profit on a loan and forbidden on the ground that to lend money to a man who needs it is a charitable act, while to demand payment for the loan is grasping and unchristian.

To traditional ideals of poverty, Italian merchants and their humanist apologists opposed a positive evaluation of wealth. They quoted Aristotle's *Ethics* and *Politics*, in which wealth is considered a necessary aid to the development of a moral life and a necessary condition for happiness. The proper life for man, they said, is action in the world, not solitary contemplation; and all things are good that increase his power to act for the good of himself, his family, his friends, and his country. Poverty leads not to

[1]*Summa theologiae*, IIa IIae, quaest. LXXVII, art. 4.

virtue, but to pettiness; it restricts the possibility of active virtue; it sordidly limits the mind instead of broadening it. Honorable riches, on the other hand, guarantee freedom of choice and give substance to family and civic responsibility.

Nevertheless, few merchants questioned the Church's prohibition of usury. To have done so openly would have exposed them to serious charges in the 'ecclesiastical courts. Nor must one exaggerate the economic importance of this prohibition. Usury was not identical with interest, which theologians and canonists defined as "compensation due in justice to a creditor because of loss he has incurred through lending."[2] If a man, it was argued, suffered a loss because he lent money to another, then he might justly claim payment in addition to the principal. By the middle of the fifteenth century, moreover, the progress of financial and commercial capitalism had forced the common acceptance of a further title to interest, called *lucrum cessans,* or profit ceasing. When a man lent money to another, it was now often said, he was kept from using it advantageously for his own benefit. He was therefore justly entitled to interest payments which would compensate him for that loss. A loan purely for profit was usury and continued to be forbidden; it remained legally prohibited in France until the French Revolution. But during the late fifteenth century and the sixteenth century, exceptions and reinterpretations proliferated to the point where interest on loans came to be considered normal and usury the exception. Nobles and widows deposited money with merchant bankers and were regularly paid 5 to 12 per cent on their demand deposits, although merchants still preferred to call this payment a "gift," "reward," or "profit," rather than interest. Merchants regularly operated on credit in international commerce. But these credit transactions were conveniently described as simple sales instead of loans. Bankers lent money to princes, and citizens bought interest-paying government bonds. These practices, like prostitution, were considered necessary in order to avoid evils even worse. A few merchants had sufficiently tender consciences on their deathbeds to instruct their heirs to restore to borrowers the interest on loans they had made for business purposes. But in the end, common practice secularized the problem. By 1560 capitalist interests were bluntly supported by the most influential theologian of the age, John Calvin. Sucking the substance of a poor man without risk to oneself is wicked usury. But on loans to the rich or to businessmen a lender's profit is no worse than a manufacturer's or shopkeeper's profit on a sale. A parson knows little about business. So let the believing banker's conscience be his guide. A few years later, the second Congregation of the Jesuit order approved 5-per-cent interest on loans for business purposes, practically

---

[2]Quoted by John Noonan, *The Scholastic Analysis of Usury* (Cambridge, Mass., 1957), p. 105.

ending the application of usury theory to business finance. The competitive individualism of the merchant had escaped ecclesiastical control and reoriented the ethical teaching of the churches.

The merchant found it more difficult to disarm aristocratic snobbery than clerical suspicion. Everywhere, the nobility retained prestige and status. Nowhere (until the nineteenth century) did manufacture and trade confer the highest social position. In a rigidly inegalitarian society, merchants occupied an honorable but median position, with unskilled manual laborers, peasants, artisans, and retail traders below them, and *gentilshommes*, seigneurs, and princes above them. They agreed with Cicero that shopkeeping was "sordid," but they could not agree with those Spanish nobles who remarked to a Florentine ambassador in 1513 that trade in general was "shameful." So a novel theoretical defense of their own merits, virtues, and achievements was from the beginning inseparable from social climbing in practice.

A popular genre of humanist ethical literature in the Renaissance was the treatise *De vera nobilitate* ("of true nobility") which put true nobility in virtue and personal merit rather than in birth and taught that virtue is acquired, not inherited. The popularity of such works should probably be expained by their usefulness in legitimizing bourgeois pretensions. The idea of virtue, moreover, was itself given a positive middle-class content. In Italy in the fifteenth century, and north of the Alps in the sixteenth, there emerged clearly for the first time the attitudes which we lump together as "bourgeois morality," attitudes which contrasted sharply with aristocratic values. A noble, insofar as he could be precisely defined at all in the sixteenth century, was "a man who lived nobly." Fundamentally, to live nobly meant to fight and not to work. Above all, the noble was thought to derogate from his nobility (this was generally true in northern continental Europe, much less so in Italy and in England) if he engaged in trade. In contrast, bourgeois morality attributed positive value to productive work. The great sin became idleness rather than dishonor. Again, nobility obliged the aristocrat to maintain a certain standard of expenditure and consumption. If his income was insufficient, he borrowed. The bourgeois, however, practiced a willing thrift and was persuaded that he should spend less than he earned. He was willing to live ascetically so that his enterprise might prosper. By insisting that spiritual athletes live in the world rather than in monasteries, Protestantism reinforced this tendency and gave the individual new incentives to plan his life rationally in the pursuit of a worldly success, which was increasingly taken to be the sign of spiritual health. The noble might squander wealth in the idle enjoyment of what it could buy. The bourgeois found his identity in a very different ideal: constant productive activity and the reinvestment of its fruits.

Merchants were pleased to know that true nobility consisted in personal merit and that willing thrift could be a moral imperative—as long as they

The Classes of Men. *Woodcut by Hans Weiditz made about 1530. The European social hierarchy is represented as a tree. Entwined among the roots, two peasants; above them, journeymen, artisans, and merchants; next, bishops and cardinals, nobles and princes; then pope, emperor, and kings; at the very top, again two peasants, a reminder that they fed everybody else.*

were merchants. In practice, however, bourgeois virtue rarely resisted the attraction of aristocratic status; and the ambition of most merchants was to exchange the social ambiguities of trade for the universally recognized prestige of nobility. The sixteenth-century merchant class was therefore extremely fluid, with trade and industry serving as the chief means by which men moved up in the social hierarchy. The kind of social mobility which had been assured by the Church during the Middle Ages (when the son of a peasant might reasonably hope to be pope) in the Renaissance was assured by mercantile enterprise. To be a noble, craftsman, or peasant was a largely hereditary condition; but few bourgeois fortunes remained invested in trade or industry for more than two or three generations. Normally, the grandson of a successful merchant abandoned the risky enterprises in which the family had made its money and invested more safely. He put his money into land, urban real estate, and government bonds. He bought a seigneury, a title and a government office. He gave his sons a humanistic education. By imitating aristocratic manners and investments, by intermarriage, simply by living "nobly," the bourgeois family displaced or merged with the older nobility.

The phenomenon was universal. In Venice in the sixteenth century the ruling class as a whole was gradually transformed from a purely mercantile oligarchy into an aristocracy whose wealth was in land and government bonds. By the early seventeenth century, the Fuggers were settled on their Swabian estates as imperial counts. In England, men of talent and modest origins made fortunes as clothiers or in the wholesale trade of woolen cloth. Their sons held administrative offices and began to buy up land in their home counties. The grandsons settled on these estates and founded gentry families. The pattern was similar in France. In one case, typical of many, a merchant in a small provincial town bought an office for his son in the royal financial administration. The son made a fortune in government finance and bought land and titles. His sons made brilliant careers in the magistracy and in the Church. In 1600, the family hired a genealogist, who traced their origins to a twelfth-century feudal baron. Success in trade and industry, in short, was the elevator which lifted the most enterprising members of lower social groups into the aristocracy. The process might take several generations; but great merchants, constantly recruited from below, ultimately gravitated to the land. Here they assumed the privileges and authority of nobles. At the same time they took on the economic problems, and opportunities, of agrarian landlords.

LANDLORD AND TENANT

During the Renaissance, as in the Middle Ages, by far the greatest part of human energy had to be devoted to producing food, and men who lived in towns were a small minority in an overwhelmingly agrarian population. The relative size of rural and urban populations naturally varied from region to region. But even in the most urbanized and economically most sophisticated parts of Europe—central and northern Italy, southern Germany, and Flanders and Brabant—over three quarters of the inhabitants were peasants. The progress of industrial capitalism, the expansion of trade, and the widening of the organized money market affected them profoundly.

Medieval agrarian society had been in flux since the early thirteenth century. The mold of manorialism, which bound serfs to work the demesne, or home farm, of their lord in exchange for protection and the hereditary use of a portion of the estate, began to loosen. As the use of money became commonplace and an exchange economy developed, lords wished and needed to buy more commodities from merchants and craftsmen than in the past. They therefore found it advantageous to commute to money some of the traditional dues and services owed them. In order to increase their cash income still more, many landlords abandoned direct exploitation of the demesne and leased it, like the rest of the estate. Where demesne farming declined, serfdom lost its economic importance. For a fee, lords were willing to free their peasants of the dishonorable ties of personal dependence; and the manorial contracts, which had promised personal protection and a subsistence living in return for labor service, gave way to rent contracts. Very gradually, economic individualism began to insinuate itself into rural life.

In the fourteenth century, pestilence and war reinforced the disrupting influences of the money economy on the manorial structure of rural life. The Black Death of 1348–1349 cut the rural population of Europe to a half, in some regions even to a third, of its former level. Wages rose, and landlords were forced to compete for new tenants. In France the devastations of the Hundred Years' War had analogous consequences. By its end the French countryside was ravished, the peasantry decimated and pauperized. Whole regions were desolate and almost abandoned. Powerful nobles reclaimed them, but again the peasants who remained were in a stronger bargaining position than their predecessors had been. The scarcity of labor hastened the abandonment of demesne farming, the commutation of labor service, and the replacement of traditional tenures by rent contracts. Manumissions multiplied, and serfdom disappeared in many parts of western Europe.

Emancipation did not necessarily benefit the peasantry economically. Nor was renting out his whole estate the only means by which a landlord could adjust to a money economy and to the scarcity of labor. In areas where crops like grain or wool could be raised on a large scale and readily sold for cash on the international market, landlords were tempted to evict their tenants and farm the whole estate themselves commercially with hired labor.

The expansion of trade between 1460 and 1560 sharpened this temptation and increased the landlords' freedom of maneuver. Agriculture shared in the general prosperity of the century. Production increased notably in many areas, and opportunities for agricultural profit multiplied as communications improved and a dense network of trade in agricultural produce covered the continent. Grain moved from Sicily to Naples, Rome, and Venice; from eastern Germany and Poland to Scandinavia, the Netherlands, and the Rhineland; from northern Europe to the Mediterranean. Ever more rapidly, the land and its products were sucked into the mainstream of an expanding exchange economy and the subsistence agriculture of the past was transformed into production for near or distant markets. What became decisive for the economic relations between landlord and peasant was precisely whether the market was near or distant,

Peasants. *Drawings by Hieronymus Bosch, about 1558. Kupferstichkabinett, Staatliche Museen Preussischer Kulturbesitz, Berlin.*

local or international. Where the market was exclusively local, agriculture remained of necessity unspecialized and landlords preferred to rent out their whole estates to tenant farmers because this was the easiest way to assure themselves a money income. Under these circumstances, the manorial lord became a rentier. Where landlords could grow wool or grain for export, they preferred to assert their absolute ownership of the estate and engage in capitalist agriculture, the rational exploitation of a large holding to produce a cash crop for commercial profit. Under these circumstances, the manorial lord became a capitalist farmer.

The transformation of the manorial lord into a capitalist farmer is well illustrated by the agricultural histories of the English Midlands and of Germany east of the Elbe River. The decisive factor in England was the expanding manufacture of woolen textiles and the industry's growing demand for wool. This demand was a powerful inducement for landlords to increase their revenues and guard against social and economic decline by raising sheep. To raise sheep they needed a large acreage under their direct control. They got it by a variety of processes called *enclosures*: taking over the common lands of the villages, consolidating scattered strips into compact properties and fencing them with hawthorn hedges, absorbing or "engrossing" small holdings into large farms, and converting arable land into pasture. They then evicted their customary tenants and proceeded to cultivate their holdings themselves. As the great sociologist

Max Weber put it, the "peasants were freed from the land and the land from the peasants." Enclosures, ran a popular proverb, "make fat beasts and lean poor people." The fat beasts were the prospering landlords, while many peasants lost their land and became agricultural laborers.

East of the Elbe, the economic basis of the great landed estates which were in the sole control of the lords included three main elements: rising grain prices (by 1600 three to four times as high as they had been at the beginning of the sixteenth century), the growing demand for eastern grain in western Europe, and the cheap and easy transportation of this grain from grower to market which was provided by the lake and river systems of northeastern Germany. But whereas sheep farming required little manpower and the enclosures therefore led to the creation of a small free agricultural proletariat (ready and anxious to spin and weave for the clothier), the raising of grain required a great deal of labor, and the revival of demesne farming in Pomerania, Brandenberg, and Prussia, (and indeed in Poland and other parts of eastern Europe as well) was accompanied by a growing subjection of the peasantry. Aristocratic landlords, or *Junkers*, grew rich and enlarged their demesnes by buying out or evicting the peasants, and after the Reformation, by appropriating monastic and parish lands. The peasants, who had been freer than those of western Europe in the high Middle Ages, were reduced to serfdom, tied to the land, and burdened with new dues and increased labor services. The great dividing line of the Elbe solidified permanently in the sixteenth century. In the middle of the nineteenth century it still separated a western Europe of small independent peasant proprietors (with the exception of England, where the enclosure movement, reaching its climax in the eighteenth century, had created individual holdings often larger than those of Prussian *Junkers*) and an eastern Europe of serfs and landed magnates. Today it divides communist and capitalist Europe.

On the other hand, in France, much of western Germany, Switzerland, the Low Countries, northern Italy, and the south of England—in the cultural heart of Europe, in short—most landlords secured a money income after 1500 by renting, and agriculture was carried on by peasant farmers working small plots. Landlord and tenant shared proprietary rights in the soil. The old burdens of dependent status were attached to the land rather than to persons, and the peasant was generally a free man. In return for his use of the land he paid rent and supplied equivalents, either in kind or in money, for the traditional manorial services; and the relative prosperity of the landlord and tenant was determined by the movement of prices and rents.

Some landlords found it possible to raise rents at will (a practice tenants called "racking" rents). They thus diverted the bulk of their tenants' profits to themselves, and did well. Many French landlords introduced a short-term contractual lease called *métayage*, similar to the *mezzadria* system common in Italy, especially in Tuscany, since the fourteenth century. Instead of paying an annual rent, peasants paid a fixed proportion of their yearly crop, usually half. This system too increased the landlord's proprietary right in the land and brought him a significant share in the benefits of rising agricultural prices. On the other hand, the long-term leases described by an English observer in 1549 benefited tenants rather than landlords: "The most part of the landes of this Realme," he wrote, "stand yet at the old Rent," unexpired leases cannot be enhanced, though the owners would, and despite raising rents as leases expire, the landlord cannot expect a third of his land to come to his disposition during his lifetime or even during that of his son.[3] In this instance real rents lagged well behind more rapidly rising prices, at least in the short run. Finally, in certain areas, especially in parts of France and western Germany, peasant tenure was heritable. The tenant could farm his holding any way he liked, sell it, divide it among his heirs. He could sell his surplus produce freely on the market. Commuted payments were often fixed in customary law. In such circumstances real rents fell, the landlord was caught in an inflationary vice, and it was the tenant who profited from rising prices.

The aggressive instability of the sixteenth-century nobility suggests that many smaller landlords were caught in the squeeze of rising prices and falling real rents. Hoping to recoup their losses with ransoms, booty, and confiscated land in conquered territory, nobles threw their weight behind royal and princely wars abroad. The pressure exerted by the French nobility was a major force behind the aggressive attacks on Italy that began in 1494. The Spanish nobility had lived for centuries on the reconquest of the peninsula from the Moors. The fall of Granada in 1492 ended the activity and plunder of that long crusade. The arrogant *hidalgos*, or lesser nobles, with small property then turned with alacrity to lead and exploit colonial expansion in the New World. By sailing west, Cortes, an indigent gentleman nourished on romances of chivalry, got a marquisate and vast estates in Mexico. In a pungent autobiography, the German knight Götz von Berlichingen (1480–1562) described how he pillaged peasants and ransomed merchants. Nobles pressured the Church, trying to tap its resources by installing their relatives in lucrative ecclesiastical positions. They pressured their tenants. Like kings, the nobles ultimately resorted to borrowing. But unlike kings, they could not repudiate their debts with impunity, and as their indebtedness grew, they were forced to mortgage and then sell their land. This is when climbing merchants bought it, seizing the opportunity to invest commercial and industrial profit in social prestige and real estate. Most noticeably in France and

[3] *A Discourse of the Common Weal of This Realm of England,* ed. by Elizabeth Lamond (Cambridge, Eng., 1893), pp. 19, 38–39.

England, a "new" aristocracy grew up beside the old, mercantile in origin, efficient agricultural managers, adaptable to changing economic circumstance. The bitter resentment of the old nobility exploded in the civil and religious wars of the second half of the century. A lively chronicler of the court of Catherine de Medici, Pierre de Brantôme (*c.* 1540–1614), writing during the last years of the French religious wars, isolated its role with admirable intelligence: "Rich merchants, usurers, bankers, and other money-grabbers have stolen everything. Gentlemen, having mortgaged or sold their property, can hardly find the wood to warm themselves. But this good civil war (this is what they call it) will put them on their feet again. The fine nobility of France will recover its own by the grace (or rather by the grease [the fat profit]) of this good civil war."

The economic condition of the peasantry was the mirror image of the economic condition of the land-owning aristocracy. Where landlords prospered—in Spain and Portugal, in southern Italy and Sicily, in parts of England, and east of the Elbe—peasants suffered. But from the Elbe to

A Country Wedding. Painting by Pieter Brueghel the Elder, about 1565. A glimpse of peasant life. The wedding feast takes place in a barn furnished with rural stick furniture and crude clay bowls and jugs. The food is bread, gruel, and beer; there is no meat. Kunsthistorisches Museum, Vienna.

the English Channel, from the Apennines to the North Sea, peasants were freer and more prosperous in the sixteenth century than they had been in the thirteenth. We should not be surprised that they nevertheless remained dissatisfied. Real misery more often deadens than sharpens discontent. It is the class on the economic upgrade that finds its burdens, though diminishing, most oppressive. Such a class was the sixteenth-century peasantry in the heart of Europe. Peasant income had risen. Peasants could sell their produce in a rapidly expanding market, while the payments they made their landlords declined in real value. What galled them was that peasant emancipation, in progress since the thirteenth century, stopped in the sixteenth. In an earlier age emancipation had benefited the landlords as much as if not more than, the peasantry. In the sixteenth century, under the pressure of rising prices and the increasing cost of living "nobly," landlords enforced every claim they still possessed and invaded peasant rights whenever circumstances allowed them to. In France, *banalités* survived: fees the peasants were forced to pay for the use of the mill, oven, and wine press, over which the lord had monopolistic control. Lords invaded the old commons of waste, forest, stream, and meadow, all traditionally open to peasant use. German peasants in the sixteenth century complained that "our lords have appropriated all the woods to themselves alone, and when the poor man needs any wood, he must buy it at double price," and that "they have taken over fishing, hunting, and grazing rights as well."[4] Where landlords successfully racked rents or introduced more favorable leases, like *métayage*, peasants actually lost ground. Finally, all peasants felt the sharper financial bite of their political rulers. In Germany, especially in the southwest, many large landlords were becoming the tiny sovereign princelings of their territories. As in much of France, tenures here had generally been hereditary and rents fixed. The new princelings restored the economic balance to their own favor by leveling new dues in the form of taxes, squeezing their tenants not as landlords but as tax collectors. In the larger states what was to be a fundamental maxim of taxation until the nineteenth century—that those who can least afford it should pay most—was already operative. The profit of the peasant became the resource of his king.

As a result, the sixteenth century was an age of permanent agrarian crisis. Where serfdom remained, it seemed a purely arbitrary bondage in a world where lack of personal freedom was no longer accompanied by any economic advantage. Free tenants resented all obligations and tried to escape the dues and services that landlords tried to enforce. Tension between landlord and peasant was endemic, and it occasionally erupted in open violence. There were minor movements in England, scattered risings

[4] Quoted by Günther Franz, *Der deutsche Bauernkrieg,* fourth ed. (Darmstadt, 1956), p. 124.

in France. In Germany there were eleven major peasant uprisings between the early fifteenth century and the great peasant revolt of 1525–1526. The peasants wistfully demanded a return to the good old days and the "good old law." Their mentality was conservative, profoundly religious, and utopian. They dreamed of freedom and a social life regulated by the precepts of the Gospel. Their attitude is perfectly reflected in a revolt of 1476 led by Hans Böhm (*c.* 1450–1476) the bagpiper of Niklashausen, known as the "holy youngster." He preached to immense crowds that he was going to make them glad with proclamations of the pure world of God. The kingdom of God, he cried, is at hand. When it comes there will be neither pope nor emperor, all class distinctions will be ended, all men will be free and equal, in bondage only to the law of brotherly love. "The princes, spiritual and lay, also the counts and knights are so rich that if all they have were shared by the community we should all have enough; and this must come to pass." Forest, water, meadows, and wastelands must be free for the use of all. It would come even to this, that princes and lords would have to work for daily wages.

The prosperity and dynamism of the European economy in the late fifteenth century and in the sixteenth century was thus inseparable from sharpening tension between landlord and tenant as well as between employer and worker. The fundamental causes of tension were structural changes in production and the organization of labor associated with the development of the capitalist mode of production in industry and, to a lesser extent, in agriculture. These changes produced a widening gap between capital and labor, rich and poor, and forced every group in the social hierarchy to adapt or suffer economic penalties. The price revolution aggravated the crisis. The results were so various as almost to defeat generalization, although certain tendencies seem reasonably clear. Merchant-bankers were coming to enjoy a larger share of wealth and economic power than in the past. Laborers, journeymen, and artisans did less well. In an inflationary period and a preindustrial, "underdeveloped" society, land remained the best and safest form of investment in the long run. For this reason the European nobility, sloughing off its weaker, incompetent members and constantly recruiting from below, did relatively well, and European society was as aristocratic in 1560 as it had been a century earlier. To be sure, the aristocrats paid a price. Gradually they forfeited political and military independence in return for tax exemptions and honorific privileges. Gradually they made service to their prince and state their principal profession, tailoring to this service their manners, mode of life, and education. These developments had important political and cultural repercussions. They form one strand in the intricate patterns of the emergence both of the sovereign territorial state and, equally powerfully though less obviously, of a lay culture based on a revived enthusiasm for classical literature.

CHAPTER 3

Renaissance Society and Humanist Culture

On December 10, 1513, Niccolò Machiavelli wrote a letter that has become famous. Exiled from Florence, he was living in reduced circumstances on a Tuscan farm. In the mornings, he told his friend, he hunted or snared thrushes, stopping occasionally to reread a few verses of Dante, Petrarch, Tibullus, or Ovid. After lunch he would go to the local inn and play dice with the yokels, only to taste again in their brutish company the "malign dregs" of his destiny.

> But when evening comes [he continued] I return home and go into my library. At the door I take off my muddy everyday clothes. I dress myself as though I were about to appear before a royal court as a Florentine envoy. Then decently attired I enter the antique courts of the great men of antiquity. They receive me with friendship; from them I derive the nourishment which alone is mine and for which I was born. Without false shame I talk with them and ask them the causes of their actions; and their humanity is so great they answer me. For four long and happy hours I lose myself in them. I forget all my troubles; I am not afraid of poverty or death. I transform myself entirely in their likeness.[1]

Few texts express so movingly the Renaissance admiration for classical antiquity and the effort of many sixteenth-century men to pattern their lives on the image of man to be found in the Greek and Latin classics.

This is a *humanist* attitude. The noun *humanista* ("humanist"), is a Renaissance word, coined toward the end of the fifteenth century in Italy to designate members of a particular professional group: teachers of subjects variously described in the texts as *studia litterarum* ("literature"); *bonae artes, humanae artes, artes liberales* (the "good arts," "human arts," or "liberal arts"); or, most frequently and expressively, *studia humanitatis* (the "humanities"). *Humanitas,* from which "humanist" derives, is a classical word and a classical idea. Cicero used it to translate the Greek *paedeia* ("education" or "culture"). The second-century gram-

[1]*Lettere*, ed. by G. Lesca (Florence, 1929) pp. 88–90.

marian Aulus Gellius defined it as *eruditio institutioque in bonas artes* ("knowledge and instruction in the good arts"). Fourteenth- and fifteenth-century Italian humanists revived the word. "To each species of creatures," wrote one, "has been alloted a peculiar and instinctive gift. To horses galloping, to birds flying comes naturally. To man only is given the desire to learn. Hence what the Greeks called *paedeia* we call *studia humanitatis*. For learning and training in virtue are peculiar to man; therefore our forefathers called them *humanitas*, the pursuit of activities proper to mankind."[2] By "literature," humanists meant Greek and Roman literature; by "learning," classical learning; by "virtue," conduct modeled on the precepts of ancient moral philosophy. "Humanism" (a useful and legitimate word in spite of the fact that Germans coined it in the early nineteenth century) thus denotes something quite specific: an educational and cultural program based on the study of the classics and colored by the notion of human dignity implicit in *humanitas*.

Classical literature no longer commands the enthusiasm it aroused in Machiavelli and his contemporaries. We find it difficult to credit that a young French scholar should have spent three hours on his wedding day studying Greek or that when a visiting Italian lectured on the second satire of Juvenal at the University of Salamanca in 1488, the press of students and professors was so thick, their reluctance to leave the hall so great after two and a half hours, that the lecturer had to be passed bodily over the heads of the audience before he could go home. Yet similar anecdotes could be multiplied. Humanism was the most important single intellectual movement of the Renaissance. Its first great representatives were Francesco Petrarch (1304–1374) and Giovanni Boccaccio (1313–1375). In the fifteenth century a host of celebrated Italians enriched and popularized its program. By the beginning of the sixteenth century, humanist values had begun to refashion the intellectual life of northern Europe. John Colet (c. 1467–1519) and Sir Thomas More (1478–1535) propagated the new ideals in England; Jacques Lefèvre d'Étaples (c. 1460–1536) and Guillaume Budé (1468–1540), in France; Conrad Celtis (1459–1508) and Johann Reuchlin (1455–1522), in Germany. Towering above them all was Desiderius Erasmus (1469–1536), of Rotterdam, who influenced his contemporaries and expressed many of their most important and typical aspirations to a degree and with a lucidity and comprehensiveness unmatched before Voltaire. Caught by the enthusiasm of these men, princes hired humanist secretaries; aristocrats and wealthy burghers entrusted their sons to humanist educators. Humanism transformed literature, art, and scholarship. It influenced medicine, law, theology, and morals. It was the cultural fashion of the day—as

[2]W. H. Woodward, *Vittorino da Feltre and Other Humanist Educators* (New York, 1963), p. 177.

recognizable, as penetrating, and as subtle as the style of a sharply individual painter or musician.

How are we to understand an intellectual passion and a cultural program apparently so remote from our own twentieth-century sensibility and needs?

THE STUDY OF HISTORY

Renaissance enthusiasm for the classics flowed from a transformation of men's sense of history. Humanists adored the classics because they had learned to read them in historical perspective, a perspective they had established by inventing the idea of the Renaissance, by creating certain of the principles and tools of modern historical writing, and by imagining a new periodization of the past.

The way a man divides the past into periods reveals some of his most basic, and often unconscious, assumptions. Medieval scholars had divided history into an age of darkness and error and an age of light and truth. Between the two ages stood the Cross of Christ. Developing hints from the Old Testament, medieval historians distinguished subsidiary periods within the age of darkness. Some used the scheme of four successive world monarchies adumbrated in the Book of Daniel; others adopted the six ages outlined by St. Augustine (354–430) in *The City of God*. Most agreed that secular history illustrated a providential plan in its movement from the creation to the Incarnation and from the Incarnation to the Last Judgment; that the final period of world history had begun with the simultaneous founding of the Roman Empire and the birth of Christ; and that they themselves were living near the end of that last age.

Humanist historians drew two sharp chronological lines rather than one. The first line divided *antiqua*, or ancient history, from the period humanists now named, for the first time, the "dark ages." The important dates became those of the emperor Constantine's conversion (312) and of the sack of Rome by the Visigoths (410). The second line, dated variously but always placed in the very recent past, distinguished their own period from the dark middle age that had preceded it. This tripartite division of European history into ancient, medieval, and modern was at the same time a judgment of value. By calling the period after the early fourth or early fifth century a dark age and by shifting the moment of crucial discontinuity in historical development from the Incarnation to the conversion of Constantine and the barbarian invasions, humanists reversed the traditional metaphor of light and darkness. Antiquity, so long considered dark because it was the time of pagan error, became in this new vision of the past an age of light; while the period after the decline of Rome was branded an age of cultural decadence and barbarism. Correspondingly, the humanists represented their own age as a new historical

The Conquest of Ignorance. *An engraving after a fresco by Rosso Fiorentino in the chateau of Fontainebleau. King Francis I opens the door of the temple of Jupiter to his blind and ignorant subjects, an allegory of the renaissance of art and letters and of the rebirth of virtue and true learning. Metropolitan Museum, New York.*

epoch of a special kind: a renaissance—an age of light after darkness, awakening after sleep, rebirth after death.

Classical poetry, they complacently maintained, had withered under the chill of monastic contempt and the onslaught of barbarian invaders. For centuries no poet sang; then Petrarch recalled the banished Muses. Ancient art had declined in the time of Constantine, and nothing that was not awkward or barbarous had emerged from the Gothic shadows until Giotto (*c.* 1276–1337) restored painting to the light. Erasmus discerned the same pattern in the history of religion. The great Church Fathers of antiquity had united wisdom and eloquence in an admirable harmony; but the same barbarian flood that had drowned "good letters" had also muddied the springs of Christian piety. Erasmus attributed the damage to monks and scholastics. Incapable of eloquence, barbarized by a contentious logic, medieval theology—in his view—was arid, presumptuous, and unedifying. Only in his own day, he felt, was sacred truth, in the company of classical letters, beginning to emerge from Cimmerian darkness. In the eyes of Renaissance humanists history was a great arc sadly sagging in the middle. On one side was the greatness of ancient achievement; on the other, the contemporary rebirth of piety, art, and literature. Between them stretched a middle age of cultural and intellectual squalor.

The conviction that they lived at the beginning of a new and brilliant period of human history (rather than near the end of the fourth and last monarchy or the sixth and last age) filled the humanists with vivid optimism. Before their hopes faded during the bitter ideological struggles of the Reformation, European intellectuals repeatedly chorused their self-congratulations on living in a golden age. To be sure, much still needed reform and restoration. But grammar, eloquence, painting, architecture, sculpture, and music were being reborn. Like Prometheus, men of genius were "seizing the splendid torch of wisdom from the heavens."[3] There seemed almost no limit to possibility and expectation, and men looked forward to an almost immediate future when all branches of knowledge would recover their pristine beauty; when Roman eloquence would be restored and a beneficial knowledge of Greek firmly reestablished; when the *studia humanitatis*, coupled with a revived and purer Christianity, would become the common treasure of a cultivated elite. Early sixteenth-century men faced the future with confidence and hope.

The humanist periodization of history transformed men's sense of the past in another way. Since the medieval historian had believed that his own historical epoch went back to the reign of Augustus (27 B.C.–14 A.D.), he had been unconscious of the intellectual and imaginative gulf that had to be crossed if the ancient world was to be understood. Apart from the inescapable fact that this world was pagan, it could have for him no special character or style. He regarded the Romans as his contemporaries. The familiarity imposed on him by a theological periodization weakened his ability to see Rome as a culture complete in itself, quite different and separate from his contemporary world. By sharply dividing medieval from ancient history and their own age from the recent past, Renaissance humanists encouraged in Europeans a very gradual development of what Nietzsche was to call the "pathos of historical distance," on which the modern sense of history depends. They came consciously to recognize that a thousand years separated them from classical Rome. They realized too that this past was dead, that it formed a distinct historical period, remote, complete, and over. This sense of historical mortality is the pathos of the past and the price of understanding it. One does not necessarily have to escape the conditioning of one's own epoch, country, and class in order to understand a contemporary. But if one imagines that an ancient Roman is essentially one's contemporary, one can never escape provincialism or be free of anachronisms.

[3]Robert Gaguin, *Epistole et orationes*, ed. by Louis Thuasne (Paris, 1904), Vol. II, p. 26.

A forger needs unusual historical sensitivity in order to avoid anachronisms. It is good evidence of a sharpening sense of history among Renaissance men that a young humanist architect could produce a clever pastiche of a Roman comedy, and that Michelangelo carved a cupid that passed for an antique. The same feeling for style and period shaped a critical method which made possible the exposure of the less skillful forgeries of the past—more evidence of historical awareness. Lorenzo Valla (1406–1457) proved the spuriousness of the Donation of Constantine, a document actually written in the eighth century but purporting to be the legal act by which Constantine recognized the superior dignity of the bishop of Rome and conferred on him extensive properties in various parts of Italy. Valla pointed out (among other less probing arguments) that the word "fief" occurred in it, although both the word and the institution were unknown in fourth-century Rome. Erasmus applied similar critical techniques to the Bible. In his Latin translation of the New Testament, published with his famous edition of the Greek text in 1516, he omitted the verse (the *Comma Johanneum*) in the First Epistle of John that is the scriptural basis of the doctrine of the Trinity. Both in the Vulgate (the Latin translation by St. Jerome, c. 340–420, which was authoritative in the Middle Ages and in the Roman Church) and in the King James version, the text of I John 5:7–8 reads as follows: "And there are three that bear record in heaven, the Father, the Word, and the Holy Ghost: and these three are one. And there are three that bear witness in earth, the spirit, and the water, and the blood: and these three agree in one." Erasmus proved the first of these verses to be apocryphal. He found it in no Greek manuscript. It was missing in several of his oldest Latin manuscripts. He discovered that it was unknown to any Christian writer before the fourth century. He argued, with perfect cogency, that if the text *had* existed, it would surely have been quoted by orthodox writers in a period when the doctrine of the Trinity was the center of theological controversy; and he concluded—modern scholarship confirms him—that the text must have been interpolated into the New Testament after the Council of Nicaea (325) in order to give biblical sanction to the Trinitarian formula adopted there.

Textual criticism of this kind is the concrete embodiment of an historical sense and represents the beginning of modern "scientific" history. It is understandable that the civilization which produced it produced also the early classics of modern historical writing: Leonardo Bruni's *History of Florence* (1420), Machiavelli's *Discourses on Livy* (1516–1517) and *Florentine History* (1525), Francesco Guicciardini's *History of Italy* (1535), and Jean Bodin's *Easy Introduction to the Study of History* (1566). Renaissance historians have obvious faults: a facile moralism, a narrow concentration on political and military narrative, an inconsistent application of the critical techniques they had themselves discovered, a tendency to conceal their sources under a flow of Ciceronian rhetoric and to sacrifice accuracy to elegance. But if there are difficulties in their assumption that history is a branch of literature, there are far greater difficulties in the medieval assumption that it is a branch of theology. The positive contribution of Renaissance historians was to secularize historical writing.

History regained its causal autonomy. Recourse to God's providential plan or to direct intervention by God in order to explain historical events became rarer. The explanations advanced by Bruni, Machiavelli, and Guicciardini are usually natural rather than supernatural, involving causes rooted in the appetites of individuals or in the ambitions of particular social or political groups. Renaissance historians also secularized historical writing in another way: by introducing novel principles of selection, new criteria of what was important, of what should and should not be included in a work of history. The most characteristic genre of medieval historical writing was the world chronicle, a universal history of mankind from the creation to the Last Judgment in which the test of relevance was the religious significance of an event and the edification to be drawn from it. The greatest Renaissance historians were laymen of wide experience in law, government, and diplomacy. They wanted to be politically rather than theologically effective. So they normally restricted their narratives to the history of a single state and selected for emphasis events which might help their contemporaries understand and control the political, diplomatic, and military situations in which they found themselves.

Finally, Renaissance historians had a more secular conception of the uses of history, one which fitted it admirably for its important place in humanist education. Instead of being an illustration and justification of God's ways to man, history was, in their view, a guide to life. The study of history incites to virtue and discourages vice. It trains future statesmen in politics and war. It is the mother of experience and the grandmother of wisdom. Old men are said to be wise because their judgment rests on the accumulated experience of a lifetime; a right reading of history builds a vicarious experience that also makes men wise. The new history was thus a secular narrative of past politics or a comparative study of ancient and contemporary institutions, elegantly written, coherently organized, practical in purpose, with causes and motives explained in human terms. The works of historians like Bruni and Guicciardini remained models for generations.

THE REDISCOVERY OF THE CLASSICS

The humanist's secular conception of history and his sense of the historical distance separating him from Greece and Rome transformed the way Europeans read the classics. Renaissance scholars claimed to have recovered ancient literature from the dust and neglect of a millennium.

One must not take their claim literally. To be sure, humanists did popularize certain Latin authors and works little read by their predecessors: Plautus, for example, Cicero's *Letters*, the histories of Livy and Tacitus. They read in the original Greek works that men in the Middle Ages had read largely in selected Latin extracts, epitomes, and translations. Above all, they completed the European appropriation of its Hellenic inheritance. Aristotle had been recovered in the twelfth and thirteenth centuries. Most of Plato's dialogues, all of Herodotus and Thucydides, and the most important works of the Greek dramatists, poets, and Church Fathers became an integral part of European culture only in the Renaissance. Humanist editions and translations of Greek works represent an enormous increment of knowledge. They stimulated intellectual life as profoundly as the discoveries of the explorers stimulated economic life. Nevertheless, it must be recognized that a large body of ancient literature had been conveniently available for centuries. The Latin classics survived at all only because they were copied and recopied in the *scriptoria*, or writing rooms, of medieval monasteries. Virgil and Ovid were universally popular in the Middle Ages. Cicero and Seneca were respected ethical teachers. A tenth-century German nun wrote little plays, imitating the style of Terence (though with a different content). From the twelfth century on Roman law was systematically studied at the University of Bologna. Medieval medical knowledge was a précis of Galen, its physics a reworking of Aristotle. The achievement of Renaissance humanists, then, was not that they read the classics, but that they read them, whether familiar or rediscovered, with eyes newly trained in the perspective of history.

What this could mean is suggested by the novel treatment of classical themes and motifs in Renaissance art. Artists of the high Middle Ages had illustrated classical themes and subjects—Dido and Aeneas, for example, and the antique gods—just as medieval scholars had read and quoted the *Aeneid* and Cicero's *De officiis*. They had often borrowed classical motifs and reproduced, sometimes with great fidelity, the classical images of Hercules, Orpheus, and Atlas. What is striking is that classical motifs were almost never used to represent classical themes, and conversely, classical themes were almost never expressed by classical motifs—a disassociation caused by a lack of historical sense and by an inability, both intellectual and emotional, to grasp the fundamentally secular assumptions of ancient thought. Thus a classical visual image was given a Christian, nonclassical meaning, while pagan themes were illustrated by Christian and medieval motifs. In the one case a depiction clearly based upon the antique figure of Orpheus might be used to portray David, or a Hercules-like figure might represent Christ. In the other case, classical subjects were illustrated by invariably anachronistic images. Dido and Aeneas appeared as a fourteenth-century couple playing chess, Venus as an aristocratic lady fully clothed and plucking a lute. One novelty of Renaissance artists was to close this gap between classical theme and classical motif. For the first time since antiquity, Mercury recaptured his youth and beauty and Venus her naked sensuality. Portrayals of classical heroes, nymphs, and divinities invaded the homes of princes, aristocrats, and bankers, and among the still far more numerous representations of the Virgin and the saints arose pictorial reflections of classical sentiment as fresh and precise as the "Galatea" of Raphael (see p. 85).

The reintegration of classical theme and classical motif in Renaissance art is one aspect of a vaster reintegration: that of the classical text and its classical meaning. Just as medieval artists Christianized classical motifs, so medieval scholars mined classical texts for information relevant to their own concerns and read into these texts Christian meanings. They interpreted Virgil's *Aeneid* as the itinerary of the human soul (Aeneas) to the promised land (Latium) and of its ascension from human love (Dido) to divine love. They identified Aristotle's First Cause with the Christian God. They equated natural law with the ten commandments of the Old Testament. A philosopher, the ancients had said, is a lover of wisdom. Christian theologians identified wisdom with the second Person of the Trinity and defined the philosopher as a lover of Christ. Aristotle's virtue of temperance came to include chastity, and monks understood Stoic detachment from the things of this world as a form of Christian asceticism. Ancient philosophers were often said to have been divinely illuminated, inspired to speak the truth by God as He had inspired Moses, Abraham, or David. Necessarily, medieval scholars found in the classics what they had already assumed to be there.

Allegorical interpretations of the *Aeneid* continued to be published in the sixteenth century, but the great epic poem was also read in historical perspective as a glorification of Augustan Rome. Some Renaissance scholars continued to pillage the ancient texts in the inevitably rewarded expectation of finding pearls in dung heaps. But others passed beyond St. Augustine's injunction that the classics were to be used and not enjoyed. They took pleasure in the melody of Catullus and the epigrammatic thrust of Tacitus, just as they took pleasure in the balance and harmony of ancient orations and ancient temples.

Some Renaissance philosophers defended the divine illumination of the ancients and used as much ingenuity Christianizing Plato as St. Thomas Aquinas had used harmonizing Christianity and Aristotelianism. Thus Renaissance Platonists located Plato's Ideas in the divine intellect. Just as the architect—they argued—has in his mind an image of the building he is erecting, which, as his model, he tries to imitate exactly, so God has in His divine mind the Ideas and patterns of all things, the Ideas of the sun and moon, of men, of all animals, plants, and stones, of the elements, and indeed of everything else as well. This divine mind—and here is the

identification on which the Christian Platonism of the Renaissance rested
—is the intelligible world, where all things exist, not in a material or
sensible manner of being, but in a truer, nobler, more beautiful way, the
ideal or intelligible. Man's contemplation of the intelligible beauty of the
Ideas is therefore a kind of celestial love, *desiderio intellettuale di ideal
bellezza*,[4] (the "intellectual desire for ideal beauty"), and once man has
turned to the eternal beauty and light of God, his soul shines with the
light of the Ideas in an esctatic vision akin to that of the mystics.

Yet at the same time that Marsilio Ficino (1433–1499), the greatest of
the Renaissance Neoplatonists, was discovering this Platonic-Christian
vision, other scholars were founding the disciplines of classical philology,
classical archaeology, numismatics, and epigraphy, and coming progressively closer to a critical understanding of institutions as different from
their own as the Greek games and the Roman senate, of the principles of
ancient jurisprudence and political theory, of the distinctive values and
moral ideals not only of Platonism, but of Aristotelianism, Stoicism, and
Epicureanism as well. Disciplined by the insight that the arts and literature of antiquity were the historical expression of a particular period and a
unique society detached from their own, they gradually built up, through
the critical and historical study of ancient texts, an image of ancient
thought and institutions more nearly approximating ancient reality than
any achieved before.

This more objective knowledge of the admired civilizations of Greece
and Rome had an impact on the European mind analogous to that of the
discoveries. Renewed contact with the cultures of antiquity, like serious
contact for the first time with the Aztecs and the Incas, the Indians and
the Chinese, encouraged in sixteenth-century Europeans a new freedom
from temporal provincialism (the conviction that the culture of one's own
age has a peculiar virtue and validity) and a more self-conscious understanding of their own society. Montaigne has described the provincialism
of a society whose values are unquestioned: "We all call barbarism that
which does not fit in with our usages. And indeed we seem to have no
other standard of truth and reason but the example and model of the
opinions and usages of the country we live in. There we always see the
perfect religion, the perfect government, the perfect and accomplished
manner of doing things."[5] That Montaigne could make such a statement is
itself an excellent demonstration of how contact with foreign cultures
widens the mind's horizons and undermines the ignorant self-satisfaction
characteristic of every society that considers its values absolute.

Correspondingly, it was no accident that the first utopia since

[4]Pico della Mirandola, *De hominis dignitate, Heptaplus, De ente et uno e scritti vari*, ed.
by Eugenio Garin (Florence, 1942), p. 500.

[5]*Essais*, I, xxxi, ed. by F. Strowski (Bordeaux, 1906), Vol. I, p. 268.

antiquity—that of the English humanist Sir Thomas More—appeared in 1516 and was inspired in part by an account of the voyages of Amerigo Vespucci (1451–1512) to the New World and in part by first-hand knowledge of Plato's *Republic*. For utopias, as Robert Burton (1577–1640) later put it in his *Anatomy of Melancholy*, are "witty fictions" describing the supposed effects which would result from imagined institutions different from one's own. By playing the utopian game, More made explicit what had been implicit in the discoveries of explorers and historians from the beginning: the extraordinary variety of possible institutions and beliefs. Just as Copernicus had shown that the earth was not necessarily the center of the universe, as Vasco da Gama and Columbus had shown that Europe was not necessarily the center of the world, as Luther was to prove that Rome was not necessarily the center of Christian Europe, so More's *Utopia* suggested that the perfection of European standards and European values could no longer be taken for granted. His point was not that foreign societies or his fictional utopian society were better than his own. On the contrary, he was certain that many of their beliefs and practices were worse. More's purpose, like that of Machiavelli and Bodin in their comparative institutional studies, was rather to exploit the variety of possible and actual societies as a means of forcing his readers to reexamine their own convictions in an unexpected perspective—from the outside as it were, across a distance analogous to the historical distance from which the humanist regarded Rome—and then to accept, reject, or modify them consciously in the light of this comparative knowledge. Knowledge of other worlds and of the past thus fostered a more detached comprehension of the virtues and corruptions of the present; while the comparison of foreign laws and customs with those of Europe suggested the revolutionary possibility of conscious choice among institutional, moral, and religious alternatives.

THE DIGNITY OF MAN

Yet the achievement of historical distance, the realization that antiquity constituted a period and a culture detached from their own was not the only reason for the humanist's ability to understand the classics more perceptively. Equally important was the fact that transformations in European society were creating objective parallels between the problems of Europeans and those of the ancients. These changes made many ancient solutions relevant to contemporary needs. Here perhaps we reach one root both of the Renaissance enthusiasm for the classics and of the sense of history with which fifteenth- and sixteenth-century men read them. They grasped again the Roman idea of sovereignty because they no longer lived in a feudal society in which public office and public powers were owned as private property, because the fact of sovereignty was again a real part of their daily lives. The English gentry had no difficulty with the Roman idea of absolute property in land because they had begun to enclose their fields and assert their sole proprietary rights to their estates. Italians could more nearly understand Plato's *Laws* and Aristotle's *Politics* because their communal life too was centered in city-states. The idea of *humanitas*, the ancient definitions of wisdom and virtue, Cicero's conception of the orator and of eloquence, the physical perfection of the classical gods—in short, the humanist ideal of man and the educational program that embodied it—attracted men of substance because they seemed to find their own conception of themselves reproduced there more nearly than it was in the ideal human types created by the priestly feudal society of the past.

The humanist philosophy of man was a complex reweaving of traditional ideas. Its novelty, like that of most innovations in intellectual history, is one of selection, arrangement, and emphasis. Professors of theology in medieval universities had normally defined man by what he lacked, by the gulf that separated him from God. (Protestant theologians would unequivocally do the same.) Humanists preferred to praise him and to define him in terms of the positive capacities generously granted him by God when He created him in His own image. "God clearly and especially manifested his wisdom in the creation of man," wrote a German humanist in 1512. "Making man the link between [the sensible and intellectual worlds], he endowed him with magnificent gifts, attributing to him reason and free will, a most excellent gift and noble vestige of that supreme liberty with which God created all things." Not all humanists trusted reason. They were suspicious of the metaphysical and logical subtlety of medieval scholastic philosophy and of the theological rationalism that had created intellectual structures like the *Summa theologiae* of St. Thomas Aquinas. Caution in scrutinizing the divine mind was usual among them, while their attitude to the claims of metaphysicians and logicians was a certain skepticism. An early fifteenth-century Italian humanist condensed the common view in an epigrammatic formula: *Scire nostrum nihil aliud est quam rationabiliter dubitare*[6] ("all our knowledge is no more than rational doubt"). But if many humanists set limits to the competence of reason, very few set any to that of the will. Indeed, they minimized the power of the speculative intellect precisely in order to emphasize the greater importance and freedom of the will. "The will alone is really ours and in our power. The rest—understanding, memory, imagination—all this can be taken from us, altered, troubled by a thousand accidents, but not the will."[7]

Man can know and will the good. On this assertion more humanists

[6]*Epistolario di Coluccio Salutati*, ed. by Francesco Novati (Rome, 1891–1905), Vol III, p. 603.

[7]Pierre Charron, *De la sagesse*, I, xviii, ed. by A. Duval (Paris, 1820–1824), Vol. 1, p. 142.

agreed than on almost any other. They repeated Aristotle's eloquent words in the third book of the *Ethics*, his statement that since it is in man's power to do good or evil acts, "being good or vicious characters is in our power." Man is the "originator or generator of his actions as he is the generator of his children." They revived the story, unused in the Middle Ages, of Hercules at the fork of the road, and made it a favorite subject of Renaissance painting. Arrived at the parting of the ways, Hercules could take either the road of vice or the road of virtue. So man at each important moment of his life is free to choose. Inspired by encomiums of man in classical literature and in the Greek Church Fathers, the Florentine philosopher Pico della Mirandola (1463–1494) wrote an *Oration on the Dignity of Man* (1498) in which he located human dignity in man's freedom from any fixed or static place in the chain of being that links him to the angels and to God above him and to the animals, plants, and inert matter below him. Man is an autonomous moral agent, containing in his own nature the possibility of the most varied development, who can by free choice become akin to any being, become like a rock or plant or beast if he turn toward evil, like the angels or like a mortal god if he turn toward good. Nature seeks to realize that perfection of which it is capable. Since human nature is free, its progress toward perfection is an offered choice. This idea of human freedom was given a coherent statement by the French humanist Charles de Bovelles (1480–1533). Our actions, he wrote in 1509, have three causes or principles: intelligence, will, and power. Through his intelligence man can know what should be done; he can will to do what should be done; he has the power, finally, to act according to his knowledge and desire because he is all things and can become all things. All three causes are necessary for a free and efficacious act. For even if one understands an action and has the power to perform it, that action will be vain if one does not want to do it; similarly, one may know and desire an object, but the knowledge and desire are vain without the power to acquire it; and if one desires something and has the capacity to get it, yet has no clear understanding of what one wants, again action is neither efficacious nor free. Freedom is the harmonious union of knowledge, capacity, and will, and this freedom is a human conquest, the result of the gradual development, through education and a long series of appropriate choices, of the habit of virtue.

The identification of human dignity with moral freedom suggested an ideal of man different from those of the Middle Ages. Medieval admiration had focused on three human types: the saint, the monk, and the chivalrous knight. The humanist conception of a desirable human being was less specialized. The ideal man was noble, but his nobility, his *gentilezza*, as Dante had called it, unlike the knight's was based not on birth but on virtue, and his virtues, unlike the monk's, were not exclusively ascetic and contemplative. The humanist idea of perfection included both mind and body, contemplation and action, the good of the soul and what contemporaries called the goods of fortune—wealth, physical beauty, and health. "Man is a mortal but happy god," wrote the humanist architect Leon Battista Alberti (1404–1472), "because he combines capacity for virtuous action with rational understanding," thus echoing a wonderful passage in Cicero's *De finibus*: "Just as the horse is born to run, the ox to plow, the dog to scent a trail, so is man, as Aristotle says, born to two things: to know and to act, and in this he is almost a mortal god." Contemplation to the exclusion of all else is the prerogative of angels. Man contemplates to the extent that his soul is divine and separate, but as a man, a composite of soul and body living in the world, he exercises the moral virtues and is useful to his family, friends, fellow citizens, and prince. Humanists quoted another famous line from Cicero: *Virtutis laus omnis in actione consistat* ("the true praise of virtue lies in doing"); and Alberti summed up the argument in a sentence equally memorable, "Man was born to be useful to man."

HUMANISM AND ART

"The good painter," wrote Leonardo da Vinci, "must paint principally two things: man and the ideas in man's mind."[8] Because Leonardo's contemporaries did indeed choose these as their subject, few sources make so attractively explicit the humanist philosophy of man as do Renaissance works of art. The poems, orations, moral essays, histories, and educational treatises of even the greatest humanists are little read today except by specialists. Since most of them are written in Latin, only specialists *can* read them. The paintings, statues, and buildings of Renaissance artists are more accessible, even to moderns more easily moved by African masks than by the Cnidian Aphrodite.

Renaissance art was a humanist art in its sources, its content, and its style. Consider the "Allegory of Philosophy" by Albrecht Dürer (1471–1528). The woodcut illustrates, perhaps with more learning than charm, a volume of love poems written by the German humanist Conrad Celtis and published in 1502. Celtis himself devised its complicated program, wrote the verses included in it, and provided the artist with a sketch showing the general arrangement of the figures. Artistic activity in the high Middle Ages had normally been an anonymous, communal enterprise controlled by the clergy and directed by ecclesiastical authority to orthodox religious ends. By the sixteenth century, humanists had replaced clerics as the typical "inventors" of the subject matter of works of art.

Dürer's woodcut is humanist in another way. It illustrates a humanist

[8]Quoted by Anthony Blunt, *Artistic Theory in Italy 1450–1600* (Oxford, 1940), p. 34.

Allegory of Philosophy. Woodcut by Dürer illustrating the
Amores of Conrad Celtis, published in 1502.

ideal of knowledge. The central figure is a woman, sumptuously gowned
and jeweled, wearing a crown and seated on a throne. A tag identifies her
as Philosophy. The literary source for both Celtis and Dürer is the
opening paragraphs of the popular *Consolation of Philosophy*, by the late
Roman moralist and scholar Boethius (*c.* 480–524). In a dream, Boethius saw a majestic woman: "In her right hand she had certain books,
and in her left hand she held a scepter," while on the lower part of her
dress was "placed the Greek letter Π, and on the upper Θ, and between
the two letters, like stairs, there were certain degrees made by which there
was a passage from the lower to the higher letter." Celtis made one
change. He replaced Boethius' Π by the letter Φ, probably intending it
to represent *phronesis*, or prudence, defined by Cicero as "practical knowledge of things to be sought for and of things to be avoided." The two
Greek letters therefore stand for the two great divisions of philosophy,
ethics and metaphysics (Θ denotes *theoria*, speculative or contemplative
philosophy). The "stairs" between them are the seven liberal arts: grammar, logic, rhetoric, arithmetic, geometry, astronomy, and music.

Celtis spelled out the meaning of the picture in verses at the top and bottom. "Everything in heaven and on earth, in the air and sea, all things human, everything the flaming god [the sun] brings to pass in the whole world [of nature], by philosophy I hold them all in my breast." And again: "The Greeks call me *sophia* [wisdom], the Latins *sapientia* [wisdom]. The Egyptians and Chaldeans discovered me, the Greeks wrote me down, the Latins translated me, the Germans have added to me." In medallions fixed to the wreath around the central figure are portraits of the "Egyptian" astronomer Ptolemy, Plato the Greek, the Latins Cicero and Virgil, and to represent the wisdom of the Germans, Albertus Magnus, the teacher of St. Thomas Aquinas. His inclusion is a touch of German nationalism, but a reminder too that the great scholastics of the Middle Ages continued to be widely read and admired throughout the sixteenth century. In each corner is one of the four winds, with accessory objects symbolizing one of the four elements (fire, air, water, and earth), one of the four humors (the choleric, the sanguine, the phlegmatic, and the melancholic), one of the four seasons, and one of the four ages of man. Finally, on each of the arms of the throne is a Greek inscription: on the left, "First honor God," on the right, "Be just to all." Celtis took them from an obscure didactic poem, actually by a first-century Hellenistic Jew, which Renaissance humanists mistakenly attributed to an early Greek poet named Phocylides of Miletus. Equally mistakenly, they believed that the poem shone with Christian doctrine, one more example of a heathen poet who had preached monotheism and Christian ethics centuries before Christ.

The wise man, clearly, should know something about everything, have some knowledge of all things divine and human. He must be both humanist and encyclopedist. For the word "encyclopedia," as more than one sixteenth-century scholar pointed out, is made up of the words *kyklos* ("circle," "orb") and *paedeia* (*humanitas*) and denotes therefore an all-embracing *humanitas*. Dürer has made his central figure the symbol of that ideal.

The idea of *humanitas* included virtue as well as knowledge; and virtue, as we have seen, was thought to be the more important. In 1502, the year that Dürer's "Allegory of Philosophy" appeared, Andrea Mantegna (1431–1506) finished his "Minerva Expelling the Vices from the Grove of Virtue," which he painted for Isabella d'Este, marchioness of Mantua, according to a program supplied by one of her humanist advisers. In it he pictured the kingdom of the will and of moral choice as fancifully and pedantically as Dürer portrayed the realm of intellect.

Vice has entered the grove of virtue, deranging a garden ordered by art. The pool has become an infected swamp. Venus, represented here as the mother of the vices, has imprisoned the mother of the virtues in a rock. (Mantegna records her call for help on the ribbon at the right: "O Gods!

Minerva Expelling the Vices from the Grove of Virtue. *Painting by Mantegna.
The Louvre, Paris.*

Come to my aid. I am the mother of the virtues.") Standing on the back
of a centaur, emblem of a humanity more beast than man, Venus surveys
her conquest. In the venereal pool wallow Sloth, Ingratitude, Ignorance,
Avarice, Hate, Suspicion, Fraud, and Malice. A female satyr with her satyr
children stands for lasciviousness. A little monkey woman carries bags of
seeds labeled "the bad," "the worse," and "the worst." Behind the garden
the mountain seems to explode, in a natural catastrophe which comments
on the destruction by vice of the order, beauty, and harmony of the moral
world and of the human soul. The spirit of the grove, a ghostly olive tree
at the left, joins its prayers to those of the imprisoned mother of the
virtues, and lifting imploring arms, calls out to the gods—in Latin, Greek,
and Hebrew—to expel the vices from the land and accompany the heavenly virtues back to earth. (The Latin inscription is correct; the Greek
reproduces the Latin in a Latin script meant to look deceptively like
Greek; the Hebrew is an arbitrary arrangement of letters. Study of Greek
and Hebrew was more preached than practiced, even in the sixteenth
century, and the Renaissance remained a fundamentally Latin culture.)

Answering these prayers, Prudence, or moral wisdom, in the guise of Minerva, rushes in from the left, preceded by Diana (with her bow) and Chastity (carrying an extinguished torch). In the sky on a cloud, waiting for their sister to open the way for their return to earth, are the three other cardinal virtues: Justice (on the left with sword and scales), Fortitude (wearing a lion's skin as a helmet), and Temperance (holding two jars). The fierceness of the fight is emphasized by a fantastic confrontation in the clouds, where an attentive eye can discern heads in profile facing each other, some light, some dark, personifying the combat of vice and virtue and giving it a cosmic resonance.

The theme of the battle of virtues and vices was an old one. But Mantegna has treated it with a typically humanist sensibility. The battle is secular, without specifically Christian references. It records the recurrent struggle of man to order his soul, to subordinate his passions to the rule of reason. It assumes freedom of choice and a significant degree of moral autonomy. As Pico della Mirandola had taught, man can become all things. Virtue is as natural as vice. Both are in man's power. The battle within him is hot and continuous precisely because the stakes are high and the choice is real.

It has been argued that the humanist emphasis on man's dignity and moral freedom weakened religious sentiment. Despite the absence of overtly Christian allusions in such works as Mantegna's painting, this is not true. No serious evidence exists that any fifteenth- or sixteenth-century European was an atheist. It is most unlikely that any Renaissance humanist was a pagan. Humanists were good Christians, quite as good Christians as thirteenth-century professors of theology had been. They were not necessarily the same *kind* of Christians. There are styles in religiosity as there are styles in art; and the one tells us a good deal about the other. The particular flavor of humanist piety is perhaps best caught and expressed in Renaissance church architecture, and especially in its greatest innovation, the circular church.

A church is the house of God. In order to be worthy of God's perfection, it must be built in God's image; that is, it must embody (and so define for us) the particular qualities that an age or culture attributes to God. The humanist architects of the Renaissance believed that the ideal church should be located at the center of the city, stand isolated and elevated on a pedestal in the middle of a spacious piazza, and be sublimely beautiful. How did they propose to achieve staggering beauty? By geometry—because only geometry can create that perfect harmony of proportion which is beauty itself. Since the noblest and most beautiful geometrical shape is the circle (an unquestioned assumption architects shared with philosophers, poets, and astronomers) and since, because of its divine simplicity, uniformity, and equality, the circle of all shapes most adequately mirrors God, the ideal church must be circular. The circular

Tempietto. *Designed by Bramante in 1502. S. Pietro in Montorio, Rome.*

temple, wrote the great architect Andrea Palladio (1518–1580), "is enclosed by one circumference only, in which is to be found neither beginning nor end, and the one is indistinguishable from the other; its parts correspond to each other and all of them participate in the shape of the whole; and moreover every part being equally distant from the center, such a building demonstrates extremely well the unity, the infinite essence, the uniformity and the justice of God."[9] As an example of what he meant, Palladio picked one of the smallest and loveliest churches in the world, the Tempietto in Rome by Donato Bramante (1444–1514). It fulfills virtually every requirement of the humanist church: it is perfectly round and domed; it stands freely on a high platform; it is virtually without decoration, perfectly simple and perfectly proportioned.

The qualities of Bramante's Tempietto are also the qualities of humanist piety: simplicity, sobriety, serenity, equilibrium. Its form and proportion make a clear statement about God, man, and nature. The harmony and symmetry of the church reflect the harmony and symmetry of the world. God has created and ordered the world according to immutable mathematical laws. The structure of the universe is therefore mathematical and harmonious.

[9]Quoted by Rudolf Wittkower, *Architectural Principles in the Age of Humanism* (London, 1949), p. 21.

In the view of the humanist, this harmony is best and most easily perceived in the human body, "because from the human body," in the words of an Italian mathematician who also wrote an early and important treatise on double-entry bookkeeping, "derive all measures and their denominations and in it is to be found all and every ratio and proportion by which God reveals the innermost secrets of nature."[10] Indeed, man is able to build a church in God's image only because God created men in His image and made him the center of a rational and harmonious world. Admiration of the harmony of his body and of the world arouses man's admiration and love of God, while the harmonies of nature teach him something about the nature of God—the one infinite, perfect, generous creator of a geometrically harmonious universe.

Since the harmony of man's body was regarded by the humanist as the measure of all other terrestrial harmonies, it is not surprising that in the Renaissance the human body, particularly the nude, became the central subject of art; art itself, in the first decade of the sixteenth century, became the harmonious arrangement of ideal forms in a rationalized geometrical space. The "Galatea" of Raphael (1483–1520) is a ravishing example.

Agostino Chigi (*c.* 1465–1520) a Sienese merchant who made his fortune and that of his family as a papal banker, commissioned this fresco about 1514 for his villa on the Tiber. Here he entertained artists, poets, cardinals, and the pope himself. After dinner in the garden he liked negligently to invite his guests to toss into the river the golden plates they had just finished eating off—only to retrieve them later in the night from nets cunningly deployed under the water.

In the fresco, Raphael chose to represent the milk-white sea nymph Galatea, the beloved of Acis, sung by Theocritus and Ovid among the ancients and by the Italian poets Angelo Poliziano (1454–1494) and Pietro Bembo (1470–1547) among contemporaries. Galatea rides a conch shell pulled by two dolphins. Against a background of sky and sea veined like an antique marble, nereids and tritons, hippocamps and cupids, celebrate her triumph. The scene is a vision of antiquity consciously disciplined by historical and archaeological expertise: the figures come directly from a nereid sarcophagus. Raphael's successful effort to make the figure of Galatea an image of ideal beauty represents a conscious revival of the similar effort of ancient art. "To paint a beautiful woman," he wrote about the "Galatea" to his friend and patron Baldassare Castiglione, "I need to see many beautiful women. . . . But since there is a dearth both of good judges of what is beautiful and of beautiful women, I use as my guide a certain idea of the beautiful that I carry in my mind."[11] This idea

[10]Quoted by Wittkower, *Architectural Principles*, p. 14.

[11]V. Golzio, *Raffaello nei documenti, nelle testimonianze dei contemporanei e nella letteratura del suo secolo* (Vatican City, 1936), pp. 30–31.

The Nymph Galatea. *Wall
painting by Raphael in the
Villa Farnesina, Rome.*

of the beautiful he derived in practice from the canons of classical art and
from the example of ancient sculpture. The same idealizing impulse
controls the tight geometry of the composition. Like every Renaissance
artist, Raphael intended to imitate nature—but he regarded nature as
ordered, harmonized by geometry, just as Copernicus, and later Johannes
Kepler (1571–1630), were certain they would find ideal geometrical patterns behind the confusing particularity of observed experience. Thus
Galatea's head is at the apex of a triangle. The horizon divides the picture
space into two equal parts, locked together in a musical harmony by
intersecting circles; the three flying *amors* outline the circumference of the
upper circle; the figures around Galatea mark the lower circumference of the
other. In the center of rational nature is a beautiful human being.

Use of the nude to determine harmonious ratios and of geometry to
rationalize nature are intimately related to the greatest artistic innovation
of the Renaissance: the systematic development of the techniques of
perspective. The use of perspective enables the artist to project a unified
three-dimensional space upon a plane. The painting surface becomes a

window through which we look into a world of rationally related solids. The objects represented seem to have the same sizes, shapes, and positions relative to each other that the actual objects located in actual space would have if seen from a single point of view. The perfection of exact perspective construction in Florence about 1420 was an extraordinary accomplishment. Unknown to any previous culture, these techniques of perspective were to dominate European painting from 1420 until the end of the nineteenth century, giving it, despite the succession of schools and styles, a remarkable cohesion and humanity. Their discovery is a chapter in the prehistory of the scientific revolution. It took place just at the time that men were developing the definition, also in Florence, of the educational and cultural program of humanism. Their abandonment—first apparent in such works as the paintings of the Postimpressionists and Picasso's "Demoiselles d'Avignon" (1906–1907)—is one aspect of the collapse of humanist values in the decades before the First World War.

THE THEORY AND PRACTICE OF EDUCATION

Because humanists believed that man's free will could be trained to virtue and that the piety and the active civic and moral virtues they particularly admired could be taught, education was central to the humanist program. The curriculum was designed to educate laymen rather than priests, to form citizens rather than monks or scholars, to produce free and civilized men, men of taste and judgment rather than professionally trained doctors, lawyers, merchants, philosophers, or theologians. It therefore concentrated on the three subjects humanists considered most suitable for achieving these purposes: Latin and Greek (including classical literature and the principles of effective discourse—rhetoric—to be learned from it), history, and moral philosophy, or ethics. These studies formed the "good and liberal arts," the *studia humanitatis*. Humanists made them the core of education because rhetoric, ethics, and history are disciplines of doing, uniquely appropriate for training useful scholar-citizens. Moral philosophy teaches the student the secret of true freedom, and defines his duty to God, family, country, and himself. It draws him from the abstract preoccupations of physics and metaphysics to fruitful activity in the world. History offers him concrete illustrations of the precepts inculcated by moral philosophy; it teaches ethics by examples. The one shows what men should do; the other what men have said and done in the past and what practical lessons we can draw for the present day. Eloquence, finally, is indispensable not only because a beautiful style is pleasurable in itself, but also because it enables us to persuade our fellow men to follow the lessons of history and the duties of ethics in their private and public lives. Literature, history, and ethics remained the core of the liberal education until the end of the nineteenth century. These studies are called liberal, wrote a humanist educator and statesman, "because they make men free," and they are called humane "because they perfect man." And again: "We call those studies liberal which are worthy of a free man; those studies by which we attain and practice virtue and wisdom; that education which calls forth, trains and develops those highest gifts of body and of mind [honor and glory], which ennoble men, and which are rightly judged to rank next in dignity to virtue only."[12]

The humanist emphasis on physical training reflects a similar human purpose. Medieval educators, suspicious of the body, had been reluctant to assign any place to physical exercise in the schools under their jurisdiction. Renaissance educators, reviving the antique ideal of a healthy mind in a sound body, wished to develop fully all an individual's potentialities, the strength and grace of his body as well as his intellectual and moral virtue. An age which redefined happiness, with Aristotle, to include money, beauty, and health as well as virtue; which redefined wisdom, with Cicero, to include knowledge of the human as well as of the divine; which, for the first time since antiquity, reestablished the portrait as a major genre and used the nude to express its image of perfect beauty—such an age was inevitably concerned to educate the body as well as the mind, to prize as peculiarly liberal and humane the harmonious cultivation of every admirable human potentiality. Thus the training of aristocratic boys in riding and fighting, which in the Middle Ages had had a strictly utilitarian purpose, acquired a new and more general signifiance when fifteenth-century schoolmasters made gymnastics and organized sports an integral part of a liberal education. "As regards a boy's physical training," wrote Pius II, pope from 1458 to 1464, "we must bear in mind that we aim at implanting habits which will prove beneficial through life. . . . Games and exercises which develop the muscular activities and general carriage of the person should be encouraged by every teacher."[13] A kind of football, for example, was very popular in Italian schools; and a member of a great Florentine family wrote a book describing its virtues: it made the body dexterous and robust and caused the sharpened mind to desire virtuous victory. This emphasis on sports was not common in northern Europe before the middle of the sixteenth century. In England, where competence in sports was ultimately to bulk so large in the ideal of the gentleman, football was considered base and mean. Football, wrote an English humanist in 1531, ought to be utterly rejected by all noblemen because there is in it "nothing but beastly furie and exstreme violence; whereof procedeth hurte, and consequently rancour and malice do remaine with them that he wounded."[14] The ideal, nevertheless, in both Italy and

[12]Woodward, *Vittorino da Feltre*, p. 102.

[13]*Ibid.*, pp. 137–138.

[14]Sir Thomas Elyot, *The Boke Named the Gouvernour*, ed. by H. H. S. Croft (London, 1880), Vol. I, pp. 295–296.

ER·ROT

TERMINVS

Pallas Apellæam nuper mirata tabellam,
Hanc ait, æternum Bibliotheca colat.
Dædaleam monstrat Musis HOLBEINNIUS artem,
Et summi Ingenii Magnus ERASMUS opes.

Erasmus of Rotterdam. *Woodcut by Hans Holbein the Younger, 1535. The old humanist rests his right hand on the head of Terminus, a Roman god whom Erasmus understood as a symbol of death.*

the north, was the man who excelled in both arms and letters, who combined contemplation and service to the state, *humanitas* and physical excellence.

Such a conception of man, the humanist believed, found its highest expression in ancient literature. A humanist education, therefore—aside from the fact that Latin was the indispensable language of the Church, diplomacy, scholarship, and the professions of law and medicine—was necessarily classical and literary. The study of letters meant the study of Latin letters. Latin, and later Greek, literature formed the core of education because, as Erasmus bluntly put it, "within these two literatures is contained all the knowledge which we recognize as of vital importance to mankind." Ancient literature was the voice itself of *humanitas*, the civilizing force which made man free and whole, refined his sensibility, molded his moral attitudes. A man was liberally educated who had achieved self-knowledge through the accurate understanding of ancient literature, whose imagination was stirred by the ideal pattern of classical humanity, who modeled his life on the image of man in the Greek and Latin classics in just the way as Scipio and Caesar had kept before their eyes the image of Alexander. The very idea of *humanitas*, indeed, suggested that a classical education was peculiarly human, that it, preeminently, civilized the rude and uncultured, that it made a human being more fully and perfectly a man. In the Renaissance a liberal education was invariably classical.

By the early sixteenth century, humanist schools were attracting students in every country of Europe. Overwhelmingly, recruitment was from two groups: the nobility and socially ambitious merchants. This particular pattern of recruitment suggests a final explanation of the Renaissance enthusiasm for the classics: a humanist education fashioned a ruling class trained to govern the early modern state in cooperation with the sovereign prince.

The declining economic resources of some of the nobility and the diminishing military and political independence of them all forced aristocrats to adapt to changing circumstance. They needed to read, write, and calculate if they were to manage their estates with the rationalism and efficiency demanded by a competitive agricultural market. They needed new standards of manners and more realistic values than the ideals of a decaying chivalry could supply if they were to become courtiers, at ease in the behavior and attitudes demanded by an evolving ceremonial. Above all they had to have adequate formal education if they were to compete successfully for royal offices and favors and represent their prince abroad or serve him profitably at home. Humanist propaganda tirelessly insisted that nobles could claim no office simply by right of birth. Only education—a humanist education—could fit a man to be a judge, councillor, governor, or military commander. Education had, in fact, become an avenue to power and influence for laymen, and many among the nobility recognized this novel situation. Adaptable nobles met the need of king and prince for educated service by sending their sons to humanist schools or adding a humanist tutor to their household. By 1500 the phenomenon was no longer unusual in Italy. Between 1500 and 1560 the reeducation of the nobility made rapid progress north of the Alps. A great Flemish noble, Jean de Lannoy, pointed out to his son what a disadvantage it had been to him not to have a Latin education: "No day passes that I do not regret this, and especially when I find myself in the council of the king or the Duke of Burgundy, and I know not nor dare to speak my opinion after the learned, eloquent legists and scholars who have spoken before me."[15] He was determined that his son should have what

[15]Quoted by J. H. Hexter, "The Education of the Aristocracy in the Renaissance," in *Reappraisals in History* (New York, 1963), p. 63.

he had lacked. Many of his peers sent their sons to a humanist college in Louvain. Nobles appeared in ever larger numbers at the universities of Salamanca, Oxford, and Paris, and at the German and Italian universities. In 1500 a humanistically educated young noble like Erasmus' pupil Lord Mountjoy was a rarity. By 1560 a modicum of cultivation was commonplace among the nobility at least in the politically more sophisticated states; and the new conception of the gentleman had been codified in one of the most important and agreeable books of the century: the *Courtier*, by Count Baldassare Castiglione (1478–1529), written between 1507 and 1510 and a best seller in Italian, French, Spanish, German, and English versions throughout the sixteenth century. A humanist education became the formal device which helped transform the members of a feudal aristocracy into diplomats, provincial governors, even customs officials. "To receive favors of princes," Castiglione wrote, "there is no better way than to deserve them." And how does one deserve them? "I would have the Courtier devote all his thought and strength of spirit," Castiglione continued, "to loving and almost adoring the prince he serves above all else, devoting his every desire and habit and manner to pleasing him."[16]

The second important source of students for the humanist educators was the urban bourgeoisie. In France, humanists educated the most active segment of the high bourgeoisie, the "Fourth Estate" of royal officers, the core—under the king—of the ruling group of the country, men who were investing their wealth and talent in the highest ecclesiastical, legal, and administrative posts, buying land and titles, and by intermarriage and the heredity of office creating the first bureaucratic nobility. Humanist schools in England and Germany showed similar patterns of recruitment. In 1496, for example, the town council of Nuremberg founded a *Poetenschule*, a humanist school distinct from the other town schools (which were run by the canons of local churches or by the Dominican order). The students were the sons of the local patriciate. They were taught the humanities in the expectation that this education would make them better citizens and rulers and would equip them for wider careers as lawyers, councillors, political secretaries, or ambassadors in the service of neighboring territorial princes or of the emperor. When the humanist John Colet founded St. Paul's School in 1509 his purpose was the same. The headmaster and teachers were married laymen and the students were sons of the London middle class. He put his school into the charge not of the church, but of "the most honest and faithful fellowship of the Mercers of London," one of the great guilds of the city. Just as the new education made courtiers out of nobles, so it made gentlemen out of merchants. The old aristocracy and the new rich were molded to a common end: royal or princely service in the sovereign territorial state.

[16]*The Book of the Courtier*, trans. by Charles Singleton (New York, 1959), pp. 110, 114.

CHAPTER 4

The Formation of the Early Modern State

THE POLITICAL ORGANIZATION of the European states reached a new level of efficiency in the century between the end of the Hundred Years' War in 1453 and the Peace of Cateau-Cambrésis, which in 1559 brought to a close the Habsburg-Valois wars. Administrative centralization had begun long before 1453, with the first efforts of medieval rulers, after the political fragmentation which had characterised the feudal age, to establish a minimum of order in their domains and to build a more widely respected authority. These efforts achieved an early partial success during the twelfth, thirteenth, and fourteenth centuries in the institution of feudal monarchy. The process was to continue long after 1559, to culminate in western Europe in the administrative reforms of the French Revolution and Napoleon and in the final unification of Germany and Italy after 1850. But it was during the late fifteenth and the sixteenth centuries that state building was most concentrated, rapid, and dramatic. Before 1453, European states were more feudal than sovereign; after 1559, they were more sovereign than feudal. Before 1453, we properly speak of the feudal state or feudal monarchy; after 1559, we speak more properly—though, as we shall see, with qualifications—of sovereign states.

The sovereign state is still the characteristic form of political organization in the contemporary world. It is our familiar reality. To understand feudalism therefore requires an act of conscious historical imagination. We must escape our temporal provincialism and imagine a society which knew no state in the modern or Roman sense; we must picture a system of government in which the normal prerogatives of the state—the authority to wage war, to tax, to administer and enforce the law—were privately owned as legal, hereditary rights by members of a military landed aristocracy. The system rested on a confusion of public power with private property. In the feudal age kings were very weak, while over much of Europe private persons exercised state powers as rights derived from their ownership of property.

By the beginning of the thirteenth century, monarchical authority had again become a significant political force. Kings passed from the defensive to the offensive. They consolidated their power and their holdings. But Europe was still clearly a feudal society and a king's great vassals continued to own important elements of public power as hereditary and legally recognized property rights. This division of power between monarch and magnate, royal lord and great vassal, was the central characteristic of feudal monarchy, an intermediate political type, standing between decentralized feudal government on the one hand and the sovereign state on the other. The feudal monarch shared with the magnates of his realm many of those powers which a Roman emperor had held intact. His relationship to all others in his realm was not that of a king to his subjects or of a republic's executive to its citizens; instead, he was linked to them by the network of personal loyalties and obligations created by the feudal bond between lord and vassal. He was chief lord, or suzerain, of a feudal hierarchy which included all members of the ruling class, and he enjoyed few powers or resources not dependent upon his position at the apex of this hierarchy. From his position in the hierarchy the king derived certain rights, privileges, and obligations—more rights, privileges, and obligations, indeed, than fell to anyone else in the hierarchy. But his vassals also had rights and privileges. In the high and late Middle Ages the forces of feudal decentralization and monarchical centralization were in precarious balance.

Between 1453 and 1559 this balance tipped in favor of the crown.

THE EMERGENCE OF THE SOVEREIGN STATE
IN WESTERN EUROPE

The pretensions of French, Spanish, and English kings in the sixteenth century were absolutist and sovereign. In 1527 the president of the highest court in France assured the reigning monarch, Francis I, that "we do not wish to dispute or minimize your power; that would be sacrilege, and we know very well that you are above the laws."[1] *Princeps legibus solutus* ("the prince is not bound by the laws"). The text is from the Roman law. Jurists cited a second ancient text: *Quicquid principi placuit legis habet vigorem* ("the will of the prince has the force of law"). These are definitions of absolutism; they also define the fundamental attribute of sovereignty: the power to make the law. The political theorist Jean Bodin (1530–1596) is explicit. *Maiestas* ("sovereignty") is the power to make law. By definition, a sovereign authority is unbound by human law and above it, for what the sovereign can make he can also unmake or change. "It is the distinguishing mark of the sovereign," wrote Bodin, "that he

---

[1] Quoted by Gaston Zeller, *Les institutions de la France au XVIe siècle* (Paris, 1948), pp. 79–80.

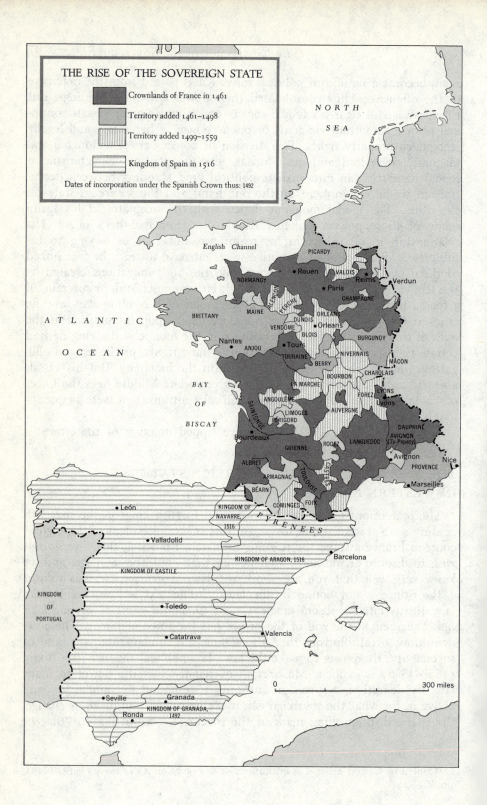

THE RISE OF THE SOVEREIGN STATE

Crownlands of France in 1461

Territory added 1461–1498

Territory added 1499–1559

Kingdom of Spain in 1516

Dates of incorporation under the Spanish Crown thus: 1492

NORTH
SEA

English Channel

PICARDY

NORMANDY • Rouen VALOIS
★ Paris Reims • Verdun
CHAMPAGNE

ATLANTIC

BRITTANY MAINE PERCHE ALENÇON
DUNOIS ORLEANS
VENDÔME • Orleans
OCEAN • Nantes BLOIS BURGUNDY
ANJOU • Tours NIVERNAIS
TOURAINE MÂCON
BERRY CHAROLAIS
BAY LA MARCHE BOURBON FOREZ LYONS
OF ANGOULÊME AUVERGNE • Lyons
BISCAY LIMOGES
SAINTONGE PÉRIGORD DAUPHINÉ
AVIGNON
• Bourdeaux (To Papacy)
RODEZ LANGUEDOC • Avignon • Nice
ALBRET GUIENNE PROVENCE
ARMAGNAC CASTRES • Marseilles
BÉARN TOULOUSE

KINGDOM OF COMINGES FOIX
NAVARRE
1516 PYRENEES

• León
KINGDOM OF ARAGON, 1516 • Barcelona

• Valladolid

KINGDOM OF CASTILE

KINGDOM
OF • Toledo
PORTUGAL • Valencia

• Catatrava

0 300 miles

• Seville • Granada
• Ronda KINGDOM OF GRANADA,
1492

The Emperor Maximilian I (1493–1519). *Engraving by Lucas van Leyden, 1510. Around the emperor's neck is the chain of the Order of the Golden Fleece.*

cannot in any way be subject to the commands of another, for it is he who makes law for the subject, abrogates laws already made, and amends obsolete law."[2] The sovereign prince is an absolute ruler limited only by divine and natural law. He monopolizes all power and justice in the state. He has drawn back into his own hands those public powers usurped from him by the magnates of the feudal age. Theoretically, he should be able to tax regularly and without consent; face his unarmed subjects with a permanent army under his sole control; command an efficient bureaucracy; dispense his justice in every case and to every subject, sharing his jurisdictional prerogatives with no one; and dominate the rival authorities of parliament, estates, and church.

Theoretical claims are one thing; practice is another. To what extent did the "new monarchs," as the Renaissance kings of France, Spain, and England have traditionally been called, exercise in fact the attributes of a sovereign ruler? To what extent had the balance of effective power shifted in their favor and away from their greater subjects? To answer these questions one must look first at what we would call today the bureaucracy—the administrative structure of the new monarchies—and more particularly, at the king's officers.

The King's Officers

At the top of the governmental hierarchy the king was supreme both in theory and in fact. He ruled through his council and great officers of state; by the middle of the sixteenth century the council was an instrument of

[2]*Six Books of the Commonwealth*, trans. by M. J. Tooley (Oxford, n.d.), p. 197.

absolute government dependent on him alone. Its composition was entirely in the king's hands. Members had no security of tenure. Their function was to carry out the wishes and policies of the king. They advised a monarch who was in no way bound by their advice. They enabled a king to do what he wished to do; they did not determine what he ought to do. Royal "ministers" could become immensely powerful; but their authority reflected exclusively the power of their royal master. They were instruments.

At the local level, on the other hand, though the king was supreme in theory, he was not always so in fact. The Castilian *corregidor* was the officer of local government most nearly approaching the bureaucratic type. The crown appointed and paid him. To prevent him from identifying himself with local interests, his term of office in one locality was limited to a maximum of five years; he was never sent to the area where he had his home; and he was forbidden to mingle in local factions, buy property, or build a house where he served. The royal council bombarded him with instructions. At the end of his term a special judge was sent down to his district to receive complaints and to prepare for the council a full report on his administration.

Justices of the peace served the Tudors of England just as efficiently as the *corregidors* served the Castilian kings. The crown appointed them and the council supervised them closely. But unlike the *corregidor*, the justice of the peace was selected for his burdensome and responsible job from among the men of substance of his own locality, and he was not paid. English local government rested on the unpaid voluntary service of wealthy amateurs. It worked remarkably well under Henry VIII (ruled 1509–1547) and Elizabeth I (ruled 1558–1603) and helped establish a valuable tradition of public service and political activity among the economically powerful. Its weakness lay in the independence implicit in voluntary service. As long as the local official was asked to enforce regulations that benefited his locality and furthered the interests of his class, he enforced them effectively and gladly. But when royal orders conflicted with his interests and convictions, he seldom resisted the temptation to disregard them.

In France, theory and practice diverged more strikingly. The principal officers of local government were the *baillis* and the *sénéchaux*, equivalent terms for the same office. They had few bureaucratic characteristics. Most were recruited from the highest nobility. They were usually absent from their administrative districts, at court or with the royal armies abroad, and the real work of administration was done by a subordinate, the *lieutenant du roi ès bailliage*. Like the *corregidor*, the *lieutenant* was an expert, a university graduate in civil or canon law, usually a bourgeois not immediately identified with the interests of the landed aristocracy. But on the crucial question of appointment bureaucratic principle, according to which an official is appointed by the sovereign authority, was constantly infringed. Sometimes the *bailli* alone appointed the *lieutenant*. Sometimes the *bailli* chose him on the advice of the notables of the district (the *gens de bien*). Sometimes the notables actually elected him themselves. Elsewhere, they selected three candidates, and the king appointed one of them. A royal edict of 1531 tried to limit the appointment of *lieutenants* exclusively to the king. In vain. The most important royal officer at the local level remained a local appointee—the client of local magnates and local interests.

It is in the context of this ambiguous relationship between the king and his officers that the selling of royal offices, the most important administrative innovation of the period, assumes its full importance. Venality of royal offices first became common in France and Spain in the early years of the sixteenth century. In return for immediate cash, kings sacrificed some of their control over the appointment of financial and judicial officers. For although the first result of the traffic in offices was an increase in royal revenue, a secondary and permanent effect was the reappearance in a new form of the feudal tendency to confuse public office and private property. This became the more obvious where venality of office led, as in France, to the inheritance of offices, and on the payment of a suitable fee they passed from father to son like feudal fiefs. The king found it very difficult to dismiss a subordinate who had bought his office and expected to pass it on to his son. Ownership of office encouraged independence of royal policy as well, and kings faced a growing inability to enforce their orders, a situation clearly indicated by the constant reiteration of commands so noticeable in any collection of sixteenth-century ordinances. By generalizing the venality of offices continental princes themselves erected obstacles to the effective exercise of royal power.

This limitation of the effective exercise of the royal will by bureaucratic inadequacy should not obscure the equally significant fact that kings were becoming noticeably stronger precisely because their officers were more numerous and more powerful. No longer were the king's officers excluded from the fiefs of powerful vassals. Royal justice touched directly, if not exclusively, each of the king's subjects. For the first time, effective political power was largely concentrated in the hands of the king and his officers instead of being fragmented among a multitude of spiritual and temporal lords. Venality itself was an essentially royal form of corruption. Its positive function was to attach thousands of magistrates to the crown by the most direct financial ties, to create indeed a "Fourth Estate" whose *esprit de corps*, ambition, and thirst for power and wealth magnified royal power at the expense of the traditional liberties and jurisdictions of the clergy, the nobility, and the towns. In this perspective, a proliferating corps of royal officers is an infallible sign of administrative centralization and the most direct institutional expression of a transfer of power from feudal magnate to sovereign prince.

The Army

A second characteristic of the new monarchies was the existence of a permanent mercenary army. Under feudalism the means of violence were privately owned and the magnates enjoyed the legal right to wage private war. In a modern sovereign state, ownership of the means of violence is a monopoly of the sovereign power, and the right to make war is limited exclusively to the state. Between 1460 and 1560 the rapidly growing wealth of Europe and the technological innovations associated with gunpowder enabled several European rulers to create armies of a new, though still intermediary, type.

The French army during the reign of Francis I is a typical example of such a force. The first steps to create it had been taken by Charles VII (ruled 1422–1461) during the last years of the Hundred Years' War. By an ordinance of 1439 he founded the *compagnies d'ordonnance*, units of heavy cavalry supported by mounted archers. The *compagnies d'ordonnance* were staffed by volunteers from the nobility, but these nobles entered the royal army in a new capacity—not as vassals performing the traditional *auxilium*, or military aid they owed their lord, but as paid volunteers in the regular and permanent service of the crown. Removed from their seigneuries, incorporated into royally recruited units where their place in an abstract military hierarchy rather than the number of feudal dependents who accompanied them to war determined their effective influence, the nobles were broken to royal discipline. They ceased to be knights and became mounted mercenaries.

In the fifteenth century, infantry was commonly conscripted by means of a semidraft. In 1448 Charles VII ordered each parish to train and furnish one archer for the royal army. These rustic reserves were not a success, and by the time Francis I became king the infantry was no longer conscripted, and had become a professional mercenary force. Captains appointed or hired by the French king organized foot soldiers—by now far more numerous than cavalry, and equipped with pikes and with arquebuses or muskets—in companies of from three to five hundred men. Recruitment was royal but not national. Some infantrymen were French, recruited in provinces like Picardy and Gascony, whose inhabitants were noted for their military brio; the majority were foreign. The archers of the king's personal bodyguard were Scots. Under a permanent agreement with Francis I, the Swiss Confederation supplied from six to sixteen thousand pikemen for each of his campaigns. After the Swiss, German *Landsknechte* were the best and most easily available mercenaries in Europe, and several thousand served regularly in the French army, reinforced by Englishmen, Italians, Poles, Greeks, and Albanians.

In France and Spain armies of this type provided the sanction of force behind royal efforts to build centralized sovereign states. Like the corps of administrative officers, however, they were imperfect mechanisms of royal control. When they were left unpaid, they became pillaging mobs, mercilessly sacking cities and ravishing the countryside. Even when paid, they did not accept their discipline from, or give their loyalty to, the crown exclusively. Although the heavy cavalry was no longer feudal, it continued to be almost exclusively aristocratic and was therefore potentially unreliable in internal struggles involving aristocratic interests. Foreign infantrymen were politically safer, but real authority over them was wielded by their captains rather than by the states that hired them. Northern monarchs, to be sure, could not be blackmailed by their mercenaries the way the Italian city-states were blackmailed by the *condotieri*; but they often found that their troops had inconveniently changed sides at the moment they needed them most.

Nor were any European king's subjects totally disarmed. The individual castle had become an anachronism, but innovations in urban fortifications soon enabled a resolute town to defend itself successfully against anything but a costly siege. Most towns retained their own militias. In the middle of the sixteenth century, even quite small places like Troyes and Amiens could field over three thousand admittedly unmartial men. The greatest nobles, finally (this was especially true of France, much less so of England), remained the centers of complex webs of patronage, famly ties, and clientage relationships with lesser nobles. Such ties enabled a Montmorency, member of one of France's greatest families, to arrive at court in 1560 with a retinue of eight hundred horsemen. The continued political and military importance of these relationships is clearly shown by the ease with which the dukes of Guise and William of Nassau, prince of Orange, raised opposition armies during the civil wars in France and the Netherlands in the second half of the century. Sixteenth-century monarchs commanded military machines far more effective than those of their medieval predecessors; but Valois and Habsburgs continued to rely on the willing support of their more powerful subjects in war as in administration.

Finances

The nature of the particular balance of power between the prince and the ruling class which was characteristic of Renaissance monarchy appears even more clearly in its financial institutions.

Renaissance princes were desperate for money. Their largest expense was warfare. Although armies were small by modern standards (the average size of the French and Spanish armies engaged during the Italian and Habsburg-Valois wars was between 20,000 and 25,000 men), war was as expensive, relatively, as it is now. "No money, no Swiss" was a sixteenth-century axiom. When Louis XII (ruled 1498–1515) was preparing to invade the duchy of Milan in 1499, he asked one of his Italian commanders what was necessary for success; the reply was blunt: "Money, more money and again more money." Peace never relieved the pressure for long; war was almost continuous. Major campaigns were mounted by the important powers in three out of every four years between the beginning of the Italian wars in 1494 and the end of the sixteenth century. To military expenditures must be added the costs of diplomacy, the sums, for example, paid by the French between 1525 and 1546 to secure the friendship of the Swiss, the German Protestant princes, and Henry VIII of England; the salaries of royal officers; the pensions given to nobles, a financial aspect of that process by which a feudal nobility was being transformed into an aristocracy in the service of the crown; the spiraling expenditures of royal households on magnificence, display, and luxury in buildings, artistic patronage, and sport (Emperor Maximilian I kept two thousand hounds)—and all this in an age of rapidly rising prices.

To meet these mounting expenses, rulers obtained revenues from a variety of sources. One, the largest in the past but of dwindling importance in the sixteenth century, was the royal domain, which yielded rents and dues owed the king in his capacity as a great landed proprietor and chief of the feudal hierarchy. A second source of revenue was indirect taxation. For all governments, the major sources of indirect taxes were customs duties and sales taxes on wine, meat, cloth, and a growing list of other commodities. To these, individual governments added others. France had the *gabelle*, the famous salt tax, collected by forcing each householder to buy a fixed minimum of salt each year from government warehouses at prices which assured the crown an enormous profit. The *alcabala*, a cornerstone of Spanish royal finance, was a tax of 10 per cent on the amount of all commercial transactions, a heavy burden on merchants and probably a contributing cause of the declining vigor of Spanish economic life in the later sixteenth century.

Kings tried to meet their expenses in a third way—by borrowing. Some loans were forced, constituting a form of disguised and extralegal taxation. The bourgeoisie of the larger cities were the most frequent victims. The case of Toulouse is typical. Louis XII asked the citizens for a "gift" of ten thousand livres. Francis I obtained twenty thousand livres from them in 1537, in 1542, and in 1544. Henry II raised seventeen thousand livres there in 1553 and again in 1555. Borrowing from the great merchant-bankers was a more orthodox but more onerous way of raising money. The French expedition against Naples in 1494 was largely financed by émigré Italian bankers in Lyons. Charles V paid for his wars during the last years of his reign with loans from Antwerp bankers. His debts there rose from half a million livres to over six million between 1551 and 1555. When royal credit fell so low that it became difficult to borrow from merchant-bankers, monarchs turned to the public and initiated two of the most interesting novelties of sixteenth-century government finance: the sale of government bonds and the floating of public loans. The Spanish government sold *juros*, annuities priced at ten to fifteen times their annual yield. Beginning in 1522 the French issued bonds, called *rentes sur l'Hôtel de Ville*, bearing 12-per-cent interest paid by the king and secured by the domains and revenues of the city of Paris, whose credit was stronger than that of the crown. The most spectacular credit operation of the period was the loan floated in 1555 by Lyons bankers for Henry II (ruled 1547–1559). This is one of the first examples outside of Italy of public borrowing on a large scale. Tempted by what a contemporary called the "sweet expectation of excessive profit," men of every class and fortune, from Swiss and German nobles to valets and charwomen, hastened to subscribe. Widows invested their dowers, ladies sold their jewels. From distant Turkey, pashas subscribed 500,000 écus through their agents. The speculative bubble burst in the great financial crisis of 1557, when both the French and Spanish governments suspended payments on their obligations. In the end subscribers were lucky to recover 30 per cent of their investment.

Taxation and Representation

European monarchs had a final major source of revenue: direct taxation. Income from the royal domain was totally inadequate. Indirect taxes were lucrative, but did not yield enough to meet the costs of war. Borrowing was a palliative. The crucial problem of every Renaissance ruler was the universal and critical disequilibrium between income and expenditure. The only possible basis for sound government finance was a regular system of direct taxation. But to collect taxes regularly a monarch had to overcome one of the most deep-seated aversions of his subjects and abrogate one of their most cherished and most firmly established rights. The common traditional view was that a king should live "on his own," that is, on revenues from the royal domain and from indirect taxation. These were the *ordinary* revenues of the crown. If a military emergency should create a need for futher and *extraordinary* revenues, the king's next step—men even more firmly believed—must be to ask his loyal subjects for them. In short, taxation was not recognized as an integral and necessary part of government finance. All direct taxation was extraordinary. And no taxation could be imposed without the consent of the subject. Medieval theorists expressed this conviction in another way when they said that to the king belonged *dominium* ("political authority"), while to the subject belonged *proprietas* ("private property").

It was unjust for the subject to interfere in political matters like diplomacy or war; the conduct of these was part of the royal prerogative. It was equally unjust for a king to tamper with the property of the subject without his consent.

Everywhere in Europe the subject consented to taxation (or withheld his consent) through representative assemblies—the English Parliament, the Castilian or Aragonese Cortes, the Estates-General and the provincial estates of France. Taxation was the subject of periodic negotiation between a king demanding money and representatives of the clergy, nobility, and commons of his realm reluctantly granting it. The dialogue between them—a complex struggle for power in which military necessity, financial need, and the defense of property all played major roles—was ultimately to determine the location of sovereignty in the state. Sovereignty itself was not at issue. More obviously even than their administrative or military institutions, the finances of the new monarchies were those of sovereign states. No one denied that the crown could tax, and only the most determinedly old-fashioned literally expected the king to live "on his own." No private individual still levied and collected taxes as a legal right of his ownership of landed property. Taxation was a government monopoly, an unshared prerogative of the state. At issue, rather, was the future of consent, and through consent, of the representative institutions in each state. In due course, the strength or weakness of the estates would determine the particular constitutional form each sovereign state would take: on the one hand, absolute monarchy, with sovereignty located in the king alone; on the other, limited monarchy, with sovereignty located in the king and estates combined, or as the English would later phrase it, in the king in Parliament.

The kings of France and Spain defeated the principle of consent in practice and seriously weakened representative institutions in their states. French constitutional history is particularly instructive. The most important direct tax was the *taille*, theoretically granted by the national and local estates. From the Estates-General, which represented the kingdom as a whole, the king secured preliminary recognition of his financial needs. Constituents did not empower their representatives in it to vote extraordinary grants, but only to agree that such grants were necessary. Only the provincial, or local, estates could actually consent to taxation. It was the achievement of Charles VII (ruled 1422–1461) to extract from the Estates-General the recognition of the continuing need of the crown for a reliable income. The circumstances are significant—it was a period of military crisis, the time of the final campaigns of the Hundred Years' War against the English. And the immediate purpose of the grant is noteworthy—to finance a royal artillery and pay for the *compagnies d'ordonnance*. Henceforth the crown treated solely with the provincial estates, assemblies much easier to manipulate and awe. Royal ministers negotiated with these provincial estates throughout the sixteenth century. The fiction of consent was maintained, but in fact it became a mere formality. Each year the crown determined unilaterally the amount of the *taille*, and collected it through royal agents. The justification for this action continued to be military necessity—at the beginning the need to repel the foreign army of occupation present in the kingdom, then between 1494 and 1559 the pressing and continuous demands of the Italian wars and the struggle against Charles V. In the meantime, between 1484 and 1560, the Estates-General did not meet. Its decline, and the mounting figure of the *taille*, especially during the reigns of Francis I and Henry II, measure the effective power of the crown, the latent threat of royal arms, the efficiency of the financial bureaucracy, and the tacit submission of the population to a policy which drained all practical substance from the traditional liberty of consent.

Submission was all the easier because the French kings taxed directly only the politically weakest sections of the population. A fundamental characteristic of the *taille* was the inequality of its incidence. Immunities to direct taxation derived originally from the functional stratification of society and the military end that direct taxation was thought to serve. The *taille* was a demand for service from those who were not already serving against the king's enemies in some other recognized and useful way. The nobles served by active participation in the fighting, the clergy by praying for victory, the Third Estate (which included everybody else) by giving money. Each order, in other words, had its special function in society—to fight, to pray, to work. This division of functions theoretically exempted

Francis I, King of France (1515–1547). *Drawing by an unknown artist. Bibliothèque Nationale, Paris.*

the clergy and the nobility from direct taxation, causing it to fall exclusively on the Third Estate. In practice, the situation was more complex. The clergy—and this fact suggests its declining strength and independence—paid a good deal. Conversely, many members of the Third Estate did in fact gain exemption either by serving in some other way—as soldiers or royal bureaucrats, for example—or, more frequently, by obtaining it as a special privilege granted or sold by the king. By paying lump sums the oligarchies of whole towns bought financial immunity. The nobility, however, remained exempt in both theory and fact, so much so that exemption from the *taille* became one of the surest proofs of aristocratic status. In France, and in most other continental countries, aristocratic exemption from taxation became one term of the political transaction at the basis of the early modern state; in exchange for financial immunity the nobility gradually forfeited independent political power. This is why "absolute" monarchies were to live largely on the taxes of peasants.

The pattern of English constitutional development was rather different. England was on the periphery of power politics. While France, as we shall see, was ringed by the territories of Charles V, England was protected by the Channel and, after the middle of the fifteenth century, rarely at war. She had no permanent army and hired few mercenaries. All free men were in theory obligated to military service, but they were recruited and trained by local notables, not by professionals. Like its local government, England's army was amateur, and it was far below the continental level in tactics and armament. As late as the reign of Elizabeth I its principal exercise was shooting longbows on the village green. In England, furthermore, everyone paid taxes, nobles as well as commons; and the universal bite of taxation, along with widespread experience in local government, encouraged in many a sense of political commitment and the ambition to influence legislation and policy. English kings thus had no overwhelming military motive to tax regularly without consent; nor, because they stood disarmed before their subjects, the richest and most powerful of whom were liable to taxation, had they the power to do so.

But the decisive event in sixteenth-century English constitutional history was the religious break with Rome. The English Parliament was able to consolidate its influence in the reign of Henry VIII because the king desperately needed to mobilize opinion and support during the political crisis of his great struggle with the pope. The Reformation Parliament sat in seven sessions between November, 1529, and April, 1536. Under Henry's skillful leadership it legislated the English church's independence of papal control, creating a national church with the king its head. Parliament emerged from the religious crisis with enhanced prestige. The House of Commons had consolidated and widened its privileges, securing freedom from arrest and limited freedom of speech. Its members had played a role in great affairs. The long sessions had helped to establish a tradition of continuity and *esprit de corps*. For the first time, membership began to confer social prestige, access to patronage, and political advantage. Men began to compete for membership. To be sure, Parliament's chief duty was still to supply money and assent to the legislative program of the crown. Under Henry VIII, and even under Elizabeth I, it was no more than a useful adjunct to the Crown's far greater power, an instrument of government, and not, as it would become in the seventeenth century, a check on government. But it existed. It met. It became firmly entrenched in the needs, interests, and ambitions of men of substance. Above all, by using Parliament to give full legal status to many of their political acts, the Tudors tended to make cooperation with Parliament indispensable for their successors. And already in the sixteenth century some members were trying to introduce bills and motions of their own—obscurely demanding, that is, to share in shaping the policy their taxes paid for. The fruitful interplay had begun in which Parliament supplied money in return for redress of grievances, and the crown tailored policy to parliamentary opinion in return for money. The way was open which would eventually lead to quite different interpretations of the nature of parliamentary authority than could be developed under the personal rule of the popular and despotic Tudors.

One should not press the contrast between the constitutional developments in France and in England. They were to diverge remarkably in the seventeenth century: toward limited monarchy in England, toward absolutism in France. In the sixteenth century what was as clear to Englishmen as to Frenchmen was the brute fact of royal power. Wearily advising the English clergy to bend their backs and principles before the king, the archbishop of Canterbury distilled the experience of his age in a lapidary phrase: *Ira principis mors est* ("the anger of the prince is death"). Conversely, it was as clear to a Frenchman as to an Englishman that royal authority rested on the active cooperation of the king's great subjects. French kings bought the cooperation of the ruling class by tax exemption; English kings, by their readiness to use Parliament. In the one perspective, Henry VIII was as "absolute" as Francis I; in the other, Francis' power was as limited by his dependence on the willing administrative service and political support of his subjects as was Henry's.

Like other sixteenth-century institutions, then, Renaissance monarchy was a transitional form, a complex amalgam of tradition and innovation. By 1560, in the key monarchies of western Europe giant steps had been taken toward territorial unification, administrative centralization, and the magnification of royal power. The rapid accumulation of exclusive prerogatives by the central governments of France, Spain, and England—to make laws, to govern through legal, financial, and administrative officers, to tax, to declare war and make peace, to exercise ultimate jurisdiction, and to coin money—defines their transformation from feudal monarchies into sovereign territorial states. Thus we call them the new monarchies not because they broke abruptly with the past or because all feudal remnants had disappeared (we have seen in detail that they did not), but because their structures were sufficiently novel to mark a new period in the history of European political institutions. On these foundations were built the great sovereign monarchies of the seventeenth and eighteenth centuries.

THE EMPIRE OF CHARLES V

Leopold Ranke, the most famous of the early nineteenth-century founders of modern "scientific" history, attributed the pleasure and fascination of historical study to the extraordinary diversity of its human object, the "living variety of mankind." There are few better examples of this variety than the political institutions of Europeans in the sixteenth century. A survey of the new monarchies does not even begin to exhaust it, though their structures are various enough. To sense, even approximately, the complexity of the ways in which kings, princes, cities, and estates exercised, shared, or competed for political authority, one must turn from France and England to the patchwork of territories that made up the empire of Charles V.

Charles of Habsburg (ruled 1519–1556) was par excellence an heir, his empire a classic example of the effects of the accidents of royal marriage, birth, and death in a dynastic age. His paternal grandfather was Emperor Maximilian I (ruled 1493–1519), who had married the only daughter of the last duke of Burgundy, the heiress of the seventeen provinces of the Netherlands and of Franche-Comté. His maternal grandparents were the Catholic kings, Ferdinand of Aragon and Isabella of Castile; their daughter, Juana, married Philip the Handsome, son of Maximilian I and Mary of Burgundy. By 1500, the year of Charles's birth, deaths in the Spanish royal family, unforeseen and untimely, had left Juana heiress of

THE HABSBURG SUCCESSION, 1493–1564

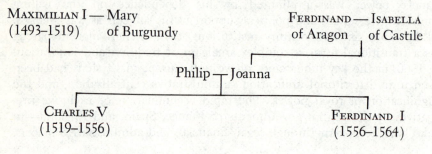

The Emperor Charles V (1519–1555). *Portrait by Titian, 1548. Alte Pinakothek, Munich.*

the Spanish kingdoms and made the match a political triumph for the Habsburgs. The result was an unprecedented concentration of territory in the hands of a single prince. At the death of his father in 1506, Charles became duke of Burgundy; at the death of Ferdinand in 1516 (the succession of Juana, now mad, had been set aside) he became king of Castile and Aragon, and of Naples, Sicily, Sardinia, and the Spanish possessions in the New World. When Maximilian died in January, 1519, Charles inherited the Austrian territories of the Habsburg archdukes. In June, 1519, the German electoral princes, moved by tradition, dynastic sentiment, and bribery, chose him king of the Romans and emperor-designate. The empire of Charles V stretched from Vienna to Peru.

Charles inherited political traditions as well as lands and titles. The ducal court of Burgundy was the European center of decaying chivalry. Charles's favorite reading consisted of courtly chronicles about his Burgundian ancestors, and his political correspondence is heavy with references to his ambition for "honor," "reputation," "glory," and "perpetual fame." In Spain he learned that crusades against the Moors were the central obligation and glory of kingship. His imperial title embodied the medieval idea of the *universitas Christiana*, a body politic, embracing theoretically the whole of Christian Europe, of which the emperor was temporal head. "Sire," his grand chancellor wrote to the young emperor after the election of 1519, "God has granted you a most wonderful grace and raised you above all the kings and all the princes of Christendom to a power hitherto enjoyed only by your ancestor Charlemagne. He has set you on the way towards a world monarchy, towards the gathering of all Christendom under a single shepherd."[3] This was rhetoric rather than a definition of policy. No European king recognized Charles as his overlord. The old notion of Christendom as a hierarchy of states headed by the emperor had given way; Europe consisted of independent, competing, equal states. Charles himself had no ambition in practice to be *dominus mundi* ("monarch of the world"), or to win kingdoms in Europe beyond those he had inherited. But he was profoundly moved by his responsibility for the spiritual unity of Christendom, which he tended to confuse with the political prosperity of his dynasty; and in his own eyes (as in the eyes of many contemporaries) he was emperor of the West, reformer of Europe, chastiser of the Turk, and defender of the Christian faith. His ideology, like his inheritance and his temperament, was ecumenical.

Yet even in the territories Charles in fact ruled, the idea of empire was a myth. His monarchy was fortuitous and personal. He ruled not a single imperial state but a heterogenous collection of autonomous kingdoms and principalities united only in the identity of their sovereign; and in each he had a different title and ruled with different powers. A Castilian jurist described the situation neatly: "These kingdoms must be ruled and governed as if the king who holds them all together were king only of each one of them."[4] Charles was conservative. He created no administrative structure common to the empire as a whole. He had no common treasury or common budget. Although his total resources in men and money were larger than those of any other single European prince, the actual power he could mobilize was determined by his strength or weakness as a ruler of separate states, each independent of the other, each with its own laws, customs, traditions, and institutions, each with particular political and economic interests it was reluctant to sacrifice to the larger interest of Habsburg ambition. Charles's empire was less than the sum of its parts.

The Germany of the Habsburgs

The emperor's constitutional position in Germany—the largest, most populous, and richest of his dominions—illustrates his predicament. The Holy Roman Empire (*Heiliges römisches Reich deutscher Nation*) was a congeries of autonomous cities and principalities. As early as the first half of the thirteenth century, the German emperor, weakened by furious struggles with the papacy, by the effort to impose his authority in central and northern Italy, and by civil war at home, had been forced to withdraw his royal officers

[3]Quoted by Karl Brandi, *Kaiser Karl V* (Munich, 1937), p. 96.
[4]Quoted by J. H. Elliott, *Imperial Spain, 1469–1716* (New York, 1964), p. 157.

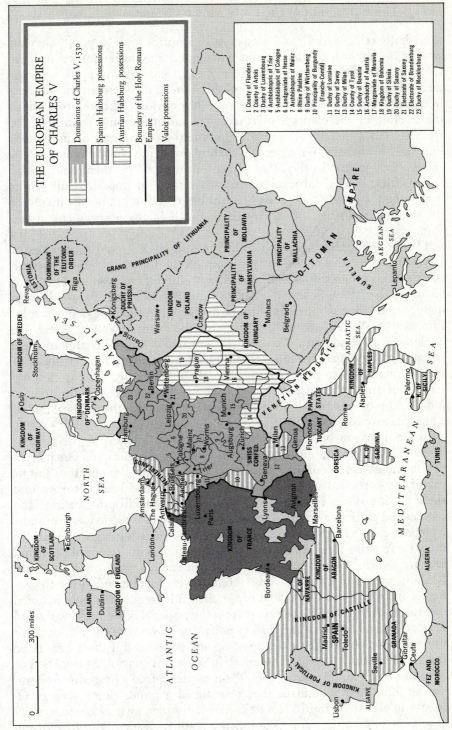

THE EUROPEAN EMPIRE
OF CHARLES V

Dominions of Charles V, 1530

Spanish Habsburg possessions

Austrian Habsburg possessions

Boundary of the Holy Roman
Empire

Valois possessions

1 County of Flanders
2 County of Artois
3 Duchy of Luxembourg
4 Archbishopric of Trier
5 Archbishopric of Cologne
6 Landgraviate of Hesse
7 Archbishopric of Mainz
8 Rhine Palatine
9 Duchy of Württemberg
10 Principality of Burgundy
   (Franche-Comté)
11 Duchy of Lorraine
12 Duchy of Savoy
13 Duchy of Milan
14 County of Tyrol
15 Duchy of Bavaria
16 Archduchy of Austria
17 Margraviate of Moravia
18 Kingdom of Bohemia
19 Duchy of Silesia
20 Duchy of Saxony
21 Electorate of Saxony
22 Electorate of Brandenburg
23 Duchy of Mecklenburg

300 miles

0

from both ecclesiastical and secular principalities and to grant German princes the exclusive right to coin money and administer justice in their territories. Princely independence of royal and imperial authority was codified in the Golden Bull of 1356, the cornerstone of the German constitution in the later Middle Ages and in the sixteenth century. The bull formalized the election of the emperor by seven electoral princes and confirmed the electors in their exercise of regalian rights and their complete immunity from imperial jurisdiction. In the decades that followed, the same immunities and rights were granted to the other princes, or usurped by them, and to the larger cities, whose patrician governments soon monopolized all power within their walls. By 1500, the princes and the free and imperial cities were the dominant partners of an elected monarch in the government of the empire.

There were approximately three hundred significant political entities in Germany on the eve of the Reformation. At the top of the hierarchy were the electoral principalities—the three archbishoprics of Mainz, Trier, and Cologne, the Rhine Palatinate, Saxony, and Brandenburg. Below them in dignity, but often as powerful, came the greater ecclesiastical and secular princes: the Wittelsbach dukes of Bavaria, the dukes of Württemberg, the landgraves of Hesse, and the dukes of Saxony. Within and around these preeminent principalities clustered in chaotic confusion the territories of several dozen lesser princes and more than a hundred counts, seventy bishoprics and abbeys, sixty-six free and imperial cities, and the minute jurisdictions of over two thousand imperial knights, each the political lord of a dilapidated castle and a few score peasants.

In Germany, in other words, centrifugal forces, curbed in the western monarchies by strong central governments, emerged victorious. The pattern of political development was characterized not by gradual unification, but by solidifying particularism. In France the great fiefs had been absorbed into the royal domain; in Germany they became independent principalities, and entrenched particularism prevented the formation of a single German state. Emperor, electors, princes, and cities recognized the advantages of workable unity for resisting foreign enemies and maintaining a minimum of order and security within the empire. But they could never agree on the means. Electors, princes, and cities, whose interests were represented in the *Reichstag*, or imperial Diet, at the end of the fifteenth century the only national institution of any significance apart from the imperial office itself, wished to have an expanded federal machinery under their own control. The emperor wanted an army and the money to equip and pay it; and if there were to be federal institutions, he wished them to be under his control. At the Diets of Worms (1495) and Augsburg (1500) the estates forced a program of reform on the indigent Maximilian: they proclaimed a public peace (the *Landfriede*) in order to halt private wars and curb disorder, instituted a federal tax (the *Gemeinpfennig*), and established a court of justice (the *Reichskam-*

mergericht) and a permanent imperial governing council (the *Reichsregiment*). On the council sat representatives of the electors, princes, and cities. No act of the king was valid without its consent, and the king had only a single vote. In short, the estates intended drastically to subordinate monarchical authority to that of local rulers. The new machinery did not work. The emperor naturally refused to recognize the authority of the council or attend its meetings. The very princes who had voted the *Gemeinpfennig* at the Diets refused to levy it in their own territories. The larger principalities would not allow appeals from their own courts to the *Reichskammergericht*. The *Landfriede* was a boon, but only because princely, not federal, authority enforced it. The outlines of a federal constitution survived throughout the reign of Maximilian's grandson; but real power in Germany remained focused at the level of the territorial prince until the nineteenth century.

Although feudalism triumphed in Germany at the level of the nation, within the several principalities political change paralleled that in the great western monarchies. German princes faced many obstacles. At the end of the fifteenth century they were still feudal lords, their power and resources those of feudal proprietors rather than of sovereigns. Nobles and towns within their territories had often usurped elements of those public powers they themselves had usurped from the emperor. Few princes had even the beginnings of an effective bureaucratic administration. Their finances were inadequate. They had no monopoly on the use of force or the administration of justice in their territories. Customary law bound every prince, and a *Landtag*, or local diet, limited and rivaled his authority. In 1508, for example, the new duke of Bavaria swore at his accession virtually the same oath Charles V would swear when he was crowned at Aachen in 1520: to secure to the estates of prelates, nobles, and cities their "freedom, ancient customs and respected rights" and not to interfere with them in any way. A contemporary observer summed up the situation when he said that "as the princes have brought the emperor to a state of dependence and allow him only certain superior rights, so in turn are they dependent on the pleasure of the Estates."[5]

During the sixteenth century, vigorous princes began to overcome these obstacles and to construct homogeneous sovereign states out of the feudal principalities they had wrested from imperial control. They worked to assure the succession of their territories according to the law of primogeniture. The Golden Bull had already established primogeniture in the electoral principalities; by the middle of the sixteenth century the succession of the oldest son to an undivided territory was common in many of the larger states. Princes also tried to consolidate, round out, and expand their territories by means of force or through suitable marriages. Most sixteenth-century German wars can be understood immediately or ultimately in terms of the princes'

---

[5] Quoted by Johannes Janssen, *Geschichte des deutschen Volkes seit dem Ausgang des Mittelalters*, ed. by L. Pastor (Freiburg-im-Breisgau, 1897), Vol. I, p. 523.

attempts to give their frontiers a rational shape and eliminate enclaves of independent territory within them. Their real problem, of course, was to make their own authority effective throughout a unified and indivisible state. To this end they began to create institutions of orderly centralized administration. They transformed their old councils of nobles and ecclesiastics into permanent and more specialized bodies staffed largely by professionals with legal training. As in the western monarchies the council, at once the supreme administrative body and the high court of justice of the principality, became the key unit of effective central government, its members appointed exclusively by the prince and responsible only to him. Princes rationalized the financial machinery of their states and regularized the collection of taxes. Their subjects, reports a sixteenth-century chronicler, "look on them as a greater curse than the robber knights of old. The knights only carried off material property, while the princes undermine the wisdom of our forefathers, change what we have heretofore held as equitable, and like a plague destroy the traditional rights of the nation."[6] a judgment which describes accurately enough the ambition of the princes, while exaggerating their success. For although German princes moved in the same direction as Francis I and Henry VIII, they moved much more slowly. The estates restricted their freedom to maneuver. They were financially dependent. Unable, like the king of France, to make consent to taxation a formality, without the colonial revenues of the king of Spain, they remained captives of tradition—under the law rather than above it. Penury circumscribed their military power. Their officers were too few to break decisively the immunities of seigneurial and municipal jurisdiction. Aristocratic opposition increased rather than diminished during the century. German princes were to exercise only in the eighteenth century the sovereign powers that the kings of France, England, and Spain had grasped two centuries before.

Charles's German dominions were just one band in the spectrum of political types formed by the component parts of his empire. If in Germany Charles was the nominal overlord of independent cities and of princes who had retained, and were consolidating, the regalian powers their predecessors had usurped from his, in Castile he ruled a compact sovereign state, enjoyed the revenues of a colonial empire rich in gold and silver, and freed by Mexican and Peruvian treasure of his financial dependence on the Cortes, dispensed with representative institutions as effectively as did Francis I and Henry II. Sicily, on the other hand, was a turbulent feudal monarchy. There a Spanish viceroy shared the attributes of sovereignty with landed magnates; on their vast estates these greater nobles monopolized civil and criminal jurisdiction, appointed local administrative and judicial officers, levied feudal dues at will, and maintained private armies. The Netherlands was a federation of semiautonomous provinces. The old nobility controlled the administration at both the central and the

[6]*Ibid.*, p. 547.

local level. Nobles monopolized the council of state. The chief officer of local government in each province was a great noble, omnicompetent and irremovable. Charles left him full liberty.

This diversity is instructive. It reminds us that the pattern of political development in France, Spain, and England was only one among several. It emphasizes the fact that the older forms of political organization survived tenaciously—just as earlier types of economic organization continued to flourish alongside the new capitalistic types. The purely dynastic unity of Charles's empire, moreover, and its looseness of structure, warn us not to overestimate the unity of any European kingdom in the sixteenth century, a period when the difficulty and slowness of communication, and the prevalence of a pattern of human habitation in which towns and the well-populated fertile areas around them were separated by immense distances of sparsely populated forests or steppes, imposed a more or less federated structure on every large state. Spain itself was a dynastic union of kingdoms united only in the person of their sovereign, and little progress was made toward imposing a common institutional and administrative structure on Castile and Aragon before the reign (1556–1598) of Philip II. Many French provinces, especially those most recently annexed to the crown, had their own particular laws and customs, their own provincial estates, their own courts. "France" could still mean only the Île-de-France (Paris and the surrounding area), and one spoke of going from Britanny to France. Each region had its own system of weights and measures, while internal customs barriers hindered the movement of goods from province to province.

Yet the emergence of the sovereign state remains the common thread that makes diversity intelligible. Everywhere in Europe the direction of political change was toward conciliar and bureaucratic government. What varied was the rate of change and the kind and size of the territorial unit controlled by a centralized administration. In the new monarchies, sovereign states crystallized at roughly the level of the nation. In the non-Spanish territories of Charles V, smaller states crystallized more slowly around great fiefs and cities, eventually forming sovereign principalities and city-states. This gradual proliferation of sovereign states within Charles's empire explains why even its dynastic unity did not survive him. Already in 1521 and 1522 he had transferred his Austrian territories and German responsibilities to his younger brother, the Archduke Ferdinand (1503–1564). At his abdication (1555–1556) he formally divided his territories between his son and his brother. Spain (with its colonial empire and its Italian dependencies) and the Netherlands went to Philip II; Austria, Bohemia, Hungary, and the imperial title went to the Austrian Habsburgs—Ferdinand and his heirs.

But until his retirement to the Gerelamite monastery of Yuste in Estremadura, Charles dominated European politics, and his empire was the focus of a struggle for power involving every European state.

THE ITALIAN STATE SYSTEM DURING THE RENAISSANCE

Between 1450 and 1560, the crystallization of sovereign territorial states in much of Europe, the ascendancy of the house of Habsburg, the bellicose expansionism of France, and the penetration of Ottoman armies up the Danube to the gates of Vienna, created new patterns of international rivalry and, for the first time, a European state system.

Italy was the prototype of the new system and the prey of its aggressions. In the high Middle Ages the peninsula had been divided into three major spheres of power: northern and much of central Italy formed the *Regnum Italicum,* an integral part of the Holy Roman Empire of the German kings; Rome and the rest of central Italy was ruled by the papacy; southern Italy and Sicily were independent kingdoms ruled in turn by Normans, Germans, Frenchmen, and Aragonese. Imperial authority in the *Regnum Italicum* collapsed in the second half of the thirteenth century. In central Italy the withdrawal of the papacy to Avignon in the fourteenth century hastened the dissolution of the old political order. The result was an atomization of the peninsula. The Italian cities profited. As the fame and memory of the German *Imperium Romanum* declined, as papal overlordship crumbled even in Rome itself, a civilization of city-states rose on the ruins. Ever since antiquity, central and northern Italy had been exceptionally dense with towns; the type of feudal baron so common in France, England, and Germany had not developed there. Enriched by commerce, commanding resources beyond those of most feudal princes, Italian cities usurped the sovereign powers of emperor and pope; refused, like the Florentines, to draw in their horns before presumptive overlords; founded independent states; and defended their liberty by force. By the early fourteenth century, Italy north of Rome was a patchwork of autonomous city-states.

During the fifteenth century aggressive warfare simplified Italian political geography. Many smaller cities lost their independence. The more powerful ones expanded to form sizable states. By 1450, five states shared the substance of power: the kingdom of Naples in the south, the Papal States, the republics of Florence and Venice, and the duchy of Milan. Naples was a feudal monarchy; the Papal States, an ecclesiastical principality most of which was independent of effective papal control; Florence's institutions were republican, but in fact it was ruled by the merchant house of Medici; Milan was a despotism, with effective political power monopolized by the duke; Venice was an aristocracy ruled by a closed circle of families who monopolized both political and economic power. All were effectively independent of any higher authority. Milan, Florence, and Venice were sovereign states. Power and justice within their territories were exercised exclusively by their governments, whatever its constitutional form. But though they were territorial states, they were rather different from the northern kingdoms and principalities. Their peculiarity was that all a state's territory except for the mother city was regarded as a colonial hinterland, in striking anticipation of

*M. — MARQUISATE

A L P S

EARLDOM OF ASTI

DUCHY OF SAVOY

Milan

DUCHY OF MILAN

Verona

Padua

Venice

VENETIAN

REPUBLIC

ISTRIA

OTTOMAN EMPIRE

MARQUISATE OF SALUZZO

*M. OF MONTFERRAT

Po R.

*M. OF MANTUA

Genoa

DUCHY OF MODENA

DUCHY OF FERRARA

Bologna

DALMATIA

REPUBLIC OF GENOA

Lucca

Florence

REPUBLIC OF LUCCA

Pisa

REPUBLIC OF FLORENCE

Siena

REP. OF SIENA

PAPAL STATES

ADRIATIC SEA

CORSICA (to Genoa)

Tiber R.

Rome

KINGDOM OF NAPLES

Naples

SARDINIA (to Spain)

TYRRHENIAN SEA

0   200 miles

Palermo

KINGDOM OF SICILY

M E D I T E R R A N E A N

SEA

the administration of the Portuguese and Spanish empires. Cities subject to
Venice, for example, were forbidden independent commercial dealings with
foreign merchants. Venetian merchants monopolized foreign trade and were
the intermediaries in all transactions. Superimposed on the institutions of
formerly autonomous city-states was the authority of governors appointed by
the Venetian senate. No representative institutions developed, and the
interests of the "colonials" rarely influenced policy. In Florence, only a small
minority even of those men who lived within the city's walls were citizens
and participated actively in political life. The rise of the Medicean principate
in the fifteenth century and its reimbodiment in the grand duchy of Tuscany
in the sixteenth resulted in the suppression not of the civic liberty of a
people, but of the privileged position of an oligarchy; while beyond the walls

stretched the political hinterland of the Tuscan territories, ruled by and in the interests of the citizens of Florence and their prince.

Between 1450 and 1494 the Italian states played a sophisticated diplomatic and military game in relative isolation from the rest of Europe. Rules for this game developed rapidly, concerning such matters as the role of the resident ambassador, offensive and defensive alliances, intervention and nonintervention treaties, guaranty and neutrality declarations, demarcation of spheres of influence, nonaggression pacts with provisions for action against disturbers of the peace, commercial treaties, and so on. Italians invented the modern techniques of international relations with the same fertility with which they invented techniques of business and styles of art. The regulating principle of the system was an early version of the balance of power. Francesco Guicciardini (1483–1540), whose histories of Italy and of Florence recaptured in the sixteenth century the intellectual ferocity of Thucydides, gave the new principle an early statement: "It was the aim of each [of the five major powers] to preserve its own territory and to defend its own interest by carefully making sure that no one of them grew strong enough to enslave the others; and to this end each gave the most careful attention to even minor political events or changes."[7] Since Venice was the most powerful and aggressive of the Italian states, Florence, Milan, and Naples united against Venice. The result, says Guicciardini, was a beneficent balance (*bilancia*), an equilibrium under relatively peaceful conditions. This is an early description of a closed state system regulated by the balance of power. Movement by one state necessarily called forth responses by all the other states. Equilibrium guaranteed the independence and security of all.

The governing class of every Italian state fought tenaciously to preserve this independence. There was no absence of national feeling for what Petrarch had called the "gentle Latin blood" and the "loveliest country of the earth." Everyone assumed that Italy's soil was sacred, its frontiers defined by the seas and mountains of nature herself. Italians had a common language, which printing was helping to standardize, and in the fifteenth century, a common culture which intellectuals rightly considered superior to that of the remainder of "barbarian" Europe. We call such attitudes cultural nationalism. They parallel the revived popularity in Germany in the sixteenth century of Tacitus's *Germania*, with its contrast of brave and virtuous Germans and decadent predatory Romans, and the French conviction that in language, piety, moral virtue, courage, and every other "rare and antique" virtue they surpassed all other peoples. This nationalism had no political or military significance. Nowhere in Europe did the state rest on or incarnate a national tradition. And certainly it did not do so in Italy. Although statesmen appealed to the "universal needs of Italy" and urged their rivals to be

[7]*Storia fiorentina*, ch. xi. *Opere inedite di Francesco Guicciardini*, ed. by P. and L. Guicciardini (Florence, 1859), Vol. III, p. 105.

"good Italians," in their view the idea of an independent Italy implied first of all the independence of their particular states. Like the Greek city-states before their conquest by Macedonia, the Italian cities would not and could not create a unity which might assure a common and Italian independence by destroying the basis of their own particular autonomy and independence. At the end of the fifteenth century the Italian states stood disunited before the new monarchies of France and Spain.

PATTERNS OF INTERNATIONAL RIVALRY

In 1494 King Charles VIII of France (ruled 1483–1498) invaded Italy and destroyed the autonomy of the Italian state system of the Renaissance. A European system replaced the Italian. Between 1519 and 1559, on this larger stage, with more ample resources and diminished subtlety, Charles V, Francis I, and Suleiman the Magnificent, the Turkish sultan, played the diplomatic and military game invented by the fifteenth-century Italian states. Charles's empire was the predominant European power. His territories, his crusading zeal, and his dynastic claims blocked the paths of French and Ottoman expansion. The two great conflicts of the period therefore opposed Habsburg to Valois and Habsburg to Ottoman. The fundamental alliance designed to balance, and to crush, Habsburg power was between the French and the Turks.

The Habsburg—Valois Struggle

The struggle between Habsburg and Valois was personal and dynastic to a degree difficult for us to understand. The new monarchies were sovereign states, not national states. The aims of their rulers were not national aims. The state was identified with the person of the monarch and with his dynasty. The Renaissance king had sole control over the conduct of foreign affairs, and although social pressures (from the nobility, for example) and even commercial considerations sometimes influenced his policies, his purpose normally was to further no interest larger than that of his own family. It is for this reason that marriage alliances were so prominent a subject of diplomatic negotiation and so rich in consequences. The empire of Charles V, as we have seen, was the result of royal marriages; and advantageous matrimony remained a fundamental and successful object of Charles's diplomacy. In 1521 he laid the basis of the future Austrian monarchy by arranging to have his sister Mary marry King Louis of Hungary and Bohemia while his brother Ferdinand married Louis' sister, who was next in the line of succession. His own marriage to a Portuguese princess opened the way for his son, Philip II, to succeed to the throne of Portugal and in 1580 unite the Spanish and Portuguese empires under a single ruler. He married Philip II to Queen Mary of England. If a son had been born to them, England would probably not be a Protestant country today.

Sixteenth-century wars were equally personal. Kings went to war to gain honor and profit, moved not by national interest—an anachronism in this context—but by personal ambition or resentment and by the "just" dynastic claims of their families. Charles VIII invaded Italy in order to prosecute a dubious claim to the kingdom of Naples inherited from a younger branch of the French royal family. The next French king, Louis XII, invaded the duchy of Milan in 1499, asserting that the Sforza, the reigning ducal house, were usurpers, while he himself was the rightful legal heir through his grandmother Valentina, daughter of an earlier Milanese ruling family, the Visconti. When Charles V succeeded Ferdinand of Aragon, Naples became his, to tax but also to defend. When he succeeded Maximilian as German king he became, like the German kings before him, the feudal overlord of the duchy of Milan and the inevitable opponent of French pretensions in northern Italy. Nor was Italy the only area where conflicting dynastic claims opposed Habsburg to Valois. At the death of the last duke of Burgundy in 1477, Louis XI of France (ruled 1461–1483) had seized the duchy and reincorporated it into the royal domain. Charles was determined to recover French Burgundy and reconstitute the totality of his Burgundian inheritance. Francis was equally determined to resist this fatal dismemberment of his kingdom. To the north and west, the counties of Flanders and Artois were at once fiefs of the king of France and, as two of the seventeen provinces of the Netherlands, in the actual possession of the Habsburgs. Francis considered them French, Charles viewed them as part of his empire. Similarly conflicting claims to provinces on the French and Spanish sides of the Pyrennees exacerbated relations there. Both monarchs, in short, considered their personal rights and their territories to be threatened. Charles saw France as an aggressive power attempting to rob him of his rightful patrimony, egotistically disrupting the peace of Europe, nullifying his divine

THE VALOIS SUCCESSION, 1461–1559

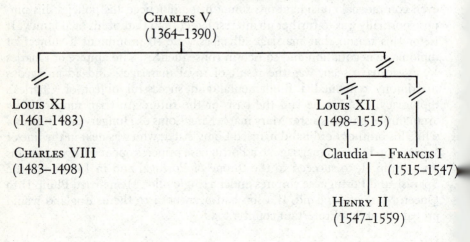

vocation to lead a united Christendom against the Turk. Francis I, conversely, saw his kingdom surrounded by Habsburg territory—Spain, the Netherlands, and Germany—and believed that possessions legitimately his were
threatened, that Charles wanted "to be master everywhere." The hostility
between Habsburg and Valois was irreducible.

The Habsburg-Ottoman Struggle

So too was the hostility between Habsburg and Ottoman. Since the
middle of the fourteenth century, Europe had looked with fear and anger,
but—except for states immediately threatened—with passivity, at the rise to
power of the Ottoman Turks. In the decades after the fall of Constantinople
in 1453 the Turks subdued much of eastern Europe south of the Danube,
including the Adriatic coast; reduced the last Genoese colonies in the East;
seized large portions of the Venetian empire; and though a vigorous trade
continued, broke the old commercial monopoly Italian merchants had so
long enjoyed in the eastern Mediterranean. Christendom, expanding so
remarkably across the western ocean, was under mounting pressure from the
Moslem East. During the reign (1520–1566) of Sultan Suleiman the Magnificent, Habsburg territories bore the brunt of Turkish aggression, and the
Ottomans, pushing up the Danube, became an integral part of the European
state system. Suleiman took Belgrade in 1521. In August, 1526, he crushed
the Hungarian army at Mohács. His diary is vividly laconic. He recorded on
August 31: "The emperor, seated on a golden throne, receives the homage of
the vizirs and beys: massacre of 2,000 prisoners: the rain falls in torrents."
And on September 2d: "Rest at Mohács: 20,000 Hungarian infantry and
4,000 of their cavalry are buried." King Louis died in the slaughter. To
succeed him, his brother-in-law, the Archduke Ferdinand, was elected king
of Bohemia in October, 1526, and king of Hungary in 1527. In the meantime, Suleiman pressed on to Vienna. In September, 1529, he appeared
before the gates of the city. The coming of winter and the enormous
overextension of his lines of communication forced his retirement. Vienna
never fell. But for decades the Turks directly threatened the hereditary
center of Habsburg power. Inevitably, Charles and Ferdinand dignified their
defense of the hereditary lands as a defense of Europe itself against the
infidel, and their determination to recover their lost Hungarian kingdom as a
crusade for which they could legitimately demand men and money from all
of Europe. Charles counterattacked in 1531. He resumed Portuguese and
Spanish crusading probes in northern Africa, captured Tunis (in his role as
"God's standard bearer"), and opened a new theater of war in the western
Mediterranean, the beginning of a campaign which reached its climax many
years later, in 1571, when his illegitimate son Don John of Austria (1547–
1578) smashed the Turkish Mediterranean fleet at Lepanto.

Around the two fundamental lines of force and opposition generated by
the conflicts of Habsburg and Valois, Habsburg and Ottoman, alliances

developed according to an abstract logic of power. The first duty of any government servant, wrote Ermolao Barbaro, a Venetian noble, diplomat, humanist, Aristotelian, and cardinal, is "to do, say, advise, and think whatever may best serve the preservation and aggrandizement of his own state."[8] Two imperatives dictated international political action: first, to preserve one's own state in the face of attacks by a stronger neighbor; second, to collect allies, counterattack, defeat, and if possible, plunder that neighbor. In an age of religious enthusiasm and doctrinal nicety, motives were notably secular. One of the three great contestants was Moslem, yet the fundamental alliance of the period was between the Most Christian King of France and the infidel sultan against their common enemy, the Holy Roman emperor, the temporal head of Christendom. From Madrid, where he was kept prisoner after his defeat and capture at the Battle of Pavia (February 24, 1525), Francis wrote secretly to the sultan asking for help. The Battle of Mohács was the answer to Pavia, the fulfillment of Suleiman's promise to deliver the bey of France from the supremacy of the bey of Spain. Contemporaries denounced the "impious alliance," but it was only final evidence of the hollowness of the crusading ideal. Already in the fifteenth century the Venetians had encouraged the Turks to attack Brindisi and Otranto in order to weaken the kingdom of Naples; and they in fact occupied a part of the Apulian coast for two years (1480–1481). Even the pope received a Turkish pension, in return for keeping a rebellious brother of the sultan in captivity.

The two Christian contestants were Catholics. They fought without quarter, while the smaller states, whether Catholic or Protestant, almost invariably decided their alignment by the logic of power rather than by the text of orthodoxy. The Italians, when they were free to act, allied with the weaker against the stronger, hoping always to expel both Habsburg and Valois from the peninsula. The aim of the German princes, both Catholic and Protestant, was to keep the emperor weak, and they reacted swiftly, by forming alliances with France, against attempts to assert imperial power in Germany. Papal policy is particularly illuminating. In the crucial decades after 1520 during which Protestantism established itself in much of Europe, the temporal position of the papacy as an Italian state, and the desperate fear of successive popes that Charles V would call a church council and settle the religious question in Germany and in Europe independently of Rome, determined papal policy. After Pavia, Charles dominated both northern and southern Italy. Irresistibly the popes were drawn into a French alliance. Even the sack of Rome in 1527 by imperial troops and the captivity of the pope blunted only temporarily a necessary attraction. The result was a pattern of alignment constantly repeated during the middle decades of the century, a pattern disastrous for Catholicism but, in the logic of power, of an elegant and inevitable symmetry. On one side was the empire of Charles V; on the

<hr/>

[8]Quoted by Garrett Mattingly, *Renaissance Diplomacy* (London, 1962), p. 117.

Henry II, King of France (1547–1559). *Engraving by Niccolò della Casa, 1547. The king wears a superb suit of dress armor. National Gallery, Washington, D.C.*

other was France, allied with the Turks, the German Protestant princes, and the Roman pontiff. "How one lives," wrote Machiavelli in the fifteenth chapter of *The Prince* (1513), "is so far distant from how one ought to live, that he who neglects what is done for what ought to be done sooner effects his ruin than his preservation." Renaissance rulers rarely made that mistake.

Financial collapse brought peace and the settlement of Cateau-Cambrésis (April, 1559). The contestants, now Henry II of France and Philip II of Spain, recognized what had been plain for some time. France was not strong enough to conquer Italy and make good its claims to Milan and Naples. The long struggle for that reservoir of power and wealth, seat of the imperial dignity, and home of everything most beautiful, original, and learned in art and letters, left the house of Habsburg master of the peninsula. Spanish viceroys ruled Sicily, Naples, and the duchy of Milan. The grand duchy of Tuscany and the Papal States were Spanish satellites. Only Venice retained a limited independence of action. On the other hand, the Habsburgs were not strong enough to dismember France or seriously to weaken a kingdom relatively so tightly organized, so rich in men and resources, so strategically located. Philip II therefore renounced his claims to French Burgundy, condemning the bones of his ancestors, resting in their magnificent tombs in a Carthusian monastery near Dijon, to foreign soil. Artois and Flanders remained part of the Spanish Netherlands. By a separate treaty, the enclave at Calais, the remnant of once vast English possessions on the continent, was returned to France. Marriages cemented the dynastic truce. Continental princes turned, momentarily, from pressing their foreign ambitions to deal with the challenge of heresy at home.

CHAPTER 5

Revolution and Reformation in the Church: The Problem of Authority

MARTIN LUTHER posted his ninety-five theses against indulgences on the door of the castle church in Wittenberg in October, 1517. John Calvin died in Geneva in 1564. Within these less than fifty years a handful of religious geniuses kindled the enthusiasm of millions, created original systems of Christian doctrine, and founded new churches hostile to Rome. Inadvertently, decisively, and permanently the Protestant reformers cracked the millennial unity of European Christendom.

The word "Protestant" has a precise and well-known origin and presents no problem of meaning or usage. In March, 1529, the Catholic majority in the Diet of Speyer called on all Germans to condemn Lutheranism and to stop making changes in their religion. On April 19, the minority of princes and towns that had gone over to Lutheranism "protested" before God that they would act in no way contrary to God's will, His Word, their consciences, or the salvation of their souls. Catholics called them the "protesting Estates." Eventually, anyone who left the Catholic church was called a Protestant, and the name came to be applied to any member of a western Christian church or sect outside the Roman communion.

The origin of the modern definition of "Reformation" is more difficult to trace. In the Middle Ages the word had had two principal meanings: it could denote the inner renewal or transformation of the individual Christian, or it could refer to the correction of ecclesiastical abuses, as in the phrase "to reform the Church in head and members." Only very gradually in the sixteenth century, and exclusively by Protestants, was the word applied to the contemporary movement, begun by Luther, of opposition to Rome and the Catholic Church; and only in the seventeenth century did it become common, again among Protestants, to speak of the Lutheran "reformation" or the Lutheran "reform" of religion. In modern historiography this usage has come to express a consistent and influential interpretation of the Protestant movement and its causes. Its thesis was trenchantly put by Henry

126

Charles Lea, the great nineteenth-century historian of the medieval Inquisition and sacerdotal celibacy, when he wrote that "the primary cause of the Reformation is to be sought in the all-pervading corruption of the Church and its oppressive exercise of its supernatural prerogatives." The Reformation, in this view, was violent and broke the unity of Christendom because the "abuses under which Christendom groaned were too inveterate, too firmly entrenched, and too profitable to be removed by any but the sternest and sharpest remedies."[1]

This is the "abuse" theory of the Reformation. It has two difficulties. First, it masks the concern of all serious contemporary Christians, both Catholics and Protestants, with the reform of abuses. Second, it misrepresents the nature of the Protestant Reformation itself.

The Church, as all medieval and sixteenth-century men knew, was a divine institution whose head was Christ; but they knew too that it was a human institution as well, staffed by rational beings with intellects and wills vitiated by Adam's fall. Abuses were inevitable, and from the earliest times, frequent. So were efforts to narrow the gap between the ideal and the actual and to restore the Church to a nearer image of the virtues of the saints. Ecclesiastical abuses were neither more widespread nor more iniquitous in the early sixteenth century than in many earlier periods. To be sure, contemporaries concerned with the spiritual condition of the Church and the religious education of the laity deplored the secularization of the episcopacy, plurality of benefices (the possession of two or more ecclesiastical livings by one man), and clerical nonresidence (the permanent absence of priests from their parishes and bishops from their dioceses), but these were venerable abuses at every level of the hierarchy. Sixteenth-century parish priests were grindingly poor. They were often ignorant and superstitious. They kept concubines. In many convents monastic life was spiritually tepid. For the past five hundred years reformers had struggled against the same evils. The Renaissance papacy, like every contemporary monarchy, was short of money, and successive popes disdained no worldly opportunity to obtain funds. As ruler of one of the five major Italian states, many a pope used excommunication and the interdict to further his temporal ambitions. Nepotism was normal. Kings learned how to manage the sale of temporal offices by observing the traffic in ecclesiastical ones. On the other hand, the degradation of the papacy was greater in the ninth and tenth centuries than in the Renaissance. The story of the "martyrs" Rufinus and Albinus—Red Gold and Pale Silver—whose relics the pope magnificently buried "in the treasury of St. Cupidity beside the mercy seat of St. Avidity her sister, not far from the basilica of their mother St. Avarice"[2] circulated in the twelfth century,

[1]*Cambridge Modern History*, Vol. I (New York and London, 1903), pp. 678–679, 691.
[2]Quoted by R. W. Southern, *The Making of the Middle Ages* (New Haven, 1953), p. 153.

Gottes wort
bleibt ewig.

Biblia/ das ist/ die
gantze Heilige Sch-
rifft Deudsch.

Mart. Luth.

Wittemberg.

Begnadet mit Kür-
furstlicher zu Sachsen
freiheit.

Gedruckt durch Hans Lufft.

M. D. XXXIIII.

Title page of the first complete edition of Luther's translation of the Bible. *Published in Wittenberg by Hans Lufft in 1534. The source book of the German Reformation. At the top, flanked by cherubs holding the four Gospels, God the Father writes down His Word.* Gottes wort bleibt ewig; God's Word endures forever.

not in the sixteenth. Dante, writing in the early fourteenth century, put several popes in hell.

Like their medieval predecessors, sixteenth-century Christians clamored for reform and tried to achieve it. Franciscan and Dominican preachers castigated the pride, the covetousness, the secular and worldly living, of monks and priests. In moral tracts, manuals of piety, and satires, humanist intellectuals tried to temper the laity's immoderate devotion to images, relics, and pilgrimages. The magistrates of the Parlement of Paris vigorously pushed monastic reform. On occasion they used troops to impose a reforming abbot on recalcitrant monks. In 1512, the archbishop of Canterbury called a convocation of the clergy of his province to correct abuses. Between 1512 and 1517, the Fifth Lateran Council sat in Rome. At its opening session the general of the Augustinian order (Luther's order) prayed God to give the clergy strength to "restore the church to its ancient splendor and purity," and the assembled prelates passed decrees on the selection of qualified bishops and legislated against heresy, blasphemy, simony, and clerical concubinage. As the council ended, a group of distinguished Roman priests and laymen founded the Oratory of Divine Love. They took no vows; they had no papal sanction or special position. They were men of learning and religious sensibility who met from time to time in order to restore the dignity and the due observance of the divine service, participate in spiritual exercises, and awaken by their example the religious life of the city and the Church. No group of men better suggests the aims and character of a reforming movement that encompassed all of Europe. Episcopal members retired from Rome to reform their own dioceses, in Verona, Chieti, Mantua, and Carpentras in the south of France. They investigated each priest and suspended the unworthy. They encouraged preaching and the more frequent celebration of the sacraments. They insisted on clerical residence and moved against pluralities. In short, from Cracow to Toledo, from Durham to Palermo, reformers were actively engaged against entrenched corruption. In every country of Europe and in every class of society in the decades before 1517, there were men for whom *reformatio* was a matter of immediate, active concern.

The leaders of the Protestant Reformation, too, were sensitive to ecclesiastical abuses and wished to reform them. Yet the reform of abuses was not their fundamental concern. The attempt to reform an institution, after all, suggests that its abuses are temporary blemishes on a body fundamentally sound and beautiful. Luther, Zwingli, and Calvin did not believe this. They attacked the corruption of the Renaissance papacy, but their aim was not merely to reform it; they identified the pope with Antichrist and wished to abolish the papacy altogether. They did not limit their attack on the sacrament of penance to the abuse of indulgences. They plucked out the sacrament itself root and branch because they believed it to have no scriptural foundation. They did not wish simply to reform monasticism; they saw the institution itself as a perversion. The Reformation was a passionate debate on the proper conditions of salvation. It concerned the very foundations of faith and doctrine. Protestants reproached the clergy not so much for living badly as for believing badly, for teaching false and dangerous things. Luther attacked not the corruption of institutions but what he believed to be the corruption of faith itself. The Protestant Reformation was not strictly a "reformation" at all. In the intention of its leaders it was a restoration of biblical Christianity. In practice it was a revolution, a full-scale attack on the traditional doctrines and sacramental structure of the Roman Church. It could say with Christ, "I came not to send peace, but a sword." In its relation to the Church as it existed in the second decade of the sixteenth century, it came not to reform, but to destroy.

MARTIN LUTHER

Luther was the son of a prosperous mining entrepreneur of peasant stock. When he was eighteen, he matriculated at the University of Erfurt. He

ÆTHERNA IPSE SVAE MENTIS SIMVLACHRA LVTHERVS
EXPRIMIT·AT VVLTVS CERA LVCAE OCCIDVOS
·M·D·X·X·

Martin Luther in 1520. *Etching by Lucas Cranach the Elder. This is the earliest portrait of Luther. The inscription:* Luther himself makes known the immortal lineaments of his thought, but Lucas drew his mortal features.

mastered the Aristotelian curriculum in record time and received the bachelor's degree in 1502 and the master's early in 1505. On his father's advice he enrolled in the faculty of law, the normal path to lucrative and responsible preferment in church or state. Then in July, 1505, Luther was caught in a thunderstorm. A terrifying bolt of lightning struck near him. In fear of death and possible damnation he cried out, "St. Anne help me, I will become a monk." He fulfilled his vow by joining the mendicant order of St. Augustine before the end of the same month. The next years were punctuated by periods of tightening spiritual and psychological anguish. In the last year of his life Luther himself described very simply the problem that had brought him close to despair and blasphemy: "Though I lived as a monk without reproach, I felt that I was a sinner before God with an extremely disturbed conscience. I could not believe that he was placated by my satisfaction. I did not love, yes, I hated the righteous God who punishes sinners, and secretly, if not blasphemously, . . . I was angry with God."[3] God is just; equally certain was Luther's conviction that he himself was weak, impure, and sinful, and

[3]*Luther's Works*, Vol. XXXIV, ed. by Lewis W. Spitz (Philadelphia, 1960), pp. 336–337.

that his desperate effort to merit salvation was a failure. Appalled by the disparity between his paltry monkish "good works" and God's demand that he be just, he trembled before the prospect of deserved damnation.

With the radicalism of genius Luther eventually found peace by totally transforming the problem. In 1511 he was transferred from Erfurt to the little town of Wittenberg, in electoral Saxony, and in 1512 he was appointed professor of Holy Scriptures at its new university. He lectured on Genesis (October, 1512–July, 1513), the Psalms (August, 1513–October, 1515), and finally Paul's Epistle to the Romans (November, 1515–September, 1516). He found his inspiration in Paul:

At last, by the mercy of God, meditating day and night, I gave heed to the context of the words, namely, "In it the righteousness of God is revealed, as it is written, 'He who through faith is righteous shall live.'" [Romans 1:17] There I began to understand that the righteousness of God is that by which the righteous lives by a gift of God, namely faith. And this is the meaning: the righteousness of God is revealed by the Gospel, namely, the passive righteousness with which merciful God justifies us by faith, as it is written, "He who through faith is righteous shall live." Here I felt that I was altogether born again and had entered paradise itself through open gates.[4]

The conception of an angry God faded before that of a God of mercy. Human struggle to *earn* salvation gave way to a total passivity and trust and faith in Christ. The justice of God became a free acquittal of the guilty. The result was a doctrine whose implications were devastating for the Church and for traditional Christian belief and practice as they had developed from the ninth to the sixteenth century.

Three formulas epitomize Luther's teaching: *sola fide* ("by faith alone"), *sola scriptura* ("by Scripture alone"), and *sola gratia* ("by grace alone"). They define a relationship between man and God in which as much as possible is attributed to God and as little as possible is attributed to man. Man is irremediably weak and evil.

It is not only the privation of a property of the will [wrote Luther] nor only the privation of light in the intellect, of virtue in the memory; but the absolute privation of all righteousness and of the power of all strengths, of body and soul, of the whole man interior and exterior. Further, there is in man a positive inclination to evil, a disgust for the good, a hatred of light and wisdom, a delight in error and darkness, a flight from and an abomination of good works, a race toward evil.[5]

Sola fide emphasizes the insignificance of reason and the primacy of

[4]*Ibid.*, p. 337.
[5]*D. Martin Luthers Werke. Kritische Gesamtausgabe*, Vol. LVI (Weimar, 1938), p. 312.

revelation. More radically, it insists that man is saved or justified by faith alone. This doctrine of justification by faith alone is the cornerstone of classical Protestantism. Its chief scriptural sources are two celebrated texts of St. Paul: "For by grace are ye saved through faith; and that not of yourselves: it is the gift of God: Not of works, lest any man should boast" (Ephesians 2:8–9); and "Therefore we conclude that a man is justified by faith without the deeds of the law" (Romans 3:28). No man is saved by his own merit. Man has no merit. Nothing that he can do with his own strength and by the exercise of his own will brings him closer to God. If God were just only, all men would be damned; but God is also merciful. His purely gratuitous mercy, which no one can do anything to deserve, mysteriously chooses some few men for salvation. These are the elect, predestined for salvation. They are accounted just—and thus saved—by faith; and faith itself is a gratuitous gift of grace. Therefore, to say that a man is justified by faith alone is to say that salvation is an inscrutable process over which man has no control and in which his merits and good works play no part. Man cannot cooperate in his own salvation.

Sola scriptura is a specific case of *sola fide*. It rigorously maintains that the only source of religious truth is the Word of God revealed in Scripture. Scripture is uniquely authoritative because it is the concrete locus of the Word of God, the written record of the revelation of God in Christ, the channel through which God reaches those to whom He has granted the grace of faith.

Sola gratia is a generalization of *sola fide*. Grace and nature are viewed as inalterably opposed. The natural man can neither know the truth nor will the good without the aid of grace. Human reason is deformed and blind. The unaided intellect is chained in darkness; knowledge of divine things comes from grace alone. Similarly, the human will is captive. The natural man is free to choose only between different degrees of sin; grace alone can grant him Christian freedom, the freedom to choose only the good. All power, all good, all virtue, come from God's grace; all wickedness, weakness, and evil come from nature, especially man's nature. "This doctrine," said Luther, "may seem hard and cruel, but it is full of sweetness; for it teaches us to seek humbly all assistance and all salvation, not from ourselves, but from without, through faith in Christ the Redeemer."[6]

Between 1517 and 1520—gradually, haphazardly, under the pressure of events—Luther discovered the radicalism implicit in his sweetly cruel doctrine of forgiveness. Astonished but undismayed, he found himself the leader of a revolutionary attack on the Roman Church.

The Roman Church was a monarchical, sacerdotal, and sacramental organization. Its secular power had shrunk since the crises of the Avignonese captivity and schism in the fourteenth century; but in the area of faith and

[6]*Ibid.*, pp. 89, 91, 382.

morals, Roman claims had become more comprehensive and sharply monarchical. Papal theorists identified the universal Church with the Roman Church and the Roman Church with its supreme and monarchical head, the pope. Just as the universal Church could not err in faith and morals, so also papal rulings, definitions, and interpretations were infallible. Moreover, the Church itself—defined now as that ecclesiastical hierarchy of which the pope was head, that "empire" ruled by the monarchical laws and ordinances of the pope—claimed a monopoly on grace. God's saving grace operated objectively and exclusively through the sacraments: baptism, confirmation, the Eucharist, penance, ordination, marriage, and extreme unction. The clergy, in turn, monopolized the administration of the sacraments. Separated from the laity by the indelible mark of ordination, the priest, according to the doctrine of transubstantiation, possessed the miraculous power, denied even to angels, of transforming the Eucharistic elements of bread and wine into the real body and blood of Christ. It is not an accident that this doctrine of transubstantiation was the only medieval contribution to dogma. The Mass lay at the heart of medieval sacerdotalism and sacramentalism. When the priest repeated the words "This is my body," he transformed the substance of the elements into the body and blood of Christ, while their accidents, all attributes perceivable by the senses, remained those of bread and wine. He reenacted the Incarnation and Crucifixion: God became flesh, and Christ died sacrificially upon the altar for man's salvation. Only through the mediation of the priest could this grace reach the laity. Here was the foundation of clerical power and of the unique position of the Church in society.

Luther's initial protest was against indulgences. An indulgence was the transfer by the pope of superfluous merit accumulated by Christ, the Virgin, and the saints to an individual sinner in order to remit all or some of the penalties for sin later to be suffered in purgatory. By Luther's time, papal doctrine held that such transfers of divine credit could benefit not only the living, but the dead as well. Because he believed that man is justified by faith alone, Luther denied that saints had superfluous credits or that merit could be stored up for subsequent use. He denied the power of the pope over purgatory. Finally, he branded indulgences as positively harmful because they induced a false sense of security and imperiled salvation. Peace and forgiveness of sins come only in the Word of Christ through faith. "But if anyone does not believe this word, even though he be pardoned a million times by the pope himself, . . . he shall never know inner peace."[7] The ninety-five theses against indulgences made Luther famous overnight.

The theses were the work of a reformer. Three devastating tracts published by Luther in 1520—*An Open Letter to the Christian Nobility of*

[7]*Luther's Works*, Vol. XXXI, ed. by Harold J. Grimm (Philadelphia, 1957), pp. 100–101.

the German Nation, *The Babylonian Captivity of the Church,* and *On Christian Liberty*—were the works of a revolutionary. In them Luther attacked every important assumption on which the medieval Church had rested. He asserted that the councils of the universal Church had erred. He called papal authority a human invention and denied the pope's infallibility in matters of doctrine. At a stroke he rejected the sacraments of confirmation, marriage, penance, holy orders, and extreme unction. In denying the sacrament of orders, Luther sought to erase the distinction between the spiritual estate (pope, bishops, the secular clergy, and the monastic clergy) and the temporal estate (princes, lords, merchants, craftsmen, and peasants), the distinction between priest and layman, thus ending, as he put it, "the detestable tyranny of the clergy over the laity." Instead Luther envisioned a priesthood of all believers. Because all of these had one baptism, one Gospel, one faith, they were all alike Christians, all alike truly members of a single spiritual estate, all priests. The alleged difference between the priesthood and the laity was, in his view, a human invention. Most important, Luther struck at the heart of sacerdotal power by redefining the sacrament of the Eucharist. He denied that the Mass was a sacrifice, a repetition of Christ's sacrifice on the cross. He denied the doctrine of transubstantiation. He denied that the sacrament worked, as medieval theologians had believed, by its own innate virtue and power. Because men were justified by faith alone, the efficacy of the sacrament was a function of the faith of the recipient. The faith that made the sacrament effective was one's own. God gave faith directly to the individual. No mediator, except the Word of Scripture, was necessary. The individual human soul stood alone before its Savior and creator.

THE FRAGMENTATION OF CLASSICAL PROTESTANTISM

Religious individualism is necessarily disruptive of established beliefs and practices. Its progress poses at once the problem of authority. By what authority, asked Luther's Catholic opponents, does a single monk presume to stand against the common faith of the entire Church and the opinion of all of Christendom? More general questions quickly followed. Where is the source of religious truth? What is our guarantee that we have found it? Luther's answers appeared to be clear. The Word of God revealed in the Bible is alone authoritative: *sola scriptura.* Scripture alone is the lord and master of all writings and doctrines on earth. No Church Father, not even St. Augustine, no theologian, not even Aquinas, no ecclesiastical dignitary, not even the pope, has the right to teach something that cannot be demonstrated from Scripture.

The difficulty with this position is that the meaning of Scripture is far from clear and that, in practice, biblical texts can be and have been interpreted in different ways. Shall we conclude that each Christian is free to interpret Scripture for himself? "God forbid," answered Luther and every responsible sixteenth-century theologian after him. Such a conclusion confuses Christian liberty with license and is, as one Protestant divine put it, "a most diabolical dogma, because it means that everyone should be left to go to hell in his own way."[8] But if the individual's reason or judgment cannot guarantee the truth and certainty of a scriptural interpretation, what can? Again Luther's answer was apparently clear. Christians must read the Bible under the guidance and inspiration of the Holy Spirit. The Holy Spirit guarantees the truth and uniformity of scriptural interpretation. The assertion was not new. What was new was that Luther denied the Spirit's authoritative guarantee to be legitimately institutionalized in the Roman Church. The objective control of interpretation by tradition and papal authority had in the past secured the doctrinal unity of western Christendom. The doctrine of *sola scriptura* dissolved this controlling link between Scripture and tradition and introduced into the definition of religious truth an element of subjectivity which not only separated Lutheran from Catholic but also gradually fragmented Protestantism itself into a multiplicity of competing faiths. The Catholic humanist Thomas More accused Luther of presuming to make his own individual interpretation of Scripture normative. (He called him an "infallible donkey.") And he predicted that once the Church's monopoly of scriptural interpretation was broken, "almost all the dogmas of the Christian faith, unchanged for so many centuries, will be called into question at the whim of upstart heretics."[9]

Events proved More right. Other reformers soon interpreted Scripture as freely and personally as Luther had done. Each claimed the guidance of the Holy Spirit. Each claimed a monopoly on Christian truth as universal as that claimed by Rome. *Sola scriptura* was the razor with which Luther cut away the "fictitious customs" and "human inventions" of the Catholic Church. Other innovators soon turned the same instrument on him; and from their divergently inspired interpretations of Holy Writ arose new varieties of Protestantism. In the sixteenth century the most important of these variant types were Zwinglianism and Calvinism.

HULDREICH ZWINGLI

Zwingli, after Luther the most creative among the Protestant theologians of the first generation, received a humanist education; he learned Greek in order to study Christ's teachings in the "original sources." In January, 1519, after several years of service as a parish priest in other towns of German

[8]Quoted by Roland H. Bainton, *The Travail of Religious Liberty* (Philadelphia, 1951), p. 114.
[9]*Responsio ad Lutherum*, trans. by Sister Gertrude J. Donnelly (*The Catholic University of America Studies in Medieval and Renaissance Latin*, Vol. XXIII, Washington, D.C., 1962), p. 147.

Switzerland, he began to preach the Gospel in the Grossmünster, or principal church, of Zurich. First Erasmus, then Luther, influenced his doctrinal development. As early as 1520, in marginal notes in his copy of the Psalms, he stated clearly the doctrine of justification by faith alone. He accepted the unique authority of Scripture, and like Luther and against all evidence, believed that the Bible was simple, clear, and easy to understand. In his view, the true Christian had to try every doctrine and usage by the touchstone of the Gospel and the fire of the apostle Paul. What agreed with Holy Writ was true; what conflicted with it, detestable. He followed Luther, too, in many of the consequences he drew from these assumptions. He disputed the efficacy of good works as a means to salvation, denied the existence of purgatory, and attacked monasticism and sacerdotal celibacy; he denied free will, and defended the predestination of the elect; he reduced the sacraments to two, and simplified the liturgy. When on Maundy Thursday, 1525, Zwingli celebrated the Lord's Supper instead of the Mass in the Grossmünster, Zurich's break with Rome was complete.

Zwingli's contribution was to push liturgical and sacramental simplification beyond the point to which Luther was prepared to go. Zwingli wished to reduce religion to its essentials, to achieve what he called a *summa religionis* (a "quintessence of religion"). Because he nursed a marked prejudice against any corporeal conception or representation of divine things, his passion for simplicity led him to an ascetic rejection of images and of every sensuous detail in the traditional ceremonial of the Church and to a denial of the Real Presence of Christ in the sacramental elements of the Eucharist. The congregation, he believed, should have ears only for the Word of God, not for the "trills" of music, and should have eyes only for the Scripture, not for female saints "luxuriously and sleekly" painted, as though their very purpose were to incite lasciviousness. Under Zwingli's influence his fellow citizens broke up the organ in the Grossmünster, removed and destroyed the stained glass windows, statues, and pictures of Zurich's churches, and whitewashed the interior walls. Zwinglians renounced liturgical magnificence and reduced their vernacular services to a reading and exposition of the Word of God. As a Catholic priest in Glarus, Zwingli had used at Mass a magnificently decorated golden chalice. As a Protestant minister in Zurich, he celebrated the Supper with a simple wooden cup.

From the same impulse came Zwingli's "sacramentarianism," his conviction that the Communion service was not a physical partaking of God, but only a commemorative, spiritual, and symbolic eating. Both Luther and Zwingli rejected the Catholic Mass, regarding it as a form of sacrificial magic. But Luther retained the Real Presence, maintaining that the actual flesh and blood of Christ coexisted in and with the natural substance of bread and wine and that the virtue of the sacrament depended on the faith of the recipient. Zwingli was more radical and more consistent. He denied the

From Catholic mass to Protestant Supper. *On the left, the chalice Zwingli used when he was a Catholic priest at Glarus; on the right, the wooden cup with which he celebrated the Lord's supper.*

objective presence of the Eucharistic Christ in the sacrament of the altar because it contradicted, in his view, the primordial idea of justification by faith alone. The bread and wine of the Supper were not the means of salvation, but only tokens of communion and symbols of duty. They conferred no grace, for the distribution of grace appertained to the Spirit alone. The Lord's Supper was a memorial service, celebrated in memory of the redemptive death of Christ.

Luther and Zwingli broke on this issue. No confrontation illuminates more clearly the problem of authority than the debate on the sacrament of the altar, or Eucharist, between Lutherans and Zwinglians at Marburg, in Hesse, in October of 1529. Zwingli came to the colloquy with Johannes Oecolampadius (1482–1531), the reformer of Basel, and the great Strasbourg theologian Martin Bucer (1491–1551). Luther came with Philip Melanchthon (1497–1560), his right-hand man and ultimately his sucessor. Luther began the debate by writing on a table in large letters Christ's words of institution: *Hoc est corpus meum* ("This is my body"—Matthew 26:26). Oecolampadius replied that the word *est* ("is") should be understood symbolically to mean *significat* ("represents"). To prove this point he cited a text from the sixth chapter of John (verses 48–54). Here Jesus says that he is the bread of life, and continues, "Whoso eateth my flesh and drinketh my blood, hath eternal life; and I will raise him up at the last day." But the Jews and disciples take him literally, and Jesus hastens to explain, "It is the spirit that quickeneth; the flesh profiteth nothing" (verse 63). Oecolampadius concluded, "Is it not then clear that Jesus would have nothing to do with the physical eating of his body?" In his splendidly one-track way, Luther answered: "I won't argue about whether *est* means *significat*. I rest content with what Christ says, and He says: *This is my body*. Not even the devil can change that. Therefore believe in the pure word of God and glorify Him." The end came in a rapid dialogue between Luther and Zwingli:

ZWINGLI: We urge you too to give up your preconceived opinion and glorify God. I do not give up my text either, and you will have to sing another song.
LUTHER: You are speaking in hatred.
ZWINGLI: Then let John 6 cure your ignorance.
LUTHER: You are trying to overwork it.
ZWINGLI: No! No! This text will break your neck.
LUTHER: Don't brag. Our necks don't break so fast. You are in Hesse now, not in Switzerland.[10]

Luther concluded that he and Zwingli each had a different kind of spirit. "I myself," he wrote later, "will in no wise hearken to aught that is contrary to my doctrine; for I am certain and persuaded through the Spirit of Christ, that my teaching . . . is true and certain."[11] He was equally persuaded that Zwingli was the victim of spiritual witchcraft. The Catholics, of course, were certain that Luther himself was inspired by the devil. With a scatological wit entirely typical of Reformation polemic, Sir Thomas More pointed out that though Luther talked as if he were "safe in Christ's bosom," in reality "he lies shut up in the devil's anus."[12]

JOHN CALVIN

Calvin was born in Noyon, in northern France, a quarter of a century later than Luther and Zwingli. He was a reformer of the second generation. Inevitably he was not an innovator in the same sense that each of them had been. But he too was certain that he read and understood the Bible under the direction of the Holy Spirit, that his own interpretation of Scripture was therefore true, that "what I have taught and written did not grow in my brain, but that I hold it from God." The result was a third variety of

[10]*D. Martin Luthers Werke*, Vol. XXX.3 (Weimar, 1910), pp. 110–123.
[11]*A Commentary on St. Paul's Epistle to the Galatians*, ed. by P. S. Watson (Westwood, N. J., n.d.), p. 195.
[12]*Responsio ad Lutherum*, p. 127.

Protestantism, an independent theology midway between Luther's and Zwingli's. Calvin's achievement was to organize Protestant doctrine into a clear, comprehensive theological system, to weld the insights of Luther, Zwingli, and Bucer into the last, and one of the greatest, of the *summae* of theology—the *Institutes of the Christian Religion.* In due course, he won over the magistrates of Geneva. In November, 1552, after long opposition, the highest secular authority in the city-state declared the *Institutes* "to be well and saintly made, and its teaching to be the holy doctrine of God."[13]

A constructive intellect, autocratic self-confidence, and an admirable education equipped Calvin supremely well for his task. He mastered scholastic philosophy at the University of Paris, read massively in patristic, medieval, and contemporary theology, studied law at Orléans and Bourges, and learned and used the humanist's historical and philological techniques of textual criticism (his first book was a commentary on Seneca's *De clementia*). When the first edition of the *Institutes* appeared in 1536, he was only twenty-six. The book is beautifully written, organized, and argued; it is clear and pungent, as sharp and well turned as a brilliant legal brief. Calvin expanded and reworked it in successive editions throughout his life. Designed to be a complete account of Christian teaching, it is the most dynamic and influential synthesis of sixteenth-century Protestant thought.

Rarely has the Protestant vision of the relation between God and man been more majestically defined. God is just and good, powerful and glorious. His will is free, sovereign, and omnipotent. Man is ignorant, vain, infirm, depraved, radically corrupt. His shameful nakedness exposes a "teeming horde of infamies." For Calvin, therefore, as for Luther, justification by faith alone is the principal article of the Christian religion. Because man is morally helpless, he cannot reestablish contact with God. God must reestablish contact with man. He does so through the Incarnation of His Son. He justifies man by mercifully and gratuitously granting him faith in His Word, that Word which is alternatively referred to as Wisdom, Christ, the Redeemer, the second Person of the Trinity, and the canonical Scriptures. Christ is the Word by whom all things were created. Christ is also the author of the written scriptural Word. In the written Word, the eternal Word is known. For this reason the Bible is the infallible book of truth when it is read under the direction of the Holy Spirit. But the Word does not move equally all who hear it preached. The action of the Holy Spirit and of God's grace is independent of man's will and works. Therefore predestination is inseparable from justification by faith alone, illuminating and reinforcing that central truth.

No fact more powerfully exalts the glory of God or more persuasively teaches humility to man than the existence of predestination. From eternity,

---

[13]Quoted by François Wendel, *Calvin. The Origins and Development of His Religious Thought,* trans. by P. Mairet (New York, 1963), p. 92.

God has decided the salvation or reprobation of every man. By His eternal and immutable counsel He freely ordains some to eternal life, others to eternal damnation. With respect to the elect, God's counsel is founded on His free mercy, without regard to human merit. He wills the rest of humanity to damnation according to a just and incomprehensible, but irreprehensible, judgment. Why, we may ask, does God take pity on some but not on others? There is, says Calvin, no other answer but that it pleased Him to do so. Nor can one argue that God's foreknowledge of a man's faith or faithlessness, of his merits or lack of them, determines His choice. The divine will is never dependent on the good will of man. God's will is free; man's is in bondage. Election does not depend on faith; faith makes election manifest. Man cannot choose faith or reject it, for grace is irresistible. God freely chooses some and rejects the rest, again "for no other reason than that he wills to exclude them." But this is not all. By definition every action of God's will is just, although man's puny reason cannot grasp this justice. The reprobate are incomprehensibly but justly condemned. And because the reprobate are justly condemned, they are condemned by their own fault. "Accordingly, man falls according as God's providence ordains, but he falls by his own fault." Calvin himself confessed the doctrine a horrible one: *Decretum quidem horribile fateor.*[14] All the more strikingly it measures the gulf between the secular imagination of the twentieth century and six-teenth-century Protestantism's intoxication with the majesty of God. We can only exercise historical sympathy to try to understand how it was that many of the most sensitive intelligences of a whole epoch found a supreme, a total, liberty in the abandonment of human weakness to the omnipotence of God.

ANABAPTISM

The crystallization of classical Protestantism into three distinct systems of doctrine—Lutheran, Zwinglian, and Calvinist—did not exhaust the six-teenth-century consequences of the idea that Scripture alone is normative in faith and morals. The classical reformers—Luther, Zwingli, and Calvin—tended to see the Bible primarily as a guiding authority in matters of doctrine. More radical groups, the most important of whom were the Anabaptists, understood *sola scriptura* to mean a minute ordering of human life according to the commandments of the Sermon on the Mount, a literal restitution of New Testament Christianity by a covenanted community of believers separated from the world and its evil works.

Anabaptism arose in Zurich among members of Zwingli's circle who

---

[14]*Institutes of the Christian Religion,* ed. by J. T. McNeill, trans. by F. L. Battles (*Library of Christian Classics,* Vols. XX–XXI, Philadelphia, 1960), Vol. 11, pp. 955, 957.

Huldreich Zwingli at the age of forty-eight. *Woodcut by an unknown artist, 1531.*

protested his gradualism and demanded a complete and immediate break with all antiscriptural ceremonies and doctrines. It crystallized as a distinct variety of Protestantism on January 21, 1525, when the layman Conrad Grebel, the son of a wealthy patrician merchant, rebaptized a former priest named Georg Blaurock, who in turn rebaptized the other men and women present in his house. Its first important doctrinal statement was the Schleitheim Confession, produced by a Synod of Swiss Brethren in February, 1527. After two decades of persecution, sporadic excesses, and near disintegration, the sect was given by Menno Simons (1496–1561) both its permanent doctrinal and organizational form and its name. (Anabaptists initially called themselves Brethren, or simply Baptists. Their enemies named them Anabaptists, or "rebaptists," in order to bring them within the jurisdiction of an ancient law of the Justinian Code carrying the death penalty for rebaptism. They were first called Mennonites in 1545.)

Jesus said, "If ye love me, keep my commandments." Anabaptists did so literally, presuming to live in the perfection of Christ. They read Matthew 5:34, "Swear not at all," and they obeyed. This seemingly innocuous refusal to take oaths isolated them in a society accustomed to confirm by oath innumerable transactions and contracts, and placed them in a posture of civil disobedience, for Swiss and south German cities normally required their inhabitants to swear a yearly oath of obedience to the municipal authorities. They read in Paul's Epistle to the Corinthians that Christians should not go to law, so they avoided lawyers and refused to go to court. They read that the early Christians had held all property in common, and in order to conform to this New Testament standard they broke the locks on the doors of their houses and cellars and lovingly shared their goods with one another. Some Anabaptists practiced evangelical communism. Because Christ said, "Resist not evil," and commanded Peter to put his sword into the sheath, Anabaptists were usually pacifists, and in the face of persecution, nonresistant. "True Christian believers," wrote Conrad Grebel, "are sheep among wolves, sheep for the slaughter; they must be baptized in anguish and affliction, tribulation, persecution, suffering, and death; they must be tried with fire, and must reach the fatherland of eternal rest, not by killing their bodily, but by mortifying their spiritual enemies. Neither do they use worldly sword or war, since all killing has ceased with them."[15]

Revolutionary biblical literalism of this kind could lead to picturesque excess. Some Anabaptists actually preached from the rooftops, or obeying Christ's command to become like little children, played and babbled like infants, or ran about naked because of a verse in Isaiah, or practiced polygamy in imitation of the Old Testament patriarchs, or persuaded credulous women that it was impossible for them to be saved without sacrificing their virtue, for, they argued, the Lord said that only he who was willing to part with all he held most dear would enter the Kingdom of Heaven. In 1532, demented by persecution, millenarian enthusiasm, and expectations of eschatological revenge, Anabaptists captured the episcopal city of Münster, in northwestern Germany, and briefly established a heavenly Jerusalem—communist, polygamous, and violent.

But these were occasional aberrations. Typically Anabaptists were peaceful, humble, patient, honest, and temperate. They originated the movement for total abstinence from alcoholic beverages. They wore coarse cloth and broad felt hats. Any brother or sister who fell into sin was first admonished, then openly disciplined or banned, that is, excluded from the sacrament of communion until he had repaired his life. Their worst enemies agreed that their lives were exemplary. Luther called them "work saints," and regarded them as legalists who disowned the principle of justification by faith alone and sought salvation through good works. Anabaptists answered that they tried to fulfill God's will not in order to be saved, but in order to obey God's express commands and to give proof of their faith by its fruit in good works. Yet fundamentally Luther was right. A profound moralism was at the heart of Anabaptism. It is for this reason that Anabaptists rejected as the "abomination of all abominations" one of the central doctrines of classical Protestantism—predestination and the bondage of the will. Like the humanist Erasmus they believed in free will, and they did so for the same reason: both considered it the indispensable basis for a responsible moral life, newly and freely chosen in Christ.

---

[15]*Spiritual and Anabaptist Writers*, ed. by G. H. Williams and A. M. Mergal (*Library of Christian Classics*, Vol. XXV, Philadelphia, 1961), p. 80.

Such a life, Anabaptists believed, was possible only apart from the world. The authors of the Schleitheim Confession put it like this: "A separation shall be made from the evil and from the wickedness which the devil planted in the world; in this manner, simply that we shall not have fellowship with them [the wicked] and not run with them in the multitude of their abominations. . . . For truly all creatures are in but two classes, good and bad, believing and unbelieving, darkness and light, the world and those who [have come] out of the world, God's temple and idols, Christ and Belial; and none have part with the other."[16] Anabaptists were separatists. They considered the state and society to be outside the perfection of Christ, and regarded themselves as citizens only of heaven. They concluded, therefore, that the realm of civil government and civil coercion must be entirely separate from the realm of conscience, religious discipline, and polity, and they rejected the possibility of a Christian magistracy. Thus Anabaptists refused to hold civil office, just as they refused to bear arms. Conversely, they denied that the civil authorities could legitimately interfere in matters of faith. Anabaptists withdrew from the world as effectively as medieval monks had done. Or rather, they moved the monastery into the world and transformed it into the "segregated Protestant community."

It is precisely because their conventicles were voluntary congregations of believers separated from the world that Anabaptists rejected infant baptism and practiced instead adult or believer's baptism. Baptism is the sociological sacrament. It links the individual Christian to society; while the manner of its definition and administration reveals at once whether he belongs to a church or a sect. Infant baptism presupposes a church that includes the entire population of a community or territory. Babies, without explicit faith or voluntary choice, are born into the church. Adult baptism creates a sect, a voluntary congregation of true Christians, a gathered society of the regenerate. It is the sign of mature repentance and rebirth in Christ, the symbol of membership in a society of believers who have consciously chosen Christ. Luther, Zwingli, and Calvin founded churches. Anabaptism was the first sixteenth-century sect.

THE CITY OF THE SAINTS

Lutherans, Zwinglians, Calvinists, and Catholics all feared, detested, and persecuted the Anabaptists. One fundamental tendency of Anabaptism penetrated classical Protestantism nonetheless: its reformist impulse, its drive to maintain the ethical purity of the segregated community by an elaborate discipline, its concern with every detail of morals and manners. When puritanical aspirations and practices of this sort, associated among Anabap-

[16]John C. Wenger, "The Schleitheim Confession of Faith," *Mennonite Quarterly Review*, Vol. XIX (1945), p. 249.

John Calvin at the age of fifty. *Woodcut by an unknown artist, 1559. In the frame*: John Calvin, faithful minister of the Word of God. *Below, Proverbs, 1, 7*: The fear of the Lord is the beginning of knowledge.

Prouerbes j.
La crainte du Seigneur eſt le commencement de Science.

tists with voluntary adherence to a sect, became a central concern of "magisterial" Protestants—that is, Protestants like Zwingli and Calvin, who retained and defended the ecumenical and authoritarian conception of the church they had inherited from the Middle Ages, regarded the church as an ally of the Christian state, and believed that reformation should proceed with the cooperation and under the protection of the secular power—the result was a penetrating and comprehensive system of social control.

The most conspicuous example of such a disciplinary system in operation was the city-state of Geneva during the long period of Calvin's ascendancy (1541–1564).

Every member of the civic community of Geneva was also a member of the church. To Anabaptists, who argued that in the visible church, as in the eternal and invisible church, membership must be restricted to true believers, to those with faith, Calvin answered that no adequate criteria exist for distinguishing the few true Christians from the hypocritical majority. Any such distinction was the more difficult because even true Christians remained sinners throughout their lives on earth. Everyone, therefore, must have an opportunity to hear the Word of God purely preached by a minister of the church. By infant baptism every child must be snatched from Satan and initiated into the ecclesiastical community, just as under the old covenant circumcision initiated infants into the holy community of Israel. Every adult must attend the Lord's Supper.

Calvin considered a comprehensive effort to discipline the beliefs and manners of the entire population necessary not only because membership in church and in state were inseparable, but also because every adult must attend the Lord's Supper worthily, unspotted by heresy, blasphemy, or wickedness. Wrong belief and immoral behavior dishonor God; since the church is the body of Christ, it "cannot be corrupted by such foul and decaying members without some disgrace falling upon its Head."[17] The purpose of Calvinist discipline was to keep the sacrament from profanation by making sure that the beliefs of every member of the community conformed to the teaching of the *Institutes* and that everyone's life and manners were exemplary. To this end, transgressors were identified and warned. If they did not mend their ways, the ministers publically denounced them. Refractory sinners were excommunicated, for just as a heretical member must be cut away so that it cannot infect the healthy body, so too must the wicked be excluded from the church to prevent the corruption of the good by the company of the bad. Cut off from his fellows and from the sacraments by excommunication, the excluded sinner was supposed to feel shame, repent, and reform; if he laughed at excommunication, he was handed over to the secular authority for punishment.

Discipline was institutionalized in the Consistory, composed of twelve elders—members of the city council, laymen of good life and good repute—who met with the pastors once a week to hear the reports of informers and busybodies about their neighbors. No man or woman, however highly placed, could escape the "fraternal correction" of the Consistory. It prosecuted a bewildering variety of offenses, from the gravest moral lapses to the most frivolous. A major category of offense was private immorality—fighting, fornication, adultery, swearing, and so on. Another concerned behavior in church. There were penalties for making a loud noise or laughing during service, and for unseemly behavior on the sabbath. The elders controlled all amusements, prohibiting promiscuous bathing, card playing, gambling, dancing. They forbade theatrical performances and tried to close the taverns and replace them with state eating houses furnished with French Bibles. Many infractions involved the remnants of popery. A goldsmith was punished for making a chalice for the Mass, a barber for tonsuring a priest, another man for saying that the pope was a good man—every "reformed" Genevan knew that the pope was Antichrist. Geneva's ecclesiastical discipline created a holy commonwealth, a city whose end was to glorify God, with the life of every citizen sanctified to that high purpose. The Scottish reformer John Knox (1505–1572) has recorded the pious astonishment of

---

[17]*Institutes*, ed. by McNeill, trans. by Battles, Vol. II, p. 1232.

the faithful: Geneva, he wrote home in December, 1556, "is the maist perfyt schoole of Chryst that ever was in the erth since the dayis of the Apostillis. In other places, I confess Chryst to be trewlie preachit; but maneris and religioun so sinceirlie reformat, I have not yit sene in any uther place."[18]

CATHOLIC REFORMATION AND COUNTER-REFORMATION

While Protestant revolutionaries founded and ordered new churches and sects, Catholic reformers repaired the fabric of the old Church. Already before 1517, as we have seen, the reformation of abuses preoccupied dedicated clerics and laymen in every country of Europe. Their efforts to reform the church gathered momentum after 1517, and became in the 1530's a vast movement of spiritual, moral, and ecclesiastical renewal, independent of Protestantism and not necessarily directed against it. This movement is appropriately called the Catholic Reformation. It was an increasingly successful effort, at every level of the hierarchy—papacy, cardinalate, diocese, parish, and monastery—to correct ecclesiastical abuses within the traditional sacramental and institutional framework of the Church. Catholic reformation culminated in mid-century in the decrees of the Council of Trent concerned with the correction of abuses. Although Catholic sovereigns enforced the decrees at the local level with more deliberation than speed, much progress was made in rationalizing Church government and jurisdiction, eliminating the chaos in ecclesiastical appointments, and improving the discipline and education of priests and monks. Such reforms made possible the revitalization of the Church which is so striking a fact of the later sixteenth century.

Intertwined with the reforming impulse of sixteenth-century Catholicism were policies and practices which took their origin from the need to repel Protestant attack, and in due course, to counterattack and recover the ground steadily being lost to Protestantism between the beginning of the Lutheran revolt and 1560. This long, and in the end remarkably successful, struggle against Protestantism is appropriately called the Counter-Reformation. It was fought on many fronts and with a variety of weapons. As Protestant ideas spread, the need to protect the faithful against heretical proselytizing and propaganda became ever more urgent. Local authorities tightened censorship; and to guide them the papacy began to issue more elaborate indexes of prohibited books. In 1542, in order more effectively to discover heretics and to try and judge them, the pope established the Roman Inquisition, which successfully rooted out every trace of Protestantism in Italy. A lively concern to bolster the doctrinal reliability of clergy and laity and to convert Protestants in Europe and heathens overseas encouraged the foundation and proliferation of new orders. The most famous was the Jesuit

[18] *The Works of John Knox*, ed. by David Laing (Edinburgh, 1864), Vol. IV, p. 240.

order, founded by the great Spanish soldier-mystic St. Ignatius of Loyola (1491–1556) and officially approved by Pope Paul III in 1540 in a bull beginning with the stirring words, *Regimini militantis ecclesiae* ("For the order of the church militant"). The best-known paragraph in Loyola's *Spiritual Exercises* (written 1522–1542) catches perfectly the commitment, passion, and discipline of mid-century Catholic militancy: "To arrive at complete certainty, this is the attitude of mind we should maintain: I will believe that the white object I see is black if that should be the decision of the hierarchical Church, for I believe that linking Christ our Lord the Bridegroom and His Bride the Church, there is one and the same Spirit, ruling and guiding us for our souls' good. For our Holy Mother the Church is guided and ruled by the same Spirit, the Lord who gave the Ten Commandments."[19]

But the most important and interesting development in sixteenth-century Catholicism was neither the reform of abuses within the Church nor the Church's successful effort to stem the spread of Protestantism; it was rather the emergence during the decades before the end of the Council of Trent of the doctrine and style of piety that have stamped Roman Catholicism in modern times.

The medieval Church was more ecumenical, more genially encompassing, more permissive doctrinally, then either the sixteenth-century Protestant churches or the post-Trentine Catholic Church. There was more room in it for doctrinal maneuver. More possibilities existed for disagreement and debate among the orthodox. Most of the doctrines propounded in Calvin's *Institutes* and all of the doctrines embodied in the decrees and canons of the Council of Trent had coexisted peacefully in the Middle Ages. Intellectual clerics could and did debate them, question them, believe them, and defend them. In a word, all the bits and pieces that were to make up the sixteenth-century theologies of Protestantism and Catholicism were in solution in medieval thought. What so dramatically happened during the age of the Reformation is that they crystallized into two distinct and opposed systems, each more exclusive, more consistent, and more rigid than the medieval theological tradition from which they both derived. First, Protestants built up a systematic theology based on Luther's three *solae*: faith, grace, and Scripture. Inevitably, Catholics felt the need to redefine and reorganize Catholic doctrine in response to this challenge. This was the task and accomplishment of the Council of Trent.

The council sat in three sessions. The first lasted from 1545 to 1547; the second met in 1551–1552; the third, in 1562–1563. The dogmatic decrees of the first and second sessions left no doubt about what Catholicism was, and little subtlety was required to distinguish it from Protestantism. Protestants

[19]*The Spiritual Exercises of Saint Ignatius,* trans. by Thomas Corbishley, S.J. (New York, 1963), p. 122.

Tomb of Pope Paul III. *Guglielmo della Porta. The Counter-Reformation took shape in Rome during the reign of this decisive and magnificent pontiff. St. Peter's, Rome.*

admitted only one authority—Scripture. The fathers at Trent reestablished two—Scripture and tradition. Moreover, they declared the Latin Vulgate translation to be an authentic text of the Bible, and they stressed the exclusive right of Holy Mother Church "to judge of the true sense and interpretation of the holy Scriptures." Protestants asserted that men were justified by faith alone, without the works of the law; in a masterly exposition, the fathers at Trent decreed that men were saved by faith in combination with good works. The decrees and canons concerning the sacraments sharply distinguished the Catholic interpretation from the views of Lutherans, Zwinglians, and Calvinists. The last session of the council redefined and reaffirmed almost every belief and practice that Catholic humanists like Erasmus had considered superstitious half a century before: the making of vows, the belief in purgatory, the invocation of saints, the veneration of relics, and the giving of indulgences. On November 13, 1564, the pope summed up the Catholic faith as taught at Trent in the Creed of Pope Pius IV.

Growing differences in their devotional practices and styles of piety and feeling created a psychological gap between Catholics and Protestants even wider than the doctrinal gap so precisely defined by Calvin and the Trent fathers. An unusually heated emotionalism is the most noticeable character-istic of Catholic piety by the mid-century. Contemporary religious paintings suggest the ideal attitudes of worship: copious weeping, distorted features, extravagant gestures, eyes turned up dramatically to heaven. A medieval literary genre, the poem of tearful contrition, was revived and enjoyed a great vogue. The purpose of such verses was to describe, for example, the remorse-ful tears of St. Peter after he had denied Christ, or those of St. Mary Magdalene deploring her early life, in order to provoke the tears of the faithful and freshen their faith and piety. To encourage the spectator to relive the sufferings of Christ on the Cross or the torments of the martyrs, the Church asked its artists to picture these holy agonies in gruesome detail: St. Agatha with her breasts being torn away, St. Dorothy branded, St. Fidelis scourged, St. Edward with his throat cut. A revival of the late medieval preoccupation with death is another aspect of this holy enthusiasm. Repre-sentations of skulls are regularly found on tombstones after Trent. Epitaphs take on a more somber tone than they had had during the fifteenth-century Renaissance. On the tomb of a cardinal who died in 1451 in Rome was inscribed, "Why fear death, which brings us rest?" but a typical epitaph of the later sixteenth century reads: "My turn yesterday, yours today."

At the heart of Catholic religious emotion was mysticism. No other period, except possibly the fourteenth century, has produced so abundant a crop of attractive visionaries as the age of the Council of Trent. One reason for this development is the harmony between the dogmatic decrees of Trent and the assumptions of mysticism. The mystic assumes that man, with the aid of God's grace, can gradually perfect himself and briefly see God face to face. Mysticism—how unlike classical Protestantism—is optimistic about God and about man. With its emphasis on planned and ordered meditation, spiritual exercises, and a rigorous training of the will, sixteenth-century mysticism admirably complemented a theology built on an affirmation of the freedom of the will, man's ability to cooperate in his own salvation, and the efficacy of charity and good works. It answered too the need of devout men and women for a more personal, warmer piety and a more direct relation between God and man. Protestantism met this need by eliminating hierar-chical and sacramental intermediaries between God and man; Trentine mysticism offered an ascending ladder of contemplation and perfection on whose upper rungs men experienced brief moments of ineffaceable sweetness and joy.

Perhaps the most striking characteristic of the new Catholic piety was its stress on just those elements in the traditional inheritance of Christian devotion which were rejected or minimized by Protestants. Protestants minimized the religious significance of the Virgin Mary and the saints. In late sixteenth-century Catholicism, on the other hand, devotion to the Virgin gained a popularity it had enjoyed at no time since the thirteenth century. The doctrine of the Immaculate Conception of Mary, vigorously attacked by late medieval and Renaissance Dominican theologians as a popular superstition, was now officially defended in Rome. New and related devotions appeared: of the Holy Family, of St. Joseph (a figure of ribald fun in the Middle Ages), of the Child Jesus. Correspondingly, increased attention was paid to the saints, and especially to St. Peter. At St. Peter's in Rome, frescoes painted during this period show him walking on the waters, raising the dead, healing sick people with his shadow, meeting Christ at the gates of Rome, vanquishing the magician Simon Magus, all episodes designed to illustrate and defend the primacy of the papal see. Protestants denied the existence of purgatory. Catholics multiplied confraternities to pray for the dead. In the *Spiritual Exercises* Loyola urged his readers to speak with particular approval of religious orders, of virginity and celibacy, of the relics of the saints, "showing reverence for them and praying to the saints themselves," of pilgrimages, indulgences, jubilees, Crusade bulls, fasting and abstinence in Lent, and the lighting of candles in churches. The iconography of the Last Supper changed, reflecting the renewed emphasis on the doctrine of the Real Presence. The normal medieval and Renaissance depiction of the Last Supper (Leonardo da Vinci's is a good example) shows Christ and the apostles at the moment when Christ says, "One of you shall betray me." After the middle of the sixteenth century, painters chose the moment when Christ says, "This is my body," that is, the institution of the Eucharist. Protestants, finally, had rejected much of the sensuousness and beauty of the medieval liturgy and of earlier church decoration. The Trentine Church did everything possible to make the Catholic service as splendid as possible. A vivid symbol of the growing differences in feeling, taste, and habits between Protestants and Catholics is the contrast between the whitewashed inside walls of the Grossmünster in Zurich and the interior of the Jesuit church in Rome—theatrical, brilliantly painted and gilded, filled with magnificent frescoes and sculptures, sounding with the serpentine polyphony of Palestrina and the massed brasses of Gabrieli.

By 1560 the religious unity of Europe had been irreparably shattered. A vigorous Catholic church, a Lutheran church, Zwinglian and Calvinist churches, an Anglican church, and a variety of sects competed for men's minds and loyalties. For the first time in many centuries, problems of religious choice and conversion became of major concern for ordinary men and women.

CHAPTER 6

Revolution and Reformation in the Church: The Problem of Conversion

FROM WITTENBERG AND ZURICH, Strasbourg and Geneva, in books, through personal contact between churchmen, commercial travelers, and students, by public and secret preaching, Protestant ideas penetrated every state in Europe.

Printing played the most important role in the spread of Protestantism. Some two thousand different editions of Luther's books and sermons appeared between 1517 and 1526 alone. To those we must add the flood of popular pamphlets, broadsides, and cartoons attacking the pope as Antichrist, satirizing the Mass, calling for the secularization of monasteries, urging the incompatibility of serfdom and Christian liberty. These simple texts and vivid images touched every social and intellectual level of the population.

Preaching was the second important channel for the communication of the new ideas. The Reformation was a doctrinal crisis. It began as a debate among professionals who took doctrine seriously. In the early sixteenth century, as in the thirteenth, almost all such men were clerics. It is not surprising, therefore, that Protestantism's earliest converts were priests and monks—members of Luther's own Augustinian order, Franciscans and Dominicans, and parish priests like Zwingli. As soon as these men heard and believed the good news of justification by faith alone and the wonderful authority of God's scriptural Word, they went forth and preached it to others. At first they had no organization, no church. In the countryside and in the towns, Lutheran and traditional practices and beliefs existed side by side. The situation was fluid, upsetting, and confusing. Ideas ordinarily confined to theological faculties were now propagandized by pastors and ministers, officially debated before princes, magistrates, and citizens, and discussed at home and in the streets by merchants, craftsmen, knights, peasants, students, bishops, and dukes.

In short, religious doctrines were in public competition, and individuals

Luther preaching. *Woodcut by Lucas Cranach the Elder. Lying before Luther is the Bible. His right hand points to the crucified Christ; his left consigns the Roman clergy to Hell. The congregation is receiving communion in both bread and wine.*

had the freedom (progressively limited, as we shall see, by persecution and the religious preferences of their rulers) to choose among them. What determined their choices? Why did some men remain attached to the old faith? Why did others become Lutherans or Calvinists? What attracted still others to Anabaptism?

Making a choice involved a personal drama of conscience. By and large, the evidence suggests that most men chose a religion among the several competing for their allegiance because they believed it was true rather than because it was in some way useful. It has sometimes been supposed that direct correspondences can be found between particular systems of theological doctrine and the interests of particular social classes, but the validity of this assumption is illusory. Luther found converts at every level of the social structure and among men of widely divergent social and economic interests. Calvinism was not in the sixteenth century a middle-class religion. It appealed equally, perhaps more, and certainly with greater political effect, to the aristocracy. This is not to say that conversion is unintelligible except in terms of personal religious psychology. A sociology of conversion is possible and can be useful—but only if it is alert to the concrete variety of local circumstances.

THE PEASANTS

The response of the peasantry offers an initial perspective on the spread of Protestantism. In 1524–1526 tension between German peasants and their landlords erupted in a peasants' revolt, the last and most desperate of a series of uprisings that had begun in the later Middle Ages. Peasant grievances were not new. The most famous peasant manifesto, the so-called Twelve Articles (January–February, 1525), listed complaints familiar for over a century—against tithes, serfdom, the invasion by landlords of the common fields, forests, streams, and meadows, the lords' disregard of manorial customs and their efforts to raise rents and increase labor services. Nor was it unusual for peasants to associate their economic and social demands with evangelical and millenarian expectations, or to justify them by scriptural texts. Lutheranism, that is, did not cause the armed and revolutionary outburst of some 300,000 peasants, miners, artisans, journeymen, and disaffected knights against their lords; on the other hand, Luther's intransigence concerning the Gospel clearly magnetized them. And of course some of his ideas could be given a radical social twist. The freedom of the Christian man, for example, though a purely religious conception in the context of Luther's theology, could be extended to mean freedom from

Peasants plundering the monastery of Weissenau. *Drawing by an unknown artist, 1525.*

serfdom. The idea of a priesthood of all believers suggested a more secular egalitarianism. Luther's repudiation of monasticism suited peasant covetousness. Here, at least, was one body of landlords who could be justifiably pillaged. Luther's primitive economic ideas, his blasts against usury and what he called *Fuggerei*, after the Augsburg bankers, harmonized with a widespread resentment. Above all, perhaps, Luther offered hope, hope that religious reformation was the initial step toward a new and juster society, one in which evangelical precepts were less obviously contradicted by reality than they had been in the past.

Peasant spokesmen therefore rephrased traditional demands in the language of evangelical Lutheranism. The first of the Twelve Articles demanded for every congregation the right to choose its own pastor to "preach to us the Holy Gospel purely and clearly, without any human addition, doctrine or commandment." Another attacked the small tithe, a traditional cattle tax due the parish priest, on the grounds that "God the Lord created cattle for the free use of men, and we regard this as an improper tithe which men have invented; therefore we will not give it any longer." The most important article was against serfdom: "It has been the custom hitherto for men to hold us as their own property; and this is pitiable, seeing that Christ has redeemed and bought us all with the precious shedding of His blood, the lowly as well as the great, excepting no one. Therefore, it agrees with Scripture that we be free, and will to be so." The peasants swore to obey the commandments of Scripture and their legitimate rulers, and concluded with unfounded optimism: "We have no doubt that, as true and real Christians, [our lords] will gladly release us from serfdom, or show us from the Gospel that we are serfs."[1]

In April, 1525, Luther answered in his *Admonition to Peace: A Reply to the Twelve Articles of the Peasants in Swabia*. The peasants, he said, had seriously misinterpreted the Gospel. Their attitude was carnal, not spiritual. They sought to give their enterprise an evangelical appearance, although in fact their single purpose was to make their properties and bodies free. His commentary on the article condemning serfdom struck bluntly home: "That is making Christian liberty an utterly carnal thing. Did not Abraham and other patriarchs and prophets have slaves? . . . Therefore this article is dead against the Gospel. It is a piece of robbery by which every man takes from his lord the body, which has become his lord's property. For a slave can be a Christian, and have Christian liberty, in the same way that a prisoner or a sick man is a Christian, and yet not free. This article would make all men equal, and turn the spiritual kingdom of Christ into a worldly external kingdom."[2] Few passages in Luther's works underscore so heavily his con-

---

[1] *Works of Martin Luther*, Vol. IV (Philadelphia, 1931), pp. 210–216 gives the Twelve Articles in an English translation by C. M. Jacobs.
[2] *Ibid.*, p. 240.

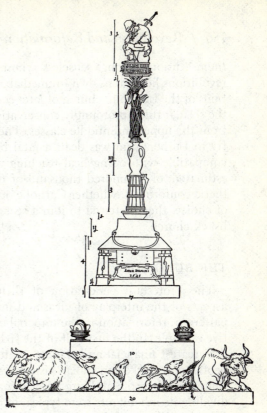

Project for a monument commemo-
rating the Peasant War. *Woodcut
from Dürer's* Unterweisung der Mes-
sung, *published in 1525. "Should
someone wish to erect a victory
monument because he has defeated
the rebellious peasants," wrote Dürer,
"let him use this design." Base and
shaft assemble the fruits and attributes of peaceful labor. At the top,
on a cage of chickens, sits a peasant
with a sword plunged between his
shoulder blades.*

tempt for secular aspiration; his conservatism and authoritarianism; his
insistence that the kingdom is supernatural and in heaven, not of this earth;
his refusal to draw any social inferences from the Gospel except that man's
external life in this world properly consists in suffering wrong, patience, and
contempt for temporal wealth and life; the utter primacy that religion had
for him and his single-minded concern for its purity.

This was not Luther's last word on the peasant war. A month later, in
May, he published his tract *Against the Robbing and Murdering Hordes of
Peasants*, the only unforgivably shameful thing he ever wrote. He said the
peasants were guilty of three sins: perjury, rebellion, and blasphemy. "Therefore let everyone who can, smite, slay, and stab, secretly or openly, remembering that nothing can be more poisonous, hurtful, or devilish than a rebel.
It is just as when one must kill a mad dog; if you do not strike him, he will
strike you, and a whole land with you."[3]

Virtually without exception princes and nobles, secular and lay, Catholic
and Lutheran, combined to crush the peasants. The gruesome repression
strengthened every despotic tendency in German political and social development. At a crucial moment, the leaders of the new religion chose not the
people, but the princes. Luther had no illusions about the princes. He called

[3]*Ibid.*, p. 249.

them "furious, raving, senseless tyrants." But in his terror of other men's revolutions he tied his own irremediably to the princes and laid the foundations of the Lutheran church of later centuries: a state church dependent on the secular ruler, profoundly conservative, its membership drawn primarily from the upper and middle classes. The attachment of the German peasantry to Lutheranism was dealt a fatal blow when their appeal for a justice compatible with evangelical teaching was answered by the slaughter, it is estimated, of a hundred thousand of their number. Peasants became apathetic conformists, whether Catholic or Lutheran. When they had freedom of choice, they preferred to join a sect, apart from the state and the established church.

THE BURGHERS

The Protestant penetration of the urban population illustrates other aspects of the interplay of ideas and interests in the Reformation era. The pattern of reformation in the imperial city of Augsburg provides an instructive example. In the first half of the sixteenth century, Augsburg was one of the greatest financial and trading centers of the continent. (The kings of Scotland, remarked an Italian visitor, would wish to be as well housed as the simple burghers of Augsburg.) Both its social structure and the antagonisms dividing its inhabitants were typical of contemporary urban life. At the top were a small group of wealthy merchant-bankers. The Fuggers are the best known, but they were not alone. The firm of Anton Welser and Conrad Vöhlin traded with Venice, lent money to the Habsburgs, dabbled in Tyrolese silver, and helped finance the first Portuguese voyages. In 1505, Welser sent three merchant ships to India with the fleet of the king of Portugal and made a profit of 175 per cent on the return cargo. The Hochstetters were the most hated monopolists of their time. Herwarts and Gossembrots, Paumgartners and Rems, were other merchant-bankers of the same stamp. In the stratum below this wealthy elite were the manufacturers of linen cloth and fustian, clothes, books, and shoes; while below these independent entrepreneurs were the very much more numerous dependent journeymen, workers, and servants. Journeymen and workers were pitted against the masters of the guilds. The masters fought on two fronts, against their workmen and against the great merchant-bankers who were coming to dominate the city's economic and political life. Themselves capitalist innovators in their relations with their journeymen, they stubbornly defended the fixing of a "just price" and the cooperative limiting of competition against what they considered the unscrupulous machinations of the oligarchs, who through their commercial and financial pressures threatened to undermine the independence of the masters in the same way as the masters had undermined that of the journeymen.

The religious choices made by the inhabitants of Augsburg reflect this pattern of competing interests and discontents. Most of the great mercantile and financial families remained Catholic. Ambrosius Hochstetter was "entirely against the Lutherans." So were the Fuggers, the Welsers, and the others. It is equally evident that the majority of independent masters, and in the early 1520's many of their workmen, were eager converts to Lutheranism. Manufacturers of fustian listened with respect to Lutheran preachers. Augsburg printers published Luther's translation of the Bible into German, as well as many of his other works. A former Franciscan preached against Rome and high prices, caused, he cried, by Jakob Fugger. When the council expelled him from the town, 1,800 weavers and journeymen tailors demonstrated in front of the town hall for his return. In Augsburg, in this first phase of its reformation, the Lutheran attack on Catholicism was inseparable from the attack on monopoly and *Fuggerei*.

During the peasants' revolt the situation changed. Anabaptist missionaries entered the city, preached secretly in cellars and gardens, and recruited some eight hundred converts, principally among the mass of impoverished weavers, the *armen Weber*. The arrival of Zwinglian preachers in 1526 complicated the religious life of the city even further. By 1530 Catholicism was in full retreat, and the council had broken Anabaptism by executions and expulsions. Lutherans remained numerous. The sympathies of the government were Zwinglian.

It is one thing to notice that in Augsburg the *armen Weber* were attracted to Anabaptism, the small-scale manufacturers were often Lutheran, and the merchant-bankers preferred to retain their old religion. It is quite another to argue that this particular pattern of correspondences is a necessary one, reflecting intrinsic affinities between certain religious beliefs and certain social classes. It was not an innate harmony between sixteenth-century Catholic teaching and the higher forms of capitalist enterprise that caused the merchant oligarchy to remain Catholic. A more plausible explanation can be found in the commitment of Augsburg merchant-bankers to the emperor. Charles V needed them; and once they had lent him money, they needed him even more. Every interest which held them to the Habsburgs held them to the traditional faith as well. It is equally hazardous to argue any inherent affinity between the principal doctrines of Luther and the psychological and ethical needs of petty manufacturers. As we have seen, Luther appealed just as much, in certain circumstances, to peasants and workers.

Moreover, other cities of Europe offer patterns of religious choice different from Augsburg's. In Lyons, for example, men of substance normally remained Catholic, while many journeymen and workers became in turn Lutheran and Calvinist. In 1529 unrest among workers in the silk and printing industries crystallized in serious social disturbances. Contemporaries attributed the difficulties to the "wicked sect," that is, to the Protestants. In the early 1550's large groups of printing and silk workers (sons of poor artisans and of agricultural laborers in the surrounding provinces or impover-

View of Augsburg. *From Hartmann Schedel's* Liber chronicarum *with wood-cuts by Michel Wohlgemuth and Wilhelm Pleydenwurff, published in Nuremberg, 1493.*

ished immigrants from Germany and Italy) customarily assembled in the streets to sing "Calvinist" psalms. In 1573 a Lyons cleric attributed the high incidence of Protestantism among the *menu peuple,* or plebeians, to their hopes for freedom from ecclesiastical government and taxes and their expectation of sacking the houses of the rich under the sanction of religion. Elsewhere the pattern was either reversed—with the urban ruling class sympathizing with Zwinglianism or Calvinism while a majority of the workers remained Catholic—or more commonly, as in Paris, modified. During the night of October 17–18, 1534, Protestants plastered the walls of Paris with placards attacking the Mass. The government reacted by burning as many of the culprits as it could catch. The fragmentary lists of men and women burned or condemned to death in absentia record their ranks or occupations. These lists suggest that the social composition of Parisian Protestantism was exceedingly varied. Most of the individuals listed were members of the working, lower-middle, and middle class. Among them were relatively small groups consisting on the one hand, of journeyman dyers, weavers, masons, cooks, and carpenters, and on the other, of substantial entrepreneurs, goldsmiths, printers, and minor civil servants. A larger group was made up of modest artisans and retail traders: bookbinders, engravers, hatters, cobblers, illuminators, cabinetmakers, bakers, grocers, and four singers from the royal chapel choir. The lists also record a scattering of quite different types: a theologian and four Augustinian monks, the poet Clément Marot, several aristocrats and their wives, and a handful of rich merchants.

What can we conclude? In the first place, in the early decades of the Reformation, Protestantism frequently mobilized social and economic discontent. The peasants of southwestern Germany, German knights making a last stand against the encroachments of princely power, journeymen and artisans in the larger European cities, all understood the Gospel "carnally" and pursued their material aspirations with evangelical zeal. This simple response gradually yielded to another as the logic of conflicting interests created more complicated patterns of religious diversity: as long as men had a reasonable freedom of choice among competing churches and sects, the members of different social groups tended to choose different religious affiliations. What particular religion a particular group in a particular place in fact adopted was accidental—the result of specific local conditions. The generalization that can be made is that the religion of the poor was very often different from the religion of the rich. By 1540 the wealthier citizens were Catholic in some towns, Lutheran in others, Zwinglian or Calvinist in still others. And in each town a religion different from that of the wealthy and dominant attracted the petty artisans, journeymen, and workers. The sixteenth-century religions possessed no inherent economic or social biases, but within the range of exceptions suggested by such statistics as those from Paris, social divisions assumed religious dimensions and men extended rivalries of class into the novel area of religious ideology.

PERSECUTION AND LIBERTY

From the very beginning of the Reformation, however, the possibility of free choice among competing faiths was limited by persecution. This forcible pressure to conformity was ultimately to be a decisive factor in the shaping of the religious geography of Europe.

Lutherans, Zwinglians, Calvinists, Anglicans, and Catholics all forcibly repressed dissent. Anabaptists were the first martyrs of Protestant persecution. As early as 1525 the Zurich authorities, with Zwingli's approval, condemned Anabaptists to death by drowning. In 1529, at the imperial Diet which met at Speyer, six Protestant princes and the representatives of fourteen Protestant south German cities joined with the Catholic majority and the Emperor Charles V in approving the revival and enforcement of an ancient law of the Justinian Code punishing rebaptism by death. The result was inhuman. Here is how Menno Simons described it:

How many pious children of God have we not seen during the space of a few years deprived of their homes and possessions for the testimony of God and their conscience; their poverty and sustenance written off to the emperor's insatiable coffers? How many have they betrayed, driven out of city and country, put to the stocks and torture? How many poor orphans and children have they turned out without a farthing? Some have they hanged, some have they punished with inhuman tyranny and afterward garroted them with cords, tied to a post. Some they have roasted and burned alive. Some, holding their own entrails in their hands, have powerfully confessed the Word of God still. Some they beheaded and gave as food to the fowls of the air. Some have they consigned to the fish. They have torn down the houses of some. Some have they thrust into muddy bogs. They cut off the feet of some, one of whom I have seen and spoken to. Others wander aimlessly hither and yon in want, misery, and discomfort, in the mountains, in deserts, holes, and clefts of the earth, as Paul says. They must take to their heels and flee away with their wives and little children, from one country to another, from one city to another—hated by all men, abused, slandered, mocked, defamed, trampled upon, styled "heretics." Their names are read from pulpits and town halls; they are kept from their livelihood, driven out into the cold winter, bereft of bread, pointed at with fingers. Yes, whoever can wrong a poor oppressed Christian thinks he has done God a service thereby, even as Christ says.[4]

Anabaptists were not the only victims of Protestant persecution. The case of Michael Servetus (1511–1553) is exemplary. In the eyes of virtually every contemporary Christian, this Spanish physician was a notorious and obstinate heretic. He rejected infant baptism and embraced the Anabaptist idea of the church as a voluntary society of the regenerate. Going even further, he attacked the Trinity, thereby embracing the second doctrinal deviation to carry the death penalty in Roman law. He was an antitrinitarian on scriptural grounds. By demonstrating the *Comma Johanneum* to be a late interpolation, Erasmus had shown that the doctrine of the Trinity had no clear scriptural foundation (p. 71). In 1523 Sir Thomas More had tried to show the absurdity of Luther's contention that nothing should be believed with certainty unless it could be proved from a clear scriptural text by pointing to the belief in the Trinity: "Nowhere in all scripture," he remarked, "is the Father called 'uncreated'; the Son nowhere called 'consubstantial'; nowhere is the Holy Spirit indicated with enough clarity as 'proceeding from the Father and Son.'"[5] Why, he asked, had Luther, having rejected so much else because it had no scriptural authority, not rejected the Trinity also?

Servetus dared to take the step at which all the great reformers balked. Because it had no biblical foundation, he called the Trinity a "three-headed Cerberus" and asserted that the Son was not coeternal with the Father. Melanchthon condemned his "detestable heresies." Calvin judged his work "a rhapsody patched together from the impious ravings of all the ages"; and when in early 1553, after living and practicing in Lyons for twenty years under an assumed identity, he secretly published his masterpiece, the *Restitution of Christianity*, and imprudently sent Calvin a copy under his own name, Calvin denounced him (through a third person) to the Catholic authorities in France. Servetus was jailed, but escaped. The Inquisition in Lyons garroted his effigy, then burned it. He planned to take refuge in Naples, but a suicidal vanity led him to travel from Lyons to Naples by way of Geneva. The day after he arrived, he went to hear Calvin preach. He was recognized, and Calvin at once instructed one of his disciples to lodge against

[4]*The Complete Writings of Menno Simons*, ed. by John C. Wenger, trans. by Leonard Verduin (Scottdale, Pa., 1956), pp. 599–600.
[5]*Responsio ad Lutherum*, trans. by Sister Gertrude J. Donnelly, (*The Catholic University of America Studies in Medieval and Renaissance Latin*, Vol. XXIII, Washington, D.C., 1962), p. 141.

him before the magistrates the capital charges of blasphemy and heresy. Within three weeks the council condemned him. On October 27, 1553, he was burned alive, suffering the penalty prescribed by Roman law for antitrinitarianism and antipedobaptism.

Catholics persecuted dissenters with equal vigor. The most celebrated engine of persecution in all of Europe was the Spanish Inquisition, established in 1478. Theoretically, the inquisitorial process was not a trial at all. The inquisitor was not a judge, but a father confessor whose object was not to punish the body but to save the soul; to plead guilty was to obtain mercy. Consequently the Inquisition did not punish. It imposed penances appropriate to the guilt confessed: a pilgrimage, flogging (generally one to two hundred lashes administered publicly), exile, imprisonment of from a few months to life, service on the galleys of the royal navy. Needless to say, penitents were excluded from all public office and their property was confiscated by the state.

For the obdurate the penalty was death, with the following classes of offender "relaxed" to the secular arm for burning: the pertinacious heretic who refused to recant (there were never many of these); the *negativo*, who persistently denied that he held any erroneous beliefs although the tribunal was satisfied that he did; and most numerous of all, the relapsed, who had once recanted and become reconciled and had then fallen back into their former errors. It is impossible to determine exactly how many thousands of persons the Inquisition relaxed to the secular arm. But there can be no doubt of its success. It ferreted out backsliders among the *conversos*, Jews converted to Christianity, many of whom had married into the first families in Spain (King Ferdinand had Jewish ancestors; so did St. Teresa of Avila) and occupied prominent positions in church and state. By 1530 no Marranos (outwardly conforming Christians who secretly remained faithful Jews at home) were left in Spain. Protestantism too found Spain uncongenial. Inquisitors suspicious enough to jail the founder of the Jesuit order and the archbishop of Toledo, primate of Spain, easily discovered and burned the few "Lutherans" there.

It is reasonably easy to understand what the victim of religious persecution died for. He died for the truth of an individual interpretation of Scripture, and to maintain the integrity of his own conscience. But why, for example, did Calvin and the magistrates of Geneva, with the unanimous approval of the Lutheran authorities in Wittenberg and the churches of Basel, Bern, Schaffhausen, and Zurich, think it necessary and desirable to kill Servetus? Why did the Catholic authorities in France strangle and burn him in effigy? Why did Servetus' own brother, an agent of the Spanish Inquisition, make a special trip out of Spain to collect evidence against him? Why did Servetus himself consider death the proper penalty for other men's heresy?

Persecution was justified by a variety of persuasive arguments. A father legitimately restrains a child from playing with fire; a son may forcibly

prevent his crazed father from jumping off a cliff; the doctor rightly ampu-
tates a diseased limb in order to save the rest of the body; the good gardener
removes rotten branches to save the tree. In the same way, the heretic must
be constrained for his own good and the good of others.

Scripture confirmed these rational analogies; for by the end of the thirteenth century, theologians had attached the Old Testament penalty for
apostasy—death—to the New Testament crime—heresy. They argued that
the enormity of an offense depended on the rank of the person against whom
the crime was committed. Since heresy was a crime against God, death was
the only adequate penalty. St. Thomas Aquinas illustrated this argument by
comparing the heretic to a false coiner. As the false coiner corrupted the
currency, which was necessary for temporal life, so the heretic corrupted the
faith, which was necessary for the life of the soul. Death was a penalty justly
meted out by the prince to false coiners; how much more just was the death
penalty for heretics, whose sin was graver to the extent that the life of the
soul was more precious than the life of the body.

But the persecutor did not only believe that heresy was a heinous crime
against God and rightly punishable by death; he also passionately believed
that his interpretation of the Bible was the only true one and that he, and
the church he represented, had a monopoly of religious truth. Commonly
allied to this conviction was the assumption, shared by virtually everyone in
Europe before the outbreak of the religious wars of the second half of the
century, that the security of the body politic demanded religious as well as
temporal obedience, religious as well as secular loyalty and uniformity. The
heretic, consequently, was more than a shameless distorter of God's truth; he
was a rebel and a political subversive as well. These convictions were
accompanied by the equally prevalent belief that coercion was effective and
that it benefited the coerced; the result, in the opinion of every man of
common sense, was an impregnable justification of persecution.

The persecutor's intransigence—and it was the intransigence also of his
victim and of his age—ultimately rested on his refusal to betray the Holy
Spirit, the guarantor of his doctrinal impeccability. Every religious leader was
persuaded that a man who denied his interpretation of Scripture, or what he
considered a fundamental doctrine of Christianity like the Trinity, was
giving the lie to God. Wrong belief is a monstrous crime against God. It
insults the Most High. We punish the slanderer. Shall we permit a blas-
phemer of the living God to go unscathed? Treason against a temporal
prince is punished by death. Shall the man who reviles God, the sovereign
emperor, suffer a less punishment? We justly execute murderers, who kill the
body. Shall we not execute blasphemers, who kill the soul? We muzzle dogs.
Shall we leave men free to open their mouths as they please and contaminate
their fellow citizens and the church with their pernicious books? "God
makes plain that the false prophet is to be stoned without mercy," wrote
Calvin in a commentary on the thirteenth chapter of Deuteronomy. "We

The Water Torture. *Engraving from Milles de Souvigny,* Praxis criminis persequendi, *published in 1541. A widespread method of interrogation, used in both criminal and inquisitorial procedures. The victim's mouth was stuffed with a cloth, his nose held, and the cloth saturated with water. The result was intermittent suffocation.*

are to crush beneath our heel all affections of nature when his honor is involved. The father should not spare his child, nor the brother his brother, nor the husband his own wife or the friend who is dearer to him than life. No human relationship is more than animal unless it be grounded in God. If a man be conjoined to his wife without regard to God, he is worthy to be cast out among the brute beasts. If friendship is contracted apart from God, what is this union but sheer bestiality?"[6] Servetus was rightly killed because he was a false prophet. His views were wrong, they might bring other souls to perdition, they disrupted the unity of the civic and ecclesiastical communities, above all, they were a scandalous blasphemy against the majesty of God.

Not quite everyone agreed that Servetus had been rightly burned. His death provoked the most eloquent defenses of toleration written in the sixteenth century: two works by the Protestant humanist Sebastianus Castellio (1515–1563): *Concerning Heretics and Whether They Should Be Punished by the Sword of the Magistrate* and *Contra libellum Calvini*

[6]Quoted by Roland H. Bainton, *The Travail of Religious Liberty* (Philadelphia, 1951), p. 70.

(1554). His conclusion is justly remembered: "To burn a heretic is not to defend a doctrine, but to kill a man."[7]

THE RELIGIOUS PREFERENCES OF THE GERMAN PRINCES

As the coercive governments of city-states, principalities, and kingdoms enforced religious uniformity within their territories—some with rapid success, some only very gradually—the religious preferences of the magistrates and princes overbore those of the citizens and subjects. Almost without exception the religion of a territory became identical with the religion of its prince; the individual's freedom of religious choice was reduced to a single right, that of emigration to a state whose ruler was a coreligionist. Just as the personal decisions of sovereigns determined war and peace, so did their personal theological convictions determine the success or failure of the Reformation in their territories. Although the consciences of emperor, kings, and princes have no more intrinsic interest than those of peasants and merchants, they have had a far larger historical importance. The conversions of princes were as important for the religious history and geography of sixteenth-century Europe as their marriages and dynastic claims were for its diplomacy and wars.

In his *Open Letter to the Christian Nobility of the German Nation,* published in August, 1520, Luther had thanked God for awakening his heart once more to hope now that He had given Germany in Charles V a young and noble ruler to reign over it. How unfounded this hope was to be became clear at the dramatic confrontation of Luther and the young emperor at the Diet of Worms. On the evening of April 18, 1521, Luther appeared in the great torchlit hall before his king and the representatives of the German nation. He was asked whether he was prepared to recant his books. He replied briefly in German. His closing words are justly famous. Turning to Charles V and the imperial electors and princes, he said:

Unless I am convinced by the testimony of the Scriptures or by clear reason (for I do not trust either in the pope or in councils, since it is well known that they have often erred and contradicted themselves), I am bound by the Scriptures I have quoted and my conscience is captive to the Word of God. I cannot and I will not retract anything, since it is neither safe nor right to go against conscience. May God help me! Amen.[8]

The next day, April 19, Charles V answered. His statement is as passion-

---

[7]Quoted by Joseph Lecler, *Toleration and the Reformation,* trans. by T. L. Westow (New York and London, 1960), Vol. I, p. 355.

[8]*Luther's Works,* Vol. XXXII, ed. by George W. Forell (Philadelphia, 1958), pp. 112–113.

ate, as moving, as true to the essential character and vision of the man who spoke it, as Luther's:

You know that I am descended from the most Christian emperors of the noble German nation, from the Catholic kings of Spain, the archduke of Austria and the dukes of Burgundy. To the honor of God, the strengthening of the faith, and the salvation of souls, they all have remained up to death faithful sons of the church and have always been defenders of the Catholic faith, the sacred rituals, decrees, ordinances and holy customs. After death they have left to us by natural right and heritage these holy Catholic observances, to live according to them and to die according to their example, in which [observances], as true followers of these our predecessors, we have up to now lived. For this reason I am determined to support everything that these predecessors and I myself have kept, up to the present. . . . For it is certain that a single friar errs in his opinion which is against all of Christendom and according to which all of Christianity will be and will always have been in error both in the past thousand years and even more in the present. For that reason I am absolutely determined to stake on this cause my kingdoms and seignories, my friends, my body and blood, my life and soul. For it would be a great shame to me and to you, who are the noble and renowned German nation, who are by privilege and pre-eminent standing singularly called to be defenders and protectors of the Catholic faith, if in our time not only heresy but suspicion of heresy or decrease of the Christian religion should through our negligence dwell after us in the hearts of men and our successors to our perpetual dishonor. And after having heard the obstinate answer which Luther gave yesterday, April 18, in the presence of us all, I declare to you that I regret having so long delayed to proceed against this Luther and his false doctrine and I am no longer willing to hear him speak more. . . . I am determined to proceed against him as a notorious heretic, requesting of you that you conduct yourselves in this matter as good Christians as you have promised it to me and are held to it.[9]

Charles spoke in French, a reminder that the German king was a foreigner in Germany. He had grown up in the Netherlands, nurtured in the French culture of the Burgundian court. He matured outside of Germany, and by the time of his death was a Spaniard in sensibility, language, and taste. To the extent that the Lutheran revolution was an expression of German cultural and religious nationalism, it was utterly foreign to him. To the extent that it expressed specifically German political aspirations, it was the ally of princely and urban particularism and threatened to limit still further his authority in Germany. Charles's policy could never be German. Taken as a whole it was imperial and therefore larger than any national German policy; with respect to specifically German matters it was locally territorial, like that of any other German prince, and therefore smaller than a national policy. His imperial policy, moreover, was inevitably rooted in Catholicism, its ideology inevitably Roman. Charles could hardly be a Catholic in Spain

[9] *Ibid.*, p. 114, note 9.

and a Protestant in Germany. Every personal and dynastic interest, every conviction and aspiration, bound Charles to Rome. He considered himself the secular head of Christendom. To abandon the traditional faith would have been to reduce the meaning, purpose, and justification of his empire, to turn it into an accident of power. The emperor remained Catholic, condemned Luther, and put him under the ban of the empire, making him an outlaw.

In practice, throughout his reign Charles was powerless to act effectively in Germany. He failed to strengthen the royal power and curtail the power of the princes. His efforts to extirpate heresy and restore the religious unity of the empire by means of a national council and then by military force also failed. His struggle against the Valois kept him almost continuously out of Germany. Constant Turkish pressure compromised the anti-Protestant zeal of his brother Ferdinand, who found it impossible to reconcile his need for subsidies from Protestant princes to fight the Turk with his Catholic duty to prosecute them for heresy. Even Charles's victory over the Protestant princes at Mühlberg, in 1547, was illusory. A league of princes, in alliance with France, immediately rose against him to defend German "liberty" against Spanish "despotism," reversed the military situation, and drove Charles across the Alps into Italy. In short, from the Diet of Worms until his abdication thirty-five years later, the independent power of the princes disarmed Charles's hostility to Luther and to the Reformation; and the princes' preferences, not the emperor's, determined in the end the religious geography of Germany.

No simple formula can explain the religious choices of the German princes. The economic and political advantages of a Lutheran conversion were substantial. The act of becoming a Protestant added religious sanction and motive to a prince's claim to be independent of the Catholic emperor. The prince's opposition to imperial interference in his territory became a defense not only of his jurisdictional autonomy but of evangelical truth as well. Furthermore, conversion to Protestantism was economically tempting. Luther condemned monasticism; a secularization of Church property, especially monastic property, was a "reform" that could lead to a significant increase in revenue. Typical is the disposition of Church wealth by Landgrave Philip of Hesse (1504–1567), one of the most important Protestant princes, after he dissolved the monasteries and nunneries in his territories. Too many vested interests were involved for him to appropriate all monastic revenue for himself; he therefore allocated 59 per cent to educational and charitable purposes—to hospitals, as dowries for poor noble ladies, to found the first German Protestant university at Marburg. But 41 per cent remained for him. Clearly, Philip's financial gain was considerable. Above all, by introducing the reformation in his state the German prince increased his control over the church. As early as the fourteenth century it had been the stated ambition of German princes to be "pope, archbishop, bishop, archdeacon, and deacon" in their own territories. Breaking openly with Rome was one way to achieve this ambition. The prince usurped the authority of pope and bishops. His courts absorbed the jurisdiction of the ecclesiastical courts. The enforcement of family law and the supervision of morals became prerogatives of the state. The prince extended his control of ecclesiastical patronage and appointments. Ecclesiastical commissioners appointed by the prince reformed abuses and dealt with the finances and physical needs of the various congregations. They enforced uniformity of faith and liturgy on the prince's subjects. In practice they even defined doctrine. Acquisition of authority over these activities increased enormously the power of the prince.

Protestant princes did not secure these advantages without risk. During the crucial decades between 1520 and the Peace of Augsburg in 1555, Catholic princes were in a majority in the Diet. Until his death in 1546 Luther remained an excommunicated heretic under the ban of the empire. To embrace Lutheranism and transform the ecclesiastical organization of a territory was a revolutionary act, an open defiance of imperial authority and the decisions of the Diet. Charles V was determined to suppress heresy, by force if necessary. In such a struggle, Protestant princes risked their lands and titles. How real that risk could be is illustrated by the fate of the Saxon elector John Frederick (1503–1554). In 1547 Charles invaded the electorate with Spanish troops and defeated the Saxon army at Mühlberg. The elector was captured and imprisoned. Forced to choose between his lands and his faith, he chose his faith. He lost his title and much of his territory.

Nor must one suppose that the religious crisis did not offer Catholic princes similar increments of power and ecclesiastical control—with less risk. The duchy of Bavaria was a bastion of Catholicism in southern Germany. The religious policy of the Bavarian dukes was supple. They remained attached to the old faith. They saw in Lutheranism a threat to law and order. "Do not fail to realize," wrote Duke William to his brother in 1527, "that a creed which allows each man to interpret his faith according to his taste and will must breed civil disobedience and ultimately rebellion and bloodshed."[10] They were prepared to stamp it out; but in their own time and way. Each move against heresy extracted concessions from Rome: an expansion of ducal jurisdiction over clerics, curtailment of jurisdictional appeals to Rome and of the competence of the ecclesiastical courts, a bull empowering the dukes to visit monasteries and remove unworthy abbots and priors, increased control over ecclesiastical appointment, permission to tax the clergy at the rate of a fifth of their yearly incomes (henceforth a pillar of the Bavarian financial system). The dukes reinforced their monopoly on the formation of religious policy. Their agents conducted the reform of ecclesiastical abuses. They reserved to themselves alone the power to arrest and

---

[10]Quoted by Gerald Strauss, "The Religious Policies of Dukes Wilhelm and Ludwig of Bavaria in the First Decade of the Protestant Era," *Church History*, Vol. XXIII (1959), p. 368.

Within the image:
AL ANDER HERSCHAFT IST VON GOT
ZVR HVLF DEM MENSCHEN IN DER NOT
ON SATAN VNDT SEIN BERSTLICH EST
SINDT HERNIV STIFTEN VNDT VNDT TODT
DER BABST HEIST RECHT DER WILDE MAN
DER DVRCH SEIN FALSCHE SCHALCKE BAN
AL VNGLVCK HAT GERICHTET AN
DAS GOT VNDT MENSCHEN NICHT LEIDEN KAN

1545
MART. LVTHER D.

The Pope as Antichrist. *Drawing by Melchior Lorch, dedicated to Luther; dated 1545. Crowned with the papal tiara and with a tree-trunk cross in one hand and the corroded keys of Peter in the other, the satanic beastman spreads fire, destruction, and abomination over the earth. It is an image of the violence, fanaticism, and cruel hatreds never far below the surface of sixteenth-century life.*

examine suspected heretics. Catholic doctrine was preserved at the expense of clerical "liberties" and papal authority. The result was a Bavarian territorial church very largely under ducal control.

The absence of any striking difference between the secular advantages secured by Lutheran princes and those obtained by Catholic princes during the religious revolution in Germany suggests that princely motives for remaining a Catholic or becoming a Lutheran were seldom exclusively political or economic. Placed in similar circumstances, with identical political and economic interests, one elector of Brandenburg was a zealous Catholic, while the next—his son—became a Lutheran. For some princes reform was cynically indistinguishable from secularization. In 1525 Albert of Hohenzollern (1490–1568) grand master of the Order of Teutonic Knights, on Luther's advice, renounced his clerical calling, secularized the order's lands, and made himself the first duke of Prussia. Another prince became a Lutheran because his wife was one. But others embraced the new faith for a simpler reason—because they were persuaded that what Luther said was true. Princes remained Catholics for reasons equally various. Duke George of Saxony was a sincere Catholic, but there seems no doubt that his attachment to the old faith was fortified by the fact that the elector of Saxony—his kinsman, rival, and bitter foe—was Luther's secular protector. Some Catholic princes, such as the dukes of Bavaria, were influenced by the fear that religious revolution would become the signal for social revolution. Few ecclesiastial princes followed the example of Albert of Hohenzollern; but even those who did not were quite prepared to use Luther against Rome—to blackmail the papacy into concessions with respect to finance, jurisdiction, and appointments—relying on their Catholicity to protect them from those elements in Lutheranism they believed to threaten their own positions. Others again were as certain as Charles V "that a single friar errs in his opinion which is against all of Christendom," and would as willingly have renounced their states as their religion. Princely conversion, in short, was a matter of conscience, dozens of individual choices molded by a complex variety of pressures, some secular, some religious, different in each particular case and harmonized by the infinite capacity of human beings for self-deception.

By the middle of the century the princes, in order to safeguard the independence, free choice, and faith of each, had agreed to build a measure of religious diversity into the German constitution. The result was the Religious Peace of Augsburg, hammered out by the imperial Diet between February and September, 1555. The Diet subordinated religious principle and the ecumenical claims of the Catholic and Lutheran churches to political expediency. The settlement allowed electors, princes, imperial knights, and cities to choose between Catholicism and Lutheranism. It excluded sacramentarians (Zwinglians and Calvinists) and sectarians (Anabaptists). Cities which had both Catholic and Lutheran citizens were required to allow each group to practice its religion freely. In the princely territories, on the other hand, the religious preferences of the ruler were binding on his subjects. The Catholic subjects of a Lutheran prince, and the Lutheran subjects of a Catholic ruler, were free only to sell their property and go. The *ius reformandi*, the right to order the religious affairs of a territory, became an attribute of princely sovereignty; the subject enjoyed the *ius emigrandi*, the right to emigrate. Lawyers of a later generation defined the principle of the settlement in an expressive phrase: *cuius regio, eius religio* ("he who rules a territory determines its religion"). Princely "liberty" was victorious in religion as in politics, and for the first time in the history of western Europe, secular law recognized two religious confessions.

THE TRIUMPH OF THE TERRITORIAL CHURCH

During the sixteenth century the unity of Roman ecclesiastical organization collapsed not only in Germany but in all of Europe. The Church, which in the high Middle Ages had been a European corporation, broke apart into a congeries of local territorial churches, their boundaries determined by the geography of political power; there were national churches, princely churches, provincial churches, even churches confined to the population of a single

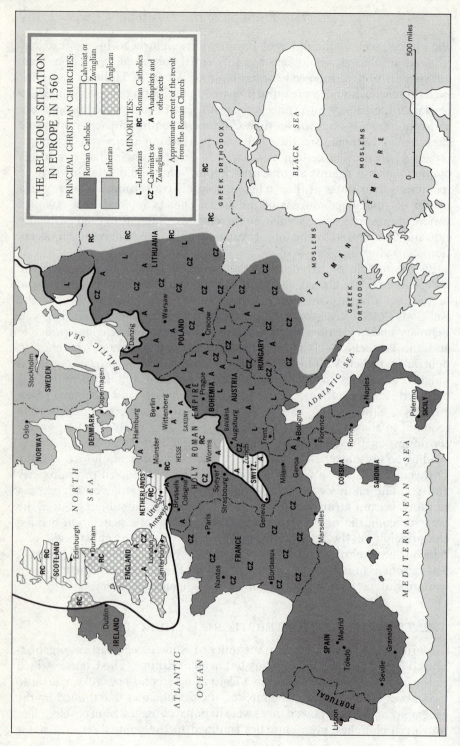

THE RELIGIOUS SITUATION
IN EUROPE IN 1560

PRINCIPAL CHRISTIAN CHURCHES:

Roman Catholic

Lutheran

Calvinist or
Zwinglian

Anglican

MINORITIES:
L —Lutherans   RC —Roman Catholics
CZ—Calvinists or   A —Anabaptists and
      Zwinglians   other sects
——— Approximate extent of the revolt
        from the Roman Church

500 miles

0

BLACK SEA

GREEK ORTHODOX

OTTOMAN

MOSLEMS

MOSLEMS

GREEK
ORTHODOX

GREEK ORTHODOX

EMPIRE

BALTIC SEA

NORTH SEA

ATLANTIC OCEAN

ADRIATIC SEA

MEDITERRANEAN SEA

Stockholm

SWEDEN

Copenhagen

DENMARK

Oslo

NORWAY

Edinburgh

SCOTLAND

Durham

ENGLAND

London

Canterbury

Dublin

IRELAND

LITHUANIA

Warsaw

POLAND

Cracow

Danzig

Berlin

Wittenberg

SAXONY

Hamburg

Münster

HESSE

Brussels

Cologne

Antwerp

Utrecht

NETHERLANDS

HOLY ROMAN EMPIRE

Worms

Speyer

Strasbourg

Paris

Nantes

Bordeaux

FRANCE

Geneva

SWITZ.

Zurich

Augsburg

BAVARIA

Prague

BOHEMIA

AUSTRIA

HUNGARY

Trent

Milan

Genoa

Bologna

Florence

Rome

Naples

Palermo

SICILY

CORSICA

SARDINIA

Marseilles

SPAIN

Madrid

Toledo

Seville

Granada

PORTUGAL

Lisbon

city or, as in Poland, to the population of a single aristocratic estate. Doctrinal variety made this consolidation of secular control of the church at the level of the territorial state more obvious than in the past, but it did not alter its essential character: the concentration of ecclesiasical appointments, taxation, jurisdiction, administration, and discipline in the hands of the secular authorities. In this context the Reformation is another aspect of the emergence of the sovereign state.

Circumstances peculiar to the Iberian peninsula, in addition to the personal devotion of Charles V to the faith of his ancestors, assured the Catholicity of the Spanish monarchs. Medieval Spanish history had been characterized by perpetual crusades, climaxed by the reconquest of Granada in 1492. The long struggle against the Moslems and the presence in the kingdom of a large Jewish population created a self-consciously Christian sensibility that was fervently Catholic and uniquely aggressive, suspicious of foreign beliefs, fearful of heresy, unswerving in its doctrinal loyalty to Rome. The same year that Granada fell and Columbus sailed for "India," the Spanish government expelled the Jews. In succeeding decades the victorious fight of the Inquisition against Marranos and "Lutherans" gradually created a doctrinal unity and an intellectual conformity unique in Europe.

The passionate orthodoxy of crown and country did not prevent the kings of Spain from asserting their authority over a powerful and wealthy church. By 1523 the crown had secured the right to present to every bishopric in Spain. In America it exercised a universal *Patronato* over the church, including a monopoly of appointments to all ecclesiastical benefices. The king also widened his authority over the Church in a second way, by limiting ecclesiastical jurisdiction. The royal council examined every papal bull received in Spain in order to make sure it contained nothing contrary to the prerogatives of the king or his kingdom. When Pope Paul IV (in office 1555–1559), as a temporary diplomatic maneuver, excommunicated Charles V and Prince Philip, the council "retained" the bull and forbade its publication on pain of exemplary chastisement. The crown severely curtailed appeals from Spanish ecclesiastical courts to the Roman curia. After the creation in 1527 of the *Nunciatura*, a high court staffed by the papal nuncio and six Spanish judges, the vast majority of cases that had formerly gone to Rome remained in Spain. The council reviewed the court's decisions as well as the nuncio's own instructions from the Vatican. Finally, the government increased its control of the Church's wealth by limiting payments to Rome and taxing the clergy far more heavily than in the past. Throughout the sixteenth century, taxation of the Church was one of the most important sources of royal revenue. By the time of the reign of Philip II, the king was head of the church in Spain almost as effectively as Henry VIII was head of the Church of England.

The situation in France was similar. By 1515, when Francis I ascended the throne, the French church claimed three kinds of liberties: administrative liberty, the right to staff itself according to the canonical principle of election; fiscal liberty, the right to tax itself for its own purposes; and jurisdictional liberty, the right to judge and discipline its own members. The French, or Gallican, clergy defended these liberties against both pope and king. They considered virtually any papal interference in the internal affairs of the French church an abuse, and with the backing of the royal courts repulsed papal efforts to appoint to French benefices, limited appeals to the Roman curia, and refused the payment of "annates," a sum equivalent to a year's income from a benefice, due in Rome when the pope confirmed the appointment. But the Gallican church presumed to be independent not only of Rome but of the crown as well. It failed to preserve its liberties against this nearer threat. In 1516 Francis I negotiated the Concordat of Bologna, a compromise between papal and royal interests achieved at the expense of the autonomy of the French church. Over the furious opposition of the clergy, the University of Paris, and the royal courts, the concordat suppressed elections and made the king master of every important ecclesiastical appointment in France. He nominated whom he chose; the pope rarely failed to confirm his choice. The pope's *quid pro quo* was financial—the restoration of annates; in this transaction the pope, the spiritual power, took the temporalities for himself and gave the spiritualities to a temporal prince. Of course, Francis had no intention of allowing the pope a monopoly on plucking the golden feathers of the Gallican goose. He tightened royal control of the Church's property and wealth and instituted policies which led to the regular taxation of the clergy by the end of the century. The Gallican church had resisted papal interference only to fall the more completely under the domination of the king.

The settlement at Bologna, just a year before the publication of Luther's theses on indulgences, became a powerful cement binding the French crown to Rome. Assured of practical supremacy over their own church, Francis I and his successor, Henry II, had little inducement to follow the example of the king of England. The logic of power also bound French kings to Rome in another way. The widening success of imperial armies in Italy during the 1520's both frustrated French ambition and curtailed papal independence. The result, as we have seen, was a Franco-papal alliance. A small price, willingly paid, was continued royal loyalty to the Catholic faith. There was to be no danger of a Protestant succession as long as the Valois occupied the throne.

THE ENGLISH REFORMATION

Unlike Francis I and Charles V, Henry VIII of England, who ascended the throne in 1509, did break with Rome. The circumstances of his defection illustrate yet another aspect of the complex interplay of politics and reformation. No religious motive complicated Henry's ecclesiastical policy. He was conservative in religion and disliked doctrinal innovation. In 1521 he wrote a book against Luther, and a grateful pope conferred on him the title *Defensor fidei* ("defender of the faith"). Before his death in 1547 Protestantism made little headway among his subjects. To be sure, many laymen were anticlerical, outspokenly hostile to abuses such as the granting of benefices to minors, burial fees, the excessive number of holy days during harvest time, and the pretensions of the ecclesiastical courts. But no more than their king did they stomach doctrinal change. Except for the rejection of papal suprem-acy, the official teaching of the Anglican Church during Henry's reign remained Catholic in every important respect.

Nor was this Catholic monarch initially tempted to break with Rome because his grip on the English church and clergy was any weaker than that of the kings of France and Spain on theirs. Papal authority was as limited in England as in the continental monarchies. Parliament had passed, and the crown enforced, statutes designed to strengthen the secular power and protect the king's rights against ecclesiastical usurpation. The Statute of Provisors (1351) limited papal appointments in England, guaranteeing the autonomy of the English church and the rights of lay and ecclesiastical patrons. The complex of laws known as the *praemunire* (passed between 1352 and 1393) restricted appeals to the papal court and protected the royal courts from papal and clerical interference. The crown had significant control over ecclesiastical revenues and over persons and documents sent from Rome. As early as 1420 the pope wryly observed, "Not the pope but the king of England governs the church in his dominions."

Henry's motive for the break with Rome was more specific: it was personal and dynastic. He wished to be rid of his wife, Catherine of Aragon. He was passionately in love with Anne Boleyn and determined to marry her. More important, Catherine had produced no male heir, only a daughter, Mary Tudor, and the absence of a male heir raised the specter of dynastic crisis. England had never been ruled by a queen. In any case, having a queen as sovereign was known to result in almost insuperable dynastic and interna-tional problems—threats of aristocratic rivalry, faction, and even civil war if she married one of her own subjects; the threat of foreign domination if she married a prince from abroad. A scruple was conveniently at hand to disturb Henry's conscience about the validity of his marriage. Scripture forbids a man to marry his brother's wife, and Catherine was the widow of Henry's older brother, Arthur. Only a papal dispensation had made it possible for Henry to marry her. Henry now wished the pope to annul the marriage his predecessor had sanctioned, and under ordinary circumstances he would have had no difficulty in securing this papal annulment. But circumstances were not ordinary; Catherine was the aunt of Charles V. In 1527 Rome fell to imperial troops, and during the next few years the pope was so securely in the emperor's power that it was impossible for him to grant Henry's request.

After failing to secure the "divorce" by negotiations with the pope between 1527 and 1529, Henry hesitated. Then, early in 1532, under the influence and guidance of his great minister Thomas Cromwell (c. 1485–1540), he set a course which by 1534 was to make him pope in his own dominions. His purpose was to create a legal authority in England that could and would annul his marriage. He had already neutralized ecclesiastical opposition by forcing the clergy to recognize him as head of the church in England "as far as the law of Christ allows" (1531). Parliament then authorized him to cut off the payment of annates to Rome (1532). Combining the threat of financial pressure with diplomatic finesse, he extracted from the curia the bulls necessary to confirm Thomas Cranmer (1489–1556), a candidate wholly sympathetic to his cause, as archbishop of Canterbury. The pregnancy of Anne Boleyn in January, 1533, made it necessary to hasten events; her issue had to be made legitimate. In February, Parliament passed the great Act of Appeals, cutting every judicial link with Rome and making Cranmer's archiepiscopal court the highest and only legitimate ecclesiastical tribunal for English cases. In May, Cranmer granted the annulment. The future Queen Elizabeth was born in the autumn. An Act of Succession confirmed her legitimacy and the rights of hoped-for sons to succeed to the throne. A final piece of legislation, the Act of Supremacy, crowned the revolutionary edifice in November, 1534. Henry became without qualification the "only supreme head in earth of the Church of England called *Anglicana Ecclesia.*"[11]

Although the crucial inducement to break with Rome was thus personal and dynastic—if not for the problem of the "divorce," the Reformation in England would at least have been long delayed—its result was the decisive subordination of church to state. The English Reformation subjected the clergy to a royal will independent of Rome. At last, after centuries of papal "usurpation," England had become a "true monarchy" and an "empire" owing allegiance to no authority except its king's. The king now exercised every power formerly wielded by the pope. He controlled the church's courts, appointments, and revenues. He made ecclesiastical law and determined doctrine. Like the German Protestant princes, he was *summus episcopus*—a lay bishop—in his dominion. It followed that the religion of the people must be the religion of the church's head: *cuius regio, eius religio.* Deviation was at once heretical and treasonable, and Henry established the Anglican "middle way" by burning heretics in pairs—papists on the one hand, Anabaptists and "Lutherans" on the other. During the last years of his reign, and again during the reign of Mary, committed Protestants found it expedient to emigrate to Switzerland and the Rhineland. Not surprisingly, the consciences of the vast majority of Englishmen were more elastic than theirs. They followed with apparent docility the rapidly altering doctrinal preferences of their sovereigns, and many thousands lived long enough to be

[11]G. R. Elton, *The Tudor Constitution* (Cambridge, Eng., 1962), 355.

Roman Catholics in 1529, Henrician Catholics from 1534 to 1547, moderate, then extreme, Protestants under Edward VI (1547–1553), Roman Catholics once more under Mary (1553–1558), and again moderate Protestants under Elizabeth I.

The very triumph of the territorial church and the emergence of the secular rulers of Europe as the religious arbiters of their dominions gave the religious struggle a new political violence. Just as economic and class tensions took on a religious coloration, so too did the fundamental political opposition of the age—that between royal and princely efforts to unify the state and centralize its administration, on the one hand, and the defense of local and corporate privilege, the "liberties" of nobles and clergy, monasteries and universities, provinces and cities, on the other. With the exception of the Tudors, the most important European monarchs ultimately became the allies of a reformed and reinvigorated Catholicism. Protestantism, by contrast, normally secured its political base at a lower level, that of the smaller principality, the province, or the city, and was supported by groups resisting the encroachments of centralizing sovereigns. In the sixteenth century, Catholicism gradually became the religion of "absolutism"; Protestantism the ideology of the feudal, urban, and corporate opposition. However, the opposition did not choose Protestantism because some political principle favorable to liberty was inherent in it; the competing religions were as neutral politically as they were economically and socially. The defenders of local autonomy and local privilege were so often Protestant simply because the Habsburgs and the Valois were Catholic. Like those German princes who found in Lutheranism and its affirmation of the rights of conscience another bulwark against imperial authority, many nobles and urban oligarchs in the Netherlands and France, in Germany, Poland, and Hungary, discovered an affinity between Calvinism and their ambition to defend, augment, or recover their political independence. But the case of England indicates clearly enough that opposition to the crown did not have to be Protestant. There, feudal reaction (for example, the rebellion under Henry VIII known as the Pilgrimage of Grace and the revolt of the northern earls under Elizabeth), this time against a Protestant prince, found an ideological program in the restoration of Catholicism. Once the struggle between centralizing "absolutism" and the defense of local "liberties" fused with the struggle between Protestantism and Catholicism, the most potent secular antagonism of the age acquired a religious dimension and the certainties of faith mixed inextricably with the passions of politics. The struggle became absolute, incapable of compromise. Europe stood on the threshold of a century of civil and religious war.

Part II

THE AGE OF RELIGIOUS WARS
1559-1689

Introduction

DURING THE 130 YEARS between 1559 and 1689, Europe passed through a tumultuous and anarchic period of civil wars and rebellions. Each upheaval had its own distinct character; each had multiple causes. The one common denominator, which constantly recurred, was Protestant-Catholic religious strife. Luther had inaugurated the ideological controversy in 1517, but it spread with heightened intensity after the Habsburg-Valois dynastic wars came to a close in 1559. The French civil wars of 1562–1598, the Dutch revolt against Philip II, the Scottish rebellion against Mary Stuart, the Spanish attack on England in 1588, the Thirty Years' War in Germany between 1618 and 1648, and the Puritan Revolution of 1640–1660 and the Glorious Revolution of 1688–1689 in England were all religious conflicts, though of course they had other causes as well. This was an age of crusaders and martyrs, of plots and assassinations, of fanatic mobs and psalm-singing armies. The most militant crusaders proved to be the disciples of John Calvin and of St. Ignatius of Loyola. Between 1559 and 1689 the Calvinists gained control of Scotland and the northern provinces of the Low Countries, temporarily seized power in England, and tried to take over in France, Germany, Poland, and Hungary. The Catholics, revitalized in the mid-sixteenth century, kept trying until the late seventeenth century to restore the seamless unity of the Christian Church. In France, Flanders, Austria, and Bohemia, at least, they successfully suppressed Protestantism. Both sides in this extraordinary contest were able to attract a high percentage of articulate, prosperous, and socially powerful people into their ranks. Both sides eventually lost their crusading zeal. But by the time the ideological conflict burned out during the seventeenth century, it had left a permanent impress on nearly every aspect of European life: on concepts of liberty and toleration, on party politics, business enterprise, social structure, science, philosophy, and the arts. At length the Glorious Revolution resolved the last active religious issues. After 1689, European international politics reverted to its secular pattern.

The people of Europe were by no means wholly addicted to religious controversy during the years between 1559 and 1689. The fanatics were generally in a minority, and many ingenious efforts were made to smother the Protestant-Catholic conflict. The turbulent insurrections and revolutions of the period compelled peace-loving people to support strong rulers who could restore order. The political trend was toward centralized, authoritarian state power. An era which opened with the reign of Philip II in Spain and closed with the reign of Louis XIV in France deserves to be labeled an age of absolutism. Yet this absolutist label cannot be applied to the English or the Dutch, who refused to abandon their medieval heritage of constitutional, representative government, and evolved strikingly effective new concepts of civil liberty and public responsibility during the sixteenth and seventeenth centuries.

In economics, the years 1559–1689 saw a long and startling inflationary spiral, the so-called price revolution. The doctrine of mercantilism, a new formula for economic planning at the state level, became widely popular. Yet the most successful businessmen of the day, the Dutch, were essentially antimercantilist. Dutch commercial capitalism reached its zenith in these years, and Amsterdam became Europe's leading shipping center, commodity market, and financial exchange.

No seventeenth-century achievement is better remembered today than the intellectual revolution in mathematics, astronomy, and physics, accomplished by Galileo, Descartes, Newton, and an international brotherhood of fellow scientists. In the arts, this was the era of the Baroque, a spectacular new style of bravura display in painting, sculpture, and architecture. At the same time, in England, Spain, and France, the drama was in its golden age; theatergoers were enjoying the plays of Shakespeare, Lope de Vega, and Molière. Obviously, the society we shall examine in the following pages was richly complex.

The years 1559–1689 saw a steadily widening disparity between western and eastern Europe. The commercial capitalism of western Europe expanded, while the agriculture of eastern Europe stagnated. The chief states of western Europe—Spain, France, England, and the new Dutch republic —developed sovereign national power, while the chief states of eastern Europe—the Holy Roman Empire, the Ottoman Empire, and Poland— slowly disintegrated. The religious wars proved to be much more destructive in Germany than in the states bordering the Atlantic, where the conflict stimulated fruitful new modes of political, economic, and artistic expression. Inevitably, therefore, our focus must be on western Europe.

Even the most prosperous countries of western Europe were hobbled by primitive production techniques. There was never enough wealth for all to share. As a result, the years 1559–1689 saw a steadily widening social disparity between the upper and the lower classes, the propertied and the propertyless. At the top of the social scale, a relatively small number of aristocrats, landlords, and merchants monopolized most of the political power, social privileges, and surplus wealth. At the bottom of the social scale (the submerged six sevenths of the iceberg, so to speak), millions of serfs in eastern Europe and wage laborers in western Europe eked out a bare subsistence, excluded from schools, skilled jobs, property ownership, and creature comforts. Yet this profoundly undemocratic society spawned many of the democratic ideas and values which we prize today. And the status-bound people of early modern Europe started a general intellectual revolt against authority which has been going strong ever since.

CHAPTER 7

Calvinism Versus Catholicism
in Western Europe

IN THE SPRING of 1559, envoys from Philip II of Spain and Henry II of France met on neutral ground in the bishop's palace at Cateau-Cambrésis, a little town on the French-Netherlands border, to arrange a peace treaty between their respective masters. Philip and Henry were the two strongest princes in Europe, but they both needed peace. Their rival dynastic houses, the Habsburgs and the Valois, had been dueling inconclusively for half a century, and their treasuries were exhausted. Futhermore, the Catholic King of Spain and the Most Christian King of France had a common enemy to deal with. The Protestant heresy was spreading from central Europe into Spanish and French territory, and Philip and Henry were determined to stamp it out. Accordingly, the diplomats at Cateau-Cambrésis worked out a peace settlement which could be expected to last for many years. The French abandoned their efforts to wrest Italy and the Low Countries from Spain; the Spaniards abandoned their efforts to dismember France. The Peace of Cateau-Cambrésis was more a Habsburg than a Valois victory, since France remained encircled by Habsburg territory. But Valois France in 1559 was rich, populous, and powerful. Surely this settlement was mutually advantageous to Philip and Henry. The reconciled Habsburg and Valois monarchs would now be able to crush Protestantism within their territories and join forces to restore the seamless unity of the Christian Church.

But to their surprise and dismay, the Peace of Cateau-Cambrésis ushered in a strange new era of civil wars and rebellions which the Habsburg and Valois kings were quite unable to cope with. The religious conflict which had racked central Europe from 1517 to 1555 moved with a new revolutionary force into western Europe between 1560 and 1600. In Germany the fighting had come to a temporary halt. The truce between the Protestants and the Catholics in the Holy Roman Empire, established in 1555 by the Peace of Augsburg, lasted into the early seventeenth century. But in western Europe,

Dutch Calvinists rebelled against Spanish Habsburg control of the Nether-lands, while French Calvinists, or Huguenots, rebelled against the Valois monarchy and plunged France into forty years of civil war. At the same time in England and Scotland, Calvinists, Catholics, and Anglicans were vying for political mastery. In essence, western Europe became a giant battleground fought over by two crusading armies, Calvinist and Catholic.

The Calvinists employed the dogma and discipline of Geneva to challenge the political *status quo* in France, the Low Countries, and the British Isles. They proved to be effective rebels, for though few in number, they were drawn chiefly from the upper and middle classes, and were zealous and self-assured. The Catholics, led by Philip II, employed all the resources of the mighty Spanish empire to crush the French Huguenots and restore Britain and the Netherlands to Rome. Calvinists and Catholics alike can be labeled "conservative" in the sense that they clung to the traditional medi-eval belief that no diversity could be tolerated within Christendom. There was just one interpretation of God's commands, just one road to salvation; only by vanquishing the forces of Satan could Christ's rule on earth be achieved. Yet what gave the Calvinists and Catholics such dynamic power was their active involvement in the world. Both sides recognized the new secular forces which were transforming western civilization—overseas expan-sion to Asia and America, commercial capitalism, dynastic rivalry, national-ism, and state sovereignty—and they harnessed these forces to the service of God. The Calvinist-Catholic struggle was in one sense the last medieval crusade, in another the first modern war between nation-states. Nothing like it has ever been seen before or since.

RELIGION AND POLITICS

From the day Martin Luther first posted his ninety-five theses in 1517, the religious controversy between Protestants and Catholics was embroiled in politics. This was inevitable. The spiritual crisis affected men's attitudes toward this world as well as the next. The Church possessed vast political and economic resources, and when the Protestants repudiated the basic doctrinal tenets of Rome, they necessarily also attacked the Church's exist-ing institutional fabric. Protestant and Catholic reformers alike looked to the secular authorities for help, and kings and princes gained political and economic advantage from participating in the conflict.

At mid-century, subtle—but crucial—religious and political changes took place. With the death of John Calvin in 1564, the initial creative work of the Protestant reformers was completed. Correspondingly, with the death of St. Ignatius of Loyola in 1556, and the termination of the Council of Trent in 1563, the Catholic internal reform program was fully spelled out. The ideological battle lines became frozen. But as the Protestants and Catholics lost their initial spiritual creativity, they developed a new political creativity.

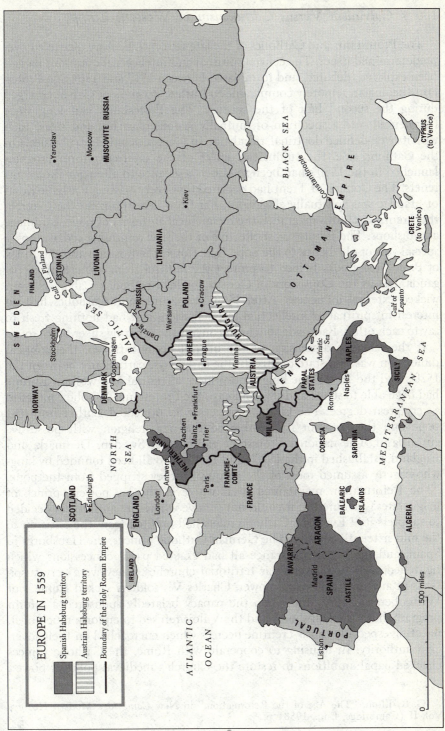

EUROPE IN 1559

- Spanish Habsburg territory
- Austrian Habsburg territory
- — Boundary of the Holy Roman Empire

0 ___ 500 miles

MUSCOVITE RUSSIA

- Yaroslav
- Moscow

BLACK SEA

CYPRUS (to Venice)

Constantinople

OTTOMAN EMPIRE

CRETE (to Venice)

SWEDEN

FINLAND

Gulf of Finland

ESTONIA

LIVONIA

LITHUANIA

- Kiev

Stockholm

BALTIC SEA

PRUSSIA

Danzig

POLAND

- Warsaw
- Cracow

HUNGARY

Gulf of Lepanto

NORWAY

DENMARK

Copenhagen

BOHEMIA

- Prague

AUSTRIA

Vienna

VENICE

Adriatic Sea

PAPAL STATES

Rome

NAPLES

Naples

SICILY

MEDITERRANEAN SEA

NORTH SEA

Aachen

Mainz · Frankfurt

Trier

NETHERLANDS

Antwerp

MILAN

CORSICA

SARDINIA

SCOTLAND

Edinburgh

ENGLAND

London

Paris

FRANCHE-COMTÉ

FRANCE

BALEARIC ISLANDS

ALGERIA

IRELAND

ATLANTIC OCEAN

NAVARRE

ARAGON

Madrid

SPAIN

CASTILE

PORTUGAL

Lisbon

The Protestants and Catholics of the late sixteenth century quarreled over predetermined issues. The central spiritual and intellectual questions had all been explored, debated, and formulated between 1517 and 1564. No Protestant theologian remotely comparable to Luther, Zwingli, or Calvin emerged during the second half of the century. The Protestants had long since fragmented into a spectrum of mutually jealous churches and sects, each with its well-defined doctrinal, ritualistic, and institutional idiosyncrasies. On the Catholic side, the cumulative effect of the internal reform program launched in the 1530's had been to stiffen resistance to all major Protestant tenets. The Council of Trent had declared that every existing Catholic ritual or practice was spiritually efficacious. Far from decentralizing the Church, the Trentine reforms magnified the hierarchical authority of pope, cardinals, and bishops. The Jesuits, most effective of the new reforming orders, took a special vow of obedience to the pope. The Roman Inquisition and the Index of Prohibited Books helped to protect the faithful from Protestant propaganda, just as the Consistory in Geneva shielded orthodox Calvinists from wicked external influences. After 1560, Protestants and Catholics had no interest in spiritual or intellectual reconciliation, and had nothing fresh to say to each other. Each side sought to convert the other by sheer brute force.

If the religious dimension of the quarrel became frozen, the political dimension was in a state of flux. In the early days, particularly between the 1520's and the 1550's, the kings and princes of central and western Europe had been able to shape and stage-manage the Protestant-Catholic conflict to a very great degree. The German princes who protected Luther from the pope and the emperor had embraced the new religion with possessive enthusiasm. The national Protestant churches of Sweden, Denmark, and England, established in the 1520's and 1530's, had all been founded by kings who eagerly assumed most of the perquisites they stripped from the pope. "The Reformation maintained itself wherever the lay power (prince or magistrates) favoured it; it could not survive where the authorities decided to suppress it."[1] Even the Catholic rulers had profited from the crisis up to the mid-sixteenth century. The German Catholic princes, the Habsburgs in Spain, and the Valois in France all had exacted papal concessions which tightened their hold over their territorial churches. They were very suspicious of any revival of papal power. Charles V's soldiers sacked Rome, not Wittenberg, in 1527, and when the papacy belatedly sponsored a reform program, both the Habsburgs and the Valois refused to endorse much of it, rejecting especially those Trentine decrees which encroached on their sovereign authority. In refusing to cooperate with Rome, the Catholic princes checked papal ambitions to restore the Church's medieval political power.

---

[1] G. R. Elton, "The Age of the Reformation," in *New Cambridge Modern History*, Vol. II (Cambridge, Eng., 1958) p. 5.

By patronizing the Protestant reformers, the Protestant princes made sure that their reforms did not go too far.

After 1560 the rulers of western Europe were no longer able to blunt the revolutionary force of the religious crisis. Both Calvinists and militant Catholics began to rebel against the political *status quo*. They organized effective opposition against rulers who did not share their religious convictions. In the name of God they launched a wave of civil wars and rebellions against constituted authority. Mary, Queen of Scots, lost her throne and her life. Catherine de Medici of France got caught between Huguenot and ultra-Catholic crusaders. Under her management, the Valois dynasty collapsed and the French central government crumbled. Philip II of Spain was a far more heroic figure than Mary or Catherine, and was the prime champion of the Church among sixteenth-century princes. His motives were mixed, for he hoped to extend his dynastic power by crushing the heretics, but at the same time, no other political leader risked so much for his faith. He risked too much, as events proved, and instead of gaining territory, he lost some. He provoked a Calvinist rebellion in the Netherlands which could not be suppressed; his intervention in the French religious wars backfired; and he failed to conquer Protestant England. It is instructive that the two western European rulers who best survived the religious crisis behaved much more circumspectly than Philip. Both Elizabeth I of England and Henry IV of France pursued policies of moderation and compromise which eventually disarmed their Calvinist and Catholic critics. But even Elizabeth and Henry were thrown on the defensive most of the time.

The Calvinists, who caused so much trouble to these princes, were never very numerous. Calvin himself had had a restricted base of operations: his little city-state of Geneva on the French border of Switzerland had only thirteen thousand inhabitants. But Calvin's teachings and his presbyterian church structure proved to be highly exportable to larger centers of population and power. Before he died in 1564, he had gained an elite following in France, the Netherlands, Scotland, and England. The movement attracted recruits from the privileged classes: noblemen, landowners, merchants, and lawyers. Persons from the unprivileged classes, peasants and urban wage laborers, were less likely to join. Today Calvinism has the reputation of being a misanthropic, repressive creed. How could it win such aristrocratic and prosperous adherents, let alone fire up a crusade? The best answer, perhaps, is that it offered a harsh but immensely exhilarating challenge. One had to accept Calvin's concept of God's absolute and all-pervading power and of Man's utter depravity, which renders him incapable of fulfilling God's law as revealed in the Bible. One had also to believe that God chooses to save some few persons, not on their merits (they have none), but solely by His grace. The person who accepted these premises, who abased himself before God's will and experienced God's irresistible grace, knew that he was among the predestinated "elect" or "saints," the only true Christians. As Calvin himself explained, "when that light of divine providence has once shone upon a godly man, he is then relieved and set free not only from the extreme anxiety and fear that were pressing him before, but from every care."[2] Despite Calvin's stress on human worthlessness, his church was an exclusive brotherhood which separated the saints from the sinners, the wheat from the chaff. Far from being fatalistic, the saints were intensely active.

It has been recently argued that the sixteenth-century Calvinists organized themselves into the first modern radical political party, analogous to the Jacobins and the Bolsheviks in more recent revolutionary times.[3] Of course, their chief goal was to reach the next world, not to remake this one. Yet the saints felt stifled by their unregenerate neighbors, and supposed that God wished them to master and reconstruct their corrupt environment. Their fellowship was bound to be socially and politically disruptive, for Calvinism was a total way of life. Their social model was Geneva: a homogeneous little city, rigidly self-disciplined, zealously self-righteous, and independent of any external authority. When Calvin's disciples began proselytizing in large and complex states like France, the Netherlands, and England, they gathered the saints into communities of Genevan purity and Genevan self-sufficiency. In France, for example, the Huguenots established congregations on the Genevan model, with pastors who preached and administered the Lord's Supper, teachers who educated the young, deacons who looked after the poor and unemployed, and elders who watched for immorality and disorder. The Huguenots united these congregations under a countrywide discipline, with local consistories and a national synod of the chief clergy and laymen. Every member of a Calvinist congregation swore to obey and help enforce God's law, and this covenant, or contract, to which all agreed, easily came to serve as a kind of constitution binding the Calvinists in a political or military confederation against their worldly enemies. Armed with the Genevan virtues of asceticism, industry, practical education, and moral responsibility, these people were hard to suppress or silence.

Calvin himself always preached obedience to the Christian prince. But in 1558, John Knox (1505–1572) sounded his *First Blast of the Trumpet Against the Monstrous Regiment of Women*, a tract denouncing the cluster of Catholic queens then coming to power. By the 1570's the Huguenots were arguing that resistance to tyrants, male or female, was divinely ordained. This sentiment was very attractive to the great noblemen within the Calvinist movement, who hoped by rebelling against their tyrannical kings to undermine monarchical government and restore the good old days of feudal

---

[2]John Calvin, *Institutes of the Christian Religion*, ed. by John T. McNeill (Philadelphia, 1960), Vol. I, p. 223.

[3]Michael Walzer, *The Revolution of the Saints* (Cambridge, Mass., 1965).

St. Peter's, Rome. *From a late seventeenth-century engraving. The immense piazza and colonnades were designed by Bernini.*

decentralization. But significantly, many Calvinists were professional and business men or small landowners, traditional proponents of strong kingship and effective central government. These men from the middle ranks were by no means trying to turn back the clock and weaken the national sovereign power of the western European states. Quite the contrary. But they refused to tolerate ungodly kings and magistrates, and they were prepared to fight for the right to participate in or even control the state.

On the Catholic side, the Society of Jesus, an order of priests founded in 1540 by St. Ignatius of Loyola, was almost equally disruptive. Calvin spoke contemptuously of "the Jesuits and like dregs," but the resemblance between Calvinist and Jesuit is a fascinating one. Working from diametrically opposite religious principles, Loyola and Calvin each built a select, cohesive, extroverted band of zealots. St. Ignatius devised a systematic emotional and intellectual discipline for the members of his society, and a highly autocratic, semimilitaristic organization, directly responsible to the pope. There were a thousand Jesuits by the time of Loyola's death in 1556, and sixteen thousand by 1624. But their influence far transcended their numbers. They established hundreds of schools to teach boys, especially upper-class boys, how to define and defend the authoritative dogmas of the Church. They excelled as

St. Ignatius of Loyola. *Engraving by Vosterman. This portrait romanticizes Loyola somewhat, but catches his psychological intensity and robust zeal.*

preachers, and in order to engage the secular authorities in the counterattack on heresy, they made a specialty of serving as confessors to Catholic princes. Jesuit militance, autonomy, and busy intervention in all phases of Church work aroused deep hostility among many Catholics. To the Protestants, "Jesuitical" meant the same thing as "Machiavellian," a curse word for the crafty intrigues and immoral tactics sponsored by these devilish priests.

The role of the Jesuits was of particular importance because they were supporters of papal supremacy. The late sixteenth-century popes, though able and energetic men, could exert little direct pressure on the Catholic rulers of western Europe. But the Jesuits, through their schools and confessionals, exercised considerable indirect influence. Jesuit confessors excelled at casuistry, the art of resolving difficult cases of conscience. The Protestants liked to believe that they winked at evil conduct, that their credo was, the end justifies the means. In fact, the Jesuits were successful at persuading others to fight for the Church because they fought so courageously themselves. Jesuit missionaries fearlessly penetrated into Protestant England and hatched a series of plots to depose Queen Elizabeth. Jesuit pamphleteers in France boldly called for the assassination of the lukewarm Catholic Henry III and the Huguenot Henry IV. Despite these inflammatory proceedings, the Jesuits had a generally conservative concept of the social order. Cardinal Bellarmine (1542–1621), the most eminent Jesuit writer in the late sixteenth century, presented a nostalgic view of the Christian commonwealth presided over by the pope. But Bellarmine, like the Calvinists, was no friend to absolute monarchy. In his view, heretical princes were liable to deposition, and even Catholic secular authority was distinctly limited.

The Protestant rebellions and Catholic assassinations of the late sixteenth century forced the proponents of strong monarchy to develop counter arguments which would bolster the prince's absolute sovereign power and make attacks upon him sacrilegious as well as treasonable. The political theory of the past was of little use on this point. Medieval theorists had generally denied that princely power was absolute, and the Renaissance theorists, like Machiavelli, who placed the prince above the law were too nakedly secular to suit the religious tastes of the late sixteenth century. It was necessary to devise a new quasi-religious doctrine of absolutism in order to answer the Jesuits and the Calvinists. The doctrine which resulted is known as the divine-right theory of kingship. According to this theory, God appoints the secular sovereign as His earthly lieutenant and invests him with absolute power over his subjects. The king has no obligation to obey the laws and customs of his state. He is answerable to God alone. Even if he rules tyrannically, he is still God's lieutenant, for God has placed him on the throne to punish the people's sins, and their only recourse is to pray for mercy. The subject has no right to rebel against his anointed king under any circumstances. This divine-right theory, absurd as it seems today, was very comforting during the religious wars to devout people who craved peace and order. It was eagerly adopted by Catholic and Protestant rulers alike. James I of England preached it; the French kings from Henry IV to Louis XIV practiced it. So did their Habsburg rivals, and most other seventeenth-century princes.

In the years of religious conflict and political upheaval between 1559 and 1689, politicians of every stripe invoked God's will to suit their particular purposes. The aristocratic and bourgeois Calvinists found divine sanction for rebellion, constitutionalism, and limited government. The Jesuits found divine sanction for the deposition of heretical rulers and a return to papal suzerainty. The secular princes found divine sanction for absolute monarchy. Radicals found divine sanction even for republicanism, democracy, and communism. Such were the effects of religion on politics, and of politics on religion.

SPAIN UNDER PHILIP II

The sixteenth century was Spain's time of power and glory. Four great rulers shaped its destiny. Ferdinand (king of Aragon, 1479–1516) and his wife Isabella (queen of Castile, 1474–1504) were the founders of modern

Spain. Their grandson Charles I (ruled 1516–1556), better known by his German imperial title of Charles V, was the mightiest European prince in the early sixteenth century. His son Philip II (ruled 1556–1598) was the mightiest European prince in the late sixteenth century.

Under Ferdinand and Isabella, the crowns of Castile and Aragon were joined, the Spanish conquered Moorish Granada, and Columbus discovered America. Under Charles V, the *conquistadores* mastered the Aztecs and Incas and began to mine Peruvian and Mexican silver, while Spanish armies drove the French out of Italy and won a reputation as the best soldiers in Europe. During his forty-year reign, Charles was able to spend only sixteen years in Spain, because of his manifold obligations in Germany, Italy, and the Low Countries. But his paternalistic style of rule suited the Spaniards, and kept them internally peaceful and stable. In 1556 he bequeathed to his son Philip the western half of his immense Habsburg patrimony: the Spanish kingdoms of Castile, Aragon, and Navarre; the Balearic Islands; several North African outposts; Sardinia, Sicily, Naples, and Milan; the Netherlands, Luxemburg, and Franche-Comté; and overseas, Mexico, Florida Central America, the West Indies, the entire coast of South America except for Brazil (held by Portugal) and lower Chile and Argentina (left to the Indians), as well as the Philippine Islands and numerous smaller Pacific islands. Philip II was really fortunate not to inherit the eastern Habsburg lands—Austria, Bohemia, and Hungary—and the Habsburg claims to the Holy Roman imperial title, which Charles passed to the Austrian branch of the family. Though Philip's domain was scarcely unified, it was much more manageable than his father's had been. It was a Spanish empire, centered in Madrid, politically absolute, fervently Catholic, shielded by unbeatable armies, and fed by an apparently boundless supply of American bullion which Philip's European rivals bitterly envied.

Sixteenth-century Spain was far from being a unified nation. Philip II was king of three distinct Spanish states—Castile, Aragon, and Navarre—each with its own separate institutions, customs, language, and culture. Philip governed each state independently, but he concentrated his attention on Castile, the biggest, richest, and most populous of them. Castile had about seven million inhabitants; Aragon and Navarre together had little more than one million. Furthermore, Castile was much easier to govern. The Castilian upper nobility were immensely rich and socially powerful, but politically harmless. The crown exempted the great magnates from taxation, and recognized their huge property holdings, and in exchange they refrained from contesting royal political authority. The lower nobility, or *hidalgos*, also exempted from taxation, were useful servants to the crown. Philip II's *corregidores*, royal officials who inspected and regulated the conduct of the sixty-six principal Castilian town councils, were drawn from the *hidalgo* class. The Castilian Cortes, or parliamentary assembly, was very weak. Only eighteen towns sent representatives, and the nobility and clergy were excluded. Philip summoned this body often, whenever he wished it to levy taxes, but did not permit the deputies to share in legislation. In Aragon, on the other hand, the nobility exercised considerable political power, and the Cortes was more independent. Philip let the Aragonese nobility alone, summoned the Aragonese Cortes rarely, and avoided asking for money. Little money could be squeezed out of Aragon in any case. Nor could Philip's Italian subjects supply much revenue; and his subjects in the Low Countries refused to contribute. The king depended heavily on silver from America, but the brunt of Philip's imperial administration was borne by the impoverished Castilian peasantry.

The sprawling Spanish empire was held together at the top by a remarkably centralized bureaucracy. The king sent viceroys, generally great Castilian noblemen, to govern his distant territories, serving as his *alter ego*. Each viceroy reported to a supervisory council in Madrid: the Council of Italy, the Council of Flanders, or the Council of the Indies. Each council was staffed by six to ten professional civil servants (again mostly Castilians) vested by the king with sweeping jurisdiction over the executive, judicial, and religious affairs of their particular territory. There was also a Council of Castile, a Council of Aragon, and councils to handle matters of state, war, finance, and the Inquisition. The king himself seldom attended any of these council sessions, but he reviewed all council decisions and often reversed them. He alone had total information—or as total as the flood of dispatches, petitions, and memoranda from all parts of his domain would permit—on every aspect of affairs. Outsiders joked about the Spanish government's grave and stately pace of operations, and it is true that Philip's elaborate system of bureaucratic checks and balances prevented quick decisions. But by playing his ministers and councillors off against one another, the king reduced the possibilities for bribery and corruption, and also preserved his personal power. As far as any one man could be, Philip II was the master of Spain.

Philip's vigorous supervision of his distant colonies in the New World demonstrates the long reach of Spanish royal government. Only a generation before he came to power, a band of tough and resourceful *conquistadores* led by Hernando Cortes (1485–1547) and Francisco Pizarro (c. 1470–1541) had conquered Mexico and Peru, acquired personal fortunes, and harnessed millions of docile Indians to work for them. But Charles V and Philip II managed to prevent the *conquistadores* and succeeding Spanish colonists from developing political autonomy, carving up the country into giant feudal estates, or crippling royal power in America. To control the colonists, the crown sent out Castilian grandees as viceroys of Peru and New Spain (Mexico). Lest they grow too strong, the crown encouraged the *audiencias*, or courts of justice, in the colonies to challenge the authority of the viceroys. Back in Madrid, the Council of the Indies kept tabs on both the viceroys and the *audiencias*. The Church, in partnership with the crown, protected the Indians from total enslavement by the colonists. The crown received one fifth of the bullion mined in America, and earned this royalty by protecting the treasure fleets from attack by French, English, and Dutch marauders. Philip II's military power kept his North Atlantic rivals from establishing permanent colonies in the Indies until after 1600. Sir Francis Drake could raid the Caribbean audaciously in the 1570's, when he caught the Spaniards by surprise, but in 1595 he was beaten off Puerto Rico and Panama; Spanish fortifications there were now too strong for him. No Spanish treasure fleet was captured until 1628.

The Spanish government insisted on closing its colonies to outside settlers or traders. Charles V had wanted to open the Indies to any inhabitant of his Hasburg domain, but this policy was speedily reversed. Castilians insisted that America—discovered by a Genoese—was their monopoly. All American commerce had to be funneled through the single Castilian port of Seville, where it was closely supervised by royal officials in the *Casa de Contratación* ("House of Trade"). Every merchant ship in the American fleet had to be licensed by the *Casa*. All incoming and outgoing cargo was registered with *Casa* officials, whose most important job was to receive and distribute the incoming silver and gold. Not only Italian or Flemish merchants but also

Philip II. *Painting by Coello. The king, true to his character, looks gravely dignified and is austerely dressed in black. Prado Museum, Madrid.*

Catalan merchants, from eastern Spain, were denied licenses to trade. Moors and Jews, so unwelcome in Spain that a half million or more were expelled from the Iberian peninsula between 1492 and 1609, found themselves rigorously excluded from asylum in America.

Spain's great weakness, which Philip II did nothing to correct, was its lopsided economy. The country was, as it still is, mountainous, barren, and parched. Although 95 percent of the people were peasants, sixteenth-century Spain did not produce enough grain to support the population and had to import wheat from the Mediterranean and Baltic areas. The nobility, who owned almost all the land, preferred raising sheep to cultivating crops, and merino wool was Spain's chief export. The Spanish exported raw wool to Flanders at a low price and imported finished Flemish cloth at a high price, giving Flemish entrepreneurs most of the profit. There were no industries to speak of in sixteenth-century Spain; most manufactured goods had to be imported. The Castilians had always valued business well below fighting and praying, and much of their commerce and banking was handled by outsiders. Within Philip's empire there were three principal trade routes: between Spain and Italy, between Spain and the Low Countries, and between Spain and the Americas. The first route was dominated by the Genoese and the second by Netherlanders; only the American trade was a closed Castilian preserve, and even here, much of the cargo shipped to America was non-Spanish in origin. In the late sixteenth century, as many as two hundred ships a year sailed between Seville and the Americas, making this far and away the busiest single route of European overseas commerce. Bullion shipments into Seville reached their peak between 1580 and 1620. In 1594, silver and gold accounted for 96 percent of the value of American exports to Spain. Unfortunately for the Spaniards, little of this treasure stayed in Spain. Because of the deficiencies in the Spanish economy, it had to be paid out to foreign farmers, manufacturers, merchants, and bankers.

Philip II's military power was handicapped by Spain's unbalanced economic and social structure. He could not raise enough money to pay for his large standing armies and his elaborate military campaigns. Throughout his reign the royal exchequer was in a virtual state of bankruptcy. Philip inherited large debts from his father, and when he suspended payment to his creditors in 1557 and again in 1575, he found it harder than ever to float new loans. He was unable to tap the wealth of his richest Spanish subjects, for the members of the nobility were exempt from taxes. Three hundred magnates owned more than half the land in Castile, and the rent-rolls of the thirteen Castilian dukes and thirteen marquises totaled nearly a million ducats a year—more than the king's annual share of American bullion until the 1580's. But this money was untouchable. Nor could Philip squeeze much from the Spanish merchant and professional class, which was notably smaller than that of other western European states. The only class which he could and did tax with impunity was the one least able to pay, the impoverished peasantry. In addition, of course, he spent his American silver as fast as it came in and even mortgaged future treasure shipments. But Philip's soldiers consumed all the American bullion and all the peasant taxes that could be scraped together. When their pay still fell into arrears, they mutinied and rioted uncontrollably. An unpaid army is worse than no army at all, as Philip found to his cost.

The Spanish ardor for fighting and praying had an old-fashioned flavor, being still largely directed against the traditional Moorish enemy. One of Philip II's major taxes was the *cruzada,* or crusade subsidy, authorized by the papacy to encourage continued Spanish warfare against Islam. Spaniards could not understand the general Catholic agitation for ecclesiastical reform, since the Spanish church had experienced its own reform movement in the fifteenth century, well before Luther. The Spanish Inquisition, dating from 1478, had been designed to root out heresy among converted Moslems and Jews. These *conversos* were generally hated and feared, and by the time of Philip II a racist campaign had been launched to bar anyone from public office whose blood was impure. The Inquisition was the one institution common to Castile, Aragon, and Navarre, and once the Protestant revolt broke out, the inquisitors went to extraordinary lengths to keep the new heresy out of Spain. Anyone deviating in the slightest particular from Catholic orthodoxy was branded a Lutheran by the Holy Office, subjected to torture and secret trial, and if found guilty and obdurate, handed over to the secular authorities for public execution at an *auto-da-fé.* Erasmus' supporters in Spain were hounded into silence. St. Ignatius of Loyola was twice imprisoned by the Spanish Inquisition on suspicion of heresy. Even the archbishop of Toledo, the primate of Spain, was held prisoner by his enemies in the Inquisition from 1559 to 1576 on trumped-up heresy charges. Despite this repressive atmosphere, two late sixteenth-century Spanish mystics, St. Teresa of Avila (1515–1582) and St. John of the Cross (1542–1591), sparked a new ardor well illustrated in the rapturous paintings of El Greco (c. 1548–1614). Spanish rapture did not extend to the papacy. Relations between Madrid and Rome were continually strained. Like every other prince of his day, Philip was jealous of outside interference with his territorial church, and besides, "in his heart he considered religion too serious a matter to be left to the Pope."[4]

What sort of man was Philip II? He was outwardly retiring and reserved, yet inwardly secure in his Catholic faith and his royal majesty. He was slim, sober, and dyspeptic in appearance, spoke slowly and softly, rarely smiled, was bookish and artistic rather than athletic, and was happiest when at his desk reading memoranda. He never personally led his troops on the bat-

[4]J. H. Elliott, *Imperial Spain, 1469–1716* (New York, 1964), p. 223.

tlefield. He disliked traveling or mingling with people, and after 1559 he never left the Iberian peninsula. But he avidly absorbed all the data his officials could collect. He was a file clerk on a heroic scale. Every day he sifted through masses of papers, many of them ludicrously trivial, and wrote voluminous marginal comments, sometimes correcting errors of grammar and spelling. The king, as some of his subjects complained, tried to govern the world from a chair. He deeply venerated his father, but he had none of Charles's cosmopolitan and ecumenical temper.

Philip II bore more than his share of private sorrows. He outlived four wives, all married for dynastic expediency, as illustrated by the fact that at the age of twenty-seven he chose a bride of thirty-eight, and when she died he married at the age of thirty-two a girl of fourteen. Six of his nine children died young. His first son, Don Carlos (1545–1568), was physically deformed and mentally unbalanced. Don Carlos passionately hated his father, and when the Dutch rebellion began, he tried to escape to the Netherlands to join the rebels. One night in 1568 the king broke into his son's bedchamber with a party of councillors, seized the startled prince's weapons and papers, and placed him under armed guard. Philip never saw Don Carlos again. Six months later, the prince died, perhaps poisoned but more likely a suicide. Philip's enemies to the north were scandalized by this episode. They called the king a cruel and secretive murderer. Ever since, Anglo-Saxon Protestant historians have generally pictured Philip in very dark colors. Spaniards, on the other hand, affectionately remember him as their Prudent King and prize his dignified, methodical, and conscientious statecraft. The Spanish view is obviously closer to the truth, yet Philip's crusade against Protestantism turned out to be far from prudent.

Philip II established his court at Madrid, in the center of Spain. But he craved a solitary retreat where he could escape from the elaborate court ceremonial and the tiresome audiences with suppliants and envoys. So he built the Escorial, a vast gray granite structure rising out of the bleak foothills of the sierras north of Madrid. The building, which took twenty years to construct, perfectly expresses Philip's taste and temper. Behind its severe facade one finds a combination of palace, church, tomb, and monastery. It is laid out in the shape of the gridiron on which the king's patron saint, Lawrence, was supposedly toasted alive. Under the great dome of the church—one of the first copies of St. Peter's in Rome—the king buried various members of his family and prepared his own grave. He found peace and privacy by going into retreat with the cloistered monks he installed in one section of the building. There are splendid public chambers in the Escorial, and a fine library and picture gallery. But Philip's favorite place was a meanly furnished little room from whose window he could peep out at the high altar of his church while Mass was being sung.

Despite his love of solitude and circumspection, the Prudent King was

The Escorial. *Painting by an unknown artist. The isolated setting, huge bulk, gridiron design, and monastic severity of Philip II's retreat are clearly shown. Standing in the center of the complex is the domed church.*

driven by his zeal and by the military strength at his disposal to play a strong hand in international affairs. The first half of his reign was dominated by warfare in the Mediterranean against Islam, the second half by warfare in the North Atlantic against the Protestants. On the Mediterranean front, Philip II did very well. Here he sent his army and navy against the traditional Mohammedan foe. When the Moors in Granada rose in rebellion in 1568, royal troops crushed the revolt and forced 150,000 Moorish prisoners to resettle in other parts of Spain. Philip fought an inconclusive series of engagements against the Barbary pirates of North Africa. He could not stop their raids against the Spanish coast and Spanish shipping, but he did strengthen Spanish naval protection for commerce in the eastern Mediterranean. Behind the Barbary pirates stood the mighty Ottoman Turks. The Ottoman Empire, like the Spanish, was at its peak in the early years of Philip's reign. The Turks occupied three quarters of the Mediterranean shoreline, from the Adriatic to Algeria, and they were still on the move. They almost took Malta in 1565 and did take Cyprus in 1571. To save the situation, Philip joined Venice and the papacy in a Holy League against the terrible Turk.

In October, 1571, a fleet of three hundred ships and eighty thousand sailors and soldiers (predominantly Spanish) sailed into the Gulf of Lepanto off the Greek coast to fight an Ottoman navy which had even more ships and men. The Battle of Lepanto was the biggest naval battle of the century, a showdown between Europe's western and eastern giants. Both fleets consisted of galleys propelled by oarsmen, and they fought in the old-fashioned close-range style, the men of each galley trying to ram, grapple, and board an enemy ship. When the Christian fleet closed for action, a crucifix was displayed in every galley, and all the warriors knelt in adoration as the Turks came up screaming and trumpeting. After a few hours of ferocious hand-to-hand combat, the Turkish fleet was annihilated. Three quarters of the Turkish ships, with their crews, were sunk or captured. Cautious as always, Philip did not follow up the smashing victory by trying to storm Constantinople. But he had stopped Turkish expansion, and he had proved who was king of the Mediterranean. Among the many Spanish soldiers wounded at Lepanto was a young man named Miguel de Cervantes (1547–1616). Many years later, in the prologue to his *Exemplary Novels*, Cervantes proudly described his sacrifice: "In the naval battle of Lepanto he lost his left hand as the result of a harquebus shot, a wound which, however unsightly it may appear, he looks upon as beautiful, for the reason that it was received on the most memorable and sublime occasion that past ages have known or those to come may hope to know."[5]

Philip II's greatest success came in 1580, when he annexed Portugal and the Portuguese empire. Philip's mother had been a Portuguese princess, and when the king of Portugal died in 1580 without a direct heir, Philip had as good a claim to the vacant throne as anyone. Portugal and Castile had long been bitter political and economic rivals, and the Portuguese people were strongly anti-Castilian. But by the judicious distribution of silver and promises of future rewards, Philip's agents won the Portuguese nobility and upper clergy to his candidacy; and more important, the Spanish king sent in an army to secure the country. In four months his soldiers overran Portugal, and Philip was soon crowned at Lisbon. His new kingdom was a small state with only a million or so inhabitants, but by joining the crowns of Portugal, Castile, Aragon, and Navarre, Philip had seemingly completed the unification of the Iberian peninsula. Furthermore, the Portuguese empire overseas was very valuable, second only to the Spanish empire in size and importance. Philip now had possession of Brazil, the Azores and other mid-Atlantic islands, slaving stations in Africa, trading posts in India, and spice islands in Malaysia. Portugal's Asian spice trade perfectly complemented Spain's American silver mines. The Portuguese had no silver of their own, and they needed Spanish bullion in order to buy spices in Asia. The Spanish colonists in America wanted slaves from Portuguese Africa, and the Spanish home government needed Lisbon (a far better Atlantic port than Seville or Cádiz) and the Portuguese navy and merchant marine.

[5] *The Portable Cervantes*, trans. and ed. by Samuel Putnam (New York, 1951), p. 706.

But the promise of 1580 was never realized. Philip's annexation of the Portuguese crown was purely personal and dynastic. To conciliate the Portuguese, he promised to preserve the country's independent institutions and independent commerce and to appoint only Portuguese officials. No effort was made to break down frontiers nor even to coordinate Spanish and Portuguese economic policy. Initially, the Portuguese accepted their new Habsburg ruler without much complaint, but as the years passed, they saw less and less advantage to the union, especially when the Spanish were unable to protect the Portuguese colonies from Dutch attack. Thus what might have been a fruitful permanent partnership lasted for only sixty years.

The annexation of Portugal helped to direct Philip II's attention west and north rather than east. Portugal, much more than Spain, faced onto the Atlantic, and for the first time Philip possessed adequate naval forces to deal with his Protestant adversaries in the North Atlantic—England and the Netherlands. Furthermore, in the 1580's, bullion imports from America suddenly doubled. Philip was now receiving two million ducats in silver ingots each year. His chronic fiscal problems seemed less pressing, and he felt that he could afford more ambitious military adventures than in the past. Now was the time to deal decisively with a situation which, from Philip's viewpoint, had been steadily deteriorating ever since 1559. As we shall see, the Spanish government had long been trying to suppress heresy and rebellion in the Netherlands. English privateers had been raiding the Spanish Indies with rising impudence. The French religious wars had entered a critical stage. Accordingly, in the 1580's Philip launched his grand design to solve all these problems by an overwhelming display of military power. His soldiers and sailors would quell the Netherlands revolt, invade and conquer England, and end the French religious wars. The Catholic-Calvinist conflict was reaching its climax.

THE FRENCH WARS OF RELIGION, 1562–1598

In striking contrast to Spain, which enjoyed internal peace and unity during the second half of the sixteenth century, France was nearly torn apart by forty years of agonizing, destructive civil war. The French collapse was many-faceted. Huguenots battled Catholics, aristocratic factions joined together to oppose the crown, the bourgeoisie strove for new political and religious rights, the Paris mob went wild, and the outer provinces reverted to their medieval autonomy. Religion was by no means the only source of trouble, but religion triggered the crisis with explosive force. The French wars exposed all the latent flaws in sixteenth-century European civilization. The French, despite their rich cultural resources, their well-balanced economy, and their impressively centralized governmental institutions, seemed to lose all sense of social community. The trouble was partly caused by the size

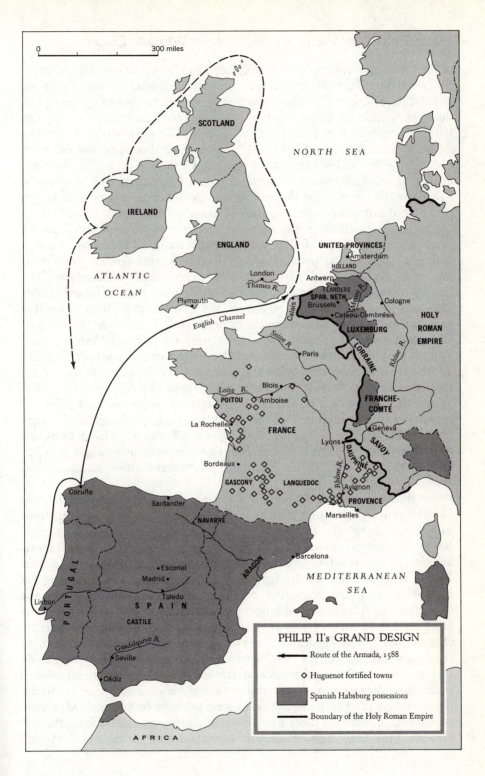

0   300 miles

SCOTLAND

NORTH SEA

IRELAND

ATLANTIC
OCEAN

ENGLAND

UNITED PROVINCES
Amsterdam
HOLLAND
Antwerp
London
Thames R.
Plymouth
Calais
FLANDERS
SPAN. NETH.
Brussels
Cateau-Cambrésis
Cologne
HOLY
ROMAN
EMPIRE
English Channel
LUXEMBURG
Seine R.
Meuse R.
Paris
LORRAINE
Rhine R.
Blois
FRANCHE-
COMTÉ
Loire R.
POITOU
Amboise
La Rochelle
FRANCE
Geneva
Lyons
SAVOY
Bordeaux
DAUPHINÉ
GASCONY
LANGUEDOC
Rhône R.
Avignon
Coruña
PROVENCE
Santander
Marseilles
NAVARRE

Barcelona

PORTUGAL
ARAGON
MEDITERRANEAN
SEA
Escorial
Madrid
Lisbon
Toledo
SPAIN
CASTILE
Guadalquivir R.
Seville
Cádiz

AFRICA

PHILIP II's GRAND DESIGN

⟵ Route of the Armada, 1588

◇ Huguenot fortified towns

Spanish Habsburg possessions

— Boundary of the Holy Roman Empire

of the country. France was awkwardly large and heterogeneous by sixteenth-century standards, with some fifteen million inhabitants, nearly twice the population of Spain. Yet the French state was certainly more closely knit than the worldwide Spanish empire. A more obvious trouble in the late sixteenth century was poor royal leadership. The four Valois kings who followed Francis I (ruled 1515–1547) were all mediocre, to say the least. Between 1559 and 1589 the queen mother, Catherine de Medici, was the central figure. Catherine had political talent, but not for the situation at hand. She tried to play the Huguenots and Catholics against each other; the result was disastrous for the house of Valois and for France.

During the first half of the sixteenth century, the French state had the characteristic attributes of a "new monarchy." Francis I exercised sovereign authority through his network of royal officials, through his permanent mercenary army, through his power to levy direct and indirect taxes. The French representative assembly, the Estates-General, did not meet between 1484 and 1560. In the outer regions of the country, the crown negotiated with the provincial estates, much easier to browbeat than the Estates-General. In central France, where there were no provincial estates, royal agents annually assessed and collected the *gabelle*, or salt tax, and the *taille*, an income tax levied mainly on the peasants. The king was master of his territorial church. In the Concordat of Bologna (1516), the papacy had agreed that all French bishops and abbots were to be nominated by the crown. Ambitious members of the nobility served as officers in the royal army, fighting Francis' frequent wars against Charles V. This activity not only kept them busy but kept them out of the country as much as possible. Clearly the tendency under Francis I was toward absolute, centralized monarchy.

But the king was not all-powerful. The *parlements,* or state courts, in Paris and the provinces insisted that he obey the established laws and to some extent substituted for the Estates-General as a brake on arbitrary royal power. Border provinces such as Brittany and Burgundy, only recently annexed to the crown, enjoyed special privileges and exemptions. The great French magnates had all the rights of the Spanish nobility, including tax exemption, and they exercised considerable political control over the *lieutenants du roi*, or royal administrators, at the local level. The crown was handicapped by lack of money, despite its taxing power. One sixteenth-century money-making device, the sale of royal offices, tended to hamper the king's control over his own bureaucracy; office holding became hereditary and semifeudal in character. A further complication was introduced when the religious controversy began to stir men's minds and emotions. One morning in 1534, good Catholics were horrified to find placards prominently posted in all the chief French cities, scurrilously denouncing the sacrament of the Mass. Some daring reformer had even nailed a placard onto the king's bedchamber door while he slept in the château of Amboise.

Opposition to centralized royal power began to mushroom during the reign of Henry II (1547–1559). This king was interested only in hunting and in his elderly mistress, Diane de Poitiers, a lady twenty years his senior. He was ashamed of his Florentine queen, Catherine de Medici, (1519–1589), because she came from a "bourgeois" family. At Henry's court three rival aristocratic factions—the Guises, the Montmorencys, and the Bourbons— began to jockey for control of royal policy. All three wanted to return to the feudal particularism of the good old days, when the great noble families ruled the various regions of France, and the king was just a figurehead. But they were bitterly jealous of each other's efforts to manipulate the king. The duke of Montmorency, constable of France, had immense landholdings and a personal retinue of several hundred knights. The Bourbons were princes of the blood, with the best claim to the French throne should Henry's sons leave no heirs. The Bourbon leaders were Louis, prince of Condé and his brother King Anthony of Navarre, whose kingdom in the Pyrenees was mostly in Spanish hands. But the Guise faction was the strongest of the three. Francis, duke of Guise, was Henry II's most brilliant general, and his brothers Charles, cardinal of Lorraine, and Louis, cardinal of Guise, led the French church. They married their niece (the future Mary, Queen of Scots) to the royal dauphin, and they persuaded Henry to continue his father's dynastic war with the Habsburgs. The heavy war taxes stirred his subjects and sent Henry deeply into debt. When he finally made peace with Spain in 1559, he had to renounce all pretensions to Italy. The nobility who had fought in this losing cause were unpaid and restless. But Henry did not have time to worry about this problem, for while jousting in a tournament during the celebrations following the Peace of Cateau-Cambrésis, he was killed when a splinter from his opponent's lance pierced his eye.

The French throne passed successively to three of Henry II's sons: Francis II (ruled 1559–1560), Charles IX (ruled 1560–1574), and Henry III (ruled 1574–1589). All three were feeble and neurotic. All three were dominated by their mother. But though Queen Catherine de Medici could rule her sons, she could not rule France. The country dissolved into anarchy and from anarchy into downright war. The war was ignited by the spread of Calvinism into France. The Huguenots not only spread heresy but challenged the power and profits of the crown. They were well organized for political subversion. Working at first in secret, they established a network of congregations throughout France. Even when Henry II organized a special court to try Huguenots and have them burned at the stake, they continued to proliferate. In 1559 they held their first national synod. They attacked convents and desecrated Catholic churches by smashing the holy relics and statuary. In 1561 there were 2,150 Huguenot congregations worshiping

Catherine de Medici in widow's weeds. *Painting by Clouet.*

openly, with roughly a million adherents out of a total French population of fifteen million. Their impact was disproportionately great, however, because most French Catholics were apathetic. Besides, the Huguenots were elite in character and strategically concentrated in the autonomous fringe provinces: Dauphiné, Languedoc, and Gascony in the south, Poitou and Britanny in the west, Normandy in the north. Merchants and lawyers, rulers of the provincial towns who were tenacious of their local privileges, joined in large numbers. Especially in the south and west, scores of walled towns became Huguenot bastions. Even more striking was the high percentage of converts among the *noblesse*. About two fifths of all the French nobility joined the Huguenot cause. Why should so many of these proud feudal magnates become smitten with a belief in original sin and predestination? In truth, few of them had authentic conversions, but they saw a wonderful chance to reverse the trend toward absolute royal power by patronizing the new religion. They wanted an arrangement in France similar to that established in Germany by the Peace of Augsburg in 1555, with each nobleman controlling the church in his own lands. When Admiral Coligny of the Montmorency faction, and the Bourbon prince of Condé were converted to the new religion, the Huguenots became a really dangerous political threat.

As early as 1560, Condé and Coligny hatched a plot to capture the boy king Francis II and "liberate" him from his Guise advisers. Conspirators converged on Amboise, where the king was staying. Here in the Loire Valley hunting country, the Valois kings and their courtiers spent as much time as possible, and here they built their great châteaux, fortress-palaces with massive battlements and gorgeously fanciful ornamentation in the Italian style, the finest Renaissance buildings in France. The Guises foiled the *coup d'état* at Amboise and festooned the crenellations of the château with the corpses of the conspirators. But Queen regent Catherine de Medici prevented the execution of the chief instigators, Condé and Coligny. The Guises were too powerful to suit her, and she needed the Bourbons as a counterweight.

Catherine hoped to reduce the tension in the situation by arranging a settlement which would bury the Huguenot-Catholic conflict, and in 1561 she actually got Calvinist and Catholic theologians to attend a joint conference, the Colloquy of Poissy, and tried to make them subscribe to a common body of doctrine. Having no real religious principles herself, Catherine supposed that she could paper over the dogmatic dispute. Her plan, as we shall see, was not far different from the English religious settlement which Elizabeth I was devising just at this time. But it worked much less well. In France there was no chance for a latitudinarian church or for religious toleration as long as both factions believed that they could win total victory.

The queen's overtures to the Huguenots shocked the more fervid French Catholics into taking up arms against Protestantism. The Guises had always been fiercely anti-Huguenot, and the religious crisis gave their faction a much wider popularity and a much greater driving force than it had possessed before. Under Guise leadership, the ultra-Catholics developed into a power bloc (like the Huguenots) very dangerous to the Valois monarchy and to the French state. They had the loyalty of Paris, far and away the biggest and most important city. They controlled large sections of northern and northwestern France, where they could recruit and pay for large armies. They were backed by the papacy, by the Jesuits, and by Philip II, who had no love for the Guises but welcomed the chance to exploit French factionalism to his own advantage. Correspondingly, Elizabeth I of England supported the Huguenots.

In 1562 the duke of Guise, passing the little town of Vassy with his troopers, was infuriated to see a congregation of Huguenots worshiping in a barn, and ordered his men to kill them. This incident triggered the French religious wars. Once started, the fighting was almost impossible to stop. The Huguenots formed far too small a minority to conquer France, but their armies became so expert at defensive campaigns that they could not be disbanded. Noncombatants suffered more than the soldiers: for every pitched battle there were numerous forays, sieges, lootings, and massacres. Peace treaties were repeatedly arranged only to be quickly broken. The original commanders on both sides were soon killed, not in battle but by assassins—the duke of Guise in 1563 and the Bourbon prince of Condé in 1569. These murders launched a blood feud in which the Catholic and Huguenot zealots strove for retaliation by ambushing and slaughtering the remaining leaders. Both sides were able to keep troops in the field for years at a time, their operations financed largely by tax money diverted from the royal treasury, and led by vagabond aristocrats who loved fighting and freebooting.

After ten years of inconclusive combat, the Huguenots seemed to be gaining the upper hand. In August, 1572, during an interval of peace, the cream of the Huguenot nobility gathered in Paris to celebrate the marriage of their chief, the young Bourbon prince Henry of Navarre (1553–1610), to the sister of King Charles IX. Not everyone joined in the rejoicing; to young Henry, duke of Guise (1550–1588), and to the queen mother, this wedding was bitter evidence that the Huguenots were capturing the king and the country. Admiral Coligny was now Charles IX's chief adviser and had just about persuaded the pliable king to reverse French foreign policy, declare war against Spain, and assist the Dutch Calvinist rebels. This was too much for Catherine de Medici. Insanely jealous of Coligny's influence over her son, she hired an assassin to murder the Admiral. On August 21, three days after the wedding, the assassin shot Coligny but merely wounded him. Now Catherine threw caution to the winds and hastily joined the Guise faction in a scheme to wipe out the entire Huguenot leadership. She insisted to Charles IX that the Huguenots, headed by Coligny, were plotting to kill him and seize power; playing upon the wretched king's jagged nerves as a musician bows his violin, she got Charles to agree to ambush *all* the traitorous Huguenot leaders.

Shortly after midnight on August 24, St. Bartholomew's Day, armed squads broke into the houses where the Huguenots lodged. The duke of Guise personally killed Coligny, in revenge for the murder of his father. Prince Henry of Navarre managed to save his life by promising to turn Catholic. By dawn the whole hysterical city was taking up the bestial cry, "Kill! Kill!" Women and children were senselessly hacked to death and dumped into the Seine. The great scholar Petrus Ramus was cut down while he knelt at prayer, and his pupils dragged his body through the streets. Debtors murdered their creditors. Looting continued for days. Such was the St. Bartholomew massacre, in which at least three thousand Huguenots were killed in Paris. As word spread throughout the country, thousands more were killed in the provincial towns. When the news reached the pope, he was so delighted that he gave a hundred crowns to the messenger. Catherine de Medici laughed exultantly when she saw Henry of Navarre attending his first Mass. Charles IX, on the other hand, sickened with guilt at having abused his royal responsibilities. Charles was wiser than his mother, for the massacre discredited the Valois monarchy without breaking the Huguenots or ending the conflict.

When Charles died in 1574, he was succeeded by his even more neurotic brother, Henry III. The new king was quickly hated for the money and affection he lavished on his *mignons*, effeminate court dandies, to say nothing of the degenerate royal ballets and masquerades, where (according to a scandalized Paris lawyer) the king "was usually dressed as a woman, with a low-cut collar which showed his throat, hung with pearls."[6] Henry's feckless extravagance was inherited from his mother, but not his sudden spasms of religiosity, during which he took up the hermit's life or walked barefoot on penitential pilgrimages. Under this last Valois king, the Catholic-Huguenot conflict reached its climax. Ultra-Catholics and Huguenots alike saw Henry as a dissembling hypocrite. They repudiated his efforts at peacemaking, and did their utmost to dismantle the French state. The Huguenots, despite their loss of many aristocratic leaders in the St. Bartholomew massacre, still held important western towns, such as La Rochelle. They were strongest in the south, and Languedoc became virtually independent. The ultra-Catholics formed a Holy League in 1576 and vowed to exterminate heresy and to seat a Catholic champion, such as Henry, duke of Guise, on the French throne. Leaders of both religions preached rebellion. In the most famous Huguenot tract, the *Vindiciae contra tyrannos*, (1578) Calvin's political theory was rewritten to show that a tyrannical king has violated his contract with the people and should be overthrown. Jesuit writers argued the League position that a king who betrays the Church must be overthrown. Both sides had strong commanders. For the League, Henry of Guise was a perfect bandit captain, brave, dashing, and arrogant, with a saber scar etched across his cheek. But the Huguenots could boast the heir apparent to the throne, Prince Henry of Navarre, who quickly renounced his forced St. Bartholomew conversion. Henry of Navarre was an easygoing extrovert with one priceless virtue: he was the only late sixteenth-century French political leader who honestly tried to serve his country as well as himself.

The turning point in the French crisis came in 1588–1589, with the War of the Three Henries: Guise versus Valois versus Navarre. The conflict began when the duke of Guise made his supreme bid to capture the monarchy. He had to move carefully, for he was in the pay of Philip II, who

[6]*The Paris of Henry of Navarre As Seen by Pierre de l'Estoile*, ed. by Nancy Lyman Roelker (Cambridge, Mass., 1958), p. 58.

The assassination of Henry, duke of Guise, in 1588. *The pro-Guise artist shows the assassins drawing their weapons (right) as they converge on the unsuspecting duke, stab him (center), and drag his body behind a tapestry (left) as Henry III looks on.*

had his own claim to the French throne! (Philip's third wife had been a Valois princess.) In 1588 the Spanish king directed Guise to stage a revolt in Paris in order to prevent Henry III from interfering with the Spanish Armada when it attacked England. Accordingly, Guise entered Paris against Henry III's express orders. He incited the city mob to disarm the king's guards and besieged him inside the Louvre palace. Before Guise could summon the nerve to assault the Louvre and kill the king, his intended victim fled the city. Nevertheless, Guise now had virtual control. He forced Henry III to make him chief minister, he dictated policy, and he managed the Estates-General which convened at Blois in 1588. The only trouble was that by this time Guise's patron, Philip II, had been badly beaten by the English and was unable to protect his French agent.

The royal château at Blois was Henry III's last retreat. This rambling palace, with its famous open staircase, myriad paneled rooms, and secret passageways, lies in the heart of the Loire Valley. Nearby are Amboise, where Henry's brother escaped conspiracy, and Chenonceaux, where his mother squandered a fortune on new construction. Catherine de Medici could no longer intervene, for she lay mortally ill. Imitating Catherine's role in the St. Bartholomew massacre, Henry III plotted to murder Guise. "He does not dare," said the duke contemptuously, but for once he underestimated the

Valois. On December 23, 1588, the king's bodyguard closed in on Guise and cut him down. The old queen mother could hear the uproar as the dying duke dragged his assassins through the royal chambers above her sickbed.

Henry III now joined the Huguenots in an all-out effort to crush the Catholic League. He threw himself into an alliance with Henry of Navarre, whom he recognized as his heir, and the two men marched together against Catholic Paris. But retribution for Guise's murder came fast: in July, 1589, Henry III was himself assassinated, by a fanatical monk who had secreted a dagger in the sleeve of his habit. Only one of the three Henries was left. Could the French Catholics be induced to accept this heretical prince as King Henry IV?

The new king's strongest asset was the mounting popular revulsion against anarchy. Many Frenchmen, derisively called *politiques* because they preferred merely political goals to spiritual ones, had long craved for peace and stability. The skeptical essayist Michel de Montaigne (1533–1592) was a *politique*, disgusted with cannibalism in the name of divinity. So was the profound political theorist Jean Bodin (1530–1596), whose *Six Books of the Republic* (1576) pleaded for the establishment of centralized sovereign authority in the hands of a purposeful prince. In Henry IV, the *politiques* saw at last a French prince who could be trusted with sovereign authority, who was a statesman of humanity and honesty (unlike Catherine de Medici), with a suitably jocose, pragmatic temper. Yet it took Henry IV a full decade to end the war. With Guise dead, the Catholic champion became Philip II, who intended once he had conquered Henry IV to put a Spanish infanta on the throne. In the early 1590's, Spanish troops repeatedly swept down from Flanders and blocked Henry IV's efforts to occupy his capital city. The Parisians continued to believe their League priests, who taught that a good Catholic would eat his own children rather than submit to a heretic. In 1593, Henry concluded that he must undergo the humiliation of abjuring Protestantism. "Today I talk to the Bishops," he told his mistress. "Sunday I take the perilous leap" (that is, attend Mass). Henry's politically motivated conversion scandalized the ultra-Catholics even more than the Huguenots, but the pope felt compelled to grant him absolution. Paris opened its gates to the king who, hat in hand, saluted all the pretty ladies in the windows as he entered the city.

In 1598, Henry IV and Philip II finally made peace, restoring the terms of 1559. Spain had gained nothing. In this same year, Henry bought off the last of the Catholic League nobility with grants of money and titles and conciliated the Huguenots with the Edict of Nantes. With this edict, Henry established a lasting religious truce. He declared Catholicism the official French religion and prohibited the reformed worship within five leagues of Paris. Yet any nobleman who chose to do so could practice the reformed religion in his own household, and bourgeois and lower-class Huguenots

The last page of the Edict of Nantes, 1598. *Henry IV's sprawling signature is in the center.*

could also worship in certain specified places. The Huguenot residents of some two hundred towns, mostly in the south and along the Bay of Biscay, were granted full religious freedom, including the right to set up schools and printing presses. About half of these towns were fortified and garrisoned by the Huguenots at royal expense. In addition, Huguenots throughout the country were promised "perpetual and irrevocable" liberty of conscience, full civil rights, and eligibility for public office. The king appointed special courts (half Catholic, half Huguenot) to adjudicate breaches of his edict.

The close of the French religious wars, with the Edict of Nantes, was to some extent a Catholic victory. France was hence forth a Catholic country with a Catholic king. Yet Henry IV temporarily expelled the Jesuits and repudiated the fanaticism of the ultra-Catholic League. At the same time, his edict was to some extent a Protestant victory, since it granted the Huguenots an entrenched position within the country. Yet the Huguenots had lost their leader; toleration was a gift of the king. In most ways, the compromise of 1598 signalized the triumph of political expediency over religion. The chief lesson of the French religious wars was a political one, that strongly centralized government was the only possible alternative to rebellion and social chaos. Upon this foundation would be built the magnificent seventeenth-century absolute monarchy of Louis XIV.

THE REVOLT OF THE NETHERLANDS

In the mid-sixteenth century, the people of the Low Countries had a style of life all their own, distinctly different from both the Spanish and the French. Theirs was a business society of towns and merchants, with the highest per-capita wealth in Europe. The Netherlanders were polyglot, particularistic, and cosmopolitan. Their country was divided into seventeen autonomous provinces, of which the most important were Flanders, Brabant, and Holland. Most of the people spoke Low German (Flemish or Dutch), but the Walloons, who lived in the southern border provinces, spoke a dialect of French. The Netherlanders lived at the crossroads of northwestern Europe, where the North Sea coast is intersected by a great river system feeding into Germany and France. The chief Flemish cloth-manufacturing towns, Bruges and Ghent, were no longer as prosperous as they had been in the late Middle Ages, but by the sixteenth century the enterprising Netherlanders were cultivating a more variegated commercial and industrial pattern. Antwerp was now the biggest city in the Low Countries and the chief financial and distribution center for western Europe. English cloth merchants, Portuguese spice merchants, Spanish wool merchants, German metalware merchants, French wine merchants, Italian silk merchants, and Baltic grain merchants congregated in Antwerp to exchange northern and southern products. Antwerp and other Netherlands towns were also leading industrial centers, and sailors from Zeeland and Holland dominated the North Sea herring fishery.

The hereditary ruler of the Low Countries was the duke of Burgundy. From 1506 to 1556, the emperor Charles V had held this title. The Netherlanders had had little to complain of during Charles's long administration, for thanks to the persistence of local customs and privileges, they had been able to manage their own affairs. The emperor had drawn heavily on the wealth of his Netherlands subjects in financing his wars, but he had left the central administration (such as it was) in the hands of the high nobility, and the government of the towns in the hands of the rich merchants. These merchant oligarchs controlled the provincial estates and the States-General as well. They refused to grant taxes unless their grievances were redressed, and they did their own tax collecting, keeping any surplus for their own purposes. The Netherlands States-General was particularly hard to handle, because the delegates from all seventeen provinces had to give their consent before anything could be done. Charles V had been unable to prevent the influx of Protestantism. Netherlanders were receptive to new religious opinions; their attitude—as exemplified in their great Christian humanist, Erasmus of Rotterdam—was tolerant and latitudinarian. Starting in the 1520's, Lutheran and Anabaptist doctrines spread widely despite savage heresy-hunting by Charles's government.

When Philip II inherited the dukedom of Burgundy from his father in 1556, he regarded the Low Countries as vital to his Spanish empire. Antwerp was the chief outlet for Spanish wool and wine, and the Netherlanders supplied Spain with grain, timber, textiles, armaments, and mercury for Philip's silver mines. But when Philip tried to introduce Spanish political and religious practices into the Low Countries, he encountered massive resistance. Philip personally disliked the Netherlands and never visited there after 1559. He could speak no Dutch, had no trusted native advisers, and he ruled by paper orders from the Escorial. He soon found that the atomistic political structure of the Netherlands left much to be desired by Spanish standards. The people of the Low Countries reciprocated Philip's feelings; Charles V had been a fellow Netherlander, but his son was an outsider. The high nobility found that their power was short-circuited by Castilian bureaucrats in Brussels and Madrid. Philip was so annoyed by the obstructionist tactics of the States-General that he vowed as early as 1559 never to convene it again. But the most explosive issue was religious. By the 1550's Calvinism was spreading from France into the Walloon provinces and Flanders. Antwerp became a Calvinist stronghold. When Philip found that his inquisitors could not eradicate this new heresy, he summarily reorganized the Netherlands church in 1561 by increasing the number of bishops from four to sixteen, nominating them all himself.

Philip II's Spanish absolutism had a traumatic effect upon the Netherlanders. Shopkeepers turned into soldiers; cosmopolites turned into patriots; latitudinarians turned into Calvinist fanatics. But as we shall see, in the end the revolt of the Netherlanders was only half successful. The seven northern provinces became independent and Protestant; the ten southern provinces (half Low German and half Walloon) remained loyal to Spain and to Catholicism. This division was largely accidental; in the 1560's the southern provinces were more Protestant and more rebellious against Philip II than the northern provinces. But accidental or not, the division became permanent. Between 1560 and 1600 the modern nations of Holland and Belgium were born.

The revolt against Spain was initiated by the Netherlands nobility. Three of the highest nobles, the prince of Orange and the counts of Egmont and Horn, all members of the Council of State, tried repeatedly to persuade Philip to alter his policy. When they failed, a group of the lesser nobility petitioned the king in 1566 to abolish the Inquisition in the Netherlands and to stop persecuting the Protestants. "Why be afraid of these beggars?" asked a courtier contemptuously, as several hundred gentry solemnly presented their petition to Philip's regent in Brussels. And "Long live the beggars!" suddenly became the rebel cry. Calvinist preachers sprang up everywhere in the Netherlands and whipped their excited auditors into a rage not only against the bishops but against all the outward trappings of Catholicism. In the summer of 1566 hundreds of churches were ravaged by iconoclasts. Some were converted into conventicles, or meetinghouses, of the Genevan type. This "Calvinist fury" shocked many Netherlanders and stung Philip into brutal reprisals. The duke of Alba arrived in 1567 with ten thousand picked Spanish troops, and he came very close to crushing all Netherlands resistance to Spanish absolutism. Alba executed Egmont and Horn, tortured and killed several thousand suspected heretics, and confiscated their property. He canceled all meaningful self-government and levied fantastically heavy new taxes. Only a forlorn band of exiles under the banner of the prince of Orange maintained active opposition to Philip.

The revolt of the Netherlands was slow to crystallize because the rebels lacked cohesion. Like the French Huguenots, the Dutch rebels were more destructive than constructive. They were not trying to mold a Netherlands nation-state; each of the seventeen provinces wanted to preserve its cherished autonomy. Nobility and merchants, Calvinists and moderate Catholics, could agree only in their distaste for Philip II. From 1567 to 1584 the rebel chief was Prince William of Orange (1533–1584), a man with many of the same character traits as the Huguenot chief, Henry of Navarre. Nicknamed William the Silent because of his skill at masking his intentions, Prince William was actually a gregarious extrovert who lived grandly and expensively. As a rebel leader he displayed alarming deficiencies. He was a mediocre general and so personally mired in debt that merchant creditors refused to lend him enough money. William was a religious opportunist who changed from Lutheran to Catholic to Calvinist as the circumstances warranted. In the 1560's he appeared to be a frivolous figure. But as he called upon his countrymen to stand up against Spanish tyranny, he revealed great courage and patriotism. Prince William appealed to the common people over the heads of the town oligarchs and his fellow nobles, yet scrupulously avoided grabbing dictatorial power. Almost single-handedly he strove to harmonize religious, sectional, and class differences, and weave the Netherlands into a nation. Thanks largely to William, the rebellion progressed, but it did not culminate in the achievement of his dream, a unified Netherlands nation-state. Instead, during the 1570's and 1580's the seventeen provinces split into two sections, the rebel north versus the Spanish south. Religion, which William wore so lightly, proved to be the great divider.

The decisive point came in 1572, the year of the St. Bartholomew massacre, when fugitive rebel ships (self-styled "sea beggars") managed to capture a number of ports in the provinces of Zeeland and Holland. These sea-beggar rebels had to overcome determined local opposition, because they were fiery Calvinists invading an area which was still predominantly Catholic. Having got possession of the territory bordering the Zuider Zee, the beggars had a permanent base of operations. The Spanish were never able to recapture Holland and Zeeland, for in this low-lying country the dikes could be opened to flood an invading army. Religious and political refugees from the southern Netherlands moved into the rebel Zuider Zee area in large numbers, and Calvinism became the established religion. Here was the beginning of the partition of the Netherlands into two separate states.

For a moment in the late 1570's, William the Silent came close to his goal of uniting all seventeen provinces, and Philip II came close to losing the south as well as the north. In 1576 the Spanish garrison in the still-loyal southern provinces ran amuck because the soldiers had been unpaid for two years. They sacked the city of Antwerp and murdered upwards of eight thousand inhabitants. This frightful "Spanish fury" persuaded the people of Brabant and Flanders that they must ally themselves with the rebel north. In 1577 all of the provinces joined the Union of Brussels, shelving religious disputes and pledging to fight Spain until Philip restored their privileges and withdrew his troops. William was recognized as their military commander. Yet the rebels were not effectively united. In 1578 a new Spanish commander, the duke of Parma, Philip II's ablest general, appeared on the scene with twenty thousand fresh troops. As soon as Parma began scoring military victories in the south, he detached the French-speaking Walloon provinces from the rebel federation. Parma appealed to these southern Netherlanders not so much on linguistic as on religious grounds. How could good Catholics associate with Calvinists? In 1579 he organized the loyal south into the Union of Arras and forced William to regroup the Calvinist north into the Union of Utrecht. In 1581 the States-General of the rebel provinces deposed Philip II as their prince and declared the independence of the United Provinces, or Dutch republic.

In the 1580's, each side tried to conquer the other, with the Spanish under Parma keeping the rebels very much on the defensive. After Parma had taken the chief Flemish towns in 1584, and Brussels and Antwerp in 1585, he held almost everything south of the Rhine River. A new wave of religious and political refugees fled north. Philip II hoped that the seven remaining rebel provinces would surrender if he could eradicate their leader. He declared William of Orange an outlaw and offered twenty-five thousand crowns as a reward for his assassination. Several efforts were made to earn this money, and in 1584 a Catholic fanatic gained entry to the prince's house in Delft, stood among a crowd of petitioners, and murdered him at point-blank pistol range.

With the death of its great founder, the Dutch republic was truly in desperate plight. The Dutch had already appealed to Germany and France for help but had received very little. Now they turned to Queen Elizabeth of England, who grudgingly sent a small army under the incompetent earl of Leicester. For two years (1585–1587), the Anglo-Dutch force precariously held the Rhine River line against Parma. Philip II, in the Escorial, remembering his mighty naval victory against the Turks at Lepanto, calculated that another such blow could crush the Dutch and the English simultaneously. Accordingly he prepared a huge new fleet, the "Invincible Armada," designed to clear the English Channel and North Sea of Dutch and English shipping, end the revolt of the Netherlands, dethrone the heretic queen of England, and eradicate North Atlantic Protestantism.

ELIZABETHAN ENGLAND

The British Isles which Philip II prepared to invade in 1588 offered three strikingly varied scenes. In England, under "good Queen Bess," there was peace and prosperity as never before. The English people, by some alchemy beyond the historian's analysis, were transforming their backwater island into a magnificently dynamic society. Scotland, by contrast, was still half wild. The Scots managed their affairs with crude abandon. This was the era of the sex-driven Mary, Queen of Scots, and the hot-gospeling John Knox. Ireland, barely on the edge of civilization, was a land of perpetual blood feuds and cattle raids, with no real government and no defense against invaders. During the late sixteenth century, the Irish slowly fell victim to English conquest and exploitation. Yet in their different styles, all three peoples experienced the western European religious crisis. Protestants and Catholics were everywhere vying for control.

When Queen Elizabeth I (ruled 1558–1603) ascended the English throne, religion was unquestionably the great issue. Back in the 1530's, when her father, Henry VIII (ruled 1509–1547), had so easily separated from Rome, the atmosphere had been worldly and cynical. Henry had invited the nobility and gentry who sat in Parliament to legislate the break with the papacy, giving them a larger share of power, and had then sold the

The Ditchley portrait of Elizabeth I. *The queen is shown as she liked to be portrayed, in fantastic costume, standing on a map of her beloved England, impervious to thunderstorms. National Portrait Gallery, London.*

confiscated Church lands to them cheap. In those days only a few Englishmen, such as Sir Thomas More, had been willing to die for the old universal Church. Only a few Englishmen, such as William Tyndale, who translated the Bible into English, had been outspoken proponents of Luther's new doctrines. But by the 1550's the atmosphere was much changed. During the reign of Elizabeth's feeble brother Edward VI (1547–1553), radical Protestants had overhauled the doctrine and ritual of the English church. In the succeeding reign, Elizabeth's fervidly Catholic sister, Queen Mary Tudor (1553–1558), had forcibly reunited the English church with Rome and burned at the stake the several hundred persons who dared to protest. This short period of violent fluctuation, reminiscent of the period of Valois rule in France, aroused deep religious passions in the English people. Would

Elizabeth follow Edward's example, or Mary's?

She did neither. Queen Elizabeth I was the only ruler in western Europe in the late sixteenth century who was able to handle the religious issue. Despite the loud fulminations of Calvinists and the conspiracies of Catholics, she unerringly pursued a policy of peace and compromise, and got away with it. This achievement alone is good reason for nominating Elizabeth the ablest politician of her time. Certainly she was more attractive as a queen than as a human being. She had a temper to match her red hair and a tongue to match her sharp features. Superficially, she was vacillating, evasive, and vague, but she was willfully stubborn underneath. Her unfortunate councillors had to take the blame for whatever went wrong. She was frugal, not to say mean, in her expenditures; though she paid plenty for clothes and cosmetics, she allowed her devoted courtiers to buy her entertainment, without offering in return the royal pageantry supplied by Catherine de Medici or public monuments like Philip II's Escorial. In an age when government was reckoned to be strictly a man's job, Elizabeth refused to marry because she would not share power, but kept the bachelor princes of western Europe dangling as her suitors. In an age when women were reckoned to be fit chiefly for childbirth, and queens for the production of male heirs, Elizabeth made a virtue of her spinsterly virginity, while behaving with ever more outlandish coquetry the older she got. And yet, she was one of the greatest rulers in English history.

Elizabeth's I's first and most important work was her religious settlement, achieved between 1559 and 1563. The new queen was confronted with a church staffed by her sister Mary's Catholic appointees, with the clamors for reinstatement of her brother Edward's ousted Protestant clergy (many of whom had returned from exile in Geneva and other Calvinist centers), and with a Parliament divided between the Catholic House of Lords and a Protestant House of Commons. Queen and Parliament worked out a compromise reorganization of the Church of England so as to combine an external Catholic structure with a broadly Protestant dogma. The intention was to satisfy as wide a spectrum of religious tastes as possible. All Englishmen were required to attend public worship in the national church, but no man's inner conscience was publicly scrutinized. Under the Elizabethan system, there was no heresy-hunting, no Inquisition, no burnings, only a system of fines for those who stayed away from church. Less than 5 per cent of the clergy resigned (they were replaced, of course, by Protestants); the remainder docilely subscribed to the required Thirty-nine Articles of belief, which affirmed all the chief Lutheran tenets and listed numerous "errors" in the Roman Church. The queen hand picked her bishops and sometimes kept bishoprics vacant for years in order to tap the revenues: the Elizabethan church was decidedly subordinate to the state. Men of strong conviction were of course offended by the expediency of a church which in its prayer book could describe the pivotal Communion service both as a miracle and as a memorial ceremony. But only the most radical Calvinists and the most committed Catholics refused to tolerate the dignified beauty of the Anglican liturgy, and soon many Englishmen were deeply loyal to their *via media*.

Having worked out a formula for English religious stability and peace, Elizabeth I spent the rest of her long reign trying to keep the *status quo*. She was a political conservative, and with good reason. England, after all, was a small state with a population of less than four million and a predominantly agrarian economy. The income of the royal government was very modest by Spanish or French standards. The queen could afford neither a standing army nor an elaborate civil service. She depended on the cooperation of the nobility and the landed gentry. The English nobility were less wealthy than their Spanish or French counterparts and enjoyed fewer privileges; they even paid taxes. Henry VII and Henry VIII had done a great deal to domesticate the feudal magnates who had controlled England in the late Middle Ages. But under Elizabeth the nobility still exercised great power: they commanded small armies of retainers, they sat in the House of Lords and got their adherents elected to the House of Commons, and they formed aristocratic factions at court dangerously similar to the Guise and Bourbon factions in Valois France. Like earlier Tudor monarchs, Elizabeth tried to bolster her position with respect to the nobility by patronizing the upper middle class: country squires and London merchants. She chose her two chief advisers—Sir William Cecil (1520–1598) and Sir Francis Walsingham (*c.* 1530–1590)—from this class, and on the local level appointed deserving squires as justices of the peace. The justice of the peace received no pay, but he had dignity, responsibility, and control over neighborhood affairs. When his interests coincided with those of the royal government, he served the queen very well.

The most obvious brake on English royal authority was Parliament. Elizabeth could neither tax nor legislate except through Parliament. Unlike the Castilian Cortes and the French Estates-General, Parliament gained power steadily throughout the sixteenth century. Henry VIII, Edward VI, Mary, and Elizabeth all worked through Parliament in their attempts to shape the English church. Much more legislation was enacted by Parliament during the Tudor era than in the Middle Ages. Parliamentary taxes were vital to the crown, and Elizabeth (unlike Philip II in Castile) had great difficulty in wheedling tax levies from Parliament even in emergencies.

In the early sixteenth century the lower house, the House of Commons, had been more tractable than the House of Lords, citadel of the nobility, but under Elizabeth, the Commons became the more independent and aggressive of the two houses. Ambitious and well-connected country gentlemen actively sought election to the Commons. Elizabethan parliamentary elections bore little resemblance to modern ones. There were no parties or platforms. Most elections were uncontested. Only candidates of high social standing, wealth, and influence presumed to stand, and they were dutifully accepted by a few hundred subservient voters. But if the electorate was subservient, the members of Parliament were not. Elizabeth was hard pressed to cope with the opinionated, self-confident gentry who crowded into the Commons chamber in St. Stephen's Chapel at Westminster, just outside the city of London, in order to question her policies and advocate their own. The queen summoned Parliament as infrequently as possible, convoking it for a session of a couple of months every three or four years. Her ministers carefully stage-managed every bit of business, but they could not prevent rude speakers in the Commons from urging Her Majesty to marry or to crush popery. Even though the government introduced legislation, members of the Commons freely debated and amended bills in committee and introduced new bills of their own. The queen became adept at seeming to surrender to Parliament, while still preserving her prerogative.

There was always a Puritan bloc in Parliament. Puritans were the English species of Calvinist. They wanted to cleanse the English church of its popish ceremonies and ritual, to abolish Elizabeth's episcopal church government, to erect a preaching ministry and a national Geneva discipline. The Puritans were less rebellious against the government than were their compeers in France and the Netherlands. Much as they disliked the queen's lukewarm Protestantism, they accepted membership in the Church of England and aimed at purifying it from within. Hence the Puritans were less easy to identify than were the Huguenots and the Dutch Calvinists. Indeed, many Anglican clergymen, including several bishops, were Puritans. The movement was attractive to articulate, educated laymen, and an increasing number of landed gentlemen and London merchants became Puritans. Cambridge University was the intellectual headquarters of the Puritans. Elizabeth intensely disliked Puritan criticism of her church. She took special pains to gag Puritan polemicists and kept the movement relatively small. But even Elizabeth could not stop the prolific Puritan pamphleteers from formulating belligerent protests against prayer books, bishops, and godless rulers, developing a line of argument which would lead—a generation after the queen's death—to the Puritan Revolution of 1640.

In the short run, the biggest challenge to the *status quo* came not from the radicals in religion, but from the conservatives. The Catholics had a very active claimant to the English throne in Mary Stuart, better known as Mary, Queen of Scots, who was everything Elizabeth was not: beautiful, alluring, passionate, and rash. Mary's reign in Scotland (1561–1567) was brief and turbulent, and suggests the chaos that might have engulfed England had she been able to take her cousin Elizabeth's place. To be sure, sixteenth-century

Scotland was not an easy place to govern. The wildly beautiful countryside was economically underdeveloped. The few small towns were frequently overrun by marauders despite their grim gray stone walls. The Scots nobility were untamed tribal chieftains, continually feuding and fighting among themselves. Roughly half the people were Catholics; the other half, Calvinists. The Calvinist leader was John Knox, a brass-tongued preacher whose "Reformed Kirk" was patterned after the Genevan presbyterian system. The General Assembly of the Reformed Kirk was a more powerful body than the Scots parliament, for it was quite independent of royal control. Mary Stuart had been queen of Scotland since she was an infant, but she had spent her girlhood at the French Valois court, her mother governing Scotland as regent until she died in 1560. One foggy, dismal day in 1561 the nineteen-year-old queen returned from France to Holyrood Palace, in Edinburgh, to be greeted by a serenade of psalms sung out of tune. She was already a widow; her first husband, the boy king Francis II of France, had died the previous year. Mary established as gay a court as possible at Edinburgh and won over many of the Protestant nobility. But her charms cast no spell on John Knox. Mary reportedly told Knox, "I will defend the kirk of Rome, for it is, I think, the true kirk of God."

"Your will, madam," came the reply, "is no reason: neither doth your thought make that Roman harlot to be the true and immaculate spouse of Jesus Christ."

Mary had no desire to settle permanently in dour Scotland. She immediately pressed Elizabeth to recognize her as heir to the English throne, and when Elizabeth procrastinated, she married her cousin Henry Stewart, Lord Darnley, who had the next-best claim to the English throne. But Mary soon lost interest in the empty-headed Darnley and adopted a court musician named David Rizzio as her paramour. Early in 1566 the jealous Darnley gathered a band of conspirators who surprised Mary and Rizzio at supper in Holyrood Palace and hacked Rizzio to death as he clung to the queen's skirts. Mary shortly got her revenge. When Darnley contracted smallpox, she installed him in a lonely house outside the walls of Edinburgh, and one night someone strangled Darnley and blew up his house with gunpowder. Who did it can never be proved, but most Scotsmen at the time suspected the earl of Bothwell, Mary's latest lover. Their suspicions became firmer when Mary married Bothwell three months after Darnley's murder. The question of Mary's guilt or innocence in this lurid affair has been endlessly debated. One fact is plain. By marrying Bothwell she lost control of Scotland. The nobility revolted against the lady and forced her to abdicate. In 1568 she fled to England, and Elizabeth imprisoned her.

Mary was still young, still bewitching. In 1569 a band of Catholic lords led an abortive rebellion on her behalf in northern England. The 1570's and 1580's were marked by a series of Catholic plots to assassinate Elizabeth and enthrone Mary—all discovered (and some perhaps planted) by Elizabeth's spies. The pope had excommunicated Elizabeth, and resolute Jesuit missionaries, such as Edmund Campion and Robert Parsons, were encouraging the remaining English Catholics to stand firm in their faith. The queen and her ministers felt compelled to crack down: during Elizabeth's reign, over two hundred priests and Catholic laymen were executed on the technical charge of treason. In 1586, government spies uncovered Mary's complicity in a new assassination plot. This time she was tried and found guilty. With a great show of reluctance, partly real and partly feigned, Elizabeth signed the death warrant. In 1587, Mary Stuart was released from her nineteen years of imprisonment by the executioner's axe. Catholics naturally saw her as a martyr and denounced the Protestant Jezebel for murdering an anointed queen.

Religion was one of the causes of mounting friction between Elizabethan England and Philip II's Spain. Another was Elizabeth's support of the Dutch rebels. A third cause, perhaps the most decisive, was English intrusion into the Spanish empire in America. Until the mid-sixteenth century, English sailors had taken practically no part in the exploration and exploitation of the New World, and English merchants were perfectly content with the traditional Flemish wool trade. By the 1560's, however, even Englishmen were becoming interested in the possibility of finding wealth in the New World. Elizabeth I encouraged private investment in overseas enterprises and offered token investments herself. Sailors from Plymouth and other southwestern ports began to reconnoiter the Atlantic. Some, such as Martin Frobisher and John Davis, searched the still unclaimed North American coastline, looking fruitlessly for a passage to Cathay, and panning fruitlessly for gold. Others ventured into the Spanish Caribbean. Between 1562 and 1568 John Hawkins sold African slaves to the Spanish planters with some success. Between 1571 and 1581 Francis Drake (c. 1540–1596), a fiery Protestant, made three piratical raids on Spanish America with much greater success. On his third voyage, Drake took his ship, the *Golden Hind*, through the Strait of Magellan, captured a Spanish treasure ship off the Pacific coast of South America, then sailed up to California and from there to the South Pacific spice islands and to the Cape of Good Hope; thus, when he returned to Plymouth after an absence of three years, he had circumnavigated the globe. The queen knighted Drake in 1581, and no wonder; his cargo of Spanish treasure was worth twice Elizabeth's annual revenue. In 1585–1586, with the official backing of his government, Sir Francis took a big fleet of thirty ships once more into the Caribbean, where he vandalized the Spanish more than he plundered them. Certainly the Elizabethan sea dogs were doing all they could to provoke the Prudent King.

So it was that the two most cautious leaders in Christendom, both fearful of change and sensitive to the burdens of war, faced each other in dramatic

The defeat of the Spanish Armada. *An old English print showing the crescent-shaped Spanish fleet in flight and one struggling Spanish ship (lower left) being hunted down. The English ships display the red cross of St. George on their ensigns. The Spanish oared galley (lower right) was better suited to the Mediterranean than the Atlantic.*

conflict. In 1586, Philip II began to plan his invasion of England. A Spanish fleet, powerful enough to hold the English navy at bay, was to sail from Lisbon to the Flemish coast, rendezvous with Parma's army, assembled on barges, and cross the English Channel, landing at the mouth of the Thames. Even with the best of luck this plan would have been extremely difficult to execute, and one misfortune after another compounded the difficulty. In 1587, Sir Francis Drake daringly raided Cádiz, Spain's chief Atlantic port. He sank enough ships to delay Philip's enterprise by a year and destroyed the Spaniards' precious store of seasoned barrel staves, thereby condemning the Armada crew to a diet of stinking water and spoiled food as a result of storage in casks made of green timber. Then, on the eve of embarkation, Philip's admiral died. His replacement, the duke of Medina-Sidonia was brave but inexperienced.

The Invincible Armada that finally neared the English coast in July, 1588, was a majestic fleet of 130 ships and thirty thousand men. The English sailed out from Plymouth with an equally impressive force. They had as many ships as the Spaniards, their seamanship and their guns were better, and they had Sir Francis Drake. This was not the biggest naval showdown of the century. Twice as many ships and men had fought at Lepanto in 1571. But the Battle of Lepanto was a land battle transferred to sea, with soldiers swarming across oared galleys which had locked together. The Anglo-Spanish confrontation in 1588 was altogether different, a mariners' duel between sailing ships armed with cannon. The Armada fight inaugurated the classical age of naval warfare, which stretched from the sixteenth into the nineteenth century, from Drake to Nelson.

The Spanish and English fleets met off Cornwall, at the southwestern tip of England. Both sides were reluctant to attack. The duke of Medina-Sidonia was dismayed to see how nimbly the English could sail around his ships. The English were baffled by the tight Spanish crescent formation, designed to force them to grapple at close quarters, to fight in the style of Mediterranean galleys, by ramming and boarding, at which the Spanish excelled. For nine days the two fleets drifted slowly up the length of the Channel, the English buzzing around the Spanish crescent, neither side doing much damage. Medina-Sidonia was approaching his rendezvous with Parma, but so far he had been continuously outmaneuvered, and he saw that if he tried to convoy Parma's men in barges from Flanders across the Channel to England, the English navy would lacerate them. He anchored off Calais, trying to think of some way to join forces with Parma. All at once, disaster struck the Armada. At midnight the English sent eight blazing fire ships into the Spanish fleet. The Spanish ships scattered to sea, their crescent formation broken. Drake and his comrades pounced on them, sank some of the ships, and pounded the rest until ammunition gave out. Then a gale swept the battered Armada into the North Sea. Medina-Sidonia had lost all hope of joining with Parma or invading England. With the English fleet chasing him north, toward Scotland, he sailed his limping, leaky galleons around the British Isles. A number of ships and thousands of men were lost off the stormy Irish coast. About half the fleet eventually straggled back to Spain. So ended the first modern naval battle. So ended Philip's plan to dethrone Elizabeth.

THE DECLINE OF SPAIN

The defeat of the Spanish Armada was a decisive event. It exposed the limitations of sixteenth-century military power. It stamped Philip II's overweening international policy with failure. It tipped the religious struggle, which underlay all western European politics during the late sixteenth century, in favor of the Protestant minority. And it closed Spain's golden century of power and glory.

After 1588, nothing went right for Philip II. The Spanish king received the news of the Armada's defeat with his customary sober stoicism—and kept on trying to conquer England and put down the Dutch rebels. In the 1590's, as has been mentioned, he took on a new opponent, invading France in an attempt to dethrone Henry of Navarre. The French, English, and Dutch formed an alliance against him, fought him to a standstill on land, and bested him at sea. The Spanish infantry was still superlative, and in northern France the duke of Parma campaigned with his usual brilliance against Henry IV. But his successes roused French patriotism against the Spanish invaders. Unwittingly, Philip II helped Henry IV to reunite his country and restore the centralized power of the French monarchy. In 1598, just a few months before his death, Philip reluctantly made peace with Henry. Though this peace treaty restored the *status quo* of 1559, psychologically it was a French victory, the first of a long series of Bourbon victories over the Habsburgs. Within a few years the agony of the French religious wars became only a memory, as Bourbon France rapidly eclipsed Habsburg Spain in political and military power.

Philip II never made peace with England. The Anglo-Spanish war continued until 1604, with the English inflicting more damage than they received. Despite the failure of the Armada, Philip doggedly kept trying to invade Britain. His last great fleet, headed for Ireland, was dispersed by storms in 1596. Through the years, the English countered by launching a series of armadas against Spain but never came close to achieving a knockout blow. In 1589, Sir Francis Drake failed to capture Lisbon; in 1596, he died while leading an abortive attack against the Spanish West Indies. The English did score some victories. In 1596, they sacked Cádiz and pillaged the surrounding Spanish countryside. Throughout the war, English privateers mercilessly plundered Spanish commercial vessels. On the whole, the long war cast a damper on the buoyant Elizabethans. They were spending too much blood and money for too little glory. Yet England emerged from this conflict in far better shape than Spain and with new ambitions for an empire of its own to rival the Spanish empire.

Philip II's bitterest legacy was the Netherlands rebellion. The Spanish-Dutch war continued until 1609, with neither side able to penetrate far beyond the Rhine River line which divided the seven Calvinist United Provinces from the ten Catholic provinces in Spanish hands. The Dutch commander, Prince Maurice of Nassau, son of William the Silent, hoped to reunite the northern and southern provinces, but many of his Calvinist supporters did not wish to join with Catholics, and the burghers of Holland and Zeeland did not wish to share their business prosperity with the towns of Flanders and Brabant. The northern provinces flourished mightily during the war; the south was in economic collapse. After Parma captured Antwerp in 1585, Amsterdam, the chief northern port, quickly became the leading entrepôt in the Low Countries. The Amsterdam businessmen did not want Antwerp's old primacy restored. Accordingly, even after the Spanish and Dutch arranged a twelve-year truce in 1609, the Dutch insisted on blockading the Scheldt River, Antwerp's avenue to the sea. The war reopened in 1621, and this time the Dutch clearly gained the advantage. Prince Frederick Henry, the youngest son of William the Silent, was now the Dutch general, and he pushed the Spaniards well south of the Rhine. But the great Dutch successes were at sea. The purpose of the Dutch West India Company, founded in 1621, was to plunder Spanish America. Company ships captured the Spanish silver fleet in 1628. By 1636, they had taken 547 enemy vessels. In 1648, Spain capitulated, and after trying for eighty years to overcome the Dutch, finally recognized the independence of the United Provinces.

By this time, Spain and its empire had sadly decayed in wealth and vigor from the great days of the sixteenth century. The decay could be found at all levels of Spanish society. Philip II's successors—Philip III (ruled 1598–1621), Philip IV (ruled 1621–1665), and Charles II (ruled 1665–1700)—were feckless kings, unable or unwilling to sustain the Prudent King's grasp on the central institutions of government. The population shrank, and there was a severe slump in the production of wool, Spain's chief export. The peasants were less able than ever to pay the high taxes their government demanded. The merchant marine never recovered from the shipping losses inflicted by English and Dutch privateers. Apathy set in, extending even to the New World. American silver production fell precipitously, until by 1660, bullion shipments to Seville were only 10 per cent of what they had been in 1595. In Spanish America, the Indian population decreased, towns decayed, and the colonists fell back on a subsistence agricultural economy closely parallel to that of the mother country. Old Spain and New Spain no longer had much to contribute to each other. Though the empire remained technically closed to outsiders, the home government was helpless to prevent the intrusions of foreign traders. It is estimated that during the second half of the seventeenth century, two thirds of the European goods sold to Spanish Americans were smuggled in by Dutch, English, or French interlopers. These illicit traders did not plunder the Spanish Main as the Elizabethan sea dogs had once done. Instead, by punctiliously bribing the local Spanish officials, they gained permission to offer their wares to the colonists, who bought eagerly because the smugglers (having evaded Spanish customs taxes) undersold the Seville monopoly. Economically, the Spanish empire had disintegrated.

The Spaniards remained as proudly autocratic, devout, and introspective as ever. Indeed, as their political power evaporated, they became ever more sensitive to questions of status and honor. And war remained the chief field of honor. There were only twenty-eight years during the seventeenth century when Spain did not have armies in combat. It fought five wars with France alone. The net result of all this fighting was that Spain had to cede territory in the southern Netherlands, the Pyrenees, and Franche-Comté to the French, and yield a number of small Caribbean islands to the English, French, and Dutch. The strain of war precipitated a chain of mid-seventeenth-century rebellions within the Spanish empire. Portugal rose up in revolt in 1640, and after long years of fighting, Spain recognized its independence in 1668. Rebellions in Catalonia, Naples, and Sicily were suppressed with difficulty. This cumulative tale of defeat and decay is not easy to explain. A formula which had worked well in the sixteenth century stopped working in the seventeenth. Philip II can be blamed for overstraining the Spanish system, but he can hardly be blamed for his people's collective loss of vitality. Spaniards were no longer swashbuckling *conquistadores*; somehow, after 1588 they lost the knack of remaking the world.

Philip II's defeat and Spain's decline signalized the collapse of the Catholic crusade against Protestantism in western Europe. The ancient unity of western Christendom had been smashed beyond redemption. Yet the Calvinist crusaders had not won an outright victory. By the time Philip died in 1598 it was apparent that neither side could conquer the other. The French religious wars resulted in a compromise: king and country remained Catholic, while the Huguenots enjoyed political autonomy and religious liberty. The Netherlands revolt also resulted in a compromise: the north became predominantly Calvinist and politically independent, while the south remained Catholic and Spanish. In England, yet another kind of compromise emerged, with both Calvinists and Catholics forced to accept a state-controlled latitudianarian church. These compromise settlements can be interpreted as moral triumphs for the Calvinists, since they had fought the Catholics, despite their far greater political and military resources, to a standstill. But the Calvinists in France and England had not achieved their Genevan ideal, and in the Dutch republic the Calvinist zeal of the 1560's was already turning by 1600 into a secular zeal for making money. Except in England, Calvinism had passed its most militant phase by the end of the century. The most effective leaders of the late sixteenth century—Henry IV, William the Silent, and Elizabeth I—were all *politiques* who did their best to bury the religious issue and keep the church subordinate to the state.

It would be a great mistake, however, to dismiss the Calvinist-Catholic conflict as unimportant because neither side won. Though the religious ideals of Calvin and of Loyola were quickly diluted in practice, the impact left by these sixteenth-century crusaders was strong and lasting. They strengthened the moral purpose and community spirit of every western European state. For the Spanish people, the sixteenth century was the golden age, illuminated by a fusion of missionary zeal, military prowess, and artistic creativity which they were never afterward able to match. For the French, Dutch, and English, the greatest days lay ahead. In the seventeenth century these three peoples would dominate Europe and give the world new definitions of individual liberty and public order, of individual prosperity and public power.

CHAPTER 8

Political Disintegration in Central and Eastern Europe

THE WARS OF RELIGION engulfed the whole of Latin Christendom, eastern as well as western Europe. Germany, birthplace of the Protestant Reformation, was a battleground between the 1520's and the 1640's. Switzerland, Bohemia, Poland, Hungary, and Transylvania were all religiously divided, with Catholics, Lutherans, Zwinglians, Calvinists, and Anabaptists pitted against one another. The Austrian Habsburgs, like the Spanish Habsburgs in the west, were Catholic champions; Gustavus Adolphus of Sweden was the chief Protestant leader. Yet the Protestant-Catholic conflict in Germany, and elsewhere in central and eastern Europe, took on quite a different style from the crusading ardor of the Atlantic peoples. East of the Rhine, the motives for fighting were less "religious," indeed in every sense less ideological. Protestants and Catholics exhibited less sense of moral regeneration, less missionary zeal, than did their counterparts in the west, and a stronger preoccupation with territorial aggrandizement. The Thirty Years' War, biggest of all the wars of religion, was fought for more obviously secular objectives than were the French and Dutch religious wars. It was also more destructive of life, property, and social vitality. How ironic that Luther's compatriots should suffer more damage, to less purpose, in the name of Protestant-Catholic rivalry than any other European people!

Political, social, and cultural factors help explain why the religious crisis of the sixteenth and seventeenth centuries worked out so differently in eastern and in western Europe. East of the Rhine, the concept of state sovereignty at the national level had not yet developed as it had in France, England, and Spain. Political units were simultaneously larger and smaller than in the west. The Holy Roman Empire, the Ottoman Empire, Poland, and Russia were each much larger than any western national state, but within these large units the most effective authority was generally held by the local magnates—the *landgrafs, beys, szlachta,* and *boyars.* The average inhabitant owed indirect allegiance to a distant emperor or king who had no personal control over him, and direct allegiance to an aristocratic landlord whose power was real but petty. No eastern European prince, great or small, could match Philip II or Elizabeth I in sovereign strength. That is, no eastern European prince could expect several million reasonably cooperative subjects (like those in Castile and England) to pay burdensome taxes, obey complex instructions, perform patriotic military service, and participate intelligently in civil obligations. Only Gustavus Adolphus could muster from his people the kind of strong community spirit which animated the Spanish, English, Dutch, and French. Community spirit or national consciousness was hard to achieve in central and eastern Europe, for the population was ethnically diverse. Some fourteen major languages were spoken, as against five in western Europe, and most of the ethnic groups were intermingled. Every large eastern state was multilingual. The Holy Roman Empire alone included eight rival ethnic groups. Ethnic rivalries cut across religious rivalries. Protestants and Catholics staged their family quarrel hemmed in by alien creeds—Islam and Greek Orthodoxy south of the Danube, and Russian Orthodoxy east of the Dnieper.

Between 1559 and 1689, during the era of the religious wars, the disparity between eastern and western Europe widened steadily. In the mid-sixteenth century this disparity had been disguised by the immense size of Charles V's empire, straddling Spain and Germany. The division of Charles's empire in 1556 into Spanish and German sections symbolized the new era. In the west, as we have seen, the religious crisis stimulated the evolution of an articulate urban capitalist class, as well as the development of national spirit and of a genuine state sovereignty. In the east the effect was almost the opposite. Political organization was splintered more than ever, commerce stagnated, and only the semifeudal class of agricultural magnates emerged as the true victor. The gains of these local landlords were made at the expense of the emperors and kings above them and of the burghers and peasants below. By the close of the seventeenth century, the largest eastern political units—the Holy Roman Empire, the Ottoman Empire, the kingdom of Poland—were in obvious decline. New power centers—the Austrian, Russian, and Prussian monarchies—were rising. But in 1689 they were far inferior to France and England in strength, wealth, and cultural vitality. In short, the religious wars accelerated the political disintegration of central and eastern Europe at the very time when the Atlantic states were consolidating their sovereign national power.

THE HOLY ROMAN EMPIRE, 1555–1618

When Charles V divided his Habsburg empire in 1556 between his son Philip and his brother Ferdinand, he arranged Ferdinand's election as Holy Roman emperor and gave him the family lands (known collectively as the

Austrian Habsburg lands) within the southern and eastern borders of the empire: the Tyrol, Carinthia, Carniola, Styria, Austria, Bohemia, Moravia and Silesia, as well as Hungary and other territories beyond the eastern imperial border. Theoretically, Emperor Ferdinand was a very strong prince. His was an empire with a population of twenty-five million, three times the population of Philip II's Spain. Actually, his power was severely limited. The Holy Roman Empire was divided into three hundred autonomous political units, of which at least three dozen had some importance. The real rulers of Germany were the local princes. During the late sixteenth century the Habsburg emperors were only nominally in charge of the Holy Roman Empire. They were only barely able to govern their own family lands and played a far more passive role in international politics than did their Spanish cousins. However, they were spared the religious warfare which engulfed western Europe; the Religious Peace of Augsburg, which Ferdinand negotiated with the German princes in 1555, preserved an uneasy truce between German Protestants and Catholics until 1618. Peace allegedly breeds prosperity, but the late sixteenth century was a period of stagnation not only for the German Habsburgs but for their subjects within the Holy Roman Empire.

The Peace of Augsburg confirmed the sovereign authority of the local princes within the empire, its guiding principle being *cuius regio, eius religio* ("he who rules a territory determines its religion"). Catholic princes were permitted to impose Catholicism upon all their subjects, and Lutheran princes to impose Lutheranism. This recognition of territorial churches within the empire was a religious compromise, but not a political one. The German princes, Catholic and Lutheran, had in effect ganged up against the Habsburgs. They had observed, correctly enough, that Charles V had been trying not only to crush Protestantism but to increase Habsburg power and check the centrifugal tendencies within the empire. They had noticed how he confiscated Lutheran princely territory much more readily than he enlarged Catholic princely territory, and how he showed real favor only to members of his own family. The princes, both Lutheran and Catholic, had also been trying to turn the Reformation crisis to their personal advantage, by asserting new authority over their local churches, tightening ecclesiastical patronage, and squeezing more profit from church revenues. In 1552–1553 the Lutheran princes, allied with Henry II of France, had beaten the imperial forces while the Catholic princes stood by, neutral. The Habsburgs were forced to accept the Peace of Augsburg, which effectively squelched any hopes for a German state with a single religion and administration.

As a device for pacifying Protestant-Catholic strife, the Peace of Augsburg was closer in spirit to Henry IV's Edict of Nantes in France than to Elizabeth I's religious settlement in Egland. The Augsburg negotiators refused to let Catholics and Lutherans live together, except in those German cities where the population already included members of both groups. The sharp delineation of the two competing confessions was in strong contrast to the deliberately amorphous character of the Anglican establishment. Calvinists, Zwinglians, and Anabaptists were not recognized, though a good many Germans belonged to these churches. In 1555, a large majority of the German population was Protestant, but the ruling Habsburg dynasty and four of the seven electors who chose each new emperor were Catholic. The old religion was largely confined to the western German Rhineland and to such south German states as Bavaria. Protestants controlled almost all of northern and central Germany, and Württemberg, Ansbach, and the Palatinate in the south. Even within the Habsburg family lands, Protestantism was very strong. Most Bohemians and Moravians were Protestants, as were the nobility and burghers in Austria. How long this precarious Protestant-Catholic balance would last depended very much on the princes. The German peasantry and urban working class, scarred by memories of the debacle of the peasants' revolt in 1524–1526, were inclined to follow orders

THE HABSBURGS, 1556–1700

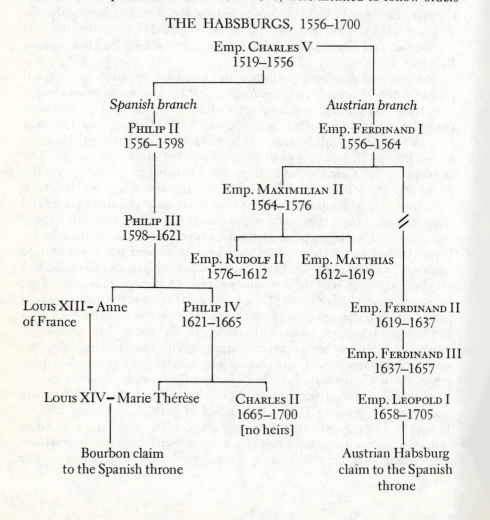

inertly on the religious issue, and switch from Lutheran to Catholic, or vice versa, as their masters required.

The emperors Ferdinand I (ruled 1556–1564), Maximilian II (ruled 1564–1576), Rudolf II (ruled 1576–1612), and Matthias (ruled 1612–1619) were all far less energetic men than Charles V or Philip II. Their highest aim was to hold off the Turks in Hungary and to administer their family holdings along the Danube. These Austrian Habsburg territories look compactly organized on the map, but they were split into a dozen distinct governments, and incorporated almost as many language groups. The greatest source of internal friction was religion. During the late sixteenth century, the Habsburg emperors' treatment of the Protestants within their Danubian lands was very gingerly compared with Philip II's treatment of his Protestant subjects in the Netherlands. Only Rudolf II made much effort to enforce the Augsburg formula: in the Tyrol, Carinthia, Carniola, and Styria, he managed to convert or deport practically all the Protestants. Some ten thousand emigrants fled from these provinces between 1598 and 1605. In Austria the task was more difficult, because the nobility and townspeople were mainly Protestant. To enforce the Trentine reform decrees, Rudolf II appointed a Jesuit bishop of Vienna and expelled all Protestant preachers from the city. He could not cow the Protestant nobility and burghers, however, nor the Austrian diet or assembly. The Austrian Protestants lost some strength, but in 1609 the diet extracted a pledge guaranteeing considerable liberty of worship.

In Bohemia, the Habsburgs faced even stronger opposition. The kingdom of Bohemia was the most populous, prosperous, and cultivated possession of the Austrian Habsburgs, and like the Netherlands for the Spanish Habsburgs, the most troublesome. The Czech people were proudly Slav and overwhelmingly Protestant. They boasted two entrenched native strains of evangelical Protestantism, the Utraquists (analogous to Lutherans) and the Bohemian Brethren (somewhat analogous to Calvinists), both stemming back to the Hussite movement of the early fifteenth century and hence quite separate from the sixteenth-century Reformation. For two hundred years the Czechs had stubbornly maintained their independence from Catholic orthodoxy and German culture. Rudolf II was hardly the man to bring them into line. Melancholic and unbalanced, the king-emperor sequestered himself in the Hradschin castle in Prague, enveloped by his art collection, dabbling in science and magic. Intermittently, he tried to restore Catholicism in Bohemia by appointing Catholic officials, encouraging Jesuit missionary work among the Utraquists, and issuing edicts against the Brethren. But in 1609 the Bohemian diet rose up in rebellion. In order to conciliate the rebels, Rudolf granted his Letter of Majesty, the fullest guarantee of religious freedom to be found anywhere on the continent. Obviously the Habsburgs had not yet accomplished much in Bohemia.

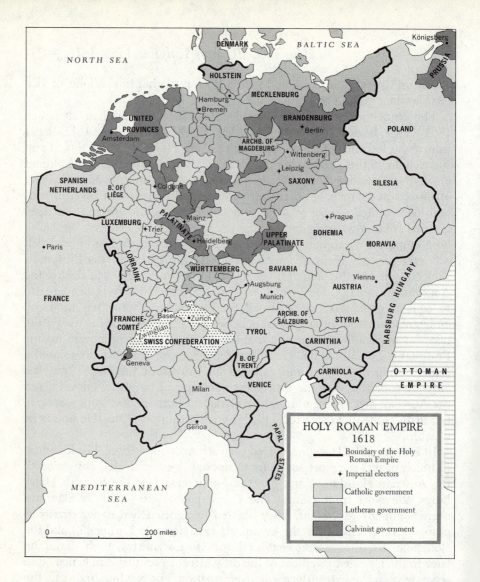

NORTH SEA

BALTIC SEA

DENMARK

Königsberg

PRUSSIA

HOLSTEIN

MECKLENBURG

Hamburg
Bremen

BRANDENBURG

Berlin

POLAND

UNITED
PROVINCES

Amsterdam

ARCHB. OF
MAGDEBURG

Wittenberg

SPANISH
NETHERLANDS

B. OF
LIÈGE

Cologne

Leipzig

SAXONY

SILESIA

Mainz

Prague

LUXEMBURG

Trier

PALATINATE

Heidelberg

UPPER
PALATINATE

BOHEMIA

MORAVIA

Paris

WÜRTTEMBERG

BAVARIA

Augsburg

Munich

Vienna

AUSTRIA

HABSBURG HUNGARY

LORRAINE

FRANCE

FRANCHE-
COMTÉ

Basel

Zwinglian

Zurich

SWISS CONFEDERATION

Geneva

ARCHB. OF
SALZBURG

STYRIA

TYROL

CARINTHIA

B. OF
TRENT

CARNIOLA

OTTOMAN

EMPIRE

VENICE

Milan

Genoa

PAPAL STATES

MEDITERRANEAN
SEA

HOLY ROMAN EMPIRE
1618

───── Boundary of the Holy
Roman Empire

＋ Imperial electors

Catholic government

Lutheran government

Calvinist government

0   200 miles

In the German heart of the Holy Roman Empire, the late sixteenth century was a time of prolonged economic depression. The Hanseatic League of north German cities, which had once dominated commerce in the Baltic and North seas, was quite unable to compete against Dutch, Danish, and English merchants. The old overland route to Italy had lost its central importance. In southwestern Germany, where the cities had been especially wealthy and enterprising in the fifteenth and early sixteenth centuries, political fragmentation was most extreme, and the economy suffered as a result. Each prince, striving for sovereign power within his petty state, levied taxes and tolls which clogged commerce and reduced manufacturing output. The Fuggers of Augsburg, the leading bankers in Europe in the mid-sixteenth century, with control of Tyrolese silver and Hungarian copper production, overstrained themselves with loans to the Habsburgs toward the end of the century, and their business empire rapidly fell apart. As the Fuggers and the other leading German entrepreneurs lost their wealth and the German cities declined in population, the princes dominated the scene more than ever.

The princes, both Protestant and Catholic, were growing dissatisfied with the religious truce they had worked out in 1555. One source of trouble was Calvinist expansion. In 1559 Elector Frederick III of the Palatinate (1515–1576) had introduced a modified version of Calvin's church organization into his central Rhineland territory. The elector's fellow princes, Catholic and Lutheran, vainly protested this clear violation of the Augsburg treaty. Heidelberg, the Palatine capital, became the Geneva of Germany. Scholars at the university formulated the Heidelberg Catechism in 1563 as a creed for the German Reformed (or Calvinist) churches. Within a generation the princes of Nassau, Hesse, and Anhalt had swung their central German states from Lutheranism to the German Reformed church. In 1613 the elector of Brandenburg announced his conversion also, though he abandoned the *cuius regio, eius religio* formula of Augsburg by letting his Lutheran subjects retain their religion. Two of the three Protestant imperial electors were now Calvinists; only the elector of Saxony remained Lutheran.

The German Reformed princes acted more aggressively than their Lutheran colleagues, because they were not included in the Lutheran-Catholic compromise of 1555. Frederick III and his Palatine successors assumed leadership of the Protestant cause within the empire, and finding the other German Protestant princes to be torpid or hostile, looked abroad to the French Huguenots and Dutch Calvinists for help in times of crisis. Yet the German Reformed church lacked dynamism. Unlike the Calvinism of western Europe it was not a spontaneous force among German merchants and gentry; it depended upon princely sponsors and was state controlled. Its growth was strictly limited. Although it made inroads into Lutheranism, it had little impact among Catholics, and it could not by itself re-ignite religious warfare.

A second, and more important, source of rising tension was the spread of the Catholic reformation within the empire. The south German state of Bavaria became the nucleus of renewed Catholic zeal and political power. Duke Albert V of Bavaria (ruled 1550–1579) enthusiastically enforced the reform decrees of the Council of Trent. He stamped out all traces of Protestant heresy by having his ecclesiastical agents inspect every Bavarian church annually, revamp the schools systematically, and censor all books. Jesuits were invited to take charge of the Bavarian schools and universities, and the duke's subjects were forbidden to study abroad. The new style of dogmatic Catholicism facilitated political autocracy in Bavaria. When Protes-

St. Michaelskirche, Munich. *The architect has boldly employed Renaissance statuary, arches, columns, and entablatures to achieve a vigorous yet balanced ensemble. This is the Mannerist style, prefiguring the Baroque. In the right rear is seen one of the Gothic Frauenkirche's capped towers.*

tant nobles and burghers tried to protest, Albert excluded them from the Bavarian diet, thereby effectively emasculating that assembly. By the close of the sixteenth century, the duke of Bavaria was governing in a more absolute fashion than any other German prince.

Elsewhere in Germany, the Catholics began to win back converts. Between 1580 and 1610, Protestants were driven out of a whole series of cities, among them Cologne, Aachen, Strasbourg, Würzberg, Bamberg, Münster, Paderborn, and Osnabrück. Everywhere, the Jesuits were in the forefront of the campaign. They established schools and universities in key German cities and made a specialty of educating young Catholic princes. Peter Canisius (1521–1597) is the best known of these sixteenth-century German Jesuit missionaries. The striking Jesuit Michaelskirche (Church of St. Michael) in Munich, built by the dukes of Bavaria, is a symbol of the Catholic reformation. This church was erected in the 1580's, when St. Peter's was nearing completion in Rome, and it introduced to Germany the sumptuous classical architecture of the reformed papacy. The Munich tourist today need only visit two churches a block apart, built a century apart—the fifteenth-century Frauenkirche (Church of Our Lady) and the sixteenth-century Michaelskirche—to catch the immense psychological distance between pre- and post-reformation German Catholicism. The Gothic Frauenkirche rises in awkward vertical bulk, austere and homely, her round capped towers reflecting the native Bavarian style, and her soaring nave expressing a questing spirit. By contrast, the Michaelskirche is international in style, harmonious in scale and proportion, and lavishly decorated to proclaim the certitude, symmetry, and power of the new Church Militant.

By 1609 all signs pointed to the end of the Augsburg truce. The imperial Diet, the one vestige of collective German government, collapsed in 1608 when the Protestant representatives boycotted its proceedings. In 1609 the most aggressive German Protestant states formed a Protestant Union for self-defense, headed by the Elector Palatine, whereupon the most aggressive Catholic states immediately formed a rival Catholic League, headed by the duke of Bavaria. Yet it must be emphasized that the German princes in their two armed camps still dreaded Armageddon. The Protestant Union was ineffectual because the Lutheran elector of Saxony would not ally himself with the Calvinist Elector Palatine. Nor was the Catholic League much stronger, thanks to hostility between the Austrian Habsburgs and the Bavarian Wittelsbachs. Both sides had pretext for war in 1609 when two Rhenish principalities, Jülich and Cleve, were contested by rival Protestant and Catholic claimants. Eventually, in 1614, a compromise was worked out by which Jülich went to the Catholic claimant and Cleve to the Protestant. But when the next crisis came in Bohemia in 1618, it could not be patched up.

The problems of these years become easier to visualize if we think of the Holy Roman Empire as being something like the mid-twentieth-century world in microcosm. The inhabitants of the empire were culture-bound to their own cities or provinces as modern man is culture-bound to his own nation. People refused to admit, then as now, that their fate depended upon cooperation with strangers who spoke and thought differently, but lived uncomfortably close by. Politicians waged ideological cold war, their motivation ostensibly religious instead of political or economic. Protestant and Catholic imperial states formed alliance systems to maintain the balance of power. Whenever a Lutheran prince converted to Catholicism or vice versa, diplomacy was required to keep the conflict local. When delegates from the various states convened in the imperial Diet, the only institution effectively embracing their whole community, they raised issues without attempting to solve them, just as the members of the United Nations do today. Gradually even this meager spirit of imperial community disappeared. The cold war grew inexorably warmer. Leaders on both sides, sick of the stalemate, began supposing that they could solve issues simply by unilateral action. And when they did take unilateral action, in 1618, they plunged the empire into thirty years of civil war.

EASTERN BORDERLANDS:

THE OTTOMAN EMPIRE, POLAND, RUSSIA, AND SWEDEN

To the east of the Holy Roman Empire, in the late sixteenth century, three extremely large states filled the map—the Ottoman Empire, Poland, and Russia. North of the Baltic Sea lay the extensive kingdom of Sweden. These states, particularly the Ottoman Empire and Muscovite Russia, seemed profoundly alien to western and central Europeans. Travelers found the Turks and Russians almost as barbaric and exotic as the Indians of America, and infinitely more dangerous because of their large armies, equipped with modern weapons. English merchants, venturing to trade with the Turks and Russians in the late sixteenth century, wrote home to describe the amazing Mohammedan and Greek Orthodox religious practices they had witnessed, the bizarre architecture, food, and dress, the stark contrast between an opulent ruling caste and an impoverished peasantry, the vast extent of these eastern lands and the herculean scale of their armies. "We arrived at the great and most stately city of Constantinople," one traveler reported, "which for the situation and proud seat thereof, for the beautiful and commodious haven, for the great and sumptuous buildings of their Temples, which they call Mosques, is to be preferred before all the cities of Europe. And there the Emperor of the Turks kept his Court and residence, at least two miles in compass." Yet no westerner forgot that the Turks were infidels. Their lavish

St. Basil's Cathedral, Moscow. *This remarkable stone church, built in the sixteenth century, with its strong colors and dizzying decorations capped by nine onion domes, is completely removed in spirit from contemporary western European Renaissance architecture.*

oriental ceremonies seemed tedious and empty. Their eunuchs and seraglios evoked incredulous contempt. Turkish warriors had an unrivaled reputation for cruelty and deceit.

As for Muscovy, the few westerners who penetrated into this land told tales of a climate too extreme for civilized man to endure. In the sub-zero Russian winter, "you shall see many drop down in the streets, many travelers brought into the towns sitting stiff and dead in their sleds. The bears and wolves issue by troops out of the woods driven by hunger, and enter the villages, tearing and ravening all they can find." The Russians, it was said, besot themselves with kvass and mead. They had strange smoky complexions because they took too many steam baths. Their primitive wooden buildings were constantly burning down. When the invading Tartars set fire to Moscow in 1571, they largely wiped out Russia's chief city within four hours. The Muscovite tsar, for all his jewels and ornate skirted garments and his giant feasts on plates of gold, seemed semicivilized at best. An English poet who visited Moscow in 1568 summed up in jogging verse the westerner's easy disdain for these eastern borderlands of European civilization:

> The cold is rare, the people rude, the prince so full of pride,
> The realm so stored with monks and nuns, and priests on every side,
> The manners are so Turkey like, the men so full of guile,
> The women wanton, Temples stuft with idols that defile
> The seats that sacred ought to be, the customs are so quaint,
> As if I would describe the whole, I fear my pen would faint.
> Wild Irish are as civil as the Russies in their kind,
> Hard choice which is the best of both, each bloody, rude and blind.

Fortunately for the west, the Turks, Poles, and Russians were all politically weak in the late sixteenth and early seventeenth centuries. Size was deceptive in these sprawling eastern states. The Turkish sultan, the Polish king, and the Muscovite tsar were all less effectual rulers than western observers supposed. Their armies were much smaller than westerners thought them to be, and in any case generally faced east in order to cope with the Persians and Tartars. Hence, despite the near paralysis of the Holy Roman Empire, its eastern neighbors did not intervene effectively in German affairs between 1555 and 1618. Nor (except for Sweden) did they participate in the Thirty Years' War. How is this uniform political softness in eastern Europe to be explained?

The Ottoman Empire

The Ottoman Empire had been anything but soft before the middle of the sixteenth century. Suleiman the Magnificent (ruled 1520–1566), the last of the great Turkish warrior sultans, held the whole Balkan peninsula and most of Hungary. He had thirty million subjects, a revenue greater than that of Charles V, and a much more efficient military system, including a permanent standing army of over ten thousand infantry (janissaries), over ten thousand cavalry (spahis), and at least a hundred thousand auxiliary cavalry available for annual campaigns. The janissaries were Moslem converts, mainly drawn from the conquered Greek Orthodox peoples of the Balkans. Taken captive as boys by the sultan's forces, they were rigorously trained to fight for Islam and to administer the Ottoman Empire. They formed an enslaved elite, permanently dependent on the sultan, given a professional schooling, never allowed to marry or to inherit lands and titles, yet freely promoted on the basis of talent and merit to the highest imperial posts. They made superb soldiers.

After the death of Suleiman the Magnificent, the Turkish fighting machine lost much of its fearsome power and its expansive drive. In 1571 the Spanish Habsburgs smashed the Turkish fleet at Lepanto. In the 1590's the Austrian Habsburgs tried to capture Hungary and Transylvania, and did keep the Ottoman armies mostly on the defensive, though the peace terms of 1606 left the Balkan frontier unchanged. Ottoman passivity gave the Habsburgs freedom to concentrate on German affairs after 1618, and when the Thirty Years' War went badly for the Habsburgs, the Turks failed to capitalize on a golden opportunity for further western expansion.

The key to Turkish success had always been strong military leadership by the sultan. After Suleiman came a long line of feckless sultans who abandoned Mars for Venus. They ceased to conduct military campaigns, ceased even to emerge from the Constantinople harem. Back in the days of tough, ruthless leadership, each new Ottoman sultan had stabilized his accession by killing his younger brothers (they were strangled with a silken bowstring so as not to shed exalted blood). Now, with the sultans' amorous proclivities resulting in numerous progeny, this custom was turning the seraglio into a slaughterhouse. In 1595 the new sultan had forty-six brothers and sisters, and he thought it necessary to strangle his nineteen brothers and fifteen pregnant harem women. In the seventeenth century this systematic fratricide was stopped, but by then the sultan himself had become a puppet, frequently deposed in palace revolutions. With no new lands to conquer and little war booty to enjoy, the Turkish soldiery became preoccupied with status and intrigue. The janissaries changed radically, becoming in the seventeenth century a closed, self-perpetuating caste. They now married, passed their jobs on to their sons, agitated for new perquisites, and engineered palace coups. As the economy stagnated and tax levies dwindled, bribery and corruption greatly increased.

In the 1650's, a drastic administrative shake-up in Constantinople temporarily revived the old militancy and efficiency. In the 1660's the Turks captured the island of Crete from Venice. They tightened their grip over Hungary and resumed their drive up the Danube into Austria. In 1683 they laid siege to Vienna. But in the closing decades of the seventeenth century, Ottoman expansion was once again stopped, this time decisively. The Turks were forced to surrender Hungary in 1699, and their huge empire began to shrink. This shrinkage continued for nearly 250 years. In the early nineteenth century the Turks still held half of Suleiman's European territory and all of his North African and Near Eastern possessions. The First World War marked the final stage: the Turks were confined at last to Anatolia, and the Ottoman Empire was dissolved. Seldom, if ever, has a decaying state disintegrated so slowly. In the seventeenth century, the Ottoman Empire had by no means yet become the Sick Man of Europe. Buttressed by total intellectual isolation from the new currents in European culture, the Turks still retained their profound contempt for the West. "Do I not know," the grand vizier told the French ambassador in 1666, "that you are a Giaour [nonbeliever], that you are a hog, a dog, a turd eater?"

Ottoman Europe—that is, the Balkan peninsula—was something of a cultural no-man's-land in the sixteenth and seventeenth centuries: only superficially Turkish, cut off from Latin Christendom, and with a very rudimentary native peasant style of life. The Turks had wiped out the native ruling class when they conquered the Balkans, but they never migrated into the area in large numbers, nor did they try to assimilate the local peasantry, which they preferred to keep as permanently unprivileged agricultural laborers. From the Turkish viewpoint, the Balkan peasants were fairly easy to subjugate as long as they remained divided into six rival language groups: Greeks, Albanians, Bulgarians, Serbo-Croatians, Rumanians, and Magyars. Instead of imposing Mohammedanism upon the subject peoples, the Turks encouraged the perpetuation of the Greek Orthodox Church, largely to keep the Balkan population hostile to western Christianity. This Ottoman policy did indeed effectively curb Balkan defection to the Catholic Habsburgs or Poles. The Orthodox patriarch in Constantinople repaid his Turkish patrons by teaching his people to submit docilely to Ottoman rule. Certainly the Ottoman Empire was more tolerant of all sorts of alien cultures and customs than any contemporaneous state in western Europe. French, English, and Dutch merchants were granted their own trading enclaves in Turkey, governed by western law. Jews flocked from Spain to enjoy Turkish freedom. The few towns in the Balkans were inhabited mainly by Turks and Jews; minarets and bazaars gave these towns an oriental atmosphere. In the Balkan countryside, the Christian peasants were confined to the lowest rung of the Ottoman social ladder; illiterate, ignorant, and silent, they paid extortionate taxes and tributes. In the sixteenth century their young sons were frequently levied as janissaries, and in the seventeenth century their farms were often pillaged by brigands. Even so, they probably fared no worse than any other peasants in eastern Europe.

Poland

North of the Ottoman Empire and east of the Holy Roman Empire lay the extensive kingdom of Poland, stretching from the Oder to the Dnieper River and from the Baltic almost to the Black Sea. Poland had no natural frontiers except for the Baltic coast to the north and the Carpathian Mountains to the south. Its six million widely scattered inhabitants raised grain and cattle. In the eastern part of the kingdom agricultural development was hindered by the attacks of wild Cossack raiders and by vast sketches of marshland. Cracow and Danzig, both on the western border, were the two chief towns. Poland did possess considerable human and natural resources, yet in the sixteenth and seventeenth centuries it played only a feeble international role, and in the eighteenth century the Polish state completely disappeared. There were ethnic and religious reasons for Poland's failure, but by far the biggest problem was political disorganization.

The dominant Polish social class was the *szlachta*, the landed gentry. Its members—like twelfth-century feudal knights in the west—were absolute masters of their rural domains; they forced the peasantry into serfdom, extracted unpaid labor from the serfs, disdained the burghers who huddled behind the town walls, and frustrated every effort by the Polish kings to consolidate power. The *szlachta* formed a numerous class—8 percent of the total population. A typical sixteenth-century Polish landlord owned a village near the Vistula River. His serfs labored two or three days a week in his wheat fields and loaded the harvested grain into barges to be shipped to Danzig for export west. He tried and punished his serfs in his own court, without fear of appeal to the king, for the *szlachta* had virtual immunity from arrest and trial. The landlord paid few taxes, saw occasional military service, sat in the local *seym*, or diet, sent delegates to the national Diet, and helped to elect the king. Poland was called a royal republic because the gentry voted their king into office and handcuffed him with constitutional limitations. It is said that fifty thousand *szlachta* assembled at Warsaw in 1573 to elect as king the French prince Henry of Valois—this was an unusually bad choice, and the Poles were lucky that he skipped the country after six months in order to take the French throne as Henry III (see p. 27). The Polish gentry were so suspicious of dynastic power that they almost always elected foreigners. Between 1548 and 1668 the winning candidates were Lithuanian, French, Hungarian, and Swedish. These kings lacked the royal lands, budget, army, and bureaucracy of western monarchs. The Polish serfs had less individual freedom than the Balkan peasantry under Turkish rule. When romantic Polish historians talk of their country's sixteenth-century "gentry democracy," one should remember that they are using a pretty special definition of democracy.

Like other eastern European states, Poland was ethnically divided, a situation which compounded its political difficulties. Poles occupied the west,

Lithuanians the northeast, White Russians the east, and Ruthenians the south, and Germans and Jews congregated in the towns. Of all these peoples, only Poles and Lithuanians were admitted to the ruling landlord class. Since 1386, the members of the Lithuanian nobility had shared a common king with the Polish gentry but in most ways had run their own affairs. In 1569 the Lithuanian nobility became so frightened by Tsar Ivan the Terrible of Russia that they surrendered their autonomy and in the Union of Lublin merged with the Polish ruling caste. Henceforth the Polish-Lithuanian landlords had a single king, a single Diet (meeting at Warsaw, near the Polish-Lithuanian border), and a single foreign policy. But the union was always superficial, for the Lithuanians continued to manage their White Russian peasants in their own fashion and kept their own laws and language. Indeed, each ethnic group had its own language. Since the *szlachta* sneered at the Polish dialect spoken by their serfs, they adopted Latin as the religious, political, and literary language of the ruling class. The *szlachta* sneered also at the German-speaking townspeople, who were excluded from the Diet and from political power. The Yiddish-speaking Jewish community was despised by everyone.

The Christians in Poland were doubly divided in the mid-sixteenth century. The people were predominantly Latin Christians, except in the south and east, where they were largely Greek Orthodox; this division was only papered over in 1596, when the Ruthenian Orthodox church agreed to obey the pope and accept the Roman dogma while retaining its Slavonic rites and practices. The second religious division was among Latin Christians—Catholic versus Protestant. In the 1550's, Polish Catholics found themselves in a very precarious majority, for about half the *szlachta* were Calvinist, and the German burghers were largely Lutheran. Even Unitarian, or anti-Trinitarian, ideas were circulating, possibly inspired by contact with Jewish and Moslem teachings. In 1555 King Sigismund Augustus (ruled 1548–1572) and the Polish Diet agreed to allow individual freedom of worship to Protestants. The heresy-hunting power of Catholic church courts was suspended. More than the contemporaneous Augsburg formula in Germany, this Polish policy weakened ecclesiastical discipline and sapped what little cultural unity there was. But the Protestant Reformation was not well rooted in Poland. The *szlachta* had adopted Calvinism as a weapon against centralized monarchy, and once assured of political victory, they lost interest in the new doctrine. During the late sixteenth century the Catholics—their efforts spearheaded by Jesuit upper-class missionary work—regained control. Numerous Jesuit schools were opened for the sons of the gentry. By the mid-seventeenth century, with Catholicism securely reestablished, education stagnated even for the upper class. Proud and touchy, the Polish gentry cultivated long mustachios and oriental sashed costumes as their badge of immunity from Italian or French standards of civility. Poland in the seventeenth century became almost as isolated as Ottoman Turkey from the intellectual currents of western Europe.

Between 1559 and 1689, Poland faced east and north rather than west in all its wars and diplomacy. It fought the Turks intermittently without permanently winning or losing any territory. It fought the Swedes constantly and generally got beaten. In 1629 it ceded the province of Livonia to Sweden, and had to accept Swedish control of the Baltic. Poland's most menacing neighbor was Russia, and the Poles were lucky that internal Muscovite turmoil in the late sixteenth and early seventeenth centuries delayed effective Russian westward expansion. In 1667 Poland ceded Smolensk, Kiev, and the eastern Ukraine to Russia.

These sizable territorial losses were less alarming than Poland's rising political anarchy, which paralyzed the state and invited further foreign encroachment. The gentry were so suspicious of centralized royal power that in the Diet legislation could not pass without the unanimous consent of the *szlachta* deputies. In the sixteenth century the majority of deputies could generally persuade or coerce the minority into accepting a policy. But in 1652, for the first time, an individual deputy declared his total opposition, his *liberum veto* against the legislative proceedings, and left the chamber— forcing the Diet to disband. Henceforth, 90 percent of the Polish Diets were "exploded" in this way, by use of the individual *liberum veto*. It became possible for the French, Prussians, or other foreign powers, by bribing refractory members of the gentry, to veto Polish tax laws or stymie Polish military preparations. To many observers, Poland's "gentry democracy" proved the folly of constitutional self-government and the necessity for absolute monarchy. To the Russians, Prussians, and Austrians, Poland's governmental paralysis offered an excellent excuse for partitioning the state in the eighteenth century.

Russia

East of Poland lay the vast tsardom of Muscovy, or Russia. In the sixteenth and seventeenth centuries it was an open question whether Russia was part of European civilization, for in scale and temper, life there differed profoundly from life in the rest of Europe. To begin with, the country was gigantic. In 1533, when Ivan the Terrible inherited the throne, Muscovy stretched 1,200 miles, from Smolensk to the Ural Mountains, and covered five times the area of France. Ivan nearly doubled his European holdings by annexing the Don and Volga river basins to the south, and launched the Russian eastward trek across the Urals into Siberia. By the time Peter the Great took power in 1689, the Russians had annexed further European land along the Dnieper and Ural rivers, and their Asian settlements were strung along the Siberian river system for five thousand miles, right to the Pacific. Russia then covered thirty times the area of France.

The climate throughout this continental sweep of territory was savage by European standards, with arctic winters, blazing summers, and a short growing season. Population estimates for sixteenth- and seventeenth-century Russia are pure guesswork, but whether one accepts the lowest, four million inhabitants, or the highest, seventeen million, it is evident that settlement was far less dense than in western and central Europe. The huge reservoir of empty land encouraged hit-and-run agricultural techniques. The peasants were extremely mobile, sometimes voluntarily migrating long distances to find better land and working conditions, sometimes forcibly transported by their landlords or the tsar. In contrast with western Europe, where people habitually tilled the same ancestral land, lived in the same village, and even occupied the same buildings for centuries, no human enterprise seemed lasting in Russia. The average wooden peasant's hut was built to last four years. An English traveler between Yaroslavl and Moscow in 1553 was impressed by the numerous villages he passed through; thirty-five years later another English visitor found the same region deserted and gone back to forest. Tartar raiders periodically swept into Muscovy from the Crimea, as Viking, Saracen, and Magyar raiders had pillaged western and central Europe in the ninth century. The Tartars carried hundreds of thousands of Russians off into slavery. Belief in the individual dignity of man—fragile enough in the sixteenth-century west—was an unobtainable luxury for Moscovites. Tsars, nobles, priests, and peasants all accepted physical brutality—flogging and torture—as staple features of society.

Russia's contact with western Europe was minimal between 1559 and 1689. Blocked by Sweden from an outlet on the Baltic during most of these years, and by Turkey from an outlet on the Black Sea, Russia had only one port—Archangel, on the White Sea—from which to trade directly with western Europe. Its commerce with the Middle East was more important. Strange as it seems, western Europeans had built closer commercial and diplomatic contact with Russia in the eleventh and twelfth centuries than they did in the sixteenth and seventeenth centuries. The Muscovites found it far easier to spread eastward into empty Siberia than to reconquer from Poland the White Russian and Ukrainian lands which had once belonged to their ancestors. Not until the reign of Peter the Great did the Russians learn how to beat a crack European army.

Russia's most meaningful tie with the west was Christianity. Yet the Russian Orthodox clergy viewed Latin Christendom with the darkest suspicion. For centuries they had accepted as spiritual overlord the Greek Orthodox patriarch at Constantinople, and when Byzantium fell to the Ottomans, the Russian Orthodox naturally supposed that the metropolitan of Moscow had inherited the role of the patriarch of Constantinople as the leader of true Christianity. In 1588 the patriarch of Constantinople grudgingly accepted the metropolitan's elevation to patriarch of Moscow. The Russians called

Moscow the third Rome. They believed that Old Rome had fallen into heresy under the popes, and that New Rome (Constantinople) had become a pawn of the infidel Turks; Moscow was the third and greatest capital of the Christian world. Because of their hostility to the papacy, the Muscovites were better disposed toward Protestant merchants and diplomats from England, the Netherlands, Scandinavia, and Germany than toward Catholics. But the Russians wanted no Reformation in their own church, nor even any discussion over the smallest details of Orthodox belief and practice.

The Russians settled Tobolsk, beyond the Urals, in 1587, two years after Sir Walter Raleigh first tried to found an English plantation at Roanoke Island, North Carolina. The Russians reached the Pacific in 1643, a few years after the English Puritans had founded Massachusetts. It would be hard to find a stronger social contrast than that between the Russian folk movement across Eurasia and the contemporaneous English folk movement into North America. Both peoples held an enormous reservoir of empty land, but while the Americans methodically inched their way inland, taking nearly three centuries to span the continent, the Russians lightly spanned Siberia in two generations. Frontier America was a paradise for the self-reliant, egalitarian free farmer, disdainful of government, unencumbered by taxes. But in Russia, frontier expansion fostered the sharpest possible social stratification, and Europe's most autocratic, oppressive government. The members of the Muscovite nobility, who held great estates in European Russia, were determined not to let their agricultural laborers move off to free land in Siberia. So they introduced new regulations which tied the laborer and his descendants to his master's soil or (better yet) to his master's person—in short, turned the peasant into a serf, virtually indistinguishable from a slave. At the same time, the tsars were determined not to let their nobility carve up the land into autonomous feudal principalities, or perpetrate political anarchy in the fashion of the Polish *szlachta*. So they ruthlessly killed all aristocratic troublemakers, confiscated their large properties, and divided them into smaller parcels suitable for the *pomeshchik*, a loyal dependent employed in the royal army or administration. Since the members of this service nobility could not own land outright, but held it from the tsar only as long as they served him, they tended to squeeze the peasants hard in order to make short-run profits. Peasants ran away from *pomeshchik* estates with special frequency. By the seventeenth century, the landlords and the tsar had reached a tacit understanding. The landlords accepted the principle that they must serve the tsar, and in return the tsar agreed that the peasants—90 percent of the population—were legally defined as serfs, bound to their master and subject to his will.

Ivan IV (ruled 1533–1584), better known as Ivan the Terrible, was the principal author of the Muscovite formula: absolute power for the tsar, state service for the nobility, thralldom for the peasantry. Far less evidence has

Ivan the Terrible. *This old print presents evidence that the prince was well named, looking very different from a western ruler.*

survived about the details of Ivan's reign than about the reigns of his western contemporaries, Philip II and Elizabeth I, but we know enough to tell that his style of rule differed utterly from theirs. Ivan was the first Muscovite ruler to have himself crowned Tsar (that is, "Caesar") of All the Russians. He handled his subjects as a cat toys with a mouse. His behavior could be described as *mad* in a half dozen distinct senses—raging, frantic, foolish, visionary, giddy, lunatic. He decimated the *boyar* class, the hereditary Russian aristocracy, by killing hundreds, probably even thousands, of its members. He pitilessly sacked Novgorod, the second city in his realm, because of a rumor of disloyalty. His deep piety did not prevent him from flogging and torturing priests or killing his victims in church during Mass. He once had an archbishop sewn into a bearskin and tossed to the dogs. He struck his oldest son and heir so hard with a pointed stick that he killed him, and it is supposed that his melancholic brooding over this crime hastened his own demise. Most of the time there was method in Ivan's madness. His wholesale confiscation and redistribution of land was economically catastrophic, depopulating much of central Russia, but it broke the *boyar* power and bolstered that of the new service nobility. The more Ivan bullied the Russian Orthodox Church, the more the clergy preached abject reverence to God's lieutenant, the tsar. Uncivilized Ivan certainly was, but he magnetized the Russian landlords and peasants alike with his awesome God-given power. The tsar of Russia had far greater psychological appeal for the mass of the people than did the elected monarchs of Poland or the seraglio sultans of Turkey.

Ivan the Terrible's successor, Fedor (ruled 1584–1598), was mad in a less complicated way than his father; he was a simpleton who chiefly delighted in ringing church bells. Fedor's reign inaugurated Muscovy's "Time of Troubles," the period of aristocratic rebellion against tsarist autocracy, which lasted from 1584 to 1613. Among the tsars in this anarchic period was Boris Godunov (ruled 1598–1605), more famous thanks to Mussorgsky's opera than his statecraft deserves. During these years the Russian landlords tried to run the country as the *szlachta* ran Poland. A national assembly, the *zemsky sobor*, assumed the authority to choose each new tsar. Marauding armies, led by would-be tsars, ransacked the countryside. During the Time of Troubles, the church was the one institution which held Russia together. People gathered in the fortresslike monasteries for protection, and left their land and wealth to the church. Eventually, as we shall see, the clergy managed to restore political order.

In 1613, the *zemsky sobor* chose Michael Romanov (ruled 1613–1645) as the new tsar because he was a youthful mediocrity—dubious accreditation for the dynasty which would rule Russia for the next three hundred years. But this first Romanov had other assets. He was a grandnephew of Ivan the Terrible, and the son of an able priest-politician named Philaret, who became patriarch of Moscow soon after Michael ascended the throne. Philaret made himself the real ruler of Russia, and the patriarchs who succeeded him after his death in 1633 were equally ambitious for secular power. The church's obtrusive political role during this period distressed many Russian clergy and laity. A crisis developed during the patriarchate of Nikon (1652–1666), for Nikon not only ruled in the name of the tsar but claimed a theoretical supremacy over the tsar, since the spiritual realm is higher than the temporal. Nikon was deposed, and the tsars regained control over the Russian church. But Nikon's policies left a bitter legacy. In order to bring Russian Orthodoxy into closer conformity with Greek Orthodoxy, Nikon had introduced certain technical revisions in ecclesiastical practice, such as making the sign of the Cross with three fingers rather than two, and spelling Christ's name *Iisus* rather than *Isus*. Many Russians supposed that these innovations blasphemed God and imperiled their immortal souls. These people, styled the Old Believers, felt that Nikon had disastrously corrupted the third Rome. We are told that twenty thousand Old Believers burned themselves alive in despair at the impending end of the world.

The first Romanov tsars, those ruling between 1613 and 1689, were much less forceful monarchs than Ivan the Terrible. But they maintained the partnership with the church and they won the cooperation of the landlords. The *zemsky sobor* faded away, though not before it ratified the final codification of serfdom. The great problem now was how to stop the serfs from running away. A decree of 1664 required that any serf owner who was caught receiving a fugitive serf must compensate the master with four peasant families of his own. Tsar and landlord aided each other in taking away the peasant's freedom and in saddling him with taxes. The cost of warfare and of government-sponsored colonization fell squarely on the people least able to pay. It is estimated that the peasant tax rate in 1640 was a hundred times what it had been in 1540![1] This certainly helps to explain why Russia was the scene of the largest European folk rising of the century, the great peasant rebellion of 1667–1671 led by Stephen Razin in the Volga basin. A hundred thousand peasants may have died in their vain struggle for liberty. Such was the starkly stratified and deeply insular society on which Peter the Great forcibly imposed western technology and cultural mores in the years following 1689.

Sweden

West of Russia and north of Poland lay the kingdom of Sweden. Seventeenth-century Sweden was a Baltic empire, double its twentieth-century size; it incorporated modern Finland, Estonia, and Latvia, and extensive Russian, Polish, and German coastal land. Sweden held 2,500 miles of Baltic shoreline. Nonetheless, its resources were puny compared with those of Turkey, Poland, or Russia. Sweden's was a simple society of a million or so peasants, who subsisted on porridge, turnips, coarse bread, and home-brewed beer. Stockholm was the one town of any size; commerce was mainly conducted by foreigners; and specie was so scarce that wages, taxes, and debts were paid in kind. The king of Sweden was the only European monarch who found it necessary to build warehouses to store his revenue of butter, fish, and hops. Sweden had always been on Europe's cultural periphery: it boasted a medieval university, but the Renaissance had scarcely touched its shores. Swedish political structure was rudimentary by western standards. Yet Sweden was the only one of the borderland states to play a vigorous international hand in the years between 1559 and 1689.

Under the leadership of a young nobleman named Gustavus Vasa, Sweden had secured independence from Denmark in the early sixteenth century. Gustavus Vasa established himself as king of Sweden and ruled purposefully from 1523 to 1560. But his three sons, who reigned between 1560 and 1611, squabbled among themselves and alienated their subjects. When sixteen-year-old Gustavus Adolphus inherited the throne in 1611, Sweden was in acute crisis. It was at war with Denmark, and the war was going so poorly that the Danes appeared likely to reconquer the country.

Gustavus Adolphus (ruled 1611–1632) shaped Sweden almost overnight into a major power. He had some good material to work with. For one thing,

[1]Jerome Blum, *Lord and Peasant in Russia* (Princeton, N.J., 1961), pp. 229–230.

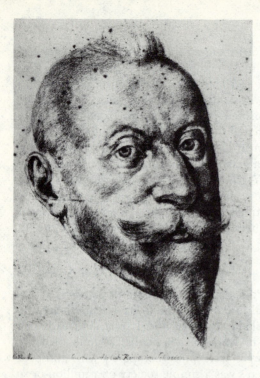

Gustavus Adolphus. *Pencil sketch by Strauch, drawn in the year of the Swedish king's death. Nationalmuseum, Stockholm.*

the Protestant Reformation had infused the early seventeenth-century Swedes with crusading ardor. As in England, the Swedish Reformation had begun in the 1520's and 1530's as a cynical maneuver to grab Church land and wealth, and only slowly did Luther's gospel cry stir the people. By the 1620's, however, Sweden's warfare with Catholic Poland and Orthodox Russia for control of the Baltic was having much the same galvanizing effect as Elizabethan England's warfare with Catholic Spain. Calvinism made small headway in Sweden; the country was solidly Lutheran. Gustavus Adolphus' clergy were more truculent than their brethren in Germany. The king's chaplain dared to reprove him publicly for his sexual laxity, whereupon Gustavus Adolphus (who deserved this reproof far less than most contemporary monarchs) gave the chaplain the next vacant bishopric—surely a commendable way to avoid hearing further sermons. Another Swedish asset was the sturdy independence of the peasant farmers. In Sweden, society was not polarized into a landlord master class and an enserfed peasantry, as in Turkey, Poland, and Russia. There were no serfs in Sweden. The peasants owned 50 per cent of the arable land. They had their own chamber in the *Riksdag*, or national assembly. The nobility were correspondingly less rich and privileged than in the great eastern European states. To be sure, they assumed political leadership, possessed large farms, hired tenant laborers, and exhibited family pride. But in style of life the

Swedish noblemen were none too distant from the peasants. From this comparatively undifferentiated, homespun, God-fearing society, Gustavus Adolphus drew a peerless army of self-reliant soldiers, militant chaplains, and officers eager to invade and plunder Sweden's wealthier neighbors.

Gustavus Adolphus is best known as a warrior, the Protestant hero in the Thirty Years' War. He began his reign by making peace with Denmark, but he soon took advantage of the internal weakess of his neighbors, wresting territory along the Gulf of Finland (the future site of St. Petersburg) from the Russians and Livonia (modern Latvia) from the Poles. The tolls he levied upon captured southern Baltic ports enabled him to finance further military operations without overtaxing the Swedish people. Swedish copper and iron mines supplied added revenue and metal for armaments. But Gustavus Adolphus was much else besides a soldier. He was easily the most creative administrator in Swedish history. Paunchy, jocose, explosive, this roughhewn Nordic figure with big blue eyes and blond Vandyke beard obviously bulged with manly energy, but he had deep reserves of religion and culture as well. He recruited the Swedish nobility, led by the extremely able Chancellor Axel Oxenstierna (1583–1654), into administrative service. He charmed the burghers and peasants in the *Riksdag*. He bolstered his doughty Lutheran clergy, and they in turn mixed patriotism with religion, performing such thankless civil jobs as collecting the local taxes. Ashamed of Sweden's backward school system, the king founded many new schools and reorganized the faltering University of Upsala.

Not being a magician, Gustavus Adolphus failed to transform Sweden into a lasting great power. When he led his army into Germany in 1630, to battle the Catholic Habsburgs, he committed his country to aims beyond its resources. After Gustavus Adolphus was killed in 1632, Chancellor Oxenstierna doggedly kept Sweden in the endless German war. Swedish armies won more often than they lost, and by peace treaties in 1645, 1648, and 1658 the Swedes gained considerable Danish and German territory. The late seventeenth century, however, saw a swift eclipse of Sweden's great-power status, and between 1700 and 1809 it lost the whole of its Baltic empire to Russia. Sweden's age of greatness was thus short—but decisive. To see how pivotal Gustavus Adolphus' Lutheran crusade was in the 1630's, let us return to the Holy Roman Empire and the international power struggle which devastated Germany.

THE THIRTY YEARS' WAR, 1618-1648

Other wars have lasted as long, have caused as much damage, and have settled as little. But the Thirty Years' War, which opened in Bohemia in 1618 and convulsed central Europe for a generation, had one peculiar feature. The chief combatants (after the first few years) were non-German, yet their combat took place almost entirely on German soil. The most populous provinces of the Holy Roman Empire became a playground for the invading armies of Spain, Denmark, Sweden, and France. How and why did the German people suffer this indignity?

In 1618, the Habsburg heir apparent to the imperial throne was Ferdinand of Styria (1578–1637), a cheerful, bustling little man of forty. Ferdinand was a rabid Catholic, educated and counseled by the Jesuits. He was frankly unwilling to tolerate Protestantism among his subjects. Clearly, this man was going to make a more energetic Holy Roman emperor than anyone since Charles V, but the Protestant imperial princes were none too alarmed. Not even the great Charles V had been able to exercise much power as emperor. Within the Austrian and Bohemian provinces held directly by the Habsburgs, however, the situation was different. Here Ferdinand did have real power. As soon as he was crowned king of Bohemia in 1617, he began to rescind the religious toleration guaranteed to the Bohemian Protestants by his cousin, Rudolf II, in 1609. The Bohemians were in much the same predicament as the Netherlanders had been in the 1560's—alienated from their autocratic Habsburg prince by language, custom, and religion. As in the Netherlands, the nobility engineered rebellion. On May 23, 1618, a hundred armed Bohemian noblemen cornered Ferdinand's two most hated Catholic advisers in the council room of the Hradschin castle, in Prague, and tossed them out the window into the castle ditch some fifty feet below. The victims survived the fall, perhaps (according to the Catholic view) because they were rescued in mid-flight by guardian angels, or perhaps (according to the Protestant view) because they landed on a dung heap. At any rate this "defenestration of Prague" put the rebels in charge of the Bohemian capital. Their announced aim was to preserve ancient Bohemian privileges and to rescue King Ferdinand from the wicked Jesuits. But they were really repudiating Habsburg rule.

The crisis quickly spread from Bohemia to the entire empire. The aged emperor, Matthias, died in 1619, giving the German Protestant princes a golden chance to join the rebellion against Habsburg rule. Seven electors had the exclusive right to choose Matthias' successor: the three Catholic archbishops of Mainz, Trier, and Cologne; the three Protestant princes of Saxony, Brandenburg, and the Palatinate; and the king of Bohemia. If the Protestant electors denied Ferdinand's right to vote as king of Bohemia, they could block his election as Holy Roman emperor. But only Elector Frederick V of the Palatinate (1596–1632) turned out to be willing to do this, and he backed down. On August 28, 1619, at Frankfurt, the electors unanimously cast their votes for Emperor Ferdinand II. A few hours after his election, Ferdinand learned that the Bohemian rebels in Prague had deposed him as their king and elected Frederick of the Palatinate in his place! Frederick accepted the Bohemian crown. A general war was now inevitable. Emperor Ferdinand prepared to crush his rebel subjects and to punish the German prince who had dared to usurp his hereditary Habsburg lands.

The Bohemian rebellion was poorly conceived from the start. The rebels sorely missed a folk hero equivalent to John Huss (*c.* 1369–1415) who had led the great Bohemian religious revolt two centuries before. The members of the Bohemian nobility did not trust one another. The Bohemian assembly hesitated to levy special taxes or build an army. Having no native candidate to replace Ferdinand, the rebels had turned to the German Calvinist Elector Palatine. But Frederick was a very poor choice. A simple young fellow of twenty-three, he had no feeling for the Slavic evangelical religion he was being asked to champion, nor could he supply men and money with which to fight the Habsburgs. The Bohemians counted on the other German princes to support King Frederick's cause, but very few did so. Frederick's foreign friends, such as his father-in-law, James I of England, also stayed neutral.

The rebels' best hope lay in the weakness of Ferdinand II. The emperor had no army of his own and little means of raising one; in the Austrian Habsburg lands, most of the nobility and the provincial estates were in league with the rebel Bohemians. But Ferdinand was able to buy the services of three allies. Maximilian (1573–1651), duke of Bavaria and the most powerful German Catholic prince, sent an army into Bohemia on the promise that the emperor would cede him Frederick's electoral dignity and some of his Palatine land. Philip III of Spain likewise sent his Habsburg cousin an army, in return for the promised cession of the remaining Palatine land. More surprising, the Lutheran elector of Saxony also helped reconquer Bohemia, his reward being the Habsburg province of Lusatia. The result of these shabby bargains was a quick military campaign (1620–1622) in which the rebels were utterly defeated. The Bavarian army easily routed the Bohemians at the Battle of White Mountain in 1620. From the Alps to the Oder, throughout the Habsburg lands, the rebels capitulated and were left to Ferdinand's tender mercies. The Bavarian and the Spanish armies next conquered the Palatinate. Foolish Frederick was dubbed the *Winterkönig* ("king of one winter"). By 1622, he had lost not merely his Bohemian crown but all his German territories as well.

The war did not end in 1622, though the original issues had now been resolved. One cause of continuing conflict was the emergence of private armies led by soldiers of fortune. Ernst von Mansfeld (1580–1626) was at first the most prominent of these mercenary captains. By birth a Belgian Catholic, Mansfeld had fought for the Spanish before turning Calvinist and selling his services to Frederick and the Bohemians. He subsequently switched sides several times, always working for the highest bidder. Since

Mansfeld supported his army by looting the towns and villages through which he passed, he preferred to keep moving into fresh territory. After Frederick's defeat in 1622, Mansfeld—a law unto himself, less bent on fighting than on plundering—took his army into northwestern Germany. Maximilian of Bavaria kept his army in the field against Mansfeld. His troops did not subdue the captain, but they harried the German Protestant civilian population of the area ruthlessly. Maximilian was doing well from the war: he had snatched much of Frederick's land, and his seat as an elector, and the emperor owed him large sums of money; so Maximilian was none too anxious for peace. Foreign Protestant princes, who had stayed neutral in 1618–1619, now started to intervene in imperial affairs. In 1625, King Christian IV of Denmark (ruled 1588–1648), whose province of Holstein was within the Holy Roman Empire, entered the war as protector of the Protestants in northern Germany. Christian was anxious to prevent a total Catholic conquest of the empire, but he also hoped to profit as Maximilian had done from the fluid situation. He was an abler leader than Frederick and had a better army, but he could find no German allies. The Protestant electors of Saxony and Brandenburg wanted the war to end, and they declined to join the Protestant cause. In 1626 Maximilian's veterans crushed Christian at the Battle of Lutter and drove him back into Denmark.

So far, Emperor Ferdinand II had gained the most from the war. The capitulation of the Bohemian rebels gave him a free hand to suppress Protestantism, redistribute land, and revamp the administration of his dynastic Habsburg possessions. The expulsion of Frederick permitted him to tinker with the imperial constitution: by shifting the Palatine electoral vote to Bavaria, Ferdinand obtained an unbreakable Catholic, pro-Habsburg majority. The spread of the war into northern Germany enabled him to eject additional rebel Protestant princes and to parcel out their territories among his family and friends. By 1626 Ferdinand envisioned what had been inconceivable in 1618, the transformation of the Holy Roman Empire into an absolute, sovereign, Catholic, Habsburg state.

Obviously, Ferdinand's war aims were not quite compatible with those of his ally Maximilian. The emperor needed a more pliant instrument than the Bavarian army. Yet he was deeply in debt to Maximilian and could not subsidize an army of his own. This situation explains his curious partnership with Albrecht von Wallenstein (1583–1634), a soldier of fortune par excellence. A Bohemian Protestant by birth, Wallenstein had sided with the Habsburgs during the Bohemian revolt, and built a fabulous private fortune in the process. Of all the leading participants in the Thirty Years' War, Wallenstein was the most enigmatic. A tall, baleful figure, he exhibited most of the unpleasant personality traits one expects in an impatient parvenu. He was unscrupulous, greedy, reckless, cruel, quarrelsome, and superstitious. A promoter on the grandest scale, Wallenstein evidently set no limits to his ambitions. All of his contemporaries feared and distrusted the man; it is impossible for a modern analyst to be sure just what he was up to. In 1625 he contracted to field an imperial army at his own expense and was authorized by Ferdinand to requisition food and shelter from the unfortunate districts he occupied. Wallenstein once asserted that he could maintain an army of fifty thousand more easily than an army of twenty thousand, because the larger force could more thoroughly squeeze the land off which it was living. For a while Wallenstein cooperated with the Bavarian general Tilly. But he preferred to campaign independently. He chased Mansfeld out of the empire, and occupied much of Denmark and much of the German Baltic coast. By 1628, he commanded 125,000 men. The emperor made him duke of Mecklenburg, one of the newly conquered Baltic provinces. Neutral princes, such as the elector of Brandenburg, were powerless to stop Wallenstein from occupying their territory. Even Maximilian, belatedly aware of the emperor's new power, pleaded with Ferdinand to dismiss his overmighty general.

By 1629, the emperor felt the time had come to issue his Edict of Restitution, perhaps his fullest expression of autocratic power. Ferdinand's edict outlawed Calvinism within the Holy Roman Empire, and required the Lutherans to disgorge all Church properties they had confiscated since 1552. Sixteen bishoprics, twenty-eight cities and towns, and over one hundred and fifty monasteries and convents scattered throughout northern and central Germany were ordered restored to Rome. Ferdinand acted unilaterally, without recourse to an imperial Diet. The Catholic princes felt almost as menaced as the Protestant princes by the Edict of Restitution, for the emperor was trampling their constitutional liberties and enhancing his centralized authority. Wallenstein's soldiers soon occupied the cities of Magdeburg, Halberstadt, Bremen, and Augsburg, which had been predominantly Protestant for many years, and forcibly converted them to Catholicism. There seemed to be no reason why, with the help of Wallenstein's army, Ferdinand could not soon abrogate the whole Augsburg formula of 1555 and transform the empire into a Catholic absolute monarchy.

It was at this crucial moment in 1630 that Gustavus Adolphus thrust his Swedish army into Germany. He announced that he was coming to protect German Protestantism and constitutional liberties from Ferdinand II's attacks, but he was also obviously looking for conquest and profit. The Swedish king suffered from the same handicap as the previous would-be Protestant champion, King Christian of Denmark: he was a foreigner without German allies. Luckily for Gustavus Adolphus, Ferdinand II played into his hands. Feeling securely in command of Germany, Ferdinand called upon the imperial Diet in 1630 to recognize his son as heir to the imperial throne and to help the Spanish Habsburgs against the Dutch and the French. The emperor's plans were recklessly ambitious, and he underesti-

Liff Ländter

Lapländter.

Schotländter.

Caricature of the Swedish army which invaded Germany in 1630. *Gustavus Adolphus'* soldiers are *represented as barbarians from Lapland, Livonia, and Scotland, bent on rape and plunder. The Livonian is mounted on a reindeer.*

mated the German princes' hostility toward him. The princes refused both of his requests, even after he tried to placate them by dismissing Wallenstein from command of the imperial army. All that Ferdinand had accomplished was to remove his best general. Meanwhile, Gustavus Adolphus had a second stroke of luck. The French government, headed by Cardinal Richelieu, agreed to subsidize his invasion of Germany. Obviously, the French cardinal had no interest in Gustavus Adolphus' Protestant crusade. Nonetheless, he agreed to pay the Swedes a million livres a year to maintain an army of thirty-six thousand in Germany, because he wanted to harass the Habsburgs, paralyze the empire, and stake out French claims to Rhenish territory. All that Gustavus Adolphus now needed was enough German support so that he could play the role of avenging hero. It was no easy task, but he finally badgered the electors of Brandenburg and Saxony into signing alliances with Sweden. Now he could take action.

In 1631 Gustavus Adolphus smashed the imperial army at Breitenfeld; this was probably the most decisive battle of the Thirty Years' War, for it wiped out at a stroke most of the Catholic gains of 1618–1629. During the next year he systematically occupied the heretofore unspoiled Catholic regions in central Germany. Bavaria was sacked with special thoroughness. The Swedish king prepared to invade Habsburg Austria and acted more and more as if he intended to usurp Ferdinand's place as Holy Roman emperor.

Gustavus Adolphus' intervention was pivotal because he saved German Protestantism and defeated Habsburg imperial centralization, but his personal triumph was very brief. In 1632 Wallenstein came out of retirement to fight him. Emperor Ferdinand had already begged his general to resume command of the imperial forces, and when Wallenstein finally took the field, his army was more than ever a personal instrument. On a dark, foggy November day in 1632 the two great commanders met at Lützen, in Saxony. Their armies locked savagely, blindly. Gustavus Adolphus galloped into the fog on a cavalry charge, and shortly his horse careered back, wounded and riderless. The Swedish troops, maddened at the loss of their king, drove Wallenstein's army from the battlefield. In the darkness and the mud they finally found Gustavus Adolphus' bullet-riddled corpse, stripped to the shirt by scavengers. "O," cried one of his grieving soldiers, "would to God I had such a leader again to fight such another day; in this old quarrel!"[2]

Old quarrel indeed, by 1632—and after Lützen a hopeless deadlock. None of the combatants was strong enough to win, or weak enough to surrender. Wallenstein, once again the most feared soldier in Germany, had a brief chance to engineer a compromise peace settlement. Unencumbered by religious passion or by loyalty to the house of Habsburg, he was ready to deal with anyone who would pay handsomely for his services. In 1633 he campaigned as little as possible for the emperor, while dickering simultaneously with all of Ferdinand's enemies: the German Protestants, the Bohemian rebels, the Swedes, and the French. But Wallenstein was by now too sickly and irresolute to play this dangerous game. In February, 1634, Ferdinand II dismissed him from command, and instructed his new general to capture Wallenstein dead or alive. Wallenstein was in winter quarters at Pilsen, in Bohemia. He appealed to his officers to fight for him rather than for the emperor, but they mutinied against him. With a few companions, he fled from Pilsen, but they were quickly cornered. The final scene was sordid enough: an Irish mercenary captain kicked open Wallenstein's bedchamber door, speared his unarmed chieftain, rolled the bloody body in a carpet, and dragged it unceremoniously down the stairs.

For the moment, Ferdinand II scarcely missed Wallenstein's military talents. In 1634 imperial forces decimated the Swedes at Nördlingen, and the following year the emperor made peace with Sweden's German allies, Saxony and Brandenburg. Yet the war was far from over. In 1635 France under Richelieu poured fresh men and money into Germany to compensate for Swedish reverses. The combatants were now France and Sweden versus

---

[2]Quoted by Michael Roberts, *Gustavus Adolphus* (London, 1953–1958), Vol. II, p. 789.

Spain and the emperor. The war had become a Habsburg-Bourbon dynastic struggle, with the original religious, ethnic, and constitutional issues laid aside. Very few Germans wanted to continue fighting after 1635; most of them tried to stay neutral. Their lands, however, continued to be the battlefields, and their property continued to be pillaged.

The final thirteen years of the war, from 1635 to 1648, were the most destructive. The Franco-Swedish armies generally maintained the upper hand, but their objective was to keep the war going rather than to strike a knockout blow against their Habsburg opponents. It is noticeable that the French and the Swedes rarely invaded Habsburg Austria and never sacked the emperor's personal lands the way they sacked central Germany and Bavaria. In this style of warfare, troops customarily expended far more energy in looting than in fighting. Every army had its train of camp followers—women and children—who kept the troops comfortable enough so that they were willing to campaign indefinitely. Except for the plague epidemics at many campsites, military life in mid-seventeenth-century Germany was definitely more safe and pleasant than civilian life. The numerous German towns were prime targets: Marburg was occupied eleven times; Magdeburg was besieged ten times. But at least town dwellers could sometimes withstand sieges behind their walls or buy off a conquering army. The exposed peasantry, on the other hand, had no defense except to run away, and hence their suffering was worst of all. The total population loss was staggering, even when one discounts the estimates of contemporaries who exaggerated their figures wildly in order to claim damages or plead tax exemption. The German cities lost one third of their population, and the rural areas two fifths of their population, during the course of the war. The empire had seven or eight million fewer inhabitants in 1648 than in 1618. Not until the twentieth century could any other European conflict boast such human butchery.

Peace negotiations opened in 1644, but four years passed before the multitude of diplomats congregated in Westphalia finally settled on terms and ended the war. After all this haggling, the Peace of Westphalia (1648) turned out to be essentially a confirmation of the long-scorned Peace of Augsburg. The Holy Roman Empire remained politically fragmented, divided into three hundred autonomous, sovereign princely states, most of them very small and weak. The emperor, now Ferdinand II's son, Ferdinand III (ruled 1637–1657), had meager executive authority beyond his own family lands. The imperial Diet, in which all the sovereign princes were represented, continued to be moribund. Thus the Habsburg hope of welding the empire into a single, absolute state was dashed once again, this time permanently. The Peace of Westphalia also reaffirmed the Augsburg formula of territorial churches. Each prince kept the right to establish Catholicism, Lutheranism, or Calvinism (prohibited in 1555) within his state. A greater effort was made now than in 1555 to guarantee private liberty of conscience to Catholics living in Protestant states and vice versa, but in fact most Germans docilely accepted the creed of their ruler. Anabaptists and members of other sects excluded from the Westphalia formula continued to suffer persecution. Thousands of them emigrated to America, especially to Pennsylvania, in the eighteenth century. After 1648 the northern half of the empire was pretty solidly Lutheran, and the southern half pretty solidly Catholic, with important pockets of Calvinism along the Rhine. In no other part of Europe did Protestants and Catholics achieve such a state of balanced deadlock.

Almost all of the major combatants in the Thirty Years' War gained some territory at the Peace of Westphalia. France annexed parts of Alsace and Lorraine. Sweden annexed western Pomerania, on the Baltic coast. Bavaria kept part of the Palatine territory and the electoral seat it had grabbed at the beginning of the war. Saxony kept Lusatia. Brandenburg, considering its passive role in the war, did exceptionally well in annexing eastern Pomerania and Magdeburg. Even the son of Frederick V, the would-be king of Bohemia, was taken care of: he was restored to his father's Palatinate (considera-

The Treaty of Munster in 1648 between Spain and the Netherlands. *Painting by Ter Borch. This treaty, in which Spain finally recognized the independence of the Dutch Republic, was part of the general peace settlement of 1648. In the painting, the Dutch delegates swear the oath of ratification with hands upraised, while the Spanish delegates (right center) place their hands on a Bible.*

bly reduced in size) and given a new eighth seat in the electoral college. The Swiss Confederation and the Dutch republic were recognized as independent of the Holy Roman Empire. Neither the Spanish nor the Austrian Habsburgs gained any territory in 1648, but the Austrian Habsburgs still had much the largest bloc of imperial land, and Ferdinand III exercised far firmer political and religious control over Austria and Bohemia than had his father before the Bohemian rebellion. It is hard to argue that anyone gained enough at the Peace of Westphalia to justify thirty years of fighting. But the settlement of 1648 did prove to be unusually stable. Except for some details, the intricate German political boundaries were not redrawn thereafter until the time of Napoleon. The religious boundaries lasted into the twentieth century.

The Peace of Westphalia ended the wars of religion in central Europe and left Germany a mere geographical expression. Ever since 1648, the Thirty Years' War has had a continuously bad reputation. Statesmen of the late seventeenth and eighteenth centuries looked back on it as a model of how *not* to conduct warfare. In their view, the Thirty Years' War demonstrated the dangers of religious passion, and of amateur armies led by soldiers of fortune. The philosophers and kings of the age of reason, having discovered a controlled style of warfare with armies professional enough to reduce brigandage and defection, and objectives limited enough to negotiate with minimum bloodshed, scorned the uncivilized, inefficient seventeenth-century wars of religion. To observers in the nineteenth century, the Thirty Years' War seemed calamitous for a different reason: because it blocked for so long the national unification of Germany. Twentieth-century observers may no longer feel so certain of the virtues of national unification, but they still criticize the Thirty Years' War for its stupid waste of human resources. A current historian has summed up her feelings about this conflict as follows: "Morally subversive, economically destructive, socially degrading, confused in its causes, devious in its course, futile in its result, it is the outstanding example in European history of meaningless conflict."[3] This judgment perhaps unduly stresses the negative aspects of the war. But it is hard to find many positive aspects. Modern critics sense an uncomfortable parallel between the ideological posturing and civilian atrocities of the mid-seventeenth century and our present style of total war. This is why the dramatist Bertolt Brecht chose the Thirty Years' War as the setting for his biting antiwar play, *Mother Courage and Her Children*, written as the Second World War was getting under way. But of course the analogy between the Thirty Years' War and the Second World War is imperfect: when everyone finally got sick of fighting, the fortunate diplomats at Westphalia could arrange a peace settlement.

[3] C. V. Wedgwood, *The Thirty Years War* (London, 1944), p. 526.

THE RISE OF AUSTRIA AND BRANDENBURG-PRUSSIA

During the second half of the seventeenth century, the Holy Roman Empire was a phantom state, a much revered and very elaborate constitutional mechanism which no longer worked. The princes' final victory over the emperor at Westphalia confirmed the imperial government's inability to enforce orders, pass laws, raise taxes, mount armies, or conduct foreign policy. Sovereignty could be found only at the local level, in the three hundred princely states and imperial cities. In these petty states (the average population was only forty thousand), there was a prevailing late seventeenth-century tendency toward political absolutism. Each prince wanted to have his own small standing army, in case another general war should break out. Many princes suppressed or restricted their representative assemblies. Many built expensive Baroque palaces, gaudy symbols of power, and surrounded themselves with courtiers and ceremonial functionaries in conscious imitation of Louis XIV at Versailles. Armies and courts cost money, which the imperial princes collected through a variety of crude taxes—excises, tariffs, and river tolls. These taxes impaired commerce. A cargo shipped four hundred miles down the Rhine from Basel to Cologne had to pass through thirty political jurisdictions and was subject to so many tariffs and tolls that the shipment was impractical. Because of the handicaps imposed upon business, German towns suffered continuing losses in population, wealth, and importance. Just as the princes exercised sovereign power in regulating (or overregulating) domestic commerce, so they exercised sovereign power in conducting international relations. The treaty of 1648 recognized their right to make alliances with foreign states. In the latter half of the seventeenth century, France was always able to buy allies among the imperial princes while she was attacking imperial territory. Thus in the 1670's, when Louis XIV invaded the Rhineland, twenty thousand Germans served in his army. Though the emperor induced the imperial Diet to declare war against France, many west German states refused to contribute to the imperial war effort, and six of the eight electors remained clients of Louis XIV.

With the empire a hollow facade, interest focuses on the several German states which were large enough after 1648 to function in the international power structure. Two German states, Austria and Brandenburg, developed vigorously during the second half of the century. The Habsburgs transformed their dynastic Austrian possessions into a great new Danubian monarchy, while in northern Germany the Hohenzollerns of Brandenburg laid the foundations for another great new state, the eighteenth-century kingdom of Prussia. Three other German states, Bavaria, Saxony, and the Palatinate, seemingly had as much chance as Brandenburg to build their strength during the late seventeenth century, but all three failed to do so. The Elector Palatine was peculiarly unlucky, for no sooner did his people begin to recover from the Thirty Years' War than the Palatinate was twice

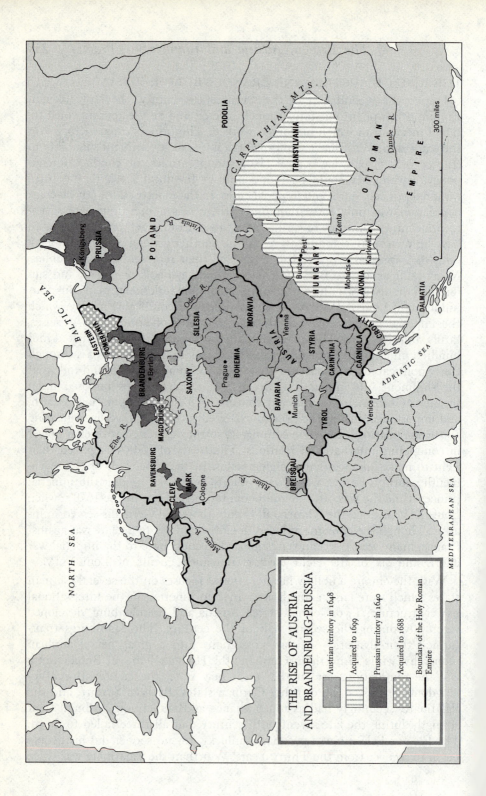

NORTH SEA

BALTIC SEA

EASTERN POMERANIA

PRUSSIA
• Königsberg

POLAND

Vistula R.

PODOLIA

CARPATHIAN MTS.

TRANSYLVANIA

OTTOMAN

Danube R.

EMPIRE

300 miles

0

BRANDENBURG
• Berlin

Oder R.

SILESIA

MORAVIA

HUNGARY

Pest
Buda•

Zenta

Mohács•

SLAVONIA

Karlowitz•

DALMATIA

MAGDEBURG

Elbe R.

SAXONY

BOHEMIA
Prague•

AUSTRIA

Vienna•

STYRIA

CARINTHIA

CROATIA

CARNIOLA

ADRIATIC SEA

RAVENSBURG

CLEVE

MARK

Cologne•

Rhine R.

BAVARIA

Munich•

TYROL

BREISGAU

Venice•

Meuse R.

MEDITERRANEAN SEA

THE RISE OF AUSTRIA
AND BRANDENBURG-PRUSSIA

Austrian territory in 1648

Acquired to 1699

Prussian territory in 1640

Acquired to 1688

Boundary of the Holy Roman
Empire

overrun and devastated by Louis XIV. The elector of Saxony dissipated his energy and his country's wealth in trying to secure election as king of Poland. The elector of Bavaria, who had earlier played a key role in the Catholic reformation and in the Thirty Years' War, now poured all his resources into his Munich court; in international affairs, Bavaria became a French satellite. The relative failure of these western and central German states, and the success of Austria and Brandenburg, meant among other things that German and imperial leadership would henceforth come from east of the Elbe. Both the Habsburgs and the Hohenzollerns ruled over territories situated on the eastern border of the empire; both faced east during the late seventeenth century and built their new states at the expense of the Ottoman Turks, Poland, and Sweden.

Austria

The rise of Austria was the most striking phenomenon in eastern Europe during the late seventeenth century. It was a story of luck as much as skill. The Habsburg dynasty which built the new Danubian monarchy—Ferdinand II (ruled 1619–1637), Ferdinand III (ruled 1637–1657), and Leopold I (ruled 1658–1705)—was not remarkable for talent. Habsburg Austria was a unique creation, a crossbreed between a centralized western nation-state like France and an old-style dynastic empire like Charles V's miscellaneous collection of territories. The reigning Habsburg prince, besides being Holy Roman emperor, was simultaneously archduke of Upper and Lower Austria, margrave of Styria, duke of Carinthia and Carniola, count of Tyrol, king of Bohemia, margrave of Moravia, duke of Upper and Lower Silesia, king of Hungary, Croatia, Slavonia, and Dalmatia, and prince of Transylvania—though in fact the last five of these territories were mainly possessed by the Turks until the end of the century. The Habsburgs managed each of these provinces separately. Every province had its individual native customs and institutional patterns. Several, notably Bohemia and Hungary, boasted long, proud histories of resistance to foreign rule. The Habsburgs' subjects spoke some ten languages and practiced at least eight religious creeds. No part of Europe was more heterogeneous ethnically and culturally. Though the Habsburg lands were physically contiguous, their peoples shared little except the accident of common allegiance to one ruling dynasty. It was the Habsburg ambition to secure absolute control over each and every province, to chase the Turks out of Hungary and adjoining areas, and to cultivate certain cultural and social uniformities which would make their subjects easier to handle. But the Habsburgs did *not* want to weld these diverse peoples into a single political unit equivalent to France or England. On the contrary, they preferred to play one province against another. The Danubian monarchy was an atomistic congeries, each province separate from its neighbors, each province bound as tightly as possible to the Habsburg crown.

Leopold I of Austria. *Engravings by van Dry-weghen. This Habsburg emperor looks less than handsome because of his protruding jaw, a common trait in his family, caused by generations of inbreeding within the Habsburg dynasty.*

This new Danubian monarchy began to take shape as early as the 1620's, when Ferdinand II reorganized Bohemia, Moravia, and Austria in the wake of the abortive Bohemian rebellion. Since the rebellion had been initiated by the nobility in these provinces, Ferdinand confiscated the huge estates of the rebel nobles and redistributed the forfeited lands among loyal Habsburg supporters. Many mercenary captains of the Thirty Years' War (Wallenstein was among them) became members of an acquisitive new landlord class in Bohemia and Moravia. Ferdinand also expelled all Protestant clergymen and school teachers, replacing them as far as possible with Jesuit missionaries. He had remarkable success in making almost all the Bohemian people rejoin the Catholic Church. Bohemia, bastion of the Hussite movement for more than two centuries, was the only thoroughly Protestantized community to be reconverted to Rome during the wars of religion.

The Austrian Habsburgs held rather fixed ideas about the good society. Devotion to the dynasty and to the Virgin Mary was supposed to give their subjects spiritual and moral strength. A big standing army provided the muscle. A small educated class provided the priests and civil servants. The German language was considered superior to the Slavic languages; hence German culture was mandatory for the ruling elite. Yet the Habsburg were cosmopolitan enough to attract men of every European nationality into their employ. Agricultural landlords were encouraged to exploit the peasantry but were discouraged from taking active part in governmental administration or legislation. Thus in Bohemia and Moravia the once-powerful estates met seldom in the middle and late seventeenth century, and did little except to legislate the imposition of serfdom on the peasant population. The new landlords, perhaps more businesslike than their rebel predecessors, saw that they could farm very profitably if they could get free agricultural labor. Despite peasant revolts, the Habsburg government required of each Bohemian peasant three days of unpaid compulsory service (*robota*) for his lord every week. Like the Polish landlords, the Bohemian and Austrian agricultural magnates produced for export. They raised grain and timber for the western European market, and meat, grain, and fish (bred in elaborate fishponds) for the Habsburg army. In this overwhelmingly rural, stratified society the Czech and Austrian towns served few functions, and during the seventeenth century they decayed even more completely than the towns of western Germany.

The Habsburgs needed outside help in order to reconquer Bohemia in the 1620's, and again to regain control of Hungary in the 1680's and 1690's. The Habsburg-Turkish demarcation line in Hungary had been fairly stable since the mid-sixteenth century. The Turkish frontier garrisons were only eighty miles east of Vienna, the Habsburg capital. In the 1660's, the Turks renewed their efforts to conquer Austria. Though the Habsburgs beat back an invading Ottoman army in 1664, Leopold I was so alarmed at the Turks' military strength that he paid the sultan a tribute of 200,000 florins in order to secure a truce. As soon as the truce expired in 1683, another huge Turkish army advanced through Hungary, crossed the Austrian border, and laid siege to Vienna. Leopold fled his capital, leaving a rather small garrison to man the stout city walls. Contemporaries supposed that the Turkish siege camp, a colorful forest of tents, mules, and camels, contained 200,000 or more soldiers. No doubt this Turkish force was larger than any army in the Thirty Years' War had been, but it lacked mobility and firing power. For two months the Viennese grimly withstood the siege. Just as the Turks were at last breaching the walls, on September 12, 1683, a relief army of Austrians, Germans, and Poles commanded by King John Sobieski of Poland (ruled 1674–1696) swept down from the heights overlooking the city, routed the Ottomans, and sent the dreaded janissaries reeling back down the Danube, leaving all their equipment behind.

This great victory shattered the legend of Turkish invincibility and opened the whole of Hungary to reconquest. In sixteen years of hard fighting, the forces of the Austrian Habsburgs, the papacy, Poland, and Venice, in a coalition known as the Holy League, drove the Turks south of the Danube and east of the Carpathians. The League armies were led at various times by

Polish, Italian, Rhenish, Bavarian, and Saxon commanders. Prince Eugene of Savoy (1663–1736) was the ablest of this international brigade of generals. In 1697, Eugene pounced on the sultan's army as it was crossing a river at Zenta, in southern Hungary, and in two hours so stampeded the Turks that the janissaries fell to massacring their own officers. At the Peace of Karlowitz in 1699, the Turks surrendered a huge belt of territory to the League: Hungary, Transylvania, Slavonia, and Croatia passed to the Habsburgs, Podolia to Poland, Dalmatia and much of Greece to Venice. The Danubian monarchy had doubled in size since 1648.

The Habsburgs' efforts at reorganization were not quite so successful in Hungary as they had been in Bohemia. The Hungarians, or Magyars, had long resented Habsburg overlordship, partly because the dynasty was foreign, partly because the Habsburgs had done little to rescue Hungary from the Turks, and partly because the Habsburgs' absolutist, Catholic program encroached upon Hungarian "liberties." These liberties were strictly confined to the nobility. Like their counterparts everywhere in eastern Europe, the Magyar landlords kept their serfs in thralldom while demanding total freedom for themselves. In Royal Hungary, the western strip which the Turks had never conquered, the nobility counted among their liberties the right to elect their king (as in Poland) and to govern themselves through their estates. In Transylvania, the eastern province which the Turks had only nominally conquered, the nobility operated an independent republic, which was staunchly Calvinist to boot. The Habsburgs had their best chance to reshape the society in central and southern Hungary, the area which had been directly under Turkish rule for 150 years. When they expelled the Turks in the 1680's and 1690's, the Habsburgs sold or gave as much as possible of the newly acquired land to their army officers and to others presumably dependent on the crown. But these new landlords quickly melted into the Magyar nobility. It was quite impossible for the Habsburgs to govern this frontier country without the cooperation of the local magnates. Because they had to convince the Magyar nobility that Austrian rule was at the very least preferable to Turkish, they dared not impose absolutism or Catholicism too nakedly. In 1687 Leopold did get the Magyars to surrender their elective monarchy; thereafter, the Hungarian crown was a hereditary Habsburg possession. But the Hungarian estates retained real power, and the Protestant nobility kept their religion. As commercial farming developed in Hungary, the peasants (many of whom were Slovaks and Croats) sank deeper into serfdom. They had to fulfill heavy obligations to their Magyar masters and pay heavy taxes to the Austrian government as well—taxes from which the landlord class was exempt. Habsburg Hungary, with its autocratic Austrian ruler, its selfish Magyar aristocracy, its downtrodden Slavic peasantry, its few small towns inhabited by Germans and Jews, was a melting pot in which nothing melted.

Brandenburg-Prussia

Compared with the growth of Habsburg Austria, the development of Hohenzollern Brandenburg during the late seventeenth century was modest. The key figure here was Frederick William, elector of Brandenburg from 1640 to 1688, who is known as the Great Elector. Frederick William was the shrewdest ruler of his day in eastern Europe, but his contemporaries may be pardoned for failing to notice his ability, since he governed a small state and did nothing spectacular during his reign. The Great Elector was an institutional innovator whose policies bore fruit long after his death. Because the later Hohenzollern princes followed his recipe in building the eighteenth-century kingdom of Prussia and the nineteenth-century German empire, the Great Elector's reign is of special historical interest.

In 1640 Frederick William inherited the Hohenzollern family's scattered collection of underdeveloped north German territories, devastated by the Thirty Years' War. He was a Calvinist; his subjects were mainly Lutherans. Brandenburg was his chief possession, a flat country with unproductive sandy soil, cut off from the Baltic coast, whose several hundred thousand inhabitants raised grain and brewed beer. Berlin, the chief town in Brandenburg, was a small place. Brandenburg was completely dominated by the *Junkers*, the noble landlords, who thwarted the Elector above them and squeezed the serfs below. More than a hundred miles east of Brandenburg, beyond the imperial border and enveloped by Poland, lay Prussia, the Elector's second most important province. Here was a region of forests and lakes, its chief center the commercial town of Königsberg. Prussia too was strongly Lutheran and dominated by the *Junkers*. More than a hundred miles west of Brandenburg, near the Dutch frontier, lay the Elector's remaining small outposts, Cleve, Mark, and Ravensburg. These provinces all had their own autonomous estates, and being widely separated from each other and only recently joined under the Hohenzollern dynasty, they shared no common interests. Eventually, under Bismarck's leadership, the Hohenzollerns would be able to conquer all the intervening territory, to form a coherent kingdom stretching from Cologne to Königsberg. But this was unthinkable in the seventeenth century. All Frederick William could hope for in 1640 was to free his diverse lands from the Swedish and imperial armies which overran them, and to learn from the horrid example of this war how to build his territory into a self-sufficient, consolidated state.

The Elector's basic decision was to create a permanent standing army. All his other political, social, and economic innovations stemmed from the army's role in centralizing the Hohenzollern state. During the closing stage of the Thirty Years' War, Frederick William fielded eight thousand efficient troops, a lilliputian display by great-power standards, but enough to clear the foreign soldiers from his land and to give him a voice at the peace conference at Westphalia. In 1648 the Great Elector rather surprisingly gained more territory than any other German prince: eastern Pomerania and several secularized bishoprics, including Magdeburg. So far so good.

Naturally, the several estates of Brandenburg, Prussia, and Cleve-Mark wanted the army disbanded once the war was over, but instead Frederick William gradually enlarged it, until he had thirty thousand professional troops by 1688. Who was going to pay for this army? The Elector knew that he could not let his soldiers live off the land in the manner of Wallenstein's mercenaries. Nor could he pay for them himself, though his large private landholdings produced enough income to cover the ordinary expenses of civil government. Foreign subsidies would help, but the cost would have to be met chiefly through taxes, which the several estates adamantly refused to approve. In 1653 the Elector worked out a compromise with the Brandenburg estates whereby he recognized the special economic and social privileges of the *Junker* landlords in return for what turned out to be a permanent tax to maintain his army. The Elector acknowledged that only *Junkers* could own land, that *Junkers* could freely evict peasants (who were all assumed to be serfs) from lands they occupied, and that *Junkers* were immune from taxation. On the other hand, he severely curtailed the political privileges of the Brandenburg *Junkers*. After the army tax expired, he kept right on collecting it and soon imposed an additional excise tax on the towns,

The Prussians swearing homage to the Great Elector at Königsberg, 1663. *The Prussian estates long refused to admit that the Elector had sovereign power over them, but finally in 1663 he persuaded them to pledge allegiance to him as overlord.*

without the consent of the estates. In his Rhineland territories, the Elector bullied the estates into levying army taxes by threatening to send his soldiers to collect the money by force. In Prussia, resistance was stouter. To force the estates to levy his taxes, Frederick William imprisoned the two chief leaders of the opposition and executed one of them; he billeted his troops in Königsberg until the taxes were collected.

Frederick William's subjects paid twice as much per capita in taxes as Louis XIV's much richer subjects; in a state with little surplus wealth, and with the only affluent class—the *Junkers*—exempted from taxation, the burden of supporting the army was truly crushing. However, the Elector's military exactions did produce some side benefits. To collect his army taxes, Frederick William created a new bureaucratic institution, the *Generalkriegs-kommissariat*, or military commissariat, which also disbursed army pay and equipment, and soon supervised all phases of the state economy. The commissariat officials, zealous servants of the Elector, worked hard to promote new state-supported industry, especially the manufacture of military supplies. Some twenty thousand persecuted Calvinist textile workers from France and the Palatinate emigrated to Brandenburg, to the great benefit of the Elector's uniform-manufacturing industry. By the close of the century, the Hohenzollern lands had recovered economically from the terrible damage of the Thirty Years' War, and the population had climbed back to its early seventeenth-century level of about 1.5 million persons.

The Great Elector's standing army could not make Brandenburg-Prussia into a great power overnight. Frederick William was at war about half the time during his long reign. He fought for purely opportunistic reasons and changed sides whenever he seemed likely to benefit thereby. Thus in the 1650's he first joined Sweden against Poland and then joined Poland against Sweden. In the 1670's and 1680's he outdid himself by switching between the Dutch and the French three times. All this effort brought the Elector one paltry acquisition after 1648, a thirty-mile sliver of Pomeranian territory. But Frederick William built enduring strength into his north German society. The Elector's army gave him and his heirs absolute political control. It encouraged the people in habits of discipline and obedience. It contributed to the unity of the state, for peasants from all the Hohenzollern provinces were recruited into the rank and file, while *Junkers* from Brandenburg and Prussia staffed the officer corps. It facilitated the growth of an efficient bureaucracy. And it enabled Frederick William to capitalize upon the existing rigid social stratification, the separation between privileged *Junkers* and unprivileged serfs. To the aspiring *Junker* squire, an officer's commission became the proudest badge of his membership in the master class. The Elector's whole policy rested on partnership with the landlords. As for the serfs, a clergyman observed in 1684, "the peasants are indeed human beings," but he went on to advise that they be treated like the stockfish, which is "best when beaten well and soft."[4]

Brandenburg-Prussia and Austria were obviously organized along somewhat differing lines by the close of the seventeenth century. The Great Elector had worked to make his state homogeneous; the Habsburgs cultivated heterogeneity. Brandenburg-Prussia was the more militaristic and bureaucratic. Austria could not, or did not, extract from its subjects as much money and service per capita as did Brandenburg-Prussia, but since the Austrian population was much larger, Austria was nevertheless a far greater power. Brandenburg-Prussia was Protestant, Austria was Catholic—but this difference was decidedly less significant than it once would have been. The two states gradually turned into strategic rivals, because both were headed by German dynasties hoping to expand eastward. In the eighteenth century Prussia (as Brandenburg-Prussia came to be called) and Austria would quarrel bitterly for the leadership of central Europe, and in the nineteenth century they would fight for the control of Germany. But this Austro-Prussian rivalry should not obscure the fact that the two societies exhibited some striking similarities in their parallel climbs to power in the seventeenth century.

For one thing, both Austria and Prussia divorced sovereignty from nationality, unlike contemporaneous western states. To be sure, Prussia was not multinational, as Austria was. But in the eighteenth century Prussia annexed more Polish territory than German, and before the French Revolution demonstrated no Pan-German desire to embrace the whole German-speaking population. Prussia and Austria were dynastic states, congeries of territories their rulers happened to have inherited or conquered. Both the Hohenzollerns and the Habsburgs achieved absolute, centralized political power by 1689. They shared executive and legislative responsibility with no one but God, who apparently did not breathe very heavily over the Great Elector's shoulder.

In both states, the rulers succeeded in breaking through the constitutional restrictions of the representative estates, or diets. This absolutism, however, could only be maintained at the cost of tacit partnership with the landed magnates. The serf-owning lords everywhere east of the Elbe, in Poland and Russia as in Austria and Prussia, consolidated their immense social and economic privileges during the seventeenth century. The whole of eastern Europe was profoundly agrarian. The town-dwelling merchants and lawyers, who had often turned Calvinist in the sixteenth-century west and fought their kings in the seventeenth-century west, had always been comparatively weak in Austria and Prussia and lost strength steadily throughout the century. Thus by 1689, though the political disintegration of central Europe had at last been arrested, the social and economic disparity between east and west had by no means been eliminated.

[4]Quoted by F. L. Carsten, "The Empire after the Thirty Years War," in *New Cambridge Modern History*, Vol. V (Cambridge, Eng., 1961), p. 438.

CHAPTER 9

The Psychology of Limited Wealth

EUROPEAN BUSINESSMEN in the years between 1559 and 1689 faced problems and developed policies characteristic of a society quite well off but very far from affluent. No longer did everyone have to concentrate on the struggle for bare survival, as in the agrarian subsistence economy of the early Middle Ages. The so-called commercial revolution was in full swing, with the merchant the key figure, distributing more goods than ever before to a worldwide market. The putting-out system of domestic manufacturing was producing a rising volume and variety of consumer commodities, especially textiles. A dramatic sixteenth-century increase in the circulation of bullion spurred purchasing power. Refinements in credit facilitated international commerce. Innovations in banking encouraged private investment and public loans. The development of specialized commercial agriculture, combined with improvements in the long-distance shipment of bulk cargo, made it possible for big cities and densely populated regions to be fed from distant farmlands. On the other hand, Europe did not yet have the economic techniques to produce as much as its people needed for comfort, to say nothing of abundance. Agriculture was still by far the largest occupation, and farming methods were crude; the agrarian populace still had to expend most of its energy in meeting its own needs rather than producing for the market. Manufacturing was still done by hand rather than by machine. Transportation remained slow and difficult. Commerce was extremely risky. Business enterprises were typically small-scale. Taken as a whole, population was static. Small wonder that in this era of rising yet limited wealth many Europeans clung to the attitudes appropriate in a subsistence economy.

Europe's wealth, such as it was, was unevenly distributed geographically. The commercial west held a vastly larger share than the agrarian east. Within western Europe, the Atlantic ports were the chief capitalist centers. Wealth was also very unevenly distributed among the various social classes; indeed it was scarcely distributed at all. Everywhere in Europe the distance between the propertied and the propertyless was widening. Great property holders such as kings and landed magnates luxuriated in unprecedented conspicuous consumption. Small and middling property holders, independ-

269

ent farmers, artisans, shopkeepers, members of the learned professions, and the like, typically got only a taste of wealth but hoped to acquire more by copying the habits of the beaver and the squirrel. The propertyless bottom half (or more) of society, the wage laborers, serfs, unemployed, and unemployables, got nothing—and were told to expect nothing—beyond bare survival. In most of Europe the laboring classes had somewhat harder working conditions and lower living standards in 1689 than in 1559.

Also noteworthy is the fact that in this period the politically consolidated national state clearly replaced the city-state as the most effective business unit. The mercantilist policies of Spain, France, and England—politically belligerent, but economically conservative and protectionist—most fully express the sixteenth- and seventeenth-century European psychology of limited wealth.

POPULATION

Demographers estimate that the population of Europe leveled off during this period at a round figure of a hundred million inhabitants—less than a sixth of the present total. Any such estimate has to be rough, since no census was taken at the time, and the first reasonably accurate population counts in most European countries date from the mid-nineteenth century. But we can tell enough from the fragmentary statistical data to be sure that Europe's total population rose very slowly, if it rose at all, during the era of the religious wars. A very high death rate counterbalanced a very high birthrate to keep the population in equilibrium. As would be expected in an agrarian society, the population was pretty evenly distributed; density was lowest in Poland, Scandinavia, and Russia, and highest in the Low Countries and Italy, both long-established urban areas. Everywhere, life expectancy was low, thanks to plague, war, and famine. Young couples could expect only a few years of marriage before one or the other partner died; parents could only hope that some of their babies would survive infancy. The poets of the day feasted on the bittersweet theme of brief young love, embellished by fading roses, drying dewdrops, and passing spring. In the most popular English lyric of the seventeenth century, Robert Herrick's song "To the Virgins, to Make Much of Time," the poet urges shy maidens to

> Gather ye rosebuds while ye may,
> Old Time is still a-flying;
> And this same flower that smiles today,
> Tomorrow will be dying.

Although the overall size of the European population remained constant between 1559 and 1689, some regions experienced considerable population growth, while others suffered corresponding losses. The three most dynamic states of the day—France, England, and the Dutch republic—each registered a considerable increase in population. On the other hand, Germany, Italy, and Spain all registered net population losses during the seventeenth century, at a time when they were suffering from political and economic dry rot. There seems to have been some correlation in the seventeenth century between population growth, political vitality, and economic prosperity.

The German population loss cannot be explained entirely by the Thirty Years' War. German business was already slumping by the end of the sixteenth century, and German cities were dwindling in size before the war began. German merchants and craftsmen clung to outmoded economic patterns developed two hundred or more years earlier. In the German cities, elaborate guild restrictions hampered industrial productivity. The cities were too small and weak to trade competitively on the world market against merchants from the big Atlantic states. The medieval concept of a commercial union among cities, such as the Hanseatic League, no longer worked well. Few German merchants took part in the immensely profitable new trade to Asia and America. Among the German merchants were some very big businessmen: in the sixteenth century, no entrepreneur in Europe could match the Fuggers of Augsburg. But when Philip II defaulted, the Fuggers were forced to liquidate their banking business. Thus the German slump antedated the Thirty Years' War. But the fearsome property damage and population losses inflicted during the war further aggravated the situation, and the settlement of 1648 did not solve any of Germany's political or economic problems.

Italy was an overcrowded country by contemporary standards, and its population loss in the sixteenth and seventeenth centuries was not very great. Nevertheless, it was symptomatic of the general political and economic malaise. Italy never recovered from the twin disasters of the 1490's: the conquest of nearly all the chief city-states—Milan, Florence, Genoa, and Naples—by French, Spanish, and German armies, and the shift in trade routes from the Mediterranean to the Atlantic. After 1559, Spain governed half the peninsula directly, and most of the other Italian states indirectly. Rome remained a mecca for pilgrims, artists, and fashionable tourists in the late sixteenth and seventeenth centuries. The popes celebrated the Catholic reformation in stone and mortar by refurbishing their city on a heroic scale. The basilica of St. Peter's, finished in the early seventeenth century, was the largest and most majestic church in Christendom. Wide new streets were cut through Rome, opening onto dramatic piazzas embellished with theatrical public buildings and colorful fountains, all perfectly attuned to the brilliant Roman sunlight. But the traveler who ventured a few miles outside Rome found the countryside infested with brigands.

Elsewhere in Italy, the story was much the same. Florence under the Medici grand dukes of Tuscany had lost most of its old vigor, but the ruling dynasty lived well. In Milan, Naples, and Sicily, the Spanish governed in partnership with the local landed nobility, who adopted the Spanish aristo-crats' contempt for commerce and industry. The peasants of southern Italy were among the most impoverished in Europe. There was much more wealth in northern Italy. The Venetian republic continued both rich and independent, though the Turks captured its two island colonies in the eastern Mediterranean—Cyprus and Crete. As the Venetian spice trade slumped during the seventeenth century, Venetian capitalists withdrew much of their money from risky foreign trade to invest it in safe farmland. Genoa was an important business center. The Genoese merchants domi-nated the trade between Italy and Spain and became Philip II's principal bankers. The sumptuous palaces of the Genoese nobility, like the sumptuous churches of the Roman papacy, were mostly built during the late sixteenth and early seventeenth centuries. Even so, Italy had lost its central impor-tance in European life. The Italian city-states, too small to fend off France and Spain in the wars of 1494–1559, were likewise too small to compete against the national economic power of France, England, and the Dutch republic in the seventeenth century.

The most dramatic demographic reversal occurred in Spain. Through most of the sixteenth century the Spanish population seems to have in-creased markedly, as the country enjoyed its imperial wealth and power. The glittering Spanish empire of Philip II was based, as we have seen, on a dangerously lopsided agrarian economy. In Spain, industry and commerce never developed as extensively as in Germany or Italy. Even during Spain's peak period of success, its chief export was raw wool. During the late sixteenth century, the Spanish peasantry began drifting from the countryside into the towns, where there was little employment for them. Plague epidem-ics ravaged the overcrowded towns, and harvest failures brought famine throughout the country. Agricultural output shrank so disastrously that Spain had to depend on imported grain for survival. The Spanish population loss of some 25 per cent during the course of the seventeenth century reflected the country's general loss of vigor as its imperial system fell apart.

The population losses in Germany, Italy, and Spain were counterbalanced by population growth in France, England, and the Dutch republic. These three states accounted for something like 20 per cent of the total European population in the mid-sixteenth century and for something like 30 per cent by the end of the seventeenth century. London and Paris were the two biggest cities by far, each with nearly half a million inhabitants by 1700. Amsterdam suddenly became one of Europe's largest cities, though the Dutch republic remained a very small state. Population figures scarcely begin to suggest the degree to which Dutch, English, and French businessmen came to dominate the seventeenth-century economy. These states had the highest per-capita agricultural and industrial output, the greatest volume of

A law office in seventeenth-century Amsterdam. *Painting by Bloot. This busy scene suggests how people from all walks of life, rich and poor, young and old, required a lawyer's services in this booming Dutch metropolis.*

trade, the most active flow of capital, the most effective tax and revenue systems, and the largest accumulation of surplus wealth. By every index they outclassed Spain, Germany, Italy, and eastern Europe.

AGRICULTURE AND INDUSTRY

The dynamism of the Dutch, English, and French can be explained only in small part by their methods of agricultural and industrial production. It is true that during the sixteenth and seventeenth centuries the Dutch made some important changes in farming practices, and the English developed some new techniques for heavy industry, but none of these innovations could compare with the scientific livestock breeding, soil chemistry, steam power, and manufacturing by machine which began to revolutionize European output in the late eighteenth century. Basic productive techniques everywhere in Europe remained all too much as they had been in 1500— indeed, as they had been in 1300. *Manufacture* still retained its Latin meaning: "to make by hand." Economic enterprise was still shackled by manual labor.

It is not easy to generalize about developments in agriculture. Broadly speaking, European food production became more commercial and capitalistic between 1559 and 1689. Farmers grew cash crops for the urban market on land they owned or rented. In western Europe, landlords could make money in several ways. They might cultivate their estates with wage labor, or lease out small plots to peasants, or take half of the tenant's crop in lieu of rent—this sharecropping system was called *métayage* in France. Sharecropping was also common on the great Italian *latifundia*, or estates, and on the *latifundios* of Spain. In Poland, Bohemia, Hungary, and Prussia, landlords were less likely to bother with money wages or rent; generally they required their serfs to farm their estates three days a week without pay. The expanding agricultural market thus turned some western European peasants into wage laborers, some into tenant farmers, and others into small free farmers, while the eastern European peasants were driven deeper into serfdom. Everywhere, the market economy was eroding traditional agrarian habits of local self-sufficiency and cooperation within a close-knit community.

Many legacies from medieval agriculture nevertheless remained. Villagers still divided their arable land into three great fields to be planted with different crops in successive years; for example, one field with wheat and one with oats, leaving the third fallow. This wasteful three-field system of crop rotation prevailed through much of England, France, and Germany. Plowing and harvesting techniques had not improved much since the twelfth century. The yield per bushel of seed remained wretchedly low. The traditional, undiversified crops were grown, mainly cereals and legumes, with little in the way of meat, dairy produce, fruit, or leafy vegetables. The staples were still bread and beer in the north, bread and wine in the south. Corn and potatoes had been introduced from the New World, but were not yet widely cultivated in Europe. Consumers were very grateful for the spices, sugar, tea, and coffee which were imported from Asia and America.

It is interesting to compare conditions in Spain, where agricultural production declined during the sixteenth and seventeenth centuries, with conditions in England, where production increased. In both Spain and England, large-scale wool raisers were converting grain fields into sheep runs. In Spain, an estimated 3 per cent of the population held 97 per cent of the land, so it was comparatively easy for the landlord class to increase the percentage of land devoted to sheep pasturage. The members of the *Mesta,* or sheep ranchers' association, owned some three million Merino sheep in the early sixteenth century. To graze this many animals, a tremendous proportion of Castile's barren land was required. The Spanish government granted the *Mesta* special privileges; in 1501, their migratory flocks were given exclusive possession of huge belts of pasture land which had formerly been used to raise grain for the Castilian towns. In consequence, the countryside was depopulated as the dispossessed farmers moved to the towns, wheat production fell, and Spain was faced with famine. Ironically, in the seventeenth century the *Mesta* flocks dwindled in size and value. During the same period, aggressive English landlords evicted their tenants from a half million acres of land and "enclosed" much of this land into great sheep pastures. But the English enclosure movement did not assume major proportions until the eighteenth and nineteenth centuries. In England the aristocracy and gentry controlled less of the land than in Spain. At the close of the seventeenth century, nearly half of the English rural population consisted of small farmers who either owned their own land or held it on long leases. A more important difference between England and Spain was that the English farmers, large and small, worked their land more efficiently. Some enterprising farmers created rich new farmland during the seventeenth century by draining the fen district near Cambridge. Others cut down large forest tracts and learned how to till areas which had hitherto been wasteland. Not only did wool production rise in seventeenth-century England, but grain and cattle production more than kept pace with the expanding population. By the close of the century, the English farmers exported a good deal of wheat.

The Dutch were probably the most enterprising agriculturists in Europe. They had to be, for they had very little farmland on which to support a dense population. Their low-lying fields were periodically inundated by the North Sea, and the soil was soggy. During the sixteenth and seventeenth centuries, the Dutch reclaimed huge tracts, known as polders, from the sea. They built dikes and drainage canals to keep the water out, and windmills to pump the land dry. They farmed the new lands intensively, planting orchards and truck gardens as well as grainfields and pasture. Raising tulips—the colorful bulbs were introduced from Turkey in the sixteenth century—became a Dutch specialty. They experimented with clover and turnips, which improved the soil yield and fattened the cattle. The Dutch were able to produce butter and cheese for export, whereas the English dairy farmers were hampered by their practice of slaughtering most of their animals every fall for lack of winter fodder. Spain, with its parched and rocky soil, badly needed some Dutch-style agricultural experiments. But all efforts to irrigate the Spanish fields were blocked by inertia. In the seventeenth century, Spanish clerics rejected a canal project which was designed to improve inland transport; if God had wanted Spain's waterways to be navigable, they reasoned, He would have made them so.

A good example of seventeenth-century agrarian enterprise is the development by grape growers in the French county of Champagne of a method for making superlative sparkling wine. French wines were already well established as the best in Europe, but Champagne was not among the great wine-producing regions. Its chalky soil grew stunted vines with small quantities of particularly sweet white and black grapes. Its northerly climate delayed the harvest season and slowed the crucial fermentation process by which the grape juice was converted into alcohol. The standard method of making wine was (and is) to harvest the grapes in September or October and press them into a mush, which fermented. Before the fermented liquid turned into vinegar, it was poured into great wooden casks. The liquid was then piped from cask to cask in order to remove the sediment and filtered to achieve a clear color. The standard seventeenth-century practice was to drink wine young, but it could be casked for several years, until it matured into old wine. A blind monk named Dom Pierre Pérignon (1638–1715), the cellarer of a Benedictine abbey, is supposed to have been the man who invented a new vintage process which turned the still red wine of Champagne into a sparkling white wine. First, Dom Pierre achieved a perfect blend by combining in the winepress grapes from various different vines (he had a famous nose for the bouquet of the grapes). Next, before the mush had completed its fermentation, Dom Pierre poured the liquid into bottles instead of casks, and stored it in the cool chalk cellars of Reims, the chief town in Champagne. The fermentation process continued inside the bottles, giving the wine a bubbly effervescence. Dom Pierre needed very strong bottles; in the early days of champagne making, a great many of the bottles exploded. He needed strongly wired cork stoppers instead of the oil-soaked wads of hemp which people had been using for bottle stoppers. The development of a foolproof technique took many years. Since bottled wine could not be piped or filtered, the producers of champagne had to find another way of removing the sediment from their wine. They set the bottles upside down in racks, and slightly twisted each bottle every day for many months, until the sediment had settled on the cork. Then they had to open each bottle, wipe off the sediment, hastily insert a pinch of sugar to give the wine its sweet-dry flavor, and recork it before the effervescence was lost. Seventeenth-century champagne may not have tasted very much like the modern beverage, but it was already the toast of kings. Louis XIV drank it copiously, and Charles II was so pleased with the bubbly stuff when he visited France as a young man that he introduced it into England.

Turning from food and drink to manufacturing, we once again find regional divergences and a prevailing tendency toward the large-scale capitalistic organization of production. In the seventeenth century, industrial production was geared to elementary consumer needs. Cloth is the most basic manufactured commodity, and in seventeenth-century Europe, as in the Middle Ages, textile manufacturing was by far the largest industry. Textile-production techniques had not changed since the early sixteenth century. Utilitarian wool cloth, from which most garments were made, was produced all over western Europe by the rural putting-out system. Large-scale clothiers hired peasants to spin, weave, and finish their cloth. Many clothiers did not attempt to dye the cloth, for dyeing required skill; half the price of the finished cloth was in its color. Dutch clothiers had the best formulas for wool dyeing (which they kept as secret as possible), and they imported much "white" cloth from England and dyed it. The enterprising clothier might buy raw wool from various strains of sheep, and experiment with various mixtures and various weaves to get a cloth which struck the public's fancy. He might employ hundreds of men and women, and when he controlled every stage by which the raw wool was converted into finished cloth, his organization of production resembled that of the modern assembly-line factory. But the actual work was performed under extremely primitive conditions, by semi skilled hand labor.

Luxury fabrics, such as silk, were produced in towns rather than in the countryside, because the work required a delicate coalition between highly skilled laborers, costly materials, and rather elaborate machinery. Only the rich could afford to buy silks and velvets, and the silk merchant strove for quality rather than quantity. Lucca had been the biggest Italian silk center since the thirteenth century; cities farther north, such as Lyons and Amsterdam, developed the craft in the sixteenth and seventeenth centuries. Naturally, the skilled silk weavers and dyers of Lucca were better organized and better paid than the semiskilled wool weavers and dyers of an English village. But they too were pieceworkers in a large-scale enterprise.

The tailors who sewed the finished cloth into garments were the most tradition-bound of the textile workers. These small, self-employed craftsmen were to be found in every European town. They were organized, as they had been for centuries, into guilds. The tailor sewed his garments according to prescribed guild standards and offered his wares to the consumer at prescribed guild prices. The wool clothier and the silk merchant abominated such protectionist, restrictive business procedures. Yet the clothier himself expected the state to protect and promote all phases of his textile production. The English government, like other governments, obligingly prohibited English farmers from selling their wool abroad. It laid heavy duties on all imported woolens. It bought domestic worsteds and serges for military uniforms, and required that every English corpse be buried in a woolen shroud. Actually, the seventeenth-century woolen industry had more in common with the medieval tailoring craft than with the cotton industry which was going to develop in England during the eighteenth cntury. Not only would cotton be cheaper and more practical than wool, not only would cotton cloth be made by machine rather than by hand, not only would cotton textile production be concentrated in great factories rather than scattered in rural cottages, but the cotton magnates would be so self-reliant that they could disdain all regulation and protection, national as well as local. The textile manufacturers of the seventeenth century, for all their aggressive organization, did not dare to risk free competition. They thought they were living in a subsistence world.

There was not much spare capital or labor, or much technical skill, for heavy industry. England was the most industrialized society during the late sixteenth and seventeenth centuries. The coal mines along the Tyne River in northern England were big affairs, with elaborate machinery for draining the shafts, though not for cutting the coal. The colliers mined and carted the coal by hand. English coal production increased from approximately 200,000 tons a year in the 1550's to 3,000,000 tons by the 1680's. During the same span of years English iron production rose fivefold. Because of these impressive gains, Professor John Nef, the chief authority on the early British coal industry, argues that the English achieved an "industrial revolution" between 1540 and 1640 comparable in importance to the better-known machine age which began after 1760.[1] But "revolution" seems too strong a term for the industrial developments in Tudor and Stuart England. The volume of seventeenth-century English coal and iron output remained very modest, so modest that it could not greatly affect techniques of production. The English did use coal fires in their dyehouses, brick and glass kilns—and breweries, despite the cry that the smell of coke gas tainted the beer. But they had not yet discovered how to smelt iron ore with coal; this was still done by charcoal. Londoners consumed much of the new coal in place of wood to heat their houses; the new iron supply was turned into pots, grates, knives, pins, and other domestic articles. England in the 1640's produced 1/250 as much coal as the United States in the 1950's, and 1/2500 as much iron and steel. The English did not yet produce enough coal and iron to substitute coal-powered, iron machinery for handicraft manufacturing—as they would start doing in the cotton mills of the late eighteenth century.

Whether or not England experienced an industrial revolution in the seventeenth century, continental Europe certainly did not. The overall European output of iron and steel remained pretty steadily at the low figure of 150,000 tons a year from the 1530's into the early eighteenth century. While English production was rising during these years, iron and steel production in Germany, Bohemia, and Hungary was declining. War is supposed to stimulate heavy industry, but the wars of religion probably had the opposite effect. They disrupted mining and metalworking more than they encouraged new enterprises. Weapons were still simple enough to be largely handmade. The muskets and cannon which Gustavus Adolphus used in the Thirty Years' War were manufactured in Swedish state factories, but the gunpowder was made in peasants' cottages.

Transportation improved somewhat, facilitating the distribution of market commodities from one European region to another. Horse-drawn carriages and wagons were equipped for the first time with spoked wheels and springs, which greatly eased overland travel and transport. The pony-express postal couriers of the elector of Brandenburg carried mail the six hundred miles from Königsberg to Cleve in only a week. But the narrow, rutted,

---

[1]John U. Nef, *War and Human Progress* (Cambridge, Mass., 1950), pp. 10, 35, 80–81, 291.

muddy roads hindered the overland conveyance of bulk cargo, as did the prevalence of highwaymen and toll collectors. It was calculated in 1675 that coal could be shipped three hundred miles by water as cheaply as fifteen miles by road. Merchant ships were no bigger in 1689 than in 1559 and sailed no faster, but there were many more of them. The cheaply built, easily handled Dutch *flute*, or flyboat, was particularly well designed for carrying awkward cargoes like coal, timber, salt, or grain. Thus seaports and riverports received goods from many parts of the world, while interior villages still had to be nearly self-sufficient. The peasant who depended upon country fairs and itinerant peddlars to supply his wants had to have modest tastes indeed.

By and large, the seventeenth-century economy suffered from chronic problems of underproduction, as our own economy now suffers from chronic problems of overproduction. Almost the entire seventeenth-century labor force was tied up in inefficient manual labor, required to provide the bare necessities of life—food, clothing, shelter. Seven or eight out of every ten members of the labor force were agricultural workers, yet the people of seventeenth-century Europe were none too well fed or dressed. By contrast, only one out of ten members of the mid-twentieth-century American labor force is an agricultural or textile worker, yet our farms and mills glut the market. Of the 440 occupational categories listed by the United States Bureau of the Census in 1950, at least two hundred (mostly of the white-collar type) did not exist in any form three hundred years ago. A seventeenth-century entrepreneur would hardly believe that in our mechanized society almost as many laborers are engaged in transportation as in agriculture.[2] Or that we have to create consumer "wants" by sales and advertising, and persuade customers to discard merchandise long before it wears out. The seventeenth-century bourgeois virtues of thrift, abstinence, and restraint have become vices in our era of built-in obsolescence.

DUTCH COMMERCIAL CAPITALISM

The Dutch were the most enterprising businessmen in seventeenth-century Europe. Their success did not stem from their superiority in agricultural and industrial production, though they were indeed good farmers and skilled manufacturers. Primarily, they were middlemen: they bought, sold, and carried other people's products. They bought great quantities of spices, tea, china, and cotton in Asia, and of sugar, tobacco, and furs in America. They bought even greater quantities of lumber, grain, cattle, and copper in northern Europe, and of wool, wine, silk, and silver in southern Europe. With their ample fleet of merchant ships, the Dutch transported all these commodities to Amsterdam and other Dutch towns, and sold them to the

[2] U. S. Bureau of the Census, *Historical Statistics of the United States, Colonial Times to 1957* (Washington, D.C., 1960), pp. 74–78, 356, 416.

buyers from all over Europe who congregated there. Whenever possible, they enhanced their profits as middlemen by converting the raw materials they imported into finished goods. The Dutch textile mills, dyehouses, breweries, distilleries, tanneries, sugar and salt refineries, tobacco-cutting factories, and soap works all depended on imported materials. By gearing their whole society to foreign trade, the Dutch overcame their lack of natural resources, manpower, and military strength. As Dutch prosperity proved, the merchant middleman was the prime catalyst in the seventeenth-century economy.

The rise of Dutch commercial capitalism is a remarkable story. When the Netherlanders began their revolt against Philip II in the 1560's, the northern provinces (the future Dutch republic) were decidedly less prosperous than the southern provinces. Amsterdam stood far behind Antwerp as a commercial entrepôt. But the inhabitants of Holland and Zeeland, the two northern provinces bordering on the North Sea, had long been seafaring folk and possessed many ships of all sizes. They already dominated the North Sea fisheries and the Baltic grain and timber trade. Once the "sea beggars" had captured ports in Holland and Zeeland in 1572, the Dutch could ward off the Spanish army by opening the dikes when necessary; and they could outsail the Spanish fleet and plunder the Spanish merchant marine. All through the years between the Dutch declaration of independence in 1581 and the final peace settlement with Spain in 1648, Dutch commerce boomed. Dutch merchants aggressively developed old avenues of trade and opened new ones. Despite the war, they kept on buying Spanish wool and selling grain to the Spaniards. They even sold military stores to the Spanish army! They capitalized on Portugal's weakness during the Portuguese union with Spain (1580–1640) by seizing the most valuable Portuguese colonies and trading posts. When the duke of Parma captured Antwerp in 1585, Amsterdam quickly replaced that city as Europe's greatest shipping center, commodity market, and financial exchange. The Dutch insisted on blockading the mouth of the Scheldt River, Antwerp's entrance to the North Sea, to guarantee that Antwerp could never regain her old commercial primacy.

The Dutch republic in the mid-seventeenth century was very small, with an area about the size of the state of Maryland and a population of two million. The eighty-year war with Spain had not caused any appreciable modernization of its particularistic political structure. The seven sovereign provinces—Holland, Zeeland, Utrecht, Gelderland, Groningen, Overyssel, and Friesland—continued to cherish their separate identities. Cynics called them the Disunited Provinces. Wealthy, crowded, cosmopolitan Holland had few economic, social, or cultural bonds with backwater, feudal, cattle-raising Gelderland. The central government, such as it was, functioned by means of negotiations among the seven autonomous provinces. Each province sent ambassadors to The Hague to meet in the States-General, a body which rarely acted energetically because its decisions required the consent of all seven constituencies. But in a crisis the other six provinces deferred to Holland, since the Hollanders contributed over half the union's financial support. Political control in Holland was vested in the merchant oligarchs who ruled Amsterdam and the other towns. There was no central executive in the Dutch republic, though William the Silent's house of Orange developed some of the attributes of a ruling dynasty. The prince of Orange was normally the commander of the federal army and navy, and *stadholder*, or chief administrator, in five of the seven provinces. The Dutch federation looked fragile and impractical—but it worked. Dutch politics became a tug of war between the house of Orange and the merchant oligarchs in Holland. Except in times of acute military emergency, the merchant oligarchs prevailed. They wanted international peace, which would facilitate the development of Dutch trade throughout the world.

Seventeenth-century Dutch commercial capitalism produced no individual titans to compare with Jacques Coeur, Cosimo de Medici, or Jakob Fugger. Nevertheless, by pooling their resources the Dutch merchants were able to undertake ventures which would have been too expensive and risky for the solitary giants of the past. Great numbers of investors, big and small, organized themselves into companies chartered by the state, in order to tackle large commercial projects. The grandest of these companies, the Dutch East India Company, was founded in 1602 with an initial capital of 6,500,000 florins. It was a joint-stock enterprise; hundreds of investors from all over the Dutch republic pooled their money to give the company working capital. The seventeen directors who operated the East India Company were drawn from among the biggest shareholders, but the small shareholders had little to complain about. The pepper, cloves, and nutmeg which the company brought to Amsterdam netted an average annual dividend of 18 per cent.

By the mid-seventeenth century, the Dutch had created a worldwide empire which differed in every way from the Spanish empire. It was a trading network owned and operated by private enterprise, with minimal government supervision. Two joint-stock companies, the East India Company and the West India Company (founded in 1621), divided the globe between them. Each of these companies had sovereign authority to possess and govern overseas territory, to negotiate treaties, and to wage war. The East India Company was the more important. In the early seventeenth century the company's soldiers and sailors drove the Portuguese out of the spice islands, the Malay Archipelago, and Ceylon, and kept the English from moving into these places. The Dutch thus secured virtually complete control over Sumatran pepper, Ceylonese cinnamon, and Moluccan nutmeg, mace, and cloves. The company also maintained a post on an island off Nagasaki, where the suspicious Japanese government gave the Dutch a monopoly on all

European trade with Japan. The company shipped home tea and porcelain from its Chinese trading posts, cotton from its Indian trading posts, silk from Persia, and coffee from Arabia. In 1652 the company established a way station at the Cape of Good Hope to break the long sea voyage between Amsterdam and Asia. The Dutch West India Company, operating in the western hemisphere, had less success because other European states were too well entrenched there. It could not capture any major Spanish colonies, and in the 1640's and 1650's the Portuguese reconquered Brazil and Angola from the Dutch. In North America, the Dutch never got much profit out of their fur-trading posts at Manhattan and Albany, and lost them to the English in 1664. However, the West India Company did get good returns from the lucrative African slave trade, and its island outposts of Curaçao and St. Eustatius proved to be useful bases for raiding and trading in the Caribbean.

The East India and West India companies were dazzling symbols of Dutch commercial capitalism, but they were actually less vital to the Dutch economy than the North Sea fishing industry and the western European carrying trade. The fisheries employed several hundred thousand Dutchmen. Many workers were needed to build, equip, and repair the fishing smacks. Others manned the North Sea fleets which fished for herring, haddock, and cod. Others manned the Arctic whaling fleets. Others pickled, smoked, and barreled the catch for export. Still others fetched from Portugal and France the salt needed to cure the herring, and from Norway the timber needed in constructing the ships and the barrels. Despite the fact that they had to import all their lumber, the Dutch built a great fleet of merchant ships. Contemporaries guessed that the Dutch possessed sixteen thousand merchant vessels in the mid-seventeenth century, something like half the European total. Danish toll records indicate that two thirds of the ships which entered the Baltic Sea during this period were Dutch. At times there were more Dutch than Spanish ships off Spanish America, and more Dutch than English ships off English America. In 1619, the first cargo of Negro slaves to Virginia was carried in a Dutch ship. This carrying fleet enabled the Dutch to collect middleman profits on nearly every branch of waterborne commerce, and caused Amsterdam to develop into the busiest trading center in Europe.

During the century following the outbreak of the Dutch revolt in 1566, the population of Amsterdam climbed from 30,000 to 200,000. The harbor was shallow and inconveniently inland from the North Sea, but the city was the most northerly and the most defensible of the Dutch ports, and was therefore safe from the Spanish. Amsterdam lay athwart the Baltic Sea, Rhine River, and English Channel shipping routes. Nobody but nobody could undersell the Amsterdam merchants because they dealt in volume. They would sail a fleet of flyboats into the Baltic laden with herring (which Dutch fishermen had caught off the English coast) and return with all of the

Amsterdam harbor in 1663. *Engraving by Dapper, showing dozens of merchant ships moored outside the city because the interior docks are jammed to capacity. Note the church steeples and windmills silhouetted against the flat Holland countryside. Scheepvart Museum, Amsterdam.*

grain surplus from a Danish island, or with twenty thousand head of lean cattle to be fattened in the Holland polders. They would buy a standing forest in Norway for timber, or contract before the grapes were harvested for the vintage of a whole French district. They would buy shiploads of undyed cloth, crude Barbados sugar, and Virginia leaf in England; have the cloth dyed, the sugar refined, and the tobacco cut and wrapped by Amsterdam craftsmen; and sell the finished commodities all over northern Europe at prices the English could not match. Foreign merchants found it worth their time to shop in Amsterdam because there they could buy anything from a precision lens to muskets for an army of five thousand. The exchange bank eased credit; marine insurance policies safeguarded transport. And no merchant could feel a stranger in a city where the presses printed books in every European tongue, and the French- and English-language newspapers were more lively and informative than the gazettes printed back home.

The Dutch republic was a Calvinist state, but John Calvin would not have felt at home in mid-seventeenth-century Amsterdam. The great Dutch merchants did not permit the Dutch Reformed clergy to interfere in politics or business. Catholics, Anabaptists, Jews, and unbelievers were tolerated in Amsterdam. The religious zeal which had stirred the Dutch into rebellion against Philip II, and nerved them into continuing the fight in the 1580's when all seemed hopeless, had turned into a secular zeal for making money. Indeed, the Dutch had lost more of their mid-sixteenth-century crusading impetus than had their old adversaries, the Spaniards. This loss of Dutch religious zeal is particularly evident if one compares seventeenth-century Dutch and Spanish mission work among the heathen overseas. Thousands of

Spanish priests and monks proselytized vigorously in the Philippines, India, Siam, and China, and maintained an elaborate network of Catholic churches, schools, seminaries, and universities. The Dutch East India Company sent a good many Calvinist ministers and schoolteachers into Asia, but their missionary efforts were singularly feeble. "Nay," lamented a Dutch Calvinist in 1683, "while the Jesuits and other locusts of the whore of Babylon apply so patiently their blind zeal to promote the Kingdom of Darkness, we do so little to make the Kingdom of Mercy come!"[3]

The moneymaking ethos was certainly more pervasive and powerful in Amsterdam than it had been in such earlier capitalist centers as Florence, Venice, Augsburg, and Antwerp. We should not, however, exaggerate the modernity of seventeenth-century Dutch commercial enterprise. Amsterdam's business structure—its bank, exchange, insurance companies, and joint-stock companies—was based on sixteenth-century models. The characteristic Amsterdam business firm continued to be a simple partnership. The Dutch joint-stock companies resembled medieval guilds in their protectionist policies. The East India Company had a monopoly on the eastern trade and forbade any Dutch merchant not a shareholder from trading in the spice islands. The company did more than just resist external competition; it deliberately destroyed some of its own Sumatran pepper plantations and Molucca nutmeg cargoes in order to keep the supply limited and the price high. Furthermore, Dutch commercial prosperity was strictly limited to the upper and middle classes. The paintings of Jan Vermeer and Pieter de Hooch, with their scenes of well-fed, well-dressed burghers living in spotlessly clean, comfortably furnished brick houses, illustrate only one side of seventeenth-century Dutch life. Half the inhabitants of Amsterdam lived under slum conditions, in squalid shanties or cellars. The Dutch wage laborer worked twelve to fourteen hours a day when he was lucky enough to have a job and subsisted on a diet of beans, peas, and rye bread. For all their enterprise, not even the Dutch could achieve an economy of abundance in the seventeenth century.

PROPERTY AND PRIVILEGE

Europe's relatively low productivity during the sixteenth and seventeenth centuries helped keep its social structure sharply stratified. Class lines were formalized to an extent hard for us to credit. While there was more social mobility than in the Middle Ages, people were no less self-conscious about their proper station in life. Every rank in the social order, from princes and aristocrats at the top to serfs and beggars at the bottom, had its own distinct

[3]Quoted by Peter Geyl, *The Netherlands in the Seventeenth Century* (London, 1961–1964), Vol. II, p. 188.

style of dress, diet, habitation, and entertainment; its own training, customs, and mental attitudes. The value systems of the aristocrat, the bourgeois, and the peasant differed profoundly. A person's vocabulary and accent, even his physical posture, instantly identified his social station, which helps explain why it was still exceptional for anyone born into a given rank (especially at the bottom or top of the scale) to climb up or down. Hierarchy was considered a measure of civilization. Social gradations might be rough and ready in frontier areas, such as Ireland, Sweden, Russia, and America, but in France, the center of civility, they were elaborated to the fullest extent. Ulysses' oft-quoted soliloquy in Shakespeare's *Troilus and Cressida* perfectly expresses the prevailing contemporary belief that social hierarchy preserves political order and economic well-being.

> The heavens themselves, the planets, and this centre,
> Observe degree, priority, and place,
> Insisture, course, proportion, season, form,
> Office, and custom, in all line of order: . . .
> Take but degree away, untune that string,
> And, hark, what discord follows! . . .
> Then every thing includes itself in power,
> Power into will, will into appetite;
> And appetite, an universal wolf,
> So doubly seconded with will and power,
> Must make perforce an universal prey,
> And last eat up himself.

Shakespeare evidently expected the growing spirit of capitalism to dissolve traditional hierarchical patterns, but in some ways it intensified them. To be sure, men of talent and enterprise now had a better chance to improve themselves. But the economic disparities between the upper, middle, and lower classes grew sharper. Had Europeans during the sixteenth and seventeenth centuries experienced an economy of abundance and of mechanized production, such as our own, no doubt the expectations of the very poor would have been leveled up and the tastes of the very rich leveled down. But an economy based on hand production and offering only limited wealth had a contrary psychological effect. For the people at the top of the social scale, the increase in wealth and income made possible an extravagant style of life undreamed of by medieval kings and lords. Luxury and waste became the necessary badges of high social status. The people at the bottom of the scale, on the other hand, remained as poorly off as they had been for centuries, prevented (by the economy's chronic underproduction) from achieving any improvement in their standard of living. In short, Europe in the era of the religious wars was divided as never before into "haves" and "have nots"— the rich and middle classes, with their total monopoly on wealth and comfort, and the servile classes who knew that they would never have anything beyond bare subsistence.

This psychological division between "haves" and "have nots" is well illustrated by a survey of English society drawn up in 1696 by an ingenious statistician named Gregory King. Using figures obtained through personal observation during extensive tours of the country, and through his analysis of tax returns and of birth, death, and marriage records, King calculated that England's total population was 5.5 million, a guess which modern demographers support. The interesting thing is the way King divided the people included in this total into two categories: 2.7 million were persons "increasing the wealth of the kingdom," and 2.8 million were persons "decreasing the wealth of the kingdom." His first category included everyone who held some stake in society—land, office, or a profession or craft. Among these were the aristocracy, country gentlemen, royal officials, merchants, military officers, lawyers, teachers, clergymen, shopkeepers, artisans, and farmers. All of these occupational groups, according to Gregory King, had some share in the country's surplus wealth. Obviously, a noble lord with ten thousand acres had a far greater share than a yeoman with fifty acres, but even the artisan or small farmer produced more than enough from his labor to support a family. For the great majority of persons in this category, land was the chief and most valued form of property. The 2.8 million persons in King's second category formed the unpropertied, submerged half of the population, having no share in the country's wealth. Among these "have nots" were agricultural wage laborers, domestic servants, soldiers, sailors, paupers, and vagabonds. Notice the remarkably low standing of seventeenth-century soldiers and sailors, recruited from the dregs of society.

In King's opinion, the wage laborers were almost as great a drain on the economy as the paupers. Their wages ate into the wealth of the kingdom, and since they generally earned too little to cover necessary living expenses, they had to be partially subsidized by public charity. The wage laborers could scarcely afford to marry. King calculated that they produced one or two fewer children per capita than their social superiors in the first category.[4] Property owners felt little compassion for the oppressed workers, better known as "the poor," because their plight seemed irremediable. There was simply not enough wealth to go around. Thus half the people in England were categorized as a necessary evil at best. If this was the situation in relatively affluent England, the psychological division was certainly even sharper east of the Elbe, where a small landlord class enjoyed all the surplus wealth and an immense servile class was excluded from possession of any property or comfort.

A society which labeled half or more of the population as hapless and burdensome was hardly geared for social or political democracy. Everywhere in Europe the property-owning upper classes had a monopoly on political

[4]Gregory King's tabulations are conveniently reproduced in Charles Wilson, *England's Apprenticeship, 1603–1763* (London, 1965), p. 239.

participation as well as on wealth and comfort. Even words like "liberty" and "freedom" had much less egalitarian connotations than they do today. "Liberty" in the sixteenth and seventeenth centuries referred to the enjoyment of special advantages not open to other men. For example, in Venice a closed circle of two thousand noblemen possessed the liberty of governing their state: they had an oligarchic monopoly on administration which prevented the Venetian middle and lower classes from choosing their legislators or holding office. When the Dutch burghers defended their ancient liberties against Philip II, they were not proclaiming the birthright of all Dutchmen to govern themselves, but rather protecting the vested interests of a privileged caste. Likewise, "freedom" meant exemption from restrictions which unprivileged persons had to observe. A cobbler's apprentice who served out his indentures for seven years obtained the freedom of his craft: he could now make shoes for his own profit instead of laboring for his master without pay. He was initiated into a privileged group with a monopoly on shoemaking, for no cobbler was allowed to set up shop without having first served his apprenticeship and won his freedom. Thus "liberty" and "freedom," far from conveying the modern notion of the right of all men to act as they see fit, were both expressions referring to special privileges. Property and privilege went hand in hand. The "haves" and "have nots" are perhaps better defined as the "privileged" and the "unprivileged" classes. There is no social concept today equivalent to "*un*privileged." The term "*under*privileged" is quite different, for we define underprivileged persons as those members of society who have been denied economic, social, or political rights properly belonging to all men. The *un*privileged members of seventeenth-century society could claim no such rights.

To keep the unprivileged classes in their place, every government employed repressive measures. Beggars were whipped and pilloried. Since long imprisonment was too expensive, convicted criminals were either summarily executed or maimed—the tongue bored, the nose slashed, the cheeks branded, a hand or foot lopped off—and then released. In England, convicts were sometimes transported to the colonies. In France they were put to forced labor in the royal galleys. Crimes against property were punished as savagely as crimes against persons. The most trifling theft might bring a penalty of death. Public executions rivaled bearbaiting and cockfighting as popular spectacles. The authorities customarily exhibited the decaying heads of executed criminals on pikes over bridges and gateways as a grim warning to would-be malefactors. One seventeenth-century traveler counted some 150 rotting carcasses of robbers and murderers swinging from gibbets along the highway between Dresden and Prague. Despite this harsh criminal code, in the absence of police forces most crimes went unpunished. But by quartering troops in the large towns, governments could at least overawe the mobs and keep rudimentary order. It is striking to see, in an overcrowded city like

Hanging Thieves. *Engraving by Callot. This grim scene illustrates seventeenth-century techniques of criminal justice: troops stand guard and priests shrive hastily, as two dozen condemned men are executed at once.*

seventeenth-century Paris, how much space was allocated to military display: massive forts, such as the Bastille; huge army barracks and hospitals, such as the Invalides; and suburban parade grounds, such as the Champ de Mars. Even more striking is the space consumed by royal palaces and aristocratic pleasure gardens. In Paris, the connecting Louvre and Tuileries palaces opened onto a mile-long garden bordering the Seine, designed for the use of the court nobility, and in addition, during the seventeenth century two more palaces were built within the city—the Palais du Luxembourg and the Palais-Royal, both surrounded by extensive formal gardens where a privileged few could take the air.

It is against this background of domestic stratification, exploitation, and repression that one must assess the institution of chattel slavery in Europe's overseas colonies. In the sixteenth and seventeenth centuries, Europeans enslaved millions of Negroes and Indians. Whenever any European—whether Portuguese, Spanish, Dutch, English, or French—first came into contact with African Negroes, Indonesians, or American Indians, he instinctively and automatically ranked these people several notches lower in the social order than the unprivileged servile classes at home. The reasons are obvious. These dark-skinned peoples lacked both the Christian culture which Europeans considered essential for salvation, and the technology to resist European mastery. When even the Turks were scorned as infidels despite their military prowess and political organization, it is small wonder that Cortes and Pizarro failed to appreciate the cultural attainments of the Aztecs and Incas whom they conquered with absurd ease. A few stay-at-home savants like Sir Thomas More might picture the New World as Utopia, or like Michel de Montaigne, suggest that cultural differences between the New World and the Old were only relative. Who are we, Montaigne asked in the

1570's, in the midst of the French religious wars, to judge the cannibals of Brazil? But the rough and energetic adventurers who staked out claims to America and trafficked with Asia and Africa felt no such inhibitions. To them, the native peoples were all barbarians, to be Christianized if possible, handled like vermin when necessary, and put to work for their white masters.

As early as 1443 the Portuguese were sending home African slaves. In 1493 Columbus brought back to Spain some Arawak Indian slaves. But slave labor was needed in America, not in Europe. In the first decades of the sixteenth century the Spaniards required unskilled manpower for their West Indian mines and plantations, the sort of brute labor done by the unprivileged classes at home, which the *conquistadores* refused to undertake themselves. They soon discovered that West Indians made very poor slaves. Forced labor killed off the gentle Arawaks, and the fierce Caribs were untrainable. The problem was solved by importing from the Guinea coast Negroes inured to hard work in tropical conditions. In 1511 the first recorded slave ship to reach Spanish America sold her black cargo, unwilling pioneers in an epic folk migration.

One estimate is that 900,000 African slaves were shipped to America during the sixteenth century, and 2.7 million during the seventeenth century. However inaccurate such figures may be, there can be no doubt that many more Africans than Europeans came to America in these years. Though the slave trade did not reach its peak until the eighteenth and early nineteenth centuries, it was already a roaring business in the seventeenth— highly dangerous, brutalizing, and lucrative to the slaver. The slave traders exploited and encouraged the endless political anarchy within West Africa. Hundreds of small tribes incessantly warred against one another, and any chieftain who could put together a string of prisoners eagerly sold them to the white man in return for firearms and trinkets. The trade was dominated by the Portuguese throughout the sixteenth century, by the Dutch in the mid-seventeenth century, and by the English in the later seventeenth century, but the French, Spanish, Swedish, Danish, and Germans were active also. A big problem for any slaver was how to transport his captives economically without losing too many of them. Packed like sardines into small, stinking ships, chained to the decks without air or exercise, many Negroes died before they could be sold in America. Records of the Royal African Company in England show that in the 1680's, when the slaver could buy Negroes for £3 apiece on the Guinea coast, 23 per cent of the slaves died during the Atlantic crossing. But by the early eighteenth century, when the initial investment in an African captive had climbed to £10, mortality during the crossing dropped to 10 per cent.[5] The slaver handled his cargo

[5]K. G. Davies, *The Royal African Company* (London, 1957), pp. 292–293.

like any perishable produce, calculating to a nicety the ratio between cost per item and tolerable spoilage.

To a great extent, the lot of the American slave depended on his master's nationality, and on whether he lived in the islands or on the mainland. Negroes in Portuguese Brazil and in the Spanish colonies had roughly the same status as serfs in eastern Europe, but in the French and English colonies (especially the Caribbean sugar colonies) they were much worse off. The reason for this difference is that the Spaniards and Portuguese were accustomed to holding Moors and Jews in slavery, and accorded the Negro the same social position which these earlier slaves had occupied. They recognized him as a moral person, insisted on his active membership in the Catholic Church, and gave him legal protection against his master's mistreatment. Many Brazilian Negroes, in particular, earned wages and bought their freedom. The English and French slaveholders were less generous. Lacking past experience with slavery, and suddenly confronted with a large force of exotic, restive, and menacing black laborers, they developed repressive law codes which froze the Negroes permanently into a subhuman category as chattel slaves without moral or legal standing or hope of manumission. English-style slavery created an agonizing psychological distinction between black and white. Furthermore, the English Protestant clergy made little effort to convert or instruct the Negroes lest they stir up notions of egalitarianism and rebellion. In the overpopulated Caribbean sugar islands, the slaves were fed so skimpily and worked so hard that their death rate far exceeded their birthrate. On one Barbados plantation for which we have records, six Negroes died for every one born. The managers of this plantation reckoned that it was cheaper and more efficient to restock regularly with fresh slaves from Africa than to raise living standards to the point where the existing slave population would maintain itself. Horses and cattle were managed on a different principle, receiving enough care to keep them healthy and fertile.

In recounting the establishment of Negro slavery it is hard to refrain from moralizing. But we must remember that an unprivileged, servile class seemed as necessary then as refrigerators and washing machines do today. When sixteenth- and seventeenth-century writers envisioned the ideal society, they found room in it for slaves and servants. Sir Thomas More's *Utopia* (1516) depicts an economically egalitarian, communistic society with a class of bondsmen to do the dirty work. Francis Bacon's *New Atlantis* (1627) portrays a cooperative community of research scientists and technologists, well served by flunkies. Some social critics, notably the Spanish priest Bartolomé de Las Casas (1474–1566), protested strenuously and successfully against the enslavement of American Indians. But almost no one (including Quakers who visited the sugar islands) protested openly against the enslavement of African Negroes. The serfdom east of the Elbe and the slavery in

America were ugly but natural by-products of Europe's strenuous search for wealth in an era of primitive productive techniques.

THE PRICE REVOLUTION

The people of Europe during the sixteenth and seventeenth centuries became more money conscious than they had ever been before. Between 1521 and 1660 the Spanish brought home from their Mexican and Peruvian mines eighteen thousand tons of bullion, enough to treble the existing European silver supply and to enlarge the European gold supply by 20 per cent. Over half of this precious metal flooded in during the forty years of peak production, 1580–1620. Great pains were taken to funnel all of the treasure into Spain. Every spring a Spanish fleet, convoyed by warships, carried a year's production of silver ingots from the Caribbean to Seville. Yet relatively little of the precious metal remained permanently in Spanish hands. A small quantity was captured by English and Dutch pirates in their raids on the Spanish treasure fleets. Quite a bit was smuggled into western Europe by the Spanish colonists, who thus evaded paying their king his royalty, or *quinto real* ("royal fifth"). The Spanish king did actually receive more than 25 per cent of the bullion which landed at Seville, but he could not keep it, since he had to pay his foreign creditors and his armies in the Low Countries, France, and Germany. Most of the remaining bullion which landed at Seville went to foreign merchants. It is estimated that in 1600 nearly a third of the Seville bullion was used to pay for French imports alone. In all these ways Spain's treasure circulated throughout western Europe. It was fluid wealth: some was hoarded; some was fashioned into goblets, plate, cutlery, and similar articles of luxury; but a great deal of it was minted into coins—Spanish gold escudos and silver reals, French gold louis and silver livres, Dutch gold ducats and silver florins, English gold guineas and silver shillings.

Since the volume of agricultural and industrial production remained comparatively unchanged, while the quantity of circulating specie increased, there was more money to spend on any given commodity. The consequence was a long and startling inflationary spiral. Between the beginning of the sixteenth century and the middle of the seventeenth, Europe experienced a veritable price revolution. Spain was hit first and hit hardest, as might have been expected. Spaniards were paying approximately four times as much for their commodities in 1600 as in 1500. After making a detailed study of Spain's annual bullion imports and price levels, Professor Earl J. Hamilton concluded that the bullion and price curves correlated very closely. In his view, the Spanish price rise throughout the sixteenth century was directly inspired by the flood of bullion; as soon as bullion imports declined in the seventeenth century, prices stabilized. This neat picture has been disputed by other economic historians, who believe that Spanish prices rose most steeply before 1565, whereas bullion imports reached their peak between 1580 and 1620.[6] But if American silver was not the sole cause of the price revolution, no one doubts that it was a principal cause.

In every state in western Europe the price of goods seems to have doubled or trebled between 1500 and 1650. In England the inflation was almost as severe as in Spain. What the price revolution meant in concrete terms is suggested by the following table, compiled from the ancient account books of Winchester College, a school attended by the sons of English aristocrats and country gentlemen. The figures are all in shillings, and show the rising prices the school purchasing agents had to pay for several representative commodities.[7]

	1500	1580	1630	1700
wine for the school chapel				
per 12 gallons	8		64	96
cloth for students' uniforms				
per piece	40	80	120	120
parchment				
per dozen	3	5	6	18
candles				
per 12 dozen	1	2	4	5
beef				
per 14 pounds		1	2	2
rabbits				
per 12 pair		9	12	18

As this table shows, the price rise was not uniform, but it was general. Winchester College paid three or four times as much for staples in 1700 as in 1500. The rise in the cost of chapel wine was particularly steep, perhaps because the boys were developing champagne tastes, but more likely because all wine had to be imported from the Continent and became subject to new customs and excise taxes in the seventeenth century. As a result, Englishmen tended to drink more home-brewed beer and less French wine. It is interesting to note that Winchester beef (unfortunately we lack a figure for 1500) seems to have become cheaper in real money. English cattle breeding had improved somewhat not only in quantity but in quality during the period; cooks in the Winchester kitchens and elsewhere no longer found it necessary to spice their meat dishes heavily in order to cover the taste.

No doubt the families of the Winchester boys could afford to pay the

[6] Earl J. Hamilton, *The American Treasure and the Price Revolution in Spain, 1501–1650* (Cambridge, Mass., 1934), p. 301. For a criticism of Hamilton, see J. H. Elliott, *Imperial Spain, 1469–1716* (New York, 1964), pp. 183–187.

[7] My figures are extracted from the detailed Winchester tables in Sir William Beveridge, *Prices and Wages in England* (London, 1939), Vol. I, pp. 81–90.

mounting bills. But many persons were profoundly distressed by the price revolution. Wages for day laborers in Spain, England, and other western states climbed more slowly than consumer prices; in other words, real wages for farm laborers and artisans fell during the late sixteenth century. Land-lords and entrepreneurs naturally wanted to avoid paying higher wages if possible, and they badgered their governments into fixing wage controls. In the late sixteenth century, unskilled laborers in Spain, England, France, and Germany must often have exhausted their entire wages in paying for minimum requirements of bread and drink. Elderly people living on savings, and those with fixed incomes, such as clergymen, teachers, and government clerks, also tended to suffer. There is a heated historical debate as to whether the large landowners were helped or hindered by the price revolution. If the landowner rented out his land on long leases, his income remained fixed and he suffered. If, on the other hand, he hired wage laborers to produce cash crops, he was more likely to prosper. It is safe to conclude that large-scale farmers, if they were energetic, efficient, and a bit ruthless, could more than keep pace with the rising prices. It is also evident that landed property, traditionally the only honorable form of wealth, was not in the sixteenth and seventeenth centuries the best source for quick profits.

Among the most important effects of the price revolution was the strain it placed upon government budgets. Traditionally, taxation had been closely tied to agriculture. Princes drew a considerable percentage of their revenue from their own private lands; the rest came largely from taxes on farms and crops. As the inflationary spiral developed, these agricultural taxes proved to be hopelessly inelastic and inadequate. The peasants, who bore the brunt of customary tax levies, were hard hit by the price rise, and their income rose more slowly than government expenses. In France, for instance, the principal source of royal revenue was the *taille,* a relatively low-yield tax on the peasants' income. It did not occur to the sixteenth-century French govern-ment that commerce offered a far more buoyant supply of capital than agriculture, and that the most effective way to increase state revenues was to encourage economic growth. On the contrary, the Valois kings imposed so many new tolls and tariffs on French commerce that they hindered business expansion—and lost additional revenue. Whenever French tax yields proved inadequate, the government borrowed money at exorbitant interest rates from the great international banking houses in Italy, Germany, and Flan-ders. The Valois kings were notorious spendthrifts, but even Elizabeth I of England, remarkable among sixteenth-century monarchs for her frugality, was forced by the expenses of her war with Spain to sell royal lands valued at £ 800,000 (equivalent to three years' peacetime revenues) and to contract large debts.

Elizabeth's great enemy, Philip II of Spain, was in a better position than any other sixteenth-century monarch to tap the new fluid capital effectively.

Yet even Philip got into terrible fiscal difficulties as soon as he undertook expensive wars. The situation he inherited in 1556 was alarming. Charles V left him a Spanish revenue of less than two million ducats a year, and a debt of more than twenty million. Twice during the early years of his reign, in 1557 and again in 1575, Philip was forced to declare bankruptcy, suspending all payments to the Fuggers and his other creditors. No wonder he felt less enthusiasm than his father had for military adventures. Yet as we have seen, the last thirty years of his reign were filled with campaigns against the Moors, the Turks, the Dutch, the French, and the English. Philip seems to have supposed that American silver would pay for all these wars. Actually, however, American silver was never his main source of income. By the 1580's he was receiving two million ducats in every treasure fleet, but this was a small sum compared with the six million annually extracted from the Castilian peasantry. Philip's subjects paid a wide range of taxes, including a sales tax (the *alcabala*) of 14 per cent on every transaction. Total Spanish revenues reached nearly ten million ducats by the 1590's. Thanks to his extortionate tax policy, the Prudent King managed to keep ahead of the price rise. But he still failed to meet the skyrocketing costs of war. All of Philip's revenues were mortgaged far in advance, and in the 1590's he was spending twelve million ducats annually. The Armada alone cost him ten million. He borrowed wildly, as his father had done, and in 1596 came another declaration of bankruptcy. When Philip died two years later, perhaps his chief legacy was a debt in the neighborhood of a hundred million ducats. Another legacy was the ruin of the house of Fugger, which went out of business shortly after 1600.

The era of inflation and fiscal crisis continued into the first half of the seventeenth century. Many of the German princes' difficulties during the Thirty Years' War were attributable to their outmoded tax systems. Even a solvent prince like Maximilian of Bavaria quickly exhausted his treasury in trying to finance his army, and once the soldiers of fortune got control, no German prince had the means to stop them from wrecking the country. But by mid-century the situation had changed radically. After 1630, American silver imports started to peter out, and the price structure stabilized fairly soon. Real wages in France, England, and the Netherlands regained or surpassed their early sixteenth-century levels. While Spain had irretrievably lost its former economic and political vitality and sank to the position of a second-rate power, the French, English, and Dutch prospered as never before, and their governments displayed unprecedented fiscal strength. In 1678 Louis XIV could pay for an army of some 270,000 men—at least four times the size of Philip II's army at its peak. Even backwater Brandenburg-Prussia maintained through tax levies an army of thirty thousand—as large as Philip's Armada force. This remarkable growth in state-supported armies was symptomatic of the vitality of governmental enterprise toward the end of the seventeenth century. What advantages did Louis XIV and the Great Elector have that Philip II lacked?

The answer lies in a combination of several factors. First, there was a general seventeenth-century rise in living standards among property holders and in the accumulation of surplus wealth, especially in the three chief Atlantic states. Second, there was a wider circulation of specie and an increased reliance on credit, both of which facilitated the use of Europe's wealth as working capital. Third, governments were devising better techniques for tapping this wealth by taxing the consumer more and the producer less.

Unlike the sixteenth-century Valois and Habsburg kings, the seventeenth-century Bourbon kings of France attempted to increase tax revenues by promoting industry and commerce. But in other respects the seventeenth-century French fiscal system, despite its ability to support Louis XIV's heroic army, was rather old-fashioned, and its yield was low by English and Dutch standards. The *taille* still brought in the greatest returns. Some regions of France were much more heavily rated than others, but everywhere the aristocrats and the bourgeoisie were in large part exempted. Jean Baptiste Colbert, Louis XIV's great minister of finance, tried without success to change the *taille* from an income tax on peasants into a real-estate tax on all property owners.

One of the 1,400 fountains in Louis XIV's gardens at Versailles. *Engraving by Mercy. This scene suggests the enormous size of Louis XIV's pleasure garden for the privileged French aristocracy and the crushing strain such building projects imposed on the state budget.*

He did manage to increase the *aides*, indirect liquor taxes which almost everyone had to pay. But French taxes were still collected principally from the poor. Colbert was unable to shake the French upper- and middle-class notion that tax payments were a badge of dishonor. It cannot be saio that the Dutch and English embraced a "soak-the rich" policy, but they did tax the propertied as well as the propertyless.

The English government in the 1680's tried abandoning land taxes altogether and drew 50 per cent of the royal revenues from customs duties on international and colonial trade. English overseas commerce suffered somewhat under this tax burden, but the Stuart monarchs drew enough money from customs levies to free them from dependence on the country gentlemen who sat in Parliament—with results which we shall observe in the next chapter. Since the Dutch depended even more heavily than the English on foreign trade, they refrained from imposing such heavy customs duties. Instead, they taxed domestic commerce, placing excise levies (similar to the French *aides*) on a wide range of staple market goods. The excise was intended, like the English customs duties, to siphon off surplus purchasing power without strangling business. It was a burdensome but practicable tax. Brandenburg-Prussia and England also made heavy use of the excise.

None of these states could survive on taxes alone; public borrowing was essential for covering the expenses of wars and other emergencies. Here again, the Dutch managed better than the French. While Louis XIV had to pay interest of 8 per cent or more, and consumed much of his budget in debt service, the Dutch were successfully floating government loans at 3 or 4 per cent. Thousands of Dutch citizens, including very humble people, subscribed to these loans to their government in the belief that they constituted a safe investment. Not so many years earlier, the Fuggers had been gambling their money on Philip II at extortionate rates in the hope of making a quick killing before the king defaulted.

England and the Dutch republic were fiscally the most effective seventeenth-century states because they were the most commercialized. In the era of the price revolution, commercial profits proved to be much more elastic than agricultural or industrial profits. The Dutch and English governments developed fruitful partnerships with the merchants of Amsterdam and London. In each instance, the state granted commercial privileges and protection to the mercantile community, and in return received excise and customs revenues, and was able to secure public loans at tolerable rates of interest. The vigorous Dutch and English traffic in domestic and foreign goods produced greater wealth than the mines of America. Merchants, traditionally disdained by the priests as moral parasites and by the knights as moral cowards, felt confident that they now formed the most dynamic social class. "Behold then the true form and worth of foreign trade," the English merchant Thomas Mun proudly wrote in the 1620's, "which is the great revenue of the king, the honor of the kingdom, the noble profession of the merchant, the school of our arts, the supply of our wants, the employment of our poor, the improvement of our lands, the nursery of our mariners, the walls of the kingdom, the means of our treasure, the sinews of our wars, the terror of our enemies."

CAPITALISM AND CALVINISM

Was there a connection between business enterprise and religious zeal? Did militant Protestantism spark capitalist expansion while reformed Catholicism discouraged it? Was it mere coincidence that the most dynamic businessmen were to be found in Protestant Holland and the most vigorous industrial growth in Protestant England, both states heavily tinctured with Calvinism? Why were the Huguenots so prominent in the business community of Catholic France? Or Protestant Brandenburg-Prussia under the Calvinist Great Elector almost the only seventeenth-century German state to exhibit increasing prosperity? Or Catholic Italy, Portugal, and Flanders, all flourishing business centers before 1559, so depressed by 1689? Or Spain, the most aggressively Catholic society of the day, the victim of startling economic collapse?

Scholars have been wrangling over these questions for the last sixty years without reaching agreement. The German sociologist Max Weber started the controversy in 1904 by publishing *The Protestant Ethic and the Spirit of Capitalism*, in which he maintained that the early Protestants—particularly Calvin and his followers—strongly influenced the beginnings of modern capitalism during the sixteenth and seventeenth centuries. Weber recognized that there had been many individual capitalists during the Middle Ages and the Renaissance, but he argued that these businessmen had not been able to instill into European society a pervasive profit-making ethos. He defined the capitalist spirit as a rationally calculated and highly systematized pursuit of profit rather than an irrational greed for gain, power, or glory. Weber did not find this rational capitalism in such pre-Reformation merchant-bankers as the Medici of Florence or the Fuggers of Augsburg. He contended that the Medici and the Fuggers exhibited irrational greed in their grandiose moneylending operations. They gambled for heroic stakes, made risky loans to kings and popes, and lavished their winnings on extraneous political projects, art patronage, or high living. Weber traced the beginnings of the modern capitalist spirit to the smaller-scale merchants of sixteenth- and seventeenth-century England and the Netherlands. These businessmen, he thought, practiced the restraint, sobriety, purposeful industry, and calculating frugality necessary for the construction of a rationally ordered profit system. And they were inspired in their business practices by the ethical teachings of Calvin. Weber made much of the Protestant idea that every man's wordly vocation or career was a "calling" assigned to him by God. If a man succeeded in his calling, this was a sign that God had predestined him for salvation. In Weber's view, Calvin's doctrine of predestination produced in his adherents character traits of inner loneliness and outer discipline, asceticism and drive. The Calvinist merchant's energy lifted him above the servile working class. His dignity was proof against the luxury and waste of aristocrats and banker princes. As Weber's supporter R. H. Tawney put it, "Calvin did for the *bourgeoisie* of the sixteenth century what Marx did for the proletariat of the nineteenth."

Weber's thesis has been challenged in a number of ways. Some critics deny his premise that there is meaningful cultural interaction between religious and economic forces. Others see little point in searching for an emerging "spirit" of capitalism. Marxists and other economic determinists generally reject Weber's contention that economic ideas and attitudes cause changes in business practice. They hold instead that business practices cause changes in economic attitudes; hence the focal point should be the economy itself and not the environmental "spirit." Still other critics object to Weber's dismissal of pre-Reformation capitalism. They point out that Renaissance Florence and Venice and sixteenth-century Antwerp employed almost all the business techniques of seventeenth-century Amsterdam and London. Many members of the Catholic bourgeoisie practiced self-discipline, frugality, and industry before Calvin came along to enshrine these virtues. Another line of attack is that Weber misconstrued the ethical teachings of Calvin. He has been accused of distorting the reformer's notion of a worldly "calling," of soft-pedaling Calvin's hostility to money and profit, and of ignoring the repressive atmosphere of Calvin's Geneva, which suffocated rather than stimulated business enterprise. Furthermore, it has been argued that the most intensely Calvinist areas of sixteenth- and seventeenth-century Europe—Scotland and the rural Netherlands—remained economically backward. In comparison with agrarian Friesland, Amsterdam was hardly Calvinist at all: it tolerated Catholics and Jews, and its Reformed preachers watered down the Founder's doctrine of predestination. Weber's more extreme critics go so far as to say that Calvinism was the enemy of capitalism.

The Weber controversy has run itself into the ground in recent years. Today most specialists in the history of the period regard Weber's thesis as far too simple. Yet however inadequately Weber formulated his proposition, it is surely naïve to doubt his premise, that the dynamic economic and religious forces of the sixteenth and seventeenth centuries had a strong mutual impact.

The exact impact of the Protestant and Catholic reformations upon the European business climate can never be determined, but there seems to be a large kernel of truth in Weber's contention that the Protestant ethic of disciplined individualism bolstered the value system of the western Euro-

The Fountain of the Four Rivers in Rome. *Designed by Bernini. A splendid example of ostentatious display in Baroque Rome.*

pean merchant community. To be sure, St. Ignatius of Loyola placed as much stress on emotional and intellectual discipline as John Calvin did, but the disciplined Calvinist practiced underconsumption and hated sinful ostentation, whereas the disciplined Jesuit lavished his resources on Baroque extravagance for the greater glory of God. Baroque Rome, transformed by the reformed papacy's building program of gorgeous churches, avenues, piazzas, stairways, statues, fountains, and palaces, was a far more telling exhibit of what Weber termed irrational, anticapitalistic display than Renaissance Florence had ever been. Seventeenth-century Amsterdam, for all its commercial prosperity, was a plain town, with few prominent public buildings. Every Amsterdam canal presented the same view: a serried double row of tall, narrow, gabled houses, looking rather homely and very solid. The Dutch businessman characteristically maintained his office on the ground floor of his house, his living quarters on the middle floors, and his warehouse on the top floors. The grandest Amsterdam capitalist was not ashamed to have a pulley projecting prominently from the ridgepole of his house, by which barrels and bales were hoisted into his upper windows from barges in the canal below.

The impact of Calvinism upon capitalism can only be gauged impression-istically; the impact of capitalism upon Calvinism is easier to trace through several chronological stages. The early Calvinists were deeply suspicious of moneymaking. The saints of mid-sixteenth-century Geneva, inhabiting a small oasis in a desert of sin, took community action to control the wicked avarice of usurers and monopolists. But by the early seventeenth century, when Calvin's disciples had penetrated into all the business centers of western Europe, they could no longer segregate themselves from the carnal practices of their unrighteous neighbors. Only in backwater places like Scotland, New England, and the rural Netherlands was it possible to maintain exclusive and pristine communities of the elect. Increasingly, the Protestant activist had to rely on individual self-discipline. The Puritan merchant in London schooled himself to maintain his stewardship to God. But his God-given business success encouraged him to value worldly labor as an end in itself. Profit making became a duty. By the late seventeenth century those London and Amsterdam capitalists who had been trained in a Calvinist heritage still dedicated themselves to hard work, but the original ethical purpose of their "calling" had been secularized. The saint of 1559 had become the privileged property holder of 1689.

The Protestant ethic was secularized, but it did not disappear. Successful Protestant businessmen felt a measure of social responsibility as stewards of God's wealth, and their extensive private charity to the poor and the sick was of great importance in an age when governments performed a minimum of social services. Dutch almshouses, orphanages, and hospitals for the sick poor, supported largely by private donors, drew high praise from all visitors. According to a recent study of English private philanthropy, the property-holding classes gave eight times as much money to charity in 1640 as in 1480. Merchants gave much more generously than anyone else, especially in the early seventeenth century, when so many of them joined the Puritan movement. Once we have made allowances for a 350-per-cent price rise and for England's commercial growth during this period, we may question whether the seventeenth-century Protestant donor was much more generous than his fifteenth-century Catholic predecessor. But there can be no doubt that his money went to a different set of charitable goals. The pre-Reforma-tion philanthropist gave 53 per cent of his bequests to the church (half of this to subsidize prayers for the dead) and only 15 per cent to poor relief, hospitals, and social-welfare schemes. The early seventeenth-century philan-thropist gave 12 per cent of his bequests to the church (none of it to subsidize prayers for the dead) and 55 per cent to poor relief and social welfare.[8] Statistics like these indicate the manifold connections between business enterprise and religious zeal in the sixteenth and seventeenth centuries.

[8]W. K. Jordan, *Philanthropy in England, 1480–1660* (London, 1959), pp. 367–387.

MERCANTILISM

The years between 1559 and 1689 saw the popularization of the quasi-economic, quasi-political doctrine which Adam Smith, a hundred years later, contemptuously branded as the mercantile system, or mercantilism. Historians have always sharply disagreed in their definition, interpretation, and estimation of mercantilism. Some prefer to drop the whole concept. Seventeenth-century economic thought, they contend, was too inchoate to be regarded as a system. Most governments may have adopted mercantilist planks, but no two built the same economic platform. Only a handful of polemicists and bureaucrats, such as Colbert in France, preached the pure mercantilist gospel. Although these objections have validity, it must nevertheless be recognized that mercantilism was pervasive and powerful. The term usefully identifies characteristic western European notions concerning the relation between business and government. The mercantilist attitude of mind was partly radical, partly conservative, and wholly consistent with the psychology of limited wealth.

Hazarding a definition, we may say that the mercantilists were those who advocated the conscious and artificial development of the sovereign state into an economic unit, for the purpose of fostering community wealth and power. The businessmen and statesmen who groped toward this goal were

The English East India Company factory at Surat, India, early in the seventeenth century. *From an old print. The English, Dutch, and French maintained factories or trading posts similar to this one in numerous Asian cities. In this scene, the Indians in the foreground are evidently carting off goods they bought at the factory. The Englishmen in the courtyard within are identifiable by their broad-brimmed hats.*

exhilarated by the new abundance of fluid capital, hungry for profit, yet still convinced that the total quantity of wealth was relatively fixed. The best way to get and keep as large a share as possible of this limited wealth, they argued, was through a planned, cooperative society. Experience had shown the dangers of rugged individualism. After all, freewheeling entrepreneurs like the Fuggers lost their fortunes faster than they made them. Self-centered princes like the Valois, obsessed with dynastic politics, disastrously mortgaged themselves to foreign moneylenders. Mercantilists applauded the concept of secular sovereignty articulated by Jean Bodin and other social theorists who were sick of political anarchy and irresponsible wars. They agreed with Bodin that final authority and power belonged to the state, not the reigning prince. The sovereign state could and should back up aggressive

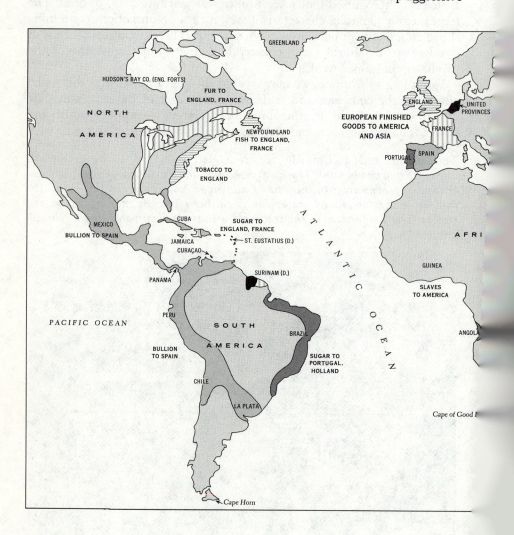

businessmen and protect their accumulated profits. This advocacy of a planned state economy was by no means new. The medieval town and the Renaissance city-state had functioned as economic units. But in the sixteenth-century political arena, the Italian and German city-states lacked the necessary size and strength. In eastern Europe, states like Austria, Poland, and Russia were certainly large enough, but they were too purely agrarian to achieve the benefits of a capitalist economy. Mercantilist attention therefore focused on Spain, Portugal, the Netherlands, Sweden, Brandenburg-Prussia, and—most particularly—on England and France.

Mercantilists tended to entertain fixed economic notions, one of which (inspired by the influx of New World treasure) was that bullion was the best measure of wealth. A state accumulated bullion by achieving a favor-

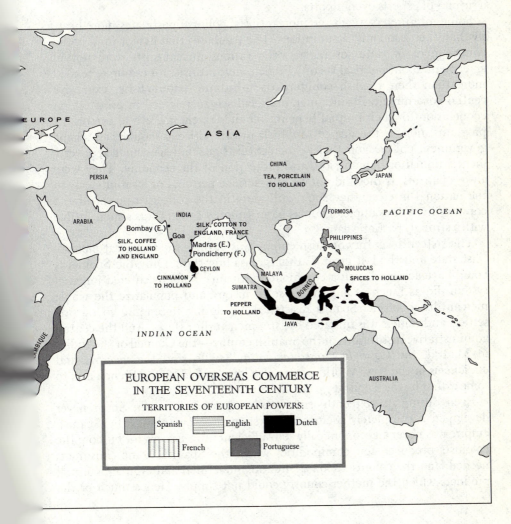

EUROPEAN OVERSEAS COMMERCE
IN THE SEVENTEENTH CENTURY

TERRITORIES OF EUROPEAN POWERS:

Spanish English Dutch

French Portuguese

able balance of trade—that is, by exporting goods of more value than those imported. It followed that a state ought to be as nearly self-sufficient as possible, so as to minimize dependence on imports. Overseas colonies could assist self-sufficiency by supplying those goods which the state would otherwise import. The larger a state's industrial production and trade were, the greater its exports and profits. It is revealing to find how indifferent the mercantilists were to the crude hand methods of production which hampered output during the sixteenth and seventeenth centuries. Hard work and full employment was their simple recipe for increasing productivity. Mercantilists were easily alarmed and dismayed by expanding domestic consumption and improvements in the living standard, which we regard as an index of wealth. They continually preached frugality and abstinence in order to assure a surplus of exports over imports.

Some interpreters weigh the mercantilists' political postulates more heavily than their economic assumptions. The trouble is that except for a broad endorsement of state sovereignty, the various mercantilists were not in agreement about political theory. French mercantilists, for example, tended more than their English counterparts to admire paternalistic, expensive central government. Businessmen and civil servants agreed in principle on cooperation for their mutual benefit, but they rarely saw eye to eye on tax programs, nor on the degree to which private citizens should help shape government policy. Nonetheless, mercantilists generally encouraged government stimulation, supervision, and protection of the economy. They were always patriots. If they did not care to sacrifice personal or local interests to the national interest, they could still glory in the collective power of the community. For example, Thomas Mun (quoted earlier) was a mercantilist with a strongly patriotic flair.

The sixteenth-century Spanish empire was at once the first great mercantilist state and the last great Catholic crusading state. Only the Spaniards could have achieved such a combination. Spain's bullion-centered imperial system did as much as anything else to inspire and popularize the whole mercantilist doctrine. Spain's insistence on closing its empire to outside settlers and traders was imitated by later mercantilist states. And the central administrative institutions of the Spanish empire—the Council of the Indies in Madrid, the *Casa de Contratación* in Seville, and the viceroys and *audiencias* in the New World—were also later copied by the French and to some extent by the English.

Even during its sixteenth-century boom period, however, Spain never developed a completely mercantilist system. For one thing, the Spanish empire was never an economically self-sufficient unit. Except for bullion, the colonists produced few commodities which the Spanish home consumers needed, and the colonists soon desired manufactured and even agricultural products which the mother country could not supply. Hence much of the cargo for the Seville-Indies trade had to be obtained from Flemish, French, or English merchants in exchange for bullion. Antwerp, not Seville, was the chief commercial entrepôt under Spanish rule—until Philip II's soldiers sacked it during the Dutch war. In the course of the seventeenth century, the Spanish empire became less and less mercantilist in character. Silver production fell off, and so did the Seville-Indies trade. The home government could not stop foreign interlopers from smuggling goods into Spanish America. The imperial administrative machinery was still intact, but the empire had disintegrated economically. From a mercantilist viewpoint, Spain had thrown away the grain and kept the chaff.

Of the three seventeenth-century Atlantic states which vied for the economic leadership abdicated by Spain, the United Provinces diverged most markedly from Spanish-style mercantilism. This was no accident. The Dutch rebelled against Philip II's business methods as well as against his Catholicism and his absolutism. They rejected, for both political and economic reasons, the mercantilist concept of the sovereign state as an economic unit. It was pointless to dream mercantilist dreams of achieving wealth through state power in a small country with only two million inhabitants. It was absurd to aim for economic self-sufficiency when the chief native products were tulips and cheese. Since the Dutch were the middlemen of Europe, their prosperity depended on wide-open trade. Dutch scholars wrote learned treatises to find legal justifications for freedom of the seas—possibly inspired by the fact that the United Provinces had by far the largest merchant marine in Europe. Dutch merchants flouted the most sacred mercantilist canons in order to stimulate trade. Orthodox bullionists were scandalized by the East India Company's shipment of specie to China and Japan in exchange for oriental luxury wares. To Dutch entrepreneurs, patriotism rarely seemed as alluring as profit. In 1622, in the midst of the war with Spain, the Dutch government found it necessary to prohibit brokers from insuring enemy ships and cargoes. The English and French governments were startled to discover Dutch investors subscribing handsomely to the English and French East India companies, which were intended to steal Asian trade from Amsterdam.

But if the Dutch rejected doctrinaire mercantilism, neither were they dogmatic advocates of *laissez-faire*. They simply adapted their economic views to fit changing circumstances. Thus in the late sixteenth and early seventeenth centuries, when the enemy was Spain, Dutch sailors could profitably plunder shipping and capture colonies, and Amsterdam thrived on war. But after the mid-seventeenth century the enemies became England and France, whose privateers could lacerate the huge Dutch shipping fleet and dislocate overseas trade. Accordingly, Dutch merchants then became advocates of international peace. The Dutch always insisted on free passage for their ships around the Danish islands to reach the Baltic; at the same time, in 1609 and again in 1648 they made the Spanish close the Scheldt River, in order to prevent Antwerp from ever again rivaling Amsterdam. Dutch belief in freedom of the seas stopped at Sumatra. The East India Company invested heavily in forts, warships, and soldiers to exclude interlopers from all the spice islands, including those not occupied by the Dutch. In 1623 the Dutch massacred some English traders who had dared to establish a post on the nutmeg island of Amboina. Nor would the company permit the native Indonesians to produce more spices than Dutch ships could handle. In the northern Moluccas they denuded whole islands, chopping down the clove plantations and killing any Indonesians who protested. The Dutch guarded their spice preserve every bit as jealously as the Spanish guarded their silver mines.

To the English and the French, the superb vitality of mid-seventeenth-century Dutch society was both impressive and annoying; the dry rot which vitiated the Spanish empire was both gratifying and puzzling. One overall conclusion seemed evident: if one could take Dutch business enterprise, combine it with Spanish centralized power, and shake thoroughly, the result would be a mercantilist's dream. After 1660, the English and the French coordinated public planning and private enterprise more consistently and self-consciously than the Spanish or the Dutch had ever done. These two great adversaries developed the mercantile system to its fullest extent. The story of their classic rivalry demands a separate chapter. Seventeenth-century England and France, competitors for wealth and power, antithetical in politics, religion, and social structure, were the two most dynamic states to emerge from the era of religious warfare.

The Spanish and the Dutch were another great pair of rivals, of course, and even the most summary review of business conditions in these two states will demonstrate the complexities and contradictions in the European economy during the sixteenth and seventeenth centuries. Both the Spanish and the Dutch were shackled by primitive techniques of hand production, both were strongly affected by the price revolution, both displayed energy in exploiting America and Asia. There is no simple explanation for Spain's economic disaster or for the Dutch boom prosperity. The Spaniards imported eighteen thousand tons of silver and gold only to wind up poorer in 1689 than they had been in 1559, while the Dutch had no gold mines or other natural resources, yet emerged in 1689 far richer than in 1559. In Spain the population shrank, farm production fell, sheep ranching declined, and the textile industry collapsed. In the Dutch republic the population grew, farm production rose, stock breeding improved, and the textile industry flourished. In Spain the government's oppressive tax policy and rigid trade regulations strangled private enterprise. The Dutch government taxed business without killing it, and Dutch merchants pooled their resources in joint-stock companies, built fleets of flyboats, developed techniques for banking, exchanging, investing, and insuring capital, and became the middlemen of Europe. Both states were at war most of the time, but while the costs of Philip II's armies drove Spain into irredeemable bankruptcy, the Dutch thrived on war until the mid-seventeenth century and could still float low-interest government loans to cover military expenses at the end of the century. Perhaps part of the answer lies in the differences between Spanish Catholicism and Dutch Calvinism. At any rate, the Spaniards and the Dutch did share three traits. Both societies were internally divided into privileged and unprivileged classes. Both readily enslaved the Negroes and Indians they encountered. And both in their own fashion expressed the psychology of limited wealth.

CHAPTER 10

Absolutism Versus Constitutionalism

SEVENTEENTH-CENTURY EUROPE saw the evolution of two strikingly effective forms of state power—absolute monarchy, best exemplified by Bourbon France, and constitutional monarchy, best exemplified by Stuart England. The contrasting development of these rival states is the subject of this chapter. The contrast was indeed dramatic. In politics and religion alike, the two societies moved toward opposite goals. In France, where the sixteenth-century Valois kings had lost control of the state during the wars of religion, a masterful succession of seventeenth-century kings and ministers—Henry IV, Richelieu, Mazarin, Colbert, and Louis XIV—built royal strength to unprecedented heights. In England, where the sixteenth-century Tudor dynasty had achieved great success and popularity, their Stuart successors were twice overthrown, in the revolutions of 1640 and 1688. Representative institutions atrophied in France, while the English Parliament gained sovereign authority. In religion, the French gradually abandoned the toleration policy set forth by Henry IV in the Edict of Nantes in favor of a unitary national Catholic church, whereas the English gradually abandoned Elizabeth I's insistence on a unitary national church in favor of toleration for minority creeds. In 1684 Louis XIV revoked the Edict of Nantes; in 1689 the English Parliament passed the Toleration Act. What caused these profoundly antithetical developments?

France and England were political and religious rivals because they were so different, but economic rivals because they were so similar. Except for such specialties as French wine and English coal, both produced much the same diversified range of goods. Both espoused mercantilism, seeking economic self-sufficiency by protecting home agriculture and industry while promoting a favorable balance of foreign trade. Frenchmen and Englishmen contested for the same products in the same places all over the world. In India they competed for cotton and calico, in West Africa for slaves, in the North Atlantic for fish, and in North America for furs and deerskins. In the West Indies they staked out rival sugar plantations on islands within sight of each other and even partitioned one miniature island—St. Christopher—into French and English zones.

Striking as this rivalry was, we must remember that the two societies shared certain basic characteristics which set them apart from their neighbors, especially those east of the Rhine. Unlike the Germans, Italians, Poles, Turks, and Russians, the French and English had already achieved national sovereignty. A comparatively homogeneous linguistic, cultural, and religious experience facilitated political cohesion and community spirit in both countries. National consciousness is no political cure-all, as recent history abundantly demonstrates, but it certainly helped the French and the English to generate more large-scale corporate energy than any other seventeenth-century society. Also, particularly in England, it tended to bridge the psychological gulf between the privileged and unprivileged classes. Agrarian magnates like those who controlled eastern Europe were decidedly less potent in France and England, where a vigorous urban capitalist class held a rising share of the wealth, and centralized institutions tended to curb local autonomy and particularism. The two Atlantic rivals could boast a wider distribution of property, a broader participation in public affairs, and a higher level of education and culture than any other contemporary state except the Dutch republic. And they far outmatched the Dutch in political power.

To most contemporary observers, France looked more impressive than England. It was the French who replaced the Renaissance Italians as arbiters of civility. Their language was spoken, their books were read, and their tastes were copied by well-bred persons everywhere. The seventeenth century was also France's *grand siècle* in international politics. Having the biggest population, the biggest army, the biggest revenue, and the best bureaucracy, France more than replaced Spain as Europe's most fearsome imperialist power. Largely because of France's glittering success, the prevailing European political trend was toward absolutism, not constitutionalism. The Bourbon style of monarchy was admired and aped not merely by petty German and Italian princes, but by the leading potentates of the day: the Spanish Habsburg kings, the Austrian Habsburg emperors, the Brandenburg Hohenzollern electors, and—most pertinent—the English Stuart kings.

THE RISE OF FRENCH ABSOLUTISM, 1598–1661

During the years between the end of the French wars of religion in 1598 and Louis XIV's assumption of personal control in 1661, France triumphantly recovered its political strength. At home, the French repaired their governmental system. Abroad, they decisively defeated the Habsburgs in Germany and Spain, and emerged as unquestionably the leading power in Europe. This achievement was no miracle, for France enjoyed splendid assets: a large population (some sixteen million people in 1600), a diversified economy, and a heritage of strong government and military prowess. But its problems during the late sixteenth-century wars of religion had seemed well-nigh insuperable. Antipathy between Huguenots and Catholics, between the aristocracy and the crown, between Paris and the provinces, had very nearly shattered the country into autonomous fragments like those of the Holy Roman Empire. That the French people not merely recovered from their civil wars, but developed a more vital society than they had known before, was due in great measure to the efforts of three purposeful statesmen—King Henry IV, Cardinal Richelieu, and Cardinal Mazarin.

Very different from one another in personality and tactics, the first Bourbon king and the two cardinals all pursued the same set of goals: to weaken local particularism, to strengthen central royal authority, and to enlarge French territory by means of an aggressive foreign policy. These aims were not new. The French Renaissance monarchs of the early sixteenth century had been trying to achieve exactly these purposes before the religious crisis and the price revolution disrupted their efforts. In taking up where Francis I and Henry II had left off, Henry IV, Richelieu, and Mazarin adroitly masked their policies through compromise and prevarication, yet they could never eradicate the centrifugal tendencies latent in French society. Opposition from Huguenots, ultra-Catholics, feudal nobility, privileged officeholders, entrenched bourgeoisie, autonomous provincials, oppressed peasantry, and the Paris mob remained constant and dangerous. Periodically—most notably in 1610–1624 and 1648–1653—several of these dissident factions coalesced to reignite the old anarchic civil tumult. But each outburst was mastered, and the centripetal process was patiently resumed. Hence while neither Henry, nor Richelieu, nor Mazarin was a conscious reformer or innovator, their sixty years of management did have great cumulative effect.

Henry IV (ruled 1589–1610) has the special distinction of being the most affectionately remembered figure in the long gallery of French kings. Stylish and witty, yet a bluff man of action, he played many roles: the soldier from Navarre with a magnificent white plume in his helmet, dramatically rallying his outmanned troops in battle; the sensual courtier with curling moustache, always in pursuit of the ladies; the conscientious administrator, absorbed by a current treatise on farming techniques—Olivier de Serres' *Théâtre d'agriculture*—read to him after dinner; and the simple, garlic-scented man of the people—*le roi de la poule au pot*, saying he hoped to live long enough to see every French peasant have a chicken in his pot each Sunday. Henry cultivated an image of himself as distinct as possible from that of the last Valois kings, the neurotic and effete sons of Catherine de Medici. In a system where so much depended on the king's character, Henry's outgoing, virile personality had immediate impact and long-range symbolic value. He never allowed the bitter war experiences of his youth to sour his temper or

Henry IV. *Painting by Pour-bus. The king looks charac-teristically skeptical and amused. Bibliothèque Pub-lique et Universitaire, Geneva.*

ossify his convictions. Raised as a Huguenot, he had twice turned Catholic. The difference between Henry's expediency and Catherine de Medici's was not great, except that his gambits worked and hers had not. Politics, like baseball, is a game of inches.

Henry IV spent the first half of his reign, from 1589 to 1598, closing the wars of religion, and the second half, from 1598 to 1610, securing domestic peace. The obstacles he overcame in terminating the wars have been described earlier. Henry bought off all internal opposition, bribing his Catholic subjects by joining their church, his Huguenot subjects by guaranteeing them civil and religious autonomy through the Edict of Nantes, and the commanders of the ultra-Catholic League by paying them 32 million livres (a sum greater than the annual royal revenue) to disband their troops. "France and I," he remarked in 1598, "both need to catch our breath." Having yielded so often in order to win acceptance, Henry endeavored thereafter to rebuild royal authority. In his view the Estates-General, which had met four times between 1560 and 1593, was a vehicle of feudal particularism. Hence he never summoned it. He could tolerate the continuation of provincial representative assemblies in Brittany, Normandy, Burgundy, Dauphiné, Provence, and Languedoc, with their privilege of taxing themselves (very lightly), since he possessed uncontested powers of direct taxation over the rest of the country. Correspondingly, he tolerated the claim of the *parlements*, or law courts, of Paris and the outlying provinces to authorize royal edicts by registering them, as long as they did in fact register all of his decrees, including unpopular ones like the Edict of Nantes. Henry staffed his administrative posts with the tractable bourgeoisie in preference to the high nobility, and he surrounded himself with able advisers like the Huguenot duke of Sully (1560–1641). On the vexed question of religion, he kept the Huguenots content by maintaining the protection and toleration pledged them in the Edict of Nantes. Meanwhile, he shrewdly played off the Italian papacy against the Gallican clergy in order to gain a firmer control over the French Catholic church than the late Valois kings had ever enjoyed. Even the Jesuits, when they were readmitted to France in 1604, became ardent supporters of the Bourbon monarchy.

Henry IV's handling of public finance aptly illustrates the achievements and limitations of his reign. He inherited a staggering burben of war debts. In 1596 the king owed his creditors 300 million livres at exorbitant interest rates, and annual expenditures were running twice as high as the royal revenues. Unlike the Spanish government, the French government avoided declaring bankruptcy. But the duke of Sully, Henry's finance minister, did repudiate part of the royal debt and rescheduled the remainder at a lower rate of interest. By drastically retrenching once the war was over and seeking out additional sources of revenue, Sully managed to balance his budget. By 1609 he had reduced the debt by 100 million livres and scraped together a royal treasure of 12 million livres in the form of barrels of gold, stored in the Bastille cellars. Sully, however, made only a superficial effort to reform the gross inequities in the French tax structure. The impoverished peasantry continued to pay most of the taxes, while the prosperous privileged classes were exempted. Sully did indeed reduce the *taille*, but he correspondingly raised the *gabelle*, or salt tax. Both *taille* and *gabelle* continued to be assessed at far higher rates in some sections of the country than in others. And as before, most taxes were collected by tax farmers, middlemen under government contract who could make fat profits by squeezing more money from the peasants than they had contracted to deliver into the treasury. Public finance was further hamstrung by the crown's long-established policy of selling financial and judicial offices for life to aspiring bourgeoisie, more intent on social climbing than on the zealous performance of duty. Sully not merely continued to sell administrative posts, but made them hereditary in return for payment of an annual fee, the *paulette*.

By 1610, Henry IV was again ready for war. His target was the traditional French enemy, Habsburg Spain. Every strong French king since the late fifteenth century had tested his mettle against Habsburg armies, more often losing than winning. France was virtually encircled by Spanish Habsburg territory, the Pyrenees on one side and Franche-Comté, Luxemburg, and Flanders—provinces Henry was eager to annex—on the other. Besides, he had not forgiven Philip II for prolonging the French civil wars in the 1590's by supporting the League with men and money. In May, 1610, on the eve of his campaign, as Henry was passing through a narrow Paris Street, his open carriage was caught momentarily in a traffic jam and a demented monk named Ravaillac leaped up onto the wheel and stabbed the king to death. To Ravaillac, Henry was an apostate who protected heretical Huguenots and went to war against good Catholics. It was probably lucky for Henry's subsequent reputation that he was martyred before his Spanish campaign could begin. He would have found the Habsburg armies very formidable, and Sully's treasure of twelve million livres would have been quickly exhausted. Nonetheless, his sudden death plunged France into an extended crisis, alarmingly reminiscent of the situation in the 1560's, when the religious wars began.

The French crisis lasted from 1610 to 1624. The new king, Louis XIII (ruled 1610–1643), was only nine years old when his father was assassinated. Henry's widow, Marie de Medici (1573–1642), was the regent during Louis' minority. A distant cousin of Catherine de Medici, Marie shared her predecessor's taste for intrigue and opulence, though she was more pious and shallow than Catherine, and did less damage to the French monarchy. She immediately canceled Henry's plans for war against Spain, and indeed soon reversed his policy completely by contracting a marriage alliance between young Louis and the daughter of the Spanish king. During Marie's regency the high French nobility grabbed control at the provincial level, and bullied her into squandering Sully's treasure among them in the form of new pensions and offices. Marie was pressed into calling the Estates-General in 1614, but when the three estates convened, hostility between the aristocratic and the bourgeois deputies was so paralyzing that they could accomplish nothing. Evidently a national representative institution was no longer of use in France; the Estates-General did not meet again until 1789.

While the country drifted aimlessly, Marie de Medici squabbled with her son. Louis XIII was whipped at the queen mother's orders until well into adolescence. In 1617 he pushed Marie aside, but though the young king understood the need for a drastic administrative shake-up far better than his mother did, he was too morose and diffident to formulate or execute any changes himself. France had become a cipher in international affairs, taking no significant part in the opening stages of the Thirty Years' War. By the early 1620's religious warfare was beginning again in southern France. The Huguenot towns of Languedoc were in open revolt against the crown. Louis XIII urgently needed a strong new minister if any part of his father's legacy was to be salvaged.

Cardinal Richelieu (1585–1642) became Louis XIII's chief minister in

1624 and directed the French government until his death. Born Armand Jean du Plessis, the son of a minor nobleman, Richelieu started his career in the family bishopric and entered state service during the regency of Marie de Medici. The queen mother, hoping to regain control of the government through Richelieu, persuaded the pope to make him a cardinal and the king to put him on the royal council. However, Richelieu was not her pawn. He looked thin and sickly, but his iron willpower, keen intelligence, and austere elegance ideally equipped him to rule in the king's name. Marie de Medici and most other members of the royal family soon hated him for ruthlessly shattering all their court intrigues against him. Richelieu drove the queen mother and Louis XIII's younger brother into exile. Five dukes and four counts were among the noblemen arrested, sentenced (several in secret courts), and executed on treason charges for challenging the cardinal's authority. Richelieu was greedy for power, no doubt, but he did devote this power to the service of France and of his royal master. For a prince of the church, Richelieu was remarkably worshipful of the state. Indeed, his foreign policy was more Protestant than Catholic whenever royal interests required. He lived by the philosophy of *raison d'état*: any workable expedient was justifiable as long as it aided the Bourbon monarchy.

Richelieu's first task was to prevent the Huguenot rebellion from expanding into another full-scale religious war. Fortunately for him, the Huguenots of his day posed much less of a threat than in the preceding century. They were less numerous, less ardent, less cohesive, and less ably led. In 1628 Richelieu captured La Rochelle, the chief Huguenot stronghold on the Atlantic coast, after a siege of fourteen months. In 1629 a royal army reduced all of the remaining rebel Huguenot towns in Languedoc. Richelieu's Edict of Alais in 1629 amended the Edict of Nantes by depriving the Huguenots of all their political and military privileges, while continuing their religious liberty. The cardinal was willing to tolerate French Protestants after 1629 because he saw that they were more likely to remain politically harmless if they were not persecuted.

In most respects Richelieu evoked the spirit of Henry IV and Sully. He constantly worked to reduce feudal and regional particularism. He managed to abolish three of the six provincial representative assemblies (those of Burgundy, Dauphiné, and Provence), though when he tried to impose direct royal taxation in Languedoc as well, opposition was so intense that he gave up the idea. He sent *intendants*, agents of the royal council, into the provinces to oversee local tax collection. He appointed himself superintendent of navigation and commerce, to focus attention on France's neglected merchant marine, navy, and coastal defenses. When Richelieu came to power, the royal navy was nonexistent, the Atlantic ports were defenseless against Spanish or English attack, and the Mediterranean coast was infested by pirates. Between 1610 and 1633, some 2500 French vessels were captured by Barbary pirates, before Richelieu launched a series of campaigns against them. One of his proudest accomplishments was the creation of effective fleets in both the Atlantic and the Mediterranean. The cardinal's program was expensive, and he constantly resorted to deficit financing, particularly after France entered the Thirty Years' War in 1635. He did manage to double the royal revenue during his term of office, mainly by raising the *taille* and thus squeezing the peasants still further. Richelieu had to suppress tax riots in many parts of France, but accepted this consequence quite cheerfully. The common people, he wrote, should not be made too comfortable, for they were like "mules, who, being accustomed to burdens, are spoiled by a long rest more than by work."[1]

The most spectacular aspect of Richelieu's administration was his foreign policy. Once he had reestablished domestic order, he picked up where Henry IV had left off in 1610 and entered into war against the Habsburgs. From Richelieu's viewpoint, the international situation in the late 1620's was thoroughly alarming. While France had stood by, neutral, during the dozen opening years of the Thirty Years' War, its Habsburg rivals had slowly gained the upper hand. Ferdinand II appeared to be well on his way to converting the Holy Roman Empire into an absolute monarchy, while his Spanish cousin, Philip IV, had added part of the Palatinate to his belt of territory which stretched from Milan to Flanders, and Spanish armies were even making some small progress in their efforts to reconquer the Dutch republic. Hence, in 1630 Richelieu subsidized Gustavus Adolphus' invasion of Germany, to the scandal of orthodox Catholics, and after the Swedish king's death in 1632, he organized a new Swedish-German league against the emperor. The Habsburgs' overwhelming victory over the Swedes at Nördlingen in 1634 abruptly liquidated this league. Richelieu was now compelled to take a more active role. He declared war against Spain in 1635 and opened a three-pronged French attack in northern Italy, the Rhineland, and the Netherlands. This bold scheme very nearly boomeranged in 1636 when counterattacking Spanish and imperial forces overran Picardy and threatened Paris. But thereafter the French kept the fighting off their own soil, while the Spanish were crippled by internal crises in Portugal and Catalonia. Richelieu did not live to see his troops annihilate a larger, veteran Spanish army at Rocroi in 1643—the first total defeat inflicted on the vaunted Spanish infantry since the accession of the Habsburg dynasty in 1516. But it was Richelieu who laid the groundwork for the French diplomatic success and the Habsburg defeat at Westphalia in 1648.

It is instructive to compare Richelieu's administration with the strikingly parallel efforts of his Spanish counterpart, the count of Olivares (1587–1645), to overhaul the Habsburg monarchy of Philip IV. Like the French

[1]Charles W. Cole, *Colbert and a Century of French Mercantilism* (New York, 1939), Vol. I, p. 139.

under Louis XIII, the Spaniards desperately needed skillful statesmanship if they were to recover their sixteenth-century heritage of effective government. There was little to choose between Louis XIII and Philip IV. Each was intelligent yet weak-willed, and each depended on a strong minister. Olivares was Philip's chief minister between 1621 and 1643. Like Richelieu, he secured control over his government by winning the confidence of his royal master and ruthlessly eliminating all rivals. He was a big man, always in a hurry, bursting with ideas and energy. He was determined to revive Spain's sixteenth-century imperial greatness by revamping its easygoing, inefficient style of rule. Like Richelieu, Olivares had to wrestle with soaring war costs, a badly unbalanced budget, and an outdated tax system which grossly overburdened the peasantry. And like Richelieu, Olivares tried to break down the entrenched regional particularism of his state. The Iberian peninsula was divided into four semiautonomous kingdoms: Castile, Aragon, Navarre, and Portugal—the latter annexed only in 1580. Under Charles V and Philip II, the Spanish empire had been the private preserve and responsibility of Castile, but Olivares wanted to broaden the responsibility and to make the outlying Iberian regions (where the taxes were comparatively light) share Castile's crushing financial and military commitments. The Portuguese and the people of Catalonia, a province in Aragon, viewed Olivares' efforts at "Castilianization" with the deepest suspicion. These people taxed themselves through their own representative assemblies, or cortes, and they repeatedly ignored Olivares' pleas for the men and money he needed in order to maintain Spanish armies in Italy, Germany, and the Netherlands. When Olivares undertook war against Richelieu's France without first making peace with the Dutch, the Swedes, and the German Protestants, he quickly met disaster. In 1640 both Portugal and Catalonia rose in rebellion and declared their independence of Habsburg rule. The Catalan revolt was at last suppressed in 1652; the Portuguese revolt was never suppressed, though the Habsburgs did not recognize Portugal's independence until 1668. Long before then, Olivares had died a broken man, and Spain's international leadership had irretrievably vanished.

The stark contrast between Richelieu's success and Olivares' failure can scarcely be accounted for by personality differences between the two men. Richelieu may have been somewhat shrewder than Olivares, or less rash. But the antithetical results from their parallel efforts at reform are better explained by fundamental differences between the two societies. Bourbon political and military effectiveness must be correlated with France's rising wealth and vigor, likewise Habsburg political and military weakness with Spain's social and economic stagnation. Seventeenth-century France was so much more prosperous and populous than Spain that Richelieu inevitably had far greater resources at his disposal. Spain was so much more particularistic and hidebound than France that Olivares' imaginative and energetic strategy shocked his people without stimulating them. In trying to arrest Spanish decay, Olivares actually hastened the process of collapse.

After Richelieu's death in 1642, France also plunged into a period of domestic turmoil, but unlike Spain, soon recovered. Louis XIII died in 1643, a few months after his great minister, leaving his five-year-old son as King Louis XIV and his widow, Anne of Austria (1601–1666), as regent. The regency was instantly unpopular, for Anne was a Habsburg princess and she entrusted the management of affairs to her paramour, a smooth and supple Italian adventurer named Guilio Mazarini (1602–1661). This Mazarin, as he was called in France, was a matchless opportunist. Starting as a papal diplomat, he entered French state service under Richelieu, was made a cardinal (though he was not a priest), collected expensive tapestries and paintings, married his beautiful Roman nieces into the high French nobility, and—what particularly galled the pamphleteers who flooded the Paris bookstalls with libels against him—became the queen's lover and very likely her secret husband. But Cardinal Mazarin did not deserve the abuse heaped on him, for he proved to be an astute administrator, entirely devoted to the continuation of Richelieu's policies and to the training of the young king. During the opening years of his administration, Mazarin kept the factious nobility occupied with the war against Spain and the Holy Roman emperor. But the mounting costs of this war strained his ingenuity. He tried various shoddy expedients for raising additional money, such as creating and selling new and useless government offices, manipulating the stock market, and levying fines on trumped-up charges. By an unhappy coincidence, the 1640's saw the worst agricultural depression of the century in France. The desperate peasants not only were unable to pay their manorial obligations to the nobility and their taxes to the crown, but were forced to surrender many of their small landholdings to their bourgeois creditors. Economic dislocation and political unrest ignited the Fronde, a series of tumults (1648–1653) directed against Mazarin's rule.

The Fronde started as a protest by royal officials against Mazarin's perverted administrative techniques; in effect, it was a protest against the whole fifty-year absolutist trend launched by Henry IV. These dissident officials felt cheated out of their rightful perquisites. Having gained privileged status by buying their posts from the crown, French officials had found over the years that Sully, Richelieu, and Mazarin in turn kept cutting back their salaries, creating rival new offices, and imposing over them *intendants* who stole away their authority. The *Parlement* of Paris, the chief law court in France, voiced these grievances in 1648, and demanded that Mazarin and the queen restore the former privileges and powers of the entrenched bureaucracy. The Paris mob rioted wildly in support of the *Parlement*—indeed, the *fronde*, which gave its name to these disorders, was a slingshot used by mischievous Paris boys to mess up the streets by flinging mud or stones. But the officials of the

Parlement of Paris disapproved of riots and rebellions; their aim was to safeguard their own privileged status within the government, not to tear the government apart. In 1649 the *Parlement* came to terms with Mazarin. By this time the Thirty Years' War was over, and the aristocratic French army officers, itching for fresh action, marched their troops against the hated cardinal. The Fronde thus suddenly turned into a feudal rebellion led by the princes of the blood who felt excluded by Richelieu and Mazarin from their rightful station. These aristocratic *frondeurs* were much more dangerous and destructive than the officials of the *Parlement* of Paris had been. They chased Mazarin out of France, and the king and his mother out of Paris. Many of them were hoping to dismantle the central government and to cut France into a mosaic of sovereign princely states like the Holy Roman Empire. For three years their private armies roamed the country, tilting against one another as if in a gigantic tournament. At last, in 1652, the fourteen-year-old Louis XIV declared his majority and was welcomed back to Paris. By 1653 Mazarin was back also, the rebel nobles had retired to their country estates or disappeared into exile, and the Fronde was over.

Like the French crises of 1560–1598 and 1610–1624, the Fronde demonstrated that there was no palatable alternative to absolute monarchy in seventeenth-century France. The *frondeurs* had plenty to complain about, but their motives were so patently and narrowly selfish that they could not mount a constructive protest movement, let alone produce a tolerable substitute for Mazarin. Throughout the crisis the various rebellious elements

An anti-Mazarin cartoon, *c.* 1652. *One of the leading* frondeurs, Mademoiselle de Montpensier, *having rallied the city of Orleans in the name of the young king, is putting the torch to the hated cardinal.*

in French society—the nobility, the bureaucracy, the peasantry, the Paris mob—worked at cross-purposes. One traditionally rebellious group, the Huguenots, took no part in the Fronde, supposing that fulsome loyalty to the crown offered the best chance for survival. Indeed, the Fronde compelled all Frenchmen who placed much value on stability and prosperity to be ardent royalists. Certainly Louis XIV believed that such anarchy must never recur. The bitter experience of 1648–1653 made an indelible impression on the young king. His memory of rampaging Parisians, particularly of the crowd which burst into his palace bedchamber one night in 1651 to make sure that he had not escaped with Mazarin, persuaded Louis to remove the royal court from Paris to Versailles. His memory of irresponsible noblemen dividing the spoils during his minority convinced Louis that he must politically emasculate the privileged aristocracy. His memory of the Paris *Parlement* daring to criticize royal policy sharpened his resolve to assert his own majesty, based upon divine right and buttressed by a phalanx of obsequious underlings.

But Louis XIV was still too young to take personal charge. Hence, Cardinal Mazarin resumed direction of affairs from 1653 until his death in 1661. Under Mazarin, France reaped the rewards of Richelieu's ambitious foreign policy. At the Peace of Westphalia in 1648, despite his preoccupation with the Fronde, Mazarin had secured very advantageous terms. Portions of Alsace and Lorraine were ceded to France, while the permanent internal paralysis of the Holy Roman Empire permitted the French government to build a network of alliances with German princely states against the Habsburg emperor. War against Spain continued for a decade longer, though both contestants were largely engrossed in domestic problems. In 1659 this war finally terminated in the Peace of the Pyrenees, another diplomatic success for Mazarin. France gained further territory—Artois, adjoining Flanders, and Roussillon, bordering the Pyrenees. The Bourbon-Habsburg conflict was papered over by the second intermarriage between the two families in two generations, this time between Louis XIV and his cousin Maria Theresa, the Spanish infanta. Through his new queen, Louis established a strong claim to the inheritance of all the Spanish Habsburg possessions in Europe and America. He could thus hope to create a new dynastic empire greater than that of Charles V. There seemed no limit to Bourbon ambition or success. The Sun King was staging his grand entry into European affairs.

THE PURITAN REVOLUTION

During the first half of the seventeenth century, while in France the Bourbons were consolidating power, in England the Stuart kings James I (ruled 1603–1625) and Charles I (ruled 1625–1649) lost control of the government. The English civil war of the 1640's, also known as the Great Rebellion or the Puritan Revolution, was a much more fundamental protest against monarchy than was the contemporaneous Fronde in France. Superficially, this English revolution is something of a puzzle. The English monarchy was immensely popular when the last Tudor sovereign, Elizabeth I, died in 1603. Elizabeth left no direct heirs, and the throne passed to James Stuart, king of Scotland. James and his son Charles were certainly inferior kings, yet they were trapped in circumstances which might well have baffled far abler rulers. England was a more cohesive community than France, less dependent on strong management from above. The country was only one quarter as large and as populous as France. Parliament was the uncontested national representative assembly, there being no regional assemblies. The nobility, gentry, and merchants, whose spokesmen sat in Parliament, were more homogeneous than in France and better able to cooperate in politics—or in opposition to their king.

After a century of Tudor paternalism, the English had grown restive during the final years of Elizabeth I's reign. The crown was handicapped by inadequate revenues, a stunted bureaucracy, and the absence of a regular army. And England was one of the few European states—the Holy Roman

SUCCESSION TO THE ENGLISH CROWN, 1558–1714

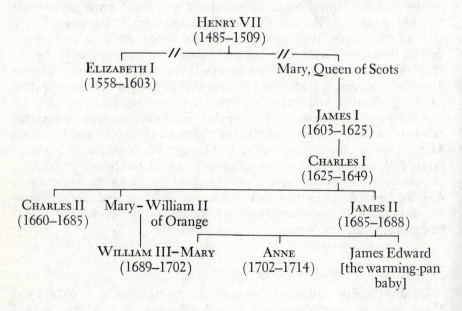

Empire and Sweden were the others—where religious tensions were rising rather than declining during the early seventeenth century. The Puritans formed a dissident Calvinist movement within the state church, agitating strenuously against the Catholic ceremonial and institutional elements in Anglicanism. Puritans could be found practically anywhere in England, but they were most evident in intellectual circles, among the lesser landed gentry (particularly in the eastern counties of Norfolk, Suffolk, Cambridge, and Essex), in the city of London, and in Parliament. It was far from easy to cope with a movement half hidden and amorphous, yet infused with righteous zeal.

The first Stuart king, James I, was a tragicomic failure despite good intentions and real abilities. He was the son of Mary, Queen of Scots, an alarming pedigree, but James had little of his mother's reckless passion—or bewitching charm. He was an erudite scholar, and proud of it. He had ruled Scotland successfully for many years, but the overbearing tactics he had used in handling wild lairds and fanatic Presbyterians were inappropriate in England. In 1598, James had published *The Trew Law of Free Monarchies*, in which he exhorted his Scottish subjects to obey their king, who was accountable to God alone. All laws were given by the king, he asserted, and all constitutional forms and assemblies existed entirely at his pleasure. Elizabeth I had tacitly subscribed to this divine-right theory of monarchy, but she carefully avoided writing a book on the subject, nor did she lecture Parliament on her God-given powers, as James did repeatedly when he took the English throne. James did not look like God's lieutenant. His tongue was too big for his mouth, and his rolling eyes gave him a perpetually apprehensive expression. He wore his clothes heavily padded against the stilettos of would-be assassins, and while stag hunting he sometimes was tied onto his horse to keep from falling off. Even sycophantic courtiers disliked these hunting parties, during which the king might exultantly slash a fallen stag's belly, shove his hands into its entrails, and slop his dogs and attendants with blood.

In the course of James's reign, the revolutionary crisis began to take clear shape. The new king quarreled publicly with the Puritans, mostly because he identified them with the Scottish Presbyterians who had tried to shackle him with Calvin's church government. "No bishop, no king," he cried out during a conference with Puritan spokesmen—a telling aphorism with which his adversaries would one day agree. "I will make them conform themselves," James warned the Puritans, "or I will harry them out of this land or else do worse." James did in fact deprive many Puritan clergy of their benefices, with the consequence that the movement spread among the laity more powerfully than before. James's fiscal policy exposed the crown to further criticism. His expenditures were double those of Elizabeth, partly because of the continuing inflationary spiral, partly because he had a wife and children to support, but mostly because he was more extravagant than the late queen. In order to increase revenue, the crown resorted to various business-damaging expedients, such as the sale of hundreds of monopolies, which artifically rigged the production, distribution, and price of such everyday commodities as soap, coal, vinegar, and pins. Elizabethan monopolists had been highly unpopular, and James's growing dependence on them greatly irked the hardheaded landowners and businessmen who sat in Parliament.

The king's relations with Parliament deteriorated steadily. He would have done well to imitate Elizabeth, who asked Parliament for as little money as possible, and saw to it that her ministers prepared programs of government proposals in advance and steered debate and legislation through both houses. James asked Parliament freely for money, without bothering to justify his needs. The initiative in debate and legislation was quickly seized by critics of the government. Ignoring the king's lectures on his divine attributes, Parliament voted him very little money and devoted a good deal of time to the formulation of statements of grievances. The House of Commons, James complained, was a body without a head—true enough, since the king had abdicated the responsibilities of headship.

Everything went wrong for James I during the closing years of his reign. As he grew older and slacker, his previously latent homosexuality asserted itself, and he handed over the direction of affairs to his favorites, young men whose only qualifications were their physical beauty and their grace. The last and most seductive of these favorites, the scatterbrained duke of Buckingham (1592–1628), had total control over the infatuated king from 1619 until his death. James's last parliaments, in 1621 and 1624, were more openly critical of the government than the earlier ones had been. The House of Commons had a great leader in Sir Edward Coke (1552-1634), the wisest jurist of the age, who had been dismissed from judicial office by the king. In 1621 Parliament revived the medieval procedure of impeachment against Coke's bitter enemy Lord Chancellor Francis Bacon, the philosopher, on charges of bribery. Bacon's impeachment was a clear step toward parliamentary regulation of the king's ministers. Parliament also denounced the government's foreign policy, which was pro-Spanish because the king hoped to arrange a Spanish Habsburg marriage for his son Charles. In 1623 he let Charles slip off secretly to Madrid with Buckingham in a romantic effort to woo and win the infanta. The doting king wrote anxiously to his "sweet boys," as he called them—"Baby Charles" and "Steenie"—and closed his letters, "your dear dad and husband, James R." But Baby Charles came home from Madrid furious at the Spaniards' refusal to let him court or marry the infanta, and Steenie secured Parliament's consent to a war against Spain, despite the senile king's protestations. Thus, by the time James died in 1625, all his hopes had been ludicrously dashed, and the opposition to the Stuart monarchy was formidable.

Charles I was more truculent than his father, and during the opening years of his reign, 1625–1629, the political and religious critics of the Stuart monarchy began to join together in a serious rebel party. In the elegant portraits by Anthony Van Dyck, Charles cuts the perfect figure of a king: he looks handsome, reserved, abstemious, cultivated. But the new king was totally insensitive to public opinion and incapable of political give-and-take. Charles I was a stalwart High Churchman, valuing the Catholic ceremonial elements in Anglicanism, and he held his father's views on divine-right monarchy. The hated duke of Buckingham continued to be chief minister. Charles immediately quarreled more violently with Parliament than his father had ever done. The new king peremptorily demanded money, but Parliament was only interested in impeaching Buckingham. So Charles levied a forced loan, which gave him as much money as he would have obtained through Parliament. Seventy-six prominent gentlemen (including several members of Parliament) were jailed for refusing to "contribute."

When Charles I, still needing money, summoned another Parliament in 1628, he found both houses united against him. Lords and Commons cooperated closely in framing the famous Petition of Right. By bribing the king with a tax grant, they extracted his promise not to levy or borrow money without parliamentary consent, nor to imprison men without due process of law. By agreeing to these conditions, Charles acknowledged that he had violated his subjects' liberties. In time, the Petition of Right became a constitutional landmark, but its immediate effect was slight, for the king

Charles I. *Painting by Van Dyck.The portrait was painted about 1635, when the king seemed to be winning his battle against Parliament and the Puritans. Louvre, Paris.*

soon resumed his nonparliamentary levies and the arbitrary punishment of persons who dared to criticize his regime. One great grievance was permanently removed in 1628; the duke of Buckingham was assassinated, to the king's grief and the public's joy. Any remaining possibility of cooperation between king and Parliament disappeared in 1629, when the tempestuous Sir John Eliot (1592–1632) started the Commons on a new hue and cry against royal policy. When the king ordered the House to adjourn, two of the more athletic members held their weeping speaker in his chair to keep the meeting in session, while the excited assembly passed by acclamation Eliot's three resolutions declaring High Church innovations and the collection of customs unauthorized by Parliament to be treasonable. This dramatic gesture alienated many moderate men and permitted the king to seem more reasonable than his adversaries. Charles vowed to govern without Parliament and did so for the next eleven years.

Charles I's personal rule between 1629 and 1640 has often been compared with Richelieu's contemporaneous administration in France. But whatever his ultimate aims, Charles never came close to erecting a Bourbon-style monarchy. To be sure, his most conspicuous ministers after Buckingham's death, Archbishop William Laud (1573–1645) and Sir Thomas Wentworth (1593–1641), thought they knew better than the people what was good for

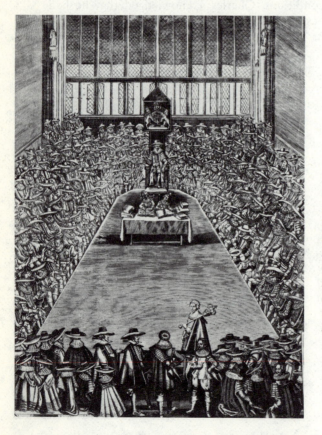

The House of Commons in 1640. *From an old print. The Commons chamber was very small and, as this picture shows, some of the members had to stand. The Speaker of the House sits in the tall chair with two clerks before him; the sergeant-at-arms, who carries the mace (lower center), has the job of keeping out strangers.*

them and urged "thorough" measures to achieve efficiency and order. But Laud and Wentworth were often frustrated by rivals within the royal council, and in any case Wentworth was mostly absent in northern England or Ireland, where he served as the king's deputy. No English minister could enforce decisions as Richelieu did. Charles I had no *intendants*, no standing army. Local administration continued to depend on the cooperation of unpaid justices of the peace, many of whom had sat in Parliament and criticized royal policy. The government lived from hand to mouth, a cipher in international politics. The king's advisers searched for legal loopholes by which to circumvent parliamentary control over taxation. For example, they discovered a long-forgotten requirement that any gentleman worth £40 or more a year should present himself to be knighted at the king's coronation, and this permitted Charles to collect £165,000 in fines from all the wealthy gentry who had not been knighted at his coronation in 1626! More crucial was Charles's manipulation of ship money, an impost which had customarily been levied on seaports in times of emergency to provide naval vessels for defense. Charles turned ship money into an annual national tax, levied on inland as well as coastal areas. John Hampden (1594–1643), a wealthy squire, challenged his £1 assessment in the courts on the ground that if a national emergency existed, Parliament should be called. The royal judges upheld the legality of ship money by the narrow majority of seven to five, but the tax could no longer be collected effectively. Charles's financial policy thus roused more troublesome opposition than Richelieu's. The French tax burden fell mainly on the unprivileged peasantry, but the Stuart extraparliamentary levies provoked the nobility, gentry, and merchants. These people could well afford to pay, for their collective wealth was vastly greater than the king's. But conscious of their rising prosperity, they deeply resented being excluded from power.

Religion, however, was the most explosive single issue. Charles I entrusted management of the state church to Archbishop Laud, a martinet with exceptional powers of industry and obstinacy. Where Cardinal Richelieu respected the religious liberty of the Huguenots, Archbishop Laud deliberately challenged the Puritans. His ambition was to elevate the power of the Anglican episcopate and the dignity of Anglican public worship. By teaching all Englishmen to revere "the beauty of holiness" as expressed in the order of worship in the Anglican prayer book, Laud hoped to foster social decorum and suppress Puritan zeal. These aims were closer in spirit to the Catholic reformation than to the Protestant and gave a new ring to James I's motto—"no bishop, no king." In fact, however, few among the bishops supported Laud, and on the parish level his wishes were freely ignored. The archbishop's efforts to bully the Puritans by prosecuting his most obnoxious Puritan critics in the royal law courts backfired painfully. In 1637, when three antiprelatical pamphleteers named Burton, Bastwick, and Prynne had their ears cropped—very mild punishment compared with the ruthless religious persecution of the sixteenth century—they were immediately hailed as martyrs. Bigger trouble came in Scotland when Charles I and Laud endeavored to impose an Anglican prayer book on the Presbyterian populace. The Scots riotously rejected the prayer book and in 1638 swore a national covenant to defend to the death their religious and political liberties. Charles tried to suppress the Scottish rebellion, but he could not raise an effective army, and by 1640 the Scots had invaded the north of England. The king was now completely cornered. With no money, no army, and no popular support, he had to summon Parliament in 1640.

The Long Parliament, so called because it remained in session from 1640 to 1653, triggered the biggest revolution in English history. Scholars have traditionally argued that the crisis of the 1640's was a contest over religious and political principles—Puritanism versus Anglicanism and parliamentary self-government versus royal absolutism. The current tendency, however, is to stress the economic and social factors underlying these religious and political issues. Marxist historians, for instance, have greatly enriched our understanding of the crisis by viewing the English revolution as an expression of class warfare, like the French and Russian revolutions. It was, they argue, the first major victory by the European bourgeoisie over the feudal class. There is considerable evidence for this argument: in the 1640's the English merchants and artisans, particularly in London, generally supported Parliament, while the aristocracy and the economically backward northern part of the country backed the king.

Yet the awkward obstacle to this class-war interpretation is the role of the gentry, or lesser landlords. These people were the chief actors in the English revolution, and they divided themselves pretty evenly between the parliamentary and the royalist camps. Whether we label the gentry as feudal or as bourgeois, how are we to explain in economic terms their prominence in the struggle and their ideological disunity? Various efforts have been made to do so. One school, adapting Marx's thesis, sees them as a rising agrarian middle class, gaining prosperity at the expense of the crown and the aristocracy between 1540 and 1640. The more prosperous and self-confident members of this class, it is argued, led the fight for Parliament and Puritanism in the 1640's in order to consolidate their power. But a contrary school insists that the most prosperous members of the gentry attached themselves to the king's court, and that those small landlords who had to live on their farm income were becoming less prosperous between 1540 and 1640. Caught by the inflation and by agricultural depression, and excluded from government patronage by the Stuarts, these declining gentry turned to Puritanism and to revolution in a desperate effort to retrieve their status. The first of these interpretations appears to fit the facts better than the second, but neither is convincing. Present evidence suggests that the gentry—like most Englishmen—were neither booming nor collapsing economically in the mid-seventeenth century.

Hence an economic or social interpretation of the English crisis is ultimately unsatisfactory. The English revolution remains less susceptible than the French and Russian revolutions to analysis in terms of economic classes. But it is certain that the English people *were* wildly excited over religious and political issues. Religion was the greatest single catalyst. The crisis of the 1640's is best called the Puritan Revolution; it constituted the last and grandest episode in Europe's age of religious wars.

The course of events in England from 1640 to 1660 is not easily summarized, for the English revolution, like all great revolutions, was a complex phenomenon with its own special heroic and tragic qualities. At the outset, in 1640, there appeared to be no possibility of civil war. Parliament had the united support of the English upper classes, and Charles I stood helplessly isolated. Exhilarated by the frenzied London atmosphere, the Lords and the Commons speedily rescued the king from the evil advisers who had perpetrated the "eleven years' tyranny" of nonparliamentary rule. Wentworth and Laud were imprisoned. Parliament sentenced Wentworth to death, and half the population of London jammed Tower Hill to watch and cheer his execution.

The members of Parliament were not conscious revolutionaries in 1640. They supposed themselves the guardians of England's ancient liberties, though in fact, under the astute management of John Pym (1584–1643), who had learned his tactics from Sir Edward Coke, Parliament circumscribed Charles I's sovereignty through a series of constitutional innovations. All of the king's recent extraparliamentary taxes were declared illegal. The royal law courts which had been used by Wentworth and Laud were abolished. Parliament was henceforth to sit every three years at least, and the present Parliament could not be dissolved without its own consent.

Having pulled down the old government, Parliament in 1641 began building a new one. Immediately, parliamentary unity dissolved. As controversial issues came to the fore—should Parliament nominate the king's ministers? control the army? reorganize the church?—many members began to ally with Charles I. The hottest question was religious: whether or not to abolish the office of bishop and eliminate the prayer book. The Puritans and the political radicals, who held a slim majority in the House of Commons, hardened into a truly revolutionary party bent on reconstructing church and state. In reaction to this, a royalist party formed, within Parliament and throughout the country, to resist further change. In January, 1642, Charles I tried to break the parliamentary radicals with a military coup. But his plan was too clumsy. When he entered the House of Commons, backed by four hundred armed men, intending to seize Pym and the other leaders, his intended victims had already escaped. Mob pressure forced Charles and his adherents to leave London. Within a few months both sides were raising troops, and the war was on.

The civil war of 1642–1646 was very modest in scale and intensity. At the peak of combat, no more than one Englishman out of every ten of fighting age was in arms (compared with one out of four in the American Civil War), and the amateurish campaigning kept damage to life and property fairly negligible. The parliamentary soldiers were nicknamed Roundheads because of the Puritan propensity for cutting the hair short; the royalists, or Cavaliers, looked swashbuckling and romantic by comparison. It was no accident that the Roundheads won the war. They held London and the wealthy and populous southeastern half of the country. Parliament collected large sums of money through excise and property taxes—far heavier levies, ironically, than Charles I had ever attempted. The Cavaliers operated out of the more sparsely populated northwestern half of England, and they were chronically short of money, manpower, and war materials. The king's troops resembled the roving bands led by soldiers of fortune in the Thirty Years' War. Prince Rupert, the most dashing Cavalier commander, could open a battle brilliantly with a madcap cavalry charge, but his undisciplined horsemen then often disappeared in search of the enemy baggage train, while the Roundheads regrouped and won the engagement. The Roundheads' greatest initial resource was their exalted moral fervor. An unprecedented torrent of pamphlets, averaging 1,500 a year throughout the 1640's, expressed in manifold ways their ardent quest for the political, religious, or social rebirth of England. John Milton's *Areopagitica* (1644), the most famous of these pamphlets, epitomized the Roundhead wartime spirit. "Methinks," the exalted Puritan poet chanted, "I see in my mind a noble and puissant nation rousing herself like a strong man after sleep, and shaking her invincible locks. Methinks I see her as an eagle mewing her mighty youth, and kindling her undazzled eyes at the full midday beam." But the parliamentary leaders were not equal to Milton's vision. For two years Charles I's troops held the upper hand, mainly because the Roundhead generals really did not want to fight and defeat their anointed king. The tide began to turn in 1643 when Pym secured a military alliance between Parliament and Presbyterian Scotland. The next year a parliamentary-Scottish army beat Prince Rupert at Marston Moor in the biggest pitched battle of the war. But even more significant in the long run was the emergence of a Puritan soldier of genius, Oliver Cromwell (1599–1658).

Nothing in Cromwell's humdrum prewar career prepares us for his preeminent role in the Puritan Revolution. When the Long Parliament convened, he was an obscure middle-aged country squire, one of the least affluent members of Commons. Few noticed this blunt, roughhewn man when he spoke out occasionally and chaotically against the Anglican bishops. Once fighting started, Cromwell enlisted in the parliamentary army and subscribed £ 500 (his annual income) to help defray military expenses. Some inner resource—Cromwell would have said it was God's redemptive grace—gave him the rock strength to master every problem he encountered from his first battle in 1642 until his death in 1658. He recruited in 1643 a cavalry regiment of "honest, godly men," who maintained strict discipline and sang psalms as they chased the Cavaliers. Most Puritans, believing (as Cromwell did) that God had predestined them for salvation, gathered themselves during or after the war into congregations or churches of the elect. Cromwell never joined a Puritan church. He saw his regiment as a kind of church, the Lord's humble instrument for rescuing England from popery and slavery. Cromwell's regiment, soon christened the Ironsides, won every engagement it fought. Cromwell and his troops were chiefly responsible for the defeat of Prince Rupert's Cavaliers at Marston Moor in 1644. "God made them as stubble to our swords," wrote Cromwell in describing the battle. At his instigation, Parliament reorganized the Roundhead army, weeding out the lukewarm generals who hated to fight the king. This "New Model" parliamentary army (with Cromwell second in command) decimated Charles I's remaining forces at Naseby in 1645. The king was taken prisoner in 1646 and remained under army guard for the next two years. The Puritans seemed to have secured a stunning victory.

It was much easier to end the war than to reach a peace settlement. The Puritans had been held together only by their common hostility to bishops, the prayer book, and arbitrary monarchy, and by 1646 they were hopelessly fragmented into three factions. Most conservative were the Presbyterians, who wanted the Church of England transformed into a tightly organized national Calvinist church on the Scottish model, and believed that the king should be subordinated to parliamentary control, but advocated no further changes in the social or political order. The Presbyterians were less strong in England than in Scotland, but they held a majority in Parliament and dominated the London mercantile community. In the center, the Independents wanted more thoroughgoing changes. They rejected any sort of compulsory state church, whether Anglican or Presbyterian, and advocated religious toleration for a variety of voluntary, autonomous Puritan churches. In their view, Parliament as well as the monarchy needed to be reformed so as to respond more effectively to the needs of the common people. The Independents had spokesmen in Parliament, but their stronghold was the officer corps of the New Model Army. Oliver Cromwell was an Independent. More extreme than the Independents were numerous radical Puritan sects, most of which had not even existed before 1640. Their members called for the total regeneration of English society. Some of them were apocalyptic, as were the Fifth Monarchy Men, who supposed that Christ's second coming was

Death warrant of Charles I, 1649. *It was signed and sealed by fifty-nine members of the High Court of Justice which found him guilty of treason. Oliver Cromwell's signature is the third in the first column. Some of the judges signed with great reluctance, and one of them later alleged that Cromwell had forcibly guided his pen.*

imminent. Others were more secular, as were the Levellers, who drafted constitutions providing for universal male suffrage and other guarantees of popular sovereignty, democratic principles not to be realized in England or anywhere else until the nineteenth century. More extreme than the Levellers were the Diggers, or agrarian communists, who believed that God forbade the ownership of private property. Naturally, these radical sects appealed more to the poor than to the rich; they drew enthusiastic support from the rank and file of the New Model Army. Thus, in the maelstrom of the English revolution, Presbyterians, Independents, and radical sectaries had developed Calvin's precepts into a full spectrum of social attitudes, from self-righteous bigotry to compassion for the unprivileged, from repressive conservatism to visionary radicalism, from autocracy to anarchy.

Between 1646 and 1648, while trying to negotiate a settlement with the captive Charles I, the Presbyterians, Independents, and radical sectaries struggled violently among themselves for control of the revolution. The Presbyterians in Parliament made the fatal mistake of trying to disband the

New Model Army without paying the soldiers. Under Cromwell's leadership, the army refused to disband. Cromwell barely managed to keep the radicals within his army under control. The shorthand notes have been preserved of a fascinating debate between army spokesmen for the Independents and the Levellers at Putney in 1647. "The poorest he that is in England hath a life to live, as the greatest he," cried one of the Levellers. "I do not find anything in the Law of God, that a lord shall choose twenty burgesses [representatives in Parliament], and a gentleman but two, or a poor man shall choose none." The Independents retorted that "the meanest man in England ought to have a voice in the election of the government he lives under—but only if he has some local interest," that is, some property to give him a stake in society. Cromwell's role in the Putney debate was to call for prayers whenever the argument grew too hot. His soldiers still shared enough spirit of common purpose to remain an invincible force. In 1648, Cromwell crushed a Presbyterian-Cavalier uprising on behalf of the king. His army entered London and executed the sort of military coup against Parliament which Charles I had failed to carry off in 1642. A certain Colonel Pride stationed his troopers around the Parliament house and permitted only those members friendly to the army—some sixty Independents—to enter. "Pride's Purge" eliminated the Presbyterian majority in Parliament and reduced the proud national assembly of 1640 to a minority "rump" session.

Now Cromwell was in a position to deal with the king. Convinced that Charles I was the chief remaining obstacle to peace, Cromwell determined that he should be killed as publicly and solemnly as possible. The "Rump" Parliament erected a High Court of Justice which sentenced Charles to death as a tyrant, traitor, murderer, and public enemy of the people of England. On January 30, 1649, he was executed outside his banqueting hall at Whitehall. "I am a martyr of the people," Charles protested to the groaning crowd, just before the masked executioner decapitated him with a single stroke of the ax.

The king's execution was very unpopular, yet Cromwell had little choice. It was pointless to negotiate any further with a man who refused to accept a Puritan state in any form, and it was unsafe to let Charles stay in prison or retire abroad. Ironically, Cromwell had tried harder than any of his adversaries—far harder than Charles himself—to find a generous settlement. But his methods had become more extreme, more tyrannical, than Charles's had ever been. The royalists, Presbyterians, and radicals all hated Cromwell's recourse to naked military rule. Though the Independents were securely in control by 1649, their liberal aims were hopelessly compromised.

From 1649 to 1660 England was a Puritan republic. In its relations with other states, the revolutionary regime acted with impressive energy. In 1649 Cromwell conquered Ireland, slaughtering Catholics much more freely than he had killed Cavaliers during the English war. In 1650–1651 he conquered

Scotland. By compelling both peoples to accept union with England, the Puritans did what no English king had been able to do; they welded Great Britain into a single political unit. In 1652–1654 the English fought a naval war with the Dutch, during which they captured 1,400 enemy ships and bolstered England's competitive position with respect to the Dutch merchant marine. In 1655–1659 they fought Spain, capturing Jamaica in the West Indies, and Dunkirk in Flanders.

Internally, however, the revolutionaries were less successful; they could find no acceptable constitutional framework. Between 1649 and 1653 the government consisted of an awkward alliance between the Rump Parliament (the sixty members who had not been purged in 1648) and the army officers. Cromwell felt increasingly frustrated by the petty spirit of his civilian partners and increasingly convinced that his all-conquering army was God's chosen instrument. "Is not this Army a lawful power," he asked, "called by God to oppose and fight against the King, and being in power, may it not oppose one name of authority as well as another?" In 1653 he disbanded Parliament in another military coup and cut his last tie with the pre-1642 constitution. Cromwell took the title of Lord Protector and operated pretty much as an absolute monarch. Most Englishmen wanted a king. Cromwell refrained from adopting the royal title only because his army officers so adamantly opposed his doing so. The Protector's standing army of fifty thousand men and his belligerent foreign policy required a budget triple the size of Charles I's in the 1630's. The gentry and merchants protested, with better reason than under Charles, that they were being overtaxed. The Protector having ejected the Long Parliament, called three Parliaments of his own, but since he would not let these assemblies control taxation or question his executive powers, he got along with Parliament no better than the Stuarts had done.

Oliver Cromwell was not a conscious dictator. Religion mattered most to him, and he offered Puritans of every description, whether Independents, Presbyterians, Baptists, Fifth Monarchy Men, or even the highly inflammatory new sect of Quakers, the liberty to quest freely for spiritual grace. The doctrine of religious liberty is the Puritans' noblest legacy. Yet there was no liberty for Anglicans, to say nothing of Catholics. As far as most Englishmen were concerned, the Puritan crusade had ossified into a killjoy code of blue laws, enforced by military police. The tonic faith of the 1640's that England could be spiritually regenerated was gone. The mood of the 1650's was better captured by Thomas Hobbes's *Leviathan* (1651), the most remarkable book to come out of the English revolution. Hobbes endorsed the Protector's dictatorship, not on religious grounds (Hobbes was a cynical materialist) but because Cromwell abridged the people's individual liberty more effectively than the Stuarts had done, and thus restrained them from their natural propensity to destroy one another.

Oliver Cromwell died in 1658. In the eighteen months following his death, a series of artificial governments were set up and overthrown. None of the army officers had the stature to succeed Cromwell, but the army could not be dislodged from power, despite the bankruptcy of the revolutionary cause. Finally, in 1660, General George Monck arranged the election of a new Parliament, which promptly invited Charles I's son to return to England as Charles II. With the restoration of the Stuart monarchy, a new era began.

Some historians like to view the Puritan Revolution as part of a wider "general crisis" which swept across western Europe in the mid-seventeenth century. The revolt against Charles I in England occurred during the same period as the Fronde directed against Mazarin in France, and the Portuguese and Catalan revolts against Olivares in Spain. In each of these contemporaneous revolutions, a parliament or equivalent assembly challenged the crown on the specific issue of taxation and the general issue of expensive, paternalistic, central government. Each was triggered to some degree by economic and social malaise, resulting from the interminable Thirty Years' War, the inflationary spiral, a series of bad harvests, a severe slump in the cloth business, and dislocations in international trade.[2] Yet this dreary picture of "general crisis" scarcely suggests the dynamic creativity of the English rebels in the 1640's. Their expression of protest was not merely larger in scale and intensity than the Fronde and the Iberian revolt. It was galvanized by a religious idealism missing in the other revolts. Unlike the reactionary *frondeurs*, and the provincial Catalan and Portuguese rebels, the Puritans launched new ideas of great motor power. They could not erect a lasting republic, but no subsequent English king dared to forget the lesson of 1649. The task the Puritans started would be completed in the English revolution of 1688–1689.

FRANCE UNDER LOUIS XIV

As England's revolutionary crisis was dying down, a very different era dawned in France. In 1661, with the death of Cardinal Mazarin, Louis XIV (ruled 1643–1715) assumed personal direction of the French government. Circumstances were ideal for a grandiose reign. No radical innovations were required of the young king, for Henry IV, Richelieu, and Mazarin had already laid down his guidelines. The French privileged classes were eager to be commanded by a king who acted the part. Louis' army and his revenues were much the largest in Europe. France had just defeated archrival Spain, and with Germany divided, England distracted, and the Dutch posing no military threat, French international preeminence was incontestable. Louis

[2]For a fuller exposition of this "general crisis" thesis, see *Crisis in Europe, 1560–1660,* ed. by Trevor Aston (New York, 1965), pp. 5–116.

Louis XIV at the age of thirty-two. *Engraving by Pitau. The king is shown when he was at the pinnacle of his success.*

XIV, being but twenty-two years old in 1661, could anticipate a long future as the first gentleman in an elaborately hierarchical society, graced by sumptuous royal pageantry and the glory of fairly easy foreign conquests. Such hopes were lavishly fulfilled. For an incredible fifty-four years, Louis held the stage as the *Grand Monarque*, the archetype of absolutism, admired and feared by all other European princes. Toward the end of the reign, to be sure, Louis' style of rule created serious problems both at home and abroad. But during the years 1661–1688, with which we are here concerned, he could aptly characterize his royal performance as "grand, noble and delicious."

Louis XIV might not have succeeded in many occupations, but he was superbly equipped to be a divine-right monarch. To begin with, he appeared majestic, with his proud demeanor, robust physique, graceful carriage, opulent costumes, and perfect manners. More important, he had the stamina and concentration to act out each tiresome detail of his role as potentate before thousands of hypercritical spectators, day after day and year after year. Finally, he had the common sense to enjoy what was given to him, without overstraining his powers in trying (like the English Puritans) to remake France. That Louis had received a very superficial education was doubtless an advantage, since it permitted him to accept his own greatness naïvely, without having to worry about the subtleties and complexities of governing a powerful state. He hated to read, but he was a good listener and enjoyed presiding over council meetings for several hours a day. Greater brilliance or intellectuality would have handicapped Louis in his crucial position as leader of the French aristocracy, a role in which breeding and ceremony counted for more than brains. Louis moved his royal court from the Louvre to Versailles, twelve miles outside Paris, partly to escape the tumultuous citizenry and partly to provide a suitably huge yet secluded social center for the aristocracy. At Versailles he built a colossal palace, the facade a third of a mile long, the echoing marble chambers embellished with Gobelin tapestries and bravura ceiling paintings celebrating his military triumphs, the vast surrounding formal gardens decorated by 1,400 fountains, the orangery stocked with 1,200 orange trees, and the halls and grounds adorned with classical statuary—most often representions of Apollo, the sun god. Today Versailles is an empty tomb. In the late seventeenth century, ten thousand noblemen, officials, and attendants lived there. Sixty per cent of the royal tax revenue was expended on Versailles and the upkeep of Louis' court.

The secret of Louis XIV's success was really very simple: he and he alone could give the French aristocracy and upper bourgeoisie what they each wanted more than anything else at the moment. The king devoted more than half of each working day to the ceremonial ballet of his court. This was time well spent, for the aristocracy had long been the most fractious and unmanageable element in French society, and would cooperate only if the king honored and glorified their exclusive world of social privilege. They alone were permitted to attend the king at Versailles. Louis shrewdly required all of the chief members of the nobility to live at court, where he could keep an eye on them. He regimented every aspect of his own daily routine, and that of his courtiers, by a strict code of palace etiquette, so as to impart order to the huge court, exalt his own person, and domesticate his semifeudal nobility. The aristocrat who might otherwise have been plotting a new Fronde at his country château was harmlessly occupied at Versailles by court scandal, his highest ambitions being to hold one sleeve of Louis' garment when he dressed, hear the king speak a few daily platitudes, and watch him eat. Louis was a hearty trencherman and preferred to dine alone, unencumbered by aristocratic attendants. By the time a guard of honor had escorted the king's dinner several blocks from the kitchens to the royal table, the food was invariably cold, but this did not stop Louis from polishing off a half dozen plates of fowl and meat at a sitting. The menu for one of his banquets included 168 distinct garnished dishes.

Only through assiduous court attendance could an aristocrat obtain favors, sinecures, and pensions. The king had numerous honorific positions in his gift; deserving aristocrats were appointed bishops, generals, provincial governors, or foreign ambassadors. Only the highest and luckiest magnates could expect such favors. Most of the 200,000 members of the French peerage lived in obscure exile on their country estates, but even they enjoyed the privilege of tax exemption. Overall, the aristocracy under Louis XIV enjoyed little real power. But the chief aristocrats, at least, preferred Louis' reflected glory to the feudal autonomy they had once known. They no longer wished to dismantle the French state, though by the close of Louis' reign they did wish to control it. In the eighteenth century, the aristocracy's bid for increased political power commensurate with their exalted social privilege was to be a root cause of the French Revolution.

While Louis XIV encouraged the aristocracy to become useless parasites, he invited the upper bourgeoisie to govern France under his direction. Louis took his executive responsibilities as seriously as his court pageantry. After Mazarin's death, he made all important decisions himself, or thought he did. "*L'état, c'est moi*," he allegedly boasted—"I am the state." Or as one of Louis' bishops put it, "all the state is in him; the will of all the people is included in his." This French concept of absolute monarchy was rather

Central courtyard, palace of Versailles. *Painting by an unknown artist. This picture shows the way Louis XIV's enormous palace looked soon after it was built. In contrast to Philip II's Escorial, Versailles was designed as a stage for courtly pageantry on the grandest possible scale.*

different from the contemporaneous version of absolutism in eastern Europe. Louis XIV thought he personified the French community; he identified his sovereign power with the collective will of his people, unlike Leopold I and Frederick William, whose subjects had no sense of national community, because Austria and Brandenburg-Prussia were congeries of unrelated territories. Moreover, the eastern monarchs' absolutism rested on a simple partnership with their landed magnates, whereas Louis XIV devised a double partnership with his aristocracy and his bourgeoisie. Like his Bourbon predecessors, Louis preferred middle-class men as his ministers, councillors, and *intendants*. His chief ministers, such as Colbert, a draper's son, worked under the king's direct supervision. No members of the royal family or the high aristocracy were admitted to the daily council sessions at Versailles, where the king presided over deliberations on war, diplomacy, finance, and justice. Council orders were transmitted to the provinces by the *intendants*, who supervised all phases of local administration, notably the courts, the police, and the collection of taxes. Louis effectively nullified the power of all remaining French institutions which might challenge his centralized bureaucracy. He never called the Estates-General. His *intendants* muzzled the three provincial estates still in existence by arresting and harassing all members who dared to criticize royal policy. The *parlements* offered no further resistance.

Louis XIV's centralized administrative system had its drawbacks. The king's orders could be enforced at the local level only by the more than forty thousand bourgeois officials who had bought from the crown lifelong possession of their posts. Despite all that the *intendants* could do, these officials continually ignored or evaded unpopular decrees. Yet the partnership worked well enough. The king's civil servants were more docile and efficient than noblemen would have been. The French bourgeoisie eagerly entered state service, finding the reflected power it conferred more satisfying than such "vulgar" occupations as commerce and industry. Only in the eighteenth century did the bourgeoisie, like the aristocracy, become dissatisfied with their position; their consequent bid for increased social privileges commensurate with their political and economic power was another root cause of the French Revolution.

Like every other seventeenth-century prince, Louis XIV offered little to the huge unprivileged sector at the base of his society. He did protect his peasantry from civil war and foreign invasion, at least until the closing years of his reign. But in a society where 80 per cent of the population were farmers, very little was done to stimulate increased agricultural productivity. There were terrible years of famine in France in the 1660's and again in the 1690's. Many French peasants owned their own land, but they still had to render feudal dues and services to their local lords. The poorer peasants were compelled to surrender their mortgaged plots to their bourgeois creditors, and the percentage of *métayers*, who rented land on the sharecropping principle, and of those who worked for wages was probably increasing during the late seventeenth century. The idle poor were conscripted into the Sun King's army, or put into workhouses. Taxes nearly doubled during Louis XIV's reign, increasing from 85 million livres in 1661 to 116 million in 1683, and 152 million in 1715. Many bourgeoisie managed to gain tax exemption during this period, so the burden on the peasantry was pitiless. Whenever the peasants attempted to rebel against new taxes, Louis XIV quartered soldiers in the rebel districts and hanged the ringleaders or condemned them to state service as galley slaves.

The money wrung from the French peasantry subsidized Louis' court and army, and also Colbert's mercantilist policy. Jean Baptiste Colbert (1619–1683), finance minister from 1661 to 1683, was exceptionally energetic and exceptionally doctrinaire. His energy is demonstrated by the way in which he plugged a gaping hole in the king's revenue system. On taking office, Colbert discovered that only 25 per cent of the tax money paid by the French people was reaching the royal treasury; the other 75 per cent disappeared in middleman profits to tax farmers and corrupt officials, and in interest payments on the royal debt. Colbert clamped down on the tax farmers and repudiated part of the debt. By the time he died, the treasury's net receipts had risen to 80 per cent of gross tax payments. With the same energy, Colbert pursued his mercantilist goal. He employed every stratagem at his disposal to turn France into a self-sufficient economic unit. Colbert equated wealth with bullion, and since the amount of bullion circulating was fairly stable in the late seventeenth century, he supposed that France could increase its wealth only by taking bullion from other states. He was particularly anxious to take from the Dutch, being jealous of their business enterprise. In order to introduce French exports into areas dominated by the Dutch, he organized a series of French trading companies, the most important being the East India Company, the West India Company, the Company of the North, and the Levant Company. He paid bounties to ship builders. He raised the tariffs on Dutch and English imports. He did what he could—which in truth was not much—to expedite internal French commerce: he improved the roads a little, built some canals, and eliminated some toll barriers. But shipping goods across the country still took a month, and cost more in transport charges than most cargoes were worth. Colbert put special effort into the promotion of new French industries. He sponsored the manufacture of goods which France had habitually imported, in particular luxury items such as silk, lace, fine woolens, tapestries, mirrors, and glass.

Was all this effort well spent? The limitations of Colbert's achievement are painfully obvious. He did not build a merchant marine to rival that of the Dutch, nor could he shut off foreign imports. French internal trade remained clogged by tolls and regional customs barriers. Since French merchants refused to invest in Colbert's overseas ventures, the king had to pay more than half the costs of the East India and West India companies. In any case, most of Colbert's companies collapsed within a few years. His pet industrial projects took better root, though his meticulous regulation of them choked initiative and hampered growth. He neglected heavy industry, such as iron manufacturing. And he neglected agriculture, because French food production was generally adequate. Yet there can be no doubt that French commerce and industry gained a great deal from Colbert's paternalistic prodding. In a society where businessmen were not socially respectable, it was important for the government to protect and dignify the role of commerce and industry. Furthermore, late seventeenth-century France was well suited to the application of Colbert's mercantilist doctrine. The French economy was more diversified than Spain's, and French businessmen tolerated government interference in private enterprise more readily than did their Dutch and English counterparts.

One of Colbert's accomplishments was to shape the scattered French overseas plantations founded earlier in the century into a huge colonial empire. By the 1680's, Louis XIV held trading posts in India, several island way stations in the Indian Ocean, slaving stations in Africa, and fourteen Caribbean sugar islands. By far his most imposing overseas possession was New France; fur traders and Jesuit missionaries were exploring the vast North American hinterland from Acadia and the St. Lawrence north to Hudson Bay, west to the Great Lakes, and south along the Mississippi to the Gulf of Mexico. To be sure, only a few thousand Frenchmen lived in these far-flung places. The amount of fur, fish, and tobacco exported from New France disappointed the crown. Only the sugar islands and the trading posts in India would develop into a great source of wealth for France. All in all, however, under Colbert the French had taken a long stride toward their impressive global economy of the eighteenth century.

So far, little has been said about religion. Louis XIV was troubled by the anomalous position which he occupied within the Catholic Church. He permitted Huguenot heretics to worship within his state, which scarcely any of his fellow Catholic princes would tolerate. And his country was the one Catholic state to ignore the reform decrees promulgated by the Council of Trent, because the French crown steadfastly refused to share control of the Gallican church with a pope or council. Certainly Louis had no thought of surrendering his ecclesiastical powers. On the contrary, in 1682 he encouraged his bishops to assert that the pope had no temporal authority over the French church. Still, Louis wanted to impose the equivalent of Trentine orthodoxy and discipline upon French religious practice, in order to promote the unity of his state and at the same time clear his conscience. It was not easy to unify French religious practice. Quite apart from the Huguenot problem, the Catholics were experiencing a highly variegated spiritual revival. The Catholic reformation had come to France in the seventeenth century, decidedly later than to Spain, Italy, and Germany. New orders sprang up, such as the Trappists and the Christian Brothers. St. Vincent de Paul (c. 1581–1660) founded the Sisters of Charity to care for the sick poor, foundlings, and prostitutes of Paris. Some of the reformers quarreled among themselves; in particular, three groups—the Jesuits, the Quietists, and the Jansenists—competed for support from the French ruling class. Louis favored the Jesuits. In their schools, pulpits, and confessionals, the Jesuits did an admirable job of instructing the faithful to shun schism and obey church and state. Many devout Catholics, however, were affronted by Jesuit casuistry and by the pragmatic implication in Jesuit teaching that God helps those who help themselves. The Quietists retreated into a religion of private mystical experience, in the optimistic belief that the soul could achieve perfectibility through passive union with God. The Jansenists went to the opposite theological pole. They rejected the Jesuit belief in free will and reaffirmed St. Augustine's—and Calvin's—doctrine of inherent human depravity and irresistible grace for the elect. The Quietist and Jansenist movements attracted some of the finest spirits in seventeenth-century France: François Fénelon is the best-known Quietist, and Blaise Pascal the best-known Jansenist. Nevertheless, Louis found Quietism and Jansenism intolerable, and he drove the members of both groups into surrender, prison, or exile.

If Louis XIV was so hostile to Catholic heterodoxy, his attitude toward the Huguenots may be easily guessed. Since the 1620's, when Richelieu had crushed their political and military independence, the Huguenots had been docile subjects and valuable citizens. They had changed from the warlike, aristocratic faction of the sixteenth-century religious wars into a respectable society of bourgeois officials and businessmen. But there were still upwards of a million of them in France when Louis undertook to eradicate Protestant heresy. He demolished Huguenot churches and schools, paid cash gratuities to converts, and billeted soldiers in the houses of those who refused to convert. In 1685, the king revoked Henry IV's Edict of Nantes. Henceforth, French Protestants had no civil rights, their children were to be raised as Catholics, and their clergy were exiled or sent to the galleys. Protestantism did survive in France after 1685, but very inconspicuously. The most stubborn Huguenots—estimates run as high as 200,000—fled to England, the Dutch republic, and other Protestant states. Louis willingly paid this price to achieve the kind of cohesive Catholicism found in Spain, Austria, and Bohemia. In the late seventeenth century, the Dutch and English were exceptional in permitting any degree of nonconformity. The French were perhaps no more bigotedly anti-Protestant than the English were anti-Catholic, but they did persecute minority creeds more savagely. Louis, like other absolute monarchs, claimed the right to dictate the consciences of his subjects. His motto was, *un roi, une loi, une foi.*

However coercive his methods, Louis XIV was far from being a modern totalitarian dictator. His autocracy was superimposed on a stratified society in which every class had its own distinct function and status. Louis had to enlarge the special privileges of the aristocracy and the bourgeoisie in order to secure their cooperation. The king rarely ventured beyond his Versailles court circle. He had no means of establishing direct contact with the great masses of unprivileged peasantry, who remained subject to their feudal lords. When the great revolution of 1789 awakened an egalitarian, national consciousness among the French people, it opened up new dimensions of state power beyond Louis' dreams. His method of governing France is most fruitfully compared with Philip II's method of governing Spain a century before. At first glance the two kings seem a world apart. The introspective, somber Philip in his tomblike Escorial versus the extroverted, worldly Louis with his gilded pageantry at Versailles. Yet these are differences between the Spanish and the French temperament. Both monarchs enjoyed the assets and endured the limitations characteristic of early modern European absolutism. Sixteenth-century Spain and seventeenth-century France were both agrarian, semifeudal societies, in which the king was as strong as his army and his bureaucracy, and as rich as peasant taxes would permit. Because Bourbon France was larger and wealthier than Habsburg Spain, Louis XIV could extract greater power out of the absolutist formula than Philip II had been able to. He raised much larger armies with which to pursue his dynastic

Capture of Cambrai in the Spanish Netherlands by Louis XIV, 1677. *This old print shows how the French siege guns breeched the city walls (left center). The king himself (lower center) is receiving an obsequious emissary from Cambrai.*

ambitions and challenge the international balance of power. But France's rivals kept pace. Louis discovered—as had Philip before him—that war could bankrupt the mightiest absolute prince.

During the first half of his reign, from 1661 to 1688, Louis XIV's foreign policy was his most glorious achievement. Building on the conquests of Mazarin, he annexed further territory all along France's northern and eastern frontiers—in Flanders, Luxemburg, Lorraine, Alsace, and Franche-Comté. His generals defeated the Spanish and the imperial armies with ease. In 1672 they invaded and almost conquered the United Provinces. French diploma-

LOUIS XIV AND WILLIAM III

→ French invasion of the United Provinces, 1672

⇢ William's invasion of England, 1688

Territory annexed by Louis XIV, 1648–1684

Territory claimed by France, 1684–1697

tists skillfully played Louis' enemies off against one another so as to prevent a coordinated anti-French coalition. England and Sweden were bribed by subsidies into alliances with France. Louis' ambitions were dynastic, not national, and it was accidental that the people in the territories he annexed were French-speaking. He claimed any land to which he could lay title through heredity or marriage. In the closing years of his reign he would attempt to annex the entire Spanish Habsburg empire on the double grounds that both his mother and his wife were Spanish infantas. But after 1688, Louis' grandiose foreign policy suddenly stopped working so smoothly. France had to wage twenty-five years of grueling warfare against an international coalition which first halted Louis' expansion and then threw him on the defensive. The organizer of this anti-French coalition was one of the master politicians of the century, William of Orange. A frail little Dutchman, whose fishlike personality masked his calculating common sense and his indomitable courage, William spent his entire career fighting Louis XIV and all that he stood for.

Prince William III of Orange (1650–1702) was *stadholder,* or chief executive officer, in the United Provinces, and the great-grandson of William the Silent, the instigator of the Dutch rebellion against Philip II. Everything in William's experience made him hostile to the absolutist style, Habsburg or Bourbon. The Dutch republic over which he presided was small and loosely structured. His countrymen had no political ambition beyond maintaining the independence which they had wrested from Spain. By the mid-seventeenth century the Dutch had already reached their economic zenith. The two political factions, the Orangists and the Regents, were both well satisfied with the *status quo.* The Regents were patrician merchants in Holland, by far the most populous and important of the seven Dutch provinces. They advocated political oligarchy, religious toleration, and international peace. The Orangists, as the name implies, wanted more power for William's princely house. In times of international crisis, the military talents of the Orange dynasty were especially in demand. William the Silent and his sons had led the long war against Spain from the 1560's to 1648. During William's boyhood, the Regents controlled Dutch politics. The Regent leader, Jan de Witt (1625–1672) based his foreign policy on friendship with France; hence his position was disastrously undermined when Louis XIV invaded the United Provinces in 1672. At the height of the invasion crisis, a hysterical mob in The Hague caught de Witt in the street and hacked him to death. Young Prince William took charge. To stop the French advance, he made a truly last-ditch effort: he opened the dikes and flooded a belt of land extending from the Zuider Zee to the Rhine. The stratagem worked; Louis withdrew his army. During and after the invasion crisis, William was content to have the substance of power without the form of kingship. He recognized that monarchy was contrary to the traditions and temper of the

Dutch people, so he preserved the established federal, republican framework while purging de Witt's adherents from all government posts. In any case, his obsession was foreign affairs, above all, the prevention of further French conquests.

In 1674 William organized the first of his anti-French coalitions. It consisted of the United Provinces, Austria, Spain, and several German states. To William's mortification, his allies fell apart under French military pressure and in 1679 sued for peace on Louis XIV's terms. A decade of ostensible peace followed, during which the French continued to advance inexorably toward the Rhine. Louis occupied Strasbourg in 1681, Luxemburg in 1684. By this time all of France's neighbors were thoroughly alarmed. A new and larger anti-French coalition took shape: the League of Augsburg included the partners of 1674 plus Sweden and all the major German states. William knew that in order to stop Louis the League of Augsburg needed the participation of England as well, and he knew that the English people were on the brink of revolution against their king, James II. William had a highly personal interest in England; indeed, he had the same kind of dynastic claim to the English throne that Louis XIV had to the Spanish throne, for both his mother and his wife were Stuart princesses. In 1688 he undertook to direct a *coup d'état* against his father-in-law, James, and thereby bring England into his grand European alliance against France. Let us follow him across the English Channel.

THE GLORIOUS REVOLUTION

There is a refreshingly farcical touch to English events between 1660 and 1688, welcome after the heavy pomp of French absolutism. The English people had worked the Puritan crusading impulse out of their system. They were sick of Cromwell's army rule and blue laws. Hence in 1660 they joyfully welcomed the restoration of the Stuart monarchy. Charles II (ruled 1660–1685), son of the martyred Charles I, was a tall young man with black curls, sensuous lips, roving eyes, and irrepressible wit. He had spent the years from 1649 to 1660 in humiliating exile in France and the United Provinces, and this experience had given him a cynical view of politics and patriotism. Charles's restoration in 1660 was unconditional. Constitutionally, this meant a return to the situation that existed in 1642, on the eve of the civil war. The king had full executive control, but he was financially dependent on Parliament. Thus the battle for sovereignty between crown and Parliament had by no means been settled. The prewar religious situation was less fully restored. After 1660 the Church of England was again the state church, with bishops and prayer book, though without Archbishop Laud's aggressive High Church leadership. The Anglican establishment, however, no longer embraced all Englishmen. The Presbyterian, Independent, Baptist, and Quaker sects were too firmly rooted to be destroyed. The Anglican majority might despise and persecute these Puritan relics, but English Protestants were permanently divided into conformists and nonconformists. Economically, crown and church lands were restored in 1660, but many a Roundhead landowner and merchant emerged in better shape than those Cavaliers who had lost their estates during the revolution. Intellectually, there was no restoration at all. The prewar milieu had been metaphysical, dogmatic, passionate, and ornate. The new age of John Dryden and the Royal Society was mechanistic, skeptical, clever, and urbane. The mood was new, but the basic political and religious issues were old and unresolved.

The 1660's saw the full-scale emergence of mercantilism in England, paralleling Colbert's efforts in France. English mercantilist policy was not shaped by a presiding genius; it sprang from the mutual needs of the business community and the government. Whereas Colbert supervised all aspects of the French economy, English mercantilists concentrated on the one area most in need of stimulation and protection: overseas trade. English foreign trade had grown during the first half of the century, but it remained dangerously dependent on one export—woolen cloth—and it was crippled by an inadequate merchant marine. English merchants needed protection against Dutch competition. The government needed increased customs revenues. The result was a series of Navigation Acts, passed between 1651 and 1673—initiated, it may be noted, by the Puritan republic and reinforced by Charles II's Parliament. The Navigation Acts stipulated that imports to England were to be carried there directly from the country of origin, in ships belonging either to that country or to England—thus the Dutch carrying trade would be excluded and the Amsterdam entrepôt bypassed. Such English colonial products as sugar and tobacco, for which there was a heavy European demand, had to be shipped first to England, and the colonists were required to buy on the English market any non-English commodities they desired—thus the English merchants would be encouraged to become middlemen, like the Dutch, and London's development as an entrepôt would be stimulated. The Dutch fought back, defending their free-trade principles. Three Anglo-Dutch naval wars took place in rapid succession, in 1652–1654, 1665–1667, and 1672–1674. The two commercial rivals battled each other to a standstill. But since the Dutch also had to ward off Louis XIV, they were exhausted by the struggle and nervous for the future. In the end they resigned themselves to England's new mercantile policy. By 1700 Dutch commerce, industry, and banking had stopped expanding, whereas by every index the English economy was growing fast. England's foreign and colonial trade were particularly flourishing. Between 1660 and 1700, the value of English imports and exports climbed 50 per cent, its merchant marine more than doubled in size, and customs revenues nearly trebled. The English had replaced the Dutch as the business leaders of Europe.

After 1660 the English colonial empire also took firm shape. In the sixteenth and early seventeenth centuries, English explorers and colonizers had been completely outflanked by the Spanish and the Dutch in their quest for quick profits from precious cargoes, such as bullion and spices. It took some time for the English to reconcile themselves to their role as the founders of basically agricultural colonies overseas. More than a century elapsed between the first English exploration of North America and the first permanent settlement, at Jamestown in 1607. Thereafter, the English made a substantial colonizing effort. Some eighty thousand emigrants crossed the Atlantic from England between 1607 and 1640, nearly as many as had gone from Spain to America during the entire previous century. The English emigrants were mainly young people from the middle classes, lured by free land and open air. Initially, the English government played a much more passive role than the Spanish government had done. James I and Charles I anticipated no quick profits from American agriculture, and since most of the early settlements were operated by Puritans, the crown declined to subsidize or supervise them. Thus it happened that without any overall plan or purpose, two dozen separate little English communities sprouted in America, scattered from Newfoundland to Guiana. Each colony functioned as an autonomous unit. Each developed its own identity. Some were sponsored by joint-stock companies; some were sponsored by individual proprietors; some lacked any authorization from the home government. In contrast to the Spaniards, with their epic conquest of the Aztecs and the Incas, the English hugged the Atlantic coast, hesitant to explore the vast continent at their backs, unable to make the Indians work for them or pray with them. But the English colonists possessed a self-reliance lacking among the Spanish in America. Each colony had its own representative assembly, with all the constitutional ambitions of Parliament at home.

In the 1670's Charles II launched a new policy toward English America, designed to shatter colonial autonomy and bind each plantation closer to the crown. Recognizing the rising commercial value of Caribbean sugar and Chesapeake tobacco, English mercantilists belatedly began to erect a central imperial administration for the colonies. After a generation of protest and rebellion throughout English America, the colonists by 1700 had adjusted to their new imperial status. They learned to live with the Navigation Acts, the sugar planters more willingly than the mainland colonists. But they prevented the home government from centralizing the empire in a thorough-going Spanish or French sense. Englishmen in America retained a larger measure of local self-determination, diversity, and democracy than could be found in any seventeenth-century European society. Meanwhile, by 1700 English merchants dominated the lucrative African slave trade. The English East India Company was doing a booming business through its trading posts at Bombay, Madras, and Calcutta. All in all, England's worldwide commercial undertakings were worth much more than the bullion and spices the English explorers had failed to find.

Though the English economy was thriving under Charles II as never before, domestic politics had seldom been so erratic. The new king greatly admired Louis XIV's absolute monarchy, and he also rather preferred French Roman Catholicism to English Protestantism. But Charles was ill equipped to be a Sun King. His court at Whitehall was far less grandiose and glittering than Versailles. The English upper classes were less dependent on royal patronage than they had been under Elizabeth or the early Stuarts. They wanted direct political power, not reflected glory. Charles was much too foxy to risk starting another revolution, and besides, he was too lazy to work seriously at building an absolute state.

During the first fifteen years of his reign, Charles II masked his views by employing a hodgepodge of ministers: old-fashioned Cavaliers, ex-Cromwellians, and opportunistic Catholics. Of these, only the Catholics enjoyed the king's confidence. Charles's first Parliament was so enthusiastically royalist that the king figured it could never be improved upon. He kept this Cavalier Parliament in session for eighteen years, from 1661 to 1679. Even so, king and Parliament were soon pursuing divergent religious policies. The Cavalier Parliament was ardently Anglican and harassed the nonconformist sects with a series of persecuting laws known as the Clarendon Code. The king meanwhile secretly promised Louis XIV (in return for an immediate subsidy) to restore England to Rome as soon as conditions were favorable. Charles moved circumspectly. In 1672 he suspended the Clarendon Code and all other penal laws against Catholics and Protestant nonconformists. But the popular outcry was so terrific that Charles decided his pledge to Louis must be abandoned. He reinstated the persecuting laws and reorganized his ministry in support of Anglicanism. In the mid-1670's, two clearly delineated political factions emerged within the English upper classes: the Tories, who supported Charles's government, and the Whigs, who criticized it. The Tories, led by the king's chief minister, the earl of Danby (1631–1712), had much in common with the Cavaliers of 1642. They championed divine-right monarchy and the established Anglican church. The Whigs, led by an ex-minister, the earl of Shaftesbury (1621–1683), had much in common with the Roundheads of 1642. They advocated parliamentary supremacy and toleration for Protestant nonconformists. Three factors, however, kept the party division of the 1670's less fundamental than that of the 1640's. Tories and Whigs were both fearful of another civil war. Both were anti-Catholic and anti-French. And both were out of step with their willowy monarch.

In the closing years of Charles II's reign, from 1678 to 1685, the Whigs and Tories grappled furiously without resorting to arms—a notable step toward the domestication of party politics. The Whigs got their big chance

James II in prayer. *This engraving of the pious king was made when he was in exile in France after the Glorious Revolution. Pepysian Library, Magdalene College, Cambridge.*

in 1678, when a shifty character named Titus Oates announced to the startled world that he had uncovered a horrendous Popish Plot. According to Oates, the Jesuits (with papal blessing) were planning to assassinate Charles, massacre the English Protestants, and install the king's brother James on the throne. Englishmen high and low avidly swallowed this preposterous story. Oates had dramatized a fatal flaw in the Stuart dynasty. Charles, with his bevy of mistresses, had sired several bastards, but no legitimate children. The heir to the throne, his brother James, was extremely unpopular because he was a zealous Catholic convert. For two years the country was swept by anti-Catholic hysteria. Charles knew that Oates was a liar, but he dared not pooh-pooh his story, lest someone uncover the real popish plot that Charles himself had engaged in with Louis XIV. Shaftesbury, the Whig leader, also guessed that Oates was a liar, but by skillfully manipulating the popular hysteria he discredited the Tory leader, Danby, and built a Whig majority in Parliament. Between 1679 and 1681 three Whig parliaments were elected in rapid succession. Each of these, under Shaftesbury's management, had a single aim: to exclude James from the royal succession. But Charles II had the last laugh. After 1681 he ruled without Parliament. The rising customs revenues, together with Louis XIV's subsidy, permitted him to dispense with parliamentary taxation, and hence to gag the Whigs. Charles restored Tory control. Shaftesbury was charged with treason and died in exile, and the king found pretexts for executing a number of other Whig leaders. He persecuted the nonconformists more heartily than before. He remodeled a great many town constitutions and parliamentary electoral districts, so as to make local governments subservient to the crown, and future Parliaments manageable. When Charles died in 1685, there was no effective opposition to James's succession.

Superficially, Charles II appeared to have achieved Louis XIV's absolutism after all. In fact, he had scarcely affected the English trend toward constitutional monarchy. Charles was not really independent of Parliament. In any fiscal emergency, such as a war, the crown would still require taxes which only Parliament could authorize. Charles had been able to punish the Whigs, persecute the nonconformists, and remodel local governments because the Tories warmly supported these policies. The Stuart dynasty was as strong as its Tory support. Should the Tories turn against the Stuarts, their autocratic policy would easily be reversed. Charles had buried the Popish Plot, but England's fear of French power, and of popery, was by no means dead. Three years of exposure to James II touched off a new revolution against the Stuarts, the Glorious Revolution.

James II (ruled 1685–1688) attempted single-handedly to reverse a whole century of history. Few kings have failed so spectacularly. James was fooled by his easy accession to power. In 1685 royal troops quickly nipped an inept Whig rebellion. The House of Commons dutifully voted the new sovereign such generous revenues that he did not need to call Parliament after his first year. He also received money from Louis XIV. But James alienated this initial support. He dismissed his brother's Tory ministers and appointed Catholics wherever possible to all government posts down to the level of justice of the peace. Since there were very few English Catholics to draw upon, James's appointees were generally untried and inferior men. The king also stationed a standing army, largely officered by Catholics, outside London. He did his best to undermine the Anglican establishment by reviving Charles II's suspension of penal laws against Catholics and nonconformists. Unlike Charles, he frankly broadcast his motives. "We cannot but heartily wish," he told his subjects, "that all the people of our dominions were members of the Catholic church." As a result, most nonconformists distrusted his toleration policy, and Anglicans were scandalized.

The breaking point came in June, 1688. When the king ordered the Anglican clergy to read his toleration decree from their pulpits, seven bishops dared to protest. James put them in the Tower and ordered them tried for seditious libel. To his amazement, the jury returned a verdict of not guilty. In this same month, James's queen bore him a son. According to the rules of royal inheritance, this infant immediately took precedence over the king's two grown daughters, both Protestant, the offspring of a previous marriage; James had the Catholic heir his subjects had been dreading. James's elder daughter was married to William of Orange. Like many Englishmen, William wanted to believe that the royal birth was an imposture. A fantastic rumor spread that the baby had been smuggled into the queen's bed in a warming pan. There is much greater truth in the well-known nursery rhyme which describes what happened to the newborn prince and his father during the closing months of 1688:

> Rock-a-bye baby, in the tree top.
> When the wind blows,* the cradle will rock.
> When the bough breaks, the cradle will fall,
> And down will come baby, cradle and all.

By June, 1688, Tories and Whigs were allied against James II. The king was more isolated than Charles I had been in 1640. But no one wanted another full-scale upheaval. In the revolution of 1688–1689, no new Cromwell rose up to crusade against the Stuarts. Instead, a cross section of Whig and Tory aristocrats discreetly invited that cool and calculating Dutchman, William of Orange, to bring a foreign army to England and restore their religion and their liberty. Nothing was said in the invitation about overthrowing James, though everyone knew that William and his wife, Mary, were the prime Protestant candidates for the throne. William accepted the invitation, primarily because it gave him leverage for pulling England into his coalition against Louis XIV. Poor James was paralyzed by the magnitude of the conspiracy against him.

In November, 1688, William landed his army unopposed in southwestern England. Despite the king's flurry of desperate, last-minute concessions, the chief men in the country deserted to the prince's camp. Had James led his army into battle against William, he might still have rallied English patriotism against the Dutch invader. But the king was incapacitated by a severe nosebleed—about the only blood shed during the Glorious Revolution. William advanced implacably toward London. James abjectly fled to France. In February, 1689, a parliamentary assembly declared that James II had abdicated and offered the vacant throne to William and Mary. The new sovereigns accepted Parliament's Bill of Rights, the Magna Charta of 1689. The Bill of Rights enumerated the elementary civil liberties of Englishmen and declared absolutist practices like those of the last Stuart kings to be illegal. It epitomized England's evolution into a constitutional monarchy, in which the king governed by parliamentary consent and was subject to law.

Strictly speaking, the Glorious Revolution was a *coup d'état*, but in the wider sense it marked the final victory for representative self-government and

*This phrase refers to the gale which blew William of Orange's invading fleet from the Netherlands to England in November, 1688.

William of Orange landing in England, 1688. *This old print shows William, unflappable as always, seated in a rowboat, his Dutch fleet to the rear, as happy Englishmen scramble to welcome their deliverer. Actually, few English joined William when he first landed, since they disliked the prospect of a Dutch king almost as much as James's Catholicism.*

religious pluralism in England. The Whig philosophy had triumphed, but only with Tory support. The revolutionary settlement of 1689 was a compromise with which almost all Englishmen could live. William and Mary still exercised great executive independence, but Parliament henceforth met annually, controlled the purse strings, and shared in the direction of public affairs. No English king after James II tried to govern without Parliament, or in defiance of Parliament. Party factionalism continued as a permanent feature of English political life, but after 1689 the Whigs and Tories contested for power within the framework of parliamentary government. In religion, the Toleration Act of 1689 permitted nonconformists to worship publicly, though in comparison with the Anglicans they remained second-class citizens. The provisions of the Toleration Act did not apply to Roman Catholics, but Catholics in England, in the latitudinarian post-revolutionary atmosphere, suffered much less persecution than Protestants in France. Economically, the revolution cemented the partnership between business and government. Henceforth, to a much greater extent than in France, merchants and landlords underwrote the costs of government through taxes and loans. The Bank of England, founded in 1694, utilized private capital to perform public services. In France, it was still risky to lend the king money, and any deficit incurred by the French government was construed as the king's personal liability. But in England, crown and Parliament floated huge war loans in the 1690's at guaranteed interest rates. The moneyed classes invested with confidence in a government they helped to control. The king's deficit was transformed into a national debt.

The Glorious Revolution had its inglorious aspects. It was carried out by and for the propertied classes, who were determined to perpetuate their privileged status. To the unprivileged, servile sectors of English society, the revolution brought no benefits. Back in the 1640's, democratic and even communistic aspirations had been loudly voiced. Such sentiments were unheard now. Only educated and prosperous Englishmen could practice the "liberties" specified in the Bill of Rights, enjoy representation in Parliament, or take advantage of the atmosphere of religious and economic emancipation. In Ireland, the revolutionary settlement was especially inglorious. Here, the downtrodden Catholic majority naturally supported their coreligionist, James, against the Calvinist William. Once William and Mary's forces gained control of Ireland in 1691, all power and most property were given over to a small ruling caste—the Protestants from England and Scotland who had been trying for 150 years to conquer and exploit the Irish. Some members of this Protestant master class lived grandly in England as absentee landlords, spending there what little surplus wealth could be extracted from Irish subsistence agriculture. Their colleagues in Dublin developed a code of vindictive penal laws which outlawed Catholic priests and schools, excluded Catholics from public life, and hindered them from holding property or pursuing trades and professions. The purpose of this code was not to wipe out Catholicism, but to keep the native Irish in a state of peasant servility. No other people in western Europe was so brutally oppressed.

The chief international consequence of the Glorious Revolution was that William III brought England into the League of Augsburg against Louis XIV. The year 1689 marks a major turning point in Anglo-French relations. Between 1559 and 1688, England and France had been almost always at peace with each other, despite the obvious contrasts in their internal development. Between 1689 and 1815, they fought against each other in seven major wars. No pair of adversaries had ever been better equipped, for both French and English strength had been tempered by 150 years of religious conflict. A long road had been traveled since the 1560's, when the Calvinists and Catholics began their battle for the mastery of western Europe. But, as has been shown, both the Calvinist and the reformed Catholic movements had great survival power. In 1689 William III was recognizably John Calvin's heir, and he drew upon Calvinist resources in the Netherlands and England. His family had led the Dutch Calvinists against Philip II. He himself brought to a successful conclusion the English Calvinists' century-long rebellion against the Stuarts. The Calvinist ethic had left its distinctive imprint on Dutch and English business enterprise and political organization. Louis XIV drew upon a different heritage, one in which the Catholic reformation was a prime stimulus. His dynasty had restored France to Catholic unity. He himself had crushed the Huguenots. His style of rule bore many of the conservative attributes of the reformed Roman Church: it was majestic, paternalistic, tightly ordered, hostile toward disruptive new ideas, and aggressive in the defense of old ones. Thus fortified, the English and French began their eighteenth-century contest for world leadership.

CHAPTER 11

The Century of Genius

IF THERE WERE no other reason for examining the years between 1559 and 1689, the galaxy of superb artists and thinkers who flourished during this period would still command our attention. This was the age of Shakespeare, Cervantes, El Greco, Montaigne, Descartes, Galileo, Rubens, Milton, Molière, Bernini, Rembrandt, Velázquez, Hobbes, Spinoza, Newton, and Locke—all men of creative genius whose work still lives today. If the ultimate measure of genius is to produce work of timeless beauty and universal significance, these great artists and thinkers can stand comparison with any in history.

It is not easy to characterize in a few words the culture of early modern Europe. The difficulty is increased by the jagged intellectual and aesthetic crosscurrents of the period. The sixteen men just listed did not share a common platform of ideas and ideals. Six or seven of them can be identified as participants in the scientific revolution of the seventeenth century. Another five or six can be identified as Baroque artists. But since Shakespeare, Cervantes, and Rembrandt can be placed in neither category, this formulation is scarcely satisfactory. In the seventeenth century, European culture was passing through an especially iconoclastic, aggressive, experimental phase. Something in the atmosphere encouraged thinkers to question rather than to synthesize, and inspired artists to wrestle with the newest, biggest, and most variegated subjects they could find. For want of a better label, the seventeenth century is often called the century of genius.

Inevitably, all branches of art and learning reflected the wide disparity—political, economic, and social—between western and eastern Europe which was such a conspicuous feature of our period. Culturally, the years from 1559 to 1689 constituted a golden age for Spain, the Dutch republic, and England, and at least a silver age for France. But for Italy the golden age was passing, and for Germany it had not yet arrived. In Italy, which had been the artistic center of Europe for three centuries, the most significant seventeenth-century figure was a scientist—Galileo. In central Europe, too, the most eminent personages were scientists—Kepler and Leibniz. Poland and Russia,

354

during the late sixteenth and seventeenth centuries, were more isolated from general European cultural trends than they had been during the Middle Ages and the Renaissance.

To facilitate our understanding of the western European culture of this time, let us focus upon three major themes. First, the scientific revolution from Copernicus to Newton. What effect did the new science have upon man's view of nature and of himself? Second, the Catholic-Protestant struggle for mastery of Europe. How did this conflict inspire new forms of religious art, and at the same time provoke new antireligious intellectual attitudes? Third, the social and economic disparity between rich and poor, privileged and unprivileged. How did the arts reflect this social polarity, and why did European culture grow more aristocratic in the course of the seventeenth century? We stand today in the shadow of these questions.

THE SCIENTIFIC REVOLUTION

Between the 1540's and the 1680's, a brilliant constellation of astronomers, physicists, and mathematicians, including Copernicus, Kepler, Galileo, Descartes, and Newton, accomplished a veritable revolution in science. They obliterated the traditional view of nature and established scientific practice on an impressive new footing. This great breakthrough equipped the physical scientist with new methods and new standards which worked exceedingly well throughout the eighteenth and nineteenth centuries. So total was the victory, that it requires an effort of imagination to understand how any intelligent man could have taken the pre-Copernican view of nature seriously. Yet this traditional view was scientific within its own terms. For many centuries thinking men had found it logical and empirical, as well as emotionally convincing. We must try to reconstitute this obliterated system in order to appreciate the magnitude of the scientific discoveries which swept it away.

The traditional view of the cosmos, accepted by almost every educated man until well into the seventeenth century, was a synthesis of Aristotelian mechanics, Ptolemaic astronomy, and Christian teleology. Commonsense observation demonstrated that Aristotle's theory of motion did indeed represent the way God operated the universe. All heavy bodies, said Aristotle, naturally fell toward the center of the universe and rested there, unless propelled by a mover in some other direction. It followed that the round earth, obviously solid and weighty, stood motionless in the center of the universe. Both Catholic and Protestant theologians associated the earth's heaviness with corruption and compared terrestrial mutability with the changeless purity of the firmament above. Thus the earth, divinely appointed to mortal man's use, was in effect the cesspool of the universe, with hell at its innermost core. Such teachings harmonized nicely with Ptolemaic astronomy. According to the second-century mathematician Ptolemy, a concentric series of transparent crystalline spheres revolved in an ascending order of purity around man's corruptible habitat. The moon, the sun, the planets, the fixed stars, and the *primum mobile* (the outermost sphere, which drove the entire system) all wheeled in perfect circles, going once around the earth every twenty-four hours. Beyond the *primum mobile* lay the purest region of all, God's heavenly abode. Everything in this picture conformed to men's experience and expectations. Anyone could see that the earth stood still and that the stars were fixed. Ptolemy's theory of harmonious celestial motion coincided as well as could be expected with the crude astronomical observations which stargazers were able to collect.

Pre-Copernican science embraced a corresponding set of biological and chemical assumptions, which again suited men's experience and expectations. It was believed that God had created all living things within an immense, purposeful, and harmoniously ascending order: the great chain of being. Inanimate objects (such as liquids and metals) belonged at the lowest level of existence. Next came the subdivisions of the vegetable class, possessing life as well as existence. Next, the various gradations of dumb animals, with feeling as well as life. Next, man (the little world, or microcosm), endowed with intelligence and a soul in addition to all the lower earthly faculties. At the top of the ladder was the hierarchy of angels, purely spiritual creatures, enjoying man's understanding without his sinful and mutable nature. The angels, it was thought, dwelt in the pure ether of the spheres, beyond the realm of scientific analysis. The composition of terrestrial matter, however, was much discussed. In chemistry, the basic assumption was that all terrestrial matter was compounded of four elements: earth, water, air, and fire. Earth was the basest element, and fire the noblest, but life required all four, and health depended on keeping them in balance. Hence in *King Lear*, when Shakespeare wanted to dramatize the chaos of the storm, he had Lear cry out that all four elements were at war:

> Blow, winds, and crack your cheeks! rage! blow!
> You cataracts and hurricanoes, spout
> Till you have drencht our steeples, drown'd the cocks!
> You sulphurous and thought-executing fires,
> Vaunt-couriers to oak-cleaving thunderbolts,
> Singe my white head! And thou, all-shaking thunder,
> Strike flat the thick rotundity o' the world!

In human physiology, the four elements had their counterparts in four fluids known as humors—melancholy, phlegm, blood, and choler—which were thought to pass through the veins from the liver to the heart. During the Middle Ages and the Renaissance, the chief object of medical and psychiatric practice was to keep the patient's humors in proper balance, and thus preserve his good health and his normal temperament.

Two features of this pre-Copernican science require special emphasis. In the first place, it rested to an extraordinary degree on past authority, not merely on ancient Greek theory, but also on the results of ancient Greek experimentation. Before the mid-sixteenth century, no anatomist tried to improve upon Galen's authoritative experiments in the dissection of the human body, nor did any astronomer dare to question Ptolemy's celestial calculations, even though Galen and Ptolemy had both done their work back in the second century. In the second place, there were major mysteries unexplained by this traditional view of the world which made it difficult to draw a line between science and superstition, between experimentation and magic. Despite Aristotle's assertion that all matter preferred rest, the whole universe was in constant motion. What drove the *primum mobile?* The elements could not be artificially isolated, and the humors could not even be seen. Why were they so unpredictable? Why should a healthy man suddenly drop dead, or a thriving crop be blasted by insects, or a city be swept by the plague? What caused storms, floods, and other natural catastrophes? What made one metal precious and another dross? What did it mean when strange comets suddenly blazed in the sky? The fickleness of life seemed to show that God had delegated a large role in nature to fate, fortune, or chance. Hence astrologers, who claimed to be able to predict human events by the position of the stars, were given as much credence as astronomers. Alchemists, who claimed to be able to transmute base metals into gold, were given as much credence as chemists. Most people absorbed the folklore of fairies and pixies, small-scale supernatural beings who meddled in human affairs for good or ill. Many believed in witchcraft, the intercession of evil spirits (fallen angels) or the devil himself. In short, there was no confidence that man, through the exercise of his God-given intelligence, could learn to master his physical environment.

The New View of the Universe

It is ironic that the first thinker to challenge this traditional view of nature was Nicolaus Copernicus (1473–1543), for Copernicus was a conservative and quiet Polish cleric who lived in an obscure East Prussian cathedral town. He published his revision of Ptolemy's geocentric theory of celestial motion in 1543, hoping to bring Ptolemaic astronomy up to date. Instead, he sapped the accepted foundations of science. Copernicus had no quarrel with the Ptolemaic vision of concentric crystalline spheres wheeling in perfect circles around the central point in the universe. What troubled him was the fact that Ptolemy's spheres were not perfectly circular. Even Ptolemy's own astronomical observations indicated that only the sun moved with perfect uniformity. The moon, the planets, and the fixed stars sometimes speeded up or changed direction. To plot all observable celestial motion around the earth in spherical form required an intricate network of eighty interlocking circles and epicycles. Copernicus believed that God must have designed a simpler, more harmonious pattern for His universe than this.

Copernicus' great discovery was that he could account for the irregularities in celestial motion much more simply by making a single elemental adjustment. He visualized the sun rather than the earth as the immobile center of the universe. Copernicus was something of a sun worshiper, considering the sun a nobler orb than the earth. His central hypothesis, that the earth rotated daily on her axis and revolved annually around the sun, temporarily bolstered the ancient doctrine of the spheres. Spherical motion could be plotted around the sun in thirty-four circles and epicycles, as against Ptolemy's eighty. But the heliocentric theory cast doubt on the ascending purity of the spheres. The earth was now seen as one of the planets, operating on the same physical principles as Jupiter or Saturn, which had previously been regarded as situated on a higher level. According to Copernicus, it was no longer necessary to believe that the distant fixed stars wheeled completely every twenty-four hours. But most men accepted the daily revolution of the stars more readily than the daily rotation of the earth, which contradicted common sense. And if Copernicus was correct, why did not centrifugal force tear the world to pieces? Copernicus had no satisfactory answer to this question, but he stimulated other scientists to work on it.

For a half century after Copernicus' death, his heliocentric theory gained few adherents. It was taught at only one university (Salamanca, in Spain), and it was not broadcast in layman's language to the general public. Such late sixteenth-century savants as Bodin and Montaigne lightly dismissed Copernicus. Tycho Brahe (1546–1601), the leading practical astronomer in the half century after Copernicus, clung to the geocentric theory. For, he argued, if the earth rotated and revolved, a stone dropped from a high tower would fall to the west, which in fact did not happen. In science-fiction parlance, Tycho Brahe was something of a mad scientist. On a Danish island he built and operated the fantastic castle of Uraniborg, equipped with outsize instruments, observatories, laboratories, and a team of research assistants; there he engaged in astronomical, astrological, and alchemical studies. Nevertheless, he was an important contributor to the scientific revolution. He tracked the positions of the planets more systematically than had ever been done before and compiled a mass of astronomical observations which reached the limits of naked-eye accuracy.

Tycho's ablest assistant, Johannes Kepler (1571–1630), was a Copernican. Kepler used Tycho's data to demonstrate beyond question the mathematical symmetry of Copernicus' heliocentric system. Kepler, like Tycho, fused science with pseudoscience. His undigested and unreadable books are stuffed with rhapsodic musings about the harmony of the universe and the magical geometry of the planets. For Kepler, "the music of the spheres" meant that Mars was a tenor, Mercury a falsetto, and so forth. But he was also a mathematician of genius. For years he puzzled over the apparently erratic orbit of Mars. According to Tycho's observations, this planet moved in a far from perfect circle, and it traveled faster when approaching the sun than when receding from it. Kepler's efforts to find mathematical expression for Mars's orbit led him to his three descriptive laws of planetary motion. He discovered that Mars, the earth, and all the other planets orbit elliptically around the sun, and that the sun is not at the center, but at one focus of the ellipse. An ellipse is less obviously perfect in shape than a circle, but it too has abstract properties, reducible to a mathematical formula. Kepler further discovered that while the planets do not travel at uniform speed, the radius vector between the sun and a planet always sweeps over equal areas in equal times. In other words, all planetary motion can be described by a single mathematical formula. Finally, he discovered that while each planet takes a different length of time to go around the sun, the square of the planetary period of orbit is always proportional to the cube of its distance from the sun. In other words, all planetary time periods can likewise be described by a single mathematical formula.

Kepler had done more than prove mathematically that Copernicus was right and Ptolemy wrong. His laws reconciled fact with theory. They stripped the cosmos of some of its old mystery and endowed it with a new mechanistic regularity. For all his mystical rapture, Kepler abandoned Copernicus' traditional belief in the crystalline spheres. He saw the planets as moving through immense empty spaces, held to their courses by some power beyond his investigation, yet always operating in accordance with simple, uniform, verifiable, mathematical principles.

The first Copernican scientist to gain wide public attention was a doughty Florentine, Galileo Galilei (1564–1642). Galileo was a Renaissance man, cast in the same larger-than-life mold as Leonardo da Vinci and Michelangelo before him. He was a wonderfully complete scientist: a lucid analytical thinker, an ingenious experimentalist, a masterful technologist, and a zestful writer. Kepler's laws were abstract and abstruse, but there was nothing abstract or abstruse about Galileo's frontal assault on Ptolemy and Aristotle.

In 1609 Galileo heard that a Dutchman had invented a spyglass through which distant objects could be seen as if close up. He soon constructed a telescope of his own, which magnified distant objects thirty times. In 1610 he jubilantly announced in his *Starry Messenger* the exciting new things he had seen in the heavens through this instrument. The moon, he reported, had a mountainous surface very much like the earth's, concrete evidence that it was composed of terrestrial matter rather than some purer substance, as Aristotle had supposed. Galileo was struck by the difference between the planets and the stars; when viewed through his telescope, the planets looked like solid globes, but the stars, far more numerous and less sparkling than when seen by the naked eye, were still without distinct size or shape. The stars, he realized, must be fantastically remote from the earth. Galileo was especially pleased to discover four satellites orbiting around Jupiter. Here was additional evidence against the uniqueness of the earth and her moon. Later, Galileo detected rings around Saturn, observed the moonlike phases of Venus, and noted spots on the surface of the sun. Each of these findings cast further doubt on the validity of the Ptolemaic cosmos. Each demonstrated how a seventeenth-century experimental scientist could learn far more about nature than was taught in ancient books. "Oh, my dear Kepler," wrote Galileo in 1610, "here at Padua is the principal professor of philosophy, whom I have repeatedly and urgently requested to look at the moon and planets through my glass, which he obstinately refuses to do. Why are you not here? What shouts of laughter we should have at this glorious folly!" When another professor who scorned his telescope died, Galileo was heard to hope that he would notice the new celestial phenomena on his way up to heaven.

Galileo knew that the professors denied the evidence of his telescope because it conflicted with the accepted Aristotelian concept of motion. Aristotle had taught that for a body to be put into motion, a mover, either internal or external, was necessary. He distinguished between *natural* motion, the result of internal self-direction, and *violent* motion, the result of artificial propulsion by an external force. For example, heavy bodies were thought to fall naturally at an accelerating rate because they were jubilant at returning home to rest at the center of the universe. Light bodies naturally rose to their proper station. To Aristotelians, it violated nature to suppose that the moon and the planets could fly permanently through outer space if they were heavy like the earth. Surely God would not permit the earth to be violently swung in perpetuity about the incorporeal sun.

Putting aside the Aristotelian concept, Galileo developed a wholly new approach to dynamics, the study of the behavior of bodies in motion. He tried to explain not why bodies move, but how they move. In a series of experiments he demonstrated that the movement of bodies through time and space can be described by mathematical equations. For instance, having shown that a pendulum of fixed length always completed its swing in a fixed time whether it moved through a long or a short distance, Galileo could express the period of the pendulum mathematically. Similarly, having worked out the parabolic trajectory of a cannonball, he could formulate a general theory of projectiles. Perhaps Galileo did not really drop a ten-pound weight and a one-pound weight simultaneously from the top of the Leaning Tower of Pisa, but he certainly did prove that a heavy body falls with no greater velocity than a light body of the same material. The behavior of all free-falling bodies, regardless of weight, is described by Galileo's law of acceleration. This series of demonstrations vitiated the Aristotelian distinction between natural and violent motion. Galileo's experiments with rolling balls on inclined planes led him toward his most fundamental achievement, the reinterpretation of inertia. Galileo was the first to see that under ideal physical conditions, with gravity and friction eliminated, a moving ball will continue to roll infinitely unless checked or hastened or deflected by another force. All past thinkers had equated inertia with rest, and the science of mechanics had always been concerned with explaining the motion of bodies. Once Galileo equated inertia with rest *or* infinite uniform motion, he saw that only *changes* of motion required explanation. In Galileo's view, it was as easy to conceive of the earth in perpetual rotation and revolution as to conceive of it at rest. Once his principles of dynamics were established, the traditional physics became as worthless as the traditional astronomy.

It is scarcely surprising that Galileo's repudiation of Aristotle and Ptolemy got him into trouble with the Church. The old science, though pagan in origin, was deeply embedded in the Christian intellectual tradition. The new science conflicted with some passages of Scripture. Galileo argued that Scripture and nature should be treated as separate truths, but he took perverse delight in mocking the stupid scientific opinions of his clerical critics. Owing largely to pressure from the Jesuits, the Holy Office in 1616 labeled the Copernican theory as "foolish and absurd, philosophically false and formally heretical." Galileo was admonished not to accept or propound Copernicanism. Nevertheless, in 1632 he thought it safe to publish his *Dialogue Concerning the Two World Systems—Ptolemaic and Copernican.* By presenting the respective merits of the old astronomy and the new in dialogue form, Galileo could pretend to be neutral. In fact, he portrayed the champion of the old science as an ignorant clown, Simplicio, who got the worst of every argument. Pope Urban VIII (ruled 1623–1644) believed that Galileo was lampooning him as Simplicio. Galileo was brought to Rome, examined by the inquisitors, made to recant his errors, and sentenced to house arrest for the remainder of his life. The *Dialogue* was put on the Index. The legend is that when Galileo retired to his Florentine villa, he looked up at the sky, stamped his foot on the ground, and muttered, *"Eppur si muove"*—"It still moves."

Galileo's trial has perhaps received undue attention. Being a good Catholic, he accepted his punishment with better grace than have modern secular liberals. The Church did not prevent him from working or writing. In 1638 the dauntless old man published his last and greatest book, the *Discourse on Two New Sciences,* in which he laid the foundation for modern physics. Yet it is not accidental that Galileo sent this manuscript to Leiden for publication. As the seventeenth century wore on, Protestant countries, particularly the United Provinces and England, provided the freest atmosphere for the exploration and discussion of the new science.

Descartes. *Painting by an unknown artist.*

The Scientific Climate of Opinion

During the first half of the century, two influential philosophers vigorously championed the scientific revolution: Francis Bacon (1561–1626), an Englishman, and René Descartes (1596–1650), a Frenchman who settled in Holland. Both Bacon and Descartes announced their contempt for the outdated old science. Like Petrarch at the dawn of the Renaissance, they saw themselves as pioneers in a glorious new age, ending 1,500 years of intellectual stagnation. Bacon and Descartes were bolder pioneers than Petrarch, for they endeavored to emancipate themselves from *all* past intellectual authority, classical as well as medieval. Descartes felt so suffocated by the dead dogmas of Aristotle and his medieval scholastic disciples that he set himself the intellectual task of doubting all past knowledge and custom. He stripped away belief in everything except his own existence as a thinking and doubting being—"I think, therefore I am." On this naked premise he erected a brand-new metaphysics and physics. Both Bacon and Descartes believed that science, properly practiced, offered the key to unprecedented human progress. "The true goal of the sciences," wrote Bacon, "is none other than this: that human life be endowed with new discoveries and power." Although he lived in an era of very slow technological development, Bacon understood that the scientific revolution would immeasurably strengthen man's control over his physical environment. He foresaw the kind of interplay between science and technology which has indeed transformed the modern world.

Both Bacon and Descartes had valuable things to say about scientific method. In his *Novum Organum* ("The New Instrument"), published in 1620, Bacon argued that the true scientist (unlike Aristotle) worked by the inductive method, moving from the particular to the general, from specific experiments to axioms which in turn pointed the way to further experiments. Bacon urged scientists to experiment as systematically as possible, to pool their knowledge and dovetail their research projects, and above all to keep open-minded about the results. Though not himself an experimentalist, Bacon advocated the kind of empirical, inductive procedure normally followed by modern chemists and biologists. But Bacon's method was not employed by the greatest scientists of his own day. The thinking of mathematicians, astronomers, and physicists is more abstract than Bacon realized.

The most important science of the seventeenth century was deductive, as when Kepler deduced his general laws of planetary motion. Here Descartes' understanding of scientific method was much more relevant. Descartes was a great mathematician in his own right. He invented analytical geometry and perfected Galileo's law of inertia. In his *Discourse on Method* (1637), Descartes laid down rules for the abstract, deductive reasoning suitable to mathematicians. The true scientist, according to Descartes, was interested not so much in concrete phenomena as in the laws which systematized and explained nature. To uncover nature's secrets, he had to search for the simplest elements making up the physical world and deduce from these elements principles which would give meaning to concrete phenomena. Descartes' method was far closer than Bacon's to the intellectual process by which Copernicus, Kepler, and Galileo arrived at their discoveries.

Both Bacon and Descartes had their limitations as philosophers of the new science. Bacon's concept of science was too crudely utilitarian; Descartes' was too divorced from experience. Bacon's defects are more obvious. His insistence on material results blinded him to the revolution in astronomy and physics. He could not appreciate the creativity of abstract thinkers who worked by intuitive leaps of the mind. He particularly condemned Galileo for expressing the problem of motion in mathematical formulas. Bacon wanted Galileo to investigate and explain the internal tensions within particular moving bodies. Like the despised scholastics, he adhered to a concept of nature which was loaded with pseudoscientific embellishments. Descartes went to the opposite extreme. He condemned Galileo for being too experimental and insufficiently abstract! Descartes confidently asserted that his comprehensive new philosophy explained why and how the universe operated much better than Galileo's experiments could.

Descartes reduced nature to two absolutely distinct elements: mind and matter, or *res cogitans* ("thinking substance") and *res extensa* ("extended substance"). He did not presume to investigate the realm of thinking substance, which included soul and spirit, the province of theologians and the Church. But his concept of extended substance enabled him to explain every aspect of physical nature in terms of an all-inclusive, self-operating mechanism. According to Descartes, the universe was continuously and completely filled with an infinite number of particles of matter. Each particle was mathematically definable, having length, breadth, and depth. There was no room for occult forces like gravity and magnetism. Descartes explained motion on mechanistic principles as incessant whirlpool contact among invisible particles. "Give me extension and motion," he bragged, "and I will construct the universe." Cartesianism was immensely popular among seventeenth-century intellectuals who had lost faith in the old Aristotelian-Ptolemaic view of nature. It incorporated every branch of science. Descartes made a useful contribution to physiology by insisting that the human body was a machine, subject to the same laws as the cosmic machine. The trouble was that he explained too much too rigidly. He was more ingenious than Aristotle, but just as dogmatic, and no truer to nature. Before the close of the century Cartesianism had been superseded by Newton's improved version of the World Machine.

Bacon and Descartes helped to create a new climate of opinion, in which the scientist became an esteemed public figure. After 1650 scientists found it easier to get money for equipment and experiments. Their findings were more widely circulated and more quickly appreciated. Most important, scientists from various countries exchanged ideas with one another as never before. Since the universities, traditional centers of intellectual life, disdained the new learning, scientists did not feel at home within the cloistered precincts of Oxford, Paris, and Padua. Bacon urged them to form their own scientific societies, in which new ideas and experiments could be freely tested. When he envisioned an ideal commonwealth in the *New Atlantis* (1627), he lovingly described the operations of Salomon's House, where a team of scientists were busily unlocking nature's secrets. And indeed, in this century scientists did begin to form societies of their own. Galileo belonged to one of the earliest, the Accademia dei Lincei ("Academy of the Lynx-Eyed"), in Rome. By the 1650's, similar informal groups were meeting regularly in Florence, Paris, and London. During the following decade, much more powerful and permanent scientific institutions were founded in England and France under government patronage. Charles II chartered the Royal Society in 1662. Colbert sponsored the Académie des Sciences in 1666. Most of the great figures in late seventeenth-century science were affiliated with these bodies. The members listened to papers, shared instruments, collected specimens, conducted experiments, and reported their findings in volumes of *Transactions* or *Mémoires*—prototypes of the modern scientific journal. The membership was an odd medley of professional scientists and gentleman *virtuosi* or dilettantes. Charles II himself enjoyed working in his chemical laboratory.

The popularity of the new science among dilettantes was easy to laugh at. In *The Virtuoso*, by Thomas Shadwell, a popular English farce of 1676, a gentleman scientist named Sir Nicholas Gimcrack was portrayed as a speculative ass. Sir Nicholas transfused sheep's blood into a man (this experiment was actually performed by the Royal Society) in order to cultivate human wool. He watched armies in battle on the moon through his telescope. He read a Geneva bible by the phosphorescent glow of a putrid leg of pork. When a skeptic asked him why he lay on a table, flailing his limbs in imitation of a frog in a bowl of water, the following exchange ensued:

GIMCRACK: I swim most exquisitely on land.
SKEPTIC: Do you intend to practice in the water, Sir?
GIMCRACK: Never, Sir. I hate the water,I never come upon the water, Sir.
SKEPTIC: Then there will be no use of swimming.
GIMCRACK: I content myself with the speculative side of swimming. I care not for the practick. I seldom bring anything to use, 'tis not my way. Knowledge is my ultimate end.

Actually, the *virtuosi* tended to make the emphasis in the new scientific societies excessively utilitarian rather than speculative. Charles II and Colbert hoped for Baconian technological improvements. Much effort was spent on designs for industrial machinery, ship models, experiments with new recipes for brewing beer, and so forth. Very little was accomplished along these lines. In the second half of the seventeenth century the most fruitful scientific research continued to be highly abstract.

Sir Isaac Newton

The supreme genius of the Englishman Isaac Newton (1642–1727) brought the scientific revolution to a majestic climax. Newton was not an exceptionally interesting or attractive personality. He was very much the absentminded professor: he forgot to eat when he was working, and had to be prodded into publishing any of his findings. He suffered from paranoia, and unjustly accused his colleagues of stealing his ideas. He expended much time and energy on alchemical studies, not to mention his laborious and inaccurate calculations of the dates of biblical events. But when Newton turned to physics and astronomy, only Galileo among seventeenth-century scientists could rival his extraordinary imagination and discipline. Only Galileo shared his mastery of the whole scientific terrain from instrument making, to experimentation, to theory. And Newton was a much better mathematician than Galileo, and a more powerful abstract thinker. Like many scientists, he did his best work as a very young man. In 1665, when he was a student at Cambridge, an epidemic of bubonic plague closed the university. Newton was forced to spend nearly two years on his mother's isolated Lincolnshire farm. In this unlikely setting, he began experiments in optics which made the study of light for the first time a branch of physics. In mathematics, he invented the differential and integral calculus. In mechanics, he began to formulate his laws of universal gravitation and motion. "In those days," he later reflected, "I was in the prime of my age for invention, and minded mathematics and philosophy [science] more than at any time since."

Newton's supreme achievement was to weld Kepler's laws of planetary motion, Galileo's laws of falling bodies, the concept of inertia developed by Galileo and Descartes, and his own concept of gravitation into a single mathematical-physical system. Newton asked what inward pull kept the planets in elliptical orbits about the sun, and the moon in orbit about the earth, when according to Galileo's concept of inertia each of them should fly off in an infinite straight line. As he sat in his orchard, the thud of a falling apple startled him into thinking that the moon must be pulled toward the earth's center by the very same force which drew the apple to the ground. He deduced that gravity must be a universal force, equally affecting all celestial and terrestrial matter, and that the action and reaction between any two masses is equal and opposite. That is, the moon draws the earth with the same force with which the earth draws the moon; the pull exerted by the moon causes the oceans' tides. In the case of the falling apple, its mass is so tiny in comparison with the earth's mass that the pull of the apple has no measurable force. Twenty years passed before Newton felt satisfied with his mathematical proofs. At last, in 1687, he set forth his theory of universal gravitation and motion (and much else) in an epochal book, *The Mathematical Principles of Natural Philosophy*, always known by its abbreviated Latin title, the *Principia*. It sold for five shillings a copy.

The *Principia* is a deliberately difficult book, addressed to those few scholars who could understand Newton's mathematics and appreciate the elegance of his theory. No brief synopsis can capture its intellectual thrust. First of all, Newton brought together the mathematical, astronomical, and mechanical findings of the preceding century, effecting a synthesis which was badly needed. In particular, he correlated Kepler's celestial mechanics with Galileo's terrestrial mechanics and distilled from this material three basic laws of universal motion, which he expressed mathematically. Next, he formulated his law of universal gravitation: every particle of matter attracts every other particle with a force proportional to the product of the two masses, and inversely proportional to the square of the distance between them. The whole *Principia* is an extended demonstration of this key discovery. Newton did not pretend to understand the mysterious force of gravity. He clashed head on with Descartes, who had denied the existence of gravity and explained mechanically how and why particles move. Newton's view of nature, like Descartes', was mechanistic and mathematical, of course, but he intensely disliked Descartes' method of inventing an intellectualized picture of the world which bore no relation to empirical observation. Like Galileo, Newton believed that the scientist should describe how the universe operates, not why. He took special delight in puncturing the Cartesian balloon. Meticulously supporting his abstract reasoning with experimental evidence, Newton concluded his book with a marvelously precise description of the structure of the celestial system. This section particularly impressed and satisfied his readers. For instance, Newton detected and calculated a conical twist in the earth's axis of rotation, so slight that the cycle takes twenty-six thousand years to complete. His general description of the universe needed no correction for more than a century, and physicists continued to work within the framework of Newtonian, or classical, mechanics until the age of Einstein. The *Principia* was immediately recognized as a masterpiece, even by Cartesians who could not accept Newton's theory of gravitation. Far from being persecuted as Galileo had been, Newton was lionized. He was knighted, made master of the English royal mint, and elected president of the Royal Society. When he died, he was given a state funeral and buried in Westminster Abbey.

Biology and Chemistry

Very little has been said so far about biology and chemistry, for there was no revolution in these sciences between 1559 and 1689. Biology remained a neglected auxiliary to medical practice, chemistry an auxiliary to medicine and metallurgy. Neither science had as yet developed rational methods, standards, or objectives. However, in some areas of biology—notably in anatomy, physiology, and botany—there were important developments. For the first time the 1,500-year-old medical teachings of Galen were corrected and amplified, mainly by professors and students at the University of Padua, Europe's leading medical center. In 1543, the year in which Copernicus announced his heliocentric theory, Andreas Vesalius (1514–1564), a Flemish professor at Padua, published a pioneering treatise on human anatomy. Vesalius had dissected many more human cadavers than Galen, and he was able to correct many—though by no means all—of Galen's mistakes. His book was a work of art as well as science, for the text was illustrated with superb drawings of muscles and bones.

A much more fundamental advance over Galen came in 1628, when William Harvey (1578–1657), an Englishman who had studied at Padua, demonstrated the circulation of the blood. It had previously been supposed that since venous blood is tinged with blue and arterial blood is bright red, the blood in each system must ebb and flow separately. Galen had taught that venous blood distributed nutrition from the liver, and arterial blood distributed an intangible vital spirit which kept man alive. Harvey rejected these views; he proved that blood is pumped into the arteries by the heart at a massive rate, travels to the veins, and returns to the heart. Harvey was a heart worshiper as Copernicus had been a sun worshiper, and he was much influenced by the Aristotelian belief that circular motion is perfect. His great discovery undermined the traditional humoral theory of medicine, but Harvey's fellow doctors did not recognize this. Even physicians who comprehended the physiology of the circulatory system continued to suppose that the sovereign remedy for almost any internal disorder was to bleed the patient copiously.

In botany, naturalists collected a great mass of new data about the plant kingdom. In the 1540's only five hundred distinct botanical species had been classified, as against eighteen thousand by the 1680's. But there was no disposition to challenge traditional views about the fixity of species and the great chain of being. During this period the Dutchman Anton von Leeuwenhoek (1632–1723) made a microscope which magnified objects three hundred times. Through this instrument he uncovered a whole new world of one-celled organisms, invisible to the naked eye. But he never understood that the microbes he delighted to watch swimming about in human spittle might be disease carriers. That fact would remain hidden until the nineteenth century.

In chemistry, it is hard to see much purposeful development during this period. There were chemists in plenty: mining engineers who assayed ores, pharmacists who compounded drugs, alchemists who tried to transmute metals, and philosophers who speculated about the atomic structure of matter. Physicians liked to purge their patients with chemical drugs like mercury and antimony especially when trying to cure such frightening new diseases as syphilis. These chemical potions may have been no more harmful than the traditional herbal recipes, but their effects were certainly more violent. The modern chemist's concept of elements and compounds had not yet been developed. Robert Boyle (1627–1691) was the leading chemical experimentalist and theorist of his day. He discarded the Aristotelian belief in four basic elements—earth, water, air and fire—but he had no better theory to offer concerning the structure of matter. The chemical revolution would not start until the late eighteenth century, when Lavoisier isolated oxygen and drew up the first table of chemical elements.

Nevertheless, the cumulative change in scientific thought and practice between 1559 and 1689 was immense. One measure of the revolution in science is the way in which Descartes and Newton persuaded the intellectual community to view the cosmos mechanistically. Newton's concept of nature as a kind of giant clockwork, the World Machine, was in its own way as satisfying intellectually and emotionally as the Aristotelian-Ptolemaic view had been. Instead of admiring perfect circles and the ascending order of purity, man could marvel at the perfect regularity of nature, at the way in which all inanimate objects, however great or small, were governed by the same timeless laws. There was certainly more romance in the old view of the world, more rationality in the new view. How can one weigh the loss in passion, imagination, and complexity against the gain in precision, elegance, and common sense? In educated circles there was no longer much room in 1689 for belief in magic and myth. During the religious wars, especially the Thirty Years' War, fear of witchcraft had risen very high. But such superstition receded for good in the closing decades of the century. The Salem witchcraft hysteria of 1692, during which twenty witches were executed in Massachusetts, was the last major outburst of this particular form of public dementia.

The new philosophy forced men to reframe their religious beliefs. Both Protestant scientists like Kepler and Newton, and Catholic scientists like Galileo and Descartes, eagerly sought to harmonize their findings with Christian teleology. Nonetheless, it was hard to see any explicitly Christian purpose in the abstract mathematical design of the Newtonian World Machine. The Great Clockmaker, however perfect His handiwork, was more remote than the Creator worshiped by Calvin or Loyola. Human incentive and achievement seemed correspondingly more significant. To be sure, man no longer lived at the center of the cosmos. He occupied a second-rate planet spinning through endless empty space. But he was learning to master his physical environment. If God set the clock in motion, man could tell the time. Here was the most pervasive long-range consequence of the seventeenth-century scientific revolution, a buoyant faith in rational human progress.

RELIGIOUS ART IN THE BAROQUE AGE

In art, as in science, the years from 1559 to 1689 saw a revolt against traditional standards and values. In the late sixteenth century the Renaissance style in painting, sculpture, and architecture was vigorously challenged. In the seventeenth century it gave way to a new style, the Baroque. At first glance this artistic revolt is puzzling, since the Renaissance style reached a majestic peak during the opening three decades of the sixteenth century, the period art historians call the High Renaissance. In these years five great masters—Leonardo da Vinci, Michelangelo, Raphael, Titian, and Dürer—were expressing the Renaissance ideal of human beauty with matchless skill. No later artist could hope to surpass their harmonious, lifelike and exalted depiction of man. How could one improve upon Leonardo's psychological insight, or Michelangelo's glorification of the male body, or Raphael's idealization of women, or Titian's vibrant color, or Dürer's mastery of design? So perfect was this High Renaissance art that by the 1520's it was reaching a dead end. Michelangelo himself, having mastered all the problems inherent in the old style, began to formulate a new style known as Mannerism, which deliberately violated Renaissance conventions.

In the 1520's the Renaissance tradition was also attacked from a very different direction, by the Protestant movement. Luther denounced the religious art of the High Renaissance. He called it more pagan than Christian, and questioned the whole Catholic tradition of religious art. Protestants found it blasphemous to worship God in lavishly decorated churches, filled with statues and paintings honoring the saints, and carnal representations of the Madonna, Christ, and God the Father. Catholics, of course, rejected this protest, asserting the efficacy of religious imagery more ardently than ever. But by the mid-sixteenth century, Catholics too were finding the Renaissance style uncomfortably pat and worldly. They needed a new artistic way of expressing old truths. The moral and aesthetic issues raised in the early sixteenth century, and the crusading ardor of Protestants versus Catholics during the religious wars, gives special interest to the religious painting, sculpture, and architecture produced by Catholic and Protestant artists between 1559 and 1689.

Painting in the Sixteenth Century
Throughout the sixteenth century the Protestant Reformation had a blighting effect upon northern European art. In Germany and the Low Countries, as in Italy, painters had always supported themselves principally by filling commissions for religious works, such as altar panels and church frescoes. But the preaching of Luther, Zwingli, and Calvin incited iconoclastic riots against such symbols of popish idolatry. Protestant mobs smashed church statuary, burned altar pieces, and whitewashed frescoes. Lutheran and Calvinist churches were kept characteristically austere and undecorated. In the sixteenth century even Catholic churches in northern Europe offered fewer ecclesiastical commissions to painters, sculptors, and architects than they had in the good old days. Albrecht Dürer (1471–1528), the greatest German artist of Luther's generation, was not much affected by this crisis. Dürer earned his living by painting portraits and illustrating books. He did simplify his style in the religious engravings of his closing years and chose biblical themes compatible with the reform spirit, for Dürer greatly admired Luther although he did not actively join his movement. Dürer's colleague Hans Holbein the Younger (c. 1497–1543) had to abandon the painting of Madonnas, at which he excelled as a young man. Holbein moved from Germany to Switzerland and from Switzerland to England in search of work. He spent the last half of his career painting portraits of Henry VIII and his courtiers. Holbein left no successor in Germany or in England, and there were few outstanding masters in sixteenth-century France or the Low Countries.
The paintings of Pieter Brueghel the Elder (c. 1525–1569) illustrate very well the changing temper of art in northern Europe. Brueghel was a Flemish Catholic who painted his greatest pictures in the 1560's, just as the Low Countries were starting to rebel against Philip II. He painted for private

Massacre of the Innocents. *Painting by Brueghel. Kunsthistorisches Museum, Vienna.*

patrons in Antwerp and Brussels rather than for the Church, specializing in noncontroversial genre paintings of everyday life, scenes of peasants at work and play, artlessly rustic in appearance, yet richly detailed and ingeniously composed. Brueghel's religious paintings are in the same style as his genre paintings. For example, his "Massacre of the Innocents" is highly unconventional. The subject, of course, is a sensational one, generally represented by a theatrical tableau of twisted bodies, with knife-wielding soldiers, wailing mothers, and naked babies expiring in pools of blood. Brueghel's picture is very different. At first glance we see a wintry Flemish street scene, then notice the invading cavalry sealing off the village with their pikes, the frantic peasants milling about helplessly in the snow, the soldiers prying open the shuttered doors. Few babies can be seen, and only one pool of blood. But Brueghel's understatement gives his picture great realism and poignancy, for the viewer knows what is going to happen and feels as helpless as the rustic crowd in the street. By catching the timeless horror or soldiers preying on civilians, Brueghel found a fresh way of illustrating a very old Christian story.

In sixteenth-century Italy the artistic crisis was more complicated. Viewing the sumptuous paintings of Titian (*c.* 1477–1576), one might conclude that there was no crisis at all. For seventy years this Venetian master filled his spacious canvases with glowing Venuses and Virgins in stately perpetuation of the High Renaissance style. But other artists betrayed moral and aesthetic tension. The sack of Rome in 1527 by Charles V's soldiers ended the High Renaissance for the papacy if not for Venice. Temporarily, the popes suspended their patronage of artists and architects. Under the reforming popes of the mid-sixteenth century, the Roman climate became austere and antihumanist. Pope Pius IV (ruled 1559–1565) was so offended by the naked figures in Michelangelo's great fresco of the Last Judgment in the Sistine Chapel that he had loincloths painted on to cover them decently. But the Church soon recovered its old confidence. In 1563 the Council of Trent decreed that religious imagery was beneficial for instructing the faithful and stimulating piety. St. Ignatius of Loyola reasserted the Church's belief that worship demanded the Christian's full physical and psychological resources. His *Spiritual Exercises* taught the reader how to use all of his senses to achieve a vividly personal spiritual experience. Gradually, the popes resumed their building program. St. Peter's was completed at immense expense in the late sixteenth and early seventeenth centuries, and the whole city of Rome was refurbished on a very grand scale. Once the Catholic reformation was in full swing, architects and artists enjoyed unparalleled ecclesiastical patronage.

Sixteenth-century Italian artists searched for a new style appropriate to the Catholic spiritual revival. Michelangelo Buonarroti (1475–1564) altered his whole approach in the 1530's, and initiated a far-reaching rebellion against Renaissance standards and values. His two celebrated frescoes in the Sistine Chapel illustrate Michelangelo's changing concept of religious art. The ceiling fresco of scenes from Genesis, painted about 1510, retains the proportion, harmony, and restraint of classical Greek sculpture, despite the immensity of its scheme. But the wall fresco of the Last Judgment, painted in the 1530's, after the sack of Rome, erupts in violence and distortion, deliberately transgressing all classical canons. It is true, of course, that no great artist would treat a joyous subject like the creation of Adam in the same spirit as a terrible theme like the end of the world. But Michelangelo changed his style drastically over the years even when handling the same subject. In his first effort to carve a statue of the dead Christ, the "Pietà" (1499) at St. Peter's, Michelangelo managed, by means of artistic sleight of hand, to achieve an exquisitely naturalistic rendering of an implausible tableau. He wanted to convey a double vision of the Mother of God sorrowing over the crucified Christ and of the young Mary cuddling her infant Jesus. So he gave Mary the face of the young Virgin and reduced the scale of Christ's body, in order to cradle Him gracefully in Mary's arms and lap. Thanks to the sculptor's mastery of Renaissance style—the anatomical perfection and harmonious modeling of the figures—we accept this artificial composition as completely realistic. As an old man, Michelangelo returned to the same subject in his anticlassical style. His "Descent from the Cross"

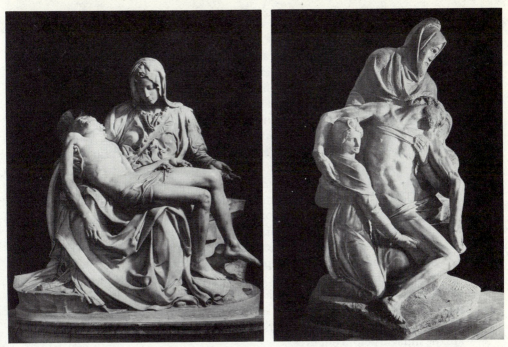

Left: Pieta. *Carved in 1499 by Michelangelo.* St. Peter's, Rome. *Right*: Descent from the Cross. *Carved in 1555 by Michelangelo.* Cathedral, Florence.

(1555), in the cathedral at Florence, is unfinished, but there is no mistaking the jagged, searing design of Christ's broken body, too heavy for three mourners to lift. Michelangelo elongated and exaggerated Christ's limbs, and flouted traditional scale and proportion, in order to evoke the tortured weight of His sacrifice.

Michelangelo's late paintings and sculpture inspired a school of imitators, known as Mannerists because they worked "in the manner of" Michelangelo. It was a dangerous manner to imitate unless one had Michelangelo's genius. Mannerist artists generally manipulated classical components to achieve anticlassical effects. In late sixteenth-century Italian churches and palaces, the columns, arches, entablatures, and pediments of Greco-Roman building design are juxtaposed unconventionally in the effort to escape the old Renaissance clichés. Mannerist painters decorated walls and ceilings with complex allegorical scenes of muscle-bound athletes in contorted attitudes. Today most of this hectic art and architecture seems jejune at best, vulgar at worst, and singularly ill suited to the Catholic revival. However, two Mannerist painters produced religious art of great power and originality. One was Tintoretto (1518–1594), of Venice, and the other was El Greco (*c.* 1548–1614), of Toledo in Spain.

It is said that Tintoretto posted this motto over his studio door: "The drawing of Michelangelo and the color of Titian." Whatever Tintoretto's coloring was originally like, his canvases are now generally much less rich than Titian's. But the electric energy and daring of his composition is still exciting. He had little interest in Titian's pagan themes, and preferred religious subjects of the sort which Protestants abominated—saints, miracles, and Madonnas. Tintoretto's output was prodigious. In emulation of Michelangelo's "Last Judgment," he painted a number of monumental panoramas, the most grandiose being his seventy-foot mural of Paradise in the Ducal Palace at Venice. In this painting, nearly five hundred figures swirl around the Virgin and Christ. For centuries Venetians bragged that they had the largest oil painting in the world until Forest Lawn Cemetery in California installed an even bigger one. Some of Tintoretto's smaller pictures are equally dramatic. His "Massacre of the Innocents" is a tumultuous avalanche of movement, the exact opposite of Brueghel's picture. He could be vulgar, as when he painted the Last Supper with the table askew and the apostles lounging and jostling like drunken louts. He could also achieve an otherworldly incandescence. In the National Gallery at Washington there is a beautiful Tintoretto painting of Christ walking on the waters with majestic yet incorporeal tread. The painter's eerie lighting and subtle rhythms recreate the miracle before our eyes.

El Greco was an even more individual artist than Tintoretto, and it is perhaps misleading to label him as a member of the Mannerist school. His real name was Domenicos Theotocopoulos; he was called "the Greek" because he came from the Greek island of Crete. He spent a long apprenticeship in Venice and Rome before moving to Spain in the 1570's. El Greco hoped to be a court painter, but Philip II did not appreciate the work of this bizarre foreigner, so utterly different from the insipid and derivative painting of sixteenth-century Spaniards. So El Greco settled down in Toledo to a busy and unspectacular career as a church painter. We think of him as the most "modern" stylist of his day; hence it is worth emphasizing that El Greco's mystical, ardent temper was entirely attuned to the sixteenth-century world, and very congenial to the Spain of Don Quixote. El Greco learned much from Tintoretto, Titian, and Michelangelo, but he was always an independent artist. Having Byzantine origins, he viewed the whole classical Renaissance tradition from the outside. He never had to strain in order to avoid the naturalistic clichés of the Renaissance style; there was no artificiality in his elongated, emaciated, sexless, two-dimensional figures, who seem to hover between heaven and earth.

El Greco called his painting of the burial of the Count of Orgaz "my sublime work," and this masterpiece does indeed epitomize his religious style. The painting commemorates a local miracle: when the pious Count of Orgaz died in Toledo, St. Stephen and St. Augustine descended from heaven to lay him gently in his tomb. A little boy, El Greco's son, shows us the miracle, and the gazing priest at the right carries our attention to the dead

The Burial of the Count of Orgaz. *Painting by El Greco. Church of San Tomé, Toledo.*

grandee's soul, being carried by an angel up to Christ. By subtle tricks of color, bodily gesture and facial delineation, the painter carefully stages three hierarchical levels of reality: the dead man in his sepulcher, the living mourners, and the heavenly spirits. It is remarkable that such a crowded composition should convey an exalted upward sweep. El Greco's silent gravity precludes false sentimentality or melodrama. His painting radiates a spirit of loving communion between Christ, the saints, and man—the quintessence of Catholic art.

Beautiful as El Greco's painting seems to us, it was too ethereal for contemporary Catholic taste. At the turn of the century, in Rome, the painter Michelangelo da Caravaggio (c. 1565–1609) cultivated a realistic and earthy approach at the opposite pole from that of El Greco. Caravaggio protested very effectively against the desiccated artificiality of the Mannerist school. He shocked people by painting Doubting Thomas as a bald and wrinkled peasant, jabbing his finger into Christ's open wound. He set the scene of the Virgin's death in a dingy cottage, with Mary's stiffened corpse attended by coarse-looking common folk. Caravaggio was a highly talented painter, and his pictures were honest and robust, but if El Greco was too rarefied for seventeenth-century sensibilities, then Caravaggio was too plebian. Art patrons, especially princes and churchmen who paid the largest commissions, craved grandeur as well as robustness. What they wanted was the Baroque, a splendiferous new style developed by seventeenth-century painters like Rubens, Van Dyck, and Velázquez, and architects like Bernini.

The Baroque

The Baroque is a notoriously difficult concept to define. Seventeenth-century Baroque art and architecture is generally characterized by magnificence, theatricality, energy, and direct emotional appeal, though as we shall see, these characteristics are more apparent in some Baroque works than in others. There is no clear dividing line between the Mannerism of the sixteenth century and the Baroque of the seventeenth; both styles are anticlassical, though Baroque artists tend to be more cheerfully extroverted and less tense than Tintoretto and El Greco. Admirers of the Baroque like to apply the label to every positive feature of European society between 1550 and 1750. They speak not only of Baroque art, music, and literature, but of Baroque thought and Baroque politics.[1] But this deprives the concept of all useful meaning. It is difficult enough to correlate with any precision the Baroque traits in seventeenth-century art and music. In music, the most obvious Baroque manifestation was the development of opera. Such seventeenth-century composers as Monteverdi in Italy, Lully in France, and Purcell in England popularized this new form of secular entertainment, which combined music, acting, dancing, and pageantry. The opera became an instant success in court circles all over Europe. In seventeenth-century church music, too, there was a new brilliance and dramatic intensity, apparent, for example, in the contrapuntal choral and organ writing of Schütz and Buxtehude. But in music the Baroque style reached its peak considerably later than in art. The best-known Baroque composers—Corelli, Vivaldi, Scarlatti, Handel, and Bach—all flourished in the early eighteenth century.

Our concern is with Baroque art and architecture. This new seventeenth-century style was more class-conscious than Renaissance art had been, for Baroque artists knew how to flatter rich patrons by celebrating the pomp and luxury of upper-class life. The new style appealed far more to kings and aristocrats than to the middle classes or the peasantry. In bourgeois Holland, painters like Rembrandt, Hals, and Vermeer had little affinity for the grand manner. It was in Habsburg territory, in Italy, Spain, Belgium, Austria, and Bohemia, that the Baroque style developed most vigorously. Habsburg territory was Catholic territory, and Catholics liked the Baroque far more

---

[1]Carl J. Friedrich is a Baroque enthusiast. His *Age of the Baroque, 1610–1660* (New York, 1952) presents an all-embracing interpretation of the movement.

The Triumph of the Name of Jesus. *Ceiling fresco by Gaulli in the Church of the Gesù, Rome. Note the Baroque device of combining fresco painting with gilded stucco and statuary so as to achieve an overpowering ensemble.*

than Protestants. What better proof of renewed Catholic vigor than the splendidly assertive Baroque churches of the seventeenth century, stunningly ornamented with bravura paintings and statuary? The principal Jesuit church in Rome, the Gesù, combines a sixteenth-century Mannerist exterior with a seventeenth-century Baroque interior. The Baroque decorations of this church have a lavish intensity hard to describe. The painting on the vaulted ceiling depicts ecstatic worshipers straining upward toward the mystical name of Jesus. The dazzling tomb of St. Ignatius, studded with lapis lazuli and bronze, expresses exultation rather than grief. The statue groups to either side show religion trampling on heresy and barbarians adoring the faith. No longer harking back to pagan classicism, Baroque Rome expressed the power and exuberance of reformed Catholicism. Unhappily, this vibrant style slowly degenerated into the sugar-and-gingerbread kitsch manner which has vitiated most religious art, Protestant as well as Catholic, since the eighteenth century.

Peter Paul Rubens (1577–1640) was the first full-scale Baroque artist. A Fleming trained in Italy, he established a fantastically successful studio in Antwerp. His breezy, florid pictures, crowded with heavily fleshed figures bathed in lush colors, were exhilarating to people accustomed to Pieter Brueghel's meticulous peasant scenes. Rubens was an artistic entrepreneur. He operated a picture factory, with an assembly line of assistants trained to execute his compositions, each assistant a specialist in figures, faces, animals, or backgrounds. Rubens himself would apply the finishing touches to each canvas, but often no more than that. For example, he sent one prospective customer a list of twenty-four paintings for sale, only five of which were entirely his own work. The choice included *"Prometheus Enchained on Mount Caucases*, with an eagle which devours his liver; an original work of my own hand, the eagle done by Snyders, 500 florins. *Christ on the Cross*, life-size, considered perhaps the best thing I have ever done, 500 florins. A *Last Judgment*, begun by one of my pupils after an original which I made of much larger size for the Prince of Neuberg, who paid me for it 3,500 florins in ready money. As the present piece is not quite finished, I will retouch it altogether by myself, so that it can pass for an original, 1,200 florins." [2] Rubens' mass-production technique was especially geared to heroic mural painting, where the general impact of his exuberant design is greater than the sum of the details. His decorating talents were highly prized by the crowned heads of Europe. Marie de Medici and Louis XIII of France, Charles I of England, and Philip IV of Spain all commissioned Rubens murals or tapestry designs for their royal palaces. While traveling from court to court, this man of the world also served the Habsburgs as a diplomatic agent. Rubens was a fervid Catholic, and almost half of his pictures treat religious themes. He often preaches the Catholic reformation, as when he shows St. Ignatius exorcising evil spirits from the sick. His religious paintings are generally festive and always vividly alive. A favorite subject is the adoration of the Magi. Rubens invariably crowds a horde of people around the manger, making the stable look like rush hour at Grand Central Station. Yet all this bustle is so spontaneous, joyful, and loving that the viewer feels himself participating in the discovery and worship of the newborn Christ Child.

The two other chief Baroque painters, Van Dyck and Velázquez, were

---

[2]*Rubens: Paintings and Drawings*, ed. by R. A. M. Stevenson (New York, 1939), p. 26.

The adoration of the Magi. *Painting by Rubens. Baroque devices here include the contorted attitudes of the spectators, to indicate their joyful amazement, and the exotic camels, which almost steal the scene from the Christ child. Royal Museum, Antwerp.*

primarily court portraitists, and did much less religious work than Rubens. They exemplify the increasingly secular character of seventeenth-century art even in Catholic countries. Anthony Van Dyck (1599–1641) was a Fleming who painted in Rubens' studio for some years before establishing his own portrait business. Few society painters have excelled Van Dyck's elegant and flattering style. He endowed his aristocratic sitters with a languid pride and poise to match their fine clothes. Like Rubens, he was a mass-production artist. During the decade he spent in England, Van Dyck, with his assistants, turned out some 350 portraits, including thirty-eight of Charles I. Van Dyck's Spanish contemporary Diego Rodríguez Velázquez (1599–1660) was an even finer portraitist, indeed, one of the giants of western painting. For thirty-seven years Velázquez was court painter to Philip IV, and his genius immortalized the mediocre men and women who ruled mid-seventeenth-century Spain. His portaits of Philip IV are much more candid than Van Dyck's glamorous portraits of Charles I, yet just as appealing. He manages to convey the king's official majesty and his personal frailty all at once.

Velázquez painted every sitter, whether king, court jester, or dwarf, with

Innocent X. *Painting by Velázquez. Galleria Doria, Rome.*

the same objective sincerity. His great portrait of Pope Innocent X illustrates his remarkable integrity and immediacy. The picture seems a caricature at first: how could such a brutal man masquerade as a pope? But the longer we study this canvas, the more we admire Innocent's scrutinizing gaze and his caged energy. Velázquez was a superb technician. In this painting, every brushstroke distributes light and shadow, gives texture to the papal robes, defines the muscles of Innocent's body, imparts life to his sweat-beaded features. Although Velázquez had an eye for color and costume, he painted in a simple, grave, and static style. Even his most theatrical work, the "Surrender of Breda," celebrating a Spanish victory over the Dutch, is as stately and restrained as a High Renaissance composition, with none of El Greco's supercharged tension nor Rubens' heroic tumult. He did, however, exhibit two important Baroque traits: artistic concentration upon the royal court, and emotional repudiation of Renaissance idealism. He was an uncompromising realist and painted life exactly as it is, not as it should be. This dissociation from the classical ideal of beauty hampered Velázquez's effectiveness as a religious painter. He found no adequate flesh-and-blood models for Mary and Jesus, and he lacked Raphael's or Holbein's Renaissance vision of perfect human form. Here he suffered from the same handicap as Van Dyck. Both artists painted gently melancholy Madonnas and Crucifixions which are reverent and handsome, yet distressingly vacuous in comparison with their court portraits inspired by real people.

In Baroque sculpture and architecture, the central figure was Gianlorenzo Bernini (1598–1680), a Neapolitan who spent most of his career in Rome, building and decorating for five popes. No other seventeenth-century artist, not even Rubens, epitomized the Baroque spirit so completely. Bernini had a genius for theatrical effects. He manipulated classical building forms with much more freedom than his Mannerist predecessors had displayed. His facades, colonnades, and stairways look like stage settings. His statues and fountains posture and prance. For example, he carved a statue of David in frenzied action, just as he is slinging his shot at Goliath. Compared with Michelangelo's noble David, standing reflectively in naked majesty, Bernini's beetle-browed actor looks a bit comic. Bernini was primarily a church architect and decorator. By the time he became papal architect, the monumental basilica of St. Peter's was nearly finished. He enclosed the immense piazza in front of the church with two semicircular colonnades, a stroke of genius, since the marching columns draw worshipers toward St. Peter's while distracting their attention from the basilica's top-heavy facade. Within the church, under Michelangelo's mighty dome, he erected a flamboyant baldacchino, or altar canopy, which stands the height of an eight-story building on four bronze corkscrew columns. Bernini appealed blatantly to the senses, for he believed that the church was a stage for the physical display of divine mysteries. In one Roman chapel he dared to stage St. Teresa's vision of being pierced through the heart by a flaming arrow of heavenly love. Leaning upon clouds suspended in mid air above the altar, Teresa swoons, her face ecstatic with blissful pain, a smiling seraph poised above her with the arrow, while bronze shafts of light cascade upon the scene. Rarely has a miracle been made so tangible. Other seventeenth-century Roman architects, sculptors, and painters followed in Bernini's footsteps. The papal city became a festival of domed churches, of curved and columned facades, of action-packed fountains, monuments, and tombs, of ceiling frescoes erupting skyward as if to dissolve earth into heaven.

Itinerant Italian architects carried the Baroque building style into central Europe and Spain during the second half of the seventeenth century. In Germany, Austria, and Bohemia, incessant warfare crippled major building projects through most of the century. The Baroque age could not begin in Bohemia until after 1648, or in Austria until the Turks were driven out of the Danube Valley in the 1680's. In Spain the new Italian fashion was initially resisted by local builders accustomed to the austere Escorial style of Philip II. Baroque architecture in central Europe and Spain was still in its heyday in the 1730's. Both Austrian and Spanish Baroque architecture had its own distinct character, compounded of local custom and Italianate borrowings. In Austria, Baroque churches sported onion steeples as well as

The Ecstasy of St. Theresa. *Sculpture by Bernini. Cornaro Chapel, Santa Maria della Vittoria, Rome.*

Roman domes. In Spain, Baroque churches displayed explosively ornamented facades and altar screens owing little to Bernini. In both central Europe and Spain the new building style was less sophisticated and more fanciful than Italian Baroque. Because the Germans, Slavs, and Spaniards had never really assimilated the classical building style of the Italian Renaissance, they could manipulate and multiply ornamental effects more spontaneously and innocently than Bernini, who was a self-conscious rebel against his architectural heritage.

The first notable Austrian Baroque builder, Fischer von Erlach (1656–1723), was trained in Italy and heavily influenced by Bernini. His chief clients were princes and noblemen who wanted imposing new palaces. To provide the necessary pomp and grandiloquence, Fischer developed what became a trademark of central European Baroque: the grand staircase supported not by conventional pillars, but on the shoulders of muscular, straining Atlas figures. Fischer also designed churches. Many Baroque churches and monasteries were built in newly converted Protestant areas like Bohemia. For example, in Prague, a city very rich in Baroque architecture, the Jesuit Church of St. Niklas has a nave whose rhythmically curving walls and vault achieve an extraordinary undulating effect. Spanish Baroque architecture was primarily ecclesiastical. It is called "churrigueresque," after José Churriguera (1650–1723), the leading Spanish Baroque architect. The convoluted sculpture of his church facades and the gilded richness of his altar screens is overpowering. The style even spread to Spanish America; the far-off Mexican city of Puebla could boast thirty-six domed churches in the 1680's, including the staggeringly churrigueresque Church of Santo Domingo.

French, English, and Dutch Art

The Baroque spirit did not triumph everywhere. In France, Bourbon absolutism required an artistic style emphasizing grandeur, monumentality, and power, yet the French never accepted the Baroque. They found Rubens' paintings and Bernini's buildings distastefully showy, passionate, and undignified, and clung to the classical values and standards against which Baroque artists were rebelling. Seventeenth-century French painters, sculptors, and architects prized clarity, simplicity, and harmony of design. French classicism is a rather frigid version of the High Renaissance style. The two chief seventeenth-century French painters, Nicolas Poussin (1594–1665) and Claude Lorrain (1600–1682), spent their careers in Rome, trying to recapture the aesthetic and moral values of the antique Romans. Poussin specialized in scenes from classical mythology which celebrated the dignity of the ancient republic or the grandeur of the empire. Compared with the paintings of Tintoretto, Caravaggio, or Rubens, his canvases appear calm, chaste, and congealed. Claude Lorrain had a warmer style than Poussin, but he too was far from boisterous. His dreamy landscapes of the countryside around Rome evoked the bucolic poetry of Virgil. All this was a far cry from the art of Bernini.

When Bernini visited Paris in 1665, Louis XIV rejected his plans for the rebuilding of the Louvre palace. The Sun King could not bear to imitate a style so intimately associated with the papacy and with Habsburg Europe, and he settled on a sober and massive design for the Louvre. Louis' architectural taste ran toward featureless monumentality. His great palace at Versailles is Baroque in scale but not in temper. The regimented facade is without flamboyance. The fountains and statuary in the garden served as formal backdrops for Louis' rigid court pageantry. In the arts, as in politics, Louis imposed order. His favorite painter, Charles Le Brun (1619–1690), laid down rules of composition, proportion, and perspective which court painters were expected to obey. At Versailles, Le Brun organized a team of builders and decorators who suppressed their individual eccentricities in order to achieve a blandly grandiose effect—the aim of most government architecture ever since.

In Protestant northern Europe, the impact of the Baroque style was relatively superficial. The English and the Dutch, in particular, were too bourgeois to appreciate the exuberant pomp of Baroque secular art and too puritanical to appreciate the brilliant theatricality of Baroque religious art. In seventeenth-century England, the Stuart court patronized Rubens, Van

Steeple of St. Bride's Church, London. *Designed by Wren.*

Dyck, and other far less talented society portraitists. Had they been able to afford it, Charles I and Charles II might have built Baroque palaces. But Sir Christopher Wren (1632–1723), the one great native English artist in the seventeenth century, drew upon the High Renaissance and French classicism rather than the Baroque in shaping his elegantly classical style. Wren was a very insular Englishman, whose one trip abroad was to Paris. By accident he became the most prolific church builder in seventeenth-century Europe; in 1666 the disastrous fire of London gutted eighty medieval churches, including St. Paul's cathedral, and Wren was commissioned to rebuild the cathedral and fifty-one of the parish churches. Wren's churches were the Protestant answer to Bernini's papal architecture. The twisted, narrow London streets offered no opportunities for vistas, colonnades, and eye-catching facades. Wren had to build his churches on crowded commercial sites, squeezing the church doors between tightly packed rows of shop fronts. Wisely, he focused all external emphasis on his tall, fanciful steeples, each one different. These steeples ingeniously combine the verticality of the Gothic spire with the classical ornamentation of the Baroque cupola. To save money, he built the interiors of his churches with plastered brick rather than stone. He was no Puritan, yet his Anglican churches look like meeting halls rather than shrines. They are sparingly decorated, and designed so that the whole congregation can see the pulpit and hear the preacher. Compared with these parish churches, the rebuilt St. Paul's cathedral is elaborate and magnificent; compared with St. Peter's in Rome, however, Wren's cathedral is modest and reticent. Though Wren stole shamelessly from other architects in designing St. Paul's, he achieved an original total effect. The Cathedral's one great ornament is the central dome, which floats over the London skyline in simple dignity, the embodiment of Wren's classical spirit.

The Dutch were even more impervious than the English to the Baroque spirit. In art, as in business, they distrusted ostentation and extravagance, and prized common sense and discipline. They were not philistines. The seventeenth century was the golden age of Dutch painting. Every self-respecting burgher had his picture painted; every drinking club and almshouse board commissioned a group portrait; the popular demand for art was so great that peddlers hawked landscapes, seascapes, and genre scenes. Dutch painters did not travel to Italy for inspiration or training. Like Brueghel and other earlier Netherlandish artists, they found beauty and significance in the humdrum details of everyday life. Their art was both anticlassical and anti-Baroque, for they neither idealized nor dramatized the bourgeois society they recorded. Their subject matter was emphatically secular. For instance, three of the best seventeenth-century Dutch painters, Frans Hals, Pieter de Hooch, and Jan Vermeer, produced no religious pictures whatsoever.

Frans Hals (*c.* 1580–1666) was a rollicking portraitist. With rapid-fire brush strokes, he painted a gallery of artlessly casual middle-class folk, sometimes catching them laughing out loud. Hals's bluff pictures were the antithesis of Van Dyck's blue-blooded society portraits. Pieter de Hooch (1629–*c.*1683) painted quiet interior and courtyard scenes. He had none of Hals's gift for bringing people to life, but his finicky style gave charm to the spotless rooms, tiled floors, and brick walls on which he dwelt so lovingly. Jan Vermeer (1632–1675) is now reckoned a more complete artist than Hals or De Hooch, though he was unappreciated in his own day. Vermeer painted only a few small-sized pictures of trivial scenes, but in these bejeweled miniatures he created a world of timeless beauty. There is certainly nothing arresting about Vermeer's representation of a painter in his studio. The artist at the easel may be Vermeer himself, but since he turns his back to us, we look at the jumble of objects in his studio. Vermeer's technique is so flawless that the plaster cast on the table can be identified as Michelangelo's "Brutus," and the elaborate map of the Low Countries on the wall is accurate to the smallest detail—the Dutch were much the best cartographers in seventeenth-century Europe. But Vermeer is not merely a photographer in paint. He endows the studio scene with a limpid purity, as if to say that the commonest things in life have beauty and significance.

The greatest of all Dutch artists was Rembrandt van Rijn (1606–1669).

The Painter in His Studio. *Painting by Jan Vermeer.* Kunsthisto- risches Mu- seum, Vienna.

He started out as a Dutch-style Rubens. Before he was thirty he was operating a fashionable studio in Amsterdam, painting opulent portraits and bombastic scenes in a richly Baroque color scheme all his own—deep browns and reds, luridly highlighted by barbaric gold. Like Rubens, he was very prolific. Over six hundred of his paintings and nearly two thousand of his etchings and drawings have survived. But Rembrandt became increasingly unwilling to curry public favor, and as his genius ripened, he gradually lost his popularity. His magnificent "Night Watch," depicting an Amsterdam company of musketeers going their rounds, displeased the militiamen who commissioned it, because many of their faces were obscured by the murky light and the tumbling pattern of pikes and charging figures. The proud artist's tragic decline from youthful prosperity to bankrupt old age is haunt- ingly recorded in his long series of self-portraits. He was a self-contained artist, who never left Holland, and fused elements of Netherlandish, Italian Renaissance, and Baroque art into his own inimitable style. Like other seventeenth-century Dutch painters, he was a realist, exploring the joys and sorrows of ordinary people. Even the works of his early Baroque phase were never theatrical, and the older he grew the more introspective his pictures became. He was a devoutly pious Mennonite, and despite the Protestant distaste for religious pictures, almost half of his paintings, etchings, and drawings illustrate biblical stories. Rembrandt was thus the one supremely great Protestant religious painter of the seventeenth century.

In his religious art, Rembrandt chose biblical themes which permitted him to dwell in Protestant fashion on the isolated individual's personal relations with God. He avoided portraying monumental scenes like the Creation, the deluge, the slaughter of the innocents, or the Last Judgment. In his youth, Rembrandt was attracted by externally dramatic subjects like the blinding of Samson, but in later life he preferred to depict men's inward failings and sufferings. Like Shakespeare, he tried to imagine a scene from the viewpoint of every participant. Some of his most sympathetic portraits are of his Jewish neighbors in Amsterdam, and he put these men and women into his biblical pictures. He visualized the life and passion of Christ not only through the Gospel record but through the eyes of Christ's Jewish critics, which adds a fresh dimension of human tragedy to his religious art. Among his private papers are hundreds of sketches of Gospel scenes, such as his drawing of Christ's arrest by a gang sent from the chief priests, a drawing which illustrates his genius in its simplest form. A few strokes of the pen can say more than acres of painted canvas. Rembrandt has caught the full drama of the confrontation: a crowd surging angrily toward the passive Jesus, confounded by His radiance. A fuller statement of Rembrandt's religious art is the last picture he ever painted, his "Return of the Prodigal Son." This very simple picture violates all the classical rules of composition, color,

The Arrest of Christ. *Drawing by Rembrandt. Nationalmuseum, Stockholm.*

Return of the Prodigal
   Son.
*Painting by Rembrandt.
Hermitage, Leningrad.*

perspective, and proportion. It is wholly at odds with the Renaissance concept of human dignity and self-reliance, and equally at odds with the Baroque concept of exuberant display. Rembrandt concentrates attention on the old father's compassionate forgiveness, and the tattered son's humble repentance. The solemn figures stand immobile, but inwardly deeply moved. It is doubtless the aged painter's own last affirmation of faith in God's loving mercy toward weary and repentant man.

Rembrandt was the first great Protestant painter—and the last. The roll of outstanding Catholic artists during the era of the Catholic reformation is much longer. Tintoretto, El Greco, Rubens, and Bernini are only the most conspicuous figures. But the works of the Baroque age turned out to be the swan song of great Catholic as well as Protestant art. Since 1700, broadly speaking, creative artists and architects have pursued secular goals. The quality of popular Christian art, divorced from the aesthetic standards and values of the modern world, has been distressingly low during the last two and a half centuries. Catholics and Protestants alike have contented themselves with mawkishly sentimental pictures and statuary, and slavishly derivative church architecture. It is hard to think of a major painter, sculptor, or architect since 1700 who has been primarily a religious artist. It is equally hard to think of a major painter, sculptor, or architect before 1500 who was not primarily a religious artist. Nothing demonstrates more plainly the secular temper of modern society, and Europe's profound cultural transformation during the sixteenth and seventeenth centuries.

FIVE PHILOSOPHICAL WRITERS: MONTAIGNE, PASCAL, HOBBES, SPINOZA, AND LOCKE

The years from 1559 to 1689 constituted an extraordinarily fertile period in moral philosophy and political theory. The general intellectual revolt against tradition and authority during these years inspired thinking men to ask fundamental questions about human nature and social organization. Such questions were essential because the humanist moral and intellectual postulates of the early sixteenth century no longer worked. Erasmus and his fellow humanists, with their touching faith in man's rationality, had supposed that through a thorough grounding in classical literature and the teachings of the Gospel, men would acquire all necessary moral virtue and intellectual discipline. But Erasmus' effort to civilize and pacify Europe through a fusion of pagan and Christian values was smashed by the Protestant Reformation. Pico della Mirandola's complacent concept of the dignity of man was subverted by Calvin's doctrine of human depravity, and to a lesser extent by Copernicus' heliocentric theory. Even the validity of Machiavelli's coolly rational analysis of political behavior was cast in doubt by the flagrantly irrational dynastic and religious wars which shook sixteenth-century Europe. Throughout the late sixteenth and seventeenth centuries, speculative thinkers and writers invented a rich variety of new approaches to old moral and intellectual issues, but they did not reach a consensus, for they quarreled violently with each other on religious, political, and scientific grounds. Only in the eighteenth century did the *philosophes* reestablish an intellectual framework roughly comparable to the discarded humanist assumptions of the Renaissance. It is quite impossible to describe early modern Europe's chaotic compound of philosophical creativity and polemical disputation in a few pages. The best we can do is to sample the intellectual range and vitality of the period by focusing on five particularly well-known philosophical writers: Montaigne, Pascal, Hobbes, Spinoza, and Locke.

Montaigne

Michel de Montaigne (1533–1592) was a classical humanist ruefully aware that his standards and values were out of place in late sixteenth-century France. His father, a prosperous country gentleman from Perigord, gave him the sort of classical education which Erasmus had wanted for all well-born boys. Until Michel was six years old, he spoke nothing but Latin, and he always preferred Latin to French literature. "I do not take much to modern authors," he said, "because the ancient seem to me fuller and more vigorous." Montaigne spent some years as a lawyer and a royal courtier, but when the French religious wars broke out, he was ill equipped by training and temperament to participate in this ferocious struggle. In 1571, at the peak of the fighting, he withdrew from public life and shut himself up in his château. There he converted a tower storeroom into a book-lined study, and began to write his *Essays*, a series of informal musings about himself and his personal experiences. When Huguenot or Catholic troopers overran his estate, he offered no resistance, and somehow shamed them into leaving him alone. The ideological posturing of Huguenots and ultra-Catholics sickened Montaigne. Each side, he felt, was trying to obliterate the other, a cheap—but false—way of coping with the complexities of life. "Greatness of soul is not so much mounting high and pressing forward, as knowing how to put oneself in order and circumscribe oneself," he wrote. "Between ourselves, these are things that I have always seen to be in remarkable agreement: supercelestial thoughts and subterranean conduct." In his view, crusaders such as the Huguenots and ultra-Catholics were victims of self-delusion: "instead of transforming themselves into angels, they transform themselves into beasts." Montaigne was too circumspect to criticize any of the combatants in the French wars by name, but in his *Essays* he continually preached moderation and toleration. His strictures against cruelty to children, servants, and animals show how revolted he must have been by the hysterical butchery of the St. Bartholomew massacre.

Montaigne is not a systematic philosopher, but few books are richer in moral reflection than his *Essays*. "I have no other aim," he says, "but to disclose myself." He is not trying to brag, nor to confess his sins. Montaigne believes, with Socrates, that self-knowledge is the starting point for purposeful human experience, and he encourages the reader to attempt his own searching self-examination. "There is no description so hard," he assures us, "nor so profitable, as the description of oneself." Montaigne details the quirks and complexities of his personality with urbane wit and charming candor. One scarcely notices what a dronelike existence this cultivated gentleman led. He treats most topics with ironic skepticism, not only questioning the moral absolutes brandished by the Protestant and Catholic crusaders, but wondering whether "civilized" Europeans are really morally superior to the "savage" Indians of the New World. Are we not all cannibals? he asks. Montaigne is an utterly secular thinker. He can write about education, repentance, death, and immortality without reference to the Christian verities. He speaks as a weary middle-aged man who knows his own limitations, dislikes violent change of any sort, yet always accommodates himself to the necessary evils in life. In essence, he presents a chastened restatement of Erasmus' Renaissance humanism, stripped of all its buoyant optimism and Christian idealism.

Yet Montaigne was not a completely passive witness to his country's agony. He became a leading spokesman for the *politique* party, which finally brought the French religious wars to a halt. Montaigne entertained Henry of Navarre at his château and in the 1580's supported him against the Valois and Guise factions. He did not live long enough to witness Henry's expedient conversion to Catholicism or his compromise Edict of Nantes. But unquestionably Montaigne would have approved of these measures, for they exemplified his moderate and tolerant philosophy.

Pascal

To Blaise Pascal, Montaigne's brand of humanism was intellectually and spiritually inadequate. Pascal (1623–1662) is a complex and controversial figure. The blinding headaches and other debilitating illnesses which he endured throughout his short life help explain his distinctive blend of toughness and delicacy. Pascal combined razor-sharp intellectual prowess with an anguished sense of man's moral predicament. His father, a French government official, encouraged the boy's precocious aptitude for mathematics and science. While still a youth, Pascal published an essay on conic sections, conducted elaborate experiments concerning atmospheric pressure, and invented a calculating machine. He was a proud and brilliant participant in the scientific revolution. Then one night in 1654 he had an experience of religious ecstasy. "FIRE!" he wrote in white heat on emerging from this vision. "God of Abraham, God of Isaac, God of Jacob, not of the philosophers and savants. Certitude. Certitude. Feeling. Joy. Peace. God of Jesus Christ."—and so on for a pageful of exclamations inadequate to express his rapture. The short remainder of his life he dedicated to austere devotions. Both of his best-known books, the *Provincial Letters* and the *Pensées* ("Thoughts") are religious apologetics.

Pascal was drawn to Jansenism, the movement within the French Catholic church which preached a semi-Calvinist doctrine of human depravity and divine predestination of the elect. He retired periodically to the Jansenist community of Port-Royal, at the very time when the Jesuits were stigmatizing the Jansenist movement as heretical, and pressing the French government to close down Port-Royal. Pascal counterattacked with the *Provincial Letters*, an anonymous series of pamphlets which accused the Jesuits of employing immoral tactics in order to gain power. The *Provincial Letters* are sensationally effective satire, written in the mocking style of Molière. In order to expose Jesuit casuistry—that is to say, the Jesuit method of handling cases of conscience—Pascal quotes (or misquotes) from various Jesuit confessional manuals which wink at evil conduct. In one of the letters, a Jesuit proudly

Pascal. *Painting by an unknown artist. This portrait conveys hauntingly Pascal's keen and suffering gaze.*

explains to Pascal the confessional technique of mental reservations: "After saying aloud *I swear that I have not done that*, add in a low voice, *today*; or after saying aloud *I swear*, interpose in a whisper *that I say*, and then continue aloud, *that I have done that*. This, you perceive, is telling the truth." "I grant it," replies Pascal, "though it might possibly be found to be telling the truth in a low key, and falsehood in a loud one." The Jesuits had the last laugh, however, for after Pascal's death, Port-Royal was closed and the Jansenist movement was crushed.

Pascal's chief target during his closing years was not the Jesuits, but the rationalist freethinkers in the tradition of Montaigne. Although he had learned from the *Essays* how to examine himself, Pascal was repelled by Montaigne's urbane skepticism toward new ideas and high ideals. As a practicing scientist, Pascal was keenly aware that the rational pursuit of mathematics and physics was shaping a scientific view of the world even more belligerently secular than Montaigne's. Unless the new seventeenth-century science could be wedded to revealed religion, the intellectual community would lapse into outright agnosticism. Accordingly, Pascal planned a monumental apology for the Christian religion which would convert rationalists by appealing simultaneously to their minds and their emotions. He did not live to write this book, but he did leave nearly a thousand scrappy notes, which were collected and published posthumously as his *Pensées*. The reader can appreciate Pascal's *Pensées* as finely chiseled fragments or piece them together into a unified argument. To demonstrate that the natural world is not our final home, Pascal dwells on the frailty and folly of man's earthly life. Much of his argument is compressed into one aphorism: "Man's condition: inconstancy, ennui, unrest." In another famous passage, he says, "Man is but a reed, the weakest thing in nature; but a thinking reed." He believes that this ability to think, honestly directed, will make us acutely aware of unbearable moral conflicts and spiritual hunger, which can only be assuaged by the grace of God. Pascal's argument has not perhaps converted many rationalists, but his *Pensées* are strangely unsettling. The eighteenth-century *philosophes* tried to bury Pascal, but he has had a continuous influence upon subsequent moral philosophers, not least upon the existentialist thinkers of the twentieth century.

Hobbes

The English philosopher Thomas Hobbes (1588–1679) shared Pascal's pessimistic view of the human condition but not his faith in a religious solution to man's problems. Hobbes was a boldly materialistic thinker. The story that he was born prematurely when his mother was scared by the noise of the Armada guns is a little hard to credit, since his birth occurred three months before the arrival of the Spanish fleet. But it is very easy to believe that young Thomas rebelled against his environment: his father was an incompetent country parson, and his teachers at Oxford had nothing fresher to offer than medieval Aristotelian scholasticism. Hobbes gradually broadened his intellectual horizon while tutoring English aristocrats and chaperoning them on grand tours of the Continent. He became friendly with such leading scientific personages as Galileo, Bacon, Descartes, and Harvey, and he was so delighted by their experimental attitude toward physical nature that he determined to apply the new scientific method to the study of human nature as well. He sharpened his understanding of human conduct by translating Thucydides' *History of the Peloponnesian War*, the deepest and most withering analysis of political behavior by any classical writer. To Hobbes, the Puritan Revolution of the 1640's appeared to be a sickening repetition of the fratricidal agony described by Thucydides. Soon after the English revolutionary crisis began, he fled from London to Paris under the exaggerated impression that his life was in danger. In exile, he tutored the Prince of Wales, the future Charles II, with no discernible effect, and wrote the *Leviathan*, his monumental treatise on how to prevent revolutionary turmoil. Although a proponent of absolutism, Hobbes was no orthodox royal absolutist. Once Cromwell had executed Charles I in 1649, he transferred his allegiance to the Puritan absolutist state. In 1651, the *Leviathan* was published and Hobbes came home to settle down under Cromwell's dictatorship. The Restoration of 1660 renewed his apprehension, but Charles II graciously gave his old tutor a small pension. Hobbes spent his remaining years answering an avalanche of critics who found his books atheistic and depraved.

Hobbes's *Leviathan* is generally reckoned the greatest treatise on political philosophy in the English language—a special compliment, since very few readers of this remarkable book have liked its argument. Hobbes's analysis of political conduct rests on his mechanistic concept of human psychology. He sees men as animals, stimulated by appetites and aversions rather than by rational calculation or moral ideals. Hobbes's picture of mankind's desperate and continuous struggle for self-preservation anticipates by two hundred years Darwin's picture of the struggle for survival in the animal world. Hobbes says that men, stripped of all social conventions, are the most formidable and rapacious of beasts. Every man in his natural state is at war with all other men, and his life in Hobbes's pungent phrase is "solitary, poor, nasty, brutish and short." Hobbes does not deny the crucial importance of man's rational powers but argues that reason can merely regulate the passions, not conquer them. Rationality persuades men to cooperate in forming civil governments which will rescue them from their natural state of war and restrain their urge to destroy one another. Each man surrenders his right of self-government to his neighbors on condition that they all do likewise. By this mutual social contract, men form a commonwealth, which Hobbes calls "that great Leviathan (or rather, to speak more reverently, that mortal god) to which we owe ... our peace and defense." The commonwealth vests its collective power in a sovereign, perferably one person, who becomes sole judge, legislator, and executor. The sovereign's sole purpose is to prevent war. He has absolute and unlimited power over his subjects, except that he cannot compel them to kill themselves, which would violate the primary human law of self-preservation. Subjects are obliged never to rebel, and the sovereign is obliged always to suppress rebellion. Should the sovereign fail to exercise power effectively, however, he loses his sovereignty, and his subjects shift their allegiance to a new sovereign who will protect them. In this fashion, Hobbes justified the transfer of English sovereignty from Charles I to Cromwell, and later from Cromwell to Charles II.

Ever since 1651 commentators have argued over the implications of Hobbes's political theory. Several points are generally accepted. Hobbes's effort to apply the scientific method to social analysis produced a train of thought much more corrosive than Montaigne's tolerant humanism or Pascal's appeal for divine grace. Not since Machiavelli had power politics been subjected to such an unsentimental, utilitarian analysis. Though Hobbes's approach, unlike Machiavelli's, was theoretical, both men judged politicians by their ability to stay in power, and governmental institutions by their effectiveness in protecting people against their own worst instincts. Hobbes justified absolute monarchy without recourse to the customary monarchist claims of historical legitimacy and honor; English royalists could not forgive him for repudiating the divine-right theory of monarchy. Like Machiavelli, Hobbes distinguished between the "ghostly" realm of revealed religion and the earthly realm of politics, and divorced spiritual from temporal power. Accordingly, he excoriated with equal vigor Catholic and Protestant crusaders who confused this world with the next, and he assigned to the secular sovereign total control over ecclesiastical institutions. In his concept of corporate state power, Hobbes went far beyond Machiavelli and even beyond the sixteenth-century French theorist Jean Bodin, the first to articulate a modern view of national sovereignty. Hobbes's sovereign has more coercive authority over his subjects than Louis XIV ever dreamed of. However, those who have labeled the *Leviathan* a manifesto for totalitarianism, have ignored Hobbes's basic premise that the commonwealth provides its individual members with peace and contentment. The *Leviathan* shocked both liberal constitutionalists and conservative monarchists in the seventeenth century, but it is evident now that Hobbes came closer than any other thinker of his day to envisioning the modern omnicompetent state.

Spinoza

Benedict Spinoza (1632–1677) was an even more controversial thinker than Hobbes. Unfortunately Spinoza's unorthodox opinions cannot be briefly summarized without grotesquely distorting them. His philosophical system is abstruse and intricate, and unlike Montaigne, Pascal, and Hobbes, he wrote in a style far from easy to understand or enjoy. In his Latin treatises, Spinoza sought to combine the metaphysical precision of medieval scholasticism with the mathematical precision of seventeenth-century science. His *Ethics,* for instance, is a long series of geometrical definitions, axioms, propositions, and corollaries. Spinoza lived the life of a social leper. He was born in Amsterdam, the son of a Jewish merchant. While still a boy, he rebelled against the cloistered Hebrew intellectual code of the Amsterdam Jewish community and learned Latin and several modern languages in order to master the new scientific knowledge of the seventeenth century. In 1656 his synagogue excommunicated him as a heretic. Thereafter Spinoza remained independent of any religious sect. Recurrently the Dutch Calvinist clergy branded him an atheist. He eked out a living by grinding optical lenses and turned down a professorship at the University of Heidelberg because it would infringe upon his solitude and intellectual freedom. However, he was no ivory-tower recluse. His *Tractatus Theologico-Politicus*, published in 1670, championed freedom of thought and speech in the teeth of the Dutch Calvinist clergy. He was almost lynched by a mob at The Hague, and when he prepared to publish his *Ethics* in Amsterdam, the outcry was so great that the book remained in manuscript until after Spinoza's death. Why was this solitary and difficult thinker so obnoxious to his contemporaries?

Spinoza was a deeply religious man, but his concept of God outraged orthodox Jews, Protestants, and Catholics more than the skepticism of Montaigne or the materialism of Hobbes. Spinoza was not satisfied with Descartes' and Hobbes's method of divorcing the realm of metaphysics from the realm of physical nature and exploring only the latter. On the contrary, he fused metaphysics with physics. He conceived of nature as unified and uniform, incorporating all thought and all things, embracing mind and body, and he defined philosophy as the knowledge of the mind's union with the whole of nature. To Spinoza, everything in nature is an attribute of God, nothing in nature is independent of God, and God cannot be conceived of as distinct from His creation. God determines all of man's actions, as everything else in nature. Yet Spinoza cannot be charged with fatalism. His view of human potentiality is considerably more buoyant than that of Calvin or Pascal or Hobbes. Most men are swayed by their passions, he says, but one passion can be mastered by another, and reason teaches us how to master hatred by love. Man's highest goal is the intellectual love of God, which gives us a vision of the infinite beauty of the universe and contentment beyond any vulgar notion of heavenly reward.

It is easy to see why people called the *Ethics* an atheistic book. Spinoza's God cannot be imagined anthropomorphically. In his pantheistic system there is little place for the Jewish and Christian concepts of divine revelation through the Scriptures or through miracles, and no room for belief in divine rewards and punishments, or in personal immortality. His heretical opinions were too rational for seventeenth-century sensibilities and too mystical for eighteenth-century sensibilities. Spinoza's first enthusiastic admirers were nineteenth-century romantics like Goethe and Shelley. Ever since, he has been accepted in the pantheon of great philosophers.

Locke

All four of the philosophical writers we have considered were somewhat lonely rebels. Hobbes worked out a political theory which scandalized his readers, while Montaigne, Pascal, and Spinoza agitated people by their probing moral arguments but did not win many converts. Our last philosopher, the Englishman John Locke (1632–1704), was more fortunate. His political philosophy was enshrined by the Glorious Revolution of 1688–1689; his commonsense morality comforted his late seventeenth-century audience; and his concept of human nature nicely complemented Newton's concept of physical nature. Locke was the son of a Puritan country lawyer who fought briefly in the parliamentary army during the English civil war. He was educated at Westminster School and at Oxford. In retrospect Locke shared Hobbes's opinion that English schools and universities were harmfully old-fashioned and restrictive, though his own academic experience was certainly open-ended enough. He was given a post at Oxford which required no teaching duties, joined the Royal Society, and traveled on the Continent. The turning point in Locke's career came in 1667, when the earl of Shaftesbury, the great Whig politician, invited him into his household as physician, secretary, and intellectual companion. Before he joined Shaftesbury, Locke had been a conventional Anglican royalist, suspicious of religious and political dissent. Shaftesbury thrust him into the rough and tumble of Whig party politics. Locke watched and perhaps helped the earl scheme against Charles II and his brother James during the stormy years of the Popish Plot and the attempts to exclude James from the succession. In 1683, after Shaftesbury and the Whigs had been defeated, Locke fled to Holland. This experience completed his education and molded him into a pragmatic champion of political liberalism, religious latitudinarianism, and intellectual toleration.

Locke composed all his major books during the 1680's, the heyday of strong-arm rule by Charles II and James II. The *Two Treatises on Civil Government*, written to justify Shaftesbury's abortive rebellion against Charles II, were laid aside unpublished when the rebellion fizzled out. The *Essay Concerning Human Understanding* and the *Letter Concerning Toleration*, written during Locke's Dutch exile, were circulated in manuscript among his friends. Suddenly the Glorious Revolution transformed him from an outcast into a celebrity. In 1689 Locke hurried home to England and published his three major books. The aptness and lucidity of his common-sense philosophy were immediately recognized, and during the closing years of his life Locke enjoyed an intellectual esteem second only to Newton's.

Locke's theory of limited parliamentary government is propounded in the *Two Treatises on Civil Government*. The first of these treatises ridicules the notion that kings possess a divine right to paternal power. The second, and much more important, treatise argues that the subjects of a state are endowed with inalienable natural rights to life, liberty, and property. This theory conveniently lent sanction to the Glorious Revolution, though it was originally framed to justify Shaftesbury's activities a decade earlier. Locke was also trying to refute Hobbes's *Leviathan*. In contrast to Hobbes, Locke supposes that man is animated by reason rather than passion. When he imagines man in a state of nature, he stresses the perfect freedom and equality of precivilized life rather than the Hobbesian natural state of war. Therefore, Locke argues, man's natural liberty should be preserved as fully as possible in civil society. He wants a minimal degree of governmental regulation, in contrast to Hobbes's all-embracing sovereignty. Locke offers no empirical proof of man's natural rights, but the doctrine and its corollary of limited government proved immensely popular throughout the eighteenth century. Among man's natural rights, according to Locke, is the right to acquire private property. He recognizes that the unequal division of property undermines man's natural equality and incites crime. Hence man needs civil government to protect his life, liberty, and property. Locke insists that government should reflect the opinion of the majority, which meant, in England, a majority of the property owners represented in Parliament. Most important, he defends the people's right to resist and overthrow tyrants. His doctrines endorsed the Bill of Rights of 1689, and in a more general way commended the post-revolutionary English social pattern of representative self-government, acquisitive capitalism, and an entrenched division between the propertied and unpropertied classes. No wonder Locke's political philosophy was so popular in England. His posthumous influence in eighteenth-century France and America was even greater.

Locke's commonsense view of religion was also welcomed by many Englishmen. His *Letter Concerning Toleration* attacks the idea that Christianity can be promoted or defended by force. He sees no harm in a wide variety of religious practices, as long as the worshipers profess faith in God, obedience to God's will, and belief in an afterlife where virtue is rewarded and sin punished. Locke has a poor opinion of Protestant "enthusiasts" such as the Quakers, whose attitude of familiarity toward God seems blasphemous to him. For political reasons he is willing to deny toleration to Roman Catholics, as subversive agents of a foreign power, and to atheists, who can not be bound by oaths to fulfill civil obligations. To some critics, Locke's own latitudinarian credo verged on atheism. One Calvinist pamphleteer sneered that Locke "took Hobbes's *Leviathan* for the New Testament" and Hobbes himself "for our Saviour and the Apostles." Indeed Locke did have a Hobbesian motive for wanting to separate the church from the state, or more accurately, rescue the state from the church. His notion of religious toleration was a far cry from the Puritan religious liberty of the 1640's. John Milton had demanded the liberty to search for spiritual truth untrammeled by secular politics; John Locke wanted to liberate man's rational powers from religious restrictions. The Toleration Act of 1689 carried Locke's theory into practice.

Locke's commonsense philosophy, so lucid on the surface, is pretty muddled underneath. Much of the confusion in his thought stems from the seventeenth-century conflict between empiricism and rationalism. As we have seen, Bacon was the apostle of the inductive, empirical intellectual method, in which knowledge is obtained through observation and experimentation. Galileo and Newton, though deviating widely from Bacon's precepts, were leading exemplars of the empirical method. Descartes was the rationalist par excellence, a deductive system builder who evolved his ideas through abstract ratiocination. Hobbes and Spinoza, however much they quarreled with Descartes' ideas, were likewise rationalist thinkers, their conclusions in no sense drawn from empirical observation. John Locke was sometimes a rationalist and sometimes an empiricist. His political philosophy is strictly rationalist. His central tenet, the existence of natural rights, is a proposition incapable of empirical proof. On the other hand, Locke's *Essay Concerning Human Understanding* presents an empirical theory of the mind. In this book Locke denies that men are born with innate ideas or principles. The human mind at birth is a *tabula rasa*, or blank slate. We furnish our minds, he says, through sensate experience. Our ignorance is always infinitely larger than our knowledge; consequently we have little reason to be dogmatic in our beliefs. The *Essay*, like Locke's other books, appeals to the reader's intellect rather than to his faith or his feelings. Locke consistently eschewed the conventional Christian emphasis on original sin and moral anguish. He preferred to show, like his friend Isaac Newton, what man could accomplish by applying his reason to the study of nature. Locke was not able to discover a system of social laws as simple, uniform, and majestic as Newton's universal laws of motion. But he offered the hope of human self-improvement through education and mental discipline. The most unspectacular of great philosophers, Locke voiced his society's growing confidence in worldly progress through freedom, individualism, and hard work.

THE GOLDEN AGE OF ENGLISH, SPANISH, AND FRENCH DRAMA

We cannot close this rapid survey of early modern European culture without saying something about late sixteenth and seventeenth-century literature, the most enduring achievement of the age. In poetry the spectrum ran from such monumental epics as Tasso's *Jerusalem Delivered*, Spenser's *Faerie Queene*, and Milton's *Paradise Lost* to daringly experimental lyric verse by Donne and the other English metaphysical poets, Góngora in Spain, and Vondel in Holland. Miguel de Cervantes wrote the first great novel, *Don Quixote*. John Bunyan wrote one of the most enduring Christian allegories, *Pilgrim's Progress*. Bunyan, Bacon, Milton, Sir Thomas Browne, and many others contributed to the amazing development of English prose style. In 1559 the English language was a clumsy instrument for the conveyance of ideas or the creation of moods, but by 1689 English prose writers could generate the utmost power or shade the most delicate nuance. Correspondingly, in France, such prose stylists as Montaigne, Pascal, La Rochefoucald, and Boileau were purifying and polishing their tongue so as to exploit its elegance, precision, and wit.

Above all, this was the golden age of the theater—the age of Marlowe, Shakespeare, and Jonson in England; of Lope de Vega and Calderón in Spain; of Corneille, Molière, and Racine in France. For both the English and the Spanish stage, the peak years can be specified rather precisely—from 1580 to 1640. The heyday of the French theater came a little later, between

1630 and 1680. Seventeenth-century drama, like its twentieth-century counterpart, was as much show business as art. The circumstances of theatrical production reveal a great deal about contemporary social and economic conditions. And the plays themselves, written to please a capricious public, illustrate most of the generalizations made in this book about the religious and intellectual climate and the political structure of European society in the late sixteenth and seventeenth centuries. To the social historian, perhaps the most interesting aspect of the English, Spanish, and French theater between 1580 and 1680 is the gradually changing character of the audience. In 1580 the playwright addressed himself to the poor as well as the rich; in 1680 he wrote only for the rich. Why did the drama become more aristocratic?

England

The professional theater which suddenly emerged in the 1570's was quite unlike any previously to be found in England. In the Middle Ages, English drama had been chiefly religious. In more than a hundred towns the local guilds annually staged plays which celebrated the Christian mysteries. There were also medieval folk plays about such figures as Robin Hood and St. George. Elaborate pageants were staged in London on state occasions. By the early sixteenth century, the spread of humanist learning had led the English schools and universities to produce plays grounded on Roman comedy and tragedy. But when in 1576 the first two professional theaters operated by acting companies for paying audiences opened in London, they caught the public attention with a repertory of richly romantic plays far more exciting and entertaining than the didactic medieval religious plays or the humanist school plays.

The first two great hits of the English professional stage were Thomas Kyd's *Spanish Tragedy* and Christopher Marlowe's *Tamburlaine*, both produced in the 1580's. Kyd's *Spanish Tragedy* fascinated the Elizabethans because of its lurid story about a father, maddened with grief at his son's murder, who filled the stage with corpses in his efforts to gain revenge. The revenge theme recurred in a majority of the great Elizabethan tragedies, *Hamlet* being the most obvious example. Christopher Marlowe (1564–1593) was a much more notable literary figure than Kyd, even though his five plays are all the work of a very young man: he died at age twenty-nine. Marlowe was the first English poet to use blank verse effectively in the theater. His protagonists, notably Tamburlaine and Faustus, were larger than life, and they poured out their outrageous demands with a propulsive force which thrilled the Elizabethan audience and which is still thrilling today. Like Kyd and Marlowe, other Elizabethan dramatists packed their plays with action. Their comedies were slapstick and bawdy. Their tragedies were passionate and gory. These plays were rarely set in contemporary England, and often in Italy, partly because the playwrights borrowed so many plots from Italian *novelle* and partly because the Elizabethans believed that anything could happen in Italy. Since every play had to be licensed by the royal censor, most playwrights (including Shakespeare) avoided controversial issues. Historical subjects were popular. Classical history afforded a safe opportunity for moralizing, and medieval English history offered a chance for displays of patriotism, as in Shakespeare's *Henry* V. Very few Elizabethan plays touched on the question of Protestantism versus Catholicism, the most explosive issue of the day.

The Elizabethan theater was a roaring business. Between 1580 and 1640 over three hundred playwrights wrote for a hundred companies of actors. In and around London, four to six professional theaters were in operation six afternoons a week, except during plague epidemics, when the players would pack up and tour the provinces. Some of these London theaters were circular unroofed structures, like Shakespeare's Globe playhouse, holding upwards of three thousand people. Half the audience at the Globe stood in the pit for an admission charge of one or two pennies. At a time when a prostitute or an evening in the tavern cost at least sixpence, the only cheaper form of entertainment was a public hanging at Tyburn. Other London theaters, like Blackfriars, where Shakespeare's company also performed, were roofed rectangular boxes, holding no more than five hundred persons, with the price of tickets high enough to exclude the rabble. It is estimated that 10 per cent of the total population of London might be found in the theaters on any given afternoon.

The Elizabethan theatrical audience was a great audience because it was so diversified. Court nobility, lawyers, shopkeepers, apprentices, and drifters all came to demand their money's worth. They formed an audience worthy of Shakespeare, and inspired him to write plays which traverse the entire range of human experience and feeling. Not all Elizabethans joined in the applause. Puritans continually bewailed the wickedness of the London stage. The city fathers considered the theaters a public nuisance, and therefore all the London playhouses were built either outside the city walls, like the Globe across the Thames, or, like Blackfriars, on crown land, which was exempt from city jurisdiction. Elizabeth I enjoyed the theater, and she countered Puritan and civic disapproval by inviting the professional troupes to present their best plays at court. But the queen was very stingy. In the 1580's and 1590's she sponsored only six to ten court performances a year, many fewer than would occur under the Stuarts. Thus the Elizabethan theater began as unsubsidized private enterprise. To make money, Elizabethan theatrical companies had to run a grueling repertory of up to fifty plays a year, including a dozen new ones. Each new play would be acted several days consecutively; then it was entered into the repertory, and if unpopular, soon forgotten. Nearly two thousand of the plays produced between 1580 and 1640 still survive, perhaps a third of the total number.

William Shakespeare (1564–1616) was of course the greatest Elizabethan dramatist and also probably the most popular playwright of his day, though the audiences at the Globe and Blackfriars certainly did not appreciate how far he towered over all other English poets. Contemporaries saw Shakespeare as a complete man of the theater, author of three dozen successful plays, and actor and shareholder in the chief theatrical troupe of the period, the Lord Chamberlain's Company, later called the King's Company. Regrettably little can be discovered about Shakespeare's career. His life is better documented, however, than that of any other Elizabethan playwright except Ben Jonson. A great many people have refused to believe that a Stratford glove maker's son, with only a grammar-school education, could possibly write *Hamlet*. It makes them happier to suppose that the plays were secretly written by some aristocrat with a university education, such as Francis Bacon or the earl of Oxford. There is no way of reasoning with people who equate genius with book learning or blue blood. But it should be emphasized that the Elizabethan stage provided a suitable career for an ambitious country boy of middling birth like young Shakespeare. Players and playwrights could make a good living, even though they ranked socially just above beggars and whores. The theatrical life could be brutal. Christopher Marlowe died in a tavern brawl, stabbed through the eye, and Ben Jonson narrowly escaped execution for killing an actor in a duel. Shakespeare was much more even tempered than Marlowe or Jonson. He worked hard in London for about twenty years, and once he had earned enough money, retired in comfort to the Warwickshire country town he loved much more. Obviously he composed his plays quickly, even if not as fast as some of the hack writers who teamed up in threes or fours to cobble together a play in a few days.

Shakespeare always carefully designed his plays for the two dozen actors in the Lord Chamberlain's Company. The protagonist in the late plays is generally older than in the early plays, because Richard Burbage, the company's leading actor, had grown older. There are never many female roles in Shakespeare's plays, since women were represented on the Elizabethan stage by boy actors, less experienced and effective than the men in the acting troupe. Shakespeare published some of his poetry, but he published none of his plays, regarding them as company property without independent literary value. Fortunately, since his plays were popular, eighteen of them were printed in pirated versions during Shakespeare's lifetime. And even more fortunately, his friends (spurred on by Ben Jonson's careful edition of *his* plays in 1616) collected the plays in a folio volume in 1623, printed "according to the True Originall Copies." Actually, some of these folio texts are quite imperfect. *Macbeth*, for instance, has survived only in a shortened, doctored acting version, perhaps used for touring in the provinces.

Even before Shakespeare's retirement from the stage in 1613, London theatrical conditions were beginning to change. His younger colleague Ben

Jonson (*c.* 1573–1637) was writing biting comedies set in contemporary London and bookish tragedies set in ancient Rome, which pleased the courtiers in the box seats much more than the groundlings in the pit. Francis Beaumont and John Fletcher were collaborating on a series of tragicomedies, a fancy new kind of escapist entertainment, far more frivolous than Shakespeare's tragedies and more exotic and farfetched than his most romantic comedies. Such plays did better in small enclosed theaters like Blackfriars than in big open arenas like the Globe. Playwrights were getting more daringly controversial. A sensational hit of 1624, Thomas Middleton's *A Game at Chess*, lampooned Prince Charles's expedition to Spain to woo the Infanta. This play ran at the Globe for nine consecutive days while the royal court was out of town, and grossed £1,000, with customers lined up for hours to get in, before James I heard about it and banned further performances.

As Puritan criticism of the London theater grew louder, the acting companies allied themselves with the Stuart court. James I and Charles I spent much more money on theatricals than had Elizabeth. James I employed Ben Jonson to write court masques, in which the songs, dances, scenery, and costumes greatly outweighed the libretto. Jonson dedicated his splendid anti-Puritan play *Bartholomew Fair* to James, who must have enjoyed Jonson's portrayal of the unctuous hypocrite Zeal-of-the-land Busy. In 1632 the real-live Puritan William Prynne produced a thousand-page diatribe against the stage called *Histriomastix*, written in a style very reminiscent of Zeal-of-the-land Busy. Prynne had seen only four plays, but he damned the theatrical profession wholesale, implied that Charles I's queen, Henrietta Maria, was a whore because she acted in court masques, and demanded that her royal husband close the theaters. "Do not Play-Poets and common Actors (the Devil's chiefest Factors) rake hell and earth itself," he asked, "so they may pollute the Theater with all hideous obscenities, with all the detestable matchless iniquities, which hitherto men or Devils have either actually perpetrated or fabulously divulged?" Prynne had his ears cropped for publishing this polemic, and the play-poets continued their pollution undisturbed for another decade. By the 1630's the London stage was certainly somewhat decadent. Dramatists provided their jaded audience with hectic spectacles of lust and debauchery. There is a corrosive brilliance to this Caroline drama quite different from the adolescent rampaging of Kyd and Marlowe in the 1580's and from the witty naughtiness of the Restoration stage after 1660. The Puritans quickly took their revenge. In 1642, as soon as they gained control of London, they closed the theaters, and they kept them closed for the eighteen years they remained in power.

When the London playhouses reopened after the return of Charles II in 1660, the theater was a strictly upper-class form of entertainment. Restoration drama was more sophisticated, more libertine, and more limited than

Elizabethan drama had ever been. Actresses now assumed the female roles, and the plays were staged within a proscenium arch, with elaborate scenery, stage machinery, and artificial lighting. But the public theater was no longer a roaring business. An average of ten new plays a year appeared on the London stage between 1660 and 1700, as against a hundred a year between 1580 and 1640. Although the Restoration playhouses were small, the audience was not large enough to support two theaters simultaneously. Charles II was an ardent playgoer, and he honored Nell Gwyn, the most popular actress of the day, by taking her as his mistress. Great aristocrats such as the second duke of Buckingham amused themselves by writing plays. The best Restoration playwrights—Etherege, Wycherley, Congreve, Vanbrugh, and Farquhar—wrote their plays when they were very young men and quickly retired from the stage. John Dryden (1631–1700) produced a series of stately heroic dramas, but the Restoration stage is best remembered for its witty, indecent comedies of manners, which perfectly mirrored the cynical, farcical temper of the late seventeenth-century English aristocracy.

Spain

The Spanish theater enjoyed its *siglo de oro*, or golden age, during exactly *those years*—1580 to 1640—when the Elizabethan public stage was flourishing. As in England, medieval Spanish drama had consisted chiefly of religious plays (*autos sacramentales*), performed by the various guilds in each Spanish town to celebrate the feast of Corpus Christi. There was also a sixteenth-century humanist drama of pastoral plays performed in noble households. The first professional theaters, which opened in Madrid and Seville in the 1570's, were operated by acting companies very similar to those in England, though the plays they put on have a much different literary character from the Elizabethan drama. When the professional theaters first opened, they produced plays composed by the great novelist Cervantes, among others, modeled on Seneca and Plautus. But the Spanish public, like the English, wanted something more romantic and entertaining. Lope de Vega began writing for the Spanish stage in the 1580's, and soon established a wildly successful formula which all the other Spanish playwrights imitated.

The Spanish *comedia*, or play, was divided into three acts, interspersed with vaudeville skits, ballads, and dances, making the total effect much more of a variety show than in England, where the plays were performed straight through without any interludes or intermissions. One great advantage the Spanish theater had over the Elizabethan was that women were allowed to act in the *comedias*, as well as dance the voluptuous *zarabanda* between acts. In place of the Elizabethans' ornate blank verse, Spanish playwrights used a medley of quickstep verse forms to give their *comedias* a spontaneous and racy stamp. The *comedia* was something like a modern television script, punctuated by commercials. Its prime purpose was to show off the actors, its appeal was immediate and obvious, and like a television script, a *comedia* was seldom repeated more than a few times. Hence the Spanish theater needed an even larger supply of new plays than the Elizabethan theater. Not surprisingly, in Spain playwrights were paid relatively less than in England, and actors relatively more. There are no towering literary masterpieces among the thousands of Spanish *comedias*, though a very high percentage of those surviving have beauty and interest. The range of subject matter is immense: comedy, tragedy, history, mythology, court life, city life, peasant life, saints' lives. Romantic love is the pervasive theme, and contemporary Spain is the characteristic setting. The Spanish drama is introverted without being introspective. Even more ardently than the Elizabethan dramatists, Lope de Vega and his fellows uncritically extol their Spanish way of life.

The whole society became play-mad. Madrid was the center of theatrical activity, but being a much smaller city than London, could only support two *corrales*, or public playhouses. However, every big town had its *corral*, even Mexico City in distant America, where touring companies introduced the latest Spanish *comedias*. Bands of strolling players performed in innyards and farmyards throughout the Iberian peninsula. Some of their escapades in the remote villages read like scenes out of *Don Quixote*. When one fly-by-night troupe was playing *Lazarus*, the director, who took the part of Christ, called "Arise, Lazarus!" several times, but nothing happened. The actor playing Lazarus had managed to sneak out of his sepulcher and run away. The director was furious because the vanished actor had stolen his costume, but the peasant audience was well satisfied, believing that Lazarus had miraculously ascended to heaven. In Madrid, the customers were much harder to please. The audience there was as variegated as in London. Philip II did nothing to encourage the popular drama, and many clergymen disapproved, but everyone else from high to low crowded into the two public theaters, which were open arenas similar in design to the Globe. If the playgoers liked the performance, they shouted *"Victor! Victor!"* If they disliked it, they whistled derisively, and the women who sat in the *cazuela* ("stewing pan") pelted the actors with fruit. Beginning playwrights were advised to write *comedias* treating saints' lives, which the audience would not hiss out of respect for the saint. Religious themes were much more conspicuous in the Spanish popular drama than in the English. The reason is obvious: the whole population was unitedly Catholic, devoted to the saints, receptive to miracles, and accustomed to seeing representations of sacred stories in the churches. The traditional *autos sacramentales*, staged at the feast of Corpus Christi, achieved their greatest magnificence and popularity in the seventeenth century. The *autos* were now written by the major dramatists, such as Lope de Vega, and produced by professional actors rather than by the amateur guilds.

Lope de Vega (1562–1635) was the Spaniards' answer to William Shakespeare. He had the same middle-class background, a better formal education, and a far more explosive temperament. He conducted a long series of passionate love affairs, generally with married women, and took up the last of these mistresses after he had become a priest. Lope de Vega was a fantastically prolific writer. In less than fifty years he turned out 1,500 *comedias*, of which nearly five hundred still survive! In his sixties he was writing two plays a week. Lope enjoyed immense celebrity and earned a fortune from his plays, but he valued them much less highly than his now-forgotten epics. "If anyone should cavil about my *comedias*," he once wrote, "and think that I wrote them for fame, undeceive him and tell him that I wrote them for money." Unlike Shakespeare, however, Lope de Vega did publish a large number of his plays. The fact that most of them follow a single pattern helps explain how he was able to turn them out so quickly. The first act introduces the action, the second act scrambles it, and the third act builds up to the denouement, delayed as long as possible, for once the audience guessed it, they walked out! Lope de Vega's *Discovery of the New World by Christopher Columbus* exemplifies his dramatic technique. In the first act of this play, Columbus secures the backing of Ferdinand and Isabella for his voyage —according to Lope, in 1492 he was looking for the New World, not a new route to Cathay. Since it was impossible to keep the audience guessing as to whether Columbus would find the New World, Lope brought his Spaniards to the West Indies early in the second act, and concentrated thereafter on their patronizing treatment of the childlike Indians. In the third-act climax, a demon inspires the Indians to kill some of the gold-crazy Spaniards and pull down their cross. Instantly a new cross miraculously rises and the stupefied savages are converted to Christ. Every scene and every speech in this drama had the authentic, trivial ring of true life. Other dramatists might feel impelled to explore the obvious moral issues raised by this story; Lope de Vega was content to amuse his audience with a sparkling, colorful romance.

By the 1630's the Spanish stage was declining, for several reasons. No playwright after Lope de Vega had his range and universal appeal. The collapsing Spanish economy shrank box-office receipts. The clergy, like the Puritans in England, criticized the immorality of actors and actresses with mounting indignation and pressed the government to close the theaters. During the reign of Philip IV (1621–1665), such clerical agitation had small effect, for this dissolute monarch—the patron of Velázquez—was an ardent lover of plays and of actresses. Philip IV turned the Spanish drama from a popular art form into a royal hobby. He built a palace theater and spent so lavishly on court productions that the leading acting companies came to depend on his patronage. The king would disrupt public performances in the Madrid theaters by commanding certain actors and actresses to come immediately to the palace to rehearse for royal performances!

The changing character of the theater is reflected in the plays of Pedro

Calderón (1600–1681), the chief Spanish dramatist after Lope de Vega. Whereas Lope wrote for the people, Calderón wrote for the court. In his youth, up to 1640, Calderón wrote comedies about lovesick grandees in pursuit of their mistresses and tragedies about jealous grandees in pursuit of their wives' lovers. His plays are more subtle and complex than Lope's, but less variegated. Everything hinges on the aristocratic code of honor, which the proud Spaniards cultivated as a substitute for their lost political power and prestige. Calderón clearly approves of the way his gentlemen fight duels at the twitch of an eyebrow and murder their adoring wives on the rumor of infidelity. During the crisis of the 1640's, with Catalonia and Portugal both in revolt, all theatrical activity ceased temporarily. Calderón himself took holy orders, and for the last thirty years of his life wrote only *autos sacramentales* and operatic court masques. He left no successors. By the close of the century, the professional theater in Spain was dying; it was in worse plight than in England, where the court circle kept the London stage alive.

France

In France, the great theatrical age began about 1630, just as it was drawing to a close in England and Spain. The first French professional acting companies had begun operating in the late sixteenth century, but they put on crude shows for uncultivated audiences and did better in the provinces than in Paris. In these early years, no Frenchman remotely comparable to Marlowe, Shakespeare, or Lope de Vega wrote for the stage. The political turmoil during the sixteenth-century wars of religion and again during Marie de Medici's regency certainly delayed the development of the French public theater. Finally, Richelieu's administration gave France the self-confident stability which England and Spain had achieved fifty years earlier. In 1629 two auspicious events occurred: an accomplished troupe of actors established fixed residence in a Paris theater, and an immensely talented dramatist, Pierre Corneille, produced his first play. When the French theater began to flourish in the 1630's under Richelieu's patronage, it provided entertainment for the elite, like the English theater of the same period, patronized by Charles I, and the Spanish theater patronized by Philip IV. The French drama remained closely tied to the royal court throughout its period of greatness, 1630–1680. Corneille, Racine, and Molière never wrote for the kind of huge and diversified audience which had thronged to the Elizabethan and Spanish playhouses at the turn of the century. Their audience was sophisticated but limited. In seventeenth-century Paris there were never more than three theaters, playing three evenings a week. Playwrights and actors could not make ends meet without royal patronage. Richelieu opened the finest theater in Paris, pensioned dramatists, and subsidized actors. Mazarin was less generous, but Louis XIV in his youth was extremely fond of the theater, and his support kept afloat five acting companies: three

French, one Italian, and one Spanish. Molière's company, for example, was not only subsidized by Louis XIV, but given the use of a royal theater. In addition, Molière held a court appointment as the king's bedmaker. Many of his plays were commissioned by the king for production at Versailles. Louis also pensioned Racine, without quite appreciating what he was paying for. The royal pension list for 1664 includes the following entries:[3]

To the Sieur Racine, a French poet	40 louis d'or
To the Sieur Chapelain, the greatest French poet who ever lived	150 louis d'or

In the drama, as in art and literature, the Bourbon monarchy wished to cultivate a pure and dignified classical style. Court patronage helped to steer seventeenth-century French playwrights away from the exuberant romanticism of the Elizabethan and Spanish stage. In the time of Richelieu, French critics adopted the Aristotelian rules for dramatic composition. Seventeenth-century French playwrights generally observed the three unities of time, place, and action, and avoided Shakespeare's rambling plots and his mixture of high tragedy and low comedy. The spectator is spared the sight of murders, duels, and similar violent acts which are instead decorously reported by messengers. This classical influence is particularly evident in seventeenth-century French tragic drama, whose themes and plots are largely derived from Greek and Roman sources. French tragedies tend to be more literary and less stageworthy than the romantic tragedies of Elizabethan England and Habsburg Spain. But the French neoclassical tragedians were not blind copyists. They always reworked ancient history and myth to suit seventeenth-century taste, expanding the love interest and expunging the pagan religious element. Racine's Greek heroines and Corneille's Roman heroes are always recognizably ladies and gentlemen of the Bourbon court.

Pierre Corneille (1606–1684), the first great French dramatist, wrote a number of effective comedies but is best remembered as a neoclassical tragedian. In 1636 his *Cid* caused a sensation. Corneille's mastery of dramatic verse, his fiery lyricism, his characterization and plot structure, thrilled and shocked his audience as Marlowe's *Tamburlaine* had hit the Elizabethans, only more so, for *Le Cid* is a much finer play. It tells a tale of star-crossed lovers, kept from each other by a feud between their families. When the boy kills the girl's father, her love conquers her sense of filial honor, and she agrees to marry him. This ending scandalized the moralists, and the resulting furor had a somewhat unhappy effect on Corneille. In his subsequent plays he tried to please the critics with safer themes, extolling family honor, patriotism, monarchy, and Christianity. His favorite setting

[3]W. H. Lewis, *The Splendid Century: Life in the France of Louis XIV* (New York, 1953), pp. 23–24.

Molière.
Painting by Coypel.

was imperial Rome, which gave him abundant opportunity to moralize on the virtues of benevolent despotism. Corneille never recaptured the verve, passion, and warmth of *Le Cid*. By the 1660's he had woefully lost his touch, and in a pitiful effort to outdo his young rival, Racine, he produced in his late years a series of grotesquely contrived melodramas.

Jean Baptiste Racine (1639–1699) was a poet of surer taste and control than Corneille, and he perfected the French neoclassical tragic style. At the age of four Racine was sent to school at the Jansenist stronghold of Port-Royal, and he emerged with an austere piety akin to Pascal's, and a deep love of the classics. He quickly established his reputation at court with a play about Alexander the Great, tactfully dedicated to Louis XIV. His next play, *Andromaque* (1667), was a great success. It told the story of Hector's widow after the fall of Troy, forced to choose between marrying her Greek captor and seeing him kill her child; in other words, here once again was Corneille's theme of love versus honor—in a presentation graced by an exquisitely euphonious and precise verse style. In later plays, Racine reworked the tragic themes of his favorite Greek poets. *Phèdre*, perhaps his best play, follows Euripides' *Hippolytus* so closely that some scenes read like translations from the Greek. Suddenly, at age thirty-seven, Racine retired from the secular stage. His last two plays are biblical dramas designed for private performance by schoolgirls, in reversion to the early sixteenth-century amateur theatrical tradition.

The great comic master of the seventeenth-century French stage was of course Molière (1622–1673), whose real name was Jean Baptiste Poquelin. His father, a prosperous Paris furniture maker, sent the boy to a Jesuit school for the sort of classical education which Descartes, Calderón, Corneille, and thousands of other Jesuit pupils had received. Young Poquelin was determined to be an actor, and he endured a strenuous apprenticeship to prove himself. In 1643, taking the stage name of Molière, he helped to organize a Paris troupe, which rapidly went bankrupt. Molière and his companions toured the provinces for twelve years before they felt ready to attempt another assault on the capital. While touring, Molière wrote his first plays. In 1658 his troupe reappeared in Paris, performed successfully before the young king, and received the use of a theater in the Louvre palace. During the remaining fifteen years of his life, Molière wrote and produced a brilliant constellation of farces, parodies, and satires for his company. He generally took the lead role of valet or comic marquis himself, for Molière was a wonderfully accomplished comic actor. He made the Paris bourgeoisie and the Versailles aristocracy laugh at themselves. He mocked bourgeois greed in *The Miser,* and social climbing in *The Bourgeois Gentleman.* He mocked the rottenness of court society in *The Misanthrope,* and the hypocrisy of canting clerical bigots in *Tartuffe.* He mocked medical quackery in *The Imaginary Invalid,* and overly educated women in *The Female Savants.* Unlike Corneille and Racine, Molière was a total man of the theater. His plays read well, but they act better, and they remain more vibrantly alive than any other seventeenth-century plays except Shakespeare's. Molière's humor is realistic and hard-hitting, like Ben Jonson's but more universal and humane. His style is witty and urbane, like that of English Restoration comedy, but less smutty and trivial. Naturally he stepped on many toes. The clergy were so incensed by *Tartuffe* that the play was banned for five years, and only the king's patronage shielded Molière from heavier punishment. No doubt Molière was lucky that he wrote *Tartuffe* before Louis XIV had become pious and persecuting. No doubt he would have been silenced fast enough had he ventured to mock Bourbon absolutism or ask his royal patron to laugh at himself. Nevertheless, it remains ironic that the best social satire of the century was sponsored by the most complacent and authoritarian monarch in Europe.

With Molière's death, Racine's retirement, and Louis XIV's growing preoccupation with international war, the great age of the French theater drew to a close. To compare the art of Molière and Racine with that of Lope de Vega and Shakespeare is to see once again the bewildering diversity of

European culture in the early modern period. Artists and intellectuals lived in closer proximity than ever before, yet the international cultural community established during the Middle Ages and the Renaissance had been shattered. Scientists, to be sure, cooperated with unprecedented fruitfulness, sharing discoveries and building on one another's experiments and theories. Painters, sculptors, and architects congregated in Italy and in a few of the large northern cities for their training and roved over Europe in search of commissions. This helps explain the spread of the Baroque style from Italy to Spain, Belgium, and Austria. But the Baroque was not all-conquering. In philosophy, as in theology, there was no consensus, scarcely even a dialogue. The art and thought of the seventeenth century has a deeply fragmented quality which reflects the loss of traditional religious unity and the rise of autonomous sovereign states. Catholics and Protestants evolved distinctly different responses to art. Literature, always the most chauvinistic art form, acquired a self-consciously national style in each vernacular language. At the close of the century, sophisticated persons everywhere wanted to copy French taste, but this attitude was symptomatic of the coming era, the Enlightenment. The seventeenth century was intellectually disorderly, contentious, intolerant. Audiences were easily unsettled by shocking ideas. Iconoclasts like Galileo and Spinoza were muzzled. Even poets like Milton and Molière risked persecution for their polemical art. Yet no censor or inquisitor could suppress the general intellectual revolt against authority, the richest legacy of the age.

Part III

KINGS AND PHILOSOPHERS
1689–1789

Introduction

On February 13, 1689, some two weeks after it had declared the throne vacant because King James II "endeavored to subvert the constitution of the kingdom" and "abdicated the government," the Convention Parliament invited William and Mary to accept the crown along with the parliamentary version of the constitution enshrined in the Declaration of Right, and thereby consummated England's Glorious Revolution. On June 17, 1789, some six weeks after it had demanded common convocation with the noble and clerical orders, the Third Estate unilaterally transformed itself into the National Assembly, and three days later it formally voted its intention of writing a constitution, thereby initiating the French Revolution. In terms of gross results, the intervening one hundred years would seem a long time for constitutional government to have taken to cross the twenty miles of channel between Britain and the Continent. And since, in these terms, the result only marked a stage in the process of homogenizing Europe politically—a process that began before and would continue after—the eighteenth century would appear not only laggard but unremarkable in its political development.

And yet it was a most remarkable age politically. Even if we look more carefully only at its gross political results we must grant that the growth of the movement for constitutional government from an insular to a general and exportable system was no mere quantitative extension but a crucial stage in the development of modern politics. We shall find, moreover, that the manner of this growth during the eighteenth century will help us to define its political effects, for the way it happened perpetuated more of the achievements of political absolutism than one would suspect from a mere registration of results. And if we look beyond the slow evolution of states in their political orbits, we see an eighteenth-century European society in full movement, spawning the economic connections, the social attitudes, and above all the ideas that met, dissolved, and recombined in associations and conflicts dramatic in themselves, contributory to political change, and prodigal with the seeds of modernity. It is, indeed, the engagement of the stable institutional structure, fixed especially in the political order, with the unsettling dynamism of the society, crystallized especially in its intellectual activity, that gives the authentic flavor of the age. From the running interaction between the political institutions that channeled the social movement and the "enlightened" ideas that challenged the institutions comes the essential outline of eighteenth-century culture. From the activities of rulers and writers come the characteristic strands of the history that filled it.

There are many valid ways of approaching the general history of an age. Historians who use a comprehensive chronological approach divide the age into periods and compose as full a picture as they can of men's assorted activities in each period. Historians who use a comprehensive functional approach analyze successively all the institutions or fields of human activity that make up the structure of the age, admitting chronological events only to show the effects or the internal development of these institutions and fields. The approach in this book will not utilize either of these familiar formats, for our purpose is not to compose a comprehensive portrait or to make a comprehensive analysis, but rather to follow the shifting course of the different institutions and fields of activity that men at different stages of the age found most important, and thus to trace the central process that both reflected and molded the character of the age. Since this process consisted in the production of a political stability that then nurtured a social and intellectual movement, we shall first focus on the formation of the state system that was in fact the cynosure of early eighteenth-century activity and then shift, along with our historical subjects, to the social and intellectual activities that were the main outlets of cultural energy during the second half of the century. We shall conclude, as the century did, with the series of confrontations, first between kings and philosophers and then between kings and societies, that ended the long status-bound epoch of European history.

CHAPTER 12

The Nature of Kingship

IT WAS AN age of kings. Never before had so much effective power accompanied the prestige of kingship and never again would this power prevail with so little resistance as in the half century that spanned the last years of the seventeenth century and the first part of the eighteenth century. For Louis XIV, that paragon of monarchs, to be a king was a "delightful" profession, and the Continent was to be crowded with colleagues who obviously enjoyed it almost as much as he. The unbridled gusto of their reigns has made Peter the Great and Charles XII the individual heroes of Russian and Swedish history. The Electors Frederick August of Saxony and Frederick III of Brandenburg were sufficiently envious of the royal title to intrigue earnestly for the acquisition of one, the Saxon ruler by converting to Catholicism and getting himself elected to the vacant Polish throne (1697) and the Hohenzollern by arranging for the recognition of his self-announced elevation from duke to king in Prussia (1701). Less spectacular but more far-reaching in their effects were the achievements of the kings Charles XI, Frederick William I, and Charles VI, in establishing bases of unified authority in Sweden, Prussia, and the Habsburg dominions respectively. And if the Glorious Revolution of 1688 had frustrated what seemed like the Stuart attempt to institute a continental type of monarchy in England, still at the start of our period William of Orange, as the English King William III, did take with him, from the covert military dictatorship which he had exercised in the Netherlands as their general *stadholder* since 1672, the jealous care for royal prerogative that helped to moderate the constitutional results of the revolution.

The vogue of kingship meant something very definite in the history of Europe. In its most general meaning, to be sure, it was simply part of that respect for order that had dominated European political life since the early

Middle Ages and that persuaded men to accept a network of undisputed authorities by the end of the seventeenth century. If we think of monarchy in its broadest sense as government by a single ruler, whatever his title, then we may well say that, with a few minor exceptions of which the Swiss cantons were the most important, Europe as a whole was organized into monarchies by 1700. But if this fact testifies to the prevalence of political authority in general, the particular emergence of kings out of the welter of monarchs testifies to the precise kind of political authority that was becoming prevalent. The practical conditions of government and the attitudes of men now converged to establish an actual hierarchy among the monarchs, and the rise of the kings to the top of the pyramid illuminated the conditions and the attitudes that were at work.

Grand dukes, dukes, counts, and Electors could exercise the same kind of supreme or even absolute dominion over their subjects as the kings over theirs, but the days were long gone since a Duke Henry of Rohan (1579–1638) could wage a regular war against and conclude a peace with a king of France, or when a duke of Bavaria (Maximilian I, 1573–1651) could be a preeminent power in Germany, or when an Albrecht von Wallenstein (1583–1634) would get himself invested as duke of Friedland, the better to play an independent role in a war between the great powers. Even more impressive in underlining the distinctive role of kingship was the relatively sad plight of emperors in this age of kings. The once-powerful Ottoman Empire entered now into the long period of decline which later led to its personification as the Sick Man of Europe: the treaties of Karlowitz (1699) and Passarowitz (1718) affirmed the military defeats that marked the definitive end of the centuries-old Turkish threat to Europe, and the sultans responsible for them were ultimately deposed. The Holy Roman Empire, which Voltaire was tellingly to characterize as neither holy nor Roman nor an empire, remained the nominal political organization of the 360-odd principalities that comprised the German nation. It was, indeed, by now more usually referred to simply as the German Empire (as it will henceforward be called here), but it added little beyond the title to the Habsburgs who were usually elected its Emperors. It was precisely during our period, indeed, during the reign of Charles VI, that the Habsburgs began deliberately to choose southeastern expansion on the basis of their real ducal and royal powers in Austria, Bohemia, and Hungary over central European hegemony on the basis of their imperial function in Germany.

Only Russia, where Peter confirmed the imperial implications of the traditional title, Tsar ("Caesar"), when he proclaimed himself Imperator (1721), seemed to escape the derogation of empires. But even here, after Peter's death in 1725, the strain of imperial expansion developed flaws in

the structure of state and society that made the position of tsar (or tsarina) unstable in a way that European kingship no longer was.

The advantage which the conditions of the time gave to kings over both
dukes and emperors was more than a matter of preferred nomenclature. In
the theoretical terms of traditional public law, kings ranked above dukes
and below the emperor. It was precisely this intermediate position, paradoxically enough, which established the preeminence of kings in the first
half of the eighteenth century, for it was the intermediate region, larger
than a city, city-state, county, province, or duchy, smaller than the multi-
nationed span of an empire, and usually identified with the "realm" of a
king, that now proved itself to be the most effective unit for the exercise of
political power abroad and the organization of social energies at home.

Internationally, the hallmark of the period was the ascendance of a
plural system of great powers which would dominate the destiny of
Europe until the Second World War of the twentieth century. This
system was a practical response to a series of real challenges. It evolved
as the fittest means of repelling the claims or aggressions of *de jure*
empires like the German and the Ottoman and of aspirants to *de facto*
empires like sixteenth-century Spain and seventeenth-century France. Just
as a system of independent realms became superior to a hegemonical
empire, so the powers which composed this system began now clearly to
dominate the several city-states and smaller principalities whose competitive position until recently had rivaled their own. England, France, Austria, Prussia, and Russia—this was the pentarchy whose relations were to
determine the issue of war and peace in Europe for two centuries, and it
was in the age of kings that it appeared as an authoritative institution on
the international scene. The countries whose political decline it signified
included, to be sure, kingdoms like Spain, Sweden, and Poland as well as
the republican Netherlands and the Electorate of Bavaria, but whatever
the titles of the excluded sovereigns the essential fact was that inclusion
within the circle of great powers henceforward required the possession of
physical and human resources great enough, and the government over
them unified enough, to be fit for a king.

Domestically, the hallmark of the period was the development of the
king's realm from a set of legal claims to an actual district of administration and of the king's government from a superior magistracy to a supreme
authority. At different times in different countries over the previous two
centuries, kings, like sovereigns by any other name, had already succeeded
in abridging the autonomy of such constituted authorities and corporations as governors, syndics, bailiffs, assemblies, churches, aristocracies, and
municipalities, and in asserting, by fair means and foul, a lawful dominion
over them. The individual constituted authorities—"subordinate magis-

trates" in customary legal parlance—were either successors of earlier royal agents who had settled down into local autonomy or the heads of self-administering corporations who exercised public functions. The corporations themselves remained, at the end of the seventeenth century, closer to what they had been in the Middle Ages than to what we now recognize by the term. Each corporation was still a combined social and political association which reflected in its organization the order of rank of a hierarchical society and in its function the interpenetration of private and public services. Each still was sanctioned by a legal charter which authorized it to exercise a monopoly of its assigned function in the community of its assigned region and which guaranteed both its right of governing its own members and its privilege of policing the community in the administration of its function. The most characteristic of the seventeenth-century corporations were the "estates," which referred to both the organized ranks of the society at large and the political organization of representative bodies ("parliaments" or "diets") by social rank; but villages, guilds, churches, and nobility (except in Russia and England, where for different historical reasons nobility as a social corps had no legal standing) equally exemplified the combination of internal hierarchy, self-governing association, and public-service administration which defined the pre-nineteenth-century corporation. At the turn of the eighteenth century most Europeans were still members of such corporations, high and low, but the tendencies were already at work which were limiting both their social monopoly and their administrative rights. As their hierarchical structure hardened into oligarchic exclusiveness the excluded men turned to individual enterprise, and whether as capitalists or day laborers increased the numbers of the unincorporated. As the political and economic demands upon public administration increased, the more mobile and open-minded response of the royal bureaucracies led to the community's acceptance of the king's sovereignty both over the members and over the functions of the corporations.

But the actual administration of this legal power had traditionally been left in the hands of the intermediate authorities and corporations except for those particular matters such as war, diplomacy, high justice, and finance, in which the sovereign had an urgent and continuous interest. As long as the public domain was shared out in this fashion, the difference between kings and other authorities was, in fact if not in law, a difference of degree rather than of kind. Toward the end of the seventeenth century, however, this system of indirect rule was increasingly overlaid by agencies of direct government responsive to the will of the sovereign. The realm of the sovereign became the effective unit for the exercise of political power, claiming jurisdiction over public business of all kinds and administering a growing share of it. The sovereign now became an authority different in kind from all others, and since this development pointed unmistakably to a single center of overall responsibility, it redounded to the advantage of kingship over the plurality of intermediate aristocracies and corporations. The key fields for the transition from particular regalian to general sovereign powers were justice and economics, for these were the activities in which the royal bureaucracies now established direct contact with the mass of the subjects and through which the state became a real force. The traditional authorities in these fields either became themselves instruments of the king's government or witnessed the appearance of new supervisory provincial and local organs that were such instruments.

Although the establishment of governmental agencies and policies that looked to the realm as a whole, and the parallel reorganization of myriad local and provincial communities into larger polities of citizens who looked to the regional state as the primary source of benefits and obligations, were the novel elements in the exaltation of kingship around the turn of the eighteenth century, they were not the only domestic factors in the veneration of kings. Historical changes rarely come in wholesale lots, and in this situation too men clung to accustomed practices and attitudes not simply out of nostalgia or inertia but because there was still a vital need for them. The bureaucratic service state that was coming into its own did not, after all, require a king at its head. That kings, with the regional scope of their legal authority and the practical convenience of their mediating position above competing social groups, should have been more appropriate to this function than more circumscribed nobles and oligarchs is clear, but other, more traditional functions explain why the new needs did not bypass kings as well. These functions were rooted in the psychology of early-eighteenth-century Europeans, in the structure of their society, and in necessary conditions of administration.

However real the activities of its organs, the state as such was an abstraction of which most Europeans were barely aware. Of the three elements that constitute a state—territory, people, and government—territories shifted with the fortunes of wars and dynasties, the people usually had no visible organs of direct participation in the state, and the government was made up of a congeries of authorities undertaking a variety of activities which added up to no visible system. For a minority of intellectuals, trained by philosophy to see abstractions as real things and by legal studies to see a rational order behind the apparent confusion of current practices, the state was the tissue of relationships that actually existed. Another small group, composed of politicians and administrators in the central governments, recognized the reality of the state as a whole because they had increasingly to deal with it in practice. The great majority of men, however, accustomed to recognize reality only in what was visible, tangible, or

incarnate, dimly sensed the effects of this new institution which was providing security and services from afar, but could identify it only through its
incorporation in the royal person who led and symbolized it. Thus the
divine right of kings, which had been replaced among the vanguard of
intellectuals by a secularized natural-law theory of sovereignty, remained
well into the eighteenth century at the root of the popular attitude toward
monarchs. The idea of divine right, in its application to *kingship*, went

EUROPE IN 1689

——— Boundary of the German Empire

Spanish Habsburg territory

Austrian Habsburg territory

DEN

SEA

PRUSSIA

RUSSIA

Warsaw

POLAND

Vistula R.

Kiev

Dnieper R.

Volga R.

PODOLIA

Dniester R.

TRANSYLVANIA

MOLDAVIA

GARY

Zenta

Karlowitz

WALLACHIA

BLACK SEA

Belgrade

OTTOMAN

EMPIRE

0   500 miles

MOREA

VENICE

back to the Middle Ages; in this sense it signified the sacred origination of the royal office, or the king's "body politic." The divine right of *kings*, however, was a more modern product, developing during the sixteenth and seventeenth centuries to extend the sanctity of the king's "body politic" into his "natural body." This extension was a response both to the psychological need for a visible symbol of the ever more palpable activities of the invisible state ("body politic") and to the political need for a distinctive blessing upon kings vis-à-vis the more indiscriminate anointment of any officeholder in the hierarchy of public authorities. Through the dynasty, personal heredity became the natural counterpart of the permanence of the state and the person of the king the embodiment of the state itself.

There were good social as well as psychological reasons for the particular exaltation of kings in the early eighteenth century. The growth of the state, with its exercise of power from one central agency or set of agencies upon all subjects alike, inevitably extended the fields where traditional social distinctions were irrelevant. Economically, this meant the official encouragement of the commerce and industry run by commoners at least as much as of the agriculture dominated by aristocrats. Legally, it implied a community of subjects equal in their common subjection to the laws of the state. Administratively, it entailed the construction of a bureaucratic apparatus which required a technical training and a standard of practical efficiency transcending class origins. In all these ways the seventeenth century had witnessed an improvement in the fortunes of the middling sectors of society in contrast with the nobility. But, not for the first time in history and not for the last, what appeared to be the linear course of an apparently simple progressive development came a cropper during the early eighteenth century. Not that the bourgeoisie either declined or diminished. Powered by the dramatic expansion of overseas trade and by the first stage of the modern population explosion that continues to this day, the European economic growth of the eighteenth century infused wealth, leisure, and culture into an ever-widening circle of enterprising burghers. Nor was the centralizing process of state making reversed. The claims and effective force of bureaucracies continued to increase, and with them the opportunities for trained and talented commoners on the way up.

What was reversed was the precipitous descent of the aristocracy, a descent that had accompanied, and that had seemed a necessary counterpart to the rise of the bourgeoisie and the emergence of national sovereigns during the sixteenth and seventeenth centuries. In the eighteenth century, surprisingly, aristocracies—or at least important parts of them— were resurgent. Appreciating the principle of what would later become a proverbial prescription for men to join what they could not beat, nobles in the several countries of Europe picked themselves up and began to appropriate commanding positions in the governmental structures of the new states and even in the network of commercial relations. The Whig oligarchy that ruled Britain without serious challenge between the accession of the Hanoverian dynasty in 1714 and George III's assertion of royal influence after 1760 represented a landowning aristocracy that was sponsoring a capitalized and scientific agriculture in response to demands of the market and that had economic ties with merchants and bankers of the

City. The French peers, refueled by Louis XIV's calculated infusion of subsidies, made a serious bid to refashion the monarchy in their own image after the death of the Sun King in 1715, and when this attempt failed, a more economically progressive and modern-minded judicial and administrative aristocracy (*noblesse de robe* and *noblesse d'office*) rose to continue the counteroffensive on behalf of the privileged. In Russia various sections of the military and landed nobility dictated the succession to the throne—in general they preferred tsarinas in the expectation that they would behave consistently as members of the "weaker sex"— and dominated the social policy of the government from the death of Peter the Great in 1725 through the accession of Catherine the Great in 1762. The long period from 1718 to 1772 that the Swedes euphemistically called their "era of liberty" was actually an age of aristocratic sovereignty, exercised constitutionally in a nominal monarchy through the nobles' oligarchic control over both the *Riksdag*, or parliament, and the bureaucracy. The Dutch gave the same high-flown label to the period from 1702 to 1747, when the small but influential class of Regents, an oligarchy comprised of urban patricians, resumed its sway after the death of William III and kept the office of *stadholder* vacant. The seven provinces that made up the Dutch "Republic" were, in this respect, expanded versions of the independent city-states in Europe. Concentrated mainly in Switzerland and Germany, they too were stabilized during the first half of the eighteenth century under the rule of exclusive patrician oligarchies.

Only in Spain—an early achiever of state building—and in Austria and Prussia—two relative latecomers to the field—did the aristocracy register no visible resurgence, but the reason was the lack of need or occasion rather than of will or capacity. With Philip V (ruled 1700–1746), the first of the Bourbon line, the attempt was indeed made to rejuvenate the Spanish monarchy through bureaucratic centralization on the French model, but Philip's own political lethargy and the persistence of the Spanish predilection for government by committee throughout the administrative system enabled the nobility to carve their niches of influence in and around the reformed bureaucracy. Austria's Charles VI did obtain the legal recognition of the variegated Habsburg dominions as a single monarchy, but the Pragmatic Sanction of 1720, which secured an indivisible succession, was finally enacted only with the approval of the sundry aristocratically dominated estates of his realms, and their power sufficed to prevent the establishment of any real institutional unity on the basis of it during his reign. When, under the pressure of military defeat, his daughter, Queen Maria Theresa (ruled 1740–1780), did create unified institutions extending throughout Austria, she had to operate through an ambiguous policy of "gentle violence" which spared both the organizations and the feelings of the different kinds of aristocrats in the various Habsburg territories. The Prussian aristocracy, finally, could offer only passive resistance to the implacable mopping-up operation conducted by Frederick William I against the remnants of their political autonomy, but despite the hostility and grim satisfaction he expressed in his statement: "I am destroying the authority of the *Junkers*," Frederick William never even attempted to divest the *Junkers* or any other section of the Prussian aristocracy either of their social privileges in the army and on their estates or of their monopoly in the exercise of the state's administrative and judicial power over the local countryside. Thence they could be returned by Frederick the Great after 1740 to their wonted posts in the upper echelons of the government.

The aristocracies' new lease on life for the eighteenth century was thus predicated upon the modernization of their premises, and they thereby shifted the arena of social conflict from outside to inside the structure of the state. Where they had formerly defended their privileged rights to land-ownership, manorial lordship, judicial immunities, and tax exemptions by denying the jurisdiction of the central governments, they now defended these privileges by occupying and controlling the governmental agencies which exercised the jurisdiction. This aristocratic penetration of the state ran counter to the standards of general law, equal citizenship, and uniform administration which had served and continued to serve bureaucrats as guides in extending the scope of central government. But the hierarchical tendency was no mere atavism. Despite the obvious and reciprocal hostility between it and the leveling tendency with which it shared the state, the coexistence of the two tendencies, however mismatched in logic, was a faithful response to a fundamental social demand of the age. European society required, for the military security of its inhabitants, for the direction and subsidization of its economy, and for the prevention of religious turbulence and popular disorder, the imposition of unified control over a larger area and more people than the contemporary instruments of government could manage. Hence the employment of the traditional social and corporate hierarchies by the government as extensions of the governing arm into the mass of inhabitants. All people were subject, but some were more subject than others.

The necessity both for a social caste and for a bureaucracy which undermined the social caste redounded to the advantage of the kings. For effective political operation an authority was required which was recognized by bureaucrats and aristocrats alike as their representative in the adjudication of rival claims and in the allotment of appropriate powers. This authority could only be the king, for only the king combined in himself a social position as the highest-ranking noble with a political position as the supreme magistrate of the community. For centuries the notion of kingship had joined the idea of a natural man who was preeminent among aristocrats with that of a political man who symbolized the unity of the entire civil society, and the development of the aristocracy as well as the growth of bureaucracy in the late seventeenth century made this two-headed monarch indispensable.

And if the king was necessary to this anomalous mixture of hierarchy and equality in early-eighteenth-century society, he had an interest in perpetuating the anomaly, for it was equally necessary to him. The king's development of organs and policies to perform services needed for the security and welfare of the whole community was an obvious means of combating the dispersion of public power among the traditional corporations, but just as essential albeit not so obvious was the interest of the king in maintaining and even sustaining the privileged corporations—not simply for his administrative convenience but in their own social right. He needed the support of a hierarchy against the dangers of leveling as much as he needed the support of middle-class officials against the ambitions of the notables. The continuous threat and frequent outbreak of popular disorders through the seventeenth and eighteenth centuries were a constant reminder of how unreliable a basis of loyalty the appreciation of governmental services could be. The existence of a hierarchy which made the inequality of rights and functions an ultimate and unquestionable necessity of social organization accustomed men to accept the relationship of inferiors to superiors as a primary fact imbedded in the very nature of things. For kings, their position at the apex of the divinely constructed social ladder called for obedience even when the benefits of their government were not in evidence, and they never dreamed of destroying a support which linked their own preeminence with the general constitution of human society.

Thus peoples were related to their kings in two different ways, one primarily political and uniform, the other primarily social and pyramidal; and each of these relations in its own way supported the king and was in turn supported by him. But such a general characterization should not mislead. The development of kingship into this form may be clear to us, but it was not so clear to the men who developed it and lived under it. For this shape of the institution was being defined as a result of piecemeal practical necessities rather than of a deliberate program. It was no accident, then, that in the period from 1690 to 1748, between Locke's *Second Treatise on Civil Government* and Montesquieu's *Spirit of the Laws*, no important political theory emerged that commanded consensus: the mixture of institutions and principles that were going into the monarchical state was too new, too loose, and too attached to the particular circumstances of its origin for contemporaries to conceive it as a system. There were standard political theories for each of the ingredients, but their basic ideas stemmed from earlier periods.

We have already noted the divergence between the natural-law doctrine to which many of the intellectuals adhered and the divine-right ideas cherished by the populace. None of the great names associated with either theory belong to the period—not Grotius, Hobbes, or Locke for the former, nor James I, Filmer, or Bossuet for the latter—and they had no successors of like stature.

Contemporary political writers attempted to combine natural law with divine right or natural law with historical institutions, but emerged with works that were too special and occasional to command influence. Of the best-known thinkers which the period produced, neither Leibniz, nor Berkeley, nor Hume, nor Voltaire succeeded in concocting a coherent political philosophy. Those who did succeed in communicating some political ideas, on the other hand, had a limited effect in their time and fell into obscurity thereafter. Samples of this genre were Henry St. John, Viscount Bolingbroke (1678–1751), who covered his confusions of nature and history under the slogan of an English "patriotism"; Archbishop Fénelon (1651–1715), who recommended a mélange of royal absolutism, popular reforms, and the restoration of the French aristocratic constitution; Jean Jacques Burlamaqui (1694–1748), who put a bewildering amalgam of individual rights, sovereign authority, and corporate privilege into the deceptive format of a legal system; and Christian Thomasius (1655–1728), who tried to bring rationalism and German Pietism together in an unstable alliance of natural law and divine right.

The inchoate quality of political thinking during the first half of the eighteenth century not only reveals the primacy of practice over theory but hints at the primacy of circumstances over policies even within the area of practice. The historical pattern of the age confirms this. From 1688 until 1713 in western Europe and until 1721 in central and northern Europe, what was important—that is, of lasting effect—in public life was crystallized into a succession of dramatic events. Thereafter, until almost mid-century, what was important in public life was the creation of new institutions, *i.e.* new agencies for and ways of doing things, that set up changed conditions for later events. Events occurred too in this second quarter of the eighteenth century, to be sure, but they were relatively insignificant alongside the reorganization of public life which provided new routines for men's daily lives. The subdivision of the period 1688–1748 into this sequence of stirring events and stabilizing institutions indicates a significant characteristic of the period: from the circumstantial events of the first phase monarchs and ministers learned the lessons that they embodied in the institutions of the second; and from this sequence came the pattern and preeminence of kingship in Europe.

To see how this development worked as a process, we shall follow each stage in turn.

CHAPTER 13

The Kings at War, 1688-1721

DURING THE generation that separated Louis XIV's invasion of the Rhine Palatinate in 1688 from the Treaty of Nystad in 1721, the states that were evolving into the great powers of recent memory enjoyed but one brief year of peace (1699-1700). In the manner of the age, the number of belligerents was never constant, the motives even of allies were frequently obscure and local if not divergent, and the actual fighting was intermittent; but when the war aims and the battles are strained through the sieve of history, they separate out into two great conflicts which had fundamental effects upon the development of European society. There was a western war and an eastern war, and the future of Europe was determined by the unity within each and the connection between the two.

The war in the west was diffused through two stages—the War of the League of Augsburg from 1688 to 1697 and the War of the Spanish Succession from 1701 to 1713. Its continuity was further disturbed by the shift of focus from Germany to Spain, the shift of some states from one side to the other, and the mutual suspicions and incessant squabbling among ostensible allies. But it was nonetheless essentially one war, pitting the Grand Alliance against Louis XIV for the domination of western and central Europe.

To the east, similarly, the renewed nameless struggle of Habsburg against Turk in the southeast from 1683 until 1699; its succession by the duel between Sweden and Russia from 1700 until 1721, celebrated under the grandiose name of the Great Northern War; the sporadic pattern of hostilities in both stages; and the complications of Venetian, papal, Polish, Saxon, and Danish participation: these ill-assorted pieces obscure the historical meaning of one long conflict. Essentially, it was the counterpart of the western war: it decided the balance of power in eastern Europe.

Considered separately, then, these wars determined which of the myriad states and principalities would be most influential in shaping European destinies for the next two and a half centuries. But the western and eastern wars can also be considered together. They were connected with each other by belligerents and motives common to both, and their political effects converged into the formation of a single European political system composed of similarly organized states.

THE WAR IN THE WEST: FIRST STAGE, 1688–1697

The war in the west broke out over the issue of Germany, was resumed over the issue of Spain, and was actually fought for purposes which transcended both. Ostensibly the War of the League of Augsburg, or the War of the Grand Alliance, as the phase of it that terminated in the peace of Ryswick of 1697 has been alternatively called, was fought to determine the possession of the German Rhineland and had its origins in the usual escalation of reciprocal suspicions about the intentions of the main powers in the area. The struggle opened in September, 1688, when Louis XIV decided to take advantage of the Austrian involvement with the Turks and to forestall the unfavorable consequences of the imminent Austrian triumph for French influence in the German Empire. He embarked upon a preventive military invasion of the Rhine Palatinate, one of the politically sensitive German Electorates (*i.e.* the eight principalities whose rulers elected the German emperor and constituted the First Estate of the Imperial Diet, or Reichstag)—ostensibly to anticipate an attack on France by the Emperor's League of Augsburg, but actually to prevent the accession of an anti-French Elector in the Palatinate. Leopold I, Habsburg ruler of the Austrian dominions and German Emperor, countered this gambit with a formal declaration of war. Not only the occasion but the underlying cause of the war seemed to be the assertion of hegemony over western Germany. For Louis, addicted like so many aggressors to the policy that may be characterized as "creeping defense," the purpose was to force, through conquests on the right bank of the Rhine, the legal recognition of the irregular holdings in Alsace and Lorraine which the French had acquired at Westphalia in 1648 and in the "reunions" of 1680 and 1681—holdings which the Emperor had refused to recognize as legal in the Truce of Regensburg (1684) and which, indeed, in Louis' eyes, were threatened by the recent addition of Hungary to the Habsburg power (1687) and by the Emperor's previous sponsorship of the League of Augsburg in 1686. Constituted by the Bavarian, Saxon, and Palatine Electors and by the Kings of Sweden and of Spain in their capacities as princes of the German Empire—plus the Emperor—the League was indeed an alliance against the presumed aggressive program of Louis XIV for Germany.

But beyond these appearances more profound causes were at work. The German situation brought into focus fundamental factors that had previously been diffuse but would henceforth play important roles in the war and its aftereffects. These factors had broken the surface of European politics only in the repeated but aborted attempts by William of Orange to organize an offensive coalition against Louis XIV. Now, with the League of Augsburg as a core, William's effort bore fruit. His Protestant, commercial initiative and the Emperor's Catholic, traditional, landed defensiveness converged into a single definite military alliance against France, thus forging the political integration of economic, religious, and dynastic interests that had been incapable, by themselves, of producing a common issue around which Europe could be organized. But now the German problem was broadened into precisely such an issue.

This first of the European "grand" alliances was effected, under William's prodding, by the formal Treaty of Vienna (May, 1689) between Austria (on behalf of the German Empire), England and the Netherlands, bringing these maritime powers into the war against France, and by the subsequent inclusion of Spain, Sweden, and Savoy in the coalition (although the Swedes would be belligerents in name only and the Savoyards would change sides in 1696). The German issue formed the initial basis for the alliance, but it obviously was not, for many of the participating powers, a sufficiently vital interest to bring about their adherence. In the Netherlands and England, for example, Louis' German demarche triggered a long-standing resentment born of the commercial war which Louis' minister Colbert had waged for so many years against them, and nurtured on French territorial aggression in the Spanish Netherlands—an area strategically vital to both maritime powers—during the Dutch war of 1672–1678. The Bourbon threat to the lifelines of their respective economies readied influential business interests in both countries for an accounting with France. The Dutch move into the German conflict was actually preceded by a new tariff war against the French in November, 1688.

It is easy to overestimate the impact of the religious animosities which followed hard upon Louis XIV's revocation of the Edict of Nantes in 1685; actually the sound and fury of the Huguenot émigrés and the wild talk of their English, Dutch, and German Calvinist coreligionists about a crusade against France hardly explain the alliance of Catholic and Protestant powers that came into play against Louis. And yet it seems clear that even if this recrudescence of sectarian rivalry was not a general cause of the war it certainly contributed sufficiently to the belligerency of some states to be a cause of the war becoming general. Thus William of Orange, whose implacable hostility to Bourbon France far antedated Louis' Huguenot persecution and far transcended religion, could exploit outraged Protestant emotions to bring such erstwhile rival bargainers for Louis' favors as Sweden and Brandenburg-Prussia into a defensive accord against France (1686), and as William III of England he could develop the English revolution against the Catholic James II into participation in the war against France (May, 1689). The religious sensibilities of Frederick William, the Great Elector of Brandenburg-Prussia (ruled 1640–1688), combined with his political disappointment in the results of his French alliance to put him into a general anti-French posture after 1685. His son, Elector Frederick III (ruled 1688–1713), could use the historic fear which associated Catholic and political aggression to found the Magdeburg Concert of north German Protestant princes (October, 1688) for the war against France, despite the absence of a direct threat to their immediate interests.

In addition to the economic and religious factors, there were also dynastic considerations that were activated by the German crisis but went far beyond it. The most potent of these was undoubtedly the Habsburg claim to the Spanish succession. This issue, which was to appear in the open and dominate the second phase of the western war after the death of the Spanish king, Charles II, in 1700, was already covertly at work a decade before. It helped to remind the Habsburg Emperor, Leopold I, of his German patriotism and to take the incursion into the Palatinate by his rival Bourbon claimant to the Spanish crown as the occasion for the declaration of war (October, 1688). Indeed, he insisted upon a secret article recognizing his own right to the Spanish succession, as a condition of his adherence to the alliance against Louis which was formalized in the Treaty of Vienna.

Nor were Leopold's the only dynastic interests at stake or the only family ties involved. Louis XIV himself was continuously concerned with asserting Bourbon rights against the Habsburgs, and the Bourbon claim to the Spanish succession. In this instance he was representing the claims of his sister-in-law, the duchess of Orléans, to holdings in the Palatinate that would have given the Bourbon family a seat in the German Reichstag. The Great Elector's turnabout against France was connected with his hope of satisfying Hohenzollern claims to western Pomerania and parts of Silesia which he had failed to obtain through his policy of French alliance. Moreover, his kinship with William of Orange, his nephew and the chief architect of the anti-French coalition, eased his change of fronts. William, in turn, acquired the possibility of directing English foreign policy toward war with France through his marriage to Mary, eldest daughter of King James II, and through his own more distant claim, as the King's nephew, to a vacated throne. His plans for intervention in England were predicated on these dynastic ties, and in fact, the cautious alliance of Tories and Whigs which made the revolution would hardly have accepted him as the new king without them. A prime motive for Sweden's accession to the coalition went back to the French appropriation, during the "reunions" of 1680 and 1681, of the Zweibrücken principality whose succession had been promised to the Vasa dynasty. Even the Spanish Habsburg, Charles II, long a plaything rather than player in the game of European power politics, bestirred himself into joining the alliance in conformity with the change in his family relations following the death of his French wife in 1689 and his remarriage to an Austrian later in the same year. Even the occasion of the war took a dynastic form, for it was set off by the election of Joseph Clement, a prince of the Bavarian Wittelsbach line that had long controlled the See, to the archbishopric of Cologne, over the candidate from the pro-French Fürstenberg family.

Thus economic, religious, and dynastic factors, activated by Louis XIV's German invasion, all entered into the opening of the war in the west. Obviously, there was nothing new or remarkable either in the martial incidence of any of these factors or in the role of Germany as the battleground of Europe. What was remarkable was the new interrelationship among these factors which could make them all operative on the same occasion. In foreign as in domestic affairs, it signified the growth of a collective interest above the special interests which fed into it. For the government of Louis XIV, the move against the Palatinate fell into line with the commercial, religious, and dynastic aggression that had preceded it, and became a piece in a general policy of expanding a unified France. It was rightly taken in the rest of Europe as a part of such a policy. Among the rest of the European powers, the French action in Germany brought various partial interests together in the general agreement that Europe should be restored to the settlement created by the treaties of Westphalia (1648) and the Pyrenees (1659), with France deprived of its several intervening acquisitions. This was the core of the consensus embodied in the Treaty of Vienna. It indicated that Europe had caught up to the French in assessing transient business, confessional, and familial concerns by the standard of long-range, political aims. However varied the spur for the different powers, the effect was common: fear and resentment at the obstruction posed by French ambitions.

The perception of an overriding political interest, different in kind from other human interests and arbitrating among them, was not so much a rational conclusion from a political ideal as a lesson of practical experience. It is true, certainly, that systematic theories along this line had become ever more influential since Jean Bodin (1530–1596) in the sixteenth century, until by the late seventeenth century, they were represented in every major country by publicists and academicians who installed them as part of the mental equipment carried about by educated administrators. But men were accustomed, in Europe, to a wide span between theory and practice, and these ideas were not applied until conditions called for their application. And even then, they were applied not systematically but piecemeal, to meet particular situations. For the decisive authorities in the late seventeenth century were not the intellectuals or the administrators, but the kings—violent, poorly educated, distracted, or pious, diligent, pettifogging, but in any case attending to particular decisions rather than to general policies.

Yet it was in this period that the kings emerged who responded to their experience by permitting larger points of view to inform these decisions. History is always the result of the meeting between a situation and a personality (whether collective or individual), and in this case the personalities relevant to history were the royal figures who, in one way or another, were sufficiently attuned to their environment to meet its challenge and exploit its possibilities.

Louis XIV

Still holding the center of the stage was the Sun King, Louis of France (ruled 1643–1715), the scourge and the envy of Europe. In many ways he seemed the same as ever, only more so. The manliness and the presence that made him "every inch a king," the unquestioning self-righteousness, the untiring conversion of his private life into the public business, the unblushing identification of the public community with his private person, the active foreign policy of creeping defense: all these marks of his regime since 1661 were indelible until his death in 1715. But however persistent these fundamentals may have proved, a subtle change in their operation took place during the decade of the 1680's that set off the subsequent years as a new era. In part, the change was external to Louis, initiated by the converging decisions of other European monarchies to meet his challenge by acting up to the standards of power and policy which he had so successfully established. But in part, too, the change was internal to Louis and his regime, a dislocation of the parts which made up the pattern of his government.

The inconsistencies in Louis' absolutism have been noted often enough, but in his office as in his policies it was precisely the fine balance between opposites that constituted the chief strength of his regime during the first twenty years of his personal rule. There were contrasts between his private pleasures and his public dedication, between his vaulting ambitions and his bureaucratic pettifoggery, between his preference for commoners to do his work and his concern for the nobility that got his pensions, between the centralized administration which he imposed and the local institutions which he preserved, between maritime and continental policies, and between the arts of peace and the arts of war. But by holding these factors in equilibrium he had managed to draw strength from each of them in an age when neither the techniques of government nor the modest tempo of change permitted radical solutions.

From the 1680's the texture of his life and his policies coarsened, the delicate balance was disturbed, and the interest of state, which, as balance wheel, had enjoyed the joint support of the countervailing parts, began now to tilt. In this historical case as in so many others, the data hardly suffice to substantiate a psychoanalytic explanation of politics, but we must at least note the coincidence that the start of Louis' political excesses was accompanied by a rupture in the intimate habits that had contributed to his emotional stability. It was said of Louis that "he could not do without women," and from adolescence to middle age his amorous disposition had

Louis XIV praying. *Sculpture by Antoine Coysevox. The aging monarch in a characteristic pose. Notre Dame, Paris.*

found ample outlet in a continuous succession of affairs with partners of high and low estate. But when, in 1684, he married the last of his mistresses, the pious and frigid Madame de Maintenon (1635–1719), he broke with the habit of extramarital dalliance that had balanced the intensity of his application to the profession of kingship. It is at least ironical, if not revealing, that Louis should have reached simultaneously the states of conjugal fidelity and political concupiscence.

Not only in his morality but in his religiosity as well did Louis alter the previous pattern of his life. Louis' piety was an unquestioning, external commitment. He subscribed to the whole panoply of Catholic formulas and rituals, which he accepted, as he accepted all established institutions, insofar as they manifested the divinely ordained order and recognized the Most Christian Majesty—*i.e.* Louis himself—as its supreme caretaker. He had always abominated Huguenots and Jansenists, both because they fomented disorder in religion and the church, respectively, and because they appealed to principles of faith above the instituted authorities of which he counted himself the chief. Both groups did indeed share the same general doctrinal tendency to stress the role of divine grace over human free will in the awakening of faith, the role of faith over good works in the attainment of salvation, and the rigorous role of good works over accommodations to human frailty in the living of the good Christian life. Both groups shared too the same general ecclesiastical tendency to resist Catholic authorities who espoused contrary doctrines. To this extent Louis' opposition to both groups as rebellious heretics of similar stripe had a basis in general fact, but the specific differences between the two groups also reflect two different dimensions in the policy of suppression which the later Louis would visit upon them. The Huguenots were French Calvinists with their own separate churches whose autonomous corporate rights were

recognized by law. Jansenism was originally a theological and ethical movement *within* the Catholic Church, claiming to represent a purified version
of traditional Catholic dogma and morals and to oppose only the particular Jesuit influence whose emphasis upon free will, good works, and adap-
tability supposedly was corrupting the tradition. Stressing religious inwardness and personal ethics, seventeenth-century Jansenists tended rather
toward reform of theology and clerical morals within the French Catholic
Church, and when threatened, toward quietism, mysticism, and passive
resistance, than toward ecclesiastical separatism or political action. Their
organization as a church party and political movement during the eighteenth century would be more a result than a cause of the Papacy's
alignment with the Jesuits and of Louis' with the Papacy at the start of
the century.

During the earlier part of his reign Louis' antipathies to religious heterodoxy had been held in check by his suspicions of the Ultramontan-
ists—advocates of papal authority in the French Catholic Church and
activists against Huguenots and Jansenists alike—on the other side of the
clerical spectrum. Then he had chosen to promote political Gallicanism, a
middle-of-the-road position which sponsored the claims of religious orthodoxy against the deviants, of the French Church against the Papacy, and
of the monarchy as the protector of French orthodoxy. In this activity as
in others, the fundamental features of Louis' policy remained constant,
but from the mid-1680's their internal relations shifted. Whatever the particular occasion that inspired Louis to end the toleration of the Reformed
(Calvinist, or Huguenot) Church in France by revoking the Edict of
Nantes in 1685—the anxiety of a literal-minded, middle-aged believer over
the eternal consequences of a misspent youth, the growing influence of an
entourage led by Madame de Maintenon and the royal confessor, Père La
Chaise (1624–1709), the momentum of the ever-expanding list of disabilities imposed upon the Huguenots since the time of Cardinal Richelieu
(1585–1642), or Louis' belief in the reported mass conversions to Catholicism of the Huguenots, whose few lagging brethren would need only the
encouragement of law to bring about a religious unanimity—the importance of the act for our purposes lies rather in the general change of attitude which it betokened and initiated. For it was followed by Louis' rapprochement with the Papacy in the 1690's and climaxed by the enthusiastic cooperation of king and pope (Clement XI) in the persecution of Jansenists. The high points of their joint campaign came in 1709, when the
community at Port-Royal, long a Jansenist haven, was evicted by royal
troops, and in 1713, when, with Louis' approval, Clement issued the bull
Unigenitus, which condemned one hundred and one propositions of
France's leading Jansenist, Father Pasquier Quesnel (1634–1719). By 1715
the bitter conflict over his acceptance of the bull awakened even Louis, in
a last flash of insight before his death, to a belated futile recognition of

the political perils entailed by the unbalanced sectarian course of his latter years.

The meaning of Louis' religious shift at mid-reign, then, was not the simple growth of his authoritarianism, for his passion for unbrooked power was as strong before as after, and indeed was more surely attained in the earlier than in the later form. Its meaning lay rather in its revelation of his growing preference, in part deliberate and in part compulsive, for uniformity over balance as the better means of enhancing his authority.

The same pattern is observable in the final change that was to mark off the second half of Louis' personal government as a new era in the history of France and Europe: the replacement of Colbert by Louvois as the king's leading political counselor. Until the 1680's Louis had balanced adroitly between his two great ministers—ennobled scions, both, of bourgeois families, but exemplifying very different qualities of their class. Jean Baptiste Colbert (1619–1683), merchant's son, was the very model of the successful burgher. Icy by temperament (he was nicknamed "the North"), unbending, parsimonious, diligent, he dedicated himself to the same kind of calculation, rationality, and orderliness in the administration of the state as he would have in the management of an established business, and even the flaws in this granite character were those of his type—the nepotic provision for the expanded family and the uncritical reverence for his king. Controller general of Finance, Minister of Commerce, of Colonies, and of the Navy, Colbert had assumed direction of economic control and development. Through these functions, he directed the general internal administration as well as an appropriate part of foreign policy. To these functions he brought, and from them he drew, an equilibrated view of French interests. In domestic affairs he held a middle line between innovation and tradition, commercial liberty and regulation, bureaucratic leveling and aristocratic hierarchy. In foreign affairs he alternated between recognition of the economic need for peace and the mercantilist advocacy of limited war, and he approached these alternatives in terms of an oceanic rather than a continental orientation.

François Michel Le Tellier, Marquis of Louvois (1641-1691), represented another branch of the ascendant bourgeoisie. Middle member of a bureaucratic dynasty—he was to pass his office on to his son just as his father had bequeathed it, extralegally, to him—Louvois ran the Ministry of War like a hard-driving entrepreneur. Tireless, obsessed, brutal, he rode roughshod over traditional restraints and fed the king's authority through the restless expansion of his means of control. He had remade the army into a reliable royal instrument by leveling aristocratic privilege and rationalizing the conditions of promotion, training and administration. He agitated incessantly against foreign neighbors and French Huguenots alike, prescribing disciplined force and unbridled terror as equally permissible means for smashing all resistance, whether actual or potential, to the royal will. He had contested the direction of French foreign policy with Colbert, seeking for it a continental orientation that would increase the contiguous territories under French dominion.

Louvois' rise to power in the government of France was an important influence in changing the tenor of Louis' reign. Colbert's death in 1683 was a fortuitous removal of a rival influence, but the role of chance was not as crucial as this circumstance might seem to indicate. Colbert's star was already on the wane at the time of his demise. Louis' acquiescence in Louvois' policy of "reunions" as early as 1680–1681 showed that the subsequent triumph of the war minister was part of a general shift in Louis' approach to politics. If the French aggression which triggered the War of the League of Augsburg was a Louvoisian act, it was of a piece with the preceding developments of the 1680's which marked Louis' turn to the drastic over the balanced, the coarse over the fine, in his politics. Louvois was himself to die in 1691, and the unofficial place of policy maker for the king which Colbert and he had occupied was henceforth to remain vacant. Relying now upon his own devices, Louis held his course for the remainder of his reign, as if through a kind of inertia, in the direction that Louvois had impelled him. Whatever moral or even political judgment may be levied upon the constant warfare and increasing oppressiveness of Louis' later years, they paradoxically manifested the growing preponderance of the institutional over the private factors in kingship. For Louis' monopolization of decision making, his adoption of unitarian and expansionist policies in the style of Louvois, and his readiness to use repression and war in pursuit of them were accompanied by his growing tendency to think of kingship rather as a responsible public charge which acted through law for the general welfare than as the office of a divinely ordained person. This anomalous combination of increased despotism in the act and increased limitation in the concept is explicable only by Louis' developing conviction that he was trustee for a body politic that required uniformity at home and absolute removal of all risks from abroad.

William III

Louis' great rival was William, coincidentally "the Third" both as prince of Orange and as king of England, where he ruled between 1689 and 1702. On the surface the conflict between the two seems like one of those spectacular personal duels which have, independently of time and place, pitted individuals of titanic mold against each other recurrently throughout the recorded history of man. The confrontation has been generalized even further by the added attribution of an epical moral dimension: Louis is the archetype of the villain, William the model of the hero. But however dramatically satisfying, the tableau is flawed. The house of Orange has had a good historical press as dynasties go, and there is reason to suspect that some of the luster indelibly associated with his great-

William III, *stadholder* of the Netherlands and King of England.

grandfather, William the Silent, protagonist in the previous century's resistance to Philip II of Spain, has rubbed off on the descendant. Despite the common traits of persistence, determination, and courage in the face of adversity, the common position of *stadholder* over the Netherlands, and the common championship of national independence and Protestantism, William III evinced, in addition, unsympathetic qualities that were wanting in his forebear. Rigid, cold, calculating, as authoritarian in his politics as he was dogmatic in his Calvinism, William was a bully in his private life and a dictator to the nominally free and formerly tolerant republic of the Netherlands.

William's ultimate political purpose, moreover, in terms of which his severity has been extenuated, was and remains doubtful. Certainly he was consumed, all through his career, by his antagonism against Louis, and certainly too he saw in Louis a threat to the very existence of the Netherlands and of Protestantism, to both of which he was equally and sincerely devoted, as he was to the traditional constitutions of the European system and its several states. But it is also clear that personal ambition played an undue role in his antipathy to the French king. The restoration in the Netherlands of the *stadholder*ship, which had been suspended between 1650 and 1672, had stemmed directly from the needs of the war against France, and the preservation of the hereditary quasi-monarchy into which William converted it depended upon continued hostility. Again, William had English expectations of his own which were rooted in his Stuart blood, encouraged by his marriage to an English royal princess, and ultimately confirmed by his insistence upon an equal share of the English crown in 1689. Hence it was perhaps as much because Louis supported the Catholic

King James and whatever Catholic male heir he might sire—including the belated son he did sire in June 1688—and thus threatened to block William's access to the most exalted of honors, as because he cherished the patriotic project of using the English crown as an additional weapon in the Dutch fight against France that the *stadholder* persisted in his hostility to the French king. It should be added, as a final touch in the disparagement of William's heroic role, that he was but an indifferent general; his triumphs were generally attributable to his mastery of the valuable but unglamorous art of diplomacy.

The meaning of William's role lay neither in the principles, whether political or religious, nor in the personal or Dutch interests that he represented. It lay rather in his will and capacity to convert a variety of principles and interests into a system of countervailing power. Against the new organization of social force from a single political center pioneered by the government of Louis XIV, he educated the sovereigns of Europe in equally novel means of associating their various centers of social force against it, thereby introducing the concert as the alternative to hegemony in the mobilization of political power.

The sphere in which William thus modernized European politics was the sphere of international relations. He had, to be sure, proved himself adept at building an effective political machine out of the motley Dutch constitution, and he drew from it more force than any single authority had ever succeeded in amassing before. But he changed no institutions here any more than he was to change any in England when he assumed royal authority there. His domestic policy in both his realms varied with the needs of his wars and his diplomacy, and it was in foreign policy alone that he was truly constructive. In this arena he broke through to the perception of *political* interests as the general currency of diplomacy into which special dynastic, religious, or economic interests must be converted if the relations among states were to be negotiable and controllable. Because William himself perceived and brought his fellow monarchs to perceive the primacy of security from aggression as the political value on which all other public values hinged, he was able to convert the heterogeneous fears of and animosities against Louis XIV into the awareness of a unified European political interest against the military extension of the French political system. Piecemeal, through the indoctrination of one prince after another through the decade of the 1680's, he built informal understandings, agreements, and partial coalitions into the great alliance that fought the war.

The Lesser Monarchs: Charles XI, Leopold I, Frederick I

Measured alongside Louis and William, the two pioneers of modern statecraft, other European rulers of the period seem puny. And yet, despite the traditional, partial, and myopic cast of their political personalities, the King of Sweden, the German Emperor, and the Elector of Brandenburg manifested, each in his own way, an admixture of political consciousness that made them at least responsive to the challenge posed by Louis and the lead offered by William.

Among the participants in the western war, it was Charles XI of Sweden (ruled 1660–1697) who was closest in political stature to the great ones and who approximated, along with them, the type of royal state builder characteristic of the period. From one point of view, Charles's personal government was simply an oscillation in the customary cycle of nobiliar and monarchical preponderance that characterized Swedish history throughout the early modern period. Personally shy, ill-educated, and opportunistic as he was, the King was certainly driven by no doctrine or plan of political reorganization, and to this extent he belongs to the traditional rather than the modern pattern of government. And yet, from the way in which he reacted to his opportunities and from the unintended integration of his piecemeal policies, a new element emerged, important enough to earn for Charles the historical credit of having established the bases of the modern Swedish state.

Only Sweden's imminent decline from great-power status, a decline already visible in the Swedes' diminishing influence upon the destinies of western Europe in the latter seventeenth century, has cast Charles into the rank of secondary political rulers. Like Louis he grew up in the disorder of a noble-ridden regency, and like William he rose to power by assuming the role of national savior which he associated with his position of military commander at a time when the ruling oligarchy was militarily impotent. The autocratic political power which was consequently vested in him after 1680 was at once analogous to Louis' and William's and something new in Swedish history. The Swedish parliament, the *Riksdag*, like the Dutch estates, continued formally in being with its wonted constitutional powers, but it now expressly recognized in Charles its "absolute sovereign King, responsible to no one on earth." Utilizing every occasion to establish his independence and increase his authority at the expense of the compliant assembly for the purpose of expanding Sweden's military resources, Charles's particular policies—hardly unfamiliar in themselves—of recovering crown lands, destroying the political and bureaucratic predominance of the old nobility, and creating a new service aristocracy alongside the old on the land, and above it in the government, took a permanent institutional form: there emerged a rational budget, a reorganized regular army, and a centralized administration staffed by officials loyal to the king as head of state.

This work of internal consolidation absorbed the bulk of the king's attention and energies after the Treaty of Nijmegen (1678–1679), in which Louis XIV's studied neglect of his Swedish ally seemed to confirm the near disaster of Sweden's military fortunes during the precedent war,

Habsburg Emperor Leopold I in
his later years.

but if Charles's foreign policy was muted its influence was nonetheless pervasive. It was, indeed, in the light of Sweden's diplomatic position that the
domestic reforms were undertaken, and Charles's approach to international relations was analogous to the pattern of his internal politics. For
internationally too, a series of particular policies added up to a general
policy which, however unconscious, testified to the reality of a state interest transcending traditional motives. Charles's resentment of French
"tutelage" at Nijmegen, his reaction to Louis' violation of the dynastic
rights he claimed in the Palatinate, and his opposition to the Huguenot
persecution all had an effect upon his policy, but they did not dominate it.
They fed into a larger attitude that did dominate it. Under their influence
Charles entered into the various anti-French combinations of the 1680's to
redress the balance upon which the restoration of Sweden's independent
role depended, and he climaxed this phase by participating in the formation of the Grand Alliance of 1689 against Louis. But once the alliance
was formed Charles deliberately repressed his own anti-French motives,
since they no longer served the Swedish interest. This depended, in his
view, upon a balance of the powers that now existed without him. Sweden
remained militarily neutral through the War of the League of Augsburg,
for Charles and his advisers now saw Swedish interests best served by a
mediator's role. As a matter of fact, the calculation was, for the short run
at least, quite correct. Sweden was instrumental in bringing about the
peace conference at Ryswick and did draw a commission for its services as
honest broker—the recognition (only until 1718, as it turned out) of its
king's dynastic claim to the German Rhenish duchy of Zweibrücken. The
real payoff for the performance of Charles XI was to come shortly there-

Pleasure-yacht of the uncharacteristically fun-loving Hohenzollern, Frederick I of Prussia.

after in the early successes of Charles XII, for the father supplied the son not only with the institutions but with the mentality appropriate to the age of power politics.

Leopold I (ruled 1658–1705), Holy Roman Emperor, *de jure* ruler of the Austrian archduchies and King of Bohemia, *de facto* ruler of Hungary (he had the royal title transferred to his son Joseph in 1687), was a monarch in the traditional Habsburg mold. Full of family pride and the sense of his own prerogatives, Leopold was yet pacific by temperament, aesthetic by taste, and sectarian by religious conviction. He was therefore, for much of his reign, the very model of the passive autocrat in which the Habsburg line has been so prolific. Interested rather in music, the theater, and Catholic piety than in royal politics, his had been rather a responsive than a provocative role on the European scene, with the characteristic exception of his energetic repression of Hungarian Protestantism.

But under the pressure of experience he developed a new political concern, which he introduced as a permanent trait into the Habsburg dynastic character. From the defections among the German principalities during the Dutch war he discovered at first hand the futility of Austria's Imperial position and from the conjunction of Hungarian revolt, Turkish invasion, and French aggression he discovered the vital military importance of the Habsburg non-German dominions, the priority of the political over the religious aspects of the confessional conflict, and the unity of Austrian interests amid the apparent multiplicity of issues. There was, then, a new political awareness in Leopold's perception of the common danger from east and west, in his decision to turn the war against the Turks into a two-front war against the French as well, and in his participation in a coalition with the Protestant powers of Europe.

Frederick III, Elector of Brandenburg (ruled 1688–1713), was undoubtedly something of a sport in the Hohenzollern line of strong rulers. Such has been the common historical judgment upon him, and it is sustained by his propensities toward extravagance, luxury, display, indecisiveness, dependence, and pessimism—traits obviously uncharacteristic of the dynasty. Dwarfed by the state-building activists who preceded and succeeded him, Frederick's reign is usually considered a hiatus, notable only for his acquisiton of the royal title of King in Prussia (as Frederick I), during 1701—and this too has been criticized as an empty form of pomp too dearly bought.

But still, even aside from the cultural innovations which were included among Frederick's diversions—the Academy of Sciences and the University of Halle were the most important of these foundations—Frederick made a positive contribution to the age. He did have a feeling, articulated both in the quest for kingship and in the emulation of the Sun King's manners and tastes, for the standards appropriate to the new appreciation of the state and its representatives, and the presence of such a feeling in such an unpolitical personality was a mark of how far the appreciation had come. It was Frederick who, immediately upon his accession in 1688, set aside his father's testament and saved the unity of the Hohenzollern dominions, which the Great Elector had willed to be divided. It was Frederick too who, just as immediately, led the northern princes into the war against France and was thereby instrumental in creating the solid front against Louis out of which the multipower international system of modern times was to come.

WESTERN LINKS WITH THE EASTERN WAR: FIRST STAGE, 1688–1699

The War of the League of Augsburg was itself as deceptive as the policies and personalities that produced it, for its events, when viewed individually, gave one impression, but when taken together, had quite a different meaning. Once the French had been driven back across the Rhine by the German Imperial victories at Mainz and Bonn in 1689 and into a defensive naval posture by the Anglo-Dutch defeat of the French fleet at La Hogue in 1692, the war seemed to drag on interminably and without direction, with the gods bestowing local victories on either side apparently at random. The campaigns were far-flung—the Rhineland, the Spanish Netherlands, Spain itself, northern Italy, Ireland, North America, the Caribbean, and India were all theaters of war—but everywhere equally without decisive issue. The conflict soon took on the familiar aspect of a stalemate, with separate peace feelers and negotiations starting as early as 1693 and gradually leading to separate agreements until the Habsburg Emperor Leopold, left isolated, was forced to acquiesce in the general peace at Ryswick in 1697.

The settlement at Ryswick confirmed the fruitless and unfocused course of the war, for not only was it articulated into several bilateral treaties between Louis XIV of France and each of his opponents but it restored, with a few apparently inessential changes, the territorial arrangements in force before the war. The only noteworthy provisions of the settlement were the French agreement to return German territories seized since the Treaty of Nijmegen with the notable exception of Strasbourg and Alsace; the French agreement to end its tariff war against England and the Netherlands; the French recognition of William III as legitimate king of England; and for the French concession, as a symbol of Dutch security, the right of the Dutch to garrison the "barrier" fortresses in the Spanish Netherlands to the south—"barrier," of course, to French invasion.

And yet, beneath the surface of these apparently aimless and fruitless maneuverings the events formed certain significant clusters. First, the war and the treaties that concluded it adumbrated the outlines of a multipower international system. French claims to hegemony were repulsed on the Continent, on the sea, and in the colonies, but in each of these arenas the French status as a great power among others was confirmed along with the recognized rise of England and Austria to a similar status. Second, beneath the apparent military and diplomatic dispersion of allied forces there remained elements of cohesion within the Grand Alliance—notably, the force of English subsidies and the influence of William III, who in fact although not in form negotiated with Louis on behalf of the whole alliance. Finally, for the first time the colonies of the European powers around the globe were drawn into a conflict initiated on the mother continent. The synchronization of these colonial conflicts attested to the power of the invisible bonds which the states were drawing around their agents and their citizens, however distant their situation and however limited their stake.

Contributing to the important long-range effects of the apparently sterile western war were its connections with the first stage of the eastern war which ran a course parallel to it. Once more we must look beneath the surface for relationships that were not obvious in the actual events. In appearance the eastern war of the 1690's was simply a continuation of the conflict which opened with the Turkish invasion of Hungary and Austria in 1683 and with the ensuing formation of the Holy League, in which Venice, and later Russia, joined the German Empire and Poland under the aegis of the Papacy in a military alliance against the Turk. In its origins this eastern war was independent of the growing tensions in western Europe: not only was the Turkish attack free of French complicity but the Christian crusade against the infidel and the territorial ambitions in eastern Europe which spurred the counteroffensive of the Holy League were equally separate from the turmoil in the west. The struggle in the east persisted without formal break through the entire War of the League of Augsburg until it was terminated by the Peace of Karlowitz in 1699, and its insulation was attested to by the refusal of the maritime powers (England and the Netherlands) to expand their alliance with the German Emperor against France into an alliance against the Turks as well.

But the two wars were related nonetheless. Their main link was the Habsburg monarchy, both through its own dominions and, to a lesser extent, through the states of the German Empire, whose foreign policies were actually—albeit not legally—controlled in this period by the Habsburg monarch in his capacity as German Emperor. The sequence of successful military campaigns in the Turkish War of the 1680's brought additional territories under Habsburg rule—particularly through the conquest of Hungary—so that Leopold was encouraged to resist Louis XIV in the west; on the other side, it was Louis' invasion of the German Empire that spurred the Turks to continue the war against the Habsburgs and the Empire despite the telling losses of Budapest in 1686 and of Belgrade in 1688. Moreover, the eastern war did take a new turn in the 1690's because of the diversion of Imperial troops to the west. The Turks took the offensive, and although stopped at the Danube in the Battle of Slankamen, reconquered during the 1690's the bulk of the Balkan territory lost during the 1680's.

Another link between the two wars developed in the successful candidature of the Austrian protégé, the Saxon elector Augustus the Strong (1670–1733), for the Polish crown (1697) against Louis' candidate, François Louis, Prince of Conti (1664–1709). As a result of this strand reaching across the continent, Poland was held in the anti-Turkish camp, Saxony in the anti-French, and the eastern Imperial army, which had been inefficiently led by Augustus before his convenient elevation to the Polish kingship, received a brilliant new commander in Eugene of Savoy (1663–1736), who crushed the Turks at the Battle of Zenta in 1697 and prepared them for the acceptance of peace.

The eastern peace itself, embodied in the Treaty of Karlowitz (1699), was conditioned by the situation in the west, for the mediation by the Dutch and the English and Leopold's acceptance of the terms of the treaty despite his commanding military position were undertaken in the light of the incipient resumption of the western war on the issue of the Spanish succession. The terms of the peace treaty indicated the inconclusiveness of this eastern settlement that was made under western influence: not only were the declining powers of Poland and Venice conceded territorial acquisitions—Podolia and the Morea respectively—that would soon have to be disgorged again, but Russia, the new power in the European constellation, refused to participate in the treaty and instead signed its own reluctant truce with the Turks at Constantinople in 1700, leaving still unsatisfied the Russian claims to free navigation of the Black Sea. The one definitive provision of Karlowitz related, significantly enough, to Austria, the swing power between east and west: by recognizing Habsburg sovereignty over Hungary and Transylvania it established the Habsburg monarchy as a power in eastern Europe and made it the pivot of the continental system of states that was aborning.

THE WAR IN THE WEST: SECOND STAGE, 1700–1713

The second stage of the western and eastern wars, running a convergent course, brought the continental system into existence. Each of the wars, formally separate from the other and from its own first stage, now took on a new name. The western conflict became the War of the Spanish Succession, the eastern, the Great Northern War—a label which obscured Russia's new orientation toward all of eastern Europe. Along with the names the character of the conflicts changed. Not only were campaigns now punctuated by decisive battles but warfare and the domestic political considerations stemming from the demands of warfare temporarily replaced diplomacy as the main fields in which fundamental decisions were taken.

The character of the new historical personages who entered upon the scene at the start and during the course of the renewed conflicts typifies the new focus of events. In the west Louis the Sun King, old and somewhat tarnished, continued in power throughout the war and provided the main thread of continuity with the past. But he outlived his opponents, whose replacements created a new atmosphere and a new historical situation. His old archrival, William III, died in 1702, shortly after he had brought his diplomatic career to a fitting climax by re-forming the Grand Alliance against Louis. Based once more on the triple entente of the two maritime powers (England and the Netherlands) and the Habsburg Emperor, the alliance was once again extended to include the bulk of the German principalities. But it had now to do without Spain (under its new Bourbon king, Philip V), Bavaria, Cologne, and Savoy (which would once again switch sides, in 1704): all these powers, for sundry hopes of dynastic and territorial gain, went over to Louis XIV.

The leadership which William had supplied was now assumed by the English commander, John Churchill, Duke of Marlborough (1650–1722), and the militant grand pensionary of Holland (the chief legal counselor of the province and the most influential civil official in the whole Netherlands), Antonius Heinsius (1641–1720). The Emperor Leopold, whose decision to resist Louis XIV once again, as in 1688, precipitated war, lived on until 1705, but once again too this singular show of determination was followed by the resumption of his chronic indecisiveness, and he turned over the active direction of Habsburg policy to the most energetic and effective of his generals, Prince Eugene of Savoy. Eugene retained his influence with Leopold's successor, the fun-loving Emperor Joseph I (ruled 1705-1711), and when it waned with the accession of Emperor Charles VI (ruled 1711–1740), it was replaced by the personal government of a monarch equally addicted to a forward course. In its unprecedented concern with the cohesion of the Habsburg dominions, Charles's reign marked a new era in the history of central Europe. Toward the end of the western war, finally, the grim Frederick William I replaced the flighty Frederick I at the helm of the Prussian state (1713), and therewith the Prussian oscillation between western and eastern orientations of foreign policy gave way to the determined construction of a highly centralized bureaucratic monarchy.

In the eastern theater, similarly, the cast changed. Augustus the Strong, unscrupulous and ineffective as ever, remained on the scene but paled into insignificance beside the two new titans whose duel was to assume epic proportions for European history: Charles XII of Sweden and Peter I of Russia. Both monarchs risked the destinies of their countries on the decision of the battlefield. Both achieved the national glory of the military hero, and through them Russia and Sweden became strong monarchies forged in war and justified by war.

The new protagonists, then, were either generals like Eugene and Marlborough, who played the role of kings, or kings like Charles and Peter, who played the role of generals. Common to this quartet was the set of beliefs which, in league with their undoubted talents at the court and on the battlefield, channeled their actions into epochal achievements: the faith in their states as the supreme agencies of earthly values, the conviction that decisive military victory was the primary condition for the effective existence and functioning of these states, and the focus upon the individual sovereign as the bearer of the state's destiny. But if these were common tenets, each of these history-making individuals held them in his own way and reflected, in his particular personality, a different feature of the age.

Eugene of Savoy

Eugene, dedicated, ascetic, self-disciplined, manifested the kind of secular conversion that was making war and politics the cynosure of men's attention toward the end of the seventeenth century. Eugene's origins reflected the variety and the insecurity of the age, and his development reflected the direction in which it sought order. Son of a Savoyard prince in the service of France and an Italian-born niece of Cardinal Mazarin, Eugene was French by birth and rearing albeit not by descent. He grew up, moreover, with an attachment to his dissolute mother and to a licentious juvenile coterie at the free-living French court of the youthful Louis XIV that comported ill with his destination for the clergy. Physically weak and unprepossessing, known sardonically as "the little Abbé," Eugene responded, at some undetermined stage in his adolescence, by transforming himself into a proud, self-driven, puritanical Spartan, wholly committed to the profession of arms. Stung by the successive humiliations of his mother's banishment and Louis' personal rejection of his application for a commission, Eugene resentfully turned his back on France and in 1683 entered the service of the Habsburgs. However much the fortuitous circumstances of momentary pique and fraternal example—his older brother entered and abandoned French service before him—contributed to Eugene's decision, it was the fundamental character of the Habsburg dynasty—its polyglot staff, multinational base, and pan-European outlook—that harnessed the lifelong loyalty of this uprooted aristocrat.

His loyalty to the Habsburgs became the constant and certain center in his life toward which Eugene of Savoy could unleash restless energies and around which he could organize them. He broke through the military conventions of his time, which were oriented around the strategies of position and of siege warfare, to act single-mindedly for the mobility of his own armies and the destruction of the enemy. At Zenta, in 1697, where he first proved himself as a commanding general, he drove his army forward in a forced march, surprised the Turks crossing a river toward the end of the day, attacked their main body in a pincers movement, and destroyed it. He exhibited the same restlessness, the same concentration on the main goal, in the realm of politics. His categorical judgments, acerbic impatience, and fanatic obsession with the conditions of military victory made him alternately indispensable and *non grata* at the easygoing court of Vienna, according to the greater or lesser degree of crisis. Although his actual influence vacillated, he was, for most of his career, president of the Imperial War Council and chairman of the Privy Conference of Ministers, posts that expanded his attention from purely military concerns to the more general problems of wartime administration and the diplomacy of war and peace. In government as in command Eugene was rigidly committed to efficiency. He worked to clarify the lines of authority; he was indifferent to inherited rank, and judged performance by results; and he concentrated, without pomp or sentiment, on the effective operation of existing institutions.

But the public life to which he was so devoted could not, in an age and a country still so reverent of tradition, absorb all the force of this dynamic and versatile personality, and the forces of inertia ruling at the court first limited and then ended his exercise of political power. But the cultural life of the era was infinitely more dynamic, and Eugene's application of the same traits in this arena was more continuously successful. He became one of the largest collectors and most appreciative patrons of the arts in history: his library, his gallery, his places, his friendships (*e.g.* with Leibniz) all manifest an intensity, a tenacity, an impatience to conquer the realm of beauty that are reminiscent of Eugene's martial disposition. It was characteristic of the late seventeenth century—and this is a trait that sets it off from the century to follow—that his two passions, government and the arts, should remain as separated as they were in Eugene. Still, the religious-style fervor that he brought to each represented something new. Earlier in the century, another Austrian general, Johan Tilly (1559–1632), like Eugene foreign-born and like Eugene single-mindedly and puristically devoted to the Habsburg cause, had been known as the "monk in armor" because of the open Catholic fervor behind his military efficiency. Eugene reflected the change of the times: the monk had become a lay brother.

Marlborough

The other guiding genius of the allied cause in the War of the Spanish Succession was John Churchill, Duke of Marlborough, a soldier-statesman whose military and political domination of the English war effort after the death of William in 1702 paralleled Eugene's position at the Habsburg court. An intriguing puzzle surrounds the relations of the two leaders, for they were collaborators in policy, partners on the battlefield, friends off as well as on it—and yet not only was each a military virtuoso, solitary in his own genius, but Marlborough's indulgent character and reputation were a far cry from those of the austere Eugene.

Born into the obscure country gentry and launched upon his career by the patronage of the duke of York, Churchill worked his way up toward wealth and power, using appointments in the military arm of the English state as his stepping-stones, and he became what the parlous political conditions of seventeenth-century England might be expected to make of a man naturally endowed with uncommon ambition and prudence. He became expert, that is, in the management of his armies and his wealth, in the enchantment and manipulation of men, in the facile assumption and discard of loyalties, depending on his estimate of the main chance.

For his manifold military and diplomatic services to the Stuarts, James II had granted to him and he had accepted an English peerage, the rank of lieutenant general, and command of the royal army against William of Orange. But Churchill had been in contact with William, and in November, 1688, on what seemed the eve of battle, deserted to him, receiving in exchange a place on the Privy Council and the earldom of Marlborough. He had indeed protested against James's Catholicizing policies, but although James's religious policies were a factor in his shift to William's side, Marlborough characteristically resumed communication with the exiled James after the revolution—a connection which was the basis for the unproved charges of treason levied against him in 1692 and again in 1696. By the turn of the century he had once more insinuated himself into William's favor, and in 1702, with the accession of the last of the Stuarts, Queen Anne (ruled 1702–1714), to whom his wife and he had long and foresightedly paid court, he became, along with his lifelong friend and political ally Sidney Godolphin (1645–1712), the effective ruler of England. His one abiding concern thereafter became the prosecution of the war against France, and he shifted nimbly from Tory to Whig collaboration in his search for support. Godolphin and the Whigs were dismissed in 1710 but Marlborough hung on for another two years, and when he was then removed, his fall was characteristically accompanied by a formal charge of peculation and the informal charge of betraying the national interest—*i.e.* prolonging a futile war for pecuniary gain.

And yet, through all these manipulations, unquestioning friendship and cooperation between the overshrewd English tactician and the direct Eugene never faltered. Behind the visible contrast between the two personalities and behind even the political bond arising out of their common implacable hostility to Bourbon France lay a fundamental sympathy of disposition. In their military as in their personal careers, both were mobile, both were aggressive, and both believed in decisive and thorough action as the only means of public survival in their age.

That men of this stripe should dominate the second stage of the western war—the War of the Spanish Succession—was an indication of the quality of the epoch that was being ushered in with the new century. Whereas Louis' triumphs had manifested French primacy in consolidating stability, order, and authority as the means of power, the repeated successes now of Marlborough and Prince Eugene in outflanking, outmaneuvering, and outracing these same French symbolized the new possibilities that would make movement, energy, and the rapid concentration of force the new means of superior power.

The War and the Peace

The origins of the war, to be sure, continued a familiar pattern. The readiness of the English and Dutch to make concessions—short of endorsing the hegemony of one continental power—where their commercial interests were not involved had produced two successive partition agreements with Louis XIV, providing for disposition of the Spanish possessions upon the death of the ailing and childless Charles II. Even when the latter issued a deathbed will bequeathing the whole of the Spanish empire to Louis' grandson, the Duke of Anjou, the maritime powers had recognized the arrangement on Louis' assurance that the crowns of France and Spain would never be united.

Representing the rival Habsburg claim to the Spanish succession, Emperor Leopold, stubborn as usual where the Habsburgs and Bourbons were concerned, had refused to accept either the treaties of partition or the Spanish will. Louis, also as usual, played into his hands by using the formalities of the law to commit actual aggressions. With the death of Charles II in November, 1700, the Duke of Anjou acceded to the Spanish throne as Philip V, and in the nominal role of agent of the new king, Louis immediately moved French troops into Italy and occupied the Spanish Netherlands, including the barrier forts. In his own name as King of France, moreover, he now recognized the rights of his grandson—who also

The Battle of Turin, 1706. *Imperial troops under Eugene of Savoy smashed the French siege of the Piedmontese city and ended the French military presence in Italy until Napoleon.*

happened to be King of Spain—to the French succession. As signatory of an agreement with the sovereign state of Spain, finally, he secured for a French trading company a temporary concession of the coveted *asiento*— the right to import Negro slaves into Spanish America—and thereby offended the mercantile susceptibilities of the maritime powers. William III's renewal of the Grand Alliance in September, 1701, was a response also in the traditional mold, for it stipulated as war aims, provisions designed to divide the opposing powers: the eternal separation of Bourbon France and Bourbon Spain, the Austrian acquisition of the Spanish Netherlands and Spanish Italy, and English and Dutch monopolization of the Spanish colonial trade. When the Elector of Bavaria remembered the old hostility of the Wittelsbachs against the Habsburgs and attached himself, like many of his ancestors before him, to the French, and when his brother, the Archbishop of Cologne, followed suit, the juncture with tradition seemed complete.

But from this point Marlborough and Eugene took over and infused a new spirit into European affairs. The premium that was now placed upon energy and initiative found expression in the new domination which England exercised both within the Grand Alliance and over the course of the war as a whole, thereby opening the era of British preponderance over Europe and the world that was to last for two centuries. Marlborough was commander in chief officially of the combined English and Dutch armies and unofficially of the whole Grand Alliance. Similarly, Eugene's solo triumphs over the French in Italy and his active participation in the most notable of the allied victories in Germany and the Low Countries reflected

Louis XIV's ratification of the separate armistice between Great Britain and France in 1712. *Detail from a stylized announcement welcoming a "happy augury of the peace" which was concluded in 1713 and 1714.*

the adroit adaptation which the Habsburg monarchy was making to a dynamic multiple-power system that was coming to life. At the same time, the timorous, defensive, and obstructionist tactics of the Dutch were a true index of the general decline in vitality that would cause the Netherlands to fall from the ranks of the first-line powers in the eighteenth-century system of states.

Thus English participation was the common element in all the decisive actions of the war, and when the English lost their verve for the war the decisiveness went out of it. Fleets under English command took Gibraltar (1704) and Minorca (1708). On land, after Imperial losses inflicted in Germany by the French and in Hungary by a rebellion under the resourceful Francis Rákóczi (1676–1735) during 1703, Marlborough and Eugene converged rapidly upon the French on August 13, 1704, to combine forces and commands in the epic victory of Blenheim on the Bavarian Danube, one of the decisive battles of history because it destroyed the aura of French military superiority and initiated the long era of British hegemony over a balanced continent. Two years later Marlborough and Eugene, at Ramillies and Turin respectively, blunted the French push north and expelled them from Italy for almost a century. In July, 1708, it was once more as a smoothly functioning team that the two generals swooped down upon the French at Audenarde on the Scheldt and destroyed Louis' hopes for the conquest of the Spanish Netherlands.

But despite these spectacular exploits an actual balance of power, which was henceforth to dominate international relations, now showed itself as an inescapable military fact. Audenarde proved to be the last decisive battle of the war. When Marlborough and Eugene pressed southward a little over a year later the French met them at Malplaquet, and although the allies were left in possession of the war's bloodiest battlefield, the Pyrrhic quality of their achievement was such that the French Marshal Claude Villars (1653–1734) could with justice remark that "the enemy would have been annihilated by another such victory." Malplaquet fed the growing war-weariness in England that edged the Tories into power as the peace party and led to the covertly negotiated Preliminary Articles of October, 1711, between the English and the French. In May 1712, the English withdrew their subsidies and armies from combat. Without the English, the Dutch and imperial armies quickly lost the initiative to the resurgent French. A series of defeats in the Low Countries and on the Rhine convinced the reluctant Dutch to join the English in making peace with the French at Utrecht (1713) and the even more reluctant Austrians to conclude the separate Treaty of Rastatt (1714).

This complex of bilateral treaties, commonly subsumed under the general title of the Peace of Utrecht, takes its place, along with Westphalia (1648) which preceded it and with Vienna (1815) and Versailles (1919) which followed it, as one of the fundamental settlements in the history of international relations. To settle the chronic international conflict stemming from the role of competing world-religions in politics the signatories at Westphalia had legislated the sovereignty of the several territorial rulers into international law. After this principle bred its own continuing international conflict stemming from the indefinite extensibility of the rulers' claims, the signatories at Utrecht broadened the principle to make the plurality of realms—that is, of settled territories and peoples—as well as of rulers subjects of international law and co-beneficiaries of its guarantees of sovereignty. In this form of an international order made up of the several sovereign states, formally equal in their rights and necessarily represented by their rulers, Utrecht's contribution would be preserved at Vienna against unsettlement in the name of world revolution and at Versailles by the merger of nationality with the traditional sovereignty of the territorial state. At Utrecht, moreover, the signatories not only registered the sovereignty of the several states but explicitly introduced the principle which would henceforward be inseparable from it: the balance of power was formally prescribed as the standard to which the mutual relations of the several sovereign states should conform.

Just as the course of the war had established the military conditions for the open recognition of balance of power as a goal of foreign policy, the preliminary negotiations leading to the peace had laid down its diplomatic base. The favorable reception which the English accorded French peace feelers ripened into agreement when the death of Emperor Joseph I in

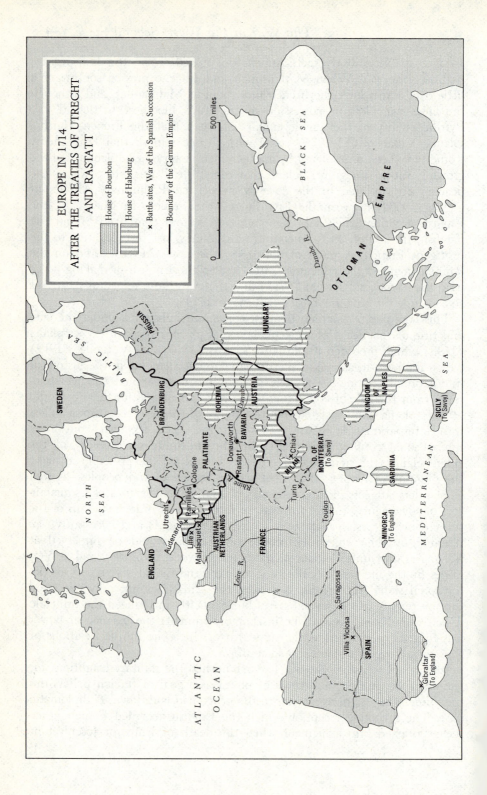

EUROPE IN 1714
AFTER THE TREATIES OF UTRECHT
AND RASTATT

House of Bourbon

House of Habsburg

× Battle sites, War of the Spanish Succession

—— Boundary of the German Empire

500 miles

0

BLACK SEA

OTTOMAN EMPIRE

Danube R.

HUNGARY

BOHEMIA

AUSTRIA

BAVARIA

Danube R.

Donauwörth

Rastatt

Rhine R.

PALATINATE

Cologne

KINGDOM OF NAPLES

SICILY (To Savoy)

SARDINIA

MEDITERRANEAN SEA

D. OF MONTFERRAT (To Savoy)

MILAN ×

× Chiari

Turin ×

Toulon ×

BRANDENBURG

PRUSSIA

SWEDEN

BALTIC SEA

NORTH SEA

Utrecht ●

Audenarde ×

Lille ×

Malplaquet ×

Ramillies ×

AUSTRIAN NETHERLANDS

ENGLAND

ATLANTIC OCEAN

FRANCE

Loire R.

MINORCA (To England)

× Saragossa

Villa Viciosa ×

SPAIN

Gibraltar (To England)

1711 made the Archduke Charles, designate of the Grand Alliance for the throne of Spain, head of the house of Habsburg and all its dominions, for the English were no more disposed to Austrian than to French hegemony over Europe. Hence in the Peace of Utrecht they recognized the Bourbon Philip V as legitimate monarch of Spain in exchange for the formal renunciations of the French succession by Philip and of the Spanish succession by Louis' French heirs, stipulated the removal of the sensitive Netherlandish and Italian territories from Spanish to Austrian control, and accepted Louis' recognition of the Protestant succession in England as established by the parliamentary Act of Settlement in 1701. This agreement revealed that in the association of dynastic with state interest the latter had become the dominant factor. The force that could be exerted by the separate sovereigns of the several European states became a more important consideration, in international law as well as practice, than the larger family connections within and between dynasties.

In addition to its factual and formal exposition of the balance of power, Utrecht also initiated the paradoxical but persistent pattern that joined this balance to English hegemony. Not only were the English the chief architects of the peace but the provisions upon which they insisted reveal the political logic in the apparent paradox of hegemony through balance. For one thing, the provisions sponsored by England to achieve a general equilibrium among the great powers obviously prevented the mobilization of continental resources against the island kingdom, but the English went further to assert a positive influence upon continental affairs by initiating local balance-of-power arrangements in the coastal areas sensitive to English naval power. At Utrecht they utilized several kinds of arrangements to check the domination of such areas by the large states. They now took from Bourbon Spain the one European possession they permitted themselves—Gibraltar—to supplement their patronage of Portugal. In the former Spanish and now Austrian Netherlands, moreover, the new Habsburg overlord submitted to English pressure and concluded a self-denying treaty with the Dutch Republic: Emperor Charles VI granted the right of garrisoning barrier forts within Austrian territory to the Dutch, whose marked decline in naval and military strength was reducing them to the status of English clients. In Italy, finally, the English made analogous arrangements for their naval security; they enlarged the role of the landlubberly Austrians whose dominion replaced that of Spain in the principalities of Milan, Sardinia, and Naples. But at the same time, the English limited any possible Habsburg pretensions to maritime power by endorsing the acquisition by Savoy (the core of the future united Italy) of the Duchy of Montferrat in the north and of Sicily in the south (later—in 1721—bartered, under English pressure, with the Habsburgs for Sardinia, after the Savoyards had shown their incapacity to defend Sicily against Britain's more pressing Mediterranean foe, Bourbon Spain). England secured, moreover, the formal declaration of "the neutrality of Italy," under general guarantee.

The free hand which this policy of interior and peripheral balance on the Continent secured to the English they chose to exercise for the acquisition of colonies and trading rights. Aside from Gibraltar and the island of Minorca, England's immediate gains at Utrecht, however modest by later eighteenth-century standards, were all of this kind, and they served as the foundation for subsequent conquests: France ceded Newfoundland, the Hudson Bay area, and Nova Scotia; the Spanish yielded the right of *asiento* and associated rights of naval protection, and gave the English an opening wedge into the Spanish colonial carrying trade. A European balance of power was indeed tailor-made for the extra-European expansion of the English.

What made possible these local agreements for British advantage was the stalemate into which the Bourbons of France and the Habsburgs of Austria had finally settled after their struggle of more than two centuries for predominance in Europe. The general lines of the settlement laid down at Utrecht were to endure for almost a century: the Rhine was formally recognized to be "the frontier between France and Germany"; German particularism was perpetuated undiminished with the restoration, at French insistence, of the anti-Imperial princes (the Electors of Bavaria and of Cologne) to their offices and possessions; Austria was compensated by a preeminent place in Italy, from which France was henceforward excluded.

At Utrecht the new mobility of the western powers, reflected in the dynamic strategies of the war, came to a temporary halt. That the halt would be only temporary was ensured by the persistence well beyond Utrecht of the eastern war and by its drift into the western orbit of international politics. For it was at this point that the European states arranged themselves into a single system of international politics in which the issues of the entire continent were mutually related. Here was the origin of that fateful pattern through which the instability of eastern Europe has time and again in the past two and a half centuries upset the more stable arrangements of the west.

THE WAR IN THE EAST: SECOND STAGE, 1700–1721

As in the west, the war in the east took a unique form from the two personages who supplied its political and military direction. Like Eugene and Marlborough, Charles XII of Sweden and Peter the Great of Russia represented that fusion of military and political considerations under whose aegis the states of Europe were beginning to assume their characteristic modern form; to all four, this fusion exalted an undogmatic and thoroughly pragmatic passion **for organization and efficiency**; for all four, mobility and aggressiveness in favorable circumstances, mobility and resilience in the face of disaster, kept organizations in being and were the marks of efficient performance.

Charles XII

Charles XII (ruled 1697–1718), the soldier-king of Sweden, presided over the definitive descent of his country into the ranks of the secondary powers, but so splendid was his defeat, so strong his grasp of what it took to be a great power, that he has remained a national hero, a symbol of what Sweden had been and of what it might have become were population and resources not the equivalent of will and intelligence in the ranking of modern states. Charles exploited and expended what his able father, Charles XI, had carefully constructed and husbanded. In particular, the wars which the elder Vasa had both prepared for and avoided the son fought unremittingly, at first by necessity, then from deliberate policy, and finally through obsession.

Effectively nurtured in the arts of government, Charles followed the spirit rather than the letter of his father's legacy in 1697 when, at the tender age of fifteen, and mere months after his father's death, he took advantage of a conflict between regents and nobility to reestablish the *de facto* autocracy of Charles XI. There is no telling what direction his government might have taken had he been left undisturbed, for his domestic administration of the next two years was fairly nondescript, compounded equally of a sovereign diligence reminiscent of Charles XI and a fresh tone of gaiety customary in the court of a teen-age monarch. The unique cast of his career, like that of so many other kings in this epoch, received its initial mold from outside, in the kiln of international politics. In 1699, the rulers of Denmark, Saxony, and Russia, foreshadowing the parallel re-formation of the Grand Alliance against French domination of the west, entered into a coalition with the aim of partitioning the Swedish empire and terminating the Swedes' hegemony over the Baltic. The following spring the allies launched a three-pronged attack against Schleswig-Holstein (a Swedish protectorate), Livonia and Ingria (Swedish possessions), thereby confronting Charles with the situation that revealed his calling and crystallized his character.

It was as a soldier that Charles XII found himself, as a soldier that he lived the rest of his life, and as a soldier that he has gone down into history. Charles's stern moral code would probably not have allowed him to start the war; but once he was convinced of the moral evil in those who had started it, this same moral code supported his professional desire not to let it end. And in truth, for the next eighteen years of this Great Northern War, Charles literally abjured capital, court, administration, marriage, civil and polite society, for the saddle and the sword—a chivalric preference that made him the last of the kings to retain personal leadership of his men in battle as the most continuous, the most characteristic, and the

Charles XII at the disastrous battle of Poltava (1709). *Characteristic representation of the wounded Swedish monarch.*

most exalted duty of a King. His atavism made his life a national epic. Like Eugene of Savoy, he was celibate, ascetic, single-minded, reserved, and blunt. Like Eugene, he focused his energies and passions upon the waging of war, and he waged it with a determination and a momentum that brought him victories beyond his resources.

But Charles was unlike Eugene in his lack of the iron self-restraint and of the cultural tastes that made the Prince of Savoy a success both as a commander and as a man. There was in Charles the passion for the infinite, the inability to rest content with any given achievement or limit, that have driven conquerors from Alexander to Hitler and that led him to ignore prudence and despise diplomacy in an age when the distribution of power was making a political necessity of both. This passion of the conqueror was joined in him, moreover, with a moral purism that ennobled it as it has rarely been ennobled in human history but that contributed nonetheless to its fateful political influence. When Charles hounded Augustus the Strong until he forced the deposition of that weaselly Saxon Elector from the throne of Poland, he undoubtedly performed an ethically satisfying act, but he also enmired himself in the bog of Polish politics and granted precious convalescent time (almost four years) to his mortal enemies, the Russians.

Just as he had rejected all peace offers from Augustus he declined them equally from Peter, and for essentially the same reason—that they came from an unworthy source. When he set off after Peter he was drawn, as by a magnet, into the boundless reaches of the Russian interior, passing up the much more reasonable and possible option of recovering the Baltic provinces. Even after he had been sucked deep into the Ukraine, had been grievously weakened by the remarkable Russian defensive combination of scorched earth and "General Winter," had been smashed by Peter at the battle of Poltava (1709), and had been reduced, as a solitary fugitive in Turkey, to an intriguer for war between Russia and the Ottoman Empire, Charles refused all offers of compromise, of mediation, or neutralization. We can guess why the Turks called him "ironhead."

The result of intransigence and weakness in combination was what might be expected—the ultimate expansion of the anti-Swedish coalition, by the time of his return to Sweden in 1714, to include all powers whose interests touched the Swedes in any way: Russia, Saxony, Denmark, Prussia, and Great Britain (in support of King George I, who as Hanoverian Elector, had covetous interest in Sweden's north German possessions). Aided by divisions among the allies, Charles performed heroically in the defense of Sweden, and he paid unprecedented lip service to the necessity of diplomatic negotiations for peace. But war had become an obsession with him, and even in these straitened circumstances he was ready to support militarily the Scottish invasion of the Stuart pretender and to embark himself upon an invasion of Danish-owned Norway. It was in the midst of this enterprise that he met his death (1718).

In many ways Charles XII was an atavism, and in these respects he reflected the anachronism of Sweden as a great power. Like his country he tended toward isolationism in diplomacy and monomania in war. Perhaps even more important, he reflected his nation's past in the ambiguous mixture of religion and morality with politics and war. In the earlier seventeenth century, under Gustavus Adolphus (ruled 1611–1632), the combination had worked to Sweden's advantage, and much of what seems inexplicable in Charles's personality and policy is attributable to his persistence in attitudes which were no longer appropriate. "Have princes the right to commit actions which in commoners are dishonorable?" he asked. "I should be incapable of it, though ten royal crowns were at stake; and could I win a hundred cities I would not do so in the manner of the King of Prussia. . . ." But the present belonged to the king of Prussia and his ilk, who recognized that politics had its own demands, its own morality, and its own limits. Charles's moral intransigence, however honorable the repute it brought him, now appeared extreme and fanatic, alienating him from reality and justifying unlimited war.

And yet there was also a modern facet in this last king of Sweden's great age. His taste and capacity for mathematics, itself in the latest mode, went into the strategy of mobility which he shared with the most advanced army commanders of the period. More fundamentally, his association of morality with the absolute inviolability of the state and its frontiers, however old-fashioned in his rigid application, did reflect the ethical and even sacred character that was passing over into the modern state.

Peter the Great

In Peter of Russia (ruled 1682–1725), Charles's great antagonist, we find the same boundless energy, the same vaulting ambition, the same dedication to the martial side of statecraft. Yet the historical destinies of the two monarchs were diametrically opposed, since the one presided over the demise of his state as a great power while the other ushered his dominion into that status. This divergence of political destiny was paralleled by the widely different traits which accompanied the common qualities of the two leaders. Where Charles was xenophobic, Peter sought out the foreigner. Where Charles was ascetic and abstemious, Peter was coarse and self-indulgent. Where Charles viewed politics from the apex of military command, Peter viewed it from the closer angle of military organization and supply. Where Charles subscribed wholeheartedly to an integral code of honor, Peter constructed his guidelines piece by piece, according to what did and what did not bring success. In short, where Charles looked to the past, Peter looked to the future, and both were right, since the greatness of their countries lay in those respective dimensions.

Like Louis XIV, Peter acceded to the throne during his minority (in 1682, on the eve of his tenth birthday) and grew up under a regency which left him in chronic want and sporadic danger. Like Louis', his youthful experience bred a lifelong mistrust of the old court and aristocracy, but under Russian conditions this mistrust found a different expression. Because the danger came from the *streltsy*, or palace guard, Peter's attention was early riveted on things military; because the regent exiled him from the Kremlin, he grew up outside the Muscovite tradition dispensed in the court; because Russian techniques were backward, he turned to foreigners within Russia.

From the age of eleven Peter absorbed himself in playing at war, but as he organized his attendants into increasingly elaborate and professional formations, staffing them with foreign officers and directing his education to mathematics, engineering, and military studies, the pastime grew into a profession and helped to frame the Tsar's career. So involved was he that even after he attained his majority in 1689, his concern was with his regiments and their "military ballets," as their exercises were called, rather than with politics and government. It is in this context, indeed, that his famous visit of 1697 to western Europe in the guise of a carpenter is to be understood. The guise was more truthful than the reality, for the artisan-tsar went more as an artisan than as a tsar. He went to learn at first hand the industrial, the military, and particularly the naval technology to which the foreign colony in Russia had alerted him and Russian naval deficiencies in the Turkish war attracted him. This addiction to the instrument,

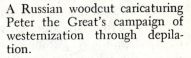

A Russian woodcut caricaturing Peter the Great's campaign of westernization through depilation.

the means, the procedure, rather than the system, the theory, or the process was to characterize his whole regime.

He returned to Russia in 1698 and immediately proceeded to demonstrate both his impulsiveness and the enthusiasm for western things that directed his impulsiveness by energetically striking out on such varied activities as exterminating the old Muscovite *streltsy*, proscribing the traditional Russian beards and dress, and building a fleet on the Sea of Azov. He made free use of torture and execution in the elimination of the *streltsy*, and he himself wielded the razor on beards of his reluctant courtiers, thereby initiating the simple and brutal resort to direct means for the attainment of an immediate result that would become the hallmark of his regime.

The Great Northern War, which followed almost immediately, had the effect of magnifying rather than submerging these tendencies. The stress of this struggle, coming hard upon the military predilections of his youth, fixed once and for all in his mind the priority of war for the state and the derivative status of all other concerns. Earthy, coarse, incontinent on the one hand and curious, sensitive, shrewd, cognizant of his official duties on the other, Peter learned through doing. Around the incessant warfare in which his own predilection and his conception of imperial responsibility coincided, he introduced, step by step, the total reorganization of the Russian state as experience revealed its necessity to military security. At first indifferent to ideas, principles, and theories, but ever more aware of western political and technical superiority, Peter applied with violence the progressive reforms which he paradoxically designed to increase the voluntary contribution of the society to the state.

Peter's participation in the Great Northern War, from which his personal rule stemmed, was itself a response to a situation rather than a deliberate change of system. He had, during the 1690's, accepted the Turkish war which he had inherited and he had directed his naval plans toward the Black Sea. The shift toward the Baltic and the north which was forced upon Peter by the Austrian defection from the anti-Turkish coalition in the Peace of Karlowitz (1699) resumed an alternate line of seventeenth-century Russian foreign policy. With no alliance against the Turks, but with an anti-Swedish alliance in the making to which he had merely to accede, the reorientation toward the north was scarcely a revolutionary act. But if Peter was not the architect of this policy, still the western orientation which was his passion before his entry into diplomacy led him to accept wholeheartedly the proposed change of fronts from the south center (on the Azov frontier, gateway to the Caucasus) to the northwest of his dominions. Although he would offer Sweden many concessions during the twenty-one continuous years of warfare upon which he now embarked, he always excepted the frontier post, near the mouth of the Neva River in the captured province of Ingria, which he began in 1703 to develop into the unofficial capital city of St. Petersburg. However fortuitous in origin, the Great Northern War provided him with the stimulus for the military, political, and social reorganization of his state because it embodied for him the fundamental decision to enter into the competitive system of the European powers.

Peter proceeded not by prearranged plan, but from measure to measure as the circumstances seemed to dictate, and these circumstances, as he intelligently perceived them, called for an ever-widening scope of governmental reorganization. Between the disaster at Narva in 1700 and the epochal triumph at Poltava in 1709, Peter devoted himself entirely to the recruitment, training, and support of a reliable and efficient army through a desperate succession of *ad hoc* decrees. The standard set by such a highly organized military power as Sweden drove him, by 1705, from the irregular induction of raw volunteers and conscripts into regular general levies, incumbent upon all classes of the population, and providing a continuing supply of trained reserves.

The civil counterpart of such an armed force, required to feed it a steady stream of loyal soldiers, uniforms, up-to-date muskets, artillery, and the tax monies to pay for it all, received in these years before Poltava the sporadic measures which military emergency obviously called for, such as the sponsorship of armaments industry and the imposition of retroactive taxation. But after Poltava, Peter by his own admission extended his purview to "the administration of civil affairs." He expanded military political reorganization into domestic affairs just as he now learned to surround military policy with a diplomatic context in foreign affairs. He utilized the temporary alleviation of the martial crisis after 1709 to rebuild the northern alliance, add Prussia to it, and embroil himself in central European affairs. To the persistent war, there was thus added a permanent entanglement in competitive international politics, and it was this new, long-range pressure that turned Peter to the enactment of basic legislation and the establishment of fundamental institutions in the effort to harness, western-style, the energies of the society to the power of the state.

What Peter said of the Senate, the organ which he created in 1711 on the Swedish model to unify and centralize the whole of internal government, held for his entire work of reform: its purpose was "to collect money, as much as possible, for money is the artery of war." Around this core he subsequently built a whole network of new or reformed agencies: the "colleges"—*i.e.* boards—into which, again on the Swedish model, the older languishing departments were reorganized to serve as the various branches of central administration; the office of procurator-general, a kind of prime minister to supervise and control the colleges; a system of provincial government newly specialized to exclude judicial and military functions (now under separate agencies) and include a host of educational and welfare activities; and a system of municipal government reorganized to promote urban self-administration by guilds under central governmental control. Accompanying these efforts to equip government for the mobilization of the society's resources was Peter's direct approach to the society itself, to galvanize its energies and direct them into governmental channels. His chief target here was, characteristically, the aristocracy—the military class par excellence—for whom he made, through punishment, education, and blandishment, the old nominal and sporadic obligation to state service a compulsory and permanent reality. The enforcement of military registration upon threat of attainder was supplemented by the imperial sponsorship of secular education for the aristocracy, at first abroad and after 1714 at home, in practical subjects that would increase its usefulness to the state. The formerly revertible and divisible service-fiefs of the aristocracy were converted into entailed hereditary estates—a measure designed to stabilize the economic basis of one part of the service nobility and to send its unpropertied siblings wholly into state service. The climax of Peter's social legislation was the enactment in 1722 of the famous Table of Ranks, which made both the nobility and the newly created distinctions of status within the nobility dependent upon service to the state—that is, upon the grade attained in military or civil office. Revelatory of the ultimate motive of this far-reaching social reform were Peter's prescription that two thirds of the nobility fill military functions and his grant of precedence to the military over the civil branch of the same rank. The reform was capped by the legislation in 1724 of the poll tax, a household levy which fell primarily upon the peasantry. This act confirmed the official function of the aristocrat as governmental administrator as well as private landlord of his serfs.

As Peter was thus led insensibly from the makeshift military measures of his early years to the fundamental political and social reforms that they entailed for him, his consciousness of the connection kept pace with the reality. The peremptory tone of the early decrees gave way to the rational explanatory prefaces of the later laws as he became increasingly aware that military security required both political unity and social cohesion. As he matured in his understanding of the network of relationships that bound governor and governed together in the modern state, his receptivity to western culture broadened from his appropriation of its techniques to the employment of the ideas which westerners used to direct their techniques. The rationales which he came to append to his laws showed more and more the influence of the western political ideas that had developed during the seventeenth century to account for and spur on the growth of the modern state. Secular and utilitarian like himself, these ideas conformed to Peter's own. They were imported, together with German and Swedish legists, to articulate the Tsar's convictions of the preeminence of "interests of state," the equal subjection of all citizens to the sovereign, the toleration of dissident—if politically loyal—religious sects, and the subordination of church to state.

And as Peter grew in political self-consciousness with the aid of western notions, his attitude toward the Russian Orthodox Church, with its traditionally ambiguous relationship to the tsar, developed apace. Where he had initially expropriated Church property and income for military purposes, he proceeded by 1721 to a fundamental reorganization of the Church which abolished the patriarchate, feared by Peter as "a second sovereign" in the eyes of his subjects, and established in its stead a Holy Synod, appointed by Peter and organized analogously to the executive colleges which ran his secular departments of state. This reform, sweeping and permanent as it proved to be, was not intended by Peter to be revolutionary, either in a religious or even an ecclesiastical sense. He was himself a believer who accepted without question, so far as we know, not only the divine governance of the world but the Orthodox doctrinal and liturgical formulations of worship. What he intended was not the principled assertion of tsarist supremacy over the spiritual organization of Russian life, but rather the tsarist authority over those aspects of clerical activity which his own experience and his western models had demonstrated to be relevant to the interests of the state—above all, over the role of the Orthodox Church in civil obedience, education, and public morals.

The institutional changes which Peter sponsored proved so fundamental that they mark the decisive turning point in Russian history down to the revolution of 1917. Obviously they could not have taken root if the soil had not been prepared for them, and as a matter of fact much of what Peter wrought had been begun before him. To this extent his statesmanship consisted in his selection, from the several possibilities available to

A picture worth a thousand words. *Depicted by an unknown artist and purporting to show the interrogation of Prince Alexis by his father, Peter the Great, because of the son's involvement in the conservative and clerical opposition to Peter's reforms. The facial expressions anticipate Alexis's fate: he was tortured and thrown into jail, where he died under mysterious circumstances in 1718.*

him, of the long-range policies that would materially strengthen the competitive western position of the Russian state, and in his ruthless execution of them.

And yet the future was to bear the marks not only of the long-range but also of the circumstantial factors that went into the policies of this age of kings. For Peter's growing realization of his state's needs betokened a broadening of his interests rather than a radical change in him. Both the violence and the despotism that were native to him continued to accompany his rule, even in its more enlightened phases. He outlived the Great Northern War, but war was as much a law of life to him as to his great rival, Charles XII of Sweden, and the year after the victorious Treaty of Nystad with Sweden (1721) he was again in the field, carrying on the struggle which he had fomented for the conquest of Persia's Caspian provinces.

His achievements at home pacified Peter no more than those abroad. He passed his last years, indeed, in a state of deepening depression, interrupted by the recurrent coarse revelries and dissipations that testified to the persistence of the unrestrained autocrat in the aging ruler. His bouts of melancholy stemmed from the conjunction of his growing conviction that only he was the reliable agent of Russia's welfare with his growing recognition of the massive scope of activities that the state, as the arena of that welfare, demanded. He imprisoned, tortured, and perhaps murdered his son Alexis, the heir apparent (the precise circumstances of Alexis' death in the prison into which Peter had cast him are unknown), and he was unable, to the day of his own death, to settle upon his successor. He despaired of the Russian will either to obey or to execute the law. During the last years he intensified the prosecution and execution of officials for malpractice, and at the time of his death he was planning a massive campaign against the bureaucracy.

When Peter died, in January, 1725, his country was as relieved as the France of 1715 and the Sweden of 1718 had been at the passing of the ·kings whom they too had nonetheless accounted great. All three countries were paying the price, as Stuart England had before them and Hohenzollern Prussia would after them, for the concession of their entire collective concerns to the care of a fallible individual. The incorporation of a whole society in one man in each case gave to that society a specious unity it could not otherwise have attained, but by the same token the confusion of the body politic with the royal person infused the still pliant structure of the new service states with a lasting tincture of arbitrary and violent compulsion.

CONVERGENCE OF THE WARS, FORMATION OF THE EUROPEAN POLITICAL SYSTEM, 1709–1721

The general course and results of the Great Northern War follow obviously from the careers of the two titanic antagonists who dominated it. Charles's early successes had driven Russia's allies from the field and turned the war into a duel for hegemony in the Baltic which Peter's decisive triumphs of 1708 and 1709 secured for Russia. Thanks in good measure to Charles's stubborn rejection of any compromise or mediation, Peter's victory held through a decade of intermittent warfare and was registered in 1721 in the Treaty of Nystad through the Swedes' cession to Russia of their eastern Baltic provinces—Livonia, Estonia, Ingria and southern Karelia, on the southeastern border of Finland. With this transfer of coastal territories Russia replaced Sweden as mistress of the Baltic Sea and as one of the European great powers as well.

These gross facts are clear enough, but a few of the more obscure details which attended the latter phases of the war give an indication of their implicit meaning.

First, the further decline of the Ottoman Empire underlined the new ascendency of the Russians. True enough, the Turks took advantage of their temporarily favorable military position when Sweden's Charles XII instigated them to attack the Russians in 1710, and in the Treaty of Pruth

(1711) Turkish power not only checked the Russian surge to the Black Sea but forced Peter to disgorge Azov (the Russians would regain it permanently in 1739) as the price for the Turks' desertion of Charles. But this fleeting triumph was overbalanced by the subsequent defeats of the Turks at the hands of the Austrians. In 1714, immediately after the conclusion of peace with France, Emperor Charles VI turned east once more against the Ottoman Empire to resume the struggle that his father had suspended in 1699. The doughty Eugene, reaching the pinnacle of his illustrious military career, led the Austrians to smashing victories at Peterwardein (1716) and Belgrade (1717). The importance of this flareup in the age-old Habsburg-Ottoman conflict was not its overt result, for however impressive the Austrian gains from the following Peace of Passarowitz (1718) may have been—and indeed, the cession of northern Serbia, parts of Bosnia and Walachia, and the Hungarian Banat seemed to open the way to the Black Sea—the bulk of them had to be surrendered again in 1739. The settlement of 1718 served indeed only to mark out the lines of future Habsburg policy. The real importance of the Austrian triumph was rather that it neutralized the prior Russian setback and allowed Peter to assert Russia's position as the eastern and not simply a Baltic power. By the spring of 1717, with the Turkish armies in retreat, Sweden's Charles XII limited to the Scandinavian peninsula, and Poland reduced to a Russian satellite, Peter could offer France an alliance against its traditional Habsburg rival in which Russia would replace all three of the eastern states with which France had traditionally cooperated. In its effects, then, the Great Northern War became an eastern war, and as such it radically simplified the international power structure of Europe.

A second set of details attendant upon the concluding phase of the Great Northern War revealed still another facet of the European system that was coming into being: the convergence of its eastern and western spheres. As might be expected from the geography of the Continent, the crucial function in this connection belonged to the central European states of the German Empire. When the western war drew toward its close at Utrecht the north German principalities of Hanover and Prussia turned their attention to the coveted possessions of stricken Sweden on the German shores of the North and Baltic seas and were drawn, on their account, into the Great Northern War as allies of Russia. Indeed, the first of the Russian-Prussian treaties that were to prove so fateful for the future history of Europe was signed in 1714 on the grave of the Swedish empire and on the basis of their common interest in the conquest of Swedish provinces. But the same favorable tide that then (between 1714 and 1720) brought Bremen and Verden to Hanover, and Stettin and western Pomerania to Prussia, also brought Peter and his army into the north German states of Mecklenburg and Holstein, which became virtual Russian protectorates.

By 1716 the shock of the Russian presence in central Europe had been transmitted through Germany into western Europe. The frightened hostility of Russia's Baltic neighbors and Germany's Habsburg Emperor to the new eastern power communicated itself to the Atlantic maritime powers. Peter's German occupation and naval preponderance, which threatened to convert the Baltic into a Russian lake, brought the western naval powers, Britain and the Netherlands, unofficially into the war as naval supporters of the Swedish cause. In response, Peter sought an alliance with France, and the first of the Franco-Russian agreements which have spanned the politics of the European continent was signed in 1717. It was not the military pact for which Peter had hoped, but it was a treaty of friendship which recognized the connection between the late western and the ongoing eastern wars, and as a matter of fact it provided for the French mediation that helped to bring about the Treaty of Nystad and thus to complete the pacification of Europe.

And so was concluded, hardly more than a century after the outbreak of the first, Europe's second thirty years' war. Together, they determined that Europe would neither be dominated by any one power nor be split up into myriad local combinations of states and issues. What emerged was a limited group of superior powers whose interests spanned the whole continent in a connected set of relations. This was the system that was to produce the decisive wars and diplomacy over the globe for more than two centuries. This was the system too that was to set the standards of national security and thus to determine the limits of what could lawfully be done by and for citizens at home.

CHAPTER 14

The Kings at Home:
The Old Powers, 1689-1748

For a whole generation the attention of the European monarchs and their governments had been fixed upon the battlefield and the conference table. Domestic policies had tended to assume convulsive and haphazard forms, since they were immediate responses to the necessities of war. And yet the effects of these domestic policies were enduring. They faithfully reflected longer-range tendencies of the respective states, and in the post-war period of the early eighteenth century many of these policies were translated into fundamental peacetime legislation which incorporated the military function into the very structure of government. The wartime generation of 1689–1721 was succeeded by the peacetime generation that focused its attention upon domestic institutions until the 1740's.

Foreign relations remained, of course, objects of continuing concern to the statesmen of the period, but they were no longer either explicit or primary for the formulation of governmental policy. The international rivalries that did break into hostilities, such as the War of the Polish Succession (1733–1735) and the Russo-Turkish war of 1736–1739, were limited in their participants, in their commitments, and in their effects. Even when, toward the end of the period, European energies were again caught up in a more general war—the intermittent and overlapping armed conflicts that have been misleadingly lumped together as *the* War of the Austrian Succession (1740–1748)—the obscurity of the war aims and the indecisiveness of the results show the struggle to have been in many ways the consequence of the domestic preoccupations which had made for peace and prepared for war. The bellicosity of the "war parties" was in part a psychic reflex from the boredom of well-solved domestic issues, in part an external explosion of internally well-ordered economic and social energies, and in part a rational determination to make use abroad of the political instruments that had been developed at home. And so, by the end of the period the European states had created the pattern of reciprocal influence between their international and internal policies which was to form so prominent a threat in their subsequent history.

There were four different kinds of domestic response to the challenge of the competitive European state system which was crystallizing out of the eastern and western wars spanning the Continent around the turn of the century. On a scale ranging from passive to active accommodation to the new international situation, we may identify: first, the states like Sweden, the Netherlands, Poland, and the Ottoman Empire, which found the strain too great and gave up on the task of forming an appropriate internal political organization; second, states like the Spanish and Habsburg empires, which adjusted only enough to maintain a stubborn but precarious defense against the dangers of partition and dissolution; third, the singular case of France, which now reached the crisis of the autocratic state as precociously, vis-à-vis the rest of Europe, as it had earlier found the key to its organization; and finally, the aggressive states of Great Britain (the official title of the island kingdom after the union of England and Wales with Scotland in 1707), Prussia, and Russia, whose rulers saw in the emergent system of international relations not simply new necessities but also new opportunities for expansion, and consequently went furthest in modernizing the constitutions of their respective states.

The differential development, in this period, of the basic institutions concerned with the security of states produced the European political system which would dominate the next two centuries. It broadened the gap between "small"—i.e. weak—states and the great powers, and it accounted for the remarkable geographical pattern which the system would assume. Henceforward the two states on Europe's periphery, Russia and Great Britain, held a balance within the continent and prosecuted aggressive designs outside it; a new central power, Prussia, would function as the organizing core for reordering the centuries-long chaos of the mid-continent; the two southern empires, Habsburg and Ottoman, would continue amid repeated convulsions to brake the forces of change; and France, that crossroads of Atlantic and continental influences, would absorb all the possible alternatives of the new state—absolutist, aristocratic, and popular—and would become the first victim of its tensions.

Success or failure in three main fields accounted for the rise or decline in power of the various European states in the eighteenth century. First, their administrations were more or less successful in mobilizing available resources. Second variations in resources, in population, and in the degree of opportunity for participating in the international seagoing trade—now a driving force in economic development—were clearly crucial factors in the rise and decline of states. But over and above these facts of political and economic geography was a variable social factor: running through the whole tendency toward the centralization of political and administrative power in the early eighteenth century was the contrapuntal resurgence of the European aristocracies. The resurgence affected ascending and declining powers alike, but the different ways in which the aristocracies met the challenge of political reorganization furnish the key to the emerging differences in the pattern of states.

THE DECLINING POWERS

The particular path of descent taken by the declining powers varied with the local conditions, but their terminus was remarkably uniform: a long era glorified as "liberty" but actually signifying a return to government by a traditional oligarchy which stifled and limited the central authority of the state in favor of aristocratic privileges and exemptions.

In the East: Poles and Turks

For Poland and the Ottoman Empire, where this oligarchic condition persisted throughout our entire period and the heights from which descent could be made lay far in the past, the decline was of a relative kind, referring to the growing gap separating these stagnant states from the active governments that were making domestic readjustments rather than to any important changes within the disorganized polities themselves. In Poland, the chronic foreign intervention and a federal constitution which conferred blessings upon aristocratic anarchy had relegated the state—if such that sanctum of nobiliar immunities may be called—to a secondary rank long before the start of our period. In the absence of any unifying institutions (the posts of what was only nominally the king's government were held by the same class of independent nobles that rendered the Diet incapable of common action) or any loyal body of citizens (the aristocracy was faction-ridden, the peasantry was enserfed, and the little there was of a middle class was composed of aliens), neither the Great Northern War of 1700–1721 nor the War of the Polish Succession of 1733–1735 could stimulate any domestic reorganization. Poland remained more a battleground than a protagonist, and only the vain dreaming of a viable Polish monarchy by its ineffectual Saxon king, Augustus, mislabeled "the Strong," affords a measure of what might have been.

For the Ottoman Turks, it was neither the constitution nor foreign intervention but military weakness stemming from the long process of *de facto* limitation of absolutism since the mid-sixteenth century that now caused the empire to drop from the ranks of the great powers. The brief surge of effective government in the third quarter of the seventeenth century, stemming from the massive enlistment of Phanariot Greeks into the Turkish administration, faded as the Greeks followed the pattern of Ottoman officialdom and built their offices into centers of independent aristocratic power. By the eighteenth century the sultan and his central government were at the mercy of the unruly corps of janissaries in the capital and of fractious warlords—Greek in the Rumanian principalities of Moldavia and Walachia, Turkish elsewhere—in the provinces. Instability at the heart of the empire manifested itself not only in the chronic insecurity of the position of the grand vizier (the sultan's chief minister) but in the violent deposition of the sultan himself—Mustafa II in 1703, and Ahmed III in 1730.

The weakness was one not so much of persons as of institutions. Even if the pacific bent and the cultural patronage of the sultans Ahmed III (ruled 1703–1730) and Mahmud I (ruled 1730–1754) be accounted political liabilities, certainly Mahmud's grand viziers, Yegen-Mohammed and Mohammed-Pascha, measured up to the current standards of statecraft. As a result of the military reorganization over which they presided, the Turks gained the surprising victories over the Austrians and the Russians in the war of 1736–1739 which brought to them the return of the Austrian Balkan conquests of 1718 (including Belgrade and excluding only the Hungarian Banat). But these successes scarcely outlasted the two grand viziers, because the Turks still had no permanent institutions that could make habitual the loyalty of the provincial paschas and hospodars, the secular collaboration of Moslems and Christians, or the impersonal devotion of the bureaucracy. Only French diplomatic and technical aid checked the descent of Turkish power during the first half of the century, but even this aid could not prevent the resumption of Turkish decline after the disastrous Russo-Turkish war of 1768–1774. Thenceforth, the Russians' presence on the shores of the Black Sea, and the acknowledgment of their claim to be protectors of the Christian population in the Ottoman Empire, effectively circumscribed Turkish freedom of action in Europe.

In the North: Dutch and Swedes

In the Netherlands, which had reached the apogee of its power only during the previous century, the decline was more perceptible, albeit hardly dramatic. The dictatorial authority which William III of Orange had wielded over the United Provinces as their *stadholder* had been rooted in his personal prestige and indispensability and administered by a personal party. It had effected no permanent institutional or constitutional change and did not survive his death in 1702. The Regents, as the urban patricians who had dominated the governments of the Dutch provinces through most of the century were appropriately called, resumed their sway, purged the Orangist partisans from the provincial and local administrations, and were able, since the succeeding Prince of Orange was still a minor, to prevent the appointment of another national *stadholder*. Behind their spokesman, Antonius Heinsius, grand pensionary (chief magistrate) of Holland, the Regents did unite in support of the alliance with the English against France in the War of the Spanish Succession, but even the Dutch share in the ultimate victory of the alliance could not long maintain the illusion that their state was still a great power, eroded as it was by the conservative administration of resources and the effects of a constitution that had fallen out of line with the requirements of the competitive system of international trade and politics. The obstructions placed by the Dutch deputies at Marlborough's headquarters in the way of that commander's dynamic strategy were symptomatic of the narrowing defensive mentality with which the Dutch ruling group was now facing its problems. Saddled with its Protestant, privileged, and particularist traditions, it made no serious effort either to expand its limited territorial base by appealing for national reunion to its former Netherlandish confederates in the Catholic but detachable Spanish (after 1714 Austrian) Netherlands to the south or to make the extraordinary levies of men and taxes demanded by the protracted warfare against Louis XIV. The result was the growing dependence upon British military subsidies and the growing proportion of British, as against Dutch, components in the nominally combined fleet. The remarkable attempt of the seven united provinces that had attained a federated independence from Spain to assert both a continental and an oceanic position of the first rank thus ended with the loss of both to Great Britain.

But it was the violent break in Swedish history at the end of the Great Northern War that made the domestic retreat of the declining states most perceptible. The Swedes had built their military power, at once awesome and exemplary to the rest of Europe, upon strict regimentation of men and resources and upon the fierce loyalty of the entire citizenry. The conversion of these relationships into the institution of absolute monarchy by Charles XI toward the end of the seventeenth century was apparently capped by Charles XII, who followed the standard practice of absolute kings when he set up his own centralized executive agencies—the Defense Commission and the Purchasing Deputation—on top of the traditional administration to carry through the conscription, special taxation, and forced loans that he required for his Great Northern War.

And yet, at Charles's death in 1718, not only the executive agencies of his own creation but the whole structure of absolute monarchy in Sweden collapsed. Aided by the fortuitous extinction of the Vasa dynasty and the advantages inherent in electing a new monarch, the *Riksdag* formally assumed supreme power and established a system of government in which the actual exercise of sovereignty lay with the aristocratized bureaucracy. Still deliberating and voting in separate houses and with the requirement of three majorities for the passage of legislation, as of yore, the four estates—nobles, clergy, burghers, and peasants—checked one another too thoroughly for the diet to function as an effective sovereign authority. Government redounded in fact to the ennobled officials who ran the Council of the Realm and who were careful to disturb neither the nobles' monopoly of high office, nor their privilege of tax exemption, nor their hostility to the further expansion of the noble class, nor the right of Crown peasants to purchase freeholds. Under the prudent leadership of the Counselor Arvid Horn (1664–1742), a Swedish oligarchy of aristocratic officials, supported by burghers and peasants, managed until Horn's fall in 1738 to endow the "era of liberty" with a pacific policy abroad and at home. Reconciled to the loss of empire and careful to respect the traditional privileges and immunities of all corporate groups, the oligarchy remained in office by avoiding the impositions and tensions of great-power status.

THE PERSISTENT EMPIRES

While the aristocracies of the declining states thus used their recovered strength to roll back the concentration of power in the sovereign authority, the aristocracies of the persistent empires struck a bargain with their monarchs. The notables of these states acceded to the extension of imperial power on condition that their own privileges and immunities would not be infringed thereby.

Spain

The fall of Spain had seemed virtually complete by the end of the seventeenth century under the combined weight of the nobiliar oligarchy whose councils frustrated the central government, the local nobility who secured the autonomy of their provinces through their domination of the influential regional cortes (diets) of Aragon, Catalonia, and the Basque Provinces, the urban oligarchies who jealously guarded the medieval immunities of their communes, and a degenerate dynasty of Spanish Habsburgs who reached their moral as well as physical conclusion under the feebleminded Charles II (ruled 1665–1700).

When the War of the Spanish Succession assumed the shape of a civil war within Spain, with Aragon and Catalonia espousing the cause of the Austrian Habsburg Charles against the Bourbon Philip, the state seemed on the verge of dissolution. But once recognized as the legitimate monarch by the powers of Utrecht the Bourbon Philip V checked the decomposition of the central authority by imposing an overlay of a French-style administrative system upon the traditional governing organs. Setting a series of ministries over the councils on the central level and placing intendants and military commandants over the cortes on the regional level, Philip reestablished royal authority over the basic functions of military security, finance, colonial relations, and general administration. He forcibly repressed the rebellious provinces and the Aragonese Cortes, but he otherwise asserted absolute power without violent alteration of the wonted constitution. The other provincial diets and the executive councils, with their corporate organization and aristocratic personnel, remained in being,

Charles II, last of the Spanish Habsburgs. *His death in 1700 triggered the War of the Spanish Succession.*

and the Councils of Castile and of the Indies even retained a considerable administrative importance.

Although the continued existence of the political preserves of the privileged classes marked the limits of change in Spain, the administrative reorganization did enable a bureaucratized monarchy to wield effective authority in the colonial and naval fields—the activities most relevant to the reassertion of Spanish power.

The Spanish empire was strengthened economically by King Philip's mercantilist policy of industrial protection, by the centralization of the financial administration, and by the encouragement of private participation, through new trading companies, in the exploitation of the colonies. Under the direction of such able ministers as Giulio Alberoni (1664–1752) and José Patiño (c. 1666-1736), the revived central government restored its navy to a third-ranking place, behind those of Great Britain and France. The result was a surprising reassertion of Spanish power, giving the state a respectable, if not preeminent, position in the shifting alignments of eighteenth-century international politics. Spain indeed was in the thick of the minor wars that kept breaking out during the generation that followed Utrecht, and emerged not only with its empire intact but with its sphere of influence modestly expanded. The primary issue of contention was Italy, the one area whose disposition had been left unresolved by the Utrecht settlement. Spurred on by Philip's domineering Italian-born queen, Elizabeth Farnese (1692–1766), Spain was an aggressive claimant to the southern and central territories of the disorganized peninsula.

The Spanish ambitions in the Mediterranean brought open conflict with the Austrians in 1717, 1733–1735, and 1741–1748, and with the British in 1718–1719, in 1727, and, abetted by Anglo-Spanish colonial rivalry in America, most seriously in 1739–1748. As long as the Spaniards had to contend with a common Anglo-French front—an unusual combination for these rival Atlantic powers, explicable by their mutual interest in preventing any change that might threaten the Utrecht settlement—their tactical victories over the Austrians in Italy were to little avail. But then, in the 1730's, the revival of the traditional French anti-Habsburg policy and the increasing colonial frictions with the British shifted the orientation of Bourbon France toward the family compact with Spain that was to persist as a stable factor in European diplomacy until the French Revolution. The Spaniards then managed to stalemate the British in America and to roll the Habsburgs back from southern Italy. In 1738, the Treaty of Vienna, which formally concluded the War of the Polish Succession, recognized a Spanish Bourbon dynasty in an independent Kingdom of Naples (including the island of Sicily). Although formal union with Spain was barred by the provision that the succession in Naples was to be through the dynasty's second sons ("secundogeniture"), southern Italy would remain within the orbit of Spanish ambition until its conquest by Napoleon, and dynastically related to Spain until the unification of Italy in 1860.

Habsburg Dominions

The other realm which was characterized by astonishing powers of survival was the empire of the Habsburgs. From the heady days of Prince Eugene's victories against the French and the Turks in the early years of the eighteenth century—victories crowned by the territorial gains registered in the treaties of Rastatt (1714) and Passarowitz (1718)—Austrian fortunes went into a rapid decline until the state seemed destined for partition in the War of the Austrian Succession, which began in 1740. For this war was not a sudden catastrophe: the groundwork for it had been laid by a whole series of losses in the international arena and by the neglect of needs at home. Between 1725 and 1728, the Habsburgs had briefly seemed to be reaping the fruit of their earlier triumphs by becoming the core of a continental bloc, which included Russia, Prussia, and Spain. But the bloc soon disintegrated, and Austria, isolated except for some inadequate support from post-Petrine Russia, lost during the disastrous decade of the 1730's the bulk of the territory acquired during the glorious decade of the teens. Through the War of the Polish Succession, Naples and Sicily were lost to the Spanish Bourbons and the satellite Duchy of Lorraine to France. As a result of the Turkish war of 1736–1739 the Serbian, Walachian, and Bosnian acquisitions of 1718 were returned to the Turks. The Habsburgs did receive Parma, Piacenza, and through an indirect dynastic arrangement, Tuscany, in partial compensation for the Italian cessions; and they did retain the Hungarian Banat. But at the time these territories seemed to be outposts in a general retreat rather than the bases for the expansion of Austrian influence that they would in fact become.

The post-Passarowitz military failures were related directly to diplomatic ineptitude and indirectly to the government's passivity in domestic affairs. On the diplomatic side, Austria's isolation in western Europe led to the defeats in the War of the Polish Succession and to a dependence upon Russia that pulled the Habsburgs into their pointless and disastrous participation in the Turkish war. On the domestic side, the *de facto* political absolutism—that is, the hereditary succession of Habsburg monarchs and the acceptance of their legislative sovereignty by all their dominions—which had been erected at the time of the Thirty Years' War on the basis of Catholic uniformity remained static while other governments were energetically extending their effective authority over their peoples. Provincial diets and county estates retained far-reaching rights of self-administration and economic privileges under royal governments in Vienna (for Austria and Bohemia) and in Pressburg (for Hungary) which were not organized actually to make the policy they had the acknowledged authority to make. In the Viennese central administration itself, only the Court Chamber for the supervision of finances and a Court War Council had general jurisdiction. Otherwise, government in Vienna was conducted by separate agencies for the various lands of the Austrian archduchy and the Bohemian monarchy. The aristocracies of the sundry dominions that made up the Habsburg realm were loyal to the dynasty, but only within the limits of a mutual respect for the traditional way of doing things. When the sovereign's ministers did make tentative efforts to effect a more intensive mobilization of the dominion's resources, the notables withheld their cooperation —a posture which their crucial role in provincial and local administration made tantamount to a successful campaign of passive resistance. Aristocratic self-government and privilege in regard to land taxes stymied financial reform; provincial and local obstructions to trade and traffic stymied economic development. Thus the growing expenses of the new political demands met a static supply of resources, and the result was a chronic financial crisis that undermined the state's capacity for decisive action.

But if the predominance of the aristocracy in the provinces and at the court helped to prevent the *extension* of the central power, this same aristocracy did acquiesce in the monarch's *retention* of the basic functions which made it possible for him to exploit his various dominions as a single state for purposes of international relations. However diverted in the execution, the central administration retained supreme control over the command and organization of the army and over federal tax assessments, and its agents levied and collected these assessments on towns, royal domains, and commodities. However divided and impotent in practice, a Privy Conference did exist as a supreme advisory council. It included the highest officials from the various branches of the government, and their deliberations were intended to form the basis for a unified policy.

The political connections among the Habsburg territories were close enough, moreover, to make Austria the original home of "cameralism," the version of mercantilism that was to become characteristic of eighteenth-century German economic policy. It was to the Habsburg monarchy of Leopold I that the typical programs of this school had been first addressed, in the last quarter of the seventeenth century, and it was in the Habsburg monarchy of Charles VI that a tentative application of them was made during the first third of the eighteenth century. What was distinctive in cameralism, vis-à-vis the more familiar versions of mercantilism which furnished the guidelines of policy in the western European countries, stemmed from the conditions of Habsburg rule, and Habsburg cameralism became the model for other German states where conditions were similar. Definitive of these distinctive conditions were an economy that was laggard in comparison with those of competing countries, a society with few traditions of cohesion, and a government in which the distinction between the definite rights of the ruler over his own domain and his indefinite rights over the rest of the state was still a real one. The cameralists, taking their name from *Kammer* ("chamber"), the territorial lord's own exchequer, responded to these conditions not only by working out a set of policies, as the mercantilists did, but by elaborating a theory, as the mercantilists did not. There were three distinctive attributes of Austrian and German cameralism. First, cameralism was not simply, like mercantilism, a set of economic policies for an operating administration, but rather an entire administrative "science" to modernize the operation of government in general, including economic policy as one of its essential parts. Economics, in this context, was central to the extension of the sovereign's control from his private domains to the very different conditions of his subjects' domains, of which he was ruler but not lord. Second, greater emphasis was put, in economic policies, on the positive role of public agencies in both stimulating and operating new economic enterprise than on their role in controlling existing private economic activities. Finally, the financial purpose and interest of the sovereign in cameralist controls were far more explicit than the covert fiscal motives lurking behind the more general political, economic, or social mercantilist goals of the more advanced societies. The adoption of cameralist standards by prominent officials in Charles VI's regime testified at least to their belief in the possibility of imposing from the top the institutions and policies that would galvanize and coalesce the separate classes and regions of the Austrian society. But until the catastrophic War of the Austrian Succession

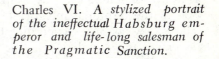

Charles VI. A *stylized portrait of the ineffectual Habsburg emperor and life-long salesman of the Pragmatic Sanction.*

(1740–1748), the notables would not accept these institutional consequences of the monarchy they did accept, and the measures initiated against internal trade barriers under Charles VI, for example, were frustrated by provincial opposition.

The balance in Austria between the general recognition of monarchical sovereignty and the limits within which the valid exercise of that sovereignty was recognized explains the history of the famous Pragmatic Sanction, the central issue in the reign of Charles VI. The Pragmatic Sanction, declared by Charles VI to his closest advisers in 1713 and submitted officially to his territorial estates for ratification from 1720, was a royal ordinance with the status of fundamental law. It made Leopold I's family compact of 1703 a constitutional amendment. This compact had provided for female succession to the Habsburg throne, and thus to the rulership over all Habsburg possessions, in default of male heirs. But the Pragmatic Sanction reversed the compact's specific order of the succession, transferring priority from the daughters of the older brother, Joseph (died 1711), to the daughters of Charles VI. The domestic importance of the Pragmatic Sanction lay in the potential conflict between the principle of the indivisibility of the Habsburg territories asserted in it and the still valid fundamental laws of those Habsburg territories which excluded female succession. Charles's protracted but successful negotiations with the estates of his territories for their consent to this amendment of their fundamental laws faithfully expressed the relations between the Habsburgs and their aristocracies: by 1732 all the estates had agreed to the Pragmatic Sanction and its principle of an indivisible empire but had underscored the voluntary basis of their assent by making the reaffirmation of their consitutional rights an essential part of their compact with the ruler. Certainly the Pragmatic Sanction represented a net gain for the unity of the Habsburg dominions, for it placed the integrity of the state beyond the accidents of succession. But the necessity of securing the consent of the aristocracy and of confirming its traditional privileges and immunities left Charles VI with little disposition or energy to struggle against this group, and without such a struggle he could not extend the authority of his central government.

The international history of the Pragmatic Sanction was similarly marked by protracted and successful negotiations for endorsement, but in this arena the result, in the final balance, was a net loss. In his diplomacy, as in his bargaining with his estates, Charles purchased the formal recognition of the territorial integrity of Habsburg lands for his heiress, Maria Theresa, by nominally conceding the long-asserted claims of his rivals. But in foreign affairs, unlike domestic, the stagnation of the monarchy invited not loyalty but attack. Prussian impatience at the Austrian failure to deliver the succession rights to the Duchy of Berg, promised in 1728 as the price for the Prussian guarantee of the Sanction, formed a grievance which, together with the conviction that Austria was impotent, impelled the young Frederick II of Prussia to attack and acquire Austrian Silesia in 1740. Similarly, the Habsburg concession of the Duchy of Lorraine to the French protégé Stanislas Leszczynski (1677–1766), in 1735—a concession that helped to buy France's recognition of the Sanction—encouraged the rise of the French war party which soon resumed expansionist policies against the apparently vulnerable Habsburgs along the Rhine and in the Austrian Netherlands. The same party urged the Franco-Prussian military alliance which was actually concluded in 1741 against Austria.

Thus the efforts to secure international agreement to the Pragmatic Sanction aroused the resentments and stimulated the greed that led to the War of the Austrian Succession. Ironically, the concessions promised by the Habsburgs to ensure the undivided succession of their dominions brought on a war that threatened to divest them of dominions to succeed to. Prussia, Spain, and Saxony sought to slice off peripheral Habsburg territories, and the French had plans to set up a Bavarian Emperor of Germany and to partition the Austrian and Czech heartlands of the Habsburg dominions.

Obviously, the Habsburg policy of bargaining was a diplomatic failure, but the entrenchment of the dynasty effected by the domestic counterpart of this policy, abetted by a military alliance with Great Britain, limited Austrian losses to Silesia and to trivial cessions in Italy. Moreover, the combination of the domestic success of the Pragmatic Sanction with the military losses which it failed to prevent nurtured the seed of Habsburg revival which was to flower in the second half of the century.

FRANCE: CROSSROADS OF EUROPE

The domestic history of France between Louis XIV's last great war and the middle of the eighteenth century uncovered the tensions which were subsequently to isolate this nation as the one revolutionary power in Europe. The gap which favorable geography, available resources, and superior political organization had opened between France and the rest of Europe during the seventeenth century began to tell against the leader. The comparative superiority of the French, which had enabled them to make martial expansion a national tradition, now imposed a serious strain upon the state. Not only did French governments fail to recognize the mounting costs of maintaining such a tradition in the face of effective foreign competition both from Great Britain on the ocean seas and from modernizing land powers on the Continent but the French position on the crossroads of the Atlantic economies and the mainland societies opened the internal organization of France fully to the paralyzing countercurrents of economic growth and social resistance.

The most convulsive symptom of this strain was the financial crisis that darkened the latter years of Louis XIV's reign and deepened during the course of the eighteenth century. The financial crisis was not simply a symptom of too much war and too much royal extravagance. It also testified to the arrival of an advanced stage of state making in which the central authority was faced with the necessity of invading areas of economic and social privilege hitherto inessential to it. The paradox whereby the most centralized state in Europe experienced, during the eighteenth century, the most effective aristocratic resurgence is explicable by the new economic and social level which the confrontation of state and aristocracy now reached in France. This conflict remained a stalemate, and the chronic financial crisis was the most prominent reflection of it. The very success of the nation in meeting the challenge of the international exchange economy made large sections of the aristocracy dependent on support by the state to meet their rising costs and their growing indebtedness. But the state in turn looked to the contributions of all classes for the support of its own officials and their activities. The financial crisis became the battlefield wherein aristocracy and bureaucracy fought for control of the state they both needed. While other states, with their socially detached bureaucracies and their relatively undeveloped economies, were still reaping the benefits of a political unity that by common consent only the central government could provide, the French were progressing to the critical stage of social politics wherein the bureaucracy and the corporations represented mature, aggressive, and opposing groups which aimed at turning political unity to their own social advantage.

France under Louis XIV: Last Phase (1689–1715)
Under the pressure of the incessant warfare that filled the last twenty-

five years of his reign, Louis XIV had extended the instrumentalities of royal absolutism ever more obtrusively into the internals of French social life. In part the extension stemmed from the expansion and specialization of the royal agencies. It was a matter rather of administrative practice than institutional change, for the system of government through central councils and functional departments of state, unified by the supreme will and common direction of the king, persisted actually to the end of Louis XIV's regime and nominally until the revolution. But wherever government affected people rather than policy, the balance between corporate and bureaucratic institutions which had made the increase in monarchial power not only acceptable but even welcome to the society of seventeenth-century France was now, in the latter stage of Louis' long reign, upset by an excess of bureaucratic pressure. The *intendants*, general regional agents of the king, extended their control over provinces and towns; the inspectorates, agencies of the central administrative departments, were multiplied for the most varied kinds of products and activities; the office and powers of the police lieutenancies, both in Paris and in the provinces, grew inexorably.

But in part, too, the increasing regimentation of the French society was an indirect product of fiscal need: the ever more frequent resort to the creation and sale of offices generated a plethora of officials whose competition for control and for fees multiplied the points of contact between government and people. The growing pressure of the state upon the society was concentrated particularly in the fields of economics and religion, and the character of this pressure set the stage for the profound divisions that tore the nation throughout the eighteenth century and beyond.

The mounting financial requirements of the state at war furnished the spur for the extension of mercantilism into an ever more rigid and inclusive system of controls. The institutions that had been designed by Colbert to trigger economic growth were now developed into a fiscal machine to siphon off all surpluses from working capital and current income. Import tariffs were raised to prohibitive proportions. Exports of food and raw materials from France and even from one region of France to another were prohibited. Internal tolls were raised as a matter of tax policy. Available resources were diverted to the industries which armed and clothed the military forces of the king. Hordes of inspectors supervised every stage in the process of production, setting standards and collecting taxes for their stamps of approval. Capital was in effect confiscated, both by the enforced circulation of paper currency and by compulsory loans to the treasury. The result of the wars and of the economic policy geared to wars was a severe depression of the French economy—affecting all its branches save the armaments industries—and the literal bankruptcy of the government, complete with the virtual repudiation of a large proportion of its debt to those citizens who by choice or under duress had invested their capital in it.

The tax needs of the state grew increasingly more critical as the tax base shrank. Louis XIV's government, consequently, sought to expand this base by canceling the age-old exemption of the aristocracy from direct taxation, and by imposing new levies upon all citizens, with capacity to pay the only principle of discrimination. A royal decree of 1695 enacted a head tax (*capitation*), dividing all French subjects into twenty-two classes according to assumed income, and proportioning the tax according to the class. Since these revenues proved inadequate, the king announced still another presumably egalitarian direct tax in 1710: the royal tithe (*dixième*), a 10 per cent income tax modeled on the church tithe. Although both taxes were limited to the duration of the war (the head tax was indeed suspended during the truce of 1697–1701), they clearly signified the intention of the monarchy, under the pressure of necessity, to breach the financial privileges of the aristocracy and the clergy, privileges whose retention had formed a crucial part of the tacit agreement which had reconciled these corporations to political obedience.

The royal policy that sought to abridge the tax immunities of the privileged classes coincided with royal infringements upon the ecclesiastical rights of clerical bodies in their own religious capacity. We have already seen what Louis' later brand of religiosity meant for him (see pp. 20–21), but in the event, it proved to be more than a personal matter, since the long-run residue of the change in Louis' religious policy was a thorn that festered in French public life as a source of conflict throughout the eighteenth century. For the country as a whole, Louis' shift away from the mixture of Gallicanism and qualified toleration that had aided the rise of both Bourbon and French power since the age of Henry IV (ruled 1589–1610) implied as fundamental a rift in the network of corporate privilege as his simultaneous financial enactments. If the spectacular suppression, by agencies of the state, of the Reformed (Calvinist, or Huguenot) Church and the Jansenist movement within the Catholic Church may be seen as the elimination of recalcitrant minorities with the aid of the official church, certainly the accompaniment of these measures by Louis' quiet revocation of the charter of Gallican liberties which had guaranteed the rights of the French Catholic Church as a national institution threw new light upon the policy. Whatever the motivation, the effect of the policy was to put the power of the state into areas that had been under the competence of corporate bodies.

The impact of the financial and religious measures of Louis' later reign was twofold: the customary privileges of traditional corporations were violated, and individuals were thus confronted directly with the state in areas of social activity which had formerly been the terrain of corporate mediation between state and individual. The immediate response of the society to the innovations was correspondingly twofold: on the one hand, the privileged orders sought to resist the royal incursions and recover their specific exemptions; on the other hand, representatives of those orders sought to redefine those exemptions, changing them to general rights which would bring the will of the whole society to bear against the overextension of state power.

The most characteristic response of the first type was the aristocracy's forceful opposition to and effective frustration of the new equalizing taxes of Louis' wartime administration. The aristocracy evaded the intended incidence of the taxation through a combination of bargains with the government for reduced rates, redistribution of the levies within the provinces on the model of the traditional and unequal *taille*, and simple noncompliance. Nor was the aristocracy the only corporation in the France of the aging Louis XIV to oppose his growing intervention in fields of vested interests. The merchants, still grouped by the myriad of privileges and obligations stemming from the palmy days of the commercial guilds, grew restive under the increasing burden of indirect taxation and direct regulation imposed by the agents of the central authorities. Their spokesmen in the royal Council of Commerce (the official advisory body of bureaucrats and elected merchant representatives which had been formed in 1699) began to complain aloud of the obstructions to and decline of trade, while in the towns they themselves initiated the practices of evasion which, during the course of the eighteenth century, undermined in fact the mercantilist policies that grew ever more stringent in the lawbooks. Presaged now, too, was the social lineup which, whatever the class frictions in other contexts, permitted aristocratic initiative against autocracy to represent other organized groups in French society until the very eve of the revolution.

Characteristic of this traditional and corporate type of response too was the reaction to Louis' religious aggressions. Against his arrangements with the Pope and his sympathy with Ultramontane Jesuits, the Gallicans rallied to the defense of the national church, and the Jansenist cause was adopted by the royal courts (*parlements*). Louis' extraordinary measures adumbrated ordinary royal policy throughout the eighteenth century, and the opposition to them adumbrated the corporate resistance to this policy. Not surprisingly, tax privileges and religion remained the two primary issues of conflict between king and notables until the revolution.

Equally prophetic of the internal struggles to come was the progressive form taken by the articulate response from the threatened groups. This kind of response was pioneered, during Louis' own lifetime, by aristocratic and religious writers who transmuted the traditional claims of corporations into general programs of political reform. In the process they rationalized and modernized their defense of privilege by reconciling it with the political sovereignty of the monarch and by connecting it with the claims of the whole community upon the monarch.

Among the spokesmen for the aristocracy, that inveterate gossip, Louis le Rouvroy, Duke of Saint-Simon (1675–1755) with his nostalgic and

The Duke of Saint-Simon. *Unreconstructed aristocrat, nostalgic grumbler, and gossipy memorialist of the court of Louis XIV.*

impotent grumbling for the good old days of noble and royal partnership in the government of France, may have been close to what his peers were thinking; and certainly the French histories of his contemporary, Henri de Boulainvilliers, Count of Saint-Saire (1658–1722), were unashamed exaltations of those days with the purpose of bringing about their restoration; but the up-to-date thinking of Archbishop François Fénelon (1651–1715), Sébastien de Vauban (1633–1707), and Pierre de Boisguillebert (1646–1714) announced the main line that the aristocracy was to take in the coming century.

Noble-born, royal tutor (of Louis XIV's grandson, the Duke of Burgundy), maverick Archbishop of Cambrai (inclining toward heterodox Quietism), Fénelon combined elements of tradition and innovation in his writing as in his life. In his banned utopian novel, *Telemachus* (1699), as well as in his essays on the responsibilities of kings, Fénelon stressed, in good traditional fashion, both the inherent obligation of the king to govern for the good of his subjects in accordance with the law of the land and the necessity of an edifying moral education to inculcate him with fitting self-restraint. Neither such pious discourse nor Fénelon's fulminations against the evils of despotism were particularly new. What was new was his project for the constitutional reform of France, in which he sought to renovate the political function of the aristocracy by making it the pivotal factor in maintaining a balance between the sovereign monarch and popular rights. He would check the king not by pleading for special class immunities, but by placing general constitutional limitations upon the sphere of recognized sovereign power which the king exercised. The guarantor of the royal limits, accordingly, was not simply the noble caste, but a whole hierarchy of assemblies, stretching from the local to the national levels, which would represent the entire people and would be led by its aristocratic section in its primary function of confining the royal authority within proper bounds. Fénelon did not shrink from giving his proposals immediate point by blaming Louis XIV's excesses of power for miseries of all classes of the population, and he thereby initiated the role of spokesman for the nation which the French aristocracy was to assume during the eighteenth century.

In Vauban and Boisguillebert, the other facet of the aristocracy's representative function during the eighteenth century was adumbrated. Where Fénelon initiated the modernization of the nobility's constitutional claims upon the state, Vauban and Boisguillebert opened the way to new versions of its administrative prerogatives within the government. Both were aristocrats by birth and bureaucrats by profession, Vauban as a military engineer and Boisguillebert as a jurist. Both were convinced monarchists who were led by their specific criticisms of Louis XIV's monarchical policies into seminal proposals for the reorientation—albeit not the reformation—of royal absolutism. Both developed their proposals in the context of avocations adjacent to their administrative careers—Vauban as a writer on military science, Boisguillebert as a political economist—and the import of both recommendations was the simultaneous limitation and strengthening of monarchy through the elimination of what was capricious and arbitrary in its policies.

The beginning of Vauban's disaffection can be traced to his precise estimate, in 1689, of France's loss—and its enemies' corresponding gain—in soldiers, cash, and industrial resources as a result of the Huguenot emigration after the revocation of the Edict of Nantes. In a crucial position to observe the destructive effects which Louis' subsequent exactions had on the military fortunes of the French state as well as on the welfare of its inhabitants, Vauban ultimately worked up his disapproval into his *Plan for a Royal Tithe* (written in 1698 and published in 1707), wherein he demanded equality of taxation and postulated as its corollary a monarchical state governed in accordance with general laws. During the same period Boisguillebert, an avowed supporter of Vauban, was making the same points in a broader economic argument. First in his *Economy of France* (1695) and again in his *Memorandum on France* (1707), Boisguillebert expanded his criticisms of the inequities of the French tax system into a general attack upon the bullionist and restrictive policies of governmental mercantilism and made a general defense of agriculture as the main source of the national wealth. What these writers resented was civil rather than social privilege. They found special rights and exemptions incompatible with the requirements of the state, and they insisted upon the contribution of all classes to the support of the state for the purpose of making the social hierarchy compatible with a state predicated upon the equal obligations of its citizens.

Not only the aristocracy but confessional Christianity too responded to Louis XIV's subversion of traditional corporate institutions by developing new intellectual bases of their rights. Among the Christian churches, it was dispersion of the Huguenots, the most persecuted of Louis' ecclesiastical corporations, which produced the most progressive theory of the free spirit. Pierre Jurieu (1637–1713), the exiled Huguenot pastor who fulminated against his former sovereign from his refuge in the Netherlands, was the transitional figure in this intellectual development, and through the ambiguities of his writings we can see how it worked. In his *Pastoral Letters* (1688-1689) and his *Sighs of Enslaved France* (1689–1690) he asserted nominal doctrines of religious liberty, natural rights, popular sovereignty, and contractual government side by side with commitments to Calvinism as the one true faith, to the sanctity of historical tradition as the basis of valid constitutions, to the hierarchy of corporate estates as the political spokesmen of the people, and to the exclusive right of this corporately organized people as a whole to defend both individual and collective liberties against violation. Thus he gave a modern libertarian cast to the old sixteenth-century monarchomachic doctrine of ecclesiastical resistance to religious oppression, but he added rather than combined the newer and the older ideas.

It was left to Jurieu's fellow Calvinist and exile, Pierre Bayle (1647–1706), to use the same kind of bitterness as a goad to the clear enunciation of a new liberal principle. Author of the *Historical and Critical Dictionary* (1697), which was to become the source book of the French Enlightenment, Bayle deepened his criticisms of Bourbon France, arriving at a general principle of doubt that was directed against all propositions, beliefs, and institutions not founded on sound reason or a solid empirical base. He broadened the special claim for toleration of the Reformed Church into a general principle of liberty of conscience, applicable by right to every religious belief and grounded in the priority of universal moral reason over particular religious dogma. Bayle's intellectual advance, so far beyond the stymied religious corporation from which he started, was an early harbinger of the philosophical breakthrough which would lead men from the defense of corporations to the assertion of individualism later in the eighteenth century.

The Regency (1715–1723)

The death of the Sun King, in September, 1715, followed hard upon the last of the conventions composing the Utrecht settlement. Both events announced the start of a new era: within France there was a visceral reaction against all that the grasping, failing Louis had stood for; outside of

France one-power hegemony was ended, and a multipower balance began to emerge. The immediate consequence of Louis' death was the swing of the pendulum in domestic political and economic affairs, for some five years, to the opposite extreme. Where autocratic wartime control had been the rule, the pursuit of peace, pleasure, and profit became general.

The shrewd but licentious Duke of Orléans (1674–1723), who had brought into focus the growing discontent under his uncle Louis XIV and now became regent for the five-year-old Louis XV, set the tone. The court moved to Paris and became the model for the relaxation of manners and morals from the recent constraints of Versailles' somber piety. The Duke himself embarked upon notable experiments in government, finance, and foreign policy quite different in tendency from the former system.

In government, he attempted to restore the political influence of the high nobility by instituting a set of central councils—from feudal times the most appropriate kind of institution for the aristocracy's participation in the business of monarchy—as the supreme executive organs of the state. But this *Polysynodie*, as the conciliar system was called, was no mere throwback to the unprofessional conciliar governments of the Middle Ages. Composed of bureaucrats as well as nobles and organized by function (war, navy, foreign affairs, interior, finance, and religion), it represented an effort to work the old-line aristocracy into the actual administration of a modern bureaucratic state. There was no inherent necessity for the experiment to fail, as the contemporaneous experience of Prussia was to show, but in France fail it did. It was dismantled as early as 1718, because, as one of its most strenuous proponents, the Duke of Saint-Simon ruefully admitted, the nobility that manned it evinced neither the taste nor the competence for the job.

The Regency thereupon accomplished the restoration of the balance between aristocracy and bureaucracy, which had been displaced in favor of the latter under Louis XIV, by deliberately returning a traditional right to an aristocratic party and inadvertently removing the crucial lever of control from the bureaucracy. On the first count, Orléans returned the right of remonstrance—*i.e.* of protest against the king's edicts—to the royal *parlements*, and he thereby conferred upon the judicial nobility that composed them the political weapon that would make them the aggressive leaders of the aristocratic resurgence. On the second count, the Regency initiated the diffraction of central authority that would prevent any unitary resolution of its internal tensions. No person or agency could replace the king as synchronizer of councils and ministries in the French system, and the failure of the *Polysynodie* brought not only the dismantling of the new councils but the gradual atrophy of the established ones. The actual work of government settled firmly in the hands of the chancellor (the chief legal officer) and the ministers (the four secretaries of state and the controller general), with their specialized departments. The Regency did revive the post of prime minister, dormant since the tenures of Richelieu

Mass anger and bitterness in Paris in 1720 after the collapse of John Law's Mississippi project.

and Mazarin in the previous century, to coordinate activities of the ministers, separately appointed and responsible as they were. For a few months before his death in 1723 Orléans took the post himself in fact and in title, but it was not revived after Louis XV (ruled 1715–1774) assumed his majority in 1723. From 1726 until 1743 Cardinal Fleury effectively occupied it in fact albeit not in title. But the post proved to be only a way station on the central government's road to confusion: not only was it discontinued both in name and in function after Fleury, but even during its revival it served more as an adjunct of the foreign office than as a source of general policy and unified control.

From the Regency on, the government operated through agents who recognized that the source of their powers lay in royal authority but who claimed that the right to exercise these same powers inhered in their offices and was inviolable by the royal authority which was its source. Here was the institutional basis of the political issue that seems so anomalous to modern minds but was to dominate the constitutional debates of eighteenth-century France: the issue of the limits that, according to fundamental law, could be imposed upon the sovereign power in the state by its own derivative agents.

Orléans' financial experiment was perhaps bolder and certainly more modern. Envious of the stability which had enabled Great Britain and the Netherlands to weather the long wars without suffering the quasi-bankruptcy that was the French memento, Orléans was persuaded by the Scottish adventurer and sometime banker John Law (1671–1729) that a two-pronged program of credit expansion and tax reform would finally resolve France's long-standing financial crisis. The Regent entrusted Law with both parts of the program. By 1720 Law had, with official approval, founded a trading company and a state bank, and united both into a single institution. He was, moreover, issuing both paper money and stock certificates on the joint basis of the trading monopoly (in North America) and of state credit. In 1720, too, Law was appointed Controller-general by Orléans, and in this capacity he sketched a progressive scheme of reform reminiscent of Vauban's in its provision for an equal tax and a uniform system of tax collection by state agencies. But the influences favoring a boom were too strong: the upward turn of the economic cycle following upon the long wartime depression, the beginnings of the spectacular growth in overseas trade that was to mark the century, the heady atmosphere of postwar abandon, and the unfamiliarity with the new credit instruments all generated the speculative fever which found expression in the scheme, which was subsequently known as the "Mississippi bubble." When it burst, in October, 1720, the downfall of Law and his projects confirmed an opposition to central banking and tax reform that was successfully to frustrate both until the end of the *ancien régime* (the shorthand term for the political and social structure of France between the fifteenth century and the revolution of 1789; in its anglicized form of "Old Regime" it can be applied to all Europe in the same era).

The financial experiments of the Regency signalized a basic problem of eighteenth-century France. Just as the administration became the arena of social conflict in absolutist France, so did the administration's tax question become the social issue appropriate to this arena. The recurrent fiscal crisis certainly had its own financial roots: the inefficient and corrupt habits of the government's semi-independent agencies; the continued shortsighted sale of public offices—and the multiplication of public offices to sell—with the effect of draining long-term revenues into private fees; the state's pensionary support of an idle and restive nobility; and its repeated foreign overcommitments on the land and on the sea. But the financial crisis was also widely believed to stem from an inadequate tax base caused by exemption of the privileged. The persistence with which the proposal for a tax upon all classes of people was raised and obstructed throughout the century indicates its status as the one issue in which the government confronted the question of social privilege.

In foreign affairs, finally, Orléans pursued a policy diametrically opposed to that of his bellicose uncle: he sought the friendship of Great Britain and in 1717 concluded a formal alliance with both of Louis' most persistent enemies—Britain and the Netherlands—to preserve the Utrecht settlement that sealed Louis' lost war. Orléans' interest was a personal one. He was interested in the continued exclusion of the Bourbon Philip V of Spain, his rival to the status of Louis XV's heir apparent, from the French succession. Coming as it did in the midst of the long period from 1689 to 1815 which, by reason of the profundity and persistence of Anglo-French hostility, has been dubbed by historians—with their customary casual arithmetic—"the second hundred years' war," the alliance with Great Britain has seemed like just another example of eccentric and unnatural dynastic diplomacy. But the entente—and the French policy that pushed it—

actually made more sense under the circumstances than its dynastic occasion indicates, for it was predicated on the coincidence of French with British interests in trade with the Spanish empire and in the Mediterranean, and of British with French interests in preventing a restoration of Austro-Spanish hegemony on the Continent. The first set of those interests was threatened by the remarkable Spanish resurgence of colonial exclusiveness and Mediterranean offensives after 1717; the second was threatened by the even more remarkable Austro-Spanish alliance of 1725, which opened the prospect of its joint domination of Italy, of Austrian participation in Spanish overseas trade (through the new Habsburg "Ostend Company"), and of dynastic union. But the results of the Anglo-French cooperation were not lasting enough to include the arrangement among the diplomatic revolutions for which the century was to become notorious. Once Spanish and Austrian designs in Italy had been checked, Austrian trading privileges canceled, and the Austro-Spanish alliance split in 1731, France resumed the independent policy that gradually fretted away the understanding with Great Britain until the resumption of actual hostilities in 1744.

Thus the Regent tried but failed to find a permanent solution for the international problem whose irresolution throughout the century was to intensify domestic social and financial problems and to strain the faulty administrative instrument to distraction. The problem was the choice between an oceanic and a continental orientation. The definite option for one would permit, on at least the other of these fronts, the preservation of the peace that France urgently required for the repair of the domestic establishment. Orléans' attempt was optimal from the point of view of prudence if not of glory: the British alignment kept the peace both at sea and—aside from an occasional skirmish—on the Continent. But the unpopularity of this policy signalized the problem that would weigh upon France as upon no other nation in the eighteenth century: the vital commitment to both colonial and European ambitions. Because the French could not choose between the options, they blundered into every conflict on either of the two fronts and had to fight in every major war on both.

France under Louis XV: First Phase (1723–1748)

After the Regency, only an undemanding foreign policy could postpone the day of reckoning. The leader primarily responsible for the persistence of this salubrious international orientation and its concomitant happy domestic inertia was André Hercule de Fleury (1653–1743), third and last of the great cardinal-statesmen who did so much to consolidate and prolong the Bourbon monarchy. Deceptively amiable and supple in demeanor, always dependent for his power on the shaky ground of Louis XV's personal, quasi-filial, reminiscent regard for his original role as the indulgent royal tutor, Fleury exhibited unexpected force, determination, and even arrogance in keeping the French state within the consistent lines of peace

Cardinal Fleury. *France's leading minister and architect of peace and prosperity in the early phase of Louis XV's reign.*

and retrenchment that he deemed necessary to the country's rehabilitation after the ruinous wars of the previous regime. Between 1726, when he succeeded to the *de facto* prime-ministership, and 1740, when his grasp began to slip, he collaborated with his like-minded British contemporary, Robert Walpole, in keeping the general peace. When dynastic ties and the growing strength of a war party at the French court embroiled France in the War of the Polish Succession, Fleury succeeded in limiting and focusing the French commitment to an extent that kept Great Britain neutral and acquired Lorraine definitively for France.

Similarly, Fleury influenced the appointment of ministers—particularly Henri d'Aguesseau (1668–1751), the law-codifying Chancellor, and Philibert Orry (1689–1747), the tightfisted Controller-general—who cooperated with him to give France the conservative and restrained domestic administration appropriate to the sobriety of the foreign policy. In internal affairs, as in foreign, when violence did break out it was quickly limited in its scope and effect as it dissipated in the placid atmosphere of an expanding economy and a government that watched benevolently over it. The social and religious conflicts that, in tandem, were to provoke corporate opposition to the royal government later in the century did not merge under Fleury. The only outbreak was occasioned during the 1730's by what has been called the "new Jansenism." Developing as an institutional and political movement in the stead of the pious, fideistic, and moralistic coterie that had been smashed by Louis XIV and the Bull *Unigenitus* (1713), the new Jansenism became the rallying point of the lower clergy, which used it against the ritualistic and Ultramontane hierarchy, and of the *parlements*, which associated it with their own Gallican claims to jurisdiction over the national church as nominal agents of the king. Between 1730 and 1732 the Archbishop of Paris, supported by Louis XV (who was already exhibiting the anti-Jansenism that, along with his passion for autocracy, represented the whole of his philosophy of government), sought to force acceptance of *Unigenitus* upon a recalcitrant lower clergy, and the subsequent disorder in the Church was paralleled in the state when the *parlements*, both in Paris and the provinces, supported the clerics who refused to accept it. But the agitation subsided in 1732, as a result of Fleury's alternation of firmness and amnesty, the notables' revulsion at the mass hysteria triggered by "miracles" around a Jansenist grave, and the absence of other grievances upon which to feed.

A decade later, the war and disorder that Fleury had kept limited and insulated began to join in the pattern of chronic crisis ultimately fateful to the monarchy. The break came, as it did so often during this century, in the field of foreign policy. In 1741 a war party led by Marshal Charles Louis de Belle-Isle (1684–1761) and constituted by court nobility of the sword gained the confidence of the king, and, taking the direction of foreign affairs away from the failing Fleury (he was a ripe ninety when he died in office during 1743), renewed the militant anti-Habsburg and anti-British policies which had for so long occupied the French warrior class. Resuming Louis XIV's lineup of a Spanish alliance and a south German clientele, the French involved themselves in the War of the Austrian Succession with an attack on Austria in 1741, extended the war to the Austrian Netherlands, and by 1744 found themselves confronted by a coalition of powers led by Great Britain and reminiscent of the Grand Alliance. The war lasted until the Peace of Aix-la-Chapelle in 1748—for the French a mere truce in the armed conflict that would drain their strength until the end of the century and beyond—and in its crucible the political chain of persistent crisis was forged.

The first link, on which all else hung, was the emergence, from behind Fleury, of the king whose character would set the conditions of government for the next thirty years. Louis XV, it turned out, was a monarch who would neither rule nor let anyone else rule. This stultifying indecision became a permanent feature of French public life, for it was the political expression of a cleft that ran deep in the king's character. Heir apparent since the age of two and king from the age of five, Louis grew up as the public ritual figure that his great-grandfather had meant the French monarch to be. But the heir reacted schizophrenically to the legacy: he clung to the plenitude of royal power and prerogatives as his by unquestionable right, and he hated all the business associated with the kingship. After Fleury's death, consequently, he would have no more chief minister, nor would he direct or coordinate the government himself. Bored with all affairs of state, he simply permitted each department to run itself, its insulation broken only by sporadic and fortuitous interference from a changing panel of favorites.

Probably the most constant and possibly the most beneficial of these

Louis XV. *The French Bourbon's alternation of political indifference with sporadic meddling in affairs of state dissipated the popular good will which good looks, native intelligence, and the peaceful prosperity of his early regime had secured for him and his dynasty.*

extra-political interlopers who entered into the political vacuum left and filled by the King's fancy was the notorious Madame de Pompadour (1721–1764), royal mistress from 1745—for five years in fact, and fourteen more in name. More intelligent than generally reputed, she balanced her well-publicized extravagance by her encouragement of literature and the arts and by her patronage of liberal intellectuals. Yet she had persons rather than policies as channels of her public influence. She practiced, indeed, a kind of royal favoritism in the second degree. Even within this personal orbit she was only moderately successful in eliciting desired actions from the King. Orry, the Controller-general whom she resented, she could get fired, but not the Count d' Argenson (1696–1754), the war minister whom she hated—at least not for twelve years. Nor was she able to get action brought against the Jesuits, whose influence at court she passionately opposed. Their expulsion in 1762 was welcome to her, but it was not a consequence of her hostility. Again, she could not protect her favorite Controller-general, Machault, when his reform policy—which she backed—was at stake, although she did succeed in getting him dismissed as naval minister later when he seemed to intrigue against her personally. Certainly it is true that her positive political power has been overestimated, but it can hardly be denied that in more senses than one she contributed to the distraction of the government.

Louis himself had but two interests that could bestir him to sporadic political activity—his hostility to Jansenism and his concern for the independence of Poland—and these stemmed more from family prejudice than

Madame de Pompadour. *Revised estimates make the mistress of Louis XV less sensual and less influential than was formerly thought and they show more appreciation for her intellectual tastes and for the real protection she afforded philosophes.*

from national policy (the first from the legacy of Louis XIV and the second from the Polish heritage of Louis XV's queen, Maria Leszczyńska, 1703–1768). To the sins of omission which were the continuing results of imperious boredom were added parallel sins of commission. On the few items of public business with which he did concern himself he tended to be devious rather than direct, a tendency which led to the proliferation rather than the coordination of agents purportedly executing the king's sovereign will. When he dabbled in foreign affairs he used a personal and covert organization of secret agents that confused and at times even opposed the regular organs and policies of French diplomacy. When domestic opposition to the policies of his own government became so strident as to disturb his indifference and sour his pleasures, he tended to remove the source of the annoyance simply by giving in to it, thereby endowing the opposition with a *de facto* veto upon the administration and preventing any consistent policy in government.

After Fleury, then, there was no force in the French state to prevent the issues of social crisis that had been suppressed by Louis XIV and assuaged thereafter from festering and erupting into sporadic political disorder. The war against Austria and Great Britain that Fleury had not wanted ended in 1748, but only to initiate the effects that Fleury had feared from it. In 1749, the Controller-general, Jean Baptiste de Machault d'Arnouville (1701–1794), member of the judicial aristocracy by birth but of the royal bureaucracy by career (he had been an *intendant*—royal district agent— before becoming controller-general), instituted a new direct tax of 5 per cent, called the *vingtième* ("twentieth"), on all incomes, from landed and mobile property alike, to succeed the wartime *dixième* ("tithe") and help pay for the late war. No doctrinaire but rather a rigid, logical, and practical administrator, Machault came to his edict from the simple observation that the deficit, once more becoming chronic with the resumption of French belligerence, could be made up only with the permanent submission of the formerly exempt classes to regular taxation. Unlike the *capitation* and the *dixième* that had preceded it, the *vingtième* was a peacetime tax and was accompanied by a newly trained corps of royal tax inspectors to provide for its equal administration. Supported in general by the merchants, Machault retained the support of the King long enough to fend off the protests from the judicial aristocracy in the *parlements* and the landed aristocracy in the provincial estates, but when the assembly of the French clergy, dominated by its hierarchy, added its remonstrance, the will of the King broke. In December, 1751, he formally exempted the clergy from the *vingtième*, and with the principle of equality thus fundamentally violated, the other privileged corporations quickly acquired their customary share of immunities, simply passing the *vingtième* along with the *taille* on to the peasantry for payment.

The resumption of the struggle over taxation, and the frustration of its reform, signalized both the growth of the financial problem into a continuing drain upon the monarchy and the united front of the privileged orders against any attempt of the bureaucracy to resolve it by equalizing the burden. But the active participation of both the entire nobility and the clergy and the overt primacy of the latter in the corporate resistance to the reform obscured a second significant development implicit in the conflict: the rise of the judicial nobility to preeminence among the privileged orders. This shift of influence within the aristocracy implied a shift of the aristocracy as such from a traditional to a popular defense of privilege, for it was precisely with its formulation now of a progressive and popular appeal that the judicial branch became spokesman for the whole aristocracy. Arguing from its distinctive constitutional position as direct organ of the sovereign power for the declaration of law, and from its distinctive social position as the most functional and most recently elevated service aristocracy out of the commonalty, the judicial nobility claimed to be the modern heirs of the ancient Estates-General and thus to represent the entire nation as the guarantor of its fundamental laws.

Having ascribed to themselves a unique position among the defenders of privilege in the tax conflict, the *parlements* assumed the same role in the renewed Jansenist conflict. Erupting in 1751, simultaneously with the climax of the tax struggle, the renewed ecclesiastical struggle pitted against each other the lay and clerical aristocracies whose collaboration was about to gain the day for their common financial exemptions. Once more, just as they had twenty years before, the Ultramontane hierarchy opened the fight by attempting to coerce the clergymen who still refused to accept the bull *Unigenitus*, and once more the *parlements* took up their defense. But here the historical resemblance stopped. The form of coercion now chosen by the clerical hierarchy—the requirement from the laity, under penalty of excommunication, of "tickets of confession" issued by priests who accepted *Unigenitus*—obviously broadened the conflict beyond the clergy and strengthened the claim of the *parlements* to a rightful jurisdiction. The *parlementaires* did not this time fall back before either the displeasure of the King or the popular disorders fomented by their resistance to King and Church. The conflict was in fact never resolved. It was prosecuted in full bitterness for some six years. Priests refused sacraments to Jansenists and were prosecuted by the *parlements*; the King threatened the *parlementaires* and issued decrees evoking all such cases to more submissive tribunals; the *parlements* refused to register such decrees, were dispersed by the King's order, and—as the court dockets overflowed, the pamphleteering war sharpened, and the urban disorders rose—were recalled by the King's order. Not until the outbreak of war in 1756 and an assassination attempt on Louis XV in January, 1757, did Madame de Pompadour's efforts at mediation bring a truce. But it was a truce that resolved none of the issues in the conflict. The internecine struggle between the Church and the courts, the two main institutions of privilege, was to continue through the expulsion of the Jesuits in 1762 until the end of the autocratic and aristocratic regime which was necessary to both but which they both thus helped to end.

By mid-century the pattern of the eighteenth-century French monarchy lay exposed. It was riven by a division between the divergent requirements of the national community and the corporate aristocracy that were its dual supports. It was riven further by a division between the different corporations of this aristocracy, and each of these corporations in turn itself issued contradictory claims both to exercise the powers of the sovereign and to enjoy immunity from control by the crown. These successive divisions not only affected the relations of the state and the society but were themselves reflected within the state itself with the result that no organ of the state was itself unified enough to reverse the process. In a France where only the accident of a strong king could compel unity, and only a policy of peace abroad could perpetuate the delicate balances of social and political division—in such a France, a Louis XV reigned over a government whose only consistent policy was commitment to war.

CHAPTER 15

The Kings at Home:
The Ascending Powers, 1714-1748

THAT STATES with internal political systems as different as Great Britain's on the one hand and Prussia's and Russia's on the other should have risen to great-power status in the first half of the eighteenth century testifies both to the stubborn variety of all historical experience and to the abstract character of what was common in the sundry examples of state building. The obvious political facts, certainly, were such as to warrant the usual classification of the constitutional island-monarchy and the two continental autocracies as opposite extremes of the European political spectrum. According to this overt scheme, the implications of the Glorious Revolution, confirmed by the circumstances of the Hanoverian succession a generation later (1714), made Great Britain into the very model of a limited monarchy at the very same time as Prussia and Russia, untroubled either by the tradition of fundamental laws or by the autonomy of the subordinate authorities nestling under them, were replacing France as the archetypes of absolute monarchy. Corresponding to these differences in political systems, moreover, were the differences in social conditions to which these political systems were the respective appropriate responses. Thus the British blend of monarchy and representative government can be seen as the most potent form of state for a commercially integrated society which specialized in the production of ships and services and which required a government authoritarian enough to defend and further trading interests abroad and respectful enough of property rights to command the confidence of the mercantile community at home. The administrative autocracies of Prussia and Russia, on the other hand, were the most efficient possible instruments of collective power for territories whose historic divisions, artificial connections, and economically localized communities offered few points of social cohesion.

The importance of the differences in conditions and institutions between the constitutional and the absolutist states can hardly be overestimated, not only for what they obviously meant in the subsequent history of east and west but less obviously for their schizophrenic effect upon the typical eighteenth-century man, who was attracted simultaneously to constitutionalism and to authoritarian monarchy. And yet, although this dual attraction complicated eighteenth-century political attitudes, the commitment of the same men to constitutionalism and absolutism at the same time pointed to a political reality common to both. This reality was the unity of the governing organs, which, regardless of the differences in their number and names in the different countries, collaborated effectively and intentionally in the common achievement of diplomatic and military power.

The distinctive organs and forms of government exhibited by each of these new great powers reflected the historic differences of location, circumstances, and cultural values that were forming each of these states into a separate nation. But the parallel coordination of these organs and forms of government also reflected an important historical process—the impact of competition among states, actualized by war or the continuous threat of war, as a general force for rationalizing and modernizing the political relations among institutions within the separate nations. The homogenizing role of international politics in the molding of the new great powers that arose during this period is easily visible in the cases of the Russian and Prussian administrative monarchies, where the new needs were literally translated into new institutions. It is discernible too in the more difficult and obscure British case, where intangible conventions and relations long prevalent among older institutions were now revised under the pressure of European war and overseas rivalries.

RUSSIA

Peter the Great had revolutionized the old Russian state and society in a series of reflex responses to international military and diplomatic competition. But his creation was so much a product of his personal force and the force of the extraordinary circumstances in which he had embroiled Russia that the form and the relations of the institutions which would make the revolution permanent remained a question for the future. Between the death of Peter in 1725 and the accession of Catherine II ("the Great") in 1762 these institutions took the basic shape which they would retain for almost two centuries. The six monarchs who ascended the throne in this interval reigned but did not rule, and thus the relations of government and society could find their own level. Of the three emperors—who reigned for a scant four years out of the thirty-seven—Peter II (ruled 1727–1730) was an adolescent dupe, Ivan VI (ruled 1740–1741) an infant, and Peter III (ruled 1762) an infantile "monster," as his aunt the Tsarina Elizabeth called him.

It was, then, an age of empresses in Russia, or more precisely—since they had personal commitments but no political interests—of favorites and factions. However varied their characters and attachments, the reigns of the ignorant and ailing Catherine I (ruled 1725–1717), the bitter and cruel Anna (ruled 1730–1740), and the charming but capricious Elizabeth (ruled 1741–1762), alternating with those of their short-lived male kin, resulted in the relaxation of actual royal authority and in the resurgence of aristocratic influence. But in Russia as in the rest of the European states which retained or acquired great-power status in the eighteenth century, the revitalization of the nobility was deceptive. In Russia no less than in France the revival took peculiar forms that made it something quite different from the regression toward the feudal decentralization with which the aristocracy had been traditionally associated.

Certainly the leading events of the period testified to the expanded public role that was being assumed by the Russian nobility. In the absence of a fixed rule of succession, the accession of emperors and empresses alike usually depended on the toleration or revolution of the palace guard—the worst kind of elective monarchy, as one contemporary characterized it. Again, not only did the older noble families strive—successfully in institutions like the exclusive cadet schools established in 1731—to reassert their precedence over the new service aristocracy, but the post-Petrine regimes progressively alleviated the service aristocracy's own compulsory obligations. Thus state service was limited to twenty-five years and leaves and exemptions to care for family estates were provided, and finally nobiliary compulsory service as such was abolished in 1762. Other edicts consolidated and extended the rights of noble lords over their serfs: the ownership of peopled estates became the exclusive privilege of the aristocracy, and a land-credit bank was set up to finance the cultivation of such estates; Peter the Great's provision for individual peasant emancipation through army enlistment was revoked; to the recruiting and taxing powers which Peter had conferred upon the lords was now added the authorization for the lords to enserf peasantry through inscription on their tax lists at their own pleasure, to supervise the conduct of their serfs, and to decree punishments for them—including deportation.

But closer inspection reveals that all these aristocratic gains were victories not at the expense of the state but in behalf of the state. They were, indeed, the results of a *de facto* agreement by monarchy and the combined nobility that the nobility would be the prime agents of the absolute state. Thus the weight of the palace guard invariably came down on the side of autocracy, crystallizing at the very center of the state the alliance between the Crown and a combination of the newer and the lower aristocracies. The decisive affirmation of this alliance came as early as 1730, when the group of old great nobles which had controlled Peter II and dominated the Supreme Privy Council tried, at Peter's death, to make Anna's accession conditional upon her subscription to the "Articles" drawn up by Prince Dimitri Golitsyn (1654–1738) and prescribing joint sovereignty of the Crown and a cooptative, oligarchic supreme council of the high nobility. In spite of Golitsyn's attempt to sweeten this plan for a nobiliar *coup d'état* by presenting it as a constitutional reform based on revived assemblies of estates, it furnished the occasion for the actual cooperation of the service and the lesser landed aristocracy with the monarchy. The palace guard and the country nobility, fortuitously in Moscow for a royal wedding that had been called off and left them with nothing to do, combined to reject the "Articles" of the old families and to install Anna as an absolute monarch. The counterpart of this commitment to absolutism, as the spoilers' projects and proposals on the occasion made clear, was their affirmation of their role as servants-in-chief of the autocracy.

The coup and countercoup of 1730 furnish the key to the meaning of the aristocratic resurgence in Russia during the era which ended in 1762 with the abolition of compulsory service and the accession of Catherine II (ruled 1762–1796). The weakness of the monarchs during this period did not signify the dissipation of sovereign authority in favor of aristocratic immunities, but the depersonalization of that authority in favor of the collective institutions of the state. Not only did the bureaucratic structure of administration by boards—the set of nine functional colleges under a Senate—instituted by Peter the Great persist and, at least in terms of quantity of business, expand during the first half of the eighteenth century, but the ambitions of favorites and factions tended to be embodied in a superinstitution which, under varying titles, was an instrument for the direction of the bureaucratic machine. Known under Catherine I and Peter II as the Supreme Privy Council, under Anna as the Cabinet of Ministers, and under Elizabeth as the Conference, it associated nobles and high bureaucrats in the formulation of unified policy.

In the country at large, similarly, the increased powers and privileges of the nobles over serfs and estates were not concessions to their corporate rights or their traditional jurisdictions—for it was the distinctive quality of the Russian aristocracy that it was invested with neither—but rather assignments of authority to them as local agents of the state. Russian serfdom has been characterized as an institution not of private law, as in the rest of Europe, but of public law, since it was a legal relationship imposed by the state to fix and to reach the floating population of a vast domain. Certainly the shift in emphasis, which accompanied the extension of Russian serfdom during the eighteenth century, from the real—*i.e.* propertied—to the personal bondage of peasant to lord confirms this interpretation, since it shows servile status to come with the development of peasant-lord relations from private obligation to civil obedience. From this point of view, the progressive alleviations of the compulsory service obligations which were granted the aristocracy after the death of Peter the Great, like the repeal of his legislation on entailed estates and the reversion to subdivision of estates, may be seen not as private or corporate exemptions extorted by a recalcitrant nobility, but rather as a shift of governmental policy changing from feudal to social the kind of service required from the aristocracy.

Several developments favored the new partnership of autocracy and aristocracy. The nobility grew into the habit of state service and made it an accepted custom in the aristocratic way of life. At the same time, the westernized education to which preparation for state service exposed the nobility began to produce an aristocratic cultural elite. Encouraged by these movements, the government tended increasingly to shift the chief weight of the aristocracy's role from compulsory service in the regular offices of the administration, where it was decreasingly needed, to the more diffuse control by the state of the society at large, where it was increasingly needed. The period between the great Peter and the great Catherine thus becomes the period in which the Russian nobility was weaned from its administrative swaddling clothes, inculcated with broader concepts of state service, and thus prepared for its subsequent role as the social complement of political autocracy.

PRUSSIA

The rise of Prussia to great-power status in the first half of the eighteenth century paralleled in many ways that of Russia. Both were "northern" monarchies—that is, benefactors of the Swedish decline and newcomers to the competitive world of European politics. Both were expansive states—externally oriented, and molded by the conditions of international competition. Both found their chief internal problem to lie in the organization of the variety of territories added piecemeal to the original centers of Brandenburg and Muscovy, respectively. Both, finally, responded to these external and domestic pressures by creating bureaucratic autocracies which were originally imposed by the imperious wills of forceful monarchs and subsequently maintained by a network of royal administrative agencies that absorbed every power of the state.

But despite the similarity of general type, there was enough variation in the situations, the social structures, and the action-sequences of the two states for them to represent different species within the same type of administrative absolutism. As old member of the Holy Roman Empire as well as new rising power on the Baltic, Brandenburg-Prussia was involved by the simple facts of past history and present geography more intimately and continuously than its eastern neighbor in the culture, society, and politics of western Europe. From this involvement stemmed the distinctiveness of the political forms which its rulers adopted—forms which were to leave a permanent impress upon the Prussian and ultimately upon the

German state. The individuality of these political forms had to do first with the special timing of the Prussian Hohenzollern dynasty's creation of centralized institutions, in comparison to the sequence of actions typical of the rest of Europe; and second, with the special relationship of the Prussian state to the Prussian society which this historical timing produced.

The actual pattern of events which marked the Prussian kings' consolidation of their power minimized the habit of empirical response to immediate competitive conditions that characterized the politics of so many European states and maximized the habit of rational planning for potential competition that was ultimately to become so prominent a feature of the German reputation. The great wars which ended the seventeenth century and created the conditions for the basic political institutions of the eighteenth in most of the European states had no such direct effect upon Prussia. Obversely, the postwar period after 1721, which in most of Europe was a time of aristocratic resurgence, with no expansion of governmental powers, fomented a drastic extension of royal controls in Prussia. This Prussian counterpoint stemmed partly from the accidents of royal succession and personality. After the shrewd and forceful Great Elector, Frederick William, had initiated Brandenburg into the European pattern of absolutism in direct response to the Thirty Years' War, the successive reigns of the ineffectual Brandenburg Elector Frederick III during the Wars of the League of Augsburg and of the Spanish Succession, and of the imperious King Frederick William I for the most part in a period of peace for Prussia, reversed the usual sequence of royal strength and weakness which other successful European states found appropriate to the sequence of war and peace. In King Frederick William's political personality, indeed, the contrast between the energetic authoritarianism of his domestic rule and the timid pacifism of his foreign policy demonstrated the Hohenzollern pattern of centralizing the government in preparation for rather than in response to war.

But factors more fundamental than accidents of personality were involved in the distinctive timing of the Prussian development. Both the state's Janus-faced involvement in the relations of eastern and western Europe and the geographic discontinuity of the Hohenzollern territories turned the Prussian rulers from the external to the internal extension of their authority and thereby reversed the usual pattern of state building.

Prussia fought in the War of the League of Augsburg, the War of the Spanish Succession, and—briefly—in the Great Northern War. The failure of this participation to produce in Prussia the kind of immediate and far-reaching political reorganization it produced elsewhere was accountable as much to the position and tradition of the state as to the frivolity or timidity of its kings. Prussian territorial ambitions at the time were directed primarily toward Swedish Pomerania in the north and Austrian-held Silesia in the east, but the exposed position of the isolated Hohenzollern possessions

Frederick William I. *Organizer of Prussian absolutism.*

along the Rhine and Brandenburg's membership in the threatened Holy Roman Empire combined to push the Brandenburg Elector Frederick III (from 1701 Frederick I, King in Prussia) into the anti-French and pro-Austrian policy of belligerency in the two western wars. It was as much because the Prussian interest in these wars was marginal and the participation of Prussians reluctant as because King Frederick's tastes were lavish and his political habits slothful that the Prussian government risked military dependence by financing the war through foreign subsidies rather than risk the domestic consequences of increased taxation and the institutional reorganization it usually required.

The entry of Frederick William I (ruled 1713–1740) into the Great Northern War during 1714 was, indeed, more conformable to the contemporary assessment of Prussian vital interests; but the Prussian participation was limited to the brief siege of Stralsund, and the Prussian acquisition of Stettin and Western Pomerania was more the gift of Peter the Great than the firm war aim of the Prussian king. Hence the immediate effect of this war too upon the state was minimal. Since, moreover, Frederick William's subsequent peace policy was centered on the now traditional Austrian entente and since his ambitions were limited to the lawful realization of equally traditional dynastic claims upon Jülich and Berg along the Rhine, the new style of power politics can scarcely be said to have infected this old-fashioned German prince.

And yet this Frederick William I was the very king who, in these same years, established the most modern administration in Europe, trained the bureaucracy to run it, and thereby fathered the Prussian state—all this, moreover, with a deliberate focus upon the growth and financial independence of a standing army for which his foreign policy envisaged no use. This riddle of a war machine created for a pacific policy, of internal innovation in the service of international tradition, was in part, of course, an expression of the ultimate riddle that was the political personality of Frederick William I. A tyrant to his family, a despot to his people, a fussbudget to his Emperor, an obedient servant to his God, and a driving executive to his officials, Frederick William merged the traits of ancestral patriarch, divine-right ruler, and rational administrator in a blend that reflects the mixed qualities of the age. He has been described as a violent, passionate, and limited man who, fundamentally unsure of himself, held all the more stubbornly and unqualifiedly to the few simple truths and precepts which the Lutheran pietism he preferred (formal Calvinist though he was) and the royal absolutism he preached and practiced afforded him. But the riddle remains: hating and fearing whatever smacked of reason and innovation, from theology to all things French, this throwback to sixteenth-century princely paternalism could yet find himself completely at home with the general policies that made a rational system of the Prussian administration. Thus he interposed between his aristocracy and himself a categorical barrier that was in everything but name the modern principle of exclusive sovereignty.

But if the surprising internal reorganization of the Prussian state in peacetime owed much to the personal accident of a weak war king and a strong postwar king, it owed even more to the basic needs and opportunities afforded by the Prussian population. The people were too poor, scattered, and caste-ridden either to supply immediate resources for piecemeal wartime levies or to resist the systematic peacetime organization and exploitation of their resources for long-range military needs.

Thus the reign of King Frederick William I established the characteristic pattern of Prussia's permanent institutions: it was military in principle even when it was pacific in fact, and it made military considerations not merely a seasonal or external, but a continuous and habitual feature of the Prussian state and society. The most spectacular tangible results of Frederick William I's reign were all connected with the army, and they were accomplished only by his making it the end and model of his government. Between the beginning and the end of his reign he doubled the size of the Prussian army from forty to eighty thousand men, guaranteed its independence from foreign subsidies by carving a secure financial base for it out of normal revenue, and even accumulated a considerable war chest for its support in the event of hostilities. To mobilize such human resources from a state of some two million people inhabiting an area poor in natural resources required a political concentration of social energies that was remarkable for the age.

Not only did the King assign an unparalleled 80 per cent of the state's revenues to the army but he exerted the entire force of his political and social position toward its conversion from a hired service into an absolutely loyal instrument of the crown. He created the Prussian officer corps and made it into the aristocratic pillar of the state it was thenceforward to be, by abolishing both recruiting contracts and the feudal type of military obligation, reserving officers' posts exclusively for the nobility, forbidding them foreign service, granting to the military a definite precedence over civil officials, and adopting the officers' uniform as his own daily habit. With the *Junkers* of the sword thus converted from feudal vassals into military bureaucrats, Frederick William acquired reliable agents for the recruitment of a native militia through the enactment of the canton system in 1733. Far from the universal conscription for which it was later to serve as a precedent, the canton system exempted the privileged classes, propertied citizens of the towns, and workers in loosely defined essential industries, but the peasant boys and journeymen who were regularly enrolled on the recruitment list of the neighborhood—*i.e.* canton—regiment and conscripted according to need anchored the state deep in the Prussian society. The incessant drill, in which this king with the proverbial sergeant's temperament delighted, worked officers and men alike into an efficient political as well as tactical machine.

The Prussian army exercised two kinds of formative influence upon the state. First, military standards entered into the civil administration, and this for the simplest of all reasons—because at the top and the bottom of the two hierarchies there was a personal identity between the military and civil officials. This was clearly the case at the apex, for the same king who created the characteristic Prussian institution of the officer corps also created, at the same time and in its image, the equally characteristic institution of the Prussian bureaucracy. Through appointment by examination, through a strict system of accountability enforced by the king's own regulations, his inspectors (the "fiscals"), and his punitive displeasure, Frederick William created an instrument of civil government that paralleled the military in its blend of personal and public loyalty to him and in its disciplined power over the rest of the society.

Nor did his system of "cabinet government" differ essentially from a chain of military command, since it consisted of the King's governing directly through the department heads whom he called individually to his *Kabinett* ("chamber") for the purpose of eliciting reports and giving orders. At the lowest end of the hierarchy, where the bureaucracy met the public, the military style had a similar personal base. The posts of the lower officialdom were habitually filled from the ranks of former noncommissioned army officers, and it is hardly surprising that the virtues of corporate devotion and honesty were balanced by the tendency to petty tyranny so often ingrained in the breed.

The second kind of military influence upon the Prussian state went through the institutions of civil government which were required by the needs of the army. Prussia, indeed, demonstrates more transparently than any other state the logical sequence that led from military requirements to the general centralization of government. Frederick William's primary concern, during the first decade of his reign, was the provision of an adequate tax base for the expanded army that he planned. For the efficient collection of what taxes there were he embarked on a throughgoing reorganization of the central and provincial financial agencies, aimed at establishing greater rationality and uniformity. But because tax yields in a poor state like Prussia were depressingly low in comparison with the scope of the military project, these financial agencies were commissioned with powers of economic development—*e.g.* the right to grant licenses, exemptions, subsidies—and control for the purpose of increasing the taxable resources. In order, finally, to secure the civic conditions required for an economy directed and in part operated by the government, the economic jurisdiction of these royal organs was broadened into a general competence over internal affairs.

This unbroken chain of cause and effect that led from the Prussian army into the very heart of the governmental system took explicit form both in the treatment of the Prussian aristocracy and in the structure of the royal administration itself. The same legislation that abolished the anachronistic feudal military obligations of the aristocracy also abolished the conjoined conditional tenure of their estates and replaced the military condition with a tax upon the same estates, which were now recognized as absolute private property. This special tax was obviously deemed the modern counterpart of the old knights' service, and was the only tax to which the aristocracy was subject.

Analogously, the development of the royal administration under Frederick William was essentially the story of the growth of military agencies into standard civilian bodies, exercising financial and economic functions which can be considered as war waged by other means. Frederick William's great administrative achievement was to merge into one uniform authority, on both the central and provincial levels, the two separate financial hierarchies which he found in existence and in competition upon his accession. The hierarchies administered, respectively, the traditional dues from the king's own domain and the public taxation which had originated in and retained the character of military levies; they were, accordingly, called "domain chambers" and "war commissariats." In establishing the supremacy of a central joint organ—the "General Directory," to abbreviate its mouthfilling German title, *General-Ober-Finanz-Kriegs-und-Domänen-Direktorium*—Frederick William assured that the standards of the war commissariats would prevail in the merger. Not only were the provincial domain chambers, which had enjoyed far-reaching autonomy, now definitely subordinated to the new central body, but the officials who were henceforward to dominate the state's administration on the local level came from the war-commissarial branch.

Even before the accession of King Frederick William the local war commissioners in town and countryside separated, as they became permanent officials. They became *Steuerräte* ("tax counselors") in the towns and *Landräte* ("county counselors") in the countryside. These officials were thus specialized because of the age-old economic differentiation and social distinction between the burgher caste which dominated the Prussian towns and the aristocratic caste which ran the Prussian countryside, and because of the difference in the kind of taxes to which each area was consequently liable. The urban tax counselors were simply royal officials whose primary job was to collect centrally imposed excise taxes. The rural county counselors combined in their persons the offices of royal appointee and local representative—in practice, of the local aristocracy—for the assessment of the "contribution," as this permanent land tax upon the county's peasantry was still misleadingly called in memory of its equally misnamed sixteenth-century origins in the occasional "contribution" voted, upon the ruler's special request, by the local assemblies of the exempt aristocracy on behalf of the peasantry who had actually to pay it. Under Frederick William I it was the urban tax counselor who made royal sovereignty a fact over the nominal rights of the decadent urban oligarchies, and it was under the same king that the royal capacity of the rural county counselor, despite all local attachments, was confirmed.

Much in these reforms recalls the political reorganization of France under Louis XIV and of Russia under Peter the Great. Like the work of these illustrious forebears, Frederick William's achievement was military in its purpose, centralizing in its means, aristocratic in its preferences for the army, bourgeois in its preferences for the civil service, and practical in its style. But there were shadings in both the purpose and the structure of the Prussian reform that set it off from precedents and contemporary parallels. Frederick William built his state around a powerful army not to fight with it, but as he said, to be able to negotiate diplomatically and make himself heard. In part this caution was a response to the temporal circumstance that saw Prussia already surrounded by powerful states even while he was only building its army, but even more it was a response to the internal conditions that were reflected in the distinctively comprehensive quality of monarchical sovereignty in Prussia. Where the conflict of bureaucratic and corporate elements within the French state obstructed any rational system of government and where the triumph of the bureaucratic service state in Russia absorbed traditional social groups wholly into the state and frustrated any direct connection between the state and the rest of the society, the Prussian system was unified in itself and, particularly through its officer corps and rural officialdom, continuous with the traditional aristocratic organization of society.

The reasons are not far to seek. Where France was rich in people and goods and Russia rich in people and land, Prussia was blessed in none of the three. Where France and Russia governed contiguous territories from the natural center that had expanded through them, Prussia was spread discontiguously across northern Germany in a congeries of distinct territories whose only center was the personal identity of a ruler who chanced to reside in Berlin. In Prussia, therefore, government had to supply, through the artifice of reason, all the connections that nature, history, or social intercourse had helped to provide elsewhere. There were, to be sure, in the municipal and aristocratic corporations autonomous social connections that Russia did not have. But in Prussia these were local, or at most provincial, connections which still had to be directed to all collective purposes by the central government of the state, whereas the aristocracy of Russia, however unorganized apart from the state, yet remained through the state a national aristocracy. Thus in the very same age that witnessed the aggressive struggle of aristocracies for national power and influence all over Europe, Frederick William I simply had no all-Prussian aristocracy with which to contend. When he excluded the aristocrats from central posts of civil administration and when he threatened them with his rights of "sovereignty," as he frequently did, it was precisely against their national ambitions rather than their local privileges that he acted. For the rest, the preferred position he gave them in his regional administration and in his peasant army and the full police powers over the peasantry that he permitted them on their estates indicate the successful juncture of the unified Prussian state with the fragmented Prussian society.

When the son—soon to be known as Frederick the Great—whom Frederick William had misunderstood and mistreated ascended the Prussian throne in 1740, he set about reversing the peculiarities of his father's position, and in respect to war, aristocracy, and western culture, put Prussia into the mainstream of European life. But the individuality of the historical and social pattern which had been forged in the first third of the eighteenth century persisted: in Prussia internal integration would precede aggression and the aristocracy would remain politically reliable and socially preferred as the primary channel between king and country.

GREAT BRITAIN

The society and politics of early-eighteenth-century Britain were closer to those of its continental contemporaries than the distinctive qualities which we have learned to associate with the island kingdom would lead us to believe. The lead in wealth over France and the Netherlands was achieved only during the eighteenth century itself. Urbanization and industrialization, together with the concomitant social traits of self-restraint and orderliness, became predominant only in the Victorian era of the nineteenth century. Parliamentary government, with its corollaries of a cabinet system, a prime minister, and the sovereignty of an elected House of Commons, was a nineteenth-century development, while the separation of powers, so famous in constitutional theory from the time of John Locke, is generally deemed to have corresponded to British political reality neither then nor ever after. The British society and polity, in the early eighteenth century, was violent in temperament, aggressive in disposition, rural in primary occupation, oligarchic in structure, conservative in the aims and royalist in the initiation of policy: it resembled, in short, one or another of its rivals across the Channel.

And yet there were gradations of national distinction, even beyond the obvious factor of geographical insularity, that foreshadowed the special role that Britain would play among the eighteenth-century powers. By the end of the seventeenth century, two of its economic developments were crystallizing into social effects that gave a peculiar slant to the British version of the common European social hierarchy. The extraordinarily large share of overseas trade in the British economy, together with an improvement of agricultural techniques, promoted the general increase of wealth, of domestic commercial and industrial activity, and of the enterprising spirit that would establish Britain's economic primacy by the end of the eighteenth century. These developments, moreover, combined with the new infusions into the aristocracy from the political convulsions of the seventeenth century to create an uncommon strand in the British governing class and in its relations with the lower orders. Although still based upon the ownership of land, the predominant section of this governing class was not only itself favorably oriented toward and actually participant in the mobile life of commerce but also joined in a *de facto* political alliance with the commoners of the mercantile community.

It was this ambiguous position of Great Britain on the periphery of the European world, at once sharing and modifying its characteristic institutions, that was given permanent shape in the legislation and conventions established in the period between the Glorious Revolution in 1688 and the resignation of Robert Walpole in 1742. Even the circumstances under which these fundamental arrangements were worked out reflected the combination of insular and European elements in the British social and political structure. For the much-touted "Britannic constitution" of the eighteenth century, usually not understood at home, misunderstood on the Continent, and prized as a model in both arenas, emerged both as a settlement of the local revolution and as a response to Britain's international involvement, first in the continental wars against Louis XIV and then in the competition with the European colonial powers. Under these general conditions, the particular British forms which this constitution enshrined developed under conditions common to all the great states of Europe.

The Revolutionary Settlement (1689–1714)

The revolutionary settlement that was gradually worked out between the Declaration of Right of 1689 (legalized as the Bill of Rights) and the Septennial Act of 1716 marked the start of a political continuity which has

persisted to this very day. It set up what looked like an inimitable constitutional pastiche. The constitution itself was a mystifying blend of law and
of conventional devices to make the law work. The law of the constitution,
moreover, was passed in the way of ordinary legislation and was formally
indistinguishable from regular revocable statute law. Although its chief pillars—the Bill of Rights, the main clauses of the Act of Settlement of 1701,
and the Septennial Act of 1716—soon came, in what has since been characterized as the English fashion, to be especially reverenced as clauses in
the unwritten constitution, it was never decided whether their special
status was one of irrevocable fundamental law or of revocable contract
between country and monarch.

The one clear political result of this mélange of prescription and convenience was the general consensus on the supremacy of Parliament. Four crucial governmental activities were subordinated to acts of Parliament: accession to the Crown (Declaration of Rights and Act of Settlement), elections (Triennial Act of 1694, replaced by Septennial Act of 1716), war and
peace (a corollary in practice of Parliament's exclusive power of taxation),
and—most important—the determination of what was and what was not
subject to legislation and therefore to Parliament (Bill of Rights)—in
legal parlance, the decisive jurisdiction over jurisdictions. But with this one
generally comprehensible fact of parliamentary sovereignty, clarity ended.
Parliament was not a thing but an abstraction, and when it came to giving
practical effect to its theoretical preeminence the new British constitution
began to seem like the obscure reshuffling of the ingredients in a peculiarly
British political recipe.

Parliament had been—and still was—composed of three independent
and equal organs—King, Lords, and Commons—each with a different root
in the nation and with a different function in Parliament. Although composed by these three organs, moreover, Parliament could not be simply
defined by them, since both King and Lords also exercised governmental
functions outside and independent of Parliament. The essence of Parliament was thus not that it was a body with three organs but that it was a
definite relationship among three authorities insofar as they were organs of
it. The relationship which linked them was the law-making function, but
beyond this function and beyond Parliament the king possessed the
supreme executive and the Lords the supreme judicial power. It was
because the King and Lords had extra-parliamentary functions and
Commons did not, that the Commons became the chief spokesman of
parliamentary claims in general and tended to be especially identified with
Parliament.

This structure, with its mixture of functions in at least two of the three
governing organs, antedated the Glorious Revolution. Although, moreover,
the revolutionary period helped to identify as legislative, executive, and
judicial, functions which had not been so classified before, still the subsequent changes in constitution did not separate in substance the powers

that it segregated in name. The revolutionary settlement did not rationalize the actual distribution of powers by assigning one kind of power to
each organ. Rather it distinguished, by name and in law, between the
powers that were exercised jointly and the powers that were not,
labeled the joint powers legislative, raised these joint legislative powers
to superiority over any and all of the powers exercised by the same organs
separately, shifted a few crucial powers from separate to joint exercise, but
for the rest left the traditional mélange of powers in each constitutional
organ as it had been. This meant that in the very process of establishing
the supremacy of Parliament as the seat of the joint legislative power, the
revolutionary settlement not only retained the mixture of powers in King
and Lords that tended to confuse legislative, executive, and judicial functions but compounded the confusion by conferring on the legislative power
a preeminence and a supervisory capacity that permitted incursions by
Parliament from its legislative base into executive and judicial functions.

Thus the King exercised both his exclusive prerogative and his joint parliamentary powers, and the line between them was tenuous indeed.
Although royal prerogative was now primarily executive and parliamentary
power primarily legislative, the prerogative still extended to such legislative
acts as the convocation, prorogation, and dissolution of Parliament; and the
Parliament of which he was a part acquired the power to fix the limits of
the sphere within which the exercise of the prerogative was, by definition,
unlimited. The House of Lords exercised both its exclusive jurisdiction as
high court of appeals and its share in parliamentary power, but here too
the line was hard to draw in view of the persistent tradition of the whole
Parliament as a "high court" for the declaration of the common law and
the protection of rights under it. The House of Commons, finally, coupled
with its share in parliamentary legislation its old judicial right to impeach
(with the approval of the Lords) the King's ministers and its new *de facto*
executive power, which stemmed from its legislative initiative in money
matters and from its legislative rights over foreign policy, the standing
army, and the conduct of war. Nor were mixtures of powers in the three
organs of government simply historical anachronisms. They were essential
to the functioning of the eighteenth-century constitution, for they were
rooted in the independent origins and powers of King, Lords, and Commons outside of Parliament—in the fundamental law of succession, the
prescriptive right of a hereditary council, and the electoral power of the
national community respectively—origins and powers which were the bases
of their mutual equality inside of Parliament.

This unwieldy structure made sense in its negative and parochial function of preventing a recurrence of the despotisms of either the King or the
Commons which had seemed so imminent during the seventeenth century.
But by the same token it seemed to run counter to the centralizing tendency which characterized the rising states of the late seventeenth and early

eighteenth centuries. The appearance, however, was deceptive, for if the legislation of the revolutionary settlement had as its primary goal and result a balance of powers that resolved a peculiarly English conflict, this same legislation also had a countervailing tendency toward the concentration of powers in response to the general European trend in this direction. And the conventions that made the laws work reinforced this tendency. Here indeed is the real meaning behind the apparently pedantic insistence on checks and balances rather than separation of powers as the underlying principle of the eighteenth-century British constitution. Whereas separation of powers would have meant divided sovereignty, checks and balances actually meant joint sovereignty. As the *Annual Register* would later summarize the system: "The impulsion, the soul . . . of the British government depends on the harmonious understanding and cooperation of all its members."

The fundamental laws of the revolutionary settlement laid down the practical basis for such cooperation by the simple device of making each of the parliamentary organs dependent upon the others. Thus not only did the dynasty owe its existence to an act of Parliament but the King was made dependent upon the houses of Parliament even in his lawful operations by virtue of the new parliamentary monopoly over the taxing power and because of the limits which the legal requirement of septennial elections placed upon the King's control over the House of Commons. Parliament itself, on the other hand, continued to owe its operational existence to the King and his prerogative, for within the limits set by the Septennial Act it was at his discretion that the Lords and Commons were convoked, prorogued, and dissolved. Thus was created a legal circuit of dependence in which each organ could fulfill its own functions only with the assistance or toleration of the others.

Within this framework of law the set of practices which hardened into persistent conventions tended overwhelmingly to be those which harmonized the operations of the three national authorities into one parliamentary sovereignty. Although these conventions assumed the precise forms which they were to hold through the eighteenth century only after the accession of the Hanoverians in 1714, they had their origins and received their characteristic unifying tenor in the wartime conditions accompanying the reigns of King William and Queen Anne between 1689 and 1714. Six important practices which were to become tacit clauses in the eighteenth-century British constitution originated during this period. The one tendency comon to them all was the conversion of divided powers into a single governing system and the assignment to each member of its own function in the activity of the whole.

First, to the King went a monopoly not only over the execution of policy but also over its initiation. The King chose and dismissed ministers, like the rest of his "servants," at his discretion, and the King's government made policy within the limits of legislative approval and financial support by Parliament. These royal functions were consolidated by William III, who insisted on keeping in his own hands military and foreign policy as well as the executive means to administer it. They became standard under the weaker Queen Anne, when, despite the monarch's personal frailty, they were sealed by the formal repeal, in 1705, of the Commons' attempt to subjugate the royal advisers through parliamentary control of the Privy Council.

Second, to the Commons went the great preponderance of the parliamentary legislative control over royal policy. The same war that confirmed the King's initiative in policy and administration expanded the Commons' legal right to initiate money bills into a general power to approve policy. The length and intensity of the war not only bred the habit of annual Parliaments to vote supplies but gave to Commons the lever to use this right as a means of expressing approval or disapproval of policy and to extend this right by a degree of parliamentary control over the expenditure of all revenues from extraordinary taxation—a continuously growing area of finance that came to include the entire military and naval budget after 1697. This *de facto* distribution of functions could, and occasionally did, lead to friction between King and Commons, but its actual effect tended more toward the complementarity than the opposition of powers. This was indicated by the actual evisceration of the monarch's discretion in the convocation of Parliament and by his (or her) surrender after 1708, in practice, of his parliamentary right to disapprove legislation.

Third, the right of the king's "placemen"—*i.e.* officeholders—to election into the Commons assured royal influence in the deliberations of that House and provided a solid core of Commons majorities in support of the King's governments. This relationship was worked out the hard way between 1692 and 1716 in a tug-of-war between the members of the Commons and supporters of the King's government. Of the sixteen bills introduced into the House during this period to assure the independence of the Commons by eliminating or significantly restricting the placemen eligible to sit in that House, only four became law—and these provided for enough exclusions (particularly of the lesser revenue officers) to prevent the Commons from being swamped by the beneficiaries of royal patronage but not enough to prevent the Commons from being continuously susceptible to management by government. However much an abuse this influence which the King's government could exercise within the House of Commons through patronage might appear, it actually operated through the eighteenth century as one of the sinews of British collective power.

Fourth, the system of royal influence in Parliament worked as well as it did essentially because it operated through still another convention that muted the potential conflict over it: the role of the Lords in mediating between King and Commons. Surprisingly, in view of their apparent eclipse during the seventeenth-century conflict between King and Commons, the Lords first established their claims to independence by playing an important part in the Glorious Revolution and then by asserting their parliamentary equality vis-à-vis both King William and the Commons. Then, with its own position thus reasserted, the House of Lords benefited from the need for a unified joint sovereign which the wars against Louis XIV demonstrated. This need stimulated practices which made the House of Lords both the reservoir of the King's ministers and the channel through which the ministers could influence elections to the House of Commons. For it was because of the Lords' influence over the boroughs (which elected almost three fourths of the members of the House of Commons) that the King's government, usually composed of coalitions among the great families in the Lords, could count on a majority in the Commons at the start of every new Parliament.

Fifth, the replacement of the Privy Council by the "cabinet" (alternatively called "cabinet council") as the monarch's chief advisory organ on policy was an extralegal development called into being by the new requirements of activity and efficiency in the central government. Ultimately it assisted in bringing about the collaboration of the houses of Parliament with the government. The existence of an unofficial group of advisers labeled "cabinet" or "cabinet council"—referring to consultations in the King's private chambers—went back to the earlier Stuarts, but only under the pressure of war did William III make frequent resort to it and did Anne institute it as a regularly convoked body. It was distinguished from the unwieldy Privy Council not only by its smaller numbers but by the exclusive focus on governmental function rather than on the traditional mixture of status and function as the criterion for attendance. Behind the shifting membership dependent on the royal discretion, it tended to be composed particularly of officeholders. Its orientation toward effective government was demonstrated both by its relegation of the Privy Council to largely honorific duties and by the emergence, already under Queen Anne, of a small inner cabinet constituted by the leading ministers to make decisions that the large cabinet simply endorsed.

To be sure, under the last Stuarts and throughout the eighteenth century this cabinet was a far cry from the modern institutions that have developed to associate the executive with the legislative powers in parliamentary systems of government. The eighteenth-century cabinet had no recognition—or even mention—in the law, no definite membership, no collective tenure or responsibility, no formal connection with political parties, and no dependence upon a prime minister beyond the informal influence which the leading minister might exercise, as a first among equals, upon the King, to whom each minister remained directly and individually responsible. As an unofficial body that smacked of cabal, moreover, the cabinet continued through the eighteenth century to be mistrusted by Commons, which saw in it an extralegal device for removing royal policy-making from parliamentary scrutiny. But if the eighteenth-century cabinet did help, in these respects, to keep the King's government independent of Parliament, it also contributed, in other respects, to their collaboration—a contribution that received reluctant recognition in the grumbling Commons' evasion of any fundamental challenge to the cabinet after that house gave up on its attempt to control the Privy Council in 1705. Behind this restraint lay the tacit acknowledgment by the Commons that the decisive role played by the heads of governmental departments and agencies in the cabinet rendered that body indirectly accountable to the Commons as the parliamentary organ that appropriated the money for those departments and agencies. The rise of the cabinet to executive preeminence thus furnished another occasion for the mutual cooperation of government and Parliament.

And finally, the distinctive shape assumed by the British party system in the wartime Parliaments of William and of Anne surprisingly abetted the harmonious relationship between monarch and Commons which it superficially seemed destined to frustrate. The Whig and Tory parties had risen during the factional strife of the restoration and were perpetuated after 1688 by the competition for preferment, the advocacy of different alternatives for the dynastic succession, and the conflict over war and peace before Utrecht. Each of these parties was based upon a combination of general principles, private loyalties, and personal ambitions which tended to work at cross purposes within each group and hence to moderate rather than to intensify party divisions. Thus, on questions of political principle, an undeniably fundamental opposition divided the Tories' belief in the divine right of kings, nonresistance to royal authority, and strict conformity to the established Anglican Church (High Church), from the Whigs' inclination toward parliamentary monarchy, resistance to royal transgressions of the law, and a latitudinarian or Low Church. And yet in practice the Tories' fidelity to the Church of England nullified their reverence for the sanctity of monarchy so thoroughly as to make possible the cooperation of their great majority with the Whigs in the crucial political actions against the Catholic Stuarts: the Glorious Revolution of 1688, the Act of Settlement of 1701 (prescribing the succession of Anne and the Hanoverians), and the actual acceptance of the Hanoverian George I in 1714. Again, the evolution of most Tory groups into the peace party and of most Whig groups into the war party under Queen Anne did not prevent the Tory Marlborough from collaborating with the Whigs for the further prosecution of the war or some Whig groups from collaborating with the Tory minister Robert Harley, Earl of Oxford (1661–1724), in the conclusion of peace.

Indeed, cutting clean across the Whig-Tory division and weakening its impact was the cleavage between the Court and Country parties, rooted primarily in the varying degrees of influence which the various members of Parliament had on the disposition of offices and favors by the Crown and its appointees. The Court party consisted of those, Whig and Tory alike, with actual or potential access to such offices and favors through their ties with ministers or other high officials. The Country party consisted of those, Whig and Tory alike, who were either gentry essentially independent of the Crown's influence or "out" politicians and their satellites with a policy of mobilizing opposition to get back "in."

The net result of these overlapping opinions and interests was a party lineup that formed, dissolved, and re-formed from issue to issue and from ministry to ministry. The bitter parliamentary debates and pamphleteering polemics that gave the illusion of a struggle between fixed party organizations actually used party labels as straw horses with which to dignify or brand the momentary position of an evanescent group, while in usual fact members of both major parties were temporarily aligned on either side of the dispute. Neither Whig nor Tory nor Court nor Country, in short, had any party organization, any party discipline, or any party program. Each was a party only in the sense that individuals so classified themselves by virtue of habitual political dispositions and/or associations. William made a deliberate policy of mixing Whigs and Tories in his ministries of the 1690's, an indication of their consensus at that time on the basic issues of the revolution and the war. Even when, in the following reign, the combination of Queen Anne's political indolence with the tendency of Whigs and Tories to divide on the issue of the war led ultimately to the all-Tory ministry of 1710–1714, the peculiar flexibility of the British party system served rather to abet than frustrate the support of the Commons for the government's peace policy. Beneath the surface of vociferous party squabbling, the mutual hostility between the two leading Tory ministers, Robert Harley and Henry St. John, Viscount Bolingbroke (1678–1751), was perhaps more serious an obstacle to forceful government than the conflict of parties. The government used the party conflict to its own advantage: Harley could attract the support of Whig groups to the ministry while the feud between Whig and Tory segments of the opposition kept them from joining forces against the ministry.

It is obvious that the function of any party system is to keep government accountable and thereby in restraint, but parties are also practical means for organizing support behind governments in a parliamentary regime—and it was this latter function that prevailed in Britain between the Glorious Revolution of 1688 and the accession of George III in 1760. The most telling evidence of this function was the fundamental attitude toward party as such held by the public figures—including party men—of the period. Party was universally denounced as "faction," connoting seditious conspiracy against the king. The British thus found themselves in the apparently paradoxical position of living with parties whose validity they rejected. But the anomaly is only apparent, and the explanation demonstrates the state-building orientation of the early parties. For parties were accepted as a means of identifying the actual or potential supporters of the King's government, and they were rejected as a means of grouping the opposition to the King's government. Only later in the eighteenth century, with the growing recognition of society's independent role as a source of political power, would the development of a "loyal opposition" permit the full acceptance of the idea of party.

Social Basis of the Settlement

These six unifying mechanisms, ensconced in the practice of the new parliamentary regime during the two and a half decades of war following upon the Glorious Revolution, outlasted both the martial influence and the dynasty under which they had been devised. Their longevity can be attributed in part to the British successes in the military and colonial competition with France and Spain, but institutions do not long draw their vitality from past achievements, and these unifying conventions had more persistent roots than the revolution and the wars that first helped mold them.

These practices could survive both the peace and the new dynasty that came to Great Britain in 1714 because they were the political expression of a social alliance whose members were to remain for more than a century fundamentally agreed on the forms and objectives of the British state. Behind the unified sovereignty of Parliament was the concord of the nobles, gentry, and propertied middle classes whom Parliament represented. By the terms of their accord, the nobles and gentry made up the governing class, supported by the consent of the propertied middle classes and oriented toward the pursuit of interests common to all three groups. These interests were a compound of political order and commercial enterprise, a compound that made for parliamentary unity since it blended a conservative reverence for authority with a progressive cast of policy. Hence there was a consensus on the vigorous prosecution of colonial acquisition, of overseas trade, and of wars against colonial and commercial rivals; on the studied neglect of restrictive mercantilist regulations (save the Navigation Acts that protected the British carrying trade); and on the toleration of Protestant dissent alongside an established Anglican Church. What made these interests common was the convergent effect of three social factors: the participation of all propertied classes, privileged and commoner alike, in the commercial net extended by the growing international trade and stimulating in its turn the capitalization of both agriculture and industry; the infusion of enterprising and progressive recruits into the aristocracy not only from the process of economic growth but from the shrewd management of high public office; and finally, the crucial mediatory role of the gentry in eighteenth-century British society.

Of these social factors the role of the gentry was perhaps the least obvious and the most far-reaching politially. These "gentlemen," or "squires," as they were alternatively called, occupied a fruitfully ambiguous position between the aristocracy and what we should call the middle class (in eighteenth-century parlance "the middling sort"). The gentry possessed no privileged status by law, but they did possess a privileged status by virtue of social prestige. Linked to the aristocracy by their common interests as estate owners, their common rights as landlords, and the reciprocal claims of gentle clients and noble patrons, they were at the same time linked to the middling sort by their common legal position as commoners, by the commercial and professional occupations of their younger sons, and by their common interests as local oligarchs—the gentry defending for the counties the same kind of investment in autonomy as the burghers defended in the towns.

Despite the many instances of parochial pride, expressed in resentment of the titled nobility and arrogance toward all of ungentle birth, the gentry supplied the cement in the British social structure. They represented the commoners of the realm in the House of Commons, and dominating that House, collaborated with the nobility in the governance of Britain. Moreover, not only did they embody, on the national level, the social consensus that made the parliamentary system work but they also manifested the invisible ties that forged the national and local authorities of Britain into a powerful unified state without the obvious clamp of a centralized bureaucracy. Because the same social group that dominated the most influential organ of the sovereign Parliament also supplied the justices of the peace who dominated the local government of Britain, the levels of government were tied together by the bonds of common interest, of common outlook, and, often enough, of common kinship.

But this social accord that formed the basis of British power was not independent of the political factors that were making for the centralization of other European states. War, for example, was a powerful and continuing influence on the modern English industrial society which began to emerge in the eighteenth century. This was a matter not simply of military stimulus to the economy and of additions to the colonies but of the cohesion worked upon British society by the common hostility to the French enemy and by the growing accord on the primacy of commercial interests as the mainspring of national power.

What distinguished Great Britain from its continental competitors, then, was not so much the obvious difference between limited and absolute sovereignty—since this difference was quite deceptive in terms of effective political power—but rather the difference between a state run by an alliance of social groups and states run by officials who mediated between social groups. Not, to be sure, that British society was immune to the popular disorders by the underprivileged, endemic to Europe during this era, but in Britain—unlike France, for example—the concord of all propertied classes sufficed to reduce such disorders to evanescent mob riots without definite goal or effect.

The social alliance forged in Britain by the Glorious Revolution and the subsequent wars against France proved to be a more permanent fount of unity than the more purely political instruments of continental absolutism. In the two and a half decades of comparative peace that followed upon the Peace of Utrecht, Britain shared in the aristocratic resurgence that affected so many European countries but not in the retrenchment of centralized power that marked this resurgence in states like Russia (after the death of Peter the Great in 1725), France, Sweden, and the Netherlands. Certainly the initial signs seemed to presage a crisis in the British government as well. The accession of the new Hanoverian dynasty in 1714 stimulated the activities of the "Jacobite" party, a small group of High Tory lords, squires, and Catholics committed to the claim of the Stuart James III upon the British succession. The Hanoverian preference for the Whig aristocracy, moreover, initiated nearly half a century of Whig ministries which seemed destined to turn Tories into Jacobites and dynastic feud into civil war and which, moreover, put into the saddle precisely the section of the aristocracy most suspicious of central power and most jealous of its own rights, privileges, and—above all—property.

But the signs were misleading. When rebellion for a Stuart restoration was attempted in Scotland by the stubborn James (the "Old Pretender," 1688–1766) in 1715 and by his infinitely more charming son "Bonnie Prince Charlie" (Charles Edward, the "Young Pretender," 1720–1788) in 1745, they were joined in both cases by a few of the Scotch lords and clans still smarting over the unwanted union of 1707 with England. Agitation by a minuscule Jacobite sect which persisted throughout the half century simply had the unintended effect of reconciling moderate men to the reign of the Hanoverians and the preeminence of the Whigs. As for these Whigs, despite their theoretical suspicion of authority, their actual domination of both the government and the houses of Parliament resulted in the peacetime consolidation of the war-born conventions that had knit the organs of the British state into an effective sovereign power.

Under the Hanoverians (1714–1748)

The tone of the approximate half century covered by the reigns of George I (ruled 1714–1727) and George II (ruled 1727–1760) was set by the Whig country gentleman, Robert Walpole (1676–1745), by whose name, indeed, the era is now known. Both out of office and in, he confirmed the conventions which limited the range of opposition and put a premium on a governing consensus. When he was excluded from government during the Hanoverian settling-down period he initiated the pattern, which was to persist through the century, of minimizing principle and of organizing the out-groups, Whigs and Tories alike, into a joint opposition to Whig ministries for the simple tactical purpose of creating a nuisance and so blackmailing their way into ministerial offices. Walpole's period in opposition (1717–1720) coincided, moreover, with the first of the deep-

Sir Robert Walpole directing a cabinet meeting. *Painting by Joseph Coopy. British Museum, London.*

seated rifts between king and crown prince that were to be a recurrent feature of the Hanoverian dynasty and were to have two important effects upon British constitutional practice.

With the first of these effects Walpole had little to do: after the King's rift—perhaps even more characteristic of royal than of ordinary families—with his son, the future George II, George I established the precedent of the king's absence from cabinet meetings, less because of his ignorance of the English language in itself (the usual reason cited) than because of the advantage his ignorance would have bestowed upon his hated bilingual son at such meetings. The second political effect of the royal feuding, however, Walpole did help to initiate: the gravitation of the opposition leaders to the household of the crown prince, with the effect of emphasizing the role of personality rather than principle in the opposition and resulting in the formation of a kind of shadow government for the next reign. Here was the beginning of the notion of a dynastically loyal opposition.

But it was in his long tenure of governmental leadership, from 1721 to 1742, that Walpole left his chief unifying impress upon British politics. The nature of this impress mirrored the combination of traits that made up his political personality. For Walpole, like Britain itself, was not so much an integral personality as a composite character that blended generally familiar purposes with distinctive ways of realizing them. Forceful, self-confident, avid of both wealth and power, skilled in the acquisition of the one and the conservation of the other, Walpole was as feared, mistrusted, and intrigued against as the leading minister of any contemporary autocracy. And yet, country gentleman on the make that he was, his conception of his own interests so abetted his unquestioning faith in the British constitution as to make the art of managing people and interests the characteristic instrument of his power.

Walpole sounded the keynote of his regime on the very occasion of its establishment: in his handling of the crisis attendant upon the bursting of the "South Sea Bubble." The South Sea Company, which had been chartered in 1711 nominally as a commercial corporation with a monopoly on trade in the South Seas, had actually functioned as a kind of investment trust, and early in 1720 its directors proposed to use the national debt for this function, issuing stock in exchange for government securities which would, in turn, form the basis for further capitalization in expectation of the profits from the South Sea monopoly. Persuaded by the prospect of a cost-saving refunding of the national debt and by the liberal gifts of stock in the right places, Commons approved the scheme, and aided by the apparent magic of credit exhibited during the successful late war, by the fever for quick gain following hard upon it, and by the Company's encouragement of buying on margin, the stock rose from 130 to over 1,000 before running out of fresh buyers and collapsing in September, 1720. The crisis that followed was more serious politically than economically, for the resentment and bitterness stemming from lost fortunes were directed at the King's government and indeed at his very household, and Walpole's solution of it, which was his springboard to power, was characteristically political as well. His financial proposals may have helped somewhat in the reestablishment of confidence but in fact stability was recovered without the necessity of their application.

What made Walpole the indispensable man was his resolute management of the question of responsibility, for at the expense of his own popularity he spared the King and the King's associates and threw to the wolves only those participants in the scheme who were minimally necessary to satisfy Commons' thirst for revenge. On this basis, as the only public figure who could hold King and Commons in harness, he was appointed by the King and accepted by the Commons as the First Lord of the Treasury and Chancellor of the Exchequer in April, 1721, the official posts from which he exercised what even then was occasionally and unofficially called the office of "prime minister" for the next two decades.

It is true enough that Walpole himself rejected the appellation of prime minister and that, as commentators on eighteenth-century Britain have cautioned *ad nauseam*, he lacked much of what the office of prime minister now connotes: he had no tenure independent of the King's favor; he had no official authority over the appointment, dismissal, or conduct of other ministers; he found no use for the cabinet as a formal vehicle of collective consultation and decision. But the one essential function of a prime ministership which he did provide was the concentration in one minister of the responsibility for achieving unison between King and Parliament.

Walpole was a royal favorite, not only because of his varied services to

Mass anger and bitterness in London in 1720. *William Hogarth's caustic view of the effect of the "South Sea Bubble" on London life and morals.*

the Crown starting with the South Sea Bubble, but because of his assiduous cultivation of the intelligent Princess Caroline (1683–1737), who was liked by her father-in-law, George I, and as Queen after 1727, revered by her husband, George II. Walpole built a reliable machine by putting his own men into as many influential governmental posts as he could reach. By 1733 he had even persuaded the King to purge the ministry in which he was legally only a first among equals, and thus Walpole did succeed to an unprecedented degree in excluding opposition from the ranks of the administration. Just as intense, finally, was his management of the Commons. He refused a peerage in order to retain his seat in the Commons. He organized a steady—although not infallible—majority through the artful blend of patronage for his faction with the deliberate display of the country squire's plain and blunt rusticity to attract the independent gentry into the ranks of his sympathizers.

The governmental policy of the Walpole era was similarly calculated to avoid offense, to avoid strain, to placate all interests, and thus to avoid the irritation of any social grievance that might disturb the collaboration of government and Parliament, a collaboration that was henceforward to be the necessary basis of any leading minister's secure possession of power. Hence Walpole's policy was simple: to keep the peace, to encourage trade, to reduce taxes—and "to let sleeping dogs lie." Not, of course, that Walpole followed this policy simply because of his overriding concern with maintaining himself in power. He was compulsively for efficiency in administration and against the extravagance of war. He believed in economy and peace, and he associated his political destiny naturally with them.

For Walpole's opponents, similarly, the desire for power did not exclude genuine considerations of policy. Their indiscriminate attacks all along the personal and political front had indeed their envy of Walpole's power as their one consistent element, paralleling the centrality of Walpole's ambition in his own makeup; but just as he associated his interests with the British interest in peace, so they connected theirs with the British interest in economic, and if need be military, competition with France and Spain.

The intimate union of private and public interests which thus came to characterize British political life was a sign of the close and direct relations that subsisted between British society and the British state. The state both reflected and shaped the common interests of the society, and the Walpole era served to show that the unifying institutions of the state worked as well in peace as in war. It created the British system which guaranteed the cooperation of the organs of sovereignty on the basic issues and reduced political conflict to the status of personal rivalries as long as consensus on the fundamental issues persisted. But by the same token, this system could and did raise these rivalries to the status of political conflicts requiring a new orientation of all the organs when the consensus on the issues changed.

Down to the accession of George III in 1760, the issue which determined the preponderance of personalities or principles in the amalgam of British politics was precisely the question of war and peace, and in terms of it the fall of Walpole was a demonstration of the workings of the British political system. Centered first in the ministry and then, after its exclusion from there during the early 1730's, in the House of Lords, the opposition to Walpole had always been vociferous enough, but it had also been localized and largely personal as long as the governing classes in country and town had remained content with the prosperity that accompanied Walpole's peace policy. But as impatience with this policy grew, aggravated by commercial conflict with Spain, the opposition, born along by the unifying force of the war issue, spread through the several organs of government.

First, in 1739, Walpole was forced to accept a declaration of war against Spain—subsequently known as the War of Jenkins' Ear for circumstances too obscure to detail—when support for it extended into both the Commons and his own ministry. Then, when his halfhearted prosecution of the war instigated patriotic fervor and factional hostility to combine against him in a fundamental challenge to his regime, Walpole came up against an opposition that was well entrenched in the royal family—by courtesy of Frederick, Prince of Wales (1707–1751)—and in the Lords, and that by 1742 attracted a majority in the Commons. Even the continuing favor of

George II could not save him: both King and minister had to yield to a new government that could harmonize the three governing organs in the waging of the Spanish war and its extension to the European continent through participation in the War of the Austrian Succession.

The regime that replaced Walpole's was a precise response to the combination of personal and political issues that had unseated him. The Pelham brothers dominated the British government for the next dozen years, Henry (*c.* 1695–1754) as policy maker and Thomas (better known as the Duke of Newcastle, 1693–1768), as Whig party manager, until Henry's death in 1754. Their tenure shows that Walpole's was more than an individual achievement, for without his forcefulness they still led a government which proved stable for the same reason that his had—because like his it harmonized King, Lords, and Commons. They had been, indeed, members of Walpole's government, and Henry, at least, acknowledged himself Walpole's disciple, but the conditions of the regime differed sufficiently from his to reveal the existence of a political system independent of the accidents of personalities and capable of accommodating changes in policy without crippling divisions.

Henry Pelham was as unassuming and ingratiating as his predecessor had been arrogant and feared, and yet the conventions of government worked as well for the Pelhams as they had for Walpole. The Pelhams' eminence was grounded both in the judicious use of political mechanics—that is, in the careful management of patronage and connections—and in the fidelity with which their policy of limited war reflected the attitude of the ruling classes. The martial enthusiasm of these classes still came from an inchoate feeling of where British power and profit lay rather than from a clear and persistent perception of Britain's national destiny as world trader and colonial power—William Pitt (1708–1778) had this vision, but his was still a voice crying in the wilderness, hated by the King and isolated in the Commons—and it was therefore a fickle enthusiasm that flagged at the point of hardship and sacrifice. The curtailed military commitment and the inconclusive Peace of Aix-la-Chapelle in 1748 which were the hallmarks of the Pelhams' policy raised no widespread opposition because, unsatisfactory as they were generally sensed to be, they conformed to unreflective British sentiment that was still but one stage removed from Walpole's pacifism.

Not until the outbreak of the Seven Years' War in 1756 and the accession of William Pitt to ministerial office a year later did there arise a permanent consensus on the direction of the national interest that could stand the test of all-out war. It was at this point, when the unifying force of government had organized society into a self-conscious unit, that collective initiative passed from the state into the society, ending one historical age and initiating another. For the accession of George III in 1760 followed hard upon the rise of Pitt to national leadership, and the conflicts that marked the new reign were important not because of the old party politics they perpetuated but because of the new social participation they inaugurated. And so, its version of state making completed, Great Britain passed, together with its western European neighbors, from the political into the social phase of eighteenth-century civilization.

CHAPTER 16

The Social Context
of the Enlightenment

HISTORICAL DATES are conveniences to mark the temporal relations of events. Historical periods are conveniences to mark the temporal relations of groups of events. Dates are, by and large, especially appropriate to the history of men's politics, since men have directed their political interests and desires to the performance of particular actions in definite times and places. Periods are, by and large, especially appropriate to the history of men's social and cultural pursuits, since what is essential to them is embodied in persistent institutions and attitudes that are constituted by whole sets of related actions. To choose a specific date as a division between two periods is thus doubly misleading if it makes historians forget both that the sequence of political events has usually continued through the critical date without a noticeable break and that changes in social and cultural orientation are too gradual to be bound by any singular dates. If, therefore, we choose the middle of the eighteenth century as its watershed, we must do so with the full realization that in politics not only did this midpoint obviously signify no fundamental shift in the domestic regimes of the European powers but it did not even alter the tendency to general warfare recently resumed in 1740, and that in society and culture the trends toward economic growth and intellectual ferment characteristic of the second half of the century were evident as well in the preceding generation.

But if due regard be had for its function as a rhetorical device, then a date—the year 1748—may be singled out as a dramatic way of marking the reversal of the proportionate weights of politics and society in determining the direction of European history. For two events of this year—one political and the other cultural—marked the intersection of a political development that was losing its former autonomy and a social development that was acquiring a new focus. The Peace of Aix-la-Chapelle, inconclusive as were its substantive provisions and short-lived as was the peace it sealed, marked the end of the significant dynastic wars triggered by crises of succession: when continental military conflict was resumed in 1756 it was preceded by a reversal of alliances—the so-called Diplomatic Revolution—which brought the old rivals, Bourbon France and Habsburg Austria, into coalition against Great Britain and Prussia and thus announced the shift from prescriptive monarchy to collective interest as the main guide to policy. In 1748, too, the Baron de Montesquieu published his *Spirit of the Laws*, a work which focused the diffusive thought of the Enlightenment upon the problems of social and political organization and thus announced the corpus of influential works in the field of public affairs that would spearhead the rising demand of a mobilized society for a reformation of the traditional ways of thinking and of doing.

From about mid-century on, then, the tone of European life gradually altered. The game of international politics went on and the domestic institutions of public order held firm, but the rules of the game were insensibly amended and the domestic institutions were pushed into an alternation of defensiveness and accommodation as the social pressures for change grew in intensity, crystallized into definite forces, and began to occupy the center of the European stage. Let us consider first the factors of social mobility that were growing through and around the stable arrangements of the traditionally organized European society, and then go on in subsequent chapters to the intellectual groups and ideas that articulated this mobility, to the new style of politics that was a response to it, and, finally, to the prerevolutionary movements of social and political protest that were the harbingers of a new age.

No economic revolution preceded the political revolution that ended the eighteenth century. During the entirety of the period with which we are concerned—that is, until 1789—by far the greater part of the European population lived, and saw no option but to live, in the same kind of corporately organized, hierarchical society that they and their forebears had inhabited since the reestablishment of religious and civil peace in the seventeenth century; and for the vast majority of men this pattern of stability held for all regions from the Urals to County Kerry. Throughout Europe, in progressive Great Britain as well as in retrograde Russia, most men were still undertaking the significant activities of their lives as members of time-honored associations which channeled these activities along the lines of well-tried custom and imbued these men with the values of the security that is attached to familiar routine. The model existence for which men strove was still to have a rich variety of protective institutions—ideally, a separate institution for each function of life. However distinct from one another in function or membership these institutions were supposed to be—like the organs of the human body to which they were still so often compared—they shared important qualities: they were bound by tradition; they were addicted to ritual; they were organized on the basis of privilege both in their internal structure and in their external relations with one another. For the guarantee of their rights in law and social custom (including the rights to political representation, where such rights were recognized), men were still grouped in a hierarchy of "ranks," "orders," or "estates," as they were variously called. For the pursuit of their occupations they were still subject in varying measure to the regulations of guilds, manors, or peasant communes. For the guidance of personal and social life, local corporations retained a far-reaching autonomy, and they continued to sanction the rules that were administered by local authorities who were powerful precisely because of the corporate tradition they administered: oligarchs were the heads of municipalities, gentry of counties, lords of villages, and in their exercise of controls they were joined by the bishops and local clergy of the established churches, who still registered the great events of personal life, sponsored the social entertainments, and articulated the public conscience.

The reality, undoubtedly, was not nearly so harmonious or stable as this model. In the first place, the neat allocation of separate corporations to separate groups and functions had never worked without friction in practice, and particularly in the second half of the eighteenth century the overlap and the competition between different corporations pursuing the same function, between complementary corporations pursuing presumably complementary functions, and between different groups in the same corporation, were exacerbated. Thus the merchants of the burgher estate and the progressive landowners of the noble estate fought over wholesale trade and rural manufacturing. The lay aristocracy came increasingly to dispute the local influence of the clerical aristocracy, in a campaign favored by the growing toleration, in fact more often than in law, of dissenting churches and by the ensuing competition between ecclesiastical establishment and dissent. And within the churches, the gulf between higher and lower clergy grew apace.

But there was also a second disturbance of corporate tradition. Distant authorities, as we have seen, had been encroaching for centuries on the judicial, financial, economic, and ecclesiastical autonomy of the local corporations, and this tendency continued throughout the eighteenth century. Responding in part to the supralocal administrative activities of the ever more numerous officials working and traveling for the central agencies and in part to the extra-corporate economic activities of merchants and factors who ignored guilds to set up their branches or their domestic industries among the rural cottagers, increasing numbers of people were escaping the traditional corporate institutions.

It is indeed the series of changes in the wonted way of doing and looking at things that makes up the history of the second half of the eighteenth century and that will be our chief concern, but these changes can only be understood if we keep always in mind the integrated structure and the static ideal of the society which contained the activities and retained the allegiance of most Europeans until the end of the Old Regime. This image of a corporately organized and traditionally motivated European people is obviously important both as the constant backdrop against which all changes must be measured and as a reminder not only that the agents of change were a minority, as agents of change usually are, but that in this case they were a minority who did not, until the explosion which ended the Old Regime toward the close of the eighteenth century, succeed in altering the fundamental rules by which men actually lived.

There are, however, two other reasons that are perhaps not so obvious but that also make the remembrance of what did not change in the eighteenth century important for the explanation of what did. First, the active minority that spread the seeds of change, whether in the policy of governments, in the pattern of trade, or in the realm of ideas, did what they did and thought what they thought in full consciousness of the predominantly static society upon which they were operating, and neither their deeds nor their theories are comprehensible without awareness of this valid consciousness of theirs. Second, the persistent commitment of most Europeans to their wonted ways and their familiar values meant that in response to the dislocations engendered in these ways and values of life by the proponents of change the conservative leaders were themselves galvanized into action to defend the social establishment. The actual course of change in the later eighteenth century makes sense only in light of the knowledge that it was powered not only by those who wanted change but also by those who unwittingly and unwillingly contributed to the process of change through the novel means they chose to fight it.

For a portrayal of Europe in the second half of the eighteenth century, then, let us turn first to the economic and social relationships which show the factors of stability and mobility in their due proportions.

POPULATION

The eighteenth century witnessed the takeoff of the population explosion that has continued to our day, surging powerfully against all social barriers in its path. Although the absolute numbers may be unimpressive by our standards, the proportional increase during this initial stage was great enough to overflow the dikes that had been constructed for a less densely packed humanity. Population figures for the eighteenth century are as unreliable as their explanation is uncertain, but their basic tendency seems clear enough: the population of Europe increased considerably, and the increase was markedly greater in the second half than in the first half of the century. According to one plausible estimate, the increase for the century totaled about three fifths, from around 120 million to around 190 million, with two thirds of the increase coming after 1750. The cause of the increase is even more uncertain than its extent. Historians now reject the older explanation of this "vital revolution" in terms of a falling death rate attributable to improvements in the practice of medicine and in sanitation, for these improvements were themselves limited in kind and restricted in incidence. The most probable explanation would seem to be a falling death rate explicable by the retreat of the age-old scourges of man—pestilence, devastation, and hunger—because of ecological changes noxious to the plague-bearing rat, the more disciplined conduct and limited depredations of eighteenth-century warfare, and the acceptance of hardy new crops like the potato as staple items of mass consumption. But a case has also been made for a rising birthrate in localities where a traditional tendency toward early and prolific marriages was given an unprecedented boost by the waning of natural calamities in the eighteenth century.

Although the causes of the population rise may still be debated, there can be little doubt that its effects were far-reaching. Population pressures increased the demand for goods and thereby initiated the chain reaction which stimulated trade and expanded the capitalization of both agriculture and industry. The expansion of the labor supply, especially in such favored areas as Britain and the Low Countries, led to the development of intensive agriculture and of urban labor reservoirs for industrial growth. But in less favored areas, the increase in population resulted in rural overpopulation that forced the subdivision of small farms to the point of agrarian crisis, and created an oversupply of wandering artisans who became tinder for popular uprisings in town and countryside alike. But however diversified its precise economic effects, the constant growth in the numbers and the density of Europe's inhabitants during the eighteenth century had a uniform social effect: whether it pushed people from the family farms into the labor pools of the countryside, from the countryside into the cities, or from the home country into the colonies, everywhere it upset established customs and began to orient men toward change rather than stability as the dominant way of life.

TRADE

.International trade, for some five hundred years one characteristic activity among many in the undulating kaleidoscope of European life, broke from its duly assigned mooring to become a second major force for economic change. Not, of course, that its incidence was evenly distributed. The growth of international commerce in the eighteenth century occurred mainly in overseas trade, with direct effects upon the great maritime and colonial nations, Great Britain and France, and with diminishing but perceptible effluence, mediated largely through these nations, into the rest of Europe. Although the statistics for trade are almost as inadequate as they are for other eighteenth-century economic activities, some notion of the

The extension of the European market economy, in which Great Britain led the way during the eighteenth century, was based largely on water transport, both at home and abroad. *Above: The Duke of Bridgewater canal in England. On the opposite page: Merchant adventurers of the East India Company in the Far East.*

orders of magnitude involved may be gleaned from such estimates as the fourfold increase in French overseas trade and the fivefold increase in the carrying capacity of the British merchant fleet during the course of the century.

The importance of international trade in European life is evident not only in the rise of the British-French commercial rivalry to the status of the single most important issue in international politics but perhaps even more clearly in the great leap which both of these powers took over such former maritime and colonial competitors as the Netherlands and Spain. For both declining powers, the relative insulation of their international economies from their domestic economies now became a comparative disadvantage. The Netherlands did continue to play an important role in European overseas and transit trade, and Spain retained its colonial system, but for both powers the stagnation of their development in relation to their own past and the decline of their competitive position in relation to their chief rivals testified to the changed role of international trade. Amsterdam, indeed, remained the center of international finance and the Netherlands the chief source of the world's capital during the eighteenth century, but since the Dutch tended increasingly to invest in the more vital economies of other countries, they themselves contributed an international movement of capital to the process of economic development in the industrialized nations. The expanding orbit of international trade came to include Scandinavians, Prussians, Russians, and other new or rejuvenated actors on the maritime mercentile scene. Their entry increased the competition in international commerce, but the economic effect which world trade had on them was limited and the social effect correspondingly different from that in the more mobilized societies of the west.

Great Britain and France, on the other hand, shared a distinctive combination of economic traits: both had a colonial basis for their foreign trade, and both felt the domestic effect of this commerce. But the precise pattern of the trade and consequently of its effects differed for the two countries. By 1789 not only was more than half of the British trade with areas outside of Europe, in comparison with France's one third, but the character of the commerce itself varied. British commerce consisted in general of the importation of raw materials in exchange for manufactured products, as indicated by the intensity of its trade flow with the North American colonies, a relatively prosperous market for manufactures, and with the Baltic region, a source of grain and naval stores. French trade involved mainly the transshipment of foreign raw materials and the export of French natural products—especially wine and spirits—accompanied by only a modicum of cloth manufactures, as was attested by the large role played in French commerce by Spain, Italy, and the Levant—areas with their own handicraft industries and a low effective demand for industrial imports. For the British, consequently, overseas trade contributed substantially to the demand for increased production and for materials to be used in production. By the last third of the century these demands were preparing the change of economic system we know as the Industrial Revolution. In France ever-expanding sectors of the society—aristocrats, peasants, merchants, bankers, and the professional classes—were caught up in the movement and dislocations of a commercialized economy, but without the alterations in economic organization needed to resolve the resulting tensions and insecurity.

Without the direct stimuli of colonies and overseas trade in massive proportions, the other large European nations fell behind Britain and France both in the affluence and in the mobility of their societies. Still, even the less advanced countries experienced the indirect effects of a modest commercial growth stimulated by the oceanic powers, which in conjunction with the direct effects of a population increase and the international political ambitions of the ruling classes, did have consequences for the mainland societies. Essentially, these consequences were of two kinds: first, influential, albeit small and isolated, groups of merchants and landowners were absorbed into the larger network of interlocal exchange; and second, the rulers of these countries adopted economic and social policies geared to the growing material bases of power in the leading mercantile states.

Both these kinds of continental economic development were visible in the pattern of urban growth, for the cities in the underdeveloped sectors of Europe that rose to international prominence in the eighteenth century were themselves of two types, corresponding to the two channels of economic stimulation. First, there were cities like Hamburg, Frankfurt, and Geneva, which through their position on the sea or on the great rivers became transit centers for the exchange of Dutch, British, and French goods and money for inland products. Second, there were the expanding cities of Vienna and Berlin, both of which increased in population to well over 100,000 in response to the demands of the royal court, the administration, and the military for the most modern goods and services. Small wonder that the cities of Europe, capital and provincial, became centers of prosperity, culture, and power that exceeded even the great urban concentrations of the Italian Renaissance.

INDUSTRY

The spurs from a growing population and a ballooning overseas trade combined to shake unprecedented numbers of Europeans out of their wonted routine and into the kaleidoscopic world of the distant marketplace. To assay what this change meant for the way in which such men earned their livelihood, let us make clear first what it did not mean. There was no "Industrial Revolution," in the proper sense of the term, during the eighteenth century. The Industrial Revolution refers to the rapid series of economic and social events that enthroned mechanized production as the determining factor in the material life of Western society. This drastic shift of economic control from the directors of natural and manual power to the managers of invested capital would, when it came, involve both the change from machines as isolated, *ad hoc* laborsaving devices to mechanization as a general process transferable to all branches of the economy, and the initiation of a self-sustaining chain reaction through which the comparative advantages of machines would continuously create the industrial and urban social conditions and attitudes favorable to their own extension.

The eighteenth century witnessed only the first of these two steps, and it witnessed this introductory phase, moreover, only in Great Britain. Not even in Britain did the second step occur, which would turn technological change into a permanent economic and social revolution. The Industrial Revolution, in short, was a product of eighteenth-century economic and social conditions, but the mechanization they sponsored did not react back upon the economy and society to consummate the revolution until well into the next century.

Because the conditions for the Industrial Revolution first appeared in late-eighteenth-century Britain, this island kingdom may be seen as the most advanced, and therefore the clearest, representative of the commercial system that still dominated the economic development of all Europe. For the inventions that initiated the economic transformation to the industrial era were British not because only the British were inventing or because invention was a different kind of activity in eighteenth-century Britain than it was in Europe then or had been in Britain before—it remained a product rather of practical craftsmanship than of theoretical science—but because Britain experienced in greater degree the factors of economic mobility that were affecting Europe as a whole, and responded in ways that became different in kind. Thus the British inventions of the latter eighteenth century were economically distinctive because here the commercial pressures for increased supplies were so pervasive and the relaxation of social and political bonds was so general that the inventions dovetailed in an economic series altering whole processes of production.

The most obvious factor making for the comparative advantage of the British was their leadership over the rest of Europe in the rate of population growth and in the expansion of international trade—elements directly relevant to the expanded market for textiles which was the primary stimulus for technological innovation. The apparently insatiable demand for cloth led to a contagious imbalance which stimulated inventions all along the production line. The comparative efficiency of cotton weaving over spinning, which had been reinforced by John Kay's flying shuttle of 1733, created the challenge that was answered by James Hargreaves' spinning jenny (1765), Richard Arkwright's water frame (1769), and Samuel Crompton's mule, a combination of jenny and water frame (1779). The consequent efficiency of yarn production, in turn, called for the mechanization of weaving, introduced gradually with the improvements upon Edmund Cartwright's first power loom (1787). The need for a reliable metal from which to make these precise machines led to the exploitation of coke smelting, after 1760, to produce the pig iron that went into the new tools. The need for mechanical power to drive them was filled by James Watt's version of the steam engine (1769), whose distinctive contribution was to extend the applicability of this engine from mining, where it was originally used, to all kinds of industry—particularly to textiles.

But if its superlative rise in population and foreign trade made Britain representative of the most obvious dynamic tendencies in Europe as a whole, the peaking of industrial change in Britain was also conditioned by other circumstances, which were apparently distinctive to the island kingdom. Yet these too, upon closer examination, turn out to be expressions of tendencies real but latent in the rest of Europe. They were also tendencies that were products of a long-established economic organization, however revolutionary their potentialities ultimately proved to be.

Even the distinctive insular geography of Britain—the small, compact land mass indented by the long, serrated shoreline—was in economic terms the most felicitous locale for the water transportation that for centuries had been the lifeline of European trade and was now exploited for commercial purposes as never before. Behind the industrial leadership that Britain was beginning for the first time to assume in Europe lay British leadership not only in oceanic and coastal trade but in the improvement of rivers and the construction of canals. The development of land transport, which was to become so signal a force in nineteenth-century economic growth, was not, interestingly enough, a prominent factor during the eighteenth century. Although there was some improvement in the building and maintenance of British roads, they remained in the hands of local turnpike trusts, and the heightened activity of these authorities after mid-century was unfortunately accompanied by corresponding increases in neither efficiency nor coordination. The most notable advances in road building were made in France, where, by the last quarter of the eighteenth century, a special corps of officials, trained at a technical School for Bridges and Roads, constructed and reconstructed some 25,000 miles of state-controlled highways. The French roads, like those of the German states which used them as models, undoubtedly contributed to the growing scope of the market economy on the European continent, but it should be remembered that none of these countries broke through to any decisively new stage or level of industrialism in the eighteenth century. The crucial physical channel of economic growth remained what it had been for centuries—the waterway— but simply exploited now to an unprecedented degree.

More peculiarly British and more apparently germane to the new industrialism was the complex of qualities associated with the British political and social system—a complex which derived from the abstractly antithetical but practically complementary connections of unity and individual liberty in Britain. By virtue of the early centralization of the British state, traditional local authorities raised no effective barriers to the movement of goods, men, and resources and hence to the formation of a national market equipped with a rapidly specializing division of labor. The effect was not only the absence of such obvious deterrents as local tolls but also the emphatic relocation of industry into the countryside, where capitalist entrepreneurs operated unencumbered by the restrictive regulations of municipal corporations and the old guilds. At the same time, the parlia-

A scene from *The Rake's Progress. Engraving by William Hogarth.*

mentary defense of property rights, manifested as early as the Patent Law of 1624, which undoubtedly encouraged the industrial inventions of the next century, led after the Glorious Revolution to the deliberate neglect and atrophy of mercantilist controls (with the exception of the Navigation Acts) and thus to a *de facto* reign of economic liberty.

Favored by this political climate, moreover, the relative fluidity of the relations among the classes not only offered incentives to the enterprise of energetic men with social ambitions but also had economic effects which redounded directly to the national demand for increased production. In the countryside the agricultural "revolution," which standardized crop rotation, fertilizing crops, and new fodders in the service of increased yields and calculated profits, was associated, to be sure, with such scientifically and commercially minded noblemen as Charles ("Turnip") Townshend (1675–1738) and Thomas William Coke of Norfolk (1754–1842), but it was also predicated upon the flexible economic and social structure of British farming. The enclosure acts, whereby an aristocratically dominated Parliament sanctioned the reorganization of scattered strips and unproductive commons into consolidated holdings, thereby encouraging the capitalization of agriculture and the raising of rural rents, accelerated an agrarian system which operated not through the direct exploitation of unitary estates by the aristocracy but through a system of long-term leases to middle-class farmers with whose interests the aristocracy associated itself.

On the urban side, the pattern was analogous. In the commercial and financial centers, as in the mushrooming industrial towns, the patriciate of inherited wealth and the oligarchy of established municipal families were at once threatened and replenished by enterprising traders, workshop owners, and professional people whose numbers and prosperity grew with the national economy.

The growth of a larger and richer middle class and the growing incidence of its upward mobility into the governing class meant not only an increase in the effective domestic demand for goods but a qualitative change in the goods that were now demanded in the market. Whereas international trade had traditionally been dominated by the luxury items called for by the tastes of a segregated court and aristocracy and their mimics among the local oligarchs, the spread of wealth and the opening of the aristocracy both to recruitment from below and to styles of a more popular kind began to make articles of mass consumption staple items of commerce and consequently of industrial production for market. The most spectacular and far-reaching of these shifts was the growing tendency of cotton to replace wool and silk as the chief material of textile manufacture. In part this change was a matter of economics and technology: the cotton supply was the most flexible in response to demand and cotton fiber was the most adaptable to mechanical spinning. But whether as cause or as effect, a change in social mores and standards of taste accompanied the shift. As the century wore on, silks and heavy brocades gave way to muslins as the preferred cloth of aristocracy and middle classes alike, and with it the materials of dress yielded to the subtler criterion of style as the mark of class distinction.

Nor was this development an isolated phenomenon. The propensity of the well-to-do in all classes to use wallpaper instead of woven tapestries, and their inclination to surround themselves with fine furniture made from plentiful overseas woods, were also obvious signs of the expanded market that was being created by an enlarged upper class, an increasingly prosperous and ambitious middle class, and the pressure on production exerted by their numbers and converging tastes. In the case of some foodstuffs—such as coffee and sugar—what had been items in the luxury trade of the sixteenth century penetrated even below the middle-class level to become items of mass consumption and demand by the end of the eighteenth.

Clearly, then, the political liberality, the social fluidity, and the material prosperity of the British scene created an economic demand and favored a technological response that proved in the event to be qualitatively different from contemporaneous tendencies on the Continent, since only on the island did they crystallize after the turn of the century into an Industrial Revolution, while on the Continent this revolution came later, the product as much of British influence as of native development. And yet, however distinctive the British origins of the distinctive British Industrial Revolution may seem in retrospect, they constituted, during the eighteenth century, only the most advanced stage of a general economic growth that in varying degrees and covert forms was affecting the whole of the European world.

The similarity in kind, albeit not in degree, of British and continental economic growth can best be understood if we illustrate the limits upon the former and the achievements of the latter. The statistics, approximate as they are, reveal a Britain only on the turn toward a new industrial system. In the 1780's Britain's production of iron was still smaller than France's. Even by the end of the century there were only some five hundred of Watt's steam engines in use, producing about 5,000 horsepower and reflecting an industrial structure still largely dependent upon water-power, upon the traditional woolen textiles as much as the revolutionary cottons, and upon the cottage and the workshop rather than the factory. Continental industrial growth, on the other hand, albeit spotty, was perceptible enough to make most contemporary observers unaware of a qualitative difference between the economic systems of the island and the mainland. France and the Austrian Netherlands (the later Belgium) were older industrial centers whose steady advance during the century seemed to keep approximate pace with Britain's, and at least in Russia and in Austrian Bohemia new industrial areas sprang into European prominence, eclipsing the more modest and artificial service industries that were mushrooming in the expanding capital cities.

In the French case, industrial production doubled, and most of the characteristics of the British economic growth were in evidence as well: extension of industry into the unregulated countryside, atrophy of controls both by guilds and by central mercantilist regulation, application of technological invention to economic processes (particularly in the silk and mining industries), and the beginnings—especially in the 1780's—of industrial concentration into large plants. By 1789, indeed, only the French necessity for using British machines in the cotton industry and the French weakness in coal deposits could have presaged the drastic lag which that nation was about to experience vis-à-vis Britain, and at that time the position of cotton and coke as the bellwethers of an Industrial Revolution was not yet clearly recognized.

Russia in the eighteenth century developed into one of the great industrial powers of Europe. As in its renewed industrialization at the end of the nineteenth century, the distinguishing trait of the Russian development was its concentration, both in plant and in region. Factories devoted to non-metallurgical manufacturing tripled in number between 1760 and 1800 (from about seven hundred to two thousand) and were grouped mainly in the Moscow area and the Urals. The latter, indeed, now became one of the great industrial regions of the world, for it was also the main seat of Russian metallurgy, the most important branch of Russian industry. As late as 1800 Russia was still the world's leading producer of pig iron, although there were already signs then of the stagnation, accountable to technological inertia, that was to last far into the nineteenth century. Even in the palmiest years of the eighteenth century the relatively limited proportions of industry in Russia were exhibited in the continuing role of agricultural raw materials as the chief Russian export and in the prevalence of metals over finished manufactured goods among the industrial products it did export. But lopsided and convulsive as its economic development may have been, the agricultural exports of flax, hemp, and—after 1780—wheat to western Europe, and of pig iron particularly to Britain, in exchange for finished manufactures made Russia an important factor in world trade and oriented a significant sector of the Russian economy to produce for and to purchase from distant markets.

Thus wherever industrial advance occurred in eighteenth-century Europe it took on a roughly similar pattern: it responded to increased demand stemming from interregional and overseas trade; it took the form primarily of an expansion of domestic industry into rural areas where traditional controls were weak, and secondarily of the growth of large plant units in the separate industries and locales where the supply of labor and power permitted; and it applied technical improvements piecemeal to the industrial process without transforming the character of that process.

THE IMPACT ON SOCIETY

Just as European economic growth in the eighteenth century can be viewed as a single economic process that varied significantly in its proportions from country to country, so too can the social facet of this growth—that is, the relations of the groups that engineered it to the groups that suffered it—be seen as a common social process whose variations from state to state hardened into the distinct nations of the European community.

The chief protagonists of commercial and industrial development were the middle-class merchants who assumed more and more the function of industrial organizers as the increasing supplies of raw materials and the expanding markets for finished products drove manufacturing into the suburbs and countryside where labor was plentiful and corporate modes of industrial organization were weak. Economically ancillary but socially crucial were the secondary agents of industrial growth: on the one hand, the artisans and the peasants who rose to the status of small-scale entrepreneurs in their own workshops, and on the other, the titled landowners whose estates became the locus of larger-scale industrial enterprises. Frequently entailing the paradoxical use of serfs as workers to assure labor discipline in modern, profit-oriented factories, such enterprises ranged from the food-processing, mining, and iron industries of the Russian nobility to the larger textile mills of the Bohemian aristocracy.

But both economically and socially the countervailing tendency toward the preservation of the old ways was far stronger on the Continent than in Great Britain. In France the guilds, however limited in their economic functions by public administrators and private entrepreneurs, persisted as a pervasive conservative influence and even increased in number as the government continued to profit from licenses for them. In Russia the notable rise of factory production shaded but did not categorically alter the preponderance of peasant handicraft and the local market in the Russian industrial picture. In both nations, moreover, even the middling sectors of society, which included the prime agents of economic change, responded to the change differently than in Britain. Where the British entrepreneurs in industry and the wholesale trades tended increasingly to set the aggressive tone for the bulk of the middle classes and ultimately for the most influential groups in the society as a whole, their French and Russian counterparts remained, in varying ways and degrees, isolated even within their class. In France, the bourgeois continued typically to yearn for status, either through investment in landed property and hence a claim on a place in the aristocracy or urban patriciate, or through investment in government obligations and acquisition of the perquisites of the leisured *rentier*. Despite the increased role of Russian merchants in both trade and industry, the active traders and industrialists among them were such a minuscule part of the urban communities that the municipal delegates to Catherine the Great's Legislative Commission of 1767 themselves complained of the paucity of merchants in their ranks and proceeded unwittingly to back their complaint through the passivity of their own behavior in the Commission.

Among the traditional groupings of the continental European population the negative response to economic growth went beyond such inertia to overt counter-action. These groups not only set limits to the dimension of change upon the Continent but triggered reactionary movements against it. The most spectacular and the most fateful of these movements was the so-called "feudal reaction" in France, where from mid-century, noble estate owners responded to the economic pressures of rising world prices by searching out old titles and seeking to enforce both manorial claims against the peasants and political immunities against the crown. Ultimately, in the portentous spring and summer of 1789, two other groups representing the conservative dimension of French society—the peasants and the artisans—rose against the campaign of the aristocracy to pass the cost of economic and social change on to the French masses.

In Russia, similarly, the most important social developments of the latter eighteenth century were reactionary movements of the traditional groups. By the reign of Catherine the Great—that is, from 1762—the Russian nobility acquired, with a decisive assist from the state, for the first time the legal status and the corporate consciousness of a caste such as had existed in western Europe since the Middle Ages. The aristocracy exploited its new legal status to extend its judicial, police, and seignorial powers over the serfs at the cost of the governmental protection formerly accorded these wards.

Pugachev in chains. *Drawing from a contemporary pamphlet designed pointedly to show readers the grim end awaiting any "rebel and traitor."*

The other prominent conservative group—the peasantry—responded in its own fashion to the new mobility in Russian affairs with the most radical of countermovements. The Pugachev rebellion of 1773 was the most widespread of eighteenth-century peasant revolts. Starting as a political rebel on the southeastern frontier of European Russia, Emelyan Pugachev, himself a Don Cossack, appealed first to a mixture of outlying groups— Russian Orthodox Old Believers, Ural Cossacks, and other ethnically non-Russian tribes—who resented the recent encroachments of the central government, but then, masquerading as a wrongfully deposed Peter III (who had actually been murdered in 1762), he raised the banner of social revolution, promised freedom and land to the peasants, and enlisted a host of private landed and factory serfs in a large area of southeastern Russia. The revolt was crushed and the retribution terrible, but it gave spectacular notice of the pattern which agrarian revolts in Europe would take until the middle of the nineteenth century in response to the ever-deeper penetration of an exchange economy. The virulence of the peasant movements stemmed from the triple stimuli that triggered them. However local the substantive issues behind it were and however untypical of western Europe the Russian tendency toward the extension of serfdom in the eighteenth century may have been, the Pugachev rebellion was representative in its accumulation of grievances: first against the state as an agency of change; second, against progressive sections of the aristocracy which caused dislocation in the countryside by bringing capitalistic enterprise to it; third, indirectly against the exchange economy and directly against the regressive sections of the aristocracy which recoiled from this economy by tightening their hold on the peasantry.

In sum, the social response to the spreading effect of the exchange economy in Europe was divided between the minority in all classes who joined the merchant pioneers in advancing it and the majority of all classes who passively or actively resisted it. But it must be emphasized, to understand this response aright, that this distinction between a progressive and a reactionary response was an economic and social, but *not* a political distinction. No more in the eighteenth than in the previous centuries of the early modern era was there the consistent lineup of social and political interests to which we have become accustomed from subsequent experience. Thus Pugachev's revolt was politically radical and socially conservative. Obversely, enterprising businessmen, particularly in Britain and France, continued to support governments which, whatever their political complexion, favored the trading interest.

The primary reason for the discrepancies between the social and the political lineups in the eighteenth century lay indeed precisely in the ambiguous relationship between society and government. The authoritarian regimes of the eighteenth century were not simply reflections of the dominant social group or tendency. Because the stability of these regimes was based on the resources they could mobilize from the whole society to meet the ever-present threat of war abroad and on the pressure they could exert among the groups of the society to meet the still-present threat of disorder within, governments required both social mobility to generate force and social hierarchy to control it. Typically, then, governments swayed from one side to the other of the social structure they sought to straddle, in response to the changing pressures of external security, internal order, and domestic lobbyists. The politics of the various social groups, in turn, often depended more upon the direction of governmental policy at any particular moment than upon any consistent attitude toward politics dictated by their abiding social interests. Government was relevant to the social classes because it required their support and because the policies it adopted affected their destinies, but government was also independent of its social base because of the specifically political dimension—external and internal security—in its policies. In addition to the various estates and classes, then, government must be considered an independent factor in the society of eighteenth-century Europe.

SOCIETY AND GOVERNMENT

Like the relationships of the classes to one another, the policies of governments varied greatly from country to country and yet, especially during the second half of the eighteenth century, manifested an increasing similarity that reflected the common European scope of the economic and social development with which these policies were designed to deal. However dissimilar in forms and however varied in specific policy, European rulers and officials tended increasingly to favor the process of industrial and commercial growth, not only in the obvious forms of financial subsidies, tax privileges, public sponsorship and public ownership of manufacturing and trading enterprises, and the like, but also in the creation of a freer environment for the prosecution of private undertakings. Thus in some measure the freewheeling atmosphere provided by the commercially interested and property-minded parliamentary sovereign of Great Britain marked the extreme point of a tendency in more modest evidence elsewhere. In country after country on the continent of Europe, the apparent incongruity of their absolute monarchies with constitutional Britain was softened by their adoption of economic policies comparable to the growing liberality of the island kingdom.

The favored field for the relaxation of controls was—as might be expected from the most expansive of the century's economic activities—the field of commerce. But not all trade was equally subject to liberalized economic attitudes. Curiously enough, in view of the enormous increase in the volume and attraction of foreign trade, it was internal rather than international commerce that was the chief beneficiary of the new policy. Aside from a slight moderation of their trading monopoly with their West Indian colonies by the French in 1784, the only notable steps toward international free trade were the Franco-American Treaty of Amity and Commerce of 1778 and, more importantly, the Anglo-French commercial treaty of 1786.

The common factor of France's participation in all these arrangements would seem to argue the prevalence of liberal commercial ideas in that country, and indeed from 1750 to the 1780's an influential school of economic reformers called the Economists, led by an administrator, Vincent de Gournay (1712–1759), and a court physician, François Quesnay (1694–1774), did have considerable effect in French official circles. But if their ideas made possible the tariff reductions that rendered the Anglo-French commercial treaty so noteworthy, they were not primarily responsible for its actuality. The French, indeed, were the initiators of the treaty, but for a political reason—to seal the peace of 1783 with Britain—and it was opposed by French industrial groups who feared inundation by British manufactures. The British negotiator, William Pitt "the Younger" (1759–1806), was an authentic disciple of Adam Smith and does seem to have been moved by the perception of the benefits of free trade for Britain, but he stood almost alone and succeeded in having the treaty ratified rather through his general influence than through any generally favorable response to this policy.

Governmental attempts at liberalizing internal trade were much more widespread, and where they took place had much stronger backing, than on the international stage. The best known of these attempts is associated with the idea of *laissez-faire*, but the policy had a far broader base than this explicit doctrine. In 1774 Anne Robert Jacques Turgot (1727–1781), long a friend of the Economists and recently appointed Controller-general of France, enacted the domestic free trade in grain as part of a far-reaching general program of liberal economic reform, an enactment that was then frustrated along with Turgot and his program. But in fact this kind of measure had a more positive career in the latter eighteenth century than the spectacular rise and fall of Turgot indicated and a more hybrid character than its association here with a general economic liberalism connoted. The positive attitude toward freer internal trade was indicated even in this context, for a successor of Turgot as Controller-general, Charles de Calonne (1734–1802), renewed his declaration of free trade in grain during 1787.

But it was the removal of barriers to domestic commerce elsewhere in Europe, where the influence of liberal doctrine was not so strong, that revealed more accurately the kind of pressure behind the free-trading policy. By edicts of 1753 and 1762 Russia abolished internal customs barriers throughout its dominions, and in 1775 the Habsburgs did the same for their crown lands (only Hungary and the Tyrol were excluded from the single-customs territory). The Russian enactment showed governmental responsiveness to pressures from merchants and market-minded nobility; the Austrian revealed the antithetical form that the relations between international and internal free trade could take in the eighteenth century. For the Habsburg decision to enlarge the Austrian domestic market was taken as a deliberate counterweight to the decision to maintain the prohibitive tariffs on foreign goods that obviously handicapped Austrian exports.

Thus the realities of eighteenth-century commercial policy belie the simple opposition that Adam Smith (1723–1790), like his fellow Scotsman David Hume before him, found between the system of economic freedom which he advocated and the set of restrictive practices which he saw all around him and to which he affixed the systematic label of mercantilism. Undoubtedly the school of liberal British economists whose ideas Smith synthesized and the school of French Economists, who coined the term *laissez-faire* for the policy of non-interference, did think in terms of a disjunction between desirable liberty and existing controls. It is true too that these ideas did invade the councils of governments in this oppositional form and set off conflicts between liberal and restrictionist officials; the younger Pitt in Britain, the economic reformers in the French administration, and the liberal young Prussian bureaucrats who expressed a rising discontent with the protectionist policies of Frederick the Great are cases in point. But the fact remains that the most characteristic effect of liberal economic ideas in the latter eighteenth century was not to replace but to redefine mercantilist practice, and this explains the pattern of domestic free trade behind a mercantilist tariff policy.

The theoretical mechanics of this pattern can be seen in the distinctive character of the doctrine that was the most influential vehicle of economic liberalism on the Continent. Physiocracy, the name attributed in the nineteenth century to the subgroup of Economists who followed François Quesnay, flourished particularly in the sixties and seventies of the eighteenth century. As the label indicates, the Physiocrats believed in a natural economic order that should be inviolable by government and to this extent shared with the general run of economic liberals the general faith in the beneficence of *laissez-faire*. But at the same time the particular emphases of the Physiocrats that distinguished them from other economic liberals were such as to permit more easily the modulation of this faith into a mercantilist framework. For the Physiocrats, a corollary of the primacy of the natural order in economics was the status of the soil as the sole source of wealth and consequently of agriculture as the sole producer of value. Exchange was important to them, to be sure, but not as a criterion of wealth. For the physician Quesnay and his disciples, the economy, like the individual human, was a body, and exchange was the means by which wealth, produced originally from the soil, circulated naturally through it. Hence the Physiocrats tended to emphasize production more than trade and because of this emphasis seldom carried their subscription to free trade beyond the national frontier. Neither Catherine II of Russia nor Joseph II of Austria found any great problem of consistency in fitting an endorsement of Physiocracy into general policies of mercantilist regulation. It simply contributed to the more liberal redefinition of mercantilism which removed intermediary units between the state and the individual.

The tendency toward the relaxation of economic controls in the second half of the eighteenth century extended to the process of production as well as to trade. In its application to production, indeed, the policy of relaxation ran directly afoul not only—like trade—of the traditional intermediate authorities but also—unlike trade—of the mercantilist central bureaucracy. On the issues of industrial and agrarian liberty, then, can be found both the bitterest conflict of reformers against guilds and aristocracies and the greatest tension, within governments, between the proponents of individual enterprise and of the supporters of centralized direction. Neither type of struggle had a decisive result in the form of dramatic and categorical transformations of policy all along the economic line, but the cumulative effect of the innumerable skirmishes was definitely toward a greater freedom of production, if freedom is taken in its eighteenth-century connotation of individualism. Here again Great Britain was the model of a process shared more inchoately by the rest of Europe. The British liberalized economic conditions tacitly and practically, with little change in literal law and institutions, and yet in this unspectacular style they showed the way to European reformers all along the productive front, detouring around the guilds, converting the British aristocracy from lords to property owners, and deliberately neglecting the governmental regulations for industry still on the books from the previous centuries.

On the Continent the scope of the changes in policy was more modest. The reformers tended to have more success against the intermediate corporate authorities than against the mercantilist officials of the central bureaucracies, and even their successes against the traditional corporations were often nullified in practice. But while the scope of economic liberty was much narrower than in Britain, in the economic fields for which the policy was adopted it was much more clearly marked by definite legislation which made it an explicit social issue. Even the rulers and bureaucracies of Russia and Austria, two of Europe's most underdeveloped areas, sought to impose the conditions of economic mobility upon their largely static societies by legal fiat. More typical were the miniature states, intermediate between the western and eastern wings of Europe both in geography and in the sociopolitical spectrum, which enjoyed liberal reform that was the resultant of action taken by enlightened governments and by spontaneously stirring social groups. In western Germany and northern Italy, the economic vitality of yesteryear had become routinized, but the towns, the burghers, and the free peasantry which had once worked these flourishing economies remained in institutional being. Here the measures of progressive governors reflected their awareness of latent social possibilities that needed to be mobilized for economic growth. In the margravate of Baden, in Piedmont-Savoy, and in the Austrian-dominated Italian territories of Lombardy and Tuscany, hereditary bondage was abolished, free trade in grain was established, and the introduction of crop rotation, the use of fertilizer, and the division of common pastures—all steps toward the commercialization of agriculture—were officially sponsored under the explicit aegis of Physiocratic doctrines. In Baden, the government of the enlightened Charles Frederick (ruled 1738–1811) frankly expressed its liberalizing intention of teaching its subjects "even against their will how to manage their own business." In Piedmont-Savoy, distinguished by an exceptional degree of freedom, government policy under King Charles Emmanuel III (ruled 1730–1773) reflected this condition by proceeding to abolish the real as well as the personal obligations of the servile past—that is, the traditional dues owed by the peasant not only for his person but also for his land. Again, in Tuscany, with its strong Florentine industrial history, the Grand Duke Leopold (ruled 1765–1790, subsequently Leopold II of Austria) proceeded to abolish the guilds in a modestly successful attempt to rejuvenate Tuscan industrial life.

Thus, whereas in eastern Europe governments were striving to create the social agents of economic growth, in western Germany and northern Italy governments encouraged an existing minority of enterprising social agents to stimulate economic growth.

In France, to complete the continental spectrum, there was an even balance between governmental initiative and social pressure that reflected the comparatively even balance between mobile and static elements within the society itself. These forces were more evenly matched in France than elsewhere in Europe, and this fact helps to explain both the French representative position as arbiter of a common European culture and the greater intensity of the political and social crisis in France which brought the Old Regime to its close. To this crisis we shall return in our final chapter.

SOCIETY AND ENLIGHTENMENT

Thus did the domestic policies of the various European states run the gamut between molding and reflecting the crucial relationship between the conservative defenders of the social establishment and the enterprising promoters of a dynamic economy. Since, as we have seen, the governments' interest in the new resources of power was always circumscribed by the constant concern for the preservation of internal order and of the privileged classes without which this order appeared inconceivable, the states' acknowledgment and encouragement of the economic and social agencies of change remained limited, indirect, and diffuse. The most substantial and crystallized expressions of this change were neither economic, nor social, nor political—they were cultural. What was new and distinctive in European society was defined primarily in its intellectual works, and only subsequently, through politicians educated in these works, did governments assume the distinctive eighteenth-century form of "enlightened" absolutism and did society begin its distinctive eighteenth-century development toward political revolution.

The culture of the Enlightenment was the most articulate product of the new social dynamism in its confrontation with Europe's inherited social torpor. Because the social confrontation was European in scope, so was the span of the Enlightenment. Because the relative strength of the active and passive opponents in the social confrontation varied from region to region, the function of intellectuals in the cultural movement did too, ranging from the production of Enlightenment in Britain and France to the various degrees and ways of consuming it in central and eastern Europe. And because the philosopher, in his eighteenth-century role as a worldly intellectual, was the most self-conscious and influential spokesman for the new society in its relations with the old, he became its uncrowned king, a partner ultimately in a kind of diplomatic correspondence with the crowned kings of Europe.

CHAPTER 17

The Worldly Philosophers, 1687-1776

AROUND THE MIDDLE of the eighteenth century the proponents of the intellectual movement which took its name from their proclaimed dedication to the cause of "Enlightenment" became the representative social leaders of the party of change and the dominant figures in the culture of the whole European society. This development was the joint result of a social process which now found its focus in the Enlightenment and of an intellectual process which had equipped the Enlightenment for both its social role and its cultural hegemony.

We have already examined the ingredients of the social process. Out of it there grew an active minority of men committed to social mobility but forced by the external pressure of traditional institutions and their own loyalty to the fundamentals of hierarchy and authority in those institutions to invest their cherished desires and values in the malleable realm of ideas and to see themselves most faithfully represented by intellectual brokers. This social environment furnished the external conditions which influenced the developing thought of the Enlightenment, and explains its popular reception. Like the Italian humanism of more than two centuries before, the European Enlightenment of the eighteenth century was essentially a movement of urban culture. The restless profusion of its ideas; its positive orientation toward change; its attraction for a whole intellectual hierarchy of innovators, diffusers, and popularizers; its sense of community, which gave to its protagonists an *esprit de corps* among themselves, a continuing rapport with a growing audience, and a practical social reference for their intellectual endeavors: these qualities of Enlightenment culture grew out of the tempo and integration of city life.

But the social environment does not entirely explain the ideas themselves. For these ideas also had their own intellectual base, and their development had its own intellectual momentum. From this base and this development we can plot the course of the Enlightenment which made it socially relevant by mid-century and socially effective subsequently. This inside story of the Enlightenment's worldly philosophers is our next assignment.

The Enlightenment was not, of course, born in 1748, although it became predominant on the European scene at that point; and it was not the only considerable cultural movement of the century, although intellectual historians have frequently enough labeled the whole era with its name. Its life was coterminous with the period of this volume. It was conceived with the publication of Newton's *Principia Mathematica* in 1687 and born—insofar as any movement within the continuous development of ideas in Western civilization can be said to be "born" at all—with the coincident publication of John Locke's *Essay Concerning Human Understanding* and his *Two Treatises on Civil Government* in 1690. It finally died, after a lingering illness, in 1789, when the French Revolution sealed the alienation of its social support and the disruption of its intellectual identity.

Made up of as many fiercely independent virtuosos as it was, the movement was organized in no definite institution and subscribed to no uniform doctrine, but it did develop a real, if intangible, supra-individual identity in which its members came to participate and which took on a life of its own. In this sense we may feel justified in applying an organic analogy to its career. It can be viewed, then, in three stages: a protracted childhood in which, until the middle of the eighteenth century, it defined itself internally by the gradual coalescence of separate perceptions into a characteristic outlook and externally by self-assertion against competing outlooks; a period of maturity in which it extended its unified outlook across the board to all kinds of natural and social reality, achieving thereby a comprehensive and powerful integrity with an enormous comparative advantage over its intellectual competitors; and finally, a period of querulous and troubled old age, in which family discord fed the recovery of former competitors and the growth of new ones.

The intellectual identity, cultural preeminence, social impact, and hence the historical role of the Enlightenment date from the second stage of its development in the latter half of the eighteenth century. But if the Enlightenment was the central cultural movement of the century it was far from the only one, and we must go back into the earlier half of our period not only to trace the elements that composed it but also to take note of its rival cultural movements at a time when they were still recognizable, before they were blurred by the blaze of the triumphant mature Enlightenment.

ORIGINS OF THE ENLIGHTENMENT, 1687–1715 −1715

Every cultural movement is both a development of and a reaction against a precedent cultural movement. The Enlightenment was no exception, but of the two dimensions the proportion of filial dependence upon the dominant science, philosophy, and jurisprudence of the seventeenth century loomed uncommonly large in its origins. The continuity is visible in some of the labels affixed to the two cultural eras. Around the middle of the eighteenth century, Etienne Bonnot de Condillac (1715–1780) and Jean Le Rond d'Alembert (*c.* 1717–1783), two of the keynoters of the Enlightenment, coined and diffused, respectively, a formula for comparison of the Enlightenment with the rationalism of the seventeenth century. The similarities between the two movements are all the more striking for the contrast they intended. Even at their most filially impious, they could make only the tenuous distinction between the "spirit of systems" and the "systematic spirit" to epitomize the difference between the cognate movement of the seventeenth century and their own. Subsequently, historians have added to the ambiguity by denominating the period of either the "age of reason," at their discretion. And when we list the generic qualities in the two phases of rationalism there is a striking degree of overlap. Both were secular in their emphasis, natural in their focus, scientific in their models, mathematical in their methods, individualist in their criticisms, and lawful in their constructions.

For the original impulse of the Enlightenment we should look to its fathers, men who grew up in the seventeenth-century world and never entirely outgrew it but who, in the generation from 1687 to 1715, added the special touches from which the Enlightenment took off. This generation produced the patron saints of the Enlightenment—Isaac Newton for science, John Locke and Gottfried Wilhelm Leibniz for philosophy, and Pierre Bayle for a little bit of everything, critically considered. These shining lights presided over what has been called a general "crisis of the European mind"—a crisis fed by political and sectarian conflict, the accumulation of scientific experience, the growing awareness of the larger world outside Christian Europe, and a resultant skeptical habit of mind.

"Crisis" is probably too strong a word to use for the Enlightenment's setting—though any historian worth his salt can find a cultural crisis wherever he has a mind to find it—for the doubts prevalent around the turn of the eighteenth century rarely extended to the fundamentals of religion and society. But with the ever greater attention paid to realities that did not fit any of the inherited systems, the final stages of seventeenth-century thought did produce the transition and the challenge that eventuated in the Enlightenment.

What, then, were the emphases of these late masters from the "century of genius"—as historians have labeled the seventeenth century—and what did their busy little successors do with them in the first half of the eighteenth century?

The first of the transitional emphases in the late seventeenth century was the shift in the center of gravity from general principles to particular facts. The dominant mode of thought in the seventeenth century, represented by Bacon, Descartes, Hobbes, and Spinoza, had validated both principle and fact by ruling out theological dependence in the knowledge of

Gottfried Wilhelm Leibniz. *German philosopher, mathematician, jurist, historian, and pioneer of the European Enlightenment.*

either, but in the absence of an ordaining divinity, these thinkers had given priority to ordering principle. Without surrendering the joint character of the framework, the generation that closed out the century tended rather to focus on the particularity and plurality of reality and on the empirical sources and inductive methods of knowing it. Thus Newton's famous "rules of reasoning in philosophy" accepted the uniformity of nature and of nature's laws but the distinctive element in his recipe was the decisive role he attributed to specific phenomena as the basis of knowledge; to observation, analysis, and experiment as the means of processing them; and to the descriptive nature of all general laws. Again, in spite of rejecting the innate "clear and distinct ideas" which Descartes had deemed the general ordering powers of the mind, Locke retained the notion of "ideas" as the constituents of mind, but he insisted upon their origin in specific perceptions of external objects and in specific mental operations upon them. Even Gottfried Wilhelm Leibniz (1646–1716), high-flown speculator and proponent of a preestablished universal harmony that he was, made his most striking contributions through his notion of "monads," the mutually independent and incomparable basic units of reality which reflected the universal order in a wholly individual way, and through his "law of sufficient reason," a special logic of probability designed especially to give a firm foundation to *factual* truth. Finally, in Pierre Bayle, whose *Historical and Critical Dictionary* (1697) was to be a treasure chest of uninhibited information and skeptical judgments for the Enlightenment, there was a large, rich, encyclopedic corpus of knowledge whose apparently simple strain of critical rationalism actually covered a deeper tolerant faith in the beneficent multiplicity and variety of natural and human creation.

Second, along with the shift in emphasis from general reason to particular facts, the generation at the turn into the eighteenth century likewise shifted its preferred fields of knowledge. Where the prime generations of the seventeenth century had systematized all fields of knowledge from natural science to politics with the connecting cables of metaphysical universals, the last generation submerged metaphysics, minimized system, and focused on the released branches of academic and intellectual concern. Both Locke and Bayle extended their condemnation of dogma to a condemnation of metaphysics, theological and secular alike, on the ground that authentic knowledge of this kind was beyond the capacity of the human mind. Locke, the most influential philosopher of the age (the influence of Leibniz, who published little, was indirect and belated), and Newton, its most influential scientist, embody the dissolution of system: after a century in which such double-barreled geniuses as Giordano Bruno, Galileo, Descartes, Hobbes, Spinoza, and Pascal had coupled science and philosophy in inseparable combinations, we find that Locke evinced little science and Newton a most naïve and confused philosophy.

Nor was this separation of the talents entirely fortuitous. Locke shifted the task of philosophy entirely to the investigation of how we know (epistemology), a concentration appropriate to the empirical approach but hardly conducive to scientific theorizing. Scholars, indeed, are still trying to fit the rationalism of Locke's natural-law political theory into the empiricism of his epistemology without much success, and the most notable philosophers of the half century that followed, Bishop George Berkeley and David Hume (again, Leibniz excepted), were—like Locke—British, empiricist, predominantly epistemological and not notably scientific. In science, analogously, Newton shifted the emphasis from mathematics, the most philosophically adaptable of the seventeenth and eighteenth-century sciences, to physics, where the greater attention to the real plurality of observed phenomena diverted men from the abstractions of philosophy in its traditional metaphysical mode. Both from our point of view and from that of his eighteenth-century successors, to be sure, Newton's achievement consisted in his miraculous synthesis of physics and mathematics, but he put the greater historical momentum into physics in two different ways: first, his emphasis upon its autonomy and upon its indispensability to mathematical laws was far greater than was that of the mathematical physicists who preceded him; and second, his equivalence of physics and mathematics undermined the belief in the absolute sovereignty of mathematical law and initiated the commitment to its necessary immanence in the facts of the actual world. It followed consistently from Newton's impulse that his great eighteenth-century successors in the world of science were distinguished for the laws and processes they discovered in the physical and life sciences and for the theories they formulated in these fields. Among these men were Joseph Priestly and Antoine Laurent Lavoisier in chemistry;

Joseph Black and Count Rumford in heat physics; Luigi Galvani, Alessandro Volta, and Charles Coulomb in electricity; Carl von Linné (Linnaeus), Denis Diderot, Georges Louis Leclerc de Buffon, and Jean Baptiste de Lamarck in biology.

A third late development of seventeenth-century culture was the extension of the critical spirit from theoretical to practical affairs. The main line of seventeenth-century intellectuals had criticized and revised the foundations of institutions rather than the institutions themselves; the last generation continued to accept both the new foundations and the old institutions, but shifted the onus of criticism to the specific operations of those institutions. Thus the church and the state became targets of intellectual discussion in the decades around the turn of the eighteenth century, but for their specific policies rather than their fundamental structure. On the church, both Locke and Bayle treated particular religious affiliation as a matter of indifference, and emphasized the nefarious moral effects of intolerant clerical practice. On the state, we have already had occasion to take notice of the particular complaints levied by Vauban, Boisguillebert, and Fénelon against the policies of Louis XIV (see pp. 71–72). Perhaps even more telling was the selection evident in the immediate reception of Locke's work on government. Men chose to see in it, not its principle of popular sovereignty or its assertion of the right of revolution, but its defense of private property and its validation of lawful as against arbitrary government—a reception which converted Locke's legacy, at least temporarily, from a model of political theory into a model of constitutional law.

A final important change of late-seventeenth-century thought, consistent with its substantive trend toward the tangible and the concrete, was perceptible in the appearance of a new level of discourse, geared to popular reception and translating the specialized language of the narrow circle of seventeenth-century scholars and thinkers into the common language of men of letters and their educated public. The popularizer who more than any other figure of his century set the tone for the century of the Enlightenment to follow was Bernard de Fontenelle (1657–1757). In works like the *History of Oracles* and *Dialogues on the Plurality of the Worlds*, both published in 1686, he put the insights of the new science and its philosophical implications relating to the lawfulness, the self-sustaining order, and the autonomy of nature, into a gracious and entertaining form which helped to make the revolution in cosmology a conversation piece. More important perhaps, the style in which he diffused seventeenth-century thought carried with it a subtle change in point of view: by presenting its results as matters of common sense he gently dismissed the metaphysics it had prized and exalted the self-evident truths of everyman's reason. With his sure touch for the dramatic issue, finally, he presented the achievements of his century in the eye-catching guise of a victorious duel: he turned what had been the purely literary feud of "the Ancients and the

Moderns" on the comparative values of ancient and contemporary tragedy into a celebration of the intellectual progress registered by the naturalism and the rationalism of the "century of genius" beyond even the highest points of past human attainment.

It was the unprecedented progress in human culture achieved by the intellectual pioneers of the seventeenth century that popularizers like Fontenelle proposed to disseminate. In England, Joseph Addison (1672–1719) and Richard Steele (1672–1729) made this campaign into an explicit program, when they published *The Spectator* daily in 1711 and 1712, with the avowed aim of bringing "Philosophy out of closets and libraries . . . to dwell in clubs and assemblies."

THE ORTHODOX REVIVAL AND THE CULT OF SENTIMENT, 1690–1740

Accompanying these final modulations of seventeenth-century rationalism in the generation that spanned the break between the centuries, two cultural tendencies of a quite different order also made a successful transition from the seventeenth century into the new era. These tendencies—religious orthodoxy and the cult of feeling—would live through the transitional generation to form the competitive cultural background against which the young Enlightenment would grow during the first half of the eighteenth century.

Despite the threat of naturalism and pantheism from the main line of seventeenth-century philosophy, religious orthodoxy had shown a formidable intellectual as well as ecclesiastical vitality in at least two of the three established Christian confessions—the Catholic and the Calvinist. And despite the threat of total regulation by the aesthetics of seventeenth-century classicism, the poetry and drama of imagination, passion, symbol, and wit had ignored, strained, or broken through the classical "unities" to create the powerful literature of Milton, Racine, and Dryden.

Occasionally, as the brilliant figures of Milton and Pascal illustrate, the two extra-rational cultural tendencies that were rooted in religious piety and in human emotion had met in creative union, but such junctures were rare and smacked of individual heresy. In general, orthodoxy had prevailed over feeling in the seventeenth century. Piety was dominated by dogmatic conformity that either repelled or subordinated spontaneous emotion just as it rejected the autonomy of reason and made it dependent. The force of feeling and imagination was diverted into the orthodox service that produced at its best the Lutheran hymns of a Paul Gerhardt (1607–1676) and at its worst the excesses of heresy hunting and witchcraft. There was not yet, in the seventeenth century, sufficient trust in the authenticity of man's imaginings or in the reliability of his feelings to do without the direction and control of them. Appreciation did grow for the cultural function of these human powers in the immediate perception of reality and in the creation of art, but within a framework set by faith or reason. By far the greatest cultural achievements of imagination and feeling during the seventeenth century—apart from the rare religious genius of a Milton or a Pascal—had come from the engagement of these faculties with the classical rules of reason, which gave them both support and challenge. The typical results of this engagement were what might be called indirect products of emotional and imaginative culture—Racine's tragedies of the noble passions and the address to "the passions and humors" of human nature in the penetrating satires of Molière and Dryden.

During the first half of the eighteenth century, these nonrational cultural currents not only maintained themselves but developed in directions that permitted them to live through even the subsequent triumph of the rational Enlightenment. These developments went essentially along two lines: first, religious orthodoxy adjusted itself to the vogue of a critical and practical reason through a combination of spirited defense in the name of tradition, shrewd appropriation of a rational dimension, and the wholehearted alliance with emotionalism. Second, the aspects of human culture rooted in the more feeling, imaginative, and intuitive faculties of men developed independent movements, both through the powerful role that emotions now began to play openly in religious piety and religious music and through the direct cultivation of a frankly sentimental literature to accompany the perfection of the satiric fantasy.

Types of Orthodox Revival

The religious orthodoxy which arose just before the turn of the century would provide fresh targets for the secular Enlightenment, but it also equipped churchmen with the means of their own preservation in this duel.

In their defense of organized churches against both rational criticism from without and "heresy" from within, the orthodox found their intellectual scope limited. But the vigor of their attacks against all presumed violators of the divine order betokened the continuing appeal of unbroken tradition. At the end of the seventeenth century Bishop Jacques Bénigne Bossuet (1627–1704), the official troubleshooter of French Catholicism, asserted against all comers the virtues of divine-right monarchy and Catholic hierarchy. He seems in retrospect a caricature of an intellectual today, but his exposition of the divine-right political principle, his scheme of providential universal history, and his analysis of Protestant sectarianism were contemporary enough to remain standard targets through much of the eighteenth century. One of his most spirited antagonists, moreover, was a kind of mirror image of Bossuet, confirming the persistence of his kind of institutional orthodoxy. The exiled Hugenot pastor Pierre Jurieu, whom we have already met as a critic of the aging Louis XIV, polemicized passionately for the nominal supremacy of the rights of free conscience over the authority of a persecuting church, as well as of a tyrannical ruler, but his insistence on assigning the protection of these rights to social and religious corporations, in a pattern reminiscent of sixteenth- and early-seventeenth-century Presbyterianism, and his savage attack upon Bayle for extending the defense of toleration and dissent beyond the interests of the true Reformed faith, confirmed the essential orthodoxy of his Calvinist position. As Bossuet perpetuated the intellectual defense of orthodoxy by associating it with the preservation of worldly order, Jurieu showed how to perpetuate it by associating it with the defense of personal liberty. In either case, they illustrated the continuity of conservative orthodoxy, of the Catholic or the Protestant variety, as an intellectual as well as institutional counterpoint of the Enlightenment.

A second kind of orthodoxy, which may be called moderate orthodoxy, became rooted in these decades around the turn of the eighteenth century by absorbing elements of the new science and philosophy into the traditional religions. The most striking Catholic influence along these lines was the subtle work of Nicolas de Malebranche (1638–1715), the Oratorian priest who argued persuasively and incessantly through some thirty volumes of writing and through years of edifying discourse in sundry aristocratic salons for the reconciliation of dogma and Descartes, faith and reason. Among Protestants, Leibniz strove for a similar kind of harmony by elevating both reason and religion above partisan considerations—that is, by making reason more inclusive than the Cartesians did and by making theology more ecumenical than either the Catholics or the Protestants were wont to do. Although he himself remained rather a philosopher than a theologian and was suspect to both confessions, his influence in the eighteenth century went into German Protestant as well as into European secular thought.

The British branch of this modernized Protestant orthodoxy also received its main impetus around the start of the century. The much-maligned Latitudinarians became the dominant party within the "established" Anglican state church—the original "Establishment"—as it was reconstituted by William III after the Glorious Revolution and perpetuated by the Hanoverian Whigs after 1714, but despite the frequent indictment of them for worldliness and superficiality they did produce an intellectual defense which diverted into orthodox clerical channels much of the fashionable deism characteristic of the British Enlightenment. In both the sophistication and profundity of their sermons and treatises they fell far short, to be sure, of the Cambridge Platonists, who had woven a delicate mesh of mystical faith and reason after the Restoration of 1660. For the Latitudinarians' reason was simple and commonsensical rather than architectonic and all-embracing, and their faith tended to be trimmed rather to the reasonable requirements of the moral practical life than to its assumptions and its source. But many of the Latitudinarians had studied with the Cambridge Platonists, and if they vulgarized the exalted rationality of the latter, Latitudinarian bishops like John Tillotson (1630–1694) and Edward Stillingfleet (1635–1699) did diffuse reasonableness, a tolerant spirit, aversion to dogma, and an ethic of social responsibility into commonplaces of the British official and educated classes.

A third kind of orthodoxy, finally, which we may term reactionary orthodoxy, also took new forms in this transitional generation and so could remain a definite, if recessive, cultural factor through the eighteenth century and beyond. The characterization of "reactionary" is meant, for this religious context, not in any pejorative sense but literally, to designate the point of view that would undo existing ecclesiastical arrangements in favor of an earlier model of establishment. For the distinctive attitude of the reactionaries was their rejection not simply of secular trends—for this was also true of the orthodox conservatives—but of the moderate adaptations of orthodoxy as well, even when such adaptations were built into the official established churches.

The two most spectacular examples of clerical reaction in this sense were the British Nonjurors and the Russian Old Believers. The Nonjurors were some four hundred Anglican clerics who accepted deprivation from their offices rather than take a new oath of allegiance to the revolutionary monarchy of William and Mary. Their original motivation was undoubtedly a mixture of politics and conscience rather than defense of distinctive principle, but in the debate that they initiated during the 1690's they asserted a principle that made them the vanguard of the High Church party within the Church of England and hence of anti-official orthodoxy in the eighteenth century. The principle was the spiritual independence of the Church, and on the basis of it, High Churchmen initiated such running disputes as the Convocation controversy, from 1697, on the right of the clergy to its own regular assemblies and the Bangorian controversy of 1717 on the corporate rights of the Anglican church vis-à-vis both individual judgment and temporal authority. Because it deemed the undogmatic and unritualistic temper of Low Church Latitudinarianism to be tainted by the politically motivated toleration of dissent, the High Church party developed its institutional defense of the Church into an assertion of literal doctrine and strict observance of ritual.

The origins of the Old Believers go back before our period to the mid-seventeenth-century reaction against Patriarch Nikon's revision of traditional Russian ritual and liturgy to conform with the sources of the Orthodox Church in the light of Greek scholarship. But it was only after 1700, when Peter the Great abolished the remnants of ecclesiastical autonomy, and like the British, associated the established church with the rational attitudes of political administration, that the cultural strain of Old

Belief took its long-range form. As the participation of Old Believers in Pugachev's revolt shows, they came to represent and to symbolize the inchoate attitude of all those who would have no truck with modernity.

A final variety of religious reaction was represented by French Jansenism. Certainly it was not as clearly reactionary as the others we have considered, but the eighteenth-century Jansenists in France showed an explicit connection between religious piety and social reaction which was obscure in the purer examples of traditional religiosity. In its origins and early career, as we may recall (see pp. 20–21), Jansenism had been a kind of Puritanism within the Catholic Church, with a logical rigor in its theology of God's omnipotence, a moral vigor in its principle of man's total commitment to God's prescriptions, and an uncompromising honesty in its penetration into human frailty which had made it a pervasive intellectual and cultural force in the seventeenth century. But after the joint papal and royal persecution of Louis XIV's last years, this movement for a reformation of the spirit tended to become, in the eighteenth century, a respectable ideological cover for sundry social and political tendencies of a reactionary kind. Its theological and moral fervor faded into an institutionalized Gallicanism (advocacy of the French national church against the Jesuits' championship of papal authority), and as Gallicans, the Jansenists became associated with the various groups in the disgruntled Church hierarchy, the lower clergy, and the aristocratic *parlementaires*, who found in Jansenist Gallicanism a pious common front for organizing opposition against centralizing tendencies within the monarchy. There was, of course, nothing reactionary in Gallicanism itself, but in the hands of these partisans the Jansenist attitude tended to become a kind of aggressive fundamentalism, directed against what was progressive in their opponents—against the Jesuits' addiction to learning and accommodation to secular culture, and against the monarchy's policy of equalizing the burdens of taxation. It is hardly surprising to find that through this development what had been inspiring in the seventeenth century became obscurantist in the eighteenth, when Jansenism became associated, not with a philosopher like Blaise Pascal or a dramatist like Jean Racine, but with mob delirium, the relentless pursuit of Jesuits, and the preservation of aristocratic privilege.

Types of Emotional Culture

Essentially independent of religious orthodoxy, and as the future was to show, even more dangerous a rival to the reasonableness of the Enlightenment, the cultural movement which we may call—for want of a better term—emotionalism also took a new lease on life in the transition from the seventeenth to the eighteenth century. But if both the transitional form and the subsequent history of this movement are to be understood, we must fix precisely—as contemporaries did not—its ambiguous relationship with religion. For one main type of it still took a religious form and through much of the eighteenth century was judged to be as traditionally dependent as always upon dogma and church when in actuality the relations of the emotions with religion were being completely transformed.

Toward the close of the seventeenth century a movement arose which deemed the emotional way of reaching the truth more important than the definition of the truth to be reached. With this shift in emphasis, emotionalism was born. Alienated from religious orthodoxy by the orthodox emphasis upon the defined truth and upon the habitual means of apprehending it, repelled from rationalism by the rationalists' intellectual approach to passion, will, and intuition, and yet unready to declare the sovereignty of the emotions, the protagonists of the emotions turned to revivalist religion as their appropriate vehicle. Quietism in France, Pietism in Germany, and Wesleyanism in England became its chief social forms, the music of Bach and Handel its chief aesthetic expression.

Quietism, a development of the highly charged Spanish mysticism associated with St. Teresa and formulated by Miguel de Molinos (1640–c.1697), became influential in the France of the 1690's, thanks mostly to the sympathy of Archbishop Fénelon. It was typical of emotionalism in its indifference to dogma and ritual and its stress on the most fervent degree of love as the only way to union with God. It was less typical in its focus on passive contemplation, inward segregation of the spirit, and self-destruction of the individual will. The vogue during the age of Enlightenment itself of the Swedish mystic Emanuel Swedenborg (1688–1772)—"dreamer of emotion," as Kant was to call him—indicated that mysticism did indeed remain an alternative in the emotional void left by orthodoxy and rationalism.

But it was not with the mystics that the future of emotionalism lay. The transition between religiosity and the autonomy of the emotions was represented rather by the kind of evangelical movement pioneered by the German Pietists and continued by the English Wesleyans (a common function that permits us to label both as "pietists" in a general sense). No more than any other intellectual current of the eighteenth century was pietism as simple or uniform as our label would imply. Thus mysticism, persistent in the German religious tradition from medieval times and recently revived in the influential writings of the early-seventeenth-century mystic, Jakob Boehme (1575–1624), remained an essential feature in the Pietism of so prominent a leader as Count Nikolaus Ludwig von Zinzendorf (1700–1760), sponsor of the most influential of all Pietist foundations—the Herrnhut Community of the Moravian Brethren. Mysticism was, moreover, a factor in the development of most pietists, from the Saxon Jakob Spener (1635–1705), more than any other single individual the founder of the movement, to John Wesley (1703–1791), founder of the Methodist Church and pietism's most famous disciple in the English-speaking world. Mysticism contributed to pietism a spiritual alienation from the arid intellectuality of dogma and an emphasis instead on personal experience and on the emotional immediacy of faith.

But the pietists added two other essential traits which distinguished their movement from mysticism and made its ultimate impact that of a general cultural force rather than merely a particular religious sect. These traits were individualism and activism: pietists were individualistic in that they regarded the religous experience as essentially personal, and they were activist in their encouragement of good social works as the only authentic expressions of piety. Such features obviously created tensions with the self-abnegation and inwardness that were other pietist values, and indeed, in their respective emphases on the transcendence of personal spirit and the immersion in communal practice, individualism and activism did not comport perfectly with each other either. Thus pietists were torn between the outer passive acceptance of a Lutheran or Anglican church and of a secular world from which they were spiritually and emotionally alienated and the inner challenge to penetrate the church and the world actively with congregations of the true faithful and with beneficient foundations of missions, hospitals, schools, workhouses, and orphanages.

Because such divisions of conscience were not threats to an original consistency but were built into the very essence of pietism, they help to account for its far-reaching historical influence and importance. For they reflected the impulse of men to reassert the ancient integrity of faith in terms appropriate to a dawning new age by withdrawing the individual soul from dependence on this world but then giving it practical effect in this world. However inconsistent from the points of view of dogma or reason, the living otherworldly faith and the living worldly deed became one in the immediacy of men's feeling for God and man. Thus the pietists fixed on human feeling as the decisive faculty in faith that could renew itself in an individualistic and practical age, and the moving and enduring qualities of Methodist hymns still attest to the fruitfulness of the new emphasis. Pietism could compete with the Enlightenment because it offered an independent alternative direction for the ideal individualism and the real worldly activity drawn by both movements from the atmosphere of their common century.

Pietism was, indeed, to outlive the Enlightenment as an identifiable cultural force. Like the early Enlightenment, it took root in the last decades of the seventeenth century and spread well into the forties of the eighteenth. But the form which it took during this period—small conventicles within the established Protestant churches of Germany and England—proved unstable, and this instability, combined with the cultural preeminence and intellectual attractiveness of the mature Enlightenment,

Handel conducting an eighteenth-century orchestra and chorus.

reduced the movement temporarily to an obscure and subterranean existence during the middle decades of the century. But then, in the seventies and eighties, as the Enlightenment began to unravel, pietism found the three forms in which it became a permanent cultural force. In England, by virtue of its revivalistic appeal to large masses of working people it had organized a myriad of independent Methodist churches. In Germany, it exercised a less crystallized but a culturally more pervasive force. Within the established Evangelical church it was asserting the validity of natural human feelings in the rejuvenation of faith, and through its influence on theologians like Friedrich Schleiermacher (1768–1834), German Pietism would prepare the way for cultural modernism in the Protestant church. And beyond the church, the Pietist influence would help to launch the creative movement in thought and the arts associated with the giant figures of Goethe and Schiller and dedicated to exalting the role of spontaneous emotion in the freedom of the individual.

What the pietists achieved in religion and contributed to literature, composers like Johann Sebastian Bach (1685–1750) and George Frederick Handel (1685–1759) were achieving in religious music and contributing to secular music. Both these composers worked during the first half of the eighteenth century to deepen the emotional life of church and society by combining the natural human feelings expressed through Italian musical forms with the themes of Protestant piety. Bach concentrated on the emotional expansion of church music, Handel on the Protestant infusions into worldly musical forms which established the oratorio to give a new freedom to choral drama. The pattern of their musical influence, like the sermons and literature of pietism, outran their own generation and their own categories. For the legacy of Bach too was submerged in the mannered music of the middle decades, but then, toward the end of the century, his influence joined that of Handel to inspire Joseph Haydn (1732–1809) and Wolfgang Amadeus Mozart (1756–1791) with the added dimension that gives their later music its most profound emotional appeal.

The sovereignty of the emotions that pietism prepared did not come to full fruition until the Protestantism and the romanticism of the nineteenth century. In the pietism of the first half of the eighteenth century the validity of human feeling was still balanced by the validity of traditional faith and church. But there was another area of culture in which, during this same period, the emotions were recognized in their own right. For the modern novel was born then precisely as the mode of analyzing human character through the depiction of an individual's sentiments and as the mode of communicating the insight through the deliberate appeal to the reader's sentiments.

Early in the century Jonathan Swift's *Tale of a Tub* (1704) and *Gulliver's Travels* (1726) had applied the seventeenth-century satiric tradition to the novel form and demonstrated the capacity of that form to make narrative coherence derivative from the power of imagination and fantasy. But it was in the decade of the 1730's that the novel of "sensibility" and with it the cult of emotionalism came into being. "Emotionalism" is an inexact term for the set of attitudes that holds the combination of passion, feeling, intuition, and will to afford an immediate access to reality superior to that attained through either the graduated steps of discursive reason or the self-denying leap of blind faith. Its appearance as an influential cultural movement apart from religious faith and independent of rational control was most prominently associated with the publication of the tremendously popular *Pamela*, by Samuel Richardson, in 1740; but this work was a representative rather than a unique cultural product, for it came on the heels of other novels in the same genre. Pierre de Marivaux's *Marianne*, published from 1731 in eleven volumes (but still left incomplete), and Antoine Prévost's more famous *Manon Lescaut* (also 1731) probed inexhaustibly, like *Pamela*, the feelings of the heroine—in each case, characteristically, the protagonist was a sensitive and articulate female—feelings that were stimulated by the conflict between instincts and morals.

The emphasis upon feeling as the most integral and authentic faculty of the individual and upon the articulation of it as the most genuine kind of communication between individuals swept through Europe and threatened to drown the continent in a sea of tears. The connection of the sentimental novel with the emotional underground that later emerged strongly in the preromanticism of Rousseau's *Nouvelle Héloïse* (1761) and Goethe's *Sorrows of Young Werther* (1774) is obvious, but what may not be so obvious is the positive influence it had upon the Enlightenment

Samuel Richardson. *His sentimental and moralizing effusion
initiated the literary form of
the modern novel.*

as well. Marivaux, to be sure, was hostile to Voltaire and the Enlightenment in general, and the tongue-in-cheek attitude toward Pamela's vapor-
ings which Henry Fielding put to work in *Joseph Andrews* (1742) smacked
strongly of the Enlightenment's aversion to excess. But men of the
Enlightenment as critical as Denis Diderot and Samuel Johnson admired
Pamela precisely for its "sentiment," and hence the literary cult of feeling
confirms the dual relationship of religious and emotional cultural tendencies in the first half of the eighteenth century with the contemporary
Enlightenment: they furnished it with a target against which the Enlightenment sharpened its critical reason, but they also supplied it with an
appreciation of human emotions as morally sanctioned forces in a providential natural order. With due moderation, the emotions and the moral
order alike were taken into the fabric of Enlightenment thought.

THE EARLY ENLIGHTENMENT, 1715–1748

Since several cultural tendencies persisted and developed during the
period, it is clear that when the hundred-year span from the end of the
seventeenth century to the end of the eighteenth is called the Age of
Enlightenment—as it usually is—the title is meant not as a summary
of the century's culture but as a judgment of what was dominant
in it and most characteristic of it. The labelers have only followed the
self-congratulatory judgment by the protagonists of one definite cultural

movement among many when these advocates named their whole century the *siècle des lumières* after the light of knowledge which they themselves purported to bring their benighted fellowmen. Pursuant to this label these advocates—and many historians after them—tended to distort the movement, attributing to it both an internal consistency and an exclusive cultural influence which it did not in fact possess. The advocates and their movement require historical definition before we can even begin to talk about them.

The most numerous and most prominent of the advocates were grouped under the label *philosophes*, but the literal reference of the term in the eighteenth century to the philosophers of the French Enlightenment did not give its full meaning, for both "French" and "philosophers" must be understood in a special way. Because the French forms of the Enlightenment dominated Europe, we can speak of its devotees as *philosophes* whether they were French or not, in recognition of the international vogue of the French fashion in culture; but we must also remember, then, that there were national distinctions among the *philosophes*. More important, the *philosophes* were philosophers in a distinctive sense, for they lacked some of the most obvious traits which we have come to associate with philosophers and they obviously possessed traits which we have come to dissociate from philosophers: the *philosophes* were addicted neither to contemplation, nor to abstraction, nor to logical consistency, nor even to the inquiry into pure ideas and their mutual relations; the *philosophes* were, on the other hand, committed to the application of ideas to social criticism, and to political change. But if they appear to be closer to twentieth-century intellectuals than to twentieth-century philosophers in these respects, they were nonetheless philosophers both in the loose eighteenth-century sense of the term and in the fundamental sense of the term generally. For the *philosophes* asked the basic questions about God, man, and nature; they sought behind effects for their causes; and they looked through phenomena for intelligible realities that underlay them. The *philosophes* combined the vocations of philosopher and intellectual which would be separated later, and they could combine these vocations simply because they felt that the most fundamental ideas were necessarily applicable, communicable, effective, and socially relevant, and that there existed no valid pure idea to be thought or separable basic reality to be analyzed. The *philosophes* admitted variety and shrugged off illogicality not because they abjured philosophy, but because of the malleable character of the world they philosophized about.

The Enlightenment was a movement which actually first assumed an identifiable form between 1715 and 1748, and then only as a loose collection of like-minded individuals, engaged in the most various kinds of intellectual enterprises but associated through mutual recognition in the common task of turning the philosophies of secular reason and natural sci-

MAJOR FIGURES OF THE ENLIGHTENMENT

1660 1680 1700 1720 1740 1760 1780 1800 1820

Thomasius (1655-1728)
Swift (1667-1745)
Vico (1668-1744)
Shaftesbury (1671-1713)
Steele (1672-1729)
Clarke (1675-1729)
Wolff (1679-1754)
Berkeley (1685-1753)
Pope (1688-1744)
Montesquieu (1689-1755)
Butler (1692-1752)
Quesnay (1694-1744)
Hutcheson (1694-1746)
Voltaire (1694-1778)
Gay (1699-1745)
Hartley (1705-1757)
Buffon (1707-1788)
LaMettrie (1709-1751)
Mably (1709-1785)
Hume (1711-1776)
Rousseau (1712-1778)
Frederick the Great (1712-1786)
Sterne (1713-1768)
Diderot (1713-1784)
Helvétius (1715-1771)
Condillac (1715-1780)
Winckelmann (1717-1768)
D'Alembert (1717-1783)
Möser (1720-1794)
Blackstone (1723-1780)
D'Holbach (1723-1789)
Adam Smith (1723-1790)
Ferguson (1723-1816)
Kant (1724-1804)
Galiani (1728-1787)
Lessing (1729-1781)
Mendelssohn (1729-1786)
Burke (1729-1797)
Hamann (1730-1788)
Priestley (1733-1804)
Wieland (1733-1813)
Coulomb (1736-1806)
Gibbon (1737-1794)
Galvani (1737-1798)
Beccaria (1738-1794)
Lavoisier (1743-1794)
Herder (1744-1803)
Lamarck (1744-1829)
Goethe (1749-1832)
Schiller (1759-1805)

ence into a real cultural force competitive with contemporary orthodoxies and the emotive arts. Not until the intellectual generation of 1748–1776 did these protagonists of Enlightenment develop the organized communication and doctrine which endowed them with a comparative unity among themselves and a clear preeminence over their cultural competitors. And even this halcyon phase was short-lived, yielding to the unraveling of the Enlightenment itself and to the cultural pluralism which featured the last quarter of the eighteenth century.

But when the *philosophes* are not regarded as a closed party and their Enlightenment as an intellectual monopoly the movement can indeed be considered as the central cultural theme of the eighteenth century. The variations in internal organization and consistency among the *philosophes* were the chief expressions of the relationship between cultural innovation and society in the eighteenth century. Competitive cultural movements, orthodox and enthusiastic alike, oriented themselves during the same century primarily according to the threats and possibilities offered by the Enlightenment at any particular time. For both the social and the intellectual history of the eighteenth century, then, we are directed to the successive stages of Enlightenment culture.

The early Enlightenment first took identifiable shape amid the changed conditions of cultural production which followed upon the passing of the Stuarts, the death of Louis XIV, and the clearing of the strife-torn atmosphere associated with both sets of royal personages. The stimulus and focus of creative endeavor shifted from the patronage and entourage of kings to the educated groups in the society at large. In both France and Great Britain, the development of wealth, leisure, and self-confidence in the middle classes coincided around 1715 with a significant reduction in the cultural influence of royal courts (owing to the death of Louis XIV and the accession of the Hanoverians, respectively), and with a shift of aristocratic culture from royal to popular standards of taste. It was precisely in France and Britain that the social organizations of intellectual life were most advanced and the early Enlightenment most concentrated. Its characteristic channels of communication were academies (capital and provincial), salons, journals, books, pamphlets, and unpublished manuscripts and correspondences, all serving at this juncture primarily a "republic of letters" within the limited circle of intellectuals by providing forums for the exchange, debate, and mutual clarification of their ideas. The literary forms in which these citizens of the republic of letters communicated were equally various; they included the formal treatise, the informal essay, poetry, drama, the novel, and literary criticism. The typical protagonist of the Enlightenment worked in several of these genres. It was part both of his new self-image as representative of the society at large and of his pragmatic approach to affairs of the mind that he adhered to no academic protocol but wrote in whatever form would attract the widest interest, be most appropriate to his subject of the moment, and act with best narcotic effect on the official censors of church and state.

The content of the new Enlightenment culture was determined in part by these conditions and in part by the intellectual ingredients which the previous, turn-of-the-century generation had left floating free and which the early *philosophes* now sought to fuse into a relevant world view. From this purely intellectual point of view, the early Enlightenment may be seen as a movement which accepted the primacy of nature, law, and reason from the legacy of seventeenth-century classicism and rationalism but modified the meaning and the direction of these principles by applying to them the critical and empirical emphases added by the generation of Newton, Locke, and Bayle and the passionate moral individualism drawn from the memory of seventeenth-century religious and aesthetic dissent. The *philosophes* combined these cultural strands, moreover, in the context of the worldly concerns and opportunities opened by their own generation of comparative peace and prosperity. The metaphysical rational order which men of the seventeenth century had made the basic character of reality receded to the status of unspoken and even unconscious assumption as the function of reason itself changed for the men of the new Enlightenment. From the dispassionate explanation of natural reality and of man as part of natural reality, reason became the weapon of a fighting creed aimed at the mastery of nature for the sake of a wiser and better humanity and against competing orthodox or emotional—that is, "fanatical"—creeds. As the function of reason shifted, so did its character. As its function shifted from the construction of a stable and necessary order of nature to the demonstration of the freedom of individuals and of the orderly mutual relations which they could construct for themselves on the model of nature, reason became more concrete, more flexible, more utilitarian, more commonsensical, more libertarian, and more dynamic.

The mechanics of this transition from the rationalism of the seventeenth century to the reasonableness of the eighteenth was more evident in the early Enlightenment of the more stagnant and traditional national societies than in the more mobile Atlantic societies like France and Britain, where the break with the past was sharper and more deliberate. In Germany, for example, representative figures of the early Enlightenment such as Christian Thomasius (1655–1728) and Christian Wolff (1679–1754) carried enough of the past with them, both in their social position as intellectuals and in their theoretical position as thinkers, to expose the seventeenth-century scaffolding of eighteenth-century Enlightenment. Both were professors, thereby prolonging the social distance and academic flavor of seventeenth-century thought into eighteenth-century Germany in contrast to the literary tone of the Enlightenment in the west. Thomasius, moreover, developed his pattern of Enlightenment thought during the first two decades of the new century by combining the influences of seventeenth-century rationalism, Lockean empiricism, and German Pietism, thereby commuting between the Pietist values—freedom of conscience, individuality of faith, and the duty of pious charity—and corresponding secular principles—freedom of expression, moral primacy of individual happiness, and a commonsense rationalism as the guide from individual to social interests. Nonetheless, he always retained a Pietist spiritualism and indifference to institutions that was quite uncharacteristic of the western Enlightenment.

A bit later, in the second quarter of the century, Christian Wolff performed an analogous service for the rationalization of the German Lutheran tradition when he developed a philosophy that went far to reconcile the tensions between faith and reason in the direction of reason. Where Leibniz had complicated reason to make it harmonious with faith, Wolff appropriated the secular and homogeneous notion of reason from the recent doctrines of natural law and accomodated faith to it. Thus he stimulated the rationalist movement in German Protestant theology that would be known as Neology and he contributed to the philosophy of the Enlightenment the ultimate goal of human "perfection" as the secular equivalent of salvation. But for all his substantive contributions to the culture of the Enlightenment, Wolff's addiction to metaphysics, and the scholastic aridity of his writing, held him apart from the men of the Enlightenment proper, not only because his style resembled rather the heavy tradition they attacked than the graceful mode they espoused but because it indicated his persistence in a contemplative posture apart from the earthly reality in the midst of which they would frolic.

But if the lethargic societies of central and southern Europe best reveal the historical conditions of the early Enlightenment, the volatile societies of France and Great Britain produced versions of it which most clearly reveal its essential contemporary features. It is not easy to get at what these were, for at this early stage the partisans of the French and British Enlightenments were many and frequently obscure; no rank order of talents or prestige had as yet developed to weave threads of influence through the intellectual maze; a good number of the contributors to the Enlightenment mentality were, at this early stage, like Alexander Pope with his ambiguous religiosity, intellectual hybrids; and their fields of literary endeavor were various and disconnected. The multiplicity and diversity of its products must indeed be accounted a characteristic trait of the early Enlightenment, but it had certain common traits as well—traits which were consistent with its variety.

In order to select those traits of the early Enlightenment which were most relevant to the history of the Enlightenment as a whole we may focus, for our illustrations, upon the early thought of figures like David Hume (1711–1776), Charles de Secondat, Baron de Montesquieu (1689–1755), and François Marie Arouet, known as Voltaire

The young Voltaire. *The look of the man —acerbic, proud, and intelligent—parallels the tone of his work. He was obviously every inch a king—of the* philosophes.

(1694–1778), whose intellectual development spanned the early and mature stages of Enlightenment. When so considered, the distinctive functions of the early Enlightenment were, first, the frank acceptance and dissemination of the critical and empirical points of view which had been proposed in special contexts by the generation of Locke and Newton; second, the construction of a general intellectual framework of physical and human nature within which new theories of the world, man, and society, at once realistic and reasonable, could be subsequently developed; and third, the preliminary and piecemeal application of the new combination of practicality and rationality to particular events, works, and activities.

The New Reason

In their diffusion of the critical and empirical ideas which they took over from the preceding generation, the early *philosophes* took two paths. The more obvious device was the popularization of their intellectual patron saints, such as Voltaire undertook in his open adulation of Pierre Bayle and his epitomes of the ideas of Locke and Newton in his *Philosophical Letters* (1734) and his *Elements of the Philosophy of Newton* (1738). Their more original device was to identify the skeptical, practical, limited kind of reason which they adopted from the previous generation, and to match it deliberately against any metaphysics, whether of faith or reason, in a way which had not been dared by their predecessors. This shift from the older juxtaposition to the newer opposition of faith and reason and of different kinds of reason to one another was first prepared in the crucial field that intersected science and philosophy. Known to the seventeenth and eighteenth centuries alike as "natural philosophy," it became the arena, after the turn of the century, of a bitter intellectual feud between Cartesians and Newtonians on the metaphysical versus the empirical derivation of natural laws. The prevalence of the Newtonian view by mid-century spelled victory for Voltaire's prescription to "let the facts prevail" and consequently for the *philosophes'* address to particular kinds of knowledge as the materials of rational truth.

The same kind of emphasis then made its appearance in philosophy itself. Although the orthodox Anglican clericalism of Bishop George Berkeley (1685–1753) places him in general outside the Enlightenment, the subjective idealism which he developed to show the derivation of all knowledge from the operation of the mind upon its sensations rather than from any logical structure in the external world was actually a radical empiricism and reflected the spirit of the age. But it was David Hume, an authentic *philosophe* and the most original philosopher of the age, who made the most throughgoing application of the new attitude to reason. He wrote his *Treatise of Human Nature* (1739–1740) to show that "the experimental method of reasoning" reduced all certain knowledge to sense impressions, demeaned all rational connections among such impressions to associations based on fortuitous psychological habits and social customs, and therefore posited an empirically derived "science of man"—consisting primarily of "moral philosophy" and history—as the necessary basis of the whole corpus of science and philosophy. Hume's *Treaties* went too far for his colleagues among the *philosophes*, since his extension of skepticism from metaphysical to all rational coherence among things struck at the assumptions they tacitly held. But they chose rather to ignore than to refute it, and he remained a *philosophe* in good standing—indeed, the most popular Briton in the camp of the Enlightenment—because his rigorous empiricism and his hypercritical use of reason simply carried to an extreme the particular emphasis of the early Enlightenment. The *philosophes* did not mean all the negative things they said about Descartes, for they carried with them more of his principles of a rational order than they knew, but they could accept Hume, even if they could not respond to him, because their early impulses were as critical as his. And Hume himself followed a common practice of the early Enlightenment when his skepticism turned him from philosophy to history. Scholars once held that this development of Hume's marked a frightened retreat from the consequences of his own philosophical position, but it is now generally agreed that he was consistent both with himself and with his age when his rejection of "refined reasoning" in the abstract left him free to pursue the actual varieties of human behavior in his quest for uniform principles of human nature.

David Hume. *He was both a formal philosopher and a* philosophe, *a comparatively rare combination in the eighteenth century.*

The New Framework

In the place of the rejected supernatural order and metaphysical unity which had for so long supported men's thinking about the world and man, the *philosophes* now built a new platform of basic principles which would be more appropriate to their immediate concern with man's life in this world and from which the rethinking about it could be launched. Their favored intellectual fields for this purpose were natural religion and morals. Declared independent of their traditional theological and metaphysical tutelage, both fields now became arenas of primary principles and served together as the mold for the worldliness, the hedonism, and the humanism which were henceforth ingrained in the Enlightenment.

In the field of natural religion the most characteristic innovation of the early Enlightenment was deism, the antitheological movement which took the form of "natural theology." Deism may be narrowly construed to signify merely the theology that holds God to act exclusively through the invariable laws He has established in the natural creation and that holds men to know God exclusively through the natural reason which understands those laws. Certainly deism meant this kind of natural theology in the eighteenth century–but it also meant something more. It meant an anticlericalism which mounted a frontal attack on every ecclesiastical dogma, ritual, practice, and influence presumably directed against the rational autonomy of the individual layman. Deism originated in Britain as a natural theology, and for the forty years of its prominence there—between 1690 and 1730—its theological character as a religion of natural reason undoubtedly continued to prevail. But even in Britain this classification fails to convey the tone of the tendency. John Locke's *Reasonableness of Christianity* (1695) furnished the fundamental arguments of the movement, but there was an essential difference between Locke's cautious endeavor to reconcile reason with revelation and the work of authentic deists like John Toland (*Christianity Not Mysterious*, 1696) and Anthony Collins (*Discourse of the Grounds and Reasons of the Christian Religion*, 1724), who attacked the unreasonableness both of dogma and of Scripture itself. Indeed, Christian though they claimed to be, the British deists not only submitted revelation to the rational judgment of the ordinary individual but resurrected the anticlerical tradition of attributing dogmatic and ritual error to priestly deception and exploitation of the laity.

In the British case, to be sure, the anticlerical motif was countered by the constitutional moderation which was only now beginning to form part of what would come to be considered the British national character. Criticism of institutions remained subordinate to the assertion of the individual's autonomy within them, and consequently the impetus of deism was absorbed after 1730 by the respectable and tolerant reasonableness of Latitudinarian Low Churchmanship. It was in France that deism had its fullest, broadest, and longest effect, for here it was not only the central theological position in the whole intellectual community of *philosophes* but it included, as an equal emphasis, a virulent attack on every institutional aspect of Christianity.

The caustic criticism which the French *philosophes* mounted on Bible, doctrine, church, and clergy alike under the aegis of facts perceivable by everyman and of rational notions conceivable by everyman distributed the deist impact along a wider front and gave it a different cultural function from its counterparts either in Britain or in Germany, where it was limited by and large to the depreciation of revealed theology in favor of natural theology. In France, the theology of deism was joined to a anticlerical campaign because in France, Catholic dogma had been indissolubly associated with a church which furnished common symbols and linkages for the social and political establishments. The struggle for natural religion against organized religion thus epitomized the general struggle for a larger individual liberty against the constructions of traditional institutions.

The representative function of religion for the protagonists of the early Enlightenment revealed an essential fact about the movement at this stage: the *philosophes* specialized in religion because religion afforded a peripheral approach to social reality at a time when the *philosophes* felt drawn toward this reality but could afford only an indirect path to it. There were several reasons for the detour. Circumstantially, the censorship in countries like France, sufficiently effective during the first half of the century to make the copying and clandestine circulation of unpublished

Charles de Secondat, Baron de Montesquieu. *The aristocrat who showed the* philosophes *the way in history, literature, and political theory, but was never considered one of them.*

manuscripts an important means of intellectual communication, was more politically than clerically sensitive. Tactically, the *philosophes* could achieve more consensus among themselves in their arguments against established religion than on any other topic. Thus despite the differences in their temperaments, styles, social status, and political loyalties, Montesquieu and Voltaire agreed on their common deism, while Hume, whose philosophy undermined the invariable laws and necessary connections so prominent in the rational faith of the *philosophes*, yet proved himself one of them by virtue of his essay on the implausibility of miracles (written in 1737 and published in 1748) and his sketch of *The Natural History of Religion* (first published in 1741 and, expanded, republished in 1757), which he designed precisely to show positive religion as the social effect of human foibles.

But political censorship was hardly a consideration in Great Britain and the Netherlands during the first half of the century and even in France would prove porous during the second half. Consensus among the *philosophes*, moreover, virtuosos that they conceived themselves to be, was not deemed a goal worthy in itself of a deliberate tactic. Behind the circumstances and the tactics of the *philosophes'* focus on religion during the early Enlightenment were crucial assumptions internal to their thinking. The early *philosophes* agreed that their shared antipathies—unexamined belief, blind obedience, unearned privilege, ignorance, superstition, intolerance, fanaticism, "enthusiasm"—had their common denominator in organized religion because they believed themselves to be the harbingers of a new age that was called first to settle accounts with the preeminently religious culture of the past by attacking its still-potent ecclesiastical residues in the present. More important, the *philosophes* concentrated on religion because their own ideas were, at this stage, concerned less with changing things than with changing the way of looking at them. For this, the relocation of point of view from the next world to this seemed decisive.

The *philosophes'* early concentration on attitude rather than on substantive theory paralleled the contemporary position of the mobile social groups of which the *philosophes* were a part. They too were altering the standards of a preponderantly static and agrarian society from its periphery, before they penetrated it. Hence the chief burden of the *philosophes'* message during the first half of the eighteenth century, conditioned in part by the apparent impenetrability of social reality and in part by their own stubborn faith that once turned toward its appropriate objects in the things of this world man's unfettered reason would do the rest, was the call for men to discard the dogmatic and ecclesiastical shackles upon free thought as the indispensable first step to any freedom whatsoever. In the two most characteristic writings of the age—Montesquieu's *Persian Letters* (1721) and Voltaire's *Philosophical Letters* (1734)—the intellectual leaders of the early Enlightenment gave an archetypal form to this message: through the indirection of an exotic model—Persia and Britain, respectively—they used the deistic principle of a universal standard implanted in nature and in man as the basis of a moral critique aimed at the fundamental institutions of French thought and society.

The second main foundation of Enlightenment culture, consistent with the deistic focus on man and this world, was humanitarian ethics. Relatively neglected in the seventeenth century, when it had tended to become merely derivative from the various combinations of the old religion and the new science, in the early Enlightenment human morals became an independent and central area of inquiry. With nature now deemed to be the only source of moral as well as of physical laws, and with the conscience now deemed as fully a part of nature as the rational order of things, the knowledge of this world became as much a matter of moral as of physical science. Since, moreover, God was deemed manifest exclusively through the laws of His creation, moral inquiry, as the probe of the laws for man's conduct implicit in this creation, assumed a new independent function in relation to religion itself. Not only had the divine rules for the good life now to be discovered in the created nature of man to replace those that had been derived from or at least guided by the prescriptions of special revelation, but morals now even acquired a positive religious function, since the only authentic worship of God lay in the knowledge of and the voluntary obedience to the fundamental laws of human nature.

Early-eighteenth-century moral philosophy, then, was simply the obverse side of deism, taking the same natural and rational view of man as the deists had of God. Consistently with deism, too, the new morality emphasized a general point of view rather than systematic ethical doctrine, and it was addressed rather to individuals for their reformation than to social or political authorities for their reform. Hence it was concerned not so much with what men should do but with the angle from which they should look at what they should do. The chief common prescriptions in the moral teachings of the early Enlightenment, consequently, were designed more for the orientation than the direction of men: the norms of human behavior must be secular in origin; they must aim at man's earthly well-being; they must include happiness, in the sense of both material and spiritual satisfaction, as an indispensable part of earthly well-being.

In these three instructions on how to devise a humanitarian morality we have the gist of what was common to the moral philosophies produced during the early Enlightenment. Specifications for such a morality abounded, of course, but none achieved a classic formulation and none commanded consensus, for in morals as in religion it was rather at the foundations than the structure of ideas that the members of this generation worked They were blocked from further construction in part by their preoccupation with clearing away the inhabited ruins that blocked moral renewal and in part by their own subscription to a secularized version of original sin. For if the typical *philosophe* was optimistic—a term reputedly coined in this period—about the moral possibilities of natural reason in humans, he was not optimistic about human nature's will to exercise that reason. Hume was, as usual, far more extreme than his friends among the *philosophes* when he declared flatly that "reason has no influence on our passions and actions" and that, consequently, "moral distinctions are not the offspring of reason." But such representative *philosophes* as Voltaire, Montesquieu, and even the young Jean Jacques Rousseau (1712–1778) similarly qualified their confidence in the potentialities of rational man with their acerbic insights into the actual tyranny of his self-seeking—and worse, his stupidly self-destructive—impulses. They did not regard natural impulses, passions, or self-interest as evil in themselves, but they did consider these drives denatured and demoralizing when they were divorced from reason and hence from the balance of nature.

The plurality of acceptable natural principles and the difficulty of harmonizing them led the first generation of Enlightenment moralists to insist rather on the common ground occupied by such secular moral principles as naturalism, individualism, utility, happiness, and benevolence than on systematic ethical formulations of the problematical relations among them. Only the Britsh, conformably with their pioneering position in the definition of deism, began early to distinguish among the new worldly principles of morality. No more than anyone else in the first half of the eighteenth century did they develop coherent moral doctrines, but they did give definition to moral principles that would later be elaborated into doctrines.

The moralists of the early British Enlightenment developed, in memorable form, the ideas that would become the building blocks of the three main moral theories of the eighteenth century. At the very start of the century, in a series of writings collected in 1711 as *Characteristics of Men, Manners, Opinions, and Times,* Anthony Ashley Cooper, Earl of Shaftesbury (1671–1713), esteemed as the "virtuoso of humanity," prepared the way for the intuitive or "sentimentalist" type of moral theory with his notion of a "natural moral sense," which impelled men to acts of benevolence and social beneficence through an innate affection for and sympathy with their fellows. The Reverend John Gay (1699–1745) published the first clear but implicit argument for utility as a moral principle (he had the idea but not the name) in his *Dissertation Concerning the Principle and Criterion of Virtue and the Origin of the Passions* (1730), where he declared happiness, defined as the achievement of pleasure and the avoidance of pain, to be the necessary and valid end of all human actions, which must therefore be assessed as means toward this end. The theologians Samuel Clarke (1675–1729) and Joseph Butler (1692–1752), finally, propounded the two standard versions of a morality based upon natural reason. In lectures of 1705, later published under the title *A Discourse Concerning the Unchangeable Obligations of Natural Religions and the Truth and Certainty of the Christian Revelation* (1706), Clarke based moral principle on the recognition of the "Fitness and Reason of Things," which were for him eternal principles of order in nature analogous to the propositions of mathematics. In his ethical discourses (published 1726), Bishop Butler, one of the great English moralists of the century, cast doubt on the rationality of nature as a whole, but he propounded instead a morality of "conscience," which he identified with "the principle of reflection" in the nature of man.

Each of these moral ideas would be taken up and developed into ethical and political doctrine later in the century, and the culture of the Enlightenment was characterized precisely by the simultaneous addiction to all three principles—sentiment, utility, and reason—and to the preservation of a balance among them. In proportion, indeed, as they were to fall out of balance toward the end of the century, the Enlightenment would dissolve as an identifiable cultural movement. But in the early Enlightenment they appeared typically and openly in combination with one another.

Indeed a chart of intellectual influences for this subject and this period in Great Britain would show a remarkable crisscrossing pattern. Protagonists of all three principles alleged their debt to John Locke, and both Shaftesbury and Gay, indeed, claimed to be his disciples. The objective rationalist, Clarke, taught the subjective rationalist, Butler, who in turn taught Hume, who first identified "utility" as an explicit moral principle. Hume took from Butler the rational conviction that morals are grounded in the constant principles of human nature, and he added to it the influence of Francis Hutcheson (1694–1746), who combined in himself the sentimentalist morality of Shaftesbury and the notion of its assessment by the utilitarian criterion of "the greatest good of the greatest number"—a phrase which, incidentally, Hutcheson coined. Nor was Hutcheson an eccentric in this respect. By the middle of the century Shaftesbury was deemed to have clothed utility in idealistic form of a moral sense, and the "Scottish school" of moralists, which included such well-known figures as Hutcheson, Hume, and Adam Smith, all characteristically united the morality of sentiment with the morality of utility. The role of reason in this ethical syndrome was, to be sure, more subdued in the early Scottish school than it was in the contemporary moralistic hedonism of Montesquieu and Voltaire in France or Thomasius and Christian Wolff in Germany. But even in Britain the moralists of the early Enlightenment sought to make a rational connection between the moral sense of individuals and the utility of society that was the object of this moral sense.

Thus the precocious formation of different schools among the British moral theorists of the early Enlightenment merely articulated what was implicit in the vaguer moralizing on the Continent: that the principles of self-interest, sympathy, utility, conscience, and reason were compatible enough to form a self-sufficient natural basis of moral doctrines. This early British ethical development also forecast what would be an essential quality of these moral doctrines during the mature Enlightenment: each would be a combination of these natural qualities, and even when they were ranged against one another—as the doctrine of utilitarianism would be against the doctrine of rational natural rights, for example—they would differ rather in the priority of the ranking than in the exclusive preference for one over another of the generally accepted moral principles.

The New History

The final common feature of the early Enlightenment lay at the other end of the intellectual spectrum from its formulation of appropriate general principles of natural religion and morality: the *philosophes* also applied themselves to the appropriate illumination of all kinds of specific realities—physical, psychic, and aesthetic alike. They described and explained gadgets and customs; they wrote and interpreted literature and art. To each thing and activity they brought their own combination of delight in detail and insistence upon rationalizing; from each thing and activity they took an added confirmation of the universal validity of their approach.

Examples of this particularizing tendency in the early Enlightenment can be taken from many fields, but perhaps the most revealing was its writing of history, since the deprecation of the *philosophes'* attitude toward history has been an important feature in the misunderstanding of the Enlightenment, and the disregard of the historical writing produced during its early stage has been an important feature in the distortion of the *philosophes'* attitude toward history. The great works of Enlightenment history would come, to be sure, in its mature stage, but they would build on the interest and the particular slant of the ideas invested in the lesser productions of the early stage. Just as the large works of interpretative and "philosophic" history would form a consistent part of the systematic and encyclopedic pattern which characterized the mature Enlightenment after 1748, so the more specialized and heterogenous interest in history which prevailed before mid-century was a contribution of the dispersed and particularized concerns inherent in the early Enlightenment.

The writing of history in the early Enlightenment contributed, indeed, more to the culture of the Enlightenment than to the discipline of history. Notable advances in the historical discipline were made during the period, it is true, but not by representatives of the Enlightenment. These advances were made by representatives of traditions that antedated the Enlightenment, and they were made in the three different kinds of historical study that were appropriate to the respective defenses of these traditions.

On the level of historical method, Benedictine monks of the Congregation of St. Maur in Paris, whose predecessors had advanced the critical study of documents in their seventeenth-century editions of ecclesiastical sources, extended their new techniques during the first half of the eighteenth century to the publication of authentic editions of sources for the study of the national and provincial history of Christian France. Nor was this extension of critical methods into secular history merely a local achievement. It was paralleled in Italy by the collections of the Maurist disciple Lodovico Muratori (1672–1750), whose edition of Italian historical sources earned him a reputation as the "father of Italian history."

If the clergy's urge to restore both the ecclesiastical and the political sources of a more religious past thus fertilized historical method, the impulse of kings and resurgent aristocracies—and of their literate minions—to buttress their respective claims with the sanctity of original right or long usage fed into a second kind of historical advance: the vogue of a constitutional history that put continuity into history through the persistent themes of a monarchical or aristocratic constitution undergoing processes of development or degeneration. The two outstanding exemplars of this history were the embittered and reactionary Count Henri de Boulainvilliers and the versatile royal agent and pensionary, the Abbè Jean Baptiste Dubos (1670–1742). Boulainvilliers' *History of the Ancient Government of France*, published posthumously in 1727, was a coherent history of the French constitution from the aristocratic point of view, unified by its theme of an original political power rightfully accruing to the French nobility as heirs of the Franks, but gradually eroded by successive generations of usurping kings. Dubos countered with his *Critical History of the Establishment of the French Monarchy in the Gauls* (1734), where he argued for constitutional continuity from the Roman emperors to the Frankish kings and thence to the modern kings, leaving no place for any autonomous Frankish right of conquest or, consequently, for any inherited aristocratic authority based on it.

The third and final level of history effectively worked during the first half of the eighteenth century was a philosophy of history produced not merely outside the Enlightenment but explicitly against it in the service of a competitive cultural tradition. The *New Science* (1725) of Giambattista Vico (1668–1744) revitalized the Christian Neo-Platonic tradition which had been strained through the Italian Renaissance, and which was in this work turned against rationalism in the Cartesian mode. His "new science" was an idealistic philosophy that incorporated history into his description of the irreducible multiplicity, the inimitable dynamism, and the essential autonomy of all living things. The only law of nature that pertained to men prescribed the organic pattern of development from infancy through old age as the common process which each organism experienced in its own way, realizing thereby a universal principle truer to life than the abstract universals of the mathematical reason common to seventeenth-century philosophy and eighteenth-century *philosophes* alike. If Vico thus invoked the history of nations, subject to a common pattern of natural growth but each realizing the design of Providence in accordance with its individual genius, to reconcile the cyclical and providential principles of philosophy, history in its turn acquired a developmental pattern that rooted it in the fundamental reality of things. Vico had no immediate influence, to be sure, on the contemporary early Enlightenment against whose rationalistic ancestors he overtly directed the substance of his philosophical history, but like the monastic progress in historical method and like the traditionalists' development of constitutional history, Vico articulated eighteenth-century tendencies toward the appreciation of individual things and of general processes within the time of this world which were also operative in the early Enlightenment and which were reflected more inarticulately in its historiography.

For the most part it was only later that the *philosophes* would make deliberate use of this threefold achievement by non-Enlightenment historians—as Voltaire would of Dubos' French history, for example, or as Herder would when he merged Vico's organic approach to the development of nations with the late Enlightenment's cosmopolitanism to create a polyphonic history of humanity (see pp. 232–34)—but the early Enlightenment did lay the foundation for the later enrichment of Enlightenment history. The representative writers of the early Enlightenment perpetuated the critical approach and the addiction to sources which had characterized their spiritual godfathers, Bayle and Leibniz, at the very beginning of the century, and they went beyond these forebears to develop a new sense of the importance of history and a concern for its connection with what they called "philosophy." They tended to express this sense and this concern rather in writing *about* history than in writing history itself, for, as with their interests in morals, the writers of the early Enlightenment were more engaged in establishing a point of view than in working it out through substantiated doctrine. The most famous of these programmatic pronouncements was undoubtedly Lord Bolingbroke's definition of history as "philosophy teaching by example," dating from the 1730's, when he was writing his *Letters on the Study of History*, and its fame rests on its faithfulness in typifying the age. By the end of the same decade Voltaire was beginning to write the *Essay on the Manners and Spirit of Nations*, for whose introduction he would later coin the term "philosophy of history," and Hume was publishing the *Treatise of Human Nature* and preparing the essays "Of the Study of History" (1741) and "Of the Rise and Progress of Arts and Sciences" (1742), which together laid the basis for the concept of history as a source of knowledge about human nature and of principles for human action—a basis which his later historical works would attempt to substantiate.

The actual history that was written from such points of view during this period tended simply to illustrate this approach to history as a casebook for the study of the universal principles of human nature. The best-known historical works of the period are probably Voltaire's *History of Charles XII* (1731) and Montesquieu's *Thoughts on the Greatness and Decline of the Romans* (1734), and both only faintly adumbrate the qualities through which their later works, Voltaire's *Age of Louis XIV* (1751) and Montesquieu's *Spirit of the Laws* (1748), would dominate the fertile historiography of the mature Enlightenment. Voltaire's earlier work lacked the historical depth, accuracy, and breadth of his later; Montesquieu's work on Rome was more traditional (in the humanist tradition of moral commentary on a classic theme), more imprecise, and more mechanical in its application of causal principle than his later study of the historically developed spirit of modern nations would be. And yet the earlier work of each man did prepare the way for the later. Voltaire's *Charles XII* was an integrated literary work, permeated with a unity at once moral and aesthetic; Montesquieu's *Romans* showed a coherent development and eventuated in a single moral on the need to adapt attitudes to circumstances.

In its scattered but programmatic works of history the early Enlightenment manifested the same general pattern as in its works of theology and morals. In all these realms the *philosophes* tested their rational faculty on sample issues of this world and made it an efficient means of separating the things that made sense and brought satisfaction from what did not. Equipped with this faculty as a cutting tool and with the raw materials of nature they had separated out from the dross of Christian tradition, the *philosophes* were ready by mid-century to carve out whole sets of ideas in conformity with their own bent.

THE MATURE ENLIGHTENMENT, 1748–1776

The change from the early to the mature stage of the Enlightenment may be dated with a precision not often permitted by the gradual changes in cultural fashions, for the mature Enlightenment both began and ended with clusters of characteristic intellectual events. The publication of Montesquieu's *Spirit of the Laws* in 1748 marked the advent of a series of remarkable works which signalized a new direction within the Enlightenment, and the coincidental appearance of Adam Smith's *Wealth of Nations,* Edward Gibbon's first volume of the *Decline and Fall of the Roman Empire,* and Gabriel Bonnet de Mably's *On Legislation* in 1776 marked a final concentration of important works along this line. The same terminal year, moreover, witnessed two events which, while not themselves intellectual, drastically altered the political circumstances in which the intellectuals wrote and thereby transformed the atmosphere in which the mature Enlightenment had flourished: the outbreak of the American Revolution and the fall of the reforming philosopher-minister, Turgot, from power in the French government combined to terminate an era of comparative stability and hopefulness and to bring into prominence the social and political turbulence that were helping to create other cultural styles and directions in the last quarter of the eighteenth century. But in the intervening third quarter of the century the Enlightenment came into its own as both the best-organized movement of European society and as the dominant theme of European culture. The two functions were related, because the informal organization of intellectuals into a "republic of letters," dedicated to the communication and the communicability of ideas, also helped to organize the exploratory reasonable principles of the early Enlightenment into the explicit, crusading, rational doctrines of the mature phase.

The Republic of Letters

The juncture of intellectual and aesthetic talents that produced the finely finished doctrines of the mature Enlightenment was encased in virtuosos of such varied temperaments as to cast doubt on the compatibility of their ideas and on the integrity of the Enlightenment as a unified intellectual movement. Certainly the works that were written during the mature Enlightenment have become classics of the major national cultures of Europe, and the authors they have immortalized evinced the social and personal waywardness of genius. Most of them, to be sure, had their social origins in what would now be called the respectable middle class and in mobile sectors of the aristocracy once removed from this middle class, if we may so classify Montesquieu's, Condillac's, and Mablys' descent from the judicial nobility, d'Alembert's knight-sired illegitimacy, and d'Holbach's probably imaginary German barony. But if these origins predisposed them toward the life-style of the urban burgher, the ways in which they actually lived were extremely varied. Diderot and Lessing eked out precarious livings as free-lance writers. By astute financial management of his income from plays and patronage Voltaire succeeded in building up a small fortune, which he used to enjoy the life of a country squire at his estate in Ferney. Hume, Gibbon, and d'Alembert lived comfortably on inherited annuities. Rousseau admired and envied the burghers of Geneva, but he himself lived the life of a vagabond: rootless, poor, dependent for both psychic and material subsistence on the favors of sympathetic women.

Nor are there overt signs of a joint personality for the *philosophes*. There was almost as large a distance between the willfulness of a Voltaire and the steady amiability of a Hume—"the good David"—as between the fastidious aesthetic tastes of the German critic, Wieland, and the grossness of the French physician, La Mettrie, who was reputed to have eaten himself to death. Nor should the cool irony so often associated with Voltaire, nor the passionless placidity reputed in Gibbon, nor the punctiliousness of Kant, by whose daily routine the citizens of Königsberg were said to set their clocks, be taken as representative of the typical personality of the rational *philosophe*. For even if we dismiss the countervailing capricious beneficence of Voltaire, the intense classical commitments of Gibbon, and Kant's persistent enthusiasm for the French Revolution, we must still reckon with the traits of the mercurial Diderot, that incessant fount of movement, ideas, and sentiments, who rarely kept an appointment, and—in a different vein—with those of Lessing, the anticlerical clergyman's son who spent a lifetime pursuing the Holy Grail of human perfection.

And yet, after all these varieties have been acknowledged and the inference drawn that they are undoubtedly connected with the diverse emphases in the doctrines of the Enlightenment—their lesser or greater radicalism, their lesser or greater rationalism, their lesser or greater materialism, their lesser or greater optimism—the fact remains that there were general features common to the *philosophes* and that these too affected their doctrines. The concentration of *philosophes* in the upwardly mobile propertied classes truly indicates their posture in favor of reform rather than revolution—in favor, that is, of an ordered society which would give due recognition to talents such as theirs. Personally, too, there were the rough outlines of a general personality which underlay the obvious individual differences. For one thing, the *philosophes* were, as a rule, restless seekers after the truths and goods of this world. Indeed, the very variety within the mature Enlightenment is explicable by the energy with which the *philosophes* pursued the different dimensions of earthly experience, and they were joined in the common desire to penetrate the reality of the here and now, calling on nature's God or man's history as auxiliaries in this enterprise.

The mature *philosophes* shared a persistent need for threads of meaning

Voltaire (hand raised) presiding over a dinner-meeting of *philosophes*. *Diderot is on his left; d'Alembert in the left foreground.*

with which to hold together their sundry experiences and make some textured sense of them. This need was a prime source of the sociability which was the most prominent of their common traits. For the *philosophes* formed a close social group and were in continual communication with one another. Aside from their voluminous correspondences, they met often and talked incessantly. The leaders of the Scottish Enlightenment—David Hume, Adam Ferguson, William Robertson, Adam Smith—were often with one another at home or with their French counterparts on the Continent. Hume and Gibbon were also accepted in the Parisian circles, where weekly attendance at salons like Madame du Deffand's and Baron d'Holbach's identified the international society of *philosophes* that might then be invited to the court of their own king, Voltaire, in Ferney or to the court of the Prussians' king, Frederick, in Berlin. The taste for one another's company which was displayed by the men of the Enlightenment was an indication of something more fundamental than the positive approach to pleasures of the world and the awareness of their own common intellectual identity—although both these indications were certainly true of them. What it indicated in addition was their conviction that experiences and ideas must be communicable and discussable to be authentic. This meant that they must be capable of being formulated in the sequential language of rational discourse, and thus behind the sociability of the Enlightenment lay the urgent requirement that the realities which it appreciated in all their variety must yet be arranged in patterns which revealed the principles common to them. When the *philosophes* drummed Rousseau out of the Enlightenment because he withdrew from participation in their club, they revealed the intellectual implication of their personal congeniality: it was both a channel and a symbol of the rational connections which gave purpose in this life to the experiences of this life.

The domination of the mature Enlightenment by *French* intellectuals favored both its communication with the society at large and the rational linkage among its ideas. The shift from the earlier British cynosure to the headquarters in France—and particularly in Paris—entailed special consequences both for the dissemination and for the intellectual character of the movement. The diffusion of ideas from their intellectual progenitors to the educated public went further in France than anywhere else in Europe, and the practice of writing for an extended reading public endowed the French Enlightenment with its special qualities of universality and social awareness which explain its preeminence in eighteenth-century European culture.

The French comparative advantage in the communication of ideas was in part a matter of intellectual institutions. Publication replaced the circulation of manuscripts as the chief means of distribution for the French Enlightenment after 1750, when the duties of chief censor were assumed by Chrétien de Lamoignon-Malesherbes (1721–1794), who was to prove himself more a friend than a judge of the *philosophes*. The salons of Paris and the academies of the French provinces, though far from French monopolies, outdistanced their British, German, and Italian counterparts in the intensity and the continuity of the intellectual interchange provided by the salons and by the breadth and progressiveness of intellectual interests evinced by the academies. The French, morever, showed a special predilection for the art of correspondence, and the tendency to circulate ideas in the form of epistolary exchanges showed, like the French addiction to incessant intellectual conversation, the new emphasis upon communicability. And in France, finally more than anywhere else on the Continent, "authorship," as a contemporary French directory of writers opined, "is a profession now, just like the army, the magistracy, the Church, and finance." As men of letters came increasingly to depend on it for their status they tended increasingly to produce a widely marketable commodity.

But none of these institutions—neither a moderately free press, nor a liberal choice of avant-garde salons and coffee houses, nor auxiliary urban centers of Enlightened culture in the provinces, nor the publication of intellectual correspondence, nor the free-lance writer—was exclusively French. Indeed, the persistent currency of the weekly general periodical in Great Britain and Germany—some hundred and fifty of them were in British circulation by 1750—indicated a mode of communication in which the French remained at a comparative disadvantage. It was, then, not only the techniques of communicating ideas but also the social structure of communication that lay behind the superior liquidity of French ideas both in the society of France and in the culture of other countries.

The French men of letters had a special place in their society that spurred them to produce and publish ideas with the widest possible appeal, a place that "engaged" them—to use a twentieth-century term for an eighteenth-century relationship—in the pressing concerns of the society. The leaders of the Enlightenment in France as elsewhere in Europe were middle-class in orientation, but the French middle class had a distinctive position which made its relations with the classes above and below at once more continuous and more problematic than anywhere else in Europe. Through the far-flung bureaucracy and the flourishing institution of purchased offices the middle class was connected with the court; through the bourgeois sixteenth- and seventeenth-century judges who sired the eighteenth-century nobility of the robe it was connected with the aristocracy; through the recruitment of wholesale merchants and members of the free professions from the ranks of the shrewder peasants, master artisans, and small traders it was increasingly connected by the prosperity of eighteenth-century France with the laboring mass of French society. More than in any other continental state, therefore, the aristocracy was infected by middle-class standards of value and taste and the masses of peasants and artisans shared in the fierce devotion to individual property-holding that was an extension of the middle-class way of life.

As part of this wide-ranging middle class, the French *philosophes* were encouraged to comport themselves as representatives of the whole society, and they were confirmed in this generalized character of their outlook by the absence of a traditional status or particular function specially appropriate to them in the society. In Germany, the representatives of the Enlightenment were often university professors or state officials. In Protestant lands generally, they were frequently clergymen. But in France none of these traditional callings diverted the *philosophes* from their image of themselves as free-lance intellectuals of the entire society. Many of them did take holy orders and carry the title of *Abbé*, but as the strictly secular writings of the *Abbés* Condillac, Mably, Morelly, and Raynal indicate, the affiliation was rather an avenue to higher education and patronage than a serious condition of an intellectual career. Again, the institution of patronage—at the royal court, in the houses of the aristocracy, and at the pleasure of the plutocracy—was still very much alive in France, as in the rest of Europe, but in France its spirit was transformed: the competition for *philosophes* was keen, the responsiveness of royal favorites and of nobles was apparently unlimited, and the advantage was on the side rather of the patronized than of the patron. These social ties served, then, not to constrain the ideas of the *philosophes*, but only to augment their effects. Although very few tried, like Diderot, to support themselves through their writing or editing, the protagonists of the French Enlightenment did in fact assume the self-appointed trusteeship for the whole society that we associate with the independent profession of letters.

The particular position which the French *philosophes* held within the middle class also helped the diffusion of what they wrote. The members of the French middle class had long been torn between the assertion of their own practical, rational, and worldly values and the desire to rise into the aristocratic echelons of the hierarchy they by and large accepted. The characteristic resultant of these two drives had been such hybrid social forms as the official aristocracy, in which middle-class aspirants were ennobled either by service or by purchase, and the patrician *rentier*, who patronized progressive culture in the cities and cultivated progressive agriculture in the countryside. By the mid-eighteenth century, however, both these outlets for middle-class ambition were being frustrated by the nobiliar reaction, ironically led often enough by middle-class converts of an older generation. In this situation, the bulk of the middle class was left in a state of embittered but impotent bewilderment. The intellectuals assumed the leadership of the class, using the flexibility of ideas to assert the bourgeois blend of criticism within the establishment and fundamental loyalty to it at a time when this mixture of attitudes frustrated definite action by the rest of the class. The French *philosophes* thus were in the anomalous position of writing on behalf of the whole society and at the same time castigating large sections of it for chronic abuses—governments for their inequities, aristocracies for their gratuitous privileges, and the masses for their servility. And yet this kind of anomaly, appealing at once to the capacities of men to love and to hate, has ever had the widest appeal.

This position of the French *philosophes* was, in relation to the intellectuals of the other European nations, at once distinctive and representative—that is, it was distinctive precisely because it combined tendencies that were one-sidedly manifest elsewhere. With their British counterparts the French intellectuals shared the wide social base and the consequent orientation of their writing toward the practical and social application of their ideas, but they did not entirely share in the transcendence of caste, the unbalanced empiricism, and the general tone of moderation that segregated the insular intellectuals as a group from the rest of Europe. With the intellectuals of the European countries to the south and east, the French *philosophes* shared the hatred directed toward the upper classes and the half-fearful, half-pitying contempt directed toward the lower, the combination of impatience with and dependence upon authoritarian government, and the tension between pride in themselves as an aristocracy of merit and their proclamation of equal citizenship as a general principle. But in the more progressive social context of France, the *philosophes* there directed this message rather to rational individuals everywhere than to a narrow political or professional elite. Their writing thus combined practical and doctrinaire motifs with a common human touch that was the envy of mid-eighteenth-century Europe.

The shift from the British to the French models that marks the transition from the early to the mature Enlightenment helped to solidify the differences in the intellectual features of the two stages. The British vogue in Europe had reflected and focused qualities that were at once characteristics of British thinking and caricatures distorted by the impossibility of reproducing on the Continent the conditions and the references of this thinking. Thus the skepticism and naturalism in deism that fed the Latitudinarian church tendency in Anglicanism became anti-Christian on French soil and a sectarian Protestant theology on German, during the early Enlightenment. For the mature European Enlightenment of the middle decades, the French inspiration had a more homogeneous effect. It exhibited the shortened distance between the conditions of those who made the cultural models and those who followed them, and it reflected the universality built into the French mode of thinking. In contrast to the empirical and relativistic emphasis of the insular British tradition, which necessarily changed when it was applied elsewhere, the French articulated their experience with a sense of form and a crusading zeal that made their ideas travel very well indeed. The absorption of British practicality into French universal doctrines is a simple way of viewing the essential balance of the mature European Enlightenment.

In addition to these social forms of the mature Enlightenment, which organized its ideas for the purpose of communicating them, its spokesmen also developed characteristic intellectual forms of organizing its ideas, for the purpose of impressing a unifying mold upon their various experiences. Two of these intellectual forms, in particular, were characteristically employed toward this end.

First, because the *philosophes* appreciated the variety of real things and real people as much as they did and also sought to organize them under flexible principles, many of them looked to an aesthetic unity as the best way of composing the idiosyncrasies of actual life into forms which bore meaning. But theirs was an aesthetic unity of style that wove together real things and ideas rather than the aesthetic unity of imagination that exalts things to a reality above ideas. For the mature Enlightenment was not an especially fruitful era for literature proper. The age of Swift and Pope, of Marivaux and Prévost had just passed, and the time of Schiller and Goethe, of Burns and Blake was still to come. Now the dictators of style, like Samuel Johnson in England and J. C. Gottsched in Germany, reigned supreme; it seemed an age rather of prescriptions for literature than of the creations of literature. The hiatus may well be only apparent, an implied tribute to the men of the Enlightenment, so many of whom blended belles-lettres into formal thought. But whether by their merit or

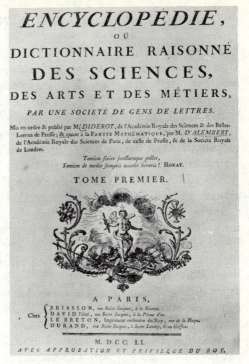

Title page of Diderot's and d'Alembert's great *Encyclopedia*, Volume I (1751). *Financed by subscription—five thousand subscribers were to pay almost two hundred dollars each for it—it had a tormented and tenuous career before the seventeenth and final volume was published in 1772. The royal approval, noted at the bottom of the title page, was withdrawn under pressure of Jesuits, Jansenists, and parlements in 1759, and only the liberal counterpressure of the uncensorious official censor Chrétien de Malesherbes, and Madame de Pompadour, as well as the circumlocutions of the* philosophes *and the quiet internal censorship of the printers enabled it to be completed.*

by chance, the literary lull redounded to their advantage, since it minimized competition with their hybrid products in the popular market. An appreciative Voltaire could say of a work as apparently technical as the *Discourse on the Grain Trade* by the Italian economist, wit, and favorite of the Parisian *philosophes*, "Abbé" Fernando Galiani (1728–1787) that it was a delightful blend of Plato and Molière!

Second, from 1748 on, the *philosophes* focused their diffuse interests on systematic publications in the grand manner. The most far-reaching of the new enterprises was Diderot's and d'Alembert's preliminary work on the *Encyclopedia*. They transformed the original plan for a translation of the mechanically organized Chambers' *Cyclopaedia* into the novel project of collecting—in Diderot's words—"all the knowledge scattered over the face of the earth" and of presenting it so as to dispel all illusions, include "the most essential details ... of each science and every mechanical and liberal art," expose the general principles connecting them, and direct the whole corpus to the end of making men "more virtuous and happier." By the time this new approach to human knowledge—at once critical, comprehensive, ordered, and useful—was announced to the public in Diderot's *Prospectus* of 1750 and d'Alembert's *Preliminary Discourse* of 1751, an impressive succession of other publications had also announced the new intellectual era that was under way.

In the interim no less than seven pioneering works had appeared, opening up various areas of human concern and initiating their reinterpretation in the light of the new skeptical, practical and commonsensical attitude. Hume's *Concerning Human Understanding* developed the standard proofs for the derivation of all knowledge—including both belief and reasoning—from experience. This philosophical primacy of perceived things in all the variety and multiplicity of their existence was applied by Hume himself, in the same work, to the disproof of miracles; by Condillac to scientific method in his *Treatise on Systems*; by Diderot to the psychological relativism of his *Letters on the Blind*; by David Hartley (1705–1757), in his *Observations on Man*, to the association of ideas as the only valid way of connecting diverse sensory perceptions; by Georges Louis Leclerc de Buffon (1707–1788) to the evolution of the individual forms of living nature in the preface of his *Natural History*; by Montesquieu to the order of society and politics in his *Spirit of the Laws*; and most stridently, by Julien Offroy de La Mettrie (1709–1751) to the materialistic doctrine of man in his *Man a Plant*, the climax of the trilogy whose earlier volumes, *The Natural History of the Soul* (1745) and *Man a Machine* (1747), had already scandalized Europe and caused their author to be exiled from his native France.

It is true enough that Hume's one-sided empiricism and La Mettrie's equally one-sided physical and mechanical determinism were neither typical of the Enlightenment nor compatible with each other. It is equally true that Montesquieu's aristocratic reverence for intermediate organs of government and his stress upon the ecological justification of political variety aroused the suspicions of the other *philosophes*. But what was common to this concentration of publications around mid-century was, at this stage, more impressive than what divided them: they proclaimed man's concrete experience of the world to be the test of their ideas about it, and stipulated that the ordering of this world, both in science and in politics, must follow from, rather than be imposed upon, the actual arrangements of its autonomous individual constituents. In field after field of knowledge they proceeded to work out the new views resulting from the assignment of reason to the linkage of things. The common emphasis, in short, was on the primacy of "facts" and on the subsequent role of reason in showing their "inner connections."

The program for a new knowledge and a new ethic that would dispense with beliefs and ideas prior to the actual experience of this world was, in itself, nothing new. As a program it had already been promulgated by Newton and Locke at the end of the previous century, and as a general approach it had already permeated the early Enlightenment. And yet, around the mid-century mark something novel was undoubtedly developing within this line of thought. The recognition of a new stage at this point in time is not simply a product of historical hindsight. The most representative figures among the *philosophes* were all aware, with Diderot, that "if one looks attentively at the middle of our century, . . . it is

A chemical laboratory, from the Diderot and d'Alembert *Encyclopedia*. This illustration exemplifies the philosophes' intense interest in experimental science.

difficult not to see that in several respects a most remarkable change has taken place in our ideas, a change which, by its rapidity, seems to promise a greater one yet." What marked this "change" at mid-century was the application of the "new method of philosophizing" to all kinds of actual issues—"from the principles of the secular sciences to the bases of revelation, from metaphysics to matters of taste, from music to ethics, from the scholastic disputes of theologians to affairs of business, from the rights of princes to those of the people, from the natural law to the discretionary laws of particular nations." What was novel at mid-century, then, was the progress from the sketchy program of the early Enlightenment to the actual reinterpretation of human knowledge in the clear light of a definitely perceived natural reality and to the actual revision of human ideals in terms of the primacy of individual freedom. Given the variety of the applications in which the *philosophes* actually invested their characteristic mode of thought and given their distaste for organizing the various applications of thought in the form of total systems on the model of Aquinas' *Summa Theologica* or even of Descartes' strict recipe of deductions from a few clear and distinct ideas, they had to find indirect ways of expressing their systematic spirit. They found these ways both in the coherent form of their writing and in the unifying function of their ideas.

Aside from the obvious device of loosely structured encyclopedias—the revealing subtitle of Diderot's great *Encyclopedia* was *Systematic Dictionary of the Sciences, Arts, and Crafts*—the *philosophes* used two other devices to organize their experiences in the light of an acceptable systematic spirit which would fall short of the spirit of systems they rejected. One consisted of the deliberate application of the same approach by the same thinker to many different fields of knowledge. D'Holbach was, as usual, too rigid and mechanical to be entirely typical when he wrote, in quick succession, a *System of Nature* (1770), a *Social System* (1773), a *Natural Politics* (1773-1774), and a *Universal Morality* (1776)—works which became notorious precisely for their attempt to apply a single doctrine of natural order to the whole range of human experience. But, again as usual, d'Holbach's system was an extreme development of a tendency generally characteristic of the mature Enlightenment. However more flexible a Voltaire, a Diderot, a Lessing, a young Rousseau, and a Prussian Prince Frederick may have been as they moved nimbly among the fields of philosophy, popular science, ethics, political theory, aesthetics, philosophical and sentimental novels, poetry, and even—in the cases of Rousseau and Frederick at least—musical composition, for each of these *philosophes* too the various fields of cultural endeavor received the consistent impress of the intellectual personality who spread himself among them.

The alternative unifying device of the mature Enlightenment was the vogue for single works on general subjects, since such subjects inevitably called for the all-inclusive and consistent arrangements of many ideas. This was the era in which the sense for the variety of all life and the sense for its inherent meaningfulness—the two intuitions which produced the blend of realism and of reasonableness that are associated with the Enlightenment—combined to produce works in the grand manner and on great themes, works in which the universal principles of reason were invoked to order vast reaches of human experience. Thus the most notable of the century's cosmic histories of humanity—a genre which we now label "philosophical history"—were penned in this middle period. Turgot's lectures on the "progress of the human spirit" (1750), Rousseau's anthropological history of the human species in his *Discourse on the Origins of Inequality* (1755), Voltaire's attempt at a genuinely universal history in his *Essay on the Manners and Spirit of Nations* (1756), and Adam Ferguson's *Essay on the History of Civil Society* (1767), became models of the Enlightenment's characteristic attempt to recognize the actual vagaries of nature's most fickle creature and still to interweave a rational pattern among them. Even when they set their sights lower than the heady vistas of all humanity, the men of the Enlightenment opted for large canvases. The first fifteen volumes of Buffon's *Natural History* (1749–1767), Samuel Johnson's epoch-making *Dictionary of the English Language* (1755), Voltaire's immortal *Candide* (1759), the first volume of Gibbon's ambitious *Decline and Fall of the Roman Empire* (1776), and Adam Smith's merger of ethics, sociology, and economics in his *Wealth of Nations* (1776) were outstanding examples of fundamental intellectual achievements in single works.

Whether in this form of a single work combining many interests or in the other form of a single set of ideas spread across several works, the *philosophes*' devices for organizing a variety of intellectual innovations in uniform molds made their doctrines irresistible to those groups in eighteenth-century society who would control change by embarking upon it from the security of a new intellectual order.

In addition to its social forms of communication and its intellectual forms of expression, the republic of letters developed two distinctive points of view in its approach to thought at the time of the mature Enlighten-

Contemporary illustration accompanying the initial tribulation of Voltaire's mock-comic hero in his satirical novel, *Candide* (1759). *Caught by the baron in the act of experimenting with the cause-effect relationship on the body of his daughter pursuant to Voltaire's version of the Leibnizian principle that "an effect cannot possibly be without a cause . . . in this best of all possible worlds,"* Candide *is expelled into the series of misadventures which demonstrates the absurdity of any metaphysical system when applied to the vagaries of physical and human nature.*

ment, and these too helped to make the period a watershed in the history of European culture.

First, the *philosophes* made social relevance a constant touchstone of all their thinking. The realm of social and political relations was an arena particularly appropriate to the blend of rational and empirical principles characteristic of the mature Enlightenment. For those who achieved a satisfactory blend in the primary realms of moral or natural philosophy, the application to society and politics meant a pragmatic confirmation of their logical achievement. For those who were not so satisfied with the logic of their moral or scientific blend, the social and political realm played an even more crucial role. Attention to social and political conditions which by their very nature were common to whole groups of men provided a practical kind of unity for the social and political theory of the Enlightenment when its principles could be unified in no other way. Thus the principles of reason (or law), of utility (or happiness), and of passion (or sentiment), which were recognized by the men of the early Enlightenment and developed into full-fledged doctrines by the men of the mature Enlightenment, were either synthesized abstractly and then applied to society and politics, or left separate in theory and synthesized in their application to society and politics.

Whichever way was chosen, the result was a fruitful juncture of devotion to moral ideals and attention to social realities that produced the classic political theories of the Enlightenment. By proceeding in the first way, Montesquieu worked out the theory of constitutions in his *Spirit of the Laws*. Priestley and Paine the theory of liberal democracy in the former's *First Principles of Government* and the latter's *Common Sense*, Helvétius and d'Holbach the politics of the right to happiness in the former's *On the Mind* and the latter's *Natural Politics*, young Edmund Burke the idea of party in his *Thoughts on the Present Discontents*, and Adam Smith the policy of *laissez-faire* in his *Wealth of Nations*. Equally fundamental were the achievements of those who approached politics in the second way and found in the practical organization of civil society a cohesive force that made their political theory the most unified sector of all their ideas. Thus Hume's political essays and political history, Diderot's political articles in the *Encyclopedia*, and Rousseau's *Social Contract* were the most notable cases of works by men who saw in politics the rational calculation of means to connect the passions of individuals with the welfare of the society and who thereby invested their political theories with a unity of reason, sentiment, and utility that their philosophies did not otherwise provide. But, either way, the social and political emphasis of the mature Enlightenment helped to spread its influence, for through its social analysis and political critique its characteristic principles were brought home to the literate nonintellectual citizenry in terms most relevant to their actual experience.

In its second distinctive point of view, the mature Enlightenment marked a fundamental break and a new departure not only from the early Enlightenment but in Western thought generally: liberty replaced order as the dominant value toward which thinking was directed. No more than in any other intellectual revolution did this change mean an absolute metamorphosis, as if men had been exclusively preoccupied with order before 1750 and would be exclusively preoccupied with liberty thereafter. Order had been preeminent among the social values, including liberty, in the sense that it had furnished the constant point of reference with which all other values, especially liberty, had to be rendered compatible. Now the priorities were reversed: men's freedom became the issue of primary concern, and the continuing respect for order in the organization of both thought and society became subservient to the concern for liberty, for which order was to provide the necessary but external condition.

The new liberal faith was held by all types of *philosophes*. The sober d'Alembert pontificated that "liberty of thought and action alone is capable of producing great things." The passionate Denis Diderot (1713–1784) caught the spirit of the age perhaps even more faithfully when he recognized the logic of naturalistic determinism and the convenience of enlightened absolutism but broke through time and again to exalt the faith which was his primary commitment: "The child of Nature abhors slavery; intransigent foe of every authority, he is shamed by his yoke, he is outraged by constraint; liberty is his desire, liberty is his call." From this appeal of the man who came closest to being everybody's *philosophe* it was but a step to the radical Rousseau, in this context a reliable son of the Enlightenment, and his famous opening of the *Social Contract*:

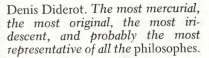

Denis Diderot. *The most mercurial, the most original, the most iridescent, and probably the most representative of all the* philosophes.

"Man is born free; and everywhere he is in chains." And from here there was a direct connection with the careful and moderate Immanuel Kant (1724–1804), who declared that behind the rigorous logic of his philosophical *Critiques*, behind his demonstration of a necessary order in nature and an imperative law in morality, lay the simple lesson taught him by Rousseau—how to use thought for the purpose of "establishing the rights of humanity." Often, indeed, the *philosophes* despaired of human liberty. They despaired of achieving it or of the use that some men would make of it. Often they qualified their concept of liberty, to make it easier of attainment or safer to use. Often they devoted more attention to the prescriptive laws of nature and the obligatory laws of absolute kings which they felt to be the necessary prerequisites of freedom than to the elucidation of the freedom itself. But freedom it was that remained the ultimate end of their thought and their propaganda.

In the final analysis the social and intellectual conditions of life in the mature Enlightenment's republic of letters left their deepest mark on the substantive doctrines which the *philosophes* developed under their influence. For the doctrines, like the conditions, were shaped by the continuing effort to associate the varieties of experience in ways that made unified sense. In the generation that followed the intellectual innovations of the late 1740's, the *philosophes* developed doctrines that bridged the extremes set forth at the start of this generation. Between the limits set by Hume's skeptical empiricism and La Mettrie's dogmatic rationalism, the mature Enlightenment developed a whole host of hybrid positions. The variety of its philosophical doctrines was paralleled, indeed, by a similar scattering of its political positions, ranging from the pragmatic conservatism of a Hume through the radical democracy of a Rousseau to the utopian communism of a Morelly. The assignment of such labels as empiricism, rationalism, conservatism, democracy, and communism to the mature Enlightenment indicates its range and its flexibility, but for its characteristic ideas—the ideas that give it a distinctive identity in the history of Western culture—the Enlightenment must be considered not from the point of view of these alternative philosophical and political categories, but rather from the point of view of the doctrines which the *philosophes* invented to connect them. These unifying doctrines were their chief concerns. For the *philosophes* believed, in varying proportions, in the whole variety of basic positions opened up by their dismantling of orthodoxy, and they were distinguished in their heyday precisely by the doctrines which they devised to make combinations of positions rational which were not in themselves rationally compatible. The doctrines of the mature Enlightenment bridge such opposite categories as fact and reason, utility and ideal, authority and liberty. These hybrid doctrines, being of the same kind, could themselves be fitted together into rigorous systems, juxtaposed in compatible patterns, or at the very least discussed within a common universe of discourse. If we line up the most characteristic of the doctrines elaborated during the mature Enlightenment according to the fields which they represented—religion, psychology, ethics, politics, and history—we should be able to sense the harmony underlying the variegation of its accomplishments. Religion, ethics, and history were interests carried over from the early Enlightenment, but now they were related to one another through the new interest in psychology and politics, and they were themselves developed from statements of abstract principles to definite religious, ethical, and historical doctrines.

Religion
In the field of religion, the earlier emphasis upon the autonomous sphere of natural theology gave way to the doctrine of anti-Christianity. Not, of course, that deism or the other early forms of rational theology died out at mid-century. They spread from Great Britain into France, where they prominently framed the thinking of *philosophes* as various as the older Voltaire and the young Rousseau. When deism reached Germany, earnest "neologists" of much assiduity and little fame painstakingly reinterpreted Protestant dogma according to the dictates of reason. But for the Enlightenment as a whole, this kind of theologizing, while still being diffused and still operative as intellectual background, was no longer in the forefront of the *philosophes'* attention nor was it the kind of thinking about religion which attracted their most original efforts. What was more prominent as an explicit concern and more characteristic therefore of the mature Enlightenment was the anti-Christian campaign epitomized by Voltaire's battle cry: *Ecrasez l'infame* ("Crush the vile thing"). Anti-Christian doctrine became Hume's main interest during the decade of the

1750's. He wrote but did not publish his skeptical credo in *Dialogues Concerning Natural Religion* (finished in 1751, but published posthumously in 1779). And he then did publish his anthropological explanation of religion in *The Natural History of Religion* (1757).

The same preoccupation became Voltaire's obsession in the decade of the 1760's, when he bitterly castigated clerical persecution and enshrined his anti-Christianity in the immortal pages of his *Philosophical Dictionary* (1764). In this decade also d'Holbach carried the same crusade to another battlefield when he blamed the priests for the faulty education of men that diverted them from the happy and beneficent paths of nature. In the 1770's, finally, Gotthold Ephraim Lessing (1729–1781) developed, under the stress of sectarian opposition, the doctrine of universal toleration that, in his famous play *Nathan the Wise* (1779), reduced Christianity to but one of the several valid ways in which religion has served the moral perfection of human nature.

In its effects, then, the anti-Christian doctrine of the mature Enlightenment served to ally the various tendencies of the *philosophes'* thinking—skepticism, rationalism, humanism, and materialism—against a common orthodox enemy. But the shift from the earlier reinterpretation of Christian dogma to the rejection of Christian doctrine and the abomination of Christian churches came from a deeper source of Enlightenment thought. What this source was may be recognized from what was common to the two main forms taken by the anti-Christian doctrine. As a representative work like Voltaire's *Philosophical Dictionary* demonstrated, anti-Christianity could take the form either of explicit criticism of ecclesiastical beliefs and practices or of belligerent argument for the entirely secular and naturalistic basis of such crucial subjects as the soul, freedom of the will, and virtue, which had been favored topics of Christian exegesis. The first of these forms of anti-Christianity was an anticlericalism that had passed a decisive stage beyond the anticlericalism of the early Enlightenment: where the anticlericalism of the early Enlightenment was a criticism of ecclesiastical practice and dogma as a perversion of churches, the anticlericalism of the mature Enlightenment, particularly in its French version, was a criticism of ecclesiastical practice and dogma as the noxious essence of churches. The second, subtler from of the anti-Christian campaign was the more pervasive and the more influential of the two. Thus the *Encyclopedia,* which was certainly designed in large measure to exclude Christian revelation as a source and Christian theology as an explanation of human knowledge, executed this design primarily by ignoring the Christian God and, in Diderot's words, making "Man ... the center around which everything revolves."

But common to both forms was the single impulse of the *philosophes* to give their ideas a practical form. The twin themes of the *Encyclopedia* were articulated with cumulative emphasis as its seventeen large volumes of text and eleven volumes of plates rolled from the presses between 1751 and 1772. These themes were the self-sufficient rational unity of all human knowledge and the usefulness of the mechanical arts and crafts that were derived from it. But between these two themes—between the general principles that explained natural reality and the practical arts that enabled men to live in accordance with these principles—neither the Encyclopedists nor the mature Enlightenment which they epitomized could find a sure and positive way. For the practical arts required, like any kind of human action, incentives that were other than the incentives to theoretical knowledge, and the *philosophes* were never able to show satisfactorily why men did not act in accordance with a natural knowledge apparently open to all, or how man could act in accordance with the dictates of nature and still retain the autonomy of his will. But what the *philosophes* could not show positively they insisted all the more on showing negatively. That is, they could show how the knowledge of secular nature was congruent with the freedom of the secular will only by showing how both principles were equally opposed to Christianity, which had certainly succeeded in linking knowledge and will with a supernatural connection. The insistent logic of their anti-Christianity was this: things that are opposed to joined things must be joined themselves. The *philosophes* sought to demonstrate the connection between the unreasonableness of Christian dogma and the tyranny, at once vicious and unhappy, of its institutional effects. Through its rejection of both sectarian dogma and clerical institutions the anti-Christian doctrine of the *philosophes* forged a link, however negative in form, between the theory and the practice of the Enlightenment.

Psychology and Ethics

In the psychology of human nature, the *philosophes* promulgated the related doctrines of sensationalism and associationism, which for more than a century would dominate the discussion of how men derived their ideas. The standard works in this field were Condillac's *Treatise on Sensations* (1754) and Priestley's tendentious abridgment of Hartley's *Observations on Man* (1775), each of which developed an earlier limited idea into a comprehensive doctrine of general application. Condillac took as his starting point his own *Essay on the Origins of Human Knowledge* (1746), which was a popularization of Locke's theory on the derivation of knowledge from both sensation and reflection. But when he popularized it, he changed it by simplifying it. Condillac now traced the construction of knowledge as a continuous process starting from a single root in sensation and developing it into a richly ramified structure wherein perceptions, ideas, and passions were all simply different ways in which sensations combined, dissolved, and recombined into new sensations.

Where Condillac stressed the analysis of experience into particular, mutually negotiable realities, Hartley and Priestley made an explicit and independent doctrine out of the synthetic aspect of the process—they made the association of ideas the essential process in the construction of knowledge and considered what went into the association to be secondary. Hartley tied his original notion of association to a physiological theory of "vibrations" in the sensory nerves to explain what the primary units of experience were that first got associated. Priestley restated Hartley without the theory of vibrations and thus made the law of association an independent natural law of the human psyche applicable to any operation constructing a more general out of a more particular level of truth.

These compatible emphases in psychology—on particular sensations and on the natural law of association—passed into the foundations of morals to support an analogous combination of values there. In the field of morals, the *philosophes* developed the doctrines of utilitarianism and of naturalism as compatible modes of relating pleasure and principle, passion and control, self-interest and social welfare—in short, what is and what ought to be. The doctrine of utilitarianism originated during the mature Enlightenment precisely as an intellectual device to connect the apparently discordant values in each of these pairs. Just before the mature Enlightenment, Hume had announced the "principle of utility" as a human motive actually involved in men's moral ideals and social values but not rationally connected with them. Just at the end of the mature Enlightenment, Jeremy Bentham's *Fragment on Government* (1776) would isolate utilitarianism as a total and self-sufficient theory and would disconnect it from any larger natural order. In between came the mature Enlightenment's invention of the utilitarian doctrine which combined the principles of utility and of natural law. In this form the doctrine stipulated a rational connection between the individual's interest in the pleasurable effects of his actions for himself and his commitment to the pleasurable effects of his actions for the whole society. This rational connection was considered to be grounded in universal laws governing all natural reality.

The classic formulation of the utilitarian doctrine appeared in *On the Mind* (1758), by Claude Adrien Helvétius (1715–1771). It was applied to law by Cesare Beccaria (1738–1794), in his influential *On Crimes and Punishments* (1764), and to politics by Joseph Priestley (1733–1804), in his *First Principles of Government* (1768). Basing his ethics on Condillac's psychology, Helvétius reduced all morality to various forms of the individual's desire for pleasure and abhorrence of pain, just as Condillac had reduced all knowledge to the various forms of particular sensation. Since in Helvétius' doctrine all pleasures were equivalent in quality, all men were equally capable of moral acts. Each of these acts, moreover, contributed to both the utility of the individual and the utility of the society by virtue of the same Newtonian natural law that harmoniously ordered individual bodies with the force of gravitation. The connection between private interest and social benefit broke down only when faulty education obscured the recognition by reason that they were necessarily associated by nature. In this event the legislator had to supply laws as the means of re-educating the unfortunate.

In admitted dependence upon this basic utilitarian position of Helvé-tius, which invoked the lawmaker as the awakener of men to the natural order of things, Beccaria worked out his utilitarian juristic doctrine. He based the validity of penal law on its conformity with the natural law which "like the force of gravity. . . makes us always tend toward our well-being," and through its natural law the sole valid function of penal ordi-nances is the deterrent use of punishment to confirm the natural tie between individual and social pain. Priestley pioneered the broader political application of utilitarianism when he made the utilitarian criterion—"the good and happiness of the members, that is, the majority of the members of any state"—the supreme principle of political action, grounded it in the "natural rights" of every individual, and associated it with the natural right of popular revolution against governments that fail to promote the good of the majority.

For the mature Enlightenment, in general, utilitarianism was a doctrine with which to bring into reasonable connections all the great forces that moved men upon this earth, and to exclude as meaningless and illusory what could not be so connected. The utilitarians accepted the whole range of realities—from the passions of individuals, through the rational interests of the society, to the compulsory edicts of governments—but they accepted only those passions, those interests, and those edicts whose results could be related to one another through the operation of a general law of human nature.

All the *philosophes* were utilitarians in some degree, for they all com-bined the beliefs, characteristic of the utilitarianism of that vintage, that actions should be measured by the happiness they brought and that this measuring by results was sanctioned by its origins in the authority of nature. Moral utilitarians were thus moral naturalists as well, just as those who made nature the source of virtue also insisted on its useful effects. Yet the distinction between utilitarians and naturalists—between the *philo-sophes* like Helvétius, Beccaria, and Priestley who stressed utility and those like Diderot, Rousseau, and Adam Smith who stressed nature—was more than a mere difference of emphasis. It was also, and more impor-tantly, a difference in the principle that connected natural origins with happy results. For the utilitarians the natural warranty of happiness was a general law, discovered by reason either directly in nature or indirectly through the state. For the naturalists what guaranteed the congruity of self-interest and the social good was not the lawfulness but the variety and creativity of nature; it implanted the complementary impulses of "egotism" and "compassion," as Rousseau called them, in the original composition of man and sponsored their reciprocal and compatible interaction in all unobstructed moral acts. In this form naturalist moral doctrine took its place alongside utilitarianism as a separate, but related, moral doctrine of the mature Enlightenment.

Politics

From utilitarianism and naturalism in ethics it was but a short step to the articulation of constitutional and democratic doctrines in politics, and of liberal and socialist doctrines about society. The ethical, political, and social doctrines, indeed, were often identical, appearing as ethics when viewed from the angle of the individual and as political and social theory when viewed from the angle of the group. Political and social doctrines in the Enlightenment thus served the same function as psychological and moral doctrines—they served to distinguish the kinds of institutions and practices that could be put together into reasonable combinations from those that could not, and to show the principles of their combination.

But social and political ideas played a special role in the general synthesizing function which characterized the doctrines of the mature Enlightenment. Ideas about society and politics had a peculiarly ambiguous status with the *philosophes*. On the one hand, the active interest of the *philosophes* in them, starting at least from the publication in 1748 of Montesquieu's *Spirit of the Laws,* is undeniable, and not without cause have modern political movements traced their ideological roots to them. On the other hand, these same *philosophes* were often not very systematic in their theorizing, and there is a curious kind of absentmindedness in their political writings—as if they were aiming at something else, that was not political. In part, the explanation lies in the *philosophes'* distinction between society and the state and in their tendency to concentrate on the former, which they regarded as the organization of what was natural, moral, and essential in the relation of man to man, and to depreciate politics to the status of a necessary evil, contingent upon the will of the society and assigned the menial chore of protecting society from its unnatural defectors. The importance of this political function varied, to be sure, with the degree of restraint deemed needful for the human species, but common to the Enlightenment as a whole were both the judgment of the negative character of politics in respect to the essential human values of liberty and brotherhood, and the relative neglect of the political function in favor of the concern with the general relations between the individual and society. Thus the *philosophes* subordinated politics both to individual freedom and to social morality. Montesquieu, Voltaire, the *Encyclopedia,* and British liberals like Priestley, Richard Price, Adam Smith, and Thomas Paine, all exemplified this tendency, whether through the French emphasis upon the social "spirit" behind laws and politics or through the British emphasis on the primacy of civil over political liberties.

But what must still be explained is the political interest that led the men of this same Enlightenment to advance the first modern theories of such influential political doctrines as government by law, the separation of powers, popular sovereignty, the "night-watchman" state, and the welfare state. However secondary in value politics may have been for the *philosophes*, they fully recognized its inescapable necessity for the implementation of their primary values. Primary for them were the rights of individuals and the benefits of voluntary association, but because they were interested in results and were realistic enough about the actual moral disposition of their fellowmen to doubt their voluntary attainment, the *philosophes* turned sporadically and fruitfully to political compulsion as the means of calling men from what they were to what they should be—or more precisely, in terms of the Enlightenment notions of human psychology and ethics—to recall men from their unintelligent private diversions to the recognition of their true social nature.

Hence the most fruitful political doctrines of the mature Enlightenment were those that proposed permanent institutional channels for directing men's self-interest toward social morality. The *philosophes* approached politics through the idea of law, since they deemed the laws of the state to be embodiments of the moral law, adjusted to men as they are and equipped with the power to make them act as they ought. Montesquieu introduced the conception of a moral connection between nature and politics by recognizing fear, honor, and virtue as the operational moral principles "which necessarily flow from the nature of things," underlying the laws of all despotisms, monarchies, and republics respectively. Subsequently, writers as different as Helvétius and Rousseau approached politics through an analogous moralizing function of the law. Helvétius appealed to the "Legislator" to enforce the order of nature by associating public pain with unsocial acts, and thereby make men virtuous. Rousseau took an opposite tack when he denied the derivation of the law of the state from any law of nature, but he too saw in the law of the state and in the "Legislator" who initiated it the expression of the general will that turned natural into moral liberty.

The separation of powers, similarly, became a widespread and fundamental doctrine of Enlightenment political thinking because it was developed as the way to make a practical possibility out of a fundamental principle. Once more the initiation of the doctrine goes back to Montesquieu, who believed it was realized in the British constitution. Certainly, as has often been pointed out, his recognition was a distorted one, since the tortuous and intricate historical growth of mutual checks in Great Britain was a far cry from the categorical separation of legislative, executive, and judicial powers that Montesquieu claimed to see in it. But the distortion is precisely what made his doctrine of their separation so influential, since it thereby seemed at once rational and real, general and specific. An accurate transcription of British practice would hardly have been transferable to any other situation, but in Montesquieu's version, it became a political incarnation of the cosmic balance of forces in the Newtonian structure of the natural universe. In this form of a constitutional balance of powers, paralleling the gravitational balance in physical nature, the age-old principle of mixed government was transmuted from a mere political preference into a basic constitutional doctrine which expounded the only valid way of guaranteeing and controlling the natural liberty of man. Thus did the doctrine pass through Diderot and d'Holbach into the *Encyclopedia*, and along with the individual freedom which it secured from violation and from license, became the characteristic political tenet of the Enlightenment.

Not nearly so widespread or characteristic for the Enlightenment itself, but momentous for the ages that followed, was the third political invention of the eighteenth century's middle decades, the modern doctrine of democracy. The emphasis here must be on the "modern," for two reasons. First, the name of "democracy" was not assigned to this invention of the mature Enlightenment until the revolutionary final two decades of the century. Second, this nameless mid-century doctrine of what would later be called democracy was a different kind of theory from the traditional ideas of democracy which the Enlightenment inherited and welded together into a new product.

We may distinguish three separate concepts associated literally or equivalently with the older notion of democracy. As a descriptive term for government by the people—that is, by the whole body of citizens—democracy had been used since the ancient Greeks as one of the valid pure forms of the state and as a constituent of mixed governments. Second, the derivative notion of popular sovereignty had been used since the ancient Romans as a legal concept to affirm the validity of those states that recognized the people as the possessors of the ultimate governing power, whatever the form of the government and whoever actually exercised this power. Third, the right of popular revolution, as asserted since the sixteenth century and embodied in John Locke's classic *Second Treatise of Civil Government* on the eve of the Enlightenment, validated the occasional assumption of the governing power by the people, whoever the possessors of sovereignty might be, in order to restore some fundamental, suprapolitical right of the people.

Common to all three traditional strands of the democratic principle was the age-old separation between the actuality and the ideal of political power. As a regular form of government, democracy had been deemed primarily a practical device best fitted to secure good government for civil societies in certain kinds of circumstances—notably those of small city-states. As the legal principle of popular sovereignty, democracy had been etherealized into an invisible sanction of visible political power. As a revolutionary ideal, democracy had been limited to sporadic moments of destructive efficacy. This traditional separation of the democratic actuality from its ideal, even among those who acknowledged its validity, had taken on added depth and meaning because it reflected a more basic separation in the tradition of political thinking–the separation between the origins and the ends of political authority. On the one hand, whether viewed as instituted by God, modeled on the hierarchical organization of nature, or authorized by contract, the origin of governments had been deemed a response to a practical need for order, varying according to the local circumstances of that need. But once originated, governments had also been deemed, on the other hand, to be a positive means to a higher good of the community than the mere preservation of order—a higher good that was variously identified as salvation, virtue, or welfare. Thus the form of government depended on its geographical, anthropological, and historical origins and was independent of the higher end of the community, which could be either approached or violated equally by any of the valid forms of government. For traditional political thought, in other words, the sanctity of the end blessed government in general and occasional revolutionary acts of popular sovereignty in particular, but it did not bless any particular form of government—not even democracy.

The political writers of the mature Enlightenment continued tradition in their literal notion of democracy as one of several valid forms of government—and as a not particularly favored form—but they prepared the way for modern democratic theory in their development of an implicitly democratic doctrine of consent. To be sure, the idea of consent too had a traditional history that paralleled notions like democracy and popular sovereignty in that the consent of the governed had been deemed historically fortuitous, occasional, or extra-governmental—but in any case politically inessential. Thus consent had been specified as a general factor in the origin of some governments, or as a particular factor in legitimating a government's power to abridge private rights by taxing property when this power was considered beyond the proper political sphere of government. But it was primarily through the convergence of these separate ideas of consent into a single doctrine associating the popular source of government with its sacred role in protecting individual rights that the *philosophes* created the pattern for the subsequent reworking of all the traditional notions of democracy into modern democratic theory.

The most transparent testimony of what happened to the idea of consent in the eighteenth century was its incorporation into Rousseau's doctrine of the general will, as he developed this doctrine in his *Social Contract* of 1762. Now it is perfectly true that by this date Rousseau was estranged from the *philosophes* and was well started on his "preromantic" path to the supersession of the Enlightenment. It is true too that the *Social Contract* was the least influential of his works during the eighteenth century. A final caveat to the democratic implications of Rousseau's general will for the Enlightenment was his own refusal to associate it literally with democracy: the general will was, in Rousseau's view, the foundation of valid law for all governments, but he viewed "democracy" in age-old terms as merely one of the many possible legitimate forms of government—the one particularly suited to small states. But after all these reservations have been made, the fact remains that Rousseau's doctrine of the general will set forth the cardinal principle on which democracy would be founded and that in respect to this principle he represented the undiluted extreme—the limiting case—of what was common to many of the *philosophes.*

The fruitful new principle that underlay the doctrine of the general will was the conversion of popular consent into a continuous and fundamental factor in government. This principle followed from three connected postulates. First, individual consent was not only prepolitical (that is, a condition for the installation of a regime or ruler) or occasionally political (that is, an agency for the deposition of despotic rulers) but permanently political, contributing to every valid act of government. Second, this continuous efficacy of political consent was grounded not so much in variable rights of custom or considerations of utility as in the fundamental rights of man that made the daily exercise of political consent a series of basic moral acts necessary to all governments. Third, the function of this permanent and fundamental political consent was to organize the free expressions of individual wills for the purpose of protecting the freedom common to them all; consent thus connected the origins and mechanics of government with the purpose of government and made the liberal ideal a determinant not of the results, as of yore, but now of the structure and operation of governments.

In Rousseau this new function of consent, which made the democratic principle the essential bridge between the actual conditions and the moral potentialities of man, was particularly clear from the two successive steps into which he analyzed his doctrine of the general will. By the first step, the general will is *formed* out of the free and actual decisions of all the participant individuals, living in a state of nature and driven by their natural needs to participate in a political community. Thereby they initiate the general will of this community into which every individual deposits all his insecure and instinctive natural rights for the purpose of confronting the similar rights of his fellow humans and distilling from the social interaction rights that are equal, certain, rational, and moral. By the second step, the general will *operates* in political communities through the virtual consent of the individual citizens. This is expressed both in the original sanction of the general will, which continues to serve as the measure of every political action, and in the will of the "people," who—usually in the form of majority voting—in every state realize the general will through their exclusive right to make laws. Rousseau did not call this model state a democracy because he identified "government" with the executive power and in this changed setting admitted democracy along with the other traditional forms of government as circumstantially variable agents of the constant legislative power of the people. But however abstract his notion of the general will and however much he doubted the fidelity of actual laws to it, Rousseau's doctrine did establish political consent to government as an essential act of moral freedom for every individual, and it did prescribe a continuing function for popular sovereignty in the making of ordinary laws. Thus he invented a democratic theory that made the continuous participation of all citizens in the exercise of political power a fundamental right of man and an essential activity in the realization of the good life.

In the specifics of his doctrine Rousseau stood alone. He was the only figure in his age to come so close to the literal democratic principle by combining absolute political equality, legislative sovereignty, and positive morality in the idea of consent. But the core of his achievement—the exaltation of political rights to an essential status among human liberties—was shared by many of his eighteenth-century contemporaries. Diderot advanced the notion of a general will before Rousseau, and Kant adopted it after Rousseau. For both Diderot and Kant it was part of a moderate design for a mixed government predicated on the limitation of active political rights to men of property. Others expounded the point of the new doctrine of political consent even when they avoided the notion of a general will, with its possible encouragement of strong and willful government. Thus in Great Britain the succession of political crises starting with the exclusion of the regularly elected John Wilkes from the House of Commons during the 1760's and climaxed in the issue of the American colonists' right of consent to taxation during the early 1770's spurred a whole group of political writers to include political liberty—that is, the right to hold public office or to be represented by those who do—among the inalienable natural rights of man. Joseph Priestley, Richard Price, Thomas Paine, and Major John Cartwright were the most prominent of these moralists turned political doctrinaires. If they were unlike Rousseau in their assessment of political society as a necessary evil and their restriction of political rights to the minimal function of securing other rights, they were like Rousseau in their grounding of these political rights in the "natural equality of mankind" and in holding that political rights were indispensable to all the other rights of mankind.

But practical as their political stimulus was and doctrinaire as their political language may have been, the British radicals ultimately, like the French, shied away from consistent democratic theory. Indeed, in the very distance they kept from it we may glimpse the characteristic contribution of this era to the subsequent formation of this theory. Only for Cartwright and his few followers did the political rights required by the equality of men mean equal political rights—that is, universal suffrage. Only for Paine did such rights mean the rejection of the independent rights of king and lords. For Priestley and Price alike the apparent inconsistency between the democratic principle and the moderate program was deliberate: they held both that "every government in its original principles, and antecedent to its present form, is an equal republic" in whose parliament "every man by natural right will have a seat" and that in the present forms of the state the political liberty of all individuals is neither necessary to nor sufficient for the civil liberty of these individuals. Thus they validated any political system that included a responsive representative organ.

This ambiguous insistence upon political equality as a fundamental principle with a persistent but impractical relevance points to the essential features of the incipient democratic doctrine promulgated in the middle decades of the eighteenth century: it was a doctrine not of democracy as a *form* of government but of democracy as an *end* of government. The mid-eighteenth-century radicals insisted upon the original equality of political rights not as a reason for an actual equality in the exercise of political rights but as the reason for requiring that political power be exercised for the sake of all men's equal rights. This first version of the modern democratic principle, in other words, grafted a political dimension onto men's fundamental liberties for the purpose of insisting that these liberties be respected by the state not as a matter of policy, but as a matter of right incumbent upon governments by their very constitution. Kant's later formulation of what we might call a "subjective democracy" was a precise expression of this Enlightenment position: all men should obey only those laws to which they "could have given consent."

Neither in Kant nor in his radical predecessors did this kind of constituent democratic principle confer on every individual a right to participate in the actual exercise of the political sovereignty that was bound hereby to cherish his rights in all other respects. But still the *philosophes* did draw from this principle one conclusion that went beyond the question of what political power was being exercised for and had bearing on the question of who should exercise it. However indifferent they may have been to precise forms of government, they were adamant on some role for the "people" in it. Since by the "people" they meant the collective association of ordinary individuals, the original political rights of the individual became the basis of the actual political rights of the "people." These actual political rights became in turn the popular basis of representative assemblies, however constituted. Through this conversion the original political rights of individuals were absorbed in the collective organs of the state and participation in these organs was no longer a matter of individual right but of utility in protecting the "people's" collective rights. This device for absorbing the political rights of the individual permitted the assignment of a democratic foundation to such oligarchic representative organs as the eighteenth-century British House of Commons and allowed for the typical *philosophes'* recommendation of a limited suffrage. Thus representative assemblies were secured a new positive function in the assertion of fundamental rights, and the democratic principle, duly camouflaged by the principle of representation, was built into the foundation of respectable institutions.

Society

The crucial notions of "people" and of "civil society" that permitted democratic principles to be connected with elitist politics lie behind the two other doctrines originated by the mature Enlightenment: the doctrines of *laissez-faire* and of socialism. We are used to thinking of economic liberty and collectivism in terms of the mutual opposition that was their most obvious relationship and that would govern their immediate future as theories and as movements. But equally important for the understanding of the Enlightenment and perhaps also of the ideas' mutual accommodation in our own time was the common attitude toward society that made these doctrines the twin products of the same conditions in the same era.

The concomitant appearance of the first modern socialist and *laissez-faire* doctrines was more than mere historical coincidence. The pioneering works of both schools appeared first in France during the same decade—the 1750's—and they shared prominent congenital tendencies. *The Code of Nature* (1755) of the mysterious Abbé Morelly attempted to bring the old dream of a communist society down to earth as a contemporary practical program. Three years later François Quesnay published his *Tableau Economique (Economic Model)*, the *laissez-faire* treatise that has caused him to be called the "founder of economic science." Indeed, as we have seen, Quesnay and his followers labeled themselves "Economists," but their intellectual connection with their contemporaries is clearer from the label "Physiocracy"—that is, "the government of nature"—which would subsequently be affixed to their doctrine.

The differences between these initial socialist and *laissez-faire* doctrines were clear enough. First, for the socialists private property was the root of all evil; it was the cause of inequality, avarice, vice, and misery. For the Physiocrats private property was the basis of natural right and the guarantor of liberty. Second, the socialists had an ambiguous doctrine, they were themselves isolated and obscure, and their subsequent influence was tenuous and sporadic. The economic liberals, on the other hand, formed a genuine school, had an immediate impact upon educated laymen and policy makers alike, and initiated a continuous tradition that soon developed into the dominant school of political economy in Europe.

The comparative alienation of the socialists from their society is abundantly clear from a few salient personal facts. Despite the occasional strictures of a Diderot or a Rousseau upon private property—strictures indicating that at least a vague tendency toward socialism responded to something real in the contemporary society—there were only two recognizable proponents of socialism during the Enlightenment and neither of these was prominent in the eyes of his contemporaries for this doctrine. Nothing was—or is still—known about the Abbé Morelly save that he was the author of the socialistic *Code of Nature,* and indeed for years the mistaken attribution of this work to Diderot denied him even this shred of identity. Gabriel Bonnet de Mably (1709–1785), whose *On Legislation* of 1776 transmitted Morelly's socialist doctrine to the generation who made the French Revolution, was certainly visible enough and popular enough in his day, but his socialism was such a mixed and unstable set of notions that it was not socialism he was visible and popular for. He was a humanist with a passion for Plato's *Republic*; he was a secularized prophet and pessimist who preached that man's fall from his original life of harmony among equals to the sinful state of self-seeking avarice, greed, and dominion made it impossible for him to recover the "community of goods and equality of conditions" necessary to the good society; he was an ascetic who counseled respect for private property and abstention from its fruits as the virtues appropriate to the fallen condition.

Undoubtedly Morelly was more optimistic, more hedonistic, more practical, and consequently more relevant in his socialist doctrine—his *Code of Nature* advanced an explicit "model of legislation" for the actual establishment of a true community of property and of citizens—but in him too the mechanical insistence upon equality, the economics of the public storehouse, the local and pyramidal basis of social organization, and the undiluted collectivization of all aspects of life seem rather reminiscent of traditional utopias than relevant to the new large-scale society aborning. Even the terms "socialism" and "communism," terms appropriate to movements of this society, were not used by these eighteenth-century precursors, but were coined more than a half century later. The frequent use of these labels to characterize their doctrines is thus an anachronism not only semantically but substantively, in that the eighteenth-century doctrines manifested neither the progressive economic connotation of the more general term "socialism" nor the radical political connotation of the more restricted term "communism." And yet both terms have been and are still retroactively applied to Morelly and Mably, to indicate that behind the obvious retrogressive features of their moralism and their utopianism there lies a new idea of social progress which links them with the modern movements to come.

The relationship of the free traders to late-eighteenth-century society was obviously closer, for no such obscurity, ambiguity, or delayed effect qualified their function. The Physiocrats were a genuine "school" of intellectuals, wholeheartedly committed to the pioneering doctrines of their schoolmasters—Quesnay and his chief collaborator, Victor Riqueti, Marquis de Mirabeau (1715–1789), who contributed the *Theory of Taxation*

(1760) and *The Rural Philosophy* (1763) to the Physiocratic canon and was the father of the Count Honoré de Mirabeau of French Revolutionary fame. That the Physiocratic principle of economic liberty struck a responsive chord was signalized by the attraction of faithful disciples like Pierre Du Pont de Nemours (1739–1817), who coined the term "Physiocracy," and Paul Pierre Mercier de la Rivière (1720–1794), whose *Natural and Essential Order of Political Societies* (1767) developed Physiocracy from a tool of economic analysis and a principle of economic policy into a complete social doctrine. It was signalized too by the organization of its own journal (the *Ephémérides*), by its demonstrable impact upon more influential figures who were disciples of a kind (such as Turgot and Adam Smith), and by its self-conscious promulgation of the label—*laissez-faire*—which would continue to identify the doctrine in its subsequent versions down to the present day.

But the patent differences between the two contemporaneous doctrines should not obscure the common traits which make them complementary indications of what was happening in mid-eighteenth-century society. Of these common traits, three stand out as particularly revealing.

First, and most important, the proponents of both doctrines saw society as a prime reality of nature, equivalent to any other reality of nature and ordered directly by its laws. What was novel in this emphasis was the finality it attributed to society as a self-enclosed process with its own structure and its own purpose: society was conceived to be a constant and reciprocal relationship among all the individuals who composed it, and this relationship was considered real, valuable, and permanent in itself rather than, as heretofore, intermediate in the ultimate formation of a political or ecclesiastical authority out of individual persons or families. From this point of view, when the Physiocrats found the natural basis of society in the economic laws governing the circular flow of goods and services among individual producers and consumers and when the socialists found the natural basis of society in the essential law of equality governing the daily relations of all individuals, both were stressing the orderliness, the meaningfulness, and the self-sufficiency of the ordinary social relations among ordinary individuals. The recourse by both groups to nature for the ground of social laws, whether of economic exchange or of communal harmony, was impelled by the conviction that only the sanction of nature could confer value on a uniform relationship among essentially independent individuals and by the confidence that this approach to society as an extension rather than a modification of nature would make social phenomena susceptible to the same kind of scientific treatment and control as other natural phenomena. Quesnay's analogy of the economic process to the circulation of the blood, and Morelly's explicit allusion to the mechanics of the "moral attraction" provided among men by nature were but literal references to a natural science that was generally deemed applicable to society. It was now,

Adam Smith. *Founder of the classical school of political economy and pioneering theorist of the free-enterprise system.*

in this context which witnessed the application of the methods and laws of natural science directly to society, that economics was invented as the form of human activity closest to nature.

Second, and more surprising, the progenitors of both these doctrines that were to flourish with the inception of an industrialized society were protagonists of none of the groups or branches of economic activity that were generating this society. Physiocrats and socialists alike went so far as to favor agriculture, the most conservative of economic activities. The Physiocrats explicitly found it the only source of economic value, stigmatizing commerce and manufactures equally as "sterile," while the socialists assumed a static, unspecialized, consumer-dominated economic mentality that had for centuries been associated with the predominance of agriculture. Even progressive economists like Turgot, his friend Vincent de Gournay, and Adam Smith, all of whom differed from the Physiocrats in admitting the productivity of trade and industry, put no special stress on these activities or the classes that performed them and that would espouse the doctrines of these very economists. Adam Smith's labor theory of value was designed, not to favor industrial producers, but to indicate the productivity of every economically active individual, whatever his activity. He meant to emphasize the equality of all classes in the exchange process as opposed to the Physiocrats' notion of the agriculturalists' superiority, which he deemed inconsistent with general economic liberty, and he meant to emphasize the economic creativity of the individual human being as opposed to the Physiocrats' focus on nature's impersonal creativity in land, which he deemed a lopsided view of nature. But having justified trade and industry in theory, Smith balanced his position by making it quite clear that in practice he mistrusted merchants and masters of industry and as a matter of fact trusted both the agriculturalist and the old-fashioned journeyman to assess their interests more rationally and therefore more in accord with the national interest.

Whatever the variations among these economic and social doctrinaires, then, it seems clear not only that they did not come out of an industrial society but that they did not speak to one. They spoke for and to no special classes at all, since the traditional groups they favored were actually unprepared to engage in the competitive economic process or the collective social process the doctrinaires prepared for them. Thus the progressive agrarian capitalism espoused by the Physiocrats found so few takers that by the 1770's the school as such was in decline, leaving its doctrine of *laissez-faire* as a detachable economic model to be carried on by less definitely committed observers. Even Adam Smith's version of the model became a real social force only when a later generation of theorists transformed his assumption of the harmonious interests of all producers into conditions of inevitable competition favoring the industrial entrepreneur.

The failure of eighteenth-century collectivists and individualists alike to recognize the proletarian and bourgeois interests with which their doctrines would some day be joined reflected not the absence of perception or foresight but the presence of a definite and distinctive stage in the development of European society. They analyzed a society in which all groups, new and old, were entering into the orbit of an exchange economy and thus into a kind of relationship that rendered every individual both indispensable to and dependent upon every other. It was not a new economy or a new society that they saw, but rather the homogenization and the emancipation of the old. It was not any particular social group, but society itself, that was now deemed autonomous, for it supplied its own power and its own direction. Individuals in society provided the former; the nature of society the latter. Thus each of the main doctrines afforded two crucial concepts, one for each function: the Physiocrats proclaimed *laissez-faire* and the natural order; Adam Smith the division of labor and nature's "invisible hand"; the socialists the equality of all individuals and the benevolent harmony of human nature. It was this attribution of initiative and value to the social process as such, rather than to any specific dynamic group in it that reflects and helps to explain the diffuse nature of the actual social movements in the second half of the eighteenth century.

The third of the features common to the individualistic and collectivist doctrines of the mature Enlightenment was one that pertained to its constitutional and democratic doctrines as well: the whole of the political, social, and economic theory of the period was practical without being practicable. The critical problem implicit in the political dogmas of the mid-eighteenth century and illuminated by its economic and social doctrine was simply this: the same principles that were advanced as the real truth of how things actually worked functioned mainly as ideals that had still, in some unspecified way, to be realized. What was new about the separation of powers, popular sovereignty, free trade, and socialism in the eighteenth century was the claim that they manifested the actual force of nature in men's social arrangements—and yet in each case they were paired with antithetical political and social institutions, such as political authoritarianism or private property, which made the doctrines seem more like utopian visions than fundamental truths.

Much has been made of Montesquieu's double inconsistency—first, in misinterpreting the British mixed government in the doctrinaire terms of the separation of powers, and second, in juxtaposing this combination, exalted as the illustration of the only guaranteed liberty, with an analysis of France as a lawful monarchy whose whole sovereignty devolved from the king. But there must have been a rationale behind the inconsistency, for it was not personal to Montesquieu. The common subscription of a Voltaire, a Diderot, a Helvétius, and even a d'Holbach to both the constitutional separation of powers and the political cooperation with enlightened autocrats indicates a problem intrinsic to the constitutional and political thinking of the Enlightenment. The vacillation which we have seen in the radical group, moreover, between a belief in the democratic principle behind all governments and a pluralistic standard of effective governmental forms is another expression of the same kind of problem. The doctrines of *laissez-faire* and socialism bring this problem to a head and point the way to its solution. They bring the problem to a head because their analyses of men's economic activities and property relations were clearly attempts to bring natural philosophy to bear upon the most concrete and practical of all human interests, but these doctrines were at the same time abstract, simplistic, and utopian models separated from the inconvenient complexities of economic and social existence. Like the ideal of constitutional government and the principle of consent, they too required political action from outside the economic and social process before they could become the economic and social realities they claimed to be.

The key to this paradox between a practical kind of human ideal and the reliance upon an extraneous means to make men practice it can be found in an analysis of the frank Physiocratic defense of "legal despotism" as the political regime most appropriate to the antipodal liberal economics of *laissez-faire*. In the form given the notion of legal despotism by its chief proponents, Mercier de la Rivière and Du Pont de Nemours, it referred to the necessary despotism of the natural law, which imposed itself on men with "the irresistible force of truth" and which could be expressed only by a corresponding "personal despotism." Their explicit argument that the "despotism" of a natural order which prescribed the economic freedom of the individual could be administered only by a hereditary monarch and not by the individuals (or their representatives) who were the prime agents of this natural order revealed the three chief assumptions of eighteenth-century political and social theory:

First, the realistic quality of this theory consisted in the incorporation of material considerations within the thought but not in the consideration of how to get this thought into practice. Thus we must distinguish, when we assess these doctrines, between the earthiness in their ideas and the applicability of their ideas.

Second, the self-proclaimed practicality of Enlightenment political and social thinking entailed the further distinction between the practice of men within an established order and the practice of men required to get an order established. In the correspondence of a Voltaire or a Diderot with such "enlightened despots" as Frederick the Great, Joseph II, or Catherine the Great, as in the later political doctrine of a Kant, the ambiguous relations between constitutionalism and enlightened absolutism in Enlightenment thought are clarified into a call for the autocrats to create the conditions for a constitutional regime which could then become an operative reality on its own.

A third and final assumption of eighteenth-century political and social thought, following in turn from this distinction between the *de jure* independent social process that would maintain justice and the *de facto* political agency required to institute a reign of justice, postulated a fundamental ambivalence in the attitude toward the individual, whose liberty was deemed on the one hand essential to the movement of the social process but on the other hand inadequate, because of its partial function within the society, to the direction of the social process as a whole. The corollary of this ambivalence was the distinction between the freedom of individuals, whether singular or in combination, as the essential goal of collective action and the authority of institutions as the contingent sponsors of collective action. Thus whether the rights were those of Rousseau's democracy, the Physiocrats' *laissez-faire*, or Morelly's equal share in the communal property, they were conceived to be not in conflict with, but on a different level from, the visible rights of governments. Democracy, *laissez-faire*, socialism, were all, for the men of the Enlightenment, guiding ideas for those who happened to be in power.

The relationship between the liberal ideal and the practice of politics varied, to be sure, from country to country. In Great Britain, as befitted the vitality of its commercialized society and its representative form of government, the connection was closest. Not only did the political views of such prominent writers as David Hume and Sir William Blackstone (1723–1780) attempt simply to rationalize the existing constitution, but even the radicals associated their doctrines with actual movements for British parliamentary or American colonial reform. In France, as befitted the gaps between the absolute state and the society and the divisions within the class-torn society itself, the gulf between theory and actuality was far wider. Writers proposed their doctrines of a just constitution and a free society as counsel which the competing ministerial and aristocratic authorities should apply as the goals toward which their respective policies would tend.

In Germany, Austria, and Russia, finally, where the gap between active autocrats and passive societies was greatest, the doctrine of a just constitution and a free society was all but divested of any reality, whether present or future, and was assigned the status of a figurative and unattainable ideal of autocratic policy. The typical forms of political and social writing in central Europe were not political, social, or economic theory as such, but jurisprudence and Cameralism. These were theories that treated the fundamental questions of the state and the economy within the framework of the government and its policy. Through the influence of Christian Wolff, perpetuated during the mature Enlightenment through no less a publicist than Frederick the Great, the proper constitution of the state was made to consist in the proper policy of the ruler. Despite some direct borrowing of Physiocratic ideas by German officials the characteristic form of economic theory continued to be Cameralistic. The two outstanding mid-eighteenth-century Cameralists, the German Johann Heinrich von Justi (1717–1771) and the Austrian Count Josef von Sonnenfels (1733–1817), were both adept at turning the Enlightenment's liberal goals of individual and social welfare into canons of efficiency for the guidance of the monarchical administration.

But behind these national variations the common features of doctrine and the common assumptions of its role remained, and from them we may draw a composite sketch of the political and social theory characteristic of Europe's mature Enlightenment. By virtue of their very nature, men become real human beings only when they collaborate as free individuals with their fellows in a free society. Because individuals are nature's primary agents they are capable of acting freely within a free society, but because they are presently misguided and inevitably partial they are incapable now of instituting and ultimately of guaranteeing the generality of the rules for the operation of such a society. Enlightened by the *philosophes* in the understanding of the general laws of a free society, the political authorities (or "Legislators," as the *philosophes* preferred to call them) must use their traditional monopoly of social force to institute such a society and participate in its permanent guarantee. Once instituted, the free society is maintained by the harmonious activity of the free individuals within it and by the constitutional balance of social representatives and political authorities to prevent excesses both of individual rights and of governmental power. And as long as such a society has not been instituted and does not yet exist—a contingency which tallied, for almost all the *phi-*

losophes, with their contemporary situation—governments must prepare the way for it by making what would be the reality of this society the present ideal of governmental policy.

Philosophical History

Like the religious and ethical doctrines of the mature Enlightenment, the historical focus of the period further developed an interest already characteristic of the preceding phase. Like the practitioners of these other fields too, the historians of the mature Enlightenment gave substance to what had been only a program and a framework, but here the substance was not memorable doctrine but immortal monuments of historical literature.

Not, to be sure, that the *philosophes* showed themselves averse either to discussing the idea of history or to working out their favorite ideas in history—they were too fond of ideas in general and too conscious of their own educational mission to avoid either of these didacticisms. In Voltaire's historical prefaces—particularly in the 1756 introduction to the *Essay on the Manners and Spirit of Nations* which he entitled "The Philosophy of History"—the Enlightenment view of history received its authoritative formulation. Such formulations, indeed, became so much the style that when toward the end of the age the German philosopher and historian Johann Gottfried von Herder wanted to attack the rationalism and the pragmatism of Enlightenment history he published a counterformulation under the title *Another Philosophy of History for the Education of Humanity: Contribution to the Many Contributions of the Century* (1774).

But more characteristic of the mature Enlightenment's idea of history than this programmatic philosophy of history was the "philosophical history" which sketched the general history of humanity in order to prove the reality of one or another principle of human nature by demonstrating its role in furnishing rational coherence to the course of human history. Voltaire's *Essay on the Manners and Spirit of Nations* was the most famous of these philosophical histories, with its renunciation of the traditional historical focus on political leaders and western Christian culture and with its affirmation that all men everywhere were the subjects of history and that their struggle for rationality was the unifying principle of history. Turgot's lectures of 1750 on the "progress of the human spirit," with their stress on innovation as the force and progress as the principle of the human species, and Adam Ferguson's *Essay on the History of Civil Society* of 1767, with its stress on the role of social instincts in the origins of organized society and on the role of the civic virtues in its preservation, indicate that Voltaire's was not an isolated performance. None of these cases of what came to be called "theoretical" history was itself a notable work of historical literature (although a forerunner's status has been accorded Voltaire's for cultural history and Ferguson's for historical sociology), but together they did contribute three features to the modern idea of history. First, there is a connectedness and a meaning in human history that comes from something constant and fundamental in men themselves. Second, not only the politics and wars of kings but all kinds of activities of all kinds of men can have significance for the understanding of human nature and therefore for history when they serve as authentic ingredients of the moral "spirit" that connects the historical actions of men. Third, such coherent actions are not only to be found in history–they are the only authentic history. Actions that are trivial and unconnected, like the traditional political chronicles, are not historical and should remain beneath the notice of an historian.

Not the abstract statement of these principles, however, but the actual historical works in which they were applied have proved to be immortal in Enlightenment historiography. Voltaire's *Age of Louis XIV* (1751), Hume's *History of England* (1754–1762), William Robertson's *History of the Reign of the Emperor Charles* V, *with a View of the Progress of Society in Europe from the Subversion of the Roman Empire to the Beginning of the Sixteenth Century* (1769), and Gibbon's *Decline and Fall of the Roman Empire* (1776–1788) can be said to mark the beginning of modern historical literature. Previous histories had been valued, and have been valued since, for the religious or political points of view they served, for the historical sources they collected, or—as accounts of contemporary events—for the historical sources they themselves were. Now, for the first time, historical commentaries on a grand scale sought both to record and explain broad swaths of a definite human past from a point of view that was designed both to understand this past and to relate the historians' present to it.

These historians were all *philosophes* in good standing, representatives par excellence of the Enlightenment, and as such they have all been indicted for an unhistorical bias at least as great as that of the tendentious predecessors they attacked. It is undeniable that the attitudes which they brought to bear upon history did limit what we have come to consider a genuine sense of history. Their operative notion that not only human nature but human motivation was constant in all ages; the exaltation of the rational principle that led them to exclude the recalcitrant detail as trivial and to deprecate ages, institutions, and men of faith as noxious; their actual persistence, despite their pretensions to the contrary, in concentrating on politics as the representative strand of cultural history: these characteristic features of the Enlightenment world view that have made for its unhistorical reputation were undoubtedly visible in even its premier historians.

But in the great histories of the period these features were combined fruitfully with other equally characteristic features of the Enlightenment—notably, with its addiction to scientific method, its attention to the specific

Edward Gibbon. *Author of* The Decline and Fall of the Roman Empire, *the greatest historical work of the eighteenth century.*

identity of any particular fact, its skepticism toward traditional truths, its fascination with the human psyche, and its awareness of the social context in which it saw its politics. Thus Gibbon's ideal of "the philosophical historian" who selects from "the vast chaos of events" the facts "that dominate the general system" and arrives thereby at "the general causes" which "change the face of the earth" is to be judged not by the statement itself but by the historical function he makes it play. Outstanding in *The Decline and Fall*, far overshadowing the occasional errors, the intrusive anti-Christianity, the aristocratic preferences, and the curious modernity of Gibbons' ancient Romans, is the blend of vast canvas with precise scholarship, of panoramic composition with the startling clarity of every detail. In an early description of his historising, Gibbon revealed his desire always to immerse his ideas in his historical materials, an immersion characteristic of all Enlightenment thought. However, his judgment that in the final analysis "we must be careful not to make the order of our thoughts subservient to that of our subjects" was equally characteristic of Enlightenment thought. And so it is that through the awesome research, the colorful drama, and the majestic style for which *The Decline and Fall* is justly celebrated, Gibbon wove a fine mesh of narrative coherence, composing all kinds of variations on a fundamental theme—the destruction of "the solid fabric of human greatness"—and fulfilling his grand purpose of connecting "the ancient and modern history of the World."

In their lesser ways the other notable historians of the mature Enlightenment manifested a similar blend of the qualities that made the movement the sire of modern history. Political as was their emphasis and distorting as was their preference for the ancient and modern over the medieval stages of Western civilization, they too avoided the extremes of compilation and of theoretical exposition. Voltaire and Hume organized historical events around the patterns of nationality, while Robertson prefaced his detailed narrative history of sixteenth-century Europe's most ambitious emperor (the Habsburg Charles V) with a comprehensive survey of the tendencies which converged into the "one great political system" characteristic of modern times. Thus did the Enlightenment's concern for general principle become, in the practicing historian, the attention to a cohesive historical process within which each event had its place.

Far from representing a soft spot in eighteenth-century thought, the best history produced by the mature Enlightenment reflected as faithfully as any other field of its culture the attitude that would become its legacy to Western civilization. This attitude engendered a profound respect for the reality of every natural and human fact that played a role in a larger structure of meaning; and conversely it taught men to look for the general principles which make up the framework of meaning only in the fabric of facts and to trim this fabric in accordance with the nature of the facts. It was a delicate balance that could last only as long as facts and principles were in equipoise and as long as all facts and principles that were respectively incompatible were excluded from consideration. But the nostalgia with which men still hearken back to this age that has recently and admiringly been labeled the age of "humanity" signalizes its unforgettable, if evanescent, success in reconciling the most fundamental of human desires: to give the individual a stable identity and to discover the unity which associates individuals in common enterprises and gives to the life of each its direction and its meaning.

CHAPTER 18

The Unworldly Philosophers, 1770-1789

ORIGINATING AT the very height of the mature Enlightenment as a kind of fugal counterpoint to it, a new cultural movement gradually arose to dominate the last third of the eighteenth century. Not, of course, that the Enlightenment simply disappeared. The familiar figures and their disciples did continue to spread illumination in their wonted way. The giants of the mature Enlightenment—Voltaire, Diderot, d'Alembert, Mably, Gibbon, Wieland, and Lessing—continued to write well into the decade of the 1770's, and in some cases, the 1780's. When they fell silent, their message was taken up by a host of lesser figures—such as the radical historian Guillaume Raynal in France, the rationalistic systematizer of utilitarian morality William Paley in Great Britain, and the Enlightened journalists August Ludwig von Schlözer and Christoph Nicolai in Germany. But the movement no longer possessed, in these protagonists, its wonted flexibility, its creativity, and its power to attract the best of the new intellectual talent. These qualities passed in part to a radically opposed group, which is now usually called "preromantic," who abominated everything the Enlightenment stood for. But an even more critical sign of the decay of the Enlightenment may be seen in the identities of the other groups who succeeded the *philosophes* in dominating the cultural life of the last third of the century: they were heirs of the Enlightenment, and their development into cultural independence demonstrated the incipient disintegration of the parent movement.

The soul of the Enlightenment and the force of its typical doctrines inhered, as we have seen, in the flexible balance which the *philosophes* poised between variety and unity, individuality and generality, reality and meaning, experience and purpose, movement and stability, pleasure and principle—equivalent but antithetical values which they had to keep adjusting within the natural realm once they had excluded a supernatural realm. Since it was rather the balance and the communication maintained by the *philosophes* among these diverse factors than any homogeneous lineup of compatible factors that was the essence of the mature Enlighten-

ment, the cultural movements which succeeded it in the last third of the
century could be powered as much by men who deliberately upset the balance by espousing the supremacy of one or another of the Enlightenment's
own values as by men who espoused the supremacy of values outside the
entire syndrome of the Enlightenment.

Thus the passing of the Enlightenment should be seen not as a simple
mechanical case of petrifaction and reaction, but as an articulated cultural
process in which developments from the Enlightenment provided a linkage between the Enlightenment itself and the revulsion against it. This
polyphonic structure of the post-Enlightenment exhibits a cultural pattern
far more integrated than the usual mechanical image of Enlightenment
action and preromantic reaction indicates. Not one but three kinds of
intellectual movements between 1770 and 1789 were putting an end to the
Enlightenment and embalming its remains for the edification of posterity.
First, what has been called the "radicalization" of the Enlightenment was
actually the one-sided development of its rational ordering principles into
the rigid systems of atheism, determinism, and inevitable progress, represented by such figures as d'Holbach, Laplace, and Condorcet. Second,
what has been erroneously included in the reaction against the Enlightenment was actually the one-sided development of its individualizing, liberalizing, and dynamic principles into the utilitarian, sentimental, idealistic,
naturalistic, and evolutionary creeds represented by such figures as Bent-

Beatrice addressing Dante from the Car (Purgatorio, Canto **XXIX**). *Painting
by William Blake, the British mystic, artist, poet whose revulsion against the
rationality and the practicality of the Enlightenment betokened the dawn of
another cultural era. National Gallery, London.*

ham, Rousseau, Kant, Godwin, and Lamarck. Third, the authentic revolt against the Enlightenment was actually a rejection of the *philosophes* and all their works on behalf of individual, anarchic, and demonic powers entirely outside the Enlightenment syndrome. Represented by the German school of *Sturm und Drang* ("storm and stress"), by organicists like Burke, and by mystics like Blake, this revolt was a preromantic movement of an aesthetic character, but it did appropriate ideas from the sentimental, classical, and dynamic offshoots of the Enlightenment for its intellectual content.

The age which was dominated in thought by this three-pronged cultural movement was an age which was dominated in action by the eruption of revolutionary situations in many of the European states. The development out of and against the Enlightenment may be seen as a kind of cultural revolution which peaked in anticipation of the subsequent political and social revolution in France. The detailed consideration of the three strands of this intellectual revolution will show the first forms taken by the typical revolutionary parties of modern times: the party that desires a radical execution of the systematic order promised by the Old Regime; the party that desires a radical execution of the freedom promised but compromised by the Old Regime; and the extreme party that wants no part of the Old Regime and would inaugurate an age categorically new.

But if this cultural revolution that climaxed the Old Regime anticipated the forms of modern revolutionary practice, and if it helped to prepare men's minds and their spirits for what they would do with political and social revolution after it came, it is also important to realize that the one revolution did not in fact cause the other. We must investigate all three parties of the intellectual revolution to understand the exclusively intellectual resolution that they gave to social tensions and the free field that they left to the more material and tangible interests of men in the initiation of the political and social revolution of 1789.

THE NEW RATIONALISM

Most closely akin to the Enlightenment and frequently characterized by posterity as its radical phase, the rigorous rationalism that flourished in the last quarter of the eighteenth century was actually a successor movement. The heirs of the *philosophes* resolved the tensions of the Enlightenment in the name of Enlightenment, but in a way that belied it. They reconverted its delicate "systematic spirit" into the rigid "spirit of systems" by developing its logical, rational, necessary facet at the expense of the individual, the experimental, and the voluntaristic.

The nodal figure in the transition from the flexible reasonableness of the *philosophes* to the intransigent rationalism of their successors was the Baron Paul Henri d'Holbach (1723–1789), author of the fashionable

Joseph Priestley. *British chemist, physicist, theologian, and democratic political theorist.*

Christianity Unmasked (1767), participant in the intellectual enterprises of the *philosophes*, and host at one of their liveliest salons. From 1770 to 1776 he published, under various pseudonyms, the series of volumes on natural and moral philosophy which developed the characteristic Enlightenment notions of reason, nature, utility, and humanity into a simple and unbending atheism, materialism, and fatalism. "All is in order in nature, no part of which can ever vary from the certain and necessary rules which issue from its inherent essence."

This renewal of dogmatic materialism earned d'Holbach refutations from such stalwarts as Voltaire and Frederick the Great, among others, but his viewpoint was increasingly shared by that intellectual barometer of the age, Denis Diderot, and independently, by that provocative blend of scientist, theologian, and philosopher, Joseph Priestley. In themselves, materialism, determinism, and even atheism—d'Holbach and Diderot were obviously atheists—were not anything new for the Enlightenment. At least La Mettrie and Helvétius had been of a similar persuasion in their conception of nature without bringing the Enlightenment to a final crisis. What gave these doctrines their lethal force in the last third of the century was their association with ideas of man's freedom and their influence in turning these ideas into radical dogmas. D'Holbach, Diderot, and Priestley all elaborated doctrines of moral or political liberty alongside their doctrines of natural necessity, and the logical rigor of the latter carried over into the former, subordinating the familiar Enlightenment notion of a moderate constitutional freedom to the categorical rational principles of an infallible general will or an unqualified and homogeneous law of nature. However modest their practical recommendations remained, the uncompromising statement of these underlying principles gave to the political doctrines of d'Holbach and

Priestley and to the moral protests of Diderot a radical tone that differed essentially from the reasonable aura of the Enlightenment. Thus, d'Holbach shared the general inclination of eighteenth-century Europeans to depend on the established rulers for the initiative in political and social reform, but his subordination of politics to the uniformity of his natural law gave a sweeping quality and trenchant tone to his demands for the removal of specific restraints and abuses. Similarly, both Diderot and Priestley shared the eighteenth-century intellectual's suspicion of the masses and tended to trust only the propertied middle classes with political rights, but once again the equal subordination of all individual things and men to their rigorous notion of natural law endowed their moderate political proposals with a radical egalitarian overtone that announced the onset of the post-Enlightenment era.

The emphatic rationalism to which d'Holbach, Priestley, and the later Diderot were the transitional figures had, like them, both a scientific and a political tendency.

The notable scientists of the post-Enlightenment era confirmed its tendency, if not to materialism specifically, at least to the rigorous rationality represented in the resurgence of mathematics. The mathematical determinism which Pierre Laplace (1749–1827) developed in this period grew ultimately into what is probably the most extreme and the most famous formulation of it ever penned: "An intellect which at any given moment would know all the forces that animate nature and would know the mutual positions of the beings that compose nature—if this intellect were vast enough to submit its data to analysis—could condense into a single formula the movement of the greatest bodies of the universe and that of the lightest atom. For such an intellect nothing could be uncertain; and the future, like the past, would be present before its eyes." Joseph Lagrange (1736–1813), Laplace's contemporary of equal mathematical genius, was impelled by the same faith in predictability on the basis of universal natural law to write his classic, *Analytical Mechanics* (1788), which abstracted from the physical and geometric (that is, spatial) properties of matter and turned the science of matter in motion—the science of mechanics—into a purely rational discipline, a perfect system of mechanical laws deduced from a few simple formulas through a sequence of differential equations.

It was in this same period, moreover, and under these same intellectual auspices that Antoine Laurent Lavoisier (1743–1794) reorganized chemistry into a modern science—notably in his *Elements of Chemistry* (1789)—essentially by quantifying and systematizing it. He reduced the phenomena of combustion to a "simple principle" ("the oxygenic principle"). He undertook a "new arrangement of chemistry" in which he recommended less attention to assembling facts and observations, and more attention "to classifying them" and to locating them in the proper

Luigi Galvani's experiments with frogs (1780). *Along with Alessandro Volta and Charles Coulomb in the same period, Galvani demonstrated the continuity of electrical current and contributed thereby to the substitution of physical for moral connections in nature.*

"part of the whole to which they pertain." He reformed the nomenclature of chemistry in conformity with "natural logic," that is, with "the natural order in the succession of ideas." By making precise experimentation and quantitative observation the basis of primary principles in a logically integrated chemistry, Lavoisier resolved the former tension between the uniformity of natural law and the multiformity of chemical phenomena in favor of the natural law. Nor was his pattern of resolution an isolated one: his contemporary Charles Coulomb (1736–1806) was performing an analogous service for the science of electricity when he worked exact measurements into "Coulomb's law" of electrical attraction on the Newtonian model. These scientific developments embodied an essential quality of the neo-rationalism which helped to dissolve the intellectual synthesis of the Enlightenment: the appreciation of particular realities and the importance of observing them precisely—values which the men of the Enlightenment had endowed with an autonomous status—were still acknowledged by the post-Enlightenment rationalists, but now they were integrated into overriding rational systems of natural law.

The characteristic note of the 1770's and 1780's in the human sciences—i.e., in the literature on human nature, society, and history—has often been defined as "radical," and in terms of emphasis, passion, and thoroughness in criticism of existing abuses the characterization undoubtedly fits. But in terms of intellectual content, this kind of writing is better understood as the social and political component of the new rationalism, imparting to the study of society a systematic quality which generalized the individual liberties of the Enlightenment in a way that was analogous to the contemporary scientific emphasis on generalizing particular observations. Like this scientific emphasis, the new social and political rationalism was in many ways continuous with the Enlightenment and was regarded by protagonists and antagonists alike as an integral part of it, but, again like the scientific emphasis of the age, it manifested a runaway universalism that actually betokened a growth out of rather than within the Enlightenment. There were, moreover, personal connections between the two branches of the new rationalism. The Marquis de Condorcet (1743–1794), one of the most prominent of the social rationalists, not only was an able mathematician but explicitly replaced teleology with science to ensure the strict lawfulness of human progress. Again, *The Philosophical and Political History of European Settlements and Trade in the East and West Indies,* whose ever more daring revisions between 1770 and 1780 made it a popular reservoir for radical sentiment and turned its presumed author, Abbé Guillaume Raynal (1713–1796), into an exile from his native France, was actually a compendium by Raynal of conversations and contributions from several sources, most notably from d'Holbach's salon and Diderot's pen.

The historic function of these so-called radicals, indeed, was not to develop new revolutionary ideologies, but rather to put a new emphasis on the drastic opposition of the Enlightenment's familiar social and political doctrines to contemporary social and political practice. The radicals were closely attuned to the agitated social and political scene of the 1770's and 1780's, and their writings registered their sympathy with the agitators— with the Americans, the British parliamentary reformers, and the anti-aristocratic French pressure group around Turgot. These sympathies took the form of a sharper tone, a more sweeping criticism, a more categorical condemnation, of established church and state than ever before, as the intellectuals became impatient with the compromise of rational principles and asserted them in ever greater purity. Thus the notorious radicalism of Raynal and his cohorts—as of the aging Voltaire—was directed primarily at the church on behalf of reason, and the rise of Freemasonry during the last decades of the Old Regime confirmed the hardening of anticlericalism into a rationalist dogma. When they did turn to practical policies, "radicals" like Mably (in his pro-American *Observations on the Government and Laws of the United States of America,* 1784), Richard Price (in his equally pro-American *Observations on the Importance of the American Revolution and the Means of Making It a Benefit to the World,* 1784), Joseph Priestley (in his utopian *Lectures on History and General Policy,* 1788), and Condorcet (in his essays of 1788 on the European relevance of the American Revolution) asserted the universality of the principles of natural rights for all men that underlay the American Revolution and the necessity of leveling European aristocratic institutions in the light of them, but they also were unanimous in limiting political rights to men of property, divided on the issue of a unicameral or bicameral legislature, and silent on the question of how the reforms would be realized. Only the future leader of the Girondin party in the French Revolution, Jacques Pierre Brissot de Warville (1754–1793), was a genuine revolutionary before the revolution, and in him it was a matter of an even more unqualified and systematic application of universal human rights than his like-minded contemporaries would face up to. In general, the swift pace, after 1776, of events they did not make left the radical rationalists further and further out of the real world they could not master.

For the most part, these political rationalists thus were prepared to welcome revolutions when they came (Raynal would not even do this), but they did not create the kind of doctrine that would start revolutions. None developed a program that called for popular political action, though all gave new emphasis to the people's right to political representation as an inviolable universal natural right that kings should grant or history realize—some day. Condorcet's formula made the attainment of civil liberty and social equality not, as formerly, the problematic issue of the struggle between personal utility and general law, but the inevitable, predictable product of the general laws that ensured the progress of humanity and the perfectibility of its nature. This formula, resolving the problem of freedom by making it a function of universal law, epitomized the physical and political rationalism that the dissolution of the Enlightenment deposited into the stream of European history.

THE NEW FREEDOM

A second principal legacy of the Enlightenment, similarly detached during the last third of the eighteenth century from its associations with the other principles of the mature Enlightenment, was the intense focus upon individual freedom and the effort to construct a system of values based entirely upon it. This tendency was intermediate between the radical rationalism that claimed to represent the Enlightenment and the preromantic revulsion aimed deliberately against the Enlightenment, and it combined characteristics from each movement. Like the rationalists, the new libertarians made predominant one of the values that had been balanced in the mature Enlightenment, and they hypostatized this value in order to resolve the tensions and frictions of its uneasy equilibrium. Thus they made primary the kind of human being that the *philosophes* had conceived—that is, one who found moral fulfillment in a social system. But like the preromantics the new libertarians rejected, as antithetical to individual freedom, the constant and universal kind of natural law that the Enlightenment had set up vis-à-vis the liberty of individual action as its controlling principle.

The result was a wholly distinctive program: the construction of a new kind of rational system, both in respect to the knowledge of nature and in the organization of society, that would realize rather than restrict the liberty of individuals. As the rationalists reduced liberty and particularity to logical functions of their rational systems, the libertarians reduced reason and society to moral functions of their individualistic systems.

One of the incongruities of European intellectual history is the number of eighteenth-century movements with some relationship to the Enlightenment that remained influential in the nineteenth century, when men were otherwise rejecting the Enlightenment. The explanation of the incongruity lies precisely in the way the Enlightenment dissolved during the last third of the eighteenth century. The movements in question—Bentham's utilitarianism, Rousseau's naturalism, Kant's idealism, and Lamarck's evolutionism—all developed from the individualistic libertarian strand of the unraveled Enlightenment, and hence they were historically both related to and independent of the Enlightenment itself. But there was an important historical distinction within this strand of movements—the distinction between those that acknowledged the Enlightenment as the source for their doctrines of individual freedom and developed beyond it unconscious of their departure from it, and those that came to revile the Enlightenment for its static and stringent laws of reason and developed beyond it unconscious of their debt to it. The founders of utilitarianism and idealism were in the first category; the progenitors of naturalism and evolutionism were in the second.

Bentham's Utilitarianism

The utilitarianism of Jeremy Bentham (1748–1832) grew naturally out of its eighteenth-century soil. The principle of utility had been announced in the early Enlightenment. The doctrine of utility had been developed in the mature Enlightenment. With all due and grateful acknowledgments to Hume for the first and to Helvétius, Beccaria, and Priestley for the second, Bentham worked the principle and the doctrine into the full-blown theory of utilitarianism, the main lines of which were laid down in works as early as his *Fragment on Government* (1776) and his *Introduction to the Principles of Morals and Legislation* (1789). Bentham has been adjudged an ambiguous intellectual figure. His utilitarian ideas, his analytical approach, and his reasonable tone all aligned him with the *philosophes*. But his starting point and his ultimate effect depended heavily upon his decisive rejection of their most cherished doctrine. The primacy of the individual-pleasure principle in the constitution of human nature, of the greatest-happiness principle in the ideal of society, of practical results in moral

Jeremy Bentham. *Founder of Utilitarianism.*

judgments, of *laissez-faire* in economics, and of a proper legislation in directing individual pleasure toward social morality—all these Benthamite ideas came straight out of the Enlightenment. They reflected not only its belief in individuals as the prime units of human reality but also its conception of the potentiality in these individuals for rational and ethical association. But in his categorical rejection of both the reality and the validity of natural law as a moral principle that guaranteed the harmony of individual and social utility, Bentham attacked the fundamental bond which the *philosophes* had used to assure this kind of association.

But this apparent ambiguity of Bentham's toward the Enlightenment disappears when Bentham is seen as one of the new libertarians who sought to free the utility-seeking individual from any a priori bondage, whether of privilege or principle, and sought only to erect a legal system based on the harmonizing of such individual utilities. Thus his fundamental convictions established the primacy of the individual: only the individual could judge what was useful to him; this judgment required the freedom to act upon it; the assumption of a priori, universal laws of nature was irrelevant and injurious to the freedom of this individual judgment. But he also erected an alternative rational system of measuring utility which he deemed consistent with individual liberty. He held that the rigorous deduction of a "calculus" of pleasures and pains to serve as the bond of a just and rational society was appropriate and salubrious for the freedom of individual judgment. Bentham thus built the self-interest of the individual into the common interest of the society through a set of moral and legal propositions which validated security and equality as well as civil liberties. Yet they remained for him derivative from individualism because they were constructed on the consequences of individual freedom rather than on the prescriptions of an a priori principle other than individual freedom.

Idealism

The German analogue of British utilitarianism was idealism, for it too had an important root in the liberal strand of the eighteenth-century Enlightenment and dominated its nation for almost half of the nineteenth century. It rose in late-eighteenth-century Germany and spanned the greatest age of thought and letters that Germany has ever known. "Idealism" in this context has both a specific and a general reference. Specifically, it refers to the philosophical position, dominant in these years, that made the world we know and act in primarily a product of ideas or mind. More generally, it refers to the cultural attitude, dominant in philosophers, men of letters, composers, and statesmen, that made the conscious infusion of spiritual ideals into neutral or refractory existence, both natural and social, the task of the generation. In its more general sense the German age of idealism was manifest in many branches of intellectual and artistic activity, and the function of the Enlightenment as an important root of German idealism is visible in each of these branches. In music, the development of both Haydn and Mozart from the melodious regularity and symmetry of their earlier works to the more moving, varied, and freely articulated mode of addressing the interior self of the individual listener in their quartets and operas from the 1780's, represent dramatic cases of the connection between the classic style of the Enlightenment and the style of spiritualized idealism in central Europe. This same connection is found in the more prosaic works of Lessing and Kant. In both, the relationship between the balanced reasonableness of the Enlightenment and the libertarian emphasis of early idealism was a matter of continuous growth and vital interaction.

Lessing, like Diderot, was one of the *philosophes* who initiated freelance writing as an independent, paid (usually underpaid) profession. Until the 1770's Lessing divided his efforts between collaborating with the leaders of the German Enlightenment in typical criticisms of the Christian establishment on behalf of reason and composing pioneer works of literature, literary criticism, and aesthetic theory in praise of individual dignity, sentiment, imagination, passion, and the individuality of the arts. In this latter line of his activity Lessing strained but did not yet rupture the orderly bounds of the Enlightenment. His epoch-making play, *Minna von Barnhelm* (1767), did indeed exalt the private honor and sensibilities of definite individuals, but it portrayed them in inevitable and equal conflict with the morality of society. In his *Laokoon* (1766), now a classic of aesthetic theory, he loosened the structure of aesthetics so as to provide for the individuality of each art form—especially for poetry in distinction from the plastic arts—but still within each of these art forms he insisted that

Gotthold Ephraim Lessing. *German playwright, literary critic, philosopher, and free-lance* philosophe.

universal criteria of beauty applied. He criticized the drama of Voltaire and declared the superiority of Shakespeare, but both on the contemporaneously acceptable grounds of fidelity to nature. Only in 1780, with the publication of his *Education of Humanity*, did the unflagging vigor, the passion for authenticity in any shape, and the elasticity of the rational impulse which had given Lessing a special place within the Enlightenment lead him beyond it. What had been a plea for toleration in *Nathan the Wise* now became a design for the internalization of the moral unity of mankind within each individual, to be realized by each in his own way.

Immanuel Kant, whose staid manner of life and placid career stood in marked contrast to Lessing's restless wandering and volatile spirit, traversed nonetheless a similar road to cultural immortality. Raised in the rationalism of Christian Wolff, the foremost philosopher of the German Enlightenment, Kant, like Lessing, spent most of his intellectual career in its service, revamping its framework of reason to sit more comfortably upon the variety of the realities it acknowledged in men and things. In the first—and the greatest—volume of his critical philosophy, the *Critique of Pure Reason* (1781), Kant took a fruitfully ambiguous stance precisely between the Enlightenment and a revolutionary position beyond it. On the one hand, he sought to save the Enlightenment's operation of reason as the unifying principle of human knowledge by defining the limits of the reality it could unify. On the other hand, he drastically shifted both the scope and the basis of this "theoretical reason" by excluding all but self-criticism and men's experience of nature from its proper field of employment and by making it entirely a common and necessary function of every individual's mind rather than, as previously, a correspondence between the mind and a natural or supernatural ordering principle outside the mind.

In the decade that followed, Kant moved definitely beyond the Enlightenment by developing an entirely different kind of reason to order the individualized kind of reality which was inaccessible to theoretical

Immanuel Kant. *Partisan of the Enlightenment who recognized its limits and went beyond them, Kant is frequently acknowledged as the most important Western philosopher since Plato. He shifted the core of human experience from something given to men from without to something that men help to make for themselves from the beginning.*

reason, but he never entirely gave up the connection with the Enlightenment, which now assumed a contrapuntal position in his thought. Indeed, in his smaller essays of 1784 he gave currency to the term "Enlightenment." He declared that "we do live in an age of Enlightenment" and he wrote a prescription for it: "Have the courage to use your own reason" (in his "What is Enlightenment?"). He also developed a theory of a rational progress toward freedom (in his "Idea for a Universal History") that has been deemed the epitome of the faith of the Enlightenment. But his major effort during this decade was expended in the construction of a system of "practical reason," a new kind of rationality that divorced the universal moral law from its familiar ground in nature and from its familiar source in man's knowledge of nature, and based it instead squarely on the ultimate reality of individual freedom by making it the necessary form of the direction the individual gave himself (chiefly in his *Critique of Practical Reason,* 1788).

At the very end of the decade which coincided with the end of Europe's Old Regime, Kant completed the final volume of his great philosophical trilogy. In it he worked his simultaneous commitment to and transcendence of the Enlightenment into a coherent pattern that both acknowledged its due place in the cultural future and led posterity beyond it. In the *Critique of Judgment,* published in 1790, Kant formulated this double-edged testimonial in two ways. First, this work climaxed the critical use of reason which his trilogy shared, as a general approach, with the Enlightenment, but it also announced the next stage of thought to be the construction of a "system . . . under the general name of Metaphysic"—a prescription for the future that the men of the Enlightenment could never have lived with. Second, in the substance of its argument the *Critique of*

Judgment asserted, just as the Enlightenment had, the validity of both natural laws and moral freedom and the necessity of finding a connection between them, but it revealed the growing tendency to go beyond the Enlightenment in satisfying this necessity. For Kant sought the connection in the judgment of individual things, and he found it in the artistic creation of men and in the self-directing organic forms of nature, both of which put the unity of reason in the service of the ultimate individuality of the free act. Only if the rational ideal of the Enlightenment is considered no longer as the goal but henceforward rather as the condition of human rights, according to Kant, is all of reality accounted for and does life have meaning. And with this step, he moved definitely beyond the Enlightenment and bore witness to its conversion from a movement into a heritage.

Naturalism

The propagators of naturalism in the last quarter of the eighteenth century exhibited a much more jaundiced view of the Enlightenment than did its loyal idealist sons, but they actually manifested essentially the same kind of legacy. The outstanding representative of the naturalist vogue was Rousseau, whose vociferous complaints against the rational universalism in the Enlightenment's view of nature obscured his own debt to the moral passion and individual freedom which the Enlightenment also derived from nature. The familiar interpretation of his development beyond the Enlightenment as a revolt against it seems confirmed by his personal estrangement from the *philosophes*. There is little doubt that he withdrew deliberately from their circle or that they considered him a "deserter" and poured contempt on him for his apostasy. But the character of the estrangement suggests not a complete separation but something rather more in the nature of a sibling rivalry. For Rousseau broke most directly and most violently with Diderot and with Voltaire, precisely the *philosophes* who influenced him most deeply in two of his most characteristic attitudes. Rousseau visited and was profoundly impressed by Diderot just before writing the *Discourse on the Arts and Sciences* (1750), whose theme of the contrast between the goodness of nature and the viciousness of artificial intellectuality was a favorite of Diderot's as well. Again, Rousseau acknowledged the shock that Voltaire's work on the 1755 Lisbon earthquake—"Poem on the Lisbon Disaster"—gave him, focusing his attention on the problem of evil that would henceforth bulk so large in his thinking and writing.

Rousseau himself claimed that all his works, from the beginning of his career to the end, were fashioned on "the same principle," but certainly he shifted his ideas of how to apply it. His break with the *philosophes* in the latter part of the 1750's—*after* his formulation of such characteristic attitudes as his exaltation of natural liberty against intellectual and social oppression in his discourses *On the Arts and Sciences* (1750) and *On the*

Jean Jacques Rousseau. *Tormented ex*-philosophe *who showed the limits of Enlightened values. Bust by Jean-Antoine Houdon. Louvre, Paris.*

Origins of Inequality (1755), and *after* his promulgation of the idea of the general will in the "Discourse on Political Economy" (1758), which he wrote for the *Encyclopedia*—symbolized the different way he would go to realize ideals which he had begun by sharing in good measure with his contemporaries. His rupture with the society of the *philosophes* was related to his conviction that the natural integrity of man was vitiated by the withdrawal of the rational faculty into a segregated realm of abstract communication, where it was associated with respectable society and divorced from action by individuals who would level this society. Rousseau continued to endorse the synthesizing ideas that the *philosophes* held to give men and things their order and direction—the reason of men, the laws of nature, the morality of society, and the deistic belief in a providential Creator—but he insisted on relocating them in the individual self and redefining them as the personal impulse, awareness, and conscience from which all social order must come. Consequently, Rousseau set himself the two-fold task of dramatizing the existing evils inherent in the artificial division of what should be united—instinct and reason, acting and thinking, individuals and society—and of constructing models of how the underlying nature of man could, were it not for psychic and social repression, develop reason, law, and society harmoniously out of the original instincts, liberties, and sovereignty of the individual. Since these tasks involved the dissolution of the loose and tolerant balance of the Enlightenment and the reorganization of its elements into a complex unity poised on its narrow individualistic and libertarian base, Rousseau's mature works mix values that were familiar to the Enlightenment with tendencies that modified them in a definite direction.

La Nouvelle Héloïse (1761), a sentimental, moralizing novel in the popular tradition of Richardson's *Pamela* and Rousseau's greatest contemporary success, departed from the Enlightenment's standards primarily in its puritanical attitude toward sex, an attitude that seemed to square so ill with Rousseau's naturalism but that would be confirmed in the guilt-ridden obsessions of his *Confessions*. In contrast to the *philosophes'* compliant enjoyment of sensuality as an intrinsic boon of nature, Rousseau's rigidity in matters of sex typified a larger rejection, exemplified as well in the disapproval of theater which led to a break with d'Alembert, of sensory pleasures in principle and of any sophisticated art or science on the ground that they were diversionary, detached from the whole man, and obstructive of his freedom of action. In *Émile* (1762), Rousseau's educational treatise in the form of a novel, he followed a well-worn path when he proposed a regular scheme of secular education as the best means of conducting individuals to morality, but he departed from the norm with his thesis that moral education consisted not in the inculcation of rationality or sociality but in the simple provision of opportunities for the individual to be undisturbed in his natural growth into rationality and sociality.

The *Social Contract* (1762), finally, was typical in its exaltation of liberty as the source, contract as the sanction, law as the standard, and collective reason as the agency of the good society, but however familiar the political function of these ideas remained, in Rousseau they no longer had quite the same status or the same meaning as they did for his contemporaries. Liberty was no longer deemed a possession to be preserved, but was regarded as the continuing condition necessary for action of any kind; contract was no longer an instrument of obligation, but of self-elevation to social action; law no longer an eternal rule of nature, but the product of social action; reason no longer the capacity to recognize universal law or calculate public welfare, but the socializing faculty that gave every individual will an equal share in the general will to act. The meaning of these terms was conditioned by the purpose of the *Social Contract*: to show how every individual could enjoy the practical and the moral advantages of society and "still obey himself alone, and remain as free as before." Hence these terms no longer referred to a stable political order compatible with freedom, but to stages in a developing process driven throughout by freedom. The *Social Contract* was thus the complement of *Emile*: its "general will" was a higher freeedom for all the individuals within a society, just as Émile's "conscience" was the higher freedom for all the faculties within the individual. In the human society as in the human psyche, freedom consisted in the never-ending interaction between the spontaneous variety and the self-controlled organization of all the elements in human nature.

It was precisely because Rousseau built a seamless continuum from the elemental drives of the isolated savage to the infallible moral will of the sovereign legislative power that he has proved so ambiguous, and has been invoked for causes ranging from primitivism to idealism, from anarchism to despotism. But this very ambiguity testifies to his historical role: he took seriously and simply the Enlightenment's commitment to both the freedom of individuals and the unity of their purpose, but where his contemporaries accepted the duality and mediated between the two, resigning themselves to compromise where need be, Rousseau strove for a total system of freedom.

Although Rousseau's major work was done well within the era of the mature Enlightenment, his positive influence began to tell only after this era had begun to wane, in the last third of the eighteenth century. This influence made itself felt in two directions. The more obvious and direct effect was on the preromantics (see pp. 642 ff.), who used his rejection of the stable rational framework of the Enlightenment to oppose the movement as a whole. Rousseau's own late development, indeed, intensified this line of influence. His *Confessions*, written in 1765–1770 but not published until the 1780's (the first part in 1782, the second in 1789), showed a derangement of his mind and his system in the direction of his exclusive absorption in the infinitely divided self so dear to the incipient romantics. In his lyrical and surprisingly serene *Day-dreams of a Solitary Stroller*, written a decade later, between 1776 and the eve of his death in 1778, he struck another preromantic chord by finally reconciling himself to himself in the immediate presence of nature. But the impact of Rousseau's work as a whole during the late eighteenth century was exercised in another direction. It was exercised on figures like Kant, William Godwin, and the notorious Marquis de Sade, heirs of the Enlightenment who confirmed Rousseau's position at its periphery through their own more patent transmission into identifiable cultural movements of the same kind of systematic freedom that he espoused.

Kant and idealism we have considered already (see pp. 633 ff.). Suffice it here to recall Kant's own acknowledgment that it was Rousseau who inspired him to devote his whole philosophical system to "establishing the rights of humanity." The bulk of both Godwin's and Sade's writings belong to the subsequent era of the French Revolution, but the formative intellectual experience of their prerevolutionary years remained with them always, and their works may stand as a kind of *reductio ad absurdum* of the attempt, so attractively ambiguous in Rousseau and so fruitfully dialectical in Kant, to construct a unitary system of freedom. Consequently, the intellectual process that was merely implicit in Rousseau and Kant became only too transparent in Godwin and Sade.

The very styles of the two *enfants terribles*—or more precisely, the defects of their styles—reveal the skeleton of their thinking. William Godwin (1756–1836), a chief transmitter of the Enlightenment to the British romantics, delivered his message on the sovereignty of the "feelings" or "affections" in essays of the most intellectual and casuistic cast, and he wrote melodramatic novels like *Caleb Williams* (1794) with avowedly didactic purposes in mind and in text. Sade, who has been elevated of late from the pornographic underground to the ranks of the pre-existentialists, alternated long sections of the most detailed and extravagant physicality with even longer sections of the most abstract and remorseless speculation on the meaning of it all.

The moral of what they taught was no more subtle than its style, for both Godwin and Sade deliberately took the idea of natural liberty out of its Enlightenment context and tried to construct unambiguous monistic systems upon it. Both espoused doctrines of extreme and unqualified individualism, and both used the idea of nature to make the sovereignty of the individual an absolute necessity by virtue of every individual's very constitution—Godwin by assigning to the individual the monopoly on universal benevolence, Sade by assigning to universal egoism a monopoly on the individual.

Godwin gathered the elements of his system in the 1780's, when he juxtaposed the natural individualism of Rousseau with the natural determinism of d'Holbach, but it was only after the shock of the French Revolution that he began to put them together in a system that would make the latter serve the former—that is, would make the order of nature furnish the underlying structure for the play of unlimited freedom among men. In his *Political Justice* (1793), Godwin compounded the negations of Swift, Hume, Rousseau, and his family tradition of religious dissent into a categorical doctrine of philosophical and political anarchism, seeing as human realities only free and independent individuals who seek happiness and who may not validly be limited in their search by any restriction whatsoever, whether its origin be in human authority, general law,' or self-binding contract. Godwin's goal, indeed, was the return of men to the sovereign individualism of the state of nature, but he wanted to avoid the limitations which the Enlightenment had imposed via the educating role of the Legislator or the moralizing role of society. Godwin sought to set up this individualism neither as a mere ideal to be realized through other means nor as one of several values to be mutually accommodated, but rather as the underlying reality necessarily and exclusively corresponding to the nature of things. It is the mechanistic, tightly determined order of nature that makes all other kinds of order both superfluous and distorted, for when it is "unloosed from shackles," the mind of every individual must receive the "impressions" of this natural truth into itself, employ its reason to regard "all things—past, present, and to come—as links of an indissoluble chain," and expand itself to universal proportions accordingly. Thus through the primacy of reason Godwin had every individual recognize the absolute natural equality of all individuals and hence expand his local affections irresistibly into universal benevolence. Feelings, while still not primary, received now, from Godwin, a functional importance in thought that they had not heretofore had. As internal replacements for the institutional stimuli of state and society they provided a spontaneous motivation for the universalizing faculty of reason and thereby made the attainment of general happiness the monopoly of individual endeavor.

The Marquis de Sade (1740–1814) provided a mirror image of Godwin's paradoxical conversion of freedom into a necessary system, revealing the single intellectual process behind the opposite literal results. Where Godwin used the authority of nature to build a logic of humanity upon the principle of individual independence, Sade used the same authority to build a logic of solipsism upon the same principle. Most of Sade's works, like Godwin's, were written after the start of the French Revolution, but again like Godwin's the elements of them came out of the preceding era. These elements, revealed in the *Dialogue Between a Priest and a Dying Man* (1782) and in *Justine* (first draft completed in 1787), consisted of three categorical propositions. First, since every variety of taste and feeling derives "directly from the kind of organization we have individually received from Nature, . . . of whom we are the involuntary instruments," every action whatsoever is physically caused and morally justified (or more precisely, amorally justified) by "the designs of Nature." Second, Nature operates its designs exclusively through individuals who pursue their own happiness in their own way. "Egoism is Nature's fundamental commandment." Even "the philosopher" considers himself "alone in the universe; he judges everything subjectively; only he is of importance." Third, the individual's pursuit of happiness reduces itself to the immediate pursuit of sensory pleasure, which is, by Nature's fundamental decree, not only the basis but the final principle of moral philosophy: "Benevolence has nothing to do with Nature, . . . who never imbued us with any desire but that of satisfying ourselves at no matter what price."

Later Sade would develop his obsession with the absolute sovereignty of individuals entirely beyond Enlightenment views, coming to regard individuals as opposed to the claim of nature, and recognizing in them an autonomous force predominant even over nature and its pleasure principle. It is not this pre-existentialist position, however, but Sade's earlier naturalism that is the more historically revealing. Sade and Godwin, making into alternative systems of nature the principles that the Enlightenment had organized as natural complements—the individual's search for pleasure and the individual's capacity for benevolence—exemplify for the field of morals the pattern of the Enlightenment's passing and the character of its legacy. Those intellectuals who, toward the end of the eighteenth century, repudiated the ordering and unifying ethical devices which the Enlightenment had typified, such as the natural law and the moral sense, in favor of individual liberty, preached a freedom which bore one indelible mark of its eighteenth-century heritage: it was not sufficient unto itself but still required integration into rational doctrine for its definition and its meaning.

Evolution

The new combination of liberty with nature in the late Enlightenment, moreover, unleashed an intellectual force powerful enough to carry over even into natural science. It was reflected in the evolutionary doctrine and ideas of Jean Baptiste de Lamarck (1744–1829). In the 1770's and 1780's Lamarck developed the chemical and botanical notions which became preliminary stages for the theory of biological evolution he would announce in 1800. These notions he developed under the influence of Diderot's natural philosophy and Buffon's natural history, with their emphasis on the incessant flux of all nature and the infinite variety of all living things, and in explicit reaction against the static unities of mathematical reason represented by Priestley and Lavoisier. Certain basic assumptions of Lamarck's evolutionary theory stemmed from this one-sided appropriation of the dynamic and individualizing aspect of Enlightenment science together with the decisive dissociation from its physical mechanics: the assumptions, namely, of organic nature as an over-flowing life-force articulated into the great variety of individual organisms; of the individual organisms as the essential centers of life, whose activities toward their own perfection make up the fundamental process of nature; and of the organisms' capacity for change through appropriation of and adaptation to the resistant forms of inorganic nature.

But if Lamarck deliberately emancipated this living nature from what he considered the bondage of contemporary physical science by insisting

Jean Baptiste de Lamarck. *The French biologist who made the vitalist philosophy of nature scientifically respectable through the doctrine of evolution and the mechanism of the inheritance of acquired characteristics.*

on the categorical distinction between organic and inorganic nature (later to grow into the categorical distinction between the organism and its environment) and on the changeability of the chemical molecule (later to grow into the capacity for integral adaptation), he would not therefore emancipate it from all system. As in other fields of thought, the individualistic character of Lamarck's natural science was such as to drive him consciously into natural philosophy, and it was from this drive toward a rationale appropriate to the individualized life of his organisms that his theory of evolution developed. He chose, for his integrating concept, the idea of "systems" of organisms, by which he meant to signify the loose connection among individual organisms that comes from their parallel response to a common environmental condition. He hoped thereby to demonstrate the operation of an organized natural movement that would leave free its vital source in the autonomous individual organism. In the post-Enlightenment doctrine of evolution, as in the doctrines of utility, of the ideal, and of nature, the eighteenth century spawned the model for organizing a whole world view around one central idea, a model which would be followed in all the "isms" of the nineteenth century.

PREROMANTICISM

The third line of thought which rose to prominence in the last third of the eighteenth century stemmed from cultural traditions older than the Enlightenment and independent of it, rebounded to new life by publicly rejecting the Enlightenment root and branch, and developed into a modern movement by covertly taking from the Enlightenment whatever it could absorb. Associated especially with the names of Burke and Blake in Great Britain and of Herder, Goethe, and Schiller in Germany, the preromantics rejuvenated the emotional, pietist, and mystical currents that had retreated before the surge of Enlightenment. These currents gained a new force and a new direction from the growing impatience with the neat, balanced, limited world of the *philosophes* and from the surge of national passions that followed the association of this intellectual world with French hegemony. The favored medium of expression for preromanticism, consequently, was soaring aesthetics rather than rational exposition, and its habitat German and—to a lesser extent—British rather than the Gallic homeland of the "age of reason."

The common cry of the preromantics was for a kind of freedom and a kind of individualism that they claimed to be different from and greater than any liberty which the *philosophes* ever even imagined in their boldest dreams. The preromantics' deprecation of the Enlightenment's obvious commitment to human liberty in the name of liberty itself seems anomalous, particularly in view of their traditional background and the conservative future of the emotional and intuitional tendencies they represented. Thus the rebellious writers of the *Sturm und Drang* reverenced as their spiritual godfathers such intermediaries to a religious past as Johann Georg Hamann (1730–1788), who combined an abiding pietism with his revulsion against the "abstract" rationality of the Enlightenment, and Friedrich Gottlieb Klopstock (1724–1803), who caged his lyricism and his German patriotism within the confines of Protestant orthodoxy. Edmund Burke (1729–1797), despite a career devoted to original defenses of civil liberty, would end by becoming the model for the attraction of romantics to political reaction.

One of the keys to the kind of freedom exalted by the preromantics may be found in their radically distinctive idea, vis-à-vis the Enlightenment, of the individual whose freedom was in question. The distinction has been signified by the use of the term "individualism" for the Enlightenment's approach and of the term "individuality" for the preromantic approach. On the one hand, the Enlightenment had thought of individuals as essentially equal to one another, as essentially commensurable with one another in their fundamental interests, and as essentially needful of guarantees for the liberty that was common to them all, while the preromantics, on the other hand, thought of individuals as severally unique, as absolutely incommensurable with one another in any essential way, and as needing an escape from the shallow limits of common experience into the infinite depths of self-discovery. What defined preromanticism as an intellectual movement was not so much the revolt against the tyranny of formal rules in the arts about which they fulminated so furiously—for many of the *philosophes* had also fought this kind of regulation—but rather the deliberate identification of the Enlightenment with such formalism. The liberty that the *philosophes* based upon the individual's capacity to reason, to communicate, and thus to enjoy the rights of humanity was to the preromantics not liberty at all; it was the reduction of individuals to interchangeable "atoms," the denial to every person of what was truly individual in him, and his subordination to the rule or the law of reason that was supposed to be the common standard of all individual rights and judgments alike.

Where the *philosophes* identified freedom with the homogeneous and compatible rights of everyman, the preromantics identified it with the incomparable and unlimited rights of genius. Through their "cult of genius" the preromantics exalted not only the need, the right, and the capacity of the creative artist to break through all rules and barriers in the development of his aesthetic powers but also the rights and the powers of great men in any walk of life, who become individuals only by pursuing their own genius against the distorting and depersonalizing laws of the outside world. "Every individual human soul that develops its powers," wrote Friedrich von Schiller (1759–1805), "is more than the greatest of human societies," and both he and Johann Wolfgang von Goethe (1749–

Johann Wolfgang von Goethe. *A literary genius ranking with the greatest produced by any age in Western culture, Goethe epitomized the development of European classicism from the reign of the rules of reason and of balance in the arts to the perception of an ultimate aesthetic meaning and unity behind the acknowledged richness and variety of all life. (By the same token, however, Goethe's very gift for applying the vitality of concrete experience to the idea of the mind perpetuated the German disinclination to apply the ideas of the mind to the formation of concrete experience.)*

1832), during the 1770's and early 1780's when they participated in the flourishing stage of *Sturm und Drang*, developed this theme in the youthful dramas that they wrote and in the initial versions of their later, more famous dramas. From these years come Goethe's *Götz von Berlichingen* and *Egmont*, Schillers's *The Robbers*, and abortive versions of Goethe's *Faust* and Schiller's *Don Carlos*. They gave the world, in Karl Moor of *The Robbers* and the title figures of the other plays, unforgettable portrayals of "demonic" individuals—heroes driven by a ceaseless inner force to assert themselves beyond all human measure and against any social consideration. At this early stage of their growth, the heroic genius represented, for Goethe and Schiller, the only true freedom, since only the self-creating individual in this mold seeks to realize his freely chosen values in a world otherwise dominated by rules, routine, and practical necessities. The cult of genius was thus a kind of metaphor of the preromantic concept of individuality, signifying both its essential antipathy to any order or system and the inevitable elitism of its incidence.

The preromantic connotation of freedom in terms of an unconfined and aristocratic individuality had three corollaries. First, it supplied the context for the emotional emphasis that would become the most obvious feature of romanticism. That such an emphasis goes back to the preromantics is undeniable. Burke's *Philosophical Inquiry into the Origin of Our Ideas of the Sublime and Beautiful*—the early essay on aesthetics in which he exercised his most important influence on Europe until his writings on the French Revolution—persuaded German critics that both the sublime and the beautiful originate in the "passions," that "the influence of reason in producing our passions is nothing near so extensive as is commonly believed," and that, to the contrary, "the great power of the sublime, . . . far from being produced by them, . . . anticipates our reasonings and hurries us on by an irresistible force." Hamann taught Herder, a charter member of *Sturm und Drang,* that "nature works through the senses and the passions. Whoever mutilates these instruments of hers—how can he experience anything?" And Goethe himself, in his *Sorrows of Young Werther* (1774) drowned susceptible Europeans in copious tears of sentimental melancholy when he novelized a kind of mirror portrait of his heroic theme: the integrity and authenticity of the sensitive man of feeling, and his destruction, through his lack of a heroic genius, under the pressure of conventional society.

The preromantic stress on passion and emotion was undoubtedly spurred by the obvious hostility explicitly demonstrated by its progenitors against the rationalism of the Enlightenment. Since the *philosophes,* as we have seen, acknowledged the valid roles of passion and emotion far more than their opponents admitted, the emotionalism of the preromantics was in this respect an exaggerated partisan reaction against the guiding and balancing role that the *philosophes* did attribute to reason. But there was also a more essential and a more justifiable cause of the one-sided concern with passion and emotion than the mere squabble over the ranking of the human faculties. Passion and emotion were crucial to the preromantic idea of individuality, just as reason had been crucial to the Enlightenment idea of individualism. For the typical position of the preromantics was not that human action and ideas stemmed directly from sensations, emotions, and passions, but rather that they stemmed from the whole person—in Goethe's terms, "from all his united powers"—and what Hamann called "immediate feeling" and Herder "inner sentiment" was deemed the unifying force among these powers. The idea that the emotions supplied the psychic unity in a fragmented world was clearly a secularization of the traditional function of religious faith, and this secularization was a product of the competition with the secularized reason of the worldly philosophers. The preromantics revived religion as well, to be sure, but rather as an appropriate medium of the emotional life than as its final purpose. For them, the naturalized emotions now became an independent factor in the cultural life of Western man. Henceforward they would rival reason as the source of the internal unity that made a human being an authentic individual.

The second corollary of the preromantic commitment to individuality was the notion that the essential issues of life were fought out within the individual, who then proceeded to form the outer world in his own image. The vogue of Shakespeare in the Germany of the late eighteenth century was accountable not only to his obvious freedom from the French rules of classical dramaturgy but also to his focusing of tragic issues upon internal conflicts within the individual. Goethe's *Götz von Berlichingen* (1773) was the first of the German tragedies on a frankly Shakespearean model. It is no coincidence that it was precisely Goethe who made both a literary form and a philosophical doctrine out of the process of first localizing conflict and resolution in the individual and then showing how a plastic macrocosm (nature) is molded by the complete microcosm (the individual). In the England of Lawrence Sterne (1713–1768), his novel *Tristram Shandy* (1759–1767) and his autobiographical *Sentimental Journey* (1768) developed prose literature in a similarly subjective direction. Dispensing with both the objective moralization and the objective narrative sequence of the Richardsonian pattern, Sterne concentrated meaning and continuity in the individual protagonist's consciousness of events and circumstances that were casual and indifferent in themselves. In Hamann's dramatic summary: "Only our descent into the hell of self-knowledge opens our way to Paradise."

This preromantic corollary that made the individual an arena before he could become an agent had the immediate effect of withdrawing intellectual attention from political and social life. There was, to be sure, no inherent necessity in this withdrawal. To a man, the leading preromantics were abundantly aware of the conflict between their assertive individualities on the one side and the stagnant combination of conventional social morality and bureaucratic political absolutism on the other, and certainly the romantics would later use attitudes similar to theirs for all kinds of social and political positions. But in the period before the French Revolution the preromantics tended to feel themselves rather alienated from than engaged in their contemporary society. In part, undoubtedly, this passive alienation had to do with the comparative social immobility of the Germany which was the headquarters of the movement. But in greater part it reflected the original impulse of the movement to urge the segregation of those individuals who were great enough to receive and to master the varied experience from without before sending them out to infuse the great world with their genius.

If the mental set of the preromantics was such as to inspire no political or social doctrine, it did produce a third and final corollary of individuality that extended it beyond the human individual and was a harbinger of romantic political and social doctrines to come. In Herder's idea of the "nation" and in Burke's justification of "party" we may glimpse the original tie between the fundamental preromantic notion of the individual and the principled defense of group life over and above the individuals of whom the group was composed.

The early doctrine of the culture-nation—which Johann Gottfried von Herder (1774–1803) developed during the 1760's and 1770's—may be best understood in terms of the ideas of individuality proffered by two of its sources: Leibniz' monadology and Hamann's symbolism. The "monad"

Johann Gottfried von Herder. *Philosopher of nationalism.*

was Leibniz' term for the metaphysical principle of individuality that made everything what it was. Because the monad lived and developed harmoniously in a world of monads it prefigured the capacity of the sovereign individual to be integrated into a group and yet retain his freedom. Because the monad applied not only to particular persons and things but also to any body, however complex, that developed its own potential in its own inimitable way, it could confer individuality as easily on collective as on personal bodies.

On this skeleton of the socialized and historicized monad, Herder hung his version of Hamann's intuitive symbolism, to emerge with the culture-nation as the primary unit of humanity. For Hamann, the only approach to human reality that could avoid the deadly distortions of abstract reasoning was the immediate intuition of linguistic symbols, particularly in folk poetry, for here the succession of concrete images brought men as close as they could come to the fleeting, elusive stuff of human reality. The feeling for language and literature thus became the key to the insight into humanity for Herder, who was concentrating, in the years that he was helping to found the movement of *Sturm und Drang,* precisely on these subjects—in his *Fragments on Recent German Literature* (1767) and *On the Origins of Speech* (1772). In Herder's hands, language and literature composed a single primary social power, shaping the attitudes of each people into a national culture that conferred an individual form upon its art, its religion, and indeed all its collective expressions. The nation as a greater individual was the immediate creation of nature, as the intimacy of the national languages and folk literatures with their direct perception of nature's evanescent reality attested, but it also was, for Herder, the natural expression of all the human individuals who were its members. Since the variety, complexity, and mobility of the natural world were such that individual persons could know it and assert themselves in it only through the common symbols created in collaboration with their neighbors, the nation was for Herder not only an individual in its own right from the point of view of nature in general but the necessary condition for the individuality of the human persons who composed it.

In the early version of his philosophy of history, *Another Philosophy of History for the Education of Humanity,* which he published in 1774 while he was still under the influence of *Sturm und Drang,* Herder gave special emphasis to the genesis of nations, when their collective personalities were first formed, and to their disparate but equal individualities, which were based upon the incomparable genius of each. In its origins cultural nationalism may thus be understood as a doctrine which applied the elitist ideas of unlimited freedom and incommensurable individuality to the mass of ordinary individual humans, whose capacities equipped them not for the creative freedom of the individual genius, but for a share in the creative freedom of the individual nation.

Others besides Herder were promulgating ideas of cultural nationalism during the last third of the eighteenth century, in contrast to the humanitarian cosmopolitanism inferred by many *philosophes* from the universal scope of reason in men. In two of Herder's like-minded contemporaries, the German historian Justus Möser (1720–1794) and the British parliamentarian Edmund Burke, the notion of culture was extended to emphasize institutional and constitutional rather than aesthetic forms, but the cultural idea of the nation as an immediate product of nature and the only permanent identity for the ordinary individual was at the basis of their constitutional nationalism and supplied what was new in it.

In addition to the cultural nation, the preromantics also created the modern idea of political party. They attributed to party, as to the nation, the personality and principles of a collective individual. Although Burke developed his classic formulation of the national constitution as "a partnership not only between those who are living, but between those who are living, those who are dead, and those who are to be born" only after the revolution broke out in France, he formulated his equally classic justification of party before that cataclysmic event. Party had for centuries been identified with faction and classified under sedition. The main ground for this condemnation had been the conviction that for each government, as once for each religion, there was but one true set of principles, which bound the sovereign and the individual citizens and which would be undermined by any other bond of political association. In the rare instances when the idea of party was defended, as it had been by Machiavelli, it was defended on grounds not of individual rights but of public effect—to wit, that the competition between parties prevents the tyranny of either. But Burke based party both on the right of individuals to combine for a political purpose and on the validity of making a "particular principle" the bond of their combination in a party. The political individual, indeed, had not only the right but the obligation to enter into such parties, for we must "model our principles to our duties and our situation" and so form "connections" which are the only means of carrying these principles into execution. From Burke's idea of party we glean the fundamental contribution of the preromantics to the modern theory of associations: the idea of a group as both an extension of its individual members and an embodiment of general principle. Hence it enables principle to be imposed on the individual without ostensible loss of his freedom.

It remains only to ask what was the actual role of the preromantics in the cultural life of the eighteenth century. Their own idea of that role, as we have seen, was that of a revolutionary opposition to the Enlightenment, and hence the inference has sometimes been drawn that a straight line of cultural development led away from the Enlightenment through the preromantics to the romantics proper, who emerged around the turn of the century to complete the revolution. But the inference is only partly valid. What went into preromanticism did not determine what came out of it. Although preromanticism originated in a revolutionary posture against every characteristic feature of the Enlightenment it did not maintain this position throughout its development. In fact, the preromantics, during the 1780's, manufactured their own brand of classicism. This classicism had its sources in the era before the French Revolution and was part of the legacy of the Enlightenment. Romanticism arose later, in the conditions produced by the French Revolution, and is no part of our story at all.

The assessment of the influences involved in the origins of preromanticism requires, like most historical assessments, a qualified rather than a categorical judgment. Undoubtedly, there were positive relations between the *philosophes* and the preromantics. Burke was impressed by Montesquieu and in his turn impressed Diderot. Moreover, the impact of Burke's aesthetics on the German *Sturm und Drang* was mediated through Lessing and Moses Mendelssohn (1729–1786), two figures variously associated with the German Enlightenment and otherwise *non grata* to this same *Sturm und Drang*. Herder studied in Königsberg under the early Kant as well as under Hamann and was influenced by the rationalist version of Leibniz that marked Kant's position before he developed his critical philosophy. As late as 1768 Geothe was under the spell of French culture and the Francophile influence of Christoph Wieland (1733–1813), before a transitional Pietist conversion and his meetings with Herder helped to usher in the *Sturm und Drang*. Rousseau was reprobated by Burke as the writer who put an emotional surcharge on the abstractions of the so-called age of reason: but Rousseau was also a powerful positive force in the development of Herder, Goethe, and Schiller alike. Wieland, who was too frothy, too hedonistic, too ironical, too French in his tastes to be generally respected by the preromantics, yet did affect them specifically through his contribution to the liberation of art from morals and was himself an appreciative connoisseur of Klopstock, Goethe, and Schiller.

But the specific contacts of the preromantics with the *philosophes* should not obscure the far more emphatic preromantic conviction that they were overthrowing simultaneously the tyranny of French civilization over German culture and the tyranny of the Enlightenment over creative freedom. The specific influences of the Enlightenment that helped to prepare the preromantic attitude were transmuted into building stones of a qualitatively different cultural attitude.

For the preromantic revolt was short-lived. Its instigators simply could not sustain the irresolution of the unlimited freedom or the loneliness of the absolute individuality in their initial posture. Herder, Goethe, Schiller—the three most prominent figures of the *Sturm und Drang*—all sought, during the 1780's, to organize ideas of a larger world in which individual men and nations would find appropriate materials and a unifying principle to provide substance and direction for their freedom. In his mature philosophy of history—the *Reflections on the Philosophy of the History of Humanity* (1784–1791)—Herder adduced notions of a common humanity and of the progress of nations toward its realization that were obvious reprises on Voltaire and the Enlightenment for the purpose of lending coherence to the aimless pluralism of his original nationalism. Ideas from the mid-century classical revival, stimulated especially by J. J. Winckelmann's excited confusion of the Greek aesthetic ideal with universal standards of culture as such, led Goethe to sketch a philosophy of nature which made the standards of art into the principles of reality and conceived the outer world to be a dynamic unity of spirit and matter serving at once as stuff, model, and form for the creative individual.

Schiller, finally, went through an analogous crisis during the 1780's. As Herder had found a world for the orientation of his sovereign individuals in a universal philosophy of history and Goethe for his in a pantheistic philosophy of nature, Schiller found a moral world for his in Kant's categorical imperative—that is, in the ethical realm created by the laws which every individual determines for himself. Insisting still on the primacy of freedom and on the role of art in synthesizing the sensual and moral natures of man into the wholly free individual, Schiller now learned both to define this freedom—*i.e.* as self-determination—and to give it form by equating morality with reason and making the rational harmony within and among individuals the measure by which freedom is assessed and the purpose to which art is directed. Thus in Schiller's *Don Carlos*, the spotlight put by the early draft upon the tempestuous hero who gives the play its title shifted in the final version (1785) to the humane and tolerant Marquis of Posa—now the central character, who, like the verse form of the drama, reflects the influence of Lessing's informed and principled *Nathan the Wise*.

The German preromantics not only were influenced by Enlightenment figures like Lessing and Kant but joined them in the same cultural movement, German classicism. This classicism was thus composed of two convergent currents—the men of the Enlightenment who detached the libertarian strand from it and developed a new kind of lawful order on this libertarian base, and the men of the *Sturm und Drang* who created a new kind of freedom and grafted on to it a rational order, taken from the Enlightenment and its heirs. This composite movement would later produce a Hegel and a Marx. Clearly, this classicism that was the last great cultural movement of Europe's Old Regime did more than merely complement the rationalist and libertarian movements. It was, together with the direct channel which links the witty, tolerant, critical, reasonable, socially concerned minds of the *philosophes* with ours, the other main conduit through which the civilization of eighteenth-century Europe passed into the contemporary world.

FROM THOUGHT TO ACTION

The balance of laws and movement, of reason and facts, of society and individuals, and of morals and politics in the thought of the mature Enlightenment came appropriately from the mid-century apogee of prerevolutionary Europe. For the society of this Europe was characterized by an analogous balance between the crust of political and social institutions that were still accepted and a movement of people from below toward levels of well-being, education, and self-assertion that was spreading from commoners to notables and producing a massive restiveness beneath the placid surface of public life. The intellectual movements of the post-Enlightenment era that arose during the two decades between 1770 and 1789 were also faithful articulations of their contemporary society. The impatience with unreasonable practices, the sense of incessant movement, and the idea of infinite freedom which were the chief solvents of the intellectual order represented by the Enlightenment had their counterparts in the local social and political unrest that began in this period to break through the institutional crust of the Old Regime.

But the interaction of thought and society was not only in the direction of thought. If the first product of the interaction was the intellectuals' translation of the social conditions in which they lived and wrote into the language of philosophy, science, and the arts, this crystallization was quickly followed by a reciprocal movement which brought this language to bear upon the concrete political and social development of the second half of the eighteenth century. The application of eighteenth-century ideas to political and social reality was carried out not by intellectuals, but by practical men who were the consumers of the ideas of the intellectuals.

There were two radically different kinds of such practitioners, corresponding to the two different stages in intellectual history of the late eighteenth century and to the two different kinds of society characteristic of the Atlantic and continental peoples respectively. The first kind of practitioners consisted of the enlightened monarchs of central and eastern Europe who sought to apply the intellectual pattern of the mature Enlightenment by finding a role for rational order and civic virtue in the welter of real interests that were their primary concerns. Both the sincerity and the result of this attempt are moot historical problems which will engage our attention, but it is clear that the ideas which the enlightened rulers professed to apply were the identifiable and integral ideas of the Enlightenment and that their political version of the Enlightenment dominated European public life until the 1780's, when another kind of practitioner rose to prominence. This second kind of practitioner of eighteenth-century ideas consisted of the notables and commoners whose use of the dynamic, radical, and libertarian tendencies spawned by the last phase of eighteenth-century culture initiated the movement toward social revolution among the Atlantic communities. With these practitioners the independent and formative force of ideas which had been cherished by all eighteenth-century intellectuals yielded to the role of ideas as supports of practical social interests and demands. Thus the rise of fundamental opposition to the kings coincided with the passage from philosophy to ideology, and it is no historical accident that if the origins of the joint movement against the kings and the philosophers can be found in the society and culture of the eighteenth century, its victory belongs to another era.

What follows, then, is the story of the men who sought to realize reason by grafting the intelligence of the *philosophes* onto the power of the kings and of the social movement that would ultimately topple both the detached philosopher and the ensconced king from their places in the traditional civilization of the West.

CHAPTER 19

Enlightened Absolutism

FOR SOME TWENTY-FIVE hundred years, when men dreamed of a better life they were caught between the hope that the better life would make men better and the fear that only better men could make a better life, and they looked to a single extraordinary figure, the philosopher king, who would break through the dilemma to improve men by his example and life by his power. He was to be a *philosopher* king because knowledge and virtue were convertible in the good life. He was to be a philosopher *king* because only a man whose force was independent of other men but yet acknowledged by them could have the leverage to initiate improvements which men as a whole were incapable of initiating and the coverage to make improvements which would be generally effective on the lives of men as a whole. Even the few periods and the few polities where republics had been preferred to monarchies contributed to the persistent ideal of the philosopher king, for in a tradition reaching from Solon to Helvétius and Rousseau the republican "Legislator" was assigned the power to impose the constitutional conditions of the subsequently good society and thus to fill the role of a constituent philosopher king. But in general, just as the model of the Greek and Roman republics had given way to the composite model of the Roman Empire and the Christian monarchy, so was the ideal of the temporary and dictatorial Legislator absorbed in the ideal of the permanent and legitimate philosopher king.

For the most part this ideal of the philosopher king remained only an ideal. The actual records of kingship afforded some examples of saintly kings who exemplified virtue, and even more of the knowledgeable kings who patronized scholarship and the arts—in the period around the beginning of the eighteenth century Louis XIV, the Habsburg Emperor Leopold I, and the Prussian Frederick I were cases in point. But there were indeed few philosopher kings who deliberately applied the principles of knowledge as means and the civic virtues as ends to a system of royal policy aimed at social improvement.

From around the middle of the eighteenth century, rulers who impressed contemporaries as belonging to this rare breed appeared in such a cluster as to indicate a remarkable convergence of the actual conditions bearing on kingship and the intellectual tendencies of contemporary philosophy—a convergence that made the marriage between the king of the realm and the queen of the sciences the most revealing political institution in Europe during the half century preceding the French Revolution. King Frederick II ("the Great") of Prussia, the Habsburg Emperor Joseph II of Germany and the Habsburg dominions, and Empress Catherine II ("the Great") of Russia were the outstanding examples of this combination by dint of the power and prominence of the states they governed, but the style of rulership which they modeled extended beyond them to become the dominant fashion for royalty in the second half of the century. The kings Charles III of Spain, Stanislas II of Poland, and Gustavus III of Sweden, the Habsburg Grand Duke Leopold of Tuscany (subsequently Emperor Leopold II), and a number of German princes—avid as ever to replicate the latest mode in European royalty—were all members of the set to which the collective label of "enlightened despotism" was later to be affixed. And where legitimate rulers were inadequately enlightened or despotic, there were leading ministers like the cultivated Prince Kaunitz in Austria, the doctrinaire Johan Struensee in Denmark, and the reforming Bernardo di Tanucci in Naples, to play an analogous role.

THE PROBLEM OF "ENLIGHTENED DESPOTISM"

But if the popularity of Enlightenment culture in some of the unlikeliest courts of Europe demonstrates beyond doubt the advent of a new vogue in government, it has also raised a serious question of what that vogue really was. Those who have called it "enlightened despotism" have tended to signify by the term a distinctive stage of absolutism, in which rulers responded to the changing social conditions of power and the congruent philosophy of the Enlightenment by making government into an unprecedentedly effective instrument of authority and by taking a deliberate interest in the civil rights and welfare of all citizens, thereby initiating a categorical extension in both the means and the ends of monarchical government.

But others have rejected the term precisely because they consider this implication of a new content as well as a new style in autocratic government to be a historical distortion. What has been called enlightened despotism, it is argued, was neither enlightened nor despotic. It was still simply absolutism as such, now adjusted to the particular tone of the later eighteenth century but essentially continuous in its forms and its goals with the absolutism that preceded it. The statements of principle, policy, or purpose that are usually taken as proof of a different, enlightened form of absolutism, these critics conclude, were, in respect of politics, either rhetorical or irrelevant: monarchs used the fashionable terms of the Enlightenment to rationalize irrational policy or to express cultural interests other than policy, but in either case such terms had, and were intended to have, little bearing on the realities of government.

Now obviously, if this were only a pedantic squabble among historians about the suitability of a label, it would be of little moment, since it does not matter whether the kings and ministers concerned are called enlightened despots or mere autocrats as long as we know what they thought and did. But the issue is worth attention because it underscores, as an issue, certain qualities about the politics of the age that are not accounted for either by the loose notion of enlightened despotism or by the undifferentiated concept of a general absolutism, taken separately. What is important, in other words, is not whether the absolutism of the later eighteenth century was actually independent enough of its past and distinctive enough from other forms of government to warrant its own label—what is important is to clarify the problematic historical reality that is reflected by the conflict in historical interpretations.

For the most part the clarification must come from the consideration of what kind of people the presumed enlightened despots were, what kind of policies they had, and what kind of measures they enacted. But before we enter into such an empirical accounting—into enlightened despotism from the inside, as it were—we must secure a certain preliminary clarification from an analysis of what is indisputable about the tendency as a whole—a view from the outside, as it were. Only from such a preliminary analysis will we know what to look for in the empirical investigaton to follow.

Three general facts about the rulers who are usually classified as enlightened despots define the issue raised by the label, and by defining it, contribute to the understanding of culture and politics in late-eighteenth-century Europe.

First, each of the major rulers so labeled had a predecessor whose policies were similar to those of "enlightened despotism" but whose political personality and rhetoric have barred him (or her) from inclusion in the set. Peter the Great in Russia, Frederick William I in Prussia, and Maria Theresa in the Habsburg lands strove for and in large measure effected fundamental reforms in the direction of the centralized welfare state, the retrenchment of aristocratic privilege, and the legislation of a common state citizenship that their "enlightened" successors could in many ways only elaborate upon. Peter and Frederick William we have already met, and we can understand how, despite the constructive policies which created the basic institutions of the modern Russian and Prussian states respectively, the tyrannical brutality of the Romanov and the sanctimonious paternalism of the Hohenzollern would seem antithetical to the notion of an enlightened ruler in any of its usual connotations.

But lest we think the distinction merely a matter of chronology or of

Empress Maria Theresa of Austria. *The domineering Habsburg pride and willfulness, the keen good sense, the attractive and self-conscious femininity, the stern but kind motherliness — all the qualities which went into Maria Theresa's mode of governing—are apparent in this portrait of the aging monarch.*

personal character we have the later case of the Habsburg Queen Maria Theresa (ruled 1740–1780), intelligent, warmhearted, beloved by her subjects, contemporary of the enlightened Frederick, mother of and coregent with the equally enlightened Emperor Joseph, promulgator of the permanent reforms which modernized the Austrian empire—and yet, by common historical consent, no enlightened despot. Nor can it be argued that in her case the problem was one of despotism rather than enlightenment, for however benign her manner and however effective her arts of persuasion, the quality of "gentle violence" which was recognized as the epitome of her policies testifies to the inexorable force behind the soft tactics and establishes her place firmly in the ranks of the autocrats. Politically shrewd and self-willed, she knew how to delegate authority, when to bargain, and what limits were set to her power by her own femininity and by the disjointedness of her polyglot dominions. But within these limits she asserted all the prerogatives of sovereignty to effect the political and military reorganization of her empire's heartland.

As in the cases of her Russian and Prussian precedent state builders, Maria Theresa's governmental reforms were a direct response to a military challenge, and like them too the response entailed not only an administrative overhaul to increase revenue but more fundamental reforms in the direction of the equalization of taxable classes, general conscription, universal elementary education, state control over the established Church, and secularization of university programs. In Maria Theresa's Austria, as in Petrine Russia and Hohenzollern Prussia, the actual progress toward these goals was slow, halting, and still unequal in its incidence upon the privileged, but enough of a start was made in the direction of equalizing the conditions of citizens and of encouraging practical initiative in the individual subjects to indicate the conformity of such tendencies to the essentials of statecraft—enlightened and unenlightened alike—in the eighteenth century. Maria Theresa has been excluded from the group of enlightened monarchs not because of what her policies did in particular but because of what her political personality guaranteed they must add up to in general. She was badly educated, had a simple, orthodox Catholic piety, and cherished the benevolent but archaic attitude of a "universal mother" toward her peoples. The political relevance of these qualities in excluding her from the ranks of enlightened absolutists to which her measures and her favorite ministers, such as the enlightened Prince Wenzel Kaunitz (1711–1794) and Count Friedrich Haugwitz (1702–1765), might otherwise have entitled her, tells us something about the genre.

The uniform presence of effective and intelligent, albeit "unenlightened," reforming rulers in the immediate background of "enlightened despotism" goes far to delimit the problem of what was distinctive to this later-eighteenth-century version of kingship. It confirms the view of the skeptics that the association of the interests of the state with the equal protection of rights within the state had become ingrained in the tradition of monarchical sovereignty as such and that there was consequently nothing particularly enlightened about the endorsement of it by the so-called enlightened despots. Their differential qualities must be sought elsewhere.

The second preliminary observation which should be made about the general conditions of enlightened despotism has to do with its political and historical geography: it tended to characterize the states of central and eastern Europe and the states—like Sweden and Spain—well along in the decline from former greatness. Undoubtedly, the accidents of birth had much to do with this geographical distribution: Great Britain's George II and France's Louis XV were not interested enough, and their successors George III and Louis XVI not bright enough, to qualify. But however fortuitous the immediate cause, the historical effect was to locate "enlightened despotism" in states where the requirements of government, both to meet the contemporary challenge of international competition and to satisfy the contemporary standards of social justice, exceeded the material and moral resources of their comparatively retrograde or stagnant societies. Ministers like Turgot and the younger William Pitt, however cultivated and however authoritarian they may have been, denoted something other than "enlightened despotism" in late-eighteenth-century politics, not because they lacked the formality of a royal title, but because they represented and articulated, constitutionally or virtually, the positive claims of a whole mobile, middling sector of the society upon the state—a function for which a royal title would have been in any case irrelevant.

Thus factors of geography and of history limited "enlightened despotism" to those monarchies in which the ruler framed his goals and his policies in a language that far transcended the terms of any existing social interest or the claims raised by any combination of existing social interests.

The third general feature of enlightened absolutism that helps to define the character of late-eighteenth-century monarchy is the restricted sense in which its "enlightened" quality must be taken. We must accept the double meaning which inevitably inheres in "enlightened" here, for it refers—and is meant to refer—both to the general quality of intelligence and to the particular passion for the culture of the Enlightenment that are to be found in the enlightened rulers of this period. In itself the ambiguity is permissible enough, for if intelligence be taken in this context to mean the rooting of political judgments in broad secular knowledge then certainly the Enlightenment may be seen as a fitting cultural form of such a quality.

But perhaps because of the moral ends that have always been associated with philosopher kings, the connection of eighteenth-century monarchs with the philosophy of the Enlightenment has tended improperly to expand from their appropriation of its ideas of knowledge to their appropriation of its moral ends. Thus enlightened despotism has been interpreted explicitly to mean "benevolent despotism" and implicitly to mean liberal despotism, in reference to the humanitarianism and the individual freedom that were supreme values in the general culture of the Enlightenment. These are the connotations that have obscured the reality of eighteenth-century monarchy and have threatened to invalidate the whole concept of enlightened despotism. The fact was that universal benevolence and individual rights were endorsed by the rulers concerned, but not as *political* principles. "Enlightened despotism" in the benevolent or liberal sense is thus self-contradictory, for it refers to the principles by which the despots defined the limits of their utilitarian and authoritarian politics. What we must look for in "enlightened despotism" is not the political realization of the Enlightenment ethic or even of the liberal political doctrines that were the corollaries of that ethic. What we must look for is the entirely distinctive form taken by the Enlightenment when kings applied it as a theory of knowledge to the realities of human politics and as a theory of value to the context of human politics.

The Enlightenment was for politics, as for many other fields of eighteenth-century endeavor, above all a way of mastering reality. What has been called enlightened despotism thus mirrored the Enlightenment at large in its belief that knowledge is power. But it also resolved the Enlightenment's ambiguous relation of the real and the ideal by affirming in principle the gap that remained between the political utility the absolute rulers could achieve and the human values they could only profess. If, then, the term "enlightened," is justified for such rulers in the triple sense that they were devotees of Enlightenment culture, that they applied the materials and method of rational knowledge to statecraft, and that they made a political principle out of the *philosophes'* moral dilemma between the reality which they appreciated and the ideals which would transform it, the term "despots" is thereby unjustified. Absolutists these monarchs certainly were, for there was nothing in their "Enlightenment" to make them welcome or acknowledge in principle any limitation by other human agencies; but despots they were not, for they were enlightened enough to perceive both the actual limits upon the will of any government and the inherent limits of all politics. Enlightened despotism in the eighteenth century is a rhetorical hyperbole. Enlightened absolutism was a historical reality.

THE ABSOLUTIST PERSONALITY

Like the *philosophes* whom they read, hosted, and mimed, the enlightened absolutists were free spirits who uninhibitedly expressed their individual tastes and temperaments. But they also shared certain general traits of a collective personality.

Frederick the Great of Prussia (ruled 1740–1786), the first of the enlightened absolutists and the model for the rest, was an amateur philosopher, poet, musician, composer, and critic, a moralist and an aesthete who was also an implacable and indefatigable general in the field, a probing, hardworking administrator in chambers, and an energetic inspector of all the phases in all the locales of his subjects' lives. However powerfully he affirmed nature, culture, and humanity in general, he just as strongly denied men in particular. His occasional acts of spontaneous generosity were increasingly overborne by the suspicious, cynical, and domineering attitudes that peer out from the grim-faced portraits of his later years.

Where Frederick was a study in contradiction, Joseph II of Austria (co-regent 1765–1780, sole ruler, 1780–1790), on the other hand, seemed a model of simplicity. He was restless and impatient, driven by human sympathy, ambition, and a passion for logical consistency to the repeated anonymous travels among his people that sponsored the legends of the "Peasants' Kaiser," to his repeated international aggressions upon weaker powers, and to the remorseless execution of doctrinaire policies that ultimately called down revolution upon him.

Catherine II of Russia (ruled 1762–1796), in apparent contrast to both of these royal contemporaries, was notoriously fickle and opportunistic. By her own admission, she was a "starter" rather than a finisher of policies. But there was a pattern that ran through the variety of her initiatives. Certainly she had to tread more warily, as befit the fragile status of a German-born widowed sovereign in the rough court of the tsars. Nor was she helped by the circumstances of her accession. She had certainly usurped the throne from her own husband (Peter III) in 1762, with the assistance of the ever unreliable palace guard; she was generally believed to have conspired in his mysterious death immediately after the deposition; and she double-crossed the old-line nobility who had looked for a compliant regency after the event. Nor did she have even the modest philosophical and literary talents of a Frederick or the spontaneous human sympathies of a Joseph. But she was, for all that, at least as vigorous and even more versatile than they. Her voracious consumption of lovers showed a kind of zest for life that was shared by neither her Prussian nor her Austrian counterpart, but it was a passion that supplemented rather than replaced worldly interests they all did share. For Catherine too consumed the writings of the *philosophes*, corresponded lengthily with the intellectual suzerains of the movement, hosted them, and even wrote plays, stories, and an abortive Russian history in inferior imitation of them. Like the other enlightened monarchs, moreover, her taste for rational discourse and aesthetic composition dignified rather than inhibited the flamboyant expression of sentimental pity for the unfortunate and of indefatigable delight in the business of ruling.

From this amalgam of distinctive and similar traits in the enlightened absolutists the outline of a collective personality emerges. It is a personality that bears a marked resemblance to the possible pencil sketch of the Enlightenment's typical French *philosophe*, for whom, indeed, these monarchs shared an unstinting admiration and to whom they owned their chief

The price of power: Frederick the Great before (left) and after (right) the royal possession of it. *The facial contrast registers not simply the aging process but also the impact of dangerous experience and the traces of the iron discipline which he came to impose on others and upon himself as well.*

Emperor Joseph II of Austria, who overreached himself with egalitarian reforms in an aristocratic society. *After a painting by Drouais.*

cultural debt. The enlightened absolutists were given a collective identity by two primary features. They were all impelled by an insatiable cultural drive to know and experience what life in this world had to offer, and they were all equally impelled by the determinate political drive to assert their mastery over it. These teamed commitments found obvious expression in their preference for the Enlightenment, which gave intellectual form to precisely this double tendency.

Politics and Culture

But it was not merely this preference for the Enlightenment combination of politics and culture that shaped the rulers' distinctive personality. What did shape it most decisively was their resolution of the duality between politics and culture in a way that made of politics the rigorously and rationally organized core of their lives, around which they could afford to dispose their carnal, sentimental, and cultural interests freely. The long hours which without exception they devoted wholeheartedly to the business of state were reminiscent of the cherished administrative labors of a Philip II or a Louis XIV, but if the hours and working conditions of all the dedicated autocrats were similar whatever the generation of the autocracy, still the spirit of the labor was not. Monarchs of the earlier stage of autocracy, like Philip and Louis, doted on all the details of government from the mixed motives of suspicion and simple pleasure. They wished to know as much as possible about their realms and to resolve by themselves as much of their business as they could humanly manage because they feared resistance and mistrusted any delegation of their powers. But they also enjoyed administrative details for their own sake, so that it has been said of both Philip and Louis that despite their fearsome repute each had

Catherine the Great of Russia in 1769. *This portrait faithfully conveys the sense of her energetic and imperious disposition.*

the soul of a petty bureaucrat. Such motives were not wholly absent from the enlightened absolutists—Frederick mistrusted his officials and Catherine certainly had reason enough to fear sedition—but in general their immersion in the details of government was spurred rather by the conviction that the organization of these details by one rational mind was necessary to consistent policy and that consistent policy was also the only sound policy. For the enlightened monarchs much more than for their illustrious predecessors, in other words, the time and energy they devoted to the business of state were aimed not simply at the control but at the direction of social life. In the rulers' own existence as in their peoples' the work of state furnished a secure base for all the activities of man.

In Catherine of Russia, undeniably, the two collective traits of the enlightened absolutist personality—the passion for varieties of experience and the passion to master them—never jibed. The hardness of her policies was obviously and tragically separate from the humanity of her cultural professions—an incongruity which indeed earned her an unenviable repute as a hypocrite. But as the opprobrium itself shows, Catherine did succeed, however reprehensibly, in relating her sensual and cultural interests to the rational core of her politics. Even in her love affairs, uninhibited as she seemed in the bestowal of her favors, the political motif was rarely absent. Not only was she quite immune to influence by her lovers but as often as not she put them to good political use.

If Catherine's duplicity represents the tenuous extreme in the relations of the energy and the control that were the two poles of the enlightened monarchs' collective personality, Joseph represents the other—integrated—extreme. He has been called the political man par excellence precisely because all the notorious signs of his spontaneity—his impulsiveness, his impatience, his forcefulness, his passion for ideas, his quick sympathies—were harnessed by political ambitions and directed toward a political goal.

Both extremes meet in showing the preeminent power of politics as the organizing principle in the lives of the enlightened absolutists. Catherine and Joseph exemplify the different ways in which politics could organize culture, but neither exemplifies clearly the autonomy of the cultural impulse and its role in the personal syndrome. For this we must turn to Frederick the Great, whose character developed in a way that lay bare the inner relations of the traits common to but not so transparent in all the rulers of his ilk.

In his early years as king, from his accession in 1740 to the outbreak of the Seven Years' War in 1756, Frederick's interest in the humanitarian culture of the Enlightenment and his commitment to a politics of sheer power were equally strong and mutually independent in him. Perhaps the fierce duress with which his austere and orthodox father, Frederick William I, had broken the young, freethinking, and irreverent Crown Prince to obedience and public administration simultaneously was responsible for the original isolation of the political power-motif in Frederick. But whatever the cause, the approximate simultaneity (around his accession in 1740) of such ill-assorted measures as his rejuvenation of the Berlin Academy as a cultural center, his publication of the *Anti-Machiavel* as a handbook of the philosopher king for the direct application of morality to politics, and his unprovoked aggression against Austria for the conquest of Silesia set the pattern for the separate tracks his interests would follow for a decade and a half.

Not, of course, that there were no connections at all. Just before he invaded Silesia, Frederick did apply culture to policy by dismantling prior censorship of the press, decreeing religious toleration, and abolishing torture in penal proceedings. In the *Anti-Machiavel*, moreover, behind Frederick's enlightened provision for a rulership contract between ruler and people which sanctioned the ruler's obligation to govern for the happiness of his subjects he was careful to settle the enforcement of the obligation only on the conscience of the king and to include a goodly measure of military security and public order in the makeup of his subjects' happiness.

But the fact remains that until the Seven Years' War the mutual independence of Frederick's cultural and political interests was much more in evidence than their sporadic connections. When he played and composed for the flute; when he protected La Mettrie, or discussed and corresponded at length with Voltaire; when he wrote his own poetry, drama, essays, history, and joyfully belabored the works of others; when he filled his court and his Academy with the bearers of the contemporary French culture he loved so well: in all these activities he was enlarging himself and his kingdom by added dimensions that were only marginal to the necessities of politics.

But the trials of the Seven Years' War, which brought Prussia to the verge of apparent destruction at the hands of an encircling continental coalition headed by Austria, France, and Russia, tempered Frederick and merged the different strands of his character into one composite whole. Preyed upon—so he felt—by a pack of neighbors, and deserted—he was convinced—by his uncertain ally, Great Britain, Frederick, along with the state for which he was responsible, survived through a combination of luck (the dim-witted Tsar Peter III, who idolized Frederick, acceded to the throne and pulled Russia out of the war in 1762) and his own desperate perseverance. But in the process Frederick lost his earlier spontaneity, manysidedness, and confidence in the capacities of his fellowman. A plurality of interests was a luxury that neither he nor his state could henceforward afford, and his former inclination toward the intellectual liberties gave way to a new stress on practical controls. Yet his cultivation of iron discipline, both for others and for himself, did not mean the exclusion of cultural interests, but only their subordination to another kind of interest. He examined them carefully for their relevance to the safety of the state, which was now, in its turn, defined more broadly than before. The upshot was his growing commitment to a Stoic way of life, which made knowledge and the arts essential to the well-being of the state, valued them according to their contribution to the state, and made their cultivation for this political purpose a public obligation of the ruler.

Perhaps the clearest expression of this development was Frederick's changed attitude toward French culture. No longer did he acknowledge the French Enlightenment to be the model culture, and no longer did he seek out the French *philosophes* to grace his Berlin Academy. He came to deplore the radicalism of the French version of Enlightenment which he associated with d'Holbach, and he came at the same time to understand the importance of encouraging German intellectual participation in letters generally and in official cultural institutions like the Academy particularly. But these changes represented something new in Frederick's idea about the function of culture rather than in his idea of culture itself. For he remained a devotee of the Enlightenment that he had learned from the French and he continued to prefer their language as the cultural medium above all others. For the distinctive German literature and the new appreciation of the German language that were the great cultural events of his last two decades, Frederick showed no appreciation. What he recommended to the Germans was their development of the same kind of rational culture and standardized language from which he felt the French were latterly defaulting. This amalgam of cultural attitudes, whatever it may mean for the interminable subsequent debate on Frederick's German patriotism or his lack thereof to which it is often applied, does reveal a definite feature of his growth: the increasing tendency to see the political relevance of culture and to make political categories the organizing principles of cultural interests.

Theory and Practice

The crucial and complex relationship in Frederick between political and cultural or humanitarian concerns which were at once distinct and connected was shared by his fellow enlightened absolutists in whom the relationship was not so clearly articulated. For all of them, culture and humanity were intellectual and natural values transcending the state. But for all of them too the call to legislate the conditions for the progress of human thought and welfare combined with the need of their state for informed administration and popular support to make politics the center of their persistent commitments to culture and humanity. The same pattern, moreover, holds for the more familiar, but essentially derivative, problem of the relationship between the liberal and the authoritarian, the ameliorative and the power-seeking, strains *within* their politics. Here we return to the crucial issue of the relations between profession and deed, between ideology and policy, that is at the heart of the dispute over the authenticity of the "enlightened" in enlightened absolutism, but now, after our insight into the structure of the absolutist personality, we may hope to shed some light upon it.

Unquestionably, the "freedom," "rights," "welfare," and "happiness" of man which all the enlightened monarchs professed to have as their primary concerns were in fact frequently and deliberately violated by the oppressiveness of their bureaucracies and their studied neglect of social inequalities. Unquestionably, too, the principles which the enlightened rulers took, often literally, from the political theory of the Enlightenment—the principles of an original natural liberty, of government founded on contract, and of sovereignty limited by natural law—were frequently negated by the practical principles of power politics and the interests of state. But if we look closely at the absolutists' formal statements of their principles—at Frederick's early *Anti-Machiavel*, his *Political Testament* of 1752, his *Essay on the Forms of Government and the Duties of Sovereigns* of 1771; at Catherine's *Instruction* to the Legislative Commission of 1767; and at Joseph's assorted correspondence and memoranda—we can see that the discrepancies between their theory and their practice were not attributable simply to hypocrisy, for the discrepancies were prepared within the theory itself.

For Frederick, the contractual public powers which natural individuals transferred to the political sovereign, and which were recompensed by the security and welfare to be delivered by the sovereign to the citizens, were irrevocable and unaccountable. For Catherine, the explicit dependence upon the liberal principles and legal doctrines of Montesquieu and Beccaria, however borne out by her endorsement of human rights in the law, equality before the law, and definition of legitimate government by the law, stopped categorically short of endorsing the separation of powers or the political right of consent, and she deliberately revised her mentors in the direction of monarchical absolutism. For Joseph, finally, the self-appointed task of legislating "philosophy," however liberal in its orientation toward religious toleration, peasant emancipation, and equality of opportunity, tended to find its rationale more in the collective than in the individual welfare of his subjects.

Rather than a mere conflict of theory and practice in the politics of eighteenth-century absolutism, the tension between humanity and power which obscures its "enlightenment" may thus be seen as a feature of political personality infecting political theory and political practice alike. These monarchs endorsed the liberal principles of natural right, rulership contract, and the general interest because they were the only available sanctions for the secular service state in which they believed and the only available substitutes for the divine right of kings, in which, as the basis of the prescriptive political hierarchy and the religiously bound state, they just as energetically disbelieved.

The rulers needed this change in principles not because the worldly service of the community at home and abroad was a new function of authority, but because they now claimed it as the exclusive function of the state. Hence it required a correspondingly categorical set of secular, rational, and utilitarian principles. But however sincere the adoption of these principles, their use was definitely limited. They were used as the grounds of political obedience and as the purposes of policy, but they were *not* used as organizing principles for the state. Thus the liberal principles of freedom of thought and conscience, sanctity of property, and equal protection of the laws served to justify autocratic legislation, but the equally liberal principles of enforceable limits upon the monarch and representative participation in the legislative process were rejected for the constitution of the state.

The enlightened monarchs rejected these constitutional principles in part because they were as subject as anyone else to the general rule of Western politics that power is not relinquished spontaneously; in part because the socially static regions in which enlightened absolutism flourished generated comparatively little pressure for such relinquishment; in part because such pressure as did exist was aristocratic and corporate, claiming influence over or exemptions from rather than division of the state's power; and in part because the persistence of international rivalries made the continued concentration of political force a continuing responsibility of the ruler.

But over and above these general considerations of public order that conditioned the thinking of enlightened as well as unenlightened monarchs there was an equally important reason for the inhibition of liberal principles that was distinctive to the enlightened monarchs who professed them: in the overwhelmingly agrarian and conservative social context of central and eastern Europe, liberal principles could not be made operational without becoming self-contradictory. In this context the religious liberty of minorities was deemed to violate the rights and sensibilities of the orthodox majority; peasant liberation, to violate the property rights of either the lords or the peasants themselves, depending on the disposition of the land; the entrepreneurial freedom of estate owners, progressive farmers, and merchants, to infringe on the communal rights of peasants and the collective rights of artisans. Hence the society could not, even in theory, be vouchsafed the right of representative government without importing the contradictory liberties into the very structure of the state. For the enlightened monarchs, then, the maximum of human rights could be achieved, even in theory, only by balancing the different kinds of rights with an impartial measure that was not itself a matter of right and that could command a larger consensus than right—in other words, with the undiluted and undivided authority of the monarch to service the amalgamated rights of the community.

Hence when Frederick the Great epitomized the political theory of enlightened absolutism in his famous description of the sovereign as "only the first servant of the state," he revealed as much about the sovereign's primacy which he did not emphasize as about the obligation to service which he did. In this theory of enlightened absolutism, the variety of individual rights required the unity of sovereign power, and the legal obligations of ordinary citizens were enforced only by the sovereign's supralegal *ethic* of responsibility. The enlightened monarchs justified absolute political authority as the only common bond among the competing rights in a diversified society and as the only power that could, by its very constitution, guarantee what was fundamental in these rights from violation by any social force whatsoever.

We may conclude that the enlightened absolutist was identifiable, first, by his espousal of intellectual interests and liberal ideas apparently indifferent to or at variance with the authoritarianism of his political calling, and second, by his deliberate integration of this neutral or antithetical political authority into his scheme of cultural and liberal values as their indispensable complement. Such a royal personality was especially relevant to the Enlightenment because he shared with the *philosophes* the Enlightenment's assumption that men's material interests, including the benefits of political power, were ultimately compatible with their ethical principles —in Frederick's frank formulation that "the original principle of virtue is interest"—and he also shared the Enlightenment's contrary insight that men's actual prosecution of these interests was usually antithetical to their ethical principles.

But the enlightened monarch did more than simply share in the culture of the Enlightenment. Because he had to act where the *philosophes* only wrote, he had to bring into confrontation the recalcitrant facts and the unrealized principles that the *philosophes* could acknowledge equally side by side. Hence he created a logic of facts to connect the actual facts he found in the world with the unity of principle that gave them meaning, and he assigned the working out of this factual logic to politics. In his accessibility to wide ranges of cultural experience and in his insistent tendency to conceive of political authority as a rational field of force which gave to this manifold experience a manageable pattern, the enlightened absolutist filled the void left in the Enlightenment by the *philosophes'* provision of an essential place for politics in the good society and their unpolitical reluctance to occupy it. The enlightened ruler was, indeed, the political *philosophe* par excellence.

But even if we grant to enlightened absolutism a distinctive psychic and ideological reality, the question of its political and social reality still remains. For it can be argued—and has been argued—that no such specific identity pertains to the actual measures and deeds of the putatively enlightened autocrats, who met problems, dealt with resistance, and embarked on practical policies that had far more in common with the traditions of absolutism than the principles of Enlightenment. For this issue of enlightened absolutism, which is important because it involves the whole nature of politics in the second half of the eighteenth century, we turn from what the enlightened absolutists thought to what they did.

CHAPTER 20

The Enlightened Absolutists Abroad

THE RECORD OF foreign affairs in the second half of the eighteenth century undoubtedly constitutes the most serious indictment of enlightened absolutism as a distinctive kind of government. If enlightenment is understood to include, as the typical *philosophe* certainly understood it to include, the explicit rejection of force, conquest, dynastic claim, interest of state, and balance of power in favor of reason, peace, international law, universal morality, and cosmopolitan unity, the foreign policies of the enlightened absolutists must be accounted infinitely more absolute than enlightened. For the eighteenth century has long enjoyed a reputation of stealth, duplicity, rapacity, and naked aggression in international relations which is second to that of no other century in Western history, save possibly our own, and the rulers most responsible for this dubious preeminence were precisely the most "enlightened."

In part, the special responsibility of the philosopher kings is a matter of rhetoric. They were more articulate than other monarchs, and they gave literal expression to some of the notorious maxims of foreign policy that have seemed to epitomize all that was unprincipled in the international practice of the age. "When one has an advantage," wrote the great Frederick rhetorically, "is he to use it or not?" The first rule of foreign policy, he wrote, is to "seize the favorable opportunity." As for "rights" in international relations, he deemed them "the business of ministers" to work up, not of sovereigns to wait upon, and his main concern with them was epitomized in his notorious cynical injunction anent the partition of Poland, that "when rights are not very good, they should not be set forth in detail." "Of all States, from the smallest to the biggest," he concluded grimly, "one can safely say that the fundamental rule of government is the principle of extending their territories.... The passions of rulers have no other curb but the limits of their power. Those are the fixed laws of European politics to which every politician submits." Joseph was more sententious, but Catherine spoke for the diplomatic and military orientation of all three philosophical monarchs with her succinct aphorism: "He who gains nothing, loses."

Again, the enlightened monarchs have been particularly associated with the generally unsavory character of old-world diplomacy by virtue of the simple fact that they dominated continental diplomacy in the second half of the eighteenth century, precisely when its moral prestige was at its nadir. The foreign policies of Great Britain and France, the leading Atlantic powers, where the accidents of royal character, the persistence of constitutional traditions, and the surge of an increasingly mobile society excluded enlightened absolutism, were alternately paralyzed and obsessed during this period by their overseas duel for colonial wealth and possessions, leaving the initiative in manipulating the European system of states to the great central and eastern European powers with the energetic, shrewd, and enlightened monarchs.

Not only the shape of continental war and diplomacy as a whole, finally, but the most influential—and notorious—events in it were the special work of the enlightened absolutists. The secretly prepared Diplomatic Revolution of 1756–1757 and the ensuing Seven Years' War, the one-sided Russo-Turkish war of 1768–1774, the cynical Polish partition of 1772, and the expansionist Austrian designs upon Bavaria which produced the War of the Bavarian Succession in 1778 and the German crisis of 1785 were the outstanding continental events of the half century. All of them were in the mold of foreign policy created by Frederick the Great's unprovoked seizure of Silesia in 1740, and like this pilot event all were initiated by one or more enlightened monarchs.

To confirm this correlation of the unprincipled side of eighteenth-century international politics with enlightened monarchs we may note that the British-American struggle and its ramification in Europe, the one notable conflict between nations involving principle at all, was the one prominent event with which these monarchs had least to do. It had to do with precisely those countries—Great Britain, the British colonies, and France—in which the culture of the Enlightenment was associated more prominently with the society than with the state. True enough, French policy was pursued primarily in the prosecution of the commercial and colonial rivalry with Britain and in conformity with the inveterate royal habit of encouraging the rebels of one's enemy, but the difference between the French government's attitude toward these goals and the attitude of the allied Spanish government, under the enlightened Charles III (ruled 1759–1788), toward the same goals in the same war confirms the difference between the moral ambiguity of traditional foreign policy and the definitely amoral cast of enlightened foreign policy in the second half of the eighteenth century.

The French foreign minister, Charles Gravier, Count of Vergennes (1717–1787), was a career diplomat with a fear of and vengefulness toward Britain that had become a French obsession after the Seven Years' War of 1756–1763 and with a respectable belief in American independence as a "weight in the balance of power." But he also had the liberal conviction that trade had superseded territory as the chief sinew of power. His was the famous declaration that "in the present state of the world commercial questions are political questions," and it was he who would be responsible for the free-trading Anglo-French commercial treaty of 1786, which would establish naval peace and commercial competition. These insights not only led him to see the war more in terms of intangible trade privileges than brutal conquests but also made him responsive to the French literate society in general—since its members were vocal proponents of these insights—and to its principled pro-Americanism in particular. It was, indeed, through his preparatory work with the Dutch party of republican Patriots that the Netherlands entered the war against Britain during 1780 in ostensible defense of the commercial freedom of the seas. It was through his initiative that in the same year Catherine the Great agreed to form the League of Armed Neutrality, in which she never did believe, on the same principle of neutral rights. Spain, on the other hand, whose dogged, heavyhanded, single-minded king was accounted enlightened precisely for the conformity of his policies with the great monarchs' of central and eastern Europe rather than for any similarity in cultural tastes or intelligence quotient, entered the war against Britain in 1779 purely and simply for the reacquisition of Gibraltar and Minorca and for the expulsion of the British from the Gulf of Mexico and the Caribbean Sea. Unlike official France, "enlightened" Spain was entirely unsympathetic to the American principles in the war, refused to ally with the former colonies, and granted them recognition only at the very end of the war.

PRINCIPLES OF FOREIGN POLICY

Let us stipulate from the start, then, that the foreign policies of the enlightened autocrats shared none of the Enlightenment's typically pacific and humanitarian principles of international relations. But there remains the question of whether there was anything distinctive in the way these sovereigns pursued the policies of aggrandizement for the home country and balance of power for everyone else which had long been the goals of monarchical foreign policy. As a matter of fact, their approach to international relations does show a constant tendency, common to all of themselves and different from their predecessors, that was not so much a reflection of as a contribution to the culture of the Enlightenment. This common tendency was composed by the combination of two persistent traits in the foreign orientation of enlightened absolutism.

First, whereas personal, dynastic, and collective considerations merged in the traditional canons of international statecraft, the enlightened monarchs distinguished among these strands and deliberately arranged them in a clear order of priority which recognized the collective interest as supreme, the personal interest as subordinate, and the dynastic interest as purely instrumental. Frederick the Great put as little store in the Hohenzollern claims to the Silesia he seized as in the Habsburg, and if he acknowledged princely "honor" or "glory" as a valid "principle" of foreign policy he also declared categorically that it must be "sacrificed" when "the safety and the greater welfare of the state demand it." Joseph was no less cavalier about the ancient Wittelsbach title to Bavaria. If he at first put forth a weak and hoary Habsburg claim to a part of that electorate, he ultimately sought to exchange the Austrian Netherlands for the whole of it, deliberately negating the reciprocal rights of dynasties and peoples in return for the "solid advantage" of an expanded Austrian heartland in central Europe.

The enlightened rulers believed, to be sure, in the superior merit of hereditary monarchy, but they believed in it rather for the orderly benefits it conferred than as something good in itself, sanctified by divine ordination or human tradition. The final measure of all political values and institutions, by which both dynastic right and individual princely honor must be assessed, was now deemed to be a single standard. The collective interest of the realm, joining the interests of ruler and people into a unity vis-a-vis other states, was now explicitly recognized by the rulers themselves to be *the* guiding principle of their policies. In Frederick's categorical terms: "The rulers must always be guided by the interest of the state. . . . The interest of the state is their law and is inviolable."

The interest of state was not only tangible and integral but also rational —and this rationality in foreign policy was the second distinguishing feature in the international attitude of the enlightened monarchs. The standard of state interest was rational not in the normative sense of conformity to a universal law or principle, but in the functional sense of its capacity to be calculated, compared, and logically linked with similarly analyzed interests of other states. Hence the tendency to view the interest of state in the quantitative terms of miles, souls, and wealth to be acquired. The Polish partition, for example, was viewed by all three enlightened rulers as the preservation of a numerical balance among the three eastern powers, and Joseph's own designs upon Bavaria were stimulated by his estimation of it as a precise equivalent for the irrevocably lost Silesia. Such considerations, moreover, were only the most literal expression of the objectivity, the regularity, and the uniformity that were deemed the general attributes of the interest of state. It was Frederick, as usual, who articulated this rational approach into appropriate maxims. "He whose conduct is best calculated," he wrote about the making of foreign policy, "triumphs over those who act with less consistency." An analogous view went into his prescriptions for the understanding of foreign policy, for he directed attention to "the fixed and lasting interests" of the various states and assigned to their "interplay" the rigor of "systems." By virtue of their commensurability, the respective interests of state permit the wise man to compare current events and, "observing the relations and similarities, . . . to be able to know everything, judge everything, predict everything."

These two main tendencies in the foreign policies of the enlightened rulers—the organization of various partial interests within the community into the single standard of an exclusive state interest, and the possibility of connecting it rationally with the analogously perceived interests of other states—shared a common assumption. Both tendencies alike postulated a world of states that was constituted entirely by facts—by political and economic conditions, by contemporary events, and by the motives of statesmen that would produce new facts. There was no place in this realm for the universal qualities of human nature that referred to what man fundamentally was rather than to how men severally acted and that in other realms of human relations provided for the authority of universal law and humane moral principle over the real actions of men.

It was, indeed, precisely in their exclusion of laws and principles common to humanity from any relevance to relations among states that the enlightened absolutists diverged signally from the *philosophes* whose rhetoric they shared. When the *philosophes* spoke of the actuality of human behavior in the international arena they usually analyzed it into the same kind of naked self-interest that formed the basis of their royal readers' policies. Voltaire's cynical reference to occasion, custom, and force as "the only laws" and Kant's dour portrait of self-seeking men in an international jungle were typical of the *philosophes'* attitude toward international affairs, past and present. But where the *philosophes* condemned this actuality by measuring it against the reality of humanity and its universal laws, which they deemed as relevant to international as to domestic affairs, the enlightened absolutists accepted the same actuality as the only reality pertinent to international affairs and committed themselves wholeheartedly to it. Catherine gloried in intrigue, Joseph threw himself enthusiastically and continuously into project after project for the expansion of his dominions, and even Frederick, who alone lamented on occasion the evil ways of his peers that compelled him to lower himself to their level, ended by making "a sacred law" out of his necessity.

But if the rulers thus segregated foreign policy from the more general political and moral considerations which the disengaged *philosophes* held to be relevant to it, they did apply the characteristic intellectual approaches of the Enlightenment within the circumscribed sphere of international politics. Kings and ministers used the skeptical, empirical, pragmatic strand of the Enlightenment as a destructive weapon of the regional service state against the residual temporal and patriarchal bonds of an older Christian Europe, and they used the Enlightenment's typical balance of reason and fact to construct rational international arrangements of actual state interests. The combination of the critical and synthetic uses of reason in war and diplomacy, the fields of politics furthest removed from the humanitarian ideas of the age, demonstrates the status of enlightened absolutism as an authentic but autonomous branch of Enlightenment culture.

The enlightened absolutists displayed their characteristic patterns of foreign policy most distinctively in the Diplomatic Revolution of 1756–1757 and the first Polish partition of 1772, the two events which most clearly were the products of enlightened-absolutist initiative and which most decisively impressed the influence of enlightened absolutism upon the emergent forms of modern international relations.

THE DIPLOMATIC REVOLUTION OF 1756

The Diplomatic Revolution of the mid-eighteenth century comprises the three successive treaties which reversed the alliances binding France and Prussia against Great Britain, Austria, and Russia—multiple and ill-assorted bilateral alliances only a generation old at most, to be sure, but generally deemed to reflect an underlying international order hallowed by both nature and tradition, and confirmed by the War of the Austrian Succession (1740–1748). The three "revolutionary" treaties were: the Convention of Westminster (January 16, 1756), which joined Great Britain and Prussia in a nonaggression pact aimed at the neutralization of the German Empire to prevent any extension of the *de facto* Anglo-French war from its actual maritime and probable Dutch theaters; the First Treaty of Versailles (May 1, 1756), which bound Austria and France in a defensive alliance providing for mutual assistance in the event of an attack upon the European possessions of either by any power but Great Britain, pledged Austria to neutrality in the event of such an attack by Great Britain, and was supplemented by Russian adherence on December 31, 1756; finally, the Second Treaty of Versailles (May 1, 1757), concluded by Austria and France well after Prussia's Frederick initiated the Seven Years' War with his invasion of Austria's ally, Saxony, on August 29, 1756. This last treaty converted the Austro-French defensive pact into an offensive alliance looking to the dismemberment of Prussia, with explicit provision for the restoration of Silesia to Austria, in return for the ultimate transfer of the Austrian Netherlands to France.

That such instruments—two defensive agreements hopeful of sparing previous alliances and one offensive treaty that was a reflex of ongoing military hostilities—should register the impact of a revolution upon contemporaries and posterity alike is a matter not so much of their specific provisions as of their implications and effects.

First, the replacement of the old Bourbon-Habsburg rivalry with a Franco-Austrian alliance signalized the supersession of dynastic interests by reasons of state.

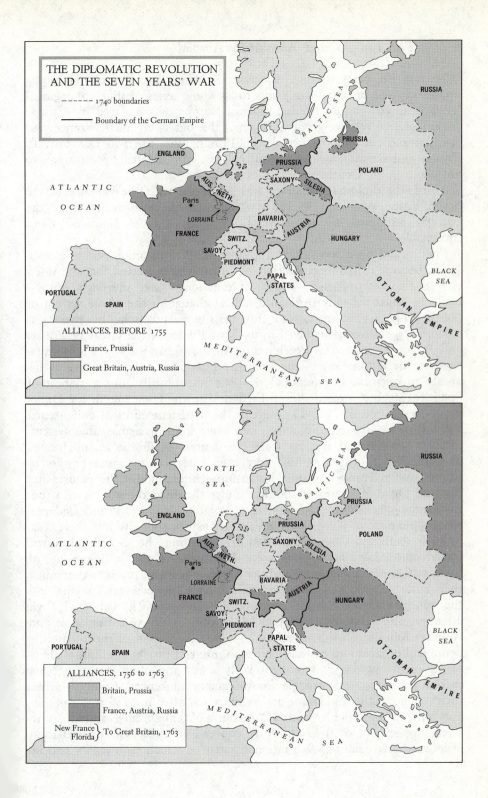

THE DIPLOMATIC REVOLUTION
AND THE SEVEN YEARS' WAR

----- 1740 boundaries

——— Boundary of the German Empire

RUSSIA

ENGLAND

PRUSSIA

PRUSSIA

SAXONY   SILESIA

POLAND

ATLANTIC

OCEAN

AUS. NETH.

Paris

LORRAINE

BAVARIA

AUSTRIA

FRANCE

SWITZ.

SAVOY

PIEDMONT

PAPAL
STATES

HUNGARY

BLACK
SEA

OTTOMAN

EMPIRE

PORTUGAL

SPAIN

MEDITERRANEAN   SEA

ALLIANCES, BEFORE 1755

France, Prussia

Great Britain, Austria, Russia

NORTH
SEA

RUSSIA

BALTIC SEA

ENGLAND

PRUSSIA

PRUSSIA

SAXONY   SILESIA

POLAND

ATLANTIC

OCEAN

AUS. NETH.

Paris

LORRAINE

BAVARIA

AUSTRIA

FRANCE

SWITZ.

SAVOY

PIEDMONT

PAPAL
STATES

HUNGARY

BLACK
SEA

OTTOMAN

EMPIRE

PORTUGAL

SPAIN

MEDITERRANEAN   SEA

ALLIANCES, 1756 to 1763

Britain, Prussia

France, Austria, Russia

New France }
Florida   } To Great Britain, 1763

Second, the older balance of power, in which the Bourbon-Habsburg opposition had provided the pivots for a whole series of different regional balances in the various trouble spots of Europe, was replaced by a single system of five relatively equal powers (the old antagonists, France and Austria, and the old balance wheel, Britain, plus the two new arrivals, Prussia and Russia), whose general balance was affected by disturbances anywhere on the Continent.

Third, the diplomatic revision was associated with the violence of the Seven Years' War of 1756–1763, which executed with armed force the changes registered by the reversal of alliances and rendered them irreversible.

Finally, and most revealingly, the shift of alliances amounted to a revolution because it had its revolutionaries, men who perceived that the interests of their own parties—in this international case, sovereign states—could be advanced only through a radical change in the whole system of politics. The revolutionaries in this crisis were precisely the two most enlightened statesmen involved in it—King Frederick the Great of Prussia and Prince Kaunitz, the freethinking Austrian chancellor whose admiration for the rationalism of the French *philosophes* and confidence in his ability to organize international relations scientifically into a system of "political algebra" exceeded even Frederick's own. Their role in the Diplomatic Revolution of 1756–1757 reveals the persistent effort of enlightened absolutism to organize diplomacy into some kind of manageable system.

Their achievement is clear from the contrast with the unenlightened diplomacy of the age. At this very time three of the great powers of Europe suffered under myopic leadership—Britain under the painstaking but dull Duke of Newcastle, France under the divided counsels of a routine-bound official diplomacy and the sporadic, dynastically obsessed personal diplomacy of King Louis XV, and Russia under the impulsive Tsarina Elizabeth and Count Alexis Bestuzhev-Ryumin, her British-subsidized foreign-office chief. These powers vacillated between the familiar issues of the Low Countries, Hanover, and the Baltic, which continued to determine their basic policies, and the developing interests in overseas colonies and the continental borderlands of eastern Europe, which distracted their attention and rendered their policies indecisive. Prussia's Frederick and Austria's Kaunitz, on the other hand, grasped the import of the apparently peripheral oceanic and eastern European interests for the traditional alignments of the powers and brought both newer and older issues together to bear on their own struggle for supremacy in central Europe. Hence their seizure of the diplomatic and military initiative in 1756 was a matter not only of the highly touted "realism" of enlightened statesmen in foreign policy but of their ability to conceive of the whole constellation of international relations as a rational system in which each reality had its

The pious Maria Theresa with her Enlightened chancellor, Prince Kaunitz.

due place. In international politics as in intellectual life, the devotees of the Enlightenment were distinctive for the constancy with which they strove to connect their two ultimate passions—their passion for perceiving the facts as they were, free of any obscuring associations, and their passion for associating these facts in patterns manageable by reason.

Again analogously with intellectual life, there were different versions of the common enlightened approach to foreign policy, and the variations served to show the range of possibilities in Enlightenment principles. A comparison of the proportions of realism and system in the respective roles played by Kaunitz and Frederick in the Diplomatic Revolution demonstrates, in general, the joint addiction of both men to both principles as such, in contrast to the combination of illusion and incoherence in their unenlightened and passive contemporaries. But it will also show a difference of proportions which betokened a difference of method between the two men, and this difference clarifies the two alternate methods bequeathed by enlightened monarchy to the making of foreign policy; for it was the play and counterplay of Kaunitz's and Frederick's methods that made the Diplomatic Revolution.

It was a notable confirmation of the connection between the real and the rational in the practical as in the theoretical culture of the eighteenth century that in his rivalry with Frederick during 1756 and 1757 Kaunitz proved to be the more realistic precisely because his system was the more inclusive. His grand design, conceived back in 1749 and accepted as official Habsburg policy in 1755, organized the various Austrian interests into a logical sequence of priorities and organized the even more various interests of all the powers concerned into a system of Austrian foreign relations which could presumably account for every contingency. The recovery of Silesia and the concomitant destruction, through dismemberment, of Prussia as a great power were the supreme immediate goals to which all else was to be subordinated, not for the reasons of revenge, damaged dynastic pride, and outraged morality that were Maria Theresa's private incentives, but because the Austrian recovery of hegemony in central Europe was a necessary prior condition for the assertion of the other Austrian interests—in the east against the Ottoman Empire and in Germany and the west against the French.

To accomplish the immediate goals. Prussia had first to be isolated and then crushed by an encircling coalition. To achieve these conditions, in turn, a clear hierarchy of priorities was set up. Most important was Austria's complete freedom of military disposition and diplomatic maneuver, based on the financial independence born of internal reform. Next in importance was the detachment of France from the Prussian alliance, purchased by the promises of support for Bourbons in Poland and of their investiture in the Austrian Netherlands. Almost as crucial was the conversion of Russian friendship into active assistance. Lowest in priority was the retention of the British alliance that had worked so poorly for Austria in the last war (of the Austrian Succession).

From 1749 on, Kaunitz pursued all the lines indicated by this system, but by the summer of 1755 only the internal policy of achieving military independence through financial reform, administrative centralization, and the equalization of the tax burden was actually beginning to bear fruit. Then, precisely because he was looking for an enlarged framework of international policy that would be more appropriate to his large-scale planning than the frustrating bilateral crisscross of existing foreign relations, he perceived the real, if still subliminal, effect of the undeclared Anglo-French colonial war in expanding the arena of international relations and making possible more rational combinations among the pentarchy of great powers. He now intensified his wooing of France, artfully combining new and old appeals to the French fears of a British-organized continental coalition, to the official French mistrust of an upstart Prussian satellite, and to Louis' dynastic cupidity. At the same time he increased his pressure on the exposed British and pushed them to promise, in the Anglo-Russian convention of September, 1755, the subsidies which would make Russia an effective partner in a Habsburg-led continental bloc. With this large preset scheme, Kaunitz established a whole network of conditions that gave to each particular action of the powers a different reality and effect than it was intended to have. Only the Anglo-Russian convention proved abortive, because of Frederick's counteraction in concluding the Convention of Westminster with the British, but Kaunitz's system endowed this defensive agreement with an offensive effect upon the French and endowed the subsequent Franco-Austrian defensive pact of May, 1756, with an offensive effect upon Frederick, even anticipating, in the words of Count Georg Adam von Starhemberg (1724–1807), Kaunitz's ambassador in Paris, the impact of Frederick himself, as "our most effective helper" in activating the desired offensive combination of Austrians, French, and Russians against Prussia.

Kaunitz's comprehensive system of conditions evoked from Frederick the incisive analysis of politics which was, in turn, ever characteristic of *him*. He would separate a complex condition into its component issues and initiate immediate action upon the issue most vital and accessible to him, with a view to isolating and resolving it before its connections with other issues made it insoluble. For Frederick, political conditions as a whole could not be mastered, but they had to be understood as a whole so that they could be rationally analyzed into their constituent parts, which could be mastered. Thus, reasoning that the Anglo-French conflict gave both powers alike a real interest in disengagement from central Europe, Frederick signed the Prusso-British nonaggression pact of January, 1756 (Convention of Westminster), in the expectation that by localizing the Anglo-French war in the colonies, the seas, and the Netherlandish coastal areas where it belonged, it would remove Britain from the hostile coalition, undermine the financial capacity of the Russians to participate, and yet not violate his alliance with France. Again, Frederick's invasion of Saxony in August, 1756, which first made a matter of fact a reversal of alliances that had heretofore been a matter of opinion, was only in part a reflex response to his perception of Kaunitz's grand design against him, triggered by the dubious reports of his intelligence agents of prearations in Austria, Russia, and Saxony for an imminent concerted attack upon him. The very real and persistent obstacles still raised by the reluctant French to Kaunitz's offensive design before August had left Frederick with a choice of policies and indicate an additional cause outside the design that persuaded him to make the choice he did. This cause was Frederick's own model of action, and the outbreak of the Seven Years' War is best seen neither as the inevitable result of the diplomatic realignment nor as the fortuitous compounding of French and Prussian mistakes, but rather as the collision of two inflexibly rational system of international relations—a collision that may well be viewed as the conflict of Frederick's analytic with Kaunitz's synthetic spirit within the Enlightenment syndrome.

For Frederick's unannounced attack upon Austria's ally, Saxony, was not simply a reflex reaction to Kaunitz's system but also a characteristic conclusion from his own chain of calculations. He came to the decision to strike when and where he did as the only valid inference from the conjunction of two of his long-cherished premises: that a hostile union could be countered only by anticipating the combination of its elements and mastering them piecemeal; and that the annexation of Electoral Saxony, with its productive industries, with its Catholic Elector's ties to Austria, Poland, and, through Poland, to Russia, and with the strategic threat of its long common frontier running up the extended western edge of Silesia and along the southern border of Brandenburg itself, was and had to be a persistent object of Prussian policy.

What was illuminating about Frederick's initiation of the Seven Years' War was his conviction that a particular Prussian advantage could be acquired through the dissolution of a general European situation into its manageable parts. Where Kaunitz would direct an entire system toward a particular claim as its necessary result, Frederick acted to break up the system on the principle that one should adjust one's claims to "the barometer of one's fortunes." So Frederick chose to attack Austria in Bohemia through Saxony rather than Austria in Moravia from Silesia because the former course seemed better calculated to attain his goal of isolating and defeating Austria before Maria Theresa's Russian and French allies could bring their concerted forces to bear and because like all wars for Frederick such a war would be worthwhile only if its costs were compensated by a permanent gain like Saxony.

Actually, the Seven Years' War achieved the goals neither of Kaunitz's synthetic nor of Frederick's analytic utilitarianism. The diversion of the French war effort to the colonial conflict against the British and the lack of coordination between the Russian armies, committed to the Baltic, and the Austrian armies, committed to Saxony and Silesia, ultimately frustrated the Austrian project of regaining Silesia and dismantling Prussia. But if Frederick did thus manage to save the integrity of his state by using his characteristic strategy of dealing separately with the coalition armies and his characteristic tactic of the oblique battle order which permitted him to concentrate his forces against a single isolated wing of the enemy, he also not only failed to acquire Saxony but came very close to complete defeat from the powerful, if sporadic, effects of successful coalition warfare. He felt, indeed, that only the Russian withdrawal from the war in 1762, occasioned by the accident of Tsarina Elizabeth's death and the accession of the admiring Peter III, rescued him from the increasingly effective encirclement.

For both Austria and Prussia, the Seven Years' War marked a decisive turning point. In 1765 Joseph II became German Emperor and coregent, with Maria Theresa, of the Habsburg dominions. Henceforward he joined Kaunitz in decision-making, and he helped to bring a new direction to Austrian policy, away from Silesia and from obsession with Prussia. Frederick, for his part, never forgot the terrible abyss of failure that the war had opened before him, and he now came to feel, as never before, the "uncertainty" that "holds sway in all operations of foreign policy."

But the failure of the Diplomatic Revolution to fulfill the requirements of either of the systems—Austrian or Prussian—which were jointly responsible for it did not mean the end of systematic foreign policy for the enlightened absolutists. So powerful was the tendency toward systematic policy for them that their response to failure was simply to adjust their systems to their experience. Frederick's became more combinatory, more synthetic; under Joseph's influence Austria's became more partial, more flexible. In conjunction with the parallel development of Russian policy toward a regional system under Catherine the Great, the convergence produced the first partition of Poland and therewith the origins of the eastern system that would play a dominant role in European history for the next century and a half.

THE FIRST PARTITION OF POLAND, 1772

The shock and disappointment which the course of the Seven Years' War brought to the expectations of its participants had the immediate effect not so much of reducing the scope of the great-power system, but of dismantling it temporarily in all its versions, traditional and revolutionary alike. Even during the last phase of the war itself international relations had been reduced to unilateral action and to exclusive bilateral arrangements. Despite treaties of mutual assistance which had bound the Russians and Austrians in February, 1757, and the British and Prussians in April, 1758, both sides during 1762 began separate negotiations in which allies were not consulted and their interests were not considered. The Anglo-French preliminary agreement of November 3, 1762, which provided for mutual withdrawal from the continental war, for Britain's retention of its mainland conquests in North America, and for its return of occupied West Indian islands and Indian bases to France and Spain (a belated belligerent since the British extension of the colonial war to the Spanish empire in January, 1762), became, with the later Spanish adherence, the basis of the final Peace of Paris on February 10, 1763. The separate Prussian-Russian peace of May, 1762, and the offensive alliance which Frederick negotiated a month later with his Russian adulator, the new but short-lived Tsar Peter III, were voided by the enforced abdication of the latter at the end of June (he was assassinated in his jail during July), but they set the stage for Catherine the Great's unilateral withdrawal of Russia from the war in July, and consequently, for the final separate Treaty of Hubertusburg of February 15, 1763, wherein Prussia and Austria (along with Saxony, the Austrian satellite), agreed to peace in central Europe on the basis of the *status quo ante bellum.*

The decomposition of the wartime alliances reflected, moreover, a growing awareness within each of the great powers of distinct long-range interests—an awareness which perpetuated the war-born pattern of segregated interests and independent initiatives, tempered only by limited bilateral arrangements, in the international relations of the postwar period. In both Great Britain and France the governing classes persisted in the conviction, which had disposed them to peacemaking, that maritime and colonial rivalry had become the primary issue of foreign policy and that it would be much more effectively pursued without the diversions of continental entanglements. This view led Britain to diplomatic isolation, and France to reliance on the Franco-Spanish Family Compact of 1761, with its provision for joint action by the Bourbon powers to satisfy their respective claims against Britain, as the mainstay of French foreign relations. Henceforward French continental connections, such as the entente with Austria and the support of Francophiles in Poland and Constantinople, were depreciated to the purely defensive purposes of maintaining a balance and preventing a diversion of French energies upon the Continent.

Prussia and Russia, similarly, focused their interests and commitments after the war. Frederick the Great inferred from that conflict the dispensability of the western powers and the indispensability of Russia to the defense of his scattered holdings in central and eastern Europe. At the same time Catherine the Great based her policies on the underpopulation of Russia and resolved to replace her predecessors' policies of European commitments and adventures with a policy of expansion into populous, contiguous Poland. This convergence of particular interests produced the Russo-Prussian agreement of 1764, which gave to Frederick the desired security of a Russian defensive alliance and to Catherine Prussian support for her unilateral diplomatic and military intervention in Poland, beginning in the same year, to secure the election of her former lover, Stanislas Poniatowski, as Polish King and to assert Russian hegemony over an unreformed Poland against the resistance of the conservative Roman Catholic Polish nobility organized in the Confederation of the Bar. Both Frederick and Catherine, significantly, opted for these limited benefits against broader alternatives—Frederick against his own expressed fears of Europe's contributing "to the rise of a people that may some day become Europe's own doom," and Catherine against the project of a Northern System set forth by her adviser Count Nikita Panin (1718–1783) to organize a multipower permanent military alliance to keep the peace in Europe.

Even the Habsburgs, whose spread of dominions across Europe from the Belgian coastline on the English Channel to the Turkish Balkan frontier continued to provide the real underpinnings for the comprehensive policy-making of their long-term Chancellor Kaunitz, contributed after 1763 to the international fragmentation that was the essential background of the Polish partition. Convinced of the necessity for a thorough internal reorganization and consolidation of the Habsburg dominions as a prior condition of any resumption of the diplomatic offensive, the Austrian authori-

ARCTIC OCEAN

SWEDEN

Nystad
Abo
KARELIA
Lake Onega
Lake Ladoga
Narva
INGRIA
St. Petersburg*
ESTONIA
LIVONIA
BALTIC SEA
N. Dvina R.
W. Dvina R.
Volga R.
Moscow
EAST PRUSSIA
POLAND
Niemen R.
Smolensk
Warsaw
RUSSIA
Ural R.
Chernigov
Kiev
Poltava
Dnieper
Bug R.
Dniester R.
Don R.
Volga R.
Azov
Danube R.
Sevastopol
Sea of Azov
BLACK SEA
CASPIAN SEA

0   500 miles

THE WESTERN EXPANSION OF RUSSIA UNDER PETER AND CATHERINE

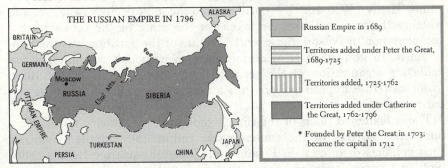

THE RUSSIAN EMPIRE IN 1796

ALASKA
BRITAIN
GERMANY
Moscow
RUSSIA
Ural Mts.
SIBERIA
OTTOMAN EMPIRE
PERSIA
TURKESTAN
CHINA
JAPAN

Russian Empire in 1689

Territories added under Peter the Great, 1689-1725

Territories added, 1725-1762

Territories added under Catherine the Great, 1762-1796

* Founded by Peter the Great in 1703; became the capital in 1712

ties—including Kaunitz himslf—shifted their main attention from the diplomatic to the domestic systematizing of the "second reform period," as the decade following the Seven Years' War has been called in comparison with the first period, the years 1749–1756, with their less absorbing and extensive reforms. When Joseph II joined his mother, Maria Theresa, as coregent in 1765, not only did he collaborate wholeheartedly with his fellow devotees of the Enlightenment in the work of internal centralization and modernization but his own thirst for personal glory brought a force for unilateral action into Habsburg diplomacy that would henceforth rival its traditional passion for combinations. Characteristically, the one fruitful initiative of the Habsburgs in the decade after the Seven Years' War was the unilateral seizure of the county of Zips in February, 1769: a place—a Polish enclave in Hungary adjacent to Polish Galicia—and a time—during the confusion attendant upon the recently opened Russo-Turkish war of 1768–1774—that would make it a precedent for further partition.

The Eastern Crisis

The general context of the first Polish partition thus consisted in a European constellation which had each power pursuing regional goals either independently or with, at most, the passive support of one neighboring ally. In this disorganized situation the fortuitous eruption of the Russo-Turkish war—it started when the Turks panicked at the violations of the Polish-Turkish frontier by pro-Russian Polish guerrillas in defiance of official Russian policy—threatened to trigger a generally destructive chain reaction, and the first partition of Poland, in 1772, can be seen as a mutually concerted organization of particular interests to prevent it. More important—and more fruitful—than the still unresolved issues of who was primarily responsible for the partition and which motive—mutual greed or the anxiety to localize the Russo-Turkish war—was its primary cause were the two indubitable facts about the decision to partition: first, all the enlightened authorities embroiled in eastern Europe—Catherine, Joseph II, Kaunitz, Frederick II, and his similarly enlightened brother, Prince Henry (1726–1802)—contributed to the joint decision; and, second, whether the war in Turkey be taken for the cause or the occasion of a compensation in Poland, the essential feature of the partition was the resolution of an immediate crisis arising out of a particular war through the deliberate organization of the separate long-range interests of the three major eastern-European powers into a permanent common stake in the entire region.

The enlightened rulers of the three major powers, following a well-worn intellectual pattern of the contemporary culture they admired, resolved their conflicts of interest in Poland and Turkey by relating them as subplots in a larger design and thereby combining the discordant elements of each arena into harmoniously balanced parts of the expanded whole. The

Destruction of the Turkish by the Russian fleet at Cesmé in the Aegean Sea, July 1770. *This naval battle was one of the notable Russian victories over the Turks which made imminent the involvement of other powers and set the stage for the first partition of Poland.*

suggestions of each government for a Polish partition had been irreconcilable as long as they reflected the incompatible long-range interests of the three powers in the limited Polish context, but were reconciled in the fact of a concerted Polish partition when the expanding Turkish crisis created the possibility of a general eastern settlement deliberately aligning the unequal Polish interests of the powers into a system of equilibrium with the unequal Turkish interests of the same powers.

Only in 1771, when the conditions of policy making were drastically altered by the imminent spread of war, owing to Russian military conquests and the Austrian promise of armed support to the Turks, did the enlightened policy makers select from the various interests the common elements that would constitute an agreed scheme of Polish partition as the core of a general eastern settlement. Frederick, with most to gain in Poland and nothing to gain in the Ottoman Empire, was the first to recognize the combination which used the Ottoman war to make possible a Polish partition and the Polish partition to limit the Ottoman war. Taking up Catherine's playful suggestion of a three-power grab in Poland and turning it into a serious policy of collective security, he spent most of 1771 urging it upon both Catherine and the Kaunitz-Joseph team as a mutual compensation for what each must concede and as a reciprocal pledge for what both parties tacitly accepted in the Turkish theater. Frederick's pressure on Poland and the Austro-Russian negotiations on the Turkish war ran on side by side, and in October, 1771, Catherine on the one side and Kaunitz and Joseph on the other came to corresponding decisions on both issues: both sides agreed on the principle of a Polish partition among the three powers, and both sides agreed on the limits of a Turkish settlement that would realize Russian war aims on the Black Sea and in the Crimea, but not in the Danubian principalities.

By February, 1772, the details were worked out, but it took a Russo-

Cartoon illustrating
the first partition
of Poland in 1772.

Prussian *fait accompli* and six months more for the representatives of the
political Enlightenment to persuade the old-fashioned Maria Theresa to
sign up, against her avowed "inability to understand" how she could be
urged "to imitate two other powers in the injustice of using their superior
force to suppress an innocent victim on the dubious grounds of prudence
and convenience," and against her avowed insistence on the contrary
principle that "the rights of the prince are not different from the rights of
any private man." But nonetheless consent she did, and the Austrians
acceded to the treaty on August 2, 1772. The event had as an incidental
by-product a rare confrontation of Christian and Enlightened judgments
on the standards of European foreign policy. When Maria Theresa moaned
that the treaty spread "a stain over my whole reign," Frederick made the
dry response that epitomized the Enlightenment's view of Christian
politics: "She cries, but she always takes."

Terms of the Partition

The instruments of the first Polish partition were several. What we
think of as one arrangement was actually the joint product of three bilateral treaties, concluded by each possible pair of the partitioning powers
with each other (in 1772); a declaration by the Russian ambassador in
Warsaw endorsed by the ambassadors of the other two partitioning powers
(also in 1772); and separate treaties concluded by Poland with each of the
three partitioning powers and confirming the provisions of the prior treaties and the declaration (in 1775). This staggered pattern of treaty making
is important because it formally sanctioned the joint stake of the three

great eastern states in both the territorial and the political terms of the Polish partition.

Almost one third of the Polish kingdom's territory and one half of its inhabitants were divided among the three neighboring great powers, with each gaining what was required by its own long-range interest. Prussia took the smallest but strategically most vital section, the West Prussian districts that now connected East Prussia with the heart of the monarchy, and Ermeland, the large Polish enclave in the middle of East Prussia—a total area of some 14,000 square miles and 600,000 inhabitants. Only the isolated port of Danzig was left dangling in Polish possession, inviting toll wars and a future repartition.

The Russians received the sections of White Russia, Lithuania, and Livonia that gave them the coveted river courses of the upper Dvina and Dnieper, adding an area of some 34,000 square miles for the support of their western armies and more than a million and a half souls to their human resources.

The Austrian gain was the least vital of the three to the partitioners' interests, as they were then conceived, but compensated by being quantitatively the most impressive of all. The Habsburgs took Lodomeria and the old kingdom of Galicia on the northern slope of the Hungarian Carpathians and the district of Red Russia to the east of the kingdom, together an area of 32,000 square miles and 2.5 million people, including Lvov (renamed Lemberg), one of Poland's largest cities. Conformably to the Habsburg pattern of accumulation, the new acquisition formed a salient protecting Hungary from the new dominant threat in the east—Russia.

Less remarked than this massive transfer of land and people but perhaps even more subversive of acknowledged rights were the political principles explicated in the treaties, for these principles belied the formal guarantee pledged by the powers to the territorial integrity of the residual Polish kingdom and legitimated in advance the complete destruction of independent Poland that was not yet intended. The signatory powers justified their annexations as security measures necessary to protect their claims in Poland, and their own adjacent territories, from Polish "anarchy," and they confirmed the implications of this promise for further intervention by requiring joint participation of the partitioning powers in the preservation of the Polish constitution that was in fact producing the anarchy. Moreover, they legitimated such intervention in advance by forcing the Polish Diet itself to endorse not only the territorial transfers but also the constitutional intrusions.

Results of the Partition

However much the facts and principles of the partition may support the subsequent moral judgments of it as a piratical conspiracy against international law, an unconscionable oppression of Polish nationality, and a suicidal model for revolutionary destruction of monarchy, these judgments tell more about the ideals, the nationalism, or the nostalgia of the later generations who did the judging than they do about the partition that was judged. A clue to the political, rather than moral, meaning of the partition lies in the stark contrast between the indifference or even mild approval prevalent among its contemporaries and the righteous indignation that would obsess their descendants. The obvious disorder of Polish conditions to which so many men of the age referred in justification of the partition pointed clearly to what was positive in the policies leading to it and what was permanent in its results. The partition adumbrated the three pillars of the great-power system which, for better or worse, would bring a degree of order into the anarchic international relations among the several states of Europe.

First, the enlightened partitioners perceived the fundamental rule of the new international relations—the necessary connection between the concert and the balance of powers—and converted it from a pious principle into a literal and permanent reality. The political notions of concert and balance stemmed from very different roots, concert from the traditional ideal of an essential Christian community among the European temporal authorities and balance from the traditional practice of preserving their contingent plurality. These divergent origins would continue to foment illusions of a necessary antithesis between the concert and the balance of powers among the naïve and the unwary from the Holy Alliance of 1815 through the United Nations of the present. In actuality the European concert and the balance of its several sovereign states would be permanent complements and mutual dependents in the great-power system which would dominate world history from the mid-eighteenth to the mid-twentieth centuries. The outstanding statesmen of this system—Metternich, Bismarck, Churchill—would understand that a secular concert of powers could be united only on the common adjustment of their several independent interests and that these interests, conversely, could be kept in balance only through the concerted acknowledgment of each by all. Not only was the Polish partition of 1772 the first deliberate and categorical example of this combination, unmitigated by either the older rhetoric of Christian unity or the older fragility of emergency coalitions against a hegemonic power, but it created a settlement whose balance required a continuous tacit concert of the partitioning powers over the next century for its preservation.

The second important principle of the great-power system which the partition crystallized into an overt and unmistakable reality was the prescription that the approach to domestic issues—both of one's own and of other countries—be made in the context of foreign policy. To be sure, some of the ways of measuring internal political relations by the standards of foreign policy were centuries old. But in the last third of the eighteenth century this relationship entered into a new phase, inaugurated by the first

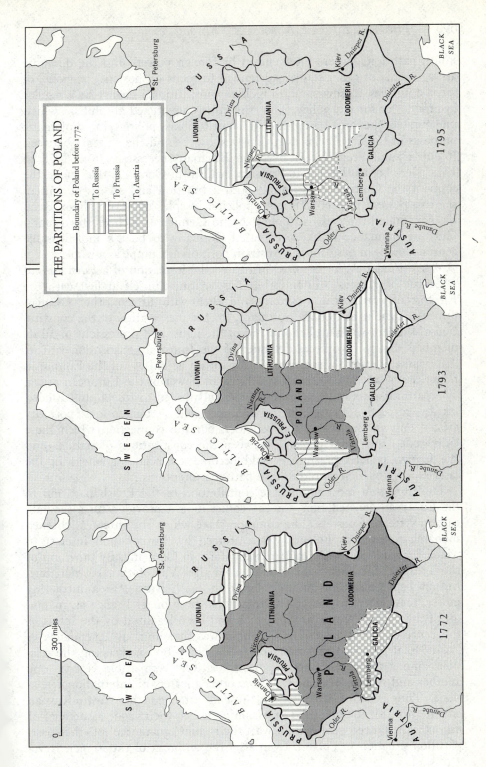

THE PARTITIONS OF POLAND

——— Boundary of Poland before 1772

To Russia
To Prussia
To Austria

Polish partition. Where intervention by foreign powers into the domestic arrangements of other states had tended to focus on persons, religions, or specific policies, it now came to include constitutional change as a regular by-product of foreign policy. Thus the same enlightened absolutism which inaugurated the broad new use of constitutional politics for diplomatic purposes in the first Polish partition was also behind the struggle between Joseph II and Frederick II over the Bavarian succession, from 1778 to 1785. Here began the Austro-Prussian dualism in Germany that made the form of the German constitution both a function and an instrument of the two powers' respective foreign policies. Joseph's efforts to annex Bavaria inaugurated the Austrian policy toward Germany which regarded Habsburg predominance in a confederated Germany to be the indispensable central-European basis for the Austrian position in Europe as a whole.

When Frederick, in response, instigated the formation of a *Fürstenbund* ("League of Princes") in July, 1785, associating himself at first with the Electors of Hanover and Saxony and then with fifteen other German princes, Catholic as well as Protestant, for the preservation of the constitution of the Holy Roman Empire and of the rights and possessions of all its members, his pious pose as defender of the Imperial constitution and its "Germanic liberties" was a mere facade for his actual use of the Empire to retain the balance of Austrian and Prussian power in the European arena. The patriotic intentions that were widely attributed to Joseph and Frederick by respective contemporary admirers and a tendentious posterity existed only in the eye of the beholder, but the connection which these enlightened rulers did perceive between the constitutions of nations and the foreign policies of states would become a crucial ingredient in the later policies of men who did have patriotic intentions.

The third and most immediate contribution of the Polish partition to the European constellation was the cornerstone it provided for a separate eastern system of powers. The common stake which the three enlightened monarchs created in Poland was reinforced by the common interest to which the same rulers committed their states in Germany. By provision of the Treaty of Teschen, which terminated the War of the Bavarian Succession between Joseph and Frederick in 1779, Russia, as a mediating power, thenceforward shared the traditional position of France as guarantor of the German constitution, which had been legalized by the terms of the Peace of Westphalia (1648). But it was their mutual dependence in Poland that exercised the most continuous attraction in keeping the relations among the three eastern powers relatively compatible vis-à-vis one another and relatively unified vis-à-vis other theaters of international relations. Thus when Catherine and Joseph arranged the Austro-Russian entente of 1781, the one solid provision on which their vague assurances of mutual assistance were based was their joint guarantee of the post-partition situation in Poland. Even after the outbreak of the French Revolution, moreover, not only did the persistent eastern orientation of the three absolute monarchies at first grant to the revolution the three years of peace it required for its own consolidation but the revolution itself had the effect of strengthening the connections within the eastern system. Absolutist as they were, Prussia's Frederick William II (Frederick the Great's nephew and successor from 1786) and Russia's Catherine were at first too preoccupied with their conflicting ambitions in rump Poland to attend seriously to the French revolutionary menace. Then, the revolution in the west recalled them, and later the Austrians as well, to the basis of their joint power in the east. Linking Polish reformers with French "Jacobins" and Polish nationalism with revolutionary anarchy, by 1795 the eastern powers completed the partition of Poland among themselves.

Thus the foreign policies of the enlightened absolutists, cynical, opportunist, and materialistic as they were, bequeathed more to subsequent European history than their obvious contributions to the definition of the long-range interests of Prussia, Austria, and Russia and to the suppression of moral conscience and dynastic rights in international affairs. They exemplified the combination of balance of powers and concert of powers that alone would organize the separate state interests into a viable system of international relations, and they glimpsed the connection of internal constitutions with foreign affairs that would remain the key to statecraft through the next century. But their most fateful achievement was to create the basis for an eastern system of absolutist powers that would provide an international solidarity for the defense of political conservatism against the currents of change.

CHAPTER 21

The Enlightened Absolutists at Home

WITHIN THEIR OWN states the enlightened monarchs never questioned either the structure of absolutism or the priority of the military and economic power whose mobilization they recognized to be the indispensable domestic requirement of their competitive foreign policies. The connection of domestic and foreign policy spurred these vigorous, restless, and arrogant rulers to organize their resources for the increase of their strength, and to this extent it reinforces the view of enlightened absolutism as simply a more intelligent and efficient mode of exercising unlimited authority. But their deliberate focus of domestic policies upon the increase of governmental power explains these policies in the sense of determining their limits rather than in the sense of determining their substance within those limits. It explains, that is, why the enlightened monarchs did not undertake policies which might diminish power rather than how they chose the policies that they deemed compatible with it. Power, however beloved by them, did not automatically prescribe definite courses of domestic action to them. What did prescribe these courses were the rulers' specific ideas about the kind of things that made for power, the kind of things that were antithetical to power, and the kind of things that were indifferent to power, and the rulers' specific decisions to maximize the first, exclude the second, and accommodate the third. The contribution of enlightened absolutism to internal politics, indeed, was not only its reduction of politics to power but its redefinition of political power in terms of its relationship to the larger life of the community.

Hence the enlightened monarchs applied themselves vigorously to all of the three main fields of internal affairs—to the structure of administration and law that was the channel of power, to the forms of education and religion that separated what was political and accessible to the exercise of power from what was not, and to the social and economic policies that would reconcile the apparently discordant aims of increasing the resources available to the state's government and increasing the resources available to its citizens. Each of the three fields of internal policy revealed the same general idea of politics in a different way, and only when all these ways are taken into consideration does the whole enlightened idea of domestic politics emerge clearly.

The pattern of a unified principle amidst diversified practice characterized the progenitors as well as the fields of enlightened domestic policy. By reason of her sex, the physical difficulties of administering her vast territories, and the special political orientation of her aristocracy toward the state as the persistent source of its privileges as well as obligations, Catherine remained the most insecure of the enlightened monarchs and the most inclined toward placating the notables of her realm. Joseph represented the opposite extreme of a radical, leveling absolutism, not only because it fit his temperament to "approve nothing that was done before his time and by others," as his own mother, doting as she was, sorrowfully admitted, but more importantly because he started from the already considerable reforms enacted under her auspices by enlightened ministers.

Despite the domestic variations among the enlightened monarchs who ruled the great states, the aggregate internal policy of each was designed to complement the foreign policy which was so similar in all, and the common context of their international great-state status made the parallel features in their respective domestic policies more essential than the divergencies. The one fundamental difference of pattern, establishing another species of enlightened monarchy, concerned not these rulers but the progressive sovereigns of small states for whom international rivalry was not a constant condition of domestic politics. In the spontaneous and wholehearted patronage of the arts by Duke Charles Augustus of Weimar (ruled 1775–1828), in the categorical abolition of serfdom and the wide-ranging application of free-trade doctrine by Margrave Charles Frederick of Baden (ruled 1738–1811), and in the combination of strict neutrality in foreign affairs with economic liberalism, tax equalization, penal reform, and even a planned representative constitution by the Habsburg Grand Duke Leopold of Tuscany (ruled 1765–1790)—in all such reforming policies of small-scale rulers there was a sensitivity to practical needs that was relatively free from the continuous pressure for the maximal mobilization of economic and military power, and there was room for cultural, doctrinal, or humanitarian considerations that were relatively free from practical needs. Such rulers were indeed set off from like-minded sovereigns of the great powers.

The presence of such a benign species of enlightened monarchy in the eighteenth century had a significance that went beyond the blessings conferred upon the inhabitants of the individual states concerned. It showed a congruity of the moral and intellectual values characteristic of the Enlightenment with the practical politics of small and pacific communities that would help to perpetuate particularism in Germany and Italy for almost a century and minor states in Europe until our own day. But both in the

quantitative terms of effect upon the lives of men then and since and in
the qualitative terms of effect upon the basic issue of resolving the conflicting claims of power and freedom in those lives, the enlightened absolutism of the great powers was the more influential and the more problematical. What follows, then, is an inquiry into the main fields of the
domestic policies promulgated by this species of enlightened rulers, with a
view to elucidating the way in which they tried to resolve in actual fact the
problem of relating political power and human freedom.

GOVERNMENT AND LAW

The enlightened absolutists approached government as a single force
and civil society as a collective whole animated by government. In Joseph's
terms, government must be organized from top to bottom in accordance
with "uniform principles," and it must act "to unite the parts of the monarchy . . . into a single province, . . . a single mass of people all subject
to impartial guidance [and] . . . joined in a common enterprise." The
resulting state he called a "universe" (*Universum*), to characterize it as
a human world revolving around a common administration as its axis and
unified by the rule of general laws. The enlightened rulers contributed
both to the administrative unity of government and to the legal unity of
the state, albeit more tangibly to the second than to the first.

In the field of governmental institutions the enlightened absolutists
were at their least distinctive, for they made comparatively few structural
changes in the administrations which they inherited from their less cultured state-building forbears. What they added tended to build on the
centralizing, professionalizing, specializing, and bureaucratizing institutions
which they had received. But they did contribute a distinctive spirit and
a changed attitude toward these institutions which put government in a
different relation to the community than heretofore. Unlike the piecemeal,
ad hoc approach of their fathers, the enlightened autocrats viewed the governmental apparatus as an integrated whole in itself and as a deliberate
force for the integration of society at large. A representative example of
their comprehensive approach to government was their contribution to
modern bureaucracy. They were responsible for merging their sundry
officials into a homogeneous bureaucratic corps, with the spirit and the
character that would dominate the public life of their respective countries
into the twentieth century. They did not create their bureaucracies any
more than they created any other of the essential administrative institutions
which they used, but in the case of the bureaucracy their distinctive attitude
took perceptible form in the shape of a definite, long-range set of practices
and standards.

Identifiable "Frederician" and "Josephinian" traditions of civil service
would mark Prussian and Austrian officials for generations to come with

the obedience, probity, industry, impersonality, professionalism, officiousness, punctilio, and hierarchical sense for which Prussian and Habsburg bureaucrats would become notorious. The merit system in recruitment and advancement and the measure of performance by regular inspection were practices bequeathed to modern civil service in general by these demanding and ubiquitous royal founders of the bureaucratic ethic. In Russia, the professional bureaucracy did not develop into its definitive mold during the eighteenth century, as in Prussia and Austria, but Catherine's modernization of the service nobility's conditions of state service from a general and unspecified military and administrative obligation to a definite monopoly of local government did seal the junction of bureaucracy and aristocracy that would persist as long as the empire. The enlightened absolutists' suspicious resort to their own spies, spot inspections, and direct interventions as checks on the work of their regular administration gave a personal cast to the governmental apparatus that did not outlive their energetic persons. But even such capricious operations left a lasting residue in the tendency toward arbitrary behavior that would accompany the mechanical functioning of nineteenth-century bureaucracies.

The second result of the enlightened monarchs' deliberately unitary approach was the codification of the law of their respective states. In this sphere, these rulers did innovate, for their codes were not simply in the administrative pattern of infusing a new spirit into old institutions but were themselves new institutions. Both Frederick and Joseph directed the compilation of the law codes that would serve as unifying bonds for the Prussian and the Habsburg monarchies through the nineteenth century. Both monarchs prefaced the preparation of the codes with judicial reforms that established a centralized hierarchy of courts, separated from the rest of the administration (rigorously in the Austrian case, imperfectly in the Prussian), and an autonomous corps of trained and salaried judges to run them.

The legal amalgamations themselves included codes of procedure (Prussian civil procedure in 1781 and Austrian criminal procedure in 1788) and the great syntheses of substantive law that were initiated by the enlightened monarchs and finished after their deaths. The *Allgemeines Landrecht* (Prussian Law Code), a composite of civil, criminal, and public (*i.e.* constitutional) law prepared by Frederick in conjunction with his chancellor J. H. von Carmer (1721–1801) and the reforming jurist Karl Suarez (1746–1798) was completed and published under the more conservative auspices of Frederick William II in 1794. The first section of the Austrian civil code was promulgated by Joseph in 1786 but completed in 1812 under Francis I. The Austrian penal code, however, was published in full during 1787.

The primary purpose of all these codifications was to homogenize, over a statewide range, the myriad of local ordinances, Germanic tradition, and

Roman law that perpetuated the particularity of the sundry provinces in each realm. To realize this purpose the laws had to be not only mutually adjusted but rooted in and measured by a constant principle which made each collection of laws something more than and different from the sum of its parts. This principle, as prominent throughout Frederick's and Joseph's actual codes as in Catherine's *Instruction* for such a code, was the proposition, authorized by the self-evidence of natural law, that the inherent right of all men to pursue their own welfare can only be secured by the equal benefit and protection of the laws dispensed by a common sovereign to them as "free citizens of the state." Since the laws guarantee men's fundamental rights and since the sovereign is the source of these laws, the community of men formed by common subjection to the law is the most essential of human associations and the good of this community becomes both the general measure of the different rights and duties of its citizens in respect to one another and the general sanction of the equal obedience owed the sovereign.

Thus the law codes that were projected in Russia (the project of 1767 did contribute to the code enacted in 1830) and enacted in Prussia and Austria under enlightened auspices helped to translate into reality the enlightened rulers' integral attitude toward their states. The codes' anomalous mixture of custom and innovation, of humanitarian reform (such as the abolition of torture and the reduction of crimes subject to the death penalty) and the retention of serfdom, of declarations of equality and affirmations of caste privileges was now rationalized by a single standard which required each right and each privilege to be assessed by the general interest of the entire community and the general interest of the community to be defined by the only citizen in a position to make such a definition—the enlightened sovereign.

RELIGION AND INTELLECTUAL LIFE

The enlightened monarchs' approach to administration and the law organized their subjects into a coherent political body. Their approach to religion and intellectual life supplied this body with a soul. Their policies in these fields were such as to absorb a whole set of spiritual values into their system of political controls. Thereby they elevated the function of the state from providing the common welfare as the external political condition of a higher suprapolitical community to providing the common welfare as a primary ethical value produced by a political community independent of and at least equivalent to any other human community.

Political sovereigns had, of course, long exercised authority over the hearts and minds of their subjects, but along with the rulers of religious and social communities and without making such authority an essential ingredient of the state. They either had trimmed the state's role in ecclesiastical

Frederick the Great playing the flute at his palace, Sans Souci.

and intellectual issues down to the mere provision of an external temporal
order or had at most claimed for this role the political community's instrumental contribution to the higher general order in which all human communities shared and for the domination of which they all competed. The
enlightened absolutists now added a new spiritual dimension to the state
itself because they claimed for the state a monopoly over human order, in
both its utilitarian and ideal aspects. The principle of liberty, on the other
hand, they now assigned to individuals outside of their relationship to the
community.

Thus the blend of repression and toleration that was the hallmark of the
enlightened absolutists' policies toward churches, schools, and publications
was not merely an *ad hoc* mixture of authoritarian disposition, religious
indifference, and practical sense for the limits of the politically possible,
that it superficially seemed to be. It was also—and in terms of its permanent effects, more significantly—the function of the complementary relationship posited by the enlightened sovereigns between the state on the
one side, now definitely conceived as the exclusive locus of the principle of
unity among men, and men's consciences and minds on the other, now
definitely conceived as the locus of liberty among men. For the enlightened absolutists, the institutions of religious and intellectual life combined both sides: churches, academies, books, all had their unitary aspects
that made them part of the expanded function of the state, and they all
also had their spontaneous aspects that made them both independent of
the state and needed by it. Authoritarian and liberal principles thus joined
in the religious, as in the intellectual, policies of the enlightened monarchs.

Religion and the Churches

In the field of religion, the enlightened autocrats combined the extension of state control over the established church with the grant of toleration to dissident churches—a combination which, in terms of the principle of religious liberty, abridged the autonomy of the one while it affirmed the autonomy of the other.

The most definite sponsor of both policies, moreover, was the same ruler—Joseph II. Indeed, "Josephinism"—a term that originally referred to his reform of the law and would later be used to epitomize the whole tradition of rational bureaucratic absolutism stemming from Joseph—was a label which contemporaries generally applied to his ecclesiastical policy alone, and as the blend of authoritarianism and liberalism in the usual connotation of "Josephinism" indicates, its subordination of the official Catholic Church and its toleration of religious minorities were deemed by Joseph and his aides to be equally contributory to the central authority of the state. Joseph's specific measures along both lines, undertaken simultaneously during the 1780's, were such as to reveal the precise nature of the common political criteria behind the apparently divergent policies.

On the one hand, Joseph conceded the right of private worship and full civil rights to Protestants, Greek Orthodox, and Jews (the concession to the latter was a particularly rare expression of liberality for the eighteenth century). On the other hand, in contrast to this relinquishment of state controls, he notably extended the control of the state over the established Catholic Church. He prohibited all communications between the Pope and the Austrian Catholic Church without the sovereign's approval. He increased, by political decree, the ecclesiastical powers of the bishops and required them to take an oath of allegiance to the sovereign. He founded new Austrian bishoprics to replace the older politically uncontrollable jurisdictions of German bishops in Austria. He abolished pious lay brotherhoods and contemplative monastic orders, and transferred their properties to a "religious fund" administered by public authority for socially useful ecclesiastical purposes. He subordinated the other—teaching and charitable—orders to the local bishops. He prohibited religious processions and pilgrimages. He regulated Church ritual, sermons, and adornments, and ordered the supervision of clerics by bureaucrats to ensure obedience to the regulations. He assigned clerical education to "general seminaries" which would be established by the government and operated under the direction of governmental appointees to train priests to be "spiritual officials of the state." He validated civil marriage.

What unified these liberal and authoritarian measures into a coherent policy were the two political functions both kinds of measures shared. Both had the fiscal function of increasing taxable population and production, and both had the governmental function of attributing to the head of the state the determination of the respective rights of church and state.

Monks leaving
their monasteries
after Joseph II's
decree of 1781.

The Josephinians themselves propounded the practical connection in the
government's joint authority to determine the rights and the limits of
ecclesiastical activity: "Toleration helps to populate lands and make them
rich; fanaticism degenerates into persecution and will depopulate and
impoverish them."

But powerful as these political criteria were in the formulation of
Joseph's ecclesiastical policy, they were not the distinctive elements in it.
The assertion of the state's authority over the Austrian Catholic Church
against the papacy had been persistent Habsburg policy since the Thirty
Years' War, and under Maria Theresa, orthodox by religious disposition
and intolerant by religious principle as she was, this policy had been
expanded in practice to include creeping encroachments upon Catholic
clerical preserves and tacit concessions to industrious religious minorities.
During her regime, indeed, advocates of Jansenism—in its eighteenth-
century German version of Febronianism, a doctrine rooted in the
published argument of "Justinus Febronius" (pseudonym of Johann von
Hontheim, 1701–1790), for the espiscopal constitution of the Catholic
Church, the supremacy of general councils over the papacy, and the solidarity of national councils and temporal princes against papal
domination—and of the Enlightenment had already collaborated tactically to further the anti-papalism, the anti-Jesuitism, and the ban on ecclesiastical extravagances that were immediate aims common to both kinds of
advocacy. What was distinctive to Joseph's regime was the fusion of the
two movements into an integral civic faith that joined the Jansenist belief
in the autonomous, inner, religious springs of the moral impulse with the
enlightened belief in the secular, rational, social organization of moral
action. The result was a theistic political rationalism that sponsored a fundamentally new position on the state and its relations with religion. It
meant the attribution to the state, in principle as well as in practice, of the
final responsibility for men's supreme ethical task in this world—the reali-

zation of their common humanity, of their essential unity as brothers under God. In frank deference to the religious dimension of this new political function, the Josephinians called religion "a political matter" (*Politicum*), and Joseph described his own position to be "fanaticism for the state."

But of equal importance with this shift of the responsibility for the moral ordering of mankind from the old partnership of state and church to the exclusive sovereignty of the state was the state's new relationship to the church. For the Josephinian, not only religion as such but "theoretical religious doctrines" and "external rites"—*i.e.*, churches—were "indispensable" to the state because they supplied to social morality an essential spiritual ingredient that the state could indeed direct but not supply by itself. This function of the churches created a twofold relationship with the state. On the one hand, the state had to regulate and reform the churches to ensure the indispensable contribution of religion to the moral unity of the community for which the state was primarily responsible. Hence the Josephinians retained the commitment to an established Catholic Church, but on the novel ground that the overlay of church and state furnished the most appropriate arrangement for channeling the religious impulse into the moral service of the state.

But the religious impulse itself, on the other hand, was viewed by the Josephinians as a force independent of the state, and their insistence that the Catholic Church be "purified" was impelled not only by the idea of reorganizing it into a proper political instrument but also by the ideal of reforming it into a religious instrument of authentic piety. Joseph himself was a convinced Catholic. Indeed, his decree on toleration excluded deists, and a contemporary Swiss observer remarked in general on "the bigotry which is rooted deep in his soul." Joseph insisted that "religion must be strengthened not only by inspirations of the heart but also by outer ceremonies," and he limited the activities of the anticlerical Masonic lodges. His piety combined the urge to good moral works commanded by the Author of humanity with the rational forms of worship appropriate to stimulate them. Reason in the religious service consisted for him in a simple ritual which excluded the appeal to miracle, terror, sentiment, and unquestioning faith and included effective exhortations to good deeds.

The appropriateness of such a moral, social, reasonable, and practical piety to the collective service purposes of the state seems obvious enough. Actually, however, Joseph's piety pointed in two very different directions: if it pointed toward the state by virtue of its forms and its effects, it pointed toward the individual by virtue of its principles and its origins. He insisted that both the feeling for humanity and the rational knowledge of human rights were originally implanted by God through nature in all men. This individual ordination, for Joseph, was the religious source of the authority and the force behind the moral community of man organized by the churches and directed by the state. Hence he admonished the Protestant ministers of Vienna that "everyone should be allowed to pray and to sing in his own way," and he accompanied this admonition both with the additional prescription of definite rites and doctrines to prevent "Christianity from degenerating into a rational paganism" and with his covert hope that the political reform of Catholic rite and doctrine toward primitive Christian simplicity would bring a mass conversion of Protestants to a single official ecclesiastical organization. For Josephinians, this was a consistent position because it reflected their belief that the individual, the church, and the state were equally indispensable to the ideal of social service and unequally disposed to the realization of that ideal. Only personal piety could supply the incentive to social service; only the church could organize the pious intentions of individuals into the civic loyalties and the foundations for the relief of the poor and the handicapped that could make a reality of social service; and only the state could keep the church to this, its primary function. Through their political control of churches whose confessional identities they acknowledged the Josephinians thus extended the power of the state over the acts of individual wills that were themselves beyond the power of the state.

Neither for Frederick nor for Catherine was church policy as central a consideration as it was for Joseph. The combination of controls and toleration which they shared with him was much more exclusively external and circumstantial in character. Frederick's chief aim in the regulation of the Lutheran church was to prevent any excess of dogmatism and fanaticism from endangering the civil peace, and prominent among the incentives of his broad-gauged toleration policy were the old Hohenzollern motives of attracting able-bodied and able-minded immigrants and of keeping peace among the minorities at home while stirring turmoil within the majorities abroad. Thus he even granted asylum—and a base of operations—to the much maligned Jesuits after their expulsion from Portugal, France, and the Habsburg dominions led to the abolition of the order (1773) under duress by Pope Clement XIV (1769–1774).

Catherine's Orthodox policy featured most notably the definitive nationalization of all the properties of the Russian Orthodox Church and the conversion of its clergy into officials paid by the state. For the rest, she remained careful to recommend external observance of Orthodox rites and to respect Orthodox sensibilities, as befit the political motives of her nominal conversion to Russian Orthodoxy. Like Frederick, she practiced *de facto* toleration, justified it by reference to the civil peace of a varied population, maliciously extended it to the Jesuits, and suspiciously abridged it for the Jews.

But if Frederick's and Catherine's indifference to denominational religion represents an enlightened approach quite distinct from Joseph's desire to reform it, the divergence was overshadowed by what was common in the relations established by all three monarchs between their states and religion in general. All shared the view of churches as political institutions specializing in the adaptation of social ethics to the ignorance, superstition, and simplicity of the mass of their subjects. All shared too the conviction that authentic religious belief resided in individuals. Thus all three attempted to legislate religious toleration as an individual right, and in the case of Frederick's Prussian Law Code the belief in the individual basis of piety inspired an unqualified declaration of religious liberty: "Every inhabitant of the state must be granted complete freedom of conscience and religion."

The shared attitudes toward church and religion effected a common contribution by enlightened absolutism to the public consciousness of what a "state" was; the attitudes that were not shared revealed the alternative policies which states could adopt toward the social organizations and the individuals within them. By regarding the churches as extensions of the state, the enlightened rulers agreed in appropriating for the state the socialized organization of individual religious beliefs that were themselves beyond the reach of the state. Religion thus became the midwife of a new politics that not only *defined* what belonged to the state *in contrast to* what did not but also *justified* what belonged to the state *in terms of* what did not. Politics was now *defined*, not as one kind of human activity among others, but as the collective and orderly dimension of all human activities in contrast to the individual and libertarian dimension of all human activities that epitomized the extrapolitical in man. Politics was now *justified* by the complementary relations that the enlightened rulers posited between the collectivity of the politics and the individuality of the religion. They posited this affirmative connection between opposites in one or both of two versions. The deistic Frederick directed the state's power especially to the defense of individual conscience against the oppression of religion's social organizations—that is, churches; the Catholic Joseph directed the state's power especially to making individual conscience practically effective in the social organizations—that is, churches—that were the state's only connections with conscience. In either case, religion contributed to the development of a politics that could regiment for the practical purposes of the community the same human activity that it held sacrosanct as the ultimate source of its individual members' moral capacity for community.

Intellectual Life

The state's relations with secular thought under enlightened absolutism exhibited the same apparent incongruity and the same kind of underlying pattern as its relations with religion. Just as the apparent contrast between the political control over churches and the acknowledgment of free conscience reflected a division of function between the community's and the individual's role in effecting the moral good of humanity, just so the political control of institutionalized education and the acknowledgment of intellectual freedom should be considered as complementary functions of state and individual in a coherent approach by the enlightened rulers to the secular culture of European society.

For all their sporadic flurries of educational activity, the effective policies of the enlightened rulers in this field, as in the field of administration, remained within the framework set up by their absolutist predecessors and contributed rather a conscious spirit than viable institutions to it. The parallel between educational and administrative policies was not fortuitous, since the training of the citizenry, in Joseph II's terms, "to become fit for service to the state" was precisely the goal of education for the enlightened sovereigns, and consequently the features which they stressed in the scholastic arrangements which they found and extended were similar to what they favored in administration generally: they stressed what was authoritarian, utilitarian, and elitist. Joseph infused the Austrian school system particularly with the first two of these qualities. He worked with the model educational pyramid, ranging from compulsory elementary schools to the universities, which the Habsburg bureaucracy had organized under his co-regent, Maria Theresa, in the General School Ordinance of 1774, and was primarily responsible for the rigid regulation of books, courses, and teachers aimed at the elimination of individual discretion and at the production of civil servants. Frederick stressed the elitist principle in education because he believed that only the aristocracy was socially and morally capable of direct service to the state. Hence he was disinterested in the education of other groups, which he thought should be designed only to keep them in their economic and social stations; he focused his energies on the founding of academies for the sons of his nobility and neglected the execution of the ordinance worked out by Johann Hecker (1707–1768), his own school planner, to put enforcement and control by the state behind the general elementary-school system which had been initiated by Fredericks' unenlightened father, Frederick William I.

Only Catherine seemed to transcend the usual limits of absolutist scholastic policy and approach the exalted aims which the *philosophes* cherished for the education of humanity. Proclaiming the goal of education to be the production of a "new breed" of Russian, transformed not only as a citizen but as an "entire man," Catherine enacted resounding general decrees in 1764 and again in 1786. They were designed not only to rejuvenate the decayed and spotty system of primary schools which had been instituted by Peter the Great but to expand it into an unbroken national network of general education in both technical and humanistic curricula. But in fact, neither of these far-reaching measures was seriously applied, partly because of Catherine's fickleness in matters not directly affecting her own power, but mostly because of the limits imposed by administrative necessity and social privilege on enlightened absolutism. Hence her most effective activities in the field of education were the founding of engineering schools, the expansion of aristocratic Cadet training, and the concession of the nobles' right to organize their own schools—activities that conformed to the technical and elitist tendencies both of Russian education since Peter the Great and of contemporary enlightened absolutism elsewhere.

But the state-oriented educational policy of the enlightened monarchs should be viewed in conjunction with the socially oriented cultural policy which balanced it, for only together do they give an undistorted picture of enlightened absolutism's characteristic approach to intellectual life.

Certainly the enlightened rulers' political approach to culture shared a common authoritarian dimension with their approach to education. In part their cultural policy too was defined by the arbitrary modes of their government and by the ever-present criterion of clear and present political danger to authority. Examples of these limits were prominent enough, indeed, to have left the dominant impression that in the field of culture, as in education, religion, and constitutional rights, absolutism overbalanced enlightenment for the rulers in which they were combined. Frederick's misanthrophy led him to conclude in principle that "enlightenment . . . is a destructive firebrand for the masses" and to censor in fact the private communications and the publications of ordinary citizens and uncelebrated pamphleteers when they engaged in political criticism. Joseph was notorious for his utilitarian deprecation of the pure arts and sciences in favor of applied knowledge. To this philistine quality he added the studied policy, between 1785 and his death in 1790, of assigning censorship to the secret police and of intensifying the suppression of "books . . . which are calculated to undermine the principles of all religion, morality, and social order." His expulsion of the radical publisher Georg Wucherer, and the destruction of his stock of books in 1789 without due process of law, was only the most sensational instance of Joseph's increasing concern to suppress criticism and control public opinion. Catherine's restrictions on intellectual freedom were the fiercest of all. When she tried her hand at journalism, during the late 1760's, in the vainglorious enterprise of raising the level of Russian culture all by herself, she first pressured the humanitarian Nikolai Novikov (1744–1818) into suspending his journal because he dared to polemicize against her, and later, in 1792, she condemned him without trial to a fifteen-year prison term because he continued to criticize the government for its failure to help the needy. In her *Instruction* to the Legislative Commission of 1767 she recommended the abatement but not the abolition of censorship, and in 1773 she refused Diderot's request to permit an uncensored Russian edition of the *Encyclopedia*. Her most celebrated suppression, finally, was her prosecution in 1790 of Alexander Radishchev (1749–1802). A disciple of the French Enlightenment in its late phase of radical criticism, Radishchev was tried for his "diffusion of dangerous reasoning" in his famous *Journey from St. Petersburg to Moscow*, a trenchant and circumstantial indictment of Russian conditions.

ЖИВОПИСЕЦЪ

ЕЖЕНЕДѢЛЬНОЕ

НА

1772 ГОДЪ

СОЧИНЕНІЕ.

ВЪ САНКТПЕТЕРБУРГѢ.

Title page of a 1772 issue of the
satirical journal *The Painter*, edited
by Nikolai Novikov. *Catherine, at
one stage a contributor, subsequently suspended the journal and jailed
its editor.*

But important as all these prominent political limits on cultural freedom were, they are quite misleading if they are not seen to be precisely that—political limits on a cultural activity for which the monarchs' own liberal policy was itself largely responsible. Frederick the Great
distinguished sharply between the intellectual elite and the literate general
public, recognizing an unprecedented freedom for the former as the producers of culture and persisting in the traditional controls over the latter as
the politicizers of culture. Thus, immediately upon his accession in 1740
Frederick encouraged the growth of a periodical press, exempting its nonpolitical organs from censorship on the ground that "if journals are to be
interesting they should not be restricted." He proceeded, analogously, to
reorganize the old Berlin Academy of Science into a broad-gauged Academy of Science and Literature, to people it with free spirits from all over
Europe under the lead of French *philosophes*, to load the Prussian universities with representatives of the natural-law school of philosophy and jurisprudence, and to affirm the freedom of both the Academy and the universities from censorship. Faithful to Frederick's notions of intellectual hierarchy, the universities exercised a self-censorship over their members while
the members of the Academy were subject to no censorship at all.

The same basic distinction was embodied in the Prussian Law Code
that was drawn up under Frederick's inspiration: it provided, on the one

hand, for the prosecution of public critics of state and church and of published authors of ideas endangering civil peace, and on the other, for the categorical distinction between external acts which could be punished and internal convictions which could not. Whether a published idea was an act or a conviction depended, apparently, on its position in the cultural scale between intellectual creation and social consumption. The failure of the Code to give fuller recognition to freedom of expression manifests the wary response of the aging Frederick to the radicalization of the Enlightenment whose dissemination he had himself sponsored.

For Joseph and Catherine too, their later reactions to radical opinions were built upon an earlier commitment to a liberalized regime of the press. In 1781, shortly after his accession, Joseph passed a law which went far toward the creation of a free press: it permitted public criticism, including criticism of the sovereign himself, and forbade only those publications that attacked public morals or religion as such. The result was a veritable flood of pamphlet literature, most of it even more rationalist, more freethinking, and more anticlerical than the government's policy. It was, indeed, the critical middle-class public opinion that the government's own liberality had spawned which triggered, in conjunction with a bloody Transylvanian peasants' uprising, Joseph's accelerating censorship and clericalism after 1785.

The young Catherine, similarly, could declaim that "nothing can bring me to fear a cultivated people," and despite her failure to amend the institution of censorship, she transformed its spirit to give Russia both an atmosphere and the materials of intellectual freedom, the like of which had never before been experienced in that nation. Catherine's concern in the 1760's was rather for the conditions of cultural creation than for the interests of political order. We must remember, she wrote, "the danger of debasing the human mind by restraint and oppression which can produce nothing but ignorance, must cramp and depress the rising efforts of genius, and must destroy the very will to write." The result of this attitude, undoubtedly attributable at least in part to Catherine's own pretensions as a writer, became apparent in the astonishing leap in the sheer quantity of published material. Whereas the decade before Catherine's accession had seen an average annual publication of a mere 23 books, the figure rose almost fivefold in the decade from 1761 to 1770, and finally reached an annual high of 366 in 1790 before Catherine's repression reversed the trend. Like Frederick, finally, Catherine revamped her capital city's Academy of Sciences to include literature and thus established an institutional link between the educational culture immediately useful to the state and the pure cultural activity external to the state but needed by it to feed its educational system.

Thus the relationship which the enlightened monarchs set up between state education and free culture paralleled their subscription to a system of state churches founded on freedom of individual conscience. The overlay confirms both the principled distinction they made between men's social activity that was subject to the state and the individual springs of this activity that were not and the complementary connection between them. For if the monarchs' exclusion of religious belief from political control could be accounted to indifference, their analogous exclusion of the intellect they cherished was certainly a matter of principle. The result of the enlightened absolutists' spiritual policies—ecclesiastical and educational, religious and cultural—was to give the state a categorical definition as the organized monopoly of collective authority and collective power and to give it a positive function in the realization of the individualized freedom that would henceforth be recognized as the fundamental principle of human activity beyond politics.

SOCIAL POLICY

Equipped with the enlightened absolutists' operational ideas of what the state was and of its relations with what it was not, we now possess the assumptions wherewith to simplify and to understand their social policy, that most controversial and ambiguous aspect of their regimes, which is almost incomprehensible without these assumptions. There was an apparent ambivalence in their treatment both of the agrarians—that is, of the intertwined claims of the landed aristocrats and the peasantry—and the burghers which requires an explanation in the context of their total approach to government and society if the place of enlightened absolutism in Western history is to be understood.

Lords and Peasants

The enlightened approach to the agrarian problem is particularly revealing because in the overwhelmingly agrarian society of central and eastern Europe lord-peasant relations were the primary social issues and because the ambiguities of policy in this field were equally visible on two different levels of enlightened absolutism. Not only were there the crucial discrepancies between the rulers whereby Joseph took measures to liberate the peasants, Catherine took measures to intensify their serfdom, and Frederick left their status virtually unchanged, but there were identifiable countercurrents within each ruler's policies.

The main thrust of Joseph's social policies was undoubtedly in the anti-aristocratic and pro-peasant legislation which ultimately earned him rebellion by the notables and veneration by the rural masses. In a whole series of decrees, starting with the famous November patent of 1781 and continuing throughout the decade of his exclusive rule, Joseph prosecuted what seemed to contemporaries a veritable agrarian revolution and what undoubtedly amounted to the most liberal peasant program of any regime before the French Revolution.

For the Habsburg dominions as a whole, the legislation emancipated peasants from the condition of "hereditary subjection"—that is, bondage to the soil—that was the residue of serfdom in the eighteenth century. This condition imposed two kinds of obligations upon the peasants, obligations which were, of course, the obverse of the manorial lords' legal rights. The first kind comprised the personal duties owed by the peasant to the lord as part of the obligations stemming from the former's attachment to the soil. They were particularly galling because they were reminiscent of the direct personal bondage of peasant to lord, the more oppressive form of serfdom which was no longer valid in the legal practice of eighteenth-century central Europe. Joseph simply abolished the most pressing of these personal liabilities that persisted in the servile property relationship: the peasant's obligation not to marry, leave his holding, or enter a vocation without the permission of his lord, and the peasant's legal incapacity to lodge complaints with the public authorities or bring suit in the state courts against his lord. The second kind of reciprocal peasant obligations and seigneurial privileges comprised the real dues stemming from the lord's blend of public and private rights in the land held by the peasants. Joseph prescribed renegotiation by lords and peasants under state supervision for some of these rights, such as the lord's milling and brewing monopolies; imposed limitations on others, such as the lord's hunting rights on the land (rights which, however, remained a seigneurial monopoly); and most important, converted the historical accumulation of assorted traditional, capricious, and servile dues on peasant tenures—customary rents and fees payable in varying dimensions and in both money and kind, and above all the hated compulsory labor services for the lord—into a single money rent amounting to 30 per cent of the peasant's gross income, divided between the state and the lord on the ratio of about 2 to 3.

The effect of the reform was to make the peasants affected by it free citizens and hereditary leaseholders, with rights to protection under the law, to freedom of movement and occupation, and to being charged a fixed and reasonable rent for the land they worked. The one obvious right that was denied them in this general legislation—the property right in the land that would make them its owners with free disposition over it—seemed promised for the future. On all demesnes immediately subject to the sovereign—dynastic, secularized, and municipal—the abolition of compulsory labor services without compensation and the easy terms granted for the peasants' full ownership of their tenures were both designed and taken by contemporaries to set up a model for the general legislation of the future.

Joseph's tax program, moreover—for him, as in general for the eighteenth century, the barometer of monarchies' social policy—anticipated a social regime of legally uniform equal property ownership on the land. Utilizing as his bases the population censuses initiated during his mother's reign for purposes of military conscription, Joseph initiated the compilation of a complete land register of his dominions in 1785, and in 1789 he fixed the rate of 12-2/9 per cent as a uniform land tax, payable by lords as well as commoners.

And yet Joseph was not nearly so univocally egalitarian as his resentful aristocracy thought, or, indeed, as the dominant tendency of his measures does suggest. For it was this same Joseph who in 1777, shortly before his initiation of his own peasant reforms (in 1781) opposed a similar project of his mother's for Bohemia alone. He described it, in terms that would fit his own legislation at least as well, as an abolition of serfdom and an "arbitrary" fixing of customary peasant dues and payments that were "without the slightest consideration for the lord" and would be the nobility's ruination. The radical difference between the two stages of his policy on land reform does not seem attributable to the obvious tactical shift from the attitude of a critical coregent to that of a glory-seeking exclusive sovereign, for the attitude behind his earlier reservations on peasant reform continued to play a role in his later legislation as well, limiting its scope and its effect.

First, the reforms did not apply at all to the "dominical" peasants—that is, to peasants with terminable tenures on the lord's own demesne—or even to the poorer of the peasants with their own hereditary tenures ("rustical" peasants). Second, the reforms left intact the lord's crucial authority to exercise patrimonial jurisdiction, which gave him local police and judicial powers over the peasantry and perpetuated the public basis of his privileges. Thus Joseph's agrarian policy limited the lord's exercise of his monopolies—above all, the vexatious hunting rights across land held by peasants—but did not abrogate them in principle precisely because they stemmed from original perquisites of the aristocracy's governmental functions, and these functions were still visible in the form of its patrimonial jurisdiction.

In Prussia and Russia, the ambiguities of agrarian policy were at least as striking as in Austria, but for Frederick and Catherine the social proportions were the reverse of Joseph's: the main tendency of their measures sustained or even, as in Catherine's case, intensified the regime of aristocratic privilege and peasant bondage, while they announced liberal principles that seemed to vitiate this regime and proposed ameliorations that would put limits upon it. The rift between Frederick's principles and his practice appeared, on the surface at least, to be categorical. Not only did his law code promulgate, as a fundamental principle of the law, the equal "natural rights of the individual" to exercise his "natural freedom to seek his own good" but Frederick himself explicitly condemned the institution of serfdom for the subservience to his lord forced upon the peasant by his bondage to the soil. But the net effect of what Frederick actually did in this field was to perpetuate the existing servile relations between peasants and lords in his Prussian dominions, and the reforms that he initiated to

A Russian peasants' school in the time of Catherine the Great.

limit the exploitation of the former by the latter tended rather to make the peasants' bonds more secure than to increase their freedom in line with his liberal principles. He attempted no general emancipation of the peasants either from their attachment to the soil or from their dues to the lords. For the country as a whole he succeeded only in preventing the lords from appropriating peasants' holdings, and even in his own royal demesne he did not go beyond assuring the peasants security of tenure on the hereditary holdings to which they remained bound by law, and attempting—with only modest success—some restrictions on the most onerous of his own peasants' compulsory labor services. But even these palliatives were more than offset by Frederick's sponsorship of cooperative credit associations, trading companies, and entailed estates for the benefit of the landed aristocracy, since these institutions encouraged the kind of large-scale agriculture which in eastern Europe extended the direct exploitation of peasant labor by the estate owners.

Catherine stood at the pro-aristocratic extreme of monarchical social policy. Although the debate still rages about the effect of this policy on the Russian aristocracy's relations with the government—that is, whether Catherine's concessions were silken bonds subjecting the aristocracy more tightly to government or real privileges purchasing the voluntary cooperation of the aristocracy with government—there is no doubt about the effect of the policy in expanding the already considerable powers of the aristocracy over the Russian peasantry. This policy was, moreover, more deeply rooted in Catherine than was conceded by the old interpretation which attributed it to her later years and to her fearful experience of the nobles' opposition to her presumed liberalism in her early years. Actually,

Catherine's declaration of policy made her pro-aristocratic position clear from the start. Immediately after her accession, in July, 1762, a decree declared her general policy to be her "resolution to preserve inviolate the estates and possessions of the landlords and to maintain the peasants in their dutiful obedience to them." She voluntarily submitted the draft of her *Instruction* of 1767 to an informal committee of noblemen and accepted their thorough emasculation of its proposals for agrarian reform. Even this draft, moreover, did not go beyond advocating "restrictions on the abuses and dangers of serfdom"; it did not question the institution itself. Indeed, she explicitly warned that "a great many serfs should not be liberated at once by a general law" and she gave, as a prominent ground of the modest amelioration of peasant conditions that she did advocate, the merely prudential need "to remove the causes for the serfs' rebelliousness against their lords."

In view of these assertions, it is hardly surprising to find that Catherine's government enacted concrete measures strengthening the hand of the aristocracy over the peasantry from the very morrow of her accession and continued to make such enactments throughout her long reign. She converted large tracts of the public domain into the property of the nobility and thereby condemned almost a million state peasants, with their comparatively larger personal freedom and lesser obligations, to the more onerous private status of serfs—first by gift to the conspirators who enthroned her and then by a series of grants to her favorites. She bound the free peasants of Little Russia (the recently conquered region in the west and southwest) to the lord whose lands they inhabited, thereby recognizing the illegal expropriations of peasant land by the nobility and establishing the actual conditions of serfdom on it, although, characteristically and uncomfortably, she avoided calling it by that name.

For Russia as a whole, moreover, the conditions of serfdom were not only extended but intensified by governmental decrees. For the most part, such measures confirmed aristocratic privileges which had been conferred by earlier legislation, or they affirmed in law encroachments upon peasant rights which the nobility had already accomplished in practice. But these apparently formal enactments had a massive social effect, for they meant the withdrawal of state control over the aristocracy's legal exercise of its social power and the abandonment of state guardianship over the remnants of serfs' rights. Thus one set of decrees acknowledged the lord's authority to sentence serfs to exile or to military service at his own discretion, not only for felonies, as formerly, but for attempted flight from the land and for insubordination, and capped this alienation of public power over agrarian relations by prohibiting petitions by the serfs to the government against the practices of the lords.

Another set of decrees gave the force of law to the aristocratic monopolies that excluded any alternatives to the servile relations between lord and peasant. Only nobles could own land. Only nobles could own serfs. Only nobles could employ serfs in factories. Only nobles could engage in the lucrative production of alcoholic beverages. Only nobles could authorize serfs to contract a loan, a lease, or outside employment. Only nobles could elect officials to the district administrations. Still another set of decrees, finally, encouraged the nobles, with their specially advantaged position, to compete favorably in activities where they did not have a monopoly. As epitomized in the decree of 1775 on provincial and district government and in the Charter of the Nobility of 1785, such preferences for the nobles included: the right to dominant posts in both town governments and peasant courts; full personal rights, based on freedom from service to the state (save by special call of the sovereign on occasions of urgent political necessity) and the right to corporate organizations as a self-administering social class; full rights of ownership and disposition over property including the purchase, sale, and entail of land, the establishment of industries on their lands, the ownership of and disposition over all timber on their lands and of the minerals beneath them, and the ownership of and disposition over habitable and industrial property in the towns; finally, the right to engage in both wholesale and export trades. Thus the nobility was authorized to participate in the activities authorized to other classes, and its participation was legally favored in activities from which the other classes were barred and the government self-excluded.

But despite the predominantly elitist tendency of Catherine's policy—she once declared that "I am an aristocrat by profession"—it had its counterpoint. Even if the pro-peasant paragraphs of her *Instruction* of 1767 are discounted for the rhetoric designed to draw the praise of the *philosophes* and for the careful preservation of serfdom as an institution, there remains a steady undercurrent of agrarian reform in Catherine's statements of policy. Her draft of the *Instruction* asserted the general principle that every citizen has a right to the equal protection of the laws and every man to food and clothing. This statement may not have been designed for literal application to the Russian peasantry, but a set of more specific declarations in the draft was so designed. Her recommendations that lords be required to moderate their dues, that serfs be assured by law of their right to their own property, and that serfs be encouraged to buy their own freedom were based on one genuinely held practical principle. "Agriculture cannot flourish," she wrote, "where the peasant or the agricultural laborer has nothing to call his own. Every man cares more for what belongs to himself than for what belongs to somebody else, and he does not care at all for what can be taken from him."

In this same category of unrealized declarations were Catherine's two projects for state peasants that were never put into execution. In 1765 she drew up a plan providing for the freedom of those peasants who would settle on crown lands, but withdrew it when it met ministerial opposition.

She was later reported to have drafted a proposed law that would have emancipated all serfs' children born after 1785. Although this draft remains undiscovered and the report unconfirmed, the general intent is supported by her project, which was definitely drawn up but never published or effected, of a charter for the state peasantry to accompany the charters of 1785 for the nobility and for the towns. In this draft charter Catherine would have granted full personal freedom and property rights to all crown peasants, and as if to prove the authenticity of her frustrated agrarian liberalism, these conditions were actually ordered into effect during 1787 for Ekaterinoslav, the new province that Catherine named after herself.

Catherine's actual record of peasant reform lagged far behind her professions of it in principle. Still, her attention to the issue on the operational as well as the planning level is attested by her boast of having issued more than a hundred decrees "for the relief of the people." Even if historians do agree that the effect of such measures was minimal in contrast with the massive impact of her pro-aristocratic policy, enough official action was taken to lend some credence at least to her abstract claims of concern for the peasantry. Decrees of a liberal cast forbade the reenserfment of freed peasants and the public auction of serfs without land, and others cited humanitarian grounds for ordering lords to feed their peasants when harvests failed, forbidding lords to liberate old serfs (and therewith abandon the seigneurial responsibility for them), and instructing officials to watch for egregious maltreatment of serfs by lords.

But more important than any of these kinds of concern for the peasant was Catherine's admission of the peasantry, free and serf alike, into the economic rights of free individual enterprise. This admission consisted not only in the government's tacit toleration of the practice by which serfs conducted their own businesses under the cover of their lords' name, but also in the explicit governmental acknowledgment in all peasants of the right to pursue both wholesale and retail trade in the countryside and both handicraft and factory production in the countryside and the towns alike. This acknowledgment, moreover, embodied though it usually was in specific decrees on particular commodities, was capped by the decree of 1775 which included serfs in the enactment of the general principle of free industrial enterprise—that "nobody from anywhere be hindered from setting up mills of any kind and from making in them manufactures of any kind without permit or order."

The Urban Sector

The economic policies of the enlightened monarchs have an ambiguity that parallels the tensions in their social attitude toward the rural classes, and because their economic ambiguity is more readily comprehensible than their social equivocations it can be used to explain them. Each and every enlightened ruler was committed simultaneously to a regime of state economic controls and the principle of individual economic liberty. In the field of commerce, they combined prohibitive protective tariffs with domestic free trade. Joseph of Austria was especially noteworthy both for the height of his duties on foreign imports and for his removal of trading restrictions within an expanded Austro-Bohemian domestic market.

In the field of industry, the combination of policies was even more startling. On the one hand, armies of inspectors continued to regulate the production and control the quality of industrial goods, governments continued to subsidize industries and tempt foreign entrepreneurs, and rulers persisted in skimming heavy excise taxes from the returns of the industries they had encouraged—all in good old mercantilist style. On the other hand, however, the industrial policies of both Joseph and Catherine, as well as of lesser monarchical lights like Charles Frederick of Baden and Joseph's brother, Leopold of Tuscany, also showed visible traces of the Physiocratic *laissez-faire* literature they imbibed. They rejected the old mercantilist predilection for either exercising or conferring industrial monopolies; Joseph went so far as to emasculate the coercive power of the Austrian guilds on the principle that "every man should be permitted to earn his bread in the way that seems best to him." Catherine, whose problem was simplified by the virtual absence of guilds in Russia, needed only to issue the antimonopolistic decree of 1767 prescribing that "no trade and handicraft by which town inhabitants can make themselves an honest living . . . be forbidden."

This combination of interventionist and liberal economic policies was held together by two assumptions which made these policies seem consistent to the enlightened rulers and their like-minded officials. First, they believed that economic growth increased political power and that government therefore had to stimulate and regulate all economic activities. In Austrian terms, ". . . the promotion of the welfare and prosperity of the community . . . is the most important object of political office." Second, the only source of the economic growth which the government had to promote was the free activity of individuals. In Joseph's words, ". . . nothing is more necessary than liberty for commerce and industry." For the enlightened sovereigns, in short, the wealth they needed had to have its source in the free activities of individuals that lay necessarily beyond the competence of the state, but the state could and should control the conditions of production and direct the allocation of resources for the financial benefit, the civil order, and the moral unity of the collective society.

The mutual congruity of these apparently opposite policies in the minds of the enlightened monarchs found its clearest expression in their attitude toward the burghers who were engaged in trade and manufacturing. Frederick complained bitterly precisely because of their lack of entrepreneurial initiative, while Catherine went beyond the familiar employment of subsi-

dies, tax rebates, and trade treaties to promote specific economic performance. She recommended governmental controls that would enforce the
conditions of economic freedom upon a stagnant burgher class—and she
saw no incongruity in such a policy for such a purpose. In her *Instruction*
for the Legislative Commission of 1767 she proclaimed the necessity for
Russia of a large and active economic bourgeoisie, and she proceeded to
entice the Russian burghers to participate in setting the legal conditions
for their own growth by grossly overrepresenting them in the Legislative
Commission. With membership in the Commission based on elections by
estate, the Russian towns were granted three-eighths of the seats—more
than any other social group, including the aristocracy—at a time when
Russia's urban population amounted only to about one twenty-fifth of
the total. To assist their cohesion, moreover, the townsmen were not
divided into subgroups, with the result that almost 200 of their 208 deputies were merchants. The burghers, however, did not rise to the opportunity which the Empress thus provided: not only did their lethargy and obse-
quiousness permit the aristocracy to dominate the proceedings of the
Commission but their own claims were limited to the restoration of their
old narrow municipal monopolies of trade and industry and to the appropriation of such aristocratic privileges as sword bearing and serf employment.

It was at least in part because the burghers thus proved ineffective both
at counterbalancing the power of the aristocracy and at developing the
conditions for their own free enterprise that Catherine abruptly adjourned
the Commission *sine die* in 1767. For the next two decades she applied
governmental goads of a purely economic kind in the effort to galvanize
the burghers into taking the initiative, catering to their old caste monopoly
of trading within the towns but otherwise exposing them to the challenges
of free commercial and industrial enterprise by courtesy of governmental
decree and of expanded foreign markets by courtesy of governmental
treaty.

In this context of Catherine's protracted effort to provoke free initiative
by state fiat, her legislation of 1785, which included a charter for the town
burghers as well as the famous Charter of the Nobility and the abortive
charter for the state peasants, can be seen as her final attempt to develop
the traditional social privileges and duties of the separate Russian castes
into generalized economic rights and governmental functions.

Like the others, the town charter sought to organize its social object—in
this instance the burghers—into a self-administering corporation which
minimized the traditional internal rankings within the estate and
established the elective institutions designed both to guard the economic
liberties of its individual members and to represent the estate's share in
the state. Where the nobles were legally recognized as provincial corporations, the burghers were legally recognized as municipal corporations.

Where the nobles were organized into provincial and district assemblies under elected marshals who together administered the common will within the corps of nobility and represented it to the provincial and district governments, the burghers were organized under elected town councils and mayors who together were to run the towns and represent their interests to the financial and police officials of the provincial and district governments. Where the nobles' charter distinguished six different sources of noble status (Imperial appointment, military and civil service, ancient birth, and so on) but prescribed the equality of all nobles in the enjoyment of the aristocracy's freedom from service and other civil and economic rights, the town charter ranked the burghers in six classes but prescribed their equal participation in the election of the municipal authorities and the district burgher courts and in the executive board nominated by the town council. Where the distinction between the service aristocracy and the aristocracy by birth was recognized in the nobles' charter by granting political rights in the provincial noble assemblies—that is, both the right to vote in them and the right to be elected to corporate or public office by them—only to aristocrats with civil or commissioned military service, the distinction of merchants from the rest of the burghers was recognized in the town charter by the granting of civil rights—that is, freedom from compulsory state service (both civil and military), immunity from corporal punishment, and the right to substitute a business tax for the servile poll (or "soul") tax—only to the merchants.

The Meaning of Enlightened Social Policy

Catherine's charter for the urban burghers thus made explicit what was implicit in her social policy toward the nobles and the peasants: the conversion of the older social regimen of particular obligations and particular rights into a combination of political function and economic liberties. Here, indeed, is the key to the ambiguities of the enlightened absolutists' social policies in general. Their attention to both aristocratic privilege and peasants' rights, like their attention to both the official tutelage over and the entrepreneurial freedom of the economic bourgeoisie, was predicated on their reorganization of incompatible social claims into the compatible combination of political function and economic right. They used political function as a valid means of favoring one or another social class for its contribution to the state. They used economic right as a valid means of favoring one or another social class for the greater enterprise of its individual members.

The parallel of these social policies with the enlightened monarchs' policies toward the religious and intellectual institutions over which they extended political control, and toward the freedom of conscience and of thought which they deemed beyond political control, is patent. But since man's practical economic and social activities were, in the eighteenth century, still considered less sacrosanct and less essential to his individuality than his spiritual activities, the emphasis on collective political privilege over individual suprapolitical rights was correspondingly greater in the practical than in the spiritual sphere of enlightened-absolutist policy. Thus the primarily pro-aristocratic orientation of both Frederick's and Catherine's social policies was geared to their view of the aristocracy as the most important social contributor to the order of the state—in Frederick's case for its essential qualities of civil and military leadership, in Catherine's for the prudential considerations of its potential for disorder and its monopoly of authority over the vast Russian countryside. In Frederick, indeed, the political ground of his preference was explicit: in addition to "the general rights of man," which are based on the natural freedom of all individuals, he acknowledged "the hierarchy of particular rights," which are appropriate to membership in the various estates, primarily because he measured such particular rights by the differential contribution of the estates to the welfare of the state.

Even behind the apparent consistency of Joseph's policy of peasant liberation with his principles of natural-rights individualism there lay not the radical dogmatism of which he has so often been accused but the coincidence of the two different criteria. Certainly his humanitarian doctrine was more authentic than his enlightened rivals', but so was his preoccupation with politics. If, then, his peasant liberation was of a piece with his far-reaching program of publicly administered social welfare—his government built and ran hospitals, orphanages, lying-in homes, and institutions for the handicapped all over Austria—in testifying to his general feelings and principles in favor of the underprivileged and the unfortunate, both the liberation and the welfare were equally effects of his political conviction that "the working class" is "the most useful class in the nation." When sympathy for the exploited classes was detached from considerations of political utility, as Joseph had been convinced it was in his mother's concern for the Bohemian peasants, he was suspicious of it, and showed an anxiety for the viability of a noble class that was also vital to the state. In general, however, Joseph favored the peasants and restricted the lords in a way that agreed with Frederick's and Catherine's principles but diverged from their policies simply because, unlike them, he judged the interests and rights of the masses to be more needful to the state than the exemptions and privileges of the classes.

In the long run, the combination of political collectivism and economic individualism that was common to the social policy of all the enlightened monarchs proved to be more important than the differences of social preference that came out of their respective applications of this double standard. For a policy that made social status a resultant of political function and economic right had the permanent effect of weakening the autonomy of all social groups and of strengthening the power of the sovereign political authority, who now could add to his categorical monopoly of collective force over all social classes his protection of the individual rights on which his resources depended. The enlightened absolutists thus equipped the autocracies of central and eastern Europe with the capacity to survive through the liberal atmosphere and the social unrest of the nineteenth century. As a matter of fact, all these autocracies without exception—including the Habsburg empire after Joseph—first appropriated the old nobility as the political governing class par excellence. Then, when subsequent industrialization in the western powers placed a greater political premium on the rights of free economic enterprise, these states were prepared to accommodate the economic and civil rights of the rising social classes—liberal aristocrats, bourgeoisie, peasant farmers—and thus to perpetuate the authoritarian state, together with its dependent nobility, through the nineteenth into the twentieth century.

RESULTS OF ENLIGHTENED ABSOLUTISM

Like its social policies in particular, the results of enlightened absolutism in general varied from country to country in their specifics, but its joint effect upon the great powers of central and eastern Europe was massive and uniform.

Joseph's measures were, by and large, undoubtedly the shortest-lived and Catherine's undoubtedly the longest. In the latter 1780's opposition to Joseph arose both from the conservative clergy, nobles, and particularists (that is, Hungarians and Belgians) who felt violated by the liberal and centralistic features of his legislation and from the liberal intellectuals and peasants who were disappointed by the utilitarian limits as well as the centralistic oppressiveness of the reforms. Joseph responded to the resistance from 1785 on by increasing the central controls and diminishing the liberty in his reforms, and after his death in 1790 his successor, Emperor Leopold II, enlightened reformer though he had proved himself to be as Grand Duke of Tuscany, rolled some of them back entirely. Except for the retention of the peasant's right to leave his holding, a dubious right when thus isolated, Joseph's measures of peasant liberation were repealed, and some of the strongholds of aristocratic and clerical influence that he had dismantled were now restored—the administrative committees of the provincial diets, the corporate constitutions of Hungary and the Austrian Netherlands, and the Church-run seminaries and Church-controlled liturgy.

In Russia, on the other hand, the reaction against Catherine's characteristic policies after her death in 1796 was brief and ineffective. Her son and heir, Paul I (ruled 1796–1801), did indeed translate his hatred for his mother into an anti-aristocratic policy that not only attacked the preeminent position of the nobility in district and local government but abridged the personal rights and tax immunity which had been guaranteed in the

Charter of the Nobility. But even he coupled this policy with a further extension and intensification of serfdom, and after he was murdered by aristocrats in 1801 his anti-aristocratic measures were repealed while his enserfments were not. True, the corporate vitality that Catherine had hoped to stimulate as a kind of social feeder of human energies to her state did not develop in the nobility any more than in the burgher group; yet through the nineteenth century the alliance of state and aristocracy that had been cemented by Catherine continued to dominate Russian public life.

The fate of the particular policies associated with Prussia's Frederick fell between the Austrian tendency to repudiate what Joseph did and the Russian tendency to continue what Catherine did. In Prussia, Frederick's achievements were built upon. The decade of reaction which followed immediately upon his death in 1786 turned out to be, like Paul's briefer reign in Russia, evanescent and inconsequential. The lasting revision of Frederick's work was taken up, under quite different auspices, by liberal bureaucrats who reacted against the rigid mercantilist side of Frederick's policies. With the accession of the diligent Frederick William III in 1797, Frederick's fundamental policy of mobilizing Prussia's intellectual and social resources on principles taken from the advanced societies of the west was resumed. After the Prussian defeat by Napoleon at Jena in 1806, the Frederician heritage was adapted to the new conditions of power created by the revolutionary French. What was rejected was not the Frederician system as such but the persistence of its literal institutions which had become anachronisms—like the personal absolutism that had degenerated into government by irresponsible private secretaries, and the association of social castes with political authority that was now squeezing life out of the society and force out of the state. The modernization of the Prussian state was undertaken by aristocrats who had been attracted into the Prussian service by Frederick and who sought to adapt the merger of authoritarian government and liberalized society which had been initiated by Frederick on the basis of intellectual principle to the new real possibilities of free economic and social endeavor.

But the net effect of enlightened absolutism went beyond the variable destinies of its specific policies to establish a pattern of domination that would pervade vast sections of the European continent and influence the lives of future generations down to the present day. The enlightened absolutists adjusted the instruments of government—that is, bureaucracies, laws, and political values—to enforce a collective power, stability, and order over a society that required spontaneity, mobility, and freedom. Thus they pioneered a mode of politics which reconciled authoritarian government with the growing self-determination of a developing society precisely by making a necessity of the antithesis between them—by demonstrating to autonomous social groups in various stages of modernization that a viable community among them was possible only if their conflicting social claims from below were transmuted into compatible political programs by adjudication from above.

In these part-archaic, part-modern societies of central and eastern Europe (measuring modernity by the usual standards of western industrial society) authoritarian governments have imposed the advanced standards of the west upon their military, diplomatic, and economic instruments to enlarge their peoples' international capacities; and across the resulting fault of static and mobile strata in their societies they have constructed overarching policies which no group or combination of groups could construct by itself. To do this work, authoritarian governments long continued to employ the two main instruments of rule from above that their "enlightened" forebears employed as a joint principle—monarchy and philosophy. Thus they perpetuated the union of kings and philosophers in new guises.

The longevity of the Romanovs, the Habsburgs, and the Hohenzollerns, as dynasties that not only reigned but ruled until the end of the First World War, was only the physical expression of the modern function of autocracy in the fissured societies of Russia, Austria-Hungary, and Germany that under other forms persisted even deeper into our century. The merger of such autocracy with philosophy has likewise proved to be something much more fundamental in these nations than the mere historical memory of their coincidence in some eighteenth-century ancestors. For these are nations which have in fact been especially susceptible to philosophies of politics—that is, to political and social theories which call for political means to realize total social systems whose validity comes from outside the contemporary societies themselves. The legitimacy of the philosophies has been precisely like the legitimacy of the kings which it has accompanied in these countries where both have governed for so long. It consists, for both, in the derivation of their authority from a source transcending the existing society as a society and the derivation of their function from a single, supreme, collective goal—whether racial, national, or social—that must be imposed upon a fragmented society.

For better or for worse, the kings' appropriation of philosophy in the eighteenth century has developed into a fundamental mode of politics.

CHAPTER 22

The End of an Era:
The Social Movement
in the West, 1763-1789

WHEN THE LAST third of the eighteenth century is reviewed from the vantage point of its climax in the great French Revolution of 1789, the most important historical strand of the whole era is the generation-long revolutionary turmoil which gave it a European context. Starting from the obscure local circumstances of a scurrilous London newspaper article in 1763, a factional squabble in the little city-republic of Geneva in 1768, and a distant colonial struggle across the sea in 1776, diffuse social movements against established authority spread erratically across Europe during the decade of the 1780's. They erupted in Ireland and England during 1780 and zig-zagged eastward across the Continent, returning to Geneva in 1782, disrupting the Netherlands from 1783 to 1787, and infecting the Austrian Netherlands, Poland, and Sweden in 1788, before the outbreak of decisive and violent revolution in France during 1789 triggered the Hungarian rising of that year.

All these movements were social (that is, they involved groups other than those actually exercising political rights and functions accorded by the established constitution), rebellious (that is, they undertook active resistance to legal authority, whether through civil disobedience, physical violence, or irregular organizations), and liberal in their appeal (that is, they resisted in the name of the rights of man). Finally, and most concretely, these movements were all revolutionary, whether they succeeded or not, in the sense that each of them sought a transfer of political power through a sudden and decisive change in its country's constitution.

TYPES OF REVOLUTIONARY MOVEMENTS

In view of the number of movements with such qualities during the final decades of the Old Regime, and in deference to our own rising con-

721

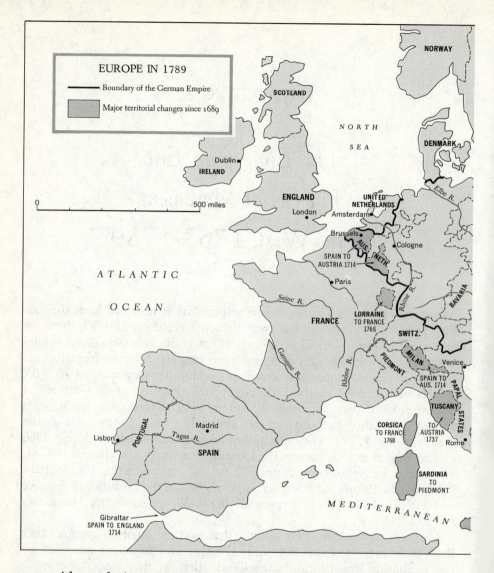

EUROPE IN 1789

Boundary of the German Empire

Major territorial changes since 1689

cern with revolutionary processes, historians have tended increasingly to stress the alienation of life in these decades from the characteristic institutions of the Old Regime and its continuity rather with the cataclysmic events of 1789 and after in a general European "Age of Revolution."

From this retrospective angle of their ultimate issue in the authentic revolutions of the 1790's, the radical events of the two preceding decades can be analyzed into four different types of revolution. Each revolutionary situation contained several types of revolutionary movements, one often setting off the others, but for clarity we shall separate in interpretation what were mixed in reality.

First, there were the interventionist revolutions, where the intrusion by

foreign powers played a crucial or determining role in the transfer of political power. This kind of revolution came in two models. The intervention of France (supported by Zurich and Bern) on behalf of the patriciate in the Genevan civil strife of 1782, the Prussian intervention in 1787 on behalf of the conservative coalition of Dutch oligarchs and monarchists loyal to the prince of Orange against an independent party of the liberal middle classes, and even, on a more modest scale, the French intervention of 1778–1783 on behalf of the North American colonists against Great Britain, were cases of *imposed* revolution, where the intervening power directly affected the result of a constitutional conflict. The progressive movement of enlightened Polish magnates (that is, upper nobility) in alliance with the equally enlightened King Stanislas II (ruled 1764–1795) and what there was of an intellectual and mercantile Polish commoner class in the towns became the outstanding case of *patriotic* revolution, where the intervening power provoked a nationalistic opposition to the satellite constitution supported by the intruder. The traditional Polish constitution, whose provisions for a severely limited elective kingship and for unanimity (*liberum veto*) in the decisions of the national Diet guaranteed the sovereignty of the provincial assemblies of local serf-owning nobles whose delegates composed the Diet, received the puppet's taint from its support by Russia under cover of the joint guarantee by the partitioning powers of 1772, and the patriotic movement in rump Poland received from the shock and the continuing humiliation of foreign intrusion the cohesion which led to the enactment of administrative, educational, and censorship reforms between 1772 and 1789 as prelude to the revolutionary establishment of a liberal constitutional monarchy in 1791. The revolutionary movements in North America (1776–1783), Ireland (1780–1785), and the Austrian Netherlands (1788–1790) also shared this quality of national resistance, albeit in diluted form since the British and Habsburg powers whose intrusions seemed alien had acknowledged if ambiguous rights of sovereignty over the nations concerned. The deliberate assumption of the name "Patriot" by all these movements symbolized the provocative power of the interventionist motif in their revolutions.

Second, there were the revolutions by enlightened monarchy—that is, by enlightened kings or by kings' enlightened ministers. These revolutions also came in two models. Gustavus III's forceful imposition of a formal new constitution upon Sweden in 1789, like the Habsburg Joseph II's equally formal abrogation of his Belgian provinces' constitutional charters of self-government during the same year, climaxed *objective* revolutions by enlightened monarchy—that is, revolutions that actually shifted constitutional powers to the monarch. Neither the timid, malleable, and well-meaning Louis XVI nor the persistent, myopic, legalistic George III can be rehabilitated into an enlightened monarch by any stretch of the term, but the successive efforts of Louis' reforming ministers at tax equalization and judicial centralization in France, and attempts by the Grenvilles and the Townshends under George III to organize a rational colonial system of controls in place of the haphazard accumulation of rights and regulations for North America, were, like Joseph II's analogous centralization of local administration and his imposition of governmental controls on serfdom in Hungary, cases of *subjective* revolutions by enlightened monarchy—that is, reforms that were taken to be despotic revolutions by the privileged groups immediately affected by them.

Third, there were the conservative revolutions. In Britain's American colonies, France, the Austrian Netherlands, and Hungary, privileged groups answered the revolutionary threat of royal centralization by going beyond mere counterrevolution for the *status quo* to their own revolution for a new permanent share in the soverign power that would preempt such threats in the future.

Finally, there were the popular revolutions, evoked by the example and appeals of the monarchical or conservative parties, temporarily joining one or another of them in its revolutionary movement, but growing essentially independent of either. The popular revolutionaries were a coalition of liberal notables (from the lower ranks of the aristocracy and from enfranchised commoners) with the insecure stake of vulnerable privileges and subordinate public functions in the old society and of commoners with no stake of either privilege or public function in the old society. They drove for the organization of a new society without privilege and with public functions based on common consent rather than distributive hierarchy. These popular revolutions came in two models. In Britain, Ireland, the Netherlands, and the Austrian Netherlands the exclusive predominance of the old society's mobile elite in the liberal coalition produced *abortive* popular revolutions. In Britain's North American colonies and in France the more balanced coalition of subordinate elite and the unprivileged produced *effective* popular revolutions.

REVOLUTIONARY MOVEMENTS AND THE OLD REGIME

This retrospective classification of the revolutionary preludes to Europe's Age of Revolution identifies the four main factors of this coming revolution, but it tells little of their connection with the European past and hence little of their real historical character. For this knowledge, we must consider the turbulent movements from 1763 to 1789 from the genetic point of view and look to their origins and growth in the Old Regime rather than to their destination beyond it. From this vantage point the radical events of the period are patterned not by the shape of the democratic revolution that was emerging but by the strands of the Old Regime that was unraveling. The political and social "revolutionaries" of the last generation before the French Revolution had, indeed, the same kind of relationship to the Old Regime in the realm of action as the "unworldly philosophers" of the same era had to the Enlightenment in the realm of thought (see pp. 208–10). Just as the thinkers were post-Enlightenment rather than anti-Enlightenment in that each of them sought to develop to a categorical extreme a single strand—such as reason, liberty, or passion—of the Enlightenment culture that had consisted in the balance of them all, so were most of the actors post-Old-Regime rather than anti-Old-Regime in that each of them sought to develop a consistent system of political authority out of one or another of the particular institutions—such as the royal bureaucracy or the aristocratic assembly—which had coexisted in time-tested, if inconsistent, equilibrium. Only the popular revolutionaries had contributed to the balanced order of the Old Regime no such particular institution that was capable of being generalized into a system of political authority, and only they, consequently, turned against the whole authoritarian and hierarchical structure of the Old Regime.

The light thrown on the four types of radical movements by their respective relations with the centrifugal tendencies of the Old Regime shows the real pattern connecting the prerevolutionary Europe of the early modern centuries to the revolutionary Europe of 1789 and after. What was decisive in this pattern was not the common social and political revolutionary effect of the four kinds of radical movements but the differences between them which made the interventionist, monarchical, and aristocratic movements crucial alternatives to the popular movement and perpetuated the regional diversities of the old Europe's political geography into the new era.

We must distinguish, therefore, between the qualified revolutionary character of the foreign intervention, the enlightened absolutism, and the social conservatism which sponsored unbalanced movements by pitting one standard institution of the Old Regime against another and the unqualified revolutionary character of the popular revolution which would transform all the standard institutions of the Old Regime. And we must note the geographical pattern of these different kinds of movements. The interventionist, monarchical, and aristocratic movements were revolutionists of Europe's political periphery. They erupted in minuscule or debilitated states like Geneva, Sweden, Poland, and the Netherlands or in the outlying dependencies of the Habsburg and British empires—in places where the combination of social hierarchy and territorial sovereignty that constituted the characteristic controls of the Old Regime was most attenuated. Of Europe's political heartland only France was struck by these revolutionary outcroppings of the Old Regime, and the exception would prove fatal. For France was also implicated in the entirely different regional pattern of popular revolution. This, the most authentic of the revolutionary movements, was spawned only by the mobile, commercialized, western societies of the Atlantic seaboard even in its abortive form of a movement by a suppressed elite, and among these societies, only in France and America in its effective form of a movement by a coalition of the subordinate elite and unenfranchised commoners.

The regional pattern created by the varying degrees of revolution from the stability of aristocratic absolutism to the popular movement against both the social and the political pillars of the traditional European order was the legacy of the Old Regime to the modern world. Just as the great powers of central and eastern Europe were the strongholds of the enlightened monarchy which equipped the balance of social hierarchy and political authoritarianism for continued viability into the twentieth century, so was the Atlantic complex of peoples the reservoir of the social movement which would again and again change elites and authorities alike in a continuing response to the growing economic and intellectual pressures for equality. These would be the two major poles of modern European history, and between them the smaller continental nations at the Old Regime's periphery would follow the pattern of partial revolution into the gradual and experimental mold of modern small-nation social politics.

Thus the political heritage of Europe's Old Regime took its final form from the absence of revolution in some nations and from the specific type of revolutionary movement, in the nations where there was revolution, during the generation preceding the epochal transformation of France in the summer of 1789. To our sketches of the stabilized regimes in Austria, Prussia, and Russia under their enlightened monarchs and to our discussion of the interventionist revolution which these domestically stabilizing rulers introduced into Europe's international relations (see chapter 9), we must now add sketches of enlightened absolutism and of aristocratic rebellion in their late posture of partial "revolutions" and a concluding discussion of the popular revolutions that initiated a new social, political, and intellectual era of European civilization.

The Revolution of Enlightened Monarchy

Of the two ways in which the later development of enlightened monarchy had revolutionary effect, the course taken in France by the enlightened ministers of Louis XVI (ruled 1774–1792) was the most important instance of the subjective model, where administrative and fiscal reforms were received as acts of constitutional revolution, and the course taken by Gustavus III in Sweden was the most prominent case of the objective model, where the enlightened ruler actually did make a forcible change in the constitution.

The French leading ministers, from Turgot in 1774 through Necker and Calonne to Loménie de Brienne in 1788, were steeped in the culture of the Enlightenment and were committed to liberal administrative change as the means of increasing the economic and social resources available to the king's government—a commitment that was actually in the best style of the reforming type of enlightened monarchy. Mortmain—the anachronism that recognized the permanently inalienable property rights of feudal corporations—was abolished on the royal domain in 1779, and the corvée—compulsory peasant labor—in 1787. Penal procedures were amended during the 1780's to prohibit the use of torture for securing confessions and to limit the use of the notorious *lettres de cachet*, which authorized imprisonment without due process. Vergennes, the foreign minister who first plotted the French intervention on behalf of the revolutionary Americans against the common British rival, subsequently initiated the negotiations with the younger William Pitt which led to the liberal—that is, low-tariff—Anglo-French commercial treaty of 1786, on the equally good royalist grounds that a larger trade for France meant a larger power for France and that a détente with England might aid the rekindled French interest in the Netherlands. Finally, the French Toleration Edict of 1787 granted civil rights to Protestants and acknowledged he validity of Protestant marriages —a reform which may be viewed as the partial restoration, on a generalized basis, of the many special Huguenot rights and liberties that had been abolished with the revocation of the Edict of Nantes a century before.

Even the two main lines of the French ministerial attempts at far-reaching reforms that could not be executed were outgrowths of older absolutist policies. Behind both was a financial crisis which was itself the culmination of the expensive old royal addiction to two-front wars and of the ruinous old royal addiction to "fiscalism"—the policy of paying for them through the creation and sale of public offices that had the effect of diverting public revenues into private fees of the office-owners and through the levying of unequal imposts that extended immunities and dried up future revenues. Hence the grave imbalance of expenditure over income which resulted from French participation in the Americans' was against Great Britain from 1778 to 1783 and which impelled the reform proposals of the 1780's climaxed both the chronic burden of royal policy on French society and the equally old paralysis of royal fiscal policy by duplicating the social conflict between privileged and commoner groups within the institutions of the state.

The first line of reform was the general land tax which Turgot devised as a solution for the chronic financial problem in 1776 and to which Calonne recurred under the immediate threat of bankruptcy in 1787. It was, for both ministers, a part of a plan for a general reorganization of the royal administration that would cut costs and increase revenue, but it also conformed to the centuries-old autocratic model of equality as the equal subjection of all citizens to the king's law. The second main line of enlightened ministerial policy—opposition to the *parlements*—also had its precedent in the French absolutist past. Even the attempt to emasculate the *parlements* in 1788 by removing their right to register royal decrees, the step that triggered uprisings against the government throughout France and led directly to the revolution of 1789, was viewed by Louis XVI as a defense of monarchy against the unlawful pretensions of an aristocracy rather than as a constitutional change (the judicial right to register was retained, and transferred to a new Plenary Court). The measure looked back, indeed, to the abolition of the *parlements* between 1771 and 1774 which had been engineered by his grandfather's imperious chancellor, René Charles de Maupeou. Louis himself had restored them upon his accession as a gesture of good will and now considered himself fully entitled to do once more what he had undone. He felt all the more authorized since he deemed the *parlements*' refusal to register his new taxes without the convo-

Anne Robert Turgot, Baron de l'Aulne. *The one French statesman who was himself a wholehearted* philosophe *and who tried to legislate Physiocratic ideas. Turgot carried down with him the hope of reforming the French monarchy from above when he fell from power in 1776.*

cation and approval of the Estates-General both unconstitutional and subversive.

Insofar as the French ministers of the decade and a half before the French Revolution thus plotted their reforms within the framework of political absolutism and limited their espousal of social change to the leveling only of those privileges directly incidental to the financial resources of the state, it would be wrong to accept the judgment of their conservative opponents and call them revolutionary. Like the Habsburg case of Joseph II, indeed, the reforms sponsored by the French autocracy had the effect of provoking conservative revolutions before the reforms could develop their own revolutionary consequences.

But one French project of the period, did indicate a possible development from reform to revolution by enlightened absolutism. Turgot's plan to associate new provincial assemblies, elected not by order or estate but by property owners as such, with the royal government for consultation on the administration of new taxes could not be implemented before he was forced from the office of Controller General in 1776 by aristocratic pressure upon the court. After Calonne adopted this project along with so many others of Turgot's some eleven years later, it was again frustrated by his enforced resignation from the same office under the same influence. When the idea was finally translated into reality under Calonne's successor, the enlightened, charming, and compliant Archbishop Loménie de Brienne, for whom the post of prime minister was resurrected, it took the old form of provincial diets which represented the three traditional estates under the chairmanship of a churchman or a noble, and in this form played a role in fomenting the conservative revolution. But in its original concept the plan for representative assemblies of the propertied citizenry in a country like France, where of the agricultural land alone some 35 per cent seems, according to the best estimates, to have been owned by peasants and some 30 per cent by burghers, does show the possible transition whereby enlightened absolutism could exchange the hierarchical for the representative principle as the final link of its administration with the body politic and thus transfer to the whole propertied citizenry the share of executive power traditionally reserved to the aristocracy. By building representative assemblies into a system of formal absolutism as the King's administrative agencies, the French plan serves to demonstrate the continuity between monarchial absolutism and monarchial revolution.

In Sweden, where the role of the aristocracy in the king's executive authority was formally guaranteed by the constitution, an enlightened monarch took the revolutionary step the French just failed to take: he forcibly changed the constitution to reduce decisively the aristocracy's share of the public power.

The Swedish monarchical revolution was consummated in two widely separated stages—the seizure of effective legislative sovereignty by the king from the mutually hostile aristocratic and commoner parties of the Swedish Diet in 1772, and the transfer of the aristocracy's dominant share of the administrative power to the commons by the king early in 1789.

A scant year after the young Gustavus III (ruled 1771–1792) had acceded to the Swedish throne, he carried through what has been called the *coup d'état* of 1772. Since it brought an immediate transfer from the estates to the king of the actual power to make laws, and anticipated the later transfer from the aristocracy to the king of the power to administer them, its implications were more revolutionary than the king's bloodless assumption of the authority of the Diet seemed to indicate. The coup itself brought Sweden a new constitution and a *de facto* absolutism to replace the "era of liberty" and its *de facto* sovereignty of aristocracy. The chief organs of aristocratic rule were the nobles' chamber of the four-chambered Swedish Diet and the civil and military services, headed by the central executive council, which the aristocrats dominated and through which they retained their social privileges over the disposition of land. Seizing the occasion of a growing social conflict between the aristocracy and the commoners, who were represented in the other three chambers of the Swedish Diet (clergy, burghers, and peasants), Gustavus enlisted the physical support of the aristocratic faction and the theoretical slogans of the popular faction against "aristocratic despotism" to take sovereign power from the Diet, where both factions had been fighting over it.

The written constitution of 1772, which he composed and imposed upon the Diet, was the ambiguous product to be expected from an

Literary conversation during the reign of Gustavus III of Sweden. *Although the king's readiness to undertake authoritarian and egalitarian coups d'état against the Swedish constitution indicated a revolutionary temperament not usually to be found in his fellow rulers, his intellectual tastes aligned him with the enlightened monarchs of the eighteenth century.*

ambitious royal disciple of Montesquieu and Voltaire who used the *philosophes'* language of constitutional monarchy to cover the distance between the absolute sovereignty he coveted and the legislative powers of the Diet he had both to acknowledge and to minimize. It granted the King full powers to govern the kingdom and the right to call the Diet at his discretion, but the Diet's concurrence was required for the imposition of new taxes, for the renewal of old taxes, and for the declaration of offensive war. Once called, moreover, it possessed the power of initiative for all legislation. As a matter of fact, the king convoked the Diet only for two regular sessions under this constitution—in 1778 and in 1786—and for the rest governed autocratically, bypassing the council for which provision had been made in the constitution and governing, like his uncle Frederick the Great, through his unofficial secretaries on the basis of decisions taken in his own "cabinet." But if the king thus minimized the legislative rights of both the aristocrats and the commons in the Diet for whose share in legislation there remained constitutional warrant, he continued to favor the aristocracy in the civil and military services that carried out his policies in the country and abroad.

The ambiguities of Gustavus' incomplete revolution came to the surface in the Diet of 1786 when he demanded approval and support for a modern army to carry out his decision to fight Russia for the control of the Baltic. When the aristocrats led the resistance in the Diet, and after his unconstitutional declaration of war against Russia in 1788, organized subversive leagues against him, Gustavus proceeded to complete his revolution by reducing to the bare minimum of an administrative instrument the rights of the Diet and by leveling the privileged position of the aristocracy in the administration. Convoking an extraordinary session of the Diet in February, 1789, Gustavus banished the nobles' chamber and issued a set of constitutional amendments—called the Act of Union and Security—in alliance with the three chambers of the lower estates. The new version of the constitution, which went into effect despite the formal disapproval of the nobles' chamber when it was later reconvened, provided for the consistent application of the king's "complete powers to govern" by denying the Diet's right of legislative initiative. The new constitution also provided for the equality of all classes in their access to the state services (with certain formal exceptions), and since civil inequalities had long been justified by the aristocracy's special role in these state services, these inequalities too were now minimized. The Act of Union provided for equal rights before the law and in the courts, and it extended to all classes the right to own and dispose of land.

The epilogue of Gustavus' monarchical revolution was an ironic demonstration of its separate identity vis-à-vis both conservative and modern revolutions. The last years of his reign were filled on the one hand by the continuing opposition of his aristocracy, resentful of the loss both of their legislative rights and their administrative and civil privileges, and on the other by his own fanatic desire to lead a monarchical crusade against the French revolutionaries. He was assassinated, finally, in 1792 by an ambiguous aristocratic coalition of conservative revolutionary nobles and of liberal aristocrats who sympathized with the French revolutionaries—a coalition which could agree only on its joint resistance to the revolutionary despot.

Aristocratic Revolutions

Because the most pervasive factors for change in the late eighteenth century—the extension of the market economy and the intellectual diffusion of liberal ideas—impinged upon the European aristocracy as both a tempting opportunity and a grave threat, aristocratic political radicalism for socially conservative purposes was the most widespread of all the revolutionary movements. Social elites were parties, indeed, to every kind of revolution. They were satellites or resisters of foreign intervention; they overreacted to royal limitations of privilege; and they paved the way for the popular movements which they had evoked for their own support. Thus the patriciates of Geneva and the Netherlands were the beneficiaries of the interventions by France and Prussia, respectively, into their civil strife against the plebeians of their cities for political supremacy. British Presbyterian and Congregationalist lawyers and merchants in North America, like factions of even more respectable lords and gentlemen in Great Britain itself, were first goaded into movements to change the British constitution by the alterations which they convinced themselves a despotic King George III had already made in it. Similarly in France, where the opposition to the crown would develop even more radically than elsewhere, the initial stage was dominated by an aristocratic revolt. The nobility of the robe (*i.e.* the judicial nobility), acting through the sovereign courts (*parlements*), first made constitutional opposition to the king's government honorable between 1763 and 1770 by defending as items in the fundamental rights of the people the tax immunities of their own lands and offices against Louis XV's bureaucratic reformers headed by Chancellor Maupeou. The *parlements* expanded this defense to the protection of privilege and the corporate hierarchy in principle against Turgot's enlightened program of 1776 for a uniform land tax and the suppression of the restrictive guilds. In both cases they developed the possession of a judicial right to register such royal legislation into the claim of a constitutional right to deliberate on its legality. When, in 1787, the most urgent of all French financial crises triggered the most imminent of all the royal threats of tax equalization, the nobility of the robe developed this claim into a general aristocratic campaign for a permanent share in the sovereign power on behalf of "the people"—and thereby took the fateful step of appealing to the masses and initiating the cycle of revolutions.

The purest conservative revolutions were in the Austrian Netherlands and Hungary, for in both of these outlying Habsburg possessions the aristocratic social groups who rose to undo the innovations of Joseph II not only initiated the resistance movement but retained their domination over it.

The Hungarian movement is outside our orbit, since neither the agitation of the Magyar magnates for the suspension of agrarian reform and for the restoration of the violated constitution of noble-dominated and self-governing estates nor the competing movements of peasants and radical gentry reached revolutionary proportions before the stimulus of the French events of 1789. But the Austrian Netherlands (later Belgium) does merit our attention, for there the outbreak of revolution was an autonomous development prior to the decisive news from France.

The Belgian movement revealed clearly a fundamental fact about social conservatism in the Old Regime which the overt preeminence of the nobility in eighteenth-century Europe obscured elsewhere: the recognition of privilege in many kinds of exclusive social corporations, of which the titled aristocracy was only the most favored and the most prominent. In the Austrian Netherlands, the Austrian Habsburgs, like the Spanish Habsburgs before them, governed a collection of the ten Lowland provinces whose political and social constitution had undergone surprisingly few changes since the halcyon era of local and corporate self-government in the Middle Ages. Unconnected save through the common Habsburg overlord, each of the provinces was administered by provincial estates representing the three self-administering social oligarchies of the community—the landed nobility, the Catholic hierarchy, and the municipal guildsmen.

Joseph's program—anti-aristocratic, anti-clerical, and anti-guild—had something socially offensive to every privileged corporation, and the result was a conservative coalition of social groups against it. But it was not until 1787, when Joseph passed from social to constitutional legislation by supplanting the traditional mixed judicial and administrative tribunals of the corporate oligarchs with his centralized system of separate judicial and administrative authorities in redrawn judicial and administrative districts, that two of the provincial estates declared a tax strike and resistance became active. When Joseph responded, in January, 1789, with the abrogation of the Belgian constitution—that is, of the paradigmatic Joyous Entry of 1355, the Brabant provincial charter confirming the historic rights of corporate self-government—his escalation of the conflict into constitutional politics brought a similar escalation of the resistance, and the whole conservative front broke into open revolution.

The Belgian movement was distinguished not only by the comparatively broad social base of its conservative parties but also by the collaboration of a genuinely liberal middle class group. Called Patriots or Vonckists (after their leader, the progressive lawyer Jean François Vonck, 1743-1792), it joined the aristocratic Estatists to expel the Austrian authorities in November and December, 1789. The coalition drew up an Act of Union, patterned on the American Articles of Confederation and designed as the constitution of a united Belgium. Both parties at this stage were committed to the revolutionary goal of an independent Belgium, but they clashed violently on the political form it should assume. The Patriots pushed for a genuinely representative constitution, based on an expanded electorate and embodying national sovereignty. The Estatists pushed for the reinstatement of the pre-Josephinian corporate constitution, returning sovereignty to the unreformed estates of each province and limiting the revolution to the substitution of a weak confederation of the estates for the mild Habsburg suzerainty. The Patriots—or the Democrats, as they now came to call themselves—undoubtedly belonged to the really new political movement which was beginning to appear in western Europe during the 1780's, but of more immediate importance was their comparative weakness, for the triumph of the Estatists over the Democrats in Belgium was symptomatic of the preponderance of conservative over liberal elements in European society until the very end of the Old Regime.

Only France proved to be an exception to this rule, and consequently it was in France, and in France alone, that the new political movement succeeded and brought down the complex of institutions and values that composed the Old Regime. A comparison of the French and Belgian patterns isolates the decisive difference in the balance of social forces between France and the rest of Europe. In Belgium, as in France, the reforming monarchy ultimately lined up with the aristocracy against the liberals: the new Habsburg Emperor, Leopold II, took advantage of the civil strife to

The revolt in Belgium. A *crowd gathers outside the Town Hall of Brussels.*

reoccupy Belgium in December, 1790, and consolidated the Habsburg return by reaching an agreement with the Estatists that restored the traditional corporate constitution of the Austrian Netherlands. But in Belgium, unlike France, this alliance of monarchy and aristocracy succeeded in ending the revolution, and it succeeded because the mass movement of peasants and artisans in Belgium, unlike the analogous mass movement in France, supported the corporate establishment. More attached to their church than their French counterparts, and far less burdened by the crushing taxation imposed by an expensive court and war machine, the Belgian rural masses rose in a form not very different from that of their risings since time immemorial. They joined their priests and their lords in the defense of their customary faith and way of life against innovation in church and state.

Since the conservative revolutionary movements of the 1780's partook so much of the age-old resistance by self-administering and privileged corporations to centralizing and leveling absolutism, the questions arise: What was new in them? What was revolutionary about them?

Two features of the movements distinguish them from the assertion of corporate rights and exemptions against bureaucratic encroachment which had been standard in the Old Regime.

First, the aristocrats of the revolutionary generation demanded the preservation of their social privileges no longer merely as chartered group liberties appropriate to their special status in the state but as particular instances of universal rights which imposed general limits on the power of the state as such. This language of natural rights, particularly in the context of the American Revolution, gave a radical flavor to the advocacy of social privilege. Thus the *Parlement* of Paris gave such an argument for its protection of corporate privilege against Turgot's reforms in 1776 when it insisted that "a fundamental rule of natural law and civil government . . . not only upholds property rights but safeguards rights attached to the person and born of prerogatives of birth and estate."

Second, and more important, the aristocrats of the revolutionary generation sought a new constitutional basis for the recovery of the public functions that monarchs had taken from them. Unlike the social privileges which they attempted merely to retain, the corporate political rights of local self-government and of participation in the central sovereign power, which the aristocrats now sought, represented a demand for immediate constitutional change, and it was only at the stage of this demand that the conservative movement became truly revolutionary. It was revolutionary, indeed, not only because it claimed for itself a shift of political power in favor of the aristocracy but also because the aristocracy's actual dependence upon the support of other social groups for the seizure of political power from the monarchy committed it to doctrines of national sovereignty and representative government that were far more revolutionary than the rhetoric of social privilege. The Belgian Estatists, as we have seen, explicitly used a constitutional model of revolutionary America to bring about the recovery of their old corporate liberties. The Hungarian country assemblies which Joseph had destroyed would reemerge upon his death in 1790 to reinstitute the traditional Hungarian constitution, and then the serf-owning magnates who dominated these assemblies would touch off a wide-ranging revolutionary movement by basing their actual monopoly of corporate power on the constitutional claim that "the social contract which creates the state places sovereignty in the hands of the people."

The French notables went a step further than the Belgians and the Hungarians in demonstrating the revolutionary implications of the aristocratic renewal of conservative constitutions. Whereas the aristocrats of the Habsburg Empire sought to save all their social privileges by taking a share of political power, the French were willing to give up the foremost of these privileges—tax exemption—for a share of political power. The Assembly of Notables of 1787 approved the principle of a uniform land tax, and during that same year the *Parlement* of Paris surrendered a bastion of the judicial nobility's special right to verify royal legislation when it denied its own long-cherished claim to virtual "representation" of the people. But both sacrifices were for the purpose of concentrating the entire weight of the conservative party and its popular support on the convocation of the Estates-General, which would restore the medieval corporate constitution of France in modernized form. Under it the aristocracy would be assured a permanent preeminent position in the representative organ of the nation and in the sovereign authority of the monarchy to tax and to legislate. The aristocracy thus hoped to translate the letter of particular social privileges

The Assembly of Notables, 1787. *On this occasion the French monarchy called upon its aristocracy for financial assistance and was refused, to the ultimate distress of both parties.*

into the substance of a political power which would guarantee the general conditions of its social superiority.

The merger of reactionary privilege and radical politics in a movement toward conservative revolution has been a recurrent feature of European history from the Reformation to National Socialism, and in each instance the combination has seemed so anomalous as to require precise social analysis of the group that led the movement. For the aristocratic revolutions of the late eighteenth century, the characterization of the leading group as "aristocrats" is only the beginning, rather than the conclusion, of such an analysis, since the contemporary eighteenth-century use of the term—a use that we have so far followed here—referred to the *political* party fighting for hierarchical constitutions and guarantees of privilege and not to the *social* group behind it. Recent studies of the social groupings in Europe on the eve of the French Revolution have stressed their internal divisions and increasing varieties, to the effect that the social group which twentieth-century analysts identify as the aristocracy was much too variegated to be represented as a single class by the political group which eighteenth-century publicists identified as aristocracy. Aristocracy, in its modern connotation, is defined as a social status actually held by all those who possess superior privilege, power, or influence over the rest of the society and who share a distinctively coded way of life, compounded of license in private, formality in public, and elegance in company. In its application to late eighteenth-century society it includes both old and recent nobility (dividing usually at four generations of hereditary title) and both traditional and new non-noble elites (such as old gentry families in Britain and parvenu banking families in France, respectively)—an assortment of social subgroups and interests that provided social aristocratic support to the politics of enlightened monarchy and of popular liberal constitutionalism as well as to the radical conservatism of the political "aristocrats."

The social grouping with which men linked the political "aristocrats" in the 1780's was thus not the aristocracy in our comprehensive sense of the term but a particular one of its subgroups, the old nobility, defined then as now as a stipulated legal status conferring definite title, hallowed by long familial possession, and guaranteeing exclusive privileges—most importantly, in our context, political access to high deliberative, judicial, or administrative offices of state. The contemporary testimony was undoubtedly correct, for the old nobility was indeed the social grouping that led the movement for conservative political "revolution," representing, defending, and followed by their clients among the old non-noble elite of country gentry and urban oligarchs. But this social identification does not, by itself, suffice to explain the movement toward a "revolutionary" reconstitution of the state on the part of lords who had hitherto preferred to move for feudal immunities from the state. The change is explicable by two novel features in the nobles' situation. First, when enlightened monarchs or the enlightened ministers of monarchs withdrew the political guarantees of social privilege from the alliance of sovereignty and hierarchy which had composed the settled order of the Old Regime, nobles rushed to fill the void of the political authority upon which they had become dependent for their security. Second, the growth and reorientation of the larger social aristocracy whose status the old nobility actually shared but consciously rejected reached dimensions, with its absorption of contemporary economic and cultural elites, which drew from the nobles a political response as ambivalent as their social position within the aristocracy. Thus both the collective aristocratic status which eighteenth-century men did not recognize and the noble status which they exclusively recognized were factors in the politics of conservative revolution. This politics grew in good measure out of the actual relations between the inclusive aristocracy and the exclusive nobility, and for a social explanation of the politics it is to these relations that we now turn.

The most prominent common attribute of the European aristocracy throughout the eighteenth century remained what it had traditionally been for the nobility it counted within its ranks: the possession of landed estates. But this formal mark of unity covered a myriad of distinctions, old and new, which actually divided both the landowning aristocracy and its partial subset, the titled nobility, into a myriad of separate, often conflicting, interests. The aristocracy still included both noble and non-noble estate owners within its ranks. Within the nobility, by the same token, aristocrats had still to be distinguished from the non-aristocrats who commanded neither power, prestige, wealth, nor, often enough, even a landed estate. As one went from east to west in Europe the coincidence of nobility and aristocracy diminished from the full overlay in Russia to the mere peerage in Great Britain, which would have been impotent without the untitled gentry that with it made up the British aristocracy.

Again, within the European landed aristocracy the distinction persisted between the eastern serf-owning noble who wielded public administrative and judicial powers over his peasants and the western landlord who collected rents and dues from free tenants. Within the eastern serf-owning nobility, in turn, there was the further distinction between those who cultivated their own demesne with servile labor and those who let it out in servile tenures. Among the western landlords there was the distinction between those who rented their own lands to farmers through terminal leases, as in Britain, and those who possessed customary obligations upon hereditary tenures legally owned by the occupying peasants, as in France. If, finally, the old legal distinction between high and low nobility persisted with diminished force, the equally hoary social differentiations of ancient from new nobility, of the nobility of blood and sword from the nobility of administrative and judicial office, of court from country nobility, persisted with increasing force.

To these familiar divisions within the aristocracy, the growth of wealth, the attractions of the great cities, and the spread of secular culture during the eighteenth century added new distinctive criteria, bringing in additional ranks of aristocrats and redrawing some of the lines among the old. If the landed estate and the manor house remained the most uniform overt marks of aristocracy, they were now much more often than previously the signs rather than the bases of aristocratic status: men acquired them to make visible the social position they had actually attained in other ways. The possession of wealth in particular now became a widespread and accepted ground of aristocracy, bringing rich commoners into the ranks of the privileged and increasing the ratio of monied aristocrats to poor nobles. If, moreover, the magnet of commercial profits still drew comparatively few landowners, outside of England, into the class of progressive farmers who applied scientific techniques to agricultural production, it did increase the class of landlords who were oriented toward a market economy, whether indirectly, by using enclosures (as in England) or the dusty old claims of the "manorial reaction" (as in France) to increase their rents, or directly, by participating or investing in manufacturing or in wholesale and international trade. Second, the vogue of Enlightenment culture changed the standards of the way of life that was deemed both common and essential to members of the aristocracy. Intelligence, knowledgeability, the arts of communication, and good taste, now brought some of the intellectual elite—like Voltaire—into the aristocracy as a distinct group and sowed a new seed of distinction within the older aristocracy between its cultured and its unlettered sectors. Finally, the development of the cities—both capital and, to a lesser extent, provincial—into centers of social concourse, intellectual discussion, and performance of the arts developed a new kind of urbanized aristocracy with an ambition, an openness, and a mobility quite distinct from the qualities of the old rural nobility.

The superimposition of the newer upon the older criteria of aristocracy pointed in two contrary directions. On the one side, it tended to break down the old aristocratic barriers, and this attenuation included both the barriers separating the aristocratic from the nonaristocratic sectors of the society and the barriers separating one kind of aristocracy from another. The accommodation of the aristocracy to the standards set by the possession and the expenditure of monetary wealth and by the participation in and consumption of a generally accessible urban culture opened it to the elite of talent and intelligence, whatever its social provenance. Through commoners' purchase of landed estates, intermarriage into the families of needy nobles, and purchase of or skillful performance in high public office, the magic circle of aristocracy was in fact expanded, and in France and Great Britain particularly, the expectation of such upward social mobility became widespread among ambitious commoners. So permeable, indeed, did the expansion of aristocracy seem to make the barrier between noble and deserving commoner that many Frenchmen awarded themselves titles as their own just desserts and simply used them on their own authority as befitting their acquired station. Under these influences, too, such older distinctions within the aristocracy as those between the military and the judicial nobility in France or between the peerage and the gentry in Britain or between the landed and the bureaucratic nobility in Germany became quite blurred in reference to both their social prestige and their political influence.

On the other side, however, this same overlay of new upon old varieties of aristocracy led to a process of segregation through which the newly joined forces of older aristocrats sealed themselves off from the threatened inundation by new aristocrats and the pressing hordes of ambitious commoners behind them. The most striking evidence of this tendency occurred in Britain, where an economic and legal situation that made the relations between commonalty and aristocracy more fluid than anywhere else was accompanied, in the second half of the eighteenth century, by surprisingly few intermarriages between commoners and the great aristocratic families, sales of estates by nobles to commoners, or entries by commoners into the peerage. Throughout Europe, indeed, the formal creation of new nobles by the kings failed to keep pace with the pressure of the new aristocratic elite which was being increasingly populated by practitioners of the noble way of life recruited from the beneficiaries of rising incomes and from the ranks of cultivated men.

The important fact about this lag was that it was not simply a matter of institutional inertia. It was part of a more general policy on the part of the ensconced nobility, who used their growing influence in the royal governments to reinforce the definite legal criteria of nobility against the flood of claimants admitted through the actual porous standards of the new aristocracy. More and more, indeed, as the century wore on, the institutions of state became the battleground of the social conflict between the new *de facto* aristocracy and the bourgeois aspirants to that status on one side and the older nobility who would reassert their preeminence on the other. Thus, of the letters of nobility that monarchs did issue in the second half of the century far more were rewards for government service than for any other cause, and to counter this pressure the older nobility tried to anchor social caste in political privilege by making noble status of ancient lineage the necessary qualification for high governmental position. The French *parlements'* reservation of their top posts to men with four quarters (*i.e.* generations) of nobility during the 1770's and the official French stipulation, by the royal edict of 1781, of the same social requirement for army commissions were clear indications of the political lever which the conservative nobility sought to use upon the shifting social basis of the aristocratic class.

The very variety of aristocratic types and the tensions between them that historians have stressed in their social analyses of the European aristocracy during the second half of the eighteenth century give the clue to the main agents of the conservative revolutions. The conservative revolutionaries were representatives of the older nobility who took account of contemporary conditions and responded to them in two related ways. They accommodated themselves to the concentration of power in central governments, to the popular culture of the Enlightenment, and to the mobile society of a mercantile economy. But they also were in mortal fear of the leveling consequences of these contemporary conditions. Hence the members of this nobility sought to take political control of the modernizing tendencies in their society in order to direct them to the support of a stabilized aristocracy.

The connection between the ambivalent social attitude of the nobility toward the broader aristocratic culture of the age and its equally ambivalent politics of conservative "revolution" was epitomized in the leadership of the political nobles: the old Whigs in England and the judicial nobility in France were precisely those aristocrats who had long since joined the old nobility and appropriated its exclusive standards but who also retained the capacity to adapt their interests and policies to changing conditions. This connection between the social and the political positions of the old nobles was epitomized too in the terminology of their liberal opponents. The liberals gave the label of "grandees" to the great noble families which used their positions of power in the high offices of state to oppose all politics of reform by the king's government, and the overtones of the label indicated precisely the balance between their exploitation of the contemporary monetary and intellectual culture and their arrogant deprecation of the society that produced it.

The schizoid attitudes of the old high nobility toward its kings and its

contemporary society explain both the limits and the result of the conservative "revolution" it led. Driven to political opposition against the sovereigns they needed by what they considered to be the royal unbalancing of
traditional constitutions, the "grandees" and their clients in the lower old
aristocracy could not take their "revolution" beyond the conquest of only
enough political power to enforce permanent cooperation upon the monarch. But the progressive and universal character of the appeals in which
the old nobles, given their contemporaneity, could not help but dress their
claims, galvanized the newer mobile elites and underprivileged commoners
first into subordinate support of the nobiliar movement and then, in the
active societies of the Atlantic coast, into independent and authentic
popular revolution.

THE POPULAR REVOLUTIONS

Because the movements which sought to shift the ultimate political
power over the general rules of the society from the hierarchies of authority
to the people as a homogeneous body organized themselves outside the
institutions of the Old Regime and opposed both the political and the
social bases of the Old Regime, they made the only integral revolution of
the revolutionary generation that closed out the eighteenth century. In
this kind of revolutionary movement, underprivileged and unprivileged
social groups did what had never been done before. They created their own
political mass movement, and they worked out their own program, appropriate to it. Instead of sovereign kings these groups demanded royal agents
symbolic of and accountable to the sovereign will of the nation. Instead of a
many-tiered social hierarchy they demanded a single body of equal citizens, differentiated only by the simple assignment of its socially independent members to participate in government on behalf of all. And instead of
exalting philosophies for the principles of explanation that justified an ultimate order of reality, they produced ideologies to serve as principles of action that would realize the ultimate rights of all men.

The distinction between the underprivileged and the unprivileged
groups in the revolutionary movements of the period was a crucial one.
The underprivileged consisted of those who had status in the existing
society, but a status that put them in the lower reaches of the privileged
hierarchy. Ranging from country gentlemen to master artisans, they consisted mainly of the merchants, professional men (especially lawyers),
larger shopkeepers, new manufacturers, middle-income farmers, and writers—the group that was called the "middling set" in Britain and that would
speak for the Third Estate in France. The unprivileged group, called the
"inferior set" in Britain and the Fourth Estate in France, consisted largely
of the unpropertied in town and country: journeymen, small shopkeepers,
peasant sharecroppers and farm workers.

These two revolutionary groups had different positions in the society, and, consequently, different aims for it. The members of the underprivileged group enjoyed some of the exemptions from obligations, and often enough, even a measure of the political rights, that the Old Regime had to offer substantial property owners, but as beneficiaries of the commercial prosperity and as avid consumers of the Enlightenment, their ambition was to extend their influence, not as of yore, by ascending the available ladder of social privilege, but by creating a new channel to political power outside the old. Whether this new road to political power—which was usually identified with representative government based on a broad propertied electorate—would be an addition to or a replacement of the traditional avenues of aristocratic and bureaucratic influence depended upon the responsiveness of the privileged groups on the one hand and the unprivileged on the other.

For the great mass of unprivileged men and women in towns and countryside who made up the overwhelming majority of Europe's population, life during the late eighteenth century remained nearly as precarious, brutal, and miserable as it had ever been, and much of their response to the exigent conditions of their existence was correspondingly as immediate, visceral, and compulsively conservative as it had ever been. Very few of these people, indeed, were practically affected by the improvements in medical science and public sanitation that were a restricted feature of the age, and the general increase of population from mid-century on, accompanied as it was by a general price rise and the persistence of sporadic crop failures, actually swelled the numbers of landless peasants, underemployed drifters, and other consumers dependent on market supplies, whose sufferings grew with the rising cost of living. Hence the bulk of the popular disturbances in the period took the traditional forms of the food riot against the inflated price of grain, the strike for higher wages by journeymen, apprentices, and common laborers, risings against real or fancied violations of customary rights by landlord or public officials, and the mass frenzy in favor of one kind of popular faith against another kind of unpopular faith. The Gordon Riots of 1780, when anti-Catholic crowds burned, looted, and took over the streets of London for more than a week in support of Lord George Gordon's protest against the grant of civil rights to Roman Catholics by the liberal Catholic Relief Act of 1778, was only the most prominent case of the preference for good old social and religious causes on the part of those who had ever been without privilege, were now increasingly numerous and insecure as well, and hankered more than ever for the familiar certainties.

But there also were changes of degree in these conditions that helped to produce, among some men in some places, a political attitude that was new in kind. If there were more of the poor and the desperate than ever, the slight ameliorations of their lot which the late eighteenth century did witness sufficed to make the familiar blind riot for material or fanatical ends somewhat more infrequent than heretofore and thus to leave some of the unprivileged disengaged and ready for a more constructive appeal. The increase in the numbers of the unprivileged meant more actual misery, but because it also meant increased longevity, it changed their attitude toward their misery. The implications of this fall in mortality were such as to divert growing numbers of men from participation in the chronic rioting of what has been called the "preindustrial mob." The psychic implications of an increased life expectancy are indeterminable for the short-run period of a single generation, but the economic corollary of an improved system of life support was confirmed by the new crops and the better means of transportation that made famine a much rarer calamity in the later eighteenth century than it had ever been before. In some of the mobile western societies of the Atlantic seaboard, morover, the same demographic and economic growth that was dislocating the lowest orders of the society from their accustomed places and readying them for novelty was also producing a special kind of unprivileged group that coud receive and transmit the liberal political appeals diffused by the literate underprivileged groups in the name of equal rights for all. Out of the ranks of sharecroppers, artisans, and small shopkeepers, a growing layer of enterprising and prosperous peasants, traders, and manufacturers emerged to join the interests of the unprivileged with the programs of the underprivileged. They were abetted by a restive group of intellectual have-nots, dissatisfied ideologists who separated themselves from the intellectual elite and translated the social needs of the unprivileged into the political language of the underprivileged.

Popular revolutionary movements of a new type, involving either the underprivileged alone or the underprivileged and the unprivileged in combination, founding political concentrations (they were still too loose and informal to be called organizations) of their own outside the regular corporate institutions of the society, and asserting goals transcending the rearrangement of the regular corporate institutions in the state, made their appearance in the Netherlands, the Austrian Netherlands, Great Britain and its American and Irish dependencies, and finally in France.

The Free Corps movement in the Netherlands and the Vonckists in the Austrian Netherlands were liberal movements of the underprivileged and enlightened middle classes who fought for the end of oligarchic domination within the provinces and for national constitutions which would give representation to the bulk of property owners. But they were not joined by the unprivileged mass, which in the Netherlands tended to remain loyal to the house of Orange and in the Austrian Netherlands supported the traditional corporations against the Vonckists.

The American and Irish developments were special cases, since the separate legislative institutions in each of these dependencies—the colonial assemblies in America and the Irish Parliament at Dublin—provided rallying points for coalitions of conservatives, liberals, and sections of a mass movement. In America the coalition persisted at least until the achievement of independence. In Ireland, however, where liberal political reform rather than national independence was the main issue, the European pattern prevailed: the coalition dissolved before the essential institutions of the Old Regime were breached. In the late 1770's the example of the American Revolution, the crippling effect of British restrictions on Irish trade, and the temporary vacuum of British military force in Ireland produced the Irish volunteers, a militia organization led by such members of the liberal Anglo-Protestant Irish gentry as Henry Grattan (1746–1820) and Henry Flood (1732–1791), including both Protestant peers and the Protestant middle class in its ranks, and drawing support from a small active sector of the unenfranchised Catholic minority. As long as the Volunteers concentrated on the issues of Irish free trade and the legislative independence of the Irish Parliament, the coalition was effective. But with the rise of the issue of parliamentary reform the process of dissolution set in. The British concession of complete legislative autonomy to the unreformed Irish Parliament in 1782 bought off the more conservative sections of the Anglo-Irish establishment, while the liberals split between those who would simply remove political disabilities from the more substantial Catholics within the existing electoral system and those who would fundamentally change the whole traditional system of voting by historic counties and incorporated boroughs. By 1785 the liberal movement had run down, enervated by its own divisions, by Catholic passivity, and by the ties between the Irish and English Protestant establishments.

The defeat of these popular revolutions by coalitions of aristocracy and monarchy was a more faithful reflection of the balance of internal power even in the waning years of the Old Regime than was the impression of democratic strength given by the frequency of such revolutions. For they achieved their greatest force, as has been noted, in the politically or geographically peripheral areas of the European political system, where the continuing traditions of the city-state kept alive the possibility of direct popular participation in government, or where the combination of great distance from the political center with viable local institutions debilitated both the physical and the moral hold of the sovereign central authority so typical of the Old Regime. Certainly the turmoil in these outlying societies did reflect, in exaggerated form, strains in the states and societies of Western Europe at large, but for the proper perspective on the role of popular revolutions in the territorial societies whose growth had been most characteristic of the Old Regime we must look to the great states of England and France. We shall find such movements, to be sure, but we must attend carefully to their spatial and social limitations in the former case and their temporal limit in the latter.

England

As might be expected from the lively memories of their seventeenth-century revolutions, the first popular revolutionary movement in eighteenth-century Europe arose among the English. Anticipating the pattern that would become standard elsewhere, the mass movement that gathered in 1763 around the slogan "Wilkes and liberty" had its origins in a situation prepared by the opposition of a politically displaced aristocratic group to what it conceived to be the despotic innovations of royalty.

George III (ruled 1760–1820) is now generally conceded to have been not nearly so authoritarian, nor the Whig opposition so libertarian, as the rhetoric of the latter and of their later advocates on both sides of the Atlantic seemed to indicate. The first of the Hanoverians to have been born in England, the new king was in accord with the fundamentals of the balanced constitution as we have seen them laid down at the revolutionary settlement after 1688 and developed by Walpole and his Whig successors. Indeed, George III's policies and problems alike stemmed from the very literalness with which he took his rights within the constitution. But despite the underlying continuity between his reign and the Whig ascendancy that preceded him, his abrupt changes of ministers after 1760 and his persistent search for managers hostile to the Whig connection until he settled down with the younger William Pitt after 1783 was caused by more than the personal pique at his father's hated entourage that has been standard for the ruling houses of Europe. His politics were an attempt to develop the constitution by restoring to the substance of the royal power the management of the constitutional keys which the Whigs had actually controlled by informal conventions in the name of the royal power. Thus the King was neither a despot nor a revolutionary, but within the flexible constitution he certainly did intend a change of system that would, as the Whigs feared, sheer them of political power. The King was interested not in asserting his royal prerogative at the expense of Parliament, as his seventeenth-century forebears had been, but in asserting his constitutional prerogative to approve the actions of his own ministers—actions which lay in the no-man's-land between King and Parliament—and to use patronage, connections, influence on the politically dependent members and persuasion on the independent members to secure a majority for his government in the House of Commons, just as the great Whig families had used these means to make the mixed constitution work when they had formed the ministries under the earlier, more passive Hanoverians.

But whatever the constitutional rights of the matter, the political effect was clear enough. Powerful factions of the Whig governing class accused the King of upsetting the balance of the constitution by using the appointments and emoluments in the possession of the Crown and the government to control Parliament by pushing the election of his "placemen"—i.e., servants of the Crown—and by corrupting members otherwise selected. The group around the elder William Pitt—his brother-in-law Richard Grenville, Earl of Temple, and his successors, William Petty, Earl of Shelbourne, and his son, William Pitt the Younger—and the group around Charles Wentworth, Marquis of Rockingham—especially the radical Charles Lennox,

Great Britain's King George III, of American ill-fame.

Duke of Richmond, and the American and Irish sympathizer, Edmund Burke—not only opposed the King's party in Parliament but encouraged and associated with the two main popular, extraparliamentary movements. These two groups pioneered revolutionary modes of political action and aimed at the radical reorganization of Parliament itself in the generation before the French Revolution.

The first of these was the movement of 1763–1774 that focused on the career and tribulations of John Wilkes (1727–1797). The unstable character of the man, the sporadic violence of his following, and the recurrent sympathy with its cause by one or another group in the Whig opposition show immediately how limited the revolutionary possibilities of the movement were. Wilkes was a profligate, dissolute, shrewd, charming, and desperate careerist who had married into the gentry and bought an election, in a style not unusual for the time, to the House of Commons. He turned to demagoguery as his only alternative for political and pecuniary salvation when his early attachment to Pitt's and Temple's following in the House of Commons failed to save him from prosecution by the King's government for seditious libel. He was prosecuted on the basis of an article which was simply a more scurrilous attack than usual against the character and credibility not of the King but of his "Minister." He was arrested on a general warrant—that is, a warrant specifying the alleged crime but not the accused—and his court appearances in London, where the empire-oriented Pitt party had a large following, were attended by unruly crowds who demonstrated under the banner of "Wilkes and Liberty." Wilkes immediately responded to them in kind by declaring that his case represented not only "the liberty of all peers and gentlemen," but "what touches me more sensibly, that of all the middling and inferior set of people, who stand most in need of protection." The "liberty" that was at stake was hardly new: it involved the legality, by the standards of the traditional rights of Englishmen, of particular instruments of governmental prosecution—in this case, the general warrant—and it involved the immunities of members of Parliament. Wilkes was released in May on the ground of his parliamentary immunity, and his case also had as a permanent, albeit indirect, result, the definitive outlawing of general warrants both by the Court of King's Bench and by the House of Commons.

But the Wilkes affair was far from over, and its subsequent course centered around a far more revolutionary issue of liberty involving Parliament—the political rights of electors. Late in 1763 Wilkes's decision to reprint the earlier indirect attack upon the King and to print a pornographic *Essay on Woman* not only brought a new prosecution on joint-charges of seditious libel, obscenity, and blasphemy but transformed the nature and backing of his cause. Wilkes went into exile to escape arrest, and his aristocratic allies, now scandalized, withdrew their support. When he finally returned to England in 1768, he made his appeal directly to the constituencies, over the heads of all the parties, for election to the House of Commons. After one false start in the City of London itself, where he was roundly defeated, Wilkes ran for a county seat in Middlesex, a suburb of London. Pitching his campaign primarily at "the middling and inferior sets," who responded enthusiastically with demonstrations and occasional riots, Wilkes was elected in March, 1768, and upon successive disqualifications by the House of Commons, was reelected three times. The House brought the issue to a climax by admitting Wilkes's defeated opponent in the fourth election (April, 1769) to Wilkes's seat as member for Middlesex.

Between 1769 and 1774, before Wilkes's election as mayor of London and his qualification by the Commons for his Middlesex seat diverted him into respectability and his support into regular institutional channels, the Wilkite movement took on its most organized and its most revolutionary form. It was revolutionary in its appeal. However legal it felt its specific demands to have been, the movement summarized them under the call for a generic "liberty" which attracted all who felt, however vaguely, that their rights of whatever kind were being violated and which made freedom, for such people, the primary principle of the constitution and the primary value in politics. Again, it was revolutionary in its method. The Society of the Supporters of the Bill of Rights, which was organized to support Wilkes's right to his seat in Parliament and campaigned in 1769 for the rights of electors, the dismissal of the king's ministers, and the dissolution of Parliament, was the first of the many political pressure groups whose organization of mass movements outside the regular institutional channels of public opinion would be instrumental in the "bloodless revolutions" of

The Battle of Temple Bar. A *Wilkite mob breaks up a merchants' procession in a scene of striking modernity.*

nineteenth-century England. There was, finally, a revolutionary factor in the social identity of the people who were mobilized. Contemporaries often referred to Wilkes's supporters, particularly in the metropolitan area, as the "mob," and if, as we shall soon see, this characterization was far too indiscriminate for accuracy, the fact is that he did bring into action under the liberal political banner the kind of unprivileged, unenfranchised, and unpropertied members of the lower orders who had been traditionally subject only to stimuli of an economic or bigoted kind.

But if the development focusing on John Wilkes is thus important as the first appearance in a great state of a popular and extraconstitutional movement for liberal change, the limits of the development are equally important, for they indicate the weighty factors militating against the success of such a movement in a viable state of eighteenth-century Europe.

The development had, first, its geographic limits. Wilkes's popular support was centered in London and was for the most part limited to the contiguous counties of Middlesex and Surrey.

Again, the development had its social limits. The crucial fact was that the social group characterized as the "mob" or "inferior set" included a large proportion of county and borough voters, since traditional electoral rights in Middlesex and London extended far down the social ladder. Consequently, Wilkes's sporadic appeal to the unprivileged journeyman and laborer, precedent though it later proved to be, was actually far less important to the contemporary movement than his continuing appeal to the enfranchised traders and craftsmen of the inferior set, and in lesser degree, to the merchants and professional men of the middling set, who felt themselves an underprivileged part of the political nation.

The Wilkite development was limited, finally, by the moderate nature of its program. The main direction of the movement was, in the early terms of the Society of the Supporters of the Bill of Rights, "to defend and maintain the legal, constitutional liberty of the subject." Thus the main effort of the movement, aside from the support of Wilkes in his trials and campaigns, lay in such respectable enterprises as extending safeguards against unjust prosecution, securing the immunities of members of Parliament against the crown, securing the rights of electors against Parliament, and extending the freedom of the press to the publication of parliamentary debates. There were proposals, to be sure, that were not so compatible with the existing constitution. The Society of the Supporters of the Bill of Rights, in particular, spawned demands for constitutional change that focused on shorter terms of Parliament than the existing seven years and on radical revisions of its popular base which would involve both the extension of suffrage and the destruction of aristocratic influence, especially in the boroughs. Wilkes himself, indeed, introduced such a measure into the House of Commons in 1776. But this aspect of the movement was a product of its fragmentation. It rose in the Society as a function of its radicalization and helped to split it both internally and from the country at large. Like Wilkes' own presentation of it to the House, in short, the radical content in the Wilkite movement was a dud.

The second stage of the English development toward popular revolution—The Association movement of 1780–1785—showed a similar blend of radical tendencies and moderate limits, but with the terms reversed. This time the aims were radical but the methods moderate. The center of the revived radical movement was a very different man from John Wilkes. Christopher Wyvill (1740–1822) was a member of an old and respected Yorkshire gentry family, a possessor of a prosperous estate in that county, and a retired clergyman. In him this background combined to make a man of independent and highly moralistic mind who abominated the "corruption" of the court, of the Parliament he deemed controlled by it, and of the aristocratic factions through which he deemed the control exercised. For him, then, the reform of corruption entailed not only the exclusion of "placemen" from Parliament but the thoroughgoing expansion of the electorate to increase the independent members of Parliament. Thus he exemplified the development of the English revolutionary movement from the traditional defense against the powers of the king to the popular offensive against the combined powers of king and aristocracy.

But Wyvill tempered the radicalism of his political morality with the caution of a country gentleman. Although he recognized the theoretical validity of annual Parliaments based on universal manhood suffrage, he worked for triennial Parliaments based on independent property owners—an accommodation which in practice came down to the demand for increasing by one hundred, in proportion to population, the eighty members who represented the forty counties equally, regardless of size, in the unre-

formed House. Similarly, he took over, for the organization of his movement, the idea of an Association of deputies from reform-minded constituencies—an idea which had first been broached in James Burgh's *Political
Disquisitions* of 1774 as a revolutionary proposal for a constituent assembly with the sovereign power to enforce reform on Parliament—but turned
it into a collaboration among the gentry of the several counties to present
commonly designed petitions to Parliament for its own reform.

Like Wilkes, Wyvill found allies both in the aristocratic opposition to
the king's government and in the radical movement of metropolitan
London. But Wyvill, who retained the initiative in what there was of the
movement outside of London, opted first for an organization of county
gentry over the appeal to the middling and lower freeholding electorate,
and then for cooperation with the aristocratic reform movement in the
Commons over the popular radical movement in the country at large.
When his aristocratic support failed him Wyvill had no resource left.

Given the respectability of Wyvill's social status and the moral fastid-
iousness of his temperament, the revolutionary qualities of the Association
movement he led stand out like beacons: like the Wilkite movement
it proposed to effect change by organizing people for action outside the
regular institutions of the society, and even more than the Wilkite movement it proposed to achieve changes in the constitution that would in
effect shift sovereignty from the Parliament (which, it will be remembered, constitutionally included king, lords, and commons) to the House
of Commons and would shift the constituent power from the corporate
interests to the propertied electorate of the kingdom.

Over and above these obvious qualities, the Association movement
produced a more subtle contribution to the modern syndrome of revolution. In the Society for Constitutional Information it produced an early
grouping of the kind of intellectuals who would play their due role in the
revolutions of all the western countries. Its leaders were intellectual activists who were distinguished not by the cogency of their theory but by the
concrete application they gave to a mixture of current political ideas. John
Jebb (1736–1786) adapted to Wyvill's movement James Burgh's theory of
a sovereign Association which would represent "the acknowledged right of
the people to new-model its constitution." John Cartwright (1740–1824)
applied the old Leveller argument for equal suffrage on the basis of the
right of "personality" to the same purpose. They represented, in general,
the eighteenth-century "Commonweathman", who perpetuated the English
seventeenth-century revolutionary tradition in simplified and modernized
form. The Society thus gathered pamphleteers and journalists who were
themselves neither philosophers nor theorists, but who created a new social
role for philosophical and theoretical ideas.

But overshadowing these revolutionary facets of the Association movement were the two crucial antirevolutionary features that ultimately under-

mined it. First—in contrast to the Wilkite movement—the social groups concerned in the Association organization not only were limited entirely to those whom we have called the underprivileged rather than the unprivileged—that is, to those with political rights, albeit not with equal political rights, in the established constitution—but also to those who had their center of gravity in the upper rather than the lower set of these underprivileged—that is, in the independent country gentry rather than in the ambitious tradesmen and craftsmen of the city.

Second, the actual effect of the movement was not to foment popular revolutionary forces, since these drained away by the mid-1780's, but rather to flow into the preestablished channels of aristocracy and king, as might have been expected from a movement which increasingly depended upon the factions in the established Parliament. In the Fox-North ministry of 1783, the former Rockingham Whigs under Burke enacted the measure of "economical reform"—that is, the reduction of governmental patronage through which the king could influence Parliament—which had been their joint plank with the Associationists, but in itself, this measure served not to make Commons less subject to influence as such or more responsible to its electorate or representative of a wider electorate, but only to reduce the king's influence in comparison with the aristocracy's. And when the younger Pitt began his long tenure as prime minister on behalf of the Crown in the waning days of 1783, the country gentry and the metropolitan trading classes that had backed the Association movement for constitutional change threw their support behind his reform of the king's administrative services, since his combination of efficiency in government and collaboration with the independent members of Parliament reconciled the underprivileged groups to the material and moral efficacy of the monarchy as a counterweight to the power of the "grandees" in the Lords and Commons.

The net result of the two decades of revolutionary unrest in England was to foreshadow the pattern of popular pressure and institutional response through which the aristocratic monarchy would ultimately reform itself. But this same unrest also demonstrated the persistent strength of both aristocracy and crown that would postpone the reform for half a century.

France

In France alone did the conditions that produced the great powers of eighteenth-century Europe also develop into the conditions of a massive popular revolution against the monarchical and aristocratic institutions characteristic of those powers. Oddly enough, in view of the profound effects of the events of 1789 in France, the prehistory of those events is brief. The French Revolution of 1789 was as convulsive as it was because in France, and only in France, an elemental explosion of the unprivileged mass groups of the society converged with a political revolution by the articulate underprivileged groups for an equalized representative constitution. The conditions making for the massive unrest of peasants, artisans, shopkeepers, and unpropertied laborers in the countryside and the towns included long-range economic developments as well as a short-range crisis, and this side of the popular revolt certainly belongs to the Old Regime. But it was the political revolt of the middling classes that turned the mass unrest into a popular revolution, and this part of the story was a sudden growth that dated back only to the closing weeks of 1788 and that gave the end of the Old Regime the form of a sudden cataclysm.

The factors making for the unrest of the unprivileged masses—that is, primarily, the peasants and artisans—in eighteenth-century France were demographic and economic rather than social. The long-range social tendencies favored the easing rather than the aggravation of social tensions. In the countryside, the recognition of the peasants' personal freedom and of their property rights in the lands to which they held hereditary tenures joined with the growing markets for agricultural products and the rising price levels of the middle half century from 1730 to 1780 to produce a growing class of free and prosperous peasant proprietors. Certainly, manorial obligations on peasant land—rents, labor services, hunting and milling rights, all in favor of the lord—persisted and were even aggravated by the rediscovered dues associated with the lords' manorial reaction of the eighteenth century, but neither they nor the continuing burden of unequal taxes galvanized the French peasantry before 1789. Agrarian risings caused by deep-seated social and political grievances, such as occurred in eastern Europe, were not a feature of eighteenth-century France. In the towns, similarly, the expansion of small-scale trade and manufacturing and the deliberate governmental neglect of the restrictive guilds were reinforcing the growth of the independent class of small-scale proprietors so that they were becoming analogous to the peasant landholders in the countryside.

But against these pacifying social tendencies the effect of the dislocating changes wrought by population growth on the stagnant sectors of the economy increased, and these changes were intensified by the effects of the economic cycle. Beneath the group of prosperous peasants, artisans, and shopkeepers there grew an ever-larger group of sharecroppers, journeymen, and laborers who had only their lagging wages to balance their consumers' status and who consistently suffered under the long curve of rising prices.

The effect, against this long-term background, of a short-term recession after 1778 and an immediate crisis triggered by the catastrophic crop failure of 1788 was to depress the marginal producers, increase unemployment, worsen the position of those who were dependent on market sales, make desperate the position of those who were dependent on market purchases, and thus to spread fear throughout the unprivileged classes, prosperous and impoverished alike. It was in this situation, with the unprivileged feeling themselves in the grip of forces beyond their control, that the political revolution of the underprivileged who were legally grouped with them in the order of the Third Estate suddenly provided the unprivileged with the notion of king and aristocracy as the controlling powers of their malign destiny.

Those belonging to the educated and literate group of merchants, lawyers, doctors, government officials, and writers whose influence, self-confidence, articulateness, and expectations had risen far faster than their legal rights and honors in eighteenth-century France were late indeed in embarking on an independent political movement. Through almost the entire century they had aligned themselves with the Crown or with aristocracy in the struggle between these two titans of the Old Regime, either backing the equalizing reforms of the monarchy along with Voltaire and Turgot, or following Montesquieu and the *parlements* and espousing the privileges of the aristocratic corporations as the bastions of the whole society against despotism. Even in the bitter struggle of 1787 and 1788 between the King's reforming ministers Calonne and Loménie de Brienne, on the one side, and the aristocratic notables, led by the *parlementaires*, on the other, over such vital issues as tax equalization and the convocation of the Estates-General, the underprivileged bourgeois groups took no independent role but contented themselves with supporting the aristocratic advocates of the constitutional cause.

The popular revolutionary movement thus rose only toward the end of 1788, after the *Parlement* of Paris affirmed the traditional procedure for the Estates-General in September and a second Assembly of Notables confirmed the decision in December. This procedure, according to the precedent of the Estates' last meeting in 1614, entailed the separate voting by the three orders and, consequently, the subordination of the commons to the clerical and lay aristocracies. To their disaffection from royal absolutism the educated and propertied bourgeoisie now added an articulate rejection of aristocratic privilege. From this sequence of oppositions there followed not only a spate of pamphlet literature for an equality of commoner representation in an Estates-General with real constitutional powers but the organization of a "patriot" party, complete with committees of correspondence, already familiar from American, English, and Netherlandish precedents of popular revolution.

But the French movement went beyond its other European counterparts in its conjunction with the restive unprivileged masses on the land and in the towns. In part this was accountable to the coincidence of the economic crisis. In part it was accountable to the mechanics of the elections to the Estates-General, for the breadth of the suffrage brought the underprivileged and literate bourgeois together with unprivileged and illiterate peasants in local or district assemblies of the Third Estate. In part, it was accountable to the social geography of France, with its myriad towns spotted through the countryside and their propertied citizens and officials in continuing contact with the small-town artisans and the surrounding peasantry. In part, finally, it was accountable to the fateful decision of the King to support the constitutional position of the aristocracy. For the merger of authorities removed the last possibility for the underprivileged or the unprivileged to rest their cases with one of the pillars of the Old Regime.

Thus was the first of the popular fronts created in France. Its program was formulated by a new kind of intellectual, a man who started from the particular practical grievances announced by the various unprivileged and underprivileged groups and used principles as the means of connecting them so that these groups might act in concert. The most notable of these ideologues was Abbé Emmanuel Joseph Sieyès, who replied to the titled question of his pamphlet, *What Is the Third Estate?* with the answer that essentially it was "everything" because he would reduce philosophy's absolute principles of universal human rights to a general appeal on behalf of the practical claims of the Third Estate.

And so, along with the age of kings, the age of the philosophers passed into history.

Part IV

THE AGE OF REVOLUTION AND REACTION
1789–1850

Introduction

Two REVOLUTIONS profoundly transformed the lives of Europeans in the years from 1789 to 1850: the great French Revolution and the Industrial Revolution. Any attempt to comprehend the history of Europe in this period requires an analysis of the subtle and complex ways in which they worked themselves out in the material existence, the institutions, and the ideas of Europeans. Some individuals and groups tried to resist or contain the revolutions; others accepted their consequences and tried to exploit them; no European was unaffected by them.

The French Revolution has traditionally been viewed as a major dividing line in modern Europe's history, an event which destroyed that complex of political, social, legal, and juridical institutions known as the "old regime" and inaugurated a new era characterized by a greater emphasis upon individual rights, the spread of representative government, and the emergence of a new kind of loyalty to the nation. These generalizations about the French Revolution still retain much of their validity as long as they are qualified in some significant ways.

The break with the past was not nearly as sharp as has often been contended. Some of the traditional institutions and conceptions associated with the old regime had already been challenged earlier in the eighteenth century. A series of lesser revolts and disturbances in Europe and her colonial possessions beginning about 1760 preceded and, in some respects, contributed to the major upheaval of 1789. After 1789, many traditional institutions and ideas persisted through the revolutionary and Napoleonic eras into the age of the Restoration, from 1815 to 1848. Indeed, in most parts of Europe the Restoration was dominated by rulers who reacted against the revolutionary doctrines and who, if they could not turn the clock back to the old regime, did their best to maintain the status quo against growing pressures for reform and change.

Not surprisingly, the French Revolution had its greatest initial impact upon France itself, where the revolutionaries proceeded to sweep aside the complex set of administrative institutions inherited from the old regime and to substitute for them a new, more efficient organizational structure that would at the same time be more responsive to the needs of the entire nation. This structure, further refined or altered by Napoleon, has endured substantially to the present day. In class terms, the revolution also wrought significant changes in France; the ultimate beneficiaries were the bourgeoisie, who, having eliminated the traditional privileges of the aristocracy, made certain that political power remained in the hands of the possessors of property.

Outside of France the French Revolution and the Napoleonic regime which succeeded it had results that were both creative and destructive. During almost a quarter century of intermittent conflict between the French armies and the powers that resisted them, Europeans suffered disruption of their lives and established institutions. Old states went out of existence; new ones came into being. Territories conquered and occupied by the French underwent significant changes. In the last analysis, however, the revolutionary ideals of the French may have had more profound and lasting effects upon Europe than did their armies. In the powerful revolutionary slogan "Liberty! Equality! Fraternity!," in the fundamental political rights enunciated in the Declaration of the Rights of Man, and in the successive constitutions drawn up by the revolutionary assemblies, nineteenth-century liberals found their political programs and their source of inspiration. Even more important, France had shown during the revolution what powerful forces could be released when a people is galvanized by loyalty to a national ideal. Many of the fundamental characteristics of modern nationalism emerged for the first time during the revolution, and France provided models that were widely imitated in the century that followed.

In the long run, the Industrial Revolution undoubtedly transformed the lives of Europeans even more thoroughly than did the French Revolution, but its principal impact in the first half of the nineteenth century was restricted to Great Britain and the states lying in the northwestern tier of the European continent. Central, southern, and eastern Europe underwent similar changes only in the second half of the century. In countries affected by industrialization, long-established patterns of life were shattered as production was mechanized and moved into factories. The need to situate factories near the sources of power led to massive shifts of population and to the phenomenal growth of towns and cities. Wherever industrialization occurred, it dramatically increased the size and strength of the older bourgeoisie and brought into existence a new social class, the industrial proletariat. That these changes in class structure would have a significant effect upon the political life of the European states was inevitable. One of the main themes of the period from 1789 to 1850 was the struggle of the new manufacturing interests for political power and influence commensurate with their rising economic status.

The revolutions of 1848 provide a striking finale to the period. In the series of uprisings that swept across Europe in that year can be discerned the combined effects of the French revolutionary legacy and the Industrial Revolution. The demands of the revolutionaries still tended most often to be couched in the political terminology of the French Revolution — constitutions, representative assemblies, and the extension of political rights — but the movements of 1848 brought into focus underlying social discontents and grievances that stemmed from the Industrial Revolution.

CHAPTER 23

The French Revolution and
Its Impact on Europe

THE GENESIS OF THE REVOLUTION

WHAT FEATURES of French society under the Old Regime help explain the outbreak of the revolution in 1789? What grievances or injustices, what aspirations or ideals, contributed to the overthrow of a political system that had lasted for centuries?

One of the most common misconceptions about revolutions is that they occur in societies that are economically depressed and on the verge of collapse. Never has this view been more clearly disproved than it was by the state of affairs in prerevolutionary France, which, during the half century before 1789, enjoyed a period of steady economic growth indicated by rising industrial production, an expansion of the volume of foreign trade, and the increasing prosperity of the merchant class. But there were certain important flaws in this generally favorable situation. First, the wealth of the country was unevenly distributed. The prosperity of the merchant class was shared, though to a less striking degree, by the nobility and the clergy who, as landowners, benefited from the rising prices of foodstuffs during the decades preceding the revolution. This price rise was largely attributable to the increased demand for foodstuffs resulting from a rapid growth of population after 1750. But prosperity did not invariably reach all elements of the population. Because wages failed to keep pace with rising prices, artisans and wage earners in the cities suffered from a decline in purchasing power. Nor do the peasants as a group appear to have profited from the rise in food prices during the prerevolutionary decades despite the fact that they owned an estimated 30 to 40 per cent of the land in France. Their problem was an inability to produce on their relatively meager landholdings crops large enough so that a surplus remained to be sold on the market after their families had been fed and their church and feudal dues and taxes had been paid. The French peasants were undoubtedly much better off in many respects than their counterparts in central and eastern Europe, but they were still far from satisfied with their lot.

Second, the general expansion of the French economy from 1730 to the 1780's was interrupted by periodic economic crises, which brought suffering to the unprivileged groups. One of the more acute of these crises struck France in 1787 following a bad harvest. The nation suffered from food shortages, sharply rising food prices, a decline in textile production, and widespread unemployment in the cities. The resulting misery, both in the country and in the cities, helped to precipitate the revolution of 1789.

Finally, in qualifying our generalization concerning the soundness of the French economy, we must note the desperate financial condition of the government, which contrasted strikingly with the condition of the country as a whole. The volume of trade was growing and the upper classes were prosperous, but the monarchy—which had been in financial straits ever since the reign of Louis XIV (1643–1715)—found itself unable to tap this wealth in order to meet its obligations. Faced with repeated refusals on the part of the privileged orders to abandon their traditional exemption from certain taxes, the king continued to borrow, until by 1788 the interest on the debt consumed more than half of the royal government's expenditures. Such a condition could not endure forever, yet attempts on the part of a succession of finance ministers during the decade prior to the revolution to discover ways out of the financial impasse met with such resistance that their proposed reforms had to be dropped. The crisis reached its climax in 1788 when the king, unable to secure either fiscal reform or further loans, reluctantly agreed to summon the Estates-General, a body which had the traditional right to institute taxes, but which had not met for 175 years. The convening of this body in the spring of 1789 and the subsequent secession of the Third Estate from the other two in order to form the "National Assembly" marked the first stage of the French Revolution.

Little needs to be said concerning the political weaknesses of the Old Regime. A government which could not raise adequate revenues clearly revealed its lack of political effectiveness. General confusion and inefficiency prevailed in the royal administration, which consisted of successive layers of offices, bureaus, and agencies that had piled up over many centuries, with jurisdictions that were now ill defined and sometimes contradictory. Dealing with this rigid bureaucracy—frustrating for everyone—was particularly exasperating for the enterprising merchant or landowner. Finally, in a regime which was still absolutist in theory, if not in fact, the character of the ruler was a matter of considerable importance. Here the Bourbon dynasty was particularly unfortunate. The times called for a ruler of intelligence and resolution—and France in 1774 got Louis XVI, honest and well intentioned, but lacking in will and unable to comprehend the dangers of the situation. Fat, dull, and slow-witted, he was the laughing stock of his

King Louis XVI. *Portrait by
Callet. Petit Trianon, Versailles.*

own courtiers. A leading historian of the revolution, speaking of Louis XVI,
concludes, "It is scarcely doubtful that events would have taken a different
turn if the throne had been occupied by a Henry IV or even a Louis XIV."[1]

In a France suffering from economic and political weaknesses, what were
the existing attitudes toward the regime? Crane Brinton, in his *Anatomy of
Revolution*, notes a phenomenon which he labels the "desertion of the
intellectuals." Analyzing four prerevolutionary societies, he argues that in
each the intellectuals (defined roughly as the "writers, artists, musicians,
actors, teachers and preachers") were close to unanimous in their opposition to the established regime, ". . . bitterly attacking existing institutions
and desirous of a considerable alteration in society, business, and government."[2] Eighteenth-century France is the classic example of a country
where almost all intellectuals were critical of existing social and political
institutions. Voltaire, Rousseau, Diderot, and Condorcet were simply the
most prominent of a vast company of *philosophes* intent upon remaking

[1] Georges Lefebvre, *The Coming of the French Revolution*, trans. by R.R. Palmer
(Princeton, N.J., 1947), p.25.
[2] Crane Brinton, *Anatomy of Revolution* (New York, 1957) pp. 44, 45.

society in accordance with the laws of nature. Their proposals for reform varied greatly, but they all were highly critical of existing institutions. Yet even it it can be established that the intellectuals were alienated from the regime to an unusual degree, one may still ask whether their discontent reflected that of the population as a whole. Such a question is impossible to answer with certainty. But it is a matter of record that many works critical of existing political and social institutions, such as Rousseau's *Social Contract* (1762), went through numerous editions in the years before the revolution and were apparently widely read by the educated. A further indication of the degree to which the *philosophes* struck a responsive chord among their contemporaries may be found in the public declarations of revolutionary leaders, who frequently echoed the sentiments of a Voltaire in their attacks upon the clergy or the views of a Condorcet in their expressions of faith in man's capacity for unlimited progress.

Finally, class antagonisms were mounting steadily during the last years of the Old Regime, and played a role in the outbreak of revolution. French society was officially divided, as it had been for centuries, into three estates. The clergy constituted the First Estate, and the nobility, the Second. The Third Estate included all the rest of the population but had traditionally been represented in the medieval assembly, the Estates-General, by members of the bourgeoisie, commonly town dwellers. To be sure, French society did not consist of neatly separated, coherent, self-conscious social groups, each pursuing its own interest. But among individuals of similar social or professional status certain common sentiments did exist; hostility was often strong toward those who were higher on the social scale and possessed greater privileges. Paradoxically, those complaining the loudest were often those best off financially—that is, the upper bourgeoisie. It was precisely because wealthy merchants and manufacturers had improved their economic position so markedly during the eighteenth century that they resented the remaining restrictions—social and political—upon their activity. For an individual of this class, two courses of action with respect to the traditional aristocracy were possible. He could try to become a noble himself, or perhaps marry his daughter to a noble, or he could set out to eliminate the privileges of the noble caste. Up to a decade or two before the revolution, many members of the bourgeoisie chose the first alternative, since it was still possible to gain entrance into the nobility, either by royal appointment or by the purchase of offices carrying noble status. Indeed, the royal courts of law and the more important administrative offices were staffed by the newer "nobility of the robe," which in contrast to the more traditional "nobility of the sword" was composed of former commoners, who were quick to forget their bourgeois origins once they received noble status. But because of an "aristocratic resurgence," it was increasingly difficult after 1760 to secure such appointments. Jealous of the centralizing and despotic tendencies of the monarchy on the one hand and of the threat to their position from the newer moneyed classes on the other, members of the French nobility did their best to defend their position and make their privileges more exclusive. Specifically, the nobles sought to regain a monopoly over appointments to high positions in the army, the church, and the government and to discourage the mingling of the aristocracy with those less wellborn. Such a campaign naturally provoked the resentment of the ambitious bourgeois hoping to improve his social status, and increased his readiness to accept affirmations of "natural rights," civil equality, equality of opportunity, and so on. The sense of frustration was perhaps greatest among wealthy financiers and merchants, because in economic position and in mode of life they were so like the nobility, but the resentment against aristocratic privilege and discrimination based on birth was shared as well by the lesser bourgeoisie—the shopkeepers, artisans, and petty bureaucrats.

The conditions of life among the peasants, who formed the great mass of the Third Estate and an estimated 80 per cent of the total population, varied widely from one region of France to another. It is particularly difficult to generalize about the sentiments of this class on the eve of the revolution. Although serfdom was rare in France by the end of the eighteenth century, many feudal or manorial obligations remained to plague the peasants—fees, dues, payments in kind to the landlords who retained ultimate jurisdiction over the peasants' holdings. To the clergy was owed the tithe, as well as a levy on grain and other farm products which was particularly resented. And a more recent burden superimposed on these traditional obligations was royal taxation, which fell most heavily upon the peasant class—direct taxes such as the *taille* (head tax) and indirect taxes like the *gabelle*, the government monopoly on salt which kept the price of this product artificially high in a good part of France. The question remains of whether peasant resentment over these obligations was any greater in the decade or so before the revolution than it had been before. Certainly France had seen peasant discontent, and even revolts, long before the eighteenth century. Yet two circumstances, in particular, appear to have sharpened the antagonism after 1750. One was a marked increase in the peasant population, which made it more difficult for peasants to support their families on the land available; the other was a tendency on the part of the landowning aristocrats to reaffirm their rights over the peasants and to make sure that they were exacting all that was due them in the way of fees and other obligations. A particular grievance in this connection was the encroachment of the landlords on various kinds of "common land," where the peasants had traditionally grazed livestock, gathered dead wood, and cut trees. Since the lords held the ultimate rights over such lands, they were permitted by the courts to break them up and put them under cultivation for their own profit. Inevitably, the result was an increase in the bitterness of the peasants toward their landlords, as the lists of peasant grievances drawn up in 1789 make clear.

To summarize, then, fairly strong class tensions had developed in France by the end of the eighteenth century. Some of the grievances of the Third Estate were long-standing, but they were sharpened after 1750 by rising food prices, by a marked growth in the peasant population, which taxed their available land resources, and finally by a reassertion of privileges and a growing exclusiveness on the part of the nobility. These ills alone were perhaps not sufficient to provoke a revolution; but they built up a sense of frustration in the unprivileged groups, and, once the revolution had begun, they caused it to turn into a mass movement of incomparable fury.

The Outbreak of the Revolution

One of the great ironies of the French Revolution is that it was most directly provoked by the class whose privileges it did much to destroy—the nobility. By their repeated refusals to submit to new taxation, the nobles finally forced the king to adopt their own proposal—that is, to summon the Estates-General, the only body they regarded as competent to levy new taxes. The nobles were convinced that they would be able to dominate this assembly and use it as an instrument for strengthening their own position at the expense of the monarchy. But the outcome was not what they had anticipated. For the election and convocation of the Estates-General in 1789 provided representatives of the Third Estate with an opportunity to assert their claim to equal status with those of the other two orders, and ultimately, when this was denied, to proclaim themselves the true representatives of the "nation."

Because the Estates-General had not met since 1614, considerable research was necessary to determine precisely how representatives should be elected to the assembly and how voting within the assembly should be conducted. The second of these questions was the more controversial. Traditionally, each estate, or order, voted as a unit. But spokesmen for the Third Estate—particularly a group known as the Patriots, who espoused the cause of constitutional reform—realizing that the Third Estate would be outvoted on questions involving the privileges of the other two orders, came up with alternative proposals. Their plan called for double representation for the Third Estate, so that the commoners would elect as many representatives as the other two orders combined; and for voting by head rather than by order, so that each individual vote would be counted. In this way they felt they could secure a majority for their reforms, since they could count on some defections from the clergy and on the support of a few liberal noblemen. At the end of 1788 the king accepted the first part of this plan, announcing that the Third Estate could have twice as many representatives as each of the other two estates, but the question of whether the voting would be by order or by head had still not been settled when the Estates-General assembled at Versailles on May 1, 1789.

Delegates to the Estates-General had been named by voters who met in the chief town of each district. Members of the clergy and nobility had voted directly for their representatives, but voters from the Third Estate— that is, almost all male citizens over twenty-five—had named their delegates through an indirect system which had the effect of eliminating as candidates all but an educated elite drawn from the middle and upper bourgeoisie. Most representatives of the Third Estate were lawyers or career bureaucrats rather than peasants or wage earners. Indeed, some of the most prominent representatives of the Third Estate were maverick aristocrats or clergymen who could not have been named by their own orders. One such, for example, was Honoré Gabriel Riqueti, count of Mirabeau (1749–1791), who became one of the most prominent statesmen during the first phase of the revolution. Born of an aristocratic family of Provence, Mirabeau as a young man estranged himself from his family by his excesses, which more than once caused him to be thrown into prison. By 1789 he had already achieved a reputation as a violent opponent of the privileges of his own class and as a critic of the Old Regime. Despite his ugly, pockmarked countenance he had a commanding presence and soon distinguished himself as an orator. Elected a representative of the Third Estate by the voters of Aix-en-Provence in 1789, he soon manifested shrewd qualities as a tactician and emerged as the principal spokesman of the Third Estate.

Emmanuel Joseph Sieyès (1748–1836) was another important representative of the Third Estate drawn from the ranks of a different order. An indifferent clergyman in the years before the revolution, Abbé Sieyès won national renown in January, 1789, through the publication of his pamphlet *What Is the Third Estate?* This spirited attack upon the privileges of the nobility and clergy began:

> The plan of this pamphlet is very simple. We have three questions to ask:
> 1st. What is the third estate? Everything.
> 2nd. What has it been heretofore in the political order? Nothing.
> 3rd. What does it demand? To become something therein.[3]

Not surprisingly, he failed to win election to the Estates-General by his fellow clergymen, but he was named by the electors of Paris a delegate of the Third Estate. In this capacity he played an important role in the initial stages of the revolution, participating in the drafting of the Declaration of

---

[3] Stewart, *A Documentary Survey of the French Revolution*, ed. by John Hall Stewart (New York, 1951), p. 42.

the Rights of Man and the Constitution of 1791. Abbé Sieyès demonstrated remarkable powers of survival during the revolutionary and Napoleonic eras. Serving in successive revolutionary assemblies, he voted for the execution of the king, lived through the Reign of Terror, reemerged as an important figure in the reaction that followed, and later helped engineer the *coup d'état* which brought Napoleon to power in 1799.

On the momentous occasion of the assembling of the Estates-General, the optimism of the commoners was tempered by the treatment they received from the king. The somber black costumes that the king required the representatives of the Third Estate to wear contrasted sharply with the rich and colorful attire of the nobility and the clergy. At a formal reception given for the delegates on May 2, Louis XVI kept the commoners waiting for hours and then received them coldly while representatives of the other two estates looked on.

At this point, the king had still announced no decision on the crucial problem of how votes would be counted, although a speech delivered by Jacques Necker (1732–1804), the king's finance minister, had intimated strongly that on certain questions the vote would be by order. In protest, the representatives of the Third Estate refused to present their credentials for verification; the resulting deadlock between the king and the Third Estate lasted for five weeks and was broken only when the commoners announced that they were presenting their credentials not as delegates of the Third Estate, but as representatives of the nation. After a number of parish priests who were delegates for the clergy had joined them, the commoners issued a statement proclaiming themselves the "National Assembly" of France, representing the entire nation. This declaration, dated June 17, has been termed the first genuinely revolutionary act of 1789; it was followed three days later by the more famous Tennis Court Oath. On June 20, the commoners found their regular meeting place barred to them, ostensibly for repairs. They adjourned therefore to a nearby indoor tennis court, and amid great enthusiasm, swore "not to separate, and to reassemble wherever circumstances require, until the constitution of the kingdom is established and consolidated upon firm foundations." Faced with this open act of defiance, the king wavered. At first he announced his intention of maintaining the distinction among the three orders, and declared the actions of the Third Estate on June 17 and June 20 invalid, but the continued resistance of the commoners, coupled with the desertion from their own assemblies of more representatives of the clergy and a minority of the nobles, forced him to recognize a *fait accompli*. On June 27 he ordered the remaining delegates of the first two estates to take their places in the

The Tennis Court Oath, June 20, 1789. *Painting by David. Members of the Third Estate raise their arms to take the oath as spectators peer through the caged windows far above.*

National Assembly alongside the representatives of the Third Estate. The National Assembly set about its self-appointed task of giving France a new constitution.

Within two weeks, however, the deliberations of the Assembly were interrupted by popular demonstrations in Paris which gave events a more violent turn and also provided Frenchmen with that great symbolic act which has been associated with the revolution ever since—the storming of the Bastille. The origins of these riots are obscure; apparently they were in part a reaction to what appeared to be an alarming concentration of royal troops around Paris and Versailles. The dismissal by the king on July 11 of his chief minister, Necker, who had a popular reputation as an advocate of reform and conciliation, and the appointment of several ministers of a more conservative outlook, seemed to give substance to the rumor that the king was planning a military *coup d'état* against the National Assembly. Whether this rumor was correct or whether the king had brought in the troops to protect the Assembly, as he contended, has never been settled; in any event, the view of many Parisians seems to have been that the Assembly was in danger. Inspired by a number of agitators, some of whom were undoubtedly in the pay of Louis Philippe Joseph, duke of Orléans (1747–1793), the popular cousin of the king, crowds paraded through the streets of Paris, carrying busts of the duke and of Necker. Among those whipping up the enthusiasm of the mob was Camille Desmoulins (1760–1794), a radical journalist, whose pamphlets and speeches were at least partially responsible for the violence that subsequently occurred. The electors of Paris (who had earlier named delegates to the Estates-General and now reconstituted themselves as an active group), were alarmed, on the one hand, by the threat of a royal attack and disturbed, on the other, by the mounting unrest of the Paris mob; they therefore improvised a provisional municipal government and organized a militia of bourgeois volunteers, later christened the National Guard.

On July 14 a search for arms and gunpowder led these bourgeois volunteers to the Bastille, the celebrated old feudal fortress on the eastern side of Paris, which had served a prison for many years. The Bastille was a symbol of royal despotism; stories were rife about the alleged mistreatment and torture of political prisoners supposed to be confined in its deep dungeons. The fortress, with ten-foot-thick walls, ninety-foot towers, and a moat, would have been easy to defend against the relatively unarmed crowd if De Launay, the governor of the prison, had not mishandled the situation. A deputation sent by the provisional municipal government of Paris from the Hôtel de Ville (city hall) to negotiate with the governor for the surrender of gunpowder was assured by him that he would not turn his cannon upon the demonstrators unless the Bastille were attacked. A short time afterward two men succeeded in lowering a drawbridge leading from

The Taking of the Bastille, July 14, 1789. *To the left of center the insurgents are seizing Delaunay, the governor of the prison, who was later beheaded.* Musée Carnavalet, Paris.

the outer to the inner courtyard surrounding the prison. Although the drawbridge at the main gate into the prison was still closed and defended, De Launay, thinking that a frontal attack was imminent, gave the order to fire on the crowd. When the volley was over, some ninety-eight of the besiegers lay dead and seventy-three had been wounded. The governor's apparent betrayal of his promise provoked the mob, which had now been joined by two detachments of French guards, to fight its way into the inner courtyard and to train five cannon against the main gate. De Launay decided to surrender and ordered the main drawbridge lowered. The crowd swarmed into the prison and slaughtered six or seven of the 110 guards defending it. De Launay himself was decapitated. Ironically, the Bastille yielded only seven prisoners—five ordinary criminals and two madmen.

The fall of the Bastille, insignificant in terms of its immediate results, was an event of great symbolic importance; it marked a deepening of the revolution. Disregarding the advice of those urging him to flee the country, the king decided to attempt a reconciliation. Only a day or two after the fall of the Bastille, Louis XVI announced that the royal troops would leave Versailles and that Necker would return to his post in the ministry. He also recognized the new municipal government of Paris and the newly established citizens' militia, the National Guard. In a final gesture, he agreed during a visit to Paris to wear the tricolor cockade, which combined the white of the Bourbons with the red and blue of the city of Paris. The Paris mob had intervened successfully, as it would on many subsequent occasions during the revolution.

Careful studies have exploded some popular myths concerning the social composition of the crowd of eight or nine hundred that took the Bastille. Far from being vagabonds or criminals drawn from the lowest elements of Paris society, the attackers appear to have been primarily small tradesmen, artisans, and wage earners, people with established occupations. Their revolutionary temper can be explained in part by their discontent over rising living costs in Paris, but also by their fear that the Assembly and the hopes they placed in it were endangered by some kind of aristocratic plot. It also appears that the storming of the Bastille was a less spontaneous affair than has been generally supposed. As has been mentioned, the crowd consisted largely of formally enrolled members of the recently organized bourgeois militia, and their actions on July 14 were guided to some degree by the provisional municipal government.

Paris was not the only site of popular disturbances in the summer of 1789. At about the same time that the Bastille fell, new municipal governments were established in a number of other major cities, a development that suggests some degree of coordination in the activities of the revolutionaries. More alarming to the large landowners was the series of disturbances in the country districts which began before July 14 and mounted steadily through the summer. These riots, which came to be known as the Great Fear, arose in part from rumors that the feudal aristocracy, the *aristos*, as they were called by the peasantry, were sending hired brigands to attack peasants and pillage their land. Actually, there is no evidence of any large-scale brigandage or of a counterrevolutionary plot, and the origin of these rumors is uncertain. But they did create a near panic—particularly in the eastern and some of the western provinces—that ultimately resulted in violence against local lords and their stewards and in the burning of châteaux and of records of feudal obligations. Local police were helpless to stop this anarchy and the king did not dare employ regular troops because he feared they might join the rebels. As the violence increased, alarm spread in the National Assembly, not only among the noble deputies but also among those members of the Third Estate whose income included feudal rents from their estates. A committee appointed by the Assembly to consider the situation recommended measures of repression, but a different solution was found during the famous night session of August 4: first the viscount of Noailles and then the duke of Aiguillon, another liberal noble, voluntarily abandoned their feudal privileges and revenues; then, one by one, other deputies followed suit, renouncing privileges and rights of various sorts. The clergy relinquished their tithes, the wealthy bourgeois their individual exemptions from taxation, the cities and provinces their ancient customs and privileges. Before that dramatic night was over the feudal regime in France had been abolished and all Frenchmen were, at least in principle, subject to the same laws and the same taxes and eligible for the same offices. What provoked this apparently spontaneous sacrifice and mass renunciation of privileges? Disinterested self-sacrifice may have been the motive of some; others may have acted on impulse. But a great many deputies probably felt that their privileges were doomed anyway and that a gesture of this sort might calm the peasantry. When the formal decrees which embodied these decisions were issued, the terms were somewhat less generous than the promises of August 4. Feudal dues were not renounced outright; such a renunciation would have been too strong a threat to the principle of private property. Rather, the peasants were to compensate their landlords through a series of direct payments for the obligations from which they had supposedly been freed. In this instance, as in others during the next two years, members of the National Assembly made revolutionary gestures but remained essentially moderates, bent on safeguarding the right of private property. After all, even the delegates elected to represent the Third Estate, though they talked of equality and natural rights, were men of the bourgeoisie, hardly ready to turn the country over to the masses.

Members of the National Assembly (also referred to as the Constituent Assembly) viewed as one of their principal tasks the drafting of a constitution which would substutute a new, rational set of political institutions for the antiquated forms of the Old Regime. Before settling down to work out the details of political organization, the Assembly, following the precedent of both English and American revolutionaries, issued the Declaration of the Rights of Man and of the Citizen, a statement of the general principles on which the new order was to rest. This historic document, approved on August 27, 1789, in a sense links the eighteenth and nineteenth centuries: it is a remarkable distillation of those political ideals of the eighteenth-century Enlightenment which became, during the first half of the nineteenth-century, the gospel of European liberals.

Central to the declaration, as its title suggests, is the concept that there exist certain "natural rights" which should be enjoyed equally by all citizens. The aim of every political association, the declaration maintains, must be to preserve the natural and inalienable rights of man—"liberty, property, security, and resistance to oppression." Five of its seventeen articles deal specifically with these rights, an enumeration which recalls the Bill of Rights of the American Constitution and the seventeenth-century English documents which inspired it: included are freedom from arbitrary arrest, trial by established laws, the presumption that a man is innocent until proven guilty, freedom of speech and of the press, and so on. In Article 6, the declaration explicitly emphasizes the equality of all men before the law.

Popular sovereignty is the second general principle asserted in the document; or, as Article 2 puts it, "The source of all sovereignty resides essentially in the nation; no group, no individual, may exercise authority not emanating expressly therefrom." Precisely how this power was to be exercised is not specified in detail, although Article 7 contains a statement concerning the law-making powers that is strongly reminiscent of the political philosophy of Rousseau: "Law is the expression of the general will; all citizens have the right to concur personally, or through their representatives, in its formation . . . ." The declaration implies the general right to vote, or universal suffrage, but we shall see that the constitution drawn up by the National Assembly interpreted the term "citizen" rather narrowly and made the right to vote dependent upon property ownership.

Indeed, the importance of property rights is reiterated in the declaration itself. It appears as one of the "natural and inalienable rights" of man, and it reappears in the final article of the declaration, "Since property is a sacred and inviolable right, no one may be deprived thereof unless a legally established public necessity obviously requires it, and upon condition of a just and previous indemnity."

Many historians, particularly Marxists, have branded the revolution of 1789 as "bourgeois," asserting that it merely substituted the rule of one privileged class for that of another. The emphasis on the "sacred" right of property found in the Declaration of the Rights of Man, the restrictions upon voting contained in the Constitution of 1791, and the actual workings of the new revolutionary regime tend to confirm the view that the regime produced by the revolution was intended to preserve the interests of the propertied classes. Yet this fact should not obscure the more radical aspects of the upheaval. Mid-twentieth-century democrats take for granted many of the rights proclaimed in 1789, but these rights had been denied to most Frenchmen for centuries. Before the revolution the mere fact that a man was born into a noble family gave him the right to receive special treatment before the law courts, to occupy certain official positions closed to others, to obtain exemption from certain taxes, and to exercise numerous other privileges. In 1789 distinctions based on birth alone were abolished forever. It is quite true that the old aristocracy of birth was replaced, in time, by a new aristocracy of wealth and that the possession of a specified minimum of property became the prerequisite for voting as well as for holding public office, but wealth and property were, in theory at least, accessible to every man. On these grounds it can be argued that this was a genuinely democratic revolution.

THE COURSE OF THE REVOLUTION, 1789–1799

After issuing the Declaration of the Rights of Man, the Assembly settled down to the more routine business of writing a constitution for France. During the two years it took to complete this task, the Assembly also acted as a legislative body, sharing with the king the responsibility for ruling the country. Before examining the problems confronting the constitutional monarchy, let us look for a moment at the subsequent development of the revolution and survey the successive phases through which it passed. Whether one should speak of a single French Revolution lasting for a decade or of several separate revolutions is a matter of interpretation, but most historians agree that the convoking of the Estates-General and the proclamation of the National Assembly in 1789 marked the beginning of the revolution and that the assumption of power by Napoleon Bonaparte in the *coup d'état* of Brumaire in 1799 marked its end.

It is easier to name France's successive governments in this crowded decade than to discern a general trend and classify the regimes accordingly. The government between 1789 and 1792 is regarded as a limited or constitutional monarchy even though the constitution was not formally completed until 1791. After issuing the Constitution of 1791 the Assembly resigned and was replaced by a Legislative Assembly elected under the provisions of the constitution. When this body had served for about a year, a "second" revolution, in August and September of 1792 resulted in the overthrow of the monarchy and the proclamation of a republic. (The French state was formally known as a republic for the remainder of the revolutionary era.) The Legislative Assembly now gave way to a newly elected National Convention, which officially ruled France until 1795 and produced a new instrument of government, the Constitution of 1793, which was never put into effect. During the period of rule by the Convention, France underwent the celebrated Reign of Terror, when power was concentrated for about a year (from the summer of 1793 to the summer of 1794) in the hands of a few men acting in the Committee of Public Safety, responsible, in theory, to the Convention. The third and final phase of the revolution, from 1795 to 1799, saw the establishment of the Directory, a regime provided for by the Constitution of 1795 (drawn up by members of the outgoing Convention), which assigned the executive power to five "directors" and the legislative power to a bicameral assembly. This was the regime which Napoleon overthrew in 1799.

In following the revolution through these successive regimes one may find it useful to keep in mind some of the interpretations of its course. One standard interpretation sees a political trend toward the left in the regimes which succeeded one another from 1789 to 1794, and a steady development back to the right from 1794 to 1799. In this connection, it is noteworthy that the political terms "right" and "left" originated during this era. It became the custom in the revolutionary assemblies for the more conservative deputies to take their places to the right of the speaker's rostrum, in the horseshoe-shaped banks of seats, while the others ranged themselves according to their political inclinations in the center or to the left of the speaker. A shift in the composition of successive assemblies did in fact occur. As the more conservative deputies of one assembly failed to be reelected to the next, those in the center moved to the right to take their places. At the same time, the leftist members of one legislative body were forced to move to the center in the next to make room for newly elected deputies of even more radical views. This trend continued up to the end of the Terror in 1794; then it was reversed and a movement in the opposite direction set in. The question to be kept in mind is whether one can legitimately refer to the government in power during the Terror as the furthest to the left because of the composition of its assembly, or whether factors other than the political complexion of the legislators must be taken into account in evaluating the nature of the several revolutionary regimes.

According to another interpretation, strongly deterministic in character, the French Revolution followed a dynamic inherent in all revolutionary disturbances: power is inevitably transferred by a series of successive shocks to ever more radical groups until the initial momentum of the revolution is finally exhausted and a turning point is reached; then the more moderate elements may begin to regain control, or a dictator, claiming to embody the will of the people, may seize power.

A third view is presented by Crane Brinton, who borrows his terms from pathology and compares a revolution to a fever or a disease. The revolutionary fever begins with the appearance of certain symptoms; it proceeds by advances and retreats to a crisis stage, or delirium. The crisis ends when the fever breaks; a period of convalescence follows, interrupted perhaps by a relapse or two before the recovery is complete. Applying his metaphor to the French Revolution, Brinton sees the revolutionary fever rising steadily after the outbreak of the illness in 1789 until a crisis is reached in the years 1793–1794, during the Reign of Terror. The end of the Terror in July, 1794, marks the breaking of the fever and the beginning of a long period of convalescence, punctuated by brief relapses during the years of the Directory, 1795–1799. Whether Napoleon's seizure of power in 1799 should be viewed as an indication of France's "recovery" is debatable, but unquestionably the country had achieved by that year a measure of the equilibrium that had been lost during the successive crises of the revolutionary decade.

One additional feature of the revolution must be mentioned before we proceed with the account of its events. This is the crucial role played by the people of Paris. We have already noted the impact upon the king of the attack upon the Bastille by a Paris mob. In the October Days of 1789, as we shall see, a Paris mob was responsible for the transfer of the court and the seat of government from Versailles to Paris. But the influence of Paris upon the course of the revolution became really evident beginning in the summer of 1792, with the advent of the "second" revolution. Had the fate of the monarchy been left to the rural population of France, it might well have survived, but an increasingly radical minority of Parisians, acting through political organizations such as the Jacobin clubs and spreading their propaganda through popular pamphlets and newspapers, provided the impetus for the overthrow of the monarchy and the establishment of the republic. In these events the elected assembly, including representatives from all over France, capitulated to the revolutionary Commune, a committee of Paris radicals who seized power from the legal government of the city on August 10, 1792. From this point on, the Commune played a leading role in the government of France, frequently dictating policy to the elected representatives of the nation. The weapon of the Paris radicals was force and the threat of force. Over and over again, carefully organized demonstrations staged outside the meeting place of the deputies succeeded in swaying the hesitant to a course of action desired by this or that faction of Paris radicals. In this way the will of a determined minority, sure of its goals, was imposed upon the more or less passive majority of Frenchmen. How this minority gained control of the government and its bureaucracy, how it enforced its decrees throughout the country, forms an important part of the story of the revolution.

Achievements of the Constitutional Monarchy, 1789–1792

After the violence of the summer and fall of 1789, a calmer period ensued; indeed, no serious disturbances erupted until the summer of 1792. The National Assembly took advantage of this interlude of relative tranquillity to initiate some of the most significant measures of the revolutionary era. Most important in terms of their long-range impact were the Constitution of 1791, the new administrative system, and the confiscation of Church lands and the promulgation of the Civil Constitution of the Clergy.

Having proclaimed in the Declaration of the Rights of Man that "men are born and remain free and equal in rights," the National Assembly immediately denied this principle in the constitution by dividing Frenchmen into "active" and "passive" citizens, a distinction based upon the amount of direct taxes one paid. Only "active" citizens—those who paid direct taxes equal in value to at least three days of labor in their particular region—had the right to vote. This arrangement denied the franchise to about a third of the adult males in France. Domestic servants were also excluded from "active" citizenship. To those who had taken the promises of the Assembly literally, this provision of the constitution naturally came as a bitter disappointment. The method of election to the Assembly further emphasized the importance of property. Citizens were denied the privilege of voting directly for their representatives. Instead they met in primary assemblies to choose "electors," for whom the property qualification was considerably higher than for the voters, and these in turn named the deputies to the Assembly. The makers of the constitution were clearly determined that the country should not be turned over to the mob.

The constitution included a system of checks and balances designed to

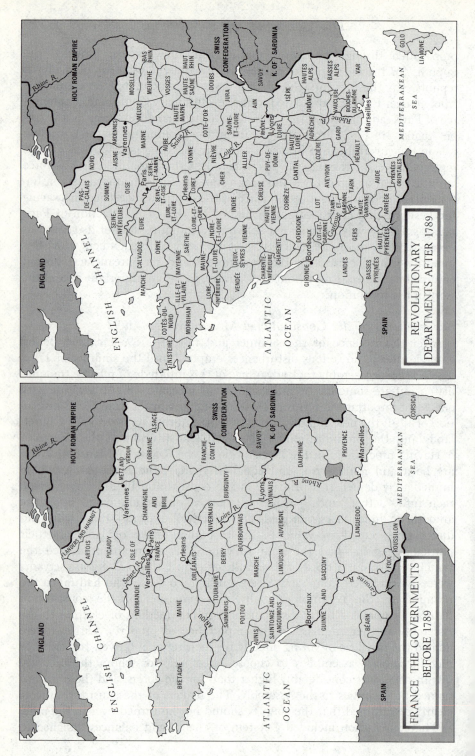

REVOLUTIONARY DEPARTMENTS AFTER 1789

HOLY ROMAN EMPIRE

SWISS CONFEDERATION

K. OF SARDINIA

Rhine R.

ENGLAND

ENGLISH CHANNEL

MEDITERRANEAN SEA

GOLO
LIAMONE

MOSELLE
BAS RHIN
MEURTHE
VOSGES
HAUT RHIN
MEUSE
HAUTE SAÔNE
DOUBS
JURA
AIN
SAVOY
HAUTES ALPS
BASSES ALPS
VAR
MARNE
HAUTE MARNE
CÔTE-D'OR
SAÔNE-ET-LOIRE
ISÈRE
BOUCHES DU RHÔNE
VAUCLUSE
DRÔME
ARDENNES
AISNE
AUBE
YONNE
NIÈVRE
RHÔNE
Lyons
LOIRE
HAUTE LOIRE
ARDÈCHE
GARD
HÉRAULT
Varennes
NORD
PAS-DE-CALAIS
SOMME
OISE
SEINE-ET-MARNE
Paris
SEINE-ET-OISE
SEINE
LOIRET
CHER
INDRE
ALLIER
PUY-DE-DÔME
CANTAL
AVEYRON
LOZÈRE
TARN
AUDE
PYRÉNÉES ORIENTALES
SEINE-INFÉRIEURE
EURE
EURE-ET-LOIR
Orleans
LOIRE-ET-CHER
INDRE-ET-LOIRE
CREUSE
HAUTE VIENNE
CORRÈZE
LOT
TARN-ET-GARONNE
HAUTE GARONNE
ARRIÈGE
CALVADOS
ORNE
SARTHE
MAYENNE
MAINE-ET-LOIRE
VIENNE
DORDOGNE
LOT-ET-GARONNE
GERS
HAUTE PYRÉNÉES
MANCHE
ILLE-ET-VILAINE
LOIRE-INFÉRIEURE
VENDÉE
DEUX-SÈVRES
CHARENTE
CHARENTE-INFÉRIEURE
GIRONDE
Bordeaux
LANDES
BASSES PYRÉNÉES
CÔTES-DU-NORD
MORBIHAN
FINISTÈRE

Seine R.
Loire R.
Rhône R.
Garonne R.

ENGLISH CHANNEL

ATLANTIC OCEAN

SPAIN

FRANCE THE GOVERNMENTS BEFORE 1789

HOLY ROMAN EMPIRE

SWISS CONFEDERATION

K. OF SARDINIA

Rhine R.

ENGLAND

CORSICA

MEDITERRANEAN SEA

FLANDERS AND HAINAUT
ARTOIS
PICARDY
ALSACE
LORRAINE
METZ AND VERDUN
Varennes
CHAMPAGNE AND BRIE
FRANCHE-COMTÉ
BURGUNDY
SAVOY
ISLE OF FRANCE
Paris
Versailles
ORLÉANAIS
Orleans
NIVERNAIS
LYONNAIS
Lyons
DAUPHINÉ
PROVENCE
Marseilles
NORMANDIE
MAINE
TOURAINE
BERRY
BOURBONNAIS
MARCHE
AUVERGNE
LANGUEDOC
ROUSSILLON
FOIX
BRETAGNE
ANJOU
SAUMUROIS
POITOU
AUNIS
SAINTONGE AND ANGOUMOIS
LIMOUSIN
GUINNE AND GASCONY
Bordeaux
BÉARN

Seine R.
Loire R.
Rhône R.
Garonne R.

ENGLISH CHANNEL

ATLANTIC OCEAN

SPAIN

prevent undue concentration of power in the hands of a single individual or governmental body. Still, the Legislative Assembly was clearly intended to be the most powerful political institution in the state. It had the exclusive right to initiate and enact legislation, fix tax assessments, and control public expenditures. No declaration of war or ratification of a treaty could be made without its consent, and it supervised the ministry and directed diplomacy. The King was given a veto over legislation, but it was merely suspensive since it could be overridden by the approval in three successive assemblies of the proposal in question.

France's administrative system was thoroughly overhauled by the National Assembly, and this revision reveals most clearly the impulse of the revolutionaries toward the kind of rationalization and systematization advocated by the *philosophes*. In place of the overlapping and confusing divisions, districts, and bureaus of the Old Regime, the revolutionary deputies established a new uniform administrative organization. France was divided into eighty-three *départements*, or departments; each department into *arrondissements*, or districts; each district into cantons; and each canton into communes. Each department was kept small enough so that its citizens could reach the *chef-lieu*, or capital, in no more than a day's journey by horse-drawn vehicle. Time-honored provinces like Normandy, Brittany, and Champagne were deprived of official status. The new departments were named after rivers, mountains, and other natural features of their respective regions. Such a measure was bound to offend many Frenchmen whose attachment to their particular regions was strong, but the revolutionaries hoped precisely to eliminate differences among their countrymen, to create unity of feeling and loyalty to the new regime.

At the same time, a substantial decentralization of government was introduced. Local and regional officials were elected (again only "active" citizens had the right to vote); at each level of government, an elected council served as both the deliberative body and the permanent executive bureau. Lacking training and experience, these officials had difficulty in carrying out all the tasks with which the royal bureaucracy had formerly been charged. The result was considerable confusion and inefficiency, particularly at the local level. Subsequently, Napoleon replaced the elected officials of the revolutionary era with a corps of appointed functionaries, carefully supervised from the capital by the minister of the interior; however, the departments and districts established in 1789–1790 survived the revolution and have persisted through numerous changes of regime to this day.

The most critical question facing the National Assembly in 1789 was how to finance the government; it was, after all, Louis XVI's failure to solve this problem that had brought on the revolution. The easiest, and in some ways the most obvious, solution would have been to repudiate the national debt, but this option was never seriously considered by the men of property who composed the Assembly, and who in many instances were themselves creditors of the government. Other alternatives were considered and some were tried. First, the Assembly imposed direct taxes upon income from land and other sources, but it failed to raise the anticipated revenue. The Assembly then instituted a "patriotic tax," a kind of voluntary capital levy, with the individual expected to give a quarter of a year's income to the government, in payments spread over three years. Since this tax was not compulsory, the results were naturally disappointing. Meanwhile the deficit in the national treasury continued to mount; the government had to find money somewhere.

The solution ultimately adopted—the confiscation of the land of the Catholic Church—was full of consequences for successive revolutionary governments and constitutes one of the most controversial decisions of the whole era. Among the most frequently voiced arguments used to justify the seizure of the Church's land was the claim that this land was not private property in the sense implied in the Declaration of the Rights of Man. Rather, the Church was a "corporation" which existed to perform certain services and which therefore had a special status under the law. If the state assumed the obligation for guaranteeing these services, it could "take back" the land from the Church. Defenders of the Church challenged such reasoning, arguing that a corporation as well as an individual had certain rights and that one could no more legitimately be deprived of its property than the other. By November, 1789, the decision had been reached. The Assembly voted to place the ecclesiastical land at the disposal of the state, which assumed the obligation of paying the clergy, meeting the expenses of worship, and relieving the poor.

The confiscation of Church lands did not solve the financial problem of the government immediately. Land could not, after all, be used to pay the state's debts. The government planned to sell the lands; in the meantime, it issued to its creditors interest-bearing notes (known as *assignats*) which had the former Church lands as security. Whoever acquired *assignats* was entitled to certain privileges in the purchase of Church lands. The state was to retire the notes as the lands were sold. But not long after the *assignats* had been issued, they began to circulate as paper currency, and the government yielded to the temptation to put more and more of them into circulation. So began the inflation that formed an important part of the history of the revolution. During the later stages of the revolution, as the government printed more and more *assignats* to meet its obligations, they lost over 99 per cent of their face value. Yet the inflation of these years was not without its benefits: it enabled successive revolutionary regimes to liquidate much of the national debt by paying off their creditors in cheap money, and it spurred the growth of a class of enterprising businessmen who acquired the *assignats* at their depreciated value and used them at their face value to purchase Church lands.

Perhaps more significant than the purely economic consequences of the confiscation of Church lands was the new relationship established between the French state and the Catholic Church. Among the obligations the National Assembly agreed to assume were payment of the clergy and maintenance of the churches. Details of this arrangement were spelled out in the Civil Constitution of the Clergy, completed by July, 1790, which not only set salary scales for the various ranks of the clergy but also reorganized the Church. Old dioceses were abolished and new ones were created to coincide with the newly formed administrative departments. Parish priests were to be elected by the district assemblies and bishops were to be named by the department assemblies, the same bodies that functioned as local and departmental governments. The pope had no voice in the appointment of the clergy; he was simply to be notified of the choices.

This arrangement was clearly unacceptable to the pope, particularly since it had been drawn up by the National Assembly without any consultation with Roman authorities. And when the Assembly decided in November, 1790, to require an oath in support of the constitution and the Civil Constitution of the Clergy from all public servants, the stage was set for a

Assignat. One of the interest-bearing notes issued by the revolutionary government using nationalized church lands as security.

bitter struggle between Pius VI, pope between 1775 and 1799, and the revolutionary government. Those priests who agreed to take the oath became a part of the new "constitutional" church; the others, a little more than half the clergy, were branded "refractory" priests by the Assembly and were subjected to intense persecution. Perhaps no single action of the revolutionary governments caused greater resentment among Frenchmen than the policy toward the Church. Though Napoleon was later to reach a compromise with the pope which resulted in improved relations, the bitterness of many French Catholics toward the revolution and toward those who carried on the revolutionary heritage dates from this era.

Decline of the Constitutional Monarchy

Despite certain errors and despite the animosity it aroused among the clergy and some other groups, the government of the National Assembly did come to grips with a number of France's fundamental problems and was responsible for most of the constructive reforms of the revolutionary era. Why did this regime survive only until 1792? Who was responsible for the failure of France's first experiment in constitutional monarchy?

Exponents of a deterministic interpretation of the revolution argue that nothing the king or his ministers might have done could have saved the constitutional monarchy from the fate it suffered in 1792, that it was only natural for control of the revolutionary government to pass from moderate to more radical leaders.

Without rejecting entirely this view, one may still single out certain mistakes made by Louis XVI and his advisers, certain actions by his opponents, and certain initiatives taken by foreign powers, which contributed to the ultimate downfall of the monarchy.

Louis XVI could hardly be expected to collaborate wholeheartedly with an assembly which had deprived him of powers traditionally held by French rulers. Moreover, as early as October, 1789, he and the members of his family were subjected to indignities, an experience which increased his hostility to the revolution. During that fall, mounting unemployment combined with a shortage of bread created renewed unrest among Parisians. Alarmed by the threat, the king summoned troops to Versailles, contending that he must protect the National Assembly from the Paris mob. But his action gave rise once more to rumors that he intended to use the troops against the Assembly and the revolutionary cause. In these circumstances a more or less spontaneous demonstration of Parisian women for bread on October 5 was transformed by popular agitators into a "march on Versailles." Along the twelve-mile route the women were joined by adventurers and curiosity seekers. The climax of the October Days came early the following morning, when some of the angry mob invaded the palace and were fired upon by troops. Entering the inner rooms, they forced the queen,

Departure of the Heroines of Paris for Versailles, October 5, 1789. *A variety of weapons was assembled for the march on Versailles.*

Marie Antoinette, to flee for her life to the king's apartments. Only by appearing on a balcony with his family was the king able to appease the crowd. Even so, he was forced to agree to leave Versailles, where he was thought to be surrounded by evil advisers, and move to Paris. Accordingly, the royal family departed the same day, in a carriage escorted by the cheering mob. The king took up residence in the Tuileries palace, in the heart of Paris, and the National Assembly followed him to the new seat of government.

Though the king outwardly collaborated with the revolutionary government in the months that followed, he had serious reservations about the regime and his position in it. He was particularly offended by the measures taken against the Church, and clearly sympathized with members of the clergy who refused to take the oath in support of the constitution. Among his advisers were many who counseled resistance to the Assembly and its decrees. And even if the king had wanted to accept his responsibilities under the constitution, such a course would have been difficult because of the activities of the *émigrés*, those who had left France in the early stages of the revolution in the hope of stirring up a counterrevolutionary crusade to restore the Old Regime. As early as July, 1789, many members of the court had fled to seek the support of the Holy Roman emperor (whose power stemmed from his rule of Austria), the king of Prussia, and other European monarchs in combating the revolution and restoring the king to his rightful position. Foremost among the *émigrés* were the count of Provence and the count of Artois, Louis' younger brothers, who were far more uncompromising than the king in their opposition to the revolution, and whose projects Louis was forced to disavow on more than one occasion. That Louis ultimately sought the aid of his brother-in-law Leopold II of Austria (ruled 1790–1792), and communicated through intermediaries with other European monarchs is beyond question, but the charges that he maintained close ties with the émigrés are without foundation; actually, their plotting more often than not proved a source of embarrassment to him. It has also been suggested that the failure of the constitutional monarchy was caused by the absence of outstanding leaders among the moderates. Had a truly skillful minister emerged, it is argued, he might have reconciled the king to his constitutional role and brought about the necessary collaboration between the king and the various factions in the Assembly. But no such individual appeared. Neither of the two most prominent statesmen in France during the constitutional monarchy, Mirabeau and the marquis de Lafayette (1757–1834), appears to have been of sufficient stature. Mirabeau, with his outstanding oratorical ability, was the unquestioned leader of the National Assembly for a time, but he was never wholly trusted by the more righteous members, who could not forgive him his dissolute past. And despite his conviction that the best regime for France would be one in which the monarch retained strong powers, he never enjoyed the full confidence of the king. His premature death at the age of forty-two in 1791 has been lamented by those who argue that he was the one statesman capable of saving France from the excesses that followed, but the consensus of modern historians is that Mirabeau's political position and prestige had so seriously deteriorated by 1791 that he could not have substantially altered the course of events.

Lafayette, despite his considerable prestige, was not a man of great intelligence or political shrewdness. He had won his reputation as a military leader in the American Revolution, and enjoyed substantial popularity during the initial phases of the French Revolution, first as a liberal noble who voted with the Third Estate, and later as commander of the National Guard of Paris. But he was a poor speaker and lacked influence in the Assembly. And despite his services to the royal family during the October Days, when he protected them from what might have been even greater violence, he was not popular with the king and queen.

The absence of effective leadership in the moderate camp was all the more important to the monarchy because of the steady growth in influence between 1789 and 1792 of radical "clubs," which ultimately came to favor a republican form of government. The most famous of these was, of course, the organization of Jacobin clubs, which after the downfall of the monarchy in 1792 became the most important political group in France and provided the revolution with some of its most celebrated leaders. The Jacobins had their origins among a group of radical deputies in the National Assembly who in 1789 formed the Society of Friends of the Constitution. This group became known as the Jacobin Club when it began to hold its meeting in the library of a former Jacobin monastery in Paris. At first it was merely a debating society, where deputies from the Assembly discussed radical policy, but it soon broadened its membership to include nondeputies as well, and established ties with similar clubs in other cities of France. Gradually, a vast network of clubs was built, with branches all over the country communicating with one another, holding district meetings, dispensing propaganda, and attempting to influence elections. The membership of the Jacobin clubs was overwhelmingly middle class, consisting primarily of professional men and educated businessmen, though a number of well-to-do artisans joined as the organization grew. With its centralized structure, its strict discipline, and its ties at the local level, the Jacobin machine resembled the single party of the twentieth-century totalitarian state. Mastery of the organization proved a considerable asset to radical leaders in undermining the monarchy, and it remained a valuable instrument of control after the establishment of the republic.

While Louis XVI's attitudes, the absence of effective moderate leaders, and the growth of the Jacobin clubs all contributed to the increasing alienation of the king from the revolutionary regime, the episode which probably sealed the fate of the monarchy was his attempt in June, 1791, to flee the country with his family. With the aid of the Swedish Count Hans Axel von Fersen, Marie Antoinette's lover, the royal family managed to escape from the heavily guarded Tuileries on the night of June 20, and the royal carriage made for a point on the border of Luxembourg. Royal troops were to ensure the safety of the king in his passage through France until he was met at the border by Austrian troops dispatched by the queen's brother, Emperor Leopold II. But the plan went awry when the royal family was recognized and their carriage was halted at Varennes, near the border. There they were detained until orders came from the Assembly to seize the king and bring the royal family back to Paris. What is perhaps most surprising about this episode is that it did not lead immediately to the dismissal of the monarch. Some radicals did indeed demand at this time that the king be declared to have abandoned his throne and that he be replaced by a new executive, but the Assembly was still moderate enough to reject this solution, recognizing that the radicals would probably gain control if the monarchy were abandoned. The moderate majority therefore adopted the fiction that the king had been abducted by enemies of France, and went ahead with plans to promulgate the Constitution of 1791, which retained the constitutional monarchy. However, after the flight to Varennes, Louis was little more than a prisoner of the Assembly.

How long the regime would have survived in peacetime it is impossible to say. The new Legislative Assembly, which met in October, 1791, was torn increasingly by factionalism. Disputes between local officials and the Assem-

The Flight to Varennes, June, 1791. *The print shows the halting of the carriage of the royal family, who were then returned to Paris. Musée Carnavalet, Paris.*

bly hampered the operation of government. But the major crisis which undermined the regime was the outbreak of war in April, 1792. The reasons for the war may be found partly in the reactions of the rest of Europe to the French Revolution. These will be discussed shortly, but first let us consider briefly those in France who desired war. Foremost among them was the king, who as early as 1790 considered asking for the intervention of foreign powers in the hope that a military demonstration by the Austrian and Prussian rulers might strengthen his own hand and enable him to intimidate the revolutionaries. By the spring of 1792 he was convinced that his only salvation lay in a war between the revolutionary government and a coalition of European rulers, a war which—he thought—would end in defeat for the French armies. He would then act as mediator between the French people and the victorious powers. The several appeals for intervention which Louis accordingly directed to his fellow monarchs did indeed help to precipitate the conflict.

The most important group desiring war was the Girondins, members of a faction within the Legislative Assembly who were so named because a number of their mainstays came from Bordeaux, in the department of the Gironde. Since their most prominent spokesman at this stage was Brissot de Warville (1754–1793), they were also known to their contemporaries as the Brissotins. Brissot and some of his Girondin associates were at this time members of the Jacobin Club, but a division developed between Jacobins and Girondins in the final months of the Legislative Assembly and the two factions openly split after the National Convention was elected in September, 1792. In the spring of 1792 the Girondins hoped to precipitate war for two reasons. First of all, unlike the king they were convinced that the revolutionary armies would prevail over their enemies and that a war would make it possible to spread the benefits of the revolution beyond France. In short, a war would become a crusade in which the French armies would carry the torch of liberty to oppressed peoples still living under absolute rulers. In this goal they were encouraged by individuals who had come to France (in a kind of reverse emigration) hoping to enlist the support of the French for the cause of revolution in their own countries. Second, although this idealistic aim was most important to the Girondins, they also believed that a declaration of war would lead to the appointment of a Girondin ministry and a corresponding rise in their influence over the Assembly and the king.

In any event, both the king and the Girondins did what they could to heighten the tensions that existed between France and its potential enemies in the spring of 1792 and thus precipitate the conflict which they thought would serve their respective purposes. Both were mistaken in their expectations; the war which began on April 20 did much to hasten the downfall of the monarchy and to strengthen the extremist elements which ultimately won control from the Girondins.

Europe and the French Revolution, 1789–1792

To the first news of the revolution in France the response of many foreigners was ecstatic. William Wordsworth's rapturous cry is one of the most celebrated: "Bliss was it in that dawn to be alive. . . ." The Whig statesman, Charles James Fox, termed the fall of the Bastille "much the greatest event . . . that ever happened in the world! and how much the best!" In Germany the philosopher Johann Gottfried von Herder pronounced the revolution the most important movement in the life of mankind since the Reformation and saw it as a no less decisive step toward human freedom. Numerous associations sympathetic to the French cause sprang up in England; their members were primarily dissenters and radicals. Some of these likened the revolution of 1789 to England's own Glorious Revolution of 1688 and linked the struggle of the French for freedom with their own strivings for parliamentary reform. Certainly the educated classes throughout Europe followed the events of the revolution with the greatest interest and were familiar to a surprising degree with what was going on in France. One must remember that at this time, France was still the leading nation in Europe, the country whose literature, art, and manners were most admired.

But this initially enthusiastic response was followed by a less favorable reaction. In England, the celebrated Whig statesman, Edmund Burke

(1729–1797), who was skeptical of the French Revolution from the start, in 1790 published his famous indictment, *Reflections on the Revolution in France*, in which he denounced the excesses of the revolutionaries and questioned the entire philosophy of "natural rights." Before long, others in England began to be disturbed by the effects of revolutionary propaganda at home and to call for measures curbing the radical associations. A similar change of heart occurred among admirers of the revolution in the German states, though their deepest disillusionment came only with the excesses associated with the Reign of Terror in 1793–1794.

The initial reactions of the rulers in Europe were complex and varied. In the light of what afterward occurred, it would be tempting to infer that all European monarchs "trembled on their thrones" at the news of the revolution and foresaw similar threats to their own positions. But this was not the case. Instead, events in France were viewed for the effect they might have on the complicated game of international politics. For the moment, France could be discounted as a major force in European diplomacy. In fact, Frederick William II, the ineffectual king of Prussia who succeeded Frederick the Great in 1786, saw the revolution at first as an opportunity for Prussia to detach France from its alliance with Austria (dating from the Seven Years' War) and to bring it into the existing alliance between Prussia, England, and the Dutch republic (Holland). Negotiations to this end proved fruitless, but they suggest that neither ideological considerations nor fear of revolution prevented the Prussian king from hoping for a tie with revolutionary France. Leopold II, the Austrian ruler, who came to the throne in 1790, sympathized with the plight of his brother-in-law and sister, the king and queen of France, but he did not undertake a crusade to rescue them from the revolutionaries. Indeed, Leopold was far more concerned at first with reestablishing order in his own Habsburg lands, which were in a state of turbulence after ten years of rule by Joseph II, his reforming predecessor. He was faced not only with demands from the Magyar nobility in Hungary for greater autonomy, and with awakening nationalist sentiment in the Bohemian part of the empire, but also with open revolt in the Austrian Netherlands (later Belgium). His principal effort, therefore, was to establish peace within the empire and to maintain peace abroad. Once he had subdued the revolt in the Netherlands, he was willing to make a gesture toward the French ruler. He joined the Prussian king, Frederick William, in the Declaration of Pillnitz (August 27, 1791), which stated that French affairs were the interest of all Europe and that the two sovereigns might intervene to protect Louis XVI if the other European powers would support them. Yet Leopold was well aware that since England would not consent to such an arrangement, he would not have to fulfill the obligation. As long as Leopold was on the Austrian throne, no war with France occurred. But his sudden death on March 1, 1792, and the succession to the throne of his less cautious young son Francis II, altered the Austrian position, bringing into prominence advisers who favored a more belligerent policy toward France.

War might still have been averted if the change in Austria had not coincided with the advent to power in France of a ministry dominated by the Girondins, who, as we have seen, were the leading advocates of a crusade of liberation. Charles François Dumouriez (1739–1823), a veteran soldier and adventurer, was minister of foreign affairs in the new government. Though not himself a Girondin, he strongly favored war, in which he hoped to play a leading role and thus achieve influence over the king. Pretexts for a conflict with Austria were not hard to find. The French government had repeatedly protested the activities of the French *émigrés* on Austrian soil and the leniency of the emperor toward them. Disagreement also existed concerning the claims of German princes who had been deprived of their feudal rights in the French province of Alsace by decrees passed on August 4, 1789. The princes had refused the indemnity offered by the French government, instead demanding the restoration of their rights and appealing for support to the Austrian emperor. Neither of these issues was important enough of itself to cause a rupture, but feeling had mounted so high in France that on April 20, 1792, the Assembly voted overwhelmingly to declare war on Austria. Almost immediately, the king of Prussia decided to join the Austrian ruler. Both were convinced that France, torn by factionalism and internal dissension, could be easily defeated.

Initially, their expectations proved correct. The French armies were ill prepared for the conflict. Half of the officer corps had emigrated, and many of the men had deserted; new recruits were enthusiastic but ill trained. Dumouriez's strategy was to invade the Austrian Netherlands, but in their first encounter, the French troops broke ranks and fled in disorder; a number of regiments even went over to the enemy. Had the Austrian and Prussian armies mounted a full-scale invasion at this point, France might have been defeated, but the German rulers were reluctant to devote all their resources to the war against France because of their concern over events in Poland, which Russian armies had entered in April, 1792. Until an agreement was reached by the Austrian and Prussian rulers with Catherine the Great over the disposition of Polish territories, they hesitated to proceed against France.

Establishment of the Republic, September, 1792

Meanwhile, the initial reverses of the war produced an internal crisis in France that culminated during the late summer of 1792 in the overthrow of the monarchy and the establishment of a republic. As news of the first defeats reached Paris, and as the military situation grew steadily worse, popular discontent over the conduct of the war mounted. French officers were charged with betraying their troops. Aristocrats and refractory priests were suspected of being enemy agents acting in collusion with the hated *émigrés*. Finally, many were convinced that the king himself was engaged in treasonable negotiations with the monarchs who were opposing France. To this tension and fear resulting from the war was added an economic crisis that manifested itself in higher prices, marked depreciation of the *assignats*, and a food shortage caused in part by the requisition of supplies for the armies.

All these circumstances created a new revolutionary mood in the country. But the real impetus for the "second" revolution came from a determined minority of Paris radicals—many of them members of the Jacobin clubs— who were prepared to exploit the situation in order to seize power.

Their first step was to secure control over the administrative districts of Paris. For purposes of administration the capital was divided into forty-eight *sections*, each with its own assembly of "active" citizens who ruled the district and chose representatives to the city council. Because many eligible citizens took no interest in the government of their *sections*, radical politicians gradually managed to gain control of the assemblies and turn them into political action groups to be used for revolutionary purposes. These Jacobin-dominated bodies played a crucial role in the insurrection of August 10, 1792.

This uprising was triggered in part by the publication in Paris on August 3 of a manifesto that had been issued by the Prussian duke of Brunswick, commander in chief of the forces allied against France. With Prussian troops poised on the border of France, the duke declared the intention of the allies to restore Louis XVI to full sovereignty, and threatened to destroy the city of Paris if any harm should come to the royal family. The manifesto seemed to confirm popular suspicions concerning the king's treason. Representatives of the Paris *sections* reacted by presenting a petition to the Legislative Assembly demanding the deposition of Louis XVI. At the same time radical leaders completed their plans for an insurrection. They abolished the distinction between "active" and "passive" citizens in the *sections* and thus secured the support of the working classes in their districts. During the night of August 9–10 the tocsin was sounded, signaling the beginning of the uprising. Delegates of a majority of the *sections* succeeded in ousting the legal municipal government from the city hall and establishing a revolutionary Commune as the government of Paris. Meanwhile the mob, carefully organized by radical leaders, laid siege to the Tuileries, which was defended only by the king's Swiss Guard and a few loyal units of the National Guard. The king, losing heart, took refuge with the deputies of the Assembly in their meeting hall. As the attack on the Tuileries was intensified he gave orders to the Swiss Guard to lay down their arms, hoping that they would be spared. Instead, the mob invaded the palace, and enraged by their own losses, butchered the Swiss Guardsmen and the royal

Georges Jacques Danton. *Anonymous portrait. Contemporaries commented on Danton's pockmarked visage and his brilliant eyes. Musée Carnavalet, Paris.*

servants as well. The king was not pursued to his place of refuge, but the Assembly, yielding to pressure from the newly formed Commune, ordered him suspended from his functions and turned him and his family over to the Commune for imprisonment.

The removal of the monarch left the nature of the regime temporarily in doubt. The Legislative Assembly was unwilling to pass judgment upon the monarch, so it decided to summon a National Convention, to be elected by universal manhood suffrage, which would decide the fate of the king and draft a new constitution. In the meantime the Assembly named a provisional council of six ministers to hold executive power until the Convention could be named. In the weeks that followed, both the Assembly and the new ministers found their authority challenged and often usurped by the Paris Commune, which not only asserted its jurisdiction over the capital but sent delegates to the provinces to oversee and interfere with government officials. For six weeks these three bodies—the Assembly, the council of ministers, and the Commune—vied for control; more often than not, the will of the Commune prevailed.

Among the ministers named by the Assembly, the most prominent was unquestionably Jacques Danton (1759–1794), a lawyer and political organizer who had risen rapidly to leadership in the Jacobin Club because of his active involvement in almost every radical plot in Paris since the beginning of the revolution. Most recently he had distinguished himself as one of the principal organizers of the insurrection of August 10. Opinions differ as to

Danton's real capabilities as a statesman, but he seems to have responded to the needs of the hour. He was an excellent orator, popular with the Parisians, and appeared to embody the patriotism required in the desperate situation in which France found herself. Prussian troops had continued their advance on French soil. With the enemy before Verdun, the last obstacle on the road to Paris, Danton called upon his countrymen to defend their country: "To triumph over the enemy . . . we must be bold, still more bold, ever bold, and France is saved."[4]

At this juncture, between the insurrection of August 10 and the assembling of the Convention on September 21, the celebrated September Massacres occurred. They must be viewed against the background of military defeats that appeared to spell imminent disaster for France. The prisons of Paris were overflowing with political prisoners—refractory priests, aristocrats, and royalist sympathizers arrested after August 10. All were suspected of treason. Somehow the rumor started that the prisoners were plotting to break out and attack from the rear the armies defending France, while the Prussians attacked from the front. To forestall this rumored conspiracy, patriotic mobs fell upon the prisoners, dragged them from their cells, and after summary trials, massacred them. More than a thousand were killed in this brutal fashion in a few days. Responsibility for the murders has never been determined, but the proceedings appear to have been carefully organized and no real attempt was made by the council of ministers or the Commune to halt them. Regardless of who was to blame, the gruesome September Massacres went far toward discrediting the revolution among its remaining sympathizers abroad.

Since the elections for the National Convention occurred at about the same time as the September Massacres, it is hardly surprising that royalist sympathizers stayed away from the polls; indeed, in Paris the Commune used terrorist methods to keep them from voting. Despite the provision for universal manhood suffrage, only 700,000 out of 7,000,000 qualified voters cast their ballots. Those whom they named to the Convention were overwhelmingly in favor of the republic. The first act of the newly assembled Convention on September 21, 1792, was the formal abolition of the monarchy in France. A supplementary decree passed the following day stated that henceforth all public documents would be dated according to a new revolutionary calendar in which September 22 became the first day of "the Year I of the French Republic."

The decrees just mentioned were passed unanimously. Before long, however, the differences which had split the left in the old Assembly reappeared among the members of the Convention. On the right now were the Girondins. On the left sat the group known as the Mountain, headed by Danton and some of the other leading Jacobins. Between these two groups,

---

[4] Quoted by Leo Gershoy, *The French Revolution and Napoleon* (New York, 1964) p. 221.

each of which held about 150 seats, lay the Plain (sometimes scornfully called the Marsh or the Belly), consisting of four hundred or more deputies who sometimes voted with the right, but usually ended by throwing their support to the Mountain. The history of the first eight months of the Convention is the story of the struggle between the Girondins and the Mountain for control, a struggle which the Mountain had won by the summer of 1793.

At first, both the Girondins and the Mountain numbered Jacobins among their members, but the leaders of the Mountain gradually forced the Girondins from the club, and eventually dominated it to such an extent that "Mountain" and "Jacobins" became almost synonymous.

To define the essential differences between the Girondins and the Jacobins is not easy. Deputies of both factions were bourgeois, not workers, though in general the Girondins may have come from somewhat higher social strata. Both voted for the republic. Both apparently favored continuation of the war against France's enemies. It has been said that the two may have differed in temperament rather than in class or doctrine. The Girondins, who would certainly have been considered dangerous radicals in any other country in Europe at this time, now occupied the moderate position in France, convinced that the revolution had gone far enough and opposed to any further social leveling. They tended to emphasize "liberty" in their speeches, advocating—among other kinds of freedom—the exemption of trade and industry from regulation by the state. Because many prominent Girondins came from the provinces, they distrusted Paris and the interference of the Commune in national politics. Though they had done nothing to prevent the September Massacres, they subsequently condemned those who were responsible for them.

The Jacobin leaders, though by no means all alike in temperament, were more inclined to emphasize "equality" in their public declarations. They favored the elimination of all civil and political distinctions, and although they were not prepared to abandon the principle of private property, they tended to be sympathetic toward the underprivileged, and to admit the right of the government in certain circumstances to intervene in the economy for the welfare of the society as a whole. Specifically, they inaugurated a system of government regulation of prices and wages in order to control the inflation from which France was suffering, and openly advocated confiscation of the wealth of *émigrés* as well as of priests. Whether they favored these measures as a matter of principle or because they appeared expedient is hard to determine. While not averse to adopting policies which would help them secure and maintain political power, the Jacobins were, it appears, genuinely convinced that they alone could save France.

Perhaps the most important reason for the victory of the Jacobins was that the Girondins had become moderates prepared to compromise or even

Execution of Louis XVI, January 21, 1793. *The executioner holds the king's head up for the crowd to see.*

vacillate in a situation that seemed to require bold, decisive measures. The position they took on the trial of the king is a good illustration of their weakness. The monarch and his family had remained prisoners in the tower of the Temple, a building formerly owned by the Knights Templars. The problem of what to do with the king was highly controversial. Some of the Girondins advocated clemency; others wanted to send him into exile; still others favored a popular referendum to determine his fate. In general, the Girondins were inclined to temporize, hoping to postpone a decision indefinitely. The position of the Mountain was clear: the king was a traitor; he should be brought to trial and suffer the penalty customary for such an offence—death.

The trial of the king was hastened by the discovery in a secret cupboard in the Tuileries of a cache of documents which proved conclusively Louis' knowledge and encouragement of foreign intervention. In December, 1792, therefore, the Convention constituted itself a court to try "Louis Capet" (as he was then called) for treason. After prolonged debate, members of the Convention were asked in January, 1793, to vote publicly on the fate of the king. All agreed that he was guilty of treason, but there was sharp division on the nature of the penalty. The Mountain demanded Louis' death and won enough support from the Plain to carry the day. Even some Girondins at the last moment joined the majority in voting for the king's execution. The final vote was 387 to 334, with twenty-six of the majority favoring a delay in carrying out the sentence. On January 21, 1793,

Louis was led under a tight security guard from the Temple to the Place de la Révolution (now the Place de la Concorde), where the guillotine had been placed. Showing courage to the end, he mounted the scaffold, and amidst the rolling of drums, was beheaded.

The vacillation of the Girondins throughout these proceedings discredited them with the minority who were shaping events in Paris. And because the Girondins were guilty of similar hesitation and disunity on other issues—the conduct of the war and the formulation of a constitution, for example—the Mountain seized the initiative and gradually consolidated its position. The climax of the struggle between the two factions did not come until June, 1793, when the Convention, under pressure from a carefully organized mob, voted the arrest of a group of Girondin deputies on charges of counterrevolution. This act paved the way for the dictatorship of the Mountain over the Convention, which began in July, 1793.

Prelude to the Terror

The celebrated era of the French Revolution known as the Reign of Terror lasted for a year, from the summer of 1793 to the summer of 1794. Because the leaders of the government justified their undemocratic procedures and harsh measures by claiming that France faced a desperate crisis, with the revolution threatened by enemies at home and abroad, we must briefly examine the nature of this crisis in the months preceding the establishment of the Terrorist regime to determine how serious it really was.

After the initial defeats of the spring and summer of 1792, the French armies enjoyed a temporary change of fortune, beginning at Valmy on September 20. At this point in northeastern France the advancing Prussian army was stopped by French forces under the leadership of General François Christophe Kellermann (1735–1820) and of Dumouriez, who had assumed command of the Army of the North after his resignation from the ministry in June. Though this victory was by no means striking, the fact that they had held against the Prussians and prevented their further advance provided a great boost in morale to French troops, whose feat was christened the "miracle" at Valmy. Encouraged, French forces took the offensive during the fall of 1792 and enjoyed a number of successes. The territory of Savoy, whose ruler had allied himself with Austria, was invaded in September and fell to the French along with the city of Nice. Farther to the north, General Adam Philippe de Custine (1740–1793) took the offensive against Austrian troops in the Rhineland and not only captured the cities of Speyer, Worms, and Mainz but crossed the Rhine and took Frankfurt. Finally, Dumouriez invaded the Austrian Netherlands and the revolutionary troops won their first great victory at Jemappes, on November 6. Brussels, Antwerp, and Liège subsequently fell, and the French occupied the whole of the Austrian Netherlands.

The response to French occupation and control varied. In general, the peasants and bourgeoisie at first welcomed the French, since their coming meant an end to the authority of reigning princes and a weakening of the position of the nobility. Before long, however, the armies of liberation began to seem more like armies of occupation as the French government took steps to annex the several territories to France and to impose upon the natives fiscal exactions designed to cover the costs of the occupying armies. This was the case, for example, in the Austrian Netherlands.

Another important consequence of the French conquests was that they provoked the opposition of certain European powers that had hitherto remained neutral. The most important of these was Great Britain. William Pitt the Younger (1759–1806), prime minister since 1783, had been determined to pursue a policy of neutrality when France went to war with Austria and Prussia in 1792, not so much because of the ideological divisions among Englishmen concerning the French Revolution, as because he saw no advantage to be gained by intervention. To be sure, British opinion was shocked by certain events in France: the insurrection of August 10, the imprisonment of the royal family, and the September Massacres. But not until the revolutionary armies took the offensive against the Low Countries in the fall of 1792 did Britain begin to see its strategic and commercial interests threatened. The capture of Antwerp, directly across the Channel, seemed to menace Britain's security. Moreover a decree of the Convention opening the Scheldt River to commercial navigation openly violated an earlier treaty which had guaranteed exclusive Dutch control over this river; a protest of the British government on this question was ignored. If the French could defy with impunity treaties affecting the maritime interests of other nations, they were, in Pitt's view, a real threat. Tension between Britain and France mounted steadily after November, 1792. The Convention's decision in January, 1793, to execute the king was used as a pretext by Pitt for expelling France's diplomatic representative. The Convention thereupon declared war upon Great Britain and its ally, Holland. Though the formal declaration of war on February 1 came from France, the British government had already decided that there was no alternative.

Britain and Holland were joined shortly by Spain and two of the Italian states, Sardinia and Naples, which came out openly against France only at this time. Along with the powers already at war with France, these came to constitute what is known as the First Coalition. During February and March, 1793, the allies began to assume the offensive against the French armies, forcing them to withdraw from some of the territories taken in the preceding year. In the Netherlands, for example, Dumouriez was confronted with a fresh Austrian offensive which resulted in two successive defeats of the French. Convinced that he had failed because of inadequate support from the war bureau and the government in Paris, Dumouriez entered into

A National Guardsman. *Drawing made in 1793. On guard duty, the guardsman holds a gong with which to sound an alarm.*

treasonable negotiations with the Austrian enemy. His plan was to evacuate the Low Countries and lead his troops on Paris, where he would seize power and restore the monarchy. When his army failed to support him in this venture, he was forced to flee across the border and join the enemy. The news of France's betrayal by one of its leading generals heightened the shock of the recent defeats in the Netherlands and in the Rhineland, where the Prussians had again taken the offensive. Dumouriez's treason also sharpened the division between Girondins and Jacobins, as each charged the other with complicity in his plots.

As if the stress of defending France against foreign invasion were not enough, the revolutionary government was faced in March with an open rebellion in the region known as the Vendée. (This included not only the department of La Vendée but also parts of the adjoining regions of Poitou, Anjou, and Brittany.) The immediate pretext for the revolt was the government's attempt to conscript additional troops. Resentment against the revolutionary government's anticlerical policies was intense in this strongly Catholic region. Now the peasants, generally loyal to Church and king, refused to be drafted into the republican army and exploded into revolt. They were supported in their resistance by a group of Catholic noblemen in the region whose counterrevolutionary conspiracy had recently been discovered. By May the rebels had established a Royal Catholic Grand Army, which caused serious concern to the Convention.

To the problems caused by the steady deterioration at the front and the outbreak of civil war in the Vendée was added a new economic crisis in the late winter and spring of 1793. Requisitions for the armies had depleted stocks of grain and other foodstuffs, causing bread riots in Paris in February. War contractors and speculators in grain profited from the situation, thus contributing to a rise in prices. The government responded by issuing a new flood of *assignats*, with the result that their value depreciated even further. When popular resentment over these hardships culminated in antigovernment riots in Paris and other major cities, members of the Mountain in the Convention realized that they had to take drastic steps.

They found a ready-made program in the proposals of the *Enragés* ("Madmen"), groups of radicals led in Paris by a man named Varlet and a constitutional priest, Jacques Roux. The *Enragés*, claiming to speak for the poor, demanded government regulation of food prices, subsidies for the poor, and a heavy graduated tax upon the wealthy to finance the costs of the war. Not all of their proposals were enacted immediately, but during the spring of 1793, the Convention passed legislation providing for public relief of the poor, imposed a war tax and a forced loan upon the rich, and on May 4 passed the First Law of the Maximum, which attempted to set maximum prices for grain and flour. The regulation proved to be unenforceable, but was a prelude to more stringent controls under the Terror.

The reluctance of the Girondin deputies in the Convention to adopt extreme measures of this sort, their earlier vacillation during the trial of the king, and their general moderation aroused suspicion among the more radical elements in Paris and elsewhere. Delegations from the Paris *sections* repeatedly petitioned for the expulsion of the Girondin deputies and hinted that the Commune was prepared to use force if the Convention failed to take action against them. The Girondins—recognizing that their principal support lay outside Paris—reacted by trying to stir up opposition to the capital among their sympathizers in the provinces. The tension reached a climax in early June. Unable to secure their demands by petitions, the Paris *sections* formed a revolutionary committtee; this body, in turn, organized a mass demonstration around the Tuileries, where the Convention was meeting. Declaring that no deputy would be allowed to leave the building until the Girondin leaders had been handed over, the mob forced the Convention to vote the arrest of twenty-nine prominent Girondin deputies. The Mountain, backed by the Commune and the Paris populace, had apparently triumphed over the Girondin opposition.

Among the arrested deputies, some refused to submit without a fight. Instead of being imprisoned, they had just been detained in their homes, and twenty of the Girondin leaders escaped from Paris and sought to organize an insurrection against the capital. At first, it appeared that their "federalist revolt" might be successful. They were joined in their rebellion by other antigovernment groups, particularly the royalists, who were only too willing to exploit the situation. The Vendée was, of course, already in arms against the republic, and the revolt spread from there to all of Poitou, Anjou, and Brittany. Some of the major cities in France, including Lyons, Marseilles, and Toulon, fell to royalist forces. Only the departments around Paris, in central France, and on the eastern frontier appeared to remain loyal to the republic. As events subsequently showed, the strength of the rebels was illusory; their forces were scattered and lacked any sort of unified command, and their various members had radically different goals.

But in the summer of 1793, republican leaders could maintain with some justice that the country was in danger, that the revolution itself was threatened by its enemies. Only the most drastic measures, they argued, could save France in this hour of crisis. The situation of the republic was never quite so desperate as the government pretended, but the combined threat of foreign invasion and civil war did exist, and was exploited to justify the ruthless measures adopted during the Terror.

The Reign of Terror, 1793–1794

The precise nature of the political system by which France was ruled during the Terror must be explained before we turn to the activities of the regime. The Convention, elected in September, 1792, remained the official sovereign assembly throughout the Terror; indeed it remained in existence until October, 1795. But the Convention had been named in part to draft a constitution that would supplant the Constitution of 1791. Such a constitution was, in fact, completed by June, 1793, and sent for ratification to the primary assemblies of citizens in the departments, but it was never put into effect. It was easy for Jacobin leaders to argue in the midsummer crisis of 1793 that the country could ill afford the upheaval that the dissolution of the Convention and the election of a new assembly would cause. The Constitution of 1793 was therefore suspended for the duration of the war; as a matter of fact, it never was put into operation.

The stillborn Constitution of 1793 was in its provisions the most democratic of the constitutions formulated during the revolutionary era. It provided for universal manhood suffrage, without property qualifications for either voters or candidates. Gone was the distinction between "active" and "passive" citizens. Representatives to the legislative body were to be named directly by all citizens who voted in primary assemblies. The legislative body was to consist of one chamber, to which an executive council would be responsible. In order to allay the fears of the provinces, the constitution provided that the departments would name the candidates for the executive council, with the legislative body selecting the twenty-four officials from these candidates.

Paradoxically, the body which adopted this most democratic constitution also supported the most dictatorial regime of the revolutionary era. For the Convention continued to sit throughout the Terror, although its power was in fact vested in two executive committees which it had set up. The Committee of Public Safety, the more important of the two, was charged with general administration; it was composed at first of nine and later of twelve members. The Committee of General Security was given control over the revolutionary police. Members of both of these committees were chosen from the Convention and were theoretically responsible to it, but they became practically independent in their jurisdiction. After the autumn of 1793, their membership was automatically renewed by the Convention every month. They reported to the Convention occasionally on their activities, but their policies were never seriously challenged by that body until the summer of 1794, when the Terror ended.

The Terrorist regime has been called a dictatorship, but it was not a one-man dictatorship. Each of the members of the Committee of Public Safety had particular interests or responsibilities and was relatively autonomous in his jurisdiction, though major policies had to be agreed upon by the group as a whole. All twelve members of the Committee were educated, middle-class radicals, members of the Mountain in the Convention, sincerely devoted to revolutionary ideals. Among them were six lawyers, two army officers, two men of letters, a civil servant, and a Protestant minister. Only gradually did Maximilien Robespierre (1758–1794), the thirty-five-year-old provincial lawyer with whose name the Terror is most closely associated, achieve a certain preeminence in the Committee, and his supremacy was frequently contested. Moreover, the power of the Committee of Public Safety was to some degree limited by the Committee of General Security, theoretically at least its equal, and by the Paris Commune, which continued to exercise considerable influence on government policies.

In regional and local administration the government of the Terror attempted to return to the tradition of centralization characteristic of the Old Regime. The administrative divisions established by the National Assembly—departments, districts, cantons, and communes—were retained, but the Terrorist government exercised its authority through appointed officials acting on behalf of the Convention. In the spring of 1793, "deputies on mission" were sent out by the Convention to the various regions of France to levy troops and stimulate revolutionary enthusiasm. When these officials threatened to become too independent, they were replaced by "national agents," one in each district or commune, directly responsible to the Committee of Public Safety. At the local level the national agents collaborated in some instances with "surveillance committees" (local revolutionary police) and with the Jacobin clubs, now termed "popular societies," but the clubs played a much less significant role than might have been expected.

Maximilien de Robespierre.
*Anonymous portrait. Musée
Carnavalet, Paris.*

This simple description of the machinery of the Terror does not begin to suggest the range of its activities or the messianic spirit of its leaders. The Terrorist regime had three basic goals: to win the war; to suppress the enemies of the republic at home; and to establish in France what Robespierre and others termed the "Republic of Virtue." A brief account of what was done to achieve each of these goals will illuminate some of the more important aspects of the Reign of Terror.

On August 23, 1793, the Convention, acting to meet the crisis caused by the war and the revolts in the provinces, issued a decree proclaiming a *levée en masse,* a plan for the universal conscription of French citizens to defend the republic:

Henceforth, until the enemies have been driven from the territory of the Republic, the French people are in permanent requisition for army service. The young men shall go to battle; the married men shall forge arms and transport provisions; the women shall make tents and clothes, and shall serve in the hospitals; the children shall turn old linen into lint; the old men shall repair to the public places, to stimulate the courage of the warriors and preach the unity of the Republic and hatred of kings.[5]

[5] *A Documentary Survey of the French Revolution,* pp. 472–473.

This document, which constitutes the first appeal in modern times for the complete wartime mobilization of a people, suggests the kind of national loyalty which the revolutionary leaders hoped to inspire. They were not disappointed, for the *levée en masse* released a remarkable outburst of popular energy, characterized by Frenchmen of a later era as the "spirit of '93." Under its impetus the French armies halted the advance of the allied forces, and by the spring of 1794 recovered territories that France had conquered in the first months of the republic and later lost. By the end of the Terror, French armies once again occupied the Austrian Netherlands and the entire left, or west, bank of the Rhine.

Patriotism is certainly not a phenomenon that appeared for the first time during the French Revolution, but the attitude of the French citizen-soldier of 1793 toward his country differed considerably from that of the professional mercenary serving the Old Regime. Instead of fighting for a dynasty or a privileged caste, he was fighting for a nation in which he felt he had a personal stake. Nowhere else can one see quite so clearly the vital role of the doctrine of popular sovereignty in the emergence of an aggressive nationalist spirit. The lesson was not lost on foreign observers. A few years later, after the French victory at Jena, the Prussian military leader Neithardt von Gneisenau remarked, "One cause above all has raised France to this pinnacle of greatness. The Revolution awakened all her powers and gave to each individual a suitable field for his activity." [6]

Part of the reason for French successes in the field lay in certain economic measures taken by the government, measures of the sort we have come to recognize as practically inevitable for a modern nation engaged in a total war. Among these were the celebrated Maximum, a law of September, 1793, which established maximum prices for certain basic commodities and also imposed controls on wages. These were essential to combat the continuing inflation which threatened the urban poor with starvation. Other measures included government requisitioning of supplies for military purposes at the maximum prices which had been set, the establishment of bread and meat rationing for civilians, and controls on foreign trade and exchange. Although these hastily improvised regulations proved hard to enforce, they worked well enough to fulfill some of the basic needs they were designed to meet; indeed, the value of the *assignat* was stabilized, and even rose, during the Terror, and the poorest classes were able to buy their own food instead of relying on charity. The armies were successfully provisioned, and as has been noted, they were generally victorious during this period.

To achieve its second goal—the suppression of the enemies of the republic at home—the Terrorist government used both its armies and a set of special revolutionary tribunals. Most of the revolts in the provinces had collapsed by the end of the summer of 1793, but opposition con-

---

[6] Quoted by G.P. Gooch, *Studies in Modern History* (London, 1931), p. 197.

ON NE CONNOÎT ICI

QUE LA DÉNOMINATION

DE CITOYEN.

Placard posted during the French Revolution reads: "Only the title of 'citizen' is employed here."

Marie Antoinette. *Drawing by David. David made this sketch while watching from a window the procession taking the queen to her execution. The Louvre, Paris.*

tinued in certain key regions, notably in the Vendée and in the cities of Lyons and Toulon, both in the hands of the royalists. A concerted drive against Lyons reduced it to submission in October; Toulon, where the royalists had the help of the English, was recaptured in December. (One of the officers of the forces that took Toulon was a young artillery captain named Napoleon Buonaparte.) Bitter fighting continued in the Vendée until the end of 1793, and even after that republican troops continued to carry out bloody reprisals against the inhabitants. Responsibility for punishment of those who had participated in these revolts lay with the deputies on mission, who organized mass executions, or with special revolutionary tribunals set up for the purpose.

In the capital sat the highest court in the system of revolutionary justice, the Revolutionary Tribunal of Paris, which had been established in the spring of 1793 to deal with enemies of the revolution. At first its procedures were similar to those of a regular court of law, but as time went on its justice became increasingly summary. Its activities were stepped up in October, 1793, when the desire for vengeance against traitors to the republic seems to have reached a peak. Among the most prominent victims at this time were the queen, Marie Antoinette (known in her trial simply as "the widow Capet"), a number of the Girondin leaders who had been arrested in June, and several former generals who had not shown sufficient enthusiasm for the republic. All met their death on the guillotine which stood on the *Place de la Révolution*. The Revolutionary Tribunal of Paris was alone responsible for imposing death sentences upon 2,639 victims in the fifteen months of its existence.[7] Estimates of the total number of victims under the Reign of Terror run as high as 20,000.

[7] Donald M. Greer, *The Incidence of the Terror During the French Revolution* (Cambridge, Mass., 1935), p. 135.

A persistent myth concerning the Reign of Terror suggests that it was strictly a class phenomenon. According to this old view, representatives of the middle and lower classes, having secured control of the government, relentlessly pursued the aristocrats and clergy over whom they had triumphed. But a careful analysis of the social origins of the victims of the Terror has led to the abandonment of this theory; only about 15 per cent of those sentenced to death by revolutionary tribunals belong to the nobility and clergy. The rest were members of the Third Estate, largely peasants and laborers. Surprising as this discovery appears at first glance, it is explained by the simple fact that the "enemies" of the republic were drawn from all social groups. In the Vendée, for example, the rank and file of the rebels (an estimated 90 per cent) were peasants loyal to king and Church, though some of their leaders were from the upper classes. Evidently, then, political necessity rather than class antagonism was the underlying motive for the mass executions of the Terror. The victims were those who had challenged the republic, or who were thought to endanger it, regardless of their social origins.

A consideration of the ways in which Robespierre and his colleagues attempted to achieve their third goal, the Republic of Virtue, takes us to the heart of the Terror—its semireligious, messianic character. For at least some of the revolutionary leaders the founding of the republic marked the beginning of a new order on earth, the establishment of the Heavenly City of the eighteenth-century *philosophes*. More specifically, they drew their inspiration from Rousseau's vision of an ideal republic, founded on virtue, where the highest aim of the citizen would be to serve the general will. Only in such a community would men be truly free, living in harmony in accordance with the precepts of justice and reason and enjoying their "natural rights."

Not surprisingly, there were a variety of views on how this utopia could be attained. For some, the French nation was so closely identified with the ideal Republic of Virtue that patriotism became all-important. Any loyalty which could be regarded as detracting from allegiance to *la patrie* was immediately suspect. As a result of this sentiment, attempts were made to supplant Catholicism with a new state religion complete with martyrs, rituals, and civic festivals. One aspect of this campaign was the further elaboration in October, 1793, of the revolutionary calendar, which assigned new names to the months and did away with the sabbath and the saints' days of the old Christian calendar. Simultaneously more aggressive dechristianization activities were carried out in the provinces by some of the deputies on mission, who closed churches or converted them into "temples of reason," ordered the unfrocking of priests, and fostered anti-Catholic demonstrations.

Members of the Committee of Public Safety soon called a halt to these proceedings, feeling that they would alienate believing Christians from the republic. Nevertheless, Robespierre was convinced that Catholicism was fundamentally incompatible with the ideals of the republic, and set about devising an official religion which would serve the needs of the state. This emerged finally in the spring of 1794 as the Cult of the Supreme Being, which seemed to him to reconcile moral values with revolutionary principles and eliminate superstition and the corrupt influence of a priesthood; it retained only two positive articles of faith: belief in a Supreme Being and belief in the immortality of the soul. On 20 Prairial (June 8, 1794), Robespierre inaugurated the new religion in a ceremony in honor of the Supreme Being held in the Tuileries gardens. On this occasion he delivered an oration in which he denounced tyrants and exalted the Supreme Being, who had decreed the republic. At the end of the speech he declared, "French republicans, it is your task to purify the earth which they [tyrants] have defiled and to recall Justice which they have banished. Liberty and Virtue issued together from the Divinity: one cannot endure among men without the other." He then proceeded to demonstrate allegorically the triumph of Wisdom by setting fire to figures of Atheism, Vice, and Folly. From the ruins emerged a statue of Wisdom triumphant.

Another way to gain understanding of the Republic of Virtue is to examine the character and ideas of Robespierre, its chief exponent. One of the most controversial figures of the revolution, Robespierre has been denounced as a blood thirsty, power-hungry tyrant and praised as "the incorruptible," the man who best embodied the cause of the underprivileged during the revolution and who sought to bring about the equality envisioned by Rousseau. In the presence of these widely diverging opinions it is difficult to arrive at a true estimate of the man. Before the revolution he was an undistinguished but reasonably successful lawyer in Arras, in northern France, unmarried, chaste, and ascetic in his manner of living. Elected to the Estates-General in 1789 as a representative of the Third Estate, he remained relatively obscure in the National Assembly, but achieved a position of prominence in the Jacobin clubs because of his "sheer persistence, dogged consistency [and] fanatical conviction in the rightness of his own ideas." [8] Elected to the Convention, he soon emerged as the leader of the Mountain and after the elimination of successive opponents, became virtual dictator in the final stages of the Terror. Contemporaries described him as small and thin. During the revolutionary era, when most men adopted clothing that was informal or even careless, Robespierre continued to dress meticulously in the style of the Old Regime, wearing a light-blue coat and breeches, a clean frilled shirt, and carefully powdered hair. Portraits reveal a small face with eyes set far apart, a mouth with corners turned up in a slight smile; to some contemporaries his features were those

[8] Gordon Wright, *France in Modern Times* (Chicago, 1950), pp. 69–70.

of a cat or a tiger. Single-minded, fanatic devotion to a cause is perhaps the key to his personality, and to his success. In Crane Brinton's words, "Robespierre survived because the Terror was in large part a religious movement, and Robespierre had many of the qualities of a second-rate religious leader."[9] He regarded his opponents not simply as personal enemies, but as wicked men determined to prevent the salvation of mankind on earth.

One of the reasons for the success of the Terrorist regime was unquestionably the existence of a national emergency which demanded drastic measures. With the gradual removal of the threat of foreign invasion, and with the end of the civil war in the provinces, the sense of crisis abated. Just as a victorious coalition is apt to dissolve when war is over, so the victorious Jacobins began to be plagued with internal divisions and factionalism. It would be an exaggeration to refer to the several factions as political parties; rather they were loosely formed groups organized around particular individuals. The Robespierrists were clearly the leading faction in the Committee of Public Safety by the beginning of 1794, but they were challenged by two other groups. One consisted of the Dantonists, or followers of Jacques Danton, the hero of the early days of the republic. Danton had remained one of the active leaders of the Mountain up to the fall of 1793, when he was outflanked by the more fanatic members of the Committee of Public Safety and forced into temporary retirement. But his belief that the revolution had proceeded far enough and that it was time for a return to a more moderate, conciliatory regime won him the support of a varied assortment of men—political adventurers, war profiteers, businessmen—at least some of whom hoped to benefit personally from a relaxation of the controls of the Terror. Danton's return to an active political role in the Convention early in 1794 appeared particularly menacing to Robespierrists. To the left of the Robespierrists emerged an even less coherent group around the Parisian demagogue Jacques Hébert (1755–1794); they called for an intensification of the Terror, further economic controls, a renewed attack on the Church, and concentration of greater power in the radical *sections* of Paris.

Aware of the threat to his position from these groups, Robespierre proceeded vigorously against them both by playing one off against the other. The turn of the Hébertists came first, in March, 1794. Capitalizing on the anti-Parisian sentiment of provincial members of the Convention, Robespierre (with Dantonist support) secured from that body the indictment of the Hébertists before the Revolutionary Tribunal; the result was death by guillotine for the Hébertist leaders. A few weeks later he turned on the Dantonists. Charging Danton and his colleagues with criminal acts commit-

[9] Crane Brinton, *A Decade of Revolution, 1789–1799* (New York, 1934), p. 108.

ted in office, Robespierre persuaded the frightened Convention to condemn them as well.

With both opposing factions eliminated, Robespierre appeared to have the situation in control, and could concentrate on creating the Republic of Virtue. But before long the dictator himself was in trouble. Many members of the Convention became fearful for their own safety after this double proscription. As if to confirm their fears, Robespierre convinced the Convention, in June, 1794, to pass a law speeding up the procedures of the Revolutionary Tribunal in Paris. With these new powers the tribunal sent some 1,300 victims to their death in the following six weeks. With the exception of the period following the suppression of the revolt in the Vendée, no stage of the Terror witnessed a greater number of executions than occurred in June and July of 1794. The result was the rallying of Robespierre's opponents to a plot conceived by Joseph Fouché (1763–1820), a former deputy on mission who had been dismissed because of his excessive brutality toward the people of Lyons. The climax came on July 27 (9 Thermidor in the revolutionary calendar). Appearing on the floor of the Convention to deliver a speech denouncing his enemies, Robespierre found himself howled down by the deputies. His last-minute attempt to rally the support of loyal Jacobins and the Paris Commune for an uprising against the hostile Convention failed. When troops of the Convention discovered him among the insurrectionists at the Hôtel de Ville, Robespierre apparently tried to shoot himself, but succeeded merely in shattering his lower jaw. The next day he was sent, along with twenty-one of his closest associates, to the guillotine.

Robespierre's death is generally viewed as a critical event in the history of the revolution, for it marked the beginning of the "Thermidorean reaction" against the extremes of the Terrorist regime. This development had not been anticipated by Fouché and his fellow conspirators, who were primarily concerned with saving their own lives, but the desire of most Frenchmen for a relaxation of tensions and an end to violence was strong enough to enable the moderates to regain control. Within the next few months the Convention, under the leadership of the moderate Thermidoreans, eliminated the Paris Commune, stripped the Committee of Public Safety of its powers, closed many of the Jacobin clubs, and removed the price and wage controls imposed by the Terrorist government. A similar reaction against the Terror appeared in the behavior of ordinary Frenchmen. For example, the Republic of Virtue had been characterized by a mode of dress that was austere and without frills. Patriotic Jacobin men—with the notable exception of Robespierre—had abandoned the *culottes*, or fancy knee breeches, of the aristocracy in favor of the simple, long trousers of the workingman. (Indeed, the term *sans-culottes* was used from 1792 to 1794 to describe the active, militant members of the Paris *sections* who played so important a role during the Terror.) Women had dressed in flowing white robes like those worn by females of the Roman republic. Both sexes had substituted for the wigs and powdered hair of the Old Regime hair styles that were simple and unaffected. During the Thermidorean reaction, fashions changed rapidly as men and women returned to more revealing and flamboyant clothing. At the same time, the French once again began to indulge in the pleasures that had been banned in the preceding months. Theaters, cafés, and ballrooms flourished in the freer atmosphere.

The Thermidorean era was not without its difficulties, however. With the relaxation of economic controls, inflation and its consequent hardships for the poorer classes returned. The spring of 1795 was marked by bread riots, and working-class agitation in Paris was exploited by the survivors of the Jacobin organization, who sought to direct it against the Convention. In the end, however, the only result of these demonstrations was the elimination of the remaining Jacobin leaders, who were shipped off to exile.

Despite the success of the Thermidoreans in ending the Jacobin threat, and despite the continued victories of the French armies, which led in 1795 to the conclusion of peace with both Prussia and Spain, the Convention was not generally popular. Its lack of support was dramatically illustrated by the reception accorded the Constitution of 1795, which was completed in August. Opponents of the new constitution objected not to its specific provisions, but to the condition that two thirds of the members of the new assembly were to be drawn from the rolls of the outgoing Convention. (These members came to be called "perpetuals.") The stipulation had been included to prevent extensive royalist victories in the forthcoming elections, but it was interpreted as merely an attempt by the members of the Convention to perpetuate their own power. Indeed, resentment against this proposal was so great that on October 4 (13 Vendémiaire) an insurrection against the Convention broke out in Paris. The uprising failed and would probably have been forgotten had it not been for the fact that the defense of the Convention was entrusted to young General Bonaparte, who dispersed the attackers with a "whiff of grapeshot." Bonaparte's success enabled the Convention to sit out its appointed term. Three weeks later the body dissolved itself and the Directory, the last government of the revolutionary era, came into being.

The Directory, 1795–1799

For the student of the revolution the years of the Directory, lasting from 1795 to 1799, have an anticlimactic quality. Following the excitement of the initial years of the revolution, the achievements of the National Assembly, and the extreme ruthlessness of the Reign of Terror, the Directory appears a prosaic interlude, finally brought to an end by the aggressive and dramatic dictatorship of Napoleon Bonaparte. Many French historians have termed the Directory incompetent in its handling of financial problems, inept in the conduct of foreign policy, and cynical in its manipulation of elections and electoral results. There is a measure of truth in each of these charges, but the tendency in recent years has been to take into account the magnitude of the problems facing the Directory, most of them inherited from the preceding regimes, and to be a little more charitable toward France's leaders during this era. And if the Directory was a government not distinguished for its positive achievements, it must be remembered that Frenchmen, after six years of revolution and three years of war, were looking more for order and stability than for innovation and excitement. Apologists for the regime have even pointed out that in a pragmatic way the Directory developed some of the techniques—administrative, electoral, and financial—which have been attributed to the Napoleonic government or which became standard in nineteenth-century bourgeois states. Finally, it should be noted that the regime collapsed in 1799 not as a result of its own inefficiency and corruption (as has often been suggested), but because a few determined individuals, with the support of the army, set out to destroy it.

In some respects the political institutions of the Directory were comparable to those of the constitutional monarchy. Power was shared by the executive and legislative branches, with the executive now consisting of five directors instead of a hereditary monarch. These five were to chosen initially by the legislative body; after the first two years the legislative body was to replace one director annually. The legislative body, instead of being a unicameral assembly, was to consist of two councils, the Council of Ancients and the Council of Five Hundred. The latter was to initiate and discuss bills; the former could adopt or reject them. As in the Constitution of 1791, the suffrage was restricted, this time to those who paid a direct tax on wealth, landed or personal, and to soldiers who had fought for the republic. Such a restriction denied the vote to less than two million adult males out of a total of seven million, but because all top officials (including representatives to the legislative councils) were elected indirectly, the real power of franchise rested with a relatively limited group of wealthy men. In addition, it turned out that on more than one occasion the directors— dissatisfied with the results of an election—simply excluded legally elected deputies and named their opponents to the vacant seats. They defended such procedures on the grounds that the regime was threatened on the right by partisans of a royalist restoration and on the left by heirs of the Jacobins anxious to establish a democratic republic. That these threats were not wholly imaginary is proved by the sizable vote which went to opposition deputies in the elections to the legislative councils in 1797 and 1799, and by the several attempts to overthrow the regime.

One of these, not very significant at the time in terms of the number of people involved or of its chances for success, was the Conspiracy of the Equals, led in 1795–1796 by François Émile Babeuf (1760–1797), who, drawing his inspiration from the celebrated social reformers of the Roman republic, called himself "Gracchus." This episode, which ended in complete failure, has been singled out for considerable attention because some people detect in the egalitarian ideas of Babeuf the germs of modern socialist doctrine. He did, in fact, go considerably beyond the Jacobins, calling for the abolition of private property and the establishment of a communal society, but he did not spell out in detail the way in which these goals were to be achieved and he was content to proclaim as his immediate goal the restoration of the Constitution of 1793. In any event, the Conspiracy of the Equals was betrayed in advance by some of its members, and its leaders were arrested, tried, and condemned to death or exile.

Considerably more dangerous to the government was the recrudescence of the right in 1797, since the conservative camp included many who favored a restoration of the monarchy. Because the young son of Louis XVI had died in prison in 1795, royalists regarded one of the former king's brothers—Louis Xavier Stanislas, count of Provence (1755–1824)—as the legitimate heir to the throne. The prospect of a restoration was certainly unwelcome to those former members of the Convention who had voted for the death of Louis XVI and therefore feared reprisals against themselves as regicides. When elections to the legislative councils in 1797 returned a large bloc of conservative deputies, the moment seemed opportune for a rightist *coup d'état*. In order to forestall such an event, the three moderates among the directors—Jean François Rewbell, Louis Marie LaRévellière-Lépeaux, and the former viscount of Barras—called troops into the capital, claiming the existence of a royalist plot. Under their leadership the "loyal" members of the legislative councils nullified the elections of almost two hundred conservative deputies and condemned to deportation the two other directors, François de Barthélemy and Lazare Carnot. Barthélemy's secret royalist sympathies had been discovered, and Carnot had made the mistake of trying to heal the rift among the directors. This was the *coup d'état* of Fructidor (September 4, 1797); it ended, for the time being, the threat from the right.

When, in elections the following year, the left wing enjoyed a dramatic rise in its representation, the directors resorted to similar tactics and restored the balance by excluding from their seats many of those who had been elected. The legislative councils, resentful of the high-handed tactics of the directors and spurred on by the revived Jacobin clubs, retaliated in June, 1799, by arbitrarily replacing four of the directors with men whose outlook was more radical. The only director who survived all these changes was the pleasure-loving ex-noble Barras, who had been responsible, along with Bonaparte, for the defense of the Convention during the uprising of 1795.

His colleagues now were Sieyès, who had served in the Convention and stayed on in the legislative body; Roger Ducos, a former Girondin; Louis Jérôme Gohier, a former minister of justice; and General Jean François Moulin. Although Sieyès had been named a director, he had nothing but contempt for the existing regime and was determined to strengthen the authority of the executive branch, by a change in the constitution if necessary. He found sympathy and support for his views among army leaders who were known to favor greater executive power, but because they had served the republic, feared the possibility of a restoration of the monarchy. Certainly these were the views of young General Bonaparte, who had made his reputation fighting in the defense of the republic, but scorned the parliamentary maneuvering that characterized the Directory.

Bonaparte, as we shall discover, had been absent from France for more than a year as commander of the celebrated Egyptian campaign, but had kept himself informed about political developments in Paris. Convinced that he could turn the disorders suffered by the Directory to his personal advantage, he slipped out of Egypt in the summer of 1799 and returned to France. Arriving unannounced on the Mediterranean coast, he established contact with the directors Sieyès and Ducos with a view to collaboration. Sieyès, as we have seen, had been contemplating a *coup d'état*, and he now determined to use Bonaparte to guarantee its success. Having reached an agreement, the two fixed 18 Brumaire (November 9; 1799) as the date for their seizure of power. A pretext for the *coup* was found in an alleged Jacobin plot against the regime. The legislative councils were summoned to meet at Saint-Cloud, outside of Paris, ostensibly because they would not be subjected there to pressure from the Paris mob. Sieyès and Ducos resigned their posts in the Directory. Of the three remaining directors, Barras was prevailed upon to resign and the other two were arrested, so the government was without an executive. At this stage Napoleon appeared before the Council of Five Hundred to ask that he be given special powers to deal with the crisis confronting the country. Some of the deputies, seeing through the conspiracy, challenged him to produce evidence of a Jacobin plot. When he was unable to do so, they were on the verge of ordering his arrest. But quick action by his younger brother Lucien, who was president of the lower house, prevented the entire venture from collapsing. Lucien rallied the troops stationed outside the hall to Napoleon's cause, assuring them that he would plunge his sword through his brother's heart if Napoleon ever plotted against the liberty of the French people. Inspired by this declaration, the troops followed Napoleon's order to clear the hall of all deputies. A rump session of those sympathetic to the conspirators later voted full powers to Bonaparte, Sieyès, and Ducos, proclaiming them "temporary consuls." The *coup d'état* of Brumaire had succeeded; France had a military dictatorship. In this way the somewhat dreary political history of the Directory came to an end. It is perhaps worth pointing out, however, that the successive changes in the composition of the government under the Directory occurred with a minimum of violence and loss of life. In this respect, at least, the Directory was an improvement over the Terror, during which dissidents were normally sent to the guillotine. For a parallel in our own era one may compare the terrorist regime of Stalin with the more moderate administrations of his successors.

An evaluation of the Directory must take into account more than its political evolution. One of the government's acute problems was economic—a financial crisis of significant proportions inherited from the preceding regime. By 1796 the *assignats* had depreciated to less than 1 per cent of their face value. In an effort to establish the paper currency on a sounder foundation, the government stabilized the *assignats* at one thirtieth of their face value and announced that they could be exchanged on that basis for new paper money, the *mandats territoriaux*. Those who acquired the *mandats* could use them to buy the remaining nationalized lands at a price set by the government. In this way the *assignats* were withdrawn from circulation, but the measure was ultimately unsuccessful since the *mandats*, in turn, depreciated to about 10 per cent of their face value. In 1797 the Directory returned to a metal-backed currency, and although this step did not end the financial difficulties of the regime, it restored a measure of confidence among French businessmen. Other measures taken to improve the financial position of the government were the sharp curtailment of expenditures and the reorganization of the servicing of the national debt. The latter step, though publicized as the "consolidation" of one third of the debt, constituted in fact a repudiation by the government of the other two thirds and temporarily undermined confidence in public credit. In the balance, however, the financial condition of the government and the country was better in 1799 than it had been in 1795. The Directory restored a measure of order to France's finances and laid the groundwork for Napoleon's subsequent fiscal reforms.

One major objective of the Directory was the conclusion of a general European peace which would at the same time guarantee France's security. This was never achieved. Prospects for peace were not bad in 1795. The Thermidorean regime had already ended the war with all of France's major enemies except Austria and Britain. In its first two years the Directory made more than one attempt to reach an agreement with Britain, but negotiations were complicated by France's determination to retain the lands that it had conquered in Belgium, Savoy, and Nice. Against Austria the Directory mounted a three-pronged attack in 1796. Two French armies were to invade the empire from the upper and lower Rhine. A third army, under the command of the twenty-seven-year-old General Bonaparte, was to drive the Austrians out of Italy and join the other two by way of the Tyrol. Although the northern armies were successful at first, they later ran into a counterattack led by the Austrian Archduke Charles Louis (1771–1847), who forced them to retreat. Bonaparte's Italian campaign was little short of phenomenal and established his reputation as France's most brilliant general. In a matter of months he advanced eastward along the Mediterranean coast, inflicted an initial defeat upon the Austrians, and managed to knock their Sardinian allies out of the war. Pursuing the Austrians farther, he ultimately gained control of most of northern Italy and then turned southward, toward Rome and the Papal States. The pope hastened to conclude a treaty with him, ceding the Romagna and the legations of Bologna and Ferrara to the French. In the spring of 1797 Bonaparte crossed the Alps to meet Archduke Charles advancing from Germany, and pushed the Austrian forces back to within seventy-five miles of the capital at Vienna. But because the Venetians had risen against French control and threatened his rear, Napoleon decided to negotiate a preliminary peace with the Austrians at Leoben. Some of the terms of his truce were incorporated six months later in the formal Treaty of Campoformio between Austria and France (October, 1797). Among the more important articles of this treaty were: first, the cession to France of Austria's Belgian provinces; second, the cession of Venice and the surrounding territory to Austria as compensation (Napoleon had crushed the revolt there and occupied the city); and third, the recognition by Austria of a new Cisalpine Republic, set up by the French, which included all of Napoleon's conquests in northern and central Italy. In secret clauses of the treaty Austria agreed to cede imperial territories on the left bank of the Rhine to France if France would support Austrian claims to Salzburg and territories in Bavaria. The German princes, thus dispossessed of territories ceded to France, would receive compensation elsewhere in the Holy Roman Empire. Lastly, Austria agreed to a congress to discuss further the execution of this treaty in the empire and to consider the problems arising from the cession of the left bank of the Rhine to France. The Treaty of Campoformio provided a temporary respite in the struggle between France and Austria, but as we shall see before the territorial ramifications of the treaty in Germany could be settled, Austria, Russia, and Britain formed the Second Coalition against the French, and a general war resumed late in 1798.

Meanwhile, peace negotiations with the British had broken down toward the end of 1797, leaving Britain the lone power, except for its ally, Portugal, at war with the French. France had the support at this time of the Batavian Republic (Holland) and had concluded a naval and commercial pact with Spain in the summer of 1796. Although the French talked of an invasion of England and even gave Bonaparte the task of training troops for this purpose, the idea was abandoned as premature in 1798, and the Directory decided to attack Britain through its empire. Bonaparte was authorized to organize an expeditionary force of about thirty-five thousand troops for an invasion of Egypt. Apparently he had contemplated such an enterprise for a number of years as part of his dream for oriental conquest on the scale of Alexander the Great. He received support from the diplomat Talleyrand, who helped to persuade the Directory of the advantages of such a plan. The acquisition of Egypt, it was argued, would be the prelude to a march to India, where Tipu Sahib (ruled 1782–1799), a powerful native prince who had recently revolted against British rule, would join the French in driving the British from India. In the meantime, the acquisition of the Isthmus of Suez could be exploited by construction of a canal; this would give the French commercial supremacy over the British, who would be forced to continue their costly voyages around the Cape of Good Hope.

The expedition was organized in great secrecy. It sailed from Toulon in May, 1798. En route, Napoleon launched a surprise attack on the island fortress of Malta, which he took without difficulty. His forces landed at Abukir in June, captured Alexandria without firing a shot, and moved on to Cairo. Egypt, nominally a part of the Ottoman Empire, was defended only by a native military elite, the Mamelukes. Despite their excellent cavalry they were no match for a trained European army with artillery, and went down to defeat in the Battle of the Pyramids. So far, the expedition had been a complete success, but shortly afterward it met disaster at sea. The French fleet that had transported the expedition to Egypt, still anchored at Abukir Bay, was surprised and completely annihilated by a British fleet under the command of Admiral Horatio Nelson (1758–1805). Despite his initial victories Napoleon found himself a virtual prisoner in Egypt, cut off from his source of supplies and unable to carry out his ambitious plans for the conquest of India. Refusing to admit defeat, he invaded Syria, another possession of the Ottoman Empire, but after early successes, his army suffered from an outbreak of the plague and was forced to retreat in haste to Egypt. Napoleon's forces were still strong enough to withstand an attack by Turkish forces at Abukir in July, 1799, but he realized that he could gain no further advantage for himself by remaining in the Near East, and he managed to slip back to France, where, as we have seen, he joined the conspiracy of the directors Ducos and Sieyès. The troops which he abandoned in Egypt in 1799 remained there until 1801, when the British finally defeated them and restored Egypt to the sultan.

FRANCE AND EUROPE

The War of the Second Coalition, 1798–1802

Napoleon's invasion of Egypt and his apparent intention of dismembering the Ottoman Empire was one cause of the formation in 1798 of the Second Coalition of European powers against France, for Paul I, tsar of

Russia (1796–1801), viewed himself as the protector of Turkish interests and was alarmed by French expansion in the east. Moreover, he resented the French seizure of the island of Malta, since he held the title of grand master of the Knights of Malta. Russia was therefore receptive to Britain's proposals for an alliance against France, which was, in fact, concluded in December, 1798. Austria was also prepared to renew the war against France, having come to realize after the Treaty of Campoformio that the French not only intended to consolidate their domination over territories already acquired but also had further ambitions, particularly in Switzerland and the Italian peninsula.

Early in 1798 the Directory used a disturbance in Rome as a pretext for intervening there, expelling the pope, and establishing a Roman Republic, which was added to the two "sister" republics in Italy already under French control (the Cisalpine Republic and the Ligurian Republic, the name given by the French to the former Republic of Genoa). In the same year the French found a pretext for extending the republican form of government to the Swiss cantons; the centralized Helvetic Republic was proclaimed and brought into the French orbit. In Holland, which the armies of the Convention had invaded and conquered in 1795 and where the Batavian Republic had been established, the provisional government was replaced in 1798 by a regime modeled on the Directory; an alliance imposed upon this new government secured for the French valuable financial and military aid.

Each of these moves added to the suspicion and distrust of the other powers and increased their willingness to enter a new coalition against the French. The most significant change in the composition of the bloc allied against France was the substitution of Russia for Prussia. The latter, having concluded a peace with France in 1795, remained neutral during the war of the Second Coalition.

Geoffrey Bruun, in *Europe and the French Imperium,* has pointed out that the aims of the Second Coalition, summarized in a set of proposals drawn up in 1798 by the English prime minister, William Pitt, foreshadowed the final settlement imposed upon France in 1814–1815.[10] Essentially, the goal of the allies at this time and throughout the Napoleonic era was to restore the balance of power that had been upset by the conquests of France's revolutionary armies. Their aims included the restoration of Holland and Switzerland to independence, the union of the Belgian provinces with Holland under the rule of the *stadholder,* and the restoration of Savoy and Piedmont to the kingdom of Sardinia. Austria was to be compensated with Italian territories for the loss of its Belgian provinces, and Prussia would be permitted annexations in northern Germany. It was tacitly assumed that Russia would acquire territories at the expense of the Ottoman Empire and that Britain would retain all of its colonial conquests.

[10] G. Bruun, *Europe and the French Imperium,* (New York, 1938), p. 38.

Such a program should have provided the powers with sufficient incentive to unite in bringing about the defeat of France, but in fact, the Second Coalition and all subsequent coalitions except for the last one, in 1814–1815, suffered from the same weakness: the inability of the allies to coordinate their efforts effectively enough to win the war. Over and over again, alliances fell apart because one or another of the powers was tempted by rewards offered by Napoleon and decided to treat separately with France. Only when France threatened to dominate all Europe, and when the powers had learned that Napoleon's promises were worthless, did they collaborate to bring about France's defeat.

It can also be argued that France's repeated victories ultimately depended upon the character of its armies, and after 1796, upon the genius of Napoleon as a general. Bonaparte's qualities as a military leader will be discussed in the next chapter. As to the character of the French armies, we have already noted the crusading spirit of the French citizen-soldier after the proclamation of the republic, his sense of fighting for a nation in which he had a personal stake. This attitude apparently inspired in the average soldier greater individual initiative, more confidence in his own resources, than was characteristic of troops fighting in the armies of the absolutist powers. Georges Lefebvre argues that the passion for equality and the hatred of aristocrats common among soldiers during the Jacobin phase of the revolution lasted into the Napoleonic era.[11] One reason for the persistence of this attitude was Napoleon's preservation of the system of promotion through the ranks that had developed in the revolutionary armies. Napoleon did ultimately create a military aristocracy with privileges of its own, but advancement in his armies depended not upon birth, nor even upon education, but upon boldness and bravery in battle. Because officers were drawn from the ranks, a kind of *camaraderie* existed between them and their troops that was found much less often in the armies of France's enemies. These, then, were some of the reasons for the frequent triumph of France's armies over forces far superior numerically.

In the war of the Second Coalition, Tsar Paul I (who had succeeded Catherine the Great in 1796) sent his armies deep into Europe to join with the Austrian and British forces in battles against the French. Russian troops under the command of General Suvorov (1729–1800) fought alongside Austrian armies in a generally successful campaign against the French in the Italian peninsula and later in Switzerland. But a joint Anglo-Russian army under the duke of York failed to drive the French out of Holland because of stiff French resistance and friction between the allied forces. The coalition's principal successes came in the spring and summer of 1799, but a new wave of Jacobin-inspired enthusiasm in the French armies turned the tide even before the *coup d'état* in November. The first ruler to defect from the

[11] Georges Lefebvre, *Napoléon,* fourth ed. (Paris, 1953), p. 192.

alliance was the tsar. Disgusted by the strategic errors of his Austrian allies and by their refusal to consult him about the disposition of Italian territories, Paul withdrew from the coalition in October, 1799, and in the following year, irritated by Britain's arrogant use of sea power, he revived the League of Armed Neutrality, a collaborative effort of Sweden, Denmark, Prussia, and Russia to protect neutral shipping against arbitrary search by British naval vessels. Paul even showed some disposition toward concluding an alliance with France, but his assassination in March, 1801, brought about an end to any such project. The other allies fought on for a while longer, but as we shall see, Austria came to terms with France in 1801 and Britain did so in 1802, thus dissolving the Second Coalition.

REACTION OUTSIDE FRANCE, 1792–1799

In discussing the history of the republic from its proclamation in September, 1792, to the *coup d'état* of Brumaire we have had occasion to see the profound influence which France's war with the First Coalition had upon its internal development. But we have said little about the spirit in which the war was fought, the policies of French governments toward conquered territories, and the continuing reaction of other powers to the revolution and to France's conquests.

With the proclamation of the republic a change occurred in Frenchmen's attitude toward the war. It was still viewed, as it had been at the outset, as a defensive war against the European monarchs bent on crushing the revolution. But a new note is detectable in some of the decrees of the Convention issued in the latter part of 1792. In November, for example, the Convention declared in the name of the French nation that it would ". . . grant fraternity and aid to all peoples who wish to recover their liberty . . ."[12] Another decree, occasioned a month later by resistance in the Austrian Netherlands to French annexation, was even more specific:

In territories which are or may be occupied by the armies of the Republic, the generals shall proclaim immediately, in the name of the French nation, the sovereignty of the people, the suppression of all established authorities and of existing imposts or taxes, the abolition of the tithe, of feudalism, of seigneurial rights, both feudal and *censuel*, fixed or contingent, of *banalités*, of real and personal servitude, of hunting and fishing privileges, of *corvées*, of nobility, and generally of all privileges.

They shall announce to the people that they bring it peace, aid, fraternity, liberty, and equality, and they shall convoke it thereafter in primary or communal assemblies, in order to create and organize a provisional administration and justice. . . .

12 *A Documentary Survey of the French Revolution*, p. 381.

The French nation declares that it will treat as an enemy of the people anyone who, refusing liberty and equality, or renouncing them, might wish to preserve, recall, or treat with the prince and the privileged castes; it promises and engages itself not to subscribe to any treaty, and not to lay down its arms until after the establishment of the sovereignty and independence of the people upon whose territory the troops of the Republic have entered, who shall have adopted the principles of equality and established a free and popular government.[3]

Clearly the war had become, as the French armies took the offensive, a crusade for the liberation of subject peoples from their royal or feudal oppressors. And here the French found a pretext for the annexation of conquered territories, which might, if left unprotected, be reconquered by their former rulers. It would be unfair to conclude that the idealistic proclamations served merely as a cloak for more cynical territorial ambitions. Some of the republican leaders were sincerely determined to bring the benefits of the revolution to the peoples of Europe, but the fact remains that the liberated peoples were not normally given an opportunity to choose between their liberators and their former oppressors. The customary procedure was for a minority of republican or French sympathizers in an occupied region to petition the Convention for annexation to the republic. Another justification for the incorporation of border regions into the republic was the claim that they lay within France's "natural frontiers"— the Pyrenees, the Alps, the Rhine, the Atlantic, and the Mediterranean. For example, when a delegation from Savoy presented its petition for annexation, the Convention accepted it on the grounds, first, that the people of Savoy shared the sentiments of France, and second, that the territory of Savoy lay within "the limits set by the hand of nature to the French Republic."[14]

The ease with which the border regions were assimilated into the republic varied from place to place. In general, the annexation of Savoy and Nice met with little resistance. The Savoyards were mostly French-speaking anyway and their way of life was quite similar to that of Frenchmen in neighboring Dauphiné. Although the inhabitants of Nice were of Italian stock and spoke an Italian dialect, they had no strong objections to incorporation in the French state. In the provinces of the Rhineland, pro-French orientation and sentiment among the bourgeoisie had been strong even before the revolution, and the granting of full ownership of the land to the peasantry won them over to French control.

The French ran into the greatest resistance in the Belgian provinces conquered from the Austrian empire. Despite their abortive revolt against Austria in 1791, the people of the Austrian Netherlands were not eager to

---

[13] *Ibid.*, pp. 382–383.

[14] Quoted by Gershoy, *The French Revolution and Napoleon*, p. 241.

submit to French domination. The leaders of a pro-French minority, exiled by Austrian authorities after the suppression of the revolt, returned with the conquering armies of Dumouriez late in 1792. Supported by the French armies, this group set up Jacobin clubs throughout the conquered provinces and embarked upon an anticlerical campaign which quickly antagonized the devout. When the Convention sent in commissioners to confiscate Church and royal lands and impose new taxes, a rash of civil disturbances and general discontent resulted. The retreat forced upon the French in 1793 meant a temporary respite, but when the armies of the republic returned in 1794, the methods of the occupying authorities were far more ruthless. Now the provinces were annexed outright and integrated completely into the French administrative structure. The republic was well on its way toward using methods later employed by the Napoleonic dictatorship in conquered territories.

The initial responses in Britain and Germany to the French Revolution, and the steps leading to the outbreak of war between France and the First Coalition, have already been described. Once they were actively involved in a war with France, the British, Prussian, and Austrian governments found it easier to deal with revolutionary sympathizers in their own countries, who could now be branded traitors. All European rulers denounced the threat of "Jacobinism," viewing it as an international conspiracy subsidized by French money and supported by French agents. To what extent an international conspiracy actually existed is very difficult to determine, but there is no question that its ramifications were exaggerated by contemporary rulers. Where revolutionary sentiment existed outside of France—and it was rare after the September Massacres, the aggressive decrees of the Convention, and the execution of the king—it was encouraged by a minority of native sympathizers rather than by paid French agents. Even governments not actively at war with France proceeded against such individuals with great vigor. In central and eastern Europe they were arrested for the most insignificant political offenses and given heavy penalties. For example, a Hungarian Jacobin who dared to translate into Magyar the "Marseillaise," the French revolutionary song, was condemned to death. To prevent the infiltration of French ideas, the most rigid censorship was instituted in the Austria of Francis II and the Russia of Catherine and Paul.

In Britain, where the legal tradition afforded greater protection for individual liberties, the government had a more difficult time proceeding against supposed Jacobins and radical societies. Even after the war with France had begun, a number of such organizations, supported primarily by artisans and tradesmen, continued to express their sympathy for the revolution and to pursue the cause of parliamentary reform. Pitt, the prime minister, increasingly exasperated by these agitators, finally decided to proceed against them. In a series of state trials in 1794 twelve leaders of the two most prominent London societies—the Corresponding Society and the Society for Promoting Constitutional Information—were charged with treason. Despite overwhelming anti-French sentiment in the country, the juries refused to condemn the accused because of insufficient evidence. The defendants were political reformers eager to change the existing regime, but no real evidence that they intended violence or were actively promoting the overthrow of the monarchy was produced in the trials. As the war continued, Pitt managed to secure legislation from Parliament which gave him greater powers in dealing with the radical opposition. The Two Acts passed in 1795–1796 widened the definition of treason to include writings and speeches as well as actions and banned all large public meetings except those held by special authority. Further regulations in 1799 forbade the existence of secret associations or federations, including trade unions, instituted press censorship, and required the registration of all printing presses. With this legislation the Tory government effectively stifled radical agitation.

By and large, the revolution was not responsible for immediate changes in the political and social institutions of the countries pitted against France. Except for a tightening of censorship restrictions and judicial procedures, the governments of Prussia, Austria, and Russia remained immune to change, their privileged aristocracies even more committed than before to preserving the *status quo*. The principal impact of the revolution in Britain was not on governmental institutions, but rather on the balance of the two political parties in Parliament. The Whigs, who were divided even before the war with France, were further split by Fox's stand of sympathy with the principles of the revolution and his opposition to Pitt's repressive measures. When the duke of Portland defected to Pitt's government in July, 1794, taking a majority of the Whigs with him, there was practically no opposition left in Parliament; the Tory government had the backing of both the landed gentry and of the newer moneyed interests. During the years of the revolution was formed the rigid Toryism, characterized by opposition to reform of any kind, that persisted until well after the defeat of Napoleon.

A FINAL APPRAISAL

Despite the initial attraction of the revolutionary ideals of liberty, equality, and fraternity to sympathizers in countries other than France, their primary impact during the decade 1789–1799 was on Frenchmen, and they have continued to affect Frenchmen ever since. In a nation highly conscious of its own history, the revolutionary tradition has come to mean different things to different groups, but it has persisted, being repeatedly invoked in the series of revolutions that France underwent during the nineteenth century and in the political crises of the twentieth. The key to a French-man's political outlook may still be found in his attitude toward the great revolution.

What impressed contemporaries more than anything else was the fact that revolution had struck in France, the state regarded as the oldest and best established on the continent. For this very reason the uprising seemed to constitute a deadly blow to the cause of absolutism and to the feudal institutions which still prevailed in most of Europe. If the venerable French monarchy and the elite of the European nobility could not withstand such assaults upon their privileges, other European rulers and aristocrats might well doubt their capacity to meet similar challenges in their own countries. The attempts of the revolutionary armies after 1792 to liberate the rest of Europe by force heightened their fears and ultimately stiffened their will to resist any changes in the old order.

In the long run, no country entirely escaped the impact of the French Revolution; indeed, its influence continues to be felt even today. It not only shattered long-standing traditions and deep rooted institutions but also proclaimed new ideals which have powerfully affected succeeding genera-tions both inside and outside of France.

For the "revolutionary virus" (as it was described by conservatives) could not be confined to France indefinitely. Despite the efforts of European rulers to quarantine the "disease," many individuals were infected by it and became its carriers in the Restoration era following the defeat of the revolutionary and Napoleonic armies. The 1789 Declaration of the Rights of Man, and the successive constitutions of revolutionary France, became major sources for ideologies and ideological movements in the nineteenth century. The debt of liberal and nationalist movements to the French Revolution is obvious. Socialists have drawn heavily upon its heritage for theory and strategy. Even conservatives have found it a source of inspira-tion, since their social and political philosophies often take as their starting point a refutation of the doctrines that inspired the great revolution. It will be the task of chapters that follow to make precise the legacy of the French Revolution to nineteenth-century Europeans, showing more particularly how it provided ideals, slogans, and models for the revolts that punctuated the era from 1815 to 1848.

CHAPTER 24

Napoleon

WHATEVER VIEW one takes of the character of Napoleon Bonaparte, whatever aspect of his achievement is emphasized, whether one admires him as a superb military leader or condemns him as the forerunner of twentieth-century dictators, one cannot deny that he dominated his age. He barely qualified as a native Frenchman, for he was born in Corsica into a family of impoverished nobles in 1769, just a year after the island had been taken over by France from Genoa. As a youth, he secured a state scholarship and studied in military schools in France. Partly because he considered himself an alien in a foreign country, he was forced to rely on his own resources and worked assiduously. He became a conscientious student of history and geography as well as of military strategy and tactics. In 1785, when he was only sixteen years old, he was appointed a second lieutenant in the artillery, but because of his foreign extraction his chances for promotion in the royal army were not particularly good. The advent of the revolution suddenly opened up new prospects for him. He returned to Corsica and devoted his energies for the next three or four years to the movement for Corsican independence, which had been his dream since childhood. This phase of his career ended when he broke with Pasquale di Paoli (1725–1807), the leading Corsican patriot, and his entire family was banished from the island. Abandoning his earlier plans, he now became an ardent French patriot and Jacobin.

His role in recapturing the port of Toulon from the royalists and the English in the winter of 1793 earned him a promotion from captain to brigadier general and attracted the notice of the influential politician Barras, who later proved of assistance to him. The fall of Robespierre brought Bonaparte a temporary reversal of fortune. He was arrested as a Terrorist, deprived of his commission, and briefly imprisoned. Subsequently, however, Barras had him put in charge of the defense of the Convention when it was threatened by the uprising of October, 1795, and his success in this enterprise led to his appointment as commander in chief of the Army of the

Interior. At this point he met Joséphine de Beauharnais (1763–1814), the attractive widow of an aristocratic general who had died on the guillotine during the Terror. She was six years his senior, had two children, and was without a fortune, but the young Napoleon fell violently in love with her and married her on March 9, 1796.

Two days before his marriage he was appointed to command the army in Italy, where he first demonstrated his qualities as a military genius; brilliant in offensive warfare, he put emphasis on great speed and mobility and on surprise attacks to disconcert the enemy. He emerged from the Italian campaign a national hero, and the failure of the Egyptian expedition in 1798–1799 did not dim his reputation, partly because the full story of its failure was not known until later.

What manner of man was Napoleon at the time of his accession to power in 1799? From the mountains of conflicting testimony written by his contemporaries, almost invariably biased, it is nearly impossible to arrive at a composite picture. Count André François Miot de Melito (1762–1841), a French councillor of state, who met Napoleon for the first time during his Italian campaign in 1796, recorded his impressions in his memoirs:

> I was quite astonished at his appearance. Nothing could be more unlike the idea my imagination had formed of him . . . I saw a man below the middle height and of an extremely spare figure. His powdered hair, oddly cut and falling squarely below the ears, reached down to his shoulders. He was dressed in a straight coat, buttoned up to the chin, and edged with very narrow gold embroidery, and he wore a tricolored feather in his hat. At first sight he did not strike me as handsome; but his strongly-marked features, his quick and piercing eyes, his brusque and animated gestures revealed an ardent spirit, while his wide and thoughtful brow was that of a profound thinker. He made me sit near him and we talked of Italy. He spoke in short sentences and, at that time of his life, very incorrectly.

Bonaparte the Consul. *Portrait by David. Though unfinished, this is one of the most celebrated portraits of Napoleon in his prime. The Louvre, Paris.*

Most of his contemporaries agreed that he had a remarkable intelligence and an unusual capacity for sustained effort and intense concentration. The following comment by Jean Chaptal (1756–1832), his minister of the interior, who knew him perhaps as well as anyone, discusses his performance as First Consul immediately after the *coup d'état* of Brumaire:

We met in the First Consul's rooms almost every evening, and deliberated fom 10 till 4 or 5 A.M. It was in these conferences that I came to know the great man to whom we had just entrusted the reins of government. Though still young, and with little experience of administrative detail, he brought to our discussions an astonishing clarity, exactness, power of argument, and width of view. An untiring worker, and full of resource, he collected and co-ordinated facts and opinions relating to every part of a huge system of administration with unrivalled sagacity.... Though he worked as much as twenty hours out of the twenty-four, he never showed signs of mental or physical fatigue.[1]

He manifested some of these same qualities as a military commander, his decisions being based on careful planning and detailed knowledge rather than intuition. What seemed to be sudden flashes of insight were actually the fruit of painstaking rational analysis. "Every operation must be done according to a system," he said, "because chance cannot bring about success."[2] This reliance upon reason led many to view Napoleon as a good son of the Enlightenment, but another side of his character made him one of the great heroes of the romantic era. Although he adhered to no established religion, he still felt that his life was guided by what he called his "star," and he referred frequently to the workings of "destiny." And although he might employ careful calculation to achieve specific goals, his ultimate aims seem to have been limitless and undefined. He admired Alexander the Great, Caesar, and Charlemagne not so much for their specific achievements as for their visions of universal empire, which fired his own imagination and inspired his actions. Georges Lefebvre, suggesting the romantic dimension in Napoleon's personality, says, ". . . [the realist] determines his goal, taking into account the possible, and if his imagination and the desire for glory drive him on, he knows where to stop."[3] Napoleon quite clearly was not a realist in this sense, for he recognized no limits to his ambition, and this, in the long run, proved his undoing.

One of the questions most often raised in discussions of Napoleon's domestic policies is whether his regime carried on and—as he said— "crowned" the revolution, or whether it constituted a reversal or denial of

[1] Quoted by James M. Thompson, *Napoleon Bonaparte: His Rise and Fall* (Oxford, 1952), p. 150.

[2] Quoted by Georges Lefebvre, *Napoléon*, fourth ed. (Paris, 1953), p. 67.

[3] *Ibid.*, p. 68.

the revolution. The answer depends in part, of course, on one's definition of the revolution: on whether one is thinking primarily of the accomplishments of the National Assembly and the Legislative Assembly during the moderate phase between 1789 and 1792, or viewing it as the whole succession of regimes between 1789 and 1799, including the Terrorist government and the Directory. Apologists for the view that Napoleon was a true "son of the revolution" argue that the constructive achievements of the initial period were cut short or interrupted during the rule of the Convention and the Directory, and that with his accession to power as First Consul, Bonaparte undertook to complete the work of the revolution. Opponents of this view grant that many measures completed during the Consulate and Empire stem from reforms initiated under the constitutional monarchy, but they argue that the character of Napoleon's political institutions, the way in which he dealt with the opposition, the strict control of opinion during his regime, and indeed the entire spirit of his administration were in direct contrast with the ideals of 1789. Some contend further that Bonaparte really had far more in common with the enlightened despots of the eighteenth century than with the revolutionaries. According to this view, he displayed the same passion for rationalization and systematization that characterized Frederick the Great and Joseph II of Austria, and whatever reforms he instituted were enacted on his initiative within the framework of a despotic government which permitted no criticism. He was, it is argued, the ruler who carried the principles of enlightened despotism to their logical extreme. Like so many other historical questions, this problem of interpretation has no simple solution; we shall be examining in the sections which follow evidence in support of these opposing views.

THE CONSULATE, 1799–1804

The government which emerged from the *coup d'état* of Brumaire was merely a provisional regime. It was up to the three victors who had been named "consuls"—Bonaparte, Sieyès, and Ducos—to provide France with a new constitution and a stable government. After a decade of revolution, civil disorders, and foreign wars, most Frenchmen were willing to sacrifice what appeared to them the illusory benefits of liberty for a regime that could ensure internal tranquility and peace. On the day following the *coup d'état*, the consuls swore to end the civil conflict which had continued sporadically in the west, stabilize finances, codify the laws, and terminate the foreign war with an honorable peace. Most of the energies of the First Consul and his government during the next five years were devoted to the fulfillment of these promises.

The Constitution of the Year VIII (1799), drafted by Sieyès with Bonaparte's collaboration, provided a set of institutions that appeared to preserve republican forms but at the same time gave considerably increased powers to the executive. Although the constitution stipulated that the three consuls who held the executive power were to be elected to ten-year terms by the Senate, it specifically designated as the first incumbents of these offices Bonaparte and the two men he had chosen as his colleagues—Jean Jacques Régis de Cambacérès (1753–1824) and Charles François Lebrun (1739–1824). Instead of two chambers, the national legislature now had three—the Senate, the Tribunate, and the Legislative Body. But their activities were circumscribed and the ways in which their members were chosen made them relatively ineffective. The Senate consisted of eighty men named for life. Initially, a majority of them were to be appointed by the outgoing second and third consuls, who became senators themselves. This group, in turn, was to select the remaining senators from lists presented to them by the Legislative Body, the Tribunate, and the First Consul. What in fact happened was that both the original list of senators and the remainder were selected, with Bonaparte's approval, by Sieyès, one of the outgoing consuls. He, too, named the members of the first Legislative Body and Tribunate.

The Senate had no direct legislative powers unless the constitutionality of a measure was at issue, but it had the power to name the members of the other two chambers from a list of "notables." The notables were chosen through universal suffrage—the only feature of the constitution that was ostensibly democratic—but the privilege of voting was now even less meaningful than it had been under the Constitution of 1791 or the Directory. The voters could elect only a group of notables in their own commune, who then elected one tenth of their number to serve as notables of the department. These, in turn, elected one tenth of *their* number to become the notables of France, from whom the Senate chose the members of the Tribunate and the Legislative Body. The Tribunate, consisting of a hundred men, had the power to discuss measures submitted to it by the First Consul or his advisers, but did not have the power to vote on them. The Legislative Body, three hundred men, had the power to accept or reject measures, but could not discuss them. Since membership in all three bodies was appointive rather than elective, the consuls had little to fear in the way of opposition.

Despite this elaborate set of legislative institutions, the actual work of drafting laws fell to the Council of State, a group of experts appointed by the First Consul and directly dependent upon him.

If there were objections to the authoritarian character of this constitution, they were hardly expressed, for the popular vote registered 3,011,007 in favor and only 1,562 opposed. There is little question that the regime was popular with a great majority of Frenchmen. The new First Consul considered the plebiscite an overwhelming vote of confidence, since his name had appeared in the constitution.

NAPOLEON'S ADMINISTRATION

Napoleon revised his initial constitution in 1802, when he had himself proclaimed consul for life, and in 1804, when he became emperor. In each case he sought approval for the increase of his powers through plebiscites which returned him overwhelming majorities. As First Consul, and later as emperor, he carried out an impressive series of administrative, financial, educational, and legal reforms.

Those who view Napoleon as a son of the revolution point out that he completed the administrative system whose main lines had been laid down by the National Assembly. It is true that he retained the basic geographical divisions established in 1789, but in many other respects, his contributions in this sphere marked a reversal of the basic principles of administration which had guided the revolutionaries. For example, he substituted for the elected officials and local self-government of the years 1789 to 1792, the centrally appointed bureaucrats who have been at the heart of France's administrative system ever since—prefects for the departments, subprefects for the districts, and mayors for the communes. Though local councils still functioned to assist the appointed officials, they too were named from Paris rather than elected. The French have apparently come to prefer such a centralized bureaucracy to the kind of federal structure found in the United States and to the decentralized institutions characteristic of Britain, but such a preference is not in harmony with the intentions of the pioneers of the revolution.

The same emphasis on centralization can be seen in Napoleon's approach to financial problems. The Directory had attempted to restore fiscal stability to France by withdrawing the inflated paper currency which had plagued preceding revolutionary governments and by repudiating two thirds of the national debt. Despite these measures no way had been found to augment revenues, and the credit of the government had been seriously impaired. Napoleon realized that an effective method of assessing and collecting taxes was essential. Therefore, instead of leaving with municipal officials the power to draw up the tax rolls and collect taxes levied by the central government, he turned this responsibility over to representatives of the central government—a general director at Paris, deputy directors for each department, and inspectors and assessors in each commune. In this way the entire machinery of taxation was tightened up, receipts were increased, and the government could predict its expected revenues more precisely. Although the French have proved remarkably ingenious in devising means of evading taxes, the basic system established by Napoleon has persisted to this day. In 1800 Napoleon decreed the creation of the Bank of France, which was intended to ease the problem of government borrowing, stabilize the currency, and facilitate the payment of annuities. In 1803 it was given the exclusive right to issue bank notes in Paris; not until 1848 could it do this for the entire country. Technically a private institution, it acquired a special status because its shareholders included the First Consul, members of his family, and leading state officials.

Napoleon is often given credit for continuing and elaborating upon the system of public education inaugurated during the revolution. The principle of free, elementary education for all children had been first proclaimed in the Constitution of 1791 and was reaffirmed by the Convention, but little progress was made during the revolutionary years in the establishment of primary schools. Nor was the Napoleonic government much more success-ful in expanding the system of primary public education. It has been estimated that only one out of every eight children of school age could be accommodated in primary schools existing in 1813.[4] At the secondary level the Convention provided for the establishment of state-supported "central schools," one for each department and five to be located in Paris. Although some difficulties were encountered in getting these into operation the quality of the teaching in them was high and they were flourishing during the early years of the Consulate. However, in 1802 Napoleon abolished the central schools and substituted for them *lycées* under more direct govern-ment supervision. He also permitted the existence of a limited number of private secondary schools. The *lycées* were intended quite frankly as "nurseries of patriotism." The Napoleonic regime prescribed the curriculum and the teaching schedules, appointed the teachers, and set up a system of inspectors to enforce the regulations. Discipline in the schools was on military lines: students wore uniforms, classes began and ended with the rolling of drums, and students received military instruction from retired officers. In 1808, Napoleon further centralized education by establishing the *Université*—not a university in the usual sense of the term, but a single system incorporating the whole range of public schools from the elementary level up through institutions of higher learning. Again, the purpose was to ensure greater control over education and promote loyalty to the regime. Private and church schools continued to exist under limited supervision by the state even after 1808, but the *Université* embodied the principle recognized during the revolution that education, controlled and supported by the state, should be available to all citizens.

In Napoleon's own opinion, and in the opinion of subsequent generations, one of the most significant achievements of his administration was the compilation of a series of five law codes, begun when he was First Consul, although not entirely completed until after the establishment of the Empire. Of these the Civil Code—referred to simply as the *Code Napo-léon*—was the most important. The revolution had prepared the way for the First Consul by sweeping away most of the statutes and legal privileges

[4] Cited by G. Bruun, *Europe and the French Imperium,* (New York, 1938), p. 146.

of the Old Regime, but the various revolutionary assemblies had made relatively little progress in the drafting of new legal codes. With his passion for order and speed Napoleon in August, 1800, appointed a committee of several of France's most prominent lawyers to draft a Civil Code, and he made sure that it was completed within six months. Keenly interested in the enterprise, the First Consul presided over about half the sessions of the Council of State in which provisions of the draft were discussed in detail. The promulgation of the code was delayed until early in 1804, however, because of opposition to certain articles by the Tribunate and the Legislative Body—one of the few instances in which these chambers delayed proposed legislation.

The finished product has been termed a compromise between some of the most important ideals of the revolution and the needs of the authoritarian Napoleonic regime. One of the fundamental principles of the revolution was retained: the equality of all citizens before the law. The code provided a uniform system of law for the entire country, guaranteed religious liberty and the supremacy of the secular state, and asserted the right of the individual to choose his own profession. In some of its other provisions the code showed the influence of Napoleon's authoritarian outlook. For example, the sections relating to family life reinforced the authority of the father over his children and provided for the subordination of the wife, whose property was legally placed at the disposal of her husband. Revolutionary legislation had required the equal division of property among heirs, but the code permitted greater freedom to the head of the family in disposing of his estate. The right of divorce by mutual consent was recognized but was restricted in the interests of family unity.

Some of the later codes—for example, the Code of Civil Procedure promulgated in 1806—bore a close resemblance to laws under the Old Regime. Both the Code of Criminal Procedure and the Penal Code, begun under the Consulate but not completed until 1810, reflected the increasing despotism of the Napoleonic regime in that they prescribed strict penalties for political offenses as well as for crimes against persons and property. Where revolutionary legislation had changed criminal procedure so that the defendant was presumed innocent until proved guilty, the code reversed this change, restoring the presumption of the defendant's guilt. A Commercial Code, drawn up in 1807, was much less complete than the other codes and merely retained many of the ordinances of the monarchy.

Criticisms have been leveled against the Napoleonic codes, but as a whole they were a remarkable achievement. For brevity and clarity of expression the Civil Code was unmatched; any citizen could look up any point with a minimum of difficulty in a volume so small that it fitted into his pocket. Although the lawmakers assumed that their codes conformed to nature and were therefore universally applicable—just as the *philosophes* and the revolutionaries had supposed that the principles they set forth were "natural laws"—the codes were in fact strongly national in their origin. They drew upon earlier distillations of Roman law that had prevailed in the south of France and upon the Teutonic customary law common to the northern provinces. These were combined and blended with the laws promulgated during the revolution which had so drastically undermined the hierarchical structure of French society and altered the status of the individual. The resulting amalgam was a set of legal codes adapted to the bourgeois-oriented society that came into being with the revolution, a society which stressed the equality of all citizens before the law but at the same preserved the principle of private property. This adaptation explains, in part, why the French codes were borrowed or imitated so widely during the nineteenth century. They were of course, applied directly by the French to many of their conquered territories, including the Austrian Netherlands, Holland, Switzerland, Luxemburg, and a number of the German states. But the influence of the codes spread farther, to the New World where it affected the laws of Canada, Louisiana, and parts of Central and South America, and even as far as Japan.

The Napoleonic Regime as a Police State

Critics of the point of view that Napoleon continued and completed the work of the revolution do not deny his achievements with respect to the administrative system, education, and law, but they emphasize aspects of the Napoleonic regime which seemed directly to reverse the intentions of the original revolutionaries. To begin with, the political system established in 1799—the Consulate—constituted a denial of the doctrine of popular sovereignty which was at the heart of the Declaration of the Rights of Man. Although French citizens were given the right to vote, their vote was essentially meaningless since members of the Napoleonic assemblies were appointed rather than elected. Moreover, the legislative bodies themselves, restricted in their functions by Napoleon's first constitution, were progressively shorn of their limited powers in the ensuing years. Bonaparte could argue that his mandate from the people came in the form of periodic plebiscites, but these plebiscites were inevitably invoked to ratify decisions already made. By contrast, the initial constitution of the revolution (the Constitution of 1791), though it too fell short of the ideal of popular sovereignty because of its restrictions on the franchise, did provide for an assembly that had genuine legislative powers and truly shared sovereignty with the king. Napoleonic parliamentary institutions were from the beginning little more than window dressing for what was essentially a dictatorship.

The Napoleonic regime was marked, too, by drastic curbs upon freedom of expression. Article II of the Declaration of the Rights of Man had proclaimed: "Free communication of ideas and opinions is one of the most precious rights of man. Consequently, every citizen may speak, write, and print freely, subject to responsibility for the abuse of such liberty in the cases determined by law." No principle was violated more consistently by the Bonapartist government. A few months after Napoleon came to power the number of Paris newspapers was reduced from seventy-three to thirteen. Eventually, the remaining papers in Paris and the provinces were little more than government organs printing official news dispatches and suppressing any information considered detrimental to the regime. The government was also on guard against literary works that might prove politically harmful. Particular attention was paid to the theater, which was placed under the general supervision of agents who subjected all plays, old and new, to rigorous censorship.

In order to enforce such regulations, a large and elaborately organized police force was necessary. Supervision of the police was entrusted to the notorious Joseph Fouché, who had been dismissed from his post as a deputy on mission under the Terror because of his excessive brutality. Fouché created what the Empress Josephine termed "a vile system of espionage" for the surveillance of the personal lives of thousands of individuals suspected of harboring subversive sentiments. The constitutional prohibition of the arbitrary detention of individuals was—in practice—consistently violated. Some political opponents of the regime were kept under close watch in assigned residences; others were detained in insane asylums. After 1810 they were held in "state prisons," where the number of political prisoners rose by 1814 to an estimated 2,500. The resulting atmosphere—reminiscent of Paris under the Terror—was certainly at odds with the principles of individual liberty and freedom of speech proclaimed in 1789.

Because he was first and foremost a soldier, Napoleon reserved a special place in French society for the military. Indeed, his top-ranking officers were showered with favors and came to form an elite which staffed his court and enjoyed special privileges in the Empire. Appointment as a marshal of France was the highest honor Napoleon could confer, and it was received by relatively few. Some were given this title as a reward for personal loyalty or to pacify a particular army clique, but the most outstanding marshals were brilliant generals like Louis Nicolas Davout (1770–1823), a superb tactician who never lost a battle; André Masséna (1758–1817), who distinguished himself in a number of battles, and particularly at Wagram (1809); and the celebrated Michel Ney (1769–1815), termed by Napoleon "the bravest of the brave" for his exploits as a general in numerous campaigns of the revolutionary and Napoleonic eras. Although many marshals had begun their lives as sons of peasants or members of the petty bourgeoisie, they were created dukes or princes, with titles recalling their victories or the

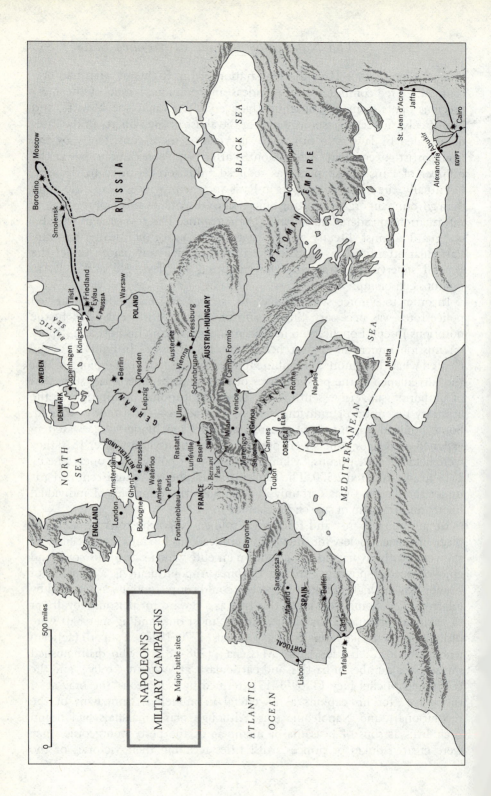

NAPOLEON'S
MILITARY CAMPAIGNS

★ Major battle sites

500 miles

ATLANTIC
OCEAN

NORTH
SEA

ENGLAND
London

BALTIC
SEA

SWEDEN

DENMARK
Copenhagen

NETHERLANDS
Amsterdam
Ghent
Brussels
Boulogne
Waterloo
Paris
Amiens
Fontainebleau
FRANCE
Lunéville
Rastatt
Basel
SWITZ.
St. Bernard Pass

GERMANY
Berlin
Dresden
Leipzig
Ulm
Schönbrunn
Vienna
Austerlitz
Pressburg

RUSSIA
Moscow
Borodino
Smolensk
Tilsit
Friedland
Eylau
Königsberg
E. PRUSSIA

POLAND
Warsaw

AUSTRIA-HUNGARY
Campo Formio

Milan
Marengo
Savona
Genoa
Cannes
ELBA
CORSICA
Toulon
Venice
ITALY
Rome
Naples

Bayonne
Saragossa
Madrid
SPAIN
Bailén
Cádiz
PORTUGAL
Lisbon
Trafalgar

BLACK SEA

OTTOMAN EMPIRE
Constantinople

MEDITERRANEAN SEA

Malta

St. Jean d'Acre
Jaffa
Alexandria
Aboukir
Cairo
EGYPT

provinces they had conquered. Holders of such titles were also rewarded with generous pensions, large bequests, and grants of "fiefs" in Germany or Italy. Some even became kings. Thus Joachim Murat (c.1767–1815), husband of Napoleon's sister Caroline and one of Napoleon's most flamboyant marshals, was named king of Naples in 1808. Napoleon's ideal of the "career open to talent" was strikingly realized in the lives of many of his marshals.

Peace with the Church: The Concordat

After his accession to power, Bonaparte made no immediate public statement about the status of the Roman Catholic Church in France. But he was convinced that the religious issue had to be settled, if possible by a concordat with the pope. The French clergy remained divided into two groups: the constitutional clergy, who had taken an oath to the revolutionary government, and the legitimate—or refractory—clergy, who were either in hiding or in exile, but who retained the sympathy of many French Catholics. Napoleon realized that to win the support of the refractory clergy he would need the aid of the pope. He was further led to seek a settlement with the Church by concern for those Frenchmen who had acquired nationalized Church lands during the revolution and were anxious to have the Church formally renounce its title to these lands. Although Napoleon had no firm religious convictions—he was the first to admit his own opportunism in this respect—he was convinced that France was fundamentally Catholic and that the support of the authority of a revealed religion would be useful in securing the submission of French citizens to law and order.

In 1800, after a successful military campaign in northern Italy had reinforced Napoleon's domination there, he opened negotiations with representatives of Pius VII, pope between 1800 and 1823. The threat of military force and the possibility of a further reduction of the papal territories loomed in the background of the discussions. Nevertheless, the pope's diplomats engaged in delaying tactics and the Concordat underwent some twenty-one drafts before it was acceptable to both Rome and the French state. While the Concordat of 1801 was something of a compromise, the Napoleonic state was the principal gainer. Catholicism was recognized not as the state religion, but as the religion of "the great majority of French citizens" and of the three consuls of the republic. The semiprivileged status given the Catholic faith sufficed to reconcile the papacy and the refractory clergy. Priests were permitted the free exercise of the Catholic worship "in conformity with the police regulations which the government shall deem necessary for the public tranquility." The pope agreed to recognize as valid the titles of all those who had bought Church lands confiscated by the revolutionary government. Since the relinquishment of these lands, together with the abolition of the tithe, left the Church with

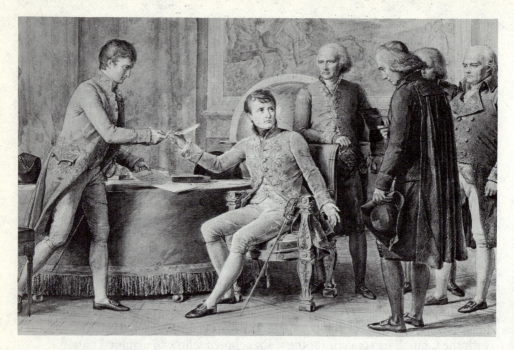

Signature of the Concordat by the First Consul (1801). *Painting by Gérard. The pope's representative stands in the right foreground. Musée de Versailles, Versailles.*

much reduced revenues, the state agreed, as it had under the Civil Constitution of the Clergy, to pay the salaries of bishops and priests, who were required, before assuming their functions, to take an oath of fidelity to the government. French bishops and archbishops were to be nominated by the government and canonically instituted by the pope; they, in turn, had the right to name members of the lower clergy.

In the Concordat, Napoleon achieved his principal goals. The agreement ended the division within the French church, reconciled the refractory clergy to the republic, and gave the necessary security to owners of former Church lands. The principal gain for the Church, in addition to state salaries for the clergy, was the assurance that Catholic worship could be practiced freely once again in France. Yet the reservation to this right—the agreement concerning police regulation—left an opening by which the government could (and did) control the Church in France. One other concession to the Church was French recognition of the Papal States; however, the pope did not regain the territories of Ferrara, Bologna, and the Romagna, which had been incorporated into the Cisalpine Republic in 1797. The Concordat was not universally popular in France, but it had the enthusiastic support of well over half the nation, and the reconciliation of France and the papacy was celebrated on Easter Sunday in 1802 by a *Te Deum* at Notre Dame.

INTERNATIONAL DEVELOPMENTS

The End of the Second Coalition: Peace with Austria and Britain

After his accession to power as First Consul, Napoleon made offers of peace to Austria and Great Britain, the two remaining members of the Second Coalition. When these were spurned he decided upon a major campaign against Austria. With his armies striking again through both Germany and Italy, Napoleon took personal command of a French force of forty thousand in a dramatic march across Great St. Bernard Pass into Italy. There he fell upon the Austrian flank and took the city of Milan. He encountered the main body of the Austrian army in the Battle of Marengo (June, 1800), where only the timely arrival of a relief force under General Louis Desaix (1768–1800) enabled him to turn what appeared to be a catastrophe for France into victory. When Napoleon followed up his defeat of the Austrian armies in Italy by pressing the invasion of Austria through Germany, the Austrian emperor was ready to sue for peace. The treaty concluded at Lunéville in February, 1801, reaffirmed the cessions Austria had made in the Treaty of Campoformio and forced Austria to abandon its remaining possessions in the Italian peninsula (with the exception of Venice and the surrounding region) and to recognize the independence of the Batavian, Helvetic, and Ligurian republics. Gone was the earlier promise of French support for Austria's claims to Bavarian territory, and France now asserted the exclusive right to settle the question of indemnification of the German princes who had lost territories along the left bank of the Rhine.

Once again Britain was the sole member of the coalition to hold out. Although the British had reconquered the island of Malta from Napoleon, had expelled the French from Egypt, and had taken a number of former Dutch and Spanish colonies, their sentiment for peace was strong, for British merchants hoped to regain access to continental markets. Napoleon, too, was anxious to secure an honorable peace, which would leave him free to consolidate his position in France and in Europe. In the ensuing negotiations, the British were at a disadvantage because Pitt had resigned as prime minister in the spring of 1801 and his successor, Henry Addington (1757–1844), was a much inferior statesman whose representatives were no match for the French. * The Treaty of Amiens (March, 1802), was greeted with dismay in Great Britain; it seemed that the British had conceded everything and the French nothing. Among the more important provisions were the following: Great Britain returned to France or to its allies (Spain and the Batavian Republic, or Holland), all the colonial territories won since the beginning of the war with the exception of Trinidad (taken from

---

* The change of prime ministers provoked the following comment from a contemporary: "Pitt is to Addington as London to Paddington."

Spain) and Ceylon (ceded by the Batavian Republic).

The French agreed to evacuate the kingdom of Naples and the Papal States and recognized the return of the island of Malta, captured by Napoleon and later retaken by the British, to the Order of the Knights of Malta. France also recognized the independence of the Ionian Islands. These seven islands lying in the Ionian Sea off the western coast of Greece had been occupied by the French in 1797. But the Russian fleet seized them in 1799 and established them as the Septinsular Republic, under Turkish protection and Russian guarantee. The Russians, in fact, occupied them until 1807. From the British point of view, the treaty's omissions were more significant than its provisions. For no mention was made of France's many conquests on the Continent. France was left in control of Holland, Belgium, the left bank of the Rhine, Switzerland, and most of the Italian peninsula. The independence of the various republics which had been set up under French authority was not guaranteed; they were clearly nothing more than satellites of the French state. Most important, France was left a free hand in reshaping Germany. Nor did British negotiators secure any agreement from the French concerning the restoration of commerce with the Continent, although most continental ports were now in French hands. British merchants who had looked forward to the revival of trade with the Continent were among the treaty's bitterest critics.

In attempting to understand why the British government accepted the terms of the Treaty of Amiens, we must recall both its overwhelming desire for peace after nine years of war and the relative weakness of the new ministry. Furthermore, the treaty did leave intact Britain's strongest weapon, its navy. Britain's mastery of the seas was unaffected; in fact, the war had heightened its superiority in this respect. Whereas the French had lost close to half of their fleet, the British had almost doubled the strength of their navy. Therefore, they were now in a position to renew hostilities against the French whenever it seemed desirable to do so. Meanwhile, they could wait to see whether Napoleon would be satisfied with his conquests or whether he was ambitious for further expansion.

The Reorganization of Germany, 1803

Napoleon profited from the brief interlude of peace afforded by the Treaty of Amiens to reshape drastically the map of Germany. His power to do this stemmed from the Treaty of Basel (concluded by France with Prussia in 1795) and from France's treaties with Austria—Campoformio in 1797 and Lunéville in 1801. Through these treaties France had acquired all the German territories lying along the left bank of the Rhine, an important step in the fulfillment of its long-standing goal of expanding to its "natural frontiers." As far as Germany was concerned the central problem created by these treaties was how to compensate or indemnify those princes who had lost territories to France. The treaties themselves had suggested a solution by proposing the secularization of at least some of the old ecclesiastical principalities of Germany—which had been ruled for centuries by archbishops or bishops with temporal as well as spiritual powers—and their annexation to states which had been promised compensation.

Prussia and many of the lesser states favored the proposed secularization, and even Austria, despite long-standing ties with the Roman Catholic Church, cast covetous eyes upon the archbishopric of Salzburg and some of the smaller ecclesiastical territories. An imperial congress summoned in 1797 at Rastatt in accordance with the provisions of the Treaty of Campoformio failed to produce agreement among the German states on the problem of indemnification. To end the deadlock, the imperial Diet agreed to turn the problem over to an imperial deputation (*Reichsdeputation*) consisting of eight members. Before this body could meet, however, Napoleon proceeded to make his own arrangements for Germany. Talleyrand, his foreign minister, having accepted bribes and gifts from German rulers who hoped to acquire this or that piece of territory, drew up the terms of the settlement. After concluding separate treaties with Prussia and some of the states of secondary rank, Napoleon imposed the entire arrangement upon the imperial deputation and eventually upon the Austrian emperor.

The final terms were embodied in a document known as the Imperial Recess of 1803. In accordance with its provisions, 112 states of the Holy Roman Empire went out of existence, their territories being incorporated into neighboring states. Of the ecclesiastical states, all but one, Mainz, were destroyed—and even the archbishop of Mainz lost some of his territory. Of approximately fifty free cities, only six remained: Frankfurt, Augsburg, and Nuremberg, and the three Hanseatic cities—Lübeck, Hamburg, and Bremen. The principal beneficiaries of the settlement in Germany were Prussia and Bavaria, each of which gained about five times as much territory as it had lost on the left bank of the Rhine, and the southwestern German states of Baden and Württemberg. Although Austria gained territory in the south to compensate for the loss of imperial possessions in the west, the overall settlement further undermined the Austrian position with respect to Germany by eliminating the ecclesiastical states which had traditionally supported the Habsburgs and by strengthening Prussia and some of the secondary states. Certainly part of Napoleon's intention in intervening in Germany had been to decrease both Austrian and Prussian influence by attracting to France's orbit a group of secondary states indebted to France for territories they had acquired and willing to accept French leadership in the hope of further favors. In this he was successful, since Bavaria, Baden, and Württemberg tended to look to France for leadership during the following decade.

THE EMPIRE, 1804–1814

In 1802 the French had reason to be grateful to Napoleon, for in less than three years he had brought about the apparent pacification not only of his own country but of Europe as well. The ratification of the Treaty of Amiens, concluding peace with France's last remaining enemy, was followed in a few days by the celebration of the Concordat with the papacy. Many of the former opponents of the regime had become reconciled to it as success followed success during the first years of the Consulate. Others—principally die-hard Jacobins and republicans who accused Bonaparte of having betrayed the revolution—had been exiled or imprisoned. Toward monarchists and *émigré* nobles Napoleon's policy was much more lenient. After the victory of Marengo in 1800, Napoleon removed the names of some fifty thousand from the list of *émigrés* drawn up during the revolution. (This list included some nobles who had not actually left the country but were nevertheless classified as *émigrés*.) In the spring of 1802, after the conclusion of peace, he extended full amnesty to another fifty thousand on condition that they return to the country by September, 1802, and take an oath of loyalty to the constitution. To those whose estates had been seized but not sold he promised full restoration of their property. Only a thousand intransigent nobles were excluded from this amnesty. These measures served to eliminate practically all organized opposition within the country. Bonaparte was now ready to take the first steps toward the establishment of the Empire.

The Proclamation of the Empire, 1804

As early as 1800 Napoleon's brother Lucien had tried to determine the popular reaction to the establishment of hereditary rule for the Bonapartes, and had concluded that such a move would be premature. In 1802 circumstances seemed more auspicious, and the Tribunate was prompted to declare that the nation owed "a signal pledge of gratitude" to the First Consul for his work of pacification. The Senate responded to the suggestion, but instead of offering to retain Napoleon as First Consul for life, merely proposed to extend his term by ten years. Keenly disappointed, Bonaparte seized the initiative and referred the decision to the people in a plebiscite. The question, as finally formulated by the all-powerful Council of State, was simply this: "Is Napoleon Bonaparte to be made Consul for life?" The French people responded with an overwhelming affirmative (3,568,885 in favor, 8,374 opposed), and the Life Consulate was proclaimed in August, 1802. To accompany this change the Senate approved alterations in the constitution which increased the powers of the First Consul and strengthened the Senate (now clearly under Bonaparte's control) at the expense of the Tribunate and the Legislative Body. Although two other consuls remained in office, ostensibly sharing power with the First Consul, the

Consulate was now a monarchy in all but name.

However, Napoleon felt that further preparations were essential before he could assume a royal title. He had to be made to appear as the indispensable ruler of the nation, the only bulwark between France and a state of anarchy. This impression, he decided, would be created by the discovery of a conspiracy, a plot to restore the Bourbon dynasty, which would appear to threaten the very existence of the regime. Many *émigrés* still in exile did indeed favor such a restoration. In due course, secret agents of the Napoleonic government, posing in England as monarchist sympathizers and supplied with funds from the treasury to finance the project, approached the leaders of a planned coup who were also receiving a subsidy from the British government, anxious to encourage any plot for the removal of the First Consul. With the conspirators now on French soil, the so-called Cadoudal conspiracy was suddenly exposed; at the proper moment early in 1804, government agents swooped down and arrested Georges Cadoudal (1771–1804), a royalist from Brittany; General Charles Pichegru (1761–1804), one of the former revolutionary generals; and General Jean Victor Moreau (1763–1813), Napoleon's chief rival as a military commander, whom the first two secretly in Paris had attempted to persuade to join the conspiracy. All three were imprisoned, and the details of the plot were bared in the newspapers. Pichegru was subsequently found strangled in his cell. Cadoudal and several other conspirators were tried and executed. General Moreau, who in point of fact refused to participate in the plan, was found guilty but permitted to go into exile in America. Even after the leaders of the plot had been exposed no specific representative of the Bourbon family could be found implicated. The only clues that were picked up seemed to lead to the duke of Enghien (1772–1804), a Bourbon prince of the collateral line of Condé, who had been living in the German state of Baden and had allegedly come to Strasbourg to communicate with English agents. On the flimsiest of evidence Napoleon ordered a contingent of troops to invade Baden, a neutral territory, arrest the duke of Enghien, and bring him to Paris. He had firmly decided on condemning the duke to death, and although he discovered even before Enghien reached the capital that the charges against him were false, he went ahead with the summary military trial and had him executed within twenty-four hours of his arrival. The speed and brutality with which this action was taken caused a temporary revulsion against Napoleon in some quarters, but most Frenchmen were relieved that the plot had been discovered and the apparent threat to the regime overcome. All who had a stake in the maintenance of the *status quo*—peasants who had acquired nationalized lands during the revolution, merchants and businessmen who benefited from the prosperity and order achieved under the Consulate, bureaucrats and military men whose fortunes were tied to those of Bonaparte—were willing to approve when the Tribunate proposed

Coronation of Napoleon, 1804. *Detail from a painting by David. Napoleon is seen raising the crown which he subsequently placed on his own head. Josephine kneels at the left and Pope Pius VII is seated at the right. The Louvre, Paris.*

that Napoleon be proclaimed emperor and that the imperial dignity should be hereditary in the Bonaparte family. A plebiscite once again approved overwhelmingly what was, in fact, a *fait accompli*.

In the newly revised constitution (sometimes referred to as the Constitution of the Year XII), the first article began, "The government of the republic is entrusted to an emperor," and the document went on to specify the method to be followed in determining the succession within the Bonaparte family. This curious amalgamation of political forms appeared also on the coinage, which subsequently bore on one side the words *République Française* and on the other, *Napoléon Empereur*. Napoleon's reasons for choosing to be "emperor" are not hard to determine. He could hardly call himself king; the Bourbon pretender had not abandoned his claims to the throne, and in any event that title would have been inconsistent with the revolutionary origins of Napoleon's government. Besides, "emperor" carried more grandiose overtones, recalling both the rulers of Rome and Charlemagne, who had been emperor as well as "king of the Franks." Certainly the title suggested that his dominion would extend far beyond the borders which had circumscribed the France of the monarchy.

Napoleon's ambitions also led him to seek a legitimization of his title greater than could be conferred by the French Senate. Accordingly, he succeeded in persuading Pope Pius VII to come to Paris to lend the papal presence to his coronation in December, 1804. Such an act required the pope to abandon certain scruples since a legitimate Catholic prince still claimed the throne of France, but the good will of the most powerful ruler in Europe was not to be dismissed lightly. Besides, Pius was assured by Napoleon's representatives that he would both anoint and crown the emperor. But a few hours before the coronation, the pope was informed that the procedure had been changed. In the climax of the impressive ceremony in Notre Dame, Napoleon took the crown from the pope, turned his back upon him, and facing the audience, placed the crown upon his own head. In this manner he proclaimed to the pope and to all others present his independence of any earthly authority.

War with Britain and the Third Coalition

Historians have speculated on what would have happened to the Napoleonic Empire if it had enjoyed a decade of peace. Frenchmen were, on the whole, satisfied with the ruler who had ended the insecurity of the revolutionary era and provided them with a stable regime and relative prosperity. But could Napoleon Bonaparte have survived a decade of peace? His reputation had been built initially upon his military victories. And despite his active program of domestic reforms in the years after 1799, his power was based essentially on his command of the army and on the military glory surrounding his name. Moreover, there was a romantic element in his character which made it impossible for him to limit his ambitions. Could one who in a few short years had achieved mastery over the French nation and had successively defeated the other major powers of Europe have settled down to the relatively prosaic tasks of government and administration? Napoleon was impelled by an almost compulsive drive toward further military exploits and the expansion of his newly founded empire.

Responsibility for the renewal of war between France and Britain in May, 1803, lay almost entirely with France. The rest of Europe may well have been ready to settle down to an era of peace after the decade of wars which had ravaged the Continent. The territories which France had annexed by 1803 could largely be regarded as lying within France's "natural frontiers." True, French influence extended to the so-called sister republics in Holland, Switzerland, and Italy, but the peoples of these regions still had a degree of autonomy, and at least some of them benefited from the introduction of French institutions into their territories. The other major European powers had apparently acquiesced in the extension of French influence into these regions; at least, they had signed treaties with France which did not specifically withhold approval of French acquisitions. Addington, the British prime minister, certainly regarded the Treaty of Amiens as more than a temporary truce, but the same cannot be said for Napoleon. For a number of reasons he regarded a resumption of the war with Britain as inevitable, or rather, he took certain steps which made it inevitable. In the first place, he revealed fairly soon that he had no intention of maintaining the *status quo* on the Continent. Even before the peace with Britain had been formally signed, he imposed a new constitution on the Cisalpine Republic (henceforth called the Italian Republic) and had himself appointed its president. A few months later France formally annexed the neighboring state of Piedmont. Dissension between centralists and federalists in the Helvetic Republic gave him a pretext for intervening there, mediating the dispute, and establishing a new state, the Swiss Confederation, which became a close military ally of France. His drastic reorganization of Germany has already been discussed.

Second, and even more alarming to the British, there was evidence of renewed French designs in the eastern Mediterranean. Napoleon sent one of his officers, Colonel Horace Sébastiani (1772–1851), to that region as a military observer, and saw to it that a report of his findings was published (January 30, 1803) in the official government newspaper, the *Moniteur*. Sébastiani's most provocative conclusion was that Egypt, because of its weakened military condition, could easily be recaptured by the French.

A third cause for continued antagonism between France and Great Britain was Napoleon's stubborn refusal to accept British commercial and colonial supremacy. He regarded his own hopes for the economic domination of the Continent as doomed to frustration as long as Britain retained this superiority. How to destroy it was a problem that occupied Napoleon for the remainder of his career.

First he tried to build up a colonial empire in the western hemisphere. His intention was to consolidate French control over the rich sugar-producing island of Haiti and to expand French influence from there into North and South America. The principal obstacle to his designs was the native Negro leader Toussaint L'Ouverture (1743–1803), who had established his control over the island in the 1790's and made it virtually independent of France. In 1802, Napoleon sent an expeditionary force to Haiti to reestablish French supremacy, and announced the restoration of slavery, which had been abolished during the revolution. These measures, and the deposition and deportation of Toussaint, provoked a violent uprising among the natives. An epidemic of yellow fever among the French soldiers completed the decimation of the military force, which finally capitulated to the natives in 1803. Faced with this catastrophe, Napoleon abandoned his plans for a western colonial empire and cut his losses by withdrawing from Haiti and selling the Louisiana Territory to the United States in 1803.

He decided to concentrate instead on undermining Britain's commercial supremacy. Having been brought up in the mercantilist tradition, he was convinced that continental markets lost to British manufacturers would go to the French and provide a further stimulus to French industry and commerce. In effect he was merely continuing policies dating from the Anglo-French commercial and colonial rivalry of the seventeenth and eighteenth centuries. His principal innovation, as we shall see, was his attempt to apply to the entire continent of Europe a policy which had hitherto been restricted to France and, during the 1790's, to those regions immediately dependent upon France. Now France would become the senior partner in a European-wide economic system. But the success of such an enterprise depended upon domination by the French of the entire Continent, and upon their ability to enforce the restrictions imposed on trade with the British. Not until 1806 did Napoleon control enough of Europe to inaugurate his famous Continental System, whose purpose was the destruction of British trade and the achievement of economic mastery of the European continent. His policy in 1802 foreshadowed the Continental System, for he refused to supplement the Treaty of Amiens with any sort of commercial agreement which would have permitted British merchants to trade with France, and he tried to extend this ban to France's allies. Probably no other action by Napoleon did more to consolidate British opinion in support of a renewal of the war with France.

Tensions between Britain and France culminated in the outbreak of war in May, 1803. Napoleon used as a pretext for renewing the conflict Britain's refusal to evacuate the island of Malta. This was a technical violation of the terms of the Treaty of Amiens, but the expansion of his own domination over Italy and his designs elsewhere on the Continent certainly provided the British with adequate grounds for retaining control over this island outpost in the Mediterranean. The war that began in 1803 dragged on indecisively for two years. Napoleon found himself unable to achieve a quick victory, partly because the French fleet was bottled up in its own ports by superior British squadrons, but also because Britain was soon joined by other nations, forming the Third Coalition.

At first, Napoleon seriously entertained the idea of invading England. In the fall of 1803 he concentrated a force of 150,000 men on the coast at Boulogne and ordered the construction of a flotilla of 1,200 flatboats to transport the troops across the Channel. Subsequently, he decided that the invasion forces required support and devised a plan for several French squadrons to escape from the blockaded ports, lure units of the British fleet to the high seas, evade them, and return to the Channel to join the invasion forces. In March, 1805, he was finally able to put this plan into operation. A French squadron under the command of Admiral Pierre Villeneuve (1763–1806) slipped out of Toulon and joined a Spanish squadron (Spain, too, had become involved in the war against Britain), and the combined fleet made for the West Indies. As Napoleon had hoped, the British took the bait. Admiral Horatio Nelson set out in pursuit with a British fleet. But when Villeneuve attempted to evade Nelson and return to Europe to support the projected invasion, the plan began to go awry. For Nelson ascertained the direction of the French fleet and managed to warn the British admiralty, which promptly stationed ships off the northwest coast of Spain to intercept Villeneuve's squadron. Villeneuve took refuge in the port of Cádiz, where he was promptly blockaded again by British units.

Although Villeneuve was blamed for the failure of the project, Napoleon had decided to abandon the invasion even before he got word of his admiral's retreat. Publicly he claimed that French troops stationed at Boulogne were needed on the Rhine to counteract the mobilization of Austrian armies, but probably the decisive factor was the return of Nelson's fleet, for he knew that the Franco-Spanish fleet would be no match for it.

Napoleon's fears were dramatically confirmed later that year. Admiral Villeneuve, contemptuously ordered by the emperor to make for a Mediterranean port, sailed out of Cádiz. Admiral Nelson intercepted Villeneuve's signals and prepared to meet him at the strait of Gibraltar. On October 21, 1805, off Cape Trafalgar, Nelson's ships overwhelmingly defeated the enemy fleet in six hours of ship-to-ship fighting. At the end of the battle only eleven of the thirty-three French and Spanish ships managed to regain their

The Death of Lord Nelson at the Battle of Trafalgar, October 21, 1805. *The British admiral was fatally wounded while commanding the battle from the quarterdeck of his ship, the* Victory.

harbor. The British lost no ships, but they did lose their admiral; Nelson was fatally wounded in the first hour of fighting. The Battle of Trafalgar was unquestionably one of the decisive battles of the Napoleonic wars, for it ended definitively all French hopes of challenging Britain's mastery of the seas.

By one of those ironic twists of history, France's defeat at Trafalgar coincided almost to the day with the surrender of twenty thousand Austrian troops to Napoleon at Ulm, in Bavaria. For Napoleon had lost no time in moving his Grand Army (as he now called the forces hitherto intended for the invasion of England) to the Rhine and invading German territory. His goal was now the defeat of the Third Coalition, which had been formed against France during 1804-1805.

Among the leaders of this coalition was Tsar Alexander I of Russia, whom the British government had approached in 1804 with a view to forming an alliance against France. Alexander, one of the most colorful individuals of this era, had ascended the throne only three years earlier, at twenty-three. His role as ruler of Russia from 1801 to 1825 will be examined in detail in a later chapter; here it is important to note that his actions as a military leader and diplomat, like his polices at home, were frequently marked by unpredictability and inconsistency. Son of the unstable autocrat Paul I, Alexander had been brought up by his grandmother, Catherine the Great, who saw to it that he was given a liberal and humanist education by his Swiss tutor, Frédéric César de La Harpe. The principles inculcated in Alexander by this training were at odds with the respect for the army and the pride in himself as a soldier which he had derived from his father. His instability (some have diagnosed his condition as schizophrenia) was further heightened by the sense of guilt he felt over his father's violent death. Although he played no direct role in Paul's assassination, he is known to have been aware of the plot to depose him and to have done nothing to stop it. Upon his accession, he surrounded himself with liberal advisers and even talked of granting Russia a constitution, but little came of his promises except for some administrative and legal reforms. As he grew older and as Russia became involved in wars against France, Alexander turned more and more conservative. Ultimately he regarded himself as a divinely appointed savior of Europe destined to defeat Napoleon, the Antichrist.

In 1804 he was receptive to Britain's proposals for an alliance for two reasons. First, he felt the French emperor was violating certain accepted standards of conduct in international relations—in his abduction of the duke of Enghien from the independent state of Baden for example. Second, he was convinced that Napoleon posed a threat to Russia's interests in the Ionian Islands, in the Balkans, and in central Europe, where Alexander looked forward to becoming an arbiter. The alliance formally concluded between Britain and Russia in 1805 reiterated some of the aims of the

Second Coalition—an independent Holland which would include the Belgian provinces and constitute a barrier against France in the north, and an independent kingdom of Sardinia, controlling Savoy, Piedmont, and the former Republic of Genoa, which would serve the same function in the south. Other goals, less carefully defined, included the elimination of French influence in both Germany and Italy and the strengthening of Prussia on the Rhine. Alexander also expressed his intention of establishing a reconstituted Polish state, and proposed that some sort of international body be set up after the war to enforce the peace settlement.

Francis II of Austria was understandably hesitant about renewing the war against France, having lost so much territory in the wars of the First and Second coalitions. Nevertheless, steps taken by Napoleon to consolidate French control over northern Italy led Austria in November, 1804, to conclude a defensive treaty with Russia which provided for joint resistance against any further French aggression in Italy or Germany. When Napoleon decided in 1805 to transform the Italian Republic into a kingdom of Italy, with himself as king, Austria prepared to join the coalition with Britain and Russia. As we have seen, Austria's mobilization of its armies gave Napoleon the excuse he needed for transferring his troops from the Channel coast to the Rhine border.

General Mack (Baron Karl Mack von Leiberich, 1752–1828), commander of the Austrian forces in Germany, played from the start into Napoleon's hands by penetrating far ahead of his reinforcements; thus the French were able to outflank and encircle his troops at Ulm. From Ulm, Napoleon moved on without hindrance to the Austrian capital of Vienna. There he heard the news of the defeat at Trafalgar and became aware that his enemies of the Third Coalition—Russia, Austria, and Britain—might be joined by another ally, Prussia. The king of Prussia had preserved his neutrality for a little more than a decade, but the expansion of Napoleon's influence in the German states and the violation of Prussian territory by French forces under General Jean Baptiste Bernadotte (*c.*1763–1844) during Napoleon's campaign against Austria drove the Prussians to threaten support of the coalition. Before these plans could materialize, however, Napoleon met the main armies of the Russians, supported by the Austrians, near the little Moravian village of Austerlitz, and on December 2, 1805, the first anniversary of his coronation as emperor, achieved one of his most brilliant victories. Weakening the right wing of his own forces in order to provoke a Russian attack upon it, he concentrated the full strength of his own attack on the Russian center. His strategy worked perfectly, for having destroyed the center, he was able to turn and annihilate the Russian forces which had advanced on his right. The defeat at Austerlitz cost the allied forces between 25,000 and 30,000 casualties; Napoleon lost fewer than 9,000, including dead and wounded.

The stunning victory at Austerlitz brought about the collapse of the Third Coalition, for the Russians pulled back their troops and informed the Austrians they could count on no more Russian support. Austria saw no alternative but to sue for peace. Prussia hastily dropped its plan for opposing France, and instead, entered into negotiations with Napoleon which resulted in an alliance and the cession to France of minor territories in return for Prussian annexation of Hanover. The terms imposed upon Austria were contained in the humiliating Treaty of Pressburg (December 26, 1805), which deprived Austria of virtually all its remaining possessions in Italy and awarded its imperial territories in western Germany to Bavaria, Württemberg, and Baden as rewards for their support of Napoleon in the war just ended.

Defeat of Prussia and Russia. The Treaties of Tilsit, 1807

The victory at Austerlitz at the end of 1805 and the formation of a Franco-Prussian alliance in February, 1806, brought little more than a brief respite for the Napoleonic armies. Within a few months Napoleon was at war with Prussia, the one power that had managed to remain at peace with France for over a decade.

One explanation for the change in Prussian policy lies in the personality of its monarch, Frederick William III, who had come to the throne in 1797.

Meeting between Napoleon and Emperor Francis II of Austria after the Battle of Austerlitz, December 4, 1805. *Painting by Gros. This interview was a prelude to the humiliating peace imposed on Austria by Napoleon in the Treaty of Pressburg. Versailles.*

Though a man of good intentions, he was characterized by weakness of will and vacillation, traits that are particularly unfortunate in an absolute ruler. Frederick William preserved the governmental institutions that had been shaped by his great-uncle, Frederick the Great, among them a cabinet of councillors. But whereas under a strong monarch these officials had executed the will of the ruler, under Frederick William they exerted their own influence upon the king. Unfortunately for the Prussian state, these officials were divided in their counsel, some favoring a policy of conciliation and compromise with Napoleon, others urging an alliance with Austria or Russia and resistance to the French. Prussian policy was consequently erratic during the first years of Frederick William's reign, though the group advocating compromise with Napoleon generally held the upper hand. By the summer of 1806, however, those favoring resistance to France could point to developments that made war with Napoleon appear the only possible course of action.

Prussia's resentment arose in part from the domination which Napoleon now exercised over all parts of Germany that lay outside the boundaries of Prussia and Austria. For it was at this time (July, 1806) that Napoleon established the Confederation of the Rhine, a union of fifteen German states, including Bavaria, Württemberg, Baden, Hesse-Darmstadt, and Berg. The rulers of the confederation states had little choice but to submit to French control since the probable alternative would have been direct absorption into the French Empire. With Napoleon as its protector, the union was later expanded to include practically every state in Germany except Austria and Prussia. One consequence followed less than a month after the establishment of the confederation, when Napoleon finally announced the end of the thousand-year-old Holy Roman Empire. When the rulers of states belonging to the confederation declared that they no longer recognized the empire, Francis II was forced to abandon his traditional title; he retained only the new title that he had assumed two years before: Francis I, emperor of Austria.

Another source of trouble between France and Prussia was to be found in the alliance itself. The treaty had awarded the state of Hanover to Prussia in return for territories on the right bank of the Rhine which Prussia turned over to France and its allies. When, in the course of the next few months, the Prussian king heard that Napoleon had offered to restore Hanover to Great Britain in exchange for the withdrawal of British protective forces from the island of Sicily, he naturally viewed this proposed bargain as a betrayal of the worst sort. The fact that the Anglo-French negotiations broke down did not diminish Frederick William's resentment over Napoleon's duplicity.

In response to these and other provocations the Prussian king concluded a secret agreement with Tsar Alexander which assured Prussia of Russian support in the event of an attack by France. Even before Russia had ratified the treaty, Prussia mobilized its army against the French. The final blow to Franco-Prussian relations was Napoleon's ruthless execution of Johann Philipp Palm, a Nuremberg bookseller who had circulated a pamphlet entitled *Germany in Her Deepest Humiliation;* the tract had called upon Saxony and Prussia to save Germany from destruction at the hands of the French emperor. The disparity between the relative insignificance of the crime and the severity of the punishment offended almost all Germans and helped to arouse Prussian sentiment against France. The war began in October, 1806.

Frederick William's decision to mobilize his troops before he had been assured of adequate Russian support was a mistake. Prussian troops were outnumbered two to one, and they turned out to be no match for the well-trained armies of Napoleon. On October 14, 1806, before the Russians could arrive to support them, the Prussians were defeated simultaneously at Jena and at Auerstedt. After this decisive victory the French pursued the Prussian armies through their own country until they had captured Berlin. The king was forced to take refuge in East Prussia.

Having extended his domination to northern as well as central Germany, Napoleon now stood face to face with Tsar Alexander's Russian armies. His inclination was to engage the Russians immediately and put an end to the war, but the terrain and general conditions were much less favorable than they had been in the Prussian campaign. Winter was approaching, and he feared the losses that would be involved in fighting on the muddy reaches of East Prussia. When he nevertheless took the chance, at Eylau in February, 1807, he lost fifteen thousand men in a battle which settled nothing. The Russians suffered even heavier casualties, and both sides were forced to fall back and wait until spring to renew the conflict.

As was so often the case, Napoleon profited more from the delay than did his enemy. While the Russians and Prussians waited for subsidies from the British and tried vainly to persuade the Austrians to join them, Napoleon called up some eighty thousand new recruits from France and Italy and thus achieved the numerical superiority which helped him to win a decisive victory at the Battle of Friedland in June, 1807.

Despite his heavy losses, Tsar Alexander could have continued the war against the French, but he decided instead to sue for peace. He had been disappointed by the reluctance of Austria and Britain to support him more actively, and feared that continued fighting might provoke an uprising by the Poles. In addition, a pro-French faction of advisers which was gaining strength in his entourage was encouraging him to reach an understanding with Bonaparte. Napoleon was receptive to the tsar's peace overtures partly because of the heavy losses his armies had suffered in the year just past, but also because he hoped that an agreement with Russia would permit him to

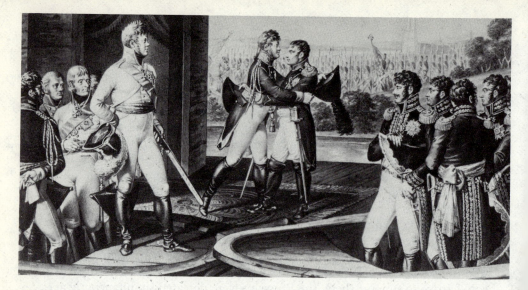

Meeting of Tsar Alexander I and Napoleon on the Niemen River, 1807. *The Treaties of Tilsit resulted from this celebrated encounter of the two emperors on a raft anchored in the middle of the river.*

close Baltic ports to British shipping and goods.

The negotiations between Napoleon and Tsar Alexander constituted one of the most dramatic episodes of the Napoleonic era. On a raft moored in the middle of the Niemen River, the two young emperors met for a series of conferences in which they appeared to contemporaries to be dividing up the European world. And as if to heighten the drama, the hapless Frederick William of Prussia was left on one of the river banks, riding up and down the shore, waiting for the outcome of conversations which would determine the fate of his country. For several days the two rulers matched wits, and in the end, each felt he had triumphed over his opponent.

Two treaties—the treaties of Tilsit (July, 1807)—resulted from the discussions: one concerned France and Prussia; the other settled issues between France and Russia. In the former, Napoleon carried out his intention of humiliating the ex-ally who had dared to oppose him. The king was allowed to retain his throne, but Prussia lost some of its most valuable territories and half its population. Prussian lands to the west of the Elbe were ceded to France; these, with some adjacent areas, formed the new kingdom of Westphalia, which was given to Napoleon's brother Jerome. In the east, Prussia lost the Polish provinces that it had secured in the eighteenth-century partitions of Poland; they were established as the duchy of Warsaw and assigned to the king of Saxony. A separate military convention reduced the Prussian army to a minimum force and provided that French troops would occupy key Prussian fortresses until an indemnity or war contribution had been paid to France.

In the treaty with Russia, the tsar formally accepted the Napoleonic conquests in central and western Europe by recognizing the Confederation of the Rhine and the claims of Napoleon's brothers to the thrones of Holland, Naples, and Westphalia. Napoleon led the Russian emperor to believe that in return for this recognition of the French hegemony in Germany and Italy, he was acknowledging Russia's claim to an eastern European empire. Specifically, the treaty provided that Napoleon would offer his good offices as a mediator in the conflict between Russia and Turkey that had broken out in 1806, a war which he had himself helped to provoke by encouraging the sultan. A secret clause stipulated that if mediation failed, Napoleon would make common cause with Russia in a war against the Ottoman Empire and that France would agree to the cession of the Turkish European provinces of Moldavia and Walachia to Russia. Meanwhile, Russia agreed to withdraw its fleet from the Mediterranean and to yield control over the Ionian Islands to the French. Finally, the tsar offered to mediate between France and Britain. But if the British refused to restore all conquests they had made since 1805 and to respect the freedom of the seas, Russia would declare war on Britain, close the Baltic ports to British products, and call upon the Baltic States, Austria, and Portugal to join in the struggle. Since there was little likelihood of Britain's accepting the suggested conditions, Napoleon thought he could count on Russian support of his efforts to eliminate British trade with the Continent.

The question of who benefited most from the treaty turns less on the actual terms than on the subsequent interpretations made of the agreement by the two rulers. We shall discover that neither Napoleon nor Alexander lived up to the promises made at Tilsit, and each rapidly became disappointed with his new ally. How much faith either ruler put in the alliance is difficult to say. Perhaps neither had too many illusions about its permanence. By 1810, both were coming to the conclusion that a renewal of the war between them was inevitable.

Napoleon's Grand Empire

After the Battle of Austerlitz, in 1805, Napoleon began to speak openly of the Grand Empire which he was constructing in Europe to replace the practically defunct Holy Roman Empire. Indeed, as we know, Francis of Austria, the Holy Roman emperor, had seen the handwriting on the wall as early as 1804, when Napoleon crowned himself emperor of France, and had taken the precaution of naming himself hereditary emperor of Austria as well.

Napoleon's Grand Empire included, first of all, the French Empire proper: metropolitan France and the areas formally annexed to France, such as a sizable strip of Italian territory extending down the western coast to a point halfway between Rome and Naples. In 1810 Holland was eliminated as a satellite state and directly incorporated into the Empire. This nucleus was administered directly from Paris; as new territories were added, they were simply divided into departments ruled by prefects, just like the original eighty-three departments. Beyond the borders of the French state, Napoleon established a series of dependent, or satellite, states; their relationships with France were not uniform, but their rulers were all appointed by Napoleon (indeed, many were members of his own family), and owed allegiance to him. Among these states were some of the "republics" created during the revolutionary era. A third category of states, later added to the Grand Empire, included those which retained their independent status but became "allies" of France, forced to submit to its economic and military directives and to join in the wars against its enemies. For a time both Prussia and Austria fell into this category.

The process of assigning rulers to the dependent states began in 1805, on the Italian peninsula. Once Napoleon had taken the title of emperor he could hardly remain merely "president" of the Italian Republic. He therefore decided to convert this republic into the kingdom of Italy, and after pretending to offer the throne first to his older brother Joseph and later to his stepson Eugène de Beauharnais, announced that because of their refusals he would assume the title himself. He added that his kingship was only provisional: ultimately the new kingdom would go to his chief heir, who would abandon his rights to the French empire as a condition of becoming king of Italy. Eugène de Beauharnais, for the time being, was named viceroy of Italy. At the end of the year, after the Battle of Austerlitz, he added a second state to the Grand Empire, the kingdom of Naples. Angry at the Bourbon ruler of Naples for having violated his promise of neutrality by inviting British and Russian forces into Neapolitan ports, Napoleon declared that "the dynasty of Naples has ceased to reign." In March, 1806, within a month after a French detachment had taken over the kingdom, Napoleon proclaimed his brother Joseph king of Naples and

"The Plumb-pudding in danger; or State Epicures taking un Petit Souper." *Cartoon, published in London, 1805, showing William Pitt and Napoleon carving up the world.*

Sicily. In 1808, Joseph moved on to Spain, and Joachim Murat, Napoleon's brother-in-law, received the crown of Naples.

The pattern established in Italy was also followed elsewhere on the Continent. In 1806 Napoleon dissolved the eleven-year-old Batavian Republic and named his younger brother Louis to the throne of the short-lived kingdom of Holland. To his brother-in-law Murat, in 1806, went the newly created duchy of Berg, in the Rhineland, which was later expanded at the expense of Prussia. To his brother Jerome he assigned the kingdom of Westphalia, created after Tilsit, in 1807. These royal relatives of the emperor were of course bound to him by personal ties, although they were nominally independent of France.

To what extent did the establishment of this sprawling empire spread French institutions to the rest of Europe? Did the dependent states of Germany and Italy, forced to contribute men and money to the support of Napoleon's armies, derive some compensating advantages from French rule? The extent to which French reforms and legislation were introduced varied as greatly from one part of the Empire to another as did the characters of the individual administrators and rulers named to govern the several territories. In regions directly annexed to France institutions were established that were, in theory, the same as those existing in metropolitan France itself, though some adjustments were inevitably made to language and local circumstances. In the newly created departments—and in the dependent states as well—the emperor or his vassal rulers attempted to introduce the Napoleonic codes, the French administrative and financial system, and forms of political representation comparable to those existing at home. It was the general policy, also, to abolish serfdom, eliminate feudal dues, and prohibit the inheritance of large estates. With respect to the church, Napoleon hoped to apply throughout the Empire the policies which had been developed in France: the insistence upon the supremacy of the lay state over the church, the abolition of monastic institutions, the establishment of a system of public instruction, and so on. Resistance to the secular control of education was, as one might expect, particularly strong in parts of Italy. Often the rulers of the dependent states, in closer touch than the emperor with the problems of their particular regions, proved more flexible in the matter of imposing French institutions. When Louis Bonaparte, the ruler of Holland, protested to Napoleon that several provisions of the *Code Napoléon* should be dropped in Holland because they ran counter to Dutch prejudices, his advice was refused with the words, "If you revise the *Code Napoléon* it will no longer be the *Code Napoléon*. . . . The Romans gave their laws to their allies; why should not France have hers adopted in Holland?" [5]

[5] Quoted by Bruun, *Europe and the French Imperium*, p. 136.

Many peoples of the Grand Empire benefited from the introduction of more efficient administrative institutions, more equitable laws, a more just distribution of the burdens of taxation, and other improvements brought by French rule. The changes were particularly advantageous to those who had been living under the antiquated hierarchical institutions of some of the petty states of Germany or in a state such as the kingdom of Naples. At the same time, the attempt to impose from above institutions that affected established prejudices, personal relationships, and daily routines met with a mixed reception even from those who might have gained most from such changes. It is one thing for a people to achieve reforms as the result of its own efforts; another, to have those reforms bestowed by a conqueror.

In the last analysis, Napoleon came to be viewed more as a conqueror than as a liberator. For membership in the Grand Empire brought disadvantages as well as rewards. As the Napoleonic wars progressed, the vassal states were required to contribute more and more heavily to their support, providing not only financial subsidies but recruits to supplement the imperial armies. (Of the 600,000 men in the forces which invaded Russia in 1812 only a third were native Frenchmen; the rest were of twenty different nationalities.) Regions which did not suffer directly the ravages of warfare were often required to support armies of occupation. Most annoying to the business and trading classes were the galling economic restrictions that formed a part of Napoleon's Continental System, and the hordes of French agents and inspectors required to enforce those restrictions.

In later years, after his defeat and exile, Napoleon tried to create the impression that during his reign he had championed the nationalist aspirations of Germans, Italians, Poles, and other scattered peoples. He could thus contrast himself with the restored rulers of Europe, who after his downfall, held these peoples in subjection or thwarted their hopes for unity. To what extent was this claim justified? Can Napoleon, as some have contended, be viewed as the architect of German and Italian unity, the defender of Polish nationalism?

In two respects he did stimulate the nationalist sentiments of certain European peoples, though perhaps not in the ways he later suggested. His rearrangement of the map of Europe, by decreasing the number of states in Germany and Italy, may have contributed to a greater sense of unity among both peoples. Where Germany consisted of some three hundred states, principalities, and lesser political entities at the end of the eighteenth century, the conquests of the revolutionary and Napoleonic armies left only the truncated states of Prussia and Austria, the Confederation of the Rhine (fifteen states at the outset), and a few lesser territories. In addition, Napoleon's decree of 1806 put an end to the anachronistic Holy Roman Empire. He thus cleared the way, unintentionally, for those who subsequently espoused the cause of a united Germany. In the Italian peninsula, the political organization established by the French was destroyed in 1815, but the fact remained that Italians could look back to a time under Napoleon's rule when the numerous states had been combined into only three separate parts: the regions directly incorporated into the French Empire, the kingdom of Italy, and the kingdom of Naples and Sicily. Italy had not known so great a measure of unity since the era of the Roman Empire. Also, by establishing the duchy of Warsaw in 1807 and adding western Galicia to it in 1809, Napoleon revived the hopes of the Polish people for an independent state.

A second, and more important, way in which Bonaparte contributed to the growth of nationalist sentiments among Europeans was by arousing patriotic resentment among the peoples subjected to French domination. How strong such feelings were among the rank and file is difficult to determine. The soldier who served in an army pitted against the French probably fought because he had to rather than out of any sense of loyalty to his nation. The peasant doubtless resented the requisition of his crops or the physical damage to his property caused by warfare, but this reaction did not necessarily result in a new allegiance to his ruler or a new sense of unity with his compatriots. However, among a minority of intellectuals during this era can be detected a new patriotic spirit. The philosopher Johann Gottlieb Fichte, for example, sought to inspire German national sentiment through his *Addresses to the German Nation*, delivered in Berlin in 1807 and 1808, and Ernst Moritz Arndt, a poet and historian, toward the end of the Napoleonic era published a series of poems calling upon Prussia to liberate all Germany from the yoke of the French tyrant. In Italy, the *Carbonari* ("Charcoal Burners"), a conspiratorial organization later devoted to the cause of Italian unity, began as a group devoted to resistance to the French occupation. None of these individuals or groups attracted a mass following before 1815, but the seeds sown during the Napoleonic era bore fruit in the nationalist movements of the nineteenth century.

As for Napoleon's own feelings toward these various national groups, his actions during his years of rule speak louder than any later words. His ruthless subjugation of the peoples of the Grand Empire to French national aims and aspirations, his imposition of French rulers and French institutions upon the dependent states, suggest no profound understanding of national differences or sympathy with nationalist goals. When he destroyed traditional institutions and upset the dynasties of petty rulers in central Europe, he did so not in order to encourage German or Italian national aspirations, but rather to rule the peoples of these territories more effectively and to exploit their resources for his own military or economic advantage. If Bonaparte was motivated in his conquests by any transcendent ideal, it was the ideal not of a federation of equal nations, but rather of a universal empire, like the Roman Empire or that of Charlemagne.

The Continental System, 1806

The Continental System did not emerge suddenly, but was the culmination of a policy of restrictions on trade with Britain adopted by France during the revolution and continued by Napoleon after his accession to power. Only at the end of 1806 did Napoleon feel secure enough in his control over Europe to undertake an all-out effort to destroy British trade with the Continent. In that year, having acquired the kingdom of Naples, he was able to close one of the major remaining points of access for the British, the Neapolitan ports. Even more important was the French defeat of Prussia, which gave Napoleon control of the north German ports, the principal entrepôts for British goods going to the Continent. With the famous Berlin Decree of November, 1806, he formally inaugurated the Continental System, banning all commerce with the British. Hereafter, British subjects on the Continent were subject to arrest; all goods belonging to Great Britain or coming from its factories or its colonies were subject to confiscation. Any vessel, regardless of nationality, coming directly from the ports of Britain or its colonies was forbidden access to continental ports. Since the decree was binding on all of France's dependent states and allies, Napoleon was, in effect, trying to establish a barrier extending from the north German ports to the tip of the Italian peninsula. Because of the condition of the French fleet, Napoleon could not hope to enforce a blockade of British ports; the principal intention of the decree was to prevent all vessels (neutral as well as British) from bringing British or colonial goods into continental ports. The emperor's aim was to secure for continental—preferably French—manufacturers and merchants, markets that had formerly been controlled by the British.

Even before the Berlin Decree, the British had instituted a blockade of their own on goods flowing in and out of continental ports on the North Sea and English Channel. After the decree, Britain retaliated by announcing that all neutral ships plying between coastal ports from which English ships were excluded would be considered liable to capture and condemnation as lawful prizes. The economic struggle between the French and British lasted until about 1812, but the principal goal of the Continental System—the destruction of British trade—was never achieved. Napoleon's plan was basically sound: if he had really succeeded in excluding British commerce from Europe, British credit would have collapsed. But British commerce never was excluded from Europe; British goods continued to flow in by a variety of means. Smuggling operations were carried out on a large scale, particularly through Holland and northwestern Germany. In many instances, customs officials were bribed to allow prohibited goods to enter. By 1810 the British were selling a great many "licenses of trade," which guaranteed neutral ships immunity from capture by British vessels and thus permitted them to carry British goods safely to the Continent. Such ships could be provided with false papers which certified their departure from a non-British port and the non-English origin of their cargo.

In the last analysis, Napoleon simply did not have the navy or the vast corps of loyal civil servants and customs inspectors required to make the system work throughout the entire continent. Frenchmen might respond to his patriotic appeals to defeat the British by adhering to the restrictions imposed by the Continental System, but there was much less reason for the natives of the dependent and allied states to heed such regulations. Merchants who saw their volume of business reduced and consumers who were deprived of products they desired were only too willing to find loopholes by which they could evade the restrictions. Most discouraging to the emperor was the fact that instead of increasing, French trade and business activity declined. For the British blockade achieved its principal purpose, which was not to prevent imports from reaching the Continent, but to weaken the enemy by destroying his commerce and shipping. Numerous French shippers and merchants went out of business as their vessels languished in continental ports blockaded by the British navy.

By 1810, the Continental System was working so badly that Napoleon decided to take advantage of its weaknesses and exploit them to the profit of France. What he did, in effect, was to become a smuggler himself: he authorized the auction of prize cargoes (including goods formally prohibited from entry) if the purchaser paid a duty of 40 per cent. Then he instructed his customs agents to admit prohibited goods on condition that they had been falsely labeled by their sellers as prize cargoes. In this way he increased the revenue from duties and permitted the entry of those goods which were particularly in demand. However, this step constituted the abandonment of the purpose of the Continental System and obviously undermined the entire operation. Thus at a time when Napoleon was still enjoying political and military victories, he had already suffered a major economic defeat.

The Peninsular War, 1808–1813

In 1807, with peace temporarily assured in central and eastern Europe, Napoleon became involved in warfare in an entirely different quarter of the Continent. He had long resented the loyalty shown by the ruler of Portugal toward his British ally and was determined to crush the Iberian kingdom and make it conform to the Continental System. To fight Portugal, Napoleon had to secure passage for French troops through Spain. This he did by vaguely promising its senile Bourbon monarch, Charles IV (ruled 1788–1808), that he would divide Portugal between France and Spain. But as we shall see, once French troops had secured a foothold in Spain, Napoleon found a pretext for overthrowing the Spanish monarchy as well. The invasion of Portugal was merely the prelude to the subjugation of the entire Iberian peninsula.

The Peninsular War is important in the context of Napoleon's entire career, for many historians have viewed the beginning of this war as the turning point in the emperor's military fortunes. For the first time he seems seriously to have underestimated the degree of resistance he would arouse and the difficult nature of the warfare he would encounter, the result, in this instance, of the mountainous terrain. Some of the initial French defeats can be ascribed to the ineptitude of the military commanders; when Napoleon took personal command, he was more successful. But the Spanish campaign proved a steady drain on his resources and dragged on indecisively until the final ejection of the French in 1813.

Although the Portuguese royal family fled to Brazil in the face of the invasion, resistance to the French continued, and the Portuguese soon had the support of a British army under the command of Sir Arthur Wellesley (1769–1852), later duke of Wellington, who defeated the French in his initial encounter with them. Meanwhile, a force of 100,000 French troops had crossed the Spanish border, ostensibly to protect the Spanish coasts against the British. In March, 1808, an opportune rebellion against King Charles IV, stemming from the unpopularity of the queen's favorite, Manuel de Godoy (1767–1851), caused Charles to abdicate in favor of his son Ferdinand VII. Profiting from the unsettled situation and from antagonisms within the royal family, Napoleon refused to recognize Ferdinand and succeeded in getting him, as well as his father and Godoy, across the Franco-Spanish border, presumably to settle the dispute among them. The outcome of this maneuver was the forced abdication of the son, which left the throne vacant. Napoleon thereupon arranged for a petition to be drawn up by a number of responsible Spanish officials requesting that the throne be given to Joseph Bonaparte. Only too happy to comply with this request, the emperor agreed, and Joseph abandoned his rights to the kingdom of Naples to become king of Spain.

What Napoleon failed to recognize was that the antipathy shown by the Spaniards toward their ruler did not necessarily imply a corresponding enthusiasm for rule by the French, for the deposition of the Bourbons was greeted by a general uprising which drove the French from Madrid. After a number of reverses during the summer of 1808, Napoleon decided to take personal command of the forces in Spain and succeeded in recapturing the capital. But failing again to understand the character of the Spanish, he undertook a series of reforms—including measures against the Catholic Church, such as ending the Inquisition and decreasing the number of monastic establishments—which merely alienated the people further. Despite a number of victories against the Spanish and the British, who had come to their aid, Napoleon was unable to bring the war to an end. Many of the inhabitants took to the hills to engage in guerilla fighting, and because the country was decentralized and disorganized, opposition was particularly difficult to overcome. Indeed, the city of Cádiz in southwestern

Spain, never submitted to French control, and it was here that a national assembly was elected in 1810 to draw up a new constitution for Spain.

The Short War with Austria, 1809

The unexpectedly strong resistance to Napoleon's armies in the Iberian peninsula, and the difficulties he encountered there, served to encourage his enemies elsewhere on the Continent. When, in 1808, Napoleon was forced to withdraw large contingents of the Grand Army from Germany for use in the Spanish campaign, the war party in the Austrian court urged Emperor Francis to seize the opportunity to embarrass his traditional enemy. After Austria's defeat at Austerlitz, Francis' younger brother, Archduke Charles Louis, had undertaken a partial reorganization of the army; this step had been matched by corresponding administrative reforms designed to strengthen the country in a future conflict with Napoleon. Francis himself was reluctant to renew the conflict with the French without allies, and he rightly guessed that no significant support would be forthcoming. Tsar Alexander was still formally allied with France; indeed, the agreements of Tilsit had been reaffirmed at a meeting between the two at Erfurt in September, 1808. Prussia, its territory still occupied by French troops, was engaged in a series of drastic reforms and was in no position to take arms against the French. Despite these misgivings, Francis was persuaded to take the risk. It was pointed out to him that France had half of its forces tied up in Spain, that the war was increasingly unpopular at home, and that the German peoples could not fail to respond to an appeal to liberate their territories from French domination.

Throwing caution to the winds, Austria began the war in April, 1809, by invading Bavaria. Napoleon was aware of the danger of his position. When it became clear that no support would be forthcoming from Russia, he hastily called up fresh recruits and ordered two divisions from Spain rushed to the east. Despite the improvised character of these forces, Napoleon's first moves showed that he had lost none of his skill as a military leader. Within a matter of days he had counterattacked and halted the Austrian advance. He followed up his advantage by marching his armies down the Danube to Vienna at a pace of twenty miles a day. Meanwhile, Archduke Charles Louis was regrouping his troops on the left bank of the Danube. When Napoleon crossed the river and attacked, he met with vicious resistance from the Austrian forces, and after two days of fighting, he was forced to recross the Danube, having lost some twenty thousand men. The Austrians also suffered heavy casualties, but they took satisfaction from the battle because they had beaten back an army commanded personally by Napoleon. After this encounter both armies remained at a standstill for seven weeks while reinforcements were brought up. When Napoleon attacked again, his was the superior force, and he carried the day with a victory at Wagram. The battle was not nearly so decisive as Austerlitz had been, but the archduke saw no purpose in continuing the war and a week later he asked for an armistice.

Austria had challenged the conqueror and had been defeated by him for the fourth time. By the Treaty of Schönbrunn (October, 1809) it lost an additional 32,000 square miles of territory, with some 3.5 million inhabitants. A good part of the ceded area went to Bavaria, and the duchy of Warsaw was strengthened by the annexation of western Galicia. To the south, Napoleon combined formerly Austrian territories with the Ionian Islands to constitute a new state, the Illyrian Provinces. A final provision of the treaty forced Austria to adhere to the Continental System and to break off all ties with Great Britain.

The Empire in 1810

In terms of square miles of territory under French control, the year 1810 marked the apogee of the Napoleonic Empire. The defeat of Austria at Wagram in 1809 extended the domination of the French southward and eastward down the Adriatic coast. Because his brother Louis had shown himself as king of Holland more sympathetic to Dutch than to French interests and had consistently violated the Continental System by allowing British goods to be smuggled in through Holland, Napoleon deprived him of his throne in 1810 and incorporated the Dutch kingdom directly into the French Empire. With other areas along the North Sea coast also added to it, the French Empire proper now consisted of 130 departments (instead of the original 83) and extended in a great arc from the Baltic Sea at the base of the Danish peninsula to a point on the Italian coast south of Rome. The Grand Empire stretched from the southwest coast of Spain to the limits of the duchy of Warsaw, on the border of the Russian empire.

Napoleon appeared to be at the height of his power, practically unchallenged throughout Europe. Except for the continuing war in the Spanish peninsula and the economic struggle with Great Britain, the period from 1810 to 1812 was relatively peaceful for the Empire. By this time he had also taken steps toward the solution of a problem which had been plaguing him for years—the absence of a son to inherit his vast domain. His marriage with Joséphine, contracted in 1796, had failed to produce an heir. More than once since becoming emperor he had considered the possibility of securing a divorce; neither partner to the marriage had remained faithful to the other. Yet Napoleon seems to have been reluctant to separate himself definitively from the woman who had inspired in him his greatest passion.

Nevertheless, marriage with the younger sister of Alexander of Russia was discussed at Tilsit in 1807 and again in 1809; the offer was finally refused by the tsar, ostensibly because the girl was too young. After the defeat of Austria in 1809, the emperor's representatives entered into negotiations with the Austrian court to arrange his marriage to the eighteen-year-old Austrian

The Empress Marie Louise. *Portrait by Gérard. The Habsburg princess married Napoleon in 1810 after his divorce from Joséphine. Musée de Versailles, Versailles.*

princess, Marie Louise (1791–1847). Prince Metternich, Austria's foreign minister, immediately took up the proposal, seeing in it a chance for Austria to achieve at least temporary security in its relations with France. For Napoleon the marriage offered not only the hope for a male heir but the prestige of affiliation with the oldest royal house on the Continent. Unable to obtain the consent of Pope Pius VII to the annulment of his marriage with Joséphine, he secured the annulment from a subservient ecclesiastical body in Paris, retired Joséphine to her château at Malmaison, and married Marie Louise in April, 1810. Within a year she had borne him a son, who was given the title of king of Rome. The dynasty now appeared secure.

Beneath the apparent stability of the Empire in the years 1810–1812 lay a number of signs of weakness and deterioration. We have spoken of the resentment aroused in the dependent states by the Continental System and the enforced levies of men and money to support Napoleon's wars. Even in France there were signs of growing discontent. A business recession in 1810–1811 diminished the regime's standing with the bourgeoisie, hitherto Napoleon's strongest supporters. The war in Spain was never popular with the French and aroused considerable opposition to the emperor. The burden of conscription in France reached down to younger and younger men during the Spanish campaign and the Austrian war of 1809, and by 1810 there were disturbing rumors of an impending war with Russia. Finally, devout Catholics, who had regarded Napoleon at the time of the Concordat as the restorer of the faith in France, were shocked by his dealings with the papacy in the years following the proclamation of the Empire. Relations between the pope and the emperor deteriorated steadily

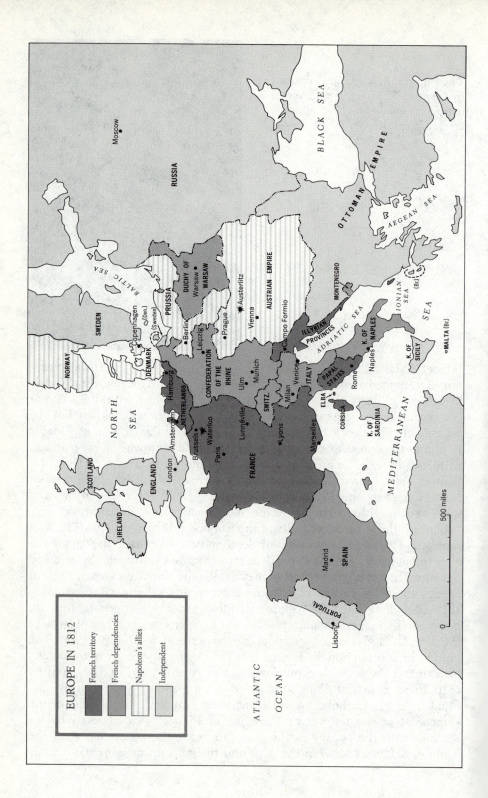

EUROPE IN 1812

French territory
French dependencies
Napoleon's allies
Independent

ATLANTIC OCEAN

NORTH SEA

BALTIC SEA

BLACK SEA

AEGEAN SEA

IONIAN SEA

ADRIATIC SEA

MEDITERRANEAN SEA

RUSSIA
Moscow

NORWAY
SWEDEN
DENMARK
Copenhagen
(Den.)
(Sweden)

PRUSSIA
Berlin
Hamburg

DUCHY OF WARSAW
Warsaw

AUSTRIAN EMPIRE
Vienna
Austerlitz
Prague
Leipzig
Campo Formio

CONFEDERATION OF THE RHINE
Munich
Ulm

SWITZ.

NETHERLANDS
Amsterdam
Brussels
Waterloo

FRANCE
Paris
Lunéville
Lyons
Marseilles

ENGLAND
London
SCOTLAND
IRELAND

SPAIN
Madrid

PORTUGAL
Lisbon

ILLYRIAN PROVINCES
MONTENEGRO

ITALY
Milan
Venice

PAPAL STATES
Rome

K. OF NAPLES
Naples

K. OF SICILY

ELBA
CORSICA

K. OF SARDINIA

MALTA (Br.)

OTTOMAN EMPIRE

(Br.)

500 miles

after 1805 because of difficulties in the administration of the Concordat and the high-handed action of Napoleon with respect to papal territories in Italy. Gradually, what had been left of the lands of the Church after the establishment of Napoleon's kingdom of Italy was either absorbed into that kingdom or occupied and administered by the French. In May, 1809, when Napoleon proposed formally to incorporate the remaining Papal States into the French Empire, the pope threatened him with excommunication. Napoleon's response was to have Pius VII arrested and taken to Savona, near Genoa, where he was held prisoner. From there he was transferred in 1812 to Fontainebleau. Such an act, culminating the entire series of aggressive moves against the Church, earned Napoleon the bitter enmity of devout Catholics throughout Europe.

As early as 1809 a number of individuals saw the handwriting on the wall and began to lay the groundwork for the regime which would succeed Bonaparte's. Among those most active in such plotting was the consummate opportunist Charles Maurice de Talleyrand, who managed to serve and to survive most of the governments that succeeded one another between 1789 and his death in 1838. Born to an aristocratic family in 1754, Talleyrand began his career as a liberal priest and was awarded the bishopric of Autun on the eve of the revolution. As a member of the Estates-General he sided with the Third Estate; in the National Assembly he supported the confiscation of Church lands and the Civil Constitution of the Clergy. In 1791, having been placed under the ban of the Church by the pope, Talleyrand entered the diplomatic service. Upon the execution of Louis XVI, he sought refuge in the United States, returning to France only after the establishment of the Directory in 1795. After serving for two years as minister of foreign affairs for the Directory, he resigned in 1799, in time to help Bonaparte to power in the *coup d'état* of Brumaire. As Napoleon's minister of foreign affairs from 1799 to 1807 he helped assure French supremacy in Europe, and in 1806 was rewarded by the emperor with the title prince of Benevento. In 1807 he resigned his post as foreign minister and in 1809 established contact with the Austrian diplomat Metternich, with a view to providing for future contingencies. He was to play an active role, as we shall discover later, in persuading the victorious allies to accept the restoration of the Bourbon dynasty in 1814, served again as foreign minister—this time for the Bourbon king, Louis XVIII—and represented France at the Congress of Vienna in 1814 and 1815. Before his death he assisted one more French ruler—Louis Philippe—to the throne, in 1830; he ended his career as French ambassador to Britain in the 1830's.

Talleyrand's reputation has suffered at the hands of historians who view him as the prototype of the Machiavellian statesman and faithless diplomat. They charge that his primary concern was enriching himself and ensuring his survival in power in the bewildering succession of French governments

Charles-Maurice de Talleyrand.
Portrait by Prudhon.

from 1789 to 1830. Even his defenders concede his egotism and attribute his
survival to the facility with which he adapted his utterances, public and
private, to the ideology prevailing at a particular moment. This was perhaps
easy for him since, in the last analysis, he adhered to no abstract ideals or
principles. But his apologists have also contended that one consistent thread
underlay his actions throughout his long career: his concern for France and
his loyalty to its interests. His skills as a diplomat and a negotiator were
always directed toward improving his country's international position. He
deserted Napoleon, it is argued, when he found himself unable to restrain
the emperor's insatiable ambition and realized it would ultimately destroy
his country. Cutting his ties with the emperor, he laid the groundwork for
the restoration of the Bourbon dynasty, and in the peace settlement following the Napoleonic wars he was remarkably successful in restoring his
defeated country almost immediately to the ranks of the great powers.

The Invasion of Russia, 1812
   Despite the evidence of mounting dissatisfaction with his regime, Napoleon began preparations in the spring of 1812 for the campaign against
Russia which ultimately was to prove disastrous for him. Like Adolf Hitler
almost 130 years later, Napoleon saw two powers blocking his plans for
complete European domination—Great Britain and Russia. Like Hitler, he
tried unsuccessfully to subdue Great Britain, and when his attempt failed,
turned eastward, convinced that if Russia were defeated, Britain must also
succumb.
   We have seen that the relationship between the two emperors, Napoleon

and Alexander, was an uneasy one from the start. The ink was hardly dry upon the agreements made at Tilsit in 1807 when Napoleon strengthened his dominion over the newly created duchy of Warsaw and sent thirty thousand troops into the region, a move that appeared very threatening to the Russian empire. His interest in consolidating his control over the Poles was further revealed when, after the defeat of Austria in 1809, he incorporated western Galicia into the duchy of Warsaw, leading Alexander to suspect his designs upon territories taken by Russia from Poland in the eighteenth-century partitions. It also became clear to Alexander that Napoleon was far from willing to concede to Russia the free hand in the dismemberment of Turkey which the tsar thought he had obtained at Tilsit. Alexander realized, as Russia's war with Turkey dragged on, that even if he were victorious, Napoleon would probably block his plans for expansion into Turkey's provinces in southeastern Europe. The nature of Napoleon's own designs in the Balkans is not entirely clear, but there can be no doubt that he was determined to prevent Russia from taking Constantinople. Finally, Napoleon's marriage with Marie Louise in 1810, and his consequent alliance with Austria, were viewed with misgivings by Alexander.

Napoleon's principal grievance against the tsar was Alexander's failure to enforce the Continental System in his own ports. True to the agreement made at Tilsit, Russia declared war on Great Britain, but Alexander never pursued the war actively and his administration of the regulations against British trade left much to be desired. When Napoleon asked Russia in 1810 to confiscate all neutral ships in its ports on the ground that they were carrying British goods, Alexander refused. Instead, he issued a decree later in the year which specifically encouraged the entry of neutral ships into Russian harbors. It was clear to Napoleon that the alliance was nearing its end. Late in 1810, Russia formally withdrew from the Continental System.

Anticipating conflict, both rulers sought allies. Each hoped for the support of Austria and Prussia, but the presence of the Napoleonic armies in Germany and the recent defeats which both Prussia and Austria had suffered at Napoleon's hands left them little choice but to submit to his demands. Accordingly, in 1812 Prussia pledged to contribute twenty thousand men, and Austria thirty thousand, to Napoleon's Grand Army. Unable to win support in Germany, Russia formed an alliance with Sweden. According to its terms, Sweden agreed to join Russia in the war against Napoleon in return for a promise of Russian assistance in annexing Norway, then in Denmark's possession, at the end of the war. Denmark was to be compensated with other territory. Ironically, Sweden's decision to join Russia was made by Crown Prince Bernadotte, once one of Napoleon's generals, who in 1810 had been named heir to the throne by the Swedish Estates. During this period, also, Russia ended the wars against Turkey and

Great Britain, and concluded an alliance with Great Britain against France.

In preparation for the invasion, Napoleon assembled his Grand Army in eastern Europe. Its strength at the time of the invasion in June, 1812, was approximately 450,000; by the time reinforcements were brought up, it numbered about 600,000—and was probably the largest military force that had ever been brought together. In its ranks were not only French soldiers but contingents of Italians, Poles, Swiss, Dutch, and Germans (from the Confederation of the Rhine, Austria, and Prussia). Napoleon planned to have the predominantly French contingents of the army advance in the center, supported by an Austrian army to the south and a Prussian army to the north. Crossing the Niemen River in June, he hoped to drive a wedge between the two main Russian armies, surround them, and defeat them separately. His objective for the campaign of 1812 was Smolensk, where he hoped to impose terms on the tsar. If Alexander refused to submit, Napoleon would winter at Smolensk and renew the war in the spring of 1813 with a drive on Moscow.

He proceeded according to this plan. What disrupted his calculations was his failure to engage the main body of the Russian armies before he was deep into Russia. The Russian generals, fearing the numerical superiority of the enemy, repeatedly avoided giving battle. Advancing relentlessly across the Russian plains under a blazing July sun, Napoleon lost thousands of men through the ravages of heat, disease, and hunger, and through desertion. When his troops finally reached Smolensk in mid-August, the Russians fought only a rearguard action and then left the city to the invader. According to his original plan Napoleon was to halt here, and he was urged to do so by some of his subordinates. Instead he made the fatal decision to press on to Moscow. General Mikhail Kutuzov (1745–1813) had been given orders to halt the advance on Moscow at Borodino, and there, on September 7, Napoleon met the main Russian force. The two armies fought bitterly, in a battle which left some seventy thousand dead and wounded. In the end, both sides claimed victory, but it was the Russians that retreated, leaving the path to Moscow open. When the French finally reached Moscow on September 14, they found it practically deserted; within a few hours, fires broke out in the city, set presumably by those who had stayed behind for this purpose by order of the retreating military governor. Because most Moscow dwellings were built of wood, the fires spread swiftly, and within a week almost three quarters of the city had burned to the ground. For five weeks Napoleon remained in the empty, devastated city, as the morale of his troops rapidly deteriorated. His offer of a truce having been rejected by Alexander, he waited in vain for the tsar to come to terms. Finally, unable to supply his troops so far from their bases, frustrated in his hope of achieving a decisive victory, and fearing the onset of the Russian winter, on October 19 he began his celebrated retreat from Moscow. His troops were harassed by attacks by Kutuzov's army and prevented from following a shorter southern route to Smolensk. At the beginning of November, cold weather set in and caused additional suffering for the hungry, beleaguered French forces. By the time they reached Smolensk, only half of the troops who had left Moscow remained. The climax of the catastrophe came in late November when the retreating forces, attempting to recross the Berezina River, were subjected to murderous fire by Russians both behind and ahead of them. From this point on, the retreat became a rout as the army lost all semblance of organization and disintegrated. On December 18, the last remnants of the Grand Army straggled across the Niemen River, from which they had set out in June. Of 600,000 men, only 100,000 remained. The rest had been killed or captured.

Napoleon had left the army early in December, before it reached the Niemen, and had hastened back to Paris. The full extent of the disaster was not known in France immediately, but rumors were trickling back and Napoleon wished to be present personally to quiet misgivings in the capital. His main reason for returning, however, was to organize a new army. Far from being shattered by the defeat he had just suffered, he was more determined than ever to renew the war against his two enemies, Russia and Great Britain. Three weeks after he got back to Paris he demanded from the Senate a draft calling up 350,000 new recruits.

The War of Liberation, 1813–1814

Fifteen months elapsed between the end of the disastrous Russian campaign and the triumphal entry of the allied armies into Paris on March 31, 1814. What is perhaps surprising is that the French managed to hold off their enemies for so long. That Napoleon succeeded in raising a

The Rout of Napoleon's army at the Bérésina River, November 26, 1813.

force of a quarter of a million men by the spring of 1813 was a miracle, but of course the men in this army were not the seasoned troops he had used at Austerlitz and Jena. Moreover, the final campaigns of the emperor were seriously handicapped by shortages of arms, ammunition, and equipment. Indeed, some military historians argue that France's defeat was caused as much by the lack of materiel as by the lack of men. A final reason for the defeat of Napoleon was that his enemies, after almost two decades of intermittent wars against France, succeeded in temporarily setting aside their differences and uniting to achieve victory.

The cornerstone of the coalition which defeated Napoleon was laid in March, 1813, when Prussia and Russia formed an alliance and called upon Austria and Great Britain to join them. The response was not immediate, but the potentialities of the coalition were augmented by an agreement at about the same time between Great Britain and Crown Prince Bernadotte of Sweden. Bernadotte promised, in return for a large subsidy from the British, to furnish thirty thousand Swedish troops to be used against the French. The war between the allies and Napoleon's reconstituted army began in the spring of 1813. Despite two nominal victories in May, Napoleon's losses were heavy, and he willingly agreed in June to an armistice, which lasted most of the summer. This pause turned out to be of greater advantage to his opponents than to himself, for when the fighting began again in August, Metternich had decided to take Austria into the war on the side of the coalition and Great Britain had signed a treaty providing the allies with heavy subsidies. Metternich's decision was reached after Napoleon refused to accept an agreement calling for the abandonment by France of most of its conquests in the interest of a balance-of-power settlement for the Continent. For the first time in his career Napoleon found himself confronted by the united forces of four major powers. Besides his French troops, he had only contingents from the Confederation of the Rhine supporting him. Nevertheless the emperor attacked, and within two weeks, had inflicted a defeat on one of the allied armies at Dresden (August, 1813), in his last major victory on German soil. From that time on, however, the campaign went badly for the emperor, as his subordinate commanders met with a series of reverses. Early in October, Bavaria withdrew from the Confederation of the Rhine and joined the alliance against the French. The climax of the fall campaign came in a series of decisive battles around Leipzig in mid-October, when all the allied armies converged upon the French in what came to be known as the Battle of the Nations. After several days of preliminary fighting, the allies, in a single nine-hour engagement, drove the French armies back to the gates of Leipzig, winning a shattering victory. Deserted by his remaining German allies, Napoleon was forced to retreat across the Rhine; the Confederation of the Rhine had come to an end.

What made the debacle in Germany even more serious was a series of setbacks in other parts of the Empire. A revolt in the Dutch provinces, followed by an allied invasion there, resulted in the restoration of the prince of Orange as ruler in Holland. An army raised by Eugène de Beauharnais in northern Italy at Napoleon's instigation met with defeat by the Austrians. Finally, the year 1813 saw one reverse after another in Spain, as the duke of Wellington advanced against a French army weakened by the transfer of important contingents to the German front. By the middle of the year, Joseph Bonaparte had fled to France and the French were retreating from region after region. In November, Wellington crossed the frontier into France and laid siege to the city of Bayonne.

Before the allies invaded France from the east, they made an offer of peace to Napoleon which would have left France with its "natural frontiers" of the Alps and the Rhine. Metternich later admitted in his memoirs that the allies had no intention of keeping this promise, that it was made in the belief that Napoleon would refuse, thereby assuming responsibility for continuing the war. Metternich's assumption proved correct. Napoleon did not reject the offer outright, but stalled in such a way that the allies could withdraw it and still blame him for the prolongation of the conflict.

In the beginning of 1814 the allied armies, 200,000 strong, crossed the Rhine. Napoleon, left with only 90,000 soldiers, many of them mere youths, fought a brilliant defensive campaign in these desperate circumstances. Shifting his troops swiftly in order to attack the divided allied forces piecemeal, he managed still to win isolated victories against the Prussian general Gebhard von Blücher (1742–1819) and the Austrian prince Karl Philipp zu Schwarzenberg (1771–1820). But the rawness of his troops, their numerical inferiority, and the lack of equipment finally decided the issue. While he made a desperate attempt to throw himself on the rear of the allied forces in Lorraine, the leading contingents of the invaders pressed on toward Paris. With the final storming of Montmartre by the allies, the French were forced to capitulate. On March 31 Tsar Alexander and King Frederick William made their triumphal entry into the capital. Napoleon had meanwhile hastened back to Paris, hoping to make a last-ditch stand, but he arrived too late and retired to Fontainebleau. Even at this stage he urged his marshals to join him in an assault on the city, but they refused. Prince Talleyrand, who had remained in Paris, now used his position as vice grand elector to summon the Senate, and influenced that body to declare that Napoleon and his family had forfeited the throne of France. Hoping to salvage something, Napoleon thereupon announced his abdication in favor of his son. But the allies would have none of it, and forced him to make his abdication unconditional. Within a month he had departed for the tiny island of Elba, off the Italian coast, where the allies, with a certain degree of irony, granted him sovereign control.

THE BOURBON RESTORATION AND THE HUNDRED DAYS

Although during the final stages of the war, there had been differences among the allied leaders about the selection of a successor to Napoleon, these had been largely resolved by the time of his defeat. Partly because of the skillful machinations of Talleyrand, who was the spokesman of a royalist minority in Paris, the allies settled upon the count of Provence, a younger brother of the beheaded Louis XVI to rule as Louis XVIII. The news that a Bourbon would occupy the throne was not greeted with particular enthusiasm by the French people, but the king's initial pledge that he would not discriminate against individuals because of their past opinions and that he intended to grant a liberal constitution to France helped reconcile those who feared the consequences of a royalist restoration. Moreover, the relatively lenient treatment given France by the allies in the Treaty of Paris (May 30, 1814) was expressly designed to facilitate the resumption of power by the Bourbons.

Despite these advantages, the regime encountered difficulties from the start. The way in which the new constitution, the Charter of 1814, was presented irritated popular sensibilities, for the king expressly stated that the Charter was a "gift" to the French people granted by the king "in the nineteenth year of our reign." By this move, Louis XVIII appeared not only to be denying the principle of popular sovereignty but also to be ignoring the fact that the revolution and the Napoleonic interlude had even existed. The provisions of the Charter itself belied this view, for the document incorporated many features of the Declaration of the Rights of Man and the Constitution of 1791 and maintained the administrative institutions of the Empire. But the uneasiness of the more liberal elements in France was enhanced by the growing influence in court circles of the king's younger brother, Charles Philippe, count of Artois (1757–1836), who was far more conservative than the king and was the unofficial leader of the faction known as the Ultraroyalists, or Ultras. This group openly regarded the Charter as a mere stopgap and called for the establishment of an absolutist regime and the restoration of the Roman Catholic Church to its former privileges. Finally, certain measures taken by the new government alienated specific groups of Frenchmen. Army officers and soldiers suffered from the conversion of the army to a peacetime footing, with a consequent reduction of pay; manufacturers resented the sudden tariff reductions, which subjected them to foreign competition; peasants looked on uneasily as the government returned large tracts of unsold national land to the original owners. Many of the ills from which Frenchmen suffered in 1814–1815 were attributable to the transition from a wartime to a peacetime economy, but the new government received the blame for them.

Napoleon Bonaparte, who had become increasingly restive under the restraints imposed upon him at Elba, was kept well informed of the mood of his former subjects and had decided by the midwinter of 1815 that the moment had come for his return to power. Taking advantage of the British commissioner's absence from the island, he commandeered several vessels and embarked for France. He landed at Cannes on March 1, 1815, and made his way northward through the mountain passes of Dauphiné, encountering practically no resistance. Indeed, most of his former soldiers rallied to his standard and the cities that lay on his route opened their gates to welcome the former emperor. By the time Napoleon reached Paris on March 20, Louis XVIII and his entourage had fled across the border to Ghent, and the Empire was once again proclaimed. In this way began the period known as the Hundred Days; it lasted until Napoleon's defeat at Waterloo in June.

In an effort to win the support of those groups which had formerly opposed his regime, Napoleon adopted during this period the liberal pose which he was to elaborate further during his final years in exile. Claiming that he had been prevented from offering reforms earlier by the need to defend France against European kings and aristocrats, he provided in his new constitution for an extension of the suffrage, the institution of a responsible ministry, and the elimination of press censorship. The announcement of these changes was greeted with a certain amount of skepticism, and Napoleon was aware that, in the last analysis, what he needed to ensure his position was a military victory.

News of Napoleon's escape from Elba struck the capitals of Europe with the force of a bombshell. March 1 found many of Europe's leaders in

Louis XVIII leaves the Tuileries. *Detail of painting by Gros. This shows the king (center) about to flee from Paris when Napoleon returned to France during the episode of the Hundred Days. Versailles.*

His Grace, the Duke of Wellington. *Engraving from a drawing by R. Cruikshank. Wellington had already distinguished himself as a military commander in the peninsular campaigns against Napoleon before his celebrated victory at Waterloo in 1815.*

Vienna, where they had assembled at a congress in the fall of 1814 to deliberate on the disposition of Napoleon's former empire. Within an hour after the reception of the news, Metternich had secured agreement from the monarchs of Austria, Russia, and Prussia to renew the war against Napoleon. Great Britain subsequently branded Napoleon an "outlaw" and joined the three eastern powers in a new alliance directed against him.

Napoleon realized that his situation was precarious. Against the combined allied forces, which were estimated at 700,000, he was able to marshal an army of only 200,000, of whom more than a third had to police the interior and defend his frontiers. Nevertheless he determined once more to strike boldly. On June 15 he crossed the Belgian border, seeking to make contact with the armies of Blücher, commanding the Prussians, and the duke of Wellington, commanding a combined force of Belgian, Dutch, German, and British troops. He hoped to split the two armies and defeat them individually. An initial victory against Blücher caused the Prussians to retreat, and Napoleon, having dispatched thirty thousand of his own troops to pursue them, turned to support Marshal Ney* against the forces of the duke of Wellington. But the emperor had miscalculated the direction of Blücher's retreat. The Prussian troops evaded the pursuing French forces, and Blücher succeeded in regrouping them in a position from which he

* Michel Ney, duke of Elchingen (1769–1815), was one of Napoleon's most celebrated generals. Created a marshal of the empire in 1804, Ney distinguished himself at the Battle of Friedland in 1807 and at Borodino in 1812. In May, 1814, he was among those who persuaded Napoleon to abdicate, and he became a peer of France upon Louis XVIII's restoration. He initially denounced Napoleon's escape from Elba, but less than two weeks later, Marshal Ney impulsively rejoined his old commander, and participated in his final campaign. After Napoleon's defeat and exile Ney was tried by the Chamber of Peers for treason, and he was executed in December, 1815.

could lend support to Wellington. Thinking that the Prussians were no longer in the area, Napoleon, handicapped by the absence of thirty thousand of his own troops, launched an attack on Wellington at Waterloo. Wellington had the numerical advantage, and because he was fighting from the shelter of a ridge, was able to conceal the strength of the forces massed at his rear. What for a time appeared to be a deadlock between the two armies was turned into an allied victory by the return of Blücher's divisions, which were thrown upon the French right. By the end of the day, there remained only half of the forces Napoleon had taken into battle at noon, and these fled in undisciplined panic. This was a defeat which even Napoleon could not survive. Four days later he abdicated once again, and frustrated in an attempt to escape to America, he surrendered to the captain of a British warship off La Rochelle. To the British fell the responsibility for serving as Napoleon's jailer and he was shipped off to the lonely island of St. Helena in the South Atlantic.

THE ACHIEVEMENT AND THE LEGACY OF NAPOLEON

During the six years that remained to Napoleon, he had little to do beyond reliving and reviewing his epic career. An individual of lesser stature might have engaged in sterile regrets over mistakes made, opportunities lost, and betrayals by trusted individuals, and indeed Napoleon's memoirs are not altogether free of regrets of this sort. But he was more concerned with arranging and ordering his version of the events of his career so as to impose an appearance of unity and coherence upon his achievements. The fruits of this effort are to be seen in his memoirs, sometimes referred to as "the gospel according to St. Helena," which often bear scant resemblance to events which actually took place and are particularly distorted when they deal with the emperor's intentions and motives. But they are nonetheless important, since the account of the emperor's life constructed at St. Helena forms the basis for the Napoleonic legend that emerged after his death and was embellished by successive biographers and admirers.

The essence of the myth which the dethroned emperor attempted to construct was that he had been a liberal and a son of the revolution, aiming to carry on and complete the reforms begun during the revolutionary era and to bring these benefits to the peoples of Europe still living under the antiquated institutions and reactionary rulers of the Old Regime. Writing during an era which witnessed the restoration of many of these very rulers and institutions, he sensed that this image would have a particular appeal.

We have already seen that a number of Napoleon's measures under the Consulate and the early Empire—the *Code Napoléon*, the overhaul of administrative structures, and the stabilization of finances—can be interpreted as bringing to completion reforms initiated during the revolutionary years. In these respects, Napoleon could pose legitimately as the consolidator of the achievements of the revolution. Furthermore, the attempt to introduce many of these changes into the vassal states as well as all of the French Empire seems to justify his claim that he was the standard-bearer of the revolution throughout Europe.

On the other hand, these reforms were made within the context of a political system that denied the individual citizen any real voice in his government and consistently stifled the free expression of opinions, through censorship and surveillance of those suspected of opposition to the regime. Such an atmosphere certainly constituted a betrayal of principles embodied in the Declaration of the Rights of Man, and its existence seems to weaken Napoleon's argument that he was a true son of the revolution.

In the assessment of Napoleon's long-range impact upon Europe as a whole, it is difficult to separate his policies and their influence from those of the revolutionary governments that preceded him. At first he merely extended to the territories he conquered the institutions that the revolutionary governments had inaugurated in France. For this reason he was initially welcomed, at least by some, as a liberator intent upon freeing the people from traditional obligations and restrictions. We have seen, however, that in the long run, enthusiasm turned to resentment as it became clear that the member states of the Grand Empire were merely satellites of France, their chief function being to supply the emperor with men, money, and supplies for his further conquests. Napoleon's new order, if considerably less brutal than Hitler's in the following century, was hardly more appealing to contemporaries. Certainly there were few Europeans outside of France who lamented his downfall in 1814.

But just as time altered the image of Bonaparte in France, so did it transform his reputation in the rest of Europe as well. To be sure, "the gospel according to St. Helena" was never universally accepted: Napoleon did not come to be viewed as the apostle of liberal and nationalist causes. What captured the popular imagination of succeeding generations instead was the vision of Napoleon as a man of the people who made his way to the top, or as the daring general, the brilliant strategist, who commanded hundreds of thousands of men and succeeded in mastering for a time an entire continent. In the relatively prosaic age that followed his downfall, an era of prolonged peace, the exploits of Napoleon the soldier, the limitless quality of his ambition, made of him a romantic hero more glamorous than any creation of fiction.

CHAPTER 25

The Concert of Europe, 1815-1848

THE VIENNA SETTLEMENT of 1815 has been ranked with the Peace of Westphalia (1648), the Peace of Utrecht (1713), and the Peace of Paris (1919) as one of the four most significant international agreements in the history of modern Europe. Merely in terms of square miles of territory affected, such a judgment appears justified; the task of the statesmen at Vienna was nothing less than to dispose of all the lands that had been conquered by the French armies over two decades. The settlement is also notable for its durability. Some adjustments were made shortly after 1830, and more significant changes accompanied the revolutions of 1848 and the movements for German and Italian unification later, but no war among the major European powers occurred until the Crimean War in the 1850's, and a general European conflict comparable to the Napoleonic wars was avoided until 1914. Perhaps even more interesting in retrospect is the fact that the allied statesmen created in 1815 the system of international relations which came, in time, to be known as the Concert of Europe. This system, which provided for periodic conferences among the so-called Great Powers (Great Britain, Russia, Austria, and Prussia) to discuss problems affecting the peace of Europe, lasted, with some alterations, until well past the middle of the century. France, after an initial probationary period, joined the ranks of the Great Powers in 1818. Ultimately the system was replaced by a diplomacy of alliances and alignments, associated with Bismarck, but the precedent of holding general international conferences for the peaceful settlement of differences had been established, and would be revived in the twentieth century.

THE SETTLEMENT OF 1815

We have referred to the settlement of 1815 as the Vienna settlement, and it is quite true that some of the major decisions concerning the disposition of territories were reached in the celebrated Vienna congress which lasted —with interruptions—from September, 1814, until June, 1815. But we shall use the term "settlement of 1815" in a broader sense, to designate the several agreements reached by the European powers during 1814 and 1815, whether or not they were actually made at Vienna.

The Treaty of Chaumont and the First Treaty of Paris

In March, 1814, even before the war with Napoleon had ended, representatives of the four major powers—Great Britain, Russia, Austria, and Prussia—met in Chaumont, France, to conclude the treaty which became the cornerstone of the Quadruple Alliance. In it the allies pledged to remain united not only until France was defeated but for twenty years after the conclusion of hostilities, in order to ensure France's observance of the forthcoming peace. Viscount Castlereagh, the British foreign minister, was primarily responsible for getting his allies to bury their differences and participate in the coalition. Each of the allies agreed to contrbute 150,000 men to the struggle against France; Britain, furthermore, pledged 5,000,000 pounds to the cause of victory.

After the coalition had achieved its initial purpose, the defeat of France, the allies concluded with the government of Louis XVIII what is known as the first Treaty of Paris (May, 1814). The most striking feature of this peace treaty is its relative leniency toward the defeated power, for which several explanations have been given. Hoping to establish a balance of power, the statesmen who drew up this treaty saw that reducing France to second- or third-rate status would serve no useful purpose. More important, perhaps, was the unwillingness of the victors to handicap the restored Bourbon dynasty with an excessively harsh peace. The new king had not, after all, been responsible for the aggressive conquests of France in the wars just ended; his government should not be required to pay the penalty. Accordingly, France was allowed to retain the territories that it had held on November 1, 1792; these included parts of Savoy, of Germany, and of the Austrian Netherlands, as well as a few enclaves such as Avignon. But France was forced to recognize the independence of the remainder of the Austrian Netherlands, Holland, the German states, the Italian states, and Switzerland. All of France's colonies, with the exception of Trinidad, Tobago, St. Lucia, and Mauritius (Ile de France) in the Indian Ocean, were returned to her by Great Britain. Britain also retained the island of Malta. Perhaps most surprising is the fact that France was not required to pay an indemnity to the victorious powers, or even to give back the art traesures that Napoleon had pirated from foreign cities during the wars.

There had been some hope that the Treaty of Paris would settle the fate of territories which France had conquered in central Europe, but disagreements among the allied statesmen prevented immediate decisions about these areas. When the disagreements persisted into the summer of 1814, it was decided to defer further discussion of the territorial settlement until the opening of the Congress of Vienna in the fall. The most important issue creating suspicion among the powers at this time, an issue which continued to be of crucial importance throughout the congress, was the fate of Poland. Russian troops had occupied the former duchy of Warsaw, and Tsar Alexander hoped to establish a Polish kingdom under Russian protection. The tsar's reconstituted Poland would include not only the duchy of Warsaw but also the territories which Prussia and Austria had acquired during the partitions in the last decades of the eighteenth century. Alexander harbored this plan for some time and encouraged Polish leaders— among them Prince Adam Czartoryski (1770–1861), whom he had appointed as his own foreign minister—with promises of a liberal constitution for the revived kingdom. Frederick William III of Prussia knew of the tsar's project and had no objections to it, even though Prussia would have to yield the lands it had taken during the partition, so long as compensation was provided in the form of other territory—preferably that of the kingdom of Saxony, whose ruler, Frederick Augustus I (ruled 1806–1827), had sided with France once too often during the final stages of the Napoleonic wars.

Fearing the reaction that his proposal would provoke, Tsar Alexander avoided making an open statement of his intentions, with respect to Poland even after the war with France was over. His reticence merely served to increase the misgivings of both Viscount Castlereagh and Prince Metternich over the entire issue. Metternich naturally viewed with distrust any proposal which would involve Austria's abandonment of territory acquired during the partitions. Both Castlereagh and Metternich were skeptical about Alexander's reassurances to the Poles that they would retain their freedom, and saw the entire scheme as a plot for extending Russian influence in central Europe. With Poland in the Russian orbit, Alexander's troops would be within easy striking distance of both Berlin and Vienna. The tsar would then replace Napoleon as the principal threat to European peace and stability. The fate of Poland was, then, one of the principal problems facing the statesmen who assembled at Vienna in the fall of 1814.

The Congress of Vienna

ORGANIZATION AND LEADERSHIP

The Congress of Vienna was not really a congress, for the delegates never met in plenary session. Invitations were extended to "all the Powers engaged on either side in the present war," but a secret article of the Treaty of Paris (where the congress was first mentioned) stipulated that the dis-

The Congress of Vienna, 1814–1815. *Seated in the left foreground: Hardenberg; standing next to him: Wellington; standing in the left foreground: Metternich; seated to the left of center foreground: Castlereagh; seated at right: Talleyrand.*

position of territories and other important decisions would be left to the four Great Powers of the Quadruple Alliance. The initial hope was that the congress would last only four weeks, after which the decisions of the major powers would be submitted to all the delegates for ratification. But the closed negotiations aroused the resentment of the lesser powers: their representatives had come to the congress under the impression that they would participate actively in its deliberations, or at least be consulted on matters affecting their own interests; now they found, instead, that though some were called to serve on committees dealing with specific problems, in general they were ignored.

One of the unforeseen consequences of this policy was the obligation which fell upon the host of the congress, Emperor Francis of Austria, to entertain the delegates of the smaller states throughout the winter of 1814–1815. Sir Harold Nicolson, in his lively study of the Congress of Vienna, describes the obligations confronting the emperor and his court officials.

In the Hofburg itself he (the Emperor) was obliged, day in and day out, to entertain an Emperor, an Empress, four Kings, one Queen, two Hereditary Princes, three Grand Duchesses and three Princes of the blood. Every night dinner at the Hofburg was laid at forty tables; special liveries and carriages were provided for all the royal guests; the horses in the stable numbered no less than 1,400. Each monarch or head of a family had brought with him a crowd of chamberlains and equerries, and the royal consorts were attended by mistresses of the robe and ladies-in-waiting .... In order to amuse this horde of miscellaneous visitors the Emperor Francis had appointed from his court officials a Festivals Committee who were driven to distraction by the task of inventing new forms of amusement and by the excruciating problems of precedence.[1]

[1] Harold Nicolson, *The Congress of Vienna* (New York, 1946), pp. 159-160.

Socially active though Vienna was that winter, accounts of the congress which emphasize only its more glamorous aspects—the balls, banquets, and theatrical performances—are misleading; the principal statesmen and their staffs regularly put in long and hard hours of work hammering out the details of the final settlement.

To a large extent the decisions were the outcome of the interaction of the chief representatives of the five major powers—France and the members of the Quadruple Alliance. The only ruler who took part personally in the negotiations was Alexander I, who was convinced that Russia's major share in the victory against Napoleon entitled him to the dominant role in drawing up the peace. Moved alternately by idealism, religious mysticism, and shrewd calculations of what would best serve Russia's interests, this erratic prince was the despair of those who had to deal with him. His determination to consolidate Russian control over Poland and generally to extend Russia's influence in Europe aroused the suspicion and antagonism of diplomats who were already wary of his professions of liberalism.

Emperor Francis of Austria, though host to the congress, preferred to leave the burden of diplomatic negotiations to his chief minister, Prince Klemens von Metternich (1773–1859). In 1814 Metternich was already an experienced diplomat. He had served the Austrian foreign office since 1801, first as minister to Saxony, then as minister to Prussia, and from 1806 to 1809 as ambassador to the court of Napoleon in Paris. In 1809 he was appointed foreign minister, a position he held without interruption until 1848. A handsome man who wore the uniform of a knight of Malta and had finely powdered hair, he was known to all his contemporaries for his conceit and pompousness. He wrote in his memoirs in 1819, "There is a wide sweep about my mind. I am always above and beyond the preoccupation of most public men; I cover a ground much vaster than they can see. I cannot keep myself from saying about twenty times a day: 'how right I am, and how wrong they are.'" He has been called a supreme opportunist, but he himself denied the charge, claiming that his actions sprang from certain "principles" to which he consistently adhered. Among these the most important was the idea of "equilibrium," which he applied to his conduct of both domestic and foreign policy. According to Metternich, all society rested ideally in a kind of equilibrium, or "repose," which was periodically upset. In his own time, the balance had shifted too far in one direction with the violence attendant upon the French Revolution and the Napoleonic conquests. Now it would be the task of Europe's rulers to restore equilibrium, for which a period of peace was essential. To some degree he felt that Europe's stability would be ensured by the return to their thrones of "legitimate" rulers who had an interest in the preservation of established institutions; however, his adherence to this principle has been exaggerated, for many parts of the Vienna settlement to which he agreed violated the principle of "legiti-

Klemens von Metternich. *Portrait by J. Ender. Metternich is wearing the regalia of a knight of the Order of the Golden Fleece.*

macy." Metternich was assisted in 1814–1815 by Friedrich von Gentz (1764–1832), who acted as secretary general for the congress and whose brilliantly written memoirs and letters are a rich source for information about the period.

Great Britain was represented in the negotiations at first by its foreign minister, Viscount Castlereagh (Robert Stewart, second marquis of Londonderry, 1769–1822), and after February, 1815, by the duke of Wellington, who came as first British plenipotentiary. Castlereagh was a fundamentally lonely individual who concealed his shyness behind a screen of formal good manners. To many he appeared aloof and condescending. We have already seen him as one of the chief architects of the final coalition against Napoleon; because of Britain's unique position among the powers, he also played an important role in the territorial settlement of Vienna. The British government was as determined as the other powers to prevent a resurgence of French aggression, and had made a heavy financial contribution to the winning of the war, but Britain, unlike the others, had no territorial ambitions on the Continent. As long as his country's maritime and commercial interests were secure, Castlereagh could play the role of a disinterested mediator among the conflicting continental states. His position was enhanced, moreover, by the fact that Britain had restored to France almost all of its colonial possessions and could therefore call for comparable generosity on the part of the other allies.

Prussia played only a small part in the deliberations at Vienna, partly because the deafness of its chief representative, Prince Karl August von Hardenberg, made it difficult for him to follow the discussions closely, and partly because the Prussian king, Frederick William III, was personally subservient to the tsar. The king was not only ready to support Alexander's claims in Poland but showed himself prepared to follow Russian dictates on other matters of policy as well.

Since the peace treaty with France had been concluded before the congress assembled, France was invited to send a representative. This turned out to be Prince Talleyrand, who had survived the downfall of Napoleon and now served Louis XVIII, whom he had assisted to the throne. Though the four allies had certainly not intended to admit the defeated power to their deliberations, Talleyrand's skill as a diplomat never showed to greater advantage than at the Congress of Vienna. By exploiting the resentment of the lesser powers over their exclusion from the discussions, and posing as their champion, the indefatigable Talleyrand gradually managed to worm his way into the councils of the big four, and to participate in the making of some of their decisions. Indeed, by the middle of the winter he was able to take advantage of a split that developed among the victorious powers in the Polish-Saxon crisis to conclude a secret agreement with Britain and Austria directed against Russia and Prussia.

THE POLISH-SAXON SETTLEMENT

The inability of the allied representatives to come to an agreement over the status of Poland and Saxony in the early summer of 1814 meant that the whole issue was still very much alive when they assembled in Vienna in the fall. Castlereagh did his best to persuade Tsar Alexander to scale down his demands for Polish territory and to arrange some sort of compromise, but he failed. Metternich's attempt at direct negotiations with Alexander resulted in a scene so violent that the tsar threatened him with a duel and refused to speak to him directly for three months thereafter. Even Hardenberg entered into discussions with Alexander which were designed to bring about a compromise, but Prussia's insistence on the acquisition of the whole of the kingdom of Saxony did not predispose the tsar to moderate his own demands. By December the atmosphere between Britain and Austria, on one side, and Russia and Prussia, on the other, was so tense that there was open talk of the possibility of war. At this point Prince Talleyrand stepped in with a stratagem which appeared at first to heighten the crisis but ultimately resulted in its solution. He proposed to Metternich and Castlereagh a secret alliance to be directed against Russia and Prussia. The agreement, signed on January 3, 1815, provided that France, Austria, and Great Britain would support one another in the event that any of them should be attacked by Russia or Prussia, and went on to specify the number of troops each would contribute to the joint defense. Although the detailed terms of the alliance remained secret, rumors of its formation were allowed to leak out, and they reached the rulers of Russia and Prussia almost immediately. The expectation that further attempts to push through their designs would result in a general European war was sufficient to convince the tsar and his Prussian supporters to back down, and the crisis was effectively ended.

Would the three signatories really have resorted to war if the tsar had persisted in his designs? It is known that Castlereagh was acting against the orders of his government in signing the agreement, and France would certainly have had difficulty in mustering the forces promised for the defense of Poland and Saxony; but the bluff worked, and the way was paved for a peaceable settlement of the dispute. Perhaps the most amazing feature of the entire episode was the fact that France, which had been defeated a mere six months before, had formed an alliance with two of its conquerors directed against the other two. Immediately after the conclusion of the agreement, Talleyrand wrote to his monarch, Louis XVIII, "The Coalition is dissolved. France is no longer isolated in Europe." [2] From this time on, Talleyrand sat with the inner group at the congress.

Late in January, Metternich made the proposal that was the basis for the final agreement on Poland and Saxony. Poland emerged as an ostensibly independent kingdom, but it was a greatly reduced version of the state Alexander had hoped for, since Prussia was allowed to retain Posen, and Austria to keep Galicia, territories they had taken during the partitions. Krakow, with the area immediately around it, was established as a free city under the joint protection of Austria, Prussia, and Russia. The rest of the former duchy of Warsaw constituted the new Polish state, with Alexander as its ruler. In time, the tsar conferred upon the Polish kingdom a liberal constitution, which guaranteed full independence and a separate political structure to the Polish people, but the preamble made clear that the constitution was being granted not as a right, but as a favor. Furthermore, the kingdom was to be a hereditary possession of the Romanov dynasty, and its foreign policy was to remain under the control of Russia.

Prussia may not have come away with all that it had hoped for, but it fared reasonably well, receiving two fifths of the territory of Saxony, with a population of 850,000; the remainder of Saxony was restored to its former ruler, who retained the title of king. Prussia also received additional territories in Germany—Swedish Pomerania, and portions of Westphalia and the Rhineland—in part, as compensation for lands ceded to Hanover and Bavaria.

THE FINAL SETTLEMENT

Once the Polish-Saxon issue had been disposed of, the diplomats at Vienna were able to reach agreement on other aspects of the territorial settlement without further crises. Their decisions were embodied in a

---

[2] Quoted by Nicolson, *The Congress of Vienna*, pp. 177-178.

document known as the Final Act, which was completed and signed in June, 1815. Traditional interpretations of the Vienna settlement have emphasized the adherence of its architects to certain fundamental principles: legitimacy, the balance of power, and compensation. According to this view, the negotiators at Vienna set as one of their tasks the restoration of "legitimate" rulers to their thrones. In fact, however, this principle was frequently disregarded, particularly with respect to the former German states, for no statesman seriously contemplated the restoration of all the petty rulers to their thrones. The intention of establishing a balance of power was unquestionably more important than considerations of legitimacy in the settlement of 1815. From it stemmed both the unwillingness of the Great Powers to weaken France unduly and the insistence by Britain that Prussia be strengthened so as to serve as a counterweight to Russia in the east and France in the west. The principle of compensation merely supplied one means for preserving the balance of power. When a victorious nation gave up a piece of territory, it received compensation in the form of other territory. Thus in the Polish-Saxon crisis Prussia received Saxon lands in return for relinquishing some of its Polish possessions. Austria acquired territories on the Italian peninsula in return for yielding the Austrian Netherlands to an enlarged kingdom of Holland.

But in the last analysis the Vienna statesmen were probably less concerned with following principles than with pragmatically ensuring that France would not trouble the peace of Europe in the future. To this end they established around France two defensive barriers made up of the neighboring states. At the northernmost end of the first of these barriers, which was formed by states touching France's borders, was the new kingdom of the Netherlands, consisting of the former Dutch republic and the Austrian Netherlands, under the rule of the ex-*stadholder* of Holland (the heir of the house of Orange), who was given the title King William I. This reunification of the two regions of the Low Countries, formally separated since the Peace of Westphalia in 1648, was one of the less durable achievements of the congress. Linguistic and religious differences contributed to the dissatisfaction of the people of the southern provinces, and in 1831 they revolted and proclaimed their independence as the new kingdom of Belgium.

Along the eastern boundary of France were ranged a number of German states (including Prussia, in that it was given control of the territories along the left bank of the Rhine); Switzerland, which was reestablished as an independent confederation of cantons; and the kingdom of Sardinia, which included not only the island of Sardinia but also the territory of Piedmont on the mainland. The kingdom of Sardinia (also referred to as the kingdom of Piedmont) was enlarged and strengthened by the addition of Genoa, Nice, and a part of Savoy. On France's southwestern border Spain was again

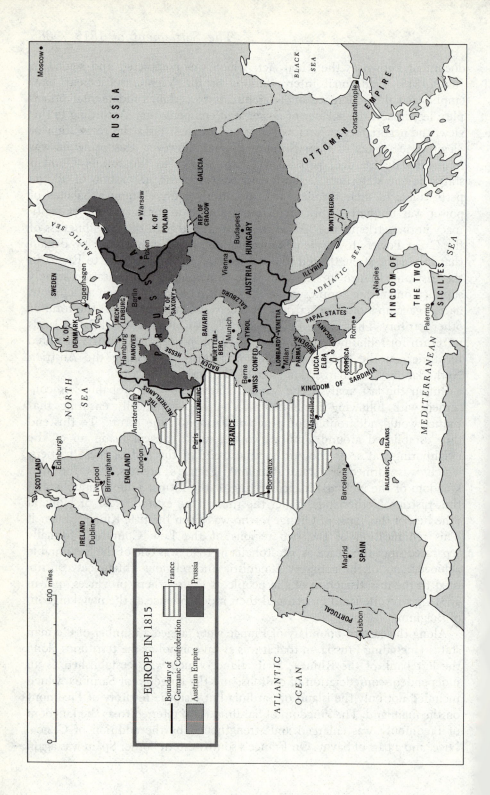

EUROPE IN 1815

Boundary of
Germanic Confederation ——
France (vertical lines)
Prussia (dark)
Austrian Empire (shaded)

500 miles

RUSSIA

Moscow

BLACK SEA

OTTOMAN EMPIRE

Constantinople

GALICIA

Warsaw

K. OF POLAND

REP. OF CRACOW

Budapest

HUNGARY

Vienna

AUSTRIA

MONTENEGRO

ILLYRIA

ADRIATIC SEA

BALTIC SEA

SWEDEN

Copenhagen

K. OF DENMARK

Berlin

Posen

P R U S S I A

MECK-LENBURG

K. OF SAXONY

SALZBURG

Hamburg

HANOVER

HESSE

BAVARIA

WÜRTTEM-BERG

BADEN

Munich

TYROL

LOMBARDY-VENETIA

Milan

MODENA

PARMA

LUCCA

TUSCANY

PAPAL STATES

Rome

Naples

KINGDOM OF THE TWO SICILIES

Palermo

MEDITERRANEAN SEA

KINGDOM OF SARDINIA

CORSICA

ELBA

Berne

SWISS CONFED.

THE NETHERLANDS

Amsterdam

LUXEMBURG

Paris

FRANCE

Bordeaux

Marseilles

Barcelona

BALEARIC ISLANDS

SPAIN

Madrid

PORTUGAL

Lisbon

ATLANTIC OCEAN

NORTH SEA

SCOTLAND

Edinburgh

IRELAND

Dublin

ENGLAND

Liverpool

Birmingham

London

under Bourbon rule; Ferdinand VII had been restored to the throne by Wellington in the final stages of the Peninsular War.

Reinforcing the states along France's borders was the second defensive barrier, lying farther to the east: Prussia proper, Austria, and the remaining German states. The British intended Prussia to emerge from the settlement as a formidable power in central Europe, standing as a bulwark against both French and Russian aggression. Ultimately Metternich agreed to support this policy even though it was strongly attacked by other Austrian statesmen as a threat to Austrian domination of the German states.

Austria received major territorial restorations in the south. These included on the Italian peninsula the provinces of Lombardy and Venetia, and on the Dalmatian coast the Illyrian Provinces—all of which were directly incorporated into the Austrian empire. Austria also recovered Salzburg and the Tyrol, both lost to Bavaria during the Napoleonic wars. A *Deutscher Bund* ("Germanic Confederation") was established as a kind of successor to the defunct Holy Roman Empire. It was composed of thirty-eight states, including four free cities, and Austria and Prussia (except for their non-German territories), bound together in a loosely organized union under the presidency of Austria.

On the Italian peninsula, beyond the second defensive barrier, a number of rulers were restored to their thrones. The Papal States were returned to the pope. In central and northern Italy, three small duchies—Tuscany, Parma, and Modena—were put under princes related to the Austrian royal family, and Austrian influence was to remain strong throughout the peninsula in the years after 1815. The kingdom of Naples and Sicily (the kingdom of the Two Sicilies) was ultimately restored to the Bourbon ruler, Ferdinand I, after remaining under Joachim Murat, Napoleon's brother-in-law, until he made the mistake of rallying to the emperor's standard during the Hundred Days.

In other provisions of the Vienna settlement, Sweden was allowed to retain Norway, acquired from Denmark in the preceding year, but was forced to accept Russia's conquest of Finland. Great Britain voluntarily abandoned all colonial conquests with the exception of those taken from France in the first Treaty of Paris, Helgoland and the former Dutch colonies of Ceylon, the Cape Colony, and Demerara, in Guiana.

The Second Treaty of Paris and the Holy Alliance

Napoleon's escape from Elba and the episode of the Hundred Days delayed the discussions at the Congress of Vienna but did not affect the overall territorial settlement. Indeed, the Final Act of the congress was signed before the Battle of Waterloo. The principal consequence of Napoleon's return for the settlement of 1815 was the change it brought about in the terms imposed upon France. The failure of the French to oppose

Napoleon—indeed, the enthusiastic reception which many Frenchmen gave him—seemed to call for harsher punishment than the first Treaty of Paris had imposed.

Quick action by the British brought about a second restoration of Louis XVIII, who returned, according to the current phrase, "in the baggage of the allies." Because they had played the principal role in the final battles against Napoleon, the British and the Prussians took the lead in drafting the second Treaty of Paris, which was signed only in November, 1815, after five months of wrangling among the allies. Hardenberg had to contend with the vigorous demands of the Prussian general staff for a treaty which would strip France of Alsace-Lorraine, the Saar Valley, and the rest of Savoy and impose a crushing indemnity. These demands for a vengeful peace were also resisted by Castlereagh, who hastened to Paris in July and remained there until November, patiently working for a moderate settlement. In his view the considerations that had made lenient treatment of France desirable a year earlier were still present. The resulting treaty, somewhat of a compromise, was nevertheless notable for its moderation. The first treaty had cut France back to the boundaries of 1792; this one specified the boundaries of 1790, which meant the loss of several fortresses, a few small strips of territory on the Belgian and Swiss frontiers, and an additional slice of Savoy, ceded to the kingdom of Sardinia. The first treaty had imposed no indemnity, this one required France to pay 700,000,000 francs to the victors and to support an army of occupation of 150,000 troops for five years. (This force was reduced to 30,000 in 1817 and removed entirely in 1818.) Finally, France was required to return the art treasures it had kept under the first treaty.

France's renewed defiance of Europe during the Hundred Days made a reaffirmation of the Quadruple Alliance appear essential. A declaration signed on the same day as the second Treaty of Paris was designed as a guarantee of that treaty. In it each of the four powers pledged to supply sixty thousand men in the event of a violation of the Treaty of Paris, particularly another attempt at a restoration of the Bonapartist dynasty. Of special interest is the article of this document calling for periodic conferences of the contracting powers for discussion of their "common interests" and for "the examination of measures which . . . will be judged most salutary for the repose and prosperity of peoples, and for the maintenance of peace in Europe." In this statement were contained the germs of the conference system which persisted well into the nineteenth century.

The Quadruple Alliance was reaffirmed for the limited purpose of preventing violations of the Treaty of Paris, not to guarantee the broader settlement made at the Congress of Vienna or the more general goals of the contracting monarchs. But it was to become confused in the popular mind with another alliance, which had been proposed by Tsar Alexander and signed by the monarchs of Prussia and Austria in September, 1815. The other rulers of Europe were invited to adhere to the three monarchs' agreement. Precisely where Alexander got the idea for this Holy Alliance has never been determined, though it is clear that considerable influence was exerted upon him by Baroness Barbara von Krüdener (1764–1824), a Pietist mystic, who had acquired temporary ascendancy over him. The concept of a general agreement among the European states for the renunciation of war and the establishment of international order seems to have been in his mind for at least ten years, and the religious sanction which underlay the proposal reflected his mood at this time.

The general reaction of European diplomats to Alexander's proposal seems to have been one of amused cynicism, summed up by Castlereagh's oft-quoted comment, "A piece of sublime mysticism and nonsense." Metternich appears to have shared this view, yet Emperor Francis joined Frederick William of Prussia in signing the document, since they felt this act could do no harm and would please the tsar. Indeed the only rulers who failed to adhere formally to the Holy Alliance were the future George IV of Great Britain, acting as prince regent, who excused himself on the ground that his signature would be unconstitutional without the accompanying signature of a minister; the sultan of the Ottoman Empire, who refused on the ground that he was not a Christian; and Pope Pius VII, who commented acidy that "from time immemorial the papacy had been in possession of Christian truth and needed no new interpretation of it."[3]

In the Holy Alliance, the three contracting monarchs declared "their fixed resolution to take no other guide for their conduct . . . than those precepts of that holy religion, namely the precepts of Justice, Charity and Peace . . . as being the only means of consolidating human institutions and remedying their imperfections." It went on to state that the three monarchs, acting as Christian brothers, would on all occasions and in all places lend each other aid and assistance to protect religion, peace, and justice.

Whatever the motives behind the Holy Alliance, there is no question that within a few years it was serving Metternich and the tsar as an instrument for the repression of liberal and revolutionary movements throughout Europe. Perhaps most unfortunate was the confusion in the public mind between the Holy Alliance and the Quadruple Alliance: the conference system delineated by the Quadruple Alliance consequently came to be viewed merely as a device for enforcing reactionary policies. The defense of reaction had certainly not been the intention of Viscount Castlereagh. Indeed, the history of Britain's relationship with its allies during the next few years consisted largely of Castlereagh's repeated

---

[3] Quoted by F. B. Artz, *Reaction and Revolution, 1814–1832* (New York, 1934), p. 118.

attempts to prevent the transformation of the Quadruple Alliance into an instrument for repression.

The Settlement of 1815 Appraised

During the nineteenth century the settlement of 1815 was widely criticized by liberals and nationalists. For one thing, it was associated in the popular mind with Metternich, who came to symbolize for his critics all that was antiliberal and antinationalist. It was also attacked because of the apparently callous way in which territories had been shifted from one state to another with no consideration for the wishes of the inhabitants. This sort of cynical maneuver, it was felt, was typified by the annexation of the Italian provinces of Lombardy and Venetia by the Austrian empire, a move which appeared to have no other justification than the principle of compensation: Austria had given up its provinces in the Netherlands in order to permit the formation of a strengthened kingdom of Holland, and therefore received territory elsewhere; whether the Italian-speaking peoples of Lombardy and Venetia favored submission to the Habsburg emperor of Austria had seemed irrelevant to the peacemakers. The continued domination of large blocs of Poles by Prussia and Austria (to say nothing of the sham character of Polish "independence" under Russian tutelage) was another example of the Vienna statesmen's indifference to nationalist aspirations.

What can be said in response to these charges against the statesmen of 1815? The most obvious reply is that the accusations were anachronistic. Such transfers of territories and peoples had been practiced for centuries and were entirely consistent with the traditions of European diplomacy. Nor did the peoples affected react as their descendants a generation or two later would have done. True, the French revolutionaries had emphasized the doctrine of popular sovereignty and the feeling of Frenchmen toward their nation changed during the revolutionary years, but it would be a mistake to assume that the attitudes of all other European peoples underwent a corresponding transformation during the same era. To be sure, as we have noted, Napoleon did arouse resentment among the peoples he conquered, and German, Italian, and Polish patriots attempted to arouse nationalist sentiments among their fellow countrymen. In Prussia and in Poland they were partially successful, but only slowly did a strong sense of national identity emerge among the masses. It is therefore unreasonable to criticize Metternich, Castlereagh, and their colleagues for failing to appreciate the potential strength of feelings which were frequently no more than embryonic in 1815.

The settlement achieved in 1815 has inevitably been compared with the one reached by the Paris Peace Conference in 1919. Both followed general European wars; both involved major territorial adjustments; both had to deal with the difficult problem of how to treat a defeated power whose aggression was believed to have been responsible for the war. The peacemakers of 1919, aware of the parallel, set out consciously to avoid the "mistakes" made by their predecessors a century earlier, and the disintegration of the Paris settlement in the 1930's after little more than a decade led to a reappraisal of the work of the Congress of Vienna and to a more favorable judgment of its achievements. Perhaps the Vienna statesmen had a less difficult task than their successors after the First World War precisely because they did not have to reckon with the strong nationalist feelings generated during the nineteenth century.

Many circumstances help to determine whether a treaty lasts, yet it is hard to escape the conclusion that the relatively judicious treatment accorded France by the peacemakers in 1815 had something to do with the permanence of the settlement. The unwillingness of the victors to handicap the restored Bourbon ruler with a punitive peace, coupled with their conviction that France must inevitably take its place once again among the major powers, led them to draw up a treaty which the French were able to live with for close to half a century. When one compares this result with the fate of the Treaty of Versailles, imposed on Germany in 1919, the peacemakers of 1815 do not appear as benighted as their critics have charged.

Finally, in assessing the positive accomplishments of the statesmen of 1815, we must return to the plan of the Quadruple Alliance for periodic conferences of the Great Powers to deal with questions affecting the peace of Europe. Beneath this proposal lay an assumption concerning international relations which differed from the view that had prevailed before 1789. This changed point of view was reflected by Metternich in 1824 when he said, "For some time Europe has had for me the character of my own country." By this statement, and perhaps more by his actions, he seemed to suggest that the Great Powers had a responsibility for maintaining the welfare of Europe as a whole—not just for pursuing their own interests—and that an important part of their obligation was the avoidance of war. This idea was at the heart of what was called the Concert of Europe.

THE FATE OF THE CONFERENCE SYSTEM

In the years immediately following 1815, the Great Powers met regularly in a series of conferences dealing with problems of mutual concern. The last of these was held in 1822. By that date—and indeed, even earlier—Great Britain's differences with Austria, Russia, and Prussia over the nature and purpose of the alliance had reached a stage where collaboration on a permanent basis was no longer possible. Yet the collapse of the plan for regular meetings did not end the Concert of Europe. For the continental powers—joined occasionally by Britain—continued to assemble whenever specific crises developed, and the idea persisted that any threat to peace in Europe was automatically of concern to all. The period following 1815 was certainly not free of tensions, but the fact that no war was fought among the major powers may be attributed at least in part to this new system of European diplomacy.

The Congress of Aix-la-Chapelle

For the first three years after the conclusion of peace the primary task of representatives of the Quadruple Alliance was to supervise the enforcement of the Treaty of Paris and the occupation of France. By 1818 France had arranged for the final payment of its indemnity and the allies decided that the time had come to evacuate the occupation troops and adjust relations between France and the other powers. This was the principal task of the Congress of Aix-la-Chapelle, which brought together in 1818 the rulers of Russia, Austria, and Prussia, along with delegations of diplomats from the four Great Powers and France. To all appearances the congress went smoothly and achieved its stated purpose. The withdrawal of troops from France was agreed upon, and as a token of complete reacceptance by the treaty nations, France was included in a newly formed Quintuple Alliance with the four other powers. Lest the French should disturb the peace again, the Quadruple Alliance was retained. But this was merely a safeguard; the diplomats generally agreed that France had fulfilled its obligations and was ready to assume its privileges and obligations as a Great Power. A number of other questions were dealt with by the powers, and the general impression was that the hopes which had been placed in the conference system were now being realized. Thus Metternich could comment, "Never have I known a prettier little congress."

Yet the testimony of others who participated in the Congress of Aix-la-Chapelle belied this general impression. For the discussions at the congress brought out sharp differences between the British and Russian views of the alliance and its purposes. Tsar Alexander had taken the opportunity to propose an *Alliance Solidaire*, by which the powers of Europe would guarantee not only each other's borders and possessions but also the security in each country of whatever form of government then existed. Castlereagh's sharp rejection of this proposal was accompanied by an explanation of the position which the British had held since 1815, and which they were to reiterate more than once in the years that followed. The British representative made it clear that the Quadruple Alliance had never been more than a specific commitment to prevent French military aggression. To interpret the alliance as a broad instrument for the preservation of established regimes and the suppression of revolutions wherever they occurred was to go far beyond the treaties to which Britain adhered. In the face of this determined stand, Tsar Alexander withdrew his proposal.

The Revolutions in Southern Europe, 1820–1823

Two years later, in 1820, the unity of the Great Powers was tested more concretely when a series of revolutions broke out in Spain and on the Italian peninsula. For the first time the differences among the Great Powers were brought into the open. The first of the revolts was directed against Ferdinand VII of Spain, the Bourbon ruler who had been restored in 1814. He had been returned on condition that he would observe the liberal Constitution of 1812, which had been drawn up by an elected national assembly, the Cortes, in Cádiz, the one region of Spain that Napoleon had never subdued. Yet as soon as he had been restored he dissolved the Cortes, abandoned the constitution, and proceeded systematically to persecute the liberals who had been responsible for it. The general inefficiency of the government, evidence of corruption in high places, and an economic crisis provoked further antipathy to the regime. The rebellion began in the army, among regiments about to be sent to the Spanish colonies in Latin America to suppress revolts which had erupted there, but it quickly gained the support of upper-middle-class merchants whose business had dwindled in the postwar era and of a handful of liberal intellectuals sympathetic with the ideals of the French Revolution. Although the revolution was in no sense a popular movement, the rebels were strong enough to force their will upon the king, who agreed in March, 1820, to respect the constitution and to summon the Cortes once again. For two years, until the French rescued him, the king remained the captive of the revolutionaries.

The response of the Great Powers to news of the revolt in Spain was far from uniform. The strongest reaction, not surprisingly, came from Tsar Alexander, who before the revolution succeeded, sent notes to the other allies suggesting some sort of joint intervention in defense of Ferdinand VII. Among the most amenable to this proposal was France, which had a particular interest in Spain because of its proximity, and saw intervention as an opportunity to counteract British influence in the Iberian peninsula. Prussia, although less directly concerned, was also willing to follow Russia's lead. Given Metternich's general horror of revolutions, it is a little surprising that he hesitated to support the tsar's proposal, but his conviction that the Iberian peninsula was Britain's particular sphere of influence led him to await the British reaction. The British position was unequivocal. Although Castlereagh had no sympathy for the revolution, the British were determined for several reasons to prevent joint allied intervention in Spain. In the first place, intervention was contrary to Britain's view of the Quadruple Alliance. Second, the presence of the allies in Spain might threaten British commercial interests there. Finally, Britain saw that intervention by the allies might lead to an attempt to wrest from the South American colonies the independence they had recently won from Spain, and in the process hinder the increasing British trade with the western hemisphere. Acting upon motives of principle and pocket, the British government on May 5,

1820, circulated a memorandum to the other powers opposing allied intervention in Spain and reiterating the view that the alliance had originally been directed against France and that it had never been intended as "an union for the government of the world or for the superintendence of the internal affairs of other States."[4] In the face of such categorical opposition, the Russian proposal was temporarily dropped.

When a series of revolts, apparently inspired by the Spanish example, erupted later in 1820 in other parts of Europe, Alexander's appeals met with more enthusiastic support. Indeed, Metternich, resorting to his most extravagant metaphors, referred to the revolutions as "conflagrations," "torrents," and "earthquakes." Spain's neighbor, Portugal, was affected in August. Here a peculiar situation existed; John VI, the king, was still in Brazil, where he had fled during the Napoleonic wars, and the government was in the hands of a regent who had the support of Marshal William Carr Beresford (1768–1854), the British general commanding troops stationed in the country. Taking advantage of the temporary absence of Beresford, a group of Portuguese army officers raised the standard of rebellion and established a provisional government which announced its support of the king, provided he returned to his country. Meanwhile, a newly summoned assembly began to draft a constitution on the Spanish model.

More alarming to the powers, particularly to Metternich, was a concurrent revolt in Naples that threatened Austrian control of the entire Italian peninsula. Metternich spoke of this as the "greatest crisis" of his career. The rebellion was directed against Ferdinand I, the restored king of Naples and Sicily, who was an uncle of the king of Spain, and resembled him in many respects. Like the Spanish king he had broken the promises made to his people upon his return in 1815 by abolishing reforms introduced during the French occupation and restoring the nobility and clergy to their privileged positions in the state. Further, since Metternich had helped place him upon the throne, he was regarded as subject to Austrian influence. Opposition to Ferdinand came in large measure from the same groups that supported the rebellion in Spain: army officers and members of the business class. They had the additional support of nationalist secret societies like the Carbonari, which had emerged during the Napoleonic occupation and now directed their attack against Austrian influence as well as the reactionary government of Ferdinand. The demands of those who revolted in Naples were vague and primarily negative. The rebels did press for a constitution based on the Spanish Constitution of 1812, but there is some evidence that they were ignorant of its actual provisions.

The Neapolitan revolt aroused great excitement throughout the peninsula, but only in the northern Italian kingdom of Sardinia did an actual

[4] Quoted by Charles K. Webster, *The Foreign Policy of Castlereagh, 1815–1822* (London, 1925), p. 238.

insurrection break out. Here the hopes of the revolutionaries were focused on Charles Albert (1798–1849), nephew of King Victor Emmanuel I and heir to the throne, but the irresolute behavior of the young prince when the rebels sought to make him their leader in March, 1821, helped doom the revolt to failure.

Metternich was horrified by the revolt in Naples; yet he delayed taking measures to suppress it. It would have been relatively simple for an Austrian army to invade the kingdom and crush the rebels, but Metternich preferred to win the support of the Concert of Europe before adopting such a course of action. Despite Britain's refusal to condone intervention in Spain, Metternich now appealed to Castlereagh for backing in Italy. The British foreign minister's reaction is interesting. While he fully sympathized with Metternich's concern over a revolt which might easily spread to the rest of the peninsula, and affirmed that Britain would have no objection to armed Austrian intervention in Naples on behalf of Ferdinand, he opposed here—as he had in Spain—the principle of joint allied intervention. Rebuffed by the British, Metternich turned somewhat reluctantly to a quarter where he knew he could get support. He arranged for a congress of the rulers of Austria, Russia, and Prussia to be held at the Austrian village of Troppau in the autumn of 1820. Both Britain and France refused to participate officially but sent observers to the meeting. Apparently Metternich would have preferred to limit the discussion to the question of intervention in Naples, but Alexander insisted that the congress draw up a more general statement. The result was the Troppau Protocol, which in effect asserted the general right of the European powers to intervene in states that had undergone revolutions and to bring them back, by force if necessary, to the "bosom of the Alliance." This document referred throughout to the "European Alliance," never specifying whether the congress was acting in the name of the Holy Alliance or the Quadruple Alliance.

In accordance with the protocol, the eastern powers agreed to authorize intervention in Naples, but they postponed determination of the form it should take until January, 1821, when the congress reconvened at Laibach, with Ferdinand of Naples invited to consult with them. There it was decided that an Austrian army, acting in the name of the allies, should be sent to Naples. Quickly dispatched, the army suppressed the revolt and restored Ferdinand to his throne. Then it moved northward to join the royalists in Sardinia, and the two forces defeated the rebels there.

Metternich had apparently achieved his goal of securing international support for the suppression of the Italian revolutions, but the victory was sealed at the cost of British friendship. For Castlereagh, incensed that the action in Italy was undertaken in the name of the allies, issued an official statement in January, 1821, dissenting from the action of the other powers and proclaiming publicly the British position. Repudiating the Troppau

Protocol, the declaration stated that the British government "cannot admit that this right [of interference in the internal affairs of another state] can receive a general and indiscriminate application to all revolutionary movements, without reference to their immediate bearing upon some particular State or States, or be made prospectively the basis of an Alliance." The statement was hailed by liberals throughout Europe with great enthusiasm. They looked upon Britain as the champion of the liberal cause against the leaders of the Holy Alliance, whose apparent intention was to police the European continent and suppress liberal movements wherever they existed.

Those who viewed Britain as the defender of liberal aspirations throughout Europe were mistaken, for the Tory government headed by Lord Liverpool (Robert Banks Jenkinson, 1770–1828) had no such intentions. Its actions reflected instead the growing rift between Britain and the three eastern powers. Castlereagh had worked more closely with his continental colleagues than any British foreign minister before him; he had been, indeed, the prime mover behind the Quadruple Alliance and the conference system which grew out of it. But when he saw that system being perverted, being exploited for purposes for which it had never been intended, he felt that there was no alternative to withdrawing Britain's support. Castlereagh had already embarked upon the policy that was later to be characterized as "splendid isolation." When he committed suicide as a result of overwork and fatigue, George Canning, his successor at the foreign office, continued with enthusiasm the policy which Castlereagh had adopted with regret.

Canning's acceptance of the post of foreign minister preceded by only a few weeks the Congress of Verona in 1822, the last in the series of regular postwar conferences among the allies, and the meeting at which the split between Britain and the other powers was formally confirmed. The congress was summoned to discuss further measures to be taken in Spain and to deal with still another revolution, the Greek war for independence from the Ottoman Empire, which had begun in the preceding year. By the time the congress met, a temporary settlement of the Greco-Turkish affair had been reached, but sentiment for intervention in Spain was strong, since Ferdinand's position was steadily worsening. In the forefront of those urging action in Spain was France. France's attitude during the 1820–1821 crisis had been ambiguous. Like Britain, it had sent only an observer to the Congress of Troppau, but, although not formally adhering to the Troppau Protocol, France had made no protest against it. In the interim between Troppau and Verona, the Ultraroyalist faction had gained the upper hand in Paris. It advocated a French invasion of Spain to restore the king and to extend French influence in the Iberian peninsula. At Verona, France got the support of all three eastern powers and was authorized by them to act on behalf of the Concert. Before the agreement was completed, however, Canning instructed the duke of Wellington, the British delegate to the congress, to inform his colleagues that the British would not be a party to any intervention in Spanish internal affairs, "come what may."

Britain could protest, but could not prevent the action decided upon by the others. When the Spanish revolutionary government refused to modify its constitution at the request of the continental powers, a French army crossed the Pyrenees (April, 1823) and drove the revolutionary government from Madrid. By autumn the last resistance of the rebels had been crushed at Cádiz and the king was restored to his throne. Ignoring the advice of the French to maintain a moderate constitutional regime, Ferdinand VII proceeded to eliminate the last vestiges of constitutionalism and to carry out mass reprisals against the liberals. Those who escaped torture and execution were imprisoned or driven into exile. Spain had been restored, in the words of the Troppau Protocol, to the "bosom of the Alliance."

Having failed to thwart intervention in Spain, Canning still hoped he could prevent the restoration of the Latin-American republics to Spain. This aim was shared by President James Monroe of the United States, which in 1822 had recognized these new republics. Somewhat suspicious of British designs on Cuba, Monroe refused a British proposal for joint action and proceeded alone. In December, 1823, in a statement which came to be known as the Monroe Doctrine, he proclaimed that the Americas were henceforth closed to European colonization and intervention. Great Britain subsequently recognized the independence of the Latin-American republics from Spain and Portugal. Because British sea power helped guarantee this independence, Canning could boast in 1826, "I called the New World into existence to redress the balance of the Old."

The Greek Revolt, 1821–1832

The revolt of the Greeks against Turkish domination and the reaction of the European powers to this revolt were aspects of a larger problem that was to plague European diplomats throughout the nineteenth century. This was the "Eastern Question," which had its origin in the continuing decline of the Ottoman Empire and the weakening of its authority over its outlying territories. Each European government had to decide whether to stem the disintegration by bolstering up the sultans, or to hasten it and exploit the decay to its own particular advantage. No power pursued a perfectly consistent course with respect to the Sublime Porte (as the court of the sultan was called). The Russians clearly hoped to profit from their proximity to the Turkish empire and from the religious tie between Russians and Greek Orthodox Christians living within the empire to acquire special privileges from Turkey. The British, suspicious of Russian ambitions in the Near East, more than once defended the sultan against his enemies; their support of the Greek revolt was an exception to this general policy.

The Greeks had been living under Turkish rule since the middle of the fifteenth century, and to most Europeans, Greece was merely a province of the Ottoman Empire. Actually, Greece had enjoyed a privileged position within the empire from the seventeenth century onward, for the sultans used educated Greeks from Constantinople (the so-called Phanariot Greeks) in their administrations and permitted Greek merchants (along with Armenians and Jews) a near monopoly of trade in the eastern Mediterranean. Moreover, within Greece the Turks permitted the teaching of the Greek language and the exercise of the Greek Orthodox faith. The Greeks, then, had never entirely lost sight of their past and their identity. In addition, a marked revival of Greek national sentiment and of interest in the past occurred at the end of the eighteenth and the beginning of the nineteenth centuries, and with this came a growing desire for independence from Turkish rule. The immediate impetus for revolt came in 1821 from a secret society known as the *Hetaíria Philiké* ("Society of Friends"); the society had been organized in 1814 and consisted primarily of Greeks living outside of Greece who hoped for a revival of the Greek empire of the early Middle Ages. The leader of the society was Prince Alexander Ypsilanti (1792–1828), son of a Greek provincial administrator and himself a former general in the Russian army. Having been given the impression by the tsar's Greek-born foreign minister, Count Johannes Antonius Capodistrias (1776–1831), that he would get Russian support for a Greek uprising, Ypsilanti led a band of volunteers into the Turkish province of Moldavia, where he summoned the native Rumanians as well as his fellow Greeks to revolt against their Turkish masters. Ypsilanti's attempt failed because the Rumanians refused to respond to his call and because the tsar disavowed him. Two weeks later a more spontaneous revolt erupted in the Morea and spread to some of the Aegean Islands and to central and northern Greece. The avowed goal of the revolutionaries was complete independence from the Ottoman Empire and the creation of a new Greek state.

Representatives of the major powers were still assembled at Laibach when they received news of the Greek revolt early in 1821. Their response was practically unanimous. They had no particular sympathy for the Greeks, and they considered the revolt one more threat to established authority that had to be suppressed. Chiefly at Metternich's urging, the tsar denounced the rebels and dismissed Capodistrias. Not even Britain, on whom some liberals had counted for support, showed any inclination to aid the Greeks. Indeed, the principal goal of Castlereagh and the British government was to see order restored in the Ottoman Empire and to forestall the possibility of Russian intervention.

But a new force became involved in the Greek revolt, a force that did not come into play in the revolutions in Spain and Italy and that gradually compelled the governments of Britain, Russia, and France to repudiate their initial stand and throw their support to the rebels. This was a ground swell of popular backing for the rebels—the movement known as Philhellenism, which included admirers of Greece all over Europe and America. To generations brought up on the classics, the Greek revolt had a romantic appeal unlike that of any other. Moreover, the fact that the Greeks were Christians struggling to free themselves from Moslem domination gave the entire movement the flavor of a crusade. Unable to express opposition to their own regimes, liberals throughout Europe rallied to the cause of Greek independence and organized committees to provide the rebels with money, supplies, and even volunteers. And the success of the Philhellenic cause was in no small part due to the fervent support of some of the leading romantic writers of the era—Byron and Shelley foremost among them. Byron had gone to Greece in 1810 and subsequently expressed his hope "that Greece might still be free." To this cause he devoted his last years, and he died in Greece in 1824.

Sympathetic to Greek independence though they were, the Philhellenes were thoroughly horrified by the brutality of the Greeks in the Morea revolt. But they were quickly stirred to renew their sympathy by the vicious retaliatory measures taken by the Turks, who on Easter Day, 1821, hanged the Greek patriarch in his sacred vestments at Constantinople, and in 1822 massacred most of the hundred thousand Greeks living on the island of Chios, an event commemorated by Delacroix in a famous painting.

Despite popular sympathy for the Greek cause, several years of public pressure and protracted negotiations were required before any European

Massacre at Chios.
Painting by Delacroix.
The Louvre, Paris.

government actively intervened. During this time Sultan Mahmud II (ruled 1808–1839), unable to defeat the Greeks with his own forces, called upon his vassal, the powerful Mehemet Ali (1769–1849), pasha of Egypt, to lend military and naval assistance. Mehemet Ali's son Ibrahim Pasha (1789–1848) was put in command of a force that invaded and subdued the Morea in 1825. Although the odds against the rebels were heavy and internal quarrels at times brought them to civil war, the Greeks continued to hold out, hoping for intervention by the European powers. Only in 1827 did this become possible. In that year, France joined Russia and Britain in signing the Treaty of London, which stated that if Turkey refused to accept an armistice, the three powers might support the Greeks with their naval forces. When Turkey did indeed reject an armistice, a joint force of British, Russian, and French ships bottled up Ibrahim's fleet in the bay of Navarino, on the west coast of the Morea, in October, 1827. Unable to force either Greeks or Moslems to stop fighting, the allied naval commanders finally moved into the bay itself, met Ibrahim's fleet in a close artillery engagement, and almost completely destroyed it. Philhellenes cheered the news of the victory at Navarino. But the conservative governments of Great Britain, France, and Russia were somewhat embarrassed by it, and the duke of Wellington, who had succeeded Canning as prime minister of Great Britain and was much less sympathetic to the Greek cause, apologized to the sultan for the action of the allied naval commanders.

A few months later, in April, 1828, Tsar Nicholas I, who had come to the throne in 1825, used a hostile statement by the sultan as a pretext for declaring war on Turkey. The tsar was interested not so much in achieving Greek independence as in capitalizing on the weaknesses of the Ottoman Empire, which appeared near collapse. Yet during the conflict, which lasted for more than a year, the Russians seemed to undergo a change of heart. Turkish resistance proved to be stronger than anticipated and the tsar came to realize that even if he succeeded in defeating the sultan, the other powers would not stand idly by while he despoiled the Ottoman Empire. Accordingly, the Russians stopped short of Constantinople and in September, 1829, in the Treaty of Adrianople, concluded with the Ottoman Empire a peace which imposed certain restrictions on the Turkish government in the administration of its European provinces of Moldavia and Walachia (present-day Rumania), making them virtually Russian protectorates, but involved no significant territorial concessions.

The Treaty of Adrianople also stipulated that the Ottoman Empire must abide by decisions which Russia, France, and Britain would reach concerning Greece. The three powers met in London in 1830 to settle the Greek situation. They declared Greece an independent kingdom under their protection, but two years of negotiations were necessary before the boundaries of the new state were definitively settled and a ruler named. The crown

Battle of Navarino, 1827. *Painting by Langlois. British, Russian, and French vessels practically destroyed the Turkish fleet in this engagement. Musée de Versailles, Versailles.*

of the new kingdom was refused by two German princes before it was finally accepted by Otto, the son of King Ludwig of Bavaria, in February, 1832, eleven years after the outbreak of the revolt.

The revolt of the Greeks and their ultimate achievement of independence made a great impression on contemporary Europeans. For this was the first successful breach of the *status quo* after 1815 and seemed to mark a significant victory for the idea of nationality as well as for the cause of liberalism. That these were not necessarily the motivating concerns of the British, French, and Russian governments is indicated by their decision to name a German-born ruler for the new Greek state, but factionalism among the Greeks would have made it difficult for the guaranteeing powers to find a native ruler whom all could support. In any event, European liberals, temporarily disillusioned by the defeat of the revolutions of 1820–1821, derived new hope from the success of the Greeks and the support given their cause by Britain, France, and Russia. The way had been prepared for a new wave of uprisings in 1830.

THE BELGIAN REVOLT, 1830–1831

Before the Greek question had been settled, the European powers were confronted by another crisis, which appeared to threaten the *status quo* much more directly. Indeed, it was the first real challenge to the territorial settlement reached at Vienna and was therefore a matter of vital concern to all the Great Powers. This was the revolt of the Belgian provinces against the Netherlands, to which they had been annexed in 1815 as a barrier to

French aggression. The Belgians had never been enthusiastic about the union. Differences in traditions, language, religion, and economic interests naturally separated the two peoples. The Dutch, proud of their two centuries of independence, were contemptuous of the Belgians, who had been subjected to Spanish, and then Austrian, rule. The policies of King William of Orange further aggravated tensions between them. The predominantly Catholic population of the Belgian provinces resented the Protestant king's policy of equality for all religious denominations. The establishment of Dutch as the official language of the realm except in the French-speaking Walloon districts of Belgium annoyed the Flemings, whose dialect was very different from Dutch. And although the economic activities of the two parts of the kingdom actually complemented each other rather well—the industry and agriculture of the southern provinces finding outlets through the commercial centers of the northern—Belgian manufacturers felt that the Dutch tariff system did not sufficiently protect their industries.

Opposition to the Dutch was concentrated mainly in two political groups, the Clericals and the Liberals, themselves often at odds. The Liberals were resentful of the constitutional structure of the state because it gave an equal number of representatives in the elected States-General to the Dutch and the Belgians, even though the Belgian population was nearly 3.5 million and the Dutch a mere 2 million. They were critical of the high-handed way in which the king dealt with the States-General and often dispensed with the advice of his ministers; they protested government persecution of the opposition press. The Clericals resented the creation of state secondary schools and the extension of state control over independent (that is, ecclesiastical) schools through a system of government inspection. In 1828, Liberals and Clericals managed to bury their differences and formed a "union of parties," which drew up a common program demanding freedom of the press, freedom of teaching, and ministerial responsibility in government. Neither group contemplated the overthrow of the dynasty; rather, they hoped to achieve their demands within the framework of the existing regime.

The success of the July Revolution (1830) in neighboring France, which overthrew the reigning monarch, Charles X, and substituted a broader constitutional regime under King Louis Philippe, quickened the spread of discontent in Belgium. Moreover, a temporary economic decline brought particular hardships to the working classes in Belgium's larger cities. But the Belgian revolt was actually touched off by the performance of an opera. After a stirring rendition in Brussels of *La Muette de Portici*, an opera by Eugène Scribe and Daniel Auber about a revolt in Naples, students left the theater shouting "Down with the Dutch!" and "Down with the Ministry!" The student riot turned into revolt, and the revolt spread. The king sent troops to Brussels, but after three days of bitter fighting, they were forced to withdraw, leaving the city in the hands of the rebels. By October a provisional government had been established and a national congress summoned to draw up a constitution for the new state. Belgium was to be a constitutional monarchy, but members of Holland's house of Orange were explicitly excluded from the throne.

The independence of Belgium clearly violated the settlement of 1815, and it was on this basis that King William of Holland appealed to the Great Powers for their help in reestablishing his authority in the Belgian provinces. As might be expected, Tsar Nicholas of Russia was eager for intervention, and he appeared to have the support of Metternich and Frederick William III of Prussia. Before they could act, however, Talleyrand, newly arrived in London as French ambassador, warned the duke of Wellington that France would not tolerate intervention by the eastern powers in a territory lying on its borders. Wellington agreed to oppose intervention and notified the eastern powers of the British and French position. He further proposed a conference of the five Great Powers in London to discuss the future of the Belgian provinces, an invitation which the eastern powers accepted reluctantly. Metternich apparently hoped that Wellington might be persuaded to support joint military action, but by the time the conference met in November, 1830, Wellington's ministry had fallen and had been succeeded by the Whig cabinet of Earl Grey.

Although Lord Palmerston, the Whig foreign minister, was hardly enthusiastic about the revolt in Belgium, he concluded in November that it could no longer be reversed. Moreover he was not eager to see troops of the eastern powers move into an area where Britain traditionally had interests. The French, having just emerged from their own revolution, were sympathetic to the cause of Belgian independence and hoped it would result in an increase of French influence in the region. At the same time, a revolt of the Poles against their Russian overlords in November distracted Tsar Nicholas from Belgian affairs; he was now far more interested in suppressing the revolution in his own territory than in intervention in the Netherlands. Both Austria and Prussia were concerned about the possible spread of the Polish revolt to subject Poles living within their own borders, and by early 1831 Metternich was also preoccupied with revolts in Italy. In the end, Russia, Prussia, and Austria played only a small role in the settlement of Belgium's status. By stipulating that Belgium would remain a neutral state under the permanent guarantee of the Great Powers, Britain and France succeeded in persuading them to accept a protocol which virtually recognized Belgium's independence.

The collaboration between Britain and France was threatened early in 1831 when the newly elected Belgian national congress offered the throne to the duke of Nemours (1814–1896), second son of the French king, Louis

Lord Palmerston. *An engraving from a photograph made in his later years.*

Philippe. The French government was not innocent of maneuvering on behalf of the duke's candidacy, seeing in it a means of making Belgium subservient to France's interests. But Palmerston's strong reaction to the offer, including a threat of war, led Louis Philippe to refuse the throne for his son. It was then offered to Leopold of Saxe-Coburg, a German prince but a British subject, the widower of Princess Charlotte of England and uncle to the future Queen Victoria. Accepted by all parties at the London conference, Leopold was proclaimed king in July, 1831. Only King William of Holland was unreconciled to this solution. In August, 1831, he sent a sizable army into Belgium in an effort to reconquer the lost provinces. The Concert thereupon authorized joint Anglo-French intervention to eject the Dutch. William continued his resistance for another year and a half and did not finally acknowledge Belgium's independence until 1839.

The handling of the Belgian revolt suggested that the Great Powers could act together in reaching a solution to a thorny diplomatic crisis despite the sharply opposing points of view of the several governments. Credit for the outcome must go to Lord Palmerston for his skillful conduct of the negotiations. But the Russian and Austrian governments may have been more willing to accept his solution for Belgium because of the restraint shown by both the British and French governments toward the revolts in Poland and the Italian states. Despite impassioned pleas from liberals in both the House of Commons and the French Chamber of Deputies for intervention on behalf of the Poles and the Italians, neither government had seriously considered going to the support of the rebels against Russia and Austria. Each of the major powers appeared determined in 1830–1831 to avoid any action which might precipitate a general European war.

THE "EASTERN QUESTION," 1832–1841

To contemporaries, one of the most notable features of the international crisis created by the Belgian revolt was the way in which it seemed to underline the growing division between the three absolutist powers of eastern Europe and the two constitutional states of western Europe. This alignment, signs of which had existed ever since the conclusion of Alexander's Holy Alliance in 1815, had not been maintained consistently throughout the 1820's. Indeed, France under the Bourbon monarchs had more than once sided with the eastern powers, as it did, for example, on the question of intervention in the Iberian peninsula. The revolution of 1830 in France appeared to heighten the chances of Anglo-French collaboration, for it brought to power a regime whose institutions were similar, at least superficially, to those of Britain, and the new monarch, Louis Philippe, paid lip service to the individual liberties and guarantees traditionally respected in Britain. Yet a close look at the relationship between France and Britain in the 1830's and the 1840's reveals that it was far from cordial; indeed, outright hostility prevailed during the diplomatic crisis which occurred in 1840. The friction between the two powers arose in part from conflicting economic interests; French manufacturers feared British competition and therefore sought to maintain tariff schedules that would exclude or limit British imports. In addition, as Louis Philippe became more firmly established on his throne, his outlook grew increasingly conservative, and he turned more frequently to Metternich, seeking an understanding between France and Austria which he hoped would heighten the legitimacy of his regime.

The revival of the so-called Eastern Question after the Greek settlement of 1830 most clearly illustrates the tenuous character of Anglo-French relations and the degree of flexibility still present in the European Concert. This time the trouble arose out of the conflict between the sultan of Turkey and his powerful vassal, Mehemet Ali, pasha of Egypt, whose aid he had secured during the Greek revolt. As a reward for his support, Mehemet Ali now demanded the cession of Syria, and when the sultan refused, he proceeded in 1832 to send an army, led by his son Ibrahim, into this territory. The sultan appealed to Britain for support against his rebellious vassal, but Palmerston, still occupied with the Belgian situation, turned him down. After a number of victories by Mehemet Ali's forces seemed to threaten the sultan's regime, Russia decided to intervene on behalf of the sultan, and early in 1833 sent a squadron to Constantinople. The French and the British, alarmed by the threat of Russian domination over Turkey, marshaled their fleets in the eastern Mediterranean and joined Russia in imposing a settlement on the sultan and his vassal. Turkey was saved from collapse, but the sultan was forced to cede Syria to Mehemet Ali. The crisis had apparently been surmounted. Soon afterward, in July, 1833, Russia and

Mehemet Ali, pasha of Egypt. *Lithograph from a drawing by the Count of Forbin at Alexandria, March, 1818.*

Turkey concluded the Treaty of Unkiar-Skelessi for mutual assistance in the event of attack. In a secret clause, Turkey was excused from fulfilling its obligation in return for closing the Dardanelles to all non-Russian vessels of war. When France and Britain discovered the existence of this clause a short time later, they protested the treaty because it gave a favored position to Russian warships in the Straits and seemed to leave Turkey at the mercy of Russia. But for the time being, they did nothing.

A second crisis developed when, in 1839–1840, the growing power of Mehemet Ali once again appeared to endanger not only the sultan but also other powers with interests in the eastern Mediterranean. Lord Palmerston, now convinced of the seriousness of the threat from Mehemet Ali and suspicious of Russia's designs on Turkey, decided that Britain should support the sultan more effectively. But France, whose interest in Egypt dated back to the Directory, was sympathetic to Mehemet Ali and encouraged him in his ambitions for an empire in the Near East. The issue came to a head in 1839 when the sultan renewed hostilities by invading Syria. His forces proved no match for those of his enemy; his army was defeated by Ibrahim, and his leading admiral shortly afterward deserted with the fleet to Mehemet Ali. At this crucial point the sultan died, leaving the Ottoman Empire in the hands of a young boy, Abdul-Medjid I, who was prepared to yield to his more powerful vassals, Mehemet Ali and Ibrahim.

The crisis brought renewed attempts to revive the Concert. Even before the outbreak of hostilities Palmerston had tried to secure a general guarantee of Turkish integrity from the Great Powers. But he encountered French hostility to the sultan and he could get no support from Russia, which was still adhering to the unilateral promise of aid to Turkey made in the Treaty of Unkiar-Skelessi. In September, 1839, after the defeat of the sultan's forces, Tsar Nicholas had his representative in London approach Lord Palmerston with a proposal for settlement of the crisis. Palmerston was initially wary of the Russian plan since he suspected that the tsar would attempt to drive a wedge between Britain and France by insisting that France's protégé, Mehemet Ali, back down despite his victories and return his conquests to the Ottoman Empire. But he welcomed the tsar's simultaneous offer to abandon the Treaty of Unkiar-Skelessi and substitute a general guarantee of Turkey's integrity.

Accordingly, Palmerston invited the other Great Powers to London to join in a general settlement. Austria and Prussia quickly agreed. But France, now under the premiership of Adolphe Thiers (1797–1877), demurred. Public opinion in France was running strongly in favor of the Egyptian pasha, and Thiers was convinced that Britain would not act independently of France in the Near East. He was soon proven wrong, for Palmerston was convinced that "for the interests of England, the preservation of the balance of power and the maintenance of peace in Europe" a settlement of the sort proposed had to be reached. Overcoming opposition within his own cabinet by threatening to resign, he forced acceptance of his position and the four-power Treaty of London was signed in July, 1840. Mehemet Ali was offered Egypt as a hereditary possession, and control over southern Syria for the remainder of his life, but he was to relinquish everything else he had conquered from the sultan and return the Turkish fleet. Counting on French support, the Egyptian pasha refused to accept the terms of the treaty and announced that he would stand firm. The result was renewed conflict in the Near East. The British bombarded the Syrian coast and landed troops. But France, despite repeated threats of war with Britain, which kept international tension at a fever pitch for three months, never did join the conflict. Realizing that war with Britain would not be in France's interest, Louis Philippe dismissed Thiers from office in October, 1840, and entered into negotiations with the other powers. No longer supported in his intransigent position by France, Mehemet Ali was persuaded to conclude an agreement with the sultan which embodied the provisions of the Treaty of London, except that it did not give him control even over southern Syria. In July, 1841, the five Great Powers signed the Straits Convention, which stipulated that the Straits, both the Bosporus and the Dardanelles, were to be closed to *all* foreign warships when Turkey was at peace. France's participation in this agreement signified its return to the Concert of European powers and the end of the diplomatic crisis.

What was perhaps most interesting about the crisis of 1839–1840 was the diplomatic alignment of powers which were at ideological extremes. The principal antagonists in the crisis were Britain and France, whose political systems were more alike than those of any other two powers. Britain's principal collaborator was Russia, whose absolutist government was anathema to liberals throughout Europe. At the height of the crisis Metternich seems to have suspected Britain and Russia of planning war against France and even considered seceding from the London agreement, drawing Prussia with him and concluding a separate agreement with France. Moreover, it was Metternich who was instrumental in bringing France back into the Concert of Europe by mediating between it and the other powers. Ideological considerations seem, then, to have played a relatively minor role in the relationship among the Great Powers in this crisis, as in others before 1850.

Perhaps the most interesting question concerning international relations during this period is why no war occurred among the major powers for almost forty years after the Vienna settlement, despite numerous diplomatic crises and threats of conflict. Gordon Craig, who has recently suggested a number of explanations for this absence of war, emphasizes particularly the remarkable consensus that existed among the powers despite their ideological differences.[5] All of them accepted the principle of the balance of power and the implied assumption that no state should expand its powers or influence without the consent of the others. Each government was therefore willing to exercise a certain degree of restraint in its dealings with others, as for example, Russia did in 1833 in exacting only one relatively minor concession from Turkey in return for support. The general respect for treaties also contributed to European stability. Finally, there was the willingness of the powers to participate in joint efforts to maintain peace. For example, though Britain's diplomats refused to make commitments to a stated policy in advance, they realized that their nation had an obligation and an interest in European affairs and therefore intervened at times when the balance of power was threatened or peace endangered. As long as the major powers were willing to adhere to such a code of behavior, peace among them could be preserved.

To these explanations may be added one more. Evidently no government saw a particular advantage to be gained by war. All except France were concerned with maintaining the settlement of 1815, and even France had been treated well enough by the victorious powers, so that it had no overwhelming desire for revenge or for rectification of its boundaries. If aggressive sentiments existed in France, they were found most often among members of the opposition, who did not exert a significant influence on government policy. Perhaps the greatest potential threats to peace in this era came from the liberals in France and Britain, eager to champion the cause of oppressed nationalities whether in Poland or in Italy, but their governments were generally unwilling to endanger the stability of Europe by undertaking crusades for the liberation of subject peoples.

[5] Gordon Craig, "The System of Alliances and the Balance of Power" in *New Cambridge Modern History*, Vol. X (Cambridge, Eng., 1960), pp. 266–267.

CHAPTER 26

Restoration and Romanticism

HISTORIANS COMMONLY employ the term "Restoration" to characterize the era in European history following the downfall of the Napoleonic Empire. Like most other historical labels, it is applied loosely, being used even in reference to states which did not undergo the restoration of a ruler or a dynasty. The period's end is placed at 1830 in some nations and at 1848 in others. The era was characterized by relative peace in international relations, but within practically every state a struggle was in progress, sometimes hidden, sometimes in the open, between those in power in 1814–1815 and those who challenged or sought to undermine them. The entrenched groups, in an effort to protect their position, tended to defend the *status quo* or to proceed slowly in making changes. Their opponents, impatient for reforms or greater liberties, took to the barricades when they found their wishes frustrated or denied. The members of each group drew upon earlier writers to justify their position and themselves developed political philosophies or ideologies designed to further their cause.

CONSERVATISM

If the era after 1815 is described as the Restoration, it is important to know what was restored. Certainly, not everything that had existed before 1789. Had the principle of legitimacy been carried to its logical extreme by the statesmen at Vienna, the Holy Roman Empire would have been reestablished, along with the more than three hundred petty states into which Germany was divided before the revolutionary era. Actually, the principle of legitimacy was so haphazardly applied that Napoleon's brother-in-law, Joachim Murat, could have remained permanently on the throne of Naples in the place of the "legitimate" Bourbon ruler if he had not sacrificed his position by rashly supporting Napoleon during the Hundred Days. Nevertheless, hereditary monarchy was regarded by the statesmen at Vienna as one of the fundamental institutions to be restored, for they felt it

909

was the only form of government capable of ensuring continuity and stability in human affairs. Metternich, who is usually viewed as the prototype of all that was conservative in the Restoration, did not subscribe to the divine-right theory of monarchy, but he was convinced that the hereditary succession of kings served as a guarantee for all other social institutions. Tsar Alexander I's Holy Alliance was a union of *monarchs* who pledged to lend each other assistance for the protection of religion, peace, and justice.

In almost every country in Europe, the Restoration also brought a revival in the status of the nobility. In France and the parts of Europe conquered by the French the members of the nobility had, during the revolution, suffered fates ranging from the loss of economic and legal privileges to exile or execution. But even in areas not ruled by the French the events of the 1790's had seriously frightened the aristocracy, who saw traditional prerogatives threatened by the advance of revolutionary ideas. With the advent of the Restoration, the nobles sought to recover the privileges and property that had been lost and allied themselves with monarchs against changes that might further endanger their position in society. There was a particular irony in this drawing together of king and nobility in defense of the established order in a country like France, where the feudal aristocracy had traditionally opposed the centralizing tendencies of the monarchy. But both monarch and aristocracy were now confronted with a strong bourgeoisie intent upon preserving the gains of the revolution and consolidating its political power. In central Europe the threat was less immediate since the bourgeoisie was still weak, but Metternich nonetheless allied himself with the imperial aristocracy against the middle class, which he found seriously infected with the "revolutionary virus." In Britain, where the aristocracy was already an amalgam of landed and commercial interests, a parallel to the conservative reaction on the Continent nonetheless can be found after 1815 in the determined resistance of the Tory leadership to attempts to widen parliamentary representation in the House of Commons to include the new class of manufacturers.

Along with the monarchy and the aristocracy, the churches regained their influence during the Restoration. Support and sympathy for the Catholic Church among the governing classes was unquestionably stronger in 1815 than in 1789, for the revolutionary years witnessed a revival of faith and religious observance among many of the educated who had succumbed during the Old Regime to the rationalism and anticlericalism of the Enlightenment. In particular, members of the nobility who had observed during the revolution the simultaneous assault upon the churches, the aristocracy, and the monarchy often concluded that their own fortunes were closely tied up with those of organized religion. Nor were they unmoved by the suffering and martyrdom of members of the clergy at the hands of rev-

Edmund Burke.

olutionary governments and the dignity with which Pope Pius VII withstood the harsh treatment inflicted upon him by Napoleon. Whatever the sources of the Catholic revival, the Church was viewed in 1815 as one of the bulwarks of the social order and enjoyed a position of favor with European rulers.

The monarch who occupied a throne in Europe in 1815 typically felt no need to justify his regime to his own people. A source of his strength lay precisely in his unquestioning acceptance of his role as a ruler to whom the subjects owed automatic obedience. Nevertheless he could hardly ignore the fact that legitimate rulers had been toppled from their thrones in many places during the preceding quarter century and that the very institution of monarchy had succumbed in more than one country to a republican regime.

And though the ruler himself may not have seen reason for elaborating theoretical justifications of his authority, many intellectuals did. As we know, the French Revolution had barely begun when one of the most gifted and influential of all conservative political philosophers, Edmund Burke, wrote his *Reflections on the Revolution in France*, which questioned the entire basis of the revolution and became a handbook of conservatism for the generations that followed. During the last decade of the eighteenth century two Frenchmen, Joseph de Maistre (1753–1821) and the viscount of Bonald (1754–1840), both *émigrés*, spent their years in exile writing elaborate treatises in defense of absolute monarchy and the authority of the Catholic Church. Less systematically, Metternich and his aide Friedrich von Gentz, both before and after 1815, joined in the attack upon revolutionary principles and the appeal to traditional institutions. And German philosophers like Fichte and Hegel certainly reflected some of the assumptions of early-nineteenth-century conservatives in their emphasis upon the importance of the state. The philosophy of conservatism that developed between 1790 and 1820 was in many respects far more original than the liberal thought of the era.

Although individual variations existed, there were several common themes and arguments running through the work of practically all the conservative intellectuals. For the most part they took the French Revolution as their springboard, presenting lengthy attacks upon revolutionary principles and criticisms of the philosophy of the Enlightenment, which they held chiefly responsible for the catastrophe of 1789. Then they went on to develop a philosophy that was largely a reaction against the ideas of the *philosophes* and the revolutionaries.

In particular, the conservatives objected to what they considered the excessive reliance of the *philosophes* on reason, especially the kind of abstract reason that was used to justify "natural rights" and the introduction of new political and social institutions. Burke, with his great admiration for Britain's unwritten constitution, took an unmistakable stand against revolutionary programs:

The science of constructing a commonwealth, or renovating it, or reforming it, is, like every other experimental science, not to be taught *a priori* . . . . The science of government being therefore so practical in itself and intended for such practical purposes — a matter which requires experience, and even more experience than any person can gain in his whole life, however sagacious and observing he may be — it is with infinite caution that any man ought to venture upon pulling down an edifice, which has answered in any tolerable degree for ages the common purposes of society, or on building it up again, without having models and patterns of approved utility before his eyes.[1]

Burke's appeal to "experience" as a guide in politics was echoed by other conservatives, particularly in Britain. It was part of a broader appeal to "tradition" and "history" that could be found at the very heart of conservative political thought. In this view, both society and government, because they are products of a long historical development, must be treated with respect. If changes or reforms are to be made in either, they must come gradually and only with proper consideration for historical antecedents and national traditions. This doctrine, carried to its logical extreme, was used to justify complete adherence to the *status quo* on the ground that tampering

---

[1] Edmund Burke, *Reflections on the Revolution in France*, ed. by Thomas H. D. Mahoney (New York, 1955), pp. 69–70.

with any part of the delicately balanced institutional structure might endanger the whole.

A second weakness that conservatives attributed to the political philosophy of the Enlightenment was its emphasis upon the individual and his rights. Under attack came the entire tradition of John Locke and his disciples, both in Britain and on the Continent—the view that society and government are necessary evils or artificial constructions for the preservation of the natural rights of the individual. For conservatives, it was meaningless to talk of "individual liberty," apart from society, since freedom could be achieved only through the community. The individual was not distinct from society, an end in himself, but part of a collectivity which was somehow more than the sum of its various members. Conservative political thinkers handled this theme in many different ways, but almost all shared the view that society was an organism which had evolved over the centuries and that the individuals who composed it were indissolubly bound with those who had preceded them as well as those who were to follow.

Conservatives deplored, in varying degrees, the lack of respect for established religion and ecclesiastical authority that had found expression during the revolution in the persecution of the clergy and attacks upon Christian dogma. Some, notably Joseph de Maistre, held the skepticism and anticlericalism of men like Voltaire directly responsible for the revolution. Many conservatives valued religion chiefly as a kind of cement which contributed to the preservation of social order; the Catholic Church was regarded as one of the traditional institutions of society whose fortunes were linked with those of the monarchy and the aristocracy. But for de Maistre, Catholic Christianity was the very foundation of the social order. He believed that all sovereignty is derived from God and is vested in the monarch. Because of the divine origin of his authority, the king is absolute in his realm; his power can be limited in no way by his subjects. Religion provides the people with a motive for obedience and submission to the king and at the same time reconciles them to the natural inequalities which exist in society. Having provided a justification for absolute monarchy, de Maistre went on to argue that church and state must collaborate in promoting man's moral welfare and in preserving order. Should a conflict between the two arise, the authority of the church is higher than that of the monarch. Indeed, de Maistre ended by regarding the pope as the supreme political and religious authority in what amounted to a universal theocracy.

These convictions—that the continuity of political and social institutions had to be respected, that the community took precedence over the individual, and that organized religion was essential to the social order—provided the justification for the conservatives' faith in hereditary monarchy, supported by the authority of the church, as the form of government best fitted to preserve social stability and order.

At least two of the conservatives' arguments came to exert considerable influence beyond their own camp. Their renewed emphasis upon the historical conditioning of all social institutions proved to be a much-needed corrective to the antihistorical outlook associated with the Enlightenment and contributed to the nineteenth-century habit of viewing almost all problems historically. Conservatives were not alone in seeking to explain the present in terms of the past. By mid-century Karl Marx had developed a theory of social evolution whose basic premise was historical. And even "classical" liberals adjusted their thinking to include a historical dimension and a heightened awareness of the past.

In the same way, the conservative stress upon the community (which had been foreshadowed by Rousseau a generation before) gradually weakened the atomistic view of society that had prevailed in the preceding century. Socialists accepted as a basic premise the need for individual self-sacrifice to the community, and some of them moved to the position that a strong state was the only agency capable of achieving social reform. Liberals—at least British liberals—persisted in the view that government was a necessary evil and sought to maximize individual liberty and freedom from social restraints. But even John Stuart Mill (1806–1873), the classical defender of individual liberty, was forced to admit the inadequacy of a totally atomistic view of society and recognized that individuals in society bore a responsibility for the welfare of their fellow citizens and that it might fall to government to see that these obligations were fulfilled.

OPPOSITION TO THE RESTORATION

It is easier to enumerate the groups that defended the *status quo* and benefited from the Restoration than it is to classify the opponents of the political and social order that prevailed after 1815. In the conservative camp were monarchs, nobles, and churchmen. But did the opposition, like the Third Estate in France before the revolution, include "everyone else"? Perhaps, if one counts among the opposition all who had a grievance against the existing order. However, there is a difference between mere dissatisfaction with the *status quo* and active opposition, involving attempts to change or even destroy it. The dominant and most vigorous opponents of established institutions were drawn from the middle class; they often referred to themselves as liberals. The middle class in the first half of the nineteenth century was far from being homogeneous in any country, but was not yet the all-embracing social group that it is today. The older financial and commercial leaders were joined at this time—at least in Great Britain, France, and the Low Countries—by a generation of "new men," enterprising manufacturers who sought more aggressively to win political influence. These two groups, along with wealthy lawyers and doctors, constituted the upper middle class, by far the most active segment politically.

Beneath lay various strata of the lower middle class—shopkeepers, artisans, prosperous small farmers—whose outlook differed from that of business and professional men, but who certainly did not share the point of view of the lowest classes. Even where elected assemblies existed, as in western Europe, the members of this group played no formal role in politics because normally they could not meet the property qualifications for voting. Yet it was from the lower middle class that various secret societies, such as the *Carbonari* in Italy and the Society for the Rights of Man in France, often recruited their membership and their leaders. And in the revolutions which occurred during and after the 1820's, representatives of this class were found joining in attacks upon the government and the established order.

The peasantry still constituted the overwhelming mass of the population in Europe during the first half of the nineteenth century. Though there was considerable variation in their status, from one country to another and within individual nations, it is safe to say that the members of this class played practically no active part in the political life of the European nations. The revolution had brought about changes in the economic and legal status of the peasantry in France and in areas under French control, and the Industrial Revolution slowly affected some details of existence in western Europe, but the mass of European peasants lived as they had for centuries—in a state of relative isolation, with few secular interests outside of their own particular locality. Only where their land tenure appeared to be threatened did the peasants show any concern about events at the national level.

As the Industrial Revolution proceeded in Britain and, more slowly, in France and the Netherlands, the nucleus of an industrial proletariat began to emerge. But except for the relatively unsophisticated Chartist agitation in Britain during the 1830's and 1840's, one can hardly speak of organized political activity by the working classes in the first half of the nineteenth century. To be sure, the workers had many specific grievances—long hours, inadequate wages, labor by women and children, seasonal unemployment, unsanitary and dangerous conditions in factories and homes—but, deprived of the vote and frustrated in their attempts to organize, they had no means for expressing their discontent except violence and revolution.

Two special groups also belonged to the opposition during the Restoration. One consisted of military men, primarily army officers. They were particularly active in the revolts of the 1820's in countries where there existed no constitutional or legal channels for the expression of opposition. In Spain, Portugal, the Italian states, and Russia, army officers played significant, and in some cases leading, roles in uprisings against their respective regimes. Their motives varied widely, but certainly the dissatisfaction with their reactionary governments stemmed in part from their contact with the more advanced societies of western and central Europe during the Napoleonic wars and their exposure to the ideals of the French Revolution.

The other special group consisted of students, at both the university and the secondary levels. They often took their places on the barricades, particularly during the revolutions of 1830–1831 and 1848, and helped to staff many of the revolutionary societies active throughout the Restoration. As we shall see, the *Burschenschaften*, or student societies, which sought to stir up nationalist enthusiasm, were in the forefront of the opposition to Metternich in the Germanic Confederation just after 1815. In Paris during the Revolution of 1830, students from the upper schools fought alongside workers to overthrow the Bourbon regime. Elsewhere during the 1830's, students flocked into liberal nationalist organizations like Young Italy, Young Ireland, and Young Poland. The repressive policies of the Holy Alliance and the stubborn resistance to change of the reactionary rulers proved particularly hateful to the generation that entered schools and universities after 1815.

Early Nineteenth-Century Liberalism

Opponents of the established order during the Restoration were usually termed "liberals," and to an extent they did share a common set of goals or ideals, which constituted the political philosophy of "liberalism." As used then, the term was perhaps not as vague or as emotion-ridden as it is today in the United States, but it was still subject to a wide variety of interpretations. A Spanish officer revolting against the inefficient absolutism of Ferdinand VII hardly shared the goals of a Whig seeking reform of the methods of choosing representatives for the House of Commons; a member of the *Burschenschaften* with hopes for a closer union among Germans differed considerably in outlook from a Russian nobleman intent upon the abolition of serfdom. But all were branded "liberals" by their opponents, and more important, they drew on a common heritage and shared certain goals.

The most obvious of these goals was simply a desire for changes in the existing order. Whether they opposed continued Tory domination in Britain or the autocratic rule of the tsar in Russia, they were dissatisfied with established institutions and disputed the conservative belief that whatever existed had the sanction of time and should therefore be preserved. The suspicions of Metternich and Tsar Alexander notwithstanding, there is little evidence to suggest that the liberals possessed an international organization or even that secret ties existed between the liberal groups of individual nations, but their discontent did give them a common point of view.

Despite the variety of their specific goals, almost all liberals drew in some form upon the heritage of the Enlightenment and the French Revolution. As men of some substance they viewed the more extreme phase of the revolution with disapproval, but most of them subscribed to the general body of ideals commonly described as the "principles of 1789." "Liberty," which was central to their credo, was certainly understood to include individual freedom—freedom from arbitrary arrest and imprisonment, freedom of speech, freedom of assembly, and freedom of the press. These were a part of almost every liberal program between 1815 and 1848. At the same time, even in the application of this concept, wide differences in interpretation and emphasis existed. More than one historian has pointed out that English liberals put a greater emphasis upon the individual and the desirability of individual liberty than did liberals on the Continent. Of tremendous influence upon British liberalism was the argument of Jeremy Bentham (1748–1832) that the "greatest good for the greatest number" would result if each individual were allowed to pursue his own self-interest with a minimum of outside interference. This fundamental principle, reinforced in the economic sphere by the doctrine of *laissez-faire*, gave a character to British liberalism which distinguished it from that on the Continent.

On the Continent, wherever there were peoples who had not yet achieved political unity or who were living under a foreign ruler, "liberty" and "freedom" were apt to denote liberty from foreign control and freedom for the nation. "Freedom" for the Greeks meant freedom from Turkish control; "liberty" for the Italians meant the overthrow of Austrian domination. And many of those in the German states who thought of themselves as liberals sought above all "freedom" for the German "nation"—some form of closer union among the German people, without which personal or individual freedom appeared meaningless. For these peoples, liberalism and nationalism were closely allied; indeed, nationalist aspirations often tended to overshadow, and occasionally overwhelmed, other liberal values.

Popular sovereignty, another of the great principles proclaimed in 1789, was an ideal which liberals generally acknowledged but were seldom ready to carry to its logical conclusion. They were quite willing to invoke it to contest the arguments of de Maistre or Bonald in favor of absolutism, but in practice they were determined to restrict sovereignty to the propertied classes, who alone possessed the right to vote in the countries with elected assemblies. Men like Benjamin Constant de Rebecque (1767–1830), a Frenchman who was one of the foremost spokesmen of the liberals, strongly opposed the principle of universal suffrage, arguing that the tyranny of the mob could be just as dangerous as the tyranny of a king. "Property alone, by giving sufficient leisure, renders a man capable of exercising his political rights." Justifying the property qualification, he argued that the vote was accessible to all men: the poor man had only to acquire the requisite amount of property in order to vote. The liberals, in short, were not democrats.

If the liberals spoke frequently of "liberty" in the first half of the nineteenth century, they spoke less often of "equality." Certainly they saw nothing essentially wrong with the gross inequalities in the distribution of property and wealth which were to be found throughout Europe. The new class of manufacturers in Britain included many who had built up fortunes through their own ambition and enterprise; they were convinced that any individual with similar initiative could better himself by means of "self-help." What liberals did insist upon, in theory at least, was equality before the law. This principle was already generally recognized in England and was now guaranteed in France by the *Code Napoléon*, but in many parts of Europe where it was still denied, the abolition of the special legal privileges of the nobility and clergy became a central part of the liberal program.

These, then, were some of the more important ideals shared by European liberals after 1815: liberty, for the individual and for the nation; representative government, though in practice this usually meant representation for the propertied classes only; and equality before the law. With respect to specific goals, however, there were wide differences among liberals in the various parts of Europe. In the states of central, eastern, and southern Europe, where constitutions and representative institutions were virtually nonexistent, the goal of liberals was a written constitution which would limit the authority of the ruler and provide for an elected parliament or assembly which would share in the formulation of laws. The word "constitution" took on an almost mystical significance for liberals in some of the German and Italian states, who assumed that by its mere existence such a document would solve all their problems. But in the countries of western Europe where a constitution and an elected assembly already existed in 1815, liberals naturally had different goals. Their primary task was to see that representative institutions functioned in such a way that the government was genuinely responsible to the people—or rather to the propertied segment of the population represented, for example, in the French Chamber of Deputies. Accordingly, they tried to limit the authority of the king and to make his ministers responsible to the elected chamber for their actions. Some even recommended broadening the base of the electorate to include men of lesser wealth.

A further explanation for the divergences among liberal goals lay in the differences in the social structure and class relationships in the various countries. Where the landed aristocracy or the clergy were still entrenched and retained unique privileges, liberals focused their attack upon these privileges. In France most of these prerogatives had been lost during the revolution but from 1815 to 1830 liberals had to remain constantly on guard against attempts by both the nobility and the clergy to recover them. In Britain, where the Industrial Revolution was already causing significant changes in the social structure, representatives of the newer manufacturing interests sought to free themselves of restrictions inherited from a preindustrial era and to compel the older landed and merchant classes to share their control of the House of Commons.

The specific goals of the liberals also depended in large measure on whether they lived in a unified, independent nation, such as Great Britain, France, or Spain, or belonged, like the Germans, Italians, and Poles, to a people that was divided or living under foreign domination. Where nationhood had yet to be achieved, liberalism was normally characterized by strong nationalist aspirations, and the transcendent goal became national unification or national independence.

Early Nineteenth-Century Nationalism

Frequently nationalist sentiments were not confined to liberals; they affected social groups and classes other than those usually identified with the liberal cause. Should nationalism be regarded as merely one strand of the liberal ideology, or did it have an identity of its own? It is difficult to say, especially since the terms "liberalism" and "nationalism" were not employed with precision during this period.

Two or three circumstances in the first half of the nineteenth century tended to draw together those working for liberal ideals and those striving primarily for nationalist goals. In the first place, they shared a common heritage; both drew, in part, upon the French Revolution for inspiration. For nineteenth-century nationalists, the French revolutionaries had provided a stunning example of what a people could achieve when they were unified under a government that they themselves had created. The tremendous release of national energy and the stirring patriotism that had characterized the revolutionary armies impressed those Europeans who were still divided or living under foreign rule after 1815. They were convinced that if only they could achieve a similar national consciousness and enthusiasm, they too could overcome the obstacles that stood in the way of independence and unity. The faith in popular sovereignty is perhaps the most important link between liberalism and nationalism. People living under a dynasty or ruling caste whose ends seemed to differ from their own could not feel quite the same stake in their country as people living under a regime which proclaimed, as did the *Declaration of the Rights of Man and the Citizen,* that "the source of all sovereignty resides essentially in the nation." Only when the government was closely identified with all the people could a nation be considered "free."

Furthermore, in the first half of the nineteenth century, liberals and nationalists could be closely allied because nationalism had not yet taken on

Giuseppe Mazzini.

the exclusive, parochial character that it assumed later. Paradoxical as it may seem, some of the leading nationalists were still influenced by the cosmopolitan heritage of the Enlightenment. Thus for Giuseppe Mazzini, one of the most famous of all nationalist propagandists before 1850, there was no incompatibility between loyalty to one's nation and loyalty to humanity: "In laboring according to true principles for our country we are laboring for Humanity; our country is the fulcrum of the lever which we have to wield for the common good." The achievement by each people of its own "national existence" was merely the prelude to the association of all in a higher community of nations. At the same time, Mazzini shared some of the views of liberals concerning the institutions which the nation should possess. The only true country for him was "a fellowship of free and equal men bound together in a brotherly concord of labor towards a single end." Indeed, he went beyond most contemporary liberals, advocating a republican form of government and a radical egalitarianism.

Finally, liberals and nationalists were drawn together after 1815 by the mere fact that both were in opposition to the *status quo*. Because the settlement of 1815 had failed to take into account the aspirations of both liberals and nationalists, both sought to undermine it and inveighed against the powers of the Holy Alliance apparently determined to maintain its integrity. Metternich, in persecuting both liberals and nationalists throughout central Europe, was at least partially responsible for the alliance that was forged between them.

Up to this point early nineteenth-century nationalism has been defined only in terms of its similarities and affinities with liberalism. But nationalism had nonliberal roots and characteristics as well. These are perhaps best revealed in the development of German nationalist thought at the end of the eighteenth and the beginning of the nineteenth centuries. There appeared fairly early in the development of German nationalism a strain of exclusiveness and intolerance and an emphasis upon the transcendence of the state over the individual that ultimately brought about its separation from liberalism. While this separation did not occur exclusively in Germany and illiberal elements could be found also in nationalist movements elsewhere in Europe, the phenomenon is best illustrated in the attitudes toward the nation of a number of highly influential German writers.

The first of these was Johann Gottfried von Herder (1744–1803), a Protestant pastor and theologian who wrote extensively on philosophy, history, and literature. When Herder was born, Germans did of course speak a common language, but because they were divided into hundreds of petty states they generally lacked any conception of Germany as a national entity. On the contrary, German intellectuals tended to share in the cosmopolitan outlook of the Enlightenment and the general admiration for the French *philosophes*. Herder was one of the first to object to what he considered the excessive dependence of the educated classes in Germany on French thought and French manners, and urged his compatriots to develop their native culture. He believed that each people—that is, the body of persons sharing a common language—possessed a unique *Geist* ("spirit," or "genius"), which had to be developed in its own particular way. The national culture, to be authentic, had to arise from the life of the V*olk*, or common people, and draw its inspiration from them. Two features of Herder's nationalism should be emphasized. One was its exclusively cultural character. Herder was not concerned with political questions and never argued that the political unification of Germany had to accompany its cultural renaissance. Second, Herder's theory of national development was applicable to peoples other than Germans; it certainly was not intended to imply that German culture was superior to any other.

Many literary figures of the German romantic school, such as the Grimm brothers, took seriously Herder's injunction to explore Germany's cultural past, and through their writings brought about an awareness of German folklore, law, and religion. But among some of Herder's disciples in the generation after 1800, the character of German nationalism began to change. The philosopher Johann Gottlieb Fichte (1762–1814), twenty years younger than Herder, did much to stimulate the more aggressive brand of German nationalism that was to emerge in the second half of the nineteenth century. His changed outlook resulted in part from his reaction to the French invasions of Germany and particularly to Prussia's humiliation by the Napoleonic armies in 1806, which occasioned his famous series of lectures, *Addresses to the German Nation*, delivered in the winter of 1807–1808. In these lectures he called for a system of national education in Germany which would ultimately result in the moral regeneration of the German people. Education was to make Germans aware of themselves as a unique people, reveal to them their national character, and teach them to

G. W. F. Hegel.

love the fatherland. In describing the kind of spirit that should prevail in a time of national crisis, Fichte wrote, "[It is] not the spirit of the peaceful citizen's love for the constitution and the laws, but the devouring flame of higher patriotism, which embraces the nation as the vestures of the eternal, for which the noble-minded man joyfully sacrifices himself, and the ignoble man, who only exists for the sake of the other, must likewise sacrifice himself."[2] In his earlier works Fichte was concerned with the problem of individual freedom, but he arrived at a point in his thinking where he regarded a strong, authoritarian state as the prerequisite for true freedom. He offered no simple definition of "freedom," but became convinced that the individual could attain it only by identifying himself with the greater personality of the nation. Moreover Fichte, unlike Herder, attributed to the Germans an originality and a genius not possessed by other peoples. He carried none of these ideas to extremes, but his *Addresses to the German Nation* became a source of inspiration and ammunition for subsequent German nationalists.

Of the numerous other writers who contributed to the broadening stream of German nationalism in this era, none was more important than the celebrated idealist philosopher and professor Georg Wilhelm Friedrich Hegel (1770–1831). Several of Hegel's conclusions, which were based on his philosophy of history, were incorporated into the German nationalist ideology. The first was his strong emphasis on the state. Reacting against eighteenth-century individualism, Hegel regarded the state as far more than

[2] Quoted in *Introduction to Contemporary Civilization in the West*, third ed. (New York, 1961), Vol. II, p. 155.

an artificial convenience for the satisfaction of individual needs. Rather, it was a manifestation of the "world spirit" operating in history, and its task was to bring a nation to self-consciousness. Since the state was the embodiment of what he termed the "divine idea," the essence of morality, the individual could lead a truly ethical life only by identifying himself with the state. By submitting to the state and rendering it unconditional obedience, the individual could realize true freedom. A second point concerned the special role that the Germanic nations were destined to play in the final stage of the unfolding of the historical process whose purpose was the realization of "freedom." According to his view of history, in the first, or oriental, stage of historical development the *monarch* alone had been free; in the Greek and Roman stages the *few* had achieved freedom; but only in the last, or Germanic, stage of history, were *all men* destined to be free. This belief in the peculiar historical destiny of the Germanic peoples (whether or not this destiny was interpreted as the realization of "freedom" in Hegel's sense) became an integral part of German national- ism. Finally, Hegel was responsible in some measure for the growing prestige of the Prussian monarchy in Germany as a whole. For although he implied that the Germanic state of the future would be constitutional in form, he threw his full support behind the powerful Prussian state as the agent destined by History to bring the Germanic people to full conscious- ness.

Like Fichte, Hegel did not attempt to deduce a concrete political program from his philosophical system. But there is no question that he provided a theoretical justification not only for the conservative nationalism of the later nineteenth century but for the state worship characteristic of twentieth-century fascism as well. Paradoxically, Hegel also affected modern socialist theory, through his influence upon Karl Marx (1818–1883). Hegel's confidence that he had discovered meaning and direction in human history and his emphasis upon the dialectical process by which the "world-spirit" realized itself are reflected in Marx's own theory of dialectical materialism.

If German writers were the leaders in the development of nationalist theory, the phenomenon itself was to be found throughout Europe in the first half of the nineteenth century. Herder's injunction to Germans to con- centrate upon their own cultural heritage was taken up by writers of other nationalities, who displayed a new interest in their own history, language, literature, and art. For example, among the Slavic peoples of southeastern Europe, many of whom had been living for centuries under the domination of the Austrian or the Ottoman empire, a cultural renaissance beginning at the end of the eighteenth century was in full swing after 1815. Slavic philolo- gists, historians, and literary men devoted themselves to unearthing their respective national traditions by compiling collections of folk legends, poems, and chronicles, and to systematizing knowledge of their languages by writing grammars and dictionaries. Where a language had gone out of use, attempts were made to revive it in the schools and in books and newspapers. Such nationalist movements were at first almost entirely cultural and their leaders were largely intellectuals—scholars, clerics, and liberal noblemen. But as the century proceeded they assumed an increasingly political character. While a revolt of the Serbs against Turkish rule in 1804 did not stem directly from such a cultural revival, the Greek revolt of 1821 was certainly inspired in part by a literary and linguistic renaissance that had begun in the last years of the eighteenth century. In the Austrian empire, the nationalist movements of the Slavic peoples remained primarily cultural, but the revival of the Magyar language and the growing Magyar literary production in Hungary stimulated the demand for greater autonomy of the Hungarian Diet. And Italians whose territories had been annexed to the empire in 1814–1815 grew increasingly restive under the impact of nationalist propaganda in the 1830's and 1840's.

ROMANTICISM

Where in the Restoration era does one place "romanticism"? Was it associated with the political and social developments of the period, or was it a purely literary and artistic movement? Is it possible to establish a workable definition of romanticism that can be applied to Germany as well as Britain, to Russia as well as France? Can one assign chronological limits to so amorphous a phenomenon? It is tempting to accept a recent description of romanticism as a "mood" that pervaded many aspects of nineteenth-century European culture but escapes any rigid definition. To each characteristic attributed to the "romantic school," individual exceptions may be found. Nevertheless, the mood existed and was widely influential.

The romantics reacted against the Enlightenment or against views which they attributed to writers of the Enlightenment. Whereas the *philosophes* had in general stressed the role of reason and the intellect in discovering truth, the romantics ascribed much more importance to feeling and emotion. The reality of human experience for them lay in the soul rather than the mind, in the heart rather than the head. Goethe's Faust, though created by a writer who defies classification as either classicist or romantic, was nevertheless the prototype for the romantic age: the scholar, disillusioned and discouraged by his long quest for intellectual understanding, who finally turns to sentiment, dreams, and action for the redemption of his soul.

How the romantic mood affected the visual arts can best be discovered through a brief discussion of some individual painters of the period: a German, Caspar David Friedrich (1774–1840); an Englishman, Joseph Mallord William Turner (1775–1851); and a Frenchman, Eugène Delacroix (1798–1863). None of these can be described as the prototype of the romantic artist, but together, their works reveal some of the most prominent features of painting during the romantic era. All of them reacted against existing artistic conventions and rules, in their choice of subjects, the composition of their paintings, or their actual painting techniques. Like almost all painters of the romantic era they believed that the artist must express himself—his instincts and his passions—through his work. A painting was to be not a formalized representation of some preexisting order, but rather the individual artist's vision of the cosmos, the vehicle for his imagination. A successful painting would play upon the feelings and emotions of the viewer and stimulate his own imagination.

Friedrich, who is most noted for his landscapes and seascapes, reflects the romantics' profound interest in nature. His drawings reveal his close familiarity with natural detail, but his paintings of mountains towering in the morning mists or gnarled trees silhouetted against the moonlight end by transforming nature and giving it an almost supernatural or spiritual quality. In his landscapes there is invariably an aura of the mysterious or sinister, a sense of foreboding. Friedrich attempts to convey his vision of the relationship of the individual to the cosmos by placing in the foreground of his landscapes one or two isolated figures with their backs to the viewer, contemplating the grandeur of the natural scene. Through his composition he appears to be indicating the smallness and insignificance of human beings before the vast forces of nature, but he also seems to convey a sense of the individual's longing for the infinite, his desire to lose himself in the cosmos.

Turner, too, is noted for his landscapes and his dramatic paintings of the sea, but a concern with the individual's relationship to nature is less obvious in his work. His subjects are varied: historical and mythological scenes, shipwrecks, dramatic episodes such as the burning of the Houses of Parliament in 1834, and above all, sunrises and sunsets over the water. While Friedrich was not particularly innovative in his painting techniques, Turner developed a new freedom in his brushstrokes and became particularly skilled in the rendering of light. Using watercolors, he succeeded in capturing nuances of light and color in nature, which he later reproduced in oils. As he grew older, he tended more and more to blur the contours of the objects he painted, so that a ship, for example, seemed to melt into the surrounding sea and sky. In these techniques he anticipated devices later to be used by the Impressionists, who like him were less concerned with objective detail than with the total impact of a scene upon the viewer.

Delacroix, perhaps the most celebrated of French romantic painters, wrote in his *Journal*, "If by my Romanticism people mean the free display of my personal impressions, my remoteness from the servile copies repeated

Liberty Leading the People. *Painting by Eugène Delacroix. The Louvre, Paris.*

ad nauseam in academies of art and my extreme distaste for academic formulae, then I am indeed a Romantic."[3] In his choice of subjects, his arrangement of figures, and his daring use of color Delacroix liberated himself from established conventions and gave full expression to his aesthetic imagination. He was particularly sensitive to the relationship between poetry, music, and the visual arts, and contended that the color harmonies of a painting could stimulate sensations comparable to those aroused by the combination of sounds produced by an orchestra. He drew many of his themes from Byron, Sir Walter Scott, and Shakespeare. In his choice of subjects, Delacroix, like many other romantic painters, was guided by the desire to tell a story or celebrate an event. An ardent political liberal, he commemorated the Revolution of 1830 in France with his "Liberty Leading the People," a dramatic painting dominated by the bare-breasted figure of a woman standing on the barricades, holding aloft the tricolor in one hand and a gun in the other, as she spurs the revolutionaries on. Beneath her lie the disheveled corpses of those who have fallen; the entire scene is illuminated by the flames of buildings burning in the background. The

[3] Quoted by Marcel Brion, *Romantic Art* (London, 1960), pp. 134–135.

same theatricality and sense of movement is revealed in many of the oriental scenes he was fond of painting, such as the famous "Massacre at Chios," depicting the slaughter by the Turks of the Greek inhabitants of the island of Chios during the Greek revolution. Delacroix's fascination with the Orient, which was shared by many of his contemporaries, is an example of the romantic taste for the exotic and the bizarre.

In music, romanticism tended to be less revolutionary than in the visual arts. Historians of music generally identify the period of classicism with the eighteenth century and that of romanticism with the nineteenth, but they stress the continuity between the two periods and point out that the classical forms, developed or refined by Haydn, Mozart, and Beethoven—the sonata, the string quartet, and the symphony—persisted into the romantic era. And though some romantic composers took liberties with it, the classical system of harmony too remained dominant in the nineteenth century. But the early romantic composers—men such as Franz Schubert (1797–1828), Robert Schumann (1810–1856), Felix Mendelssohn (1809–1847), and Hector Berlioz (1803–1869)—infused the traditional forms with new meaning and reinterpreted the function of music. They tried to work directly on the mind and the senses of the listener so as to evoke an infinite range of impressions, emotions, and thoughts. Some, such as Berlioz, sought to do this by using a much more varied and complex orchestration and by developing "program music," in which they attempted to convey, by means of imaginative suggestion, descriptive or poetic subject matter. Mendelssohn, for example, imparted a sunny and vibrant mood to his *Italian Symphony*, while the mood of his *Scotch Symphony* was gray and somber, with a suggestion of the skirling of bagpipes and the sound of heroic ballads. A more explicit attempt to achieve the fusion of poetry and music was made by the German romantics, particularly Schubert and Schumann, in the *Lied* ("song"), an art form in which words and melody are blended in perfect harmony. There is hardly a mood or a nuance of feeling that does not find expression in Schubert's *Lieder*, but the dominant impression is one of sadness, nostalgia, or yearning.

In literature, the revolt against the Enlightenment began as early as the mid-eighteenth century, although romanticism as a literary movement did not come to fruition in most countries until the first half of the nineteenth century. For example, in the growth after 1740 of English Methodism one finds a reaction against the prevalent Deism of the eighteenth century and a return to enthusiasm and emotion in religion. The writings of Jean Jacques Rousseau (1712–1778), himself a *philosophe,* also foreshadowed various aspects of romanticism: extreme sensitivity to nuances of feeling, concern with the individual personality, preoccupation with nature and the "natural." In Germany, the literary movement known as *Sturm und*

Drang ("storm and stress") out of which German romanticism developed, dates from the 1770's. By the early 1800's, romanticism as a literary movement was in full sway in Germany and had its representatives in Britain and France as well.

In matters of style, the romantics revolted against strict adherence to discipline and form that had characterized the classical tradition in literature. The measured Alexandrine verses of the seventeenth-century dramas of Racine and Corneille were now considered stilted and "artificial." The romantics regarded their own literary creations as freer and more "natural." The attitude of most romantic writers toward the individual also differed from the point of view prevalent in the Enlightenment. Although the *philosophes* had expressed an interest in the individual and his rights, their main concern had been to discover what qualities men had in common, what characteristics united them. In other words, they sought to generalize about human nature. Most romantic writers, on the other hand, were convinced of the uniqueness of the individual personality and suspicious of the kind of generalizations made by their predecessors. To them, diversity was not only natural but right and desirable. Carried to an extreme, this attitude led to a sense of isolation or alienation on the part of the individual, to self-dramatization and self-pity. Many a romantic figure, like the hero of Goethe's novel *The Sorrows of Young Werther* (1774), suffered from this sense of isolation and self-pity, though not all resorted, like Werther, to suicide as the only way out. The emphasis on individuality also found expression, in some of the romantics, in revolt against society and its conventions.

For others romanticism meant a return to the past and a sentimental nostalgia for earlier eras of history, particularly for the Middle Ages. Where writers of the Enlightenment like Voltaire had felt nothing but contempt for the Middle Ages as an era of superstition and obscurantism, François René de Chateaubriand (1768–1848) in France, Novalis (Friedrich von Hardenberg, 1772–1801), in Germany, and Sir Walter Scott (1771–1832) in Britain all romanticized the medieval period and compared it favorably with their own. Not all of them found the same virtues in the medieval past, nor did they all object to the same things in their own age. But the vogue of the Middle Ages was in part a reaction against the ugly, materialistic, and heartless industrial civilization that seemed to be emerging. In the Middle Ages the romantics thought they found a society in which the individual had security and a sense of belonging, an organic community in which the poor were contented with their station and deferred to their betters and the noble lords recognized their responsibility to protect those dependent upon them.

Perhaps, above all, they saw the Middle Ages as a time when faith prevailed, not the cold reason and skepticism of the Enlightenment. Romantic writers of a conservative turn were especially likely to look back nostalgically to an era in which faith had provided a sense of cohesion and unity that was missing from their own society. Certainly a return to religion, and particularly to Catholicism, was an important feature of romanticism. For many, it was less the beliefs than the colorful ceremonial, or ritualistic, aspects of Christianity that exercised a particular appeal. In this period also can be found the roots of the Gothic revival in architecture, which a few decades later saw the construction of the British Houses of Parliament and other monuments in Gothic style and the restoration of long-neglected Gothic cathedrals.

The romantic mood affected writers of practically all political and ideological persuasions and cannot be identified exclusively with any one group. Clearly, political conservatives shared many of the assumptions and points of view that have been attributed to the romantics: the reaction against the Enlightenment and its undue emphasis on reason, the return to the past, and the reversion to orthodox forms of Christianity. Particularly in Germany the major writers of the romantic school were conservative in their outlook; indeed, the German conservative tradition owes a great deal to romanticism. The admiration of romantic writers like Novalis for the organic society of the Middle Ages led them away from another romantic trait, the stress on the individual, and prepared the ground for the doctrine of the total submission of the individual to the state. Romanticism in Germany was both conservative and nationalist in tone. Yet exceptions may be found even to this generalization. The romantic writer Heinrich Heine (1797–1856), often called modern Germany's greatest lyric poet, was devoted to the cause of individual liberty and violently opposed the extreme positions taken by German nationalist writers in the first half of the nineteenth century. In Great Britain, some of the most noted romantic poets began their careers as radicals and ended as conservatives. William Wordsworth (1770–1850), an outspoken admirer of the French Revolution in its early stages, gradually turned against it, and in the end became a die-hard conservative opposed even to parliamentary reform. Samuel Taylor Coleridge (1772–1834) experienced a similar change of views. But in the second generation of English romantic poets, George Gordon, Lord Byron (1788–1824) championed the cause of oppressed nationalities everywhere and led the movement for Greek independence, and Percy Bysshe Shelley (1792–1822) shocked his contemporaries with views that caused him to be branded an atheist and an anarchist.

The element of nationalism in the romantic point of view was another expression of the reaction against the Enlightenment. Whereas the *philosophes* tended to be cosmopolitan in their outlook and to emphasize the similarities among men and nations, romantic writers turned with curiosity to their own national origins and traditions. As creative writers they were naturally interested in their native languages and often sought inspiration from folk tales and legends. Consequently, they became increasingly aware of differences among cultures, and tended to stress their national distinctiveness.

Finally, the romantic mood influenced the cause of social reform particularly during the 1830's and 1840's. Reformers appealed to the humanitarian feelings of their contemporaries by dramatizing the plight of Negro slaves and the sufferings of their own poor. The sense of conspiracy and adventure associated with the activities of republican secret societies in France after 1830 was consonant with the current romantic atmosphere and contrasted strongly with the prosaic qualities of the established order. The dreams of socialists for the creation of Utopian communities, perfect societies here on earth, though comparable in some ways to the visions of the *philosophes,* had an irrational appeal that distinguished them from the Utopias of their eighteenth-century predecessors.

Romanticism was a many-faceted, pervasive phenomenon that left almost no doctrine or ideology untouched. Some have attributed to the influence of the romantic mood the soft-mindedness and fuzziness of so much of the thinking and writing of the first half of the nineteenth century. In this view the romantic era marked an interlude between the more disciplined, rationalist *Weltanschauung* of the eighteenth century, which reflected the order and regularity of the Newtonian universe, and the positivist, science-oriented outlook that was to triumph in the second half of the nineteenth century. But whether one was a romantic conservative yearning for the rebirth of a society that had disappeared, a romantic liberal serving the cause of freedom for oppressed peoples, or a socialist reformer dreaming of the establishment of a society free of poverty and social ills, what remained of the romantic mood was shattered by the mid-century revolutions of 1848. For the abortive uprisings of that year seemed to prove that ideals were not enough, that in the last analysis physical force, material resources, and power were what counted in human relations.

CHAPTER 27

Political Change During the Restoration

ATTEMPTS TO PRESERVE the *status quo* during the Restoration era lasted longer in some parts of Europe than in others. In Great Britain, France, and the Low Countries, major changes in the political climate or alterations of the 1815 settlement took place in 1830 and 1831. In the rest of Europe, despite temporary and isolated disturbances in the 1820's and about 1830, the political arrangements of Vienna persisted at least until the revolutions of 1848. Economic and social changes did occur in central and eastern Europe during this era, but they proceeded more slowly than in western Europe and their political consequences were not openly manifested until at least the middle of the century.

TORY RULE IN GREAT BRITAIN, 1815–1830

The end of the Napoleonic wars found George III, who had assumed the crown in 1760, still on the throne in Great Britain. But since he was subject to recurrent fits of insanity, his son had become prince regent in 1811, and after his father's death, ruled in his own right as George IV, from 1820 to 1830. During this reign the prestige of the British monarchy sank. A clever but disreputable individual, George earned the enmity of a good part of the nation when he attempted to divorce his wife Caroline, from whom he had been separated for many years, and prevented her from being crowned as queen in 1820.

The irresponsibility of the ruler served to increase the importance of the Tory ministers, who had held office almost without interruption during the three decades prior to 1815. Although both Whig and Tory parties were still dominated in 1815 by members of the aristocracy, the Tories were more inclined to sympathize with the conservative view of British society and institutions that Burke had praised in his *Reflections on the French*

Revolution. Moreover, their leadership of Britain during the prolonged wars against France had made them profoundly suspicious of radicalism and movements for reform. The Whigs received support from the newer moneyed interests and from Protestant dissenters. They were therefore more amenable to the gradual reform of laws and governmental institutions and the removal of mercantilist restrictions on commerce and industry.

In the years immediately after 1815 the Tory view prevailed; indeed, the government of Lord Liverpool, which lasted from 1812 until 1827, was one of the most reactionary in modern British history. Its actions and policies between 1815 and 1820 must be seen against the background of the severe depression that attended the transition from a wartime to a peacetime economy. The sudden drop in government expenditures and the loss of wartime markets for British manufactures and grain brought a period of falling prices, unstable currency, and widespread unemployment. The government's remedy for this situation, hardly calculated to meet with general approval, was a protective tariff, the Corn Law of 1815, which prohibited the importation of foreign grain until the price of English grain rose above a specified level (eighty shillings per quarter). This measure, unabashedly favoring the landowners, naturally antagonized urban laborers who were forced to pay a higher price for their bread in circumstances that were already difficult. No one in either party came forward to champion the cause of the working classes, so the task fell to radical agitators and writers and to clubs organized for reform. Some men, among them William Cobbett (1763–1835), the most famous of the radical pamphleteers, attacked all kinds of abuses, but most radicals concentrated on trying to reform the methods of selecting representatives to the House of Commons. For they were convinced that as long as control of the lower chamber remained in the hands of the aristocracy, which also controlled the House of Lords, there was no hope for legislation that would benefit the country as a whole.

Acute economic distress after 1815 led to a series of public meetings at which radical orators called for the repeal of the Corn Law of 1815 (along with earlier corn laws still on the statute books) and for parliamentary reform. Although almost no violence was associated with these demonstrations, the Tory ministry, taking alarm and seeing the danger of revolution everywhere, acted against the reform societies in 1817 by temporarily forbidding all public meetings, suppressing all societies not licensed by government, and suspending the Habeas Corpus Act. These measures brought a brief lull in popular agitation, but a new economic slump the following year resulted in a series of mass meetings in some of the larger cities of the north and Midlands. The most famous of these was held, despite a government ban, in St. Peter's Fields in Manchester in August, 1819. Local authorities sent a squadron of cavalry into the crowd of sixty

Peterloo Massacre, 1819. *A contemporary caption to this print referred to the* "*wanton and furious attack by that brutal armed force The Manchester &* *Cheshire Yeomanry Cavalry.*"

thousand to arrest the fiery radical orator, Henry Hunt (1773–1835). In the resulting panic, eleven people were killed and several hundred injured. The incident was immediately branded the Battle of Peterloo, or the Peterloo Massacre. To the popular outcry that greeted this episode the government responded only with further measures of repression. In November, Parliament passed the famous Six Acts, a series of drastic restrictions intended to eliminate large public meetings, suppress or seriously weaken the radical press, and speed up conviction of offenders against the public order. As if to justify these measures, the government three months later uncovered a radical plot organized by one Arthur Thistlewood (1770–1820) for the assassination of the entire cabinet, the seizure of the Bank of England, and the establishment of a provisional government. Betrayed by an agent provocateur, the conspirators were arrested in a house on Cato Street in London; as might be expected, the Tory ministry gave widespread publicity to the Cato Street Conspiracy, pointing out how narrowly the country had escaped disaster.

Perhaps because of the repressive measures, perhaps because the economy picked up, after 1820 the radical movement in Britain subsided for almost a decade. During this period the Tory ministry was broadened considerably when Lord Liverpool, upon the death in 1822 of the foreign minister, Castlereagh, added to his cabinet three men who were a good deal more amenable to change than their colleagues: George Canning (1770–1827) as foreign minister and leader of the House of Commons; William Huskisson (1770–1830) as head of the Board of Trade; and Sir Robert Peel (1788–1850) as secretary for home affairs, the beginning of his long career. None of these men went so far as to favor major parliamentary reform at this time, but they were ready to carry out a series of pragmatic, piecemeal changes in laws and institutions that helped bring the British government into closer touch with economic and social realities.

Peel was responsible for a long-needed revision of the criminal code, which still carried the death penalty for some two hundred offenses, among them pocket picking, sheep stealing, and forgery. Because juries refused to convict offenders for such petty crimes when the punishment was death, disregard for the law had become widespread. Peel reduced the number of capital crimes and made the penalties more nearly commensurate with the offenses. This achievement, combined with his introduction in 1829 of a regular metropolitan police force in London (called "Bobbies" after him), led to a considerable reduction in the crime rate in Britain.

Huskisson was primarily responsible for the elimination of restrictions on British trade inherited from the mercantilist era. He was able to reduce the tariff on many items needed by British manufacturers as well as on some consumer goods, such as wine, coffee, and sugar. Many restrictions (including those on the importation of corn) still remained, but his policy was continued by subsequent ministries and in the 1840's culminated in complete free trade.

Although others prepared the way, Peel and Huskisson also deserve some credit for the repeal in 1824 of the Combination Acts, which had prohibited the formation of labor organizations. The impact of this repeal was reduced somewhat when, after a year of strikes and violence, Parliament in 1825 passed a law that restricted labor unions to bargaining over wages and hours and effectively prevented them from striking. But the right of labor to organize had been recognized.

Despite the gains achieved through these laws, the Tory ministry remained unpopular. Lord Liverpool's death in 1827 opened the way for the brief ministries of Canning (who died after a few months in office) and the ineffectual Lord Goderich (Frederick John Robinson, 1782–1859). The appointment in 1828 of the duke of Wellington, the celebrated national hero, as prime minister prolonged the Tories' incumbency, but Wellington's alliance with the most reactionary elements in the party alienated young Tory liberals and contributed to the growth of the Whig opposition. During Wellington's ministry one more major reform was achieved, despite his personal distaste. This was the passage in 1829 of the bill for Catholic emancipation, which permitted Catholics to sit in Parliament and to hold all public offices except those of lord chancellor of England and lord lieutenant of Ireland. This reform, proposed many times before, had been repeatedly thwarted by the opposition of the king or the House of Lords.

Now the pressure from an active movement in Ireland, led by the Irish barrister Daniel O'Connell (1775–1847), forced the issue. Wellington and Peel, convinced that civil war would result if they tried to hold out, pushed the bill through the House of Lords, and Wellington's threat to resign brought the king's assent. Passage of the bill did not solve the problem of England's relationship with Ireland, particularly since the ministry immediately raised the property qualification for voting there, but it was an important step in the long process of eliminating religious discrimination.

The Catholic Emancipation Act was the last significant contribution of the Tories before they left office after almost a half century of rule. Two events in 1830 helped to topple the Wellington ministry and prepare the way for passage of the Reform Bill of 1832. One was the news of the July Revolution in France, which overthrew the restored Bourbon regime and brought to power a government supported by the middle class. The other was the death of King George IV and the accession of his brother William IV, an event which according to constitutional tradition required the holding of a general election. The election resulted in sizable gains for those favoring reform. But more significant than either of these events was the cumulative effect of the Industrial Revolution upon British society; it had created social groups, forces, and problems which the old Tory leaders were incapable of handling. To the Whigs fell the task of breaching the old order and of taking into partnership with the older aristocracy the new "captains of industry."

THE BOURBON RESTORATION IN FRANCE

It is hardly surprising that some of the bitterest political struggles between 1815 and 1830 took place in France, the birthplace of the revolution and the most important country in which the restoration of a monarch occurred. The opposing forces were the Ultraroyalists, who sought to wipe out all the revolution had achieved, and the liberals and their allies, who were intent upon preserving the reforms secured between 1789 and 1814. Between them stood Louis XVIII (ruled 1814–1824), basically sympathetic with the Ultras, but shrewd enough to realize that any attempt to wipe out the gains of the revolution would end in disaster for his dynasty. The new constitution—the Charter of 1814, Louis' "gift" to the people— recognized the major achievements of the revolutionary years. It specifically guaranteed the principle of equality before the law and the retention of the Civil Code. It confirmed the titles to their property of those who had purchased national land during the revolution, and preserved the Napoleonic Concordat, along with the principle of religious toleration.

The Charter did not determine where the real power should lie, and this question was debated by political theorists, whose views ranged from the defense of absolute monarchy to the assertion of popular sovereignty, and fought out at a less theoretical level by politicians. Specifically at issue were the powers of the bicameral Assembly: the Chamber of Peers, whose members were appointed to hereditary tenure, and the Chamber of Deputies, whose members were elected in accordance with a highly restricted franchise based on property ownership. What was to be the relationship of the Assembly to the king? Executive power was vested in the king and his ministers, but legislative power did not clearly rest with the chambers. The king (or his ministers) had the sole power to initiate legislation; the chambers could only petition the king to do so. According to the Charter, the chambers could reject a bill proposed by the king but could not amend it without royal consent. Nor was the position of the ministers clearly defined. According to the Charter the ministers were officers of the king, appointed by him and charged with the execution of his policy. Nowhere did the Charter say that the ministers must represent the majority in the legislature. Yet, in fact, between 1815 and 1830 the leading minister did represent the majority group in the Chamber of Deputies except on two occasions, one in 1815–1816 and the other in 1829–1830. The principle of ministerial responsibility was thus gradually established, although it was never explicitly conceded by the king.

Some fundamental procedures of parliamentary government developed in France during the Restoration, and a generation of statesmen gained valuable political experience. But the basic issue was left unresolved, for the restored Bourbon rulers failed to establish a working compromise between the traditional claims of monarchy and the revolutionary principle of popular sovereignty. The regime foundered over this issue in 1830.

Politically, the fifteen-year era falls into three periods. During the first, which lasted for only a year (1815–1816), the Assembly was dominated by the Ultraroyalists, who won a majority in the Chamber of Deputies and embarrassed the king and the moderate-royalist ministry by announcing their intention of sweeping away a number of institutions inherited from the revolutionary and Napoleonic eras and restoring confiscated estates to their prerevolutionary owners. Actually they achieved very few of their goals, though they did set up special courts to try Bonapartists and revolutionaries whom they charged with treason. Even before the Ultraroyalist Chamber of Deputies was elected, an unofficial White Terror erupted, a counterpart of the Terror of 1793–1794, carried out by royalists during the summer of 1815 in the south of France. Bands of royalist volunteers, remnants of an army organized at the time of Napoleon's escape from Elba by a nephew of the king—Louis Antoine de Bourbon, duke of Angoulême (1775–1844)—now arrested, imprisoned, or massacred hundreds of individuals suspected of Jacobin or Bonapartist sympathies. The White Terror spread from Marseilles to other parts of Provence and Languedoc. At Nîmes and in the department of the Gard the victims included many Protestants suspected by the Catholic royalists of disloyalty to the Bourbon monarchy. It appears that the White Terror was neither instigated nor directed by the restored monarchy, but government officials looked the other way as the royalist bands carried out their vigilante purges. When Louis XVIII realized that the extremism of the Ultraroyalists was alienating the nation from the monarchy, he dissolved the Chamber of Deputies, in September, 1816, and called for new elections.

In the new chamber the majority consisted of moderate royalists, and between 1816 and 1820 they supported the ministries headed by the duke of Richelieu (1766–1822) and his successor, Duke Élie Decazes (1780–1860). This second period of the Restoration was one of relative calm despite frequent verbal attacks on the ministry by both Ultraroyalists and liberals. New electoral laws extended the franchise somewhat, though there were still only about 100,000 voters out of a total population of 30,000,000.

This tranquility was shattered in 1820—the year of revolutions in Spain, Portugal, and Italy—by the assassination of the duke of Berry, the son of Louis' younger brother and presumably the last of the Bourbon line. (The hope of the assassin that he was putting an end to the Bourbon dynasty was frustrated when the duke's widow was discovered to be pregnant, and in due course produced a male heir.) Although the murder was the act of an isolated fanatic, the Ultras charged the king's minister, Decazes, with responsibility for the crime because of his alleged laxity in dealing with the opposition. So strong was the pressure put on the king that he was forced to abandon Decazes and appoint a new ministry. At this point began the final period of the Restoration in France, an era of growing reaction that lasted until 1830. During this period Louis took a less active role in government, and the initiative gradually passed to his younger brother, the count of Artois, who became Charles X upon Louis' death in 1824.

The assassination of the duke of Berry was used as an excuse for imposing restrictions on the press and for revising the electoral law to give increased influence to the landed aristocracy at the expense of the bourgeoisie. Between 1822 and 1828, under the ministry of the count of Villèle (1773–1854), the Ultras were finally able to secure legislation favorable to their own interests. For example, the Law of Indemnity (1825) compensated nobles who had emigrated during the revolution for the loss of their landed estates. This measure was doubly offensive to the members of the bourgeois opposition because they were the principal holders of the government bonds whose interest rate was reduced to provide funds for the indemnity. Although the Law of Indemnity finally ended the controversy over the revolutionary land settlement, it was not viewed in this favorable light in 1825.

One of the principal features of Charles X's reign was the close tie established between throne and altar. The Law of Sacrilege (1825) imposed the death penalty for offenses of an allegedly sacrilegious character and for the theft of sacred objects from churches. The law was particularly odious to liberals because it appeared to put the state at the service of the Church in a manner reminiscent of the Old Regime. Villèle also did his best to undermine the *Université*, the state educational system founded by Napoleon, by placing a bishop at its head and dismissing many of its liberal teachers. At the same time he encouraged the growth of Catholic seminaries outside the state system. Their function was ostensibly to train priests, but in fact they competed with the state secondary schools for students. Finally, although the Jesuit order was still formally banned in France, the government openly countenanced the presence of Jesuits as teachers in Catholic schools. Indeed, liberals were convinced that Jesuits had infiltrated everywhere and were secretly directing government policy.

Developments like these resulted in steadily mounting opposition to the Villèle ministry. Liberal newspapers, such as the *Constitutionnel* and the *Journal des Débats*, contributed to the struggle. In 1827 was formed a liberal political society called *Aide-toi, et le ciel t'aidera* ("Heaven help those who help themselves") whose goals were to prevent falsification of electoral lists by government officials and to spread liberal propaganda. Formerly enthusiastic backers of the regime now began to join the opposition. So too did a number of wealthy bankers and manufacturers who resented legislation that favored the nobility and the clergy.

In 1827 Charles X made the error of dissolving the Chamber of Deputies and calling for new elections. When a majority of moderate royalists was returned, the king reluctantly yielded to the principle of ministerial responsibility by dismissing Villèle and summoning the moderate viscount of Martignac (1778–1832) to take his place. Martignac relaxed the restrictions on the press and dismissed some of the more notoriously reactionary Ultraroyalists from the civil service. However, the heckling of this ministry by both the Ultra and the liberal extremes made its existence difficult and ultimately provided the king with a pretext for dismissing Martignac in 1829. He then named the prince of Polignac (1780–1847), clearly flouting the will of the Assembly. For Polignac, who in 1816 had refused to swear to uphold the Charter, was one of the most notorious of the Ultras and could not possibly command a majority in the Chamber of Deputies.

From this time on, the alternatives for France seemed to be royal despotism and revolution. A protest against the Polignac ministry by a majority of the deputies in the spring of 1830 merely provoked the king to dissolve the chamber and call for new elections. But the result was an even larger majority for the opposition.

Confronted with the prospect of a recalcitrant Assembly, Charles decided

July, 1830. *Scene from the July Revolution of 1830 in France. Musée Carnavalet, Paris.*

to seize the initiative, and before the new body could meet, issued the royal decrees known as the July Ordinances. The decrees dissolved the newly elected Assembly, established a new electoral system, arbitrarily deprived the wealthy bourgeoisie of the right to vote, and imposed a rigid censorship on the press. Though the king could argue that the Charter gave him the right to issue such decrees, the opposition correctly interpreted the July Ordinances as an attempt to abandon the Charter. The promulgation of the decrees gave rise to an insurrection—the July Revolution of 1830.

The revolution occurred with a minimum of violence, partly because the government, not anticipating trouble, had made few preparations to resist. What fighting there was occurred in Paris and was all over in three days. It began in Paris on July 26, when spontaneous demonstrations greeted publication of the royal ordinances. The following day unemployed workers, joined by students and some republican agitators, threw up barricades in the streets of Paris to prevent the passage of government troops. On July 28 the insurrectionists captured the Hôtel de Ville and raised the tricolor flag. The king, who was hunting on his estate at Saint-Cloud, offered to withdraw the ordinances and dismiss the ministry, but it was already too late. A group of liberal leaders, who had been meeting daily since July 26, fearing a republican seizure of power, announced the formation of a provisional government. Favoring a constitutional monarchy, this group proposed giving the crown to the duke of Orléans, cousin of Charles X. The duke was a natural rallying point for monarchists dissatisfied with Charles X. He had remained in France during the first stages of the great revolution, fought with the revolutionary armies before going into exile early in 1793, and professed liberal views. At first, he hesitated because the legitimate king had not abandoned his title to the throne, but he agreed to serve as "lieutenant-general" of the realm until the succession was settled. Then the agreement of the marquis de Lafayette, the aged hero of the American and French revolutions and an unofficial leader of republican forces in Paris, was secured. In a dramatic scene on July 31, the duke of Orléans entered the capital and paraded through streets lined with silent and sullen workers until he reached the Hôtel de Ville. There he met Lafayette for an interview, and then they appeared together before the crowds with a tricolor flag draped over their shoulders. Lafayette had satisfied himself that the duke would sit on a "throne surrounded by republican institutions." To no avail did Charles X announce that he was abdicating in favor of his young grandson. Next, a majority of the old Chamber of Deputies met and formally offered the throne to the duke of Orléans, so Charles had no

Deputies calling the duke of Orléans to the throne. *Painting by Heim. Musée de Versailles, Versailles.*

alternative but to go into exile in England. Within a few days the new king accepted a revised version of the Charter which eliminated the preamble stating that the document was the "gift" of the king to his people. Instead, his title—"king of the French People"—clearly implied that he owed his throne to the popular will. The July Revolution had put an end to the Restoration in France.

METTERNICH'S REPRESSION IN CENTRAL EUROPE

The various peoples inhabiting the central part of the European continent, from the Baltic Sea in the north to the island of Sicily in the south, fell under the domination during the Restoration era of the Habsburg dynasty, or rather of its chief agent, Prince Klemens von Metternich. The Austrian chancellor had his emissaries or his spies everywhere, sending back reports to Vienna, constantly on the alert for evidence of liberalism or subversion that might threaten the *status quo*. In point of fact, in the years immediately after 1815, active opposition was confined to a small minority of students, army officers, liberal nobles, and merchants. The peasants who constituted the great mass of the population were little concerned with political questions. Such grievances as they had were directed primarily against their landlords, not the government. Since industrialization did not get under way until the 1830's and 1840's, and then only in the Rhineland and northern Italy, there existed no numerically significant middle class to assume the leadership of a liberal opposition.

The opposition that did exist in central Europe was as often nationalist as liberal, though no clear-cut distinction between the two was made by Metternich or, indeed, by those who agitated against the *status quo*. In Austria, nationalist sentiment normally took the form of demands by representatives of non-German groups for greater use of their language in schools and administrative offices. In Italy and the German states, nationalism meant the desire for freedom from Austrian domination and a greater measure of unity for the respective peoples. To all these aspirations, Metternich's answer was the same. They were ruthlessly suppressed as threats to the delicate equilibrium of existing institutions. He was convinced that—particularly within the Austrian empire proper—any attempt to tamper with the elaborate structure might bring the entire edifice tumbling down. If the chancellor's goal was the maintenance of order and a reasonable degree of calm, his policy worked remarkably well during the better part of the period between 1815 and 1848. But by refusing to face up to the real and complex problems existing in the Habsburg realms, and by stifling the growing nationalist desires of Germans and Italians, he merely postponed the explosion, which finally erupted in 1848.

The Germanic Confederation

The Germanic Confederation, created by the Congress of Vienna, consisted of thirty-eight states; Austria and Prussia were the largest of these, though their non-German territory was not included. The institutional embodiment of this loose federation was a federal diet, or assembly, consisting of delegates appointed by the rulers of each of the member states, which met in the free city of Frankfurt am Main. The function of the diet was ill defined, especially since the Confederation had no executive to implement its decisions, but it soon became clear that the Confederation had been set up as an instrument for the exercise of Metternich's influence throughout the German states. While Metternich seems to have viewed it initially as a kind of defensive alliance against encroachment on German territory by France or Russia, in fact it came to be used primarily for the repression of liberal movements throughout Germany.

Not all of the thirty-eight states had governments quite as reactionary as Austria's. Although Metternich had discouraged them from doing so, rulers in a number of states granted constitutions to their subjects to fulfill promises made during the final years of the Napoleonic era; among them were the medium-sized states of southern Germany—Bavaria, Württemberg, and Baden. These constitutions, like the French Charter, did not acknowledge the principle of popular sovereignty; indeed, in the virtual absence of a middle class, suffrage was confined primarily to the landed aristocracy and the administrative bureaucracy. Where elected assemblies existed, their primary function was merely to ratify legislation proposed by the sovereign.

At first, liberals throughout Germany looked hopefully to Prussia for imspiration. King Frederick William III not only had promised a constitution to his people, on the eve of Waterloo, but had agreed between 1807 and 1814 to a series of reforms that made Prussia appear to be one of the more progressive states in Germany. Leadership in initiating these reforms came from Baron Heinrich vom und zum Stein (1757–1831), who was chief minister in 1807–1808. Although he was dismissed from office in 1808 because of pressure from Napoleon upon the king, Stein's program of reforms was carried on by his successors. Among these, the most important was Baron (later Prince) Karl August von Hardenberg (1750–1822), who served as chief minister beginning in 1810. Stein, and Hardenberg after him, were convinced that Prussia's recovery from the defeat inflicted by Napoleon could occur only as the result of a series of political and institutional reforms comparable, in some respects, to those undertaken by the French during the revolution. After the humiliating defeat of Prussia at Jena in 1806, Hardenberg is alleged to have told the king, "Your Majesty! We must do from above what the French have done from below."[1] By giving its

[1] Quoted by K. S. Pinson, *Modern Germany*, (New York, 1954), p. 33.

citizens greater opportunity for participation in the affairs of state, Prussia could develop a new patriotic spirit.

Among the reforms were the abolition of serfdom, though landlords retained manorial jurisdiction over the peasants. Some of the more rigid class distinctions were abolished by decrees making it possible for non-nobles to buy land formerly restricted to noble ownership and permitting members of the noble class to go into trade. Stein's Municipal Ordinance of 1808 introduced a system of municipal self-government which permitted towns to control their own affairs through town councils and salaried magistrates. Opportunities in primary and secondary education were broadened by Wilhelm von Humboldt (1767–1835), Prussian minister of education in 1809–1810. Humboldt was also responsible for founding the University of Berlin in 1809. Inspired by a new humanistic educational philosophy, the university became the rallying point of intellectuals seeking Prussia's regeneration and liberation from foreign control. Finally, an important series of reforms in the army was undertaken by Gerhard von Scharnhorst (1755–1813) and Neithardt von Gneisenau (1760–1831), who eliminated some of the barbarous punishments hitherto inflicted upon enlisted men, encouraged promotion by merit in the officer corps, and introduced universal military conscription to create a truly national army. A new emphasis upon infantry and artillery tended to weaken the traditional, feudal character of the Prussian army.

Both Stein and Hardenberg had looked forward to the creation of a legislative assembly as the culmination of this program of reforms, and the king's promise of a constitution establishing some sort of representative government appeared to confirm their hopes. But no constitution was forthcoming. After 1815 Hardenberg and others with similar views gradually lost their influence over the king to a more reactionary group. In 1817, when it was announced that the king would form a council of state composed of the royal princes, ministers, heads of departments, and army commanders, the liberals temporarily abandoned their hope for a representative assembly and a constitution. The Prussian government became more efficient than that of any other German state, but it remained absolutist.

Those who had hoped for a closer measure of unity among Germans after the Napoleonic wars were far from satisfied with the Austrian-sponsored Germanic Confederation and resented the particularism of the rulers of the individual states. To spread the ideal of unity and "freedom" for Germans, students organized *Burschenschaften,* or student societies, in a number of German universities. These drew their inspiration from men like Joseph von Görres (1776–1848), an ardent nationalist who edited *Der Rheinische Merkur;* Ernst Moritz Arndt (1769–1860), a poet and Prussian patriot; and Friedrich Ludwig Jahn (1778–1852), who had become famous during the Napoleonic Wars when he organized an association of *Turngemeinden* or

The festival of the Burschenschaften at the Wartburg Castle, October 18, 1817. *Engraving by Ferdinand Flor. Some of the students can be seen burning books of anti-nationalist writers in the background.*

gymnastic societies, whose aim was to bring about the physical and moral regeneration of German youth. "Turnvater Jahn" was perhaps the noisiest and most aggressive of the German nationalists of his time and foreshadowed some of the traits of twentieth-century Nazism. Preaching hatred of foreign influence and even of foreign dress, he urged young Germans to return to their Teutonic heritage. His followers wore gray shirts, and he encouraged such unruly behavior as the disruption of lectures by professors who were insufficiently nationalist in their outlook. Jahn was also responsible, along with others, for injecting anti-Semitism into the doctrines of the *Burschenschaften,* though some members of the societies resisted this tendency.

During their brief history the *Burschenschaften* staged a number of popular demonstrations. An assembly in 1817 brought young people from all over Germany to the Wartburg Castle, near Eisenach, where Luther had taken refuge from his persecutors. Timed to coincide with the three-hundredth anniversary of Luther's posting of his ninety-five theses and the fourth anniversary of the German victory at the Battle of Leipzig, the assembly opened with speeches exhorting the students to dedicate their lives to the "holy cause of union and freedom." The group then marched in a torchlight parade to a nearby hilltop to witness the burning of books by conservative and antinationalist writers. Eighteen months later, Karl Sand, a mentally unbalanced theological student who was a *Burschenschaft* member, assassinated the dramatist August von Kotzebue, known for his reactionary views. Sand was condemned to death and Metternich decided the time had come to proceed against the *Burschenschaften*. Acting with representatives of the nine most important German states, Metternich drew up the celebrated Carlsbad Decrees (1819) and submitted them to the diet of the Germanic Confederation for ratification. These decrees dissolved the *Burschenschaften*, set up rigid censorship and press control throughout the Confederation, and created an elaborate system for rooting out subversive individuals in schools and universities.

The enforcement of the Carlsbad Decrees was a serious blow to the liberal and nationalist movements, which had never been very strong, and political opposition to the Metternichian system was practically nonexistent for several years after 1819. With the collaboration of Frederick William III of Prussia, Metternich actively intervened in those states of the Confederation where legislative bodies still existed in order to restrict their influence and to stifle potential opposition. Only in the latter part of the 1820's did nationalist student societies reappear, meeting clandestinely to avoid the secret police.

In 1830 news of the July Revolution in France touched off a flurry of excitement in Germany and inspired minor revolutions in Brunswick, Saxony, and Hesse-Cassel, where the rulers were forced to abdicate in favor of sons or brothers who then granted constitutions to the people. Metternich was convinced that these revolts were part of an international radical conspiracy. In 1832, at an all-German festival at Hambach, twenty-five thousand people drank to Lafayette and denounced the principles of the Holy Alliance; and once again Metternich seized the occasion of a demonstration as the pretext for issuing series of decrees which strengthened the princes in dealing with their parliaments, brought the universities under renewed surveillance, and prohibited all public meetings. Within a year or two, all open opposition had ceased.

Italy

Events in Italy between 1815 and 1830 were similar in many ways to those in the German states. For the mass of Italians, the change from French to Austrian domination made very little difference. But for the small, educated middle class in the cities of northern Italy and for other groups which had benefited from the introduction of French institutions, the restoration of petty despotic governments taking their directions from Austria proved a disappointment. Those who had hoped during the Napoleonic era for a closer union among Italian-speaking peoples were reluctant to accept Metternich's view of Italy as a mere "geographical expression." The peninsula was once again divided into a number of lesser states: the kingdom of Naples and Sicily (the Two Sicilies) under the restored Bourbon Ferdinand I; the Papal States, to which Pope Pius VII returned after several years of exile; the smaller principalities of Parma, Modena, and Tuscany, all ruled by relatives of the Austrian emperor who took their directions from Metternich; the provinces of Lombardy and Venetia, directly incorporated into the Austrian empire and administered from Vienna; and the kingdom of Sardinia, ruled until 1821 by Victor Emmanuel I, of the house of Savoy. None of these states possessed constitutions or representative assemblies in 1815 and the restored rulers retained only those French institutions which tended to strengthen their despotic regimes. Then, as now, the northern half of the peninsula was better off economically than the southern. Only in Sardinia, Lombardy, and Venetia was there significant industrialization before 1850, and only in these areas were attempts made to increase agricultural production through experimentation with new techniques.

The failure of the revolutions of 1820–1821 in Naples and Sardinia and the reprisals taken against the rebels tended to weaken and discourage nationalist and liberal opposition. As in Germany, the decade of 1820–1830 saw little overt resistance to established authority, although secret societies like the *Carbonari* continued to operate underground. Again as in Germany, the July Revolution in France was the signal for a series of minor revolts; these occurred in Modena, Parma, and the Papal States, beginning in December, 1830. But unlike their German counterparts, the Italian revolutionaries of 1830–1831 counted on the active support of the new government of Louis Philippe in France, hoping it would oppose any Austrian attempt at intervention. However, Louis Philippe was not willing to risk his international position, and the French Assembly was not prepared to risk a war with Austria. Metternich therefore had a free hand; he sent troops to Modena, Parma, and the Papal States, put down the revolts, and restored their legitimate rulers.

The Austrian Empire

Within the Austrian empire proper, Metternich's main problem, though he may not have recognized it, was the emergence of a growing national consciousness among the various peoples under Habsburg rule. This was to remain the central problem for the empire throughout the nineteenth century and was resolved only with the breaking up of the empire at the end of the First World War. For Austria in 1815 was not a national state like France or Britain, but a collection of peoples and territories united only by their common allegiance to the Habsburg ruler. The broad territorial outlines of the Habsburg empire had been set since the sixteenth century, but only at the beginning of the nineteenth century was it given a name. Until Francis adopted the title emperor of Austria in 1804, anticipating Napoleon's dissolution of the Holy Roman Empire, the territories of Austria were simply referred to as the "lands of the House of Habsburg" or the "lands of the Holy Roman Emperor." Most of the peoples in the empire thought of themselves not as Austrians, but as subjects of the Habsburg emperor.

It is difficult to find agreement on the precise national identities of the peoples that composed the Habsburg empire. However, three major national groups can be specified. The first of these consisted of the Germans; forming no more than a quarter of the population, they were concentrated primarily in the western part of the empire in the old Habsburg lands around Vienna. Large groups of Germans also lived on the fringes of Bohemia, the territory to the north which had once been a separate kingdom, and in all the major cities of the empire. To the extent that there was a middle class in Austria, it was made up of Germans. The growth of German nationalism in the first half of the nineteenth century caused division among the Germans in Austria. The strong nationalists were prepared to sacrifice the Austrian empire, if necessary, in order to join a unified German nation. The moderates hoped to see other states of Germany merge with Austria under the continued rule of the Habsburgs.

The national group second in importance—in influence if not in numbers—consisted of the Magyars, who lived in the crown lands of St. Stephen, in the eastern half of the empire, which included Hungary, Transylvania, and Croatia. The Magyars were proud of their origins, which could be traced to the Middle Ages: their first crowned ruler, Stephen ascended the throne in the year 1001. Traditionally the most independent people in the empire, they maintained their own Diet and their own local administration. Every emperor was still required, by tradition, to go to Budapest to be invested separately with the crown of St. Stephen. Even before 1815, the cultural revival had begun among the Magyars which was to grow into a movement for greater autonomy within the Austrian empire. At the same time, the Magyars constituted a minority in their own lands and were faced with nationalist movements among the Slavic peoples and the other groups subject to them.

The third major group consisted of the Slavs. Including almost half the population of the Austrian empire, the Slavs formed its largest single national group. But they were divided into a number of subgroups and before the nineteenth century had little national consciousness. Of the greatest potential political importance among the Slavs were the Poles, who had been attached to the empire only at the end of the eighteenth century and therefore retained a strong sense of national identity, and the Czechs,

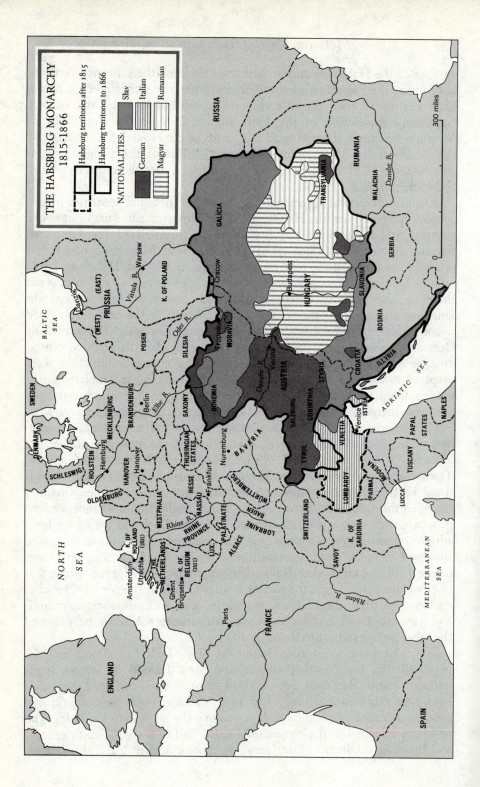

THE HABSBURG MONARCHY
1815-1866

Habsburg territories after 1815
Habsburg territories to 1866

NATIONALITIES:
Slav
Italian
Rumanian
German
Magyar

300 miles

RUSSIA

RUMANIA

WALACHIA

Danube R.

GALICIA

TRANSYLVANIA

Cracow

SERBIA

Vistula R. Warsaw

K. OF POLAND

Budapest

HUNGARY

SLAVONIA

Danzig

(EAST)

PRUSSIA

BOSNIA

(WEST)

POSEN

Oder R.

SILESIA

Troppau

MORAVIA

Vienna

BALTIC
SEA

CROATIA

ILLYRIA

SWEDEN

STYRIA

ADRIATIC
SEA

MECKLENBURG

BRANDENBURG

Berlin

SAXONY

BOHEMIA

AUSTRIA

Elbe R.

SALZBURG

CARINTHIA

Venice

ISTRIA

DENMARK

Hamburg

HOLSTEIN

HANOVER

Hanover

THURINGIAN
STATES

Nuremberg

BAVARIA

TYROL

VENETIA

NAPLES

SCHLESWIG

Frankfurt

PAPAL
STATES

OLDENBURG

HESSE

WÜRTEMBERG

LOMBARDY

MODENA

PARMA

TUSCANY

K. OF
HOLLAND
(1831)

WESTPHALIA

NASSAU

Rhine R.

BADEN

SWITZERLAND

LUCCA

Amsterdam

Utrecht

THE
NETHERLANDS

RHINE
PROVINCE

PALATINATE

K. OF
SARDINIA

NORTH
SEA

Ghent

K. OF
BELGIUM
(1831)

LUX.

ALSACE

LORRAINE

SAVOY

Brussels

Paris

FRANCE

Rhône R.

MEDITERRANEAN
SEA

ENGLAND

SPAIN

who had earlier ruled the independent kingdom of Bohemia. Because the great majority of the Slavs were peasants working the estates of German or Magyar masters, their nationalist aspirations were often mingled with social grievances.

To these three major groups should be added the Italians of the provinces of Lombardy and Venetia, which had been annexed to the Habsburg lands by the settlement of 1815, and the Rumanians, a sizable minority concentrated in the eastern part of the Hungarian kingdom.

What policies did Metternich adopt in governing this congeries of peoples under Habsburgs control? In general, he tried to avoid the problems posed by the emerging nationalism, and in the early part of the century, such an attitude served reasonably well. By the 1830's, however, it had become increasingly difficult for the government to ignore the demands of nationalist groups for greater autonomy. Still Metternich did not propose a broad solution; rather he resorted to a number of temporary expedients for neutralizing nationalist sentiment and tried to play off one national group against another. Certainly he did little to forestall the explosion of 1848, which resulted from a combination of nationalism and social discontent. In his defense it may be said that Metternich had the misfortune of serving under two emperors—Francis I and his successor Ferdinand I—who had neither the will nor the capacity to support any program of constructive reform. Ferdinand, in fact, was an imbecile and an epileptic who was allowed to inherit the throne in 1835 because of his father's wish that the direct line of succession not be interrupted. During his reign, which lasted until December, 1848, he was authorized to sign documents presented to him and reacted, on occasion, to events that occurred; but Austria was, in fact, ruled by a body of councillors (of whom Metternich was the most important) acting in the emperor's name. But Metternich did not take full advantage of the opportunities this situation offered for exercising his personal control. Indeed, there was much truth in his own admission, "I have governed Europe on occasion; Austria, never."

RUSSIA

Alexander I and the Decembrist Revolt

Despite her reputation as an "enlightened" monarch, Catherine the Great (ruler of Russia from 1762 to 1796) never relaxed her control over her subjects. At the beginning of the nineteenth century, Russia was the most autocratic of the European states. Catherine's son Paul I (ruled 1796–1801) recognized no limitations on his authority and possessed a strong sense of his position as a divine-right monarch. To a foreign envoy he is supposed to have remarked, "Know that no one in Russia is important except the person who is speaking with me; and that, only while he is

View of Moscow from a terrace in the Kremlin. *Engraving by Gabriel Lory, 1799.*

speaking." In practice, however, the authority of the tsar had certain limits. One of them resulted simply from the size of the vast empire under his rule; it extended from the Baltic Sea to the Caucasus, from the borders of Poland to the Pacific. With the modes of transportation and communication then in existence, it was impossible for the central government to extend its control into every corner of the realm.

Recognizing the danger to absolutism posed by western ideas and influences, Paul did his best to isolate Russia, restricting foreign travel by his subjects and forbidding the importation of European, and particularly French, books. He rightly estimated that the greatest threat to his autocratic control came not from the masses—peasants and serfs—but rather from the educated aristocracy, which had been exposed to French culture during the reign of Catherine. And indeed, it was this group that brought his brief tyrannical reign to an end. In 1801 he was assassinated by a cabal of aristocrats seeking to bring to the throne his twenty-four-year-old son Alexander, whose outlook was known to be much more liberal than his father's.

As we have seen, Tsar Alexander I was an unstable figure, characterized by changing moods and inconsistent actions. Viewed by some as a hypocrite and a traitor to the ideals of his youth, he seems rather to have been genuinely torn between the liberal, humanitarian impulses acquired during his unorthodox schooling and the more traditional authoritarian policies of his father. His struggle against the armies of Napoleon undoubtedly contributed to his abandonment of liberal projects after 1812. But in 1801 his accession was welcomed by those who hoped for a liberalization of the regime, and they took heart from his immediate relaxation of many of the restrictions Paul had imposed. At the outset, Alexander surrounded himself with an "unofficial committee" of advisers, men of known liberal views like Frédéric César de La Harpe (his former tutor) and Prince Adam Czartoryski, the Polish patriot who served for a time as foreign minister. The task of this committee was no less than to bring about the regeneration of Russia, and Alexander made it clear to his intimates that the granting of a constitution and the abolition of the institution of serfdom were important parts of his overall program. Despite these laudable intentions, the reforms he did in fact achieve were very limited, partly because he and his advisers failed to appreciate the complexities and practical difficulties involved. The reforms actually carried through were made in two periods in the first half of Alexander's reign, each brought to an end by the renewal of the war against Napoleon.

The most significant reforms of the first period (1801–1805) included changes in the governmental structure, among them the establishment of western-style ministries each headed by a minister responsible to the tsar; the founding of six new universities; and an increase in the number of secondary schools. As for Russia's principal social problem, serfdom, no substantial steps toward abolition were undertaken, probably because the tsar and his advisers were reluctant to mount a full-scale attack on the privileges of the landed aristocracy. However, a government decree of 1803 encouraged the voluntary liberation of serfs by their masters under government supervision. Although fewer than fifty thousand male serfs (about 1 per cent of the total serf population) were freed during Alexander's reign, this was the first step toward the emancipation in 1861.

The second period of reforms (1807–1812) was dominated by Count Mikhail Speranski (1772–1839), who served as a kind of unofficial prime minister to the tsar during these years. The results were again disappointing to those who expected any significant change in the character of the regime. Instructed to draft a constitution, Speranski prepared a moderate scheme which would have introduced self-government in stages, beginning with electoral assemblies at the local level and culminating with a state assembly at the top. However, his plan did not envisage giving real legislative initiative to the state assembly; the law-making powers were to rest rather with a council of state composed of high dignitaries and presided over by the tsar. The establishment of the council of state was, in fact, the only part of the proposal that was realized. Whatever additional reforms Speranski undertook resulted from his thorough familiarity with Russia's bureaucracy, and tended toward improving the efficiency of its operation.

Even if Napoleon had not invaded Russia in 1812, it is doubtful whether Speranski would have remained in office much longer. For in an effort to meet the serious financial crisis from which the Russian government was suffering, he proposed financial reforms and new taxes that aroused the bitter antagonism of the landed nobility. Branded a "Russian Jacobin" by his opponents, he was suddenly dismissed by Alexander in 1812 and sent into exile. He was later recalled to government service and became a member of the council of state in 1821.

Speranski's dismissal did not result in a sudden reversal of imperial policy. The transition from liberalism to reaction was rather gradual and uneven, reflecting the tsar's erratic and even inconsistent behavior. In general, Alexander appeared more liberal abroad and in the outlying parts of his empire than he was at home. To the Polish state reconstituted under Russian hegemony by the Congress of Vienna he gave a liberal constitution modeled in part on Speranski's proposal which had been rejected for Russia. The constitution of 1818 guaranteed individual liberties, including free speech and a free press, and provided for a diet to be elected on a broad franchise. Poland was permitted to maintain its own army and administrative personnel and to use Polish as the official language.

In St. Petersburg, however, the nobility of an older generation—some of whom had been associated with Tsar Paul's government—recovered influence, particularly after 1815, and the regime became increasingly repressive. The changed policy was felt especially in the educational system, which served as a kind of barometer of reaction in nineteenth-century Russia. Universities and schools were put under the control of religious bigots who established an elaborate system of surveillance, expelled professors on the slightest pretext, and prohibited study at foreign universities. Censorship regulations were complex, arbitrary, and absurd. The government not only forbade writing on political and constitutional questions but also sought to pass judgment on the alleged morality or immorality of artistic productions. The measure that aroused the most widespread resentment, however, was the establishment in 1816 of military colonies. Their original purpose was to reduce the cost of keeping an army by setting up self-supporting units of soldiers and their families to cultivate the land. But in many areas peasants were put into uniform and subjected, along with their families, to strict military discipline under the command of troops from the regular army. Bitterly resented by the peasants, the military colonies provoked movements of protest and became one of the principal grievances of opponents of the regime.

The mounting reaction of the last decade of Alexander's reign could hardly fail to arouse opposition among member of the educated classes who had placed such high hopes in the young monarch. Numerous influences helped to create this liberal opposition. To the influx of western ideas during Catherine's reign was added the stimulation of French revolutionary doctrines. During the wars against Napoleon, Russian officers and soldiers, exposed to other European cultures, could not help contrasting the relative freedom of the average western European with the absence of liberty at

St. Petersburg. *Parade in front of the royal palace. From a print made in 1815.*

home. Disappointed by Alexander's failure to provide Russia with a constitution or representative institutions, they were frustrated by their inability to express their criticisms openly. Almost inevitably the opposition was forced to act after 1815 through the secret societies that eventually engineered what has come to be known as the Decembrist Revolt.

From the outset two general tendencies were present in the movement for reform. The more moderate aims eventually found expression in the Northern Union, a group composed primarily of young aristocrats and literary men who sought to establish a constitutional monarchy on the British model. More radical measures were favored by the Southern Union, consisting mainly of impoverished army officers and led by Colonel Paul Pestel, who advocated the assassination of the tsar and the establishment of a highly centralized republican regime patterned after the Jacobin dictatorship of 1793. In some respects Pestel anticipated the Soviet regime. He favored drastic powers for the revolutionary government, to prevent counterrevolution. His program of agrarian reform included the abolition of serfdom and the state confiscation of all land. Thereafter, the land would be divided into a public and a private sector and every citizen would be guaranteed his allotment within the public sector.

The two societies were not tightly organized or disciplined, and little was done to coordinate their activities. The sudden death of Tsar Alexander I late in 1825 found them ill prepared for the revolt which followed, triggered by the confusion that arose over the succession. Constantine, the brother nearest in age to Alexander, was serving as governor-general of Poland and had secretly renounced his claim to the throne in 1823 in favor of the youngest brother, Nicholas. When Alexander died, each proclaimed the other tsar, and a period of uncertainty ensued. Since Nicholas was known to be much more conservative than his older brother, the insurgent leaders of the Northern Union decided to press for the accession of Constantine and in December persuaded two thousand troops of the St. Petersburg garrison to refuse their allegiance to Nicholas. The soldiers marched to the Senate Square shouting "Constantine and Constitution," with many of them apparently under the impression that Constitution was Constantine's wife. Once on the square they were given no further orders, and remained there in the cold all day. It was Nicholas who finally took action, bringing in loyal troops who fired upon the mutinous soldiers and killed many of them. Another uprising, by the Southern Union, also failed.

Not only was the Decembrist Revolt of 1825 badly prepared and badly led; it also lacked real popular support. Its only immediate consequence was to intensify the new tsar's antiliberal sentiments. Hundreds of those involved were arrested, and five of the leaders, including Pestel, were summarily tried and executed. Nevertheless it was a significant episode in Russian history, for it marked the first open challenge to Russian autocracy and this challenge came from some of the best-educated men in Russia— young army officers, including some of the elite Grenadier Guard, and representatives of the liberal nobility. Most important of all, it provided a revolutionary legend and a host of martyrs, for later groups that sought the overthrow of the tsarist regime.

Russia under Nicholas I, 1825–1855

Tsar Nicholas I, who assumed the throne during the Decembrist Revolt and ruled Russia until 1855, is traditionally viewed as the most reactionary of Russia's nineteenth-century autocrats. Strongly impressed by the events at the outset of his reign, he was determined to prevent their recurrence. Personally meticulous and conscientious in the performance of his duties, he carried out a prolonged investigation of the origins of the revolt, interrogating prisoners himself in some instances in order to get an idea of the true nature of the opposition. But this activity, which might have led to reform or the elimination of abuses, resulted instead in an intensification of the repressive policies pursued in the later years of Alexander's reign. Indeed, Nicholas developed an almost pathological fear of revolution at home and abroad, leading contemporary liberals to call him the Gendarme of Europe.

Under Nicholas an attempt was made to freeze the social structure of Russia by discouraging or actively preventing members of any but the upper classes from securing an education. The educational system itself was put under even closer surveillance and suffered a further decline of standards. S.S. Uvarov, Nicholas' minister of education for the better part of his reign, formulated the principles to be inculcated by the schools: autocracy (a

Tsar Nicholas I.

belief in the unlimited powers of the tsar), orthodoxy (adherence to the official church and the morality for which it stood), and nationalism (devotion to the traditions of "Russian national life").

Nicholas' particular innovation was the concentration of power in His Majesty's Own Chancery, a bureau that had originally been organized to deal with matters requiring the sovereign's personal participation. He expanded the functions of this body and divided it into several sections. One of these, the notorious Third Section, or political police, was given almost unlimited powers of surveillance over every aspect of Russian life, with the duty of arresting and exiling any "suspicious or dangerous persons," of reporting on the state of public opinion, and of keeping a close watch on all foreigners living or traveling in Russia. The tsar particularly distrusted the intelligentsia—largely writers, teachers, and liberal nobles—since many of them had been involved in the secret societies. The system of preliminary censorship (which required approval by the government censor of all written material before publication) was particularly intense after the revolutions of 1830–1831 and the revolutions of 1848, and effectively stifled the discussion of all political or potentially dangerous social questions.

It is tempting to compare the police state of Nicholas I with the totalitarian regimes of the twentieth century, but such a parallel is false and misleading. In the first place, tsarist control was limited by its own inefficiency. When Nicholas broadened his chancery and established the Third Section, he left numerous existing bureaus and administrative units intact; consequently there was extensive overlapping of functions and confusion of jurisdiction. Second, though the elaborate censorship made clear what subjects were forbidden, it did not attempt to prescribe the subjects writers *should* discuss. The atmosphere of Russia under Nicholas was unquestionably stifling, yet this era paradoxically saw the beginning of Russia's golden age of literature, and counted among its luminaries the poets Alexander Pushkin (1799–1837) and Mikhail Lermontov (1814–1841), the novelist and dramatist Nikolai Gogol (1809–1852), and finally the novelists Ivan Turgenev (1818–1883) and Fëdor Dostoevski (1821–1881), some of whose earlier works were published during Nicholas' reign. True, both Turgenev and Dostoevski were arrested in the reaction following the revolutions of 1848, but until then they had been left relatively undisturbed. As long as writers avoided discussion of proscribed subjects and direct criticism of the autocratic regime, they were allowed to publish their works.

Despite these compensating features, which made Nicholas' reign less oppressive than it has sometimes been thought, the refusal of the tsar to deal with such basic problems as the discontent of the serfs, the low productivity of the farms, and the backwardness of technology and communications meant that Russia lagged seriously behind the western European nations in economic and social development. Its weaknesses in this respect were illustrated dramatically at the end of Nicholas' reign when Russia suffered defeat by France and Great Britain in the Crimean War (1854–1856).

Though Nicholas did succeed in preventing further revolts in Russia, he was faced in 1830 by an uprising in Poland, which drastically altered the status of that country. As we have seen, the kingdom of Poland sanctioned by the Congress of Vienna had received from Tsar Alexander I one of the most liberal constitutions in Europe. In practice, however, the autonomy of the Poles was restricted and the will of the diet thwarted by Alexander's brother, Constantine (1779–1831), who commanded the Polish army and interfered frequently in the administration of the country. Compared with the Russians or with those Poles living in territory directly annexed by Russia, the inhabitants of "Congress Poland" were well off; but the violation of their constitution by the tsar, combined with a revival of Polish national sentiment after 1815, made them restive even during Alexander's reign. With the accession of Nicholas in 1825, tension between the Poles and their Russian masters increased. In November, 1830, when a rumor circulated that the tsar was about to march a joint Russian-Polish army into France and Belgium to suppress the revolutions there, a group of army cadets supported by university students revolted in Warsaw.

Only a handful of rebels was involved at first, but the departure of the

Grand Duke Constantine opened the way for the establishment of a provisional government dominated by Polish landed aristocrats. Had the Poles been unified, their revolution might well have succeeded, for they controlled a well-disciplined military force. But after the initial victory the revolutionaries divided into the Whites, feudal aristocrats who tried to negotiate with the tsar for moderate reforms, and the Reds, a more radical element drawn from the gentry, who opposed any sort of compromise. The peasants who constituted the mass of the population saw no reason to support the revolt since they had been exploited by both landowning groups. The Polish rebels had counted strongly upon intervention on their behalf by France or Britain, since liberals in these states were clamoring loudly for support of the Polish cause, but neither government was willing to commit itself to such action.

The Poles did win some initial victories, but in September, 1831, the Russians captured Warsaw and ended the revolt. Ruthless reprisals were taken by Nicholas. The constitution granted by Alexander was withdrawn, thousands of Poles were executed or banished to western Europe, and Poland was governed thenceforth by what amounted to a military dictatorship.

Despite two successive waves of revolution, in the early 1820's and in 1830–1831, the Restoration was still intact after 1830 and the old order persisted in most of Europe. Only in France, Belgium, and Greece had successful revolutions occurred, and in the latter two, the revolutionaries had succeeded because they were supported by certain of the Great Powers. Elsewhere in Europe—in Spain and Portugal, on the Italian peninsula and in some of the German states, in Russia and Poland—the revolutions had collapsed or been suppressed. Despite the rallying power of liberal ideals and goals, the revolutionaries had proved no match for the regimes they challenged. Against the secret societies composed of disaffected soldiers, liberal nobles, artisans, students, teachers, writers, and adventurers the rulers could usually muster loyal troops, and they could count on the backing of nobility and clergy in the suppression of the revolts. Often a lack of unity among the revolutionaries, along with poor organization and leadership, turned initial victory into defeat.

But the strength of the dissatisfied groups continued to mount after 1830 under the impact of the two most powerful forces of the age: the Industrial Revolution, which was significantly changing Europe's economic and social structure by bringing new classes into existence and weakening old ones; and the legacy of the French Revolution, which continued to inspire opponents of the old regimes with the ideals of liberty, equality, and fraternity.

CHAPTER 28

The Industrial Revolution and the
Triumph of the Bourgeoisie

MOST OF THE POLITICAL and international developments in Europe before 1830 can be discussed without specific reference to the Industrial Revolution. In Great Britain, where industrialization was greatest, technological change had affected the daily lives of the people by 1830, but even there it had not significantly altered the thinking of the governing classes, whose wealth and position were based largely upon agriculture and whose attitudes tended to remain those of their eighteenth-century forebears. The persistence of traditional attitudes was even greater on the Continent, where in 1830 industrialization was just getting under way, if it had begun at all. But it becomes increasingly difficult to comprehend the policies and motives of the European powers in the years after 1830 without understanding the fundamental economic changes that were transforming society and thrusting to the foreground groups with new goals and new needs.

The Restoration had brought to the aristocracy a temporary recovery of its fortunes and a return, though in many ways an illusory one, to its privileged status. During the 1830's and 1840's, however, the position of the aristocracy was challenged anew by the rapidly expanding bourgeoisie, seeking not only status equal to that of the older ruling groups, but political control as well. In Britain, France, and the Low Countries, where their economic strength was greatest, the middle classes succeeded—sometimes gradually, sometimes abruptly—in gaining control of the machinery of state. Elsewhere in Europe they had to wait until 1848 to make their bid for political power, and even then they encountered stubborn resistance from the monarchs and the older privileged groups. In the long run, however, their drive for power was irresistible and all European governments had to come to terms with the bourgeoisie, whether by granting them political representation or by enacting legislation favorable to their economic interests.

958

Yet in the victory of the bourgeoisie over the aristocracy lay a certain irony. The power of the bourgeoisie rested ultimately on the other great class created by the Industrial Revolution, the proletariat; the bourgeois success clearly would have been impossible without working-class support. The working class, essential to the production of the new manufacturers' wealth, fought on the same side of the barricades as the bourgeoisie during the revolutionary upheavals in 1830 and in 1848. Once the common enemy had been defeated, however, and the industrialists and financiers were themselves entrenched in power, their relationship with the working class began to change. Now they became defenders of the *status quo*, jealous of the privileges they had wrested from the older aristocracy. And it was now the turn of the workers, organized in socialist or working-class parties, to challenge the supremacy of the bourgeoisie and demand a share in the control of the state.

THE INDUSTRIAL REVOLUTION

Like many capsule phrases, "Industrial Revolution" has been the subject of considerable controversy and a wide variety of interpretations.* Traditionally, the Industrial Revolution is seen as a relatively sudden flurry of technical innovations that occurred in Britain during the second half of the eighteenth century. But the speed with which industrialization proceeded was greatly exaggerated by those who first described the phenomenon in Britain. Technological innovations in textile manufacturing were indeed developed quite rapidly after 1750, but they came into general use only gradually, over a period of several decades. Many kinds of manufacturing underwent no significant changes until the middle of the nineteenth century. The Industrial Revolution in Britain is now generally regarded as extending over a period of at least a century, from 1750 to 1850. Further, while certain key changes did occur first in England, these developments were not confined to the British Isles. Similar revolutions in technology took place on the European continent and in the United States during the nineteenth century. Finally, the Industrial Revolution was far more than a "wave of gadgets." If the transition from simple tools operated by hand or foot to machines driven by waterpower or steam was a key aspect of the process of industrialization, just as important were certain associated changes in the organization of production. For example, the shift in textile manufacturing from production in the homes of individual laborers to production in large factories employing scores of individuals was a change

* T. S. Ashton in *The Industrial Revolution, 1760–1830* (New York, 1964, p. 42) suggests the traditional, or popular, conception of the phenomenon when he quotes the English schoolboy who began his description of the Industrial Revolution with the statement, "About 1760 a wave of gadgets swept over England."

Stockport Viaduct. *Stockport, located six miles southeast of Manchester, became an important industrial and rail center in the nineteenth century. The railway viaduct was considered an outstanding engineering feat.*

fraught with material and psychological consequences. It required, for one thing, mass migrations of population to areas where ample supplies of power were most readily available, and resulted in the creation of new cities and the expansion of old ones. Higher levels of productivity could not be sustained by machines alone; the Industrial Revolution spurred the exploitation of fresh sources of raw materials, the opening up of new markets, and the development of new methods of trade. An integral part of the Industrial Revolution in Britain (and elsewhere) was the revolution in methods of transportation which permitted raw materials and finished products to be moved quickly.

Why did the Industrial Revolution begin in Great Britain? What peculiar features of the British society and economy explain the head start of this nation? No single answer can be given, for a number of factors, taken together, help explain Britain's primacy.

The Industrial Revolution was closely related to the changes in methods of farming and stock breeding in eighteenth-century England which had constituted an agricultural revolution. These came about when the large landowners, politically secure after their victory over the crown during the revolutions of the seventeenth century, sought to exploit their dominant position and to increase their money incomes. Their efforts to cultivate the land more efficiently and to introduce improved methods of stock breeding were hampered by the system of open fields, common lands, and semicollective methods of farming inherited from an earlier era. For success, their experiments needed large enclosed fields, so the landowners tried to speed up the process of "enclosing," or fencing in, their land by having the so-called acts of enclosure passed. As a result of these acts, which were unopposed in Parliament, vast areas were brought under more efficient cultivation and the landlords did achieve greater productivity—at the expense of thousands of small farmers who were forcibly ejected from their homes and from lands their families had cultivated for centuries. The enclosures brought about a marked increase in food production; British farms could now support a larger population with the work of fewer individuals. Some of those displaced from their farms ultimately sought employment in the new manufacturing centers and thus provided some of the surplus labor without which no industrial revolution can gain momentum.

On the Continent, no comparable source of labor was available until the nineteenth century; in France for example, the persistence of a system of small landholding probably handicapped the development of industry.

Two other requirements for an industrial revolution are adequate sources of the raw materials needed in the manufacturing process and markets to absorb the finished goods. Here, too, Great Britain had several advantages: a long-established fleet of merchant vessels and a vast and growing colonial empire. Although Britain definitely triumphed over France, its closest rival for an overseas empire, only with the defeat of Napoleon, its supremacy in North America had been established by the series of wars fought with France in the mid-eighteenth century. Britain had a thriving class of merchants ready to transport finished goods and raw materials and a reserve of potential customers for the products of its industries.

One more precondition for industrialization is the availability of capital for investment in the development of machinery and the construction of factories. Britain had a banking system and credit facilities that were better developed and more flexible than those on the Continent, and prosperous merchants and landowners who were willing to put up funds to finance new industrial enterprises.

That some of the key inventions which revolutionized the textile industry were British achievements was owing not so much to the native genius of the people as to the demand for greater quantities of goods produced more efficiently and cheaply. British hand labor could not compete successfully with Asian labor in the production of cotton cloth. But if cotton could be spun and woven by machines, British manufacturers could clearly capture the market. This was the stimulus that led to improved spinning devices and more efficient looms.

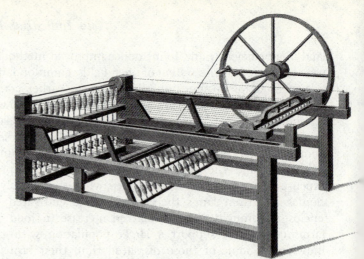

Hargreaves' Spinning Jenny. *Engraving. One of the key innovations in the revolutionizing of textile manufacturing.*

It was to be expected, therefore, that in the early years of the Industrial Revolution the innovations would be most obvious and the results most striking in the manufacture of textiles, particularly cotton cloth. Of special interest is the way in which improvements in one part of the manufacturing process stimulated advances in another part. The first notable invention, a hand loom which halved the time required for weaving, came in 1733. This loom stimulated the demand for yarn, and thus for a spinning process which could produce yarn in great quantities; the need was filled by James Hargreaves (d. 1778), who developed the spinning jenny, a simple hand device by which six or seven threads could be spun simultaneously. About 1770 Richard Arkwright (1732–1792), a Lancashire barber, further accelerated the spinning process by inventing the water frame, which used waterpower to spin many threads at a time. The introduction of the cumbersome water frame and the later substitution of steam for waterpower required that the spinning process be moved into a mill or factory. Arkwright's first water-driven factory, established in 1771, gave employment to almost six hundred workers. The revolutionary developments in spinning soon caused the production of yarn to outstrip the weaving capacity of the hand looms and thus stimulated the development of a power loom. Within a half century both spinning and weaving had been mechanized. But it took some time for these inventions to be put into general use and for textile production as a whole to be brought within factory walls. Even as late as the 1830's some cloth was still being produced in cottages.

The new technology also found early expression in Britain in two other key industries: coal mining and metallurgy. Coal was a source of fuel for the new engines, and iron was the raw material essential for building the machines themselves. Clearly, advances in textile manufacturing depended upon improvements in both coal production and iron manufacturing. The rich coal deposits of the British Isles had been largely untapped as long as wood was available as fuel. In the early eighteenth century the near exhaustion of the forests meant that wood was too precious to be used for fuel and charcoal too scarce to be used in smelting iron; a new source of fuel and a new process for smelting iron were required, and coal filled both of these needs. By 1700 the first coal-mining shafts had been sunk, but their depth was limited by the presence of underground water. Until a successful method for removing this water could be found, coal production was restricted. A steam-driven pump invented in 1705 by Thomas Newcomen (1663–1729), and improved upon in the two succeeding decades, made possible the working of seams in and below the watery layers and thus increased the output of the mines. Because of its limitations, Newcomen's invention was used solely for pumping water from the mines. In the 1770's the Scotsman James Watt (1736–1819), with the financial backing of Matthew Boulton (1728–1809), perfected a much more versatile steam engine that was to serve as a new source of power for a great variety of industries.

Britain had adequate resources of iron ore, but until a method of smelting iron without reliance on charcoal (and hence wood) could be found, these supplies could not be exploited. The pioneer in developing a new smelting process for iron was Abraham Darby (1678–1717) of Coalbrookdale. In 1709 he succeeded in smelting quality pig iron with coke instead of charcoal. The consequences of his discovery did not immediately transform the industry, however, because Darby's iron was suitable only for castings and was not thought to be pure enough to serve as material for forges. Only in 1783–1784 did Henry Cort (1740–1800) develop puddling, or rolling, a process in which he used coke to burn away the impurities in pig iron,

Coalbrookdale. *Engraving by W. Lowry after G. Robertson. View of the celebrated iron works in Shropshire in 1788.*

The Rocket. *Print of Robert Stephenson's famous steam locomotive, 1829.*

making it suitable for use in forges. Cort's discovery freed the forgemasters from reliance upon charcoal-produced iron and thus led to a remarkable expansion of the iron industry.

By 1800 then, all of the elements essential for a technological revolution were present. Fuel, in the form of coal, was plentiful; iron of a high quality was available for machines and other uses; and the steam engine provided abundant and dependable power. Perhaps the greatest single remaining need was for speedier and more efficient methods of transportation to bring together the various elements involved in production. Between 1760 and 1830 the building of an extensive system of canals greatly facilitated the movement of goods from one part of England to another and drastically reduced the cost of transporting such heavy commodities as coal, iron, timber, stone, and clay. But it was the advent of the railroad in the 1830's and 1840's that made possible the rapid distribution of raw materials and finished products so characteristic of modern industrial societies. Coal had been transported by horse-drawn vehicles on rails for several decades, but not until the 1820's when a practicable steam locomotive was constructed, could the possibilities of the railway be realized. The successful run in 1829 of George Stephenson's *Rocket* at a speed ranging up to sixteen miles an hour on the newly constructed Liverpool and Manchester Railway marked the real beginning of the railroad age in Great Britain. Within two short decades after 1830 some 6,500 miles of rails were laid, and the impact of the railroad began to be felt in almost every phase of British life.

The Social Impact of the Industrial Revolution

The revolution in technology and in the organization of production inevitably had a tremendous impact upon the societies in which it occurred. Some reference has already been made to changes in class structure caused by the Industrial Revolution: the rapid expansion of the bourgeoisie and the emergence of a new urban proletariat. But it is important to look more closely at the effect of these changes upon the lives of individuals, particularly those whose destiny it was to spend their lives digging coal or operating the machines in the factories. Perhaps never before in human history had so radical a transformation occurred in men's occupations or in their physical environment. In one country after another an increasing proportion of the working people spent their lives not cultivating the fields and living in small, isolated villages, but toiling in factories or mines and living in large, crowded cities.

It is easy to exaggerate the speed of this transformation even in Great Britain, where it appeared to occur most rapidly. Englishmen did not simply move from farm to city overnight. Although the enclosure of common lands accelerated in the last decades of the eighteenth century, many small farmers stayed on as landless agricultural laborers or tried to eke out a living by spinning or weaving in their cottages. Only gradually did they start drifting to the mills, which were at first located near the streams that supplied the waterpower. Initially, cotton manufacturers in the north had so much difficulty attracting laborers that they resorted to the employ- ment as "apprentices" of groups of pauper children from London and the south. But with the general application of steam power to the cotton industry after 1800, factories tended to be located in towns and cities near the sources of coal, and there a labor supply was more readily available. The phenomenal growth of certain key industrial cities occurred in the first half of the nineteenth century. Between 1801 and 1850, for example, the population of Manchester rose from 77,000 to 303,000; that of Liverpool, from 82,000 to 397,000; and that of Birmingham, from 71,000 to 242,000.

Among students of the Industrial Revolution one of the most disputed questions has concerned the material and psychological condition of the factory hands employed in the burgeoning industrial cities. Some have contended that workers in the new industries were little better than slaves at the mercy of their employers, suffering physical and psychological privations of the worst sort.[1] Adherents of this view dwell on the long working hours, relatively low wages, and poor housing of the workers. But this interpretation has a built-in bias; it is based heavily on reports of parliamentary commissions set up in the early nineteenth century by reformers bent on exposing the abuses of the system. That evils existed, particularly in the earlier stages of the Industrial Revolution, no historian denies. But the condition of workers varied even within a given industry and certainly from one region of the country to another. Furthermore, the hardships of the British working class in this era cannot be blamed entirely on industrialization; such factors as the depressions following the revolution- ary and Napoleonic wars and short-term fluctuations of the economy were

---

[1] Leading exponents of this point of view are John L. Hammond and Barbara Ham- mond in a series of studies: *The Town Labourer*, second ed. (London, 1925); *The Vil- lage Labourer*, fourth ed. (London, 1927); and so on.

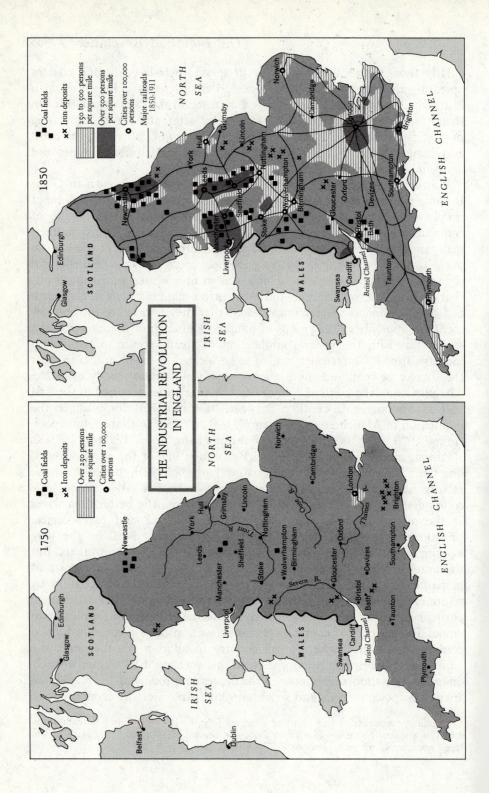

THE INDUSTRIAL REVOLUTION
IN ENGLAND

1750

- ■ Coal fields
- ×× Iron deposits
- ▨ Over 250 persons per square mile
- ○ Cities over 100,000 persons

1850

- ■ Coal fields
- ×× Iron deposits
- ▨ 250 to 500 persons per square mile
- ▨ Over 500 persons per square mile
- ○ Cities over 100,000 persons
- —— Major railroads 1850-1911

Children sent to work in the cotton factories, 1840. *Engraving*.

also responsible. Life had been hard for the agricultural worker and farmer in the eighteenth century; the nineteenth-century factory hand probably enjoyed a higher standard of living and higher standards of health than his eighteenth-century rural counterpart.

These modifications of the traditional view have come to be accepted and are perhaps a necessary corrective to the impressions gained from novels like Dickens' *Hard Times*. But even if one assumes that the city worker's standard of living was higher than that of his rural ancestor, certain intangibles must still be taken into account. The farmer or the agricultural laborer may have worked just as many hours as the factory hand, his living conditions were undoubtedly crude and primitive, and he was probably subject to just as great a variety of diseases. But he worked out of doors, his daily tasks were more varied, and his opportunities for recreation were normally greater. It was in part to the sheer monotony of his routine and to the mill discipline that the early factory hand objected. The crowding together of human beings in ugly, hastily built cities tended to sharpen their discontent. Finally, the extensive employment of women and children in the textile mills and in the mines is an aspect of industrialization which should not be forgotten and which weighed on the consciences of some industrialists as well as of humanitarians and reformers. The revelation that child apprentices, some as young as seven, were forced to work up to twelve and fifteen hours a day, six days a week, in the cotton mills of the north, came as a shock to many Englishmen and inspired legislation to restrict child labor as early as 1802. Yet because of inadequate enforcement of the laws, the exploitation of children continued at least until 1833, when the first effective Factory Act forbade the employment in textile mills of children under nine years of age and restricted the labor of those between nine and thirteen to forty-eight hours a week. Though one cannot contest the long-range benefits accruing from the Industrial Revolution, it must be recognized that the price paid in human suffering during its early stages was great.

One other noteworthy development in this period—a phenomenon which both affected the Industrial Revolution and was affected by it—was the remarkable growth in Europe's population. The number of inhabitants in England and Wales rose from an estimated six million in 1750 to approximately nine million in 1800 and eighteen million in 1850. This trebling of the population within a century resulted not from a significant rise in the birthrate, but rather from a dramatic drop in the death rate. Better diet, greater cleanliness, and improved sanitation meant that more human beings survived infancy and childhood and in time raised families of their own. That they did so was in part the result of the higher standard of living produced by the Industrial Revolution. At the same time, the additional millions of people provided workers for expanding factories and consumers for the manufactured products.

THE TRIUMPH OF ECONOMIC LIBERALISM IN GREAT BRITAIN

Of crucial importance to the success of the Industrial Revolution was the growing influence of the doctrines of economic liberalism, or *laissez-faire*, in Britain during the first half of the nineteenth century. Industrialization has, of course, taken place in societies where such doctrines do not prevail, in the planned economies of the Soviet Union and Communist China, for example. But proponents of capitalism, the system of free enterprise, argue that the initial success of the Industrial Revolution in Great Britain resulted in large part from the progressive liberation of English manufacturers from government restrictions and their relative freedom from government control. Whether or not one sees a direct causal relationship between *laissez-faire* and industrialization, there is no question that they developed concurrently in Britain. To be sure, capitalism did not emerge only at the end of the eighteenth century. Capitalist forms of organization had existed at least since the end of the Middle Ages, but the incentive for individual enterprise had been thwarted to some degree by the prevailing economic philosophy of mercantilism, according to which the state had extensive powers to control the trade and regulate the economic life of the nation. In the eighteenth century greater opportunities for commercial initiative existed in Britain than in France partly because the new mercantile interests shared control of Parliament, yet the dominant view was still mercantilist.

Toward the end of the eighteenth century, however, mercantilist policies and restrictions on trade came increasingly under attack. Their principal critic was Adam Smith (1723–1790), whose *Wealth of Nations*, published in 1776, proposed instead a "system of natural liberty" which, for the most part, denied to government the right to regulate economic life. Government's primary function, according to Smith, was to maintain competitive conditions, for only within such a framework would the unrestricted self-interest of the individual be forced to operate for the general good. Although the *Wealth of Nations* became the single most influential and widely read economic treatise of its time, the most effective opposition to Britain's restrictive trade policies probably came from manufacturers objecting not so much on theoretical grounds, as because these policies provoked retaliatory measures from other nations and thus hindered the expansion of British trade. Shortly before the French Revolution, William Pitt the Younger made a start toward removing the restrictions on British commerce, but the dislocation of trade caused by the wars with France postponed further action until after 1815.

By the end of the Napoleonic wars, British industry had gained a commanding lead; the British could produce cotton goods, for example, in greater quantities and more cheaply than any continental rivals. A lowering of British tariffs, it was hoped, would lead to a corresponding reduction by foreign powers of tariffs on British manufactured goods. During the severe economic depression that immediately followed the Napoleonic Wars, British manufacturers, burdened with surpluses of goods they could not sell abroad, intensified their pleas for tariff reductions. But the Tory Parliament, heeding only the landowners, who sought not less but more protection, passed the Corn Law of 1815, which virtually excluded foreign grain from England until the price of native grain reached a specified level.

As we have seen, the growing sentiment for free trade among both manufacturers and the working class met with some response in 1823–1825, when William Huskisson, a liberal financier in the Tory cabinet, secured a reduction of duties on certain imports and thus set a precedent for further reductions. Only in 1828 was any significant change made in the corn laws; the new law allowed the importation of grain according to a sliding scale of duties. Yet as long as landowners remained dominant in both houses of Parliament, the new manufacturers (the "Manchester men") could not hope to achieve free trade. For this reason, reform of the methods for choosing representatives to the House of Commons became the overriding concern of the manufacturers.

The Reform Bill of 1832, passed under Whig leadership, constituted the first recognition in British political life of the tremendous changes wrought in British society by the Industrial Revolution. In the years before 1832, the migration of workers from one region to another as industrialization progressed, the emergence of new cities, and the dramatic growth of some old cities accentuated the injustices of a system that had remained practically unaltered since the seventeenth century. The most glaring weakness was the underrepresentation, and sometimes the lack of representation, of new centers of population in the northern and western parts of England. Old boroughs lying in the eastern and southern counties had declined markedly in population but still sent two members each to the House of Commons. Among the most celebrated of the "rotten boroughs" was Old Sarum, which was still represented although no town existed there at all. Thriving new cities like Manchester, Birmingham, Leeds, and Sheffield, on the other hand, sent no representatives to Parliament. There were also "pocket boroughs," in which no real election took place because the seats were "in the pocket" of powerful landlords who used their influence to name their own candidates. As long as the Tories remained in office the cause of reform was stalled. But in 1830 the death of King George IV and the accession of William IV made a general election necessary, and the campaign was fought at least in part on the issue of reform. The Tories lost some fifty seats in the House of Commons, most of them to Whigs or to other advocates of reform; Commons was now in the control of the Whigs. The duke of Wellington, who had remained adamant in his opposition to reform, finally left office in November, 1830, and was succeeded by Earl Grey (1764–1845), a Whig committed to the cause. But for Grey to get the Reform Bill through Parliament took another year and a half—a stormy period characterized by mounting popular violence, strenuous measures on the part of the Whig leadership, and last-ditch resistance by Tory peers in the House of Lords. Only the threat of the king, under pressure from Grey, to create enough new peers to secure passage of the bill in the House of Lords finally persuaded the intransigents to abandon their opposition.

The Reform Bill of 1832 did not immediately revolutionize British political life. Indeed, one contemporary admitted that the House of Commons named in the first general election after the act turned out "to be very much like every other parliament."[2] Certainly those who voted for the bill had no intention of creating a thoroughly democratic political system in Great Britain. While the electorate increased by about 50 per cent after 1832, only one in five Englishmen had the privilege of voting and the franchise still depended upon possession of a minimum of property. Yet the Reform Bill of 1832 was one of the most significant measures in the evolution of modern Britain. By redistributing seats in the House of Commons to increase representation of the new towns and cities, it admitted to partnership with the older landed and commercial aristocracy the new class of industrialists and manufacturers. The latter certainly did not take over the government of Britain in 1832, but in succeeding decades

[2] Charles Greville, quoted by A. Briggs, *The Age of Improvement* (London, 1959), p. 261.

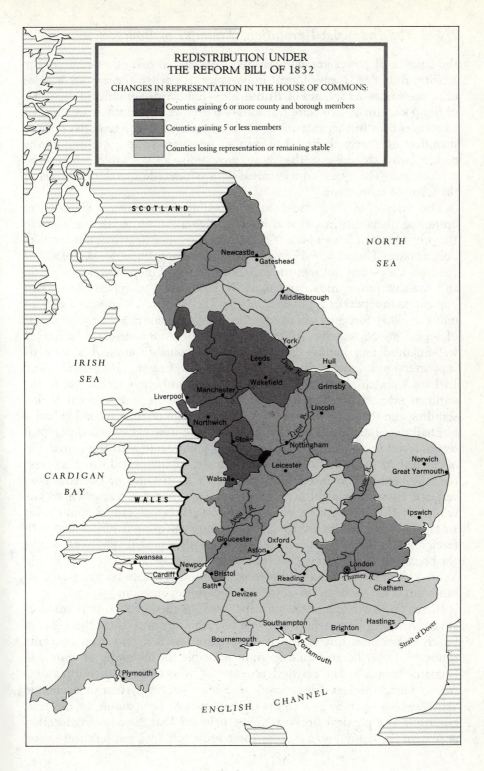

REDISTRIBUTION UNDER
THE REFORM BILL OF 1832

CHANGES IN REPRESENTATION IN THE HOUSE OF COMMONS:

Counties gaining 6 or more county and borough members

Counties gaining 5 or less members

Counties losing representation or remaining stable

SCOTLAND

NORTH SEA

Newcastle
Gateshead

Middlesbrough

IRISH SEA

York
Leeds
Hull
Wakefield
Grimsby
Liverpool
Manchester
Lincoln
Northwich
Trent R.
Stoke
Nottingham
Leicester
Norwich
Great Yarmouth
Walsall
Ouse R.
Ipswich

CARDIGAN BAY

WALES

Avon R.

Gloucester
Oxford
Aston
Swansea
Newport
London
Cardiff
Bristol
Reading
Thames R.
Chatham
Bath
Devizes

Southampton
Hastings
Brighton
Bournemouth
Portsmouth
Strait of Dover

Plymouth

ENGLISH CHANNEL

the balance of power gradually shifted to them. In two other respects the Reform Bill of 1832 was of great importance. It opened the way for a series of reforms in other spheres of British life—municipal administration, relief of the poor, and church-state relations—and more important, it established a precedent for further extensions of the franchise. If representatives of the manufacturers were to be taken into partnership in the governing of the nation, why should not the more prosperous and reliable workers be represented? This question was raised within a decade by the organizers of the Chartist movement.

The reform of Parliament made possible the eventual triumph of economic liberalism in Great Britain by giving greater legislative voice to the proponents of *laissez-faire*. Yet the new economic doctrines did not take hold at once. The principal demand of the economic liberals—the repeal of the corn laws—was not met for a decade and a half despite vigorous action and massive propaganda campaigns by proponents of repeal. The main opposition to repeal came, of course, from the landlords, who feared that an influx of cheap foreign grain would ruin British agriculture. The proponents of repeal joined together in 1838 to form the Anti-Corn-Law League, a well-financed and highly effective pressure group. Prominent among its supporters were such manufacturers as John Bright (1811–1889) and Richard Cobden (1804-1865), who argued not only that repeal was in the national interest but that free trade would promote international under-standing and the cause of peace. Yet the campaign might have failed had it not had the support of the laboring classes, who were convinced that repeal would lower the price of bread. A turning point came with the conversion of Sir Robert Peel, the leading Tory minister of the period, to this cause, once he became convinced that continued maintenance of the corn laws was not essential to British prosperity. Further impetus was given by the failure of the Irish potato crop in 1845; a threat of famine hung over Britain, which could be dispelled only by supplementing British wheat with foreign grain. In 1846 the corn laws were finally repealed. That year marks the beginning of a free-trade era for Britain that lasted until the First World War. The abolition or reduction to a minimum of duties on practically all other imported goods followed the repeal of duties on grain.

If free trade was one of the principal goals of the liberals, elimination of government regulation of the domestic economy was the other. Adam Smith emphasized this aspect of *laissez-faire* less than has been generally supposed, but it became an important principle for the group of writers in England known as the classical economists, who elaborated Smith's doc-trines. These thinkers "discovered" a comprehensive system of economic "laws" which operate in a competitive economy, comparable to the laws governing the physical universe. They believed that government interfer-ence with the natural operation of these economic laws was harmful to the economy. This point of view was adopted, for example, by the economist David Ricardo (1772–1823). Although his ideas concerning wages were interpreted more rigidly by his followers than he intended, he did advocate a strict *laissez-faire* position with respect to the rise and fall of the price of labor. Workmen might be doomed to an eternal cycle in which higher wages resulted in larger families and an increased supply of labor, followed by a corresponding increase in competition for jobs and an inevitable drop in wages, but it was not the function of government to try to interfere with free competition in order to maintain wages at a high level; the fluctuation of wages would be determined by the law of supply and demand operating in the labor market.

To what extent did a *laissez-faire* attitude prevail in Britain in the first half of the nineteenth century? This view, without question, became increasingly influential during this period. Yet a closer look at the role played by government in the British economy of the mid-nineteenth century reveals that during the years of expansion of the free-enterprise system there developed also a tradition of state intervention and regulation of industry on behalf of the working class which was clearly at odds with the *laissez-faire* position. There was never a lack of critics to attack the excesses of a system which seemed to leave the wage earner at the mercy of economic "laws." Ironically, a year after the Reform Bill, when manufacturing interests had increased their representation in the House of Commons, Parliament passed the first effective Factory Act, curbing the hours of employment of children in the textile mills and prescribing other regulations for their treatment. The following decade saw the passage of further legislation, restricting the employment of women and children in the mines and enforcing the introduction of safety devices and of better methods of sanitation in the factories. The Ten Hours Act of 1847 applied officially only to women and young persons, but had the practical effect of limiting the working day of adult males as well. Such statutes, involving interference by government with the functioning of free competition, were generally opposed by manufacturers. But the fact that they were passed and enforced suggests that the philosophy of *laissez-faire* never held undisputed sway in Great Britain.

It would be tempting for the sake of simplicity to view the opposition to economic liberalism in purely class terms. Thus, it could be argued that while bourgeois manufacturers clearly favored the application of *laissez-faire* doctrines and opposed restrictions upon their activity, members of the landowning aristocracy, seeing their political and economic domination threatened, sought to retain government restrictions or impose new ones upon the rapidly growing industries. According to this view, the members of the working class were in an ambiguous position. They sided with their employers on the issue of free trade, in the hope that lowered tariffs would reduce the cost of living; on the other hand, they viewed the manufacturers as exploiters bent on securing maximum profits at labor's expense, and consequently sought an alliance with the landowners as a means of imposing regulations on industry.

There is just enough truth in this interpretation to make it appealing. Landowners did stubbornly resist the repeal of the corn laws until finally forced to capitulate by growing pressures from the manufacturers and workers. The Tory leaders, who defended the property holders' interests, did support legislation regulating working conditions in retaliation against the manufacturers for their opposition to the corn laws. Finally, the working-class movement was indeed divided over its goals.

But the divisions on class lines were not so clear-cut as this interpretation suggests. The movement for restricting the working day of women and young persons to ten hours, for example, had the support of a variety of individuals. The two principal leaders of the movement in Parliament, Michael Sadler (1780–1835) and Lord Ashley (Anthony Ashley Cooper, later earl of Shaftesbury, 1801–1885) were Tories. Sadler had been a businessman before becoming a social reformer, and Ashley, though a landowning aristocrat, appears to have been motivated not so much by a desire for revenge against the manufacturers as by religious and humanitarian impulses linked with a traditional sense of *noblesse oblige*. The campaign for the Ten Hours Act had the active support of many who called themselves radicals, but it also was backed by some maverick manufacturers, such as John Wood of Yorkshire, and John Fielden of Lancashire. Reform was not, therefore, exclusively the goal of one social class or group.

The most important single manifestation of working-class sentiment in these years, the Chartist movement, seems to have sprung not from discontent with *laissez-faire* economic policies or from specific grievances against the new manufacturers, but rather from a generalized distress in the 1830's and 1840's for which the workers saw one principal remedy—political representation. Finding inadequate the Reform Bill of 1832, for which they had agitated along with the middle classes, they sought further parliamentary reform. Chartism drew its support from at least three different groups among the working classes. One of these consisted of the rather moderate, quite respectable artisans of the London Workingmen's Association founded in 1836 by a cabinetmaker, William Lovett (1800–1877). They were joined by members of the more radical Birmingham Political Union, a propagandist group dating back to 1816, which, was revived in the 1830's by a radical Birmingham banker, Thomas Attwood (1783–1856). The third group, led by Feargus O'Connor (1794–1855), a fiery Irish landowner and demagogue, appealed to the most distressed elements of the population of Leeds and the northern counties. All three groups threw their support behind the People's Charter, the document which gave its name to the Chartist movement. The Charter, a list of political demands to be presented to Parliament, called for universal manhood suffrage, equal electoral districts (that is, districts with equal numbers of inhabitants), vote by secret ballot, annual elections to Parliament, the abolition of the property qualification for members of Parliament, and the payment of stipends to those elected to the House of Commons. The last demand was important since workers or those representing them could hardly afford to run for Parliament as long as its members were unpaid.

During 1838–1839 a massive campaign to enlist support for the Charter was organized, complete with large public meetings, inflammatory speeches, and torchlight processions. This culminated in the spring of 1839 in the assembling in London of a National Convention (the name was chosen for its associations with the French Revolution) and the presentation to Parliament of a huge petition on behalf of the Charter signed by several hundred thousand individuals. Despite this wave of agitation which was attended by great publicity, Parliament refused even to consider the petition. The Chartists found themselves in a dilemma. Some of the more radical branches of the movement staged riots and local strikes, but the majority were not prepared to resort to violence to gain their ends. After 1839 the movement split into rival factions and temporarily collapsed. The National Chartist Association continued to uphold the principles of the Charter and presented the demands again in 1842 and in 1848, the year of revolutions on the Continent, but Chartism was never as strong in the 1840's as it had been at the outset and fell into the hands of less responsible leaders, such as Feargus O'Connor, ready to use the movement for the advancement of personal ends.

The Chartist movement failed in its own time, but the goals of the Chartists, were realized between 1858 and 1918. Only the requirement of

A Chartist Procession in London, April 10, 1848.

annual elections to Parliament has not become a part of the English electoral system. Perhaps most interesting about the Chartist agitation is the fact that although it arose from severe economic distress, the average English workingman was convinced that he could improve his condition not by direct action against his employer or a generalized attack on *laissez-faire* policies, but rather by peaceful, legal means and direct representation in Parliament. His counterpart on the Continent resorted to more violent tactics.

FRANCE UNDER THE JULY MONARCHY

Although those who had engineered the July Revolution of 1830, which overthrew the legitimate Bourbon ruler, Charles X, were under the impression that they had carried out a genuine revolution, the constitutional changes that resulted in France from the change of dynasty were relatively slight. As "king of the French People" Louis Philippe presumably recognized the principle of popular sovereignty, but in point of fact he never fully accepted this doctrine. The Charter of 1814 was retained with only slight modifications, and the right to vote was still restricted to substantial property owners. The suffrage was extended from about 100,000 to 170,000 in a nation of 30,000,000. Nonetheless, the July Revolution represented the final triumph of the *haute* ("upper") *bourgeoisie* over the nobility. It was, after all, representatives of the bourgeoisie who had helped bring the new king to power and who thereafter held a privileged position in his regime. The constitutional embodiment of their victory lay in the provision that appointments to the Chamber of Peers, the upper house, would henceforth be held for life only, instead of being hereditary. A few liberal members of the noble class continued to play a role in politics but most of them viewed the new regime with contempt and retired to their homes in the exclusive Faubourg Saint-Germain of Paris or to their country estates.

Louis Philippe's regime is often termed "the bourgeois monarchy." It drew its principal support and its allegedly drab, materialistic character from the middle class, and the monarch himself appeared to embody many of the virtues exalted by this class—thrift, sobriety, a propensity to hard work. The policies of the government favored the interests of the wealthier manufacturers and tradesmen, and after an initial wave of enthusiasm for the new regime, disillusionment began to set in among the *petite* ("lesser") *bourgeoisie*, who were still excluded from political participation, and among the Parisian working class, whose contribution to the Revolution of 1830 had apparently counted for nothing. The history of the July Monarchy is, in large part, the history of the mounting dissatisfaction of these social groups with the government and the consolidation of opposition to it which culminated in the Revolution of 1848.

Even among the upper bourgeoisie who were represented in the Chamber of Deputies there were different opinions about the direction the regime should take. Led by François Guizot (1787–1874), a group designated as the right-center which came to be known as the Party of Resistance, supported the view that France had now arrived at the perfect and final form of government, a balanced system in which the monarch, the peers, and the elected representatives of the propertied classes each played their allotted role. Anyone excluded from political participation had only to "get rich" (in a phrase often attributed to Guizot) in order to secure the privilege of voting. Now that France had achieved this state of perfection, further changes in its institutions were unnecessary. The other group, the left-center, or the Party of Movement, was represented by Adolphe Thiers, a statesman whose political career spanned the better part of the nineteenth century; its members argued that the Revolution of 1830 was merely a stage in the political evolution of France and that the electoral base should be gradually broadened. At first these two factions were evenly matched, but by 1840 the right-center (with which the king was in sympathy) had won the day. Guizot was the premier during the last eight years of the king's reign and effectively suppressed opposition to the regime in the Chamber of Deputies.

Outside of the chamber the opposition was vigorous, particularly in the early years of the regime. It came from a number of sources. There were the Legitimists, who remained loyal to the dynasty which had been overthrown and hoped for a restoration of its heir. Then there were the Bonapartists, and in these years the Napoleonic legend won increasing popularity among Frenchmen. The death without heirs of the duke of Reichstadt, Napoleon's son, in 1832, temporarily weakened the cause and at first nobody took very seriously the claims of the emperor's nephew, Louis Napoleon, as his successor. Two ill-planned and rather ridiculous attempts by the young pretender to seize power, one in 1836 and another in 1840, were quickly thwarted by the government. Arrested and tried after the second of these, he was condemned to life imprisonment, but he escaped to England in 1846 and remained there until 1848.

The only group that appeared potentially dangerous to the July Monarchy consisted of those who favored the establishment of a republic. In 1830 they were still few, mainly students and young radicals drawn from the lesser bourgeoisie. Having initially accepted the new regime, they quickly became disillusioned with it and began to renew their republican propaganda, multiply their secret societies, and attract new recruits from the discontented. Except for the aim of eliminating the monarchy, their program was not particularly extreme; they advocated extension of the suffrage, salaries for members of the Chamber of Deputies, and free public education.

King Louis-Philippe. *Satirical coin proposed by Daumier.*

Since censorship was one of the issues about which the Revolution of 1830 was fought, the July Monarchy began by allowing considerable freedom of expression in the press. The result was an outburst of political commentary and criticism. In this age political and social satire was a powerful weapon, and the caricaturist Honoré Daumier (1808–1879) was only one of the more successful social satirists. Daumier's caricatures of Louis Philippe shaped like a pear were so popular that opposition newspapers could be sure of being understood when they spoke simply of *La Poire.* Before long the tolerance of the government (and of the king) began to wear thin and steps were taken to curb the excesses of the opposition press. As we shall see, in defense of its restrictions the government pointed to public demonstrations and riots allegedly inspired by press attacks on the regime and to a series of attempts upon the life of the king which more than once came dangerously close to success.*

In a country where the Industrial Revolution was still in its infant stages, no sizable urban proletariat existed in 1830. But the rapid expansion of French industry in the 1830's and 1840's, and its concentration in a few regions, led to the development of an urban working class. Conditions in industrial areas were as bad, and in some cases worse, than in the corresponding parts of England. The labor of women and children was used extensively in the textile mills of the north, where a fifteen-hour working day was not uncommon. Epidemics were frequent, particularly among children, because of poor hygienic conditions in homes and factories. Periodic economic crises led to temporary unemployment and consequent suffering for laborers living at a bare subsistence level. In contrast with

* The fact that the king was the target of attempted assassinations on ten different occasions during the first decade of his reign led him to remark, ". . . there seems to be a closed season on all kinds of game except me."—Quoted by Gordon Wright, *France in Modern Times* (Chicago, 1960), p. 152.

Great Britain, France made practically no effort to regulate conditions in the factories and mines. With the bourgeoisie firmly in control, the government's *laissez-faire* policy went largely unchallenged. The few reforms that reached the statute books such as a child-labor law passed in 1841, were unenforced. In these circumstances, the working class in France behaved with remarkable restraint.

The only significant working-class disturbances under the July Monarchy took place in 1831 and 1834 at Lyons, the center of the silk industry and the second largest city in France, but their repercussions were felt elsewhere. Because the silk industry was well established, the workers were relatively class-conscious and receptive to programs of political and social reform. The first insurrection seems to have been a largely spontaneous affair resulting from discontent over low wages, but there is evidence of collaboration between the workers and republican secret societies in a more generalized protest during the uprising in 1834. Both outbreaks were suppressed by government troops. In the second one the workers held Lyons for five days and the government had to bombard sections of the city before the rebellion could be quelled. The Lyons insurrections, the most important social uprisings in France since the French Revolution, marked the beginning of an alliance between republicans and the working class against the July Monarchy. One month after the insurrection of 1834, an attempted republican uprising in Paris led to brutal reprisals by government forces. This was the occasion memorialized by Daumier in his famous drawing "The Massacre in the Rue Transnonain," showing a victim of a government raid, clad in his nightshirt and cap, stretched out at the foot of his bed and covered with bayonet wounds.

Massacre in the rue Transnonain, 1834. *Honoré Daumier.*

These insurrections were followed by the mass arrest and trial of republican and radical leaders, and the republican opposition was driven completely underground. The government used the uprisings and the attempts on the life of the king as pretexts for the September Laws of 1835. These brought the press under strict censorship and simplified and speeded up judicial proceedings against those accused of provoking insurrection against the state. The September Laws marked a turning point in the history of the July Monarchy: they did not end criticism but they drastically curbed the opportunities for its expression. With the safety valve of a free press no longer available, pressure built up steadily in the final years of the regime, until it finally exploded in the Revolution of 1848.

Perhaps the most serious charge that can be brought against the leaders of the July Monarchy is that they made no real effort to understand the underlying causes of the insurrections and demonstrations against the regime. Refusing to recognize the legitimacy of republican demands for broader political representation and of working-class demands for an amelioration of social conditions, they simply chose to ignore popular unrest. As premier from 1840 to 1848, François Guizot bears much of the responsibility for the failure of the July Monarchy. Though a brilliant historian and one of the instigators of the Revolution of 1830, he seems to have been incapable of understanding the forces active in his own time. In an era when important economic changes were taking place in French society, he adopted a policy of almost total immobility and resistance to change. In the realm of foreign affairs, his do-nothing policy could be justified on the ground that peace was in France's self-interest, but the absence of adventure and the drabness of France's role in the international scene contributed to the unpopularity of the government. In economic matters he retained the *laissez-faire* policy pursued by the July Monarchy from the outset, though the government did take the initiative in establishing a plan for a national network of railroads in 1842, offering subsidies to private firms which undertook their construction. No serious attempts were made to regulate or improve working conditions even though abuses were widespread. Where Guizot particularly excelled was in the manipulation of elections and the corruption of elected representatives, activities which were essential if he was to maintain a majority in the Chamber of Deputies. By carefully selecting the time at which elections were to be held, choosing the towns where the voters were to meet, and promising patronage where it would do the most good, he could secure the return of a favorable majority. And to ensure the continuing support of those elected, lucrative government posts, which they could hold while serving as deputies, were offered to them. Political devices like these are employed to some extent in all parliamentary regimes, but Guizot so abused them that the representative system became a farce. One of the most serious consequences of Guizot's method was that the king and the government were prevented from discovering the true sentiments of the French people. Repeated proposals from a minority of deputies for a reform of the electoral system or the elimination of officeholding by deputies were overridden or disregarded by Guizot's majority. With a growing sense of frustration, liberal reformers in the Assembly finally decided they must turn to extra-parliamentary means for achieving their ends. From this resolve were to originate the electoral banquets held in the winter of 1847–1848 throughout the country, in the propaganda campaign for electoral reform which helped precipitate the Revolution of 1848.

THE EMERGENCE OF SOCIALISM

Among the more vigorous critics of the bourgeois industrial societies emerging in western Europe in the first half of the nineteenth century were a number of writers who referred to themselves as socialists. Without any significant influence on the working classes, they did call attention to the inequities and injustices of unrestricted competition and proposed alternative methods of economic and social organization. Despite the great variations in their schemes, they are usually grouped together as Utopian Socialists. The term is used in part because they, or their disciples, tried to establish model communities of a Utopian character—many of them in the United States; it also distinguishes these socialists from the followers of Karl Marx, a little later in the century. In Marx's view, the socialism of the Utopians was excessively abstract, not sufficiently grounded in the facts of history.

What was common to all the Utopian Socialists—men like Henri de Saint-Simon, Charles Fourier, and Robert Owen—was the belief that under the existing economic system there was far too much emphasis on the production of goods and far too little on their distribution. The result was that those who were most in need of the products of industry were frequently unable to secure them. This is the way an Owenite publication put the problem in 1821:

England possesses the means and the power of creating more Manufactured Goods than the world can consume; and her soil is capable of furnishing several times the number of her present population with food.

Notwithstanding this power, and this inalienable source of superabundant subsistence, millions of her own people are but imperfectly supplied with some, and are entirely destitute of most, of the necessaries and comforts of life, and of the numberless articles of convenience or of elegance which inventive skill has contrived for the accommodation or embellishment of society.[3]

Socialist writers could also point to the frequent crises, attended by

[3] Prospectus to *The Economist* (1821).

large-scale unemployment and suffering, that seemed to be inherent in a system of unrestricted competition. Where was the basic flaw in the system? The Utopians offered no single answer, but they generally shared the view that excessive individualism and self-seeking were characteristic of capitalism, and proposed in its place systems of social organization based on cooperation and mutual respect.

Henri de Saint-Simon (1760–1825), one of the pioneer socialists in France, maintained that industrial society should be organized on a "scientific" basis, in accordance with certain social "laws" which could be discovered through the study of history. Rejecting ideals of political and social equality, he proposed a hierarchy of classes; the dominant class was to be an intellectual and moral elite concerned with the general improvement of humanity. Below it he placed the propertied class—the captains of industry, charged also with governmental and administrative functions. Finally, at the bottom, was the "most numerous" class, the unpropertied laborers, whose welfare was to be the responsibility of those above them. The most important feature of Saint-Simon's cooperative commonwealth was its goal: the improved material condition and moral and intellectual regeneration of the lowest class.

Charles Fourier (1772–1837), another French socialist, was admired by later socialists for his systematic exposure of some of the glaring abuses and wasteful practices of the capitalism of his day. But he is perhaps better remembered for his blueprint of a cooperative community which he believed would so transform men's environment as to bring about a fundamental change in human behavior. His theory was based on the view that men's actions were governed by a set of "passions," or instincts, which under existing conditions were misused or misdirected because of the faulty environment. Accordingly, he proposed the establishment of a number of small communities or self-contained societies, called *phalanges* ("phalanxes"), in which work would be performed and social life organized so as to make the most effective use of the "passions." To make work attractive (*i.e.* satisfying to the passions) jobs would be rotated, giving everyone an opportunity to perform "agreeable" as well as "necessary" tasks in the community.* Despite the communal nature of these enterprises, Fourier did not intend to abolish private property. Indeed, he anticipated that considerable differences in wealth might remain. Fourier, whose own means were modest, announced after the publication of his proposals that he would be at home daily at noon, ready to discuss them with anyone interested in financing a phalanx. He hoped to establish a limited number of phalanxes which would prove so successful that they would be imitated

* One of Fourier's ingenious proposals concerned garbage disposal in the phalanxes: since little boys and girls love dirt, this and other disagreeable jobs in the community would be assigned to the children.—Alexander Gray, *The Socialist Tradition* (London, 1946), p. 188.

throughout the world. Reportedly, he returned home punctually at noon every day for ten years, but no patron ever appeared.

Utopian Socialism was not confined to France. One leading socialist who had an opportunity to put his theories into practice was the Welshman Robert Owen (1771–1858), a self-made manufacturer who bought a cotton mill at New Lanark, in Scotland, and turned the town into a model community organized on cooperative principles. Like Fourier, Owen believed in man's natural goodness and was convinced that he was corrupted only by an improper environment. If man could live in a society based upon cooperation and mutual respect rather than self-interest and competition his true nature would reveal itself. At New Lanark, beginning about 1800, Owen converted a miserable factory town into a clean, orderly community with educational facilities for children and a remarkably high standard of living. The extent to which this achievement resulted from the application of cooperative principles and not from Owen's own benevolent rule is a matter of dispute, but the project has been viewed as one of the first successful socialist experiments. Like Fourier, Owen tried to interest others, particularly his fellow manufacturers, in establishing cooperative communities, but he met with little response. Believing that his ideas might have greater success in the less tradition-bound atmosphere of the United States, he took over an existing community in Indiana in the 1820's and rechristened it New Harmony, but this experiment was marked by internal dissension and collapsed after three years. Owen was subsequently active in the trade-union movement in Great Britain and in founding consumers' cooperatives for workers, but experienced failure and disillusionment in his later years.

Louis Blanc (1811–1882), a Frenchman, has been described as a figure of

Louis Blanc. *The socialist author of* The Organization of Labor *who was named to the Provisional Government in February, 1848.*

transition between the Utopian Socialism of the first half of the century and the "proletarian socialism" of the second half. His ideas—as expressed, for example, in his essay "The Organization of Labor" (1839)—were simpler and had a more direct appeal to the working class in France than those of either Saint-Simon or Fourier. Writing in an era plagued by depressions, he charged that under the system of *laissez-faire* the worker was often denied one of his basic rights, the right to work and earn a decent living. To the state belonged the responsibility of guaranteeing this right. Aware that the bourgeois-dominated July Monarchy would never fulfill this obligation, Blanc viewed political reform and the broadening of the franchise as essential prerequisites to social reform. Once the state was sympathetic to the cause of the laboring classes, it would subsidize the formation of "social workshops," cooperative enterprises for production which would in time dominate the most important branches of industry. The workers themselves would assume control of the workshops, repaying the government loans over a period of years. Blanc further hoped that the association of workers for economic ends would lead them into voluntary associations for the satisfaction of other needs as well. In other words, the social workshops would form the nucleus of a fully cooperative society. The simplicity of Blanc's ideas—particularly his emphasis on the right to work and the responsibility of the state to provide work—constituted their appeal. *The Organization of Labor* went through numerous editions in the 1840's and seems to have reached a fairly wide audience. In the Revolution of 1848, Blanc's propaganda was reflected in the demand of Paris laborers for recognition of the "right to work" and in the revolutionary government's establishment of "National Workshops." These turned out, however, to be little more than caricatures of Blanc's original proposal.

With the possible exception of Louis Blanc, these early socialists had relatively little influence upon their contemporaries. Aside from small bands of disciples and a few attempts, almost all abortive, to establish model socialist communities, they were ignored. For this neglect there is a variety of explanations. Yet one assumption, common to all of the Utopian Socialists, may help to explain their failure; this was their belief, derived from certain of the *philosophes* of the eighteenth century, that man was naturally good, so that once his social environment and institutions were changed, all evil and suffering would automatically be eliminated. Adherence to this view clearly resulted in their underestimating the complexity of human institutions and the obstacles to social change.

Later socialists led by Marx and Engels specifically attacked the Utopian conviction that a socialist society could be brought into existence at will, at any time or place, and that if one only propagandized widely enough, or set up enough model communities, socialism would be accepted and substituted for the existing social framework. The Marxists believed instead that to try to establish socialism before conditions were ripe was an exercise doomed to failure. Yet even Marxists were willing to give credit to the Utopian Socialists for a number of insights, and to draw on their critique of the capitalist system. All of the Utopians challenged the principle of economic competition, arguing that it resulted at best in a kind of anarchy of waste and inefficiency, at worst in serious social injustice and acute suffering for the working classes. Saint-Simon, anticipating the Marxist analysis, recognized the importance of social classes and class divisions in history and pointed out the diverging class interests in industrial society.

Finally, all of the Utopians in one way or another felt that the state bore some responsibility for the material welfare of its citizens and concluded that the reform of society was a proper task for government. All of these notions have, of course, become a part of subsequent socialist thought, and one need hardly point out that their influence has also spread beyond the circle of socialists, that they have been accepted in some degree by all democratic industrial societies.

GERMANY IN THE VORMÄRZ ERA

Because the revolutions that disrupted the German states in 1848 occurred in March, the decades in Germany preceding these mid-century upheavals are often referred to as the *Vormärz* ("pre-March") era. Politically, this was a period of relative stagnation. The German princes, with Metternich's encouragement, clung stubbornly to established institutions and rigorously suppressed dissent. Economically, however, the years between 1815 and 1848 were of great importance for Germany's subsequent progress. Although the development of German industry at this time can hardly be compared with that of Great Britain, France, and Belgium, the groundwork was laid for the major advance that occurred in the second half of the century. Even in these early years, industrial progress was great enough to disturb the existing equilibrium of social forces in certain regions of Germany, thereby creating significant sources of unrest. In addition, the steps taken to break down the economic barriers between the various states of Germany were to have important political as well as economic consequences.

German economic development in the first half of the nineteenth century varied greatly from one region to another. What industrialization there was tended to be concentrated in certain regions, such as the Rhineland and Saxony, while other areas were almost entirely unaffected. Even in Prussia there were vast differences between the Rhine provinces of the west, which enjoyed an industrial development comparable to that of France, and the provinces of the east, where an almost feudal agrarian society persisted well into the nineteenth century. Obstacles to industrialization were many. Although events of the French revolutionary and Napoleonic eras had shattered traditional economic patterns and modes of organization, the period after 1815 brought a revival of the authority of the guilds in many regions, and the handicraft system persisted in most industries. Governments were still dominated by the landed interests, and manufacturers found it difficult to secure the removal of restrictions on business enterprises and trade. Many conservative Germans associated economic liberalism with political liberalism and therefore viewed it with suspicion.

Despite these difficulties significant advances in German industrial development occurred after 1830, particularly in the coal-mining and metallurgical industries. Deep mine shafts were sunk in the Ruhr Valley and coal production increased substantially. By the early 1840's the Krupp works at Essen was producing high-grade steel. Developments in the textile industry were slower since Germany produced mainly linen and woolen cloth, both less adapted to manufacture by machinery than cotton and silk. But there were advances here as well. Industrial growth was supported by new transportation systems; by 1850 the German states could boast of three thousand miles of railroad track, although the first line had been laid only in 1835.

To the German manufacturer or merchant seeking customers beyond his local market, the most serious obstacle was the vast network of tariff barriers that separated the German states and hampered trade even within some of the larger states, such as Prussia. In the early nineteenth century goods shipped from Hamburg, on the North Sea, to Austria had to cross ten different states with ten different customs systems, all exacting transit duties. No wonder the German manufacturer, unlike his French counterpart, was reluctant to produce for national consumption. For this reason the most important single economic development in this era was the establishment of a *Zollverein* ("customs union"), which by 1844 included most of the states of Germany. Prussia took the lead in 1818 by abolishing all tariff barriers among the provinces within its own borders and establishing a uniform tariff rate on imports. Within the next few years Prussia concluded tariff treaties with a number of neighboring states and provoked the negotiation of similar treaties among some of its rivals. In 1834, seventeen states with a population of 26,000,000, came together in the *Zollverein*, a union which established free trade among them and provided for annual meetings of their delegates. By 1844 all German states except Austria, Hanover, Oldenburg, and the Hanse cities (Hamburg, Bremen, and Lübeck) adhered to the union; the result was a remarkable expansion of the volume of trade among them. Gradually the political implications of this economic collaboration became clear: Prussia's leadership of the *Zollverein* was undermining the hitherto dominant position of the Habsburg monar-

View of a factory where machinery was manufactured near Munich, 1849.

chy. The *Zollverein* turned out to be of decisive importance in preparing Germany for unification under Prussian leadership.

In estimating the effects of these economic changes upon German society one must remember that as late as 1848 at least two out of three Germans still made their living from the land. Yet even in rural areas the years from 1815 to 1848 were characterized by change and unrest, for in many regions the peasants were trying to adjust to legislation, introduced during the revolutionary and Napoleonic eras, which radically altered their status. Serfdom had been abolished in the parts of Germany under French control and even in some areas, such as Prussia, not annexed by the French. But freedom from personal servitude did not necessarily mean improvement of the peasants' material status, for many were still saddled with manorial dues or other obligations, and only in certain regions and under certain circumstances did they receive clear title to the land they farmed. Indeed, in Prussia the legislation abolishing serfdom strengthened the great landholding *Junker* aristocrat. Freed from his feudal obligation to protect the serf and to provide him with lodging and other necessities of life, the *Junker* took possession of his land and exploited it for his own profit, employing his former serfs, now landless, as agricultural laborers. The condition of the "free" peasant of East Prussia was far worse after his so-called emancipation than before. When the peasant did secure title to a piece of land, it was often so small that he could not farm it productively. Whether the peasant was a freeholder, a tenant farmer, or a landless laborer, he had grievances. And he could hardly hope to secure redress of them from a government dominated by the large landowners.

Among the workers living in the towns and cities, those employed in factories were still in a minority as late as 1848. The majority were artisans working under the traditional handicraft system and it was among this group that there was the greatest unrest. Suffering from the competition of new industries in Germany and abroad, the old craft guilds went into a decline and the artisans found themselves either unemployed or earning starvation-level wages. Their discontent found occasional expression in riots and blind onslaughts upon the machinery which they held responsible for their situation. For example, Silesian linen weavers rioted in 1844, attacking factories and destroying the homes of the owners. By comparison, factory workers in Germany enjoyed steady employment and relatively high wages.

As elsewhere, the impact of industrialism brought a rapid expansion of the middle class during the Vormärz era. Neither as large nor as concentrated as the bourgeoisie of England and France, this class assumed in Germany an economic influence far out of proportion to its size. German manufacturers and merchants, denied the right to participate actively in the governing of their respective states, managed to win concessions as their rulers began to be aware of their potential strength. The Zollverein, for example, was established largely in response to their pressure. The cause of national unification had no stronger supporters than German businessmen anxious to promote greater efficiency of government and smoother economic operations. A comment in the Düsseldorfer Zeitung in 1843 gives an indication of their outlook, "Thus we have instead of one Germany, thirty-eight German states, an equal number of governments, almost the same number of courts, as many representative bodies, thirty-eight distinct legal codes and administrations, embassies and consulates. What an enormous saving it would be, if all of that were taken care of by one central government. . . ."[4]

Comparisons have been made between Germany at the beginning of 1848 and France in 1789, and there are indeed certain superficial resemblances. In both, the nobility was still dominant; if anything, the German nobility was probably more strongly entrenched than its French counterpart under the Old Regime. In both, a rising bourgeoisie had gained significant economic influence but was still excluded from political privileges. In both, there was widespread dissatisfaction among the lower classes, which made them potential supporters of the middle class in the event of revolution. But the parallel begins to break down when one looks at the nature of the grievances

[4] Quoted by T. S. Hamerow, Restoration, Revolution, Reaction (Princeton, N.J., 1958), p. 17.

of the peasantry and the urban workers. And an even greater difference appears in the organization of the two countries: the decentralization, if not fragmentation, of Germany on the eve of 1848 contrasts markedly with the relatively high degree of centralization in France, where a development in Paris might carry the entire country with it. In the *Vormärz* era Germans were still seeking the unity which the French monarchy had achieved long before 1789.

THE RISORGIMENTO AND THE REVOLUTIONS OF 1848 IN ITALY

To understand the revolutions of 1848 in Italy we must look briefly at the development of the *Risorgimento* ("Resurgence"), the movement for Italian unification, during the 1830's and 1840's. The failure of revolutionary movements in 1830–1831, following the suppression of the revolts in Naples and Sardinia ten years earlier, served to discredit the methods used by such secret societies as the *Carbonari*. The *Risorgimento* now entered a new phase, with different leaders and techniques.

Among the leaders before 1848, Giuseppe Mazzini (1805–1872) is unquestionably the most renowned, though recently historians have suggested that the classic accounts of the *Risorgimento* exaggerate his role. With his idealistic, semireligious faith in Italian nationalism, he was undoubtedly the chief inspiration for radical students and intellectuals who hoped to see Italy emerge as a unified republic. Mazzini was born in Genoa, in the kingdom of Sardinia. During his youth he was active in secret societies. In 1821, when he saw refugees streaming northward from Naples after the suppression of the revolt there, he put on a black suit to signify his mourning for the condition of Italy, and he affected this costume for the rest of his life. He participated in the revolts of 1830–1831, and was imprisoned for six months, being released on the condition that he remain outside of Genoa. Instead, he chose exile from all of Italy, and spent most of the remaining forty years of his life in Switzerland, France, and Great Britain. There he wrote inspirational tracts and pamphlets that were circulated in his homeland, and founded Young Italy, the organization particularly associated with his name. The goal of this movement, in which membership was restricted to men under forty living either in Italy or in exile, was the expulsion of foreign tyrants from the Italian peninsula and the establishment of a united republic. However, Mazzini's skills at organization and administration fell short of his ability as a propagandist, and his few attempts to foment uprisings in his native land failed.

Schooled in the writings of the French revolutionaries, Mazzini believed strongly in the principle of popular sovereignty. At the same time, he felt that during the French Revolution the *rights* of man had been emphasized too much and his *duties* too little. Drawing on the heritage of Rousseau and to some extent on the German idealist tradition, he was convinced that a person could be happy only while devoting himself to a collective enterprise. In the work which he appropriately called *The Duties of Man* (published in two parts, 1844 and 1858), Mazzini argued that the highest collective enterprise to which the individual could dedicate his life was the nation. In a lyrical passage typical of his prose, he wrote, "O my Brothers! love your Country. Our Country is our home, the home which God has given us, placing therein a numerous family which we love and are loved by, and with which we have a more intimate and quicker communion of feeling and thought than with others; a family which by its concentration upon a given spot, and by the homogeneous nature of its elements, is destined for a special kind of activity." Yet important as love for the nation was to Mazzini, he regarded national loyalty as part of a higher duty toward "Humanity," to whom men owed primary allegiance. "You are *men* before you are either *citizens* or *fathers*." The nation was for him the vehicle through which men fulfilled their obligations toward humanity as a whole. His concern for other nationalities led him to found in 1834 a movement known as Young Europe, which was to establish national committees for patriotic agitation in Germany, Poland, and Switzerland. Mazzini was convinced that by encouraging nationalist movements among the peoples still divided or living under foreign domination, he was working toward the day when all nations, having realized their national aspirations, would work for humanity at large. For this reason Mazzini is often viewed as the prophet of the ideals that President Woodrow Wilson (1856–1924) tried to embody in the peace settlement of 1919: national self-determination and the association of all peoples in a League of Nations.

Many Italians who desired the unification of the peninsula viewed Mazzini as a dangerous radical whose ideal of a democratic republic implied social revolution and a threat to property. Some of these rallied to the Neo-Guelph movement, which took its name from the papal faction in the medieval struggle between popes and emperors. The principal impetus to the Neo-Guelph cause came from the publication in 1843 of *The Civil and Moral Primacy of the Italians*, by Vincenzo Gioberti (1801–1852), which called for the establishment of a federation of Italian states under the leadership of the papacy, with executive authority vested in a college of princes. To those who were skeptical about the willingness of the pope to lead a crusade for Italian unity, the election of a new pope in 1846 seemed to offer hope, for the man who took the name Pius IX had a reputation as a liberal. His initial measures in the Papal States—granting an amnesty to political offenders and relaxing restrictions on freedom of speech and of the press—suggested that he might indeed become the rallying point for a liberal Italian federation.

A third faction working for the cause of unification consisted of the

so-called Moderates, most active in the kingdom of Sardinia, with supporters in Lombardy and Venetia. Principally liberal nobles and members of
the bourgeoisie, the Moderates looked to Sardinia for leadership in unification and foresaw the establishment of a constitutional monarchy. They
believed that economic unification had to precede political unity. Accordingly, they strove for the elimination of tariff barriers and the stimulation of
commerce among the Italian states. While urging industrial development,
they nevertheless realized that they must concentrate on improving and
modernizing agricultural methods since farming was still Italy's principal
industry. Young aristocrats like Count Camillo Benso di Cavour (1810–
1861), later prime minister of Sardinia, set up model farms and established
agricultural societies to disseminate knowledge of new techniques. Some
historians argue that the efforts of northern Italian liberals and Moderates
for economic reform contributed more than all the propaganda of Mazzini
toward the unification of the peninsula.[5] An elite of educated, influential
individuals in a number of Italian states became accustomed to exchanging
ideas and collaborating in the attainment of certain limited goals. Their
efforts were partially rewarded when Charles Albert, the king of Sardinia,
lowered tariffs, reformed the finances of his country, and officially encouraged agricultural improvements, but his liberalism did not extend to
political matters until the eve of the revolutions of 1848.

Thus, at least three different movements had been organized in the
peninsula before 1848, each working in its own way for greater unity among
the Italian peoples. Yet it should be emphasized that the strength of the
Neo-Guelphs and the Moderates was concentrated almost exclusively in
the northern regions of Italy and that even Mazzini's Young Italy won
the support of only a small minority of the population. As yet most Italians
were untouched by the *Risorgimento.*

[5] For example, Kent R. Greenfield, *Economics and Liberalism in the Risorgimento*
(Baltimore, 1934).

CHAPTER 29

The Revolutions of 1848

ON JANUARY 12, 1848, the people of Palermo revolted against their ruler, Ferdinand II, since 1830 king of Naples and Sicily. At the moment, the uprising attracted little attention; yet it was the first of almost fifty revolutions that occurred within the first four months of 1848, disturbances that rocked France, Austria, Prussia, and almost all of the lesser German and Italian states. By April, 1848, no European ruler appeared to be safe on his throne, and Tsar Nicholas I, horrified at the spread of revolution, could write to the English queen, Victoria: "What remains standing in Europe? Great Britain and Russia."[1] Despite differences in language and nationality, in political and economic development, the countries of Europe showed remarkable uniformity in their response to the revolutionary impulse.

Tensions had been mounting throughout the 1830's and 1840's. In France there had been growing resentment of Guizot's manipulation of the electoral machinery, his corruption of the deputies, and his almost total disregard of the distress of the working class. In the German states the bourgeoisie had long been dissatisfied by the continued political division, and the handicraft workers and peasants had been suffering economic deprivation. Within the Habsburg empire and Italy nationalist aspirations had been continually thwarted. With all this combustible material, only a spark was needed to set off the conflagration. A particularly acute economic crisis helped to precipitate the revolutions. The crisis had its origins in low grain production in Britain and Europe in 1845 and 1846 and in the failure of the potato crop in Ireland in 1845. Harvests in the British Isles improved somewhat in 1847, but in France and Germany they were again bad. Food prices, particularly the price of bread, the staple of the lower classes' diet, rose markedly during 1847. The crisis in agriculture had repercussions in the world of finance, with bankruptcies and bank closings. In France, where industrial expansion had not been accompanied by a corresponding development of new markets, overproduction in a number of industries led to

[1] Quoted by L. B. Namier, *1848: The Revolution of the Intellectuals* (London, 1946), p. 3.

992

falling prices for manufactured goods, business failures, and widespread unemployment.

Many have asserted, however, that the revolutions of 1848 were born of hope as much as of despair. Behind them was a whole range of ideals and aspirations for a better world. So pervasive was the idealism of the revolts that it has been argued that they had a common denominator in a uniform ideological outlook developed during the first half of the nineteenth century. Thus, Sir Lewis Namier refers to the events of 1848 as "the Revolution of the Intellectuals". Yet there was no single revolutionary organization or movement encompassing all of Europe, and although revolutionaries everywhere mouthed similar phrases and slogans, the words meant quite different things to different peoples. A broad spectrum of goals motivated the revolutionaries of 1848.

In general, all of the revolutions took much the same course. Though France's February Revolution followed the revolt in Palermo by more than a month, it was this outbreak in Paris that sparked revolts elsewhere in Europe, and the subsequent fate of the revolution in France seemed to foreshadow developments in central Europe. The overthrow of Louis Philippe in February triggered successful revolts during March, first in the Austrian empire, then in many of the lesser German states, and finally in Prussia. During the same period revolts spread northward in the Italian peninsula from Naples and Sicily into Sardinia, Tuscany, the Papal States, and finally the regions directly under Austrian control. In this initial stage the frightened rulers capitulated with practically no resistance to the revolutionary demands, promising their subjects constitutions and representative assemblies and hastily granting the freedoms which had been denied their peoples. Unlike Louis Philippe, the central European rulers managed to retain their thrones while their more unpopular ministers were dismissed or, like Metternich, forced to flee. For the moment the revolutionaries appeared triumphant.

The turning point in the course of the revolts came during the summer of 1848. In France, an insurrection of disillusioned workers against the new government in June was decisively defeated. The victory of "forces of order" in France encouraged counterrevolutionary forces elsewhere in Europe. In most instances the armies of the central European states had remained loyal to their respective rulers during the revolts, and now they were ordered to attack the revolutionaries, whose ranks were weakened by the divisions that inevitably appeared after their initial successes. In this counterrevolutionary assault the rulers were supported by the landowning aristocracy and in some states also by elements of the bourgeoisie who, though they had participated on the side of the revolutionaries at the outset, were now alarmed at the possibility of thoroughgoing social revolution.

By December, 1848, the revolutionaries had been defeated or were fighting rearguard actions almost everywhere in Europe. The overthrown dynasty was not restored in France, but in December the first presidential election under the new republican constitution resulted in an overwhelming victory for Louis Napoleon Bonaparte, who emerged as a savior and symbol of order for many Frenchmen frightened by the bloodshed and social upheaval that had occurred earlier in the year. Another eight months passed before the Habsburg monarchy, with the aid of Russian troops, suppressed the revolt in Hungary. In the early months of 1849 the Sardinians renewed their struggle against Austria for the liberation of Italian territory, and elsewhere in the peninsula the Roman Republic was proclaimed. But these were short-lived episodes which merely prolonged the revolutionary agony but could not reverse the general trend. By the end of 1849 the counterrevolution was everywhere triumphant. To the bitterly disillusioned revolutionaries it seemed that nothing had been gained. In fact, the situation in many countries appeared worse than it had been before the revolts. Where constitutions had been granted they were either suspended or rendered ineffectual. Revolutionary leaders were imprisoned or exiled and the freedoms for which they had fought were systematically denied.

Such were the general outlines of this period of upheaval. But a closer look at the separate revolutions is needed, for 1848 proved to be a watershed in the history of nineteenth-century Europe; in the writings and speeches of the 1850's a new atmosphere can be detected, setting this decade off from those which preceded it.

THE FEBRUARY REVOLUTION IN FRANCE

On January 29, 1848, a little more than three weeks before revolution erupted in France, Alexis de Tocqueville (1805–1859), a noted writer and member of the parliamentary opposition, addressed his colleagues in the Chamber of Deputies:

...I am told that there is no danger because there are no riots; I am told that, because there is no visible disorder on the surface of society, there is no revolution at hand. Gentlemen, permit me to say that I believe you are mistaken. True, there is no actual disorder; but it has entered deeply into men's minds. See what is preparing itself amongst the working classes, who, I grant, are at present quiet. No doubt they are not disturbed by political passions, properly so-called, to the same extent that they have been; but can you not see that their passions, instead of political, have become social? Do you not see that they are gradually forming opinions and ideas which are destined not only to upset this or that law, ministry, or even form of government, but society itself, until it totters upon the foundations on which it rests today? . . . This, gentlemen, is my profound conviction: I believe that we are at this moment sleeping on a volcano. I am profoundly convinced of it....[2]

[2] Alexis de Tocqueville, *The Recollections of Alexis de Tocqueville*, trans. by Alexander Teixeira de Mattos (London, 1948), pp. 12–13.

De Tocqueville's speech was greeted with ironical cheers from the majority; no one took seriously his prophecy of catastrophe.

Yet signs of the forthcoming troubles were certainly not lacking. The combination of food shortages, a rising cost of living, and widespread unemployment had led to an increasing number of working-class demonstrations during the winter of 1847–1848. Sometimes sheer hunger was to blame. Yet because the workers were not effectively organized, their demonstrations attracted relatively little attention. The most obvious expressions of opposition to the July Monarchy were banquets to popularize the cause of electoral reform. Political leaders, frustrated in their attempt to effect changes through normal legislative channels and forbidden by law from organizing political rallies, used the device of the dinner meeting to focus opposition to the regime. Participating in these dinners were not only members of the so-called parliamentary opposition, such as Adolphe Thiers, but also men of known republican views. Some seventy banquets were held all over France during the winter, and this campaign was to culminate in a large banquet scheduled for February 22, 1848, in Paris. On the very day of the banquet, Guizot's government banned both the dinner and the procession that was to precede it. This was the episode that precipitated the revolution.

The revolt lasted only four days. At first the crowds that gathered on the Paris boulevards were dispersed without difficulty. Gradually the movement gathered momentum, as regiments of the bourgeois National Guard joined the opposition. Inhabitants of working-class districts began to tear up the paving stones in the streets in order to erect barricades.

Louis Philippe, now seventy-five, refused to take the first demonstrations seriously. But by February 23 the situation had become so acute that he dismissed the unpopular Guizot and replaced him with an old personal friend, Count Louis Molé (1781–1855). Guizot's dismissal might have placated the middle-class opposition; it did not satisfy the Parisian working class, which became ever more radical in its demands. By February 24 the situation in the capital was so serious that the king decided to abdicate in favor of his ten-year-old grandson, the count of Paris. But his decision came too late, for the popular forces now controlled most of the city and were approaching the Tuileries, the royal residence. The king escaped through the garden to a waiting carriage, which started him toward exile in England.

A crucial point in the revolution had been reached. The symbol of authority was gone, and the new form of the French government had to be determined. The Chamber of Deputies was still in session, and the king's daughter-in-law, the duchess of Orléans, decided to attempt to have herself proclaimed regent for the count of Paris. When the duchess appeared on the rostrum with the young count and her brother-in-law, the duke of Nemours, the poet-turned-politician Alphonse de Lamartine (1790–1869)

The "February Days" in Paris, 1848. *This engraving shows a young insurgent bearing the banner of reform surrounded by workers and members of the National Guard.*

was speaking. Some members of a mob had forced their way into the assembly hall and stood menacingly at the rear, behind the deputies. The fate of the royal family rested with Lamartine, who at this point abandoned the dynasty and declared his support of a republic. The crowd responded by swarming over the hall; deputies retreated hastily, and the duchess fled with her son. In this chaos a provisional government was chosen. As Lamartine read aloud names that had been proposed for the new government, the mob shouted its acceptance or rejection of each, in a kind of impromptu election. When the list was complete, the crowd adjourned to the Hôtel de Ville, where revolutionary ritual demanded that the republic be proclaimed.

Those who had been named to the provisional government at the Chamber of Deputies were moderate republicans, men generally sympathetic to the program advocated by the republican newspaper *Le National*, which had called for electoral reform in the last years of the July Monarchy. When they arrived at the Hôtel de Ville, however, they found a delegation from a more radical republican newspaper, *La Réforme*, which was far more concerned than *Le National* with social issues. Since the radical republican group had named its own provisional government, the two lists had to be combined. To the original moderate republicans, therefore, were added three men supported by the radical faction: the socialist Louis Blanc, a mechanic named Albert, and the astronomer François Arago.

In the moment of victory the moderate and the radical republicans had closed ranks and agreed on the provisional government for the Second French Republic. But in the months that followed the cleavage between the two factions broadened. The moderates were concerned primarily with political questions, such as the nature of representation, qualifications for suffrage, and the working of the electoral system. The radicals, while they did not neglect political issues, talked largely of social reform. They had no well-formulated program—indeed, their proposals were vague and amorphous —but their basic concern was improvement of the condition of the working classes. The history of the first four months of the republic is the history of a growing divergence between the moderate republicans, who had the confidence of a majority of the French, and the radical republicans, who had the support of the Paris working class.

One question which confronted the provisional government immediately, and about which moderates and radicals disagreed, was what to do with the vast numbers of unemployed who were concentrated in Paris and who had contributed to the success of the revolution. One of the few coherent demands of the members of the Paris mob in the February Revolution had been for recognition of the "right to work"; they expected the new government to provide employment for all who wanted it. Pressed by the Paris mob for an immediate solution, the provisional government announced the establishment of "National Workshops," on the pattern outlined by the socialist Louis Blanc in his *Organization of Labor*. It would have seemed natural to confide the direction of this project to Blanc himself, especially since he was already a member of the new government. But the task of establishing the National Workshops was given to Alexandre Marie, the minister of public works, while Louis Blanc was sidetracked in a newly created "Workers' Commission." Instead of being autonomous cooperative enterprises operated by the workers, as envisioned by Blanc, the National Workshops became in fact vast relief projects in which the unemployed were put to work on hastily contrived road-construction jobs. To complicate matters, the number of unemployed far exceeded the number of jobs the government was able to provide and the surplus laborers were put on what amounted to a dole. Although the moderate republicans in the government may have been sincere in their desire to provide jobs, their decision to entrust the program to Marie, an avowed antisocialist, proved that they had no intention of making the National Workshops the nucleus of a social transformation. Instead, one of their motives was to immobilize the Paris mob and thus avert the threat of further social revolution. Ironically, this is precisely what they failed to do. The enrollment in the National Workshops jumped from an initial 10,000 in March, to 70,000 in April, 100,000 in May, and an estimated 120,000 in June. Unable to provide employment for such vast numbers, the government discovered it had created a huge army of idle proletarians in Paris ready to support radical leaders and demagogues in further demands upon the republic.

The split between moderates and radicals was further widened in a national election held on April 23, to name the National Assembly, which was to draw up a constitution for the republic. In the general state of euphoria immediately following the February Revolution, the provisional government had proclaimed universal manhood suffrage. By a stroke of a pen the electorate was increased from the 200,000 qualified to vote by the end of the July Monarchy to 9,000,000. How would this vastly expanded electorate vote? The results of the election showed the essentially moderate and even conservative character of the country as a whole as opposed to the radical complexion of the capital. Out of nine hundred seats, approximately five hundred went to moderate republicans and only one hundred to radicals. Most surprisingly, the remaining three hundred seats were won by avowed monarchists, supporters of either the Legitimist Bourbon dynasty or the recently overthrown Orléanist succession. The elections had proved conclusively that the provinces of France were far more conservative than the capital; the French peasantry, alarmed by radical statements that implied a threat to property, had united with the bourgeoisie against the radical republicans and the Paris proletariat. The new five-man executive committee chosen by the National Assembly to replace the provisional government included no representative of the working class. Indeed, Lamartine, the committee's head, was an outspoken opponent of Blanc.

In the face of direct defeat in the elections, the workers of Paris staged a demonstration on May 15 that looked at first like a repetition of the February Revolution. Again the workers overpowered guards and invaded the hall where the assembly was meeting. After listening to harangues by Armand Barbès and Auguste Blanqui, leaders of two revolutionary clubs, they moved to the Hôtel de Ville, where a provisional government was proclaimed. But the established government was better prepared than its predecessor had been in February and used the National Guard and a newly formed mobile guard to clear the assembly hall and reoccupy the Hôtel de Ville. Barbès, Blanqui, and a number of other leaders were imprisoned, and their radical clubs were dissolved. The abortive uprising increased the government's fear of the left and precipitated a decision to dissolve the National Workshops. Anticipating a violent reaction, the government delayed announcing the liquidation of the workshops until reinforcements had been mobilized. On June 22, just four months after the outbreak of the February Revolution, the termination of the National Workshops was proclaimed. The reaction of the Paris workers was immediate and spontaneous. Disillusioned by the government's failure to fulfill its promise of work for all, many workers disobeyed the order to disband and took up arms instead. So began the bloody June Days.

In February workers and members of the lesser bourgeoisie had fought side by side. Now the class lines between them were rigidly drawn. For three days Europe witnessed some of the bloodiest street fighting of the nineteenth century, as the Paris proletariat battled the government forces. A state of martial law was declared in the capital and General Louis Cavaignac (1802–1857), former governor of Algeria, became virtual dictator of Paris. Benefiting from the experiences of 1830 and of February, 1848, Cavaignac allowed the fighting to spread before moving in with guns trained on the barricades. At the end of three days, the toll of dead and injured was estimated at ten thousand. And this was not all. Cavaignac used his emergency powers to carry out vigorous reprisals against those suspected of leading the insurrection. Most of the eleven thousand prisoners taken were deported to the French colony of Algeria. Cavaignac could boast that order had been restored.

The June Days constituted a clear-cut victory for the moderate republicans over the radicals. But it was an expensive victory, for it left great bitterness among the working classes and opened up wounds that took many years to heal. The propertied classes were convinced that they had barely escaped the overthrow of the entire social order; thus the June Days strengthened what came to be known vaguely as the Red Fear. In the months that followed, conservatives capitalized upon this fear by introducing legislation to curb the freedom of the press, limit the right of political association, and outlaw secret societies. The reaction to the June Days was also reflected in the constitution of the Second Republic, which was finally completed in November. In providing that the president should be elected by universal manhood suffrage and that the executive and legislative powers should be separated, the framers of the constitution intended to create a strong executive who could deal effectively with any future proletarian uprisings.

A final effect of the June Days was to strengthen the appeal of one of the candidates for the presidency in the first election, held under the new constitution on December 10, 1848. Charles Louis Napoleon Bonaparte (1808–1873), who had returned from exile in England, entered the lists against candidates whose names were associated with the early months of the Second Republic. These included, in addition to Lamartine and General Cavaignac, Alexandre Auguste Ledru-Rollin (1807–1874), who had been minister of the interior in the provisional government, and François Raspail (1794–1878), who had been active as a republican as early as the Revolution of 1830. Posing as the defender of order, Napoleon's nephew won a landslide victory: 5,500,000 votes compared with the 1,500,000 of his nearest opponent, Cavaignac.

Louis Napoleon had not been taken very seriously by his opponents. In his two personal appearances before the National Assembly his awkward bearing, his German accent, and his halting speech had made him a subject of ridicule. Apparently some monarchists voted for him, as a harmless stopgap who could serve as president until France was ripe for a royalist restoration. Although he had written vaguely socialist tracts during his years of imprisonment and exile, it is doubtful that these views won him many working-class votes. His great appeal unquestionably lay in the magic of his name. In the more than three decades that had elapsed since the defeat of the first Napoleon, Frenchmen had had an opportunity to forget the unpleasant aspects of the Napoleonic regime. The Napoleonic legend had grown particularly during the drab years of the July Monarchy, when Louis Philippe's foreign policy had appeared timorous and inglorious. In contrast, the name Napoleon symbolized an era when France's power had been second to none. But the three years following his election revealed that Louis Napoleon had been greatly underestimated by those who hoped to use him. Like his uncle before him, Louis Napoleon saw himself as the instrument of destiny, and he was determined to make himself the master of France.

THE REVOLUTIONS OF 1848 IN THE GERMAN STATES

When news of France's successful February Revolution crossed the Rhine, a wave of popular discontent spread through the states of Germany, beginning in the south and west, then extending into the central areas, and reaching Prussia and the north by the middle of March. Most of the German rulers, frightened by the fate of the French king, capitulated even before the opposition had a chance to organize, and replaced their conservative ministers with men of known liberal views. Many promised constitutions and other reforms, and offered to give their subjects a share in government. These concessions did not eliminate the threat of violence, however, for the causes of the revolutions in Germany were social as well as political. The smoldering bitterness of handicraft workers against the industrialization which had deprived them of a livelihood burst forth in attacks upon machinery and factories. In rural areas the peasants' pent-up resentment of manorial dues and obligations, the hunting and forest privileges of the nobility, and inadequate land allotments, found expression in orgies of looting and burning. The first task faced by the new liberal ministers in many states was the suppression of popular disturbances and the restoration of order.

Prussia

Prussia was most seriously affected at the outset, in part because of the irresolute behavior of King Frederick William IV (ruled 1840–1861). The king's accession to the throne had given rise to hopes for constitutional changes and for Prussia's leadership in a movement for national unification,

King Frederick William IV of Prussia. *Lithograph, 1849.*

but these hopes proved groundless. Although the king talked of national unity for the Germans, he appears to have had merely a romantic feeling for a common German past, and even retained his loyalty to the Habsburgs as the traditional imperial dynasty. His conception of political representation was not based on any current liberal theory, but rather on an idealized medieval view of the state as a structure in which the various estates of the realm were to be grouped under a king whose position derived from divine right. In 1847 Prussian liberals were temporarily encouraged when the king summoned the *Landtag*, or United Diet, which brought together representatives of provincial diets named by the long-established estates. But in his first speech to the diet he showed that he had no intention of relinquishing any real control over legislation or the budget, and the diet was prorogued shortly afterward, to the disillusionment of the liberals.

When popular demonstrations broke out in Berlin in the middle of March, 1848, the king refused to believe that they were directed against himself and ordered his troops not to fire on his "beloved Berliners." Nevertheless he decided that concessions were in order; on March 18 he announced his readiness to participate in the drawing up of an all-German constitution, indicating also that the United Diet would be reconvened. Serious trouble for the government might have been averted had it not been

Revolution of 1848 in Berlin. *One individual is writing "National Eigenthum"* *(National Property) on the palace of the prince of Prussia in order to protect it* *from the mob.*

for an episode which occurred later the same day. An apparently good-natured crowd that had gathered outside the royal palace was being dispersed by the cavalry when two shots rang out from an unknown quarter. Within minutes, the crowd had been transformed into an angry mob, which engaged the troops in eight hours of bitter street fighting. So disturbed was the king over the violence and loss of life that he yielded to popular demands and ordered the departure of the troops from the city. Without armed protection, he was left in Berlin a captive of the aroused citizenry and was subjected to a series of humiliating experiences which he was never to forget. On one occasion he was summoned to the palace balcony with the queen to view the mutilated corpses of those who had died in the street fighting. As each body was thrust toward the monarch, the name of the victim and the manner of his death were intoned.

During this crisis the king issued a proclamation declaring his willingness to assume leadership among the German princes and added that Prussia would "merge itself" into a new German empire. For the moment he was not called upon to fulfill this promise. But he did agree to the election by universal manhood suffrage of an assembly, which met in May to draw up a constitution for Prussia. This constituent assembly, which included a generous representation of liberals and democrats, became increasingly radical in its deliberations during the summer and fall. Meanwhile the king, encouraged by the mounting counterrevolutionary trend elsewhere in Europe, regained his nerve and consolidated the conservative groups around him. In November he was strong enough to order troops back into the capital and to banish the constituent assembly to a nearby town, where it was finally dissolved on December 5. Curiously enough, the efforts of this body were not entirely without results. For Frederick William in December, 1848, promulgated a constitution of his own which was quite similar in many respects to the one drafted by the assembly. It included safeguards for the liberties of Prussian subjects and provided for a bicameral legislature whose lower house would be chosen by universal manhood suffrage though through a system of indirect election. However, in the following year modifications of the electoral system made the provision for universal suffrage almost meaningless. The voters were divided into three categories, or classes, according to the amount of taxes they paid, and the votes of the wealthy counted far more heavily than those of the poor. Indeed, two thirds of the delegates to the lower house were chosen by about 15 per cent of the population. In this way the authority of the king and the privileged orders was preserved in the lower as well as in the upper house, whose members inherited their seats or were appointed to them by the king. Prussia retained this constitution until 1918.

The Frankfurt Parliament

The revolution in Prussia had its counterpart in virtually every one of the thirty-eight German states, including Austria. During 1848 liberals from all over Germany made a concerted attempt to establish a unified nation under liberal auspices. The vehicle for unification was to be the Frankfurt Parliament (sometimes called the Frankfurt Assembly), and the failure of this body to unify Germany in 1848 marked a significant defeat for German liberalism and a major turning point in the development of modern Germany.

The origins of the Frankfurt Parliament help, in part, to explain its weakness. It emerged not from any official action by the governments of the German states but from a spontaneous gathering of about fifty German liberals inspired by the March revolts, who met in Heidelberg. They issued invitations to a preliminary parliament (*Vorparlament*); this group, in turn, arranged for elections to be held in each of the German states for delegates to an all-German national parliament. Voting was to be by universal manhood suffrage, and each delegate was to represent fifty thousand Germans. The elections were duly held, though the electoral laws and methods varied considerably from state to state. When the delegates came

German National Assembly, Frankfurt am Main, 1848. *Contemporary wood engraving. The procession moves into the Paulskirche (St. Paul's Church) for the opening of the Frankfurt Parliament on May 18, 1848.*

together for the first time on May 18, 1848, in the free city of Frankfurt am Main, the event attracted great excitement. The galleries of the old St. Paul's Church, where the assembly met, were crowded with journalists from all over Europe; the altar was draped with a huge portrait representing "Germania." The spectators and delegates believed that they were witnessing the birth of a new nation.

The professions and social origins of the 830 delegates are of particular interest. The overwhelming majority were university-educated members of the upper bourgeoisie. Among those elected were more than a hundred professors and teachers and numerous lawyers, doctors, ministers, bankers, merchants, and manufacturers. Some of Germany's leading scholars, writers, and publicists were present. Particularly noteworthy was the paucity of statesmen and of men with experience in practical politics, a shortcoming which handicapped the assembly throughout its brief history: far too much time was spent in arguments over theoretical or doctrinaire issues, while practical problems tended to be neglected.

The assembly was also hampered from the start by the conflicting aims of its members. With no established political parties to marshal a consensus on particular issues, it was extremely difficult for the assembly to take any concerted action. The delegates did all agree that their goal was a unified German nation. But they disagreed on the form of government—whether it should be a federation or a unitary state, a monarchy, an empire, or a republic—and on who, if a monarchical or imperial regime was selected, would be the German ruler. They disagreed, furthermore, on what the boundaries of the new state should be; indeed, this proved to be a particularly divisive issue.

Perhaps the most serious weakness of the Frankfurt Parliament was its anomalous position in regard to existing German governments and their princes. For the assembly did not conceive of its purpose as merely the drafting of a constitution for a united Germany but claimed to be a government speaking and acting for the German people as a whole. Yet its relationship to the rulers and governments of the German states was undefined, and these did not accept its leadership. The diet of the old Germanic Confederation, for example, continued to meet for several weeks after the formation of the Frankfurt Parliament. At the root of this general question of sovereignty was the fact that the Frankfurt Parliament had no armed forces at its disposal. The armies of the individual states were left intact. When it became necessary for the assembly to use force—as, for example, when it declared war on Denmark in response to the appeal of German-speaking inhabitants of the territories of Schleswig and Holstein for protection against the Danes—Frankfurt had to call upon Prussia to supply the necessary troops. The lack of a consolidated armed force under its control also hampered the new German government's dealings with foreign powers. Nevertheless the assembly did attempt to pursue an independent foreign policy, to the annoyance of the Prussian and Austrian governments, which maintained their own foreign offices and diplomatic relations.

There were other fundamental weaknesses. In their excitement and enthusiasm over the prospect of founding a new nation, the delegates to the Frankfurt Parliament failed to take into account the power relationships in Germany. With Austria and Prussia the strongest states, no enduring nation could be founded without the approval and support of at least one of these. Misled by the temporary weakness of the Prussian and Austrian governments after the March revolts, the delegates assumed that the two rulers would follow Frankfurt's lead and permit their states to be absorbed into a new German nation. They were wrong. In the end, neither government was willing to merge with the new nation and neither ruler was willing to accept its leadership.

The delegates considered the drafting of a constitution for the new Germany their principal task, and because so many of them were scholars, professors, and lawyers, they threw themselves into this project with great enthusiasm. Members of the committee writing the constitution spent six

1006 / *The Revolutions of 1848*

months constructing a statement of the "Fundamental Rights of the German People." Drawing on the French Declaration of the Rights of Man, the American Declaration of Independence, and other similar documents, they incorporated into their statement the major principles of mid-nineteenth-century liberal philosophy. The result became a part of the constitution completed in March, 1849, which guaranteed the basic liberties of speech, assembly, and the press; it was particularly advanced in its provisions for public education and religious toleration. But by the time the deliberations were over and the draft was completed, circumstances in Germany had changed so significantly that there was little chance for its acceptance.

One issue divided the members of the assembly and prevented them from concluding their task sooner—the question of the boundaries of the new state. One group of delegates favored what came to be known as the *Kleindeutsch* ("Little-German") solution: the inclusion in the new Germany only of Prussia and the lesser German states. Another group of delegates favored the *Grossdeutsch* ("Big-German") solution: the incorporation into the new state, in addition to the territories just named, of the German provinces of Austria (including Bohemia, with its large Slavic population). A compromise was reached in October, 1848: all German territory would be joined in the new nation, but any state with non-German possessions (*i.e.* Austria) would be accepted as part of the new Germany only by abandoning its non-German possessions or by holding them exclusively through a personal union in the crown. This condition meant that Austria could not join the German nation unless the emperor abandoned his Hungarian territories as an integral part of his empire. Such a possibility was remote, and Francis Joseph I (ruled 1848–1916) indicated his attitude toward this solution early in March, 1849, by promulgating a new constitution that reaffirmed the unity and integrity of the Habsburg empire and thus precluded any possibility of the inclusion of Austrian territory in the new Germany. The *Kleindeutsch* faction appeared to have won out, and the Frankfurt Parliament voted not long afterward to offer the crown of the "emperor of the Germans" to the king of Prussia. At first Frederick William IV refused to give a direct reply to the offer, on the grounds that he needed the consent of the princes of the lesser German states. But when twenty-eight princes indicated their willingness to accept the constitution, the king rejected the offer outright and ordered the Prussian delegates to quit the Frankfurt Parliament. He refused to accept what he had earlier termed a "crown picked up from the gutter," like that worn by Louis Philippe.

Austria, too, withdrew its delegates, and a number of lesser states followed. There remained only a "rump" parliament of radicals; these subsequently moved to Stuttgart, in Württemberg, whence they issued appeals to the German people and tried to foment new uprisings. Revolts did occur in a few of the lesser states of Germany in May, 1849, but these were quickly suppressed—in some instances with the support of Prussian troops. The remaining members of the Frankfurt Parliament finally dispersed ignominiously in June, 1849.

Thus ended the attempt of the liberals to establish a united Germany. Had the nation been unified under liberal auspices in 1848 rather than under Prussian leadership, by Bismarck, in the 1860's, the subsequent history of Germany might have been different. It is often argued that instead of becoming an aggressively nationalistic and militaristic state, Germany would then have joined the company of peace-loving nations. But how peace-loving were German liberals? An examination of the deliberations and actions of the Frankfurt Parliament with respect to other nationalities and national groups shows that these liberals were far from tolerant and peace-loving; on the contrary, their speeches reveal exactly the strain of aggressiveness and contempt for other nationalities that recurred in the declarations of succeeding German statesmen.

A case in point involves the attitude of the assembly members toward the Polish minority in the eastern provinces of Prussia. Before 1848 German liberals, like other European liberals, were sympathetic to Polish aspirations for an independent state. As late as April, 1848, in the *Vorparlament,* they talked of a restored Poland with the boundaries of 1772. But, when put to the test, these German liberals reversed their stand. The Poles living in the Prussian province of Posen (where they outnumbered Germans 8 to 5) became restive after the king made some vague promises. They began to demand the autonomy or independence of Posen as a preliminary to the restoration of an independent Poland. A Polish National Committee was set up, but Polish peasants became impatient and rose up against Prussian officials administering the region. When the Prussian government responded by sending in troops, the Poles appealed to the Frankfurt Parliament for support. In the ensuing full-scale debate, in July, 1848, one speaker after another denounced the Polish pretensions and supported Prussian suppression of the revolt. The overwhelming majority of the assembly renounced their earlier sympathy for Polish nationalism because it now appeared to conflict with German national aims. If the eastern provinces of Prussia (such as Posen) were abandoned to the Poles, they would be lost forever to the new German nation. Some of those most emphatic in their speeches were precisely the liberals who had a few months earlier spoken in favor of Polish independence. To justify their position some argued that the Poles had shown themselves unable to maintain their existence as an independent nation and therefore deserved to be subjected to the rule of another people. One delegate declared that Germany's right to dominate the Poles was "the right of the stronger, the right of conquest." Only a small minority of extreme left-wing deputies held out; the Frankfurt Parliament voted 342 to 31 to support Prussian suppression of the Polish bid for independence.

This was not an isolated episode. Another test of German liberalism developed with respect to the Austrian empire. Because of the large German-speaking population in Bohemia, the Frankfurt Parliament considered its inclusion in the new German state. But the even larger Czech population in Bohemia not unnaturally objected to this proposal and talked of a closer union with other Slavic peoples. Where Czech nationalism conflicted with German nationalist goals, most Frankfurt delegates were willing to sacrifice Czech aspirations.

It is impossible to say what kind of Germany the liberals might have established had the Frankfurt Parliament succeeded. But evidence suggests that in 1848 German liberals were no less nationalistic than other Germans. The fact that in the 1860's many liberals rallied to Bismarck when it became clear that he was achieving the unification of Germany seems to confirm this judgment.

The Austrian Empire

Metternich's attempt to stem the tide of change by insulating Austria from the rest of Europe became increasingly difficult in the 1840's. Though the Habsburg empire lagged behind Prussia and some of the other German states in economic development, its chief cities—Vienna, Prague, and Budapest—did not remain immune to industrialization, with its consequent pattern of social change. In the large cities a growing bourgeois class became restive under the backward economic policies of Metternich's government and impatient with the intrusion of the bureaucracy into its business affairs. The small urban proletariat was subject to the same hardships and uncertainties that plagued the working classes elsewhere. Handicraft workers, resentful of the introduction of machines which deprived them of employment, were particularly discontented. The peasants, the overwhelming mass of the population, showed increasing annoyance with one of the few remaining obligations to their landlords, the *robota*, a form of labor rent. When a revolt broke out in Galicia in 1846, the imperial government had to promise to abolish the *robota* in this region, thereby provoking demands during the revolutions of 1848 for its abolition in other parts of the empire.

Subversive political ideas managed to seep into the Austrian empire despite Metternich's strict censorship. Books and pamphlets, smuggled into Bohemia, found their way to universities throughout the empire, which became centers of opposition to the regime. Students exposed to the egalitarian ideas of Rousseau and to the constitutional studies of the German writer Friedrich Dahlmann (1785–1860) envisaged a greater measure of political freedom for Austrians.

Revolution of 1848 in Austria. A *barricade on the Michaeler Platz (St. Michael's Square), Vienna.*

Perhaps the greatest threat to the regime, however, lay in the growing nationalist aspirations of the various peoples of the empire. More than one movement which at the outset had been purely cultural, emphasizing the revival of a national language or literature, had by the 1840's become political, its aim being greater autonomy for a particular national group within the empire. The most noteworthy was the Magyar, or Hungarian, national revival. Under the leadership of Louis Kossuth (1802–1894), a dynamic journalist and orator, Hungarian nationalists in the 1840's demanded the complete autonomy of Hungary and the establishment of a Hungarian national parliament. In 1844 the Hungarian Diet, consisting of representatives of the semifeudal Magyar nobility, abolished Latin as its official language and decreed that Magyar would henceforth be used in all government transactions and in the schools. Similar nationalist revivals occurred among the Czechs of Bohemia, the Croatians on the Adriatic, and the Rumanians of Transylvania, in the eastern region of the empire.

News of the February Revolution in France was the spark dropped into this combustible mass of grievances—social, political, and nationalist. Revolts broke out in the major cities of the empire. In Budapest, Kossuth addressed the Hungarian Diet, denouncing the Metternichian system and calling for a constitution for the empire granting responsible government to Hungary. In Vienna, students drew up a petition to the emperor requesting freedom of speech and the abolition of censorship. When news of Kossuth's speech arrived from Budapest they added, as an afterthought, the demand for a constitution. Despite the relative mildness of their demands the students feared the government's reaction to their petition and therefore enlisted the support of Viennese workers for their demonstrations. On March 13 a clash between the crowd and troops resulted in bloodshed. Fearing further loss of life, Emperor Ferdinand I, like Frederick William IV of Prussia, called off the troops and announced his consent to the demands, including the demand for the convocation of a constituent assembly. On the same day the aged Metternich resigned, after more than half a century of service to the Habsburgs; he left Vienna by common cab and made his way into exile in London. His departure symbolized the end of an era.

From this point on it is difficult to follow events in detail. In Italy, as we shall see, outbreaks in the Austrian territories of Lombardy and Venetia led to an attempt at a war of liberation from the empire. The revolts occurred in several parts of the empire, pursuing a more or less independent course in each. In Budapest the Hungarian Diet moved boldly; it adopted the March Laws, which left Hungary almost independent, joined to the rest of the empire only through allegiance to the emperor. Hungary was to have a regular parliament in place of the Diet, and its own army, budget, and foreign policy. In deference to the peasantry the *robota* was abolished. Though asserting their own autonomy, the Magyars were unwilling to grant it to their subject nationalities. Both Transylvania and Croatia were absorbed into the Hungarian kingdom and their diets were abolished. Ferdinand I, on the defensive throughout the empire, had no alternative for the moment but to accept the new status of his Hungarian possessions.

Prague, the capital of Bohemia and the center of Czech national aspirations, was also the seat of a revolt in March. The initial demands of the revolutionaries were relatively modest; only after the Magyar Diet had passed its March Laws did the Czechs decide to demand their own constitution and virtual autonomy. The imperial government responded with a promise to convoke a constituent assembly and granted the equality of the Czech and German languages in Bohemia. In June the first Pan-Slav Congress assembled in Prague. This body was dominated by Czechs who hoped to demonstrate their solidarity against a proposal of the Frankfurt Parliament to incorporate Bohemia into the new German national state. Though they clearly opposed union with Germany, the Czechs had few specific proposals. They appeared to favor the transformation of the Austrian empire into a federation of nationalities in which the Slavs would have an honorable place along with other national groups. Yet neither the preferences of the Pan-Slav Congress nor the demands of the Czechs for a responsible government of their own received further consideration from the imperial government. A new radical demonstration during June gave General Alfred Windischgrätz (1787–1862), at that time military commander in Prague, a pretext for bringing in reinforcements and ruthlessly suppressing the Czech revolutionary movement. The Pan-Slav Congress was dissolved and Prague was put under a military dictatorship. The seizure of Prague was, in fact, the first victory of the counterrevolutionary forces in the Austrian empire and strengthened the determination of the imperial goverment to proceed against the revolution elsewhere.

In Vienna, despite the revolt in March, there was at first no radical change in the character of the regime. Though the emperor had permitted the establishment there of a national guard composed of civilians and an Academic Legion representing university students, the government remained in the hands of conservative statesmen. Ignoring the emperor's promise to call a constituent assembly, the imperial government in April simply promulgated a new constitution. But this document was not liberal enough to satisfy the radical elements in the capital, and when, in addition, the government attempted to disband the national guard and dissolve the Academic Legion, there was a second uprising, in May, by students, workers and the national guard. The emperor and his family were forced to flee the capital, and took refuge at Innsbruck. The government now agreed to convoke a constituent assembly. This body met in Vienna in July and set to work on a constitution, which turned out to be a far more democratic than the one issued in April. One lasting accomplishment of the assembly, achieved in September, was the abolition of the *robota* in all parts of the empire where this reform had not previously been undertaken. On the surface the revolution seemed to have triumphed in Austria.

But the actual situation was not so clear-cut. From May to October, Vienna remained in the hands of the revolutionaries and the assembly worked at giving constitutional embodiment to the gains of the revolution. But the dynasty had not been overthrown and the army remained loyal to it. While pretending to play along with the constituent assembly, the emperor—or rather the Court party, composed of conservative statesmen and military leaders—encouraged General Windischgrätz to drill his troops in preparation for the recapture of the capital and the suppression of the revolution. In October he had the opportunity to strike. The Viennese radicals, learning that the Court party was moving against the Hungarian revolutionary movement, staged a third insurrection, in the course of which they seized the unpopular minister of war and beat him to death in the streets. This act of violence was used by Windischgrätz as a pretext for treating Vienna as he had treated Prague. He bombarded the city with artillery and by the end of the month had occupied it. Many of the radical leaders were executed on the spot. The constituent assembly was exiled to the Moravian town of Kremsier. To all intents and purposes the revolution in Vienna had been defeated by October, 1848.

Among the adherents to the counterrevolutionary cause in Austria the conviction had grown during 1848 that it was essential to secure the abdication of the feebleminded Emperor Ferdinand I if the power of the Habsburgs was to be restored. After the October revolt, Prince Felix zu Schwarzenberg (1800–1852), the new principal leader of the government, succeeded in convincing the emperor to yield the throne to his eighteen-year-old nephew. Assuming the crown in December, 1848, Francis Joseph I ruled Austria for sixty-eight years, until his death during the First World War. The young emperor was unhampered by the promises Ferdinand had made to the revolutionaries. With Schwarzenberg, who remained as the chief minister, he was determined to restore the power of the imperial house. They did not immediately feel strong enough to dismiss the constituent assembly meeting at Kremsier, but allowed it to complete its deliberations before dissolving it in March, 1849. However, Schwarzenberg rejected the constitution drawn up by this body, which would have established a decentralized, federal government, and instead issued his own. Like Frederick William's constitution in Prussia, this document contained liberal features, such as a diet of elected representatives and a responsible ministry, but having issued it, Schwarzenberg announced that it would come into operation only when the "provisional emergency" confronting Austria had ended. Meanwhile he governed the country autocratically. Schwarzenberg also put an end for the time being to the aspirations of non-German nationalities for greater autonomy by establishing a highly centralized administrative system.

There remained one last smoldering of the outbreaks in the Habsburg empire—the Hungarian revolt. Efforts to suppress this revolt had begun before Francis Joseph came to the throne in December. The way in which the counterrevolutionary Court party handled this problem is particularly complex. At first they merely gave unofficial encouragement to the Croatians, a dissident south Slavic people living under Magyar rule, when they revolted against the new Hungarian regime and sought autonomy from it. But by the end of 1848, the government at Vienna had decided on an all-out effort to suppress the Hungarian revolutionary movement, and ordered an invasion of Hungary by imperial troops. The invaders were no match for the Hungarian defenders, who under Kossuth's leadership, drove them out of the country. Had the suppression of the Magyar revolt been left exclusively to the Austrian armies, Hungary might have emerged an independent state in 1849. In April, the Hungarian parliament proclaimed a Hungarian republic, ending the tie with the Habsburgs and made Kossuth president. At this juncture, however, Tsar Nicholas I of Russia, always the enemy of revolutionary movements and fearful that the success of the Hungarian movement might set off a revolt in Poland, offered military assistance to the Austrian emperor. A joint invasion of Hungary by Austrian troops from the west and 140,000 Russian troops from the north took place in June, 1849. The Hungarians, commanded by General Arthur von Görgey (1818–1916), resisted fiercely, but weakened by further revolts of national minorities at home, they surrendered in August. Despite promises by the Austrian general, Baron Julius von Haynau (1786–1853), of clemency for the defenders, the victors wrought a bloody vengeance, flogging, hanging and shooting their victims. Kossuth managed to escape to Turkey and eventually reached the United States, where he made a prolonged speaking tour in an effort to raise money for Hungary's liberation.

The defeat of the Hungarians marked the end of the revolutions of 1848–1849 in the Austrian empire. Hungary, along with the rest of the empire, lost all semblance of autonomy and was thenceforth controlled absolutely from Vienna. Despite the provisions for a responsible ministry and a representative diet in the constitution promulgated by Schwarzenberg in 1849, Austria was thereafter ruled just as autocratically and a good deal more efficiently than under Metternich. In the end, the revolutions of 1848–1849 brought no improvement in the situation of the various nationalities within the empire, and in fact, sharpened the tensions among them. One of the few lasting results of the revolutions was the abolition of the *robota*; this benefited the peasantry, but it may also be one explanation for the failure of the uprisings. For once the peasants had secured this concession they were no longer interested in the fate of the revolutions, which faltered without the support of the masses, and could ultimately be suppressed by the emperor.

THE REVOLUTIONS OF 1848 IN ITALY

The events of 1848–1849 in Italy fall naturally into three phases: first, the separate revolts that took place in many of the states and in the territories under Austrian rule; second, the war for Italian independence from Austrian domination, led by King Charles Albert of Sardinia; and third, the short-lived attempt by Mazzini and others to establish the Roman Republic. As elsewhere in Europe, all the revolutions in Italy apparently ended in failure; yet in fact they marked a significant step forward in the process of Italian unification, for through them the revolutionaries learned certain important lessons.

The series of revolts began with the January uprising in Sicily. Ferdinand II, king of Naples and Sicily, the first ruler in Europe affected by a revolution in 1848, granted a constitution to his people much like the French Charter of 1830. From the southernmost state in Italy the revolts spread northward. Grand Duke Leopold of Tuscany (1797–1870) was the next to yield to the demands of his people for a constitution. In Sardinia, the Moderates, including Count Cavour, prevailed upon Charles Albert to promulgate the constitution known as the *Statuto*, which a decade later became the basis for the constitution of the unified kingdom of Italy. Pope Pius IX, who had already given some evidence of liberal tendencies, followed suit by granting a constitution to the Papal States, though he took care to reserve to the pope and the College of Cardinals the power to veto the acts of an elective council of deputies. Finally, the revolts spread into Lombardy and Venetia, the regions directly under Austrian rule. In January, the chief city of Lombardy, Milan, had experienced riots directed against an unpopular tax on tobacco. In March, the news of the revolt in Vienna and the flight of Metternich precipitated in Milan what came to be known as the Five Glorious Days (March 18–22), an outbreak of fierce street fighting which forced the Austrian general, Joseph Radetzky (1766–1858), to abandon Lombardy. At about the same time a republic was declared in Venice after a short uprising; its first president was Daniele Manin (1804–1857), a political prisoner released by Austrian authorities upon the outbreak of the revolt there. By the latter part of March, then, each of the major Italian states had experienced a significant political crisis, though only in Milan had serious fighting occurred.

The spirit and courage shown by the Milanese inspired the liberals and moderates of Sardinia to call for an Italian war of liberation from Austrian domination. King Charles Albert, far from enthusiastic about allying himself with the revolutionary cause, was nevertheless persuaded by his advisers to assume leadership and accordingly invaded Lombardy on March 22. At the same time, he appealed for the support of all the other Italian rulers in ridding the peninsula of the hated Austrians. So great was the enthusiasm for the national cause at the outset that even Ferdinand of Naples felt obligated to supply a contingent of troops to the Sardinians, and what was more surprising, a force from the Papal States joined briefly in the war for independence, although it was withdrawn almost immediately in the face of Austrian protests. Despite his enthusiasm for the cause of Italian unity, Pius IX, as spiritual leader of Catholics throughout the world, could hardly undertake a war against Catholic Austria. The Italian forces led by Sardinia fought against heavy odds. Although enthusiastic and patriotic, they suffered from a lack of discipline, and before long dissension developed between the moderate Sardinians, whose goal was a constitutional monarchy under Charles Albert, and the republican forces which had joined them. The newly established Venetian republic had no intention of dissolving itself in order to submit to the rule of Sardinia. By May, the contingent from Naples had been withdrawn; a counterrevolution had restored absolute control there to Ferdinand. Though Charles Albert's armies won some important victories, in the last analysis they were no match for the better-disciplined armies of General Radetzky. By July, 1848, Radetzky had consolidated his forces, and he inflicted an overwhelming defeat on the Sardinians at Custoza.Within ten days he had driven them from Austrian territory and imposed an armistice by which Charles Albert agreed to abandon any claim to Lombardy. A brief epilogue occurred the following spring when Charles Albert, charging the Austrians with having violated the terms of the armistice, once again attacked, but he suffered a decisive defeat at the Battle of Novara in March, 1849. The Austrian government was now free to complete the counterrevolution in territories under its control. Last to succumb was the Venetian republic, which yielded in August, 1849, after heroically resisting a five-week siege.

The most radical event during the Italian revolutions was unquestionably the establishment of the Roman Republic in February, 1849. Despite Pope Pius IX's initial concessions, radical elements in Rome became increasingly dissatisfied with his regime and particularly with the prime minister, Count Pellegrino Rossi, who was appointed in September, 1848. In November a fanatical democrat assassinated Rossi and Pius fled Rome, taking refuge in Naples. With the pope gone, the Romans elected a constituent assembly, which met in February, 1849, proclaimed the overthrow of the pope as temporal ruler, and established the Roman Republic. Although the revolutionaries controlled only Rome and its immediate environs, the Roman Republic was to be the nucleus of a unified Italian state. Giuseppe Mazzini was summoned to head a triumvirate which would rule the new republic. This was the fulfillment of his lifelong dream; Mazzini issued decrees calling for the confiscation of Church lands for distribution to the peasantry, public housing for the poor, and other humanitarian measures. But from the first the government was beset by serious inflation and appeared unable to solve its economic difficulties. Even if foreign intervention had not ended the Roman Republic, it would probably have collapsed in a matter of months.

Intervention on behalf of the pope came, surprisingly enough, not from a conservative central European state, but from the Second French Republic of Louis Napoleon. Leading the French assembly to believe that the move was being undertaken to forestall Austrian ambitions in Italy, Louis Napoleon secured approval for an expeditionary force. His real motive seems to have been a desire to win the support of French Catholics for his regime. In any case, he underestimated the difficulties of the enterprise and the strength of feeling in Rome for the republic; French forces attacking Rome met fierce resistance. Defenders of the city had been hastily organized by Giuseppe Garibaldi (1807–1882), whose exploits at this time won him a reputation throughout Europe. Unquestionably the most colorful figure of the *Risorgimento,* Garibaldi had been forced into exile in 1834 for his role in a plot against the government of Sardinia. With a price on his head he fled to South America, where he fought for revolutionary movements in Brazil and Uruguay. Garibaldi, the son of a sailor, consciously identified himself throughout his life with the cause of oppressed peoples everywhere, but his highest dream remained the establishment of a unified Italian republic. When he returned to Italy during the revolutions of 1848, his countrymen found him a striking figure, with his long blond hair, somewhat rough manner, and the distinctive red shirt which he and his followers adopted as part of their uniform. After leading a volunteer legion in Charles Albert's unsuccessful war against Austria, Garibaldi rallied to the Roman Republic. Despite their initial successes, his ill-equipped and ill-trained forces were in the long run no match for the more numerous and better-disciplined French armies. In July, 1849, after an existence of only five months, the Roman Republic capitulated. Garibaldi led his band in a heroic retreat across the Italian peninsula. Most of his followers died or were captured, but he ultimately escaped to the United States, where he remained until he could return to Italy in the 1850's to help complete Italian unification. After the collapse of the Roman Republic the pope returned to Rome under the protection of a French garrison, which Louis Napoleon maintained there until 1870.

By the end of the summer of 1849 the revolutionary movement appeared to have been defeated everywhere in the Italian peninsula. Only in Sardinia a moderate regime remained. There Charles Albert, after his second defeat by the Austrians at Novara in March, 1849, had abdicated in favor of his son Victor Emmanuel II, and retired to a Portuguese monastery. The new young monarch succeeded in winning less harsh terms than had been expected from the Austrian empire, including permission to retain the constitution granted by his father the year before.

Despite the apparent failure of the revolutionaries in most of Italy, the events of 1848–1849 provided at least three valuable lessons for patriots striving for Italian unification. First, this unification could not be accomplished under papal leadership, as those in the Neo-Guelph movement had hoped before 1848. The pope's withdrawal of his troops from the Italian army of liberation just after the initial attack on the Austrian forces discredited him as a potential leader of a unified Italy, though his defenders might argue that he had had no alternative because of his position as spiritual leader of the Catholic world. If the Neo-Guelph cause suffered in 1848, the chances of Sardinian leadership in the unification of Italy certainly improved. Here was the second important lesson of the events of 1848–1849. The Sardinians had resisted Austria, and the new king, Victor Emmanuel II, in refusing to renounce the liberal constitution of 1848 as Radetzky demanded, further enhanced the prestige of Sardinia among liberals everywhere in Italy. But the final, and perhaps most important, lesson learned in

1848 was this: Italians alone could not eject the Austrians from Italy. Though the Austrian armies had retreated initially in 1848 and the Austrians had made certain concessions, their power in Italy had never been destroyed. Among those who recognized that foreign help would be necessary was Count Cavour, who in 1851 became the prime minister of Sardinia. Convinced that Sardinia alone was not up to the task, he made his principal diplomatic goal in the 1850's the acquisition of allies for the war against Austria which he considered essential for the unification of Italy under Sardinia's rule.

CONSEQUENCES OF THE REVOLUTIONS OF 1848

Not long after the failure of the revolutions of 1848, the French anarchist Pierre Joseph Proudhon (1809–1865) wrote, ". . . we have been beaten and humiliated . . . scattered, imprisoned, disarmed and gagged. The fate of European democracy has slipped from our hands. . . ."[3] Most of the revolutionaries throughout Europe must have reacted in this way. Begun with such high hopes, the uprisings produced results that were indeed disappointing. Almost without exception the rulers who were challenged in 1848 managed to reassert their authority by 1849. Where constitutions had been granted, they were withdrawn or replaced by documents which denied the very principles for which the revolutionaries had struggled. The revolutions appeared to have been fought in vain; yet they were certainly not without their consequences, both immediate and long-range. In the judgment of one historian, the revolutions "crystallized ideas and projected the pattern of things to come."[4]

The long-range impact of the revolutions was to be felt for at least the next fifty years. The experience of 1848–1849 certainly crystallized and focused the urge toward national unity that was already present during the first half of the nineteenth century. Whether the revolutions provided a comparable impetus to the ultimate achievement of *liberal* goals is more debatable. The dissolution of elected assemblies, as in Prussia and Austria, the rejection by the monarchs of the constitutions drafted by these bodies, and the suppression of individual freedoms that characterized the postrevolutionary era suggest that the defeat of liberalism was nearly total. But the revolutionaries set precedents for subsequent generations of European liberals and democrats. And certain institutions managed to survive the conservative reaction of 1849—for example, universal manhood suffrage in France. Louis Napoleon came to power in France by means of universal suffrage, and no subsequent regime there has attempted to dispense with it. The prin-

[3] Quoted in *The Opening of an Era: 1848*, ed. by François Fejtö (London, 1948), p. 414.

[4] Lewis B. Namier, *Avenues of History* (London, 1952), p. 55.

Manifest

der

Kommunistischen Partei.

Veröffentlicht im Februar 1848.

Proletarier aller Länder vereinigt euch.

London.
Gedruckt in der Office der „Bildungs-Gesellschaft für Arbeiter"
von J. E. Burghard.
46, Liverpool Street. Bishopsgate.

Title page of the Communist Manifesto, 1848. *The final words of the Manifesto appear on the title page: "Proletarians of all countries! Unite!"*

ciple, once established in France, became the goal of democrats and radicals throughout Europe. Indeed, the trust put in universal suffrage after the mid-century revolutions corresponds to the faith put in constitutions during the first half of the nineteenth century.

Perhaps the most unequivocal consequence of the failure of the revolutions of 1848 was the destruction of working-class hopes and illusions. With their leaders dead, in hiding, or in exile, the workers did indeed appear "beaten and humiliated...scattered, imprisoned, disarmed and gagged." But even here the revolts served an important function: they foreshadowed a significant change in the character of European socialism and the working-class movement by creating a strong sense of class consciousness among the proletariat. Karl Marx, writing of the revolt in France, declared, "The February republic finally brought the rule of the bourgeoisie clearly into prominence, since it struck off the crown behind which Capital kept itself concealed."[5] Perhaps Marx exaggerated, but clearly events such as the

[5] Karl Marx, *The Class Struggles in France* (1848–50) (New York, 1934), p. 41.

June Days in France and the brutal suppression of the Vienna insurrection in October could not help sharpening the class consciousness of European workers. Up to 1848 they had more often than not been allied with the middle class against the old order, and they fought on the same side of the barricades in many places during the initial phases of the uprisings. But as the revolts progressed, the bourgeoisie, increasingly concerned over the extremism of the mob and the alleged threat to private property, tended to line up with the old order or at least with those intent upon suppressing the threat of a thoroughgoing social revolution. In time, the bitterness and class antagonisms created by the events of 1848 declined, but the possibilities for genuine collaboration between capitalist and proletarian, employer and employee, were never quite the same. It is significant that the First International Workingmen's Association, dedicated to the overthrow of the bourgeoisie, came into being in 1864, a mere decade and a half after 1848.

Finally, a less tangible but no less important consequence of the revolts was the change in the climate of opinion in Europe. Such changes of mood are, of course, difficult to define, and even more difficult to substantiate. But the literature of a given era certainly provides a clue to its mood; other forms of art may reflect it as well. And there is general agreement that the era following the revolutions was characterized by a marked change of atmosphere, frequently reflected in the writings of the time. If one word may be singled out to characterize this new atmosphere, it is "realism." The realistic attitude can be seen in politics, in the conduct of international relations, in class relationships, in a new emphasis on science and technology, as well as in literature.

To tie this new attitude directly to the failure of the revolutions of 1848 is, of course, to raise a host of problems concerning historical causation. Yet it is undeniable that the shattering of the romantic hopes of the revolutionaries and the discrediting of pre-1848 utopian illusions resulted in a more sober evaluation by contemporaries of the world in which they found themselves. The goals of Europeans did not change radically after the experience of 1848–1849, but individuals and groups came to view their goals from a different perspective. Instead of envisioning their ends idealistically, they now tended to evaluate more realistically the concrete means for achieving them. And they very often reached the conclusion that abstract ideals and principles were less important in securing their goals than were power and force. A new tough-mindedness characterized the generation of the 1850's and 1860's, and this mood resulted largely from the disillusionment of 1848–1849. For these reasons the revolutions constituted a significant turning point in the history of nineteenth-century Europe.

Part V

THE AGE OF NATIONALISM
AND REFORM
1850–1890

Introduction

ALMOST EVERY PERIOD in the history of modern Europe can be described as an age of revolution of some kind, and the last half of the nineteenth century is no exception. These years saw a continuation and acceleration of the scientific, technological, and social revolutions that were already well under way in many parts of Europe, but their distinguishing feature was the eruption of national revolutions in every part of the continent: in Ireland and Poland, the Balkans and Hungary, Italy and Germany.

National revolution was no new phenomenon in European history. There had been a strong element of nationalism in the struggle of Joan of Arc against the English, in the Protestant Reformation, and in the French Revolution. In the later nineteenth century, however, the spirit of nationalism flared with new intensity, and it is not too much to say that the mystique of nationalism was the major ideological force making for change in European politics and society.

Between 1815 and 1848 the forces of change had been held in check with considerable success by the European governments. Some historians categorically reject the term "Concert of Europe" to describe the cooperation among the powers in these years, and indeed their dissonances were frequently more in evidence than their harmony. Yet the statesmen of this period, whose political ideas had been shaped by the French Revolution and the Napoleonic wars, generally felt that it was safer to settle their differences by diplomacy than by war, for it seemed to them that even a successful war might unleash revolutionary forces they would be unable to control. Even the British, who are supposed to have seceded from the Concert when it became an instrument of oppression, pursued an independent course only when they could do so with impunity. Whenever British interests were seriously affected by events on the Continent, British statesmen took a prominent place in the councils of the major powers.

The international system established in 1815 survived the revolutions of 1848, but in the course of those revolutions some of the foremost champions

1023

of international conservatism, including Klemens von Metternich, whose name had become synonymous with the old order, were swept away, and were succeeded by statesmen whose memories of 1789 were dim, or whose ambitions transcended the common interests of the European monarchies.

Foremost among the new leaders was Napoleon III, whose principal foreign-policy objective was to release France from the restrictions imposed by the 1815 treaties. His big opportunity came with the Crimean War, which temporarily put an end to effective co-operation among the great powers. He attempted to follow up this success by encouraging national revolutions in the spheres of interest of rival powers, hoping through the leadership of these national movements to re-establish French ascendancy on the Continent. He was to find, however, that he had conjured up forces he was unable to control, and that the breakdown of the Concert of Europe had cleared the way for political opportunists more ruthless and skillful than he. In the end he was destroyed by the forces he had done so much to release.

By 1871 the Italians and Germans had achieved political unification in independent national states, and the Hungarians had been granted quasi-independence within a new Austro-Hungarian empire. The successful example of these nations gave fresh impetus to others. The Irish became a major problem in Great Britain; Russia and Austria-Hungary were racked by national dissension; and the Ottoman empire in the Balkans began to fall asunder as Montenegrins and Serbs, Rumanians and Bulgars, followed the lead of the Greeks in overthrowing Turkish overlordship and gaining partial or complete independence. By far the most important of the new nation-states was the German empire, whose emergence on the political scene as the foremost military power in Europe invalidated all previous conceptions of the relations among the powers. After the establishment of the German empire, however, the governments of Europe began to cooperate anew, and developed the precarious international stability that endured until 1914.

Meanwhile, nationalism itself exploded into expansionism. Hardly had some of the new nations asserted their own identity than they aspired to conquest over others. Italians and Germans vied with British, French, and Russians for the spoils of empire, while on a smaller scale the new Balkan nations sought to expand at the expense of Turkey, Austria and one another.

The national revolutions were not caused by nationalism alone. They took place in a period of unprecedented social and economic dislocation. Industrialization, population increases, the mass migration of people from the country to the city, wrought a fundamental transformation in European life and society. To deal with these social and economic changes, all European governments were obliged to recognize the need for far-reaching revisions in their policies, laws, and institutions—in short, for reform.

In Great Britain, with its strong traditions of parliamentary government, most advocates of reform looked to Parliament to bring about the necessary changes through legislation; their most significant political agitation was for a further extension of the franchise, which would enable people to influence this legislation. The confidence of British reformers in parliamentary government was justified; their country passed through the social and economic crises of the nineteenth century without major upheavals. The British government served as a model for people of all states who wished to bring about political changes by peaceful means.

On the Continent, most of the parliamentary governments established in 1848 or earlier were discredited by their inability to satisfy the needs and aspirations of the people they represented. Instead, the requirements of a changing society were generally met by authoritarian governments, many of them operating behind a constitutional-parliamentary façade. The failure of genuine parliamentary government among the continental great powers was due not only to the weakness of parliamentary forces and traditions, but to the absence of the feature most necessary for its successful operation: broad agreement among the main power groups in a country about fundamental issues. Britain experienced the effect of this lack of agreement in dealing with the Irish, who by the end of the nineteenth century demanded national independence, which the English were not prepared to concede. Most continental governments were faced with many Irelands. The new German empire, for example, was forced to deal with a centuries-old heritage of political and religious cleavage—hostility between Bavarians and Prussians, Prussians and Poles, Protestants and Catholics—in addition to the social and class conflicts between landlords and peasants, factory owners and workers. These were differences so great that it seemed impossible to maintain the new empire, much less to govern it effectively, without a strong, centralized executive authority.

Whether the government of a state was parliamentary or authoritarian, however, its policies were carried out by the professional bureaucracy that staffed the various administrative departments. Although the bureaucracy was the indispensable tool of government leadership, it should not be confused with leadership itself. The professional bureaucrats ensured the continuous functioning of government processes; they might exercise enormous influence on government heads; but the crucial power to determine government policy remained in the hands of the executive leadership. Hence the quality of leadership in every country was at all times of paramount importance. In states where supreme power was vested in an authoritarian executive, no single aspect of life or society was more significant than the personality of this ruler.

As the nineteenth century progressed, the state assumed, or was obliged to assume, ever greater powers and responsibilities. It was the state that enacted—and enforced—laws for freeing the serfs, that supervised working conditions in mines and factories, that built sewers and water lines for the new cities, that provided facilities for free (and compulsory) elementary education. Finally, it was the state that protected its citizens from disorder at home and threats from abroad, that realized the aspirations of patriots for national unity, that responded to demands of people in all countries for glory and empire.

As the functions of the state expanded, so did the bureaucracy. The innovations of science and technology were bent to its needs. The telegraph and the printing press, the railroad and the steamship, the machine gun and the rifled steel cannon, became instruments of government departments, secret police, armies, navies, and tax collectors. Programs of compulsory military training by all continental great powers forced every able-bodied man into the service of the state; compulsory education provided the opportunity to indoctrinate each citizen with principles of patriotism and loyalty to the state.

By the end of the nineteenth century, the state had acquired unprecedented power to establish control over the minds and bodies of men, control actually welcomed by many nationalists and reformers who saw in the state the most effective instrument for the realization of their ideals. In countries where the government was traditionally associated with political oppression—for example, in Russia—anarchism and related political doctrines rejecting every kind of state authority claimed numerous adherents. But only a few isolated prophets like the German philosopher Friedrich Nietzsche and the Russian novelist Fëdor Dostoevski envisaged clearly what the ultimate consequences of state control might be. For the most part the growth of state power went unheeded in the atmosphere of optimism and confidence in human progress that characterized the era.

CHAPTER 30

The Civilization of Industrialism

By 1850 the Industrial Revolution had already been under way in Europe for well over a hundred years, primarily in Great Britain. During the second half of the nineteenth century this revolution gathered momentum and spread to every part of the Europeanized world. In no previous period in history did man's ability to produce increase more rapidly or more dramatically.

THE REVOLUTION IN PRODUCTION

The revolution in production was the result of a large number of interrelated factors. Fundamental among these was the development of new sources of power. The steam engine, which had freed man from dependence on human or animal labor, or on such natural forces as wind and water, was steadily improved. The compound engine came into general use after 1850, and the even more efficient turbine engine was developed in 1884. Since the principal fuel of the steam engine was coal, the general employment of steam power was closely connected with the improvement of mining machinery, which made possible substantial expansion in the production of coal.

Coal and the steam engine were soon to be supplemented or supplanted by new sources of power and new engines. Natural gas had been used for street lighting and fuel since the beginning of the nineteenth century. An internal-combustion engine, powered by natural gas, was invented in 1862, but the relative lightness and mobility of this machine were not fully exploited until the 1880's, when liquid petroleum, more easily stored and transported than natural gas, was successfully used as its fuel. The success of the petroleum-driven internal-combustion engine soon swelled the demand for oil, which was found in abundant quantities in such diverse places as southern Russia (Baku), Borneo, and Texas, and was tapped with the aid of new oil-drilling machinery. In the twentieth century petroleum became a major rival to coal as a source of power.

A more immediate rival was electricity. As early as 1831 Michael Faraday (1791–1867) had demonstrated that the movement of a coil of wire through a magnetic field produces a flow of electric current through the wire, but it was not until 1870 that an efficient electric generator was produced. The importance of this invention was greatly enhanced soon afterward by the discovery of the rotating magnetic field, which made possible the long-distance transmission of electric power. During the following decade, alternators and transformers for producing high-voltage alternating currents were developed, and central stations for the production of electric power were established in many parts of Europe. Electricity was a particular boon to countries without large supplies of coal, for water and even wind could be harnessed to generate electric current. The perfection in 1879 of the incandescent electric light by Thomas A. Edison (1847–1931) inaugurated the era in which electricity became the principal source of artificial light. In that same year Werner von Siemens (1816–1892) demonstrated the application of electric power to the railway. Besides serving as an increasingly important source of light and power, electricity made possible numerous scientific and industrial processes, such as electroplating, and entire new industries, such as the manufacture of aluminum.

New engines and new sources of power were harnessed to an ever-growing variety of new machines. The importance of coal-mining and oil-drilling machinery has already been mentioned. Equally vital was machinery for mining iron ore, the principal metal of industrial construction. At the same time, more sophisticated machinery was constantly being introduced in the textile industry, where the Industrial Revolution had begun. By the end of the nineteenth century there was scarcely any industry that had not been revolutionized by machine technology, including the manufacture of machines themselves. The private household, too, began to experience the effects of this revolution with the invention in 1846 of the sewing machine, the first of the myriad of household gadgets that were to ease the labors of the housewife.

Inseparable from the revolution in power and machinery was the revolution in construction materials. Steel, heretofore rare and expensive, was essential in the manufacture of the precision, high-compression engine and many of the other new machines. In 1856 Sir Henry Bessemer (1813–1898) perfected a process for making steel by blowing oxygen through molten iron, and thereby made possible the mass production of steel. Steel manufacture was aided further by the development between 1864 and 1868 of the Siemens-Martin process for refining low-grade ores and scrap iron, and in 1878 of the Thomas-Gilchrist process for removing the phosphorus that had previously rendered large ore deposits in Europe unsuitable for steel production. By the end of the century, steel had supplanted other forms of iron as the chief metal in industrial construction.

Manufacturing steel by the Bessemer process. *This 1875 engraving shows molten pig iron (top, center) being poured into a metal mixer (right), while in the converter (left) a blast of oxygen causes the reactions that transform the mixture of low-grade ores into steel. Workers pour the molten steel by ladle into ingot molds (bottom, center).*

New mining machinery and refining techniques had meanwhile increased the availability of other metals, such as copper and lead. In 1886 came the revolutionary discovery of the Hall-Héroult electrolytic process for deriving aluminum from bauxite, which permitted the mass production of this light, malleable, noncorrosive, yet sturdy metal.

Scarcely less significant than the discoveries in the field of metallurgy was the development by the mid-nineteenth century of a high quality of Portland cement. Its superior strength as a mortar facilitated construction with such traditional materials as stone and brick, but its greatest importance was in the production of concrete, an ancient building material consisting of cement, sand, and stone or gravel. With the new, high-grade Portland cement, concrete could be molded into manifold sizes and shapes, with varying degrees of hardness and resiliency. Unlike earlier concrete, it would harden under water and was thus especially valuable for installations such as dams and harbors. The practice of strengthening concrete with iron or steel bars (resulting in "reinforced concrete") further extended the possibilities of its use.

The development of Portland cement and of techniques for the mass production of steel and aluminum were aspects of the revolution taking place in the field of chemistry. By the end of the nineteenth century the manufacture of chemicals had become a major industry in its own right as a result of the discovery of relatively economical methods for producing critical and heretofore scarce items, and the invention of an impressive array of new ones. Sulfuric and hydrochloric acid, ammonia, alkalis, soaps, bleaches, animal and vegetable oils, drugs, and photographic agents were all produced at prices that permitted their large-scale use in the industrial and domestic economy. Synthetic dyes were manufactured from coal tar, cheap paper and artificial silk (rayon) from wood pulp. In 1867 Alfred Nobel (1833–1896) invented a safe method for making dynamite from nitroglycerin, and twenty years later, combining nitroglycerin with guncotton, he developed a powerful and almost smokeless powder that was to revolutionize the armament industry.

Chemistry's most important contribution, however, was the discovery of methods for producing cheap artificial fertilizers, which contributed to a revolution in agricultural production that was in many ways even more important than the Industrial Revolution. This agricultural revolution put an end, at least temporarily, to the chronic threat of famine in Europe. For the first time in history it became possible to support a significant growth of population on a fixed amount of land.

The agricultural revolution was not brought about by artificial fertilizers alone. It owed much to changes in farming equipment—the use of steel for such traditional tools as the plow and the cultivator, and the invention of the reaper and the threshing machine—and to scientific experiments that led to improvements in seed strains and in the breeds of domestic animals. In northern and eastern Europe no innovation was more important than the widespread cultivation of the potato, a plant that could be grown on poor soil, that was comparatively insensitive to the vicissitudes of weather, and that yielded from two to four times as much food as wheat and other cereals.

At the same time that its own agricultural production was increasing, Europe began to have access to immense supplies of food from abroad. Vast new acreages were brought under cultivation in Asiatic Russia, the Americas, and Australia. The products of these and other lands were now made available to Europe in abundant quantities and at prices most people could afford as a result of yet another nineteenth-century revolution, this one in transportation.

Better road construction, the paving of a few highways, and the extension of Europe's canal network had brought about some improvement, but the principal revolutionizing agent of transportation in the nineteenth century was the railroad. For the first time the large-scale, economical, and rapid distribution of goods overland became possible, and even the secluded interiors of the larger European countries developed into producing areas and markets. Perishable goods were shipped long distances packed in ice and sawdust (the first refrigerator car was used on railroads in 1851). A

The Great Eastern, launched in 1857. *Built of iron and equipped with a screw propeller as well as paddle wheels, this "Wonder of the Seas" was five times larger than any ship ever built and in terms of displacement the largest to be built until 1907. It was from this ship that the first transatlantic cable was laid in 1866.*

Gottlieb Daimler (1834–1900) in his first "horseless carriage." *It was driven by a petroleum-powered internal-combustion engine.*

mechanical method of refrigeration, invented in 1867, was introduced on ships in 1880 and soon became standard equipment on oceangoing vessels, but railroads continued to use ice-and-sawdust refrigeration for many years because it was cheaper. The railroads were crucial to the growth of great urban industrial centers, for they provided a means of transporting large supplies of coal and raw materials to the cities, and of distributing finished products to other areas.

Most of the great railroad lines in western Europe were built in the second half of the nineteenth century. During this same period the steamship, equipped with a compound engine and driven by a screw propeller, supplanted the sailing vessel for water transport, while iron, and by 1870 steel, replaced wood in the construction of ships. In 1879 the electric streetcar made its first appearance and rapidly displaced horsedrawn vehicles as the chief means of urban public transport. In 1887 the internal-combustion engine, with petroleum as its fuel, was successfully used in an automobile, which was to revolutionize transportation in the next century. More immediately important was the invention in 1876 of the safety bicycle, driven by the rear wheel, which became the most popular mechanical means of private transportation. To the development of both the bicycle and the automobile, the invention of the pneumatic tire in 1889 was fundamental.

Changes and progress in the field of communication were equally rapid. The electric telegraph was invented in 1844. In 1851 the first submarine cable was laid, between Dover and Calais. A transatlantic cable in 1866 was followed by a cable from Europe to India in 1870 and one from Europe to Hong Kong in 1872. In 1876 came the invention of the telephone, which by the end of the century had become a standard fixture in most government and business offices and in some private homes. The typewriter came into general commercial use in the 1870's. In all European countries there were great improvements in the postal services. In 1875 the Universal Postal Union, with headquarters in Switzerland, was established to regulate and supervise international mail service.

The mass communication of news was facilitated by the perfection of high-speed printing presses and machines for the rapid setting of type—the rotary press in 1875, the linotype and monotype machines in 1885, and the straight-line press in 1889. These inventions, with the simultaneous development of an inexpensive process for making paper, meant that news-papers could be produced cheaply, at least in countries where the taxes on them had been abolished. By the end of the century the newspaper was more influential in molding public opinion than ever before.

The pace of industrial production was quickened by the formation of great corporations—joint-stock companies, trusts, and cartels, which made possible the large-scale and more efficient manufacture of goods. Although often more shoddy than articles fabricated by hand in small shops, mass-produced goods were far cheaper. Mass production thus made many items available to large numbers of people and was decisive in the creation of a mass market. The European economy continued to be dominated by small business establishments, but large companies provided the chief impetus for industrial expansion.

The founding of investment banks and the use of new credit devices made greater supplies of money available for business expansion. But the most important factor in the growth of big business in the nineteenth century was the general recognition accorded to the principle of limited liability, which meant that investors were not threatened with the loss of all their resources when a company failed. With the risk of investment lowered, individuals and institutions with surplus capital were tempted by the prospect of large profits to invest in business enterprises. Entrepreneurs thus found it easier to sell stocks and bonds to raise the money needed for expansion. Governments, too, began to sell bonds to the public, thus freeing themselves from dependence on loans from private banks. The stock exchange, where securities were bought and sold, became the center of the European business world. By the end of the nineteenth century the focus of European investment had changed from land to securities.

A major reason for the relaxation of official restrictions on business enterprises was that in the later nineteenth century most European governments became aware of the contribution such enterprises could make to their countries' strength and welfare. To an increasing extent governments not only eased economic restrictions, but actively aided the development of business and agriculture through state-sponsored banks, direct subsidies, tax concessions, and tariffs.

Despite the marked rise in protective tariffs toward the end of the century, international trade flourished as never before. Linked by an international monetary system based on the gold standard, the economies of the various European countries became so interwoven that all of them went through similar cycles of prosperity and depression. The depression of the 1840's, so significant a part of the background of the revolutions of 1848, was followed by prosperity in the 1850's. Then in 1857 came a financial crash, and what has been called the first worldwide economic depression. The bank failures in Europe had been set off by overexpansion and unsound banking practices in the United States, where much European money was invested. The resulting financial chaos struck both industry and agriculture and affected the markets of South America and the Far East. Economic revival in Europe came quickly after 1859, to be followed by another slump in 1866, another revival, and in 1873, another great financial crash. The European economy remained depressed throughout the 1870's; agriculture in particular suffered from an influx of cheap grain from America. It revived with the widespread introduction of protective tariffs in the 1880's, and by 1890 a large part of Europe was enjoying relative prosperity.

SOCIAL CONSEQUENCES OF THE INDUSTRIAL REVOLUTION

Demographic Changes

The new abundance of agricultural and manufactured goods in the nineteenth century was accompanied by a large population increase, which provided the labor force—and the consumer demand—to sustain the industrial expansion. A rise in the birthrate in some parts of Europe was accompanied by a marked fall in the death rate, as a result of advances in medical knowledge and improvements in public and private sanitation.

Pasteur in his laboratory.

The application of the theories of Joseph Lister (1827–1912) concerning the need for antiseptic surgery lowered the incidence of death due to blood poisoning in surgical operations, and was particularly important in reducing infant mortality, hitherto one of the major causes of premature death in Europe. Robert Koch (1843–1910) and Louis Pasteur (1822–1895), after years of experimentation, demonstrated the validity of Lister's theories by proving that many diseases are caused by germs. During the last two decades of the century, the microorganisms responsible for malaria, tuberculosis, diphtheria, cholera, bubonic plague, and typhoid were identified. The germ theory of disease created a new public attitude toward sanitation and resulted in the passage of public-health laws by most central and local governments.

Pasteur went beyond the identification of bacteria. Bulding on the work of Edward Jenner (1749–1823), who in 1798 had announced a means of immunization against smallpox, he began experimenting in methods of inoculation against other diseases. He found a vaccine for anthrax in 1881 and one for rabies in 1885; these led to a succession of similar discoveries. By the end of the nineteenth century the major endemic diseases had been brought under control in western Europe.

The availability of greater supplies of food also contributed to the growth of population. At the same time, the stability of governments in the major European states reduced the number of deaths through civil strife and disorder and provided a large measure of personal and economic security, which may have encouraged the raising of large families. For almost a century, from 1815 to 1914, there was no general European war.

Unlike many regions that have experienced great and sudden increases in population, western Europe was able to absorb most of its new members. Men were displaced by machines in many old industries, but the Industrial Revolution created far more jobs than it eliminated. The Industrial Revolution did not spread uniformly over Europe, however. In Ireland, southern Italy, and other areas relatively unaffected by industrialization, the surplus population starved or was forced to leave the country. The total population of Ireland declined by as much as 50 per cent when the failure of the potato crop led to famine and large-scale emigration.

In the countries of western and northern Europe the rate of population increase began to drop in the 1880's, a process that had already begun in France some fifty years earlier, as growing numbers of people, especially in the middle classes, began to restrict the size of their families to allow themselves greater freedom and a higher standard of living. Once the major causes of infant mortality had been removed, the rise or decline of the birthrate was largely determined by social and religious attitudes rather than by economic and political factors. Not until the twentieth century did certain European governments actively encourage population growth by direct or indirect subsidies.

The Industrial Revolution and the population explosion produced the greatest and probably the most important human migrations in history. In numbers at least, the movement of populations in Europe in the nineteenth century dwarfed the vast folk migrations of the late Roman Empire.

This movement of peoples in Europe was due in part to the abolition of serfdom in all European countries except Russia by 1848 (even after the freeing of the serfs in Russia in 1861, the Russian peasant was not entirely free to leave his land) and to improvements in transportation, which opened the interiors of continents to large-scale settlement. The nineteenth-century migrations involved approximately 85 per cent of all the people in Europe. Seventy per cent of the population moved from the country to the cities, causing so great an increase in the size and number of European cities that western Europe was transformed from a predominantly rural to a predominantly urban society.

About 15 per cent of the population left Europe altogether. Approximately 45 million settled in the Americas, Australia, New Zealand, and South Africa. Another 6 million moved from Europe to the sparsely populated areas of Asiatic Russia, in a migration as dramatic and important in many ways as the European settlement of the western part of North America. These migrations Europeanized some parts of Russia, and they reinforced the European quality of other areas.

While the migrations were vast in scale, they followed no plan or pattern, and were almost completely lacking in organization. They resulted from personal decisions by individuals and small groups, decisions occasionally made under threat of political or religious persecution or because of economic necessity, but for the most part voluntary. Most people seem to have moved to the cities when times were good, when jobs were plentiful and the pay (by the standards of rural labor) high. They emigrated abroad when they could save money to pay for their passage and accumulate enough capital to make a start in a new land. In periods of prosperity big business and industry in the United States—the railroads, steel companies, and later, petroleum companies—offered attractive inducements to immigrants in order to obtain fresh supplies of cheap, and unorganized, labor.

Economic reasons alone, however, do not explain why the traditional inertia and conservatism of the European peasant were overcome to such a remarkable degree in the last part of the nineteenth century. Political and social ideas stirred up by revolution and the Napoleonic wars may have played their part, and the freeing of the serfs removed the legal obstacles to migration. But most important was probably the self-generating quality of the migration movement. As adventurous young men went to the cities and found jobs and a more exciting life, their example stimulated others, until movement to the cities became a natural and accepted pattern of behavior—as it has remained ever since. In the same way, emigration abroad was fostered by the example of pioneers who found land and opportunity in other countries and then encouraged friends and relatives to follow their lead.

Urbanization and the Transformation of Society

The dislocation of European society brought about by the Industrial Revolution inevitably caused much human misery. The movement of peasants from the soil to alien enviroments, the crowding of people into squalid and unsanitary tenements, the wretched working conditions in mines and factories, the long hours and low wages, the exploitation of child and female labor, the absence of safety precautions, the lack of accident and sickness insurance—all these abuses of the Industrial Revolution were exposed and angrily denounced, and with reason. This was an era when men and women worked fourteen to sixteen hours a day in unheated factories; when little children were used to draw coal carts in the mines because they were a cheap source of labor and were small enough to crawl through the narrow shafts; when a single drowsy moment at a machine might result in the loss of an arm or a leg for which there was no insurance or compensation, even though it might put an end to a man's ability to work. The system of unrestricted free enterprise brought great wealth and power to nations and to a number of individuals, but for the common man it meant freedom to be ill paid, ill housed, and ill fed, and when times were bad, freedom to be unemployed and to go hungry.

Economic misery was nothing new in Europe, however, and if work in factories and mines was oppressive, so also had been work in the cottage industries. It is easy to romanticize rural life, but the existence of the average farm laborer in the nineteenth century was generally even more wretched than that of the city worker. The dwellings of the rural poor were often little more than mud huts, as cramped, dark, and unsanitary as any city tenement. Wages were even lower than in the city, and work was more seasonal. Few farm laborers could afford to eat meat or cheese regularly; their diet often consisted of little more than bread, potatoes, turnips, and such fruits or vegetables as might be in season. They were seldom allowed to hunt or fish in local woods or streams, and poaching was severely punished. One of the reasons for the drift to the cities was the desire for a better standard of living, and toward the end of the century the cities began to provide it.

By this time the flagrant abuses of the Industrial Revolution in big cities had forced many governments to recognize the need to remedy them. The concentration of people in the cities had made it possible for the workers themselves to agitate more effectively for reforms, and trade unions and labor parties had been organized to give common voice to their grievances. During the second half of the nineteenth century a long series of government regulations gradually improved working conditions in the larger industries of western Europe. As a result of legislation requiring higher standards in housing and sanitation, and of the introduction of amenities such as gas and electric lights, the cities became more bearable places in which to live.

The Industrial Revolution did more than free man from economic dependence on relatively static methods of production; it increased the total amount of food and goods available to every individual. Many people enjoyed a more ample and varied diet than ever before. For the first time a large number of laborers could afford to eat meat regularly. Sugar, citrus fruits, cocoa, were made available to a mass market. Tea and coffee, once luxury items, became standard drinks for every class. Shoes, clothing, furniture, toys, all were produced in increasing quantities at prices most people could afford. Industrial workers formed the chief market as well as the labor force of the new industrial society. On balance it can be said that the Industrial Revolution, with all its evils, brought a great increase in material prosperity to a majority of the members of the societies which it transformed. It is only necessary to compare the living conditions of laborers in nonindustrial areas with those of industrial workers, miserable as these may be in some cases, to be aware of the material benefits of the conversion to machine technology.

The revolution in the economy of Europe produced important changes in European society. Land, for centuries the economic base of the aristocracy, was no longer the chief source of wealth. New industries, finance capitalism, and commerce brought ever-increasing wealth to the middle classes. With

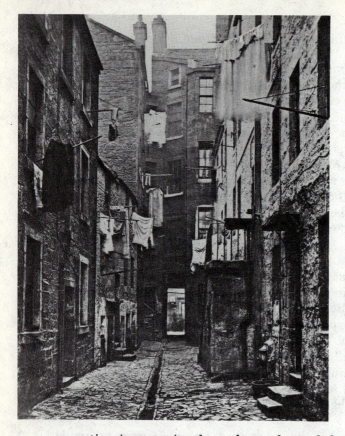

An urban slum in Glasgow, Scotland. *In the right foreground is a hydrant, often the sole source of water for the tenements. By the end of the nineteenth century water piped in from municipal reservoirs had generally supplanted local wells, which had almost always been badly polluted, because usually the only toilet facilities for these tenements were constructed over holes in a corner of this same courtyard. Other sewage flowed through the open gutter, shown in this photograph, to similar gutters in the streets, and thence to a local stream or other body of water.*

mounting importunity these classes demanded political power to match their economic power, and through the greater part of the nineteenth century they challenged the political authority of the landed aristocracy.

A growing segment of the population of the new industrial society consisted of the urban proletariat, the great reservoir of industrial labor, but also a great reservoir of potential political strength. In the early part of the century most industrial workers were content to accept middle-class political leadership. After the collapse of the revolutions of 1848, however, workers became increasingly aware of the divergence between their interests and those of the middle classes, and they began to turn to economic and political organizations—trade unions and socialist parties—designed to promote their interests.

The change in western Europe from a predominantly rural to a predominantly urban society had other important effects. A population concentrated in cities was more accessible to the influence of new ideological trends than a population scattered through the countryside. The man who had severed his traditional local ties to live in the impersonal and anonymous city searched for something he could identify with, for new loyalties and attachments. The city became the great center of the mass movements of the industrial age, the breeding ground of nationalist and socialist doctrines, of new religious sects, temperance societies, reform movements, and revolutionary associations. It was the city that gave birth, in the late nineteenth century, to the cheap daily newspaper, which thereafter helped mold public opinion on political and social issues.

THE INTELLECTUAL CLIMATE

Materialism and Realism

So great was the material progress in the latter part of the nineteenth century and so profoundly did men appear to be dominated by material considerations that this period in history has been called an age of materialism. In all classes of society people seemed obsessed with the desire to amass goods, and judged themselves and their neighbors by standards of material wealth. Many intellectual leaders embraced the philosophy of positivism originated by Auguste Comte (1798–1857), which held that everything, including mental and spiritual qualities, was the product of natural forces. In 1864 Pius IX, pope from 1846 to 1878, thought it necessary to condemn the view "that no other forces are recognized than those which reside in matter and which . . . are summed up in the accumulation and increase of riches by every possible means and the satisfaction of every pleasure."

The pope had reason for concern. Yet the nineteenth century was an extremely moralistic if not always a moral age. Rarely has pleasure been more generally condemned by the classes most capable of pursuing it. The accumulation of riches was regarded not as a means of enjoying life, but as a sign that a man had not spent his time in idleness or frivolous pursuits. In this respect the attitudes of the middle class in the nineteenth century resembled those of the Calvinist world in the sixteenth and seventeenth centuries.

To many men of the time, material progress indicated human progress, and this belief itself functioned as a religion. They were convinced that scientific advances and improved living standards were steps toward a higher civilization and the general improvement of mankind, and that in time all human problems could be solved and all abuses eliminated. Faith in human progress, joined with the strong emphasis on good works in many of the popular religious movements of the period, did much to make the nineteenth century a humanitarian age. There was widespread agreement throughout Europe that the world should be rid of slavery and torture, of hunger and disease. Humanitarianism frequently lay behind government legislation to alleviate the social distress caused by the Industrial Revolution. Public opinion could be shocked by revelations of the wretched conditions of child labor and similar abuses; in no part of Europe could the demands of public opinion for reform be totally ignored.

Closely associated with the materialistic outlook was a belief in the necessity of viewing the world and its problems "realistically." Impressed by the triumphs of science, which were regarded, at least in the popular mind, as the result of objective analyses of factual evidence, many people turned away from abstract ideals and took pride in their ability to face facts, to see the world as it actually was. This point of view was widely adopted by politicians in the period of disillusionment following the failure of the revolutions of 1848, which was generally ascribed to the excessively visionary idealism of revolutionary leaders. So great was the emphasis on realism by articulate members of late-nineteenth-century society that subsequent historians have tended to accept contemporary estimates of this attitude at face value. They find a new realistic understanding of politics in the statecraft of Bismarck and Cavour—a recognition of the preeminence of force in achieving political success, and a willingness to brush aside morality and idealism as unrealistic and hence irrelevant. This political realism has been seen to correspond with realism in the sciences and with a new realism in the arts.

But did a new realism in fact prevail in the later nineteenth century? Were Bismarck and Cavour more realistic in their appraisal of the interests of their governments than diplomats of earlier decades, such as Metternich or Castlereagh? Did they have a more acute sense of the importance of power than Napoleon? Were they more willing to disregard conventional standards of morality than Talleyrand?

There is even more reason to wonder whether any of the distinctive ideological forces of the period—liberalism, nationalism, social Darwinism, Marxian socialism—can be called realistic, despite their scientific pretensions. Belief in representative government, in national uniqueness or superiority, in the triumph of the proletariat and the withering away of the state—all depended on faith quite as much as did religious convictions; indeed more so, because these secular beliefs could so readily be challenged by facts.

In the arts, too, the realism of the period was neither so realistic, so original, nor so generally accepted as many contemporary and later interpreters have assumed. The novelist Émile Zola and the painter Gustave Courbet, who made realism something of a cult, formed part of a long tradition of European genre art. Moreover, there was a strong element of romanticism in their celebration of the sordid and the commonplace.

The genuinely popular art of the era, far from being realistic, was frankly sentimental and escapist, and popular taste was profoundly shocked (or pretended to be) by the realistic writers and painters. Gustave Flaubert, who wrote a novel about adultery without overtly moralizing on the subject,

Le Déjeuner sur l'Herbe. *Painting by Manet. The realistic representation of a naked woman profoundly shocked contemporary viewers. Louvre, Paris.*

was sent into exile by Napoleon III, himself hardly a model of sexual morality, while another Frenchman, the painter Édouard Manet, who dared to depict naked women without disguising them as nymphs or allegorical figures, was branded a moral pervert and hounded out of the country.

In short, the men and women of the nineteenth century, with all their emphasis on material values and realism, were as hypocritical and as much influenced by emotional and ideological forces as those of any other period in history.

Faith in Science; Darwin and Darwinism

Europeans during the later nineteenth century were surrounded to an ever-increasing extent by products of scientific discovery; science was steadily providing explanations for natural phenomena that had once been considered miraculous. Hence it was natural that a growing interest in science should develop among members of all classes. Public lectures on new discoveries and theories were in great vogue, and the lecturers themselves were often imbued with missionary zeal. The efforts of the popularizers of science, together with the remarkable scientific achievements of the era, produced a common impression that science could explain everything and in time eradicate poverty, disease, even death itself. The optimism of the more sophisticated did not go so far; yet, although they recognized that science would probably never be able to explain such mysteries as the origins of the universe or of life, many categorically rejected the explanations of revealed religion, adopting the view that what could not be ascertained rationally and scientifically was forever unknowable.

Faith in science and faith in revealed religion were not necessarily incompatible, as Pope Leo XIII had emphasized; and many scientist, fully aware of their own limitations, still looked to revealed religion for the ultimate explanation of existence. Similarly, many deeply religious men were engaged in scientific investigation. It was an Augustinian monk, Gregor Mendel (1822–1884), who in the 1860's unraveled the first principles of heredity.

Scientific discoveries in the later nineteenth century were characterized by the formulation of major generalizations based on an accumulated fund of facts. Among the most important were the theories of the indestructibility of matter, the conservation of energy, the atomic structure of the universe. Scientific methods were also applied to the study of man and human society in the belief that general principles or laws could be discovered for human as well as natural phenomena.

From a social-historical point of view, the most important scientific generalizations of the era were advanced by the naturalist Charles Darwin (1809–1882), whose theory of biological evolution supplied a scientific explanation for the development of life on earth. The idea of evolution did not originate with Darwin. Philosophers had long thought in evolutionary terms, and geologists and naturalists had already accumulated a great deal of evidence on the subject. It was Darwin, however, who compiled—in his *On the Origin of Species by Means of Natural Selection*, published in 1859 —the first large-scale body of information to support the hypothesis that living organisms evolve. He was also the first to link evolution to the theory of natural selection (another theory that did not originate with him) to explain how evolutionary changes take place. In Darwin's view the world is far from well ordered or harmonious. On the contrary; all living things are engaged in a constant struggle for existence, and in this struggle the organisms with the best-developed qualities for obtaining food, for reproduction, or for self-defense are "naturally selected" to survive. From this theory came the formula "survival of the fittest," which Darwin's popularizers put forward as a scientific law governing all aspects of life.

In considering the impact of Darwin's ideas on nineteenth-century thought, one must distinguish between Darwin and Darwinism. Darwin himself advanced his theories with caution and surrounded his main propositions with reservations and qualifications. In poor health during the later part of his life, he shunned scientific meetings and rarely became involved in the bitter controversies his views aroused. Darwinism was created by Darwin's popularizers, who reduced his theories to oversimplified and easily comprehensible slogans. "Your boldness sometimes makes me tremble," Darwin told one of his followers. It was Darwinism, not Darwin the man, that had the greatest influence on the intellectual climate of the period.

To many of Darwin's contemporaries the chief significance of Darwinism lay in its threat to the Christian religion and public morality. By denying the account of the creation in the Book of Genesis and by equating man with other animals, Darwinism seemed to strike at the root of Christianity and to undercut the concept of Christian morality based on belief in man's uniqueness in a divine world order. In reality, Darwinism was not so great a threat to Christianity as many feared. Sophisticated theologians had long interpreted parts of the Bible in a symbolic sense, and the majority of Christians had little difficulty in reconciling the theory of evolution with their religious beliefs after the first shock had worn off.

The influence of Darwinism on popular social attitudes was far more profound. The theory of the survival of the fittest gained tremendous vogue and in the form of "social Darwinism" was used to explain every kind of social phenomenon, including the existence of various classes. According to convinced Darwinists, the poor were poor because they lacked the intelligence, the initiative, and the energy of the more favored members of society; the rich were rich because of their natural endowments. In an era

Charles Darwin.

when consciences were disturbed by the problem of poverty and social distress, this was a comforting assumption—unless one happened to be poor.

Darwin's theories were used to explain not only inequalities within a society but inequalities among societies. His ideas were eagerly seized by nationalists, racists, and imperialists to prove the superiority of entire nations or social groups over others. The concept of the survival of the fittest led many Frenchmen, Englishmen, and Germans to believe that their present positions of international power were proof of their respective nations' fitness to survive and to rule. Perhaps most important was the fact that this view engendered a moral compulsion in these nations to provide further proof of their fitness, which many nationalists believed could be demonstrated conclusively only on the field of battle. As a result of their victory in the Franco-Prussian War of 1870–1871, many Germans smugly assumed that they were intellectually, morally, and physically superior to the French; the French, in turn, harbored a desire to regain their self-respect through a successful war of revenge. Theories of racial fitness asserted the superiority of whites over blacks, of Anglo-Saxons over Gauls, of Teutons over Slavs. These nationalist-racist ideas were not necessary consequences of Darwinism, but this viewpoint did seem to provide a rational and scientific justification for one of the oldest and most cherished of human beliefs, the conviction that one's own group is a chosen people. The popular acceptance of social Darwinism does much to explain the force of European imperialism and the strident nationalism in the years before 1914.

The Continued Importance of the Christian Churches

It is commonly assumed that the economic and social changes of the nineteenth century, the impact of scientific thought, the emphasis on materialism and realism, produced a sharp decline in religious faith. In every country a substantial percentage of the working class, especially migrants to the big cities, did indeed lose contact with the church, and there is no doubt that for many Europeans the authority of the Bible was irretrievably undermined by scientific refutations of the literal truth of the Book of Genesis and by textual criticisms showing apparent inconsistencies in both the Old and New Testaments. Yet in view of the political importance of the churches after 1850, their ability to resist pressure and persecution, and the vitality and scope of their missionary activity in Europe and overseas, the conclusion is inescapable that the Christian churches continued to exercise a powerful hold over the loyalties of men.

The Roman Catholic Church remained the strongest and most important church in Europe. Pius IX, hailed as the Pope of Progress soon after his accession in 1846 because of the reforms he introduced in the Roman government, was denounced as a traitor two years later for his refusal to support the Italian national cause in the war against Austria. Forced into exile by a republican revolution in his territories, he returned to Rome in 1850 as an uncompromising foe of liberalism and a defender of traditional institutions and values. In the period of political reaction following the 1848 revolutions, he was able to conclude advantageous treaties with a number of secular governments, which now looked to the Roman Catholic Church as an ally against revolution.

In the encyclical *Quanta cura* issued in 1864, and the appended *Syllabus of Errors*, Pius IX launched an attack on the major intellectual tendencies of his day: nationalism, socialism, communism, Freemasonry, natural science, religious indifference, religious tolerance, secular education, and the separation of church and state. It was an error to believe "that the Roman Pontiff can and ought to reconcile himself to and agree with progress, liberalism and contemporary civilization."

While defending the *status quo* in all other spheres, Pius IX carried out a revolution within the Church itself. In 1869 he convened an ecumenical council at the Vatican, the first since the Council of Trent in the sixteenth century. The Council proclaimed that a pope cannot err, when speaking officially (*ex cathedra*) on matters of faith and morals, because at such times he is endowed with divine authority. Acceptance of the dogma of papal infallibility by the council marked the triumph of the pope over movements within the Church to limit papal authority by transferring substantial powers to the councils or the bishops, and represented the victory of centralized authoritarian government in the Church.

The assertion of papal supremacy in spiritual affairs was made even as the Church was losing the last vestiges of its temporal power. The greater part of the Papal States had been lost in 1860 during the wars of Italian unification. French troops protected Rome itself from Italian nationalists, but in 1870 these soldiers were withdrawn to fight against Prussia. While the Vatican Council was in session, troops of the Italian national government occupied Rome and made it the capital of the newly united Italy. The pope was left only the territory containing the Vatican and St. Peter's. Pius IX and his successors refused to recognize the loss of Rome, and until 1929 the popes followed a policy of self-imprisonment in the Vatican.

The loss of Rome and the Papal States, although at the time regarded as a disaster by the papacy, actually gave it new opportunity to assert its spiritual authority. The papacy could now become what Pope Gregory the Great, more than a thousand years before, had thought it should be, the conscience of the world, without the need to consider the effect of its actions on its earthly holdings.

Pius IX's assertion of papal authority and his violent denunciations of all contemporary political and intellectual trends alarmed and alienated many secular governments and liberal Catholics. Leo XIII, pope from 1878 to

1903, adhered to his predecessor's views on papal authority, but was diplomatic in his presentation of papal claims and more willing to recognize the problems of his age. He promoted a revival of the study of St. Thomas Aquinas (c. 1225–1274), whose writings dealt with many moral questions still alive in the nineteenth century; Aquinas had taught, for example, that there is no conflict between true science and true religion. On his authority, Leo relaxed the Church's opposition to science and encouraged the work of Catholic scientists.

Leo XIII realized that the Church was discrediting itself in many countries by its support of extremist conservatives and lost monarchist causes. He argued that democracy was as compatible with Catholicism as more authoritarian types of government, and that genuine personal liberty had its firmest basis in Catholic Christianity. He believed that the Church could accomplish its purposes far more effectively by forming political parties, and working through representative governments instead of opposing them, and that the Church should take a deeper interest in social problems. In his encyclical *Rerum novarum* (1891), the pope urged the application of Christian principles to the great social issues of the age. He deplored the abuses of unrestricted free enterprise and the consequent degradation of the worker. Although he defended the institution of private property, he acknowledged that there was much in socialism that was Christian in principle. State, Church, and employer had the duty of improving the condition of the worker, but the worker should also be encouraged to help himself, through the formation of Catholic political parties and Catholic labor unions.

The Roman Catholic Church could not be dismissed as an elaborate superstructure maintained on dead or decaying foundations. In its frequent and bitter conflicts with secular authorities between 1850 and 1890 it revealed a capacity to draw on popular support rivaled only by that of the new ideology of nationalism. In Italy, where the Church clashed directly with the nationalist movement, it succeeded in holding its own against the attacks of the secular government, and in Ireland and Poland, where the Church's interests often coincided with national interests, it played a leading role in efforts to shake off foreign rule. Napoleon III, a weather vane of public opinion, granted extensive powers to the Church in order to gain support for his regime, and made some of his most critical decisions in both domestic and foreign policy in response to the pressure of Roman Catholic opinion. During the first years of the Third Republic in France, the Church lost a number of valuable privileges, but by 1890 it had made a strong comeback through its newly founded political and labor organizations. In Austria the government sought Church support of its efforts to impose a centralized administration on the Habsburg empire. During the period of anticlerical liberal government in Austria after 1867, the Church retained its hold on the country's national minorities by cooperating with regional national movements; after 1879 it was one of the bulwarks of the Taaffe regime, which attempted to conciliate these minorities. In Germany the Roman Catholic Church proved to be the only organization capable of thwarting Bismarck. His campaign to break the power of the Church, one of his few political failures, resulted in the consolidation of the Catholic Center Party, which was to become the most powerful and stable political party in the German Reichstag. In resisting Bismarck and the new German national state, Roman Catholic leaders exhibited a courage and adherence to principle that put liberal and radical intellectuals to shame, and in doing so they received firm and ungrudging support from the majority of Germany's Roman Catholic population.

The Protestant churches were more seriously affected than the Catholic by scientific and textual criticisms of the Bible because Protestant faith had always depended more heavily on biblical authority. Scholarly criticism of the Bible was nothing new, however, and Protestant as well as Catholic theologians had long dealt with seemingly inconsistent or irrational passages by interpreting them in a symbolic sense. Biblical criticism does not seem to have shaken the faith of the majority of Protestants, and church membership grew at least at the same rate as the overall population. In the major Protestant countries the role of religion in everyday life did not change appreciably except among town laborers and a minority of intellectuals. In Russia the Orthodox Church, controlled by the tsar, continued to play a major role in politics and society.

The loyalty of Protestant congregations was less demonstrable than that of members of the Catholic Church. Since the largest Protestant churches were state churches, their adherents were not subject to persecution. But in areas where they did suffer official harassment, Protestants, too, exhibited courage and tenacity in standing by their beliefs. In Great Britain the Protestant dissenters—Methodists, Baptists, and members of other sects that rejected the authority of the Church of England—were a strong force in the Liberal party, especially in Wales and Scotland. Failure of Liberal leadership to pay sufficient regard to the religious feelings of this group was an important cause of the liberal election defeat in 1874.

Further evidence of the continued strength of the Christian churches can be found in the remarkable upsurge of Christian missionary movements in the last decades of the nineteenth century. Overseas missionary activity was facilitated by improvements in transportation and by the concomitant new accessibility of territories once closed to all but the most intrepid traveler. But the fact that missionaries went out in large numbers and risked their lives in unknown, unhealthy, and often hostile lands indicates that in addition to the prevailing optimism regarding the human capacity for improvement, a spirit of faith and sacrifice persisted in Europe.

The most important missionary work of the age was done by the French, who supplied more missionaries and more money to support them than all the other peoples of Europe put together. Largely through the activity of French missionaries, the Roman Catholic Church established full-fledged Church hierarchies for China in 1875, for North Africa in 1884, for India in 1886, and for Japan in 1891.

By the end of the nineteenth century approximately forty thousand Roman Catholics, eighteen thousand Protestants (of all denominations) and two thousand of the Russian Orthodox faith were missionaries in Africa, Asia, and the Pacific area. The Christian churches estimated that they had converted some forty million people in these territories. This figure in itself means little, for the statistics of most churches tended to be inflated and the quality of the conversions varied widely. Yet there can be no doubt of the vigor of the European missionary movement and of the strong support it received from congregations at home.

Nor should the activity of missionaries within Europe itself be overlooked. The Roman Catholics claimed large-scale conversions in Protestant countries, but the Protestant churches also claimed sizable gains in membership. Statistics on conversions in Europe, like those on conversions overseas, tended to be exaggerated, but the fact that conversions did take place in large numbers is another indication of the continued appeal of Christianity.

Nationalism and Liberalism

Strong as the hold of the Christian churches on men's loyalties during the later nineteenth century may have been, there is no doubt that the most dynamic ideological force during this period was nationalism, whose importance in the modern world can hardly be exaggerated. On the basis of this idea, Germany and Italy were unified; the independence of Hungary was recognized within a new Austro-Hungarian empire; Serbia, Montenegro, and Rumania were conceded complete independence from Turkish rule. In areas where the national principle did not win recognition, it became one of the most disruptive forces in domestic and international politics.

There was nothing inevitable about the triumph of the new nation-states. Germany, for instance, might have remained divided as a result of the effective operation of the international balance of power—that is, France and Russia might have joined forces to prevent the establishment of a new great power directly on their borders. Or Germany might have been united under Austria, in which case the entire Austrian empire, with all its national minorities, might have survived. Today Germany is again divided, and there is little prospect of its reunification. Russia has extended its imperial dominion over most of the national minorities once governed by Austria, and has ruthlessly suppressed national uprisings in the areas under its control.

Nor is there anything inevitable about nationalism itself. Man is not born with feelings of national self-consciousness. During the early development of national feeling in a particular society, national self-consciousness is generally restricted to a minority consisting of the educated and the politically aware. This was the situation in Germany and Italy in the early nineteenth century, and it exists in the Congo and in Indonesia today. The majority of the population is only gradually imbued with the spirit of nationalism, often as the result of deliberate programs of indoctrination.

A frequent accompaniment to the development of national self-consciousness is the formulation of theories of a common origin which reinforce national ties by adding a fund of tradition. It was no accident that the nineteenth century witnessed a great increase in the study of history, with emphasis on the national origins of the European peoples, together with an intensive investigation of national myths and folklore. For example, in Germany the brothers Jacob and Wilhelm Grimm (1785–1863; 1786–1859) collected old and almost forgotten folk tales, and Richard Wagner (1813–1883) based his music dramas on Teutonic legends.

In the course of the nineteenth century, the cultural nationalism represented by Johann Gottfried von Herder (1744–1803) and his followers, which held that each people has a unique folk spirit worthy of preservation, gave way to political nationalism, the belief that to maintain national values effectively each nation must establish itself as a sovereign state. At the same time the liberal nationalism of political idealists, who saw in the nation-state a means of achieving constitutional representative government that would ensure liberty and justice for all citizens, gave way to arrogant nationalism, a belief in the superiority of one nation over another, in which racism played a prominent part. Advocates of this view were increasingly willing to sacrifice the rule of law and the protection of individual rights to the greater power and glory of the national state.

The breakdown of traditional local and social ties resulting from population movements in the later nineteenth century, and the profound social and economic changes that then took place, may have intensified the need for individuals to feel part of a community. Membership in a national community was made particularly attractive by the concept that this community was in some way superior to others. Convinced nationalists generally put forward historical evidence to support a belief in national uniqueness or superiority. Fundamentally, however, this belief was an act of faith, and nationalism accordingly took on the character of a religion. For it met not only the need to belong but also the need to believe in something greater than self, in this case in a mystical national mission.

During the early part of the nineteenth century, nationalism was closely linked with liberalism, another of the great ideological forces of the era.

There were almost as many varieties of liberalism as there were liberals.

As the name implies, liberalism was a philosophy of freedom, a belief that man can be trusted to govern himself and deal with his affairs with a minimum of interference from any outside authority—church, state, guild, or labor union. Left to his own devices, each man pursues his own best interests, and the sum of these individual efforts makes for the greater welfare of all.

Because liberalism, the struggle for political freedom, often coincided with the struggle for national freedom, nationalism and liberalism were frequently regarded as a single revolutionary movement. It was Bismarck who demonstrated that liberalism and nationalism were not ideological Siamese twins, that nationalists could be separated from their liberal principles once their national aspirations had been satisfied.

Most liberals believed in self-government through representative institutions, and in the desirability of a written constitution as a guarantee of political rights and liberties. Yet only a minority of them advocated complete democracy and universal suffrage. Moderate liberals generally thought that political representation should be extended just to educated property owners, who could be trusted to use their political power wisely and responsibly—in other words, to men like themselves. There was widespread fear that if those without education or poverty were given the vote they would be easily swayed by demagogues. Many liberals had a strong faith in education, however, and were willing to consider the extension of voting privileges as literacy increased.

Liberalism has been called the political ideology of the middle class, for most of the active liberals belonged to this class and their political doctrines reflected middle-class interests. After the failure of the revolutions of 1848, liberals tended to renounce the use of tactics of violence to achieve their political aims. These revolutions had demonstrated the ineffectiveness of violence, and they had also exposed the dangers of revolution by the propertyless masses. Radical revolutionary programs demanding the abolition of private property and an equitable distribution of economic and political power had alarmed the members of the middle class, who had too much at stake in the existing order of society to desire a social as well as a political revolution. After 1848 they therefore emphasized the need to create or strengthen institutions of representative government as a means of gaining a greater share of political power, still largely monopolized by the landed aristocracy in most European countries. With the acquisition of political power, they intended to carry out the political and social reforms they considered desirable by orderly, legal, and peaceful means.

In theory most liberals believed in free enterprise in economic affairs (*laissez-faire*). They wanted to remove government constraints at home to permit maximum scope for their economic activities, and they wanted free trade among nations to create the largest possible market for their products.

But at the same time liberals expected government protection of private property. Moreover, despite their objections to government interference, liberal businessmen seldom hesitated to ask the government for subsidies and loans, and they were quick to agitate for tariff protection when international competition became too intense, and to demand government military intervention when their investments abroad were threatened.

Whether for religious, humanitarian, or practical reasons, many liberals were among the foremost advocates of social as well as political reform in the nineteenth century. Liberals worked for the abolition of slavery and serfdom; they sought to alleviate the miseries of the working class; they recognized the need for broader popular education and improved sanitation facilities. The introduction of social reforms necessarily meant added government interference in the affairs of the individual, and liberals wrestled with their consciences over the problem. By the end of the century, however, many of them were willing to advocate increased government controls in the interest of human betterment. Indeed, their association with social reform grew so strong that today liberals are often confused with socialists or communists, whose doctrines are the antithesis of liberalism.

Socialism: Marx and Marxism

Socialist theories, which gained rapidly in influence after 1848, were essentially a denial of the liberal view that, given maximum freedom, man could work out his problems to the greatest benefit of society. Although there were as many shades of opinion among socialists as among liberals, socialists generally believed in a greater regulation of society. They viewed the free-enterprise system as chaotic and unjust, and favored some kind of control over the means of production and distribution to give the workers a fairer share of the fruits of their labor. Many socialist political thinkers, like many liberals, believed that there were certain natural laws at work in society, but unlike the liberals they did not consider government regulation the chief obstacle to the ideal operation of these laws. Instead, they regarded it as man's duty to discover the laws and, by means of government action, to organize society in conformity with them.

The outstanding figure in the history of socialism was Karl Marx (1818–1883), who formulated a theory of history that provided a key—*the* key, Marx was convinced—to understanding the past, present, and future of human society. Marx viewed history in evolutionary terms, and in describing the evolutionary process in human society he claimed to have done for human history what Darwin had done for natural history. Marx's friend and frequent collaborator, Friedrich Engels (1820–1895), echoed this belief in his funeral speech at Marx's grave: "Just as Darwin discovered the law of development of organic nature, so Marx discovered the law of development of human history." Marx wanted to dedicate the first volume of his major work, *Das Kapital*, published in 1867, to Darwin, an honor which Darwin, with characteristic caution, declined.

Marx's ideas, like those of Darwin, were not entirely original, nor were his theories altogether clear or systematic. His writings contain many puzzling ambiguities and paradoxes. It has therefore been possible for Marx's followers and popularizers frequently to tailor his ideas to their own needs and prejudices. As in the case of Darwin, it is necessary to distinguish carefully between the master and his interpreters, between Marx and Marxism—or anti-Marxism.

Marx's first principle, on which his other ideas were based, was that the economy was the mainspring of human activity. His world view has therefore been called economic determinism. In all societies, he said, "the mode of production in material life determines the general character of the social, political and spiritual processes of life." Through his economic interpretation of society, Marx believed, he had discovered a fundamental pattern in history: the class struggle. The truly significant conflicts in history, he maintained, were not political or national rivalries but conflicts between slaves and slaveholders, plebeians and patricians, serfs and landlords, workers and bourgeois-capitalists.

Although Marx regarded the class struggle as the key to all historical conflicts, he did not expect it to continue indefinitely or regard it as a permanent historical phenomenon. On the contrary, he believed that the final cataclysmic struggle between the classes, the economic Armageddon, was at hand; the capitalist system was creating conditions for the ultimate clash between workers and capitalists. The total amount of the world's

Karl Marx.

wealth was being concentrated in ever fewer hands, with the result that an ever smaller number of capitalists were growing richer, while more and more people were being pressed into the ranks of the wretched proletariat. The consequent social tensions would inevitably produce a revolution. This, however, would be the final revolution, for the new society would be organized according to the scientific economic laws Marx had discovered and hence the fundamental causes of conflict and revolution would be eliminated.

One of the most important of Marx's economic formulations was the theory of surplus value. This theory held that the real value of any commodity could only be measured by the labor used to produce it. Under capitalism, labor was not given just compensation, and the surplus went into the pockets of the capitalists. After the revolution the worker, the actual producer of wealth, would control the means of production and distribution and would receive full value for his work. With that, presumably, he would be content.

Marx saw that to organize society according to scientific economic laws, some sort of supervisory control would be necessary, and he assigned a definite place to the state in the period immediately following the revolution. Once this organization had been carried out, economic classes would no longer exist and the class struggle would come to an end. The state would then become unnecessary and would gradually wither away. This new society, completely freed from state controls, was described by Marx as an association "in which the free development of each is the condition for the free development of all." His vision of the social order was remarkably similar to the ideal conception of the free-enterprise system, although not even the most optimistic liberal believed that a society operating freely according to natural laws would be so perfect that there would no longer be any need for the state. Marx did not think that human controversy would cease after the social conflict had been resolved, but he suggested that future disagreements would involve the merits of abstract values instead of wealth and power.

Besides supplying the socialist movement with a theoretical foundation, Marx imbued it with a revolutionary dynamism. He urged the working class to prepare constantly and systematically for the revolution and the overthrow of the bourgeois-capitalist system. Conditioned by centuries of subjugation and ignorance, the workers would need help in recognizing their true interests. Providing this help was to be the task of the socialist parties, which would educate the masses and take the lead in preparing for the revolution. The people had to be taught that government, law, religion, and traditional standards of morality were all bourgeois creations meant to deceive and subjugate them. The workers had to learn to see through such artifices, to identify themselves with their class and realize that efforts to improve their status within the capitalist system were a betrayal of class interests, that petty gains in wages or working conditions achieved through trade unions or government legislation were actually harmful. Such minor benefits only delayed the revolution, which alone could give them their just share of worldly goods. The workers had to be welded into a disciplined fighting force to wage continuous class war until the final revolution had been won.

Marx's basic error was his failure to appreciate the importance of noneconomic forces in society: religion, emotion, prestige, genius, stupidity, and such factors as climate and geography. His economic theories themselves were based on antiquated conceptions of a static economy. The theory of surplus value did not take sufficient account of the importance of capitalist equipment, administrative ability, initiative, and the willingness to take risks. The capitalist-industrial revolution, far from pressing more and more people into proletarian poverty, increased production to such an extent that it improved the general standard of living of all men; indeed, in the most highly industrialized countries the proletarian class is rapidly disappearing. The great revolutions inspired by Marxist doctrines have taken place not in industrial societies, where Marx expected them to occur, but in societies still overwhelmingly agricultural, beset by very real economic hardships. In all the revolutions inspired by Marxism, the state has played a dominant role in the reorganization of society, but nowhere is there any sign of its withering away.

Like many intellectuals, Marx misjudged the responses of the working class. Socialist parties were to find it difficult to keep workers in a constant state of belligerent excitement. Moreover, there was a fundamental contradiction between Marx's theory of the inevitability of revolution and his appeal to the workers to get ready for it. If revolution was inevitable, why was there so much need for preparation?

The fallacies and contradictions in Marx's theories, the obvious incorrectness of his prophecies, the perversion of Marxist doctrine in modern Russia and China, should not blind us to the fact that his ideas are among the most significant ever produced by the human mind. His economic interpretation of history, although by no means original, was presented with such cogency and such a wealth of supporting evidence that it has compelled a recognition of the role of the economy in every aspect of human affairs. The economy may not be generally accepted as the basic motivating force in society, but its importance can no longer be ignored even by the most violent anti-Marxist. His theory of the class struggle, too, has provided valuable new insights for the study of history and society, and has led to important reinterpretations of past events and present problems. His call to revolution and his definition of the role of socialist parties has supplied a rationale and a dynamism for insurgent parties in every part of the world.

Marx was more than a political or economic theorist. He was a prophet, and in a very real sense, the founder of a faith. His prediction of the coming revolutionary holocaust from which a new and perfect society would emerge was not political theory; it was political theology, with the allure of a religion. But Marxism did not depend on faith alone. With its scientific apparatus it appealed to would-be rationalists; with its promise of social justice it appealed to humanitarians; with its call to revolution it appealed to that imporant segment of society formed by the discontented and the maladjusted, who looked to revolution to provide scope for their energies. Marxism, with all its fallacies and inconsistencies, has qualities that have gripped the hearts and minds of men of every race and nationality, and like nationalism, remains one of the most potent revolutionary forces in the modern world.

Voices of Protest: Nietzsche

In every age there are independent spirits who react against the dominant political or intellectual currents of their time. Since the late eighteenth century, many artists and writers, imbued with the spirit of romanticism, had considered it almost obligatory to assume a pose of protest against society. By the last decades of the nineteenth century, however, the belief in the necessity of protest had become deadly serious. The all-encompassing state, mass conscription, mass education, the mass cults of nationalism, materialism, social Darwinism, and various forms of socialism—all seemed designed to crush individuality and creativity. In various ways anarchists and artists, philosophers and poets, expressed their hatred for the contemporary world, but none did so more passionately or eloquently than the German philosopher Friedrich Nietzsche.

Nietzsche (1844–1900) was actually no more representative of his age than are rebels at any time, but in his case the society he loathed committed the ultimate crime against a thinker, the perversion and distortion of his ideas. This was largely the work of his sister, who gained custody of his papers after his insanity and death, and falsified his unpublished manuscripts to make him appear as a spokesman for German nationalism and racism. Not until after the death in 1935 of Elisabeth Förster-Nietzsche did reliable scholars gain access to these papers, and since then a new and very different picture of Nietzsche has emerged.

Far from being an apostle of Nordic superiority and racism, Nietzsche denounced German nationalism and race hatred as "a scabies of the heart and blood poisoning." He refused to share "the utterly false racial self-admiration and perversion which today displays itself in Germany," an attitude he deemed doubly worthy of scorn in a people with a sense of history. The new German national state, he predicted, would annihilate the German spirit. Obsessed with a sense of power, the Germans would soon surrender what was left of their culture to prophets of national greatness, a contemptible and self-destructive ideal.

At the same time, Nietzsche was not in sympathy with the prevailing intellectual climate in Europe: the mediocrity, hypocrisy, complacent smugness, and superficiality that seemed to permeate society. The scholars involved in myopic literary criticism or in investigating the minutiae of the past, the scientists with their sensational discoveries about the natural world—none seemed to be concerned with universal, timeless questions. What did their discoveries amount to? What were they trying to achieve? What, above all, were their values?

The search for values—this, in Nietzsche's opinion, should be the fundamental and permanent concern of thoughtful men; for values cannot be defined once and for all, but must be submitted to constant reexamination. Not to those who have the courage of their convictions should honor be paid, but to those who have the courage to question their own convictions.

Nietzsche's own supreme value was culture and the creation of culture. His famous Superman was no crude German racist or conqueror, but the creative spirit: the artist, philosopher, or statesman whose genius lifted him above the common level of mankind, and whose thoughts and works infused life with new beauty and meaning. Michelangelo, Goeth, Beethoven, Caesar—these were Nietzsche's Supermen.

Nietzsche made his own contribution to culture by propounding a theory of human behavior in many ways more profound than the ideas of either

Nietzsche and his mother, about 1890.

Marx or Freud. Not economics or sex is the basic drive in man, Nietzsche said, but the Will to Power, an urge to which all other human instincts are subordinate. This Will to Power is also the basic ingredient in human creativity, and it is the strength of that quality in the Superman that distinguishes him from other human beings. The person without strong will, without passionate feelings and impulses, can no more create the beautiful than a castrated man can beget children. Nietzsche did not eulogize power for its own sake. The supreme evidence of man's possession of power is his ability to control it, to direct his impulses into creative channels, to "sublimate" his energies. "It is the weak characters without power over themselves who hate the constraint of style . . . and who find it necessary to interpret themselves and their environment as *free* nature—wild, arbitrary, fantastic, disorderly, astonishing." The truly creative spirit will override old traditions, he will break laws of style and composition, as Beethoven and Michelangelo broke laws, but he will feel compelled to create and submit to new laws, new forms. "It will be the strong and domineering natures who find their greatest satisfaction in such compulsion, in such restraint and perfection under laws of their own."

Nietzsche felt nothing but contempt for contemporary optimists who regarded evolution as progress and believed in the ultimate perfectibility of mankind. Had the worth of man increased? Had beauty progressed? Had aesthetic values advanced to a higher plane? What could another ten or twenty centuries bring that could be interpreted as progress over the life and works of Socrates and Jesus, Shakespeare and Goethe? In them and through them the events of history had been "intensified into symbols." History itself was not a progression but a timeless allegory, with the great problems of history its unchanging themes.

Culture and the Industrial Civilization

Subsequent events have shown that Nietzsche's pessimism about progress and human perfectibility was justified, but as he demonstrated through his own example, the political and intellectual climate of the later nineteenth century did not halt the flow of human creativity. Artists might be alienated from society, or subjected to censorship and ridicule, but both the quantity and the quality of the cultural production of the period were impressive.

The era saw new heights in the art of the novel. Rarely had so many countries produced so many talented writers: Turgenev, Dostoevski, Tolstoi, in Russia; Dickens, Thackeray, Trollope, in England; Flaubert and Zola in France; Raabe and Fontane in Germany; Manzoni and Verga in Italy; Stifter in Austria, to name only a few. In music there were the towering figures of Verdi, Wagner, Brahms, Debussy; in poetry, Hugo, Baudelaire, Heine, Browning, Tennyson, Hopkins, Mallarmé, Verlaine; in painting, Courbet, Manet, Renoir, Cézanne; in drama, Ibsen and Hauptmann—the list could be extended almost indefinitely to cover all fields of human endeavor.

Not to be forgotten are the revolutionary discoveries in science and technology, themselves significant products of the human spirit, which made the greatest contribution in history toward raising the standard of living of the European masses. If a civilization is judged by the number of people sharing its benefits, that of nineteenth-century Europe may well have been the greatest the world had so far produced, for never before had so large a proportion of the population been able to enjoy the material and cultural advantages of their age. This was the unique contribution of the civilization of industrialism.

The industrial civilization had other effects, however. In the later nineteenth century a distinct cleavage took place between popular art and what can only be called art-for-art's-sake. Mass production for the first time created a mass market, and perhaps inevitably, it formed and catered to the mass taste. In the visual and practical arts, this taste ran to ornamentation; in literature, to escapism.

Among the newly affluent of all classes, there was an unabashed enjoyment of comfort and ostentation. Architecture, perhaps the best mirror of the taste of a period, produced elaborate imitations of Gothic castles and Chinese pagodas, Swiss chalets and Greek temples. Interior decoration matched the flourishes of architecture. Bright mosaics and stained-glass windows, copies of ancient masterpieces of sculpture and painting, graced the walls and vestibules of public and private buildings. Furniture, of wood or iron, was elaborately decorated and well upholstered; frills and flounces dangled from beds and sofas, lamps and chandeliers. Stuffed birds and animals, pastorals in porcelain, and potted palms and ostrich plumes filled corners and covered tables, against a background of intricately patterned shawls and oriental rugs.

In popular journals, moral aphorisms and household hints shared prominence with stories of chivalry and romance, in which the typical heroine was weak and chaste, the typical hero strong and virile. *The Loves of the Harem, The Seamstress, or The White Slave of England*, and similar sagas made G. W. M. Reynolds (1814–1879) the best-selling English writer of his day. Painting and sculpture were supposed to be not only decorative but morally uplifting, according to the precepts of John Ruskin (1819–1900), the most influential contemporary aesthetic authority, but the pictures in greatest demand were those that also told a story—"The Soldier's Farewell," "Waiting for the Doctor," or "The Gambler's Wife."

This popular art, some of it executed with great technical skill and a fine aesthetic sense, most of it imbued with a lively gusto, represents for the historian important material for establishing contact with another age. The best-selling novel, the widely circulated journal or art reproduction, may provide a far more accurate reflection of contemporary attitudes and opinions than works of art that appeal to later or more sophisticated tastes.

Moreover, much of the art that was popular, for example, the novels of Charles Dickens (1812–1870) and the music of Giuseppe Verdi (1813–1901), possessed from the beginning, and still retains, a universal appeal. Nevertheless, many nineteenth-century artists whose works have stood the test of time remained outside the mainstream of popular culture—not necessarily because they were in revolt against society, although that was often the case, but because they followed their own artistic bent without regard to popular taste. The artistic production of the later nineteenth century was primarily distinguished not by its much-vaunted realism, but by the desire of its creators to experiment, to discover new techniques and forms of expression, to explore new dimensions of human experience. In this respect the writers and painters of the era were akin to the scientists and inventors, who must after all be regarded as artists in their own right.

Henrik Ibsen (1828–1906) in the drama and Fëdor Dostoevski (1821–1881) in the novel led the way to new psychological insights in literature through their relentless probing into what they deemed to be the inner motivations of man. New avenues of literary expression were explored by the poet Stéphane Mallarmé (1842–1898). "It is not description which can unveil the purpose and beauty of monuments, seas, or the human visage in all their depth and quality," he said, "but rather evocation, allusion, suggestion." Mallarmé's concept of poetic expression through images and symbols found adherents in every part of Europe. In their search for methods of conveying thoughts and emotions the Symbolist poets began to find radically different ways of using not only words, but rhythms, rhymes, punctuation, the position of the words on the page, and the very material on which the poems were reproduced. New techniques in poetry passed almost simultaneously into prose, with the result that the self-conscious use of imagery and symbols became part of the equipment of every creative writer.

Similar experimentation took place in painting. Nineteenth-century realists had tried to demonstrate, as Rembrandt had done with his famous painting of the carcass of an ox, that sensitive artists could discover beauty in any subject, no matter how commonplace or sordid. The French realists Gustave Courbet (1819–1877) and Édouard Manet (1832–1883) went further, insisting on the need to paint outdoor scenes on the spot so as to infuse them with a sense of real sunlight and air, a procedure facilitated by the technical innovation of packaging colors in tubes. To achieve more striking effects of color and light through oils, Manet experimented with the application of light colors first, in "fat, flowing" pigments, subsequently adding the medium and dark tones while the light pigment was still wet, a reversal of the usual practice. The example of Manet inspired other painters

The Card Players. *Painting by Cézanne. Musée de Jeu de Paume, Paris.*

to experiment further in the application of pigments to capture the quality of sunlight and atmosphere. Realizing that this quality was constantly changing, they attempted to work as rapidly as possible to record almost photographic impressions of the scenes before them. These "impressionist" painters were reviled by academicians as unskilled botchers, indeed as enemies of society, but a few perceptive critics understood what they were attempting to do, and over the years this understanding has been communicated to the majority of art lovers.

The greatest of the Impressionists did not remain content with the results achieved through the rapid application of pigments and a relative disregard of line and contour. Auguste Renoir (1841–1919), while retaining the luminosity achieved through new color techniques, developed a purity of line and an emphasis on form that amounted to a return to classical ideals. Paul Cézanne (1839–1906), who had always paid great attention to form as well as color, began to see these as the essential qualities in all painting, and to eliminate detail that distracted attention from architectonic and coloristic effects, in a technique that has been labeled Post-Impressionism. Some of his followers, pressing his ideas to their extreme conclusion, concentrated on form and color alone, and abandoned all pretense of objective representation.

Georges Seurat (1859–1891), following another line of development in painting, attempted to make use of scientific principles of color and vision in a method known as pointillism. Instead of mixing his colors on a palette and applying them rapidly, he placed them on the canvas in tiny dots intended to blend when seen from a distance. Paul Gauguin (1848–1903) moved in yet another direction. Rejecting society, he turned to a form of mysticism and arrived at an appreciation of primitive art that he was to convey to the entire Europeanized world.

In the field of music, the French composer Claude Debussy (1862– 1918) abandoned familiar concepts of melody, tonality, and form. Through delicately shimmering tonal effects, the clashing dissonances of brasses and percussions, the cry of the human voice, he sought to evoke moods and images in the imagination of the listener.

The innovations in the arts broke new ground for artistic expression and understanding in every field. But in one important way their effect was unfortunate. The new poetry, art, and music, with their unfamiliar techniques, their obscure and frequently incomprehensible terminology, not only failed to appeal to the general public but awakened feelings of hostility and fear. The consequence was a marked separation of the artist from society, and a decline in appreciation of the importance of art and aesthetics in daily life that is one of the most unfortunate aspects of the modern world.

THE GROWING POWERS OF THE STATE

The Extension of Bureaucratic Government

One of the most prominent features of the industrial-urban society has been the accelerated growth of the responsibilities and consequently of the powers of the state. In the later nineteenth century government supervision was needed to carry through such major reforms as the abolition of serfdom, the regulation of child and female labor, the introduction of safety procedures in mines and factories. Public transportation, provisions for sanitary facilities and clean water supplies, the maintenance and equipment of armies and navies—all had to be administered and regulated. The government was frequently called upon to stimulate the national economy, to help build the railroads, pave the highways, construct harbor installations, open mines, operate the postal and telegraph systems. For all these purposes the state required money, which could only be raised through an elaborate taxation system. The steadily growing demands on the services of the state, and the corresponding growth of the state's demands on its citizenry, necessitated the recruitment of ever larger numbers of civil servants and resulted everywhere in an enormous expansion of the bureaucracy.*

The extension of bureaucratic government was not only required but also made easier by the economic and technological development of the era.

---

* The problem of imperialism and the extension of the authority of European states overseas during this period is treated in detail on pp. 1254–1259 and 1323–1336.

Improved business methods and accounting systems made for more efficient taxation procedures; improved methods of transportation and communication permitted governments to supervise more effectively the activities of their agents, especially those concerned with taxation. And the general increase in productivity made more money available to be taxed and to pay for the increasing costs of government.

The Army and the New Arsenal

Behind the government agent and the tax collector stood the army, equipped with weapons embodying the scientific and technological developments of the age. Since only the state could afford the large-scale purchase of the new armaments, the increasing effectiveness of weapons contributed primarily to the augmentation of the power of the state.

The breech-loading gun, which allowed for a much faster rate of fire than the old muzzle-loader and permitted reloading and firing from a prone position, was introduced in the Prussian army in 1840. The grooved-bore rifle, with far greater range and accuracy than smoothbore guns, was invented soon afterwards. A repeater rifle came into use toward the end of the American Civil War. In artillery, too, rifled and breech-loading weapons replaced smoothbore muzzle-loaders, and shells replaced round shot. The Gatling gun, a primitive machine gun, was developed during the American Civil War, and in 1867 the French army acquired the *mitrailleuse*, an artillery weapon capable of firing 125 rounds a minute. Meanwhile, the telegraph provided a means of coordinating the movements of mass armies, and the railroad made possible a new strategy of mobility that compelled planners in all countries to reorganize existing military installations and draw up new mobilization and campaign programs. A large number of the new railway lines in Europe were laid down primarily for military reasons.

Navies changed even more fundamentally than armies. Sail gave way to steam, wood to iron and steel. Like the armies, the navies adopted rifled, breech-loading guns; the resulting offensive advantage was partly offset by the iron and steel plating that became standard armor for all ships of war. The invention of the mine, the torpedo, and the submarine should have created even greater changes in the navies, but not until the First World War was the significance of these new weapons fully appreciated by naval strategists.

To secure the manpower to utilize the quantities of weapons made available by mass production, and to train their citizens in the workings of the new types of armament, all the major continental states of Europe adopted programs of compulsory military service soon after 1871, when Prussia's victory over France seemed to demonstrate the necessity of such a system.

Mass armies and the introduction of more lethal weapons made war more costly in human lives and in money than it had ever been before. As the century drew to a close a number of statesmen and military men, alarmed at the prospect of war and at the danger that the involvement of mass armies might set off social revolution, began to search for effective means to preserve peace. Others believed that a balance of terror might be maintained indefinitely among the great powers because none would dare risk a major conflict. On the whole, however, there was still a general acceptance of war as a feasible, legitimate, and honorable method of prosecuting national policies.

Whatever their views on war, military strategists were agreed on the need for careful defensive and offensive military preparations. Great importance was attached to strategy, on the assumption that the state that mobilized first and struck most speedily against its enemy would win the next war. Almost nobody considered the possibility of a long war; it seemed inconceivable that any national economy could bear the cost, or any people the sacrifices, of such a conflict.

On the domestic scene, the new arsenal made it easy for a small body of trained men to deal with undisciplined mobs. Between 1850 and 1890 no successful revolution took place in any of the great European states except after a government and its army had been defeated in foreign war, as in France in 1871.

Compulsory Education

Governments did not depend altogether on physical force to maintain themselves. Through official censorship, and manipulation of the press, they had means to control the minds as well as the bodies of men. But their most effective instrument for this purpose was compulsory education, which was instituted in all major European states during the second half of the nineteenth century.

The introduction of compulsory education was not necessarily the result of cynical political calculation. Among people of all countries there was widespread faith in the elevating and remedial powers of education, and sponsors of education programs were often motivated by a spirit of altruism. Liberals and democrats looked upon education as the most effective means of providing all people with equality of opportunity, and even such a conservative as the French statesman and historian François Guizot (1787–1874), declared that "the opening of every schoolhouse closes a jail." In countries with representative governments there was a growing belief that education was essential to train men to make intelligent and responsible use of their political rights. Everywhere men of affairs began to recognize that education had become a practical necessity for workers in the industrial age and for soldiers who had to cope with the increasing complexities of modern warfare.

From the beginning, however, there were those who saw in state control of education an ideal instrument for indoctrination, and in practice government-sponsored education programs (in which compulsory military service played an important part) generally instilled in the citizen a feeling of loyalty toward the state. This feature of state education was at once apparent to leaders of the Christian churches, which prior to the nineteenth century had been the major and often the sole source of education in Europe. As the state assumed more and more educational functions, the struggle for the control of education, and hence for the minds and loyalties of men, became crucial in conflicts between church and state.

The state was to discover, as had the church on numerous occasions, that education could produce unexpected and not always desired results. In Austria-Hungary, for example, it did much to arouse national self-conciousness among the various peoples of the empire, as it was to do later in the British and French imperial territories. In all countries, education made the masses accessible to socialist, revolutionary, and every other kind of antigovernment propaganda, and thus facilitated the development of subversive political organizations.

An important aspect of compulsory education was the provision for the schooling of girls as well as boys, which not only helped women become literate but opened teaching as a new profession for women. These developments were major steps in the political and social emancipation of women.

All programs of compulsory education were originally limited to the elementary level. By 1890 only a beginning had been made in extending compulsory education beyond this level and in establishing free trade and technical schools.

The New Stature of the State

By the end of the nineteenth century the growing power of the state loomed over all human activity. Increased bureaucratic authority, compulsory military service, compulsory education, the new weapons for mass destruction, and the flourishing mass media provided the governments of Europe with means to control and manipulate their populations more effectively than ever before. Pessimistic prophets such as the historian Jakob Burckhardt (1818–1897) wondered how long it would be before all aspects of human endeavor were absorbed or utilized as tools by the new Leviathan.

For most people, however, material progress obscured all evil portents. So impressive were the products of human ingenuity that they seemed to overshadow politics and political ideas. But precisely because of the power for good or evil now placed in the hands of the state, politics and political ideas had never been more important.

CHAPTER 31

The Disruption of the Concert of Europe

AFTER THE defeat of Napoleon in 1815, there was no major war in Europe until 1853. The Concert of Europe established after 1815, with all its weaknesses and defects, proved to be an effective league of princes, who recognized their common interests and stood together against the revolutionary forces of the era. They supported the international settlements of 1815 with considerable consistency and united against attempts to disturb the *status quo*. As a means of maintaining stability in Europe, the policy of monarchical solidarity represented a sense of realism in politics far more profound than that of the so-called realistic statesmen who emerged after 1848—men like Schwarzenberg, Cavour, and Bismarck. The policies of these later realists were revolutionary; they permanently shattered the confidence of the monarchs in one another, and nothing they could do could restore that confidence or reestablish a genuine harmony among them.

The revolutions of 1848 should have given the Concert of Europe a new lease on life by warning the princes of the developing threats to their authority and of the greater need for unity and vigilance. Furthermore, a new and uncertain factor had been introduced into European politics in the person of Louis Napoleon of France. The Concert of Europe had originally been formed to safeguard the states of Europe from French domination, and the rise of a new Napoleon, like the revolutions themselves, might have been expected to encourage the other monarchs to close ranks. That this did not happen was due above all to fear of the growing power of Russia, which obscured the emergence in France of a renewed threat to the old order.

LOUIS NAPOLEON AND THE NEW ASCENDANCY OF FRANCE

When Charles Louis Napoleon Bonaparte, nephew of the first Napoleon, became president of the Second French Republic in December, 1848, he was contemptuously dismissed by many of his contemporaries as a nonen-

Napoleon III. *Contemporary photograph.*

tity. Dull, heavy-lidded eyes and an expressionless face gave him an appearance of stupidity, and his refusal to reveal his thoughts gained him the reputation of being a man of mystery without any secret. By the most famous writer of the age, Victor Hugo, he was branded indelibly as *Napoléon le Petit*.

This low estimate proved to be a serious error. Louis Napoleon (1808–1873) was never a great statesman, but he was one of the most able politicians of the nineteenth century. He possessed a remarkable flair for sensing and exploiting the popular forces of his age, and a stubborn tenacity in pursuing his goals. He also had an unshakable faith in his mission to rule France.

It was neither political ability nor faith, however, that catapulted Louis Napoleon into the presidency of the newly created republic. It was his name. The republican legislators, with more idealism than political wisdom, had included a provision for universal suffrage in their constitution of November, 1848. In the subsequent elections, Louis Napoleon was the only candidate whose name was familiar to the majority of French voters. But the name Napoleon, although a major political asset, was also a fateful legacy, for it possessed a dynamism of its own. "Napoleon" stood for political stability, for law and order; but to a far greater extent it stood for military triumph, for glory, and for empire. In the attempt to live up to his name, Louis Napoleon was to reestablish the empire at home and to engage in foreign adventures that would plunge France into political catastrophe.

Although he concealed his thoughts so well that some people wondered whether he had any ideas at all, there can be little doubt that from the time he became president he intended to do away with the republic and revive his uncle's empire. "We are not at the summit yet," he told an old friend on the day he took the presidential oath of office. "This is only a stop on the way, a terrace where we may rest a moment to gaze at the horizon." It was some time before Louis Napoleon took a further step. In the first period of his presidency he trod warily through the unfamiliar fields of French politics, not yet ready to challenge the recently created republican institutions.

President and Parliament

Louis Napoleon's most obvious political opponents were to be found among the deputies in the legislature. In January, 1849, the predominantly republican assembly that had drawn up the 1848 constitution reluctantly voted to dissolve. New elections in May resulted in the return of a large conservative-monarchist majority, a reflection of the people's general fear of radicalism and political unrest. Victory for the monarchists did not mean a victory for Bonapartism, however. On the contrary, most of the new deputies favored the restoration of a Bourbon or Orleanist candidate, and were decidedly hostile to the pretensions of the new Napoleon.

For three years Louis Napoleon worked steadily to build up his personal following and political power by placing trusted lieutenants in key positions in the government, the army, and the police; by distributing political favors astutely; and by convincing the people of France that he represented their best guarantee of order against the forces of revolution. In the manner of a modern political campaigner he made frequent public appearances on national holidays, at military reviews, at the opening of new bridges and railway lines. His speeches on these occasions were calculated to appeal to the interests and prejudices of the particular audience he was addressing. He spoke to financiers and industrialists about building projects and commercial expansion; to landowners and peasants about agricultural subsidies and higher farm prices; to military men about past glories and the prospect of new ones; and to all he emphasized the virtues of public order and good government.

On a more practical level he won over an important number of army officers by key promotions; he ensured the loyalty of the army rank and file by pay increases and extra rations; he gained favor with the Church by sending an army to Rome to support the pope against republican revolutionaries and by backing legislation to give the Church greater control over education at home. He suppressed every threat of social revolution or political unrest. "It is time that the good should be reassured and that the wicked should tremble," he declared.

By the end of October, 1849, Louis Napoleon felt strong enough to dismiss the Orleanist ministry he had selected the previous December, when the legislature was still predominantly republican, and to appoint a ministry "devoted to his own person." In January, 1851, he relieved an outspoken champion of the legislature, General Nicolas Changarnier (1793–1877), as military commander in Paris. Later in the year he appointed his own henchmen to the crucial posts of minister of war, prefect of police, and minister of the interior.

The monarchist-dominated Legislative Assembly meanwhile was conducting a campaign against the president. Recognizing the advantages to Louis Napoleon of universal suffrage, the monarchists passed legislation that deprived some three million men of the franchise and imposed numerous restrictions on freedom of assembly and of the press. Louis Napoleon acquiesced to these measures and at the time made no move to abrogate the power of the legislature. Instead, he allowed the monarchists by their actions to discredit themselves with liberals and republicans, the natural supporters of parliamentary government. The president's request in May, 1850, for repeal of the new electoral law and a return to universal suffrage was denied by the conservative majority in the assembly. On July 15, 1851, the legislature directly challenged the president by rejecting a proposal to revise the constitution to allow him to stand for reelection. This meant that Louis Napoleon would be compelled to relinquish office in 1852 at the end of his four-year term, and that his career as head of state would be over.

The Coup d'État of 1851

The refusal of the legislature to let him stand for reelection ended whatever intentions Louis Napoleon may have had of trying to extend his power by legal means. On the night of December 1, 1851, Paris was occupied by troops loyal to the president. The main government buildings, military installations, and strategic points were seized; police agents arrested seventy-eight key political figures who might have become leaders of an opposition movement. On the morning of December 2, the anniversary of the coronation of Napoleon I and of the Battle of Austerlitz, Paris was placarded with announcements that the president had dissolved the legislature, which—the notices alleged—had robbed the people of their right to vote and throttled their political liberties. It was declared that the president was restoring universal suffrage and would seek the people's approval of fundamental changes in the constitution.

The coup d'état of December 2, 1851, made Louis Napoleon dictator of France. Opposition was ruthlessly suppressed in Paris and in the provinces. Throughout the country approximately a hundred thousand people were arrested; by the end of the year about twenty thousand had been sentenced to terms of imprisonment or exile. On December 21 a plebiscite was held asking the French people to approve the *coup d'état* and grant the president the right to draw up a new constitution. Napoleon made full use of his powers to influence the voters, but there is no reason to doubt that the overwhelming preponderance of "Yes" votes represented the sentiments of the majority of the French people.

The new constitution of January 14, 1852, was modeled directly on the constitution of the Consulate of the first Napoleon. It declared that the chief of state was "responsible to the nation," but at the same time it gave him "free and unfettered authority" to conduct the nation's affairs. There was to be a Council of State, appointed by the president, to draw up laws proposed by the president; a Senate, appointed by the president, had the duty to guard and amend the constitution. A legislative body was to be elected by universal manhood suffrage, but its presiding officers were to be appointed by the president. No public debate was permitted, and only government-approved summaries of the legislature's proceedings could be released to the press. One of Napoleon's ministers and the chief author of the constitution informed the Austrian ambassador: "I am willing enough to be baptized with the water of universal suffrage, but I don't intend to live with my feet in it."

The actual administration of France was carried on by the professional civil service through the highly centralized bureaucratic system created during the French Revolution and perfected by Napoleon I. The prefects, appointed by the central government, were the administrative heads of the departments into which the nation was divided. Through the prefects and their departmental bureaucrats, the legislation of the central government was transmitted to the entire country. As in Prussia, the government was based fundamentally on the civil service and on the army.

THE CRIMEAN WAR, 1854–1856

Louis Napoleon had yet to fulfill the promises of national glory associated with his name. The French ruler recognized that to gain this glory and to restore France's old position of ascendancy in Europe, he would have to break the restrictions imposed on France by the treaties of 1815. He also recognized that the chief supporter of those treaties in the mid-nineteenth century was Russia, which was using them to establish its own ascendancy on the Continent. It was Napoleon's good fortune that he came to power at a time when fear of Russia overshadowed fear of France among the states of Europe, and he soon discovered that France would not lack allies in pursuing an anti-Russian policy.

Fear of Russia was no new phenomenon in European history. Since the days of Peter the Great, European statesmen had looked with increasing apprehension at the mammoth power rising in the east and at the gradual but steady extension of Russia's frontiers in every direction. Finland, the east coast of the Baltic, and a large part of Poland came under Russian control in the late eighteenth and early nineteenth centuries. For two centuries there had been a war between Russia and Turkey almost every twenty years, as Russia extended its influence at the expense of the Ottoman Empire into the Middle East, the Balkans, and the Mediterranean. As long as Russia was economically and technically backward, containment by the smaller states of Europe remained feasible. But were this backwardness to be overcome, Russia, with great natural resources and a large population, might prove more than a match for the countries of western Europe, especially if by that time its power had been solidly established not only on the Baltic but in the Balkans and at the great naval base of Constantinople, from which the entire Mediterranean basin could be dominated.

It was to prevent Russia from controlling the Balkans and Constantinople that the Crimean War was fought. The tragedy of the war was that its purpose could have been, and in fact was, accomplished by diplomacy. The one significant result of the Crimean War was that it permanently destroyed the Concert of Europe.

Russia had emerged from the revolutionary era of 1848 as the apparent arbiter of Europe: the friend of Prussia, the protector of Austria, the reservoir of support for all monarchical and conservative governments. Russia's strength, or semblance of strength, was to prove a serious political handicap, for it tended to make other countries suspicious of Russian policies and anxious to prevent any extension of Russian influence. Austria, though deeply indebted to Russia for military aid against Hungary in 1849 and for diplomatic support against Prussia in 1850, had no desire to become a Russian protectorate. To maintain their nation's political independence, Austria's leaders sought to strengthen their diplomatic ties with other powers. Their attitude toward Russia was summed up by the Austrian prime minister, Prince Schwarzenberg: "We will astonish the world by our ingratitude." Prussia, under the irresolute leadership of King Frederick William IV (ruled 1840–1861), played a negible role in the diplomacy of the period, but Prussia too had reason to fear Russian power, and was resentful of Russia's support of Austria in German affairs.

Curiously enough it was Great Britain, farthest away and least menaced, that was to become the most rabid opponent of Russia in Europe. The British feared the Russian threat to the European balance of power, the possible establishment of Russian control over the Ottoman Empire, and the consequent danger to their routes to India, their trade in the Near East, and their sea power in the Mediterranean. These British fears were compounded by the belief that Russia had gained control of the Concert of

Europe and that Austria, Prussia, and the other conservative powers had fallen under its domination. The British therefore welcomed Louis Napoleon's anti-Russian policy and his efforts in 1851 to challenge Russia as the chief protector of the Christian holy places in the Ottoman Empire.

The dispute over the holy places was no empty issue of national prestige but a question of power and influence in the Near East. By establishing its role as protector of the holy places and the Christian population, a state could obtain an excuse to intervene in the internal affairs of the Ottoman Empire and thus gain a valuable means of improving its position in areas under Turkish control.

France already exerted considerable influence in the Near East through trade, missionary work, and financial assistance to the Turkish government. In 1851 Napoleon took advantage of this influence to press for special privileges in connection with the holy places. These were granted by the sultan, who was not blind to the fact that faraway France was a less dangerous protector of Christianity than neighboring Russia. The tsar retaliated by demanding new concessions for Russia. When the Turks, on the advice of Britain, rejected the Russian demands, the tsar occupied the Turkish provinces of Moldavia and Walachia (later reunited as the state of Rumania) to back up his claims. The French and British replied by sending their fleets into the eastern Mediterranean. The situation was tense, but it seemed the difficulties could be resolved by diplomacy as they had been so often since 1815. After complicated negotiations, the tsar promised to evacuate Moldavia and Walachia and to refrain from direct intervention in Turkey; he insisted only that Russia's existing treaty rights in the Ottoman Empire be observed. So moderate were the Russian conditions that Louis Napoleon could find no good reason for rejecting them. But the British cabinet was divided on the question, and anti-Russian influences in London prevailed. The Russian proposal was rejected, and at the end of September, 1853, the British fleet was ordered to Constantinople. Confident of British support, the Turks declared war on Russia on October 4, 1853.

The Turkish armies temporarily held their own against Russia, but on November 30 a Turkish naval squadron was destroyed by the Russians at Sinop, a port on the Black Sea. The battle at Sinop demonstrated conclusively the vulnerability of wooden warships; a Russian fleet equipped with the most recent type of shell-firing guns blasted the Turkish ships to pieces. But the Russians themselves failed to learn the lesson of Sinop; otherwise, the course and outcome of the Crimean War might have been very different. British and French naval vessels were still built entirely of wood. Had the Russians blocked the entry of a hostile fleet into the Black Sea and taken up a defensive position at the mouth of the Bosporus, they might have prevented, or at least rendered far more difficult, allied domination of the sea-lanes to the Crimea.

As it was, the most important result of Sinop was its effect on British public opinion. Russia's perfectly legitimate act of war was denounced in Britain as a treacherous massacre; British newspapers called for war against the "inhuman" Russians and demanded the reinstatement of Lord Palmerston, the most bellicose and anti-Russian member of the cabinet, who had resigned (in opposition to a franchise-reform bill) on the day the news of Sinop arrived in London. The French reaction was more restrained, but Napoleon could not afford to neglect this opportunity to move against Russia in alliance with Britain.

In December, 1853, the British and the French fleets were sent into the Black Sea to protect the Turkish coast and clear the Black Sea of Russian warships. On March 28, 1854, Great Britain and France formally declared war on Russia.

The greatest puzzle in the origin of the Crimean War is the attitude of Britain. For France the war was a blow against the peace treaties of 1815 and a step in the reestablishment of French political predominance in Europe. For Turkey the support of Britain and France provided a unique opportunity to open a counteroffensive against Russia, which had long been encroaching on Ottoman territory. But why should Britain have sought war after the tsar had agreed to Britain's principal conditions for the settlement of the Near Eastern question? Even after Sinop, the tsar offered to withdraw his troops from Moldavia and Walachia and to negotiate a settlement satisfactory to the powers, and still Britain went to war.

There were two obvious reasons for this British behavior. The first was the fervent desire for war by a British public that wished to see the nation reassert its influence on the Continent. The second was the attitude of a few influential British statesmen, notably Palmerston and the British ambassador in Constantinople, Lord Stratford de Redcliffe, who had no faith in Russian promises and believed war was the only certain means of restoring the European balance of power. On May 26, 1854, Palmerston wrote to Lord John Russell, a member of the cabinet, that just to expel the Russians from Moldavia and Walachia "would be only like turning a burglar out of your house, to break in again at a more fitting opportunity. The best and most effectual security for the future peace of Europe would be the severance from Russia of some of the frontier territories acquired by her in later times, Georgia, Circassia, the Crimea, Bessarabia, Poland and Finland . . . she would still remain an enormous Power, but far less advantageously posted for aggression on her neighbors." Palmerston's reasoning resembles that of most advocates of preventive war. He forgot, however, that Britain and its allies might not have the strength to impose such terms on Russia, and that even if Russia could be permanently deprived of the power of aggression, which was practically impossible, there would be other states to take its place. Palmerston himself was one of the first to be dismayed by the emergence of French power after the Crimean War and was soon talking in terms of preventive war against France.

"At the camp of the Fourth Dragoon Guards: a convivial party of French and English." *A Photograph by Roger Fenton, who took the first successful war pictures. Although Fenton had ample material to show the horrors of war in the Crimea, he was uncertain whether the British public would buy pictures of mutilated bodies and unsanitary field hospitals. He concentrated instead on officers and groups of soldiers. The woman in the picture is a* cantinière *who sold refreshments.*

The Conduct of the War

The strategy of the Crimean War was as senseless as its causes. The major problem for Britain and France in a war against Russia was to find a geographical target for an offensive. In August, 1854, under diplomatic pressure from Austria, the Russians withdrew from Moldavia and Walachia. The provinces were promptly occupied by Austria, which remained neutral, thereby making impossible either an allied campaign against Russia or a Russian campaign against Turkey through the Balkans. The British sent a naval squadron to attack Russian strongholds in the Baltic and White seas, and an allied fleet threatened Russian possessions in the Pacific, but nothing significant was accomplished. The allies finally settled on an attack on Russia's Crimean peninsula, which was accessible to allied armies because their navies controlled the Black Sea.

The allied leaders, presumably after a superficial study of maps of the Crimea, reasoned that their fleets could easily cut the peninsula off from the mainland by dominating the narrow isthmus with their guns. The strategy might have worked but for the fact that the waters on either side of the isthmus were only two to three feet deep. When this awkward fact was discovered, it became evident that an actual invasion of the Crimea would be necessary.

Allied forces landed in the Crimea on September 14, 1854, and on September 20 they defeated a Russian army on the Alma River. Had they pressed home their victory they might well have captured Sevastopol, the great Russian naval base in the Crimea, which was the major objective of the campaign. As it proved, however, the failure to capture Sevastopol in the first offensive was a stroke of luck for the allies. Their delay gave the

Russians time to strengthen the city's defenses and bring up reinforcements. The resulting siege of Sevastopol was probably the most effective drain on Russian resources that could have been devised. The allies could be supplied and reinforced relatively easily by sea, whereas the Russians, although fighting on their own territory, were forced to deal with the problems of long supply lines, bad roads, and weather. Men and matériel were sent overland to the Crimea at fearful cost. So severe were the rigors of the long journey, especially in winter, that only one Russian soldier in ten actually reached the front, after a three-month march. The Russian medical department estimated the nation's losses at half a million men; in comparison, the British and French lost about sixty thousand, two thirds of whom died of disease. The drain on the Russian economy was on a comparable scale. The defense of Sevastopol bled the country white. The allies could have adopted no better strategy, but it was unplanned and undesired, for the politicians in London and Paris wanted dramatic victories to satisfy the public. A tedious siege offers few opportunities for glory.

No military commander emerged from the war with credit except the Russian engineer Count Eduard Ivanovich Totleben (1818–1884), who organized the defense of Sevastopol. Symptomatic of the low quality of military leadership was the disastrous charge of the British Light Brigade, whose slaughter resulted from confused orders transmitted by a confused orderly to an officer foolish enough to carry them out. Only one person, a woman, gained a heroic reputation from the Crimean War—Florence Nightingale (1820–1910), the nurse who reorganized the military field hospitals and later inspired the reorganization of the entire British hospital system. Her activity led to the opening of the nursing profession as a respected public career for women, the first big step toward the more equal status of women in public life.

The Crimean War had a significant effect on methods of warfare. Indeed, it brought about a revolution in naval procedures. The operations in the Black Sea demonstrated conclusively the superiority of steam over sail and of the ship driven by a screw propeller over the side-wheeler. They also revealed the inability of wooden warships to withstand the firepower of rifled, shell-firing cannon. To meet this difficulty, the French developed the first ironclad warships, which they used as floating fortresses in the siege of Sevastopol.

The innovations in land warfare were less dramatic. The allies had the advantage of being equipped with Minié breech-loading rifles, while the Russians still used smoothbore muzzle-loaders. The railroad was used for the first time for military purposes, to bring allied troops and equipment to the front lines before Sevastopol. An attempt was made to employ another new invention, the telegraph, to direct military operations in the Crimean from London and Paris, but the results of such long-distance leadership were sufficiently unfortunate to end this experiment quickly. The telegraph

The interior of a fortress guarding Sevastopol after its evacuation by the Russians, who destroyed it before withdrawing. *The photograph is by James Robertson, an amateur photographer who was superintendent and chief engraver of the Imperial Mint at Constantinople.*

was put to more significant use by British war correspondents, whose descriptions of the inadequacies of the military supply system and the consequent suffering of the soldiers aroused public opinion and led to a demand for large-scale reforms in the military system.

Tsar Nicholas I died in March, 1855; Sevastopol fell in September; and in December, Austria threatened to join the allies unless Russia surrendered. The new tsar, Alexander II, his resources exhausted, faced with revolt at home and the prospect of an Austrian invasion, decided to yield. An armistice was arranged on February 25, 1856.

The Aftermath of the War

In the Treaty of Paris of March 30, 1856, the Russians surrendered only one piece of territory that they had not been willing to renounce before the war began—the strategic province of Bessarabia, at the mouth of the Danube. They agreed to the internationalization of the Danube and relinquished their claim to the right to protect Christians in the Ottoman Empire. Most important of all, they accepted the neutralization of the Black Sea, which meant that Russia could not maintain a navy or naval bases on the Black Sea and was consequently deprived of offensive and

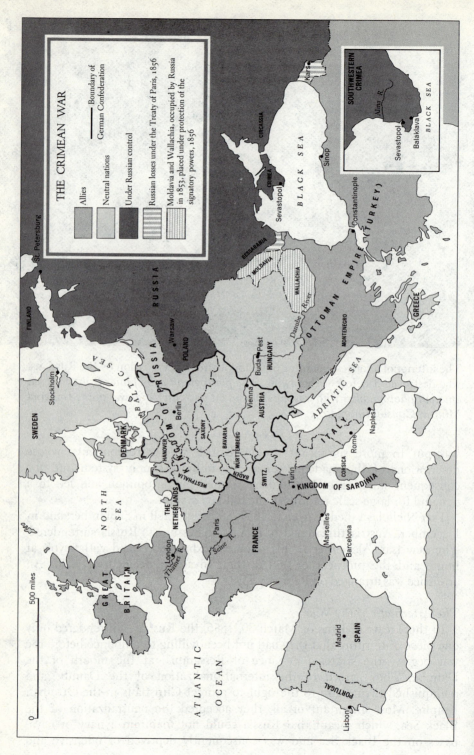

THE CRIMEAN WAR

- Allies
- Neutral nations
- Under Russian control
- Russian losses under the Treaty of Paris, 1856
- Moldavia and Wallachia, occupied by Russia in 1853, placed under protection of the signatory powers, 1856

—— Boundary of German Confederation

SOUTHWESTERN CRIMEA

Kars
Alma R.
Sevastopol
Balaklava
BLACK SEA

St. Petersburg

FINLAND

RUSSIA

BALTIC SEA

Warsaw
POLAND

Stockholm

SWEDEN

DENMARK

KINGDOM OF PRUSSIA

Berlin

HANOVER

WESTPHALIA

THE NETHERLANDS

SAXONY

BAVARIA

WÜRTEMBERG

BADEN

SWITZ.

Vienna

Buda Pest

HUNGARY

AUSTRIA

BESSARABIA

MOLDAVIA

Danube River

WALLACHIA

OTTOMAN EMPIRE (TURKEY)

Constantinople

Sinop

BLACK SEA

CRIMEA

Sevastopol

CIRCASSIA

Kars

MONTENEGRO

GREECE

ADRIATIC SEA

ITALY

Rome

Naples

CORSICA

KINGDOM OF SARDINIA

Turin

Marseilles

Barcelona

SPAIN

Madrid

PORTUGAL

Lisbon

FRANCE

Paris

Seine R.

London

Thames R.

GREAT BRITAIN

NORTH SEA

ATLANTIC OCEAN

500 miles

0

defensive weapons in this area. They also agreed to leave the Aaland Islands in the Gulf of Bothnia unfortified and to restore to Turkey the fortress city of Kars, near the east coast of the Black Sea, which they had captured in the course of the war. The Danubian principalities of Moldavia and Walachia were placed under the protection of the signatory powers, who further promised to respect the independence and territorial integrity of the Ottoman Empire.

These provisions might have created a permanent obstacle to further Russian expansion at the expense of Europe and Turkey had they been permanently enforced, but international settlements are never permanent. The coalition that imposed the Treaty of Paris on Russia had already begun to break apart during the peace negotiations. Russia repudiated the Black Sea clauses of the treaty in 1870, was again at war with Turkey in 1877, and had regained both Bessarabia and Kars by 1878.

The most permanent result of the Crimean War was the disruption of the Concert of Europe. Forty years of peace were now followed by four wars (1859–1871) that revolutionized the power structure of the Continent. Defeated and humiliated, Russia was determined to break the restrictions imposed by the Treaty of Paris, and thus became a revisionist state, although it refrained from active intervention in European affairs during the next two decades, while setting its own house in order. "Russia is not sulking," the Russian chancellor Prince Gorchakov explained. "She is quietly gathering her forces—*la Russie se recueille*." Great Britain, disillusioned by an inglorious war and an inconclusive peace, adopted an attitude similar to that of Russia by withdrawing from European affairs. Austria was isolated. During the Crimean War both sides had confidently anticipated Austrian backing: Russia had expected Austria to support the 1815 peace settlement against France and to repay a debt of gratitude for recent military and diplomatic aid; Britian and France had been certain that Austria would recognize the necessity of halting Russian expansion in southeastern Europe, where vital Austrian interests were at stake. Austria's neutrality antagonized all the belligerents, with the result that until 1879 Austria was without friends among the great powers. Prussia's policy during the war was so flaccid and its strength seemed so inconsequential that it was almost dismissed as a major power.

France was the state that seemed to have gained most from the war. French armies had won the most impressive victories in the final attacks on Sevastopol; the international system of 1815 and its restrictions had been swept away; France had supplanted Russia as the dominant power in Europe. But France's position was not so strong as it appeared. Britain was apprehensive about the revival of French power and the renewed danger of French hegemony on the Continent. Russia, already antagonized by the Crimean War, was further alarmed by Napoleon's talk of an independent

Polish state, which would deprive Russia of its Polish provinces. A similar reaction occurred in Austria and Prussia, with large Polish minorities of their own, and these states also resented Napoleon's interference in German and Italian affairs. France was as isolated among the great powers as Austria, a situation Napoleon never seemed to understand. He pursued an ambitious foreign policy, confident that French strength and prestige could overcome all obstacles. He was to be cruelly disillusioned.

Only one state gained a diplomatic advantage from the Crimean War. The north Italian kingdom of Sardinia had entered the war on the side of the allies in January, 1855, as a move in its struggle against Austria for supremacy in Italy. Cavour, the astute Sardinian prime minister, had seen clearly that his country's Italian ambitions might be permanently jeopardized if an exclusive alliance between Austria and the western powers were formed. To forestall this danger and to stay in favor with his sovereign, who was eager to win military glory, Cavour had agreed to send Sardinian troops to the Crimea. "Once our soldiers have mixed with yours," King Victor Emmanuel II told the French ambassador, "I will laugh at Austria."

Cavour's policy was successful. In the eyes of Britain and France, Sardinia's unconditional participation in the war contrasted favorably with Austria's neutrality. Sardinia was therefore admitted to the peace conference on an equal footing with the great powers. The British and French delegates supported Cavour's denunciation of political conditions in Italy, which was, in effect, an indictment of Austrian influence in that country. Although Sardinia gained nothing concrete from the Crimean War, it established goodwill with France and Britain which would prove of considerable value in subsequent maneuvers against Austria.

With the Concert of Europe in shambles, Russia and Britain temporarily withdrawing from the international scene, and Austria in isolation, the field was open to political opportunists of every kind. Foremost among them was Louis Napoleon, whose ambitious but ill-defined and inconsistent policies kept European politics in ferment until the fall of his regime.

THE SECOND EMPIRE

In 1852, while the Crimean War was brewing, Napoleon finally dropped the mask of republicanism. On November 21 another plebiscite was held, to ask public approval for the restoration of the empire. Again the government secured an enormous majority, and on December 2, 1852, the anniversary of the *coup d'état*, Louis Napoleon was proclaimed emperor of the French. He took the title Napoleon III, thus recognizing the reign of the first Napoleon's little son, in whose favor Napoleon I had abdicated on April 6, 1814.

On January 30, 1853, Napoleon III married Eugénie de Montijo (1826–1920), the daughter of an impoverished Spanish-Scots family. The Empress Eugénie was never really popular in France, but she provided the empire with a male heir. She also provided French society with a glittering court, the most dazzling, if not the most exclusive or cultivated, in Europe. Women enjoyed a special eminence there, as did the representatives of the bourgeoisie—the stock promoters and business magnates who played so prominent a part in the economic life of the Second Empire. It was a court of the *nouveaux riches*, whose vitality and self-indulgence is well reflected in the music of Jacques Offenbach (1819–1880), the most popular composer of the time.

Economic Policy

The first half decade of the reign of Napoleon III was, on the whole, a period of prosperity for France, as it was for the other countries of western Europe. The policies of the imperial government undoubtedly contributed to the French economic revival. The emperor took a genuine interest in economic questions, especially as they related to social welfare. As head of state he put the power and authority of the central government behind programs to stimulate the national economy and improve the standard of living of the French worker. The emperor was strongly influenced by the socialist theories of Henri de Saint-Simon (1760–1825), a leading advocate of economic planning. Napoleon III believed with Saint-Simon that society should organize its resources scientifically for the benefit of its members. His was a program of state socialism, but to fulfill it he employed all the resources of the rapidly developing capitalist system.

The basis of this imperial economic program was the expansion of credit: money was made available on easy terms to entrepreneurs of every kind— farmers, manufacturers, builders, shippers—to permit them to take full advantage of the developments of the agricultural and industrial revolutions. They, in turn, were expected to produce more goods and services for the French people, to provide employment for French labor, and to create an expanding market for French products. The government floated public bond issues for major construction programs and encouraged private investment by providing state guarantees for government-sponsored credit companies. The Crédit Mobilier was founded with official backing in 1852 to promote large-scale industrial enterprises: railroad and harbor construction, the installation of gas-lighting in urban centers, the expansion of mining and shipping companies. The Crédit Foncier, also founded in 1852, was originally conceived as a national mortgage bank to provide long-term loans to peasants for agricultural improvements, but the conservative French peasant was suspicious of the innovation. The Crédit Foncier became instead a major source of capital for public and private building, above all for the great urban-reconstruction programs of the Second Empire.

The government's easy-credit policy provided a breeding ground for shady

The reconstruction of Paris. *Shown here is the demolition of the area near the Panthéon in the Latin Quarter. Under the plan of Baron Haussmann, slums were torn down and replaced by broad boulevards and open spaces that afforded majestic vistas of the city and its monuments.*

speculators and financial manipulators, but it did indeed stimulate the national economy. The major French railway lines, planned during the reign of Louis Philippe, were built or completed, together with an impressive network of branch lines. The harbors of Marseilles, Le Havre, Brest, and Cherbourg were developed into centers of world shipping. French shipyards were equipped to build iron steamboats in place of wooden sailing ships. The Suez Canal, largely a product of French enterprise, was built between 1859 and 1869. The adoption of new inventions and methods of manufacture stimulated a boom in the mining and metallurgical industries. Coal production doubled. France remained behind Britain in steel production, but in 1870 was still ahead of the states of Germany in this crucial industry.

The economic policies of the Second Empire prompted the greatest building boom up to that time in French history. Under the direction of Baron Georges Eugène Haussmann (1809–1891), the prefect of the Seine, Paris was transformed from a picturesque medieval city of narrow, winding streets into the present city of air and light, with broad, straight boulevards, great circular plazas with avenues radiating from them, and superb architectural vistas. Paris was provided with an adequate public water supply, an underground sewage system, gas illumination. A new central market was built, construction on the lavish opera house was begun, a public park was created in the Bois de Boulogne. The rebuilding of Paris was a major enterprise in city planning. The vast construction program supplied employment to large numbers of skilled and unskilled workers, and materially improved the living conditions of Parisians. The new city plan also facilitated the suppression of revolts and street fighting by making the erection of barricades more difficult and by providing easy access to every quarter of the city for artillery and troops. As one observer put it, the new broad streets were beautifully accessible to light, air—and infantry. Paris is the best-known example of civic reconstruction undertaken during the Second Empire, but the work of the emperor's planners in other cities, especially Marseilles, was equally noteworthy.

As a further stimulus to the French economy, Napoleon lowered import duties to provide industry with cheaper raw materials and labor with cheaper food. This policy was also designed to compel French producers, including the peasants, to adopt more efficient and economic methods in order to compete with foreign manufacturers and growers. In 1853 tariffs were lowered on food and on basic raw materials such as iron and coal. In 1860 the Cobden-Chevalier trade treaty with Britain significantly reduced French tariffs on British goods and opened the British market to French products. In the next six years France concluded similar reciprocal-trade agreements with Belgium, the German customs union, Italy, Austria, Sweden, Switzerland, the Netherlands, Spain and Turkey.

Napoleon's trade treaties provoked the first widespread opposition to the imperial regime. This arose even though the government provided subsidies for agriculture and industries that had been injured by the tariff agreements, thereby undercutting its own efforts to compel French producers to adopt more efficient methods. The emperor was unlucky in that his reciprocal-trade program was instituted at a time when the general prosperity in Europe was in sharp decline after the financial crash of 1857 and the French economy itself was suffering a succession of severe blows. Crop failures at the end of the 1850's were accompanied by the incidence of a disease of the silkworm, which badly damaged the silk industry, and of the attack of the phylloxera plant louse on French vineyards, which temporarily ruined the French wine industry. The blockade of southern United States ports by the Union navy during the American Civil War cut off a vital source of raw cotton and seriously hurt the French textile industry.

The French economy in the 1860's was also affected by a change in government financial policy. In 1859 Pierre Magne (1806–1879) was replaced as minister of finance by Achille Fould (1800–1867), a conservative banker who favored tighter credit, a balanced national budget, and severe curtailment of government spending. Fould's policies did put an end to loose speculation, but at the same time they ruined many marginal enterprises and depressed the national economy just when it was in need of stimulus. Drastic retrenchments were also made in expenditures for the army. The government did allocate 113 million francs to equip the army with a rapid-firing breech-loading rifle, the *chassepot*, but it did not provide adequate funds to modernize the artillery, a serious oversight. For the inferiority of French artillery was to be a major factor in France's defeat by Prussia in 1870–1871. The ministry of finance was not alone to blame for the cuts in the French military budget; a program of government economy was a prominent feature of the period of political liberalization in the final years of the empire.

The Liberal Empire

Opposition to the imperial regime aroused by government tariff policies, the economic slump, and various aspects of the imperial foreign policy prompted Napoleon III to seek new bases of popular support. His efforts to secure this support did not really represent a fundamental change in his approach, but rather constituted an extension of methods he had used since the beginning of his reign. As he had once won over landlords and businessmen by offering them political stability and economic opportunity, he now attempted to win over republicans, workers, and other disaffected groups by a lavish use of the spoils system and by political and economic concessions. During the 1860's many restrictions on personal freedom were relaxed, trade unions were legalized, workers were granted the right to strike.

To gain more active parliamentary support for his regime, the emperor increased the voice of the legislature in affairs of state and enlarged its control over the budget. Publication of the complete records of legislative debates was authorized, and members of parliament were granted the right to question government ministers on official policies. In making these concessions, Napoleon appears to have been motivated primarily by a desire to find men of talent to support his regime: politicians willing and able to aid him in governing France, ministers who might assume some of the work and responsibility now burdening him.

One fateful result of the liberalization policies was that the emperor was rendered powerless to force through reforms in the French army to match recent military reforms in Prussia. Many members of the legislature objected on principle to strengthening the army and to the higher taxes which doing so would entail. They looked upon the army as a bulwark of the Napoleonic dictatorship and upon compulsory military service as an instrument of political indoctrination and oppression. Between 1863 and 1870 the legislature relentlessly pared military expenditures. But a large share of the responsibility for the inadequate reorganization of the French army belonged to government and military leaders: an economy-minded ministry of finance; conservative generals reluctant to accept innovations; high-ranking imperial officials who, fearing the revolutionary outlook of the population, hesitated to arm what might eventually become the instrument of their own downfall.

The so-called Liberal Empire did not last long enough to make possible a sound evaluation of its ultimate aims and potential. Over the short run the emperor's liberalization policies evidently produced the results he desired. Opposition was undercut; the government strengthened its hold on old supporters and won important new ones; republicans and socialists as well as financiers and industrialists gained an interest in preserving the imperial regime. In January, 1870, Émile Ollivier (1825–1913), former leader of the radical opposition in the legislature, became the chief minister in the imperial government. Ollivier was told that the emperor needed his assistance in "organizing liberty." In May, 1870, the French people were asked to approve by plebiscite the recent liberalizing legislation, and thus, in effect, to cast a vote of confidence in the imperial regime. The returns gave Napoleon III a victory as great as any he had scored at the beginning of his reign.

These triumphs in the domestic arena were short-lived. Five months later the Second Empire was swept away as a result of mistakes in the conduct of foreign affairs.

Imperial Foreign Policy

In foreign policy, as in domestic, Napoleon III showed a rare ability to understand the popular forces of his day, but his efforts to exploit or placate these forces, instead of increasing his power or improving the international position of his country, involved him in ruinous political adventures. It was above all in international relations that the name Napoleon played him false. The French people had given him their overwhelming endorsement in the 1848 elections and had enthusiastically approved the restoration of the empire in 1852, but with that restoration they anticipated a new succession of military victories, a revival of French glory, the reestablishment of France as the Great Nation of Europe. These expectations too Napoleon understood, and fatefully, he undertook to satisfy them.

The most astute feature of the emperor's foreign policy was his effort to improve relations with Great Britain. Having brooded long over the history of the First Empire, Napoleon III had concluded that Britain had been the greatest obstacle to his uncle's success and that the hindrance exerted on France's freedom of action on the Continent by this state should be removed by winning its friendship. Accordingly, he sought to break down tariff barriers and establish closer trade relations with Britain. He backed

British policy in the Near East, and during the Crimean War, French troops fought alongside instead of against British troops in a European campaign for the first time since the days of Cromwell. In 1860, in cooperation with Britain, France brought pressure to bear on China to open eleven new treaty ports to European commerce. In 1861, again in cooperation with Britain, France compelled the Mexican government to recognize European property rights, a prelude to the ill-fated Mexican expedition shortly thereafter.

Especially after the experiences of the Crimean War, Napoleon recognized that he had neither the military nor the organizing genius of his uncle, but he believed that there were other ways to European leadership than military conquest. Just as he was one of the first modern statesmen to exploit mass public opinion, so he was one of the first to appreciate the power that the explosive force of nationalism might give to the man who could harness it to his own interests. His uncle had supplied the formula: "The first ruler who appeals to the peoples of Europe will be able to accomplish anything he wishes." But Napoleon I had failed to apply his own ideas, and the peoples of Europe had overthrown him. The opportunity now fell to the new Napoleon. If he became the champion of the cause of nationalism, if he led the peoples of Europe to freedom from foreign and domestic tyranny, he, the emperor of the French, would be regarded as the natural leader of a free Europe, and France would acquire a political and moral ascendancy on the Continent unmatched in history. Napoleon III's program to liberate the peoples of Europe was not the product of cynical calculation. Inspired by the Italian nationalist Giuseppe Mazzini, he believed in the cause of national liberation as ardently as he believed in the cause of eradicating poverty, and he looked forward to an era when free nations would live together harmoniously under the leadership of France.

Napoleon's vision of a society of free nations under French leadership was undeniably a grand conception. As a program of foreign policy, however, it was not only impractical but also directly contrary to French national interests. His encouragement of the Polish rebellion against Russia in 1863 gave rise to cruelly false hopes among Polish patriots, to whom he was unable to give effective aid. At the same time he gratuitously drew upon France the wrath of the tsar. The encouragement of nationalism, and hence inevitably of national unification movements in Germany and Italy, proved disastrous, for it contributed to the creation of great powers directly on the French border in place of weak and impotent neighbors.

In 1859, Napoleon went to war with Austria in support of the efforts of the Italian kingdom of Sardinia to drive Austria out of Italy. The French emperor undoubtedly sympathized with the Italian national cause, and he was grateful to Sardinia for its recent participation in the Crimean War. But he also had more selfish reasons for entering the Italian arena. The situation in Italy offered him a dramatic opportunity to place himself at the head of the European nationalist movement. On a more practical level, it gave him a chance to supplant Austrian by French influence in Italy.

As a move to establish paramount French influence in Italy, Napoleon's action made sense, but in all other respects his Italian policies were ill-conceived, ill-executed, and inconsistent. His armies failed to score a quick victory over the Austrians, and in the Italian nationalist movement he found he had released passions he was unable to control. Alarmed at what was happening in Italy and fearful that Prussia and other German states might come to the aid of Austria, he made peace with Austria without consulting his Italian allies. He left Venetia under Austrian rule and at first refused to permit the states of central Italy, which had revolted against their Austrian-supported rulers, to unite with Sardinia. Unable to stem the tide of national feeling without resorting to force, he finally agreed to this union, but forced Sardinia in return to give up Nice and Savoy to France.

All this time French troops had remained in Rome, where they had been sent in 1849 to support the Pope against republican revolutionaries. These troops now blocked the aspirations of Italian nationalists, who looked upon Rome as the natural capital of a united Italy. Thus Napoleon was cast in the ridiculous position of simultaneously supporting Italian nationalists against Austria and thwarting them in Rome. As a result of his separate treaty with Austria, his acquisition of Nice and Savoy, and his policy concerning Rome, Napoleon found that instead of winning the gratitude of Italian patriots for his aid against Austria, he had reaped hatred and abuse. It was an inauspicious beginning to France's spiritual conquest of Europe.

The emperor's policy with respect to Germany was even less fortunate and more confused. Napoleon saw the danger of a Germany united into one strong state, but he believed he could maintain a balance of power between the two major states of Germany—Prussia and Austria. As in the case of Italy, he hoped to establish in Germany a loose national confederation in which the weaker states would look to France for protection. In pursuing this policy he believed he would be able to round out France's "natural frontiers" by gaining control of the territory on the left bank of the Rhine. His calculations went completely awry. Prussia's victory over Austria in 1866 ended any hope for a balance of power. To compensate for the fiasco of his German policy and to offset the increase in Prussian strength, Napoleon now made territorial demands hardly befitting the champion of national freedom. Ineptly and unsuccessfully he claimed for France the Rhineland, Belgium, and Luxemburg.

Napoleon's search for successes in foreign policy became all the more frantic after the Second Empire suffered a serious setback in Mexico. Napoleon's Mexican expedition began after a joint diplomatic campaign by Great Britain, France, and Spain to force the revolutionary government of Benito Juárez (1806–1872) to recognize European property rights. Taking advantage of the fact that the Civil War left the United States government unable to intervene in Mexico, Napoleon sent an army to establish Archduke Maximilian (1832–1867), brother of the emperor of Austria, as emperor of Mexico. Napoleon appears to have been motivated by the desire to curry favor with the Catholic Church by overthrowing Juárez's anticlerical regime, to conciliate Austria, which had been antagonized by his Italian policy, and to give France a great new political and economic sphere of influence in the western hemisphere. (The first Napoleon, too, had dreamed of a Mexican empire.) With the end of the Civil War, the United States government forced Napoleon to withdraw his troops from Mexico, and the French Mexican empire collapsed. In 1867 the unfortunate Maximilian was executed by Juárez's troops at Querétaro.

The Fall of the Second Empire

"There are no mistakes left to commit," said the veteran Orleanist statesman Adolphe Thiers, but he was wrong. In 1870, after scoring a diplomatic victory by persuading the Prussian king to withdraw the candidacy of a member of his family for the Spanish throne, Napoleon III yielded to the demands of French public opinion, and of his empress and his ministers, and posed further conditions, which Prussia found unacceptable. The result was war and national disaster. Poorly organized, poorly equipped, and miserably led, the French armies went down to defeat; at Sedan on September 2, 1870, the Second Empire collapsed under the pounding blows of the Prussian artillery.

Napoleon III left France with better railroads, better ships, better harbors, a stronger economy—and with two new great powers, Italy and Germany, on its frontiers. This was a heavy price to pay.

Autograph letter of Napoleon III to King William of Prussia, September 1, 1870, after the French defeat at Sedan. *The text reads: "Not having been able to die in the midst of my troops, there is nothing left for me to do but place my sword in the hands of your Majesty."*

CHAPTER 32

The National Revolutions, 1850-1870

AFTER THE withdrawal of Russia from the Concert of Europe, the principal defender of the *status quo* on the Continent was Austria, the multinational empire of the Habsburgs, which was to be the major victim of the disruption of the 1815 treaty system and Napoleon III's policy of encouraging nationalism. The 1815 treaties had restored the Habsburgs' control over much of central Europe and had given them preponderant influence in Italy and Germany. In the later years of the century their favorable position in these various areas was either destroyed or seriously undermined by nationalist revolution and agitation. The unification of Italy and Germany was achieved largely at the Habsburgs' expense; within what was left of their territories they were obliged to recognize the quasi-independent national status of the Hungarians; and the agitation of other nationalities for special rights or outright independence threatened the empire's very existence.

THE HABSBURG EMPIRE

So serious was the nationalities problem that many historians have tended to regard the Habsburg empire as an anachronism, an institution containing within itself forces that would bring about its inevitable collapse. It is well, however, to be cautious about the concept of inevitability in history. The Habsburgs had been emperors in Europe since the thirteenth century, and their empire had already faced and survived many disasters—the rending effects of the Reformation, the Thirty Years' War, Turkish invasions that had reached the gates of Vienna, the program of dismemberment of Frederick the Great, four decisive defeats by Napoleon, and the revolutions of 1848. By its very survival the empire had demonstrated that there was an unusual resilience in its character and institutions, and throughout its worst crises it had managed to retain to a remarkable degree the loyalty of its diverse peoples.

The unifying forces within the empire were the crown, the army, the bureaucracy, the Roman Catholic Church, and to a limited extent, the economy and the culture.

The imperial idea, associated with the Habsburgs for six hundred years, held sway over members of all nations and all classes. Until the empire was swept away after the First World War it was possible to undertake the most drastic kind of political and social reform under the imperial banner. The house of Habsburg had developed its own mystique, a belief that its rulers were not only kings by divine right but executors of a divine will. This certainty of its right to rule helps explain the impersonal quality of so many of its leaders, the unscrupulousness of their policies, their cold-blooded use of men and nations which made "the ingratitude of the house of Habsburg" proverbial over the centuries.

The army was the main pillar of the Habsburg state, the force which protected the empire from foreign foes and imposed internal political unity. It was also an effective instrument for indoctrinating a large body of men of every class and nationality with dynastic sentiments and the idea of imperial unity, especially after the introduction of compulsory military service in 1868. To the army, the fatherland was the whole empire, not some province or region, and more particularly it was embodied in the sovereign himself, a concept underlying the maxim "If my emperor is in Baden, then my fatherland is there also." Officers and men were rotated regularly from one part of the empire to another to promote the feeling of unity and overcome regional loyalties.

The bureaucracy, including the police and the secret service, was the civilian army of the Habsburgs. Through this administrative apparatus the central government could bypass feudal magnates and local governments, and impose imperial policies on every part of the empire. Careers in the imperial civil service, including the highest posts, were open to men of talent of every class and nationality and attracted some of the ablest people in the empire. Like all bureaucracies, that of the Habsburgs was characterized by pedantry, thoughtless routine, and secrecy, and not infrequently, by haughty incompetence and inefficiency. "An absolutism tempered by slovenliness," a prominent socialist leader called it. Yet even the severest critics of the imperial bureaucracy admitted that it was far superior to former feudal administrations, and that, compared with other governments of the nineteenth century, especially those of eastern and southern Europe, it represented an honorable degree of integrity and humanitarianism. It remained remarkably free of corruption and could seldom be accused of brutality toward the poor and oppressed.

The Roman Catholic Church had acted as a unifying influence in the empire in the years following the Reformation, when Church and state had cooperated to stamp out Protestantism and impose a considerable measure of religious unity on the realm. Since the eighteenth century, the Church had lost some of its political influence and it was often in conflict with the government, but it remained a strong force in society, and on the whole considered that its interests were served by supporting rather than undermining imperial rule.

The empire was never a natural economic unit—few states are—but by its very size it formed a large free-trade area in central Europe, particularly after the abolition of tariff barriers between Hungary and the other parts of the realm in 1850. The agricultural regions formed a valuable hinterland for the developing industries of German Austria, Bohemia, and Galicia.

Finally, there was the unifying quality of Viennese culture. In Vienna, melting pot of the empire, years of synthesis had produced a predominantly German culture with a strong admixture of Slav, Magyar, Italian, and other ethnic influences. German was still the lingua franca of the empire in 1850, but even after German gave way to local national languages later in the century, Vienna remained the cultural heart of the monarchy. For generations the imperial court had been the chief sponsor of talent and ambition. To Vienna flocked Czechs and Magyars, Rumanians and Croatians, Poles and Slovenes, representatives of every class and profession, all with a desire to make a name in the world. These people were absorbed into Viennese culture and in turn made their contributions to it.

The greatest weakness of the empire was its lack of organic unity in administration and in the composition of its population. It was a patchwork of provinces brought together over the centuries by conquest, diplomacy, or marriage alliances. Each province retained in large measure its local government, rights, traditions, and customs. The empire included the seventeen hereditary lands of Austria; the territories inhabited by the Slovenes in the south; the predominantly Czech lands of the crown of Bohemia, including Moravia and part of Silesia; the Polish province of Galicia, acquired in the partitions of Poland; the provinces of Venetia and Lombardy with their distinctly Italian population; and the lands of the crown of St. Stephen (Hungary, Transylvania, Croatia). Within this conglomerate of provinces there were some twenty more or less distinct nationalities.

The awakening of self-consciousness among the many nationalities of the Habsburg dominions was the most disruptive force in the empire in the nineteenth century. It is important to remember, however, that nationalism was not a mass movement in central Europe in 1850. In most parts of the empire the peasantry and town laborers were hardly touched by the nationalist spirit; to many members of the nobility espousal of the nationalist cause was little more than a means of safeguarding or extending local privileges. The Hungarian nationalist movement, for instance, attracted Magyar nobles who resented the restraints on their authority imposed by the Vienna government. The same motives characterized many members of the Polish nobility. During the Polish revolt in 1846 and the Hungarian revolt in 1848 it was the house of Habsburg that enjoyed the "popular" support of the peasants, who looked to the imperial government for protection against the local landlords of their own nationality. Once the rights of the Polish and Hungarian nobles had been guaranteed by the Vienna government, many of them became staunch supporters of the monarchy. Having secured "freedom" for themselves, they proved far more intolerant of national minorities within their own territories than the Habsburgs had been, and their policy toward the peasantry was often one of harsh oppression. In Italy, too, the common people still supported the Habsburgs in the mid-nineteenth century. The Italian patriot Giuseppe Garibaldi saw with dismay how the peasants of Lombardy rejoiced when the Austrians returned after a brief period of national "liberation" in 1849. The unimaginative but honest Austrian administration had treated them only with rough justice, but at least not with the crass injustice displayed by the kingdom of Sardinia. Nationalist sentiment was to become a steadily stronger disruptive force, however, and was undoubtedly the single greatest threat to imperial unity during the later nineteenth century.

The persistence of traditions confined to particular regions or groups, the jealous guarding of feudal and local privileges, the presence of economic inequalities and of dissension among the various social classes as well as the several nationalities, made for further weaknesses in the imperial structure. These weaknesses were clearly recognized at the time. Many Austrian leaders were infected with pessimism and accepted the general view that their empire was doomed. This opinion was already prevalent in the period following the French Revolution and the Napoleonic Wars. Prince Metternich, the chief engineer of political reconstruction after 1815, was so obsessed with fear of revolution that he has been described as suffering from a "dissolution complex." The gloom persisted and became more widespread as the signs of national disaffection increased and the problems of government seemed to grow more difficult. Pessimism permeated the entire population. Austrians accepted crisis at home and defeat abroad with a certain fatalism, an attitude summed up in the expression *Es ist passiert* ("well, it has happened"), suggesting that they had expected "it" all along.

The revolutions of 1848 seemed to confirm the view of the worst pessimists. The process of dissolution went forward rapidly, and Metternich, long a prophet of disaster, fled the country. But recovery followed, national and social revolts were suppressed, and in 1850 the empire seemed to have emerged from its agonies stronger than ever.

The Emancipation of the Peasants and the Industrial Revolution

The most important and lasting result of the revolution of 1848 was the final emancipation of the serfs. The act of emancipation of September 7, 1848, put an end to all rights of the lords over the peasants and abolished the compulsory labor service (the *robota*). Compensation to the lords for the loss of this free labor was paid in part by the state, in part by the peasants who held the land.

The emancipation of the peasants gave great impetus to agricultural production and economic life generally. The peasants worked harder for themselves than they had for their landlords, produced more than ever before, and became consumers with significant purchasing power. The great estates, freed from the wasteful system of forced peasant labor, could be run more efficiently and economically. The compensation paid to the great lords allowed them to develop their estates as capitalistic enterprises, to invest in mechanical farm equipment, to build breweries, beet-sugar factories, and sawmills, to exploit mines. The petty nobles, on the other hand, did not own enough land to run their estates profitably without free labor, nor did they receive enough money in compensation to become agricultural entrepreneurs. For many of them the emancipation of the serfs meant economic ruin, and they became competitors for positions in the service of the state. Because these poorer nobles were of many nationalities, their competition did much to intensify national antagonism in the empire.

The richer peasants, like the great landlords, profited from the emancipation. An act of Emperor Joseph II (ruled 1780–1790) had forbidden the acquisition by the nobility of traditional peasant holdings ("rustic land"). This measure was still in force, not so much to protect the peasants as to prevent this rustic land from falling into the hands of the nobility, who paid lower taxes than the peasants, or, as in Hungary, no taxes at all. The land law gave the peasant class security of tenure, but it did not prevent richer peasants from buying out poorer ones. Like their counterparts in western Europe, the richer peasants tended toward political conservatism, but during this period they also became more nationality-conscious and began to identify their interests with those of their national groups. The poorer peasants, with little or no land, supplemented their incomes by working on the land of others or subsisted altogether as farm laborers. Many were attracted to the towns, where they supplied the manpower for industry and swelled the ranks of the industrial proletariat. The great influx of unskilled peasant labor to the towns after 1848 laid the basis for future class antagonisms and also contributed to the conflict of nationalities. Before 1848 the majority of the townspeople in the empire were Germans. The arrival of Czech, Polish, or Croatian peasants destroyed the predominantly German character of the towns, but the Germans generally remained in control of the economy and were the chief employers of labor. Thus the class and nationality struggles reinforced each other, and laborers too, became nationality-conscious.

Perhaps the most significant result of peasant emancipation in Austria was the creation of a supply of mobile labor, which sped the progress of the

Industrial Revolution. The Industrial Revolution was the great force behind economic change in the Habsburg empire, as it was everywhere in Europe at this time. The government stimulated industrial development by abolishing trade and tariff barriers within the empire in 1850, by sponsoring a large-scale program of public works and railroad building, by providing official encouragement to manufacturing and trade. The main impetus for the industrial boom that took place after 1850, however, appears to have been the rapid growth of finance capitalism. Before 1848 the chief sources of capital in the empire had been the Austrian National Bank, which dealt almost exclusively with the state, and the house of Rothschild, which still operated conservatively and was far from generous with loans and credit.

The first bank to make credit available on a large scale in Austria was the Crédit Mobilier, founded in Paris in 1852 to promote industrial joint-stock enterprises and open new fields of business. In 1853 the first private Austrian bank, the Diskonto-Gesellschaft, was established for the same purpose. In 1855 the Rothschilds opened the Creditanstalt to compete with the highly successful Crédit Mobilier. These institutions provided the financial stimulus for the expansion of Austrian industry, which flourished particularly in Vienna and in the provinces of Bohemia and Galicia.

The Industrial Revolution brought to Austria the usual problems of city growth: an urban proletariat, slums, and labor unrest. But it also brought wealth and prosperity to a large section of the population and created a new middle class. Above all, it provided the money and material required by the administration and the army. And the strength of the army enabled Austria to remain among the great powers in spite of the disruptive forces operating within the empire.

Francis Joseph

At the head of the heterogeneous Habsburg realm was Emperor Francis Joseph I (ruled 1848–1916), who had been summoned to the throne during the revolutions of 1848 at the age of eighteen, with little preparation for his complicated duties. Despite his consequent need for good advisers, he seldom appointed men of outstanding ability to top government positions. Fearful of delegating authority, he insisted on himself formulating the major policy decisions affecting his empire. And because he was ponderously slow in making up his mind, important decisions might be delayed for months or even years. Yet when he did see the necessity for quick action, he could move with thoughtless haste. His life was a long record of misfortune. His only son killed himself; his wife was assassinated; his empire was in a chronic state of crisis; his foreign policy led from defeat to defeat. After his first major setback in the Italian war of 1859, he never regained his self-confidence. "I have an unlucky hand," he once confessed.

Yet Francis Joseph, through his office and through his personal qualities,

The Emperor Francis Joseph of Austria and his brothers. *From left to right: Archduke Charles Louis, a passionately pious man who died of dysentery after drinking water straight out of the River Jordan on a trip to the Holy Land; Archduke Louis Victor, who retired in a cloud of scandal to the castle of Klessheim near Salzburg; the emperor; Archduke Ferdinand Maximilian, the ill-fated Emperor Maximilian of Mexico.*

probably did more than any other man or institution to hold the Habsburg empire together. His dignity and his unwavering sense of obligation to his position made him the embodiment of the imperial idea; during the sixty-eight years of his reign he won and retained deep personal loyalty among the many peoples of his empire. His profound consciousness of his imperial mission, of the tradition and greatness of his house, gave him the moral strength to push on through a lifetime of difficulties and personal tragedies. It is symbolic that his empire did not collapse until after his death.

Upon becoming emperor of Austria in 1848, the young monarch attached to his original name of Francis the name of his popular predecessor, Joseph II. This, too, was symbolic, for in his rule Francis Joseph was to fluctuate between the principles of Francis I, whose chief minister, Metternich, had defended the *status quo*, and of Joseph, who had pressed ruthlessly for change, seeking a more rational, centralized system of government of the kind advocated by the political theorists of the Enlightenment. The outstanding characteristic of Francis Joseph's reign was his experimentation with a variety of governmental techniques in the interest of preserving his empire. Far from being rigid in his political ideas, as his critics have frequently maintained, he was all too ready to jettison a system when it met with setbacks and to experiment freely with the process of government.

The Schwarzenberg Government and the Bach System

The first governmental system adopted after Francis Joseph came to the throne on December 2, 1848, was introduced not by the emperor, but by the ministers who had restored order in Austria during the last months of 1848 under the leadership of Prince Felix zu Schwarzenberg (1800–1852). In 1851 the Schwarzenberg government formally abolished the various constitutions introduced as a result of the 1848 revolutions and instituted a system of imperial autocracy.

Schwarzenberg's attention was devoted primarily to foreign affairs. The chief architect of Austrian domestic policy after 1848 was Alexander von Bach (1813–1893), a German lawyer and former liberal, who was more interested in efficient government than in political freedom. To break the power of the feudal nobility and overcome regional particularism, he flooded the empire with German, Czech, and Polish officials, the notorious Bach "hussars." Behind the bureaucracy stood the army, the police, and a network of spies and informers as extensive as Metternich's. Unlike Joseph II, Bach did not hesitate to use the Roman Catholic Church as an instrument for consolidating state power. In an 1855 Concordat the Church was given extensive control over education and censorship, ecclesiastical courts were restored, the property of the Church was declared sacred and inviolable, civil marriage was abolished, and the government agreed not to alter confessional laws without the consent of the Vatican; in return, the government expected clerical support in carrying out its unification policies. The Bach regime, according to a bitter socialist critic, consisted of "a standing army of soldiers, a sitting army of officials, a kneeling army of priests, and a creeping army of denunciators."

Under Bach the Habsburg empire became for the first, and last, time a centralized state. He ruthlessly swept aside local rights and privileges and introduced a unified administration, a single system of law and taxation. He made German the official tongue of government in order to simplify administration and at the same time utilize language as a means of unification. The judiciary was separated from the executive branch of government to give it greater independence. Trial by jury was introduced. Every citizen was accorded equal rights and could move about within the empire without a passport. Bach's bureaucracy enforced the legislation freeing the serfs, a move that required strong pressure on the part of the central government to overcome the opposition and inertia of the nobility in every part of the realm.

The economy, too, was centralized. In 1850 all tariff barriers within the empire were removed, and for the first time the entire empire became a free-trade area. Karl Ludwig von Bruck (1798–1860), the minister of commerce, tried to extend this customs union to include all of Germany and to establish a central European empire of seventy million people under Habsburg leadership. His plans failed because of the opposition of Prussia and the smaller German states, and of Russia, which feared so great an increase in Habsburg power.

The state took over the construction of railways; communications were generally improved; the merchant fleet was expanded; the postal services were reorganized. Chambers of trade and industry were founded in an attempt to expand industry and encourage exports. Extensive public works and a stepped-up armaments program provided workers with employment and industry with lucrative contracts.

The economy nevertheless remained the weakest and most vulnerable aspect of the Bach regime. Mounting expenditures for the army and the bureaucracy, the outlays for the large-scale public works, the compensation paid to landowners for the emancipation of the serfs, produced a staggering rise in the costs of government. Mobilization during the Crimean War was unexpectedly expensive. At the same time, Bach's officials found it increasingly difficult to collect taxes. In the many parts of the empire where the centralization policies were unpopular, especially in Hungary, rich and poor alike displayed unexampled ingenuity in evading payment of taxes, and the costs of collection rose sharply. To secure the necessary funds to run the government, the state borrowed from the National Bank, sold crown property and the state railways, generally on very unfavorable terms, and floated loans at ever higher rates of interest. A stock-exchange crash in 1857 plunged the empire into economic depression. The Bach regime was in serious economic trouble by the end of the 1850's.

It was also in serious political trouble. The Bach system aroused widespread hostility in many segments of the population. The policy of centralization clashed with local administrative, legal, and economic rights. Non-German peoples objected to the German character of the government. The German middle classes, who welcomed the predominance given to the German language and German officialdom, resented the antiliberalism of the government, its concessions to the Church, and the heavy tax burden it imposed.

But it was blunders in foreign policy that brought the Bach system to an end. Under Schwarzenberg's forceful leadership the Habsburg empire had recovered from the shock of 1848 with remarkable speed and once again ranked as a great power in Europe. But Austrian leaders forgot that their recovery had been due in large measure to Russian support, and that to maintain their position they would have to retain the goodwill of Russia or secure similar backing from other states. Austrian diplomats did neither, with grave consequences for the realm.

With the sudden and unexpected death of Schwarzenberg in April, 1852, foreign affairs were placed in the hands of Count Karl Ferdinand von Buol-Schauenstein (1797–1865). His appointment proved to be disastrous. His policy of irresolute neutrality during the Crimean War cost Austria the friendship not only of Russia but of Britain and France as well. Then in 1859 he fell into the trap the Italian statesman Cavour had set for Austria in Italy.

THE UNIFICATION OF ITALY

At the midpoint of the nineteenth century, Austria was the chief power blocking Italian unification. Besides controlling the wealthy and populous provinces of Lombardy and Venetia, the Habsburg empire stood behind the "legitimate" rulers of the Italian petty states, and behind the pope, who governed Rome and much of central Italy. The ruling families of Modena and Tuscany were members of Austria's house of Habsburg, and after the 1848 revolution even the Bourbon rulers of Parma and Naples looked to Austria for protection.

In Italy, as in many other parts of Europe in the mid-nineteenth century, the concept of national freedom and unification was meaningful to only a minority of politically conscious people. Neither nationalism nor liberalism was in any sense a mass movement at this time. Successful national revolts in Italy were organized by small groups, and generally won widespread popular support only when they were able to exploit local grievances.

The most striking achievement of the Italian nationalists was their propaganda, by which they convinced others, Italian princes as well as foreign powers, of the deep-seated desire of the whole Italian people for political freedom and national unification, and of the inevitable triumph of these causes.

Although Italian patriots generally agreed about the broad goals of their movement, they differed widely on how Italian unification was to be achieved and on what form of government the new Italian nation should assume. Some favored a confederation of Italian states under the leadership of the pope, others a republic. After 1848, however, a growing number of Italian nationalists looked for leadership to the state of Sardinia.

The kingdom of Sardinia, which included the island of Sardinia and the mainland provinces of Piedmont, Nice, and Savoy, was ruled by the house of Savoy, the only native Italian dynasty. In 1848 Sardinia had been granted a constitution by its sovereign, and had attempted to wrest Lombardy and

Venetia from Austria. Despite the far from liberal nature of its new constitution and its utter defeat in the conflict with Austria, Sardinia emerged from the 1848 revolutions as the foremost standard-bearer of Italian liberal-nationalist aspirations. Shortly afterward, the Sardinian government came under the leadership of one of the outstanding statesmen of the nineteenth century, Count Camillo Benso di Cavour.

Cavour

Before devoting himself entirely to politics, Cavour (1810–1861) enjoyed a highly successful career in several fields. By employing scientific and efficient methods of farming on his private estates, he made a fortune in agriculture. He acquired additional wealth in banking, railroads, and shipping. He traveled much and learned much, especially from the political and economic system of England.

Cavour's entry into political life began with the publication in December, 1847, of his newspaper, *Il Risorgimento* ("The Resurgence"), which gave its name to the entire Italian nationalist movement of the nineteenth century. Cavour was no revolutionary firebrand, but rather an aloof and somewhat detached intellectual. In his political orientation he was a moderate liberal and a moderate nationalist. He believed in constitutional government and sought to improve the existing social system by means of orderly reform. As a nationalist, he wished to free Italy of foreign domina-

Count Camillo Benso di Cavour.

tion and to bring about some kind of political unification of the peninsula, but he had no rigid views on how Italian liberty and unification were to be achieved and was doubtful whether these ideals could be realized in his lifetime.

Cavour's moderate political views and his cold intellectuality did not make him popular with his king or with the majority of Sardinia's politicians, but Cavour did not depend on popularity for political influence. His energy and resourcefulness were combined with a rare ability to take advantage of political opportunities. He displayed exceptional skill as a parliamentarian. His speeches, replete with facts and statistics, conveyed a sense of inevitability which, as a rule, won support for his policies. He was at his best in debate: after summing up all the arguments on a question, he would present his views with such cogency that his own conclusion seemed the only one possible. In the course of his life Cavour not only dominated his own government but changed the political configuration of most of the Italian peninsula. By the time of his death in 1861, all of Italy with the exception of Rome and the province of Venetia had been united under the leadership of Sardinia.

Cavour's first concern when he became prime minister of Sardinia in 1852 was to strenghten the country economically and militarily. He reorganized the treasury, reformed the taxation system, and borrowed heavily from abroad to stimulate the national economy and raise the funds to maintain and equip a large modern army. He concluded trade treaties with foreign governments and sponsored the construction of highways and railroads, harbors and canals. He reformed the banking system, encouraged the expansion of credit, and stimulated investment in new industrial and agricultural enterprises. The result was a remarkable spurt in Sardinia's economy and a considerable rise in the state's revenues.

Despite the kingdom's increased power and prosperity, Cavour, unlike many of his countrymen, realized that Sardinia alone could not vie with Austria for supremacy in Italy. His country had failed to defeat Austria in 1848, when the entire Habsburg empire was in revolt; its chances against a stabilized Austria would be considerably worse. Sardinia needed powerful allies. To secure them, Cavour engaged in a series of brilliant diplomatic maneuvers.

Cavour's Diplomacy

Although Sardinia's entry in the Crimean War appears to have taken place against the wishes of Cavour, he made skillful use of his country's participation in the subsequent peace negotiations with Russia to win recognition among the great powers and draw attention to the Italian problem. "We have gained two things," he announced to the Sardinian Chamber of Deputies upon his return from the Paris peace conference. "In the first place, the unhappy and abnormal condition of Italy has been denounced to Europe, not by demagogues, not by hot-headed revolutionaries or passionate journalists, but by representatives of the foremost powers of Europe. . . . In the second place, those very powers have declared that it was not only useful to Italy but to Europe to apply some remedy to the ills of Italy. I cannot believe that the judgments expressed, the counsels given, by powers like France and England can long remain sterile."

Four years after the Crimean War, Cavour succeeded in forming an alliance with Napoleon III against Austria. This alliance was concluded in a secret and informal agreement on July 20, 1858, at the spa of Plombières. Napoleon promised to join Sardinia in a war against Austria provided the war "could be justified in the eyes of diplomacy and even more in the eyes of the public opinion of France and Europe." Following a successful conclusion of hostilities, Italy was to be reorganized as a confederation of four states under the presidency of the pope. Sardinia was to become the kingdom of Upper Italy and would annex the Austrian provinces of Lombardy and Venetia, along with the duchies of Parma and Modena and a large section of the Papal States. In central Italy a new state would be created, envisaged by Napoleon as a kingdom for his cousin Prince Napoleon Bonaparte (1822–1891), who would form an alliance with the house of Savoy by marrying the daughter of King Victor Emmanuel II of Sardinia. Evidently the pope was expected to be satisfied with the presidency of the new confederation, for he was to be stripped of most of his territories, those not turned over to Sardinia going to Prince Napoleon Bonaparte's new kingdom. The pope's temporal authority was to be restricted to Rome and its immediate surroundings. The boundaries of the fourth member of the confederation, the kingdom of Naples, were to remain unchanged.

On the face of it the Plombières agreement, which was further defined and strengthened by later treaties, gave Napoleon a variety of means for exercising future control over Italy: he would be able to do so through the pope, who depended on French military support to maintain his temporal power; through Sardinia, which would need French aid against a vengeful Austria; through his cousin, who would be king of central Italy; and through his hold on the sentiments of the Italian nation, which would be grateful for French aid against Austria and look to France for leadership. To cap these advantages, Cavour agreed to cede to France the Sardinian provinces of Nice and Savoy, which lay on the French side of the Alps and which the French had long desired to round out their "natural frontiers"—the Alps, the Pyrenees, and the Rhine.

Great as were the apparent advantages of the pact of Plombières for France, the real winner in the negotiations was Cavour. The agreement gave him the alliance he needed against Austria and assured him of the support of the strongest military power in Europe. Nice and Savoy, the price to be paid for French aid, could not be compared in value to Lombardy and Venetia, Parma and Modena, and the large section of the Papal States that

Sardinia would acquire. Cavour's only problem now was to "justify" a war with Austria in order to realize the terms of the agreement. This could be done most easily by making Austria appear as the aggressor. Cavour accordingly did his best to goad Austria by such tactics as encouraging revolt in Austria's Italian provinces and sheltering deserters from the Austrian army on Sardinian territory. The Austrians foolishly played into his hands, and on April 23, 1859, sent an ultimatum to Sardinia, which Cavour naturally rejected. The Austrian invasion of Sardinia four days later brought France into the war.

The War of 1859 and Its Aftermath

Napoleon III soon found that he had made serious miscalculations in his Italian policy. The war with Austria proved to be more costly and more difficult than he had expected. After two major battles, at Magenta and Solferino, the Austrians had still not been decisively defeated, and France was faced with grave danger from another quarter. The war in Italy had aroused anti-French sentiment in Germany, and it seemed likely that public opinion in Prussia and other German states would compel their governments to come to Austria's aid. Prussia mobilized its army; with the bulk of the French forces in Italy, the road to Paris from the east lay open.

Events in Italy also took an unexpected turn. Shortly after the war began, nationalist revolts broke out against the Austrian-supported governments in central Italy. These revolts were encouraged by Cavour, who had sent Sardinian commissioners into the central Italian states to organize them for the war effort against Austria and to bring them into a closer political relationship with Sardinia. The rapid spread of the Italian nationalist movement alarmed Napoleon, who feared that Sardinia might absorb enough territory to become a rival instead of a satellite state. Faced with this accumulation of dangers, Napoleon decided that his best course was to make peace with Austria as soon as possible. On July 11, 1859, he concluded an armistice with Austria at Villafranca, in northeastern Italy, without troubling to consult his Italian allies.

At Villafranca, Austria agreed to give up the greater part of Lombardy, but kept Venetia and the strategic Lombard fortresses. The various rulers who had been deposed by the revolts in central Italy were to be restored to their thrones. Napoleon turned Lombardy over to Sardinia, and with considerable restraint relinquished his claim to Nice and Savoy, but these gestures failed to win him the gratitude of Italian nationalists, who were indignant that Venetia had been left under Austrian rule and that the Austrian-supported governments of central Italy were to be restored. Even the normally cool Cavour was furious at being deprived of the full fruits of the Plombières agreement, and he resigned his prime-ministership in a rage.

It was soon evident to Napoleon that, short of using force, he would be

Giuseppe Garibaldi. *The uniform, which he habitually wore, derived from his days as a guerrilla fighter in South America. From a contemporary lithograph.*

unable to restore the rulers of the central Italian states or prevent the union of these states with Sardinia. To make the best of the situation he concluded another bargain with Cavour, who had returned as prime minister in January, 1860. By the Treaty of Turin of March 24, 1860, Napoleon secured Nice and Savoy for France in return for his consent to Sardinia's annexation of the states of central Italy. Thus Napoleon finally achieved some gains for France, but at the price of further antagonizing Italian nationalists.

Garibaldi and the Conquest of Southern Italy

The next chapter in the history of Italian unification was written by a man whose character and methods differed in almost every respect from those of Cavour. Giuseppe Garibaldi (1807–1882) was a single-minded Italian patriot: simple, blunt, devoid of guile or selfish ambition. A colorful and romantic military hero, he was capable of arousing immense enthusiasm in the men who served under him. Whereas Cavour applied a highly sophisticated intelligence to politics and prepared every political move with extreme care, Garibaldi believed in direct action; and he had the courage to take such action no matter how great the odds against him. He professed to be a radical republican and a believer in the freedom of the individual, but like many men of action he was willing to employ dictatorial methods to achieve his ends.

In 1833, at the age of twenty-six, he had fallen under the influence of Mazzini and had joined the Young Italy movement, taking an oath to fight against injustice and tyranny and for the unification of Italy. Exiled from Sardinia in the following year for revolutionary activity, he became a soldier of fortune in South America, where he acquired exceptional skill as a guerrilla leader. During the revolutions of 1848–1849 he led an army of volunteers against Austria in Lombardy. In 1849 he conducted the defense of the Roman Republic against the professional armies of France with ability and courage.

Garibaldi was back on the battlefield in the 1859 war with Austria. He shared the disgust of most Italian patriots at the Peace of Villafranca. The subsequent transfer to France of Savoy and Nice, the place of his birth, again spurred him to action. He organized an army of volunteers to defend these provinces against the French, at the same time initiating preparations to free Venetia from Austria and to expel the French forces from Rome. These activities were most embarrassing to Cavour. To divert Garibaldi from northern Italy, he secretly contrived to have him take his volunteer army to Sicily in support of a revolt that had broken out against King Francis II (ruled 1859–1861), the Bourbon monarch of Naples and Sicily. It was a clever move. If Garibaldi succeeded, Sardinia might profit from his victory. If he failed, Sardinia could disavow him, for officially the government knew nothing about this Sicilian undertaking. Cavour even alleged that he done his best to stop it, ignoring the fact that Garibaldi's expedition sailed from Quarto, near Genoa, and picked up arms in Tuscany, both of which were under Sardinian control. On May 11, 1860, Garibaldi and his volunteer army—the Thousand Red Shirts—landed in Sicily.

Garibaldi advanced against an organized army that outnumbered his 20 to 1. By daring and resourceful tactics, and with the support of revolutionaries on the island, he outmaneuvered the Neapolitan forces. On May 27 he captured the Sicilian capital of Palermo. Success led to success. Thousands of volunteers and deserters from the Neapolitan army joined his forces. The Sicilian peasants, most of whom had little or no feeling for the Italian nationalist movement, were converted into enthusiastic Garibaldians by the dramatic personality of Garibaldi himself and by his promises of land and tax reforms.

Widespread peasant unrest in Sicily played an important part in Garibaldi's victory. Many of the peasant bands that had terrorized the island and in some areas had brought local government to a standstill joined Garibaldi's army. At the same time, many property owners also found it necessary to support him, since he offered their only hope for the reestablishment of law and order. They, at least, were not disappointed. Garibaldi proclaimed himself dictator of Sicily in the name of Victor Emmanuel II, "the constitutional king of Italy." If only for reasons of military necessity, he at once set about establishing effective control over the country. To facilitate the requisitioning of supplies for his troops, he restored the authority of local government, and his edict conscripting all male Sicilians between the ages of seventeen and fifty into his army temporarily drained the area of the manpower heretofore available to terrorist bands.

By the end of July, 1860, most of Sicily had been conquered. On August 22 Garibaldi crossed to the mainland and began a triumphal campaign up the Italian peninsula. The city of Naples fell on September 7, and Francis II withdrew with what remained of his army to the fortress of Gaeta, in the northern part of his kingdom.

Cavour and Garibaldi

Garibaldi's success placed Cavour once again in an awkward position. The general's exploits had captured the imagination of people in every part of the peninsula, and it was conceivable that he might establish permanent authority over southern Italy. As a power and an ideal, Garibaldi had become a dangerous rival to King Victor Emmanuel II and the state of Sardinia, despite his professions of allegiance to the house of Savoy. Garibaldi had also become a danger in the field of diplomacy. If he continued his drive to the north and attacked Rome, as he had announced intentions of doing, war with France would result. An attack on Venetia, which Garibaldi also envisaged, would mean renewal of the conflict with Austria—this time without French support. Cavour realized that war with France or Austria would hardly be as simple as war with the demoralized forces of Francis II. He accordingly decided to take measures to put a decisive check on Garibaldi's activity by sending a Sardinian army to join Garibaldi in the south. On the flimsiest of excuses, Cavour invaded the Papal States, having convinced Napoleon that it was preferable for Sardinian rather than French troops to deal with Garibaldi. *"Fatte ma fatte presto"* ("act, but act quickly"), the emperor told Cavour.

The Sardinians easily defeated the papal army. They then moved into the kingdom of Naples, where they joined Garibaldi in the final stages of the campaign against the Bourbon regime. By this action Cavour not only checked Garibaldi but also regained the initiative in the Italian unification movement. On October 21 and 22, 1860, plebiscites were held in Naples and Sicily, and the people voted overwhelmingly—according to the official count—for union with Sardinia. Similar plebiscites were held in the former papal states of Umbria and the Marches, with similar results. Only the city of Rome, garrisoned by French troops, was left to the pope. Garibaldi might have attempted to resist Sardinia's absorption of the fruits of his exploits, but he chose to subordinate himself to the cause of Italian unity. He went

THE UNIFICATION OF ITALY

Kingdom of Sardinia at the time of the Congress of Vienna, 1815

Territories acquired, 1859–1860

Territories acquired, 1860–1870

into temporary retirement at Caprera, his island home off the coast of Sardinia, leaving to others the political reorganization of the areas he had conquered.

On March 17, 1861, the kingdom of Italy was proclaimed by an Italian parliament, and King Victor Emmanuel II of Sardinia became the first king of Italy. On June 6 of the same year Cavour died at the age of fifty-one. His death was a grievous loss to the new state, which badly needed his leadership and political resourcefulness during the period of its consolidation.

The final steps in the unification of Italy were primarily the result of Prussian rather than Italian enterprise. In 1866 Italy was Prussia's ally in the war with Austria and was given Venetia in the wake of Prussia's military victories—the Italians themselves had been defeated on land and sea. On September 20, 1870, after the withdrawal of French troops from Rome in the course of the Franco-Prussian War, Italian forces occupied Rome, which was henceforth to be the capital of the united Italy. Thus, almost from the start, the new Italian nation was dwarfed by the rising power of Bismarck's Germany.

THE UNIFICATION OF GERMANY

The Germanic Confederation and the Austro-Prussian Rivalry

The Germanic Confederation established in 1815 consisted almost exclusively of the states inhabited by German-speaking people; thus in an ethnic sense at least it came close to being a perfect German union. Austria exercised a preponderant influence in the affairs of the Confederation during the first half of the nineteenth century, but was never able to impinge seriously on the sovereignty of its members. Even the smallest of the German states jealously guarded its independence, and joined with the others to prevent effective domination of the Confederation by either Austria or Prussia, Austria's only serious rival to predominance in Germany.

Toward the middle of the nineteenth century this balance of power among the German states was threatened by the rise of national feeling among politically conscious members of the German population, many of whom desired the unification of the entire German people under a single government. In Germany, as in Italy, nationalists disagreed widely about how unification was to be achieved and about what form of government was desirable for their country. There were advocates of a stronger confederation, of union under Austria or Prussia, of union through an all-German, popularly elected parliament.

During the revolutions of 1848, the Germanic Confederation was discredited by its inability to give effective support to the German national cause in a quarrel with Denmark over Schleswig-Holstein; in the same period an attempt to achieve German unity through the popularly elected Frankfurt Parliament failed. The result was that after 1850 the hopes of German nationalists came to focus on Austria and Prussia, which alone seemed to possess the power to bring the rest of the country under their dominion.

In the rivalry between these two states, Austria had the advantage of a long tradition of supremacy; it dominated the existing confederation, and as a Catholic country appealed to the largely Catholic population of southern Germany. Above all, Austria was commonly believed to possess a stronger army and greater natural resources than Prussia. Austria's weakness lay in the multinational character of the empire; it had barely survived the recent revolutionary crises, and most of its subjects were not Germans at all. Further, although Austria's Catholicism was attractive to the Catholics of southern Germany, it alienated the Protestants of the north.

Prussia had the advantage of possessing an almost exclusively German population, its own autocratic tradition had been sufficiently tempered by reform to make its leadership more acceptable to German liberals, and its Protestantism was an asset with respect to Germany's Protestant population. Prussia's greatest strength lay in its economic domination of Germany through the customs union (*Zollverein*), and in the rapid development of its own economic power, especially in the Rhineland provinces.

Prussia to 1862

As the nucleus of a future great power, few states could have been more unpromising than Brandenburg-Prussia in the seventeenth century, when its rise began. Its territories were scattered, its population sparse; it lacked both natural resources and natural frontiers. These weaknesses, typical of most German states in this period, were overcome in Prussia by a few strong rulers, who with unusual firmness of purpose centralized the government and built up a strong army, thereafter devoting a large part of the state's resources to its maintenance. In carrying out their aims, they ruthlessly crushed the power of the landowning nobility (the *Junkers*), and channeled the energies of the members of this class into the service of the state. *Junkers* became the chief ministers of the Prussian government, the mainstays of the bureaucracy, and the officers of the army.

By the late eighteenth century, the rulers of Prussia had expanded their territories and raised their country to the status of a great power. Their success was the result of skillful and often unscrupulous leadership, aided by a bureaucracy that had become proverbial for its honesty, efficiency, and willingness to work hard for little pay. Most obviously significant in Prussia's rise, however, was the army, which was regarded as the central pillar of the state, its main line of defense, its only true frontier. This importance in the development of Prussia makes understandable the high status enjoyed by the army in that country, and the corresponding prestige of its leaders, almost all of them members of the *Junker* aristocracy.

After the Napoleonic wars, Prussia was given a large part of the Rhineland, the territory that was to become the principal center of the Industrial Revolution in Germany, and thus obtained unprecedented economic strength to harness to the Prussian political-military organization. With the Rhineland, Prussia also acquired a population with a more liberal political tradition, including an influential group of financiers, industrialists, and professional men who resented the monopolization of political power by the landed aristocracy and who joined forces with the rising middle classes in other parts of the state. These people desired the establishment in Prussia of

King Frederick William IV of Prussia in his study in the palace in Berlin. *Painting by Franz Krüger. The paintings and artifacts in the background reflect the king's varied and far from military tastes, an atmosphere that was to change during the reign of his brother William I. Potsdam, Sans Souci Palace.*

parliamentary government on the English model, and during the early years of the reign of King Frederick William IV (ruled 1840–1861) it seemed that this desire might be fulfilled.

Frederick William, however, proved to be an unstable romantic visionary, whose impractical schemes and political vacillation were to be recalled during the reign of his great-nephew Emperor William II. He was one of the few nineteenth-century monarchs who still appears to have believed sincerely in the divine right of kings. Upon coming to the throne, he spoke of satisfying the desires of the middle classes for representative government, but what he actually had in mind was a revival of medieval estates—which had never existed in Prussia. In 1848, submitting ignominiously to the demands of revolutionaries for genuine representative government, he granted his country a constitution. But once the revolution was crushed, he failed to honor the most important provisions of this constitution, and ruled autocratically, with a small group of reactionary advisers. In domestic affairs, his reign was characterized by repressive legislation. In foreign affairs, his pusillanimity and inconsistency led to a marked decline in Prussia's international influence.

That the reign of Frederick William IV was not totally barren of constructive action was due in large measure to the efforts of the Prussian bureaucracy, especially with respect to economic affairs. Prussia's control of the German customs union was successfully defended against a vigorous Austrian attack, and some important legislation was enacted to implement provisions for freeing the serfs. For Prussia, as for the rest of Europe, the early 1850's were years of prosperity, of economic and industrial expansion, and the Prussian government did much to foster this growth. In these years was inaugurated the remarkable cooperation between industry and universities and technical schools under government auspices that contributed significantly to Germany's later economic progress. Within Prussia and the area of the customs union, tolls on rivers and roads were abolished to encourage the free flow of trade, while a system of tariffs protected Prussia's infant industries from competition by states outside the union. Roads were improved, rivers and canals widened and deepened. The government sponsored banking programs on a limited scale to provide the capital for these projects. Although Prussia, unlike other German states, relied mainly on private enterprise to finance and manage its railroads, it did encourage the building of lines that were economically and militarily essential by guaranteeing interest on investments in them and by other financial devices. Furthermore, the government exercised close supervision over the construction of all railroads in order to prevent wasteful competition and to ensure that they would meet strategic requirements. Throughout the territory of the German customs union the rate of railroad construction was more rapid than in any other part of the Continent.

In the struggle for leadership in Germany, the Prussian government had attempted to take advantage of Austria's weakness during the 1848 revolutions by putting forward a proposal for unification through a federal union of German princes under Prussian domination. Austria soon recovered, however, and in November, 1850, compelled Prussia to withdraw the proposal through the Treaty of Olmütz, which patriotic Prussians subsequently branded as the Humiliation of Olmütz.

In the Olmütz treaty, Austria scored a major diplomatic victory over Prussia. Yet Austria was no more successful than Prussia in establishing control over the smaller German states. The stalemate between Austria and Prussia in Germany might have continued indefinitely, with the smaller states throwing their support from one side to the other to prevent either from gaining a decisive advantage. Above all, both France and Russia were vitally interested in preventing the unification of Germany under a single great power. Actually, the stalemate persisted for sixteen years after Olmütz. Then the struggle was decisively settled in Prussia's favor through the political genius of Otto von Bismarck, who became prime minister of Prussia in 1862.

The Constitutional Conflict in Prussia

The political history of Prussia after the revolutions of 1848 turned largely on the constitution granted to his people by King Frederick William IV in December, 1848, but subjected to several conservative revisions before its final promulgation in 1850. The constitution established a system of government very different from that desired by most Prussian liberals. The government remained authoritarian; executive power was vested in the king, and the royal ministers were responsible to the king alone. The constitution did provide for a parliament, but it was obviously intended to be little more than a façade. The upper house could be packed by royal appointments. Voting for representatives to the lower house, although ostensibly based on universal suffrage, was weighted to favor the biggest taxpayers. The establishment of this system of weighted votes proved to be a serious miscalculation on the part of the conservatives: it gave little voting strength to peasants and artisans, who by and large remained conservative during this period, and accorded the major representation to the rising middle classes, who now wanted more political power to match their new economic status.

Despite its authoritarian character, the constitution had given parliament important legislative and taxation powers, which liberal representatives might have used to acquire a strategic position in the government if the king and his ministers had honestly respected their own constitution. But they did not. The most important constitutional rights and guarantees were simply disregarded. Freedom of the press was curtailed, public meetings and demonstrations were forbidden, liberal political clubs were dissolved, and the government removed inconvenient critics by arbitrary arrest and imprisonment.

The situation changed when, in September, 1858, King Frederick William IV suffered a mental breakdown and was declared insane. He was succeeded by his brother William, first as regent, then, upon the death of Frederick William in 1861, as king. William was a direct contrast to his dreamy and impractical brother. He possessed what family chroniclers liked to think were typical Hohenzollern virtues: industry, sound common sense, and a profound feeling of responsibility for the welfare of his people. He was also a man of honor. Although a staunch conservative and certainly no champion of constitutional government, he regarded the constitution granted to Prussia by the crown as a contract between the king and his people that was as inviolable as any other moral obligation. He accordingly put an end to many of the restrictive measures introduced during the last years of his brother's reign, dismissed his brother's ministers, and selected a cabinet that included men with liberal sympathies. It seemed as though a profound change were about to take place in Prussian politics, and hopeful liberals designated this first period of William's rule as the New Era.

Those who believed the prince regent would move in the direction of genuine parliamentary government were sorely disappointed. Although he meant to respect the constitution, he had no intention of surrendering his executive authority to parliament. His defense of his royal powers led to one of the bitterest and most important constitutional conflicts in German history. The issue was clear-cut: would the country be governed by king or by parliament?

The constitutional conflict in Prussia centered on control of taxation and of the army. Before becoming head of state, William had made his career in the Prussian army, and the army remained the chief object of his concern. It seemed to the prince and his military advisers that Prussia's main weakness in dealing with Austria in 1850 and in its overall foreign policy during the past decade had stemmed from military inadequacy. No important changes had been made in the Prussian army since 1815, and both its organization and its equipment were in dire need of renovation. Mobilization in 1859 during the war in Italy between France and Austria had glaringly exposed Prussia's military deficiencies. A drastic reform of the army seemed essential if Prussia were to return to the ranks of the great powers. In December, 1859, William appointed Albrecht von Roon (1803–1879) minister of war and authorized him to execute the necessary reforms. With the assistance of Helmuth von Moltke (1800–1891), chief of the army general staff, Roon was to make the Prussian army the most effective military machine in Europe.

It was over the question of army reform that the Prussian parliament came into direct conflict with the crown. According to the constitution, parliament's consent was required for the additional taxes needed to pay for the reorganization and reequipment of Prussian forces. Besides sharing the usual reluctance of legislative representatives to vote new taxes, liberals in the Prussian parliament feared that the proposed reforms, with their provisions extending the period of compulsory military service, would bolster the authority of the monarchy and strengthen the influence of the conservative-military clique, which might use the reformed army as much against domestic as against foreign foes.

Despite the opposition of many liberals, the Prussian parliament did agree to new taxes in 1860 and 1861, but in order to retain its strategic control over the government's powers of taxation, it refused to vote for a permanent increase in military appropriations. Elections in December, 1861, brought a more determined group of liberals into the Prussian parliament, and the new military budget submitted in March, 1862, was rejected. A dissolution of parliament and new elections failed to return more pliant representatives. The conflict between crown and parliament had reached a deadlock.

William, who had become King William I in January, 1861, could have dealt with the situation most easily by basing his authority squarely on the army, repudiating the constitution, and ordering the parliamentary deputies to go home. But this was a course William could not bring himself to pursue. He seriously considered abdicating in favor of his son, Crown Prince Frederick William, who sympathized with the liberal cause and under the influence of his strong-minded English wife (the daughter of Queen Victoria), favored the establishment of English parliamentary institutions in Prussia. But Frederick William was destined not to come to the throne for another twenty-six years; by that time the cause of genuine representative government in Prussia had been lost.

Bismarck

It was Roon, the minister of war, who persuaded William I to remain on the throne and to entrust the government leadership to the conservative statesman apparently offering the last hope for a solution of the constitutional conflict on terms acceptable to the monarchy. On September 23, 1862, Otto von Bismarck (1815–1898) was made provisional head of the Prussian government. His official appointment as prime minister followed on October 8.

The decision was difficult for the king because he distrusted Bismarck, who at this time was generally known only as an extreme conservative. So audacious were his views that even men who sympathized with his opinions feared he might plunge Prussia into civil war. Others, among them many liberals, refused to take him seriously. They reasoned that a man with such extreme ideas, so out of step with the times, would soon face political bankruptcy and be forced to yield to more moderate elements. Bismarck's political genius became apparent only after he had been in office for several years.

Bismarck was born in 1815, the son of a dull, unenterprising Prussian *Junker,* from whom he inherited his massive physique and prodigious strength. His middle-class mother was the daughter of a distinguished Prussian civil servant, whose sponsorship of reform had earned him a reputation for Jacobinism. In contrast to her stolid husband, she was high-strung, often ill-tempered, with a restless, inquisitive mind. It was from his mother that Bismarck inherited his temperament—and his brains.

The young Bismarck did not distinguish himself at school. At the university he adopted the current pose of rebellious romanticism, joined briefly one of the radical *Burschenschaften,* engaged in passionate love affairs, drank, and dueled. Yet, while affecting to scorn his studies, he read widely in history and the German classics. After taking a degree in law, he entered the service of the Prussian state, but he resented the tedium and discipline of a bureaucratic career and soon resigned to manage his country estates. Still bored, he found release in wild escapades, which earned him local notoriety as "the mad Bismarck."

At this stage of his life he came into contact with a group of Pietists, among them Johanna von Puttkamer (1824–1894), whom he later married. Under their influence he appears to have experienced a genuine religious conversion. The belief that he was an instrument of God's will gave him a

Bismarck, Roon, Moltke. *The political and military forgers of German unification.*

new feeling of confidence and purpose, but also a sense of responsibility for his actions to which he was to refer at many major crises of his life.

Bismarck entered public life in 1847, but was given little opportunity to prove himself until 1851, when the king appointed him Prussian delegate to the diet of the Germanic Confederation in Frankfurt. Here he gained his first experience in diplomacy and a detailed knowledge of German affairs. Later, as Prussian ambassador to St. Petersburg, and then to Paris, he had an opportunity to study the political situation in Russia and France and to size up the character of the rulers of these states.

Bismarck has been called a realist in politics, the exponent of a peculiarly modern and amoral *Realpolitik*. But most statesmen, even the most self-consciously idealistic, look upon themselves as realists. The distinctive quality of Bismarck's realism resulted from his ability to recognize the limitations of his own powers and those of the state he governed. In the tradition of Richelieu and Talleyrand, he regarded politics as the art of the possible, and his maneuvers to achieve the possible were masterful.

Bismarck was an artist in statecraft as Napoleon had been an artist in war. Like Napoleon's campaign strategy, Bismarck's policy was never bound by fixed rules or preconceptions. While remaining aware of long-term goals and broad perspectives, he concentrated on the exigencies of the moment. His plans retained a resilience which allowed for error, for misinformation, for accident—the *imponderabilia*, as Bismarck called them. He did not only take into account the most obvious moves of his opponents; he was prepared to deal with every conceivable move, even the most stupid, which if unanticipated might upset the cleverest calculations. Much of his success depended on patience and timing. He once compared himself to a hunter inching forward through a swamp to shoot a grouse while one false step might cause him to sink into a bog.

Bismarck's outstanding quality, and the one he himself valued most highly in a statesman, was the ability to choose the most opportune and least dangerous political course. He was keenly aware that politics presents a constant succession of alternatives, that there is rarely a single solution to a specific political problem; and he would explore simultaneously a wide range of possibilities until the moment came for a final choice. Even then, except when the choice was war, he left alternatives open and never committed himself irretrievably. Although frequently checked, Bismarck thus always remained in a position to abandon an unsuccessful policy and embark on some new course by which he might regain the political initiative and recoup his losses.

The absence of doctrinaire rigidity in Bismarck's politics is reflected in the shifts his personal values underwent in the course of his career. He was born a Pomeranian *Junker* into a society not distinguished for its political sophistication or breadth of vision. Bismarck's fellow squires were loyal to the king, to the kingdom of Prussia, and to the *Junker* class. Bismarck gradually emancipated himself from the standards of this society, and in due time moved from a Prussian, to a German, to a European, and ultimately even to a global, point of view. But it would be a mistake to think that Bismarck had no fixed values or loyalties. He was loyal to the Prussian state, which provided the means of his self-realization. At the height of his career, the keystone of his system of values was the German empire, which he regarded as his creation. To maintain and defend that creation became the aim of all his policies and the focus of all his energies.

Bismarck possessed that most rare quality of men of political genius—moderation, the ability to recognize where to draw the line. Unlike Napoleon, he was never a political gambler; he never staked the future of the state or his own career on the outcome of a battle or a political experiment. He did not wage war until he had ascertained that all other means had been exhausted and that all possible odds—military, diplomatic, and moral—were on his side. Each of his wars was fought with a clear, limited purpose. When he decided that the advantages to be gained by war no longer justified the risks involved, he became Europe's staunchest defender of peace.

Bismarck's Policies

Bismarck's most immediate problem upon becoming head of the Prussian government was the conflict with parliament. His approach to this crisis was characteristic. He first tried to compromise, and literally offered parliament an olive branch he had plucked at Avignon. When his various proposals for a compromise were rejected, he seized the moral initiative and accused parliament of violating the constitution by claiming exclusive control over the budget. By refusing to negotiate with the crown, which had also been given budgetary powers in the constitution, parliament itself had caused the breakdown of constitutional government. Therefore the crown had both the right and the duty to carry on the business of state without parliamentary cooperation.

From 1863 to 1866 Bismarck simply ignored parliament. He solved the financial problem by collecting the taxes already voted in 1861 and 1862. From these funds money was allocated to the army to carry through the projected military reforms.

To counteract Bismarck's tactics, parliament would have had either to engage in open revolt or to persuade a majority of the citizens to refuse to pay taxes. The weakness of the parliamentary position was immediately apparent. As long as the army remained loyal to the king, no revolt could be successful; and as long as the army stood behind the tax collector, it was inconceivable that any large number of Prussian citizens would withhold their taxes. Furthermore, the liberals of the 1860's, mindful of the grim lessons of 1848, were not prone to violence. Most of them were confident that human reason and the inevitable march of progress were on their side; they had only to wait until Bismarck's policies had been discredited. While they waited, Bismarck was free to concentrate on foreign affairs, which, he was convinced, would decide the crucial questions of Prussia's future.

Bismarck was well aware that most politically conscious Germans craved some kind of national unification; in his youth he himself had fallen under the influence of romantic nationalism. He therefore could not fail to see the advantage to Prussia of gaining the leadership of the nationalist movement. He also recognized that there were two major obstacles to Prussia's domination of Germany: Austria and France. Neither of these could be expected to concede Prussia the leadership of a united Germany unless compelled to do so, and such compulsion would very probably involve armed conflict.

Unlike many of the German liberals, Bismarck did not eschew the use of force. In one of his first speeches as prime minister—an appeal to the parliamentary finance committee to grant funds for army reforms— Bismarck said: "Germany is not looking to Prussia's liberalism but to her power . . . The great questions of our time will not be decided by speeches and majority resolutions—that was the mistake of 1848–1849—but by iron and blood." This statement, the most famous of all Bismarck's political pronouncements, disclosed a crucial aspect of his thinking. But it did not mean that Bismarck considered iron and blood the only means of establishing Prussia's leadership in Germany. The speech was primarily an appeal for military appropriations, and necessarily its emphasis fell on the importance of military power. Bismarck was aware of the hazards of war, and of the danger that victories on the battlefield might create military heroes who could become serious political rivals. Moreover, he realized that Prussia needed more than military power. It needed allies, and a diplomacy that would undercut the alliances of its opponents and secure the maximum moral advantage in any international controversy. Iron and blood, if used at all, should be employed only under the most favorable possible circumstances. Even then he believed the risks to be so great that he never abandoned his efforts to attain his ends by peaceful means.

The Polish Revolt

A revolt in the Russian part of Poland in February, 1863, gave Bismarck an opportunity to secure the goodwill of Russia. European public opinion was generally sympathetic to the Poles. France, Great Britain, and Austria made motions to intervene on behalf of the rebels. The pro-Polish position of France and Britain was understandable, especially since the French sympathized with the Polish Catholics and the British felt concern for an oppressed people. Austria's support of the rebels was motivated by a desire to conciliate its own large Polish population and to establish closer diplomatic ties with Britain and France. But in view of its festering minority problems and its need for Russian goodwill to bolster its position in central Europe, Austria's policy was a piece of arch-foolishness.

Bismarck made no such error. Disregarding the protests of liberals in the parliament, Bismarck sent a mission to St. Petersburg to assure the tsar of Prussian support, and he dispatched four army corps to the frontier. Prussian interests in any case demanded cooperation with Russia in order to prevent the revolt from spreading to Prussia's Polish provinces. The revolt was quelled, and as a result of these events, Prussia supplanted Austria as Russia's protégé in German affairs.

The Schleswig-Holstein Question and the Danish War

The revival of the complicated Schleswig-Holstein question in 1863 provided Bismarck further and far broader scope for maneuvering in foreign affairs. In 1848 the two duchies had rebelled against their dynastic overlord, the king of Denmark, who had tried to integrate Schleswig, with its large German population, into Denmark. An international treaty signed in London in 1852 restored Schleswig and Holstein to the king of Denmark on a dynastic (personal) basis but specifically forbade their integration with Denmark. In 1863 the Danish government enacted a new constitution which was widely interpreted as a step toward the incorporation of Schleswig into Denmark. The Danish action aroused the anger of German nationalists, who regarded both Schleswig and Holstein as German states. In response to the pressure of nationalist opinion, the diet of the Germanic

A Prussian coastal battery at Almor during the Austro-Prussian war against Denmark, 1864.

Confederation resolved to send troops into Holstein, which was a member of the Confederation, to defend the independence of both duchies. Since both Austria and Prussia were also members of the Confederation, the action of the diet automatically involved them in the controversy.

Bismarck had no intention of subordinating Prussian policy to the decisions of the Austrian-dominated German federal diet, but neither could he afford to alienate German opinion by remaining aloof from the Schleswig-Holstein question. To secure independence of action and to gain the political initiative, he came forward in defense of international law as represented by the treaty concluded in London in 1852, which had been violated by both Denmark and the German federal diet. He then maneuvered Austria into joining Prussia in sending an ultimatum, on January 16, 1864, demanding that Denmark abide by the terms of the London treaty by abrogating its new constitution within forty-eight hours, a condition he knew the Danes could not fulfill. Thus he dissociated himself from the action of the federal diet, destroyed Austria's advantage as leader of that body, and appeared in Germany as the champion of the German national cause. At the same time, by making impossible demands on Denmark, he obtained a reason for war while posing as the champion of international law.

But the Danes, too, were anxious for a showdown on the Schleswig-Holstein question. They rejected the ultimatum not only because of its impossible conditions but because they had confidence in the strength of their military and diplomatic position. They believed that they could contain an Austro-Prussian invasion until they received aid from other powers. And they had no doubt that such aid would be forthcoming, being convinced that neither Great Britain nor Russia would tolerate the conquest of the strategic Danish peninsula by the most powerful German states, and expecting support from Sweden and possibly from France as well. The Danes seriously misjudged the situation. Austria and Prussia declared war on Denmark on February 1, 1864. The Danes received no outside military support, and alone they were no match for the German powers. On April 18 German troops stormed the strategic fortifications at Düppel, which guarded the crossing to the principal Danish islands.

The British tried to rescue the Danes by diplomatic intervention. On April 25 an international conference met in London to deal with the Schleswig-Holstein question. Bismarck, in possession of the disputed territories, was in a strong bargaining position. His proposals for a settlement were rejected by the Danes, who thus incurred the blame for the failure of the conference. The war was renewed at the end of June, and by the middle of July the Danes had been completely defeated. In the Treaty of Vienna of October 30, 1864, they surrendered both Schleswig and Holstein to Austria and Prussia.

In determining the final status of the duchies, Bismarck again persuaded Austria to ignore the German federal diet. In the Convention of Gastein of August 14, 1865, Austria and Prussia agreed to maintain joint sovereignty, with Prussia administering Schleswig and Austria administering Holstein, which lay between Schleswig and Prussia. A situation was thereby created which would make it possible to engineer an incident between Austria and Prussia whenever it was required.

The Austro-Prussian War of 1866

There can be no doubt that when Bismarck arranged the Convention of Gastein in the summer of 1865, he had in mind the possibility that war with Austria for the leadership of Germany might become necessary. In the months that followed, his policies, as usual, were flexible and he tested a variety of possible courses. He tried to persuade Austria to agree to a division of influence in Germany, with Prussia dominating the area north of the Main, and he conducted a vigorous political campaign to persuade the German population and the governments of the smaller German states to accept Prussian leadership peacefully. At the same time, he began to lay the groundwork for success in a future conflict by securing support for Prussia among the great powers and by isolating Austria.

He had no difficulty with Russia. The Russians had no desire to see a single power dominate Germany, but they did not expect a complete Prussian victory; moreover, they welcomed a war likely to weaken their German neighbors. Tsar Alexander II remained grateful for Prussian support during the recent Polish insurrection and resentful of Austria's position in the Polish crisis and in the Crimean War. After ascertaining the tsar's attitude, Bismarck concluded that he could count on the benevolent neutrality of Russia in a war with Austria, at least during its first stages.

Great Britain, which had not actively intervened in the Danish war even though important British interests were at stake, might be expected to stay out of a conflict over Germany.

The main problem was the attitude of France. In dealing with Napoleon III, Bismarck played a brilliant diplomatic game. He realized that the French emperor badly needed an international success to balance the increasingly obvious failure of the Mexican expedition and to quiet mounting criticism of his regime at home. Napoleon could only welcome a war between Prussia and Austria, which might be expected to exhaust the two major German powers, and give France the opportunity to extend its influence into the Rhineland and perhaps into the Low Countries as well. In October, 1865, Bismarck met Napoleon at Biarritz, where he hinted that France would receive territory in the Rhineland in exchange for Napoleon's promise of benevolent neutrality in the event of an Austro-Prussian war. Napoleon was willing to give this assurance. His only fear was that Prussia would be defeated by Austria before France could gain sufficient advantage from the conflict, for his military observers during the Danish war had reported that the Austrian army was far superior to the Prussian. To balance the opposing forces, Napoleon helped Bismarck arrange an alliance with the new kingdom of Italy, which was looking for an opportunity to wrest Venetia from Austria as a further step toward Italian unification. To make sure of winning no matter what the outcome of the conflict in Germany, Napoleon also concluded a secret treaty with Austria, on June 12, 1866, whereby Austria agreed, that if victorious, it would cede Venetia to France, and consented to the establishment of a new independent state along the Rhine, which would presumably be a French protectorate.

By the spring of 1866 Bismarck had evidently decided that a war with Austria was unavoidable. His attempts to extend Prussian authority in Germany were being steadfastly opposed by Austria, which had strong backing from the smaller German states. Meanwhile, Bismarck had completed his diplomatic preparations, and the Prussian army had been reorganized and modernized. So far as Bismarck was concerned, everything now depended on timing; his alliance with Italy, signed on April 8, 1866, assured him of Italian support only if war with Austria broke out within three months.

Immediately after concluding the Italian alliance Bismarck set about forcing a crisis in German affairs. The Austrians were not reluctant to take up the challenge. They believed their army was superior, and they were assured of the support of the most important of the smaller German states. Early in June, 1866, using as a pretext the Austrian effort to reorganize the government of Holstein, Bismarck declared that Austria had violated the Convention of Gastein and sent Prussian troops into the duchy. Austria replied by persuading the diet of the Germanic Confederation to order federal mobilization against Prussia for violating the federal territory of Holstein. War between Prussia and Austria was now certain, and the smaller German states with any freedom of choice hastened to align themselves with Austria, which they expected to be the victor.

None of the prophets of Prussian defeat had reckoned with the new Prussian army. In training and equipment the Prussian army was now far superior to the Austrian. The Prussian breech-loading needle gun, which could be loaded and fired in a prone position, was more accurate and had a higher rate of fire than the Austrian muzzle-loader. In addition, the Prussian network of strategic military railroads gave the army a high degree of mobility.

The Prussians also possessed superior leadership. Moltke, chief of the army general staff, was employing bold new conceptions in strategic planning—among them the use of technical innovations such as the railroad and the telegraph—in his attempt to solve the problem of military operations with mass armies. Instead of adhering to the traditional strategy of concentrating forces at one point to achieve a military decision, he divided his troops, but kept them in a position to converge on a single point at the opportune time. "The main task of good army leadership is to keep the masses separate without losing the possibility of uniting them at the right moment," he said. "If on the day of battle the forces can be brought from separate points and concentrated on the battlefield itself; if the operations are directed in such a way that from different sides a last short march strikes simultaneously against the enemy's front and flank: then strategy has achieved the most that it can achieve, and great results must follow."

From the beginning of the war the Prussians seized the initiative. On June 15, 1866, the day after war was declared, a Prussian army invaded Hanover, Saxony, and Hesse-Cassel, which had entered the conflict on the side of Austria. Meanwhile, the bulk of the Prussian forces advanced against the Austrians, who had been forced to divide their armies to meet a simultaneous invasion by Prussia's ally, Italy. On June 29 the Hanoverian army capitulated following its defeat at the Battle of Langensalza. Four days later, on July 3, 1866, the Austrian army was decisively beaten in the Battle of Königgrätz (or Sadowa). In just over two weeks the Prussians had scored a complete victory. It was one of the shortest and most decisive wars in history.

Moltke's strategy was much criticized by military experts despite the crushing victories of his armies. The Prussian victory was ascribed to the needle gun, to the superior quality of the Prussian troops, to the incompetence of the Austrian commanders, to luck. Only a few military observers appreciated the significance of Moltke's handling of mass armies. Although both Austria and Prussia had been obliged to divide their forces, each side had sent almost half a million men into the field at Königgrätz, which in terms of numbers, remained the biggest battle in history until the First World War. Moltke's method of deploying so large a force to encircle and destroy an army maneuvered according to conventional tactics was a military innovation quite as important as the needle gun. The cast-steel rifled cannon developed by the great armaments firm of Alfred Krupp (1812–1887) were badly handled at Königgrätz, and would not demonstrate their worth until the war with France in 1870.

Bismarck's superb sense of proportion in international affairs was never more evident than in the period following the Battle of Königgrätz. Before the war, Bismarck had been obliged to overcome the doubts of his king and several of his military advisers about undertaking a conflict with Austria. Now he had to restrain their desire to exploit their victory by annexing vast stretches of Austrian territory and staging a triumphal march through Vienna. With Russia on one side and France on the other, Prussia could not afford to prolong the war, giving these great powers a chance to intervene, or to make Austria and the other defeated German states into bitter and irreconcilable opponents. Bismarck's one big aim in the war had been the expulsion of Austria from German affairs. This aim could be realized without annexing Austrian territory and without a victory march through Vienna, which would wound Austrian pride while accomplishing no political purpose.

The preliminary Peace of Nikolsburg of July 26, 1866, was followed on August 23 by the final Peace of Prague. Austria was deprived of all influence among the other German states, and the states of northern Germany, while retaining their old identities, were organized into the North German Confederation under Prussian leadership. The vanquished states of southern Germany were allowed to remain independent, but they were forced to sign treaties with Prussia that would bring their armies under Prussian leadership in the event of war with a foreign power. Only the rulers of Hanover and Hesse-Cassel, who refused to accept the Prussian terms, were deposed and deprived of their territories. These areas, together with Schleswig and Holstein and the free city of Frankfurt, were annexed by Prussia.

The End of the Constitutional Conflict in Prussia

The Prussian victory over Austria decided more than the question of supremacy in Germany. It also marked the final victory of authoritarian over representative government in Prussia. Bismarck was the hero of the hour. Now, at the height of his success and popularity, he came before the Prussian parliament to end the constitutional conflict. He appealed to the liberal majority for a bill of indemnity retroactively making legal the taxes whose collection had made possible the reorganization of the Prussian army and the consequent victories over Denmark and Austria. A surprisingly large number of deputies (75 out of 285) stood by their principles and refused to be swayed by Bismarck's achievements. In so doing, they risked repudiation by their constituents, for public opinion was enthusiastically on Bismarck's side. However, most of the liberals were enthusiastic about the Prussian victories and went over without hesitation to the Bismarck camp. National sentiment had triumphed over liberalism.

At the same time, Bismarck outdid the liberals at their own game. In the constitution of the North German Confederation he provided for a parliament that would be elected by universal manhood suffrage, a political democratization that went beyond most liberal programs. Bismarck made this move in the belief that the peasants and artisans who constituted the majority of the population were more conservative than the middle classes who dominated the existing electoral system in Prussia. The rapid growth of a volatile urban proletariat was to upset Bismarck's calculations, and the parties that appealed to the masses were to become his most determined opponents. Bismarck's concession of universal suffrage also lost him the support of a powerful body of conservatives. Much of his opposition henceforth was to come from his former conservative allies, who felt he had betrayed them. In addition, he was still opposed by discerning liberal idealists, who denounced his concessions as a sham and deplored the fact that the new representative bodies he had created lacked real legislative authority. After 1867 Bismarck's main support came from the nationalists, both liberal and conservative, and from interest groups that were reaping profits as a result of German unification or of governmental policies.

THE FRANCO-PRUSSIAN WAR

Prussia's remarkably rapid victory over Austria in 1866 ruined the plans of Napoleon III, who had counted on a long war in Germany that would exhaust the belligerents and permit France to dictate terms to the German states. Two days after Königgrätz, the French emperor attempted to salvage something from his German policy by offering to mediate between Prussia and Austria. Bismarck's fear that Napoleon might now seek to intervene actively in German affairs was his principal reason for concluding a swift and lenient peace with Austria. The danger from France, however, was slight. Many of Napoleon's troops were still in Mexico; the emperor himself was ill and lacked the strength and will power to pursue an energetic policy. In August, 1866, he tried to persuade Bismarck to honor his vague promise, made in Biarritz in 1865, to give Rhineland territory to France in exchange for French neutrality during the war against Austria. When Bismarck rejected this claim on the ground that such a concession would never be sanctioned by German public opinion, Napoleon put forward a request for Belgium and Luxembourg. At Bismarck's suggestion he made the terrible blunder of allowing his ambassador to put this proposal into writing. Bismarck was to avail himself of this document to influence British opinion during Prussia's war with France in 1870. He made immediate use of Napoleon's request for compensation in the Rhineland to persuade the south German states to enter into a close military alliance with Prussia for their mutual security.

It is commonly assumed that Napoleon's failure to gain compensation for Prussia's victories in 1866, and his need for prestige to bolster his tottering regime, forced him to adopt the desperate expedient of going to war with Prussia, and that Bismarck was eager to meet the emperor's bellicosity halfway. A remarkable amount of popular as well as official opposition to any extension of Prussian authority had manifested itself in southern Germany between 1867 and 1870, and Bismarck is supposed to have concluded that German unification could only be completed by exploiting the patriotic sentiment that would be generated by a national war against France.

This interpretation of the origin of the Franco-Prussian War is plausible, but it again raises the question of Bismarck's ultimate political objective in Germany. Was he consciously aiming to bring about the immediate political unification of Germany under Prussia, or would he have been content with a gradual extension of Prussian influence in southern Germany which would have avoided a direct challenge to France? War with a great power such as France was a hazardous undertaking under any circumstances, no matter how confident of victory the Prussian generals might be. In addition, there was always the possibility of outside intervention. If the war went at all badly for Prussia, a vengeful Austria might be expected to join forces with France. In the event of a Prussian victory, Great Britain, Russia, Austria, and other states might intervene to prevent the creation of the new great power which a united Germany would represent. It is hard to believe that Bismarck, who is credited with so much political realism, would have provoked a war with France that involved so many obvious dangers, especially as there seemed so little to be gained from such a war. By 1867 the south German states were already bound to Prussia by military and economic alliances. The fact that they currently opposed further Prussian encroachments on their sovereignty did not mean that they would always do so, or that their resistance could not be worn down over the years by skillful diplomacy.

There was a chance that the opposition of France, too, might be worn down or neutralized, and in 1868 Bismarck was presented with an opportunity to test this possibility. In that year Prince Leopold of Hohenzollern-Sigmaringen (1835–1905), a member of a Catholic branch of the Protestant ruling house in Prussia, was offered the throne of Spain after a revolution there. The establishment of a Hohenzollern in Spain, which would be another serious blow to the prestige of the French government, might be expected to precipitate a domestic crisis that would prevent effective French intervention in German affairs for some time to come. Furthermore, the presence of a Hohenzollern in Spain would force the French to keep part of their army on guard along the Pyrenees and thus would weaken the pressure they could bring to bear on Germany.

The French were certain to protest the Hohenzollern candidacy, but their objections could be turned aside as unjustifiable interference in the affairs of another country. If they directed their wrath against Prussia, Prussia could be made to appear as the innocent victim of French bullying and aggression. If they chose to go to war with Prussia over the issue, their diplomatic case and hence their international position would be very weak indeed.

Bismarck's diplomatic campaign built around the Hohenzollern candidacy broke down by sheer accident—a coding error by a clerk in the Prussian legation in Madrid. Bismarck had counted on keeping the matter secret until Prince Leopold was formally elected by the Spanish parliament, so that the cabinets of Europe would be presented with an accomplished fact. Instead, as a result of the coding error, the Spanish parliament was allowed to adjourn on July 2, 1870, before the *pro forma* vote had been held, the news of Prince Leopold's candidacy leaked out, and the French were given ample opportunity to take countermeasures. They at once brought pressure to bear on the leaders of the Spanish government to withdraw the offer and on the Hohenzollern family to decline it. But powerful elements within the French government wanted more than an elimination of the candidacy; they wanted to exploit the incident to humiliate Prussia and thereby bolster the prestige of their own government.

In the beginning, the French were successful in this endeavor. They totally ignored Spain and thrust Prussia to the fore as their chief target. On July 6 the French foreign minister, the duke of Gramont (1819–1880), set the public tone of the campaign with a statement in the Chamber of Deputies threatening war unless Prussia withdrew the candidacy of Prince Leopold. At the same time the French government urged the king of Prussia, as head of the house of Hohenzollern, to order his relative to abandon the Spanish project in the interests of European peace. To Bismarck's chagrin, the king yielded to the French arguments. On July 12, Prince Karl Anton (1811–1885), father of Prince Leopold, withdrew his son's candidacy.

The French had scored a great diplomatic triumph, but Gramont wanted to underline the fact that this victory had been achieved at the expense of Prussia. The French accordingly demanded that the king of Prussia write Napoleon a letter of apology for the trouble his relative had caused. The letter was to state that the king was animated by feelings of respectful friendship for France; it was specifically to disavow the candidacy of the king's relative to the throne of Spain and promise that this candidacy would never be renewed. On July 13, Count Vincent Benedetti (1817–1900), the French ambassador to Prussia, tried to bring these demands to the attention of the king of Prussia, who was at the spa of Ems. When the king understood the nature of the French proposals, he politely dismissed Benedetti and resisted all further efforts by the French ambassador to see him. On the same day the king sent Bismarck an account of what had happened.

Gramont had overplayed his hand, and in so doing he gave Bismarck the opportunity to turn the tables in the Hohenzollern affair. Upon receiving the royal telegram from Ems describing the incident with Benedetti, Bismarck edited it to make the king's dismissal of the French ambassador seem more brusque and rude than it had been. He then released the edited dispatch to the press. The French effort to inflict humiliation on Prussia was now made to appear the source of humiliation for France.

Bismarck was fully aware of the risk he was taking, but by this time he was evidently convinced that a peaceful settlement was no longer possible. If the French now chose to declare war on Prussia, as Bismarck expected, they would appear to be the aggressors, and Prussia might therefore hope to secure the benevolent neutrality of the moralistic Gladstone government in Great Britain. Bismarck had already arranged for the neutrality of Russia, which engaged to keep Austria uninvolved, and he had military alliances with the states of southern Germany. The Prussian generals assured him of the preparedness of the Prussian army. Diplomatically and militarily, Prussia was ready for war. But to the end Bismarck remained cautious, and he waited for the French to make the decisive move.

In France voices of caution were raised against war with Prussia. The emperor vacillated. He lacked confidence in the French army and feared a long, inconclusive struggle. But French public opinion was clamoring for war, Gramont and the Empress Eugénie declared that the empire could not survive if it accepted the latest humiliation from Prussia, and French military leaders were confident of victory. On July 15, 1870, the French government decided to declare war on Prussia. "The army is ready down to the last gaiter-button," said the French minister of war. "We go to war with a light heart," said Émile Ollivier, the French prime minister.

The ensuing conflict showed that the Prussian political and military calculations had been far more accurate than the French. Bismarck had managed to put France into diplomatic isolation. The Austrians were still suffering financially from the 1866 war; they were still angry with Napoleon for his support of Italy in 1859; and they were held in check by Russia. The majority of the German Austrians were enthusiastically on the side of their fellow Germans. The Hungarians, too, were opposed to an alliance with France against Prussia, for the reestablishment of Habsburg influence

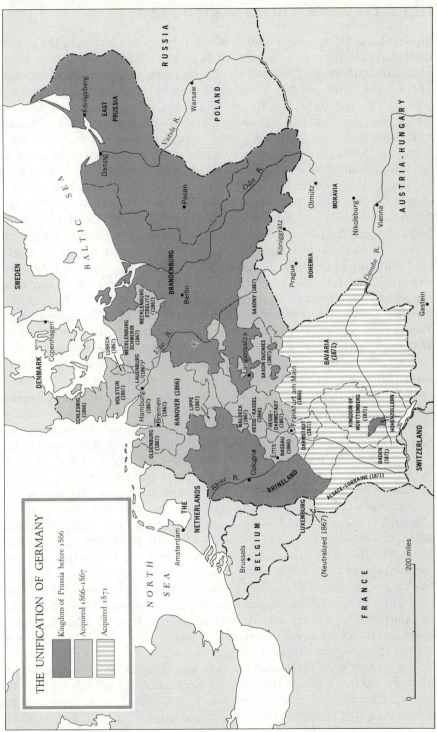

THE UNIFICATION OF GERMANY

Kingdom of Prussia before 1866

Acquired 1866–1867

Acquired 1871

RUSSIA

POLAND

AUSTRIA - HUNGARY

Königsberg

EAST PRUSSIA

Warsaw

Danzig

Vistula R.

Posen

Oder R.

Olmütz

MORAVIA

Nikolsburg

Vienna

BALTIC SEA

SWEDEN

BRANDENBURG

Königgrätz

Berlin

Prague

BOHEMIA

Gastein

Danube R.

DENMARK

Copenhagen

MECKLENBURG STRELITZ (1867)

MECKLENBURG SCHWERIN (1867)

LÜBECK

LAUENBURG (1867)

Elbe R.

SAXONY (1867)

SAXON DUCHIES (1867)

Langensalza

BAVARIA (1871)

SCHLESWIG (1866)

HOLSTEIN (1867)

Hamburg (1867)

Bremen (1867)

OLDENBURG (1867)

HANOVER (1866)

LIPPE (1867)

WALDECK (1867)

HESSE-KASSEL (1866)

HESSE-DARMSTADT (1867)

Frankfurt am Main (1866)

DARMSTADT (1871)

KINGDOM OF WÜRTTEMBERG (1871)

HOHENZOLLERN

SWITZERLAND

Ems

NASSAU (1866)

BADEN (1871)

THE NETHERLANDS

Amsterdam

Cologne

Rhine R.

RHINELAND

ALSACE-LORRAINE (1871)

NORTH SEA

Brussels

BELGIUM

LUXEMBURG

(Neutralized 1867)

FRANCE

0   200 miles

among the German states would diminish their own influence in the newly created Austro-Hungarian empire. In Italy, the king was tempted to help Napoleon, but Italian nationalists had been alienated by the French seizure of Nice and Savoy, and they were now anxious to take advantage of France's war with Prussia to occupy Rome, which was still garrisoned by French troops. Any efforts of the Italian king to side with France would probably have been met by a republican revolt, and Bismarck was in touch with republican leaders to lend support to such a revolt. Russia remained grateful for Prussian support during the Polish insurrection, and was anxious as well to take advantage of French involvement in war to abrogate the Black Sea clauses of the Treaty of Paris imposed by France and Britain after the Crimean War. Toward the end of the Franco-Prussian War the Russians began to realize that a united Germany might be a greater danger to Russia than France had been, but in the early stages of the war Russian neutrality was assured. The British had for centuries regarded the French as the chief threat to the peace of Europe, and Bismarck reinforced this impression by releasing Napoleon's demands for Belgian territory to the London *Times*, which published them on July 25, 1870. In Britain as in Russia there was grave concern about the change in the balance of power that might result from Prussia's victories, but the Gladstone government was chiefly occupied with domestic reform, so the danger of British intervention was at all times slight.

In the military sphere, too, the Prussian preparations proved to be far superior to the French. The reorganization of the French army had been intelligently conceived, but had barely begun. France's secret weapon, the rapid-firing *mitrailleuse* cannon, had been kept so secret that most of the French troops did not know how to use it. The French *chassepot* rifle was better than the Prussian needle gun, but this advantage was offset by the superiority of the Prussian artillery, which was decisive in a large number of engagements. The Prussian army surpassed the French in organization, mobility, and leadership. The rapid advance of the Prussian forces through southern Germany prevented the south German governments from even attempting to evade their military commitments, and meant that the war was fought on French rather than on German territory.

The actual conduct of the war, however, showed that Bismarck had been wise to try to accomplish his purposes by peaceful means. Had the French been better led, had they made full use of their superior weapons, had they taken advantage of Prussian errors, they might have fought the war to a stalemate or at least secured foreign mediation. As it was, the French generals made even more mistakes than the Prussian. Within a fortnight after the outbreak of war the Prussian armies had penetrated deeply into French territory and split the French forces. One French army, under General Achille Bazaine (1811–1888), was bottled up in the fortress of

Metz. While attempting to relieve Bazaine's forces, a second French army, under Marshal Marie Edmé de MacMahon (1808–1893) was surrounded by the Prussians at Sedan. On September 2, 1870, after a day of heavy fighting, this entire army surrendered and the emperor was captured. The French defeat at Sedan brought the Second French Empire to a close.

The collapse of the empire did not end the war. Bazaine's army held out in Metz until October 27, and the French continued a dogged resistance from the provinces. They organized new armies that fought effectively despite their lack of training and equipment. The great French hope at this stage was foreign intervention, but Bismarck had laid his diplomatic foundations well and no aid was forthcoming. On January 28, 1871, after a siege of over four months, Paris capitulated. At the end of February representatives of the provisional French government appealed for an

King William I of Prussia proclaimed German Emperor in the Hall of Mirrors at Versailles, January 18, 1871. *Painting by Anton von Werner. This self-consciously symbolic act was held in the palace of Louis XIV, who in the opinion of patriotic Germans had inflicted so many humiliations on their country. The painting shows the King of Prussia flanked by his son, Crown Prince Frederick William, and his son-in-law, Frederick I, Grand Duke of Baden, whose hand is raised in calling for a cheer for the new emperor. Bismarck stands prominently in the foreground in a white uniform, with Moltke on his left.*

armistice. The final peace treaty between France and Germany was signed at Frankfurt on May 10, 1871. France was compelled to give up Alsace and part of Lorraine, to pay an indemnity of five billion francs, and to support a German army of occupation until the indemnity had been paid.

On January 18, 1871, shortly before the war had come to an end, King William I of Prussia was proclaimed German emperor, or kaiser, in the Hall of Mirrors of Louis XIV's palace at Versailles.

The French defeat, the establishment of the German empire, and the loss of Alsace-Lorraine created a hatred between France and Germany that would prevail until well after the Second World War. Bismarck has been charged with a major political error in aggravating the animosity of the French by annexing territory they regarded as their own, and the question is frequently raised of why he abandoned his restraint in this instance. As in all aspects of Bismarck's statecraft, there is no simple answer. With respect to Alsace-Lorraine, he had German as well as French opinion to consider. To the French the region might be part of their nation's sacred soil, but to the Germans it was a segment of the medieval German empire that had been stolen by France when Germany was weak and divided. Bismarck himself did much to incite German national feeling on this issue, for nationalism was his only weapon in overcoming the religious and political particularism of the German people. There was also the pressing and cogent argument of the army that these provinces were strategically essential. Bismarck realized that the loss of Alsace-Lorraine would arouse hostility in France, but he did not foresee how intense and lasting that resentment would be. He probably considered that the real reason for future French hostility would not be the loss of territory, but the fact of defeat itself and the creation of a German empire that would represent a constant threat to French security. For the first time since their victory over the Spaniards at Rocroi in 1643, with the exception of the brief interlude after 1814, the French had lost their position of political and military superiority in Europe.

A contemporary French cartoon showing French bitterness over the loss of Alsace-Lorraine. *It reflects the popular resentment toward the French peace negotiators, Jules Favre (left) and Adolphe Thiers, who had agreed to the cession of the provinces.*

CHAPTER 33

The Course of Reform:
Great Britain and Russia

Two states at opposite ends of Europe, Great Britain and Russia, were not seriously affected by the revolutions of 1848, and for opposite reasons. In Russia a consistent policy of political repression had succeeded in controlling popular movements; in Britain the institutions of representative government gave men who might otherwise have led revolutionary movements the hope of accomplishing their purposes by legal means.

After 1850 the British continued to meet (if not always to solve) the problems confronting their country by reform legislation enacted by a Parliament that by 1884 represented almost all adult males. But in Russia, too, especially after the Crimean War, it was recognized that repression alone was no longer enough, and that major reforms of government and society were necessary. In Russia, however, reforms were enacted not by a popularly elected parliament, but by the autocratic government of the tsar.

GREAT BRITAIN IN THE MID-NINETEENTH CENTURY

For Britain, a more significant date than 1848 was 1851, the year of the first great international exhibition in London's Crystal Palace, where Britain paraded its prosperity and material achievements before an admiring world. The exhibition reflected a feeling general in the country of satisfaction with the present and confidence in the future, and a belief that given enough time all problems affecting human life and society could be solved by human reason.

The symbol of this mood was Queen Victoria, who ruled Britain and its colonies for sixty-four years (1837–1901). With her strong sense of moral respectability, her national pride and self-satisfaction, she represented to a remarkable degree the values and attitudes of her countrymen and of an age that has appropriately been named after her.

The Crystal Palace in London. *Designed by a greenhouse builder, it housed England's 1851 exhibition of the technical achievements of the age. With its 300,000 panes of glass and 5,000 columns and girders, it was in itself a monument to the new technology. The photograph shows the interior of the building after it was disassembled and rebuilt at Sydenham.*

The British had grounds for satisfaction with their achievements. Despite the continued existence of widespread poverty, slums, and poor working conditions, the vast majority were better housed and better fed than ever before, and enjoyed more of life's amenities. By 1851 Britain was not only the workshop of the world but also its shipper and trader, insurer, and major investor. During the second half of the nineteenth century the prosperity of the people steadily increased, as did Britain's national wealth and productivity. It is estimated that in the course of these decades, the real wages of all workmen rose as much as 30 per cent, while the increase for skilled workmen was considerably greater. Only toward the end of the century did Britain begin to face serious competition from other parts of the world, especially Germany and the United States.

British politics after 1850 must be viewed against this background of national prosperity and optimism. Although voices were raised against the smug self-satisfaction and philistinism of the era, and although there were prophets of disaster, the prevailing sentiment was one of confidence in the nation and in its institutions.

For British politics in the second half of the nineteenth century, the Reform Bill of 1867 serves as a watershed. In the years before the bill, political parties and political loyalties were in a state of flux; after 1867, the

parliamentary system settled firmly into the pattern of two-party government. The terms Whig and Tory gave way to Liberal and Conservative to
describe the major British political parties, and it began to seem part of the
natural order of things, as a character in a Gilbert-and-Sullivan operetta
observed, "that every boy and every gal, that's born into the world alive, is
either a little Liberal, or else a little Conservative."

The era of political instability began with the collapse of the Tory
(Conservative) Peel government in 1846, when Peel's conversion to free
trade and the repeal of the major agricultural tariffs (corn laws) shattered
the unity of the Tory party. A period of Whig (Liberal) supremacy
followed, but the Whig party too was weakened by internal strife. Between
Peel's fall in 1846 and the formation of Gladstone's first government in 1868
there were eight separate ministries, none of them backed by strong party
support or committed to carrying out a particular political program. Party
ideas and party memberships changed rapidly; politicians who felt betrayed
by their leaders formed new political groups or transferred their allegiance
to other parties. Individual politicians underwent astounding transformations in their views. Gladstone, the giant of nineteenth-century British
liberalism, began his parliamentary career as a high Tory and defender of
slavery and imperialism. His conservative counterpart, Disraeli, began his
parliamentary career as something of a radical.

Queen Victoria and the Prince Consort, 1854. *Roger Fenton's candid photograph
is a far cry from the flattering court portraits of Winterhalter.*

Palmerston

In this period of political confusion and shifting loyalties, of weak governments and lax party discipline, politics tended to be dominated by individuals rather than by parties or principles. The most prominent statesman of the era was Henry John Temple, viscount Palmerston (1784–1865). Although a leader of the Whig party, Palmerston was without fixed political ideas or party loyalties. His strength lay in his astounding energy, his ability to work with men of widely different opinions, and his popularity with the voter. His personality embodied to a remarkable degree the tastes and prejudices of the British: his patriotism coupled with a distrust of foreigners, his good humor and courage, his love of horses and hunting, all combined to make him the most popular statesman of the day. His success was partly the result of longevity and of undiminished vitality in old age. At seventy, he still rode to hounds, he still relished long debates in Parliament, and he astounded younger colleagues by walking home from all-night parliament sessions buoyant, alert, and apparently as fresh as ever.

Palmerston's easygoing manner and willingness to compromise were major assets in conciliating political opponents and in winning personal support in Parliament, but they also aroused the contempt and distrust of men with more rigid opinions. George Canning, Britain's foreign secretary and prime minister earlier in the century, said that Palmerston "almost reached the summit of mediocrity," and Gladstone called him "by far the worst minister the country has had during our time"; yet Canning included Palmerston in his government and Gladstone joined a Palmerston government.

In contrast to many of his colleagues, Palmerston recognized the importance of public opinion in British politics, especially after the passage of the Reform Bill of 1832. When he was unable to win support within an existing Parliament he appealed directly to the British voter. Disraeli complained that in the election campaign of 1857 appeals for Palmerston were made "in favor of a *name*, and not a *policy*." The name was sufficient, however. The elections resulted in a great victory for Palmerston.

Palmerston's bombastic foreign policy and his militant defense of British honor and national interests enhanced his popularity at home. His assertion of British rights occasionally became ludicrous. In 1850 he risked war with Greece and France to defend the doubtful claims against the Greek government of a certain Don Pacifico (a Gibraltar-born Portuguese Jew whose house had been burned down by a rioting Athens mob) on the ground that the man had been born a British subject and was therefore entitled to the protection of the British government. Palmerston shared—and fanned—the bellicose attitude of the British public at the time of the Crimean War, and rode to the premiership on the strength of his war policy. He honestly feared the Russian threat in the Near East, but before the Crimean War was over his apprehensions were focused on the growing strength of his ally Napoleon III. By 1860, with the French annexation of Nice and Savoy, the rapid development of the French Atlantic ports, and the modernization of the French navy, he began to speak about the probable necessity of war with France.

After the disasters and disillusionments of the Crimean War, however, the British were no longer so eager to engage in foreign military adventures, and Palmerston was too shrewd a politician to ignore this sentiment. During the Austro-Prussian war against Denmark in 1864 he wanted to intervene on the side of the Danes to prevent the key to the Baltic Sea from falling into the hands of a great power, but because of the apathy of British public opinion, he restricted his intervention to diplomatic maneuvers and protests. Public sentiment also affected his policies with respect to the American Civil War. Although he professed neutrality, Palmerston in fact supported the South in the belief that an independent Confederacy that could negotiate its own treaties might provide not only raw materials, particularly cotton for the textile mills of England, but also an open market for British manufactured goods. From a long-range point of view perhaps his most important consideration was that the dissolution of the Union would weaken a potential political and economic rival, and create a balance of power in North America comparable to the situation in Europe which had proved so great a benefit to Britain over the centuries.

The American Civil War attracted greater attention and aroused far deeper passions in Britain than the wars that transformed the power structure of Europe in the later nineteenth century. Not only British political and economic interests were involved, but fundamental questions of principle. The British were deeply divided in their views, with some admiring the aristocratic-oligarchic system of government of the South and others favoring the greater degree of democracy that seemed to prevail in the North and feeling a moral and emotional commitment to the abolition of slavery. In the light of theories of economic determinism, it is interesting to note that popular opinion was most fervently on the side of the North in the British textile regions, which were most adversely affected by the northern blockade of southern cotton. Palmerston eventually gave in to the preponderance of British sentiment for the cause of the North, as he was to yield to popular feeling on many other foreign-policy issues following the Crimean War. Britain did not intervene on the side of the South any more than it intervened on the side of Denmark.

Palmerston's domestic policy was aimed at preserving the *status quo.* "One cannot always be legislating," he said. He especially disliked proposals for further franchise reform. "I cannot be a party to the extensive transfer of representation from one class to another . . . We should by such an arrangement increase the number of Bribeable Electors and overpower Intelligence and Property by Ignorance and Poverty." This attitude reflected the views of many middle-class voters emancipated by the 1832 reform bill, who considered their interests safeguarded by the existing laws. They had no desire to see their privileges undermined by new legislation or their political influence diluted by the extension of the franchise which was desired by reformers.

Domestic Reforms before 1867

The period before 1867 was not altogether barren of domestic reform. Palmerston himself, as home secretary, made vigorous efforts to combat air pollution and improve sanitation. He devised a system of tickets-of-leave for convicts (a kind of parole), and adopted the ideas of the great reformer, Lord Ashley, now Earl of Shaftesbury (1801–1885), for combating juvenile delinquency. Shaftesbury said of him: "I have never known any Home Secretary equal to Palmerston for readiness to undertake every good work of kindness, humanity and social good, especially to the child and the working class. No fear of wealth, capital, or election terrors; prepared at all time to run a-tilt if he could do good by it."

At mid-century, during the Whig government of Lord John Russell (1792–1878), the administration of the Poor Law was transferred from arbitrary local control to a government board under the direction of a cabinet minister. A Public Health Act established a central directorate to create local boards of health. In 1850 a Factories Act set a maximum 10½-hour day for factory workers, with a 7½-hour day on Saturday. Workers employed in establishments too small to be subject to government inspection were not affected, nor were shop assistants and domestic servants, whose hours of work were still unlimited. In 1855 a Civil Service Commission was created to obtain candidates for the home civil service by competitive examination instead of through patronage, but since final responsibility for appointments still rested with the heads of the various departments, the effect of the reform was limited. An act of June, 1858, put an end to property qualifications for members of Parliament. An act of the following month removed disabilities on Jews, permitting them to hold seats in Parliament.

Some of the most notable government reforms were undertaken by Gladstone, chancellor of the exchequer in several administrations between 1852 and 1865. By simplifying the taxation system and the collection of various levies, he was able simultaneously to increase the national revenue and to lower taxes. He disapproved of the income tax, believing that the ease with which it could be collected would encourage government extravagance, and thought it should be used only in periods of national emergency; it was in fact levied during the Crimean War. In 1861 Gladstone began to combine all money bills for the year into a single budget bill; henceforth opponents of a particular item could reject it only by opposing the budget as a whole, a step which they might be reluctant to take. By this stratagem he succeeded in abolishing the tax on paper and thereby made possible the publication of cheap newspapers and magazines, the first of the mass media. Gladstone was a champion of free trade, and his influence was decisive in securing the passage of Richard Cobden's trade treaty with France in 1860, a move that did much to ease diplomatic tension with France at this time. Gladstone regarded the trade treaty as the only alternative to the "high probability of war," and he made it an integral part of his 1860 budget, which he conceived as a "European operation." Following in the footsteps of Peel, Gladstone tried to stimulate trade and national productivity by reducing taxes and tariffs of every kind. Using the French treaty as a lever, he abolished or substantially lowered duties on all imports.

The Reform Bill of 1867

These reforms scarcely even began to fulfill the needs of a rapidly changing British society. The remarkable feature of British politics, however, was the confidence of most advocates of reform that necessary changes could be effected through the existing parliamentary institutions, and that what the country required above all was an extension of the franchise. Throughout the nation there were mass meetings—some of the crowds were estimated at 200,000 or more—demanding not revolution, but voting rights. Several attempts were made by governments of both major parties to secure the passage of innocuous franchise-reform bills, but they were regularly defeated. With the death of Palmerston in October, 1865, Gladstone believed the Whig party could at last be transformed into a genuinely liberal body which would push through the necessary reform legislation. The time had come, he wrote, for a "new commencement."

It was a Conservative government, however, that took the lead in extending the franchise. Although genuinely concerned about social questions, Benjamin Disraeli, the Conservative leader in the House of Commons, was above all a politician, and his attitude toward franchise reform appears to have been determined primarily by expediency. His tactics and expressions of opinion were anything but consistent, being characterized instead by improvisation, and often reflecting his efforts to respond to the political moods of the moment. It is possible, however, as he contended later, that he recognized at an early stage that a radical extension of the franchise, so ardently advocated by the more extreme liberals, would in fact benefit his own party because it would create new voters among the more prosperous artisans and farmers, who would be more likely to vote Conservative than the middle-class citizens enfranchised by the Reform Bill of 1832. If this was the case, his reasoning was similar to that of Bismarck, who

The young Disraeli criticizing Gladstone's war budget in the House of Commons. *A contemporary sketch.*

in 1867 conceded universal manhood suffrage to the voters of the North German Confederation. Both men were undoubtedly influenced by the success of Napoleon III's plebiscites. The extension of the franchise in Britain would be a gamble for the Conservative party—"a leap in the dark," as Lord Derby (1799–1869), the Conservative prime minister, later described it, but after twenty years in a minority party with only interludes of power as a result of splits among the Liberals, the more realistic among the Conservatives were ready to gamble. At the same time, the huge mass meetings in every part of the country had begun to shake even the more rigid Conservatives, as did a riot that broke out on July 23, 1867, in London's Hyde Park, within full view of the residents of fashionable Park Lane. To many Conservatives it began to appear that the alternative to franchise reform might be revolution. Once Disraeli was certain of the backing of his own party, he was assured of the passage of a franchise-reform bill. The Liberals would be forced to support it, since opposition would be construed as repudiation of their own reform program, and the House of Lords could be expected to pass the measure because a Conservative government had introduced it.

The original franchise bill submitted to Parliament by the Conservatives was a cautious document filled with reservations, but Disraeli apparently expected—and hoped—that the Liberal opposition would eliminate many of these reservations and greatly increase the size of the proposed electorate. This was, in fact, what happened. The final Reform Bill of 1867 was a major step in the democratization of the country. It provided for a wide extension of the franchise for elections to Parliament and almost doubled the number of voters, which went from about one million to two million. In the boroughs it gave the vote to all men who paid taxes on property or paid an annual rent of at least ten pounds, and in the counties to all who received an income of five pounds or more from their land or paid an annual rent of at least twelve pounds. The vote was withheld from the urban poor, from domestic servants, from the majority of agricultural workers, and from women (whose political rights John Stuart Mill supported in a spirited plea soon afterward). There was also a large-scale though still inequitable redistribution of parliamentary seats to allow for population increases and movements that had taken place since 1832. Boroughs with populations of less than ten thousand would henceforth send one member to Parliament instead of two; larger towns were given two or three members; nine new boroughs were created; twenty-five additional members were allotted to the counties. In 1868 franchise-reform bills for Scotland and Ireland were enacted. The Scottish bill was very similar to the English bill of 1867. The Irish bill reduced income requirements for voting in the boroughs, but left the county franchise unaltered.

In 1868 Disraeli succeeded Derby and Gladstone replaced Russell as heads of the Conservative and Liberal parties, respectively. Under the leadership of these powerful personalities the two parties emerged as the only significant political organizations in Britain, and were therefore able to enforce a great degree of party discipline on their members. Parliamentary politics became more than ever a national game, with unwritten rules and procedures that came to be clearly recognized. Parliament itself gained new prestige as a result of its significant accomplishments and of the high intellectual level of its debates during the Gladstone-Disraeli era, and in contrast to parliamentary bodies in Germany after 1871, it attracted exceptionally gifted men to its ranks.

For the Conservatives the Reform Bill of 1867 indeed proved a leap in the dark. Industrial workers did not rally to the Conservative party as anticipated, and the first elections after the passage of the bill resulted in a tremendous victory for the Liberals. In December, 1868, Gladstone formed his first ministry at the head of what was now unequivocally the Liberal party. The power of the right wing of the party had been shattered in the last elections, Palmerston was gone, and the radicals were willing to rally under Gladstone's banner.

Gladstone's First Ministry, 1868–1874

William Ewart Gladstone (1809–1898) served his country in the House of Commons for over sixty years. One of the most efficient administrators of his age and a brilliant financier, he combined personal vigor with remarkable powers of concentration and a retentive memory. He was a superb

Gladstone in later years.

debater, whose eloquence was backed up by an uncanny mastery of facts and figures. Like many statesmen of his time, he pursued interests which ranged far beyond politics. He was a distinguished classical scholar, author of the three-volume *Studies on Homer and the Homeric Age* (1859). But the chief influence on his life was biblical literature and the writings of Protestant theologians. He earnestly tried to act as a moral and upright Christian in his personal and in his political life. Typical of his seriousness of purpose and humanitarian impulses was his project to redeem prostitutes by persuading them to enter a home for moral rehabilitation maintained by himself and his wife.

During Gladstone's first administration an impressive amount of reform legislation was passed. The prime minister first turned his attention to Ireland, where the need for reform was more desperate than in any other part of the United Kingdom and where hatred of English rule was being manifested in terrorism and open rebellion. "My mission is to pacify Ireland," Gladstone declared before taking office. He did his best to achieve that purpose, and during his four terms as prime minister devoted much time and energy to the matter, finally exposing himself to political defeat and his party to political annihilation for the Irish cause.

The problem was an old one. The Irish had never totally submitted to English rule, and the Act of Union of 1801, which provided for the union of the Irish and English parliaments and for religious union under the Church of England, had not made the Irish more amenable to English leadership. Irish discontent was the product of national self-consciousness, of the religious division between Protestant England and Roman Catholic Ireland, and of sheer economic misery. Englishmen owned a large part of the land of Ireland. In most instances, the landlord lived in England and left the administration of his Irish estate to a local agent, who was expected to obtain for his employer a specified annual income from the property. This system led to many abuses. The refusal of the large majority of landlords and their agents to give long leases or other guarantees of tenure to their landless tenants stifled the initiative of the Irish peasants, who had no incentive to improve property from which they might be evicted at any time without compensation.

Gladstone set out to remove what he believed to be the major causes of Irish discontent. The Disestablishment Act of July 26, 1869, ended the dominion of the Anglican church as the official church in Ireland; henceforth the Irish Roman Catholics were not obliged to support a church they did not attend. The Anglican church was stripped of about half its Irish property, the income from which was subsequently allocated for poor relief, education, and other local needs. Gladstone then attacked the problems of land tenure and absentee landlordism. The Irish Land Act of August 1, 1870, provided that an evicted tenant receive some compensation for improvements he had made. If, however, his payments were in arrears, he would receive nothing unless the rent could be proved "exorbitant." In practice the new law hardly touched the evils it was supposed to remedy. It failed to establish fair rents or security of land tenure, and a landlord could avoid payment of compensation for improvements by increasing the rent sufficiently to force his tenant into default. Gladstone tried hard to achieve more for Ireland, but was unable to overcome the apathy and opposition in his own party.

Gladstone's reforms in England were more successful. An Education Act of August 9, 1870, was designed to improve the standard of elementary education, which was far inferior to that available in France and Prussia. Approximately half the four million children of school age at this time did not attend school at all, and the majority of those who did left by the age of eleven. About a million children went to schools run by the Church of England, which were supported in part by voluntary contributions supplemented by government grants. Another million attended schools that received no government support and that were not controlled or inspected in any way, a situation that had produced the type of institution represented, apparently without much exaggeration, by Dotheboys Hall in Dickens' *Nicholas Nickleby* (1838–1839). The aim of the new Education Act was to make elementary education available to all, and to do so as quickly and as cheaply as possible. Voluntary schools were retained if they could demonstrate their adequacy. Many were given government financial support, and all were subject to government inspection. New schools were set up

"The internal economy of Dotheboys Hall." *An illustration by "Phiz" from Dickens' Nicholas Nickleby.*

wherever they were needed under the control of locally elected education boards. They were to be maintained by government grants, local taxes, and fees paid by parents. The great difficulty in connection with the school law was religion. Dissenters (Protestant Christians who did not belong to the Church of England) strongly objected to state support of Church of England schools, especially because the new law permitted these schools to continue their religious instruction. On the other hand, all denominations objected to the secular character of the new board schools, which were not to give religious instruction of any kind. The act itself left much to be desired, for it did not provide for compulsory or free education. It nevertheless represented a big step forward in raising educational standards, and paved the way for further reforms. In 1880 elementary education was made compulsory, and in 1891 all school fees for public education were abolished. At the university level, a University Tests Act passed in 1871 freed students at Oxford and Cambridge from the need to submit to religious tests in order to obtain degrees.

An Order in Council of June 4, 1870, extended the reform of the civil service begun in 1855. Recruitment based on competitive examinations was made compulsory in all major government departments with the exception of the foreign office, and was thus no longer subject to the whims and favors of department heads. The Army Regulation Bill of June, 1871, ended the system of buying commissions, and in theory, made merit and seniority the prerequisites for promotion. The long twelve-year enlistment period of military service was abolished in favor of a six-year enlistment period followed by six years in the reserves. An important part of the bill was the subordination of the commander in chief of the army to the minister of war in the cabinet; the army was thus removed from the control of the crown and placed directly under the control of Parliament. The Ballot Act of 1872 made voting secret for the first time and ended the possibility of exercising direct pressure on voters. The Judicature Act of 1873 simplified the British legal system and put an end to abuses such as those described by Dickens in *Bleak House* (1852–1853), which permitted lawyers to consume the bulk of a client's estate before bringing his case to court.

One of Gladstone's more important political moves was his unsuccessful effort to secure a temperance bill. In an age when alcohol was clearly the chief opiate of the masses, and when the low price and constant availability of spirits encouraged drunkenness, a moderate bill might have been beneficial. But the advocates of temperance went too far. The licensing bill of 1872 proposed not just a restriction of the consumption of spirits but total prohibition. The bill was defeated, but its mere introduction did much to injure Gladstone at the polls. The powerful brewery and distillery interests united against him, as did the owners of the public houses (pubs), the Englishmen's neighborhood forums. "We have been borne down in a torrent of gin and beer," Gladstone said after his election defeat in 1874.

There were other reasons for the Liberal defeat. The Liberal party was badly split and Gladstone was having trouble holding his cabinet together. Disraeli contemptuously called the Liberal leaders a "range of exhausted volcanoes." The Church of England had been alienated by the Irish Disestablishment Act. Anglicans and dissenters, the latter a major source of Liberal strength at the polls, had been alienated by the Education Act. Advocates of temperance resented the government's failure to pass a temperance bill; their opponents were angry that such a bill had been introduced at all.

Hostility aroused by Gladstone's domestic policies was reinforced by patriotic resentment of his slack foreign policy. Bismarck had been allowed to shift the balance of power on the Continent without the slightest regard for Britain or British interests. In 1872 Gladstone had acceded to the demands of a truculent American government for the settlement of claims in connection with the damage caused by the Confederate raider *Alabama*, a ship which had been equipped in Liverpool and had been allowed to sail from that harbor to prey on Union shipping during the American Civil War. In retrospect, it appears that the fifteen million dollars paid to the United States in settlement of the *Alabama* affair probably constituted one of the best investments Britain ever made; Americans were impressed by the moderation and fairness of the British government, and the incident, which might have had ugly consequences, became instead a landmark in the restoration of goodwill between the two nations. Gladstone's policy was not seen in this light at the time, however, and he was bitterly criticized for his failure to defend British interests more vigorously.

Disraeli's Second Ministry, 1874–1880

The Conservative victory in the elections of February, 1874, the first in which the secret ballot was used, resulted in the formation of Disraeli's second ministry. Now for the first time Disraeli enjoyed an independent majority in the House of Commons; previously he had been associated only with coalition governments.

The great tragedy in the political career of Benjamin Disraeli (1804–1881) was that he came to power so late in life. In 1874 he was seventy and ailing; in two years poor health would force him to give up his leadership of the House of Commons and move to the House of Lords as the earl of Beaconsfield, although he nevertheless stayed on as prime minister. He had long been suspected of being a political opportunist and adventurer, and his dandified dress and social affectations increased the distrust of his critics. Moreover, although he was a baptized Christian, he took considerable pride in his Jewish background. In this age of strong religious feeling and social prejudice, the remarkable thing is that Disraeli ever came to power at all. The fact that he did so suggests something of the tolerance and scope for talent present in the British political system. And Disraeli did have talent. He was a shrewd parliamentary tactician, an able administrator, a match for Gladstone in debate. Like Napoleon III he had the ability to sense and exploit the popular movements of his day, but in contrast to the French emperor he did not indulge in chimerical schemes.

As a Conservative, Disraeli thought the primary mission of his party should be to preserve the best features of British society, but he did not believe the party should be merely negative and obstructionist. On the contrary, he felt it should repair and construct; it should accept change— indeed, it should take the leadership in change by building on existing institutions. Its strength should lie in confidence and calm; it should have the moral power to attract idealistic youth as well as traditionalists; it should appeal to intellect as well as to interest.

While injecting new vitality into the Conservative party's philosophy, Disraeli introduced some practical and badly needed reforms into its machinery. During the period of Liberal ascendancy after 1868, the Conservative Central Office was established. Its task was to get in touch with local Conservatives and encourage them to form democratically run local associations which would suggest candidates in preparation for the next elections. The Central Office compiled a classified list of candidates and undertook to supply local associations with the type of candidates required by local conditions. Thus the foundations were laid for the election victory

The Disraeli cabinet in 1876. *Disraeli is standing at the extreme right. Standing, third from the left, is Lord Salisbury, Disraeli's successor as head of the Conservative party and three times prime minister.*

of 1874, and party machinery was created which was to serve as a model for other British parties.

Disraeli did not value political power just for its own sake; he sincerely desired—and in this he again resembled Napoleon III—to use that power to improve the lot of humanity. His concern for social justice is evident in his novels, above all in *Sybil, or The Two Nations* (1845), which contrasts the life of the upper classes and the wretched condition of the workers in the depression of the 1840's. During his parliamentary career Disraeli repeatedly tried to give concrete expression to this concern, and his second ministry (his first with an independent majority) was in many ways as productive of reform as Gladstone's.

In 1875 the Conservative government passed two labor laws, which, Disraeli assured the queen, were the most important pieces of social legislation of her reign. The first, the Employers and Workmen Bill, gave labor the same legal status as the employer with regard to breaches of contract. Previously, a workman who broke a contract with his employer could be sent to prison, whereas an employer who broke a contract with his workman was liable only to a civil action for damages. The second, the Trade Union Act, abolished many restrictions on union activity by giving unions the same rights as individuals. Thus, peaceful picketing and similar labor tactics became legal. The Factory Act, also of 1875, set a maximum fifty-six hour week for factory workers. (Again, shop assistants and employees in plants too small to be inspected were not affected.) Other legislation of 1875 included a Public Health Act, which furnished the nation with a badly needed sanitary code, and an Artisans' Dwellings Act, which established a minimum housing standard and made a start at providing adequate housing for the poor. This act was a new departure, for it called upon public authorities to remedy the defects of housing built by private enterprise, empowering them to raze existing structures for sanitary or other reasons and to replace them with new buildings for the use of artisans (workmen). The year 1875 also saw the passage of a Sale of Food and Drugs Act to prevent adulteration, and an Agricultural Holdings Act to give tenants compensation for property improvements in case of eviction. The Merchant Shipping Act of 1876 was an attempt to improve living and working conditions for merchant seamen, and to halt the use of unseaworthy vessels, which were often sent forth so well insured that the owners made a profit when they sank. Sponsored by Samuel Plimsoll (1824–1898), this act sought to prevent the overloading of ships by requiring placement of a mark on the side of every cargo vessel—the "Plimsoll line"—that had to appear above the water level at all times.

Disraeli's most spectacular achievements, however, were in the field of foreign affairs. In November, 1875, he made the brilliant stroke of purchasing the controlling shares in the Suez Canal from the khedive of Egypt, borrowing the money from the Rothschilds and subsequently securing parliamentary approval. The great problem in foreign affairs in the late 1870's was the crisis in the Near East, where Disraeli pursued the traditional British policy of preserving the Ottoman Empire as a bulwark against Russian expansion. By astute negotiations he persuaded Russia to give up substantial gains in the Balkans and a foothold on the Mediterranean, and in 1878 he acquired from Turkey the island of Cyprus as a naval base to protect the Suez Canal and British interests in the Near East. In exchange for Cyprus, Disraeli agreed to guarantee Turkey's Asiatic territories, thereby obtaining for the British an excuse to send troops into the Ottoman Empire whenever they saw fit. In July, 1878, Disraeli returned in triumph from the Congress of Berlin, bringing his country "peace . . . with honour."

Disraeli's last years in office were not so fortunate. Troubles with the Afghans, Zulus, Boers, and Irish discredited the government and were exploited by the opposition. In 1879 Great Britain experienced a severe agricultural depression, accompanied by the worst harvest of the century. The agricultural crisis of 1879 capped several years of economic hardship, which had begun with the general European economic depression of 1873 and had plagued the entire course of the Disraeli administration. In March, 1880, Disraeli dissolved Parliament and called for new elections.

Gladstone made the election campaign of 1880 memorable by abandoning the aloof attitude heretofore considered proper for party leaders, and addressing his constituents in Midlothian in a series of speeches on the major issues confronting the nation. Gladstone's method of stumping the country and presenting his own and his party's case directly to the voters was a natural outcome of the extension of the franchise, and set a precedent which members of all parties soon found themselves obliged to follow. With ringing eloquence Gladstone denounced Disraeli's imperialistic and aggressive foreign policy and represented the disaffected colonial peoples as victims of Tory oppression. The elections themselves, however, turned far more on the British voters' anxiety over economic depression at home than on their concern with political oppression abroad. The Conservatives suffered the fate of almost every government caught in an economic slump, and were turned out of office.

Gladstone's Second Ministry, 1880–1885

Gladstone's second ministry was not nearly so successful as his first. There was a lack of cohesion and purpose among the members of his cabinet. Within his party he was faced with the task of reconciling right-wing liberals with radicals, Anglicans with dissenters, and of accommodating the aggressive, quasi-socialist new radicalism represented by Joseph Chamberlain (1836–1914), who had built up a reputation as a social reformer while lord mayor of Birmingham.

The administration got off to a poor start when Charles Bradlaugh (1833–1891), an atheist elected to Parliament, refused to take the oath of office because it included the words "so help me God." The Bradlaugh case created a personal dilemma for Gladstone, who was a deeply religious man but believed in freedom of thought. It created an even greater dilemma for the Liberal party. Many uncompromising Christians in the party refused to follow Gladstone's lead in supporting a bill permitting a simple affirmation of allegiance as an alternative to the normal parliamentary oath. The case dragged on until 1888, when the passage of the Affirmation Bill removed the last religious restriction on membership in the House of Commons.

During his second administration Gladstone attempted to achieve passage of additional reform measures, but his efforts were hampered by his difficulty in finding proposals on which the majority of his party could agree. He did succeed in obtaining one major piece of legislation: the Reform Bill of 1884, which gave the vote to all males who paid regular rents or taxes. The largest group to be enfranchised by the new act consisted of agricultural laborers—who generally voted Conservative. Domestic servants, migrant workers, bachelors living under the parental roof, and women were the only sizable groups that still did not have the right to vote. About two million new voters were created, and the total electorate was almost doubled. A redistribution bill of 1885 gave more representation to the larger towns and set up county constituencies with one representative each, putting an end to the traditional two-member constituencies. Inhabitants of boroughs with populations of less than fifteen thousand were deprived of their separate representation and were merged into the electorate of the local county. The historic boroughs and counties thus ceased to be the basis of representation in the House of Commons. Some less sweeping legislation also was passed during the second Gladstone ministry. The Employers' Liability Act of 1880 provided for compensation to employees injured at work, and a measure of 1883 initiated electioneering reform by limiting the funds parties and candidates might spend in campaigns.

Ireland remained Gladstone's major concern. His Land Act of 1870 had not succeeded in pacifying Ireland or in stopping the eviction of tenants by absentee landlords. On the contrary, both terrorism and evictions had increased markedly during the agricultural depression of the 1870's. The Irish question was further complicated by the creation of an Irish Home Rule party in the British Parliament, where Irish members had been given the right to sit through the Act of Union of 1801. In the late 1870's this party came under the leadership of an Irish Protestant named Charles Stewart Parnell (1846–1891), an able politician and a masterful parliamentary strategist. Parnell used two sets of tactics in working for Irish independence. In Parliament he manipulated the solid bloc of Irish votes to extract concessions from both major parties in exchange for Irish support; if concessions were not forthcoming, he used the Irish vote to block legislation altogether. In Ireland, he encouraged local agitation to make British rule as difficult as possible and to keep the Irish question before the public. However, though a fanatic in the cause of Irish independence, Parnell was against the more extreme forms of violence and terrorism. The technique he recommended in dealing with tenant evictions was social ostracism rather than the barn burning, cattle mutilation, and murder adopted on a large scale by his countrymen. Anyone who assisted an unjust eviction or took over a farm made available by such an eviction was to be treated as a social leper. One of the first victims of this treatment was a land agent named Charles Boycott, whose ostracism added a new word to the English language.

To halt the epidemic of terrorist outrages, Gladstone was persuaded to grant increased coercive powers to the agents of the English government in Ireland; the Habeas Corpus Act was suspended, and the executive authority in Ireland was given absolute power of arbitrary and preventive arrest. At the same time, however, Gladstone tried to secure the passage of a new land act for Ireland that would remedy some of the defects of the act of 1870. His new bill, passed in August, 1881, met old Irish demands for the so-called three F's—fair rent, fixity of tenure, and free sale by a tenant of his investment in a rented property. But by this time Irish leaders were no longer satisfied with reform; they wanted political independence. Parnell continued his agitation. In October, 1881, he was sent to jail for his activities; the imprisonment made him a martyr but did nothing to pacify the Irish. The new and more severe coercive measures of the English government were also ineffective in restraining Irish terrorism. At last

Gladstone decided that his only course would be to work with Parnell. By the so-called Kilmainham Treaty of May 2, 1882, named after the prison in which Parnell was held, Gladstone agreed to release Parnell in return for his promise to aid in the pacification of Ireland. Gladstone apparently gave Parnell clear indications that he intended to work for home rule for Ireland. But hopes for a peaceful solution of the Irish problem were short-lived. Before Gladstone could take action in Parliament, any prospects for success were destroyed by the action of Irish terrorists. On May 6, four days after Parnell's release, the new chief secretary for Ireland, Lord Frederick Cavendish, and the permanent undersecretary, Thomas Burke, were brutally murdered in broad daylight in Phoenix Park, Dublin. The resulting indignation in England made a policy of concession to Ireland impossible. Instead, Parliament passed new coercion acts, which in turn set off a new wave of Irish terrorism. For the time being, Gladstone's Irish policy was a failure.

Failure in Ireland was accompanied by failures in foreign policy. To be sure, the Gladstone government scored something of a triumph by securing control of Egypt in 1882. The prime minister gained little credit for this action, however, because he promised that Britain would evacuate Egypt as soon as order had been restored—a promise that only the British voters appear to have believed. In South Africa, British troops were defeated by the Boers, the Dutch settlers in the Transvaal, who had revolted against British rule in 1880. By the Treaty of Pretoria of April 5, 1881, Gladstone conceded independence to the Boers, but they were to remain under British "suzerainty": they would have authority in their internal affairs, but their foreign relations would be controlled by Britain. A dispute with Russia over the frontiers of Afghanistan almost led to war in April, 1885, when Russian forces clashed with Afghan border troops at Penjdeh. Gladstone avoided war by submitting the case to arbitration, and was accused by the opposition and by some members of his own party of truckling to Russia. The worst blow of all came in the Sudan, where Anglo-Egyptian efforts to subdue a revolt against Egyptian overlordship were proving so costly and unsuccessful that the British government decided to evacuate the territory. General Charles George Gordon, who had been sent to the Sudan to investigate the means of evacuation, instead attempted to subdue the area with inadequate forces and found himself besieged in the city of Khartoum. Gladstone hesitated to send a relief army into the Sudan "against a people rightly struggling to be free"—although the people in this case were Moslem fanatics, struggling to maintain the slave trade and a brutal despotism. While Gladstone hesitated, reinforcements for Gordon were delayed. On January 26, 1885, Khartoum fell, and Gordon and his troops were massacred. A censure motion in Parliament failed by just fourteen votes. In June, 1885, Gladstone resigned over a budget amendment, and Lord Robert Cecil, third Marquis of Salisbury (1830–1903), the head of the Conservative party since the death of Disraeli in 1881, formed his first ministry.

Alternation of Ministries, 1885–1892

Salisbury's first ministry lasted only seven months, Gladstone's third ministry only five (to July 20, 1886). Both were made possible by the support of Parnell, who held the balance of power in the House of Commons and extracted concessions from the major parties in exchange for his Irish votes.

Gladstone's third ministry was remarkable chiefly for the introduction of the first home-rule bill for Ireland, which was bitterly attacked by the Conservatives and was the cause of a permanent rift in the Liberal party as well. Gladstone was deserted by the so-called Liberal Unionists, who favored the preservation of union with Ireland; these included members of both the right and the left wings of the party—the aristocratic Whig faction under Lord Hartington and the young radicals under Joseph Chamberlain.

With the defeat of his home-rule bill, Gladstone dissolved Parliament and appealed to the British voter. Although now seventy-seven, he stumped the country with his old vigor, full of enthusiasm for what he believed to be a righteous cause. But the forces against him were too great. The sorry record of the Liberal government in foreign affairs, the hostility of public opinion to Ireland as a result of Irish terrorism, the reluctance to desert the Ulster Irish (for the most part Protestants loyal to Britain), and the divisions within the Liberal party all contributed to Gladstone's defeat.

During Salisbury's second ministry (to August 13, 1892) a new coercion act directed at Ireland was passed by a coalition of Conservatives and Liberal Unionists. At the same time, Parnell became involved in a succession of political and personal scandals that ruined his career. He died in 1891. The scandals surrounding Parnell, and the struggle to succeed him as leader, split the Irish Home Rule party and drastically reduced its political effectiveness. The Irish national cause did not regain its momentum for many years.

The failure to settle the Irish question demonstrated that even the British Parliament, with its powerful traditions and able leadership, had difficulty in dealing with national and economically depressed minorities and was compelled to resort to repression. But for Britain as a whole, the policy of gradual reform through parliamentary institutions was proving its worth. The lot of the average British subject was steadily improving, extremist parties of the right and left found few adherents, and there was never any serious threat of revolution against the established political and social order.

The British system of government was admired and envied by many foreign observers, but it was not generally emulated. The reluctance to adopt British methods was not simply an indication of conservatism or political immaturity, as patriotic Britains often assumed. Many continental statesmen felt that the problems confronting their countries were just too complex to be solved by parliamentary consensus. This was especially true in Russia, where political and social reform took a very different course.

RUSSIA AFTER 1850

In Russia the massive apparatus of autocratic government—army, secret police, censorship, repression—had prevented the outbreak of revolution in 1848. While the thrones of other monarchs crumbled, the Russian autocracy had stood firm and inflexible. The tsar had put his troops at the disposal of the emperor of Austria to crush the revolutions in Hungary and Austrian Poland. He had given his political and diplomatic support to the suppression of liberal movements in every part of Europe. Russia appeared to have taken the place of Austria as the arsenal of autocracy. It was Russian power that had preserved the Austrian empire, that had stood behind the authoritarian governments of Italy and Germany, that had kept the Poles, the Magyars, the Czechs, the Finns, in thrall to foreign despotisms.

The Crimean War exposed the inadequacies behind the imposing façade of Russian autocracy. The mighty empire of Russia was unable to repel a localized invasion on its own soil by two western powers that had invested but a fraction of their potential strength in the conflict. Even the most obscurantist conservative could no longer ignore the fact that Russia's impervious resistance to change had left it far behind the states of western Europe, not only in science and technology but in social and administrative developments. Russia's backwardness was the major problem recognized by most Russians who realistically appraised the lessons of the Crimean War. But in their efforts to overcome this backwardness the advocates of change met enormous inertia in every department of the government and at every level of Russian society.

Alexander II and the Problem of Reform

Tsar Nicholas I (ruled 1825–1855), the standard-bearer of uncompromising autocracy, died during the Crimean War and was succeeded by his son, Alexander II (ruled 1855–1881). Although given the title of Tsar Liberator because of the reforms that took place during his reign, Alexander II was anything but a liberal in the western sense. He was as staunch a believer in autocratic government as his father, and it was as an autocrat that he introduced, or rather imposed, his great reforms. The tsar remained the supreme authority in the state. He ruled through a vast bureaucracy that was responsible to him alone. In a country as large as Russia, with its poor transportation and communications, a good deal of power passed by default to the local authorities, but no changes could be made on a national scale unless they had been initiated or approved by the tsar. There existed no government machinery through which the ordinary Russian citizen could introduce improvements or suggest reforms. This lack of an outlet for the expression of political opinion fostered the development of the many illegal political societies that flourished in Russia in the nineteenth century, and created an atmosphere of frustration in which politically conscious people turned to extremist ideas and methods, to bombings and assassinations, as the only means of bringing about change.

Alexander II was not a forceful person. He frequently yielded to the pressures around him, and failed to carry through in a consistent or logical manner the reforms that he inaugurated. But the problems he faced were staggeringly complex, and unlike his father, Nicholas I, or his son, Alexander III, he made a determined and on the whole intelligent effort to solve them. His policies met with opposition on every hand: from reformers, who wanted him to do a great deal more; from conservatives, who thought he was undermining the foundations of Russian society; from the peasants, who wanted greater freedom and more land. Alexander himself was disillusioned by the hostility with which his reforms were received, by their failure to stem revolutionary agitation, terrorist outrages, and assassinations of leaders of his government. It was his own fate to be assassinated in 1881. His successors concluded that his efforts at reform had been a mistake and that the only correct course was to revert to a policy of coercion and repression.

THE EMANCIPATION OF THE SERFS

The most obvious and most pressing problem of Russian society at the accession of Alexander II was serfdom, which in Russia was frequently nothing less than slavery. Plans for the abolition of serfdom had already been under consideration in Nicholas I's reign, not for humanitarian reasons but because the system simply was not working. Compared with the peasant of western Europe, the Russian serf was unenterprising and inefficient, confined to antiquated methods of production. The Russian landowner was having trouble meeting agricultural competition from abroad. Many estates were heavily in debt, the land mortgaged. Serfdom was also impeding the progress of Russian industrialization. The new factories required workers, and since serfdom bound the peasants to the soil, large-scale migration from rural to urban centers was impossible.

The effect of serfdom was seen not only in the stagnating economy but in the army, where serfs supplied the bulk of the manpower. The Russian serf-soldier was tough and brave, but his was a bravery of stolid acquiescence. He was uneducated, difficult to train, and generally unable to handle the new weapons and technological devices of modern warfare. This problem became grimly evident to Russian officers during the Crimean War.

Moreover, the government was constantly and forcibly reminded of peasant discontent. No major revolution occurred in Russia in 1848, but between 1848 and the outbreak of the Crimean War there were more than a hundred serious local peasant revolts. Such revolts were nothing new in Russia, but they were increasing alarmingly in scope and number. Stressing the need for reform, in a speech to the Moscow nobility, Alexander II said: "The existing order of serfdom cannot remain unchanged. It is better to abolish serfdom from above than to wait until it is abolished from below." It was in response to popular agitation and the threat of revolution as much as anything else that the great reforms were at last undertaken and carried through.

The problems of peasant emancipation in so vast and varied a state as Russia were extremely complex, and they were carefully studied by government committees that collected information and evidence from every class and every part of the country. The emancipation edict was largely the work of the bureaucracy, which included many men passionately interested in reform. These zealous bureaucrats were the driving force in the emancipation movement. But it was the tsar who imposed the edict on the reluctant nobility, although not before the members of this class had secured major modifications in the proposals.

The emancipation edict of March 3, 1861 (two years earlier than President Lincoln's), was a massive document that reflected the complexities of the subject. The law gave the serf some personal freedom and attempted to provide a means of livelihood for the liberated peasant in the form of land purchased by the state from the landlord. The division of land between peasant and landlord differed widely in the various regions of Russia, depending on topography, climate, and similar considerations, and was often settled locally because it was necessary to deal with questions concerning rights to water, pasturage, forests, roads, and the like.

The emancipation proved to be a boon to the landlords, who generally secured the best land and the most important rights connected with it. Landlords whose estates were mortgaged profited the most. They received generous compensation from the government for the land they relinquished; they were given clear possession of what was left of their property (generally about half); they were relieved of the responsibility of caring for the serfs on their estates. For the peasants, emancipation was a mixed blessing. In theory they were now free to own property, to marry as they pleased, and to resort to law. But from the beginning the great majority of them lacked sufficient land on which to support themselves, especially as the peasant population was increasing rapidly while agricultural productivity remained relatively static.

Two peasants photographed in 1878. *The picture shows the kind of agricultural implements available at that time to the peasantry. Only large estates had more up-to-date technical equipment.*

The most notable defect in the emancipation law was the fact that the majority of the peasants were not granted full personal liberty. The state paid the landowner for the land that was allotted to the peasant. The peasant, in turn, was now expected to reimburse the state for this land, and for the value represented by his person, through long-term installment payments. To make certain that the peasant paid this debt and did not desert the land for a job in the city or another part of the country, the state bound him to the *mir*, or village commune, which was held responsible for the payments the villagers owed. The peasant could not leave the land without the consent of the commune, which in theory was governed by the peasants themselves but in reality was closely supervised by government officials. As there was no dearth of labor in most rural areas, peasants who gave up their share of the land were generally allowed to leave the *mir*. These, on the whole the poorest and least skilled, now moved to the cities to swell the ranks of the urban proletariat.

Peasants who remained in the commune usually did not own outright the land for which they were paying. The majority of the communes could reallocate the property under their control according to the requirements of their members. Thus the father of a large family might be allocated a comparatively large amount of land, but as his children grew up, some of his fields might be handed over to another member of the commune whose needs were greater. The result was that peasant emancipation in Russia produced not the independent and conservative peasant landowner characteristic of western Europe, but a discontented, land-hungry peasant population still bound to the soil. Not until 1906 were the majority of the peasants allowed to own their land outright and to withdraw from the communes at will. The tradition of a free landowning peasantry therefore never had a proper chance to develop in Russia. Periodic redistribution of the land deprived the peasants of any incentive to improve their holdings. They continued to follow wasteful timeworn procedures, and almost nothing was done to teach them more efficient methods of agricultural production. The rapid growth of the peasant population in the late nineteenth century, static agricultural production, the fact that the peasants now had to subsist on a smaller land base, meant that emancipation, instead of improving the lot of the peasants, had made their condition worse.

The edict of 1861 was originally intended as only a step toward genuine peasant emancipation. The tragedy for Russia and for the Russian peasant was that this first step was not followed quickly by others giving the peasant complete personal freedom, outright ownership of land, and the means to acquire more land and to cultivate it more effectively. There were some additional measures, but none of them penetrated to the basic problems of the peasantry until Peter Stolypin's reforms early in the twentieth century.

REFORMS IN LOCAL GOVERNMENT, THE JUDICIARY AND THE ARMY

Inadequate as were the provisions for the emancipation of the serfs, they had a profound effect on the structure of Russian local government. The liberation of the great mass of the rural population from the administration and jurisdiction of the local landlords meant that an entirely new system of local government had to be created. By a law of January 13, 1864, the inhabitants of each rural district were empowered to elect representatives to a zemstvo, or local council, which was to assume responsibility for the maintenance of roads and bridges, poor relief, and later, for primary education and public-health services. To finance these functions, the zemstvos were given the right to levy taxes. Three classes were represented in the zemstvo: landowners, townspeople, and peasants; a system of voting according to class gave the gentry a predominant influence.

Even so, the zemstvos constituted a genuine form of self-government and attracted men who had long been anxious to have a voice in local administration. The more enterprising zemstvos established primary schools and hospitals, improved local methods of agriculture, encouraged commerce. To carry out their programs, they engaged teachers and doctors, agronomists, veterinarians, and engineers, many of them liberal or radical in their political outlook. These professionals in turn exerted a strong influence on the political orientation of the zemstvos, which frequently became lively centers of agitation for further reforms by the national government. Important in this connection was the establishment of provincial zemstvos, consisting of representatives from the district councils, to deal with problems beyond the local level. From this point the next logical step would have been a national zemstvo, which would constitute a Russian parliament representing every district and every class in the country. To achieve such national self-government was a goal not only of social reformers, but of noblemen and rich businessmen, whose political instincts and ambitions had long been stifled by the agents of the centralized bureaucracy. Like their counterparts in western Europe, most of these reformers had no wish to overthrow the existing government; they simply wanted a greater share of political power and influence within it.

The effectiveness of the zemstvos as centers of political opinion aroused the suspicion of government bureaucrats. Almost from the start the zemstvos were faced with all sorts of official obstruction. Their powers of taxation were so reduced that they were in constant financial difficulty and lacked the resources to carry out proper education or technical-assistance programs.

Reform of local rural administration was followed by a reorganization of municipal administration in June, 1870. The towns were now also granted a certain measure of self-government in dealing with local problems. Again there was a three-class system of voting, but because representation in the towns was based on the amount of taxes paid rather than on class, the rich, whether members of the nobility or of the middle class, dominated the dumas, or municipal councils. Although these councils were severely limited in their power to levy taxes and were subjected to oppressive restrictions, they were a distinct improvement on the administration that had preceded them. Like the zemstvos, they provided valuable lessons in self-government and built up public services on a scale Russia had never known.

Important reforms in the judicial system were undertaken in 1864. Petty offenses were henceforth to be handled not by local landlords, but by justices of the peace elected by the zemstvos, and the more important cases were to be brought to higher courts whose judges were appointed by the crown. The legal code was revised according to the principles of western jurisprudence; the principles of equality before the law, of legal uniformity, of the independence of law courts, of the irremovability of judges, and of public trial, were recognized. Court proceedings were to be conducted according to a strictly regulated system of prosecution and defense, and trial by jury was introduced for criminal cases.

In 1874 came a reform of the army. Military service was made compulsory for all men of all social classes, although the provisions for exemption were so numerous that only about a third of those eligible actually served. The period of service was reduced from twenty-five to six years, with an additional nine years in the reserves and five in the militia. Training was revised, discipline humanized, the cruelest forms of corporal punishment abolished. The preparation of officers was improved, and all ranks were provided with some form of education to enable them to use the complicated weapons of modern warfare. It was chiefly in the army that the Russian peasant learned to read and write, and it was in the army that a large portion of the Russian population was exposed to the revolutionary propaganda of Russian intellectuals.

The Industrial Revolution in Russia

It was not until 1890 that the great boom in industrialization began in Russia. Until about 1870 industrial development was slow and retarded by frequent depressions. Except in a few industries, manual labor and technical backwardness were the rule; antiquated methods prevailed in such basic enterprises as mining and metal production. The two decades after 1870 have been called the period of the final struggle in Russia's industrial development. By 1890 factory and machine production had won a definite victory over cottage industry and primitive types of manufacture. The foundation had been laid for dramatic industrial growth.

In view of later developments in Russia, it is noteworthy that private enterprise never flourished in that country as it did in western Europe and the United States. The chief enterpreneur in Russia was the state. Government action brought about what was achieved in other countries by the forces of an expanding free market. The state was the principal borrower of foreign capital to finance the new enterprises, the chief builder and operator of railways, the biggest developer of mines. The state founded new industries itself or supplied funds and furnished the necessary guarantees for the development of private industries.

A landmark in Russian economic history was the establishment in May, 1860, of a state bank to take over the assets and liabilities of the many private banks that had foundered in the depression of 1858. The original purpose of the bank was to promote commerce and stabilize the ruble, but in time it became the central financial institution of the empire. It played an important part in financing the emancipation of the serfs, and served as the main channel for the concentration and distribution of capital within Russia and for borrowing funds from abroad. The pace of Russian industrialization can be measured by the flow of foreign capital into the country. In 1850 foreign investments in Russia totaled 2.7 million rubles; by 1880 the figure had risen to 98 million, by 1890 to 215 million, and by 1900 to 911 million.

The state erected tariff barriers to protect Russia's native infant industries. There was a sharp increase in tariffs after 1868, and progressively higher tariffs were imposed in the 1870's and 1880's, until an all-time high was reached in 1891.

The state was also the chief mover in the building of railroads, the barometers of the progress of the Industrial Revolution. Nowhere was the improvement of overland transportation more crucial than in the farflung reaches of Russia. The first major line from Moscow to St. Petersburg was built in 1851, during the reign of Nicholas I. In the next two decades private firms were allowed to dominate the field of railway development. Progress was slow, however, and after 1870 the government assumed the biggest role in railway construction and operation both by acting directly and by giving loans or guarantees to private companies. By 1877 almost 2 billion rubles of government money had been invested in railways, compared with the 698 million rubles of private capital invested in 1870. Government-sponsored foreign loans were essential, for during the early stages of industrialization Russia had to buy almost all its railway equipment abroad.

The emancipation of the serfs and the consequent availability of a large labor supply has often been considered a major factor in the development of the Industrial Revolution in Russia, but this theory is open to question. Between 1850 and 1890 the population of Russia almost doubled. The growth of industry, however, generally appears to have been too slow to absorb the swelling supply of labor. Far from stimulating the process of industrialization, the availability of cheap labor encouraged the countinued use of antiquated methods of production. What Russia needed most was not mass labor, but skilled labor, which often had to be hired from abroad.

The government's interest in industrialization was not accompanied by a proportionate concern with the living conditions of industrial laborers. Factories and mines were unsanitary and dangerous. Nothing was done to protect workers from moving machinery; chemical fumes, dust, and smoke dangerous to eyes and lungs polluted the atmosphere. Almost no provision was made for workers' housing. Laborers were frequently obliged to sleep on the floor of the factory, or they were housed in barracks where they slept on the floor or on bare bunks arranged in tiers. A 15-hour working day was the rule; in some cases it was as long as 18 hours. Wages were at a bare subsistence level. Workers were customarily paid only three or four times a year, and wages could be withheld at the whim of the employer. Frequently, payment was made not in cash, but in food or clothing from the company store at prices fixed by the company. Heavy fines were imposed for the most trivial offenses, and a fine of three months wages was not uncommon. Strikes were prohibited by law; striking workers could be fined, imprisoned, or sent to Siberia.

Since the beginning of the reign of Alexander II, government committees had studied the need for factory reform. Nothing was done until 1882, when an epidemic of illegal strikes compelled the government to recognize the need for some kind of legislation. A law of 1882 prohibited the employment of children under twelve, and a corps of factory inspectors was created to enforce it. A law of 1885 prohibited night work in textile mills for women and for children under 17; the same restriction was later extended to other industries. In 1886 a law concerning labor contracts stipulated that wages be paid at least once a month, in cash. Factory inspectors were given new powers to enforce legislation and arbitrate labor disputes. At the same time, penalties for striking were stiffened.

Even if these labor laws had been strictly enforced—and they were not—they would have been miserably inadequate. The condition of the Russian worker remained deplorable, judged by even the worst standards of the west.

Between 1865 and 1890 the number of workers employed in large factories in Russia doubled (from 706,000 to 1,433,000); between 1890 and 1900 the number almost doubled again (to 2,208,000). This industrial proletariat was small in comparison with that of western Europe or with the Russian population as a whole. Yet its importance was greater than its numbers indicate, because Russian industry, and consequently Russia's industrial population, was concentrated in relatively limited areas. The members of the Russian industrial proletariat were thus accessible to political agitators and were more readily available for political action than the Russian peasants.

The government did much in the late nineteenth century to encourage the development of industry, but nothing was done on a large scale to improve Russian agriculture. New farm machinery and methods of cultivation were introduced in some areas, but on the whole Russian agriculture remained substantially the same as it had been during previous centuries. Whereas the Russian population rose from 40 million in 1850 to about 75 million in 1890, the yield of the land did not notably increase. This discrepancy between population growth and agricultural production explains the constant land hunger of the Russian peasant and the revolutionary force of appeals for a redistribution of land, much of which was technically still in the hands of the crown, the nobility, and the church.

Revolutionary Ferment

The relaxation of government censorship during the early part of Alexander II's reign resulted in a dramatic increase in the spread of revolutionary progaganda. The result was that after a few years government authorities imposed new restrictions, which were made especially stringent after an attempt on the tsar's life in April, 1866. But despite repression and censorship, new intellectual and revolutionary movements continued to flourish. Especially influential were the radical writings of Alexander Herzen (1812–1870), which were published abroad and smuggled into Russia on a remarkably wide scale. Herzen sounded the battle cry "land and freedom" and urged intellectuals to go "to the people" to spread their ideas. His mystic faith in the Russian peasant as the vehicle of social reform was to have a profound effect on the subsequent course of the Russian revolutionary movement. Herzen's ideas provided the intellectual foundation of populism, a peculiarly Russian form of socialism that advocated revolution and a reorganization of society on the basis of such specifically Russian institutions as communal land tenure and popular associations of peasants and artisans. The peasants were to be the core of the movement, for they were already "communists by instinct and tradition." Yet the peasant masses, around whom everything was to be built, were almost completely apathetic to the populist ideology.

Populist ideas were to be challenged by Marxism toward the end of the century. Meanwhile, extremist doctrines such as anarchism, terrorism, and nihilism claimed large numbers of adherents among intellectuals of the upper and middle classes who despaired of accomplishing significant reform within the existing framework of society. Nihilism, for example, contained some constructive features, but its principal emphasis was on the need to destroy established economic and social institutions by any means, no matter how violent.

As government repression increased, so did the appeal of terrorist methods of opposing the regime. In the 1870's the number of political assassinations mounted rapidly; high-ranking police and other officials fell victim to terrorist activities, and several attempts were made on the life of Alexander II. Government officials were divided on how to deal with the situation. The heir to the throne called for police dictatorship, but Mikhail Loris-Melikov (*c.* 1825–1888), the official entrusted with enforcement of the new security regulations, did not think that police methods alone were enough. He believed that the government should make a determined effort to win over the moderate advocates of social and constitutional reforms, the social classes that had a stake in the existing social order and were the government's natural allies against revolution. As minister of the interior, Loris-Melikov somewhat relaxed government censorship, and dismissed the foremost advocates of repressive measures. In an obvious bid for liberal support, he proposed to set up a commission composed of representatives of

Alexander Herzen.

the zemstvos and the dumas to cooperate with the imperial council of state in the discussion of new laws. Innocuous as this measure was, it would have created a legal channel for the expression of opinion by a large and important section of the population. But on the day the tsar gave his approval to the proposal, March 13, 1881, he was assassinated by a bomb thrown into his carriage by a member of a revolutionary terrorist organization.

Alexander III

Alexander III (ruled 1881–1894), brought to the throne through the assassination of Alexander II, the Tsar Liberator and reformer, drew the moral from his father's life and violent death that reform and change of any kind were a mistake. To save Russia and the monarchy, he believed, he would have to revert to the procedures of his more autocratic ancestors. The new tsar pursued his reactionary policies with stubborn tenacity.

A dominant figure in the court was his former tutor, Konstantin Pobedonostsev (1827–1907), who developed an entire philosophical and theological system to support the concepts of autocratic government. Pobedonostsev distrusted and condemned "western" ideas concerning freedom of thought, civil liberties, and constitutions, which were corrupting the morality of Holy Russia. Like the revolutionary populists, Pobedonostsev saw a mystic quality in the Russian people, but in his eyes they were the font of autocracy and Christian orthodoxy. As procurator of the Holy Synod and thus, after the tsar, head of the Russian Orthodox Church, he proposed to use religion to restore the spiritual communion between the Russian people and their tsar, making religious unity the framework and support of political unity. Dissenters of every kind were persecuted and deprived of legal status. Partial exceptions were made for Roman Catholics and Lutherans because of the protection they received from Russia's allies, Austria and Germany, but even they were subject to numerous restrictions. An almost racial concept of Russianism played a strong role in Pobedonostsev's thinking. He believed that Muscovite Russia was the core of the Russian state and that the Muscovite Russians were the bearers of the true Russian spirit. Poles, Germans, Turks, Mongols, Jews, were treated as inferior peoples, a fact which explains the responsiveness of many of these minorities to revolutionary doctrines proclaiming racial and national equality.

Pobedonostsev's influence on imperial policies was soon manifest. Almost immediately after Alexander III's accession, the Loris-Melikov reform program was abandoned and Loris-Melikov himself was replaced as minister of the interior by the Russian nationalist Nikolai Ignatiev (1832–1908), who was soon succeeded by the notorious absolutist Count Dmitri Tolstoi (1823–1889). The secret police were given new powers, and a ruthless campaign of persecution was directed against advocates of constitutional

Tsar Alexander III. *From a contemporary engraving.*

government and social reform as well as against revolutionary societies. "Exceptional measures," enacted in August, 1881, gave provincial governors and police officials extraordinary powers to proceed against suspected enemies of the state and permitted them to place entire districts under martial law. There was a notable increase in censorship, in passport regulations limiting both movement within Russia and travel abroad, in government supervision of all phases of education. A statute of July 12, 1889, put rural districts under the control of so-called land captains appointed by the minister of the interior. Justices of the peace were eliminated in rural areas and their functions transferred to the land captains, who thus exercised both administrative and judicial authority. Because the land captains were selected for the most part from among the local landowners and hereditary nobility, the new law, in effect, restored many of the powers the nobility had lost through the reforms of the 1860's. A law of June 12, 1890, modified election procedures to make the zemstvos even less representative than before and imposed restrictions on their powers. Approval of the provincial governor was henceforth required for all personnel engaged by the zemstvos—teachers, doctors, veterinarians—and all zemstvo decisions were subject to review by the provincial governor or by the minister of the interior. Similar restrictions were imposed on municipal governments in 1892.

Every autocrat is dependent on the agents who carry out his policies. Alexander III relied less than his predecessor on the professional bureaucracy composed primarily of middle-class civil servants, reverting instead to dependence on members of the nobility, who were given greater authority in local administration and were consistently preferred over middle-class candidates in official appointments. This policy did not result in more effective or even more loyal administrators. As many of Alexander's ancestors had discovered, the nobles tended to be more independent than middle-class administrators, who relied on the government for their livelihood. The Russian autocracy was, indeed, ludicrously inefficient and slovenly, a fact which explains how despite the many repressive measures so much revolutionary agitation could flourish on so wide a scale.

Territorial Expansion

In the long run, perhaps the most significant feature of Russian history during the second half of the nineteenth century was the continuation of expansion along almost every frontier of the already enormous empire. Russia was the most important and the most successful imperialist power in Europe during this era, and unlike Britain, France, or Germany, has since succeeded in holding on to most of the conquered land.

The Russian drive to Constantinople and to the Mediterranean was stopped temporarily by the Crimean War, but scarcely fifteen years later Russia resumed its push southwest, repudiating the Black Sea clauses of the Treaty of Paris and restoring its naval bases in the Black Sea area. Revolts by the Slavic peoples in the Balkans against Turkish rule in 1875 gave Russia an excuse to resume pressure on the Ottoman Empire. This pressure was now strongly reinforced by the doctrine of Pan-Slavism, a nationalist-racist belief that all Slavs were members of the same race. According to the Russian version of Pan-Slavism, it was Russia's mission to bring all Slavs together. The Pan-Slav movement became a driving force in Russian foreign policy, exploited but not always controlled by the government. In 1877 Russia again went to war with Turkey, but the presence of the British fleet in the Dardanelles prevented the capture of Constantinople, and in the months that followed, the Russians were compelled by diplomatic pressure to give up most of their gains in the Balkans. They nevertheless acquired Bessarabia, strategically located at the mouth of the Danube; a sphere of influence in Bulgaria, north of the Balkan Mountains; and an extension of territory on the east coast of the Black Sea. To the dismay of Russian Pan-Slavists, the Balkan Slavs failed to show any strong desire to replace Turkish with Russian domination. The Bulgarians, for example, resented Russian interference in their country and turned to Britain and Austria for protection. The Russians expanded no more in the Balkans in the nineteenth century, but their rivalry with Austria in this area was to be one of the major causes of the First World War.

Russian expansion in central and eastern Asia was on a far greater scale

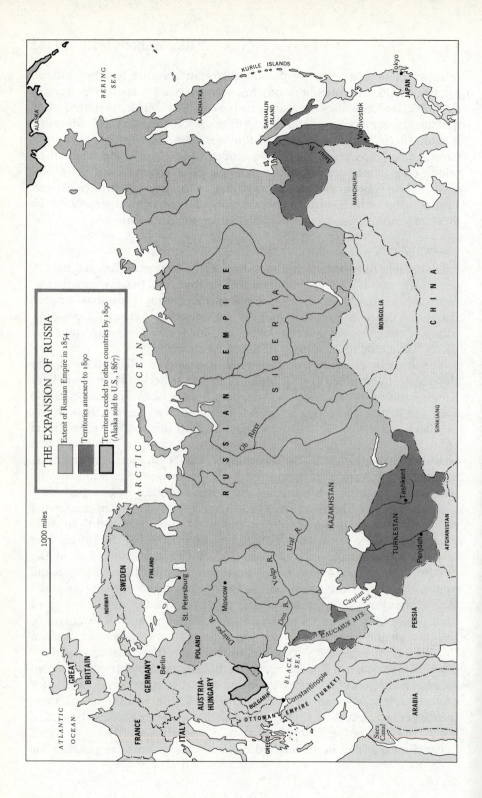

THE EXPANSION OF RUSSIA

Extent of Russian Empire in 1854

Territories annexed to 1890

Territories ceded to other countries by 1890
(Alaska sold to U.S., 1867)

1000 miles

ALASKA

BERING
SEA

KAMCHATKA

KURILE ISLANDS

Tokyo
JAPAN

SAKHALIN
ISLAND

Vladivostok

Amur R.

MANCHURIA

R U S S I A N   E M P I R E

S I B E R I A

MONGOLIA

C H I N A

A R C T I C   O C E A N

Ob River

SINKIANG

KAZAKHSTAN

Tashkent

Ural R.

TURKESTAN

AFGHANISTAN

Penjdeh

Volga R.

Caspian
Sea

Don R.

PERSIA

ATLANTIC
OCEAN

NORWAY

SWEDEN

FINLAND

St. Petersburg

Moscow

Dnieper R.

CAUCASUS MTS.

GREAT
BRITAIN

GERMANY

Berlin

POLAND

AUSTRIA-
HUNGARY

BLACK
SEA

ARABIA

FRANCE

ITALY

BULGARIA

Constantinople

O T T O M A N   E M P I R E   (T U R K E Y)

Suez
Canal

GREECE

and met with far less resistance. On the whole, acquisition of territory there appears to have been the work of ambitious and enterprising local administrators rather than a matter of policy of the central government. A striking feature of these eastern conquests was the small size of the Russian forces involved. The Russians owed their success to the superiority of their weapons and of their military and political organization.

The subjugation of the greater part of Kazakhstan, the region east of the Ural River in central Asia, was followed in 1865 by the capture of Tashkent, which became the capital of the new province of Turkestan, a vast area stretching from the Aral Sea to the borders of India, Tibet, and the Chinese province of Sinkiang. In the 1870's the Russians began the conquest of the eastern littoral of the Caspian Sea, and by 1884 they had reached the borders of Afghanistan.

Not until Russia had pushed to the Caucasus and the Himalayas, and touched the frontiers or spheres of influence of other great powers, did the expansion in central Asia come to a halt. In 1881 Russia concluded a treaty with China settling the boundary between Russia and Chinese Turkestan (Sinkiang); and in 1885, after a dispute that almost led to war, an agreement was reached with Britain concerning the boundaries of Afghanistan, which the British regarded as a buffer state for India.

Meanwhile, in the Far East, the Russians had expanded in Siberia, taking Kamchatka and the Kuril Islands, but their further movement south was blocked by Japan. By the Treaty of St. Petersburg (1875) Russia ceded the Kuril Islands to Japan, receiving in return clear possession of the entire island of Sakhalin, which lies off the Siberian coast and dominates the mouth of the Amur River.

In the eighteenth century the Russians had crossed into Alaska from northern Siberia and had set up trading stations and forts along the Pacific coast, reaching almost as far south as San Francisco. Eventually they realized that they were overextended in North America. The activity of British and French warships along the Alaskan coast during the Crimean War showed the Russian government how tenuous was its hold over the region, and in 1867 it sold Alaska to the United States for just over seven million dollars—a purchase strongly opposed by many economy-minded American congressmen.

Elsewhere in the Far East the Russians were expanding at the expense of China. Taking advantage of China's wars with Britain and France in the 1850's, Russia succeeded in forcing China's formal renunciation of the entire region north of the Amur River in 1858, and acquired another great block of territory, south of the Amur, in 1860. At the southern end of this area the Russians founded the city of Vladivostok ("Lord of the East") in 1860. The beginning of construction on the trans-Siberian railway in 1891 was to give this region greatly increased significance.

CHAPTER 34

The New Governments

THE NATIONAL revolutions of the mid-nineteenth century brought about fundamental changes in the governments of four of the six major powers of Europe. The states of the Italian peninsula, including Sicily, were absorbed by Sardinia to form the kingdom of Italy, while the majority of the German states were absorbed or "mediatized" by Prussia to form the German empire. The Habsburg empire, excluded from Italy and Germany, was transformed into the Austro-Hungarian empire as the result of a bargain with the Hungarians, and separate governments were set up for each section of what came to be known as the Dual Monarchy. In France the empire of Napoleon III, that ardent champion of the cause of nationalities, was defeated by a German national army and ousted by a national revolution at home that led to the establishment of the Third Republic. In each of these states, the leaders of the new governments were to find that the problems of consolidating power and actually running the country were complex and persistent, and that popular enthusiasm for the new national governments soon gave way to the humdrum conflict of domestic interests.

FRANCE, 1870–1890

The Beginnings of the Third Republic

With the French defeat in the Franco-Prussian War at Sedan on September 2, 1870, and the capture of Napoleon III, the Second Empire collapsed. Two days after Sedan the republican deputies in the imperial parliament proclaimed the establishment of a republic and set up an emergency government of national defense. The head of the new government was General Louis Jules Trochu (1815–1896), the governor of Paris, but the real leadership was provided by the fiery radical Léon Gambetta (1838–1882), who took the post of minister of the interior. While German troops besieged Paris, Gambetta escaped dramatically from the capital in a balloon on October 7 and began large-scale organization of French resistance in the provinces. Spurred by memories of 1793, when the armies of

1164

the French Revolution had hurled back the foreign foe, and with unshakable faith in the French nation, Gambetta succeeded in putting new French armies into the field. Despite their lack of training and equipment the new soldiers fought well. Guerilla forces harassed the German supply lines, and to the amazement and annoyance of the Germans, the war which had seemed to be over dragged on. Finally, the surrender of General Bazaine at Metz on October 27, which released a veteran German army for action elsewhere, the successful siege of Paris, and the failure of French diplomats to secure foreign intervention, ended Gambetta's chances of achieving a military stalemate. With Paris in a state of starvation, the provisional French government signed an armistice on January 28, 1871.

Before Bismarck would proceed with final peace negotiations, he demanded that the French establish a government that represented all of France. At his insistence elections on the basis of universal manhood suffrage

The flight of Léon Gambetta from the siege of Paris, October 7, 1870. *The balloon* L'Armand Barbès *carried Gambetta over the German troops, who with cannons and small-arms fire tried to shoot it down.*

were held for a National Assembly that was to make peace with Germany in the name of the French people.

The elections of February, 1871, showed that a large majority of the French people wanted peace. They gave an overwhelming endorsement to monarchist candidates, who promised the restoration of peace and political stability, and repudiated the republicans, whose foremost spokesmen advocated continuation of the war against Germany at any cost. The veteran Orleanist statesman Adolphe Thiers was made "chief of the executive power of the French Republic" by the new National Assembly, and under his leadership the final peace terms with Germany were arranged. France agreed to surrender the greater part of Alsace and Lorraine, to pay an indemnity of five billion francs, and to support a German army of occupation until the debt was paid. The final Peace of Frankfurt was signed on May 10, 1871.

After the conclusion of peace, the National Assembly could concentrate on the question of providing France with a permanent government. With a large monarchist majority in the assembly, it seemed certain that a monarchy would soon be restored. Early in March the delegates gave a strong indication of this intention by voting to move the seat of the government from Bordeaux, where it had been located since the last months of the war, to Versailles, the traditional royalist capital of France. Restoration was prevented at this time only by the fact that the support of the monarchists in the assembly was almost equally divided between the Legitimist Bourbon pretender, the count of Chambord, grandson of Charles X, and the Orleanist candidate, the count of Paris, grandson of Louis Philippe—the Bonapartists were still discredited by defeat. While the monarchists wrangled, the republic continued.

The activity of the National Assembly was viewed with hostility and alarm by the radical and militant citizens of Paris, embittered by the grueling four-month siege by the Germans and the subsequent humiliation of a German triumphal march through their city. Parisians resented the terms of the peace treaty with Germany; they resented the transfer of the government to Versailles; they resented the leadership of the conservative National Assembly, and its legislation on behalf of property owners.

Shortly after the end of the war the assembly canceled the pay of the National Guard, thereby depriving many workers of their only means of subsistence. It was in the National Guard of Paris that resistance to the National Assembly began to crystallize. Under the direction of a central committee of the guard, the chief arsenals of Paris were secured, and cannon belonging to the regular army were seized. Thiers saw the danger. On March 18 he sent troops of the regular army into Paris to capture the guns and bring the city under control. But the soldiers of the regular army, when confronted with the resistance of the Parisians, refused to fire on their

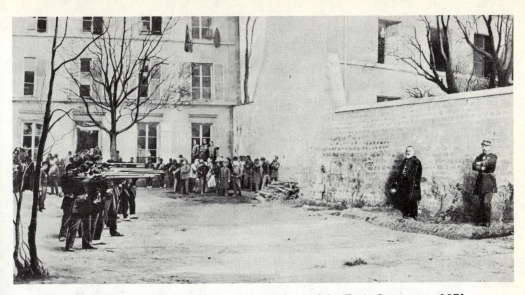

The execution of two French generals by members of the Paris Commune, 1871. *Although the location of the scene is genuine, the photograph itself appears to have been staged later, possibly for propaganda purposes, for according to eyewitnesses the generals were not shot simultaneously, but one at a time.*

fellow citizens. Instead, they fraternized with the mob and allowed the people of Paris to kill two of their generals. Government forces withdrew; the Parisians repudiated the authority of the National Assembly, and on March 26 they elected their own government, the Commune of Paris.

Marxists customarily regard the establishment of the Paris Commune of 1871 as the first proletarian socialist revolution, the first uprising to bear out Karl Marx's prophecy. However, the government of the Commune was in fact far more influenced by the precedents of 1793 than by Marxist ideology, and its leaders were a mixed group of old-style Jacobins, anticlericals, socialists of various persuasions (including a few genuine Marxists), and political adventurers. The legislation of the Commune reflected these several influences, and the passions and exigencies of the moment, rather than any distinct ideological pattern. It called for decentralization of the French government, an increase in the powers of the municipalities, the separation of church and state, the abolition of the regular army and its replacement by the citizen-controlled National Guard. None of these provisions could be carried out because the authority of the Commune was confined to Paris. The only practical legislation enacted by the Commune was the renewal of the wartime moratorium on rents and debts, which had been canceled by the assembly, and the abolition of night work in bakeries. No steps were taken to seize the resources of the Bank of France or to crush the weak forces of the National Assembly at Versailles before they could be reinforced, and very little was done to strengthen the defenses of the city of Paris.

While the leaders of Paris did nothing, Thiers steadily built up the military strength of the Versailles government. Aided by the premature release of large numbers of prisoners of war by Germany, he had a sufficiently strong force to lay siege to Paris at the beginning of April. In the final week of May, Paris was stormed in a battle more brutal and bloody than any waged in the recent war against the Germans. In the last days of the struggle the soldiers of the Commune, seeing that their cause was lost, shot their prisoners and hostages, including the archbishop of Paris, and set fire to the public buildings of the city—the Louvre and Notre Dame were barely saved. The troops of the National Assembly exacted a grim revenge. On May 28, 1871, the last organized defenders of the Commune were rounded up and massacred in the cemetery of Père-Lachaise, and in every part of the city men suspected of having fought for the Commune were arrested and shot without trial. In all, some twenty thousand were killed during that bloody week in May, and about half that number were deported to the penal colony of New Caledonia. The horrors of the suppression of the Commune left a legacy of hatred in French political life that has never been fully obliterated, and for many years it was successfully exploited by rival political parties. To conservatives the Commune represented anarchy and disorder, a horrible example to be avoided in the future; to radicals and socialists it was a landmark in the struggle for social justice, and its suppression epitomized the ruthlessness of the propertied classes in defending their unjust privileges.

The severity of the Thiers government in quashing political disorder and civil war convinced French property owners that the new regime could be trusted. Because of the confidence he inspired in French financial circles, Thiers was able to secure the funds necessary to place the French currency on a sound basis and to prime the national economy. By September, 1873, two years ahead of schedule, the entire French war debt to Germany had been paid and the last German troops were withdrawn from French soil. In July, 1872, Theirs had secured legislation reorganizing the French military system and making all Frenchmen liable to five years of military service. So effective was this reorganization that by 1875 France's standing army was almost as large as Germany's, and it was equipped with the most modern weapons.

Within France, Thiers worked to heal the wounds of civil war and to prevent new political rifts among his countrymen. Although an Orleanist, he became convinced of the desirability of continuing the republican form of government "as the system that divides us least." As time went on he became so frank in expressing republican opinions that monarchists began to regard him as a menace to their cause. A crisis came in May, 1873, when one of Thiers' lieutenants submitted to the assembly the draft of a republican constitution. A motion condemning Thiers for not being sufficiently conservative was carried by a narrow margin. Confident of his own indispensability, and meaning to strengthen his position by forcing the assembly to recall him, Thiers resigned on May 24. He underestimated the hostility of his opponents, who at once accepted his resignation. At the same session they elected Marshal MacMahon, the hero against the Austrians at Magenta in 1859 (and the loser at Sedan) to succeed him. A staunch monarchist, conscientious and well meaning. MacMahon was a political nullity, clearly chosen to keep the throne warm until the monarchists had finally selected a royal candidate.

In August, 1873, it seemed that MacMahon's tenure would soon be over, for the monarchists at last reached agreement on a candidate for the throne—the Bourbon, Henry, count of Chambord (1820–1883). As he was without heirs, he was to be succeeded by the Orleanist, the count of Paris (1838–1894). It was a sensible arrangement, but the count of Chambord was not a sensible man. He insisted on the restoration of the white fleur-de-lis flag of the Bourbons as the emblem of France in place of the tricolor, which had been the national flag since the revolution. "Henry V cannot abandon the flag of Henry IV," said the high-minded candidate, referring to his ancestor who had changed his religion three times in the process of becoming king. The flag issue proved to be insurmountable. The French nation would not give up the banner that had flown at Austerlitz and Jena, at Sevastopol and Solferino. Even the loyal MacMahon admitted that if the white flag of the Bourbons were run up, the *chassepots* would go off of their own accord. In November, 1873, the monarchists in the assembly voted to give MacMahon the "executive power" in France for seven years, in the hope that by that time the count of Chambord would be dead and the candidate succeeding him would be more reasonable. But the monarchists had missed their opportunity. Their election victory in 1871 had been a mandate for peace rather than for a royal restoration; ever since, the tide had been running strongly against them in by-elections, and practical politicians in the assembly were beginning to shift their public attitudes in accordance with the changing mood of public opinion. It was in an atmosphere of uncertain political loyalties and values that the assembly finally completed the drafting of a constitution for France.

The Constitution of 1875

The Constitution of 1875 reflected the political dissension surrounding its creation. It was a patchwork affair, the result of much compromise and haggling, as each faction in the assembly tried to reserve for itself the greatest possible leeway for future maneuvering. It contained no statement of general principles, no bill of rights. The proposition designating the new government a republic was passed by only a one-vote margin.

The choice of the president, who had a seven-year term, was left to the two houses of the legislature because it was feared that direct election by popular vote might bring a potential dictator into office. The experience with Louis Napoleon had not been forgotten. Nominally the president's powers were extensive. He could initiate legislation, he was head of the armed forces, and he appointed the top civil and military officials. With the consent of the upper house, the Senate, he could dissolve the lower house, the Chamber of Deputies, and call for new elections. However, despite the apparently substantial authority of the executive, the legislature retained firm control over affairs of state. Every act of the president had to be countersigned by a minister, who in turn was responsible to the legislature. In practice this restriction came to mean that the real power of government was vested in the legislature.

In the bicameral legislature, the Senate consisted of seventy-five life members, chosen in the first instance by the National Assembly, and of three hundred members elected for nine-year terms, one third of them every three years, by the representatives of the municipal governments of France. In the beginning the smallest town had the same vote as the biggest city, but in 1884 the procedure was changed to give the towns representation according to size and the appointment of life senators was abandoned.

Members of the Chamber of Deputies were elected for four-year terms by universal manhood suffrage. Both the Senate and the Chamber of Deputies had the right to initiate legislation, but all laws had to be passed in the lower house before they were sent to the Senate for a final vote. Moreover, the lower house had the special right to initiate all financial legislation. As a result of these powers, and because the great majority of government ministers tended to be selected from the lower house, the Chamber of Deputies came to be the center of political power in the new French government. The prime minister, although appointed by the president, had to be a political leader who could organize a majority in the Chamber of Deputies, and it was he who appointed all the other ministers, usually with a view to getting the necessary support in the Chamber for his government.

There was no plebiscite to ratify the new constitution, but the fact that a majority of Frenchmen went to the polls in February, 1876, showed that they accepted the system. The republicans won an overwhelming victory in the Chamber of Deputies, and they would have carried the Senate as well had not more than two thirds of the senators been holdovers from the conservative period.

The Triumph of Parliamentarianism

MacMahon was still president—his seven-year term had another four years to run—and it was he who instigated the first important conflict of power under the new constitution. Influenced by his monarchist and clerical supporters, who were alarmed by the strength of republicanism, the president on May 16, 1877, dismissed the ministry of Jules Simon (1814–1896), which represented a majority in the Chamber of Deputies, and appointed a new ministry headed by the Orleanist duke of Broglie (1821–1901). This crisis of May 16 set the stage for a struggle between the advocates of authoritarian and of representative government which was similar to the conflict in Prussia in the 1860's. In France the issue was never seriously in doubt. Neither MacMahon nor Broglie was willing to risk a *coup d'état* and base an authoritarian regime squarely on the monarchist-dominated army. Instead, Broglie tried to secure a popular mandate for his government by employing methods similar to those of Napoleon III for influencing the vote. On July 19 MacMahon, with the consent of the monarchist-controlled Senate, dissolved the Chamber of Deputies and called for new elections. During the ensuing election campaign Broglie put all the machinery of the central government to work. To secure expert assistance, he put a Bonapartist in charge of "making" the elections. He made unabashed use of the government's power to appoint reliable men in key administrative positions. Seventy-seven of eighty-seven prefects were changed, the republican press was persecuted, republican clubs were closed, freedom of assembly was severely restricted. Meanwhile the official press deluged the country with propaganda. The government received strong support from the church, which feared, with good reason, the anticlerical attitude of many republican candidates.

The Broglie campaign was a failure. His exploitation of the machinery of government annoyed the French voters, but did not intimidate them. In the elections of October, 1877, the republicans lost only thirty-six seats, and in November, Broglie was greeted by a vote of no confidence in the new Chamber of Deputies. Broglie resigned, as did MacMahon's next appointee, and on December 13 the president at last named a prime minister who enjoyed the Chamber's confidence. The cause of representative government had won a crucial test. In the elections of January, 1879, the republicans won a majority in the Senate for the first time, and at the end of that month MacMahon himself resigned. As a result of the crisis of May 16 the president was relegated to the role of a figurehead in the French government, and ministers became responsible solely to the Chamber of Deputies. After 1879 the president could no longer even exert his right to dissolve that body.

Symbolic of the republican triumph was the transfer of the seat of the French government from Versailles to Paris in 1880. The fourteenth of July, the anniversary of the fall of the Bastille, was made a national holiday, and the "Marseillaise," the battle hymn of the revolution, became the national anthem.

The Republic of the Republicans

Having survived the threat of an authoritarian reaction, the republican majority in the Chamber of Deputies showed a pathological fear of strong leadership of any kind. The outstanding figure among the republican deputies was Léon Gambetta, the gallant organizer of French national defense in 1870 and the chief engineer of the republican election victory of 1877. Influenced by the example of parliamentary government in Britain, Gambetta saw that a political party had to be able to count on a certain voting strength in the Chamber if it was to carry through a vigorous legislative program. He proposed to unite the moderate republicans in a single party with sufficient power to govern France effectively and provide the country with strong and stable leadership. He wanted greater party discipline and advocated changing the electoral system along British lines to encourage the development of fewer but stronger parties.

Gambetta's ideas on party organization and election reform alienated republican deputies who feared the loss of their seats or their political independence. Jealous colleagues had no desire to concede authority to him. His old radical supporters disliked his new moderation and his abandonment of programs dear to the French left, such as the immediate separation of church and state and the abolition of the regular army in favor of a citizens' militia. Conservatives, clericals, the great industrialists, and financiers looked upon him as a dangerous radical and were only too happy to join forces with his republican enemies. Because of the strength of the parliamentary forces ranged against him, Gambetta had only one opportunity to form a ministry, and his government lasted a bare three months. His death on December 31, 1882, removed the one statesman who might have transformed the government of the Third Republic into a stable parliamentary system capable of giving the country strong and purposeful leadership.

Under the republican administration, laws restricting freedom of the press, public assembly, and the sale of printed material were relaxed. The control of the central government over provincial and municipal governments was eased. Amnesty was granted to all men sentenced to prison or exile for participation in the Paris Commune. Trade unions were given greater freedom to organize and conduct their own affairs.

However, the only major program upon which the republican deputies could agree was anticlericalism. The Jesuits were expelled from France, and restrictive measures against the church and religious organizations were enacted, though subsequently not always enforced. The central feature of the anticlerical program was the campaign against church control of education. The struggle over education was bitter, for both sides believed the issue at stake was the control of the minds and loyalties of future generations of Frenchmen. The aim of republican legislators was to bring the youth of France into a state-controlled, republican educational system that would be free, universal, and compulsory. The accomplishment of this program, which would ensure equality of educational opportunity for all citizens, would be not only a great social reform but a great patriotic reform as well: it would enable France to rival Prussia in the schoolroom, where, many republican educators confidently believed, the war of 1870 had been won. A law of March 29, 1882, made primary education in some kind of school, whether state, church, or private, compulsory for all children between the ages of six and thirteen. Because state schools were free, they had the advantage in attracting students, for even among good Catholics the temptation was great to avoid the payment of fees to church schools. Officially, the state schools were neutral, which meant that they gave no religious instruction. Politically, however, they were far from neutral, for they indoctrinated students with republican, nationalist, and anticlerical principles.

To implement the program of state education, the government founded teacher-training schools and imposed greater restrictions on teachers trained by the church. No religious teaching order could maintain a school not authorized by the state, and no one was permitted to teach in a state school without a state teacher's certificate. Less was done in the field of higher education, although the state took steps to improve the educational standards in secondary schools and laid the foundation for the great reforms of the French university system that took place toward the end of the century.

In the early 1880's the French government was forced to deal with pressing economic problems arising from the general European economic depression that had begun in 1873. The peasants, faced with the competition of grain from eastern Europe and America, and of wine from Italy and Spain, were protected by an agricultural tariff enacted in 1881. Taxes on agricultural land were reduced and a program of farm subsidies was inaugurated. Agricultural schools and model farms were set up to introduce modern methods of production, and the government subsidized research for the improvement of farm products. In the same year, new industrial tariffs gave French industry added protection from foreign competition, and the tax schedule was revised to aid French business.

Encouragement of business was a prominent feature of the third Republic, as it had been of the July Monarchy and the Second Empire. The government recognized the political advantages of securing the support of this immensely powerful section of French society and the desirability of maintaining a healthy national economy, which flourishing business enterprises seemed to foster. Under the republic the expansion of France's network of railroads and waterways and the development of its natural resources was continued, and France remained one of the strongest financial powers in the world.

But despite the encouragement given to business by the state—the lucrative construction contracts and concessions, the favorable taxation system, and the protective tariffs—French industry did not experience the boom that occurred in Germany in response to similar government stimuli. After 1880 France began to fall behind Great Britain and Germany as an industrial power. One reason for this lag in industrial development was France's comparative poverty in raw materials, especially coal. Another was the absence of the kind of government leadership and coordination of financial and industrial enterprises which had been prominent during the Second Empire and was now playing a major role in German economic development. Moreover, between a third and a half of France's available capital was invested abroad, an unhealthy situation in view of the underdeveloped condition of the French domestic economy.

The magnitude of French overseas investments had other important results. A good part of these funds went into countries with weak or unstable governments, where the interest rates were high but the risks great. When political or economic chaos in these areas threatened the security of their investments, French financiers called upon their government for protection. State intervention in response to such appeals was part of the process of financial, or economic, imperialism of the era, and resulted in a considerable extension of the French colonial empire.

But overseas expansion failed to release France from the grip of economic depression. Phylloxera ruined the French wine industry in many districts, and despite government tariffs, subsidies, and tax reductions both agriculture and industry had difficulty meeting foreign competition. The economic depression, along with setbacks in colonial policy in Indochina, was probably the major reason for the defeat of the republicans in the general elections of 1885. The monarchists more than doubled their strength in the new Chamber of Deputies. A serious split between moderates and radicals divided what was left of the republican majority.

The moderate republicans, called "opportunists" because they thought new laws should be introduced only when they were expedient, wanted to avoid disruptive issues, to limit the scope of reform, and to deal with one problem at a time. "Nothing must be put in the republican program that the majority of the nation cannot be induced to accept immediately," Gambetta had said, as spokesman of the opportunist point of view. The radicals, on the other hand, wanted to carry through sweeping reforms at once. They demanded a revision of the constitution to make it more democratic, the election of judges, a graded income tax, greater local self-government, and the immediate separation of church and state. The radicals were also among the most vociferous champions of a war of revenge against Germany; indeed, many of them were so intensely obsessed with this idea that they were willing to subordinate their reform program to the cause of patriotism—thus envincing the attitude that has been called the original sin of the French left.

The election setback of the republicans and the gains of the monarchists came just when the monarchists were in a particularly strong position. For the first time in many years their ranks seemed united. The deaths of the son of Napoleon III in 1879 and of the count of Chambord in 1883 had left the Orleanist candidate, the count of Paris, as the only serious pretender to the French throne. The peasants and businessmen who had suffered in the economic depression, the propertied classes alarmed at demands of the radical republicans for social reform, and the church, angered by the anticlerical legislation of the republicans, all rallied to support the monarchists. They were joined by the most rabid nationalists, including many radicals, who believed that a monarchy or some other form of authoritarian government would be more capable of leading France to victory against Germany than a weak and divided republic. The republic was threatened. Cynics noted that since 1789 no government in France had lasted more than twenty years.

The Boulanger Crisis

Contrary to general expectation, the danger to the republic that actually materialized came not from the monarchists directly, but from an avowed republican, General Georges Boulanger (1837–1891), appointed minister of war in January, 1886, because he was thought to be the only republican general in the monarchist-dominated army. As minister he caught the public attention through his measures to improve living conditions in the army, which won him great popularity with the troops, while his mild efforts to republicanize the army won the applause of the radicals. His remarkable flair for publicity soon made him a national figure. The real basis of his appeal, however, and the quality that united so many diverse segments of French society in his support, was his embodiment of French hopes for a successful war of revenge against Germany. Here, at last, was the strong man the nation had been seeking, the French answer to Bismarck. As if to confirm French patriots in their opinion, Bismarck in a speech of January, 1887, named Boulanger as the greatest obstacle to good relations between France and Germany.

In May, 1887, moderate republicans, alarmed by Boulanger's popularity, dismissed him from the cabinet and assigned him to a military command in the provinces. Boulanger's dismissal and exile made him a martyr and only increased his popularity. Enthusiasm for him reached new heights when his supporters were able to exploit a scandal involving the son-in-law of the president of the republic, who had been selling national honors and decorations, including medals of the Legion of Honor. Although President

General Boulanger.

Jules Grévy (1807–1891) was not directly implicated in the scandal, he was obliged to resign, while Boulanger gained new luster as a man of integrity among sordid politicians.

The rise of Boulangism in France coincided with a period of serious tension between Russia and Germany in the Balkans. The prospect of a collapse of the old diplomatic partnership between Germany and Russia aroused new hopes in France. Only the most myopic French patriot believed that France alone could defeat the German empire in war, but a France allied with Russia—especially a France under the inspired guidance of Boulanger—might well be a match for the Kaiser's legions. It was well known in France that a major obstacle to a Franco-Russian alliance was the tsar's aversion to the republican form of government. Restoration of the monarchy now began to appear to many Frenchmen as a national necessity and a patriotic duty. Republicans began to speak in terms of a constitutional monarchy under Boulangist auspices, and many monarchists seemed willing to concede to Boulanger a large measure of authority in a restoration government.

At the same time, the ministers of the republican government played into Boulanger's hands. In March, 1888, they committed the blunder of dismissing him from the army for engaging illegally in politics while in military service. As a result, Boulanger was no longer a soldier under government orders, and was free to stand for election to the Chamber of Deputies. In the following weeks he entered one by-election after another, as the French electoral system made it possible for him to do, and in each case he was triumphantly elected. The crucial test of Boulanger's popularity came on January 27, 1889, when he stood as a candidate in radical, skeptical Paris. The government threw all its resources into the campaign to defeat him, but again he won a tremendous victory. It was now generally expected that he would seize the opportunity offered by this popular mandate to overthrow the government. Plans for a *coup d'état* were made by his supporters; the commanders of the key regiments in Paris waited for his orders. But instead of leading the troops against the government, he spent the night of January 27 with his mistress. Afterward, alarmed by the news of the government's intention to arrest him for treason, he fled abroad. With his flight, the Boulanger myth and Boulangism collapsed.

The elections of 1889 following the flight of Boulanger resulted in a rout of the Boulangist candidates, a severe defeat for the monarchists, and a surprisingly great triumph for the moderate republicans. The republic had survived another in a long series of severe political crises.

The Boulanger episode had important consequences for French politics. It reinforced the fear among republican legislators of strong men and strong governments. Realistic monarchist politicians recognized, once the monarchists' dubious dealings with Boulanger had been exposed, that to exert any influence at all they would have to join the republican ranks. Realistic statesmen in the Church, too, saw that they would have to reckon with the republic for some time to come. The year after the collapse of Boulangism, Pope Leo XIII inaugurated the *ralliement*—the "rally" to the republic—in the belief that more could be achieved for the Church by working through republican parliamentary institutions than by adamantly opposing them. On the left, radicals had also been discredited by their association with Boulanger; their major reform proposal, a revision of the constitution, had been rendered suspect because Boulanger had supported it.

The republic of the moderates seemed to have won a new lease on life, but the strong position gained in 1889 was soon to be lost in new crises.

ITALY TO 1890

The Problems of Unification

Difficult as were the problems confronting the leaders of France, they at least were dealing with a state with ancient political traditions, and they had at their disposal the most centralized and effective administrative apparatus in Europe. In contrast, the new Italian national government faced the problem of ruling a country that had not been under one administration for over fifteen centuries, a country in which local loyalties and local political traditions were strongly entrenched.

In Rome, Pope Pius IX refused to accept the loss of his temporal power

Victor Emmanuel II. *The first king of Italy, he ruled from 1861 to 1878.*

and maintained an uncompromising hostility toward the new national state. When in 1871 the Italian government tried to regulate its relations with the papacy by offering the pope and the Church certain guarantees, the pope denounced these proposals and refused to abandon his self-imposed imprisonment in the Vatican. He called upon the Catholic powers of the world to help him regain his territories, and ordered Italian Catholics to refrain from all participation in the affairs of the secular state. The pope received no direct support from abroad, and politically minded Italian Catholics for the most part disregarded the prohibition on political activity, but the hostility of the papacy was nevertheless a constant danger and embarrassment to the government.

Challenging the new government, too, was the omnipresent fact of poverty, aggravated by the heavy taxes levied to achieve a balanced budget—at the expense of the poor.

Nowhere were economic hardships more severe than in the south. A large-scale civil war developed in southern Italy even before the process of Italian unification had been completed. The southerners resented the rule of the Sardinian "foreigners," with their centralized administration, higher taxes, and military conscription. The Bourbons now became the popular party and began to stir up rebellion against the Sardinians. Neopolitan royalist leaders became the new Garibaldis. They were joined by the unemployed, by hungry peasants who felt cheated by unfulfilled promises of land reform, by brigands who took advantage of the general turmoil to harass the countryside. In some areas the revolt against the national government assumed the character of a religious war in response to government measures directed against the Church. Shortly after the proclamation of the kingdom of Italy in 1861, the new state found it necessary to concentrate almost half the national army in the south. It has been estimated that more men died in the campaign to subdue the south than in all the wars of Italian unification. The struggle raged until 1866. Even after the worst fighting was over, the scars of civil war remained and the problems of the south continued to foment unrest.

Italian superpatriots were another source of danger and embarrassment to the government. The major work of Italian unification had hardly been completed when clamor began for the return of Nice and Savoy from France, and for the cession by Austria of Trent, Trieste, the Dalmatian coast, and other areas regarded as *Italia irredenta*, or unredeemed territory. Imperialism was to involve Italy in awkward and costly international complications, which would reach their climax in the twentieth century under Benito Mussolini. More immediately, efforts to establish Italy as a great power involved the state in ruinous military expenditures.

Italy's political institutions were not sufficiently developed to cope with the problems facing the nation. Although the constitution made the king supreme head of the state, with sole executive authority, the lower house of the Italian parliament, the Chamber of Deputies, was the real center of political power. The king's actual position was not strong. Republicanism was a constant threat; he faced the steady and uncompromising hostility of the Church; he was opposed by the regional nobility, many of whom remained loyal to the dynasts he had displaced and resented Sardinian restrictions on their traditional privileges. Lacking the support of the Church and a large section of the aristocracy, the bulwarks of monarchical government in other countries, the king of Italy was forced to rely heavily on the army and on the support or sufferance of the vested interests represented in the Chamber of Deputies.

The political foundations of the Chamber of Deputies itself, however, were unsteady. In Italy, as in France, no clear-cut party system developed. Since the time of Cavour, Italian governments had been based largely on political alliances rather than on a single party with a consistent political program. The system encouraged political moderation, but it prevented the formation of a strong government—and of a strong and responsible opposition. Election rigging, the political indifference of an uneducated populace, and the Church's prohibition on participation in politics helped to sustain the system and to impede the formation of a vigorous parliamentary tradition in Italy. The enthusiasm and generous impulses kindled in the period of unification were stifled by narrow-minded calculations of political or economic expediency. Patriots who had devoted their lives to the Italian national cause and now came forward with programs for political and social reform were shunted aside as dangerous revolutionaries. Garibaldi went into self-imposed exile. The disillusionment of the idealists was expressed by the greatest idealist of them all, Giuseppe Mazzini. "I had hoped to evoke the soul of Italy," he said shortly before his death in 1872, "but all I can see is its corpse."

The Politics of Trasformismo

Agostino Depretis (1813–1887), the leading figure in the Italian government from 1876 until his death, was a natural product of Italian politics. Depretis' method of "transforming" opposition parties and interest groups into allies by political and economic bribery was used so consistently and so successfully that the word *trasformismo* came to describe an entire system of government. Ministries rose and fell with disconcerting rapidity after 1876, but Depretis generally managed to remain in control. The measures

The elderly Garibaldi. *Garibaldi is seated before a plaque bearing the name Aspromonte, where in 1862 his attempt to capture Rome from the Pope was halted by troops of the regular Italian army. For many Italian super-patriots Aspromonte marked the beginning of disillusionment with the new national government.*

concerning education, franchise reform, and public health which were enacted during his administrations were never adequately implemented, and the net effect of his government was a further deterioration of the tone and prestige of Italian parliamentary life.

Depretis' most significant successor in Italian politics was Francesco Crispi (1819–1901). A former Garibaldian radical, Crispi was seduced by the prospect of power into adopting Depretis' system of *trasformismo*, but he nevertheless retained a good deal of radical idealism. Like his hero Garibaldi, he believed in the efficacy of dictatorial methods to accomplish his goals. And accomplish them he did—to the later admiration of Mussolini. In 1888 his government enacted measures concerning public health, prison reform, and franchise reform in municipal elections. In 1889 the criminal code was amended, special tribunals were set up for the redress of administrative abuses, and workers were granted a limited right to strike. Salutary as some of Crispi's reforms were, his dictatorial tactics further stifled the development of genuine parliamentary government in Italy. He sharply raised taxes to pay for increased armaments required for the support of his ambitious foreign policy. He ruthlessly suppressed revolts in his native Sicily. And he permitted a notable amount of political and financial corruption. His high-tariff policy and his abrogation of Italy's trade treaty with France in 1887 helped bring about a serious economic depression.

An economic crisis had been developing for some time. The construction of railroads, the opening of new routes to Italy through the Mont Cenis and Brenner passes in the Alps, and the reduction of charges for transporting freight by ships encouraged the large-scale importation of cheap agricultural and industrial products from America and from other parts of Europe. The resulting drop in prices in Italy provoked a demand for tariff protection. But Crispi's protectionism went to extremes; it dealt a crippling blow to Italy's economic relations with France, and the consequent heavy withdrawal of French capital from Italy was partly responsible for the collapse of several important banks, followed by a serious inflation. The high cost of food, a consequence of high agricultural tariffs, caused actual starvation in some areas and was a principal reason for serious revolts in Sicily in the late 1880's.

In 1890 the Italian government was still confronted with many of the problems it had faced in 1861. The cleavage between north and south was, if anything, worse than before unification. The national economy was still unstable. Taxes were high and the taxation system was unfairly administered. The budget had finally been balanced in 1876, but soon after, the state was again heavily in debt. Inflationary policies had reduced Italian credit abroad and caused the flight of hard currency from the country. Almost nothing had been done to aid Italian agriculture, the source of livelihood for the majority of the population, and Italian farmers were unable to meet foreign competition. Crispi's high tariffs helped the Italian peasants to some extent, but they also raised the price of food for all members of the population.

The picture was not entirely bleak. In the late 1870's great progress had been made in the textile, silk, and rubber industries, and above all in the production of armaments, which was generously subsidized by the state. Industry, like agriculture, was aided by Crispi's protectionist policies, but again at immense cost to the country. Prices remained abnormally high, and outmoded and inefficient methods of production prevailed.

Italian political life was dominated by the pursuit of special interests. No respected tradition of parliamentary or democratic government had been established. The system worked well enough to carry on the routine business of government, but it proved incapable of dealing purposefully or effectively with the fundamental evils besetting the nation.

THE HABSBURG EMPIRE TO 1890

The Creation of Austria-Hungary

In the wake of the Italian war of 1859, fundamental changes were introduced in the government and structure of the Habsburg empire. The war had revealed the dubious loyalty of many of the empire's non-German troops, especially the Magyars, who had deserted in large numbers and had proved unreliable in battle. The nationalities problem thus stood exposed as one of the empire's gravest difficulties.

Following the defeats in Italy, Emperor Francis Joseph dismissed Bach and other ministers who had favored a policy of bureaucratic centralization dominated by the German element in the empire, and inaugurated his first personal experiment aimed at solving the nationalities problem. Under the influence of the Polish nobleman Count Agenor von Goluchowski (1812–1875), the emperor in 1860 issued a new constitution, the so-called October Diploma, which gave the major share of power to the provincial assemblies dominated by the local nobility. In theory it ended the policy of centralization that had favored the German population, and it represented an effort to win over the feudal nobility of every national group, and especially to regain the support of the Hungarians.

The October Diploma satisfied certain feudal elements among the Slavs, to whom it gave considerable local autonomy, but the Hungarians objected that it did not give them enough independence, and the Germans resented the diminution of their power and importance. The combined opposition of the Germans and the Hungarians made government under the October Diploma impossible, and it was never really put into effect.

The emperor now entrusted domestic policy to a new minister of the interior, Anton von Schmerling (1805–1893), who in 1861 proposed another experiment intended to take care of the nationalities problem. His February Patent, supposed to reinterpret and supplement the October Diploma, actually changed it altogether. Instead of conceding power to the provincial assemblies, the February Patent provided for an imperial parliament in which all the nationalities of the empire were to be represented. The idea was sound, but the election procedures were arranged to give the Germans the dominant share of the votes. So little representation was accorded to the non-German elements that most of them boycotted the new parliament, dubbing it Schmerling's Theater. In operation, Schmerling's system proved very similar to Bach's, for the real power was concentrated in a centralized bureaucracy and the German element in the empire was again ascendant.

Schmerling's government, like that of Bach, fell as a result of mistakes in foreign policy. To conciliate their own Polish population and to establish closer diplomatic ties with the western powers, the Austrians joined Great Britain and France in expressing sympathy for the Poles who revolted against Russia in 1863. It was a futile gesture, for it did not help the Poles and further alienated Russia. In 1864 Austria antagonized Britain and France by joining Prussia in the war against Denmark over Schleswig and Holstein. Thus in 1866 Austria was without allies among the great powers in its contest with Prussia for hegemony in central Europe.

As tension between Prussia and Austria mounted after the Danish war in 1864, Emperor Francis Joseph of Austria became alarmed at the efforts of German liberals to increase the powers of the Austrian parliament at the expense of the crown, and at their apparent willingness to cooperate with disaffected groups in Hungary to achieve this aim.

The most fiercely nationalistic group in Hungary consisted of the Magyars, a Finno-Ugrian people who had settled there in the ninth century, and who predominated over the numerous other nationalities inhabiting the country. To undercut German parliamentarians and to win Hungarian support, the emperor encouraged Magyar leaders to draw up a program that would satisfy their national aspirations and enable them to cooperate with the imperial government.

This offer was accepted with some eagerness by the more realistic Hungarian politicians, who disliked the aims of the Independence party, which wanted to sever all ties with the Habsburg empire. They realized that an independent Hungary could never be a great power, and that all alone, and opposed by the Habsburgs, Hungary might not be able to control its many subject nationalities. In response to the emperor's conciliatory approach, the Hungarian statesmen Ferencz Deák (1803–1876) and Count Gyula Andrássy (1823–1890) worked out a program that would allow Hungary to enjoy a large measure of national autonomy while retaining the

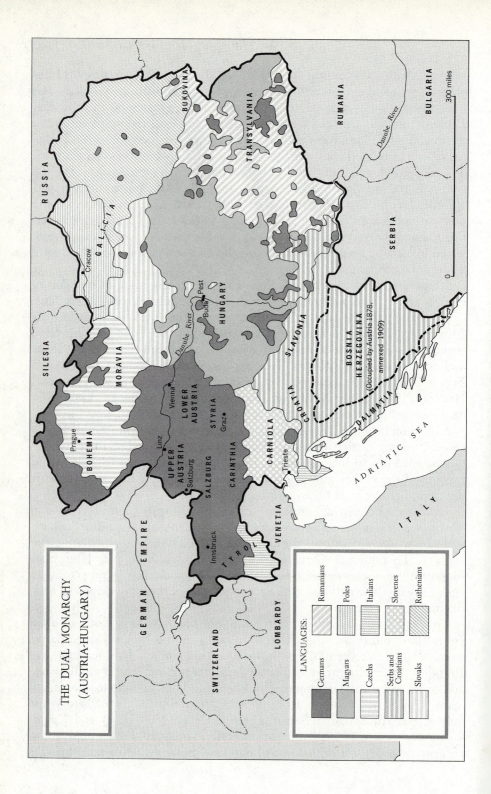

THE DUAL MONARCHY
(AUSTRIA-HUNGARY)

LANGUAGES:

Germans
Magyars
Czechs
Serbs and Croatians
Slovaks
Rumanians
Poles
Italians
Slovenes
Ruthenians

RUSSIA

GALICIA

Cracow

SILESIA

MORAVIA

Prague
BOHEMIA

GERMAN EMPIRE

SWITZERLAND

Linz
UPPER AUSTRIA
Salzburg
SALZBURG

Vienna
LOWER AUSTRIA
STYRIA
Graz

Innsbruck
TYROL

CARINTHIA

CARNIOLA

Trieste

VENETIA

LOMBARDY

ITALY

Danube River

Buda
Pest
HUNGARY

BUKOVINA

TRANSYLVANIA

RUMANIA

Danube River

BULGARIA

SERBIA

SLAVONIA

CROATIA

BOSNIA
HERZEGOVINA
(Occupied by Austria 1878,
annexed 1909)

DALMATIA

ADRIATIC SEA

300 miles

advantages of affiliation with a great power. The emperor expressed his willingness to negotiate along these lines, but the war with Prussia broke out before anything definite had been arranged.

After Austria's defeat in 1866 an *Ausgleich*, or settlement, with the Hungarians was negotiated by Count Ferdinand von Beust (1809–1886), who became Austrian foreign minister in October, 1866. Beust's primary object was to prepare Austria politically and diplomatically for a war of revenge against Prussia. His main motive in sponsoring the *Ausgleich* was to regain Magyar loyalty, for Hungarian support was an essential precondition for a renewal of the contest with Prussia.

But he failed to recognize that the Magyars were the people least likely to support a war of revenge. To them, Austrian victory in such a war would mean the restoration of Habsburg influence in Germany and the consequent reestablishment of German influence in the empire. The *Ausgleich* was to mark the permanent defeat of the Germanizers in the empire, which from now on had to be governed to a far greater extent with and through the non-German elements. The settlement with Hungary of 1867 was to be the one lasting constitutional reform of Francis Joseph's reign.

By the terms of the *Ausgleich*, the Habsburg empire remained under a single ruler, who now presided over a newly formed Dual Monarchy as emperor of Austria and king of Hungary. The emperor was still the supreme authority; he personally continued to make major policy decisions affecting the empire as a whole. The unity of the empire was maintained in the three crucial fields of foreign policy, war, and finance, each under the jurisdiction of an imperial ministry whose head was appointed by the emperor. There was a common postal system, common currency, and after 1878, a common bank.

In all other respects the two parts of the empire were separate. Each had its own constitution, its own parliament, its own ministry for domestic affairs. The administrative language in the Austrian section of the empire was German, in the Hungarian, Magyar. Common problems were discussed by representatives of the parliaments of both states. In economic affairs agreement was reached through direct negotiation between the two parliaments. The Hungarians had the right to renegotiate tariff policies and the amount of their financial contribution to the empire every ten years.

So far as their domestic affairs were concerned, the Magyars had achieved the status of an independent nation.

Austria after the Ausgleich

After 1867, the non-Hungarian part of the Habsburg empire was known officially as the "kingdoms and lands represented in the Reichsrat" (the Austrian parliament), but for the sake of convenience was generally called Austria. Following the *Ausgleich*, attempts to deal through constitutional experiments with the problems of government, especially the nationalities question, were confined to the Austrian part of the empire.

In 1867 a new constitution was prepared for Austria. It recognized the equality of all nationalities, and the right of each to preserve its own language and culture; it contained an extensive bill of rights, which guaranteed equality before the law, and freedom of speech, press, and assembly; it provided for the independence of judges; and it recognized the principle of ministerial responsibility to parliament. This constitution remained in force until 1918, the only important change being the gradual extension of the franchise, culminating in universal manhood suffrage in 1907.

In theory the Austrian constitution seemed to provide every necessary guarantee of national and personal liberty, but its provisions were not always put into practice. The principle of equality among the nationalities was violated by an electoral system giving the Germans a disproportionate share of the seats in parliament. The principle of ministerial responsibility to parliament was ignored by the emperor, who assumed the power to appoint and dismiss ministers. Moreover, the constitution gave the emperor the right to rule by decree when parliament was not in session, and his signature was necessary to validate all legislation. Thus the emperor could legislate without parliamentary consent and could veto parliamentary action.

The policies of the first Austrian ministries under the new constitution reflected the views of German liberals, the largest group in the new parliament. Laws providing for compulsory military service and compulsory elementary education were enacted, along with some anticlerical measures. The 1855 Concordat with the Vatican was abrogated in 1870 in protest against the proclamation of papal infallibility, the right of civil marriage was restored, the education system was removed from Church control, and all Christian creeds were given equal legal status. The liberal regime also introduced a number of humanitarian reforms in the penal code, and abolished religious and legal discrimination against Jews.

The Prussian victory over France in 1871 ended all immediate hope of a successful Austrian war of revenge against Prussia. The danger now was that Prussia would try to complete the process of German unification by absorbing the German-speaking parts of the Habsburg realm. The enthusiasm with which Austrian Germans greeted Bismarck's achievements seemed to indicate that many of them would not be opposed to a closer political union with Prussia. Apprehensive about the loyalty of his German subjects and alienated by the liberalizing policies of his German-dominated government, the emperor early in 1871 appointed a new ministry led by Count Karl Sigismund von Hohenwart, who advocated greater autonomy for Austria's national minorities and believed that conciliation of the large Slavic population was essential to the preservation of the monarchy.

The dominant influence in the new cabinet was the minister of commerce, Professor Albert Schäffle (1831–1903), a German Protestant econo-mist who had been a radical in 1848. Dismayed by the human misery in the industrial slums, Schäffle rejected the liberal concept of economic freedom, which he regarded as merely freedom for the entrepreneur to exploit the worker. In place of the *laissez-faire* capitalist system, he recommended reforms that amounted to a program of state socialism. Schäffle also resented the German assumption of racial superiority over the Slavs. To break the power of the Germans and of the capitalist entrepreneurs at the same time, he proposed the introduction of universal manhood suffrage. This, he felt, would give each individual and each nationality in Austria proper representation and end the artificial German-capitalist domination of the Austrian parliament.

The new ministry granted numerous privileges to the Poles, who were confirmed as the dominant element in Galicia. Henceforth, they were comparatively loyal supporters of the Habsburg government. But the most important part of Schäffle's nationalities program concerned the Czechs. With the emperor's approval, he began negotiations with Czech leaders aimed at granting the Czechs of Bohemia a status in the empire similar to that of the Magyars. These efforts were opposed by the Germans in Austria, who feared the dilution of their own influence. At the same time, objections were voiced by the Hungarians, who saw a threat to their unique position. Schäffle's purpose might still have been carried out with imperial support had not the Czechs insisted on being given jurisdiction over the "historic" kingdom of Bohemia, an area far larger than the one actually occupied by Czech-speaking peoples. The Czechs would thus have gained control over non-Czech national groups, including many Germans. The extent of the Czech demands, the threat of revolution by the Germans in Vienna, the adamant opposition of the Hungarians (who protested that granting the Czechs a status similar to their own would destroy the "unity" of the empire), persuaded the emperor not to grant the Czechs autonomy. On October 28, 1871, the Hohenwart ministry resigned.

There followed another era of German-liberal domination of Austrian politics, under Prince Adolf Auersperg (1821–1885). Changes in the elec-toral law gave townspeople—and thus Germans—greater representation, and hence aroused bitter Slavic opposition, above all from the Poles and Czechs. The latter boycotted the elections to parliament in protest against the new electoral legislation.

Economic problems were the most pressing concern of the Auersperg ministry. Austria's economic boom of the early 1870's ended in the great financial crash of 1873, which was followed by a severe depression. The government attempted to pump new life into the economy by financing public-works projects. To ease the hardship of the workers and create more jobs, it restricted employment of women and children and passed laws requiring safer working conditions. These laws were not strictly enforced, however, and there was little real improvement in the lot of the working classes. The depression spurred the growth of labor organizations, which had been developing rapidly in the previous decade. Government legislation to curb trade unions and socialist political parties was ineffective; instead of hindering their expansion, it only made them more radical.

The depression and the steady opposition of non-German national groups weakened the Auersperg ministry. Church opposition had been aroused by anticlerical measures giving the government the power to tax Church property and *de facto* control over clerical education and the appointment of priests. The ministry was further weakened by revelations that many of its supporters in parliament had been involved in financial scandals during the economic boom. The emperor was disillusioned by the failures of the government in domestic affairs, and as usual, he resented the efforts of liberal legislators to increase their power at his expense. In August, 1879, he dismissed Auersperg. German liberals never again occupied a dominant position in the Austrian government. The collapse of their domestic influence coincided with the conclusion of a military alliance with Germany and the establishment of a close alignment between Germany and Austria-Hungary in foreign affairs.

Count Eduard von Taaffe (1833–1895), the man appointed to succeed Auersperg, was a childhood friend of the emperor. A conservative bureaucrat of wide experience, he professed to stand above party and nationality (he was of Irish descent), and to owe allegiance only to the crown. Like the emperor himself, Taaffe was suspicious of theorists and preferred to govern by expedients and by conciliation. Long before it became fashionable in England, he used the term "muddling through" (*fortwursteln*) to describe his method of operation.

Although his government made many concessions to the various nationalities, Taaffe never worked out a comprehensive program to deal with the minority question, nor did he develop any programs to resolve the financial, labor, and other major problems affecting Austria. His method of keeping rival forces in the country "in a balanced state of mild dissatisfaction" allowed him to govern Austria for fourteen years without major upheavals. But beneath the surface, Austria's national and social problems continued to fester.

To gain support for his government and break the power of the German liberals, Taaffe persuaded the Czechs and other Slavic groups to abandon their boycott of the Austrian parliament; he also secured the backing of the clericals, who represented the Catholic peasants of the empire, and of conservatives of every class and nationality who had disliked the liberalizing policies of the Auersperg government. Taaffe's coalition of Slavs, clericals, and conservatives gave him a comfortable majority in parliament that came to be known as Taaffe's Iron Ring. In 1882 he further strengthened his position by obtaining passage of an electoral law which increased the representation of the Slavic minorities at the expense of the Germans.

To retain the support of the non-Germans, Taaffe made a series of concessions to the national minorities. In Bohemia, Galicia, and Slovenia, for example, the Slavic languages as well as German might be used in education and administration.

Instead of conciliating the Slavs, however, such measures only increased their self-confidence and belligerence. The Czech leaders of the older generation were pushed to the background by nationalist extremists, who demanded the complete exclusion of German influence from Bohemia and national independence within the boundaries of the "historic" kingdom, an attitude that rendered an *Ausgleich* with the Czechs virtually impossible. Unlike the Hungarian leaders in the 1860's, the Czech nationalists failed to see the advantages to themselves in the existing imperial system. As an older Czech leader pointed out, Bohemia was too small to stand alone. If the Habsburg empire collapsed, the Czechs were bound to fall under German or Russian control—a prophecy that was tragically fulfilled.

Despite the Czech nationalists' complaints about political oppression and the economic impositions of the Vienna government, Bohemia enjoyed considerable prosperity under Habsburg rule. It became the most highly

Count Eduard von Taaffe.

industrialized part of the empire and one of the major manufacturing centers of Europe. Czech textiles, leather goods, porcelain, and lace became world famous, as did the Skoda machine and armaments works.

Taaffe's concessions not only failed to conciliate the Slavs but infuriated the Germans, who saw their influence steadily eroded in the parts of the empire where they were in a minority. In 1890 militant German and Slavic nationalists combined to prevent the passage of government-sponsored legislation aimed at securing some kind of compromise on the nationalities question. In 1891 both Czech and German moderates were routed in the parliamentary elections.

Taaffe's failure to solve the minority problems was accompanied by failure to solve the serious financial problems of the empire. Expenditures for the army, bureaucracy, and public services were constantly increasing. The existing tax revenues were inadequate and the means of collecting taxes difficult and complex. Indirect taxes on consumer goods, documents, and newspapers were the principal sources of state funds. Instead of meeting the problem with a large-scale program of tax and financial reform, Taaffe simply increased the rate of state borrowing, thereby raising the cost of servicing the national debt.

Government efforts at social reform were also ineffective. New laws were passed regulating working conditions in mines and factories; the working day was limited to eleven hours in factories and to ten hours in mines; child and female labor was more strictly controlled; provisions were made for sickness and accident insurance. The enactment of these laws, most of them modeled on German examples, was a step toward the improvement of working conditions. Like so many laws in Austria, however, they lacked adequate means of enforcement. They failed to satisfy labor or to stem the growth of the socialist and trade-union movements.

Taaffe's government fell in 1893 as a result of his effort to introduce universal manhood suffrage. He had hoped by extending the franchise to undercut nationalist opposition, which he—by then mistakenly—believed to be a middle-class phenomenon, and to draw on the support of the conservative and loyal peasantry. He had also hoped to win over the workers, by introducing a new, large-scale labor-reform program. But Taaffe's proposals for universal suffrage and labor reform offended every vested interest in the country. His new policies were opposed not only by his old enemies—the German liberals and nationalists—but by conservatives and businessmen of every nationality, and by the Church. Most important of all, Taaffe's radical program alarmed the emperor. With the loss of the emperor's support, Taaffe was obliged to resign.

The threat of Taaffe's legislation to the position of the Germans in Austria gave rise to a new and virulent form of German nationalism, particularly in areas where Germans felt themselves most under pressure from the non-German nationalities. This was the case in Vienna, which attracted enterprising persons from every part of the Habsburg realm and was the scene of more direct confrontations between the nationalities than any other part of the empire. Here the Germans felt the hot breath of competition from new Slavic neighbors, who were generally willing to work for lower wages and frequently proved to be disconcertingly able. Here Germans and Slavs came into contact with Jews, many of whom had risen to positions of prominence in financial, commerical, and cultural circles.

The political response to this situation was the spectacular growth in Vienna of the Christian Socialist movement, a product of German nationalism and labor distress. Dr. Karl Lueger (1844–1910), the outstanding leader of the movement, championed the rights of the worker, peasant, and small businessman against big business and "Jewish" capitalism. He advocated a socialist welfare state, but it was to be a peculiarly German and Catholic state, where Slavs, Jews, and Protestants would not be welcome. Lueger was enormously popular and was repeatedly elected mayor of Vienna.

The wealth of talent that poured into Vienna, the crosscurrents of culture, the competition among the nationalities, made the Habsburg capital a lively and exciting place, a rival to Paris as an intellectual and artistic center. At the same time it was a place where Germans felt threatened, where Slavs and Jews sought assimilation while struggling to preserve a sense of identity, where incompetents and mediocrities of all nationalities had every reason to feel a sense of inferiority. Lueger's Vienna was the city of Bruckner and Mahler, of Johann Strauss and Arthur Schnitzler. It was also the city of Sigmund Freud—and of Adolf Hitler.

Hungary after 1867

The real winners in the *Ausgleich* of 1867 were the Hungarian nobles. They not only gained a large measure of independence in domestic matters, and control over their own national minorities, but also retained an important and often decisive voice in the affairs of the empire as a whole.

The Hungarian constitution adopted after the 1867 settlement was based on the constitution drawn up in 1848. It declared the Habsburg monarch to be king of Hungary, with the right to summon and dissolve parliament, to initiate legislation, to appoint ministers of state and other high officials. But although the Hungarian constitution seemed to give the monarch greater powers than the constitution of Austria, his actual authority was more limited. All royal acts and appointments had to be approved by the ministers concerned, and Hungarian ministers of state were responsible to the lower house of the Hungarian parliament, not to the crown. To a great extent the real power in Hungary lay in the lower house, and ministers able to secure majority support from that body could generally exercise decisive authority in Hungarian domestic affairs. This lower house, like the British

House of Commons in the eighteenth century, in no way represented the majority of the inhabitants of Hungary. It was an oligarchic body elected by oral vote by the Hungarian propertied classes. The lower house shared with the king the right to initiate legislation, and because there existed almost unlimited freedom of debate, the opposition of a few members could block the passage of any legislation. The power of the upper house, composed of great nobles, high officials of Church and state, and crown appointees, was slight. It could veto but not initiate legislation, and it exercised no legal control over the appointment of ministers.

As in Austria, the nationalities question was one of the great problems facing the government. In 1880 the population of Hungary, classified according to language, consisted mainly of Magyars (47 per cent), Germans (14 per cent), Slovaks (14 per cent), and Rumanians (18 per cent), with Ruthenians, Croatians, and Serbs forming 7 per cent. Unlike the Austrians, the Hungarians met the problem not by concessions but by suppression and a systematic program of Magyarization. An act of 1879 made the Magyar language obligatory in all state-supported elementary schools, and in 1883 this act was extended to include all state secondary schools. Magyar was the only language authorized for use by government administrators, the postal and telegraph services, the army, and even the workers on the railroads. The one important region which was spared Magyarization was Croatia, which was allowed to preserve its separate existence, its parliament, and its language.

The Hungarian policy of suppressing national minority movements prevented some of the chronic manifestations of national hostility evident in Austria, but in the long run suppression was no more successful than conciliation in quelling the spirit of nationalism.

During the latter part of the nineteenth century, the Industrial Revolution reached Hungary along with the other countries of central Europe, but Hungary remained primarily an agricultural state and the chief granary of the Habsburg empire. Some of the big landowners bought farm machinery and introduced scientific methods of agricultural production, but the mass of the peasantry adhered to traditional methods, and Hungary therefore had difficulty in meeting competition from abroad. Through their influence in the imperial government, however, the Magyars succeeded in imposing high agricultural tariffs on the entire empire, which protected antiquated agricultural techniques and raised food prices for all the peoples of the realm. These tariffs permitted some big landowners to realize large profits and enabled the peasants to maintain themselves at least at a subsistence level.

But tariffs did not save the Magyar petty nobles, who had been in economic difficulties since the abolition of forced peasant labor in 1848. They did not own enough land to run their estates profitably without forced labor, and they had not received enough compensation for the loss of their peasant labor to become agricultural entrepreneurs. Between 1867 and 1900 some 100,000 independent landlords were forced to sell their estates. Their lands were taken over by the great nobles, who by 1900 owned about a third of the land of the country. Most of the petty nobles entered government service to gain a livelihood. Their consequent dependence on the government does much to explain their loyalty to the settlement of 1867 and their jealous defense of the privileged status of their nation. In 1900 about 95 per cent of the state officials, 92 per cent of the county officials, and 90 per cent of the judges in Hungary were Magyar.

Industrial and financial affairs in Hungary were to a large extent in the hands of Germans and Jews. The Magyar gentry considered trade and commerce beneath their dignity. Jews were accorded full civil rights in 1867 and on the whole became enthusiastic and patriotic citizens.

The majority of industrial laborers in Hungary were landless peasants who had come to the city in search of work. Unlike the peasant migrants of other countries, the Magyar laborers had difficulty adapting to city life; the great ambition of most of them was to earn enough money to buy land and return to the soil. This sense of transiency prevented the growth of a strong class consciousness among the workers and obstructed the formation of powerful trade unions or labor parties. In 1872 trade unions were declared legal provided they were nonpolitical. Toward the end of the century they became closely but illegally associated with Marxian socialism.

The government did little to improve working conditions. A factory act of 1872 fixed the maximum working day at sixteen hours and placed certain restrictions on the employment of children. An act passed in 1884 regulated the hours and conditions of female workers and prescribed safety measures in factories and mines. Neither act was conscientiously enforced.

The most important figure in Hungarian politics in the last part of the nineteenth century was Kálmán Tisza (1830–1902). As head of the Liberal party, he was prime minister from 1875 to 1890. A fervent advocate of Hungarian independence in his early years, he became one of the staunchest supporters of the settlement of 1867, although he worked constantly to change it to Hungary's benefit. In pursuing this policy he represented the interests of the petty nobility, the dominant influence in the lower house of the Hungarian parliament. He consistently opposed agrarian and labor reforms, as well as the extension of the suffrage, and he ruthlessly defended the political supremacy of the Magyar nobility against encroachment by other classes and nationalities.

Tisza devoted his chief attention to financial problems. The Hungarian national debt had risen sharply after 1867 because of financial mismanagement, large-scale spending on the construction of railroads, and the costs of a growing bureaucracy and army. In 1875 about a third of the national revenue was being used to finance the national debt, and the government was having trouble finding money to meet current operating expenses. Tisza's major step toward solvency was to refund the national debt at lower interest rates; he also introduced more efficient methods of collecting taxes. During negotiations between Austria and Hungary in 1877 over their shares of the running expenses of the empire, he refused to increase Hungary's contribution, despite the growing costs of the imperial government and army. At the same time he persuaded the Austrians to agree to the reorganization of the Austrian National Bank as the Austro-Hungarian National Bank, thereby obtaining for Hungarians a greater voice in imperial financial affairs.

Tisza's administration fell in 1890 over the issue of the Magyarization of the army. Hungarian patriots demanded that Magyar be made the official language of regiments raised in their half of the empire, and that the Hungarian army leadership be given greater independence. Although Tisza had pursued a firm policy of Magyarization in domestic affairs, he saw that these demands were a threat to the security of the empire. His refusal to yield on the army issue furnished ammunition to the extreme nationalists. In 1890 Tisza's Liberal party gave way to the revived Independence party under the leadership of Francis Kossuth (1841–1914), son of the Hungarian nationalist leader of 1848, Louis Kossuth.

Count Kálmán Tisza.

THE GERMAN EMPIRE, 1871–1890

In contrast to the Habsburg empire, the new German empire consisted largely of people of one nationality, but here too centrifugal forces seemed to threaten the stability of the state. Unlike France, the empire was not tightly centralized; it was a federal union based on treaties between Prussia and the other states of Germany which permitted the individual states to preserve their separate identities and a large measure of local autonomy. Most of them maintained a good deal of financial independence; some of the larger states kept nominal control of their armies in peacetime; Bavaria and Württemberg retained their own postal systems. So great were the concessions to particularism and so numerous the powers held by local governments that many statesmen in Berlin seriously believed that the empire could not survive a severe crisis, a fear that often loomed large in their political calculations. Their apprehension was not altogether unjustified, for particularism remained a strong force in German politics.

The constitution of the empire was very similar to the constitution of the North German Confederation of 1867, and like the earlier document, it was largely the work of Bismarck. The supreme authority in the empire was vested in the emperor (kaiser), who, as king of Prussia, had the largest and most powerful state in Germany behind him. He had the right to appoint all imperial officials; he was the director of imperial foreign policy, the commander of all German armies in time of war; he had the authority to convoke and adjourn the imperial legislature, and through the chancellor, to initiate domestic legislation.

The representative of the emperor in all affairs of the empire as a whole was the imperial chancellor, who was responsible to the emperor alone. This position Bismarck created for himself, and during the reign of William I, who generally accepted his political guidance, the office gave Bismarck supreme authority in the state.

The individual states of the empire were represented according to size and population in the Bundesrat, the upper house of the imperial parliament, whose members were nominated by the governments of the states. The Bundesrat had the power to initiate legislation, and government measures affecting the entire empire were, as a rule, launched through this body. Because the Bundesrat was dominated by Prussia, which controlled enough votes to veto constitutional amendments, legislation was rarely introduced before the approval of the Prussian government had been secured. Only by uniting could the smaller states block Prussian measures, and thus preserve a certain balance of power in the Bundesrat.

The national and popular will was represented in the Reichstag, the lower house of the imperial parliament, whose members were elected from constituencies throughout the empire by universal manhood suffrage. The

William I and Bismarck. *This painting indicates the relationship between the two men: Bismarck, the subject, appears to be lecturing to his sovereign rather than simply presenting a report. The cluttered interior decoration is typical of the period.*

Reichstag, too, had the power to initiate legislation, but since measures passed by this body had to be approved by the Bundesrat, the governments of the federal states could block any proposal. The legislative initiative of the lower house was therefore severely limited. The Reichstag for its part, however, could veto all legislation passed by the Bundesrat, and by threatening to exercise this right it could force through amendments to Bundesrat enactments or bargain for the passage of its own legislation. Moreover, the Reichstag controlled financial appropriations not already fixed by the constitution, and its approval was necessary for new or extraordinary expenditures, including those for the army and navy. Thus the Reichstag was in no sense a meaningless body or a mere facade for Prussian autocracy. The importance of the Reichstag is reflected in the strenuous efforts of successive imperial chancellors to secure majorities in this body to ensure the passage of their legislation.

The actual administration of the German empire was complicated by its federal nature. The administration of each of the individual states, including Prussia, was carried on by the government and bureaucracy of that state, and legislation for a particular German state did not apply to the empire as a whole. The empire itself, on the other hand, did not have a complete bureaucratic apparatus of its own, but was obliged to rely on the civil servants of the individual German states to carry out imperial legislation. In fact, certain key departments of the empire, notably the army and the foreign office, were merely extensions of those departments in the Prussian government. There was no imperial cabinet, and only one imperial minister, the chancellor. Imperial administrative departments were headed not by ministers, but by civil servants with the title of state secretaries, who might also be ministers of the Prussian government for the same departments. Thus the imperial and Prussian governments were closely intertwined, yet separate, a situation that allowed Bismarck, who except for two years was both imperial chancellor and prime minister of Prussia, to work through either administration as circumstances required and thus to keep the threads of authority in his own hands.

The lack of distinct spheres of authority was to create serious complications in the final years of the Bismarck regime and was subsequently to be a major source of conflict. It was unclear, for example, whether the Prussian ministers of state were responsible in the first instance to the prime minister of Prussia or to the monarch in his role as king of Prussia, and whether the imperial state secretaries were responsible to the imperial chancellor or to the monarch in his role as emperor. Only one thing was certain: the ministers and state secretaries were not responsible to any parliament or to public opinion.

Perhaps the greatest weakness of the Bismarck government, and of Bismarck himself as an administrator, was the lack of opportunity for other men to gain experience in the actual process of governing. Bismarck's refusal to delegate any real power to his subordinates and to allow others to make major policy decisions meant that a whole generation of German civil servants and politicians passed decisions along to a higher authority as a matter of course. As one official expressed it, no sturdy second growth was allowed to flourish under the Bismarck oak. The lack of politicians trained in leadership and having confidence in their capacity—and right—to rule was to be sorely felt after Bismarck's dismissal and was one of the chancellor's more unfortunate political legacies.

During the first years of the German Empire, Bismarck devoted his energies to consolidating the new state and providing it with an effective administration. Until 1878 a coalition of National Liberals (pro-Bismarck liberals) and members of the Reich party (pro-Bismarck conservatives) gave the chancellor a working majority in the Reichstag. Although these parties withheld support for a number of significant pieces of legislation, they did ensure the passage of many constructive measures that contributed to greater national unity. A system of uniform coinage, a commercial code

"Bismarck As Wild Animal Trainer." *This Hungarian cartoon shows a typical foreign view of the chancellor's relationship with the Reichstag. Bismarck himself frequently regretted that the Reichstag deputies were neither so muzzled nor so firmly under his control as the cartoon made it appear.*

for trade and industry, uniform methods of procedure for the civil and criminal courts, a national bank, an imperial bureau of railroads, were all products of Bismarck's alliance with national-minded members of the Reichstag.

The Kulturkampf

Bismarck's most important campaign conducted in alliance with the National Liberals was an attack on the power of the Roman Catholic Church in Germany, aimed at overcoming what he regarded as an antinational and potentially disruptive force in the new empire. To Bismarck and many other German nationalists, it appeared that the Roman Catholics owed spiritual allegiance to a foreign power which might support and encourage their opposition to Prussian rule in the areas they inhabited—in Prussian Poland, in Alsace and Lorraine, and in the German states so recently united. A further danger in Bismarck's view was the possible formation of an anti-Prussian alliance between the two vengeful Catholic powers, Austria and France, which might call upon Catholics within Germany to aid them by throwing off the yoke of Protestant Prussia.

In his campaign against the Catholic Church, Bismarck appears to have sought to bring it under government control and thereby to make it a unifying rather than a divisive force in the empire. He was encouraged in his policy by the conflict within the Church itself over the recent proclamation of the dogma of papal infallibility. A number of prominent German clerics, the Old Catholics, had seceded from the Church in protest, and Bismarck saw reason to hope that he could exploit this division in forming the national church he desired.

Bismarck's attack on the Catholic Church, called the *Kulturkampf* ("cultural struggle," or "struggle for civilization") by his liberal followers, resulted almost immediately in a consolidation of Catholic political forces in Germany in the Center party. This party, previously a minor factor in German politics, was to become one of the most powerful and stable influences in German party politics, a role it would continue to play until the Nazi era. The opposition of the Center party in the Reichstag made it almost impossible for the government to secure the passage of anti-Catholic legislation for the empire as a whole. The Jesuits were expelled from the empire in 1872, and in 1875 civil marriage was made compulsory, but there were no other moves of this sort on a national scale. Significant laws against the Church were passed only in Prussia. Of these the most noteworthy were the so-called May Laws of 1873, which were a patent attempt to place the Catholic Church under state control. The Church fought back with grim tenacity; all the bishops and over half the parish priests in Prussia preferred prison or deposition to acceptance of the state laws, and they were loyally supported by their congregations.

The *Kulturkampf* was a failure. The Center party won strength in the Reichstag elections of 1874, gaining even in Prussia, despite government hostility. Bismarck recognized his mistake and attempted to rectify it. In 1878 Pope Pius IX was succeeded by the more conciliatory and diplomatic Leo XIII, and shortly afterward Bismarck opened negotiations with the Vatican to put an end to the *Kulturkampf*. He had strong political reasons for doing so. In the course of the *Kulturkampf* he had gained a healthy respect for the strength and organization of the Catholic Church and for the political power represented by the Center party. By striking a bargain with the Church about the *Kulturkampf* legislation, he hoped to gain the support of the Center party for his own political purposes.

New Conflicts with the Liberals and the Antisocialist Campaign

By 1878 Bismarck was definitely on the lookout for new political allies, for he was finding it increasingly difficult to work with the National Liberals. In 1874 he had clashed with them over the familiar question of the military budget. The chancellor had wanted a long-term budget so that the army leaders could plan far ahead, but the liberals in the Reichstag had insisted on retaining parliamentary control over military expenditures, for this was their greatest source of political power. A government bill providing for a seven-year military budget (the "septennate") was finally passed with the support of the National Liberal leadership, but the issue had caused a rift in liberal ranks and weakened the effectiveness of the National Liberals as a progovernment party.

Bismarck had failed altogether to win liberal support for certain economic measures designed to make the government less dependent financially on the Reichstag. He had asked for direct taxes on beer and sugar, and for a government monopoly on tobacco, which would have yielded a large and steady revenue independent of Reichstag or state-government appropriations. But the liberals refused, realizing that the passage of such measures would result in a serious diminution of their control over imperial finances and hence in a serious loss of power. Moreover, many of them adhered to the doctrine of free competition and objected on principle to a government monopoly. The most serious split between Bismarck and the liberals, however, followed dissension over the policy to be adopted toward the socialists.

Since 1870, following their refusal to vote for war appropriations, Bismarck had carried on a campaign against the socialists, who like the Catholics appeared to sustain loyalties extending beyond the national state. With the union of all German socialist groups in the Social Democratic party at the Gotha Congress of 1875, and their gains in local and state elections in 1876, Bismarck intensified his opposition, on the grounds that the socialists' international revolutionary programs threatened national security and the existing political and social order. In 1876 he introduced legislation that would have made it a criminal offense to attack in print "family, property, universal military service, or other foundations of public order, in such manner as to undermine morality, respect for law, or love of the fatherland." This measure was ostensibly aimed against the socialists, but the liberals saw that it might easily be turned against any critics of the government, and much to Bismarck's annoyance, they voted against it.

Bismarck returned to the attack in 1878 after an attempt was made to assassinate the emperor. Although the would-be assassin was not a socialist, the chancellor tried to exploit the indignation aroused by the incident to obtain passage by the Reichstag of a new antisocialist proposal. The liberals on the whole disliked and feared socialism, but they regarded Bismarck's bill as an infringement of political freedom, and again they rejected it. Unfortunately for the liberals, a month later another attempt was made to kill the emperor, and this time the aged ruler was seriously wounded. Again the assassin was not a socialist, but Bismarck used the occasion to launch a fierce attack on the opponents of his antisocialist law. Accusing the liberals of indifference to the life of the emperor, he dissolved the Reichstag, and fought the ensuing election campaign on the issues of public order and patriotism. His propaganda was effective; the liberals were defeated and the conservatives made gains.

By this time Bismarck had clearly resolved to form new political combinations to support his domestic programs. The National Liberals had failed to become the obedient government party he had hoped to fashion, and their political usefulness was declining because of splits in their ranks. But Bismarck's main reason for turning away from the liberals at this time may have been his fear that they would become the political allies of the German crown prince, who professed to be a liberal himself. Since the emperor was already eighty-one, the succession of the crown prince could be expected at any moment. If the new sovereign should prove serious about wanting genuine representative government, he might wish to appoint a chancellor who had the backing of a majority in the Reichstag. It would therefore be desirable that he should find not a strong liberal group in parliament, but a majority that would support Bismarck, along with a public thoroughly alarmed by the socialist threat and hence hostile to any drastic changes in government leadership.

The antisocialist law over which the election campaign had been fought was passed in October, 1878, this time supported even by many of the National Liberals, under pressure from their constituents or convinced by Bismarck's arguments. The Social Democratic party was declared illegal, its meetings and publications prohibited; socialists found guilty of breaking the law could be expelled from certain key cities of the empire and exiled to other parts of the country. Bismarck's antisocialist law horrified genuine liberals in Germany and abroad, but in some respects it was so lenient as to raise the question of whether the chancellor was really serious about suppressing socialism, or was merely using it as a political bogey to frighten property owners and make himself appear indispensable as a bulwark against the "democratic" tendencies of the heir to the throne. Socialist candidates were still allowed to stand for election to the Reichstag and to sit if elected; socialist literature poured over the German border from Switzerland; the Social Democratic party formed a highly effective underground organization, and socialist agitators expelled from their homes went into the countryside and carried on their propaganda from there. Socialism throve on persecution. Between 1878 and 1890 the socialists increased their popular vote from 300,000 to 1,500,000, and increased their seats in the Reichstag from nine to thirty-five. As a measure to combat socialism, the antisocialist law was a failure. As a means of dramatizing the desirability of keeping Bismarck in power, the antisocialist campaign was most effective.

New Political Combinations; Protectionism and Economic Expansion

Bismarck next made a direct bid for the political support of the Center party. In 1878 he began his negotiations with the Vatican to end the *Kulturkampf,* and in June, 1879, he forced the resignation of Adalbert Falk (1827–1900), the Prussian minister whose name was most closely associated with the May Laws. By the summer of 1879 the chancellor had brought together an uneasy parliamentary coalition of Center-party members and progovernment conservatives, along with a number of National Liberals. With this support he embarked on a political course that differed radically from the one he had pursued during the preceding nine years.

He abandoned the policy of free trade and introduced protective tariffs for German agriculture and industry. Germany had been suffering from a serious depression since 1873, when the speculative boom that had accompanied the creation of the empire had suddenly come to an end in a catastrophic series of bank and business failures. German industry, faced with powerful competition from Great Britain, was slow to recover. German agriculture did not recover at all, but continued in a steady decline because of the influx of cheap grain from America and Russia. A German tariff law of July 13, 1879, gave protection to both agriculture and industry. It was supported by the Center party, by the many conservative landowners whose economic interests were primarily agrarian, and by both conservative and liberal representatives of business interests. It was opposed by those liberals to whom free trade was still an article of faith.

The tariffs brought about a notable economic recovery and marked the beginning of a period of industrial expansion that was to make Germany the most powerful industrial country in Europe. Germany soon passed both France and Great Britain as a producer of iron and steel; railway mileage was trebled between 1870 and 1914; its merchant marine came to be second only to that of Britain.

The Germans had the advantage of rich natural resources—coal, iron ore, lignite, potash—and they used these resources skillfully and efficiently. They made an intensive study of the production methods of other industrial countries, especially Britain, and profited from the lessons and mistakes of others. They purchased or manufactured the best and most modern machinery. With the creation of a national bank (the Reichsbank) in 1875 there began the kind of cooperation between government and industry that had brought such prosperity to France during the Second Empire. The government supplied long-term loans at reasonable rates to launch new industrial enterprises, and provided financial and political backing for the German drive to break Britain's domination of foreign markets. At the same time, the formation of great trusts (cartels) that controlled the major German industries facilitated the introduction of increasingly efficient manufacturing methods, including mass-production techniques. Furthermore, only industry organized on this large scale could afford to set up laboratories and engage research scientists from the universities to experiment in the creation of new and better products. German industrialists were the first to establish a close working relationship with scientists and technologists. The most spectacular result was the rise of the chemical industry, which pioneered in the development of drugs, synthetic dyes, and photography, and revolutionized German agriculture by making available cheap supplies of chemical fertilizers that enormously increased the yields per acre and brought new prosperity to the German landowner. The great trusts thus contributed substantially to Germany's rise as a major industrial power, but like the giant British and American corporations, these quasi-monopolistic institutions made a mockery of the idea of free enterprise.

The rapid-industrialization of Germany during the 1880's was accompanied by all the familiar miseries of the Industrial Revolution. Hence it was chiefly after Bismarck's tariff law had set off the new German industrial boom that socialism in Germany became a serious political force. For socialist propaganda was primarily directed at the new urban proletariat, swelled by immigrants from rural areas, and the steady rise in the socialist vote showed that this propaganda was taking effect.

State Socialism

Bismarck met the socialist threat by continuing his repressive legislation—the antisocialist law was periodically renewed until 1890—but he also sought to correct some of the abuses on which socialism was thriving. In his social legislation, as in his economic measures, he rejected the *laissez-faire* theories of liberalism. By his government-sponsored tariff law and by government encouragement of German industry and agriculture he had succeeded in gaining the sympathy of powerful business and agricultural interests. Accordingly, perhaps a government-sponsored welfare program could win the allegiance of the working classes. Revolutionary socialism was to be undercut by state socialism.

The government's intention of inaugurating a social-welfare program was announced in an imperial message to the Reichstag in November, 1881. "A remedy cannot be sought merely in the repression of socialist excesses," the emperor said. "There must be at the same time a positive advancement of the welfare of the working classes." Between 1883 and 1889 the Reichstag passed government-sponsored laws establishing health, accident, old-age, and invalidism insurance which provided the most comprehensive protection of the working man yet introduced in any country. Bismarck resisted efforts to introduce legislation that would regulate the hours and conditions of work. His ideas on labor had been formed by his observations in the countryside, where women and children worked with men in the fields as long as there was daylight, and he disliked the idea of fixing maximum hours or forbidding the employment of women and children.

Bismarck's welfare program was continued and extended under his successors, but it never achieved the political results the government had expected. Socialism was not killed with kindness. The workers accepted the benefits conferred by the state, but they continued to agitate for more. The socialist vote, and socialist representation in the Reichstag, continued to rise steadily despite the welfare program and the antisocialist law. One important purpose of the program, however, was achieved. Although the socialist political party continued to thrive, revolutionary socialism was undermined as more and more workers were given a stake in the existing system.

"Blown Up, But Not Blown Out." *This 1884 cartoon from the German satirical magazine* Kladderadatsch *comments on the ineffectiveness of the anti-socialist law.*

The Succession Crisis and the Fall of Bismarck

Revival of prosperity in the 1880's and the general success of German foreign policy made it possible for Bismarck to govern with a coalition of conservatives, members of the Center party, and liberal protectionists. But in December, 1886, he again found himself in conflict with the Reichstag over the familiar issue of army appropriations. Once again Bismarck wanted enactment of a long-term military-appropriations bill, and once again the Reichstag rejected his bill in order to retain strategic control over military expenditures. His position was difficult. The old emperor's death was expected at any moment. The succession of Crown Prince Frederick William during a conflict with the Reichstag might provide the prince's liberal advisers with the long-awaited opportunity to bring about Bismarck's dismissal. During this same period the chancellor was faced with a serious crisis in international affairs. Anti-German sentiment was rampant in both Russia and France, and there was a strong possibility that these powers would form an alliance against Germany.

Upon the rejection of his military-appropriations bill, the chancellor dissolved the Reichstag and called for new elections. To carry on the election campaign, he succeeded in patching together the old patriotic alliance of moderate conservatives and National Liberals, which became known as the Bismarck Cartel. Patriotism was his keynote. The fatherland was in danger; opponents of the military-appropriations bill were betraying their country; it was the duty of all good Germans to vote for pro-Bismarck candidates who would support the bill.

The elections of 1887 resulted in a clear-cut victory for the Bismarck candidates. For the first time since the formation of the empire the chancellor seemed to have secured a loyal parliamentary majority which would guarantee the passage of his domestic legislation. If, upon becoming emperor, Frederick William were bent on selecting a chancellor who enjoyed the support of a majority in parliament, he would find that the head of this majority was none other than Bismarck. But Bismarck's election success proved to be a hollow victory, for it was won against a dying man. In the spring of 1887 it was learned that the crown prince was mortally ill with cancer. It was doubtful whether he would outlive his aged father.

Emperor William I died on March 9, 1888. The crown prince took the title of Emperor Frederick III. But his fatal illness made the title a mere formality. In his brief reign of ninety-nine days Frederick III was not able to carry out the liberal program that he had dreamed of during his seventeen years of waiting for the imperial crown. He died on June 15, 1888, and was succeeded by his son, William II, who was destined to be the last German emperor.

William II (ruled 1888–1918) was twenty-nine when he came to the throne, but was still immature in his conduct and thought. The great tragedy for Germany was that he never grew up. An arm crippled at birth may have contributed to a feeling of inadequacy or inferiority, which he attempted to offset by bombastic self-assertion. Disliking opposition, he surrounded himself with sycophants and mediocrities, yet he could be won over to almost any policy by a person able and willing to handle him in the right way.

With his sense of self-importance and his dislike of contradiction, William II was not the man to submit indefinitely to the authority of a Bismarck, despite a professed admiration for the chancellor. It was only a matter of time before he would use the power Bismarck himself had given the emperor in the German constitution to exercise supreme authority in the state. Bismarck's only means of retaining his influence was to use the utmost tact in dealing with the young man, or to engineer a *coup d'état* that would give him an excuse to introduce changes in the constitution granting the chancellor greater power at the expense of the throne.

Bismarck tried both courses during his final months in office, and in both he failed. The chancellor's fine political touch deserted him at several critical moments, and he made the crucial error of spending too much time at his estates in the country in the mistaken belief that his son Herbert, state secretary of the German foreign office since 1886, had the new emperor safely under control.

The final clash between the emperor and the chancellor ostensibly concerned labor policy. Actually, it was a clash over power. William II had been warned from many quarters that Bismarck was preparing to foment a domestic crisis so that he could prove himself indispensable to the inexperienced young ruler and then dictate his terms. In March, 1890, the emperor demanded that Bismarck submit his resignation. On March 20, 1890, the fateful document was signed. An era had come to an end.

CHAPTER 35

The Search
for a New Stability, 1871-1890

SHORTLY AFTER PRUSSIA's victory over France in 1871 and the formation of the German empire, the British statesman Benjamin Disraeli declared:

> This war represents the German revolution, a greater political event than the French Revolution of the last century. .... Not a single principle in the management of our foreign affairs, accepted by statesmen for guidance up to six months ago, any longer exists. There is not a diplomatic tradition which has not been swept away. You have a new world, new influences at work, new and unknown objects and dangers with which to cope. . . . The balance of power has been entirely destroyed, and the country which suffers most, and feels the effect of the change most, is England.

Disraeli's statements were somewhat extravagant. As leader of Her Majesty's loyal opposition, he was criticizing the foreign policy of his rival Gladstone, who was in power when the final unification of Germany took place. But he was nevertheless expressing a concern felt by many European statesmen. Prussia now stood at the head of an empire which was unquestionably the greatest military power on the Continent. How would Prussia use that power? Would the principle of German unification now be extended to the Netherlands, Belgium, or Switzerland? What was to be the fate of the Germans in the Habsburg empire, in Russia's Baltic provinces, in Scandinavia?

Bismarck was well aware of Europe's apprehensions, and he also saw the dangers they implied for the new German empire. In their dread of Germany, all the states anxious to restore the European balance of power might join forces with the recently defeated foes of Prussia in a great anti-German coalition. Bismarck's first concern, therefore, was to reassure Europe.

The new German empire, he said, was a satiated state whose principal

1206

foreign-policy objective henceforth would be the preservation of peace and the *status quo*.

Bismarck meant what he said. The operation of the European balance of power would make further German conquests impossible, at least in the foreseeable future, and he did not believe there was any area where expansion for Germany would be profitable in relation to the costs and risks involved. By far the most important reason for his pacific policy, however, was his conviction that the preservation of peace was the most certain and least costly means of safeguarding the state he had created. Bismarck's conception of the future course of German policy was of fundamental importance. As leader of the most powerful state in Europe, and as one of the most talented diplomats of his age, he was to dominate the European international scene until his dismissal in 1890. And because he saw his country's best interests in the preservation of the peace of Europe, he was one of the few political leaders before 1914 to pursue a European as opposed to a narrowly national or dynastic foreign policy.

THE SEARCH FOR STABILITY IN EASTERN EUROPE

The First Three Emperors' League

Bismarck's first move to stabilize the European states system established in 1871 was an attempt to revive the Metternichian Concert among the conservative powers of Europe. He looked upon Russia and Austria as natural allies in working toward this goal. In both states the threat of revolution was constant, and both might be expected to join Germany in a policy of preserving the international as well as the domestic *status quo*, for a major war, with all the risks it entailed, could only benefit the forces of revolution.

In the course of 1873, several treaties concluded among the three imperial powers resulted in the formation of what came to be known as the first Three Emperors' League. Germany, Austria, and Russia agreed to combat subversive activities in their respective countries and to consult in case other powers threatened the peace of Europe. Thus the league, which was joined by Italy in September, 1873, was based on little more than a mutual interest in suppressing revolution at home and preventing the formation of a coalition against any one of its members. It worked as long as the interests of the conservative powers were in harmony; it cracked the moment their interests began to diverge.

The Balkan Crisis, 1875–1878

As an instrument of international stability, the Three Emperors' League proved useless when in 1875 and 1876 revolts against Turkish rule erupted throughout the Balkan peninsula. All the great powers of Europe, but especially Russia and Austria, had interests in this area. For Russia, the Balkans represented the shortest overland route to Constantinople and the Straits; for Austria, now excluded from Germany and Italy, they were the last available avenue for an extension of influence. Great Britain and France, as at the time of the Crimean War, were concerned lest Russia use the Balkans as a stepping stone toward establishing influence in the Mediterranean and the Middle East, a possibility all the more threatening for both powers because of the opening in 1869 of the Suez Canal.

Germany had no vital interests in the Balkans themselves. Its concern, as conceived by Bismarck, lay in preventing a war between the great powers over the spoils of the Balkans in which Germany might be compelled to participate to prevent a serious disruption of the balance of power in eastern Europe. Because he believed Germany had little to gain and much to lose from such a conflict, Bismarck put the strongest kind of diplomatic pressure on Russia and Austria to arrange a peaceful partition of the Balkans, and warned that if they did go to war he would intervene to prevent either power from gaining a decisive victory.

Bismarck's diplomacy temporarily restrained Russia and Austria, but in the summer of 1876 the Balkan states of Serbia and Montenegro declared war on Turkey. Despite the aid of Russian volunteers and supplies, Serbia and Montenegro were soundly beaten. The Russians now took Bismarck's advice, made a treaty with Austria defining their respective spheres of influence in the Balkans, and in April, 1877, went to war against the Turks to ensure their final expulsion from the peninsula. After being held in check throughout the summer of 1877 before the fortress of Plevna in the Balkan Mountains, the Russians overcame Turkish resistance by the end of the year and on March 8, 1878, imposed the Treaty of San Stefano on Turkey.

The most important provision of the Treaty of San Stefano was the creation of a large Bulgarian state stretching from the Black Sea to the mountains of Albania on the west, and from the Danube to the Aegean Sea. As the new Bulgaria was clearly intended to be a Russian satellite, the treaty in effect gave the Russians the outlet to the Mediterranean they had so long desired. The treaty was thus a blow to both Britain and France, who wanted to keep Russia out of the Mediterranean; but it also violated Russia's prewar agreement with Austria concerning the Balkans.

By concluding a treaty with Turkey which impinged on the interests of three great powers, the Russians made a serious blunder. Only three days after the treaty was signed the Austrian foreign minister issued an invitation to the European powers to attend a conference in Berlin to discuss its revision. The Russians, their resources exhausted by the conflict with Turkey, were obliged to accept the invitation or face a war against a European coalition.

To salvage as many as possible of their gains in the Turkish war, the Russians tried to buy the support of a majority of the great powers before the conference convened. They first tried Austria, but the Austrians were wary about another betrayal and posed too many conditions. They had better luck with Great Britain. The British could never be sure that the three imperial powers might not join forces at the expense of British interests and hence seized the opportunity to safeguard those interests. On May 30, 1878, they concluded a secret treaty with the Russians that pushed the frontier of the new Bulgaria away from the Aegean Sea, thus preventing the establishment of a Russian naval base on the Mediterranean.

British diplomatic activity did not end with the Russian treaty. The British had consented to Russia's retention of its Turkish conquests east of the Black Sea, and this meant a decided extension of Russian power into the Middle East and a consequent threat to British interests in that area. Therefore, to safeguard their position in the Middle East, the British on June 4, 1878, concluded a secret treaty with Turkey in which they guaranteed Turkey's Asiatic territories, in effect obtaining an excuse to send troops into Turkey at any time they felt their own interests threatened. In exchange for this Asian guarantee, the Turks were persuaded to give them the strategic island of Cyprus. Britain thereby acquired a splendid naval base in the eastern Mediterranean, within reach of the Balkans, Constantinople, Asiatic Turkey, and the Suez Canal.

Britain made yet a third preconference agreement. The Austrians had learned from Bismarck of the secret Anglo-Russian negotiations and feared that Russia would indeed gain the support of the majority, leaving Austria in the minority at the forthcoming conference. They therefore hastened to strike a bargain of their own with Britain. The Austrians wanted above all to keep open an avenue for their economic and political influence in southeastern Europe and to prevent the formation of any large state in the Balkans that would close this avenue or threaten Austrian security. The treaty they concluded with Britain on June 6, 1878, gave them the assurances they needed.

Thus before the Congress of Berlin even met, agreement had been reached among the great powers on the most important revisions of the Treaty of San Stefano. It remained for the congress to set the seal on these preconference decisions and to work out the details.

The Congress of Berlin

The Congress of Berlin (June 13–July 13, 1878) was one of the most brilliant diplomatic assemblies of the nineteenth century. Great Britain was represented by its prime minister, Benjamin Disraeli, and his foreign secretary, Lord Salisbury; Russia by its chancellor, Prince Gorchakov, and his ambassador to London, Count Peter Shuvalov; the Habsburg monarchy,

The Congress of Berlin, 1878. *Painting by Anton von Werner. At the left, seated, is Prince Gorchakov, the Russian chancellor, with Disraeli, the British prime minister, on his left, and Count Károlyi, the Austro-Hungarian ambassador to Berlin, on his right. Behind him stand Baron von Haymerle, Austro-Hungarian ambassador to Rome; Count Launay, the Italian ambassador to Berlin; and M. Waddington, the French foreign minister. Bismarck, the chairman and host of the conference, is in the center foreground, with Count Andrássy, the Austro-Hungarian foreign minister on his right, and Count Shuvalov, the Russian ambassador to Berlin on his left. Lord Salisbury, British foreign secretary, and at his right Lord Odo Russell, the British ambassador to Berlin, are standing at the far right flanked by the Turkish emissaries. Seated in front of them is Bernhard Ernst von Bülow, State Secretary of the German foreign office.*

France, and Italy by their foreign ministers—Count Andrássy, William Henry Waddington, and Count Corti. All the plenipotentiaries were supported by their ambassadors to Berlin and by distinguished staffs. The location of the conference in Berlin was an indication of the importance of the new German empire in the European states system. Bismarck, the head of the government playing host to the congress, was elected its president, in accordance with diplomatic custom. But Bismarck was head of the congress in more than name. He dominated the meetings and set the pace and tone of the negotiations.

By the terms of the final Treaty of Berlin, the large Bulgarian state created by the Treaty of San Stefano was divided into three parts. The largest of these parts was Bulgaria proper, bounded on the north by the Danube, on the west by the mountains of Albania, and on the south by the Balkan

Mountains. This nominally became a separate principality under Turkish suzerainty, but it was in fact tacitly conceded to Russia as a satellite. The second part, the area south of the Balkan Mountains, was to be called Eastern Rumelia, so that even in name it would be distinct from Russia's Bulgaria. Eastern Rumelia was placed under the administration of a Turkish governor-general, but a reform of the government was to be carried out by a European commission. The rest of Bulgaria, including the territory bordering the Aegean Sea, was left directly under Turkish rule.

The three Balkan states of Serbia, Montenegro, and Rumania, hitherto still nominally part of the Turkish empire, were recognized as completely independent, but they lost some of the territory assigned to them at San Stefano. Rumania, which had been Russia's ally in the recent war against Turkey, was forced to cede to Russia the fertile province of Bessarabia and control of the mouth of the Danube, receiving in exchange the arid Dobruja, which was detached from Turkey.

Among the great powers, Austria was given the right to occupy (but not to annex) Bosnia and Herzegovina, and to garrison the Turkish administrative district (sanjak) of Novi Pazar, a strategic area lying between Serbia and Montenegro. Thus Austria pushed a military wedge between Serbia and Montenegro, frustrated Serbian ambitions to form and dominate a large Balkan state, and kept its own routes to the south open. Russia received Batum, Kars, and Ardahan, at the eastern end of the Black Sea, and control of what was left of Bulgaria. Britain received Cyprus. France was secretly given permission to take Tunis, also nominally part of the Turkish empire. The Italian delegates came home with clean but empty hands, and were stoned in the streets by their less scrupulous compatriots. Germany received no territory, but was relieved of the necessity of choosing between Russia and Austria in eastern Europe or of engaging in a costly and dangerous conflict where vital German interests were not at stake. The preservation of peace was in itself a major gain for Germany.

The German-Austrian Alliance of 1879

By refusing to allow the balance of power in eastern Europe to be upset by either Russia or Austria, by playing midwife to many of the individual agreements modifying the Treaty of San Stefano, and by assuming the role of "honest broker" at the Congress of Berlin, Bismarck contributed much to the prevention of a general European war during the Near Eastern crisis. But he paid a heavy price for his success. The Russians had expected to receive German support at the congress and bitterly resented the fact that Germany allowed them to sustain what they regarded as a severe diplomatic setback. The wrath of the Russians after the congress was turned not against Austria or Britain, their real opponents in the recent crisis, but against

0   300 miles

RUSSIA

AUSTRIA-HUNGARY

BESSARABIA

(To Russia)

RUMANIA

Bucharest

Danube River

Belgrade

BOSNIA
HERZEGOVINA
(Occupied by
Austria, 1878)

•Sarajevo

SERBIA

*NOVI PAZAR

DOBRUJA

(To Rumania)

BULGARIA

BLACK
SEA

MONTENEGRO

•Sofia

ADRIATIC
SEA

ALBANIA

EASTERN RUMELIA
(Administered by Turkey)

MACEDONIA

Constantinople

OTTOMAN EMPIRE (TURKEY)

•Salonica

IONIAN
SEA

AEGEAN SEA

Athens
•
GREECE

MEDITERRANEAN   SEA

TURKEY

CYPRUS
(To Britain)

MEDITERRANEAN   SEA

TREATY OF BERLIN · 1878

———— Ottoman boundary in 1800

━ ━ ━ Boundary proposed by Treaty
of San Stefano, 1878

Ottoman Empire after 1878

Independent after 1878

*(Garrisoned by Austria, 1878)

Germany, the false friend. Russia was swept by a wave of anti-German sentiment, with the result that Germany now faced the hostility of Russia in addition to that of France. If these powers were to form an anti-German alliance, they might be joined by an Austria anxious to regain its lost supremacy in central Europe.

Bismarck's reply to Russian hostility was a defensive alliance with Austria against attack by Russia or by a power supported by Russia. Concluded on October 7, 1879, this alliance served a multiplicity of purposes. It assured both powers of support in case of Russian aggression. For Austria it reduced the danger of an agreement between Germany, Russia, and Italy to partition the Habsburg empire, while for Germany it lessened the possibility of an Austrian alliance with Russia and France. For Bismarck another advantage of the treaty was the control it gave him over Austrian foreign policy. Any aggressive move by Austria in eastern Europe involved the danger of war with Russia, and Austria did not dare risk a clash with Russia without the certainty of German support. As long as Germany remained in a position to withhold that support, it would be able to exercise a strong if not decisive check on Austrian aggression in eastern Europe.

The Second Three Emperors' League

In view of the alliances subsequently concluded by Bismarck, it is safe to assume that he did not intend to restrict his treaty making at this time to Austria, but hoped to return to some kind of treaty relationship with Russia as well, in order to avoid driving Russia into the arms of France. But he evidently realized that this could not be achieved immediately, for the hysterical anti-German attitude then prevalent in Russia meant that any German effort to establish closer relations would almost certainly be interpreted by the Russians as a sign of fear. A German agreement with Russia, if it could be arranged at all, would have to be purchased at an extremely high price. It seems likely that Bismarck therefore decided on an indirect approach in dealing with the Russians. The German-Austrian alliance was supposed to be secret, but the secret was badly kept and the Russians learned of its existence even before the treaty was signed. They now found themselves in an awkward position, for the two great central-European powers were forming an alliance, with a friendly Britain in the wings.

The next turn of events in Russia may well have been what Bismarck had been counting on. News of the Austrian alliance had a chastening effect on the anti-German agitation. The Russian leaders began to realize that their anti-German attitude had been not only pointless but extremely dangerous. Consequently, while negotiations for the German-Austrian treaty were still in progress, the Russians were at Bismarck's door as suppliants for a renewal of the Three Emperors' League in some form. Thus Bismarck's bargaining

The representatives of the Second Three Emperors' League meeting in Skierniewice in 1884. *From left to right: Count Giers, the Russian foreign minister; Bismarck; and Count Kálnoky, the Austro-Hungarian foreign minister.*

position was far better than it would have been if he had approached Russia directly.

The request to revive the Three Emperors' League was well received in Berlin. Bismarck assured the Russian ambassador that his main purpose in making the Austrian alliance was "to dig a ditch between [Austria] and the western powers," and that he would be glad to reestablish the Three Emperors' League "as the only system offering the maximum stability for the peace of Europe."

Bismarck's chief difficulty in reviving the Three Emperors' League lay in persuading the Austrians to admit Russia into the German-Austrian partnership, which many Austrian statesmen had hoped to exploit against Russia. In his efforts to persuade Austria to accept the Russian alliance, Bismarck was aided by the victory of Gladstone in the British elections of March, 1880. Gladstone had violently denounced Austria during the election campaign, and his victory temporarily ended Austrian hopes of gaining British support against Russia in eastern Europe. Even so, it was not until Bismarck ostentatiously threw his diplomatic support on the side of Russia and against Austria on every current issue concerning eastern Europe that the Austrians finally yielded.

The second Three Emperors' League, in contrast to the first, was based on an agreement that contained definite, clear-cut terms. The treaty, which was secret, was signed on June 18, 1881, and was to be in force for three years. Most significant was the stipulation that if one member of the league warred with a fourth power (except Turkey) the other two were to remain neutral, a provision that safeguarded all members from the danger of hostile coalitions. The other articles of the treaty were primarily aimed at removing the major possibilities for friction between the signatory powers: the western Balkans were recognized as an Austrian and the eastern Balkans as a Russian sphere of influence.

The treaty by no means ended tensions between Russia and Austria, nor did it settle all the problems of eastern Europe. It simply eased the tensions and provided a basis for negotiation among the imperial powers in the event of a crisis. The second Three Emperors' League, for all its weaknesses, was considerably better than no league at all.

Austria's Balkan Policy

To reduce further the danger of international friction in the Balkans, Bismarck made several efforts to secure an agreement for a definite partition of the Balkans between Austria and Russia. He reasoned that both powers would then be fully occupied for several years in assimilating their respective spheres. But the partition scheme never materialized. Austrian leaders feared any permanent extension of Russian power in the Balkans, and the Hungarians disliked the prospect because the inclusion of more Slavs in the Habsburg empire would diminish their own importance.

In the meantime, Austrian interests were being advanced successfully without territorial annexations. The rapid construction of railroads in the Balkans permitted Austria to extend its economic influence in southeastern Europe to areas which were not readily accessible to the sea and hence were relatively untouched by British and French economic influence. Austria also succeeded in extending its political influence. By bribing the prince of Serbia with loans and dangling before him the prospect of recognition as king of Serbia, Austria was able to gain agreement in 1881 to political and economic treaties with Serbia which reduced that nation to the status of an Austrian dependency. In 1883 Austria and Rumania concluded a defensive alliance, which was later expanded to include Germany.

The Problem of Bulgaria

Austria's most spectacular success in the Balkans—or more properly, Russia's most spectacular failure—came in Bulgaria. The Russians used their influence in Bulgaria tactlessly in dealing with a people experiencing an awakening of national self-consciousness and highly sensitive about honor and prestige. The Russian choice of Alexander of Battenberg (1857–1893) as prince of Bulgaria was also unfortunate. Prince Alexander disliked playing the part of a Russian puppet, and wanted to establish himself as the independent ruler of an independent state. Although Bismarck warned the prince in the strongest possible terms that he could expect no help from Germany, Alexander was encouraged to pursue his quest for independence by the Austrians and by Queen Victoria of Great Britain.

In 1883 the prince's ambitions received a further powerful stimulus when he was allowed to become engaged to Princess Victoria of Prussia, the daughter of the heir to the German throne and the granddaughter of Queen Victoria. From a political standpoint the marriage would have been most welcome to the British, who were anxious to push Russian influence out of Bulgaria and must have seen in this union a means of using Germany to help them do so. Even if Germany refused to back up Prince Alexander against Russia, his marriage to a Prussian princess would arouse serious doubts in Russia about the honesty of German's policy in the Balkans, and would shake Russia's confidence in the German government, which Bismarck was trying to regain with so much effort.

These dangers were only too evident to Bismarck, who did everything in his power to prevent the so-called Battenberg marriage from taking place. He pointed out to the Austrian foreign minister that by opposing the establishment of Russian influence in Bulgaria, Austria was disregarding its treaties with Russia and creating a situation of extreme danger in the Balkans. To compensate for Austria's attitude, Bismarck made very effort to reassure Russia of Germany's good faith. He denounced Prince Alexander and applied heavy pressure to force Austria to desist from its Balkan policy.

Despite Bismarck's efforts, the Bulgarian problem came very close to involving the European powers in war. In September, 1885, a revolution broke out in Eastern Rumelia. The aim of the revolutionaries was to unite their province with Bulgaria, and Prince Alexander found himself compelled by Bulgarian national sentiment to assume leadership of the movement or to forfeit his throne.

The union of Bulgaria and Eastern Rumelia constituted a violation of the Treaty of Berlin and affected the interests of all the great powers. To complicate matters, the Serbs, jealous of the potential enlargement of their neighbor, invaded Bulgaria with the intention of securing territorial compensation. Peace between Serbia and Bulgaria was finally restored on the basis of the prewar *status quo*, and in April, 1886, the powers recognized the union of Bulgaria and Eastern Rumelia. Even then international tension did not die down. The Russians, unable to tolerate the rule of Prince Alexander any longer, had him kidnapped, and finally secured his abdication in August, 1886. But their position in Bulgaria did not improve. The new Bulgarian government proved just as unwilling as Prince Alexander had been to submit to Russian overlordship.

The Russians seethed with frustration. They were indignant with Austria for violating both the spirit and the letter of the Three Emperors' agreement; many Russians were convinced that Austria would not have dared to act in that way without assurances of support from Germany. Russian Pan-Slavists, always hostile to the Teutonic empires of Germany and Austria, proclaimed that Russia could never hope to score solid gains in the Balkans while remaining committed to the Three Emperors' League, and should therefore look elsewhere for support.

THE SEARCH FOR STABILITY IN WESTERN EUROPE

Germany and France

The surge of anti-German feeling in Russia coincided with a powerful revival of anti-German feeling in France. Since the Congress of Berlin, Bismarck had been working to reduce French animosity toward Germany and to compensate France for the loss of Alsace-Lorraine by helping it to acquire an overseas colonial empire. He hoped in this way to divert French attention from Germany and embroil France with other colonial powers. French statesmen were aware of Bismarck's motives, but some of them thought France should nevertheless take advantage of German support and strengthen its colonial holdings. The colonialists were opposed in France by the politicians of the continental school, who feared that a colonial policy would lead to disputes with other European powers and delay the reestablishment of French supremacy in Europe.

In 1881, under the leadership of the colonialist Jules Ferry (1832–1893), the French made their bid for Tunis, which had been promised to them by Bismarck and Salisbury at the Congress of Berlin. They knew that the seizure of Tunis would involve them in a quarrel with the Italians, who had large investments in this area and regarded it as a natural sphere for Italian expansion. But the French, too, had large investments in Tunis. Spurred by signs that the Italians were about to take Tunis themselves, the French on May 12 forced the Bey of Tunis to sign the Treaty of Bardo, which established a virtual protectorate over the country.

The Triple Alliance of 1882

Just as the French anticolonialists had feared, the seizure of Tunis involved France in a bitter dispute with Italy, and drove Italy into an alliance with Germany and Austria. The Tunis incident showed the Italians that their old policy of diplomatic independence, which had enabled them to sell their friendship to the highest bidder, was no longer profitable. Within Italy a strong element, primarily republican, advocated friendship with republican France despite Tunis, hoping with French aid to acquire the Italian-speaking territories still under Austrian control. But an even more influential political group favored collaboration with Germany, which because of its superior military power would be a more valuable ally than France, and better able to aid Italy in acquiring colonial territory. As a Protestant state, Germany would be of assistance against the papacy, which was still intent on recovering the Papal States. As a monarchy it would support the existing Italian government against republicanism and the forces of revolution.

Bismarck, for his part, was interested in preserving the Italian monarchy, which was less likely than an Italian republic to seek an alliance with France Above all, he saw that an Italian alliance would be valuable for Austria. The Italian desire for the Austrian territories of Trent and Trieste was always a danger, and should Austria become involved in war with Russia it would be well to have some assurance of Italian neutrality.

In the negotiations leading to the alliance between Italy, Austria, and Germany, Bismarck forced the Italians to work through Vienna. He had no intention of acting as a buffer between these old enemies, although he was always available to help the negotiations along. The treaty of May 20, 1882, establishing the Triple Alliance, was a general agreement to support the monarchical principle and the existing political and social order. It also provided for a defensive alliance which would function against France or against "two or more great powers not members of the alliance"—in other words, any combination of France, Great Britain, and Russia. This treaty improved the prospects for stable government in Italy and assured Germany of Italian neutrality in the event of a German war with France. Austria secured Italian neutrality in the event of a war with Russia and the hope of a diminution of Italian nationalist agitation for "unredeemed" territory still under Austrian control. The Italian monarchy gained badly needed prestige, two powerful defensive allies, support against efforts of the Vatican to regain the Papal States, and support against revolution.

The newly created Triple Alliance was destined to become a fixture in the international politics of Europe. Intended originally to run for five years, it was renewed periodically until 1915, when the Italians deserted the Germans and Austrians in the First World War.

The British Occupation of Egypt

Shortly after the treaty establishing the Triple Alliance was signed, an international crisis erupted in Egypt. With the opening of the Suez Canal in 1869, Egypt had become an area of prime strategic importance, but even before the building of the canal it had been a target of European economic imperialism. The khedives of Egypt, nominally under the suzerainty of the sultan of Turkey, had for years behaved as independent rulers and had contracted huge debts with European banking houses, often at usurious rates. It was the need for money to pay the interest on his debts that forced the khedive to sell his Suez Canal stock to Great Britain in 1875. But this sale failed to stabilize Egyptian finances, and in November, 1876, the British and French governments established what amount to joint control over the Egyptian government on behalf of the holders of Egyptian bonds. This move aroused deep animosity among the Egyptians, who found themselves

Dredging and construction vessels on the Suez Canal. *Begun in 1859 and completed a decade later, the canal cut the length of the sea route to India by more than half and enormously increased the strategic importance of the eastern Mediterranean and the surrounding lands. especially Egypt.*

heavily taxed simply to pay the interest on foreign debts. In January, 1882, a group of Egyptian army officers overthrew European control, and established an Egyptian national government.

The British responded in July by bombarding Alexandria and landing troops to protect the Suez Canal. In September, 1882, these British forces clashed with an Egyptian army at Tel el-Kebir. The Egyptians were routed, and somewhat to the embarrassment of the anticolonial Gladstone government, the British found themselves in sole control of Egypt.

Gladstone was against colonialism, but he was also a sound financier and a firm believer in law and order. He therefore resolved to use the opportunity afforded by Britain's occupation of Egypt to restore order and stabilize Egypt's finances. He assured the other European powers that the occupation was temporary and that the British forces would be withdrawn "as soon as the state of the country and the organization of proper means for the maintenance of khedival authority will admit of it." But to the fury of the French and the Italians, who also had important strategic and economic interests in Egypt, the British were never satisfied that a proper state of order had been established; they remained in control of Egypt until they were pushed out by a more successful Egyptian nationalist movement after the Second World War.

During the entire Egyptian crisis, Bismarck had urged agreement among the powers to prevent the problem from erupting in a general European war. As the crisis dragged on without any agreement being reached, he encouraged the British to act alone, and used his influence to prevent intervention by other states. The consequent tension between Britain, France, and Italy was not unwelcome to him. He feared an entente between the liberal government of Gladstone and republican France, which the volatile Italians might be tempted to join. The Egyptian affair temporarily put an end to these possibilities.

Bismarck's Colonial Policy

Bismarck was soon to use Britain's awkward diplomatic position for political purposes of his own. Early in 1884 he suggested to the British government that in return for Germany's continued diplomatic support in Egypt and elsewhere, Britain should cede Germany the island of Helgoland, a strategic base off the German coast in the North Sea, and agree to Germany's acquisition of a few overseas colonial territories. In making this bid for colonies, Bismarck was adopting a policy he had heretofore opposed because he did not believe overseas possessions would contribute in any way to Germany's national security or prosperity. His change of attitude appears to have been motivated primarily by domestic political considerations, above all by his fear that upon succeeding the octogenarian William I as German emperor, the liberal-minded German crown prince would seek his ouster as chancellor. By acquiring colonies, Bismarck undoubtedly hoped to enhance his own popularity with the growing number of imperialists in Germany and to undercut the position of the crown prince, whose English wife made no secret of her hostility to German colonial ambitions. As one of Bismarck's aides put it, "No other question is so liable to put the future empress, with her Anglophile tendencies, in a false position vis-à-vis the German nation. For it is precisely the liberals and democrats who want colonies."

Bismarck had no desire for serious tension with Britain, and under ordinary circumstances he would probably have dropped the entire colonial business when he found that the Gladstone government failed to respond favorably to his bid. But the circumstances in 1884 were far from ordinary. Germany was allied with all the great powers on the Continent with the exception of France, and the French, like the Germans, were smarting from British opposition to their attempts to acquire new colonies. Moreover, the government of France was at this time under the leadership of Jules Ferry, who was prepared to cooperate with Bismarck on the colonial issue. The German chancellor was therefore in an admirable position to bring pressure to bear on Britain, which he was all the more willing to do because Britain was currently under the leadership of Gladstone, whom he despised and would have been glad to bring down.

The British found that they were helpless against Bismarck's continental coalition. They were compelled to abandon a treaty with Portugal whereby

they had sought to ensure their influence in the Congo area. The claims of
the several European powers in the Congo were defined instead by an
international conference on African matters that met in Berlin in 1884–
1885 under the auspices of Bismarck and Ferry. At this conference too, the
powers agreed to cooperate to suppress slavery and the slave trade in Africa,
and the principle was laid down that an imperial state had to establish
effective control over a colonial territory before it could claim ownership.

By 1885, largely as a result of diplomatic agreements imposed on Britain
through Franco-German cooperation, Bismarck had succeeded in securing
international recognition of Germany's claims to Southwest Africa, Togo-
land, the Cameroons, East Africa, and part of New Guinea. The French for
their part were conceded French Guinea, part of the Red Sea coast, and
predominant influence in southeast Asia.

In cooperating with France on colonial questions, Bismarck may also have
had another purpose in view. He was disturbed by the uncompromising
French hostility toward Germany and tried to allay this antagonism by
supporting French policy in a variety of ways. There is no way of knowing
whether Bismarck seriously believed he could change the French attitude
toward Germany, but the situation in 1884–1885 gave him an excellent
means of testing the possibility of doing so.

The attempt to conciliate France failed. At the end of March, 1885,
Ferry's ministry fell as a result of a military setback in Indochina, and this
change in government marked the end of Franco-German cooperation. For
Bismarck the short-lived entente had served its purpose. He had proved to
himself that a genuine reconciliation with France would be impossible for
some time to come, he had taught the British that they could not ignore
German requests with impunity, and he had acquired a colonial empire for
Germany. Throughout the period of his cooperation with France, Bismarck
had recognized the probable limitations of French friendship, and for this
reason he had never gone so far in putting pressure on the British as to risk
alienating them permanently.

THE CLIMAX OF BISMARCK'S ALLIANCE SYSTEM

With the fall of Ferry, there was a sharp reaction in France against his
policies. Colonial affairs had involved France in costly conflicts overseas and
had aroused a great deal of opposition. To many patriotic Frenchmen the
whole colonial business appeared to be a German plot to divert French
resources and French attention from the recovery of Alsace-Lorraine, and
they regarded Ferry's cooperation with Bismarck as nothing less than
treason. French defeats in Indochina, along with the agitation of French
patriotic societies demanding the return of Alsace-Lorraine, brought about a
powerful resurgence of anti-German feeling in France. It was largely this

sentiment that thrust General Boulanger into prominence as the man who could lead a successful war of revenge against Germany.

The wave of anti-German feeling and the rise of Boulanger in France coincided with Russian frustration in Bulgaria and a similar wave of anti-German feeling in Russia. Bismarck again found himself in a dangerous diplomatic position. The Three Emperors' League was due to lapse in 1887, and the Russians had made it clear that they would not renew it. There was a strong possibility that Russia would now form an alliance with France, despite the tsar's dislike of France's republican government, and if such an alliance were concluded, hotheaded leaders in either country might decide that the time had come to settle accounts with Germany and Austria. Germany would then be faced with a war on two fronts which would threaten its very existence. Even a German victory in such a war could not possibly yield benefits that would in any way compensate for the costs and hazards it would involve. By far the best policy for Germany would be to keep the peace. How this was to be done posed one of the most difficult problems of Bismarck's career.

The problem was solved by Bismarck through the development of his most complicated and brilliant set of alliances. The Russians did indeed refuse to renew the Three Emperors' League when sounded on the subject in 1886, and it was clear that their present distrust of Austria made an agreement between Russia and Austria as impossible as an agreement between Germany and France. Hence, it appeared that Germany might best prevent a Franco-Russian alliance and avoid the danger of a two-front war by itself concluding an alliance with Russia. To achieve this end the Germans would have to remove all possible reasons for Russian suspicion of their policy and offer the Russians the prospect of gaining more concrete advantages from cooperation with Germany than they could hope to acquire in association with France.

At the same time, Bismarck had no intention of abandoning Austria or of allowing Russia to achieve a political domination in eastern Europe that would upset the balance of power. If Germany had to throw its weight on the side of Russia, Austria would have to be given additional support for its position in eastern Europe. Austria, in fact, would have to become the nucleus of an anti-Russian coalition, from which Germany would be rigidly excluded so that it could have a free hand to bargain with Russia.

The most obvious ally for Austria among the great powers was Great Britain, but if the isolationism of the British was to be overcome, they would have to be convinced that unless they assumed their share of the burden in containing Russia, Germany and Austria would allow Russian power to flow into the Mediterranean. Turkey could be counted on as an ally against Russia as long as outside support was assured. Austria already had defensive alliances with Serbia, Rumania, and Italy, and Bulgaria was still hostile to Russia. With the backing of Britain, Italy, Turkey, and the Balkan states, Austria would be in an excellent position. Germany could then make any necessary concessions to Russia, knowing that Russia would be blocked by the Austrian coalition. Such a grouping of alliances would have the further advantage for Germany of leaving France in isolation.

In the last weeks of 1886 and the early part of 1887, Bismarck was engaged in fostering four sets of negotiations: for the renewal of the Triple Alliance, to safeguard Austria from a stab in the back by Italy; for an agreement primarily involving Austria and Britain, to preserve the *status quo* in the Balkans and the Near East; for an agreement centering around Britain, Italy, and Austria, to preserve the *status quo* in the Mediterranean; and for an agreement between Germany and Russia.

The first tangible result of this complicated network of negotiations was the so-called First Mediterranean Agreement of 1887, which in form was not a full-dress treaty, but a confidential exchange of notes between the powers concerned. It provided for the maintenance of the *status quo* in the Mediterranean, Turkey, and the Balkans. Italy was to support British policy in Egypt; Britain was to support Italian policy in North Africa. The Anglo-Austrian note stressed the common interests of Britain and Austria in the Near East. The various notes were somewhat loosely worded and admitted differences of interpretation, but they did provide a basis for cooperation and a definition of the mutual interests of the powers involved.

On February 20, 1887, the Triple Alliance was renewed for another five years. The Italians saw clearly that anti-German agitation in France and Russia had enhanced their value as an ally, and they consequently raised the price of their partnership. The old Triple Alliance treaty was renewed without change, but it was supplemented by separate, secret Austro-Italian and German-Italian notes that met the added Italian demands. The Austro-Italian note provided for the maintenance of the *status quo* in the Near East, with the stipulation that if the *status quo* could not be preserved, Italy would participate in settling the affairs of that region. Thus Italy gained a diplomatic foothold in any future partition of the Balkans or of the Ottoman Empire. The German-Italian note provided for the maintenance of the *status quo* in North Africa, and Germany promised to aid Italy if French activity in that area threatened Italian interests. Britain had provided Italy with similar assurances, and Bismarck felt confident that Germany and Britain together could prevent any Italian abuse of these promises of support.

With the conclusion of the First Mediterranean Agreement and the renewal of the Triple Alliance, the decks were clear for Bismarck to make whatever arrangement he could with Russia. As Bismarck had hoped, the tsar, although he flatly refused to renew any kind of treaty relationship with Austria, was not averse to a treaty with Germany. Even so, the negotiations between Germany and Russia proved to be very difficult, for the Russians hesitated to give Bismarck the assurance he most needed, namely a promise of Russian neutrality in the event of a French attack on Germany.

Finally, on June 18, 1887, a three-year secret treaty between Russia and Germany was signed. In this Reinsurance Treaty, each agreed to remain neutral if the other became involved in war with a third power, but these terms did not apply to an aggressive war by Germany against France, or by Russia against Austria. Both powers promised to support the *status quo* in the Balkans; Germany specifically recognized Russia's interest in Bulgaria. The principle of the closure of the Straits in time of war was affirmed. The most important part of the treaty was contained in a top-secret protocol. Germany promised to support Russian efforts to regain influence in Bulgaria and to oppose the restoration of Prince Alexander of Battenberg. Germany also promised Russia moral and diplomatic support for any measures the tsar might find necessary to control the "key of his empire"—Constantinople and the Straits. Thus Bismarck offered Russia freedom of action and diplomatic support in areas where German interests were not directly affected, but only after he had helped Austria form a coalition of powers to preserve the *status quo* in these areas.

The main achievement of the Reinsurance Treaty was that it reduced the chances of a Franco-Russian alliance, or at least of an aggressive Franco-Russian alliance directed against Germany. As long as France was not certain of Russian support in an aggressive war against Germany, the likelihood of a French attack was greatly diminished.

The value of the treaty was evident in the months immediately after its ratification. Boulangism reached its peak in France in mid-1887 and 1888, and Russia's frustration in Bulgaria reached new heights with the election in 1887 of a German, Prince Ferdinand of Saxe-Coburg (1861–1948), as prince of Bulgaria, despite strenuous Russian opposition. Had the Reinsurance Treaty not existed, it is highly probable that a Franco-Russian alliance would have been formed.

The intensification of anti-German agitation in France and Russia in 1887 persuaded Bismarck not to place all his trust in the Reinsurance Treaty, but to do what he could to strengthen the Mediterranean coalition against these two powers. The cooperation of France and Russia against Britain in colonial affairs during this same period aided him in this endeavor, for it made British statesmen conscious of the dangerous potentialities of the Franco-Russian combination and receptive to arguments that they should make more definite commitments in the Near East.

The Second Mediterranean Agreement, concluded on December 12, 1887, took the form of an exchange of notes between Austria, Britain, and Italy. The principle of maintaining the *status quo* in the Near East was reaffirmed. Above all, the agreement stressed the importance of keeping

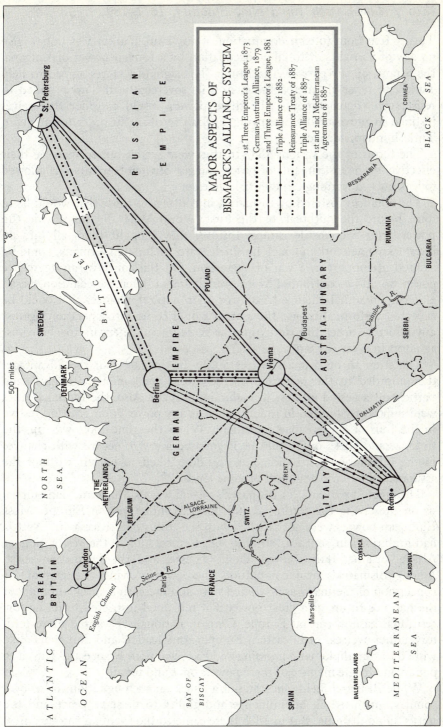

MAJOR ASPECTS OF
BISMARCK'S ALLIANCE SYSTEM

1st Three Emperor's League, 1873
German-Austrian Alliance, 1879
2nd Three Emperor's League, 1881
Triple Alliance of 1882
Reinsurance Treaty of 1887
Triple Alliance of 1887
1st and 2nd Mediterranean
  Agreements of 1887

St. Petersburg

RUSSIAN EMPIRE

CRIMEA

BLACK SEA

BESSARABIA

RUMANIA

BULGARIA

SWEDEN

BALTIC SEA

POLAND

SERBIA

AUSTRIA-HUNGARY

Budapest

Danube R.

DENMARK

GERMAN EMPIRE

Berlin

Vienna

DALMATIA

500 miles

NORTH SEA

THE NETHERLANDS

BELGIUM

ALSACE-LORRAINE

SWITZ.

TRENT

ITALY

Rome

London

GREAT BRITAIN

ATLANTIC OCEAN

English Channel

Seine R.

Paris

FRANCE

CORSICA

SARDINIA

Marseille

MEDITERRANEAN SEA

BAY OF BISCAY

SPAIN

BALEARIC ISLANDS

Turkey free from foreign domination of any kind. Turkey was not to give up any of its rights or to allow occupation by a foreign power of Bulgaria, the Straits, or any part of Asia Minor. The signatory states agreed to help Turkey to resist all encroachments on its sovereignty; if Turkey failed to resist such encroachments, the three powers would consider themselves justified in provisionally occupying Turkish territory, in order to safeguard Turkish independence.

The terms of the various 1887 treaties were secret, but to increase their effectiveness as instruments of peace, the gist of their contents was allowed to leak out—a warning to potential aggressors.

The alliances fostered by Bismarck, in contrast to those that would be in force before the outbreak of the First World War, did not divide the powers into two hostile camps. Instead, they brought them all into an interlocking network in which no single state, including Germany, could be assured of support in a war of aggression. On the contrary, an aggressive power would be confronted by an overwhelming defensive coalition, based either upon actual alliance treaties or upon natural alliances that could be expected to form. Because the system would come into operation against any effort to upset the *status quo*, it served as a deterrent to chauvinist agitators in every country.

The strength of Bismarck's treaties lay in the fact that the advantages they afforded to the powers concerned were great enough to give each participant a vested interest in maintaining them. Also, the formal treaties were sufficiently limited in time to prevent any power from growing restive in the toils of a particular agreement. When the time limit was up, the treaty would lapse; or it could be negotiated anew to accord with changes in the international situation, for no power liked to be left without the assurance of defensive support of some kind.

The greatest weakness of Bismarck's system was its Metternichian emphasis on preserving the territorial and political *status quo* in Europe. Most European powers were not satisfied with the *status quo*. Russia and Austria had ambitions in southeastern Europe; France sought the restoration of Alsace-Lorraine; Italy wanted Trent, Trieste, and the Dalmatian coast. Among Bismarck's own compatriots there was growing criticism of his conception of Germany as a satiated state and increasing speculation about the nation's future as a great power if it remained restricted to its narrow territorial base in central Europe. German nationalists wanted more territory, either overseas or in eastern Europe; army leaders and diplomats alike wished to stop diplomatic finessing and go to war with France and Russia to put an end to the menace of these powers once and for all.

While Bismarck held office he put a check on such agitation in his own country, and used all his influence and ability to preserve peace and the *status quo* in Europe. But in 1888 there came to the German throne a new emperor, receptive to the most irresponsible demands for national expansion. After the dismissal of Bismarck in 1890 his alliance system was allowed to collapse, and the formation began of new alliances, which were to divide Europe into two armed camps. In international affairs even more than in domestic, his dismissal marked the end of an era.

A GOLDEN AGE OF HOPE

The historian examining the last decades of the nineteenth century can readily identify the forces that were to explode so soon in war and revolution. Such forces exist in every society, however, and in the Europe of 1890 there seemed no cause for undue alarm. On the contrary, the preceding forty years had been a great age. The material achievements seemed to prove that evolution was synonymous with progress, and recent manifestations of the human spirit encouraged the belief that the quality of man was improving with each new generation. The selfless devotion of a Garibaldi in the cause of nationalism had been matched by the exploits of humanitarians in the cause of reform. As a result of the efforts of national leaders, new political units had been established throughout a large part of the Continent on the basis of the principle of nationalism, which many theorists and practical politicians had come to accept as the natural and hence the only sound foundation of a state. As a result of the efforts of reformers, the condition of the population of all countries was steadily being improved. The most obvious forms of serfdom and slavery had been abolished, great strides had been made in combating hunger and disease. Moreover, these reformers, at one time voices crying in the wilderness, could now count on broad support from enlightened public opinion in their struggles against illiteracy, social injustice, and all forms of human cruelty. Despite national hatreds and rivalries, international intercourse had never been more general. People could travel throughout western and central Europe easily and safely, without passports. Artists and scholars of all nationalities went to foreign cities and universities to study and exchange ideas.

Thoughtful Europeans were fully aware of the gravity of the many problems still besetting their society and there was no lack of prophets of disaster among them, but the prevailing mood in Europe as the nineteenth century drew to a close was one of optimism. Human reason seemed to have demonstrated its capacity to cope with human problems. After three quarters of a century without a general European war, people had begun to count on the future. In the light of later events this confidence may seem naïve, but it is easy to understand how those who grew up during these years could look back upon them after the First World War as a golden age, perhaps not a golden age of reality, but certainly a golden age of hope.

Part VI

THE END OF THE EUROPEAN ERA
1890 TO THE PRESENT

Introduction

WHAT FOLLOWS IS the story of the twentieth century. In the terminology of historical science, this is "contemporary history." But this term immediately raises questions and doubts, because it often has been asserted that contemporary history cannot be considered a serious scholarly undertaking. The traditional argument against the pursuit of contemporary history is that nearness of the events in time makes access to vital documents impossible for the historian; the archives are still closed to him. Another argument bears particularly upon the history of the twentieth century: developments have come so fast, the geographical limits of history have been extended so widely, the problems of the various areas of history—political, economic, social, intellectual—have become so complex that, until the dust has settled and much monographic work has been done, no one can have sufficient control over the material to give a comprehensive account of the present century.

It would be a declaration of bankruptcy on the part of historical scholarship if the work of the historian stopped short of the most burning issues of the day. And there are good reasons why the objections against the writing of contemporary history should be rejected. The arguments take much too limited a view of the historian's work. Even if contemporary history cannot be written strictly according to the methods which are applied to the history of earlier centuries, this does not mean that contemporary history is not a scholarly undertaking; it means only that contemporary history has aims and methods of its own.

There is no lack of source material. The twentieth century has been an increasingly democratic age; political actions have been preceded by public debate or at least subjected to public scrutiny. It is possible to reconstruct, partly on the basis of newspapers and parliamentary debates, not only what happened but also why it happened. Moreover, since the two world wars, the archives of the foreign offices of some of the European powers and, in some cases, of all the government agencies have been opened. War-crime trials have brought many further official documents to light. Although the inaccessibility of eastern European, and particularly of Russian, archives remains a serious gap, no historian has ever possessed complete knowledge of all the relevant documents. In writing twentieth-century history the historian is in danger of suffocating in material rather than of being handicapped by scarcity.

The overabundance of material; the disappearance of clear boundaries among geographical regions; the great variety of political, social, technical, and ideological factors which enter into a decision—these indeed are difficulties in the writing of contemporary history. But they are not insuperable, though they do show that, in writing contemporary history, an historian cannot do everything; he must keep possibilities and limitations clearly in mind.

The following presentation of European twentieth-century history does not depict European life in all its aspects. Its primary aim is to make crowded and confused events comprehensible by organizing them clearly around the predominant trends of political change, with developments in other spheres taken up only insofar as they encroach upon or illuminate political events. For the period before the First World War the conflicts which industrialization and competition had produced in all the great European powers and the relation of these internal tensions to foreign policy become the focus of the narrative. For the interwar period the decline of European hegemony over the world, the attempts to restore some measure of European influence, and the failure of these attempts are central themes. For the period after the Second World War the transformation of political life under the impact of scientific discoveries and technological advances has emerged as the crucial issue; this is a transformation which placed the conduct of politics in the European countries in a new setting and which went far to erase the boundaries between Europe and the rest of the world. It sealed the end of the European era.

CHAPTER 36

The New Industrial Society

ONE AFTERNOON early in the twentieth century a member of the British aristocracy, a great landowner, stood with one of his guests on the terrace extending along the back of his large country house. In the valley at their feet lay farms, cottages, a railway, a colliery, and streets densely teeming with workingmen. Beyond the valley, a hill with another large country house at its top was visible. Pointing to this house the host said to his guest, "You see there is no one between us and them."

Eccentric as this gentleman may have been, his remark does express the feelings of people of his social standing and wealth at the beginning of the twentieth century. A great distance separated the upper classes from the working population. Social and economic differences and distinctions had always existed in European society, but in earlier centuries noble and peasant, wealthy patrician and small tradesman, ruler and ruled, rich and poor lived in a community which was an integrated whole. Economic inequality and dependence were complemented and mitigated by personal bonds. Servants knew their masters and the masters knew the men working for them.

However, since the end of the eighteenth century, industrialization and the growth of population had been steadily reducing the personal element in the relationship between the owning classes and their dependents, between employers and employees. The Industrial Revolution, which started in Great Britain and France, penetrated in the second part of the nineteenth century into central, southern, and eastern Europe. Competition accelerated industrialization. Most city dwellers became industrial workers living in quarters distant from the elegant and older parts of the cities. The big city was both an accompaniment and a result of industrialization. Without railroads, steamboats, and streetcars, without innovations in the building industry, without street lighting by gas and then by electricity, the assembling and maintenance of masses in cities would have been impossible. Industrialization made the distance which separated the possessing classes from the proletariat more noticeable. Hotels became palaces; the rich could indulge in exotic foods and flowers brought by railroads from distant areas; their motorcars appeared on the roads; their private yachts cruised the Mediterranean and the North Sea.

At the end of the nineteenth century many people believed that the future would see a complete polarization of society. A small number of individuals would possess all wealth, while everyone else would become steadily more impoverished and more dependent. The assumption of an inevitable schism in society—a few wealthy men on the one hand and a mass of oppressed, poor people on the other—was the basic tenet of socialist theory. This view of the future was shared by many thoughtful observers. Pope Leo XIII spoke of the danger of such a polarization in the encyclical *Rerum novarum*, the first encyclical devoted to the problems of industrial society.

Actually, the fear that society would become polarized was exaggerated. Not all the members of the ruling group were immensely wealthy, and the concentration of wealth in the hands of a few was not proceeding as quickly as many around the turn of the century believed or feared. A large segment of society was neither very rich nor very poor. Although small independent entrepreneurs faced increasing difficulties in maintaining their ventures, members of the middle classes could make a satisfactory living as white-collar workers, as officials, or in the professions. But while the dividing line between the wealthy upper classes and the middle classes remained fluid, the distance between these groups and the fast-expanding industrial proletariat was wide and unbridgeable. Railroads had at least three classes, and sometimes four. The wealthiest people might travel first class, or even in their own private railroad cars, while their maids and valets traveled second class. But the well-to-do would never travel third class, and even the waiting rooms of the first and second classes were strictly separated from those of the third class; every contact was to be avoided. No less important than the divisions and conflicts between nations was this separation of the working classes from the other groups of society. Therefore, in order to understand what happened in Europe in the twentieth century, we must give close attention to its social divisions and class structure.

THE RULING GROUP IN EUROPE

Around the turn of the century the prevalent form of government in Europe was the monarchy. There were only two republics: France and Switzerland. The degree to which monarchical rulers possessed concrete political power varied. But whether or not they had sufficient power to exert real influence on state policy, the monarchs were justified in considering themselves the most important persons on the European political stage. In

A royal jamboree. *Among those present are King Edward* VII *of Great Britain (seated left) and standing behind him, the German Emperor William II. The Spanish King Alfonso XIII has his arm on the shoulder of the future King George V of Great Britain.*

each country the monarch was the apex of society, and the status of both individuals and groups was dependent on their relationship to the throne. Among themselves, royalty formed a kind of gigantic family which seemed to tie European society together into one great unit.

Members of ruling dynasties could marry only members of other ruling dynasties, unless they were willing to relinquish all their rights and status. At the beginning of the twentieth century even the members of the British royal family, who with the ruling monarch's permission might marry commoners, were for the most part married to members of princely families. Religion somewhat separated the dynasties into two groups. Almost all of the Catholic princes were related to the Habsburgs and the Bourbons. The Protestant ruling families, into which the Eastern Orthodox rulers, particularly the Russian tsars, also liked to marry, were tied together through the numerous small German dynasties, which provided marriageable princes and princesses for almost any contingency. In the nineteenth century the remarkable fertility of the admirable couple Victoria and Albert had bound the Protestant rulers still more tightly together. Thus the British king, Edward VII, was the uncle both of the German emperor, William II, and of the wife of the Russian tsar, Nicholas II. The birthdays, weddings, and funerals of monarchs were not only state occasions but also family reunions. It was natural that at the wedding of the daughter of William II in 1912 the tsar and tsarina of Russia and the king and queen of England would come to Berlin, and that almost all of Europe's rulers would be present at the funeral of Queen Victoria in 1901 and of her son Edward VII in 1910.

After the death of Queen Victoria the oldest ruling monarch in Europe was the Emperor Francis Joseph of Austria-Hungary, born in 1830, who had

The funeral procession of Queen Victoria. *King Edward VII leads the entourage, followed by the German Emperor William II.*

ascended the throne in 1848. He was venerated as a kind of patriarch by all the rulers and his seventieth birthday in 1900, his eightieth in 1910, and the sixtieth jubilee of his reign in 1908 were all occasions for royal meetings. Visits among cousins were frequent. The German emperor often met with the tsar. Edward VII, in order to lose weight and to remain in shape for the gastronomic feats which he loved, regularly visited the spa of Marienbad, and when he passed through Germany on his way, it would have been impolite for him not to arrange a meeting with his nephew, William II, though there was little love between them. On their travels the monarchs were accompanied by high officials, and unavoidably, political subjects were discussed. Most of all, this network of princely relations and connections gave the monarchs a feeling of solidarity against the common danger of revolution, although, as the First World War would show, this feeling of standing together against a common danger did not guarantee peace.

The monarchs were also the leaders of the society in their respective countries. In holding court they reinforced a traditional hierarchy and determined its order by giving titles and decorations and by receiving or excluding people according to the standards of the crown. That the monarchy fulfilled the function of guaranteeing the existence of an established order was the view not only of its adherents but of the enemies of the existing system, the advocates of revolution, as well. For them the monarchs were an important target. Although attacks on the lives of the princely heads of state were fewer than in the 1870's and 1880's the monarchs were still on the firing line in the first two decades of the twentieth century. In 1900, King Humbert of Italy was assassinated. In 1906, at the wedding of the king of Spain, an assassination attempt was made which had many victims although the king and his bride escaped. In 1908 the king of Portugal and his oldest son were killed. In June, 1914, a Serbian nationalist killed the heir to the Habsburg throne, the Archduke Francis Ferdinand. This assassination precipitated the outbreak of the First World War.

The existence of a monarchy presupposed the existence of a ruling group closely connected with the throne. In the eighteenth century the princes of continental Europe had become absolute by gaining direct control of the armed forces and by allying themselves with the landowning nobility. This alliance of the monarchs with the army and the landed aristocracy lasted into the twentieth century. Although by that time an elected parliament had become an influential factor in politics, the arbiter of social status remained the court, with its officialdom of ministers, chamberlains, masters of ceremonies—all nobles and mostly descendants of the oldest families. The monarchs kept up their special closeness to the army by insisting on a voice in the promotion of officers. Moreover, the monarchs stood in particularly intimate relation to certain regiments—the guard regiments. These were stationed in or near the capital, and in them the heirs of the throne and other princes received their military education. The officers of these regiments, almost exclusively the sons of aristocratic families, were among the few who were on familiar terms with members of the royal families. Thus in the monarchy a landed aristocracy with military values and a military code of honor continued to set the social standard.

The eminence of a landed aristocracy, which had been justified by the economic and political conditions of previous centuries, seemed an anomaly in the twentieth century, when industry and commerce became dominating factors in economic life. The heads of the large banks, the owners and managers of the great industrial enterprises, were the creators of the prosperity and power of a nation. But even in those countries in which industrialization was most advanced, agriculture still retained an important place in the economy. To be sure, it was losing ground to industry and commerce. Despite a steady population increase, the number of people in agriculture remained stable. Nevertheless—with the exception of Great Britain—in northern and western Europe about 50 per cent of the population still followed agricultural pursuits during the first decades of the

The assassination attempt on King Alfonso. *The bomb had been thrown at the wedding procession of the Spanish king on May 31, 1906.*

twentieth century. And in the Balkans and in eastern Europe this figure was around 70 per cent. Moreover, in many parts of Europe the possessor of a large landed estate was still very wealthy. Although the Dohnas, an old noble family with vast estates in East Prussia, were not as rich as the Krupps, the great armament manufacturers of the Ruhr, they were still among the richest families of Germany. The estates of the Esterházy and Károlyi families in Hungary yielded incomes which permitted them to indulge themselves in every luxury resort of Europe. The fabulous wealth of the Russian aristocracy came from agriculture. A Prince Yussupoff even as a teen-ager traveled in his special train through Europe. Moreover, many of the aristocrats had lands on which coal, the most precious raw material of that time, was discovered and mined. Lord Derby, of the Stanley family; in England, the princes Pless and Henckel-Donnersmarck in Germany, the Hohenlohes in Bohemia were landowners and industrialists at the same time. Moreover, in France, Italy, and Germany the cultivation of vineyards and the installation of breweries yielded the owners of landed estates an income often equal to that of the great bankers and captains of industry.

There remained differences, however, between the industrial and agricultural sectors of European society, and these differences were most clearly reflected in the bourgeois advocacy of free trade and the aristocratic demand for tariffs. Moreover, the less well-situated members of the nobility looked with envy and disdain on the increasing wealth of the bourgeoisie. The owners of smaller industrial enterprises usually retained many of the antiaristocratic views of the early nineteenth century, when the bourgeoisie had been struggling against the Old Regime. Yet, between the upper strata of the landed aristocracy and the wealthiest members of the industrial and commercial society there were many links; and gradually these two elements came to be joined together in a single ruling group. The monarchs furthered this process by receiving the important personages of the commercial and industrial world at court and giving them titles, ennobling such bankers and industrialists as the Rothschilds, the Sassoons, and Ernest Cassel in Great Britain, the Krupps and the Siemenses in Germany, the Rothschilds and the Gutmanns in Austria, the Franchettis in Italy. The manner and the extent of the amalgamation into the ruling classes of these two—the old landed aristocracy and the new leaders of the commercial and industrial world—varied in the different European countries. But generally the business class became closely tied to the policies of their governments. Authoritarian concepts and aristocratic mores and interests pervaded the thinking and the aims of the owners and managers of industry. And the dominance among them of this point of view hardened the tensions and conflicts within an industrial society.

A preindustrial, antimodern element persisted in the European society of the early twentieth century. The code of honor of the nobility—its duels, its concern for rank and for gentlemanly behavior—the social preeminence of the military profession, and the prestige of the life of leisure, along with a certain contempt for moneymaking activities, were characteristic of the period. Symbolic was the importance of the horse in this society. It would be reasonable to assume that in a technical and industrial age the horse, previously important for agriculture, transport, and war, would become obsolete. But horse racing remained the most elegant sport, and its great events were honored by the presence of royalty. Establishing a stable of race horses was the surest way for a wealthy man to advance into the upper strata of society. Admission to membership in the jockey clubs, founded for the promotion of horse racing, was a sign of having entered the Upper Ten Thousand, as the ruling group was called. In the armies the guard-cavalry regiments were the most elegant: the blue-and-red tunics and the helmets with drooping horsehair plumes of the English Royal Horse Guards, the black caps with death's-heads and the fur-trimmed jackets of the Prussian "black" hussars, the light-blue coats and the golden froggings of the Austrian imperial chasseurs—these were the uniforms of the cream of the European armies. In all Europe, cavalry regiments were maintained in a strength hardly compatible with the changes in warfare which the technical age required and strategic thinkers envisaged. Soon after the First World War had started, the uselessness of these trappings became obvious. Colorful uniforms were replaced by drab gray; horses bred and trained for the cavalry were left behind and cavalrymen had to fight as foot soldiers.

THE WORKERS

In previous centuries a number of social groups—household servants, serfs and half-free peasants, craftsmen, artisans—had formed the economically weakest class of society, but at the end of the nineteenth century the lowest stratum was made up of the industrial workers—the proletariat. The manpower required by industry had to be housed in the cities near the factories. Whereas few effects of industrialization could be seen in the countryside in the years before the First World War, immense changes took place in urban life. The population of most of the existing cities increased and new urban centers developed. In Great Britain and France, where the Industrial Revolution had started more than a hundred years earlier, the rate of urban growth began to slow down by the end of the nineteenth century. Nevertheless, Greater London grew from five million inhabitants in 1880 to seven million in 1914; Paris, from two million to almost three million. Cities in those countries which entered the industrial age in the fifty years before the First World War grew even more strikingly. Berlin, with about 500,000 inhabitants in 1866, had more than two million in 1914. Barcelona and Milan, the industrial capitals of Spain and Italy, both surpassed the half-million figure by 1914. Most significant was the rise in population and the growth of urban settlements in the great coal- and iron-mining districts. In northern France, Lille doubled its population between 1850 and 1914. In 1914 Lille had 200,000 inhabitants and the population in neighboring cities so increased that northeastern France began to form one megalopolis. The same phenomenon could be observed in Germany in the Ruhr area, where Essen, Gelsenkirchen, Bochum, and Mülheim began to run into each other, and in the coal-mining districts of upper Silesia around Kattowitz. Russia entered the industrialization race last. But the urban development was rapid. In 1863 Russia had only three cities with more than 100,000 inhabitants. Forty years later there were more than fifteen. Around the coal and iron-ore mines of the Donetz Basin and in the oil areas of the Caucasus densely populated districts were formed.

In Great Britain people continued to live in small one-family houses, but numerous families were herded into houses which had been built for one family, and became slums. In other countries workers were housed in large apartment buildings four to six floors high, each floor containing five or six apartments. Built side by side with no intervening space, centered around small dark courtyards, these buildings had no gardens, no green areas, and even the streets were treeless.

Factories were generally tall structures without adequate air and light. Working conditions usually improved after the first cruel years of the beginning of industrialization. But even at best sanitary conditions in the

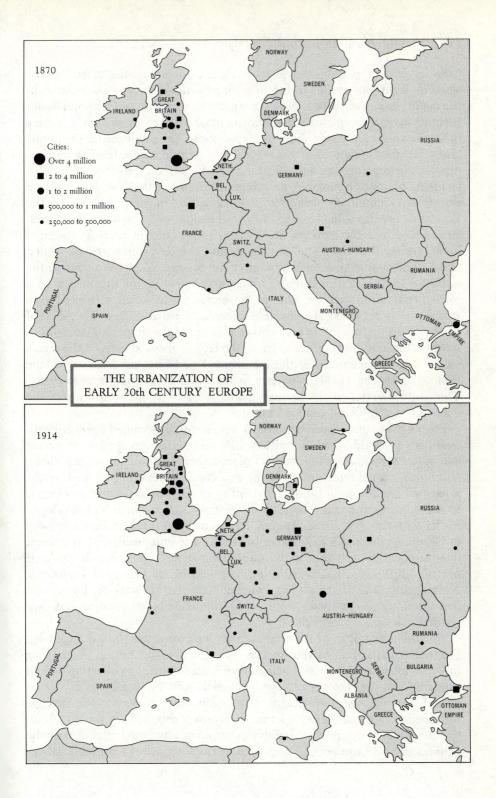

1870

Cities:
⬤ Over 4 million
■ 2 to 4 million
● 1 to 2 million
▪ 500,000 to 1 million
• 250,000 to 500,000

THE URBANIZATION OF
EARLY 20th CENTURY EUROPE

1914

factories were appalling and little was done to ensure the safety of the workers from occupational hazards. Safety precautions, particularly in the coal mines, were disastrously unsatisfactory. In Russia, Italy, and Spain there were no laws against the employment of children or women, nor were their working conditions different from those for adult men. Economic crises, frequent dismissal of workers, and a considerable rate of unemployment were regarded as unavoidable. There was no provision for these recurring periods of hardship, and wages were so low that the workers were unable to accumulate savings to fall back on. In the oil fields of the Caucasus, workers like young Iosif Vissarionovich Dzhugashvili, who later would take the name of Stalin, were imprisoned in barracks for eight hours during the night and worked during the day supervised by armed police. The young Aneurin Bevan, after the Second World War one of the inspiring leaders of the British Labor party, grew up in the misery of a Welsh coal-mining village. One of his brothers was killed in what Bevan was always to regard as an avoidable mine accident, and his mother died of starvation. A picture of life in a worker's house, of the desperate struggles of mothers for food for their children, of the lack of medical care, of the men's escape into drunkenness, of the recruitment of teen-agers for work in the mines is given by D. H. Lawrence in his novel *Sons and Lovers* (1913). This British writer, with his message of a free life, grew up amidst the collieries of a midland mining village.

People living under such conditions were naturally inclined to regard with hostility the world which permitted such misery. Realizing their economic and social weakness, many workers placed their hope in organizing themselves and formed trade unions in the expectation that unified action would improve their common lot. In the 1890's the trade-union movement began to make great strides, and by 1905 the British unions, which had developed earlier than those on the Continent, had more than three million members; in Germany one and a half million workers were unionized; and in France, one million. These figures sound impressive; actually not even 25 per cent of the adult industrial workers in these countries belonged to unions. Nevertheless, the trade unions benefited the entire working population because employers gradually were forced to provide better conditions if they wanted to keep their workers.

The main activities of the trade unions were directed toward improving the material situation of the workers by collective bargaining, by granting financial assistance to strikers when negotiations failed, by collecting benefit funds with which the unemployed, the sick, and the aged could be supported. But unions also attempted to equip the workers for the struggle for social betterment. They organized training schools, they set up educational courses, they arranged holiday excursions. They made the lives of the workers more meaningful, liberating them from a sense of helpless isolation.

It was soon noticed that the trade unions exerted considerable influence on the minds of the workers. Ministers and priests became aware of the extent to which these organizations were successfully competing with the churches. Many Catholics, among them the bishop of Mainz, Wilhelm von Ketteler, in Germany, and Albert de Mun in France, realized that if the Church was to maintain any influence among the broad masses, it would have to introduce an active social program. In his encyclical *Rerum novarum* (1891), Pope Leo XIII expressed approval of the attempts to form Christian trade unions. Although the Catholic trade unions never were as powerful as the "free" trade unions, they became a significant political and social factor in Germany and Austria.

Yet the existence of trade unions was by no means secure. They had to fight for recognition, which they achieved only slowly and gradually: in Great Britain between 1870 and 1876, in France in 1884, in Germany after 1890. In some countries only local trade unions or trade unions for particular industrial activities were permitted. In Russia trade unions remained illegal until 1906. Few countries recognized the right of collective bargaining. Strikes and picketing were frequently prohibited. Since the activities by which the trade unions tried to improve the lot of their members met with only limited success, many workers came to feel that a real improvement of their situation required a change in the entire political system: action in the economic sphere had to be complemented by action in the political sphere. Many trade-union leaders shared this view and took a leading role in political movements that attempted to organize the workers for revolution.

The last quarter of the nineteenth century saw the formation in almost all European countries of political parties which called themselves socialist or social democratic. These parties shared the main tenets of the political creed which Karl Marx (1818–1883) had formulated. Before the First World War the most powerful socialist party was the German Social Democratic party. Its program, named after Erfurt, the town where it was adopted in 1891, was written with the cooperation of the aged Friedrich Engels (1820–1895), Marx's friend and collaborator. The Erfurt Program, which became the model for the programs of all the European socialist parties, was based on a few clear and simple tenets. Fundamental was the Marxist assumption that every society consisted of classes determined by economic interests, and every political struggle was actually a struggle between different economic classes. Thus, no improvement of the economic situation of the workers could be expected without a political revolution in which the workers would wrest power from the capitalist ruling group. Then the means of production would fall into the hands of the proletariat; private property would be replaced by common possession of all goods; and the results of labor could be distributed to the benefit of all. Everyone would receive according to his needs.

"Dangerous Enemies of Society." This picture was taken in 1910 at the Annual Congress of the German Social Democratic Party. The man sitting in the center is Karl Liebknecht, one of the prominent Socialists, who in 1918 became leader of the most radical wing and was assassinated in 1919.

These developments were presented not as a desirable utopia but as the sequence of events which scientific investigation showed to be necessary and inevitable. Marxists believed that under capitalism wealth was becoming increasingly concentrated among fewer and fewer people, and therefore more and more people were being pushed down into the proletariat. Consequently, because fewer people would have the means to buy goods and to stimulate the economy, the economic crises which were considered to be inherent in the capitalist system would become progressively more frequent and severe. However, the Marxists urged the workers not to stand idly by waiting for the final crisis and the collapse of capitalism. The capitalists would defend themselves by force, so the workers had to strive for a position from which they could seize power. They were to work for a democratization of political life in capitalist society in order to undermine the existing state and to defeat the last stand of capitalism. Since capitalism dominated the world, its overthrow presupposed an international revolution. In 1889 the socialist parties of all countries therefore formed an alliance, called the International, and representatives from these parties met regularly. Although the decisions of the International were recommendations only and not binding on the individual socialist parties, the International did create the impression of a great supranational force working toward a single goal.

The socialist doctrine had obvious attractions for the workers who lived as outsiders in prewar society. But the doctrine had inner contradictions. If society had to be entirely transformed, was it meaningful to work for its democratization? If the collapse of capitalism was historically inevitable, what were the reasons for forming political parties and for undertaking a political struggle? These contradictions became the more puzzling because the actual political and economic situation in the prewar years did not develop according to the Marxian scheme. Economic crises did not become more frequent or more serious. Indeed, no serious economic crisis arose between 1890 and 1914. And although a number of economic recessions occurred, in general there was an upward trend in the standard of living on the Continent. By 1900 the wages of skilled workers were almost double those of unskilled workers, and the skilled workers were able to accumulate some reserves.

The growth of socialist parties and of trade unions led to the creation of large bureaucratic apparatuses. They employed numerous officers; they acquired publishing houses and newspapers; some of their leaders were elected to parliaments. Consequently, many party and trade-union officers became more interested in keeping their organizations alive than in risking their existence by political action. Some socialists suggested that evolution rather than revolution was the way to socialism. Since the workers would slowly become a majority, it might be possible, they thought, to achieve the transition to socialism gradually, by a democratic process. The originator of this theory was a German socialist, Eduard Bernstein (1850–1932), who had been impressed by improvements in the situation of the working classes in Great Britain during the nineteenth century. Revisionism, as the movement was called, was particularly influential in Great Britain and Germany, countries with highly developed industrial systems, where the workers received some of the benefits of economic progress. In Spain, France, and Russia, where industrialization was still in its infancy, and where the governments looked with disfavor upon demands of the workers which might retard the process of industrialization, socialists rejected the entire doctrine of Revisionism. In the meetings of the International, the views of the Revisionists were debated, but they never became official socialist doctrine. The demand for revolution was maintained.

THE MIDDLE CLASSES

"Middle classes" is a useful but tricky term. In European society a large number of people belonged neither to the upper strata nor to the proletariat, and for the characterization of this group "middle classes" seems literally correct and appropriate. But it is difficult to find common concerns and common aims among those who were neither noble nor workers. In

The middle classes reveling at the beach in the first summer of the twentieth century.

preindustrial Europe this segment of society had usually possessed a considerable degree of economic independence. Engaging in commerce or in the trades, the merchants, artisans, and shop owners had recognized their common economic bond and frequently had shared a common political outlook. But the homogeneity of the middle classes was shattered by industrialization. Industrialization favored concentration and bigness in economic life; it became increasingly difficult for the middle classes to maintain a moderate degree of economic independence. Some shop owners and artisans, of course, succeeded in adjusting to the times; they developed their trade or business into a small factory or chain stores. Over some shops, particularly those of a wine merchant or a butcher or a greengrocer, signs still proclaimed ownership in the same family extending over several centuries, but such cases became increasingly rare. In most countries the small family-owned business sooner or later was changed into a joint-stock company or absorbed by the larger companies working in the same field. The directors or managers of large factories and banks had higher incomes than the owners of small enterprises struggling to remain independent. Thus the economic basis of the middle classes was thoroughly changed. The independent small entrepreneur disappeared or was pushed down to the lower levels of the economic scale. The leaders of the great industrial and commercial enterprises could no longer be regarded as members of the middle classes; they had become part of the ruling group. Even the salaried managers and directors just below the top business leaders were highly paid, and a wide gap separated them from their employees, the white-collar workers.

Because of the white-collar workers, the middle group of society remained

numerically strong, and its ranks have steadily increased in the course
of the twentieth century. White-collar workers were in demand not only
in commerce and industry but in the modern industrial state, which needed
the services of an expanding bureaucracy. As the population grew, more
and more post-office and railroad employees, police officers, administrators,
and civil servants were required. Similarly, the need rose for members of the
so-called free professions—doctors, lawyers, teachers. Increased demand
made these professions so attractive and rewarding that they quickly became overcrowded. As supply outraced demand, wide differences in financial position appeared within the professional groups. The great corporation and criminal lawyers and the renowned medical specialists had very
high incomes; many lawyers and doctors, however, had to scrape by on
meager earnings.

Thus, the middle group in society was composed of people of different
callings and of greatly varying economic status. Some were wealthy or at
least well off; others had not much more than a minimum subsistence.
Some could still consider themselves independent, but most were employees whose opportunities were closely tied to changes in the economic
situation. To them the uncertainties of economic life made dependence a
concrete reality.

The members of the middle group varied in more than their economic
status, however; they also lacked a common intellectual bond. Their
divergent interests created great differences in outlook and education. Until
far into the nineteenth century men engaging in economic activities had not
needed higher education; the universities had served to train the relatively
limited number of doctors, lawyers, ministers, teachers, and civil servants.
But because industrial society required highly trained specialists—
economists, engineers, chemists—the content of higher education underwent a change. Secondary schools introduced programs concentrating on
natural science and modern languages; in the universities emphasis began to
shift away from a general education in arts and letters, toward scientific
training and technical instruction; technical colleges were founded which,
like the universities, received the right to grant higher degrees. Philosophers
and historians no longer dominated the universities as they had in the early
and middle decades of the nineteenth century. The most prominent and
admired figures were the great scientific discoverers—men like Helmholtz,
Pasteur, Lister.

Because of the instruction provided in the natural sciences, in economics,
and technology, university training and a university degree were of the
greatest practical use to the members of the middle classes. The wealthy
upper group of the leaders of industrial and commercial life was small and
entry into their circle was difficult, but it was not impossible. The best,
almost the only, means for economic and social advancement was the

possession of special knowledge and techniques. And these could only be acquired at a university or technical college. Middle-class parents were naturally eager to give their sons these educational opportunities, but only the relatively affluent could afford the preparatory schools and universities. Despite the value of the university degree the number of those who enjoyed a higher education remained small; statistics from the year 1913 show that in the various countries of Europe before the First World War the number of university students among each ten thousand of the population ranged between seven and eleven.

Disparity of economic status, interests, and education resulted in divergent political aims. In the eighteenth and the first half of the nineteenth century the members of the middle classes were united in their struggle for a legal and constitutional order which would end the economic and political privileges of the nobility, give protection against arbitrary rule by the monarch, and permit the people some influence in the government. As the nineteenth century wore on, members of the middle classes for the most part continued to believe that the status and rights of the individual had to be protected by law, that no legal order was secure unless it was embedded in a fundamental law or constitution, and that the best guarantee of the maintenance of the constitution was the existence of an elected parliament with some control over the government. In the 1890's the condemnation of Captain Alfred Dreyfus in France in secret military-court proceedings, and in the following decade the execution of the anarchist Francisco Ferrer in Spain without sufficient proof of his participation in revolutionary activities, aroused an excitement all over the western world that reflected the tenacity of such ideas.

Openly and consciously few members of the middle classes doubted the validity of a basically liberal outlook. But leaders of big business, independent entrepreneurs, dependent employees, small shopkeepers, officials, men of the free professions held differing views on such fundamental questions as the right of the state to intervene in economic affairs, the need for protection of the economically weak and helpless, and the desirability of extending parliamentary powers. What at the beginning of the nineteenth century had been a unified liberal movement at the end of the century started to fragment in most countries, and a number of new liberal parties were formed—some of them tending more to the right, others more to the left. These political divisions not only weakened liberalism as a political force but also opened the door to the acceptance of notions and policies which undermined the tenets of the faith which the older middle-class generation had held.

All the political parties representing the interests of the middle class felt themselves to be sharply separated from the socialists. The socialist attack on private property united the various nonsocialist groups—disparate in their status or interests though they might be—in self-defense; hostility against the proletariat was a common trait of the rest of capitalist society—of the bourgeoisie. Nowhere was this hostility greater than among those of the bourgeoisie whose economic situation was precarious. The more the members of the middle class lost their economic independence, the more they were inclined to stress their superiority over the working man. Thus the door was opened for the acceptance of ideas which were in stark contradiction to the original liberal belief in the equality and dignity of all men.

Thinking in terms of racial differences began to gain importance in this period. Racism often took the form of anti-Semitism, and indeed anti-Semitism, not as the social attitude of individuals but as a political movement, gained a certain mass appeal in these years. Racism also underlay the acceptance of the notion that birth or race made one segment of society superior to others; this view rationalized the exclusion of large groups—like the workers—from the right to participate in government. Differences in social status were believed to follow from natural selection, from having "better blood"; the existence of a ruling group, of an elite, in every society was not an accident, but a natural necessity.

Doubts were voiced as to whether the masses could be trusted and whether full democracy, in which every citizen had the same vote and the majority ruled, was the best form of government. Movements for extending the franchise slowed down; and there was little inclination to limit the powers of the upper houses of parliaments, whose members generally gained their seats either by heredity or by weighted elections in which the wealthier classes preserved control. The march of democracy seemed to falter.

The most striking break with liberal tenets occurred in the economic realm. Originally the middle classes had wanted to keep the government out of this sphere, but in the latter part of the nineteenth century their attitude changed. One of the links which brought government and industry together was the armament industry. Commissions for the production of guns or the building of warships were eagerly sought by heavy industry. Armament manufacturers wanted steady orders from their own governments. Hence, steel and coal industrialists often became allied with those elements of society which were wedded to the expansion of the military. Moreover, the great armament concerns—Krupp in Germany, Schneider-Creusot in France, Skoda in Austria—were anxious to sell their goods all over the world. They frequently needed government support because they were unable to expand their businesses without protection against foreign competitors. In the last quarter of the nineteenth century most states hesitantly and gradually turned away from free trade and introduced protective tariffs. Customs walls rose, closing nations off from their neighbors.

As a result of these developments, nationalism acquired a new explosive and aggressive character. In the first half of the nineteenth century the expression of nationalism and the demands for national unification were part of a broad liberal political program; it was assumed that, united by their belief in the same human values, the various national states would harmoniously live together as one great family. But with the weakening of the faith in liberalism and democratization, nationalism served to emphasize what was unique and different in each nation rather than what was common to them and bound them together.

By the turn of the century nationalism had become a divisive force, and racism was a factor not only in domestic, but also in foreign policy. The idea of Europe as a community lost its appeal. If nations looked for outside support they considered as their "natural" allies those of the same "race." The views on the nature and importance of racial differences had no scientific basis; they were a myth, built of crude observations and prejudices. Still, they had a significant political influence. Frenchmen and Italians advocated closer ties between their countries because they were "Latin sisters," the only true heirs of the classical tradition. Germans, Englishmen, and Americans felt themselves to belong together because they came from the same "superior" Teutonic stock. Cecil Rhodes (1853–1902) left in his will a fund for endowing scholarships for Germans and Americans at Oxford in order to establish closer relations among the elite of the three "Germanic" nations. In this period the "pan" movements flourished; they aimed at establishing cooperation among "all" people of the same race, wherever they might live. At the congresses of these "pan" movements, vehement protests against the oppression of racial brethren by foreign governments were issued and the various states were urged to undertake policies which would unite all the members of the same race in a great federation. The statesmen of the day were less impressed by the concept of "natural" allies than the masses, and the practical effects of the "pan" movements should not be overestimated, but some of them did work as strong pressure groups. Pan-Slavism, for example, forced the Russian government into an aggressive foreign policy.

The situation was paradoxical. Europe dominated the world more than ever before or ever after. But the forces which held European society together had become increasingly tenuous. The mass of the working population had no part in the government and believed in an internationalism encompassing the whole world and extinguishing all national boundaries. At the other end of the social hierarchy, royalty and aristocracy still formed a supranational element united by personal relationships and a common style of life. But the most important constituents in the social life of the period, the industrial and commercial groups, became more and more closely tied to the national state and placed their hopes on its strength and on its support in the competition against others. Thus, industrialization increased rather than diminished tensions among the great powers.

FOREIGN AFFAIRS

In all the countries of Europe diplomacy was by tradition an aristocratic profession. Even in France, where after the establishment of the republic the aristocracy refrained from participation in the government or in politics, members of the nobility continued to pursue diplomatic careers. Because diplomats were accredited to the head of the state and closely connected with the court, there was justification for the aristocratic monopoly in diplomacy. Furthermore, diplomacy was an expensive career and could be afforded only by those belonging to the wealthiest stratum of the nobility. Usually diplomats—as members of the landowning classes—were more closely connected with the agrarian part of economic life than with the industrial and commercial sectors.

Tradition, therefore, was a powerful force in the practice and the assumptions of European diplomacy before 1914. The world of states was regarded as a hierarchy with seven great powers at its summit: Great Britain, France, Italy, Spain, Germany, Austria-Hungary, and Russia. The highest rank in the diplomatic profession was that of ambassador, and this title was reserved for those diplomats of great powers who served at the courts of other great powers. In its forms and ceremonials, in its ideas and assumptions, diplomacy remained wedded to the traditions of former centuries. Most of the diplomats who advanced to high positions in the period before the First World War had received their training under the great masters of nineteenth-century diplomacy: Bismarck in Germany, Gorchakov in Russia, Disraeli in Great Britain, Cavour in Italy, and Andrássy in Austria-Hungary. Diplomats in the early twentieth century held firmly to the ideas which had dominated diplomatic thinking in the two previous centuries: balance of power and *raison d'état*. They believed in a "concert of Europe," which really meant that the smaller nations were coerced into carrying out what the great powers had agreed upon among themselves. Without openly acknowledging it, the great powers still assumed the right of intervention propounded a century earlier by Prince Metternich. They did not subscribe to the principle of national self-determination, for it threatened to lead to a disturbance of the balance of power.

But the traditional concepts no longer corresponded to the situation which had developed in industrialized Europe. The states which were numbered among the great powers were in truth very unequal in strength. For instance, Spain, which had rightly enjoyed the distinction of being a great power up to the end of the eighteenth century, had become an almost negligible element in the balance of power by the beginning of the twentieth century. For at this time the political strength of a state was dependent on the extent of its industrialization.

The intimate relationship between industrial development and political

The Krupp gun factory in Essen in 1904.

strength was particularly evident in the military sphere. The processes which Alfred Nobel had invented for the development of explosives were applied to small caliber weapons, particularly machine guns, and to new models of heavy long-range artillery. On the sea ironclad ships replaced the older wooden vessels and increased in strength, size, and mobility. The new armaments could be produced on a sizable scale only in a country which had developed a modern industrial apparatus and possessed or could obtain the necessary raw materials. Moreover, speed in the mobilization of mass armies, on which military success was believed to depend, could be achieved only if there existed a well-developed railroad system. The military establishment thus became an integral part of industrial society and encroached upon the freedom of action of the diplomats in a way of which they seem to have been almost unaware.

The distinction between mobilization and war became increasingly difficult in the industrial age. Whereas in the preindustrial age a country could mobilize its troops, march them to the frontier, and stop them there, now mobilization and war became almost identical. For the mobilization and the deployment of mass armies a timetable had to be established well in advance, and once the military plans had been worked out, last-minute modifications could not be made without leading to chaos. In the crisis of 1914 almost all the European states were bound to military plans worked out many years before and to the arrangements with other powers which had been set up by their military staffs. But no country had coordinated its diplomatic strategy and its military planning. Political leaders were shocked to discover how restricted their freedom of action was. They all seemed to have believed that, as in earlier times, mobilization and military action could be turned on and off at a moment's notice.

Diplomacy was also modified and limited by the pressures of popular interest in the making and conduct of foreign policy. As illiteracy was steadily reduced, and in some countries almost entirely eliminated, newspapers gained in circulation and in influence. Both newspapers and the newer forms of communication—telegraph, telephone, photography—bridged distances and gave events in foreign and distant lands concreteness and immediacy. The popular media often placed special emphasis on the exploits of men of their audience's own nation. People followed breathlessly the expeditions into darkest Africa, full of pride if their own countrymen made new discoveries; the attempts to reach the North and South Poles became competitions of nation against nation. In the race to the North Pole the Americans Peary and Cook were pitted against the Norwegian Amundsen, and Amundsen made the race to the South Pole against the British explorer Scott. Scott's notes, found after his death in the Antarctic, give an affecting picture of the suffering and heroism involved in these enterprises in which scientific curiosity, romanticism, and national pride were strangely combined. Seeing the flag of his own nation implanted in the polar snow or flying among the palm trees of an island in the South Seas filled the common man with pride. The prestige of one's country became a popular concern, and diplomacy could not remain aloof from this national competitiveness. Even those diplomats who did not share these sentiments were aware that they could not ignore them. In the quest for national prestige, diplomats became anxious to achieve resounding successes without regard for the lasting hostility which temporary triumphs might arouse.

The popular concern with international affairs was effectively used by economic interest groups to exert pressure on the direction of foreign policy. By means of newspapers and other communications media they aroused public attention to their causes and created active propaganda lobbies. Thus industrialists and naval officers might unite to found a naval league; others might create organizations for colonial propaganda. Manufacturers and landowners might form societies to promote their particular interests and obtain popular backing. Neither political parties nor governments were able to keep free from such influences and entanglements.

The most popular cry was for overseas expansion. Every great European state wanted to become a "world power." At the beginning of the twentieth century, this phrase dazzled even cool and critical minds. The demand that one's nation should become a world power reflected simultaneously the heated climate of national competitiveness and the pressures of industrial and commercial interests. Bound by the idea of their race's superiority, European diplomats in their forays into the non-European world sought success and prestige rather than concrete advantages. Their lack of feeling for their limitations induced a ruthlessness which often led to crises and military clashes. The international scene was kept in continuous tension.

IMPERIALISM

The European preoccupation with world politics in the decades before the outbreak of the First World War made this period the "Age of Imperialism." In the literal sense "imperialism" meant that the policies of the great powers were directed toward the creation of overseas empires, but the term usually contained the further suggestion that these policies were determined by an economic motive: the intention of acquiring control over the sources of raw materials for industrial development and over new markets for the sale of finished products.

The economic aspect of imperialism has been most strikingly presented by Lenin in his famous pamphlet *Imperialism, the Highest Stage of Capitalism.* According to Lenin, the industrial and financial forces in each country were united in one large combine and the few men at its head determined the foreign policy of their nation. After the undiscovered and unexplored areas of the world had been divided among the great powers, a period of world wars was inevitable because the states would clash with one another in their efforts to increase their markets and stave off economic crises at home. It is true that the concerns of big business played an important role in the foreign policy of this period. But Lenin's picture of the foreign offices of the great powers serving as the tools of large private companies was exaggerated. He used ideas which the British political scientist H. J. A. Hobson (1858–1940) had developed, and he gave them a sharply Marxist turn. As an analysis of the situation in Germany, from which Lenin took almost all his examples, his thesis might have been somewhat justified. But even with regard to Germany his picture was oversimplified.

If foreign policy often followed the lead of industrialists and bankers, sometimes the relationship was the reverse. A government might ask businessmen to make investments in a foreign country to supply a pretext for the presentation of political demands. Moreover, the financiers of the various European nations did not always compete against one another. Frequently, as in their loans to Russia, Turkey, and Persia, they cooperated in order to distribute the risks. And such cooperation was sometimes achieved against the will of the irrespective governments.

Contrary to widespread belief, imperialism did not always lead to the creation of overseas empires by colonization. The economic expansion of

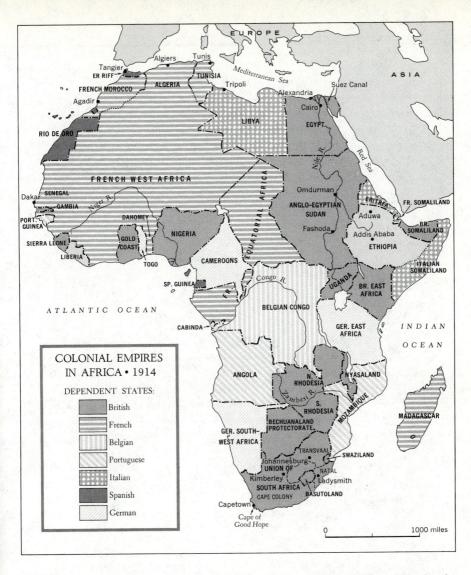

EUROPE

Tangier
ER RIFF
Algiers
Tunis
TUNISIA
Mediterranean Sea
Tripoli
ASIA
Suez Canal
FRENCH MOROCCO
Agadir
ALGERIA
Alexandria
Cairo
RIO DE ORO
LIBYA
EGYPT
Nile R.
Red Sea

FRENCH WEST AFRICA
Dakar
SENEGAL
Niger R.
GAMBIA
PORT.
GUINEA
DAHOMEY
SIERRA LEONE
GOLD
COAST
LIBERIA
TOGO
NIGERIA
Omdurman
ANGLO-EGYPTIAN
SUDAN
Fashoda
Aduwa
Addis Ababa
ETHIOPIA
ERITREA
FR. SOMALILAND
BR.
SOMALILAND
ITALIAN
SOMALILAND

SP. GUINEA
CAMEROONS
EQUATORIAL AFRICA
Congo R.
UGANDA
BR. EAST
AFRICA

ATLANTIC OCEAN
CABINDA
BELGIAN CONGO
GER. EAST
AFRICA
INDIAN

OCEAN

COLONIAL EMPIRES
IN AFRICA • 1914

DEPENDENT STATES:

British
French
Belgian
Portuguese
Italian
Spanish
German

ANGOLA
N.
RHODESIA
NYASALAND
Zambesi R.
S.
RHODESIA
MOZAMBIQUE
MADAGASCAR
BECHUANALAND
PROTECTORATE
GER. SOUTH-
WEST AFRICA
TRANSVAAL
SWAZILAND
Johannesburg
UNION OF
Kimberley
NATAL
Ladysmith
SOUTH AFRICA
BASUTOLAND
CAPE COLONY
Capetown
Cape of
Good Hope

0   1000 miles

the European nations extended over the entire world, but the political rule
of these powers was limited to only a small part of it. British and German
investments in Latin America were large and formed a sizable part of their
overall investments. Yet neither the British nor the Germans attempted to
transform their economic influence into direct political control in this area.
Economic domination did frequently result in *de facto* political dependence
while *de jure* the autonomy of the economically inferior power was
maintained. Turkey remained a sovereign state; it was sometimes even
counted among the great powers. But actually, as a result of German
investments, notably the supplying of capital for the building of the
Baghdad Railway, Turkey became a German satellite. The degree to which
the nations of the non-European world were dependent on the great
European powers varied widely.

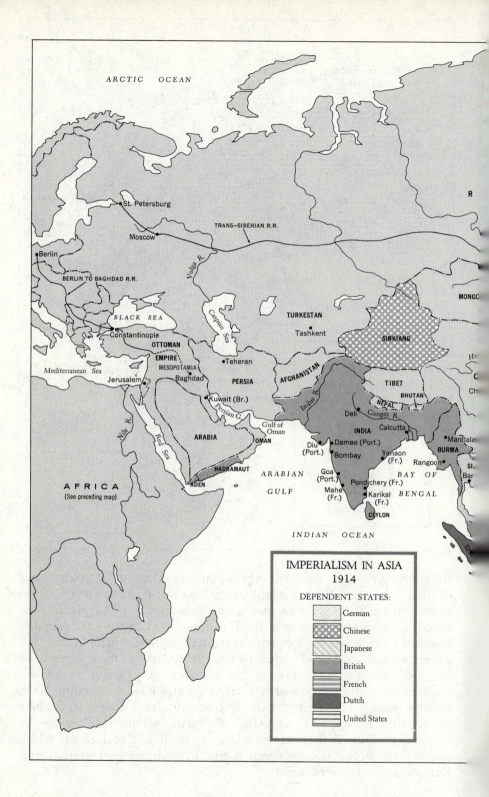

ARCTIC OCEAN

St. Petersburg

Moscow

TRANS–SIBERIAN R.R.

R

Berlin

BERLIN TO BAGHDAD R.R.

Volga R.

Caspian Sea

TURKESTAN

Tashkent

MONGO

BLACK SEA

Constantinople

OTTOMAN
EMPIRE

MESOPOTAMIA

Mediterranean Sea

Jerusalem

Baghdad

Teheran

PERSIA

AFGHANISTAN

Indus R.

SINKIANG

TIBET

BHUTAN

NEPAL

Hi

C

Ch

Kuwait (Br.)

Persian G.

Gulf of
Oman

Deli

Ganges R.

Calcutta

INDIA

Mandala

Nile R.

Red Sea

ARABIA

OMAN

Diu
(Port.)

Damao (Port.)

Bombay

Yanaon
(Fr.)

BURMA

Rangoon

HADRAMAUT

ARABIAN
GULF

Goa
(Port.)

Mahe
(Fr.)

Pondichery (Fr.)

Karikal
(Fr.)

BAY OF

BENGAL

SI

Bar

AFRICA
(See preceding map)

ADEN

CEYLON

INDIAN OCEAN

SU

IMPERIALISM IN ASIA
1914

DEPENDENT STATES:

German

Chinese

Japanese

British

French

Dutch

United States

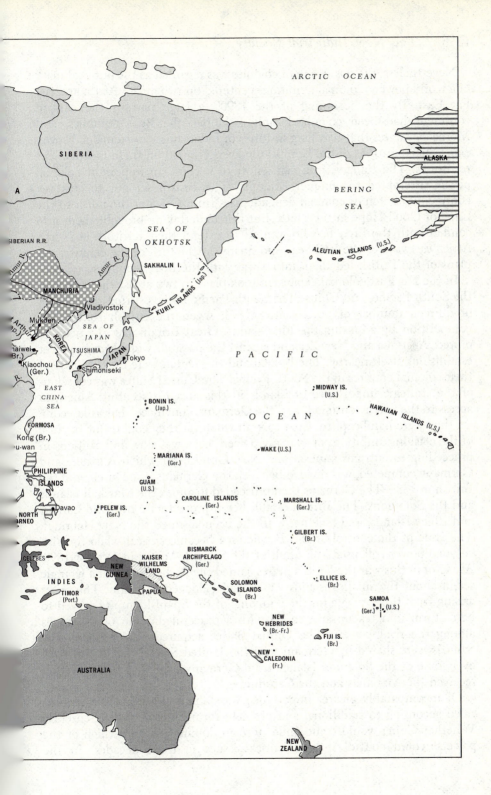

ARCTIC OCEAN

SIBERIA

ALASKA

BERING
SEA

SEA OF
OKHOTSK

SIBERIAN R.R.

Amur R.

Amur R.

MANCHURIA

SAKHALIN I.

Vladivostok

KURIL ISLANDS (Jap.)

ALEUTIAN ISLANDS (U.S.)

Mukden

Arthur
(Jap.)

KOREA

SEA OF
JAPAN

aiwei
(Br.)

TSUSHIMA

JAPAN

Tokyo

PACIFIC

Kiaochou
(Ger.)

Shimoniseki

EAST
CHINA
SEA

MIDWAY IS.
(U.S.)

BONIN IS.
(Jap.)

OCEAN

HAWAIIAN ISLANDS (U.S.)

FORMOSA

Kong (Br.)

u-wan

MARIANA IS.
(Ger.)

WAKE (U.S.)

PHILIPPINE
ISLANDS

GUAM
(U.S.)

CAROLINE ISLANDS
(Ger.)

MARSHALL IS.
(Ger.)

Davao

PELEW IS.
(Ger.)

NORTH
RNEO

GILBERT IS.
(Br.)

CELEBES

KAISER
WILHELMS
LAND

BISMARCK
ARCHIPELAGO
(Ger.)

NEW
GUINEA

ELLICE IS.
(Br.)

INDIES

SOLOMON
ISLANDS
(Br.)

TIMOR
(Port.)

PAPUA

SAMOA
(Ger.) (U.S.)

NEW
HEBRIDES
(Br.-Fr.)

FIJI IS.
(Br.)

AUSTRALIA

NEW
CALEDONIA
(Fr.)

NEW
ZEALAND

Nevertheless, the possession of colonies was regarded as the outward mark of a world power. Colonial ambitions centered on two areas: Africa and the Far East. By the beginning of the 1890's a large part of the African continent had been colonized; only Ethiopia, the Boer republics, and Morocco—states that had long histories of independence—remained sovereign. The ambitions of the European powers focused on these independent territories. The Italians, in a vain effort to become an important colonial power, attempted to conquer Ethiopia. The British set out to create a contiguous stretch of colonial dependencies from Cairo in the north to the Cape of Good Hope in the south. But this undertaking brought them into conflict with the French, who wanted to extend their territory in North Africa eastward to the Red Sea. And finally, at the turn of the century, the plans of the British led them into a war with the Boer republics.

In the Far East colonial expansion took place in two areas: the islands of the South Pacific, and China. The South Pacific islands stirred the interest of quite a number of powers after 1874, when the British started the competition by annexing the Fiji Islands. Great Britain saw the need to protect Australia and New Zealand against the possibility of a foreign power establishing itself nearby. The French and the Dutch were eager to extend their colonial empires in the South Pacific. The United States was conscious of the strategic importance of islands in this area for securing American access to the Asian continent; and the Germans, convinced that as latecomers they were handicapped, tried to grab whatever they could. But because of the clashing ambitions of so many powers, each was slow and cautious in proceeding to outright annexations. New Guinea, for which Australia and Germany competed, was divided between the Germans, the Dutch, and the British in 1885. The Germans then proceeded to annex the Marshall Islands and the Solomons. The British established a protectorate over the Gilbert and Ellice Islands, and together with the French, ruled the New Hebrides. The issue of the control of this Pacific area became critical when Spanish colonial power collapsed as a result of the Spanish-American War of 1898. As victor in this war the United States gained the Philippines, but a wrangle set in about the smaller islands which had belonged to Spain. The crises arising from this struggle for the remnants of the Spanish empire proved to be a storm in a teacup and ended with a peaceful division of the spoils among the rival powers. The United States acquired Wake Island; the Samoas were shared by Germany and the United States; the British took over some of the Solomon Islands from Germany, which as compensation received the Marianas and the Carolines.

Of incomparably greater importance was China. This gigantic empire, ruled according to traditional and obsolete forms, was almost defenseless. Whether China would come under foreign domination and which of the powers would control it were critical issues in these decades. In the treatment of the Chinese question European diplomacy showed its worst aspects: brutality, inconsistency, and shortsightedness. All of the powers involved asserted that their aim was to preserve the integrity of China and to provide the opportunity for trade with China to all states—that is, to maintain an "open-door" policy, to use a term introduced by the American secretary of state, John Hay. If accompanied by support for modern reforms in China, such a policy might in the long run have brought greater advantages than attempts by individual powers to secure exclusive control of parts of China for themselves. However, none of the states could resist the temptation of occupying Chinese ports when the opportunity offered itself. "The various powers cast upon us looks of tiger-like voracity, hustling each other in their endeavors to be the first to seize upon our innermost territories." Thus did a secret edict of the imperial Chinese government in November, 1899, describe the behavior of the white powers. The result was that all Chinese movements for reform and modernization assumed a decidedly antiforeign, nationalist character. A violent expression of this Chinese nationalism was the Boxer Rebellion of 1900; the European military intervention, which saved the encircled legations in Peking, defeated the Boxers, and forced the Chinese government to pay an indemnity, only pushed antiforeign feeling underground.

The struggle in the Far East for influence in China had peculiar features. Whereas the Russian government had no interest in the division of Africa, it regarded the Far East, and particularly China, as an eventual area for Russian colonial expansion. Moreover, two non-European powers, Japan and the United States, were vitally concerned. China had come into the forefront of the considerations of the European powers because, after a resounding victory over China in the war of 1894–1895, the Japanese had obtained in the peace treaty of Shimonoseki territorial cessions which made their nation supremely powerful in China. Russia, France, and Germany intervened in favor of China, and Japan looked for support to Great Britain, the one great naval power which had refused to back up China. These tensions and conflicts came to a head ten years later, in 1905, in the Russo-Japanese War, which resulted in the first defeat of a major European nation by a non-European state. Thus the struggle for China revealed that the great powers of Europe could no longer freely dispose of the rest of the globe. Here was a portent of times to come.

Nevertheless, though the struggles for control and colonies in Africa and the Far East did have the effect of sowing distrust, creating tensions, and maintaining an atmosphere of rivalry and hostility among the European states, the characterization of the entire age as an "Age of Imperialism" is somewhat misleading. The crucial conflicts among the European powers arose from issues within Europe.

CHAPTER 37

The Great Powers, 1890-1914

GENERALIZATIONS in history are dangerous. When closely examined, historical events and developments almost invariably reveal aspects which are
individual and unique. For a true picture of the past, a grasp of the general
pattern of development must be combined with an understanding of the
individual features which in each country modified the pattern and gave to
each nation's history its particular shape. Thus, after a broad survey of the
factors determining the course of European history at the beginning of the
twentieth century, we now turn our attention to the developments in
the individual European nations.

THE PARLIAMENTARY GOVERNMENTS

Great Britain

Of the great powers Great Britain had advanced furthest in democratic
evolution and in industrialization. Having made progress while preserving
continuity, Britain gave the impression of remarkable political and social
stability. The "miracle of its constitution"—the British two-party system,
British parliamentarism—seemed to offer an example of how the problems
and tensions of the twentieth century could be overcome.

Yet at the close of the nineteenth century even in Britain one epoch
seemed to come to an end and a new one to begin. Queen Victoria died in
1901. A famous cartoon by Max Beerbohm illustrates the difference
between Victoria and her heir, King Edward VII (ruled 1901–1910). No
more striking contrast can be imagined than that between the strict and
dignified queen and her flamboyant son. Edward indulged in all the
pleasures of a gilded society. He was devoted to beautiful women and good
food. In his youth he gambled; in later years he played bridge from
afternoon until late at night during his weekend visits to the country houses
of the British rich. He had a stable of race horses, and he was also a
motorist. When he died, the *Illustrated London News* praised him for his

1260

support of the motorcar industry: "When public opposition was at its height, when the outlook was dark indeed for the industry, when rumors and signs portended repressive legislation, His Majesty's accepted patronage of the then Automobile Club of Great Britain and Ireland—by which it became the Royal Automobile Club—came in the very nick of time." Together with his wife, Queen Alexandra, one of the great beauties of the age, the king was the recognized social leader of an ostentatiously opulent and luxurious society.

The sudden change from the dignified and aloof court of Victoria to the pleasure-loving and indulgent court of Edward VII had the effect not of impairing the position of the monarchy, but of strengthening it. During Victoria's reign the bourgeoisie through hard work—slowly and steadily—had transformed Great Britain into the leading industrial country of the world. By the turn of the century this work was done and its fruits could be enjoyed. Edward was the perfect representative of this stage of British economic development, and he was extremely popular.

With the wisdom of hindsight it is easy to see that the British economic position in the first decade of the twentieth century was not as brilliant as it appeared. In the last quarter of the nineteenth century the tempo of British economic development had slowed down. If there was no absolute decline, certainly growth decelerated. Between 1885 and 1913 the rate of increase in Britain's industrial production was 2.11 per cent, while Germany's increased by 4.5 per cent and that of the United States by 5.2 per cent. The actual output of steel, iron, and coal, the chief sources of Britain's strength as an industrial and commercial power, was still very high. But Great Britain was

King Edward VII as advocate of the motorcar.

no longer the leading producer of these goods. By 1906 it had been overtaken by the United States in the production of steel, iron, and coal and by Germany in the production of steel. Similarly, in the development of innovations connected with electricity, the motorcar, and chemicals Britain lagged behind Germany and the United States. Besides, these two countries possessed more modern industrial equipment than Great Britain. Other aspects of economic life were more favorable. In the shipping industry, in textile production, and as a center of trade, Britain remained the leading power. Above all, during its period of economic growth, Britain had made immense investments in foreign countries, which now paid off and generated new investment possibilities. Thus, it was the world's greatest capital market. Its banks enjoyed enormous prestige. The gold standard and the pound were almost synonymous. But Britain did not produce as much as it imported, although the receipts from its foreign investments concealed this deficit in the balance of trade. The basis for the economic difficulties which it had to face after the First World War, and still more threateningly after the Second World War, had already been laid.

The golden glimmer of the Edwardian era was an evening glow, but few were aware of this. To most people, London was the capital of the world in the decades before the First World War, the embodiment of a luxurious style of life unequaled since the Roman Empire. The harmoniousness of the ruling group confirmed this impression of stable prosperity. Conflicts between the attitudes of a feudal and authoritarian military class and that of a bourgeois society did not exist in Great Britain. The British people had successfully fought against the standing army which they viewed as an instrument of princely absolutism and their insular position made conscription unnecessary. Moreover, the economic basis of a military caste— agriculture—had been almost eliminated. If in the first half of the nineteenth century the repeal of the corn laws and the establishment of free trade had signified the victory of the industrial and commercial classes over agricultural interests, this development was completed by the agricultural crisis of the 1880's. In a country unprotected by tariffs, competition against grain imported from Russia or America became impossible; the cultivation of grain was virtually abandoned and the soil was used for grazing, dairyfarming, or fruitfarming. But the landowners remained wealthy. Many found that their soil was rich in coal; industrial settlements sprang up on their land, and they drew large incomes from rents. Landowners frequently became involved in industrial and financial activities. The amalgamation of the rising classes of businessmen with the old aristocratic ruling group represented no problem in Britain: "While business men were becoming peers, peers were becoming business men, so that when the new rich reached the Upper House they found themselves on familiar ground."[1]

---

[1] Élie Halévy, *A History of the English People, Epilogue*, trans. by E. I. Watkin, Vol. II (London, 1934), p. 306.

THE POLITICS OF THE RULING CLASS

Politics mirrored this homogeneity of the ruling class. Although strife between the Unionists, as the Conservatives were officially named, and the Liberals was quite vehement, the social composition of the leadership in each of the parties was very much alike. After William Gladstone's resignation in 1894 and the short-lived Liberal government under Lord Rosebery, the Conservatives held power for ten years, from 1895 to 1905: until 1902 the marquis of Salisbury (1830–1903) was prime minister; from 1902 to 1905 Salisbury's nephew Arthur Balfour (1848–1930). In both parties, descendants of the aristocratic families who had ruled Britain in previous centuries continued to be prominent. Salisbury and Balfour were Cecils; Greys and Ponsonbys were to be found on the councils of the Liberals. The leadership of both parties included aristocrats with industrial and financial connections, like the Liberal Rosebery, who was married to a Rothschild, and the Conservative earl of Derby, who had large coal-mine holdings. In both parties, businessmen played significant roles. Conservative and Liberal politicians enjoyed the same strictly classical education. Attendance at one of the great public schools—Eton, Harrow, Rugby—followed by Oxford or Cambridge was the usual background for a political career and almost a requirement for it; prominence in the debating society of one of the two universities marked a young man for political success. In this period, Oxford's Balliol College was the breeding ground of statesmen. Its master, Benjamin Jowett, the translator of Plato, attracted the most brilliant minds to his college and infused them with the idea that public service was the duty of the social elite.

Leaders of both parties were also knit together by strong common intellectual interests. Among the Liberals, John Morley (1838–1923) was an eminent literary historian; Richard Burdon Haldane (1856–1928) a distinguished student of German philosophy. The philosopher among the Conservatives was Arthur Balfour, who as a young man wrote the stimulating *Defence of Philosophical Doubt.* Balfour is the most puzzling and fascinating figure among Britain's statemen of the early twentieth century. Although he never became prime minister again after 1905, he remained influential in the inner councils of the Conservative party. His mind was open to all that was new and modern in the social, literary, and artistic scene, and politics was only one of his many interests. He considered politics a game rather than a vocation and kept aloof from the enthusiasms and nationalist passions of the masses. Skeptical, ironical, and languidly elegant, he never lost the instincts of a member of the ruling class.

The British ruling class had no doubt of the nation's right to rule over other peoples, to maintain the empire, and to continue imperial expansion despite the increasing competition of other states. The most important leaders of both parties were conscious imperialists. The Conservative government of Salisbury used the occasion of Queen Victoria's Diamond

Arthur James Balfour. *States-man, philosopher, and Magister Elegantiarum.*

Jubilee in 1897 to glorify Britain's world-spanning empire. But Liberals like Rosebery and Haldane were equally enthusiastic advocates of Britain's imperial role. Conservatives might be more concerned with maintaining their nation as the world's foremost power, while Liberals might emphasize its mission of guiding the colonial peoples to self-government and the other blessings of British society, but leaders of both parties were firmly resolved not to be content with what Britain possessed and to compete actively for the African and Asian lands which were up for grabs.

This was the time when the visionary dream of a British empire in Africa reaching from the Cape to Cairo made its impact on British policy. The first consequence was a serious clash between the British and the French. Seeking to enlarge their African holdings, the French had organized two expeditions, one starting from Ethiopia in the east and moving west, the other moving from Lake Chad to the east. They were to meet in the upper Nile Valley and there establish the French claim to this area, the possession of which would link French Somaliland in the east with the French colonies of Algeria in the north and Senegal in the west. This empire would cut straight across the continuous territory stretching from the Cape to Cairo which was sought by the British. Hence they quickly decided on countermeasures. They ordered General Herbert Kitchener (1850–1916) to move up the Nile into the Sudan, which, since the defeat of General Gordon in 1885, had remained in the control of the Mahdi. In 1898 the army of the Mahdi was overcome in two battles, at the Atbara River (April 8) and at Omdurman (September 2), and "the whole mass of the dervishes dissolved into fragments and into particles and streamed away into the fantastic mirages of the desert," according to a description of the battle of Omdurman by a participant, the young supernumerary Lieutenant Winston Churchill. Kitchener moved quickly ahead along the upper Nile, for the French expedition under Colonel Jean Baptiste Marchand, coming from the west, had reached Fashoda, in the southeastern Sudan, and had planted a French flag there on July 10, 1898. With a few of his troops Kitchener sailed up the Nile, arriving at Fashoda on September 18. He asked Marchand to withdraw; Marchand refused. Kitchener and Marchand conferred and agreed to await the decision of their home governments; then they drank whiskey and soda together. Public opinion in Great Britain was so enraged by the French audacity in placing obstacles in the path of the British imperial plans that even if the government had wanted to make concessions it could not have done so. The French were faced with the alternative of going to war against Great Britain or giving in. On November 3 the French government decided to surrender and ordered the unconditional evacuation of Fashoda.

THE LABOR MOVEMENT AND SOCIAL REFORM

The Diamond Jubilee of Queen Victoria in 1897 and Omdurman and Fashoda in 1898 represented the apex of British imperial power. Nevertheless, the coherence of society, the grasp of the ruling classes over the mass of the nation, was less firm and secure than one might have expected as a result of the unbroken success of British policy in the nineteenth century. Although Great Britain had passed the worst hardships and sufferings which accompanied industrialization in its early stages, misery among the masses of the working population was still great. The sacrifice of agriculture to industry, accelerated by a severe agricultural crisis in the 1880's, had forced small farmers and farm hands to migrate to the cities, thus increasing the number of unskilled workers. Housing conditions in the great industrial centers were bad. In the East End of London, families of eight or ten people often lived in one room.

From the middle of the 1890's to the outbreak of the First World War no severe economic crisis occurred in Great Britain. But wages, which had been steadily rising until the turn of the century, then began to stagnate—while prices increased. Moreover, the shadow of unemployment hovered perpetually over the industrial workers. At the end of their lives they were almost unavoidably dependent on charity and the very insufficient provisions of the Poor Law. The trade unions, which supplied almost the only protection the workers had, were handicapped by their limited financial means, and their rights were not clearly determined. Hence, a new, more militant spirit arose in the trade unions: the conviction grew that a change of the economic system to provide "collective ownership and control over production, distribution and exchange"[2] was necessary and that to effect this change labor had to enter the political arena as an independent force. The driving personality in the new movement was James Keir Hardie (1856–1915), a Scottish miner and trade-union organizer. Whereas previously trade-union men elected to Parliament had joined the Liberals, Keir Hardie and his friends had succeeded by 1900 in persuading the trade unions to finance and to support at the forthcoming elections a slate of candidates who would represent the interests of the workers in Parliament. The Labor party, then called the Labor Representation Committee, had come into life.

This development was helped by a movement among middle-class British intellectuals whose social consciences were deeply stirred by the contrast between the wealth of the ruling group and the misery of the workers. Calling themselves Fabians after the Roman dictator Fabius, whom they admired because he had waited patiently for the right moment but then had struck hard, the influential members of this movement were rather disparate. Among them were reform-minded radicals like Annie Besant, successful literary figures like the novelist H. G. Wells and George Bernard Shaw, at that time not yet a dramatist, but a music and literary critic, and scholars like the political scientist Graham Wallas. But the guiding spirit was that of a husband and wife whose closeness of aims is well testified by the fact that they are usually named together as "the Webbs." Sidney Webb (1859–1947) began as a civil servant, but soon decided to devote himself to the problems of industrial society: Beatrice Webb (1858–1943) was a woman of great beauty from a socially prominent family, and had a sensitive social conscience. Under her husband's influence, her somewhat sporadic welfare activities became more serious and systematic.

The Webbs' house served as a kind of headquarters for intellectuals concerned with social questions. The Fabians began by publishing a series of studies on the problems of modern industrial life. The Webbs' *History of Trade Unionism* (1897) is a classic. One of the Webbs' most lasting achievements was the founding of the London School of Economics, later a division of the University of London, which has been particularly devoted to the investigation of political and social problems in the modern world. The Fabians believed that the march of modern society was irrevocably set toward greater democratization. But democratization could be complete

---

[2] From the program issued at the foundation of the Independent Labor Party in Bradford in 1893.

only if it was economic as well as political. And economic democratization meant socialization: the public authorities—local, regional, or central—were to have the right to organize basic industries and to determine how capital income would be used. Fabianism was socialism, but not Marxism. It did not presuppose a revolution which would give all power to one class, the proletariat, and it did not advocate the end of the national state. The socialist transformation of society was to be brought about democratically, by the will of the people. The Fabians felt that their goals were in accordance with the British political tradition, constituting the natural destination toward which their nation's political life had been moving since the beginning of the nineteenth century.

For a while the Fabians tried to convince the leaders of the existing political parties that they ought to adopt the Fabian program. Sidney Webb, who disapproved of spending money on clothes or jewels, permitted Beatrice (to her inner delight) to buy a new dress if doing so might help make one of the socially prominent political leaders more willing to listen to the exposition of Fabian ideas. But when both Conservative and Liberal leaders proved unresponsive, some of the Fabians turned to the idea of establishing a third party, which would realize socialism in Britain. They joined forces with Keir Hardie's Labor Representation Committee, and their ideas soon began to dominate the young Labor party; the combination of intellectuals and trade unionists has remained a characteristic of the British Labor party. When in the 1920's the Labor party came to power, several of the Fabians received high government positions. So prominent had some of their leaders become that on the occasion of their fiftieth anniversary in 1933, George Bernard Shaw, the principal speaker, began by saying, "Ladies and Gentlemen," but then, looking to his right and left on the podium, where the early members of the Fabian movement were seated, he quickly added, "Oh, I see I have to say My Lords, Ladies and Gentlemen."

Both the Conservatives and the Liberals were aware that the founding of an independent Labor party was a threat to the two-party system. They recognized that they had to make a greater effort to satisfy the demands of the laboring classes. Ever since Disraeli had coined the slogan "Tory Democracy," a wing of the Conservative party had placed emphasis on social reform. This movement received new impetus when in 1886 Joseph Chamberlain (1836–1914), with a group of followers, broke with Gladstone and the Liberals and joined the Conservatives. Chamberlain, coming from industrial Birmingham, had made a name for himself as an advocate of radical reforms. As lord mayor of Birmingham he had introduced "municipal socialism"; he had improved public services and made them less expensive by placing streetcars, street lighting, and public utilities under the administration of the city government. Chamberlain had also modernized party politics by creating wards with party organizers who would get the masses to the polls. For a politician of this outlook "Conservative" seemed hardly the right label, and following his alliance with the Conservatives they were officially named "Unionists."

A similar tendency toward social reform could be observed in the Liberal party. Nonconformists and radicals had always formed a strong element in this party. Such Liberals felt that leaders like Rosebery and the imperialists did not represent the true Liberal tradition, and many thought they ought to oppose the imperial expansionism which oppressed other peoples. They believed that the Liberal party ought to concentrate on domestic problems and work toward the solution of the Irish question by seeking to obtain for Ireland its own government and parliament: home rule. The members of this group were sometimes called Little Englanders because of their doubts about the value of the empire. Their most respected leader, Sir Henry Campbell-Bannerman (1836–1908), had held high government office under Gladstone and was regarded as Gladstone's authentic heir, the man who would continue his reform policy. Among this group a new leader arose in a young lawyer and brilliant orator from Wales, David Lloyd George (1863–1945), whose political passion was fired by the misery which he saw among the Welsh mine workers.

IMPERIALISM VERSUS DOMESTIC REFORM

The tensions between the imperialists and the domestic reformers were sharpened by Britain's conflict with the Boer republics in South Africa. In Salisbury's government Joseph Chamberlain had become secretary for the colonies. Partly because he saw little chance to move his Conservative colleagues toward social reform, and partly because of the demands of his office, Chamberlain turned his great energies to the realization of an empire extending from the Cape to Cairo. French ambitions for the upper Nile Valley had been thwarted at Fashoda, but Transvaal and the Orange Free State, the independent Boer republics in southern Africa, still remained a barrier to these plans. A conflict between these independent states and Great Britain seemed unavoidable; its outbreak was accelerated by the discovery of gold in the Transvaal. The Boers feared that the immigrants streaming to the Transvaal in search of quick riches would soon outnumber them, limiting Boer political influence, and—since most of the immigrants (known as Uitlanders) were British—that they might decide to make the Boer republics part of the British empire. There is no doubt that Cecil Rhodes, the dominating figure in the British Cape Colony, aimed at an absorption of the Boer republics by the empire. He believed that the unrest created by the tension between Boers and Uitlanders might provide the opportune moment. In 1896 he organized an invasion by a small force of 470 men under the leadership of a Dr. Jameson, an adventurer. The expectation was that the march of this force into the interior of

An incident of the Boer War. *An armored train destroyed by the Boers.*

the Transvaal would give the signal for a rebellion in Johannesburg by the Uitlander against the Boers. But no such upheaval occurred; Jameson and his men were quickly defeated and surrendered to the Boers. Rhodes's responsibility for the raid was incontestable and he was forced to resign as prime minister of the Cape Colony. But the much-discussed question was whether Chamberlain, the British colonial secretary, had previous knowledge of the raid. The British government immediately declined all responsibility for the raid and a committee of the House of Commons gave Chamberlain a clean bill of health. But doubts about Chamberlain's role were never entirely removed and recent investigations have revealed that he knew much more about what was planned than he admitted at the time.

People outside England had no doubt that the Jameson Raid was a British defeat. The German emperor, William II, sent a telegram to the president of the Transvaal republic, Paul Krüger, congratulating him upon his success "in restoring peace and in maintaining the independence of the country against attacks from without." This message, which rubbed salt in Britain's wounds, may have been unwise politically, but in giving vent to his indignation about British ruthlessness, William expressed the feelings not only of the German nation but of all the European continent. The Jameson Raid and the telegram of the German emperor made war between the Boers and Great Britain almost certain. To the British, conquest of the Boer republics had become a matter of prestige. On the other hand, the raid confirmed the Boers in their fear of the influence of the immigrants, while at the same time the public acknowledgement of the Boers' right to independence encouraged them to resist the British. Hence, they continued their discriminatory policy against the Uitlanders, while the British took up the cause of these new immigrants and insisted that they should receive the right to vote. When negotiations proved fruitless, Britain sent troop reinforcements to the Cape Colony; and on the demand of the Boers for withdrawal of these troops, the British cut off all discussion. In October, 1899, war broke out between the Boer republics (Transvaal and the Orange Free State) on the one hand and the British on the other.

The Boer War followed a pattern common to many colonial wars. The resistance of the indigenous forces proved to be more effective than had been expected, and initially the British had severe losses. But when the full force of the British was brought into play, the difference in strength proved decisive. Where the Boer War differed from most other colonial engagements was in the severity of the reverses suffered by the invading British forces, which were first repulsed, then encircled at Ladysmith and Kimberley and there besieged. They were relieved only at the end of February, 1900, after large reinforcements from England had arrived and a change in command had taken place. The British offensive ended with the conquest and annexation of the Transvaal in September, 1900. But military action continued for another year and a half. The Boers engaged in guerilla warfare, and Kitchener, the British commander, proceeded against them ruthlessly, burning the farms of Boer guerrillas and interning the women and children of Boer soldiers in specially constructed camps. Finally, on May 31, 1902, a peace treaty was signed in which the Boers acknowledged British sovereignty.

The Boer War was a terrible shock to the British people. Since the colonial army was not sufficiently large, troops had to be sent from England; 350,000 men were needed to subdue 60,000 Boers. In England families grew increasingly anxious over the fate of relatives and friends whose lives had been unexpectedly endangered by a colonial war. Moreover, all over Europe there was an outburst of fury against Great Britain. This sudden revelation of their unpopularity was a great surprise to the British, and although the European governments did not take any common action against them, they began to fear that their country might be confronted by a combination of all the continental powers. Thereafter British foreign policy gradually began to veer away from "splendid isolation" and into an acceptance of cooperation with other states. The Boer War had shown the obsoleteness and clumsiness of British military organization, and raised serious doubts about the aims of British policy and the efficiency of British political processes.

Was the imperial expansion worth the loss of life and the expenditure of money exacted by the Boer War? At first, the opponents of the policy which had led to war were shouted down and socially boycotted. But as the conflict dragged on, the politicians who had resisted the wave of imperialist enthusiasm—men like Campbell-Bannerman and Lloyd George—gained in political stature. They found increasing support for their arguments that attention should be focused upon domestic problems. Events confirmed the view that internal tensions were reaching a dangerous state. The newly militant trade unions had encountered fierce resistance by employers, and had retaliated with local strikes against the employment of "free," or nonunion, labor. The tenseness of this situation was aggravated by the Taff Vale decision (1901), which asserted that a trade union was financially liable for damage caused by all strikes in which its members took part. Indignation among the working population was immense because the decision underlined the precarious position of the trade unions and the helplessness of the working classes. The government also lost popularity as a result of the measures it instituted for reform in education. The need for such reform was generally recognized. Great Britain had only a limited number of elementary schools maintained by the state, that is, by the counties and towns. More than half of the children of England and Wales received their elementary education at voluntary schools which were unable to maintain reasonable standards. The Education Act of 1902 placed all these schools under county and town control so that they were forced to adhere to recognized standards; if necessary they would receive financial support from local taxes. The measure undoubtedly represented a great improvement in English education. But because it implied that tax money would be used to support Anglican and Roman Catholic schools, it aroused the vehement opposition of an important segment of the British population, the nonconformists.

THE TRIUMPH OF THE LIBERAL PARTY

The final cause for the end of ten years of Conservative rule was a split among the Conservatives themselves. Joseph Chamberlain had not abandoned his original radicalism when he turned from internal reforms to imperial expansion. On the contrary, he regarded a resolute imperial policy as a means for improving the lot of the masses. He believed that his country's continued economic prosperity depended on the expansion of opportunities to emigrate to the colonies. He advocated protective tariffs which would limit foreign competition in the British market, and by giving preferences to the British colonies, would tie the empire together as a great economic unit. To promote these aims Chamberlain organized the Tariff Reform League, and to devote himself to this campaign he left the government. In Prime Minister Balfour's view, British public opinion was not ready to accept protective tariffs. In a country dependent on the importation of agricultural goods the first result of protection would be an increase in the price of food, which would place another burden on the masses. Split over the tariff question, the Conservatives seemed to lack an economic policy, while the Liberals adhered to the hallowed tradition of free trade. Unable to control his own party, Balfour resigned in December, 1905, and the Liberals took over. Campbell-Bannerman became prime minister, not without the displeasure of the imperialist elements in his own party. But he reconciled them by giving them strong representation in the cabinet. Sir Edward Grey (1862–1933) became foreign secretary; Herbert Asquith (1852–1928), chancellor of the exchequer; and Haldane, secretary of state for war. The radical wing of the reformers was also well represented. Lloyd George became president of the Board of Trade, and John Burns (1858–1943), president of the Local Government Board. The new government was an incongruous mixture of imperialists and social reformers. But at this time Great Britain was still prosperous enough to attempt simultaneously to maintain a powerful position in foreign affairs and to undertake reforms at home. In the elections of January, 1906, the Liberals gained a sweeping victory, but it was a sign of the times that the new Labor party gained twenty-nine seats. Ten years of Liberal rule followed the Conservative defeat of 1906; it would be a decade of wide-ranging reforms.

Actually, in the eight years of Liberal rule before 1914, two periods must be distinguished. In the first years of the Liberal government, legislation was somewhat cautious and tentative; the government was mainly concerned with revising those measures of the preceding Conservative governments which had aroused the greatest resentment and with improving those aspects of the administration which were inefficient or defective. The Liberal government contributed to the healing of the wounds of the Boer War by giving self-government to the Transvaal. A Trade Disputes Act legalized peaceful picketing and relieved trade unions from liability for damages caused by their members—thereby annulling the Taff Vale decision—and Haldane carried through an army reform which fully proved itself in the First World War. The army was divided into two parts, an expeditionary force ready for immediate action on the Continent, and a territorial force into which were merged traditional organizations such as the volunteers and the yeomanry; moreover, Haldane created a general staff after the Prussian example. Like most successful military reforms his measures also resulted in financial economies.

The first years of Liberal rule yielded meager results, partly because many measures which the government advocated—among them a change in the Education Act which would have removed the objections of the nonconformists—were rejected by the House of Lords, which was controlled by the Conservatives. Moreover, Asquith, the chancellor of the exchequer, pursued a traditional line in his financial policy and was disinclined to finance social experiments. This situation changed in 1908 when Asquith succeeded Campbell-Bannerman as prime minister and entrusted the office of chancellor of the exchequer to Lloyd George in order to reconcile the radical wing of the Liberal party with the leadership of an imperialist. These changes ushered in a new period of energetic legislation. Lloyd George resolutely used the power of the purse for social reform. The most important feature was the National Insurance Act (1911), patterned after the social legis-

Radicals of the Edwardian era. *Lloyd George and Churchill on the way to the House of Commons on Budget Day, 1910.*

lation which Bismarck had sponsored in Germany. Contributions made on a compulsory basis by workers, employers, and the state were to provide payments to workers in case of sickness and unemployment. Social reforms were to be paid for by means of a revised system of taxation which placed the chief burden for the expenses of the new programs on the wealthy classes. Thus Lloyd George's first budget, that of 1909, represented a radical departure. He raised the death duties, made a sharp distinction between earned and unearned income, and introduced a supertax to be levied on the possessors of large incomes. He also increased the taxes on tobacco and liquor.

In present day terms, Lloyd George's proposals were moderate. The payments given to workers in case of sickness or disability were low, and the small unemployment benefits were granted for only a limited period, a maximum of fifteen weeks in any one year. On the other hand the supertax started only on a yearly income of over £5,000 (which might be compared to an income today of more than $100,000) and the general income tax for unearned income and for earned income above £2,000 was raised only from one shilling to one shilling two pence in the pound. Nevertheless, on a very small scale Lloyd George's budget incorporated all the essential features of the future British welfare state; in the benefits provided and in the methods of financing them the government of present-day Britain continues the policy initiated by Lloyd George in 1909.

Lloyd George emphasized the novel character of his budget by introducing it with a four-hour speech. Opposition formed at once. The Conservatives were particularly upset by a suggestion which later proved to be impractical and was abandoned—the taxing of increases in land value. Since much of the wealth of the British landowners came from estates having mineral resources like coal, this tax was regarded as a direct attack on the position of the propertied classes.

The Conservatives fought the budget vigorously, and when it reached the House of Lords it was rejected. Since the Liberals had been constantly balked in their legislative proposals by the House of Lords, they were deeply aroused by this further frustration of their plans, particularly since tradition had established that the handling of finance bills was primarily a function of the House of Commons. The rejection of the budget by the House of Lords was regarded as a breach of the constitution.

As a next step the Liberal government introduced the Parliament Bill, designed to eliminate the House of Lords as a partner equal to the House of Commons in the law-making process. If it passed, the House of Lords would be able only to delay legislation, not to veto it absolutely. The great problem which faced the Liberal government was how to persuade the House of Lords to agree to its own diminution of power. This matter now began to overshadow the budget conflict.

The Liberals were not unhappy about this course of events. After the somewhat unspectacular results of their first years of rule, their electoral chances were insecure, and they hoped that an issue of consequence would help them to retain the support of the electorate. Lloyd George aimed at transforming the parliamentary controversies into a great constitutional conflict which could be represented as a fight of the people against the lords. In a number of speeches, and with great oratorical force, he castigated the unequal distribution of wealth in England due to "the fraud of the few and the folly of the many." Lloyd George was happily seconded by Winston Churchill, who in 1904, had moved from the Conservatives to the Liberals and in 1908 had been made president of the Board of Trade in the Liberal government. But the Conservatives fought back with equal vehemence, characterizing the Liberal proposal as a subversive attack on the entire English tradition. The fight over the Parliament Bill took on aspects of a class conflict and brought a bitterness and animosity previously unknown into the modern English political scene. The struggle lasted for over two years and ended only after two dissolutions of the House of Commons, new elections, and the threat that the government would create enough Liberal peers to get the proposal through the House of Lords. The final vote, on August 10, 1911, took place with immense excitement because the outcome seemed quite uncertain; the bill was passed only after thirty-seven Conservatives and thirteen bishops decided not to abstain and cast their votes with the government.

THE WANING OF CONFIDENCE

Edward VII died on May 6, 1910, in the midst of the struggle over the Parliament Bill. With his death, British life seemed to lose some of its splendor. His son and successor, King George V (ruled 1910–1936), was a much less glamorous figure; in a sense his somberness corresponded to the dark and threatening atmosphere which prevailed in Great Britain in the two or three years before the outbreak of the First World War. It is difficult to judge whether the fight over the Parliament Bill had heightened political tensions or whether the bitterness of this struggle was a reflection of a change in the political climate. The fact is that the end of the parliamentary struggle was followed by conflicts outside parliament. The victory of the Liberals might have been expected to strengthen confidence in progress by democratic means, but instead the long uncertainties about the outcome seem to have shaken the British people's faith in the efficiency of traditional parliamentary methods. Many became convinced that they would be heard and receive their due only if they used other means, perhaps even violent ones. For example, the advocates of female suffrage, the suffragettes, believed that the ruling males would give up their monopoly over political power only if forced to do so. Therefore, they pursued a policy of violent disruptions. They broke windows in shops and clubs and slashed pictures in the National Gallery; at the Epsom Derby one suffragette threw herself in front of the favorite, the king's horse, ending not only the chances of the horse, but also her own life.

Contempt for legally established authorities and procedures became evident also in the negotiations about the most ticklish issue of British policy, the Irish question. Home rule for Ireland was part of the program of the Liberal party and the Liberals were bound to fulfill this promise because, since the elections of 1910, they had no clear majority in the House of Commons and were dependent for their majority on the vote of the Irish nationalists. The Irish steadfastly supported the government in the consitutional crisis because they were aware that until the power of the House of Lords was limited, no home-rule bill would ever become law. But now they wanted to receive what they believed they had earned. Accordingly, a Home Rule Bill was drafted by the government in 1912. As in the past, home rule aroused passionate opposition. The center of this opposition, of course, was Northern Ireland (Ulster) which was Protestant and where preparations were made to fight against integration with the south which was Catholic. A less expected and more astounding sign of political extremism was the fact that the people of Ulster received clear encourage-

A violent protest. *The suffragette Emily Davison throwing herself in front of the king's horse at the Derby on June 4, 1913. At this time, action photographs were rare and usually obtained only by chance.*

ment for revolt from the leaders of the Conservatives. One of them, Sir Edward Carson, openly advocated armed resistance in Ulster if home rule should become law. Moreover, encouraged by Carson and the Conservatives, army officers, most of them Conservative and many of them descended from the Protestant Irish, demanded a government pledge that they would not be asked to coerce Ulster; otherwise they preferred to resign rather than follow orders to go to Ireland; the government seemed faced with mutiny. Only the outbreak of the First World War prevented a test of the resolve and power of the government to carry through its Irish policy.

A further expression of failing confidence in the possibility of obtaining reform through parliamentary action was the wave of strikes which rocked Great Britain between 1911 and 1913. They reflected serious weaknesses in the nation's economic structure. The period from 1911 to the outbreak of the First World War was characterized by economic prosperity. Unemployment represented no serious problem. Yet prices had been rising much more quickly than wages, and in those industries, notably coal mining, which were faced by serious foreign competition, wages had not risen at all. The workers were all the more dissatisfied because the chance of achieving results by political action seemed to be fading rather than improving.

The success of the Labor party in the elections of 1906 had not been repeated in subsequent elections. The party's parliamentary prospects had been further weakened by a court decision which prevented trade unions from levying political contributions. Disillusionment about the efficacy of the pressure exerted by their party led elements of the labor movement to look favorably upon other recipes for the ills of their economic situation. They became attracted by the idea, which reached Britain from the Continent, particularly from France, that "direct action"—strikes—was the appropriate weapon for workers seeking to improve their situation. Thus, economic and political motives lay behind a number of strikes in 1911 and 1912. The most notable were a seamen's strike, a general railway strike, a strike of the coal miners, and a strike of the dockers. Most of them were accompanied by violence, looting, and sabotage of the machinery in the factories. Frequently troops had to be used, since the police were not able to keep order. Some of the strikes were ended quickly by concessions on the part of the employers. The miners' strike resulted in the introduction of the Miners' Minimum Wage Act, which was a tacit admission by the government of the hardships faced by the mine workers. But some of the strikes simply collapsed, partly because the wage lag began to be made up and partly because the public, tired of economic unrest, began to turn sharply against the trade unions. In the debate accompanying these social tensions and conflicts the statistics of a contemporary best-seller were frequently quoted: in Great Britain, it was stated, 38,000,000 people had hardly more than half of the national income, whereas 1,250,000 "rich" had more than a third. Even if these figures were rough and somewhat exaggerated, the social unrest of these years confirmed that a deep cleavage existed in Great Britain. It was yet to be proved whether the British political system could meet the new demands placed upon it.

France

During the decade before the First World War France was the most democratic of the powers on the continent. France, too, had a parliamentary system. The head of the state, the president, had little power and the executive arm of the government, led by a prime minister, was dependent on the confidence of elected representatives—the Senate and the Chamber of Deputies. In a formal sense, France was even more democratic than Great Britain, for the French upper house, the Senate, was elected, whereas in Britain membership in the upper house was hereditary. However, the voting system by which French senators were chosen favored rural districts and the well-to-do, so the Senate functioned as a conservative counterweight to the more liberal Chamber of Deputies.

In contrast to the British system, French political life was not characterized by the dominance of a two-party system. The French parliament was composed of a large number of small parties; every government was a coalition, and governments changed frequently. In the twenty-four years between 1890 and 1914 there were forty-three governments and twenty-six prime ministers. Yet these statistics are deceptive; stability was greater than the figures imply. The multiplicity of French political parties was not a reflection of irreconcilable internal tensions. The French population was socially quite homogeneous. France was a country of small businessmen and farmers. Industrial enterprises were generally limited in size and frequently family owned. Until the First World War, more than half of the entire population was occupied in agriculture, which accounted even in 1890 for more than a third of the national income. The multifariousness of the political groupings was chiefly a reflection of tiny differences in economic interests and of variations stemming from local and regional particularities. Politicians moved easily from one party to the other. The center of the political spectrum formed the basis of almost all governments. A number of the same politicians were to be found in almost every cabinet, although they were usually assigned different ministries each time a change in government took place. The various governments differed mainly in whether the center ruled with support of the left or with support of the right.

Ironically, the strength of the center in French politics was an indication that France was lagging in the industrial race. France had entered the industrial age almost simultaneously with Great Britain. But after the spurt given by the French Revolution and Napoleon, the rate of industrial growth slowed down in the nineteenth century and France trailed far behind the United States and Germany. By its accumulated wealth the nation remained a great financial power. However, the French were inclined to invest their capital not in industrial enterprises, but—more cautiously—in public loans. In the market for government loans French banks played a particularly great role. The heavy industries were mainly centered in the northeast, where there were rich coal mines and a textile industry, and in the problems arising from modern industrialization were concentrated in relatively small areas and aroused little interest in the rest of the country. Health and safety precautions in industrial enterprises, particularly in the mines, were unsatisfactory. Collective bargaining was forbidden, and trade-union activities were restricted.

France had an active Socialist party, but it was small and many of its deputies could not have been elected without support from the rural population. Thus the Socialists, despite theoretical radicalism, were inclined to be conciliatory in practice. Since the workers could not expect much from parliamentary action, theories which recommended direct action and emphasized the efficacy of purely economic weapons—such as strikes—

were appealing. As the propagandist of the myth that the general strike was the proper instrument for the overthrow of capitalism, Georges Sorel became an influential figure among radical intellectuals through his book entitled *Reflections on Violence* (1908). His views increased the appeal of syndicalism, a revolutionary doctrine which preached direct action with the goal of building a new society through the cooperation of the trade unions of individual factories. Syndicalism was popular among workers in France and spread from there to Italy and Spain. Among the workers of these countries it was a serious competitor to Marxian socialism.

THE CONFLICT BETWEEN THE REPUBLICAN REGIME AND MONARCHIST TRADITIONS

Because the progress of industrialization in France was slow, political life was not dominated by social conflicts. The main divisions were ideological: they concerned issues which the French Revolution had raised. It has been said that after the French Revolution there were two Frances, an aristocratic monarchical France and a republican France. Defeat in the Franco-Prussian War had strengthened the feeling of malaise about the unavoidable decline of the deeply divided nation. The republic, which had been born in the times of the heroic resistance at the end of the Franco-Prussian War, was now beset by scandals and corruption and appeared unable to give an impulse to a regeneration of power. The enemies of the republican and revolutionary tradition felt justified in their conviction that the democratic form of the French government was the reason for the decline of their nation's power and that what France needed was a more authoritarian regime. Moreover, the enemies of the republic were firmly entrenched in two institutions: the army and the Church.

In the last decade of the nineteenth century a crucial event brought about an open confrontation of the two Frances. The impact of the Dreyfus Affair on French thinking was so profound that it took decades to digest and absorb it. This is strikingly indicated by the role which the Affair played in the work of the great French novelists of the twentieth century. Roger Martin Du Gard inserted in his novel *Jean Barois* an almost stenographic report of some of the high points of the Affair. In *Remembrance of Things Past* by Marcel Proust the Affair serves to question the values of the brilliant society which the novel pictures. Anatole France in his *Penguin Island* pictured the Affair as an example of the eternal struggle between reason and human weakness.

The importance of the events beginning in 1894 became clear only slowly. On October 15, 1894, Alfred Dreyfus (1859–1935), a captain in the French general staff, was placed under arrest for high treason. After some weeks Dreyfus was found guilty at a secret military trial, and a few days later, on January 5, 1895, he was sentenced in a solemn ceremony in the

AFFAIRE DREYFUS,
Document No. 1.
Le Bordereau. Fragement)

The Dreyfus Affair. *Above: Dreyfus leaving the court building after his trial.*

Right: Le Bordereau. *This famous document, on which the Dreyfus Affair turned, was given to the German military attaché.*

courtyard of the general-staff building; he was deprived of his rank, his sword was broken, and he was sent for life to Devil's Island, in French Guiana. The trial had been full of legal irregularities. The main proof used against Dreyfus was a small piece of blue paper, which became famous as the *bordereau.* It had been found by a cleaning woman in the wastepaper basket of the German military attaché; it contained information about the French army; and handwriting experts maintained that it had been written by Dreyfus.

A republican and a Jew, Dreyfus had been an outsider among the aristocratic and Catholic officers of the French general staff; his fellow officers were easily convinced, therefore, that if a traitor was among them, it could only be Dreyfus. He belonged to a wealthy Alsatian family, which made every effort to obtain a new trial. A few journalists and lawyers who opposed the military caste were active on Dreyfus' behalf. But for a long while no one could make headway.

In 1896 the counterespionage section of the French general staff received a new chief, Colonel Georges Picquart, who must be considered the true hero of the Dreyfus Affair. Picquart noticed that the removal of Dreyfus had not ended the leakage of military secrets. He also became aware that the handwriting of the *bordereau* was much more similar to that of Walsin Esterhazy, another member of the general staff, than to that of Dreyfus. Moreover, Esterhazy was in continuous financial difficulties. But when Picquart insisted on proceedings against Esterhazy, nobody in the general staff was willing to listen to him and he was transferred from Paris to Algiers. Before leaving Paris he confidentially informed a few people, among them the vice president of the Senate, Scheurer-Kestner, of his suspicions about Esterhazy. Now a number of influential voices joined the campaign for Dreyfus. In addition to Scheurer-Kestner, there were Georges Clemenceau (1841–1929), a journalist and politician; Anatole France; and others. Still, this was not a popular cause. The Socialist leader Jean Jaurès (1859–1914) was for a long time doubtful of Dreyfus' innocence, and when he finally became convinced that a miscarriage of justice had occurred, and was ready to take up the fight, he met reluctance and hesitation in his own party. The Socialist leaders doubted that their adherents, the workers, would perceive a connection between their own interests and the cause of a wealthy Jewish officer.

It is hard to say what would have happened if the army leaders had not got rattled and overplayed their hand. In order to quell once and for all the agitation for Dreyfus, they ordered a trial of Esterhazy, and he was acquitted. Picquart, one of the witnesses against Esterhazy, was arrested and imprisoned. This arbitrary procedure provoked one of the great political documents of modern times—*J'accuse* (1898). In this open letter addressed to the president of the republic, Émile Zola (1840–1902) stated the case against the army leaders briefly and concisely, singling out the responsible officers by name and devoting to each of them a single paragraph beginning *J'accuse*. The publication led to proceedings against Zola, and rightly expecting that he would be condemned, he fled to England, where he continued the fight. Zola's intervention represented the turning point in the Dreyfus Affair. Immense public interest had been aroused, and every step taken in the proceedings was carefully scrutinized. It emerged that in order to strengthen the case against Dreyfus, documents had been falsified. Colonel Hubert Henry, who had done this falsification, committed suicide; Esterhazy fled to England. Under these circumstances the highest court of appeal on June 3, 1899, set aside the previous condemnation of Dreyfus and ordered a new trial. But the military were unwilling to accept the humiliation of the rehabilitation of Dreyfus. It was widely assumed that the officers were preparing a *coup d'état* to overthrow the republican regime.

This threat against the existing regime made all the adherents of the republic realize that they had to act and to act quickly. For the first time in European history Socialists declared their willingness to support a bourgeois government. On June 22, 1899, René Waldeck-Rousseau, a member of a well-known family that was both republican and Catholic, and a man who had proved himself an able administrator in previous governments, formed a coalition government reaching from the right of center to the left, with the suppressor of the Paris Commune of 1871, Gaston de Galliffet, as minister of war and the left-wing Socialist Alexandre Millerand (1859–1943) as minister of commerce. When the new trial culminated in a grotesque verdict which confirmed Dreyfus' guilt while conceding him "extenuating circumstances," the Waldeck-Rousseau government was strong enough to pardon him.

In the course of the Affair the personal fate of Dreyfus became relatively insignificant. When Dreyfus accepted pardon from the Waldeck-Rousseau government, Charles Péguy, a young French writer, wrote: "We would have died for Dreyfus. Dreyfus did not die for Dreyfus."[3] In Péguy's opinion Dreyfus was no Dreyfusard; he should have continued to insist on his full rehabilitation because the fight had involved irreconcilable principles and ought therefore to have ended with the full victory of the right principles over the wrong ones—of the republican over the authoritarian ideas.

THE EMERGENCE OF A NEW IDEOLOGY ON THE RIGHT

The obstinacy of the anti-Dreyfusards, which appeared to be stupid, if not downright criminal, becomes more comprehensible when the Affair is seen as a struggle for principles. The most influential advocate of a monarchical revival in France was Charles Maurras (1868–1952), who fought for his idea in a number of brilliantly written essays and articles, notably his *Enquête sur la monarchie* (1900). But Maurras' concept of monarchy had little to do with the institution as it had existed in France. In his view monarchy, army, and church were necessary because they formed and maintained discipline and order. Discipline and order were the conditions of national strength. National power and vitality depended on the completeness with which the individual was willing to identify and subordinate himself to the national organization of which he was part. Against the revolutionary doctrines of individual rights, Maurras set the idea of a hierarchically organized society. Therefore to him the question of Dreyfus' actual guilt or innocence was unimportant. The individual had to be sacrificed if his rehabilitation would damage the prestige of institutions—like the army—which were essential for the life of the nation. Similar views were championed by another great figure of that period, Maurice Barrès. He placed particular emphasis on the idea that every nation was a racial unit and that those of other races have no rights as citizens. One of Barrès' novels bears the characteristic title *Les Déracinés* (1897). Gifted as these

[3] Charles Péguy, "Notre Jeunesse," in *Oeuvres en prose 1909–1914* (Paris, 1957), p. 541.

The chief editors of the *Action Française*. *Charles Maurras and Leon Daudet, and some of their collaborators shown together in 1917. The* Action Française *was a newspaper that promulgated the ideas of the French nationalist right.*

writers were, they must be counted among the intellectual ancestors of all the antiliberal and antidemocratic movements of the twentieth century. Their intense nationalism and racism, their attacks against Jews as an alien internationally minded force, their praise of discipline and military values, their contempt for law and right in favor of strength and vitality contained the germs of Fascist philosophy.

The Dreyfus Affair gave to the republic and to the republicans a prestige which they had never possessed before. High courage had been necessary to defend Dreyfus, for the Affair had aroused violent emotions. If Zola had not fled to England he might have been assassinated. Scheurer-Kestner was beaten in the streets; Dreyfus' lawyer was shot at; stones were thrown at windows in the houses of Dreyfus supporters; and the police were very slow in protecting the Dreyfusards. But after the Affair was over, the individuals who had risked their careers and their lives for the sake of justice were highly esteemed. In the following decades most of those who played a leading role in French politics were men who had first attracted public attention as defenders of Dreyfus: Clemenceau, Briand, Millerand, Viviani, Caillaux, Blum.

As a result of the Dreyfus Affair the political right acquired an ideology; the left received a new sense of direction, becoming aware that the aims of the French Revolution had not been realized, that the social problems inherent in the rise of industrial society involved new tasks to which the structure of government must be adapted. It was characteristic that the history of the French Revolution, previously a rather neglected field of study, now became a topic of scholarly interest. Indicative was the establishment of a chair for the history of the French Revolution at the Sorbonne.

THE CONSOLIDATION OF THE REPUBLIC

Obviously, progress toward a more democratic society could be achieved only if those institutions which had shown themselves open enemies of the government and obstructed its policy were deprived of power. The chief target was the army, which was now brought under civilian control: promotions to the rank of general in the army were taken out of the hands of a military council and placed in those of the minister of war, a civilian. He was inclined to favor those officers whom he considered to be reliable republicans. But while this measure did eliminate the danger of an antirepublican military coup, it also had the effect of splitting the officer corps into monarchist and republican groups. Moreover, the influence of political considerations did not always bring the most capable generals into the forefront; for instance, the selection of Maurice Gamelin (1872–1958), an officer popular among republican politicians but of moderate military gifts, as commander in chief at the beginning of the Second World War demonstrates the disadvantages of these political appointments.

The other force which had shown itself openly hostile to the republic was the Church, and the attempts at curbing its influence became the crucial issue in French politics in the first decade of the twentieth century. The problem had two aspects. One was the legal relationship between the Roman Catholic Church and the state; this was regulated by Napoleon's Concordat, according to which members of the secular clergy were paid by the state, and bishops were appointed by the Church from a list of names approved by the government. Another problem arose from the leading role which the Church had in education. A large number of French schools were controlled by Roman Catholic religious orders, which provided most of the teaching personnel. Even before the Dreyfus Affair the government had undertaken to build additional state schools and to increase their attractiveness by offering free primary education. The religious orders, however, continued to control a great many schools. After the Dreyfus Affair the government decided on a policy of reducing the number and influence of these schools. The means which the government used was a more rigid interpretation of the law regulating the existence of associations. Religious orders were declared to be associations; to exist legally, they had to obtain authorization, which required a legislative act. In 1902 Waldeck-Rousseau, whose policy had been to limit the influence of the Church on education, but who had not been anxious to eliminate all Catholic schools, resigned and was succeeded by Émile Combes (1835–1921), a fanatic anti-Catholic. Combes decided to refuse authorization to most of the religious orders. They had no choice but to leave France. The measures against the orders were vehemently denounced by the Church and the entire Catholic clergy, and provoked widespread demonstrations against the government all over France. The possibilities of a compromise between the anti-Catholic political powers and the Church began to disappear. In 1904 a law was passed that prohibited all teaching by religious orders. The relations between France and the Vatican were broken off and the Concordat was terminated. Diplomatic relations between France and the Holy See were restored only after the First World War, and then the religious orders were permitted to return.

The outcome of this conflict was the separation of church and state in 1906. The state guaranteed freedom of conscience but refused to pay the clergy. In France, where for centuries the Catholic Church and the state had been closely linked, this break between the two was revolutionary. Certain practical issues kept tensions alive until the First World War. The most difficult problem concerned the ownership of Church buildings. The state claimed them, but was willing to give them to private societies organized for this purpose, which might lease them to the Church. The Church, however, maintained that it must have the right of ownership. Because of the pressure of the Church, the private societies were not formed, and the state closed Church buildings, a step that resulted in excited demonstrations, with the police guarding Church doors. On Sundays Catholic worshipers knelt outside the closed churches, on the steps and in the streets, stopping all traffic.

Only slowly and gradually were compromises reached. In the long run, however, the situation created by the separation of Church and state did no serious damage to the Church. French Catholicism survived, and the hostility between Church and state died down. A man like Aristide Briand, who had guided the law of separation through the Chamber of Deputies and had been denounced by Catholics as an irresponsible revolutionary, would become in later years a leader respected by all groups.

The educational policy of the government could not be confined to eliminating the influence of the Church. The vacuum had to be filled, and the importance of infusing education with republican ideals was apparent. New schools had to be created; more teachers had to be trained, and they had to be guided by new educational ideas. The center from which the government's educational philosophy spread was the École Normale Supérieure, which prepared the future professors of high schools and universities. It provided an anticlerical, secular education, inspired by a belief in human rights and scientific progress. Whether taught directly at the École Normale Supérieure or by professors trained there, school teachers became the protagonists of the spirit of the Third Republic. Many novels describe the situation in the villages where the aristocratic landowner and the priest represented the Old Regime, while the mayor and the school teacher embodied the spirit of the French Revolution.

THE RISE OF NEW TENSIONS

The governments that carried through the rehabilitation of Dreyfus and the separation of church and state—those of Waldeck-Rousseau and Combes—were left-center coalitions, and their measures were prepared by the *cartel des gauches,* a committee including representatives of all the center and leftist parties. After limiting the political role of the army and the Church, the government had to determine to what extent it would undertake social reform in favor of the masses of the people, particularly the workers. On this question the *cartel des gauches* broke up; this was a demonstration of the validity of the old proverb that "Frenchmen wear their hearts on the left and their pocketbooks on the right." Some improvements in the situation of the workers were made, such as the setting of minimum standards for safety and hygiene in factories and mines, but in the crucial issues of modern industrialization—social security, the legalization of collective bargaining—little was done; France was far behind Great Britain and Germany. The failure to harvest concrete advantages from their support of the left during and after the Dreyfus Affair created dissatisfaction among the workers and increased their susceptibility to revolutionary appeals. The trade unions encouraged soldiers to mutiny. From 1906 on, there were frequent strikes, some of which had significant political consequences. In 1906 a mining disaster for which the workers held the mine owners responsible led to a strike in which, to the indignation of the Socialists and other radicals of the left, Prime Minister Clemenceau ordered troops to protect the strikebreakers. A strike of the postal workers resulted in the adoption of a law forbidding state employees to strike. And this law was regarded as a further demonstration that the power of the state was being brutally used against the masses. In 1911 the government defeated a strike of railway workers by ordering mobilization; the workers were forced to run the railroads under military command. These events weakened the political center: indignation over the government's lack of zeal for social reform and over its support for antilabor forces strengthened the left. Fear arising from the radicalization of the workers and resentment aroused by labor unrest helped the right to recover from its defeat in the Dreyfus Affair.

In the years immediately before the outbreak of the First World War the political struggle in France developed into a fight between right and left. Among the many issues over which they clashed, the most important were a modernization of the taxation system, particularly the institution of a progressive income tax, and an extension of conscription from two to three years. The left wanted an income tax which would fall mainly on the well-to-do

Jean Jaurès. *The French Socialist leader speaking in 1913 against the law requiring three-year military service.*

classes and might pay for social legislation, and was unwilling to see more money go for military expenses, of which its members disapproved in any case. But the tax reform failed, while the prolongation of military service was adopted. The main opponents in these struggles were Joseph Caillaux (1863–1944), a wealthy financier of progressive outlook, and Raymond Poincaré (1860–1934), a lawyer from Lorraine. The trend toward the right was indicated also by the election of Poincaré to the presidency of the republic in January, 1913. Yet, as the elections to the Chamber in the following spring showed, a countertrend soon set in, and the further course of French policy seemed undecided when war broke out in 1914.

FOREIGN POLICY

In the decade before the outbreak of the war, left and right were beginning also to differ about foreign policy. In the years of the Dreyfus Affair and the struggle over the separation of church and state the conduct of foreign policy had been almost independent of the domestic party struggles. From 1898 to 1905 the foreign ministry had been held by one man—Théophile Delcassé (1852–1923)—and France had a number of extremely capable ambassadors who remained at the same post for unusually long periods—Paul Cambon in London for over twenty years (1898–1920), Camille Barrère in Rome for more than twenty-five (1897–1924). Foreign policy was not subjected to pressure from economic interest groups because France was almost self-sufficient, at least more self-sufficient than any other industrial nation. This situation made for the ready acceptance of the protective tariffs which the agricultural interests desired. From 1892, when a new tariff was adopted, France was a highly protected country. Undoubtedly as a result of this protection, French agricultural prices were above those in the world market and agriculture remained highly profitable. France's export trade was not much affected by the adoption of a protective tariff because the exports were primarily luxury goods—wine, leatherware, textiles—and their sales suffered little from countermeasures by other countries.

France had already aquired an extended colonial empire and there was no pronounced economic interest in further colonial expansion. Although France did participate in the imperialist race of the 1890's, it quickly abandoned this policy after the setback at Fashoda. France retained, however, a serious concern in the countries on the North African shore across the Mediterranean: Tunisia and Morocco. This interest was political and strategic rather than economic, because in case of war the control of these countries by another power might make the transport of troops from Algeria to France impossible, and might even open France to an attack from the south. In the interest of securing domination in this area the French were willing to abandon other colonial claims. They conceded to the British their rights in Egypt and recognized the Italian demands on Tripoli. In compensation Great Britain and Italy acknowledged France's predominant interest in Morocco. Since neither of these states had claims on Morocco their concrete gains from these agreements were greater than those of France. But the ties with Great Britain and Italy gave France increased weight in Europe. This was the chief aim of French foreign policy: the nation was to become again a factor to be reckoned with in Europe. In the pursuit of this policy, financial strength was a precious asset. By means of loans France was able to establish close ties with Russia. French firms invested widely in Russian private industry, particularly in mining and metallurgy. Indeed, one third of all foreign investments in nongovernmental enterprises in Russia were of French origin. But the French banks also took up a substantial proportion of Russian government loans. At the time of the outbreak of the First World War almost half of the loans which the Russian government issued were held by foreigners and the French people held 80 per cent of this amount.

Thus France had again become powerful in European politics, a situation disadvantageous to Germany, which since the war of 1870–1871 had attempted to keep France isolated. Indicative of the tension between the two states is the fact that between 1871 and the outbreak of the First World War no official visit between French and German statesmen ever took place. Whether the maintenance of such a rigidly hostile posture was unavoidable, or whether after France had reasserted its position in Europe some gradual lessening of the tension could have been effected remains an open question. There were French financial circles interested in economic cooperation with Germany. Left-wing groups would have liked the government to spend less on defense and more on social reform. Moreover, the French Socialists were pacifists and their leader, Jean Jaurès, gave eloquent voice to their ideals. Yet there was deep emotional resistance to any attempt at reconciliation with Germany. Throughout this period, on the Place de la Concorde in Paris, where each large French city was represented by a statue, the statue of Strasbourg remained veiled in black. The French did not envisage a war to reconquer Alsace-Lorraine, but there was strong feeling that as long as Germany held Alsace-Lorraine, cooperation between the two States was impossible. French foreign policy, it was felt, ought to hold the line against Germany. And this indeed remained the prevailing tendency of that policy.

The Mediterranean Powers

The constitutional arrangements in Spain and Italy were externally very similar to those of Great Britain. But below the surface the differences were great. In Spain and Italy the kings could exert some influence of their own by means of the army, commanded by generals conservative in outlook and bound by deep loyalty to the crown. Moreover, the political systems of Spain and Italy, despite two-chamber parliaments and the dependence of the governments on securing votes of confidence from these chambers, were actually pseudoparliamentary. The parliamentary form served to disguise the rule of a relatively small social group; the majority of the people were powerless, and in both countries the Church was a powerful force resisting change.

In both Italy and Spain the middle classes, the chief protagonists of liberalism, formed only a small section of the population; in Spain Catalonia almost alone possessed a middle class. Both countries were predominantly agricultural, and the rural areas, dominated and controlled by the owners of large landed estates, retained a feudal aspect. There were a few highly industrialized regions: in Italy, around Turin and Milan; in Spain, Barcelona and wide stretches of Catalonia around it in the northeast, Andalusia with its coal and zinc mines in the south, and the rich, foreign-owned copper mines of Riotinto in the southwest. Even in these districts industrial development was still embryonic, however, and the workers were subjected to all the hardships of the beginnings of industrialization. Wages were so low that not only the father of a family but the wife and the children had to work. Treated with ruthlessness and forming a small minority, the workers were receptive to ideas of revolutionary change, and this radical activism is indicated by the fact that a high proportion— almost one third of them—were members of labor organizations. Those who were organized were divided among various movements. Marxism, anarchism, and syndicalism all had adherents, and the radicalism of the workers was frequently expressed in violence. The rest of Europe regarded Italy and Spain as unstable and threatened by revolution.

SPAIN

In Spain the rule of a small group—great landowners allied to a few wealthy industrialists—behind a parliamentary façade had been secured by agreements made in the 1870's between the Conservative leader Antonio Canovas and the Liberal leader Mateo Sagasta. They arranged that each party would constitute a government for a number of years and then hand it over to the other party, which would arrange new elections. It was a foregone conclusion that these elections would produce the desired majority for the party in power. Suffrage was limited to the propertied classes, and in the rural areas the *cacique,* a government official, determined who should vote and how to vote. By the end of the century, discontent with the system was increasing. A group of young writers, known as the Generation of 1898, was particularly vocal in advocating political and social reforms. In an article which soon became famous one of the leaders of this group, Miguel de Unamuno (1864–1936), made a distinction between the political nation and the real nation, stating that the real nation was entirely unrepresented in politics.

Dissatisfaction increased with the defeat suffered by Spain in the Spanish-American War and the resultant loss of Cuba and the Philippines. In addition to being a national humiliation, the defeat created serious economic problems. Officials, military officers, priests, entire religious orders, had to be settled and reestablished after their return to Spain. Moreover, Cuba and the Philippines had absorbed a certain part of Spain's industrial production. Faced with a rising wave of discontent, the ruling group began to feel insecure. In both parties, the Liberals and the Conservatives, the feeling grew that revolution could be avoided only if broader groups of the population were drawn more closely to the state. A competition for the masses set in between the two parties, and the tacit understanding which had secured the tenures of successive Conservative and Liberal governments broke down. Among the Conservatives, the leader of a group urging an energetic policy of renovation and social reform was Antonio Maura (1853–1925), who was prime minister in 1903–1904 and returned to that office in 1907. But because Maura was not willing to observe any longer the agreed rules of the political game, unrest set in and a revolutionary outbreak, triggered by protests against the conscription of young workers for a campaign in Morocco, occurred in Barcelona.

During the so-called Tragic Week of Barcelona, in July, 1909, the masses seized the city, and their long-endured suppression and sufferings exploded in acts of violence. Twenty-two churches were destroyed and thirty-four convents burned to the ground. After the revolt had been defeated by military forces, the government carried out a number of executions; that of Francisco Ferrer, a well-known intellectual anarchist, aroused wide indignation because valid proofs of his role in the uprising were lacking. The entire revolt was a spontaneous outbreak of dissatisfaction rather than a well-planned conspiracy. The actions of the masses as well as the reaction of the government strongly revealed the violence underlying Spanish political life.

Moreover, the Tragic Week of Barcelona disclosed the two basic difficulties militating against effective opposition to the established order in Spain. One was the unavoidable connection of all reform movements with anticlericalism. As in France—and what had happened in France was highly influential in Spain—the extension of the state school system and restriction of the influence of the teaching orders became the most essential demand of the reformers. The anticlericalism of the intellectuals in the urban centers reinforced the bond between the Church and the conservative landowners, but the Church had strong supporters also among the masses, for the clergy and the numerous religious orders were frequently the refuge of the sons and daughters of the poor.

At the same time, reformers were handicapped by the fact that the most industrialized part of the country, and hence the center of liberal and progressive movements, was Catalonia, with its capital Barcelona. With some justification the Catalans were suspected by the rest of Spain of separatist tendencies, and for this reason the revolt of July, 1909, did not spread beyond Barcelona. It was difficult to organize a unified opposition on a national basis. Thus the regime was able to survive. Maura, the Conservative prime minister, was overthrown soon after the Tragic Week of Barcelona because his plans for social reform were believed to have seduced the revolutionaries to action. The Liberal leader, Jose Canalejas, who made an attempt to carry out an anticlerical program with the help of all the forces of the left, was assassinated in 1912. With the wisdom of hindsight it is not difficult to see that the alternatives in Spain were dictatorship and revolution.

ITALY

The loss of Cuba and the Philippines exemplified Spain's decline as an imperial power. If it was still counted among the great powers this status had its basis in tradition rather than in the nation's actual strength. In contrast, Italy was a newcomer among the great powers and the recent struggles, through which unification had been achieved, left Italian political life strongly tinged with nationalism, which now manifested itself in the urge to demonstrate that Italy could be rightly counted among the great powers.

The Italian social structure showed the same sharp contrasts as that of Spain. In the south were large landed estates owned by an old nobility which was allied with the Church. Little industry existed in the south, and the percentage of the people going to school or receiving some technical training was smaller than in the rest of Italy. In the north, industry extended over a wider area than in Spain. Italy's performance as an industrial and military power was limited by the fact that its resources of pig iron and steel were insignificant, but with the help of waterpower a modern textile industry had been developed. Northern Italy had a large working population and a prosperous middle class. The nation's social stresses were increased by the great fecundity of the peasants of the south. For them the only possibility was immigration either to the industrial districts of the north, where the steady influx of unskilled workers held down wages and nourished revolutionary radicalism, or to foreign countries. National unification had primarily been the work of the middle classes in northern and central Italy, and after unification had been achieved the contrast between the firmly entrenched feudal nobility in the south and the revolutionary proletariat in the north stifled further liberal advances.

The outstanding figure among Italian statesmen in the last decades of the nineteenth century was Francesco Crispi (1819–1901), one of the heroes of the *Risorgimento* period. Crispi decided to turn Italian energies to colonial expansion, a policy that corresponded with Italy's ambition to be a great power. Many Italians still lived under the rule of the Habsburg empire in South Tyrol, Gorizia, and Istria. Crispi, however, wanted to turn Italian nationalist ambitions away from these areas because he was anxious to avoid a clash with Austria-Hungary and its ally, Germany; the only support for Italy in an anti-Austrian policy could come from France, and such an alliance would be inferior in strength to the German-Austrian combination. Moreover, Italian colonial expansion might overcome the feeling that Italian policy had reached a dead end. Crispi decided to enter the race with the other great powers for the control of African areas which had not yet been subjected to European rule; because Italy had a small colonial possession along the Red Sea, he wanted to extend its rule in the area to neighboring Ethiopia. A first Italian advance from the Red Sea toward Ethiopia had suffered a setback at Dogali (1887). But then the Italians helped Menelik (1844–1913), one of the tribal chiefs, to make good his claim to the imperial throne. In return, so Crispi claimed, Menelik had recognized an Italian protectorate over Ethiopia. But neither Menelik nor the other Ethiopian tribal chiefs acknowledged this claim and there were frequent military encounters between Italian troops and local Ethiopian forces along the frontier between Eritrea and Ethiopia. In 1896, against the better judgment of his military advisers, Crispi ordered the advance into Ethiopia of the troops stationed in Eritrea. Crispi miscalculated his opponent's military strength. The Ethiopians were good warriors; they had received some training from French officers and had been equipped with guns by the French. At Aduwa, in difficult mountainous terrain, the Italian army of 20,000 men—half of them Italians, half of them natives— encountered a well-directed force of about 100,000 Ethiopians. The Italians were completely defeated; about 6,000 were killed, 2,000 wounded, and 2,000 taken prisoner. When the news of the defeat reached Rome, the Crispi government resigned amid immense public demonstrations demanding the immediate end of the African adventure. Crispi's successor, Antonio Rudinì (1839–1908), made peace with Menelik immediately, thus recognizing the independence of Ethiopia. Italy's status among the European states plunged. Instead of solidifying Italian national unity, the attempt to become a world power had only increased discontent, and the Ethiopian adventure was followed by years of unrest.

Moreover, the protective tariffs adopted by France had provoked Italian countermeasures and the ensuing tariff war diminished Italian exports and impeded industrial expansion by cutting off loans from French banks. Unemployment rose in the industrial areas, and in May, 1898, bread riots broke out in Milan, barricades were erected in the streets, and order was restored only after some fighting and a declaration of martial law. A general, Luigi Pelloux (1839–1924), became prime minister. He ruled by royal decree and tried to establish a military dictatorship. He was defeated in the elections of 1900, and a month later King Humbert, who had appointed Pelloux and had supported his dictatorial policy, was assassinated.

Thereafter, the situation quieted. An important reason for the improvement was a gradual upward trend in the economic situation. Moreover, the radical left had overplayed its hand. Railway strikes in 1902 and a general strike in 1904 aroused widespread indignation. They appeared inspired by political motives rather than by economic hardships, and were viewed as an attempt at revolution. In consequence, all the moderate forces drew more closely together; the threat of revolution even led to a softening of the hostility between the Italian state and Roman Catholicism. Previously no Roman Catholic was supposed to participate in Italian political life, but Pope Pius X now permitted Catholics to enter the party struggle because the safety of the social order was threatened. In the elections of October, 1904, the radical left suffered harsh defeat. Moreover, in 1903 an unusually clever parliamentary tactician, Giovanni Giolitti (1842–1928), became prime minister. His consummate political skill assured a remarkable degree of political stability. Between the turn of the century and the beginning of the war Giolitti was prime minister three times—from 1903 to 1905, from 1906 to 1909, from 1911 to 1914. And even when out of office he remained the dominant figure in the Italian political scene. His main concern was the modernization of Italian economic life, and this meant industrialization. In this policy Giolitti had success. In the twenty years before the outbreak of the First World War industry in the national production increased its share from 20 to 25 per cent. Most important was the development of the silk industry, and favored by protective tariffs, some heavy industry began to develop.

For Giolitti industrialization also meant democratization. He inaugurated numerous measures of social reform. Trade unions were legalized and collective bargaining was promoted. Minimal standards for hygienic conditions in factories were laid down and working conditions for women and children were improved. The railroads, previously privately owned, were taken over by the state and in consequence both the situation of the railroad workers and the functioning of the transportation system improved. By such means Giolitti tried to provide the government with a broader democratic basis; he was anxious to draw the Socialists into collaboration with the government. The Italian Socialists were split into a revolutionary and a reformist wing and Giolitti aimed at strengthening the reformist group. The climax of Giolitti's democratization policy was, in 1912, an electoral reform which raised the number of voters from 3.5 to 8 million and made universal suffrage of males over thirty years old a reality. Only illiterates who had done no military service were denied the right to vote.

But his regime had its less progressive, dark side. His fundamental aim might have been the strengthening of democracy, but in the handling of the parliamentary machinery he was cynical and opportunistic. To the disgust of his liberal supporters, he accepted the support of the Catholics when this seemed to promise electoral success, and he permitted the south to remain in a state which made a sham out of parliamentarism and democracy. He made no serious attempt to institute agrarian reform in the south, to dissolve the great *latifundia* and provide land for the numerous peasants living there in abject poverty. Instead, the opponents of change—the great landowners and the Church—were left in control of the south. Giolitti even made some concession to Church interests by facilitating religious education in those localities where the parents demanded it. This meant that in practice the schools in the south were in the hands of the priests, who were themselves only half educated, and the masses there remained superstitiously pious and illiterate. The illiteracy rate in some areas was more than 90 per cent.

Giolitti's surrender of the south to vested interests had sinister consequences. The people remained bitterly poor. If possible they emigrated. More than half a million Italians, out of a population of about thirty million, left the country in 1910. Those who remained could not be employed in work which demanded even a minimum of skill; nor did they have the money to buy industrial goods. The internal market, and the entire industrial development of Italy, was retarded by the south. Giolitti had reasons for ignoring this problem; in return for being left in control in their areas, the southern deputies—representing the conservative land-owning group—supported his proposals for economic reforms in the industrial north. But because the south remained underdeveloped Giolitti's policy of forcing the industrial development of the north had only limited results.

For what went on in Italian parliamentary life in the times of Giolitti's domination, the Italians used the word *trasformismo,* after the political maneuver by which a deputy to parliament—even if he did not belong to the parties which composed the government—voted in favor of a govern-ment proposal and in return obtained special advantages for the district he represented. Thus the government ruled with fluctuating majorities. Ideals and principles became a façade behind which the deputies bargained for political and material advantages. This debasement of liberal and demo-cratic values and principles kept alive discontent with the existing system. The most devastating attack against Giolitti's regime was launched by a young Italian historian, Gaetano Salvemini. In a pamphlet character-istically entitled *Il ministro della mala vita* ("The Minister for Misery") he formulated the program which Italian liberalism ought to adopt: partition of the *latifundia,* spread of secular education, honest elections.

Thus, the means which Giolitti employed worked against the goal which he wanted to reach: a secure democratic basis for the regime. Contempt for democracy and parliamentarism and demands for a change of system became widespread on the left and on the right. In the Socialist party the reformist wing had the upper hand only for a brief period. In general the radical wing, which had anarchist tendencies and argued for revolutionary actions, strikes, and sabotage, set the tone, and at the party congress of 1912 the radicals gained control. One of their leaders, Benito Mussolini, became editor of the *Avanti,* the official paper of the Socialist party.

Because Giolitti's support on the left was insecure, he was willing to make concessions to the right. Diplomatic preparation for the war against Turkey for the conquest of Tripoli, which began in 1911, had been going on since the end of the nineteenth century; Giolitti's decision to embark on this enterprise at this particular time was meant to take the wind out of the sails of the nationalists on the right. They ascribed the defeats of Dogali and Aduwa to the lack of heroism inherent in democratic government, and nationalism became imbued with hostility toward parliamentarism and democracy. These resentments and aspirations found expression in a nation-alistic political movement organized by Enrico Corradini, which had a powerful spokesman in Gabriele D'Annunzio, Italy's most famous writer; he proclaimed the need for one great man to rule the country, and found many adherents among the younger generation.

Giolitti's expectations proved incorrect; the conquest of Tripoli increased the appeal of antiparliamentary nationalism instead of weakening it. The elections in 1913, based on the new law establishing universal suffrage, demonstrated the strength of radicalism on the left and on the right. It cannot be claimed that Giolitti's system resulted in the firm establishment of parliamentary democracy in Italy in 1914.

THE AUTHORITARIAN GOVERNMENTS

To what extent Great Britain, France, Spain, and Italy were democracies can be disputed, but in all of them parliaments existed which decided on the composition of the government. This was not the case in Germany, Austria-Hungary, or Russia, in the sense that their governments were not dependent on parliaments. Russia at the beginning of the twentieth century was an autocracy; the system of government in the various parts of the Habsburg monarchy varied; the German empire had a constitution, the rights of the citizens in Germany were legally secured, and elected representatives had a part, although not a decisive one, in the government. However, because the power of the parliaments insofar as they existed was limited, the rulers of these three countries— Nicholas II, Francis Joseph, William II—were highly influential in determining policy.

Germany

The authoritarian system of the German empire was primarily a product of its historical development in the preceding century. Because the unification of Germany had been accomplished by Prussia, the political structure of the German Reich bore a Prussian pattern.

Prussia had successfully withstood the middle-class revolution of the nineteenth century. Its constitution was highly authoritarian; the army was outside civilian control, under direct command of the king, and the Prussian parliament was elected by a method which guaranteed control to the great landowners from east of the Elbe, the *Junkers*.

The Prussian monarch and the Prussian leaders did not want to see their system of government submerged in a wider Reich. Hence, the German empire became not a unitary state but a federal state composed of twenty-five individual states. With the exception of three free cities, the rulers of these states were princes; the government of each of these states appointed a delegate to a federal council, the Bundesrat, which met in Berlin under the chairmanship of the delegate appointed by the Prussian king, who regularly designated the Prussian prime minister for this post. It was as president of this federation of princes that the king of Prussia held the title of German emperor. Since the number of votes which each state possessed within the council was determined by its geographical extent and

A military review in Berlin in 1900. *The street is Berlin's chief avenue, "Unter den Linden," and the building in the background is the University.*

the size of its population, the Bundesrat was dominated by Prussia.

The leaders of Prussian policy at the time of German unification had to take into account, however, that the chief resistance to unification had come from the princely rulers of the German states and the groups bound to them through interest or loyalty. The chief protagonists of unification had been the masses of the people, particularly the middle class. Thus, in order to check separatist tendencies which might come into the foreground in the Bundesrat, a parliament—the Reichstag—was created, with members elected on the basis of a most progressive voting system: universal suffrage of all males above twenty-five years of age.

Legislation for the Reich had to be passed by both the Bundesrat and the Reichstag. The areas over which the Reich could decide and legislate were strictly limited: foreign affairs, naval affairs, the mail and the telegraph, customs, colonies. And it had the right to establish common standards for the administration of justice and military affairs, although the armies remained under the control of the rulers of the individual states and were placed under a unified command only in wartime. The Reich was to receive a certain percentage of the taxes raised by the states, and it had the right to levy indirect taxes.

Although the tasks of the Reich were limited, they were extended enough to require governmental agencies, and the manner in which the federal administration was organized reinforced the dominating position of Prussia.

The control and supervision of the federal administration was entrusted to the chairman of the Bundesrat, who was expected to explain and to defend new legislation in the Reichstag. Since this chairman was always the Prussian prime minister, he combined in his person two functions. As head of the federal administration he had the title of chancellor—*Reichskanzler*—and had under him a number of high officials, "secretaries," who administered the various areas under federal control: foreign affairs, naval affairs, colonies, and so on. As Prussian prime minister he directed Prussian policy and presided over the Prussian cabinet, composed of "ministers": of the interior, of war, of education, of finance, and so on. This arrangement gave the chancellor a remarkable amount of independence. He was appointed by the Prussian king and could be removed neither by the Bundesrat nor by the Reichstag. Despite the strength of his position, the chancellor could more easily prevent a new departure in politics than initiate one. He could frustrate measures of which he disapproved by playing against each other the Reich and Prussia, the Bundesrat and the Reichstag. But he had to maneuver carefully to move these different forces in the same direction. Thus, the complicated political structure of the Reich led to strange contradictions. It made it possible for Prussia to take the leading role without having to give up its system of government and its autonomy. But in providing guarantees against meddling in Prussian affairs, the constitution of the Reich also secured the other German states against interference in their systems of government. Hence, within the German empire great political diversity existed. In contrast to the conservative north, the southern German states—Bavaria, Württemberg, Baden—were liberal, even democratic, and they had parliamentary governments. The majority of the German population was Protestant but the Catholic minority was very considerable; in 1900 there were 35 million Protestants and 20 million Roman Catholics in Germany. Some of the German states were prevailingly Protestant; in others Catholicism had an important political influence.

The complex constitution doubtless required of the Reich's leaders great art in balancing the divergent forces which constituted the German empire. The unified Reich was Bismarck's creation and its constitution had been tailored to his forceful but prudent personality. He was also favored by the fact that in the first decade after unification, an equilibrium of social forces still existed: the conflict between the interests of agriculture and industry was still muted. But toward the close of the nineteenth century the conditions for a successful functioning of the German constitution began to disappear: Bismark was dismissed in 1890, and at the end of the century there was a rapid and striking change in the German social structure which upset the delicate balance of social forces. The extent of the changes in Germany between 1870 and 1914 can best be illustrated by a few statistics. The population increased from 41 million to 65 million; whereas in 1870 more than half of the population had been employed in agriculture, by 1914 this proportion had been reduced to less than a third. Germany had become a highly industrialized and commercial country.

At the outbreak of the First World War, Germany's merchant marine was the second largest in the world, surpassed only by that of Great Britain. By then, too, Germany was the third largest coal-producing power—behind the United States and only slightly behind Great Britain. Germany produced considerably more pig iron and steel than any other European power, Great Britain included, and almost half as much as the United States. Germany's rich mineral resources favored the development of an armament industry. Krupp, the leading German armament manufacturer, together with Skoda in Austria and the French firm of Schneider-Creusot, dominated the armament market of the world. The electrical and chemical industries also flourished. Some of the German dyestuffs and pharmaceuticals enjoyed a kind of monopoly on the world market. In contrast to the United States and the British empire, Germany produced much more than could be consumed on the domestic market. Between 1887 and 1912 the value of German exports increased 185 per cent. Germany's rise as an industrial world power thus involved a rapid penetration into foreign markets; until 1880 it had traded almost exclusively with other European countries; thereafter Germany began to exchange goods increasingly with other continents.

The mineral resources on which industrial development was based could be found in almost every part of the nation. Most important was the Ruhr, where coal and iron were available. In the southwest, in the areas ceded by France in 1871, were iron and potash; in the east, Upper Silesia was rich in coal; and in central Germany, lignite deposits served the electrical and chemical industries. Thus the impact of industrialization was felt over all the country. Since industrial development in Germany started later than in Great Britain and in France, large capital investments were needed to facilitate competition with the more advanced nations. Such quantities of capital could be provided only by banks, not by the industrial entrepreneurs themselves or by private financiers. In German economic development banking and industrial enterprises became closely interconnected. This alliance promoted the formation of big companies possessing greater efficiency than smaller ones that produced the same goods. In some fields the large enterprises achieved a monopoly; in others a few big industrial companies banded together in cartel agreements that enabled them to fix prices and delimit markets. The members of a cartel could establish high price levels at home to maintain profits while they attempted to conquer foreign markets by "dumping" goods there at low prices. For this reason the German government not only permitted monopolies and cartels but even gave legal protection to cartel agreements;

violators could be brought to court and punished.

Small and middle-sized economic enterprises did not entirely disappear from German economic life, but in Germany there was some truth in the picture, given by Lenin in his treatise on *Imperialism, the Highest Stage of Capitalism,* of the domination of a nation's economic life by a small group of financiers and industrialists.

The rapid development of Germany into a great economic power, and the accompanying rise in wealth in almost all groups of the population, had a dangerously intoxicating effect on the German upper and middle classes. Most of them succumbed to the fatal fascination of the idea of becoming a "world power": Germany ought to have a navy; it ought to have colonies; German passenger ships had to be the largest and fastest. German bankers and industrialists were convinced that wherever they found the opportunity for economic penetration—in Turkey, in China, or anywhere else—they ought to make use of it, regardless of the claims, rights, or interests of other nations. Since Germany was a latecomer on the world scene, they felt, it had to be pushy to gain its due "place in the sun," as William II characterized his realm's political ambitions.

Nevertheless, industrial development in Germany did not progress without conflicts. Wherever industrial and agrarian interests clashed, the *Junkers* were able to put up strong resistance for they dominated the political system of Germany's most powerful state. Moreover, the transition to industrialization was unavoidably accompanied by social tensions, and the gap between entrepreneur and workers was widened by the resentment which Bismarck's repressive antisocialist laws had created. After these laws had lapsed, and as a consequence of the rapid progress of industrialization, the socialists made great strides. The Social Democrats increased their number of deputies in the Reichstag from 35 in 1890 to 110 in 1911 and became the strongest political party. Although by then the Social Democratic party and the allied trade unions had become big bureaucracies inclined to move slowly and cautiously, the Marxian view of the need for a revolution remained dominant among the workers, especially since the government continued to proceed vigorously against all subversive agitation and propaganda.

After 1890 instability was further increased by the fact that the role which the constitution assigned to the emperor, but which actually had been filled by Bismarck, had fallen to a monarch who wanted to rule, but lacked the qualities necessary for doing so.

THE EMPIRE UNDER WILLIAM II

In the public mind, particularly in those countries which fought against Germany in the First World War, William II (ruled 1888–1919) is usually pictured as the prototype of the warlord—imperious, brutal, barbarian.

Indeed, William did like to appear in full military panoply, preferably in the uniform of an officer of the cuirassier guards, in silvery, shining mail and a helmet crowned by a golden eagle. He talked to his ministers and to his people as an officer talks to his soldiers, giving them orders and commands. William felt himself the heir and successor of the absolutist Hohenzollern kings of the eighteenth century. He believed that his power came from God and considered himself, as he said in one of his bombastic speeches, "an instrument of God." Most of all, he felt obliged to maintain the Prussian military tradition. He was hardly aware that the army was no longer an army of mercenaries, the personal property of the monarch, but was now based on general conscription. Addressing a Berlin regiment about the socialist opposition, he told the soldiers that they would have to shoot their fathers and mothers if he ordered them to do so. Because he disapproved of modern dances he forbade all men in uniform to dance the tango, when it became popular in 1913. Since the inner organization of the army, and the appointment of officers, were entirely outside of civilian control, William had some legal justification for believing he could demand absolute obedience.

Nevertheless, he wanted to be more than the preserver of an absolutist tradition. He wanted to be a modern monarch who would lead Germany into a new era of history. He surrounded himself not only with members of the Prussian aristocracy but also with industrialists and bankers. Albert Ballin, the leading spirit of the largest German shipping line, was his friend. Rhenish industrialists such as the Stumms and the Krupps were his favorites. Although in his youth William had participated in meetings of an anti-Semitic group, he was later inclined to favor wealthy Jews and to grant them titles, to the great disgust of the Prussian aristocracy. He was fascinated by discoveries in the natural sciences and delighted in bestowing decorations on outstanding scientists, and occasionally nobilitating them. He preached enthusiastically the need for making Germany a world power. William was a zealous reader of Mahan and accepted his view that sea power was the crucial factor in the struggle of nations and the competition for empire.

This combination of Prussian authoritarianism with faith in technological progress and capitalist expansion corresponded to the inclinations of the German bourgeoisie. In the earlier years of his reign William II was extremely popular. There is some justification for the brilliant satire of the German middle-class mind in Heinrich Mann's novel *The Patrioteer* (1918), in which the hero, a bourgeois parvenu, is depicted as modeling his life in every detail according to that of his ideal, the emperor.

But William II also had many opponents, and their number increased over the years. His adversaries and critics were to be found not only among the socialists, who condemned the entire regime, but also among those who

William II, left, with Admiral von Tirpitz, center, and Admiral von Holzendorf, in 1910.

knew him best. Some considered him to be the gravedigger of the German monarchy. They were aware of his superficiality; his various intellectual and aesthetic enthusiasms were short-lived and he was incapable of sustained effort and serious work. Nervous and restless, he traveled continually from one place to another and expected to be constantly entertained. And these entertainments were not very refined. Quite a public scandal developed when one of his chamberlains, elderly and fat, died of a heart attack while dancing before him in the costume of a ballet girl. Most of all, despite his martial appearance and powerful gestures, William II was weak, easily influenced by men with stronger wills, especially when they presented their ideas in amusing and flattering forms. A kind of Byzantine atmosphere permeated the court. Military men, industrialists, bankers, and courtiers could sway the emperor. In the first decade of his reign William's great favorite was Count Philipp Eulenburg (1847–1921); his homosexual inclinations, which were unknown to the emperor, led to a scandal that severely damaged the prestige of the court. In later years a powerful influence was the secretary of the navy, Admiral Alfred von Tirpitz (1849–1930), who kept alive William's interest in the building of a great navy.

Although he failed to provide unifying direction to the nation, William II was unwilling to concede to his chancellors that decisive influence which Bismarck had possessed. Each chancellor had to struggle against military, naval, and personal influences, and the course of German policy became erratic.

Of Bismarck's successors, the first, Count Leo von Caprivi (chancellor from 1890 to 1894) was a military man; the others were civil servants. Prince Chlodwig von Hohenlohe, (from 1894 to 1900) had been the administrative head of Alsace-Lorraine; Bernhard von Bülow (from 1900 to 1909) came from the diplomatic corps; Theobald von Bethmann-Hollweg (from 1909 to 1917) from the Prussian administration. The appointment of civil servants to high positions of political leadership emphasized the independence of the government from parliamentary influence. But as we have seen, although the role of the Reichstag was limited, its approval of new legislation and taxation was necessary. The Social Democrats, as opponents of the entire system, always voted against the government, which therefore had to seek support from the parties to the right of the socialists. And these were of greatly varying political shadings. The Conservatives spoke chiefly for the agrarian interests, while the Center party included members of every stratum of society since its unifying bond was religion: Roman Catholicism. The bourgeois world was represented by two groups: the National Liberals, who championed the interests of heavy industry; and the Progressives, supported by small entrepreneurs and white-collar workers, and retaining the nineteenth-century ideal of a liberal and democratic Germany.

Cooperation among parties of such varied interests was difficult to achieve, and German domestic policy remained singularly weak in creative legislation. Laws which could be justified by an appeal to nationalism had the best chance to find support among all the nonsocialist parties. The most significant legislation was a finance bill, accepted in 1913, which, in order to permit an increase in the strength of the army, instituted a capital levy that could be raised directly by the federal government. Previously the federal government had been limited to indirect taxes and contributions from the individual states. Measures and laws which had been introduced under Bismarck were perfected. One general law code for the whole of Germany was established. The social-insurance system was extended to additional groups and payments to the elderly and invalids were increased. Working hours for women and children were strictly limited. Although politically Germany remained authoritarian, its administration was efficient and was concerned with the well-being of the citizens.

For the passage of any legislation the government always had to have the vote of both the Conservatives and the National Liberals in addition to the backing of either the Center party or the Progressives to obtain a majority. This support could usually be bought by some concessions to the particular interests of one party or the other. In particular, the Center party was willing to vote with the government in return for obtaining positions for Catholics in the administration.

The crucial aim was to achieve an alliance between the Conservatives and the National Liberals, that is, between agricultural and industrial interests. On one hand this was an economic problem. There was the conflict between the landowner's demand for protective tariffs against American and Russian grain and the industrialist's desire for low food prices which would allow low wages and facilitate competition on the world market. At the beginning of the reign of William II, under Bismarck's

William II with Chancellor von Bethmann - Hollweg in 1910.

successor, Caprivi, agricultural tariffs were lowered in the interest of industrial expansion. But the *Junkers* forced Caprivi's fall and the government changed its course and embarked on a policy of agricultural protection, buying the agreement of the National Liberals by concessions to industrial interests. Thus the rise in agricultural tariffs in 1899 was complementary to the acceptance of a law initiating the building of a fleet of battleships. A large navy provided heavy industry with a continuous flow of government orders, and in the eyes of the leaders of heavy industry this advantage outweighed the disadvantages of protective tariffs; in compensation for obtaining protective tariffs the Conservatives gave up their opposition to a large fleet. The origin of the naval program has to be ascribed to William II's envious admiration of Great Britain and to the influence of Admiral von Tirpitz on the emperor. But it was continuously pursued because it cemented the alliance between agricultural and industrial interests.

This alliance between industry and agriculture also presented a social problem. The Prussian *Junkers* were reluctant to admit members of the bourgeoisie into the ruling group. As in Great Britain, however, there were many points of contact among the wealthiest groups of society, and William II's favorable attitude toward members of the rich bourgeoisie was politically significant in creating bridges between them and the old aristocracy. But in Germany the agricultural and feudal forces continued to dominate the ruling group because German economic development needed government support and the Prussian *Junker* was firmly entrenched in the government. The adjustment of the sons of the bourgeoisie to the feudal and militaristic values of the Prussian nobility was promoted by the control which the government exerted over education. But the crucial factor was the institution of the reserve officer. Service in the army as a reserve officer was an admission ticket to society and to government positions. A commission in the officer corps of a regiment was like membership in a club. Those who were officers would accept only those who shared their standards of behavior. Thus, in Germany aristocratic values were not replaced by bourgeois values; instead, the German high bourgeoisie became feudalized.

However, it should not be assumed that Germany was a totalitarian state. The government was not despotic. On the contrary, the Germans prided themselves on living in a society which was ruled according to law—in a *Rechtsstaat*. In court proceedings legal forms were strictly observed and the individual could be sure of having his rights carefully protected. There was no censorship. The satirical weekly *Simplicissimus*, which attacked the ruling group and the stereotype of the Prussian lieutenant in a witty but savage way, circulated freely and was widely read. If intellectual life in Berlin and in Prussia was stifled by the narrowness and the conservatism of the outlook of the Prussian ruling group, a livelier and freer intellectual climate could be found in other parts of Germany. The cultural life in Munich, the capital of Bavaria, stood in stark contrast to that of Berlin. Munich was the home of the leading German exponents of Expressionism, and of literary figures like the novelist Thomas Mann and the dramatist Frank Wedekind, who advocated a new, freer morality in his plays. If Berlin was the political capital, Munich was the center of modern movements in German art and literature. Nevertheless, opposition to the prevailing militaristic tendencies was essentially powerless. This was strikingly shown in 1913 when popular demonstrations took place in the Alsatian town of Zabern against the troops stationed there. In an arbitrary extension of their functions the military authorities placed the town under martial law, and all the protests of political moderates did not help. William II even congratulated the responsible officer for his energetic behavior.

The amalgamation of the outlook of the rich industrial and financial bourgeoisie with feudal military traditions had a dangerous effect on foreign policy. In Germany's struggle for a "place in the sun," the accent was very much on power politics. Wherever some acquisition of territory seemed possible—in Africa or China or the Pacific—Germany raised claims, and these widespread claims brought about conflicts of interest with almost all the other major European states. The influence of the Prussian Conservatives made it certain that Germany would remain the strongest military power in Europe. But the building of a first-rank navy, combined with the economic competition arising from Germany's growing industrial strength, complicated German relations with Great Britain, traditionally the strongest naval power. Moreover, in order not to endanger the alliance between

"The Lieutenant the Day before Yesterday, Yesterday and Today," a caricature from *Simplicissimus. The caption was presented in slang which is difficult to reproduce in English. The lieutenant says "Yesterday, gambled at the jockey club, improved my finances; then champagne, nothing but champagne."*

agrarian and industrial interests, the government tended to yield to their pressures. Thus, for example, it supported the building of the Baghdad Railway in Turkey by German financial groups, thereby stepping into an area which previously Great Britain and Russia had regarded as exclusively theirs. Because of its ambitious rush into world politics Germany became exposed to pressure from all sides.

The Habsburg Monarchy and the Balkan States

FRANCIS JOSEPH AND THE DISINTEGRATION OF THE HABSBURG EMPIRE

Of the seven great European powers which existed at the turn of the century, Austria-Hungary alone failed to survive the First World War. Even before that conflict, the Habsburg monarchy, including the most different nationalities—Germans, Magyars, Slovaks, Croatians, Czechs, Rumanians, Italians, Poles—was an anachronism. Much of the time, despite feeble and inconsistent attempts at constitutional forms and parliamentarism, it was ruled dictatorially. The anachronistic nature of this monarchy gave to Austria-Hungary, and particularly to the Vienna of the prewar years, a peculiar attraction. Aristocratic and cosmopolitan Vienna seemed to preserve a refined cultural tradition which was disappearing in the rest of Europe. Vienna was the center of the music world, attracting the most famous singers to its opera, and the best orchestra conductors and composers. Johannes Brahms might be seen sitting next to the wife of Johann Strauss; and while Strauss was conducting his waltzes, Brahms wrote on

Mrs. Strauss' fan: "Unfortunately not by Johannes Brahms." The best German actors and actresses performed in the Burgtheater. Vienna was the center of literary trends exploring the complexities of human psychology, and in the coffeehouses the representatives of this modern literary approach—Arthur Schnitzler and Harmann Bahr—might be found talking respectfully to a fragile youth, not yet twenty years old, who had just become famous as the author of a small volume of exquisite poems: Hugo von Hofmannsthal, later to write the libretto of Richard Strauss' *Rosenkavalier* (1911). And there were the elegant Baroque palaces, from which issued carriages drawn by beautiful horses taking their noble and wealthy owners—the Liechtensteins, the Esterházys, the Schwarzenbergs —to Vienna's famous park, the Prater. They all contributed to making the life of the Vienna court the most brilliant in Europe, and because of the scandals in which the wild young Habsburg archdukes became involved, it was also the most romantic.

The embodiment of this anachronism was Emperor Francis Joseph (ruled 1848–1916). In 1900, he had ruled for more than fifty years, and he would go on ruling into the First World War. Having lived through political and personal disasters—having been forced to abandon part of his heritage to Italy, having been pushed out of Germany, having lost his son by suicide and his wife by assassination—he still continued to get up every morning at five to begin the study of the files on his desk and went on to preside over his court, in which the most rigid Spanish etiquette was observed. It is typical of the strength as well as the weakness of this regime that when in June, 1914, Francis Joseph's nephew and presumptive heir, Francis Ferdinand, and his morganatic wife were assassinated at Sarajevo, the emperor's primary reaction was not sorrow about the death of a close relation, but relief that this event would avert the danger that the son of this misalliance might become ruler of Austria-Hungary. "A higher Power has restored the order that I was unhappily unable to maintain" were the words with which he reacted to the news from Sarajevo.

It is not difficult to see why this composite of different nationalities did not survive. Rather, it is difficult to explain why the Habsburg empire continued to exist as long as it did. One reason was that all the great European powers believed that the destruction of this empire would result in a frightening disturbance of the European balance of power. It was feared that if the Habsburg empire collapsed, its Slavic nationals—its Poles, Czechs, Slovaks, Serbs, and Croatians—would turn to Russia thereby allowing it to gain an overwhelmingly strong position in Europe. Moreover, the considerable influence of the Roman Catholic Church was exerted to maintain the Habsburg realm. The frontier between the Roman Catholic and the Eastern Orthodox churches ran through the empire, and the continuing strength of the Roman Catholic Habsburgs seemed

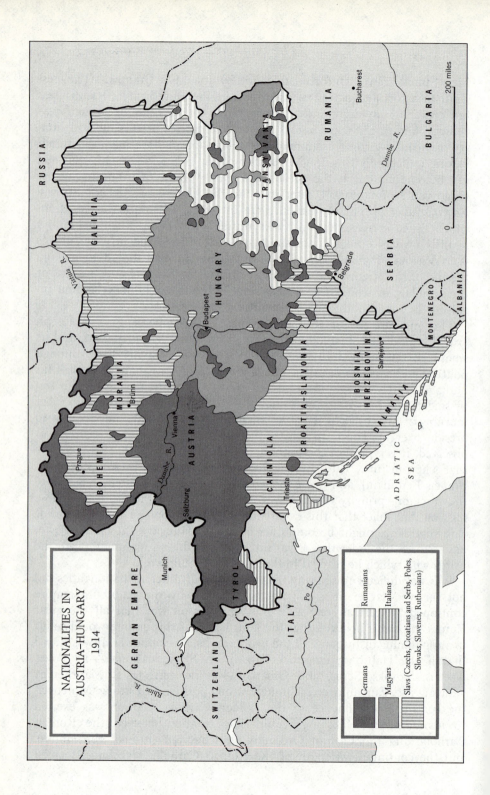

NATIONALITIES IN
AUSTRIA–HUNGARY
1914

RUSSIA

GALICIA

Vistula R.

BOHEMIA

Prague

MORAVIA

Brünn

Danube R.

Vienna

AUSTRIA

Salzburg

GERMAN EMPIRE

Munich

TYROL

SWITZERLAND

Rhine R.

HUNGARY

Budapest

TRANSYLVANIA

RUMANIA

Bucharest

Danube R.

BULGARIA

200 miles

0

Belgrade

SERBIA

BOSNIA–
HERZEGOVINA

Sarajevo

CARNIOLA

CROATIA–SLAVONIA

Trieste

DALMATIA

ADRIATIC
SEA

MONTENEGRO

ALBANIA

ITALY

Po R.

Germans

Magyars

Slavs (Czechs, Croatians and Serbs, Poles,
Slovaks, Slovenes, Ruthenians)

Rumanians

Italians

to the Roman Church a better guarantee for maintaining its position than Slavic states oriented toward the Orthodox tsar.

Furthermore, Austria-Hungary was held together by economic forces. It was a geographic unit; the Danube, which formed the great link between northwestern and southeastern Europe, facilitated an exchange of goods among the regions of the empire. The economy was well balanced. Agricultural production was sufficient to provide food for the areas where natural resources—particularly coal in Bohemia and iron in Styria—stimulated industrial activity.

Despite this development of industry Austria-Hungary remained a predominantly agrarian state. The forms of land ownership forged a further bond within the empire. For the land was in the hands of the nobility. This was particularly true in Hungary, where in 1895, 4,000 landowners—0.16 per cent of all landowners—possessed 33 per cent of the total farming area. Of these, less than 150 owned more than half of this area. The wealthiest among them—the Károlyis and the Esterházys—had immense *latifundia*. On the other hand, there were 1,300,000 peasants with holdings of less than seven acres, hardly enough to squeeze out a livelihood, and in addition the rural population included 2,000,000 farmhands and itinerant farm workers without any land of their own. In other parts of the Habsburg monarchy the social differences were not quite as deep, but the situation was not entirely dissimilar. There were extended *latifundia* also in Galicia and Bohemia. In Bohemia the great landlords were German while the bulk of the population was Czech. Serfdom had ended, but the prosperity of the aristocrats still depended on their keeping the masses of the agricultural population dependent so that they would have to work for the great landowners. Hence the great nobility, fearing economic change, gave firm support to the Habsburg monarchy. The close relationship maintained with the monarchy by the aristocracy from all parts of the empire can be seen in the diverse national origins of the men holding the most important position in the imperial government, that of foreign minister: Count Gustav Siegmund Kálnoky (in office from 1881 to 1895) was a Magyar; Count Goluchowski (1895 to 1906) was a Pole; Baron von Aehrenthal (1906 to 1912) was a Bohemian; Count Berchtold (1912 to 1915) was a German.

Finally, the most effective but also the most dangerous instrument in maintaining the coherence of the empire was the policy of playing one nationality out against the others.

THE DUAL MONARCHY

The Habsburg empire was a Dual Monarchy. In one part—the empire of Austria—the Germans predominated; in the other—Hungary—the Magyars. These two parts had in common only the person of the emperor, foreign policy, customs policy, and the army. But Austria was not purely

German, nor was Hungary purely Magyar, and the maintenance of German or Magyar rule over the subordinate nationalities became more difficult from decade to decade. The widening distribution of printed materials —newspapers and literary works—made the various nationalities conscious of their particular cultural heritage. Industrialization drew many peasants into the cities and gave them economic strength. Social tensions inherent in the general economic changes of this period were heightened by the resistance against German and Magyar rule. In the Austrian part of the empire the most dramatic crisis occurred at the end of the 1890's, when the prime minister, Count Badeni, tried to calm national unrest by a series of decrees which ordered that in districts with a non-German majority, officials had to be able to use two languages: that of the majority group and German. The Germans were vehemently resentful, since these decrees meant the loss of the privileged position which they had held in the civil service because they could be employed all over the country. A nationalist movement proclaiming German racial superiority arose, and staging violent demonstrations, its members threatened to break away from the Habsburgs and join the German empire. Under the pressure of the German agitation, Badeni was dismissed and his language decrees were withdrawn. At this point, government based on the support of the majority of the Austrian parliament ended. After 1897 the prime ministers more and more frequently had recourse to rule by emergency decrees.

In Hungary the crisis came somewhat later. From 1903 to 1905 Hungary had a parliamentary system, but voting was restricted in such a way that the Magyars and the great landowners could be assured of a majority. The fiercely nationalistic Magyars wanted to increase their power in the empire by separating the Hungarian regiments from the rest of the army. They proposed that these regiments have their own insignia; and that the language of military command for them be Hungarian instead of German. When Emperor Francis Joseph rejected these demands, regarding them as direct interference with his powers, the Magyars refused to recognize the government which the emperor had appointed. This Magyar revolt was broken by the threat of the emperor to introduce universal suffrage, which would have destroyed both the Magyar domination and the power of the landowners. The Hungarian leaders realized that they had gone too far. Henceforth, the dominant figure in Hungarian politics, a man who also had an influential voice in the general affairs of the Habsburg empire, was Count Istvàn Tisza (1861–1918); he was a strong defender of Magyar superiority, but he knew that Magyar rule in Hungary was inextricably tied up with the maintenance of the empire as a whole and might suffer from changes or a general upheaval.

The crises in Austria and in Hungary revealed the lack of underlying principles in Habsburg policy. Sometimes the government would seem to favor the non-German or non-Magyar nationalities; sometimes it would rely exclusively on Germans or Magyars; sometimes it would exert power dictatorially; sometimes it played with democratic suggestions. Its only aim was to maintain the *status quo*.

It may be the inherent logic of a fundamentally illogical situation that some of the most energetic leaders in the Habsburg empire turned away from ideas of domestic change and reform and came to believe that the empire could best be maintained by a policy of expansion. Their hope was that the pride aroused by military successes might form a bond among the various nationalities. But Austria-Hungary was without access to an ocean; world politics, sea power, and colonies had no attraction. As in previous centuries, the Balkans were the crucial area for Habsburg foreign policy. Because of the relationship between some of the Balkan nations and the peoples in Austria-Hungary, the nationalism of the Balkan states created unrest and dissatisfaction among the minorities living in the Dual Monarchy; at the same time, the Austrian concern with the Balkans kept alive the tension with Russia, which had its own ambitions in this area.

THE BALKAN STATES AND THE GREAT POWERS

In the early twentieth century, the situation in the Balkans became explosive. The Ottoman Empire still reached far into Europe, straight through to the Adriatic Sea. The Christian Balkan states—Rumania, Bulgaria, Serbia, Montenegro—were anxious to end Turkish rule over European territories, *i.e.* in the Balkans. Greece claimed from Turkey the islands in the Aegean Sea, particularly Crete. But when an insurrection on Crete resulted in war against Turkey in 1896–1897, Greece was saved from complete defeat only by the intervention of the Great Powers. In the northern part of the Balkans, Rumania, Serbia, and the small mountain kingdom of Montenegro possessed full independence. Bulgaria, although autonomous under its own ruler, Prince Ferdinand of the Saxe-Coburg family, was still not fully sovereign, being legally part of the Ottoman Empire. Rumania, especially after its oil fields were discovered, had great wealth, but exhausted most of it in the maintenance of a strong military force. Rumania resented both Russia and Austria-Hungary—Russia because it had annexed Bessarabia, and Austria-Hungary because it possessed Transylvania, which had a large Rumanian population. Thus, Rumanian foreign policy vacillated between Russia and Austria-Hungary.

The main protagonists of nationalist aspirations against the Ottoman Empire were Serbia and Bulgaria. As long as these aspirations were directed toward liberation of the Slavic people in the Ottoman Empire, the rulers of Serbia enjoyed the protection of the Habsburg monarchy. But when, in 1903, the pro-Austrian King Alexander of Serbia, despised because of a foolish marriage, was assassinated by a group of officers, Serbia began to turn to Russia and became hostile to Austria-Hungary. Although both Bulgaria and Serbia were anxious to drive the Turks out of Europe, they were at loggerheads with each other over Macedonia: both supported its aspirations to independence from the Turks, but both planned to annex it, once liberation was achieved. When Serbia turned to Russia, the Austrian government gave support to Bulgaria. The Serbs began to see in Austria-Hungary the main obstacle to their becoming a great national state composed of Croatians, Slovenes, and Serbs—briefly, of all South Slavs. Thus Serbian agitation became increasingly vehement not only for liberation from the Turks but also for the liberation of the South Slavs from Habsburg rule.

In this situation Austrian politicians began to adopt the view that military action might solve all their problems. Some Austrian statesmen—and among them was thought to be Francis Ferdinand, the heir to the throne —seemed to believe that Austria-Hungary might take over the leadership of the South Slavs and add to the Hungarian and German parts of the empire a Yugoslav part. The Dual Monarchy might become a triadic empire. Others, probably with a more realistic appreciation of the possibilities, supposed that a defeat of Serbia might help to cool off the heat of nationalist movements in the Balkans and thereby relieve the pressure from this quarter. The Austrian chief of staff, Franz Conrad von Hötzendorf (1852–1925), favored a preventive war. These men, deeply imbued with the traditions of the Habsburg empire, hoped that by a show of strength the empire would prove the value of its traditional rule as the protagonist of civilization and Christianity against the Turks in the Balkans. As in its entire social structure, so also in its foreign policy, the Habsburg empire— insofar as its leader had any intentions beyond the maintenance of the *status quo*—was still animated by the ideas through which the Habsburgs had become powerful in the eighteenth century.

Russia

Tense and unstable though the situation was in many European countries, the only state in which the tensions led to a full-scale revolution before the First World War was Russia. In its political development Russia was less advanced than any other European nation; at the end of the nineteenth century it was still ruled by an absolute monarch. Moreover, the man who held this formidable power was in character the most insignificant of all the monarchs of his time. The diary of Tsar Nicholas II (ruled 1894–1917), with its monotonous notices about the weather and visits of relations, even on days when the fate of his country and dynasty was being decided, gives the impression that for this monarch the world was confined to the precincts of his palaces. Like other weak and stupid men he clung with a desperate obstinacy to the few ideas with which he had been indoctrinated

Tsar Nicholas II and the tsarina in their coronation robes.

in his youth, and primary among these was the conviction that the absolute power which he had inherited should be left, intact and unlimited, to his son.

Nicholas was easily dominated by stronger personalities who shared this belief. In the first ten years of his reign he was under the influence of the procurator of the Holy Synod, Konstantin Pobedonostsev (1827–1907), who had been his tutor and who in his religious zeal expected that the salvation of Russia would be achieved by shutting the nation off from all liberal Western ideas. In the tsar's later years he was dominated by his wife and the monk Rasputin. The tsarina believed that Rasputin possessed healing powers which could keep her hemophilic son alive. And since Rasputin's grasping and corrupting manners were generally resented and despised, the tsarina felt that he could be kept at court if the tsar remained an autocrat. Thus, it was in the interest of both the tsarina and Rasputin to reinforce the tsar's absolutist notions. But since many ministers opposed Rasputin's political ideas and he was frequently able to force the dismissal of his opponents, Rasputin's presence at the court represented a serious political issue. In rejecting the attacks against Rasputin, the tsar and tsarina convinced themselves that their "friend" was a "holy man," through whom they heard the "voice of the people."

It was hardly feasible for one man to govern the immense Russian empire at the beginning of the twentieth century. The real ruler of Russia was a gigantic bureaucracy—slow, clumsy, uncontrolled, and corrupt. If administrators of talent and energy did emerge—as for instance, Count Sergei Witte (1849–1915), who was finance minister between 1892 and 1903, and, after the Revolution of 1905, Peter Stolypin (1863–1911), prime minister between 1906 and 1911—they soon found themselves entangled in bureaucratic intrigues. Furthermore, the tsar became distrustful of the new ideas advocated by such men, and saw in their popularity a threat to his power; thus, neither Witte nor Stolypin enjoyed the full support of the tsar and he was soon anxious to get rid of them. The obvious weakness of an absolutist system in modern times was augmented by the tsar's personal defects.

THE DRIVE TOWARD INDUSTRIALIZATION

The problems which the Russian government faced were staggering. Russia was predominantly agricultural but after the Crimean War it had been realized that the nation would have to develop industries in order to remain a great power. It did possess the natural resources necessary for industrialization: coal and iron in the Donets Basin, oil in the Caucasus, cotton in Turkestan. But the obstacles to industrialization were also formidable. Before 1860 Moscow, St. Petersburg, and Kiev were the only great cities; Russia lacked the social strata which in other countries provided the capital and the skills needed for industrial development. Most of the capital therefore had to come from abroad. In 1900 more than 50 per cent of the capital of Russian industrial companies was foreign; about 90 per cent of the capital invested in mining and over 60 per cent of the capital in metal industries was foreign. The Royal Dutch Oil Company of Henri Deterding led in the exploitation of Caucasian oil; British capital played a major role in the development of the iron industry in the Ukraine.

A requisite for industrial development was the improvement of communications through the construction of a countrywide network of railroads. In the wide steppes of Russia, some of them hardly inhabited or explored, railroad construction was a complicated and difficult task which naturally fell to the state and gave the state a direct share in the development of the iron and coal industries. Thus the government was an important entrepreneur; the capital necessary for its enterprises was derived from loans and they again were largely taken up by foreign banks, particularly the French. Almost 50 per cent of all the interest paid on Russian state loans went out of Russia.

Obtaining the manpower needed for industrialization was difficult. One of the principal motives behind Alexander II's famous emancipation of the serfs in 1861 had been that of making it possible for peasants to emigrate to the urban areas to become industrial workers. But this purpose was partly defeated by details in the emancipation regulations. The former serfs had to pay for the land which had been granted to them. To fulfill this obligation,

A first-class compartment on the Trans-Siberian Railroad.

village committees, *mirs*, were formed; these undertook to make the payments, but they needed men to work the land and were unwilling to permit emigration to the cities. In order to move to the industrial centers the peasants either had to give up all claims to land or had to return for the harvest, spending only part of the year in the cities. Unable to work continuously in industry, they remained unskilled and had to take any job given to them. Their wages were extremely low; in 1880 Russian workers in Moscow received only 25 per cent as much as their British counterparts. The workers were housed in barracks, awakened by bells, marched to the factories, and marched back again after work, and then the gates of the barracks were closed. These conditions created unrest and dissatisfaction; when the workers returned to their villages and families they gave vent to their feelings and spread revolutionary propaganda among the rural population. Moreover, Russia's industrialization suffered from the ills common to the beginnings of industrialization in all countries: the absence of health and safety precautions in the factories, and of limitations on working hours, even for women and children. For instance, in the textile industries workers were expected to work twelve to fifteen hours a day. There was no collective bargaining and no right to strike. In addition, the change in Russian social life brought about by industrialization was deeply upsetting. With the sudden eruption of big cities, industrialization in Russia was not only an economic event but an emotional experience.

Russia was the home of many nationalities. The great masses of the population in the center of the country were Russians, but the situation in the outlying districts was very different. In the west the population was Polish; in the north the Finns had been annexed to Russia only in the early nineteenth century; in the Baltic states German nobles ruled as landowners over Estonians, Latvians, and Lithuanians. The Caucasus was populated by Georgians. Most of these national groups, particularly the Poles and the Finns but also the inhabitants of the Baltic states, had formed part of the European world at the time when Russia was still isolated. Hence they were very different from the Russians in their social structure and their intellectual outlook. They had old medieval towns and a middle class. They had been active in trade and industry; the manufacture of textiles, for example, had been carried on in Poland while Russia was still purely agrarian. They had old universities, and their intellectual life was oriented toward the West. The Poles were Catholics; the Finns and the Balts were Lutherans. Religious differences reinforced the tensions arising from differences of nationality. All these non-Russians, close to the West in their outlook, felt humiliated by the absence of institutions which the West possessed: constitutional government and self-administration. On the other hand, the Russian government feared that the granting of a constitution and of self-administration would increase the centrifugal tendencies in these areas, and was brutal enough to make various attempts at Russification, demanding the use of the Russian language and placing obstacles in the way of all those churches which were not Orthodox. Moreover, the great landowners were favored at the expense of the rest of the population. All of these policies only increased national feeling and social tension.

THE OPPOSITION

The usual outlets for political dissatisfaction, the usual means for testing the strength of opposition, were absent in Russia. Political parties were not permitted. Even associations like trade unions did not exist. A few professional organizations enjoyed approval, but even their meetings were supervised. There was rigorous censorship. Some critical views and plans for change and reform might be inserted in larger theoretical treatises, where they escaped the eyes of the censor, but political literature or even newspapers expressing criticism of the government had to be secretly printed and distributed. Frequently, such publications were the work of exiles and were smuggled over the frontiers.

Switzerland and Great Britain were the chief destinations of Russian political émigrées. *Iskra* ("The Spark"), the main organ of the Russian Social Democratic party, which was an underground organization, was edited and printed in Switzerland. The party's first congress, at Minsk in 1898, had resulted in the arrest of some of the leaders, and the next one, in 1903, was held first in Brussels and then in London; it was attended largely by exiles. One of the chief points of debate of the 1903 congress concerned the organization of the party: whether it should be limited to people who were active revolutionaries or should also admit those who were just sympathizers. Clearly, a small party could be directed and controlled from the outside, whereas a larger organization would be affected by the changing moods in Russia and would be less serviceable as an instrument for conspiratorial activities. The dispute also involved a broader issue. Would the overthrow of absolutism be immediately followed by a socialist state, or would socialism have to be preceded by a bourgeois liberal regime? The division on this point was the Russian version of the split in European socialism between the orthodox Marxists and the Revisionists.

The advocates of a small revolutionary party were led by Vladimir Ilich Lenin (1870–1924), a young émigré who had escaped from Siberia to Switzerland and had attracted attention by a number of brilliant articles in *Iskra*. In a vote which was of doubtful validity because a number of the principal members of the congress were absent, Lenin's faction won out, and thereafter it called itself the Bolsheviks ("majority group"). Lenin's leadership was soon bitterly attacked, and the control of the party came into the hands of his opponents, the Mensheviks ("minority group"); the Bolsheviks, led by Lenin, essentially became a socialist splinter faction. The policy of the Mensheviks, aiming at closer collaboration with other opposition elements, seemed much more realistic than that of the Bolsheviks because the workers were only a small part of the population. Dissatisfaction was not restricted to them; it was particularly strong among the peasantry. The Social Revolutionaries, who worked chiefly among the rural population, were almost more powerful than the Social Democrats. A successful revolution seemed more likely to come about through collaboration between peasants and workers than through the exclusive efforts of the proletariat on which Lenin wanted to rely.

All these opposition movements worked underground. The threat of punishment, usually exile to Siberia, hung over the heads of everyone involved. Violence was the only effective expression of dissatisfaction with the government. Attempts on the lives of high officials and of members of the ruling dynasty were frequent. To discover prohibited meetings, investigate forbidden activities, detect conspiracies, a large police force was a necessity. The police department was one of the most extended and most feared institutions of the Russian bureaucracy. The police were said to have spies in every block of houses. They infiltrated opposition groups, and the revolutionaries countered by offering themselves as spies to the police, in order to find out about police plans. In some cases it seems impossible to establish whether a man was a police spy or a genuine revolutionary. Typical of these enigmatic figures was Azev (1869–1918), an influential member of the Social Revolutionary party who was deeply involved in organizing the assassination of an uncle of the tsar, Grand Duke Sergius, the governor general of Moscow. Later it was revealed that Azev had been in the service of the police and participated in assassination attempts only in order to gain the full confidence of the revolutionaries.

When Prime Minister Stolypin, who had become unpopular with the reactionaries of the court, was assassinated in 1911, it was widely believed that the police had had some hand in the act. These rumors were characteristic of the atmosphere of suspicion and insecurity which permeated the entire Russian political scene.

Yet if belonging to the Russian ruling group had dangers, there were also compensations. It has been said that anyone wanting to taste the full sweetness and pleasure of life at the end of the nineteenth century should have lived among the Russian nobility. In Russia at this time land ownership meant great wealth because recent innovations in transportation facilitated the export of Russian wheat to other European countries, and wheat prices were rising. The aristocrats lived in palaces in St. Petersburg and Moscow. During the year they moved from their great city palaces to their estates and to the Crimea; they traveled in private railroad cars to the Riviera, to Paris, and to London. A characteristic expression of the luxury of the Russian nobility was the popularity of the works of Fabergé: miniature sculptures constructed of precious jewels, which the members of the aristocracy found fashionable and amusing to give one another as Easter presents. From all over the world the Russian nobles imported the most famous singers and musicians for private entertainments. Some of them were remarkably sensitive to the current trends in art. Georges Braque and André Derain painted backdrops for the Russian ballet; a wealthy Russian assembled the most complete collection of early paintings by Pablo Picasso; Russian poets experimented in the most advanced literary forms.

If the Russian aristocrats appeared to indulge in senseless luxuries, one reason was that they too suffered from the distrust of the absolutist ruler and his bureaucrats, and were excluded from responsible participation in political life. Thus it should not be assumed that all the members of the Russian nobility were frivolous and unaware of the seriousness of their country's political situation. Tolstoi, with his radical ideas of returning to a life of pristine Christian virtues, was one such exception. And Russian aristocrats were active in the *zemstvos*, regional councils established by Alexander II, which represented the nearest approach to local self-administration in Russia. Many tried to work in the *zemstvos* for improvements in the economic situation and attempted to extend the sphere of activities of the *zemstvos*, legally limited to local and charitable tasks, to political matters. But they were always rebuffed by the government.

THE RUSSO-JAPANESE WAR

Resentment about the continued absolutism of the tsars permeated almost all strata of society, and though the opposition groups differed in

Kuropatkin, commander of the Russian forces in the Far East, with Chinese officials in Mukden.

their concrete aims, only a spark was needed to unite them in a general revolutionary explosion. This spark was provided by the Russian defeats in the Russo-Japanese War. The war started on February 8, 1904, with a surprise attack by Japanese torpedo boats against the Russian Far Eastern squadron anchored in the harbor of Port Arthur. But the attack had been preceded by negotiations in which the Japanese had shown their willingness to reach a peaceful solution if the Russians relinquished a Far Eastern policy which would prevent Japanese expansion on the Asian mainland. Responsible Russian statesmen had been inclined to give the Japanese assurances that a penetration into Manchuria and Korea which the Russians had started in the preceding years would remain limited. But a Russo-Japanese understanding was blocked by the tsar. Nicholas II, since his travels in the Far East in his youth, had had vague ideas about making Russia a great naval power by extending its boundaries to the Pacific. These ideas had been fed by William II, who liked to call himself Admiral of the Atlantic and to address the tsar as Admiral of the Pacific. And the tsar listened to military men and financial speculators who urged him to bring all of Korea under Russian control. Probably he was also dazzled by the thought that Russian expansion in the Far East would help silence critics of his absolutist regime.

So the Japanese struck. The defeat of the Russian land forces in the Battle of Mukden was a great surprise. Few had foreseen that a great

Bloody Sunday. *Russian guard troops shooting at the demonstrators marching to the Winter Palace on January 22, 1905.*

European power could succumb to an Asiatic state. With the wisdom of hindsight, one can recognize the reasons for the Japanese victory. The Japanese had been prepared for the war, while the supplying and strengthening of Russian forces in the Far East had been slow and difficult because the trans-Siberian railway had only one track and did not yet extend to the Pacific. Before Russia could bring the full weight of its military forces into play, the Russians agreed to accept the mediation of President Theodore Roosevelt of the United States in arranging a peace with Japan. A treaty with the Japanese was signed on September 5, 1905 in Portsmouth, New Hampshire.

THE REVOLUTION OF 1905

An early conclusion of peace had been forced upon Russia because of upheavals in the interior. The Russo-Japanese War placed an immense strain on the Russian system of transportation, and the provisioning of the great urban centers broke down. Bread prices soared and the wages of the workers proved insufficient. Spontaneous strikes broke out in many places. When on January 22, 1905, a procession of workers approached the Winter Palace of the tsar to submit to him their grievances, the way was blocked by troops, whose commander lost his head and fired on the masses. This Bloody Sunday set in motion the revolution. A general strike was declared in St. Petersburg, and most industrial centers followed suit. The workers combined into unions; the professional organizations which had been allowed a supervised existence now became politically active, electing new leaders and drawing up programs of political reform. The *zemstvos* formulated political demands. The general cry was for the creation of a parliamentary government based on universal suffrage.

Progress toward this goal was achieved in stages. In March the tsar was forced to declare that a consultative assembly would be established. In August he conceded that this assembly would be elected, but he insisted that suffrage would be limited and the power of this assembly, the Duma, would be purely deliberative. Then a new wave of strikes and revolutionary outbreaks occurred; in October, under the pressure of a breakdown of public order, with cities like St. Petersburg and Moscow in the hands of the workers, the tsar made a further concession: the Duma would be elected on the basis of a wide franchise and it would have legislative functions. Civil liberties would be guaranteed. The change in the political system was indicated by the appointment of a prime minister; this office was given to Count Witte. But revolutionary agitation among the workers continued and peasant unrest began to spread. In the southern parts of Russia peasants burned the houses of landowners and occupied the land. Under the threat of this peasant revolt the tsar, on Witte's advice, in December conceded universal and secret suffrage. But this was his last concession. Troops returning from the Far East bolstered the government; the leaders of the workers in St. Petersburg were arrested, and an insurrection of the workers in Moscow was defeated. Boris Pasternak's *Doctor Zhivago* (1957) contains a graphic description of the Cossacks riding down the masses in Moscow in the winter of 1905.

The Revolution of 1905 did not seal the fate of tsarism. It might be called a turning point which did not turn. A constitutional system was introduced. Although universal suffrage was not maintained and the voting structure favored the wealthier classes, large groups of the population were willing to cooperate with the government to make the constitution work. Moreover, the peasants were freed from making further payments for their land, and under Stolypin the dissolution of the *mirs* opened the way to an agricultural development based on private ownership; wealthy peasants— kulaks—began to appear. But the tsar, far from welcoming these developments, obstructed them in every way. In March, 1906, he dismissed Witte, whom he believed to have made unnecessary concessions; Stolypin, who came to office later in 1906, had lost the tsar's favor by the time he was assassinated in 1911. Whenever possible, Nicholas appointed reactionary ministers. He openly bestowed his favor on the most reactionary groups, among them the Black Hundreds, who with the support of the troops embarked on barbaric punitive actions against the peasants. The tsar also encouraged anti-Semitic pogroms. As before, the influence of the crown remained the chief target of all liberal forces.

Actually, the tsar might have utilized the revolution and its consequences to broaden the basis of support for his government. Through the summer of 1905, almost all social groups except for the extreme reactionaries had favored the revolutionary movement. This unified front broke down in the autumn, as agrarian unrest continued and the workers began to fight more openly for a socialist republic. Liberal aristocrats, professional groups, the middle classes—all were by then satisfied with the concessions made by the tsar in the October decree. Revolutionary activity between October and December faltered because it began to lose general support and became restricted to workers and peasants. For a moderately liberal policy the tsar could have counted on the backing of a large segment of society.

Except for the Paris Commune of 1871, previous revolutions had been bourgeois in character. The Russian Revolution of 1905 can be regarded as the first socialist revolution. It showed the immense importance of the general strike as a political weapon. Moreover, it revealed new techniques for effecting a social revolution. For the first time workers' councils, composed of men elected by the workers of the various factories, exerted a directing influence upon events and in certain critical periods functioned as an effective government. The leading spirit of the workers' council in St. Petersburg was a young socialist writer named Leon Trotsky. Like Lenin, he realized that in revolutionary times these workers' councils could serve as the authority which could prevent chaos and at the same time keep power in the hands of the proletariat.

The Russian Revolution of 1905 had a great impact all over Europe. Fear of revolution became tangible in the political atmosphere; governments became more concerned about maintaining their authority and their prestige than they had ever been before. The result was an increase in tensions within the nations of Europe and also a more intensive pursuit of success in foreign policy. And the dangers and opportunities in the international arena were abruptly expanded, for the sudden revelation of Russia's weakness changed the entire European scene.

CHAPTER 38

The End of the Concert and the
First World War

THE YEAR 1905 was crucial in the development of European diplomacy. It concluded a period in which—in the Fashoda crisis, the Boer War, the Italian adventure in Ethiopia, the Russo-Japanese War—the degree of control that the European powers had exercised in the non-European world was in dispute; with the events of 1905 the positions of the European nations in Europe and the balance of power among them became the crucial issues. The events of 1905 represent a return to Europe as the center of action, and this is why the conflicts which the partitioning of Africa and Asia evoked could be composed without war among the European powers, whereas the crises in the year 1905 and those which followed resulted in the outbreak of the First World War.

A period of diplomacy dominated by imperialist crises was followed by a period of diplomacy focused upon issues concerning the European balance of power. But it should not be assumed that the period of imperialist expansion was an interlude without importance for what happened later.

THE RIGIDIFICATION OF THE ALLIANCE SYSTEM

By 1905 the entire political atmosphere had become much more tense and heated than it had been in the late nineteenth century. The masses had begun to take an intense interest in foreign policy, and the enterprises and adventures of their conationals in foreign lands and unexplored areas had fired their imagination and their sense of national competitiveness. The conceptions which they had formed of other nations were usually unflattering. The Boer War had created a somewhat contradictory but always unfavorable image of Great Britain: ruthless in its pursuit of worldly treasures on the one hand, and decadent on the other. Perhaps the German emperor seriously believed that Germany wanted nothing but its deserved "place in the sun"; he had certainly convinced many of his subjects that this was the case. But other nations had seen in the German advances into Africa, China, and the South Seas the actions of a spoiled and brutal young man who wanted to grab everything he could lay his hands on. Moreover, the events of these imperialist years had set the policy of some of the great powers into channels from which later there was no escape.

This is particularly true with regard to Germany and Great Britain and their relations with each other.

The principal enterprises of German policy which had a fatal effect on relations with Great Britain were the construction of a powerful navy and the financing and building of the Baghdad Railway. When the building of the German navy began, there was probably little awareness of what its later consequences would be. Because sea power was regarded as essential for effective participation in world politics the navy soon became popular among the German bourgeoisie; in contrast to the predominantly aristocratic officers of the army, naval officers came mainly from bourgeois families. The popular backing for the navy was efficiently promoted by the secretary of the navy, Admiral von Tirpitz, who established a special office which edited pamphlets, helped to organize navy leagues, and arranged meetings where speakers discussed the importance of naval power: this office was the forerunner of all later propaganda ministries. In 1898 the Reichstag had sanctioned a navy bill which was a new departure for Germany in that it proposed not only cruisers which might defend the German coast but also battleships fit for combat on the open sea: the bill provided for the building of eleven battleships and five first-class cruisers by 1905. The German navy envisaged here was still rather small. However, two years later, in 1900, Tirpitz carried through the adoption of a second bill which would expand the building program, calling for the construction of thirty-eight battleships to be completed in twenty years. The anti-British tendency of this second bill was evident. Tirpitz' goal was a fleet of such strength that the British would hesitate to attack Germany.

The German project for a railroad to Baghdad developed from innocuous beginnings into an enterprise with dangerous political consequences. The capital needed and the financial risks involved were so large that the Deutsche Bank, the German financial house interested in the undertaking, obtained concessions for the project from the Turkish government in 1899 almost by default of other competitors. The leaders of the Deutsche Bank tried without success to obtain the cooperation of financiers of other countries for this enterprise. The only serious opponents of the project were the Russians. The French supported the Germans, and the British raised no objections; both Great Britain and France were anxious to bar Russian

The Baghdad Railroad. *German and Turkish officials celebrate the launching of the enterprise.*

expansion in the Near East and to involve Germany in the preservation of Turkey. However, their attitude changed when, almost unavoidably, the construction of the railroad gave Germany economic and then political control in Turkey.

As a result of Germany's striving for world power, German and British interests, which in the past had not confronted each other, began to clash. Just at this time Britain was recognizing the need for moving away from its "splendid isolation." The British had been surprised and worried by their unpopularity, demonstrated in reactions first to the Jameson Raid and then to the Boer War. They wondered whether the formation of an anti-British continental league, of which German and Russian statesmen sometimes spoke in the 1890's, might not really be in the making. Britain's first countermeasure was the treaty with Japan which was directed against Russia. The British also became aware of the advantages for the security of their imperial position which would result from backing by a continental power. To British feelers, particularly those of the colonial secretary, Joseph Chamberlain, Germany gave a very cool reception. The German statesmen in power, especially Chancellor Bernhard von Bülow (1849–1929) and his political adviser Friedrich von Holstein, felt sure that Britain could turn to no other power but Germany which could therefore refuse to be satisfied with an agreement merely delimiting German and British colonial interests, waiting instead until the time was ripe to demand a defensive alliance.

But the British government, having no intention of going that far, turned to France and the result was the Entente Cordiale, concluded on April 8, 1904. Formally, this treaty was an agreement on all the issues concerning colonies that had occasioned disputes between Great Britain and France; the chief points were that France abandoned all its claims in Egypt and Britain recognized that France had a dominating interest in Morocco and promised diplomatic support of French plans for achieving control of Morocco. The marquis of Lansdowne (1845–1927), the British foreign secretary who concluded this agreement, always maintained that the treaty had no aim except that of moderating the tensions which had arisen from colonial conflicts. The Entente Cordiale developed into a close political partnership as a result of the events of the following year—the crisis of 1905.

THE SUCCESSION OF CRISES, 1905–1914

From the German point of view the Entente Cordiale represented a serious loss of prestige; the German statesmen felt that their nation's diplomatic situation had deteriorated and that they must take action to improve it. Accordingly, German policy began to follow two different although not contradictory lines. One was to humiliate France and to show to the French that the Entente Cordiale was without value. The other aim was to reestablish friendly relations with Russia in order to reconstruct the situation which had existed in Bismarck's time, before the abandonment of the Reinsurance Treaty.

The First Moroccan Crisis

The Germans opened their action against France by claiming that the arrangements about Morocco violated German interests. This was just a pretense; German economic activities hardly existed in Morocco, and indeed the German government had found it necessary to exert pressure on the Mannesmann Company, a metallurgical and mining company, to make investments in Morocco so that there could be some substance for the assertions concerning the violation of German interests.

The Moroccan crisis started when William II, on a Mediterranean trip in March, 1905, debarked briefly in Tangier and solemnly declared that the Germans were willing to maintain the independence and integrity of Morocco. German and French claims clearly confronted each other. France regarded Morocco as belonging to the French sphere of interest and planned to absorb the country; the Germans insisted that it was an independent and sovereign state in which all nations should have equal opportunities. From the point of view of international law the French were in a weak position. So they tried to come to some arrangement with Germany, indicating their willingness to make concessions in other colonial areas. The Germans countered by demanding an international conference.

They were not interested in getting advantages to compensate for French rule in Morocco; rather they were concerned with demonstrating French political impotence. They refused to enter into any bilateral negotiations with France, and made it clear that they considered the French foreign minister Théophile Delcassé—whose policy had raised French prestige by establishing close connections first with Russia and then with Great Britain—so hostile to Germany that negotiations with him were purposeless. The situation became increasingly tense. Delcassé insisted that he had a commitment from Great Britain to support France in case of war, but the other French ministers rightly maintained that the close consultation to which Britain had agreed in the Entente Cordiale did not mean that it had any obligation to enter combat on the French side. France without Britain would not be able to hold out against Germany. These questions were thrashed out in a dramatic meeting of the French cabinet. On June 6, 1905, Delcassé resigned.

Germany had achieved a resounding diplomatic triumph. But the Germans did not know what to do with their victory. The French were now willing to agree to an international conference about Morocco but proposed that Germany and France should first work out a settlement between themselves, to be then ratified by the conference. For such a preliminary settlement the French were willing to pay a high price; for a free hand in Morocco they were prepared to make far-reaching concessions to Germany in other colonial disputes. But the German government still refused to enter into bilateral negotiations with France and demanded unconditional acceptance of the convocation of an international conference. This attitude was widely interpreted as a sign that Germany was not content with having shown its superior strength but was driving toward a war against France. Indeed, Count Alfred von Schlieffen (1833–1913), the chief of the German general staff, did want a preventive war, but there are no indications that either Chancellor Bülow or Holstein shared this view. It appears that after they had solemnly declared that the Moroccan problem ought to be submitted to an international conference they found it difficult to withdraw from this position; to make a prior settlement with France would have been to turn the conference into a farce. Furthermore the Germans believed that they would dominate the conference and that France would be unable to offer serious opposition to their demands.

The German statesmen had grounds for optimism; in the summer of 1905, they seemed close to success in their efforts to renew friendship with Russia.

During the war with Japan, Russia felt the need for German support because it feared that Great Britain, Japan's ally, might also enter the war, especially after an incident at Dogger Bank, in the North Sea, in which Russian ships sailing from the Baltic to the Far East had fired erroneously on British trawlers. The tsar and the Russian ruling group were also anxious to move close to Germany because this was the one state from which they expected sympathy and support for their attempts to maintain an authoritarian system. Accordingly, negotiations were begun between Russia and Germany, and in July, 1905, the tsar and William II met at Björkö, on the Baltic coast. Russia, losing to Japan, was then in the midst of revolutionary turmoil, and William II persuaded, almost forced, his dispirited cousin to sign an alliance treaty which, although discussed for months, had never been concluded.

Just when Germany seemed at the high point of power, with Delcassé eliminated and Russia as an ally, things began to go wrong. The Russian statesmen were disgusted with their tsar's weakness in yielding to the German emperor's demands. They began to raise objections to the treaty and to delay its finalization. After the peace treaty with Japan was signed in September, Russia had less need for German support. Moreover, a French loan helped to alleviate Russia's acute financial difficulties and increased the authority of the government. Under these circumstances the Russians had no reason any longer not to give diplomatic support to their French ally in the Moroccan crisis. Moreover, the British had begun to fear that the French might be forced to align themselves with Germany and Russia. The new British foreign secretary, Sir Edward Grey, a Liberal more inclined toward France than toward Germany, encouraged the French by permitting consultations between the French and British military staffs regarding common action in wartime, and promised the French support in the negotiations over Morocco. Thus, although the French in September, 1905, gave in and agreed to an international conference without prior accords with Germany, they could look forward to the conference with confidence.

In January, 1906, when the conference over Morocco convened in the Spanish city of Algeciras, it was not France but Germany that was in an almost isolated position. Characteristic of the polite, subtle, and indirect ways of the diplomacy of this period is the fact that there was no dramatic indictment of German policy. A test vote on a minor question revealed that Russia, France, Great Britain, Italy, even the United States, all sided with France; only Austria-Hungary voted with Germany. This was proof enough: if Germany decided to unleash a war against France it would now be opposed by almost every great power. Chancellor Bülow realized that Germany had to give in. The final agreement was couched in terms which concealed the German defeat. There was confirmation of the independence of Morocco and assurance of an economic open door for other powers. But the police in Morocco were put under the combined authority of France and Spain, and France was given control of the state bank, and thereby the finances, of Morocco. The conference had established that France would be the ruling power in Morocco.

The affair had been primarily a struggle among the European powers for hegemony, and the details of the regulations of the Moroccan situation were less significant than what the conference revealed about the diplomatic constellation in Europe: at Algeciras the powers which would confront one another in the First World War found themselves for the first time grouped in opposing camps.

The Moroccan crisis of 1905–1906 was followed by a chain of further crises and wars—the Bosnian crisis of 1908–1909, a second Moroccan crisis and the Tripolitan War between Italy and Turkey in 1911, the first Balkan War in 1912, the second Balkan War and the Liman von Sanders crisis in 1913—until, in the summer of 1914, tensions exploded into the First World War.

With the renewed concentration of the competition for power in the European continent, the region which in earlier centuries, and particularly in the nineteenth century, had been a chief object of dispute—the Balkans and the Near East—became acutely sensitive once more. In the course of the gradual economic development of this area, which was accomplished largely with the help of foreign capital, the middle classes had become stronger; professional men—lawyers, doctors, teachers—were needed in increasing numbers. Rumanians, Serbs, Greeks, Bulgars, studied in foreign countries, particularly in Germany and France, and absorbed an almost religious faith in nationalism. Contact with the powerful national states of central and western Europe could only increase dissatisfaction with the situation at home, with the subjection of the Balkan peoples to the Ottoman Empire and the Habsburg monarchy. The demand for the elimination of Turkish rule in Europe became more general and more urgent. In earlier times the great powers had always been aware of a last recourse in case the illness of the Sick Man proved fatal—partition. But this means of escape from a clash among the European powers over the spoils of the Ottoman Empire was now barred, for Germany made the maintenance of the Ottoman Empire the cornerstone of its policy. Whereas in Bismarck's time Germany could act as a mediator between the two great powers which bordered the Balkan peninsula—Austria-Hungary and Russia—as they competed for influence there, now Germany itself had become an interested participant in the affairs of this area. This change in Germany's role constituted a new and dangerous element in the situation.

The Bosnian Crisis

After the humiliation suffered in the war against Japan, the Russian government was eager for a success in foreign policy. The Slavic brethren in the Balkans were popular with the Russian public, and Russian ruling circles believed that a policy favoring independence of the Balkan nations would strengthen the authority of the tsar and weaken the trends toward parliamentarianism and democratic government. Quick action seemed appropriate because in July, 1908, a revolution had taken place in the Ottoman Empire; the tyrannical Sultan Abdul-Hamid II had been forced to abdicate, and the Young Turks, advocates of modernization and parliamentary government, had come to power. Concessions from a Turkey strengthened by reforms would be difficult to obtain. Hence, in September, 1908, the Russian foreign minister, Alexander Izvolski (1856–1919), set out to visit the courts of the European great powers, hoping to obtain their permission to open the Dardanelles to Russian warships, a move which would strengthen Russian influence in Turkey and in the Balkans. Izvolski's first stop was at Buchlau, in Bohemia, where he met the Austrian foreign minister Aehrenthal. The exact nature of the exchange between Izvolski and Aehrenthal has never become entirely clear because the accounts of the two ministers diverge widely. However, there can be little doubt that Aehrenthal promised to raise no objections against the opening of the Dardanelles to Russian warships. As a *quid pro quo*, Izvolski agreed not to oppose Austrian annexation of the Turkish provinces of Bosnia and Herzegovina, which Austria-Hungary had occupied since the Congress of Berlin. Aehrenthal was a clever and ruthless diplomat and Izvolski was not his equal. For while Izvolski continued his round of visits to the European capitals, seeking to work out a general agreement on the opening of the Dardanelles, the Austrian government, on October 6, proclaimed the annexation of Bosnia and Herzegovina. One day earlier, in collusion with Austria, Bulgaria—hitherto under the sovereignty of the sultan—had declared its full independence. The crisis had come about before Izvolski could get agreement from the other great powers, and he had to return to St. Petersburg empty-handed. Austria-Hungary had strengthened its position in the Balkan area without the Russians' receiving any compensation. In order to reassert Russian influence in Balkan affairs, and also driven by passionate hatred of Aehrenthal, Izvolski tried in every way to prevent international recognition of Austria's annexation of Bosnia and Herzegovina. The Turks, under German pressure, accepted the annexation when they were offered financial compensation. The country which was most indignant over the Austrian action was Serbia. Because the peoples of Bosnia and Herzegovina were primarily South Slavs, the Serbs felt that they, not the Austrians, ought to rule these provinces. Thus the crisis dragged on. Encouraged by Russian backing, Serbia made military preparations, and Austria followed suit. Finally, in March, 1909, the German government sent a sharp note to Russia demanding that it abandon its support of Serbia and recognize Austria's annexation of Bosnia and Herzegovina. Still too weak to risk a war against the great European powers, Russia gave in. The crisis was over.

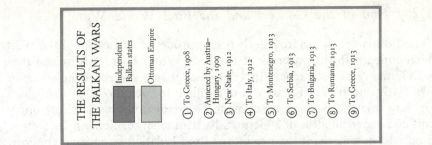

THE RESULTS OF
THE BALKAN WARS

Independent
Balkan states

Ottoman Empire

① To Greece, 1908
② Annexed by Austria–
Hungary, 1909
③ New State, 1912
④ To Italy, 1912
⑤ To Montenegro, 1913
⑥ To Serbia, 1913
⑦ To Bulgaria, 1913
⑧ To Rumania, 1913
⑨ To Greece, 1913

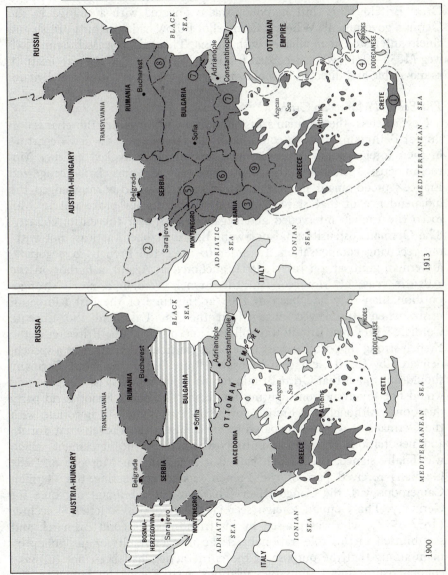

1913

RUSSIA

BLACK SEA

OTTOMAN
EMPIRE

Bucharest

RUMANIA ⑧

Adrianople ⑦

Constantinople

TRANSYLVANIA

BULGARIA ⑦

Sofia

RHODES

DODECANESE ④

AUSTRIA-HUNGARY

Belgrade

SERBIA ⑤ ⑥ ⑨

GREECE

Athens

CRETE ①

MEDITERRANEAN SEA

Sarajevo ②

MONTENEGRO

ALBANIA ③

ADRIATIC SEA

IONIAN SEA

ITALY

Aegean
Sea

1900

RUSSIA

BLACK SEA

Bucharest

RUMANIA

Adrianople

Constantinople

OTTOMAN EMPIRE

TRANSYLVANIA

BULGARIA

Sofia

RHODES

DODECANESE

AUSTRIA-HUNGARY

Belgrade

SERBIA

MACEDONIA

GREECE

Athens

CRETE

MEDITERRANEAN SEA

BOSNIA-
HERZEGOVINA

Sarajevo

MONTENEGRO

ADRIATIC SEA

IONIAN SEA

ITALY

Aegean
Sea

The Bosnian crisis has frequently been considered a rehearsal of the crisis which ended with the outbreak of the First World War. It is indeed true that Germany tried to repeat in 1914 what it had succeeded in doing in 1908–1909. But in 1914 Russia was not willing to back down.

In any case the Bosnian crisis made Germany and Russia direct opponents and ended all ideas of a German-Russian alliance. Germany's reaction was almost automatic; it tried to escape from isolation by moving closer to Great Britain. This shift in policy was connected with a change in the German government. Whereas Chancellor Bülow had been anti-British and chiefly interested in an alliance with Russia, Theobald von Bethmann-Hollweg (1856–1921), who succeeded Bülow in 1909, accepted Russian hostility as inevitable and directed his policy toward cooperation with Great Britain.

The Second Moroccan Crisis

Nevertheless, the German's first important move under the chancellorship of Bethmann-Hollweg could hardly be interpreted as a new departure in their foreign policy. The German government provoked another Moroccan crisis. Although the conference at Algeciras had recognized France's predominant interest in Morocco it had also acknowledged the independence of that state. When internal struggles broke out in Morocco the French intervened and began to take over the entire country. The Germans ostensibly did not want this to happen, at least not without receiving compensation. In order to force the French to negotiate, a German gunboat, on July 1, 1911, anchored in Agadir, a harbor on the Atlantic coast of Morocco. But the French were in a much stronger position than they had been in 1905 at the time of the first Moroccan crisis, when Russia was engaged in the Far East and the Entente Cordiale with Great Britain was still new and untried. The British gave the French strong support, their attitude being particularly evident in a speech, delivered by Lloyd George in Mansion House. He warned that Germany should not forget that Great Britain too had vital interests in Morocco and would not shy away from fighting for them: "National honor is no party question." Although the French government consented to negotiate with the Germans, it was not prepared to yield much; the French were tough, and negotiations dragged on until November. In the agreement which was finally signed, the French gained a free hand in Morocco and the Germans received part of the French Congo connecting the German Cameroons with the Congo River. This was not a brilliant outcome for Germany. The German foreign secretary, Alfred von Kiderlen-Waechter (1852–1912), who was praised by his friends as a second Bismarck and saw himself in this role, rationalized the meager results of his policy by maintaining that the purpose of the entire action had been not to make colonial gains, but to improve relations with France by removing the festering wound of Morocco with one sharp incision of the knife. Also, Germany would now be able to draw closer to Great Britain, which would no longer consider a German-British rapprochement incompatible with the Entente Cordiale. Whatever the actual aims of Kiderlen-Waechter's policy, the impression which the sudden appearance of a German warship in Moroccan waters made on other countries was not that of a country striving for appeasement. On the contrary, both statesmen and the general public chiefly remembered that since 1905 Germany had three times tried to get its way by sudden and brutal action: in Morocco in the summer of 1905; by the ultimatum to Russia in 1909; and finally, at Agadir.

Nevertheless, negotiations between Germany and Great Britain did finally take place. Frightened by the drift toward war which the Agadir crisis had indicated, the British government was also aware that military preparations in response to international tensions would diminish the financial resources available for its program of domestic reform. Hence, the British decided to probe German intentions once more; the secretary of state for war, Haldane, was sent to Berlin. The aim of his mission was to prevent the Germans from carrying out their plan for increased naval construction. Tirpitz had declared that three great battleships (dreadnoughts) would be built instead of the previously announced two. But Haldane did not obtain any modification of German naval plans. Actually, the German chancellor and the German foreign secretary, Bethmann-Hollweg and Kiderlen-Waechter, were willing to slow down the naval program and tried to keep negotiations going even after Haldane left Berlin. But Tirpitz, who entirely dominated William II, was able to prevent any concession. The naval race between Germany and Great Britain was not stopped.

Since 1905 British policies had lost much of their flexibility, and they gave the Germans some reason to distrust British intentions. After the agreement with France in 1904, Britain concluded an agreement with Russia in 1907. Like the Entente Cordiale this concerned colonial questions and settled the most urgent imperialist disputes between the two countries. Persia was divided: the north fell into the Russian sphere of influence, the south into the British sphere, and a neutral zone remained in the middle. Moreover, in the Agadir crisis Britain had not only given diplomatic support to France but agreed to military discussions, which resulted in an understanding between the French and British general staffs that in case of war a British expeditionary force would be sent to France; plans were made concerning transportation, troop-concentration areas, and command organization. While these arrangements did not constitute a definite military alliance and the political commitments between Great Britain and France did not go beyond close consultation, it was clear that the position of the European powers was becoming more rigid. Triple Entente, as the

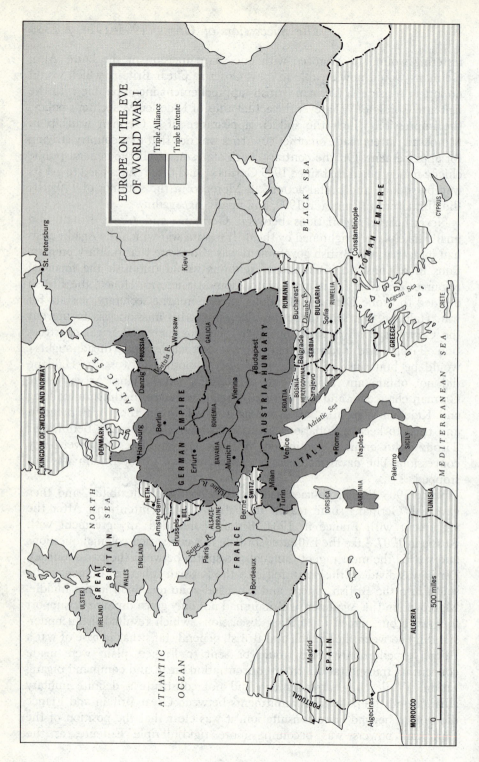

EUROPE ON THE EVE
OF WORLD WAR I

Triple Alliance

Triple Entente

somewhat loose combination of Great Britain, France, and Russia was called, confronted the Triple Alliance of Germany, Austria, and Italy.

War and Crisis in the Balkans

The possibility of avoiding war if tensions continued became increasingly less likely. After the Agadir crisis the focus of tension shifted to the East. From 1912 on the affairs of the Ottoman Empire and the national aspirations of the Balkan nations evoked one crisis after the other. The prelude was the war which began in September, 1911, between Turkey and Italy. All the great powers had recognized that Tripoli was in the Italian sphere of interest; when France finally absorbed Morocco, the Italian government decided to take action and proclaimed the annexation of Tripoli. Turkey answered with a declaration of war against Italy. The Italians won a quick victory, but in the meantime the Tripolitan War triggered action in the Balkans. Serbia and Bulgaria believed that if they did not take action before the end of Turkey's conflict with Italy, they might miss an opportunity for driving the Turks out of Europe. They succeeded in getting the support of Montenegro and Greece, and war against Turkey broke out in October, 1912. The Turkish troops in the Balkans were defeated in a number of battles in which the Bulgarian and Serbian soldiers proved themselves to be excellent warriors.

But a diplomatic settlement was much more difficult to achieve than military victory. There was dissension among the victors about the drawing of the frontiers after the war had assured the end of Turkish rule in Europe. The two areas about which disposition had to be made were Macedonia and Albania.

Bulgaria, Greece, and Serbia all demanded parts of Macedonia, and the claims of Greece and Bulgaria were particularly irreconcilable because both were anxious to control the northern coast of the Aegean Sea. The result was a second Balkan War, in which Greece, Serbia, Rumania, and Turkey rallied against Bulgaria. The outcome of this war determined that only a very small part of Macedonia fell to Bulgaria. Most of it was divided between Serbia and Greece, and the Turks regained Adrianople.

The Serbs were less successful in their demand for Albanian territory which would give them a direct access to the Adriatic Sea. The great powers, meeting with the Balkan nations and Turkey in London, forced Serbia and Montenegro to accept the creation of an independent Albania. Serbia remained cut off from the Adriatic.

In the meetings in London, Russia had backed the claims of Serbia whereas Austria-Hungary advocated those of Bulgaria, and together with Italy, sharply opposed the Serbian demand for access to the Adriatic Sea. To underline the seriousness with which they looked upon the situation, both—Russia and Austria-Hungary—made some military preparations.

Great Britain and Germany cooperated to obtain a peaceful solution of the conflict. Nevertheless, the Balkan wars accumulated new explosive material which the compromise worked out by the great powers in London concealed rather than eliminated. Turkey, in need of military reorganization, called in a German general, Otto Liman von Sanders, but this move evoked violent Russian protests because it appeared to be a further step in the establishment of German control over Turkey. Both Russia and Austria indicated that in the negotiations about the final settlement of the Balkan wars they should have received stronger support from their respective friends, Great Britain and Germany. Consequently, in both Britain and Germany the government leaders felt that their alliances might be endangered if in the next emergency they did not give stronger support to their allies. But the most dangerous consequence of the Balkan wars was that all the resentment of Serbian nationalism was now focused on the Habsburg monarchy. The Serbs had considered the Austrian annexation of Bosnia and Herzegovina in 1908 as a blow to Serbia's aspirations to become the home of all South Slavs. Now in 1913, Austria-Hungary had again been the chief obstacle to Serbia's ambitions and had deprived it of the fruits of victory: access to the Adriatic Sea. To the nationalistic Serbs the Habsburg monarchy was an old evil monster which prevented their nation from becoming a great and powerful state. On June 28, 1914, a young Serbian nationalist, Gavrilo Princip, assassinated the heir of the Habsburg monarchy, the Archduke Francis Ferdinand, and his wife at Sarajevo.

THE OUTBREAK OF THE FIRST WORLD WAR

The events of the five weeks between the assassination of the Archduke Francis Ferdinand and the outbreak of the First World War have been more carefully investigated than almost any others in world history. An endless number of books and articles have reviewed and probed all aspects of the question of responsibility for the outbreak of the war: whether the Serbian government had knowledge of the plans for the assassination of the archduke; whether Germany encouraged Austria-Hungary to take action against Serbia and deliberately instigated a general war in 1914; whether France believed this crisis would be a favorable opportunity for starting a war in order to regain Alsace-Lorraine, and therefore stiffened the attitude of its Russian ally; whether military requirements restricted and eliminated the freedom of decision of the political leaders; and whether British policy was mistaken in not taking a clear stand.

Most of the facts bearing on these questions have been clarified. The responsible leaders of the Serbian government did not know about the plans for the attempt on the life of the archduke. On the other hand, the assassination was the work not of an individual, but of a group of Bosnian

The Murder at Sarajevo. *Archduke Francis Ferdinand on his visit to Bosnia a few hours before his assassination. Right: The police seizing the assassin, Princip.*

and Serbian nationalists who were encouraged and promoted by a Serbian secret society, the Black Hand, in which the chief of the intelligence department of the Serbian general staff was a leading figure. However, when in an ultimatum of July 23, 1914 the Austrian government accused Serbian government officials of being involved in the plot, it had no proof, based its accusation on falsified documents, and did not mention the Black Hand, specifying only individuals and organizations that in truth had nothing to do with the assassination. Thus, the assassination was consciously used by the Austrian government for the purposes of power politics: to remove the threat which Serbia represented to the existence of the Habsburg monarchy. Further proof that this was Austria's intention is the fact that although the Serbian government accepted almost all the demands of the exceedingly harsh and humiliating ultimatum, the Austrian minister in Belgrade, acting on instructions given to him before he had received the Serbian note, declared the Serbian answer unsatisfactory and left Belgrade, making war between the two states inevitable.

However, without the certainty of German backing, the Austrian leaders would not have embarked on the war against Serbia. Actually, Austrian governmental circles were divided in their views on the course to follow; influential men, notably the Hungarian prime minister, Tisza, were opposed to any action which might lead to war. However, the German government urged the Austrians to resolute action against Serbia, and Tisza's hesitations were overcome when he was given proof that Germany desired Austria to proceed against Serbia and had promised support if other powers became involved in the conflict.

The Germans encouraged Austria because they regarded the death of the heir of the Habsburg throne as a danger signal foreshadowing a possible collapse of the Habsburg monarchy, which would leave Germany without allies. The Germans hoped that a successful show of strength against Serbia might revitalize the Habsburg monarchy. Since the assassination of the archduke and his wife had aroused general indignation and widespread sympathy for the Austrian emperor, there seemed to be a chance that the war between Austria and Serbia might remain localized. However, from the outset the Germans were aware that the Austrian action against Serbia ran the risk of a general war in which Russia, France, and Great Britain might be allied against Germany and Austria, and the justifiable indictment against the German leaders might be made that they willingly accepted this risk. Their attitude was the result of a variety of circumstances. A predominant part of the German ruling group was obsessed by the idea that the future belonged to the great world powers and that Germany would become a world power only through a war which would show it to be equal to the strongest and which would gain for the German people and for German economic expansion a broader territorial basis than it possessed. And if war were long delayed, Germany's chances for ascending to the small circle of world powers might be missed forever. Once Russia, with its large population and great mineral resources, became fully developed, it would tower over all its neighbors and Germany's opportunities for development would disappear. From a purely military point of view, too, time seemed to be running against Germany. In a few years Russia's recovery from losses and defeat and France's three-year conscription law would tilt the military balance against Germany. Historical speculations, economic expansionism, military calculations reinforced one another to create a climate in which war became acceptable. Such considerations guided the policy of the German government. Chancellor Bethmann-Hollweg was an earnest and responsible man inclined to pessimism and he was aware that the consequences of a world war were unforeseeable. Yet he encouraged Austria to take action and he gave the Austrian statesmen a free hand, fully conscious of the risk that a great European conflict might result. Bethmann-Hollweg was not simply bowing to the demands of the military who carried such a powerful weight in imperial Germany; he was himself among those who saw the growing Russian power as a threat to Germany's future, and he had an almost fatalistic belief that a world war was coming. In 1914 Germany's chances would be better than in later years. In the last critical days, when the prophesied world war threatened to become reality, Bethmann-Hollweg seems to have become frightened by his own courage and he made some desperate attempts to keep the conflict between Austria and Serbia localized, but in his heart he must have been aware that these efforts were condemned to failure.

If for no other reason, these last attempts could not succeed because the

Austrians had wasted in an almost incredible manner the sympathy which the assassination had aroused. They sent their ultimatum to Serbia only on July 23—after more than three weeks—when the excitement about the murder of the archduke had begun to die down. The reason for the delay was Austrian dilatoriness (*Schlamperei*), although they rationalized these delays by maintaining that the harvest in Hungary had to be gathered in before they could call the men to arms. In the end, there was a further postponement of three days because the French president, Poincaré, was visiting the tsar and the Austrians did not want to present the ultimatum until Poincaré had left Russia, so that the Russian and French governments would not be able to agree immediately upon joint action.

Poincaré and the French prime minister, Viviani, were in St. Petersburg from July 20 to July 23, 1914. It is not known what they said in private to their Russian hosts about the course which ought to be pursued in the approaching crisis between Austria-Hungary and Serbia. The emphasis which in their public declarations the French and Russian statesmen placed on the close bonds uniting the Russian empire and the French republic must have strengthened the Russian will to oppose the Austrian action. And in the following critical week the French ambassador in Russia, Maurice Paléologue (1859–1944), certainly encouraged the Russian government to take a firm line. The Russians were in a better military position than they had been in 1908; their army had been built up and transport had been improved by the development of the railroad system in western Russia. Unquestionably, the Russian rulers, under the pressure of an excited public and of military men eager to avenge the defeat of 1905, felt unable to accept another diplomatic setback, and decided to prevent Austria from encroaching upon Serbian integrity and sovereignty. When, on July 24, they were informed of the contents of the Austrian ultimatum, they decided that if Austria took action against Serbia, they would institute partial mobilization —which meant mobilization of the military districts close to the Austrian border. But on July 30, after Austria had rejected the Serbian answers, had declared war against Serbia, and had mobilized part of its forces, the Russian government persuaded the tsar to declare general mobilization. The reasons for this change of plan were in part technical; the Russian general staff believed that, after a partial mobilization was under way, it would be difficult and slow to organize a general mobilization. It also seems clear, however, that this step must have been necessitated by Russian-French military agreements. The Russians and the French had some general knowledge of the German war plans. They were aware that at the outset most of the German military forces would be concentrated against France and that the possibility of successful French resistance depended on a quick advance of Russian troops into Germany.

After the Russians had ordered a general mobilization on July 30, the military timetables which the various general staffs had worked out began to dominate political action. The Russian mobilization impelled the German military leaders to demand immediate mobilization and to urge full mobilization on Austria. According to the military plans agreed upon by the German and Austrian chiefs of staff, the Austrian armies were to slow down the Russian advances toward Germany while the bulk of the German army, engaged in the attempt to knock France out of the war, would be unable to protect Germany's eastern frontier. With the Russians mobilizing, Austrian general mobilization, which would make possible quick counteraction, was required; but it was also necessary that the German campaign against France be started immediately and ended in time for German troops to be moved from the west to the east before the Austrian resistance against the superior Russian forces broke down. Thus, the German military leaders were anxious to terminate all further diplomatic negotiations so that they could invade France. Neither the monarchs of the three empires— Francis Joseph, Nicholas II, and William II—nor their chief civilian advisers had the courage to resist the military leaders who declared that without mobilization their campaign plans would be ruined and the existence of their nations would be endangered. Germany sent an ultimatum to Russia demanding immediate cessation of military preparations, and when no satisfactory answer had been received, declared war on Russia, on August 1. This move was followed on August 3 by a declaration of war against France, which the Germans justified with the palpably false statement that French forces had violated the German frontier.

The irrevocability of the military timetables condemned to failure the last-minute attempts of Sir Edward Grey, the British foreign secretary, to halt mobilization and convoke a conference. British diplomacy had worked hard to save the peace, but the question has been raised of whether it followed the right tactics. Could peace have been maintained if at an early state of the crisis Grey had declared that Great Britain would back France and Russia in case of war? An early British commitment might have gained time for a conference. Austria might have hesitated to take action against Serbia, and Russia, secure in the promise of British help, might have been less anxious to order general mobilization. Those who defend Grey's attitude argue that an assurance of British support might have had the contrary effect of encouraging Russia and France to assume an aggressive attitude and that such a British declaration would not have restrained Germany from its course because the German leaders expected Britain's entry into the war and discounted its importance, doubting that Britain would be able to act quickly enough to prevent the defeat of France.

Moreover, Grey might have hesitated to make any definite statement on what Britain would do in case of war because he could not be sure whether the British people would follow his lead. British public opinion was split on the issue. Decision was brought about only by the German invasion of Belgium on August 3. Belgium's neutrality had been guaranteed by an international treaty to which Germany was a party, and this violation of international law by Germany convinced both the British government and the British people of the necessity of entering the conflict. War was declared on August 4.

During the critical week before the German violation of Belgian neutrality, the Conservatives had favored the participation of Britain because of its ties with France and its interest in maintaining the balance of power. The Labor party opposed intervention. This view was shared by the radical wing of the Liberal party; thus the Liberals lacked any uniform policy on the issue. The Liberal government, like the Liberal party, was divided; even after the violation of Belgian neutrality two members of the government resigned to demonstrate their opposition to Britain's participation. In the debates and discussions on this issue Sir Edward Grey favored British entry into the war, but maintained that Britain had a free hand and was not obligated to support France and Russia. Formally, he was right, in that a binding political alliance had not been concluded. The agreements between the British and French general staff were purely military. Nevertheless, Grey's contention that Britain was free to choose its course was questionable. On the basis of the conversations between the two general staffs the French could expect the arrival of a British expeditionary force on French soil. No general staff would make such arrangements without informing its government and having its approval. In denying the existence of a commitment to France, Grey either was incredibly naïve about the possibility of separating political and military planning or was bending the truth in order to avoid arousing the resentment of the radicals in his party. The French ambassador in London, Paul Cambon, in demanding a British declaration of war against Germany, said that the British answer to this request would show whether "the word 'honor' will not have to be stricken out of the British vocabulary." Grey himself felt immensely relieved when, after the invasion of Belgium, the cabinet decided to enter the war. Waverers were won over by the argument that Britain's participation had now become a moral necessity.

The European Attitude Toward War in 1914

The First World War revealed the frightfulness of warfare in the industrial age. But the terrible losses in human life and material resources caused by the war have colored and distorted the interpretation of the events of July and August, 1914. The discussion of the origins of the First World War has been dominated by the question of guilt: historical research has been essentially an effort to determine the distribution of guilt among the individuals and nations involved. It should therefore be emphasized that in 1914 war was not considered to be a crime but was regarded as a legitimate though unpleasant and dangerous instrument of politics.

Certainly a few people did have some notion of the changes in warfare brought about by the enormously increased destructiveness of modern weapons. Courageous and farseeing individuals—such as Bertha von Suttner, author of the famous book *Lay Down Your Arms!* (1889)—had tried to arouse the public to the dangers of modern war by organizing pacifist movements. The destructiveness of war had also been underlined by the two International Peace Conferences held in The Hague in 1899 and 1907. But these conferences had been concerned with the limitation of armaments and with the humanizing of war rather than with its abolition. Up to 1914 no attempt had been made to prohibit war itself. Moreover, almost everyone was convinced that because the European economy had become a complex integrated structure, a war could last for only a few weeks or months and would be quickly decided in a few great battles. Nobody in 1914 was able to envisage the possibilities which would become stark reality in the next few years.

If government leaders hesitated to embark on the adventure of military conflict they were not deterred by fear of being stamped as criminals. Rather, after the experiences of the Franco-Prussian War and the Russo-Japanese War they saw lurking behind each war the danger of revolution. They were aware that they might unleash forces which the existing ruling group might be unable to control. The governments of the European nations had another equally weighty reason for refraining from obvious aggression. Their armies were based on conscription of the male population. It seemed difficult, if not impossible, to ask people to abandon civilian life and peaceful occupations when the necessity of war was not obvious. Separated by a deep rift from the bourgeois world, the workers were thought to be unwilling to accept war unless convinced that an attack had been made upon a peaceful country by external enemies.

Thus, in the course of the summer of 1914, all the European governments were eager to appear as the innocent victims of aggression. In the course of the First World War this moralistic element, this insistence on the righteousness of one's own cause, grew steadily in emphasis; increasing hatred of the enemy bolstered internal strength. It helped stiffen the will to resist and minimized social and political friction. The war became a struggle of good against evil which had to be fought through until the enemy was completely destroyed.

The fear in government circles that the lower classes would resist mobilization had been primarily caused by the declaration of the Socialist Second International that the workers ought to respond to a call to arms with a general strike. On July 30, 1914, a nationalist fanatic assassinated Jean Jaurès, the French Socialist leader, because he was expected to pronounce an appeal against the war. But it has now been proved that Jaurès never intended to issue such an appeal. Actually none of the European socialist parties heeded the recommendation of the Second International. Each of them backed the war policy of its government. Not only did opposition fail to materialize, the outbreak of war was greeted with an almost delirious enthusiasm. This astonishing response points to causes of war which went deeper than the calculations and miscalculations of foreign ministers and diplomats.

In most European countries the war seemed like a liberation from an unbearable situation. The feeling that political developments had reached a dead end was widespread among the ruling groups—not only in tsarist Russia and in Austria-Hungary, where the governments were involved in a desperate struggle to maintain outmoded forms of rule, but all over Europe. In Great Britain the reforms of the Liberal government did not mitigate social tensions; labor conflicts and strikes had been particularly vehement in the years immediately before the outbreak of the war. And although an attempt to solve the Irish question could no longer be postponed it endangered the authority of the government. In France politics had again become polarized between right and left, which opposed each other with renewed vehemence. In Italy impatience with the government's cautious policy of industrialization and democratization had stirred up extreme antiparliamentary movements on the right and left. And in Germany the elections to the Reichstag in 1912, from which the Social Democrats emerged as the strongest political party, had demonstrated that the masses could not be reconciled to their lack of political power by orderly administration and measures of social welfare.

The years before the First World War are usually regarded as having been full of sun and light in contrast to the darkness which descended on Europe in 1914. But actually the unrest in the years immediately preceding the outbreak of the war was great. The traditional politics of the ruling groups could not reconcile the alienated segments of society and had not resulted in a broadening of the bases of the existing order. The war was a way out from what had become a deadlock.

In the view of the German sociologist Max Weber rational organization and bureaucratization, which made man a cog in the wheel of a disciplined mass society, was the unavoidable future faced by the modern industrial world; to the people of the middle classes, immured in what was still a rather new phenomenon, the war came as an opportunity to break out of this industrial society. The workers were in an ambiguous situation; they, or at least many of them, were gaining a greater share in a society from which they were alienated. But the revolution which was to make them the masters of the social order seemed far removed, certainly more distant than when the socialist parties had been founded.

In the minds of almost all classes the discontent with the existing social order made the war, with its sudden release from the bonds of daily routine and with its forging of new ties, the harbinger of a highly desirable new social order. Behind the obvious shock and fear there were also hope and expectation—this should not be forgotten in explaining the causes of the catastrophe which resulted in 37.5 million casualties, in the annihilation of nearly an entire male generation, and in the loss of European hegemony over the world.

THE NATURE OF TOTAL WAR

As time has passed since the days of August, 1914, it has become increasingly clear that the outbreak of the First World War meant the end of an age. To be sure, if we consider carefully the developments of the decades preceding the war we can distinguish trends and tendencies which were steering European politics and social life into new waters. But the First World War reinforced these trends and thus accelerated the tempo of change.

It would be a mistake to assume that the new era began only in 1918, with the end of hostilities. The First World War was not just a violent interlude separating the old era from the new. The new age came about during the war years, and what happened between 1914 and 1918 helps to make the period that followed comprehensible.

Most immediately apparent were the changes effected by the conflict itself, by innovations in the techniques and the conduct of the war. When the European powers mobilized in the radiant late-summer days of 1914, the troops marching through the streets to the railroad stations, accompanied by jubilant crowds, offered an impressive and colorful sight. Flowers were strewn before the men who were expected to return triumphant after a few weeks. Flags flew; bands played; and the soldiers went singing into the war. In the first months military action was conducted in a traditional manner. Extended columns of infantry marched along the roads. The cavalry scouted enemy positions; officers led their men to storm a town or village. But after the initial battles in the west the lines became weirdly silent. Soldiers dug themselves into deep trenches fortified by barbed wire; a no-man's-land between the opposing positions was illuminated at night by rockets, intended to reveal any enemy patrols trying to penetrate the lines. The graceful, elegant horses of the cavalry became superfluous. Reconnaissance was most efficient from the air, and sometimes these scouting planes armed with machine guns engaged in air battles. Pilots became the popular war heroes. The infantry soldier, clad in mud-colored gray or khaki, still had his rifle and bayonet but his most valuable weapons were the hand grenade and the machine gun. Before the war was over poison gas was being directed against enemy lines, and tanks moved clumsily over fields and trenches.

War enthusiasm in Germany. *Soldiers on the way to the front in 1914.*

The changes in sea warfare were no less considerable. With one exception—the indecisive meeting of the British and German fleets at Jutland (1916)—no naval battles took place. Warships were used to protect convoys against the attacks of submarines, which became the supreme weapon in the struggle for control of the seas.

These changes indicate that in the twentieth century war was becoming more than the struggle of armed forces: not without reason does the term "total war" appear. To maintain a flow of the weapons which had become decisive, the continuous functioning of a sophisticated industrial complex was required. When the war broke out, only a very few had an inkling of the importance of a steady supply of raw materials and manpower, and it took some time for political and military leaders to be convinced of this fact.

The Home Front

In the question of manpower the crucial problem was to reconcile military and industrial needs. Miners and steelworkers might be perfectly suited for military service, but they possessed the skills and the physical abilities needed in mines and industry. Priorities had to be established. As the war dragged on and casualties became heavy, the tapping of new sources of manpower became a constant concern of the governments. The age limits for military service were extended; and women were employed in jobs previously reserved for men, working in offices and factories, as streetcar conductors and farmhands.

Every industry not immediately serving military ends had to be reduced to a minimum. One reason was the need for conserving manpower; another, the scarcity of raw materials. Before the conflict no European country had been self-sufficient. France, which had been less dependent on imports than other European powers, soon lost this advantageous position because a great part of its most industrialized regions was occupied by the Germans. International trade, through which raw materials had been obtained in peacetime, was interrupted by military action. Moreover, the importation of raw materials represented a drain on the gold reserves of each country because the manufacture of the exports which had brought in foreign currency was no longer possible. Strict control over raw materials—their conservation, collection, and distribution to factories according to military needs—became necessary.

Maintenance of the supply of food was the most burning problem, not only in great industrial countries like Great Britain and Germany which, in peacetime, had relied on imported wheat and other foodstuffs, but also in agrarian countries like Austria and France, where conscription denuded the land of agricultural workers. Moreover, the transportation of food to the urban centers was difficult because the railroads were overtaxed by military needs. All of the governments resorted to rationing, which usually began with bread and meat, then extended to other foodstuffs, and finally included clothes, soap, and so on. Thus, manpower, raw materials, consumer goods, all were placed under government control.

Ministries for directing economic activities were established. Strikes were outlawed, working hours prolonged. Certainly government intervention in economic affairs and government regulation of economic life were more thorough in some countries than in others—more complete in Germany and Great Britain than in Austria-Hungary, Russia, and Italy, with their ineffective bureaucracies. Nevertheless, the subjection of economic activities to government regulation all over Europe represented a radical break with the notion that the economy could function only when free from government intervention. Unquestionably, rationing and government regulations were the only possible means of assuring the existence of all the people. Even so, on the Continent, particularly in Russia, Austria, and Germany, these measures provided hardly a subsistence minimum; people were hungry and easily exhausted, and "black markets," from which the wealthy added to their rations, resulted in a spread of corruption and a decline in morale.

No longer confined to the battlefield, war became total as belligerent activities affected the entire life of the nation. To be sure, airplane construction was not yet advanced enough to permit mass bombing. A few raids by airplanes over enemy cities and a few flights of the big German airship, the Zeppelin, over the English east coast and London were more effective in inspiring terror than in inflicting serious damage. But they were signs of the form of wars to come.

The chief instrument used to throttle the economic life of the enemy was the blockade. The British controlled the North Sea and prevented Germany from receiving supplies from the other side of the Atlantic. The Germans suddenly recognized that their strongest weapon in sea warfare was the submarine and they declared the entire British Isles to be blockaded territory and claimed the right to search and sink all ships approaching British ports.

In the First World War the activities and the morale of the civilian population acquired crucial importance. There now existed not only a military front but also a home front. And to maintain the spirit of the home front became essential. In all countries censorship was used, both to prevent the spreading of news which might be helpful to the enemy and to control and direct all news media toward the strengthening of civilian morale. It was as a consequence of the First World War that "propaganda" came to be a pejorative term: all governments installed propaganda offices and all of them falsified news. One of the chief duties of the war propagandists was to discredit the enemy, to paint him in the darkest colors, so that the populace would become convinced that defeat would mean the destruction of all that was worth living for. The practice of viewing the war as a struggle against evil increased steadily. Anti-German propaganda was particularly effective because the conduct of the Germans provided a factual basis for reports of their atrocities. The brutal behavior of the German armies in Belgium was undeniable. Because they had expected to pass through unmolested, the Belgian resistance infuriated them. The suddenness of the German invasion made it impossible for the Belgians to mobilize and many fought in civilian clothes, identified as soldiers only by armbands. This practice was accepted in international law, but the Germans considered all those fighting out of uniform as *franc-tireurs*, to be shot when captured. The impression that the entire civilian population of Belgium was resisting made the Germans jittery; they took hostages and executed them when they found opposition. In the last week of August the London *Times* called the Germans "Huns," in reference to events in Louvain. There, in the belief that sniping had occurred and that Louvain was full of *franc-tireurs*, the Germans shot a large number of citizens and set the town on fire. The famous old library of the university was entirely destroyed. The "vandalism of Louvain" was soon aggravated by the "crime of Rheims." In September, 1914, the Germans, convinced that the tower of the cathedral of Rheims served as a French observation post, fired on the cathedral, severely damaging the roof and the nave. Even if the tower was being used, the destruction wrought on a great monument of European art was indefensible. The Germans provided further food for propaganda against them by their ruthless occupation policy in Belgium. They executed Edith Cavell, a nurse who had helped British and French soldiers to escape over the borders into the neutral Netherlands, ignoring the fact—recognized by some of their own occupation officers—that as head of a hospital she had selflessly worked to mitigate the sufferings of soldiers of all nations, and deserved mercy rather

THE VETERAN'S FAREWELL.

"Good Bye, my lad,
I only wish I were young enough
to go with you!"

ENLIST NOW!

War enthusiasm in Great Britain. *A famous enlistment poster.*

than justice. Another incident, called by President Wilson "one of the most distressing and I think one of the most unjustifiable incidents of the present war," was the deportation of more than 100,000 Belgian workers into Germany.

The War Aims

The ideological and moralistic approach which determined the attitude toward the war in all countries made impossible a negotiated peace aimed at reestablishing a balance of power and restoring international collaboration. Each side was convinced that the war could end only with the complete defeat of the enemy, so that an entirely new world could be created. Each therefore attempted to present its war aims in generalized idealistic terms showing that victory would serve the interest of all mankind. Formulation of such war aims was relatively easy for Great Britain, France, and their allies in the last two years of the conflict. The war was declared to be a struggle for a new world order based on the principles of democracy and national self-determination, its purpose succinctly summarized in the famous slogan "to make the world safe for democracy." As long as Russia with its authoritarian government, was a member of the coalition against Germany, the assertion about fighting for democracy had a hollow sound. But after the overthrow of the tsar in March, 1917, the notion of a struggle between democracy and authoritarianism gained meaning, particularly since the overthrow coincided with the entrance into the war against Germany of the greatest democracy in the world, the United States. The fact that men and women of all classes contributed to the military effort gave force to the demand that they should have the right to decide the political fate of their country. Where before the First World War the demand for suffrage for women had been regarded as utopian and even ridiculous, it now became more urgent. In Great Britain, Germany, and the United States, female suffrage was achieved soon after the war. In Italy and France its adversaries were able to delay giving women the vote until after the Second World War. But even there the final victory of female suffrage was never seriously in doubt.

It was difficult for Germany and its allies to place the war on a broad ideological level. The German Social Democratic party had been the largest and best organized of all socialist parties. Socialist approval of the money bills required for the financing of the war was the most striking and also the most surprising example of the abandonment of revolutionary international-ism by Social Democrats in favor of defense of the homeland. The German government gained the support of socialist and progressive forces without taking them into the government. Thus, during most of the war Germany continued to be ruled by the members of the conservative bureaucracy Their innate resistance to liberal and democratic reforms was reinforced by the military, whose power now increased immensely. William II, who even in peacetime had failed to exercise steady leadership, did not dare to challenge the men of the hour. Thus the German military leaders Paul von Hindenburg (1847–1934) and Erich Ludendorff (1865–1937), who were enormously popular because of victories against the Russians, began to exert—if not in form, at least in fact—a military dictatorship. As allies of the Conservatives they resisted political reforms, and the tensions which had existed in peacetime came again out into the open during the last few years of the war, expressing themselves in a bitter struggle about the war aims between those who wanted to fight for total victory so that Germany could make extended annexations and those who believed that peace ought to be concluded on the basis of the *status quo* and that every effort should be made to reach a peace of understanding. Thus in Germany the united front which had been established in August, 1914, began to show fissures, which became deeper month by month.

THE TIDES OF BATTLE

The Expanding Theater of War

The conflict that took place between 1914 and 1918 is rightly called a world war, for it assumed global dimensions. At the start, however, it was confined to the great European powers: Great Britain, France, Russia,

The German Military High Command. *Hindenburg, William II, Ludendorff.*

Germany, and Austria-Hungary. Only two of the smaller European states participated from the outset in this struggle of the great powers: Serbia, whose conflict with Austria had led to the explosion, and Belgium, which had been forced to resist by the German violation of its internationally guaranteed neutrality. The first non-European power, Japan, entered the war in August. But its military contribution was limited to the conquest and occupation of the German colonial possessions in the Far East. A real enlargement of the theater of war took place with the entry of Turkey on the German side in November, 1914. Turkey occupied a key position. By allying itself with the western powers and Russia, it could have closed the ring around the Central Powers—as Austria and Germany were called—and ensured coordinated action against them from the west, east, and south. On the other hand, as an ally of Germany and Austria, Turkey could prevent the shipping of supplies to Russia through the Mediterranean and the Black Sea. Hence, a fierce diplomatic struggle for the favors of Turkey took place in Constantinople, but the hold which Germany had developed over Turkey through the building of the Baghdad Railway, reinforced by the appearance of two German naval ships in the Dardanelles, proved to be the stronger. The entry of Turkey extended the war into Mesopotamia and Persia, where British and Russian forces on the one hand and Turkish troops under German command on the other fought with alternating success. In order to relieve the pressure on Turkey, Germany and Austria became anxious to establish direct communication with the Ottoman Empire. Promising the cession of large parts of Macedonia, now in Serbian hands, they persuaded Bulgaria to enter the war in October, 1915. In counteraction, the Allies—France, Great Britain, and Russia—induced Rumania in August, 1916, and then Greece in June, 1917, to declare war on the Central Powers, although by that time Serbia had succumbed to the joint attacks from the west and the north, so that the Central Powers dominated a broad connected stretch of territory from the North Sea to Mesopotamia and the Suez Canal. However, in 1915 the Allies had gained an important partner in Italy. Originally the Italians had declared themselves to be neutral because in their view the Austrians had started the war and had not acted in self-defense, requiring Italian assistance under the Triple Alliance. The Italians were courted by both sides, but the Central Powers could not make any promises that outweighed Italy's interest in using this war for the liberation of people of Italian nationality living under Austrian rule. The Allies in a secret agreement concluded in London in April, 1915, promised Italy, in addition to the Austrian provinces inhabited by Italians, a wide expanse on the eastern side of the Adriatic Sea, including northern Albania; the Dodecanese in the Aegean Sea; and—if Turkey was partitioned—a part of Asia Minor. Later, even Portugal and San Marino entered the war; by 1917, with exception of the Scandinavian countries, the Netherlands, Switzerland, and Spain, all the European nations were engaged on one side or the other. With the entry of the United States in April, 1917, the war finally took on a global character. Then a number of Latin-American states, among them Brazil, declared war on Germany, and others, such as Bolivia, Peru, and Ecuador, severed relations with Germany. In Asia, China and Siam and in Africa, Liberia joined the coalition against the Central Powers. In many of these cases the reason for participation was purely economic. The rupture with Germany served to tighten loopholes in the blockade, to prevent the transference of German capital, and to permit the confiscation of German assets. In any event, the war had become global.

The small size of the area occupied by the Central Powers in comparison with the vast extent of the territory represented by their enemies might lead one to believe that the defeat of the Central Powers was almost inevitable. But the actual fact is that many times Germany seemed near victory and the German collapse in 1918 was sudden and unexpected.

Stalemate in the West

When the war broke out, the German general staff planned to defeat France within six weeks and then to turn against Russia. A quick victory in the west was to be attained by concentrating almost all the German forces against France, most of them on the right wing, which was to advance in a great wheeling movement through Belgium and northern France and then turn south and finally east, trapping the French forces in a gigantic ring. The strategy used by Hannibal in his defeat of the Romans at Cannae was to be repeated on an immensely enlarged scale. This was the famous Schlieffen Plan, named after the German chief of staff who had conceived it about 1905. The plan failed; the German advances were halted in the Battle of the Marne, which takes its place as one of the decisive battles of history.

1914–1915

—— Fronts, end of 1914

----- Fronts, end of 1915

NORWAY

SWEDEN

JAPAN
(AUG 23, 1914)

NORTH SEA

DENMARK

BRITISH BLOCKADE, NOV. 1914

BALTIC SEA

• Riga

GREAT BRITAIN
(AUG 4, 1914)

Kiel •

× MASURIAN LAKES, SEPT. 1914

ATLANTIC

London •

Hamburg •

× TANNENBERG, AUG 27–30, 1914

The Hague

NETH.

GERMANY
(AUG 1, 1914)

POLAND

RUSSIA
(AUG 1, 1914)

LIMIT OF GERMAN ADVANCE, 1915

• Berlin

Warsaw •

• Brest-Litovsk

OCEAN

BEL. (AUG 4, 1914)

INVASION, AUG. 1914

• Kiev

BATTLE OF THE MARNE, SEPT. 1915

LUX.

Prague •

GALICIA

ALLIED OFFENSIVE, SEPT–NOV, 1915

× Paris

FRANCE
(AUG 3, 1914)

Munich •

Vienna •

Budapest •

Bordeaux •

SWITZ.

AUSTRIA–HUNGARY
(JULY 28, 1914)

Milan •

RUMANIA

PORT.

SAN MARINO ✣
(JUNE 3, 1915)

Adriatic Sea

Belgrade •

• Bucharest

BLACK SEA

SPAIN

Marseilles •

Sarajevo •

SERBIA
(JULY 28, 1914)

BULGARIA
(OCT 14, 1915)

0 _____ 500 miles

ITALY
(MAY 23, 1915)

• Rome

MONTENEGRO
(AUG 5, 1915)

• Sofia

Constantinople

ALBANIA

Salonika •

OTTOMAN EMP.
(NOV 2, 1914)

Gallipoli •

CORFU

GREECE

Dardanelles

ALLIED OFFENSIVE, FEB. 1915–JAN. 1916

THE FIRST WORLD WAR

▨ Allied Powers ▩ Central Powers

☐ Neutral nations

Dates of entry into the war thus: (AUG 1, 1914)

NORWAY

SWEDEN

JUTLAND, MAY–JUNE, 1916 ×

NORTH SEA

DENMARK

BALTIC SEA

• Riga

GREAT BRITAIN

Kiel •

RUSSIA

ATLANTIC

London •

Hamburg •

The Hague •

NETH.

• Berlin

POLAND INDEPENDENT, NOV 5, 1916

RUSSIAN OFFENSIVE, JUNE–DEC, 1916

SOMME, JUNE–NOV, 1916

BEL.

GERMANY

Warsaw •

• Brest-Litovsk

OCEAN

LUX.

× Paris

Prague •

CARPATHIAN MTS.

GALICIA

VERDUN, JULY–DEC, 1916

Munich •

Vienna •

FRANCE

SWITZ.

Budapest •

PORT.
(MAR 9, 1916)

Milan •

AUSTRIA–HUNGARY

RUMANIA
(AUG 27, 1916)

BLACK SEA

SPAIN

Marseilles •

Belgrade •

• Bucharest

0 _____ 500 miles

ITALY

Adriatic Sea

SURRENDER, JAN. 1916

SERBIA

BULGARIA

• Rome

MONTENEGRO

• Sofia

ALBANIA

Constantinople

1916

—— Fronts, Aug 31, 1916

----- Fronts, Dec 31, 1916

MEDITERRANEAN SEA

Salonika •

CORFU

GREECE
(OCT 18, 1916)

OTTOMAN EMP.

There were many reasons for the failure. First, the Belgian resistance delayed the German advance. Also, the Germans had not counted on the appearance of a British expeditionary corps which, although thrown back in the battles of Mons and Le Cateau, seriously retarded their movement forward. Alexander von Kluck, the commander of the German First Army, operating on the extreme right, believed that the presence of the British forces made it impossible to include Paris in the wide encircling movement which had been envisaged. He ordered his troops to turn sharply to the south, leaving Paris at their right. And this gave the French their opportunity. Although forced to retreat throughout August, the French army had not disintegrated. The commander of the French forces, Joseph Joffre, was an adherent of the doctrine of continuous attack and had been less concerned with arranging a defensive position than with seizing an opportunity to attack. Kluck's move to the south made it possible for Joffre to attack the German flank and rear. A famous episode of the ensuing battle was that under orders from Gallieni, the commandant of Paris, the city's taxi drivers transported men directly from Paris to the front. On September 9, Kluck's army was ordered to retreat from the Marne to the Aisne. The German campaign plan had failed.

The German military command contributed to the defeat. It had watered down the original Schlieffen Plan; the right wing was weaker than it ought to have been. Moreover, the German army on the left had been engaged in a battle in Lorraine and could therefore spare no troops to reinforce the right wing at the decisive moment. Helmuth von Moltke, the German chief of staff, following the precepts of his uncle, the great strategist of the nineteenth century, gave his field commanders freedom of decision. But he followed this principle too literally and too slavishly. There was little leadership from above, nor was there much communication among the various German commanders. Thus, between the First German Army, operating on the extreme right, and the Second German Army, operating further left, a gap opened at the critical time when the French counterattack began. And Moltke, alarmed by the dangers which might result from French advances into this gap, ordered retreat.

Whatever responsibility for the outcome of the Battle of the Marne one assigns to the energy and courage of the French and British generals, or to the mistakes committed by the German military leaders, the entire Schlieffen Plan was probably not feasible. In 1914 armies were not yet motorized and the distances involved in encircling the armed forces of an entire nation were too large to be covered by foot soldiers, at least with the speed and precision required for success.

The Battle of the Marne was followed by a race for the channel ports. Each side tried to regain freedom of movement by outflanking the other; but despite a bloody struggle along the seacoast in Flanders, neither was dislodged. The front now became stabilized: it began at the North Sea, in Flanders; then bulged out into France, with Germany retaining control of important French industrial areas; and then swung back to the Franco-German frontier along Alsace-Lorraine, ending at the Swiss border. The armies dug in. For the next four years, until the spring of 1918, the lines remained almost unchanged, although sporadic and bloody attempts were made to end the stalemate and break through the enemy's lines. In February, 1916, the Germans launched an attack on Verdun. This was intended to be a battle of attrition. The Germans wanted to draw the flower of the French army into this battle and destroy the morale of the French troops. But in June, when the battle was broken off, the German losses were hardly less great than the French and the German territorial gains were insignificant. In July, 1916, the French and the British attacked along the Somme, their main purpose being to draw German troops away from the eastern front, where the Russians were in dire straits; again, only small territorial gains had been made by November, when the battle at the Somme got stuck in the mud. The French and British attempted a breakthrough in the spring of 1917 by simultaneous attacks at two different points, Arras and along the Aisne; the general responsible for this offensive was the French commander in chief Nivelle. His main success was the conquering of the Chemin des Dames, a height in the center of the front line, but the losses were so terrible that mutiny broke out in the French army and General Henri Philippe Pétain (1856–1951), who was called in to replace Nivelle, decided on a purely defensive conduct of the war in the west. However the British commander, Douglas Haig, believed that Nivelle's offensive had failed because of tactical mistakes and that he, Haig could do better. Despite great doubts in the British cabinet, Haig ordered an offensive in Flanders, around Ypres, which began on July 31 and lasted until November. Again the territorial gains were small and the casualties staggering. The rain and mud of autumn slowed down every step so that the advancing troops offered easy targets. Passchendaele, as this battle is usually called, together "with the Somme and Verdun, will always rank as the most gigantic, tenacious, grim, futile and bloody fight ever waged in the history of war"[1]—an entirely useless slaughter. If any further proof was needed, Passchendaele showed that new weapons and new methods had to be introduced if the superiority of the defense over the offense was to be overcome.

German Success in the East

The failure at Verdun sufficiently proved to the Germans the futility of an offensive in the west. Those German military leaders who had believed

---

[1] David Lloyd George, *War Memoirs*, Vol. IV (London, 1934), p. 2110.

The political and military leaders of Great Britain and France. *Haig, Joffre, Lloyd George are shown on the left. Foch, Haig, Clemenceau, and Weigand on the right.*

since the failure in the Battle of the Marne that victory could be obtained only through defeat of Russia now gained the upper hand. The most influential and effective representatives of this view were Hindenburg and Ludendorff. They had acquired immense popularity in Germany because in August and September of 1914, in the battles of Tannenberg and the Masurian Lakes, they had defeated and annihilated two Russian armies advancing into East Prussia. Hindenburg's and Ludendorff's responsibility for these victories is somewhat diminished by the fact that they arrived— Hindenburg from retirement, Ludendorff from the west—when the German commanders on the spot had already made the arrangements for the battles. Nevertheless, Hindenburg and Ludendorff, as saviors of Germany from the Russian barbarians, became popular heroes. In September, 1914, Hindenburg was made commander in chief of the German armies in the east and in 1916 he became chief of staff, with Ludendorff as his main assistant. The German conduct of the war in the east was brilliant. In 1915 a great offensive was started in Galicia, which the Russians had occupied, and soon the operations extended over the entire eastern frontier; by the time military activity halted in the fall the lines reached from the eastern part of Galicia straight to the north, with the Central Powers having conquered Poland, Lithuania, and Kurland.

These German victories were facilitated by the Russians' lack of munitions and equipment. At the beginning of 1915 the British had made an ingenious attempt to open a direct route to Russia through the Dardanelles. This operation—the Gallipoli campaign—failed mainly through lack of cooperation between the naval and the land forces. Thus, materials could be sent to the Russians only through Siberia; the Russians were forced to rely on their own resources for the 1916 summer campaign, which became decisive for the war in the east. The Russians had planned an offensive which would be coordinated with the entry of Rumania into the war. But Rumania was quickly defeated and occupied by the Germans, and although the Russians drove the Austrians back more than eighty miles to the Carpathians and into Galicia, they suffered such serious losses that, with the coming of the winter, they were at the end of their strength. In March, 1917, revolution broke out, the tsar abdicated, and a republic was proclaimed. Since the new liberal leaders of Russia felt close to the parliamentary democracies of Great Britain and France and were anxious to continue the war, the change in government was of no advantage to Germany. The Germans were interested in weakening or overthrowing the new liberal government and the German high command agreed to permit a group of radical revolutionaries, among them Lenin and other principal Bolsheviks, to travel in a sealed railroad coach from Switzerland, where they were living in exile, through Germany to Russia. On April 16, 1917, the Bolshevik leaders arrived in Petrograd, the former St. Petersburg, whose name had been russified during the war. Their chance came in the summer of 1917 with the collapse, after some initial success, of an offensive ordered by the liberal Russian government. Making full use of the war-weariness of the masses, the Bolsheviks succeeded in seizing power. Shortly afterward an armistice was concluded, and militarily helpless and under the pressure of further German advances, the Bolshevik government was forced to sign a separate peace treaty with the Central Powers at Brest-Litovsk in March, 1918.

Thus, in the early spring of 1918 the Central Powers had freed themselves from the danger of a two-front war and seemed in a brilliant position. Half a year later the German high command was to declare to its government that

The signing of the armistice that ended the war in the east. *On the left, the German, Austrian, and Bulgarian representatives; on the right, Bolshevik representatives.*

the war must be considered lost. And in November, 1918, a Germany transformed by revolution into a republic agreed to an armistice which could only lead to a peace dictated by the western powers. What had happened to bring about this reversal of fortune?

Decision in the West

All of Germany's successes in the east could not outweigh the fact that its strongest adversaries were in the west and that victory was impossible without defeating them. It seemed clear that action at sea would be required to subdue Great Britain, the most formidable of the western enemies. Early in the war, a naval blockade to deprive Germany of raw materials had been instituted by Britain and France. In international law a distinction is made between contraband—munitions and raw materials needed for the manufacture of military equipment—and noncontraband, notably food and clothing. Only contraband is subject to confiscation by a blockading power. But the British refused to recognize this distinction. No ships of any neutral power were permitted to go to a German port, and imports into the Scandinavian countries and the Netherlands were limited to quantities which assured that the goods would be used in the importing countries and not be reshipped to Germany.

The British violation of recognized international law created serious trouble between the United States and Great Britain. But the United States finally sided with Great Britain against Germany because the Germans too violated international law—flagrantly and even more brutally than the British. The Germans felt that they could counterbalance the British blockade by a more effective form of economic warfare, a submarine blockade. Submarines could not remove goods or people from merchant ships; they could only sink the ships. The Germans declared the waters surrounding the British Isles to be a war zone in which all enemy vessels would be torpedoed and even those of neutral nations, if suspected of carrying goods, might be sunk. In February, 1915, a German submarine torpedoed the *Lusitania*, a British passenger liner; almost 1,200 people drowned, among them 118 American citizens. While it was true that the *Lusitania* carried ammunition, the death of more than a thousand civilians, many from neutral countries, seemed incredibly brutal. Indignation in the United States mounted. After a severe warning by President Wilson, the Germans relented and for two years they modified their conduct of submarine warfare. But pressure against Chancellor Bethmann-Hollweg and those of his advisers who advocated caution in using the submarine steadily mounted. It was difficult for the public to bear the hardships of the British blockade when Germany was believed to be in possession of a weapon with which it could retaliate. Moreover, the German navy had built many new submarines and the naval high command, supported by experts anxious to please the admirals, maintained that Great Britain could be starved out and forced to surrender in a short time. Hindenburg and Ludendorff gave full support to the demands of the navy. On January 31, 1917, the Germans proclaimed the resumption of unrestricted submarine warfare. President Wilson severed diplomatic relations with Germany, and provoked by the sinking of American ships, the United States declared war on Germany on April 6, 1917.

The effect of America's entry into the war was immense. British shipping losses, especially since the declaration of unrestricted submarine warfare, had risen dangerously. In April, 1917, alone, 875,000 tons of shipping were sunk. By organizing a convoy system, the British had tried to master this threat. But the entry of the United States into the war made the German submarine warfare an evident failure, because thereafter the number of ships convoyed and the number of ships protecting the convoys was increased steadily. Convoys of ships transporting food, war materials, and troops arrived safely in Britain, and the rate of shipping construction soon exceeded the rate of loss. Moreover, the entry of the United States into the war blunted the uplift in morale which the breakdown of Russia would otherwise have produced in Germany. Indeed, Wilson's insistence on a just and democratic peace increased internal tension in Germany. The demand grew for a guarantee that the war would not be fought to achieve the aims and ambitions of the ruling group but would be terminated as soon as the existence of the German people was no longer threatened. Both at home and abroad, distrust of the policy of the German leaders was reinforced by events connected with the negotiations in Brest-Litovsk about peace with the Bolsheviks. The Bolshevik delegation, under the leadership of Leon Trotsky (1877–1940), embarked upon a heated discussion of war aims with the foreign ministers of Germany and Austria, and widespread reports of this debate disseminated the Bolshevik formula of "peace without annexations or indemnities." The treaty which was finally forced upon Russia early

War in the air. *Two planes collide during a dogfight.*

in 1918 was dictated by the German military high command, and it was harsh. Its main effect was to push Russia out of Europe. Russia was forced to abandon Finland, the Baltic provinces, Poland, the Ukraine, and Trans-caucasia. The Central Powers established in these countries regimes con-trolled by small wealthy groups: German landowners in the Baltic states, a small pro-German military clique in the Ukraine. German princes were placed on the thrones of such newly established states as Lithuania, Kurland, and Finland. The Treaty of Brest-Litovsk imposed a peace of annexation and of power politics.

Despite the apparent military advantage of the Central Powers at the beginning of 1918, their situation had grave weaknesses. The brutal German policy in the east kept the conquered areas restless and in revolt. Large military forces had to remain in the east, and the transportation of food, especially of wheat from the Ukraine, met many obstacles. Increasingly, the governments of the Central Powers were being criticized as overweening in their ambitions and unwilling or unable to terminate the war. The Allies had become strong enough to mount offensives at various fronts. In the fall of 1917 the British had thrown the Turks back from the Egyptian frontier and advanced into Palestine, taking Jerusalem on December 8, 1917. Greece's entry into the war in June, 1917, had made possible an offensive against Bulgaria. On the other hand in October, 1917, Austrian and German troops had broken the Italian front in the Battle of Caporetto, brilliantly described by Ernest Hemingway in A *Farewell to Arms* (1929). To stem the panic among Italian troops, Italian military police were ordered to shoot every tenth man of any formation that was fleeing. Significantly, even the German victory at Caporetto did not eliminate Italy from the war. The British and French were able to send in enough reinforcements to re-construct an Italian front along the Piave.

Thus, at the beginning of 1918, despite the Treaty of Brest-Litovsk, Germany was not in an unassailable position, able to wait for the Allies to force the issue. The arrival of American troops and increasing disaffection within Germany necessitated action leading to a quick end to the war. The German military leaders responded with an offensive in the west which they believed, with the help of reinforcements from the east, would bring victory. But in its outcome this offensive, which started on March 21, 1918, was no different from previous ones in the west. Initially, territorial gains were large. But when the German soldiers advanced beyond the zone where they enjoyed protection from their artillery, they again found that in trench warfare defense was superior to attack, and the German offensive got stuck. German attacks in other areas of the front lacked even the force of the March offensive. The Germans were halted—by the French at Compiègne and by the Americans and the French at Château-Thierry. Starting in July, 1918, the Allies, now led by Ferdinand Foch, commander in chief of all the armies in France, began to attack. And their advances were power-

War on land. *Dugouts on the Western Front.*

fully supported by use of the tank—a new weapon which brought an element of movement into the war of position. At the same time, the Allied armies in Salonika and the Italians at the Piave began to advance and both the Bulgarian and the Austrian fronts collapsed; Bulgaria and Austria asked for peace.

At this point Ludendorff urged the German government to seek an armistice. German political leaders now lost all confidence in the German high command, and the German people and the troops were no longer willing to accept the leadership of the military or of the rulers who had supported them. Revolution spread from town to town. By November 9 all the German princes, William II included, had abdicated, and on November 11 the armistice was signed. The First World War was at an end.

A GENERATION LOST

In western Europe the losses and casualties of the First World War were considerably larger than those suffered by the same states in the Second World War. Altogether, about 8.5 million men were dead. More than twice that number were wounded, many of them maimed for life. The total number of casualties, including killed, wounded, and missing, is figured as 37.5 million. The greatest number of war dead and wounded—about 6 million—was suffered by Germany. France's losses were 5.5 million, but with a population less than two thirds that of Germany, France suffered proportionately more in the First World War than any other belligerent. The losses in single battles were horrendous. In the Battle of Verdun the Germans and the French each lost more than 300,000 men. Passchendaele cost the British 245,000 men. An entire generation rotted on the battlefields. Modern warfare does not lead to a survival of the strongest or the best. Many who might have been leaders in the coming decade never returned from the war.

In considering the developments following the holocaust, it is important to remember that the usual transition from one generation to the next did not take place in the interwar period. It is true that at the end of the 1920's a few men of the war generation did advance to political leadership: Anthony Eden in Great Britain, Edouard Daladier in France, Heinrich Brüning in Germany. But the distinction which they enjoyed as members of the war generation emphasizes how few of those who could become national leaders survived. Benito Mussolini and Adolf Hitler made a great play over having been frontline soldiers fighting in the trenches. They pretended to be the representatives of the generation which the old men tried to keep down and to suffocate. Exaggerated as such claims were, the leading statesmen of Europe, far into the 1930's, almost up to the Second World War, were for the most part men who had come into positions before the First World War. Moreover, because the memory of the events and experiences of this war persisted long after 1918, people continued to look upon the wartime military leaders as father figures to whom they could entrust their fate. Instead of fading away, the generals, the Hindenburgs and the Pétains—whether victorious or defeated—remained important personages on the political scene. There was a strange incongruity between the new issues which the First World War had created and the aged political leaders whose task it was to grapple with these problems.

War crimes. *The cathedral of Rheims after artillery bombardment.*

CHAPTER 39

The World at the End of the
First World War

THE CONFLICT which had begun in August, 1914, as a struggle between the great European powers had become a world war by the time it drew to a close. That the future of Europe was now linked with the future of the rest of the world was apparent at the Paris Peace Conference which met in January, 1919. Statesmen assembled from all parts of the world, and they redrew boundaries not only in Europe but also in Africa and Asia. The role which political leaders of other continents now played in the making of war and peace was a striking sign that the time when the European statesmen could arrange among themselves the affairs of the entire globe had passed. Moreover, the decrease of Europe's weight in international affairs was indicated not only by the weakening of European rule over other parts of the world, but by the fact that developments elsewhere began increasingly to impinge on the political situation in Europe; the impact of global events on the European political scene grew steadily during the twenty years between the two world wars. These events would contribute to the final breakdown of the European postwar settlement. Therefore, before we enter upon a detailed discussion of the European peace settlement we shall examine briefly the new forces which emerged in other continents and which undermined the rule of European powers over the globe.

THE LEAGUE OF NATIONS

The most visible sign of the changed relationship between the European and the non-European parts of the world was the establishment of the League of Nations. In contrast to the nineteenth-century concert of a few great European powers, the League was expected to embrace all the states of the world, and large and small were to have the same voice. The idea of the League owed its origin to a widespread rejection of prewar diplomacy, which with its concern for the balance of power, its eagerness for secret treaties and systems of alliances, and its insistence on strong armaments was considered to have been responsible for the outbreak of the First World War. During the war the need for a "new diplomacy" was particularly

The Big Four. *The prime ministers of Italy, Great Britain, France—Orlando, Lloyd George, Clemenceau—and President Wilson.*

emphasized by writers and politicians of the Anglo-Saxon countries, and their ideas found an eloquent advocate in President Woodrow Wilson (1856–1924), who incorporated them in his peace program.

President Wilson provided the Allied cause with a persuasive justification. They were fighting for the creation of a new world. Boundaries should be drawn according to the principle of national self-determination, so that conflicts over expansion would not arise. Freedom of the seas and removal of economic restrictions should raise the level of economic well-being in all nations, and bind them together in cooperation. The single states should establish democratic forms of government so that the peaceful intentions of the people would prevail over the designs of small authoritarian militaristic groups. Abolition of secret treaties and "open diplomacy" would further assure the coming of a peaceful era in international relations, and a world-embracing organization of nations would supervise the maintenance of this new order. Wilson summarized these democratic war aims in his so-called "Fourteen Points" that made a deep impression all over the world.

At the Paris Peace Conference, Wilson regarded the organization of the League of Nations as his most important task; in return for agreement to this project he was willing to make many concessions, for he was convinced that if the League were established it would be able in the course of time to rectify any errors in the peace treaties.

The life of the League was short. Its first meeting took place in 1920 and its last in 1939, although the official dissolution did not occur until April 18, 1946. Since the League did not succeed in preventing war, it can hardly be called a success; nevertheless, as the first attempt to create a world-embracing organization of states for the preservation of peace it represented a landmark. Its original members came from every part of the globe. Moreover, in the League Assembly, which met regularly every year, each member—whether great or small—had the same rights. The executive business was entrusted to a Council whose composition did preserve something of the old idea of the rule of the world by great powers: Great

Britain, France, Italy, and Japan were its permanent members. But the Council also included a number of elected temporary members (originally four, later this number was steadily enlarged) and among them there regularly were representatives from Latin America, from Asia, and from the British dominions. Recognition of the equality of all nations and of their right to self-rule was also reflected in the fact that German and Ottoman territories in Asia and Africa which the victors had taken over were retained by them only as mandates, to be administered under supervision of the League with the aim of preparing their inhabitants for full independence.

Nevertheless, the League failed to prevent aggression and to preserve peace. And the reasons can be traced back to its beginnings. Although it claimed to be a world-encompassing organization, it was not. President Wilson was unable to overcome American fears that membership in the League might lead to involvement in "foreign quarrels," and the United States remained outside the League. Moreover, both Russia, because of its antidemocratic regime, and Germany, because of its role in starting the war and because of its war crimes, were excluded. The Bolshevik leaders of Russia therefore considered the League primarily as the center of a capitalist conspiracy for the encirclement of Russia and the overthrow of Communism; and the Germans viewed the League as an instrument for enforcing the peace treaty and keeping Germany down. Even when Germany (in September, 1926) and Russia (in September, 1934) finally entered the League, they did so primarily to strengthen their political position; neither the rulers nor their people ever became convinced believers in a new peaceful system of international relations which the League was to usher in. But the failure of the League has to be explained by more than the non-inclusion of important powers. Even those states which had participated in the founding of this organization and belonged to it from the beginning were hesitant to agree to arrangements which would limit their sovereignty. Thus, from the outset the League's chances of success in preserving peace were limited, for it had no "teeth." Membership involved commitments to avoid war, to respect the territorial integrity of other powers, and to submit disputes to investigation, arbitration, and settlement by the Permanent Court of International Justice in The Hague or by the Council of the League. If a government refused to honor these commitments and became an aggressor, the members of the League were to apply economic sanctions: to sever all economic intercourse with the aggressor state. Clear prescriptions for military action against the offender did not exist. Moreover, in questions of conflicts between states, decisions by the Council of the League required unanimity and were therefore almost impossible to obtain.

The most effective work of the League was done in promoting international cooperation in the technical and economic spheres. Its greatest successes were achieved by its health organization, which helped to control epidemics, to standardize drugs and vaccines, to promote worldwide studies

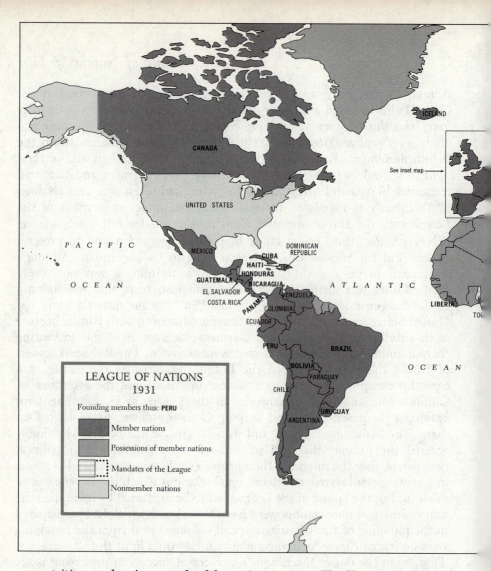

LEAGUE OF NATIONS
1931

Founding members thus: **PERU**

Member nations

Possessions of member nations

Mandates of the League

Nonmember nations

on nutrition, and to improve health services in Asia. The Economic Section of the League provided valuable analyses and statistics. The League Organization on Communications and Transit furthered collaboration concerning such matters as electric power and inland navigation. The International Labor Organization, working under the League, had some success in improving working conditions.

THE WANING OF EUROPEAN ECONOMIC SUPREMACY

The establishment of the League of Nations reflected the rise of the non-European countries, and this development was rooted in hard facts. Principal among them was the changed economic situation. The costs of the war had been fantastically high and resulted in a wasteful drain on the economic resources of the states involved. For instance, in 1917 the German war expenditure amounted to two thirds of the total German national

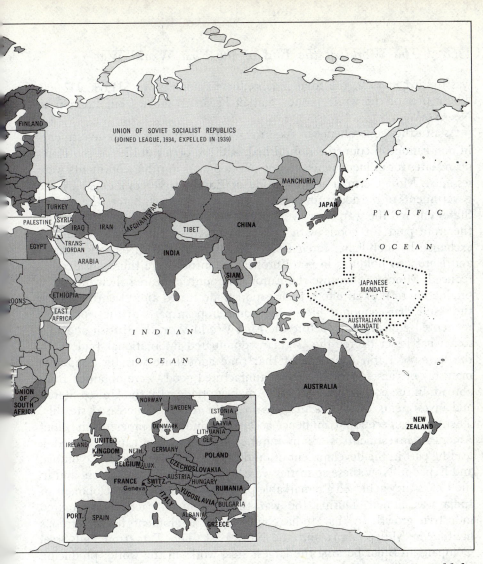

Within the map:

FINLAND

UNION OF SOVIET SOCIALIST REPUBLICS
(JOINED LEAGUE, 1934, EXPELLED IN 1939)

MANCHURIA

JAPAN

PACIFIC

TURKEY
PALESTINE SYRIA
IRAQ   IRAN   AFGHANISTAN
EGYPT TRANS-
JORDAN
ARABIA

TIBET   CHINA

INDIA

OCEAN

JAPANESE
MANDATE

SIAM

OONS

ETHIOPIA

EAST
AFRICA

INDIAN

OCEAN

AUSTRALIAN
MANDATE

UNION
OF
SOUTH
AFRICA

AUSTRALIA

NEW
ZEALAND

Inset map (Europe):

NORWAY
SWEDEN
ESTONIA
DENMARK
LATVIA
LITHUANIA
IRELAND   GER.
UNITED
KINGDOM   NETH.   GERMANY
POLAND
BELGIUM LUX.
CZECHOSLOVAKIA
AUSTRIA HUNGARY
FRANCE SWITZ.
Geneva
RUMANIA
ITALY YUGOSLAVIA BULGARIA
PORT.   SPAIN   ALBANIA
GREECE

income of prewar years. Only a small part of these vast sums could be obtained through taxation. All the governments resorted to loans; for the Allies a particularly important source of funds was the United States. By means of loans the European countries paid for the war materials which they bought from the United States; cash payments would have quickly exhausted their gold reserves.

Thus, in addition to the waste of capital and resources, there occurred a decline of the European economic position in comparison to that of the United States. The European powers were transformed from creditor nations into debtor nations. By the end of the war Great Britain's indebtedness to the United States government amounted to $3,696,000,000; that of France to $1,970,000,000; and that of Italy to $1,031,000,000. Altogether, the Allied powers of Europe owed the United States more than $7,000,000,000. In addition many loans were made in the period just after the end of the war; when the debt of the Allied nations to the United States was funded in 1922, the total indebtedness amounted to $11,656,932,900. The center of the world money market began to move from London to New York.

As a further consequence of the First World War, European investments in non-European countries diminished, and the opportunities of the European states for influencing economic development in other continents were lessened. Most German assets outside of Europe were confiscated by the governments of the countries in which they were located. Before the United States entered the war, loans were not easily obtainable, and Great Britain therefore paid for goods with gold and procured the necessary foreign exchange by mobilizing foreign securities held by British citizens. British and European holdings in non-European countries were thus considerably reduced. Moreover, because the European countries geared their industrial production to the war effort, their export trade ceased almost entirely, with the result that economic life in the non-European parts of the world was reoriented. For instance, before the First World War, the British and to a somewhat lesser degree the Germans dominated international trade with the states of Latin America. At that time agriculture was the economic mainstay of these countries, and manufactured goods were obtained from abroad. In the postwar period Latin-American trade with the United States, and investments by American firms in Latin America, increased steadily. The American economic influence accelerated industrial progress: the chief American investments were in mining, and American capital played a leading part in the development of oil fields in Venezuela, Peru, Colombia, and Ecuador. Now these countries were set toward industrialization, and in the 1920's they achieved a remarkable prosperity. Economic development in India was similar. During the war the government actively promoted industrial growth so that India could supply equipment for the troops fighting in Mesopotamia and the Near East. The Tata Iron and Steel Company in Bihar became the largest steel works in the world, producing almost a million tons annually. Production figures around the world revealed the diminished economic role of the European continent. In 1925 the world output of manufactured goods was 20 per cent higher than in 1913, and this rise can be attributed primarily to the expansion of production in the non-European world.

NATIONALIST MOVEMENTS IN THE COLONIES

More important, however, than the weakening of the European economic position was the change which took place as a result of the First World War in the relationship between white men and natives, between the European rulers and the colonial peoples. Men of different races had fought side by side; the distance which the white men had kept from other races diminished. Where native movements for autonomy or independence had existed they gained a stronger impetus, and where nationalism had been sleeping it was now awakened. The areas in which antagonism between the European ruler and settler and the native population began to play an increasingly important role were Africa and southern Asia.

Africa

In Africa one must distinguish between the Northern Arc, which the Arabs had conquered many centuries ago, and central and southern Africa. In central and southern Africa the British and French governments tried to establish in their colonies advisory councils which would gradually give the native population some part in the government. These measures had to be taken because British and French control over the former German colonies in Africa (Tanganyika, Togo, the Cameroons) was exercised in the form of a mandate, carried out under supervision of the League of Nations, with the purpose of educating the natives for self-government. Naturally, the concessions made to the natives in the former German colonies had to be extended to other areas as well. But in these parts self-government or even independence was a very distant goal.

In North Africa and the Near East the movement against European imperialism had much deeper roots. Since the Egyptian Jamal-ud-Din al-Afghani (1838–1897) had raised national and liberal claims for the Moslems in the nineteenth century, nationalist movements had taken hold in North Africa and the Near East. Even before the First World War the Arabs had begun to react against Ottoman rule. When the Turks entered the First World War this Arab nationalism received support from the British and the French, and with the encouragement of agents like T. E. Lawrence (1888–1935), the famous Lawrence of Arabia, hopes were high for the establishment of a larger Arab kingdom reaching from Arabia to Damascus and Baghdad. But these hopes were crushed in 1920—the year which the Arabs called *âm an-nakba* ("the year of the catastrophe"). The French drove the Arabs out of Damascus and took control in Lebanon and Syria, which were assigned to them as mandates. Anti-Jewish riots were crushed in Palestine, which the British government in the so-called Balfour Declaration (1917) had promised as a national home for the Jewish people and which the British administered as a mandate. The British tried to reconcile the Arabs by creating a number of Arab states—Transjordania, Iraq, and Hejaz—but Arab hostility to European imperialism remained alive, and the British and French could maintain their control in this area only by playing upon religious and racial antagonisms, like those of the Christian Arabs toward the Mohammedans and the Druzes toward the Moslems, or by using force. Nationalism also reached the westernmost of the Arab settlements. Starting in the 1920's the "young Tunisians," as the Tunisian nationalists called themselves, exerted increasing pressure, and in the 1930's a nationalist movement became active in Morocco as well. Nevertheless, only slowly and gradually, during the 1920's and 1930's, did these anti-imperialist movements become a serious threat to the control of this part of Africa by Great Britain and France; there was only one area—Egypt—where Arab nationalism became politically significant immediately after the war.

Anti-British feeling in Egypt had intensified during the war when the British entirely took over Egyptian rule and interfered in Egyptian life, requisitioning cattle and foodstuffs and forcing Egyptians to work on railroads and other installations needed for the campaign in the Near East. The resentment created by these harsh measures promoted the emergence of the Wafd, a well-organized movement whose goal was complete Egyptian independence. Disorders were frequent from March, 1919, when Britain refused the demands of the Wafd, until 1922, and under the impact of these revolts the British were forced in 1921 to release the organizer and leader of the Wafd, Saad Zaghlul Pasha (*c.* 1860–1927), whom they had exiled to Malta. After his triumphal return a certain stabilization was finally achieved. The British recognized Egyptian sovereignty but retained the right to intervene in Egyptian affairs. They kept the Sudan under their control and assumed responsibility for the defense of Egypt and the protection of foreigners living there. Even after this compromise the situation remained precarious. Zaghlul continued to press for the abolition of all the special rights which the British had preserved, and the Wafd was regularly victorious in elections. The British, however, had the support of the Egyptian king, who disliked the democratic tendencies of the Wafd. Although the British were forced to make further concessions, their retreat was slow. Nevertheless, throughout the interwar years Egypt remained a serious political concern for Britain, and the maintenance of a position there absorbed part of Britain's military strength.

India

While Arab nationalism was gaining ground only slowly, a most serious challenge to the rule of the white man arose in India at just about the time the First World War came to an end. The events in India provided the most striking example of the mounting strength gained by the movements of non-European peoples for liberation from the rule of the white man. More than half a million Indians fought in the First World War, and both princes and commoners distinguished themselves by their bravery. Even before the war ended, the British government realized that this active participation in battle gave justification to the Indians' claims for participation in the government of their country. In August, 1917, Edwin Montagu, the secretary of state for India, announced in the House of Commons that the British government planned "not only the increasing association of Indians in every branch of the administration but also the granting of self-governing institutions with a view to the progressive realization of responsible government in India as an integral part of the British Empire."

The British believed that in effecting changes in the status of India they would be dealing chiefly with the British-educated upper classes and with

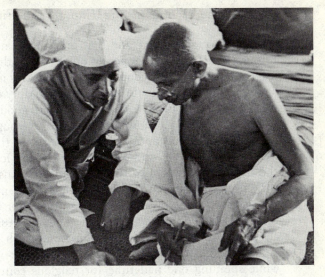

Nehru and Gandhi. *The leaders of the Indian independence movement.*

the rulers of the princely states. They felt sure that they could proceed slowly and cautiously. But the movement toward Indian independence assumed a quick tempo and became a dramatic conflict because of the inspiring personality of its leader, Mohandas Gandhi (1869–1948).

For twenty years Gandhi had lived in South Africa, where he had been the acknowledged leader of the large number of Indian workers who had gone there as indentured laborers. Gandhi had brought about remarkable improvements in their legal and economic position. The methods he had employed in achieving these gains had involved strikes, demonstrations, and hunger marches; but he had kept his followers from committing any violence, and when the police took action he and his followers had gone to prison willingly, without offering resistance. Gandhi's struggle for the Indians in South Africa had made him a well-known and highly respected figure, and when he returned to India in 1916, leadership in the nationalist movement devolved upon him almost automatically.

Gandhi infused two crucial new ideas into the movement for independence. First, its basis had to be broadened. It was not to be limited to the educated upper classes, but was to include members of all social classes, particularly the poor agricultural and industrial workers. Second, the method to be employed in obtaining independence was to be the one which he had successfully used in South Africa—nonviolence.

The broadening of the social basis required a revolutionary step: the breaking down of the barriers between caste members and "untouchables." When Gandhi began to live among "untouchables" and adopted an "untouchable" girl as his daughter, his people were deeply shocked. But gradually his moral courage aroused admiration and reinforced his political leadership. His insistence on nonviolence gave the movement a strong moral basis. Gandhi himself stated that his campaign constituted "an attempt to revolutionize politics and restore moral force to its organic station. We hope by our action to show that physical force is nothing compared to moral force and that moral force never fails." The instrument through which Gandhi hoped to obtain a withdrawal of the British without using violence was noncooperation. Again, this idea was powerful because it contained a strong moral element. As Gandhi said: "Non-cooperation with evil is as much a duty as is cooperation with good."

Noncooperation also implied practical measures which greatly weakened the British hold over India. Lawyers, among them future leaders such as Nehru (1889–1964) and Patel (1875–1950), left the courts; students left the universities; and like the *Narodniki* in Russia in the nineteenth century, professional men and intellectuals went into the villages, to educate the people and to preach noncooperation. For the success of noncooperation the rejection of all imported goods was essential, and the symbol of autarky became the wearing of homespun cloth. Gandhi admonished every Indian to spin daily. He attributed particular value to this work because while spinning one had time for religious contemplation.

Organization of the movement for Indian independence was in the hands of the All-India Home Rule League, of which Gandhi became president in 1920. Under him a democratic mass organization was created, with village units, city districts, and provincial sections, all culminating in the All-Indian Congress Committee. The fight for Indian independence became a struggle between Congress and the British. Congress adopted the policy of noncooperation, declaring that "it is the duty of every Indian soldier and civilian to sever his connections with the government and find some other means of livelihood." Noncooperation, however, developed into civil disobedience, and the latter was frequently accompanied by riots and violence. Gandhi's response to the outbreaks of violence was a fast, which he ended only when the disturbances had stopped. Indicative of the religious veneration in which the Indians held Gandhi is the fact that he could almost always control them by means of a fast; the people accepted Gandhi's demands because a prolonged fast might endanger his life.

The British were rather insecure in their handling of Gandhi. In 1922 they arrested him as the author of a number of seditious articles, and condemned him to six years in prison, but they released him after two years in order to quiet the resentment which his imprisonment had caused.

A crisis occurred in 1930. Because the British government had refused to give a definite promise of independence, a new campaign of civil disobedience was started, and Gandhi, after some years of withdrawal from politics, agreed to lead it. He decided to dramatize this campaign by an action breaking the government's salt monopoly, and accordingly he organized and led a march to the sea, covering two hundred miles in twenty-four days. At the shore he picked up and ate some salt which the waves had left, as a demonstration that he did not feel bound by the regulations concerning it. Again, Gandhi was arrested. But the British government realized that some agreement had to be reached, and released him. In appreciation of this gesture Gandhi expressed the wish to see the viceroy, Lord Irwin, later earl of Halifax (1881–1959). In the course of this famous visit, the viceroy offered Gandhi a cup of tea and Gandhi, taking a paper bag out of his shawl, answered: "Thank you. I will put some salt into my tea to remind us of the famous Boston Tea Party." Gandhi's meeting with Lord Irwin resulted in the cessation of civil disobedience, the release of all political prisoners, the abandonment of the British salt monopoly, and the agreement of the Congress party to participate in a round-table conference in London. Gandhi himself went to London as a Congress representative. In London the immense difficulties which the internal situation of India put in the way of independence became strikingly apparent. The conference produced a dramatic split between Hindus and Moslems; the Moslems, a minority in India, demanded separate electorates, an arrangement which would prevent them from being outvoted; the Hindus insisted on a single electorate. The British government's decision for separate electorates inflamed the struggle anew, and it moved in a quickened tempo through the 1930's: campaigns of civil disobedience, arrests, fasts by Gandhi, British concessions, followed one upon the other. The solution—independence accompanied by the division of India into two states, one largely Hindu, the other largely Moslem, within the British Commonwealth of Nations—was achieved only after the Second World War.

THE CHANGE IN THE FAR EAST

As a consequence of the First World War, two non-European powers—the United States and Japan—became equal in strength and importance to the European great powers; without their participation the affairs of the globe could no longer be decided. Indeed, developments in the Far East showed the extent to which in this particular area the United States and Japan now not only equaled the European great powers but even overshadowed them.

The involvement of the European nations and the United States in the European theater of war had given Japan opportunities of which it knew how to make full use. Japan was particularly anxious to strengthen its hold over China. China was forced to recognize Japan as the heir of Germany's rights in China and to give Japan extended economic privileges in Manchuria. Moreover, having taken over Germany's island possessions in the Pacific, Japan intended to keep them.

But Japanese policy ran counter to the interests of the United States. The occupied islands, particularly Yap, were so situated that control of them implied control of communications in the Pacific, and the Japanese hold over China nullified the American open-door policy. A naval armament race seemed unavoidable. But in the difficult economic circumstances after the First World War this aggravation of financial burdens seemed so senseless that the great naval powers were willing to make a serious attempt to settle their differences by negotiations. Accordingly, on December 12, 1921, they met in Washington, D.C. to discuss naval armament and the situation in the Pacific. In the opening speech, the American secretary of state, Charles Evans Hughes, made a number of concrete proposals for the limitation of naval armaments. On February 4, 1922, the conference ended with a settlement which in essence embodied these proposals in a series of complicated arrangements. One was the establishment of a definite ratio controlling the tonnage of the battleships of the great naval powers. Great Britain abandoned its claim to having the strongest navy in the world, and agreed to an American navy equal to its own. Britain and the United States were each allowed 525,000 tons of capital ships, Japan 350,000 tons, and France and Italy 175,000 tons each. Moreover, during the next ten years no new capital ships, i.e., ships of 10,000 or more tons, were to be built. This naval agreement was supplemented by the Nine Power Treaty, signed by the United States, Great Britain, France, Italy, Japan, Belgium, the Netherlands, Portugal, and China, guaranteeing the integrity and sovereignty of China and promising maintenance of the open door. In consequence of this treaty, Japan returned the former German colony of Kiaochow to China. Finally, in another treaty—the Four Power Treaty—the United States, Great Britain, France, and Japan acknowledged one another's insular possessions in the Pacific and agreed to mutual consultation if their possessions were threatened. The Four Power Treaty is usually regarded as the most important diplomatic achievement of the Washington conference. At the time of the conference the old alliance between Japan and Great Britain was due for renewal. The United States looked with distrust upon this special bond between Great Britain and Japan, and the British were reluctant to retain a commitment which might place them in opposition to the United States. The Four Power Treaty was to replace the British-Japanese alliance and initiate an era of cooperation among all the powers interested in the Far East, preventing Japan from taking isolated action.

Taken together, these agreements reveal a remarkable shift of power in the Pacific. In that area Great Britain clearly had become secondary to the United States. It had bowed to American wishes in abandoning its old alliance with Japan, and because it could keep only a part of its navy in the Far East, the arrangements about naval strength made any unilateral involvement of Britain in a Far Eastern war an impossibility. Britain's efforts now had to be directed toward gaining cooperation, and if necessary common action, among all the powers interested in the Far East. But it is very doubtful whether the policy worked out at the Washington conference was suited to this goal and whether the consequences of the replacement of a British-Japanese alliance by the Four Power Treaty were beneficial.

The Japanese withdrew from China and for a number of years adhered scrupulously to the Washington agreements. But feeling became strong in Japan that the nation had gained little from its participation in the First World War, and the moderate Japanese statesmen anxious to cooperate with Great Britain, the European powers, and the United States, lost influence, while a militaristic group bent on imperialist expansion and opposed to the parliamentary regime gained in appeal.

These developments were furthered by events in China itself. The Revolution of 1911, brought about by the Chinese resentment against foreigners and indignation about the impotence of the imperial regime, was followed by a confused period of civil war, with the various provincial governors, the so-called warlords, fighting one another. The First World War gave events a new turn. For China the crucial development was the seizure of power in Russia by the Bolsheviks, which meant that instead of being faced by a united front of powerful foreign states, China now had a defender among them. While the other nations were slow to give up the concession made to them by the Chinese imperial government, the Bolsheviks gained popularity by abandoning these privileges without hesitation. Moreover, the intellectual leader of the Chinese revolution, Sun Yat-sen (1866–1925), regarded many of the revolutionary changes which had been made in Russia, particularly in the distribution of land, as a pattern for China. Thus, Communists were admitted to the Kuomintang, the party which had led the overthrow of the imperial regime; the assistance of Russian advisers was accepted in the reorganization of the party and the reform of the army. With Russian help the process of political disintegration was halted and a central government was established in Nanking. But conflict broke out between the Communists and the more conservative members of the Kuomintang under Chiang Kai-shek (born 1886), and the Communists were driven out of the party and the government, although—under the leadership of Mao Tse-tung (born 1893) and Chu Teh (born 1886)—they remained in control in various areas. By 1928 the Nanking government was powerful enough to begin a series of political and economic reforms. The western powers, anxious to maintain trade with China, and to avoid this time the mistake of throwing the Chinese into the arms of the Bolsheviks, gave up their special privileges and evacuated the harbors which they had occupied in their imperialist days. But in contrast to the western powers, the Japanese did not consider a consolidation of the Chinese government as being in their interest. They feared that a politically strengthened China pursuing a nationalistic economic policy might exclude Japanese industrial goods from the Chinese market and make the Japanese economic situation critical. Thus, tension between China and Japan increased until, after a number of clashes along the Korean-Chinese border, there occurred in September, 1931, the so-called Mukden Incident—a railway explosion for which the Japanese made the Chinese responsible; this led to the Japanese invasion of Manchuria and to the beginning of a war which ended only with the Second World War. The European powers were unable to prevent the outbreak of the conflict or—even with the help of the League of Nations—to compose it. The helplessness which the European powers showed in this Far Eastern crisis is the most striking indication of the reduction in European influence and power.

RUSSIA UNDER THE BOLSHEVIKS

The interwar years were characterized not only by the rising antagonism of the colonial peoples toward European rule and by the emancipation of non-European powers from the European hegemony but by changes in Europe itself which had the effect of making it smaller. Probably most decisive in the weakening of European rule, and in the entire international situation in the postwar world, was the fact that Russia could no longer be counted as a member of the concert of Europe, that, on the contrary, it gave assistance to those who, like China, revolted against the European hegemony.

Since the Bolshevik take-over in 1917, Russia had been separated ideologically from the rest of Europe. But the peace settlements removed it to the periphery of the European scene geographically as well.

First, in the Treaty of Brest-Litovsk the Germans separated so much territory from Russia in the north—the Baltic provinces and Finland—and in the south—the Ukraine—that it became almost an inland state, isolated from the rest of Europe. After the German defeat, the arrangements of the Treaty of Brest-Litovsk were changed, but the Paris Peace Conference, to which Russia was not invited, confirmed the formation of a number of independent states in those areas of Europe which before 1914 had formed part of the Russian empire. In the bitter fighting of the so-called Great Civil War from 1918 to 1920 the Russians succeeded in reestablishing their authority over the Ukraine, the Caucasus, Siberia, and eastern Russia. And finally, in a war against Poland they regained some territory which had been assigned to Poland. Nevertheless, the Baltic states, Finland, Poland—all formerly parts of the Russian empire—remained independent, and Russia was thrown back to the edge of the European continent.

The victorious western powers sought to keep Russia as weak as possible because of the antidemocratic, anticapitalist character of the Bolshevik regime. With Lenin and his group, the most revolutionary and radical wing of the Russian prewar Social Democratic party came to power in Russia. During the war, which he had spent in exile in Switzerland, Lenin had not

NORWAY

SWEDEN

FINLAND

Murmansk

White Sea

Archangel

WHITE RUSSIAN
ADVANCE
1919

BALTIC SEA

Gulf of Finland

Petrograd

ESTONIA

LATVIA

LITHUANIA

GERMANY

POLAND

(TO POLAND,
1921)

Brest-
Litovsk

Minsk

UNION OF SOVIET

SOCIALIST REPUBLICS

(1922)

Moscow

1919
WHITE RUSSIAN
ADVANCES
1918

Kiev

Volga R.

AUSTRIA-HUNGARY

BESSARABIA

UKRAINE
(TO SOVIETS, 1920)

Kharkov

Dnieper R.

Tzaritsyn (Stalingrad)

1919
WHITE RUSSIAN
ADVANCES
1918

RUMANIA

(TO RUMANIA,
1918)

Sevastopol

Sea of
Azov

CRIMEA

(TO SOVIETS,
1920)

CASPIAN SEA

SERBIA

BULGARIA

BLACK SEA

GREECE

Constantinople

TURKEY
(OTTOMAN EMPIRE)

(TO TURKEY, 1918)

PERSIA

0 ———— 500 miles

MOVEMENTS OF
COUNTERREVOLUTIONARY FORCES

GER

1919

Moscow

1918

RUSSIA

Ural Mts.

1919

1918

1918

1919

Omsk

1919

SIBERIA

Irkutsk

1918

OUTER
MONGOLIA

Vladivostock

JAPAN

PERSIA

CHINA

RUSSIA IN REVOLUTION
1917-1922

—·—·— 1914 boundaries

– – – – 1921 boundaries

———— Brest Litovsk Treaty Line, 1918

▨ Territory lost by Russia in 1918

▲ ▲ ▲ ▲ 1918 } Limits of counterrevolu-
△ △ △ △ 1919 } tionary movements

only scorned those socialists who backed the war effort of their countries, but had also opposed the policy of those small socialist splinter groups which refused to support the war and urged a quick restoration of peace. To Lenin the only correct Marxist approach was to use the war to bring about revolution. At the time of the tsar's abdication, Lenin was fretting impatiently in his Swiss isolation. Then by taking advantage of the offer of the German military to transport him and his close associates through Germany, he reached Russia by way of Sweden. On April 16 Lenin, with a small group of followers—Grigori Zinoviev, Karl Radek, Anatoli Lunacharski—arrived in Petrograd, at the Finland Railroad Station. Greeted by a leader of the Mensheviks who in his speech demanded "a closing of the ranks of democracy" in defense of revolution, Lenin turned away from the official welcoming party and said to the crowds: "Any day, if not today or tomorrow, the crash of the whole of European imperialism may come. The Russian Revolution made by you has begun it and opened a new epoch. Hail the world-wide socialist revolution." Thus Lenin indicated that he regarded what had happened in Russia so far as a bourgeois revolution, which ought to be followed immediately by another revolution, giving power to the workers and peasants. Within six months the Bolsheviks would have achieved this aim.

Throughout the summer they gained steadily in appeal among the war-tired masses because they emphasized that Russia should conclude peace, while the government insisted on continuing the war. In addition, the Bolsheviks supported immediate seizure of land by the peasants, while the other political groups tended to postpone the issue of agrarian reform. Moreover, the government had failed to establish effective authority. In September, Kornilov, a popular war hero who had been appointed commander in chief, attempted a military coup to overthrow the government controlled by Mensheviks and Social Revolutionaries under Prime Minister Alexander Kerenski. The help of the Bolsheviks was needed to defeat this counterrevolutionary attempt. And as defenders of the revolution, the Bolsheviks now gained a majority in the workers' councils of Petrograd and Moscow. Rightly, Lenin thought that the time was ripe for a Bolshevik seizure of power. Trotsky played a leading part in the preparation of this coup. All the government buildings were quickly occupied, and the members of the previous government were arrested. In Petrograd and Moscow the central administrative apparatus of Russia, insofar as it existed and functioned, fell into the hands of the Bolsheviks; at the head of the government they placed a Council of People's Commissars, with Lenin as chairman.

For the next seven years, until his death in 1924, Lenin dominated Russian politics and exerted a crucial influence over developments in the rest of the world as well. The reasons for Lenin's success in achieving and

The Russian Revolution. *Street fighting in Petrograd.*

exercising power are complex. Before he came to office his study of Marxist theory had provided him with what he considered an infallible guide to the course to be followed, and his work as a party organizer had taught him to use men as instruments for definite purposes. Hence, after his return to Russia he was able to pursue the conquest of power, the secure establishment of his regime, and the social and political transformation of Russian life with ruthless single-mindedness and with a complete disregard for human life and legal restrictions. Furthermore, Lenin could count on a large number of followers who had studied his writings and accepted his leadership because they recognized his intellectual superiority. He demanded complete obedience only after a line of policy had been established; before any decision was made, he was willing to hear the views of his close followers and to discuss with them the various possibilities. Unlike Stalin, Lenin did not harbor resentment against those who gave advice contrary to the line finally adopted. However, after the decision had been made, opposition was no longer tolerated.

His hold over the masses of the workers is more difficult to understand than his eminent position among Bolshevik leaders. He was no great orator and his speeches, when read, seem monotonous. However, he never spoke down to the masses; he revealed to them with brutal frankness his views about the demands of the hour, explaining rather nakedly, but with strict logic, how he had arrived at his proposals; the masses had reason to believe

Lenin speaking to the crowds.

that he took them into his confidence and that they could rely on him. They had no doubt of his selflessness; even as ruler of Russia he continued to live modestly, claiming no exceptions or privileges. Thus, the most powerful man of Russia wrote humbly to the director of the library and asked for permission to keep a book overnight, against the rules of the library, because he had no other time for reading. Lenin inherited something of the father image which the tsars had possessed. But a principal reason for his rise to power was that he recognized, first in contrast to the revolutionary governments preceding the Bolsheviks, and later in contrast to some of his own adherents, that what the masses wanted above anything else was peace.

This resolution to end the war brought the Bolshevik regime immediately into conflict with Russia's former allies. They were anxious to prevent the supplies and ammunition which they had been sending to Russia from falling into the hands of the Germans. Thus, British and French troops were sent to such harbors as Arkhangelsk and Vladivostok. Inevitably, in the areas occupied by the Allies and therefore outside Bolshevik control, the enemies of the Bolsheviks began to organize. From the north and from the east, later also from the Baltic states and from the Ukraine, tsarist generals advanced, halfheartedly supported by the western powers. For two years, from 1918 to 1920, civil war raged. The Bolsheviks had the advantage of controlling the interior lines, which permitted them to move their troops rapidly from one threatened frontier to another. On the Bolshevik side the military hero of this civil war was Trotsky, the commissar of war. He succeeded in organizing an efficient and disciplined Red Army. He personally appeared at the most threatened points of the front, living in a railroad car which moved from one endangered sector to the other. Moreover, the leaders of the White Russians, as the opponents of the Bolsheviks were called, were disunited. Some, like Admiral Kolchak who advanced through Siberia into eastern Russia, wanted to restore the tsarist regime. Others realized the necessity for a more liberal and democratic program. Against the White Russians with their contradictory aims, the Bolsheviks were able to keep the support of large parts of the population. The peasants feared that if reaction were victorious they would have to return the land which they had seized to its former owners. The assistance which the White Russians received from Great Britain and France, though minor and insufficient, made the Bolsheviks appear to be defenders of Russian national interest against foreign intervention. Officials of previous governments placed themselves at the service of the Bolsheviks and, strictly supervised by political commissars, were used by them as "technical experts." Bolshevik attempts—with the help of native Communist parties—to reconquer Finland, the Baltic states, and Poland failed. But in the rest of the former tsarist territories, the Bolsheviks gained control.

When the civil war ended, no reintegration of Russia into the European state system occurred. The internal policy which the Bolsheviks had pursued since coming to power had opened a wide, almost unbridgeable gap between Russia and the western world.

The Bolsheviks had started their rule with a number of startling and, to the rest of the world, shocking measures and decrees. They retained civil servants who accepted the new government, but they also gave positions in the bureaucracy to reliable party members without demanding examinations or special knowledge. Likewise, courts were staffed by judges who lacked legal training. Thus the obstacles which a conservative bureaucracy usually places in the path of a revolutionary regime were immediately removed—to the horror of the rest of Europe, which regarded civil servants as members of an exclusive higher order. But the measures which of course caused the greatest abhorrence outside of Russia lay in the economic field. The Bolsheviks confiscated all private bank accounts and nationalized all banks. They repudiated the entire national debt. Factories were handed over to the workers; all land was declared national property; private trade was abolished, and retail shops were closed. To be sure, the economic policy announced in these early decrees was soon modified. Larger estates were divided up, but the peasants remained in possession of their land, although they were forced

A Russian poster. *The Bolshevik knight slaying the capitalist dragon.*

to give certain quotas of their production to the government for distribution among other sectors of the population. The chaos which resulted when the workers directed the factories was soon replaced by planning. In 1921, after the civil war had ended, there was even an openly acknowledged change from the early Communism to a New Economic Policy (NEP), which permitted a remarkable amount of freedom of trade within the country. However, heavy industry, transportation, and the credit system remained nationalized, and foreign trade remained a government monopoly. Russia had abandoned the principles of capitalist economy, and the government's grip over economic life was firm enough to permit an enforcement of stricter controls at any time. Moreover, the original measures confiscating bank accounts, socializing factories, and nationalizing land had completely impoverished the middle classes and the nobility. The appropriation of industrial enterprises and the repudiation of state loans also hit foreigners—individuals, banks, governments—who had investments in Russia. And in all further negotiations with the Bolshevik leaders the claims of these foreign investors for compensation and for the repayment of debts contracted by tsarist Russia formed an insurmountable obstacle. In particular the French, because of the large loans which they had given to the tsarist government, for a long time remained adamant in refusing contact with the Bolshevik regime until they had received compensation for their losses.

But these conflicts over financial matters were only one aspect of the differences between Bolshevik Russia and the rest of the world. The Bolsheviks rejected all the liberal and democratic values for which the western powers had claimed to be fighting. Like the tsars, the Bolsheviks refused to permit freedom of the press and freedom of expression. The Russian leaders pursued a sharply antireligious policy, and church property was confiscated. Furthermore, attempts to establish a democratic basis for the regime were soon abandoned. After their seizure of power the Bolshevik leaders had been proclaimed the legitimate Russian government by a Congress of Soldiers' and Workers' Councils (Soviets). But the previous government had ordered elections to a constituent assembly which would create a final constitution, and before seizing power the Bolsheviks had accused the government of delaying these elections; they therefore felt constrained to let them take place. But the voting, on November 25, 1917, left the Bolsheviks still a minority. When the constituent assembly opened on January 18, 1918, they declared that, because the voter lists had been made out before the Bolshevik revolution, the constituent assembly "represented the old order." With the help of troops the assembly was dissolved. The soviets remained the popular basis of the regime. Within the soviets the Bolsheviks, who represented the industrial proletariat, shared power with the left-wing Social Revolutionaries, who represented the peasants.

The dissolution of the constituent assembly sharpened internal tensions. The Bolsheviks saw themselves as surrounded by enemies within the nation. In December, 1917, they had established the All-Russian Extraordinary Commission (Cheka) for the purpose of "combating counterrevolution and sabotage." With the organization of the Cheka, terror became a consciously used, openly recognized instrument of government. In the summer of 1918 the Bolshevik leaders broke with their only partner in government, the Social Revolutionaries. As representatives of the peasant population the Social Revolutionaries had opposed the acceptance of the Treaty of Brest-Litovsk, which deprived Russia of the Ukraine, one of its most important agricultural areas. In an effort to nullify this treaty and to effect a break with Germany, Social Revolutionaries on July 6, 1918, assassinated Count Wilhelm von Mirbach, the German ambassador in Moscow. There remain puzzling questions about this event. It is difficult to understand how the murderers could get easy access to Count Mirbach, and it has been suggested that the Bolsheviks themselves, who had received information about the plans of the Social Revolutionaries, made this possible. Lenin and the Bolsheviks were eager to effect a break with the Social Revolutionaries; the murder of the German ambassador would give justification for such a break. At the same time, the Bolsheviks would have gotten rid of an ambassador whom they knew had reported home that their regime was weak and near collapse. Even if not true, such rumors were indicative of the

The Communist International. *Lenin presiding at its first meeting in 1919.*

confused and desperate situation in Moscow at this time. The Bolsheviks succeeded, however, in defeating the attempt of the Social Revolutionaries to overthrow the government, to which the assassination of Mirbach had given the signal. But the struggle went on. Like the revolutionaries of tsarist times, the Social Revolutionaries tried to shake the regime through a series of assassinations. On August 30, 1918, Lenin himself was severely wounded. The Bolshevik answer was increased terror, directed by the Cheka. Exact figures about the number of victims of this Red Terror are lacking. From Bolshevik sources we know that at the beginning of September in Petrograd 512 "counterrevolutionaries and White guards" were shot in one day. Many were killed not for the commission of a specific crime, but because as members of the propertied classes they were regarded as enemies of the state. The indignation of the non-Russian world was great; representatives of foreign powers in Petrograd and Moscow protested, accusing the Bolsheviks of "barbarous oppression" and "unwarranted slaughter" which aroused "the indignation of the civilized world."

In the fall of 1918, when the weapon of terror was unleashed with utter ruthlessness, the Bolshevik position was precarious. The conflict with the Social Revolutionaries coincided with the beginning of the civil war—the attacks of the tsarist generals, supported by the western powers, from the north and east. But although circumstances were almost desperate, the Bolshevik leaders believed that if they could hold on somewhat longer the entire situation might be reversed. For the European war was drawing to a close. The German government was tottering, dissatisfaction was widespread in other countries, and there was some reason to assume that the end of the war would be accompanied by revolution in several European states. At this time the Russian leaders could not imagine that Russia could become a socialist country while the rest of the world remained capitalist. As Lenin had proclaimed at the Finland Station, they supposed the Bolshevik revolution in Russia to be the first step of a revolutionary process which would extend over the whole globe. They believed that their own position depended quite as much on the spread of the revolution into other countries as on their staying in power in Russia. Thus, while involved in a deadly struggle within Russia, they established a Communist International, intended to stimulate revolution elsewhere. The First Congress of the Communist International, or Comintern, took place in Moscow in March, 1919; it was a rather tame affair, for the only delegates from abroad were a few leaders of extremist groups that had split off from the socialist parties. More important was the Second Congress of the Communist International, which met in Moscow in August, 1920. Including representatives of the extreme left from a large number of countries, this congress gave a more definite form to the organization of the Communist International.

The establishment of the Communist International had far-reaching consequences. One of these was a definite split within the various Marxist-inspired workers' movements. Even before the First World War most of the socialist parties in Europe had included a left and a right—a revolutionary and a revisionist wing—but the unity of the socialist movement had been maintained. From 1919 on, there were two different Marxist parties: Socialists and Communists. Moreover, the structure of the Communist International was essentially different from that of the Second Socialist International. In the latter, the socialist parties of the various nations remained sovereign; the organization which included them all—the Second International—gave advice only. In the Communist International, supreme authority was held by the World Congress of the Communist Parties which met every year, or more precisely, by an executive committee which this congress elected. The decisions of this congress or its executive committee were binding upon all Communist parties; they had to follow the "line" laid down by the Communist International. The influence of the Russian Bolsheviks was predominant because the headquarters of the executive committee were in Moscow and its permanent secretary, Zinoviev, was a Bolshevik leader. One of the basic principles of the Communist International was that all Communist parties must regard the maintenance, defense, and strengthening of the Bolshevik regime in Russia as their paramount aim. The goal of the Communist International was world revolution, and the Communist parties in the various countries were to build up support for the revolutionary movement by forming special youth organizations, Communist trade unions, and the like, all subject to the same discipline as the Communist parties themselves. Whether these organizations would work openly and freely or secretly and illegally, or whether open and clandestine organizations would work side by side, was to be determined by the situation in each country.

At the time of its formation the Communist International had as its chief goal the overthrow of the governments in the great capitalist states of western Europe. From the beginning, however, the Communist leaders were aware that the European nations drew much of their strength from the control which they exerted over the non-European parts of the world. Therefore, the undermining of European rule over colonial areas was from the outset an openly declared aim of the Communist International. Its first manifesto, issued on April 6, 1919, already included the statement that "the colonial question in its fullest extent has been placed on the agenda.... Colonial slaves of Africa and Asia! The hour of proletariat dictatorship in Europe will also be the hour of your own liberation." This point was emphasized and elaborated in 1920, when special "theses on the national and colonial question" were presented. It was proclaimed that "our policy must be to bring into being a close alliance of all national and colonial liberation movements with Soviet Russia.... The task of the Communist International is to liberate the working people of the entire world. In its ranks the white, the yellow and the black-skinned peoples—the working people of the entire world—are fraternally united."

In the West, the existence of the Communist International was interpreted as the sign of a Communist effort to continue the war against the West even after peace had been restored along the borders. The western states were hesitant to recognize the Bolsheviks as constituting the legitimate government of Russia. On the other hand, the Russians considered the reluctance of the western nations to enter into normal diplomatic relations with Russia to be a sign of their resolution to resume military intervention at the first favorable opportunity. Russia and the rest of Europe remained in opposite camps, and Russia was the ally of all those movements which were directed against European control of the globe.

THE PARIS PEACE CONFERENCE

The new forces which the First World War had released in all parts of the world contributed to the weakening and ultimately the destruction of the peace settlement which was made after the war. At a distance of fifty years the work and the procedures of the Paris Peace Conference appear rather futile and anachronistic. Many aspects of the peace settlement originated in attitudes which now seem inappropriate or obsolete. But the conference did represent a serious effort to come to grips with the needs of modern industrial society. The Europe which existed before the First World War could not be restored; and the question that hangs over the entire interwar period is whether the transition into a new world could have been achieved without the catastrophe of a Second World War.

The problem of whether a traditional or a progressive outlook would determine the nature of the peace settlement was reflected in the great differences among the leaders who assembled in Paris at the end of 1918.

Arthur Balfour, the British foreign secretary, had attended the Berlin Conference of 1878, and regarded the proceedings in Paris with the detachment of an old man; as a diplomat of the old school he was chiefly concerned with the reestablishment of a balance of power. But Balfour's attitude was an exception. The prevailing mood at the Paris Peace Conference was that of nineteenth-century nationalism. This emotion burned, for example, in the French prime minister, Clemenceau, for whom the French defeat in 1870–1871 was still a personal, unforgotten experience, so that his main concern now was to make a resumption of the Franco-German duel impossible. The principal representatives of nationalism, however, were the leaders and delegates of those nations which as a result of the war had emerged from the rule of—or dependence upon—other powers, and now strove to establish independent national states. Nikola Pasic (*c.* 1845–1926), the Serbian Bismarck, and Eleutherios Venizelos (1864–1936), the popular and influential Greek statesman, worked for the fulfillment of Greek and Serbian national aims; they wanted to create a greater Serbia and a greater Greece. The Czech and Polish representatives, Eduard Beneš (1884–1948) and Ignace Paderewski (1860–1941), based the demands for their new states on the new principle that each nationality had the right to self-determination. But they could be obdurate and ruthless when the interests of their nations clashed with those of others.

At the same time, advocates of the "new diplomacy"—those who aimed at overcoming old conflicts and tensions by building a supranational organization and strengthening international law—were also strongly represented. They came chiefly from non-European countries, as did General Jan Christiaan Smuts (1870–1950), the influential South African statesman. The leader of these idealists was, of course, Woodrow Wilson. For the first time an American president went to Europe while in office. Wilson was enthusiastically and tumultuously received in Paris, in London, and in Rome. He was welcomed as the savior who would bring about a new and better age. And though many of the leaders of the European states may have been skeptical, Wilson had numerous adherents among the younger members of their delegations. However, the variety of views and approaches represented at the Paris Peace Conference meant that the settlement which would result could not be a full realization of Wilsonian ideals, but a compromise in which the principles of a new diplomacy would be watered down by considerations of power politics and nationalist passions.

Decisive in weakening the influence of Wilsonian idealism and reinforcing the weight of political realism was the absence of Russia. A new global system could hardly be established without the inclusion of a country which covered so immense an area of the globe. The existence of Communist Russia also had a very important indirect effect on the shape which the peace settlement took. Fear of Bolshevism and of the spread of Communism into central and western Europe weakened the forces supporting Wilson's ideas of a magnanimous peace and an international peace organization. In all countries the workers now were split into two groups: the Communists, who actively sought world revolution; and the socialists, generally much more numerous, who violently opposed the extremists on their left and were willing to operate within a democratic framework. Moreover, the appeal of the left-wing bourgeois parties in England, France, and Italy diminished because they seemed to lack the hardheadedness needed to suppress subversive movements. In reaction to the fear aroused by the ruthless political proceedings and the confiscatory economic measures of the Bolsheviks, a trend toward conservatism developed in Great Britain, France, and the United States, and the statesmen in Paris were aware that the stability of their governments depended on their paying heed to nationalistic and counterrevolutionary tendencies at home. Thus, domestic policy exerted a powerful impact on the making of the peace.

Adherents of a Wilsonian peace were aware of the difficulties created by the absence of Russia, and several attempts were made—for instance, through a mission of the American diplomat William Bullitt—to get in contact with the leaders of Russia. But these efforts were not followed up energetically, for every attempt to come to an understanding with Russia immediately aroused the opposition of the influential groups in France and Great Britain which advocated intervention to overthrow the Bolshevik regime. Furthermore, just at the time of critical negotiations at the Paris Peace Conference, the fear of world revolution did appear to have some reality behind it. Communist revolts broke out in various parts of eastern and central Europe. From March to August, 1919, the Communists, under Béla Kun, ruled in Hungary. Throughout April, 1919, a Soviet republic existed in Bavaria. It was believed in Paris that only a decided anti-Bolshevik stand could save large parts of Europe from falling to the Communists. Hence the Paris Peace Conference adopted the policy of constructing a stout dam against the Bolsheviks in eastern Europe, a *cordon sanitaire* which would separate Bolshevik Russia from the democratic states. Finland had acquired independence by its own efforts. But the various Baltic nations—Estonia, Latvia, Lithuania—needed and received support in their resistance to Russian attempts at reconquest. Because it was believed that Poland and Rumania could become firm bulwarks against Communism, these states were deliberately strengthened by the makers of the peace settlement, even in violation of the principle of national self-determination. Rumania received what had been Russian Bessarabia; Poland tried to push its eastern frontiers as far as possible into Russia and claimed the entire Ukraine. Although the Russo-Polish War of 1920 stemmed the Polish advance, western diplomatic help and economic aid gave the Poles a border extending far into Russian territory.

These arrangements and considerations also influenced the main business of the Paris Peace Conference: to conclude treaties with the Central Powers—Turkey, Bulgaria, Austria-Hungary, and Germany. These settlements bear elegant-sounding and historic names because they were signed in various palaces in the suburbs of Paris. The short-lived Treaty of Sèvres (1920) terminated the war with Turkey. The Treaty of Neuilly (1919) established peace with Bulgaria. The situation resulting from the disintegration of the Habsburg empire was resolved by the Treaty of St.-Germain (1919) with Austria and the Treaty of Trianon (1920) with Hungary. The most important of the peace settlements was the Treaty of Versailles (1919), ending the war with Germany.

The Treaty of Sèvres and Developments in Turkey

The Treaty of Sèvres was the last treaty arranged at the Paris Peace Conference, being signed only on April 20, 1920. It is treated here first, however, for the reason that, strictly speaking, it dealt not with Europe, but with a non-European part of the world. Hence this treaty—or, to be exact, the failure of this treaty—was closely connected with the rise of antiimperialism and anticolonialism in the Near East and with Russia's efforts to emancipate the nonwhite races from the tutelage of the great capitalist powers of the West. In the settlement of the peace with Turkey the last chapter of one story, that of the First World War, is immediately joined with the first chapter of a new story, that of the anti-European revolt.

When the victors, absorbed in the disposition of the European situation, finally came around to deciding the fate of the Ottoman Empire, they dealt with it as if it were a colony, although actually they were facing a nation which was conscious of its great past and in addition was now inspired by the new anti-European nationalism. During the war the western powers had made a number of agreements concerning the partitioning of the Ottoman Empire. There had been a general understanding that the Arab portions would be separated from Turkey, but the arrangements made by the Allies during the war also envisaged a partition of the Turkish heartland of Asia Minor. Even after the collapse of tsarism had made the details of this agreement obsolete, the notion of a partition was maintained. In April, 1919, the Italians appeared in Adalia, in southern Asia Minor, and a month later the Greeks landed in Smyrna. The Greek occupation bore, to quote from an official report of an investigating committee, "more resemblance to a conquest and a crusade than to any civilizing mission." An Allied force controlled Constantinople and its surrounding areas.

In the Treaty of Sèvres, Smyrna and Thrace were given to Greece, large areas in Asia Minor were assigned to Italy and France as their spheres of interest, and Constantinople was internationalized. The sultan, residing in occupied Constantinople, signed the treaty under protest. But the foreign advances into Asia Minor encountered a vehement Turkish reaction, and Turkish nationalism found a leader in a hero of the First World War, Mustafa Kemal Pasha (1881–1938), who began to organize resistance in the interior of the country. Kemal Pasha set up a countergovernment in Angora (now Ankara) and refused to recognize the treaty. To enforce the treaty, the Allies permitted the Greeks to advance from Smyrna into the interior. The Turco-Greek war, lasting from 1920 to 1922, ended with the complete defeat of Greece. The Turkish success was chiefly due to the brilliant military and political leadership of Kemal. But Turkey was also aided by supplies from Bolshevik Russia, which was glad to help this revolt against the dominance of the western powers. Most important, instead of rallying to the support of Greece, the Allies were competing against one another. Italy resented the increase of Greek power in Asia Minor, and France wanted to limit the British influence in the Near East. Hence, Italy and France were willing to withdraw from Asia Minor when they received the promise of economic concessions by the Turks. Only the British, particularly the prime minister, Lloyd George, remained passionate supporters of the Greeks. But although Lloyd George was inclined toward active intervention to assist the Greeks and to hold Constantinople, the British people were too tired of war to accept this policy. Left alone, the Greeks were defeated, and in the summer of 1923 the Treaty of Lausanne, replacing the Treaty of Sèvres, was concluded. The Turks lost most of the Aegean Islands, some to Italy, others to Greece. The Straits remained demilitarized and open to ships of all nations, but the Turks regained the strip of European territory, including Adrianople, which they had possessed before the First World War. They were again complete rulers all of Asia Minor, including Constantinople.

Kemal became the creator of a modern state. The close association between the Turkish government and Islam was ended; indeed, the wearing of the fez was forbidden, and women were encouraged to abandon the veil. The Latin alphabet was introduced, school attendance became compulsory, and a policy of industrialization and of agricultural modernization was initiated. The Turkish republic became officially a parliamentary state based on popular elections, although for many years no opposition party existed and Kemal and his group of victorious officers ruled. Turkey proved that, despite European claims to the contrary, the nations of the Near East were able to develop quickly to the levels of political, economic, and social life which existed in the western world.

The Treaties of Neuilly, Trianon, and St.-Germain and the Interwar Developments in Southeastern and Eastern Europe

The immediate purpose of the treaties of Neuilly, Trianon, and St.-Germain was to conclude peace with Bulgaria, Hungary, and Austria. But these treaties involved the settlement of the entire area of eastern Europe, from the Aegean Sea in the south to the Baltic Sea in the north. The political, territorial, and economic questions with which the treaties had to deal were extremely complex. For one thing, the area was inhabited by a large number of different nationalities, with relations between some of them poisoned by the fact that before the First World War certain groups, such as the Magyars and the Germans, had dominated the others. Moreover, the reorganization of this area cut deeply into the existing economic structure. Austria-Hungary, which the treaties of Trianon and St.-Germain destroyed, had formed a natural economic unit that was now torn into parts. The various sovereign states among which the territory of the former Danube monarchy was divided needed financial resources, and the settlements therefore involved a distribution among them of the economic assets of the former Austria-Hungary.

The postwar settlements were to be made in accordance with the principles which Wilson had outlined in his Fourteen Points—national self-determination and democracy—and the victors regarded the treaties of Neuilly, Trianon, and St.-Germain as applying these principles. But in the course of time they did not pass the test: in fifteen years, with the exception of Czechoslovakia, not one of the states created or reorganized at the Paris Peace Conference remained a democracy. What were the reasons for this situation? What were the weaknesses in the peace settlement which allowed developments so different from those envisaged at the end of the war?

It is easy to understand that democracy was a weak plant in those countries which, having been defeated, had to cede territories and pay damages. Actually the territorial renunciations which the Treaty of Neuilly forced upon Bulgaria were not considerable. In addition to a few small border revisions in favor of Serbia, Bulgaria had to surrender to Greece an area along the Aegean Sea which she had conquered in the Balkan Wars and which had provided Bulgaria with an access to the Mediterranean. Bulgaria also had to pay reparations and to accept the limitation of her army to twenty thousand men. Although not crippling, these conditions were sufficiently hard to keep alive in the proud and ambitious Bulgarian nation a feeling of resentment against neighboring Rumania and Yugoslavia (the enlarged kingdom of Serbia). The officers of the diminished Bulgarian army were particularly eager for revenge. They kept a protecting hand over Macedonian nationalists who, dissatisfied because Macedonia had not been established as an independent state but had been divided between Yugoslavia and Greece, had fled to Bulgaria and operated from Bulgarian soil against Yugoslavia. Bulgarian officers allied to Macedonian nationalists

TERRITORIAL CHANGES AS
A RESULT OF WORLD WAR I

——— Line of Treaty of Brest–Litovsk

TERRITORIES LOST:

By Russia

By Austria–Hungary

By Germany

By Bulgaria

Plebiscite areas

—·—·— 1914 boundaries

Murmansk

White
Sea

FINLAND

Helsinki

Petrograd

Oslo

NORWAY

Stockholm

SWEDEN

BALTIC SEA

Moscow

NORTH
SEA

DENMARK

Danzig

U.S.S.R.

UNITED
KINGDOM

Hamburg

EAST
PRUSSIA

London

The
Hague

NETH.

Berlin

Warsaw

Brest–Litovsk

Kiev

BELGIUM

GERMANY

POLAND

LUX.

SAAR

Paris

ALSACE

Prague

Cracow

Lemberg

UKRAINE

LORRAINE

Munich

Vienna

FRANCE

SWITZ.

Budapest

Geneva

Milan

Trieste

Venice

Fiume

AUSTRIA–HUNGARY

RUMANIA

Bucharest

Marseilles

ITALY

Belgrade

BLACK SEA

ADRIATIC SEA

SERBIA

BULGARIA

Barcelona

CORSICA

MONTENEGRO

Sofia

Rome

Naples

ALBANIA

Constantinople

SARDINIA

GREECE

Aegean
Sea

TURKEY
(OTTOMAN EMPIRE)

CORFU

Athens

Algiers

SICILY

Tunis

MALTA (Br.)

CRETE

ALGERIA

TUNISIA

MEDITERRANEAN   SEA

0   500 miles

TERRITORIAL SETTLEMENTS AFTER WORLD WAR I

— 1926 boundaries
New independent nations
Zone of Allied occupation
Demilitarized zone

Murmansk

White Sea

FINLAND

Helsinki

Petrograd

NORWAY

Oslo

Stockholm

SWEDEN

ESTONIA

LATVIA

Moscow

NORTH SEA

DENMARK

Danzig (Free state)

BALTIC SEA

LITHUANIA

EAST PRUSSIA

U.S.S.R.

UNITED KINGDOM

Hamburg

London

The Hague

NETH.

BELGIUM

Berlin

Warsaw

Brest-Litovsk

GERMANY

POLAND

Kiev

Paris

LUX.

SAAR

ALSACE

Prague

Cracow

Lemberg

UKRAINE

CZECHOSLOVAKIA

FRANCE

LORRAINE

Munich

Vienna

SWITZ.

AUSTRIA

HUNGARY

Budapest

Geneva

RUMANIA

Milan

Trieste

Venice

Fiume

YUGOSLAVIA

Belgrade

Bucharest

BLACK SEA

Marseilles

ITALY

ADRIATIC SEA

Barcelona

CORSICA

Rome

BULGARIA

Sofia

SARDINIA

Naples

ALBANIA

Constantinople

GREECE

Aegean Sea

TURKEY

Algiers

CORFU

Athens

Tunis

SICILY

CRETE

ALGERIA

☐ MALTA (Br.)

TUNISIA

MEDITERRANEAN SEA

0   500 miles

vehemently opposed any policy which implied recognition of the peace settlement, and hence clashed with those who wanted to concentrate on domestic reforms.

Discredited by defeat, Bulgaria's leaders were replaced when the war ended. King Ferdinand abdicated in favor of his son Boris (ruled 1918–1943) and a new party, the Agrarian party, came into power. The Agrarian leader, Alexander Stamboliski, advocated cooperation among the peasants of southeastern Europe and aimed at a Balkan federation in which Serbians and Bulgarians would be reconciled. In Bulgaria, he introduced land reforms, dividing the extended agrarian estates. Although the number of large landowners hurt by these measures was small, Stamboliski's agrarian program was widely considered as a step toward Communism, especially since many members of his party expressed sympathy for the Bolshevik social and economic policy. Hence, the Bulgarian bourgeoisie, the military, and the king all became upset by Stamboliski's reforms. But since he had a firm grip over the peasants, who formed 80 per cent of the Bulgarian population, he could not be removed by democratic means. His enemies therefore resorted to violence. In the early summer of 1923 his government was overthrown by a military coup. Stamboliski was captured by Macedonian terrorists, cruelly mutilated, tortured, and finally killed. This military coup ended democracy in Bulgaria. Behind the façade of a series of impotent bourgeois governments, Macedonian nationalists and Bulgarian officers, sometimes in alliance, sometimes quarreling, maintained control and terrorized the country. Finally, in 1935, King Boris, who had played an important role behind the scenes all along, came into the foreground and established a dictatorship, supported by the army and the police.

In the peace settlements, Hungary suffered more extensive territorial losses than Bulgaria and Austria. The Treaty of Trianon provided that in addition to paying reparations and limiting its army to 35,000 men, Hungary would have to cede to Czechoslovakia, Yugoslavia, and Rumania, three quarters of its former territory, with two thirds of its population. These harsh conditions could hardly arouse in the defeated nation great enthusiasm for the principles, such as democracy, advocated by the victors. Moreover, through a change of regime in the last stages of the war the Hungarians had expected to gain the favor of the western democracies. Two weeks before the end of the war they had pronounced the union with Austria dissolved and had declared themselves independent. Power had been taken over by Count Mihely Károlyi, who as an enemy of Tisza and a sympathizer with democratic western ideas had been a lonely figure among the Hungarian aristocrats. Károlyi had immediately taken steps to initiate a radical land reform; he ceded himself his own vast land holdings —more than fifty thousand acres—to his peasants for distribution among them and his government began to arrange for the dissolution of large estates. Károlyi also supported the convocation of a constitutional assembly, to be elected by universal and secret suffrage of men and women. But the elections for this assembly never took place. Károlyi, who had opposed Austria-Hungary's participation in the war, was a sincere believer in Wilsonian principles, and his popularity declined when the victors treated Hungary not as a newly arisen nation, but as a defeated enemy, and supported the claims of Yugoslavia, Rumania, and Czechoslovakia to Hungarian territory. Under these circumstances Károlyi felt that he could no longer be useful, and in March, 1919, he resigned in favor of the radicals of the left. From March to August, 1919, Hungary was a Communist republic, with Béla Kun as the leading political figure. Although representing a small extremist minority, the government of Béla Kun originally enjoyed broad support. The Hungarians hoped and expected that with the help of Bolshevik Russia they might be able to repulse Rumanian and Czechoslovakian encroachments on what they regarded as Hungarian territory. Officers and soldiers of the old Habsburg army served under Kun, whose government was careful not to antagonize the non-Communist groups of society. The great landed estates were collectivized, but the management of these collectives was frequently entrusted to the former landowners or their administrators; thus, at first the old ruling group and the bourgeoisie were willing to tolerate the Communist government. However, after a few initial military successes, the Kun government was forced by Allied pressure to evacuate Slovakia, and Rumanian troops, backed by the French, advanced toward Budapest. Realizing that even the Communists were unable to save the territorial integrity of Hungary, the old ruling group and the bourgeoisie withdrew their support from Béla Kun and rallied around a former officer of the Austro-Hungarian navy, Admiral Nicholas Horthy (1868–1957). The Communists tried to retain power through terrorist measures, but under the pressure of external and internal foes their regime collapsed; Kun fled to Russia, where he was later executed in one of Stalin's purges. Horthy and his reactionary supporters took over; by the autumn of 1919, the old ruling group was in power again in Hungary, and Communists, those suspected of radical views, spokesmen for workers and peasants, and particularly Jews, were rounded up, tortured, and killed. After some months the terror ended and political life returned to its prewar pseudoconstitutionalism. Horthy reigned as regent. Legally the monarchy was restored, but Hungary's neighbors vetoed the return of the last Habsburg ruler as king, so the throne remained empty. Parliament was reestablished, but the right to vote remained limited and the elections were managed by the group in power. The landowners, large and small, were all-powerful in Hungary until the Second World War. Horthy and his group had bought the assistance of the Allies against the Communists by accepting the Treaty of Trianon, which was signed on June 4, 1920. Yet indignation about the treaty was immense. Hungarians resented the reduction of their nation to a minor power. Moreover, the loss of many of Hungary's former markets created great difficulties for industry and agriculture. The constant aim of Hungarian foreign policy was to change the peace settlement and to regain the areas which once had been under the crown of St. Stephen. During the interwar period, Hungary remained a constant factor of unrest and was the natural ally of any power seeking to revise the peace settlement.

In contrast to Bulgaria and Hungary—nations with strong national traditions—the Austria which emerged from the First World War had little relationship to the Austria of the Habsburgs. Since its territory was limited to the German-speaking part of the Habsburg empire, it became a small country, with about 6.5 million inhabitants. One German-speaking area, South Tyrol, was given to Italy. And the unwillingness of the South Tyroleans to adjust themselves to Italian rule created continual friction between Austria and Italy. In other respects, the Austrians had little cause to resent the manner in which their frontiers were drawn. The complaint which they could make against the Treaty of St.-Germain was that their nation was not permitted to join Germany, that it was deprived of the right of self-determination. This prohibition against *Anschluss* created a festering wound, for though the enthusiasm of the Austrians to become part of the German Reich may have been limited, they recognized that as a separate state Austria was economically hardly viable. Vienna, formerly the capital of an empire, was one of the world's larger cities, much too large now for the small state of which it was the capital. After the war the inhabitants of Vienna formed a third of the entire population of Austria. This disproportion between the rural and the urban populations created constant economic difficulties and political tensions. In Vienna the socialists prevailed and established an effective municipal administration. The rest of the country was conservative and Catholic and this outlook dominated the government of the republic. Thus, the political situation was inherently unstable, and when in the 1930's economic difficulties and pressure from the north endangered Austrian independence, the rulers dared no longer trust the fate of Austria to the outcome of popular elections but turned to dictatorial forms of government.

The disposition of the non-German parts of Austria and the territories relinquished by Hungary resulted in the creation of a new system of states in eastern and southeastern Europe. Galicia was given to Poland; Transylvania and part of the Banat to Rumania; another part of the Banat, Bosnia, Herzegovina, and Dalmatia to Yugoslavia, which also absorbed Montenegro. Finally, out of Bohemia, Moravia, and Slovakia a new state was formed, the republic of Czechoslovakia. Poland, Rumania, Yugoslavia, and Czechoslovakia were known as the Successor States because, through the possession of territories which had formed part of the Austro-Hungarian empire, they inherited claims and obligations which were only slowly settled in international negotiations. The justification for the distribution of these territories in the Balkans and eastern Europe was the principle of self-determination. Whether newly formed, like Poland and Czechoslovakia, or already in existence, like Rumania and Serbia, each of these states was supposed to be the independent homeland of a previously suppressed nation. Actually, however, the application of the principle of self-determination in this area was complicated; it raised as many problems as it was assumed to solve.

A case in point is Yugoslavia, the enlarged kingdom of Serbia. The new name was intended to indicate that all the people living in this state were South Slavs—Yugoslavs—members of the various branches of the South Slav family. But though they were all South Slavs, the Serbs, Croatians, and Slovenes of Yugoslavia regarded themselves as distinct national groups, and this attitude created problems which impeded the working of democracy there. The Serbs and their leader, Pasic, considered themselves the creators of this new national state and were not ready to share power with the others. They clamored for a Greater Serbia, not for a federal state of several nationalities. Because a federal principle was rejected by the government, the Croatians refused to take seats in the constituent assembly elected in November, 1919, and in their absence a constitution was adopted which established a centralized state dominated by the Serbs. The consequent resentment of the Croatians and Slovenes was reinforced by religious contrasts and social friction. While the Serbs were Greek Orthodox, the Croatians and Slovenes were largely Roman Catholic. Moreover, the great majority of the Croatians were peasants, while the controlling element among the Serbs was a bourgeoisie favoring industrialization. When in 1928 the political leader of the Croatians, Stefan Radic, was assassinated, disintegration threatened and the king, relying on the support of the army, ended parliamentary rule and established a military dictatorship. The ensuing quiet in the political scene was deceiving, for although the Croatians were forcibly suppressed, they remained dissatisfied. Throughout the 1930's, the choice seemed to be between political disintegration and the continuation of a brutal dictatorship.

Democracy did not long survive either in Poland or in Rumania. There was no nationality problem in these countries, for the minority peoples (some Magyars and Germans in Transylvania) were powerless. A virulent anti-Semitism existed in both states; governments even tried to gain popularity by permitting and stimulating anti-Semitic disturbances. But the Jews carried little political weight and could defend themselves only by economic means. In Poland, as in many countries, a primary source of unrest and dissatisfaction was the agrarian problem. New regulations limited the maximum area which a single owner could hold to a hundred hectares (or well over two hundred acres), with a total of four hundred hectares permitted in the eastern border region. But the application of these laws encountered the obdurate resistance of the Polish nobility, who owned immense landed estates, and the laws remained chiefly on the books. The landowners found allies in the members of the bourgeoisie, who feared Communist influences among peasants and workers and were reluctant to allow them greater power. The deadlock resulting from this division of Polish political life into two hostile camps provided the opportunity for a *coup d'état* in 1926. Its leader was Józef Pilsudski (1867–1935), who was recognized as a patriot and military hero by all groups of society. He had struggled for Polish independence under tsarism; he had organized a Polish legion during the First World War; and with its help he had established an independent Polish government in the last phase of the war. In 1920, as leader of the Polish army, he had stopped the Russian advance before Warsaw and saved the country from Bolshevism. In his early years Pilsudski had been a socialist, and when he undertook the military coup of 1926 he was supported by the workers of Warsaw, who expected that he would reactivate the stalled movement toward democracy and social reform. But Pilsudski disappointed them. Once in power he allied himself with the bourgeoisie and the landowners, and the rule of these relatively small groups inevitably led to restrictions on liberty. In 1935 a constitution was forced upon the people which gave the president and the government unlimited powers. In the same year Pilsudski died, and power now remained in the hands of his confidants, chiefly men who had been officers in his Polish legion during the First World War. This group of colonels, less selfless than Pilsudski, and not beyond corruption, ruled in Poland in the years before the outbreak of the Second World War.

In Rumania, as in Poland, there was antagonism between the peasant party—anxious for agrarian reform and protective tariffs—and the wealthy urban bourgeoisie, who sought to maintain lower tariffs so that other nations would reciprocate and Rumania's industrial products, particularly oil, could be sold easily on foreign markets. The bourgeoisie could produce a parliamentary majority only by rigging elections, and retained power chiefly by using force. On the other hand the agrarian party, when it acquired control, showed itself remarkably inept in conducting political affairs. In this situation, in 1930 King Carol II returned from exile, into which he had been forced because of a morganatic marriage, so that his small son Michael had ruled under a regency. King Carol's hostility to the political leaders who had opposed him led him systematically to diminish their prestige by playing one against the other. The resulting stagnation of political life made the abolition of parliament and the establishment of a dictatorship appear to be the simple solution for getting things done.

But by the time the royal dictatorship was established in Rumania, Fascism and Nazism had already appeared on the scene; imitating the Italian and German leaders, Carol tried to establish a one-party system. He believed that he was riding the wave of the future, and certainly the Rumanian dictatorial regime was not far behind Fascism and Nazism in brutality and terror.

Only in Czechoslovakia did democracy continue to function throughout the entire interwar period. Like Yugoslavia, Czechoslovakia included people of several different nationalities: Czechs, Slovaks, Ruthenians, Germans. If in Czechoslovakia nationality conflicts were less sharp than in Yugoslavia, one reason may be found in the developments which preceded the foundation of the state. During the war, leaders of the Czechs and the Slovaks, among them Tomás Masaryk (1850–1937), an internationally known scholar of proved political courage and integrity, formed a committee which propagandized the cause of Czech independence and organized a military force fighting on the side of the Allies. Even before the war had ended the Allies recognized this committee as a provisional government. From the outset Czechs and Slovaks had worked together on this committee, and they were aware of the need for building a state based on cooperation among different nationalities. Thus, when parties were formed and parliamentary elections took place, the largest and most important political parties—the Social Democrats and the Agrarian party—included members of all nationalities, from all parts of the republic. One of the first measures of the new state, the dismemberment of the large landed estates, created among the peasants throughout the country a vested interest in the maintenance of the new republic. Furthermore, since Czechoslovakia had coal and iron mines and modern brewing and textile industries, its economy was better balanced between industry and agriculture than that of any other country in this area. Finally, as president of the republic, Masaryk, himself a Slovak, worked steadily for fairness toward all sections of the population. As a professor at the University of Prague before the war, Masaryk had educated the intellectual elite of the entire area, and he enjoyed immense respect and authority. Nonetheless, Czechoslovakia was by no means free of internal tensions. The Ruthenian and Slovak parts of the country were chiefly agrarian, and their inhabitants believed that the government neglected the agrarian sector of the economy in favor of the industrial parts in Bohemia. Moreover, most of the Ruthenians and Slovaks were Roman Catholic; their antagonism to the administration was sharpened by friction which developed between the anticlerical government and the Roman Catholic Church. Finally, many of the Germans living in Czechoslovakia, particularly in the Sudeten area, had before 1918 regarded themselves as the ruling element of the population; they accepted their sudden demotion with bad grace. But these centrifugal forces became dangerous and destructive to Czech democracy only when in the second part of the 1930's they were supported and stimulated by an outside power—Nazi Germany.

Thus, in the Balkans and in the former Habsburg empire two groups of powers developed as a result of the war: on the one hand were the defeated—Bulgaria and Hungary—both dissatisfied with the peace settlement; on the other were the victors—Rumania, Czechoslovakia, and Yugoslavia—who wished to maintain the *status quo* and formed a little entente to defend the situation created by the peace settlement. The antagonism between these two groups in foreign affairs increased the internal political instability of the various states because it prevented economic cooperation. An attempt to obtain through a Danube federation the economic cohesion formerly provided by the empire was in vain. The defeated saw in such an organization an effort to stabilize the *status quo*. The victors feared that it might be a first step toward the restoration of the Habsburg monarchy. In the end each country directed its economic policy toward autarky, in the hope that it could become independent of its neighbors. The artificial stimulation of industry resulted in stiff competition and low prices— a precarious and vulnerable economic situation.

The situation in the Balkans and eastern Europe held two particular dangers for the stability of Europe as a whole. Democracy there had succumbed because of contrasts between nationalities, conflicts between a radical peasantry and a bourgeoisie anxious to foster industrialization, resistance of a landowning class to agrarian reform, fear of revolution and of Communism. The dictatorial or pseudodictatorial regimes which followed the democratic governments clamped the lid on these problems; they did not solve them. Thus, they were themselves unstable, and having come to power by force, they were threatened by force. They would rather take risks than endanger their position by retreat.

If the great powers of Europe had been united, they might have been able to work out a common policy for this area which would have improved the economic situation and relieved tension. But the great European powers were divided, and each side sought for support among the eastern European states, with the result that the antagonisms in eastern Europe deepened. On the other hand, the prestige of the great powers became tied up with the fortunes of their Balkan allies, and the conflicts over the Balkan area placed a severe handicap on all attempts to overcome tensions among the great powers.

The Treaty of Versailles and Its Aftermath

In its various provisions, the settlement concluded at the Paris Peace Conference affected the entire world. But most attention has doubtless been directed to the part of the settlement which arranged the peace with the western powers' principal enemy—Germany. This treaty was signed at

Versailles on June 28, 1919, in the Hall of Mirrors, where in 1871 the German empire had been proclaimed. Its territorial provisions included the return of Alsace-Lorraine to France and the cession of areas with Polish populations—notably Poznán and the larger part of West Prussia—to Poland, so that a stretch of territory under Polish sovereignty, the so-called Polish Corridor, would separate East Prussia from the rest of Germany. Danzig, a German seaport at the northern end of the Polish Corridor, was established as a free city under supervision of the League of Nations, which was intended to guarantee Poland unimpeded access to the Baltic Sea. Memel, at the northern tip of East Prussia was also placed under the League of Nations; later it was seized by Lithuania. Plesbiscites were ordered in Schleswig and Upper Silesia and the southern part of East Prussia, and as a result of these, Germany had to give up some additional territory, although only the loss of the rich coal mines of Upper Silesia was of significance. Finally, Germany had to relinquish its colonies. Altogether, 13.1 per cent of Germany's prewar territory and 10 per cent of its population in 1910 were lost.

These territorial arrangements were complemented by clauses dealing with military and economic matters. The German army was limited to 100,000 officers and men. It was not to utilize aircraft, tanks, or aggressive weapons, and their production was prohibited. Artillery, aircraft, and tanks still in German possession were to be handed over to the victors. Also, the German navy was to be surrendered to the British; however, the Germans succeeded in scuttling most of their ships. In the future the German navy was to be restricted to twelve ships, none more than ten thousand tons; submarines were forbidden. The general staff and the officers' schools were to be abolished. Finally, as a guarantee for the fulfillment of the military clauses, the Rhineland would be occupied by Allied forces for up to fifteen years and would remain permanently demilitarized.

The Allies had great difficulty in reaching agreement about the economic aspects of the settlement. In the end, Article 231 of the Treaty of Versailles stated that the Germans must accept "responsibility of Germany and her allies for causing all the loss and damage to which the Allied and Associated Governments and their nationals have been subjected as a consequence of the war imposed upon them by the aggression of Germany and her allies." The far-reaching nature of this formulation was obvious. It might be interpreted as requiring Germany to finance pensions for officers, demobilization payments, and compensations for the wounded and maimed. The exact determination of how much, on the basis of this article, Germany would have to pay was difficult to reach, and no figure was specified in the treaty because the amount the experts believed Germany could pay was very different from the sum the people in the victorious countries had been led to expect. The treaty did state that in the next few years Germany was to pay five billion dollars, pending a definite settlement in 1921. However, the treaty included various provisions which weakened the German economy and hence reduced the nation's subsequent capacity to make payments. Germany had to hand over to the Allies most of its merchant marine, a quarter of its fishing fleet, and a good part of its railroad stock. For five years Germany had to build annually 200,000 tons of shipping for the victors. It had to make yearly deliveries of coal to France, Italy, and Belgium, and to pay the costs of the occupation of the Rhineland by the Allied armies. In addition, France received economic control over the Saar area, rich in coal and iron; for fifteen years this area was to be administered by the League of Nations; then a plebiscite was to decide its fate.

The strong moral condemnation of Germany and the German people that was contained in Article 231, with its statement that the war had been caused by German aggression, was also implied in other arrangements. Germany was not permitted to join the League of Nations; the Germans were to hand over their former political and military leaders to the Allies so that they could be judged by an international court for their crimes against international morality; the political union of Austria and Germany was prohibited, that is, the German-speaking people were not permitted to exert the principle of national self-determination. The impression that the Germans were treated as outcasts was reinforced by the manner in which the treaty was presented to them. The German delegation which had come to Versailles on April 29 was kept in isolation behind barbed wire. On May 7 the treaty was presented to the Germans without previous negotiations, and after they had received it, only an exchange of written notes took place. On June 16 the Allies presented an ultimatum in which they declared that they would resume hostilities if the Germans had not agreed to sign the treaty within a week. They did so on June 23, and five days later the ceremony in the Hall of Mirrors took place.

The harshness of the Treaty of Versailles has been sharply criticized and is frequently mentioned as a reason for the rise of Nazism in Germany. It is probably more correct to say that the fault of the Treaty of Versailles was that it was a compromise, neither fully generous nor totally destructive. The French wanted to destroy German unity, or at least to separate the Rhineland from Germany, and to keep Germany disarmed and economically weak in the foreseeable future. Great Britain and the United States were opposed to these French aims, partly because they considered them to be immoral, partly because they regarded them as impossible to realize. All the victorious powers were agreed that if the conditions were unbearably harsh Germany might throw itself into the arms of the Bolsheviks and Communism might penetrate into the center of Europe. Thus the French aims were resisted by Great Britain and the United States. But in order to persuade the French to abandon their plans, the British and the Americans had to make concessions. The result was a treaty which appeared to be an attempt to cripple Germany permanently rather than to make possible its further existence in the society of states.

In view of the hatreds aroused in the war, perhaps nothing better than the Treaty of Versailles could have been arranged. By and large, it did establish frontiers according to the principle of national self-determination. And the necessity of revising and mitigating the military and economic clauses of the treaty was soon accepted. But the impression received by the Germans in the summer of 1919, when the treaty was presented to them, was that of unrelenting harshness. This impression was particularly strong because they believed that they had been assured generous treatment. The Germans thought that they had laid down their arms under the condition that the peace treaty would be concluded on the basis of Wilson's Fourteen Points. Actually, at the signing of the armistice, the Germans were hardly in a position to make conditions. Their armies were in full retreat, their people were in revolt, and further resistance was hopeless.

BEGINNINGS OF THE WEIMAR REPUBLIC

When in October, 1918, the German front in the west began to weaken, a new German government was formed, headed by Prince Max of Baden, a man of humane outlook and liberal principles whose activities on behalf of prisoners of war had earned him a high reputation even in the non-German world. His task as chancellor was to direct the political transition of Germany; the military failure had compromised the existing ruling group in the eyes of the German people. The constitutional changes made during October transformed Germany into a parliamentary democracy. Its government was made dependent on a vote of confidence in the Reichstag. The introduction of universal suffrage in Prussia meant that the dominating influence of the *Junkers* on the policy of the Reich was broken. Moreover, the leaders of the political parties of the center and left of center—the parties that had always urged a democratization of German political life—entered the government. Given time, perhaps the government could have persuaded the world that a new democratic Germany had arisen. But these changes and reforms took place under the shadow of imminent military catastrophe. When Prince Max of Baden formed his government, Ludendorff, despairing of the military situation, demanded the opening of negotiations which would lead to an immediate ending of hostilities. The government therefore informed President Wilson of its readiness for peace negotiations based on the Fourteen Points. An exchange of notes followed, lasting through October. Because the European allies distrusted the sincerity of this sudden conversion to democracy at the moment of defeat, Wilson demanded clear proof of the change in Germany. But meanwhile the government's appeal to Wilson was having an immense impact on the German people. They became suddenly aware of what had been concealed by optimistic military communiqués—the fact that the war was lost. The belief became widespread that the old leaders ought to give up power so that Wilson and his allies would have undeniable proof of the change in Germany. When William II hesitated to abdicate, mutinies—first in the navy—broke out. Unrest spread in the cities. Demonstrations and strikes indicated that the government could no longer rely on police or military force. On November 9, 1918, a republic for Germany was proclaimed in Berlin. Two days later the armistice was signed.

The revolution within Germany threw power into the laps of the socialists. But if they wanted to use the fall of the monarchy for a transformation of their country into a socialist state, the chaotic situation in Germany frustrated them. The socialists themselves were divided, and the next month saw a struggle between moderates and radicals. The moderate majority of the Social Democratic leaders, known as Majority Socialists to distinguish them from the dissident Independent Socialists, believed that radical social changes would result in the dissolution of the Reich, especially since separatist movements had begun to arise in Bavaria and the Rhineland. The Majority Socialists pushed the radicals out of the government, and the latter resumed revolutionary action. The driving force toward this revolutionary action was an extreme leftist organization, the Spartacus group, from which later the German Communist party developed. In the winter of 1918–1919 its leaders were Karl Liebknecht and Rosa Luxemburg, both of whom had been influential in the socialist movement before the First World War. There was fierce street fighting in Berlin, particularly vehement in the last weeks of 1918 and the first weeks of 1919. Uprisings spread in the Ruhr area and in Hamburg and in April a Soviet Republic was established in Bavaria. All these revolutionary movements were defeated.

In order to fight off the radical left, the Majority Socialists felt constrained to accept help from the elements to their right. They were particularly anxious to gain control over an organized military force. Immediately after the proclamation of the republic in November, 1918, Friedrich Ebert (1871–1925), the leader of the socialists and head of the new federal government, approached Field Marshal von Hindenburg and General Groener, of the military high command—the latter having replaced Ludendorff—and the generals agreed to cooperate with the socialist leaders in order to maintain German unity.

The alliance between the Majority Socialists and the military high command had important consequences. Following Hindenburg's example the German civil servants recognized the legitimacy of the new government and placed their services at its disposal. The resulting administrative

Revolution in Germany. *Adherents of the Spartacus group occupying a government building in Berlin.*

continuity helped to overcome the difficulties of demobilization and to ease the transition to a peacetime economy. But the advantages to the new government of gaining the support of the military high command for military action against the extremists on the left were less than might have appeared at the time of the proclamation of the republic and had a fatal influence on future developments. When the troops returned to German soil from the occupied territories in the west and east, discipline dissolved; they left the ranks and went to their homes. This created a critical situation in the last months of 1918. The high command responded by starting to organize volunteer units (*Freikorps*) in which former officers had a leading role; these *Freikorps* played their part in the fight against the extremists. The weight of the conservative allies pushed the government strongly in the direction of ending the revolutionary situation in which Councils of Workers and Soldiers interfered in the process of government. The government was urged to arrange as soon as possible elections through which the bourgeoisie and the more conservative part of the population could make their voices heard. At the end of January, 1919, when most of the revolutionary movements of the radical left had been defeated, elections to a constituent assembly took place. The new assembly met in Weimar on February 6, 1919.

However, the shotgun wedding between the socialists and the high command had consequences which extended far beyond the winter of 1918–1919, and stultified the development of democracy in Germany. Because the socialists relied on the old civil servants, the republic was obligated to preserve the rights which these functionaries had possessed under the empire. Thus, during the entire existence of the republic its administrative apparatus was in the hands of conservative, usually monarchist, civil servants who could not be dismissed and who exerted a controlling influence on the admission of new members to their ranks. Furthermore, when the new 100,000-man army was created, the task of selecting its officer corps remained in the hands of the officers of the old general staff. This reliance on conservative forces prevented the destruction or even the weakening of the powerful position of the landowners and industrialists. Promises of agrarian reform, made in the initial burst of revolutionary enthusiasm, were not kept. The industrialists fended off all attempts at socialization, although the trade unions did gain the assurance that employers would accept the principle of collective bargaining and refrain from obstructing the functioning of the unions in the factories. It has been argued that the socialists were unable to undertake a thorough transformation of German society because if they had acted against the bourgeoisie the resulting conflict would have destroyed the unity of the Reich. But the unity of the Reich withstood severe crises in the following years. The fact is that most of the leaders of the Majority Socialists were bureaucrats rather than revolutionaries and did not know what to do with the power which had fallen to them.

That in November, 1918, the German people were ready for far-reaching changes was shown by the elections which took place when reaction had already begun to set in. In the constituent assembly, those who advocated democratization of German political life obtained a striking majority: 328 deputies out of a total of 423. Within this republican group the moderate socialists, with 165 members, were strongest, but lacking a majority, they had to collaborate with the two bourgeois republican parties, the Catholic Center party and the left-liberal Democratic party, which together were not quite as strong as the socialists. Thus the constitution resulting from the deliberations of this assembly established not a socialist system, but a parliamentary democracy. All power was concentrated in the hands of a parliament (the Reichstag), elected through secret ballot by all men and women of at least twenty-one years of age, on the basis of proportional representation. The federal government of the republic was given more power than had been enjoyed by its counterpart in the empire; a provision for which a member of the Center party, Matthias Erzberger, was mainly responsible gave the right to raise direct taxes to the federal government, which then assigned funds to the various states. As in the United States, the president—the head of the republic—was to be elected directly by the people. The government, with a chancellor as its head, was responsible to the Reichstag. Thus, both the Reichstag and the president could claim to represent the people and to enjoy democratic legitimation. When they clashed, the door was opened for the overthrow of parliamentary democracy: in emergency situations the president had the right to rule by decree without previous approval of the parliament, and no law ever defined

Acceptance of the Republican Constitution in Weimar in 1919. *President Ebert and other leaders of the Republic on the balcony of the building in which the Constituent Assembly met.*

what an emergency situation was.

Despite internal conflicts and economic misery, the changes in the forms of political life and the emergence of new political leaders raised hopes in Germany. But when the draft of the peace treaty was handed to the German delegation in Versailles, these hopes turned into disappointment and vehement indignation. In the face of violent opposition, the treaty was accepted in the Reichstag by a small majority consisting of the moderate socialists and the Center party. A resumption of hostilities, as the military leaders admitted, was impossible. And it was feared that an occupation of Germany by the Allied armies might result in the disintegration of the Reich. The acceptance of the peace treaty led to a strengthening of the monarchical right and the radical left, the right accusing the republican government of a lack of feeling for national honor, the left advocating cooperation with Bolshevik Russia as a means of "liberation." After the summer of 1919 those parties that were the protagonists of a democratic republic and the true authors of the new constitution—the Center party, the Democratic party, and the Majority Socialists—did not again constitute a majority in the Reich. It has been said about the rise of the Nazis that, as long as there were free elections in Germany, the Nazis never gained a majority among the voters. And this is true. But it must also be said that after 1919, during the fourteen years of the Weimar Republic, those parties that were convinced supporters of the republican regime never had a clear majority either.

The parliamentary system never really functioned in Germany. The governments changed frequently; several of them were minority governments or governments of experts, ruling with ever-shifting majorities. Those which were based on a parliamentary majority, such as the two governments of the Great Coalition, in 1923 and 1928, were possible only with right-wing support: these governments included—in addition to the three republican parties (Social Democrats, Democrats, Center party)—the monarchist German People's party. And the governments of Heinrich Brüning and Franz von Papen, preceding Hitler's rise to power, ruled by presidential emergency decrees without a secure parliamentary basis.

THE STRUGGLE OVER FULFILLMENT OF THE PEACE TREATY

Problems connected with the execution of the peace treaty dominated the policy of the Weimar Republic throughout its existence. In the first five years after the signing of the Treaty of Versailles the two principal issues concerned the reduction of the army to 100,000 men and the payment of reparations. These questions kept alive the conflicts which had developed over the acceptance of the peace treaty. Opponents of the treaty recommended an obstructionist policy, suggesting that changes in the world situation would make enforcement of the terms impossible. The republican parties believed that Germany should attempt to fulfill the clauses of the peace treaty and hereby create a confidence in German trustworthiness that would lead to the mitigation of the treaty's requirements.

The most vehement opponents of adherence to the military clauses were the career officers, who had in the defense minister, the socialist Noske, an all too trusting chief. The general staff continued to function in disguised form as a section of the defense ministry. The military assisted the formation of unofficial, secret military organizations, provided them with weapons, and participated in their training. Among the men used by the army for keeping alive the military spirit was a corporal named Adolf Hitler, whose oratorical gifts seemed suited for this task.

The wave of military obstructionism reached its high point in March, 1920, when the reduction of the army to its accepted size could no longer be delayed. In a putsch organized by a former imperial civil servant, Wolfgang Kapp, the generals attempted to overthrow the government. Although the government had to flee Berlin, a general strike forced the putschists to surrender. The army was reduced to its prescribed strength and the illegal military organizations gradually disbanded. But the disorder of the Kapp Putsch led to Communist revolts, particularly in the Ruhr area, that could be suppressed only with the help of the military. The republican government, therefore, felt unable to take advantage of its victory over the rightists for a purge of the army of monarchist elements. The new 100,000-man army, the Reichswehr, remained firmly in the hands of the old officers' group.

The Treaty of Versailles had left determination of the exact amount of reparations and the details of their payment to later negotiations. These questions were thrashed out in a number of meetings and conferences which showed a wide gap between Allied demands and the Germans' estimate of their ability to pay; this disagreement served to maintain a poisoned atmosphere between the opponents. Germany was finally forced to accept an ultimatum in which the amount of damages for which reparations were required was fixed at 132 billion marks (31.5 billion dollars), due in annual installments of 2 billion marks (close to 500 million dollars).

All the German political parties were convinced that their country could not pay this sum. But German politicians disagreed on how a reduction could be achieved. Once again the rightist parties advocated obstruction; the republican parties wanted to go as far as possible in fulfilling the demands of the victors. The most prominent protagonist of this fulfillment policy was Walter Rathenau (1867–1922). Rathenau was an uncommon figure: an aesthete who was close to many figures of modern art and literature, and a writer who in a number of widely read books had discussed the impact of modern technology on human existence, he was also a man of action who had proved his practical abilities as chairman of the great German electricity trust. And Rathenau was a good German patriot. At the beginning of the war he had suggested that the government inventory all raw materials—a most necessary measure—and had been entrusted with the task. In the difficult postwar situation Rathenau again put himself at the disposal of the government, serving as minister of reconstruction (May, 1921) and subsequently as foreign minister (February, 1922). His primary aim was to halt the inflationary trend of the German economy by substituting deliveries of goods for payments in gold; he hoped that economic cooperation, particularly between German and French industry, would gradually lead to a feasible reparations settlement. However, Rathenau was not master in his own foreign ministry, in which influential officials believed that western pressure on their nation would be weakened only if Germany exerted some counterpressure; they favored close connections with Soviet Russia. On April 16, 1922, when no improvement in the reparations arrangements seemed obtainable, Rathenau, the advocate of a western orientation in German foreign policy, was persuaded to conclude at Rapallo a treaty with Russia which provided for closer political and economic collaboration with the East. Nevertheless, because the German public regarded Rathenau as the embodiment of a policy of concessions to the victor, he became the chief target of the extremists of the right. On June 24, 1922, he was assassinated by members of a secret organization consisting chiefly of former officers who sought to eliminate as traitors the principal exponents of the fulfillment policy. Rathenau's assassination was only one in a long chain of political murders. Early in 1919, Karl Liebknecht and Rosa Luxemburg, who as leaders of the Spartacus group had been involved in the extremist revolt against the Majority socialists, had been killed without trial after falling into the hands of the military. Matthias Erzberger, the leader of the Center party who had signed the armistice, had been asassinated in 1921, and in 1922 an attempt had been made on the life of the socialist Philipp Scheidemann, who in November, 1918, had proclaimed the republic in Berlin from the balcony of the Reichstag building. The members of the judiciary were conservative and nationalistic and refrained from probing the nationalistic organizations to which the murderers belonged.

With Rathenau's elimination, the enemies of the fulfillment policy gained the upper hand. A government of experts under the business leader Heinrich Cuno, supported by the parties of the right, deliberately refused to make the deliveries to which Germany was obligated. The French reaction was quick and sharp. French troops moved into the Ruhr area, so that the mines of the district would now produce for France. But encouraged by the German government, the miners refused to work and embarked on a policy

The occupation of the Ruhr area in 1923. *French troops enter Essen.*

of passive resistance. To provide the money which the workers needed to live on, the German presses began to turn out currency with accelerated speed, and the mark plunged to unimaginable depths. At the beginning of 1923, the American dollar, which in 1914 had been the equivalent of 4.2 marks, brought 1,800 marks. By the fall of 1923 one American dollar was worth 4.2 trillion marks. Currency of this sort had no real value. When people received their wages they hastened to transform them into goods before their buying power diminished even further. Workers were hard hit because their wages, although steadily increased, did not keep up with the rising prices. Civil servants, with fixed salaries that only slowly adjusted to the upward trend, were in dire straits. Those dependent upon pensions, rents, or investment in government loans existed by selling whatever pieces of value they possessed. That the middle classes, usually a stabilizing social force, suffered most gravely and became embittered and increasingly radical was a fatal blow to the prestige of the republican regime. The inflation had a deeply demoralizing effect. While most people did not understand what was going on, those who did were able to make great amounts of money. Boys of seventeen and eighteen left school, turned to financial speculation, and quickly earned ten times as much as their fathers, who had been slowly working their way up through the bureaucratic hierarchy.

Conditions in Germany became chaotic. Separatist movements sprang up in the Rhineland. In Saxony, the radical left came into power. Bavaria was dominated by Bavarian monarchists and radical rightist organizations led by Ludendorff and Hitler. If a unified Reich and an ordered social life were to be maintained, the printing of money would have to be stopped, the passive resistance in the Ruhr would have to be abandoned, and Germany would have to resume reparations payments.

The necessity for admitting defeat was realized not only by those who had advocated the fulfillment policy but also by a leader of the rightist German People's party, Gustav Stresemann (1878–1929). Stresemann looked like a typical German petit bourgeois. Before 1914 he had been an enthusiastic admirer of William II and as a member of the Reichstag during the war years, he had been a rabid nationalist and annexationist and supported the high command in all its demands. But Stresemann had been deeply shaken by the way the military leaders had deceived themselves and the German people about their chances in the war. He became convinced that a reorganization of German political life on a democratic basis was unavoidable, and when the republican German Democratic party failed to accept him, he founded his own party, which aimed at the restoration of the monarchy but accepted the parliamentary system of government. In asserting the hopelessness of the contest over the Ruhr, Stresemann risked his popularity, but he was aware that by assuming leadership in this matter he was opening the door to a positive role for

Inflation in Germany. A *kohlrabi* (*a type of turnip*) *cost fifty million marks in 1923.*

himself in the political life of the Weimar Republic. In a number of speeches made all over Germany during the early summer of 1923, he prepared the public for the necessity of abandoning the Ruhr struggle. And in August, 1923, he became chancellor, with the program of stabilizing the German currency and resuming the fulfillment policy. As a first step he ended the passive resistance in the Ruhr. He was helped by the fact that the chaotic situation which had developed in central Europe was having a damaging economic effect throughout the continent. All the great powers now recognized that for the sake of their own economic stability some compromise about German reparations payments had to be worked out; they agreed to the reopening of the question by a committee of experts headed by an American, Charles G. Dawes

Defects and Strengths of the Weimar Republic

Between the proclamation of the republic in 1918 and the economic collapse of 1923, events in Germany crowded one upon the other. There was a long procession of personalities who came forward and then disappeared from the scene after a short time: Liebknecht, Noske, Rathenau, Erzberger, Cuno, Kapp. There were strikes and unrest, sometimes developing into civil war, in Berlin, in Bavaria, in the Rhineland, and in Saxony. There were moments when it seemed questionable whether the federal government could enforce its authority in all parts of the Reich, especially since the army and the judiciary kept their protecting hands over secret military organizations bitterly hostile to the republic. In critical situations like that of the Ruhr occupation, hostility to the western powers created an alliance—called National Bolshevism—between the extreme right and the extreme left. The economic upheaval brought new economic leaders into the foreground. The most powerful of these was Hugo Stinnes (1870–1924), a coal merchant, an owner of coal mines in the Ruhr, who built up a gigantic concern consisting of ironworks, banks, merchant ships, newspapers, and hotels, and who was one of the strongest adversaries of the fulfillment policy; however, Stinnes' phenomenal rise to economic power and political influence was quickly followed by the disintegration of his firm after the stabilization of the mark: the debts which he had contracted in building up his enterprises, easily repaid during the inflation, became a stifling burden after stabilization.

It was a turbulent period, but the very turbulence of these years concealed the fact that the changes which the overthrow of the monarchy had brought about were not very far-reaching. Germany had become a republic, with a parliamentary system. The functions of the Reich had been enlarged at the expense of the individual states, and the power of the Reichstag had been increased so that the government—the executive branch—was now dependent on the legislative branch. General suffrage and the parliamentary system had also been introduced in the individual German states, so that, for instance, Prussia had a government headed by a Social Democrat until 1932. The position of the trade unions had been legally fortified, and as a result of the influence of the Social Democrats, governmental intervention and arbitration in labor conflicts secured a fair hearing for the cause of the trade unions. These were much-needed reforms and improvements. But they did not represent a revolutionary change, the creation of a new truly democratic society; and they left the social structure of Germany almost untouched. The strength which the traditional organizations and institutions preserved would be a serious danger to the existence of the Weimar Republic in years to come.

However, German life did assume a new shape in one area—that of culture. Frustrated in more far-reaching plans by the consequences of defeat and economic difficulties, the liberal and socialist ministers were anxious to demonstrate that at least in the field of culture a new era had opened. They supported the modern tendencies in art and literature which had been fought by conservative ministers of education under the empire. At the same time, the turmoil and the insecurity of these years created an excitement which was a spur to artistic and intellectual experiments. Furthermore, inflation had somehow shaken the belief in traditional values. And as we have seen, some people profited considerably from speculations during the inflationary period. They put their money into things of lasting worth, such as works of art; they spent freely and quickly, anticipating the rapid depreciation of paper money. Thus, masking the grimness of the social reality there was a glittering façade, particularly in Berlin and other large cities. The amusement industry flourished. Art exhibitions, operas, theaters, and concerts were well attended. There was much experimentation in opera, drama, and art. At this time the first plays of the young Bertolt Brecht appeared on the German stage; the opera *Wozzeck*, by Alban Berg, had its first triumph; movies like *The Cabinet of Dr. Caligari* demonstrated the possibilities inherent in this new form of art; and the Bauhaus, first in Weimar and later in Dessau, inaugurated a new functional style in architecture and interior design. The absence of social stability fostered cynicism, as well as a sharpening of social criticism, both reflected in the drawings and paintings of George Grosz. Even after the economic crisis of the immediate postwar period had been overcome, a critical spirit remained alive and eagerness for experimentation continued. The intellectual atmosphere of Berlin after the First World War was electrifying; it attracted journalists, writers, and artists from all over the world. Such figures as Sinclair Lewis, Dorothy Thompson, Stephen Spender, Christopher Isherwood, and Ilya Ehrenburg were to look back nostalgically upon life in Berlin in the 1920's as one of their great experiences.

But because of their rejection of traditional forms of art, and because of their conscious cultivation of contacts with the most advanced intellectual movements in other countries, these cultural activities aroused opposition among many Germans. Conservatives regarded them as further proof that the Weimar regime represented a break with German tradition and was an alien element in German history. The distance widened between Berlin, the modern capital of the republic, and the rural areas, far removed from the rapid changes of modern life. This alienation of Berlin and other large urban centers from the rest of the country strengthened the appeal which in later years the Nazi propaganda against the Weimar "system" would have among wide circles of the population.

Modern architecture in Germany. *The Bauhaus in Dessau.*

CHAPTER 40

Era of Stabilization and Its Breakdown

In 1923 THE POLICY of the victorious powers changed direction. Until 1923 unrest and tension had been increasing, and pressure on Germany had been mounting steadily, but now steps were taken toward liquidating the consequences of the war and restoring cooperation among the European powers. This shift in attitude must be explained partly as an attempt to end the rifts which had developed among the wartime allies, and partly as a consequence of economic and social developments within the victorious states.

ITALY IN THE POSTWAR WORLD

The postwar relations between France and Great Britain were not smooth. Still, the distance between these two states was less wide than that which separated Italy from them both. In the postwar world Italy did not regard itself as a victorious power; it was anxious to see the peace treaties modified, and tended to support revisionist movements. This separation from the other Allies, already evident at the Paris Peace Conference, had its roots in the events accompanying Italy's entry into the war in 1915.

Unlike the other great powers, which were drawn into the hostilities in consequence of a chain of events over which they had lost control, Italy entered the war deliberately, with the aim of aggrandizement. In the secret Treaty of London of 1915, Great Britain, France, and Russia had promised Italy wide territorial gains. But the fulfillment of this treaty had encountered difficulties at the Paris Peace Conference, especially with regard to the extended Austrian territories which Italy was to receive: the Trentino and South Tyrol up to the Brenner Pass, Trieste, Istria, the islands along the Dalmatian coast, and a great part of Dalmatia. These acquisitions were intended to give Italy security against the Habsburg empire, which in 1915 nobody expected to disappear. But when the war ended, Austria-Hungary no longer existed and adherence to the arrange-

ments of the Treaty of London was incompatible with the principle of
self-determination for it would have placed more than a million Yugoslavs under Italian rule. Nevertheless, the Italians occupied Austrian
territory up to the line assigned to them in the treaty of 1915, and when
the Paris Peace Conference convened they insisted on their pound of
flesh—the fulfillment of the treaty. Aware, however, of the obstacles
which in these changed circumstances the execution of the early promises would encounter, the Italians intimated that they might be willing
to accept less if they were given Fiume, which had not been assigned
to them in the Treaty of London. But Fiume had a large Yugoslav
population, and the Yugoslavs vehemently refused this Italian demand,
since they did not want to see the two good ports on the eastern side of the
Adriatic Sea—Trieste and Fiume—in Italian hands. The question of Fiume
became one of the stumbling blocks at the Paris Peace Conference.
President Wilson's appeal to the Italian people to accept the principle of
self-determination was rejected. For three weeks the Italian delegates
absented themselves from the negotiations. Even after their return, the
Fiume question remained undecided.

The Paris Peace Conference allowed Italy to extend its frontiers to the
Brenner Pass and to take over the Istrian Peninsula, including the city of
Trieste. Italy thus acquired all the Habsburg territories which had been
regarded as *Italia irredenta* in the prewar years, but the government, in order
to get backing for its additional claims, had whipped up nationalist
excitement to such a degree that the joy over the fulfillment of these
national aspirations was overshadowed by disappointment over the failure to
obtain Fiume and Dalmatia. All over Italy, people spoke of "the mutilated
victory." Contempt for the feebleness of parliamentary politics had arisen in
Italy before the First World War and these events reinforced this attitude.
Nationalist organizations of an antiparliamentary character sprang up everywhere. The fiery poet Gabriele D'Annunzio became an influential political
leader in Italy. In the fall of 1919, while the negotiations over Fiume were
still going on, he organized a troop of volunteers, who seized power in
Fiume. There they remained until December, 1920. By then, Italy's foreign
minister, Count Carlo Sforza (1873–1952), had negotiated a treaty
according to which Fiume became an independent city-state and in
compensation Italy received a number of islands on the Dalmatian coast.
Now Italian troops turned D'Annunzio and his volunteers out of Fiume.
But D'Annunzio had exposed the weak and vacillating character of the
Italian government, which first made great demands and then hesitated to
enforce them. Among the nationalist leaders of this period, the most
efficient was the former Socialist leader Benito Mussolini (1883–1945), who
had left the Socialist party because it had resisted Italian entry into the war.
He had served in the war as a volunteer and was now seeking a platform

from which to reenter political life. On March 23, 1919, in a building on the Piazza San Sepolcro in Milan, he founded his own organization, the *Fasci di Combattimento,* whose members came to be known as Fascists.

Resentment over thwarted nationalist aims was fed by economic misery and discontent. In Italy more than 50 per cent of the country's tax revenues came from consumer taxes, which fell off when the war caused a decrease in the production of consumer goods. An attempt was made to finance the Italian war effort through internal and foreign loans, and when these proved insufficient the government resorted to the printing of paper money. The consequence was inflation; in 1920 the lira had less than a fifth of its prewar value. The financial problems were increased by a growing deficit in the balance of trade. During the war, agricultural production had decreased drastically, and after the war Italy had to import not only coal and oil but also great quantities of grain.

Most directly hit by the inflation were the members of the middle classes: people with fixed incomes, such as civil servants, landlords prevented by law from raising rents, and rentiers who had invested their money in government bonds. But economic distress was also felt by the rural classes and the workers. After the war more than 50 per cent of all Italians were engaged in agriculture. Nine tenths of those who owned land possessed less than three acres, not nearly enough even for subsistence. And a great part of the rural population was entirely landless, working for wages on the great estates. During the war the government had promised a redistribution of the land; rumors—many exaggerated—about what had been done in Russia stimulated the impatience of the Italian peasants and raised their expectations. The war also increased unrest among the industrial workers. Hitherto industrial activity had largely taken the form of very small enterprises, employing less than ten workers. But in response to the needs of war production, large-scale industrial establishments had become much more numerous. News from Russia, coupled with the inflationary price rise with which wages could not keep up, intensified the demand for social reform by the workers, and the long-standing influence of syndicalism and anarchism contributed to their radicalization. Dissatisfaction among the rural and industrial proletariat erupted in direct action. In dramatic fashion bands of peasants and agricultural workers, marching to the accompaniment of martial music and the pealing of church bells, occupied uncultivated land belonging to the great landowners. In cities and towns strikes increased. The strike wave reached its high point in the summer of 1920, when dismissals in the metallurgical industries led to an occupation of the factories by the workers in industrial regions. However, these demonstrations had no long-lasting effect. The police removed the peasants from the land which they had appropriated, and the workers, lacking raw materials, capital, and salesmen, were unable to keep the industries going and evacuated the factories. Nevertheless, the political activity of peasants and workers contributed significantly to the transformation of the Italian party system. Before the war the Italian political parties were rather loose in structure; the individual deputy owed his election to his reputation and his standing in his own district, not to his party label. After the war, the socialists, in close alliance with the trade unions, built an efficient, centrally directed organization. Furthermore, Pope Benedict XV gave permission for the foundation of a Catholic political party, and the Catholic People's party appeared on the scene. Eager for mass support, it looked beyond the Catholic bourgeoisie for adherents, seeking to attract the peasants of the south and the industrial workers, among whom Catholic trade unions began to compete with socialist trade unions. The guiding spirit of the Catholic People's party was a Sicilian priest, Don Luigi Sturzo, whose experience in the stagnant Italian south had made him aware of the need for social —particularly agrarian—reform. The influence of the two mass parties —the Socialists and the Catholic People's party—was strengthened by the adoption of the proportional voting system, which the government had introduced as a concession to the demands for reform: the number of deputies allowed each party was determined by the total number of votes received by the party throughout Italy. The bourgeois parties of the center and the left, Liberals and Democrats, were seriously threatened. This was the situation when the Fascists came to power in October, 1922.

Mussolini's claim that Fascism saved Italy from Bolshevism is palpably untrue. If there ever was danger of a successful Communist take-over in Italy after the First World War—and this is most doubtful—the revolutionary wave had certainly passed its crest by the spring of 1921. The new mass parties, now firmly entrenched, did not advocate revolution. However, they did agree on the need for far-reaching social and economic reform. Reform was deeply feared by the industrialists and landowners, still suffering from the shock of the occupation of factories and land by workers and peasants. In their anxiety they turned to the opponents of parliamentary democracy, hoping to gain support in their fight against reform. Mussolini's Fascists offered themselves as a most suitable instrument. Throughout Italy the party had formed paramilitary organizations, consisting chiefly of young unemployed war veterans. In the industrial centers of the north these Fascist organizations made themselves popular with the bourgeoisie by protecting strikebreakers and disrupting Socialist street demonstrations. The young Fascists were ruthless but effective. Moreover, Mussolini, their leader, inspired some confidence; he was a journalist of gifts and a remarkable orator. Although his boasts of intensive study of Marx and Nietzsche were considerably exaggerated, his acquaintance with Marxist thought and modern philosophy was sufficient to give his writings and speeches intellectual respectability. Through his advocacy of Italy's entry into the war, and through his war service, he had demonstrated his patriotism, but Mussolini was too much of a Marxist to believe that the world could stand still and be satisfied with the same old ideas. He was therefore not only a nationalist but also a revolutionary activist. And this combination constituted his strength in the eyes of the Italian upper classes. On the one hand Mussolini seemed to have a hold over the masses which they had lost; on the other, he seemed to share their own nationalist ideals and their rejection of international socialism. They expected that Mussolini might develop his organization into a counterforce to the new mass parties. Leaders of the old political groups, such as Giolitti, regarded Mussolini's rise with benevolence. They believed that he would be useful and that cooperation with him would be feasible.

The test came with the Fascist seizure of power—the March on Rome on October 27, 1922. The version of this event which the Fascists later spread was that the Fascist organizations had converged on Rome and the government, faced by this revolutionary force, capitulated. Actually, negotiations about Fascist participation in the government had been going on for some time. Leaders of various political parties—Giolitti as well as the more conservative Antonio Salandra (1853–1931)—were willing to form a coalition government which included the Fascists. To clinch these negotiations Mussolini organized the March on Rome; his paramilitary organizations approached the capital from four directions. The government felt sure that it could defeat this Fascist revolt with the help of the army, and the king was willing to sign the order declaring a state of siege. But on the night of October 27, he changed his mind because—as he revealed after the fall of Mussolini—he had received exaggerated reports of the Fascists' military strength. When Mussolini heard of the king's attitude he was no longer content with a subordinate partnership in a coalition government, and insisted that he be made prime minister. Only after this demand had been granted did he come to Rome; arriving on October 30 after traveling from Milan by sleeping car, he appeared before the king and was commissioned to form a government. The Fascist organizations now entered Rome and held a victory parade. Mussolini's government included, in addition to Fascist leaders, members of the parties of the right and even some members of the Catholic People's party. The March on Rome shows all the features characteristic of Mussolini's policy in the first decade of Fascist rule: on the one hand, the dramatic gesture directed toward the outside world; on the other, cautious preparation and careful calculation.

In the first years of his regime Mussolini's policy was rather ambiguous. The Fascist paramilitary organizations became a militia paid by the state and were effectively used to eliminate opposition. Mussolini placed Fascists in key positions in his administration, and they controlled the police. But since his government included not only Fascists but also Liberals, Conserva-

The March on Rome. *Mussolini in the middle; on the extreme left, Balbo, later Italian air minister.*

tives, and some members of the Catholic People's party, parliament continued to function, and Mussolini gave repeated assurances that he would remain within the framework of the constitution in his conduct of affairs. Thus in the first few years of his prime ministership, Mussolini's system of government was not very different from that of Giolitti in the prewar years. However, because the mass of workers and peasants had become more vocal and better organized, such a parliamentary dictatorship was now much more difficult to maintain, and accordingly the men in power had fewer hesitations about the use of ruthless and brutal methods. Moreover, Mussolini was determined to remain in power, and in 1923, under the threat of a second wave of revolution, he forced parliament to accept a change in the electoral law according to which the party with the largest number of votes would receive two thirds of the seats in the Chamber of Deputies. Hence, in the elections of 1924 the government received 374 of the 535 seats.

The abandonment of the parliamentary façade and the establishment of an undisguised dictatorship came in 1924 as a result of the conflict following the assassination of Giacomo Matteotti, a young, highly respected Socialist deputy; in his writings and speeches Matteotti had presented extended proof of Fascist terrorist acts. In particular, he had demonstrated how violence had been used to intimidate voters in the recent election. And Matteotti's revelations had been highly compromising to several members of the Fascist hierarchy. It soon emerged that Matteotti's abduction and murder had been instigated by prominent Fascists, close to Mussolini. Even if Mussolini was not directly involved, the murder was a manifestation of the atmosphere of brutality and violence which had developed with the toleration and encouragement of government leaders. The excitement over these disclosures was immense. The parliamentary opposition—about a hundred deputies, among them the various socialist groups, some members of the Catholic People's party, and left-wing liberals—demanded the dissolution of the Fascist militia and refused to have any contact with the Fascists, members of a party including murderers. They therefore withdrew from the Chamber of Deputies and set up their own counterparliament on the opposite side of the Tiber, on the Aventine. The demands of the opposition were strongly supported by the large Italian newspapers, which called for Mussolini's resignation. He seems to have thought of retirement, but the king, whom the opposition expected to take the initiative in dismissing Mussolini, did not act. Mussolini remained in power, and from this time on he steered energetically toward a one-party system and a totalitarian dictatorship.

The powers of parliament were increasingly curtailed and finally almost eliminated. It could no longer overthrow a government by a vote of lack of confidence. Its members could not propose a question for discussion, the head of the government determined the subjects to be debated in parliament. The position of the head of the government, or prime minister, was raised above that of other members of the cabinet. He was to appoint and dismiss the ministers and to direct their work. Neither individually nor collectively could the ministers remonstrate against his decisions. The prime minister also became almost independent of the crown, for if it should be necessary to appoint a new head of the government, the king was now obliged to choose him from a list of candidates put together by the Great Council of the Fascist party. Thus the Fascist party became an officially recognized institution and the decisive element in Italian political life. Soon it was the only legal political party; the other parties, having become entirely impotent, were forcibly dissolved. Since the list of candidates which the voters could accept or reject was put together by the Great Council of the Fascist party, only Fascists were elected to the Chamber of Deputies. The Fascist party was carefully organized at local and provincial levels as well as nationally; all party officials were appointed, not elected. The highest authority in the party was the Great Council, consisting of about thirty members selected by Mussolini as his most loyal followers.

Mussolini was at once the prime minister—chief executive of the government—and the leader (*duce*) of the party. Through the channels of the party organization, local party officers reported to him about the efficiency and loyalty of government officials. By "supervising"—or informing on—administrative functionaries at all levels, the Fascists held a heavy club over the heads of civil servants, who soon saw the futility, if not the danger, of questioning the actions of party members. Little or nothing was done when members of the Fascist militia committed acts of violence. Terror became an instrument of rule. Many prominent political leaders of the pre-Fascist era went into exile. Some who remained in Italy were physically attacked and gravely wounded; some were imprisoned without trial, or banished to small islands in the Mediterranean or to isolated villages in the Calabrian mountains. Among the prominent political exiles were the brothers Carlo and Nello Rosselli, who in France founded a journal advocating liberal and socialist ideas. But the long arm of Mussolini reached even into France, and in 1937 the brothers Rosselli were assassinated by men hired by the Fascists.

Police supervision, reinforced by terror, was supplemented as a means of control by censorship, introduced immediately after the assassination of Matteotti. The censorship laws created so many obstacles in the way of privately owned and independent newspapers that these publications began to disappear. The owners were forced to sell them; some were taken over by the government; local papers were bought cheaply by local party officials. And censorship extended to every aspect of literature and scholarship. Writers and scholars were forced either to desist from writing on contemporary issues or to promote Fascist ideas. And the Fascists were very conscious of the importance and value of propaganda. They offered great spectacles to the masses; they embodied their doctrine in slogans, which appeared on posters all over the country; they impressed intellectuals by demonstrating interest in modern literary and artistic movements, such as Futurism; and by having the railroads run on time they showed foreigners that order had been restored.

Mussolini was aware that his regime needed support beyond what could be provided by police, terror, and propaganda. Despite the repeated assertions in his speeches that Fascism represented neither capitalism nor Marxian socialism but a new social system, Mussolini kept close to the financial and industrial leaders who had helped him into power. His famous "corporate state," which was supposed to realize the new Fascist ideas in social and economic life, actually served the purposes of the wealthier classes. According to the charter which established this corporate state, the employers and employees of each branch of industry were to form a corporation; for each corporation, committees including representatives of the employers, the employees, and the government would decide questions of wages, working hours, and the like. The decisions of the committees were to be binding, and therefore strikes were forbidden. But since only Fascist trade unions were permitted to exist, the union leaders who represented the workers in the committees followed the line set by the government representatives, who usually sided with the industrialists. The economic recovery which took place all over Europe in the 1920's caused a reduction in unemployment and disguised the fact that the workers had become powerless. Moreover, impressed by Mussolini's claim to have saved his country from Bolshevism, both Italian and foreign bankers regarded Fascist Italy as trustworthy and stable and gave loans to the Fascist government which provided additional stimulus to Italian economic life.

The respectability of the regime and its popularity among the various groups of Italian society was also increased by the reconciliation, sealed in the Lateran Treaty of February 11, 1929, of the Italian state with the Roman Catholic Church. Mussolini had initiated negotiations with the Vatican almost immediately after coming to power. In the 1929 agreement the pope was recognized as the independent ruler of a small state—Vatican City—and the Church received a large financial sum as restitution for the expropriations at the time of Italy's unification. The relations between the Church and the state were regulated by a concordat which declared Roman Catholicism to be the official religion of the state, permitted the pope to appoint the Italian bishops after he had received the approval of the government for his candidates, guaranteed religious education in schools, and made a religious marriage ceremony mandatory. Two days after the conclusion of the Lateran Treaty, Pope Pius XI (pope from 1922 to 1939) declared that he regarded Mussolini as "a man sent by Providence."

Reconciliation with the Church may seem a strange step for one who in earlier years had flaunted his atheism and his contempt for the Church. But with the adoption of Fascism, Mussolini had accepted the view that the politician should not be bound by a system or principles. He emphasized the novelty of Fascist ideas, but when he came to power it was by no means clear what these new Fascist ideas actually were. In later years, when attempts were made to formulate the system of Fascism, this lack of a consistent framework of thought was justified by the assertion that thought independent from action did not exist.

It has always been easier to discover what Fascism rejected than what it stood for. In their statements about Fascist concepts of politics and government, Mussolini and his adherents emphasized that Fascism stood against the individualistic and rationalistic philosophy of the French Revolution. The law of politics, like the law of nature, was struggle; continued existence required continued growth and could be achieved only through action, not thought. Nations were living, viable units in politics, and man's function was to be an instrument in the hands of his nation's leader. Having turned from socialism and internationalism to nationalism, Mussolini preached the subordination of the individual to the nation with the excessive zeal of a convert. But he was also aware that the pursuit of a strictly nationalistic policy offered the best opportunity to conceal the contradictions of a regime which claimed to be revolutionary but actually defended and maintained the *status quo*. Thus personal inclination and political calculation combined to make the conduct of a forceful foreign policy, expressive of national egotism, the cornerstone of Mussolini's rule. He set the new tone of Italian foreign policy as early as 1923, when he used the assassination of a group of Italian officers on the Greek-Albanian border as pretext for an ultimatum to Greece. He demanded an indemnity of fifty million lire, an inquiry with the assistance of the Italian military attaché, ceremonial apologies, and funeral honors. When the Greeks hesitated to comply he bombarded and occupied the island of Corfu, evacuating it only after the Greeks, on the advice of the Great Powers, had given in to the Italian demands. The tangible result of Mussolini's first adventure in foreign policy was small, and could have been obtained without force. But his aim had been to show the Italians that their state was no longer ruled by a weak, timid, internationally minded government, and he used every opportunity to demonstrate that Italy had embarked on a new active course in foreign policy. Through bilateral negotiations with Yugoslavia he obtained a further change in the status of Fiume. In 1924 the town became Italian, while the rest of the free state was given to Yugoslavia. Mussolini also took some concrete steps toward expansion through the establishment of an Italian protectorate over Albania, in 1927. He always emphasized his disbelief in eternal peace and stressed that Italy must possess not only a powerful army and navy but also "an airforce that dominates the skies." He was proud to have shown with his action in the Corfu incident that Italy had freed itself from the tutelage of Great Britain and France, and—as in his negotiations with Yugoslavia —he did not shy away from asking for the support of Germany.

Mussolini disliked collective action and stabilization and wanted a fluid situation in which, by making use of the changing relations among various states, Italy could advance its own national interests. He stressed that Italy was not a satisfied nation, but "a nation hungry for land because we are prolific and intend to remain so." But in the 1920's the bark of Fascism was more threatening than its bite. Mussolini was careful to avoid moves which might lead to serious complications, such as a conflict with one of the great powers. The fateful consequences of his emphasis on action and national prestige became apparent only in the 1930's, when the Nazis had come to power in Germany and pursued an aggressive course. Then Mussolini was hoisted with his own petard. He did not want to appear less virile and martial than the Fascist leader of Germany. By then the prosperity of the 1920's had passed and Italians had begun to notice how little the Fascist regime had changed the economic and social life of their nation. The only way out, it seemed to Mussolini, was to tie the fortunes of his country to the rising power of Nazi Germany.

THE POSTWAR YEARS IN FRANCE AND GREAT BRITAIN

After the conflict over Fiume, and still more, after the Fascist seizure of power, Great Britain and France could no longer count upon Italy to join in common action to enforce the peace treaties. Great Britain and France in these years and throughout the entire interwar period were aware that in European affairs they were dependent upon each other. Nevertheless, rifts did develop in the relations between them. France entered the peace conference convinced that it had to avoid at any price a situation in which it would confront Germany alone. It had to have security, and therefore tried to obtain from the United States and Great Britain a commitment for common defense in the case of attack. When it failed to get such assurances, France next sought to weaken Germany beyond recovery, even to the extent of splitting it up. But Great Britain opposed French proposals for the dismemberment of Germany. The most the French were able to obtain was a compromise which left the final solution of the reparations question open and allowed Germany to retain the Rhineland, under the occupation of Allied troops.

Germany remained the center of friction between Great Britain and France in the following years, when the arrangements of the Treaty of Versailles—especially those about reparations and disarmament—had to be given practical shape. But tension between the British and the French extended also to other areas. Each of them wanted to prevent the other from growing in strength. The Near Eastern crisis of 1922, in which the British backed the Greeks while the French favored the Turks widened the rift. A year later the British denounced the French occupation of the Ruhr. But in 1924 close cooperation and a general European understanding was reached. These developments can only be understood in the context of the political and social situation which existed in the two countries after the war.

France

The end of the First World War was a high point in French history. Alsace-Lorraine had been regained and the defeat in the Franco-Prussian War of 1870–1871 had been revenged. The First World War had been won by Allied forces under the command of a French general, Marshall Foch. The French army was looked upon as the first army of the world. Before the First World War the German army had formed the model for the military forces of many of the smaller states, but now French officers became instructors in the newly organized states, and the officers and soldiers in these new armies wore uniforms patterned after French uniforms.

It was in recognition of the role which France had played in the war that the peace conference met in Paris. With statesmen and politicians from all over the globe assembling there, Paris could claim, at least for the duration of the conference, to be capital of the world. In Paris all the world learned that French civilization was entering a new era of greatness; with Marcel Proust, Paul Claudel, André Gide, and Paul Valéry, a new generation of significant French writers had emerged.

But there was a reverse side to this picture of a France radiant in the joy of victory. The nation had lost 1,320,000 military men and 250,000 civilians in the war. Because the French birthrate was low these losses would be replaced only slowly and it was evident that in the number of males of military age France would remain inferior to Germany. Moreover, for four years the northern part of the country had been a theater of war and on their retreat in 1918 the Germans had devastated much of this area in which France's most important industries were situated. French finances, like those of other belligerents, had suffered from the war. Despite foreign loans, chiefly from the United States but also from Great Britain, France had been forced to print money; by the end of the war more than five times as much money was in circulation as in 1914, and prices were three and a half times as high as they had been before the war.

It is not astonishing that a country that had suffered as much as France would expect that its material losses would be paid for by the defeated opponent—Germany. The French were not overly concerned about the hardships which such demands would cause in German economic life. Inferior to Germany in manpower and in natural resources, France advocated the use of Germany's economic resources for rebuilding the economy of the victors, a measure that would weaken Germany's competitive capacities. And if the pressure on Germany also destroyed the unity of the Reich, this was not a development which the French would regret.

A military mentality was reflected in the elections which took place in November, 1919: known as *horizon bleu* elections, after the color of French uniforms, they resulted in a great victory of the conservative *bloc national*, which obtained two thirds of the seats in the Chamber: 437 out of 613. The *cartel des gauches*, led by Édouard Herriot (1872–1957), and the Socialists lost heavily. This swing to the right was not purely the result of nationalist enthusiasm caused by victory; in France almost more than in any other country the coming to power of the Bolsheviks in Russia had aroused deep fears and hostility. The Bolshevik repudiation of the French prewar loans to Russia had provided the French bourgeoisie with some practical experience of what a revolution could involve. Alarm was reinforced by a change in the French economic system. The war had started a trend toward concentration in industry, with large corporations overshadowing the small family enterprises characteristic of the prewar economy. The acquisition of Lorraine, with its rich iron-ore mines, strengthened the position of heavy industry within the industrial structure. A new social force in French political life emerged as membership in the Confédération Générale du Travail, the most important trade-union organization, soared from 600,000 in 1914 to 2,000,000 in 1920. In recognition of the strength of the workers the government under Clemenceau pushed through an eight-hour day and legal status for collective agreements before the 1919 elections. But this courting of labor appeared dangerous to the other strata of society because, in 1919, the French Socialist party was still in close contact with the Bolsheviks. Only in 1920, at the Socialist congress in Tours, did the party split: the larger group declared its adherence to the Communist International; the smaller, under Léon Blum, remained loyal to the Second Socialist International as it had been reconstructed after the war.

In the triumphant *bloc national* the most influential leader was Raymond Poincaré. His term as president of the republic ended in February, 1920, but he was elected to the Senate and continued political activities. As president he had supported Foch, who advocated separation of the Rhineland from Germany, and he had been hostile to Clemenceau because of the latter's willingness to make concessions to the British and the United States and to content himself with a long-term occupation of the Rhineland. Poincaré favored the most adamant enforcement of the Treaty of Versailles. When the negotiations about reparations dragged on, he took over as prime minister and foreign minister, in 1922, and embarked on a policy in which France abandoned common action with its former allies, and followed an independent course. This policy culminated in the invasion of the Ruhr in January, 1923. Poincaré expected that this combination of military and economic pressure would strengthen the centrifugal forces in the Reich and might lead to the foundation of a separate republic in the Rhineland. In such aims, his policy was unsuccessful. The Germans were forced to give up their passive resistance in the Ruhr and to declare their intention in principle to resume payments and deliveries under the Versailles treaty, but the Reich remained unified, and capitulation was followed in December by the establishment of an international committee of experts to examine the German economic situation and the possibilities for reparations.

With his agreement to the formation of this committee Poincaré abandoned his policy of single-handed French action. Probably he had underestimated the "painful impression of intransigence"—to quote from a note to the French government by the British foreign secretary, George Curzon—which French policy had made all over the world. Poincaré and his adherents also had misjudged the French economic position. Reconstruction had given a stimulus to the French economy and France had withstood relatively well the postwar depression of 1921, which had severe effects in Great Britain and the United States. But the reconstruction of the devastated areas in France was financed by extensive government credits and it was expected that these outlays would be paid for by German reparations. When German cash payments did not take place or only in much smaller amounts than had been expected, and when the occupation of the Ruhr area resulted in a considerable rise in government expenses, the inflationary tendency which was part of the legacy of the war was reinforced. In 1914, 5.2 francs would buy a dollar, but 16.5 francs were required in 1923, 18.5 francs in 1925, and 26.5 francs in 1926. Although the loss in the value was moderate, the psychological impact on the French bourgeoisie who had suffered greatly through the default of the Russian loans was very strong. This was probably the decisive factor in forcing Poincaré back into a policy of cooperation; a great change in French public opinion certainly had taken place. In the elections of the year following the Ruhr occupation the *cartel des gauches* won: Poincaré resigned. The new prime minister was Herriot, and the foreign minister in the government of the left was Aristide Briand (1862–1932).

Briand remained foreign minister from 1925 to 1932. The early years of his political career, when he had been feared as a radical for his role in effecting the separation of church and state, were far behind him. He had subsequently served in many French cabinets, as minister of education, minister of justice, and prime minister. As prime minister during the German offensive against Verdun, Briand had experienced the horrors of this battle and his interests in the postwar years turned toward foreign affairs and the problems of peace. Briand was no less convinced than his predecessors that France needed guaranties against attack, but he hoped to achieve them through agreements and alliances embedded in a system of collective security which would automatically align the members of the League of Nations against any aggressor. Briand was a great orator and his speeches, always high points at meetings of the League of Nations in Geneva, created a great deal of international good will for France. Nevertheless, the acceptance of his foreign policy in France represented a resigned acknowledgment of the limitations of French power. Despite victory in war, and despite possession of the greatest European army, France was not able to go it alone in foreign policy during the postwar years.

Great Britain

Although Great Britain came to advocate a more lenient treatment of Germany than France, the British people did not have any sympathy for the Germans at the end of the war. Indeed, the hatred had grown so strong that it took years before personal contacts between the British and German

Aristide Briand. *The French foreign minister delivers a speech during the great days of the League of Nations.*

people were resumed. The elections which took place in December 1918, and in which for the first time women were entitled to vote, were known as khaki elections, for the campaign and the voting both reflected the spirit of the khaki-clad soldier. In the campaign, the government promised to prosecute William II and all those Germans responsible for war atrocities and to make Germany pay the entire costs of war. With Lloyd George, the prime minister, assuring the people that he would "exact the last penny we can get out of Germany up to the limit of her capacity," the government gained an overwhelming victory, winning 478 seats while the opposition secured only 87. The government was a coalition of Conservatives (still called Unionists) and of Liberal adherents of Lloyd George and reflected the nationalist mood of this period in that the Conservatives, with 335 seats, were much stronger than their Liberal coalition partners.

Nevertheless, in Great Britain the expectations for the postwar world were different from those in France. The French had achieved concrete gains, such as the recovery of Alsace-Lorraine, and nurtured concrete aims, notably liberation from the incubus of German superiority and aggression. The British had much vaguer notions. They expected a peaceful world and a better life for all the people in the British Isles. The idea of a new order in international affairs went hand in hand with demands for reform in domestic life. The crucial importance of making the postwar world an era of social reforms was reflected in the address of the king at the opening of the postwar Parliament: "The aspirations for a better social order which have been quickened in the hearts of My people by the experience of the war must be encouraged by prompt and comprehensive action. . . .since the outbreak of the war every party and every class have worked and fought together for a great ideal . . . we must continue to manifest the same spirit. We must stop at no sacrifice of interest or prestige to stamp out unmerited poverty, to diminish unemployment, to provide decent homes, to improve the nation's health, and to raise the standard of well-being throughout the country." And these notions were underlined by Lloyd George in a speech in the House of Commons in February, 1919, in which he stated that there was no member in the House who was not pledged to the cause of social reform. "If we fail, history will condemn not merely the perfidy but the egregious folly of such failure."

The war effort had involved all classes of British society, and those who had participated in the war now expected fulfillment of their needs in peacetime. The government had given women of thirty and over the right to vote, and extended the male suffrage by removing property qualifications. But its record in instituting social reforms was unsatisfactory, despite such steps as the extension of unemployment insurance to almost all workers earning less than five pounds a week. The most important issue in postwar Britain was housing. Building had stopped during the war years, and it was estimated that at least 300,000 new houses were needed within one year after the war. But two years later the housing policy of the government had produced only 14,594 new houses, and when in 1923 budgetary cutbacks ended government subsidies for home construction, the shortage of houses was even worse than it had been in 1918. Slums remained an indelible and spreading blot on English industrial centers.

The disappointment of the expectations which victory and the promises of the government had aroused raised questions also about the past. It transformed enthusiasm for the wartime statesmen into doubts and criticism and aroused skepticism about the policy pursued toward Germany.

The failure to achieve social reform was partly a failure of the government, but also due in part to circumstances beyond its control. For one thing, the government was made up of prima donnas. Besides Lloyd George, who had acquired immense authority because of his war leadership, there were such formidable figures as the former prime minister Arthur Balfour, Alfred Milner of South African fame, and George Curzon, a former viceroy of India. Also included were the stars of a younger generation, among them the arrogant and witty F. E. Smith (later earl of Birkenhead),

Winston Churchill, and Austen Chamberlain, Joseph Chamberlain's son and political heir. These and other leaders seemed more interested in maneuvering against one another for public favor than in carrying out a unified policy. Their ambitions and intrigues were fed by the press, particularly by the newspapers belonging to the press "Lords"—Northcliffe, Rothermere, Beaverbrook—who themselves were eager for a political role.

As a coalition of Conservatives and Liberals the government was beset by conflicting principals whenever it strove to establish a definite line of policy. The old conflict about free trade revived with the Liberals eager to maintain an open trade policy and the Conservatives favoring preferential tariffs for the members of the British empire. There was also a conflict over the maintenance of government control over economic life within Great Britain. Without the possibility of some such control, the Liberals' demands for an active policy of social reforms could not be carried out. The Conservatives, however, used their strength in the House of Commons to force Lloyd George to abolish the economic restrictions and regulations introduced during wartime.

Other problems confronted the government as well. The turmoil which the war had raised did not easily subside; instead, unrest was widespread through the British empire. The peace conference, the question of the intervention in Russia, the struggle in the Near East absorbed much of the attention of British statesmen. Closer to home, a settlement of the Irish question, which had disturbed British political life for almost a century, could no longer be postponed. During the war the government had hesitated to take energetic steps toward the introduction of home rule in Ireland, and the result had been a rebellion at Easter time in 1916. It was quickly defeated, but the ruthlessness of its suppression destroyed the influence of the moderates in Ireland. The dominating force in Irish policy now became the Sinn Fein; the name, which means "we ourselves," indicated that the goal of this group was complete independence. The Sinn Fein engaged in guerrilla warfare; British officers were attacked, manor houses belonging to those opposed to independence were burned, banks were robbed. To replace Irishmen who had resigned, the police force was strengthened by recruits from England, derisively called the Black and Tans, after the colors of their uniform. Their brutality aroused indignation even in England.

The Conservatives believed that dealings with the Sinn Fein should start only after the Black and Tans had reestablished order. But the Liberals wanted to enter upon negotiations immediately, and their view prevailed. In December, 1921, a treaty was signed which divided Ireland into a northern part, Ulster, which remained within the United Kingdom, and a southern part, the Irish Free State, with dominion status. Some members of the Sinn Fein, led by Eamon de Valera (born 1882), were not content with this arrangement; they fought bitterly against the moderate Irish government, and finally attained power. In 1937, they succeeded in gaining complete independence for the Irish Free State.

The most serious blow to all plans of social reform was an economic depression that engulfed Britain in 1921. The pent-up demand for goods that had not been available during the war had resulted in a boom which soon led to overexpansion and overspeculation. In consequence, a great rise in prices immediately after the war was suddenly followed by a decline, which led to a shrinking of production and a diminution of buying power. In 1921 British exports to France fell by 65.2 per cent and to the United States by 42.6 per cent from the previous year's level. Altogether, British exports in 1921 were less than half of what they had been in 1920. The nadir of this depression was reached in June, 1921, with 23.1 per cent (2,185,000) of Britain's workers unemployed. The full extent of this misery was not reflected in this figure, however. Certain industries suffered more than others and in some localities unemployment climbed to 40 or 50 per cent of the labor force. After 1922 the situation improved, but not until the outbreak of the Second World War did the number of unemployed in Britain drop below a million. One of the permanent features in British economic life became the "dole," the benefits which the unemployed received under the Unemployment Insurance Act. They were strictly limited to two periods of sixteen weeks each and were paid only to those who proved to be in need. Unemployment and the dole seemed strange compensation for the hardships and sacrifices of a victorious war.

The 1920's in Great Britain became a time of disillusionment. The most flamboyant of the war leaders lost much of their appeal. Winston Churchill had to struggle hard to maintain his place in politics. Lloyd George aroused the greatest distrust. In 1922, in a famous speech in the Carleton Club, the very heart of the Conservative party, Stanley Baldwin, then president of the Board of Trade, said of Lloyd George that he was "a great dynamic force" but that a dynamic force could be a "a very terrible thing." After the Conservatives then voted against continuation of the coalition, Lloyd George never returned to a position in the government.

The view that no victory could compensate for the losses and damages of war became widespread. Pacifist organizations proliferated. Expenditure for the armed forces became unpopular. The government required the military services to base their budget estimates on the assumption that "the British Empire will not be engaged in any general war during the next ten years and that no expeditionary force will be required." Disarmament was regarded as the panacea.

The country which profited most from this change of view was Germany. It was believed that wartime propaganda had painted an exaggerated and false picture of Germany. Back in 1919 Keynes's *Economic Consequences of the Peace* had opened the attack upon the peace settlement, and now German demands for revision of the Treaty of Versailles began to find a hearing in Great Britain.

Because so many young men had been lost in the war, the older men remained in power much longer than their counterparts in the prewar days. It seemed impossible to make a dent in their closed ranks. Viewing the traditions and customs of political life with disgust young men turned away from politics. Rejection of accepted forms and values became characteristic of the most gifted writers and artists of the new generation. The great literary monument of the disillusionment and desperation of the postwar world in England was T. S. Eliot's *The Waste Land* (1922).

The abandonment, in pursuit of victory, of attitudes deeply rooted in liberal beliefs, and the disillusionment of the postwar era, aroused skepticism toward the traditions and the achievements of the past, and this changed political mood played a role in what, from the point of view of political history, might be regarded as the most striking event in the years after the war: the rise of the Labor party. In 1914 the replacement of the Liberal party by the Labor party would have been regarded as most improbable. The war had markedly changed the situation. With the ousting of Asquith as prime minister in 1916, and his replacement by the dynamic Lloyd George, the Liberal party had been split into two hostile groups. Moreover, the war had strengthened the power of the Labor party. The shift of industries to war production, and the need for using all available manpower, required cooperation of the government with trade unions. Their power and therefore also their appeal had increased. By 1919 the membership of the trade unions had almost doubled, and amounted to more than eight million. In order to assure the support of the workers, two leading figures in the Labor party, Arthur Henderson and John Robert Clynes, had entered the war government and their activities disproved the thesis that Labor leaders were wild radicals who could not be entrusted with government responsibility. On the other hand, the kind of opposition to the war which had existed in the Liberal party in 1914 continued to dominate the thinking of some groups in the Labor party. Most prominent among the opponents of the war was Ramsay MacDonald (1866–1937).

An intellectual who looked like a peer of the realm, MacDonald was rather removed from the down-to-earth trade-union leaders who dominated the party organization. But MacDonald showed remarkable courage during the war, struggling against the tide of national hysteria and sponsoring meetings at which conscientious objectors expressed their pacifist views. MacDonald argued eloquently that the war would have meaning only if it was the beginning of a changed and better world. In 1917, he greeted the Russian Revolution as an inspiration for labor movements all over the globe and advocated the formation of workers' and soldiers' councils in Britain.

In the disillusionment of the postwar years Labor benefited from the fact that, in contrast to the Conservatives and Liberals, it represented the possibility of change and, at the same time, the war seemed to have proved that Labor was able to govern. This worked to Labor's advantage in the elections which were held in December, 1923. The coalition government under Lloyd George had been succeeded by a Conservative government, headed first by Bonar Law (1858–1923) and then by Stanley Baldwin (1867–1947). Baldwin decided on new elections in order to get a mandate for the realization of the old Conservative demand for protective tariffs, which he believed would alleviate unemployment. In the elections the Conservatives remained the strongest party, but they lost their majority. The Liberals and Labor combined had more votes than the Conservatives, and since Labor held more seats than the Liberals, Ramsay MacDonald was asked by King George V to form the government. Because this first Labor government lacked a majority and needed the support of the Liberals, its potential for action was strictly limited, and its accomplishments were meager. A housing act, providing state subsidies for the building of houses with controlled rents, was the main domestic achievement. In foreign affairs, the government established diplomatic relations with Soviet Russia and promptly signed a commercial treaty with the Russians. Storms of protest greeted these moves. On a minor issue—the somewhat questionable dropping of the prosecution of a Communist journalist—the Liberals voted against the government, and in the elections which followed, Labor was defeated. This loss was chiefly due to anti-Communist hysteria. The middle classes, who had been upset by MacDonald's negotiations with Soviet Russia, were turned decisively against Labor by the publication during the election campaign of a letter allegedly written by Zinoviev, the head of the Communist International, outlining a strategy for revolution in England. Although a clever falsification, the letter did compromise the Labor party. The Labor government lasted only ten months, but its tenure, though short, established Labor as the alternative to the Conservatives. Moreover, although Labor's domestic record had been unexciting, it could claim that in foreign affairs its rule had been an undisputed success—a success which had to be primarily attributed to Ramsay MacDonald. MacDonald had been foreign secretary as well as prime minister, and it was while he was foreign secretary that agreement on the reparations question was achieved.

When Labor came to power a committee of experts was examining the reparations question but it was still not settled whether the states involved, and particularly France, would consider the result of the committee's deliberations as binding on them. In a letter to Poincaré in February, 1924, MacDonald made a statement almost undiplomatic in its frankness: "It is widely felt in England that, contrary to the provisions of the Treaty of Versailles, France is endeavoring to create a situation which gains for it

The first British Labor government. *In the middle of the first row, Ramsay MacDonald; in the last row on the extreme left, Lord Passfield, the former Sidney Webb.*

what it failed to get during the allied peace negotiations. . . . The people in this country regard with anxiety what appears to them to be the determination of France to ruin Germany and to dominate the continent without consideration of our reasonable interests and future consequences to European settlement." MacDonald clearly implied that England expected France to accept the report of the experts, and was not willing to bargain about this. The French people could have little doubt about the dangerous consequences of British hostility for French economic life in times of rising inflationary pressure. Fortunately for MacDonald, Herriot and the *cartel des gauches* came into power in May, 1924, and the new government participated in a conference in London over which MacDonald presided. The report of the committee of experts formed the basis for an agreement on reparations which was signed on August 31 by all powers concerned.

The policy of MacDonald was not very different from that of the Conservative foreign secretaries who preceded and followed him. But Labor and Conservatives arrived at the same policy from somewhat different points of departure. MacDonald's approach was idealistic. He had been an opponent of the war and he wanted to liquidate the consequences of the war as quickly and as thoroughly as possible as a prerequisite for the building of a peaceful international order. The Conservatives were more realistic. They were concerned about the deterioration and the difficulties of the British economic situation, and they regarded an improvement of the economic conditions in central Europe as necessary for Britain's own recovery. These considerations were particularly powerful among the Conservatives, who had become a party of businessmen. Moreover, financial circles in the United States which had been exerting a great influence on British economic policy since the war, were demanding a settlement of the reparations question. In the first months of 1923 Stanley Baldwin, then chancellor of the exchequer, had negotiated an agreement with the American government on the repayment of the loans which Britain had received from the United States during the war. Officially the American government maintained that there was no connection between German reparations and the repayment of war loans given to the Allies. But it was evident that the European states would not repay their war debts until they received reparations from Germany. Thus, a settlement of the reparations question which would allow an economic recovery of Europe was in the American interest, and became a common goal of the two English-speaking countries. American financial circles were willing to assume a positive role. They participated in the committee of experts, which was chaired by an American, Charles Dawes, and they were ready to make the proposals of the report work by giving a loan. It was this active interest and assistance which gave Europe the possibility of a breathing space.

THE ERA OF EUROPEAN STABILIZATION, 1925–1929

An era of political stabilization was achieved in Europe through two closely connected events. One was the attainment of agreement on reparations in the Dawes Plan; the other was the conclusion of a political agreement among the principal European powers, embodied in the Locarno treaties, arranged in Locarno, Switzerland, in October, 1925, and signed in London on December 1, 1925.

After abandoning passive resistance in the Ruhr, Germany stabilized its currency by introducing a new basic unit, the *Rentenmark*, equivalent to a trillion of the old marks. This was an operation on paper, purely an elimination of a number of zeros. It assumed some reality because Hjalmar Schacht, president of the German Reichsbank since December, 1923, managed to obtain credits from British banks and a loan from Montagu Norman, the governor of the Bank of England. On the other hand he started a strictly deflationary policy by refusing to give any further credits to the German government or to German economic enterprises. The printing of money had ended. However, renewed pressure for reparations payments would have restored the inflationary trend if the stabilization of the German currency had not been complemented by the acceptance of the Dawes Plan.

The Dawes Plan fixed the German reparations payments for the next five years; the installments were then gradually to increase as Germany's economy recovered with the aid of a large foreign loan. An American commissioner was to make certain that Germany paid to the limits of its capacity. He was to control the remittance of reparations and to establish the transfer of payments in gold. It would be in his power to exert a far-reaching influence on German economic life, for he would supervise the policy of the Reichsbank and the financial administration of the railroads, as well as other state-run enterprises. The presence of this commissioner assured the Germans of a hearing if the payments envisaged in the Dawes Plan went beyond their capacity. Furthermore, the existence of the accompanying foreign loan meant that the financial interests of other nations were connected with German economic recovery and prosperity.

John Maynard Keynes (1883–1946) described the reparations settlement as follows: "Reparations and interallied debts are being mostly settled on paper and not in goods. The United States lends money to Germany, Germany transfers its equivalent to the allies, the allies pass it back to the United States government. Nothing real passes—no one is a pennyworse." In this brilliant satirical summary Keynes did not mention one issue which in the following years would become highly important. The loans had to be repaid with interest and the Germans had to earn this interest through exports. Because German wages had been low since the end of the war, and because the world economy was again expanding, after the economic nadir of 1921, the earnings of German exports were sufficient to pay the scheduled amount of reparations and the interest on the loans. The system functioned for a number of years, but it ran into trouble when the requisite combination of low German wages and world prosperity began to disappear.

With the establishment of an international stake in the economic recovery of Germany it became important for the victors of the First World War to tie Germany also to the political settlement made at the Paris Peace Conference. To the Germans this meant a chance to regain a place among the great powers. These were the considerations which underlay the arrangements made at Locarno. The most important of them was a treaty concluded by Great Britain, Germany, France, Belgium, and Italy. Germany recognized that its western frontier, as defined in the Treaty of Versailles, was permanent. If there occurred an "unprovoked attack" by Germany against France or by France against Germany, the victim would be helped by Great Britain and Italy; especially noteworthy was the stipulation that not only a violation of the frontiers but also a "flagrant violation" of the demilitarization of the Rhineland was regarded as an act of aggression. This stipulation became important after the occupation of the Rhineland had ended in 1930, for six years later, when German troops marched into the Rhineland, the expressions "flagrant violation" and "unprovoked attack" became loopholes through which remilitarization of the

Rhineland was condoned. Although nobody could deny that the Germans had broken the Locarno treaties, it was argued that this violation was neither "flagrant" nor "unprovoked." But in 1925 the general opinion was that the frontiers between Germany, France, and Belgium—and the permanent demilitarization of the Rhineland—were now recognized as final.

This treaty, the core of the Locarno arrangements, was complemented by a number of other agreements. Treaties concluded by Germany with France, Belgium, Poland, and Czechoslovakia established that all disputes which could not be resolved by diplomatic negotiations would be submitted to arbitration. Moreover, agreements between France and Poland and France and Czechoslovakia determined that if Germany refused arbitration, these states would assist one another against Germany, by force of arms, if necessary. Finally, Germany was to be admitted to the League of Nations and receive a permanent seat on the Council of the League. Germany declared, however, if the League imposed military sanctions on some state, Germany's participation would be limited by its military and geographical situation, because military clauses of the Treaty of Versailles had left the country too weak to join in military actions. Practically, this meant that Germany would not have to participate in military action against Soviet Russia.

To what extent did the Locarno agreements change the existing political situation, and to whose advantage were they? The admission to the League of Nations and the acquisition of a permanent seat on the Council meant that Germany was again recognized as an equal of other nations and as a great European power. For the Germans, abandonment of the claims to Alsace-Lorraine on their western frontier and the acknowledgment of restrictions on the exercise of sovereignty in the Rhineland were painful. However, there was no comparable acceptance of the permanence of the eastern borders; Germany abjured the use of force for revising these frontiers, but was not prevented from urging such revision. Moreover, Germany was able to maintain its special relationship with Russia, which had been established in 1922 with the Treaty of Rapallo; in April, 1926, in the Treaty of Berlin the two states confirmed the Treaty of Rapallo. Germany had not opted between east and west. It certainly was in no worse a bargaining position than before, perhaps in a better one.

France also had not lost. Ever since the end of the First World War, France had been insisting that its security demanded a firm alliance with the United States and Great Britain against Germany. Now it had finally obtained assurances of aid from Great Britain. To be sure, the Locarno treaty was not a special Franco-British alliance, just a guarantee of the existing frontiers of both France and Germany. But since nobody expected France to want to change the frontiers, it actually amounted to a promise of British support in case of a German attack. France would have liked a

similar guarantee of the eastern frontiers of Germany. But the demilitarization of the Rhineland, coupled with France's military alliances with Poland
and Czechoslovakia, had left Germany militarily powerless, unable to
expand either to the east or to the west. Thus the Locarno treaties did not
weaken the French position. If anything, they reinforced French military
security.

For both France and Germany two ways were open. They could regard
the Locarno arrangements as a new departure, the beginning of a cooperation which slowly and gradually might remove distrust and create a
European community. Or they could fall back into antagonistic positions,
their relative strength neither weakened nor increased.

The Locarno agreements were bitterly criticized in Germany and France.
Briand and Stresemann, the foreign ministers who had concluded them,
were accused of having abandoned essential national interests. Each of these
men trusted the other and was convinced of the other's good will. But each
had to demonstrate to his people that the treaties had advantages for their
nation. To bring about a gradual recognition of these advantages, much
could be done by Great Britain. If Britain cautiously balanced France
against Germany and Germany against France by opposing every resurrec-
tion of German military power and every French attempt to use its military
strength for keeping Germany economically weak, it might help to bring
the old antagonists together. For a number of years Britain did indeed
follow this course.

When the Locarno treaties were signed in London the portrait of
Castlereagh was brought down from an attic in the British foreign office and
hung in the room in which the solemn ceremony took place. The gesture
was appropriate. Castlereagh had been banished to the attic because during
the period of Britain's splendid isolation his policy of cooperation with the
great European powers had seemed contradictory to the British tradition.
But his aim of maintaining peace and stability in Europe by a diplomacy
based upon conferences with the continent's leading statesmen appeared
very similar to the policy which Austen Chamberlain, the British foreign
secretary, was now pursuing. Indeed, the effect of the Locarno agreements
was not limited to the mitigation of tensions between Germany and France.
Their main effect was to reestablish a concert of the great European powers
thereby restoring some order within Europe and extending the influence of
the European powers through the entire world.

Mussolini was well aware of this development; Italy had kept back from
the discussions preceding the Locarno agreements, but Mussolini had
appeared in person when the success of the negotiations was assured. He
realized that their result would be the creation of a kind of ruling group
among the European powers and he wanted to demonstrate that Italy
belonged to this group. The concert of powers which the Locarno agree-

ments established was less extended and less comprehensive than the nineteenth-century Concert of Europe had been. Spain was no longer counted among the great powers, Austria-Hungary no longer existed, and Russia was excluded. Moreover, the global influence of the new European concert depended on cooperation with non-European states, such as the United States. Nevertheless, in the years following the Locarno agreements Europe again played the decisive role in world politics. Officially the League of Nations was supposed to be the center of international decision making; but the three statesmen who had concluded the Locarno agreements—Briand, Chamberlain, and Stresemann—usually held preparatory discussions in which they agreed on a common line, and this was then generally accepted by the other members of the League. Even the Russians realized that the time of revolutionary upheavals was over; they made agreements with their neighbors—Poland, Rumania, Estonia, and Latvia—in which they rejected war, and they participated in a general pact renouncing the use of war which had resulted from negotiations between France and the United States—the Kellogg-Briand Pact (1928). In this relaxed atmosphere preparations for a conference on general disarmament went happily ahead.

Nevertheless, the sky was not without clouds. The Kellogg-Briand Pact did not provide for sanctions, if, in violation of the pact, a power resorted to war. Nor did it exclude wars undertaken in self-defense. A conference held in Geneva in 1927 to arrange further naval disarmament failed. Great Britain recognized Soviet Russia in 1924, but the commercial treaties following this diplomatic recognition were soon abrogated because of strong resentment aroused by Communist agitation in Britain. Finally, Franco-German relations remained precarious. The Germans demanded modification of the Dawes Plan. They stepped up their campaign to free themselves from the restrictions of the Treaty of Versailles by publicly repudiating the war-guilt clause and by building pocket battleships. The French, alarmed by Germany's quick recovery, were reluctant to consent to revision of the Dawes Plan and tried to delay the evacuation of the Rhineland. Nevertheless, between 1925 and 1930 such tensions seemed to be the unpleasant aftereffects of the upheavals caused by the First World War rather than signs of the beginning of a new period of political tension.

THE WORLD ECONOMIC CRISIS

The relative stability achieved after 1925 was soon shattered by a world economic crisis. As the 1920's passed, people had gradually become confident that the wounds left by the First World War could be healed, that the prosperity of the years before 1914 would again be reached, and that the march toward progress which the war had interrupted could be resumed. The economic crisis destroyed these expectations and hopes; the prewar world now appeared irretrievably lost, and many were convinced that the new course of events was leading inexorably downhill and would end in a holocaust more dangerous and devastating for the continuity of European life than the First World War had been. Thus the decade of the 1930's was a period full of anxiety and insecurity. A full recovery from the world economic crisis had still not occurred when the Second World War broke out in 1939.

The really acute phase of the economic breakdown lasted from 1929 to 1933; before its underlying causes are discussed, it might be well to recapitulate the dramatic events of these years. The actual beginning of the crisis was the collapse of the New York Stock Exchange under a wave of speculation in the last week of October, 1929, although some danger signs pointing to a decline in production had appeared earlier. In Europe the height of the crisis occurred in the summer of 1931. In May, 1931, the most important Austrian bank, the *Kreditanstalt*, which was controlled by the Rothschilds, declared itself unable to fulfill its obligations. This failure shook confidence in the solvency of banks in Germany; there was an accelerated recall of money from them, and the main German banks soon found themselves insolvent and were forced to close. They were able to reopen only with the help of a government guarantee. In this critical economic situation the payment of international debts was clearly impossible, and the American president Herbert Hoover (1874–1964) suggested a one-year moratorium on reparations and war debts; after tedious negotiations, this was agreed upon in August. But the moratorium came too late to remedy the British financial situation, which had been seriously impaired by the economic collapse in central Europe. On September 21, 1931, Britain abandoned the gold standard; this event seemed to mark the end of an epoch, for hitherto the pound had enjoyed the reputation of being as good as gold. In the next years the level of economic activity remained low, although from 1934 on, slowly and gradually recovery began, especially in the industrial countries. Agricultural prices remained depressed, and the Balkan states, which were dependent on the export of agricultural products, continued to suffer severely. Moreover, France, which at the outset had seemed unaffected by the crisis, began to experience economic difficulties in 1933, and the French recession played its part in retarding recovery in the rest of Europe.

To understand the nature of this economic catastrophe—its severity, length, and spread—one must realize that two factors were at work. First, there was the decline in production, which led to a decrease in trade and created unemployment; second, there was the financial crisis.

The decline in production set in from what was a rather low plateau, for after the First World War production had remained sluggish. By 1929 the prewar level had indeed been reached, but the rate of economic growth ought to have been much larger to meet the needs of an increased population. Moreover, the European share in world trade was smaller than it had been in 1914, as European nations faced competition from the rising economies of the non-European nations. To the diminished share of Europe in non-European markets the elimination of Russia from the world economic system must be added as a further restricting and damaging factor. There was an economic boom in the second part of the 1920's, but it was built on a narrow base and lacked strength to resist any serious blow.

Even before 1929 falling prices for agricultural goods indicated the onset of an unfavorable economic trend. This decline in prices immediately affected the peasant countries of southeastern Europe—especially Rumania, Bulgaria, and Yugoslavia, where—by tradition or as a result of agrarian reforms after the war—small farms with rather high production costs were the prevailing form of land ownership. For the farmers of these countries the falling agricultural prices made competition on the European market outside the Balkans impossible. Even within these Balkan states the price of wheat fell by almost half. Since the prices of industrial goods did not decline to the same degree, the people of these countries were caught in a disparity between industrial and agricultural prices—a "price scissor"—and they were unable to purchase manufactured goods from industrial countries. Hence a shrinking of industrial production throughout Europe took place, and it was aggravated by the widespread introduction of protective measures against foreign goods, by which each country tried to defend its own industries at the expense of all others.

This crisis in production took an extraordinary and dramatic form because its difficulties were compounded by a financial crisis. Its center was Wall Street, where in 1929 a speculative boom ended in a stock-market crash which ushered in a long depression. The American economic collapse had its immediate repercussions in Europe, particularly in Germany. American loans had been granted not only to the German government for the settlement of reparations but also to many private and semipublic enterprises within Germany—industrial companies, public utilities, and municipal governments. Foreign capital had been drawn into Germany by high interest rates, which the German economy had been able to sustain because labor costs were relatively low. With the stock-market crash the influx of American money ended and American banks demanded the repayment of loans as soon as they became due. In a time of shrinking production and declining prices the abrupt withdrawal of American loans was a severe blow to the German economy; the situation was particularly critical because German businessmen, relying on the continuous availability of American capital, had used money borrowed on short terms for long-term investments. Despite the warnings of men like Schacht, the president of the

The Depression. *Workers' living quarters in northern France.*

Reichsbank, against this unsound practice, neither German businessmen nor foreign bankers had been able to resist the allure of easy gains.

With the withdrawal of American money from the German economy the liquid reserves of German banks and businesses came under steadily increasing pressure. In addition, because loans from abroad had to be repaid in foreign currency, the withdrawal endangered the German currency by absorbing the gold reserves of the Reichsbank; by 1931 they amounted to only 10 per cent of what they had been before the onset of the crisis. These developments reached their culmination in the summer of 1931 when the German public, becoming aware of the catastrophic financial situation, started a run on the banks. Because Germany had been the center for the investment of foreign money, the difficulties of the German banks meant great losses for the banks of other countries, particularly Great Britain and the United States. The result was a general restriction of credit, with capital for investments difficult or even impossible to obtain. The consequent lack of new investments prolonged the depression and slowed down recovery.

At this time the view of Keynes that in periods of depression new money ought to be pumped into the economy was regarded as a dangerous heresy by almost all economists. A deflationary policy marked by a balanced budget, with expenses limited to the absolute minimum, was the economists' prescription for the handling of both public and private finances in times of crisis; it was not realized that unemployment reinforced the depression because people without money could not buy goods. The generally sluggish economic development of the 1920's had created pockets of unemployment all over Europe; with the depression the numbers of unemployed increased rapidly. In Great Britain almost three million were jobless in 1931; in Germany at the beginning of 1933 industrial production was half of what it had been in 1929, while there were three times as many—six million—unemployed.

The economic crisis was a turning point in the interwar years because it changed the political climate and the political constellation in Europe. Even when economic life became less turbulent, there was no return to the situation which had existed before 1929.

With the end of the First World War the deep chasm, which before 1914 separated the workers from the ruling classes and the proponents of international socialism from the adherents of national states, seemed closed. The workers had supported their governments during the war and in acknowledgment of this show of willingness to recognize the value of the national state, the political rights of the masses had been extended: the lowering of the voting age, suffrage for women, elimination of property qualifications, proportional representation—some, or all, of these measures had been adopted in every state of western and central Europe after the war. Almost all the demands for political democratization which radicals had raised before the war were fulfilled.

With the struggle for political democratization eliminated as a major concern, the problem of reconciling the economic interests of all classes of society came to the forefront. In this area too the war seemed to have opened new perspectives. The socialists had lost some of their enthusiasm for revolution—partly because they rejected vigorously the theories and actions of the leftist radicals who had come to power in Russia, partly because the introduction of economic controls and regulations by the various governments during the war had demonstrated that the change from a free economy to a controlled and planned economy could be obtained within the existing system. Correspondingly, the members of the bourgeoisie had become aware during the war of the beneficial consequences of smooth collaboration with the workers, and they were frightened by the specter of the Russian Revolution, which seemed to show what might happen if the workers were driven to desperation. Hence the socialists and the bourgeoisie were willing to take some steps to meet each other. It was acknowledged that the workers were entitled to such concessions as the eight-hour day, increased unemployment benefits, recognition of the right to strike, and the establishment of the closed shop, which made trade unions the only legitimate representatives of the workers in the factories. In exchange, the socialists toned down their revolutionary propaganda, emphasized the possibility of achieving their aims by democratic means, accepted some arbitration machinery in labor disputes, and acknowledged the need for the maintenance of national armed forces until disarmament was achieved.

This period of compromise was short-lived. The economic crisis reopened the gap between the classes. With governments drafting budgets in which, to save money, unemployment benefits were cut, and with industrial enterprises dismissing workers ruthlessly, the hope of achieving socialist goals through a gradual transformation of the capitalist system appeared increasingly illusory. There was a renewed trend toward revolutionary radicalism. At the same time industrial entrepreneurs tended to become more antilabor, regarding the trade unions as obstacles to retrenchment by means of lower wages and a reduced labor force. Reactionary and authoritarian notions received new impetus, and their resurgence was accompanied by a revival of nationalism. In the grim climate of depression each government thought first of its own people and introduced measures of economic protection to fend off foreign competition. Concessions to other nations were condemned as signs of weakness.

Two areas of the European scene were particularly affected by intensified nationalist attitudes. In the Balkans hostilities among the various states sharpened and the exhortations of the greater powers for cooperation and toleration were no longer heeded, especially since they were no longer reinforced by loans. The French influence which had been predominant in this area lost ground and Italian and German influence increased. But tension also became more acute among the great powers of western Europe. Because the economic crisis had left Great Britain too weak to exert the role of intermediary and arbiter which it had assumed in the Locarno agreements, the resurgence of Franco-German hostility was almost unavoidable.

Thus all over Europe the economic crisis awakened and strengthened extremist tendencies on the left and on the right, and undermined the moderate center which clung to the ideals of democracy.

To understand the events of the 1930's, however, one must go beyond the effects of the economic crisis on the development of party politics. The entire political climate of the 1930's was different from that of the 1920's. One might say that only during the depression years did the full consequences of the shock represented by the First World War come to the surface. In large part this shock resulted from the collapse of assumptions once taken for granted. Before 1914 the steady progress of civilization had seemed assured, and the general principles of European morality were spread and accepted in widening areas of the world. The experience of the war, in which men ruthlessly attempted to create the most efficient machinery of death and destruction and to apply it against whole nations, disregarding conventions and morality when they stood in the way of national victory, could not easily be reconciled with the old principles, which with the return of peace were again proclaimed to be the acknowledged forms of civilized existence. Moreover, the young men who had been thrown straight from school into the conflict had learned that they had instincts and powers which the world of their parents seemed to have suppressed and which found no fulfillment or expression in the pattern of life to which their parents wished them to conform. It is no accident that after the war Lytton Strachey revealed the concealed hypocrisy of the Victorian age, that Freud's theories of repression and of the strength of the unconscious permeated art and literature, and that the views of Nietzsche, with his attack against conventional morality and his appeal to the new ethics of the Superman, became a reigning philosophy. Nevertheless, in the period just after the coming of peace, the belief that the postwar years provided a chance for building a new and better democratic world prevailed over the mood whose essence was rejection of historical values and traditions. But when in the 1930's the disillusionment of the postwar world was combined with the miseries of the depression, it became much more difficult to deny the voices of those who preached that the forces which the experiences of the war had revealed—violence, ruthlessness, the drive for power—were the truly effective factors in society. In social and political life the use of war and warlike weapons seemed possible and permissible. With the strength of a delayed effect, the shock administered by the experiences of the First World War transformed the psychological approach to politics and social life.

This change in the European climate helps to explain a surprising and shocking development. Not much more than ten years after Great Britain and France had completed the arrangements which were meant to establish them safely as leaders of a democratic Europe, these two powers were in retreat; initiative had devolved to antidemocratic powers.

THE RISE OF NAZISM

The emergence of the Nazis in Germany signifies the great change which took place between the 1920's and the 1930's in Europe. This development received a decisive impetus from the economic crisis, but the economic crisis was certainly not the only—and perhaps not even the most important—cause for the rise of Nazism. To a large extent Nazism was an inner German phenomenon, reviving old political attitudes which had been dominant in imperial Germany: authoritarianism and nationalism.

Decline of Parliamentary Government in the Weimar Republic

As we have seen, the leaders of the Weimar Republic had felt constrained to retain the monarchical civil servants, antagonistic to parliamentarism and democracy, and to rely on an equally authoritarian officer corps which despised pacifism and internationalism. Thus a strongly antirepublican and antidemocratic influence emanated from men holding key positions in the republic, Furthermore, the popular support which the republic possessed at the outset was soon whittled down under the impact of the Treaty of Versailles.

Along with the Communists on the extreme left and some small parties on the extreme right there were five important political parties in Germany during the 1920's: three republican—the Social Democratic party, the Democratic party, and the Catholic Center party—and two monarchist—the German People's party and the German Nationalist party. The tenuousness of the hold of the republican regime became evident in 1925 when Friedrich Ebert, the leader of the Social Democrats, died and popular elections for a new president of the republic were held. The people elected Field Marshal von Hindenburg, who received 800,000 votes more than Wilhelm Marx, the moderate Catholic who was the candidate of the republican parties. The Communist candidate, Ernst Thälmann, won almost two million votes. The republican center was weaker than the combined forces of the right and the left.

Nevertheless, in the three or four years of increasing prosperity which followed the acceptance of the Dawes Plan and the conclusion of the Locarno agreements, the republican regime seemed to gain ground. The 1928 elections for the Reichstag strengthened the moderate left. It was a sign of the prevailing temper that after the election of 1928 the monarchist People's party entered a coalition with the three republican parties. However, the situation changed quickly. One year after the elections the economic depression began to make itself felt. In September, 1929, Germany had 1,320,000 unemployed; one year later, 3,000,000; in September 1931, 4,350,000; and in 1932 the peak was reached with over 6,000,000. In Germany the widespread poverty and wretched conditions caused by the depression had an especially devastating psychological effect because they came so soon after the hardships of the inflation. Republican governments seemed unable to create a secure economic foundation for society. Leftwing and right-wing radicalism increased, with a resultant sharpening of tension between the left and right wings of the ruling coalition. The socialists, fearful that their adherents would go over to the Communists, became increasingly unwilling to agree to economic measures which might increase unemployment; and the German People's party tried to strengthen its appeal by adopting a more nationalist line in foreign policy. Particularly unfortunate was the death in October, 1929, of Gustav Stresemann, who had exerted a moderating influence in the German People's party. Shortly before his death he had achieved an important success: the acceptance of the Young Plan developed by a commission headed by the American Owen D. Young, which reduced the amount of the annual German reparations payments, eliminated the international controls over German economy, and brought to an immediate end the military occupation of the Rhineland. But because this agreement had been preceded by bitter diplomatic struggles, its acceptance aroused nationalist passions and resentment and weakened rather than helped the advocates of a policy of international understanding.

With Stresemann gone, the gap between the right and the left in the government widened steadily, and in March, 1930, the coalition disintegrated. The parties were unable to agree upon measures to overcome the accelerating economic crisis. The particular issue which led to the resignation of the government was very similar to one which brought about the fall of the Labor government in Great Britain a year later: payments to the unemployed. The socialists wanted to maintain unemployment benefits but in order to minimize the budget deficit they proposed raising the contributions.

Although never concealing his monarchist convictions, Hindenburg carried out his duties in accordance with the constitution during his first years. But he was surrounded by monarchist officers and friends who believed that the collapse of the coalition government might afford an opportunity for a change to a more authoritarian system, paving the way for a new monarchy. In 1930 they picked a rather nationalist member of the Center party, Heinrich Brüning (1885–1970), as chancellor. Brüning's political views had been formed by the experiences of the war. Despite physical disabilities he had volunteered for the army and served as an officer at the front; he preserved an almost childish adoration for officers and for military values and virtues. A strict Catholic, he lived ascetically, and tended toward obstinacy and self-righteousness. He was an administrator rather than a politician, an authoritarian rather than a democrat. Although at first Brüning impressed people as a new and interesting figure on the political scene, his lugubrious character did not inspire confidence and hope. He had made his career in the Center party as an expert in financial affairs and was a strict adherent of orthodox views on economics. He believed that the crisis could be overcome only by deflation and strict economies, including cuts in unemployment insurance. Fully aware that such a policy would never be approved by the socialists, he expected to draw his support from the center and the right; he was willing to woo the right by effecting a constitutional change which would result in a more authoritarian form of government. When the Reichstag refused to approve his financial proposals, Brüning dissolved that body and put his financial proposals into effect by emergency decrees.

The elections which took place on September 14, 1930, showed the expected shift to the right, but not to the German People's party and the German Nationalist party, which might have cooperated with Brüning; instead, gains were made by the extremist National Socialists, or Nazis, who increased their seats from 15 to 107. From this time until January 30, 1933, when their leader, Adolf Hitler (1889–1945), became chancellor, German

From the early history of the Nazi movement. *Hitler and Ludendorff in 1924.*

politics was dominated by one issue: whether or not the National Socialists would come to power.

The outcome of the elections did not deter Brüning from his course; he rejected all suggestions that he resume cooperation with the socialists. The constitution in Paragraph 48 had provided that in emergency situations the president could rule by decree. It had hardly been envisaged that an emergency situation could last for several years, but Brüning, sure of presidential support, believed that if he could go on ruling by emergency decrees he would be able to demonstrate that the government would function much better with a less powerful parliament and a more independent executive. The ground would be prepared for a constitutional change in the direction of authoritarianism. He seems to have expected that such a fulfillment of demands of the right would take the wind out of the sails of the extremists and tame the National Socialists so that they would support his government. According to the constitution, emergency decrees became invalid if a majority of the Reichstag voted against them. However, Brüning anticipated correctly that although the socialists might not like this government they would regard it as a lesser evil than a government of the National Socialists. Thus, whenever the Reichstag voted on Brüning's emergency decrees the socialists abstained from voting, and the parties of the middle and the moderate right, which supported Brüning, defeated by a small margin the radicals of the right and left. A rather doubtful interpretation of the notion of emergency, combined with socialist tolerance, kept the Brüning government in power.

Brüning further ingratiated himself with the forces of the right by giving a nationalist turn to German foreign policy. In June, 1930, when the last French troops evacuated the Rhineland, official speeches celebrating this event expressed no appreciation of the French concessions, but instead raised demands for further revisions of the peace treaty. The British ambassador in Berlin wrote: "It is an unattractive feature of the German character to display little gratitude for favors received but when the receipt of favors is followed up by fresh demands there are grounds for feeling impatient." If the British government had followed the advice of its ambassador and had stood with France, the Germans might have become more cautious in making complaints and raising new demands. But Great Britain just tried to smooth things over without taking any definite stand and Germany went ahead with its policy of seeking revision.

The most disastrous German step in this campaign was the conclusion of a customs union with Austria in March, 1931. Such an agreement was hardly compatible with the 1919 prohibition against Anschluss, and it was in direct contradiction to stipulations which Austria had accepted in 1922 in order to receive financial support from France, Great Britain, and Italy. France brought the issue before the Permanent Court of International Justice in The Hague and the customs union was declared invalid. The prestige of the Brüning government waned in the face of nationalist resentment, of which the radical right made good use. Moreover, the political uncertainty created by the conflict over the customs union triggered in the summer of 1931 the dramatic explosion of the financial crisis which began in Vienna, then moved to Germany, and finally extended to London.

During that summer, Brüning and the president of the Reichsbank were forced to make desperate trips to London and Paris to plead for financial relief, and these appeals to former enemies further damaged the prestige of the government in the eyes of the nationalists. In the winter of 1931–1932, the nationalist opposition was still gaining in strength, and unemployment reached frightening proportions.

Brüning was further handicapped by the fact that he could rule by emergency decrees only as long as he had the confidence of the president, to whom the power to issue the decrees actually belonged. In March, 1932, Hindenburg's first presidential term ended. In the subsequent election he received 53 per cent of the votes; Hitler received 36.8 per cent. Despite Hindenburg's imposing majority the result was a disappointment to him. The figures showed that right-wing radicalism had continued to grow; Brüning had failed to gain the cooperation of the rightist groups, and at the end of May, 1932, he was curtly dismissed by Hindenburg.

The details of what happened in Germany between Brüning's dismissal and Hitler's assumption of power in January, 1933, are intricate. There were intrigues centering around the president and the men who most influenced him: his son, Oskar, and his secretary, Otto Meissner. But the general pattern was constant. The continuing increase in popularity of nationalist extremism on the right made moderate conservatives less than ever inclined to resume cooperation with the socialists. Moreover, Hindenburg, getting old and dependent, decided against a return to parliamentarism. These authoritarian tendencies were strongly supported by the generals of the Reichswehr, particularly their representatives in the defense ministry, Kurt von Schleicher (1882–1934) and Kurt Freiherr von Hammerstein-Equord (1878–1943). They were sympathetic, if not to the National Socialist leaders, at least to the revival of nationalism and militarism which National Socialism preached. In their eyes the Nazis would be valuable material to be incorporated into the army when the hour arrived to break the chains of the disarmament clauses of Versailles. They were not willing to risk a serious political conflict in which the Reichswehr might have to fight the National Socialists with their paramilitary organizations. Indeed, they were not even sure that officers ordered to attack the Nazis would obey the command. Thus, all the men around the president wanted to cooperate with the National Socialists. The only stumbling block was the demand of their leader, Hitler, that he must be chancellor of any government supported by his party. Hindenburg's advisers wanted to use the National Socialists for their own purpose, but they did not want to get into a position in which the National Socialists might be able to call the tune. Brüning's successor, Papen, an ambitious and elegant former officer who through his great wealth had acquired newspapers and political influence, was disappointed in his lighthearted expectation that the National Socialists would cooperate with him. His successor, General Schleicher, was equally unsuccessful. By December, 1932, however, the situation began to change. Elections in November showed for the first time a slight decrease in the National Socialist vote; it became clear that the economic crisis had reached its peak. The conservatives and nationalists feared that if these trends continued, the occasion for the establishment of an authoritarian government and for a restoration of the monarchy might be missed. Likewise the National Socialist leaders began to feel that they might have waited too long. The masses might defect, having become convinced that National Socialism would never come to power. Under these circumstances, driven by ambition and stimulated by hatred of his successor Schleicher, Papen attempted once again to form a coalition with the National Socialists. He conceded to their leaders that Hitler should become chancellor, but only two other Nazis, Wilhelm Frick (1877–1946) and Hermann Göring (1893–1946), would become members of the cabinet, and Göring was to be minister without portfolio. The other members were to be either conservative politicians like Alfred Hugenberg (1865–1951), leader of the German

Nationalist party, or experts. Papen himself, as vice-chancellor, would be present at all Hitler's audiences with the president. In such a government, Papen and his friends believed, Hitler's chancellorship would be of no danger. Completely surrounded by sound conservatives, Hitler would have no freedom of action. With these arguments Papen, supported by Hindenburg's son and by his secretary, overcame the president's resistance. On January 30, 1933, Hitler was appointed chancellor.

Nazism in Germany

On the evening of January 30 the Nazis celebrated Hitler's appointment with a gigantic torch light parade in which they marched, along with organizations of military veterans, through the government quarter of Berlin. This demonstration was meant to emphasize that the formation of the Hitler government signified a new beginning and represented a revolution. The parallel with the rise of Fascism in Italy is striking. The formation of the government by Mussolini had been preceded by negotiations with other parties and by court intrigues; the outcome was a coalition. The traditional nature of the methods employed by Mussolini to gain office was concealed by the March on Rome, which made the seizure of power a conquest by force—a revolution. The torchlight parade on the evening of January 30 in Berlin was Hitler's "March on Rome." That the people around Hindenburg and the reactionary non-Nazi members of Hitler's government expected to control Hitler and to use the Nazis for their own purposes indicated that they had no understanding of Hitler's personality or of the reasons why so many people had been attracted to the National Socialist party. For though their final rise to power was due to the intrigues and subtle calculations of the military and the reactionaries, the Nazis had become a force in German politics because large masses of the German people approved of their radical demands for a new departure and saw in Hitler a messiah.

The rise of the Nazis reflected the disappearance of the bourgeois parties which had stood at the center in the German political scene. Among those who voted for the Nazis before 1933 were hardly any workers. There had been some shift of votes from the Socialists to the Communists, but the sum of votes given to these two parties remained constant even during the depression. The Catholic Center party too kept most of its adherents, but the German Democratic party and the German People's party disintegrated. Certainly the Nazis had many kinds of supporters. With the help of Hjalmar Schacht, who had turned against the government because in his opinion the Young Plan was still too burdensome and ought not to have been accepted, they received money from industrialists, who expected that the Nazis would put an end to concessions to the workers. Members of the nobility and of the Wilhelminian ruling group lent their prestige and their support to the

The Nazis in power. *Parade before Hindenburg on the evening of Hitler's appointment as chancellor.*

Nazis because they wanted to overthrow the despised republic. For the youth, particularly for students who believed they had little chance in the future and feared that they would become an academic proletariat, the Nazi demand for a new social order had great appeal. Farmers and small-town residents were antagonistic to the big cities and the trend toward industrialization, which they believed were dominating the policy of the republic. Most of the Nazi votes came from the middle classes, particularly the lower middle classes. They had been hit hard by the inflation. Despite some improvement in the later 1920's the economic situation remained precarious for the owners of small industries faced with overwhelming competition from large-scale industries organized into trusts and cartels. Shopkeepers found their businesses suffering from the increasing popularity of department stores. Moreover, the depression fell heavily on the white-collar workers in factories, offices, and stores, who did not even enjoy the minimum protection afforded by the trade unions. Most members of the lower middle classes became convinced of the incompetence and corruption of those whom the republican form of government had brought into power. This view of the republican government had been fed by the monarchist parties of the right, particularly the German Nationalist party. But the gains were harvested not by the Nationalists, but by the Nazis. The National Socialist party had a strong appeal because it claimed that it was entirely different from other political parties and that it took part in elections only in order to overthrow the entire existing political setup.

THE STRUCTURE OF THE NAZI PARTY

The character of Nazi propaganda and the form of the party organization emphasized the distinctiveness of National Socialism. At meetings, the paramilitary storm troopers first marched into the hall and flanked the podium; martial music was played until the main speaker appeared, greeting and being greeted by a raised right arm, the so-called Hitler salute. After an inflammatory speech he left immediately, again giving and receiving the Hitler salute. No questions were asked. Hecklers and people who tried to raise objections were thrown out of the meeting room by the storm troopers. The fact that such gatherings had the aspect of a religious revival meeting made them all the more appealing to Germans of the lower middle classes, who in their economic helplessness and isolation were drawn to a movement which seemed to make them part of a powerful world.

The structure of the party was hierarchical. At the top was the leader, Adolf Hitler. Below him was the *Gauleiter*, or subleader, having command of his own *Gau*, or region, and the *Gau* in turn divided into districts, each directed by a party official subordinate to the *Gauleiter*. The chain of command led strictly from above to below. Hitler gave the orders, and they were transmitted through the party hierarchy to the rank and file. From the beginning, Hitler considered this leadership principle to be crucial. Even in the 1920's, when the fortunes of the party were low, he refused to amalgamate with other small parties of nationalist extremism because such a move might threaten his position as the one and only leader. In the confusion of the German parliamentary system, with its numerous bourgeois parties and its many intrigues, the quality of decisiveness inherent in the leadership principle had attraction as promising a way out of chaos.

Resoluteness and decisiveness were communicated also by another feature peculiar to the National Socialist party: its paramilitary organizations, the *Sturmabteilung*, known as the S.A., or storm troopers, and the *Schutzstaffel*, or S.S. The S.S. gained importance only in later years, after Hitler's seizure of power; it began as a bodyguard for Hitler and his chief lieutenants. In earlier years the important and active military organization of the party was the S.A. Its original function was to protect Nazi speakers at open meetings. But this defensive role was soon superseded by an aggressive one, that of breaking up the meetings of Communists and other "enemies" of the nation. At first the S.A. men were given only uniforms and some food. Later, when the party became large and rich through membership dues and financial contributions, the storm troopers received regular wages. When unemployment was widespread, young men flocked to the S.A. The organization became strong enough to parade through the streets of the towns and to impede demonstrations of other groups and parties. Street fights, in which the S.A. excelled in roughness and violence, became frequent. The storm troopers committed a number of murders of political opponents, and their brutality—openly encouraged by Hitler—was one of the reasons why, until January, 1933, even nationalists who were sympathetic to Hitler's cause hesitated to entrust him with the government. On the other hand, the ruthlessness of the S.A. helped to strengthen the Nazis. In many smaller towns the S.A. became all-powerful, and citizens found it easier and less dangerous to go along with the National Socialists than to oppose them. Moreover, through the violence of the S.A. a kind of undeclared civil war developed in Germany, and the local governments which did not seem able to keep peace lost in prestige to the National Socialists, who guaranteed that they would maintain order if they came to power.

Hitler's Political Technique

Hitler's originality lay in his understanding of the art of directing the minds of the masses. He explained his views about the techniques of propaganda at some length in *Mein Kampf* ("My Battle"), written in 1924: "The driving force of the most important changes in this world had been found less in scientific knowledge animating the masses but rather in a fanaticism dominating them and in a hysteria which drives them forward." Thus the intellectual content of political propaganda must be as simple as possible: "All effective propaganda has to limit itself to a very few points and to use them like slogans. . . . It has to confine itself to little and to repeat this eternally." A political leader should not discuss an issue in all facets and complications. Everything ought to be painted in either black or white: a "suggestively biased attitude. . . . towards the questions to be dealt with." Because the masses are not acting upon intellectual considerations, are not "thinking," a political leader need not fear to speak a lie if this might be effective. But the lie must be a "big lie." Small lies the people might recognize, for they themselves tell them, but "it would never come into their heads to fabricate colossal untruths and they would not believe that others could have the impudence to distort the truth so infamously." Thus the effectiveness of a message depends not on its truth, but only on the fanaticism and the passion with which it is conveyed; to a properly presented appeal the masses will respond by accepting what they are told.

Hitler followed these rules carefully in his speeches. His oratory was his strength, and the important stepping-stones in his rise to power were the great mass meetings at which, among flags and uniformed men, under a sharp spotlight in an otherwise darkened hall, the leader spoke. Deliberately he built up an image of himself as the embodiment of the mission of the German nation. He represented himself as a man with no family and no women, living ascetically so that he could devote himself exclusively to the German nation. But he did not want to appear inhuman either. He loved dogs; he smiled at children and gave them chocolate. All this was artfully fabricated—a "big lie." Actually, his sister conducted his household. For fifteen years he lived with a mistress, Eva Braun. He spent hours looking at movies in his own theater. The photographs representing his private life which were published in German newspapers were carefully selected from the many taken by his official photographer.

Hitler's political ideas were crude and represented a mixture of Darwinism, Wagnerian romanticism, and Nietzschean philosophy, all simplified and vulgarized. "The whole work of nature is a mighty struggle between strength and weakness—an eternal victory of the strong over the weak," he said. Politics was to Hitler a struggle among races, but in his view the races were not equal; the "Aryan race"—and he never clearly defined this term—was superior to all others. Hitler believed in the importance of elites. Among the Aryans, the Germans were the elite. And among the Germans, the National Socialists were the elite, with the right and the duty to lead and to rule. Because struggle was the law of life, war was a necessity and the main task of a national leader was to make his state militarily strong so that it could win in battle and could expand.

In its political application this ideology resulted in certain concrete aims. Despite some shifts in his thought, Hitler always regarded France and Great Britain as Germany's enemies. However, he held them in contempt. As aging democracies they lacked the rule of an elite and were therefore weak and declining. The particular foe of the German nation, he believed, was Bolshevik Russia. For Russia was dangerous. It was not a democracy but a dictatorship. It showed no signs of age. Moreover, a military defeat of Russia would mean that its southwestern plains could provide the living space for which Germany had a great need. Finally, Hitler maintained that Communism was Jewish in origin, and to him the Jews were the most dangerous, the most fatal, enemies of the Aryans.

Anti-Semitism was central in Hitler's political thought. It was an effective propaganda device in Germany; the Jew could be blamed for those incomprehensible economic forces which destroyed the independence of small entrepreneurs and shop owners. But the usefulness of anti-Semitism as propaganda was secondary for Hitler; he was a convinced, passionate hater of the Jews. An admirer of Wagner's operas, Hitler was obsessed by the drama of Teutonic heroes, caught in a net by the dark dwarfs with their hoard of gold. There is no possibility of finding a rational explanation for such elements of Hitler's thought as anti-Semitism; it would be a mistake even to try to do so. As his whole career was to show, and as he himself frequently stated, in his crucial decisions he followed his intuition.

It is not difficult to determine where Hitler's ideas came from. He himself said in *Mein Kampf* that in his years in Vienna he "formed an image of the world and a view of life which became the granite foundation of my action.

Vienna was and remained for me the hardest but also the most thorough school of my life." Adolf Hitler was born in Braunau, Austria, on April 20, 1889. His father, who had been a customs official, died when his son was fourteen. His mother spoiled him; he grew up undisciplined and with a very spotty education. He was always distrustful of people with learning and imagined himself to be something better, an artist. The great tragedy of his early years was the death of his mother in 1908. Immediately thereafter, he went to Vienna, where, lacking financial resources, he drifted through various menial jobs without ever setting out on a definite career. He slept on park benches and in flophouses and wore shabby and torn clothes which people gave him out of pity. Hitler later said that the Vienna years had been very lonely. He had contact only with tramps and drunkards; he never learned to discuss or to exchange thoughts with others. His way of expressing himself was to monologize, and as the transcripts of meetings with his ministers and advisers during the Second World War would show, he retained this mode of speech to the end. But monologizing provided good training for a public speaker.

As an outsider without any special trade Hitler found himself unable to compete for jobs with organized labor, and he developed an intense hatred of Marxism. Moreover, at this time the Germans in the Habsburg monarchy were vehement nationalists, using racist theories to justify their right to rule over the other nationalities. All the German nationalist parties in Austria-Hungary were passionately anti-Slavonic and anti-Semitic. Hitler's opposition to Marxism, his belief in the value of race and in the superiority of the Germanic race, his anti-Semitism were all echoes, and mostly pure repetitions, of notions that flourished in Vienna around the turn of the century.

The one further element important in the formation of Hitler's mind was the war experience. In 1913, he moved from Vienna to Munich. As he later said, he preferred a real German city to Vienna with its "promiscuous swarm of foreign people." But in Munich his existence was quite as uncertain and miserable as it had been in Vienna. When the war broke out he volunteered for a Bavarian regiment. Hitler was a good soldier and for the first time he found some recognition and felt himself to be a member of a community. Indeed, he met in his regiment men who later became his most devoted friends and followers: Rudolph Hess, who became party secretary, and Max Amann, who was the press chief in Nazi Germany. The war experience made Hitler an admirer of all things military; he was impressed by the hierarchical structure of an army, with its chain of command. After years of rootlessness, he found a home in the army. The collapse of Germany was a personal catastrophe for him. He could not admit that the defeat had been caused by the admired military leaders; in his view it was the result of a stab in the back by those dark forces which he had seen in Vienna—Marxists and Jews. He returned to Munich, and as we have seen, was employed by the army as a propaganda speaker to keep the military spirit alive in the disheartened and defeated German nation. In the course of this activity Hitler came into contact with a small group calling itself the National Socialist German Workers' party, which pursued a somewhat confused mixture of nationalist and socialist ideals. Hitler became a member, and was soon the leader of this group. He had found his calling.

In Hitler's system of values those social ideas for which he had no feeling were no less significant than those which he emphasized. Hitler had no sense of the importance of morality or law. He was willing to stand up for murderers. He closed his eyes to the sexual aberrations of many of his companions, but he did not hesitate to make use of his knowledge of their weaknesses when he wanted to get rid of them. In politics, and probably also in his personal life, Hitler knew only friends and foes—and those who were his friends became his foes when they did not offer him blind allegiance. He used every weapon to eliminate his enemies. When in the summer of 1934 the S.A. had become an obstacle, he had the leaders—his enthusiastic followers—executed without recourse to the regular courts, explaining that he was "the supreme justiciar" of the German people. He had people placed in "protective custody" without giving them any opportunity to defend themselves in the courts. The result was the establishment of the dreaded concentration camps, where many were kept without legal recourse for unlimited periods. He established special courts, like those of the S.S., which made their own laws, and he issued retroactive laws. The lack of sense of morality, the inability to grasp the value of a system of law, were deeply rooted in Hitler's personality. In Vienna he lived as a lone wolf among outcasts fighting against each other for a minimum subsistence; his experience had been that "it is not by the principles of humanity that man lives, or is able to preserve himself above the animal world, but solely by means of the most brutal struggle." He never grasped that life in a community is possible only if recognized standards of morality and of law exist.

Almost inevitably Hitler's personality carried the seeds of his destruction. It has been debated why he could not be content with the success which he achieved. There were moments under his rule when Germany seemed to have obtained all that its people could have desired. But a halt would have meant the return to some legal order and the acceptance of some moral values permitting the existence of a stable communal life. In such a world neither the men who surrounded the leader, nor Hitler himself, would have fitted. Hence he drove restlessly on to new conquests until the chase ended in nothing. It is truly appropriate to call the Nazi revolution, as did Hermann Rauschning, at first Hitler's adherent and then his enemy, "the revolution of nihilism."

The Implementation of the Nazi Program

Hitler's aim was to obtain full power and then to launch Germany on a course of expansion, thereby fulfilling what he regarded as the natural law of politics. When he became chancellor in January, 1933, such an aim seemed far beyond his grasp. His government was a coalition in which the National Socialists were a minority. In foreign policy Germany's freedom of action was still restricted by the treaties of Versailles and Locarno. The size of the German army was limited and the Rhineland was demilitarized. One may reject Hitler's aims and detest his brutal methods, but still find remarkable the technical virtuosity with which he quickly freed himself from these internal and external restraints. A year and a half after he became chancellor, Hitler was the all-powerful dictator of Germany, and less than two years after that, in March, 1936, he made the treaties of Versailles and Locarno valueless pieces of paper.

At first, Hitler made use of the coalition with the German Nationalist party in order to stress the moderate and conservative character of his "national revolution." The black, white, and red of the German empire replaced the black, red, and gold of the national flag of the Weimar Republic; carefully staged celebrations emphasized the continuity between the old imperial Germany and the new National Socialist state. In March, 1933, the artfully contrived climax of the opening of the Reichstag in the Hohenzollern residence at Potsdam was Hitler's bow before President Hindenburg.

Hitler and the National Socialists had several reasons for the temporary adoption of a conservative line. First of all, Hitler had to win the confidence of old Hindenburg, who by refusing to sign emergency decrees could still bring about the fall of the government. Also, the new chancellor was anxious to avoid any obstruction by the bureaucracy and to make sure that the military leadership would not turn against him. Moreover, popular support of National Socialism would be strengthened if the members of the various conservative and nationalist parties and organizations, who had stayed away from the Nazis, could be lured into enrolling in the Nazi party. The conservative line also helped to secure the continuation of financial support for the Nazi party from the leaders of industrial trusts and banks, such as the Krupp metals empire and the I. G. Farben chemical works.

When the government was formed, Hitler insisted that the Reichstag be dissolved and new elections take place. The National Socialists entered the election campaign with immense advantages. They enjoyed the prestige of having their leader as head of the government. They could use the government machinery for propaganda, and on the basis of Paragraph 48 of the constitution they issued emergency decrees which limited the right of assembly of opposition parties and suppressed their newspapers and political publications. However, the decisive turn in the election campaign was

The burning of the Reichstag. *The main hall after the fire.*

brought about on the night of February 27, 1933, when the building in which the Reichstag met went up in flames. Though Marinus van der Lubbe, the young Dutchman who was caught in the building, never denied the deed, it was immediately assumed that he alone could not have caused the immense fire.

The Nazi leaders immediately accused the Communists, maintaining that the Reichstag fire was intended as the signal for a Communist revolt; but they never produced any proof, and it is certain that the Communists were not involved. We do know that the Nazis were only waiting for a Communist provocation which would give them the opportunity to suppress the Communist party and impose further restrictions on the other opposition parties. It has been suggested, therefore, that the National Socialists themselves used Lubbe as a cat's paw and were responsible for the Reichstag fire. In any event, the Nazi leaders welcomed the fire and utilized it most efficiently.

On February 28, the day after the burning of the Reichstag, the government issued a number of emergency decrees which were not rescinded until the end of Hitler's Third Reich in 1945. As a "defensive measure against Communist acts of violence," the government rescinded the guarantees of such basic rights as personal freedom, the free expression of opinion, the freedom of assembly and association, the privacy of postal and telephone communications, and the inviolability of property. In addition the number of crimes to which the death penalty could be applied was increased, and the spreading of rumors or false news was classified as treason. Finally, the Reich government was empowered to take over the government of the various federal states if necessary.

The elections, a week after the Reichstag fire, gave the National Socialists 43.9 per cent of the vote. It has been argued in favor of the political maturity of the German people that although the elections took place under severe pressure and restrictions, the National Socialists did not receive a clear majority. It is perhaps more significant that even after the dictatorial character of the Hitler regime had revealed itself, almost 44 per cent of the German people voted for the Nazis. Together with the German Nationalist party, with 8 per cent of the vote, the National Socialist party had the majority.

But application of the emergency decrees soon made this alliance unnecessary. The Communist deputies, representing 12.2 per cent of the vote, were arrested and not permitted to enter the Reichstag. Now even without the German Nationalist party the Nazis had a majority.

For Hitler this was only a first step. He wanted to eliminate entirely both parliament and elections. His government therefore proposed an Enabling Law, which would transfer the legislative power from the Reichstag to the government for four years; as a change in the constitution, such a law had to be approved by two thirds of the Reichstag. Hitler obtained the support of the Catholic Center party by threatening to use the emergency decrees against this party as he had used them against the Communists. The members of the Center party reasoned that by agreeing to the Enabling Law they might save their party and retain some influence. The Enabling Law was accepted on March 23; only the Social Democrats voted against it, while outside the hall the storm troopers shouted, "We want the bill or fire and murder."

With the emergency decrees of February 28 and the Enabling Law of March 23 all legislative and executive power was concentrated in the hands of the Hitler government, and all guarantees against transgressions by the executive had been removed. This was the "legal" framework for Hitler's dictatorship from 1933 to 1945.

However, the possession of the legal instruments for establishing a dictatorship did not overcome all obstacles to Hitler's unlimited control. Although his party now constituted a majority in the Reichstag, he was committed to retaining the coalition government. The prestige of the president, Hindenburg, was superior to his. Opposition parties and newspapers, though hampered, continued to exist. And the traditional spokesmen for educated public opinion—civil servants, professors, clergymen—could still make themselves heard. Hitler's technique for weakening and finally eliminating these remaining centers of independence was masterly. His approach was always the same. Instead of moving against all his opponents at once, he attacked one at a time, in each case proceeding gradually.

Characteristic was the way in which he ended the multiparty system. After the Communist party had been eliminated, Hitler's first target was the Social Democratic party. In this effort his coalition partners were willing helpers, and few objections were raised by the other bourgeois parties. The strength of the Social Democrats lay in their close relation to the trade unions, whose strikes could severely handicap the work of the government. Hence, Hitler's first move was to separate the trade unions from the Social Democrats; he did so by promising the unions undisturbed, continued existence if they abandoned political activities and concentrated exclusively on economic goals. Timid and bureaucratic, the union leaders fell into this trap and accepted the restrictions. Next, the Nazis declared that independent trade unions were unnecessary. The unions ought to become part of a great comprehensive organization which would include employers as well as workers. With a great celebration on May 1, which was declared to be a national holiday, a German labor front was founded. The next day the buildings of the unions were occupied, their funds were confiscated, and some of their leaders were arrested. With the elimination of the trade unions the Social Democrats lost all their remaining power to exert pressure. And when some important socialists, threatened by imprisonment, left Germany and attacked the regime from outside, the Nazis used their conduct as an excuse to declare Social Democratic activities treasonous; they prohibited the party and imprisoned many of its leaders.

Next, Hitler proceeded against the bourgeois parties outside his government. Most important among them was the Catholic Center party. Hitler again applied the tactics which he had used against the socialists: he destroyed his antagonist's source of power. A basic reason for the existence of the Center party was the need to maintain and protect the position of the Roman Catholic Church and its members. Hitler sent Papen to Rome to negotiate a concordat; for many years the Vatican had been eager for such an agreement, which would secure the legal status of the Catholic Church in Germany and would guarantee the bishops freedom of communication with the Vatican. But no previous federal government had been willing to conclude a concordat. The Vatican accepted Hitler's offer, probably as a result of the authoritarian inclinations of Pope Pius XI and the pro-German bias of his secretary of state Eugenio Pacelli, later Pope Pius XII. It was a fatal mistake. The concordat gave the first international approval to the Nazi regime and raised its prestige. It did not secure the position of Roman Catholicism in Germany, which Hitler went on to attack and undermine as soon as his immediate aim, the dissolution of the Center party, had been achieved. At the time, however, German Catholics, assured by the concordat that their religion would not suffer under the Nazi regime, abandoned membership in the Center party, and under pressure from the Vatican the party's leaders on July 8 agreed to its dissolution.

Hitler still had to dispose of his coalition partner—the German National-ist party. When he became chancellor, he had promised not to change the composition of the government, which was to include, besides himself, only two National Socialists. However, he managed to increase the influence of his own party in the coalition by creating new departments headed by Nazis: Göring, who had distinguished himself in the war as pilot and was the most respectable of Hitler's close collaborators, became air minister; Joseph Goebbels (1897–1945), who had been head of the Nazi party in Berlin and was the most intellectual and also the most cynical of the Nazi leaders, became minister of propaganda. Moreover, members of the German Nationalist party who went over to the National Socialists were rewarded with advantageous positions in the administration and in the party. Those who refused, encountered endless difficulties. Therefore, strong pressure developed within the German Nationalist party to assure its members of continued influence in the government and administration by amalgamat-ing with the Nazi party. Thus the party began to disintegrate and was finally dissolved. On July 14 a government enactment proclaimed that "the National Socialist German Workers' Party constitutes the only political party in Germany"; to attempt to maintain or organize any other political party became a crime. Germany was a one-party state. The elimination of the multiparty system was certainly Germany's most decisive step toward totalitarianism. But it was only one among many. Nazi commissars were placed at the head of the various federal states and appointed state governments dominated by Nazis. The press and the publishing houses were coordinated by the formation of a comprehensive Nazi-controlled association. Only members of this association were permitted to own, edit, or work on newspapers. A similar take-over occurred in the universities. New chairs were created for fields like racial science, and these were filled by National Socialists. The politically oriented newcomers were supported by the rectors of the universities, now not elected, but appointed by the Nazi minister of education. The expression of pronounced Nazi views became the prerequisite for obtaining tenure and promotion. No excuse is possible for the lack of resistance shown by the German intellectual community to the abolition of academic freedom. But because the Nazi infiltration of the universities happened gradually, many professors became aware of the systematic destruction of their independence only after it had been lost.

Similarly, the full aims of Hitler's anti-Semitic policy were only gradually apparent. It is certain that from the outset his mind was set on what during the Second World War became the "final solution"—the annihilation of the Jews. But at the beginning of the Nazi regime, Hitler created the impression that Jews would be permitted to continue their activities in economic life and in the professions; they were to be excluded from government service except for those who had done military service during the First World War. Soon, however, the screws were tightened. The exemption of war veterans from dismissal was rescinded. Doctors, lawyers, journalists, writers were organized in associations from which Jews were excluded; those who did not belong to these associations met increasing difficulties in the exercise of their professions. Admission to schools and universities was denied to Jewish youth. Gradually the same method was applied to business and economic life. Such activities required membership in organizations from which Jews were excluded.

The anti-Semitic policy reached a climax in the Nuremberg Laws of September 15, 1935, which deprived Jews and people with Jewish blood of German citizenship, prohibited marriage and sexual intercourse between people with Jewish blood and non-Jewish Germans, and denied Jews the right to employ non-Jewish female servants. Jews were forced to wear a yellow Star of David on their clothing whenever they went into the streets. They were pushed back into the ghetto. Protests against these measures were of no avail. As a matter of fact, few dared to endanger themselves by indicating disapproval.

All these changes were accompanied by a systematic policy of terror. When the Nazis came to power one of their first moves was to obtain control of the police. Since the ministers of the interior in the federal states were in command of the police the Nazis made sure that these posts were filled by reliable party members. Nazis also were appointed as police presidents in the larger urban centers. These officials arranged for the storm troopers to serve as an auxiliary police force. The emergency decrees passed after the Reichstag fire gave the police the right to arrest and keep in custody anyone suspected of disloyalty to the state. Nobody was secure; an incautious remark or the personal hostility of a storm trooper might result in imprisonment. People disappeared and were never heard of again. The police refused to interfere with Nazi demonstrations, as on April 1, 1933, when the Nazis marched unhindered through the streets of the center of Berlin, throwing stones into the windows of department stores and shops owned by Jews. Similar outbreaks by Nazi students in the universities forced professors regarded as unfriendly to the new regime to abandon their courses. In the atmosphere of terror, made more nightmarish by the official silence about these dark happenings, people gave up asking questions and closed their eyes and ears to what was going on around them. Moreover, the terror did not recede after the first few months; instead, it was embodied in an organization—the Secret State Police, or Gestapo—that developed into a large institution with headquarters in Berlin and offices all over Germany. The Gestapo devoted itself to the task of ferreting out the enemies of Nazism, who were arrested, interrogated, tortured, and placed in detention camps, without any legal recourse.

Under these circumstances the only serious threat to Hitler's leadership came from within—from the Nazi party itself. Many of those prominent in the party, like the fanatic but colorless Heinrich Himmler (1900–1945), the leader of the S.S., and the intelligent but generally despised Goebbels, the minister of propaganda, were aware that they had little personal following and were entirely dependent on Hitler. Göring, whose primitive enjoyment of luxury and power gave him a certain human appeal, was entirely satisfied with the power and riches he obtained as second in command and as Hitler's designated heir. But many of the early party members sincerely believed that the Nazi assumption of power would bring about a social revolution and that they would be the leaders of a new society very different from the old. A center of such aspirations was the S.A., and the main advocate of these ideas was the leader of the S.A., Ernst Röhm (1887–1934). His concrete aim was to have the S.A. become part of the army, with the S.A. leaders receiving officers' ranks. Such demands disquieted the generals of the Reichswehr, who did not want to see their control of the training and organization of the army disturbed by the "wild men" of the S.A. Hitler was anxious not to arouse the distrust of the military leaders because he anticipated needing army support for his plan to combine the position of president with that of chancellor after the death of Hindenburg, which in 1934 was imminent. The situation was further complicated by the activities of the conservatives, who were fully aware that without Hindenburg they would lack the power to halt a second revolution and were therefore trying to put a stop to Nazi radicalism before Hindenburg's death.

Out of this tangle of motives arose the blood bath of June 30, 1934. Hitler himself led the action against Röhm and other leaders of the S.A. whom he surprised in a small summer resort in Bavaria. Röhm and his associates were executed without trial; in his speech of justification Hitler emphasized his having discovered them in bed with young S.A. men. Actually he had known for a long time of the prevalence of homosexuality within the S.A. In Berlin, Göring proceeded not only against the leaders of the S.A. but also against other adversaries of the Nazis, like Schleicher, the former chancellor; he also arranged the execution of two of vice-chancellor Papen's secretaries, who had acted as spokesmen of the conservatives. Papen himself was placed under house arrest. Thus, Hitler shook off the radical wing of his party and earned the gratitude of the military leaders; he also demonstrated that he had not become a prisoner of the conservatives. The events of June 30 were both an expression of Hitler's utter disregard for law and morality and a sign of the omnipotence which he had reached. When Hindenburg died on August 2, Hitler combined the offices of president and chancellor without encountering objections.

In two sectors of social life—in economic affairs and in military affairs—the changes brought about by the Nazi dictatorship were less

The Nazi Party Congress in Nuremberg in 1934. *In the middle, Hitler, between Himmler, the leader of the S.S. (left) and Lutze, leader of the S.A.*

pronounced than in others. From the beginning the interests of the economic and military leaders harmonized with Hitler's aims. Economic life became strictly organized and controlled; industrial and commercial activities were coordinated by the trade associations to which all the entrepreneurs had to belong and from which, as we have seen, Jews—and also Freemasons—were excluded. The intermediary between the government and business was Hjalmar Schacht, who served Hitler as president of the Reichsbank and as minister of economics. Schacht abandoned the deflationary policy of previous governments; he pumped new money into the economy by initiating public works, such as the construction of the system of Autobahns, and by providing industry with armament contracts. The inflationary consequences of this policy were kept to a minimum by strict currency controls and import restrictions. Moreover, the secrecy with which German rearmament was surrounded kept the public in the dark about the extent of government expenditures and pump priming.

As the entire world has now learned, government support of economic activity—pump priming—can prove an effective means of overcoming economic depression. However, there are limits to the successful pursuit of an inflationary policy. Schacht himself believed that they had been reached by 1938, and he left the government because Hitler insisted on continuing this course. The damaging consequences did not come out into the open before the outbreak of the war in 1939. By then Germany was faced by the alternative of either a recession or a war and the Nazi leaders were entirely aware of this problem.

Once the danger of S.A. interference had been removed, the military leaders were quite content with Hitler's rule. In Hitler, Germany had a head of state who not only approved of rearmament but was anxious to accelerate the process. Thus, the military leaders no longer encountered government opposition to their desire for rearmament. However, their independence of the Nazi control was more apparent than real. The air force, created only after 1933, was under the command of Göring, and its officers were enthusiastic Nazis. Moreover, the quick promotions resulting from the expansion of the army made the younger officers favorably inclined toward the Nazi regime. In 1938, when the old army leaders began to fear that Hitler's foreign policy might be too risky, Hitler had no difficulty in replacing with more subservient generals those whom he regarded as obstructionists.

By 1936, Hitler could claim with justification that he had established a totalitarian state; with the exception of some pockets of resistance by small groups in the Roman Catholic and Protestant churches, all activities, organizations, and institutions had been adjusted (*gleichgeschaltet*) to the Nazi regime and were subject to the direction by the Nazi leader. But was there equal justification for the claim—which Hitler and the party chiefs made with still greater emphasis—that the Nazi conquest of power represented a revolution? "Revolution" may be understood as the overthrow of a ruling class and its replacement by another; in what respects, and to what extent, did the Nazi regime transform the basic structure of German social life?

The Nazi movement cannot be identified with a particular class or stratum of German society. Farmers and members of the lower middle class formed its backbone. But in the period of economic misery the unemployed swelled the Nazi ranks, and civil servants and white-collar workers joined them. Within these groups the younger generation in particular became Nazis; in 1930, the year of the party's first great electoral victory, more than two thirds of its members were under forty and more than one third under thirty years of age. Those who saw before them only a hard and bleak future were enticed by the Nazi promise of a complete change; the varied membership of the party was united only by common dissafection with the present.

Consequently, when the Nazis came to power they had no economic or social program aimed at changing the German social structure. They had promised their middle-class adherents protection against the absorption of small businesses by department and chain stores, and indeed they issued decrees which restricted the kinds of merchandise which these stores might sell and subjected them to a special tax. But the opposition of banks and other credit institutions which had invested in these enterprises led gradually to mitigation of the measures against chain and department stores. Beyond this somewhat ephemeral concession to the small middle-class businessman, the Nazis when they came to power had no concrete economic or social plans. Their "revolution" consisted in infusing a new "spirit" into the entire social body. Their apparently revolutionary actions were primarily propagandistic. They aimed at showing that a new nation had arisen in which all groups and classes harmoniously cooperated for the common good. The first of May became a national holiday intended to recognize the importance of the workers; this was only one of the many holidays created to emphasize the solidarity of the German nation. With the establishment of comradeship among the classes, "German Socialism," it was proclaimed, would become a reality. Organizations like the Hitler Youth and the Labor Service were meant to serve this purpose. The Hitler Youth consisted of boys and girls in their early years. The Labor Service was obligatory for students, voluntary for others; its disciplinary and educational effects were more highly appreciated by visiting foreigners than by those who had to undergo this training.

For Hitler the dividing lines in modern society were created not by differing education, differing professions, differing economic status, but by race. However, even within a superior race like the Germans there was an elite which alone had the right to rule; those few who came from the right stock and had excelled in their activities in the Hitler Youth were prepared for their tasks of leadership in special training schools, housed in buildings modeled after the castles of the knightly orders of the Middle Ages; the training—and these surroundings—were intended to awaken in the trainees the qualities of obedience, physical prowess, instinctivity, and will power.

The mixture of propaganda and racial romanticism in the social policy of the Nazis reflected the absence of concrete ideas about desirable changes in the German social structure. But this lack had its advantages for the Nazi regime. Since no revolution had occurred which changed the German class structure, and no ruling class had been toppled and replaced, each group of society seemed to have kept the position which it had held before the Nazis had obtained power. Except for the obvious victims of the change of regime—Jews, and politicians who had fought the Nazis—the individual did not experience an immediate diminution of status; the tenor of his life was not perceptibly changed, and this apparent stability was one reason for the lack of resistance to the Nazi regime in all levels of society.

The emphasis which Nazi propaganda placed on the establishment of a new national community was to a large extent directed toward mitigating the resentment arising from the realization of political powerlessness. The Nazi rulers took particular care to keep the industrial workers content. The

Hitler's artistic taste. *The Chancellery in Berlin built by Hitler's architect, Speer.*

labor front gave much attention to conditions in the factories, secured regular vacations for the workers, and through a special organization, called "Strength Through Joy," subsidized travel for the workers and their families during these vacations.

Nevertheless, it might be doubted whether propagandistic flattery and handouts would have been effective if employers and employees had not been consoled for their loss of political influence by economic prosperity. At the time the Nazis took over, recovery from the depression was beginning, and this trend the Nazis aided by their policy of military rearmament. In 1938 the federal budget was seven times as large as it had been before the Nazis came to power, and 74 per cent of this budget was used for military purposes. Enterprises carrying out government contracts were given credit or were assured of orders for a fixed number of years. For example, in December, 1933, the government contracted to buy motor fuel from the large German chemical concern of I.G. Farben for ten years at fixed prices. By such arrangements, industry gradually surrendered its independence and granted the government control over production and prices. But as a collaborator with the regime, industry—and particularly the large companies—began to flourish.

The spurt in economic life which resulted from rearmament also transformed the situation on the labor market. In 1936–1937 the number of employed was greater than the number of employed and unemployed together had been in 1933. Soon there was a labor shortage in Germany. Although on the average, wages were even lower than they had been in the 1920's, the unskilled worker in Nazi Germany in the 1930's had the advantage of being sure of finding a job, and the skilled worker was so much sought after that his wages were kept high. After the haunting experiences of the depression, economic security seemed to both employers and employees a benefit worth paying for.

The question was, however, how long the prosperity produced by rearmament could last. Necessarily, this economic policy was accompanied by currency restrictions and limitations on imports, and the Nazi rulers were all the more willing to utilize such measures because they cut off the German people from the outside world. Nevertheless, because rearmament is economically unproductive, the inflationary consequences of the extension of credit which this policy required could not remain concealed indefinitely. Hitler had little fear that an end of economic prosperity would disrupt the new spirit of national community which the Nazi revolution claimed to have created; he was not concerned with stabilizing the situation which existed. His economic measures were never intended to provide a lasting solution. They were aimed at a change through territorial expansion, for which the rearmament policy was the requisite.

CHAPTER 41

Toward the Inevitable Conflict

For HITLER the establishment of a totalitarian dictatorship was a means to a greater end: the expansion of Germany by war. In *Mein Kampf* he had written that along with the abrogation of the Treaty of Versailles and the restoration of the pre-1914 frontiers, Germany required additional "living space"; these goals were to be achieved, if necessary, by war. The rise to power of a man with such a program of expansion aroused fears in the non-German world. Yet Hitler succeeded in preventing common action, utilizing tactics very similar to those he had employed in domestic policy: proceeding slowly and gradually and dividing his enemies.

THE NEW POSTURE OF AGGRESSION

The Beginning of Nazi Foreign Policy

Hitler began his conduct of foreign policy with loud protestations of peaceful intentions: he was willing to disarm, if only Germany received equal treatment. Nevertheless, in October, 1933, he withdrew from the disarmament conference which had been meeting since 1932 because, as he stated, the plans for disarmament were still discriminatory against Germany. This first step toward a new foreign policy was simultaneous with Germany's withdrawal from the League of Nations. Hitler softened this blow by declaring that his nation would be willing to reenter if its claims to equality in armament were recognized. The British government, occupied with the pursuit of economic recovery, refused to participate in any strong counteraction and began to explore the possibility of coming to some agreement on armament limitations. The British felt encouraged in these attempts to bring Germany back to international cooperation when on January 26, 1934, in a sudden reversal of foreign policy, Hitler concluded a nonaggression pact with Poland. The German demands for a return of Danzig and the Polish Corridor had always been regarded as a serious danger to European peace. In coming to an agreement with Poland the new ruler of Germany, however brutal his domestic policy might be, seemed to show that he was aware that methods of violence were inappropriate in international relations. The first year of Hitler's conduct of foreign policy ended with a great plus for the Reich. Germany had indicated that it no longer felt bound by the military clauses of the Treaty of Versailles, and yet was still courted as a participant in international negotiations.

In 1934 the skies darkened for Germany. Himself an Austrian, Hitler felt emotional about the *Anschluss*. He reacted sharply to measures of the Austrian chancellor, Engelbert Dollfuss, who established a Catholic authoritarian regime with the purpose of keeping Austria independent. By prohibiting Germans from traveling to Austria Hitler ruined the Austrian tourist industry, and he gave active support to the Austrian Nazi party, which Dollfuss had outlawed. Austrian Nazis who fled to Germany were organized into a military legion stationed near the border. On July 25, 1934, the Austrian Nazis tried to seize power by force. They succeeded in assassinating Dollfuss, but the putsch failed. Another Catholic chancellor, Kurt von Schuschnigg (born 1897) took over and continued Dollfus' anti-Nazi policy. The German government tried to shake off responsibility for the putsch and dissolved the Austrian legion, but the disclaimers were not believed and the image of Hitler as a man of peace was severely damaged.

The revelation of Hitler's aggressiveness had two important consequences. France strengthened its bonds with the eastern neighbors of Germany and began to cooperate with Soviet Russia, which was thoroughly alarmed by Hitler's vehement anti-Communism and suspected that his pact with Poland might mean the preparation of a Polish-German war against Russia. Sponsored by the French, the Russians entered the League of Nations in September, 1934, and eight months later a Franco-Russian alliance was concluded in which each promised to come to the other's aid against unprovoked aggression.

Hitler's Austrian policy also brought about a change in Italy's attitude. Mussolini had regarded the rise of Hitler with satisfaction, and in the first months of 1933 had done his best to calm the fears which the Nazi seizure of power had raised in Europe and to dissuade France and Great Britain from taking action. Mussolini shared Hitler's dislike of disarmament and of the League of Nations. He saw definite advantages in a strengthened Germany, envisioning Italy as a balance wheel between Britain and France on one side and Germany on the other. But he recognized that the absorption of Austria by Germany would be counter to Italy's interests. Germany might then interfere in Italy's sphere of interest in the Danube Valley and the Balkans. Moreover, with a greater Germany on the other side of the Brenner Pass, the Germans under Italian rule in South Tyrol would become entirely intractable. Mussolini therefore helped Dollfuss to establish his anti-Nazi dictatorship, and when the news of Dollfuss' assassination came, he sent troops to the Brenner frontier, in order to show that

The Stresa Conference. *Laval, then French foreign minister; Mussolini; Mac-Donald; and the French prime minister, Flandin.*

he would not permit the *Anschluss*. From cautious support of Hitler, Mussolini had moved into the anti-Nazi camp. In January, 1935, negotiations in Rome with the French foreign minister, Pierre Laval (1883–1945), led to an agreement which even envisaged conversations between the French and Italian military staffs with the purpose of arranging for concerted action in case of war with Germany. The deterioration of the German position became evident when Hitler made his next move. In March, 1935, he declared the disarmament clauses of the Treaty of Versailles abolished, and announced a great augmentation of the German army and the introduction of general conscription. In a conference at Stresa, Great Britain, France, and Italy agreed to a sharp condemnation of this unilateral violation of an international treaty, declared their interest in the maintenance of Austrian independence, and threatened that further aggressive actions would evoke not only protests but counteraction. At this time Germany, except for the understanding with Poland, was isolated and seemed unable to move.

But the situation changed rapidly. Two months later, in June, Great Britain and Germany signed a naval agreement which defined the relative strength of their navies. Germany was permitted to have as many submarines as Britain, while the strength of the rest of the German fleet was to be restricted to one third that of the British fleet. Among the many mistakes of British foreign policy with respect to Nazi Germany the conclusion of the Anglo-German naval agreement is the most incomprehensible. The practical advantages for Britain were slight, for Germany was more interested in building a strong force of submarines than in creating a high-seas navy. The political disadvantages were immense, since by recognizing this departure from the military provisions of the Treaty of Versailles, Britain undermined the basis on which the Stresa front had been formed. Strangely enough, the British government seems not to have foreseen the implications of this naval agreement with Germany, and was apparently guided by purely technical considerations, notably the belief that the fixed strength of the German navy would facilitate negotiations with other powers about naval limitations.

The Italian Conquest of Ethiopia

Hitler, however, was encouraged to continue an aggressive foreign policy, and Mussolini began to realize that not much reliance could be placed on the western democracies. Military conversations between the French and Italian staffs were postponed. Moreover, although Mussolini had found cooperation with France and Great Britain useful for the preservation of Austrian independence, he expected to be paid for his support, and he decided to cash in as quickly as possible. The result was the Italo-Ethiopian War. The Italian conquest of Ethiopia, completed in May, 1936, in a sense constituted revenge for the old defeat at Adowa, a visible demonstration that Fascist Italy had become a great imperial power, stronger and more influential than democratic and parliamentary Italy had been. Also, Mussolini hoped to settle some of Italy's surplus population in Ethiopia. In his negotiations with Mussolini in January, 1935, Laval had indicated that France would have no objection to extension of the Italian influence over Ethiopia, and Mussolini expected a similar attitude from Great Britain. But strangely enough, while Hitler's actions had always found defenders in Britain, Mussolini's invasion of Ethiopia met vehement indignation. To the British people this seemed the occasion to set in motion the machinery of the League of Nations against aggression. When in December, 1935, it appeared that the British foreign secretary, Sir Samuel Hoare (1880–1959), was willing to make a bargain with Mussolini, popular excitement in Britain was so great that Hoare was dismissed and replaced by Anthony Eden (born 1897), a strong advocate of the League of Nations and of collective security. But this did not mean that, after the rejection of the bargain with Mussolini by the British public, the government had now decided to carry out a policy of collective security even if it should result in war. The British continued to pursue an ineffectual middle course; they were not too unhappy when the French tried to slow down their attempts to use sanctions against Italy, and they hesitated to insist on the application of the one effective sanction—the cutting off of Italy's oil supplies. The result was that in the League of Nations the British demanded only halfhearted measures, which embittered the Italians against Great Britain and France without preventing their advance in Ethiopia.

The March into the Rhineland

It was in this situation, on March 7, 1936, that Hitler ended the demilitarization of the Rhineland by ordering his troops to march into the region, and thus violated not only the Treaty of Versailles but also the Locarno pact. Hitler counted on the disarray into which the Ethiopian war had put the Stresa front to prevent action by the western powers. Nevertheless, he was aware that he was gambling. As he later stated, the twenty-four hours while he was waiting for the reaction of the French were the most exciting and nerve-racking of his life. If the French had answered by sending troops into the Rhineland, the German forces would have been withdrawn to the right bank of the Rhine. This was the condition which the German military leaders had forced upon Hitler before agreeing to this move. But there was no French military response. Hitler's gamble had come off, and the political balance in Europe was entirely altered. As long as the Rhineland had been demilitarized and the important industrial areas of the Ruhr had remained unprotected, France had held the military advantage and had been in no real danger of attack. Now, with German troops near the French border and the Ruhr area in the hinterland, a conflict with Germany would mean bitter and serious war. Germany was again the strongest military power on the European continent.

THE WESTERN DEMOCRACIES IN RETREAT

Why did the great western powers—Great Britain and France—permit this change in the balance of power? Why did they not crush the revival of German military might in the early years of Hitler's rule, when Germany was still weak? Why did they miss the opportunity for intervention which the Rhineland crisis offered, and why did they then embark on a policy of appeasement?

In both Great Britain and France, the weakness in foreign policy corresponded to internal weakness; hence understanding of their attitude to the rise of Nazism requires a consideration of their domestic situation in the 1930's.

Great Britain

In Great Britain the major domestic issue in this decade was recovery from the depression into which the nation had been thrown by the economic crisis of 1929. The seriousness of this crisis made people aware of an economic vulnerability with which Britain had actually been affected since the First World War. During the war, the diminution of foreign assets as a result of the overseas procurement of war materials had sapped the strength of an economy in which imports exceeded exports. Furthermore, after the war, the British government adopted two courses of action which, though they seemed safe and appropriate in the relatively prosperous period of the middle 1920's, turned out in the subsequent depression to have the effect of severely aggravating the economic crisis and retarding recovery: one was the industrial policy which centered in the handling of the general strike in 1926; the other was the return to the gold standard in 1925.

THE GENERAL STRIKE

The general strike of 1926 developed out of a crisis in the British coal industry, which had been lagging behind its German and American competitors even before the First World War and was now also hit severely by the increasing use of oil. During the war, coal mining had been controlled by the government; the return of the mines to private ownership led, unavoidably, to a crisis. The miners' trade union demanded guarantees that a general wage level would be maintained. The owners were not willing to give these guarantees because some of the mines were considerably less profitable than others and many were not profitable at all. Three fourths of all British coal was produced at a loss. With the help of government subsidies a showdown was postponed, and the French occupation of the Ruhr, which temporarily eliminated the competition of German coal, gave relief to the British coal industry. But in 1923, after the German passive resistance in the Ruhr had ended, a crisis could no longer be avoided. When wage contracts had to be renegotiated, the owners and the miners' trade union were at loggerheads about a reduction of wages, an extension of working hours, and so on. A commission established by the government under Sir Herbert Samuel sided with the workers rather than the owners in its report and recommended a thorough reorganization of the coal-mining industry. But though in its general tenor the Samuel report was favorable to the workers, it did suggest that they accept wage reductions pending reorganization. On this issue negotiations broke down. The miners were backed by all the British trade unions and the consequence was a general strike lasting ten days, in May, 1926. Prime Minister Baldwin had probably been anxious to avoid this gigantic industrial conflict. But some members of his government, eager to put labor in its place, considered a showdown desirable.

The government was well prepared for a general strike. A state of emergency was declared; the country was divided into districts under civil commissioners supported by civil servants; and a force of volunteers trained for such an emergency was mobilized. The most urgently needed services were maintained and food supplies reached the cities. Thus the government gradually neutralized the major effects of the work stoppage, and some members of the cabinet, among them Neville Chamberlain and Winston Churchill, urged that the strike be declared illegal, its instigators imprisoned, and the funds of the trade unions confiscated. The union leaders

The general strike of 1926. *A street in London shows the impact of the lack of public transportation.*

feared that when the financial reserves of the unions were depleted, either the strike would peter out or the workers in their desperation would resort to force, perhaps causing civil war. Therefore, relying on a compromise formula which Sir Herbert Samuel had worked out and which envisaged wage reductions only after measures of reorganization in the coal industry had been effectively adopted, they called off the general strike. It was a defeat for the workers, all the more humiliating because the miners, infuriated by the suggestion of wage reductions in the compromise formula, continued to strike throughout the summer. But then their powers of resistance were exhausted. Increasingly discouraged, they returned to work. They had no national contract, only local and regional contracts; the overall result was that they had to work longer hours for lower wages.

In the prosperity of the second part of the 1920's English life took on something of the glamor of the prewar years, and the general strike soon seemed a thing of the past. But its consequences were far-reaching. The opportunity for a thorough overhauling of the coal industry had been missed; it continued to ail and the mining regions remained centers of low wages and unemployment. The bleakness, hardships, and dangers of life among British coal miners have found literary expression in George Orwell's realistic and moving *Road to Wigan Pier* (1937).

Moreover, the general strike increased distrust between the working class and the rest of the population. The failure of the government to force upon the employers concessions which would have prevented the stoppage raised suspicions about the intentions of the ruling group, and they were reinforced by the intransigent and vehement pronouncements of some of its members while the strike was in progress. After its collapse Baldwin took a conciliatory attitude, urging that industry reinstate the workers without reducing wages. But he lacked energy in the pursuit of this policy and was not able to restrain his antilabor colleagues. In 1927 the Conservative majority in Parliament struck a blow against the trade unions by passing a bill which limited the right to strike to trade disputes; sympathy strikes became illegal. Furthermore the unions were no longer allowed to collect money for political purposes. The intransigence of the government stiffened the resistance of the workers against all measures which might involve a temporary reduction in wages or a temporary increase in unemployment through the closing of unprofitable enterprises. To compete effectively on the world market British industry required modernization, but this was not feasible without the workers' cooperation, which was unobtainable after the general strike.

Equally fatal for Britain's economy was the return to the gold standard which Winston Churchill, Conservative chancellor of the exchequer, announced in his first budget speech, in April, 1925. At this time nobody questioned the principle that the basic unit in a currency must be defined as equivalent to a stated quantity of gold. The mistake of Churchill's measure was not so much that the pound was tied again to a fixed weight of gold, but that the ratio chosen, namely the prewar parity, was too high. Churchill was acting on the advice of the governor of the Bank of England, Montagu Norman, who hoped that by returning to the prewar standard London would regain the dominating position in the money market which it had lost to New York during the First World War. However, the result of this step was an increase in the price of British goods on the world market and hence a weakening of Britain's position in international trade. This effect was the more dangerous because of Great Britain's adverse balance of trade. Financiers would now view every further widening of the gap between exports and imports as seriously endangering British economic life. Furthermore, lulled into false security by the prosperity of the nineteenth century, British industrialists had been remiss in renewing and modernizing their equipment; now the decline in profits made investments for these purposes impossible. Keynes was one of the few who realized that the return to prewar parity represented a further "competitive handicap." In general, these difficulties were fully recognized only after it was too late, when the prosperity of the later 1920's had ended in depression.

From 1924 to 1929, a Conservative government was in power, headed by Stanley Baldwin. He had risen to a leading position in the Conservative party only after the war. He was very different from the great aristocrats, Salisbury and Balfour, who had been Conservative prime ministers earlier in

Stanley Baldwin. *"How Good He Is, How Just. And Fit for Highest Trust."* Motto of a Baldwin biography by Arthur Bryant published in 1937.

the century and who might have had a sharper understanding of the change in the distribution of political and economic power brought about by the war. Baldwin was a rich industrialist, and his assumption of the Conservative leadership indicates the importance which businessmen had gained in the party. However, Baldwin was not the conventional businessman—unsentimental, purposeful and efficient; he was lazy and had no clear program or plans. He acted only when action was unavoidable, and then his conduct was determined by intuition rather than cold reason. In his expressions of longing for a quiet and peaceful life, remote from the turbulence of industrial society, he reflected perfectly the nostalgic mood of the middle classes, which were frightened by the size of the problems of the postwar world and constructed an idealized picture of the stability and prosperity of Victorian and Edwardian England. Thus, Baldwin was content to see some of the splendor of prewar England return in the later 1920's without questioning how firm and deep-rooted the prosperity of this period was. Moreover, Baldwin's easygoing attitude permitted his cabinet a free hand; energetic ministers were able to make their own policy. The tenure of Austen Chamberlain as foreign secretary was a success. His half brother Neville Chamberlain (1869–1940), minister of health, enlarged the system of social security by gaining passage of an old-age-pension bill. Churchill, chancellor of the exchequer, tried to stimulate industry by lowering income taxes and increasing death duties. But the manner in which, against Baldwin's expressed desire, Churchill and Chamberlain insisted on making use of the defeat of the general strike to obtain passage of legislation curtailing the power of labor showed the tension which existed below the surface during these few fat years.

When signs of an incipient depression appeared, the popularity of the Conservatives was immediately reduced, and as a result of elections held in June, 1929, another Labor government under Ramsay MacDonald came into power. Actually, the Conservatives still remained the strongest in the popular vote; but the boundaries of the electoral districts were drawn in such a way that Labor received 280 seats in the House of Commons and the Conservatives only 261; the 59 Liberal members turned the scales. Because, as in 1924, the Labor government relied on Liberal support, radical measures involving socialization were precluded, but Labor had no real program for solving the unemployment problem within the existing economic system. The government's freedom of action was further limited because MacDonald had given the chancellorship of the exchequer to Philip Snowden (1864–1937), an old member of the Labor party and a convinced adherent of free trade and economic orthodoxy. Meanwhile, with the spread of the depression unemployment increased until in December, 1930, it reached 2.5 million, about 1.5 million more than when Labor had come into power eighteen months previously. With income from taxation declining and payments to the unemployed rising, the budget became unbalanced. A committee which investigated the economic situation took a very gloomy view. Its report recommended economies in government and particularly a reduction in unemployment benefits. This pessimistic evaluation of the British economy coincided with the financial crisis in Germany, in which British banking interests were deeply involved. A panic followed, and the consequence was that those who owned pounds transformed them into other currencies: a flight from the pound set in; a currency crisis was added to the budget crisis. Because Labor had no majority in the House of Commons, negotiations with the leaders of the other parties became necessary; urged on by British and American bankers, these leaders made their further support contingent upon a reduction in unemployment benefits. This was a bitter pill, hard to swallow for members of a Labor government. When the members of the government could come to no agreement on whether to accept such a cut, resignation seemed inevitable; a coalition of Conservatives and Liberals was expected to take over. But instead of submitting his resignation, MacDonald astonished his party with the announcement that he had agreed to remain as prime minister, heading a national government which would include the leaders of all three parties. Most members of the Labor party refused to follow him; only two Labor politicians of reputation—Snowden and J. H. Thomas (1874–1949)—accepted positions in the new government. A national Labor party which

MacDonald founded remained insignificant. Nevertheless, MacDonald's "treason"—as his action was regarded by his former party associates—was a blow from which the Labor party began to recover only at the end of the 1930's.

MacDonald's behavior in this crisis is a puzzle. Many ascribe it to defects in his character, particularly to his vanity and social snobbery. When after the formation of the national government MacDonald was told that he would find himself popular in unfamiliar circles, he is reported to have exclaimed, "Yes, tomorrow every duchess in London will be wanting to kiss me." But it should not be forgotten that his socialist beliefs arose from a vague political idealism. He had never been a Marxist, and had never concerned himself with economic analysis. In economic questions he was accustomed to follow the views of experts, and he was probably honestly persuaded that he was placing country before party.

The new government began by introducing severe measures of economy: a reduction in the salaries of civil servants and a cut in unemployment benefits, which were now limited to twenty-six weeks a year and given only after a means test. Wage reductions in the armed services led to a mutiny in the British navy at Invergordon, Scotland, and although the mutiny ended quickly, it triggered a new financial panic. The government reacted with a step which a few months before would have been considered out of the question: taking the pound off the gold standard. As a result the share of British exports in world trade remained relatively stable. Elections held on October 27, 1931, to provide a popular mandate for the government resulted in its overwhelming triumph; Labor received 46 seats, while the parties in the national government now had 556, of which 472 were Conservative. Although the label of national government was retained and MacDonald ended his tenure only in 1935, actually the Conservative party ruled in Britain until the Second World War.

Stanley Baldwin remained leader of the Conservative party and as such was the most powerful figure in the national government, even while MacDonald was prime minister. After MacDonald's withdrawal, Baldwin took over the prime ministership. He resigned two years later, in 1937, at the height of his influence and fame. These had been immensely increased by his skillful handling of the crisis brought about by King Edward VIII's insistence on marrying a divorcee, a matter that ended with the abdication of the King. Baldwin's successor as prime minister was Neville Chamberlain, a son of Joseph Chamberlain. In his family Neville had been regarded as inferior in political talent to his older brother Austen; Neville therefore had been destined for a business career. When he finally entered political life, he became concerned primarily with affairs of economic policy. After he had been minister of health in the Conservative government of the 1920's, he served as chancellor of the exchequer in the national government; as such he was chiefly responsible for the manner in which the national government tried to lift Great Britain out of the depression.

The economic policy of the national government was strictly orthodox. The main aim was to keep the budget balanced and, as far as was compatible with this aim, to stimulate industry by keeping taxes low. Under the shield of a national government, the Conservatives were able to carry through a measure that symbolized the death of the liberal England of the nineteenth century: they introduced protective tariffs. For the party of Joseph Chamberlain, and especially for his son, this was a unique opportunity to establish closer economic ties between Great Britain and its empire by means of preferential tariffs. To do so seemed the more desirable because, in the course of the twentieth century, the cohesion of the British Empire had steadily weakened. The bond between Great Britain and the dominions (Australia, Canada, New Zealand, the Union of South Africa, and the Irish Free State) had become tenuous, sentimental rather than legal. A formula accepted by Great Britain and the dominions at a conference in 1926 stated that the dominions were "autonomous communities within the British Empire, equal in status, in no way subordinate one to another in any aspect of their domestic or external affairs, though united by a common allegiance to the Crown, and freely associated as members of the British Commonwealth of Nations." In 1931 the Statute of Westminster defined this new notion of a "British Commonwealth of Nations" in contractual constitutional terms. Because the dominions regarded themselves as fully independent in domestic and foreign policy, they gave a cool reception to the British government's suggestion to improve the economic situation by preferential tariffs among the members of the empire. The negotiations in Ottawa during the summer of 1932 were difficult, and the results fell far short of Joseph Chamberlain's dream of free trade within the empire; essentially, it was agreed that the dominions would retain their existing duties on industrial products from Great Britain but would raise duties on industrial products from other countries.

Thus the economic policy of the British government remained cautious. Neville Chamberlain himself called the course which he pursued a "pegging away." British economic activity reached its low-point in the late summer of 1932. Then, assisted by a general improvement in the world economic situation, a slow recovery took place. It was interrupted by relapses. The British industrial apparatus was never thoroughly overhauled; in the severely depressed areas people continued to live close to starvation and unemployment never went below a million.

The issues the British government had to handle in the 1930's—independence of the dominions, unrest in India, shocks like the abdication crisis, and, most importantly, the economic difficulties of Great Britain—were diverse and complex. Since a balanced budget was the cornerstone of

British economic policy, the government shied away from new, additional burdens that could easily unbalance the budget and might halt the march toward recovery. There was great reluctance, therefore, to embark on a policy of rearmament or to pursue a foreign policy that demanded a strengthening of Britain's military forces. To justify this reluctance, most members of the ruling Conservative party tended to minimize the dangers which threatened from the dictators, particularly from the rise of Hitler, and to take an overly optimistic view of the possibility of coming to peaceful terms with them. Churchill, almost alone among the Conservatives, raised a warning voice against Hitler's aggressive tendencies. But at this time his political influence was at its lowest. While Labor's opposition to the dictators was clear and definite, the pacifist tradition in the party made the Laborites unwilling to accept the necessity of military rearmament; their recommendation of relying on collective security was rather unrealistic.

There was an influential group in the British ruling class, however, which regarded the rise of Nazism with a favorable eye. To this group belonged Dawson, the influential editor of the London *Times* who since the early 1920's had been fighting a pretended pro-French orientation of British foreign policy; and empire-minded politicians like Lord Lothian, who wanted to free England from bonds to the continent; and Germanophile aristocrats like the Astors who saw Hitler as a restorer of the good German society of imperial days. The benevolent attitude of this group toward Hitler arose from a variety of sources. The members of the group accepted the revisionist thesis that Germany had been unfairly treated in the Treaty of Versailles and that Germany would be a satisfied and peaceful power if these injustices were removed. They had a certain admiration for the disciplined and orderly German ways which Hitler was supposed to have reintroduced; moreover, because Germany was the strongest nation in Europe, they believed that Germany was entitled to a hegemony in Europe and would then keep that restless continent orderly and quiet. They were inclined to believe the Nazi propaganda thesis which held that, before the Nazi seizure of power, Germany had been in danger of becoming Communist; and they were anxious to have on the European continent a powerful force that would form a dam against the spread of Communism. The importance of this group—the Cliveden set, as it has been called after the country place of the Astors—lies in the fact that it influenced, almost prescribed, the policy Neville Chamberlain followed after he became prime minister in 1937.

Neville Chamberlain turned his particular attention to foreign policy because he was impatient with the disturbances of economic life by political crises. He possessed a naïve arrogance that considered all other peoples inferior to the British, so that there was not much difference whether they were democracies or dictatorships. He saw no reason, therefore, why Britain should not come to an understanding with the dictators, and, lacking in imagination, he had no inkling of the dynamic expansionism inherent in Nazism. Neville Chamberlain approached the negotiations with Hitler as a businessman approaches a deal with other businessmen, trusting that among men of property and common sense a bargain to reciprocal advantage should always be possible. If Great Britain showed Hitler goodwill by a number of concessions, he assumed, Hitler would be willing to cooperate with Great Britain in maintaining peace. With such misconceptions, Neville Chamberlain embarked hopefully on a policy of appeasement. The original view of the Chamberlain family that Neville lacked political talents proved fully justified.

France

Although the French reaction to Nazi expansion was as weak as that of Great Britain the weakness of French foreign policy had very different origins. In the 1930's a net drop in population and a shift in the French economic structure contributed to a sense of national decline, unrest, and tension.

Although France had acquired Alsace-Lorraine as a result of the war, its losses had been so heavy that in 1921, when the first postwar census was taken, its population—39,210,000 people—was smaller than in 1914. This decrease, particularly the loss of young men, resulted in a decline in births, and just in the middle of the 1930's—in 1935—the number of births became smaller than the number of deaths. The following year the population began to increase again, but only because of the immigration of foreigners into France.

While the demographic statistics presented a somber picture, the tension which accompanied the shift in the French economic structure might be regarded as a kind of growing pains. At the beginning of the decade, in 1931, 45.1 per cent of the labor force was employed in industry, in contrast to 36.1 per cent twenty-five years before; clearly there had been a shift from agriculture to industry. Particularly noticeable was the growth of heavy industry, such as mining, iron and steel production, and the manufacture of machinery; for instance, in 1931 the iron and steel industry employed over 100,000 more men than in 1906. Accompanying this development, during the interwar years, was a trend toward industrial concentration. The increasing importance of the workers led to demands for an active social policy, while the French bourgeoisie, frightened by the Russian Revolution, the loss of Russian investments, and the inflation of the early 1920's, tended to regard labor's claims as the beginning of a dangerous revolutionary development.

During the 1930's these tensions were sharpened by a deterioration of the economic and financial situation. Throughout the preceding decade French economic development had been favorable. Reconstruction of the destroyed areas, completed by 1926, had resulted in a modernization of industrial installations. Poincaré, who in 1926 had returned as prime minister, though without influence on foreign policy, had quickly ended the inflation by drastic economies which balanced the budget. The nation entered the depression period in an economically strong position, and because France was more self-sufficient than other highly industrialized powers it remained, at least at first, relatively immune to the effects of the depression. The French government made use of this economic strength in the critical political and financial negotiations about the *Anschluss* and the Hoover moratorium during the hectic summer of 1931. In the following years, however, the general weakness of the international markets had repercussions on France. Exports declined rapidly. If those of 1912 are taken as a base and represented by 100, they had risen to 125 in 1929, but declined to 59 in 1936. The decrease in exports resulted in a steadily widening deficit in the balance of trade, reaching 64 per cent in 1936, and was accompanied by a lower rate of industrial production, which in 1935 was back at the prewar level. Because of the demographic situation unemployment was a less serious problem in France than in Germany or Great Britain; nevertheless, in 1935 the number of unemployed had reached half a million. A degree of waste in government spending, of slight consequence in the days of prosperity, now resulted in budget deficits. Fear of inflation led to a flight from the franc. The parties of the left regarded these problems chiefly as the result of the selfish attempts of the rich to save their own fortunes; economic difficulties would end if the flight from the franc could be stopped. Thus it was difficult, if not impossible, for the government to get parliament to accept measures of economy and tax increases. Because only stopgap actions were taken the situation continued to deteriorate, and the politicians were accused of incompetence and corruption. By the end of 1934 both Poincaré and Briand were dead, and the political leaders of this period—Édouard Herriot, Édouard Daladier, André Tardieu—lacked the prestige and the authority enjoyed by their predecessors—the heroes of the Dreyfus Affair and the French victory.

A striking indication of the tension which was developing in French society was the Stavisky affair of 1934. In comparison to the Dreyfus Affair, which had involved great questions of principle, this was a murky business, a small financial swindle revealing some corruption. But the Stavisky scandal has its place in history because it showed that the old conflict between right and left—existing since the French Revolution, surfacing in the Dreyfus Affair but seemingly overcome by the national revival brought on by the First World War—had broken out again, in renewed strength. The eagerness with which the scandal was blown up into a crisis of republican and democratic institutions was an expression of the desperate feeling of the French middle classes that they were losing out against the forces of big business and labor. The explosion caused by the Stavisky affair must also be regarded as a sign of the malaise arising from the impression that the successive French governments had wasted the brilliant position which France had gained with its victory in the First World War.

Serge Alexander Stavisky was a financial swindler of tremendous charm and ingenuity. He had managed to make many acquaintances among politicians, and because he had served as an informer, his relations with the police were good. If not for these contacts the fraudulence of his financial dealings would have been discovered earlier. When finally his enterprise collapsed, puzzling things happened. The police surrounded his house, but reached Stavisky only after he had shot himself. One of the judges investigating the scandal was found dead on the railroad tracks. Rumors spread that Stavisky had not committed suicide but had been shot by the police because he knew too much and that the investigating judge had been eliminated for the same reason. A high official, a brother-in-law of Camille Chautemps, one of the most influential leaders of the Radical Socialists, was suspected of responsibility for silencing the scandal. The rightists boiled over in indignation about the corruption among the parliamentary leaders of the left. When the prime minister, Daladier, dismissed the president of the Paris police, who with little justification was regarded as an embodiment of energy and integrity, war veterans and other organizations of the right arranged demonstrations, marched to the parliament building, and tried to storm it. The police fired, but Marshal Lyautey, one of France's most distinguished military leaders, announced that on the following day he himself would march at the head of the demonstrators. Unable or unwilling to face this outburst, Daladier resigned, and a new government of national unity was formed.

The head of the new government was Gaston Doumergue (1863–1937), who had been president of the republic from 1924 to 1931, and it included all the surviving former prime ministers as well as military heroes such as Marshal Pétain. It was a last—rather ephemeral—attempt to hold together the divergent forces of French society by an appeal to national solidarity, and to infuse new life into French foreign policy. Louis Barthou (1862–1934), the foreign minister under Doumergue, tried to make full use of the decline in Hitler's prestige in the summer of 1934 which had resulted from the purge of the S.A. and the murder by Nazis of the Austrian chancellor Engelbert Dollfuss. Barthou cold-shouldered British attempts to resume negotiations about armament limitations with Germany and visited the capitals of Czechoslovakia, Yugoslavia, and Rumania—which were allied in the so-called Little Entente—and of Russia in order to forge a firm alliance between these powers and France. An "eastern" Locarno, which would prevent German expansion toward the east, was to supplement the "western" Locarno, with its guarantee of the permanence of the Franco-German frontier. But on October 9, 1934, King Alexander of Yugoslavia, on a visit to strengthen his nation's ties with France, was assassinated in Marseilles by a Macedonian nationalist; another victim was Barthou himself, who was seated in the car next to the king. With Barthou's death French foreign policy returned quickly to a dependence on Great Britain.

The Doumergue government made an attempt to overcome the most evident weaknesses of French political life. It concentrated on plans to strengthen the executive at the expense of the legislative, chiefly by facilitating the dissolution of parliament and by depriving deputies of the right to augment suggested financial legislation. But Doumergue overplayed his hand; he tried to overcome resistance by appealing through radio addresses directly to the people. This authoritarian technique went against all republican tradition and the parliamentarians gained broad support as defenders of democracy against the penetration of "Fascist" ideas into French political life. The Doumergue government fell and the succeeding governments mainly marked time until the elections scheduled for the spring of 1936. In this period of weak transitional governments Hitler marched into the Rhineland. The French government in power was not strong enough to make a decision which would have demanded an abandonment of the dogma that France could not march alone, that she had to keep in line with England. So instead of ordering its troops into the Rhineland the French government acceded to the urging of England that the issue ought to be solved by negotiations.

The election campaign of 1936 was entirely a struggle between the right and the left. And the left fought the election as a Popular Front which reached from the middle-class Radical Socialists to the Communists. The Popular Front won an impressive victory. While the Communists agreed to support the government without actively participating in it, the Socialists, for the first time in French history, entered the government as a party, and their leader, Léon Blum (1872–1950), became prime minister. Blum was a strange figure to be leader of the Socialist party. He was neither a tough politician nor a Marxist. He was an intellectual, a man of wide culture, and a humanitarian. His sympathies with the underprivileged had brought him into the Socialist camp. His human qualities would shine brilliantly in his courageous stand against the Nazis during the German occupation of France. After the Second World War he would be prime minister again, and at the end of his life he was to be recognized as a major national figure. But when Blum became prime minister for the first time in June, 1936, his particular qualities were little suited to the situation. He was a pacifist, an internationalist, with little interest in the details of foreign policy. His main concern was social reform; he expected to improve the situation of the poorer classes by modernizing French life. A wave of strikes underlining the

Léon Blum, French prime minister, being interviewed during a meeting.

urgent need for social reform accompanied the formation of the Popular Front government. These strikes were of a new type—the sit-down: the workers refused to work but remained in the factories, making the use of strikebreakers impossible. Removal of the strikers would have required force, which the Popular Front government did not want to employ against its own supporters. Hence the industrialists were forced to make a number of concessions, granting the workers rights which their counterparts in most other European industrial countries already possessed—compulsory collective bargaining, the forty-hour week, paid holidays—and also wage increases of from 12 to 15 per cent. These arrangements were negotiated under government auspices and were supplemented by legislative measures intended to restrict the influence of high finance and big business on French policy. The Bank of France was brought under government control; its credit policy could no longer obstruct the financial measures of the government. The armament industry was nationalized, and the government inaugurated a series of public works to fight unemployment. Such reforms were long overdue. Thus, if France was to develop a strong air force, the nationalization of the armament industry was necessary, since it would make possible concentration on a few types of mass-produced airplanes. Even so, because time was needed to harvest the advantages of the change, airplane production in France remained dangerously weak for some years.

Meanwhile, the direct consequences of the measures taken by the Blum government were a sharpening of internal conflicts and then also a weakening of the coherence of the Popular Front. Industrialists and bankers, deeply resentful of the concessions to which they had been forced, continued the flight from the franc and sharply attacked the government policy of spending freely without attempting to balance the budget. The government had promised to maintain the value of the franc, but was soon forced to devaluate. This measure spurred fear of inflation among the middle classes, and the Radical Socialists, their representatives in the government, became doubtful about continued cooperation with the parties on the left. First Blum had to declare a "breathing spell" in social reforms, in order to restore confidence among the bourgeois partners in his coalition; then he was replaced as prime minister by a Radical Socialist, although the Socialists still remained members of the government. Then the Socialists left the government, although they continued to support it in parliament. But in 1938 Daladier, the Radical Socialist prime minister, turned to the right, and the Communists and Socialists resumed their old roles as members of the opposition.

One reason for the formation of the Popular Front, and the main motive underlying the Communist participation in it, had been to establish a firm stand against the advance of Nazism and Fascism. Unavoidably, many of those who resisted the social program of the Popular Front also opposed its ideas on foreign policy; they complained that both the domestic reforms and the international action against Fascism served the aims of international Communism rather than the national interests of France. "Better Hitler than Blum" was a slogan which spread among the rightists. Only a few organizations, although rather noisy ones, favored a Fascist regime in France, but many adherents of the right believed that because of its terrible losses in the First World War their nation should avoid involvement in another conflict at almost any cost; they saw no reason why France should obstruct Germany's ambitions in the east. France had built along the German frontier a strong defense line, called the Maginot Line after the politician responsible for its construction. And the French military leaders expressed full confidence in the ability of their army to hold firm behind this line, which, it was believed, the Germans would not be so foolish as to attack. Officially no French government ever admitted that it was willing to write off the alliances with the eastern European states. But the governments of the right which succeeded the Popular Front were inclined to minimize French commitments rather than to reinforce them. French foreign policy remained strong in words but timid in deeds. Its only serious concern was to avoid separation from Great Britain.

FROM THE RHINELAND OCCUPATION
TO THE OUTBREAK OF WAR

The militarization of the Rhineland upset the assumptions on which European statesmen had based their foreign policy. Germany was no longer open to French attack, and the great industrial area of the Ruhr was no longer exposed to the fire of French guns. The weakening of the French position had immediate repercussions in eastern and southeastern Europe. Except for Czechoslovakia, which continued to rely on the support of Great

Britain and France, the states of this region began to drift into the German orbit; this development was assisted by the German economic policy under the clever direction of Hjalmar Schacht. The eastern European countries, suffering acutely from the slump in agricultural prices, welcomed the opportunity offered by Germany to conclude barter agreements by which they could exchange agricultural products for German manufactured goods. Moreover, the German success in the Rhineland and the Italian triumph in Ethiopia had increased the prestige and appeal of the totalitarian systems. Mussolini, who in the 1920's had declared that Fascism was not an export article, was now proudly proclaiming that the democracies were obsolete and decaying and that Fascism represented the wave of the future. The various dictatorial regimes in Poland, Yugoslavia, Hungary, Rumania, and Bulgaria now began to imitate Fascist or National Socialist forms and methods, and claimed that their systems of government embodied a new political spirit, appropriate to the twentieth century.

Mussolini's praise of Fascism as a young international force which would triumph over the dying world of the democracies indicated that he had moved into the German camp. Close cooperation between Italy and Nazi Germany was established by October, 1936, after the trip to Germany of Count Galeazzo Ciano (1903–1944)—Mussolini's foreign minister and son-in-law. The so-called Rome-Berlin Axis was then confirmed by an exchange of visits, with Mussolini going to Berlin in September, 1937, and Hitler to Rome in May, 1938. The meetings of the two dictators were accompanied by immense military reviews, which were recorded on film so that the world could be impressed with the might of the Fascist powers. The western democracies were confronted by the alternatives of opposition by force and negotiations ending in concessions. Appeasement began.

The Spanish Civil War

The event in which the Axis powers first tested the democracies' will to resist was the Spanish Civil War. The contest in Spain was bitter, vehement, and long because it represented the clash of forces deeply rooted in Spanish social and intellectual life. Essentially a struggle of modern industrial and democratic forces against the continued existence of agrarian feudalism, it became enmeshed with the traditional movements for regional independence against Castilian centralism and with the age-old dispute about the position of the Church in Spanish social life.

In 1931 the inability of the Spanish army to put down a Moroccan uprising compromised the monarchy and the ruling group; revolt followed, and a republic was established in which full power was held by a democratically elected parliament. From the beginning the republican regime led a precarious existence. The new constitution separated church and state, but attempts to remove the Church from all activities which were not strictly religious aroused the resistance of the Catholic hierarchy and of many Catholics among the population. The workers, by tradition radical and anarchist, were dissatisfied by the failure of the republican government to put through anticapitalist measures. Riots, strikes, burnings of churches occurred in various parts of the country; violence led to a resurgence of rightist parties, and the counterrevolutionaries organized themselves into a movement on the Fascist pattern—the Falange. To fight reaction, all the parties from the center to the extreme left joined together in a Popular Front, which triumphed in the elections of February, 1936, more than two months before the victory of the French Popular Front.

The victors regarded their success as a mandate to purge the administration of reactionaries and to go ahead with a program of modernization and social reform. The Popular Front government took steps to divide up the great estates; it forced industrialists to take back workers who had been dismissed because of participation in strikes; and it closed Catholic schools. But the far-reaching nature of these measures spurred the rightist opposition to action. The military had been considering a *coup d'état* for a long time; now the Spanish antirepublicans received encouragement from Mussolini, who promised money and weapons. A putsch was planned for the middle of July, 1936. On July 12, 1936, the murder of the monarchist leader José Calvo Sotelo by a republican who was captain of the police played right into the hands of the conspirators. This crime seemed to show that the government was unable to guarantee order and security, and gave some justification for the rebellion, which erupted on July 17. Although the revolt was popular among upper- and middle-class groups and had the active support of organizations like the Falange, it began primarily as an officers' conspiracy. The officers ordered their troops to occupy government buildings and took over the administration of various towns, or entrusted it to rightist political leaders.

The course of the Spanish Civil War was long and confused. Originally the military coup was not a success. The generals seized power in extended areas of northern and northwestern Spain. But the entire southwest (except for a few small isolated areas), the center of Spain, and even the Basque coast in the north remained loyal to the republic. To strengthen their forces, the republican leaders, after some hesitation, distributed weapons to the workers. The resulting dependence on the masses led to a government shift toward the left, with the socialists, Communists, and anarchists becoming increasingly influential.

After the incomplete success of the military putsch both sides appealed for foreign aid: the republicans to France and Russia, the military to Italy and Germany. The Fascist powers were quick to respond. Mussolini sent bombing planes; Hitler authorized the immediate dispatch of some twenty transport planes. The acquisition of these airplanes was crucial; the Spanish

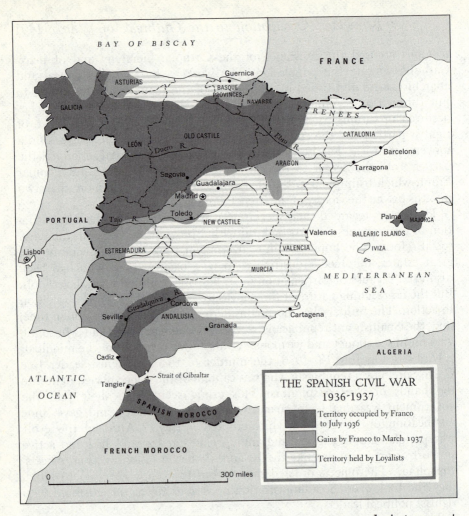

BAY OF BISCAY

FRANCE

Guernica

ASTURIAS

BASQUE
PROVINCES

NAVARRE

GALICIA

PYRENEES

CATALONIA

OLD CASTILE

Barcelona

LEÓN

Duero R.

Ebro R.

ARAGON

Tarragona

Segovia

Guadalajara

Madrid ⊛

PORTUGAL

Tajo R.

Toledo

NEW CASTILE

Valencia

Palma

MAJORCA

BALEARIC ISLANDS

VALENCIA

IVIZA

ESTREMADURA

Lisbon ⊛

MURCIA

MEDITERRANEAN
SEA

Guadalquivir R.

Cordova

Seville

ANDALUSIA

Cartagena

Granada

Cadiz

ALGERIA

ATLANTIC
OCEAN

Tangier

Strait of Gibraltar

SPANISH MOROCCO

THE SPANISH CIVIL WAR
1936-1937

Territory occupied by Franco
to July 1936

Gains by Franco to March 1937

Territory held by Loyalists

FRENCH MOROCCO

0   300 miles

navy had remained loyal to the republican government, and air transport
was the only means for bringing the well-disciplined Moroccan troops from
Africa into Spain. Hitler said correctly, some years later: "Franco ought to
erect a monument to the glory of the German transport aircraft. The
Spanish Revolution of Franco has to thank this aircraft for its victory." By
means of the Moroccan troops led by Francisco Franco (born 1892), one of
the conspiring generals, the Spanish Fascists succeeded in extending their
rule over the south of Spain and in establishing a bridge to the territory
which they controlled in the north. By the end of September the republicans no longer had a common frontier with Portugal. But even though the
Fascists advanced in four columns into the suburbs of Madrid and had a
"fifth column" of adherents within the city, their attempt to take the
capital failed as the Spanish republicans rose heroically to its defense in the
winter 1936–1937. The Fascists halted outside Madrid, and from there

extended their rule toward the west. Only three regions remained under republican control. One of these stretched from Madrid to southeastern Spain. It was connected by a small coastal strip with the second center of republican power, Catalonia. Finally, the Basque country in the north, along the Atlantic coast, remained republican. Isolated as they were, these centers of republican strength were no match for the Fascists, who conquered one after the other. The anti-Fascist regime in the Basque area fell in the summer of 1937. Then the war dragged on. Barcelona, the chief city of Catalonia, was taken in January, 1939; and thousands of freezing and starving Spanish republicans along with the remaining republican troops—altogether almost 400,000 people—crossed the frontiers to France, where on open land, fenced in by wires, lacking shelter and food, they dragged on their lives. Two months later, in March, 1939, Madrid surrendered. By then Spain was no longer a center of international politics.

The Spanish Civil War and European Diplomacy

The war was not just an internal Spanish affair. It was a struggle in which directly or indirectly the whole of Europe was involved. If the dispatch of German and Italian planes had been crucial in revitalizing the military revolt after its initial setback, the arrival of Russian tanks and aircraft in the fall of 1936 decisively helped the republican defense of Madrid against the renewed attack of the Fascists; moreover, Russian advisers gave coherence to the somewhat disorganized military effort of the republicans. Germany and Italy responded by boosting the Spanish Fascist regime with diplomatic recognition. But they also gave concrete assistance. The Germans sent more aircraft, and pilots as well—bomber squadrons of the so-called Condor Legion. The most famous—or infamous—exploit of the German fliers was the attack on Guernica during Franco's campaign against the Basque country (April, 1937). First they bombed the small rural town, then they machine-gunned the streets, killing and wounding about 2,500 of the 7,000 inhabitants. Later, the Germans would admit that this assault had been an experiment to test the effects of terror bombing. The Italian experiments were less devastating and less instructive; in trying out tank attacks they received a severe setback at Guadalajara, near Madrid (March, 1937). This loss of prestige impelled Mussolini to send additional Italian troops to Spain; at one point about forty thousand Italians were fighting there.

Undoubtedly the German and the Italian assistance to the Fascists was more effective than the Russian aid to the republicans, especially since the long route through the Mediterranean from the Black Sea was threatened by German and Italian submarines and warships. A balance could have been struck if the republicans had received airplanes, tanks, and supplies from the north, from France. But though Léon Blum, the French prime minister, was willing to send assistance, he was opposed by the British leaders and the nonsocialist members of his own government, who feared international complications, particularly the strengthening of Communism. Blum yielded to these pressures despite the indignation of the Communists and of many members of his own Socialist party.

Disagreement concerning the Spanish Civil War was an important factor in breaking up the French Popular Front. Hoping to localize the conflict, France and Great Britain suggested to the other powers a policy of nonintervention. The negotiations to implement this policy were long and drawn-out, and even after Russia, Germany, and Italy had been won over and a committee entrusted with the supervision of nonintervention had been established, Germany and Italy raised endless difficulties; they finally withdrew their troops only when they felt sure that doing so would not endanger the victory of Fascism in Spain.

For Hitler and Mussolini the Spanish Civil War was heartening proof of the weakness of their adversaries; they learned that although Russia, France, and Great Britain might be opposed to any disturbance of the *status quo*, they did not agree about how to control Fascist aggression. Evidently the main concern of the western powers was to avoid war.

But the Spanish Civil War did more than reveal the immense strength which the Fascist powers had gained. With the failure of the democracies, the opposition to Fascism lost its drive. When the Spanish Civil War began it had seemed évident that the democratic forces had right on their side and that democracy and Fascism met in Spain in a situation of equality—not prejudiced in favor of Fascism. It had appeared that if Fascism received a check in Spain the myth of its inevitable progress would be destroyed. After this one great effort the Fascist nightmare under which Europe lived might disappear.

> Tomorrow for the young the poets exploding like bombs,
> The walks by the lake, the weeks of perfect communion;
> Tomorrow the bicycle races
> Through the suburbs on summer evenings. But today the struggle.[1]

Men from all over the globe volunteered to fight for the Spanish republic. One of the most efficient of the republican military units was the International Brigade, in which Communists, socialists, and liberals served. Writers of many nationalities—George Orwell, who was British; Ernest Hemingway, an American; André Malraux, of France; Arthur Koestler, a Hungarian—came to Spain, fought with the republicans, and advocated their cause in their writings. Their hour of triumph was the heroic defense of Madrid. But they also experienced the dissension which broke out with

[1] W. H. Auden, "Spain 1937," quoted by Hugh Thomas, *The Spanish Civil War* (New York, 1961), p. 221.

Guernica. *Mural by Pablo Picasso, 1937, on extended loan from the artist to the Museum of Modern Art, New York.*

the approach of defeat—particularly a bitter struggle between Communists and anarchists in which many sincere fighters against Fascism were brutally killed.

In the years of appeasement that followed, those who had served in defense of the Spanish republic had a hard time. The governments of the western democracies looked with disfavor on these freedom fighters—"premature anti-Fascists," they were later termed by American officials. In Russia, after Stalin had turned away from the idea of a Communist-democratic alliance against Fascism, many of the participants in the Spanish Civil War were treated as criminals. However, some of the fighters for the Spanish republic survived, and were able to begin new political careers after the Second World War. Among the Communists, Ernö Gerö became one of the political leaders of Hungary. Palmiro Togliatti and Luigi Longo gained prominence in the Communist party in Italy. Of the non-Communists Pietro Nenni and Randolfo Pacciardi became ministers in Italy; André Malraux, in France. But in the years immediately following the Spanish Civil War the spirit of the fight against Fascism in Spain seemed to remain alive only in works of art; the painting "Guernica" (1937) by Pablo Picasso and Ernest Hemingway's novel *For Whom the Bell Tolls* (1940) expressed the tragic hopelessness of man's struggle against inhuman forces.

Anschluss *and the Invasion of Czechoslovakia*

The weakness which the western democracies had shown—first in the Rhineland crisis and then in the Spanish Civil War—gave Hitler the green light to proceed with his aggressive and expansionist foreign policy. In a meeting with his chief military and civilian advisers in November, 1937, he announced that Germany needed more living space, which could be secured only through war; such a war ought to take place in the early 1940's because German rearmament would then reach its peak. Preconditions for a successful war were the elimination of Czechoslovakia and the achievement of the *Anschluss*. Hitler also intimated that the situation which had developed in the Mediterranean as a result of the Spanish Civil War might afford an opportunity for quick action. Although subsequently he adjusted his tactics to changing circumstances, and the actual sequence of events was different from the one envisaged at this meeting, this speech did reveal his fundamental aims. When his chief military advisers expressed some reservations and doubts, they paid for their hesitation with loss of their positions. One of them, Werner von Fritsch, was charged with homosexuality; by the time the groundlessness of this accusation was proved it was too late to reinstate him. The other, Werner von Blomberg, the minister of war, was declared to have violated the officers' code of honor by marrying a former prostitute, even though Hitler had approved of the marriage and attended the wedding. The dismissal of these two generals demonstrated that the army had lost its independence. At the same time the foreign minister, Konstantin von Neurath (1873–1956), a professional diplomat who had been a compliant servant of the Nazis but was somewhat too cautious in Hitler's views, was replaced by a Nazi, Joachim von Ribbentrop (1893–1946). All obstacles to action had been removed.

Hitler's first victim was Austria. Stepped-up Nazi propaganda in Austria for *Anschluss* with Germany had led to increased measures of suppression by the Austrian government. In an interview with Chancellor Schuschnigg on February 4, 1938, Hitler demanded that these measures be lifted and that some of the Austrian Nazis be included in the government. Intimidated by Hitler's vehemence and by the threat of German troop movements toward the Austrian border, Schuschnigg gave in. But he soon realized that once the Nazis had entered the government they would take complete control. On March 9, in desperation, he announced a plebiscite in which the people were asked to vote on whether they wanted to keep Austrian independence. On March 11, Hitler sent an ultimatum demanding postponement of the plebiscite, and on March 12, dispatched his troops into Austria under the pretext that Schuschnigg's government was unable to maintain order. On March 14, 1938, Vienna, where Hitler in his youth had lived in utter misery, saw him return in triumph: the *Anschluss* creating a greater Germany had been achieved. The western powers did nothing except protest feebly on paper; Mussolini, who in 1934, when the first Nazi putsch took place in Austria, had moved his troops to the Brenner frontier, now declared that he was uninterested in the fate of Austria; he had gone too far to deviate from his pro-German course. Overjoyed, Hitler told Mussolini that he would never forget what he had done for him.

The next victim was Czechoslovakia. Hitler wanted the incorporation into Germany of the Sudeten region, a broad stretch of northern Czechoslovakia populated chiefly by Germans. Because this area was south of the mountains separating Germany from Czechoslovakia and included the Czechoslovakian line of fortifications, its loss would mean the end of Czechoslovakia as an independent factor in European power politics. Here again, the western powers put up only weak resistance against Hitler's expansionist policy. The crisis first erupted in the spring of 1938, and several times in the months that followed Europe seemed to be on the brink of war. Although the British government of Neville Chamberlain was little concerned about the fate of the Sudeten Germans and of Czechoslovakia—the affair being, in Chamberlain's words, "a quarrel in a faraway country between people of whom we know nothing"—the British were aware that they could not remain on the sidelines of a European conflict developing from Hitler's demands on Czechoslovakia. This danger was great, for since 1924 France had been tied to Czechoslovakia through a clear and definite defensive alliance, and Soviet Russia was obligated to support France and Czechoslovakia if they had to defend themselves against German aggression. Hence, the British government's main concern was to prevent a clash by force which would make fulfillment of the alliance commitments by France and Russia an automatic consequence. The British tried to persuade Hitler to be content with autonomy for the Sudeten Germans within the Czechoslovak state, and pressed Czechoslovakia to agree to this concession. But Hitler spurred the Nazis in the Sudeten area to demonstrations which led to clashes with the police; he then declared that Czechoslovakian brutality made further existence of the Sudeten Germans under Czechoslovak rule impossible and demanded complete separation of this region from Czechoslovakia, threatening to back his demand by military action.

At this critical moment Chamberlain decided to fly to Berchtesgaden, where he met Hitler on September 15, 1938. There Chamberlain gave Hitler what he wanted, the Sudeten area, in return for a promise that Germany would refrain from immediate military action. The British and French governments forced the Czechs to accept this solution by threatening to withdraw all support if they refused. But Hitler was still not satisfied; in a second meeting between Hitler and Chamberlain, in Bad Godesberg on September 22, Hitler declared that the procedure envisaged at Berchtesgaden for the German take-over was too slow. The transfer would have to be completed by October 1—if necessary, by military invasion. The deadlock seemed complete, and Chamberlain returned to London with little hope that peace could be maintained. But Mussolini, anxious to avoid war and eager to increase his prestige by appearing as Europe's arbiter, intervened, persuading Hitler to convene a conference at Munich on September 29.

The Munich Conference was a shocking demonstration of the extent to which the methods of international politics had deviated from those envisioned for the new world order at the end of the First World War.

The Munich Conference. *In the front row, Neville Chamberlain, Daladier, Hitler, Mussolini, and Ciano, Mussolini's son-in-law and Italian foreign minister; in the second row, Bonnet, French foreign minister (between Chamberlain and Daladier), Ribbentropp (between Hitler and Mussolini), Alexis Leger, general secretary in the French Foreign Office (between Mussolini and Ciano); as poet Leger is known under the name St.-John Perse.*

Then, the expectation had been that the great and the small nations would have an equal voice. But at Munich, the leaders of the four great European powers—Hitler, Mussolini, Daladier, and Chamberlain—conferred alone; only after all decisions had been made were the representatives of Czechoslovakia, the state most concerned, informed of the agreement by a yawning Chamberlain and a nervous Daladier. Hitler had made one concession; the deadline for the complete occupation of the Sudeten area was postponed to October 10. One may wonder what would have happened if the Czechoslovaks had rejected the Munich agreement and fought, whether then public opinion in Britain and France might have forced these powers to come to the rescue. But the Czechoslovaks and their president, Benes exhausted from endless negotiations and broken promises, felt that they could not risk such a gamble. They gave in; Benes abdicated, leaving the government of the country to men he believed might get along better with the triumphant Nazis.

In an eloquent attack on British foreign policy in the House of Commons, Winston Churchill characterized the Munich Conference as "a disaster of the first magnitude." But his was a lonely voice. Returning from Munich, Chamberlain was received like a victorious conquerer. To the enthusiastic crowds he said, "This is the second time in our history that there has come back from Germany to Downing Street, peace with honour. I believe it is peace for our time." Perhaps no remark shows more clearly the erroneous assumptions of Chamberlain's appeasement policy. Later he tried to defend the Munich agreement by explaining that it gave Great Britain and France time to rearm. But this justification was palpably false. In the year between Munich and the outbreak of the Second World War the gap in armed strength between Germany and the western powers did not narrow; it widened. The elimination of Czechoslovakia freed numerous German forces for service elsewhere, and the substantial military equipment installed in the fortifications of the Sudeten area now fell into German hands. Chamberlain did not put enough energy into the drive for British rearmament to compensate for this increase in German military strength. He regarded Hitler as a great German patriot who wanted only to complete Bismarck's work by uniting all Germans in one national state and would then rule happily and peacefully ever after. Defending the Munich settlement in the House of Commons, Chamberlain said, "There is sincerity and goodwill on both sides."

During the winter of 1938–1939 European politicians were in a euphoric mood. The French signed a pact which provided for consultation in all questions of dispute with Germany and indicated that the Germans could have a free hand in southeastern Europe. The British also expressed their willingness to regard southeastern Europe as a German sphere of interest. The harmony between the western democracies and the Axis powers was somewhat disturbed by Mussolini, who suddenly made loud claims for Nice, Savoy, and Tunisia, but the British recognized the Italian conquest of Ethiopia and hoped to act as mediators between the French and the Italians.

None of the men in control in France and Great Britain was very much bothered by events in Germany showing that Nazi brutality had not abated; in one night all the synagogues were burned and destroyed; the Jews were eliminated from German economic life and deprived of their property. At the beginning of 1939 the British government was convinced that political appeasement could now be strengthened by close economic cooperation between Germany and Great Britain. Chamberlain stated on March 10 that Europe was settling down to a period of tranquillity. Six months later Great Britain and France were at war with Germany.

The End of Appeasement

The event which changed British policy from appeasement to resistance was the incorporation of what had been left of Czechoslovakia into Greater Germany. The Nazis stimulated agitation for independence of the Slovakian region of the Czechoslovak state, and when the Czechoslovakian government took measures to suppress this movement Hitler ordered Emil Hácha (1872–1945), as Benes' successor as president of the republic, to Berlin and forced him to recognize a German protectorate over Czechoslovakia. The next morning, on March 16, 1939, German troops poured over the borders and Hitler entered Prague.

Suddenly British public opinion turned against Germany. This abrupt

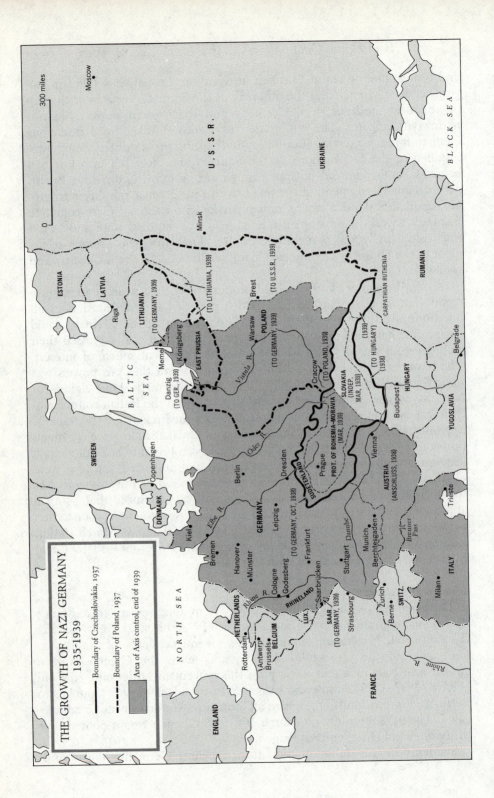

THE GROWTH OF NAZI GERMANY
1935-1939

Boundary of Czechoslovakia, 1937
Boundary of Poland, 1937
Area of Axis control, end of 1939

300 miles

Moscow

U.S.S.R.

BLACK SEA

UKRAINE

RUMANIA

Minsk

ESTONIA

LATVIA

Riga

LITHUANIA

(TO GERMANY, 1939)

(TO LITHUANIA, 1939)

Memel

Königsberg

EAST PRUSSIA

Danzig
(TO GER., 1939)

BALTIC
SEA

Vistula R.

Warsaw

Brest

POLAND

(TO GERMANY, 1939)

(TO U.S.S.R., 1939)

CARPATHIAN RUTHENIA

Belgrade

SWEDEN

Copenhagen

DENMARK

Kiel

Odor R.

Cracow

(TO POLAND, 1939)

SLOVAKIA
(INDEP.
MAR. 1939)

(1939)

(TO HUNGARY)

(1938)

HUNGARY

Budapest

YUGOSLAVIA

Berlin

Dresden

SUDETENLAND

Prague

PROT. OF BOHEMIA-MORAVIA
(MAR. 1939)

Vienna

AUSTRIA
(ANSCHLUSS, 1938)

Trieste

NORTH
SEA

Bremen

Hanover

Münster

Leipzig

GERMANY

Godesberg

Frankfurt

(TO GERMANY, OCT. 1938)

Stuttgart

Danube

Munich

Berchtesgaden

Brenner
Pass

ITALY

Milan

NETHERLANDS

Rotterdam

Antwerp

Brussels

BELGIUM

LUX.

Cologne

Rhine R.

RHINELAND

Saarbrücken

SAAR
(TO GERMANY, 1939)

Strasbourg

Zurich

SWITZ.

Berne

ENGLAND

FRANCE

Rhône R.

Elbe R.

German troops entering Prague in 1939.

explosion of British anger—after so many retreats—is difficult to understand. It has been said that British indignation was aroused because with this action Hitler demonstrated that he was not content with uniting Germans under his rule, and showed that his previous appeals for national self-determination had been hollow pretense disguising a brutal policy of expansion. It is true that the occupation of Czechoslovakia showed up the misconception of those who had presented Hitler as a great German patriot. It is more likely, however, that many people in Great Britain were simply tired of being faced by one crisis after the other, of being bullied. And it appeared unlikely that a Hitler dominating Europe would leave the British empire undisturbed.

Chamberlain now reversed his policy, but because of the pressure of public opinion rather than because he had changed his mind. Indeed, he tried until the last moment to renew contacts with Hitler. Publicly, however, he gave the impression of having abandoned appeasement, and dramatized this shift with a spectacular diplomatic move. His government gave guarantees to the two states which were now most directly in the way of further German expansion and therefore most immediately threatened—Poland and Rumania. Many Frenchmen might have preferred to evade their obligations to Poland, behaving as they had toward Czechoslovakia, but the British support of Poland meant that French retreat was impossible. When Hitler marched his troops into Poland, on the pretext that the Poles had not accepted his demands for restoration to the Reich of Danzig and the Polish Corridor, Great Britain and then France declared war on Germany, on September 3, 1939.

Hitler does not seem to have expected that his action against Poland would result in war with Great Britain and France. Lacking all sense of

The signing of the German-Soviet Pact in 1939. *Behind Ribbentropp, Molotov and Stalin.*

moral values he had no appreciation of the revulsion which his march into Prague had aroused, nor did he understand why powers which had refused to fight for strategically important and relatively accessible Czechoslovakia would undertake war for distant and indefensible Poland. On the other hand, it appears that in his quarrel with Poland, Hitler was not willing to agree to another peaceful settlement. Hitler was convinced that to restore German prestige, damaged by the defeat in the First World War, a successful military campaign was needed. Instead of being exhilarated by the results of the Munich Conference, he had been depressed. He had felt that in yielding to Mussolini's demands for a conference he had let slip the opportunity for a victorious war. Nevertheless, although he did not fear war if his actions against Poland involved him in a conflict with Great Britain and France, he would have preferred these powers to remain neutral, so that the campaign against Poland could be kept localized. He had a trump card which in his opinion would secure British and French neutrality. On August 23, 1939, a week before the attack on Poland, Germany had signed a nonaggression pact with Soviet Russia.

In all the calculations of the policy makers the insuperability of the contrast between Nazi Germany and Communist Russia had been taken for granted. When after the German march into Prague, Great Britain gave guarantees to Poland and Rumania, the British and French governments believed that they would be able to gain Soviet Russia's help in stemming further German expansion. British and French missions were sent to Moscow, but after a period of fruitless negotiations they heard the news that instead of tying Russia to the western powers, Stalin had made a pact with Nazi Germany.

SOVIET RUSSIA DURING THE INTERWAR YEARS

It is a strange reversal of fortunes that in the weeks preceding the outbreak of the Second World War, Soviet Russia's friendship and assistance were eagerly sought by the great European powers. History seemed to have turned full circle. Twenty years before, the statesmen arranging in Paris the future of Europe and of the world had been anxious to move Russia out of Europe. And indeed, during most of the interwar years Russia had remained on the periphery of international events. In the 1930's, with Hitler gaining increasing power, Russia gradually took a more active role in European affairs; but still in 1938 it had been allowed no voice in the arrangements for settling the Czech crisis.

If now in 1939 Russia's support was eagerly sought by both of the antagonistic groups, this was proof of the breakdown of the principles on which the settlements reached at the Paris Peace Conference had been based: the notion that the exercise of democracy, and obedience to international law were requisites for acceptance as an equal partner in international life. Statesmen were aware that in the emergencies of wartime Russia's wealth in natural resources—in foodstuffs and minerals—could become decisive, but the courting of Russia was also an indication that people recognized that the Bolshevik rule there was securely established. During the interwar years European intellectual and scholarly circles had never lacked an interest in the developments in Russia, and the chances of success or failure of the Soviet experiment had been the object of vehement, rather partisan, discussion. But an appreciation of the system in its entirety began only when Russia emerged as a necessary, almost crucial, factor in the European balance of power. Only then did people in the other parts of Europe begin really to grasp what had happened within the Soviet borders and to realize that in the preceding twenty years a new Russia had been formed.

The Rise of Stalin

The developments which led to this situation were inextricably tied up with the fortunes of Joseph Stalin (1879–1953). The 1920's were dominated by the fight for Lenin's successorship, which ended in Stalin's victory; and the 1930's saw the economic and political reorganization of Russia, which

A characteristic product of pro-Stalinist propaganda. A *painting intended to show the close collaboration between Lenin and the young Stalin.*

was accompanied by the purges in which all possible rivals of Stalin were eliminated.

Stalin's rise to supreme power in Soviet Russia owed much to luck. In May, 1922, Lenin suffered a stroke, and from that time until his death on January 21, 1924, he was able to work only intermittently. In his last years Lenin clashed with Stalin but was no longer able to follow up the orders by which he tried to curb him. He inserted in his last will a statement that Stalin was too ruthless and should be removed from office. But Lenin's suggestion was not carried out; many of the Bolshevik leaders were more in fear of Trotsky than of Stalin. They prefered to ally themselves with the solid and plodding Stalin against the brilliant but erratic Trotsky, whom they regarded as an unstable intellectual. Thus, when Lenin's will was read in a meeting of the Central Committee of the Communist party, a great majority—forty against ten—voted to suppress publication of the passage directed against Stalin.

In the early years of Bolshevik rule Stalin held a number of positions, highest in the official hierarchy being that of the people's commissar of nationalities. In this office he was instrumental in effecting the transformation of Russia into the federal Union of Soviet Socialist Republics; in 1922 the members of the Union were Russia, Byelorussia, the Ukraine, and Transcaucasia; to these, subsequently the Uzbek and Turkmen republics were added. The major fields of governmental activity—foreign policy, international trade, defense, economic planning, the organization of justice and education—were under federal control, but within this framework the governments of the various Soviet republics could adjust the school system, the administration of justice, the organization of agriculture, to the particular needs and demands of their regions and citizens.

Stalin was also the general secretary of the Central Committee of the Communist party; it was about this position that Lenin was primarily concerned, because Stalin's ruthlessness seemed to him to endanger the Communist party's coherence and enthusiasm. As general secretary of the Central Committee, Stalin, as Lenin wrote, "concentrated an enormous power in his hands." Understanding of the key role played by the general secretary of the Central Committee of the Communist party requires some acquaintance with the constitutional structure of Soviet Russia. The basic elements of the Bolshevik government were the Councils of the Workers and Peasants. Such councils existed on local, provincial, and regional levels, the higher councils consisting of members deputized by the lower councils. Every two years an all-union congress of councils elected a Central Executive Committee composed of two chambers, one representing the people, the other the governments of the member republics of the Soviet Union. This Central Executive Committee met every year, roughly fulfilling the role of a European parliament. It appointed the Council of People's Commissars, which exercised the highest executive power. The government thus appeared to be a pyramidal structure, rising from a broad base to a small peak. But the twelve people's commissars who directed policy were almost independent of the elected body which had appointed them. One reason was that the infrequent and relatively short meetings of the all-union congress of councils and the Central Executive Committee did not allow true supervision of the people's commissars, who had to make important decisions daily. Another reason was that the people's commissars drew their strength from their prominent position in the Communist party, for it was the party that was the controlling element within the Soviet structure. Legally, every man in the Soviet Union earning his livelihood through productive labor had the right to vote. But the lists of council candidates for whom the people could vote were assembled by the Communist party.

The Communist party was relatively small, comprising not more than 1 per cent of the population; in 1930 the party had 1,192,000 members. In sharp contrast to the pyramidal structure of the council system, the party was directed from above, by a Central Committee of about twenty of the most prominent Communists. While the most brilliant and active of these concentrated on work in a special committee—the Politburo—which laid down the general lines of Russian and Communist policy, Stalin immersed himself in the drudgery of party administration. As general secretary of the Central Committee of the Communist Party Stalin had a decisive voice in determining admission to the party and promotion within its ranks. Since the party determined who could be council candidates, he thus exerted control over personnel throughout the government. The result was that he knew intimately the rank-and-file Communists, and they, being dependent on him for promotion, were willing to accept his leadership.

The firm hold over the party organization represented Stalin's main strength in the struggle to succeed Lenin. His rivals—particularly Trotsky, the hero of the civil war—were much better known. The struggle is generally described as a conflict between adherents of the "idea of permanent revolution," grouped around Trotsky, and advocates of "socialism in one country," who followed Stalin. The conflict between the Trotskyites and the Stalinists intensified in 1923, when the end of inflation in Germany terminated the revolutionary ferment in central Europe. Any hopes that the revolution might spread beyond the Russian borders were crushed. To most Bolsheviks it was almost unthinkable that the Russian Revolution would not spark an international revolution. To maintain an isolated socialist state within a capitalist world seemed impossible. At first Stalin accepted this view. But when—after some hesitation—he had convinced himself of the solidity of the capitalist regimes in the face of Communist attacks, he set his course firmly toward the construction of a new Russian society able to stand on its own. During the Fourteenth Communist Party Congress, in March, 1925, Stalin obtained official approval of the doctrine of "socialism in one country."

Other Bolshevik leaders found abandonment of the idea of world revolution more difficult. Many of them, during long years in exile, had established close relations with extremists in other countries. Stalin had been outside of Russia just once—and then for a few weeks—and had no real acquaintance with social and industrial developments in other countries. Moreover, some of the Bolshevik leaders, such as Grigori Zinoviev, the head of the Communist International, and Karl Radek were motivated by ideological considerations in contrast to the empirical Stalin, who was aware that concentration on an economic transformation in Russia would strengthen his own position since an increasing number of party officials would be needed to direct and control the process.

Opposition to Stalin's policy of "socialism in one country" became pronounced only after it was evident that it resulted in the creation of an immense new bureaucracy. Trotsky, for instance, attacked Stalin because instead of leading to the disappearance of the state, in accordance with Marxist theory, his course of action resulted in an aggrandized bureaucratic machinery. But Stalin's views had become the accepted "line" of the Communist party, and Stalin stamped Trotsky's opposition as antirevolutionary and subversive. In 1927 Trotsky was divested of all his functions and expelled from the party, with seventy-five other leading members of the opposition. Exiled to Siberia, he continued his agitation there. In 1929 he was expelled from Russia, and found refuge in Mexico. Eleven years later he was assassinated by a man unquestionably acting on Stalin's orders.

The defeated in the struggle for Lenin's succession. *Trotsky in exile.*

"Socialism in One Country"

Pursuit of the policy of "socialism in one country" resulted in a major social upheaval accompanied by economic hardship and suffering. The golden age which theoretically was supposed to follow the defeat of capitalism seemed still far away, and the Bolshevik leaders were anxious to emphasize that a truly communist society could become reality only after the capitalist system had been overthrown all over the world; at the moment they were at work to create a system of transition, a socialist society.

The underlying aim of "socialism in one country" was to transform Russia into a highly industrialized state, able to compete with more advanced countries, such as Great Britain and the United States, and capable of putting up a good fight against aggression by capitalist nations. In Russia industrialization also involved a transformation of agriculture, which had to be made more efficient, so that the increasing number of industrial workers in the cities could be fed and a surplus could be produced for export, which alone could provide needed foreign currency. The vast changes had to be accomplished without impairment of the fundamental principle of a socialist regime—control of the state over economic life—and without the help of private or foreign capital. To achieve these aims the Russians devised a method that was entirely novel: the drafting of an economic plan which encompassed all fields of economic activity in all parts of the country. Thus, in the following years Russian life was dominated by the efforts to achieve the goals which were set in two Five-Year

Plans. The first was initiated in 1928, but as the Russian leadership proudly proclaimed, it was carried out in four years, so the second Five-Year Plan could begin in 1932.

During the Second World War, Winston Churchill once asked Stalin whether he had found the stresses of the war as bad as those arising from carrying through the policy of the collective farms. " 'Oh, no,' he said, 'the Collective Farm policy was a terrible struggle.' "[2] The Russian economic planners ordered collectivization of agriculture primarily because it would facilitate the use of modern methods and machines which would increase production. But collectivization was expected also to strengthen the grip of the government over rural life. The somewhat wealthier peasants, the kulaks, who had been favored by Stolypin's reforms and later had flourished under the New Economic Policy, became disenchanted with the Bolshevik regime in the course of the 1920's. Because rationing and fixed food prices made agricultural production unremunerative, many peasants refused to deliver their produce to the cities and limited production to their own personal needs. When the government decided on collectivization, the kulaks regarded this policy as a direct attack on their property rights and on their very existence, and they resisted in all possible ways. They burned collective farms, they destroyed tractors and other agricultural machinery, and when integration into the collective-farm system finally became unavoidable, they slaughtered their animals; almost three million horses and cattle—nearly half of their entire stock—were killed. The government then decided to eliminate the kulaks as a class, and incited the poorer peasants against them, assisting this class warfare with police and military forces. The land owned by kulaks was confiscated; their houses were transformed into clubs or schools, and an estimated two million were deported to remote areas, where they were used as forced labor.

The requirements for modernizing agriculture were important in determining the plans set up for industry. For example, the annual production of tractors increased from 6,000 at the beginning of the first Five-Year Plan to 150,000 at its end. Next to the needs of agriculture those of defense were most influential in shaping the industrialization program. The emphasis was on heavy industry. Large new cities sprang up in the vicinity of coal and iron mines; Magnitogorsk, in the midst of rich mineral deposits in the southern Urals, owed its existence to the Five-Year Plans; at the end of the first Five-Year Plan it had about 65,000 inhabitants; seven years later the population had grown to more than 150,000. The concentration on heavy industry necessarily limited the production of consumer goods; for instance, the Five-Year Plan envisaged a shoe industry which would give each person two new pairs every three years. This paucity of consumer goods meant that

[2] Winston S. Churchill, *The Second World War*, Vol. IV, *The Hinge of Fate* (Boston, 1950), p. 498.

wages could be kept down and that the general standard of living remained low. From the point of view of the planners, the shortage in consumer goods had the advantage that workers were unable to spend all their wages and would place some of their earnings in the state bonds which helped to finance industrialization. The Five-Year Plans were also financed by the profits of the state stores and by taxes, notably a turnover tax, a form of sales tax.

Although Russian pronouncements and statistics tended to paint an exaggerated picture of the success of the Five-Year Plans, the main goals were undoubtedly achieved. Russia was transformed from an agrarian into an industrial country. In 1932, 70.7 per cent of the Russian national product came from industry. In addition, as a consequence of the centralized organization of Russian economic life, private enterprise disappeared almost completely.

The Soviet rulers, as firm believers in the theories of Marx, regarded intellectual achievements as a superstructure resting on the economic system; they attached great importance to intellectuals and their training. They were aware that an industrial society required a large corps of trained personnel—technicians, engineers, doctors, economists, teachers—and that the great bulk of the people ought to have an education which would enable them to handle modern machinery. Hence the Bolshevik regime established schools all over the country to eliminate illiteracy, which at the time of the revolution was widespread; in 1923, 27,000,000 people in Russia still could neither write nor read.

Workers took evening courses to prepare for university study; universities proliferated, emphasizing technical subjects and the natural sciences. With the reduction of illiteracy, publishing activities grew in extent and importance; newspapers and periodicals dispensed knowledge useful for increasing industrial and agricultural productivity, and they also spread propaganda. The Russian rulers recognized that the work the masses were forced to do and the privations they were asked to undergo were made bearable only by the conviction that the end result would be a life safer and better than ever before. The Russian people had to be sure, however, that their leaders were steering toward this goal with utmost speed on the only possible route. Confidence in the state's leaders was emphasized; Stalin was shown to be omniscient and farseeing. What was later called the "personality cult" began to develop.

The years of the transformation into an industrial society have been called Russia's "iron age." In this period life in Russia was very different in spirit from what it had been for a brief time after the Bolsheviks came to power. Daring revolutionary intellectuals like Trotsky and Radek were now replaced by careful bureaucrats and technical experts. The experiments in avant-garde art and literature which had been promoted by Anatoli Lunacharski, commissar for education under Lenin, were now abandoned, and the government required artists to provide easily understandable, realistic representations of the achievements of the Five-Year Plans and of other events showing Russia's progress under Bolshevism. The fight of the militant atheists against religion was continued because the influence of the church formed an obstacle to the modernization of rural life. Free love and divorce, however, were no longer encouraged, as they had been in the first years of Bolshevik rule, and abortions were once again prohibited. It was hoped, however, that after the successful completion of the two Five-Year Plans, the production of consumer goods would be increased and the disciplined monotony which had become customary would gradually give way to an easier and more varied life. Furthermore, on June 12, 1936, there appeared in *Pravda* ("Truth"), the most widely distributed official newspaper, the draft of a new constitution, which seemed to indicate the beginning of a period in which the Soviet citizens would possess enlarged, well-defined rights.

The Purge Trials

The hope that Soviet Russia was entering a period of liberalization was soon destroyed by Stalin's purges, which made him a dreaded absolute ruler, with the secret police his most important and most feared instrument of government. The number of people who became victims of these purges—who were imprisoned, exiled, or executed—runs into the millions. The most prominent among them were condemned in "show trials," the first of which took place in August, 1936, two months after the publication of the new constitution. Best known among the sixteen defendants in this trial were Grigori Zinoviev and Lev B. Kamenev, both former members of the Politburo. The second great trial was staged in 1937. Among the seventeen defendants was Karl Radek, Soviet Russia's leading political writer. Between the second and the third trials there occurred a secret purge of the Russian general staff; its victims included Mikhail Tukhachevski, a hero of the civil war and the Russo-Polish War, and a number of generals. The third and last trial, in March, 1938, was the most sensational; among its twenty-one defendants were Nikolai Bukharin, who had edited the newspaper *Izvestia* ("News") and was recognized as a leading Bolshevik theoretician; Aleksei Rykov, who had been chairman of the Council of People's Commissars, H. G. Yagoda, a former head of the secret police, N. M. Krestinski, a deputy commissar for foreign affairs, and a number of high diplomats. At all these trials the defendants made "confessions," perhaps obtained through pressure. Most of the defendants were condemned to death and executed, and even those, like Radek, who received only prison sentences never reappeared in public life.

In the light of revelations made after the death of Stalin, the purges have

Zinoviev before the purge trials.

usually been ascribed to his abnormal psychology. Undoubtedly Stalin's pathological distrust and suspicion did play a role in the organization of these trials and the cruelty of the punishments meted out to the defendants. Before 1936, and then again after Stalin's death, Bolshevik leaders who recommended a line of policy which the majority rejected were demoted or removed from power; but they were not killed. The use of the death penalty for political opposition was limited to the time of Stalin's reign. Although the manner of procedure against the defendants in the purge trials was determined by Stalin's abnormal mentality, he did have rational cause to fear the influence of these men. Most of them had been prominent under Lenin in the early years of Bolshevik rule. As "old Bolsheviks" they enjoyed prestige. Some of them, like Bukharin, had opposed Stalin's agrarian policy and maintained that agricultural production could have been increased more effectively by working with the kulaks than by eliminating them. These men were probably more popular than the strict bureaucrats and experts—Stalin's loyal followers—who imposed the hardships of the Five-Year Plans.

Most of those who doubted or opposed Stalin's economic policy recommended a change toward greater production of consumer goods, and the occurrence of such a change might have been expected to promote their chances for a successful political comeback. Stalin was unwilling to permit any loosening of controls or any alterations in economic policy, anticipating that the result would be a threat to his position; at the same time, he believed that continued emphasis on heavy industry was made necessary by the international situation. With the rise of the Nazis in Germany, the possibility of war had been greatly increased. Armament production had to be augmented and accelerated, not slowed down. Every possible obstacle to a uniform direction of policy, appropriate to the dangerous situation, had to be removed. This consideration was probably a motive in the execution of Tukhachevski and the other military leaders. Under Tukhachevski the army had developed into an almost independent power factor and Stalin may have wondered to what extent he would be able to rely on the army if his policy was contradictory to the views of the military leaders. Stalin's distrust of Tukhachevski seems to have been fomented by the Nazis, who expected that Tukhachevski's fall would weaken the Russian military organization. Through Eduard Benes, the president of Czechoslovakia, they succeeded in placing before Stalin cleverly falsified documents compromising Tukhachevski. Significantly, the elimination of Tukhachevski and his followers was accompanied by the reintroduction of political commissars into the army.

Stalin's Foreign Policy

In the threatening atmosphere of the middle 1930's, continued economic austerity and a tightening of the reins of government seemed appropriate. But the ruthlessness with which these policies were pursued had a dubious effect on Russia's relations with other powers.

When the Russian leaders had embarked on a policy of "socialism in one country" they were naturally anxious to remain undisturbed by the outside world. They had normalized diplomatic relations with their neighbors in the west and participated in international efforts toward securing peace, including the Kellogg-Briand pact and the Disarmament Conference. Because of Hitler's emphatically pronounced anti-Communism, his rise to power was disquieting to the rulers of Soviet Russia and they began to seek closer ties with countries that might be equally interested in checking Nazi expansionism. After Russia joined the League of Nations in September, 1934, the Soviet foreign minister, Maxim Litvinov (1876–1952), became a chief advocate of strict sanctions against aggressors. In 1935 Soviet Russia concluded with France and Czechoslovakia agreements promising mutual assistance in case of unprovoked aggression. Correspondingly, on orders from Moscow the policies of the Communist parties in western Europe began to change. At the Seventh Congress of the Comintern, in the summer of 1935, the formula was proclaimed which initiated the new policy of the Popular Front: Communists were now willing to cooperate with the leaders of any group—socialist or rightist—which took a line of resistance to the Nazis.

Just when these broad movements of opposition to Nazism and Fascism seemed to be gaining impetus and the Popular Front obtained electoral victories in Spain and France, the occurrence of the Russian purges resulted in renewed doubts among the democratic forces about the possibility of cooperation with the Bolsheviks. The Russians even extended the purges to the various Communist parties outside of the Soviet Union, attempting to eliminate from power those whom they considered allies of the purge victims and to establish as leaders of the Communist parties men of proven loyalty to Stalin. Russia intervened in the Spanish Civil War not only to defeat Franco but also to eliminate the leaders of the left who were not Stalinists. Such developments strengthened the hands of those politicians in Great Britain and France who from the outset—for ideological and economic reasons—had opposed cooperation with the Soviet Union. It was said that a regime which had to take recourse to terroristic measures could hardly be regarded as a stable and reliable ally, and the question was raised of whether the Russian government was any more humane or civilized than the Nazi and Fascist dictatorships. In the negotiations on the Czechoslovakian crisis during the summer of 1938 Great Britain and France cold-shouldered Russia as they steered openly toward appeasement with Nazi Germany.

We do not know whether Stalin ever had much interest or confidence in an alliance with the western democracies. It is certain, however, that the Munich Conference and the appeasement policy of the western powers increased his fear that these states might come to an agreement with Germany at the expense of the Soviet Union, perhaps giving Hitler a free hand to attack Russia. Moreover, Stalin was enough of a Marxist to regard as negligible the difference between capitalist Nazi Germany and the capitalist democracies of the west. Thus, when in the summer of 1939 British and French missions appeared in Moscow, and at the same time the Nazis expressed eager interest in a pact with Russia, Stalin's main interest was to make sure that these various powers did not unite against the Soviet Union. An agreement with Nazi Germany had the advantage that the Nazis were willing to hand over to Russia the Baltic states and parts of Poland, which Britain and France refused to do. Stalin may also have found the single-minded, ruthless Hitler more attractive than the vacillating western statesmen, who until recently had embraced appeasement. Everything points to the conclusion that Stalin favored an agreement with Hitler. If he continued the negotiations with Great Britain and France, the chief reason was that otherwise the western powers, despairing of Russian support, might drop Poland; Russia would then be faced alone by a Nazi Germany strengthened by victory over Poland. In short, the purpose of Stalin's diplomacy was to bring about war between Germany and the West.

Like all the other statesmen of the time, Stalin miscalculated. If Great Britain and France were slow and not very forthright in their approach to Russia the reason was that they believed erroneously that Soviet Russia and Nazi Germany could never come to an understanding. Meanwhile, Hitler had been persuaded by his foreign minister, Ribbentrop, that a German agreement with Russia would intimidate Great Britain and France into

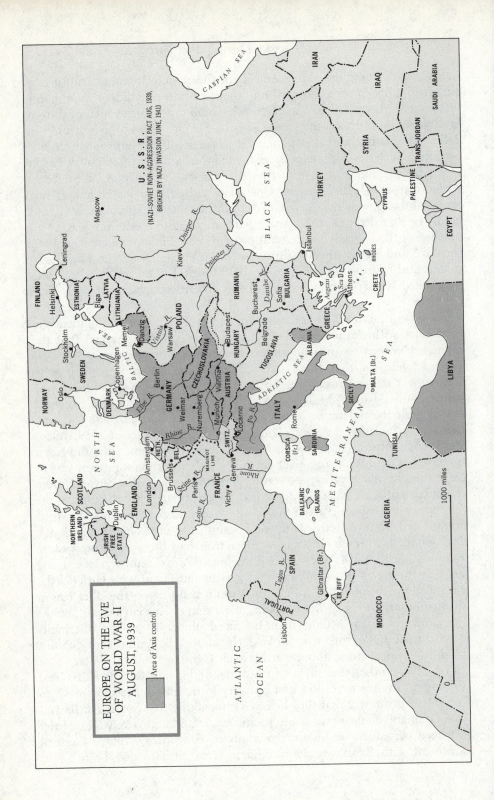

EUROPE ON THE EVE
OF WORLD WAR II
AUGUST, 1939

◼ Area of Axis control

abandoning Poland, so that his forces would have a quick and easy victory. And Stalin believed that the western democracies and Nazi Germany were almost equal in strength and would exhaust themselves in a long and bitter war; Russia—remaining at peace—would emerge as the strongest power on the European continent. The tragedy of the Second World War began with a comedy of errors.

If the war had not broken out over Poland in the summer of 1939, it probably would have been triggered by some other issue. Hitler was straining for control of the continent, and from 1933 on, Europe had been disturbed by crisis after crisis, each more serious than the one before. With everyone living under the threat of an imminent war, the situation had become almost unbearable. Yet when hostilities finally erupted over the German invasion of Poland on September 1, 1939, the public reaction was very different from what it had been at the outbreak of the First World War twenty-five years before. In 1939 there was no enthusiasm, no feeling of liberation. The dreary procession of democratic retreats and defeats, the demonstrated inability to subordinate social conflicts and divergent class interests to the common aim of preserving the basis of freedom had weakened confidence in the strength of the western powers. There seemed validity in the claim of the totalitarian states that they were the wave of the future. Behind the acceptance of the necessity of the war by the people in democratic countries there was a feeling of doom. In the face of terrible defeats, it would require the awakening of a primitive feeling of national pride to shake off this fatalism and to restore hope and confidence.

CHAPTER 42

The Second World War

Winston Churchill entitled the fourth volume of his history of the Second World War, which describes developments from January, 1942, to the spring of 1943, *The Hinge of Fate*, for Churchill saw this period as "the turning point" of the war.[1] Until the end of the summer of 1942 Germany attacked and advanced. Thereafter, the initiative was held by the opponents of Fascism.

Within this general trend of events—the Fascists first on the offensive, then on the defensive—there were movements and countermovements. Thus although the Fascists seemed overwhelmingly superior in the first half of the war, even then their power did receive certain checks, without which the subsequent attack against them could not have been mounted.

THE GERMANS ON THE OFFENSIVE

Until the autumn of 1940 the Germans marched from triumph to triumph. Poland, whose resistance to Hitler's demands had ended the period of appeasement, was eliminated in a campaign of just one month, which provided the first glimpse of the military weapons and tactics which would dominate the conduct of the war. The Germans used their tremendous air superiority to destroy the Polish air force on the ground and then to bomb roads and railroads and interrupt communications so that the Polish troops lost any possibility of movement. There was no such thing as a relatively safe rear. By concentrating an overwhelming force of tanks at certain points the Germans broke through the Polish lines; they then secured their flanks at the breakthrough points and sent the tanks, followed by motorized infantry, streaming into the open countryside, where they turned to the right or left, dividing the enemy forces into isolated segments which were encircled and annihilated one after the other. In the confusion

[1] Winston S. Churchill, *The Second World War*, Vol. IV, *The Hinge of Fate* (Boston, 1950), p. 830.

created by this lightning attack, or *Blitzkrieg,* only the big cities maintained organized resistance. Warsaw was heroically defended, the German answer was a bombardment from the air which reduced it to ruins—the first example of the destruction of a large city by air attack.

On September 27, hardly four weeks after the outbreak of the war, Polish resistance was at an end; and Poland was partitioned between Germany and Soviet Russia. The Russians quickly occupied the eastern half of Poland, which had been promised to them in the German-Soviet treaty, and they also advanced into the Baltic states—Lithuania, Estonia, and Latvia. Thus they gained control of a long stretch of the southern coast of the Baltic Sea. The Germans annexed a large part of Poland and for the remainder created a Polish protectorate ruled by a German government. The delimitation of the German and Russian spheres was settled in Moscow on September 28 in what was called the German-Soviet Boundary and Friendship Treaty.

The "Phony War"

French and British military leaders were slow to learn the lessons of the Polish campaign. They believed that the *Blitzkrieg* tactics had been effective only because of Poland's military weakness and could not be applied against armies of greater power. Although German strength in the west was limited, the British and French had not supported the Poles by an attack on Germany, being satisfied to gain time for building up their forces.

What followed was the period of the "phony war." In the west the

The beginning of the Second World War. *German motorized troops driving into Poland. Note the boundary sign with the Polish eagle which the Germans removed and took along.*

French troops manning the Maginot Line.

enemies confronted each other without engaging in serious fighting. German inactivity lulled the French and British into false security. They placed unjustifiably high hopes on the effects of economic warfare; from the outset they set up a tight blockade to prevent Germany from getting goods from abroad. Because they doubted that the Germans would dare to attack in the west, their measures for strengthening the defenses in France lacked the necessary energy. The Maginot Line was not extended along the Belgian frontier to the coast. The French and British governments felt so secure in the west that their attention focused on other areas. When the Russians invaded Finland in November, 1939, in order to improve their military defense line in the north, the French and British decided to assemble an expeditionary force to aid the Finns. But before this assistance could be sent, the war ended, in March, 1940, with the Finns conceding to the Russians the demanded frontier revision.

Concerned by the British and French interest in this northern area Hitler decided to eliminate the possibility of military action by the western Allies from the north. On April 9 German troops drove over the Danish frontier and occupied Denmark; at the same time they attacked Norway. The Norwegians resisted but were overwhelmed. The German success was due to a brilliantly executed combination of action by naval and air forces and paratroops. The British and French countermeasures were fumbling; troops were thrown in without antiaircraft protection and artillery and were quickly destroyed by the Germans.

From the British point of view the Norwegian defeat had one favorable consequence. A dramatic session of the House of Commons showed that Neville Chamberlain had lost the confidence of his countrymen. He resigned on May 10 and was succeeded by Winston Churchill, who formed a government in which all three parties—Conservative, Liberal, and Labor —participated. Churchill writes that he went to bed that night with "a profound sense of relief. At last I had the authority to give directions over the whole scene. I felt as if I were walking with Destiny, and that all my past life had been but a preparation for this hour and for this trial."[2]

The Opening of the Western Offensive

On the very day this change of government took place, the German offensive in the west began. While the Maginot Line remained quiet, the northern wing of the German armies advanced on a broad front, invading the Netherlands and Belgium. German paratroops seized the Dutch airfields and bridges and made an orderly defense of the country impossible. An air raid on Rotterdam obliterated the center of the city, and on May 14 the Dutch army capitulated after Queen Wilhelmina (ruled 1890–1948) and the government had succeeded in escaping to England. Belgian resistance lasted longer, thanks to British and French support. But the Germans, utilizing the same tactics as in Poland, achieved a breakthrough in the Ardennes and their tanks raced ahead into France, toward Amiens and Abbeville, splitting the defending forces into two parts. The northern part, including the entire Belgian army, most of the British troops in France, and a portion of the French army, was then enclosed in a steadily contracting ring. On May 27 the Belgian King Leopold III (ruled 1934–1951) capitulated with his army. British and French troops were pushed back to the beaches of Dunkerque and evacuated from there. Waiting on the beaches, the Allied forces were subjected to steady bombing from the air. A German tank attack probably would have been disastrous, but Hitler evidently believed that the destruction of the exposed troops could be left to the air force, and kept his tanks back. Nevertheless, the saving of these forces required an immense effort; the miracle of Dunkerque was made possible by the strength of the British navy, under whose protection an endless number of small craft brought the soldiers over the Channel. Between May 27 and June 4, 338,226 men reached England.

The tanks which Hitler did not employ at Dunkerque were used in the attack against the other half of the Allied forces, consisting of the bulk of the French army, which had formed a front along the Somme. Again, the German tanks succeeded in breaking through the defenders' lines. Roads were clogged with refugees; German airplanes strafed people scurrying along, creating panic and confusion. The collapse of communications prevented French airplanes and antitank guns from reaching the front, and the enemy was able to advance rapidly.

On June 14 the Germans entered Paris. The French government had fled southward. In hurried visits, Churchill tried to persuade the French to remain in the war. Prime Minister Paul Reynaud (1878–1966) was willing

---

[2] *Ibid*, Vol. I, *The Gathering Storm* (Boston, 1948), p. 667.

After the Nazi triumph in France. *Hitler with his generals in Compiègne.*

to do so. But with Germans advancing over the Loire and attacking from the rear the Maginot Line, where the last well-organized French military force was stationed, the military leaders declared all further resistance useless and demanded that the government end the war. Reynaud resigned and was succeeded by Marshall Pétain, who on June 17 asked for an armistice. Most of the country was occupied by the Germans; only southeastern France and North Africa remained under French control. In the unoccupied part of France, with Vichy as capital, a French government under Pétain as head of state was established; in the later parts of the war, starting in April, 1942, the directing spirit of this government was Pierre Laval, who expected a German victory and regarded close cooperation with the Nazis as the only possible French policy.

North Africa's freedom from German occupation subsequently proved of great value to the Allied forces, but in the spring and summer of 1940 the French surrender appeared an unmitigated disaster. This impression was reinforced by the establishment under Pétain of a new authoritarian government in Vichy, so that even unoccupied France was absorbed into the antidemocratic camp. There is no doubt that in the shock of defeat many Frenchman shared Pétain's belief that an abandonment of the ideas of the Third Republic, and a new hierarchical organization of society, were desirable. Few remained convinced, with Charles de Gaulle, that France had lost a battle but not the war. "The outcome of the struggle has not been decided by the Battle of France. This is a world war."[3] This statement was part of de Gaulle's first appeal from London, in June, 1940, to form a

[3] Quoted in *The Complete War Memoirs of Charles de Gaulle,* Vol. I, *The Call to Honour,* trans. by Jonathan Griffins (New York, 1955), p. 84.

movement for the liberation of France. De Gaulle had made a name for himself through writings in which he had stressed the importance of tanks and motorized forces in future wars. In the campaign of 1940 he had proved himself as a tank commander against the Germans; he was named under secretary of war by Reynaud on June 6 because he could be relied on to support the prime minister's efforts to keep France in the war. When these proved abortive. De Gaulle escaped in a British plane to London. There he organized the Free French movement, insisting that he alone spoke for France and that France was still a great power. He kept a proud distance from the various governments-in-exile which, after the German occupation of their countries, were set up in London.

The Battle of Britain

On June 10, before the French campaign had ended, Italy entered the war. The Italians had been resentful that Hitler had gone ahead even though they had told him that Italy was not ready for war in 1939. As long as the "phony war" lasted, neutrality seemed appropriate, since it might give Italy a chance to act as a mediator. But as Germany progressed unchecked, Mussolini became increasingly restless. His proud claims of having created a new disciplined and powerful state would seem idle boasts if Italy remained outside the war. For the outcome of the campaign in France, Italy's entry into the conflict was irrelevant. But it presented a serious threat to British communication through the Mediterranean and to the British position in the Near East.

Great Britain was dangerously alone. The German high command was sure that "the final German victory over England is only a question of time,"[4] and plans were made for invading England. But German strategy had always centered on land warfare and the military leaders, including Hitler, felt insecure in planning for a campaign combining naval and land operations. According to the German military leaders a successful invasion first required air attacks to eliminate all serious British resistance. And Göring, the commander of the German air force, gave assurances that his bombers and fighter planes could force Great Britain to its knees.

The German air fleet was superior to the British, although anti-aircraft artillery and the concentration of air squadrons in southern England compensated somewhat for the difference in numbers. The Germans began in July with an attack on airfields and military installations in an effort to destroy the Royal Air Force. And indeed the R.A.F. did lose continuously in strength. Then, at the beginning of September—in a change which is generally considered to have been a crucial mistake—the Germans switched to bombing attacks on London. The decisive days of the "Battle of Britain" were in the middle of

---

[4] From entry dated June 30, 1940, *War Diary of General Jodl.*

After the air raids in London. *Tumbling ruins with St. Paul's Cathedral in the background.*

September, when the British had to put their reserves into the defense of London. The British inflicted heavy losses on the German air fleet; on September 16 alone they destroyed 185 German planes. These blows made the Germans aware that full air protection for a landing operation was unobtainable, and they abandoned their invasion plans. However, they continued night raids on London until November, averaging two hundred bombers on each mission. These had no direct strategic purpose; they were intended to weaken British morale and will to resist. The *Blitz* on London was followed by attacks on other cities; the most devastating being the raid on Coventry on November 14, in which four hundred people were killed and the center of the city, including its historic cathedral, was completely destroyed. At the end of the year London again became the target of an air attack; incendiary bombs were used and many of the city's most ancient monuments, including Guildhall and numerous churches designed by Sir Christopher Wren, were badly damaged or destroyed. But the morale of the people was not broken nor was the production of war materials interrupted. Britain actually managed to produce more airplanes than Germany in 1940. In the Battle of Britain, Hitler had received his first check; he was forced to abandon the plan to achieve quick victory through a direct attack on Great Britain. As Churchill said of the British pilots who were instrumental in this triumph: "Never in the field of human conflict was so much owed by so many to so few."

The Opening of the Eastern Offensive

After the failure to achieve a quick decision against Great Britain, Hitler had to decide on his next move. It was then that the plan of a campaign against Russia began to take definite form. German expansion toward the east had always been Hitler's aim, but he had intended to postpone this enterprise until the western nations had been defeated. However, after the victory in France, Great Britain's aggressive potential seemed negligible, and Hitler concluded that the subjection of Russia could be achieved while the war against Great Britain continued. His hostility toward Russia had been reinforced by the energy with which the Bolshevik leaders had acted after the defeat of Poland, taking immediate possession of those areas which had been defined in the German-Soviet treaty as belonging to the Russian sphere of interest. In a visit to Berlin in November, 1940, the Soviet foreign minister, Vyacheslav Molotov (born 1890), showed that the Russians were by no means willing to give the Germans a free hand in the Balkans. Even earlier, Hitler had ordered the German general staff to work out plans for an attack against Russia; after Molotov's visit he decided to carry out these plans in 1941.

Action against Russia was delayed, however, because in the first part of 1941 Germany was drawn into military campaigns started by the Italians in the Balkans and the eastern Mediterranean. Dissatisfied with the minor role which his country was playing in the European conflict, Mussolini had decided to gain military laurels by attacking Greece. But the Italian troops which moved from Albania toward Greece were not prepared for the valiant resistance they encountered. Instead of the Italians occupying Greece, the Greeks conquered a fourth of Italian-controlled Albania.

The Italian plight in the winter of 1940–1941 was made even worse by defeats inflicted by the British in North Africa, where Hitler finally felt that he had to come to the assistance of his fellow dictator by sending German tanks, under one of the best German tank commanders, Erwin Rommel. But Hitler's main attention was directed toward the Balkans. The Italian difficulties gave him the opportunity to extend German control over this area. He forced Hungary, Rumania, and Bulgaria into alliances with the Axis, and when Yugoslavia refused a similar arrangement, he overwhelmed the country in a quick campaign which he continued into Greece. The Greeks were unable to hold off the Germans, and their country was occupied in a few weeks. Finally, through the daring use of paratroops, even Crete was conquered and in German hands by May 31, 1941. In vain had the British sent support to Greece from Africa.

The resultant weakening of their forces in Africa left the British unable

The Nazi invasion of Russia. *After the Germans had passed.*

to resist Rommel, who drove them back to the Egyptian frontier. The entire area seemed helpless and open to a German onslaught, and it is difficult to imagine what would have happened if Hitler had moved into Egypt, Turkey, and other states of the Near East. But Hitler's target was the Soviet Union. Despite delays caused by the Balkan campaign, he gave orders to carry out the plans for an attack, and on June 22, 1941, German troops marched over the borders of Russia. At the same time the Finns resumed military operations against Russia.

The Soviet rulers had received warnings of what was coming, but up to the last moment they made desperate attempts to avoid a break with Germany. They had no illusions about how precarious their situation would be in case of war with Germany.

At first, the campaign against Russia seemed to lead to a quick and complete triumph, even discounting Nazi exaggeration of the number of Russian prisoners of war taken in the early weeks of the campaign. The Russians conceded after the war that "Soviet strategic theory as propounded by the Draft Field Regulations of 1939 and other documents did not prove to be entirely realistic. For one thing, they denied the effectiveness of the *Blitzkrieg* which tended to be dismissed as a lopsided bourgeois theory."[5] The Russians were surprised by the German use of tank formations for breakthroughs and encirclement. The Germans' air superiority enabled their

[5] This citation is from the Russian official *History of the War* (1960). Quoted by Alexander Werth, *Russia at War, 1941–1945* (New York, 1964), p. 133.

air force to attack Russian airfields and destroy Russian planes on the ground. The Russian debacle was magnified by orders ascribed to Stalin to hold out in advance positions, causing the troops to miss opportunities to retreat before the ring of encirclement was closed. At Kiev, in one such encirclement of Russian forces, the Germans took 175,000 prisoners of war.

By October the Germans were before Moscow and Leningrad, and in a speech on October 2 Hitler announced a "final drive" against Moscow. People began to flee the city. Trains were packed; officials set out in their cars; and although some factories worked day and night to produce anti-tank defenses, or "hedgehogs," which were immediately placed in the roads around Moscow, other factories were evacuated. Doubts grew that the capital could be held.

The official will to defend the city was underlined by an announcement that Stalin was in Moscow. His firmness in this desperate situation muted all criticism and established him in undisputed authority as the supreme military leader. He began to be presented as a second Peter the Great. In newspapers and literature there was a deliberate stimulation of interest in the Russian past, even in tsarist history, and the war came to be called the "Great Patriot War." The Bolshevik leaders wanted the struggle to be seen as an event which concerned not only Communists, but all the Russian people. At the beginning of November, in two great speeches, Stalin invoked Russian nationalism as the inspiration for resistance to the hordes of invading barbarians. By then, the German offensive had lost its impetus, probably less because of the strength of the Russian stand than because of logistical difficulties: the necessary supplies for the tanks, artillery, and men had not kept up with the rapid advance. When the Germans started a second push in November, the Russians were prepared; their embittered resistance, together with an early onset of winter, which severely hurt the insufficiently clad German troops, caused this second offensive against Moscow to fail.

Nevertheless, the Russian situation remained serious. By the end of the campaign of 1941 the Germans had conquered most of the Ukraine, were close to Moscow, and had surrounded Leningrad, which remained under siege for eighteen months. These advances had been bought with very heavy losses—between 700,000 and 800,000 men. The Russians were quick to learn from their defeats. Generals who had been promoted because of their political merits were replaced by brilliant professionals, such as Georgi Zhukov, Semion Timoshenko, and Boris Shaposhnikov. The Russians showed great ingenuity in transporting factories from threatened areas into the safe hinterland of the Urals and Siberia. They were able to accelerate the production of tanks, airplanes, and artillery; and the Russian heavy artillery proved to be superior to that of the Germans. Moreover, supplies from Great Britain and the United States began to arrive on convoys that

AXIS EXPANSION IN THE WEST
1942

Greatest extent of Axis occupation
or control

Areas controlled by Vichy France

ARCTIC   OCEAN

Petsamo

FINLAND

NORWAY

Helsinki

Oslo   Stockholm

SWEDEN   ESTONIA

SCOTLAND   LATVIA

NORTH   LITHUANIA
SEA
DENMARK   Copenhagen
IRELAND   EAST
                                     PRUSSIA
ENGLAND   Hamburg
•Coventry   Berlin   Warsaw
London   NETH.
        Rotterdam   GERMANY   POLAND
ATLANTIC   Brussels
        Abbeville BEL.   CARPATHIAN MTS
OCEAN   Dunkirk LUX.   Lidice
        Amiens   Prague
                Paris   CZECHOSLOVAKIA
        Loire R.   Munich Vienna
                FRANCE   Budapest
Oradour-sur-Glane   SWITZ. AUSTRIA HUNGARY
        Vichy   RUMANIA
        •Bordeaux   Belgrade
                        ITALY   YUGOSLAVIA   BULGARIA
                •Marseilles   ADRIATIC SEA
PORTUGAL   CORSICA   Rome
        Madrid   Barcelona   •Naples   ALBANIA
Lisbon   GREECE
        SPAIN   SARDINIA
•Seville   MEDITERRANEAN   SICILY
ER RIFF   MALTA   SEA
                            (Br.)
•Casablanca   TUNISIA
                ALGERIA
MOROCCO
IFNI

                            LIBYA

0   500 miles

traveled on hazardous sea lanes to Murmansk. These supplies filled the gaps in production that occurred while factories were being moved to safe areas. In contrast to what had happened in Poland, France, and the Balkans, victory in one quick campaign escaped the Germans in Russia.

THE WAR AT ITS HEIGHT

The Global War

At the beginning of 1942 the entire war changed in character. It stopped being a purely European conflict, and became global. To Japanese advocates of expansionism the European struggle seemed to offer a unique opportunity for establishing a Japanese empire in the Far East. Great Britain was unable to intervene, and the German occupation of the Netherlands and France made the Far Eastern possessions of these countries an easy prey. From French Indochina, which they occupied in 1940, the Japanese prepared to move against Burma, the East Indies, and Singapore. The United States, which wanted to help Britain, and in addition had a vital interest in preventing the domination of this area by a single power, opposed these Japanese moves by diplomatic representations and economic pressures. Negotiations conducted in Washington between the two states were unsuccessful, however, and were near collapse when, on December 7, 1941, the Japanese made a surprise attack on the United States fleet in Pearl Harbor, sinking three battleships and severely damaging five others. The next day the United States formally declared war on Japan.

The outbreak of hostilities between Japan and the United States was followed on December 11 by declarations of war on the United States by Germany and Italy. The Axis powers were bound by a treaty concluded in 1940 to assist Japan in case of attack by a state not involved in the European war; it remains strange, however, that Hitler, who had few inclinations to honor treaty obligations, believed that he had to fulfill this one. To declare war on the United States was his personal decision, and his hatred of President Roosevelt, the protagonist of the democratic world, was probably a prime motive. Most of all, Hitler's decision showed that despite the setbacks in Russia he felt supremely confident. His lack of knowledge of American politics also played its role. He seems never to have considered that without this declaration of war, American military action might have focused on the Far East rather than Europe.

Ever since the outbreak of the war in Europe, President Roosevelt had left no doubt that the sympathies of the United States were with those who resisted the onslaught of Nazism and Fascism. In November, 1939, American neutrality legislation had been modified to permit belligerents to buy war materials in the United States, provided they paid cash and carried their purchases back in their own ships. The fall of France in the summer of

1940 stimulated American preparedness; the military budget was raised and conscription was introduced. Moreover, in the same summer Roosevelt gave direct encouragement to British resistance by an arrangement in which, in return for granting the United States a 99-year lease of certain of their bases in the western hemisphere, the British received a number of American destroyers. In a broadcast on December 29, 1940, Roosevelt declared formally that it was the task of the United States to serve as "the arsenal of democracy," and Congress responded by passing in March, 1941, the Lend-Lease Act, which permitted the president to provide war materials to those states whose survival was vital to the security of the United States; after the Nazi invasion of Russia this act was applied also to Soviet Russia. The identity of American and British interests was publicly announced in the Atlantic Charter, a document issued after a meeting between Roosevelt and Churchill on a warship off the coast of Newfoundland in August, 1941. In the Atlantic Charter, the two leaders emphasized that the war must result in freedom, independence, and an improvement in living standards for all peoples. Thus, even before the German and Italian declarations of war on the United States a firm bond tied the United States to Great Britain. On December 22, Churchill and a number of his military advisors arrived in Washington, and except for a trip to Canada he stayed in the United States until January 14, 1942. In the meetings in Washington two important decisions were made, one strategical, the other organizational. It was agreed that a defeat of Hitler was the first goal; the European theater of war was given precedence over the Far East. In addition, a unified command was created: within each of the various theaters of war the British and American troops were placed under a single commander, either British or American. The direction of the strategy of the war was entrusted to a committee, the Combined Chiefs of Staff, in which the outstanding figures were General George C. Marshall (1880–1959), the chief of staff of the army, on the American side, and Sir John Dill (1881–1944) on the British side.

There was never close cooperation in military planning between the Combined Chiefs of Staff and the Russian general staff. On the contrary, the Russians were most reluctant to give information to the British and American military representatives in Moscow. The organizational unification of British and American military effort helped to prevent the delays, frictions, and disorders which usually occur in the conduct of a coalition war; even so, some decisions were reached only after long debates. It was the bond of friendship and respect which existed between Roosevelt and Churchill—together with their interest in and understanding of military affairs—that served to smooth out the difficulties which arose from differences among the generals.

The main issue under dispute throughout the war years was the timing of the invasion of France. The Americans were eager to embark on this enterprise in 1942, the British were probably right in considering such an undertaking premature at a time when the Germans were at the height of their power and the American troops were inexperienced. The British idea of abandoning the plan of a continental invasion in 1942 and substituting a landing in North Africa was appropriate, just as at a later stage the Americans were probably justified in opposing British plans to extend operation in the Mediterranean area by an attack through the Balkan Peninsula—the "soft underbelly of the Axis"—and in insisting instead on invasion of France across the English Channel.

The Turning Point

Although the entry of the United States into the war provided the anti-Fascist powers with a productive capacity which would assure them material superiority, the situation in 1942 was still precarious. It was by no means clear that the American industrial potential could be mobilized before the Fascist states had placed themselves in an almost invincible position—before Japan had gained full control in the Far East and the Axis powers in Europe had driven the British from the Mediterranean and knocked Russia out of the war.

In the first months of 1942, the advance of the Japanese in the Far East was awesome. They took the Philippines from the Americans; they conquered British forces on the Malay Peninsula and by February 15 were in Singapore, where they took sixty thousand prisoners. In combined land and sea operations they overran the Netherlands East Indies, reaching Batavia in March. They occupied Burma, and took Mandalay on May 2. The road to India seemed open to them, and the barriers against their advance into Australia appeared to have fallen.

In Europe the campaigns of 1942 were of crucial importance. Hitler counted on accomplishing in a second Russian campaign what he had not succeeded in doing in 1941. The reserves which he could put into this fight were formidable. For almost a year he had been in control of the entire European continent except for the Iberian Peninsula, and during this period he had organized the continent according to Nazi aims. In the occupied territories of the East the Germans acted as if they were permanent rulers. Many of the inhabitants were removed and resettled, and large landed estates were given to German generals and Nazi leaders. Yugoslavia was divided, with one part forming the kingdom of Croatia, ruled by an Italian prince, and the rest remaining under direct German administration. Bulgaria, Rumania, and Hungary, being Nazi allies, retained their old rulers but were dominated by German-supported parties patterned after the Nazis.

AXIS EXPANSION IN THE EAST
1942

Greatest extent of Axis control

ARCTIC OCEAN

Petsamo
Murmansk

URAL MTS.

Archangel

NORWAY
Oslo

FINLAND

Stockholm
Helsinki
SWEDEN
Leningrad

ESTONIA
Volga R.
LATVIA

DENMARK
Copenhagen
LITHUANIA
Danzig

Moscow
Kuybyshev

Berlin
GERMANY
Warsaw
POLAND

UNION OF SOVIET SOCIALIST REPUBLICS

Prague
CZECHOSLOVAKIA
Kiev
Kharkov

Vienna
AUSTRIA
Budapest
HUNGARY
UKRAINE
Stalingrad

CARPATHIAN MTS.

RUMANIA
Odessa
YUGOSLAVIA
Belgrade
Bucharest

CASPIAN SEA

ITALY
Danube R.
Sofia
BULGARIA
BLACK SEA
CAUCASUS MTS.

ALBANIA
Istanbul
Batum
Baku

GREECE
Ankara

Athens
TURKEY
Teheran

CRETE
Euphrates
SYRIA
Tigris R.
IRAN

MEDITERRANEAN SEA
CYPRUS
Damascus
Baghdad

PALESTINE
IRAQ
Jerusalem

El Alamein
Cairo
TRANS-JORDAN

LIBYA
SAUDI ARABIA

EGYPT
0   500 miles

Norway, the Netherlands, Belgium, and part of France were under German occupation. Puppet governments were installed, which came to be known as Quisling governments, after the Norwegian Nazi leader, Vidkun Quisling.

The conquered countries were forced to place their economic resources at the service of the German war effort and to accept the Nazi ideology. Their cooperation was required in the execution of anti-Semitic measures. This was the time when the "final solution" of the Jewish question was undertaken. Jews from all parts of Europe were taken into custody and shipped like cattle in crowded freight trains to concentration camps, where they met their death in gas chambers. The number of those who were killed —about six million—is almost beyond imagination. And one must add that the policy of the "final solution" was carried out with a ruthlessness and brutality which afflicted its victims before their death with the most terrible sufferings and torture.

Strict controls over the economic life of the occupied countries made it possible to maintain a fairly high standard of living in Germany. Men of the subject countries were conscripted and transported to work in German factories and labor battalions. The propaganda intended to justify these measures emphasized that German arms were defending Europe against Communism and that German domination would usher in a new period in which Europe would be unified. In all the subject countries parties organized in the pattern of the German Nazi party were established, and military units were formed to join in the fight against Communism. Thus when the offensive against Russia started in 1942 Rumanian, Hungarian, and Italian armies, as well as legions of volunteers from all over Europe— even from Spain—fought under the German command.

With the tightening of German controls over Europe, resistance movements arose in almost all of the occupied countries. Originally these movements consisted of isolated groups, such as the remnants of the former political parties, among which the Socialists and Communists had particularly kept some cohesion, or of groups of nationalists, Catholics, and Protestants, who felt that they dishonored themselves if they allowed the brutal and un-Christian behavior of the Nazis to go on without taking some action. In the course of time these various units began to cooperate with one another and combine into coordinated resistance organizations. All these movements worked underground; for several years their activities consisted mainly of giving help and protection to those who, for political or racial reasons, were persecuted by the Nazis; *Anne Frank: The Diary of a Young Girl* (1947) gives a moving portrayal of the existence of a Jewish family hidden by Dutch friends, but in the end found by the Nazis.

Another function of the resistance was the transmission of intelligence, particularly about German military movements; the French were able to maintain secret contacts with Great Britain, and the headquarters of De

Gaulle's Free French movement in London were extremely well informed about developments in France. The various resistance groups kept in contact through secretly printed newspapers, many of a very high intellectual level. They contained not only uncensored news but also lively debates on what the political structure of the occupied countries should be after liberation. The generally accepted aim was a thorough reorganization of political and social life. This demand for radical changes was only partly the result of the importance of Socialists and Communists in the resistance; repudiation of the prewar ruling groups, whose policies had led to defeat and occupation, was general, and contempt for the men of the former ruling circles was intensified by the willingness of many financial and industrial leaders to collaborate with the Germans.

Throughout the occupation, the men of the resistance undertook single acts of sabotage, but the introduction of more elaborate guerrilla operations depended on circumstances. The Germans never succeeded in completely controlling the wild and inaccessible mountain regions of Yugoslavia; Yugoslav military organizations—the Communists under Marshal Tito (born 1892), the royalists under Draza Mihajlovic—remained active, usually fighting the Germans but sometimes fighting each other. In the wide forests and swamps of Russia, units composed of peasants and of soldiers who had escaped German encirclements operated behind the front, substantially damaging the German lines of communications. Resistance armies in Italy and France went into action when the invasion by American and British forces was imminent, contributing considerably to the collapse of German rule in the occupied areas.

Those participating in the resistance constituted a relatively small part of the populations, and they were exposed to great danger up to the end. The German secret police ruthlessly tortured people believed to possess information about underground activities, and the German troops, particularly the fanatic members of the S.S., tried to stamp out sabotage and resistance by brute force. They made arrests in the middle of the night, took hostages and killed them on the smallest provocation, and shot people for the slightest suspicious moves.

The names of Lidice and Oradour are testimonies of Nazi terrorism. In revenge for the assassination of the Gestapo leader Reinhard Heydrich in 1942, the Czech village of Lidice was destroyed; its entire adult male population was killed, the women were placed in camps, and the children, separated from their families and nameless, were dispersed. In the French town of Oradour, in punishment for presumed support of partisans, the men were shot and the women and the children were herded into the church and burned. Because the conqueror's controls were so thorough and brutal, the resistance movement could exert effective pressure on the Nazis only when their reserves became strained and their grip started to loosen.

THE ALLIES ON THE OFFENSIVE

The Reversal of Fortune

Hitler's campaign against Russia in the summer of 1942 seemed to offer the Germans their last opportunity for victory. It was undertaken before the United States could effectively intervene in the war, and at a time when, despite the failure before Moscow, German power was still at its peak. The offensive began in June. It was mainly directed toward the southern half of the Russian front, its purpose being to deprive the Russians of the agricultural areas of the Ukraine, the industrial areas of the Donets Basin, and the oil fields of the Caucasus. The Nazis expected that Moscow and Leningrad, cut off from supplies, would be taken from the rear by encircling movements. The German armies succeeded in penetrating into the Caucasus, but their advance to the Volga was stopped at Stalingrad, and the battle for Stalingrad developed into one of the decisive battles of the war. Stalingrad was strategically important because its conquest would have cut communications between Moscow and the south. Moreover, the name had great symbolic value to both Germans and Russians.

At the beginning of the winter, except for a few buildings on the right bank of the Volga, all of Stalingrad had been taken, and Hitler announced on November 9 that the city was "firmly in German hands." But the Russians resisted obstinately, using heavy artillery from the other side of the

The battle for Stalingrad. *One of the last German airplanes to take off from Paulus' encircled army.*

river. Then they succeeded in breaking through the front north and south of Stalingrad, and by the end of November the Germans, led by General Friedrich Paulus, were no longer attacking the Russians but defending themselves; the army before Stalingrad, 300,000 men strong, was encircled. Hitler forbade any attempt at withdrawal by a breakthrough toward the west, assuring Paulus of provisions by air. But this proved impossible, and slowly but steadily the ring around Paulus' army was drawn closer, until the German forces were reduced to a few isolated groups. On January 31, 1943, Paulus surrendered, with the 123,000 men who were left of his army. Hitler's reaction was an emotional outburst of reproach that Paulus had not committed suicide.

The hole torn in the German front through the encirclement of the army before Stalingrad made the Germans' situation in southern Russia untenable and forced them to draw back. By the spring of 1943 the lines on the eastern front were roughly the same as they had been one year earlier.

In the fall of 1942, while the German military situation was deteriorating in Russia, there was a reversal of fortune in the Mediterranean area as well. In the winter of 1941–1942 the British had succeeded in forcing their opponents back from the Egyptian frontier, but in 1942 Rommel, commander of the German-Italian forces, had pushed the British back into Egypt, where overextended supply lines forced him to a halt. A lull permitted the British to strengthen their position through reinforcements sent by sea around Africa; at the end of October the British Eighth Army under a new commander, Bernard Montgomery, was able to take the offensive. The Battle of El Alamein became the first victory of British troops over a German army in the Second World War. The fighting began on October 23, 1942, with a heavy artillery barrage which opened some holes in the German lines; British tanks penetrated these gaps and forced the Germans to withdraw. The front was small, consisting of hardly forty miles between sea and desert; because of British air superiority and control of the sea, the German supply lines, which ran along this narrow stretch between sea and desert, became unusable, and Rommel's troops were forced back from one position to another, finally from Libya into Tunisia.

While the British were exploiting their victory at El Alamein, a combined force of British and American troops under General Dwight D. Eisenhower landed in French North Africa on November 8. The Americans had yielded to the British insistence that an invasion of the European continent was not feasible in 1942, but some action which would divert German forces from the Russian front seemed necessary, and North Africa was chosen as the site for a surprise invasion. The operation was entirely successful. The French in Morocco offered only token resistance and then transferred their support to the British and Americans. The Germans in Tunisia had to fight not only Montgomery's Eighth Army coming from the south but also the British-American forces coming from the west. Encircled, the German beachhead in Tunisia was eliminated by the middle of May, 1943.

During this same period, the summer of 1943, the Allies were also beginning to make gains in the Pacific theater. In three great sea and air battles—of the Coral Sea in May, of Midway in June, and of the Solomon Islands in August—the Japanese fleet was crippled, and further advances toward the south were checked. The British succeeded in bolstering the defenses of India, and Chinese resistance on the Asian mainland remained alive. Despite amazing conquests, Japan was still enclosed in a ring of hostile forces. By the end of the summer the offensives of Japan and the Axis forces had been halted and the initiative was held by the anti-Fascist coalition.

Germany Before Surrender

Now the outcome of the war was inevitable. The American industrial machine was in full gear and was producing planes, ships, and tanks at a rate which would have seemed impossible at the beginning of the war. The Russian factories which had been transported into the Urals and Siberia were working to capacity. British war production increased steadily because air superiority gained with American help meant protection from sustained German air attacks. Now it was Germany that suffered from steady bombings; by the end of the war most of the larger German cities were in ruins. Clearly the decisive factor in warfare had become superiority in weapons and equipment, based on industrial mass production. Even Hitler recognized this fact and in the final stages of the war expected a favorable outcome only from new miracle weapons. But the guided missiles, the V-1 and the V-2 rockets which Germany was able to put into use in 1944, were of limited effectiveness, and work on jet engines had not been completed when the war ended.

For the Germans, the sole rational hope for victory lay in the possibility of breaking up the coalition which was closing in on them from all sides. The relations of the United States and Great Britain with their Russian ally had been troubled from the start. When the Germans invaded Russia in 1941, Britain and the United States promised to give the Soviet Union all possible support, and indeed the supplies sent there were of crucial importance in maintaining Russian resistance in the critical first years of the German-Russian struggle. But the Russian leaders did little to publicize this outside help among their people; in their public statements about their allies they blew hot and cold. Their main interest was to promote a "second front," an Allied invasion of western Europe. Sometimes the Russians accused Britain and the United States of timidity and lack of energy in their pursuit of the anti-Fascist war; sometimes they praised them—depending

The Yalta Conference. *Churchill, Roosevelt and Stalin with their foreign ministers—Eden, Stettinius, Molotov—behind them.*

on what approach seemed more likely at the moment to accelerate the opening of this second front.

Relations were further troubled because the Russians were unwilling to recognize the governments-in-exile, particularly the Polish government. They wanted to avoid any commitments which might affect the settlement of frontiers after the war. In eastern Europe they supported only the resistance movements led by Communists. When in January, 1943, after the successful landing in North Africa, Churchill and Roosevelt met in Casablanca, one of their purposes in demanding from Germany "unconditional surrender" was to dispel Russian fears that the western powers might make a "deal" with Nazi Germany at the expense of the Soviet Union. At the meetings of Roosevelt and Churchill with Stalin in December, 1943, in Tehran and in February, 1945, in Yalta, the discussion was largely confined to problems of strategy; statements about postwar boundaries and peace plans were so vague that the lack of any definite agreement on these issues between Russia and the western powers was obvious.

Nevertheless, there was no real reason for the Nazis to hope that the anti-Fascist coalition could be broken up before Germany was completely defeated. Neither the Russians nor the western powers were willing to negotiate as long as Hitler was in power. Germans with political insight believed that better peace terms or a separate settlement with either the West or the East might be obtained if Hitler was removed. The result was a conspiracy by socialists and liberals, high civil servants and generals, which culminated on July 20, 1944, in an attempt on Hitler's life. But the attempt failed; just a moment too soon, Hitler moved away from the place where a bomb exploded. The war was thus destined to last for almost another year.

Why did the German people go on fighting though their situation was clearly hopeless? Obviously the Allies were unwilling to negotiate with Hitler and the men around him, so for the Nazi leaders there was no alternative to struggling on. German troops on the eastern front fought willingly and obstinately until the surrender because Nazi propaganda had drummed into them a passionate hatred of Bolshevism, and they feared the retribution which might be exacted for what had been done to the Russian people; a Russian invasion and occupation of German soil seemed worse than death.

Although the decline in the German fortunes after 1942 weakened the hold of Hitler and of Nazism over the minds of the German people, a corps of loyal Nazis survived until the end. Members of the S.S. particularly stayed firmly tied to the Nazi regime and their military units remained a valuable fighting force, which was thrown into combat at critical points until the final weeks of the war. Moreover, many of the teen-age members of the Nazi youth organization, who were conscripted in the last winter of the war, continued to regard Hitler as a man of destiny. The fanaticism of the S.S. guaranteed to the Nazi rulers an instrument for control by terror, and toward the end it was primarily fear and terror that kept the German people in the war. Himmler and his police imprisoned and tortured everyone suspected of holding anti-Nazi opinions or defeatist views. Such crimes—judged in Nazi-staffed People's Courts from which there was no appeal—were punished by death. The ruthlessness of the S.S. police increased after the attempt on Hitler's life. Entire families of persons suspected of political crimes were placed in custody. There was a grisly report in the last days of the war about corpses of soldiers by the hundreds dangling from the trees of one of Berlin's streets because they had absented themselves from their military units.

Organization of resistance to the Nazi rule was impeded only by the thoroughness and the terror methods of the police but ironically also by Allied bombing attacks. The saturation bombing of German cities disrupted communications and thereby strengthened the control of the Nazi rulers, who had priority use of roads, railroads, telegraph, and telephone. In coping with civil disasters, the Nazis made certain that water and food were given only to those who had appropriate identification papers. The Nazis were in charge of evacuating people from bombed quarters, and for weeks the whereabouts of the evacuees might be unknown even to close relatives and friends. The Nazi leaders and the Nazi apparatus alone maintained awareness of the situation as a whole; for the rest of the population life became atomized.

Even though the end seemed in sight in the spring of 1943, after the victories at Stalingrad and in North Africa, the military operations of the last two years of the Second World War were bitterly fought. Severely mauled, the German war machine was still formidable, and the Japanese still controlled a vast area of great natural resources and great defensive strength. A serious Allied defeat might have raised a cry for negotiations with the enemy, which would inevitably have been accompanied by all the difficulties involved in gaining cooperation among members of a coalition.

The Overthrow of Mussolini

The first of the Axis powers to collapse was Italy. After the defeat of the Germans in Tunisia the American-British forces, now in control of air and sea in the Mediterranean, landed in Sicily, and soon conquered the island. During the Sicilian invasion, on July 25, 1943, Mussolini was overthrown by a group which included leaders of the anti-Fascist underground, some prominent Fascists, and the military high command. Although the new government under Pietro Badoglio (1871–1956), a military man, officially declared it would continue the war, secret negotiations for an armistice were started immediately. The Nazi leaders were prepared for such an event. When the armistice was announced on September 8, German tank divisions closed in on Rome and plans for an Allied landing on the beaches near Rome had to be abandoned as too risky. During the winter the fronts stabilized between Rome and Naples; even the landing of Allied troops in Anzio did not lead beyond the formation of a beachhead. Central and northern Italy remained under Axis control.

After being overthrown Mussolini had been imprisoned, but German paratroopers succeeded in liberating him. He was induced by the Germans to establish a Fascist government in northern Italy, where he proclaimed that, free from conservative and monarchist restraints, he could now pursue the original Fascist ideas of social reform. But actually his government called the Republic of Salò after the small town where some of its offices were installed, was controlled by the Germans. It was the Germans who insisted on holding trials at Verona for six Fascist leaders who had participated in the overthrow of Mussolini, among them his son-in-law Count Ciano. They were condemned to death and executed.

The End of the War in Europe

The collapse of Fascism did not end the fighting in Italy, but it had a great moral effect, spurring anti-German activities all over Europe, and in addition was of military significance for all the theaters of war. The Allies could give more effective support to the partisans fighting in Yugoslavia; German manpower resources became severely strained because the

Derailment of a train. *The work of the French resistance.*

Italian occupation troops in the Balkans now had to be replaced by German forces. Moreover, the necessity of sending German tank divisions from the Russian front to Italy in July, at the time of the overthrow of the Fascist regime, had its impact on the eastern theater. The Germans were then undertaking another offensive, their last, in the east, in the center of the Russian front. But the Russians, in a counteroffensive, forced them back on a broad front, reaching the Dnieper and reconquering Kiev in November, 1943.

From this time on, the Allies held the initiative entirely, and in 1944 they advanced everywhere. The Russians continued to attack throughout the winter and by the beginning of the summer of 1944 were driving on to the borders of Poland and Rumania. By the end of the summer they had reached East Prussia, forced Finland out of the war, and shifted the chief weight of their attack to the southern part of the front, where they brought about the surrender of Rumania and Bulgaria. The Russian armies thus were approaching the frontiers of Nazi Germany from the southeast as well as from the east, their advances facilitated by the increasing pressure which Great Britain and the United States were able to exert.

The stalemate on the Italian front was broken; Rome and Florence were taken, so only northern Italy remained in German hands. And Greece was liberated.

The decisive accomplishment, however, of the United States and Great Britain in 1944 was the invasion of western Europe. On June 6, 1944, American and British forces crossed the English Channel and established beachheads on the Normandy coast. The success of this daring operation was primarily due to the complete Allied domination of the air, which largely

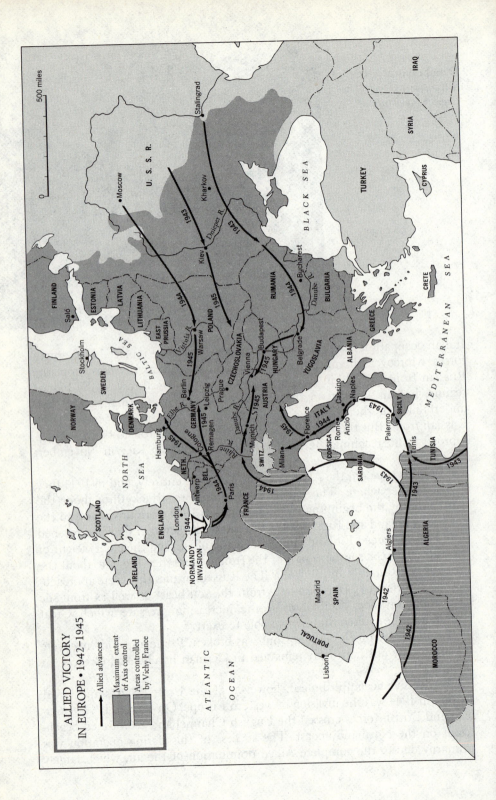

ALLIED VICTORY
IN EUROPE · 1942–1945

Allied advances
Maximum extent
of Axis control
Areas controlled
by Vichy France

500 miles

ATLANTIC

OCEAN

IRELAND

SCOTLAND

ENGLAND
London

NORMANDY
INVASION
1944

NORTH
SEA

NORWAY

SWEDEN
Stockholm

Saló

FINLAND

BALTIC SEA

ESTONIA

LATVIA

LITHUANIA

EAST
PRUSSIA

DENMARK

NETH.
Antwerp
BEL.
Paris
FRANCE

Hamburg
Bremen
GERMANY
Cologne
Remagen
Leipzig
Berlin
Elbe R.
Prague
Rhine R.
1944
SWITZ.
Milan
Munich
Danube R.
AUSTRIA
Vienna
1945

CZECHOSLOVAKIA

POLAND
Warsaw
Vistula R.

U. S. S. R.

Moscow

Stalingrad

Kharkov

Kiev
Dnieper R.
1943

1944

1945

Budapest
HUNGARY
1945

YUGOSLAVIA

Belgrade
1944

RUMANIA
Bucharest
Danube

BULGARIA

BLACK SEA

TURKEY

Florence
ITALY
1944
Rome
Cassino
Anzio
Naples
1943

CORSICA
1943

SARDINIA
1943

SPAIN
Madrid

PORTUGAL
Lisbon

ALBANIA

GREECE

CRETE

CYPRUS

SYRIA

IRAQ

MEDITERRANEAN   SEA

Palermo
SICILY
1943
Tunis
TUNISIA
1943

Algiers
ALGERIA
1943

MOROCCO
1942

1942

frustrated German efforts to reinforce and supply their front lines. Moreover, the landings were protected by the heavy guns of the British and American ships, their fire directed in accordance with the excellent information about the German positions provided by the French underground. Artificial harbors brought over from England solved the problem of establishing a continuous stream of supplies for the invading troops—a problem which had appeared to stand in the way of any landing on a great scale. Nevertheless, it was a difficult operation which had been meticulously planned and brilliantly executed under the supreme command of General Eisenhower, with the British General Montgomery and the American General Omar Bradley as field commanders.

The hours after the initial waves of American and British troops had landed on the beaches were critical. But the German military leadership proved to be uncertain and faulty. The German generals could not agree on whether to defend the entire coastline or to permit the Allies to move into the interior and draw them into a battle while they were still relatively weak. Moreover, at the crucial moment Hitler refused to allow the employment of the German tank reserves because he was convinced that the landing in Normandy was a feint and that a stronger force would attack elsewhere on the coast. Once landed in strength, the Allies were able to effect a breakthrough with their tanks and to fan out in the rear, driving the Germans to retreat. By September, the liberation of France and Belgium was nearing completion, and the Allied armies were establishing themselves along the former German frontiers, where they were forced to stop because supplies were running short. A question which has been raised but can never be answered is whether the war might have been ended in 1944, if the Allies, instead of advancing on a broad front had kept their northern wing back and given all their supplies to the advancing tank forces of Patton on their southern wing, which then might have crossed the Rhine and penetrated into southern Germany.

As it was, a further campaign in 1945 was needed. Before the Allies could resume their advance in the west, Hitler ordered a last German offensive, with troops and tanks brought together from all parts of the front. In December, 1944, the Germans attempted to break through the center of the American-British line in the Ardennes. On the first two days of their attack the Germans advanced quickly and inflicted heavy losses upon the Americans. Moreover, the initial German success shook Anglo-American morale because it seemed to demonstrate the illusory nature of the assumption that the war was almost over; the alliance with Russia rose in value. But after moving forward two days the Germans were halted; the western allies were able to regain the initiative, and in two weeks of fighting the German armies were pushed back to the line from which they had started. German losses in men and particularly in tanks were so severe that

Germany in defeat. *Tanks entering Magdeburg near the Elbe where Russian and American troops met.*

probably the effect of the "Battle of the Bulge" was to shorten the war. To relieve the pressure on the Allies on the western front, the Russians resumed the offensive in Poland early in January, and by the end of February they had driven the Germans out of Poland and were within fifty miles of Berlin. The British and American forces were able to mount an offensive in February, and on March 8 the American First Army crossed the Rhine at Remagen, south of Bonn. While the Germans were still fighting desperately in the east, the Allies in the west were mainly conducting mopping-up operations. On April 26 Russian and Allied forces met at the Elbe River. Three days later the German troops in Italy surrendered. On April 30, with Russian troops converging on Berlin from all sides, Hitler committed suicide in his bunker in the center of the city. With Hitler's death, German resistance ended. The German military commanders surrendered unconditionally on May 7 in Rheims to Eisenhower and one day later in Berlin to Zhukov, the Russian conqueror of Berlin.

The complete defeat of the German military forces after their series of stunning victories has raised many questions about the nature of Hitler's military talents and leadership. German generals, anxious to maintain the prestige of the German general staff, have claimed for themselves the credit for all the successes, while putting the blame for the defeats on Hitler. Their explanation is too simple. Hitler rightly emphasized, contrary to traditional military thought, the importance of tanks and airplanes in modern warfare. He made certain that due attention was given to the construction of these weapons and to training in their use. Unlike many of his generals, Hitler was aware of the daring ways in which these new weapons could be employed, and he took an active part in the planning of the successful Norwegian and French campaigns of 1940, which showed the possibilities of the modern *Blitzkrieg*. And Hitler's strategic judgment was not much worse than that of his generals. He was undoubtedly right when, against their advice, he insisted on defending an advanced front line in Russia during the winter of 1941–1942; retreat would have brought certain disaster. But Hitler lacked technical training and the patience for logistic details; he was inclined to plan and order operations without taking such factors as supplies and communications fully into account. He relied on his intuition, particularly after the early successes of the German army had confirmed his own and his followers' faith in his supreme military talents. His intuition, however, played him false at two critical moments: in 1940, when he refused to use his tanks against the encircled British army at Dunkerque; and in 1944, when he believed that the invasion in Normandy was a feint and reserves had to be kept back to repulse a landing elsewhere. But there were other signs of deterioration in Hitler's military leadership during the last three years of the war. Confident of his intuition and unable to grasp fully the technical difficulties involved in fighting in Russia or in the desert, he regarded each reverse as the fault of cowardly or treasonous subordinates; he denied his generals any freedom of action and reserved all decisions, even at the local level, for himself. By prohibiting withdrawals he sacrificed troops which could have been saved. He lived shut off in his headquarters, avoiding all encounters which might deter him from indulging in his strategic daydreams. Because he seldom visited the front and the bombed German cities, he lost contact with the crude reality of totalitarian war. In the final months he gave orders to armies which did not exist or existed only on paper. It seems that not until April 22, when he was informed of the failure of S.S. troops to attack the Russians, did he realize the hopelessness of the situation and decide to stay in Berlin to the end.

One of the last scraps of news Hitler received was of the end of his

The commanders of the British, American, Russian, and French armies. *Montgomery, Eisenhower, Zhukov, Lattré de Tassigny in Berlin after the Allied victory.*

fellow dictator, Mussolini, on April 28. When the German army in Italy surrendered, Mussolini and his mistress had tried to escape to Switzerland, but at Lake Como, near the Swiss border, Italian resistance fighters caught and shot them. Then their bodies were brought to Milan, and hung head downward in the Piazza Loreto. The news of Mussolini's death confirmed Hitler in his decision to commit suicide. At this last moment he married his mistress, Eva Braun, and then dictated a long verbose testament which repeated the usual accusations against "international Jewry"; having poisoned his favorite dog so that it would not have to live with another master, he shot himself and together with Eva Braun, who had taken poison, was burned. The facts of Hitler's melodramatic end are well proven.

The Fall of Japan

The German surrender made it possible for the British and Americans to concentrate their final effort on the Far East. In May, 1945, when the war in Europe ended, Japan found itself in roughly the same position in which Germany had been five months before. By the beginning of May, just before the monsoon season would have forced a halt in military operations, British, Indian, and Chinese troops under the command of Lord Louis Mountbatten, reconquered Burma in a difficult and risky operation; most of the supplies had to be brought in by air, and more than 200,000 engineers and laborers were employed in building the airfields and roads needed to maintain the impetus of the advance.

A similar success was registered by the Americans in the Philippines. Their operations to recover these islands had started in October, 1944. In a brilliant strategic stroke the Americans passed up the most southern Philippine island, Mindanao and began their offensive with an operation against the central Philippine island of Leyte. The landing there on October 20 was made possible by a naval victory in Leyte Gulf, which severely crippled the Japanese air force and eliminated the Japanese fleet as a factor of military importance. The battle was of great significance for naval history, demonstrating that the time had passed when victory at sea could be decided by encounters among heavy battleships. At Leyte Gulf aircraft carriers, airplanes, destroyers, and torpedo boats were the chief instruments of destruction. The defeat of their navy prevented the Japanese from getting supplies to their troops in the Philippines, and the American forces under General Douglas MacArthur (1880–1964) proceeded without setback to victory in the islands.

Having gained control of the Philippines, the Americans could advance to Iwo Jima and Okinawa, islands closer to Japan, which might serve as bases for a direct attack on the Japanese mainland. Well aware of the strategic importance of these two islands, which formed their homeland's outer line of defense, the Japanese resisted tenaciously, and the fighting was sharp and bloody. However, in the middle of March, Iwo Jima was conquered, and on May 21, two weeks after the surrender of Germany, Sugar Loaf Hill, the key to the Japanese position on Okinawa, was taken.

Japan was now subjected to continuous intensive bombing by American planes. The loss of shipping resulting from these air attacks was fatal to the Japanese war effort, for Japan was dependent on imported coal, oil, and food. Recognizing that their situation was hopeless, the Japanese were ready to surrender; their decision was accelerated on August 6 and 8 by the dropping of two atomic bombs, one on Hiroshima and one on Nagasaki, which burned out more than half of these cities, killed 130,000 people, and injured an equal number. Japan accepted the Allied terms of surrender on August 14. On September 2, 1945, the Second World War officially came to an end on the deck of the battleship *Missouri* in Tokyo Bay, as the Japanese signed the articles of surrender in the presence of General MacArthur.

The decision to drop the atomic bomb aroused a dispute which is still going on. Scientists had counseled against its use because of its terrifying destructive power. An initial explosion of the bomb on a deserted island, which would have demonstrated its efficacy to the Japanese, would have been more in line with American ideas about morality and law in international relations. Yet, when the decision was made American leaders were not aware of how near Japan was to surrender, and believed that heavy fighting was still ahead. It is perhaps instructive that the last military action in the Second World War demonstrated that, as devastating as the war had been, the limits of destruction which modern technology could achieve had not yet been reached.

CHAPTER 43

The New Setting of Political Life

THE SECOND WORLD WAR, which began in September, 1939, with the invasion of Poland by German forces, had been brought to a close nearly six years later when an American airplane dropped an atomic bomb on a Japanese city. The way the war ended clearly demonstrated that Europe had been absorbed into a much more extended political system, embracing the entire globe, and that science and technology had become dominant in the development of human affairs. These two phenomena—the evolution of a global political system and the attainment of scientific achievements of a revolutionary character—were intimately linked. A close interconnection of the nations of the world could never have been reached without the technical innovations based on the discoveries of the scientists. Science and technology had created an entirely new setting for the forms of political life and the conduct of political affairs.

THE SECOND INDUSTRIAL REVOLUTION

The proper position of a scientific discovery in a chronological historical account is often difficult to determine. The time at which the scientist makes his discovery may be distant from the period in which its full significance for the structure of the scientific world view becomes evident and still more remote from the point where a realization occurs of the practical application which industry can make of such a discovery. But modern warfare has shortened the distance between scientific discoveries and their practical applications; money, manpower, and raw materials are made available for any experiment which may be of some use in a war effort. Hence, the two world wars became powerful engines accelerating the transformation of the external conditions of life.

That such a transformation was underway was obvious before 1914. In the nineteenth century the decisive steps had been taken for the production and harnessing of new sources of energy: research on the nature of electricity, the realization of the usefulness of gas and oil as fuel, and invention of the turbine and the internal-combustion engine.

Thus, scientific discoveries and technological innovations led to the creation of vast new industries centering on electricity and on chemicals. In the later part of the nineteenth and the first decade of the twentieth century, these industries transformed in a startling way both everyday life and the structure of the European economy. Houses and streets were illuminated by electric lights; advertising made use of brilliantly lighted billboards that often towered over the cities. Chemical fertilizers increased the yields from soil which had lost much of its richness over centuries of planting and replanting. New medicines and new vaccines began to limit the spread of dread diseases such as syphilis, smallpox, and rabies.

The First World War accelerated research and development in the chemical industry. The most important consequence of wartime needs was probably the discovery that atmospheric nitrogen could be made into ammonia, which is an essential ingredient both for the manufacture of explosives and for fertilizers. Their production was no longer dependent on imports from those countries—primarily Chile—which possessed deposits of natural sodium nitrates. Actually, without the industrial production of sodium nitrates, Germany could not have carried on the war for a great length of time. The chemical industry also benefited from the challenge to create substitutes for goods which could not be produced during wartime because of difficulties in obtaining raw materials; the manufacture of plastics and artificial yarns steadily expanded after the war.

The First World War also exerted a great impetus in the areas of transportation and communication. A revolutionary change already had begun to take place in the decades before the First World War. Although, technically, ocean travel remained much as it had been for a century, the luxury offered to first-class passengers in the period before 1914 reached a high point. A glimpse of the opulent life on the great ocean-going liners can be gained from descriptions of the sinking of the *Titanic* which, on its maiden voyage in 1912, raced to obtain the blue ribbon for the speediest Atlantic

The first flight of an airplane. *The Wright brothers near Kitty Hawk in 1903.*

Marconi in 1901 with instruments for wireless reception.

crossing and crashed into an iceberg. The two inventions which were starting a revolution in transportation before the First World War were the
automobile and the airplane. Before 1914, automobiles were not yet in
wide use, but they had become the preferred mode of transportation of the
rich and powerful and could be seen on the roads. Airplanes were still in
a developmental stage, although great strides had been made since 1903,
when the brothers Orville and Wilbur Wright had been able to keep their
flying machine in the air for 59 seconds at Kitty Hawk, North Carolina.
The potential of aircraft was strikingly demonstrated by the flight of the
Frenchman Louis Blériot over the English Channel in 1909. In the field
of communication, telegraph and telephone, of course, had been in use
since the second half of the nineteenth century, but new developments
were ushered in by Marconi's sucecssful experiments in wireless telegraphy
in 1895.

The impact of the First World War on developments in the fields of
transportation and communication differed. Warfare was not yet motorized; tanks made their first appearance only in the final phase of the
conflict. Larger military units, if not on foot, were transported by railroad;
smaller groups, however, particularly officers, moved around in automobiles;
the resulting increase in automobile construction prepared the postwar
expansion of the auto industry. In the case of the airplane and the radio,
the war was of decisive importance in effecting a quick transition from the
experimental stage to general use. Because of its role in the war the great
possibilities of airplane transportation became recognized. Passenger service
was installed between London and Paris in 1919, and between Amsterdam
and London a year later. Soon all larger European cities had airfields and
were connected by scheduled commercial flights. Nevertheless, in the public
mind there remained something dangerous and romantic about fliers and

flying, and no other event in the 1920's caught the imagination of the world as did the daring and lonely flight to Paris of Charles Lindbergh in May, 1927—the first crossing of the Atlantic by air in an eastward direction. While Lindbergh's achievement dramatized the possibilities of air travel, the beginning of regular transatlantic air service was delayed until more than ten years later, to the eve of the outbreak of the Second World War.

Once the First World War had proved the varied applicability of wireless communications, first amateurs and then experts began to experiment in this field and financiers invested heavily, leading to the development in the 1920's of a radio industry. Sensitive receiving instruments replaced primitive earphones; radio stations presented programs lasting throughout the day. Every European state had a broadcasting company working under government control, and international conventions established the wavelengths which each country was entitled to use. In 1927 wireless-telephone service between England and America was inaugurated.

The new means of communication diminished the distance which in the previous century had separated private life and the world of politics and business. With voices from radio present in the home the individual was subjected to constant demands from the outside world. Powerful propaganda efforts had been exerted during the First World War to keep spirits from sagging on the home front—wherever he went the citizen encountered posters urging service in the army or the buying of war bonds, or warning about enemy spies. After the war the technical devices of propaganda were taken up by advertisers in print, on billboards, in the cinema, and on the radio.

The war had revealed that the human mind could be influenced and patterned; it had undermined the previously prevalent view that feeling and action are controlled by reason, and had shown the strength of appeals to the emotions and basic drives. These insights and observations stimulated an increasing concern with psychology, which developed on two levels after the First World War. At one level was a sophisticated interest in the views and theories which psychology and medical science had developed. Characteristic was the rise to fame of Sigmund Freud, who had made his discoveries about the power of the unconscious at the beginning of the century in Vienna. In the 1920's his views—and those of his pupils (subsequently his adversaries), Alfred Adler and Carl Gustav Jung—were widely discussed, and permeated the views of man presented in novels and plays. At the other level was a practical concern with psychology which inquired into man's reactions to external stimuli and the possibility of conditioning human behavior, as investigators tried to find the psychologically most effective means of mass control.

The changes in man's surroundings brought about by science, technology, and industry created new possibilities in the conduct of public affairs. But

The first television camera in 1929.

to what extent they were realized depended on the particular situation in each country, especially on the strength of its political tradition. Although the technique of radio "fireside chats" contributed to the popularity of Franklin Delano Roosevelt, its imitation by Doumergue in France was regarded as a sign of arrogance and authoritarianism and played a role in the overthrow of the Doumergue government. It was natural that those political movements which arose in opposition to the established political structure were most ready to use new political techniques. Mussolini and Hitler both stressed that they were leaders of modern movements. Mussolini liked to be photographed piloting an airplane; Hitler was seen frequently in his Mercedes Benz. In the western democracies there was much admiration for the courage of Neville Chamberlain when in September, 1938—in order to meet Hitler in Berchtesgaden—he entered an airplane for the first time in his life, with an umbrella on his arm. But the Nazis and Fascists considered Chamberlain's reluctance to use modern means of transportation contemptible—a sign of the backwardness of the democracies.

Without the existence of modern techniques Hitler's rise to power would hardly have been possible. His appearance during election campaigns in every part of Germany, in big cities, small towns, and villages, could be accomplished only by means of airplanes and motorcars, and his ubiquitousness served as proof that the new Nazi party had greater vitality and strength than the other old parties because it was directed by the will of one man. After he came to power Hitler quickly made use of the opportunities provided by modern technology. In the propaganda methods of the Nazi government, broadcasting was of central importance. The German people were cut off from all information which did not originate from official Nazi sources and they were ordered to turn on the radio when Hitler spoke, so that they would absorb his interpretation of events. When

Hitler made an aggressive move, such as ordering the German troops into the Rhineland, he accompanied this action with a broadcasted speech in which he emphasized his wish for peace and made proposals for negotiations. Such speeches were quite effective in preventing counter-actions because enough people in other countries, particularly in Great Britain, preferred to believe his words and to overlook his deeds.

Hitler's enthusiasm for technical innovations was a strength of his regime. In German rearmament he placed the emphasis strongly on modern weapons. He took a great interest in the construction of a network of roads (*Autobahnen*) which not only would help the development of the German motorcar industry but in wartime would permit the motorized transportation of troops and the quick movement of tanks. Shoddy as their ideas were, the leaders of the Nazi movement had grasped early the use to which modern technology could be put in establishing political control and building up military strength.

The Second World War transformed the external conditions of life even more thoroughly and radically than the First World War had done, and many of the implements of war were later converted to peacetime uses. On land and sea, for bombing the hinterland or for the support of soldiers in combat, for the transportation of men and of materials, the airplane was decisive in the Second World War. The gigantic bombers which had been built in response to wartime emergencies prepared the way for the transoceanic passenger air travel which developed after the war. The jet engine was invented during the war and nearly perfected by its end. Rockets, used as weapons by the Germans in the last year of the war, thereafter became important parts of the military equipment of all modern armies, but their most spectacular employment was in space exploration. The theoretical problems of constructing a device which would permit the location and detection of objects at distances not visible to the eye had been solved previously, but radar was fully developed only during the war years.

The creating of substitute (*Ersatz*) materials was almost more important in the Second World War than in the First. The extension of the war to the Far East led to an acute shortage of raw materials. For example, the Japanese occupation of Indonesia cut off the United States and Great Britain from a major source of natural rubber; as a substitute, a durable synthetic rubber was developed. The conduct of war in hot and humid climates and in areas afflicted by dangerous epidemics necessitated special attention to the problems of health and sanitation. Food refrigeration was improved. Under pressure of war new methods of immunization against contagious diseases were developed. The first antibiotic, penicillin, had been discovered in 1929 but its effectiveness against infections was established only during the war, and then its large-scale production was started in the United States. The invention of a process to extract plasma from the blood helped to reduce mortality from wounds. The damages and sufferings of the Second World War were very different from what the experiences of previous wars might have suggested.

THE NUCLEAR AGE

The greatest impact which the Second World War had on the conditions of life, however, was connected with its final event: the dropping of the atomic bomb, which ushered in the nuclear age. The atomic bomb was awesome proof that modern physics had unlocked a new source of power with almost unlimited potential for destruction, or—if applied to peacetime pursuits—for the good of man. This new weapon was developed under wartime conditions, but the scientific discoveries that made it possible had begun nearly a half century earlier.

The "understanding of atomic physics ... had its origins at the turn of the century and its great synthesis and resolutions in the nineteen twenties."[5] Thus did J. Robert Oppenheimer, one of the principals in this scientific revolution, characterize the main stages of its development. Its great events at the turn of the century were Max Planck's publication in 1900 of "On the Theory of the Law of Energy Distribution in a Normal Spectrum," which presented the thesis of the quantum theory, and Albert Einstein's publication in 1905 of the papers which set forth the special theory of relativity. By 1903 the need for a new theoretical outlook had been confirmed by experiments in the course of which Pierre and Marie Curie isolated radium and Antoine Henri Becquerel recognized the extent of radioactivity. After the First World War, the implications of these theories and discoveries were explored by a score of young scientists. The great centers of this absorbing intellectual adventure were Copenhagen, where Niels Bohr, the guiding spirit of the entire field of atomic reasearch, worked; Göttingen, where Max Born, James Franck, and David Hilbert maintained the tradition of this university as a center of mathematics and natural science; and Cambridge, where Ernest Rutherford continued his study of radioactivity and then, together with Sir James Chadwick, turned to the investigation of the composition of the atom. There was a lively exchange among all these groups, and the genesis of a new physical world view which, although it did not invalidate the classical Newtonian physics, limited its applicability, was the common achievement of scientists from many countries.

The creative excitement of these decades was caused by the necessity of revising the basic assumptions of classical physics, notably the supposition that through observation and experiments it is possible to establish the laws

[5] J. Robert Oppenheimer, *Science and the Common Understanding* (New York, 1953), p. 35.

Meeting of physicists in Göttingen in 1921. *Sitting, Max Born; standing from left to right: Wilhelm Oseen, Niels Bohr, James Franck, Oscar Klein.*

which demonstrate the causal connection determining the processes of nature. When Planck showed that certain incongruities in the radiation of energy can be explained if one assumes that energy goes out not in continuous waves but in flashes, like a stream of bullets of fixed size ("quantum"), his theory suggested that the assumption of complete continuity in the process of nature was untenable. Nature is discontinuous; that a certain sequence of events will result from the release of a quantum of energy is probable but it is not predetermined. Similarly, Einstein's demonstration in his theory of relativity of the bonds between the dimensions of space and of time forced a reexamination of the value of the material provided by observation. It was found that when measurements of a small elementary particle like the electron focus on speed, those of its precise position become uncertain, while measurements of position reduce precision in the measurement of speed. The conclusion was that in the description of nature there remains an element of uncertainty.

The disclosure that discontinuity and uncertainty are inherent in nature nullified the expectation of earlier scientists that immutable laws would someday be discovered which could explain all known phenomena. The work of the physicist became limited to the exploration of relations among the phenomena. But this limitation actually gave the investigator scope for greater creative efforts.

The basis for this change in theoretical assumptions which was worked out in the 1920's and 1930's was concrete investigation; the intellectual speculations were accompaniments of the discoveries resulting from a study of the atom. Already in the nineteenth century there had been some research which showed that the atom did not form an indivisible basic unit of matter, as had been assumed. The investigations of the twentieth century gradually revealed that the atom is composed of a very small nucleus (usually consisting of positively charged protons and electrically neutral neutrons) which is surrounded by negatively charged electrons. The problem was that, despite the radioactivity of certain elements, which ought to have led to a loss of energy, their atoms remained stable. And the explanation of this fact with the help of the new theoretical insights led to the discovery of nuclear energy. The freeing of this energy through the splitting of the atom—the result of bombarding uranium with neutrons—was first achieved in January, 1939, by Otto Hahn and Fritz Strassmann in Germany.

By then the United States had become the chief center of modern physical research, partly because laboratories equipped for such research on a major scale had been developed in places like Berkeley and Pasadena, partly because the totalitarian regimes had forced many of the leading Italian and German physicists to seek sanctuary in the United States. When information arrived that the Nazis might use the achievement of nuclear fission for the construction of a bomb, the activity of many of the physicists in the United States became concentrated on the problem of producing such a weapon before the Nazis could do so. The obstacles to such an enterprise were immense. The development of an atomic bomb required the cooperation of investigators from virtually all the fields of science. A by-product of this undertaking was the construction of a computer to accomplish the needed complicated mathematical calculations. The expenses were immense; the outlay for the Manhattan Project, as it was called, amounted to two billion dollars. Moreover, because complete secrecy had to be maintained, the teams of scientists and technicians, under the direction of J. Robert Oppenheimer and the military control of General Leslie Groves, lived and worked entirely cut off from the outside world. Without the pressure of the war emergency these difficulties could not have been overcome. But on July 16, 1945, after two years of work, the first atomic explosion was successfully achieved in New Mexico. It filled witnesses who could appreciate the possibilities and the dangers of the harnessing of nuclear energy with "terror as well as exultation."

"ONE WORLD" AND THE ESTABLISHMENT OF PEACE

The Second World War and the technical innovations connected with it gave rise to a new international outlook. The world had really become "one world." During the war powers like the United States, Great Britain, and Russia were involved in military action on a global scale. Technological advances in the postwar period have reinforced the interconnection among all parts of the world. Troops can be transported to distant areas in a matter of hours; missiles can be directed to remote targets; and nuclear rockets can be fired by nuclear submarines suddenly emerging at distant coasts. There is now a global balance of power which can be affected by events at almost any place.

The leaders of the wartime coalition were aware of the extent to which the world had been drawn together. The first conference at which Roosevelt, Churchill, and Stalin met was held at Teheran in November, 1943. Although discussions were chiefly concerned with military planning, and particularly with the establishment of a second front in the West, postwar developments were adumbrated in general terms. A second Big Three conference took place at Yalta, in the Crimea, in February, 1945. Again military questions stood in the forefront. But the approaching end of the war made the consideration of the postwar settlement a necessity, although the decisions remained rather vague and general. The liberated and the defeated countries were to become democracies. Germany and Austria were to be occupied, with each of the victorious powers receiving a zone of occupation, although in the capitals—Berlin and Vienna—a central administration assuring uniformity of occupation policies was to be established. But the American government was also urging the creation of an international organization to guarantee the maintenance of peace in the future; hence the American delegation regarded as valuable the Russian agreement, obtained at the Yalta meeting, to the establishment of such an organization. On April 25, 1945, a conference opened in San Francisco attended by all nations which had declared war on Germany and Japan; it ended on June 26 with the signing of the United Nations Charter.

From the start the most important members of the United Nations were two powers which after the First World War had remained outside the League of Nations: the United States and Russia. The League of Nations, though aimed to embrace the entire world, had always remained Europe-centered; the United Nations can claim to be global. Its headquarters were established not in Europe but in New York. The first two heads of its permanent international staff—Trygve Lie and Dag Hammarskjöld—came from the Scandinavian countries, but in 1962 a Burmese statesman—U Thant—became secretary-general.

The Economic and Social Council, one of its important organs, and the various specialized agencies working with and under the United Nations, make significant contributions by studying such problems as nutrition, overpopulation, and disease in what are regarded as the underdeveloped areas of Asia and Africa, by indicating the remedies which modern technology can provide, and by directing attention to the need for action. The International Bank for Reconstruction and Development, which is also connected with the Economic and Social Council, can provide these countries some of the requisite financial assistance.

In the political area the United Nations, with more members than the League of Nations ever had, appears much more egalitarian than the League because in the annual meetings of the General Assembly each of the numerous members has just one vote. Nevertheless, the greater powers exert a dominating influence. The Security Council, which is the crucial organ in decisions regarding critical political problems, has the United States, Great Britain, Russia, France, and China as permanent members; in addition six other members are elected by the Assembly for two-year terms, and these elections usually assure wide geographical representation. Since concurrence of all the permanent members is necessary for any decision of the Security Council which is not purely procedural, the permanent members have the power of veto.

But the actual power relationship existing in the present world is not fully reflected in the organization of the United Nations. In addition to the circle of states distinguished by membership in the Security Council, there is another exclusive circle, consisting of those possessing nuclear bombs: the United States (since 1945), Russia (since 1949), Great Britan (since 1952), Communist China, which is not a member of the United Nations (since 1964), and France (since 1966). Of these states, the United States and Russia have the largest number of nuclear weapons and are most advanced in the scientific exploration of the field. Their great natural and financial resources constitute an advantage which in the course of time will increase the distance which exists between these two and the other members of the nuclear club. Thus, science and technology have created two superpowers which can force all other nations to their will. The role which other states play in the United Nations is limited; they can take the initiative and shape policy only as long as the two superpowers neither clash nor combine.

The United Nations and the Maintenance of Peace

After attempts to establish international control of nuclear weapons failed, and Russia and the United States became involved in a competition for nuclear superiority, the United Nations was clearly divided between adherents of Russia and adherents of the United States. This division dominated the organization in the first decade after the end of the Second World War. These were years of crisis and tension because the problems of the postwar settlements and the rise of the peoples of Asia and Africa against their European rulers created continuously dangerous situations which led to confrontations between Russia and the United States. But when in the 1950's some nuclear balance between the superpowers was achieved, an increasing number of members of the United Nations began to feel able to move into an uncommitted position.

Has the United Nations been effective in guaranteeing peace; has it played its role in preventing the crises of the postwar epoch from developing into war? This is a difficult question to answer. The formal meetings of the General Assembly and of the Security Council have hardly contributed to lowering the temperature in critical situations. The various delegates attack one another's speeches acidly. Each accuses his opponent of distortions and lies, and criticizes him as representing an aggressive and oppressive power. The debates rigidify the antagonistic positions of the adversaries and serve self-justification and propaganda rather than defining a middle ground for negotiations. On the other hand, with modern means of communication statesmen can assemble from the most different parts of the earth within hours and the Security Council provides a recognized meeting place in critical situations. The speeches may serve to let off steam and to give the people at home the impression that their government is taking a resolute stand for its righteous cause, so that, freed from the pressure of excited public opinion, serious negotiations can begin. The United Nations fulfills the important function of bringing antagonists together behind closed doors, behind the façade of the public meetings. For instance, it provided the opportunities for initiating the secret negotiations which ended the crisis of the Berlin blockade in 1949. Perhaps instead of regarding the United Nations as a supranational government entrusted with preserving peace and order, one should view it as an instrument created to adjust diplomatic machinery to the requirements of the twentieth century. The niceties of traditional diplomatic language may not be appropriate to the more robust age of mass participation in public affairs. But the new roughness in the forms of diplomacy is counterbalanced by a willingness to make use of all available means for discussing differences in personal meetings which in earlier times frequently were not possible or were rejected because of considerations of prestige.

Although the United Nations provides diplomatic machinery appropriate to the modern age, the final decisions on war and peace are still left to the statesmen of the leading powers. It is the utter terror of the weapons which modern science and technology has created, rather than the moral force of an international organization, that—fortunately—has weighted the scale on the side of increasing restraint.

CHAPTER 44

Between Surrender and Cold War

EUROPE AFTER THE ALLIED VICTORY

THE COMPLETENESS of the Allied triumph, signified in the acceptance of "unconditional surrender," meant that the victors had to assume responsibility for life in the defeated nations. This awesome task was complicated by the misery and devastation which prevailed not just in Germany and Italy but in Europe as a whole.

The Legacy of Total War

The most visible imprint left by the Second World War was the physical destruction in the urban areas. Except for the university towns of Oxford, Cambridge, and Heidelberg, which out of consideration for cultural values had been left intact, all the larger towns of England and Germany had suffered extensive damage, with many areas, particularly in their centers, completely razed. Warsaw, Vienna, Budapest, Rotterdam were in ruins. In France most of the harbors along the channel coast had been hit severely.

In contrast, the European countryside, except where it had been the site of military operations, was untouched. But communications between rural and urban areas had been severed, and the various parts of a country existed almost in isolation. Roads, bridges, and railroad lines had been demolished or damaged. Locomotives and railroad equipment had been broken or stalled at the military fronts or had so deteriorated that they were almost unusable. The factories which produced the equipment needed for reconstruction had been wrecked, and manpower was not immediately available.

The Germans had been adequately fed during most of the war, but they had been supplied at the expense of the Nazi-occupied countries. Hence, in most of Europe people were near starvation and their capacity for work was small: The male inhabitants of the Nazi-occupied countries, having served as forced laborers, were dispersed in labor camps all over Europe. Moreover, during the war the populations of entire regions had been moved; thus the Nazis had transferred the inhabitants out of parts of Poland and the

Ukraine so that Germans could be settled there. At the end of the war an analogous policy was carried out by Hungarians, Serbs, and Czechs who were unwilling to tolerate troublesome German minorities within their borders. In addition, Germans of East Prussia and Silesia, in fear of the approaching Russian armies, fled toward the west. Roads were clogged with people trying either to return to their own countries or to find new homes. To those who saw the European continent in the spring and early summer of 1945 it seemed incredible that within a few years life might again become normal.

Impoverishment and economic and social disorder were not confined to Germany, Austria, and Italy. The plight of the liberated countries was equally serious. Life in the whole of Europe had to be reorganized and brought back to health. Initially this task fell upon the victors. Their troops were stationed all over Europe, since military occupation of the defeated countries required secure lines of communications through the adjacent areas. The control which the victors exerted by military means was reinforced by the fact that only they could supply the food and the basic resources needed by the European countries for reconstruction.

The task of providing for military requirements and economic assistance involved a certain amount of political interference even in areas where the victors did not possess exclusive control, as they did in Germany and Austria. In most of the liberated countries the political situation was tense, almost revolutionary. The leading politicians of the prewar era, who had withdrawn or gone into exile during the period of Nazi rule, came forward in the expectation that they again would play a leading role. Their aim was restoration of the prewar situation in their respective states. But they were confronted by new leaders, who had come to prominence through their activities in the resistance movements and now wanted social and political changes which would weaken the influence of the previously ruling circles.

After the war. *Displaced people returning to their former homes.*

After the war. *The Krupp works in ruins.*

The victors could not permit their troops to live among the starving and despairing population and under the threat of civil war. Hence, all over Europe the Americans, the British, and the Russians became involved in the revival of political and social life. Almost unavoidably the political ideas and traditions of each of these powers patterned the political revival in the areas in which it maintained a strong military posture.

Wartime negotiations and conferences, and particularly the conference at Yalta, had established only general and somewhat vague principles concerning the treatment of the Germans after surrender. It had been agreed, however, that Austria would again be separated from Germany, that both Germany and Austria would be entirely occupied, and that each of the victorious powers—Russia, Great Britain, and the United States—would receive a zone of occupation in Germany and in Austria. France was later added to the three victors and was given occupation zones cut out of those originally assigned to Great Britain and the United States. The capitals— Berlin and Vienna—were to be placed under the common administration of all the victors; it was envisaged that these cities would serve again as national capitals, each housing a central administration subject to the control of the occupying powers.

The rest of Europe was clearly divided into two different spheres of influence. Eastern Europe and the Balkans had been freed from Nazi rule by Russian armies and these forces remained stationed there ostensibly to maintain communication with the Russian-occupied zones of central Europe. But the Russians soon impressed their political patterns on the countries in these regions. Northern and western Europe—Norway, Denmark, the Netherlands, Belgium, France, and in the south, Italy and Greece—had been liberated by American and British troops, and those parts of Europe were organized in conformity with the concepts of western democracy. Thus, political revival in eastern and western Europe took very different forms, but the road was clearly staked out and the process of reconstruction started quickly.

The Settlement of the Frontiers

The victorious powers took care that within their spheres of influence no serious conflicts about boundaries arose. Readjustments were relatively minor. In the east Rumania had to cede northern Bucovina and Bessarabia to Soviet Russia, and part of Dobruja to Bulgaria. But Rumania received northern Transylvania from Hungary, which also had to relinquish some land to Czechoslovakia. Finland lost to Russia the territory of Petsamo in the north and the Karelian Isthmus in the south. Russia kept the Baltic states and extended its dominance southward along the Baltic Sea by annexing the northern part of what had been East Prussia; Poland recognized the frontiers which Russia had established in 1939 as a result of the Nazi-Soviet pact, but was promised some extension of its frontiers in the west as compensation.

The boundary changes in the areas controlled by the United States and Great Britain were still less significant. It was recognized that the former frontiers of France had to be restored, and after some negotiations it was agreed that the Saar region would be economically attached to France so that France would have priority in the use of Saar coal; the territory itself would remain under German sovereignty. Slight frontier revisions in favor of Belgium and Denmark were arranged at the expense of Germany. Italy ceded some border territory to France, lost all of its overseas possessions, and returned the Dodecanese to Greece.

The determination of frontiers was complicated only along the line where the Russian and western spheres of occupation touched each other; that is, the line which led from the Baltic Sea through the center of Germany along Czechoslovakia and Austria to the region between Yugoslavia and Italy. The final settlement of these boundaries required years of hard negotiations, and in the case of Germany, agreement has not yet been reached.

The course of political reconstruction could differ greatly in the various countries of the Russian and the Anglo-American spheres because during the war no clear and definite agreement about the form of the postwar settlement had been obtained. The Big Three—the United States, Great Britain, and Soviet Russia—had limited themselves to proclaiming that the European countries should be democracies; a precise interpretation of this term, however, had not been given.

Soviet Control of Eastern Europe

The Soviet rulers established "people's democracies" in the countries they controlled, but to the west the forms of government emerging in eastern Europe seemed hardly democratic. For the Communists regarded the workers and peasants as the only sectors of the population with the right to exert control over the government. They alone constituted "the people." Even among the workers and peasants only the politically conscious and active members—those in the Communist parties—deserved to have a voice. As in Soviet Russia, the candidates for the committees and councils which constituted the government and the administration had to be members of the Communist party. And the party was a strictly hierarchical structure directed from above, with its secretary, as in Russia, holding the key position. Thus, the "people's democracies" which the Soviets organized were actually Communist dictatorships.

The achievement of complete Communist rule took some time, and the methods employed by the Russians varied according to the situation in each particular country. Usually, the Russian occupying troops began by forming a coalition government, called a United Front government, in which the Communists were partners and held key positions. From this government the non-Communist members were gradually eliminated by methods in which psychological pressure and propaganda were combined with brute power; the presence of Russian troops made resistance to Russian demands almost impossible. Meanwhile, large parts of the population, workers and peasants in particular, acquired a vested interest in the maintenance of the system; in all the Russian-controlled areas large landed estates were divided among the peasants and the important industrial enterprises were nationalized. Undoubtedly such measures created a certain amount of popular support.

In Bulgaria and Rumania the Communists were dominant in the government by the summer of 1945, although the young monarchs of these countries were deposed only in 1946 and 1947. In Poland the Russians proceeded more circumspectly. They could not disregard the particular interest which Great Britain and the United States took in the fate of Poland; the Second World War had started in order to save the independence of Poland. After its defeat the Polish government had gone into exile in London, and it was recognized by Great Britain and the United States. Nor could Great Britain and the United States have any doubt about the great increase in power which domination over Poland would give to Russia; they were well aware that it would place Soviet might in the center of Europe. But in the end the vehement protests of the United States and Britain against the Communist pressure in Poland only slowed down the Russian abandonment of the pretense of democratic procedure. A Communist monopoly of power was achieved there in

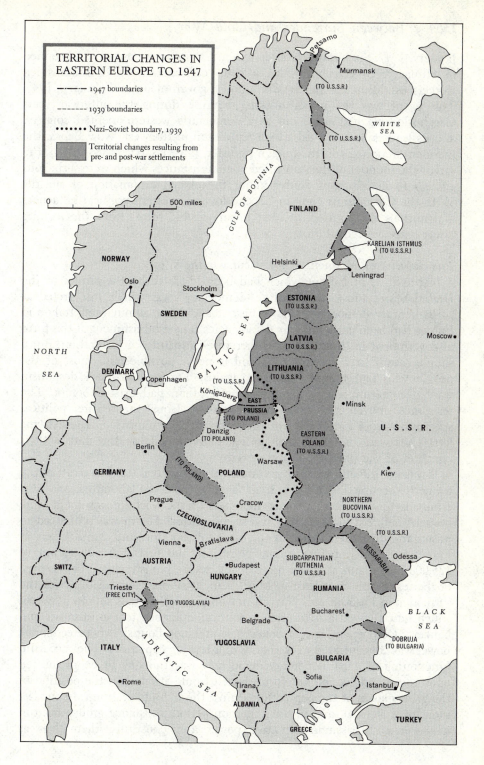

TERRITORIAL CHANGES IN
EASTERN EUROPE TO 1947

— · — · — 1947 boundaries

— — — — 1939 boundaries

• • • • • Nazi–Soviet boundary, 1939

Territorial changes resulting from
pre- and post-war settlements

0   500 miles

NORWAY

Oslo

SWEDEN

Stockholm

GULF OF BOTHNIA

FINLAND

Helsinki

Petsamo
(TO U.S.S.R.)

Murmansk

(TO U.S.S.R.)

WHITE
SEA

KARELIAN ISTHMUS
(TO U.S.S.R.)

Leningrad

NORTH
SEA

DENMARK

Copenhagen

BALTIC SEA

ESTONIA
(TO U.S.S.R.)

LATVIA
(TO U.S.S.R.)

LITHUANIA
(TO U.S.S.R.)

Moscow

(TO U.S.S.R.)
Königsberg

EAST
PRUSSIA
(TO POLAND)

Danzig
(TO POLAND)

Berlin

(TO POLAND)

GERMANY

POLAND

Warsaw

EASTERN
POLAND
(TO U.S.S.R.)

Minsk

U.S.S.R.

Kiev

Prague

CZECHOSLOVAKIA

Cracow

NORTHERN
BUCOVINA
(TO U.S.S.R.)

Vienna

Bratislava

SWITZ.

AUSTRIA

Budapest

HUNGARY

SUBCARPATHIAN
RUTHENIA
(TO U.S.S.R.)

(TO U.S.S.R.)

BESSARABIA

Odessa

RUMANIA

Bucharest

BLACK
SEA

Trieste
(FREE CITY)

(TO YUGOSLAVIA)

ITALY

ADRIATIC SEA

YUGOSLAVIA

Belgrade

DOBRUJA
(TO BULGARIA)

BULGARIA

Sofia

Istanbul

Rome

Tirana

ALBANIA

GREECE

TURKEY

January, 1947. Six months later complete Communist control was attained in Hungary. In Czechoslovakia a coup carried out by Communist-led workers established a purely Communist government in February, 1948. This event was the more shocking because during the interwar years Czechoslovakia had stood out as a democratic western-oriented country, and its leaders had enjoyed a high reputation in the west. Now Benes, the president, resigned and the foreign minister, Jan Masaryk (1886–1948), the son of the founder of the state, died in circumstances which were suspicious enough to raise serious doubts about the official explanation of suicide. With the Communist coup in Czechoslovakia, western political influences and notions disappeared, at least in any visible form, from the regimes under Russian occupation.

The Return to Parliamentary Democracy in the West

In the areas of Europe which had been liberated by the armies of the United States and Great Britain, "democracy" was widely interpreted as parliamentary democracy. Before Fascist and Nazi domination, Italy and France had been parliamentary democracies. The establishment of this form of government in these countries therefore constituted a restoration. But a simple return to a previous situation is never possible, and most of the people who had fought heroically against Fascist and Nazi despotism wanted something new, something better than had existed before. The resistance movements had included men from the entire political spectrum—from nationalists of the right to Communists on the extreme left. They were united in their hatred of Nazi collaborators and in their rejection of the prewar political system.

It was not difficult to settle accounts with individual traitors; in all of the formerly occupied countries trials against Nazi collaborators and war criminals took place. In France members of the Vichy government were brought before a high court. Laval was executed; Pétain was sentenced to prison and died there. Most of the Nazi collaborators and sympathizers in France were tried before special courts; in the first year 40,000 out of 125,000 defendants received more or less severe punishment. But the men of the resistance, or at least most of them, attributed responsibility for the surrender to Fascism and Nazism not only to individuals but to a system which had allowed a determining political influence to industrialists and bankers. Democracy, it was believed, could not flourish where economic power was concentrated in the hands of a few big capitalists. The successful functioning of a parliamentary democracy was thought to be predicated upon social and economic reforms which would strengthen the position of the great masses of the population against the rich upper group. In the last months of the war, and in the liberation period, resistance groups tried in many areas to assume executive power and constitute themselves as governments. They were balked by the military leaders of the victorious American and British armies, who were primarily interested in smoothly functioning supply and communications lines, and feared disorder and chaos. Furthermore, De Gaulle, the acknowledged head of the French resistance, opposed the encroachment of individual groups on what he considered to be the paramount authority of the state.

Yet despite the failure of the resistance to effect changes and reforms during the fluid situation at the war's end, it was generally recognized that neither France nor Italy could just reactivate its former constitution. In France a plebiscite determined that it was necessary, as De Gaulle declared in a broadcast in September, 1945, "to adopt a different system in order to revive the spirit of clarity, justice and efficiency which is the true spirit of the republic." And in both countries constituent assemblies were elected to develop new constitutions—in France on October 21, 1945, and in Italy on June 2, 1946.

The elections for these assemblies saw the rise of two newly powerful parties, a Catholic party at the center of the political spectrum and the Communist party at the extreme left. Italy changed from a monarchy to a republic, but in other respects the constitution adopted by the constituent assembly was very similar to the one which had existed before Fascism. Only the anticlerical emphasis of the nineteenth-century liberal constitution was eliminated, with Mussolini's concordat with the pope becoming an integral part of the new constitution. Roman Catholicism remained in Italy "the sole religion of the state." The new French constitution was more democratic than that of the Third Republic had been; a second chamber, an indirectly elected Council of the Republic, replacing the Senate, remained in existence but its functions were insignificant. The National Assembly, replacing the former Chamber of Deputies, was all-powerful, and it was expected that the removal of the conservative counterweight which the Senate had represented in the Third Republic would help to create greater governmental stability in the Fourth Republic.

In the years immediately following the end of the war, both Italy and France were ruled by left-center coalitions composed of the new Catholic party, the socialists, and the Communists. Despite continuous friction between the Catholic and Communist parties, a working collaboration was maintained among all three groups, based on the lesson, drawn from the years of Fascist rule, that the power of the great capitalists had to be curbed if democracy was to work. In Italy, the state retained the share which, under Fascism, it had acquired in many of the more important industrial enterprises; but whereas under Mussolini, the influence which control of industries gave to the government had been used in favor of big business, the governments of democratic Italy were expected to use this power to restrain this group. In France indignation about the "rule of the two hundred families," which before the war had exploded in the Popular Front election of 1936, had only been deepened by the events under the Nazis and the Vichy regime. And the parties in the government had no difficulty in agreeing on a wide program of economic and social reforms. They embarked on a policy of nationalization which included the credit system (banks and insurance companies), the fuel and power industries (coal, gas, and electricity), strategically important enterprises (airlines, the merchant marine), and a number of large industrial concerns which had been working for the Germans, the best known being the Renault automobile works. The economic situation of the workers was improved by the introduction of a comprehensive social-security scheme. Also, employees could form works committees, with an advisory function in the running of the factories. Finally, the role of the trade unions in collective bargaining was strengthened.

By the end of 1946 French and Italian political life had been set on its new course. At that time the contrast between western and eastern Europe—the states of the one forming their political decisions by means of parliaments and a multiparty system, those of the other having their policy directed and controlled by the leadership of one party—had not yet been fully developed, and the differences did not seem as definite and as unbridgeable as they now appear: with members of socialist and bourgeois parties participating in the governments of Poland, Hungary, and Czechoslovakia, and with Communists in the French and Italian coalition governments, the situation in the first two postwar years still seemed rather fluid. Moreover, after difficult negotiations which extended through a series of conferences—in London in September, 1945, in Moscow in December, 1945, and in Paris during the spring and summer of 1946—the situation which had developed in the defeated countries was given recognition through peace treaties, with Italy, Bulgaria, Rumania, Finland, and Poland. Yet, appearances that a trend toward stabilization was setting in and that a halfway meeting between East and West might be possible were deceptive. On the question of Germany, the most important issue in the settlement of European affairs, no understanding between East and West was reached. On the contrary, the negotiations about the treatment of Germany which had taken place since the end of hostilities had steadily widened the gap between East and West.

The Pivotal Question of Germany

It was natural that the question of Germany's future should become decisive in breaking up the wartime alliance and in dividing West and East. Germany's position in the center of Europe, and its wealth in mineral resources, made it a critical area even in defeat.

During the war the Allies had outlined only a very general framework for

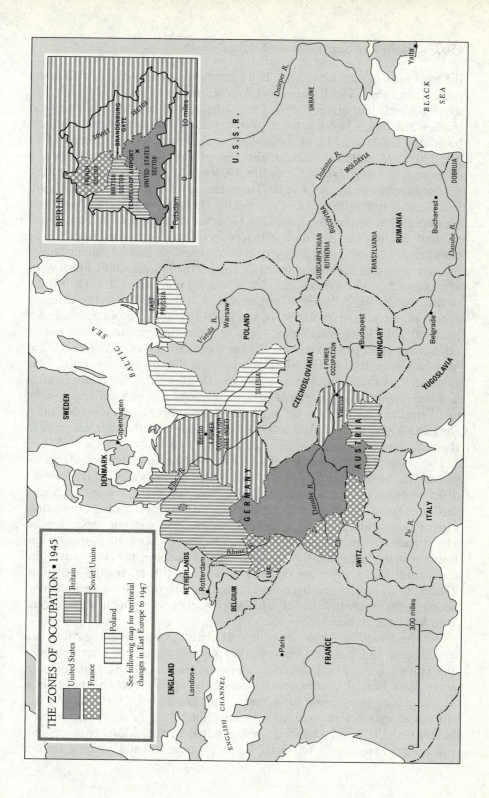

THE ZONES OF OCCUPATION • 1945

United States
France

Britain
Soviet Union

Poland

See following map for territorial changes in East Europe to 1947

ENGLAND

London •

ENGLISH CHANNEL

Paris •

FRANCE

NETHERLANDS

Rotterdam •

BELGIUM

Lux.

Rhine R.

SWITZ.

G E R M A N Y

Elbe R.

DENMARK

Copenhagen •

SWEDEN

BALTIC SEA

EAST PRUSSIA

Warsaw •

Vistula R.

POLAND

SILESIA

Berlin
4-POWER OCCUPATION
(SEE INSET)

CZECHOSLOVAKIA

Danube R.

Vienna

A U S T R I A

4 POWER OCCUPATION

Budapest •

HUNGARY

YUGOSLAVIA

Belgrade •

ITALY

Po R.

SUBCARPATHIAN RUTHENIA

BUCOVINA

Dniester R.

MOLDAVIA

TRANSYLVANIA

RUMANIA

Bucharest •

Danube R.

DOBRUJA

U. S. S. R.

UKRAINE

Dnieper R.

Yalta •

BLACK SEA

300 miles

0

BERLIN

SOVIET SECTOR

BRANDENBURG GATE
×

FRENCH SECTOR

BRITISH SECTOR

TEMPELHOF AIRPORT

UNITED STATES SECTOR

Potsdam •

10 miles

0

the treatment of Germany. They had agreed on occupation zones, and now these were set up. The Russian and American zones were roughly equal in size, and each had about 7.25 million inhabitants. The British zone was smaller but had 5 million more people because it included the densely populated Ruhr area. The French zone was the smallest in extent and in population (5 million). The main aim of the victors, as stated in a communiqué issued after the Yalta Conference, was to prevent future military aggression by Germany: "To insure that Germany will never again be able to disturb the peace of the world." Hence the powers agreed that Nazis ought to be punished and that German society ought to be changed so that militarism could no longer prosper. Germany was to be demilitarized; production was to be kept down to a level which would prevent industrial expansion and shift the balance in economic life toward agriculture. Living conditions in Germany were not to be better than those of the neighboring countries. Germany was to compensate for the damages caused in the Second World War, but in an attempt to avoid the mistakes made after the First World War it was specified that payments were not to be made in gold. Implementation of these principles was to be worked out in a peace treaty, which would also define Germany's frontiers. One important territorial change was envisaged. Because Poland's eastern borders had been modified in favor of Russia, the German-Polish frontier would be along the Oder and Neisse rivers. Until the final peace treaty was concluded the Poles would exert control as an occupying power in the areas assigned to them.

The principles established by the Allies for the treatment of Germany proved to be insufficient. First of all, they envisaged a situation very different from the one actually found by the occupying armies. Germany was crowded with refugees from East Prussia, West Prussia, Pomerania, Poznán, and Silesia, people without means and without employment. Destruction through bombing had caused a severe lack of housing. The breakdown of transportation created food shortages in the towns. The occupation forces were not staffed to deal with this emergency situation. The establishment of indigenous authorities, the promotion of industrial activities for reconstruction and for employment were much more urgent than had been assumed.

But the principles for the treatment of Germany on which the Allies had agreed were deficient also because they permitted varying interpretations and consequently were applied in different ways in the several zones of occupation. Indeed, there was only one area in which successful cooperation of the coalition partners continued: the punishment of the major war crimes. A trial before an international tribunal at Nuremberg between November, 1945, and October, 1946, resulted in the death sentence, and subsequent hanging, of ten Nazi leaders, among them Foreign Minister

The Nuremberg Trials. *Among the Nazi leaders in the front row are Göring (at the extreme left), Hess (second from left), Ribbentrop (third from left), and Schacht (at the extreme right). In the second row Papen is third from left and Speer third from right.*

Joachim von Ribbentropp, Hitler's military advisers Wilhelm Keitel and Alfred Jodl, Minister of the Interior Wilhelm Frick, and the Jew-baiter Julius Streicher. Göring committed suicide in prison. Himmler had killed himself after capture. Perhaps never before was a group of men, who five years earlier had strutted around as rulers of an entire continent and had ruthlessly sealed the fate of millions, so quickly eliminated.

Most of the other issues, however, were handled by the wartime partners in accordance with their particular political traditions and customs, and the cleavages which developed in consequence were particularly deep between the Russian and the western zones. For instance, all the occupying powers were obligated to eradicate Nazism from German life. But east and west had entirely different approaches to the problem of denazification. To the Russians denazification meant the destruction of the system—bourgeois capitalism—which had permitted the rise of Nazism, and denazification would be considered accomplished when the laboring classes were firmly established in power. Thus, the Russians in their zone of occupation terminated private ownership of big industrial and financial enterprises and divided up the large landed estates in the areas east of the Elbe. They quickly revived political life and created for their zone a German government dominated by an anticapitalist Socialist Unity party, although for some years participation of a left-wing bourgeois party in the government was tolerated. With the establishment of a new ruling class of workers and peasants, the Russians considered denazification successfully completed.

In the west, denazification was taken to mean that those who had been active in the Nazi regime were to be deprived of participation in politics and economic life. Denazification was directed against individuals; it did not imply a change in the German social structure. The denazification proceedings in the west had the disadvantage of being slow and bureaucratic; every German had to fill out a long questionnaire about his activities during the Nazi period, and the paper work became so unmanageable that sweeping amnesties had to be granted.

The two approaches to denazification typify the fundamental differences between the political and social concepts which determined occupation policies in the eastern and in the western zones.

With the emergence of widely differentiated social structures in the two halves of Germany, the conclusion of a peace treaty which would encompass the nation as a whole became increasingly complicated. Aware of the danger of such a development, the wartime leaders had agreed to establish in Berlin a central German administration which would act under the supervision of an Allied Control Council. Berlin, in the midst of the Russian zone, was placed under direct four-power control, with each power—the Americans, the British, the French, and the Russians— quartered in a different part of the city.

It is not clear whether the Russians were ever willing to permit the formation of a central German administration not dominated by Communists. The regime which they had set up in their zone was rather shaky, and they must have feared that it might not survive if the establishment of a central administration should open the door to the west. Thus acceptance of a single government for all of Germany might cost them their grip over even the eastern part of the country. A continued division of Germany into various zones might have appeared to them preferable to the establishment of a unified state in which the Communists had no control.

The issue which ended all plans for a central German administration and actually terminated the effective functioning of the Allied Control Council was the matter of reparations.

Here again the devastation which the victors found in Germany made previously conceived plans unrealizable. It had been agreed that in compensation for the immense damage caused by the German invaders, the Russians would have the right to transfer German industrial installations to the Soviet Union and to receive as reparations a proportion of the goods currently produced by German industry; they were expected in return to deliver food stocks to the western zones of Germany from the agricultural areas which they were occupying. The presupposition of this plan was that the whole of Germany would be treated as an economic unit. However, the scarcities in the eastern zone, which were the result of war devastation but were aggravated by Russian exploitation of the zone, made delivery of food to the western zones impossible; therefore, the United States and Great Britain had to export food at their own expense to western Germany in order to feed their troops and to keep the German working population at least on a subsistence minimum. This meant that deliveries from the western zones to the Russians would be financed by the United States and Great Britain—that the reparations which the Germans were to make to the Russians would actually be paid by the western powers. As a result, no deliveries to Russia of industrial products from the western zones ever took place, and the conflict on this issue totally disrupted the work of the Allied Control Council; thereafter the western occupying powers and Russia handled economic affairs in their zones independently. Attempts to overcome the deadlock on the level of foreign ministers' conferences were unsuccessful. On the contrary, such a conference in Moscow in April, 1947, not only lacked positive results but even widened the gap between Russia and the West.

The Marshall Plan

Two years after the German surrender all of Europe still suffered from the destruction of the war, from the interruption of communications and commerce, from a lack of capital to stimulate industrial productivity. After the high expectations of victory, many people were disappointed and dissatisfied. Russian intransigence was probably heightened by the expectation that Communism would gain in strength if Europe remained in this unsettled state. In this situation the American secretary of state, George C. Marshall, who had been deeply disturbed by the failure of the foreign ministers' conference in Moscow, made a speech at Harvard University on June 5, 1947, in which he promised American support if the European powers would work out plans for economic reconstruction. The result was the European Recovery Program, usually called the Marshall Plan. Over the next years—until 1952, when the plan officially ended—12.4 billion dollars were given as economic aid to the participating countries: Austria, Belgium, Denmark, France, Great Britain, Greece, Iceland, Ireland, Italy, Luxemburg, the Netherlands, Norway, Portugal, Sweden, Switzerland, and Turkey. Economic recovery set in rapidly and the outlook in western Europe changed.

Originally the assistance of the recovery program was also made available to the various countries under Russian control, and Czechoslovakia accepted the offer, but under the pressure of Molotov, the Russian foreign minister, the Czechs withdrew. No country in the Russian sphere of interest participated in the program. In March, 1946, Winston Churchill had warned that "from Stettin in the Baltic to Trieste in the Adriatic, an iron curtain has descended across the continent." By the time another year had passed, eastern and western Europe really were separated; the next event was a direct confrontation in a "Cold War."

THE FAR EAST AFTER THE JAPANESE SURRENDER

Since the Second World War had been a global conflict, the European developments after the end of the war cannot be understood apart from events in other parts of the world. The unwillingness of Russia and the United States to make concessions on the question of Germany, the rapidity with which wartime cooperation changed into tension and conflict, can be comprehended only if we realize that during the same period a clash between Russian and the American interests developed in the Far East.

When Japan surrendered on August 14, 1945, friction between Russia and the West in this area seemed unlikely. During the war Russia had been anxious to concentrate all its military efforts upon Germany and had carefully avoided embroilment with Japan. However, at the Yalta Conference, Stalin had promised that his nation would enter the war against Japan after the termination of military operations in Europe. Accordingly, Russian forces were assembled near the Manchurian border and Russia declared war on Japan on August 8. Since the Japanese military situation had become hopeless by then, and the atomic bomb dropped on Hiroshima on August 6 had broken the Japanese will to resist, Russia's entry into the war played no part in the Japanese defeat. The procedures followed by the Americans in negotiating and accepting the Japanese surrender showed clearly that they regarded the settlement with Japan exclusively as their own. And during the following years, the United States remained the only outside force to exert control and influence over the reconstruction of Japan as a political power.

But Japanese troops had penetrated far into China and had occupied most of southeast Asia. The Japanese surrender had wide repercussions in these regions. In these areas not only the United States but also China and Great Britain had fought, and America's allies were unprepared for Japan's sudden collapse.

The size of the area, the number of inhabitants, the variety of peoples, made the handling of the problems of southeast Asia a complex task. These inherent difficulties were aggravated by revolutionary ferment resulting from Japanese rule and occupation.

Japan had treated the nations of southeast Asia in various ways. For instance, Thailand had been considered an ally, and had been permitted to enlarge its frontiers at the expense of its neighbor, French Indochina. In other areas, in Malaya and in the islands of Indonesia—Java, Sumatra, Borneo, Celebes—the Japanese had ruled through military administrations. In China, in the Philippines, and in Burma they had established puppet governments. French Indochina was a special case. As long as France was in the Nazi orbit, the French administrators of Indochina had collaborated with Japan. But after the liberation of France, the French turned against Japan and the Japanese established a puppet government.

Japan exploited all these areas brutally. Yet the Japanese occupation had revolutionary and lasting consequences. The Japanese invasion of this area demonstrated that Asian people were able to shake off the yoke of European rulers; nationalism had received a powerful impetus. The attitude of the nationalist leaders of these peoples to the Japanese rule was rather ambiguous. Some regarded the formation of a national government, even if limited in its freedom of action by Japanese power, as a first step toward independence, and were willing to cooperate with the Japanese in setting up the puppet regimes. Others considered Japanese rule to be quite as oppressive as that of the western powers, and organized resistance movements. In the course of these developments indigenous leaders gained a strong hold over the masses. The nationalist leader in Indochina, Ho Chi Minh (1890–1969), fought against the Japanese; in Indonesia, Achmed Sukarno (born 1901–1970) cooperated with the Japanese, but held out against their plans to divide the region into independent units, championing a united Indonesia.

The Retreat from Colonialism

Since the Allied forces in southeast Asia were under British command during the war, the British took charge of the area after hostilities ended. The first task of the British was to organize the surrender of the Japanese forces which were stationed in this area and burdened its economy. The presence of large armies, the disturbances of war, the flight of people from their homes, and the interruption of communications had restricted cultivation of the land, and in many regions people were starving. Therefore, a foremost concern of the British authorities was to increase the production of food, particularly rice, and to arrange for its distribution. In attempting to accomplish this task the British were confronted with an unpleasant political dilemma. Undoubtedly cooperation with the indigenous governments and forces would have been most effective. But this would have strengthened the governments which the French and the Dutch, who had formerly been the rulers in these regions and were anxious to resume control, wanted to eliminate. The French and the Dutch were Britain's allies and Britain itself had colonies in southeast Asia. This contradiction between short-range and long-range interests prevented the development of a uniform policy for the entire area. Settlements were difficult to arrive at, and they varied from one region to the other. The Dutch were unable to reinstate themselves and were forced to recognize the independent Republic of Indonesia in 1946. The French reestablished their rule in Indochina, but fighting against them never ceased and after long and costly campaigns, climaxed by the defeat at Dien Bien Phu in 1954, the French withdrew and left three independent states: Laos, Cambodia, and Vietnam. The British returned to Malaya and Singapore and promoted a political evolution through which Malaya became independent but remained part of the British empire. In southeast Asia the Japanese defeat started a process of revolution which has not yet been completed.

The first manifestoes of the Communist International had stated that the liberation of the peoples of Asia and Africa from colonial rule formed an integral part of the Communist fight against capitalism. Thus, the Russians, although not directly involved in the struggle in southeast Asia, clearly favored nationalist movements in this region, and they had close contacts with some of the nationalist leaders. For instance, Ho Chi Minh was trained in Moscow and worked in the Communist movements in Europe before returning to his native Indochina.

Since American foreign policy too had an anticolonial tradition, the rise of nationalist movements in southeast Asia did not necessarily place Russia and America on opposite sides. However, the United States acted in close cooperation with Great Britain and France in Europe, and there was danger, therefore, that the United States would be stamped as an ally of traditional European imperialism. This actually did happen in China, the nation which presented the most difficult problems of the Asian postwar situation.

The Struggle in China

That China would be a source of conflict between Russia and the United States was not apparent at the end of the war. Here again the most urgent task was to effect the disarmament and withdrawal of the Japanese armies, stationed in the vast regions along the Yangtze and the Yellow rivers. The fact that much time had to be spent arranging the removal of these troops proved to be a disadvantage to the Chinese Nationalist government under Chiang Kai-shek. In the interim period the Communist armies of Mao Tse-tung in the north had the opportunity to expand their power. In August, 1945, Russia had recognized Chiang Kai-shek's regime as the central government of China, so it seemed justifiable to assume that the Russians were anxious to establish cooperation between the Communists in the north and Chiang Kai-shek's government in the south. The United States had a similar aim. The Chiang Kai-shek government had been frequently criticized in the United States for its lack of energy in pursuing the war against the Japanese, and many Americans hoped and believed that cooperation with the Communists would stimulate the Nationalists and provide an impetus to social and agricultural reform which would be highly desirable for China. But protracted negotiations failed to settle the differences between the Nationalist government of Chiang Kai-shek and Mao Tse-tung's Communist forces. Instead, there developed a sharp contest between the two opposing Chinese governments for the control of Manchuria, and in this conflict the Russians decided to back Mao. At the time of the Japanese surrender, the Russians had occupied Manchuria— temporarily, they declared. In the next months, they made no effort to evacuate the area, but in April, 1946, when the struggle over German reparations became critical, they moved their troops from Manchuria very suddenly, and the rapidity of their retreat gave the Chinese Communists the opportunity to move in.

The American government continued its efforts to establish peace in China, but neither of the warring factions really wanted an agreement, because each believed that it could win over the entire country. When General Marshall, who had been sent to China in December, 1945, abandoned his peace efforts in January, 1947, he assigned responsibility for the failure of his mission to both sides: the "dominant group of reactionaries" in Chiang Kai-shek's government and the "dyed in the wool"[1] Communists in the other camp. The final result was an open confrontation and civil war between Chiang Kai-shek's forces, somewhat reluctantly and halfheartedly backed by the United States, and Mao Tse-tung's Communists, supported by Russia. With conflict between Russia and the United States developing over China, the differences between these two powers concerning settlement in Europe gained in significance and sharpness.

[1] These phrases are from General Marshall's statement on China on February 7, 1947.

CHAPTER 45

The Cold War and its Consequences

THE TERM "COLD WAR" is widely used in discussions of recent history, but it has remained a rather vague and indefinite notion. It is not clear when the Cold War began, nor how long it lasted. Some see its beginning in the famous statement issued on March 12, 1947, by President Harry S. Truman (born 1884) in response to a note from the British declaring that they were no longer able to give assistance to the Greek government in its fight against Communist guerillas; the Truman Doctrine declared that "it must be the foreign policy of the United States to support free peoples who are resisting attempted subjugation by armed minorities or by outside pressures." Some regard the Berlin blockade of 1948–1949, with which the Russians tried to end the four-power rule of Berlin, as the beginning of the Cold War. Others consider the outbreak of the Korean War to be the crucial event.

THE POLARIZATION OF POWER

Like the causes of other wars the origins of the Cold War have been much discussed. Who was responsible for the development of this critical situation? There was actually a certain inevitability in its coming about. After the war, power was largely divided between Soviet Russia and the United States, and polarization of power between two states has almost always led to war. Moreover, in the years since the Bolsheviks gained control, the two nations had come to represent, for their citizens, opposing sets of values: to Americans, Soviet Russia was a country of criminal lawlessness, with no regard for the values of civilization; to Communists, the United States was the embodiment of their chief enemy—capitalism.

These ideological contrasts were solidified by a conflict in economic interests. The traditional policy of the United States was to encourage free trade throughout the world. And Communist Russia's withdrawal from international commerce was considered an important reason for the economic difficulties of the interwar years. The Russians, however, regarded every attempt to force the opening of the commercial barriers and to entangle their nation in the workings of the capitalist system as an aggressive act aimed at undermining the Communist regime. The cooperation of the Russians with the western powers in the Second World War was not sufficient to eradicate reciprocal distrust. In the Russian press, praise of the British-American war effort was mixed with complaints about western slowness in opening a second front. And the Russian masses were quite inadequately informed about the amount of aid which the Soviet Union received through Lend-Lease. In the United States, on the other hand, people were kept in the dark about the great difficulties which western diplomats and military leaders encountered in achieving a minimum of concerted action with their Communist partners. And because many Americans had optimistic illusions about the possibilities of an alliance with Russia, their disappointment was great when cooperation broke down.

In addition, the wartime conferences, particularly the conference at Yalta, had shown divergences in the views of the western and Russian statesmen concerning the postwar settlement. American diplomats were anxious to postpone arrangement of the details of the peace until after the end of hostilities, and they hoped and expected that the foundation of an international organization embracing the entire world would then smooth the path for agreement on particular issues; the American negotiators, therefore, were pleased when, at Yalta, they obtained Russia's agreement to the foundation of the United Nations. Yet the hesitant attitude of the Russians made it clear that they were not willing to concede to the United Nations supranational authority, and it is questionable whether they were ever prepared to grant to it any political function beyond that of providing, in times of crisis, a meeting place where tensions could be aired and

Winston Churchill delivers a famous address. *On March 5, 1946, in a speech delivered in Fulton, Missouri, the former British prime minister warned that an "iron curtain" separated eastern Europe from the rest of the continent. The phrase "iron curtain" was to be often repeated during the Cold War years.*

Scene from the Greek civil war. *Mules carrying munitions into the mountains.*

negotiations could be initiated. But while the Russians' interest in the establishment of the United Nations was limited, they were anxious to gain security against aggression and to expand their territorial frontiers toward the west. They were determined that no foreign power should have any influence in the entire area now considered as lying behind the Iron Curtain.

Churchill at Yalta was ready to accept a division of Europe into spheres of interest. But the United States was not. It was argued in the American delegation that such a plan suggested a revival of the balance of power and of all those concepts of traditional diplomacy which Americans abhor. Nevertheless, it might have been better if an understanding had been achieved about where the several victorious nations were to exert their influence. Certainly, it is impossible to state with any assurance that the Russians would not have tried to create unrest in western Europe if the United States had not attempted to stave off Communist control of Poland. But without any delimitation of spheres of interest, the Russian concern with Italian and French affairs may have appeared to the Russians not very different from the American concern with Polish affairs.

Thus, at the end of hostilities, there had still been no real clarification of the issues between the United States and Russia. Each could only speculate about the intentions of the other and indulge in guesses as to how far the other would go. In the period of the Cold War the generally accepted opinion in the West was that Russia wanted to extend Communist rule as far as possible, and from the events preceding the Cold War an impressive case was built up to show that an aggressive expansionism was the constant and dominating motive of the actions of the Russian leaders. For example, the control achieved by the Communists over the governments of Bulgaria, Rumania, Hungary, and Poland was cited. In addition, it was noted that the Communists did not desist from the attempt to achieve power in Greece, where Communist guerrillas supported from the north were able to maintain a civil war until October, 1949. Moreover, while the western powers agreed to the signing of peace treaties with the countries in the Soviet sphere, the Russians raised obstacles to the formal conclusion of peace with Austria and Germany, countries in which the influence of the western powers was strong. In their zone of Germany, the Russians conducted affairs without much regard to the principles previously laid down; they quickly revived political life so that Communist influence would be secured; they reorganized economic life in accordance with Communist ideas; and when the western powers opposed the Russian reparations policy the Russians prevented the formation of a central German administration. Their intervention to stop participation of any of the eastern countries in the Marshall Plan in 1947, and their backing of the Chinese Communists against the Nationalist Chinese under Chiang Kai-shek, were further proof of their unwillingness to come to any accommodation with the West by means of reciprocal concessions. The veto with which in 1947 they killed in the United Nations the American plan for control of atomic weapons strengthened the view that there existed an insuperable antagonism between Russia and the Russian-controlled areas on one side, and the rest of the world, the "free world," on the other.

While the people of the West regarded the Russians as aggressors, they believed the policies of their own governments toward Russia to be purely defensive and motivated by good will. After the tension of the Cold War had lessened, however, the simplistic character of this view became apparent. It was realized that the American government had taken a number of steps which to the Russians might have seemed less than friendly. Lend-Lease was abruptly terminated at the end of the war, and the Russian request for American credit for the purposes of postwar reconstruction, made in August, 1945, was "mislaid" and discovered only seven months later. Moreover, it must be realized that just as the United States regarded the measures of agrarian reform and socialization introduced in the Russian-controlled countries as an attempt to exclude western influence, so the Russians regarded the restoration of free enterprise in the states of western Europe as an attempt to rebuild these countries in a strictly anti-Communist "imperialist" spirit. Some analysts have even maintained that the United States not Russia, was the aggressor in this period—that the explosion of the atomic bomb was addressed to Russia rather than Japan. American policy makers, it has been argued, wanted to bring about a showdown with Russia at a time when American troops were still in Europe and Asia, and America possessed a monopoly in atomic weapons. In this context it is of some significance that, generous as it was, the American plan for the banning of atomic weapons presented to the United Nations in 1946 by Bernard Baruch left the United States in possession of its atomic monopoly until the envisaged inspection and control apparatus could be set in motion. American atomic superiority was to be maintained, at least for a time.

Nevertheless, it seems unlikely that the United States—in 1945, when it had an atomic monopoly and Russia was still weakened as a result of the war—had a considered strategy for forcing a showdown with Russia. It is probably more correct to say that in both the United States and the Soviet Union those in the ruling groups were divided about the policy to be pursued toward the other power; in each country there were proponents of a soft line and of a hard line. In Russia most of the economists were in favor of seeking American aid for reconstruction since the alternative would be to postpone indefinitely once again the production of consumer goods which Russia had been unable to initiate in the emergencies of the 1930's. In the United States some politicians, including a former vice president under Roosevelt, Henry A. Wallace, were perhaps overoptimistic about the chances for cooperation with the Soviet Union, but others too were convinced that a steadily conciliatory attitude, together with agreements on single isolated issues, might slowly effect a softening of Russian antagonism. Yet in both countries, policy came to be dominated by the hard line advocates, who believed that the contrasts between the two were insuperable and that any concession to the other must mean a loss of power for oneself.

In the United States men who must be counted as advocates of a hard line—Secretary of Defense James Forrestal (1892–1949), military men, and members of the State Department—were certainly in a powerful position. In Russia, those who recommended cooperation with the United States had little if any chance. Stalin, who remained the decisive figure, inclined toward a hard line. We have seen how in the 1930's an economic policy which emphasized heavy industry at the expense of consumer goods not only increased Russia's military strength but also made necessary the maintenance of strict controls and thereby served Stalin's aim of concentrating power in his own hands. It is true indeed that the victory in the war had immensely raised Stalin's stature. But the war had created other heroes as well, and the participation of the entire population in the national struggle against the invaders had loosened the dominance of the party. A new period of economic hardship which would demand strict discipline and a tightening of controls would reinforce Stalin's position; if it could be shown that Russia was threatened from the outside, people would be willing to accept the sacrifices required for the restoration of their nation's economic strength without foreign help. Hence Stalin not only rejected continuance of the slight cooperation with the capitalist world which the war had produced, but placed on the United States the responsibility for the burden involved in his country's consequent economic isolation. Andrei Zhdanov (1896–1948), one of Stalin's most trusted lieutenants, explained: "The United States proclaimed a new, frankly predatory and expansionist course. The purpose of this new, frankly expansionist course is to establish the world supremacy of American imperialism." With the Truman Doctrine of March, 1947, and the Zhdanov speech of September, 1947, the fronts were clearly drawn.

Whenever international relations are critically strained, the occurrence of any provocative incident may spark an explosion, and in this sense the period of the Cold War was a dangerous one. Nevertheless, there were reasons why the Cold War did not become hot. In both the United States and Russia considerations of domestic policy helped make it desirable to emphasize the aggressive aims of the adversary. The inconveniences and hardships involved in the maintenance of a strong military posture would be accepted more easily if people felt they were living under a direct threat. But actually neither the United States nor Soviet Russia intended to attack the other. Unwilling to be placed in the position of submitting, each contested any move by the other which might extend its territorial control and upset the balance of power. But each was cautious with respect to areas and issues which the other might consider vital for its existence. Thus, the crises of the Cold War led repeatedly to the brink, but never over the brink.

The Berlin Blockade

The event which might be regarded as ushering in the critical years of the Cold War was the blockade of Berlin. After the collapse of efforts to establish a central administration for the whole of Germany, the powers occupying western Germany—the United States, Great Britain, and France—began to build a common political and economic organization for their three zones. When the first measures for this unified administration were taken, the reaction of the Russians was unexpectedly vehement. On June 24, 1948, by cutting off all land and water communications, the Russians isolated the parts of Berlin under western control. It is not quite clear what they sought to achieve by provoking this test of strength. Perhaps they hoped to force the western powers out of Berlin, so that a clean separation of western and eastern spheres of interest could be effected in Europe. Or they may have expected that the unsettling effect of this Berlin blockade would frustrate the working of the European Recovery Program and give new strength to the Communist movements in western Europe. Whatever their motives, the Russians assumed that the western powers, particularly the British and the French, would be most reluctant to take measures which would involve a risk of war; and they were convinced that if no military clash occurred, the blockade would force Berlin into starvation and surrender. They overlooked the possibility that the two million people of West Berlin might be supplied by air. But that is what happened. An airlift broke the blockade, negotiations were started, and on May 12, 1949,

The Berlin blockade. *An airplane with provisions arriving over the Berlin airfield. The spectators are standing on the rubble of destroyed houses.*

the Russians removed the restrictions on communications between western Germany and West Berlin. After almost a year, the blockade was over.

The Korean War

After the Berlin blockade, Asia became the scene of the Cold War. By the beginning of 1949 the victory of the Chinese Communists under Mao Tse-tung was a certainty, and by the end of the year the Nationalist government under Chiang Kai-shek had withdrawn to Formosa (Taiwan). The United States refused to recognize the Communists as the legitimate rulers of China and continued to give recognition and protection to the Nationalist government. The tension between the United States and Communist China became the crucial element in the next dangerous crisis of the Cold War, that of Korea.

After the Second World War the area of Korea north of latitude 38 had been occupied by the Russians, that south of the thirty-eighth parallel by the Americans. As in Germany, agreement on a common government for the entire country had been impossible to reach. Eventually, the occupying forces were withdrawn, the Russians leaving a Communist regime in North Korea, the Americans a western-oriented democracy in South Korea. On June 25, 1950, North Korean troops began to invade South Korea, attempting to unify their divided nation. American military leaders had gradually become aware that a non-Communist South Korea was indispensable for the defense of Japan, and the United States government ordered American troops into South Korea to support the faltering South Korean government. The matter was brought before the United Nations at a time when the Russians were boycotting the Security Council, and a resolution was passed which condemned the North Korean aggression. A United Nations Command was set up, headed by General Douglas

MacArthur, and although most of the troops were American they were supported by contingents from many other countries. The U.N. military operations were conducted with wavering success. Having succeeded in driving the North Koreans out of the south, the Americans advanced beyond the thirty-eighth parallel, but there they encountered opposition by strong North Korean forces aided by Communist Chinese armies, and were driven back into South Korea. Finally a front along the thirty-eighth parallel was established and armistice negotiations were initiated. In July, 1953, after almost two years of negotiations, an armistice was concluded which ended the war and virtually restored the *status quo ante:* Korea remained divided along the thirty-eighth parallel.

War in Indochina

While the Korean War slowly petered out, another dangerous military clash developed on the southern frontier of China. There, a nationalist movement known as the Viet Minh, under the leadership of Ho Chi-Minh, was fighting the French for greater autonomy in that part of Indochina which, after the separation of Laos and Cambodia, was called Vietnam.

The Viet Minh received recognition and aid from Communist China and Soviet Russia, while France and the puppet regime which it had established were supported by Great Britain and the United States. Modern weapons and bombing from the air were unable to destroy the guerrilla forces fighting in millet fields and rice paddies, and when the French advanced into the north, a part of their forces was cut off and finally forced to surrender at Dien Bien Phu, in May, 1954; ten thousand French soldiers became prisoners. At this point mediation by Russia, the United States, and Great Britain resulted in an armistice; among its terms were provisions for an election to be held in 1956, to unify Vietnam. Until then Vietnam was to be divided along the seventeenth parallel, with the northern half Communist-controlled and the southern half western-oriented.

The Nuclear Stalemate

With the Korean armistice in 1953, and the settlement of the conflict in Indochina in 1954, the Cold War abated. The next few years were free of military clashes in which Russia and the United States were backing opposite sides or in which, as in the Korean War, one of them was directly involved. Moreover, developments in the field of nuclear weapons helped to reduce tension from 1954 on. After the negotiations about atomic control in the United Nations had failed, the Russians had gone ahead with their own search for nuclear weapons and in August, 1949, had succeeded in producing their first atomic explosion. This event came earlier than had been expected and aroused great concern in the United States. The sharp American reaction stimulated fears in Russia that America might start a preventive war before Russia had accumulated an arsenal of atomic weapons. The Russians therefore pursued their development of nuclear arms with increased energy.

Correspondingly, fearing that the Russians' advances would give them superiority, President Truman, early in 1950, ordered a crash program to develop a hydrogen bomb; the first such device was successfully tested in November, 1952. Nine months later the Russians constructed their own hydrogen bomb. The nuclear armament race between Russia and the United States augmented the nervousness and tension of this period. By 1954, with both Russia and the United States in possession of the hydrogen bomb, the continuation of the nuclear-arms race became meaningless. The incredibly destructive force of this weapon made the leaders of both states realize that in a war the two superpowers could only destroy each other. Neither of them could win.

In the quieter atmosphere of the following years, views about the reasons for the military conflicts of the critical period of the Cold War changed. These wars came to be regarded as having been caused by local conditions or by misunderstandings. For instance, the North Koreans seem not to have expected that their attempt to unify the country by force would encounter strong American opposition, for high American military and diplomatic officials had made pronouncements suggesting that America considered Korea to be of little strategic value. The particular reasons for the conflict in Indochina also became apparent: it was seen to have been a national revolt against foreign rule and a civil war of the suppressed classes against the French-oriented wealthy ruling groups. But at the time, there were very different explanations for the genesis of the struggles in Korea and Indochina. The various conflicts appeared to be integral parts of a grand design—understood by the Americans as a Communist drive for control of the world, and by the Russians as an American attempt to encircle and strangle Communism. But both powers desisted from embarking on actions which would have provoked a direct military struggle between Russia and the United States, and afterwards the grand design appeared less definite and its execution less imminent than it had seemed at the high point of the crisis.

THE FORMATION OF OPPOSING ALLIANCE SYSTEMS

During the Cold War years of highest tension, the emergency seemed so great that each of the opposing powers tried to strengthen its position by uniting in a tight organization the powers which it controlled or with which it was allied. The resulting division of large portions of the world into antagonistic blocs profoundly affected the character of developments in Europe.

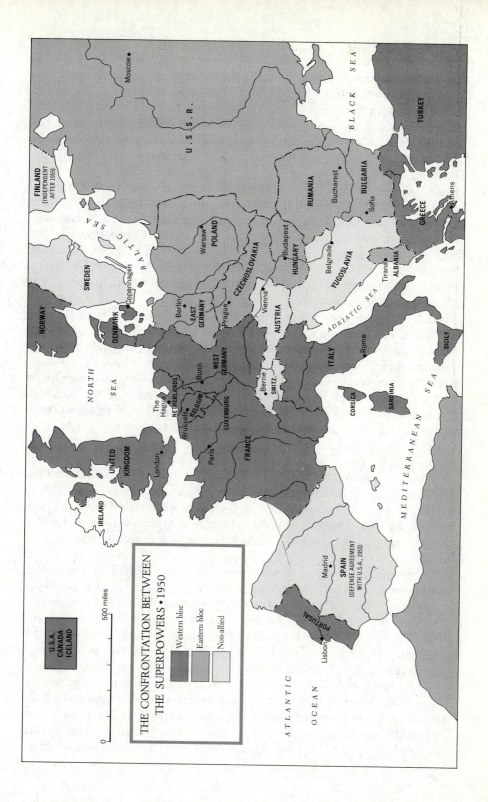

THE CONFRONTATION BETWEEN
THE SUPERPOWERS • 1950

Western bloc

Eastern bloc

Non-allied

U.S.A.
CANADA
ICELAND

500 miles

ATLANTIC OCEAN

NORTH SEA

BALTIC SEA

U.S.S.R.

Moscow

FINLAND
(INDEPENDENT
AFTER 1955)

SWEDEN

NORWAY

DENMARK
Copenhagen

IRELAND

UNITED KINGDOM
London

NETHERLANDS
The Hague
BELGIUM
Brussels
LUXEMBURG

WEST GERMANY
Bonn

EAST GERMANY
Berlin

POLAND
Warsaw

CZECHOSLOVAKIA
Prague

FRANCE
Paris

SWITZ.
Berne

AUSTRIA
Vienna

HUNGARY
Budapest

RUMANIA
Bucharest

BULGARIA
Sofia

YUGOSLAVIA
Belgrade

ALBANIA
Tirana

ITALY
Rome

CORSICA

SARDINIA

SICILY

ADRIATIC SEA

BLACK SEA

GREECE
Athens

TURKEY

MEDITERRANEAN SEA

SPAIN
(DEFENSE AGREEMENT
WITH U.S.A., 1953)
Madrid

PORTUGAL
Lisbon

The fundamental basis for the pursuit of a common line by the Communist powers was provided by the Communist Information Bureau (Cominform), created in 1947, as a replacement for the Comintern, which, as a concession to the western allies, had been dissolved during the war. The Cominform comprised only representatives of the Communist parties of the European states, and its activities were chiefly propagandistic. In addition, however, Soviet Russia created particular ties with all the Communist-controlled states. During the war Russia had concluded mutual-assistance treaties with the governments-in-exile which guaranteed help in case of future German aggression and provided for close economic, cultural, and political cooperation with Yugoslavia, Czechoslovakia, and Poland. Similar pacts were negotiated in 1948 with Bulgaria, Rumania, Hungary, and Finland, the former Axis satellites. A comparable treaty, assuring assistance against attack by Japan or by powers allied to Japan, was signed with China in 1950. Chinese agreements with North Korea and North Vietnam tied these countries to the Russian bloc. Finally, in 1955 the relation of the Communist states in Europe to one another and to Soviet Russia was redefined by a pact concluded in Warsaw; in addition to the partners of previous mutual-assistance agreements—Soviet Russia, Albania, Bulgaria, Hungary, Poland, Rumania, Czechoslovakia—the treaty included East Germany, which now advanced to full membership in the Soviet alliance system. The Warsaw Pact precluded participation of its members in any other coalition or alliance and assured members of immediate assistance, including the use of armed force, in the event of armed aggression, establishing for this purpose a joint command for the armed forces of the members, as well as a consultative committee to harmonize political action. The stationing of Russian troops in eastern European countries, notably in Rumania, Hungary, Poland, and East Germany, which until then had been justified by the need to maintain communications with the Russian occupation zones in Germany and Austria, was now guaranteed by bilateral treaties.

A similar comprehensive alliance system was established by the United States. One might say that the Russian bloc and the western bloc developed in response to each other. Wartime cooperation had brought the western European states—Belgium, France, Luxemburg, the Netherlands, and Great Britain—close together, and in Brussels in 1948, they embodied this relationship in a treaty in which they committed themselves to a common defense against attack. As a counterweight against the East this alliance was obviously weak and in the following year, a larger system was developed which, with the exception of Spain and Switzerland, encompassed all the countries of northern and western Europe, as well as Italy, and most importantly, included the United States. In the North Atlantic Treaty, concluded on April 4, 1949, the signers stated that "an armed attack against

The signing of the North Atlantic Treaty. *President Truman addresses the assembled delegates on April 4, 1949.*

one or more of them in Europe or North America shall be considered an attack against them all." In the event of such an attack they promised immediately to take whatever action was deemed necessary, including the use of armed force. As a result of this treaty the signers agreed to build up a common military organization—the North Atlantic Treaty Organization, or NATO. In 1952 Greece and Turkey became participants in NATO. Turkey was the easternmost member of this alliance, but the chain was continued by a Middle East Treaty Organization, established in 1955, which included Turkey and Britain (NATO powers) and Pakistan, Iraq (until 1959), and Iran. The last link in this ring around Communism was the Southeast Asia Collective Defense Treaty of 1954, in which Great Britain, the United States, France, Pakistan, Australia, New Zealand, the Philippines, and Thailand participated. Thus, by 1955, when the most critical phase of the Cold War was over, both Russia and the United States had organized firmly tied blocs.

Despite the globe-encircling nature of these alliances both camps were aware that the critical area was Europe. Control over Europe would mean an incontestable superiority over the other side. Hence, each of the superpowers—Russia and the United States—was anxious to firm up its partners in Europe so that they would form a solid unit able to resist attack from the other side. These aims patterned political and social life in both eastern and western Europe.

The Solidification of the Soviet Bloc, 1948–1953

By 1948 the governments of the countries in the Russian orbit were entirely Communist. Through factory and village committees the Communist party exerted its authority on the local level. Its youth organizations, backed by the power of the minister of education, guaranteed the Marxist character and ideological orthodoxy of the education system; a clash with the Catholic Church was therefore unavoidable, and indeed in every satellite country with a strong Roman Catholic population sensational proceedings against the leaders of the Roman Catholic Church were instigated: in 1946 against Archbishop Stepinac in Yugoslavia, in 1949 against Cardinal Mindszenty in Hungary, and in 1951 against Archbishop Beran in Czechoslovakia. Thus, the uniformity of Communist party strategy and tactics tied the various eastern European states to Russia. The Russians also possessed more direct means of exerting authority and control. Russian troops remained in Hungary and Poland and the military forces of these countries were built up under Russian surveillance. Moreover, the secret police in the several eastern European countries formed an almost autonomous body independent of their respective governments; they worked in close contact with the Russian secret police. Ideologically and institutionally Bolshevik Russia deeply interpenetrated the life of eastern Europe.

The all-important aim, of course, was to change the economic structure of the states of the Soviet bloc according to Bolshevik concepts, and doing this involved three tasks: to divert the trade of these countries from the West to the East, to collectivize their agriculture, and to industrialize them. It ought to be said that if one takes an overall view, these goals were attained. By 1951, 92 per cent of Bulgaria's trade was with Soviet Russia. Even Poland's trade with Russia, which before the war amounted to only 7 per cent of the country's foreign trade, had reached 58 per cent by 1951. At the same time, industrial production increased remarkably. By 1952, annual production in Poland and Czechoslovakia, the two most industrialized countries of the bloc, was double its prewar level, and the total steel production in eastern Europe was then roughly equal to that of West Germany, and twice what it had been before the war. The labor force employed in industry in eastern Europe increased about 33 per cent by the early 1950's.

The issue which created the greatest difficulties was the collectivization of agriculture; Russia's insistence on applying the Soviet pattern took little account of the situation existing in eastern Europe. Since agricultural reforms resulting in the dismemberment of the large estates had already taken place, most of the land was divided into small or middle-sized farms, and their owners were reluctant or unwilling to join collectives. Moral and economic pressure and even violence had to be used to attain collectivization. And progress in the various countries was very uneven, rather quick in Bulgaria and Czechoslovakia, but slow in Poland and Hungary.

Tensions arising from a strict application of the Soviet pattern to eastern Europe were exacerbated by Russia's adding to its imposition of overall economic control a policy of direct economic exploitation. Even after Hungary and Rumania had become purely Communist, they continued to pay reparations to Russia. Moreover, the Russians seized all German property in these countries and dismantled all German industrial installations, which they then transferred to Russia. The Russians also participated in a number of joint companies controlling such enterprises as the Rumanian merchant marine and the Hungarian bauxite mines. Thus, a portion of the earnings of these companies went directly to Russia. Moreover, the Russians forced upon these countries agreements to deliver certain goods, such as coal, at extremely low prices.

It is no wonder that the rigid exploitative economic policy pursued by Soviet Russia created dissatisfaction and unrest. Between 1948 and 1954 the eastern bloc underwent some serious crises.

In 1948 peasant resistance to collectivization and a general resentment over Russian interference in Yugoslav affairs led to a break between the rulers in the Kremlin and Marshal Tito, the head of the Yugoslav Communist party. As the military leader of the partisans during the war, Tito had become a national hero, with a very strong hold over the people. Moreover, because the partisans had been able to maintain some organized resistance throughout the entire war the Yugoslavs did not wait to be liberated by the Allied armies; the partisans took over the country when the Nazi power collapsed. Yugoslavia was the only country of eastern Europe which Russian troops never entered. Thus, when Yugoslavia resisted Soviet demands, Russia had no strong levers within the nation.

The Russians were not ready to risk the general war which might result from military intervention, and they evidently expected that exclusion from the Cominform, which implied writing off Yugoslavia as a member of the Communist bloc, would force Tito to submit. But Tito's popularity with his people, together with some economic help from the West, made it possible for him to retain power, and the Russians resigned themselves to this situation although they continued vehement vocal attacks against Tito and maintained an economic blockade of Yugoslavia. Under Tito, Yugoslavia developed a special form of Communism—a mixed economy. There was no overall economic planning for the entire country. In agriculture, collective farms coexisted with privately owned farms. Industry was nationalized, but control was exercised by the workers in the individual factories, and there was a free market for the sale of many consumer goods.

Tito's defection aroused in Stalin and the Russian leaders fears that other eastern European countries might follow the Yugoslav example, with each country forging its own inidvidual type of Communism. Consequently, under pressure from the Russians, widespread purges took place in these states. One aim of the purges was to make the Communist party an absolutely reliable instrument for the execution of directives given from above. In every eastern European country the size of the Communist party had greatly increased as many who had belonged to the dissolved and suppressed non-Communist parties had thought it useful to enter Communist ranks; this influx of incompletely trained and untested members was especially dangerous for the efficiency of the party because even the upper strata contained discordant elements—on the one hand those who had taken refuge in Moscow during the war, and on the other those who had remained in their country, working in the underground. These two groups now competed for control of the party. In danger of becoming unwieldy and divided, the Communist parties in eastern Europe instituted mass purges. Hundreds of thousands were deprived of membership in the party as "alien" or "hostile" elements. Another aim of the purges was to eliminate those Communist leaders who might be inclined to follow the example of Tito, and the consequence was a substantial change in the composition of the Central Committees of the Communist parties in the various states. Leaders who might be inclined toward Titoist deviations were brought before tribunals in sensational procedures patterned after the Russian purge trials of the 1930's, complete with accusations of treason, confessions, and finally the imposition of the death penalty. The most outstanding victims of these trials, starting in 1949, were Traicho Kostov, the vice premier of the Bulgarian government; Laszlo Rajk, the minister of the interior in Hungary; and in Czechoslovakia, Vladimir Clementis, the foreign minister, and Rudolf Slansky, general secretary of the Communist party and deputy prime minister. Wladyslaw Gomulka, the general secretary of the Polish Communist party, was deposed and later imprisoned, but he escaped execution.

The purges and trials of the leadership in the Russian satellite countries continued until 1953, and in the course of time their purposes went beyond those of party discipline and the elimination of Titoists. The motives for the persecution of individuals are frequently obscure. These were the years when Stalin's suspiciousness had clearly become pathological and when anticipation of his approaching death sharpened the conflicts among Russian Communist leaders anxious to eliminate possible rivals. The trials in the satellite countries appear to have been repercussions of the struggles in the Russian leadership group, as is suggested by the fact that some of these trials, like some of those in Russia, had anti-Semitic overtones. In his dealings with the various eastern European nations Stalin preferred to work through one person entirely devoted and obedient to him. And the purges served to concentrate power in each country in the hands of one entirely pro-Stalin Communist leader: Mátyás Rákosi in Hungary; Walter Ulbricht in East Germany; Klement Gottwald in Czechoslovakia; Boleslarv Bierut in Poland. Like Stalin himself, though to a slighter extent, each of these leaders became the center of a cult of personality. By the time Stalin died in 1953, the various means which had been applied to unify the Russian-controlled areas of Europe—ideological uniformity, institutional identity, economic integration, force—appeared to have transformed them into a monolithic bloc ruled and directed by Russia, and most of the member states seemed to be on the way to reaping the fruits of the economic transformation to which they had been submitted. But the tensions produced in these countries by the changes which they had undergone had been suppressed rather than eliminated, as the events of the later 1950's would show.

Integration in the West

The term "free world" is frequently applied to that part of Europe which lies outside the zone of Russian control and influence, and it is indeed true that certain values and institutions regarded as basic for a life in freedom have been maintained in most countries of western Europe. A system of law which gives assurances against arbitrariness in the persecution of crimes, a guarantee of freedom of thought and expression, and a representative government based on a multiparty system—recognition of the paramount importance of these formed the unifying ideological bond in the West. It would be an error, however, to conclude that all the countries of western Europe were able to develop according to their own interests and traditions without outside pressure; in a political constellation dominated by two superpowers, rejection of one meant dependence on the other. The influence of the United States and the needs of the Cold War were crucial in patterning the forms of political development in western Europe.

First of all, cooperation with the United States required removal of the Communists from political power. In West Germany the Communist party was declared unconstitutional and forbidden. In May, 1947, more or less at the time that the Russians were eliminating the non-Communist parties in eastern Europe, governments were formed in France and Italy excluding the Communists, who had hitherto been members of the ruling coalition. Within the Italian and French governments, conflicts between Communists and non-Communists about the course of foreign policy and economic policy had been constant, and the end of the period of cooperation with the Communists was not unexpected. Because Italy and France were parliamentary democracies, however, the elimination of the Communists was not considered accomplished until the people had spoken in the next elections.

Particular importance was attached to the Italian elections of April, 1948, because in contrast to France, where a wide gap separated Communists and socialists, in Italy there was a possibility that the Communists, together with their allies, the left-wing socialists, would gain a majority over supporters of the prime minister, Alcide de Gasperi (1881–1954), a Christian Democrat who enjoyed the active and energetic backing of the Roman Catholic Church. The Marshall Plan, initiated in the previous summer, had begun to demonstrate the advantages of American support, and American diplomats were not reluctant to indicate that a victory of Communism would end this assistance. In addition, the United States, together with Great Britain and France, in a statement issued a few weeks before the election, promised to support the Italian claims to Trieste and its surroundings—an area where the Russian and American zones of influence touched, and a subject of dispute between Italy and Yugoslavia since the end of the war. The direct participation of Catholic priests and foreign diplomats gave these Italian elections an unusual aspect. The disregard of the traditional rule that foreign powers ought not to interfere in the internal affairs of another country showed the supranational nature of the conflict then evolving, and the results justified the extraordinary efforts which had been made to keep the Communists out of power; the Christian Democrats won an absolute majority, with 305 seats out of 574.

But the elimination of the Communists from political power was only the beginning in the process of making western Europe a bulwark against the East in the Cold War. Just as the Russians were securing their position in eastern Europe by economic reorganization and by the development of a unified military command, so the United States set about to stabilize economic life and create an integrated military force in western Europe. The Marshall Plan and NATO represented important first steps toward achieving these aims. But all further progress encountered a difficult obstacle—the peculiar situation of western Germany within the free world. The states which had defeated the Nazis had agreed that Germany ought to be deprived of the means of again becoming an aggressor. It was to be permanently demilitarized, and the great industrial power which it possessed through the rich iron and coal mines of the Ruhr area was to be reduced. However, these notions about a demilitarized and deindustrialized Germany came into conflict with the demands arising from the Cold War: German manpower and German industrial resources were required to maintain and strengthen the military organization of the west, and in all plans for halting an attack from the east the territory of western Germany, abutting the Soviet zone, was crucial. It was hardly possible to envisage military operations among people who felt themselves to be discriminated against, who were dissatisfied and hostile. Nevertheless, Germany's western neighbors regarded a revival of its military and industrial power with great distrust. Western Germany in 1947 had 6 million more inhabitants than France (47.5 million against 41 million). The most appropriate means of overcoming the difficulty posed by the German problem seemed to be integration through the creation of common organizations which would equally limit each nation's freedom of action and weaken traditional national contrasts.

The economic and political unification of the occupation zones in western Germany—first the integration of the American and British zones and then the merger of the French zone with them—had slowly progressed since 1946. A decisive step was the introduction of a new currency in June, 1948, which halted inflation and affirmed the economic unity of western Germany; the next logical measure was the establishment of a unified political organization. On the local and regional level, political activity had been permitted since 1946, with local German administrations working under the control and supervision of the Allied powers. After the establishment of economic unity through currency reform, a parliamentary council consisting of delegates of the various German state governments worked out a constitution for a federal government. The West German Federal Republic came into being in May, 1949.

But the political revival of Germany renewed fears of what Germany might do with its power, and before Germany was resuscitated as a sovereign state, steps were taken to ensure Allied control of its industrial development. In 1948 the Ruhr Statute was concluded; this agreement was signed by the United States, Great Britain, France, Belgium, the Netherlands, and Luxemburg; and Germany joined in 1949. It gave the signatory powers authority to limit the output, and allocate the exports, of coal and iron from the Ruhr. The next step was the creation of a European free market for coal and steel. The initiative for this development was taken by the French foreign minister, Robert Schuman (1886–1963). Great Britain stayed aside, but Belgium, the Netherlands, Luxemburg, Italy, and West Germany reacted favorably to the French suggestion, and the European Coal and Steel Community, superseding the arrangements of the Ruhr Statute, was established in 1951. An assembly consisting of representatives elected by the parliaments of the member states was to appoint an executive body, the High Authority, to supervise the functioning of the coal and steel community, with the right to set maximum and minimum prices and even to limit production, if necessary.

With the subordination of the industrial production of the Ruhr area to a European economic program, one of the dangers inherent in the revival of Germany as an independent power was arrested. A similar solution was found for the question of German rearmament, although for some time a positive outcome seemed to be lost in a maze of negotiations. The North Atlantic Treaty had provided for a joint military organization of the member nations. Eisenhower was made supreme commander of the NATO forces in Europe in 1950, and American troops retained bases in western Europe in accordance with NATO planning. When the outbreak of the

Korean War made the United States government fear that its resources might become overstrained, it demanded that Germany be permitted to rearm to strengthen the western military presence in Europe. America's allies, particularly the French, responded with a remarkable lack of enthusiasm to this American eagerness to forget the past. But unable to resist the request of their powerful ally, the French suggested an integrated European army, in which they hoped the German contribution would be kept to a minimum. After lengthy negotiations, a treaty for a European Defense Community was concluded in May, 1952. But most of the signatory powers felt doubtful about the abandonment of sovereignty over their military forces implied in an integrated army. The French themselves in August, 1954, rejected ratification of the treaty, and suddenly a different and much simpler solution was obtained. West Germany became a member of NATO and was recognized as a sovereign state. Foreign troops stationed on German soil could now be regarded not as occupation forces but as allies, present on the basis of NATO membership. The French were reconciled to German rearmament by a British promise to leave several divisions on the Continent; thus, the French felt, if war did break out the British would be immediately involved. Moreover, the French obtained the establishment of a Western European Union which united Belgium, France, Luxemburg, the Netherlands, Great Britain, West Germany, and Italy in defense against attack and committed the participants to a "progressive integration of Europe." The Western European Union was also entrusted with control over the size of the military forces and the armaments of the individual nations; the French had some guarantees, therefore, that Germany's military strength would not go beyond the contribution which NATO assigned to it.

CHAPTER 46

Reconstruction and Change in
Western Europe

THE ESTABLISHMENT of close cooperation among the powers of western Europe, and the founding of supranational European institutions—in short, the acceptance of a policy of European unification—was made possible by the significant fact that in France, Italy, and West Germany during the first decade after the end of the Second World War, parties of very similar political aims and outlook were in power, namely, political parties which emphasized Christianity and Roman Catholicism as a common feature. In Italy the party was called *Democrazia Cristiana* (Christian Democracy), and from 1948 to 1953 it had the absolute majority in parliament. In West Germany the name of the party was *Christlich-Demokratische Union* (Christian Democratic Union) and it was the largest German political party ever since the first German parliamentary elections, in 1949; it obtained an absolute majority in 1953. In France the M.R.P. (for *Mouvement Républicain Populaire*), as the Catholic party was called, had its greatest strength immediately after the war and then declined, first slowly, later rather rapidly; in 1946 the M.R.P. received one vote in four; five years later, only one in eight. Nevertheless, no government in France was formed in this period without the participation of the M.R.P.

As Catholic parties their members and leaders were used to view national life embedded in a supranatural organization; the idea of a unified Europe, of building a Christian fortress against the attack of barbarians, had strong historical roots for them. The party leaders followed a policy of close European collaboration not only because it was dictated by the practical needs of the Cold War but also because it corresponded to their aims and convictions. The men chiefly responsible for the European direction of French, Italian, and West German foreign policy in these critical years were Robert Schuman, between 1947 and 1953 first prime minister, then foreign minister, in France; Alcide de Gasperi, Italian prime minister from 1945 to

1953; and Konrad Adenauer, German chancellor from 1949 to 1963.

De Gasperi and Adenauer impressed themselves upon the history of their countries by charting the political course of postwar Italy and Germany. Both leaders were very different from the idealistic statesmen of the early years of the twentieth century, with their passionate commitment to the great causes of social reform or national expansion. Their speeches emphasized concrete points and justified their policies with practical, commonsense reasons. What they wrote or said tended to be monotonous and pedestrian—Adenauer's chief saving grace was a dry wit which revealed his sharp eye for the weaknesses of his fellow men. De Gasperi and Adenauer appeared disinclined to embark on a discussion of broad principles and seemed to consider a good style and beautiful phrases as unnecessary embroidery. They gave the impression of being always in a rush, always exclusively concerned with settling the business at hand. The matter-of-factness of these two may have been rooted in their feeling that they no longer had much time to accomplish what they felt destined to do. De Gasperi had been at the beginning of a promising political career when Fascism came to power in Italy; he spent the next twenty years partly in prison, partly as an employee in the library of the Vatican. He was in his sixties when he reentered politics as a leader of the Italian resistance. Adenauer was close to seventy when, after twelve years in a political wilderness during the Nazi regime, he was reinstituted as lord mayor of Cologne by the occupying American forces and could resume a political career.

THE RECOVERY OF THE DEFEATED POWERS

The situation in Italy and Germany when De Gasperi and Adenauer took over was hardly suited for men of great plans and imagination. In the years right after the Second World War policy in these nations had to be primarily concerned with securing the basic requirements of social existence: with setting economic life again in motion and with reestablishing membership in the society of states. In economic matters De Gasperi and Adenauer had extremely capable helpers: Luigi Einaudi, Italy's leading economist, first as director of the Bank of Italy and then as minister of the budget, balanced the Italian budget by rigorous means; in 1948 he became the first president of the Italian republic. Adenauer's minister of economic affairs, Ludwig Erhard, relied courageously and successfully on the workings of free competition to stimulate production.

As a result of the impulse given by the Marshall Plan, European economic life soon began to recover. Progress was particularly pronounced in the countries of the Coal and Steel Community, and since in the early 1950's some of France's economic resources were still being absorbed by the struggle to preserve its colonial empire, West Germany and Italy, the defeated of the Second World War, were most benefitted by the economic upswing. In both countries economic miracles were achieved. In Germany the average annual rate of economic growth was 6 per cent; in Italy it was even higher. Yet in each of these countries the course of economic recovery showed different features.

Postwar Italy

Thanks to the rapid progress of the Allied armies into the Italian industrial north, and thanks to the activities of the partisans, the damage done by the war to industrial installations was a relatively low 15 per cent. Italy therefore was able quickly to restore industrial production and to export consumer goods to the rest of Europe. But as other countries set their own industrial machinery in motion, the demand for Italian goods decreased. Then the Marshall Plan provided a new stimulus, and the Italian government used the industrial and financial holdings inherited from the Fascist government to provide capital for industrial modernization. The results were startling indeed. The index of industrial production in 1954 was 71 per cent above that of 1938, the last prewar year. And electric-power production—because of Italy's lack of coal, probably the most important of the country's industries—had increased in 1953 by more than 100 per cent over 1938. By 1954 real wages were more than five times what they had been at the end of the war and almost 50 per cent higher than they had been in 1938. Nevertheless, the Italian economic situation still had great weaknesses. The domestic market remained rather undeveloped because of the poverty of the agrarian south. Although in 1954, 40 per cent of the national income came from industrial activities and only 26 per cent from agriculture, 42.4 per cent of the working population were engaged in agriculture. These figures show that the rural population had remained utterly poor, unable to buy any manufactured goods. Many of these people tried to leave the land and find work in the industrial centers of the north, where they swelled the labor market. Although unemployment had decreased, Italy still had more than four million jobless in 1954. This problem could be solved only by land reform in the south which would give more land to the peasants, but would also bring industry into this region. In dealing with this issue, the De Gasperi regime failed. Land reform had been promised at the end of the war, but the government proceeded with this task only slowly and hesitatingly. The industrial revival neither destroyed nor changed the previously existing social structure; the members of the old ruling group—industrialists allied with landowners—remained powerful throughout the early years of reconstruction. They were willing to support the Christian Democratic government because it controlled the financial resources needed by industry; they were willing to raise the wages of the

Alcide de Gasperi addresses a crowd before the 1948 elections.

workers in order to ease industrial recovery; they even accepted the introduction of an income tax, which had not previously existed in Italy—although it should be remarked that the tax law permitted declarations which had only a very remote relation to actuality. But the old ruling group opposed changes—such as land reform—which would fundamentally alter the social structure.

In consequence of the strength of the opposition to any social change, the Communists and their left-socialist allies continued to exercise strong appeal among the lower classes and made gains among the peasants and rural workers in the south. The Christian Democrats themselves split into a right wing which was willing to cooperate even with monarchists and former Fascists to prevent any change in the social structure, and a left wing which believed in the necessity of cooperation with the socialists to effect thorough social reforms. This split, together with discontent about the inertia of the government, resulted in elections in 1953 which denied De Gasperi his desired absolute majority, and he was forced to retire.

West Germany

In West Germany, the break with the past, not only with Nazism but also with the pre-Nazi past, was more thorough than in Italy. The severance of eastern Germany meant the disappearance of the *Junkers*, the owners of large estates east of the Elbe, who had continuously pressed for protective tariffs and government subsidies. And the creation of the Coal and Steel Community kept the industrial barons of the Ruhr in check. Thus the German ruling group was freed of its socially most reactionary and politically most aggressive elements. One result was a change in the composition of the German civil service, since the classes from which its members had been recruited no longer existed; although still a power within the state, the civil service became less authoritarian.

Germany's situation also differed from Italy's in that its cities and industries had been thoroughly destroyed. The huge task of reconstruction required the cooperation of all strata of the population—of government, employers, and employees, of capitalists and workers. At the same time, the scarcity of goods of all kinds made production, once begun, highly profitable; in the first years the Germans themselves eagerly bought all they could produce. Workers were therefore in great demand, and unemployment disappeared almost completely. The economy of West Germany was able to absorb the refugees from the eastern part of Germany; they turned out to be less of a discontented nationalist pressure group than had been expected and feared. The shortage of workers made employers willing to accept improvements in the status of labor. Maintenance of full employment and social security were recognized as legitimate government functions, and "codetermination," which gave the workers a share in the management of industry, was established by law. After the dictatorial handling of social questions by the Nazis, such government intervention in labor relations was considered entirely compatible with the principles of the "free market policy" advocated by Erhard, Adenauer's minister of economic affairs. If employers shared a willingness to improve the status of labor, the workers too were in a cooperative mood. They were anxious to work, so that with their earnings, they could begin to obtain the necessities of life. Thus although wages at the outset were low, the attitude of the trade unions in wage negotiations was conciliatory and no strikes of significance occurred in Germany in the first years after the war. Consequently German goods quickly reconquered a position on foreign markets.

The prevailing eagerness to prevent conflicts which might delay reconstruction and economic recovery goes far to explain the popularity of the majority party, the Christian Democratic Union, in Germany. Another reason, of course, was that the loss of the eastern part of Germany meant a great increase in the percentage of Catholics in the population, since the south and west of Germany had always been predominantly Catholic (in 1933 Catholics constituted 32.5 per cent of the German population; in West Germany in 1950 the figure was 43.8 per cent). However, the Christian Democratic Union was strong even in the northern, predominantly Protestant areas. The predecessor of the Christian Democratic Union, the old Center party, had always included a variety of social groups, ranging from the workers in the Catholic trade unions to industrialists and landowners. After the Nazi collapse, when external circumstances as well as emotional needs required a new beginning through common action, the appeal of a party which could be regarded as a microcosm of the entire population was obviously great; in contrast to Christian Democracy in Italy, which achieved

Konrad Adenauer on the day of his election. *The chancellor of the German Federal Republic signs autographs in the Bonn parliament building, September 15, 1949.*

its majority by mobilizing one part of society against the other, the German Democratic Union could be characterized as an organized consensus.

The position of Chancellor Adenauer, the leader of the Christian Democratic Union, was strong also for constitutional reasons. In an effort to avoid the instability characteristic of the Weimar Republic, the constitution of West Germany had sharply restricted the rights of parliament. Once a chancellor had been appointed and had received a vote of confidence, the vote of a majority against him could force him to resign only if his opponents had agreed on who would replace him. The only two other parties were a small bourgeois party on the right of the Christian Democratic Union and a Socialist party on the left, and it seemed most unlikely that these two extremes would come together and agree on a candidate for the chancellorship.

The opposition was ineffective also because it had no clear alternative policy to offer. The Socialist demand for socialization of key industries aroused little enthusiasm even among the workers—partly because the swollen bureaucracy of the Nazi dictatorship had produced a deep dislike of the red tape connected with all government-controlled enterprises, partly because the trade unions were concentrating on the immediate problem of getting the economy moving again, and were not bothering about an ideal society in a distant future. Moreover, West Germany had retained a federal structure, and in some of the states composing the Federal Republic the Socialists ruled in coalition with the Christian Democratic Union. As long as the concrete, practical tasks of reconstruction were urgent and in the foreground of interest, the differences between Socialists and the Christian Democratic Union were of little significance in domestic affairs.

For the Socialists the chief target of criticism was Adenauer's foreign policy. The chancellor was said to toe the American line, destroying all possibilities for agreement with the east and all chances for German reunification by adopting an anti-Russian course. Yet, to the majority of the German people these objections against the foreign policy of Adenauer's government seemed rather theoretical. Still numbed by defeat and conscious of the immense military strength of the two superpowers, the German people in these early years had little interest in resuming a role in international affairs. They were content to devote themselves, under American protection, to the tasks of material improvement.

It is ironical that as a result of the Cold War, which made the economic and military strengthening of western Europe an urgent necessity, the two European countries which most quickly returned to prosperity were those which had lost the war. Germany and Italy were able to draw strength out of weakness. And their lack of colonial possessions was an advantage in that they were not involved in the expensive efforts to subdue non-European peoples revolting against European rule.

THE DECLINE OF THE EMPIRES

At the end of the Second World War four European powers still retained empires; the Netherlands, Great Britain, France, and Belgium. The breakup of the British and French empires were the decisive historical events, but the Dutch loss of Indonesia was a prelude of some significance for it revealed that the revolt of the colonial peoples was linked to the Cold War.

After the Second World War, Dutch officials were able to return to Indonesia only after their government had declared its willingness to recognize the native government formed under the Japanese and to establish a Netherlands-Indonesian union. But conflict soon developed over the division of functions between the Dutch and the Indonesians and led to military action in which the Dutch supported separatist movements against the republican government. Finally, in 1949, the Dutch recognized the sovereignty and independence of the Republic of Indonesia. The abdication of the Netherlands as a colonial power was to a large extent a result of the Cold War. In negotiations in the United Nations, Indonesia had been strongly supported by Russia; and with the exception of France, which took the Dutch side because of its own colonial interests in this area, no power—not even Great Britain or the United States—was willing to back the Dutch fully, because of the danger of driving the Asian nations into Russia's arms. The Dutch defeat was a clear indication of the strength

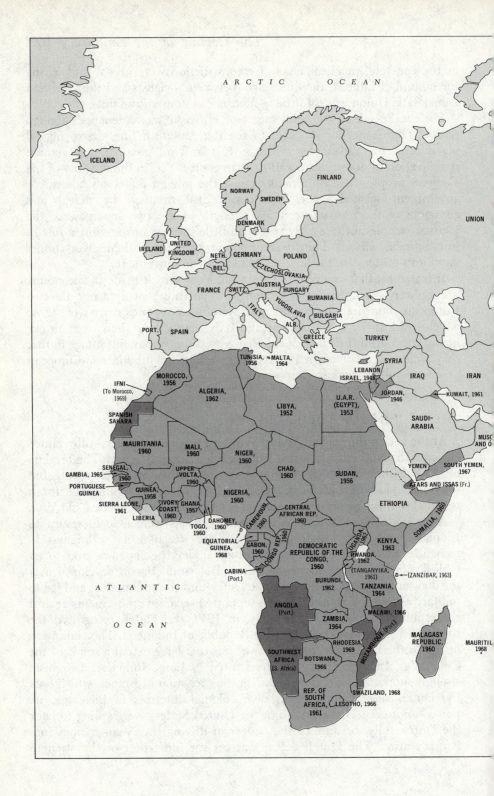

ARCTIC OCEAN

ICELAND

NORWAY
SWEDEN
FINLAND

DENMARK

UNION

IRELAND
UNITED
KINGDOM
NETH.
BEL.
GERMANY
POLAND
CZECHOSLOVAKIA
FRANCE
SWITZ.
AUSTRIA
HUNGARY
ITALY
YUGOSLAVIA
RUMANIA
BULGARIA
ALB.
GREECE
TURKEY

PORT.
SPAIN

TUNISIA,
1956
MALTA,
1964

SYRIA
LEBANON
ISRAEL, 1948
IRAQ
IRAN

MOROCCO,
1956
IFNI
(To Morocco,
1969)
ALGERIA,
1962
LIBYA,
1952
U.A.R.
(EGYPT),
1953
JORDAN,
1946
KUWAIT, 1961

SPANISH
SAHARA
SAUDI-
ARABIA

MAURITANIA,
1960
MALI,
1960
NIGER,
1960
CHAD,
1960
SUDAN,
1956
MUSC
AND Ó

SENEGAL,
1960
GAMBIA, 1965
PORTUGUESE
GUINEA
UPPER
VOLTA,
1960
YEMEN
SOUTH YEMEN,
1967

GUINEA,
1958
NIGERIA,
1960
CENTRAL
AFRICAN REP.
1960
AFARS AND ISSAS (Fr.)

SIERRA LEONE,
1961
IVORY
COAST,
1960
GHANA,
1957
CAMEROUN,
1960
ETHIOPIA
SOMALIA, 1960

LIBERIA
DAHOMEY,
1960
TOGO,
1960
GABON,
1960
CONGO REP.
1960
UGANDA,
1962
KENYA,
1963

EQUATORIAL
GUINEA,
1968
DEMOCRATIC
REPUBLIC OF THE
CONGO,
1960
RWANDA,
1962
(TANGANYIKA,
1961)
(ZANZIBAR, 1963)

CABINA
(Port.)
BURUNDI,
1962
TANZANIA,
1964

ATLANTIC

OCEAN
ANGOLA
(Port.)
ZAMBIA,
1964
MALAWI, 1966

MALAGASY
REPUBLIC,
1960
MAURITIL
1968

RHODESIA,
1969
MOZAMBIQUE (Port.)

SOUTHWEST
AFRICA
(S. Africa)
BOTSWANA,
1966
SWAZILAND, 1968

REP. OF
SOUTH
AFRICA,
1961
LESOTHO, 1966

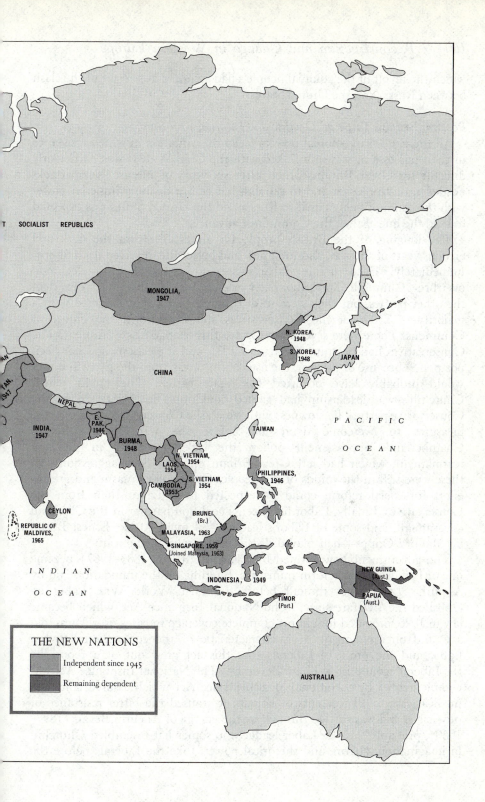

SOCIALIST REPUBLICS

MONGOLIA,
1947

N. KOREA,
1948

S. KOREA,
1948

JAPAN

CHINA

TAIWAN

PACIFIC

OCEAN

NEPAL

E.
PAK.
1946

INDIA,
1947

BURMA,
1948

N. VIETNAM,
1954

LAOS,
1954

S. VIETNAM,
1954

CAMBODIA,
1953

PHILIPPINES,
1946

CEYLON

BRUNEI
(Br.)

REPUBLIC OF
MALDIVES,
1965

MALAYSIA, 1963

SINGAPORE, 1959
(Joined Malaysia, 1963)

INDONESIA, 1949

NEW GUINEA
(Aust.)

PAPUA
(Aust.)

INDIAN

OCEAN

TIMOR
(Port.)

THE NEW NATIONS

Independent since 1945

Remaining dependent

AUSTRALIA

which the revolt of the colonial people's had acquired as a result of the clash between Russia and the United States.

Postwar Britain: Imperial Decline and Internal Reform

All the European colonial powers faced this situation in which resistance in their possessions was interlinked with the Cold War. It was particularly difficult for Great Britain, which after six years of intense Nazi attacks needed time to recover and to rebuild, but as a wide-flung imperial power with the claim of being equal to Russia and the United States was expected to hold the line against the Communist advance.

The longing of the British people for an escape from the dark and anxious years of the war, and for a new and better life, revealed itself almost immediately. Even before Japan's surrender, the British electorate overthrew Churchill. The Labor party received just 100,000 more votes than the other parties, but they were so distributed that Labor emerged with a majority of 250 over the Conservatives and Liberals in the House of Commons. There were several reasons for this change in government. The Conservatives had been in power since 1931, and if elections had not been postponed because of the war, the usual swing away from the party in power would probably have occurred five years earlier. The credit which Churchill's war leadership had gained could not be transferred to the Conservative party. The slowness with which the Conservatives had enacted measures to overcome depression before the war, the failure of Chamberlain's appeasement policy, the lack of energy in pursuing rearmament, which had left Great Britain open to Nazi aggression—all these were still in the minds of the people. Greater enthusiasm and greater effort for social reform could be expected from Labor than from the Conservatives. Finally, Labor had been a coalition partner in the Churchill government, and some of Labor's leaders—Clement Attlee, Ernest Bevin, Sir Stafford Cripps—had played distinguished roles in the war.

The government now formed by Clement Attlee (1883–1967) became one of Britain's great reform ministries. Building on the foundation laid by Asquith's Liberal government before the First World War, Labor established the "welfare state." The National Insurance Act, which became law in 1946, provided for almost complete coverage in cases of sickness, old age, and unemployment. It is characteristic of the connection between Labor and the pre-1914 Liberals that this act grew out of a report by the Liberal economist William Beveridge. The National Insurance Act was complemented by a National Health Service Act which assured complete medical care to all residents of Britain; it aroused the bitter resistance of physicians and was carried through by the energy of Aneurin Bevan (1897–1960), probably the one Labor leader who somewhat resembled Churchill in imagination, charm, and rhetorical power. Like the Liberals before the

First World War, the Labor party encountered resistance in the House of Lords. The result was further curtailment of the power of the upper chamber with respect to legislation; henceforth it could only impose a veto effecting a brief delay.

In economic policy Labor went far beyond anything the Liberals had ever envisaged, undertaking to create a socialist society, although the term used was "nationalization" rather than "socialization." The Bank of England, the road-transport system, coal mines, civil aviation, canals and docks, the electrical supply industry, and the iron industry were placed under state control and managed by government-appointed boards. The previous owners received compensation.

Through such measures Labor expected to provide a new impetus to British economic life and increased opportunity to the masses. However, these reforms did not provide the expected stimulus to society because the British people were exhausted after the tensions of the long war. Moreover, the beneficial effects of these reforms were counteracted by their coincidence with a severe economic crisis.

The developments of the Second World War had aggravated the long-standing difficulties of British economic life, particularly the problem of its unfavorable balance of trade. British foreign assets had disappeared and foreign debts had increased. Some temporary relief and some improvement in the competitive position of British goods on foreign markets was achieved through loans from the United States and a devaluation of the currency in September, 1949. But a lasting remedy could come only from a limitation of imports and an increase in exports—restriction of the production of consumer goods for the home market and forced production of goods for foreign markets. The Labor government, whose socialist ideology justified a controlled economy, continued rationing of food, fuel, and clothing, and restricted the amount of currency which a traveler might take out of the country. The architect of this austerity policy was Sir Stafford Cripps (1889–1952), a brilliant technician, ascetic, and little inclined to acknowledge the need for human amenities. The time of Labor rule was constraining rather than liberating, gloomy rather than exhilarating.

In this economically precarious situation, the question of whether possession of an empire was more an advantage than a disadvantage became a subject for sharp dispute. Colonies facilitated access to raw materials such as oil, rubber, and cotton and to foodstuffs such as coffee, tea, and rice. But they also burdened the mother country with the need to maintain a strong military posture all over the globe. Indeed, of the many justifications for colonial rule produced by the Victorians, the one which still had some validity was that only a modern industrial power could adequately defend a colony against attack. The preservation of an empire required an extended

Fuel shortage in Great Britain. *During the bitterly cold winter of 1948, the British people stood in long queues to draw their meager coal rations.*

military establishment, with all the expenses necessary for the equipment of a modern army, navy, and air force. And in a time of shrinking distances successful military protection also involved participation in the politics of the entire area in which the colonial territory was situated. Indeed, at the end of the war British troops were distributed all over the world; they were to be found in Germany, Italy, and Greece; in the Near East, Egypt, and Africa; and in the extended regions of southeast Asia. There was no conflict on the globe in which Britain was not involved. Unquestionably the occupation forces in Germany, expensive as they were, had to be maintained if Great Britain was to continue to play a role in Europe. But in the nation's straitened economic circumstances, an increase of the working force at home and a reduction in military expenses were evidently desirable, and the Labor government became anxious to decrease non-European military obligations as far as possible.

Abandonment of Britain's colonies was entirely compatible with Labor's fundamental principles. The party had always opposed imperialism and its concomitant, power politics. Although in the wartime conferences Churchill had emphasized the special interest of Great Britain in the eastern Mediterranean, the Labor government in 1948 declared itself unable to defend Greece and Turkey against Communism and left this task to the United States. The result was the Truman Doctrine (see p. 344). Moreover, the Labor government was anxious to give independence to those British colonies and dependencies which had fully developed political institutions and to introduce self-government for those which were still ruled by British governors because they were believed to be unready for independence. The most spectacular result of this policy was the granting of independence to India. The Labor government offered full freedom to India in March, 1946, but implementation was delayed by difficulties chiefly of an internal nature, caused by the differences between Hindus and Moslems. After long negotiations, the only feasible solution appeared to be the establishment of two states, one Hindu and one Moslem. The creation of India and Pakistan involved an exchange of population, the moving of millions of refugees, accompanied by terrible hardships. Moreover, the delineation of the frontiers did not cleanly separate Hindus from Moslems, and some controversies, such as the dispute over the control of Kashmir, led to bitter and long-lasting tension between the two states. The most distinguished victim of the hatred aroused by the division of India was Gandhi, the founder of the modern Indian nationalist movement; in 1948 he was assassinated by a fanatic Hindu who resented his agreement to the establishment of two states. Nevertheless, the creation of an independent India and Pakistan ended an explosive situation which had troubled the British empire for decades, and Labor had the added satisfaction that India decided to remain a member of the British Commonwealth. The granting of independence to India led unavoidably to the same change in status for the other states of this area. Burma became independent on January 4, 1948, the day and the time for the celebration of this event having been carefully chosen by astrologers. Burma left the Commonwealth; however, Ceylon, which gained sovereignty the same year, remained within the Commonwealth. The rapidity with which these changes took place reflected Communist pressure. The hope was that achievement of independence would diminish the attraction of Communism for nationalist groups. Nevertheless, Burma's emancipation was followed by a long civil war against Communist-inspired factions, and fighting between Communist-directed Chinese in Malaya and anti-Communist Malayans delayed until 1963 the establishment of the Federation of Malaysia. After a short time as a member of this federation, Singapore became independent, though remaining in the British Commonwealth.

Labor envisaged similar developments for Britain's colonies in Africa, but was convinced that further preparations were needed for the granting of independence there. The government accordingly established legislative assemblies in the Gold Coast and Nigeria and increased the number of nonwhite members in the legislative council of Kenya. The goal was the formation of independent states in which the natives would enjoy full citizenship.

The Conservatives regarded Labor's dissolution of the British imperial position with a critical eye. At the same time, the continued restrictions on economic life were diminishing the government's popularity, and Labor began to lose ground. Elections in 1950 resulted in a Labor majority so small that it was almost unmanageable. In October, 1951, the Conservatives were returned to power and Churchill again became prime minister. Some Labor measures—the nationalization of the iron and steel industries and of road transport—were revoked. But the Conservatives were aware that they had received no mandate to eliminate the main features of the welfare state. Moreover, the possibilities for initiating a new economic policy were limited because payments of pensions, compensation for war damage, expenses for the welfare state, and interest on public loans formed large, irremovable items in the budget. Nor were the Conservatives able to solve the basic problem of the deficit in the balance of trade. Yet life in Britain did become less constricted. The Conservatives were helped by the general prosperity of the 1950's; they succeeded in cutting red tape and in accelerating housing construction. But the Conservatives only improved upon the domestic policy of the Labor government; they did not alter it.

On the other hand, the Conservative government was less inclined than Labor to abandon Britain's imperial aspirations. The Labor ministry had not been able to resolve the issues in dispute between Great Britain and Egypt. Labor had declared its readiness to withdraw British forces from Egypt, as desired by the Egyptian government, but had refused to let the Sudan come under Egyptian rule against the wishes of the Sudanese people. Egypt's pride had been further hurt by the failure of its army to crush the state of Israel, which had arisen after the British mandate ended in 1948. The United States and Soviet Russia granted immediate recognition to Israel and after a successful defense against the surrounding Arab states Israel was taken into the United Nations. The withdrawal of British troops from Palestine weakened Britain's military posture in the Near East and this stimulated Egyptian nationalist demands. Nationalist students and an aroused populace engaged in fierce demonstrations against foreigners and put the Egyptian government under pressure to force the withdrawal of British troops from Egypt, the Sudan, and Suez. Clashes between British troops and Egyptian volunteers, the looting and burning of buildings and shops in Cairo by the excited masses, and the power struggle between a discredited government and a luxury-loving king brought Egypt to the brink of chaos. In 1952 a revolution by nationalist army officers deposed the king, ended the rule of the old party politicians, and established an authoritarian republic. The new regime was anxious for a success in foreign relations; the Conservatives now in power in Britain used this opportunity to arrive at a settlement. They agreed to a complete withdrawal of British forces from

Egypt and the Suez Canal, in exchange for guarantees that free passage through the canal and its control through the international Suez Canal Company would be maintained. Moreover, in case of war the British received the right to reenter the canal area with their troops. The Sudan became an independent state. Opposition to this agreement came from Conservative diehards who regarded the treaty as a British defeat. But the government explained that with the growing importance of air transport and air warfare, the Suez Canal had lost its strategic significance.

It is evident, however, that the British policy makers had still other reasons for seeking an understanding with the new Egyptian rulers. No longer burdened with the mandate over Palestine which had poisoned British relations with the Arab states, Britain's Conservative rulers were anxious again to establish Great Britain as the great ally of the Arab nations and the leading power in the Near East. The wealth of this area—notably oil, with pipelines running to the Mediterranean—and its geographical situation as a link between the Mediterranean and India, meant that the power controlling it was an important force in world politics. Gamal Abdel Nasser (born 1918), who had emerged as the leader of the new Egypt, was trying to combine the Arab nations in a unified bloc, and the British regarded their agreement with him as a step toward strengthening their nation's hold in the entire region. But they seem to have been too confident of Arab backing. When in 1955 Britain made a defense pact with Turkey and Iraq, the so-called Baghdad Pact, Egypt reacted sharply against this western interference in Near Eastern policy, particularly in the plans for a common Arab defense league. And Nasser showed his independence from the West by recognizing Communist China and ordering armaments from Czechoslovakia. This Egyptian flirtation with the East was taken amiss by the United States, which on July 19, 1956, withdrew its offer to help finance the building of a dam at Aswan. A week later, on July 26, Nasser declared that Egypt was nationalizing the Suez Canal Company and would use the revenue for the building of the Aswan Dam.

The Suez affair of October, 1956, must be seen against this background. The Conservative government wanted to maintain a strong British position in the Near East and had agreed to a troop withdrawal from Egypt and the Suez area because it expected to gain Arab cooperation. When Nasser showed more independence than had been expected, the British saw in his breach of the agreement on the Suez Canal an opportunity to crush him. Anthony Eden, who had followed Churchill as prime minister in 1955, joined the leaders of Israel and France in secretly preparing a military operation which would begin with a clash between Israel and Egypt and then lead to the intervention of French and British troops, which would occupy the Suez Canal to separate the Egyptian and Israeli forces. Militarily the operation was executed as planned, but diplomatically the plot failed.

The Suez affair. *British transports land equipment in Port Said. The scene is shown through a bullet-shattered window.*

The British miscalculated the American attitude. An explanation of the zigzag course of American policy in the Suez affair, if an explanation is possible, must be left to specialists in the history of American diplomacy. The fact is that the United States and Soviet Russia, cooperating in the United Nations, forced the British and French to accept a cease fire on November 3, 1956, and to evacuate the canal area. The Suez affair meant the end of a chapter in British imperial history.

In 1958 a *coup d'état* overthrew the pro-British regime in Iraq, killing King Faisal II, his heir, and the prime minister, Nuri as-Said. Britain had lost its most reliable ally in the Near East. When the pro-western president of Lebanon felt threatened, his position was upheld by the landing not of British but of American troops. In 1959, Britain conceded independence to Cyprus, thereby abandoning its last important military stronghold in this region. Henceforth, if outside powers played a role in the rivalries and maneuverings of the Arab countries, they were Soviet Russia and the United States; they no longer included Great Britain.

Britain now also accelerated the termination of its responsibilities in Africa. In 1957 Ghana, the former Gold Coast, became independent; at the celebration the duchess of Kent, the queen's cousin, danced the fox-trot with President Kwame Nkrumah under the admiring gaze of the American vice president, Richard Nixon. Nigeria gained independence in 1960; Sierra Leone and Tanganyika, in 1961; Uganda, in 1962: Kenya, in 1963. All these new republics remained members of the Commonwealth. Only British Somaliland, which in 1960 united with Italian Somaliland, became an independent state outside the Commonwealth. The Conservative conversion to anticolonialism was dramatically underlined by a speech made in Cape Town, South Africa, by Harold Macmillan (born 1894), who replaced Anthony Eden as prime minister after the Suez debacle. Macmillan spoke of the "wind of change" sweeping through the African continent, unmistakably dissociating himself from the white man's belief in his superiority over the black.

The refusal to continue bearing the white man's burden brought financial relief to Great Britain. The nation's military role in the Far East had been steadily reduced and plans were made to withdraw British forces completely from all territories east of Suez by 1970.

Although the termination of British colonial rule had positive effects—giving relief from the pressure of Communist anticolonialism, decreasing possible friction with the United States, and simplifying relations with Europe—the decline of the empire did not solve the problems of British domestic and foreign policy. The reduction of political and military commitments has failed to eliminate the basic weaknesses of the British economic situation. It has proved extremely difficult to overcome the unfavorable balance of trade because a relatively high standard of living makes British goods costly and limits the possibilities for selling them on foreign markets. On the other hand, the need for imports—raw materials and foodstuffs—remains constant and high. Both political parties, Conservatives and Labor, have worked with temporary expedients, like currency restrictions, foreign loans, devaluation, export incentives. But the strenuous efforts which must be made to keep the British economy afloat create no favorable climate for the needed far-reaching changes in the economic structure. They are also unpopular because some of the required measures—industrial concentration, limitation of the right to strike, flexibility in working conditions—impinge upon the power of the trade unions and might appear to be tampering with the achievements of the welfare state. Moreover, economic measures form only one part of the needed reforms; it is recognized that they must extend into the educational area and must include therefore a change in the composition of the British ruling group. The role of Great Britain as an industrial power is dependent on broadening the possibilities of higher education and on shifting, at least to a certain extent, from a broad general education to the training of specialists and technicians. Plans for a great increase in the number of institutions of higher education have been made in the sixties. But it is doubtful whether these plans went deep enough. This is the more serious because even the execution of the existing plans has been slowed down by the need for economies. But it is evident that such fundamental reforms are needed if improvements, which are permanent rather than temporary, are to be obtained.

The precariousness of the British economic situation is obvious abroad but is less noticeable to people in Great Britain where full employment, good wages, and the welfare state guarantee a satisfactory standard of living. This disproportion between the evaluation of the British position by outside powers and by the British people themselves presents a difficulty in achieving the solution which, as it is widely assumed, is best suited to overcome British economic weaknesses: Britain's entry in the European Common Market.

Adjustment to the decline in imperial power represents not only a political and economic but also a psychological problem. The legacy of Britain's imperial era is more than a shell which can be sloughed off. It is a concrete concern of British policy. Britain's policy in the post-war era has been weak not only because of economic difficulties. Despite its loss in imperial strength and its withdrawal from global obligations Britain has remained the center of a commonwealth and its foreign policy has to take the interests of the nations of the Commonwealth into account. Important members of the Commonwealth, particularly the self-governing dominions of Canada, Australia, and New Zealand, now have to look for protection to the United States and consequently Britain has to maintain a special relationship with the United States. Britain is also obligated to keep substantial military forces on the European continent, and it needs close ties with Europe for its own military security as well as for economic reasons. Britain's operations in the field of foreign policy have become increasingly limited because Britain has to chart a difficult course between its global and its European interests.

Postwar France

The dissolution of the French colonial empire created for France an entirely new situation as well as new opportunities. At the end of the war the situation in France was significantly different from that in Great Britain. The successful British resistance to the Nazi onslaught had confirmed the soundness of the nation's political institutions, and the reforms initiated by the Labor government were carried through by means of the existing parliamentary machinery. But the French defeat in 1940 had demonstrated the defective character of the constitution of the Third Republic. Most of the members of the constituent assembly which was elected in 1945 to draft a new constitution agreed that government instability had been the chief weakness of the Third Republic. De Gaulle, who returned to France with immense prestige, emphasized the necessity of strengthening the power and independence of the executive branch. But the left wing—the Communists and Socialists—which dominated the constituent assembly attempted to ensure stability in the government by means of a complete subordination of the executive to the legislative branch; the Chamber of Deputies became all-powerful. De Gaulle saw in this arrangement a disturbing sign that the period of party squabbles was returning, and he resigned as head of the Provisional Government in January, 1946.

He was right, in that government stability turned out to be no greater in the Fourth Republic than it had been in the Third. There were prolonged government crises and an endless succession of ministries. In 1946 the Communists had emerged as the strongest political party. But after they had been eliminated from the government in May, 1947, they never received much more than 25 per cent of the vote. The majority was formed by a left-center coalition of Catholic democrats, the M.R.P., Socialists, and left-liberal groups; almost every French government under the Fourth Republic obtained its support from these parties. Frequent changes in administration were caused less by political conflicts and disagreement over issues than by the maneuverings of ambitious politicians eager to become ministers and inclined to intrigue against one another. In the 1950's French political life found itself in a depressing rut. When the same men or groups remain in power for a very long time opposition tends to increase in strength and shrillness. Majorities for the existing government became increasingly precarious; but no alternative was in sight. Extremists, particularly of the right, were gaining in popular appeal; and the left and right wings of the coalition began to pull in opposite directions in their efforts to pacify the radicals on their fringes.

Yet, the troubles of the Fourth Republic cannot be blamed just on the resentment of the "outs" against the "ins" or on the bickering of the politicians, who in truth did not quite deserve the harsh criticism which they have received. The obvious difficulties of the transition from a wartime to a peacetime economy were augmented by the need to fulfill demands for social change. As we have seen, works committees in all establishments with more than a hundred workers were introduced to give the employees some part in the organization of the work in the factories, and a number of key industries—fuel and power, insurance and large financial concerns, air transport and the merchant marine—were nationalized. But there was also the fundamental question of how to renew the outmoded French industrial apparatus, which with its numerous small family enterprises was resistant to modern technology. The Fourth Republic did handle this matter well. It set up a special office under Jean Monnet (born 1888) to draw up a comprehensive scheme of economic modernization. The Monnet plan established voluntary programs for updating the basic industries, for improving farming methods, and for furthering reconstruction and new building. The government was to provide advice by experts, facilitate the procurement of the necessary labor, and make available the capital needed for investments. Marshall Plan aid, coming at a very opportune moment, was used to help carry out this policy of modernization. Nevertheless, time was needed for the results to become evident, since—as in the Russian Five-Year Plans—the emphasis was placed on heavy industry and the production of machinery. The plan gave priority to coal, electricity, transport, steel, cement, and agricultural machinery. And it would be the Fifth Republic, of Charles de Gaulle, that would harvest much of what the Fourth Republic planted in the field of economic improvement and modernization.

By 1956 French industrial production was 50 per cent higher than it had been in 1929, France's best year during the interwar period, and 87 per cent higher than in 1938, the last year before the war. But this progress in modernizing industry went relatively unnoticed, while the failure of the French government to handle urgent pocketbook issues was all too obvious. The development which hurt the French people most was inflation, produced by the scarcity of goods after the war, by large government loans to industry, and by a series of budgetary deficits. The rapid course of inflation was marked by a steep rise in prices. Wages, although rising, did not keep step, and the purchasing power of both the workers and the middle classes was low; in 1951 the average working-class family spent a third of its weekly budget on meat. Attempts to stem the inflation were futile because the government was unable to get along without a rising deficit. The nationalized industries were unprofitable at this time: the introduction of new forms of management had been costly; the government lacked the courage to brave the indignation which dismissal of superfluous personnel would arouse; and in view of the inflation, the government felt unable to burden the populace further by increases in the costs of railroads and electricity. The social-security system also showed a high deficit because its funds came from a percentage of the workers' wages, but the size of its benefits was determined in relation to prices. In addition the French system of taxation was unsatisfactory, and the left and right wings of the governments were unable to agree on reform.

But even without these many difficulties, it is unlikely that the budget could have been balanced, for funds spent in the effort to preserve French colonial power seemed to pour into a bottomless hole. During the war the French empire had been thrown into confusion. The colonial administrators, possessing a freedom of action which had been lost by the inhabitants of Axis-controlled Europe, were torn between Vichy France and the Free France of De Gaulle. Some segments of the French empire, such as Indochina, were taken by the Japanese; others, such as Madagascar, Syria, and North Africa, were occupied by British and American forces. The loosening of ties with France during the war revealed widespread dissatisfaction with the French colonial system: the chief targets were the authoritarianism with which the colonies were ruled from Paris and the economic exploitation which had cut off the colonies from trade with all countries but France. In all the colonies dissatisfaction was fed by the nationalist movements which had been active since the First World War and received new impetus during the Second World War.

The members of the French constituent assembly realized the necessity of redefining the relationship between France and its overseas possessions. But the arrangements which resulted were a compromise and lacked clarity: the new constitution provided for a French Union, to consist of metropolitan France, its overseas departments (that is, the administrative units of Algeria, which was regarded as part of France proper), protectorates (Tunisia and Morocco), its colonies (primarily in West Africa), and its associate states (Vietnam, Cambodia, Laos—together constituting Indochina). The president of the French republic was also to be the president of this French Union, and he was assisted by an assembly. But the assembly had only advisory functions, and half of its members represented metropolitan France, so real power remained with the Paris government. A promise for elected assemblies in each of the overseas territories was also rather deceptive, since the composition and the powers of these assemblies were to be determined by the French parliament. Certainly the influence of the natives remained carefully hedged in, and the very limited concessions to the desire for self-rule could not stem the colonial movements toward nationalism and independence.

Yet preservation of the empire bore not only upon French financial interests and economic power but upon the most sensitive nerve of the French political body: the army. The French army had never been entirely integrated into the life of the republic. Against the anticlerical and individualistic spirit of the French Revolution it had regarded itself as the guardian of discipline and of national tradition. With the victory in the First World War the contrasts between the army and the republic had receded into the background, and in the 1920's one of France's greatest soldiers, the monarchist Marshal Lyautey, pacified Morocco and accomplished in the service of the Third Republic what has been characterized as "the masterpiece of French colonization." Lyautey, in whose school many of the officers of the two world wars were trained, composed a famous essay "On the Colonial Role of the Army" (1900). If the spirit of the republic was not very favorable toward the ideas of the army, outside the republic—in the colonies—the army could play a great role in the service of France. Moreover, there were a number of elite regiments, with distinguished military records, consisting of Africans.

Postwar developments strengthened the ties between the officer corps and the French colonial empire. In 1940 the military had suffered a crushing loss of prestige, and at the end of the Second World War cadres of the French resistance demanded a place in the army; for the regular officers they were intruders, an alien and unpalatable element. And the entire atmosphere of postwar France was antagonistic to the traditions of the army. The political climate in which socialists were regarded as a moderating force and the intellectual climate in which the value of revolution was accepted by the most prominent intellectual leaders of postwar France whatever their political views might be—by the Communist Jean-Paul Sartre (born 1905) or the anti-Communist Albert Camus (1913–1960)—were contrary to the ideas in which French officers were trained. The close military collaboration in Europe with officers of other nationalities, particularly with Americans, resulted in an emphasis on new weapons and the technological aspects of warfare and a tendency to overlook the values of the past; and the joint European military organization did not grant French officers that prominent place to which they felt entitled by the great military history of France. But in the colonies the army could be what it had always been; it could maintain—or regain—its identity.

Consequently, when at the end of the war in Germany, a French force was sent to the Far East to assert France's claims to its former possessions and to a voice in the affairs of Asia, the army accepted its new role with enthusiasm. The French officers were convinced that in the guerrilla war in Indochina, in which modern technology was of limited usefulness, France would be able to prove that it was still the leading military power of the world. The end of the conflict, the debacle at Dien Bien Phu, was a terrible blow for the army, and was followed by recriminations in which civilian leaders characterized the military as strategically inept, and military leaders blamed the civilians for having refused to provide needed reinforcements.

In November, 1954, only four months after the settlement of the hostilities in Indochina, negotiated by Prime Minister Pierre Mendès-France (born 1907) in Geneva, an outbreak of terrorism in Algeria opened a new theater for colonial warfare. The army was sure that now it had the opportunity of revenging its defeat in the Far East and of proving its value for France. Moslem nationalists had become increasingly active in French North Africa: Morocco, Tunisia, and Algeria. In Morocco and Tunisia the French government decided to yield to the movements for independence. Arrangements were initiated by Mendès-France immediately after the settlement in Indochina, and although French rightists, with the support of the army, succeeded in overthrowing Mendès-France and delaying the conclusion of the necessary agreements, Morocco received independence on March 2, 1956, and Tunisia on March 20, 1956. The defenders of French colonial interests found some justification for the abandonment of Morocco and Tunisia in the expectation that these two countries would now refrain from supporting the Algerian nationalists.

There was no intention of giving up Algeria, where the situation was judged to be fundamentally different from that in Tunisia and Morocco. Algeria had been a French possession for more than a hundred years. Many

Frenchmen had settled there, and administratively Algeria, which was divided into the departments of Algiers, Oran, and Constantine, formed part of continental France. Dissatisfaction with French rule arose from the fact that the role of the Moslems was subordinate to that of the *colons*, or European settlers. There were two electoral colleges, each choosing the same number of deputies, but the electorate of one consisted of 1.2 million settlers, that of the other of 8.5 million Moslems. Because Algeria essentially formed part of France, the granting of independence was vehemently opposed not only by the army and the extreme right but also by many adherents of the government parties. The government therefore jogged a weary course. Together with Israel and Great Britain, France engineered the action against Egypt after the nationalization of the Suez Canal, hoping that this blow to Arab nationalism would discourage the Moslems in Algeria. However, when the Suez affair ended in a fiasco, the movement for Algerian independence grew in strength. Guerrilla warfare, which the Moslems conducted with great skill, absorbed more than 400,000 French soldiers, who were unable to put an end to terroristic acts or to restore safety in the hinterland. The mounting costs of the war increased the French budgetary deficit and accelerated inflation.

The barbaric cruelty with which the war was pursued aroused sharp criticism among French intellectuals and men of the church. A left-wing opposition to the war began to develop. The various governments tried to restore peace by offering the Moslems increased political influence but fearing the strength of the French opposition to surrender, they did not go very far in their concessions; and the Frenchmen in Algiers, with the full backing of the officers in command there, were adamant in refusing to accept any diminution of their power. Orders of the French government which ran against the wishes of the *colons* and the army were barely obeyed.

In the spring of 1958 the crisis came to a head. Weak and frequently changing governments slowly moved in the direction of further concessions to the nationalists. On May 13, 1958, during a government crisis in Paris, in the course of a demonstration by the *colons* against the vacillations of Paris the government building in Algiers was occupied, and the army agreed to spearhead the move against further concessions. A new government quickly established in Paris proved unable to assert its authority over the military in Algiers. On the contrary, the Algiers rebels were in direct contact with officers and deputies in metropolitan France; to show the helplessness of the government, troops under order of the generals in Algiers occupied Corsica. Without means to suppress the rebellion the parliamentary politicians gave in, and on May 29, 1958, Charles de Gaulle was installed as prime minister.

Those who brought De Gaulle into power—army officers in Algiers and metropolitan France, *colons* in North Africa, politicians of the right and center such as Jacques Soustelle and Georges Bidault—later had reason to regret what they had done. But in 1958, De Gaulle, who was both an officer and the leader of a popular movement, seemed the only person who might be able to inspire the French people to the efforts required to bring the Algerian war to a victorious end. Much psychological insight would have been needed to realize that he was not the man to serve a movement, that he was accustomed to stand for himself and to chart his own course.

De Gaulle had a remarkable record of independence. During the interwar years he had differed from the overwhelming majority of his military colleagues in advocating a highly motorized professional army. In the dark days of the spring of 1940 he had been stamped as a traitor by his comrades because he refused to accept Marshal Pétain's verdict of the necessity for surrender. During the war—photographs showing De Gaulle with Churchill and Roosevelt notwithstanding—the Anglo-Saxon leaders had found cooperation with him extremely difficult. Even when De Gaulle had no real power he had insisted on the inviolability of every right that France possessed, and he could not be deflected from what he regarded as the appropriate course. When he was deliriously received in the liberated Paris and unanimously elected president of the provisional government by the constituent assembly, this general approval had little effect. He did not become more pliable, and resigned four months later, in January, 1946.

This inflexible independence was deeply rooted in De Gaulle's nature. He came from a noble family that traced its origins back to the thirteenth century but in the twentieth century had no clearly defined position in French social life. Because the De Gaulles had suffered financial losses and had only limited means, they could not take their place in the upper ranks of society. Charles de Gaulle's father was not able to follow the usual career of a French aristocrat—as an officer or a landowner—but had to earn his living as a professor of philosophy, history, and literature. Despite these intellectual activities Henri de Gaulle never became a member of the ruling group of the Third Republic. The De Gaulles were Catholics and Henri de Gaulle taught at a Jesuit college. The Dreyfus Affair and the separation of church and state must have widened the gap between the Third Republic and this family of Catholic monarchical aristocrats. Nevertheless, Henri de Gaulle was too much of an intellectual to share the primitive prejudices of his class; he was no anti-Semite, nor did he believe Dreyfus guilty. Clearly, the De Gaulles were more or less outsiders in the French Third Republic, and their position apart seems to have given them a remarkable independence.

It was natural for a member of this family to chart his own course and to look for the principles behind every action. Charles de Gaulle's entire career showed his disinclination to accept any compromise—because in a compromise immediate practical usefulness often is placed above principle.

As was demonstrated by his attitude in 1940 when he separated from his fellow officers, or again in 1946 when he cut himself off from his comrades in the resistance, De Gaulle was a man acting on principles and inclined to radical "yes" or "no" decisions.

This attitude was not only inborn in Charles de Gaulle but reinforced by education. One of the most important intellectual influences on him was Henri Bergson (1859–1941), the philosopher of creative evolution. For De Gaulle history did not progress slowly and gradually in a steady stream, but must be directed by great decisions taken at critical moments. De Gaulle came to believe that the turmoil of a crisis is the best moment for giving a new impetus to events; the greater the crisis, the more propitious the time for the intervention of a creative statesman. This was the fitting approach for a man who despite his awareness of his right to rule felt distant from the political reality of his day. What De Gaulle wrote in his memoirs about another French general appears to be almost a self-portrait: "Too proud for intrigue, too forceful for mediocrity, too ambitious to be a time-server, he nourished in his solitude a passion for domination, which had long been hardened by his consciousness of his own value, the setbacks he had encountered, and the contempt he had for others."[2]

De Gaulle's conviction of superiority, his self-righteousness, his egotism were kept under control and made bearable by his love for France. In his memoirs he wrote that he imagined France, "like the princess in the fairy stories or the Madonna in the frescoes, as dedicated to an exalted and exceptional destiny. . . . Providence had created her either for complete successes or for exemplary misfortunes. If, in spite of this, mediocrity shows in her acts," this is "an absurd anomaly. . . . France is not really herself unless in the front rank. . . . In short, to my mind, France cannot be France without greatness."[3]

Despite his high estimate of his own value, De Gaulle's actions were never inspired by concern for his own fame; he always had as his criterion the greatness of France; in ruling, he served. The religious fervor of his patriotism brought him into conflict with the internationalist tendencies —both ideological and institutional—of the twentieth century. But it would be quite erroneous to see him as dominated by the aggressive nationalism of the nineteenth century, which aimed to elevate one nation at the cost of all others. De Gaulle's concern was with preserving the integrity of France —the inviolability of its territory, the uniqueness of its spirit. He was aware that this presupposes a strength which can be acquired only through using the means of modern technology. The integrity of France must be main-

---

[2] *The Complete War Memoirs of Charles de Gaulle*, Vol. 1, *The Call to Honour*, trans. by Jonathan Griffin (New York, 1955), p. 72.
[3] *Ibid.*, p. 3.

tained within the twentieth century. While rejecting a united Europe which would submerge individual nations, he favored a closer alliance among all the nations of the continent, so that "Europe" would mean "the Europe of the fatherlands."

In his first measures as prime minister in 1958 De Gaulle acted according to expectations. He accepted office on condition that he be permitted to rule by decree for the next six months and to draft a new constitution, which would be submitted to the people for approval in a referendum. As could be foreseen, the constitution, which was adopted by a clear majority in September, 1958, strengthened the executive branch of the government. The president was to be elected for seven years by the members of the parliament (consisting of a Senate and a National Assembly) and by representatives of the local and regional councils. But a few years later, in 1962, this law was changed, and by a referendum, popular election was introduced. The president was a powerful figure. He had the right to appoint the prime minister and to dissolve the National Assembly. The powers of parliament were weakened in that a vote to overthrow the government required a majority of the total membership of the National Assembly, not just of the members present. Moreover, with the approval of the Assembly the government could, for a limited time, rule by decree; only after this period had ended, which would frequently be after the decrees had fulfilled their purpose, did they have to be ratified by parliament. Assured of being able to carry out what he had in mind, De Gaulle, in January, 1959, assumed the presidency of the Fifth Republic, to which he had been elected late in December.

THE DISSOLUTION OF THE EMPIRE

De Gaulle's constitution also provided a settlement of the colonial question. And this aspect of his constitution showed an unexpected adventurousness. It envisaged a French community in which the various colonies would be autonomous, although in matters of defense, foreign affairs, and overall economic policy, they would act jointly. Actually, this plan for a French community never fully materialized. De Gaulle permitted the colonies to vote on whether they wanted to become members of the community or to enjoy complete independence. In 1960 the French colonies (Dahomey, Cameroun, Ubangi-Shari, Chad, Gabon, Ivory Coast, Mali, Niger, Senegal, Upper Volta) achieved full independence; but cultural and economic ties with France remained close. Algeria, however, was excluded from these arrangements, and the war there dragged on. While De Gaulle continued to insist that Algeria had to remain French, he cautiously and gradually moved into a more flexible position, and on September 16, 1959, announced that self-determination for Algeria was the only dignified method by which France could discharge its obligations

Charles de Gaulle in a characteristic pose during a campaign rally.

toward North Africa. In a referendum, the Algerians were to be given the choice of assimilation, full independence, or—as a middle way—close association with France. De Gaulle tried to placate the opposition by stating that such a referendum could be held only after the area had been pacified. Nevertheless, his acceptance of self-determination opened the floodgates. The movement toward the separation of Algeria from France became irresistible. On July 8, 1961, the French people approved in a referendum the principle of self-determination for Algeria. The army officers there, in a last desperate move, tried to repeat the game which they had played in 1958. But now they received no support from France, and their own soldiers began to refuse to obey them. The insurrection collapsed; prominent generals, among them Raoul Salan and Maurice Challe, who had led the rebellion, and politicians such as Jacques Soustelle and George Bidault, who were passionate protagonists of a French Algeria, fled and were condemned *in absentia*. Negotiations with Algerian nationalist leaders now began, and although they were interrupted by recurrent crises, a settlement was reached in March, 1962. Algeria was officially named independent on July 3, 1962.

In terminating the Algerian war De Gaulle succeeded in doing what no other French government had been able to do. He had made people aware that the burdens of the war were too heavy and the price to be paid was too high; at the same time, he proclaimed that the real opportunities for French greatness were in Europe. For this reason the break with the leadership of the army was less dangerous than it might appear; in a France oriented exclusively toward Europe an army based on the traditions of colonial warfare was of little relevance. A modernized force equipped with atomic weapons was appropriate to the goals which De Gaulle had set and De Gaulle spared no expense to make France a nuclear power. For France, the abandonment of the colonies made possible full concentration on Europe. The loss of the empire was a definite end and a new beginning.

The End of Belgium's Rule in the Congo

The movements for emancipation in the various colonial territories of Africa affected one another. Ghana's achievement of sovereignty in 1957 gave impetus to the drives for autonomy and independence in the French colonies, and their success in turn strengthened and accelerated nationalism all over central Africa. In this political climate Belgium, the last of the powers with a large colonial empire, felt unable to keep control over its colonies; in 1960, in a precipitate move, Belgium granted independence to the Congo, and in the same year the Republic of the Congo was admitted to the United Nations. During their rule in the Congo, the Belgians were frequently criticized for exploiting the people, and indeed they cared little about educating or giving rights to their colonial subjects. When the Belgian administration withdrew, the Congolese were insufficiently prepared to take over. The country had rich mineral resources; its mines yielded copper, diamonds, and 90 per cent of the world's supply of uranium. Coffee and cotton were the major products of its agriculture. But the people of this economically important and wealthy region still lived in a tribal society. The sudden relinquishment of power by the Belgian rulers led to outbreaks against the whites, to turmoil and internal war. The central government in Leopoldville was opposed by separatist movements, backed by white businessmen who wanted to protect their lives, their properties, and their investments and were assisted in their struggle by white mercenaries. The central government appealed to Soviet Russia for help against the white capitalists, and the Congo conflict threatened to cause a serious crisis between East and West. Its course was punctuated by bitter debates in the United Nations. By 1963 the struggle had died down, and with the help of the United Nations a settled state was obtained. The Russians had lost their most prominent adherent, Patrice Lumumba, who in 1961 had been murdered by his enemies, but the United States also abandoned support of the prowhite separatist regime in Katanga. Moreover, by then the Cold War had lost its sharp edge.

The Congo crisis strikingly illustrated the fact that in central Africa, the struggle was not just between colonials and their foreign rulers but between black men and white. The conflict had a strongly racial element. The racial issue became decisive in the most southern regions of Africa—South Africa and Rhodesia—where the whites, although their number is not inconsiderable, form a small minority within the total population. Here the white inhabitants vehemently refuse constitutional concessions or changes which might gradually lead to some black participation in the government. Instead they separate blacks and whites completely, preserve the monopoly of power for the whites, and keep the blacks in a state of subjugation.

CHAPTER 47

The New Europe
in the Global System

THE WANING OF THE COLD WAR

JUST AS THE RISE of the Cold War tension resulted in the formation of a solid Eastern and solid Western bloc, the ending of the Cold War led to a weakening of the Russian and American alliance systems.

We have said that it is impossible to connect the beginning of the Cold War with a definite event. It is equally difficult to set a definite date for its ending; the decrease in tension occurred gradually, almost unnoticeably.

If seen in wide perspective, the developments which influenced most decisively the relations of the two superpowers and created a new climate in international relations were those in the field of nuclear weapons. From 1953 on both the United States and Russia were in possession of hydrogen bombs, and the leaders of both states recognized the impossibility of war between powers with strong nuclear armaments. In 1957 Russia's successful launching of *Sputnik*, a satellite directed from the ground, renewed fears that a war might be attempted because devices operating in space might give Russia military superiority; American efforts to overtake the Russian technological advance were hastened. Likewise, the threat of the development of a "missile gap," which some American military leaders pretended to be imminent, led to fears of an attack by Russia and accelerated the American missile program. But the conclusion was inescapable that the nuclear armament of the two superpowers was so strong that attack by one could not so cripple the other that it would be unable to carry out a nuclear counterblow. In a nuclear war the United States and Russia would destroy each other. The prospect of such a war could not rationally be envisaged or defended. Acceptance of the view that the alternative created by nuclear technology was either disarmament or annihilation was reflected in the beginning of negotiations about nuclear disarmament: a nuclear test-ban treaty was concluded in 1963 and a nuclear non-proliferation treaty in 1968.

The establishment of a nuclear balance of power was the crucial reason for the gradual reduction in tension between Russia and the United States. Nevertheless, 1953, as we have seen, marked a turning point in the Cold War: military activities in Korea ended in armistice. In the following years bonds between the superpowers and their satellites or allies began to slacken until developments were accelerated by events in the critical year of 1956 which, with the Hungarian Revolt and the Suez affair changed the situation in East and West.

The Soviet Bloc, 1953–1956

For the Eastern bloc the year 1953 was important not only because of the Korean armistice; it was also the year of Stalin's death. When Stalin died he was hated in the West because he was held responsible for the tense and critical situation in which the world found itself. But only a speech by Nikita Khrushchev (born 1894) before the Twentieth Congress of the Communist Party of the Soviet Union in a closed session on February 24–25, 1956, revealed that in Stalin's last years his rule had become a personal despotism so irrational that no one felt safe, and that even in Russia he had been an object of hatred and fear. Stalin's death was of immediate political importance because the struggle to succeed him affected the entire Russian-controlled part of the globe. The most tyrannical figures of Stalin's time disappeared: Lavrenti Beria, the chief of police and Stalin's hangman, was executed, but others defeated in the struggle for power— Malenkov, on whom first Stalin's mantle seemed to have fallen, and Molotov, who insisted on unchanging continuation of Stalin's policy— were only demoted and perhaps removed from Moscow; they were not killed. Georgi Malenkov, who was premier from 1953 to 1955, favored the production of consumer goods in Russia, and even after his fall, this orientation persisted, though somewhat modified. Between 1950 and the middle of the 1960's, production of washing machines increased from 300 to 4.2 million; of television sets, from 11,900 to 4.9 million; and of refrigerators, from 1,200 to 2.8 million. Malenkov's promotion of the production of consumer goods was accompanied by a decision to permit a new economic course in the eastern European countries. A change in investment policy was to modify the emphasis on heavy industry; prices and wages were to be kept down; and in compliance with the requests of the rural population, the collectivization of agriculture was to be slowed. However, the introduction of the new wage policy led to a revolt of workers in East Berlin in the summer of 1953, and this was taken as a sign that tension had become more dangerous than had been assumed and that a change of course in economic policy was urgent and had to be undertaken as quickly as possible. The state which embarked on the changes with greatest energy was Hungary; Mátyás Rákosi, who had risen to the prime ministership of Hungary as a loyal Stalinist, remained general secretary of the party but lost the prime ministership to Imre Nagy, an advocate of the new course. In other eastern European countries the shift in direction was more moderate. In Poland the all-powerful Stalinist Boleslarv Bierut prevented any radical change.

Obviously, the establishment of a new leadership and a new political line could proceed more easily in an atmosphere of lowered international tension. Accordingly, at the Geneva Conference in 1954, the Russians helped negotiate the settlement which ended warfare in Indochina. And in the spring of 1955, to almost everyone's surprise, they agreed to a treaty which terminated the occupation of Austria and restored Austrian sovereignty, thus removing one of the sources of friction along the line where American and Russian spheres of interest touched. The various facets of the new Russian policy were clearly indicated by Khrushchev in his speech to the Twentieth Congress of the Communist party. He admitted the possibility of different "forms of transition of various countries to socialism" and he revised the traditional Marxist thesis that "war is inevitable so long as imperialism exists." This speech showed clearly that Khrushchev, the first secretary of the Central Committee of the Russian Communist party, had become the acknowledged leader of Russian policy.

The Russian leaders were not unaware that the relaxation of tensions between East and West, combined with an economic policy which permitted the eastern European states considerable variation within the prescribed general framework, might endanger Russian domination. The Warsaw Pact of 1955 was primarily intended as a countermeasure to the military strengthening of the West indicated by the formation of NATO and by West Germany's rearmament and admission to NATO. But it served also to counterbalance the economic autonomy which the satellites had gained, by tightening their military and political bonds with one another and with Russia. Thus, while the Warsaw Pact was still partly conceived as an instrument of the Cold War, it was also a measure intended to minimize the dangers of a lessening of tensions. At the same time, the Russians were anxious to counteract the centrifugal consequences of greater economic autonomy in the satellite countries. Correspondingly, the Council for Mutual Assistance, established in 1949 in answer to the Marshall Plan, began to work out plans for a division of labor and specialization in industrial production so that while complete identity of the economic policy of each country with that of Russia was no longer demanded, the economic interdependence of the entire area would be maintained. The formation early in 1956 of a Joint Nuclear Research Institute including all the Communist states reflected the same trend. There can be little doubt that the uniformity which Stalin had pressed upon the European Communist world had brought things almost to a breaking point; the attempt of the new Russian leaders to modify his policy was almost unavoidable, but because of the explosive tensions which had accumulated under Stalin, "controlled transition" proved to be a complicated process full of dangers for the coherence of the Russian alliance system.

The Western Bloc, 1953–1956

The Korean War had strengthened the bonds between the United States and its chief European allies, Great Britain and France. Although there had been some friction between the United States and its European allies about how this war was to be pursued—how far the campaign should be extended into the neighborhood of the Chinese borders, and whether the use of the atomic bomb should be considered—both France and Great Britain were anxious to stem the Russian advance into areas of the Far East in which they had interests, and they shared with the Americans the erroneous belief that the attack by the North Koreans was part of a great Russian design; repulsed in Europe, the Russians—it appeared—were now concentrating on Asia. With the end of the Korean War in a stalemate, a divergence appeared between the Far Eastern policies of the United States on the one hand and of Great Britain and France on the other. Great Britain believed that with the armistice in Korea, and the emergence of new independent states in this area, a stable political situation would develop. The British did not regard Communist China as strong enough to pursue a policy of expansion, and gave it diplomatic recognition. The French had favored the action in Korea because they expected it to relieve the pressure exerted on them in Indochina. With the ending of the Korean War, followed by their defeat a year later in Vietnam, the French were anxious to move out of the Far East and devote their military forces to the preservation of their threatened possessions in North Africa. The United States, however, regarded Communist China as a dangerous, aggressive power controlled by Soviet Russia; containment of China therefore became one of the primary concerns of American foreign policy. The United States refused to give diplomatic recognition to China and prevented its admission to the United Nations; it held its protective shield over Formosa, where Chiang Kai-shek was established, and promised to support him if the Communist Chinese should attack Quemoy and Matsu, islands a few miles off the mainland in the Formosa Straits. America's European allies did not share these deep feelings of hostility toward Communist China. They had no particular interest in Chinese affairs and they feared that America's Far Eastern policy might lead to a war in which Europe, and the whole world, would become involved.

There were two other reasons why American ties with western Europe weakened at this time. The military aspects of the NATO alliance acquired primary importance in the American mind. And the United States was increasingly inclined to align itself with any power able to strengthen the

American military posture, whatever its system of government might be. The American attitude toward Spain was typical. During the Second World War, Spanish volunteers had fought on the side of the Axis against Russia, although Franco, emphasizing the poverty of his country, avoided direct participation; after the war the victorious governments seriously considered taking steps to overthrow the Franco regime. But in 1953, after vainly trying to overcome the resistance of its European allies to the admission of Spain to NATO, the United States made agreements with Spain by which in return for assistance to the Spanish army, navy, and air force it obtained military bases in Spain. If at the beginning of the Cold War the notion of defending the traditions and values of western civilization had helped to cement the western alliance system, the ideological bond was now losing significance. When in 1955 after a visit to Spain the American secretary of state, John Foster Dulles, joined Franco to issue a communiqué stating that they "found themselves in mutual understanding" with regard to "the principal problems that affected the peace and security of free nations," the term "free world," which western statesmen liked to apply to the American alliance system, acquired a somewhat hollow sound.

American policy makers courted Franco because United States military strength was needed in Asia, and they were anxious to increase the share of the European nations in the defense of western Europe against Russia. After the Marshall Plan had ended in 1952, further American assistance was given chiefly for military purposes and was channeled through the Mutual Security Agency, which was concerned with military needs.

With the United States giving increased attention to the Far East and centering its effort on reinforcing the military position against Russia, the European nations realized that they had to take more initiative of their own. The Organization of European Economic Cooperation (OEEC), which had been formed by the nations participating in the European Recovery Program to draft plans for the use of Marshall Plan funds, remained in existence after the expiration of the Marshall Plan. Its purpose was to facilitate the transfer of currency and the exchange of goods among its members and to coordinate their efforts in fields like atomic research; in 1958 a European Nuclear Energy Agency came into existence.

Thus, the overall result of the American involvement in the Far East was that the European policy makers became convinced that they could not rely on American support, but must act on their own if they wanted to preserve their interests in other parts of the world.

THE CRISIS OF 1956 IN EAST AND WEST

The centrifugal forces working in the American and Russian alliance systems came out into the open in two dramatic events of October, 1956: the Suez affair and the Hungarian revolt. The British and French acted in

The Hungarian revolution. *The Stalin statue is pulled down and destroyed.*

the Suez affair because they were convinced that American policy took little account of their interests and that only an independent initiative could safeguard their position in the Near East and Africa.

The reasons for the Hungarian revolt were more complicated. The possibility of a revolt arose from a struggle between Stalinists and the adherents of the new Communist line. When Nagy became prime minister, his Stalinist predecessor, Rákosi, remained party secretary. In the first year of Nagy's regime, 51 per cent of the collective-farm members left the collective system, and 12 per cent of the collective farms had to be dissolved; Nagy intended to continue the policy of abandoning concentration on heavy industry and instead strengthening the development of the other sectors of the economy. Since the war, the working classes in Hungary had increased by almost 50 per cent, and a thorough training of these masses in Communist doctrine had not been possible. With the slowing down of collectivization in agriculture, Communist control of the rural population also became weakened. Accordingly, the Communist party regarded the measures introduced by Nagy with suspicion and feared that it might be losing its grip over the workers and peasants. When Khrushchev succeeded Malenkov, and accused Malenkov of mistakes in the direction of industrial and agricultural policy, Rákosi, who controlled the Central Committee of the Hungarian Communist party, incriminated Nagy as a follower of Malenkov. Taking advantage of Nagy's temporary illness, he succeeded in deposing him as prime minister and expelling him from the party. Rákosi returned to power as prime minister in the spring of 1955. But the clock could not be turned back. In the meetings of clubs named for the poet Sandor Petöfi, which had been set up by the government for intellectual improvement, students and intellectuals debated political issues; both industrial workers and the rural population remained critical and suspicious of the Rákosi government. When in the summer of 1956 Rákosi moved to arrest Nagy and four hundred of his associates, he encountered opposition in the Central Committee, and some members of this opposition turned to the Soviet embassy for help. Perturbed by the revolutionary ferment in Hungary, the Russians decided to drop Rákosi and install a new prime minister, Ernö Gerö, who was expected to steer a middle line between Rákosi's Stalinism and Nagy's new course.

That this attempt at "controlled transition" failed was to a large extent the result of external events. Just at this time, Khrushchev moved to improve relations with Yugoslavia. The rejection of Stalin's policy, which early in 1956 had been publicly proclaimed at the Twentieth Congress of the Communist party, included a condemnation of Stalin's treatment of Tito, and in consequence meetings between the Russian and Yugoslav leaders took place, which resulted on June 20, 1956, in a communiqué declaring "that the ways of socialist development vary in different countries and conditions," and "that the wealth of the forms of socialist development contributes to its strength." Naturally, the Russian satellites in eastern Europe asked why they also should not have that freedom of choice in the form of socialist development which had been granted to Yugoslavia. The first country in which demands for autonomy in domestic affairs were raised was Poland. There, the changed Russian attitude after Stalin's death had not resulted in any great shift in leadership or any dramatic reversal in economic policy; it had largely meant a general relaxation which curtailed the power of the secret police and permitted greater freedom in intellectual expression. In March, 1956, the sudden death of Bierut, who had dominated the Polish Communist party since the war, gave new impetus to the liberalizing trend. In April, amnesty was granted to thirty thousand prisoners, among them nine thousand political offenders. And it became evident that demands for a change had spread widely among the workers. In June, a strike in Poznán had to be suppressed by military forces. Impressed by the amount of dissatisfaction which had come to the fore in the Poznán strike, the majority of the government, including Bierut's successor as party secretary, accepted the need to accelerate liberalization. Wladyslaw Gomulka (born 1905), who had been released from prison, was permitted to participate in the deliberations of the Central Committee and became a member of the Polish Politburo, while Marshal Konstantin Rokossovski, the commander of the Russian troops in Poland, was relieved of his membership in the Polish Politburo. The great question was whether the Soviet leaders would regard these actions as provocative. However, in negotiations with the Russians, Gomulka was able to overcome their distrust. Though he had always been critical of the precipitate collectivization of agriculture which the Russians had imposed on the satellites, he was a loyal Marxist-Leninist, convinced of the need for the Communist party to keep control and exert leadership, and persuaded that Russia and Poland had to stand together. Briefly, he assured the Russians that Poland would remain a reliable member of the Warsaw Pact. Assured of Polish loyalty in foreign policy, the Russian leaders were willing to permit Poland autonomy in seeking its "ways of socialist development." On October 21, 1956, Gomulka was elected general secretary of the Polish Communist party.

The Russian concessions to Yugoslavia and Poland provided the spark for events in Hungary. When the Hungarians heard of the success of the Polish move, they felt that they too should try to gain greater independence. At the universities of Budapest, Pécs, and Szeged, in the Budapest technical college, and in other public buildings, heated debates took place about the means to force the government into greater activity; it was agreed to hold a "silent sympathy demonstration" before the Polish embassy on October 23. It is estimated that more than fifty thousand people participated in this demonstration. In the evening Prime Minister Gerö made a broadcast. He had been expected to accept the need for a more independent and liberal policy, but instead, surprisingly, Gerö took a hard Stalinist line in his speech. In response, the public demonstrations assumed a sharply antigovernment character. The gigantic statue of Stalin in the city park was demolished, and students attempted to take over the radio station, in order to broadcast the demands of the opposition. To protect the building, the police began to shoot. Troops were sent against the crowds surrounding the station, but instead of dispersing the demonstrators they fraternized with them. The government proved powerless to control the opposition.

The distinguishing feature of the Hungarian revolution was that, in contrast to the Polish events of the same month, it did not remain limited to a struggle within the party between the Stalinists and the adherents of a new course, but developed into a movement against Communist rule in general. Encouraging broadcasts from the West, which seemed to promise outside support, played their role in transforming the intraparty conflict into an anti-Communist revolt. But the reasons for the broadening impact of the revolt were manifold. On the night of October 23 the government, in panicky desperation, appealed to the Russian troops for help and announced at the same time that Imre Nagy had become prime minister. Nagy's appointment was expected to appease the demonstrators, but he was also expected to share the powers of government with Gerö and other Stalinists. The Russian military forces in Hungary were weak and their advance into Budapest resulted in bitter, indecisive fighting, while in the countryside, now free of troops, revolutionary committees were formed. The frontier between Hungary and Austria was opened.

Nagy, whose appointment had been announced without his own approval, was in a thoroughly untenable position. Because of the government appeal for help to Russian troops, and his presumed cooperation with Gerö, the opposition leaders regarded Nagy with the greatest distrust. They believed that his assumption of office could not be considered a guarantee of the beginning of a new course, and that therefore this was not the time to relax pressure on the government. Complying with the demands of the anti-Stalinists, Nagy got rid of Gerö and formed a government composed chiefly of members of the Communist opposition; György Lukács, the famous Marxist scholar, became minister of education. But by then many non-Communists had joined the opposition movement, and they were not content to abandon the struggle without further liberation measures. For instance, Cardinal Mindszenty, who was freed from prison and whose courageous stand against the government gave him great authority, demanded the formation of a Christian Democratic party similar to Adenauer's party in Germany. He stated that he "rejected *en bloc* everything Hungary had done since 1945, not only since 1949, and the establishment of dictatorship." And he came out in favor of "private ownership."

Nagy was rightly afraid that the Russians might interfere if order were not quickly reestablished. He tried to appease the non-Communist opposition by taking into the government leaders of the former Social Democratic, Small Holder, and National Peasant parties. But they were willing to cooperate with him and the Communists only if he made further concessions. On October 30 Nagy announced the restoration of a multiparty system, and on October 31 he declared that Hungary proposed to withdraw from the Warsaw Pact.

It is evident that the Russians could not permit a break in their bloc. They had been waiting and vacillating in their attitude to the events in Hungary. Probably they would have followed the kind of policy they adopted toward Poland, permitting Nagy freedom to undertake economic and cultural changes, if there had been no doubt of Hungary's adherence to the basic principles of Communism and of its loyalty to the Warsaw Pact. The Russians agreed to withdraw their troops from Hungary on October 30, but at the same time they began to assemble strong forces along the Hungarian frontier, preparing for any eventuality. When Nagy announced Hungary's secession from the Warsaw Pact, they decided to intervene. In the early morning of November 4, Russian troops entered Budapest, and by nightfall the revolt had ended. Mindszenty found asylum in the American embassy. Nagy sought refuge in the Yugoslav embassy, but was handed over to the Hungarians, and he and other leaders of the revolt were executed. Some of the participants managed to escape over the Austrian frontier, and there, as along the Franco-Spanish border seventeen years before, camps were established to house the disillusioned and impoverished refugees whose desperate stand for freedom had been crushed by the pitilessly functioning machines of totalitarian dictatorship.

It has frequently been said that the Suez affair, which began on October 30 and therefore coincided with the events in Hungary, caused the failure of the Hungarian revolt. Perhaps the developments in the Near East did hasten the Russians' decision to intervene, for surely they did not want to have an exposed flank in southeastern Europe in the event of a serious international crisis; without Suez there might have been a chance for the Hungarians to negotiate a less brutal surrender. But there can be no doubt that as soon as the opposition movement had developed into an anti-Communist revolt, the Russians were forced to reestablish their authority over Hungary. And it is certainly nonsense to maintain that if the West had been united, the uprising might have succeeded. Neither the United States nor any western European power was willing at this moment to undertake war with Russia, and since the Russians could not tolerate Hungary's defection to the West, active support of the revolt by the West would have meant war. Actually, the American government owed a certain amount of gratitude to the British and French because the Suez affair provided a justification for America's inactivity in Hungary. The Suez affair concealed the fact that the Russians had called the bluff of the American liberation policy.

The events of October–November, 1956, despite the upheaval which they caused in international relations, ultimately had the effect of reducing tension between the United States and Russia. The unwillingness of the western powers to give more than vocal support to the Hungarian revolt could be taken by Russia as a sign that although they had refused officially to acknowledge that eastern Europe was a Soviet sphere of interest, they did actually recognize Russia's control over this area. In the handling of the Suez affair—in forcing the British and French to evacuate the area which they had occupied—the United States cooperated with the Soviet Union, and although an underlying American motive may have been to prevent the Arab nations from throwing themselves into Russia's arms, the Russians must have regarded the American attitude as a sign of the weakening of imperialist aggression. Most of all, however, both superpowers had to concentrate on restoring order in their badly disorganized camps. Reestablishment of common purpose and common action within these spheres was difficult and was fully achieved by neither Russia nor the United States.

THE TRANSFORMATION IN THE ALLIANCE SYSTEMS

The Soviet Bloc Since 1956

The fact that Gomulka remained in power in Poland demonstrated that there was no return to the policy of forcing uniformity upon the states in

The end of the Czech liberalization movement. *Russian tanks entering Prague.*

the eastern bloc. In many respects each country followed its own economic and cultural course. Thus by 1960, when Gomulka's policy of restraining the collectivization of agriculture had been in force for three years, there was a wide difference among the various eastern countries in the proportion of collectivized arable land. East Germany with 96 per cent and Czechoslovakia with 85.2 per cent were in the lead; while Poland with 13.2 per cent brought up the rear. In general, East Germany and Czechoslovakia still adhered closely to Stalinist policies, and in Ulbricht and Gottwald and then in Gottwald's successor Antonin Novotny, they had leaders who had been personally close to Stalin. But in both countries the rigidity of the political and economic policy resulted in accumulated discontent, and in 1968 this brought about a change of course in Czechoslovakia. The movement toward democratization in Czechoslovakia was not dissimilar to that which had exploded in Hungary twelve years before, although particular emphasis on political and economic decentralization and insistence on the importance of intellectual freedom gave the Czech events their special coloring. The Russians reacted toward the change in Czechoslovakia more slowly than in the case of Hungary. After some hesitation they moved troops in, partly because Czechoslovakia seemed to be sliding out of the eastern camp into a neutralist position, partly because the closeness of Czechoslovakia to the West made its control strategically crucial. Nevertheless, in the Communist parties of the West—in France and Italy—indignation about the Russian invasion was great. However, the Russians took their own counsel; slowly but unalterably, they eased the Czech leaders of the reform movement out of power. The strategic position of Czechoslovakia, and concern for the stability of their own regimes, prompted leaders of several Soviet satellites—Hungary, Poland, East Germany—to support the Russian invasion of Czechoslovakia. Ulbricht in particular was a driving force in the suppression of the Czech reform movement. He has since emerged as one of the most important figures in the eastern bloc.

Ulbricht's position in East Germany had been firmer than that of other Communist leaders of the Stalinist brand because, after 1956, he gradually allowed a larger production of consumer goods, and the economic situation in East Germany did improve remarkably. Of the other satellites, in economic policy it was Poland under Gomulka that went furthest in following its own particular line of socialist development. In Hungary after the suppression of the revolt the government which the Russians established tried to follow a middle course.

Why did these satellite countries, despite the variety of their "ways of socialist development," retain their bonds with one another and with Russia? A chief reason was economic. Overall economic planning for the entire area, while it did not force the establishment of any industries, did help to organize the distribution of the goods which were being produced. For instance, East Germany, building on Germany's prewar accomplishments, became the chief center of the chemical industry for Russia and eastern Europe. Moreover, in purchasing goods from the satellites Russia, after 1956, paid not arbitrarily fixed low prices but world market prices. And while just after the war Russia had moved economic assets from eastern Europe into its own territory, it subsequently made sizable investments in this area. Economic interdependence was deliberately accelerated.

The absence of friction between some satellite countries and Russia was due also to the realization by the Communist leaders of eastern Europe that without Russian support their rule might become precarious. Once the settlement of their frontiers had been imposed by Russia the eastern European states felt that their territorial integrity was safe only as long as they remained within the Russian orbit; for instance, the placing of the Polish-German frontier along the Oder-Neisse line bound the Poles closely to Russia. Thus, although these countries developed somewhat divergent economic policies they retained a uniform ideological outlook and common political-military interests which forged strong bonds among them and with Russia. The fruits of industrialization have begun to appear, and all of the countries have shared in an economic upswing. Exact figures are difficult to obtain but the annual rate of postwar growth in eastern Europe seems to have been at least 6 per cent. The masses of the people have gained considerable advantages from the government policies. Consequently there has been less discontent, and a relaxation of police controls and cultural supervision has been possible. Thus, although these countries are still tied together by strong bonds, their situation has changed since the first decade after the Second World War, when Russia was clearly the head of the alliance and gave orders which everyone obeyed. Now there are frequent meetings of the leaders of all these states; although Russia's voice remains very powerful, the decisions are presented as the results of common deliberations.

There is still another reason why Russia proceeded with careful regard for the views and interests of the eastern European nations, why they have become allies rather than satellites. In the 1960's the Communist world was agitated by the antagonism of the two most powerful Communist nations—Russia and China. The Sino-Soviet conflict was hardly a part of European history, yet it had an important bearing on the European states. It provided the Communist nations of Europe with an alternative, and although probably none of the rest was inclined to follow the example of small Albania, which, separated from the Russian bloc by neutralist Yugoslavia, could afford to side with the Chinese, their bargaining strength was increased. The unity of the eastern European bloc is now maintained by a complicated system of pressures and counterpressures.

The Western Alliance Since 1956

Despite the absence of violent conflicts, signs of disintegration became clearly noticeable in the alliance between the United States and the nations of western Europe. Assuming a role like that of China in the Communist camp, France under De Gaulle, without repudiating friendship with the United States, took an openly anti-American course. De Gaulle declared that the United States had become too powerful and that a counterweight had to be created, that Europe ought to stop following American direction and stand by itself. And he saw to it that France took steps to carry out this program. For example, American troops were forced to leave French soil, and the headquarters of NATO had to be moved from Paris to Belgium.

The independent stance taken by De Gaulle presupposed the liberation of France from the burdens of colonial warfare. But it was made possible only by economic developments in Europe which had been initiated before he seized power. The European Coal and Steel Community, established in 1951, had proved a success; after a shaky beginning, production rose impressively from 1954 on. West German steel production between 1954 and 1957 increased from 17 million to 24 million tons; French steel production, from 10 million to 14 million tons. In view of this success the six countries of the European Coal and Steel Community—France, West Germany, Belgium, Luxemburg, the Netherlands, and Italy—decided to embark on a policy of European unification. In treaties concluded in Rome on March 25, 1957, they founded a European Atomic Energy Community (EURATOM), which would make the uses of atomic energy available to all the participating countries. More important, they agreed on the establishment of a Common Market (European Economic Community). Its aims were to abolish all trade barriers among the six, to establish a common external tariff, to permit the free movement of labor and capital among the member states, and—by equalizing wage rates and social-security systems—to bring about uniform working conditions in the Common Market area without creating unemployment. Clearly, these goals could not be achieved in a single stroke; for instance, in some of the participating countries agriculture was highly protected and would collapse if customs barriers were removed suddenly. The Rome agreement therefore envisaged a development in stages, to be completed within fifteen years. A European Commission with headquarters in Brussels, acting under the instructions of a regularly meeting council of ministers, was entrusted with the administration of the Common Market and the guidance of its development. On January 1, 1959, the Common Market began to function by lowering tariffs 10 per cent among the member countries, and thereafter, despite difficult negotiations and crises, steady progress was made in realizing its program.

The effect of the Common Market on the economy of the six participants was most beneficial. Between 1959 and 1962 production rose 35 per cent in West Germany, 29 per cent in France, 58 per cent in Italy. The increase in French production was particularly significant, for while Germany had shown a steady and marked economic growth since 1950, the French growth rate had been low. A special advantage for the Italian economy was the added mobility given to labor. Large numbers of Italian workers were able to obtain temporary employment in Germany and France, and between 1959 and 1963 unemployment in Italy fell from 1,500,000 to 500,000. The wage level rose correspondingly, and the improving economic and budgetary situation made it possible for the Christian Democrats to undertake a reform program to eliminate the economic disparity between northern and southern Italy. Politically, the adoption of this policy meant a turn to the left and a willingness to cooperate with the left-wing socialists, led by Pietro Nenni.

One of the most significant effects of the Common Market, however, was the impetus that it gave to trade among the six participants. Between 1958 and 1962 intracommunity trade rose by 97 per cent; by contrast, imports from outside the Common Market grew only 38 per cent, and exports to non-Market countries increased by 29 per cent. This "little Europe" began to form a vital and stable basis for the economic life of its six members.

Great Britain did not participate in the Common Market. Its response was to initiate the creation of the European Free Trade Association, with Sweden, Norway, Denmark, Switzerland, Austria, and Portugal. This organization was purely a customs union and did not envisage any further integration of economic life, for taken as a group the participating states were too diverse in their economic interests. However, the connection of the Scandinavian countries with Great Britain did have some geographical, economic, and political justification. Great Britain was one of the most important customers of the Scandinavian countries, and their currencies were tied to the value of the pound. Moreover, they had developed into welfare states with features similar to those of Great Britain. But the chief purpose of the foundation of the Free Trade Association was to strengthen Britain's bargaining position in its attempt to join the European Economic Community without relinquishing her role in the British Commonwealth of Nations.

De Gaulle was opposed to Britain's entry into the European Economic

Community, which he regarded as an independent organization which might serve to remove the American influence from European affairs. Great Britain had close economic and political ties with the United States, and this dependence had been increased by the Suez affair, with its damaging consequences for the British position in Asia, and by Britain's precarious economic situation. And some of the members of the British Common-wealth—notably Australia and New Zealand—looked to the United States for military protection.

De Gaulle's veto of Britain's entry into the Common Market (1963) was opposed by some of the other members, who expected economic advantages from the enlargement of the Common Market. But their resistance to De Gaulle exhausted itself in efforts to keep the door open for further negotiations. Adenauer probably supported De Gaulle because he feared that the widening of the Common Market might delay or prevent the further political integration of Europe, which was his particular interest; moreover, De Gaulle guaranteed him French support for the West German position in the question of Berlin. The other member countries were probably not without reservations about the British application; they had misgivings about getting involved in affairs of the world outside Europe. For while the question of Britain's entry into the Common Market was under discussion, the United States was becoming more and more deeply involved in a war in Vietnam, where it considered itself to be holding the line against Communism. Although Europeans regarded the Cold War as a thing of the past, it was still very real to Americans. Most Europeans were unable to share the view, widespread in America, that the activities of the Vietcong formed part of a great Communist offensive against the "free world." To them, social and nationalist discontent and the division of the country seemed adequately to explain the conflict between the north and the south in Vietnam. Moreover, Europeans believed that the Americans were exaggerating the threat of China, as they had ten years earlier in the Korean conflict. Hence, the United States action in Vietnam had no support from America's European allies, and the strains which the war placed on American financial resources weakened the influence that the United States could exert by economic means; at least temporarily the United States was no longer extending favors, but asking them. It wanted higher payments for the expenses involved in keeping troops stationed in Europe, so that the deficit in the American balance of payments would be decreased, and it was anxious to forestall any autarkic tendency in the Common Market which might place obstacles in the way of American investments in Europe.

The developments in the Russian alliance system and in the American alliance system were strikingly similar insofar as closer economic integration took place in both eastern and western Europe. However, the effect in each area was different. In the East it created a firmer tie with the leading power; in the West it resulted in more independence from the leading power.

The Superpowers in a Multinational System

In the years immediately after the Second World War the United States and Russia appeared to be the only powers able to make decisions and to influence the course of world affairs, but by the 1960's a number of other states could throw some weight on the scales. Perhaps there was no more striking indication of this change from bipolarization to a multinational system than the increase in membership of the United Nations. Between 1946 and 1967 the number of states in the United Nations more than doubled (from 55 to 115), largely as a result of the entrance of the newly independent nations of Asia and Africa and the powers defeated in the Second World War. In the years just after the war the great majority of the members of the United Nations almost automatically voted for the American position, and the Russians replied with frequent recourse to the veto, but now the outcome of voting often cannot be foreseen.

Nevertheless, a world divided into two hostile power blocs has not suddenly turned into a society made up of numerous equal members. Both the United States and Russia are far superior in strength to the entire rest of the world. In resources and technology the United States and Russia are so much ahead that the distance between the superpowers and the other states is likely to increase rather than diminish. The other states—particularly the European nations, which because of their own advanced technological stage can recognize the gap between themselves and the superpowers—are well aware that their influence and their freedom of action are limited. They cannot survive a serious crisis. In a clash between the two superpowers each European nation would be forced to take sides in one camp or the other. Thus, although the various nations in eastern and western Europe have made great, almost unexpected, strides toward autonomy and independence, they nevertheless remain within the gravitational fields of Russian and American power. Leaders in Russia and America are not unaware of this fact, and in the recurrent crises in the relations between these two states it is sometimes difficult to tell whether the policies of the superpowers are primarily directed against each other or are intended mainly to enhance the coherence of their respective blocs. As long as oil remains the most precious and most important raw material of modern industrial society, the oil-rich Near East will be a critical area, and a direct clash between Russia and the United States over its control must remain to be considered a possibility. When the two superpowers oppose each other in other parts of the world—in Cuba, in the Far East, in Berlin—an important reason for confrontation is to demonstrate the vitality of their alliance systems. The policy of the superpowers is mainly directed toward maintaining the established balance of power, not changing it. The continued existence of a balance of power in a state system which is not multinational, but polarized between two superpowers is a novelty and disproves the frequently expressed view that international relations never change.

EPILOGUE

The Outlook

WHEN THE TWENTIETH CENTURY began, Europeans felt that they had reason to be proud. They dominated the globe, and the achievements of their science and technology provided steady proof of continuing progress. One great problem, however, darkened this bright picture. Would the intricate fabric of European civilization be destroyed in a revolution caused by the deep gap which separated the rulers from the ruled?

In our description of the political developments in Europe during the first two thirds of the twentieth century, we have given particular attention to the three areas which constituted the source of European pride and fears: the impact of technology on the conduct of politics; the relations between Europe and the non-European world; and the evolution of the social conflict. Probably nobody at the beginning of the twentieth century foresaw the course which these developments were to take. Science and technology have not only justified the expectations of further progress but revolutionized the external and the internal world of man. Their spread from Europe to the various corners of the globe has even been decisive in what might be regarded as the most unexpected and at the same time the most significant event in Europe's political history during the twentieth century: the ending of European hegemony over the rest of the globe; the restriction of the rule of the European nations to their own continent. As we have seen, the loss of control over Africa and Asia was a complicated and painful process. But it might be said that after industrialization had spread over the world, and Europe no longer possessed a monopoly of advanced technology, the end of the domination of 450 million Europeans over three billion non-Europeans became unavoidable. But while developments in the field of technology and in the relations between Europe and the rest of the world during the first sixty years of the twentieth century had clearly definable results, it is much more difficult to say whether and to what extent the accompanying social changes modified the division into two antagonistic classes which characterized European society at the beginning of the twentieth century.

THE NEW SOCIAL STRUCTURE OF EUROPE

Certainly, the sharpness of the contrast between the classes has been mitigated. Both the composition of the ruling group and the economic situation of the working people have been significantly altered. The role of the landed aristocracy in the European nations has largely ended. In Spain and perhaps in certain parts of Italy the aristocracy still represents an element of power and influence, but even in these countries industrialization and technological progress are loosening the grip of the landowning nobility.

It is perhaps a sign of the vanishing role of the aristocracy that a new expression replacing the notion of the ruling group is now frequently used: the "establishment." This vague and hardly scientific term points to a significant feature determining the character of the policy-making group in the present age of industrialization and technology: to the domination of economic and political activity by large organizations of an institutional nature, and to the interlocking relationships of these established institutions. Their leaders are forced to cooperate and support one another because the weakness of one might lead to the collapse of all. The ideals of the liberal age which demanded that the economy be free of government interference, that the relations between employer and employee be regulated by demand and supply, and that scientists do their research disinterestedly on problems of their own choice, have long passed. In the twentieth century the trend has been in the opposite direction, toward coordination and systematic, organized planning.

The experiences of two world wars made planning in modern industrial Europe acceptable; and the interdependence of the military and industry has remained the central justification for planning on a nationwide basis. Because of the complicated nature of modern weapons and the size of the installations they require, defense preparations have become a key factor in the economic and social life of a nation; they involve far-reaching decisions concerning the distribution of manpower and of financial and scientific resources. Of course, economy and war have always been closely connected. The novelty in the twentieth century is the impact of defense requirements on the entire economic structure of a country and their influence on the field of science, through government support of research that is militarily useful—in preference to all other lines of research.

Next to the pressures of military requirements, the most important reason for the extension of planning has been the general acceptance of the view that the modern state should take an active role in determining social policy. Whether the aim of the welfare state is seen as full employment, the establishment of insurance systems covering health and old age, the protection of the workers from capitalist exploitation through nationalization of key enterprises, or all of these, the achievement of its goals requires direction of the economic process, i.e., planning. A result of this widening of the state's functions has been the creation of new government departments. Almost all European nations now have ministries or committees for planning, ministries of social security or social insurance, of technology or scientific research.

Certainly, there is a difference between the centralized planning in eastern Europe, which includes every detail of economic life, and the much less direct guidance and control of economic processes in western Europe by means of public works and government purchases, state-owned enterprises, control of the money market, schemes for regional development, and economic guidelines and production quotas. But though the form of organization and planning is less rigid in the West, the manageability of the economic process as a result of the interdependence of the forces involved in it is clearly recognized and used.

As a integral part of the working of the planned economy, the workers have become an acknowledged power within the existing system. If the vanishing influence of the landed aristocracy may be regarded as inherent in the rise of industrialized society, the acquisition of a share in power by labor is the most evident sign of the decreasing significance in Europe of the concept of the class struggle.

European workers in the second half of the twentieth century no longer constitute a proletariat; they are no longer looked down on as they were at the beginning of the century. In accordance with the revolution in economic theory which Keynes triggered in his books, particularly his *General Theory of Employment, Interest and Money* (1936), the workers are now regarded as consumers. Entrepreneurs recognize that as long as a margin is left for profit, high wages are useful. Increased income for the workers means an increased demand for mass produced goods. The economic situation of the workers also has improved because modern industrial technology requires a large number of skilled workers who receive high wages. Under the conditions of modern technology the skilled worker has the added advantage that his skills can be utilized in more than one kind of job. He can find employment in a number of industries producing different goods.

The living conditions of European workers have been improved by the progressive limitation of working hours and the introduction of guaranteed paid vacations, and above all, by benefits of the welfare state. Unskilled workers with few resources and little bargaining power have not disappeared; in all the European states there are still masses of the semiskilled and unskilled eking out marginal livings. But most workers now have a stake in the existing society. They are no longer convinced that their only chance lies in collective action, but see possibilities of advancing their positions individually. Thus, they do not hesitate to cooperate with the existing political and social system, and—it might be added—such cooperation seems the best way to obtain job security. Job security remains a serious concern. Although many former reasons for unemployment have disappeared, there is no assurance that it may not again become a problem in the future: the situation which will be created by automation cannot yet be clearly appraised.

In contrast to the situation in the early twentieth century, in which a member of the ruling group was expected to adapt to an aristocratic feudal pattern, the "establishment" of modern postwar society has no uniform style of life. In composition, it includes the leaders of all the enterprises, organizations, and activities which must be linked together in a systematically organized economic structure: heads of industrial and financial concerns; trade-union officials; directors of institutes of scientific research; specialists in economics, education, and administration; military experts. Inherited wealth is probably still an advantage in reaching the top in business, but in general membership in the ruling group is no longer hereditary.

Because the new ruling group is composed of men active in the most varied fields, the opportunities for entering the policy-making upper stratum of society have been much enlarged. Education—the acquisition of special knowledge and techniques—is the surest way to advancement. But the foreman in a factory, the minor civil servant, the clerk in an office, can all hope to reach the top through their work or through activities in their professional organization.

The upper group is now largely recruited from the middle class, but—like today's working class—the middle stratum of society in Europe differs markedly from what it was at the beginning of the century. Before the First World War the middle class constituted a mixture of different elements with the independent businessman and farmer as the backbone, although the new element of professional men and white-collar workers was increasing in numbers and importance. In the 1960's men who are independent in the sense that they own their own shop, farm, or business are no longer a significant component of the middle class, which is now primarily formed by the employees of large, usually impersonal organizations.

This new middle class has appropriately been called the service class. While the small independent businessman represented a remnant of an earlier economic situation and was in danger of being crushed by industrial giants, the service class is well ensconced in modern industrialized society. Within the general social structure, it forms a link or bridge between the new upper stratum and the workers. Some statistical figures about the German developments provide a striking illustration. In the first decade of the twentieth century 37.6 per cent of the gainfully employed were still independent. By 1967 this figure was halved (18.8 per cent). The percentage of industrial workers among the gainfully employed has remained rather constant, somewhat below 50 per cent, but the number of white-collar workers has increased from 7.5 per cent to 33 per cent. On the other hand the differences in income between workers and employees has steadily diminished; in 1966 the average wage of an industrial worker was only six per cent less than the average salary of a member of the service class. For a large part of the working class the move into the service class is not very difficult and can be achieved in one generation.

Thus, society has not been split into antagonistic groups; instead, under the direction of a broadened and more easily accessible ruling group, the trend has been toward cooperation. However, increased social mobility and easier entrance into the ruling group must be regarded as an underlying tendency rather than an accomplished fact. The degree of realization in a particular western European state depends on the traditions of that state and on the nature of its political and economic problems. For instance, Great Britain is accustomed to gradual reforms along constitutional channels, and factors which determined the composition of its ruling group in the past are still alive. Despite a system which tries to restrict to gifted children attendance at schools preparing for the university, and despite the foundation of many universities intended to widen the availability of academic training, an easy start in business or politics is still facilitated by inherited titles and wealth, education in the public schools, and attendance at Oxford or Cambridge. In Italy the conditions in the south, which has only begun to be drawn into the age of industrialization, promote an alliance of poor peasants and unskilled workers for the purpose of an anticapitalist revolution. Class struggle has remained a reality although the Italian Communist party, because of the improved circumstances of workers in other parts of Italy, walks a tightrope between revolutionary Marxism and revisionism. In France the nationalism and authoritarianism of De Gaulle with its emphasis on subordinating economic measures to a policy of prestige and power kept the workers less well paid and more discontented than in other countries and accordingly less willing to accept compromises. Insofar as class conflicts between workers and the middle classes still exist (as in Italy and France), they can be attributed to circumstances created by history or by a particular political situation. Yet the rigid social stratification which existed in Europe at the beginning of the twentieth century has become almost incomprehensible from the present point of view.

POLITICAL AND SOCIAL DISCORD

The readiness to accept the need for economic cooperation and social integration does not mean, however, that after decades of upheaval and war

Europe has reached a state of contentment and stability. The political temper of a country or a continent is almost impossible to measure, but it is certainly true that western Europe has remained restless and tense.

Dissatisfaction and a sense of uncertainty have remained widespread among many sectors of the European population. The developments which have placed economic life in a new setting have repercussions on every aspect of life and demand a reorientation of the goals and procedures of many established institutions. But because such readjustments sometimes mean a loss of power or a conflict with traditional aims, rights, and customs, the adaptation of these institutions to a planned and organized world has been difficult and incomplete. This has been particularly true in France where De Gaulle's ambition and energy promoted a rapid tempo of modernization. Tall buildings with all modern comforts were erected for the population drawn into the towns but they were constructed around urban centers in which people still lived and worked under the conditions of pre-industrial times. It is rather typical for the entire French situation that after some stretches of broad modern highways roads suddenly narrow down to two lanes. In France, it has been said, there are two economies that uneasily co-exist: a modern one, most of it implanted since the war by the technocrats and a few big state and private firms; and below it, an old creaking infrastructure, based on artisanship, low turnover with high profits, and the ideal of the small family business. The contrasts which this industrializing and modernizing activity created were certainly a factor in bringing about the end of the disquieting regime of De Gaulle in 1969. But all over Europe planning and modernization has created friction and has raised doubts and criticisms. In the center of questioning are the functions of parliament and of political parties and the forms and aims of education. Because the alterations in society have come about under the pressure of external needs rather than in consequence of an evolution or a change in ideas a wide gap has opened between the political and social reality and the ideology which is appealed to in justification of this reality. The result has been the emergence of a radically critical attitude among intellectuals.

After two world wars against authoritarianism and despotism it has become a dogma in the West that democracy is the only justifiable political order. Indeed, the political rights which the individual citizen possesses in most of western Europe go far beyond the most radical demands raised at the beginning of the century. The voting age has been steadily lowered. It is nowhere higher than twenty-five; in Germany and Italy it is twenty-one, and in Great Britain eighteen. Women have received the right to vote. Inequalities in voting, whether of a financial or an educational character, have been eliminated. The parliaments of the various states can be regarded as fully representative. One might have expected that in these circumstances the people of a nation would feel that by means of their parliament they could control their own fate. But one of Europe's problems is that the belief of the people in their capacity to determine the course of events has been shaken. The reputation and the influence of the parliaments has decreased. This phenomenon has its source in various factors, one of which is closely connected with the invention of new and expensive weapons, such as airplanes, rockets, and nuclear bombs. Since their construction is a costly and lengthy process, orders must be given years ahead, and the research necessary for developing these weapons requires steady financial support. Together with outlays for war pensions, military expenses represent a large fixed amount in each year's budget. Parliamentary command of the purse, originally the basis of parliamentary power, exists only to a very limited extent. Connected with the decline of parliament's control over the budget is the rise of the expert at the expense of the elected representative. The scientific problems involved in the maintenance of military preparedness and in the evaluation of the effectiveness and usefulness of weapons and weapons systems have become so complicated that they can be solved only by experts. In many disputes, the voice of the scientist carries more weight than the view of the elected representative. Economic planning too has come into the hands of experts. The members of parliaments frequently lack both the authority to reject the judgment of experts and the will to obstruct projects on which agreement has been reached among the experts and the representatives of business and labor. As long as there is antagonism and conflict in economic life, the holders of political power can choose among alternatives. But when interlocking economic interests establish a consensus, the task of the politicians becomes limited to ratifying the decisions made in other spheres.

The participation of almost all social groups in decision making has been accompanied by the disappearance of radical political forces. There seems to be no basis for parties working for fundamental changes because no groups are excluded from power. Differences between parties have become blurred. In elections choice is frequently determined by the personality and the appeal of the party leader rather than by the voters' preference for a particular policy. The leadership principle has penetrated the politics of democratic countries. This change has resulted partly from a shift in constitutional thinking. During the interwar years the executive was weak and the legislative was strong; at the end of the Second World War it was hoped that a reversal of this situation might help to bring about a less unfortunate political course. But primarily the diminished influence of parliament is due to advances in communication technology. Modern communication techniques focus attention on the leading statesmen. The head of the government appears on television to outline the program of his government or present his country's case during a crisis. He is viewed almost daily welcoming foreign visitors or inaugurating a new power station or a new hospital. His face and figure become familiar to the majority of the citizens. While the leaders of France, Germany, and Italy in the postwar years—De Gaulle, Adenauer, De Gasperi—have certainly been remarkable men, their extended tenure of office in countries inclined toward quick government changes has been to some extent due to the availability of technical devices permitting them to establish direct contact with the people; with the help of radio and television each has acquired a definite "image"—selfless, paternalistic, unflappable—which has inspired confidence. The concentration of power in the executive has the consequence that the far-reaching democratic rights which the individual has gained no longer assure him that he has real control over the course of events.

Questions and doubts about the functioning of the democratic system have emerged very slowly. In the first decades after the Second World War the reconstruction of economic life and the rebuilding of a new political order went hand in hand; realization of the rigidity of the system which had been established came later, coinciding with the rise of a new generation, which feels it stands outside.

THE NEW GENERATION

The problem of the new generation has been especially important because of the striking developments which, after the Second World War, transformed the demographic structure of Europe. Until 1940 the influence of population changes on political events was limited. To be sure, a steady increase in the German population heightened French fears of German rearmament, since France, with 41 million inhabitants, had only two thirds as many people as Germany, and the French population was almost stagnant. The French were also overtaken by the Italians, spurred by Mussolini to produce large families even though Italy was unable to feed its own people. But on the whole, population growth in Europe was slow, particularly in the 1920's. After the Second World War the entire picture changed; all over the continent a remarkable increase took place. It is true that the European rate of growth has remained moderate in comparison with that of other areas of the globe, but it is now considerably higher than it was in the first quarter of the century and double what it was in the 1920's. Italy, which before the Second World War had 42 million inhabitants, in the 1960's has 53 million; West Germany has about 60 million—not much less than East and West Germany combined before the Second World War—although it must be said that refugees from the east form part of the recent German population increase. The most astounding population rise has occurred in France: from 40 million after the Second

The events of May 1968 in Paris. *Students throwing pavement stones at the police on the Boulevard St. Michel.*

World War, to over 50 million. Certainly, some percentage of the increase in population is due to medical advances which have prolonged life. But the principal reason for the European population growth is a rise in the birthrate. For instance, in France the increase of births over deaths has been between 300,000 and 350,000 in every year since the Second World War. The result is a significant change in the age-structure of the population. This shift in the age structure has occurred also in the other nations of western Europe and given a focal point to the discontent which exists despite full employment and economic well-being. The problems of education, particularly those of the universities, have become the testing ground for the viability of postwar western democracy. The crisis in education has revealed the contrast between the requirements of Europe's modernized society and its system of education.

In the early decades of the century, the educational system reflected the class structure, with primary schools for the great bulk of the people, and higher education for only a small group. Higher education was expensive, and in its form and content was calculated to impress upon the students the ideas and behavior standards of the ruling group. Since the end of the Second World War there have been efforts to make higher education accessible to a greater number of young people, by government grants and by facilitating the transition from the primary schools to those preparing for the universities. Before the First World War in the most developed European countries not more than eleven of 10,000 people attended the universities. In 1934 this number had tripled. At the beginning of the 1960's fifty of 10,000 were students and the number has steadily grown since then. Despite this remarkable increase, however, these figures demonstrate that the percentage of the population attending higher schools and universities is still very small. Since a university training provides the means for social improvement, educational institutions form an obstacle to making use of the opportunities for social and economic ascent which modern industrial society could offer.

The universities in their present form do not come up to the requirements of the times. They have not been able to handle the increase in the number of the student population which, although insufficient in relation to the growth in overall population, has been staggering. The most startling increase has occurred in France, where the number of students has risen from 122,000 in 1939 to 247,000 in 1960 and to 514,000 in 1967; similar, although less startling figures can be given for all European nations. The extension of staff and facilities has not kept up with the needs of these masses; the students do not receive the training which they deserve. Difficulties are caused, however, not only by technical problems of adjustments to greater numbers. Because of their traditions the universities find it difficult to respond to the needs of modern industrial society. Because industry requires a scientifically and technically trained personnel, and because such specialized knowledge provides the best possibilities for advancement into the decision-making group, the universities will have to concentrate on professional training for practical life. But this pressure for a professional mass education runs counter to the assumptions which, consciously or unconsciously, have determined the character of the European universities. Among them is the view that the well-educated person can fulfill almost any task; it was only in 1968 that the report of a British civil-service committee admitted that in preparation for the civil service, the acquisition of specialized knowledge may be more useful than a classical education. Another assumption, one which, it must be conceded, has played its part in establishing the reputation of the European universities, is that the university is a place for scientific research and scholarly discoveries and that only a small elite can be taught to accomplish these tasks. Admittedly, the resistance customary to innovations in any academic community has complicated the solution of these problems. But the lack of adjustment of higher education to social changes raises doubts about whether the revolutionary alterations which Europe has undergone since the Second World War have penetrated far below the surface and modified basic traditions and attitudes.

The significance of the educational problem in postwar Europe—the maintenance of an elitist structure in a democratic society—lies in the fact that it has provided the large generation of postwar youth with a practical experience which has focussed attention on the striking contrast between the world as it is and the claims which are made for it, between the claim that the people rule in a democracy and the powerlessness of parliaments to enforce their will against the "establishment"; between the appeal of workers' parties to revolution and their pursuit of advantages for the workers within the existing system. One of the main objections of the new generation to life in Europe—it has been said—is that it is "an institutionalization of hypocrisy."

But these issues and questions concern not only the young generation but most European intellectuals. Although Europe in the 1960's is well functioning and relatively prosperous, it does not provide the leisure, the freedom, and the cultural values of which intellectuals have dreamt. But because all elements of society are drawn as active partners into the economic and social order, there is no group, no class, no progressive political force, with which the intellectuals can easily identify. Thus, behind the smooth façade of a prosperous western Europe there is an intense intellectual crisis. The leading writers of the first decade after the Second World War—Brecht, who became almost more popular in the West than in the East, where he directed his theater; and Sartre, whose voice carried great weight in the political discussions of the postwar world—had been deeply concerned with social and political issues. They were committed to action in the political arena. For the following generation of writers, the entire structure of society makes no sense. The expectation aroused by prospects of reform or revolution is seen as an illusion—like Godot, for whom people wait in Samuel Beckett's play, but who doesn't exist. The task of art has become to demonstrate the absurdity of the world. The argument by reason comes to be replaced by appeals to emotion and imagination, and traditional morals are rejected. Thus, there has been a breakdown in communication. Those who are established in the existing world no longer have anything to say to those who reject this world in its entirety and find in it nothing with which they can identify. One might see in this rejection, however, not only a withdrawal but also a new beginning—the dawn of an awareness that we cannot chart a course for the future unless we take a probing look at the conditions of existence created by the revolution of our time.

Suggestions for Further Reading

(Books marked * are available in paperback.)

PART I

THE FOUNDATIONS OF EARLY MODERN EUROPE, 1460–1559

GENERAL

Several good manuals survey the period: W. K. Ferguson, *Europe in Transition, 1300–1520* (Boston, 1962); Erich Hassinger, *Das Werden des neuzeitlichen Europa, 1300–1600* (Braunschweig, 1959); *Denys Hay, *The Italian Renaissance* (Cambridge, Eng., 1962) (Cambridge University Press); *Myron P. Gilmore, *The World of Humanism, 1453–1517* (New York, 1952) (Harper Torchbook); *The Reformation, 1520–1559*, ed. by G. R. Elton (*New Cambridge Modern History*, Vol. II, Cambridge, Eng., 1958).

European history in the fourteenth, fifteenth, and sixteenth centuries raises unusually interesting problems of terminology and periodization. When does modern history begin? Does the word "Renaissance" usefully describe a particular historical period? What are the dates of the "late Middle Ages"? W. K. Ferguson, *The Rennaissance in Historical Thought* (Boston, 1948) studies the answers historians have given these and similar questions between the fifteenth century and the present. Two collections of papers read at symposia in 1951–1952 and in 1959 supplement Ferguson and introduce the reader to current literature and debate in the fields of economic, political, and intellectual history and the history of literature, art, and science: *The Renaissance. Six Essays* (New York, 1962) (Harper Torchbook) and *The Renaissance. A Reconsideration of the Theories and Interpretations of the Age* (Madison, Wis., 1961) (Univ. of Wisconsin Press).

POLITICAL HISTORY

Historians continue to organize their narratives of European political history on national lines. The following histories lay the groundwork nicely: *J. H. Elliott, *Imperial Spain, 1469–1716* (New York, 1964) (Mentor); John Lynch, *Spain under the Habsburgs*, Vol. I (Oxford, 1964); *S. T. Bindoff, *Tudor England* (London, 1950) (Penguin Pelican); Hajo Holborn, *The Reformation* (New York, 1959), vol. I of his *History of Modern Germany*; Robert Mandrou, *Introduction à la France moderne, 1500–1640* (Paris, 1961). *Karl Brandi, *The Em-

peror Charles V, trans. by C. V. Wedgwood (London, and New York, 1939) (Humanities), surveys the Netherlands, Spain, Italy, Germany, and indeed all Europe from the perspective of the dominating political personality of the age.

Beneath the rapid flow of the political narrative is the rocky bed of political institutions. For England, see Kenneth W. M. Pickthorn, *Early Tudor Government*, 2 vols. (Cambridge, Eng., 1934) and *G. R. Elton, *The Tudor Revolution in Government* (Cambridge, Eng., 1953) (Cambridge Univ. Press). For France, Gaston Zeller, *Les Institutions de la France au XVIe siècle* (Paris, 1948); J. Russell Major, *Representative Institutions in Renaissance France* (Madison, Wis., 1960); and William F. Church, *Constitutional Thought in Sixteenth-Century France* (Cambridge, Mass., 1941). For Germany, F. L. Carsten, *Princes and Parliaments in Germany* (Oxford, 1959). For Spain, J. Gounon-Loubens, *Essais sur l'administration de la Castile au XVIe siècle* (Paris, 1860).

*Garrett Mattingly brilliantly describes the peacetime relations of these states in his *Renaissance Diplomacy* (New York, 1955) (Penguin Peregrine). J. R. Partington, *A History of Greek Fire and Gunpowder* (Cambridge, Eng., 1960), gives a most interesting account of the changes in military technology which revolutionized their wartime relations and put so intense a pressure on sixteenth-century political and financial institutions. See also F. L. Taylor, *The Art of War in Italy, 1494–1529* (Cambridge, Eng., 1921) and Sir Charles Oman, *The Art of War in the Sixteenth Century*, 2 vols. (London, 1937).

ECONOMIC AND SOCIAL HISTORY

The best guide is W. K. Ferguson, "Recent Trends in the Economic Historiography of the Renaissance," *Studies in the Renaissance*, Vol. VII (1960), pp. 7–26; while the *Cambridge Economic History*, especially Vol. IV (Cambridge, Eng., 1967), on the sixteenth century, provides an admirable synthesis of present knowledge. A stimulating introduction to many of the problems preoccupying social historians today is *J. H. Hexter's *Reappraisals in History. New Views on History and Society in Early Modern Europe* (New York, 1961) (Harper Torchbook). Some exceptional monographs offer more detailed treatment of salient features of a complicated and fascinating social and economic landscape: *Raymond de Roover, *The Rise and Decline of the Medici Bank, 1397–1494* (Cambridge, Mass., 1963) (Norton); Richard Ehrenberg, *Capital and Finance in the Age of the Renaissance* (New York, 1928); J. U. Nef, "Industrial Europe on the Eve of the Reformation," *Journal of Political Economy*, Vol. XLIX (1941), pp. 1–40, 183–224; Florence Elder de Roover, "Andrea Banchi, Florentine Silk Manufacturer and Merchant in the Fifteenth Century," *Studies in Medieval and Renaissance History*, Vol. III (1966), pp. 223–285; Frederick C. Lane, *Andrea Barbarigo, Merchant of Venice, 1418–1449* (Baltimore, 1944); Henri Lepeyre, *Une Famille de marchands: les Ruiz* (Peris, 1955); Emile Coornaert, *Les Français et le commerce international à Anvers, fin du XVe–XVIe siècle*, 2 vols. (Paris, 1961); Goetz Freiherr von Pölnitz, *Die Fugger* (Frankfurt am Main, 1960).

Three dynamic factors in sixteenth-century economic life were demographic expansion, the spice trade, and the great price rise. For orientation see E. F. Rice, "Recent Studies on the Population of Europe, 1348–1620," *Renaissance News*,

Vol. XVIII (1965), pp. 180–187; the chapter on the spice trade in Donald F. Lach, *Asia in the Making of Europe* (Chicago, 1965), Vol. I (1), pp. 91–147; and E. J. Hamilton, "The History of Prices before 1750," *XIe Congrès International des sciences historiques, Rapports,* Vol. I (Stockholm, 1960), pp. 144-164. All three are closely linked to the discoveries and European expansion in the New World and in the Far East. *Boise Penrose, *Travel and Discovery in the Renaissance, 1420–1620* (New York, 1962) (Atheneum) is a readable and authoritative survey.

There is a large and important literature on the meaning, origins, and development of capitalism. One may usefully begin with *Maurice Dobb, *Studies in the Development of Capitalism,* second ed. (New York, 1963) (New World Paperbacks). *Kurt Samuelsson, *Religion and Economic Action,* trans. by E. G. French (New York, 1961) (Harper Torchbook) is a recent discussion of the relation between capitalism and religion and of the controversial literature the problem has provoked since the publication in 1905 of Max Weber's celebrated essay on the Protestant ethic and the spirit of capitalism. At the heart of the controversy was the idea and practice of usury. See the illuminating book of Benjamin N. Nelson, *The Idea of Usury* (Princeton, N.J., 1949).

INTELLECTUAL HISTORY

The best introductions to Italian Renaissance thought are *W. H. Woodward, *Vittorino da Feltre and Other Humanist Educators* (Cambridge, Eng., 1897) (Teachers College Press); Eugenio Garin, *Italian Humanism. Philosophy and Civic Life in the Renaissance,* trans. by Peter Munz (New York, 1965); and two books by *Paul Oskar Kristeller: *Renaissance Thought. The Classic, Scholastic, and Humanist Strains* (New York, 1961) (Harper Torchbook) and *Eight Philosophers of the Italian Renaissance* (Stanford, Calif., 1964) (Stanford Univ. Press).

Among the many books on humanism in northern Europe, the following are reliable and attractive: *R. W. Chambers, *Thomas More* (London, 1935) (Ann Arbor Books); Fritz Caspari, *Humanism and the Social Order in Tudor England* (Chicago, 1954); Lewis Spitz, *The Religious Renaissance of the German Humanists* (Cambridge, Mass., 1963); *Hajo Holborn, *Ulrich von Hutten and the German Reformation,* trans. by Roland Bainton, (New Haven, 1937) (Harper Torchbook); Augustin Renaudet, *Préréforme et humanisme à Paris pendant les premières guerres d'Italie (1494–1517),* second ed. (Paris, 1953); Lucien Febvre, *Le Problème de l'incroyance au XVIe siècle. La religion de Rabelais* (Paris, 1942); *Johan Huizinga, *Erasmus and the Age of the Reformation* (New York, 1957) (Harper Torchbook).

Readers interested in historical writing will consult with profit Felix Gilbert, *Machiavelli and Guicciardini. Politics and History in Sixteenth Century Florence* (Princeton, N.J., 1965). For the history of science, see *Alistair C. Crombie, *Medieval and Early Modern Science,* 2 vols. (New York, 1959) (Doubleday Anchor); *Herbert Butterfield, *The Origins of Modern Science, 1300–1800* (London, 1949) (Free Press); and *Thomas S. Kuhn, *The Copernican Revolution* (Cambridge, Mass., 1957) (Random House Vintage). Pierce Butler, *The Origins of Printing in Europe* (Chicago, 1940) is an expert introduction to a technological innovation with profound consequences for European intellectual life.

Finally, a regrettably small selection of important and exciting books on the history of art: *Bernard Berenson, *The Italian Painters of the Renaissance* (London, 1952) (Meridian); Erwin Panofsky, *Renaissance and Renascences in Western Art*, second ed. (Stockholm, 1965); *Jean Seznec, *The Survival of the Pagan Gods. The Mythological Tradition and Its Place in Renaissance Humanism and Art*, trans. by Barbara Sessions (New York, 1953) (Harper Torchbook); Rudolf Wittkower, *Architectural Principles in the Age of Humanism*, third ed. (London, 1962); *Walter Friedländer, *Mannerism and Anti-Mannerism in Italian Painting* (New York, 1957) (Schocken); Otto Benesch, *The Art of the Rennaisance in Northern Europe* (London, 1965); *Kenneth Clark, *The Nude. A Study of Ideal Form* (New York, 1956) (Doubleday Anchor).

CHURCH AND REFORMATION

On the late medieval and Renaissance church, see W. K. Ferguson, "The Church in a Changing World," *American Historical Review*, Vol. LIX (1953), pp. 1–18; A. C. Flick, *The Decline of the Medieval Church*, 2 vols. (London, 1930); *G. Mollat, *The Popes at Avignon, 1305–1378*, trans. by Janet Love (New York, 1963) (Harper Torchbook); Walter Ullmann, *The Origins of the Great Schism* (London, 1948); Hubert Jedin, *A History of the Council of Trent*, trans. by Ernest Graf, 2 vols. (London and New York, 1957–1961).

A vivid introduction to the Protestant revolution is *Hans Hillerbrand, *The Reformation. A Narrative History Related by Contemporary Observers and Participants* (New York, 1964) (Harper Torchbook). *Roland Bainton, *The Reformation of the Sixteenth Century* (Boston, 1952) (Beacon) sketches the development of Protestant doctrine with sympathy and precision. *Norman Sykes, *The Crisis of the Reformation* (London, 1946) (Norton) clarifies the issues of faith and practice at the heart of the theological controversy. For the lives and teachings of the principal reformers, see *Bainton, *Here I Stand. A Life of Martin Luther* (New York, 1950) (Mentor); *Erik H. Erikson, *Young Man Luther* (New York, 1958) (Norton); E. G. Rupp, *Luther's Progress to the Diet of Worms* (London, 1951); P. S. Watson, *Let God Be God* (London, 1947), a well-balanced presentation of Luther's theology; Oskar Farner, *Zwingli the Reformer. His Life and Work* (London, 1952), a short account by the author of the definitive biography (4 vols., Zurich, 1943–1960); J. V. Pollet, *Huldrych Zwingli et la Réforme en Suisse d'après les recherches récentes* (Paris, 1963); François Wendel, *Calvin. The Origins and Development of His Religious Thought*, trans. by P. Mairet (New York, 1963); George H. Williams, *The Radical Reformation* (Philadelphia, 1962).

The following books survey the history of the Reformation in Europe and in individual countries: Emile G. Léonard, *A History of Protestantism* (London, 1965) Vol. I; A. C. Dickens, *The English Reformation* (London, 1964); G. Donaldson, *The Scottish Reformation* (Cambridge, Eng., 1960); Jean Viénot, *Histoire de la Réforme française des origines à l'Edit de Nantes* (Paris, 1926); Lucien Febvre, *Au Coeur religieux du XVIe siècle* (Paris, 1957).

PART II

THE AGE OF RELIGIOUS WARS,
1559–1689

GENERAL

There are two recent surveys of late sixteenth-century European history: *J. H. Elliott, *Europe Divided, 1559–1598* (New York, 1968) (Harper Torchbook), and *The Counter-Reformation and Price Revolution, 1559–1610*, ed. by R. B. Wernham (Cambridge, Eng., 1968) Vol. III of *The New Cambridge Modern History*. For the seventeenth century, *C. J. Friedrich, *The Age of the Baroque, 1610–1660* (New York, 1952) (Harper Torchbook) and *F. L. Nussbaum, *The Triumph of Science and Reason, 1660–1685* (New York, 1953) (Harper Torchbook) provide compact surveys; both authors have strong opinions and supply extensive bibliographies. *The Ascendancy of France, 1648–1688*, ed. by F. L. Carsten (Cambridge, Eng., 1961), Vol. V of *The New Cambridge Modern History*, is more balanced and more detailed than Friedrich or Nussbaum. *Sir George Clark, *The Seventeenth Century*, second ed. (Oxford, 1947) (Oxford Galaxy) is a series of topical essays by a master historian.

Four less conventional books attempt to delineate the subsurface transformation of early modern European society. Fernand Braudel, *La Méditerranée et le monde méditerranéen à l'époque de Philippe II* (Paris, 1949) is one of the great works of modern historical scholarship, a massive, richly suggestive study of all the societies bordering the Mediterranean in the age of Philip II. *Crisis in Europe, 1560–1660*, ed. by Trevor Aston (London, 1965) (Doubleday Anchor) is a symposium of provocative essays, stressing the social and economic tensions of the period. *R. H. Tawney, *Religion and the Rise of Capitalism* (New York, 1926) (Mentor) is a classic effort to correlate religious and economic developments. *Michael Walzer, *The Revolution of the Saints* (Cambridge, Mass., 1965) (Atheneum) is a parallel effort to correlate religion and politics. Both Tawney and Walzer deal mainly, though not exclusively, with English Puritanism.

POLITICAL HISTORY

There are several first-class recent books on Habsburg Spain. *J. H. Elliott, *Imperial Spain, 1469–1716* (New York, 1964) (Mentor) and John Lynch, *Spain under the Habsburgs*, Vol. I, 1516–1598 (Oxford, 1964) are both outstanding. *R. Trevor Davies, *The Golden Century of Spain, 1501–1621* (London, 1937) (Harper Torchbook) is partisan (pro-Philip II) and rather outdated, but highly readable. *Charles Gibson, *Spain in America* (New York, 1966) (Harper Torchbook) is a model survey of the Spanish colonial system, and J. H.

Parry, *The Spanish Seaborne Empire* (New York, 1966) is almost as good. There is no adequate biography of Philip II in English, but *Garrett Mattingly, *The Armada* (Boston, 1959) (Houghton Mifflin Sentry) is a superb presentation of the Spanish-English confrontation in 1588.

For France, *Albert Guérard, *France in the Classical Age: The Life and Death of an Ideal* (New York, 1928) (Harper Torchbook) and Georges Pagès, *La Monarchie d'Ancien Régime*, fifth ed. (Paris, 1952) are helpful introductions. J. R. Major, *The Estates General of 1560* (Princeton, N. J., 1951) and *Sir John Neale, *The Age of Catherine de Medici* (New York, 1943) (Harper Torchbook) offer two approaches to the late sixteenth-century Valois collapse. *Geoffrey Treasure, *Seventeenth Century France* (New York, 1966) (Doubleday Anchor) is the most recent survey of Bourbon absolutism. *C. V. Wedgwood, *Richelieu and the French Monarchy* (New York, 1950) (Collier) and *Maurice Ashley, *Louis XIV and the Greatness of France* (New York, 1953) (Free Press) are useful short biographies. *John B. Wolf, *Louis XIV* (New York, 1968) (Norton) is much more detailed. French mercantilism is examined from differing viewpoints in two large-scale works: C. W. Cole, *Colbert and a Century of French Mercantilism*, 2 vols. (New York, 1939) and Lionel Rothkrug, *Opposition to Louis XIV* (Princeton, N.J., 1965). *W. H. Lewis, *The Splendid Century* (New York, 1953) (Doubleday Anchor) is highly entertaining.

On England, only a few of the many good books can be listed here. G. R. Elton, *England under the Tudors* (New York, 1955) is less admiring of Elizabethan England than *A. L. Rowse, *The England of Elizabeth* (New York, 1950) (Collier). *Sir John Neale, *Queen Elizabeth I* (New York, 1934) (Doubleday Anchor) and *D. H. Willson, *King James VI and I* (London, 1956) (Oxford Galaxy) are excellent biographies. *Christopher Hill, *The Century of Revolution* (London, 1961) (Norton) is the liveliest survey of seventeenth-century England. *William Haller, *The Rise of Puritanism* (New York, 1938) (Harper Torchbook); Sir Charles Firth, *Oliver Cromwell* (Oxford, 1900); and a collection of Leveller documents, *Puritanism and Liberty*, ed. by A. S. P. Woodhouse (Chicago, 1938) illuminate various aspects of the Puritan movement. C. V. Wedgwood, *The King's Peace* (London, 1955), *The King's War* (London, 1958), and *A Coffin for King Charles* (New York, 1964) present the revolution of 1640 as a royal tragedy. David Ogg, *England in the Reigns of Charles II, James II and William III*, 3 vols. (Oxford, 1955) presents the revolution of 1688 as a Whig triumph. Charles Wilson, *England's Apprenticeship, 1603–1763* (New York, 1965) surveys economic developments authoritatively.

For the Netherlands, one should start with Peter Geyl's two books: *The Revolt of the Netherlands, 1555–1609*, second ed. (New York, 1958) (Barnes & Noble) and *The Netherlands in the Seventeenth Century*, 2 vols. (New York, 1961–1964). C. R. Boxer, *The Dutch Seaborne Empire, 1600–1800* (New York, 1965) and *Violet Barbour, *Capitalism in Amsterdam* (Baltimore, 1950) (Ann Arbor) discuss the Dutch economy; Boxer is especially interesting and informative. Two members of the house of Orange have admiring biographies in English: *C. V. Wedgwood's *William the Silent* (London, 1944) (Norton) and S. B. Baxter's *William III* (New York, 1966).

On the Holy Roman Empire, the best introduction is supplied by the first two volumes of Hajo Holborn's *History of Modern Germany*; these are *The Reformation* (New York, 1959) and *The Age of Absolutism* (New York, 1964). *C. V. Wedgwood, *The Thirty Years' War* (London, 1939) (Doubleday Anchor) is very well written, like all her books. *S. B. Fay, *The Rise of Brandenburg Prussia*, second ed. (New York, 1964) (Holt, Rinehart and Winston) is a useful sketch; F. L. Carsten, *The Origins of Prussia* (Oxford, 1954) is far fuller. Oswald Redlich, *Weltmach des Barock: Österreich in der Zeit Kaiser Leopolds I* (Vienna, 1961) is the best—indeed, almost the only—account of the rise of the Austrian Habsburg empire, 1648–1699.

On eastern Europe, W. H. McNeill, *Europe's Steppe Frontier, 1500–1800* (Chicago, 1964) is a suggestive new look at Slavic developments. L. S. Stavrianos, *The Balkans since 1453* (New York, 1958) is good on Ottoman Turkey. *The Cambridge History of Poland*, ed. by W. F. Reddaway, 2 vols. (Cambridge, Eng., 1941–1950) is the best introduction to that state. *Jerome Blum, *Lord and Peasant in Russia* (Princeton, N. J., 1961) (Atheneum) and M. T. Florinsky, *Russia*, 2 vols. (New York, 1953) offer contrasting approaches to pre-Petrine Russia. Michael Roberts, *Gustavus Adolphus, 1611–1632*, 2 vols. (London, 1953–1958) is a splendid biography with much data on seventeenth-century Sweden.

ECONOMIC HISTORY

E. J. Hamilton, *American Treasure and the Price Revolution in Spain* (Cambridge, Mass., 1934) and *J. U. Nef, *Industry and Government in France and England, 1540–1640* (Oxford, 1940) (Cornell) are pioneering works whose conclusions have been challenged. *D. P. Mannix and Malcolm Cowley, *Black Cargoes* (New York, 1962) (Viking Compass) discusses the African slave trade. Eli Heckscher, *Mercantilism*, second ed. (New York, 1955) and Charles Wilson, *Profit and Power* (London, 1957) present contrasting approaches to mercantilism. The controversy over the Weber thesis is conveniently summarized in *Protestantism and Capitalism*, ed. by R. W. Green (Boston, 1959) (Heath). Three valuable social studies deserve special mention. Pierre Goubert, *Beauvais et le Beauvaisis de 1600 à 1730*, 2 vols. (Paris, 1960) gives a depressing picture of peasant and town life in northern France. *Lawrence Stone, *The Crisis of the Aristocracy, 1558–1641* (Oxford, 1967) (abridged, Oxford Galaxy) explores the declining power and prestige of the English peerage. D. B. Davis, *The Problem of Slavery in Western Culture* (Ithaca, N.Y., 1966) examines why early modern Europeans were so ready to enslave Negroes.

INTELLECTUAL HISTORY

The following three books are very helpful studies of the scientific revolution: *A. R. Hall, *The Scientific Revolution, 1500–1800*, second ed. (London, 1956) (Beacon); *Herbert Butterfield, *The Origins of Modern Science, 1300–1800* (London, 1949) (Free Press); and *E. A. Burtt, *The Metaphysical Foundations of Modern Physical Science* (London, 1925) (Doubleday Anchor).

The art and architecture of the period are best surveyed through the splendid

*Pelican History of Art (London, 1953–   ), which includes the following pertinent volumes, all well illustrated: Jakob Rosenberg, *Dutch Art and Architecture, 1600–1800* (1966); Sir Anthony Blunt, *France, 1500–1700* (1954); Rudolf Wittkower, *Italy, 1600–1750* (1958); H. K. Gerson and E. H. ter Kuile, *Belgium, 1600–1800* (1960); George Kubler and Martin Soria, *Spain and Portugal, 1500–1800* (1959); Eberhard Hempel, *Central Europe, 1600–1800* (1965); and J. H. Summerson, *Britain, 1530–1830* (1953).

The best way to study the philosophers and dramatists is to read their works. E. A. Burtt, *The English Philosophers from Bacon to Mill* (New York, 1939) conveniently assembles generous selections from Bacon, Hobbes, and Locke. Descartes' *Discourse on Method*, Montaigne's *Essays*, Pascal's *Pensées*, Spinoza's *Ethics*, and representative plays by Lope de Vega, Calderón, Corneille, Racine, and Molière are all available in paperback in modern translations. The plays of Marlowe, Shakespeare, and Jonson are available in myriad editions.

PART III

KINGS AND PHILOSOPHERS,
1689–1789

GENERAL

Single-volume surveys of the approximate period covered in this book tend to begin from the Peace of Utrecht in 1713 or the death of Louis XIV in 1715. Of these, the most valuable by recent standards is *M. S. Anderson, *Eighteenth Century Europe, 1713–1789* (New York, 1966) (Oxford Galaxy) because of its attention to economic, social, and political institutions and despite its comparative neglect of intellectual history. For political narrative, see *David Ogg, *Europe of the Ancien Régime, 1715–1783* (New York, 1966) (Harper Torchbook). For analytical chapters, see *R. J. White, *Europe in the Eighteenth Century* (New York, 1965) (St. Martin's). For light essays on eighteenth-century "states of mind," see Sir Harold Nicolson, *The Age of Reason* (Garden City, N.Y., 1961). For a good brief survey, see *Frank Manuel, *The Age of Reason* (Ithaca, N.Y., 1957) (Cornell). For the last generation of Europe in the Old Regime, R. R. Palmer, *The Age of the Democratic Revolution: A Political History of Europe and America, 1760–1800,* 2 vols. (Princeton, N.J., 1959–1964) is now required reading.

The more familiar and more minutely subdivided series on European history have entries for our whole period. It is covered for the *Rise of Modern Europe series (Harper & Row) by John B. Wolf, *The Emergence of the Great Powers, 1685–1715* (New York, 1951); Penfield Roberts, *The Quest for Security, 1715–1740* (New York, 1947); Walter L. Dorn, *Competition for Empire, 1740–1763* (New York, 1940); and Leo Gershoy, *From Despotism to Revolution, 1763–1789* (New York, 1944). The latter two volumes are particularly useful for their analysis of the relationships between politics and administration and between politics and society, respectively. From the *New Cambridge Modern History* we have Vol. VII, *The Old Regime, 1713–1763*, ed. by J. O. Lindsay (Cambridge, Eng., 1957) and Vol. VIII, *The American and French Revolutions, 1763–1793*, ed. by Albert Goodwin (Cambridge, Eng., 1965). What can be said for these series as a whole holds for their volumes covering our period in particular: their strength lies rather in their intensive descriptions or their particular essays than in their historical continuity or their development of themes over a considerable time span. The same disjointed and uneven excellence holds for the collection of essays in the sumptuously illustrated volume, *The Eighteenth Century: Europe in the Age of the Enlightenment*, ed. by Alfred Cobban (London, 1969).

There are satisfactory general national histories for the major countries of western and central Europe in the period. British developments are covered by one volume in Dorothy Marshall, *Eighteenth Century England* (New York, 1962) and by three volumes in the Oxford History of England series: George Clark, *The Later Stuarts, 1660–1714* (Oxford, 1955); Basil Williams, *The Whig Supremacy, 1714–1760* (Oxford, 1939); and J. Steven Watson, *The Reign of George III, 1760–1815* (Oxford, 1960). See also *J. H. Plumb, *England in the Eighteenth Century* (Harmondsworth, 1950) (Pelican) and *R. J. White, *The Age of George III* (New York, 1969) (Doubleday Anchor). Among the recent general works on eighteenth-century France, both *Alfred Cobban, *A History of Modern France*, Vol. I, *1715–1799* (New York, 1965) (Penguin) and Gordon Wright, *France in Modern Times: 1760 to the Present* (Chicago, 1960) are recommended for the coverage indicated in their titles, and among the classics *Alexis de Tocqueville, *The Old Regime and the French Revolution* (New York, 1955) (Doubleday Anchor) remains important. For central Europe Hajo Holborn's *A History of Modern Germany: 1648–1840* (New York, 1964) covers both Germany and Austria in a work that remains alone in its field.

POLITICAL HISTORY

On Europe as a whole, the most recent work is E. N. Williams, *The Ancien Régime in Europe: Government and Society in the Major States, 1648–1789* (New York, 1970), a state-by-state survey in social context. For the rest, the history of eighteenth-century politics has been devoted either to absolutism or to diplomacy. *Max Beloff, *The Age of Absolutism, 1660–1815* (New York, 1966) (Harper Torchbook) is a political survey which includes the entire period, while Ronald W. Harris, *Absolutism and Enlightenment, 1660–1789* (London, 1964) deals far more with absolutism than with Enlightenment. *John G. Gagliardo, *Enlightened Despotism* (New York, 1967) (T. Y. Crowell) is a recent essay on the same aspect of the age which was covered earlier in *Geoffrey Brunn, *Enlightened Despots*, second ed. (New York, 1967) (Holt, Rinehart and Winston). On the diplomatic history of the age, *Ludwig Dehio, *The Precarious Balance* (New York, 1962) (Vintage) shows the long-range effects of the duel between Louis XIV and William III; *Albert Sorel, *Europe under the Old Regime* (Harper Torchbook), the first section of *L'Europe et la Révolution française*, 9 vols. (Paris, 1895–1911), is the classical cynical view of eighteenth-century diplomacy; Harold Temperley, *Frederick the Great and Kaiser Joseph*, second ed. (New York, 1968) is an intriguing account of the European policies and relations of the two monarchs; and Herbert Kaplan, *The First Partition of Poland* (New York, 1962) is a detailed case study of eighteenth-century diplomacy in its most notorious case.

What is available in English of national political history for the eighteenth century tends to revolve around political biography. For Great Britain, see especially two books by J. H. Plumb: *Sir Robert Walpole*, 2 vols. (Boston, 1956–1960) and *The First Four Georges* (New York, 1956); Sir Lewis B. Namier's two pioneering works in collective biography, **The Structure of Politics at the Accession of George III*, second ed. (New York, 1957) (St. Martin's Papermac) and **England in the Age of the American Revolution*, second ed. (New York, 1961) (St. Martin's Papermac); his classic essay on George III in *Personalities and Powers* (New York, 1955); and the development of his methods by Robert Walcott, *English Politics in the Early Eighteenth Century* (Cambridge, Mass., 1956); John B. Owen, *The Rise of the Pelhams* (London, 1957); John Brooke, *The Chatham Administration* (New York, 1956) and **The House of Commons, 1754–1790* (New York, 1968) (Oxford). On the side of conflict rather than consensus, Richard Pares, *King George and the Politicians* (Oxford, 1953) Herbert Butterfield, *King George, Lord North and the People* (London, 1949); **George Rudé, *Wilkes and Liberty* (New York, 1962) (Oxford); and I. R. Christie, *Wilkes, Wyville and Reform* (New York, 1963), all relate political personalities to the upheavals of George III's reign. For France, see **John B. Wolf, *Louis XIV* (New York, 1968) (Norton); George P. Gooch, *Louis XV: Monarchy in Decline* (London, 1956); Bernard Fay, *Louis XVI: The End of a World* (Chicago, 1968); Arthur M. Wilson, *French Foreign Policy during the Administration of Cardinal Fleury* (Cambridge, Mass., 1936); John M. S. Allison, *Lamoignon de Malesherbes* (New Haven, 1938); and Douglas Dakin, *Turgot and the Ancien Régime in France* (London, 1939). On Germany, see Pierre Gaxotte, *Frederick the Great* (London, 1941); George P. Gooch, *Frederick the Great* (London, 1947). On Austria, see Nicholas Henderson, *Prince Eugen of Savoy* (London, 1964); Edward Crankshaw, *Maria Theresa* (New York, 1970); Robert Pick, *Empress Maria Theresa: The Early Years* (New York, 1966); and, for Joseph II, Saul Padover, *The Revolutionary Emperor*, revised ed. (Hamden, Conn., 1967). On Russia's chief autocrats, N. Kliuchevski, *Peter the Great* (London, 1958) is a selection from a larger classic, and **G. S. Thomson, *Catherine the Great and the Expansion of Russia* (New York, 1962) (Collier-Macmillan) is a useful survey.

Among the impersonal studies of national political events and institutions which are of more than monographic interest the following may be singled out for special attention. For Great Britain, **E. N. Williams, *Eighteenth Century Constitution* (New York, 1960) (Cambridge U.); **D. L. Keir, *Constitutional History of Modern Britain since 1485* (New York, 1967) (Norton); Betty Kemp, *Kings and Commons, 1660–1832* (New York, 1957); J. H. Plumb, *The Origins of Political Stability in England, 1675–1725* (Boston, 1967); and Vol. X of William Holdsworth's *History of English Law*, third ed., 16 vols.

(London, 1922–1932) give standard accounts of the eighteenth-century constitution and its consolidation, while G. S. Veitch, *Genesis of Parliamentary Reform* (Hamden, Conn., 1967) and the first two volumes of Simon Maccoby, *English Radicalism*, 4 vols. (London, 1935–1961) give standard accounts of the rise of opposition to it. For France, aside from older narrative histories like J. B. Perkins, *France under the Regency* (Boston, 1892) and *France under Louis XV*, two vols. (Boston, 1897), English-language works on prerevolutionary politics have tended to focus on the limits of absolutism, as in Lionel Rothkrug, *Opposition to Louis XIV* (Princeton, N.J., 1965); Vivian R. Gruder, *The Royal Provincial Intendants: A Governing Elite in Eighteenth Century France* (Ithaca, N.Y., 1968); James D. Hardy, *Judicial Politics in the Old Regime: The Parliament of Paris under the Regency* (Baton Rouge, La., 1967); and *The Brittany Affair and the Crisis of the Ancien Regime*, ed. by John Rothney (New York, 1969). For Germany, as one might expect, the structure of Prussian government has attracted special scholarly concern, as in *Hans Rosenberg, *Bureaucracy, Aristocracy, and Autocracy* (Boston, 1966) (Beacon); *Sidney B. Fay, *The Rise of Brandenburg-Prussia*, second ed. (New York, 1964) (Holt, Rinehart and Winston); and R. A. Dorwart, *Administrative Reform under Frederick William I* (Cambridge, Mass., 1953). But the reader's particular attention should be called to F. L. Carsten, *Princes and Parliaments* (New York, 1959) and Helen P. Liebel, *Enlightened Bureaucracy versus Enlightened Absolutism in Baden, 1750–1792* (Philadelphia, 1965), rare analyses of political relations in German states apart from both Prussia and Austria, and to Klaus Epstein, *The Genesis of German Conservatism* (Princeton, N.J., 1966), an analysis of the social and intellectual basis of conservative politics in all of eighteenth-century Germany. For the Habsburg dominions, see P. Frischauer, *The Imperial Crown* (London, 1939); H. J. Kerner, *Bohemia in the Eighteenth Century* (New York, 1932); H. Marczali, *Hungary in the Eighteenth Century* (New York, 1910); and Bela Kiraly, *Hungary in the late Eighteenth Century: The Decline of Enlightened Despotism* (New York, 1969). For Russia, Vol. IV and V of N. Kliuchevski, *History of Russia*, 5 vols. (New York, 1911–1931) remain brilliant and profound, albeit hobbled by a poor translation.

ECONOMIC AND SOCIAL HISTORY

Although students of modern history are accustomed to the close connection between economic development and social structure which has characterized industrial society and has been reflected in the historical writing about Europe in the nineteenth and twentieth centuries, such a connection does not hold for the historical writing about Europe in the eighteenth century. Economic history, especially in the English language, tends to be sparse, but social history is rich.

For economic history proper, the available literature—aside from isolated chapters in works of general history (see above)—is focused primarily on the origins of the agricultural and industrial revolutions, starting in the latter part of the eighteenth century. Thus the standard economic-history texts are too unspecific about the eighteenth century to be very useful to historians of the period, and the two outstanding economic histories cover, at the date of this writing, only aspects of the second half of the century. *The Cambridge Economic History of Europe* still lacks Vol. V, the eighteenth-century volume. Vol. VI (in two parts), *The Industrial Revolutions and After*, ed. by M. M. Postan and H. J. Habakkuk (Cambridge, Eng., 1965), reaches back into the eighteenth century for the beginnings of the Industrial Revolution, most valuably in David S. Landes, "Technological Change and Development in Western Europe, 1750-1914," a chapter which has been expanded in the same author's *Unbound Prometheus* (London, 1969). The other, much briefer and much older general work which historians have found especially appropriate to their own work—Witt Bowden, Michael Karpovich, and A. P. Usher, *Economic History of Europe since* 1750 (New York, 1937)—also begins, as the title indicates, in the middle of our period. So do *W. W. Rostow's schematic *Stages of Economic Growth* (New York, 1960) (Cambridge U.) and W. O. Henderson's comparative *Britain and Industrial Europe, 1750–1870*, second ed. (New York, 1965). In a more specialized vein, Vols. III and IV of Charles Singer, *et al.*, *History of Technology*, 5 vols. (Oxford, 1954–1958) is most informative on the details of technical innovation. Eli Heckscher, *Mercantilism*, second ed., 2 vols. (New York, 1955) is another larger work on a special economic function—in this case, governmental economic policy—which includes the eighteenth century in its purview.

Most of what is available on the national economic history of the period deals with Great Britain, both because of linguistic accessibility and because of the indisputable focus of primary economic growth there. Two books by Thomas S. Ashton—*An Economic History of England: The Eighteenth Century* (London, 1955) and *The Industrial Revolution, 1760–1830* (London and New York, 1948) (Oxford Galaxy)—and J. D. Chambers and G. E. Mingay, *The Agrarian Revolution, 1750–1880* (New York, 1966) are recent and substantial works along the future looking line. Only sporadic special studies are available to English-language readers on French economic history of the period: Warren C. Scoville, *The Persecution of the Huguenots and French Economic Development, 1680–1720* (Berkeley, Calif., 1960) and Shelby McCloy, *French Inventions of the Eighteenth Century* (Lexington, Ky., 1952). For central Europe the economic literature is similarly scattered. W. O. Henderson has two overlapping books on Prussian policy and economic growth—*The State and the Industrial Revolution in Prussia, 1740–1870* (New York, 1958) and *Studies in the Economic Policy of Frederick the Great* (New York, 1963). For Austrian and German economic thinking Albion Small, *The Cameralists* (Chicago, 1909) should still be consulted. For Russia, the eighteenth-century chapters of *Jerome Blum's important *Lord and Peasant in Russia* (Princeton, N.J., 1961) (Atheneum) should be read for the economic basis of Russian agrarian relations.

Social history has traditionally been an amorphous field which has tended to shade off either into irrelevant details of daily existence or into politics and economics. But the historiography of eighteenth-century Europe has been benefited by the recent emphasis upon the independence of social history as the study of the kind of ordinary relations within and between groups of men and women which are prior to politics, connected with economics but not derivative from it, and definitive of the real life lived by most human beings in the past. On the European level, relevant documents and commentary for many groups are collected in *European Society in the Eighteenth Century*, ed. by Robert Forster and Elborg Forster (New York, 1969) (Harper Torchbook). For particular groups, we have *The European Nobility in the Eighteenth Century*, ed. by Albert Goodwin (New York, 1967) (Harper Torchbook); *Charles Moraze, Triumph of the Middle Classes* (New York, 1968) (Doubleday Anchor), which, however, as the title implies, emphasizes the nineteenth century; and for France and England, *George Rudé, The Crowd in History, 1730–1884* (New York, 1964) (Wiley).

Of the rich historical literature on social groups within the major European countries—in addition to the above-mentioned works by Namier on the politics of the British aristocracy, by Rudé on popular upheaval in Wilkite England, by Rosenberg on the interaction of Prussian aristocracy with Prussian monarchy, by Landes on the social impact of early industrialization, and by Blum on the social impact of agricultural change—the following are especially illuminating for the conditions of social life as such. For Great Britain, Dorothy Marshall, *English People in the Eighteenth Century* (New York, 1956); *Dorothy George, England in Transition* (London, 1951) (Pelican); A. R. Humphreys, *The Augustan World* (London, 1954); and *Man versus Society in Eighteenth Century Britain*, ed. by James L. Clifford (Cambridge, Eng., 1968) have superseded, in substance if not in style, Vol. III of George M. Trevelyan, *Illustrated Social History*, 4 vols. (New York, 1949–1952). On particular aspects of British social life, see G. E. Mingay, *English Landed Society in the Eighteenth Century* (Toronto, 1963) for the stabilizing factor; the opening chapter of *Asa Briggs, The Making of Modern England, 1783–1867: The Age of Improvement* (New York, 1965) (Harper Torchbook) sketches the social basis of change late in the century.

For France, *Franklin L. Ford, Robe and Sword* (New York, 1953) (Harper Torchbook) and Robert Forster, *The Nobility of Toulouse in the Eighteenth Century* (Baltimore, 1960) are important studies of the French aristocracy; *Elinor G. Barber, Bourgeoisie in Eighteenth Century France* (Princeton, N.J., 1955) (Princeton) is an equally important study of the urban commoners; George Rudé, *The Crowd in the French Revolution* (New York, 1959) gives background on the French masses in the *ancien régime*; *C. B. Behrens, The Ancien Régime* (New York, 1967) (Voyager) and *Georges Lefebvre, The Coming of the French Revolution*, trans. by R. R. Palmer (New York, 1957) (Vintage) give the social background of all classes. Shelby McCloy, in *The Humanitarian Movement in Eighteenth Century France* (Lexington, Ky., 1957) and *Government Assistance in Eighteenth Century France* (Durham, N.C., 1946), deals with national movements for social welfare. On the local level, *Franklin L. Ford, Strasbourg in Transition, 1648–1789* (New York, 1966) (Norton) is a microcosm of social development; John McManners, *French Ecclesiastical Society under the Ancient Regime* (New York, 1961) is a microcosm of social stability.

For German society, the standard works in English are two books by W. H. Bruford: *Germany in the Eighteenth Century* (Cambridge, Eng., 1935) (Cambridge U.) and *Culture and Society in Classical Weimar, 1775–1806* (Cambridge, Eng., 1962). See too the recent study on the German peasantry by John Gagliardo, *From Pariah to Patriot* (Lexington, Ky., 1969). On the Austrian peasantry, see Edith M. Link. *The Emancipation of the Austrian Peasant, 1740–1798* (New York, 1949).

For Russian society in the eighteenth century, the outstanding recent work is *Marc Raeff, *Origins of the Russian Intelligentsia: The Eighteenth Century Nobility* (New York, 1966) (Harbinger), but P. Dukes, *Catherine the Great and the Russian Nobility* (Cambridge, Eng., 1968) and the relevant sections of *G. T. Robinson *Rural Russia under the Old Regime* (Berkeley, Calif., 1967) (U. of California) can also be consulted with profit. Valentine Bill, *The Forgotten Class: The Russian Bourgeoisie from the Earliest Beginnings to 1900* (New York, 1959) is disappointingly thin on a promising subject.

INTELLECTUAL HISTORY

The main theme in the recent literature on the intellectual history of the eighteenth century is the refutation, both for the culture as a whole and for its individual representatives, of its homogeneous characterization as an age of secularized reason, the characterization often inferred from such formerly standard works as *Carl Becker, *The Heavenly City of the Eighteenth Century Philosophers* (New Haven, 1932) (Yale) and *Basil Willey, *The Eighteenth Century Background* (New York, 1941) (Beacon). These refutations insist both that the particular intellectual movement called "the Enlightenment" was far from being co-extensive with the entire variegated culture of eighteenth-century Europe and that the Enlightenment was itself far too variegated a movement to admit of simple definition, or indeed, for some historians, of any definition at all. Such recent refutations are exemplified by the cultural diversity shown in the essays of *The Age of Enlightenment*, ed. by W. H. Barber, *et al.* (Edinburgh, 1967) and *Aspects of the Eighteenth Century*, ed. by Earl R. Wasserman (Baltimore, 1965); by the plurality of Enlightenment motifs shown in Alfred Cobban, *In Search of Humanity* (New York, 1960); by the existentialist variety of eighteenth-century attitudes in Lester G. Crocker, *An Age of Crisis: Man and World in Eighteenth Century French Thought* (Baltimore, 1959); and by the unexpected views of some eighteenth-century intellectuals on religion in *Frank Manuel, *The Eighteenth Century Confronts the Gods* (New York, 1967) (Atheneum), and on social science in Louis I. Bredvold, *The Brave New World of the Enlightenment* (Ann Arbor, Mich., 1961). The great modern synthesis, which accounts for all such critiques and reconstructs the Enlightenment in the light of them as a coherent movement, is Peter Gay, *The Enlightenment: An Interpretation*, 2 vols. (New York, 1966–1969). Vol. I ,has appeared in paperback as *The Enlightenment: The Rise of Modern Paganism* (Vintage). This work is a mobile intellectual portrait, in contrast to *Ernst Cassirer, *The Philosophy of the Enlightenment* (Boston, 1955) (Beacon),

which also argues for the integrity of the Enlightenment, but helped to provoke the challenges to it by imposing a rigid dialectical logic upon eighteenth-
century culture. Similar to Gay in their flexible reconstructions of eighteenth-
century thought are two volumes by Paul Hazard—*The European Mind*
(New York, 1963) (Meridian), on the 1680–1715 generation, and *European
Thought in the Eighteenth Century* (New York, 1963) (Meridian) for the
succeeding period—and the recent convenient survey by Norman Hampson,
The Enlightenment (Baltimore, 1968) (Penguin).

For the various special branches of Enlightenment thought, the following readings may be recommended:

On religion and the churches in general, see *Gerald R. Cragg, *The
Church and the Age of Reason, 1648–1789* (London, 1962) (Pelican) and
the relevant chapters of J. H. Nichols, *A History of Christianity,
1650–1950* (New York, 1956). For Catholicism in general, Vol.
XXX–XL of Ludwig von Pastor, *History of the Popes* (London,
1938–   ) and the introduction of F. Nielson, *The History of the
Papacy in the Nineteenth Century* (New York, 1906) are still instructive,
while *R. R. Palmer, *Catholics and Unbelievers in Eighteenth Century
France* (Princeton, N.J., 1939) and *Richard Herr, *The Eighteenth Century Revolution in Spain* (Princeton, N.J., 1969) (Princeton) consider the
responses of Catholic churchmen to the secular attack in those countries.
On the sundry denominations and locales of Protestants, there are B. C.
Poland, *French Protestantism and the French Revolution, 1685–1815*
(Princeton, N.J., 1957); A. L. Drummond, *German Protestantism since
Luther* (London, 1951); Koppel S. Pinson, *Pietism as a Factor in the Rise
of German Nationalism* (New York, 1934); Norman Sykes, *Church and
State in England in the Eighteenth Century* (London, 1934); Roland N.
Stromberg, *Religious Liberalism in Eighteenth Century England* (New York,
1954), and on English Wesleyanism, *Methodism and the Common People
of the Eighteenth Century* (London, 1945); and *Elie Halévy, *England in
1815* (Barnes & Noble), the first volume of his *History of the English
People in the Nineteenth Century*, second revised ed., 6 vols. (London,
1949–1952).

On natural science in the eighteenth century—in addition to the above-
cited general works on the Enlightenment—see the appropriate chapters
in *Charles Gillispie, *The Edge of Objectivity* (Princeton, N.J., 1960)
(Princeton); *Natural Philosophy through the Eighteenth Century*, ed. by
Allan Ferguson (London, 1948); *Alexander Koyre, *From the Closed
World to the Infinite Universe* (Baltimore, 1968) (Johns Hopkins), and
*Alfred R. Hall, *The Scientific Revolution, 1500–1800*, revised ed. (Boston,
1966) (Beacon). The detailed A. Wolf, *A History of Science, Technology,
and Philosophy in the Eighteenth Century*, revised ed., 2 vols., (London,
1952) is the one extensive book on the general subject for the period, but
Aram Vartanian, *Diderot and Descartes* (Princeton, N.J., 1953) and Philip
C. Ritterbush, *Overtures to Biology* (New Haven, 1964) are interesting
treatments of particular eighteenth-century scientific subjects.

For special inquiries into eighteenth-century views of human nature (*i.e.*
psychology and morals), in addition to Lester G. Crocker's *Age of Crisis*

(cited above), reference should be made to the same author's *Nature and Culture: Ethical Thought in the French Enlightenment* (Baltimore, 1963) and to *Elie Halévy, *The Growth of Philosophic Radicalism* (Boston, 1955) (Beacon), the standard work on the origins and early history of utilitarianism.

Much of the available literature on the political and social ideas of the eighteenth century focuses on individual thinkers (see below). For what there is of more general treatments, see especially *Kingsley Martin, *French Liberal Thought in the Eighteenth Century* (New York, 1963) (Harper Torchbook); *J. L. Talmon, *The Origins of Totalitarian Democracy* (New York, 1960) (Norton); Elizabeth V. Souleyman, *The Vision of World Peace in Seventeenth and Eighteenth Century France* (New York, 1941); *Caroline Robbins, *Eighteenth-century Commonwealthman* (New York, 1959) (Atheneum); Harold J. Laski, *Political Thought in England: Locke to Bentham* (London, 1919); Gladys Bryson, *Man and Society: The Scottish Inquiry of the Eighteenth Century* (Princeton, N.J., 1945); and Leonard Krieger, *The German Idea of Freedom* (Boston, 1957). On economic ideas, see William Letwin, *The Origin of Scientific Economics* (Garden City, N.Y., 1963) and *The Economics of Physiocracy*, ed. by Ronald L. Meek (Cambridge, Mass., 1962). On the main line of Enlightenment ideas of history, see J. B. Black, *The Art of History* (New York, 1926). On the related ideas of historical progress and regress, see *Frank Manuel, *The Prophets of Paris* (New York, 1962) (Harper Torchbook); Charles Frankel, *The Faith of Reason* (New York, 1969); Charles Vereker, *Eighteenth-Century Optimism* (Liverpool, 1967); and Henry Vyverberg, *Historical Pessimism in the French Enlightenment* (Cambridge, Mass., 1958).

The bulk of the available general literature on the Enlightenment is, like the Enlightenment itself, oriented toward France, and until recently there has been little on the shape of the movement in other national contexts. But now for England *Leslie Stephen's old but still informative *History of English Thought in the Eighteenth Century,* new ed., 2 vols. (New York, 1962) (Harbinger) can be supplemented with Gerald R. Cragg, *Reason and Authority in the Eighteenth Century* (Cambridge, Eng., 1964) and Ronald W. Harris, *Reason and Nature in the Eighteenth Century, 1714–1780* (London, 1968). For the Spanish Enlightenment, Richard Herr (cited above) is excellent. For Germany, two of the essays in *Introduction to Modernity: A Symposium on Eighteenth-Century Thought,* ed. by Robert Mollenauer (Austin, Tex., 1965) are relevant, and so is, for Austria, the middle section of Robert A. Kann, *A Study in Austrian Intellectual History: From Late Baroque to Romanticism* (New York, 1960). Of particular interest for the distinctive intellectual development of France are Ira O. Wade, *The Clandestine Organization and Diffusion of Philosophic Ideas in France from 1700 to 1750* (New York, 1967), for the early spread of Enlightenment in France, and Robert Darnton, *Mesmerism and the End of the Enlightenment in France* (Cambridge, Mass., 1968) for the radical temper in the generation before the revolution which grew out of it.

We may conclude this bibliographical essay with a list of particularly

noteworthy recent works on individual intellectuals. On main-line repre-
sentatives of the Enlightenment: Ronald Grimsley, *Jean D'Alembert,
1717–1783* (New York, 1963); Isabel Knight, *The Geometric Spirit: The
Abbé de Condillac and the French Enlightenment* (New Haven, 1968);
Arthur Wilson, *Diderot: The Testing Years, 1713–1759* (New York, 1957);
Lester G. Crocker, *Diderot: The Embattled Philosopher* (New York, 1966);
David Kettler, *The Social and Political Thought of Adam Ferguson* (Colum-
bus, Ohio, 1965); John B. Stewart, *The Moral and Political Philosophy of
David Hume* (New York, 1963); David W. Smith, *Helvétius* (New York,
1965); Henry S. Allison, *Lessing and the Enlightenment* (Ann Arbor, Mich.,
1966); Robert Shackleton, *Montesquieu* (New York, 1961); Ira O. Wade,
The Intellectual Development of Voltaire (Princeton, N.J., 1969); and
*Peter Gay, *Voltaire's Politics* (New York, 1965) (Vintage). On figures
who developed away from the main line: Mary P. Mack, *Jeremy Bentham: An
Odyssey of Ideas* (London, 1962); F. M. Barnard, *Herder's Social and National
Thought* (New York, 1965); Karl Vietor, *Goethe the Thinker* (Cambridge,
Mass., 1950); *Ernst Cassirer, *The Question of Jean-Jacques Rousseau* (Bloom-
ington, Ind., 1963) (Midland), Judith Shklar, *Men and Citizens: A Study of
Rousseau's Social Theory* (New York, 1969); Alfred Cobban, *Edmund Burke
and the Revolt Against the Eighteenth Century*, second ed. (New York, 1960);
and *Peter Stanlis, *Edmund Burke and the Natural Law* (Ann Arbor,
Mich., 1958) (Ann Arbor).

PART IV

THE AGE OF REVOLUTION AND REACTION,
1789–1850

THE FRENCH REVOLUTION AND THE NAPOLEONIC ERA

The volume of historical literature on the French Revolution and the Napoleonic era alone is staggering. For the nonspecialist, English-speaking reader the
best annotated bibliography is contained in a new edition of Leo Gershoy, *The
French Revolution and Napoleon* (New York, 1964), which, incidentally, remains one of the outstanding surveys of the period. The original edition of this
book was published in 1933 (New York). The title of the edition reprinted in
1964 adds "with new annotated bibliography." Other general works on the revolution available in English are *James M. Thompson, *The French Revolution*
(Oxford, 1943) (Oxford Galaxy Books); Louis R. Gottschalk, *The Era of the
French Revolution* (New York, 1929); and a stimulating volume in the Rise of
Modern Europe series edited by William L. Langer. *Crane Brinton, *A Decade
of Revolution, 1789–1799*. Original edition published in New York, 1934. Bibliographical essay revised as of November, 1958; supplemented October, 1962.

Harper Torchbook edition published in 1963 (New York). See also the pioneering study of R. R. Palmer, *The Age of the Democratic Revolution: A Political History of Europe and America, 1760–1800*, 2 vols. (Princeton, N.J., 1959–1964), which views the French Revolution as part of a broader democratic revolution in the Western world beginning around 1760. Available in a paperback edition, 2 vols. (Princeton University Press). Works by some of the major twentieth-century French historians of the revolution are now available in English; for example, Georges Lefebvre, *La Révolution française*, third edition (Paris, 1951), and revised editions (1963, 1968) in the *Peuples et civilisations* series has been translated in two volumes, *The French Revolution: From Its Origins to 1793* trans. by Elizabeth Moss Evanson (New York, 1962) and *The French Revolution: From 1793 to 1799*, trans. by John Hall Stewart and James Friguglietti (New York, 1964). Available in a paperback edition, 2 vols. (Columbia University Press). See also *Lefebvre's *The Coming of the French Revolution*, trans. by R. R. Palmer (Princeton, N.J., 1947) (Princeton). Two of Lefebvre's most distinguished predecessors were François V. A. Aulard, who wrote in the last decades of the nineteenth century his strongly republican *The French Revolution, a Political History, 1789–1804*, 4 vols. (New York, 1910), and Albert Mathiez, whose more economically oriented works, published in 1928 and 1931 (New York) have been translated by Catherine Alison Phillips as *The French Revolution (New York, 1962) (Universal Library) and *After Robespierre, the Thermidorian Reaction* (New York, 1965) (Universal Library).

On the impact of the revolution upon Europe the classic work remains Albert Sorel, *L'Europe et la Révolution française*, 9 vols. (Paris, 1895–1911), the celebrated first chapter of which is available in English in paperback as *Europe under the Old Regime*, trans. by Francis H. Herrick (Harper Torchbook). A more recent work by one of the best contemporary scholars of the revolution is Jacques L. Godechot, *La Grande Nation: l'expansion révolutionnaire de la France dans le monde de 1789 à 1799,* 2 vols. (Paris, 1956). See also by the same author, in the *Nouvelle Clio* series, *Les Révolutions, 1770–1799*, second edition, revised and augmented (Paris, 1965); available in English as *France and the Atlantic Revolution of the Eighteenth Century, 1770–1799*, translated by Herbert H. Rowen (New York, 1965). On another aspect of the revolution Professor Godechot has published *Les Institutions de la France sous la Révolution et l'empire* (Paris, 1951) and second revised edition (1968). Good studies in English of more specialized topics are the following: Crane Brinton, *The Jacobins* (New York, 1930; reprinted, New York, 1961); Donald M. Greer, *The Incidence of the Terror during the French Revolution: A Statistical Interpretation* (Cambridge, Mass., 1935; reprinted, Gloucester, Mass., 1966) and *The Incidence of the Emigration during the French Revolution* (Cambridge, Mass., 1951; reprinted 1966); *R. R. Palmer, *Twelve Who Ruled: The Committee of Public Safety during the Terror* (Princeton, N.J., 1941) (Atheneum); and *George Rudé, *The Crowd in the French Revolution* (New York, 1959) (Oxford Galaxy Books).

On Napoleon and the Napoleonic era as a whole, see *Geoffrey Bruun, *Europe and the French Imperium, 1799–1814*, Rise of Modern Europe series (New York, 1938) (Harper Torchbook, 1963), which contains a bibliographical essay (revised November, 1957) and George Rudé, *Revolutionary Europe,*

1783–1815 (New York, 1966). Georges Lefebvre is the author of *Napoléon,* fourth ed. (Paris, 1953) in the *Peuples et civilisations* series. This work is available in English in two volumes: *Napoleon, from Brumaire to Tilsit, 1799–1807,* translated by Henry F. Stockhold (New York, 1969) and *Napoleon, from Tilsit to Waterloo, 1807–1815,* trans. by J. E. Anderson (New York, 1969). In the *Nouvelle Clio* series, see Jacques L. Godechot, *L'Europe et l'Amerique à l'époque napoléonienne (1800–1815)* (Paris, 1967). Older biographies of Napoleon include an authoritative nine-volume study by F. M. Kircheisen, *Napoleon I: sein Leben und seine Zeit* (Munich and Leipzig, 1911–34), which has been abridged and translated into English by Henry St. Lawrence as *Napoleon* (New York, 1932). See also J. Holland Rose, *Life of Napoleon I,* 2 vols. (New York, 1907). An interesting study of the evolution of the historical interpretation of Napoleon is *Pieter Geyl, *Napoleon: For and Against,* trans. by Olive Renier (New Haven, 1949) (Yale). Some good recent studies of the Napoleonic era include James M. Thompson, *Napoleon Bonaparte: His Rise and Fall* (Oxford, 1952) and *Felix M. H. Markham, *Napoleon and the Awakening of Europe,* (London, 1954) (Collier).

THE RESTORATION, GENERAL

General bibliographies covering the years 1815–1850 are Lowell J. Ragatz, A *Bibliography for the Study of European History, 1815–1939,* second ed. (Washington, D.C., 1946) and Alan L. C. Bullock and A. J. P. Taylor, *A Select List of Books on European History, 1815–1914,* second ed. (Oxford, 1957). General works on this period include the relevant volumes in the *Cambridge Modern History* (London, 1902–1911) and the *New Cambridge Modern History* (Cambridge, Eng., 1957–　). In the Rise of Modern Europe series are the useful volumes of *Frederick B. Artz, *Reaction and Revolution, 1814–1832* (New York, 1934) (Harper Torchbook) and *William L. Langer, *Political and Social Upheaval, 1832–1852* (New York, 1969) (Harper Torchbook), both with excellent up-to-date bibliographies. The *Peuples et civilisations* series includes a new edition (1960) of Georges Weill, *L'Éveil des nationalités et le mouvement libéral (1815–1848)* (Paris, 1930). See also, in the French series *Clio,* the volume by Jacques Droz and others, *Restaurations et révolutions, 1815–1871* (Paris, 1953). An interesting new Marxist-oriented interpretation of this period is *E. J. Hobsbawm, *The Age of Revolution, 1789–1848* (Cleveland and New York, 1962) (New American Library).

On the history of international relations and diplomacy, there is a brief survey by René Albrecht-Carrié, *A Diplomatic History of Europe Since the Congress of Vienna* (New York, 1958). A more substantial work, included in the series *Histoire des relations internationales,* is Pierre Renouvin, *Le XIXe Siècle,* Vol. 1, *De 1815 à 1871: l'Europe des nationalités et l'éveil de nouveaux mondes* (Paris, 1954). There are numerous studies of the settlement of 1815 and the subsequent development of the alliance system. One of the most readable is *Sir Harold Nicolson, *The Congress of Vienna: A Study in Allied Unity, 1812–1822* (New York, 1946) (Viking Compass Books). See also *Edward Vose Gulick, *Europe's Classical Balance of Power* (Ithaca, 1955) (Norton Library). An older work on the same subject is W. Alison Phillips, *The Confederation of Europe: A*

Study of the European Alliance, 1813–1823, second ed. (London and New York, 1920). On the Holy Alliance, the standard work is Jacques H. Pirenne, *La Sainte-Alliance*, 2 vols. (Neuchâtel, 1946–1949). Some of the best works on the diplomatic history of the Restoration era are by Sir Charles K. Webster: *The Congress of Vienna, 1814–1815*, second ed. (London, 1934); *The Foreign Policy of Castlereagh, 1815–1822*, second ed. (London, 1934), the best study of British foreign policy in the post-Napoleonic era; *Palmerston, Metternich and the European System, 1830–1841* (London, 1934); and *The Foreign Policy of Palmerston*, 2 vols. (London, 1951). On the achievement of another British foreign minister in this era, see Harold W. V. Temperley, *The Foreign Policy of Canning, 1822–1827*, second ed. (London, 1966). The standard work on the major continental diplomat of the period is Heinrich, Ritter von Srbik, *Metternich: der Staatsmann und der Mensch*, 3 vols. (Munich, 1925–1954). Two briefer but not entirely satisfactory studies of Metternich in English are A. Cecil, *Metternich, 1773–1859: A Study of His Period and Personality*, third ed. (London, 1947) and H. du Coudray, *Metternich* (London, 1935). On the diplomatic career of Talleyrand, see *Crane Brinton, *The Lives of Talleyrand* (New York, 1936) (Norton Library). On the "Eastern Question" and the involvment of the major powers in it see C. W. Crawley, *The Question of Greek Independence* (Cambridge, Eng., 1930) and C. M. Woodhouse, *The Greek War of Independence* (London, 1952).

THE REVOLUTIONS OF 1848

Studies of the revolutions of 1848 which transcend national boundaries are *Priscilla S. Robertson, *Revolutions of 1848* (Princeton, N. J., 1952) (Princeton), which attempts quite successfully to convey the reactions of individuals and groups to the revolts; *The Opening of an Era: 1848—An Historical Symposium*, ed. by François Fejtö (London, 1948); Arnold Whitridge, *Men in Crisis: The Revolutions of 1848* (New York, 1948); and the stimulating essay of *Sir Lewis B. Namier, *1848: The Revolution of the Intellectuals* (London, 1946) (Doubleday Anchor), which concentrates primarily on the nationalism of German intellectual leaders in the revolts.

NATIONAL HISTORY

On Great Britain during the era 1789-1850, standard works with good bibliographies are two volumes in the Oxford History of England series: J. Steven Watson, *The Reign of George III, 1760–1815* (New York, 1960) and Ernest L. Woodward, *The Age of Reform, 1815–1870* (Oxford, 1938; new ed., 1962). More stimulating in their interpretations are *Asa Briggs, *The Age of Improvement, 1783–1867* (London, 1959) (Harper Torchbook) and *David Thomson, *England in the Nineteenth Century*, in the *Pelican History of England* (Harmondsworth, 1950–1955). On Britain during the revolutionary and Napoleonic eras consult the two works of J. Holland Rose: *William Pitt and the National Revival* (London, 1911) and *William Pitt and the Great War* (London, 1911). Two newer and more popularly written surveys are by Sir Arthur Bryant: *The Years of Endurance, 1793–1802* (London, 1942) and *The Years of Victory*,

1802–1812 (London, 1944). The great classic on England in the nineteenth century is the work of a Frenchman: *Elie Halévy, History of the English People in the Nineteenth Century*, trans. by E. I. Watkin, second revised ed., 6 vols. (London, 1949–1952) (University Paperbacks). The first volume of this work, *England in 1815*, is particularly brilliant. Another stimulating, though brief, essay is *G. M. Young, *Victorian England: Portrait of an Age*, second ed. (Oxford, 1953) (Galaxy Books). Numerous studies of politics and politicians in this period include Arthur Aspinall, *Lord Brougham and the Whig Party* (Manchester, 1927);William R. Brock, *Lord Liverpool and Liberal Toryism, 1820–1827* (Cambridge, Eng., 1941); George M. Trevelyan, *Lord Grey and the Reform Bill* (London, 1920); and the excellent recent works of Norman Gash: *Politics in the Age of Peel* (London and New York, 1953) and *Mr. Secretary Peel: The Life of Sir Robert Peel to 1830* (Cambridge, Mass., 1961). On economic and social developments, a good introduction, despite its bias, remains John L. Hammond and Barbara Hammond, *The Age of the Chartists, 1832–1854* (London, 1930). In addition to works listed on the Industrial Revolution (below), see Sir John H. Clapham's classic *An Economic History of Modern Britain, 1820–1929*, second ed., 3 vols. (Cambridge, Eng., 1930–1938; *George D. H. Cole, *A Short History of the British Working-Class Movement, 1789–1947* (London, 1948) (Papermac); George D. H. Cole and Raymond W. Postgate, *The Common People, 1744–1946*, fourth ed. (London, 1949) (University Paperbacks); and *George M. Trevelyan, *English Social History: A Survey of Six Centuries*, third ed. (London, 1946) (Tartan). A more recent study is *E. P. Thompson, *The Making of the English Working Class* (New York, 1964) (Random House Vintage). A good survey of political thought is *Crane Brinton, *English Political Thought in the Nineteenth Century*, second ed. (Cambridge, Mass., 1949) (Harper Torchbook). On the development of Benthamite thought in England, see *Elie Halévy, *The Growth of Philosophical Radicalism*, trans. by Mary Morris, new ed. (London, 1949) (Beacon).

There are still relatively few good general works available in English on France during the Restoration era. See the relevant chapters in the best textbook on modern France, Gordon Wright, *France in Modern Times: 1760 to the Present* (Chicago, 1960). On the period up to 1830, there is the good, topical survey of Frederick B. Artz, *France under the Bourbon Restoration* (Cambridge, Mass., 1931). Much less satisfactory is Jean Lucas-Dubreton, *The Restoration and the July Monarchy* (New York, 1929). A good recent biography providing interesting insights into the July Monarchy is Thomas E. B. Howarth, *Citizen King: Louis-Philippe* (London, 1961). In French, see the volumes IV and V of *Histoire de France contemporaine*, ed. by Ernest Lavisse: these are S. Charléty, *La Restauration* (Paris, 1921) and the same author's *La Monarchie de Juillet* (Paris, 1921). More recent works include Guillaume de Bertier de Sauvigny's excellent study *The Bourbon Restoration*, translated by Lynn M. Case (Philadelphia, 1967) and Félix Ponteil, *La Monarchie parlementaire, 1815–1848* (Paris, 1949). On the Revolution of 1848, consult Donald C. McKay, *The National Workshops: A Study in the French Revolution of 1848* (Cambridge, Mass., 1933) and the more general treatment of John Plamenatz, *The Revolutionary Movement in France, 1815–1871* (London, 1952). Two accounts in French are Félix Ponteil, *1848* (Paris, 1937) and Jean Dautry,

Histoire de la révolution de 1848 en France (Paris, 1948). On the emergence of Louis Napoleon are two works by Frederick A. Simpson: *The Rise of Louis Napoleon,* third ed. (New York and London, 1950) and *Louis Napoleon and the Recovery of France, 1848–1856,* third ed. (New York and London, 1951). On French economic development in the nineteenth century, see Shepard B. Clough, *France: A History of National Economics, 1789–1939* (New York, 1939) and Arthur L. Dunham, *The Industrial Revolution in France, 1815–1848* (New York, 1955). Standard works in French are Henri Sée, *La Vie économique de la France sous la monarchie censitaire (1815–1848)* (Paris, 1927) and the same author's *Histoire économique de la France,* 2 vols. (Paris, 1948–1951). More specialized is Frank A. Haight, *A History of French Commercial Policies* (Paris, 1941). Two excellent studies of French socialists are *Frank Manuel, *The New World of Henri Saint-Simon* (Cambridge, Mass.,1956) (Notre Dame Paperback) and Leo A. Loubère, *Louis Blanc: His Life and His Contribution to the Rise of French Jacobin-Socialism* (Evanston, Ill., 1961). On the working-class movement there is the old classic: Emile Levasseur, *Histoire des classes ouvrières et de l'industrie en France de 1789 à 1870,* second revised ed., 2 vols. (Paris, 1903–1904). On two other aspects of nineteenth-century France, see Roger Soltau, *French Political Thought in the Nineteenth Century* (New Haven, 1931; reissued, 1959) and C. S. Phillips, *The Church in France: 1789–1848* (London, 1929).

On Germany, two good general surveys are Ralph Flenley, *Modern German History* (London, 1953), which emphasizes intellectual and social history, and Koppel S. Pinson, *Modern Germany, Its History and Civilization,* second ed. (New York, 1966), which is relatively brief on the pre-1848 period. In Hajo Holborn's *History of Modern Germany* (New York, 1959–1968) vol. II (1648–1840) and vol. III (1840–1945) are relevant to this period. Specifically on the nineteenth century are Heinrich von Treitschke, *History of Germany in the Nineteenth Century,* 7 vols. (New York, 1915–1919), a strongly nationalistic older work, and Franz Schnabel, *Deutche Geschichte im neunzehnten Jahrhundert,* 4 vols. (Freiburg, 1929–1937), which narrates general developments only to the 1820's. A celebrated work on the development of German nationalism is Friedrich Meinecke, *Weltbürgertum und Nationalstaat,* seventh ed. (Munich and Berlin, 1928). This work has recently been translated by B. Kimber as *Cosmopolitanism and the National State* (Princeton, N.J., 1969). On Germany during the era of the French Revolution see George P. Gooch, *Germany and the French Revolution* (London and New York, 1920) and the more recent Jacques Droz, *L'Allemagne et la Révolution française* (Paris, 1949). See also Klaus Epstein, *The Genesis of German Conservatism* (Princeton, N.J., 1966) which deals with the period from 1770 to 1806. On various intellectual developments prior to 1815 see Reinhold Aris, *History of Political Thought in Germany from 1789–1815* (London, 1936); Robert R. Ergang, *Herder and the Foundations of German Nationalism* (New York, 1931); and Koppel S. Pinson, *Pietism as a Factor in the Rise of German Nationalism* (New York, 1934). On the Prussian reform movement, in addition to the older introduction of Guy Stanton Ford, *Stein and the Era of Reform in Prussia, 1807–1815* (Princeton, N.J., 1922), see Walter M. Simon, *The Failure of the Prussian Reform Movement, 1807–1819* (Ithaca, N.Y., 1955) and Peter Paret, *Yorck and the Era of*

Prussian Reform, 1807–1815 (Princeton, N.J., 1966). On problems of Germany's intellectual development during the nineteenth century there is the extremely perceptive analysis of Leonard Krieger, *The German Idea of Freedom* (Boston, 1957), which traces this conception from the eighteenth to the twentieth centuries. See also the more controversial *Peter Viereck, *Metapolitics: Roots of the Nazi Mind* (New York, 1941) (Capricorn), which finds some quite specific antecedents of Nazism in the early nineteenth century. Also, Richard H. Thomas, *Liberalism, Nationalism, and the German Intellectuals (1822–1847)* (Cambridge, Eng., 1952). An excellent study of certain economic and social transformations occurring during the Restoration is contained in *Theodore Hamerow, *Restoration, Revolution, Reaction: Economics and Politics in Germany, 1815–1871* (Princeton, N.J., 1958) (Princeton). The best study of the German customs union is William O. Henderson, *The Zollverein* (Cambridge, Eng., 1939; reissued, Chicago, 1959). On the revolutions of 1848 in Germany, see in addition to the work of Sir Lewis B. Namier, cited earlier, Veit Valentin, *1848: Chapters of German History* (London, 1940); Jacques Droz, *Les Révolutions allemandes de 1848* (Paris, 1957); and P. H. Noyes, *Organization and Revolution: Working-Class Associations in the German Revolutions of 1848–1849* (Princeton, N.J., 1966). On the Austrian empire, in addition to works on Metternich mentioned earlier, see *A. J. P. Taylor, *The Habsburg Monarchy, 1809–1918* (London, 1948) (Harper Torchbook) and Robert A. Kann, *A Study in Austrian Intellectual History* (New York, 1960).

An outline of the history of Italy from the eighteenth to the twentieth centuries is provided by *Arthur J. Whyte, *The Evolution of Modern Italy* (Oxford, 1944) (Norton Library). The most comprehensive survey in English of the *Risorgimento* is still Bolton King, *A History of Italian Unity, Being a Political History of Italy From 1814 to 1871*, 2 vols. (London, 1912). A work with Catholic sympathies is George F. Berkeley and Joan Berkeley, *Italy in the Making, 1815–1848*, 3 vols. (Cambridge, Eng., 1932–1940). See also Kent R. Greenfield, *Economics and Liberalism in the Risorgimento: A Study of Nationalism in Lombardy, 1814–1848* (Baltimore, 1934), which challenges older political interpretations of the movement for national unification. For discussions of the most prominent leaders of the *Risorgimento* consult Gwilym O. Griffith, *Mazzini: Prophet of Modern Europe* (London, 1932) and *Gaetano Salvemini, *Mazzini* (London, 1956) (Collier), which includes selections from Mazzini's writings. The best biography of Cavour remains William R. Thayer, *The Life and Times of Cavour*, 2 vols. (Boston, 1911). A good recent study of Garibaldi is Denis Mack Smith, *Garibaldi: A Great Life in Brief* (New York, 1956). An account of another important figure in nineteenth-century Italian history is Edward E. Y. Hales, *Pio Nono: A Study in European Politics and Religion in the Nineteenth Century* (New York, 1954). On the revolutions of 1848, see the classic work of George M. Trevelyan, *Manin and the Venetian Revolution of 1848* (London, 1923) as well as his *Garibaldi's Defence of the Roman Republic* (London and New York, 1907).

For the history of Russia, there are three good, general surveys: *Sir Bernard Pares, *A History of Russia*, fifth ed., revised and enlarged (New York, 1947) (Random House Vintage), definitive ed. (New York, 1960) (Random House Vintage); *George Vernadsky, *A History of Russia*, fourth ed. (New Haven,

1954) (Yale), fifth revised edition (New Haven, 1961) (Yale); and *Benedict Sumner, *A Short History of Russia*, revised ed. (New York, 1949) (Harvest Books). An excellent recent text is Nicholas V. Riasanovsky, *A History of Russia* (New York, 1963); second edition (New York, 1969). Concerning a more limited period in Russia's relations with Europe, see Andrei A. Lobanov-Rostovsky, *Russia and Europe, 1789–1825* (Durham, N.C., 1947). An excellent study of the Decembrist Revolt is *Anatole G. Mazour, *The First Russian Revolution, 1825: The Decembrist Movement, Its Origins, Development and Significance* (Berkeley, Calif., 1937) (Stanford). One of the leading statesmen of the first half of the century is treated in Marc Raeff, *Michael Speransky, Statesman of Imperial Russia, 1772–1839* (The Hague, 1957). On the reign of Nicholas I, there are several good studies in English: Sidney Monas, *The Third Section: Police and Society in Russia under Nicholas I* (Cambridge, Mass., 1961), not quite as specialized as the title might suggest; *Nicholas V. Riasanovsky, *Nicholas I and Official Nationality in Russia, 1825–1855* (Berkeley, Calif., 1959) (University of California); and the same author's *Russia and the West in the Teaching of the Slavophiles: A Study of Romantic Ideology* (Cambridge, Mass., 1952). For Russian economic development, see J. Mavor, *Economic History of Russia*, second ed., rev. and enl. (New York, 1965) and a Soviet historian's treatment, Petr I. Liashchenko, *History of the National Economy of Russia to the 1917 Revolution* (New York, 1949). Finally, good studies of special topics include Philip E. Mosely, *Russian Diplomacy and the Opening of the Eastern Question in 1838 and 1839* (Cambridge, Mass., 1934); *Hans Kohn, *Pan-Slavism, Its History and Ideology* (Notre Dame, Ind., 1953) (Random House Vintage); and Avrahm Yarmolinsky, *Road to Revolution: A Century of Russian Radicalism* (New York, 1959).

POLITICAL AND SOCIAL THEORY

For political movements and ideologies, one of the best introductory works is *John Bowle, *Politics and Opinion in the Nineteenth Century* (London, 1954) (Galaxy Books). On conservatism there is no good single work. Ernest L. Woodward, *Three Studies in European Conservatism* (London, 1929) contains excellent studies of Metternich's views on international relations and of Guizot's political ideas, and an essay on the Catholic Church in the nineteenth century. See also Alfred Cobban, *Edmund Burke and the Revolt against the Eighteenth Century* (London, 1929) and *Herbert Marcuse, *Reason and Revolution: Hegel and the Rise of Social Theory* (New York, 1941) (Beacon). For discussion of nineteenth-century nationalism see Carlton J. H. Hayes, *The Historical Evolution of Modern Nationalism* (New York, 1931) and *Boyd C. Shafer, *Nationalism, Myth and Reality* (New York, 1955) (Harvest Books). General studies of liberalism include Guido de Ruggiero, *The History of European Liberalism* (London, 1927), available in a paperback edition (Beacon Press); and a provocative work by Jacob S. Schapiro, *Liberalism and the Challenge of Fascism: Social Forces in England and France, 1815–1870* (New York, 1949). A good introduction to socialist thought is *Alexander Gray, *The Socialist Tradition: From Moses to Lenin* (London, 1946) (Harper Torchbook). Illuminating discussions of some of the Utopian Socialists are contained in *Edmund Wilson, *To the Finland Station: A Study in the Writing and Acting of History* (New York, 1940) (Doubleday Anchor).

ECONOMIC HISTORY

Standard economic histories include Shepard B. Clough and Charles W. Cole, *Economic History of Europe*, third ed. (New York, 1952); Herbert Heaton, *Economic History of Europe*, revised ed. (New York, 1948); and Witt Bowden, Michael Karpovich, and Abbot Payson Usher, *Economic History of Europe since 1750* (New York, 1937). On the Industrial Revolution, especially in Great Britain, *Thomas S. Ashton, *The Industrial Revolution, 1760–1830* (London and New York, 1948) (Galaxy Books), provides an admirable introduction. See also Ashton's *Economic History of England: The Eighteenth Century* (London, 1955)and the older study by *Paul J. Mantoux, *The Industrial Revolution in the Eighteenth Century: An Outline of the Beginnings of the Modern Factory System in England* (New York, 1928) (Harper Torchbook). On the economic ties between Britain and the Continent there is William O. Henderson, *Britain and Industrial Europe, 1750–1870* (Liverpool, 1954), and specifically on the two most important continental countries is *John H. Clapham, *The Economic Development of France and Germany, 1815–1914*, fourth ed. (Cambridge, Eng., 1936) (Cambridge).

CULTURAL HISTORY

On literature and the arts, a standard older work is Georg M. C. Brandes, *Main Currents in Nineteenth Century Literature*, 6 vols. (New York, 1901–1905). Two good works on romanticism are *Jacques Barzun, *Romanticism and the Modern Ego* (Boston, 1943) (Doubleday Anchor) , which has been re-titled in a new edition: *Classic, Romantic and Modern*, second revised edition (Boston, 1961) (Anchor Doubleday) and P. Van Tieghem, *Le Romantisme dans la littérature européenne* (Paris, 1948). For the art of the period consult Edgar P. Richardson, *The Way of Western Art, 1776–1914* (Cambridge, Mass., 1939) and the standard works of Thomas Craven, *Modern Art* (New York, 1934); Lionello Venturi, *Modern Painters*, 2 vols. (New York, 1947–1950); Henri Focillon, *La Peinture au XIXe et XXe siècles* (Paris, 1928); and Marcel Brion, *Romantic Art* (London, 1960). This work is now available in paperback as *Art of the Romantic Era: Classicism, Romanticism, Realism* (Praeger). See also the appropriate chapters in *Arnold Hauser, *The Social History of Art*, translated in collaboration with the author by Stanley Godman, 2 vols. (New York, 1951) (Random House Vintage). On music, the best works are Alfred Einstein, *Music in the Romantic Era* (New York, 1947) and the outstanding book by Paul H. Lang, *Music in Western Civilization* (New York, 1941). See also Donald J. Grout, *A History of Western Music* (New York, 1960).

PART V

THE AGE OF NATIONALISM AND REFORM, 1850–1890

GENERAL

Two volumes of the *New Cambridge Modern History* cover the later nineteenth century: Vol. X, *The Zenith of European Power, 1830–1870*, ed. J. P. T. Bury (Cambridge, Eng., 1960) and Vol. XI, *Material Progress and World-Wide Problems, 1870–1898*, ed. by F. H. Hinsley (Cambridge, Eng., 1962). They consist of separate essays of uneven quality on a variety of topics, including intellectual developments, armies and navies, art and literature, as well as political and economic history. A convenient survey of church history is *A. R. Vidler, *The Church in an Age of Revolution, 1789 to the Present Day* (London, 1961) (Penguin). For military history, *Theodore Ropp, *War in the Modern World* (Durham, N.C., 1959) (Collier) is a useful survey with excellent bibliographies. Also valuable are two works by Cyril Falls: *A Hundred Years of War, 1850–1950* (New York, 1953) Collier); and *The Art of War from the Age of Napoleon to the Present Day* (New York, 1961) (Hesperides).

ECONOMIC AND SOCIAL HISTORY

The most useful and authoritative work for all the countries of Europe is the *Cambridge Economic History of Europe*, ed. by M. M. Postan and H. J. Habakkuk, Vol. VI (in two parts), *The Industrial Revolutions and After* (Cambridge, Eng., 1965), which includes a splendid bibliography.

Other valuable works on special aspects of economic history are N. J. G. Pounds and W. N. Parker, *Coal and Steel in Western Europe* (Bloomington, Ind., 1957); G. R. Taylor, *The Transportation Revolution, 1815–1860* (New York, 1951); L. F. Haber, *The Chemical Industry during the Nineteenth Century* (Oxford, 1958); W. Ashworth, *A Short History of the International Economy, 1850–1950* (London, 1951); and *Herbert Feis, *Europe: The World's Banker, 1870–1914* (New Haven, 1930) (Norton).

The American Historical Association pamphlet by *Franklin D. Scott, *Emigration and Immigration* (New York, 1963) is a useful bibliographical guide on this important subject. *Population Movements in Modern European History*, ed. by *Herbert Moller, (New York, 1964) (Collier-Macmillan) contains several suggestive articles, as does *Population in History: Essays in Historical Demography*, ed. by D. V. Glass and D. E. C. Eversley (London, 1965). The effects of population movements on the city are treated in R. E. Dickinson, *The West European City: A Geographical Interpretation* (London, 1951).

INTELLECTUAL AND CULTURAL HISTORY

J. T. Merz, A *History of European Thought in the Nineteenth Century*, 4 vols. (Edinburgh and London, 1896–1914) is a detailed, comprehensive survey with emphasis on science and philosophy.

W. C. D. Dampier, A *History of Science and its Relations with Philosophy and Religion* (New York, 1949) is useful, although not so comprehensive as its title suggests. W. P. D. Wightman, *The Growth of Scientific Ideas* (New Haven, 1951) provides a competent survey of nineteenth-century developments. A. D. White, A *History of the Warfare of Science with Theology* (New York, 1896) remains of great value, especially as a reflection of the opinions of its time. There are many editions of Darwin's writings. Among the most interesting is his brief and revealing *Autobiography*, ed. by Nora Barlow (New York, 1958) (Norton). Of the many excellent works on the impact of Darwin's thought, one of the best is *Gertrude Himmelfarb, Darwin and the Darwinian Revolution* (New York, 1959) (Norton).

*John Bowle, *Politics and Opinion in the Nineteenth Century* (London, 1954) (Oxford Galaxy) is a stimulating survey of major ideas of the age. The American Historical Association pamphlet by *Boyd C. Shafer, *Nationalism: Interpretors and Interpretations* (Washington, D.C., 1959) is a good bibliographical guide on this important and controversial subject. H. M. Chadwick, *The Nationalities of Europe and the Growth of National Ideologies* (Cambridge, Eng., 1945) is a historical survey while *E. Kedourie, *Nationalism* (London, 1960) (Praeger) provides an analytical approach. Walter M. Simon, *European Positivism in the Nineteenth Century* (Ithaca, N.Y., 1963) is an excellent study of Comte and his influence. On liberalism there are the works of Frederick M. Watkins: *The Political Tradition of the West: A Study in the Development of Modern Liberalism* (Cambridge, Mass., 1948) and Guido de Ruggiero, A *History of European Liberalism* (London, 1927) (Beacon). On socialism, see Carl Landauer, *European Socialism: A History of Ideas and Movements from the Industrial Revolution to Hitler's Seizure of Power*, 2 vols. (Berkeley, Calif., 1959). One of the best analyses of Marx is *George Lichtheim, *Marxism: An Historical and Critical Study* (London, 1961) (Praeger).

The important problem of education is surveyed in William Boyd, *The History of Western Education* (London, 1921), and in H. M. Pollard, *Pioneers of Popular Education, 1760–1850* (London, 1956).

On art, a good analytical survey is E. P. Richardson, *The Way of Western Art, 1776–1914* (Cambridge, Mass., 1939). Fritz Novotny, *Painting and Sculpture in Europe, 1780–1880* (London, 1960) does not include the art of Great Britain, but is otherwise excellent. It contains a fine collection of illustrations, as does the Phaidon Press publication *The French Impressionists* (London, 1952), with an introduction by Clive Bell. *Herbert Read, A *Concise History of Modern Painting* (London, 1959) (Praeger) is a competent brief analysis.

The literature and music of the period should be read and heard. The works of the major writers are available in many editions, those of the major composers, on records and tapes. For the literature, W. E. Houghton, *The Victorian Frame of Mind, 1830–1870* (New Haven, 1957) is an interesting analysis.

Among the general histories of music, Donald Jay Grout, A *History of Western Music* (New York, 1960) is a competent survey.

NATIONAL HISTORY

For Great Britain, the American Historical Association pamphlet by *Robert K. Webb, *English History, 1815–1914*, (Washington, D.C. 1967) is a useful bibliographical guide. The same author has written a general history, *Modern England: From the Eighteenth Century to the Present* (New York, 1968) (Dodd, Mead), which embodies the most recent research. Two volumes in the Oxford History of England, Ernest L. Woodward, *The Age of Reform, 1815–1870* (Oxford, 1938); new ed., 1962) and R. C. K. Ensor, *England, 1870–1914* (Oxford, 1936), are well-written, comprehensive treatments. *David Thomson's brief *England in the Nineteenth Century, 1815–1914* (London, 1950) (Penguin) stresses social and economic trends, as does *Asa Briggs, *The Making of Modern England, 1783–1867: The Age of Improvement* (New York, 1959) (Harper Torchbook), an admirable work. The most detailed biography of Queen Victoria is Elizabeth Longford, *Queen Victoria: Born to Succeed* (New York, 1965). See also the brilliant literary portrait by Lytton Strachey, *Queen Victoria* (London, 1921) (Capricorn). For an appreciation of the queen, nothing can replace the reading of her letters, large selections of which have been published in many volumes. Lytton Strachey's *Eminent Victorians* (London, 1918) (Capricorn) contains a group of delightful biographical sketches. More substantial biographies of Victorian notables include H. C. Bell, *Lord Palmerston*, 2 vols. (Hamden, Conn., 1936); John Morley, *The Life of William Ewart Gladstone*, 3 vols. (1903); *Philip Magnus, *Gladstone: A Biography* (New York, 1964) (Dutton); *Robert Blake, *Disraeli* (New York, 1967) (Doubleday Anchor); and Gwendolyn Cecil, *Life of Robert, Marquis of Salisbury*, 4 vols. (London, 1921–1931). On Irish politics, there are two interesting works: L. P. Curtis, *Coercion and Conciliation in Ireland, 1880–1892* (Princeton, N.J., 1963) and C. C. O'Brien, *Parnell and his Party, 1880–90*, (Oxford, 1957).

For France, the American Historical Association pamphlet by *Jean T. Joughin, *France in the Nineteenth Century: Selected Studies in English since 1956* (Washington, D.C., 1968) is a useful bibliographical essay. Among the excellent general histories of France, the following are brief and well written: Gordon Wright, *France in Modern Times: 1760 to the Present* (Chicago, 1960), with excellent bibliographies; *Alfred Cobban, *A History of Modern France*, Vol. II, *1799–1871* (London, 1961) (Penguin); *John B. Wolf, *France, 1814–1919* (New York, 1963) (Harper Torchbook). Lively but somewhat elliptical is *D. W. Brogan, *The French Nation: From Napoleon to Pétain, 1814–1940* (London, 1961) (Colophon). On the controversial figure of Napoleon III, Albert Guérard, *Napoleon III: A Great Life in Brief* (New York, 1955) is sympathetic toward its subject, while *James M. Thompson, *Louis Napoleon and the Second Empire* (Oxford, 1954) (Norton) is somewhat more critical. *Roger L. Williams, *The World of Napoleon III, 1815–1870* (New York, 1962) (Collier) is a delightful collection of essays originally published under the title *Gaslight and Shadow*. The best account of the war with Prussia is *Michael Howard, *The Franco-Prussian War* (New York, 1961) (Collier). On the Paris Commune the most recent work is *Roger L. Williams, *The French Revolution of 1870–1871* (New York, 1969) (Norton). On the Third Republic, the brief work by *David Thomson, *Democracy in France since 1870* (New York, 1964) (Oxford) is outstanding. Among the longer studies, there is the lively history by *D. W. Brogan, *France under the Republic, 1870–1939* (New York, 1940) (Harper Torchbook, in two volumes), also published under the title *The Development of Modern France*, which assumes a good deal of background knowledge. A more recent account is Guy Chapman, *The Third Republic of France: The First Phase, 1871–1894* (New York, 1962).

For Germany, the American Historical Association pamphlet by *Norman Rich, *Germany, 1815–1914* (Washington, D.C., 1968) is a useful bibliographical guide. Walter Simon, *Germany: A Brief History* (New York, 1966) is an excellent short survey. More detailed are Koppel S. Pinson, *Modern Germany, Its History and Civilization*, second ed. (New York, 1966), which stresses cultural and social forces; W. H. Dawson, *The German Empire, 1867–1914, and the Unity Movement*, 2 vols. (New York, 1919), which emphasizes political history; and Hajo Holborn, *A History of Modern Germany*, Vol. III (New York, 1968), dealing with the years 1840–1945, which embodies the most recent research. Otto Pflanze, *Bismarck and the Development of Germany: The Period of Unification, 1815–1871* (Princeton, N.J., 1963) is the most detailed recent biography in English. The excellent older work of Charles G. Robertson, *Bismarck* (New York, 1919) remains valuable. See also Erich Eyck, *Bismarck and the German Empire* (London, 1950) (Norton). Among special studies on modern German history, *Theodore S. Hamerow, *Restoration, Revolution, Reaction: Economics and Politics in Germany, 1815–1871* (Princeton, N.J., 1958) (Princeton) deals with the economic background of German politics; *Gordon Craig, *The Politics of the Prussian Army, 1640–1945* (New York, 1955) (Oxford Galaxy) analyzes the fateful impact of military thinking on politics; Henry Cord Meyer, *Mitteleuropa in German Thought and Action, 1815–1945* (The Hague, 1955) examines the important subject of German policies and attitudes toward central Europe.

For the Habsburg empire, a new and useful work is C. A. Macartney, *The Habsburg Empire, 1790–1918* (London, 1969). *A. J. May, *The Habsburg Monarchy, 1867–1914* (Cambridge, Mass., 1951) (Norton) is balanced, scholarly, and reliable. *Oscar Jaszi, *The Dissolution of the Habsburg Monarchy* (Chicago, 1929) (Phoenix) contains much valuable information.

For Italy, the American Historical Association pamphlet by *Charles F. Delzell, *Italy in Modern Times: An Introduction to the Historical Literature in English* (Washington, D.C., 1964) is a useful bibliographical guide. *Arthur J. Whyte, *The Evolution of Modern Italy* (New York, 1959) (Norton) is the best of the brief general histories. More detailed is Bolton King, *A History of Italian Unity, Being a Political History of Italy from 1814 to 1871*, 2 vols. (London, 1912), which remains outstanding. Also of great interest is the work of the eminent liberal philosopher-historian Benedetto Croce, *A History of Italy, 1871–1915* (Oxford, 1929). On Cavour, William R. Thayer, *The*

Life and Times of Cavour, 2 vols. (Boston, 1911) is detailed and reliable. Denis Mack Smith, *Cavour and Garibaldi, 1860: A Study in Political Conflict* (Cambridge, Eng., 1954) is an important monograph, critical of Cavour. The same author's *Garibaldi: A Great Life in Brief* (New York, 1956) is a short biography. Arthur C. Jemolo, *Church and State in Italy, 1850–1950* (Oxford, 1960) is a translated abridgment of a major Italian study on this important topic.

For Russia, *Hugh Seton-Watson, *The Decline of Imperial Russia, 1855–1914* (New York, 1952) (Praeger) is a competent brief survey. More detailed is Vol. II of M. T. Florinsky, *Russia: A History and an Interpretation* (New York, 1953). **Imperial Russia after 1861: Peaceful Modernization or Revolution?*, ed. by Arthur E. Adams, (New York, 1965) is a collection of historical interpretations with a useful bibliography. There are a number of excellent studies on special aspects of Russian history: *G. T. Robinson, *Rural Russia under the Old Regime: A History of the Landlord-Peasant World and a Prologue to the Peasant Revolution of 1917* (New York, 1930) (U. of California); Jacob Walkin, *The Rise of Democracy in Pre-Revolutionary Russia: Political and Social Institutions under the Last Three Tsars* (New York, 1962); *Franco Venturi, *The Roots of Revolution: A History of the Populist and Socialist Movements in Nineteenth Century Russia* (New York, 1960) (Universal Library); B. H. Summer, *Russia and the Balkans, 1870–1880,* (Oxford, 1937); B. H. Summer, *Tsardom and Imperialism in the Far and Middle East, 1880–1914* (London, 1942); Michael B. Petrovich, *The Emergence of Russian Panslavism, 1856–1870* (New York, 1956); and R. F. Leslie, *Reform and Insurrection in Russian Poland, 1856–1865* (London, 1963).

INTERNATIONAL RELATIONS

A. J. P. Taylor, *The Struggle for Mastery in Europe, 1848–1914* (Oxford, 1954), although erratic and contradictory, is full of illuminating insights.

B. D. Gooch, "A Century of Historiography on the Origins of the Crimean War," *American Historical Review,* Vol. LXII (October, 1956), pp. 33–58, is a valuable though incomplete evaluation of the evidence, but unfortunately fails to come to any conclusion of its own. Peter Gibbs, *Crimean Blunder: The Story of War with Russia a Hundred Years Ago* (New York, 1960) is a straightforward popular history. *C. Woodham-Smith's excitingly written *The Reason Why* (New York, 1954) (Dutton) deals with Britain's military leadership.

The most authoritative general work on the period after 1871 is *William L. Langer, *European Alliances and Alignments, 1871–1890* (New York, 1931) (Knopf), which includes a splendid bibliography brought up to date in 1950. The best brief study is R. J. Sontag, *European Diplomatic History, 1871–1932* (New York, 1933). The same author's *Germany and England: Background of Conflict, 1848–1894* (New York, 1938) (Norton) brilliantly explains why the "natural alliance" between these countries did not materialize.

PART VI

THE END OF THE EUROPEAN ERA, 1890 TO THE PRESENT

The printed material on the history of the twentieth century—documentary publications, memoirs, comprehensive histories, historical monographs—would fill a library; the following bibliography is severely selective. It is limited to works published in English, with the emphasis on titles of recent date. Included are books providing a general orientation, as well as those describing in detail events which were treated only briefly in the text because of limitations of space. Special attention has been given to books which permit insight into the conditions of life and to writings which contain interpretations different from those presented in the text.

Printed collections of documentary sources are not listed, but most of the works mentioned contain detailed bibliographies which indicate source material and may serve as guides for further reading.

GENERAL

Contemporary history poses particular problems for both research and presentation. These are well outlined in *Geoffrey Barraclough, *An Introduction to Contemporary History* (New York, 1964) (Penguin). There are few comprehensive treatments of the entire period from 1890 to the present or to the end of the Second World War; one of those is found in the *New Cambridge Modern History*, but the relevant Vol. XII exists in both an original and a revised version—*The Era of Violence*, ed. by David Thomson (Cambridge, Eng., 1960) and *The Shifting Balance of World Forces, 1898–1945*, ed. by C. L. Mowat (Cambridge, Eng., 1968)—and since these versions are not identical both of them must be considered. Illuminating essays on the outstanding problems of international politics are to be found in *Ludwig Dehio, *Germany and World Politics in the Twentieth Century* (New York, 1959) (Norton). For a broad treatment of social developments see *Peter N. Stearns, *European Society in Upheaval* (New York and London, 1967) (Macmillan) and for a brief outline of economic developments see Paul Alpert, *Twentieth Century Economic History of Europe* (New York, 1951). The basic factors determining the economic developments are analyzed in the *Cambridge Economic History of Europe*, Vol. VI, *The Industrial Revolutions and After*, ed. by M. M. Postan and H. J. Habakkuk (Cambridge, Eng., 1965).

FROM 1890 TO THE BEGINNING OF THE FIRST WORLD WAR

A lively description of the political scene in Europe before the First World
War is given in *Barbara W. Tuchman, *The Proud Tower* (New York, 1966)
(Bantam); the reader should be aware, however, that although the general
picture stands up well, details are not always correct and the author has an
anti-German bias. Much discussion has been aroused by the question of the
extent to which intellectual developments in this period prepared the way for the
new intellectual trends in the postwar world; for perceptive descriptions of the
intellectual climate of this period see *H. Stuart Hughes, *Consciousness and
Society* (New York, 1958) (Vintage) and *Gerhard Masur, *Prophets of
Yesterday* (New York, 1961) (Harper Colophon); Christopher Caudwell,
Studies in a Dying Culture (New York, 1938) is also pertinent, although it is
concerned exclusively with the literary scene. A brilliant analysis, limited to the
intellectual antecedents of later developments, is *Hannah Arendt, *The Origins
of Totalitarianism* (New York, 1951) (Meridian). The facts concerning the
economic influence of Europe in the non-European parts of the world can be
learned from *Herbert Feis, *Europe: The World's Banker, 1870–1914* (New
Haven, 1930) (Norton). The two most important works concerning the
development of the concept of imperialism are *John A. Hobson, *Imperialism:
A Study* (London, 1902) (Ann Arbor) and *V. I. Lenin, *Imperialism, the
Highest Stage of Capitalism* (written 1916) (China Books; also International
Publishers); for the crisis in Marxism brought about by the economic progress
of this period, see Peter Gay, *The Dilemma of Democratic Socialism: Eduard
Bernstein's Challenge to Marx* (New York, 1952) (Collier).

For all the great European powers there exist national histories covering
this period, some of them reaching up to the Second World War or to the
present. For Great Britain, see R. C. K. Ensor, *England, 1817–1914* (Oxford,
1936) and *Robert K. Webb, *Modern England: From the Eighteenth Century
to the Present* (New York, 1968) (Dodd, Mead); for France, *D. W. Brogan,
France Under the Republic, 1870–1939 (New York, 1940) (Harper Torchbook,
in two volumes), also published under the title *The Development of Modern
France*, and *Modern France: Problems of the Third and Fourth Republics*, ed.
by Edward Mead Earle (Princeton, N.J., 1951); for Spain, Raymond Carr,
Spain, 1808–1939 (Oxford, 1966); for Italy, Christopher Seton-Watson, *Italy
from Liberalism to Fascism, 1870–1925* (London, 1967); for Germany, Hajo
Holborn, *A History of Modern Germany*, Vol. III (New York, 1969), on the
years 1840–1945; for Austria, *A. J. P. Taylor, *The Habsburg Monarchy,
1809–1918* (London, 1948) (Harper Torchbook); for Russia, *Sir Bernard
Pares, *A History of Russia*, revised ed. (New York, 1953) (Vintage).

In addition, for an understanding of particular aspects of British history
during this period one may turn to a number of illuminating biographies and
autobiographies. *Roy Jenkins, *Asquith: Portrait of a Man and an Era* (New
York, 1965) (Dutton), is the biography of the leading British statesman of the
period by a prominent member of the Labor party who describes the problem
of political leadership in a parliamentary system with deep understanding.
The first two volumes of *Winston S. Churchill*, by Randolph S. Churchill—

Youth, 1874–1900 (Boston, 1966) and *Young Statesman, 1901–1914* (Boston, 1967)—deserve attention not only because of their significance in explaining Churchill's early development but also because of the light which they shed on the English ruling group. The power of the British monarch was limited, but Sir Harold Nicolson, in *King George the Fifth: His Life and Reign* (London, 1952), contributes to the analysis of important political developments in his account of the crisis over the House of Lords. Samuel Hynes, *The Edwardian Turn of Mind* (Princeton, 1968) is full of interesting details throwing light on unknown or forgotten aspects of the world before the First World War. The contrast between the autobiographies of two women prominent in politics, Margot Asquith, *Autobiography*, ed. by Mark Bonham Carter (Boston, 1962) and Beatrice Webb, *Our Partnership* (New York, London, and Toronto, 1948), is highly amusing. Among the many good British autobiographies the best is the five-volume series by Leonard Sidney Woolf, consisting of *Sowing* (New York, 1960), covering the years 1880–1904; *Growing* (New York, 1961), on 1904–1911; *Beginning Again* (New York, 1963, 1964), on 1911–1918; *Downhill All the Way* (New York, 1967), on 1919–1939; and *The Journey Not the Arrival Matters* (New York, 1969). It reaches from the beginning of the twentieth century to the present and is a moving commentary on the decline of the English liberal tradition.

For the two leading French statesmen we have good biographical treatments, Geoffrey Bruun, *Clemenceau* (Cambridge, Mass., 1943) and Gordon Wright, *Raymond Poincaré and the French Presidency* (Stanford, 1942). On the details of the Dreyfus case and the present evaluation of the importance of this affair, see Douglas Johnson, *France and the Dreyfus Affair* (London, 1966) and Guy Chapman, *The Dreyfus Case: A Reassessment* (London, 1955). For the background of the affair and some of its consequences see David B. Ralston, *The Army of the Republic: The Place of the Military in the Political Evolution of France, 1871–1914* (Cambridge, Mass., and London, 1967) and Eugen Joseph Weber, *The Nationalist Revival in France, 1905–1914* (Berkeley, Calif., 1959). Roger Henry Soltau, *French Political Thought in the Nineteenth Century* (New Haven, 1931), although not a recent book, is distinguished by its understanding of the tension which led to the separation of church and state.

For Spain, see Joan Connelly Ullman, *The Tragic Week: A Study of Anticlericalism in Spain, 1875–1912* (Cambridge, Mass., 1968), which describes in detail the crisis which frustrated attempts at reform.

The particular character of the Italian parliamentary system is well presented in A. William Salomone, *Italy in the Giolittian Era: Italian Democracy in the Making* (Philadelphia, 1960). For the concrete issues involved in the problem of the Italian south, see Denis Mack Smith, *A History of Sicily: Modern Sicily after 1713* (New York, 1968).

Considering the crucial importance of Germany before 1914, the available historical treatments are meager. Michael Balfour, *The Kaiser and His Times* (London, 1964) is probably the best biography of William II. Norman Rich, *Friedrich von Holstein: Politics and Diplomacy in the Era of Bismarck and Wilhelm II* (Cambridge, Eng., 1965) gives an interesting picture of the German ruling group; for an understanding of the mentality of the German bourgeoisie in this period one turns best to a novel, Heinrich Mann, *Little Superman* (*Der Untertan*, 1918; originally trans. as *The Patrioteer*). For the impact of German industrial development on attitudes in the social democracy, see *Carl E. Schorske, *German Social Democracy, 1905–1917: The Development of the Great Schism* (Cambridge, Mass., 1955) (Wiley).

On Austria-Hungary, see Robert A. Kann, *The Habsburg Empire: A Study in Integration and Disintegration* (New York, 1957) and C. A. Macartney, *Hungary: A Short History* (Chicago, 1962), which provide details on the complex structure of the Habsburg monarchy.

In Russia, personal factors played a decisive role in the fall of tsarism. For a picture of the relevant political personalities of this period, see *Sir Bernard Pares, *The Fall of the Russian Monarchy* (London, 1939) (Vintage), and for the origin of the ideas dominating the rulers, see Robert F. Byrnes, *Pobedonostsev: His Life and Thought* (Bloomington, Ind., and London, 1968). The description of industrial life given in the first chapters of *I. Deutscher, *Stalin: A Political Biography* (New York and London, 1949) (Oxford Galaxy) and the discussion of *Theodore H. von Laue, *Why Lenin? Why Stalin? A Reappraisal of the Russian Revolution, 1900–1930* (Philadelphia and New York, 1964) (Lippincott) rightly stress the immense difficulties in the way of solving Russian economic and social problems.

DIPLOMATIC EVENTS AND THE FIRST WORLD WAR

The diplomatic history of the thirty-five years before the First World War has been examined in minute detail because archives of the foreign offices became accessible soon after 1918. The decisive years for the formation of new constellations among the powers are treated in William L. Langer, *The Diplomacy of Imperialism, 1890–1902*, 2 vols. (New York, 1935), which contains a discussion of the literature and concept of imperialism; articles by the same author collected in *Explorations in Crisis: Papers on International History* (Cambridge, Mass., 1969) study main events in the following decade. The methods and techniques of prewar diplomacy emerge clearly from Sir Harold Nicolson, *Portrait of a Diplomatist* (Boston and New York, 1930). The most comprehensive description of the events leading to the outbreak of the First World War will be found in Luigi Albertini, *The Origins of the War of 1914*, 3 vols. (London, New York, and Toronto, 1952–1957). For those who find these three volumes heavy going, *Laurence Lafore, *The Long Fuse* (Philadelphia and New York, 1965) (Lippincott) can be recommended as a brief and reliable account which also reviews previous literature. Vladimir Dedijer, *The Road to Sarajevo* (New York, 1966) has interest as a very detailed investigation of a special problem, that of responsibility for the events in Sarajevo. *Fritz Fischer, *Germany's Aims in the First World War* (New York, 1967) (Norton) is a study of German war aims but also throws much light on German responsibility for the outbreak of the war. The history of the war itself has been treated in many memoirs, among them those of Lloyd George and Churchill, and also in studies of military history. A valuable analysis of the connection between military planning and political necessities is Paul Guinn, *British Strategy and Politics, 1914–1918* (London, 1965), and the relationship between war and economic developments is investigated in Gerald D. Feldman, *Army Industry and Labor in Germany, 1914–1918* (Princeton, N.J., 1966), which deals with Germany but is of general interest because similar situations existed in other countries. The First World War is placed in a wider historical context in Hajo Holborn, *The Political Collapse of Europe* (New York, 1951).

THE INTERWAR PERIOD

A number of works supply good general views of important aspects of these decades. The connections which linked the two world wars are emphasized in *Raymond Aron, *The Century of Total War* (New York, 1954) (Beacon). The great divide in the interwar years affecting the role of Europe was the depression which began in 1929; for a review of its effects see *Survey of International Affairs, 1931*, ed. by Arnold J. Toynbee (London, 1932), and for a more detailed analysis of its impact in the various European countries see "The Great Depression," *Journal of Contemporary History*, Vol. IV, No. 4 (1969). Fascism is examined as a general European phenomenon in *European Fascism*, ed. by S. J. Woolf (New York, 1968) (Vintage). *E. H. Carr, *The Twenty Years' Crisis, 1919–1939* (London, 1939) (Harper Torchbook) is noteworthy as a document of the time rather than as a valid statement of the significance of these years. Those novels of André Malraux which have the crucial political events of this period as background suggest something of the revolutionary radicalism which the hesitating and wavering policy of the ruling groups produced.

The ideas and interests which influenced and determined the peace settlement have been thoroughly discussed and analyzed by Arno J. Mayer in *Political Origins of the New Diplomacy, 1917–1918* (New Haven, 1959) (Meridian) and *Politics and Diplomacy of Peacemaking. Containment and Counterrevolution at Versailles, 1918–1919* (New York, 1967) (Vintage). *Sir Harold Nicolson, *Peacemaking, 1919* (New York, 1939) (Universal Library) gives a report of the peace conference from a human angle. The results of all the peace negotiations are succinctly summarized in Arnold J. Toynbee, *The World after the Peace Conference* (London, 1925), and throughout the entire following period the yearly volumes of the *Survey of International Affairs*, to which the preceding Toynbee book is a prologue, are a helpful guide. The role of the Russian problem in the politics of the postwar years is clarified in Richard H. Ullman, *Britain and the Russian Civil War* (Princeton, N.J., 1968), at least insofar as Great Britain is concerned.

For a comprehensive treatment of the conduct of foreign affairs during the interwar years see *The Diplomats, 1919–1939*, ed. by Gordon Craig and Felix Gilbert (Princeton, N.J., 1953) (Atheneum). Sir Harold Nicolson, *Curzon: The Last Phase, 1919–1925* (New York, 1939) demonstrates the possibilities and advantages of traditional diplomacy in the settlement of the postwar world. *Louis Fischer, *The Soviets in World Affairs: A History of*

Relations Between the Soviet Union and the Rest of the World, 1917–1929 (Princeton, N.J., 1951) (Vintage) and James Barros, *The Corfu Incident of 1923: Mussolini and the League of Nations* (Princeton, N.J., 1965) show the techniques used by Communist and Fascist diplomacy in the 1920's. For a brilliant summarization of the failure of diplomacy in the 1930's see *Winston S. Churchill, *The Second World War*, Vol. I, *The Gathering Storm* (Boston, 1948) (Bantam). In general, the events of foreign policy in the 1930's cannot be separated from the internal history of the various European countries, extensively treated in books listed in the following paragraphs.

The two states on which we have an overabundance of historical literature are Germany and Great Britain. This is natural because their policies were crucial for the development of the interwar years.

For a survey of the history of the Weimar Republic, see *S. William Halperin, *Germany Tried Democracy* (New York, 1946) (Norton). Two leading statesmen of the Weimar Republic are treated in Klaus Epstein, *Matthias Erzberger and the Dilemma of Germany Democracy* (Princeton, N.J., 1959) and *Henry Ashby Turner, Jr., *Stresemann and the Politics of the Weimar Republic* (Princeton, N.J., 1963) (Princeton); these books indicate how precarious the hold of the democratic forces was. The strength of the opponents of the republic is delineated in *Gordon Craig, *The Politics of the Prussian Army, 1640–1945* (New York, 1955) (Oxford Galaxy) and also in Andreas Dorpalen, *Hindenburg and the Weimar Republic* (Princeton, N.J., 1964), which portrays the surrender of power to the Nazis. For intellectual trends which contributed to the rise of the Nazis see *George L. Mosse. *The Crisis of German Ideology* (New York, 1964) (Universal Library). On Germany under the Nazis only a few books will be mentioned, works which throw light on the diverse aspects of the regime. *Alan Bullock, *Hitler: A Study in Tyranny* (London, 1952) (Harper Torchbook) is the best biography of Hitler, and Hermann Rauschning, *The Voice of Destruction* (New York, 1940) the best report about Hitler by a former adherent. An example of the establishment and functioning of Nazi control is presented in Oron J. Hale, *The Captive Press in the Third Reich* (Princeton, N.J., 1964). For the cultural policy of the Nazis see Barbara Miller Lane, *Architecture and Politics in Germany, 1918–1945* (Cambridge, Mass., 1968). The impact of the Nazi regime on the German social structure is carefully analyzed in *David Schoenbaum, *Hitler's Social Revolution: Class and Status in Nazi Germany, 1933–1939* (New York, 1966) (Doubleday Anchor). A colorful but rather simplified account of the Nazi years, with a very full bibliography, is *William L. Shirer, *The Rise and Fall of the Third Reich: A History of Nazi Germany* (New York, 1960) (Fawcett Crest also Simon and Schuster, in two volumes).

On Great Britain, a lively, amusingly prejudiced history of the interwar years is A. J. P. Taylor, *English History, 1914–1945* (New York and Oxford, 1965); the social problems of this period are well presented in *Robert Graves and Alan Hodge, *The Long Week-End: A Social History of Great Britain, 1918–1939* (New York, 1941) (Norton), and for a discussion of British policy from the point of view of Labor see Alan Bullock, *The Life and Times of Ernest Bevin*, Vol. I, *Trade Union Leader, 1881–1940* (London, Melbourne,

and Toronto, 1960). A central issue of historical discussion is the appeasement
policy of the 1930's. For the problems of decision making in British policy,
see D. C. Watt, *Personalities and Policies: Studies in the Formulation of
British Foreign Policy in the Twentieth Century* (Notre Dame, Ind., 1965).
The attitude of the entire group of appeasers emerges brilliantly from *A. L.
Rowse, *Appeasement: A Study in Political Decline, 1933–1939* (New York,
1961) (Norton). For biographies of two of the main appeasers see Andrew
Boyle, *Montagu Norman: A Biography* (London, 1967) and William R. Rock,
Neville Chamberlain (New York, 1969). The latter book discusses the entire
dispute about the appeasement policy and tries hard to be fair to the appeasers
—too hard, in my opinion. The desperation among the young produced by
the policy of the ruling group is movingly evoked in *Peter Stansky and
William Abrahams, *Journey to the Frontier: Two Roads to the Spanish Civil
War* (Boston, 1966) (Norton). Hugh Dalton, *The Fateful Years: Memoirs,
1931–1945* (London, 1957) must be mentioned as the best book of political
memoirs on this period.

To gain an understanding of the policy of France in the interwar years,
see the reports of one of the best-informed journalists of the time, collected
in Alexander Werth, *The Twilight of France, 1933–1940* (New York, 1942).
Joel G. Colton, *Léon Blum: Humanist in Politics* (New York, 1966) gives a
good picture of the most interesting French statesman of this period. Geoffrey
Warner, *Pierre Laval and the Eclipse of France* (New York, 1968) represents
a very substantial contribution to our understanding of the evolution of French
appeasement and defeatism.

On Russia, for an understanding of the situation which existed before
Stalin's rise to power see *Adam B. Ulam, *The Bolsheviks: The Intellectual
and Political History of the Triumph of Communism in Russia* (New York
and London, 1965) (Collier). Because of Stalin's predominance in this period
the previously mentioned, detailed biography by *I. Deutscher, *Stalin: A
Political Biography* (New York and London, 1949) (Oxford Galaxy), is
useful. *Ilya Ehrenburg, *Memoirs, 1921–1941* (Cleveland and New York,
1964) (Universal Library) shows the conditions of intellectual work in Stalin's
time.

On Italy, for the rise of Fascism see the book, previously mentioned, by
Christopher Seton-Watson, *Italy from Liberalism to Fascism, 1870–1925*
(London, 1967). *H. Stuart Hughes, *The United States and Italy* (Cambridge, Mass., 1953) (Norton) places this development in a broader context,
and Charles F. Delzell, *Mussolini's Enemies: The Italian Anti-Fascist Resistance* (Princeton, N.J., 1961) shows the oppressive nature of the regime—
even before Mussolini came under Nazi influence.

The Spanish Civil War was an international event, but also the climax of
the internal developments in Spain during the 1920's and 1930's; as such
it is presented in *Gabriel Jackson, *The Spanish Republic and the Civil War,
1931–1939* (Princeton, N.J., 1965) (Princeton) and in *Stanley Payne, *The
Spanish Revolution* (New York, 1970) (Norton). A clear, general account
of the war will be found in *Hugh Thomas, *The Spanish Civil War* (New
York, 1961) (Harper Colophon).

For an exposition of developments in the Balkan countries and their dependence on the policy of the great European powers, see *Hugh Seton-Watson, *Eastern Europe Between the Wars, 1918–1941* (Cambridge, Eng., 1945) (Harper Torchbook). This dependence emerged clearly in the Czech crisis. *John W. Wheeler-Bennett, *Munich: Prologue to Tragedy* (London, 1948) (Viking Compass), although no longer quite up-to-date, remains valuable as a testimony of the emotional atmosphere surrounding the Czech crisis and Munich.

THE SECOND WORLD WAR

The events of the Second World War are fully described in *Gordon Wright, *The Ordeal of Total War, 1939–1945* (New York, Evanston, Ill., and London, 1968) (Harper Torchbook); this book has an excellent bibliography. It should be mentioned that two of the main actors in the Second World War have written memoirs that not only have great historical interest but are also remarkable literary achievements: *Winston S. Churchill, *The Second World War*, 6 vols. (Boston, 1948–1953) (Bantam) and *Charles de Gaulle, *The Complete War Memoirs of Charles de Gaulle, 1940–1946*, 3 vols. in one, Vol. I trans. by Jonathan Griffin, Vols. II–III trans. by Richard Howard (New York, 1955–1960) (Simon and Schuster). Sir Llewellyn Woodward, *British Foreign Policy in the Second World War* (London, 1962) provides an illustration of the interaction of political and military events. The psychological attitude of the British people to the war emerges from Isaiah Berlin, *Mr. Churchill in 1940* (Boston and Cambridge, n.d.), and of the Russian people from *Alexander Werth, *Russia at War, 1941–1945* (New York, 1964) (Avon). An outstanding story of intelligence operations is presented in F. W. Deakin and G. R. Storry, *The Case of Richard Sorge* (New York, 1966). For the German side of the war see Harold C. Deutsch, *The Conspiracy Against Hitler in the Twilight War* (Minneapolis, 1968); F. H. Hinsley, *Hitler's Strategy* (Cambridge, Eng., 1951); and *Hugh R. Trevor-Roper, *The Last Days of Hitler* (New York, 1947) (Collier).

AFTER THE SECOND WORLD WAR

Developments in Europe since the Second World War have been so closely interconnected that a separation into different chronological periods is not feasible. From the point of view of foreign policy, Germany represented the most crucial issue; the international aspects of the German problem are well presented in John L. Snell, *Dilemma over Germany* (New Orleans, 1959). Clear, connected accounts of the Cold War are to be found in Louis J. Halle, *The Cold War as History* (New York and Evanston, Ill., 1967) and *John Lukacs, *A History of the Cold War* (New York, 1961) (Doubleday Anchor). The reasons for the Cold War are now hotly debated. The official American point of view that the war was a defense against Communist aggression has recently been strongly restated by Dean Acheson, *Present at the Creation* (New York, 1969). This view is no longer as generally accepted as it was at that time; many are convinced that American foreign policy was not free from aggressive and imperialist elements. See *Gar Alperovitz, *Atomic Diplomacy:*

Hiroshima and Potsdam (New York, 1965) (Vintage), and for a more balanced statement Gabriel Kolko, *The Politics of War: The World and United States Foreign Policy, 1943–1945* (New York, 1968). For a general survey of Russian foreign policy in this period, see *Adam B. Ulam, *Expansion and Coexistence: The History of Soviet Foreign Policy, 1917–1967* (New York and Washington, D.C., 1968) (Praeger). The manner in which the Bolsheviks established control in eastern Europe has been described in Hugh Seton-Watson, *The Pattern of Communist Revolution* (London, 1953). For a more detailed discussion of the events in the Balkans see *Robert Lee Wolff, *The Balkans in Our Time* (Cambridge, Mass., 1967) (Norton). A most informative description of the situation within the eastern bloc is Zbigniew K. Brzezinski, *The Soviet Bloc: Unity and Conflict* (Cambridge, Mass., 1960).

Regarding western Europe, the most striking development, the emergence of cooperation between Germany and France, is described in *F. Roy Willis, *France, Germany, and the New Europe, 1945–1967* (Stanford and London, 1968) (Oxford Galaxy). The changes in France since the Second World War have been startling. A novel by *Simone de Beauvoir, *The Mandarins* (1954) (Popular Library; also Meridian), is an interesting reproduction of the intellectual atmosphere in France at the time of the end of the war; the principal figures of the novel, although under disguised names, are Sartre and Camus. For a general survey of the economic and political developments in France after the war, see Donald C. McKay, *The United States and France* (Cambridge, Mass., 1951). A special study of the problems created by the colonial wars and the military opposition to the Fourth Republic is George Armstrong Kelly, *Lost Soldiers: The French Army and Empire in Crisis, 1947–1962* (Cambridge, Mass., 1965). An outstanding analysis of the entire French situation is *John Ardagh, *The New French Revolution* (New York, 1968) (Harper Colophon).

Writings in English on postwar Germany are less satisfactory. For German foreign policy in the postwar period see *Gordon Craig, *From Bismarck to Adenauer: Aspects of German Statecraft* (Baltimore, 1958) (Harper Torchbook). Lewis J. Edinger, *Kurt Schumacher: A Study in Personality and Political Behavior* (Stanford, 1965) provides a good introduction to the party struggles of the years immediately after the war, although since then a somewhat new situation has developed. The astounding Italian recovery has been carefully studied; see *H. Stuart Hughes, *The United States and Italy* (Cambridge, Mass, 1953) (Norton) and *Muriel Grindrod, *The Rebuilding of Italy: Politics and Economics, 1945–1955* (London and New York, 1955) (Oxford).

For Great Britain it might be well to refer to the above-mentioned book by *Robert K. Webb, *Modern England: From the Eighteenth Century to the Present* (New York, 1968) (Dodd, Mead), which uses the somewhat dispersed literature in a critical way. As an amusing and enlightening, although not always quite reliable, analysis of the British social structure, *Anthony Sampson, *Anatomy of Britain* (London, 1962) (Harper Colophon) deserves to be read. For the issues which may dominate British and European policy in the coming years see Robert L. Pfaltzgraff, Jr., *Britain Faces Europe* (Philadelphia, 1969).

Index

Bunyan, John, 399
Buol-Schauenstein, Count Karl Ferdinand von, 1096
Burbage, Richard, 402
Burgh, James, 751
Burghers, 714, 719
Burgundy, ducal court of, 111
Burgundy, dukes of, 211
Burke, Edmund, 587, 624, 642, 643, 644–45, 646, 648–49, 747, 752, 790–91, 911, 912, 931–32
Burke, Thomas, 1147
Burlamaqui, Jean Jacques, 428–29
Burma, 1527, 1529, 1573
  gains independence (1948), 1607
  see also Asia
Burns, John, 1272
Burns, Robert, 594
Burton, Robert, 80
Butler, Joseph, 579
Byron, George Gordon (Lord), 899, 926, 929

Cabinet of Dr. Caligari, The, 1413
Cadoudal, Georges, 841
Caesar, Julius, 826, 1056
Caillaux, Joseph, 1283, 1287
Calderón, Pedro, 399, 406–7, 410
Caleb Williams, 639
Calonne, Charles de, 547, 727, 728, 729
Calvin, John, 59, 129, 147, 186, 226, 283, 330, 340, 353, 369, 370, 389, 396
  biographical, 138, 139
  death, 126, 184
  denounces Michael Servetus, 160–61
  doctrines of, 139–40, 187–88
  on inseparability of church and state, 144–45
  on the Jesuits, 189
  justifies persecution of dissenters, 162–63
  political theory, 207
  see also Calvinism
Calvinism, 134, 148, 149, 150, 152, 157–58, 169, 175, 227, 230, 432, 557, 559
  capitalism and, 297–300, 307
  decline of militant zeal of, 226
  in the Dutch Republic, 283–84
  in Germany, 233, 235
  in the Holy Roman Empire, 256
  in the Netherlands, 212, 213
  in Poland, 241
  privileged classes and, 187–88
  as radical political party, 188–89
  in Scotland, 220
  spreads into Western Europe, 183–84, 187–88, 203
  in Sweden, 248
  see also Calvinist-Catholic struggle; Huguenots; Puritanism
Calvinist-Catholic struggle: effect on religious art, 370
  effect of Spanish decline on, 223, 226
  in Elizabethan England, 217–21
  fosters divine-right theory of kingship, 191
  Glorious Revolution and, 352–53
  mass denounced in French cities, 202–3
  in the Netherlands, 212–15, 224
  political character of, 184, 187
  question of politics and divine sanction, 191
  religious issues, irreconcilability of, 186
  settlement of, implications for Western Europe, 226
  see also France, religious wars in; Huguenots; Jesuits; Puritan Revolution; Thirty Years' War
Cambacéres, Jean Jacques Régis de, 828
Cambodia, 1574, 1583, 1615
  see also Indochina
Cambon, Paul, 1287, 1341
Cambrai, Archbishop of, *see* Fénelon, François
Cambridge, Platonists, 559, 560
Cambridge University, 219
Cameralism, 480–81, 617
Cameroons, the, 1369
  see also Africa
Campbell-Bannerman, Sir Henry, 1268, 1270, 1271–72
Campion, Edmund, 221
Campoformio, Treaty of (1797), 815, 817, 837, 838, 839
Camus, Albert, 1616

Canada, 1482, 1612
Canalejas, José, 1291
Candide, 597
Canisius, Peter, 234
Canning, George, 896–97, 933–34, 1132
Canovas, Antonio, 1290
Capitalism: cleavage between capital and labor, 57–58
  defined, 50–51
  effect on agrarian society, 62–69
  first labor unions and strikes, 53
  journeymen transformed to wage laborers, 52–53, 56
  secularization of economic ethic of churches, 58, 59–60
  state controlled, 51, 52
  see also Dutch Republic; Europe; Merchant-capitalist(s)
Capodistrias, Johannes Antonius, 898
Caporetto, Battle of (1917), 1360
Caprivi, Leo von, 1302, 1304
Caravaggio, Michelangelo da, 375–76
Carlos, Don, 197
Carmer, J. H. von, 695
Carnot, Lazare, 812
Carol II (of *Rumania*), 1398–99
Caroline of Anspach, 525
Caroline of Brunswick, 931
Carson, Sir Edward, 1276
Cartwright, Edmund, 537
Cartwright, John, 608–9, 751
Casa de Contratación, 194, 304
Cassel, Ernest, 1239
Castellio, Sebastianus, 163–64
Castiglione, Baldassare, 89, 95
Castile, *see* Spain
Castlereagh, Viscount, 878, 879, 882, 883, 884, 888, 889–90, 892, 893, 895–96, 898, 933, 1040
Cateau-Cambrésis, Peace of, 96, 125, 183, 203
Catherine I (of *Russia*), 502, 503
Catherine II (of *Russia*), 425, 501, 503, 504, 543, 548, 616, 669, 673, 681, 682, 791, 818, 821, 847, 949, 952
  Austro-Russian entente (1781), 690
  domestic policies, 693, 695, 696
    agrarian, 707, 709, 710, 713; censorship, 704, 705–6; economic and industrial, 714–16; education, 703–4; meaning of, 717; religion, 701–2; results of, 718–19
  League of Armed Neutrality and, 671
  partition of Poland (1772), 682, 684–86
    results of, 687–91; terms of, 686–87
  see also Absolutism, enlightened
Catherine of Aragon, 173
Catholic League (in France), 311
Catholic League (in Germany), 235
Catullus, 78
Cavaignac, Louis, 999
Cavaliers, defined, 328
Cavell, Edith, 1347
Cavendish, Lord Frederick, 1147
Cavour, Camillo Benso di, 991, 1014, 1040, 1065, 1078, 1096, 1179, 1251
  background and ideology, 1097–98
  death of, 1104
  diplomacy of, 1098–1101
  domestic policies of, 1098
  sends Garibaldi to Sicily, 1102
Cecil, Lord Robert, 1148
Cecil, Sir William, 218
Celtis, Conrad, 71, 83–85
Cervantes, Miguel de, 199, 354, 399, 404
Ceuta, capture of, 30
Ceylon, 838, 1607
  see also Asia
Cézanne, Paul, 1057, 1060
Chadwick, Sir James, 1552
Challe, Maurice, 1621
Chamberlain, Austen, 1431, 1439, 1440, 1479, 1480
Chamberlain, Joseph, 1145, 1148, 1267–68, 1269, 1271, 1325, 1431, 1482
Chamberlain, Neville, 1476, 1479, 1481–84, 1497, 1498–99, 1518, 1550, 1604
Chambord, count of, 1166, 1169, 1175
Changarnier, Nicolas, 1068
Chaptal, Jean, 826